Copyright © 2014 National Fire Protection Association®. All Rights Reserved.

NFPA® 1

Fire Code

2015 Edition

This edition of NFPA 1, *Fire Code*, was prepared by the Technical Committee on Fire Code and acted on by NFPA at its June Association Technical Meeting held June 9–12, 2014, in Las Vegas, NV. It was issued by the Standards Council on August 14, 2014, with an effective date of September 3, 2014, and supersedes all previous editions.

An extensive Tentative Interim Amendment (TIA), indicated by boxed notices at the appropriate areas within the document, was issued on August 14, 2014. This TIA implements Standards Council Decision D#14-1 to temporarily withdraw NFPA 1124 and end all NFPA standards development activities relating to the storage and retail sales of consumer fireworks. For further information, see Decision D#14-1 at http://www.nfpa.org/sc2014.

For further information on Tentative Interim Amendments, see Section 5 of the *Regulations Governing the Development of NFPA Standards*, available at http://www.nfpa.org/regs.

This edition of NFPA 1 was approved as an American National Standard on September 3, 2014.

Origin and Development of NFPA 1

This *Code* was originally developed as a result of the requests of many members of the National Fire Protection Association for a document covering all aspects of fire protection and prevention that used the other developed NFPA codes and standards. NFPA staff initiated this work in 1971 upon a directive from the NFPA Board of Directors.

The original code was written around a format that served as a guide for the development of a local fire prevention code. Prerogatives of local officials were excluded from the main text of the document but included within appendices as guidance for exercising desired prerogatives.

In the late 1980s, the Fire Marshals Association of North America undertook the task of developing a code that was more self-contained, adding administrative sections and extracting heavily from other NFPA codes and standards. The draft was submitted to the Fire Prevention Code Committee. The Committee examined changes in the built environment as it is affected by fire and incorporated significant portions of the *Life Safety Code*®. A special task group on hazardous materials examined technological changes in the handling, storage, and use of flammable and combustible materials. Chapters extracting hazardous material requirements placed a greater emphasis on protection of life and property from chemical products made and used in the environment. A major rewrite resulted in the 1992 edition of the *Fire Prevention Code*.

The 1997 edition updated the text extracted from other NFPA codes and standards and added compliance with additional NFPA codes and standards as part of the requirements of NFPA 1.

The 2000 edition of NFPA 1 was a complete revision that updated the text extracted from other NFPA codes and standards. Additional direct references from NFPA codes and standards that are essential to a code official's use of the document were added. The Committee also added a new section on performance-based design as a valuable tool for code officials and design professionals. NFPA 1 was restructured to be more functional with respect to administration, code enforcement, and regulatory adoption processes.

The 2003 edition of NFPA 1, *Uniform Fire Code*™, was a complete revision. It incorporated provisions from the Western Fire Chiefs, *Uniform Fire Code*™, under a partnership between NFPA and Western Fire Chiefs, while it updated and expanded the provisions extracted from other key NFPA codes and standards. To emphasize the partnership, the document was renamed NFPA 1, *Uniform Fire Code*™. The *Uniform Fire Code* is a trademark of the Western Fire Chiefs Association.

NFPA 1, *Uniform Fire Code*™, was restructured into parts to be more compatible with the regulatory adoption procedures, including administration and code enforcement, occupancies, processes, equipment, and hazardous materials provisions. The Committee included a newly expanded chapter on performance-based design as an enhanced tool for code officials and design professionals. Additional extracts and references from NFPA codes and standards that are essential to a code official's use of the document were added, bringing the number of referenced NFPA codes and standards to over 125. Additional chapters on hazardous materials were included that incorporate the provisions covered in the *Uniform Fire Code*™.

The 2006 edition of NFPA 1, *Uniform Fire Code*™, was a complete revision of the *Code* that incorporated the provisions from NFPA 230, *Standard for the Fire Protection of Storage*. The Technical Committee on Uniform Fire Code had been given responsibility for NFPA 230 by the NFPA Standards Council, so they incorporated the requirements into NFPA 1 UFC rather than maintain a separate standard.

The 2006 edition of NFPA 1 included new chapters on classification of occupancy, motion picture studios, outdoor tire storage, and general storage, along with other extracted provisions updated and expanded the from other key NFPA codes and standards that were essential to a code official's use of the document. The number of NFPA codes and standards referenced in this edition was 117.

With the 2009 edition of NFPA 1, the title of the document was changed from *Uniform Fire Code* to *Fire Code*. The revision updated all the extracted provisions from the 117 codes and standards that were included as mandatory reference publications in the 2006 edition. The revisions also included an expansion of Section 12.5 on interior finish to contain extracted provisions from NFPA *101*; an expansion of Section 12.6 on furnishings, contents, decorations, and treated fabrics to contain extracted provisions from NFPA *101*; a new Section 18.4, which moved fire flow requirements for buildings from Annex H; a new Section 32.5 for regulating locations for motion picture and television production studios, soundstages, and approved production facilities with extracted provisions from NFPA 140; and new Sections 40.3 through 40.7 on combustible dust explosion protection and fire prevention with extracted provisions from NFPA 654. Additional information on hazardous materials classifications was added to Annex B. This revision also added three annexes to the 2009 edition, including Annex O, In-Building Public Safety Radio Enhancement Systems; Annex P, Fire Department Service Delivery Concurrency Evaluation; and Annex Q, Fire Fighter Safety Building Marking System. The number of NFPA codes and standards referenced in this edition was 119.

Six annexes published in the 2006 edition were deleted from the 2009 edition, including Annex E, Model Citation Program; Annex F, Model Fees and Charges Program; Annex H, Fire Flow Requirements for Buildings; Annex J, Protection of Outdoor Storage; Annex M, Recommendations for Fighting Rubber Tire Fires in Sprinklered Buildings; and Annex N, AHJ Minimum Qualifications and Job Descriptions for Code Enforcement Personnel.

The 2012 edition of NFPA 1 included revisions to requirements for the fire code board of appeals (Section 1.10); certificates of fitness (Section 1.13); application limits of referenced standards (Section 2.1); emergency plan provisions (Section 10.9); prohibited storage of grills on balconies (10.11.6.2); new requirements for standardized elevator keys (11.3.6); new requirements for determination of fire department communication capabilities in buildings and two-way radio communication enhancement systems and deleted former Annex O (Section 11.10); medical gas and vacuum systems (Section 11.11); photovoltaic systems (Section 11.12); quality assurance of fire barrier penetrations and joints (12.3.2); and automatic sprinkler system requirement for new buildings three or more stories in height above grade (13.3.2.4). The 2012 edition also relocated former Annex P to the new Chapter 15, Fire Department Service Delivery Concurrency Evaluation; expanded Chapter 17, Wildland Urban Interface; added a new Chapter 36, Telecommunication Facilities and Information Technology Equipment; added a new Chapter 37, Fixed Guideway Transit and Passenger Rail Systems; added requirements for carbon monoxide detection in residential occupancies; relocated former Annex G to the new Chapter 54, Ozone Gas-Generating Equipment; extensively revised Chapter 60, Hazardous Materials, to extract from NFPA 400, *Hazardous Materials Code*; updated Chapter 66, Flammable and Combustible Liquids, per the current edition of NFPA 30, *Flammable and Combustible Liquids Code*; revised Chapter 67, Flammable Solids, to reference NFPA 400; revised Chapter 68, Highly Toxic and Toxic Solids and Liquids, to reference NFPA 400; completely revised Chapter 70, Oxidizer Solids and Liquids; revised Chapter 71, Pyrophoric Solids and Liquids, to reference NFPA 400; revised Chapter 72, Unstable (Reactive) Solids and Liquids, to reference NFPA 400; added a new Chapter 74, Ammonium Nitrate; added a new Chapter 75, Organic Peroxide Solids and Liquids; deleted Annex K, Explanation of Rack Storage Test Data and Procedures; deleted Annex L, Protection of Baled Cotton: History of Guidelines; and updated all extracts through the Annual 2011 revision cycle.

Key revisions for the 2015 edition of NFPA 1 include the prohibition of the use of sky lanterns (10.10.9.3); expanded application of photovoltaic system requirements to existing installations (Section 11.12); AHJ authorization to permit the removal of nonrequired, existing occupant-use hose (13.2.2.6); mandatory automatic sprinkler requirement for all new hotels without exception (13.3.2.15); enhanced attic protection for residential board and care occupancies with residential sprinkler systems (13.3.2.21.2.7); expanded occupancy-based fire alarm system provisions to correlate with NFPA *101* (Section 13.7); new occupant load factor for concentrated business use (14.8.1.2); completely revised fire hydrant location and distribution requirements and deleted former Annex E (Section 18.5); revisions to NFPA 654 extracts for dust explosion prevention (Chapter 40); new hot work permit limits from NFPA 51B (41.3.4.4); expanded existing commercial cooking equipment extinguishing system requirements from NFPA 96 (50.4.4.3.2); expanded ammonia refrigeration system maintenance and testing requirements (Section 53.3); updated hazardous materials maximum allowable quantities from NFPA 400 (60.4.2); new provisions for alcohol-based hand rub dispensers from NFPA *101* (60.5.2); revisions to aerosol product classifications from NFPA 30B (61.1.3); new requirements for cleaning and purging gas piping systems from NFPA 55 (63.3.1.19); new provisions for cooking oil storage tank systems in commercial kitchens from NFPA 30 (66.19.7); and updates of all extracts through the Annual 2014 revision cycle.

NFPA 1 reflects the technical knowledge of the committees who are responsible for the codes and standards that are referenced in and from which text is extracted and incorporated into the technical provisions of NFPA 1. This *Code* is intended to provide state, county, and local jurisdictions with an effective fire code.

Technical Committee on Fire Code

Jeffrey P. Collins, Chair
Palm Beach County Fire/Rescue, FL [E]
Rep. NFPA Fire Service Section

Scott W. Adams, Park City Fire Service District, UT [E]
    Rep. Western Fire Chiefs Association
Anthony C. Apfelbeck, Altamonte Springs Building/Fire Safety Division, FL [E]
    Rep. NFPA Architects, Engineers, & Building Officials Section
Carl F. Baldassarra, The RJA Group, IL [SE]
Jim Budzinski, Lake Worth, FL [E]
    Rep. International Association of Fire Chiefs
Kenneth E. Bush, Maryland State Fire Marshals Office, MD [E]
Sean DeCrane, City of Cleveland-Division of Fire, OH [E]
John F. Devlin, Aon Fire Protection Engineering Corporation, MD [I]
F. Tom Fangmann, SunCoke Energy, IL [U]
    Rep. NFPA Industrial Fire Protection Section
Keith L. Farmer, The DuPont Company, Inc., DE [U]
Ronald R. Farr, UL LLC, MI [RT]
Robert Fash, Las Vegas Fire & Rescue, NV [E]
Sam W. Francis, American Wood Council, PA [U]
Reinhard Hanselka, aidi, Inc., FL [SE]
Douglas Michael Hipp, Sr., Baltimore City Fire Department, MD [L]
    Rep. International Association of Fire Fighters
Richard S. Kraus, API/Petroleum Safety Consultants, VA [U]
    Rep. American Petroleum Institute

James K. Lathrop, Koffel Associates, Inc., CT [SE]
Vickie J. Lovell, InterCode Incorporated, FL [M]
    Rep. Alliance for Fire & Smoke Containment & Control, Inc.
Valeriano F. Martin, County of Maui, HI [E]
    Rep. Western Fire Chiefs Association
Richard W. Miller, Michigan Department of Fire Services, MI [E]
    Rep. International Fire Marshals Association
Wayne D. Moore, Hughes Associates, Inc., RI [M]
    Rep. Automatic Fire Alarm Association, Inc.
Joseph L. Navarra, Pepco Holdings Inc., DC [U]
    Rep. Edison Electric Institute
Steven Orlowski, National Association of Home Builders, DC [U]
James S. Peterkin, Heery International, PA [U]
    Rep. NFPA Health Care Section
John A. Sharry, Lawrence Livermore National Laboratory, CA [U]
Catherine L. Stashak, Office of the Illinois State Fire Marshal, IL [E]
J. L. (Jim) Tidwell, Tidwell Code Consulting, TX [M]
    Rep. Fire Equipment Manufacturers' Association
Randolph W. Tucker, ccrd partners, TX [SE]
Wayne Waggoner, National Fire Sprinkler Association, Inc., TN [M]
Peter J. Willse, XL Global Asset Protection Services, CT [I]

Alternates

Brent L. Christopherson, Missoula Rural Fire District, MT [E]
    (Alt. to S. W. Adams)
Shane M. Clary, Bay Alarm Company, CA [M]
    (Alt. to W. D. Moore)
Robert J. Davidson, Davidson Code Concepts, LLC, SC [E]
    (Alt. to J. Budzinski)
Brandon C. Ekberg, M+W US, Inc., AZ [SE]
    (Alt. to R. Hanselka)
Sarina L. Hart, Koffel Associates, Inc., MD [SE]
    (Alt. to J. K. Lathrop)
Jeffrey M. Hugo, National Fire Sprinkler Association, Inc., MI [M]
    (Alt. to W. Waggoner)
Roy C. Kimball, Brooks Equipment Company, Inc., NC [M]
    (Alt. to J. L. (Jim) Tidwell)

John Lake, City of Gainesville, FL [E]
    (Alt. to J. P. Collins)
Scott T. Laramee, Aon Fire Protection Engineering Corporation, CA [I]
    (Alt. to J. F. Devlin)
Morton L. Myers, City of Chico Fire Department, CA [E]
    (Alt. to V. F. Martin)
Tony Sanfilippo, Michigan Dept. of Labor & Economic Growth, MI [E]
    (Alt. to R. W. Miller)
Steven Taulbee, Las Vegas Fire Department, NV [E]
    (Alt. to R. Fash)
Kenneth Wood, Office of the Illinois State Fire Marshal, IL [E]
    (Alt. to C. L. Stashak)

Nonvoting

Mohd Moeed Al Arim Al Qahatni, Dar Alkawashif Company (DACO), Saudi Arabia [SE]
John E. Chartier, Rhode Island State Fire Marshal, RI [E]
    Rep. Northeast Regional Fire Code Development Committee
Bill Galloway, West Florence Fire & Rescue, SC [E]
    Rep. Southern Regional Fire Code Development Committee

Doug Hohbein, Nebraska State Fire Marshal, NB [E]
    Rep. North Central Regional Fire Code Development Committee
Kelly Nicolello, Alaska Department of Public Safety, AK [E]
    Rep. Western Regional Fire Code Development Committee
Walter Smittle, III, Ripley, WV [SE]
    (Member Emeritus)

Gregory E. Harrington, NFPA Staff Liaison

This list represents the membership at the time the Committee was balloted on the final text of this edition. Since that time, changes in the membership may have occurred. A key to classifications is found at the back of the document.

NOTE: Membership on a committee shall not in and of itself constitute an endorsement of the Association or any document developed by the committee on which the member serves.

Committee Scope: This Committee shall have primary responsibility for documents on a Fire Prevention Code that includes appropriate administrative provisions, to be used with the National Fire Codes for the installation, operation, and maintenance of buildings, structures, and premises for the purpose of providing safety to life and property from fire and explosion. This includes development of requirements for, and maintenance of, systems and equipment for fire control and extinguishment. Safety to life of occupants of buildings and structures is under the primary jurisdiction of the Committee on Safety to Life.

Contents

Chapter 1	Administration	1– 11
1.1	Scope	1– 11
1.2	Purpose	1– 11
1.3	Application	1– 11
1.4	Equivalencies, Alternatives, and Modifications	1– 12
1.5	Units	1– 12
1.6	Enforcement	1– 12
1.7	Authority	1– 12
1.8	Duties and Powers of the Incident Commander	1– 14
1.9	Liability	1– 14
1.10	Fire Code Board of Appeals	1– 14
1.11	Records and Reports	1– 16
1.12	Permits and Approvals	1– 16
1.13	Certificates of Fitness	1– 22
1.14	Plan Review	1– 23
1.15	Technical Assistance	1– 23
1.16	Notice of Violations and Penalties	1– 23

Chapter 2	Referenced Publications	1– 24
2.1	General	1– 24
2.2	NFPA Publications	1– 24
2.3	Other Publications	1– 26
2.4	References for Extracts in Mandatory Sections	1– 30

Chapter 3	Definitions	1– 30
3.1	General	1– 30
3.2	NFPA Official Definitions	1– 30
3.3	General Definitions	1– 31
3.4	Special Performance-Based Definitions	1– 48

Chapter 4	General Requirements	1– 49
4.1	Goals and Objectives	1– 49
4.2	Assumptions	1– 50
4.3	Compliance Options	1– 50
4.4	Fundamental Requirements	1– 50
4.5	General Requirements	1– 51

Chapter 5	Performance-Based Option	1– 52
5.1	General	1– 52
5.2	Performance Criteria	1– 54
5.3	Retained Prescriptive Requirements	1– 54
5.4	Design Scenarios	1– 54
5.5	Evaluation of Proposed Designs	1– 56
5.6	Safety Factors	1– 56
5.7	Documentation Requirements	1– 56

Chapter 6	Classification of Occupancy	1– 57
6.1	Classification of Occupancy	1– 57

Chapter 7	Reserved	1– 61
Chapter 8	Reserved	1– 61
Chapter 9	Reserved	1– 61

Chapter 10	General Safety Requirements	1– 61
10.1	Fundamental Requirements	1– 61
10.2	Owner/Occupant Responsibilities	1– 61
10.3	Occupancy	1– 61
10.4	Building Evacuation	1– 62
10.5	Fire Drills	1– 62
10.6	Reporting of Fires and Other Emergencies	1– 62
10.7	Tampering with Fire Safety Equipment	1– 62
10.8	Emergency Action Plans	1– 62
10.9	Smoking	1– 63
10.10	Open Flames, Candles, Open Fires, and Incinerators	1– 63
10.11	Fire Protection Markings	1– 63
10.12	Seasonal and Vacant Buildings and Premises	1– 64
10.13	Combustible Vegetation	1– 65
10.14	Special Outdoor Events, Carnivals, and Fairs	1– 65
10.15	Outside Storage	1– 69
10.16	Parade Floats	1– 69
10.17	Powered Industrial Trucks	1– 69
10.18	Storage of Combustible Materials	1– 69
10.19	Indoor Children's Playground Structures	1– 69

Chapter 11	Building Services	1– 70
11.1	Electrical Fire Safety	1– 70
11.2	Heating, Ventilation, and Air-Conditioning	1– 71
11.3	Elevators, Escalators, and Conveyors	1– 71
11.4	Utilities	1– 72
11.5	Heating Appliances	1– 72
11.6	Waste Chutes, Incinerators, and Laundry Chutes	1– 73
11.7	Stationary Generators and Standby Power Systems	1– 73
11.8	Smoke Control	1– 74
11.9	Emergency Command Center	1– 74
11.10	Two-Way Radio Communication Enhancement Systems	1– 74
11.11	Medical Gas and Vacuum Systems	1– 75
11.12	Photovoltaic Systems	1– 75

Chapter 12	Features of Fire Protection	1– 76
12.1	General	1– 76
12.2	Construction	1– 76

12.3	Fire-Resistive Materials and Construction	1–76
12.4	Fire Doors and Other Opening Protectives	1–77
12.5	Interior Finish	1–79
12.6	Contents and Furnishings	1–82
12.7	Fire Barriers	1–83
12.8	Smoke Partitions	1–88
12.9	Smoke Barriers	1–89

Chapter 13 Fire Protection Systems 1–90
- 13.1 General 1–90
- 13.2 Standpipe Systems 1–91
- 13.3 Automatic Sprinklers 1–91
- 13.4 Fire Pumps 1–105
- 13.5 Water Supply 1–110
- 13.6 Portable Fire Extinguishers 1–110
- 13.7 Detection, Alarm, and Communications Systems 1–123
- 13.8 Other Fire Protection Systems 1–176
- 13.9 Non-Listed Fire Protection or Suppression Devices and Equipment 1–176

Chapter 14 Means of Egress 1–177
- 14.1 Application 1–177
- 14.2 Exit Access Corridors 1–177
- 14.3 Exits 1–177
- 14.4 Means of Egress Reliability 1–178
- 14.5 Door Openings 1–178
- 14.6 Enclosure and Protection of Stairs 1–182
- 14.7 Exit Passageways 1–183
- 14.8 Capacity of Means of Egress 1–183
- 14.9 Number of Means of Egress 1–186
- 14.10 Arrangement of Means of Egress 1–186
- 14.11 Discharge from Exits 1–188
- 14.12 Illumination of Means of Egress 1–189
- 14.13 Emergency Lighting 1–190
- 14.14 Marking of Means of Egress 1–191
- 14.15 Secondary Means of Escape 1–192

Chapter 15 Fire Department Service Delivery Concurrency Evaluation 1–193
- 15.1 Application 1–193
- 15.2 Level of Service Objectives 1–193
- 15.3 Evaluator Qualifications 1–193
- 15.4 Fire Department Service Delivery Concurrency Evaluation Documentation 1–193
- 15.5 Independent Review 1–193
- 15.6 Approval 1–193

Chapter 16 Safeguarding Construction, Alteration, and Demolition Operations 1–193
- 16.1 General Requirements 1–193
- 16.2 Processes and Hazards 1–193
- 16.3 Fire Protection 1–194
- 16.4 Safeguarding Construction and Alteration Operations 1–196
- 16.5 Fire Safety During Demolition 1–197
- 16.6 Torch-Applied Roofing Systems 1–197
- 16.7 Tar Kettles 1–197
- 16.8 Asbestos Removal 1–198

Chapter 17 Wildland Urban Interface 1–198
- 17.1 General 1–198
- 17.2 Plans 1–200
- 17.3 Wildland Fire–Prone Areas 1–200

Chapter 18 Fire Department Access and Water Supply 1–202
- 18.1 General 1–202
- 18.2 Fire Department Access 1–202
- 18.3 Water Supplies 1–204
- 18.4 Fire Flow Requirements for Buildings 1–204
- 18.5 Fire Hydrants 1–205

Chapter 19 Combustible Waste and Refuse 1–207
- 19.1 General 1–207
- 19.2 Combustible Waste and Refuse 1–207

Chapter 20 Occupancy Fire Safety 1–208
- 20.1 Assembly Occupancies 1–208
- 20.2 Educational Occupancies 1–213
- 20.3 Day-Care Occupancies 1–214
- 20.4 Health Care Occupancies 1–216
- 20.5 Residential Board and Care Occupancies 1–219
- 20.6 Ambulatory Health Care Centers 1–221
- 20.7 Detention and Correctional Occupancies 1–222
- 20.8 Hotels and Dormitories 1–224
- 20.9 Apartment Buildings 1–225
- 20.10 Lodging or Rooming Houses 1–225
- 20.11 One- and Two-Family Dwellings and Manufactured Housing 1–225
- 20.12 Mercantile Occupancies 1–226
- 20.13 Business Occupancies 1–226
- 20.14 Industrial Occupancies 1–226
- 20.15 Storage Occupancies 1–226
- 20.16 Special Structures and High-Rise Buildings 1–227
- 20.17 Historic Buildings and Cultural Resources 1–227

Chapter 21 Airports and Heliports 1–228
- 21.1 Hangars 1–228
- 21.2 Terminals 1–228
- 21.3 Rooftop Heliport Construction and Protection 1–230

Chapter	Section	Title	Page
Chapter 22		**Automobile Wrecking Yards**	1–232
	22.1	General	1–232
	22.2	Permits	1–232
	22.3	Fire Department Access Roads	1–232
	22.4	Welding and Cutting	1–232
	22.5	Housekeeping	1–232
	22.6	Fire Extinguishers	1–232
	22.7	Tire Storage	1–232
	22.8	Burning Operations	1–232
	22.9	Motor Vehicle Fluids and Hazardous Materials	1–232
Chapter 23		**Cleanrooms**	1–232
	23.1	General	1–232
	23.2	Applicability	1–232
	23.3	Permits	1–233
Chapter 24		**Drycleaning**	1–233
	24.1	General	1–233
	24.2	Permits	1–233
Chapter 25		**Grandstands and Bleachers, Folding and Telescopic Seating, Tents, and Membrane Structures**	1–233
	25.1	General	1–233
	25.2	Tents	1–234
	25.3	Grandstands	1–235
	25.4	Folding and Telescopic Seating	1–236
	25.5	Permanent Membrane Structures	1–237
	25.6	Temporary Membrane Structures	1–238
Chapter 26		**Laboratories Using Chemicals**	1–239
	26.1	General	1–239
	26.2	Permits	1–239
Chapter 27		**Manufactured Home and Recreational Vehicle Sites**	1–239
	27.1	General	1–239
	27.2	Manufactured Home Sites	1–240
	27.3	Recreational Vehicle Parks and Campgrounds	1–240
Chapter 28		**Marinas, Boatyards, Marine Terminals, Piers, and Wharves**	1–240
	28.1	Marinas, Boatyards, and Other Recreational Marine Facilities	1–240
	28.2	Marine Terminals, Piers, and Wharves	1–243
	28.3	Construction, Conversion, Repair, and Lay-Up of Vessels	1–243
Chapter 29		**Parking Garages**	1–243
	29.1	General	1–243
Chapter 30		**Motor Fuel Dispensing Facilities and Repair Garages**	1–243
	30.1	Motor Fuel Dispensing Facilities	1–243
	30.2	Repair Garages	1–244
	30.3	Operational Requirements	1–246
Chapter 31		**Forest Products**	1–246
	31.1	General	1–246
	31.2	Permits	1–246
	31.3	Protection of Storage of Forest Products	1–246
Chapter 32		**Motion Picture and Television Production Studio Soundstages and Approved Production Facilities**	1–250
	32.1	General	1–250
	32.2	Permits	1–250
	32.3	Housekeeping	1–250
	32.4	Soundstages and Approved Production Facilities	1–250
	32.5	Production Locations	1–252
	32.6	Operating Features	1–253
Chapter 33		**Outside Storage of Tires**	1–253
	33.1	General	1–253
	33.2	Individual Piles	1–253
	33.3	Emergency Response Plan	1–254
	33.4	Fire Control Measures	1–254
	33.5	Site Access	1–254
	33.6	Signs and Security	1–254
	33.7	Outdoor Storage of Altered Tire Material	1–254
Chapter 34		**General Storage**	1–254
	34.1	General	1–254
	34.2	Classification of Commodities	1–255
	34.3	Building Construction	1–256
	34.4	Storage Arrangement	1–256
	34.5	General Fire Protection	1–257
	34.6	Building Equipment, Maintenance, and Operations	1–258
	34.7	Protection of Rack Storage	1–258
	34.8	Protection of Rubber Tires	1–259
	34.9	Protection of Roll Paper	1–259
	34.10	Storage of Idle Pallets	1–259
Chapter 35		**Reserved**	1–260
Chapter 36		**Telecommunication Facilities and Information Technology Equipment**	1–260
	36.1	General	1–260
Chapter 37		**Fixed Guideway Transit and Passenger Rail Systems**	1–260
	37.1	General	1–260

Chapter 38	Reserved	1–260
Chapter 39	Reserved	1–260
Chapter 40	**Dust Explosion and Fire Prevention**	**1–260**
40.1	General	1–260
40.2	Permits	1–260
40.3	Fugitive Dust Control and Housekeeping	1–260
40.4	Ignition Sources	1–261
40.5	Fire Protection	1–263
40.6	Training and Procedures	1–265
40.7	Inspection and Maintenance	1–265
Chapter 41	**Welding, Cutting, and Other Hot Work**	**1–266**
41.1	General	1–266
41.2	Responsibility for Hot Work	1–266
41.3	Fire Prevention Precautions	1–267
41.4	Sole Proprietors and Individual Operators	1–269
41.5	Public Exhibitions and Demonstrations	1–269
41.6	Arc Welding Equipment	1–269
Chapter 42	**Refueling**	**1–270**
42.1	General	1–270
42.2	Automotive Fuel Servicing	1–270
42.3	Storage of Liquids	1–270
42.4	Piping for Liquids	1–274
42.5	Fuel Dispensing Systems	1–274
42.6	Building Construction Requirements	1–276
42.7	Operational Requirements	1–276
42.8	Additional Requirements for CNG, LNG, Hydrogen, and LPG	1–278
42.9	Marine Fueling	1–279
42.10	Aircraft Fuel Servicing	1–282
42.11	Alternate Fuels	1–289
Chapter 43	**Spraying, Dipping, and Coating Using Flammable or Combustible Materials**	**1–290**
43.1	Application	1–290
43.2	Automated Electrostatic Spray Equipment	1–303
43.3	Handheld Electrostatic Spray Equipment	1–303
43.4	Drying, Curing, or Fusion Processes	1–303
43.5	Miscellaneous Spray Operations	1–303
43.6	Powder Coating	1–304
43.7	Organic Peroxides and Plural Component Coatings	1–304
43.8	Styrene Cross-Linked Composites Manufacturing (Glass Fiber–Reinforced Plastics)	1–305
43.9	Dipping, Coating, and Printing Processes	1–305
43.10	Training	1–306
Chapter 44	**Solvent Extraction**	**1–306**
44.1	General	1–306
44.2	Application	1–306
44.3	Permits	1–306
44.4	Special Requirements	1–306
Chapter 45	**Combustible Fibers**	**1–306**
45.1	General	1–306
45.2	Electrical Wiring	1–306
45.3	No Smoking	1–306
45.4	Vehicles and Material Handling Equipment	1–306
45.5	Loose Storage of Combustible Fibers	1–306
45.6	Baled Storage	1–307
45.7	Storage of Hay, Straw, and Other Similar Agricultural Products	1–307
45.8	Hazardous Materials	1–307
Chapter 46	Reserved	1–307
Chapter 47	Reserved	1–307
Chapter 48	Reserved	1–307
Chapter 49	Reserved	1–307
Chapter 50	**Commercial Cooking**	**1–307**
50.1	Application	1–307
50.2	General Requirements	1–308
50.3	Protection of Coverings and Enclosure Materials	1–308
50.4	Fire-Extinguishing Equipment	1–309
50.5	Procedures for the Use, Inspection, Testing, and Maintenance of Equipment	1–311
50.6	Minimum Safety Requirements for Cooking Equipment	1–313
Chapter 51	**Industrial Ovens and Furnaces**	**1–313**
51.1	General	1–313
51.2	Location	1–313
51.3	Safety Controls	1–313
Chapter 52	**Stationary Storage Battery Systems**	**1–313**
52.1	General	1–313
52.2	Permits	1–313
52.3	Safety Features	1–314
Chapter 53	**Mechanical Refrigeration**	**1–315**
53.1	General	1–315
53.2	Safety Features	1–315
53.3	Operations, Maintenance, and Testing	1–317

Chapter 54	**Ozone Gas–Generating Equipment**	**1–318**
54.1	Scope	1–318
54.2	Location	1–318
54.3	Piping, Valves, and Fittings	1–319
54.4	Automatic Shutdown	1–319
54.5	Manual Shutdown	1–319
Chapter 55	**Reserved**	**1–319**
Chapter 56	**Reserved**	**1–319**
Chapter 57	**Reserved**	**1–319**
Chapter 58	**Reserved**	**1–319**
Chapter 59	**Reserved**	**1–319**
Chapter 60	**Hazardous Materials**	**1–319**
60.1	General Requirements	1–319
60.2	Special Definitions	1–320
60.3	Classification of Materials, Wastes, and Hazard of Contents	1–320
60.4	Permissible Storage and Use Locations	1–321
60.5	Fundamental Requirements	1–334
60.6	Emergency Action Planning, Fire Risk Control and Chemical Hazard Requirements for Industrial Processes	1–341
60.7	Performance Alternative	1–341
Chapter 61	**Aerosol Products**	**1–341**
61.1	General Provisions	1–341
61.2	Basic Requirements	1–342
61.3	Storage in Warehouses and Storage Areas	1–343
61.4	Mercantile Occupancies	1–346
61.5	Operations and Maintenance	1–347
Chapter 62	**Reserved**	**1–348**
Chapter 63	**Compressed Gases and Cryogenic Fluids**	**1–348**
63.1	General Provisions	1–348
63.2	Building-Related Controls	1–350
63.3	Compressed Gases	1–355
63.4	Cryogenic Fluids	1–369
63.5	Bulk Oxygen Systems	1–377
63.6	Bulk Gaseous Hydrogen Systems	1–377
63.7	Bulk Liquefied Hydrogen Systems	1–377
63.8	Gas Generation Systems	1–377
63.9	Insulated Liquid Carbon Dioxide Systems	1–377
63.10	Storage, Handling, and Use of Ethylene Oxide for Sterilization and Fumigation	1–377
63.11	Liquid Oxygen in Home Care	1–378
Chapter 64	**Corrosive Solids and Liquids**	**1–378**
64.1	General	1–378
Chapter 65	**Explosives, Fireworks, and Model Rocketry**	**1–378**
65.1	General	1–378
65.2	Display Fireworks	1–379
65.3	Pyrotechnics Before a Proximate Audience	1–379
65.4	Flame Effects Before an Audience	1–379
65.5	Fireworks Manufacturing	1–379
65.6	Model Rocketry	1–379
65.7	Rocketry Manufacturing	1–379
65.8	High Power Rocketry	1–379
65.9	Explosives	1–379
Chapter 66	**Flammable and Combustible Liquids**	**1–379**
66.1	General	1–379
66.2	Reserved	1–380
66.3	Definitions	1–380
66.4	Definition and Classification of Liquids	1–381
66.5	Reserved	1–381
66.6	Fire and Explosion Prevention and Risk Control	1–381
66.7	Electrical Systems	1–384
66.8	Application of Area Classification	1–387
66.9	Storage of Liquids in Containers — General Requirements	1–387
66.10	Reserved	1–393
66.11	Reserved	1–393
66.12	Reserved	1–393
66.13	Reserved	1–393
66.14	Hazardous Materials Storage Lockers	1–393
66.15	Outdoor Storage	1–394
66.16	Automatic Fire Protection for Inside Liquid Storage Areas	1–395
66.17	Processing Facilities	1–415
66.18	Dispensing, Handling, Transfer, and Use of Liquids	1–419
66.19	Specific Operations	1–421
66.20	Reserved	1–425
66.21	Storage of Liquids in Tanks — Requirements for All Storage Tanks	1–425
66.22	Storage of Liquids in Tanks — Aboveground Storage Tanks	1–431
66.23	Storage of Liquids in Tanks — Underground Tanks	1–440
66.24	Storage Tank Buildings	1–441
66.25	Storage Tank Vaults	1–445
66.26	Reserved	1–446
66.27	Piping Systems	1–446

2015 Edition

66.28	Bulk Loading and Unloading Facilities for Tank Cars and Tank Vehicles	1–449
66.29	Wharves	1–451

Chapter 67 Flammable Solids 1–453
  67.1 General 1–453

Chapter 68 Highly Toxic and Toxic Solids and Liquids 1–453
  68.1 General 1–453

Chapter 69 Liquefied Petroleum Gases and Liquefied Natural Gases 1–453
  69.1 General Provisions 1–453
  69.2 LP-Gas Equipment and Appliances 1–454
  69.3 Installation of LP-Gas Systems 1–456
  69.4 LP-Gas Liquid Transfer 1–468
  69.5 Storage of Cylinders Awaiting Use, Resale, or Exchange 1–470
  69.6 Vehicular Transportation of LP-Gas 1–473
  69.7 LP-Gases at Utility Plants 1–474
  69.8 Liquefied Natural Gas (LNG) Facilities 1–474

Chapter 70 Oxidizer Solids and Liquids 1–475
  70.1 General 1–475

Chapter 71 Pyrophoric Solids and Liquids 1–475
  71.1 General 1–475

Chapter 72 Unstable (Reactive) Solids and Liquids 1–475
  72.1 General 1–475

Chapter 73 Water-Reactive Solids and Liquids 1–475
  73.1 General 1–475

Chapter 74 Ammonium Nitrate 1–475
  74.1 General 1–475

Chapter 75 Organic Peroxide Solids and Liquids 1–475
  75.1 General 1–475

Annex A Explanatory Material 1–475

Annex B Hazardous Materials Classifications 1–646

Annex C Sample Ordinance Adopting the NFPA 1, *Fire Code* 1–658

Annex D Hazardous Materials Management Plans and Hazardous Materials Inventory Statements 1–659

Annex E Fire Fighter Safety Building Marking System 1–668

Annex F Informational References 1–670

Index 1–676

NFPA 1

Fire Code

2015 Edition

IMPORTANT NOTE: This NFPA document is made available for use subject to important notices and legal disclaimers. These notices and disclaimers appear in all publications containing this document and may be found under the heading "Important Notices and Disclaimers Concerning NFPA Standards." They can also be obtained on request from NFPA or viewed at www.nfpa.org/disclaimers.

NOTICE: An asterisk (*) following the number or letter designating a paragraph indicates that explanatory material on the paragraph can be found in Annex A.

A reference in brackets [ ] following a section or paragraph indicates material that has been extracted from another NFPA document. As an aid to the user, the complete title and edition of the source documents for extracts in mandatory sections of the document are given in Chapter 2 and those for extracts in informational sections are given in Annex F. Extracted text may be edited for consistency and style and may include the revision of internal paragraph references and other references as appropriate. Requests for interpretations or revisions of extracted text shall be sent to the technical committee responsible for the source document.

Information on referenced publications can be found in Chapter 2 and Annex F.

Chapter 1 Administration

1.1 Scope.

1.1.1 The scope includes, but is not limited to, the following:

(1) Inspection of permanent and temporary buildings, processes, equipment, systems, and other fire and related life safety situations
(2) Investigation of fires, explosions, hazardous materials incidents, and other related emergency incidents
(3) Review of construction plans, drawings, and specifications for life safety systems, fire protection systems, access, water supplies, processes, hazardous materials, and other fire and life safety issues
(4) Fire and life safety education of fire brigades, employees, responsible parties, and the general public
(5) Existing occupancies and conditions, the design and construction of new buildings, remodeling of existing buildings, and additions to existing buildings
(6) Design, installation, alteration, modification, construction, maintenance, repairs, servicing, and testing of fire protection systems and equipment
(7) Installation, use, storage, and handling of medical gas systems
(8) Access requirements for fire department operations
(9) Hazards from outside fires in vegetation, trash, building debris, and other materials
(10) Regulation and control of special events including, but not limited to, assemblage of people, exhibits, trade shows, amusement parks, haunted houses, outdoor events, and other similar special temporary and permanent occupancies
(11) Interior finish, decorations, furnishings, and other combustibles that contribute to fire spread, fire load, and smoke production
(12) Storage, use, processing, handling, and on-site transportation of flammable and combustible gases, liquids, and solids
(13) Storage, use, processing, handling, and on-site transportation of hazardous materials
(14) Control of emergency operations and scenes
(15) Conditions affecting fire fighter safety
(16) Arrangement, design, construction, and alteration of new and existing means of egress

1.1.2 Title. The title of this *Code* shall be NFPA 1, *Fire Code*, of the National Fire Protection Association (NFPA).

1.2* Purpose. The purpose of this *Code* is to prescribe minimum requirements necessary to establish a reasonable level of fire and life safety and property protection from the hazards created by fire, explosion, and dangerous conditions.

1.3 Application.

1.3.1 This *Code* shall apply to both new and existing conditions.

1.3.2* Referenced Standards.

1.3.2.1 Details regarding processes, methods, specifications, equipment testing and maintenance, design standards, performance, installation, or other pertinent criteria contained in those codes and standards listed in Chapter 2 of this *Code* shall be considered a part of this *Code*.

1.3.2.2 Where no applicable codes, standards, or requirements are set forth in this *Code* or contained within other laws, codes, regulations, ordinances, or bylaws adopted by the authority having jurisdiction (AHJ), compliance with applicable codes and standards of NFPA or other nationally recognized standards as are approved shall be deemed as prima facie evidence of compliance with the intent of this *Code*.

1.3.2.3 Nothing herein shall diminish the authority of the AHJ to determine compliance with codes or standards for those activities or installations within the AHJ's responsibility.

1.3.2.4 Retroactivity of Referenced Standards to Existing Conditions. Unless otherwise specified by 1.3.2.4.1 through 1.3.2.4.3, the current provisions of the referenced standards shall not apply to facilities, equipment, structures, or installations that existed or were approved for construction or installation prior to the effective date of this *Code*.

1.3.2.4.1 Where specified by a reference standard for existing occupancies, conditions, or systems, the provisions of the referenced standards shall be retroactive.

1.3.2.4.2 Facilities, equipment, structures, and installations, installed in accordance with a reference standard, shall be maintained in accordance with the edition of the standard in effect at the time of installation.

1.3.2.4.3 In those cases where the AHJ determines that the existing situation constitutes an imminent danger, the AHJ shall be permitted to apply retroactively any portions of the current referenced standards deemed appropriate.

1.3.3 Conflicts.

1.3.3.1 When a requirement differs between this *Code* and a referenced document, the requirement of this *Code* shall apply.

1.3.3.2 When a conflict between a general requirement and a specific requirement occurs, the specific requirement shall apply.

1.3.4 Multiple Occupancies. Where two or more classes of occupancy occur in the same building or structure and are so intermingled that separate safeguards are impractical, means of egress facilities, construction, protection, and other safeguards shall comply with the most restrictive fire safety requirements of the occupancies involved.

1.3.5 Vehicles and Vessels. Vehicles, vessels, or other similar conveyances, when in fixed locations and occupied as buildings, as described by Section 11.6 of NFPA *101, Life Safety Code,* shall be treated as buildings and comply with this *Code*.

1.3.6 Buildings.

1.3.6.1 Buildings permitted for construction after the adoption of this *Code* shall comply with the provisions stated herein for new buildings.

1.3.6.2* Buildings in existence or permitted for construction prior to the adoption of this *Code* shall comply with the provisions stated herein or referenced for existing buildings *(see 10.3.2).*

1.3.6.3 Repairs, renovations, alterations, reconstruction, change of occupancy, and additions to buildings shall conform to this *Code*, NFPA *101,* and the building code.

1.3.6.4 Newly introduced equipment, materials, and operations regulated by this *Code* shall comply with the requirements for new construction or processes.

1.3.7 Severability. If any provision of this *Code* or the application thereof to any person or circumstance is held invalid, the remainder of the *Code* and the application of such provision to other persons or circumstances shall not be affected thereby.

1.4 Equivalencies, Alternatives, and Modifications.

1.4.1 Equivalencies. Nothing in this *Code* is intended to prevent the use of systems, methods, or devices of equivalent or superior quality, strength, fire resistance, effectiveness, durability, and safety to those prescribed by this *Code*, provided technical documentation is submitted to the AHJ to demonstrate equivalency and the system, method, or device is approved for the intended purpose.

1.4.2 Alternatives. The specific requirements of this *Code* shall be permitted to be altered by the AHJ to allow alternative methods that will secure equivalent fire safety, but in no case shall the alternative afford less fire safety than, in the judgment of the AHJ, that which would be provided by compliance with the provisions contained in this *Code*.

1.4.3 Modifications. The AHJ is authorized to modify any of the provisions of this *Code* upon application in writing by the owner, a lessee, or a duly authorized representative where there are practical difficulties in the way of carrying out the provisions of the *Code*, provided that the intent of the *Code* shall be complied with, public safety secured, and substantial justice done.

1.4.4 Buildings with equivalency, alternatives, or modifications approved by the AHJ shall be considered as conforming with this *Code*.

1.4.5 Each application for an alternative fire protection feature shall be filed with the AHJ and shall be accompanied by such evidence, letters, statements, results of tests, or other supporting information as required to justify the request. The AHJ shall keep a record of actions on such applications, and a signed copy of the AHJ's decision shall be provided for the applicant.

1.4.6 Approval. The AHJ shall approve such alternative construction systems, materials, or methods of design when it is substantiated that the standards of this *Code* are at least equaled. If, in the opinion of the AHJ, the standards of this *Code* shall not be equaled by the alternative requested, approval for permanent work shall be refused. Consideration shall be given to test or prototype installations.

1.4.7 Tests.

1.4.7.1 Whenever evidence of compliance with the requirements of this *Code* is insufficient or evidence that any material or method of construction does not conform to the requirements of this *Code*, or to substantiate claims for alternative construction systems, materials, or methods of construction, the AHJ shall be permitted to require tests for proof of compliance to be made by an approved agency at the expense of the owner or his/her agent.

1.4.7.2 Test methods shall be as specified by this *Code* for the material in question. If appropriate test methods are not specified in this *Code*, the AHJ is authorized to accept an applicable test procedure from another recognized source.

1.4.7.3 Copies of the results of all such tests shall be retained in accordance with Section 1.11.

1.5 Units.

1.5.1 International System of Units. Metric units of measurement in this *Code* are in accordance with the modernized metric system known as the International System of Units (SI).

1.5.2 Primary and Equivalent Values. If a value for a measurement as given in this *Code* is followed by an equivalent value in other units, the first stated value shall be regarded as the requirement. A given equivalent value could be approximate.

1.6 Enforcement. This *Code* shall be administered and enforced by the AHJ designated by the governing authority. *(See Annex C for sample wording for enabling legislation.)*

1.7 Authority.

1.7.1 Administration. The provisions of this *Code* shall apply without restriction, unless specifically exempted.

1.7.2* Minimum Qualifications to Enforce this *Code*. The AHJ shall establish minimum qualifications for all persons assigned the responsibility of enforcing this *Code*.

1.7.3 Interpretations.

1.7.3.1 The AHJ is authorized to render interpretations of this *Code* and to make and enforce rules and supplemental regulations in order to carry out the application and intent of its provisions.

1.7.3.2 Such interpretations, rules, and regulations shall be in conformance with the intent and purpose of this *Code* and shall be available to the public during normal business hours.

1.7.4 Enforcement Assistance. Police and other enforcement agencies shall have authority to render necessary assistance in the enforcement of this *Code* when requested to do so by the AHJ.

1.7.5 Delegation of Authority. The AHJ shall be permitted to delegate to other qualified individuals such powers as necessary for the administration and enforcement of this *Code*.

1.7.6 Reliance on Other Enforcement Officials.

1.7.6.1* The AHJ shall be authorized to rely on plan reviews, inspections, opinions, and approvals rendered by other enforcement officials in determining compliance with this *Code*.

1.7.6.2 When the AHJ relies on inspections, plan reviews, opinions, and approvals rendered by other enforcement officials in determining compliance with this *Code*, the other enforcement officials shall be deemed to be acting as agents under their own authority and not as agents of the AHJ enforcing this *Code*.

1.7.7 Inspection.

1.7.7.1 The AHJ shall be authorized to inspect, at all reasonable times, any building or premises for dangerous or hazardous conditions or materials as set forth in this *Code*.

1.7.7.2 The AHJ shall have authority to order any person(s) to remove or remedy such dangerous or hazardous condition or material. Any person(s) failing to comply with such order shall be in violation of this *Code*.

1.7.7.3 To the full extent permitted by law, any AHJ engaged in fire prevention and inspection work shall be authorized at all reasonable times to enter and examine any building, structure, marine vessel, vehicle, or premises for the purpose of making fire safety inspections.

1.7.7.4 Before entering, the AHJ shall obtain the consent of the occupant thereof or obtain a court warrant authorizing entry for the purpose of inspection except in those instances where an emergency exists.

1.7.7.5 As used in 1.7.7.4, emergency shall mean circumstances that the AHJ knows, or has reason to believe, exist and that can constitute imminent danger.

1.7.7.6 Persons authorized to enter and inspect buildings, structures, marine vessels, vehicles, and premises as herein set forth shall be identified by credentials issued by the governing authority.

1.7.8 Where conditions exist and are deemed hazardous to life or property by the AHJ, the AHJ shall have the authority to summarily abate such hazardous conditions that are in violation of this *Code*.

1.7.9 Interference with Enforcement. Persons shall not interfere or cause conditions that would interfere with an AHJ carrying out any duties or functions prescribed by this *Code*.

1.7.10 Impersonation. Persons shall not use a badge, uniform, or other credentials to impersonate the AHJ.

1.7.11 Investigation.

1.7.11.1 Authority. The AHJ shall have the authority to investigate the cause, origin, and circumstances of any fire, explosion, release of hazardous materials, or other hazardous condition.

1.7.11.2 Evidence. The AHJ shall have the authority to take custody of all physical evidence relating to the cause of the fire, explosion, release of hazardous materials, or other hazardous condition.

1.7.11.3 Limiting Access. The AHJ shall have the authority to limit access to emergencies or other similar situations.

1.7.11.4 Trade Secret. Information that could be related to trade secrets or processes shall not be made part of the public record except as could be directed by a court of law.

1.7.12 Plans and Specifications.

1.7.12.1 The AHJ shall have the authority to require plans and specifications to ensure compliance with applicable codes and standards.

1.7.12.2 Plans shall be submitted to the AHJ prior to construction unless otherwise permitted by 1.7.12.4.

1.7.12.3 The construction documents for each phase shall be complete in themselves, so that review and inspection can properly be made. Preliminary plans of the total building shall be submitted with the construction documents, and with sufficient detail, so that proper evaluation can be made. Areas and items not included in the phase to be permitted shall be shown as not included. [5000:1.7.6.3.3.3]

1.7.12.4 The AHJ is authorized to exempt detached one- and two-family dwellings and accessory structures from the submittal of plans.

1.7.12.5 Plans shall be submitted to the AHJ prior to the change of occupancy of any existing building.

1.7.12.6 Plans shall be submitted to the AHJ prior to the alteration of the means of egress or fire protection systems of any existing building.

1.7.12.7 Plans shall be submitted to the AHJ for other conditions as deemed necessary by the AHJ to determine compliance with the applicable codes and standards.

1.7.12.8 The AHJ shall be authorized to require permits for conditions listed in 1.7.12.2, 1.7.12.5, and 1.7.12.6, unless otherwise permitted by 1.7.12.9.

1.7.12.9 The AHJ is authorized to exempt detached one- and two-family dwellings and accessory structures from the permit requirement of 1.7.12.8.

1.7.12.10 No construction work shall proceed until the AHJ has reviewed the plans for compliance with the applicable codes and standards and the applicable permits have been issued.

1.7.13 Inspection of Construction and Installation.

1.7.13.1 The AHJ shall be notified by the person performing the work when the installation is ready for a required inspection.

1.7.13.2 Whenever any installation subject to inspection prior to use is covered or concealed without having first been inspected, the AHJ shall have the authority to require that such work be exposed for inspection.

1.7.13.3 When any construction or installation work is being performed in violation of the plans and specifications as approved by the AHJ, a written notice shall be issued to the responsible party to stop work on that portion of the work that is in violation.

1.7.13.4 The notice shall state the nature of the violation, and no work shall be continued on that portion until the violation has been corrected.

1.7.14 Certificate of Occupancy. When the building code requires a certificate of occupancy, the certificate of occupancy shall not be issued until approved by the AHJ for fire code enforcement.

1.7.15 Stop Work Order. The AHJ shall have the authority to order an operation, construction, or use stopped when any of the following conditions exists:

(1) Work is being done contrary to provision of this *Code*.
(2) Work is occurring without a permit required by Section 1.12.
(3) An imminent danger has been created.

1.7.16 Imminent Dangers and Evacuation.

1.7.16.1 When, in the opinion of the AHJ, an imminent danger exists, the AHJ shall be authorized to order the occupants to vacate, or temporarily close for use or occupancy, a building, the right-of-way, sidewalks, streets, or adjacent buildings or nearby areas.

1.7.16.2 The AHJ shall be authorized to employ the necessary resources to perform the required work in order to mitigate the imminent danger.

1.7.16.3 Costs incurred by the AHJ in the performance of emergency work shall be the responsibility of the property owner or other responsible party creating such imminent danger.

1.7.17 Standby and Fire Watch Personnel.

1.7.17.1 The AHJ shall have the authority to require standby fire personnel or an approved fire watch when potentially hazardous conditions or a reduction in a life safety feature exist due to the type of performance, display, exhibit, occupancy, contest, or activity; an impairment to a fire protection feature; or the number of persons present.

1.7.17.2 The owner, agent, or lessee shall employ one or more qualified persons, as required and approved, to be on duty.

1.7.17.2.1 The cost of standby fire personnel shall be at no cost to the AHJ.

1.7.17.3* Such standby fire personnel or fire watch personnel shall be subject to the AHJ's orders at all times and shall be identifiable and remain on duty during the times such places are open to the public, when such activity is being conducted, or as required by the AHJ.

1.7.18 Public Fire Education.

1.7.18.1 The AHJ shall have the authority to develop and implement a public fire safety education program as deemed necessary for the general welfare with respect to the potential fire hazards within the jurisdiction.

1.7.18.2 The AHJ shall have the authority to ensure duly authorized public fire safety education programs or public fire safety messages are disseminated to the general public.

1.8 Duties and Powers of the Incident Commander.

1.8.1 Authority. The incident commander conducting operations in connection with the extinguishment and control of any fire, explosion, hazardous materials incident, natural disaster, rescue, and/or other emergency shall have authority to direct all operations of fire extinguishment, mitigation of a hazardous materials incident, natural disaster, rescue, and/or control and to take necessary precautions to save life, protect property, and prevent further injury or damage.

1.8.2 Controlling Scene. During any emergency described in 1.8.1, including the investigation of the cause of such emergency, the incident commander or authorized representative shall be permitted to control or prohibit the approach to the scene of such emergency by any vehicle, vessel, or person.

1.8.3 Obstruction of Operations. Persons shall not obstruct the operations of the fire department or disobey any command of the incident commander or authorized representative or any part thereof, or any order of a police officer assisting the fire department.

1.8.4 Scene Barrier. The incident commander or authorized representative in charge of an emergency scene shall have the authority to establish barriers to control access in the vicinity of such emergency and to place, or cause to be placed, ropes, guards, barricades, or other obstructions across any street or alley to delineate such emergency scene barrier.

1.8.5 Persons, except as authorized by the incident commander in charge of the emergency, shall not be permitted to cross barriers established in accordance with 1.8.4.

1.9 Liability.

1.9.1 The AHJ, and other individuals charged by the AHJ, or the incident commander of emergency operations, charged with the enforcement of this *Code* or any other official duties, acting in good faith and without malice in the discharge of their duties, shall not thereby be rendered personally liable for any damage that could accrue to persons or property as a result of any act or by reason of any act or omission in the discharge of their duties.

1.9.2 The fire department and AHJ, acting in good faith and without malice in the discharge of the organizations' public duty, shall not thereby be rendered liable for any damage that could accrue to persons or property as a result of any act or by reason of any act or omission in the discharge of such duties.

1.9.3 Any suit brought against the AHJ, the incident commander, or such individuals because of such act or omission performed in the enforcement of any provision of such codes or other pertinent laws or ordinances implemented through the enforcement of this *Code* or enforced by the code enforcement agency shall be defended by this jurisdiction until final termination of such proceedings, and any judgment resulting therefrom shall be assumed by this jurisdiction.

1.9.4 This *Code* shall not be construed to relieve from or lessen the responsibility of any person owning, operating, or controlling any building or structure for any damages to persons or property caused by defects, nor shall the code enforcement agency or its parent jurisdiction be held as assuming any such liability by reason of the inspections authorized by this *Code* or any permits or certificates issued under this *Code*.

1.10 Fire Code Board of Appeals.

1.10.1 Establishment of Fire Code Board of Appeals. A Board of Appeals shall be established to rule on matters relating to the fire code and its enforcement.

1.10.1.1 Membership.

1.10.1.1.1 The members of the Board of Appeals shall be appointed by the governing body of the jurisdiction.

1.10.1.1.2 The Board of Appeals shall consist of five or seven principal members and one ex officio member representative of the AHJ. Each principal member shall be permitted to have an alternate with similar experience to serve in his or her stead when necessary.

1.10.1.1.2.1 The jurisdiction governing body shall have the authority to appoint alternates who shall serve when a principal member is unable to fulfill their obligations. Alternates shall have the full authority and responsibility of principal members when serving in place of a principal member.

1.10.1.1.3 Members and alternate members shall be appointed based on their education, experience, and knowledge.

1.10.1.1.4 Members and alternates shall be appointed to a 3-year term.

1.10.1.1.5 Members and alternates shall be composed of individuals experienced in the following fields or professions:

(1) Engineering or architectural design
(2) General contracting
(3) Fire protection contracting
(4) Fire department operations or fire code enforcement
(5) Building code enforcement
(6) Legal
(7) General public

1.10.1.1.5.1 Members and alternates shall not be employees, agents, or officers of the jurisdiction.

1.10.1.1.5.2 Members and alternates shall be residents of the jurisdiction.

1.10.1.1.5.3 No more than one member shall represent the same field or provision listed in 1.10.1.1.5.

1.10.1.1.6 The representative of the AHJ shall be an ex officio member and shall be entitled to participate in all discussions. The ex officio member shall not be entitled to a vote.

1.10.1.1.7 No member of the Board of Appeals shall sit in judgment on any case in which the member holds a direct or indirect property or financial interest in the case.

1.10.1.1.8 The board shall select one of its members to serve as chair and one member to serve as vice chair.

1.10.2 Rules and Procedures of the Board of Appeals. The Board of Appeals shall have the authority to establish rules and regulations for conducting its business that are consistent with the provisions of this *Code*.

1.10.3 Authority of the Board of Appeals.

1.10.3.1 The Board of Appeals shall provide for the reasonable interpretation of the provisions of this *Code* and issue rulings on appeals of the decisions of the AHJ.

1.10.3.2 The ruling of the Board of Appeals shall be consistent with the letter of the *Code* or when involving issues of clarity, ensuring that the intent of the *Code* is met with due consideration for public safety and fire fighter safety.

1.10.3.3 The Board of Appeals shall have the authority to grant alternatives or modifications through procedures outlined in Section 1.4 of the *Code*.

1.10.3.4 The Board of Appeals shall not have the authority to waive the requirements of the *Code*.

1.10.3.5 The Board of Appeals decisions shall not be precedent setting.

1.10.4 Means of Appeals.

1.10.4.1 Any person with standing shall be permitted to appeal a decision of the AHJ to the Board of Appeals when it is claimed that any one or more of the following conditions exist:

(1) The true intent of the *Code* has been incorrectly interpreted.
(2) The provisions of the *Code* do not fully apply.
(3) A decision is unreasonable or arbitrary as it applies to alternatives or new materials.

1.10.4.2 An appeal shall be submitted to the AHJ in writing within 30 calendar days of notification of violation. The appeal shall outline all of the following:

(1) The *Code* provision(s) from which relief is sought
(2) A statement indicating which provisions of 1.10.4.1 apply
(3) Justification as to the applicability of the provision(s) cited in 1.10.4.1
(4) A requested remedy
(5) Justification for the requested remedy stating specifically how the *Code* is complied with, public safety is secured, and fire fighter safety is secured

1.10.4.3* Documentation supporting an appeal shall be submitted to the AHJ at least 7 calendar days prior to the Board of Appeals hearing.

1.10.5 Meetings and Records.

1.10.5.1 Meetings of the Board of Appeals shall be held at the call of the chair, at such other times as the board determines, and within 30 calendar days of the filing of a notice of appeal.

1.10.5.2 All hearings before the Board of Appeals shall be open to the public.

1.10.5.3 The Board of Appeals shall keep minutes of its proceedings showing the vote of each member on every question or, if the member is absent or fails to vote, these actions shall be recorded.

1.10.5.4 The Board of Appeals shall keep records of its examinations and other official actions.

1.10.5.5 Minutes and records of the Board of Appeals shall be public record.

1.10.5.6 A quorum shall consist of not less than 5 members or alternates.

1.10.5.7 In varying the application of any provision of this *Code*, or in modifying an order of the AHJ, a two-thirds vote of the quorum shall be required.

1.10.6 Decisions.

1.10.6.1 Every decision of the Board of Appeals shall be entered in the minutes of the board meeting.

1.10.6.2 A decision of the Board of Appeals to modify an order of the AHJ shall be in writing and shall specify the manner in which such modification is made, the conditions upon which it is made, the reasons therefore, and justification linked to specific code sections.

1.10.6.3 Every decision shall be promptly filed in the office of the AHJ and shall be open for public inspection.

1.10.6.4 A certified copy shall be sent by mail or delivered in person to the appellant, and a copy shall be publicly posted in the office of the AHJ for 2 weeks after filing.

1.10.6.5 The decision of the Board of Appeals shall be final, subject to such remedy as any aggrieved party might have through legal, equity, or other avenues of appeal or petition.

1.10.6.6 If a decision of the Board of Appeals reverses or modifies a refusal, order, or disallowance of the AHJ, or varies the application of any provision of this *Code*, the AHJ shall take action immediately in accordance with such decision.

1.11 Records and Reports.

1.11.1 A record of examinations, approvals, equivalencies, and alternates shall be maintained by the AHJ and shall be available for public inspection during business hours in accordance with applicable laws.

1.11.2 The AHJ shall keep a record of all fire prevention inspections, including the date of such inspections and a summary of any violations found to exist, the date of the services of notices, and a record of the final disposition of all violations.

1.11.3 Emergency Response Records.

1.11.3.1 The fire department shall keep a record of fire and other emergency responses occurring within its jurisdiction and of facts concerning the same, including statistics as to the extent and damage caused by such fires or emergencies.

1.11.3.2 The fire department shall report its incident record data, collected in accordance with 1.11.3, to the recognized state agency responsible for collecting such data.

1.11.4 All records required to be kept shall be maintained until their usefulness has been served or as required by law.

1.12 Permits and Approvals.

1.12.1 The AHJ shall be authorized to establish and issue permits, certificates, and approvals pertaining to conditions, operations, or materials hazardous to life or property pursuant to Section 1.12.

1.12.2 Applications for permits shall be made to the AHJ on forms provided by the jurisdiction and shall include the applicant's answers in full to inquiries set forth on such forms.

1.12.2.1 Applications for permits shall be accompanied by such data as required by the AHJ and fees as required by the jurisdiction.

1.12.2.2 The AHJ shall review all applications submitted and issue permits as required.

1.12.2.3 If an application for a permit is rejected by the AHJ, the applicant shall be advised of the reasons for such rejection.

1.12.2.4 Permits for activities requiring evidence of financial responsibility by the jurisdiction shall not be issued unless proof of required financial responsibility is furnished.

1.12.3 Conditions of Approval.

1.12.3.1 Any conditions of the initial approval by the AHJ of a use, occupancy, permit, or construction shall remain with the use, occupancy, permit, or construction unless modified by the AHJ.

1.12.3.2 The AHJ shall be permitted to require conditions of approval be memorialized via recording in the public records, as part of the plat, permit, or other method as approved by the AHJ.

1.12.4 Approvals by Other AHJs.

1.12.4.1 The AHJ shall have the authority to require evidence to show that other regulatory agencies having jurisdiction over the design, construction, alteration, repair, equipment, maintenance, process, and relocation of structures have issued appropriate approvals.

1.12.4.2 The AHJ shall not be held responsible for enforcement of the regulations of such other regulatory agencies unless specifically mandated to enforce those agencies' regulations.

1.12.5 Misrepresentation.

1.12.5.1 Any attempt to misrepresent or otherwise deliberately or knowingly design; install; service; maintain; operate; sell; represent for sale; falsify records, reports, or applications; or other related activity in violation of the requirements prescribed by this *Code* shall be a violation of this *Code*.

1.12.5.2 Such violations shall be cause for immediate suspension or revocation of any related approvals, certificates, or permits issued by this jurisdiction.

1.12.5.3 Such violations shall be subject to any other criminal or civil penalties as available by the laws of this jurisdiction.

1.12.6 Permits.

1.12.6.1 A permit shall be predicated upon compliance with the requirements of this *Code* and shall constitute written authority issued by the AHJ to maintain, store, use, or handle materials; to conduct processes that could produce conditions hazardous to life or property; or to install equipment used in connection with such activities.

1.12.6.2 Any permit issued under this *Code* shall not take the place of any other approval, certificate, license, or permit required by other regulations or laws of this jurisdiction.

1.12.6.3 Where additional permits, approvals, certificates, or licenses are required by other agencies, approval shall be obtained from those other agencies.

1.12.6.4 The AHJ shall have the authority to require an inspection prior to the issuance of a permit.

1.12.6.5 A permit issued under this *Code* shall continue until revoked or for the period of time designated on the permit.

1.12.6.6 The permit shall be issued to one person or business only and for the location or purpose described in the permit.

1.12.6.7 Any change that affects any of the conditions of the permit shall require a new or amended permit.

1.12.6.8 The AHJ shall have the authority to grant an extension of the permit time period upon presentation by the permittee of a satisfactory reason for failure to start or complete the work or activity authorized by the permit.

1.12.6.9 A copy of the permit shall be posted or otherwise readily accessible at each place of operation and shall be subject to inspection as specified by the AHJ.

1.12.6.10 Any activity authorized by any permit issued under this *Code* shall be conducted by the permittee or the permittee's agents or employees in compliance with all requirements of this *Code* applicable thereto and in accordance with the approved plans and specifications.

1.12.6.11 No permit issued under this *Code* shall be interpreted to justify a violation of any provision of this *Code* or any other applicable law or regulation.

1.12.6.12 Any addition or alteration of approved plans or specifications shall be approved in advance by the AHJ, as evidenced by the issuance of a new or amended permit.

1.12.6.13* Permits shall be issued by the AHJ and shall indicate the following:

(1) Operation, activities, or construction for which the permit is issued
(2) Address or location where the operation, activity, or construction is to be conducted

(3) Name, address, and phone number of the permittee
(4) Permit number
(5) Period of validity of the permit
(6) Inspection requirements
(7) Name of the agency authorizing the permit (AHJ)
(8) Date of issuance
(9) Permit conditions as determined by the AHJ

1.12.6.14 Any application for, or acceptance of, any permit requested or issued pursuant to this *Code* shall constitute agreement and consent by the person making the application or accepting the permit to allow the AHJ to enter the premises at any reasonable time to conduct such inspections as required by this *Code*.

1.12.7 Revocation or Suspension of Permits.

1.12.7.1 The AHJ shall be permitted to revoke or suspend a permit or approval issued if any violation of this *Code* is found upon inspection or in case any false statements or misrepresentations have been submitted in the application or plans on which the permit or approval was based.

1.12.7.2 Revocation or suspension shall be constituted when the permittee is duly notified by the AHJ.

1.12.7.3 Any person who engages in any business, operation, or occupation, or uses any premises, after the permit issued therefore has been suspended or revoked pursuant to the provisions of this *Code*, and before such suspended permit has been reinstated or a new permit issued, shall be in violation of this *Code*.

1.12.8 Permits shall be required in accordance with Table 1.12.8(a) through Table 1.12.8(d).

> Tables 1.12.8(a) and 1.12.8(d) were revised by a tentative interim amendment. (TIA). See page 1.

Table 1.12.8(a) Permit Requirements

Operations and Materials	Permit Required	Cross Reference Section Number
Aerosol products	To store or handle an aggregate quantity of Level 2 or Level 3 aerosol products in excess of 500 lb (226.8 kg)	61.1.2
Aircraft fuel servicing	To provide aircraft fuel servicing	42.10.1.2
Aircraft hangars	For servicing or repairing aircraft	21.1.1
Aircraft refueling vehicles	To operate aircraft refueling vehicles	42.10.1.2
Airport terminal buildings	For construction and alteration	21.2.2.1
Ammonium nitrate	For storage	Chapter 74
Amusement parks	For construction, alteration, or operation of amusement park fire protection safety features	10.15.1
Asbestos removal	For the removal of asbestos	16.8.2
Automatic fire suppression systems	For installation, modification, or removal from service of any automatic fire suppression system*	13.1.1.1; 50.4.2
Automobile wrecking yards	To operate automobile wrecking yards	22.2
Automotive fuel servicing	To provide automotive fuel servicing	42.2.2.1; 42.11.2.2.4; 42.11.3.1
Battery systems	To install or operate stationary lead-acid battery systems having an electrolyte capacity of more than 100 gal (378.5 L) in sprinklered buildings or 50 gal (189.3 L) in nonsprinklered buildings	52.2
Candles, open flames, and portable cooking	To use in connection with assembly areas, dining areas of restaurants, or drinking establishments	17.3.2; 20.1.1.1
Carnivals and fairs	To conduct a carnival or fair	10.15.1
Cellulose nitrate film	To store, handle, use, or display	20.15.7.2
Cellulose nitrate plastic	To store or handle more than 25 lb (11.3 kg)	43.1.1.4
Change of occupancy	For the change of occupancy classification of an existing building	1.7.11.5

(continues)

Table 1.12.8(a) *Continued*

Operations and Materials	Permit Required	Cross Reference Section Number
Cleanrooms	For construction, alteration, or operation	23.3
Combustible fibers	For storage or handling of combustible fibers greater than 100 ft^3 (2.8 m^3)	45.1.3
Combustible material storage	To store more than 2500 ft^3 (70.8 m^3) gross volume	10.19.2; 19.1.1; 31.2
Commercial rubbish-handling operation	To operate	19.1.1
Compressed gases	1. To store, use, or handle compressed gases in excess of the amounts listed in Table 1.12.8(b) 2. When the compressed gases in use or storage exceed the amounts listed in Table 1.12.8(b), a permit is required to install, repair damage to, abandon, remove, place temporarily out of service, close, or substantially modify a compressed gas system 3. For additional permit requirements for compressed gases facility closures, see 63.1.2	63.1.2
Construction	For the construction of a building or structure	1.7.11.8
Covered mall buildings	Annual requirement for facilities that utilize mall area for exhibits or displays with 4 conditions	20.1.5.5.1
Crop maze	To operate a crop maze	10.15.11.1
Cryogens	To produce, store, or handle cryogens in excess of amounts listed in Table 1.12.8(c) *Exception: Where federal or state regulations apply or for fuel systems of a vehicle.*	63.1.2
Cutting and welding operation	For operations within a jurisdiction	41.1.5; 41.3.2.2; 41.3.2.2.2
Display fireworks (1.3G)	For possession, transportation, storage, manufacture, sale, handling, and discharge of display fireworks within the jurisdiction	65.2.3; 65.5.2
Drycleaning plants	To engage in business of drycleaning or to change to a more hazardous cleaning solvent	24.2
Dust-producing operations	To operate a grain elevator, flour mill, starch mill, feed mill, or plant pulverizing aluminum, coal, cocoa, magnesium, spices, sugar, or other similar combustible material	40.2
Exhibit and trade shows	For operation of all exhibits and trade shows held within a jurisdiction	20.1.5.5.1
Explosives	1. Manufacture, sell, dispose, purchase, storage, use, possess, or transport of explosives within the jurisdiction 2. For additional permit requirements for blasting operations, see 65.9.2	65.9.2
Fire alarm and detection systems and related equipment	For installation, modification, or removal from service of any fire alarm and detection systems and related equipment*	13.1.1.1
Fire apparatus access roads	For the construction of a fire apparatus access road	18.1.2
Fire hydrants and water-control valves	To use a fire hydrant or operate a water-control valve intended for fire suppression purposes	13.1.1.1
Fire pumps and related equipment	For installation of, modification to, or removal from service of any fire pumps, jockey pumps, controllers, and generators*	13.1.1.1

Table 1.12.8(a) *Continued*

Operations and Materials	Permit Required	Cross Reference Section Number
Flame effects	Use of flame effects before an audience	65.4.2
Flammable and combustible liquids	1. To use or operate, repair, or modify a pipeline for the on-site transportation of flammable or combustible liquids 2. To store, handle, or use Class I liquids in excess of 5 gal (18.9 L) in a building or in excess of 10 gal (37.9 L) outside of a building *Exception to item (2): A permit is not required for the following:* *(a) The storage or use of Class I liquids in the fuel tank of a motor vehicle, aircraft, motorboat, mobile power plant, or mobile heating plant unless such storage in the opinion of the chief would cause an unsafe condition* *(b) The storage or use of paints, oils, varnishes, or similar flammable mixtures when such liquids are stored for maintenance, painting, or similar purposes for a period of not more than 30 days* 3. To store, handle, or use Class II or Class III-A liquids in excess of 25 gal (94.6 L) in a building or in excess of 60 gal (227.1 L) outside a building *Exception to item (3): Fuel oil used in connection with oil-burning equipment* 4. To remove Class I or Class II liquids from an underground storage tank used for fueling motor vehicles by any means other than the approved, stationary on-site pumps normally used for dispensing purposes 5. To install, construct, alter, or operate tank vehicles, equipment, tanks, plants, terminals, wells, fuel-dispensing stations, refineries, distilleries, and similar facilities where flammable and combustible liquids are produced, processed, transported, stored, dispensed, or used 6. To install, alter, clean, repair, line with a protective coating, remove, abandon, place temporarily out of service, or otherwise dispose of a flammable or combustible liquid tank 7. To change the type of contents stored in a flammable or combustible liquid tank to a material other than those for which the tank was designed and constructed	66.1.5
Fruit ripening	To operate a fruit-ripening process	63.1.2
General storage	To store materials indoors or outdoors, representing a broad range of combustibles, including plastics, rubber tires, and roll paper	34.1.2
Grandstands, bleachers, and folding and telescopic seating	For construction, location, erection, or placement of grandstands, bleachers, and folding and telescopic seating	25.1.2
Hazardous materials	1. To store, transport on site, dispense, use, or handle hazardous materials in excess of the amounts listed in Table 1.12.8(d) 2. To install, repair, abandon, remove, place temporarily out of service, close, or substantially modify a storage facility or other area regulated by Chapter 60 when the hazardous materials in use or storage exceed the amounts listed in Table 1.12.8(d)	Chapter 60
High-piled combustible storage	To use any building or portion thereof as a high-piled storage area exceeding 500 ft² (46.45 m²)	20.15.8.2
High-powered rocketry	For the manufacture, sale, and use of high-powered rocketry	65.8.2; 65.7.2
Hot work operations	To conduct hot work	17.3.2; 41.1.5; 41.3.4
Industrial ovens and furnaces	For operation of industrial ovens and furnaces covered by Chapter 51	51.1.2
Laboratories	For construction, alteration, or operation	26.3
Liquefied petroleum gases	1. To store, use, handle, or dispense LP-Gas of 125 gal (0.5 m³) (water capacity) aggregate capacity or greater	42.11.2.2.4
	2. To install or modify LP-Gas systems	69.1.2

(continues)

Table 1.12.8(a) *Continued*

Operations and Materials	Permit Required	Cross Reference Section Number
Liquid- or gas-fueled vehicles	To display, compete, or demonstrate liquid- or gas-fueled vehicles or equipment in assembly buildings	20.1.5.5.1
Lumberyards and woodworking plants	For storage of lumber exceeding 100,000 board ft	31.2
Marine craft fuel servicing	To provide marine craft fuel servicing	42.9.1.4
Means of egress	For the modification of a means of egress system in an existing building	1.7.11.6
Membrane structures, tents, and canopies — permanent	For construction, location, erection, or placement	25.1.2
Membrane structures, tents, and canopies — temporary	To erect or operate an air-supported temporary membrane structure or tent having an area in excess of 200 ft^2 (18.6 m^2) or a canopy in excess of 400 ft^2 (37.2 m^2) *Exception: Temporary membrane structures, tents, or canopy structures used exclusively for camping.*	25.1.2
Motion picture and television production studio soundstages and approved production facilities	To design, construct, operate, and maintain soundstages and approved production facilities used in motion picture and television industry productions	32.2
Oil- and gas-fueled heating appliances	To install oil- and gas-fired heating appliances	11.5.1.8
Open burning	1. To conduct open burning 2. For additional permit requirements for open burning, see 10.11.1	10.11.1
Open fires	1. For kindling or maintaining an open fire 2. For additional permit requirements for open fires, see 10.11.4[†]	10.11.1
Organic coatings	For operation and maintenance of a facility that manufactures organic coatings	43.1.1.4
Organic peroxide formulations	To store, transport on site, use, or handle materials in excess of amounts listed in Tables 1.12.8(c) and (d)	Chapter 75
Outside storage of tires	To store more than 500 tires outside	33.1.2
Oxidizers	To store, transport on site, use, or handle materials in excess of amounts listed in Tables 1.12.8(c) and (d)	Chapter 70
Parade floats	To use a parade float for public performance, presentation, spectacle, entertainment, or parade	10.17.1
Places of assembly	To operate a place of assembly	10.15.1; 20.1.1.1
Pyrotechnic articles	For the manufacture, storage, sale, or use of pyrotechnic articles within the jurisdiction	65.2.3; 65.3.3; 65.5.2
Pyrotechnics before a proximate audience	For the display and use of pyrotechnic materials before a proximate audience	65.3.3
Pyroxylin plastics	For storage, handling, assembly, or manufacture of pyroxylin plastics	43.1.1.4
Private fire hydrants	For installation, modification, or removal from service of any private fire hydrants	13.1.1.1

Table 1.12.8(a) *Continued*

Operations and Materials	Permit Required	Cross Reference Section Number
Refrigeration equipment	To install or operate a mechanical refrigeration unit or system regulated by this *Code*	53.1.3
Repair garages and service stations	For operation of service stations and repair garages	30.1.1.3; 30.2.1.1
Rocketry manufacturing	For the manufacture of model rocket motors	65.7.2
Rooftop heliports	For construction, modification, or operation of a rooftop heliport	21.3.2.1
Solvent extraction	For storage, use, and handling	44.3
Spraying or dipping of flammable finish	For installation or modification of any spray room, spray booth, or preparation work station, or to conduct a spraying or dipping operation utilizing flammable or combustible liquids or powder coating	43.1.1.4
Standpipe systems	For installation, modification, or removal from service of any standpipe system*	13.1.1.1
Special outdoor events	For the location and operation of special outdoor events	10.15.1
Tar kettles	To place a tar kettle, a permit must be obtained prior to the placement of a tar kettle	16.7.1.2; 17.3.2
Tire storage	To use an open area or portion thereof to store tires in excess of 500 tires	33.1.2; 34.1.2
Torch-applied roofing operation	For the use of a torch for application of roofing materials	16.6.1
Water supply system for fire flow	For the construction of a water supply system for fire flow	18.1.2
Wildland fire–prone areas	For use of hazardous areas within fire-prone areas	17.3.2
Wood products	To store wood chips, hogged material, wood by-products, lumber, or plywood in excess of 200 ft^3 (5.7 m^3)	31.2

*Maintenance performed in accordance with this *Code* is not considered a modification and does not require a permit.
†Cooking and recreational fires are exempt an6d do not require a permit.

Table 1.12.8(b) Permit Amounts for Compressed Gases

Type of Gas	Amount* ft^3	Amount* m^3
Corrosive	200	0.57
Flammable	200	0.57
Highly toxic	Any amount	
Inert and simple asphyxiant	6000	169.9
Oxidizing (including oxygen)	504	14.3
Pyrophoric	Any amount	
Toxic	Any amount	
Unstable (reactive)	Any amount	

Note: See Chapters 41, 42, 60, 63, and 69 for additional requirements and exceptions.
*Cubic feet measured at normal temperature and pressure.

Table 1.12.8(c) Permit Amounts for Cryogens

Type of Cryogen	Inside Building (gal)	Outside Building (gal)
Corrosive	Over 1	Over 1
Flammable	Over 1	60
Toxic/highly toxic	Over 1	Over 1
Nonflammable	60	500
Oxidizer (includes oxygen)	10	50

Note: See Chapter 63.

Table 1.12.8(d) Permit Amounts for Hazardous Materials

Type of Material	Amount U.S. Unit	Amount Metric Unit
Cellulose nitrate	25 lb	11.3 kg
Combustible fiber	100 ft^3	2.8 m^3
Combustible liquids	See Table 1.12.8(a)	
Corrosive gases	See Table 1.12.8(b)	
Corrosive liquids	55 gal	208 L
Corrosive solids	500 lb	227 kg
Cryogens	See Table 1.12.8(c)	
Display fireworks (1.3G)	Any amount	
Explosives	Any amount	
Flammable gases	See Table 1.12.8(b)	
Flammable liquids	See Table 1.12.8(a)	
Flammable solids	100 lb	45.4 kg
Highly toxic gases	See Table 1.12.8(b)	
Highly toxic liquids	Any amount	
Highly toxic solids	Any amount	
LP-Gas	See Table 1.12.8(b)	
Nitrate film (cellulose)	Any amount	
Organic peroxides:	See Table 1.12.8(a)	
Class I	Any amount	
Class II	Any amount	
Class III	10 lb	4.5 kg
Class IV	20 lb	9 kg
Class V	Not required	
Unclassified detonatable	Any amount	
Oxidizing gases	See Table 1.12.8(b)	
Oxidizing liquids:	See Table 1.12.8(a)	
Class 4	Any amount	
Class 3	1 gal	3.8 L
Class 2	10 gal	38 L
Class 1	55 gal	208 L
Oxidizing solids:	See Table 1.12.8(a)	
Class 4	Any amount	
Class 3	10 lb	4.5 kg
Class 2	100 lb	45 kg
Class 1	500 lb	227 kg
Pyrophoric gases	See Table 1.12.8(b)	
Pyrophoric liquids	Any amount	
Pyrophoric solids	Any amount	
Toxic gases	See Table 1.12.8(b)	
Toxic liquids	10 gal	38 L
Toxic solids	100 lb	45 kg
Unstable (reactive) gases	See Table 1.12.8(b)	
Unstable (reactive) liquids:		
Class 4	Any amount	
Class 3	Any amount	
Class 2	5 gal	19 L
Class 1	10 gal	38 L
Unstable (reactive) solids:		
Class 4	Any amount	
Class 3	Any amount	
Class 2	50 lb	22.7 kg
Class 1	100 lb	45 kg
Water reactive liquids:		
Class 3	Any amount	
Class 2	5 gal	19 L
Class 1	10 gal	38 L
Water reactive solids:		
Class 3	Any amount	
Class 2	50 lb	22.7 kg
Class 1	100 lb	45 kg

Note: See Chapter 60 for additional requirements and exceptions.

1.13 Certificates of Fitness.

1.13.1 Authorization. The AHJ shall have the authority to require certificates of fitness and collect fees for individuals or companies performing any of the following activities:

(1) Inspection, servicing, or recharging of portable fire extinguishers
(2) Installation, servicing, modification, or recharging of fixed fire extinguishing systems
(3) Installation, servicing, or modification of fire alarm or fire communication systems
(4) Installation, modification, or servicing of gas- or oil-burning heating systems
(5) Chimney sweep operations
(6) Installation, inspection, servicing, or modification of range-hood systems
(7) Installation or servicing of private fire service mains and their appurtenances
(8) Crowd management services required by the *Code*
(9) Utilization of pyrotechnics before a proximate audience
(10) Installation, modification, or maintenance of liquefied petroleum gas or liquefied natural gas tanks or systems
(11) Installation or modification of medical gas systems where a permit is required by Table 1.12.8(a)
(12) Installation, modification, or maintenance of standpipe systems
(13) Installation, modification, or maintenance of automatic sprinkler systems
(14) Installation, modification, or maintenance of fire pumps
(15) Installation, modification, or maintenance of tanks, wells, or drafting points used for fire protection water supplies

1.13.2 Mandatory. The AHJ shall require certificates of fitness and collect fees for individuals or companies performing any of the following activities:

(1) Use of explosive materials
(2) Fireworks displays involving display fireworks, 1.3G

1.13.3 The AHJ shall be responsible for the issuance of certificates of fitness required by the AHJ.

1.13.4 All applications for a certificate of fitness shall be filed with the AHJ on forms provided by the AHJ.

1.13.5 Certification of Applicant.

1.13.5.1 Every individual or company applying for a certificate of fitness shall furnish to the AHJ evidence of a familiarity with applicable codes, regulations, standards, listings, guidelines, and construction and safety practices for the activity for which the certificate of fitness is issued.

1.13.5.2* The AHJ shall also utilize certification programs provided by national organizations acceptable to the AHJ, where available, to determine evidence of compliance with 1.13.5.1.

1.13.5.3 The AHJ shall investigate every application for a certificate of fitness.

1.13.5.4* The investigation shall include an examination of the applicant's experience and training in the field of the certificate of fitness for which application has been made.

1.13.5.5 When the AHJ determines that an applicant is not fit to receive the certificate of fitness because of the applicant's inability to comply with the provisions of this *Code*, the AHJ shall refuse to issue the certificate of fitness.

1.13.5.6 If the refusal is based on the applicant's inability to pass an examination given to determine competency, the applicant shall not be permitted to apply again for the certificate of fitness within a 10-day period following the examination.

1.13.6 Certificates of fitness shall not be transferable.

1.13.7 Certificates of fitness shall be issued for the period of time as indicated on the certificate of fitness as determined by the AHJ, but such period of time shall not exceed 3 years.

1.13.8 Applications for renewal of a certificate of fitness shall be filed in the same manner as an application for an original certificate.

1.13.9 Each individual or company holding a certificate of fitness shall notify the AHJ in writing of any address change within 10 days after such change.

1.13.10 A certificate of fitness shall be in the form of an identification card. The card shall contain the following information:

(1) Purpose for which the certificate of fitness is issued
(2) Date of expiration
(3) Information necessary to easily identify the individual to whom the certificate of fitness is issued
(4) Signature of the individual to whom the certificate of fitness is issued
(5) Name and signature of the AHJ or a designated representative
(6) Statement printed thereon in bold type the following: THIS CERTIFICATE IS NOT AN ENDORSEMENT OF THIS INDIVIDUAL OR COMPANY BY THE AUTHORITY HAVING JURISDICTION.

1.13.11 Any individual or company to whom a certificate of fitness has been granted shall, upon request, produce and show proper identification and the certificate of fitness to anyone for whom that individual seeks to render services or to the AHJ.

1.13.12 Revocation or Suspension of Certificates of Fitness.

1.13.12.1 The AHJ shall be permitted to revoke or suspend a certificate of fitness issued if any violation of this *Code* is found upon inspection or where any false statements or misrepresentations are submitted in the application on which the approval was based.

1.13.12.2 Revocation or suspension shall be constituted when notification is served, posted, or mailed to the address of record for the certificate holder.

1.13.12.3 Failure on the part of an individual to give such notification of a change of address required by 1.13.9 shall constitute grounds for revocation of the certificate of fitness.

1.13.12.4 Revocations or suspensions of a certificate of fitness by the AHJ are appealable to the Board of Appeals as established in Section 1.10.

1.14 Plan Review.

1.14.1 Where required by the AHJ for new construction, modification, or rehabilitation, construction documents and shop drawings shall be submitted, reviewed, and approved prior to the start of such work as provided in Section 1.14.

1.14.2 The applicant shall be responsible to ensure that the following conditions are met:

(1) The construction documents include all of the fire protection requirements.
(2) The shop drawings are correct and in compliance with the applicable codes and standards.
(3) The contractor maintains an approved set of construction documents on site.

1.14.3 It shall be the responsibility of the AHJ to promulgate rules that cover the following:

(1) Criteria to meet the requirements of Section 1.14
(2) Review of documents and construction documents within established time frames for the purpose of acceptance or providing reasons for nonacceptance

1.14.4 Review and approval by the AHJ shall not relieve the applicant of the responsibility of compliance with this *Code*.

1.14.5 When required by the AHJ, revised construction documents or shop drawings shall be prepared and submitted for review and approval to illustrate corrections or modifications necessitated by field conditions or other revisions to approved plans.

1.15 Technical Assistance.

1.15.1 The AHJ shall be permitted to require a review by an approved independent third party with expertise in the matter to be reviewed at the submitter's expense.

1.15.2 The independent reviewer shall provide an evaluation and recommend necessary changes of the proposed design, operation, process, or new technology to the AHJ.

1.15.3 The AHJ shall be authorized to require design submittals to bear the stamp of a registered design professional.

1.15.4 The AHJ shall make the final determination as to whether the provisions of this *Code* have been met.

1.16 Notice of Violations and Penalties.

1.16.1 Where Required. Whenever the AHJ determines violations of this *Code*, a written notice shall be issued to confirm such findings.

1.16.2 Serving Notice of Violation.

1.16.2.1 Any order or notice of violation issued pursuant to this *Code* shall be served upon the owner, operator, occupant, registered agent, or other person responsible for the condition or violation by one of the following means:

(1) Personal service
(2) Mail to last known address of the owner, operator, or registered agent

1.16.2.2 For unattended or abandoned locations, a copy of such order or notice of violation shall be posted on the premises in a conspicuous place at or near the entrance to such premises, and the order or notice shall be disseminated in accordance with one of the following:

(1) Mailed to the last known address of the owner, occupant, or registered agent
(2) Published in a newspaper of general circulation wherein the property in violation is located

1.16.2.3 Refusal of an owner, occupant, operator, or other person responsible for the violation to accept the violation notice shall not be cause to invalidate the violation or the notice of violation. When acceptance of a notice of violation is refused, valid notice shall have deemed to have been served under this section provided the methods of service in 1.16.2.1 or 1.16.2.2 have been followed.

1.16.3 Destruction or Removal of Notice. The mutilation, destruction, or removal of a posted order or violation notice without authorization by the AHJ shall be a separate violation of this *Code* and punishable by the penalties established by the AHJ.

1.16.4 Penalties.

1.16.4.1 Any person who fails to comply with the provisions of this *Code*, fails to carry out an order made pursuant to this *Code*, or violates any condition attached to a permit, approval, or certificate shall be subject to the penalties established by the AHJ.

1.16.4.2 Where the AHJ establishes a separate penalty schedule, violations of this *Code* shall be subject to a $250.00 penalty.

1.16.4.3 Failure to comply with the time limits of an order or notice of violation issued by the AHJ shall result in each day that the violation continues being regarded as a separate offense and shall be subject to a separate penalty.

1.16.4.4 A separate notice of violation shall not be required to be served each day for a violation to be deemed a separate offense.

1.16.5 Abatement. Where a violation creates an imminent danger, the AHJ is authorized to abate such hazard in accordance with 1.7.16.

Chapter 2   Referenced Publications

2.1 General. The documents referenced in this chapter or portions of such documents are referenced within this Code and shall be considered part of the requirements of this document.

(1)*Documents referenced in this chapter or portion of such documents shall only be applicable to the extent called for within other chapters of this *Code*.
(2) Where the requirements of a referenced code or standard differ from the requirements of this Code, the requirements of this Code shall govern.

> Sections 2.2 and 2.4 were revised by a tentative interim amendment. (TIA). See page 1.

2.2 NFPA Publications. National Fire Protection Association, 1 Batterymarch Park, Quincy, MA 02169-7471.

NFPA 2, *Hydrogen Technologies Code*, 2011 edition.
NFPA 10, *Standard for Portable Fire Extinguishers*, 2013 edition.
NFPA 11, *Standard for Low-, Medium-, and High-Expansion Foam*, 2010 edition.
NFPA 12, *Standard on Carbon Dioxide Extinguishing Systems*, 2011 edition.
NFPA 12A, *Standard on Halon 1301 Fire Extinguishing Systems*, 2009 edition.
NFPA 13, *Standard for the Installation of Sprinkler Systems*, 2013 edition.
NFPA 13D, *Standard for the Installation of Sprinkler Systems in One- and Two-Family Dwellings and Manufactured Homes*, 2013 edition.
NFPA 13R, *Standard for the Installation of Sprinkler Systems in Low-Rise Residential Occupancies*, 2013 edition.
NFPA 14, *Standard for the Installation of Standpipe and Hose Systems*, 2013 edition.
NFPA 15, *Standard for Water Spray Fixed Systems for Fire Protection*, 2012 edition.
NFPA 16, *Standard for the Installation of Foam-Water Sprinkler and Foam-Water Spray Systems*, 2011 edition.
NFPA 17, *Standard for Dry Chemical Extinguishing Systems*, 2013 edition.
NFPA 17A, *Standard for Wet Chemical Extinguishing Systems*, 2013 edition.
NFPA 20, *Standard for the Installation of Stationary Pumps for Fire Protection*, 2013 edition.
NFPA 22, *Standard for Water Tanks for Private Fire Protection*, 2013 edition.
NFPA 24, *Standard for the Installation of Private Fire Service Mains and Their Appurtenances*, 2013 edition.
NFPA 25, *Standard for the Inspection, Testing, and Maintenance of Water-Based Fire Protection Systems*, 2014 edition.
NFPA 30, *Flammable and Combustible Liquids Code*, 2015 edition.
NFPA 30A, *Code for Motor Fuel Dispensing Facilities and Repair Garages*, 2015 edition.
NFPA 30B, *Code for the Manufacture and Storage of Aerosol Products*, 2015 edition.
NFPA 31, *Standard for the Installation of Oil-Burning Equipment*, 2011 edition.
NFPA 32, *Standard for Drycleaning Plants*, 2011 edition.
NFPA 33, *Standard for Spray Application Using Flammable or Combustible Materials*, 2011 edition.
NFPA 34, *Standard for Dipping, Coating, and Printing Processes Using Flammable or Combustible Liquids*, 2011 edition.
NFPA 35, *Standard for the Manufacture of Organic Coatings*, 2011 edition.
NFPA 36, *Standard for Solvent Extraction Plants*, 2013 edition.
NFPA 37, *Standard for the Installation and Use of Stationary Combustion Engines and Gas Turbines*, 2014 edition.
NFPA 40, *Standard for the Storage and Handling of Cellulose Nitrate Film*, 2011 edition.
NFPA 45, *Standard on Fire Protection for Laboratories Using Chemicals*, 2011 edition.
NFPA 51, *Standard for the Design and Installation of Oxygen–Fuel Gas Systems for Welding, Cutting, and Allied Processes*, 2013 edition.
NFPA 51A, *Standard for Acetylene Cylinder Charging Plants*, 2012 edition.
NFPA 51B, *Standard for Fire Prevention During Welding, Cutting, and Other Hot Work*, 2014 edition.
NFPA 52, *Vehicular Gaseous Fuel Systems Code*, 2013 edition.
NFPA 54, *National Fuel Gas Code*, 2015 edition.
NFPA 55, *Compressed Gases and Cryogenic Fluids Code*, 2013 edition.
NFPA 58, *Liquefied Petroleum Gas Code*, 2014 edition.
NFPA 59, *Utility LP-Gas Plant Code*, 2015 edition.

NFPA 59A, *Standard for the Production, Storage, and Handling of Liquefied Natural Gas (LNG)*, 2013 edition.

NFPA 61, *Standard for the Prevention of Fires and Dust Explosions in Agricultural and Food Processing Facilities*, 2013 edition.

NFPA 68, *Standard on Explosion Protection by Deflagration Venting*, 2013 edition.

NFPA 69, *Standard on Explosion Prevention Systems*, 2014 edition.

NFPA 70®, *National Electrical Code®*, 2014 edition.

NFPA 72®, *National Fire Alarm and Signaling Code*, 2013 edition.

NFPA 75, *Standard for the Protection of Information Technology Equipment*, 2013 edition.

NFPA 76, *Standard for the Fire Protection of Telecommunications Facilities*, 2012 edition.

NFPA 80, *Standard for Fire Doors and Other Opening Protectives*, 2013 edition.

NFPA 82, *Standard on Incinerators and Waste and Linen Handling Systems and Equipment*, 2014 edition.

NFPA 85, *Boiler and Combustion Systems Hazards Code*, 2011 edition.

NFPA 86, *Standard for Ovens and Furnaces*, 2015 edition.

NFPA 88A, *Standard for Parking Structures*, 2015 edition.

NFPA 90A, *Standard for the Installation of Air-Conditioning and Ventilating Systems*, 2015 edition.

NFPA 90B, *Standard for the Installation of Warm Air Heating and Air-Conditioning Systems*, 2015 edition.

NFPA 91, *Standard for Exhaust Systems for Air Conveying of Vapors, Gases, Mists, and Noncombustible Particulate Solids*, 2010 edition.

NFPA 92, *Standard for Smoke Control Systems*, 2012 edition.

NFPA 96, *Standard for Ventilation Control and Fire Protection of Commercial Cooking Operations*, 2014 edition.

NFPA 99, *Health Care Facilities Code*, 2015 edition.

NFPA 101®, *Life Safety Code®*, 2015 edition.

NFPA 102, *Standard for Grandstands, Folding and Telescopic Seating, Tents, and Membrane Structures*, 2011 edition.

NFPA 105, *Standard for Smoke Door Assemblies and Other Opening Protectives*, 2013 edition.

NFPA 110, *Standard for Emergency and Standby Power Systems*, 2013 edition.

NFPA 111, *Standard on Stored Electrical Energy Emergency and Standby Power Systems*, 2013 edition.

NFPA 120, *Standard for Fire Prevention and Control in Coal Mines*, 2010 edition.

NFPA 122, *Standard for Fire Prevention and Control in Metal/Nonmetal Mining and Metal Mineral Processing Facilities*, 2010 edition.

NFPA 130, *Standard for Fixed Guideway Transit and Passenger Rail Systems*, 2014 edition.

NFPA 140, *Standard on Motion Picture and Television Production Studio Soundstages, Approved Production Facilities, and Production Locations*, 2013 edition.

NFPA 150, *Standard on Fire and Life Safety in Animal Housing Facilities*, 2013 edition.

NFPA 160, *Standard for the Use of Flame Effects Before an Audience*, 2011 edition.

NFPA 170, *Standard for Fire Safety and Emergency Symbols*, 2012 edition.

NFPA 204, *Standard for Smoke and Heat Venting*, 2012 edition.

NFPA 211, *Standard for Chimneys, Fireplaces, Vents, and Solid Fuel-Burning Appliances*, 2013 edition.

NFPA 220, *Standard on Types of Building Construction*, 2015 edition.

NFPA 221, *Standard for High Challenge Fire Walls, Fire Walls, and Fire Barrier Walls*, 2015 edition.

NFPA 232, *Standard for the Protection of Records*, 2012 edition.

NFPA 241, *Standard for Safeguarding Construction, Alteration, and Demolition Operations*, 2013 edition.

NFPA 252, *Standard Methods of Fire Tests of Door Assemblies*, 2012 edition.

NFPA 253, *Standard Method of Test for Critical Radiant Flux of Floor Covering Systems Using a Radiant Heat Energy Source*, 2011 edition.

NFPA 257, *Standard on Fire Test for Window and Glass Block Assemblies*, 2012 edition.

NFPA 259, *Standard Test Method for Potential Heat of Building Materials*, 2013 edition.

NFPA 260, *Standard Methods of Tests and Classification System for Cigarette Ignition Resistance of Components of Upholstered Furniture*, 2013 edition.

NFPA 261, *Standard Method of Test for Determining Resistance of Mock-Up Upholstered Furniture Material Assemblies to Ignition by Smoldering Cigarettes*, 2013 edition.

NFPA 265, *Standard Methods of Fire Tests for Evaluating Room Fire Growth Contribution of Textile or Expanded Vinyl Wall Coverings on Full Height Panels and Walls*, 2011 edition.

NFPA 286, *Standard Methods of Fire Tests for Evaluating Contribution of Wall and Ceiling Interior Finish to Room Fire Growth*, 2011 edition.

NFPA 288, *Standard Methods of Fire Tests of Horizontal Fire Door Assemblies Installed in Horizontal Fire Resistance–Rated Assemblies*, 2012 edition.

NFPA 289, *Standard Method of Fire Test for Individual Fuel Packages*, 2013 edition.

NFPA 302, *Fire Protection Standard for Pleasure and Commercial Motor Craft*, 2015 edition.

NFPA 303, *Fire Protection Standard for Marinas and Boatyards*, 2011 edition.

NFPA 307, *Standard for the Construction and Fire Protection of Marine Terminals, Piers, and Wharves*, 2011 edition.

NFPA 312, *Standard for Fire Protection of Vessels During Construction, Conversion, Repair, and Lay-Up*, 2011 edition.

NFPA 318, *Standard for the Protection of Semiconductor Fabrication Facilities*, 2015 edition.

NFPA 326, *Standard for the Safeguarding of Tanks and Containers for Entry, Cleaning, or Repair*, 2010 edition.

NFPA 385, *Standard for Tank Vehicles for Flammable and Combustible Liquids*, 2012 edition.

NFPA 400, *Hazardous Materials Code*, 2013 edition.

NFPA 407, *Standard for Aircraft Fuel Servicing*, 2012 edition.

NFPA 408, *Standard for Aircraft Hand Portable Fire Extinguishers*, 2010 edition.

NFPA 409, *Standard on Aircraft Hangars*, 2011 edition.

NFPA 410, *Standard on Aircraft Maintenance*, 2010 edition.

NFPA 415, *Standard on Airport Terminal Buildings, Fueling Ramp Drainage, and Loading Walkways*, 2013 edition.

NFPA 418, *Standard for Heliports*, 2011 edition.

NFPA 472, *Standard for Competence of Responders to Hazardous Materials/Weapons of Mass Destruction Incidents*, 2013 edition.

NFPA 484, *Standard for Combustible Metals*, 2015 edition.

NFPA 495, *Explosive Materials Code*, 2013 edition.

NFPA 498, *Standard for Safe Havens and Interchange Lots for Vehicles Transporting Explosives*, 2013 edition.

NFPA 501, *Standard on Manufactured Housing*, 2013 edition.

NFPA 501A, *Standard for Fire Safety Criteria for Manufactured Home Installations, Sites, and Communities*, 2013 edition.

NFPA 505, *Fire Safety Standard for Powered Industrial Trucks Including Type Designations, Areas of Use, Conversions, Maintenance, and Operations*, 2013 edition.

NFPA 601, *Standard for Security Services in Fire Loss Prevention*, 2010 edition.

NFPA 654, *Standard for the Prevention of Fire and Dust Explosions from the Manufacturing, Processing, and Handling of Combustible Particulate Solids*, 2013 edition.

NFPA 655, *Standard for Prevention of Sulfur Fires and Explosions*, 2012 edition.

NFPA 664, *Standard for the Prevention of Fires and Explosions in Wood Processing and Woodworking Facilities*, 2012 edition.

NFPA 701, *Standard Methods of Fire Tests for Flame Propagation of Textiles and Films*, 2010 edition.

NFPA 703, *Standard for Fire Retardant–Treated Wood and Fire-Retardant Coatings for Building Materials*, 2015 edition.

NFPA 704, *Standard System for the Identification of the Hazards of Materials for Emergency Response*, 2012 edition.

NFPA 720, *Standard for the Installation of Carbon Monoxide (CO) Detection and Warning Equipment*, 2015 edition.

NFPA 750, *Standard on Water Mist Fire Protection Systems*, 2014 edition.

NFPA 801, *Standard for Fire Protection for Facilities Handling Radioactive Materials*, 2013 edition.

NFPA 909, *Code for the Protection of Cultural Resource Properties — Museums, Libraries, and Places of Worship*, 2013 edition.

NFPA 914, *Code for Fire Protection of Historic Structures*, 2010 edition.

NFPA 1031, *Standard for Professional Qualifications for Fire Inspector and Plan Examiner*, 2014 edition.

NFPA 1122, *Code for Model Rocketry*, 2013 edition.

NFPA 1125, *Code for the Manufacture of Model Rocket and High Power Rocket Motors*, 2012 edition.

NFPA 1126, *Standard for the Use of Pyrotechnics Before a Proximate Audience*, 2011 edition.

NFPA 1127, *Code for High Power Rocketry*, 2013 edition.

NFPA 1142, *Standard on Water Supplies for Suburban and Rural Fire Fighting*, 2012 edition.

NFPA 1144, *Standard for Reducing Structure Ignition Hazards from Wildland Fire*, 2013 edition.

NFPA 1192, *Standard on Recreational Vehicles*, 2014 edition.

NFPA 1194, *Standard for Recreational Vehicle Parks and Campgrounds*, 2014 edition.

NFPA 1963, *Standard for Fire Hose Connections*, 2014 edition.

NFPA 2001, *Standard on Clean Agent Fire Extinguishing Systems*, 2012 edition.

NFPA 2010, *Standard for Fixed Aerosol Fire Extinguishing Systems*, 2010 edition.

NFPA 2113, *Standard on Selection, Care, Use, and Maintenance of Flame-Resistant Garments for Protection of Industrial Personnel Against Flash Fire*, 2012 edition.

NFPA 5000®, *Building Construction and Safety Code®*, 2015 edition.

2.3 Other Publications.

2.3.1 ANSI Publications.
American National Standards Institute, Inc., 25 West 43rd Street, 4th floor, New York, NY 10036.

ICC/ANSI A117.1 *American National Standard for Accessible and Usable Buildings and Facilities*, 2009.

ANSI/AIHA Z9.7 *Recirculation of Air from Industrial Process Exhaust Systems*, 2007.

ANSI B15.1 *Mechanical Power Transmission Apparatus*, 2000.

2.3.2 APA Publication.
American Pyrotechnics Association, P.O. Box 30438, Bethesda, MD 20824.

APA 87-1, *Standard for the Construction and Approval for Transportation of Fireworks, Novelties, and Theatrical Pyrotechnics*, 2004 edition.

2.3.3 API Publications.
American Petroleum Institute, 1220 L Street, NW, Washington, DC 20005-4070.

API-ASME Code for Unfired Pressure Vessels for Petroleum Liquids and Gases, Pre-July 1, 1961.

API Specification 12B, *Bolted Tanks for Storage of Production Liquids*, 15th edition, 2008.

API Specification 12D, *Field Welded Tanks for Storage of Production Liquids*, 11th edition, 2008.

API Specification 12F, *Shop Welded Tanks for Storage of Production Liquids* 12th edition, 2008.

API 620, *Recommended Rules for the Design and Construction of Large, Welded, Low-Pressure Storage Tanks*, 11th edition, Addendum 2, 2010.

API Standard 650, *Welded Steel Tanks for Oil Storage*, 11th edition, Addendum 2, 2009.

API Standard 653, *Tank Inspection, Repair, Alteration, and Reconstruction*, 4th edition, 2012.

API Standard 2000, *Venting Atmospheric and Low-Pressure Storage Tanks* 5th edition, 1998.

API 2350, *Overfill Protection for Storage Tanks in Petroleum Facilities*, 4th edition, 2012.

API BULL 1529, *Aviation Fueling Hose*, 1998.

API 607, *Fire Test for Soft-Seated Quarter-Turn Valves*, 1993.

2.3.4 ASHRAE Publications.
American Society of Heating, Refrigerating and Air Conditioning Engineers, Inc., 1791 Tullie Circle, NE, Atlanta, GA 30329-2305.

ANSI/ASHRAE 15, *Safety Standard for Refrigeration Systems*, 2010.

2.3.5 ASME Publications.
American Society of Mechanical Engineers, Two Park Avenue, New York, NY 10016-5990.

ASME A13.1, *Scheme for the Identification of Piping Systems*, 2007.

ASME A17.1/CSA B44, *Safety Code for Elevators and Escalators*, 2007.

ASME A17.3, *Safety Code for Existing Elevators and Escalators*, 2008.

ASME B31, *Code for Pressure Piping*, 2012.

ANSI/ASME B31.3, *Process Piping*, 2008.

ASME B56.1, *Safety Standard for Low-Lift and High-Lift Trucks*, 2008.

ASME *Boiler and Pressure Vessel Code*, Section VIII, "Rules for the Construction of Unfired Pressure Vessels," 2010.

ASME *Code for Unfired Pressure Vessels*, 2010.

2.3.6 ASTM Publications.
ASTM International, 100 Barr Harbor Drive, P.O. Box C700, West Conshohocken, PA 19428-2959.

ASTM A 395, *Standard Specification for Ferritic Ductile Iron Pressure-Retaining Castings for Use at Elevated Temperatures*, 1999 (reaffirmed 2009).

ASTM D5/D5M, *Standard Test Method for Penetration of Bituminous Materials*, 2013.

ASTM D 56, *Standard Test Method for Flash Point by Tag Closed Cup Tester*, 2005 (reaffirmed 2010).

ASTM D 92, *Standard Test Method for Flash and Fire Points by Cleveland Open Cup Tester*, 2012b.

ASTM D 93, *Standard Test Methods for Flash Point by Pensky-Martens Closed Cup Tester*, 2012.

ASTM D 323, *Standard Method of Test for Vapor Pressure of Petroleum Products (Reid Method)*, 2008.

ASTM D 396, *Standard Specification for Fuel Oils*, 2010.

ASTM D 635, *Standard Test Method for Rate of Burning and/or Extent and Time of Burning of Plastics in a Horizontal Position*, 2010.

ASTM D 1929, *Standard Test Method for Determining Ignition Temperature of Plastics*, 2012.

ASTM D 2843, *Standard Test Method for Density of Smoke from the Burning or Decomposition of Plastics*, 2010.

ASTM D 2859, *Standard Test Method for Ignition Characteristics of Finished Textile Floor Covering Materials*, 2006 (2011).

ASTM D 2898, *Standard Test Methods for Accelerated Weathering of Fire-Retardant-Treated Wood for Fire Testing*, 2010.

ASTM D 3278, *Standard Test Methods for Flash Point of Liquids by Small Scale Closed-Cup Apparatus*, 1996 (reaffirmed 2011).

ASTM D 3699, *Standard Specification for Kerosene*, 2008.

ASTM D 3828, *Standard Test Methods for Flash Point by Small Scale Closed Cup Tester*, 2012a.

ASTM D 4359, *Standard Test for Determining Whether a Material is a Liquid or a Solid*, 1990 (reaffirmed 2012).

ASTM D 5391, *Standard Test for Electrical Conductivity and Resistivity of a Flowing High Purity Water Sample*, 1999 (2009).

ASTM D 6448, *Industrial Burner Fuels from Used Lube Oils*, 2009.

ASTM D 6751, *Standard Specification for Biodiesel Fuel Blend Stock (B100) for Middle Distillate Fuel*, 2010.

ASTM D 6823, *Commercial Burner Fuels from Used Lube Oils*, 2008.

ASTM E 84, *Standard Test Method for Surface Burning Characteristics of Building Materials*, 2013.

ASTM E 108, *Standard Test Methods for Fire Tests of Roof Coverings*, 2011.

ASTM E 119, *Standard Test Methods for Fire Tests of Building Construction and Materials*, 2012a.

ASTM E 136, *Standard Test Method for Behavior of Materials in a Vertical Tube Furnace at 750 Degrees C*, 2012.

ASTM E 648, *Standard Test Method for Critical Radiant Flux of Floor-Covering Systems Using a Radiant Heat Energy Source*, 2010 e1.

ASTM E 681, *Standard Test Method for Concentration Limits of Flammability of Chemicals (Vapors and Gases)*, 2009.

ASTM E 814, *Standard Test Method for Fire Tests of Through-Penetration Fire Stops*, 2011a.

ASTM E 1354, *Standard Test Method for Heat and Visible Smoke Release Rates for Materials and Products Using an Oxygen Consumption Calorimeter*, 2013.

ASTM E 1537, *Standard Test Method for Fire Testing of Upholstered Furniture*, 2012.

ASTM E 1590, *Standard Test Method for Fire Testing of Mattresses*, 2012.

ASTM E 1591, *Standard Guide for Obtaining Data for Deterministic Fire Models*, 2007.

ASTM E 1966, *Standard Test Method for Fire-Resistive Joint Systems*, 2007 (2011).

ASTM E 2074, *Standard Test Method for Fire Tests of Door Assemblies, Including Positive Pressure Testing of Side-Hinged and Pivoted Swinging Door Assemblies*, 2000e1 (withdrawn 2007).

ASTM E 2174, *Standard Practice for On-Site Inspection of Installed Fire Stops*, 2010a e1.

ASTM E 2307, *Standard Test Method for Determining Fire Resistance of Perimeter Fire Barrier Systems Using Intermediate-Scale, Multi-story Test Apparatus*, 2010.

ASTM E 2393, *Standard Practice for On-Site Inspection of Installed Fire Resistive Joint Systems and Perimeter Fire Barriers*, 2010a.

ASTM E 2404, *Standard Practice for Specimen Preparation and Mounting of Textile, Paper or Polymeric (Including Vinyl) Wall or Ceiling Coverings, and of Facings and Wood Veneers Intended to be Applied on Site Over a Wood Substrate, to Assess Surface Burning Characteristics*, 2012.

ASTM E 2573, *Standard Practice for Specimen Preparation and Mounting of Site-Fabricated Stretch Systems to Assess Surface Burning Characteristics*, 2012.

ASTM E 2599, *Standard Practice for Specimen Preparation and Mounting of Reflective Insulation, Radiant Barrier, and Vinyl Stretch Ceiling Materials for Building Applications to Assess Surface Burning Characteristics*, 2011.

ASTM E 2652, *Standard Test Method for Behavior of Materials in a Tube Furnace with a Cone-Shaped Airflow Stabilizer, at 750 Degrees C*, 2012.

ASTM F 852, *Standard for Portable Gasoline Containers for Consumer Use*, 2008.

ASTM F 976, *Standard for Portable Kerosene Containers for Consumer Use*, 2008.

2.3.7 CGA Publications. Compressed Gas Association, 4221 Walney Road, 5th Floor, Chantilly, VA 20151-2923.

CGA C-7, *Guide to the Preparation of Precautionary Labeling and Marking of Compressed Gas Containers*, 2004.

ANSI/CGA G-13, *Storage and Handling of Silane and Silane Mixtures*, 2006.

CGA M-1, *Guide for Medical Gas Installations at Consumer Sites*, 2007.

CGA P-1, *Safe Handling of Compressed Gases in Containers*, 2008.

ANSI/CGA P-18, *Standard for Bulk Inert Gas Systems at Consumer Sites*, 2006.

CGA P-20, *Standard for the Classification of Toxic Gas Mixtures*, 2009.

CGA P-23, *Standard for Categorizing Gas Mixtures Containing Flammable and Nonflammable Components,* 2008.

CGA S-1.1, *Pressure Relief Device Standards — Part 1 — Cylinders for Compressed Gases,* 2007.

CGA S-1.2, *Pressure Relief Device Standards — Part 2 — Cargo and Portable Tanks for Compressed Gases,* 2009.

CGA S-1.3, *Pressure Relief Device Standards — Part 3 — Stationary Storage Containers for Compressed Gases,* 2008.

CGA-V6, *Standard Cryogenic Liquid Transfer Connections,* 2008.

2.3.8 CTA Publications. Canadian Transportation Agency, Queen's Printer, Ottawa, Ontario, Canada. (Available from the Canadian Communications Group Publication Centre, Ordering Department, Ottawa, Canada K1A 0S9.)

Transportation of Dangerous Goods Regulations.

2.3.9 FM Publications. FM Global, 1301 Atwood Avenue, P.O. Box 7500, Johnston, RI 02919.

Approval Standard for Safety Containers and Filling, Supply, and Disposal Containers — Class Number 6051 and 6052, May 1976.

ANSI/FM 4880, *American National Standard for Evaluating Insulated Wall or Wall and Roof/Ceiling Assemblies, Plastic Interior Finish Materials, Plastic Exterior Building Panels, Wall/Ceiling Coating Systems, Interior or Exterior Finish Systems,* 2007.

Approval Standard for Plastic Plugs for Steel Drums, Class Number 6083, October 2006.

Approval Standard 6921, Containers for Combustible Waste, 2004.

2.3.10 IEC Publication. International Electrotechnical Commission, 3, rue de Varembé, P.O. Box 131, CH-1211 Geneva 20, Switzerland.

IEC 61340-4-4, *Electrostatics — Part 4-4: Standard Test Methods for Specific Applications — Electrostatic Classification of Flexible Intermediate Bulk Containers (FIBC),* 2005.

2.3.11 IIAR Publications. International Institute of Ammonia Refrigeration, 1001 N. Fairfax Street, Suite 503, Alexandria, VA 22314.

ANSI/IIAR 2, *Equipment, Design, and Installation of Closed-Circuit Ammonia Mechanical Refrigerating Systems,* 2008.

ANSI/IIAR 7, *Developing Operating Procedures for Closed-Circuit Ammonia Mechanical Refrigerating Systems,* 2013.

2.3.12 ISO Publications. International Organization for Standardization, 1, ch. de la Voie-Creuse, Case postale 56, CH-1211 Geneve 20, Switzerland.

ISO 10156, *Gases and gas mixtures — Determination of fire potential and oxidizing ability for the selection of cylinder valve outlets,* 2010.

ISO 10298, *Determination of toxicity of a gas or gas mixture,* 2010.

2.3.13 NBBPVI Publications. National Board of Boiler and Pressure Vessel Inspectors, 1055 Crupper Avenue, Columbus, OH 43229.

ANSI/NB23, *National Board Inspection Code,* 2007.

2.3.14 NRFC Publications. National Railroad Freight Committee, 222 South Riverside Plaza, Chicago, IL 60606-5945.

Uniform Freight Classification (UFC), 2005.

2.3.15 RVIA Publications. Recreation Vehicle Industry Association, 1896 Preston White Drive, P.O. Box 2999, Reston, VA 20195-0999.

RVIA/ANSI A119.5, *Standard for Recreational Park Trailers,* 2009.

2.3.16 STI Publications. Steel Tank Institute, 570 Oakwood Road, Lake Zurich, IL 60047.

STI SP001, *Standard for the Inspection of Aboveground Storage Tanks,* 5th edition, 2011.

2.3.17 UL Publications. Underwriters Laboratories Inc., 333 Pfingsten Road, Northbrook, IL 60062-2096.

ANSI/UL 8, *Standard for Water Based Agent Fire Extinguishers,* 2005, Revised 2009.

ANSI/UL 9, *Standard for Fire Tests of Window Assemblies,* 2009.

ANSI/UL 10B, *Standard for Fire Tests of Door Assemblies,* 2008, Revised 2009.

ANSI/UL 10C, *Standard for Positive Pressure Fire Tests of Door Assemblies,* 2009.

ANSI/UL 30, *Standard for Metal Safety Cans,* 1995, Revised 2009.

UL 58, *Standard for Steel Underground Tanks for Flammable and Combustible Liquids,* 1996, Revised 1998.

ANSI/UL 80, *Standard for Steel Tanks for Oil Burner Fuels and Other Combustible Liquids,* 2007, Revised 2009.

ANSI/UL 142, *Standard for Steel Aboveground Tanks for Flammable and Combustible Liquids,* 2006, Revised 2010.

ANSI/UL 147A, *Standard for Nonrefillable (Disposable) Type Fuel Gas Cylinder Assemblies,* 2005, Revised 2009.

ANSI/UL 147B, *Standard for Nonrefillable (Disposable) Type Metal Container Assemblies for Butane,* 2005, Revised 2008.

ANSI/UL 154, *Standard for Carbon Dioxide Fire Extinguishers,* 2005, Revised 2009.

UL 162, *Standard for Safety for Foam Equipment and Liquid Concentrates,* 1994.

ANSI/UL 197, *Standard for Commercial Electric Cooking Appliances,* 2010, Revised 2011.

ANSI/UL 263, *Standard for Fire Tests of Building Construction and Materials,* 2011.

ANSI/UL 294, *Standard for Access Control System Units,* 1999, Revised 2010.

ANSI/UL 296A, *Standard for Waste Oil-Burning Air-Heating Appliances,* 2010.

ANSI/UL 299, *Standard for Dry Chemical Fire Extinguishers,* 2012.

ANSI/UL 300, *Standard for Fire Testing of Fire Extinguishing Systems for Protection of Restaurant Cooking Areas,* 2005, Revised 2010.

ANSI/UL 340, *Test for Comparative Flammability of Liquids,* 2009.

ANSI/UL 499, *Standard for Electric Heating Appliances,* 2005.

ANSI/UL 555, *Standard for Fire Dampers,* 2006, Revised 2012.

ANSI/UL 555S, *Standard for Smoke Dampers,* 1999, Revised 2012.

ANSI/UL 567, *Standard for Emergency Breakaway Fittings, Swivel Connectors and Pipe Connection Fittings for Petroleum Products and LP-Gas*, 2003, Revised 2011.

ANSI/UL 626, *Standard for Water Fire Extinguishers*, 2005, Revised 2012.

ANSI/UL 710B, *Standard for Recirculating Exhaust Systems*, 2004, Revised 2009.

ANSI/UL 711, *Standard for Rating and Fire Testing of Fire Extinguishers*, 2004, Revised 2009.

ANSI/UL 723, *Standard for Test for Surface Burning Characteristics of Building Materials*, 2008, Revised 2010.

ANSI/UL 790, *Standard for Safety for Tests for Fire Resistance of Roof Covering Materials*, 2004, Revised 2008.

ANSI/UL 842, *Standard for Valves for Flammable Fluids*, 2007, Revised 2011.

ANSI/UL 900, *Standard for Air Filter Units*, 2004, Revised 2009.

ANSI/UL 913, *Standard for Intrinsically Safe Apparatus and Associated Apparatus for Use in Class I, II, and III Division 1, Hazardous (Classified) Locations*, 2006, Revised 2010.

ANSI/UL 924, *Standard for Emergency Lighting and Power Equipment*, 2006, Revised 2011.

UL 971, *Standard for Nonmetallic Underground Piping for Flammable Liquids*, 1995, Revised 2006.

ANSI/UL 1037, *Standard for Antitheft Alarms and Devices*, 1999, Revised 2009.

ANSI/UL 1040, *Standard for Fire Test of Insulated Wall Construction*, 1996, Revised 2007.

ANSI/UL 1313, *Standard for Nonmetallic Safety Cans for Petroleum Products*, 1993, Revised 2007.

UL 1316, *Standard for Glass-Fiber Reinforced Plastic Underground Storage Tanks for Petroleum Products, Alcohols, and Alcohol-Gasoline Mixtures*, 2006.

UL 1479, *Standard for Fire Tests of Through-Penetration Firestops*, 2003, Revised 2010.

UL 1573, *Standard for Stage and Studio Luminaires and Connector Strips*, 2003.

UL 1640, *Standard for Portable Power-Distribution Equipment*, 2007.

ANSI/UL 1715, *Standard for Fire Test of Interior Finish Material*, 1997, Revised 2008.

ANSI/UL 1746, *Standard for External Corrosion Protection Systems for Steel Underground Storage Tanks*, 2007.

UL 1803, *Standard for Factory Follow-up on Third Party Certified Portable Fire Extinguishers*, 2012.

UL 1975, *Standard for Fire Tests for Foamed Plastics Used for Decorative Purposes*, 2006.

ANSI/UL 1994, *Standard for Luminous Egress Path Marking Systems*, 2004, Revised 2010.

UL 2079, *Standard for Tests for Fire Resistance of Building Joint Systems*, 2004, Revised 2008.

UL 2080, *Standard for Fire Resistant Tanks for Flammable and Combustible Liquids*, 2000.

ANSI/UL 2085, *Standard for Protected Aboveground Tanks for Flammable and Combustible Liquids*, 1997, Revised 2010.

ANSI/UL 2129, *Standard for Halocarbon Clean Agent Fire Extinguishers*, 2005, Revised 2012.

ANSI/UL 2208, *Standard for Solvent Distillation Units*, 2005, Revised 2011.

UL 2245, *Standard for Below-Grade Vaults for Flammable Liquid Storage Tanks*, 2006.

UL 2368, *Standard for Fire Exposure Testing of Intermediate Bulk Containers for Flammable and Combustible Liquids*, 2012.

ANSI/UL 2586, *Standard for Hose Nozzle Valves*, 2011, Revised 2012.

2.3.18 ULC Publications. Underwriters' Laboratories of Canada, 7 Underwriters Road, Toronto, Ontario M1R 3B4, Canada.

CAN/ULC-S503, *Standard for Carbon-Dioxide Fire Extinguishers*, 2005, Revised 2010.

CAN/ULC-S504, *Standard for Dry Chemical Fire Extinguishers*, 2002, Revised 2009.

CAN/ULC-S507, *Standard for Water Fire Extinguishers*, 2005, Revised 2010.

CAN/ULC-S508, *Standard for Rating and Testing of Fire Extinguishers and Fire Extinguishing Agents*, 2004, Revised 2009.

CAN/ULC-S512, *Standard for Halogenated Agent Hand and Wheeled Fire Extinguishers*, 2007.

CAN/ULC-S554, *Standard for Water Based Agent Fire Extinguishers*, 2005, Reaffirmed 2010.

CAN/ULC-S566, *Standard for Halocarbon Clean Agent Fire Extinguishers*, 2005, Revised 2007.

2.3.19 UN Publications. United Nations Headquarters, New York, NY 10017.

Recommendations on the Transport of Dangerous Goods, 17th revised edition, 2011.

2.3.20 U.S. Government Publications. U.S. Government Printing Office, Washington, DC 20402.

FAAA/C 150/5390-2B, *Heliport Design Advisory Circular*, September 30, 2004.

Interstate Commerce Commission (ICC), *Rules for Construction of Unfired Pressure Vessels*, U.S. Department of Transportation, Washington, DC.

Title 16, Code of Federal Regulations, Part 1632, "Standard for the Flammability of Mattresses and Mattress Pads," January 1, 1990.

Title 18, United States Code, "Importation, Manufacture, Distribution and Storage of Explosive Materials," 1970.

Title 21, Code of Federal Regulations, Part 210, "Processing, Packing, or Holding Drugs; General."

Title 21, Code of Federal Regulations, Part 211, "Current Good Manufacturing Practice for Finished Pharmaceuticals."

Title 27, Code of Federal Regulations, Part 555, Bureau of Alcohol, Tobacco, Firearms, and Explosives, U.S. Department of Justice.

Title 29, Code of Federal Regulations, Parts 1910.1000 and 1910.1200, "Hazard Communication," U.S. Department of Labor.

Title 49, Code of Federal Regulations, Part 100 to end, U.S. Department of Transportation.

2.3.21 Other Publications.

Merriam-Webster's Collegiate Dictionary, 11th edition, Merriam-Webster, Inc., Springfield, MA, 2003.

2.4 References for Extracts in Mandatory Sections.

NFPA 10, *Standard for Portable Fire Extinguishers*, 2013 edition.

NFPA 13, *Standard for the Installation of Sprinkler Systems*, 2013 edition.

NFPA 14, *Standard for the Installation of Standpipe and Hose Systems*, 2013 edition.

NFPA 20, *Standard for the Installation of Stationary Pumps for Fire Protection*, 2013 edition.

NFPA 25, *Standard for the Inspection, Testing, and Maintenance of Water-Based Fire Protection Systems*, 2014 edition.

NFPA 30, *Flammable and Combustible Liquids Code*, 2015 edition.

NFPA 30A, *Code for Motor Fuel Dispensing Facilities and Repair Garages*, 2015 edition.

NFPA 30B, *Code for the Manufacture and Storage of Aerosol Products*, 2015 edition.

NFPA 31, *Standard for the Installation of Oil-Burning Equipment*, 2011 edition.

NFPA 33, *Standard for Spray Application Using Flammable or Combustible Materials*, 2011 edition.

NFPA 34, *Standard for Dipping, Coating, and Printing Processes Using Flammable or Combustible Liquids*, 2011 edition.

NFPA 45, *Standard on Fire Protection for Laboratories Using Chemicals*, 2011 edition.

NFPA 51B, *Standard for Fire Prevention During Welding, Cutting, and Other Hot Work*, 2014 edition.

NFPA 52, *Vehicular Gaseous Fuel Systems Code*, 2013 edition.

NFPA 55, *Compressed Gases and Cryogenic Fluids Code*, 2013 edition.

NFPA 58, *Liquefied Petroleum Gas Code*, 2014 edition.

NFPA 59A, *Standard for the Production, Storage, and Handling of Liquefied Natural Gas (LNG)*, 2013 edition.

NFPA 61, *Standard for the Prevention of Fires and Dust Explosions in Agricultural and Food Processing Facilities*, 2013 edition.

NFPA 68, *Standard on Explosion Protection by Deflagration Venting*, 2013 edition.

NFPA 69, *Standard on Explosion Prevention Systems*, 2014 edition.

NFPA 70®, National Electrical Code®, 2014 edition.

NFPA 72®, National Fire Alarm and Signaling Code, 2013 edition.

NFPA 80, *Standard for Fire Doors and Other Opening Protectives*, 2013 edition.

NFPA 88A, *Standard for Parking Structures*, 2015 edition.

NFPA 90A, *Standard for the Installation of Air-Conditioning and Ventilating Systems*, 2015 edition.

NFPA 96, *Standard for Ventilation Control and Fire Protection of Commercial Cooking Operations*, 2014 edition.

NFPA 101®, Life Safety Code®, 2015 edition.

NFPA 102, *Standard for Grandstands, Folding and Telescopic Seating, Tents, and Membrane Structures*, 2011 edition.

NFPA 140, *Standard on Motion Picture and Television Production Studio Soundstages, Approved Production Facilities, and Production Locations*, 2013 edition.

NFPA 211, *Standard for Chimneys, Fireplaces, Vents, and Solid Fuel–Burning Appliances*, 2013 edition.

NFPA 220, *Standard on Types of Building Construction*, 2015 edition.

NFPA 241, *Standard for Safeguarding Construction, Alteration, and Demolition Operations*, 2013 edition.

NFPA 303, *Fire Protection Standard for Marinas and Boatyards*, 2011 edition.

NFPA 307, *Standard for the Construction and Fire Protection of Marine Terminals, Piers, and Wharves*, 2011 edition.

NFPA 312, *Standard for Fire Protection of Vessels During Construction, Conversion, Repair, and Lay-Up*, 2011 edition.

NFPA 318, *Standard for the Protection of Semiconductor Fabrication Facilities*, 2015 edition.

NFPA 400, *Hazardous Materials Code*, 2013 edition.

NFPA 402, *Guide for Aircraft Rescue and Fire-Fighting Operations*, 2013 edition.

NFPA 407, *Standard for Aircraft Fuel Servicing*, 2012 edition.

NFPA 415, *Standard on Airport Terminal Buildings, Fueling Ramp Drainage, and Loading Walkways*, 2013 edition.

NFPA 418, *Standard for Heliports*, 2011 edition.

NFPA 472, *Standard for Competence of Responders to Hazardous Materials/Weapons of Mass Destruction Incidents*, 2013 edition.

NFPA 654, *Standard for the Prevention of Fire and Dust Explosions from the Manufacturing, Processing, and Handling of Combustible Particulate Solids*, 2013 edition.

NFPA 805, *Performance-Based Standard for Fire Protection for Light Water Reactor Electric Generating Plants*, 2010 edition.

NFPA 914, *Code for Fire Protection of Historic Structures*, 2010 edition.

NFPA 1031, *Standard for Professional Qualifications for Fire Inspector and Plan Examiner*, 2014 edition.

NFPA 1141, *Standard for Fire Protection Infrastructure for Land Development in Wildland, Rural, and Suburban Areas*, 2012 edition.

NFPA 1144, *Standard for Reducing Structure Ignition Hazards from Wildland Fire*, 2013 edition.

NFPA 5000®, Building Construction and Safety Code®, 2015 edition.

> Multiple definitions in Chapter 3 were deleted by a tentative interim amendment (TIA). See page 1.

Chapter 3 Definitions

3.1 General. The definitions contained in this chapter shall apply to the terms used in this *Code*. Where terms are not defined in this chapter or within another chapter, they shall be defined using their ordinarily accepted meanings within the context in which they are used. *Merriam-Webster's Collegiate Dictionary*, 11th edition, shall be the source for the ordinarily accepted meaning.

3.2 NFPA Official Definitions.

3.2.1* Approved. Acceptable to the AHJ.

3.2.2* Authority Having Jurisdiction (AHJ). An organization, office, or individual responsible for enforcing the requirements of a code or standard, or for approving equipment, materials, an installation, or a procedure.

3.2.3* Code. A standard that is an extensive compilation of provisions covering broad subject matter or that is suitable for adoption into law independently of other codes and standards.

3.2.4 Guide. A document that is advisory or informative in nature and that contains only nonmandatory provisions. A guide may contain mandatory statements such as when a guide can be used, but the document as a whole is not suitable for adoption into law.

3.2.5 Labeled. Equipment or materials to which has been attached a label, symbol, or other identifying mark of an organization that is acceptable to the AHJ and concerned with product evaluation, that maintains periodic inspection of production of labeled equipment or materials, and by whose labeling the manufacturer indicates compliance with appropriate standards or performance in a specified manner.

3.2.6* Listed. Equipment, materials, or services included in a list published by an organization that is acceptable to the AHJ and concerned with evaluation of products or services, that maintains periodic inspection of production of listed equipment or materials or periodic evaluation of services, and whose listing states that either the equipment, material, or service meets appropriate designated standards or has been tested and found suitable for a specified purpose.

3.2.7 Recommended Practice. A document that is similar in content and structure to a code or standard but that contains only nonmandatory provisions using the word "should" to indicate recommendations in the body of the text.

3.2.8 Shall. Indicates a mandatory requirement.

3.2.9 Should. Indicates a recommendation or that which is advised but not required.

3.2.10 Standard. A document, the main text of which contains only mandatory provisions using the word "shall" to indicate requirements and which is in a form generally suitable for mandatory reference by another standard or code or for adoption into law. Nonmandatory provisions shall be located in an appendix or annex, footnote, or fine-print note and are not to be considered a part of the requirements of a standard.

3.3 General Definitions.

3.3.1* Absolute Pressure. Pressure based on a zero reference point, the perfect vacuum. [**55**, 2013]

3.3.2 Access Box. An approved secure box, accessible by the AHJ's master key or control, containing entrance keys or other devices to gain access to a structure or area.

3.3.3 Addition. An increase in building area, aggregate floor area, building height or number of stories of a structure. [**5000**, 2015]

3.3.4* Aerosol Product. A combination of a container, a propellant, and a material that is dispensed. [**30B**, 2015]

3.3.5 Airport (Aerodrome). An area on land or water that is used or intended to be used for the landing and takeoff of aircraft and includes buildings and facilities. [**402**, 2013]

3.3.6 Airport Ramp. Any outdoor area, including aprons and hardstands, where aircraft can be positioned, stored, serviced, or maintained, irrespective of the nature of the surface of the area. [**415**, 2013]

3.3.7* Aisle Width. The horizontal dimension between the face of the loads in racks under consideration. [**13**, 2013]

3.3.8 Alarm. A warning of danger. [**72**, 2013]

3.3.9 Alarm Signal. See 3.3.228.1.

3.3.10 Alcohol-Based Hand Rub. An alcohol-containing preparation designed for application to the hands for reducing the number of visible microorganisms on the hands and containing ethanol or isopropanol in an amount not exceeding 95 percent by volume.

3.3.11 Alleyway. An accessible clear space between storage piles or groups of piles suitable for housekeeping operations, visual inspection of piling areas, and initial fire-fighting operations.

3.3.12 Alternative. A system, condition, arrangement, material, or equipment submitted to the AHJ as a substitute for a requirement in a standard. [**1144**, 2013]

3.3.13 ANSI/ASME. The designation for American National Standards Institute publication sponsored and published by the American Society of Mechanical Engineers.

3.3.14 Area.

3.3.14.1 *Back Stock Area.* The area of a mercantile occupancy that is physically separated from the sales area and not intended to be accessible to the public. [**30B**, 2015]

3.3.14.2 *Control Area.* A building or portion of a building or outdoor area within which hazardous materials are allowed to be stored, dispensed, used, or handled in quantities not exceeding the maximum allowable quantities (MAQ). [**400**, 2013]

3.3.14.3 *Fire Area.* An area of a building separated from the remainder of the building by construction having a fire resistance of at least 1 hour and having all communicating openings properly protected by an assembly having a fire resistance rating of at least 1 hour. [**30**, 2015]

3.3.14.4 *Fire Flow Area.* The floor area, in square feet, used to determine the required fire flow.

3.3.14.5 *Indoor Area.* An area that is within a building or structure having overhead cover, other than a structure qualifying as "weather protection" in accordance with Section 6.6 of NFPA 55, *Compressed Gases and Cryogenic Fluids Code*. [**55**, 2013]

3.3.14.6 *Inside Liquid Storage Area.* A room or building used for the storage of liquids in containers or portable tanks, separated from other types of occupancies. [**30**, 2015]

3.3.14.7 *Organic Peroxide Storage Area.* An area used for the storage of organic peroxide formulations. [**400**, 2013]

3.3.14.8 *Outdoor Area.* An area that is not an indoor area. [**55**, 2013]

3.3.14.9 *Permissible Areas.*

3.3.14.9.1 *Designated Area.* A specific location designed and approved for hot work operations that is maintained fire safe such as a maintenance shop or a detached outside location that is of noncombustible or fire-resistive construction, essentially free of combustible and flammable contents, and suitably segregated from adjacent areas. [**51B**, 2014]

3.3.14.9.2 *Permit-Required Area.* Any location other than a designated area that is approved for hot work. A permit-required area is an area that is made fire safe by removing or protecting combustibles from ignition sources. [**51B**, 2014]

3.3.14.10 *Sales Display Area.* The area of a mercantile occupancy that is open to the public for the purpose of viewing and purchasing goods, wares, and merchandise.

2015 Edition

Individuals are free to circulate among the items, which are typically displayed on shelves, on racks, or on the floor. [**30B**, 2015]

3.3.14.11 *Smoking Area.* A designated area where smoking is permitted within a premises in which smoking is otherwise generally prohibited.

3.3.14.12* *Spray Area.* Any fully enclosed, partly enclosed, or unenclosed area in which dangerous quantities of flammable or combustible vapors, mists, residues, dusts, or deposits are present due to the operation of spray processes, including (1) any area in the direct path of a spray application process; (2) the interior of a spray booth or spray room or limited finishing workstation, as herein defined; (3) the interior of any exhaust plenum, eliminator section, or scrubber section; (4) the interior of any exhaust duct or exhaust stack leading from a spray application process; (5) the interior of any air recirculation filter house or enclosure, including secondary recirculation particulate filters; (6) any solvent concentrator (pollution abatement) unit or solvent recovery (distillation) unit. The following shall not be considered part of the spray area: (1) Fresh air make-up units; (2) Air supply ducts and air supply plenums; (3) Recirculation air supply ducts downstream of secondary filters; (4) Exhaust ducts from solvent concentrator (pollution abatement) units. [33, 2011]

3.3.15 ASME. American Society of Mechanical Engineers. [58, 2014]

3.3.16 ASME Container (or Tank). See 3.3.69.1.

3.3.17 ASTM. American Society for Testing and Materials, now known as "ASTM International." [55, 2013]

3.3.18 Automatic Emergency Shutoff Valve. A designated failsafe automatic closing valve designed to shut off the flow of gases or liquids that is initiated by a control system where the control system is activated by either manual or automatic means. [55, 2013]

3.3.19* Available Height for Storage. The maximum height at which commodities can be stored above the floor and still maintain necessary clearance from structural members and the required clearance below sprinklers. [13, 2013]

3.3.20* Baled Cotton. A natural seed fiber wrapped and secured in industry-accepted materials, usually consisting of burlap, woven polypropylene, or sheet polyethylene, and secured with steel, synthetic, or wire bands, or wire; also includes linters (lint removed from the cottonseed) and motes (residual materials from the ginning process).

3.3.20.1 *Block.* A basic yard storage unit for baled cotton comprising multiple-row storage with clear spaces on all sides.

3.3.20.2* *Densely Packed Baled Cotton.* Cotton, made into banded bales, with a packing density of at least 22 lb/ft^3 (360 kg/m^3), and dimensions complying with the following: a length of 55 in. (ca. 1400 mm ± 20 mm), a width of 21 in. (ca. 530 mm ± 20 mm), and a height of 27.6 in. to 35.4 in. (700 mm to 900 mm).

3.3.20.3 *Fire-Packed Baled Cotton.* A cotton bale within which a fire has been packed as a result of a process in which ginning is the most frequent cause.

3.3.20.4 *Naked Cotton Bale.* An unwrapped cotton bale secured with wire or steel straps.

3.3.21 Barrel. A unit of volume used in the petroleum industry that is equal to 42 gal (159 L). [30, 2015]

3.3.22 Basement. Any story of a building wholly or partly below grade plane that is not considered the first story above grade plane. [5000, 2015]

3.3.23 Battery System. A system that consists of these interconnected subsystems: (1) stationary storage batteries, (2) battery chargers, and (3) a collection of rectifiers, inverters, converters, and associated electrical equipment as required for a particular application.

3.3.24 Battery Types, Stationary.

3.3.24.1 *Lithium-Ion Battery.* A storage battery that consists of lithium ions imbedded in a carbon graphite or nickel metal-oxide substrate. The electrolyte is a carbonate mixture or a gelled polymer. The lithium ions are the charge carriers of the battery.

3.3.24.2 *Lithium Metal Polymer Battery.* A storage battery that is comprised of nonaqueous liquid or polymerized electrolytes, which provide ionic conductivity between lithiated positive active material electrically separated from metallic lithium or lithiated negative active material.

3.3.24.3 *Nickel Cadmium (NiCad) Battery.* An alkaline storage battery in which the positive active material is nickel oxide, the negative contains the cadmium, and the electrolyte is potassium hydroxide.

3.3.24.4* *Valve-Regulated (VRLA).* A lead-acid battery consisting of sealed cells furnished with a valve that opens to vent the battery whenever the internal pressure of the battery exceeds the ambient pressure by a set amount.

3.3.24.5* *Vented (Flooded).* A lead-acid battery consisting of cells that have electrodes immersed in liquid electrolyte.

3.3.25 Block. See 3.3.20.1.

3.3.26 Board of Appeals. A group of persons appointed by the governing body of the jurisdiction adopting this *Code* for the purpose of hearing and adjudicating differences of opinion between the AHJ and the citizenry in the interpretation, application, and enforcement of this *Code*.

3.3.27* Boiling Point. The temperature at which the vapor pressure of a liquid equals the surrounding atmospheric pressure. [30, 2015]

3.3.28* Boil-Over. An event in the burning of certain oils in an open-top tank when, after a long period of quiescent burning, there is a sudden increase in fire intensity associated with expulsion of burning oil from the tank. [30, 2015]

3.3.29* Building. Any structure used or intended for supporting or sheltering any use or occupancy. [*101*, 2015]

3.3.29.1* *Airport Terminal Building.* A structure used primarily for air passenger enplaning or deplaning, including ticket sales, flight information, baggage handling, and other necessary functions in connection with air transport operations. This term includes any extensions and satellite buildings used for passenger handling or aircraft flight service functions. Aircraft loading walkways and "mobile lounges" are excluded. [*415*, 2013]

3.3.29.2 *Apartment Building.* See 3.3.183.2.

3.3.29.3 *Attached Building.* A building having only one common wall with another building having other types of occupancies.

3.3.29.4 *Bulk Merchandising Retail Building.* See 3.3.183.4.

3.3.29.5* *Existing Building.* A building erected or officially authorized prior to the effective date of the adoption of this edition of the *Code* by the agency or jurisdiction. [*101*, 2015]

3.3.29.6* *High-Rise Building.* A building where the floor of an occupiable story is greater than 75 ft (23 m) above the lowest level of fire department vehicle access. [**5000**, 2015]

3.3.29.7* *Important Building.* A building that is considered not expendable in an exposure fire. [**30**, 2015]

3.3.29.8 *Mini-Storage Building.* See 3.3.183.28.1.

3.3.29.9 *Satellite.* A structure that can be adjacent to but separated from the airport terminal building, accessible above ground or through subway passages, and used to provide flight service operations, such as passenger check-in, waiting rooms, food service, enplaning or deplaning, etc. [**415**, 2013]

3.3.29.10* *Special Amusement Building.* A building that is temporary, permanent, or mobile and contains a device or system that conveys passengers or provides a walkway along, around, or over a course in any direction as a form of amusement arranged so that the egress path is not readily apparent due to visual or audio distractions or an intentionally confounded egress path, or is not readily available due to the mode of conveyance through the building or structure. [*101*, 2015]

3.3.29.11 *Storage Tank Building.* A three-dimensional space that is enclosed by a roof and walls that cover more than one-half of the possible area of the sides of the space, is of sufficient size to allow entry by personnel, will likely limit the dissipation of heat or dispersion of vapors, and restricts access for fire fighting. [**30**, 2015]

3.3.30 Bulk Hydrogen Compressed Gas System. See 3.3.254.1.

3.3.31 Bulk Inert Gas System. See 3.3.254.2.

3.3.32 Bulk Liquefied Hydrogen Gas System. See 3.3.254.3.

3.3.33 Bulk Oxygen System. See 3.3.254.4.

3.3.34 Bulk Plant or Terminal. That portion of a property where liquids are received by tank vessel, pipelines, tank car, or tank vehicle and are stored or blended in bulk for the purpose of distributing such liquids by tank vessel, pipeline, tank car, tank vehicle, portable tank, or container.

3.3.35 Burn-It. A fire-fighting strategy that allows for the free-burn of a tire fire.

3.3.36 Bury-It. A fire-fighting strategy in which a tire pile is buried with soil, sand, gravel, cement dust, or other cover material.

3.3.37* Cathodic Protection. A technique to resist the corrosion of a metal surface by making the surface the cathode of an electrochemical cell. [**55**, 2013]

3.3.38 Cathodic Protection Tester. A person who demonstrates an understanding of the principles and measurements of all common types of cathodic protection systems applicable to metal piping and container systems and who has education and experience in soil resistivity, stray current, structure-to-soil potential, and component electrical isolation measurements of metal piping and container systems. [**55**, 2013]

3.3.39 Certificate of Fitness. A written document issued by the AHJ to any person for the purpose of granting permission to such person to conduct or engage in any operation or act for which certification is required.

3.3.40 CFR. The Code of Federal Regulations of the United States Government.

3.3.41 CGA. Compressed Gas Association.

3.3.42 Chemical Heat of Combustion (H_c). The amount of heat released, in Btu/lb (kJ/g), when a substance is oxidized to yield stable end products, including water as a vapor, as measured under actual fire conditions in a normal ambient (air) atmosphere. [**30B**, 2015]

3.3.43 Chemical Name. The scientific designation of a chemical in accordance with the nomenclature system developed by the International Union of Pure and Applied Chemistry or the Chemical Abstracts Service rules of nomenclature, or a name that clearly identifies a chemical for the purpose of conducting an evaluation.

3.3.44 Chemical Plant. A large integrated plant or that portion of such a plant, other than a refinery or distillery, where liquids are produced by chemical reactions or used in chemical reactions. [**30**, 2015]

3.3.45* Chip. A wood chip of various species used in the manufacture of pulp.

3.3.46* Cleaning Media. Materials used to clean piping systems. [**55**, 2013]

3.3.47 Clean Zone. A defined space in which the concentration of airborne particles is controlled to specified limits. [**318**, 2015]

3.3.48 Cleanroom. A room in which the concentration of airborne particles is controlled to specified limits, including areas below the raised floor and above the ceiling grid if these areas are part of the air path and within the rated construction. [**5000**, 2015]

3.3.49 Clear Space. An area free of combustible materials but that can contain noncombustible materials that cannot transmit an exposure fire.

3.3.50 Closed System Use. See 3.3.267.1.

3.3.51 Closed-Top Diking. A dike with a cover intended to minimize the entrance of precipitation into the diked area. [**30**, 2015]

3.3.52 Clothes Dryer. A device used to dry wet laundry by means of heat derived from the combustion of fuel or from electric heating elements. [**211**, 2013]

3.3.53 Code.

3.3.53.1 *Building Code.* The building or construction code adopted by the jurisdiction. [**55**, 2013]

3.3.53.2 *Electrical Code.* The electrical code referenced in Section 2.2.

3.3.53.3 *Mechanical Code.* The mechanical or mechanical construction code adopted by the jurisdiction. [**55**, 2013]

3.3.53.4 *Plumbing Code.* The plumbing code referenced in Section 2.2.

3.3.54 Cold Deck. A single ranked pile of logs with individual logs of regular or irregular length usually 20 ft to 50 ft (6.1 m to 15.2 m) long, but greater than 8 ft (2.4 m) long.

3.3.55 Column (Paper). A single vertical stack of rolls of paper.

3.3.56 Combustible (Material). A material that, in the form in which it is used and under the conditions anticipated, will ignite and burn; a material that does not meet the definition of noncombustible or limited-combustible. [*101,* 2015]

3.3.57* Combustible Dust. A finely divided combustible particulate solid that presents a flash fire hazard or explosion hazard when suspended in air or the process-specific oxidizing medium over a range of concentrations. [**654,** 2013]

3.3.58* Combustible Fiber. Any material in a fibrous or shredded form that readily ignites when heat sources are present.

3.3.59 Combustible Liquid. See 3.3.164.1.

3.3.60 Combustible Particulate Solid. See 3.3.236.1.

3.3.61 Combustible Refuse. All combustible or loose rubbish, litter, or waste materials generated by an occupancy that are refused, rejected, or considered worthless and are disposed of by incineration on the premises where generated or periodically transported from the premises.

3.3.62* Combustible Waste. Combustible or loose waste material that is generated by an establishment or process and, if salvageable, is retained for scrap or reprocessing on the premises where generated or transported to a plant for processing.

3.3.63 Combustion. A chemical process of oxidation that occurs at a rate fast enough to produce heat and usually light in the form of either a glow or flame.

3.3.64 Commodity. The combination of products, packing material, and container that determines commodity classification. [**13,**2013]

3.3.65* Common Path of Travel. The portion of exit access that must be traversed before two separate and distinct paths of travel to two exits are available. [*101,* 2015]

3.3.66 Compartment.

3.3.66.1* *Fire Compartment.* A space within a building that is enclosed by fire barriers on all sides, including the top and bottom. [*101,* 2015]

3.3.66.2* *Smoke Compartment.* A space within a building enclosed by smoke barriers on all sides, including the top and bottom. [*101,* 2015]

3.3.67 Condition, Existing. See 3.3.101.

3.3.68 Construction Documents. Documents that consist of scaled design drawings and specifications for the purpose of construction of new facilities or modification to existing facilities. *(See also 3.3.227, Shop Drawings.)*

3.3.69 Container. A vessel, including cylinders, tanks, portable tanks, and cargo tanks, used for transporting or storing materials.

3.3.69.1 *ASME Container.* A container constructed in accordance with the ASME Code. [**58,** 2014]

3.3.69.2 *Closed Container.* A container as herein defined, so sealed by means of a lid or other device that neither liquid nor vapor will escape from it at ordinary temperatures. [**30,** 2015]

3.3.69.3 *Compressed Gas Container.* A pressure vessel designed to hold compressed gas at an absolute pressure greater than 1 atmosphere at 68°F (20°C) that includes cylinders, containers, and tanks. [**55,** 2013]

3.3.69.4* *Container (Flammable or Combustible Liquid).* Any vessel of 119 gal (450 L) or less capacity used for transporting or storing liquids. [**30,** 2015]

3.3.69.5 *Cryogenic Fluids Container.* A cryogenic vessel used for transportation, handling, or storage.

3.3.69.6 *Intermediate Bulk Container.* Any closed vessel having a liquid capacity not exceeding 3000 L (793 gal) and intended for storing and transporting liquids, as defined in Title 49, Code of Federal Regulations, Parts 100 through 199 or in Part 6 of the United Nations *Recommendations on the Transport of Dangerous Goods.* [**30,** 2015]

3.3.69.7 *[LP-Gas] Container.* Any vessel, including cylinders, tanks, portable tanks, and cargo tanks, used for the transporting or storing of LP-Gases. [**58,** 2014]

3.3.70 Control Area. See 3.3.14.2.

3.3.71* Conventional Pallets. A material-handling aid designed to support a unit load with openings to provide access for material-handling devices. *(See Figure A.3.3.71.)* [**13,** 2013]

3.3.72 Cooking Fire. The noncommercial, residential burning of materials not exceeding 3 ft (0.9 m) in diameter and 2 ft (0.6 m) in height, other than rubbish in which the fuel burned is contained in an outdoor fireplace, a barbecue grill, or a barbecue pit for the purpose of preparing food.

3.3.73 Cordwood. Logs 8 ft (2.4 m) or less in length customarily intended for pulpwood or fuel uses.

3.3.74 Core. The central tube around which paper is wound to form a roll. [**13,** 2013]

3.3.75* Corrosive Material. See 3.3.173.3.

3.3.76 Crude Petroleum. Hydrocarbon mixtures that have a flash point below 150°F (65.6°C) and that have not been processed in a refinery. [**30,** 2015]

3.3.77 Cryogenic Fluid. A fluid with a boiling point lower than −130°F (−90°C) at an absolute pressure of 14.7 psi (101.3 kPa). [**55,** 2013]

3.3.77.1 *Flammable Cryogenic Fluid.* A cryogenic fluid that forms flammable mixtures in air when in its vapor state. [**55,** 2013]

3.3.77.2 *Inert Cryogenic Fluid.* A cryogenic fluid that vaporizes to produce an intert gas when in its vapor state. [**55,** 2013]

3.3.77.3 *Oxidizing Cryogenic Fluid.* An oxidizing gas in the cryogenic state. [**55,** 2013]

3.3.78* Cultural Resource Properties. Buildings, structures, or sites, or portions thereof, that are culturally significant, or that house culturally significant collections. [**914,** 2010]

3.3.79 Cylinder. A pressure vessel designed for absolute pressures higher than 40 psi (276 kPa) and having a circular cross-section. It does not include a portable tank, multiunit tank car tank, cargo tank, or tank car. [**55,** 2013]

3.3.80 Cylinder Containment Vessel. A gastight recovery vessel designed so that a leaking compressed gas container can be placed within its confines, thereby encapsulating the leaking container. [55, 2013]

3.3.81* Cylinder Pack. An arrangement of cylinders into a cluster where the cylinders are confined into a grouping or arrangement with a strapping or frame system and connections are made to a common manifold. The frame system is allowed to be on skids or wheels to permit movement. [55, 2013]

3.3.82 Damage-Limiting Construction. For the purposes of this code, any set of construction elements, used individually or in combination, which will act to limit damage from an explosion, including open structures, pressure relieving construction, or pressure resistant construction. [30, 2015]

3.3.83 Deflagration. Propagation of a combustion zone at a velocity that is less than the speed of sound in the unreacted medium. [68, 2013]

3.3.84 Detector. A device suitable for connection to a circuit that has a sensor that responds to a physical stimulus such as gas, heat or smoke. [72, 2013]

3.3.84.1 *Air Sampling–Type Detector.* A detector that consists of a piping or tubing distribution network that runs from the detector to the area(s) to be protected. An aspiration fan in the detector housing draws air from the protected area back to the detector through air sampling ports, piping, or tubing. At the detector, the air is analyzed for fire products. [72, 2013]

3.3.84.2 *Automatic Fire Detector.* A device designed to detect the presence of a fire signature and to initiate action. For the purpose of this *Code*, automatic fire detectors are classified as follows: Automatic Fire Extinguishing or Suppression System Operation Detector, Fire–Gas Detector, Heat Detector, Other Fire Detectors, Radiant Energy–Sensing Fire Detector, and Smoke Detector. [72, 2013]

3.3.84.3 *Automatic Fire Extinguishing or Suppression System Operation Detector.* A device that automatically detects the operation of a fire extinguishing or suppression system by means appropriate to the system employed. [72, 2013]

3.3.84.4* *Combination Detector.* A device that either responds to more than one of the fire phenomena or employs more than one operating principle to sense one of these phenomena. Typical examples are a combination of a heat detector with a smoke detector or a combination rate-of-rise and fixed-temperature heat detector. This device has listings for each sensing method employed. [72, 2013]

3.3.84.5 *Electrical Conductivity Heat Detector.* A line-type or spot-type sensing element in which resistance varies as a function of temperature. [72, 2013]

3.3.84.6 *Fire–Gas Detector.* A device that detects gases produced by a fire. [72, 2013]

3.3.84.7* *Fixed-Temperature Detector.* A device that responds when its operating element becomes heated to a predetermined level. [72, 2013]

3.3.84.8* *Flame Detector.* A radiant energy–sensing fire detector that detects the radiant energy emitted by a flame. (*Refer to A.17.8.2 of NFPA 72.*) [72, 2013]

3.3.84.9 *Gas Detector.* A device that detects the presence of a specified gas concentration. Gas detectors can be either spot-type or line-type detectors. [72, 2013]

3.3.84.10 *Heat Detector.* A fire detector that detects either abnormally high temperature or rate of temperature rise, or both. [72, 2013]

3.3.84.11 *Line-Type Detector.* A device in which detection is continuous along a path. Typical examples are rate-of-rise pneumatic tubing detectors, projected beam smoke detectors, and heat-sensitive cable. [72, 2013]

3.3.84.12* *Multi-Criteria Detector.* A device that contains multiple sensors that separately respond to physical stimulus such as heat, smoke, or fire gases, or employs more than one sensor to sense the same stimulus. This sensor is capable of generating only one alarm signal from the sensors employed in the design either independently or in combination. The sensor output signal is mathematically evaluated to determine when an alarm signal is warranted. The evaluation can be performed either at the detector or at the control unit. This detector has a single listing that establishes the primary function of the detector. [72, 2013]

3.3.84.13* *Multi-Sensor Detector.* A device that contains multiple sensors that separately respond to physical stimulus such as heat, smoke, or fire gases, or employs more than one sensor to sense the same stimulus. A device capable of generating multiple alarm signals from any one of the sensors employed in the design, independently or in combination. The sensor output signals are mathematically evaluated to determine when an alarm signal is warranted. The evaluation can be performed either at the detector or at the control unit. This device has listings for each sensing method employed. [72, 2013]

3.3.84.14 *Other Fire Detectors.* Devices that detect a phenomenon other than heat, smoke, flame, or gases produced by a fire. [72, 2013]

3.3.84.15 *Pneumatic Rate-of-Rise Tubing Heat Detector.* A line-type detector comprising small-diameter tubing, usually copper, that is installed on the ceiling or high on the walls throughout the protected area. The tubing is terminated in a detector unit containing diaphragms and associated contacts set to actuate at a predetermined pressure. The system is sealed except for calibrated vents that compensate for normal changes in temperature. [72, 2013]

3.3.84.16 *Projected Beam–Type Detector.* A type of photoelectric light obscuration smoke detector wherein the beam spans the protected area. [72, 2013]

3.3.84.17 *Radiant Energy–Sensing Fire Detector.* A device that detects radiant energy, such as ultraviolet, visible, or infrared, that is emitted as a product of combustion reaction and obeys the laws of optics. [72, 2013]

3.3.84.18* *Rate Compensation Detector.* A device that responds when the temperature of the air surrounding the device reaches a predetermined level, regardless of the rate of temperature rise. [72, 2013]

3.3.84.19* *Rate-of-Rise Detector.* A device that responds when the temperature rises at a rate exceeding a predetermined value. [72, 2013]

3.3.84.20 *Smoke Detector.* A device that detects visible or invisible particles of combustion. [72, 2013]

3.3.84.21 Spark/Ember Detector. A radiant energy–sensing fire detector that is designed to detect sparks or embers, or both. These devices are normally intended to operate in dark environments and in the infrared part of the spectrum. [*72*, 2013]

3.3.84.22 Spot-Type Detector. A device in which the detecting element is concentrated at a particular location. Typical examples are bimetallic detectors, fusible alloy detectors, certain pneumatic rate-of-rise detectors, certain smoke detectors, and thermoelectric detectors. [*72*, 2013]

3.3.85 Detonation. Propagation of a combustion zone at a velocity that is greater than the speed of sound in the unreacted medium. [*68*, 2013]

3.3.86 Dispensing. The pouring or transferring of a material from a container tank, or similar vessel whereby vapors, dusts, fumes, mists, or gases could be liberated to the atmosphere. [*5000*, 2015]

3.3.87 Distillery. A plant or that portion of a plant where liquids produced by fermentation are concentrated and where the concentrated products are also mixed, stored, or packaged. [*30*, 2015]

3.3.88 Distributor. A business engaged in the sale or resale, or both, of compressed gases or cryogenic fluids, or both. [*55*, 2013]

3.3.89 Dormitory. See 3.3.183.9

3.3.90 DOT. U.S. Department of Transportation.

3.3.91 Driveway. A clear space suitable for fire-fighting operations by motorized fire apparatus.

3.3.92 Dwelling Unit. One or more rooms arranged for complete, independent housekeeping purposes, with space for eating, living, and sleeping; facilities for cooking; and provisions for sanitation. [*5000*, 2015]

   3.3.92.1 *One- and Two-Family Dwelling Unit.* See 3.3.183.22.1.

3.3.93 Emergency. A fire, explosion, or hazardous condition that poses an immediate threat to the safety of life or damage to property.

3.3.94 Emergency Relief Vent. An opening, construction method, or device that will automatically relieve excessive internal pressure due to an exposure fire. [*30*, 2015]

3.3.95 Emergency Shutoff Valve. A designated valve designed to shut off the flow of gases or liquids. [*55*, 2013]

3.3.96 Ethylene Oxide Drum. For the purposes of this code, containers built to UN specification 1A1. [*55*, 2013]

3.3.97 Excess Flow Control. A fail-safe system or approved means designed to shut off flow due to a rupture in pressurized piping systems. [*55*, 2013]

3.3.98 Excess Flow Valve. A valve inserted into a compressed gas cylinder, portable tank, or stationary tank that is designed to positively shut off the flow of gas in the event that its predetermined flow is exceeded.

3.3.99* Exhausted Enclosure. An appliance or piece of equipment that consists of a top, a back, and two sides that provides a means of local exhaust for capturing gases, fumes, vapors, and mists. [*55*, 2013]

3.3.100* Existing. That which is already in existence on the date this edition of the *Code* goes into effect. [*101*, 2015]

3.3.101 Existing Condition. Any situation, circumstance, or physical makeup of any structure, premise, or process that was ongoing or in effect prior to the adoption of this *Code*.

3.3.102* Exit. That portion of a means of egress that is separated from all other spaces of a building or structure by construction, location, or equipment as required to provide a protected way of travel to the exit discharge. [*101*, 2015]

   3.3.102.1* *Horizontal Exit.* A way of passage from one building to an area of refuge in another building on approximately the same level, or a way of passage through or around a fire barrier to an area of refuge on approximately the same level in the same building that affords safety from fire and smoke originating from the area of incidence and areas communicating therewith. [*101*, 2015]

3.3.103 Exit Access. That portion of a means of egress that leads to an exit. [*101*, 2015]

3.3.104 Exit Discharge. That portion of a means of egress between the termination of an exit and a public way. [*101*, 2015]

3.3.105 Explosion. The bursting or rupture of an enclosure or a container due to the development of internal pressure from a deflagration. [*69*, 2014]

3.3.106* Explosion Control. A means of either preventing an explosion through the use of explosion suppression, fuel reduction, or oxidant reduction systems or a means to prevent the structural collapse of a building in the event of an explosion through the use of deflagration venting, barricades, or related construction methods. [*55*, 2013]

3.3.107* Explosive Material. A chemical compound, mixture, or device, the primary or common purpose of which is to function by explosion. [*5000*, 2015]

3.3.108 Facility. As applied to access and water supply, a structure or use in a fixed location including exterior storage, use, and handling areas that relates to the occupancies and operations covered by this *Code*.

   3.3.108.1 *Hazardous Material Storage Facility.* See 3.3.145.

   3.3.108.2 *Limited Care Facility.* See 3.3.183.15.

   3.3.108.3 *Motor Fuel Dispensing Facility.* See 3.3.183.19.

   3.3.108.3.1 *Fleet Vehicle Motor Fuel Dispensing Facility.* See 3.3.183.19.1.

   3.3.108.3.2 *Marine Motor Fuel Dispensing Facility.* See 3.3.183.19.2.

   3.3.108.3.3 *Motor Fuel Dispensing Facility Located Inside a Building.* See 3.3.183.19.3.

3.3.109 Fail-Safe. A design arrangement incorporating one or more features that automatically counteracts the effect of an anticipated source of failure or which includes a design arrangement that eliminates or mitigates a hazardous condition by compensating automatically for a failure or malfunction.

3.3.110 Festival Seating. A form of audience/spectator accommodation in which no seating, other than a floor or finished ground level, is provided for the audience/spectators gathered to observe a performance. [*101*, 2015]

3.3.111 Fines (Wood). Small pieces or splinters of wood by-products that can pass through a 0.25 in. (6.4 mm) screen.

3.3.112 Finish.

3.3.112.1 *Interior Ceiling Finish.* The interior finish of ceilings. [*101*, 2015]

3.3.112.2* *Interior Finish.* The exposed surfaces of walls, ceilings, and floors within buildings. [*101*, 2015]

3.3.112.3* *Interior Floor Finish.* The interior finish of floors, ramps, stair treads and risers, and other walking surfaces. [*101*, 2015]

3.3.112.4 *Interior Wall Finish.* The interior finish of columns, fixed or movable walls, and fixed or movable partitions. [*101*, 2015]

3.3.113 Fires, Classification of.

3.3.113.1 *Class A Fires.* Class A fires are fires in ordinary combustible materials, such as wood, cloth, paper, rubber, and many plastics. [**10**, 2013]

3.3.113.2 *Class B Fires.* Class B fires are fires in flammable liquids, combustible liquids, petroleum greases, tars, oils, oil-based paints, solvents, lacquers, alcohols, and flammable gases. [**10**, 2013]

3.3.113.3 *Class C Fires.* Class C fires are fires that involve energized electrical equipment. [**10**, 2013]

3.3.113.4 *Class D Fires.* Class D fires are fires in combustible metals, such as magnesium, titanium, zirconium, sodium, lithium, and potassium. [**10**, 2013]

3.3.113.5 *Class K Fires.* Class K fires are fires in cooking appliances that involve combustible cooking media (vegetable or animal oils and fats). [**10**, 2013]

3.3.114 Fire, Recreational. See 3.3.217.

3.3.115 Fire Alarm System. See 3.3.254.10.

3.3.116 Fire Compartment. See 3.3.66.1.

3.3.117 Fire Department Access Road. The road or other means developed to allow access and operational setup for fire-fighting and rescue apparatus.

3.3.118 Fire Door Assembly. Any combination of a fire door, a frame, hardware, and other accessories that together provide a specific degree of fire protection to the opening. [**80**, 2013]

3.3.119 Fire Flow. The flow rate of a water supply, measured at 20 psi (137.9 kPa) residual pressure, that is available for fire fighting.

3.3.120 Fire Hazard. Any situation, process, material, or condition that, on the basis of applicable data, can cause a fire or explosion or that can provide a ready fuel supply to augment the spread or intensity of a fire or explosion, all of which pose a threat to life or property. [**914**, 2010]

3.3.121* **Fire Hydrant.** A valved connection on a water supply system having one or more outlets and that is used to supply hose and fire department pumpers with water. [**1141**, 2012]

3.3.122* **Fire Lane.** A fire department access road, which is marked with approved signs or other approved notices.

3.3.123 Fire Point. The lowest temperature at which a liquid will ignite and achieve sustained burning when exposed to a test flame in accordance with ASTM D 92, *Standard Test Method for Flash and Fire Points by Cleveland Open Cup Tester*. [**30**, 2015]

3.3.124 Fire Retardant. A liquid, solid, or gas that tends to inhibit combustion when applied on, mixed in, or combined with combustible materials.

3.3.125 Fire Watch. The assignment of a person or persons to an area for the express purpose of notifying the fire department, the building occupants, or both of an emergency; preventing a fire from occurring; extinguishing small fires; or protecting the public from fire or life safety dangers.

3.3.126* **Flame Spread.** The propagation of flame over a surface. [*101*, 2015]

3.3.127 Flame Spread Index. A comparative measure, expressed as a dimensionless number, derived from visual measurements of the spread of flame versus time for a material tested in accordance with ASTM E 84, *Standard Test Method for Surface Burning Characteristics of Building Materials*, or ANSI/UL 723, *Standard for Test for Surface Burning Characteristics of Building Materials*. [*101*, 2015]

3.3.128 Flammable Vapors. Flammable vapors are the concentration of flammable constituents in air that exceed 25 percent of their lower flammability limit (LFL).

3.3.129* **Flash Point.** The minimum temperature of a liquid at which sufficient vapor is given off to form an ignitible mixture with the air, near the surface of the liquid or within the vessel used, as determined by the appropriate test procedure and apparatus specified in Section 4.4 of NFPA 30, *Flammable and Combustible Liquids Code*. [**30**, 2015]

3.3.130 Floor Area.

3.3.130.1* *Gross Floor Area.* The floor area within the inside perimeter of the outside walls of the building under consideration with no deduction for hallways, stairs, closets, thickness of interior walls, columns, elevator and building services shafts, or other features, but excluding floor openings associated with atriums and communicating spaces. [**5000**, 2015]

3.3.130.2 *Net Floor Area.* The floor area within the inside perimeter of the outside walls, or the outside walls and fire walls of the building, or outside and/or inside walls that bound an occupancy or incidental use area requiring the occupant load to be calculated using net floor area under consideration with deductions for hallways, stairs, closets, thickness of interior walls, columns, or other features. [**5000**, 2015]

3.3.131 Forecasting. The ability to predict fire progression in a scrap tire storage location prior to the completion of the inventory fire break using heavy equipment.

3.3.132* **Fugitive Emissions.** Releases of flammable vapor that continuously or intermittently occur from process equipment during normal operations. [**30**, 2015]

3.3.133 Gallon, U.S. Standard. 1 U.S. gal = 0.833 Imperial gal = 231 in.^{3} = 3.785 L. [**58**, 2014]

3.3.134 Garage. A building or portion of a building in which one or more self-propelled vehicles carrying volatile flammable liquid for fuel or power are kept for use, sale, storage, rental, repair, exhibition, or demonstrating purposes, and all that portion of a building that is on or below the floor or floors in which such vehicles are kept and that is not separated therefrom by suitable cutoffs. [**5000**, 2015]

3.3.135 Gas.

3.3.135.1* Compressed Gas. A material, or mixture of materials, that (1) is a gas at 68°F (20°C) or less at 14.7 psi (101.3 kPa) and (2) has a boiling point of 68°F (20°C) or less at 14.7 psi (101.3 kPa) that is liquefied, nonliquefied, or in solution, except those gases that have no other health or physical hazard properties are not considered to be compressed until the pressure in the packaging exceeds an absolute pressure of 40.6 psi (280 kPa) at 68°F (20°C). [55, 2013]

3.3.135.1.1 Compressed Gas Mixtures. A mixture of two or more compressed gases contained in a packaging, the hazard properties of which are represented by the properties of the mixture as a whole.

3.3.135.1.2 Compressed Gases in Solution. Nonliquefied gases that are dissolved in a solvent.

3.3.135.1.3 Liquefied Compressed Gases. Gases that are contained in a packaging under the charged pressure and are partially liquid at a temperature of 68°F (20°C).

3.3.135.1.4 Nonliquefied Compressed Gases. Gases, other than those in solution, that are contained in a packaging under the charged pressure and are entirely gaseous at a temperature of 68°F (20°C).

3.3.135.2 Corrosive Gas. A gas that causes visible destruction of or irreversible alterations in living tissue by chemical action at the site of contact. [55, 2013]

3.3.135.3 Flammable Gas. A material that is a gas at 68°F (20°C) or less at an absolute pressure of 14.7 psi (101.3 kPa), that is ignitable at an absolute pressure of 14.7 psi (101.3 kPa) when in a mixture of 13 percent or less by volume with air, or that has a flammable range at an absolute pressure of 14.7 psi (101.3 kPa) with air of at least 12 percent, regardless of the lower limit. [55, 2013]

3.3.135.4 Flammable Liquefied Gas. A liquefied compressed gas that, when under a charged pressure, is partially liquid at a temperature of 68°F (20°C) and is flammable. [55, 2013]

3.3.135.5 Highly Toxic Gas. A chemical that has a median lethal concentration (LC_{50}) in air of 200 ppm by volume or less of gas or vapor, or 2 mg/L or less of mist, fume, or dust, when administered by continuous inhalation for 1 hour (or less if death occurs within 1 hour) to albino rats weighing between 0.44 lb and 0.66 lb (200 g and 300 g) each. [55, 2013]

3.3.135.6* Inert Gas. A nonreactive, nonflammable, noncorrosive gas such as argon, helium, krypton, neon, nitrogen, and xenon. [55, 2013]

3.3.135.7 Irritant Gas. A chemical that is not corrosive, but that causes a reversible inflammatory effect on living tissue by chemical action at the site of contact. A chemical is a skin irritant if, when tested on the intact skin of albino rabbits by the methods of 16 CFR 1500.41, for an exposure of 4 or more hours or by other appropriate techniques, it results in an empirical score of 5 or more. A chemical is classified as an eye irritant if so determined under the procedure listed in 16 CFR 1500.42, or other appropriate techniques. [55, 2013]

3.3.135.8 Liquefied Gas. A gas, other than in solution, that in a packaging under the charged pressure exists both as a liquid and a gas at a temperature of 68°F (20°C). [30, 2012]

3.3.135.9 Liquefied Natural Gas (LNG). A fluid in the cryogenic liquid state that is composed predominantly of methane and that can contain minor quantities of ethane, propane, nitrogen, and other components normally found in natural gas. [59A, 2013]

3.3.135.10* Liquefied Petroleum Gas (LP-Gas). Any material having a vapor pressure not exceeding that allowed for commercial propane that is composed predominantly of the following hydrocarbons, either by themselves (except propylene) or as mixtures: propane, propylene, butane (normal butane or isobutane), and butylenes. [58, 2014]

3.3.135.11 Nonflammable Gas. A gas that does not meet the definition of a flammable gas. [55, 2013]

3.3.135.12* Other Gas. A gas that is not a corrosive gas, flammable gas, highly toxic gas, oxidizing gas, pyrophoric gas, toxic gas, or unstable reactive gas with a hazard rating of Class 2, Class 3, or Class 4 gas. [55, 2013]

3.3.135.13 Oxidizing Gas. A gas that can support and accelerate combustion of other materials more than air does. [55, 2013]

3.3.135.14 Pyrophoric Gas. A gas with an autoignition temperature in air at or below 130°F (54.4°C). [55, 2013]

3.3.135.15 Scavenged Gas. A residual process gas that is collected for treatment or release at a location remote from the site of use.

3.3.135.16 Simple Asphyxiant Gas. A gas that does not provide sufficient oxygen to support life and that has none of the other physical or health hazards.

3.3.135.17 Toxic Gas. A gas with a median lethal concentration (LC_{50}) in air of more than 200 ppm but not more than 2000 ppm by volume of gas or vapor, or more than 2 mg/L but not more than 20 mg/L of mist, fume, or dust, when administered by continuous inhalation for 1 hour (or less if death occurs within 1 hour) to albino rats weighing between 0.44 lb and 0.66 lb (200 g and 300 g) each. [55, 2013]

3.3.135.18* Unstable Reactive Gas. A gas that, in the pure state or as commercially produced, will vigorously polymerize, decompose, or condense; become self-reactive; or otherwise undergo a violent chemical change under conditions of shock, pressure, or temperature. [55, 2013]

3.3.136* Gas Cabinet. A fully enclosed, noncombustible enclosure used to provide an isolated environment for compressed gas cylinders in storage or use. [55, 2013]

3.3.137 Gas Manufacturer/Producer. A business that produces compressed gases or cryogenic fluids, or both, or fills portable or stationary gas containers, cylinders, or tanks. [55, 2013]

3.3.138 Gas Room. A separately ventilated, fully enclosed room in which only compressed gases, cryogenic fluids, associated equipment, and supplies are stored or used. [55, 2013]

3.3.139* Gaseous Hydrogen System. A system in which hydrogen is delivered, stored, and discharged in the gaseous form to a piping system. The gaseous hydrogen system terminates at the point where hydrogen at service pressure first enters the distribution piping. [55, 2013]

3.3.140 Ground Kettle. A container that could be mounted on wheels and is used for heating tar, asphalt, or similar substances.

3.3.141 Handling. The deliberate movement of material by any means to a point of storage or use.

3.3.142* Hazard of Contents.

3.3.142.1 *High Hazard.* High hazard contents shall include materials defined as hazardous materials in 3.3.173.4, whether stored, used, or handled. [**5000:**6.3.2.4.1.1]

3.3.142.1.1 *High Hazard Level 1 Contents.* High hazard Level 1 contents shall include materials that present a detonation hazard including, but not limited to, the following: (1) Explosives; (2) Unclassified detonable organic peroxides; (3) Class 4 oxidizers; (4) Detonable pyrophoric materials; (5) Class 3 detonable and Class 4 unstable (reactive) materials. [**5000:**6.3.2.4.2]

3.3.142.1.2 *High Hazard Level 2 Contents.* High hazard Level 2 contents shall include materials that present a deflagration hazard or a hazard from accelerated burning including, but not limited to, the following: (1) Class I, Class II, or Class III-A flammable or combustible liquids that are used or stored in normally open containers or systems, or in closed containers or systems at gauge pressures of more than 15 psi (103 kPa); (2) Combustible dusts stored, used, or generated in a manner creating a severe fire or explosion hazard; (3) Flammable gases and flammable cryogenic liquids; (4) Class I organic peroxides; (5) Class 3 solid or liquid oxidizers that are used or stored in normally open containers or systems, or in closed containers or systems at gauge pressures of more than 15 psi (103 kPa); (6) Nondetonable pyrophoric materials; (7) Class 3 nondetonable unstable (reactive) materials; (8) Class 3 water-reactive materials [**5000:**6.3.2.4.3]

3.3.142.1.3 *High Hazard Level 3 Contents.* High hazard Level 3 contents shall include materials that readily support combustion or present a physical hazard including, but not limited to, the following: (1) Level 2 and Level 3 aerosols; (2) Class I, Class II, or Class III-A flammable or combustible liquids that are used or stored in normally closed containers or systems at gauge pressures of less than 15 psi (103 kPa); (3) Flammable solids, other than dusts classified as high hazard Level 2, stored, used, or generated in a manner creating a high fire hazard; (4) Class II and Class III organic peroxides; (5) Class 2 solid or liquid oxidizers; (6) Class 3 solid or liquid oxidizers that are used or stored in normally closed containers or systems at gauge pressures of less than 15 psi (103 kPa); (7) Oxidizing gases and oxidizing cryogenic liquids; (8) Class 2 unstable (reactive) materials; (9) Class 2 water-reactive materials [**5000:**6.3.2.4.4]

3.3.142.1.4 *High Hazard Level 4 Contents.* High hazard Level 4 contents shall include materials that are acute health hazards including, but not limited to, the following: (1) Corrosives; (2) Highly toxic materials; (3) Toxic materials [**5000:**6.3.2.4.5]

3.3.142.1.5 *High Hazard Level 5 Contents.* High hazard Level 5 contents include hazardous production materials (HPM) used in the fabrication of semiconductors or semiconductor research and development. [**5000:**6.3.2.4.6]

3.3.142.2* *Low Hazard Contents.* Low hazard contents shall be classified as those of such low combustibility that no self-propagating fire therein can occur. [**5000:**6.3.2.2]

3.3.142.3* *Ordinary Hazard Contents.* Ordinary hazard contents shall be classified as those that are likely to burn with moderate rapidity or to give off a considerable volume of smoke. [**5000:**6.3.2.3]

3.3.143* Hazard Rating. The numerical rating of the health, flammability, self-reactivity, and other hazards of the material, including its reaction with water. [**55,** 2013]

3.3.144 Hazardous Material. See 3.3.173.4.

3.3.145 Hazardous Material Storage Facility. A building, a portion of a building, or exterior area used for the storage of hazardous materials in excess of exempt amounts.

3.3.146 Hazardous Materials Storage Locker. A movable prefabricated structure, manufactured primarily at a site other than the final location of the structure and transported completely assembled or in a ready-to-assemble package to the final location, and intended to meet local, state, and federal requirements for outside storage of hazardous materials. [**30,** 2015]

3.3.147* Hazardous Reaction or Hazardous Chemical Reaction. Reactions that result in dangers beyond the fire problems relating to flash point and boiling point of either the reactants or of the products. [**30,** 2015]

3.3.148 Heat Transfer Fluid (HTF). A liquid that is used as a medium to transfer heat energy from a heater or vaporizer to a remote heat consumer (e.g., injection molding machine, oven, or dryer, or jacketed chemical reactor). [**30,** 2015]

3.3.149* Heliport. An identifiable area located on land, on water, or on a structure, that also includes any existing buildings or facilities thereon, used or intended to be used for landing and takeoff of helicopters. [**418,** 2011]

3.3.150 Hogged Material. Mill waste consisting mainly of hogged bark but possibly including a mixture of bark, chips, dust, or other by-products from trees; also includes material designated as hogged fuel.

3.3.151 Home.

3.3.151.1 *Day-Care Home.* See 3.3.183.6.

3.3.151.2 *Nursing Home.* See 3.3.183.21.

3.3.152 Horizontal Exit. See 3.3.102.1.

3.3.153* Immediately Dangerous to Life and Health (IDLH). A concentration of airborne contaminants, normally expressed in parts per million (ppm) or milligrams per cubic meter, that represents the maximum level from which one could escape within 30 minutes without any escape-impairing symptoms or irreversible health effects. [**55,** 2013]

3.3.154 Imminent Danger. A condition or practice in an occupancy or structure that poses a danger that could reasonably be expected to cause death, serious physical harm, or serious property loss.

3.3.155* Incident Commander (IC). The individual responsible for all incident activities, including the development of strategies and tactics and the ordering and the release of resources. [**472,** 2013]

3.3.156 Incidental Liquid Use or Storage. Use or storage as a subordinate activity to that which establishes the occupancy or area classification. [**30**, 2015]

3.3.157 Indicating Valve. See 3.3.268.1.

3.3.158 Initiating Device Circuit. A circuit to which automatic or manual initiating devices are connected where the signal received does not identify the individual device operated. [**72**, 2013]

3.3.159 Inside Liquid Storage Area. See 3.3.14.6.

3.3.160* ISO Module. An assembly of tanks or tubular cylinders permanently mounted in a frame conforming to International Organization for Standardization (ISO) requirements. [**55**, 2013]

3.3.161 Jurisdiction. A governmental unit or political division or a subdivision.

3.3.162 Limit.

   3.3.162.1* *Ceiling Limit*. The maximum concentration of an airborne contaminant to which one can be exposed. [**5000**, 2015]

   3.3.162.2* *Permissible Exposure Limit (PEL)*. The maximum permitted 8-hour, time-weighted average concentration of an airborne contaminant. [**55**, 2013]

   3.3.162.3* *Short-Term Exposure Limit (STEL)*. The concentration to which it is believed that workers can be exposed continuously for a short period of time without suffering from irritation, chronic or irreversible tissue damage, or narcosis of a degree sufficient to increase the likelihood of accidental injury, impairment of self-rescue, or the material reduction of work efficiency, without exceeding the daily permissible exposure limit (PEL). [**55**, 2013]

3.3.163 Limited-Combustible (Material). *See 4.5.10.* [**5000**, 2015]

3.3.164 Liquid. A material that has a melting point that is equal to or less than 68°F (20°C) and a boiling point that is greater than 68°F (20°C) and 14.7 psia (101.3 kPa). When not otherwise identified, the term liquid shall mean both flammable and combustible liquids. [**5000**, 2015]

   3.3.164.1 *Combustible Liquid*. Any liquid that has a closed-cup flash point at or above 100°F (37.8°C), as determined by the test procedures and apparatus set forth in Section 4.4 of NFPA 30, *Flammable and Combustible Liquids Code*. Combustible liquids are classified according to Section 4.3 of NFPA 30. [**30**, 2015]

   3.3.164.2* *Flammable Liquid*. Any liquid that has a closed-cup flash point below 100°F (37.8°C), as determined by the test procedures and apparatus set forth in Section 4.4 of NFPA 30, *Flammable and Combustible Liquids Code*, and a Reid vapor pressure that does not exceed an absolute pressure of 40 psi (276 kPa) at 100°F (37.8°C), as determined by ASTM D 323, *Standard Test Method for Vapor Pressure of Petroleum Products (Reid Method)*. Flammable liquids are classified according to Section 4.3 of NFPA 30. [**30**, 2015]

   3.3.164.3 *Highly Volatile Liquid*. A liquid with a boiling point of less than 68°F (20°C).

   3.3.164.4 *Stable Liquid*. Any liquid not defined as unstable. [**30**, 2015]

3.3.165 Log. Felled tree from which all the branches have been removed.

3.3.166 Loose House. A separate detached building in which unbaled combustible fibers are stored.

3.3.167 Lumber. Wood from felled trees having a section produced by lengthwise sawing or chipping of logs or other solid wood of large dimensions and possible crosscutting and/or further machining to obtain a certain size and includes boards, dimension lumber, timber, and similar wood products.

3.3.168 Manual Emergency Shutoff Valve. A designated valve designed to shut off the flow of gases or liquids that is manually operated. [**55**, 2013]

3.3.169 Manual Fire Alarm Box. A manually operated device used to initiate a fire alarm signal. [**72**, 2013]

3.3.170 Manual Pull Station. See 3.3.169, Manual Fire Alarm Box.

3.3.171 Marine Terminal. A facility comprised of one or more berths, piers, wharves, loading and unloading areas, warehouses, and storage yards and used for transfer of people and/or cargo between waterborne and land transportation modes. [**307**, 2011]

3.3.172 Marine Vessel. A water craft or other artificial contrivance used as a means of transportation in or on the water.

3.3.173 Material.

   3.3.173.1 *Combustible (Material)*. See 3.3.56.

   3.3.173.2 *Compatible Material*. A material that, when in contact with an oxidizer, will not react with the oxidizer or promote or initiate its decomposition.

   3.3.173.3 *Corrosive Material*. A chemical that causes visible destruction of, or irreversible alterations in, living tissue by chemical action at the site of contact. [**400**, 2013]

   3.3.173.4 *Hazardous Material*. A chemical or substance that is classified as a physical hazard material or a health hazard material, whether the chemical or substance is in usable or waste condition. *(See also 3.3.173.6, Health Hazard Material, and 3.3.173.12, Physical Hazard Material.)* [**400**, 2013]

   3.3.173.5 *Hazardous Production Material (HPM)*. A solid, liquid, or gas associated with semiconductor manufacturing that has a degree-of-hazard rating of 3 or 4 in health, flammability, instability, or water reactivity in accordance with NFPA 704 and that is used directly in research, laboratory, or production processes that have as their end product materials that are not hazardous. [**5000**, 2015]

   3.3.173.6 *Health Hazard Material*. A chemical or substance classified as a toxic, highly toxic, or corrosive material in accordance with definitions set forth in this *Code*. [**400**, 2013]

   3.3.173.7* *Highly Toxic Material*. A material that produces a lethal dose or lethal concentration that falls within any of following categories: (1) a chemical that has a median lethal dose (LD_{50}) of 50 mg/kg or less of body weight when administered orally to albino rats weighing between 200 g and 300 g each; (2) a chemical that has a median lethal dose (LD_{50}) of 200 mg/kg or less of body weight when administered by continuous contact for 24 hours, or less if death occurs within 24 hours, with the bare skin of albino rabbits weighing between 2 kg and 3 kg each or albino rats weighing 200 g to 300 g each; (3) a chemical that has a median lethal concentration (LC_{50}) in air of 200 parts per million by volume or less of gas or vapor, or 2 mg/L or less of mist, fume, or dust, when administered by continuous inhalation for 1 hour, or less if death occurs within 1 hour, to albino rats weighing between 200 g and 300 g each. [**400,** 2013]

3.3.173.8 *Hogged Material.* See 3.3.150.

3.3.173.9* *Incompatible Material.* Materials that, when in contact with each other, have the potential to react in a manner that generates heat, fumes, gases or by-products that are hazardous to life or property. [**400,** 2013]

3.3.173.10 *Limited-Combustible Material.* See 4.5.10. [**5000,** 2015]

3.3.173.11 *Noncombustible Material.* See 4.5.9. [**5000,** 2015]

3.3.173.12 *Physical Hazard Material.* A chemical or substance classified as a combustible liquid, explosive, flammable cryogen, flammable gas, flammable liquid, flammable solid, organic peroxide, oxidizer, oxidizing cryogen, pyrophoric, unstable (reactive), or water-reactive material. [**400,** 2013]

3.3.173.13 *Pyrophoric Material.* A chemical with an auto-ignition temperature in air at or below 130°F (54.4°C). [**400,** 2013]

3.3.173.14* *Toxic Material.* A material that produces a lethal dose or a lethal concentration within any of the following categories: (1) a chemical or substance that has a median lethal dose (LD_{50}) of more than 50 mg/kg but not more than 500 mg/kg of body weight when administered orally to albino rats weighing between 200 g and 300 g each; (2) a chemical or substance that has a median lethal dose (LD_{50}) of more than 200 mg/kg but not more than 1000 mg/kg of body weight when administered by continuous contact for 24 hours, or less if death occurs within 24 hours, with the bare skin of albino rabbits weighing between 2 kg and 3 kg each; (3) a chemical or substance that has a median lethal concentration (LC_{50}) in air of more than 200 parts per million but not more than 2000 parts per million by volume of gas or vapor, or more than 2 mg/L but not more than 20 mg/L, of mist, fume, or dust when administered by continuous inhalation for 1 hour, or less if death occurs within 1 hour, to albino rats weighing between 200 g and 300 g each. [**400,** 2013]

3.3.173.15* *Unstable (Reactive) Material.* A material that, in the pure state or as commercially produced, will vigorously polymerize, decompose or condense, become self-reactive, or otherwise undergo a violent chemical change under conditions of shock, pressure, or temperature. [**400,** 2013]

3.3.173.16* *Water-Reactive Material.* A material that explodes, violently reacts, produces flammable, toxic, or other hazardous gases; or evolves enough heat to cause self-ignition or ignition of nearby combustibles upon exposure to water or moisture. [**400,** 2013]

3.3.174 Material Safety Data Sheet (MSDS). Written or printed material concerning a hazardous material that is prepared in accordance with the provisions of OSHA 29 CFR 1910.1200.

3.3.175* Maximum Allowable Quantity (MAQ). The quantity of hazardous material permitted in a control area.

3.3.176* Means of Egress. A continuous and unobstructed way of travel from any point in a building or structure to a public way consisting of three separate and distinct parts: (1) the exit access, (2) the exit, and (3) the exit discharge. [*101,* 2015]

3.3.177 Means of Escape. A way out of a building or structure that does not conform to the strict definition of means of egress but does provide an alternate way out. [*101,* 2015]

3.3.178 Mezzanine. An intermediate level between the floor and the ceiling of any room or space. [*101,* 2015]

3.3.179* Mobile Supply Unit. Any supply source that is equipped with wheels so it is able to be moved around. [*55,* 2013]

3.3.180 Motor Vehicle Fluid. A fluid that is a flammable, combustible, or hazardous material, such as crankcase fluids, fuel, brake fluids, transmission fluids, radiator fluids, and gear oil.

3.3.181 Nesting. A method of securing cylinders upright in a tight mass using a contiguous three-point contact system whereby all cylinders in a group have a minimum of three contact points with other cylinders or a solid support structure (e.g., a wall or railing). [*55,* 2013]

3.3.182* Normal Temperature and Pressure (NTP). A temperature of 70°F (21°C) at an absolute pressure of 14.7 psi (101.3 kPa). [*55,* 2013]

3.3.183 Occupancy. The purpose for which a building or other structure, or part thereof, is used or intended to be used. [ASCE/SEI 7:1.2]

3.3.183.1* *Ambulatory Health Care Occupancy.* An occupancy used to provide services or treatment simultaneously to four or more patients that provides, on an outpatient basis, one or more of the following: (1) treatment for patients that renders the patients incapable of taking action for self-preservation under emergency conditions without the assistance of others; (2) anesthesia that renders the patients incapable of taking action for self-preservation under emergency conditions without the assistance of others; (3) emergency or urgent care for patients who, due to the nature of their injury or illness, are incapable of taking action for self-preservation under emergency conditions without the assistance of others [*101,* 2015]

3.3.183.2* *Apartment Building.* A building or portion thereof containing three or more dwelling units with independent cooking and bathroom facilities. [*101,* 2015]

3.3.183.3* *Assembly Occupancy.* An occupancy (1) used for a gathering of 50 or more persons for deliberation, worship, entertainment, eating, drinking, amusement, awaiting transportation, or similar uses; or (2) used as a special amusement building, regardless of occupant load. [*101,* 2015]

3.3.183.4 *Bulk Merchandising Retail Building.* A building in which the sales area includes the storage of combustible materials on pallets, in solid piles, or in racks in excess of 12 ft (3660 mm) in storage height. [*101,* 2015]

3.3.183.5* *Business Occupancy.* An occupancy used for the transaction of business other than mercantile. [*101*, 2015]

3.3.183.6* *Day-Care Home.* A building or portion of a building in which more than 3 but not more than 12 clients receive care, maintenance, and supervision, by other than their relative(s) or legal guardian(s), for less than 24 hours per day. [*101*, 2015]

3.3.183.7* *Day-Care Occupancy.* An occupancy in which four or more clients receive care, maintenance, and supervision, by other than their relatives or legal guardians, for less than 24 hours per day. [*101*, 2015]

3.3.183.8* *Detention and Correctional Occupancy.* An occupancy used to house one or more persons under varied degrees of restraint or security where such occupants are mostly incapable of self-preservation because of security measures not under the occupants' control. [*101*, 2015]

3.3.183.8.1 *Detention and Correctional Use Condition.* For application of the life safety requirements in Section 20.7, the resident user category is divided into the five use conditions.

3.3.183.8.1.1 *Use Condition I — Free Egress.* A condition under which free movement is allowed from sleeping areas and other spaces where access or occupancy is permitted to the exterior via means of egress that meet the requirements of NFPA *101, Life Safety Code*. [*101*: 22.1.2.1.1]

3.3.183.8.1.2 *Use Condition II — Zoned Egress.* A condition under which free movement is allowed from sleeping areas and any other occupied smoke compartment to one or more other smoke compartments. [*101*: 22.1.2.1.2]

3.3.183.8.1.3 *Use Condition III — Zoned Impeded Egress.* A condition under which free movement is allowed within individual smoke compartments, such as within a residential unit comprised of individual sleeping rooms and a group activity space, with egress impeded by remote-controlled release of means of egress from such a smoke compartment to another smoke compartment. [*101*: 22.1.2.1.3]

3.3.183.8.1.4 *Use Condition IV — Impeded Egress.* A condition under which free movement is restricted from an occupied space, and remote-controlled release is provided to allow movement from all sleeping rooms, activity spaces, and other occupied areas within the smoke compartment to another smoke compartment. [*101*: 22.1.2.1.4]

3.3.183.8.1.5 *Use Condition V — Contained.* A condition under which free movement is restricted from an occupied space, and staff-controlled manual release at each door is provided to allow movement from all sleeping rooms, activity spaces, and other occupied areas within the smoke compartment to another smoke compartment. [*101*: 22.1.2.1.5]

3.3.183.9* *Dormitory.* A building or a space in a building in which group sleeping accommodations are provided for more than 16 persons who are not members of the same family in one room, or a series of closely associated rooms under joint occupancy and single management, with or without meals, but without individual cooking facilities. [*101*, 2015]

3.3.183.10* *Educational Occupancy.* An occupancy used for educational purposes through the twelfth grade by six or more persons for 4 or more hours per day or more than 12 hours per week. [*101*, 2015]

3.3.183.11* *Health Care Occupancy.* An occupancy used to provide medical or other treatment or care simultaneously to four or more patients on an inpatient basis, where such patients are mostly incapable of self-preservation due to age, physical or mental disability, or because of security measures not under the occupants' control. [*101*, 2015]

3.3.183.12 *Hospital.* A building or portion thereof used on a 24-hour basis for the medical, psychiatric, obstetrical, or surgical care of four or more inpatients. [*101*, 2015]

3.3.183.13* *Hotel.* A building or groups of buildings under the same management in which there are sleeping accommodations for more than 16 persons and primarily used by transients for lodging with or without meals. [*101*, 2015]

3.3.183.14* *Industrial Occupancy.* An occupancy in which products are manufactured or in which processing, assembling, mixing, packaging, finishing, decorating, or repair operations are conducted. [*101*, 2015]

3.3.183.15* *Limited Care Facility.* A building or portion of a building used on a 24-hour basis for the housing of four or more persons who are incapable of self-preservation because of age; physical limitations due to accident or illness; or limitations such as mental retardation/developmental disability, mental illness, or chemical dependency. [*101*, 2015]

3.3.183.16 *Lodging or Rooming House.* A building or portion thereof that does not qualify as a one- or two-family dwelling, that provides sleeping accommodations for a total of 16 or fewer people on a transient or permanent basis, without personal care services, with or without meals, but without separate cooking facilities for individual occupants. [*101*, 2015]

3.3.183.17* *Mercantile Occupancy.* An occupancy used for the display and sale of merchandise. [*101*, 2015]

3.3.183.17.1 *Class A Mercantile Occupancy.* All mercantile occupancies having an aggregate gross area of more than 30,000 ft^2 (2800 m^2) or occupying more than three stories for sales purposes. [*101*, 2015]

3.3.183.17.2 *Class B Mercantile Occupancy.* All mercantile occupancies of more than 3000 ft^2 (280 m^2), but not more than 30,000 ft^2 (2800 m^2), aggregate gross area and occupying not more than three stories for sales purposes. Class B also includes all mercantile occupancies of not more than 3000 ft^2 (280 m^2) gross area and occupying two or three stories for sales purposes. [*101*, 2015]

3.3.183.17.3 *Class C Mercantile Occupancy.* All mercantile occupancies of not more than 3000 ft^2 (280 m^2) gross area and used for sales purposes occupying one story only. [*101*, 2015]

3.3.183.18 *Mixed Occupancy.* A multiple occupancy where the occupancies are intermingled. [*101*, 2015]

3.3.183.19 *Motor Fuel Dispensing Facility.* That portion of a property where motor fuels are stored and dispensed from fixed equipment into the fuel tanks of motor vehicles or marine craft or into approved containers, including all equipment used in connection therewith. [**30A**, 2015]

3.3.183.19.1 *Fleet Vehicle Motor Fuel Dispensing Facility.* A motor fuel dispensing facility at a commercial, industrial, governmental, or manufacturing property where motor fuels are dispensed into the fuel tanks of motor vehicles that are used in connection with the business or operation of that property by persons within the employ of such business or operation. [**30A**, 2015]

3.3.183.19.2 *Marine Motor Fuel Dispensing Facility.* A motor fuel dispensing facility at or adjacent to shore, a pier, a wharf, or a floating dock where motor fuels are dispensed into the fuel tanks of marine craft. [**30A**, 2015]

3.3.183.19.3* *Motor Fuel Dispensing Facility Located Inside a Building.* That portion of a motor fuel dispensing facility located within the perimeter of a building or building structure that also contains other occupancies. [**30A**, 2015]

3.3.183.20 *Multiple Occupancy.* A building or structure in which two or more classes of occupancy exist. [**101**, 2015]

3.3.183.21 *Nursing Home.* A building or portion of a building used on a 24-hour basis for the housing and nursing care of four or more persons who, because of mental or physical incapacity, might be unable to provide for their own needs and safety without the assistance of another person. [**101**, 2015]

3.3.183.22 *One- and Two-Family Dwelling.* One- and two-family dwellings include buildings containing not more than two dwelling units in which each dwelling unit is occupied by members of a single family with not more than three outsiders, if any, accommodated in rented rooms.

3.3.183.22.1 *One- and Two-Family Dwelling Unit.* A building that contains not more than two dwelling units with independent cooking and bathroom facilities. [**101**, 2015]

3.3.183.23* *Parking Structure.* A building, structure, or portion thereof used for the parking, storage, or both, of motor vehicles. [**88A**, 2015]

3.3.183.23.1 *Basement and Underground Parking Structures.* Parking structures that are located below grade. A basement parking structure has other occupancies above it and an underground parking structure has no occupancy other than parking above it. Basement and underground parking structures are considered as specific cases of enclosed parking structures.

3.3.183.23.2 *Enclosed Parking Structure.* Any parking structure that is not an open parking structure. [**88A**, 2015]

3.3.183.23.3 *Open Parking Structure.* A parking structure that meets the requirements of Section 5.5 of NFPA 88A. [**88A**, 2015]

3.3.183.24 *Repair Garages.*

3.3.183.24.1 *Major Repair Garage.* A building or portions of a building where major repairs, such as engine overhauls, painting, body and fender work, and repairs that require draining of the motor vehicle fuel tank are performed on motor vehicles, including associated floor space used for offices, parking, or showrooms.

3.3.183.24.2 *Minor Repair Garage.* A building or portions of a building used for lubrication, inspection, and minor automotive maintenance work, such as engine tune-ups, replacement of parts, fluid changes (e.g., oil, antifreeze, transmission fluid, brake fluid, air conditioning refrigerants, etc.), brake system repairs, tire rotation, and similar routine maintenance work, including associated floor space used for offices, parking, or showrooms.

3.3.183.25* *Residential Board and Care Occupancy.* An occupancy used for lodging and boarding of four or more residents, not related by blood or marriage to the owners or operators, for the purpose of providing personal care services. [**101**, 2015]

3.3.183.26* *Residential Occupancy.* An occupancy that provides sleeping accommodations for purposes other than health care or detention and correctional. [**101**, 2015]

3.3.183.27 *Separated Occupancy.* A multiple occupancy where the occupancies are separated by fire resistance–rated assemblies. [**101**, 2015]

3.3.183.28* *Storage Occupancy.* An occupancy used primarily for the storage or sheltering of goods, merchandise, products, or vehicles. [**101**, 2015]

3.3.183.28.1* *Mini-Storage Building.* A storage occupancy partitioned into individual storage units, with a majority of the individual units not greater than 750 ft^2 in area, that are rented or leased for the purposes of storing personal or business items where all of the following apply: (1) the storage units are separated from each other by less than a 1-hour fire resistance rated barrier, (2) the owner of the facility does not have unrestricted access to the storage units, and (3) the items being stored are concealed from view from outside the storage unit.

3.3.184 **Occupant Load.** The total number of persons that might occupy a building or portion thereof at any one time. [**101**, 2015]

3.3.185 **Open System Use.** See 3.3.267.2.

3.3.186 **Operating Pressure.** The pressure at which a system operates.

3.3.187* **Operating Unit (Vessel) or Process Unit (Vessel).** The equipment in which a unit operation or unit process is conducted. *(See also 3.3.263, Unit Operation or Unit Process.)* [**30**, 2015]

3.3.188 **Operations.** A general term that includes, but is not limited to, the use, transfer, storage, and processing of liquids. [**30**, 2015]

3.3.189 **Organic Peroxide.** Any organic compound having a double oxygen or peroxy (-O-O-) group in its chemical structure. [**400**, 2013]

3.3.189.1* *Organic Peroxide Formulation.* A pure or technically pure organic peroxide or a mixture of organic peroxides alone or in combination with one or more materials in various combinations and concentrations. [**400**, 2013]

3.3.189.1.1 *Class I.* Class I shall describe those formulations that are more severe than a Class II but do not detonate. [**400**, 2013]

3.3.189.1.2 *Class II.* Class II shall describe those formulations that burn very rapidly and that present a severe reactivity hazard. [**400**, 2013]

3.3.189.1.3 *Class III.* Class III shall describe those formulations that burn rapidly and that present a moderate reactivity hazard. [**400**, 2013]

3.3.189.1.4 *Class IV.* Class IV shall describe those formulations that burn in the same manner as ordinary combustibles and that present a minimal reactivity hazard. [**400**, 2013]

3.3.189.1.5* Class V.* Class V shall describe those formulations that burn with less intensity than ordinary combustibles or do not sustain combustion and that present no reactivity hazard. [400,** 2013]

3.3.189.2 *Organic Peroxide Storage Area.* See 3.3.14.7.

3.3.190 OSHA. The Occupational Safety and Health Administration of the U.S. Department of Labor. [**55,** 2013]

3.3.191 Overcrowded. A situation where the occupant load exceeds the exit capacity or the posted occupant load.

3.3.192* Oxidizer. Any solid or liquid material that readily yields oxygen or other oxidizing gas or that readily reacts to promote or initiate combustion of combustible materials and that can, under some circumstances undergo a vigorous self-sustained decomposition due to contamination or heat exposure. [**400,** 2013]

3.3.192.1* Class 1. An oxidizer that does not moderately increase the burning rate of combustible materials with which it comes into contact or a solid oxidizer classified as Class 1 when tested in accordance with the test protocol set forth in G.1 of NFPA 400. [**400,** 2013]

3.3.192.2* Class 2. An oxidizer that causes a moderate increase in the burning rate of combustible materials with which it comes into contact or a solid oxidizer classified as Class 2 when tested in accordance with the test protocol set forth in G.1 of NFPA 400. [**400,** 2013]

3.3.192.3* Class 3. An oxidizer that causes a severe increase in the burning rate of combustible materials with which it comes into contact or a solid oxidizer classified as Class 3 when tested in accordance with the test protocol set forth in G.1 of NFPA 400. [**400,** 2013]

3.3.192.4* Class 4. An oxidizer that can undergo an explosive reaction due to contamination or exposure to thermal or physical shock and that causes a severe increase in the burning rate of combustible materials with which it comes into contact. [**400,** 2013]

3.3.193 Ozone Generator. Equipment that causes the production of ozone.

3.3.194 Packaging. A commodity wrapping, cushioning, or container. [**13,** 2013]

3.3.195 Paper. Felted sheets made from natural fibrous materials, usually vegetable but sometimes mineral or animal, and formed on a fine wire screen by means of water suspension.

3.3.196 Patch Kettle. Any pot or container with a capacity of less than 6 gal (22.7 L) used for preheating tar, asphalt, pitch, or similar substances for the repair of roofs, streets, floors, pipes, or similar objects.

3.3.197 Permissible Exposure Limit (PEL). See 3.3.162.2.

3.3.198 Permit. A document issued by the AHJ for the purpose of authorizing performance of a specified activity.

3.3.199 Peroxide-Forming Chemical. A chemical that, when exposed to air, forms explosive peroxides that are shock sensitive, pressure sensitive, or heat sensitive.

3.3.200* Personal Care. The care of residents who do not require chronic or convalescent medical or nursing care. [*101,* 2015]

3.3.201 Pesticide. Any substance or mixture of substances intended for preventing, destroying, repelling, or mitigating any pest or for use as a plant regulator, defoliant, or desiccant.

3.3.202 Physical Hazard. A chemical for which there is scientifically valid evidence that the chemical is an organic peroxide or oxidizer.

3.3.203* Pier. A structure, usually of greater length than width and projecting from the shore into a body of water with direct access from land, that can be either open deck or provided with a superstructure. [**307,** 2011]

3.3.204* Pressure Vessel. A container, process vessel, or other component designed in accordance with the ASME Boiler and Pressure Vessel Code, DOT, or other approved standards. [**400,** 2013]

3.3.205 Primary Containment. The first level of containment, consisting of the inside portion of that container that comes into immediate contact on its inner surface with the material being contained.

3.3.206* Process or Processing. An integrated sequence of operations. [**30,** 2015]

3.3.207 Process Unit (Vessel). See 3.3.187, Operating Unit (Vessel) or Process Unit (Vessel).

3.3.208 Proprietary Information. Information regarding compounds or ingredients used in a process or production that do not qualify as trade secrets but that provide an industry or business with a competitive advantage.

3.3.209 Protection for Exposures. Fire protection for structures on property adjacent to liquid storage that is provided by (1) a public fire department or (2) a private fire brigade maintained on the property adjacent to the liquid storage, either of which is capable of providing cooling water streams to protect the property adjacent to the liquid storage. [**30,** 2015]

3.3.210 Public Way. A street, alley, or other similar parcel of land essentially open to the outside air deeded, dedicated, or otherwise permanently appropriated to the public for public use and having a clear width and height of not less than 10 ft (3050 mm). [*101,* 2015]

3.3.211 Purging. A method used to free the internal volume of a piping system of unwanted contents that results in the existing contents being removed or replaced. [**55,** 2013]

3.3.212 Pyrophoric. A chemical that spontaneously ignites in air at or below a temperature of 130°F (54.5°C).

3.3.213 Quality Assurance. The procedures conducted by the registered design professionals (RDPs) responsible for design and the registered design professionals responsible for inspection that provide evidence and documentation to the RDPs, the owner, and the AHJ that the work is being constructed in accordance with the approved construction documents. [**5000,** 2015]

3.3.214 Quality Assurance Program. A predefined set of observations, special inspections, tests, and other procedures that provide an independent record to the owner, AHJ, and RDP responsible for design that the construction is in general conformance with the approved construction documents. [**5000,** 2015]

3.3.215* Rack. Any combination of vertical, horizontal, and diagonal members that supports stored materials.

3.3.215.1 *Double-Row Racks.* Racks less than or equal to 12 ft (3.7 m) in depth or single-row racks placed back to back having an aggregate depth up to 12 ft (3.7 m), with aisles having an aisle width of at least 3.5 ft (1.1 m) between loads on racks. [**13**, 2013]

3.3.215.2* *Movable Racks.* Racks on fixed rails or guides.

3.3.215.3 *Multiple-Row Racks.* Racks greater than 12 ft (3.7 m) in depth or single- or double-row racks separated by aisles less than 3.5 ft (1.1 m) wide having an overall width greater than 12 ft (3.7 m). [**13**, 2013]

3.3.215.4* *Portable Racks.* Racks that are not fixed in place and can be arranged in any number of configurations. [**13**, 2013]

3.3.215.5 *Single-Row Racks.* Racks that have no longitudinal flue space and that have a depth up to 6 ft (1.8 m) with aisles having a width of at least 3.5 ft (1.1 m) between loads on racks. [**13**, 2013]

3.3.216* Ramp. A walking surface that has a slope steeper than 1 in 20. [***101**, 2015*]

3.3.217 Recreational Fire. The noncommercial burning of materials other than rubbish for pleasure, religious, ceremonial, cooking, or similar purposes in which the fuel burned is not contained in an incinerator, a barbecue grill, or a barbecue pit, and the total fuel area is not exceeding 3 ft (0.9 m) in diameter and 2 ft (0.6 m) in height.

3.3.218 Refinery. A plant in which flammable or combustible liquids are produced on a commercial scale from crude petroleum, natural gasoline, or other hydrocarbon sources. [**30**, 2015]

3.3.219 Registered Design Professional (RDP). An individual who is registered or licensed to practice his/her respective design profession as defined by the statutory requirements of the professional registration laws of the state or jurisdiction in which the project is to be constructed. [**5000**, 2015]

3.3.220 Relocatable Power Tap. A device for indoor use consisting of an attachment plug on one end of a flexible cord and two or more receptacles on the opposite end, and has overcurrent protection.

3.3.221 Row. A minimum yard storage unit comprised of adjoining cotton bales.

3.3.222* Safety Can. A listed container of not more than 5.3 gal (20 L) capacity having a screen or strainer in each fill and pour opening, and having a spring-closing lid and spout cover, designed to safely relieve internal pressure when exposed to fire. [**30**, 2015]

3.3.223 Sales Display Area. See 3.3.14.10.

3.3.224 Salvage Vehicle. A vehicle that is dismantled for parts or awaiting destruction.

3.3.225 Self-Closing. Equipped with an approved device that ensures closing after opening. [***101**, 2015*]

3.3.226 Separation of Hazards. Physically separated by a specified distance, construction, or appliance. [**55**, 2013]

3.3.227 Shop Drawings. Scaled working drawings, equipment cutsheets, and design calculations. *(See 3.3.12, Plan, of NFPA 1031.)* [***1031**, 2014*]

3.3.228* Signal.

3.3.228.1* *Alarm Signal.* A signal that results from the manual or automatic detection of an alarm condition. [**72**, 2013]

3.3.228.2* *Fire Alarm Signal.* A signal that results from the manual or automatic detection of a fire alarm condition. [**72**, 2013]

3.3.228.3* *Supervisory Signal.* A signal that results from the detection of a supervisory condition. [**72**, 2013]

3.3.228.4* *Trouble Signal.* A signal that results from the detection of a trouble condition. [**72**, 2013]

3.3.229 Simple Asphyxiant Gas. See 3.3.135.16.

3.3.230 Smoke Alarm. A single or multiple-station alarm responsive to smoke. [**72**, 2013]

3.3.231* Smoke Barrier. A continuous membrane, or a membrane with discontinuities created by protected openings, where such membrane is designed and constructed to restrict the movement of smoke. [**5000**, 2015]

3.3.232 Smoke Compartment. See 3.3.66.2

3.3.233* Smoke Partition. A continuous membrane that is designed to form a barrier to limit the transfer of smoke. [***101**, 2015*]

3.3.234 Smoking. The use or carrying of a lighted pipe, cigar, cigarette, tobacco, or any other type of smoking substance.

3.3.235 Smoking Area. See 3.3.14.11.

3.3.236 Solid.

3.3.236.1* *Combustible Particulate Solid.* An oxidizable, solid-phase material comprising distinct particles or pieces. [**69**, 2014]

3.3.236.2* *Flammable Solid.* A solid substance, other than a substance defined as a blasting agent or explosive, that is liable to cause fire resulting from friction or retained heat from manufacture, that has an ignition temperature below 212°F (100°C), or that burns so vigorously or persistently when ignited that it creates a serious hazard. [**400**, 2013]

3.3.237 Solid Material. A material that has a melting point, decomposes, or sublimes at a temperature greater than 68°F (20°C). [**5000**, 2015]

3.3.238 Solid Shelving. Solid shelving is fixed in place, slatted, wire mesh, or other type of shelves located within racks. The area of a solid shelf is defined by perimeter aisle or flue space on all four sides. Solid shelves having an area equal to or less than 20 ft^2 (1.9 m^2) shall be defined as open racks. Shelves of wire mesh, slats, or other materials more than 50 percent open and where the flue spaces are maintained shall be defined as open racks. [**13**, 2013]

3.3.239 Special Use. See 3.3.267.3.

3.3.240 Spray Area. See 3.3.14.12.

3.3.241* Spray Booth. A power-ventilated enclosure for a spray application operation or process that confines and limits the escape of the material being sprayed, including vapors, mists, dusts, and residues that are produced by the spraying operation and conducts or directs these materials to an exhaust system. [**33**, 2011]

3.3.242* Spray Room. A power-ventilated fully enclosed room used exclusively for open spraying of flammable or combustible materials. [**33**, 2011]

3.3.243 Standard Cubic Foot (scf) of Gas. An amount of gas that occupies one cubic foot at an absolute pressure of 14.7 psi (101 kPa) and a temperature of 70°F (21°C). [**55**, 2013]

3.3.244 Standard Temperature and Pressure (STP). A temperature of 70°F (21°C) and a pressure of 1 atmosphere (14.7 psi or 760 mm Hg).

3.3.245 Standpipe System. See 3.3.254.13.

3.3.246 Storage.

    3.3.246.1 *Banded Tire Storage.* Storage in which a number of tires are strapped together.

    3.3.246.2 *Cartoned Storage.* Storage consisting of corrugated cardboard or paperboard containers that fully enclose the commodity.

    3.3.246.3 *Detached Storage.* Storage in a separate building or in an outside area located away from all structures.

    3.3.246.4 *High-Piled Storage.* Solid-piled, palletized, rack storage, bin box, and shelf storage in excess of 12 ft (3.7 m) in height. [**13**, 2013]

    3.3.246.5 *Isolated Storage.* Storage in a different storage room or in a separate and detached building located at a safe distance.

    3.3.246.6 *Laced Tire Storage.* Tires stored where the sides of the tires overlap, creating a woven or laced appearance. [*See Figure A.34.8.1(g).*] [**13**, 2013]

    3.3.246.7* *Miscellaneous Tire Storage.* The storage of rubber tires that is incidental to the main use of the building. Storage areas shall not exceed 2000 ft^2 (186 m^2). On-tread storage piles, regardless of storage method, shall not exceed 25 ft (7.6 m) in the direction of the wheel holes. Acceptable storage arrangements include (a) on-floor, on-side storage up to 12 ft (3.7 m) high; (b) on-floor, on-tread storage up to 5 ft (1.5 m) high; (c) double-row or multirow fixed or portable rack storage on-side or on-tread up to 5 ft (1.5 m) high; (d) single row fixed or portable rack storage on-side or on-tread up to 12 ft (3.7 m) high; and (e) laced tires in racks up to 5 ft (1.5 m) in height. [**13**, 2013]

    3.3.246.8 *On-Side Tire Storage.* Tires stored horizontally or flat. [**13**, 2013]

    3.3.246.9 *On-Tread Tire Storage.* Tires stored vertically or on their treads. [**13**, 2013]

    3.3.246.10 *Palletized Tire Storage.* Storage on portable racks of various types utilizing a conventional pallet as a base. [**13**, 2013]

    3.3.246.11 *Segregated Storage.* Storage located in the same room or inside area that is physically separated by distance from incompatible materials.

    3.3.246.12 *Yard Storage.* Storage of commodities in outdoor areas.

3.3.247 Storage Aids. Commodity storage devices, such as pallets, dunnage, separators, and skids. [**13**, 2013]

3.3.248 Story. The portion of a building located between the upper surface of a floor and the upper surface of the floor or roof next above. [**5000**, 2015]

3.3.248.1* *Occupiable Story.* A story occupied by people on a regular basis. [***101***, 2015]

3.3.249 Street. A public thoroughfare that has been dedicated for vehicular use by the public and can be used for access by fire department vehicles. [***101***, 2015]

3.3.250* Street Floor. A story or floor level accessible from the street or from outside the building at the finished ground level, with the floor level at the main entrance located not more than three risers above or below the finished ground level, and arranged and utilized to qualify as the main floor. [***101***, 2015]

3.3.251 Structural Element. The columns and girders, beams, trusses, joists, braced frames, moment-resistant frames, and vertical and lateral resisting elements, and other framing members that are designed to carry any portion of the dead or live load and lateral forces, that are essential to the stability of the building or structure. [**5000**, 2015]

3.3.252* Structure. That which is built or constructed. [***101***, 2015]

3.3.253 Summarily Abate. To immediately judge a condition to be a fire hazard to life or property and to order immediate correction of such condition.

3.3.254 System. Several items of equipment assembled, grouped, or otherwise interconnected for the accomplishment of a purpose or function.

    3.3.254.1 *Bulk Hydrogen Compressed Gas System.* An assembly of equipment that consists of, but is not limited to, storage containers, pressure regulators, pressure relief devices, compressors, manifolds, and piping, with a storage capacity of more than (5000 scf) (141.6 Nm^3) of compressed hydrogen gas and that terminates at the source valve. [**55**, 2013]

    3.3.254.2 *Bulk Inert Gas System.* An assembly of equipment that consists of, but is not limited to, storage containers, pressure regulators, pressure relief devices, vaporizers, manifolds, and piping, with a storage capacity of more than 20,000 scf (566 Nm^3) of inert gas, including unconnected reserves on hand at the site, and that terminates at the source valve. [**55**, 2013]

    3.3.254.3 *Bulk Liquefied Hydrogen System.* An assembly of equipment that consists of, but is not limited to, storage containers, pressure regulators, pressure relief devices, vaporizers, liquid pumps, compressors, manifolds, and piping, with a storage capacity of more than 39.7 gal (150 L) of liquefied hydrogen that terminates at the source valve. [**55**, 2013]

    3.3.254.4* *Bulk Oxygen System.* An assembly of equipment, such as oxygen storage containers, pressure regulators, pressure relief devices, vaporizers, manifolds, and interconnecting piping, that has a storage capacity of more than 20,000 scf (566 Nm^3) of oxygen and that terminates at the source valve. [**55**, 2013]

    3.3.254.5 *Central Station Service Alarm System.* A system or group of systems in which the operations of circuits and devices are transmitted automatically to, recorded in, maintained by, and supervised from a listed central station that has competent and experienced servers and operators who, upon receipt of a signal, take such action as required by *NFPA 72*. Such service is to be controlled and operated by a person, firm, or corporation whose business is the furnishing, maintaining, or monitoring of supervised alarm systems. [72, 2013]

3.3.254.6 Compressed Gas System. An assembly of equipment designed to contain, distribute, or transport compressed gases. [318, 2015]

3.3.254.7 Continuous Gas Detection System. A gas detection system in which the instrument is maintained in continuous operation and the interval between sampling of any point does not exceed 30 minutes. [55, 2013]

3.3.254.8 Cylinder Containment System. A gastight recovery system comprising equipment or devices that can be placed over a leak in a compressed gas container, thereby stopping or controlling the escape of gas from the leaking container. [55, 2013]

3.3.254.9 Dedicated Smoke-Control System. A system that is intended for the purpose of smoke control only, which are separate systems of air moving and distribution equipment that do not function under normal building operating conditions.

3.3.254.10 Fire Alarm System. A system or portion of a combination system that consists of components and circuits arranged to monitor and annunciate the status of fire alarm or supervisory signal-initiating devices and to initiate the appropriate response to those signals. [72, 2013]

3.3.254.11 Fire Protection System. Any fire alarm device or system or fire-extinguishing device or system, or combination thereof, that is designed and installed for detecting, controlling, or extinguishing a fire or otherwise alerting occupants, or the fire department, or both, that a fire has occurred. [1141, 2012]

3.3.254.12 Nondedicated Smoke-Control System. A smoke-control system that shares components with some other system(s), such as the building HVAC system, which changes its mode of operation to achieve the smoke-control objective.

3.3.254.13* Standpipe System. An arrangement of piping, valves, hose connections, and allied equipment installed in a building or structure, with the hose connections located in such a manner that water can be discharged in streams or spray patterns through attached hose and nozzles, for the purpose of extinguishing a fire, thereby protecting a building or structure and its contents in addition to protecting the occupants. [14, 2013]

3.3.254.14 Treatment System. An assembly of equipment capable of processing a hazardous gas and reducing the gas concentration to a predetermined level at the point of discharge from the system to the atmosphere. [55, 2013]

3.3.254.15* Vapor Processing System. A system designed to capture and process vapors displaced during transfer or filling operations by use of mechanical or chemical means. [30, 2015]

3.3.254.16* Vapor Recovery System. A system designed to capture and retain, without processing, vapors displaced during transfer or filling operations. [30, 2015]

3.3.255 Tank.

  3.3.255.1 Aboveground Storage Tank. A horizontal or vertical tank that is listed and intended for fixed installation, without backfill, above or below grade and is used within the scope of its approval or listing. [30A, 2015]

  3.3.255.2 Aboveground Tank. A tank that is installed above grade, at grade, or below grade without backfill. [30, 2012]

  3.3.255.2.1 Protected Aboveground Tank. An atmospheric aboveground storage tank with integral secondary containment and thermal insulation that has been evaluated for resistance to physical damage and for limiting the heat transferred to the primary tank when exposed to a hydrocarbon pool fire and is listed in accordance with ANSI/UL 2085, *Standard for Protected Aboveground Tanks for Flammable and Combustible Liquids,* or an equivalent test procedure. [30:22.2.3]

  3.3.255.3 ASME Tank. See 3.3.69.1, ASME Container.

  3.3.255.4* Portable Tank. (Compressed Gases and Cryogenic Fluids) Any vessel having a liquid capacity over 60 gal (230 L) intended for storing liquids and not intended for fixed installation. [30, 2015]

  3.3.255.5 Secondary Containment Tank. A tank that has an inner and outer wall with an interstitial space (annulus) between the walls and that has a means for monitoring the interstitial space for a leak. [30, 2015]

  3.3.255.6* Stationary Tank. A packaging designed primarily for stationary installations not intended for loading, unloading, or attachment to a transport vehicle as part of its normal operation in the process of use. [55, 2010]

  3.3.255.7 Storage Tank. Any vessel having a liquid capacity that exceeds 60 gal (230 L), is intended for fixed installation, and is not used for processing. [30, 2015]

3.3.256 Temporary Wiring. Approved wiring for power and lighting during a period of construction, remodeling, maintenance, repair, or demolition, and decorative lighting, carnival power and lighting, and similar purposes.

3.3.257 Tire.

  3.3.257.1 Rubber Tires. Pneumatic tires for passenger automobiles, aircraft, light and heavy trucks, trailers, farm equipment, construction equipment (off-the-road), and buses. [13, 2013]

  3.3.257.2 Scrap Tire. A tire that can no longer be used for its original purpose due to wear or damage.

3.3.258 TC. Transport Canada. [55, 2013]

3.3.259 Toxic Material. See 3.3.173.14.

3.3.260* Traffic Calming Device. A roadway design element utilized to reduce vehicle speeds, decrease motor vehicle volumes, and increase safety for pedestrians and nonmotorized vehicles.

3.3.261* Tube Trailer. A truck or semitrailer on which a number of very long compressed gas tubular cylinders have been mounted and manifolded into a common piping system. [55, 2013]

3.3.262 Unauthorized Discharge. A release or emission of materials in a manner that does not conform to the provisions of this *Code* or applicable public health and safety regulations.

3.3.263 Unit Operation or Unit Process. A segment of a physical or chemical process that might or might not be integrated with other segments to constitute the manufacturing sequence. [30, 2015]

3.3.264 Unit Process. See 3.3.263, Unit Operation or Unit Process.

3.3.265 Unit (Vessel), Operating or Process. See 3.3.187.

3.3.266 Unstable (Reactive) Material. See 3.3.173.15.

3.3.267* Use. To place a material, including solids, liquids, and gases into action. [**400**, 2013]

3.3.267.1* *Closed System Use.* Use of a solid or liquid hazardous material in a closed vessel or system that remains closed during normal operations where vapors emitted by the product are not liberated outside of the vessel or system and the product is not exposed to the atmosphere during normal operations, and all uses of compressed gases. [**400**, 2013]

3.3.267.2* *Open System Use.* Use of a solid or liquid hazardous material in a vessel or system that is continuously open to the atmosphere during normal operations and where vapors are liberated, or the product is exposed to the atmosphere during normal operations. [**400**, 2013]

3.3.267.3 *Special Use.* A use that includes, but is not limited to, events or occurrences during which life safety–threatening situations or fire hazards exist or are likely to exist as determined by the AHJ.

3.3.268 Valve.

3.3.268.1 *Indicating Valve.* A valve that has components that show if the valve is open or closed. Examples are outside screw and yoke (OS&Y) gate valves and underground gate valves with indicator posts.

3.3.268.2 *Reduced Flow Valve.* A valve equipped with a restricted flow orifice that is designed to reduce the maximum flow from the valve under full flow conditions.

3.3.268.3 *Valve Outlet Cap or Plug.* A removable device that forms a gastight seal on the outlet to the control valve that is provided on a source containing a compressed gas or cryogenic fluid. [**55**, 2013]

3.3.268.4 *Valve Protection Cap.* A rigid, removable cover provided for container valve protection during handling, transportation, and storage. [**55**, 2013]

3.3.268.5 *Valve Protection Device.* A device attached to the neck ring or body of a cylinder for the purpose of protecting the cylinder valve from being struck or from being damaged by the impact resulting from a fall or an object striking the cylinder.

3.3.269* Vapor Pressure. The pressure, measured in pounds per square inch, absolute (psia), exerted by a liquid, as determined by ASTM D 323, *Standard Test Method for Vapor Pressure of Petroleum Products (Reid Method)*. [**30**, 2015]

3.3.270 Vapor Processing System. See 3.3.254.15.

3.3.271 Vapor Recovery System. See 3.3.254.16.

3.3.272 Warehouse.

3.3.272.1 *General-Purpose Warehouse.* A separate, detached building or portion of a building used only for warehousing-type operations and classified as a "storage — low hazard" or "storage — ordinary hazard" occupancy by the building code and by NFPA *101, Life Safety Code*. [**30**, 2015]

3.3.272.2 *Liquid Warehouse.* A separate, detached building or an attached building that is used for warehousing-type operations for liquids and whose exterior wall comprises at least 25 percent of the building perimeter. [**30**, 2015]

3.3.273 Water Capacity. The amount of water at 60°F (16°C) required to fill a container. [**58**, 2014]

3.3.274* Wharf. A structure at the shoreline that has a platform built along and parallel to a body of water with either an open deck or a superstructure. [**307**, 2011]

3.3.275 Wildland/Urban Interface. The presence of structures in locations in which the AHJ determines that topographical features, vegetation fuel types, local weather conditions, and prevailing winds result in the potential for ignition of the structures within the area from flames and firebrands of a wildland fire. [**1144**, 2013]

3.3.276 Wood Panel. Board or sheet made from veneers, particles, or fibers of wood and includes plywood, oriented strandboard, and similar wood products.

3.3.277 Written Notice. A notification in writing delivered in person to the individual or parties intended, or delivered at, or sent by certified or registered mail to, the last residential or business address of legal record.

3.4 Special Performance-Based Definitions.

3.4.1 Alternative Calculation Procedure. A calculation procedure that differs from the procedure originally employed by the design team but that provides predictions for the same variables of interest. [*101*, 2015]

3.4.2 Analysis.

3.4.2.1 *Sensitivity Analysis.* An analysis performed to determine the degree to which a predicted output will vary given a specified change in an input parameter, usually in relation to models. [**5000**, 2015]

3.4.2.2 *Uncertainty Analysis.* An analysis intended to (1) identify key sources of uncertainties in the predictions of a model, (2) assess the potential impacts of these uncertainties on the predictions, and (3) assess the likelihood of these potential impacts. Per this definition, sensitivity analysis performs some but not all of the functions of uncertainty analysis. [**805**, 2010]

3.4.3 Data Conversion. The process of developing the input data set for the assessment method of choice. [*101*, 2015]

3.4.4 Design Fire Scenario. See 3.4.9.1.

3.4.5* Design Specification. A building characteristic and other conditions that are under the control of the design team. [**5000**, 2015]

3.4.6 Design Team. A group of stakeholders including, but not limited to, representatives of the architect, client, and any pertinent engineers and other designers. [*101*, 2015]

3.4.7* Exposure Fire. A fire that starts at a location that is remote from the area being protected and grows to expose that which is being protected. [*101*, 2015]

3.4.8* Fire Model. Mathematical prediction of fire growth, environmental conditions, and potential effects on structures, systems, or components based on the conservation equations or empirical data. [**805**, 2010]

3.4.9* Fire Scenario. A set of conditions that defines the development of fire, the spread of combustion products throughout a building or portion of a building, the reactions of people to fire, and the effects of combustion products. [*101*, 2015]

3.4.9.1 *Design Fire Scenario.* A fire scenario selected for evaluation of a proposed design. [**914**, 2010]

3.4.10* Fuel Load. The total quantity of combustible contents of a building, space, or fire area. [**5000**, 2015]

3.4.11 Incapacitation. A condition under which humans do not function adequately and become unable to escape untenable conditions. [*101*, 2015]

3.4.12 Input Data Specification. Information required by the verification method. [*101*, 2015]

3.4.13 Occupant Characteristics. The abilities or behaviors of people before and during a fire. [*101*, 2015]

3.4.14* Performance Criteria. Threshold values on measurement scales that are based on quantified performance objectives. [*101*, 2015]

3.4.15* Proposed Design. A design developed by a design team and submitted to the AHJ for approval. [*101*, 2015]

3.4.16 Safe Location. A location remote or separated from the effects of a fire so that such effects no longer pose a threat. [*101*, 2015]

3.4.17 Safety Factor. A factor applied to a predicted value to ensure that a sufficient safety margin is maintained. [*101*, 2015]

3.4.18 Safety Margin. The difference between a predicted value and the actual value where a fault condition is expected. [*101*, 2015]

3.4.19 Sensitivity Analysis. See 3.4.2.1.

3.4.20 Stakeholder. An individual, or representative of same, having an interest in the successful completion of a project. [*101*, 2015]

3.4.21 Uncertainty Analysis. See 3.4.2.2.

3.4.22 Verification Method. A procedure or process used to demonstrate or confirm that the proposed design meets the specified criteria. [*101*, 2015]

Chapter 4   General Requirements

4.1* Goals and Objectives.

4.1.1* Goals. The goals of this *Code* shall be to provide a reasonable level of safety, property protection, and public welfare from the hazards created by fire, explosion, and other hazardous conditions.

4.1.2* Objectives. To achieve the goals stated in 4.1.1, the goals and objectives of 4.1.3 through 4.1.5 shall be used to determine the intent of this *Code*.

4.1.3* Safety. This *Code* shall provide for life safety by reducing the probability of injury or death from fire, explosions, or events involving hazardous materials.

4.1.3.1 Safety from Fire.

4.1.3.1.1* Safety-from-Fire Goals. The fire safety goals of this *Code* shall be as follows:

(1) To provide an environment for the occupants in a building or facility and for the public near a building or facility that is reasonably safe from fire and similar emergencies
(2) To protect fire fighters and emergency responders

4.1.3.1.2 Safety-from-Fire Objectives.

4.1.3.1.2.1 Buildings and facilities shall be designed, constructed, and maintained to protect occupants who are not intimate with the initial fire development for the amount of time needed to evacuate, relocate, or defend in place.

4.1.3.1.2.2* Buildings shall be designed and constructed to provide reasonable safety for fire fighters and emergency responders during search and rescue operations.

4.1.3.1.2.3 Buildings shall be designed, located, and constructed to reasonably protect adjacent persons from injury or death as a result of a fire.

4.1.3.1.2.4 Buildings shall be designed, located, and constructed to provide reasonable access to the building for emergency responders.

4.1.3.1.2.5* Operations shall be conducted at facilities in a safe manner that minimizes, reduces, controls, or mitigates the risk of fire injury or death for the operators, while protecting the occupants not intimate with initial fire development for the amount of time needed to evacuate, relocate, or defend in place.

4.1.3.2 Safety During Building Use.

4.1.3.2.1* Safety-During-Building-Use Goal. The safety-during-building-use goal of this *Code* shall be to provide an environment for the occupants of the building that is reasonably safe during the normal use of the building.

4.1.3.2.2 Safety-During-Building-Use Objectives.

4.1.3.2.2.1 Buildings shall be designed and constructed to reduce the probability of death or injury of persons from falling during normal use of the building.

4.1.3.2.2.2 Buildings shall be designed and constructed to provide for reasonably safe crowd movement during emergency and nonemergency conditions.

4.1.3.2.2.3 Buildings shall be designed and constructed to provide reasonable life safety for occupants and workers during construction and demolition.

4.1.3.2.2.4 Buildings shall be designed and constructed to provide reasonable notification to occupants of fire and other emergency situations.

4.1.3.2.2.5 Buildings shall be designed and constructed to provide reasonable signage and lighting to identify hazards, exits, means of egress, and other building safety features.

4.1.3.3 Safety from Hazardous Materials.

4.1.3.3.1 Safety-from-Hazardous-Materials Goal. The safety-from-hazardous-materials goal of this *Code* shall be to provide an environment for the occupants in a building or facility and to those adjacent to a building or facility that is reasonably safe from exposures to adverse affects from hazardous materials present therein.

4.1.3.3.2 Safety-from-Hazardous-Materials Objectives.

4.1.3.3.2.1 The storage, use, or handling of hazardous materials in a building or facility shall be accomplished in a manner that provides a reasonable level of safety for occupants and for those adjacent to a building or facility from health hazards, illness, injury, or death during normal storage, use, or handling operations and conditions.

4.1.3.3.2.2* The storage, use, or handling of hazardous materials in a building or facility shall be accomplished in a manner that provides a reasonable level of safety for occupants and for those adjacent to a building or facility from illness, injury, or death due to the following conditions:

(1) An unplanned release of the hazardous material
(2) A fire impinging upon the hazardous material or the involvement of the material in a fire
(3) The application of an external force on the hazardous material that is likely to result in an unsafe condition

4.1.4 Property Protection.

4.1.4.1 Property Protection Goal. The property protection goal of this *Code* shall be to limit damage created by a fire, explosion, or event associated with hazardous materials to a reasonable level to the building or facility and adjacent property.

4.1.4.2 Property Protection Objectives.

4.1.4.2.1* Prevention of Ignition. The facility shall be designed, constructed, and maintained, and operations associated with the facility shall be conducted, to prevent unintentional explosions and fires that result in failure of or damage to adjacent compartments, emergency life safety systems, adjacent properties, adjacent outside storage, and the facility's structural elements.

4.1.4.2.2* Fire Spread and Explosions. In the event that a fire or explosion occurs, the building or facility shall be sited, designed, constructed, or maintained, and operations associated with the facility shall be conducted and protected, to reasonably reduce the impact of unwanted fires and explosions on the adjacent compartments, emergency life safety systems, adjacent properties, adjacent outside storage, and the facility's structural elements.

4.1.4.2.3 Structural Integrity. The facility shall be designed, constructed, protected, and maintained, and operations associated with the facility shall be conducted, to provide a reasonable level of protection for the facility, its contents, and adjacent properties from building collapse due to a loss of structural integrity resulting from a fire.

4.1.4.2.4 Hazardous Materials. The facility shall be designed, constructed, and maintained, and operations associated with the facility shall be conducted, to provide reasonable property protection from damage resulting from fires, explosions, and other unsafe conditions associated with the storage, use, and handling of hazardous materials therein.

4.1.5 Public Welfare.

4.1.5.1* Public Welfare Goal. The public welfare goal of this *Code* shall be to maintain a high probability that buildings and facilities that provide a public welfare role for a community continue to perform the function for their intended purpose following a fire, explosion, or hazardous materials event.

4.1.5.2* Public Welfare Objective. Buildings and facilities that provide a public welfare role for a community shall be designed, constructed, maintained, and operated to provide reasonable assurance of continued function following a fire, explosion, or hazardous materials event.

4.2 Assumptions.

4.2.1* Single Fire Source.

4.2.1.1 The fire protection methods of this *Code* shall assume that multiple simultaneous fire incidents will not occur.

4.2.1.2 The single fire source assumption shall not preclude the evaluation of multiple design fire scenarios as required by Section 5.4.

4.2.2* Single Hazardous Material Release.

4.2.2.1 The protection methods of this *Code* shall assume that multiple simultaneous unauthorized releases of hazardous materials from different locations will not occur.

4.2.2.2 The single hazardous material release assumption shall not preclude the evaluation of multiple design scenarios as required by Section 5.4.

4.2.3* Incidents Impinging on Hazardous Materials. The protection methods of this *Code* shall assume that a fire, explosion, hazardous materials release, or external force that creates a dangerous condition has the potential to impinge on hazardous materials being stored, handled, or used in the building or facility under normal conditions. *(See Section 5.4 for performance-based design scenarios.)*

4.3 Compliance Options. Compliance with the goals and objectives of Section 4.1 shall be provided in accordance with either of the following:

(1) The prescriptive-based provisions per 4.3.1
(2) The performance-based provisions per 4.3.2

4.3.1 Prescriptive-Based Option.

4.3.1.1 A prescriptive-based option shall be in accordance with Chapter 1 through Chapter 4, Chapter 6, and Chapter 10 through Chapter 75 of this *Code*.

4.3.1.2 Where specific requirements contained in Chapter 20 for occupancies differ from general requirements contained in Chapter 1 through Chapter 4 and Chapter 10 through Chapter 75, the requirements of Chapter 20 shall govern.

4.3.2 Performance-Based Option.

4.3.2.1 A performance-based option shall be in accordance with Chapter 1 through Chapter 5 of this *Code*.

4.3.2.2 Prescriptive requirements shall be permitted to be used as part of the performance approach, if they, in conjunction with the performance features, meet the overall goals and objectives of this *Code*.

4.4 Fundamental Requirements.

4.4.1 Multiple Safeguards.

4.4.1.1 The design of every building or structure intended for human occupancy shall be such that reliance for property protection and safety to life does not depend solely on any single safeguard.

4.4.1.2 Additional safeguard(s) shall be provided for property protection and life safety in the event that any single safeguard is ineffective due to inappropriate human actions, building failure, or system failure.

4.4.2 Appropriateness of Safeguards. Every building or structure shall be provided with means of egress and other safeguards of the kinds, numbers, locations, and capacities appropriate to the individual building or structure, with due regard to the following:

(1) Characteristics of the occupancy
(2) Capabilities of the occupants
(3) Number of persons exposed
(4) Fire protection available
(5) Capabilities of response personnel
(6) Height and type of construction of the building or structure
(7) Other factors necessary to provide occupants with a reasonable degree of safety
(8) Other factors necessary to protect the building and contents from damage

4.4.3 Means of Egress.

4.4.3.1 Unobstructed Egress.

4.4.3.1.1 In every occupied building or structure, means of egress from all parts of the building shall be maintained free and unobstructed.

4.4.3.1.2 No lock or fastening shall be permitted that prevents free escape from the inside of any building other than in health care occupancies and detention and correctional occupancies where staff are continually on duty and effective provisions are made to remove occupants in case of fire or other emergency.

4.4.3.1.3 Means of egress shall be accessible to the extent necessary to ensure reasonable safety for occupants having impaired mobility.

4.4.3.2 Awareness of Egress System.

4.4.3.2.1 Every exit shall be clearly visible, or the route to reach every exit shall be conspicuously indicated.

4.4.3.2.2 Each means of egress, in its entirety, shall be arranged or marked so that the way to a place of safety is indicated in a clear manner.

4.4.3.2.3 Lighting. Illumination of means of egress shall be provided. [See 5.3.4(10).]

4.4.4* Occupant Notification. In every building or structure of such size, arrangement, or occupancy that a fire itself could not provide adequate occupant warning, fire alarm systems shall be provided where necessary to warn occupants of the existence of fire.

4.4.5 Vertical Openings. Every vertical opening between the floors of a building shall be suitably enclosed or protected, as necessary, to provide the following:

(1) Reasonable safety to occupants while using the means of egress by preventing spread of fire, smoke, or fumes through vertical openings from floor to floor to allow occupants to complete their use of the means of egress
(2) Limitation of damage to the buildings and its contents

4.4.6 System Design/Installation. Any fire protection system, building service equipment, feature of protection, or safeguard provided to achieve the goals of this *Code* shall be designed, installed, and approved in accordance with applicable codes and standards referenced in Chapter 2.

4.5 General Requirements.

4.5.1 Authority Having Jurisdiction (AHJ).

4.5.1.1 The AHJ shall determine whether the provisions of this *Code* are met.

4.5.1.2 Where it is evident that a reasonable degree of safety is provided, any requirement shall be permitted to be modified if its application would be hazardous under normal occupancy conditions in the judgment of the AHJ.

4.5.2 Historic Structures and Cultural Resource Buildings. The provisions of this *Code* shall be permitted to be modified by the AHJ for buildings or structures identified and classified as historic structures in accordance with Section 20.17.

4.5.3 Provisions in Excess of *Code* Requirements. Nothing in this *Code* shall be construed to prohibit a better type of building construction, an additional means of egress, or an otherwise more safe condition than that specified by the minimum requirements of this *Code*.

4.5.4 Conditions for Occupancy. No new construction or existing building shall be occupied in whole or in part in violation of the provisions of this *Code* unless the following conditions exist:

(1) A plan of correction has been approved.
(2) The occupancy classification remains the same.
(3) No serious life safety hazard exists as judged by the AHJ.

4.5.5 Warrant of Fitness.

4.5.5.1 Where compliance with this *Code* is effected by means of a performance-based design, the owner shall annually certify compliance with the conditions and limitations of the design by submitting a warrant of fitness acceptable to the AHJ.

4.5.5.2 The warrant of fitness shall attest that the building features, systems, and use have been inspected and confirmed to remain consistent with design specifications outlined in the documentation required by 5.1.8 and 5.7.3 and that they continue to satisfy the goals and objectives specified in Section 4.1. *(See 5.1.11.)*

4.5.6 Construction, Repair, and Improvement Operations.

4.5.6.1 Buildings or portions of buildings shall be permitted to be occupied during construction, repair, alterations, or additions only where required means of egress and required fire protection features are in place and continuously maintained for the portion occupied or where alternative life safety measures and building protection measures acceptable to the AHJ are in place.

4.5.6.2 Escape Facilities.

4.5.6.2.1 In buildings under construction, adequate escape facilities shall be maintained at all times for the use of construction workers.

4.5.6.2.2 Escape facilities shall consist of doors, walkways, stairs, ramps, fire escapes, ladders, or other approved means or devices arranged in accordance with the general principles of the *Code* insofar as they can reasonably be applied to buildings under construction.

4.5.6.3 Flammable, hazardous, or explosive substances or equipment for repairs or alterations shall be permitted in a building while the building is occupied if the condition of use and safeguards provided do not create any additional danger or impediment to egress beyond the normally permissible conditions in the building and is such that materials are safeguarded when the building is unoccupied.

4.5.7* Changes of Occupancy.

4.5.7.1 In any building or structure, whether or not a physical alteration is needed, a change from one occupancy classification to another shall be permitted only where such a structure, building, or portion thereof conforms with the requirements of this *Code* that apply to new construction for the proposed new use, except as follows:

(1) Where, in the opinion of the AHJ, the proposed occupancy or change in use is not more hazardous than the existing use, based on life safety and fire risk, the AHJ shall be permitted to approve such change of occupancy provided compliance with the requirements of this *Code* for buildings of like occupancy or use are specifically incorporated to safeguard the life, health, and welfare of persons.

(2) Change of tenants or ownership shall not be construed to be a change of occupancy classification where the nature of use and assigned occupancy classification remain the same.

4.5.7.2 Where specifically permitted elsewhere in the *Code*, existing construction features shall be permitted to be continued in use in conversions.

4.5.8 Maintenance, Inspection, and Testing.

4.5.8.1 Whenever or wherever any device, equipment, system, condition, arrangement, level of protection, fire-resistive construction, or any other feature is required for compliance with the provisions of this *Code*, such device, equipment, system, condition, arrangement, level of protection, fire-resistive construction, or other feature shall thereafter be continuously maintained. Maintenance shall be provided in accordance with applicable NFPA requirements or requirements developed as part of a performance-based design, or as directed by the AHJ. [*101:* 4.6.12.1]

4.5.8.2 No existing life safety feature shall be removed or reduced where such feature is a requirement for new construction. [*101:* 4.6.12.2]

4.5.8.3* Existing life safety features obvious to the public, if not required by the *Code*, shall be either maintained or removed. [*101:* 4.6.12.3]

4.5.8.4* Existing life safety features that exceed the requirements for new buildings shall be permitted to be decreased to those required for new buildings. [*101:* 4.6.7.4]

4.5.8.5* Existing life safety features that do not meet the requirements for new buildings, but that exceed the requirements for existing buildings, shall not be further diminished. [*101:* 4.6.7.5]

4.5.8.6 Any device, equipment, system, condition, arrangement, level of protection, fire-resistive construction, or any other feature requiring periodic testing, inspection, or operation to ensure its maintenance shall be tested, inspected, or operated as specified elsewhere in this *Code* or as directed by the AHJ. [*101:* 4.6.12.4]

4.5.8.7 Maintenance, inspection, and testing shall be performed under the supervision of a responsible person who shall ensure that testing, inspection, and maintenance are made at specified intervals in accordance with applicable NFPA standards or as directed by the AHJ. [*101:* 4.6.12.5]

4.5.9 Noncombustible Material.

4.5.9.1 A material that complies with any one of the following shall be considered a noncombustible material:

(1)*The material, in the form in which it is used and under the conditions anticipated, will not ignite, burn, support combustion, or release flammable vapors when subjected to fire or heat.

(2) The material is reported as passing ASTM E 136, *Standard Test Method for Behavior of Materials in a Vertical Tube Furnace at 750 Degrees C.*

(3) The material is reported as complying with the pass/fail criteria of ASTM E 136 when tested in accordance with the test method and procedure in ASTM E 2652, *Standard Test Method for Behavior of Materials in a Tube Furnace with a Cone-shaped Airflow Stabilizer, at 750 Degrees C.* [**5000:** 7.1.4.1.1]

4.5.9.2 Where the term *limited-combustible* is used in this *Code*, it shall also include the term *noncombustible*. [**5000:** 7.1.4.1.2]

4.5.10 Limited-Combustible Material. A material shall be considered a limited-combustible material where both of the following conditions of 4.5.10.1, and 4.5.10.2, and the conditions of either 4.5.10.3 or 4.5.10.4, are met. [**5000:** 7.1.4.2]

4.5.10.1 The material does not comply with the requirements for a noncombustible material in accordance with 4.5.9. [**5000:** 7.1.4.2(1)]

4.5.10.2 The material, in the form in which it is used, exhibits a potential heat value not exceeding 3500 Btu/lb (8141 kJ/kg) where tested in accordance with NFPA 259, *Standard Test Method for Potential Heat of Building Materials.* [**5000:**7.1.4.2(2)]

4.5.10.3 The material has a structural base of a noncombustible material with a surfacing not exceeding a thickness of ⅛ in. (3.2 mm) where the surfacing exhibits a flame spread index not greater than 50 when tested in accordance with ASTM E 84, *Standard Test Method for Surface Burning Characteristics of Building Materials,* or ANSI/UL 723, *Standard for Test for Surface Burning Characteristics of Building Materials.* [**5000:**7.1.4.2.1]

4.5.10.4 The material is composed of materials which, in the form and thickness used, neither exhibit a flame spread index greater than 25 nor evidence of continued progressive combustion when tested in accordance with ASTM E 84 or ANSI/UL 723, and are of such composition that all surfaces that would be exposed by cutting through the material on any plane would neither exhibit a flame spread index greater than 25 nor evidence of continued progressive combustion when tested in accordance with ASTM E 84 or ANSI/UL 723. [**5000:** 7.1.4.2.2]

4.5.10.5 Where the term *limited-combustible* is used in this *Code*, it shall also include the term *noncombustible*. [**5000:**7.1.4.2.3]

Chapter 5   Performance-Based Option

5.1* General.

5.1.1 Application. The requirements of this chapter shall apply to facilities designed to the performance-based option permitted by Section 4.3.

5.1.2 Goals and Objectives. The performance-based design shall meet the goals and objectives of this *Code* in accordance with Section 4.1 and Section 4.2.

5.1.3* Approved Qualifications. The performance-based design shall be prepared by a person with qualifications acceptable to the AHJ.

5.1.4* Plan Submittal Documentation. When a performance-based design is submitted to the AHJ for review and approval, the owner shall document, in an approved format, each performance objective and applicable scenario, including any calculation methods or models used in establishing the proposed design's fire and life safety performance.

5.1.5* Independent Review. The AHJ shall be permitted to require an approved, independent third party to review the proposed design and provide an evaluation of the design to the AHJ at the expense of the owner.

5.1.6 Sources of Data. Data sources shall be identified and documented for each input data requirement that is required to be met using a source other than a required design scenario, an assumption, or a facility design specification.

5.1.6.1 The degree of conservatism reflected in such data shall be specified, and a justification for the source shall be provided.

5.1.6.2 Copies of all references relied upon by the performance-based design to support assumptions, design features, or any other part of the design shall be made available to the AHJ if requested.

5.1.7 Final Determination. The AHJ shall make the final determination as to whether the performance objectives have been met.

5.1.8* Operations and Maintenance Manual. An approved Operations and Maintenance (O&M) Manual shall be provided by the owner to the AHJ and the fire department and shall be maintained at the facility in an approved location.

5.1.9* Information Transfer to the Fire Service. Where a performance-based design is approved and used, the designer shall ensure that information regarding the operating procedures of the performance-based designed fire protection system is transferred to the owner and to the local fire service for inclusion in the pre-fire plan.

5.1.10* Design Feature Maintenance.

5.1.10.1 The design features required for the facility to meet the performance goals and objectives shall be maintained by the owner and be readily accessible to the AHJ for the life of the facility.

5.1.10.2 The facility shall be maintained in accordance with all documented assumptions and design specifications.

5.1.10.2.1 Any proposed changes or variations from the approved design shall be approved by the AHJ prior to the actual change.

5.1.10.2.2 Any approved changes to the original design shall be maintained in the same manner as the original design.

5.1.11* Annual Certification. Where a performance-based design is approved and used, the property owner shall annually certify that the design features and systems have been maintained in accordance with the approved original performance-based design and assumptions and any subsequent approved changes or modifications to the original performance-based design.

5.1.12 Hazardous Materials.

5.1.12.1 Performance-based designs for facilities containing high hazard contents shall identify the properties of hazardous materials to be stored, used, or handled and shall provide adequate and reliable safeguards to accomplish the following objectives, considering both normal operations and possible abnormal conditions:

(1) Minimize the potential occurrence of unwanted releases, fire, or other emergency incidents resulting from the storage, use, or handling of hazardous materials
(2) Minimize the potential failure of buildings, equipment, or processes involving hazardous materials by ensuring that such buildings, equipment, or processes are reliably designed and are suitable for the hazards present
(3) Minimize the potential exposure of people or property to unsafe conditions or events involving an unintended reaction or release of hazardous materials
(4) Minimize the potential for an unintentional reaction that results in a fire, explosion, or other dangerous condition
(5) Provide a means to contain, treat, neutralize, or otherwise handle plausible releases of hazardous materials to minimize the potential for adverse impacts to persons or property outside of the immediate area of a release
(6) Provide appropriate safeguards to minimize the risk of and limit damage and injury that could result from an explosion involving hazardous materials that present explosion hazards
(7) Detect hazardous levels of gases or vapors that are dangerous to health and alert appropriate persons or mitigate the hazard when the physiological warning properties for such gases or vapors are inadequate to warn of danger prior to personal injury
(8) Maintain power to provide for continued operation of safeguards and important systems that are relied upon to prevent or control an emergency condition involving hazardous materials
(9) Maintain ventilation where ventilation is relied upon to minimize the risk of emergency conditions involving hazardous materials
(10) Minimize the potential for exposing combustible hazardous materials to unintended sources of ignition and for exposing any hazardous material to fire or physical damage that can lead to endangerment of people or property

5.1.12.2 A process hazard analysis and off-site consequence analysis shall be conducted when required by the AHJ to ensure that people and property are satisfactorily protected from potentially dangerous conditions involving hazardous materials. The results of such analyses shall be considered when determining active and passive mitigation measures used in accomplishing the objectives of 4.1.3.3.2 and 4.1.4.2.

5.1.12.3 Written procedures for pre-start-up safety reviews, normal and emergency operations, management of change, emergency response, and accident investigation shall be developed prior to beginning operations at a facility designed in accordance with Section 5.1. Such procedures shall be developed with the participation of employees.

5.1.13 Special Definitions. A list of special terms used in this chapter shall be as follows:

(1) Design Fire Scenario. *(See 3.4.9.1.)*
(2) Design Specification. *(See 3.4.5.)*
(3) Design Team. *(See 3.4.6.)*
(4) Exposure Fire. *(See 3.4.7.)*
(5) Fire Model. *(See 3.4.8.)*
(6) Fire Scenario. *(See 3.4.9.)*
(7) Fuel Load. *(See 3.4.10.)*
(8) Input Data Specification. *(See 3.4.12.)*
(9) Occupant Characteristics. *(See 3.4.13.)*

(10) Performance Criteria. *(See 3.4.14.)*
(11) Proposed Design. *(See 3.4.15.)*
(12) Safety Factor. *(See 3.4.17.)*
(13) Safety Margin. *(See 3.4.18.)*
(14) Sensitivity Analysis. *(See 3.4.2.1.)*
(15) Stakeholder. *(See 3.4.20.)*
(16) Uncertainty Analysis. *(See 3.4.2.2.)*
(17) Verification Method. *(See 3.4.22.)*

5.2 Performance Criteria.

5.2.1 General. A design shall meet the objectives specified in Section 4.1 if, for each required design scenario, assumption, and design specification, the performance criteria of 5.2.2 are met.

5.2.2* Specific Performance Criteria.

5.2.2.1* Fire Conditions. No occupant who is not intimate with ignition shall be exposed to instantaneous or cumulative untenable conditions.

5.2.2.2* Explosion Conditions. The facility design shall provide an acceptable level of safety for occupants and for individuals immediately adjacent to the property from the effects of unintentional detonation or deflagration.

5.2.2.3* Hazardous Materials Exposure. The facility design shall provide an acceptable level of safety for occupants and for individuals immediately adjacent to the property from the effects of an unauthorized release of hazardous materials or the unintentional reaction of hazardous materials.

5.2.2.4* Property Protection. The facility design shall limit the effects of all required design scenarios from causing an unacceptable level of property damage.

5.2.2.5* Public Welfare. For facilities that serve a public welfare role as defined in 4.1.5, the facility design shall limit the effects of all required design scenarios from causing an unacceptable interruption of the facility's mission.

5.2.2.6 Occupant Protection from Untenable Conditions. Means shall be provided to evacuate, relocate, or defend in place occupants not intimate with ignition for sufficient time so that they are not exposed to instantaneous or cumulative untenable conditions from smoke, heat, or flames.

5.2.2.7 Emergency Responder Protection. Buildings shall be designed and constructed to reasonably prevent structural failure under fire conditions for sufficient time to enable fire fighters and emergency responders to conduct search and rescue operations.

5.2.2.8 Occupant Protection from Structural Failure. Buildings shall be designed and constructed to reasonably prevent structural failure under fire conditions for sufficient time to protect the occupants.

5.3 Retained Prescriptive Requirements.

5.3.1 Systems and Features. All fire protection systems and features of the building shall comply with applicable NFPA standards for those systems and features.

5.3.2 Electrical Systems. Electrical systems shall comply with applicable NFPA standards for those systems.

5.3.3 General. The design shall comply with the following requirements in addition to the performance criteria of Section 5.2 and the methods of Section 5.4 through Section 5.7:

(1) Fundamental requirements in Section 10.1
(2) Fire drills in Section 10.5
(3) Smoking in Section 10.9
(4) Open flame, candles, open fires, and incinerators in Section 10.10
(5) Fire protection markings in Section 10.11
(6) Seasonal and vacant buildings and premises in Section 10.12
(7) Combustible vegetation in Section 10.13
(8) Safeguards during building construction, alteration, and demolition operations in Chapter 16

5.3.4 Means of Egress. The design shall comply with the following NFPA *101, Life Safety Code,* requirements in addition to the performance criteria of Section 5.2 and the methods of Section 5.4 through Section 5.7:

(1) Changes in level in means of egress: 7.1.7 of NFPA *101*
(2) Guards: 7.1.8 of NFPA *101*
(3) Door openings: 7.2.1 of NFPA *101*
(4) Stairs: 7.2.2 of NFPA *101*

Exception: The provisions of 7.2.2.5.1, 7.2.2.5.2, 7.2.2.6.2, 7.2.2.6.3, and 7.2.2.6.4 of NFPA 101 shall be exempted.

(5) Ramps: 7.2.5 of NFPA *101*

Exception: The provisions of 7.2.5.3.1, 7.2.5.5, and 7.2.5.6.1 of NFPA 101 shall be exempted.

(6) Fire escape ladders: 7.2.9 of NFPA *101*
(7) Alternating tread devices: 7.2.11 of NFPA *101*
(8) Capacity of means of egress: Section 7.3 of NFPA *101*

Exception: The provisions of 7.3.3 and 7.3.4 of NFPA 101 shall be exempted.

(9) Impediments to egress: 7.5.2 of NFPA *101*
(10) Illumination of means of egress: Section 7.8 of NFPA *101*
(11) Emergency lighting: Section 7.9 of NFPA *101*
(12) Marking of means of egress: Section 7.10 of NFPA *101*

5.3.5 Equivalency. Equivalent designs for the features covered in the retained prescriptive requirements mandated by 5.3.1 through 5.3.4 shall be addressed in accordance with the equivalency provisions of Section 1.4.

5.4* Design Scenarios.

5.4.1 General.

5.4.1.1 The proposed design shall be considered to meet the goals and objectives if it achieves the performance criteria for each required design scenario. The AHJ shall approve the parameters involved with required design scenarios.

5.4.1.2* Design scenarios shall be evaluated for each required scenario using a method acceptable to the AHJ and appropriate for the conditions. Each scenario shall be as challenging and realistic as any that could realistically occur in the building.

5.4.1.3* Scenarios selected as design scenarios shall include, but not be limited to, those specified in 5.4.2 through 5.4.5.

5.4.1.3.1 Design fire scenarios demonstrated by the design team to the satisfaction of the AHJ as inappropriate for the building use and conditions shall not be required to be evaluated fully.

5.4.1.3.2 Fire Design Scenario 8 *(see 5.4.2.8)* shall not be required to be applied to fire protection systems or features for which both the level of reliability and the design performance in the absence of the system or feature are acceptable to the AHJ.

5.4.1.4 Each design scenario used in the performance-based design proposal shall be translated into input data specifications, as appropriate for the calculation method or model.

5.4.1.5 Any design scenario specifications that the design analyses do not explicitly address or incorporate and that are, therefore, omitted from input data specifications shall be identified, and a sensitivity analysis of the consequences of that omission shall be performed.

5.4.1.6 Any design scenario specifications modified in input data specifications, because of limitations in test methods or other data generation procedures, shall be identified, and a sensitivity analysis of the consequences of the modification shall be performed.

5.4.2 Required Design Scenarios — Fire.

5.4.2.1* Fire Design Scenario 1. Fire Design Scenario 1 involves an occupancy-specific design scenario representative of a typical fire for the occupancy.

5.4.2.1.1 This design scenario shall explicitly account for the following:

(1) Occupant activities
(2) Number and location of occupants
(3) Room size
(4) Furnishings and contents
(5) Fuel properties and ignition sources
(6) Ventilation conditions

5.4.2.1.2 The first item ignited and its location shall be explicitly defined.

5.4.2.2* Fire Design Scenario 2. Fire Design Scenario 2 involves an ultrafast-developing fire in the primary means of egress with interior doors open at the start of the fire. This design scenario shall address the concern regarding a reduction in the number of available means of egress.

5.4.2.3* Fire Design Scenario 3. Fire Design Scenario 3 involves a fire that starts in a normally unoccupied room that can potentially endanger a large number of occupants in a large room or other area. This design scenario shall address the concern regarding a fire starting in a normally unoccupied room and migrating into the space that can, potentially, hold the greatest number of occupants in the building.

5.4.2.4* Fire Design Scenario 4. Fire Design Scenario 4 involves a fire that originates in a concealed wall or ceiling space adjacent to a large occupied room. This design scenario shall address the concern regarding a fire originating in a concealed space that does not have either a detection system or suppression system and then spreading into the room within the building that can, potentially, hold the greatest number of occupants.

5.4.2.5* Fire Design Scenario 5. Fire Design Scenario 5 involves a slow-developing fire, shielded from fire protection systems, in close proximity to a high occupancy area. This design scenario shall address the concern regarding a relatively small ignition source causing a significant fire.

5.4.2.6* Fire Design Scenario 6. Fire Design Scenario 6 involves the most severe fire resulting from the largest possible fuel load characteristic of the normal operation of the building. This design scenario shall address the concern regarding a rapidly developing fire with occupants present.

5.4.2.7* Fire Design Scenario 7. Fire Design Scenario 7 involves an outside exposure fire. This design scenario shall address the concern regarding a fire starting at a location remote from the area of concern and either spreading into the area, blocking escape from the area, or developing untenable conditions within the area.

5.4.2.8* Fire Design Scenario 8. Fire Design Scenario 8 involves a fire originating in ordinary combustibles in a room or area with each passive or active fire protection system or feature independently rendered ineffective. This set of design scenarios shall address concerns regarding each fire protection system or fire protection feature, considered individually, being unreliable or becoming unavailable. This scenario shall not be required to be applied to fire protection systems or features for which both the level of reliability and the design performance in the absence of the system are acceptable to the AHJ.

5.4.3 Required Design Scenarios — Explosion.

5.4.3.1* Explosion Design Scenario 1.

5.4.3.1.1 Explosion Design Scenario 1 is the detonation or deflagration of explosive materials being manufactured, stored, handled, or used in a facility.

5.4.3.1.2 Explosion Design Scenario 1 shall address the concern regarding safety of individuals not intimate with the explosion and property protection of adjacent properties and buildings.

5.4.4* Required Design Scenarios — Hazardous Materials.

5.4.4.1 Hazardous Materials Design Scenario 1. Hazardous Materials Design Scenario 1 involves an unauthorized release of hazardous materials from a single control area. This design scenario shall address the concern regarding the spread of hazardous conditions from the point of release.

5.4.4.2 Hazardous Materials Design Scenario 2. Hazardous Materials Design Scenario 2 involves an exposure fire on a location where hazardous materials are stored, used, handled, or dispensed. This design scenario shall address the concern regarding how a fire in a facility affects the safe storage, handling, or use of hazardous materials.

5.4.4.3 Hazardous Materials Design Scenario 3. Hazardous Materials Design Scenario 3 involves the application of an external factor to the hazardous material that is likely to result in a fire, explosion, toxic release, or other unsafe condition. This design scenario shall address the concern regarding the initiation of a hazardous materials event by the application of heat, shock, impact, or water onto a hazardous material being stored, used, handled, or dispensed in the facility.

5.4.4.4 Hazardous Materials Design Scenario 4.

5.4.4.4.1 Hazardous Materials Design Scenario 4 involves an unauthorized discharge with each protection system independently rendered ineffective. This set of design hazardous materials scenarios shall address concern regarding each protection system or protection feature, considered individually, being unreliable or becoming unavailable.

5.4.4.4.2* Hazardous Materials Design Scenario 4 shall not be required to be applied to protection systems or features for which both the level of reliability and the design performance in the absence of the system are acceptable to the AHJ.

5.4.5 Required Design Scenarios — Safety During Building Use.

5.4.5.1* Building Use Design Scenario 1. Building Use Design Scenario 1 involves an event in which the maximum occupant load is in the assembly building and an emergency event occurs blocking the principal exit/entrance to the building. This design scenario shall address the concern of occupants having to take alternative exit routes under crowded conditions.

5.4.5.2 Building Use Design Scenario 2. Building Use Design Scenario 2 involves a fire in an area of a building undergoing construction or demolition while the remainder of the building is occupied. The normal fire suppression system in the area undergoing construction or demolition has been taken out of service. This design scenario shall address the concern regarding the inoperability of certain building fire safety features during construction and demolition in a partially occupied building.

5.5 Evaluation of Proposed Designs.

5.5.1 General.

5.5.1.1 A proposed design's performance shall be assessed relative to each performance objective in Section 4.1 and each applicable scenario in Section 5.4, with the assessment conducted through the use of appropriate calculation methods.

5.5.1.2 The choice of assessment methods shall require the approval of the AHJ.

5.5.2 Use. The design professional shall use the assessment methods to demonstrate that the proposed design achieves the goals and objectives, as measured by the performance criteria in light of the safety margins and uncertainty analysis, for each scenario, given the assumptions.

5.5.3 Input Data.

5.5.3.1 Data.

5.5.3.1.1 Input data for computer fire models shall be obtained in accordance with ASTM E 1591, *Standard Guide for Data for Fire Models*.

5.5.3.1.2 Data for use in analytical models that are not computer-based fire models shall be obtained using appropriate measurement, recording, and storage techniques to ensure the applicability of the data to the analytical method being used.

5.5.3.2 Data Requirements. A complete listing of input data requirements for all models, engineering methods, and other calculation or verification methods required or proposed as part of the performance-based design shall be provided.

5.5.3.3 Uncertainty and Conservatism of Data. Uncertainty in input data shall be analyzed and, as determined appropriate by the AHJ, addressed through the use of conservative values.

5.5.4 Output Data. The assessment methods used shall accurately and appropriately produce the required output data from input data based on the design specifications, assumptions, and scenarios.

5.5.5 Validity. Evidence shall be provided confirming that the assessment methods are valid and appropriate for the proposed facility, use, and conditions.

5.6* Safety Factors. Approved safety factors shall be included in the design methods and calculations to reflect uncertainty in the assumptions, data, and other factors associated with the performance-based design.

5.7 Documentation Requirements.

5.7.1* General.

5.7.1.1 All aspects of the design, including those described in 5.7.2 through 5.7.14, shall be documented.

5.7.1.2 The format and content of the documentation shall be acceptable to the AHJ.

5.7.2* Technical References and Resources.

5.7.2.1 The AHJ shall be provided with sufficient documentation to support the validity, accuracy, relevance, and precision of the proposed methods.

5.7.2.2 The engineering standards, calculation methods, and other forms of scientific information provided shall be appropriate for the particular application and methodologies used.

5.7.3 Facility Design Specifications. All details of the proposed facility design that affect the ability of the facility to meet the stated goals and objectives shall be documented.

5.7.4 Performance Criteria. Performance criteria, with sources, shall be documented.

5.7.5 Occupant Characteristics. Assumptions about occupant characteristics shall be documented.

5.7.6 Design Scenarios. Descriptions of design hazard scenarios shall be documented.

5.7.7 Input Data. Input data to models and assessment methods, including sensitivity analysis, shall be documented.

5.7.8 Output Data. Output data from models and assessment methods, including sensitivity analysis, shall be documented.

5.7.9 Safety Factors. Safety factors utilized shall be documented.

5.7.10 Prescriptive Requirements. Retained prescriptive requirements shall be documented.

5.7.11* Modeling Features.

5.7.11.1 Assumptions made by the model user, and descriptions of models and methods used, including known limitations, shall be documented.

5.7.11.2 Documentation shall be provided that the assessment methods have been used validly and appropriately to address the design specifications, assumptions, and scenarios.

5.7.12 Evidence of Modeler Capability. The design team's relevant experience with the models, test methods, databases, and other assessment methods used in the performance-based design proposal shall be documented.

5.7.13 Performance Evaluation. The performance evaluation summary shall be documented.

5.7.14 Use of Performance-Based Design Option. Design proposals shall include documentation that provides anyone involved in ownership or management of the facility with all of the following notification:

(1) The facility was approved as a performance-based design with certain specified design criteria and assumptions.
(2) Any remodeling, modification, renovation, change in use, or change in the established assumptions requires a re-evaluation and re-approval.

Chapter 6   Classification of Occupancy

6.1 Classification of Occupancy.

6.1.1 General.

6.1.1.1 Occupancy Classification. The occupancy of a building or structure, or portion of a building or structure, shall be classified in accordance with 6.1.2 through 6.1.13. Occupancy classification shall be subject to the ruling of the AHJ where there is a question of proper classification in any individual case. [*101*: 6.1.1.1]

6.1.1.2 Special Structures. Occupancies in special structures shall conform to the requirements of Section 20.16. [*101*: 6.1.1.2]

6.1.2 Assembly. For requirements, see Section 20.1. [*101*: 6.1.2]

6.1.2.1* Definition — Assembly Occupancy. An occupancy (1) used for a gathering of 50 or more persons for deliberation, worship, entertainment, eating, drinking, amusement, awaiting transportation, or similar uses; or (2) used as a special amusement building, regardless of occupant load. [*101:* 6.1.2.1]

6.1.2.2 Other. (Reserved)

6.1.3 Educational. For requirements, see Section 20.2. [*101*: 6.1.3]

6.1.3.1* Definition — Educational Occupancy. An occupancy used for educational purposes through the twelfth grade by six or more persons for 4 or more hours per day or more than 12 hours per week. [*101*: 6.1.3.1]

6.1.3.2 Other Occupancies. Other occupancies associated with educational institutions shall be in accordance with the appropriate parts of this *Code* and NFPA *101*. [*101*: 6.1.3.2]

6.1.3.3 Incidental Instruction. In cases where instruction is incidental to some other occupancy, the section of this *Code* and NFPA *101* governing such other occupancy shall apply. [*101*: 6.1.3.3]

6.1.4 Day Care. For requirements, see Section 20.3. [*101*:6.1.4]

6.1.4.1* Definition — Day-Care Occupancy. An occupancy in which four or more clients receive care, maintenance, and supervision, by other than their relatives or legal guardians, for less than 24 hours per day. [*101*: 6.1.4.1]

6.1.4.2 Other. (Reserved)

6.1.5 Health Care. For requirements, see Section 20.4. [*101*: 6.1.5]

6.1.5.1* Definition — Health Care Occupancy. An occupancy used to provide medical or other treatment or care simultaneously to four or more patients on an inpatient basis, where such patients are mostly incapable of self-preservation due to age, physical or mental disability, or because of security measures not under the occupants' control. [*101*: 6.1.5.1]

6.1.5.2 Other. (Reserved)

6.1.6 Ambulatory Health Care. For requirements, see Section 20.6. [*101*: 6.1.6]

6.1.6.1* Definition — Ambulatory Health Care Occupancy. An occupancy used to provide services or treatment simultaneously to four or more patients that provides, on an outpatient basis, one or more of the following:

(1) Treatment for patients that renders the patients incapable of taking action for self-preservation under emergency conditions without the assistance of others
(2) Anesthesia that renders the patients incapable of taking action for self-preservation under emergency conditions without the assistance of others
(3) Emergency or urgent care for patients who, due to the nature of their injury or illness, are incapable of taking action for self-preservation under emergency conditions without the assistance of others [*101*: 6.1.6.1]

6.1.6.2 Other. (Reserved)

6.1.7 Detention and Correctional. For requirements, see Section 20.7. [*101*: 6.1.7]

6.1.7.1* Definition — Detention and Correctional Occupancy. An occupancy used to house one or more persons under varied degrees of restraint or security where such occupants are mostly incapable of self-preservation because of security measures not under the occupants' control. [*101*: 6.1.7.1]

6.1.7.2* Nonresidential Uses. Within detention and correctional facilities, uses other than residential housing shall be in accordance with the appropriate chapter of this *Code* and NFPA *101*. (*See 22.1.2.3 and 23.1.2.3 of NFPA 101.*) [*101*: 6.1.7.2]

6.1.8 Residential. For requirements, see Sections 20.5 and 20.8 through 20.11. [*101*: 6.1.8]

6.1.8.1 Definition — Residential Occupancy. An occupancy that provides sleeping accommodations for purposes other than health care or detention and correctional. [*101*: 6.1.8.1]

6.1.8.1.1* Definition — One- and Two-Family Dwelling Unit. A building that contains not more than two dwelling units with independent cooking and bathroom facilities. [*101*: 6.1.8.1.1]

6.1.8.1.2 Definition — Lodging or Rooming House. A building or portion thereof that does not qualify as a one- or two-family dwelling, that provides sleeping accommodations for a total of 16 or fewer people on a transient or permanent basis, without personal care services, with or without meals, but without separate cooking facilities for individual occupants. [*101*: 6.1.8.1.2]

6.1.8.1.3* Definition — Hotel. A building or groups of buildings under the same management in which there are sleeping accommodations for more than 16 persons and primarily used by transients for lodging with or without meals. [*101*: 6.1.8.1.3]

6.1.8.1.4* Definition — Dormitory. A building or a space in a building in which group sleeping accommodations are provided for more than 16 persons who are not members of the same family in one room, or a series of closely associated rooms, under joint occupancy and single management, with or without meals, but without individual cooking facilities. [*101*: 6.1.8.1.4]

6.1.8.1.5 Definition — Apartment Building. A building or portion thereof containing three or more dwelling units with independent cooking and bathroom facilities. [*101*: 6.1.8.1.5]

6.1.8.2 Other. (Reserved)

6.1.9 Residential Board and Care. For requirements, see Section 20.5. [*101*: 6.1.9]

6.1.9.1* Definition — Residential Board and Care Occupancy. An occupancy used for lodging and boarding of four or more residents, not related by blood or marriage to the owners or operators, for the purpose of providing personal care services. [*101:* 6.1.9.1]

6.1.9.2 Other. (Reserved)

6.1.10 Mercantile. For requirements, see Section 20.12. [*101:* 6.1.10]

6.1.10.1* Definition — Mercantile Occupancy. An occupancy used for the display and sale of merchandise. [*101:* 6.1.10.1]

6.1.10.2 Other. (Reserved)

6.1.11 Business. For requirements, see Section 20.13. [*101:* 6.1.11]

6.1.11.1* Definition — Business Occupancy. An occupancy used for the transaction of business other than mercantile. [*101:* 6.1.11.1]

6.1.11.2 Other. (Reserved)

6.1.12 Industrial. For requirements, see Section 20.14. [*101:* 6.1.12]

6.1.12.1* Definition — Industrial Occupancy. An occupancy in which products are manufactured or in which processing, assembling, mixing, packaging, finishing, decorating, or repair operations are conducted. [*101:* 6.1.12.1]

6.1.12.2 Other. (Reserved)

6.1.13 Storage. For requirements, see Section 20.15. [*101:* 6.1.13]

6.1.13.1* Definition — Storage Occupancy. An occupancy used primarily for the storage or sheltering of goods, merchandise, products, vehicles, or animals. [*101:* 6.1.13.1]

6.1.13.2 Other. (Reserved)

6.1.14 Multiple Occupancies.

6.1.14.1 General.

6.1.14.1.1 Multiple occupancies shall comply with the requirements of 6.1.14.1 and one of the following:

(1) Mixed occupancies — 6.1.14.3
(2) Separated occupancies — 6.1.14.4 [*101:* 6.1.14.1.1]

6.1.14.1.2 Where exit access from an occupancy traverses another occupancy, the multiple occupancy shall be treated as a mixed occupancy. [*101:* 6.1.14.1.2]

6.1.14.1.3* Where incidental to another occupancy, areas used as follows shall be permitted to be considered part of the predominant occupancy and shall be subject to the provisions of this *Code* and NFPA *101* that apply to the predominant occupancy:

(1) Mercantile, business, industrial, or storage use
(2)*Nonresidential use with an occupant load fewer than that established by Section 6.1 for the occupancy threshold [*101:* 6.1.14.1.3]

6.1.14.2 Definitions.

6.1.14.2.1 Multiple Occupancy. A building or structure in which two or more classes of occupancy exist. [*101:* 6.1.14.2.1]

6.1.14.2.2 Mixed Occupancy. A multiple occupancy where the occupancies are intermingled. [*101:* 6.1.14.2.2]

6.1.14.2.3 Separated Occupancy. A multiple occupancy where the occupancies are separated by fire resistance–rated assemblies. [*101:* 6.1.14.2.3]

6.1.14.3 Mixed Occupancies.

6.1.14.3.1 Each portion of the building shall be classified as to its use in accordance with Section 6.1. [*101:* 6.1.14.3.1]

6.1.14.3.2 The building shall comply with the most restrictive requirements of the occupancies involved unless separate safeguards are approved. [*101:* 6.1.14.3.2]

6.1.14.4 Separated Occupancies. (See also 6.1.14.4.2.) [*101:* 6.1.14.4]

6.1.14.4.1 Where separated occupancies are provided, each part of the building comprising a distinct occupancy, as described in this chapter, shall be completely separated from other occupancies by fire-resistive assemblies as specified in 6.1.14.4.2, 6.1.14.4.3, and Table 6.1.14.4.1(a) and Table 6.1.14.4.1(b), unless separation is provided by approved existing separations or as otherwise permitted by 6.1.14.4.6. [*101:* 6.1.14.4.1]

Table 6.1.14.4.1(a) Required Separation of Occupancies (hours),† Part 1

Occupancy	Assembly ≤300	Assembly >300 to ≤1000	Assembly >1000	Educational	Day-Care >12 Clients	Day-Care Homes	Health Care	Ambulatory Health Care	Detention & Correctional	One- & Two-Family Dwellings	Lodging or Rooming Houses	Hotels & Dormitories
Assembly ≤300	—	0	0	2	2	1	2‡	2	2‡	2	2	2
Assembly >300 to ≤1000	0	—	0	2	2	2	2‡	2	2‡	2	2	2
Assembly >1000	0	0	—	2	2	2	2‡	2	2‡	2	2	2
Educational	2	2	2	—	2	2	2‡	2	2‡	2	2	2
Day-Care >12 Clients	2	2	2	2	—	1	2‡	2	2‡	2	2	2
Day-Care Homes	1	2	2	2	1	—	2‡	2	2‡	2	2	2
Health Care	2‡	2‡	2‡	2‡	2‡	2‡	—	2‡	2‡	2‡	2‡	2‡

Table 6.1.14.4.1(a) *Continued*

Occupancy	Assembly ≤300	Assembly >300 to ≤1000	Assembly >1000	Educational	Day-Care >12 Clients	Day-Care Homes	Health Care	Ambulatory Health Care	Detention & Correctional	One- & Two-Family Dwellings	Lodging or Rooming Houses	Hotels & Dormitories
Ambulatory Health Care	2	2	2	2	2	2	2‡	—	2‡	2	2	2
Detention & Correctional	2‡	2‡	2‡	2‡	2‡	2‡	2‡	2‡	—	2‡	2‡	2‡
One- & Two-Family Dwellings	2	2	2	2	2	2	2‡	2	2‡	—	1	1
Lodging or Rooming Houses	2	2	2	2	2	2	2‡	2	2‡	1	—	1
Hotels & Dormitories	2	2	2	2	2	2	2‡	2	2‡	1	1	—
Apartment Buildings	2	2	2	2	2	2	2‡	2	2‡	1	1	1
Board & Care, Small	2	2	2	2	2	2	2‡	2	2‡	1	2	2
Board & Care, Large	2	2	2	2	2	2	2‡	2	2‡	2	2	2
Mercantile	2	2	2	2	2	2	2‡	2	2‡	2	2	2
Mercantile, Mall	2	2	2	2	2	2	2‡	2	2‡	2	2	2
Mercantile, Bulk Retail	3	3	3	3	3	3	2‡	2‡	2‡	3	3	3
Business	1	2	2	2	2	2	2‡	1	2‡	2	2	2
Industrial, General Purpose	2	2	3	3	3	3	2‡	2	2‡	2	2	2
Industrial, Special-Purpose	2	2	2	3	3	3	2‡	2	2‡	2	2	2
Industrial, High Hazard	3	3	3	3	3	3	2‡	2‡	NP	3	3	3
Storage, Low & Ordinary Hazard	2	2	3	3	3	2	2‡	2	2‡	2	2	2
Storage, High Hazard	3	3	3	3	3	3	2‡	2‡	NP	3	3	3

NP: Not permitted.

†*Minimum Fire Resistance Rating.* The fire resistance rating is permitted to be reduced by 1 hour, but in no case to less than 1 hour, where the building is protected throughout by an approved automatic sprinkler system in accordance with NFPA 13 and supervised in accordance with 13.3.1.7.

‡The 1-hour reduction due to the presence of sprinklers in accordance with the single-dagger footnote is not permitted. [*101*: Table 6.1.14.4.1(a)]

Table 6.1.14.4.1(b) Required Separation of Occupancies (hours)†, Part 2

Occupancy	Apartment Buildings	Board & Care, Small	Board & Care, Large	Mercantile	Mercantile, Mall	Mercantile, Bulk Retail	Business	Industrial, General Purpose	Industrial, Special-Purpose	Industrial, High Hazard	Storage, Low & Ordinary Hazard	Storage, High Hazard
Assembly ≤ 300	2	2	2	2	2	3	1	2	2	3	2	3
Assembly >300 to ≤1000	2	2	2	2	2	3	2	2	2	3	2	3
Assembly >1000	2	2	2	2	2	3	2	3	2	3	3	3
Educational	2	2	2	2	2	3	2	3	3	3	3	3
Day-Care >12 Clients	2	2	2	2	2	3	2	3	3	3	3	3
Day-Care Homes	2	2	2	2	2	3	2	3	3	3	2	3
Health Care	2‡	2‡	2‡	2‡	2‡	2‡	2‡	2‡	2‡	2‡	2‡	2‡
Ambulatory Health Care	2	2	2	2	2	2‡	1	2	2	2‡	2	2‡
Detention & Correctional	2‡	2‡	2‡	2‡	2‡	2‡	2‡	2‡	2‡	NP	2‡	NP
One- & Two-Family Dwellings	1	1	2	2	2	3	2	2	2	3	2	3
Lodging or Rooming Houses	1	2	2	2	2	3	2	2	2	3	2	3
Hotels & Dormitories	1	2	2	2	2	3	2	2	2	3	2	3
Apartment Buildings	—	2	2	2	2	3	2	2	2	3	2	3
Board & Care, Small	2	—	1	2	2	3	2	3	3	3	3	3
Board & Care, Large	2	1	—	2	2	3	2	3	3	3	3	3
Mercantile	2	2	2	—	0	3	2	2	2	3	2	3
Mercantile, Mall	2	2	2	0	—	3	2	3	3	3	2	3
Mercantile, Bulk Retail	3	3	3	3	3	—	2	2	2	3	2	2
Business	2	2	2	2	2	2	—	2	2	2	2	2
Industrial, General Purpose	2	3	3	2	3	2	2	—	1	1	1	1
Industrial, Special-Purpose	2	3	3	2	3	2	2	1	—	1	1	1
Industrial, High Hazard	3	3	3	3	3	3	2	1	1	—	1	1
Storage, Low & Ordinary Hazard	2	3	3	2	2	2	2	1	1	1	—	1
Storage, High Hazard	3	3	3	3	3	2	2	1	1	1	1	—

NP: Not permitted.

†*Minimum Fire Resistance Rating.* The fire resistance rating is permitted to be reduced by 1 hour, but in no case to less than 1 hour, where the building is protected throughout by an approved automatic sprinkler system in accordance with NFPA 13 and supervised in accordance with 13.3.1.7.

‡The 1-hour reduction due to the presence of sprinklers in accordance with the single-dagger footnote is not permitted. [*101*: Table 6.1.14.4.1(b)]

6.1.14.4.2 Occupancy separations shall be classified as 3-hour fire resistance–rated, 2-hour fire resistance–rated, or 1-hour fire resistance–rated and shall meet the requirements of Chapter 8 of NFPA *101*. [*101:* 6.1.14.4.2]

6.1.14.4.3 The fire resistance rating specified in Table 6.1.14.4.1(a) and Table 6.1.14.4.1(b) shall be permitted to be reduced by 1 hour, but in no case shall it be reduced to less than 1 hour, where the building is protected throughout by an approved automatic sprinkler system in accordance with NFPA 13 and supervised in accordance with 13.3.1.8, unless prohibited by the double-dagger footnote entries in the tables. [*101:* 6.1.14.4.3]

6.1.14.4.4 Occupancy separations shall be vertical, horizontal, or both or, when necessary, of such other form as required to provide complete separation between occupancy divisions in the building. [*101:* 6.1.14.4.4]

6.1.14.4.5* Each separated portion of the building shall comply with the requirements for the occupancy therein. [*101:* 6.1.14.4.5]

6.1.14.4.6 Where permitted in Chapters 11 through 43 of NFPA *101*, atrium walls shall be permitted to serve as part of the separation required by 6.1.14.4.1 for creating separated occupancies on a story-by-story basis, provided all of the following are met:

(1) The atrium is separated from adjacent areas by walls that are smoke partitions in accordance with Section 8.4 of NFPA *101*.
(2) Doors in the smoke partitions required by 6.1.14.4.6(1) are equipped with positive latching hardware.
(3) The atrium meets the provisions of 8.6.7 of NFPA *101* that are applicable to new atriums.
[*101:* 6.1.14.4.6]

Chapter 7   Reserved

Chapter 8   Reserved

Chapter 9   Reserved

Chapter 10   General Safety Requirements

10.1 Fundamental Requirements.

10.1.1 Every new and existing building or structure shall be constructed, arranged, equipped, maintained, and operated in accordance with this *Code* so as to provide a reasonable level of life safety, property protection, and public welfare from the actual and potential hazards created by fire, explosion, and other hazardous conditions.

10.1.2* *Life Safety Code.* Every new and existing building shall comply with this *Code* and NFPA *101, Life Safety Code.*

10.1.3 Building Code. Where a building code has been adopted, all new construction shall comply with this *Code* and the building code.

10.1.4 Structural Hazards.

10.1.4.1 Where structural elements have visible damage, the AHJ shall be permitted to require a technical analysis prepared in accordance with Section 1.15 to determine if repairs are necessary to restore structural integrity.

10.1.4.2 Where the technical analysis recommends repairs to the structure, such repairs shall be made.

10.1.5 Any person who deliberately, or through negligence, sets fire to or causes the burning of any combustible material in such a manner as to endanger the safety of any person or property shall be deemed to be in violation of this *Code*.

10.1.6 The AHJ shall have the authority to prohibit any or all open flames or other sources of ignition where circumstances make such conditions hazardous.

10.1.7 Listed and Labeled. Listed and labeled equipment, devices, and materials shall be installed and used in accordance with the listing limitations and the manufacturers' instructions.

10.2 Owner/Occupant Responsibilities.

10.2.1 The owner, operator, or occupant shall be responsible for compliance with this *Code*.

10.2.2 The owner, operator, or occupant of a building shall notify the AHJ prior to a change of occupancy as specified in 4.5.7 and 10.3.4.

10.2.3 The AHJ shall be permitted to require the owner, operator, or occupant to provide tests or test reports, without expense to the AHJ, as proof of compliance with the intent of this *Code*.

10.2.4 The owner, operator, or occupant of a building that is deemed unsafe by the AHJ shall abate, through corrective action approved by the AHJ, the condition causing the building to be unsafe either by repair, rehabilitation, demolition, or other corrective action approved by the AHJ.

10.2.5 The owner, operator, or occupant, or any person in control of a building or premises shall keep records of all maintenance, inspections, and testing of fire protection systems, fire alarm systems, smoke control systems, emergency evacuation and relocation drills, emergency action plans, emergency power, elevators, and other equipment as required by the AHJ.

10.2.6 All records required to be kept shall be maintained until their useful life has been served, as required by law, or as required by the AHJ.

10.3 Occupancy.

10.3.1 No new construction or existing building shall be occupied in whole or in part in violation of the provisions of this *Code*.

10.3.2 Existing buildings that are occupied at the time of adoption of this *Code* shall remain in use provided that the following conditions are met:

(1) The occupancy classification remains the same.
(2) No condition deemed hazardous to life or property exists that would constitute an imminent danger.

10.3.3* Buildings or portions of buildings, except for routine maintenance or repair, shall not be occupied during construction, repair, or alteration without the approval of the AHJ if required means of egress are impaired or required fire protection systems are out of service.

10.3.4 Change of Use or Occupancy Classification.

10.3.4.1 In any building or structure, whether or not a physical alteration is needed, a change from one use or occupancy classification to another shall comply with 4.6.7 of NFPA *101*. [*101:* 4.6.11]

10.3.4.2 Occupancy classifications and subclassifications, as defined, shall be in accordance with Chapter 6.

10.4 Building Evacuation.

10.4.1 Persons shall not fail to leave a building when notified to do so or when directed by the AHJ as a result of a known or perceived emergency.

10.4.2* Persons shall not fail to leave any overcrowded premises when ordered to do so by the AHJ.

10.4.3* Persons shall not fail to leave a building when a fire alarm system is activated, unless otherwise provided for in an approved building fire evacuation plan or during routine testing or maintenance.

10.5* Fire Drills.

10.5.1 Where Required. Emergency egress and relocation drills conforming to the provisions of this *Code* shall be conducted as specified by the provisions of Chapter 20 of this *Code* or Chapters 11 through 42 of NFPA *101*, or by appropriate action of the AHJ. Drills shall be designed in cooperation with the local authorities. [*101*:4.7.1]

10.5.2* Drill Frequency. Emergency egress and relocation drills, where required by Chapter 20 of this *Code* or Chapters 11 through 42 of NFPA *101*, or the AHJ, shall be held with sufficient frequency to familiarize occupants with the drill procedure and to establish conduct of the drill as a matter of routine. Drills shall include suitable procedures to ensure that all persons subject to the drill participate. [*101:* 4.7.2]

10.5.3 Orderly Evacuation. When conducting drills, emphasis shall be placed on orderly evacuation rather than on speed. [*101:* 4.7.3]

10.5.4* Simulated Conditions. Drills shall be held at expected and unexpected times and under varying conditions to simulate the unusual conditions that can occur in an actual emergency. [*101:* 4.7.4]

10.5.5 Relocation Area. Drill participants shall relocate to a predetermined location and remain at such location until a recall or dismissal signal is given. [*101:* 4.7.5]

10.5.6* A written record of each drill shall be completed by the person responsible for conducting the drill and maintained in an approved manner. [*101:* 4.7.6]

10.6 Reporting of Fires and Other Emergencies.

10.6.1 Fire Reporting.

10.6.1.1 The person discovering any unwanted fire, regardless of magnitude, shall immediately notify the fire department.

10.6.1.2 Facilities that have established on-premises firefighting organizations and have coordinated and arranged procedures approved by the AHJ shall not need to notify the fire department.

10.6.1.3* The owner, manager, occupant, or any person in control of such building or premises, upon discovery of an unwanted fire or evidence of a previous unwanted fire that had apparently been extinguished, shall immediately notify the fire department.

10.6.1.4 Persons shall not make, issue, post, or maintain any regulation or order, written or verbal, that would require any person to take any unnecessary delaying action prior to reporting a fire to the fire department.

10.6.2 Persons shall not deliberately or maliciously turn in an alarm of fire when in fact that person knows that no fire exists.

10.6.3 Notification of unauthorized discharge of hazardous materials shall be in accordance with Chapter 60.

10.6.4 Any person who willfully makes any false, fraudulent, misleading, or unfounded report or statement or willfully misrepresents any fact with the intention of misleading any fire department personnel or who interferes with the operation of the fire department shall be in violation of this *Code*.

10.7 Tampering with Fire Safety Equipment.

10.7.1 Persons shall not render any portable or fixed fire-extinguishing system or device or any fire-warning system or device inoperative or inaccessible.

10.7.1.1 As necessary during emergencies, maintenance, drills, prescribed testing, alterations, or renovations, portable or fixed fire-extinguishing systems or devices or any fire-warning system or device shall be permitted to be made inoperative or inaccessible.

10.7.2 Persons shall not render a fire protection system or device inoperative during an emergency unless by direction of the incident commander.

10.7.3 Persons, except a person authorized by the AHJ, shall not remove, unlock, destroy, or tamper with in any manner any locked gate, door, or barricade; chain; enclosure; sign; tag; or seal that has been required by the AHJ pursuant to this *Code*.

10.8 Emergency Action Plans.

10.8.1 Where Required. Emergency action plans shall be provided for high-rise, health care, ambulatory health care, residential board and care, assembly, day-care centers, special amusement buildings, hotels and dormitories, detention and correctional occupancies, educational, underground and windowless structures, facilities storing or handling materials covered by Chapter 60, or where required by the AHJ.

10.8.2 Plan Requirements.

10.8.2.1* Emergency plans shall include the following:

(1) Procedures for reporting of emergencies
(2) Occupant and staff response to emergencies
(3)*Evacuation, relocation and shelter-in-place procedures appropriate to the building, its occupancy, emergencies, and hazards
(4) Appropriateness of the use of elevators
(5) Design and conduct of fire drills
(6) Type and coverage of building fire protection systems
(7) Other items required by the AHJ [*101*:4.8.2.1]

10.8.2.2 Emergency action plans shall be submitted to the AHJ for review when required by the AHJ.

10.8.2.3* Emergency action plans shall be reviewed and updated as required by the AHJ. [*101:* 4.8.2.3]

10.9 Smoking.

10.9.1 Where smoking is considered a fire hazard, the AHJ shall be authorized to order the owner in writing to post "No Smoking" signs in conspicuous, designated locations where smoking is prohibited.

10.9.2 In areas where smoking is permitted, noncombustible ashtrays shall be provided.

10.9.3 Removal or destruction of any required "No Smoking" sign shall be prohibited.

10.9.4 Smoking or depositing any lighted or smoldering substance in a place where required "No Smoking" signs are posted shall be prohibited.

10.10 Open Flames, Candles, Open Fires, and Incinerators.

10.10.1 Permits. Permits, where required, shall comply with Section 1.12.

10.10.1.1 Permits shall not be required for cooking and recreational fires.

10.10.1.2 Where burning is conducted on public property or the property of someone other than the permit applicant, the permit applicant shall demonstrate that permission has been obtained by the appropriate government agency, the owner, or the owner's authorized agent.

10.10.1.3 When limits for atmospheric conditions or hours restrict burning, such limits shall be designated in the permit restrictions.

10.10.1.4 Instructions or stipulations of permit shall be followed.

10.10.2 The AHJ shall have the authority to prohibit any or all open flames, candles, and open, recreational, and cooking fires or other sources of ignition, or establish special regulations on the use of any form of fire or smoking material where circumstances make such conditions hazardous.

10.10.3 Outdoor Fires.

10.10.3.1* Outdoor fires shall not be built, ignited, or maintained in or upon hazardous fire areas, except by permit from the AHJ.

10.10.3.2 Permanent barbecues, portable barbecues, outdoor fireplaces, or grills shall not be used for the disposal of rubbish, trash, or combustible waste material.

10.10.4 Open Fires.

10.10.4.1 Permitted open fires shall be located not less than 50 ft (15 m) from any structure.

10.10.4.2 Burning hours shall be prescribed by the AHJ.

10.10.4.3 Recreational fires shall not be located within 25 ft (7.6 m) of a structure or combustible material unless contained in an approved manner.

10.10.4.4 Conditions that could cause a fire to spread to within 25 ft (7.6 m) of a structure shall be eliminated prior to ignition.

10.10.5 Fire Attendant.

10.10.5.1 Open, recreational, and cooking fires shall be constantly attended by a competent person until such fire is extinguished.

10.10.5.2 This person shall have a garden hose connected to the water supply or other fire-extinguishing equipment readily available for use.

10.10.6 Cooking Equipment.

10.10.6.1 For other than one- and two-family dwellings, no hibachi, grill, or other similar devices used for cooking, heating, or any other purpose shall be used or kindled on any balcony, under any overhanging portion, or within 10 ft (3 m) of any structure.

10.10.6.2 For other than one-and two-family dwellings, no hibachi, grill, or other similar devices used for cooking shall be stored on a balcony.

10.10.6.3* Listed equipment permanently installed in accordance with its listing, applicable codes, and manufacturer's instructions shall be permitted.

10.10.7 Installation of Patio Heaters. The installation of patio heaters shall comply with 69.3.11.

10.10.8 Incinerators and Fireplaces.

10.10.8.1 Incinerators, outdoor fireplaces, permanent barbecues, and grills shall not be built, installed, or maintained without prior approval of the AHJ.

10.10.8.2 Incinerators, outdoor fireplaces, permanent barbecues, and grills shall be maintained in good repair and in a safe condition at all times.

10.10.8.3 Openings in incinerators, outdoor fireplaces, permanent barbecues, and grills shall be provided with an approved spark arrester, screen, or door.

10.10.9 Open-Flame Devices.

10.10.9.1* Welding torches, tar pots, decorative torches, and other devices, machines, or processes liable to start or cause fire shall not be operated or used in or upon any areas, except by permit from the AHJ.

10.10.9.2 Flame-employing devices, such as lanterns or kerosene road flares, and fuses shall not be operated or used as a signal or marker in or upon any areas unless at the scene of emergencies or railroad operations. *(See Chapter 16 and Chapter 65 for additional guidance.)*

10.10.9.3 The use of unmanned, free-floating sky lanterns and similar devices utilizing an open flame shall be prohibited.

10.10.10 Discontinuance. The AHJ shall be authorized to require any fire to be immediately discontinued if the fire is determined to constitute a hazardous condition.

10.11 Fire Protection Markings.

10.11.1 Premises Identification.

10.11.1.1* New and existing buildings shall have approved address numbers placed in a position to be plainly legible and visible from the street or road fronting the property.

10.11.1.2 Address numbers shall contrast with their background.

10.11.1.3 Address numbers shall be arabic numerals or alphabet letters.

10.11.2 Shaftways to Be Marked for Fire Fighter Safety.

10.11.2.1 Every outside opening accessible to the fire department that opens directly on any hoistway or shaftway communicating between two or more floors in a building shall be plainly marked with a sign in accordance with 10.11.2.2 and 10.11.2.3.

10.11.2.2 Shaftway signs shall be in red letters at least 6 in. (152 mm) high on a white background stating "SHAFTWAY."

10.11.2.3 Such warning signs shall be placed so as to be readily discernible from the outside of the building.

10.11.3* Stairway Identification.

10.11.3.1 New enclosed stairs serving three or more stories and existing enclosed stairs other than those addressed in 10.11.3.1.16, serving five or more stories shall comply with 10.11.3.1.1 through 10.11.3.1.15. [*101*:7.2.2.5.4.1]

10.11.3.1.1 The stairs shall be provided with special signage within the enclosure at each floor landing. [*101*:7.2.2.5.4.1(A)]

10.11.3.1.2 The signage shall indicate the floor level. [*101*:7.2.2.5.4.1(B)]

10.11.3.1.3 The signage shall indicate the terminus of the top and bottom of the stair enclosure. [*101*:7.2.2.5.4.1(C)]

10.11.3.1.4 The signage shall indicate the identification of the stair enclosure. [*101*:7.2.2.5.4.1(D)]

10.11.3.1.5 The signage shall indicate the floor level of, and the direction to, exit discharge. [*101*:7.2.2.5.4.1(E)]

10.11.3.1.6 The signage shall be located inside the stair enclosure. [*101*:7.2.2.5.4.1(F)]

10.11.3.1.7 The bottom of the signage shall be located a minimum of 48 in. (1220 mm) above the floor landing and the top of the signage shall be located a maximum of 84 in. (2135 mm) above the floor landing. [*101*:7.2.2.5.4.1(G)]

10.11.3.1.8 The signage shall be in a position that is visible when the door is in the open or closed position. [*101*:7.2.2.5.4.1(H)]

10.11.3.1.9 The signage shall comply with 14.14.8.1 and 14.14.8.2. [*101*:7.2.2.5.4.1(I)]

10.11.3.1.10 The floor level designation shall also be tactile in accordance with ICC/ANSI A117.1, *American National Standard for Accessible and Usable Buildings and Facilities*. [*101*:7.2.2.5.4.1(J)]

10.11.3.1.11 The signage shall be painted or stenciled on the wall or on a separate sign securely attached to the wall. [*101*:7.2.2.5.4.1(K)]

10.11.3.1.12 The stairway identification shall be located at the top of the sign in minimum 1 in. (25 mm) high lettering and shall be in accordance with 14.14.8.2. [*101*:7.2.2.5.4.1(L)]

10.11.3.1.13* Signage that reads NO ROOF ACCESS shall designate stairways that do not provide roof access. Lettering shall be a minimum of 1 in. (25 mm) high and shall be in accordance with 14.14.8.2. [*101*:7.2.2.5.4.1(M)]

10.11.3.1.14 The floor level number shall be located below the stairway identifier in minimum 5 in. (125 mm) high numbers and shall be in accordance with 14.14.8.2. Mezzanine levels shall have the letter "M" or other appropriate identification letter preceding the floor number, while basement levels shall have the letter "B" or other appropriate identification letter preceding the floor level number. [*101*:7.2.2.5.4.1(N)]

10.11.3.1.15 Identification of the lower and upper terminus of the stairway shall be on the sign in minimum 1 in. (25 mm) high letters or numbers and shall be in accordance with 14.14.8.2. [*101*:7.2.2.5.4.1(O)]

10.11.3.1.16 Previously approved, existing signage shall not be required to comply with 10.11.3.1.12 through 10.11.3.1.15. [*101*:7.2.2.5.4.1(P)]

10.11.3.2 Wherever an enclosed stair requires travel in an upward direction to reach the level of exit discharge, special signs with directional indicators showing the direction to the level of exit discharge shall be provided at each floor level landing from which upward direction of travel is required, unless otherwise provided in 10.11.3.2.1 and 10.11.3.2.2, and the following also shall apply:

(1) Such signage shall comply with 14.14.8.1 and 14.14.8.2.
(2) Such signage shall be visible when the door is in the open or closed position. [*101*:7.2.2.5.4.2]

10.11.3.2.1 The requirement of 10.11.3.2 shall not apply where signs required by 10.11.3.1.1 are provided. [*101*:7.2.2.5.4.2(A)]

10.11.3.2.2 The requirement of 10.11.3.2 shall not apply to stairs extending not more than one story below the level of exit discharge where the exit discharge is clearly obvious. [*101*: 7.2.2.5.4.2(B)]

10.11.3.3* Stairway Tread Marking. Where new contrasting marking is applied to stairs, such marking shall comply with all of the following:

(1) The marking shall include a continuous strip as a coating on, or as a material integral with, the full width of the leading edge of each tread.
(2) The marking shall include a continuous strip as a coating on, or as a material integral with, the full width of the leading edge of each landing nosing.
(3) The marking strip width, measured horizontally from the leading vertical edge of the nosing, shall be consistent at all nosings.
(4) The marking strip width shall be 1 in. to 2 in. (25 mm to 51 mm).
[*101*:7.2.2.5.4.3]

10.11.3.4* Where new contrast marking is provided for stairway handrails, it shall be applied to, or be part of, at least the upper surface of the handrail; have a minimum width of ½ in. (13 mm); and extend the full length of each handrail. After marking, the handrail shall comply with 7.2.2.4.4 of NFPA *101*. Where handrails or handrail extensions bend or turn corners, the stripe shall be permitted to have a gap of not more than 4 in. (100 mm). [*101*:7.2.2.5.4.4]

10.11.3.5 These signs shall be maintained in an approved manner.

10.11.3.6 Existing approved signs shall be permitted.

10.12 Seasonal and Vacant Buildings and Premises.

10.12.1 Every person owning or having charge or control of any vacant building, premises, or portion thereof shall remove all combustible storage, waste, refuse, and vegetation and shall lock, barricade, or otherwise secure the building or premises to prohibit entry by unauthorized persons.

10.12.1.1 The requirement of 10.12.1 shall not apply to buildings used on a seasonal basis, or the temporary vacancy of a building for tenant change or remodeling purposes.

10.12.2 All fire protection systems shall be maintained in service in seasonal and vacant buildings, unless otherwise approved by the AHJ.

10.12.2.1* With the approval of the AHJ, fire protection and fire alarm systems in seasonal and vacant buildings shall be permitted to be removed from service.

10.12.2.2 When required by the AHJ, other systems or components pertaining to fire protection shall be maintained.

10.12.3 The AHJ shall have the authority to require an inspection and test of any fire protection system or fire alarm system that has been out of service for 30 days or more before restored back into service.

10.13 Combustible Vegetation.

10.13.1 Combustible vegetation, including natural cut Christmas trees, shall be in accordance with Section 10.13.

10.13.1.1 Christmas tree placement within buildings shall comply with Table 10.13.1.1.

10.13.2 In any occupancy, limited quantities of combustible vegetation shall be permitted where the AHJ determines that adequate safeguards are provided based on the quantity and nature of the combustible vegetation.

10.13.3* Provisions for Fire Retardance for Artificial Vegetation.

10.13.3.1 Artificial vegetation and artificial Christmas trees shall be labeled or otherwise identified or certified by the manufacturer as being fire retardant.

10.13.3.2 Such fire retardance shall be demonstrated by each individual decorative vegetation item, including any decorative lighting, in an approved manner.

10.13.4 Vegetation and Christmas trees shall not obstruct corridors, exit ways, or other means of egress.

10.13.5 Only listed electrical lights and wiring shall be used on natural or artificial combustible vegetation, natural or artificial Christmas trees, and other similar decorations.

10.13.6 Electrical lights shall be prohibited on metal artificial trees.

10.13.7 Open flames such as from candles, lanterns, kerosene heaters, and gas-fired heaters shall not be located on or near combustible vegetation, Christmas trees, or other similar combustible materials.

10.13.8 Combustible vegetation and natural cut Christmas trees shall not be located near heating vents or other fixed or portable heating devices that could cause it to dry out prematurely or to be ignited.

10.13.9 Provisions for Natural Cut Trees.

10.13.9.1 Where a natural cut tree is permitted, the bottom end of the trunk shall be cut off with a straight fresh cut at least ½ in. (13 mm) above the end prior to placing the tree in a stand to allow the tree to absorb water.

10.13.9.2 The tree shall be placed in a suitable stand with water.

10.13.9.3 The water level shall be maintained above the fresh cut and checked at least once daily.

10.13.9.4* The tree shall be removed from the building immediately upon evidence of dryness.

Table 10.13.1.1 Provisions for Christmas Trees by Occupancy

Occupancy	No Trees Permitted	Cut Tree Permitted With Automatic Sprinkler Systems	Cut Tree Permitted Without Automatic Sprinkler Systems	Balled Tree Permitted
Ambulatory health care				X
Apartment buildings		Within unit	Within unit	X
Assembly	X			
Board and care	X			
Business		X		X
Day-care		X		X
Detention and correctional	X			
Dormitories	X			
Educational	X			
Health care				X
Hotels	X			
Industrial		X	X	X
Lodging and rooming				X
Mercantile		X		X
One and two family		X	X	X
Storage		X	X	X

10.13.10 Exterior Vegetation.

10.13.10.1 Cut or uncut weeds, grass, vines, and other vegetation shall be removed when determined by the AHJ to be a fire hazard.

10.13.10.2 When the AHJ determines that total removal of growth is impractical due to size or environmental factors, approved fuel breaks shall be established.

10.13.10.3 Designated areas shall be cleared of combustible vegetation to establish the fuel breaks.

10.14 Special Outdoor Events, Carnivals, and Fairs.

10.14.1 Permits. Permits, where required, shall comply with Section 1.12.

10.14.2 The AHJ shall be permitted to regulate all outdoor events such as carnivals and fairs as it pertains to access for emergency vehicles; access to fire protection equipment; placement of stands, concession booths, and exhibits; and the control of hazardous conditions dangerous to life and property.

10.14.3 Life Safety Evaluation. The AHJ shall be permitted to order a life safety evaluation in accordance with this subsection.

10.14.3.1* General. Where a life safety evaluation is required by other provisions of the *Code*, it shall comply with all of the following:

(1) The life safety evaluation shall be performed by persons acceptable to the AHJ.
(2) The life safety evaluation shall include a written assessment of safety measures for conditions listed in 10.14.3.2 and of the building systems and facility management in accordance with 10.14.3.3.
(3) The life safety evaluation shall be approved annually by the AHJ and shall be updated for special or unusual conditions in accordance with the provisions of 13.4.1 of NFPA *101* for existing assembly occupancies. [*101*:12.4.1.1]

10.14.3.2 Conditions to be Assessed. Life safety evaluations shall include an assessment of all of the following conditions and related appropriate safety measures:

(1) Nature of the events and the participants and attendees
(2) Access and egress movement, including crowd density problems
(3) Medical emergencies
(4) Fire hazards
(5) Permanent and temporary structural systems
(6) Severe weather conditions
(7) Earthquakes
(8) Civil or other disturbances
(9) Hazardous materials incidents within and near the facility
(10) Relationships among facility management, event participants, emergency response agencies, and others having a role in the events accommodated in the facility [*101:* 12.4.1.2]

10.14.3.3* Building Systems and Facility Management Assessments. Life safety evaluations shall include assessments of both building systems and facility management upon which reliance is placed for the safety of facility occupants, and such assessments shall consider scenarios appropriate to the facility. [*101:* 12.4.1.3]

10.14.3.3.1 Building Systems. Prior to issuance of the building permit, the design team shall provide the AHJ with building systems documentation in accordance with 10.14.3.4. [*101:* 12.4.1.3.1]

10.14.3.3.2 Facility Management. Prior to issuance of the certificate of occupancy, the facility management shall provide the AHJ with facility management documentation in accordance with 10.14.3.5. [*101:* 12.4.1.3.2]

10.14.3.3.3 Life Safety Evaluation.

10.14.3.3.3.1 Prior to issuance of the building permit, the persons performing the life safety evaluation shall confirm that the building systems provide safety measures. [*101:* 12.4.1.3.3.1]

10.14.3.3.3.2 Prior to issuance of the certificate of occupancy, the persons performing the life safety evaluation shall confirm that the facility management and operational plans provide appropriate safety measures. [*101:* 12.4.1.3.3.2]

10.14.3.3.3.3 The AHJ shall determine the acceptable persons performing the life safety evaluation in a timely manner to enable the design team and facility management to resolve concerns to the satisfaction of the persons performing the life safety evaluation prior to their submission. [*101:* 12.4.1.3.3.3]

10.14.3.4 Life Safety Building Systems Document. The AHJ shall be provided with a life safety building systems document providing the information required in 10.14.3.4.2 through 10.14.3.4.4. [*101:* 12.4.1.4]

10.14.3.4.1 Document Distribution. The persons performing the life safety evaluation, the AHJ, the A/E design team and the building owner shall receive a copy of the life safety building systems document prior to issuance of the building permit. [*101:* 12.4.1.4.1]

10.14.3.4.2 Life Safety Narrative. A life safety narrative shall be provided describing the following:

(1) Building occupancy, construction type, and intended uses and events
(2) Building area and population capacity of the proposed facility
(3) Principal fire and life safety features/strategies for the building, including the following:
   (a) Sprinkler protection
   (b) Smoke control/protection
   (c) Fire alarm - visual and audible
   (d) PA system
   (e) Emergency power and lighting
   (f) Provisions for patrons with disabilities
   (g) Fire department access
   (h) Fire/Emergency command center
(4) Exterior construction design parameters used/applied [*101:* 12.4.1.4.2]

10.14.3.4.3 Life Safety Floor Plans. Life safety floor plans of each level shall be provided with the following:

(1) Occupant load, exit location, exit capacity, main exit/entry, horizontal exits, travel distance and exit discharge
(2) Fire and smoke barriers
(3) Areas of smoke protected assembly occupancy
(4) Separate smoke protected areas or zones if applicable
(5) Areas of other occupancy type and separations if required
(6) Unprotected vertical openings, including atriums, communicating spaces, and convenience openings
(7) Event plans for each anticipated type of event depicting the following:
   (a) Seating configuration
   (b) Exhibit booth layout
   (c) Stage location
   (d) Occupant load, exit capacity required, exits provided and travel distance
   (e) Any floor or stage use restrictions
   (f) Plan and/or section drawing indicating areas where the roof construction is more than 50 feet and limits of sprinkler protection.
   (g) Areas of refuge — interior and exterior [*101:* 12.4.1.4.3]

10.14.3.4.4 Engineering Analysis and Calculations. An engineering analysis and calculations shall be provided with the following:

(1) Smoke protection calculations as follows:
   (a) Smoke exhaust and fresh air requirements per NFPA 92, *Standard for Smoke Control Systems*
   (b) Smoke maintained at a level six ft above the floor of the means of egress
   (c) Proposed testing protocol for smoke system and pass/fail criteria
   (d) Calculations for performance-based design methods accepted by the AHJ
   (e) Smoke and fire modeling
   (f) Timed egress analysis
   (g) Assumed flow rates and travel speed
(2) Sprinkler protection calculations, including an engineering analysis substantiating locations in accordance with 13.3.2.7.3 where sprinkler protection would be ineffective due to height and combustible loading
(3) Load diagram of rigging/load capacity of gridiron, fly loft or long span roof structure used for hanging overhead objects [*101:* 12.4.1.4.4]

10.14.3.5 Life Safety Management Document. The AHJ shall be provided with a life safety management document providing the information required in 10.14.3.5.2 through 10.14.3.5.7. [*101:* 12.4.1.5]

10.14.3.5.1 Document Distribution. The persons performing the life safety evaluation, the AHJ, the A/E design team and the building owner shall receive a copy of the life safety management document prior to issuance of the certificate of occupancy. [*101:* 12.4.1.5.1]

10.14.3.5.2 Facility Management and Operational Plans. Facility management and operational plans shall address the following:

(1) Best practices adopted or recognized
(2) Emergency plans
(3) Evacuation plans
(4) Shelter-in-place plans, including capacities and protection considerations
(5) Crowd management training plans
(6) Safety plans, which include the following:
   (a) Training plans
   (b) Safety equipment plans
(7) Fire alarm, smoke system protocol and testing plans
(8) First aid or medical treatment plans, which include the following:
   (a) Defined levels of service
   (b) Standing orders adopted
   (c) Supply and equipment plan
(9) Housekeeping plans – biological, medical, hazardous materials cleaning
(10) Emergency communication plans, which include the following:
   (a) Chain of authority and incident command system employed
   (b) Contact information for the following:
      i. Venue personnel
      ii. Emergency management and response organizations (e.g., fire, police, medical, utility, transportation, key stakeholders)
   (c) Communication systems
   (d) Standard announcement for incidents or emergency situations
(11) Risk and threat assessment for venue and surrounding area for the following:
   (a) Severe weather
   (b) Hazardous materials
   (c) Terrorism
   (d) Hostile intruder
(12) Operating procedures and protocols for risks, such as the following:
   (a) Severe weather preparedness and monitoring plans
   (b) Hazardous materials incidence response plans
   (c) Terrorism response plans
   (d) Hostile intruder response plans
(13) First responder response/arrival routes plans
(14) Alcohol management plans
(15) Food safety plans
(16) Rigging and temporary performance structure, which includes the following:
   (a) Design and safety review plans
   (b) Emergency action plans
(17) Chemical and hazardous materials information and data
(18) Barrier and wall protection plans for motor sports or similar events [*101:* 12.4.1.5.2]

10.14.3.5.3 Records. Records of the facility management plans, including procedures and location, shall be maintained, for the following:

(1) Crowd management training
(2) Safety training
(3) Fire alarm, smoke system maintenance and test records
(4) First aid or medical treatment and regulation compliance [*101:* 12.4.1.5.3]

10.14.3.5.4 Building Systems Reference Guide. A building systems reference guide shall be provided in accordance with 10.14.3.5.4.1 through 10.14.3.5.4.3. [*101:* 12.4.1.5.4]

10.14.3.5.4.1 A basic life safety building systems reference guide shall be developed and maintained. [*101:* 12.4.1.5.4.1]

10.14.3.5.4.2 The life safety building systems reference guide shall contain the important and key information for the venue management's use when planning events/activities for the safety of patrons, performers/participants, employees and vendors. [*101:* 12.4.1.5.4.2]

10.14.3.5.4.3 The life safety building systems document in accordance with 10.14.3.4 shall be permitted to be used, but the life safety building systems reference guide shall include the following:

(1) Occupant capacity of every space/room
(2) Egress flow diagrams, including assumed flow rates, and capacities of all aisles and hallways, including public and non-public areas
(3) Capacities of all exterior doors and/or choke points in immediate perimeter areas
(4) Limitations or assumptions for ingress control that could be in place during an emergency egress/evacuation, including control gates, queuing barriers, and turnstiles
(5) Capacities of immediate perimeter exterior walkways, including assumed flow rates for exterior areas

(6) Assumed egress paths for normal conditions–transportation modes
(7) Management level (lay) sequencing charts for alarm and emergency communication systems, the manual or override options/instructions that include the following:
   (a) List of codes or alarm signals
   (b) Location of manual overrides
   (c) Description of what exactly happens during an alarm, such as exhaust fans or doors open
(8) Principal fire and life safety features/strategies, such as sprinklers, smoke control, fire alarm notifications, PA system, fire department access
(9) Assumptions when developing occupancy plans for venue floor, open areas, and non-event spaces, such as the following:
   (a) Event floor plans/set up diagrams for each typical event/activity
   (b) Fire sprinkler and smoke protection capabilities
(10) Severe weather shelter areas, locations, structure considerations (limitations), capacities (occupancy and density factor)
(11) Command center, which includes the following:
   (a) Location (formal or informal)
   (b) Structural integrity considerations
   (c) Redundant locations and/or capabilities
   (d) Jurisdictional rights — assumed and/or applied
(12) Locations and capacities of wheelchair and mobility-impaired seating
(13) Locations and capacities of "Safe Haven" areas
(14) Rigging or structural load capacities of grids, truss structure, fly lofts, ceilings, floors, ramps, staging, etc.
(15) List of locations of emergency equipment (i.e., fire extinguishers, fire hose cabinets, fire hydrants, AEDs, etc.)
(16) Sequencing of electrical service, such as the following:
   (a) Emergency generators and charts of all areas illuminated during power outages
   (b) Multiple electrical feed capabilities
(17) List of mechanical, moveable equipment in the facility
(18) Potential hazards in the surrounding neighborhood, including train tracks and propane stations
(19) Assumptions or accommodations considered and used in design [*101:* 12.4.1.5.4.3]

10.14.3.5.5 The facility management plans shall be maintained and adjusted as necessary for changes to the venue structure, operating purposes and style, and event occupancy. [*101:* 12.4.1.5.5]

10.14.3.5.6 Facility management and operational plans shall be reviewed by the AHJ annually. [*101:* 12.4.1.5.6]

10.14.3.5.7 For events and activities at the venue that are outside the normal operating conditions or vary from the normal facility management plans, the following shall apply:
(1) Facility management shall perform an event/activity specific facility management plan for the AHJ to review.
(2) The AHJ shall provide guidance as needed, but approval of the AHJ for the specific facility management plan shall occur prior to such event. [*101:* 12.4.1.5.7]

10.14.4 Standby Fire Personnel. Where required by the AHJ, standby fire personnel shall be provided and comply with 1.7.17.

10.14.5 Portable Fire Extinguishers. A minimum of one portable fire extinguisher shall be provided for each concession stand where required by the AHJ in accordance with Section 13.6.

10.14.6 Smoke Alarms. A minimum of one single station smoke alarm shall be located in all stock or equipment trailers when they are used for sleeping purposes.

10.14.7 Electrical Equipment. Electrical equipment and installations shall comply with Section 11.1.

10.14.8 Cooking. Concession stands utilized for cooking shall have a minimum of 10 ft (3 m) of clearance on two sides and shall not be located within 10 ft (3 m) of amusement rides or devices.

10.14.9 Communications. Where required by the AHJ, a method of notifying the fire department in the event of an emergency shall be provided.

10.14.9.1 Methods of notifying the fire department shall consist of a telephone, an alarm system connected to the fire department or other approved agency, or other approved means.

10.14.9.2 Methods of notifying the fire department shall be readily available to the public.

10.14.10 Internal Combustion Power Sources.

10.14.10.1 Fueling. Fuel tanks shall be of adequate capacity to permit uninterrupted operation during normal operating hours.

10.14.10.2 Refueling. Refueling shall be conducted only when not in use.

10.14.10.3 Protection. Internal combustion power sources shall be isolated from contact with the public by either physical guards, fencing, or an enclosure.

10.14.10.4 Fire Extinguishers. A minimum of one portable fire extinguisher with a rating of not less than 2-A:10-B:C shall be provided.

10.14.11 Crop Maze.

10.14.11.1 Permits. Permits, where required, shall comply with Section 1.12.

10.14.11.2 General.

10.14.11.2.1 The owner or operator of a crop maze amusement attraction shall advise all employees of the fire and life safety regulations established in this subsection prior to the employees assuming their respective duties.

10.14.11.2.2 The owner or operator of a crop maze or their employees shall provide safety instructions to the visitors and patrons of a crop maze prior to their entrance to the maze.

10.14.11.2.3 Employee Monitor.

10.14.11.2.3.1 A minimum of two employees shall be on duty to monitor a crop maze during hours of operation.

10.14.11.2.3.2 A minimum of one of the employees shall be located on an elevated platform a minimum of 10 ft (3 m) above the maze.

10.14.11.2.4 The owner or operator of a crop maze shall contact the local fire department and provide the fire department with the opportunity to prepare a pre-plan of the crop maze amusement attraction prior to the start of seasonal operations.

10.14.11.2.5 Motorized vehicles shall not be parked within 75 ft (23 m) of a crop maze.

10.14.11.2.6 A fuel break of a minimum of 20 ft (6 m) wide shall be cleared between a crop maze and any vehicles or vegetation outside the maze.

10.14.11.2.7 Public Address System.

10.14.11.2.7.1 A public address system shall be readily available to employees at a crop maze to assist them in making announcements to the visitors or patrons of a crop maze in the event of an emergency.

10.14.11.2.7.2 A bull horn or loud speaker shall suffice as a public address system.

10.14.11.2.8 The entrance and exit from a crop maze shall not be blocked or obstructed at any time the maze is open for business and occupied by the public.

10.14.11.2.9 No more than 200 persons per acre, including adults and children, shall occupy the crop maze at any one time.

10.14.11.3 Prohibited.

10.14.11.3.1* No open flame-producing devices or equipment shall be permitted within the confines of the crop maze.

10.14.11.3.2 No smoking shall be permitted within the confines of the crop maze.

10.14.11.4 Fireworks.

10.14.11.4.1 Fireworks shall not be discharged within a minimum of 300 ft (91 m) of any crop maze at any time.

10.14.11.4.2 The use of display fireworks shall comply with Chapter 65 in addition to the requirements of 10.14.11.4.

10.15* Outside Storage.

10.15.1 Outside storage of combustible materials shall not be located within 10 ft (3 m) of a property line.

10.15.2 The separation distance shall be allowed to be reduced to 3 ft (0.9 m) for storage not exceeding 6 ft (1.8 m) in height.

10.15.3 The separation distance shall be allowed to be reduced where the AHJ determines that no hazard to the adjoining property exists.

10.15.4 Combustible material shall not be stored beneath a building or structure unless specifically constructed or protected for this purpose.

10.15.5 Combustible storage in the open shall not exceed 20 ft (6.1 m) in height.

10.16 Parade Floats.

10.16.1 Permits. Permits, where required, shall comply with Section 1.12.

10.16.2 Fire Protection. Motorized parade floats and towing apparatus shall be provided with a minimum 2-A:10-B:C-rated portable fire extinguisher readily accessible to the operator.

10.17 Powered Industrial Trucks. Powered industrial trucks shall be operated and maintained in accordance with NFPA 505, *Fire Safety Standard for Powered Industrial Trucks Including Type Designations, Areas of Use, Conversions, Maintenance, and Operations.*

10.18* Storage of Combustible Materials.

10.18.1 General. Storage of combustible materials shall be orderly.

10.18.2 Permits. Permits, where required, shall comply with Section 1.12.

10.18.3 Ceiling Clearance.

10.18.3.1 Storage shall be maintained 2 ft (0.61 m) or more from the ceiling in nonsprinklered areas of buildings.

10.18.3.2 The clearance between the deflector and the top of storage shall be 18 in. (457 mm) or greater. [13:8.6.6.1]

10.18.3.3 The 18 in. (457 mm) dimension shall not limit the height of shelving on a wall or shelving against a wall in accordance with 10.19.3, and 8.7.6, 8.8.6, and Section 8.9 of NFPA 13. [13:8.6.6.2]

10.18.3.3.1 Where shelving is installed on a wall and is not directly below sprinklers, the shelves, including storage thereon, shall extend above the level of a plane located 18 in. (457 mm) below ceiling sprinkler deflectors. [13:8.6.6.2.1]

10.18.3.3.2 Shelving, and any storage thereon, directly below the sprinklers shall not extend above a plane located 18 in. (457 mm) below the ceiling sprinkler deflectors. [13:8.6.6.2.2]

10.18.3.4 Where other standards specify greater clearance to storage minimums, they shall be followed. [13:8.6.6.3]

10.18.4 Means of Egress. Combustible material shall not be stored in exits.

10.18.5 Equipment Rooms.

10.18.5.1 Combustible material shall not be stored in boiler rooms, mechanical rooms, or electrical equipment rooms.

10.18.5.2 Materials and supplies for the operation and maintenance of the equipment in the room shall be permitted.

10.18.6 Attic, Under-Floor, and Concealed Spaces. Attic, under-floor, and concealed spaces used for storage of combustible materials shall comply with the protection from hazards requirements for storage rooms in NFPA *101*.

10.18.7 Fueled Equipment. Fueled equipment, including but not limited to motorcycles, mopeds, lawn-care equipment, and portable cooking equipment, shall not be stored, operated, or repaired within a building except under one of the following conditions:

(1) The building or room has been constructed for such use in accordance with the building code.
(2) The use is allowed by other provisions of this *Code*.

10.19 Indoor Children's Playground Structures.

10.19.1 Structures intended as children's playgrounds, installed indoors and that which exceed 10 ft (3.1 m) in height and 160 ft^2 (14.9 m^2) in area, shall comply with the specifications in 10.19.1.1.

10.19.1.1 Indoor children's playground structures shall be constructed of noncombustible materials or of combustible materials that comply with the following:

(1) Fire retardant–treated wood.
(2) Light-transmitting plastics complying with the requirements in 10.19.1.2.
(3) Foam plastics (including the pipe foam used in soft-contained play equipment structures) having a maximum

heat-release rate not greater than 100 kW when tested in accordance with UL 1975 or NFPA 289, *Standard Method of Fire Test for Individual Fuel Packages*, using the 20 kW ignition source.

(4) Aluminum composite material (ACM) meeting the requirements of Class A interior finish in accordance with Chapter 10 of NFPA *101, Life Safety Code*, when tested as an assembly in the maximum thickness intended for use.

(5) Textiles and films complying with the flame propagation performance criteria contained in Test Method 1 or Test Method 2, as appropriate, of NFPA 701.

(6) Plastic materials used to construct rigid components of soft-contained play equipment structures (such as tubes, windows, panels, junction boxes, pipes, slides, and decks) exhibiting a peak rate of heat release not exceeding 400 kW/m^2 when tested in accordance with ASTM E 1354 at an incident heat flux of 0.24 in. (50 kW/m^2) in the horizontal orientation at a thickness of 0.24 in. (6 mm).

(7) Balls used in ball pools, in soft-contained play equipment structures, shall have a maximum heat release rate not greater than 100 kW when tested in accordance with UL 1975 or NFPA 289 using the 20 kW ignition source. The minimum specimen test size shall be 36 in. × 36 in. (0.91 m × 0.91 m) by an average of 21 in. (0.56 m) deep, and the balls shall be held in a box constructed of galvanized steel poultry netting wire mesh.

(8) Foam plastics shall be covered by a fabric, coating, or film meeting the flame propagation performance criteria contained in Test Method 1 or Test Method 2, as appropriate, of NFPA 701.

(9) The floor covering within the children's playground structure shall exhibit a Class I interior floor finish classification, as described in Chapter 10 of NFPA *101* when tested in accordance with NFPA 253, *Standard Method of Test for Critical Radiant Flux of Floor Covering Systems Using a Radiant Heat Energy Source*.

10.19.1.2* Light-transmitting plastics used for children's playgrounds shall meet all of the following criteria:

(1) They shall have a self-ignition temperature of 650°F (343°C) or greater when tested in accordance with ASTM D 1929.

(2) They shall have a smoke developed index not greater than 450 when tested in the manner intended for use in accordance with ASTM E 84, *Standard Test Method of Surface Burning Characteristics of Building Materials*, or ANSI/UL 723, *Standard for Test for Surface Burning Characteristics of Building Materials*, or not greater than 75 when tested in the thickness intended for use in accordance with ASTM D 2843, *Standard Test Method for Density of Smoke from the Burning or Decomposition of Plastics*.

(3) They shall meet the criteria of one of the following classifications:

(a) CC1 — Plastic materials that have a burn length of 1 in. (25 mm) or less and flame extinguishment when tested at a nominal thickness of 0.060 in. (1.5 mm), or in the thickness intended for use, in accordance with ASTM D 635, *Standard Test Method for Rate of Burning and/or Extent and Time of Burning of Plastics in a Horizontal Position*

(b) CC2 — Plastic materials that have a burning rate of 2½ in./min (64 mm/min) or less when tested at a nominal thickness of 0.060 in. (1.5 mm), or at a thickness intended for use, in accordance with ASTM D 635

10.19.1.3 Indoor children's playground structures shall have a minimum horizontal separation from other structures of 20 ft (6.1 m).

10.19.1.4 Indoor children's playground structures shall not exceed 300 ft^2 (28 m^2) in area, unless approved by the AHJ.

Chapter 11 Building Services

11.1 Electrical Fire Safety.

11.1.1 General. Section 11.1 shall apply to permanent and temporary electrical appliances, equipment, fixtures, and wiring.

11.1.2 Permanent Wiring, Fixtures, and Equipment.

11.1.2.1 All new electrical wiring, fixtures, appliances and equipment shall be installed in accordance with *NFPA 70, National Electrical Code*.

11.1.2.2 Unless determined to present an imminent danger, existing electrical wiring, fixtures, appliances, and equipment shall be permitted to be maintained in accordance with the edition of *NFPA 70, National Electrical Code*, in effect at the time of the installation.

11.1.2.3 Permanent wiring abandoned in place shall be tagged or otherwise identified at its termination and junction points as "Abandoned in Place" or removed from all accessible areas and insulated from contact with other live electrical wiring or devices.

11.1.3 Multiplug Adapters.

11.1.3.1 Multiplug adapters, such as multiplug extension cords, cube adapters, strip plugs, and other devices, shall be listed and used in accordance with their listing.

11.1.3.2 Multiplug adapters shall not be used as a substitute for permanent wiring or receptacles.

11.1.4 Relocatable Power Taps.

11.1.4.1 Relocatable power taps shall be of the polarized or grounded type with overcurrent protection and shall be listed.

11.1.4.2 The relocatable power taps shall be directly connected to a permanently installed receptacle.

11.1.4.3 Relocatable power tap cords shall not extend through walls, ceilings, or floors; under doors or floor coverings; or be subject to environmental or physical damage.

11.1.5 Extension Cords.

11.1.5.1 Extension cords shall be plugged directly into an approved receptacle, power tap, or multiplug adapter and shall, except for approved multiplug extension cords, serve only one portable appliance.

11.1.5.2* The ampacity of the extension cords shall not be less than the rated capacity of the portable appliance supplied by the cord.

11.1.5.3 The extension cords shall be maintained in good condition without splices, deterioration, or damage.

11.1.5.4 Extension cords shall be grounded when servicing grounded portable appliances.

11.1.5.5 Extension cords and flexible cords shall not be affixed to structures; extend through walls, ceilings, or floors, or under doors or floor coverings; or be subject to environmental or physical damage.

11.1.5.6 Extension cords shall not be used as a substitute for permanent wiring.

11.1.6 Temporary Installations.

11.1.6.1 Scope. The provisions of 11.1.6 shall apply to temporary electric power and lighting installations. [**70:**590.1]

11.1.6.2 All Wiring Installations.

11.1.6.2.1 Other Articles. Except as specifically modified in Article 590 of *NFPA 70*, all other requirements of *NFPA 70* for permanent wiring shall apply to temporary wiring installations. [**70:**590.2(A)]

11.1.6.2.2 Approval. Temporary wiring methods shall be acceptable only if approved based on the conditions of use and any special requirements of the temporary installation. [**70:** 590.2(B)]

11.1.6.3 Time Constraints.

11.1.6.3.1 During the Period of Construction. Temporary electric power and lighting installations shall be permitted during the period of construction, remodeling, maintenance, repair, or demolition of buildings, structures, equipment, or similar activities. [**70:** 590.3(A)]

11.1.6.3.2 90 Days. Temporary electric power and lighting installations shall be permitted for a period not to exceed 90 days for holiday decorative lighting and similar purposes. [**70:** 590.3(B)]

11.1.6.3.3 Emergencies and Tests. Temporary electric power and lighting installations shall be permitted during emergencies and for tests, experiments, and developmental work. [**70:** 590.3(C)]

11.1.6.3.4 Removal. Temporary wiring shall be removed immediately upon completion of construction or purpose for which the wiring was installed. [**70:** 590.3(D)]

11.1.7 Building Disconnect.

11.1.7.1* Means shall be provided for the fire department to disconnect the electrical service to a building, structure, or facility when the electrical installation is covered under the scope of NFPA 70.

11.1.7.2 The disconnecting means shall be maintained accessible to the fire department.

11.1.7.3 Identification of Disconnecting Means.

11.1.7.3.1 Each disconnecting means shall be legibly marked to indicate its purpose unless located and arranged so the purpose is evident. The marking shall be of sufficient durability to withstand the environment involved. [**70:** 110.22(A)]

11.1.8 Covers. All panelboard and switchboards, pull boxes, junction boxes, switches, receptacles, and conduit bodies shall be provided with covers compatible with the box or conduit body construction and suitable for the conditions of use.

11.2 Heating, Ventilation, and Air-Conditioning.

11.2.1 Air-Conditioning, Heating, Ventilating Ductwork, and Related Equipment. Air-conditioning, heating, ventilating ductwork, and related equipment shall be in accordance with NFPA 90A, *Standard for the Installation of Air-Conditioning and Ventilating Systems*, or NFPA 90B, *Standard for the Installation of Warm Air Heating and Air-Conditioning Systems*, as applicable, unless such installations are approved existing installations, which shall be permitted to be continued in service. [*101:* 9.2.1]

11.2.2 Ventilating or Heat-Producing Equipment. Ventilating or heat-producing equipment shall be in accordance with NFPA 91, *Standard for Exhaust Systems for Air Conveying of Vapors, Gases, Mists, and Noncombustible Particulate Solids*; NFPA 211, *Standard for Chimneys, Fireplaces, Vents, and Solid Fuel–Burning Appliances*; NFPA 31, *Standard for the Installation of Oil-Burning Equipment*; NFPA 54, *National Fuel Gas Code*; or NFPA 70, as applicable, unless such installations are approved existing installations, which shall be permitted to be continued in service. [*101:* 9.2.2]

11.3 Elevators, Escalators, and Conveyors.

11.3.1 Fire Fighters' Emergency Operations.

11.3.1.1 All new elevators shall conform to the Fire Fighters' Emergency Operations requirements of ASME A17.1/CSA B44, *Safety Code for Elevators and Escalators*. [*101:* 9.4.3.1]

11.3.1.2 All existing elevators having a travel distance of 25 ft (7620 mm) or more above or below the level that best serves the needs of emergency personnel for fire-fighting or rescue purposes shall conform to the Fire Fighters' Emergency Operations requirements of ASME A17.3, *Safety Code for Existing Elevators and Escalators*. [*101:* 9.4.3.2]

11.3.2 Number of Cars. The number of elevator cars permitted in a hoistway shall be in accordance with 8.6.9.4 of NFPA *101*. [*101:* 9.4.4]

11.3.3* Elevator Machine Rooms. Elevator machine rooms that contain solid-state equipment for elevators, other than existing elevators, having a travel distance exceeding 50 ft (15 m) above the level of exit discharge or exceeding 30 ft (9.1 m) below the level of exit discharge shall be provided with independent ventilation or air-conditioning systems to maintain temperature during fire fighters' emergency operations for elevator operation *(see 11.3.1)*. The operating temperature shall be established by the elevator equipment manufacturer's specifications. When standby power is connected to the elevator, the machine room ventilation or air-conditioning shall be connected to standby power. [*101:* 9.4.5]

11.3.4 Elevator Testing.

11.3.4.1 Elevators shall be subject to periodic inspections and tests as specified in ASME A17.1/CSA B44, *Safety Code for Elevators and Escalators*. [*101:* 9.4.6.1]

11.3.4.2 All elevators equipped with fire fighters' emergency operations in accordance with 11.3.1 shall be subject to a monthly operation with a written record of the findings made and kept on the premises as required by ASME A17.1/CSA B44, *Safety Code for Elevators and Escalators*. [*101:* 9.4.6.2]

11.3.4.3 The elevator inspections and tests required by 11.3.4.1 shall be performed at frequencies complying with one of the following:

(1) Inspection and test frequencies specified in Appendix N of ASME A17.1/CSA B44, *Safety Code for Elevators and Escalators*
(2) Inspection and test frequencies specified by the AHJ [*101:* 9.4.6.3]

11.3.5 Openings to Exit Enclosures. Conveyors, elevators, dumbwaiters, and pneumatic conveyors serving various stories of a building shall not open to an exit enclosure. [*101:* 9.4.7]

11.3.6 Standardized Fire Service Elevator Keys.

11.3.6.1 Buildings with elevators equipped with Phase I emergency recall, Phase II emergency in-car operation, or a fire service access elevator shall be equipped to operate with a standardized fire service key complying with ASME A17.1/CSA B44, *Safety Code for Elevators and Escalators*, except as otherwise permitted by 11.3.6.

11.3.6.2 Existing buildings with elevators equipped with Phase I emergency recall or Phase II emergency in-car operation shall be permitted to comply with 11.3.6.3.

11.3.6.3 Existing Buildings. Existing buildings shall be in compliance with the provisions of 11.3.6.3.1.1one year after adoption by the AHJ.

11.3.6.3.1 Where a standardized key cylinder cannot be installed in an existing elevator key switch assembly, the building's nonstandardized fire service elevator keys shall be provided in an access box in accordance with 11.3.6.3.1.1 through 11.3.6.3.1.6.

11.3.6.3.1.1 The access box shall be compatible with an existing rapid-entry access box system in use in the jurisdiction and approved by the AHJ.

11.3.6.3.1.2 The front cover shall be permanently labeled with the words "Fire Department Use Only — Elevator Keys."

11.3.6.3.1.3 The access box shall be mounted at each elevator bank at the lobby nearest to the lowest level of fire department access.

11.3.6.3.1.4 The access box shall be mounted at a location approved by the AHJ.

11.3.6.3.1.5 Contents of the access box shall be limited to the fire service elevator key. Additional elevator access tools, keys, and information pertinent to emergency planning or elevator access shall be permitted when authorized by the AHJ.

11.3.6.3.1.6 In buildings with two or more elevator banks, a single access box shall be permitted to be used where such elevator banks are separated by not more than 30 ft (9140 mm). Additional access boxes shall be provided for each individual elevator or elevator bank separated by more than 30 ft (9140 mm).

11.3.6.3.1.7 A single access box shall be permitted to be located adjacent to a fire command center, or the nonstandard fire service elevator key shall be secured in an access box used for other purposes and located in accordance with 18.2.2.1 when approved by the AHJ.

11.3.7 Elevators for Occupant-Controlled Evacuation Prior to Phase I Emergency Recall Operations and Fire Service Access Elevators.
An approved method to prevent automatic sprinkler water from infiltrating into the hoistway enclosure from the operation of the automatic sprinkler system outside the enclosed occupant evacuation elevator lobby shall be provided where the hoistway serves elevators in accordance with any of the following:

(1) Occupant-controlled evacuation elevators in accordance with Section 7.14 of NFPA *101, Life Safety Code*
(2) Occupant-controlled evacuation elevators in accordance with the building code
(3) Fire service access elevators in accordance with the building code

11.4 Utilities. Equipment using fuel gas and related gas piping shall be in accordance with NFPA 54, *National Fuel Gas Code*, or NFPA 58, *Liquefied Petroleum Gas Code*. *(See Chapter 69 for LP-Gas fuel supply and storage installations.)*

11.4.1 Existing installations shall be permitted to be continued in service, subject to approval by the AHJ.

11.4.2 Aboveground gas meters, regulators, and piping exposed to vehicular damage shall be protected in accordance with 60.5.1.9.

11.5 Heating Appliances.

11.5.1 General.

11.5.1.1 The installation of stationary liquid fuel–burning appliances, including but not limited to industrial-, commercial-, and residential-type steam, hot water, or warm air heating appliances; domestic-type range burners; space heaters; and portable liquid fuel–burning equipment shall comply with Section 11.5 and NFPA 31, *Standard for the Installation of Oil-Burning Equipment*.

11.5.1.2 Section 11.5 shall also apply to all accessories and control systems, whether electric, thermostatic, or mechanical, and all electrical wiring connected to liquid fuel–burning appliances, and shall comply with Section 11.5 and NFPA 31, *Standard for the Installation of Oil-Burning Equipment*. [**31:**1.1.2]

11.5.1.3 Section 11.5 shall also apply to the installation of liquid fuel storage and supply systems connected to liquid fuel–burning appliances, and shall comply with Section 11.5 and NFPA 31, *Standard for the Installation of Oil-Burning Equipment*. [**31:**1.1.3]

11.5.1.4 Section 11.5 shall also apply to those multifueled appliances in which a liquid fuel is one of the standard or optional fuels. [**31:**1.1.4]

11.5.1.5* Section 11.5 shall not apply to internal combustion engines, oil lamps, or portable devices not specifically covered in NFPA 31. *(See Chapter 11 of NFPA 31 for portable devices that are covered in NFPA 31.)* [**31:**1.1.5]

11.5.1.6 The installation of gas-fired heating appliances shall comply with Section 11.5 and NFPA 54. *(See Chapter 69 for LP-Gas fuel supply and storage installations.)*

11.5.1.7 All heating appliances shall be approved or listed.

11.5.1.8 Permits. Permits, where required, shall comply with Section 1.12.

11.5.1.9 Electrical wiring and utilization equipment used in connection with oil-burning appliances or equipment shall be installed in accordance with Section 11.1. [**31:**4.4.1]

11.5.1.10 Acceptable Liquid Fuels.

11.5.1.10.1* The type and grade of liquid fuel used in a liquid fuel–burning appliance shall be that liquid fuel for which the appliance is listed and approved or is stipulated by the manufacturer. Liquid fuels shall meet one of the following specifications and shall not contain gasoline or any other flammable liquid:

(1) ASTM D 396, *Standard Specification for Fuel Oils*
(2) ASTM D 3699, *Standard Specification for Kerosene*
(3) ASTM D 6448, *Industrial Burner Fuels from Used Lube Oils*
(4) ASTM D 6751, *Standard Specification for Biodiesel Fuel Blend Stock (B100) for Middle Distillate Fuel*
(5) ASTM D 6823, *Commercial Burner Fuels from Used Lube Oils*
[**31:**4.5.1]

11.5.1.10.2 Crankcase oil or used oil shall not be used as fuel unless all of the following conditions are met:

(1) The installation is in a commercial or industrial occupancy.
(2) The oil-burning appliance is designed to burn crankcase oil or used oil and is listed for such use.
(3) The appliance is installed in accordance with the manufacturer's instructions and with the terms of its listing.
(4) The installation meets the applicable requirements of Section 4.6 and Chapter 12 of NFPA 31. [31:4.5.2]

11.5.1.10.3* Where heavy oils are used, the following shall be required:

(1) The oil-burning appliance shall be designed to burn such fuels.
(2) Means shall be provided to maintain the oil at its proper atomizing temperature.
(3) Automatically operated burners that require preheating of oil shall be arranged so that no oil can be delivered for combustion until the oil is at the proper atomizing temperature.
(4)*Use of an oil-fired appliance that is listed in accordance with ANSI/UL 296A, *Standard for Waste Oil-Burning Air-Heating Appliances*, shall be deemed as meeting the intent of 11.5.1.10.3(1) through 11.5.1.10.3(3). [31:4.5.3]

11.5.1.10.4 A properly sized and rated oil filter or strainer shall be installed in the oil supply line to an oil burner. [31:4.5.4]

11.5.1.11 Clothes Dryers.

11.5.1.11.1 Clothes dryers shall be cleaned to maintain the lint trap and keep the mechanical and heating components free from excessive accumulations of lint.

11.5.1.11.2 The requirements of 11.5.1.11.1 shall not apply to clothes dryers in individual dwelling units of residential occupancies.

11.5.2 Kerosene Burners and Oil Stoves.

11.5.2.1 Kerosene burners and oil stoves shall be equipped with a primary safety control furnished as an integral part of the appliance by the manufacturer to stop the flow of oil in the event of flame failure. Barometric oil feed shall not be considered a primary safety control.

11.5.2.2 A conversion range oil burner shall be equipped with a thermal (heat-actuated) valve in the oil supply line, located in the burner compartment of the stove.

11.5.2.3 Only listed kerosene heaters shall be used. The following safeguards shall apply:

(1) Provide adequate ventilation
(2) Do not place on carpeting
(3) Keep 3 ft (0.9 m) away from combustible furnishings or drapes
(4) Use only approved Type 1-K water clear kerosene
(5) Allow to cool before refueling

11.5.3 Portable Electric Heater.

11.5.3.1 The AHJ shall be permitted to prohibit use of portable electric heaters in occupancies or situations where such use or operation would present an undue danger to life or property.

11.5.3.2 Portable electric heaters shall be designed and located so that they cannot be easily overturned.

11.5.3.3 All portable electric heaters shall be listed.

11.5.4 Vents. All chimneys, smokestacks, or similar devices for conveying smoke or hot gases to the outer air and the stoves, furnaces, incinerators, boilers, or any other heat-producing devices or appliances shall be installed and maintained in accordance with NFPA 54 and NFPA 211.

11.6 Waste Chutes, Incinerators, and Laundry Chutes.

11.6.1 Enclosure.

11.6.1.1 Waste chutes and laundry chutes shall be separately enclosed by walls or partitions in accordance with the provisions of Section 12.7. [101:9.5.1.1]

11.6.1.2 Chute intake openings shall be protected in accordance with Section 12.7. [101:9.5.1.2]

11.6.1.3 The doors of chutes specified in 11.6.1.2 shall open only to a room that is designed and used exclusively for accessing the chute opening. [101:9.5.1.3]

11.6.1.4 Chute service opening rooms shall be separated from other spaces in accordance with Section 8.7 of NFPA *101*. [101:9.5.1.4]

11.6.1.5 The requirements of 11.6.1.1 through 11.6.1.4 shall not apply where otherwise permitted by the following:

(1) Existing installations having properly enclosed service chutes and properly installed and maintained chute intake doors shall be permitted to have chute intake doors open to a corridor or normally occupied space.
(2) Waste chutes and laundry chutes shall be permitted to open into rooms not exceeding 400 ft^2 (37 m^2) that are used for storage, provided that the room is protected by automatic sprinklers. [101:9.5.1.5]

11.6.2 Installation and Maintenance. Waste chutes, laundry chutes, and incinerators shall be installed and maintained in accordance with NFPA 82, *Standard on Incinerators and Waste and Linen Handling Systems and Equipment*, unless such installations are approved existing installations, which shall be permitted to be continued in service. [101:9.5.2]

11.7 Stationary Generators and Standby Power Systems.

11.7.1 Stationary Combustion Engines and Gas Turbines Installation. Stationary generator sets shall be installed in accordance with NFPA 37, *Standard for the Installation and Use of Stationary Combustion Engines and Gas Turbines*, and NFPA 70.

11.7.2 Portable Generators.

11.7.2.1* Portable generators shall not be operated or refueled within buildings, on balconies, or on roofs.

11.7.2.1.1 Portable generators shall be permitted to be operated or refueled in a building or room that has been constructed for such use in accordance with the building code.

11.7.2.1.2 Fueling from a container shall be permitted when the engine is shut down and engine surface temperature is below the autoignition temperature of the fuel.

11.7.2.2 Portable generators shall be positioned so that the exhaust is directed as follows:

(1) At least 5 ft (1.5 m) in any direction away from any openings or air intakes
(2) Away from the building

11.7.3 Emergency and Legally Required Standby Power Systems.

11.7.3.1 General. New stationary generators for emergency use or for legally required standby power required by this *Code*, the building code, or other codes and standards shall be installed in accordance with NFPA 110, *Standard for Emergency and Standby Power Systems*.

11.7.3.2 Acceptance. Newly installed stationary generators for emergency use or for legally required standby power for fire protection systems and features shall demonstrate the capacity of the energy converter, with its controls and accessories, to survive without damage from common and abnormal disturbances in actual load circuits by any of the following means:

(1) By tests on separate prototype models
(2) By acceptance tests on the system components as performed by the component suppliers
(3) By listing for emergency service as a completely factory-assembled and factory-tested apparatus

11.7.4 Stored Electrical Energy Emergency and Legally Required Standby Power System Installation. Stored electrical energy systems required by this *Code*, the building code, or other NFPA codes and standards shall be installed in accordance with NFPA 111, *Standard on Stored Electrical Energy Emergency and Standby Power Systems*, and NFPA 70.

11.7.5 Maintenance and Testing.

11.7.5.1 Stationary generators used for emergency or legally required standby power shall be tested and maintained in accordance with NFPA 110 and NFPA 37.

11.7.5.2 Stationary generators required by this *Code*, the building code, or other NFPA codes and standards shall be maintained in accordance with NFPA 110.

11.7.5.3 Stored electrical energy systems required by this *Code*, the building code, or other NFPA codes and standards shall be maintained in accordance with NFPA 111.

11.8* Smoke Control.

11.8.1 Newly installed smoke-control systems shall be inspected by the AHJ and tested in accordance with the criteria established in the approved design documents, NFPA 204 and NFPA 92.

11.8.2 Smoke-control systems shall have an approved maintenance and testing program to ensure operational integrity in accordance with this section. Components of such systems shall be operated, maintained, and tested in accordance with their operation and maintenance manuals.

11.8.2.1 Testing. Operational testing of the smoke-control system shall be in accordance with NFPA 92, and shall include all equipment related to the system including, but not limited to, initiating devices, fans, dampers, controls, doors, and windows.

11.8.2.1.1 An approved written schedule for such operational tests shall be established.

11.8.2.2 Test records shall be maintained on the premises and must indicate the date of such testing, the qualified service personnel, and any corrective measures needed or taken.

11.8.3 All smoke-control systems and devices shall be maintained in a reliable operating condition and shall be replaced or repaired where defective.

11.8.4 The AHJ shall be notified when any smoke-control system is out of service for more than 4 hours in a 24-hour period and again upon restoration of service of such systems.

11.8.5 The AHJ shall be permitted to require the building to be evacuated or an approved fire watch to be provided for all portions left unprotected by the fire protection system shutdown until the fire protection system has been returned to service.

11.9 Emergency Command Center. Where required, emergency command centers shall comply with Section 11.9.

11.9.1 The location, design, content, and fire department access of the emergency command center shall be approved by the fire department.

11.9.2 The emergency command center shall be separated from the remainder of the building by a fire barrier having a fire resistance rating of not less than 1 hour.

11.9.3 The emergency command center room shall be a minimum of 96 ft^2 (8.9 m^2) with a minimum dimension of 8 ft (2.4 m).

11.9.4 The following shall be provided in the emergency command center:

(1) The fire department communication unit
(2) A telephone for fire department use with controlled access to the public telephone system
(3) Schematic building plans indicating the typical floor plan and detailing the building core means of egress, fire protection systems, fire-fighting equipment, and fire department access
(4) Work table
(5) If applicable, hazardous material management plans for the building

11.9.5 Where otherwise required, the following devices or functions shall be provided within the emergency command center:

(1) The emergency voice/alarm communication system unit
(2) Fire detection and alarm system annunciator unit
(3) Annunciator visually indicating the location of the elevators and whether they are operational
(4) Status indicators and controls for air-handling systems
(5) Controls for unlocking stairway doors simultaneously
(6) Sprinkler valve and waterflow detector display panels
(7) Emergency and standby power status indicators
(8) Fire pump status indicators
(9) Generator supervision devices and manual start and transfer features
(10) Public address system, where specifically required by other sections of this *Code*
(11) Controls required for smoke control

11.9.6 Emergency Command Center Acceptance Testing. Devices, equipment, components, and sequences shall be individually tested in accordance with appropriate standards and manufacturers' documented instructions.

11.10* Two-Way Radio Communication Enhancement Systems.

11.10.1 In all new and existing buildings, minimum radio signal strength for fire department communications shall be maintained at a level determined by the AHJ.

11.10.2 Where required by the AHJ, two-way radio communication enhancement systems shall comply with *NFPA 72*.

11.10.3 Where a two-way radio communication enhancement system is required and such system, components, or equipment has a negative impact on the normal operations of the facility at which it is installed, the AHJ shall have the authority to accept an automatically activated responder system.

11.11 Medical Gas and Vacuum Systems. Medical gas and vacuum systems shall comply with NFPA 99, *Health Care Facilities Code*.

11.12 Photovoltaic Systems.

11.12.1 Photovoltaic systems shall be in accordance with Section 11.12 and NFPA 70.

11.12.2 Building-Mounted Photovoltaic Installations.

11.12.2.1* Marking. Photovoltaic systems shall be permanently marked as specified in this subsection.

11.12.2.1.1 Main Service Disconnect Marking. A label shall be permanently affixed to the main service disconnect panel serving alternating current (ac) and direct current (dc) photovoltaic systems. The label shall be red with white capital letters at least ¾ in. (19 mm) in height and in a nonserif font, to read: "WARNING: PHOTOVOLTAIC POWER SOURCE." The materials used for the label shall be reflective, weather resistant, and suitable for the environment.

11.12.2.1.2 Circuit Disconnecting Means Marking. A permanent label shall be affixed adjacent to the circuit breaker controlling the inverter or other photovoltaic system electrical controller serving ac and dc photovoltaic systems. The label shall have contrasting color with capital letters at least ⅜ in. (10 mm) in height and in a nonserif font, to read: "PHOTOVOLTAIC DISCONNECT." The label shall be constructed of durable adhesive material or other approved material.

11.12.2.1.3* Conduit, Raceway, Enclosure, Cable Assembly, and Junction Box Markings. Marking shall be required on all interior and exterior dc conduits, raceways, enclosures, cable assemblies, and junction boxes.

11.12.2.1.3.1 Marking Locations. Marking shall be placed on all dc conduits, raceways, enclosures, and cable assemblies every 10 ft (3048 mm), at turns, and above and below penetrations. Marking shall be placed on all dc combiner and junction boxes.

11.12.2.1.3.2* Marking Content and Format. Marking for dc conduits, raceways, enclosures, cable assemblies, and junction boxes shall be red with white lettering with minimum ⅜ in. (10 mm) capital letters in a nonserif font, to read: "WARNING: PHOTOVOLTAIC POWER SOURCE." Marking shall be reflective, weather resistant, and suitable for the environment.

11.12.2.1.4 Secondary Power Source Markings. Where photovoltaic systems are interconnected to battery systems, generator backup systems, or other secondary power systems, additional signage acceptable to the AHJ shall be required indicating the location of the secondary power source shutoff switch.

11.12.2.1.5 Installer Information. Signage, acceptable to the AHJ, shall be installed adjacent to the main disconnect indicating the name and emergency telephone number of the installing contractor.

11.12.2.1.6* Inverter Marking. Markings shall not be required for inverters.

11.12.2.2 Access, Pathways, and Smoke Ventilation.

11.12.2.2.1 General. Access and spacing requirements shall be required to provide emergency access to the roof, provide pathways to specific areas of the roof, provide for smoke ventilation opportunity areas, and to provide emergency egress from the roof.

11.12.2.2.1.1 Exceptions. The AHJ shall be permitted to grant exceptions where access, pathway, or ventilation requirements are reduced due to any of the following circumstances:

(1) Proximity and type of adjacent exposures
(2) Alternative access opportunities, as from adjoining roofs
(3) Ground level access to the roof
(4) Adequate ventilation opportunities beneath photovoltaic module arrays
(5) Adequate ventilation opportunities afforded by module set back from other rooftop equipment
(6) Automatic ventilation devices
(7) New technologies, methods, or other innovations that ensure adequate fire department access, pathways, and ventilation opportunities

11.12.2.2.1.2 Pitch. Designation of ridge, hip, and valley shall not apply to roofs with 2-in-12 or less pitch.

11.12.2.2.1.3 Roof Access Points. Roof access points shall be defined as areas where fire department ladders are not placed over openings (windows or doors), are located at strong points of building construction, and are in locations where they will not conflict with overhead obstructions (tree limbs, wires, or signs).

11.12.2.2.2 One- and Two-Family Dwellings and Townhouses. Photovoltaic systems installed in one- and two-family dwellings and townhouses shall be in accordance with this section.

11.12.2.2.2.1 Access and Pathways.

11.12.2.2.2.1.1 Hip Roof Layouts. Photovoltaic modules shall be located in a manner that provides a 3 ft (914 mm) wide clear access pathway from the eave to the ridge of each roof slope where the photovoltaic modules are located. The access pathway shall be located at a structurally strong location of the building, such as a bearing wall.

Exception: The requirement of 11.12.2.2.2.1.1 shall not apply where adjoining roof planes provide a 3 ft (914 mm) wide clear access pathway.

11.12.2.2.2.1.2 Single Ridge Layouts. Photovoltaic modules shall be located in a manner that provides two 3 ft (914 mm) wide access pathways from the eave to the ridge on each roof slope where the modules are located.

11.12.2.2.2.1.3 Hip and Valley Layouts. Photovoltaic modules shall be located no closer than 1½ ft (457 mm) to a hip or valley if modules are to be placed on both sides of the hip or valley. Where modules are located on only one side of a hip or valley of equal length, the photovoltaic modules shall be allowed to be placed directly adjacent to the hip or valley.

11.12.2.2.2.2 Ridge Setback. Photovoltaic modules shall be located not less than 3 ft (914 mm) below the ridge.

11.12.2.2.3 Buildings Other Than One- and Two-Family Dwellings and Townhouses. Photovoltaic energy systems installed in any building other than one- and two-family dwellings and townhouses shall be in accordance with this section. Where the AHJ determines that the roof configuration is similar to a one- and two-family dwelling or townhouse, the AHJ shall allow the requirements of 11.12.2.2.2.

11.12.2.2.3.1 Access. A minimum 4 ft (1219 mm) wide clear perimeter shall be provided around the edges of the roof for buildings with a length or width of 250 ft (76.2 m) or less along either axis. A minimum 6 ft (1829 mm) wide clear perimeter shall be provided around the edges of the roof for buildings having length or width greater than 250 ft (76.2 m) along either axis.

11.12.2.2.3.2 Pathways. Pathways shall be established as follows:

(1) Pathways shall be over areas capable of supporting the live load of fire fighters accessing the roof.
(2) Centerline axis pathways shall be provided in both axes of the roof.
(3) Centerline axis pathways shall run where the roof structure is capable of supporting the live load of fire fighters accessing the roof.
(4) Pathways shall be in a straight line not less than 4 ft (1219 mm) clear to skylights, ventilation hatches, and roof standpipes.
(5) Pathways shall provide not less than 4 ft (1219 mm) clear around roof access hatches with at least one not less than 4 ft (1219 mm) clear pathway to the parapet or roof edge.

11.12.2.2.3.3 Smoke Ventilation. Ability for fire department smoke ventilation shall be provided in accordance with this section.

11.12.2.2.3.3.1 Maximum Array. Arrays of photovoltaic modules shall be no greater than 150 ft (45.7 m) × 150 ft (45.7 m) in distance in either axis.

11.12.2.2.3.3.2 Ventilation Options. Ventilation options between array sections shall be one of the following:

(1) A pathway 8 ft (2438 mm) or greater in width
(2) A pathway 4 ft (1219 mm) or greater in width and bordering on existing roof skylights or ventilation hatches
(3) A pathway 4 ft (1219 mm) or greater in width and bordering 4 ft (1219 mm) × 8 ft (2438 mm) venting cutouts options every 20 ft (6096 mm) on alternating sides of the pathway

11.12.2.2.4 Location of Direct Current (DC) Conductors.

11.12.2.2.4.1 Exterior-mounted dc conduits, wiring systems, and raceways for photovoltaic circuits shall be located as close as possible to the ridge, hip, or valley and from the hip or valley as directly as possible to an outside wall to reduce trip hazards and maximize ventilation opportunities.

11.12.2.2.4.2 Conduit runs between subarrays and to dc combiner boxes shall be designed to take the shortest path from the array to the dc combiner box.

11.12.2.2.4.3 DC combiner boxes shall be located so that conduit runs are minimized in the pathways between arrays.

11.12.2.2.4.4 DC wiring shall be run in metallic conduit or raceways where located within enclosed spaces in a building.

11.12.2.2.4.4.1 Where dc wiring is run perpendicular or parallel to load-bearing members, a minimum 10 in. (254 mm) space below roof decking or sheathing shall be maintained.

11.12.3 Ground-Mounted Photovoltaic System Installations. Ground-mounted photovoltaic systems shall be installed in accordance with 11.12.3.1 through 11.12.3.3.

11.12.3.1* Clearances. A clear area of 10 ft (3048 mm) around ground-mounted photovoltaic installations shall be provided.

11.12.3.2* Noncombustible Base. A gravel base or other noncombustible base acceptable to the AHJ shall be installed and maintained under and around the installation.

11.12.3.3* Security Barriers. Fencing, skirting, or other suitable security barriers shall be installed when required by the AHJ.

Chapter 12 Features of Fire Protection

12.1 General. This chapter shall apply to new, existing, permanent, or temporary buildings.

12.2* Construction.

12.2.1* Where required by this *Code*, a type of building construction shall comply with NFPA 220, *Standard on Types of Building Construction*.

12.2.2 Fire safety construction features for new and existing occupancies shall comply with this *Code* and the referenced edition of NFPA *101*.

12.3 Fire-Resistive Materials and Construction.

12.3.1 The design and construction of fire walls and fire barrier walls that are required to separate buildings or subdivide a building to prevent the spread of fire shall comply with Section 12.3 and NFPA 221, *Standard for High Challenge Fire Walls, Fire Walls, and Fire Barrier Walls*.

12.3.2* Quality Assurance for Penetrations and Joints. In new buildings three stories or greater in height, a quality assurance program for the installation of devices and systems installed to protect penetration and joints shall be prepared and monitored by the RDP responsible for design. Inspections of firestop systems and fire-resistive joint systems shall be in accordance with 12.3.2.1 and 12.3.2.2.

12.3.2.1 Inspection of firestop systems of the types tested in accordance with ASTM E 814, *Standard Test Method for Fire Tests of Through-Penetration Fire Stops*, or /UL 1479, *Standard for Fire Tests of Through-Penetration Firestops*, shall be conducted in accordance with ASTM E 2174, *Standard Practice for On-Site Inspection of Installed Fire Stops*. [**5000:**40.9.1]

12.3.2.2 Inspection of fire-resistive joint systems of the types tested in accordance with ASTM E 1966, *Standard Test Method for Fire-Resistive Joint Systems*, or UL 2079, *Standard for Tests for Fire Resistance of Buildings Joint Systems*, shall be conducted in accordance with ASTM E 2393, *Standard Practice for On-Site Inspection of Installed Fire Resistive Joint Systems and Perimeter Fire Barriers*. [**5000:**40.9.2]

12.3.3* Maintenance of Fire-Resistive Construction.

12.3.3.1 Required fire-resistive construction, including fire barriers, fire walls, exterior walls due to location on property, fire-resistive requirements based on type of construction, draft-stop partitions, and roof coverings, shall be maintained and shall be properly repaired, restored, or replaced where damaged, altered, breached, penetrated, removed, or improperly installed.

12.3.3.2 Where required, fire-rated gypsum wallboard walls or ceilings that are damaged to the extent that through openings exist, the damaged gypsum wallboard shall be replaced or returned to the required level of fire resistance using a listed repair system or using materials and methods equivalent to the original construction.

12.3.3.3 Where readily accessible, required fire-resistance-rated assemblies in high-rise buildings shall be visually inspected for integrity at least once every 5 years.

12.3.3.3.1 The person responsible for conducting the visual inspection shall demonstrate appropriate technical knowledge and experience in fire-resistance-rated design and construction acceptable to the AHJ.

12.3.3.3.2 A written report prepared by the person responsible for conducting the visual inspection shall be submitted to the AHJ documenting the results of the visual inspection.

12.4 Fire Doors and Other Opening Protectives.

12.4.1* The installation and maintenance of assemblies and devices used to protect openings in walls, floors, and ceilings against the spread of fire and smoke within, into, or out of buildings shall comply with Section 12.4 and NFPA 80, *Standard for Fire Doors and Other Opening Protectives.* [**80**:1.1]

12.4.2* With the exception of fabric fire safety curtain assemblies, Section 12.4 addresses assemblies that have been subjected to standardized fire tests. *(See Chapter 20 of* NFPA 80, *Standard for Fire Doors and Other Opening Protectives.)* [**80**:1.1.1]

12.4.3* Incinerator doors, record room doors, and vault doors are not covered in Section 12.4. [**80**:1.1.2]

12.4.4* Requirements for horizontally sliding, vertically sliding, and swinging doors as used in this *Code* do not apply to hoistway doors for elevators and dumbwaiters. [**80**:1.1.3]

12.4.5* Section 12.4 shall not cover fire resistance rated glazing materials and horizontally sliding accordion or folding assemblies fabricated for use as walls and tested as wall assemblies in accordance with ASTM E 119. [**80**:1.1.4]

12.4.6 Care and Maintenance of Fire Doors and Other Opening Protectives.

12.4.6.1 Subsection 12.4.6 shall cover the inspection, testing, and maintenance of fire doors, fire shutters, fire windows, and opening protectives other than fire dampers and fabric fire safety curtains. [**80**:5.1.1.1]

12.4.6.2 Operability.

12.4.6.2.1 Doors, shutters, and windows shall be operable at all times. [**80**:5.1.2.1]

12.4.6.2.2 Doors, shutters, and windows shall be kept closed and latched or arranged for automatic closing. [**80**:5.1.2.2]

12.4.6.3 Replacement. Where it is necessary to replace fire doors, shutters, windows or their frames, glazing materials, hardware, and closing mechanisms, replacements shall meet the requirements for fire protection and shall be installed and tested as required by this section for new installations. [**80**:5.1.3]

12.4.6.4 Field Modifications.

12.4.6.4.1* In cases where a field modification to a fire door or a fire door assembly is desired and is not permitted by 4.1.3.2 through 4.1.3.4 of NFPA 80, the laboratory with which the product or component being modified is listed shall be contacted through the manufacturer and a written or graphic description of the modifications shall be presented to that laboratory. [**80**:5.1.4.1]

12.4.6.4.2 Field modifications shall be permitted without a field visit from the laboratory upon written authorization from that laboratory. [**80**:5.1.4.2]

12.4.6.4.3 When the manufacturer is no longer available, the laboratory shall be permitted to provide an engineering evaluation supporting the field modification. [**80**:5.1.4.3]

12.4.6.5 Removal of Door or Window. Where a fire door or fire window opening no longer functions as an opening, or the door or window is removed and not replaced, the opening shall be filled to maintain the required rating of the wall assembly. [**80**:5.1.5]

12.4.6.6* Inspection and Testing.

12.4.6.6.1* Upon completion of the installation, door, shutters, and window assemblies shall be inspected and tested in accordance with 5.2.4 of NFPA 80. [**80**:5.2.1]

12.4.6.6.2* A record of all inspections and testing shall be signed by the inspector and kept for inspection by the AHJ. [**80**:5.2.2]

12.4.6.6.2.1 Records of acceptance tests shall be retained for the life of the assembly. [**80**:5.2.2.1]

12.4.6.6.2.2* Unless a longer period is required by Section 5.4 of NFPA 80, records shall be retained for a period of at least 3 years. [**80**:5.2.2.2]

12.4.6.6.2.3* The records shall be on a medium that will survive the retention period. Paper or electronic media shall be permitted. [**72**:14.6.2.3]

12.4.6.6.2.4 A record of all inspections and testing shall be provided that includes, but is not limited to, the following information:

(1) Date of inspection
(2) Name of facility
(3) Address of facility
(4) Name of person(s) performing inspections and testing
(5) Company name and address of inspecting company
(6) Signature of inspector of record
(7) Individual record of each inspected and tested fire door assembly
(8)*Opening identifier and location of each inspected and tested fire door assembly
(9)*Type and description of each inspected and tested fire door assembly
(10)*Verification of visual inspection and functional operation
(11) Listing of deficiencies in accordance with 12.4.6.6.3, 12.4.6.7, and 12.4.6.8 [**80**:5.2.2.4]

12.4.6.6.2.5* Upon completion of maintenance work, fire door assemblies shall be inspected and tested in accordance with 5.2.3 of NFPA 80. [**80**:5.2.2.5]

12.4.6.6.3 Acceptance Testing.

12.4.6.6.3.1* Acceptance testing of fire door and window assemblies shall be performed by a qualified person with knowledge and understanding of the operating components of the type of assembly being subject to testing. [**80**:5.2.3.1]

12.4.6.6.3.2* Before testing, a visual inspection shall be performed to identify any damaged or missing parts that can create a hazard during testing or affect operation or resetting. [**80**:5.2.3.2]

12.4.6.6.3.3 Acceptance testing shall include the closing of the door by all means of activation. [**80**:5.2.3.3]

12.4.6.6.3.4 A record of these inspections and testing shall be made in accordance with 5.2.2 of NFPA 80. [**80**:5.2.3.4]

12.4.6.6.3.5 Swinging Doors with Builders Hardware or Fire Door Hardware.

12.4.6.6.3.5.1 Fire door assemblies shall be visually inspected from both sides to assess the overall condition of door assembly. [**80**:5.2.3.5.1]

12.4.6.6.3.5.2 As a minimum, the following items shall be verified:

(1) Labels are clearly visible and legible.
(2) No open holes or breaks exist in surfaces of either the door or frame.
(3) Glazing, vision light frames, and glazing beads are intact and securely fastened in place, if so equipped.
(4) The door, frame, hinges, hardware, and noncombustible threshold are secured, aligned, and in working order with no visible signs of damage.
(5) No parts are missing or broken.
(6) Door clearances do not exceed clearances listed in 4.8.4 and 6.3.1.7 of NFPA 80.
(7) The self-closing device is operational; that is, the active door completely closes when operated from the full open position.
(8) If a coordinator is installed, the inactive leaf closes before the active leaf.
(9) Latching hardware operates and secures the door when it is in the closed position.
(10) Auxiliary hardware items that interfere or prohibit operation are not installed on the door or frame.
(11) No field modifications to the door assembly have been performed that void the label.
(12) Meeting edge protection, gasketing and edge seals, where required, are inspected to verify their presence and integrity.
(13) Signage affixed to a door meets the requirements listed in 4.1.4 of NFPA 80. [**80:**5.2.3.5.2]

12.4.6.6.3.6 Horizontally Sliding, Vertically Sliding, and Rolling Doors.

12.4.6.6.3.6.1 Fire door assemblies shall be visually inspected from both sides to assess the overall condition of door assembly. [**80:**5.2.3.6.1]

12.4.6.6.3.6.2 The following items shall be verified:

(1) Labels are clearly visible and legible.
(2) No open holes or breaks exist in surfaces of either the door or frame.
(3) Slats, endlocks, bottom bar, guide assembly, curtain entry hood, and flame baffle are correctly installed and intact for rolling steel fire doors.
(4) Glazing, vision light frames, and glazing beads are intact and securely fastened in place, if so equipped.
(5) Curtain, barrel, and guides are aligned, level, plumb, and true for rolling steel fire doors.
(6) Expansion clearance is maintained in accordance with manufacturer's listing.
(7) Drop release arms and weights are not blocked or wedged.
(8) Mounting and assembly bolts are intact and secured.
(9) Attachment to jambs are with bolts, expansion anchors, or as otherwise required by the listing.
(10) Smoke detectors, if equipped, are installed and operational.
(11) No parts are missing or broken.
(12)*Fusible links, if equipped, are in the location; chain/cable, s-hooks, eyes, and so forth, are in good condition; the cable or chain are not kinked, pinched, twisted, or inflexible; and links are not painted or coated with dust or grease.
(13) Auxiliary hardware items that interfere or prohibit operation are not installed on the door or frame.
(14) No field modifications to the door assembly have been performed that void the label.
(15) Doors have an average closing speed of not less than 6 in./sec (152 mm/sec) or more than 24 in./sec (610 mm/sec). [**80:**5.2.3.6.2]

12.4.6.6.3.7 Closing Devices.

12.4.6.6.3.7.1 All fire doors, fire shutters, and fire window assemblies shall be inspected and tested to check for proper operation and full closure. [**80:**5.2.3.7.1]

12.4.6.6.3.7.2 Resetting of the automatic-closing device shall be done in accordance with the manufacturer's instructions. [**80:**5.2.3.7.2]

12.4.6.6.3.7.3 Rolling Steel Fire Doors.

12.4.6.6.3.7.3.1 Rolling steel fire doors shall be drop-tested twice. [**80:**5.2.3.7.3.1]

12.4.6.6.3.7.3.2 The first test shall be to check for proper operation and full closure. [**80:**5.2.3.7.3.2]

12.4.6.6.3.7.3.3 A second test shall be done to verify that the automatic-closing device has been reset correctly. [**80:**5.2.3.7.3.3]

12.4.6.6.3.8* Fusible links, release devices, and any other movable parts shall not be painted or coated with other materials that could interfere with the operation of the assembly. [**80:**5.2.3.8]

12.4.6.6.4 Periodic Inspection and Testing.

12.4.6.6.4.1* Periodic inspections and testing shall be performed not less than annually. [**80:**5.2.4.1]

12.4.6.6.4.2 As a minimum, the provisions of 12.4.6.6.3 shall be included in the periodic inspection and testing procedure. [**80:**5.2.4.2]

12.4.6.6.4.3 Inspection shall include an operational test for automatic-closing doors and windows to verify that the assembly will close under fire conditions. [**80:**5.2.4.3]

12.4.6.6.4.4 The assembly shall be reset after a successful test. [**80:**5.2.4.4]

12.4.6.6.4.5 Resetting of the release mechanism shall be done in accordance with the manufacturer's instructions. [**80:**5.2.4.5]

12.4.6.6.4.6* Hardware shall be examined, and inoperative hardware, parts, or other defective items shall be replaced without delay. [**80:**5.2.4.6]

12.4.6.6.4.7 Tin-clad and kalamein doors shall be inspected for dry rot of the wood core. [**80:**5.2.4.7]

12.4.6.6.4.8 Chains or cables employed shall be inspected for excessive wear, stretching, and binding. [**80:**5.2.4.8]

12.4.6.7 Retrofit Operators.

12.4.6.7.1 The operator, governor, and automatic-closing device on rolling steel fire doors shall be permitted to be retrofitted with a labeled retrofit operator under the conditions specified in 12.4.6.7.2 through 12.4.6.7.5. [**80:**5.3.1]

12.4.6.7.2 The retrofit operator shall be labeled as such. [**80:**5.3.2]

12.4.6.7.3 The retrofit operator shall be installed in accordance with its installation instructions and listing. [**80:**5.3.3]

12.4.6.7.4 The installation shall be acceptable to the AHJ. [**80:**5.3.4]

12.4.6.7.5 The retrofit operator shall be permitted to be provided by a manufacturer other than the original manufacturer of the rolling steel fire door on which it is retrofitted, provided its listing allows it to be retrofitted on that manufacturer's doors. [80:5.3.5]

12.4.6.8* Performance-Based Option.

12.4.6.8.1 As an alternate means of compliance with 12.4.6.6.4, subject to the AHJ, fire door assemblies shall be permitted to be inspected, tested, and maintained under a written performance-based program. [80:5.4.1]

12.4.6.8.2 Goals established under a performance-based program shall provide assurance that the fire door assembly will perform its intended function when exposed to fire conditions. [80:5.4.2]

12.4.6.8.3 Technical justification for inspection, testing, and maintenance intervals shall be documented in writing. [80:5.4.3]

12.4.6.8.4 The performance-based option shall include historical data acceptable to the AHJ. [80:5.4.4]

12.4.6.9 Maintenance.

12.4.6.9.1* Repairs shall be made, and defects that could interfere with operation shall be corrected without delay. [80:5.5.1]

12.4.6.9.2 Damaged glazing material shall be replaced with labeled glazing. [80:5.5.2.]

12.4.6.9.3 Replacement glazing materials shall be installed in accordance with their individual listing. [80:5.5.3]

12.4.6.9.4 Any breaks in the face covering of doors shall be repaired without delay. [80:5.5.4]

12.4.6.9.5 Where a fire door, frame, or any part of its appurtenances is damaged to the extent that it could impair the door's proper emergency function, the following actions shall be performed:

(1) The fire door, frame, door assembly, or any part of its appurtenances shall be repaired with labeled parts or parts obtained from the original manufacturer.
(2) The door shall be tested to ensure emergency operation and closing upon completion of the repairs. [80:5.5.5]

12.4.6.9.6 If repairs cannot be made with labeled components or parts obtained from the original manufacturer or retrofitted in accordance with 12.4.6.7, the fire door frame, fire door assembly, or appurtenances shall be replaced. [80:5.5.6]

12.4.6.9.7 When holes are left in a door or frame due to changes or removal of hardware or plant-ons, the holes shall be repaired by the following methods:

(1) Install steel fasteners that completely fill the holes
(2) Fill the screw or bolt holes with the same material as the door or frame [80:5.5.7]

12.5* Interior Finish.

12.5.1 Interior finish in buildings and structures shall meet the requirements of NFPA *101* and this *Code*.

12.5.2* General.

12.5.2.1 Classification of interior finish materials shall be in accordance with tests made under conditions simulating actual installations, provided that the AHJ is permitted to establish the classification of any material on which classification by a standard test is not available, unless otherwise provided in 12.5.2.2 or 12.5.2.4. [*101*:10.2.1.1]

12.5.2.2 The provisions of 12.5.2.1 shall not apply to materials having a total thickness of less than $\frac{1}{28}$ in. (0.9 mm) that are applied directly to the surface of walls and ceilings where both of the following conditions are met:

(1) The wall or ceiling surface is a noncombustible or limited combustible material.
(2) The materials applied meet the requirements of Class A interior wall or ceiling finish when tested in accordance with 12.5.4 using fiber cement board as the substrate material. [*101*:10.2.1.2]

12.5.2.3 If a material having a total thickness of less than $\frac{1}{28}$ in. (0.9 mm) is applied to a surface that is not noncombustible or not limited-combustible, the provisions of 12.5.2.1 shall apply. [*101*:10.2.1.3]

12.5.2.4 Approved existing installations of materials applied directly to the surface of walls and ceilings in a total thickness of less than $\frac{1}{28}$ in. (0.9 mm) shall be permitted to remain in use, and the provisions of 12.5.3 through 12.5.4.7.2 shall not apply. [*101*:10.2.1.4]

12.5.2.5* Fixed or movable walls and partitions, paneling, wall pads, and crash pads applied structurally or for decoration, acoustical correction, surface insulation, or other purposes shall be considered interior finish and shall not be considered decorations or furnishings. [*101*:10.2.1.5]

12.5.2.6 Lockers constructed of combustible materials shall be considered interior finish. [*101*:10.2.1.6]

12.5.3* Use of Interior Finishes.

12.5.3.1 Requirements for interior wall and ceiling finish shall apply as follows:

(1) Where specified elsewhere in this *Code* for specific occupancies in Chapter 20 and NFPA *101* (*see Chapter 7 and Chapter 11 through Chapter 43 of NFPA 101*)
(2) As specified in 12.5.4 through 12.5.7. [*101*:10.2.2.1]

12.5.3.2* Interior floor finish shall comply with 12.5.8 under any of the following conditions:

(1) Where floor finish requirements are specified elsewhere in the *Code*
(2) Where the fire performance of the floor finish cannot be demonstrated to be equivalent to floor finishes with a critical radiant flux of at least 0.1 W/cm^2 [*101*:10.2.2.2]

12.5.4* Interior Wall or Ceiling Finish Testing and Classification. Interior wall or ceiling finish that is required elsewhere in this *Code* to be Class A, Class B, or Class C shall be classified based on test results from ASTM E 84, *Standard Test Method for Surface Burning Characteristics of Building Materials*, or ANSI/UL 723, *Standard for Test of Surface Burning Characteristics of Building Materials*, except as indicated in 12.5.4.1 or 12.5.4.2. [*101*:10.2.3]

12.5.4.1 Exposed portions of structural members complying with the requirements for Type IV (2HH) construction in accordance with NFPA 220, *Standard on Types of Building Construction*, or with the building code shall be exempt from testing and classification in accordance with ASTM E 84, or ANSI/UL 723. [*101*:10.2.3.1]

12.5.4.2 Interior wall and ceiling finish tested in accordance with NFPA 286, *Standard Methods of Fire Tests for Evaluating Contribution of Wall and Ceiling Interior Finish to Room Fire Growth*, and meeting the conditions of 12.5.4.7.2 shall be permitted to be used where interior wall and ceiling finish is required to be Class A in accordance with ASTM E 84 or ANSI/UL 723. [*101:* 10.2.3.2]

12.5.4.3 For fire-retardant coatings, see 12.5.7. [*101:* 10.2.3.3]

12.5.4.4* Products required to be tested in accordance with ASTM E 84 or ANSI/UL 723 shall be grouped in the classes described in 12.5.4.4.1 through 12.5.4.4.3 accordance with their flame spread and smoke development, except as indicated in 12.5.4.4.4. [*101:* 10.2.3.4]

12.5.4.4.1 Class A Interior Wall and Ceiling Finish. Class A interior wall and ceiling finishes shall be those finishes with a flame spread index of 0–25 and a smoke developed index of 0–450 and shall include any material classified at 25 or less on the flame spread index test scale and 450 or less on the smoke developed index test scale. [*101:* 10.2.3.4.1]

12.5.4.4.2 Class B Interior Wall and Ceiling Finish. Class B interior wall and ceiling finishes shall be those finishes with a flame spread index of 26–75 and a smoke developed index of 0–450 and shall include any material classified at more than 25 but not more than 75 on the flame spread index test scale and 450 or less on the smoke developed index test scale. [*101:* 10.2.3.4.2]

12.5.4.4.3 Class C Interior Wall and Ceiling Finish. Class C interior wall and ceiling finishes shall be those finishes with a flame of 76–200 and a smoke developed index of 0–450 and shall include any material classified at more than 75 but not more than 200 on the flame spread index test scale and 450 or less on the smoke developed index test scale. [*101:* 10.2.3.4.3]

12.5.4.4.4 Existing interior finish shall be exempt from the smoke developed index criteria of 12.5.4.4.1 through 12.5.4.4.3. [*101:* 10.2.3.4.4]

12.5.4.5 The classification of interior finish specified in 12.5.4.4 shall be that of the basic material used by itself or in combination with other materials. [*101:* 10.2.3.5]

12.5.4.6 Wherever the use of Class C interior wall and ceiling finish is required, Class A or Class B shall be permitted. Where Class B interior wall and ceiling finish is required, Class A shall be permitted. [*101:* 10.2.3.6]

12.5.4.7* Products tested in accordance with NFPA 265, *Standard Methods of Fire Tests for Evaluating Room Fire Growth Contribution of Textile or Expanded Vinyl Wall Coverings on Full Height Panels and Walls*, shall comply with the criteria of 12.5.4.7.1. Products tested in accordance with NFPA 286, *Standard Methods of Fire Tests for Evaluating Contribution of Wall and Ceiling Interior Finish to Room Fire Growth*, shall comply with the criteria of 12.5.4.7.2. [*101:* 10.2.3.7]

12.5.4.7.1 The interior finish shall comply with all of the following when tested using method B of the test protocol of NFPA 265, *Standard Methods of Fire Tests for Evaluating Room Fire Growth Contribution of Textile or Expanded Vinyl Wall Coverings on Full Height Panels and Walls*:

(1) During the 40 kW exposure, flames shall not spread to the ceiling.
(2) The flame shall not spread to the outer extremities of the samples on the 8 ft × 12 ft (2440 mm × 3660 mm) walls.
(3) Flashover, as described in NFPA 265, shall not occur.
(4) For new installations, the total smoke released throughout the test shall not exceed 1000 m^2. [*101:* 10.2.3.7.1]

12.5.4.7.2 The interior finish shall comply with all of the following when tested using the test protocol of NFPA 286, *Standard Methods of Fire Tests for Evaluating Contribution of Wall and Ceiling Interior Finish to Room Fire Growth*:

(1) During the 40 kW exposure, flames shall not spread to the ceiling.
(2) The flame shall not spread to the outer extremity of the sample on any wall or ceiling.
(3) Flashover, as described in NFPA 286, shall not occur.
(4) The peak heat release rate throughout the test shall not exceed 800 kW.
(5) For new installations, the total smoke released throughout the test shall not exceed 1000 m^2. [*101:* 10.2.3.7.2]

12.5.5* Specific Materials.

12.5.5.1* Textile Wall and Textile Ceiling Materials. The use of textile materials on walls or ceilings shall comply with one of the following conditions:

(1) Textile materials meeting the requirements of Class A when tested in accordance with ASTM E 84, *Standard Test Method for Surface Burning Characteristics of Building Materials*, or ANSI/UL 723, *Standard for Test for Surface Burning Characteristics of Building Materials*, using the specimen preparation and mounting method of ASTM E 2404, *Standard Practice for Specimen Preparation and Mounting of Textile, Paper or Polymeric (Including Vinyl) Wall or Ceiling Coverings, and of Facings and Wood Veneers Intended to be Applied on Site Over a Wood Substrate, to Assess Surface Burning Characteristics (see 12.5.4.4)*, shall be permitted on the walls or ceilings of rooms or areas protected by an approved automatic sprinkler system.
(2) Textile materials meeting the requirements of Class A when tested in accordance with ASTM E 84 or ANSI/UL 723, using the specimen preparation and mounting method of ASTM E 2404 (*see 12.5.4.4*), shall be permitted on partitions that do not exceed three-quarters of the floor-to-ceiling height or do not exceed 8 ft (2440 mm) in height, whichever is less.
(3) Textile materials meeting the requirements of Class A when tested in accordance with ASTM E 84 or ANSI/UL 723, using the specimen preparation and mounting method of ASTM E 2404 (*see 12.5.4.4*), shall be permitted to extend not more than 48 in. (1220 mm) above the finished floor on ceiling-height walls and ceiling-height partitions.
(4) Previously approved existing installations of textile material meeting the requirements of Class A when tested in accordance with ASTM E 84 or ANSI/UL 723 (*see 12.5.4.4*) shall be permitted to be continued to be used.
(5) Textile materials shall be permitted on walls and partitions where tested in accordance with NFPA 265, *Standard Methods of Fire Tests for Evaluating Room Fire Growth Contribution of Textile or Expanded Vinyl Wall Coverings on Full Height Panels and Walls*. (See 12.5.4.7.)
(6) Textile materials shall be permitted on walls, partitions, and ceilings where tested in accordance with NFPA 286, *Standard Methods of Fire Tests for Evaluating Contribution of Wall and Ceiling Interior Finish to Room Fire Growth*. (See 12.5.4.7.) [*101:* 10.2.4.1]

12.5.5.2* Expanded Vinyl Wall and Expanded Vinyl Ceiling Materials. The use of expanded vinyl wall or expanded vinyl ceiling materials shall comply with one of the following conditions:

(1) Materials meeting the requirements of Class A when tested in accordance with ASTM E 84, *Standard Test Method for Surface Burning Characteristics of Building Materials*, or ANSI/UL 723, *Standard for Test for Surface Burning Characteristics of Building Materials*, using the specimen preparation and mounting method of ASTM E 2404, *Standard Practice for Specimen Preparation and Mounting of Textile, Paper, or Polymeric (Including Vinyl) Wall or Ceiling Coverings, and of Facings and Wood Veneers Intended to be Applied on Site Over a Wood Substrate, to Assess Surface Burning Characteristics (see 12.5.4.4)*, shall be permitted on the walls or ceilings of rooms or areas protected by an approved automatic sprinkler system.
(2) Materials meeting the requirements of Class A when tested in accordance with ASTM E 84 or ANSI/UL 723, using the specimen preparation and mounting method of ASTM E 2404 *(see 12.5.4.4)*, shall be permitted on partitions that do not exceed three-quarters of the floor-to-ceiling height or do not exceed 8 ft (2440 mm) in height, whichever is less.
(3) Materials meeting the requirements of Class A when tested in accordance with ASTM E 84 or ANSI/UL 723, using the specimen preparation and mounting method of ASTM E 2404 *(see 12.5.4.4)*, shall be permitted to extend not more than 48 in. (1220 mm) above the finished floor on ceiling-height walls and ceiling-height partitions.
(4) Previously approved existing installations of materials meeting the requirements for the occupancy involved, when tested in accordance with ASTM E 84 or ANSI/UL 723 *(see 12.5.4.4)*, shall be permitted to be continued to be used.
(5) Materials shall be permitted on walls and partitions where tested in accordance with NFPA 265, *Standard Methods of Fire Tests for Evaluating Room Fire Growth Contribution of Textile or Expanded Vinyl Wall Coverings on Full Height Panels and Walls. (See 12.5.4.7.)*
(6) Materials shall be permitted on walls, partitions, and ceilings where tested in accordance with NFPA 286, *Standard Methods of Fire Tests for Evaluating Contribution of Wall and Ceiling Interior Finish to Room Fire Growth. (See 12.5.4.7.)* [*101:* 10.2.4.2]

12.5.5.3 Cellular or Foamed Plastic. Cellular or foamed plastic materials shall not be used as interior wall and ceiling finish unless specifically permitted by 12.5.5.3.1 or 12.5.5.3.2. The requirements of 12.5.5.3 through 12.5.5.3.2 shall apply both to exposed foamed plastics and to foamed plastics used in conjunction with a textile or vinyl facing or cover. [*101:* 10.2.4.3]

12.5.5.3.1* Cellular or foamed plastic materials shall be permitted where subjected to large-scale fire tests that substantiate their combustibility and smoke release characteristics for the use intended under actual fire conditions. [*101:* 10.2.4.3.1]

12.5.5.3.1.1 One of the following fire tests shall be used for assessing the combustibility of cellular or foamed plastic materials as interior finish:

(1) NFPA 286, *Standard Methods of Fire Tests for Evaluating Contribution of Wall and Ceiling Interior Finish to Room Fire Growth*, with the acceptance criteria of 12.5.4.7.2.
(2) ANSI/UL 1715, *Standard for Fire Test of Interior Finish Material* (including smoke measurements, with total smoke release not to exceed 1000 m²)
(3) ANSI/UL 1040, *Standard for Fire Test of Insulated Wall Construction*
(4) ANSI/FM 4880, *American National Standard for Evaluating Insulated Wall or Wall and Roof/Ceiling Panels, Plastic Interior Finish Materials, Plastic Exterior Building Panels, Wall/Ceiling Coating Systems, Interior or Exterior Finish Systems* [*101:*10.2.4.3.1.1]

12.5.5.3.1.2* The tests shall be performed on a finished foamed plastic assembly related to the actual end-use configuration, including any cover or facing, and at the maximum thickness intended for use. [*101:* 10.2.4.3.1.2]

12.5.5.3.1.3 New installations of cellular or foamed plastic materials tested in accordance with ANSI/UL 1040, *Standard for Fire Test of Insulated Wall Construction*, or ANSI/FM 4880, *American National Standard for Evaluating Insulated Wall or Wall and Roof/Ceiling Panels, Plastic Interior Finish Materials, Plastic Exterior Building Panels, Wall/Ceiling Coating Systems, Interior or Exterior Finish Systems*, shall also be tested for smoke release using NFPA 286, *Standard Methods of Fire Tests for Evaluating Contribution of Wall and Ceiling Interior Finish to Room Fire Growth*, with the acceptance criterion of 12.5.4.7.2. [*101:* 10.2.4.3.1.3]

12.5.5.3.2 Cellular or foamed plastic shall be permitted for trim not in excess of 10 percent of the specific wall or ceiling area to which it is applied, provided that it is not less than 20 lb/ft³ (320 kg/m³) in density, is limited to ½ in. (13 mm) in thickness and 4 in. (100 mm) in width, and complies with the requirements for Class A or Class B interior wall and ceiling finish as described in 12.5.4.4; however, the smoke developed index shall not be limited. [*101:* 10.2.4.3.2]

12.5.5.4* Light-Transmitting Plastics. Light-transmitting plastics shall be permitted to be used as interior wall and ceiling finish if approved by the AHJ. [*101:* 10.2.4.4]

12.5.5.5 Decorations and Furnishings. Decorations and furnishings that do not meet the definition of interior finish, as defined in 3.3.112.2, shall be regulated by the provisions of Section 12.6. [*101:* 10.2.4.5]

12.5.5.6 Metal Ceiling and Wall Panels. Listed factory finished metal ceiling and wall panels meeting the requirements of Class A when tested in accordance with ASTM E 84, *Standard Test Method for Surface Burning Characteristics of Building Materials*, or ANSI/UL 723, *Standard for Test for Surface Burning Characteristics of Building Materials (see 12.5.4.4)*, shall be permitted to be finished with one additional application of paint. Such painted panels shall be permitted for use in areas where Class A interior finishes are required. The total paint thickness shall not exceed ¹⁄₂₈ in. (0.9 mm). [*101:* 10.2.4.6]

12.5.5.7 Polypropylene (PP) and High-Density Polyethylene (HDPE). Polypropylene and high-density polyethylene materials shall not be permitted as interior wall or ceiling finish unless the material complies with the requirements of 12.5.4.7.2. The tests shall be performed on a finished assembly and on the maximum thickness intended for use. [*101:* 10.2.4.7]

12.5.5.8 Site-Fabricated Stretch Systems. For new installations, site-fabricated stretch systems containing all three components described in the definition in Chapter 3 of NFPA *101* shall be tested in the manner intended for use and shall comply with the requirements of 12.5.4 or 12.5.4.2. If the materials are tested in accordance with ASTM E 84, *Standard Test Method for Surface Burning Characteristics of Building Materials*, or ANSI/UL 723, *Standard for Test for Surface Burning Characteristics of Building Materials*, specimen preparation and mounting shall be in accordance with ASTM E 2573, *Standard Practice for*

Specimen Preparation and Mounting of Site-Fabricated Stretch Systems to Assess Surface Burning Characteristics. [*101:* 10.2.4.8]

12.5.5.9 Reflective Insulation Materials. Reflective insulation materials shall be tested in the manner intended for use and shall comply with the requirements of 10.2.3 of NFPA *101*. If the materials are tested in accordance with ASTM E 84, *Standard Test Method for Surface Burning Characteristics of Building Materials,* or ANSI/UL 723, *Standard for Test for Surface Burning Characteristics of Building Materials,* specimen preparation and mounting shall be in accordance with ASTM E 2599, *Standard Practice for Specimen Preparation and Mounting of Reflective Insulation, Radiant Barrier, and Vinyl Stretch Ceiling Materials for Building Applications to Assess Surface Burning Characteristics.* [*101:* 10.2.4.9]

12.5.6 Trim and Incidental Finish.

12.5.6.1 General. Interior wall and ceiling trim and incidental finish, other than wall base in accordance with 12.5.6.2 and bulletin boards, posters, and paper in accordance with 12.5.6.3, not in excess of 10 percent of the specific wall and ceiling areas of any room or space to which it is applied shall be permitted to be Class C materials in occupancies where interior wall and ceiling finish of Class A or Class B is required. [*101:* 10.2.5.1]

12.5.6.2 Wall Base. Interior floor trim material used at the junction of the wall and the floor to provide a functional or decorative border, and not exceeding 6 in. (150 mm) in height, shall meet the requirements for interior wall finish for its location or the requirements for Class II interior floor finish as described in 12.5.8.4 using the test described in 12.5.8.3. If a Class I floor finish is required, the interior floor trim shall be Class I. [*101:* 10.2.5.2]

12.5.6.3 Bulletin Boards, Posters, and Paper.

12.5.6.3.1 Bulletin boards, posters, and paper attached directly to the wall shall not exceed 20 percent of the aggregate wall area to which they are applied. [*101:* 10.2.5.3.1]

12.5.6.3.2 The provision of shall not apply to artwork and teaching materials in sprinklered educational or day-care occupancies in accordance with 20.2.4.4.3 and 20.3.4.2.3.5.3. [*101:* 10.2.5.3.2]

12.5.7* Fire-Retardant Coatings.

12.5.7.1* The required flame spread or smoke development classification of existing surfaces of walls, partitions, columns, and ceilings shall be permitted to be secured by applying approved fire-retardant coatings to surfaces having higher flame spread ratings than permitted. Such treatments shall be tested, or shall be listed and labeled for application to the material to which they are applied, and shall comply with the requirements of NFPA 703, *Standard for Fire Retardant–Treated Wood and Fire-Retardant Coatings for Building Materials.* [*101:* 10.2.6.1]

12.5.7.2 Surfaces of walls, partitions, columns, and ceilings shall be permitted to be finished with factory-applied fire-retardant coated products that have been listed and labeled to demonstrate compliance with the requirements of ASTM E 2768, *Standard Test Method for Extended Duration Surface Burning Characteristics of Building Materials,* on the coated surface. [*101:* 10.2.6.2]

12.5.7.3 Fire-retardant coatings or factory-applied fire-retardant coated assemblies shall possess the desired degree of permanency and shall be maintained so as to retain the effectiveness of the treatment under the service conditions encountered in actual use. [*101:* 10.2.6.3]

12.5.8* Interior Floor Finish Testing and Classification.

12.5.8.1* Carpet and carpet-like interior floor finishes shall comply with ASTM D 2859, *Standard Test Method for Ignition Characteristics of Finished Textile Floor Covering Materials.* [*101:* 10.2.7.1]

12.5.8.2* Floor coverings, other than carpet for which 12.5.3.2 establishes requirements for fire performance, shall have a minimum critical radiant flux of 0.1 W/cm^2. [*101:* 10.2.7.2]

12.5.8.3* Interior floor finishes shall be classified in accordance with 12.5.8.4, based on test results from NFPA 253, *Standard Method of Test for Critical Radiant Flux of Floor Covering Systems Using a Radiant Heat Energy Source,* or ASTM E 648, *Standard Test Method for Critical Radiant Flux of Floor Covering Systems Using a Radiant Heat Energy Source.* [*101:* 10.2.7.3]

12.5.8.4 Interior floor finishes shall be grouped in the classes specified in 12.5.8.4.1 and 12.5.8.4.2 in accordance with the critical radiant flux requirements. [*101:* 10.2.7.4]

12.5.8.4.1 Class I Interior Floor Finish. Class I interior floor finish shall have a critical radiant flux of not less than 0.45 W/cm^2, as determined by the test described in 12.5.8.3. [*101:* 10.2.7.4.1]

12.5.8.4.2 Class II Interior Floor Finish. Class II interior floor finish shall have a critical radiant flux of not less than 0.22 W/cm^2, but less than 0.45 W/cm^2, as determined by the test described in 12.5.8.3. [*101:* 10.2.7.4.2]

12.5.8.5 Wherever the use of Class II interior floor finish is required, Class I interior floor finish shall be permitted. [*101:* 10.2.7.5]

12.5.9 Automatic Sprinklers.

12.5.9.1 Other than as required in 12.5.5, where an approved automatic sprinkler system is installed in accordance with Section 13.3, Class C interior wall and ceiling finish materials shall be permitted in any location where Class B is required, and Class B interior wall and ceiling finish materials shall be permitted in any location where Class A is required. [*101:* 10.2.8.1]

12.5.9.2 Where an approved automatic sprinkler system is installed in accordance with Section 13.3, throughout the fire compartment or smoke compartment containing the interior floor finish, Class II interior floor finish shall be permitted in any location where Class I interior floor finish is required, and where Class II is required, the provisions of 12.5.8.2 shall apply. [*101:* 10.2.8.2]

12.6 Contents and Furnishings.

12.6.1 Furnishings, contents, decorations, and treated finishes in buildings and structures shall meet the requirements of NFPA *101* and this *Code*.

12.6.2* Where required by the applicable provisions of this *Code*, draperies, curtains, and other similar loosely hanging furnishings and decorations shall meet the flame propagation performance criteria contained in Test Method 1 or Test Method 2, as appropriate, of NFPA 701, *Standard Methods of Fire Tests for Flame Propagation of Textiles and Films.* [*101:* 10.3.1]

12.6.3 Smoldering Ignition of Upholstered Furniture and Mattresses.

12.6.3.1* Upholstered Furniture. Newly introduced upholstered furniture, except as otherwise permitted by Chapter 20, shall be resistant to a cigarette ignition (i.e., smoldering) in accordance with one of the following:

(1) The components of the upholstered furniture shall meet the requirements for Class I when tested in accordance with NFPA 260, *Standard Methods of Tests and Classification System for Cigarette Ignition Resistance of Components of Upholstered Furniture.*
(2) Mocked-up composites of the upholstered furniture shall have a char length not exceeding 1½ in. (38 mm) when tested in accordance with NFPA 261, *Standard Method of Test for Determining Resistance of Mock-Up Upholstered Furniture Material Assemblies to Ignition by Smoldering Cigarettes.* [*101:* 10.3.2.1]

12.6.3.2* Mattresses. Newly introduced mattresses, except as otherwise permitted by Chapter 20, shall have a char length not exceeding 2 in. (51 mm) when tested in accordance with 16 CFR 1632, "Standard for the Flammability of Mattresses and Mattress Pads" (FF 4-72). [*101:* 10.3.2.2]

12.6.3.2.1* Where required by the applicable provisions of this *Code*, upholstered furniture, unless the furniture is located in a building protected throughout by an approved automatic sprinkler system, shall have limited rates of heat release when tested in accordance with ASTM E 1537, *Standard Test Method for Fire Testing of Upholstered Furniture*, as follows:

(1) The peak rate of heat release for the single upholstered furniture item shall not exceed 80 kW.
(2) The total heat released by the single upholstered furniture item during the first 10 minutes of the test shall not exceed 25 MJ. [*101:* 10.3.3]

12.6.3.2.2* Where required by the applicable provisions of this *Code*, mattresses, unless the mattress is located in a building protected throughout by an approved automatic sprinkler system, shall have limited rates of heat release when tested in accordance with ASTM E 1590, *Standard Test Method for Fire Testing of Mattresses*, as follows:

(1) The peak rate of heat release for the mattress shall not exceed 100 kW.
(2) The total heat released by the mattress during the first 10 minutes of the test shall not exceed 25 MJ. [*101:* 10.3.4]

12.6.4* Furnishings or decorations of an explosive or highly flammable character shall not be used. [*101:* 10.3.5]

12.6.5 Fire-retardant coatings shall be maintained to retain the effectiveness of the treatment under service conditions encountered in actual use. [*101:* 10.3.6]

12.6.6* Where required by the applicable provisions of this *Code*, furnishings and contents made with foamed plastic materials that are unprotected from ignition shall have a heat release rate not exceeding 100 kW when tested in accordance with UL 1975, *Standard for Fire Tests for Foamed Plastics Used for Decorative Purposes*, or when tested in accordance with NFPA 289, *Standard Method of Fire Test for Individual Fuel Packages*, using the 20 kW ignition source. [*101:* 10.3.7]

12.6.7 Lockers.

12.6.7.1 Combustible Lockers. Where lockers constructed of combustible materials other than wood are used, the lockers shall be considered interior finish and shall comply with Section 12.5, except as permitted by 12.6.7.2. [*101:* 10.3.8.1]

12.6.7.2 Wood Lockers. Lockers constructed entirely of wood and of noncombustible materials shall be permitted to be used in any location where interior finish materials are required to meet a Class C classification in accordance with 12.5.4. [*101:* 10.3.8.2]

12.7 Fire Barriers.

12.7.1 General. Fire barriers used to provide enclosure, subdivision, or protection under NFPA *101* and this *Code* shall be classified in accordance with one of the following fire resistance ratings:

(1) 3-hour fire resistance rating
(2) 2-hour fire resistance rating
(3) 1-hour fire resistance rating
(4)*½-hour fire resistance rating [*101:* 8.3.1.1]

12.7.2 Walls.

12.7.2.1 The fire-resistive materials, assemblies, and systems used shall be limited to those permitted in this *Code* and this subsection. [*101:* 8.3.2.1]

12.7.2.1.1* Fire resistance–rated glazing tested in accordance with ASTM E 119, *Standard Test Methods for Fire Tests of Building Construction and Materials*, or ANSI/UL 263, *Standard for Fire Tests of Building Construction and Materials*, shall be permitted. [*101:* 8.3.2.1.1]

12.7.2.1.2 New fire resistance–rated glazing shall bear the identifier "W-XXX" where "XXX" is the fire resistance rating in minutes. Such identification shall be permanently affixed. [*101:* 8.3.2.1.2]

12.7.2.2 The construction materials and details for fire-resistive assemblies and systems for walls described shall comply with all other provisions of this *Code*, except as modified herein. [*101:* 8.3.2.2]

12.7.2.3 Interior walls and partitions of nonsymmetrical construction shall be evaluated from both directions and assigned a fire resistance rating based on the shorter duration obtained in accordance with ASTM E 119, *Standard Test Methods for Fire Tests of Building Construction and Materials* or ANSI/UL 263, *Standard for Fire Tests of Building Construction and Materials*. When the wall is tested with the least fire-resistive side exposed to the furnace, the wall shall not be required to be subjected to tests from the opposite side. [*101:* 8.3.2.3]

12.7.3 Fire Doors and Windows.

12.7.3.1 Openings required to have a fire protection rating by Table 12.7.4.2 shall be protected by approved, listed, labeled fire door assemblies and fire window assemblies and their accompanying hardware, including all frames, closing devices, anchorage, and sills in accordance with the requirements of Section 12.4, except as otherwise specified in this *Code*. [*101:* 8.3.3.1]

12.7.3.1.1 Fire resistance–rated glazing tested in accordance with ASTM E 119, *Standard Test Methods for Fire Tests of Building Construction and Materials*, or ANSI/UL 263, *Standard for Fire Tests of Building Construction and Materials*, shall be permitted in fire door assemblies and fire window assemblies where tested and installed in accordance with their listings. [*101:* 8.3.3.1.1]

12.7.3.1.2 New fire resistance–rated glazing shall be marked in accordance with Table 12.7.3.12 and Table 12.7.4.2. Such marking shall be permanently affixed. [*101:* 8.3.3.1.2]

12.7.3.2 Fire protection ratings for products required to comply with 12.7.3 shall be as determined and reported by a nationally recognized testing agency in accordance with NFPA 252; ANSI/UL 10B, *Standard for Fire Tests of Door Assemblies*; or ANSI/UL 10C, *Standard for Positive Pressure Fire Tests of Door Assemblies*; NFPA 257; or ANSI/UL 9, *Standard for Fire Tests of Window Assemblies*. [*101:* 8.3.3.2]

12.7.3.2.1* Fire protection–rated glazing shall be evaluated under positive pressure in accordance with NFPA 257. [*101:* 8.3.3.2.1]

12.7.3.2.2 All products required to comply with 12.7.3.2 shall bear an approved label. [*101:* 8.3.3.2.2]

12.7.3.2.3 Labels.

12.7.3.2.3.1* Labels on fire door assemblies shall be maintained in a legible condition. [*101:* 8.3.3.2.3.1]

12.7.3.2.3.2 In existing installations, steel door frames without a label shall be permitted where approved by the AHJ. [*101:* 8.3.3.2.3.2]

12.7.3.3 Unless otherwise specified, fire doors shall be self-closing or automatic-closing in accordance with 14.5.4. [*101:* 8.3.3.3]

12.7.3.4 Floor fire door assemblies shall be tested in accordance with NFPA 288, *Standard Methods of Fire Tests of Horizontal Fire Door Assemblies Installed in Horizontal Fire Resistance–Rated Assemblies*, and shall achieve a fire resistance rating not less than the assembly being penetrated. Floor fire doors assemblies shall be listed and labeled. [*101:* 8.3.3.4]

12.7.3.5 Fire protection–rated glazing shall be permitted in fire barriers having a required fire resistance rating of 1 hour or less and shall be of an approved type with the appropriate fire protection rating for the location in which the barriers are installed. [*101:* 8.3.3.5]

12.7.3.6* Glazing in fire window assemblies, other than in existing fire window installations of wired glass and other fire-rated glazing material, shall be of a design that has been tested to meet the conditions of acceptance of NFPA 257; or ANSI/UL 9, *Standard for Fire Tests of Window Assemblies*. Fire protection–rated glazing in fire door assemblies, other than in existing fire-rated door assemblies, shall be of a design that has been tested to meet the conditions of acceptance of NFPA 252; ANSI/UL 10B, *Standard for Fire Tests of Door Assemblies*; or ANSI/UL 10C, *Standard for Positive Pressure Fire Tests of Door Assemblies*. [*101:* 8.3.3.6]

12.7.3.7 Fire resistance–rated glazing complying with 12.7.2.1.1 shall be permitted in fire doors and fire window assemblies in accordance with their listings. [*101:* 8.3.3.7]

12.7.3.8 Glazing materials that have been tested, listed, and labeled to indicate the type of opening to be protected for fire protection purposes shall be permitted to be used in approved opening protectives in accordance with Table 8.3.4.2 of NFPA 101 and in sizes in accordance with NFPA 80, *Standard for Fire Doors and Other Opening Protectives*. [*101:* 8.3.3.8]

12.7.3.9 Existing installations of wired glass of ¼ in. (6.3 mm) thickness and labeled for fire protection purposes shall be permitted to be used in approved opening protectives, provided that the maximum size specified by the listing is not exceeded. [*101:* 8.3.3.9]

12.7.3.10 Nonsymmetrical fire protection–rated glazing systems shall be tested with each face exposed to the furnace, and the assigned fire protection rating shall be that of the shortest duration obtained from the two tests conducted in compliance with NFPA 257; or ANSI/UL 9, *Standard for Fire Tests of Window Assemblies*. [*101:* 8.3.3.10]

12.7.3.11 The total combined area of glazing in fire-rated window assemblies and fire-rated door assemblies used in fire barriers shall not exceed 25 percent of the area of the fire barrier that is common with any room, unless the installation meets one of the following criteria:

(1) The installation is an existing fire window installation of wired glass and other fire-rated glazing materials in approved frames.
(2) The fire protection–rated glazing material is installed in approved existing frames. [*101:* 8.3.3.11]

12.7.3.12 New fire protection-rated glazing shall be marked in accordance with Table 12.7.3.12 and Table 12.7.4.2, and such marking shall be permanently affixed. [*101:* 8.3.3.12]

Table 12.7.3.12 Marking Fire-Rated Glazing Assemblies

Fire Test Standard	Marking	Definition of Marking
ASTM E119, or ANSI/UL 263[a]	W	Meets wall assembly criteria
NFPA 257	OH	Meets fire window assembly criteria, including the hose stream test
NFPA 252	D	Meets fire door assembly criteria
	H	Meets fire door assembly hose stream test
	T	Meets 450°F (232°C) temperature rise criteria for 30 minutes
	XXX	The time, in minutes, of fire resistance or fire protection rating of the glazing assembly

[a]ASTM E 119, *Standard Test Methods for Fire Tests of Building Construction and Materials*, and ANSI/UL 263, *Standard for Fire Tests of Building Construction and Materials*. [*101:* Table 8.3.3.12]

12.7.3.13 Fire-rated door assemblies shall be inspected and tested in accordance with NFPA 80, *Standard for Fire Doors and Other Opening Protectives*. [*101:* 8.3.3.13]

12.7.4 Opening Protectives.

12.7.4.1 Every opening in a fire barrier shall be protected to limit the spread of fire and restrict the movement of smoke from one side of the fire barrier to the other. [*101:* 8.3.4.1]

12.7.4.2* The fire protection rating for opening protectives in fire barriers, fire-rated smoke barriers, and fire-rated smoke partitions shall be in accordance with Table 12.7.4.2, except as otherwise permitted in 12.7.4.3 or 12.7.4.4. [*101:* 8.3.4.2].

Table 12.7.4.2 Minimum Fire Protection Ratings for Opening Protectives in Fire Resistance–Rated Assemblies and Fire-Rated Glazing Markings

Component	Walls and Partitions (hr)	Fire Door Assemblies (hr)	Door Vision Panel Maximum Size (in.²)	Fire-Rated Glazing Marking Door Vision Panel	Minimum Side Light/Transom Assembly Rating (hr) Fire Protection	Minimum Side Light/Transom Assembly Rating (hr) Fire Resistance	Fire-Rated Glazing Marking Side Light/Transom Panel Fire Protection	Fire-Rated Glazing Marking Side Light/Transom Panel Fire Resistance	Minimum Fire-Rated Windows Rating[a,b] (hr) Fire Protection	Minimum Fire-Rated Windows Rating[a,b] (hr) Fire Resistance	Fire Window Marking Fire Protection	Fire Window Marking Fire Resistance
Elevator hoistways	2	1½	155 in.² [cc]	D-H-90 or D-H-W-90	NP	2	NP	D-H-W-120	NP	2	NP	W-120
	1	1	155 in.² [cc]	D-H-60 or D-H-W-60	NP	1	NP	D-H-W-60	NP	1	NP	W-60
	½	⅓	85 in.² [d]	D-20 or D-W-20	⅓	⅓	D-H-20	D-W-20	⅓	⅓	OH-20	W-30
Elevator lobby (per 7.2.13.4 of NFPA *101*)	1	1	100 in.² [a]	≤100 in.², D-H-T-60 or D-H-W-60[a] >100 in.², D-H-W-60	NP	1	NP	D-H-W-60			NP	W-60
Vertical shafts, including stairways, exits, and refuse chutes	2	1½	Maximum size tested	D-H-90 or D-H-W-90	NP	2	NP	D-H-W-120	NP	2	NP	W-120
	1	1	Maximum size tested	D-H-60 or D-H-W-60	NP	1	NP	D-H-W-60	NP	1	NP	W-60
Replacement panels in existing vertical shafts	½	⅓	Maximum size tested	D-20 or D-W-20	⅓	⅓	D-H-20	D-W-20	⅓	⅓	OH-20	W-30
Fire barriers	3	3	100 in.² [a]	≤100 in.², D-H-180 or D-H-W-180 >100 in.², D-H-W-180	NP	3	NP	D-H-W-180	NP	3	NP	W-180
	2	1½	Maximum size tested	D-H-90 or D-H-W-90	NP	2	NP	D-H-W-120	NP	2	NP	W-120
	1	¾	Maximum size tested[e]	D-H-45 or D-H-W-45	¾[e]	¾[e]	D-H-45	D-H-W-45	¾	¾	OH-45	W-60
	½	⅓	Maximum size tested	D-20 or D-W-20	⅓	⅓	D-H-20	D-W-20	⅓	⅓	OH-20	W-30
Horizontal exits	2	1½	Maximum size tested	D-H-90 or D-H-W-90	NP	2	NP	D-H-W-120	NP	2	NP	W-120
Horizontal exits served by bridges between buildings	2	¾	Maximum size tested[e]	D-H-45 or D-H-W-45	¾[e]	¾[e]	D-H-45	D-H-W-45	¾	¾	OH-45	W-120
Exit access corridors[f]	1	⅓	Maximum size tested	D-20 or D-W-20	¾	¾	D-H-45	D-H-W-20	¾	¾	OH-45	W-60
	½	⅓	Maximum size tested	D-20 or D-W-20	⅓	⅓	D-H-20	D-H-W-20	⅓	⅓	OH-20	W-30

(continues)

Table 12.7.4.2 *Continued*

Component	Walls and Partitions (hr)	Fire Door Assemblies (hr)	Door Vision Panel Maximum Size (in.²)	Fire-Rated Glazing Marking Door Vision Panel	Minimum Side Light/Transom Assembly Rating (hr)		Fire-Rated Glazing Marking Side Light/Transom Panel		Minimum Fire-Rated Windows Rating[a,b] (hr)		Fire Window Marking	
					Fire Protection	Fire Resistance	Fire Protection	Fire Resistance	Fire Protection	Fire Resistance	Fire Protection	Fire Resistance
Smoke barriers[f]	1	⅓	Maximum size tested	D-20 or D-W-20	¾	¾	D-H-45	D-H-W-20	¾	¾	OH-45	W-60
Smoke partitions[f,g]	½	⅓	Maximum size tested	D-20 or D-W-20	⅓	⅓	D-H-20	D-H-W-20	⅓	⅓	OH-20	W-30

For SI units, 1 in.² = .00064516 m².
NP: Not permitted.
[a]Fire resistance–rated glazing tested to ASTM E 119, *Standard Test Methods for Fire Tests of Building Construction and Materials*, or ANSI/UL 263, *Standard for Fire Tests of Building Construction and Materials*, shall be permitted in the maximum size tested. *(See 12.7.3.7.)*
[b]Fire-rated glazing in exterior windows shall be marked in accordance with Table 12.7.3.11.
[c]See ASME A17.1, *Safety Code for Elevators and Escalators*, for additional information.
[d]See ASTM A17.3, *Safety Code for Existing Elevators and Escalators*, for additional information.
[e]Maximum area of individual exposed lights shall be 1296 in.² (0.84 m²) with no dimension exceeding 54 in. (1.37 m) unless otherwise tested. [80: Table 4.4.5, Note b, and 80:4.4.5.1]
[f]Fire doors are not required to have a hose stream test per ANSI/UL 10B, *Standard for Fire Tests of Door Assemblies*, or ANSI/UL 10C, *Standard for Positive Pressure Fire Tests of Door Assemblies*.
[h]For residential board and care, see 32.2.3.1 and 33.2.3.1 of NFPA *101*.
[*101:* Table 8.3.4.2]

12.7.4.2.1 Fire-rated glazing assemblies marked as complying with hose stream requirements (H) shall be permitted in applications that do not require compliance with hose stream requirements. Fire-rated glazing assemblies marked as complying with temperature rise requirements (T) shall be permitted in applications that do not require compliance with temperature rise requirements. Fire-rated glazing assemblies marked with ratings that exceed the ratings required by this *Code* (XXX) shall be permitted. [*101:* 8.3.4.2.1]

12.7.4.3 Existing fire door assemblies having a minimum ¾-hour fire protection rating shall be permitted to continue to be used in vertical openings and in exit enclosures in lieu of the minimum 1-hour fire protection rating required by Table 12.7.4.2. [*101:* 8.3.4.3]

12.7.4.4 Where a 20-minute fire protection–rated door is required in existing buildings, an existing 1¾ in. (44 mm) solid-bonded wood-core door, an existing steel-clad (tin-clad) wood door, or an existing solid-core steel door with positive latch and closer shall be permitted, unless otherwise specified by Chapters 11 through 43 of NFPA *101*. [*101:* 8.3.4.4]

12.7.5 Penetrations. The provisions of 12.7.5 shall govern the materials and methods of construction used to protect through-penetrations and membrane penetrations in fire walls, fire barrier walls, and fire resistance–rated horizontal assemblies. The provisions of 12.7.5 shall not apply to approved existing materials and methods of construction used to protect existing through-penetrations and existing membrane penetrations in fire walls, fire barrier walls, or fire resistance–rated horizontal assemblies, unless otherwise required by Chapter 11 through 43 of NFPA *101*. [*101:* 8.3.5]

12.7.5.1* Firestop Systems and Devices Required. Penetrations for cables, cable trays, conduits, pipes, tubes, combustion vents and exhaust vents, wires, and similar items to accommodate electrical, mechanical, plumbing, and communications systems that pass through a wall, floor, or floor/ceiling assembly constructed as a fire barrier shall be protected by a firestop system or device. The firestop system or device shall be tested in accordance with ASTM E 814, *Standard Test Method for Fire Tests of Through Penetration Fire Stops*, or ANSI/UL 1479, *Standard for Fire Tests of Through-Penetration Firestops*, at a minimum positive pressure differential of 0.01 in. water column (2.5 N/m²) between the exposed and the unexposed surface of the test assembly. [*101:*8.3.5.1]

12.7.5.1.1 The requirements of 12.7.5.1 shall not apply where otherwise permitted by any one of the following:

(1) Where penetrations are tested and installed as part of an assembly tested and rated in accordance with ASTM E 119, *Standard Test Methods for Fire Tests of Building Construction and Materials* or ANSI/UL 263, *Standard for Fire Tests of Building Construction and Materials*
(2) Where penetrations through floors are enclosed in a shaft enclosure designed as a fire barrier
(3) Where concrete, grout, or mortar has been used to fill the annular spaces around cast-iron, copper, or steel piping that penetrates one or more concrete or masonry fire resistance–rated assemblies and both of the following criteria are also met:
   (a) The nominal diameter of each penetrating item shall not exceed 6 in. (150 mm), and the opening size shall not exceed 1 ft² (0.09 m²).
   (b) The thickness of the concrete, grout, or mortar shall be the full thickness of the assembly.
(4) Where firestopping materials are used with the following penetrating items, the penetration is limited to one floor, and the firestopping material is capable of preventing the passage of flame and hot gases sufficient to ignite cotton waste when subjected to the time–temperature fire conditions of NFPA 251 under a minimum positive pressure differential of 0.01 in. water column (2.5 Pa) at the location of the penetration for the time period equivalent to the required fire resistance rating of the assembly penetrated:
   (a) Steel, ferrous, or copper cables
   (b) Cable or wire with steel jackets

(c) Cast-iron, steel, or copper pipes
(d) Steel conduit or tubing [*101:* 8.3.5.1.1]

12.7.5.1.2 The maximum nominal diameter of the penetrating item, as indicated in 12.7.5.1.1(4)(a) through (d), shall not be greater than 4 in. (100 mm) and shall not exceed an aggregate 100 in.^{2} (64,520 mm^2) opening in any 100 ft^2 (9.3 m^2) of floor or wall area. [*101:* 8.3.5.1.2]

12.7.5.1.3 Firestop systems and devices shall have a minimum 1-hour F rating, but not less than the required fire resistance rating of the fire barrier penetrated. [*101:* 8.3.5.1.3]

12.7.5.1.4 T Ratings. Penetrations in fire resistance–rated horizontal assemblies shall be required to have a T rating of at least 1 hour, but not less than the fire resistance rating of the horizontal assembly, and shall not be required for either of the following:

(1) Floor penetrations contained within the cavity of a wall assembly
(2) Penetrations through floors or floor assemblies where the penetration is not in direct contact with combustible material [*101:* 8.3.5.1.4]

12.7.5.2 Sleeves. Where the penetrating item uses a sleeve to penetrate the wall or floor, the sleeve shall be securely set in the wall or floor, and the space between the item and the sleeve shall be filled with a material that complies with 12.7.5.1. [*101:* 8.3.5.2]

12.7.5.3 Insulation and Coverings. Insulation and coverings for penetrating items shall not pass through the wall or floor unless the insulation or covering has been tested as part of the firestop system or device. [*101:* 8.3.5.3]

12.7.5.4 Transmission of Vibrations. Where designs take transmission of vibrations into consideration, any vibration isolation shall meet one of the following conditions:

(1) It shall be provided on either side of the wall or floor.
(2) It shall be designed for the specific purpose. [*101:* 8.3.5.4]

12.7.5.5 Transitions.

12.7.5.5.1 Where piping penetrates a fire resistance–rated wall or floor assembly, combustible piping shall not connect to noncombustible piping within 36 in. (915 mm) of the firestop system or device without demonstration that the transition will not reduce the fire resistance rating, except in the case of previously approved installations. [*101:* 8.3.5.5.1]

12.7.5.5.2 Unshielded couplings shall not be used to connect noncombustible piping to combustible piping unless it can be demonstrated that the transition complies with the fire-resistive requirements of 12.7.5.1. [*101:* 8.3.5.5.2]

12.7.5.6 Membrane Penetrations.

12.7.5.6.1 Membrane penetrations for cables, cable trays, conduits, pipes, tubes, combustion vents and exhaust vents, wires, and similar items to accommodate electrical, mechanical, plumbing, and communications systems that pass through a membrane of a wall, floor, or floor/ceiling assembly constructed as a fire barrier shall be protected by a firestop system or device and shall comply with 12.7.5.1 through 12.7.5.5.2. [*101:* 8.3.5.6.1]

12.7.5.6.2 The firestop system or device shall be tested in accordance with ASTM E 814, *Standard Test Method for Fire Tests of Through Penetration Fire Stops*, or ANSI/UL 1479, *Standard for Fire Tests of Through-Penetration Firestops*, at a minimum positive pressure differential of 0.01 in. water column (2.5 N/m^2) between the exposed and the unexposed surface of the test assembly, unless one of the following applies:

(1) Membrane penetrations of ceilings that are not an integral part of a fire resistance–rated floor/ceiling or roof/ceiling assembly shall be permitted.
(2) Membrane penetrations of steel, ferrous, or copper conduits, pipes, tubes, or combustion vents or exhaust vents shall be permitted where the annular space is protected with an approved material, and the aggregate area of the openings does not exceed 0.7 ft^2 (0.06 m^2) in any 100 ft^2 (9.3 m^2) of ceiling area.
(3) Electrical outlet boxes and fittings shall be permitted, provided that such devices are listed for use in fire resistance–rated assemblies and are installed in accordance with their listing.
(4) The annular space created by the membrane penetration of a fire sprinkler shall be permitted, provided that the space is covered by a metal escutcheon plate. [*101:*8.3.5.6.2]

12.7.5.6.3 Where walls or partitions are required to have a minimum 1-hour fire resistance rating, recessed fixtures shall be installed in the wall or partition in such a manner that the required fire resistance is not reduced, unless one of the following is met:

(1) Any steel electrical box not exceeding 0.1 ft^2 (0.01 m^2) shall be permitted where the aggregate area of the openings provided for the boxes does not exceed 0.7 ft^2 (0.06 m^2) in any 100 ft^2 (9.3 m^2) of wall area, and, where outlet boxes are installed on opposite sides of the wall, the boxes shall be separated by one of the following:
  (a) Horizontal distance of not less than 24 in. (610 mm)
  (b) Horizontal distance of not less than the depth of the wall cavity, where the wall cavity is filled with cellulose loose-fill, rock wool, or slag wool insulation
  (c)*Solid fireblocking
  (d) Other listed materials and methods
(2) Membrane penetrations for any listed electrical outlet box made of any material shall be permitted, provided that such boxes have been tested for use in fire resistance–rated assemblies and are installed in accordance with the instructions included in the listing.
(3) The annular space created by the membrane penetration of a fire sprinkler shall be permitted, provided that the space is covered by a metal escutcheon plate.
(4) Membrane penetrations by electrical boxes of any size or type, which have been listed as part of a wall opening protective material system for use in fire-resistance-rated assemblies and are installed in accordance with the instructions included in the listing shall be permitted. [*101:* 8.3.5.6.3]

12.7.5.7 Openings for Air-Handling Ductwork. Openings in fire barriers for air-handling ductwork or air movement shall be protected in accordance with 11.2.1. [*101:* 8.3.5.7]

12.7.5.8 Joints.

12.7.5.8.1 The provisions of 12.7.5.8 shall govern the materials and methods of construction used to protect joints in between and at the perimeter of fire barriers or, where fire barriers meet other fire barriers, the floor or roof deck above, or the outside walls. The provisions of 12.7.5.8 shall not apply to approved existing materials and methods of construction used to protect existing joints in fire barriers, unless otherwise required by Chapters 11 through 43 of NFPA *101*. [*101:* 8.3.6.1]

12.7.5.8.2 Joints made within or at the perimeter of fire barriers shall be protected with a joint system that is capable of limiting the transfer of smoke. [*101:* 8.3.6.2]

12.7.5.8.3 Joints made within or between fire barriers shall be protected with a smoke-tight joint system that is capable of limiting the transfer of smoke. [*101:* 8.3.6.3]

12.7.5.8.4 Testing of the joint system in a fire barrier shall be representative of the actual installation suitable for the required engineering demand without compromising the fire resistance rating of the assembly or the structural integrity of the assembly. [*101:* 8.3.6.4]

12.7.5.8.5 Joints made within or between fire resistance–rated assemblies shall be protected with a joint system that is designed and tested to prevent the spread of fire for a time period equal to that of the assembly in which the joint is located. Such materials, systems, or devices shall be tested as part of the assembly in accordance with the requirements of ASTM E 1966, *Standard Test Method for Fire-Resistive Joint Systems,* or ANSI/UL 2079, *Standard for Tests for Fire Resistance of Building Joint Systems.* [*101:* 8.3.6.5]

12.7.5.8.6 All joint systems shall be tested at their maximum joint width in accordance with the requirements of ASTM E 1966 or ANSI/UL 2079, under a minimum positive pressure differential of 0.01 in. water column (2.5 N/m^2) for a time period equal to that of the assembly. All test specimens shall comply with the minimum height or length required by the standard. Wall assemblies shall be subjected to a hose stream test in accordance with ASTM E 119 or ANSI/UL 263. [*101:* 8.3.6.6]

12.7.5.8.7 Exterior Curtain Walls and Perimeter Joints.

12.7.5.8.7.1 Voids created between the fire resistance–rated floor assembly and the exterior curtain wall shall be protected with a perimeter joint system that is designed and tested in accordance with ASTM E 2307, *Standard Test Method for Fire Resistance of Perimeter Fire Barriers Using Intermediate-Scale, Multistory Apparatus.* [*101:* 8.3.6.7.1]

12.7.5.8.7.2 The perimeter joint system shall have an F rating equal to the fire resistance rating of the floor assembly. [*101:*8.3.6.7.2]

12.8 Smoke Partitions.

12.8.1* General. Where required elsewhere in this *Code,* smoke partitions shall be provided to limit the transfer of smoke. [*101:* 8.4.1]

12.8.2 Continuity. The following shall apply to smoke partitions:

(1) They shall extend from the floor to the underside of the floor or roof deck above, through any concealed spaces, such as those above suspended ceilings, and through interstitial structural and mechanical spaces.
(2)*They shall be permitted to extend from the floor to the underside of a monolithic or suspended ceiling system where the following conditions are met:
   (a) The ceiling system forms a continuous membrane.
   (b) A smoke-tight joint is provided between the top of the smoke partition and the bottom of the suspended ceiling.
   (c) The space above the ceiling is not used as a plenum.
(3) Smoke partitions enclosing hazardous areas shall be permitted to terminate at the underside of a monolithic or suspended ceiling system where the following conditions are met:
   (a) The ceiling system forms a continuous membrane.
   (b) A smoke-tight joint is provided between the top of the smoke partition and the bottom of the suspended ceiling.
   (c) Where the space above the ceiling is used as a plenum, return grilles from the hazardous area into the plenums are not permitted. [*101:* 8.4.2]

12.8.3 Opening Protectives.

12.8.3.1 Doors in smoke partitions shall comply with 12.8.3.2 through 12.8.3.5. [*101:* 8.4.3.1]

12.8.3.2 Doors shall comply with the provisions of 7.2.1 of NFPA *101.* [*101:* 8.4.3.2]

12.8.3.3 Doors shall not include louvers. [*101:* 8.4.3.3]

12.8.3.4* Door clearances shall be in accordance with NFPA 80. [*101:* 8.4.3.4]

12.8.3.5 Doors shall be self-closing or automatic-closing in accordance with 14.5.4. [*101:* 8.4.3.5]

12.8.4 Penetrations. The provisions of 12.8.4 shall govern the materials and methods of construction used to protect through-penetrations and membrane penetrations of smoke partitions. [*101:* 8.4.4]

12.8.4.1 Penetrations for cables, cable trays, conduits, pipes, tubes, vents, wires, and similar items to accommodate electrical, mechanical, plumbing, and communications systems that pass through a smoke partition shall be protected by a system or material that is capable of limiting the transfer of smoke. [*101:* 8.4.4.1]

12.8.4.2 Where designs take transmission of vibrations into consideration, any vibration isolation shall meet one of the following conditions:

(1) It shall be provided on either side of the smoke partition.
(2) It shall be designed for the specific purpose. [*101:*8.4.4.2]

12.8.5 Joints.

12.8.5.1 The provisions of 12.8.5 shall govern the materials and methods of construction used to protect joints in between and at the perimeter of smoke partitions or, where smoke partitions meet other smoke partitions, the floor or roof deck above, or the outside walls. The provisions of 12.8.5 shall not apply to approved existing materials and methods of construction used to protect existing joints in smoke partitions, unless otherwise required by Chapters 11 through 43 of NFPA *101.* [*101:* 8.4.5.1]

12.8.5.2 Joints made within or at the perimeter of smoke partitions shall be protected with a joint system that is capable of limiting the transfer of smoke. [*101:* 8.4.5.2]

12.8.6 Air-Transfer Openings.

12.8.6.1 General. The provisions of 12.8.6 shall govern the materials and methods of construction used to protect air-transfer openings in smoke partitions. [*101:* 8.4.6.1]

12.8.6.2* Smoke Dampers. Air-transfer openings in smoke partitions shall be provided with approved smoke dampers designed and tested in accordance with the requirements of ANSI/UL 555S, *Standard for Smoke Dampers,* to limit the transfer of smoke. [*101:* 8.4.6.2]

12.8.6.3 Smoke Damper Ratings. Smoke damper leakage ratings shall be not less than Class II. Elevated temperature ratings shall be not less than 250°F (140°C). [*101:* 8.4.6.3]

12.8.6.4 Smoke Detectors. Dampers in air-transfer openings shall close upon detection of smoke by approved smoke detectors installed in accordance with *NFPA 72, National Fire Alarm and Signaling Code* and Section 13.7. [*101:* 8.4.6.4]

12.9 Smoke Barriers.

12.9.1* General. Where required by Chapters 11 through 43 of NFPA *101*, smoke barriers shall be provided to subdivide building spaces for the purpose of restricting the movement of smoke. [*101:* 8.5.1]

12.9.2* Continuity.

12.9.2.1 Smoke barriers required by NFPA *101* shall be continuous from an outside wall to an outside wall, from a floor to a floor, or from a smoke barrier to a smoke barrier, or by use of a combination thereof. [*101:* 8.5.2.1]

12.9.2.2 Smoke barriers required by NFPA *101* shall be continuous through all concealed spaces, such as those found above a ceiling, including interstitial spaces. [*101:* 8.5.2.2]

12.9.2.3 A smoke barrier required for an occupied space below an interstitial space shall not be required to extend through the interstitial space, provided that the construction assembly forming the bottom of the interstitial space provides resistance to the passage of smoke equal to that provided by the smoke barrier. [*101:* 8.5.2.3]

12.9.3 Fire Barrier Used as Smoke Barrier. A fire barrier shall be permitted to be used as a smoke barrier, provided that it meets the requirements of Section 12.9. [*101:* 8.5.3]

12.9.4 Opening Protectives.

12.9.4.1* Doors in smoke barriers shall close the opening, leaving only the minimum clearance necessary for proper operation, and shall be without louvers or grilles. For other than previously approved existing doors, the clearance under the bottom of the doors shall be a maximum of ¾ in. (19 mm). [*101:* 8.5.4.1]

12.9.4.2 Where required by Chapters 11 through 43 of NFPA *101*, doors in smoke barriers that are required to be smoke leakage–rated shall comply with the requirements of 8.2.2.5 of NFPA *101*. [*101:* 8.5.4.2]

12.9.4.3 Latching hardware shall be required on doors in smoke barriers unless specifically exempted by Chapters 11 through 43 of NFPA *101*. [*101:* 8.5.4.3]

12.9.4.4* Doors in smoke barriers shall be self-closing or automatic-closing in accordance with 14.5.4 and shall comply with the provisions of 7.2.1 of NFPA *101*. [*101:* 8.5.4.4]

12.9.4.5 Fire window assemblies shall comply with 12.7.3. [*101:* 8.5.4.5]

12.9.5 Ducts and Air-Transfer Openings.

12.9.5.1 General. The provisions of 12.9.5 shall govern the materials and methods of construction used to protect ducts and air-transfer openings in smoke barriers. [*101:* 8.5.5.1]

12.9.5.2 Smoke Dampers.

12.9.5.2.1 Where a smoke barrier is penetrated by a duct or air-transfer opening, a smoke damper designed and tested in accordance with the requirements of ANSI/UL 555S shall be installed. [*101:* 8.5.5.2.1]

12.9.5.2.2 Where a smoke barrier is also constructed as a fire barrier, a combination fire/smoke damper designed and tested in accordance with the requirements of ANSI/UL 555 and ANSI/UL 555S shall be installed. [*101:* 8.5.5.2.2]

12.9.5.3 Smoke Damper Exemptions. Smoke dampers shall not be required under any of the following conditions:

(1) Where specifically exempted by provisions in Chapters 11 through 43 of NFPA *101*
(2) Where ducts or air-transfer openings are part of an engineered smoke control system and the smoke damper will interfere with the operation of a smoke control system
(3) Where the air in ducts continues to move and the air-handling system installed is arranged to prevent recirculation of exhaust or return air under fire emergency conditions
(4) Where the air inlet or outlet openings in ducts are limited to a single smoke compartment
(5) Where ducts penetrate floors that serve as smoke barriers
(6) Where ducts penetrate smoke barriers forming a communicating space separation in accordance with 8.6.6(4)(a) of NFPA *101* [*101:* 8.5.5.3]

12.9.5.4 Installation, Testing, and Maintenance.

12.9.5.4.1 Air-conditioning, heating, ventilating ductwork, and related equipment, including smoke dampers and combination fire and smoke dampers, shall be installed in accordance with NFPA 90A, *Standard for the Installation of Air-Conditioning and Ventilating Systems*; NFPA 90B, *Standard for the Installation of Warm Air Heating and Air-Conditioning Systems*; NFPA 105, *Standard for Smoke Door Assemblies and Other Opening Protectives*; or NFPA 80, *Standard for Fire Doors and Other Opening Protectives*, as applicable. [*101:* 8.5.5.4.1]

12.9.5.4.2 Smoke dampers and combination fire and smoke dampers required by this code shall be inspected, tested, and maintained in accordance with NFPA 105. [*101:* 8.5.5.4.2]

12.9.5.4.3 The equipment specified in 12.9.5.4.1 shall be installed in accordance with the requirements of 12.9.5, the manufacturer's installation instructions, and the equipment listing. [*101:* 8.5.5.4.3]

12.9.5.5 Access and Identification.

12.9.5.5.1 Access to the dampers shall be provided for inspection, testing, and maintenance. [*101:* 8.5.5.5.1]

12.9.5.5.2 Smoke and combination fire and smoke dampers in new construction shall be provided with an approved means of access, as follows:

(1) The means of access shall be large enough to allow inspection and maintenance of the damper and its operating parts.
(2) The access shall not affect the integrity of fire resistance–rated assemblies or smoke barrier continuity.
(3) The access openings shall not reduce the fire resistance rating of the assembly.
(4) Access doors in ducts shall be tight-fitting and suitable for the required duct construction.
(5) Access and maintenance shall comply with the requirements of the mechanical code. [*101:* 8.5.5.5.2]

12.9.5.5.3 Identification. Access points to fire and smoke dampers in new construction shall be permanently identified by one of the following:

(1) A label having letters not less than ½ in. (13 mm) in height and reading as one of the following:
 (a) FIRE/SMOKE DAMPER
 (b) SMOKE DAMPER
 (c) FIRE DAMPER
(2) Symbols as approved by the AHJ [*101:* 8.5.5.5.3]

12.9.5.6 Smoke Damper Ratings. Smoke damper leakage ratings shall be not less than Class II. Elevated temperature ratings shall be not less than 250°F (140°C). [*101:* 8.5.5.6]

12.9.5.7 Smoke Detectors.

12.9.5.7.1 Required smoke dampers in ducts penetrating smoke barriers shall close upon detection of smoke by approved smoke detectors in accordance with *NFPA 72*, unless one of the following conditions exists:

(1) The ducts penetrate smoke barriers above the smoke barrier doors, and the door release detector actuates the damper.
(2) Approved smoke detector installations are located within the ducts in existing installations. [*101:* 8.5.5.7.1]

12.9.5.7.2 Where a duct is provided on one side of the smoke barrier, the smoke detectors on the duct side shall be in accordance with 12.9.5.7.1. [*101:* 8.5.5.7.2]

12.9.5.7.3 Required smoke dampers in air-transfer openings shall close upon detection of smoke by approved smoke detectors in accordance with *NFPA 72*. [*101:* 8.5.5.7.3]

12.9.6 Penetrations.

12.9.6.1 The provisions of 12.9.6 shall govern the materials and methods of construction used to protect through-penetrations and membrane penetrations of smoke barriers. [*101:* 8.5.6.1]

12.9.6.2 Penetrations for cables, cable trays, conduits, pipes, tubes, vents, wires, and similar items to accommodate electrical, mechanical, plumbing, and communications systems that pass through a wall, floor, or floor/ceiling assembly constructed as a smoke barrier, or through the ceiling membrane of the roof/ceiling of a smoke barrier assembly, shall be protected by a system or material capable of restricting the transfer of smoke. [*101:* 8.5.6.2]

12.9.6.3 Where a smoke barrier is also constructed as a fire barrier, the penetrations shall be protected in accordance with the requirements of 12.7.5 to limit the spread of fire for a time period equal to the fire resistance rating of the assembly and 12.9.6 to restrict the transfer of smoke, unless the requirements of 12.9.6.4 are met. [*101:* 8.5.6.3]

12.9.6.4 Where sprinklers penetrate a single membrane of a fire resistance–rated assembly in buildings equipped throughout with an approved automatic fire sprinkler system, noncombustible escutcheon plates shall be permitted, provided that the space around each sprinkler penetration does not exceed ½ in. (13 mm), measured between the edge of the membrane and the sprinkler. [*101:* 8.5.6.4]

12.9.6.5 Where the penetrating item uses a sleeve to penetrate the smoke barrier, the sleeve shall be securely set in the smoke barrier, and the space between the item and the sleeve shall be filled with a listed system or with a material capable of restricting the transfer of smoke. [*101:* 8.5.6.5]

12.9.6.6 Where designs take transmission of vibrations into consideration, any vibration isolation shall meet one of the following conditions:

(1) It shall be provided on either side of the smoke barrier.
(2) It shall be designed for the specific purpose. [*101:* 8.5.6.6]

12.9.7 Joints.

12.9.7.1 The provisions of 12.9.7 shall govern the materials and methods of construction used to protect joints in between and at the perimeter of smoke barriers or, where smoke barriers meet other smoke barriers, the floor or roof deck above, or the outside walls. The provisions of 12.9.7 shall not apply to approved existing materials and methods of construction used to protect existing joints in smoke barriers, unless otherwise required by Chapters 11 through 43 of NFPA *101*. [*101:* 8.5.7.1]

12.9.7.2 Joints made within or at the perimeter of smoke barriers shall be protected with a joint system that is capable of limiting the transfer of smoke. [*101:* 8.5.7.2]

12.9.7.3 Joints made within or between smoke barriers shall be protected with a smoke-tight joint system that is capable of limiting the transfer of smoke. [*101:* 8.5.7.3]

12.9.7.4 Smoke barriers that are also constructed as fire barriers shall be protected with a joint system that is designed and tested to resist the spread of fire for a time period equal to the required fire resistance rating of the assembly and restrict the transfer of smoke. [*101:* 8.5.7.4]

12.9.7.5 Testing of the joint system in a smoke barrier that also serves as fire barrier shall be representative of the actual installation. [*101:* 8.5.7.5]

Chapter 13 Fire Protection Systems

13.1 General.

13.1.1 The AHJ shall have the authority to require that construction documents for all fire protection systems be submitted for review and approval and a permit be issued prior to the installation, rehabilitation, or modification. *(For additional information concerning construction documents, see Section 1.14.)* Further, the AHJ shall have the authority to require that full acceptance tests of the systems be performed in the AHJ's presence prior to final system certification.

13.1.1.1 Permits. Permits, where required, shall comply with Section 1.12.

13.1.2 The property owner shall be responsible for the proper testing and maintenance of the equipment and systems.

13.1.3 Obstructions shall not be placed or kept near fire hydrants, fire department inlet connections, or fire protection system control valves in a manner that would prevent such equipment or fire hydrants from being immediately visible and accessible.

13.1.4 A minimum 36 in. (91 mm) of clear space shall be maintained to permit access to and operation of fire protection equipment, fire department inlet connections, or fire protection system control valves. The fire department shall not be deterred or hindered from gaining immediate access to fire protection equipment.

13.1.4.1 An approved clear and unobstructed path shall be provided and maintained for access to the fire department inlet connections.

13.1.5 Detailed records documenting all systems and equipment testing and maintenance shall be kept by the property owner and shall be made available upon request for review by the AHJ.

13.1.6 Existing systems shall be in accordance with 1.3.6.2 and 10.3.2.

13.1.7 All fire protection systems and devices shall be maintained in a reliable operating condition and shall be replaced or repaired where defective or recalled.

13.1.8 The AHJ shall be notified when any fire protection system is out of service and on restoration of service.

13.1.9 When a fire protection system is out of service for more than 4 hours in a 24-hour period, the AHJ shall be permitted to require the building to be evacuated or an approved fire watch to be provided for all portions left unprotected by the fire protection system shutdown until the fire protection system has been returned to service.

13.1.10 In the event of a failure of a fire protection system or an excessive number of accidental activations, the AHJ shall be permitted to require an approved fire watch until the system is repaired.

13.1.11* For occupancies of an especially hazardous nature or where special hazards exist in addition to the normal hazard of the occupancy, or where access for fire apparatus is unduly difficult, or where the size or configuration of the building or contents limits normal fire suppression efforts, the AHJ shall have the authority to require additional safeguards consisting of additional fire safety equipment, more than one type of fire safety equipment, or special systems suitable for the protection of the hazard involved.

13.1.12 The AHJ shall have the authority to require locking fire department connection (FDC) plugs or caps on all water-based fire protection systems.

13.2 Standpipe Systems.

13.2.1 General. The design and installation of standpipe systems shall be in accordance with Section 13.2 and NFPA 14, *Standard for the Installation of Standpipe and Hose Systems*.

13.2.2 Where Required.

13.2.2.1 Where required by this *Code* or the referenced codes and standards listed in Chapter 2, standpipe systems shall be installed in accordance with 13.2.1.

13.2.2.2 New buildings shall be equipped with a Class I standpipe system installed in accordance with the provisions of Section 13.2 where any of the following conditions exist:

(1) More than three stories above grade where the building is protected by an approved automatic sprinkler system
(2) More than two stories above grade where the building is not protected by an approved automatic sprinkler system
(3) More than 50 ft (15 m) above grade and containing intermediate stories or balconies
(4) More than one story below grade
(5) More than 20 ft (6.1 m) below grade

13.2.2.3 High-rise buildings shall be protected throughout by a Class I standpipe system in accordance with 13.2.2. [*101:* 11.8.3.2]

13.2.2.4* In new assembly occupancies, regular stages over 1000 ft^2 (93 m^2) in area and all legitimate stages shall be equipped with 1½ in. (38 mm) hose lines for first aid fire fighting at each side of the stage. [*101:* 12.4.6.12.1]

13.2.2.4.1 In existing assembly occupancies, stages over 1000 ft^2 (93 m^2) in area shall be equipped with 1½ in. (38 mm) hose lines for first aid fire fighting at each side of the stage. [*101:* 13.4.6.12.1]

13.2.2.4.2 Hose connections shall be in accordance with NFPA 13, *Standard for the Installation of Sprinkler Systems*, unless Class II or Class III standpipes in accordance with NFPA 14 are used. [*101:* 12.4.6.12.2; *101:* 13.4.6.12.2]

13.2.2.5 New and Existing Detention and Correctional Facilities. Standpipe and hose systems shall be provided in accordance with 9.7.4.2 of NFPA *101* as follows, unless otherwise permitted by 13.2.2.5.1:

(1) Class I standpipe systems shall be provided for any building three or more stories in height.
(2) Class III standpipe and hose systems shall be provided for all nonsprinklered buildings three or more stories in height. [*101:* 22.3.5.5; *101:* 23.3.5.5]

13.2.2.5.1 The requirements of 13.2.2.5 shall not apply where otherwise permitted by the following:

(1) Formed hose, 1 in. (25 mm) in diameter, on hose reels shall be permitted to provide Class II service.
(2) Separate Class I and Class II systems shall be permitted in lieu of a Class III system. [*101:* 22.3.5.6; *101:* 23.3.5.6]

13.2.2.6* The AHJ shall be authorized to permit the removal of existing occupant-use hose lines where all of the following are met:

(1) This *Code* does not require their installation.
(2) The current building code does not require their installation.
(3) The AHJ determines that the occupant-use hose line will not be utilized by trained personnel or the fire department.

13.2.3 Inspection, Testing, and Maintenance.

13.2.3.1 A standpipe system installed in accordance with this *Code* shall be properly maintained to provide at least the same level of performance and protection as designed.

13.2.3.2 The owner shall be responsible for maintaining the standpipe system and keeping it in good working condition.

13.2.3.3 A standpipe system installed in accordance with this *Code* shall be inspected, tested, and maintained in accordance with NFPA 25, *Standard for the Inspection, Testing, and Maintenance of Water-Based Fire Protection Systems*.

13.2.3.4 Existing Systems.

13.2.3.4.1 Where an existing standpipe system, including yard piping and fire department connection, is modified, the new piping shall be independently tested in accordance with 11.4.1 of NFPA 14. [*14:*11.4.7.1]

13.2.3.4.2 Modifications that cannot be isolated, such as new valves or the point of connection for new piping, shall not require testing in excess of system static pressure. [*14:*11.4.7.2]

13.3 Automatic Sprinklers.

13.3.1 General.

13.3.1.1* Automatic sprinklers shall be installed and maintained in full operating condition in the occupancies specified in this *Code* or in the codes or standards referenced in Chapter 2.

13.3.1.2 Installations shall be in accordance with NFPA 13, *Standard for the Installation of Sprinkler Systems*; NFPA 13R, *Standard for the Installation of Sprinkler Systems in Low-Rise Residential Occupancies*; or NFPA 13D, *Standard for the Installation of Sprinkler Systems in One- and Two-Family Dwellings and Manufactured Homes*, as appropriate.

13.3.1.3 Existing systems shall be in accordance with 1.3.6.2 and 10.3.2.

13.3.1.4 Sprinkler piping serving not more than six sprinklers for any hazardous area shall be permitted to be connected directly to a domestic water supply system having a capacity sufficient to provide 0.15 gpm/ft^2 (6.1 mm/min) throughout the entire enclosed area. [*101:* 9.7.1.2]

13.3.1.5 Sprinkler piping serving hazardous areas as described in 13.3.1.4 shall be provided with an indicating shutoff valve, supervised in accordance with 13.3.1.8 or NFPA 13, *Standard for the Installation of Sprinkler Systems*, and installed in an accessible, visible location between the sprinklers and the connection to the domestic water supply. [*101:* 9.7.1.3]

13.3.1.6* In areas protected by automatic sprinklers, automatic water mist heat-detection devices required by other sections of this *Code* shall not be required. [*101:* 9.7.1.4]

13.3.1.7 Automatic sprinkler systems installed to make use of an alternative permitted by this *Code* shall be considered required systems and shall meet the provisions of this *Code* that apply to required systems. [*101:* 9.7.1.5]

13.3.1.8 Supervision.

13.3.1.8.1* Supervisory Signals.

13.3.1.8.1.1 Where supervised automatic sprinkler systems are required by another section of this *Code*, supervisory attachments shall be installed and monitored for integrity in accordance with *NFPA 72, National Fire Alarm and Signaling Code*, and a distinctive supervisory signal shall be provided to indicate a condition that would impair the satisfactory operation of the sprinkler system. [*101:* 9.7.2.1.1]

13.3.1.8.1.2 Supervisory signals shall sound and shall be displayed either at a location within the protected building that is constantly attended by qualified personnel or at an approved, remotely located receiving facility. [*101:* 9.7.2.1.2]

13.3.1.8.2 Alarm Signal Transmission.

13.3.1.8.2.1 Where supervision of automatic sprinkler systems is required by another section of this *Code*, waterflow alarms shall be transmitted to an approved, proprietary alarm-receiving facility, a remote station, a central station, or the fire department. [*101:* 9.7.2.2.1]

13.3.1.8.2.2 The connection described in 13.3.1.8.2.1 shall be in accordance with 13.7.1.1. [*101:* 9.7.2.2.2]

13.3.1.9* The following practices shall be observed to provide sprinklers of other than ordinary-temperature classification unless other temperatures are determined or unless high-temperature sprinklers are used throughout, and temperature selection shall be in accordance with Table 13.3.1.9(a), Table 13.3.1.9(b), and Figure 13.3.1.9:

(1) Sprinklers in the high-temperature zone shall be of the high-temperature classification, and sprinklers in the intermediate-temperature zone shall be of the intermediate-temperature classification.

(2) Sprinklers located within 12 in. (305 mm) to one side or 30 in. (762 mm) above an uncovered steam main, heating coil, or radiator shall be of the intermediate-temperature classification.

(3) Sprinklers within 7 ft (2.1 m) of a low-pressure blowoff valve that discharges free in a large room shall be of the high-temperature classification.

(4) Sprinklers under glass or plastic skylights exposed to the direct rays of the sun shall be of the intermediate-temperature classification.

(5) Sprinklers in an unventilated, concealed space, under an uninsulated roof, or in an unventilated attic shall be of the intermediate-temperature classification.

(6) Sprinklers in unventilated show windows having high-powered electric lights near the ceiling shall be of the intermediate-temperature classification.

(7) Sprinklers protecting commercial-type cooking equipment and ventilation systems shall be of the high- or extra high-temperature classification as determined by use of a temperature-measuring device. (See 7.10.6 of NFPA 13.)

(8) Sprinklers protecting residential areas installed near specific heat sources identified in Table 13.3.1.9(c) shall be installed in accordance with Table 13.3.1.9(c).

(9) Ordinary-temperature sprinklers located adjacent to a heating duct that discharges air that is less than 100°F (38°C) are not required to be separated in accordance with Table 13.3.1.9(a).

(10) Sprinklers in walk-in type coolers and freezers with automatic defrosting shall be of the intermediate-temperature classification or higher. [**13:**8.3.2.5]

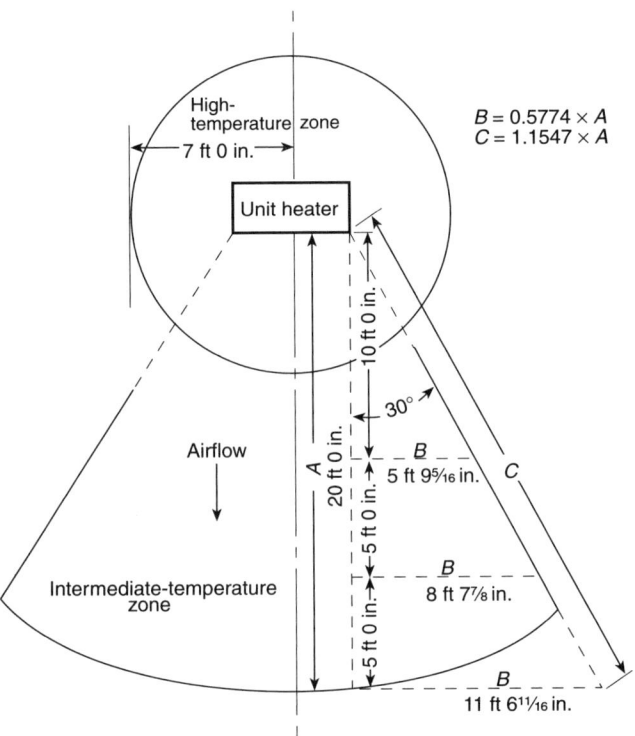

FIGURE 13.3.1.9 High-Temperature and Intermediate-Temperature Zones at Unit Heaters. [13:Figure 8.3.2.5]

Table 13.3.1.9(a) Temperature Ratings of Sprinklers Based on Distance from Heat Sources

Type of Heat Condition	Ordinary-Temperature Rating	Intermediate-Temperature Rating	High-Temperature Rating
(1) Heating ducts			
(a) Above	More than 2 ft 6 in.	2 ft 6 in. or less	
(b) Side and below	More than 1 ft 0 in.	1 ft 0 in. or less	
(c) Diffuser	Any distance except as shown under Intermediate-Temperature Rating column	*Downward discharge:* Cylinder with 1 ft 0 in. radius from edge extending 1 ft 0 in. below and 2 ft 6 in. above *Horizontal discharge:* Semicylinder or cylinder with 2 ft 6 in. radius in direction of flow extending 1 ft 0 in. below and 2 ft 6 in. above	
(2) Unit heater			
(a) Horizontal discharge		*Discharge side:* 7 ft 0 in. to 20 ft 0 in. radius pie-shaped cylinder *(see Figure 13.3.1.8)* extending 7 ft 0 in. above and 2 ft 0 in. below heater; also 7 ft 0 in. radius cylinder more than 7 ft 0 in. above unit heater	7 ft 0 in. radius cylinder extending 7 ft 0 in. above and 2 ft 0 in. below unit heater
(b) Vertical downward discharge *(for sprinklers below unit heater, see Figure 13.3.1.9)*		7 ft 0 in. radius cylinder extending upward from an elevation 7 ft 0 in. above unit heater	7 ft 0 in. radius cylinder extending from the top of the unit heater to an elevation 7 ft 0 in. above unit heater
(3) Steam mains (uncovered)			
(a) Above	More than 2 ft 6 in.	2 ft 6 in. or less	
(b) Side and below	More than 1 ft 0 in.	1 ft 0 in. or less	
(c) Blowoff valve	More than 7 ft 0 in.		7 ft 0 in. or less

For SI units, 1 in. = 25.4 mm; 1 ft = 0.3048 m.
[**13:** Table 8.3.2.5(a)]

Table 13.3.1.9(b) Temperature Ratings of Sprinklers in Specified Locations

Location	Ordinary-Temperature Rating	Intermediate-Temperature Rating	High-Temperature Rating
Skylights		Glass or plastic	
Attics	Do not use	Ventilated or unventilated	
Peaked roof: metal or thin boards, concealed or not concealed, insulated or uninsulated	Ventilated	Unventilated	
Flat roof: metal, not concealed	Ventilated or unventilated	Note: For uninsulated roof, climate and insulated or uninsulated occupancy can necessitate intermediate sprinklers. Check on job.	
Flat roof: metal, concealed, insulated, or uninsulated	Ventilated	Unventilated	
Show windows	Ventilated	Unventilated	

Note: A check of job condition by means of thermometers might be necessary.
[**13:** Table 8.3.2.5(b)]

Table 13.3.1.9(c) Ratings of Sprinklers in Specified Residential Areas

Heat Source	Minimum Distance from Edge of Source to Ordinary-Temperature Sprinkler		Minimum Distance from Edge of Source to Intermediate-Temperature Sprinkler	
	in.	mm	in.	mm
Side of open or recessed fireplace	36	914	12	305
Front of recessed fireplace	60	1524	36	914
Coal- or wood-burning stove	42	1067	12	305
Kitchen range	18	457	9	229
Wall oven	18	457	9	229
Hot air flues	18	457	9	229
Uninsulated heat ducts	18	457	9	229
Uninsulated hot water pipes	12	305	6	152
Side of ceiling- or wall-mounted hot air diffusers	24	607	12	305
Front of wall-mounted hot air diffusers	36	914	18	457
Hot water heater or furnace	6	152	3	76
Light fixture:				
0 W–250 W	6	152	3	76
250 W–499 W	12	305	6	152

[**13:** Table 8.3.2.5(c)]

13.3.2 Where Required.

13.3.2.1 Where required by this *Code* or the referenced codes and standards listed in Chapter 2, automatic sprinkler systems shall be installed in accordance with 13.3.1.

13.3.2.2 Basements exceeding 2500 ft² (232 m²) in new buildings shall be protected throughout by an approved automatic sprinkler system.

13.3.2.3 New buildings housing emergency fire, rescue, or ambulance services shall be protected throughout by approved supervised automatic sprinkler systems.

13.3.2.4 New buildings three or more stories in height above grade shall be protected throughout by an approved automatic sprinkler system in accordance with Section 13.3 unless otherwise permitted by 13.3.2.5.

13.3.2.5 Stand-alone open parking structures that are detached from other occupancies shall not be required to be protected by an automatic sprinkler system.

13.3.2.6* Exterior Roofs, Canopies, Porte-Cocheres, Balconies, Decks, or Similar Projections. In buildings protected throughout by automatic sprinklers in accordance with NFPA 13, automatic sprinkler protection shall be provided for the exterior spaces in accordance with 13.3.2.6.

13.3.2.6.1 Unless the requirements of 13.3.2.6.2, 13.3.2.6.3, or 13.3.2.6.4 are met, sprinklers shall be installed under exterior projections exceeding 4 ft (1.2 m) in width. [**13:**8.15.7.1]

13.3.2.6.2* Sprinklers shall be permitted to be omitted where the exterior projections are constructed with materials that are noncombustible, limited-combustible, or fire retardant–treated wood as defined in NFPA 703, *Standard for Fire Retardant–Treated Wood and Fire-Retardant Coatings for Building Materials*. [**13:**8.15.7.2]

13.3.2.6.3 Sprinklers shall be permitted to be omitted from below the exterior projections of combustible construction, provided the exposed finish material on the exterior projections are noncombustible, limited-combustible, or fire retardant–treated wood as defined in NFPA 703, *Standard for Fire Retardant–Treated Wood and Fire-Retardant Coatings for Building Materials*, and the exterior projections contain only sprinklered concealed spaces or any of the following unsprinklered combustible concealed spaces:

(1) Combustible concealed spaces filled entirely with noncombustible insulation
(2) Light or ordinary hazard occupancies where noncombustible or limited-combustible ceilings are directly attached to the bottom of solid wood joists so as to create enclosed joist spaces 160 ft³ (4.5 m³) or less in volume, including space below insulation that is laid directly on top or within the ceiling joists in an otherwise sprinklered attic *[see 11.2.3.1.4(4)(d) of NFPA 13]*
(3) Concealed spaces over isolated small exterior projections not exceeding 55 ft² (5.1 m²) in area [**13:**8.15.7.3]

13.3.2.6.4 Sprinklers shall be permitted to be omitted from exterior exit corridors when the exterior walls of the corridor are at least 50 percent open and when the corridor is entirely of noncombustible construction. [**13:**8.15.7.4]

13.3.2.6.5* Sprinklers shall be installed under exterior projections greater than 2 ft (0.6 m) wide over areas where combustibles are stored. [**13:**8.15.7.5]

13.3.2.7 New Assembly Occupancies.

13.3.2.7.1 The following assembly occupancies shall be protected throughout by an approved, supervised automatic sprinkler system in accordance with 13.3.1.2:

(1) Dance halls
(2) Discotheques
(3) Nightclubs
(4) Assembly occupancies with festival seating [*101:* 12.3.5.1]

13.3.2.7.2 Any building containing one or more assembly occupancies where the aggregate occupant load of the assembly occupancies exceeds 300 shall be protected by an approved, supervised automatic sprinkler system in accordance with NFPA 13 as follows *(see also 12.1.6, 12.2.6, 12.3.2, and 12.3.6 of NFPA 101)*:

(1) Throughout the story containing the assembly occupancy
(2) Throughout all stories below the story containing the assembly occupancy
(3) In the case of an assembly occupancy located below the level of exit discharge, throughout all stories intervening between that story and the level of exit discharge, including the level of exit discharge [*101:* 12.3.5.2]

13.3.2.7.3 The requirements of 13.3.2.7.2 shall not apply to the following:

(1)*Assembly occupancies consisting of a single multipurpose room of less than 12,000 ft^2 (1115 m^2) that are not used for exhibition or display and are not part of a mixed occupancy
(2) Gymnasiums, skating rinks, and swimming pools used exclusively for participant sports with no audience facilities for more than 300 persons
(3)*Locations in stadia and arenas as follows:
   (a) Over the floor area used for contest, performance, or entertainment, provided that the roof construction is more than 50 ft (15 m) above the floor level, and use is restricted to low fire hazard uses
   (b) Over the seating areas, provided that use is restricted to low fire hazard uses
   (c) Over open-air concourses where an approved engineering analysis substantiates the ineffectiveness of the sprinkler protection due to building height and combustible loading
(4) Locations in unenclosed stadia and arenas as follows:
   (a) Press boxes of less than 1000 ft^2 (93 m^2)
   (b) Storage facilities of less than 1000 ft^2 (93 m^2) if enclosed with not less than 1-hour fire resistance–rated construction
   (c) Enclosed areas underneath grandstands that comply with 25.3.4 [*101:*12.3.5.3]

13.3.2.7.4 Where another provision of Chapter 12 of NFPA *101* requires an automatic sprinkler system, the sprinkler system shall be installed in accordance with NFPA 13. [*101:* 12.3.5.4]

13.3.2.7.5 Stages. Every stage shall be protected by an approved, supervised automatic sprinkler system in compliance with Section 13.3. [*101:* 12.4.6.10]

13.3.2.7.5.1 Protection shall be provided throughout the stage and in storerooms, workshops, permanent dressing rooms, and other accessory spaces contiguous to stages. [*101:* 12.4.6.10.1]

13.3.2.7.5.2 Sprinklers shall not be required for stages 1000 ft^2 (93 m^2) or less in area and 50 ft (15 m) or less in height where the following criteria are met:

(1) Curtains, scenery, or other combustible hangings are not retractable vertically.
(2) Combustible hangings are limited to borders, legs, a single main curtain, and a single backdrop. [*101:* 12.4.6.10.2]

13.3.2.7.5.3 Sprinklers shall not be required under stage areas less than 48 in. (1220 mm) in clear height that are used exclusively for chair or table storage and lined on the inside with ⅝ in. (16 mm) Type X gypsum wallboard or the approved equivalent. [*101:* 12.4.6.10.3]

13.3.2.8 Existing Assembly Occupancies.

13.3.2.8.1 Where the occupant load exceeds 100, the following assembly occupancies shall be protected throughout by an approved, supervised automatic sprinkler system in accordance with NFPA 13:

(1) Dance halls
(2) Discotheques
(3) Nightclubs
(4) Assembly occupancies with festival seating [*101:* 13.3.5.1]

13.3.2.8.2 Any assembly occupancy used or capable of being used for exhibition or display purposes shall be protected throughout by an approved automatic sprinkler system in accordance with Section 13.3 where the exhibition or display area exceeds 15,000 ft^2 (1400 m^2). [*101:* 13.3.5.2]

13.3.2.8.3 The sprinklers specified by 13.3.2.8.2 shall not be required where otherwise permitted in the following locations:

(1) Locations in stadia and arenas as follows:
   (a) Over the floor area used for contest, performance, or entertainment
   (b) Over the seating areas
   (c) Over open-air concourses where an approved engineering analysis substantiates the ineffectiveness of the sprinkler protection due to building height and combustible loading
(2) Locations in unenclosed stadia and arenas as follows:
   (a) Press boxes of less than 1000 ft^2 (93 m^2)
   (b) Storage facilities of less than 1000 ft^2 (93 m^2) if enclosed with not less than 1-hour fire resistance–rated construction
   (c) Enclosed areas underneath grandstands that comply with 25.3.4 [*101:* 13.3.5.3]

13.3.2.8.4 Where another provision of this chapter and Chapter 13 of NFPA *101* requires an automatic sprinkler system, the sprinkler system shall be installed in accordance with NFPA 13. [*101:* 13.3.5.4]

13.3.2.8.5 Stages. Every stage shall be protected by an approved automatic sprinkler system in compliance with Section 13.3. [*101:* 13.4.6.10]

13.3.2.8.5.1 Protection shall be provided throughout the stage and in storerooms, workshops, permanent dressing rooms, and other accessory spaces contiguous to such stages. [*101:* 13.4.6.10.1]

13.3.2.8.5.2 Sprinklers shall not be required for stages 1000 ft^2 (93 m^2) or less in area where the following criteria are met:

(1) Curtains, scenery, or other combustible hangings are not retractable vertically.
(2) Combustible hangings are limited to borders, legs, a single main curtain, and a single backdrop. [*101:* 13.4.6.10.2]

13.3.2.8.5.3 Sprinklers shall not be required under stage areas less than 48 in. (1220 mm) in clear height that are used exclusively for chair or table storage and lined on the inside with ⅝ in. (16 mm) Type X gypsum wallboard or the approved equivalent. [*101:* 13.4.6.10.3]

13.3.2.9 New Educational Occupancies.

13.3.2.9.1* Educational occupancy buildings exceeding 12,000 ft^2 (1120 m^2) shall be protected throughout by an approved, supervised automatic sprinkler system in accordance with Section 13.3. [*101:* 14.3.5.1]

13.3.2.9.2 Educational occupancy buildings four or more stories in height shall be protected throughout by an approved, supervised automatic sprinkler system in accordance with Section 13.3. [*101:* 14.3.5.2]

13.3.2.9.3 Every portion of educational buildings below the level of exit discharge shall be protected throughout by an approved, supervised automatic sprinkler system in accordance with Section 13.3. [*101:* 14.3.5.3]

13.3.2.9.4 Buildings with unprotected openings in accordance with 8.6.6 of NFPA *101* shall be protected throughout by an approved, supervised automatic sprinkler system in accordance with Section 13.3. [*101:* 14.3.5.4]

13.3.2.9.5 Where another provision of Chapter 14 of NFPA *101* requires an automatic sprinkler system, the sprinkler system shall be installed in accordance with NFPA 13. [*101:* 14.3.5.5]

13.3.2.10 Existing Educational Occupancies.

13.3.2.10.1 Where student occupancy exists below the level of exit discharge, every portion of such floor shall be protected throughout by an approved automatic sprinkler system in accordance with Section 13.3. [*101:* 15.3.5.1]

13.3.2.10.2 Where student occupancy does not exist on floors below the level of exit discharge, such floors shall be separated from the rest of the building by 1-hour fire resistance–rated construction or shall be protected throughout by an approved automatic sprinkler system in accordance with Section 13.3. [*101:* 15.3.5.2]

13.3.2.10.3 Automatic sprinkler protection shall not be required where student occupancy exists below the level of exit discharge, provided that both of the following criteria are met:

(1) The approval of the AHJ shall be required.
(2) Windows for rescue and ventilation shall be provided in accordance with 15.2.11.1 of NFPA *101*. [*101:* 15.3.5.3]

13.3.2.10.4 Buildings with unprotected openings in accordance with 8.6.6 of NFPA *101* shall be protected throughout by an approved, supervised automatic sprinkler system in accordance with Section 13.3. [*101:* 15.3.5.4]

13.3.2.10.5 Where another provision of Chapter 15 of NFPA *101* requires an automatic sprinkler system, the sprinkler system shall be installed in accordance with NFPA 13. [*101:* 15.3.5.5]

13.3.2.11 New Health Care Occupancies.

13.3.2.11.1* Buildings containing health care occupancies shall be protected throughout by an approved, supervised automatic sprinkler system in accordance with Section 13.3, unless otherwise permitted by 13.3.2.11.3. [*101:* 18.3.5.1]

13.3.2.11.2 The sprinkler system required by 13.3.2.11.1 shall be installed in accordance with NFPA 13. [*101:* 18.3.5.4]

13.3.2.11.3 In Type I and Type II construction, alternative protection measures shall be permitted to be substituted for sprinkler protection, without causing a building to be classified as nonsprinklered, in specified areas where the AHJ has prohibited sprinklers. [*101:* 18.3.5.5]

13.3.2.11.4* Listed quick-response or listed residential sprinklers shall be used throughout smoke compartments containing patient sleeping rooms. [*101:* 18.3.5.6]

13.3.2.11.5* Sprinklers shall not be required in clothes closets of patient sleeping rooms in hospitals where the area of the closet does not exceed 6 ft^2 (0.55 m^2), provided that the distance from the sprinkler in the patient sleeping room to the back wall of the closet does not exceed the maximum distance permitted by NFPA 13. [*101:* 18.3.5.10]

13.3.2.11.6* Sprinklers in areas where cubicle curtains are installed shall be in accordance with NFPA 13. [*101:* 18.3.5.11]

13.3.2.12 Existing Health Care Occupancies.

13.3.2.12.1 Buildings containing nursing homes shall be protected throughout by an approved, supervised automatic sprinkler system in accordance with Section 13.3 and Section 9.7 of NFPA *101*, unless otherwise permitted by 13.3.2.12.7. [*101:* 19.3.5.1]

13.3.2.12.2 All high-rise buildings containing health care occupancies shall be protected throughout by an approved, supervised automatic sprinkler system installed in accordance with Section 13.3 within 12 years of the adoption of this *Code*, except as otherwise provided in 13.3.2.12.3 or 13.3.2.12.4. [*101:* 19.4.2.1]

13.3.2.12.3 Where a jurisdiction adopts this edition of the *Code* and previously adopted the 2012 edition, the sprinklering required by 13.3.2.12.2 shall be installed within 9 years of the adoption of this *Code*. [*101:* 19.4.2.2]

13.3.2.12.4 Where a jurisdiction adopts this edition of the *Code* and previously adopted the 2009 edition, the sprinklering required by 13.3.2.12.2 shall be installed within 6 years of the adoption of this *Code*. [*101:* 19.4.2.3]

13.3.2.12.5 Where required by 19.1.6 of NFPA *101*, buildings containing hospitals or limited care facilities shall be protected throughout by an approved, supervised automatic sprinkler system in accordance with Section 13.3 and Section 9.7 of NFPA *101*, unless otherwise permitted by 13.3.2.12.7. [*101:* 19.3.5.3]

13.3.2.12.6* The sprinkler system required by 13.3.2.12.1 or 13.3.2.12.5 shall be installed in accordance with NFPA 13. [*101:* 19.3.5.4]

13.3.2.12.7 In Type I and Type II construction, alternative protection measures shall be permitted to be substituted for sprinkler protection in specified areas where the AHJ has prohibited sprinklers, without causing a building to be classified as nonsprinklered. [*101:* 19.3.5.5]

13.3.2.12.8* Where this *Code* permits exceptions for fully sprinklered buildings or smoke compartments, the sprinkler system shall meet the following criteria:

(1) It shall be in accordance with Section 13.3.
(2) It shall be installed in accordance with NFPA 13, unless it is an approved existing system.
(3) It shall be electrically connected to the fire alarm system.
(4) It shall be fully supervised.
(5) In Type I and Type II construction, where the AHJ has prohibited sprinklers, approved alternative protection measures shall be permitted to be substituted for sprinkler protection in specified areas without causing a building to be classified as nonsprinklered. [*101:* 19.3.5.7]

13.3.2.12.9* Where this *Code* permits exceptions for fully sprinklered buildings or smoke compartments and specifically references this paragraph, the sprinkler system shall meet the following criteria:

(1) It shall be installed throughout the building or smoke compartment in accordance with Section 13.3.
(2) It shall be installed in accordance with NFPA 13, unless it is an approved existing system.
(3) It shall be electrically connected to the fire alarm system.
(4) It shall be fully supervised.
(5) It shall be equipped with listed quick-response or listed residential sprinklers throughout all smoke compartments containing patient sleeping rooms.
(6) Standard-response sprinklers shall be permitted to be continued to be used in approved existing sprinkler systems where quick-response and residential sprinklers were not listed for use in such locations at the time of installation.
(7) Standard-response sprinklers shall be permitted for use in hazardous areas protected in accordance with 19.3.2.1 of NFPA *101*. [*101:* 19.3.5.8]

13.3.2.12.10 Isolated hazardous areas shall be permitted to be protected in accordance with 13.3.1.4. For new installations in existing health care occupancies, where more than two sprinklers are installed in a single area, waterflow detection shall be provided to sound the building fire alarm or to notify, by a signal, any constantly attended location, such as PBX, security, or emergency room, at which the necessary corrective action shall be taken. [*101:* 19.3.5.9]

13.3.2.12.11* Sprinklers shall not be required in clothes closets of patient sleeping rooms in hospitals where the area of the closet does not exceed 6 ft^2 (0.55 m^2), provided that the distance from the sprinkler in the patient sleeping room to the back wall of the closet does not exceed the maximum distance permitted by NFPA 13, *Standard for the Installation of Sprinkler Systems*. [*101:* 19.3.5.10]

13.3.2.12.12* Newly introduced cubicle curtains in sprinklered areas shall be installed in accordance with NFPA 13. [*101:* 19.3.5.11]

13.3.2.13 New Detention and Correctional Facilities.

13.3.2.13.1 All buildings classified as Use Condition II, Use Condition III, Use Condition IV, or Use Condition V shall be protected throughout by an approved, supervised automatic sprinkler system in accordance with 13.3.2.13.2. [*101:* 22.3.5.2]

13.3.2.13.2 The automatic sprinkler system required by 13.3.2.13.1 shall meet all of the following criteria:

(1) It shall be in accordance with Section 13.3.
(2) It shall be installed in accordance with NFPA 13.
(3) It shall be electrically connected to the fire alarm system.
(4) It shall be fully supervised. [*101:* 22.3.5.3]

13.3.2.14 Existing Detention and Correctional Facilities.

13.3.2.14.1* Where required by Table 23.1.6.1 of NFPA *101*, facilities shall be protected throughout by an approved, supervised automatic sprinkler system in accordance with 13.3.2.14.2. [*101:* 23.3.5.2]

13.3.2.14.2 Where this *Code* permits exceptions for fully sprinklered detention and correctional occupancies or sprinklered smoke compartments, the sprinkler system shall meet all of the following criteria:

(1) It shall be in accordance with Section 13.3.
(2) It shall be installed in accordance with NFPA 13.
(3) It shall be electrically connected to the fire alarm system.
(4) It shall be fully supervised. [*101:* 23.3.5.3]

13.3.2.15 New Hotels and Dormitories.

13.3.2.15.1 All buildings shall be protected throughout by an approved, supervised automatic sprinkler system in accordance with 13.3.2.15.2. [*101:* 28.3.5.1]

13.3.2.15.2 Where an automatic sprinkler system is installed, either for total or partial building coverage, the system shall be in accordance with Section 13.3, as modified by 13.3.2.15.3. In buildings four or fewer stories above grade plane, systems in accordance with NFPA 13R shall be permitted. [*101:* 28.3.5.3]

13.3.2.15.3 The provisions for draft stops and closely spaced sprinklers in NFPA 13 shall not be required for openings complying with 8.6.9.1 of NFPA *101* where the opening is within the guest room or guest suite. [*101:* 28.3.5.4]

13.3.2.15.4 Listed quick-response or listed residential sprinklers shall be used throughout guest rooms and guest room suites. [*101:* 28.3.5.6]

13.3.2.15.5 Open parking structures that comply with NFPA 88A, *Standard for Parking Structures*, and are contiguous with hotels or dormitories shall be exempt from the sprinkler requirements of 13.3.2.15.1. [*101:* 28.3.5.7]

13.3.2.16 Existing Hotels and Dormitories.

13.3.2.16.1 All high-rise buildings, other than those where each guest room or guest suite has exterior exit access in accordance with 7.5.3 of NFPA *101*, shall be protected throughout by an approved, supervised automatic sprinkler system in accordance with 13.3.2.16.2. [*101:* 29.3.5.1]

13.3.2.16.2* Where an automatic sprinkler system is installed, either for total or partial building coverage, the system shall be in accordance with Section 13.3, as modified by 13.3.2.16.3 and 13.3.2.16.4; in buildings up to and including four stories in height above grade, systems in accordance with NFPA 13R shall be permitted. [*101:* 29.3.5.3]

13.3.2.16.3 The provisions for draft stops and closely spaced sprinklers in NFPA 13 shall not be required for openings complying with 8.6.9.1 of NFPA *101* where the opening is within the guest room or guest suite. [*101:* 29.3.5.4]

13.3.2.16.4 In guest rooms and in guest room suites, sprinkler installations shall not be required in closets not exceeding 24 ft^2 (2.2 m^2) and in bathrooms not exceeding 55 ft^2 (5.1 m^2). [*101:* 29.3.5.5]

13.3.2.17 New Apartment Buildings.

13.3.2.17.1 All buildings shall be protected throughout by an approved, supervised automatic sprinkler system installed in accordance with 13.3.2.17.2. [*101:* 30.3.5.1]

13.3.2.17.2 Where an automatic sprinkler system is installed, either for total or partial building coverage, the system shall be installed in accordance with Section 13.3, as modified by 13.3.2.17.3 and 13.3.2.17.5. In buildings four or fewer stories above grade plane, systems in accordance with NFPA 13R shall be permitted. [*101:* 30.3.5.2]

13.3.2.17.3 In buildings sprinklered in accordance with NFPA 13, closets less than 12 ft² (1.1 m²) in area in individual dwelling units shall not be required to be sprinklered. Closets that contain equipment such as washers, dryers, furnaces, or water heaters shall be sprinklered regardless of size. [*101:* 30.3.5.3]

13.3.2.17.4 In buildings sprinklered in accordance with NFPA 13, *Standard for the Installation of Sprinkler Systems*, bathrooms not greater than 55 ft² (5.1 m²) in individual dwelling units shall not be required to be sprinklered. [*101:* 30.3.5.4]

13.3.2.17.5 The draft stop and closely spaced sprinkler requirements of NFPA 13 shall not be required for convenience openings complying with 8.6.9.1 of NFPA *101* where the convenience opening is within the dwelling unit. [*101:* 30.3.5.5]

13.3.2.17.6 Listed quick-response or listed residential sprinklers shall be used throughout all dwelling units. [*101:* 30.3.5.6]

13.3.2.17.7 Open parking structures complying with NFPA 88A, *Standard for Parking Structures*, that are contiguous with apartment buildings shall be exempt from the sprinkler requirements of 13.3.2.17.1. [*101:* 30.3.5.7]

13.3.2.17.8 Buildings with unprotected openings in accordance with 8.6.6 of NFPA *101* shall be protected throughout by an approved, supervised automatic sprinkler system in accordance with 13.3.2.17.1. [*101:* 30.3.5.8]

13.3.2.18 Existing Apartment Buildings.

13.3.2.18.1* Where an automatic sprinkler system is installed, either for total or partial building coverage, the system shall be installed in accordance with Section 13.3, as modified by 13.3.2.18.2 and 13.3.2.18.4. In buildings four or fewer stories above grade plane, systems in accordance with NFPA 13R shall be permitted. [*101:* 31.3.5.2]

13.3.2.18.2 In individual dwelling units, sprinkler installation shall not be required in closets not exceeding 24 ft² (2.2 m²) and in bathrooms not exceeding 55 ft² (5.1 m²). Closets that contain equipment such as washers, dryers, furnaces, or water heaters shall be sprinklered regardless of size. [*101:* 31.3.5.3]

13.3.2.18.3* In buildings sprinklered in accordance with NFPA 13, *Standard for the Installation of Sprinkler Systems*, bathrooms not greater than 55 ft² (5.1 m²) in individual dwelling units shall not be required to be sprinklered. [*101:* 31.3.5.4]

13.3.2.18.4 The draft stop and closely spaced sprinkler requirements of NFPA 13 shall not be required for convenience openings complying with 8.6.9.1 of NFPA *101* where the convenience opening is within the dwelling unit. [*101:* 31.3.5.5]

13.3.2.18.5 Buildings using Option 3 in accordance with NFPA *101* shall be provided with automatic sprinkler protection installed in accordance with 13.3.2.18.5.1 through 13.3.2.18.5.4. [*101:* 31.3.5.9]

13.3.2.18.5.1 Automatic sprinklers shall be installed in the corridor, along the corridor ceiling, utilizing the maximum spacing requirements of the standards referenced in 13.3.1.2. [*101:* 31.3.5.9.1]

13.3.2.18.5.2 An automatic sprinkler shall be installed within every dwelling unit that has a door opening to the corridor, with such sprinkler positioned over the center of the door, unless the door to the dwelling unit has not less than a 20-minute fire protection rating and is self-closing. [*101:* 31.3.5.9.2]

13.3.2.18.5.3 The workmanship and materials of the sprinkler installation specified in 13.3.2.18.5 shall meet the requirements of 13.3.1.2. [*101:* 31.3.5.9.3]

13.3.2.18.5.4 Where Option 3 is being used to permit the use of 1¾ in. (44 mm) thick, solid-bonded wood-core doors in accordance with 31.2.2.1.3 of NFPA *101*, sprinklers shall be provided within the exit enclosures in accordance with NFPA 13. [*101:* 31.3.5.9.4]

13.3.2.18.6 Buildings using Option 4 in accordance with NFPA *101* shall be protected throughout by an approved automatic sprinkler system in accordance with 13.3.2.18.1 and meeting the requirements of Section 13.3 for supervision for buildings seven or more stories in height. [*101:* 31.3.5.10]

13.3.2.18.7* Where sprinklers are being used as an option to any requirement in this *Code*, the sprinklers shall be installed throughout the space in accordance with the requirements of that option. [*101:* 31.3.5.11]

13.3.2.19 Lodging or Rooming Houses.

13.3.2.19.1 All new lodging or rooming houses shall be protected throughout by an approved automatic sprinkler system in accordance with 13.3.2.19.2. [*101:* 26.3.6.1]

13.3.2.19.2 Where an automatic sprinkler system is required or is used as an alternative method of protection, either for total or partial building coverage, the system shall be in accordance with Section 13.3 and 13.3.2.19.2.1 through 13.3.2.19.2.6. [*101:* 26.3.6.2]

13.3.2.19.2.1 Activation of the automatic sprinkler system shall actuate the fire alarm system in accordance with Section 13.7. [*101:* 26.3.6.2.1]

13.3.2.19.2.2 In buildings four or fewer stories above grade plane, systems in accordance with NFPA 13R shall be permitted. [*101:* 26.3.6.2.2]

13.3.2.19.2.3* Systems in accordance with NFPA 13D shall be permitted where all of the following requirements are met:

(1) The lodging or rooming house shall not be part of a mixed occupancy.
(2) Entrance foyers shall be sprinklered.
(3) Lodging or rooming houses with sleeping accommodations for more than eight occupants shall be treated as two-family dwellings with regard to the water supply. [*101:* 26.3.6.2.3]

13.3.2.19.2.4 In buildings sprinklered in accordance with NFPA 13, closets less than 12 ft² (1.1 m²) in area in individual dwelling units shall not be required to be sprinklered. [*101:* 26.3.6.2.4]

13.3.2.19.2.5 In buildings sprinklered in accordance with NFPA 13, closets that contain equipment such as washers, dryers, furnaces, or water heaters shall be sprinklered, regardless of size. [*101:* 26.3.6.2.5]

13.3.2.19.2.6 In existing lodging or rooming houses, sprinkler installations shall not be required in closets not exceeding 24 ft² (2.2 m²) and in bathrooms not exceeding 55 ft² (5.1 m²). [*101:* 26.3.6.2.6]

13.3.2.20 One- and Two-Family Dwellings.

13.3.2.20.1 All new one- and two-family dwellings shall be protected throughout by an approved automatic sprinkler system in accordance with 13.3.2.20.2. [*101:* 24.3.5.1]

13.3.2.20.2 Where an automatic sprinkler system is installed, either for total or partial building coverage, the system shall be in accordance with Section 13.3; in buildings of four or fewer stories in height above grade plane, systems in accordance with NFPA 13R and with NFPA 13D shall also be permitted. [*101:* 24.3.5.2]

13.3.2.21 New Residential Board and Care Occupancies.

13.3.2.21.1 Large Facilities.

13.3.2.21.1.1 General. All buildings shall be protected throughout by an approved automatic sprinkler system installed in accordance with NFPA 13 and provided with quick-response or residential sprinklers throughout. [*101:* 32.3.3.5.1]

13.3.2.21.1.2 Supervision. Automatic sprinkler systems shall be provided with electrical supervision in accordance with 13.3.1.8. [*101:* 32.3.3.5.5]

13.3.2.21.2 Small Facilities.

13.3.2.21.2.1* All facilities, other than those meeting the requirement of 13.3.2.21.2.2, shall be protected throughout by an approved automatic sprinkler system, installed in accordance with 13.3.2.21.2.3, using quick-response or residential sprinklers. [*101:* 32.2.3.5.1]

13.3.2.21.2.2* In conversions, sprinklers shall not be required in small board and care homes serving eight or fewer residents when all occupants have the ability as a group to move reliably to a point of safety within 3 minutes. [*101:* 32.2.3.5.2]

13.3.2.21.2.3 Where an automatic sprinkler system is installed, for either total or partial building coverage, all of the following requirements shall be met:

(1) The system shall be in accordance with NFPA 13 and shall initiate the fire alarm system in accordance with 13.7.2.19.
(2) The adequacy of the water supply shall be documented to the AHJ. [*101:* 32.2.3.5.3]

13.3.2.21.2.3.1 In buildings four or fewer stories above grade plane, systems in accordance with NFPA 13R shall be permitted. All habitable areas, closets, roofed porches, roofed decks, and roofed balconies shall be sprinklered. [*101:* 32.2.3.5.3.1]

13.3.2.21.2.3.2* An automatic sprinkler system with a 30-minute water supply, and complying with the following requirements and with NFPA 13D, shall be permitted:

(1) All habitable areas, closets, roofed porches, roofed decks, and roofed balconies shall be sprinklered.
(2) Facilities with more than eight residents shall be treated as two-family dwellings with regard to water supply. [*101:* 32.2.3.5.3.2]

13.3.2.21.2.4 Automatic sprinkler systems installed in accordance with NFPA 13 and NFPA 13R shall be provided with electrical supervision in accordance with 13.3.1.8. [*101:* 32.2.3.5.4]

13.3.2.21.2.5 Automatic sprinkler systems installed in accordance with NFPA 13D shall be provided with valve supervision by one of the following methods:

(1) Single listed control valve that shuts off both domestic and sprinkler systems and separate shutoff for the domestic system only
(2) Electrical supervision in accordance with 13.3.1.8
(3) Valve closure that causes the sounding of an audible signal in the facility [*101:* 32.2.3.5.5]

13.3.2.21.2.6 Sprinkler piping serving not more than six sprinklers for any isolated hazardous area shall be permitted to be installed in accordance with 13.3.1.4 and shall meet all of the following requirements:

(1) In new installations, where more than two sprinklers are installed in a single area, waterflow detection shall be provided to initiate the fire alarm system required by 13.7.2.19.
(2) The duration of water supplies shall be as required by 13.3.2.21.2.3.2. [*101:* 32.2.3.5.6]

13.3.2.21.2.7 Attics shall be protected in accordance with 13.3.2.21.2.7.1 or 13.3.2.21.2.7.2. [*101:* 32.2.3.5.7]

13.3.2.21.2.7.1 Where an automatic sprinkler system is required by 13.3.2.21.2, attics used for living purposes, storage, or fuel fired equipment shall be protected with automatic sprinklers that are part of the required, approved automatic sprinkler system in accordance with 13.3.1.2. [*101:*32.2.3.5.7.1]

13.3.2.21.2.7.2 Where an automatic sprinkler system is required by 13.3.2.21.2, attics not used for living purposes, storage, or fuel -fired equipment shall meet one of the following criteria:

(1) Attics shall be protected throughout by a heat detection system arranged to activate the building fire alarm system in accordance with Section 13.7.
(2) Attics shall be protected with automatic sprinklers that are part of the required, approved automatic sprinkler system in accordance with 13.3.1.2.
(3) Attics shall be of noncombustible or limited-combustible construction.
(4) Attics shall be constructed of fire retardant–treated wood in accordance with NFPA 703, *Standard for Fire Retardant–Treated Wood and Fire Retardant Coatings for Building Materials.* [*101:* 32.2.3.5.7.2]

13.3.2.22 Existing Residential Board and Care Facilities.

13.3.2.22.1 Large Facilities.

13.3.2.22.1.1* General. Where an automatic sprinkler system is installed, for either total or partial building coverage, the system shall be installed in accordance with Section 13.3, as modified by 13.3.2.22.1.1.1 through 13.3.2.22.1.1.3. [*101:* 33.3.3.5.1]

13.3.2.22.1.1.1 In buildings four or fewer stories above grade plane, systems in accordance with NFPA 13R shall be permitted. [*101:* 33.3.3.5.1.1]

13.3.2.22.1.1.2 In facilities having prompt or slow evacuation capability, automatic sprinklers shall not be required in closets not exceeding 24 ft^2 (2.2 m^2) and in bathrooms not exceeding 55 ft^2 (5.1 m^2), provided that such spaces are finished with noncombustible or limited-combustible materials. [*101:* 33.3.3.5.1.2]

13.3.2.22.1.1.3 Initiation of the fire alarm system shall not be required for existing installations in accordance with 13.3.2.22.1.6. [*101:* 33.3.3.5.1.3]

13.3.2.22.1.2 Impractical Evacuation Capability. All facilities having impractical evacuation capability shall be protected throughout by an approved, supervised automatic sprinkler system in accordance with NFPA 13. [*101:* 33.3.3.5.2]

13.3.2.22.1.3 High-Rise Buildings. All high-rise buildings shall be protected throughout by an approved, supervised automatic sprinkler system in accordance with 13.3.2.22.1. Such systems shall initiate the fire alarm system in accordance with 13.7.1.4. [*101:* 33.3.3.5.3]

13.3.2.22.1.4 Attics shall be protected in accordance with 13.3.2.22.1.4.1 or 13.3.2.22.1.4.2. [*101:* 33.3.3.5.4]

13.3.2.22.1.4.1 Where an automatic sprinkler system is installed, attics used for living purposes, storage, or fuel-fired equipment shall be protected with automatic sprinklers that are part of the required, approved automatic sprinkler system in accordance with 13.3.1.2. [*101:* 33.3.3.5.4.1]

13.3.2.22.1.4.2 Where an automatic sprinkler system is installed, attics not used for living purposes, storage, or fuel-fired equipment shall meet one of the following criteria:

(1) Attics shall be protected throughout by a heat detection system arranged to activate the building fire alarm system in accordance with Section 13.7.
(2) Attics shall be protected with automatic sprinklers that are part of the required, approved automatic sprinkler system in accordance with 13.3.1.2.
(3) Attics shall be of noncombustible or limited-combustible construction.
(4) Attics shall be constructed of fire-retardant-treated wood in accordance with NFPA 703, *Standard for Fire Retardant–Treated Wood and Fire-Retardant Coatings for Building Materials*. [*101:* 33.3.3.5.4.2]

13.3.2.22.1.5 Supervision. Automatic sprinkler systems shall be supervised in accordance with Section 13.3; waterflow alarms shall not be required to be transmitted off-site. [*101:* 33.3.3.5.5]

13.3.2.22.1.6 Domestic Water Supply Option. Sprinkler piping serving not more than six sprinklers for any isolated hazardous area in accordance with 13.3.1.4 shall be permitted; in new installations where more than two sprinklers are installed in a single area, waterflow detection shall be provided to initiate the fire alarm system required by 13.7.2.22. [*101:* 33.3.3.5.6]

13.3.2.22.2 Small Facilities.

13.3.2.22.2.1 Where an automatic sprinkler system is installed, for either total or partial building coverage, the following requirements shall be met:

(1) The system shall be in accordance with Section 13.3 and shall initiate the fire alarm system in accordance with 13.7.2.21, as modified by 13.3.2.22.2.1.1 through 13.3.2.22.2.1.6.
(2) The adequacy of the water supply shall be documented to the AHJ. [*101:* 33.2.3.5.3]

13.3.2.22.2.1.1* In prompt evacuation capability facilities, all of the following shall apply:

(1) An automatic sprinkler system in accordance with NFPA 13D shall be permitted.
(2) Automatic sprinklers shall not be required in closets not exceeding 24 ft^2 (2.2 m^2) and in bathrooms not exceeding 55 ft^2 (5.1 m^2), provided that such spaces are finished with lath and plaster or materials providing a 15-minute thermal barrier. [*101:* 33.2.3.5.3.1]

13.3.2.22.2.1.2 In slow and impractical evacuation capability facilities, all of the following shall apply:

(1) An automatic sprinkler system in accordance with NFPA 13D, with a 30-minute water supply, shall be permitted.
(2) All habitable areas and closets shall be sprinklered.
(3) Automatic sprinklers shall not be required in bathrooms not exceeding 55 ft^2 (5.1 m^2), provided that such spaces are finished with lath and plaster or materials providing a 15-minute thermal barrier. [*101:* 33.2.3.5.3.2]

13.3.2.22.2.1.3 In prompt and slow evacuation capability facilities, where an automatic sprinkler system is in accordance with NFPA 13, sprinklers shall not be required in closets not exceeding 24 ft^2 (2.2 m^2) and in bathrooms not exceeding 55 ft^2 (5.1 m^2), provided that such spaces are finished with lath and plaster or materials providing a 15-minute thermal barrier. [*101:* 33.2.3.5.3.3]

13.3.2.22.2.1.4 In prompt and slow evacuation capability facilities in buildings four or fewer stories above grade plane, systems in accordance with NFPA 13R shall be permitted. [*101:* 33.2.3.5.3.4]

13.3.2.22.2.1.5 In impractical evacuation capability facilities in buildings four or fewer stories above grade plane, systems in accordance with NFPA 13R shall be permitted. All habitable areas and closets shall be sprinklered. Automatic sprinklers shall not be required in bathrooms not exceeding 55 ft^2 (5.1 m^2), provided that such spaces are finished with lath and plaster or materials providing a 15-minute thermal barrier. [*101:* 33.2.3.5.3.5]

13.3.2.22.2.1.6 Initiation of the fire alarm system shall not be required for existing installations in accordance with 13.3.2.22.3. [*101:* 33.2.3.5.3.6]

13.3.2.22.2.2 All impractical evacuation capability facilities shall be protected throughout by an approved, supervised automatic sprinkler system in accordance with 13.3.2.22.2.1. [*101:* 33.2.3.5.3.7]

13.3.2.22.3 Sprinkler piping serving not more than six sprinklers for any isolated hazardous area shall be permitted to be installed in accordance with 13.3.1.4 and shall meet the following requirements:

(1) In new installations, where more than two sprinklers are installed in a single area, waterflow detection shall be provided to initiate the fire alarm system required by 13.7.2.21.
(2) The duration of water supplies shall be as required for the sprinkler systems addressed in 13.3.2.22.2.1. [*101:*33.2.3.5.6]

13.3.2.22.4 Attics shall be protected in accordance with 13.3.2.22.4.1 or 13.3.2.22.4.2. [*101:* 33.2.3.5.7]

13.3.2.22.4.1 Where an automatic sprinkler system is installed, attics used for living purposes, storage, or fuel-fired equipment shall be protected with automatic sprinklers that are part of the required, approved automatic sprinkler system in accordance with 13.3.1.2. [*101:* 33.2.3.5.7.1]

13.3.2.22.4.2 Where an automatic sprinkler system is installed, attics not used for living purposes, storage, or fuel-fired equipment shall meet one of the following criteria:

(1) Attics shall be protected throughout by a heat detection system arranged to activate the building fire alarm system in accordance with Section 13.7.

(2) Attics shall be protected with automatic sprinklers that are part of the required, approved automatic sprinkler system in accordance with 13.3.1.2.
(3) Attics shall be of noncombustible or limited-combustible construction.
(4) Attics shall be constructed of fire-retardant-treated wood in accordance with NFPA 703, *Standard for Fire Retardant–Treated Wood and Fire-Retardant Coatings for Building Materials*.
(5) Attics shall be protected by heat alarms arranged to provide occupant notification in accordance with 33.2.3.4.2. [*101:* 33.2.3.5.7.2]

13.3.2.23 New Mercantile Occupancies.

13.3.2.23.1 Mercantile occupancies shall be protected by an approved automatic sprinkler system in accordance with NFPA 13 in any of the following specified locations:

(1) Throughout all mercantile occupancies three or more stories in height
(2) Throughout all mercantile occupancies exceeding 12,000 ft^2 (1115 m^2) in gross area
(3) Throughout stories below the level of exit discharge where such stories have an area exceeding 2500 ft^2 (232 m^2) and are used for the sale, storage, or handling of combustible goods and merchandise
(4) Throughout multiple occupancies protected as mixed occupancies in accordance with 6.1.14 where the conditions of 13.3.2.23.1(1), (2), or (3) apply to the mercantile occupancy [*101:* 36.3.5.1]

13.3.2.23.2 Automatic sprinkler systems in Class A mercantile occupancies shall be supervised in accordance with 13.3.1.8. [*101:* 36.3.5.2]

13.3.2.23.3 Extinguishing Requirements. Bulk merchandising retail buildings shall be protected throughout by an approved, supervised automatic sprinkler system in accordance with Section 13.3 and the applicable provisions of the following:

(1) This *Code*
(2) NFPA 13, *Standard for the Installation of Sprinkler Systems*
(3) NFPA 30, *Flammable and Combustible Liquids Code*
(4) NFPA 30B, *Code for the Manufacture and Storage of Aerosol Products*
[*101:* 36.4.5.5]

13.3.2.23.4 Mall Buildings.

13.3.2.23.4.1 Automatic Extinguishing Systems.

13.3.2.23.4.1.1 The mall building and all anchor buildings shall be protected throughout by an approved, supervised automatic sprinkler system in accordance with NFPA 13 and 13.3.2.23.4.1.2. [*101:* 36.4.4.13.1]

13.3.2.23.4.1.2 The system shall be installed in such a manner that any portion of the system serving tenant spaces can be taken out of service without affecting the operating of the portion of the system serving the mall. [*101:* 36.4.4.13.2]

13.3.2.23.4.2 Hose Connections.

13.3.2.23.4.2.1 There shall be a hose outlet connected to a system sized to deliver 250 gal/min (946 L/min) at the most hydraulically remote outlet. [*5000:*27.4.4.7.2.1]

13.3.2.23.4.2.2 The outlet shall be supplied from the mall zone sprinkler system and shall be hydraulically calculated. [*5000:*27.4.4.7.2.2]

13.3.2.23.4.2.3 Hose outlets shall be provided at each of the following locations:

(1) Within the mall at the entrance to each exit passage or corridor
(2) At each floor level landing within enclosed stairways opening directly onto the mall
(3) At exterior public entrances to the mall [*5000:*27.4.4.7.2.3]

13.3.2.24 Existing Mercantile Occupancies.

13.3.2.24.1 Mercantile occupancies, other than one-story buildings that meet the requirements of a street floor, as defined in 3.3.183.17, shall be protected by an approved automatic sprinkler system in accordance with NFPA 13 in any of the following specified locations:

(1) Throughout all mercantile occupancies with a story over 15,000 ft^2 (1400 m^2) in area
(2) Throughout all mercantile occupancies exceeding 30,000 ft^2 (2800 m^2) in gross area
(3) Throughout stories below the level of exit discharge where such stories have an area exceeding 2500 ft^2 (232 m^2) and are used for the sale, storage, or handling of combustible goods and merchandise
(4) Throughout multiple occupancies protected as mixed occupancies in accordance with 6.1.14 where the conditions of 13.3.2.24.1(1), (2), or (3) apply to the mercantile occupancy
[*101:* 37.3.5.1]

13.3.2.24.2 Bulk merchandising retail buildings shall be protected throughout by an approved, supervised automatic sprinkler system in accordance with Section 13.3 and the applicable provisions of the following:

(1) This *Code*
(2) NFPA 13, *Standard for the Installation of Sprinkler Systems*
(3) NFPA 30, *Flammable and Combustible Liquids Code*
(4) NFPA 30B, *Code for the Manufacture and Storage of Aerosol Products* [*101:* 37.4.5.5]

13.3.2.25 Underground and Limited Access Structures. Underground and limited access structures, and all areas and floor levels traversed in traveling to the exit discharge, shall be protected by an approved, supervised automatic sprinkler system in accordance with Section 13.3, unless such structures meet one of the following criteria:

(1) They have an occupant load of 50 or fewer persons in new underground or limited access portions of the structure.
(2) They have an occupant load of 100 or fewer persons in existing underground or limited access portions of the structure.
(3) The structure is a one-story underground or limited access structure that is permitted to have a single exit, per Chapters 12 through 43 of NFPA *101*, with a common path of travel not greater than 50 ft (15 m).
[*101:* 11.7.3.4]

13.3.2.26 High-Rise Buildings.

13.3.2.26.1 New high-rise buildings shall be protected throughout by an approved automatic sprinkler system in accordance with Section 13.3.

13.3.2.26.2* Existing high-rise buildings shall be protected throughout by an approved automatic sprinkler system in accordance with this chapter and 13.3.2.26.2.1 through 13.3.2.26.2.3.

13.3.2.26.2.1 Each building owner shall, within 180 days of receiving notice, file an intent to comply with this regulation with the AHJ for approval.

13.3.2.26.2.2 The AHJ shall review and respond to the intent-to-comply submittal within 60 days of receipt.

13.3.2.26.2.3* The entire building shall be required to be protected by an approved automatic sprinkler system within 12 years of adoption of this *Code*.

13.3.2.27* New Storage Occupancies.

13.3.2.27.1 High-Piled Storage. An automatic sprinkler system shall be installed throughout all occupancies containing areas greater than 2500 ft^2 (232 m^2) for the high-piled storage of combustibles.

13.3.2.27.2* General Storage. An automatic sprinkler system shall be installed throughout all occupancies containing areas greater than 12,000 ft^2 (1115 m^2) for the storage of combustibles.

13.3.2.27.3 An automatic sprinkler system shall be installed throughout all occupancies containing storage commodities classified as Group A Plastics in excess of 5 ft (1.5 m) in height over an area exceeding 2500 ft^2 (232 m^2) in area.

13.3.2.27.4 Mini-Storage Building. An automatic sprinkler system shall be installed throughout all mini-storage buildings greater than 2500 ft^2 (232 m^2) and where any of the individual storage units are separated by less than a 1-hour fire resistance–rated barrier. [**5000**:30.3.5.3]

13.3.2.27.5 Bulk Storage of Tires. Buildings and structures where the volume for the storage of tires exceeds 20,000 ft^3 (566 m^3) shall be equipped throughout with an approved automatic fire sprinkler system. [**5000**:30.3.5.2]

13.3.2.28 Woodworking Operations. An approved automatic fire sprinkler system shall be installed in buildings containing woodworking operations exceeding 2500 ft^2 (232 m^2) that use equipment, machinery, or appliances; that generate finely divided combustible waste; or that use finely divided combustible materials. [**5000**:29.3.5.1.2]

13.3.2.29 New and Existing Day Care. Buildings with unprotected openings in accordance with 8.6.6 of NFPA *101* shall be protected throughout by an approved, supervised automatic sprinkler system in accordance with Section 13.3. [*101*:16.3.5.3; *101*:17.3.5.3]

13.3.2.30 New Industrial Occupancies. New industrial occupancies, other than low-hazard industrial occupancies, shall be protected by an approved automatic sprinkler system in accordance with NFPA 13 in any of the following locations:

(1) Throughout all industrial occupancies three or more stories in height
(2) Throughout all industrial occupancies exceeding 12,000 ft^2 (1115 m^2) in fire area
(3) Where the total area of all floors, including mezzanines, exceeds 24,000 ft^2 (2230 m^2) [**5000**:29.3.5.1.1]

13.3.3 Inspection, Testing, and Maintenance.

13.3.3.1 A sprinkler system installed in accordance with this *Code* shall be properly maintained to provide at least the same level of performance and protection as designed. The owner shall be responsible for maintaining the system and keeping it in good working condition.

13.3.3.2 A sprinkler system installed in accordance with this *Code* shall be inspected, tested, and maintained in accordance with NFPA 25.

13.3.3.3 Ceiling Tiles and Ceiling Assemblies. Where automatic sprinklers are installed, ceilings necessary for the proper actuation of the fire protection device in accordance with NFPA 13 shall be maintained.

13.3.3.4 General Requirements.

13.3.3.4.1 Responsibility of the Property Owner or Designated Representative.

13.3.3.4.1.1* Responsibility for Inspection, Testing, Maintenance, and Impairment. The property owner or designated representative shall be responsible for properly maintaining a water-based fire protection system. [**25**:4.1.1]

(A)* Inspection, testing, maintenance, and impairment procedures shall be implemented in accordance those established in this document and in accordance with the manufacturer's instructions. [**25**:4.1.1.1]

(B) Inspection, testing, and maintenance shall be performed by qualified personnel. [**25**:4.1.1.2]

(C)* Where the property owner or designated representative is not the occupant, the property owner or designated representative shall be permitted to delegate the authority for inspecting, testing, maintenance, and the managing of impairments of the fire protection system to a designated representative. [**25**:4.1.1.3]

(D) Where a designated representative has received the authority for inspecting, testing, maintenance, and the managing of impairments, the designated representative shall comply with the requirements identified for the property owner or designated representative throughout this *Code*. [**25**:4.1.1.4]

13.3.3.4.1.2* Freeze Protection. The property owner or designated representative shall ensure that water-filled piping is maintained at a minimum temperature of 40°F (4.4°C) unless an approved anti-freeze solution is utilized. [**25**:4.1.2]

13.3.3.4.1.2.1 All areas of the building containing water-filled piping that does not have another means of freeze protection shall be maintained at a minimum temperature of 40°F (4.4°C). [**25**:4.1.2.1]

13.3.3.4.1.2.2 Aboveground water-filled pipes that pass through open areas, cold rooms, passageways, or other areas exposed to temperatures below 40°F (4°C), protected against freezing by insulating coverings, frostproof casings, listed heat tracing systems, or other reliable means shall be maintained at temperatures between 40°F (4°C) and 120°F (48.9°C). [**25**:4.1.2.2]

13.3.3.4.1.2.3 Where other approved means of freeze protection for water-filled piping as described in 13.3.3.4.1.2.2 are utilized they shall be inspected, tested, and maintained in accordance with NFPA 25. [**25**:4.1.2.3]

13.3.3.4.1.3* Accessibility. The property owner or designated representative shall provide ready accessibility to components of water-based fire protection systems that require inspection, testing, and maintenance. [**25**:4.1.3]

13.3.3.4.1.4 Notification of System Shutdown or Testing. The property owner or designated representative shall notify the AHJ, the fire department, if required, and the alarm-receiving facility before testing or shutting down a system or its supply. [**25**:4.1.4]

13.3.3.4.1.4.1 The notification of system shutdown or test shall include the purpose for the shutdown, the system or component involved, the estimated time of shutdown or test, and the expected duration of the shutdown or test. [**25**:4.1.4.1]

13.3.3.4.1.4.2 The AHJ, the fire department, and the alarm-receiving facility shall be notified when the system, supply, or component is returned to service or when the test is complete. [**25**:4.1.4.2]

13.3.3.4.1.5* Corrections and Repairs.

13.3.3.4.1.5.1* The property owner or designated representative shall correct or repair deficiencies or impairments that are found during the inspection, test, and maintenance required by this *Code*. [**25**:4.1.5.1]

13.3.3.4.1.5.2 Corrections and repairs shall be performed by qualified maintenance personnel or a qualified contractor. [**25**:4.1.5.2]

13.3.3.4.1.6* Changes in Occupancy, Use, Process, or Materials. The property owner or designated representative shall not make changes in the occupancy, the use or process, or the materials used or stored in the building without evaluation of the fire protection systems for their capability to protect the new occupancy, use, or materials. [**25**:4.1.6]

13.3.3.4.1.6.1 The evaluation required by 13.3.3.4.1.6 shall not be considered part of the normal inspection, testing, and maintenance required by this *Code*. [**25**:4.1.6.1]

13.3.3.4.1.6.2 The evaluation shall consider factors that include, but are not limited to, the following:

(1) Occupancy changes such as converting office or production space into warehousing
(2) Process or material changes such as metal stamping to molded plastics
(3) Building revisions such as relocated walls, added mezzanines, and ceilings added below sprinklers
(4) Removal of heating systems in spaces with piping subject to freezing [**25**:4.1.6.2]

13.3.3.4.1.7* Addressing Changes in Hazards.

13.3.3.4.1.7.1 Where changes in the occupancy, hazard, water supply, storage commodity, storage arrangement, building modification, or other condition that affects the installation criteria of the system are identified, the property owner or designated representative shall promptly take steps to evaluate the adequacy of the installed system in order to protect the building or hazard in question. [**25**:4.1.7.1]

13.3.3.4.1.7.2 Where the evaluation reveals that the installed system is inadequate to protect the building or hazard in question, the property owner or designated representative shall make the required corrections. [**25**:4.1.7.2]

13.3.3.4.1.7.3 Corrections shall be approved. [**25**:4.1.7.3]

13.3.3.4.1.8 Valve Location. The location of shutoff valves shall be identified at the system riser or other approved locations. [**25**:4.1.8]

13.3.3.4.1.9 Information Sign.

13.3.3.4.1.9.1 A permanently marked metal or rigid plastic information sign shall be placed at the system control riser supplying an antifreeze loop, dry system, preaction system, or auxiliary system control valve. [**25**:4.1.9.1]

13.3.3.4.1.9.2 Each sign shall be secured with a corrosion-resistant wire, chain, or other approved means and shall indicate at least the following information:

(1) Location of the design area or areas
(2) Discharge densities over the design area or areas
(3) Required flow and residual pressure demand at the base of riser
(4) Occupancy classification or commodity classification and maximum permitted storage height and configuration
(5) Hose stream allowance included in addition to the sprinkler demand
(6) The name of the installing contractor or person providing the information [**25**:4.1.9.2]

13.3.3.4.1.10 Impairments.

13.3.3.4.1.10.1 Where an impairment to a water-based fire protection system occurs or is identified during inspection, testing, or maintenance activities, the procedures outlined in Chapter 15 of NFPA 25 shall be followed, including the attachment of a tag to the impaired system. [**25**:4.1.10.1]

13.3.3.4.1.10.2 Where a water-based fire protection system is returned to service following an impairment, the system shall be verified to be working properly by means of an appropriate inspection or test as described in the table, "Summary of Component Replacement [Action] Requirements" in the applicable chapters of NFPA 25. [**25**:4.1.10.2]

13.3.3.4.2 Manufacturer's Corrective Action. Manufacturers shall be permitted to make modifications to their own listed product in the field with listed devices that restore the original performance as intended by the listing, where acceptable to the AHJ. [**25**:4.2]

13.3.3.4.3 Records.

13.3.3.4.3.1* Records shall be made for all inspections, tests, and maintenance of the system and its components and shall be made available to the AHJ upon request. [**25**:4.3.1]

13.3.3.4.3.1.1* Records shall be permitted to be stored and accessed electronically. [**25**:4.3.1.1]

13.3.3.4.3.2 Records shall indicate the following:

(1) The procedure/activity performed (e.g., inspection, test, or maintenance)
(2) The organization that performed the activity
(3) The required frequency of the activity
(4) The results and date of the activity
(5) The name and contact information of the qualified contractor or owner, including lead person for activity [**25**:4.3.2]

13.3.3.4.3.3* Records shall be maintained by the property owner. [**25**:4.3.3]

13.3.3.4.3.4 As-built system installation drawings, hydraulic calculations, original acceptance test records, and device manufacturer's data sheets shall be retained for the life of the system. [**25**:4.3.4]

13.3.3.4.3.5 Subsequent records shall be retained for a period of 1 year after the next inspection, test, or maintenance of that type required by the *Code*. [**25:**4.3.5]

13.3.3.5 Sprinkler Systems.

13.3.3.5.1 Maintenance — Sprinklers.

13.3.3.5.1.1 Where a sprinkler has been removed for any reason, it shall not be reinstalled. [**25:**5.4.1.1]

13.3.3.5.1.2* Replacement sprinklers shall have the proper characteristics for the application intended, which include the following:

(1) Style
(2) Orifice size and K-factor
(3) Temperature rating
(4) Coating, if any
(5) Deflector type (e.g., upright, pendent, sidewall)
(6) Design requirements [**25:**5.4.1.2]

13.3.3.5.1.2.1* Spray sprinklers shall be permitted to replace old-style sprinklers. [**25:**5.4.1.2.1]

13.3.3.5.1.2.2 Replacement sprinklers for piers and wharves shall comply with NFPA 307, *Standard for the Construction and Fire Protection of Marine Terminals, Piers, and Wharves*. [**25:**5.4.1.2.2]

13.3.3.5.1.3 Only new, listed sprinklers shall be used to replace existing sprinklers. [**25:**5.4.1.3]

13.3.3.5.1.4* Special and quick-response sprinklers as defined by NFPA 13, *Standard for the Installation of Sprinkler Systems*, shall be replaced with sprinklers of the same orifice, size, temperature range and thermal response characteristics, and K-factor. [**25:**5.4.1.4]

13.3.3.5.1.5* Stock of Spare Sprinklers. A supply of at least six spare sprinklers shall be maintained on the premises so that any sprinklers that have operated or been damaged in any way can be promptly replaced. [**25:**5.4.1.5]

13.3.3.5.1.5.1 The sprinklers shall correspond to the types and temperature ratings of the sprinklers in the property. [**25:**5.4.1.5.1]

13.3.3.5.1.5.2 The sprinklers shall be kept in a cabinet located where the temperature in which they are subjected will at no time exceed 100°F (38°C). [**25:**5.4.1.5.2]

13.3.3.5.1.5.3 Where dry sprinklers of different lengths are installed, spare dry sprinklers shall not be required, provided that a means of returning the system to service is furnished. [**25:**5.4.1.5.3]

13.3.3.5.1.5.4 The stock of spare sprinklers shall include all types and ratings installed and shall be as follows:

(1) For protected facilities having under 300 sprinklers — no fewer than 6 sprinklers
(2) For protected facilities having 300 to 1000 sprinklers — no fewer than 12 sprinklers
(3) For protected facilities having over 1000 sprinklers — no fewer than 24 sprinklers
[**25:**5.4.1.5.4]

13.3.3.5.1.5.5* One sprinkler wrench as specified by the sprinkler manufacturer shall be provided in the cabinet for each type of sprinkler installed to be used for the removal and installation of sprinklers in the system. [**25:**5.4.1.5.5]

13.3.3.5.1.5.6 A list of the sprinklers installed in the property shall be posted in the sprinkler cabinet. [**25:**5.4.1.5.6]

13.3.3.5.1.5.6.1* The list shall include the following:

(1) Sprinkler Identification Number (SIN) if equipped; or the manufacturer, model, orifice, deflector type, thermal sensitivity, and pressure rating
(2) General description
(3) Quantity of each type to be contained in the cabinet
(4) Issue or revision date of the list
[**25:**5.4.1.5.6.1]

13.3.3.5.1.6* Sprinklers shall not be altered in any respect or have any type of ornamentation, paint, or coatings applied after shipment from the place of manufacture. [**25:**5.4.1.6]

13.3.3.5.1.7 Sprinklers and automatic spray nozzles used for protecting commercial-type cooking equipment and ventilating systems shall be replaced annually. [**25:**5.4.1.7]

13.3.3.5.1.7.1 Where automatic bulb-type sprinklers or spray nozzles are used and annual examination shows no buildup of grease or other material on the sprinklers or spray nozzles, such sprinklers and spray nozzles shall not be required to be replaced. [**25:**5.4.1.7.1]

13.3.3.5.1.8 Protective Coverings.

13.3.3.5.1.8.1* Sprinklers protecting spray areas and mixing rooms in resin application areas installed with protective coverings shall continue to be protected against overspray residue so that they will operate in the event of fire. [**25:**5.4.1.8.1]

13.3.3.5.1.8.2 Sprinklers installed as described in 13.3.3.5.1.8.1 shall be protected using cellophane bags having a thickness of 0.003 in. (0.076 mm) or less or thin paper bags. [**25:**5.4.1.8.2]

13.3.3.5.1.8.3 Coverings shall be replaced periodically so that heavy deposits of residue do not accumulate. [**25:**5.4.1.8.3]

13.3.3.5.2* Dry Pipe Systems. Dry pipe systems shall be kept dry at all times. [**25:**5.4.2]

13.3.3.5.2.1 During nonfreezing weather, a dry pipe system shall be permitted to be left wet if the only other option is to remove the system from service while waiting for parts or during repair activities. [**25:**5.4.2.1]

13.3.3.5.2.2 Refrigerated spaces or other areas within the building interior where temperatures are maintained at or below 40°F (4.4°C) shall not be permitted to be left wet. [**25:**5.4.2.2]

13.3.3.5.2.3 Air driers shall be maintained in accordance with the manufacturer's instructions. [**25:**5.4.2.3]

13.3.3.5.2.4 Compressors used in conjunction with dry pipe sprinkler systems shall be maintained in accordance with the manufacturer's instructions. [**25:**5.4.2.4]

13.3.3.6 Impairments.

13.3.3.6.1 General.

13.3.3.6.1.1 Minimum Requirements.

13.3.3.6.1.1.1 Subsection 13.3.3.6 shall provide the minimum requirements for a water-based fire protection system impairment program. [**25:**15.1.1.1]

13.3.3.6.1.1.2 Measures shall be taken during the impairment to ensure that increased risks are minimized and the duration of the impairment is limited. [**25**:15.1.1.2]

13.3.3.6.2 Impairment Coordinator.

13.3.3.6.2.1 The property owner or designated representative shall assign an impairment coordinator to comply with the requirements of 13.3.3.6. [**25**:15.2.1]

13.3.3.6.2.2 In the absence of a specific designee, the property owner or designated representative shall be considered the impairment coordinator. [**25**:15.2.2]

13.3.3.6.2.3 Where the lease, written use agreement, or management contract specifically grants the authority for inspection, testing, and maintenance of the fire protection system(s) to the tenant, management firm, or managing individual, the tenant, management firm, or managing individual shall assign a person as impairment coordinator. [**25**:15.2.3]

13.3.3.6.3 Tag Impairment System.

13.3.3.6.3.1* A tag shall be used to indicate that a system, or part thereof, has been removed from service. [**25**:15.3.1]

13.3.3.6.3.2* The tag shall be posted at each fire department connection and the system control valve, and other locations required by the AHJ indicating which system, or part thereof, has been removed from service. [**25**:15.3.2]

13.3.3.6.4 Impaired Equipment.

13.3.3.6.4.1 The impaired equipment shall be considered to be the water-based fire protection system, or part thereof, that is removed from service. [**25**:15.4.1]

13.3.3.6.4.2 The impaired equipment shall include, but shall not be limited to, the following:

(1) Sprinkler systems
(2) Standpipe systems
(3) Fire hose systems
(4) Underground fire service mains
(5) Fire pumps
(6) Water storage tanks
(7) Water spray fixed systems
(8) Foam-water systems
(9) Water mist systems
(10) Fire service control valves
[**25**:15.4.2]

13.3.3.6.5* Preplanned Impairment Programs.

13.3.3.6.5.1 All preplanned impairments shall be authorized by the impairment coordinator. [**25**:15.5.1]

13.3.3.6.5.2 Before authorization is given, the impairment coordinator shall be responsible for verifying that the following procedures have been implemented:

(1) The extent and expected duration of the impairment have been determined.
(2) The areas or buildings involved have been inspected and the increased risks determined.
(3) Recommendations to mitigate any increased risks have been submitted to management or the property owner or designated representative.
(4) Where a fire protection system is out of service for more than 10 hours in a 24-hour period, the impairment coordinator shall arrange for one of the following:

　(a) Evacuation of the building or portion of the building affected by the system out of service
　(b)*An approved fire watch
　(c)*Establishment of a temporary water supply
　(d)*Establishment and implementation of an approved program to eliminate potential ignition sources and limit the amount of fuel available to the fire

(5) The fire department has been notified.
(6) The insurance carrier, the alarm company, property owner or designated representative, and other AHJs have been notified.
(7) The supervisors in the areas to be affected have been notified.
(8) A tag impairment system has been implemented. *(See 13.3.3.6.3.)*
(9) All necessary tools and materials have been assembled on the impairment site.
[**25**:15.5.2]

13.3.3.6.6* Emergency Impairments.

13.3.3.6.6.1 Emergency impairments shall include, but are not limited to, interruption of water supply, frozen or ruptured piping, and equipment failure, and includes impairments found during inspection, testing, or maintenance activities. [**25**:15.6.1]

13.3.3.6.6.2* The coordinator shall implement the steps outlined in 13.3.3.6.5. [**25**:15.6.2]

13.3.3.6.7* Restoring Systems to Service. When all impaired equipment is restored to normal working order, the impairment coordinator shall verify that the following procedures have been implemented:

(1) Any necessary inspections and tests have been conducted to verify that affected systems are operational. The appropriate chapter of NFPA 25 shall be consulted for guidance on the type of inspection and test required.
(2) Supervisors have been advised that protection is restored.
(3) The fire department has been advised that protection is restored.
(4) The property owner or designated representative, insurance carrier, alarm company, and other AHJs have been advised that protection is restored.
(5) The impairment tag has been removed.
[**25**:15.7]

13.4 Fire Pumps.

13.4.1 General.

13.4.1.1 Where provided, fire pumps shall be installed in accordance with NFPA 20, *Standard for the Installation of Stationary Pumps for Fire Protection*, and Section 13.4.

13.4.1.2 Permits. Permits, where required, shall comply with Section 1.12.

13.4.1.3 Retroactivity. The provisions of this section reflect a consensus of what is necessary to provide an acceptable degree of protection from the hazards addressed in this section at the time the section was issued. [**20**:1.4]

13.4.1.3.1 Unless otherwise specified, the provisions of this section shall not apply to facilities, equipment, structures, or installations that existed or were approved for construction or installation prior to the effective date of the section. Where specified, the provisions of this section shall be retroactive. [**20**:1.4.1]

13.4.1.3.2 In those cases where the AHJ determines that the existing situation presents an unacceptable degree of risk, the AHJ shall be permitted to apply retroactively any portion of this section deemed appropriate. [**20**:1.4.2]

13.4.1.3.3 The retroactive requirements of this section shall be permitted to be modified if their application clearly would be impractical in the judgment of the AHJ, and only where it is clearly evident that a reasonable degree of safety is provided. [**20**:1.4.3]

13.4.1.4* Approval Required.

13.4.1.4.1 Stationary pumps shall be selected based on the conditions under which they are to be installed and used. [**20**:4.2.1]

13.4.1.4.2 The pump manufacturer or its authorized representative shall be given complete information concerning the liquid and power supply characteristics. [**20**:4.2.2]

13.4.1.4.3 A complete plan and detailed data describing pump, driver, controller, power supply, fittings, suction and discharge connections, and liquid supply conditions shall be prepared for approval. [**20**:4.2.3]

13.4.1.4.3.1 Plans shall be drawn to an indicated scale, on sheets of uniform size, and shall indicate, as a minimum, the items from the following list that pertain to the design of the system:

(1) Name of owner and occupant
(2) Location, including street address
(3) Point of compass
(4) Name and address of installing contractor
(5) Pump make and model number
(6) Pump rating _____ gpm @ _____ psi _____ rpm
(7) Suction main size, length, location, weight, type of material, and point of connection to water supply, as well as size and type of valves, valve indicators, regulators, meters, and valve pits, and depth to top of pipe below grade
(8) Water supply capacity information including the following:
   (a) Location and elevation of static and residual test gauge with relation to the riser reference point
   (b) Flow location
   (c) Static pressure, psi (bar)
   (d) Residual pressure, psi (bar)
   (e) Flow, gpm (L/min)
   (f) Date
   (g) Time
   (h) Name of person who conducted the test or supplied the information
   (i) Other sources of water supply, with pressure or elevation
(9) Pump driver details including manufacturer, horsepower, voltage, or fuel system details
(10) Controller manufacturer, type, and rating
(11) Suction and discharge pipe, fitting, and valve types
(12) Test connection piping and valves
(13) Flow meter details (if used)
(14) Jockey pump and controller arrangement, including sensing line details
[**20**:4.2.3.1]

13.4.1.4.4 Each pump, driver, controlling equipment, power supply and arrangement, and liquid supply shall be approved by the AHJ for the specific field conditions encountered. [**20**:4.2.4]

13.4.1.5 Pump Operation.

13.4.1.5.1 In the event of fire pump operation, qualified personnel shall respond to the fire pump location to determine that the fire pump is operating in a satisfactory manner. [**20**:4.3.1]

13.4.1.5.2 System Designer.

13.4.1.5.2.1 The system designer shall be identified on the system design documents. [**20**:4.3.2.1]

13.4.1.5.2.2 Acceptable minimum evidence of qualifications or certification shall be provided when requested by the AHJ. [**20**:4.3.2.2]

13.4.1.5.2.3 Qualified personnel shall include, but not be limited to, one or more of the following:

(1) Personnel who are factory trained and certified for fire pump system design of the specific type and brand of system being designed
(2) Personnel who are certified by a nationally recognized fire protection certification organization acceptable to the AHJ
(3) Personnel who are registered, licensed, or certified by a state or local authority [**20**:4.3.2.3]

13.4.1.5.2.4 Additional evidence of qualification or certification shall be permitted to be required by the AHJ. [**20**:4.3.2.4]

13.4.1.5.3 System Installer.

13.4.1.5.3.1 Installation personnel shall be qualified or shall be supervised by persons who are qualified in the installation, inspection, and testing of fire protection systems [**20**:4.3.3.1].

13.4.1.5.3.2 Minimum evidence of qualifications or certification shall be provided when requested by the AHJ. [**20**:4.3.3.2]

13.4.1.5.3.3 Qualified personnel shall include, but not be limited to, one or more of the following:

(1) Personnel who are factory trained and certified for fire pump system designed of the specific type and brand of system being designed
(2) Personnel who are certified by a nationally recognized fire protection certification organization acceptable to the AHJ
(3) Personnel who are registered, licensed, or certified by a state or local authority
[**20**:4.3.3.3]

13.4.1.5.3.4 Additional evidence of qualification or certification shall be permitted to be required by the AHJ. [**20**:4.3.3.4]

13.4.1.5.4 Service Personnel Qualifications and Experience.

13.4.1.5.4.1 Service personnel shall be qualified and experienced in the inspection, testing, and maintenance of fire protection systems. [**20**:4.3.4.1]

13.4.1.5.4.2 Qualified personnel shall include, but not be limited to, one or more of the following:

(1) Personnel who are factory trained and certified for fire pump system design of the specific type and brand of system being designed
(2) Personnel who are certified by a nationally recognized fire protection certification organization acceptable to the AHJ
(3) Personnel who are registered, licensed, or certified by a state or local authority

(4) Personnel who are employed and qualified by an organization listed by a nationally recognized testing laboratory for the servicing of fire protection systems [**20:**4.3.4.2]

13.4.1.5.4.3 Additional evidence of qualification or certification shall be permitted to be required by the AHJ. [**20:**4.3.4.3]

13.4.2* Equipment Protection.

13.4.2.1* General Requirements. The fire pump, driver, controller, water supply, and power supply shall be protected against possible interruption of service through damage caused by explosion, fire, flood, earthquake, rodents, insects, windstorm, freezing, vandalism, and other adverse conditions. [**20:**4.12.1]

13.4.2.1.1* Indoor Fire Pump Units.

13.4.2.1.1.1 Fire pump units serving high-rise buildings shall be protected from surrounding occupancies by a minimum of 2-hour fire-rated construction or physically separated from the protected building by a minimum of 50 ft (15.3 m). [**20:**4.12.1.1.1]

13.4.2.1.1.2* Indoor fire pump rooms in non-high-rise buildings or in separate fire pump buildings shall be physically separated or protected by fire-rated construction in accordance with Table 13.4.2.1.1.2. [**20:**4.12.1.1.2]

Table 13.4.2.1.1.2 Equipment Protection

Pump Room/House	Building(s) Exposing Pump Room/House	Required Separation
Not sprinklered	Not sprinklered	2 hour fire-rated
Not sprinklered	Fully sprinklered	or
Fully sprinklered	Not sprinklered	50 ft (15.3 m)
Fully sprinklered	Fully sprinklered	1 hour fire-rated or 50 ft (15.3 m)

[**20:** Table 4.12.1.1.2]

13.4.2.1.1.3 The location of and access to the fire pump room shall be preplanned with the fire department. [**20:**4.12.1.1.3]

13.4.2.1.1.4* Except as permitted in 13.4.2.1.1.5, rooms containing fire pumps shall be free from storage, equipment, and penetrations not essential to the operation of the pump and related components. [**20:**4.12.1.1.4]

13.4.2.1.1.5 Equipment related to domestic water distribution shall be permitted to be located within the same room as the fire pump equipment. [**20:**4.12.1.1.5]

13.4.2.1.1.6 The pump room or pump house shall be sized to fit all of the components necessary for the operation of the fire pump and to accommodate the following:

(1) Clearance between components for installation and maintenance
(2) Clearance between a component and the wall for installation and maintenance
(3) Clearance between energized electrical equipment and other equipment in accordance with *NFPA 70, National Electrical Code*
(4) Orientation of the pump to the suction piping to allow compliance with 4.14.6.3 of NFPA 20 [**20:** 4.12.1.1.6]

13.4.2.1.2 Outdoor Fire Pump Units.

13.4.2.1.2.1 Fire pump units that are outdoors shall be located at least 50 ft (15.3 m) away from any buildings and other fire exposures exposing the building. [**20:** 4.12.1.2.1]

13.4.2.1.2.2 Outdoor installations shall be required to be provided with protection against possible interruption, in accordance with 13.4.2.1. [**20:** 4.12.1.2.2]

13.4.2.2 Equipment Access.

13.4.2.2.1 The location of and access to the fire pump room(s) shall be pre-planned with the fire department. [**20:**4.12.2.1]

13.4.2.2.1.1 Fire pump rooms not directly accessible from the outside shall be accessible through an enclosed passageway from an enclosed stairway or exterior exit. [**20:** 4.12.2.1.1]

13.4.2.2.1.2 The enclosed passageway shall have a fire-resistance rating not less than the fire-resistance rating of the fire pump room. [**20:** 4.12.2.1.2]

13.4.2.3 Heat.

13.4.2.3.1 An approved or listed source of heat shall be provided for maintaining the temperature of a pump room or pump house, where required, above 40°F (5°C). [**20:**4.12.3.1]

13.4.2.3.2 The requirements of 13.4.4.5 shall be followed for higher temperature requirements for internal combustion engines. [**20:**4.12.3.2]

13.4.2.4 Normal Lighting. Artificial light shall be provided in a pump room or pump house. [**20:**4.12.4]

13.4.2.5 Emergency Lighting.

13.4.2.5.1 Emergency lighting shall be provided in accordance with NFPA *101, Life Safety Code.* [**20:**4.12.5.1]

13.4.2.5.2 Emergency lights shall not be connected to an engine-starting battery. [**20:**4.12.5.2]

13.4.2.6 Ventilation. Provision shall be made for ventilation of a pump room or pump house. [**20:**4.12.6]

13.4.2.7* Drainage.

13.4.2.7.1 Floors shall be pitched for adequate drainage of escaping water away from critical equipment such as the pump, driver, controller, and so forth. [**20:**4.12.7.1]

13.4.2.7.2 The pump room or pump house shall be provided with a floor drain that will discharge to a frost-free location. [**20:**4.12.7.2]

13.4.2.8 Guards. Couplings and flexible connecting shafts shall be installed with a coupling guard in accordance with Section 8 of ANSI B15.1, *Safety Standard for Mechanical Power Transmission Apparatus.* [**20:**4.12.8]

13.4.3* Valve Supervision.

13.4.3.1 Supervised Open. Where provided, the suction valve, discharge valve, bypass valves, and isolation valves on the backflow prevention device or assembly shall be supervised open by one of the following methods:

(1) Central station, proprietary, or remote station signaling service
(2) Local signaling service that will cause the sounding of an audible signal at a constantly attended point
(3) Locking valves open
(4) Sealing of valves and approved weekly recorded inspection where valves are located within fenced enclosures under the control of the owner
[**20**:4.16.1]

13.4.3.2 Supervised Closed. Control valves located in the pipeline to the hose valve header shall be supervised closed by one of the methods allowed in 13.4.3.1. [**20**:4.16.2]

13.4.4* Diesel Engine Driver System Operation.

13.4.4.1 Weekly Run.

13.4.4.1.1 Engines shall be designed and installed so that they can be started no less than once a week and run for no less than 30 minutes to attain normal running temperature. [**20**:11.6.1.1]

13.4.4.1.2 Engines shall run smoothly at rated speed, except for engines addressed in 13.4.4.1.3. [**20**:11.6.1.2]

13.4.4.1.3 Engines equipped with variable speed pressure limiting control shall be permitted to run at reduced speeds provided factory-set pressure is maintained and they run smoothly. [**20**:11.6.1.3]

13.4.4.2* Engine Maintenance. Engines shall be designed and installed so that they can be kept clean, dry, and well lubricated to ensure adequate performance. [**20**:11.6.2]

13.4.4.3 Battery Maintenance.

13.4.4.3.1 Storage batteries shall be designed and installed so that they can be kept charged at all times. [**20**:11.6.3.1]

13.4.4.3.2 Storage batteries shall be designed and installed so that they can be tested frequently to determine the condition of the battery cells and the amount of charge in the battery. [**20**:11.6.3.2]

13.4.4.3.3 Only distilled water shall be used in battery cells. [**20**:11.6.3.3]

13.4.4.3.4 Battery plates shall be kept submerged at all times. [**20**:11.6.3.4]

13.4.4.3.5 The automatic feature of a battery charger shall not be a substitute for proper maintenance of battery and charger. [**20**:11.6.3.5]

13.4.4.3.6 The battery and charger shall be designed and installed so that periodic inspection of both battery and charger is physically possible. [**20**:11.6.3.6]

13.4.4.3.6.1 This inspection shall determine that the charger is operating correctly, the water level in the battery is correct, and the battery is holding its proper charge. [**20**:11.6.3.6.1]

13.4.4.4* Fuel Supply Maintenance.

13.4.4.4.1 The fuel storage tanks shall be designed and installed so that they can be kept as full as practical at all times but never below 66 percent (two-thirds) of tank capacity. [**20**:11.6.4.1]

13.4.4.4.2 The tanks shall be designed and installed so that they can always be filled by means that will ensure removal of all water and foreign material. [**20**:11.6.4.2]

13.4.4.5* Temperature Maintenance.

13.4.4.5.1 The temperature of the pump room, pump house, or area where engines are installed shall be designed so that the temperature is maintained at the minimum recommended by the engine manufacturer and is never less than the minimum recommended by the engine manufacturer. [**20**:11.6.5.1]

13.4.4.6 Emergency Starting and Stopping.

13.4.4.6.1 The sequence for emergency manual operation, arranged in a step-by-step manner, shall be posted on the fire pump engine. [**20**:11.6.6.1]

13.4.4.6.2 It shall be the engine manufacturer's responsibility to list any specific instructions pertaining to the operation of this equipment during the emergency operation. [**20**:11.6.6.2]

13.4.5 Components.

13.4.5.1 Indicators on Controller.

13.4.5.1.1 All visible indicators shall be plainly visible. [**20**:12.4.1.1]

13.4.5.1.2* Visible indication shall be provided to indicate that the controller is in the automatic position. If the visible indicator is a pilot lamp, it shall be accessible for replacement. [**20**:12.4.1.2]

13.4.5.1.3 Separate visible indicators and a common audible fire pump alarm capable of being heard while the engine is running and operable in all positions of the main switch except the off position shall be provided to immediately indicate the following conditions:

(1) Critically low oil pressure in the lubrication system.
(2) High engine temperature.
(3) Failure of engine to start automatically.
(4) Shutdown from overspeed.
[**20**:12.4.1.3]

13.4.5.1.3.1 The controller shall provide means for testing the low oil pressure alarms and circuit in conjunction with the engine circuit testing method. [**20**:12.4.1.3.1]

13.4.5.1.3.2 Instructions shall be provided on how to test the operation of the signals in 13.4.5.1.3. [**20**:12.4.1.3.2]

13.4.5.1.4 Separate visible indicators and a common audible signal capable of being heard while the engine is running and operable in all positions of the main switch except the off position shall be provided to immediately indicate the following conditions:

(1)*Battery failure or missing battery. Each controller shall be provided with a separate visible indicator for each battery. The battery failure signal shall initiate at no lower than two-thirds of battery nominal voltage rating (8.0 V dc on a 12 V dc system). Sensing shall be delayed to prevent nuisance signals.
(2) Battery charger failure. Each controller shall be provided with a separate visible indicator for battery charger failure and shall not require the audible signal for battery charger failure.

(3) Low air or hydraulic pressure. Where air or hydraulic starting is provided *(see 11.2.7 and 11.2.7.4 of NFPA 20)*, each pressure tank shall provide to the controller separate visible indicators to indicate low pressure.
(4) System overpressure, for engines equipped with variable speed pressure limiting controls, to actuate at 115 percent of set pressure.
(5) ECM selector switch in alternate ECM position (for engines with ECM controls only).
(6) Fuel injection malfunction (for engines with ECM only).
(7) Low fuel level. Signal at two-thirds tank capacity.
(8) Low air pressure (air-starting engine controllers only). The air supply container shall be provided with a separate visible indicator to indicate low air pressure.
(9) Low engine temperature.
(10) Supervisory signal for interstitial space liquid intrusion.
(11) High cooling water temperature.
[**20:**12.4.1.4]

13.4.5.1.5 A separate signal silencing switch or valve, other than the controller main switch, shall be provided for the conditions reflected in 13.4.5.1.3 and 13.4.5.1.4. [**20:**12.4.1.5]

13.4.5.1.5.1 The switch or valve shall allow the audible device to be silenced for up to 4 hours and then re-sound repeatedly for the conditions in 13.4.5.1.3, [**20:**12.4.1.1.]

13.4.5.1.5.2 The switch or valve shall allow the audible device to be silenced for up to 24 hours and then re-sound repeatedly for the conditions in 13.4.5.1.4. [**20:**12.4.1.5.2]

13.4.5.1.5.3 The audible device shall re-sound until the condition is corrected or the main switch is placed in the off position. [**20:**12.4.1.5.3]

13.4.5.1.6* The controller shall automatically return to the nonsilenced state when the alarm(s) have cleared (returned to normal). [**20:**12.4.1.6]

13.4.5.1.6.1 This switch shall be clearly marked as to its function. [**20:**12.4.1.6.1]

13.4.5.2 Signal Devices Remote from Controller.

13.4.5.2.1 Where the pump room is not constantly attended, audible or visible signals powered by a source other than the engine starting batteries and not exceeding 125 V shall be provided at a point of constant attendance. [**20:**12.4.2.1]

13.4.5.2.2 Remote Indication. Controllers shall be equipped to operate circuits for remote indication of the conditions covered in 13.4.5.1.3, 13.4.5.1.4, and 13.4.5.2.3. [**20:**12.4.2.2]

13.4.5.2.3 The remote panel shall indicate the following:

(1) The engine is running (separate signal).
(2) The controller main switch has been turned to the off or manual position (separate signal).
(3)*There is trouble on the controller or engine (separate or common signals). *(See 13.4.5.1.4 and 13.4.5.1.5.)*
[**20:**12.4.2.3]

13.4.5.3 Controller Contacts for Remote Indication. Controllers shall be equipped with open or closed contacts to operate circuits for the conditions covered in 13.4.5.2. [**20:**12.4.3]

13.4.6 Field Acceptance Tests.

13.4.6.1* The pump manufacturer, the engine manufacturer (when supplied), the controller manufacturer, and the transfer switch manufacturer (when supplied) or their factory-authorized representatives shall be present for the field acceptance test. *(See Section 4.4 of NFPA 20.)* [**20:**14.2.1]

13.4.6.2 The date, time, and location of the field acceptance test shall be coordinated with the AHJ. [**20:**14.2.2]

13.4.6.3 Pump Room Electrical Wiring. All electric wiring to the fire pump motor(s), including control (multiple pumps) interwiring, normal power supply, alternate power supply where provided, and jockey pump, shall be completed and checked by the electrical contractor prior to the initial startup and acceptance test. [**20:**14.2.3]

13.4.6.4* Certified Pump Curve.

13.4.6.4.1 A copy of the manufacturer's certified pump test characteristic curve shall be available for comparison of the results of the field acceptance test. [**20:**14.2.4.1]

13.4.6.4.1.1 For water mist positive displacement pumping units, a copy of the manufacturer's certified shop test data for both variable speed and non-variable speed operation shall be available for comparison of the results of the field acceptance test. [**20:**14.2.4.1.1]

13.4.6.4.2 At all flow conditions, including those required to be tested in 14.2.6.2 of NFPA 20, the fire pump as installed shall equal the performance as indicated on the manufacturer's certified shop test curve within the accuracy limits of the test equipment. [**20:**14.2.4.2]

13.4.6.4.2.1 For water mist positive displacement pumping units with variable speed features, the pump unit as installed shall equal the performance as indicated on the fire pump unit manufacturer's certified shop test data, with variable speed features deactivated within the accuracy limits of the test equipment. [**20:**14.2.4.2.1]

13.4.6.4.2.2 For water mist positive displacement pumping units, the pump unit as installed shall equal the performance as indicated on the fire pump unit manufacturer's certified shop test data, with variable speed features activated within the accuracy limits of the test equipment. [**20:**14.2.4.2.2]

13.4.6.5 System Demand. The actual unadjusted fire pump discharge flows and pressures installed shall meet or exceed the fire protection system's demand. [**20:**14.2.5]

13.4.7* Record Drawings, Test Reports, Manuals, Special Tools, and Spare Parts.

13.4.7.1 One set of record drawings shall be provided to the building owner. [**20:**14.3.1]

13.4.7.2 One copy of the completed test report shall be provided to the building owner. [**20:**14.3.2]

13.4.7.3* One set of instruction manuals for all major components of the fire pump system shall be supplied by the manufacturer of each major component. [**20:**14.3.3]

13.4.7.4 The manual shall contain the following:

(1) A detailed explanation of the operation of the component
(2) Instructions for routine maintenance
(3) Detailed instructions concerning repairs
(4) Parts list and parts identification
(5) Schematic electrical drawings of controller, transfer switch, and fire pump control panels
(6)*List of recommended spare parts and lubricants
[**20:**14.3.4]

13.4.7.5 Any special tools and testing devices required for routine maintenance shall be available for inspection by the AHJ at the time of the field acceptance test. [20:14.3.5]

13.4.8 Periodic Inspection, Testing, and Maintenance. Fire pumps shall be inspected, tested, and maintained in accordance with NFPA 25, *Standard for the Inspection, Testing, and Maintenance of Water-Based Fire Protection Systems*. [20:14.4]

13.4.9 Component Replacement.

13.4.9.1 Positive Displacement Pumps.

13.4.9.1.1 Whenever a critical path component in a positive displacement fire pump is replaced, as defined in 14.5.2.5 of NFPA 20, a field test of the pump shall be performed. [20:14.5.1.1]

13.4.9.1.2 If components that do not affect performance are replaced, such as shafts, then only a functional test shall be required to ensure proper installation and reassembly. [20:14.5.1.2]

13.4.9.1.3 If components that affect performance are replaced, such as rotors, plungers, and so forth, then a retest shall be conducted by the pump manufacturer or designated representative or qualified persons acceptable to the AHJ. [20:14.5.1.3]

13.4.9.1.3.1 For water mist positive displacement pumping units, the retest shall include the pump unit as a whole. [20:14.5.1.3.1]

13.4.9.1.4 Field Retest Results.

13.4.9.1.4.1 The field retest results shall be compared to the original pump performance as indicated by the fire pump manufacturer's original factory-certified test curve, whenever it is available. [20:14.5.1.4.1]

13.4.9.1.4.2 The field retest results shall meet or exceed the performance characteristics as indicated on the pump nameplate, and the results shall be within the accuracy limits of field testing as stated elsewhere in NFPA 20. [20:14.5.1.4.2]

13.5 Water Supply.

13.5.1 Private fire service mains shall be installed in accordance with NFPA 13, *Standard for the Installation of Sprinkler Systems*, and NFPA 24, *Standard for the Installation of Private Fire Service Mains and Their Appurtenances*.

13.5.2 Where no adequate and reliable water supply exists for fire-fighting purposes, the requirements of NFPA 1142, *Standard on Water Supplies for Suburban and Rural Fire Fighting*, shall apply.

13.5.3* The installation of devices to protect the public water supply from contamination shall comply with the provisions of NFPA 13, *Standard for the Installation of Sprinkler Systems*; NFPA 13D, *Standard for the Installation of Sprinkler Systems in One- and Two-Family Dwellings and Manufactured Homes*; NFPA 13R, *Standard for the Installation of Sprinkler Systems in Low-Rise Residential Occupancies*; NFPA 24, *Standard for the Installation of Private Fire Service Mains and Their Appurtenances*; and the plumbing code.

13.5.3.1 Backflow prevention devices shall be inspected, tested, and maintained in accordance with the requirements of NFPA 25, *Standard for the Inspection, Testing, and Maintenance of Water-Based Fire Protection Systems*.

13.5.4 Inspection, Testing, and Maintenance.

13.5.4.1 A private fire service main installed in accordance with this *Code* shall be properly maintained to provide at least the same level of performance and protection as designed. The owner shall be responsible for maintaining the system and keeping it in good working condition.

13.5.4.2 A private fire service main installed in accordance with this *Code* shall be inspected, tested, and maintained in accordance with NFPA 25.

13.6 Portable Fire Extinguishers.

13.6.1 General Requirements.

13.6.1.1 Scope. The selection, installation, inspection, maintenance, recharging, and testing of portable fire extinguishers shall be in accordance with NFPA 10 and Section 13.6.

13.6.1.1.1 The requirements given herein are minimum. [10:1.1.1]

13.6.1.1.2 The requirements shall not apply to permanently installed systems for fire extinguishment, even where portions of such systems are portable (such as hose and nozzles attached to a fixed supply of extinguishing agent). [10:1.1.2]

13.6.1.2* Where Required. Fire extinguishers shall be provided where required by this *Code* as specified in Table 13.6.1.2 and the referenced codes and standards listed in Chapter 2.

13.6.1.3 Listing and Labeling.

13.6.1.3.1* Portable fire extinguishers used to comply with Section 13.6 shall be listed and labeled and shall meet or exceed all the requirements of one of the following fire test standards and one of the following applicable performance standards:

(1) Fire test standards: ANSI/UL 711, CAN/ULC S508, *Standard for Rating and Testing of Fire Extinguishers*
(2) Performance standards:
   (a) Carbon dioxide types: ANSI/UL 154, CAN/ULC-S503, *Standard for Carbon-Dioxide Fire Extinguishers*
   (b) Dry chemical types: ANSI/UL 299, CAN/ULC-S504, *Standard for Dry Chemical Fire Extinguishers*
   (c) Water types: ANSI/UL 626, CAN/ULC-S507, *Standard for Water Fire Extinguishers*
   (d) Halon types: CAN/ULC-S512, *Standard for Halogenated Agent Hand and Wheeled Fire Extinguishers*
   (e) Film-forming foam types: ANSI/UL 8, CAN/ULC-S554, *Water Based Agent Fire Extinguishers*
   (f) Halocarbon types: ANSI/UL 2129, CAN/ULC-S566, *Standard for Halocarbon Clean Agent Fire Extinguishers* [10:4.1.1]

13.6.1.3.2* Each fire extinguisher shall be marked with the following:

(1) Identification of the listing and labeling organization
(2) Product category indicating the type of extinguisher
(3) Extinguisher classification as indicated in Section 5.3 of NFPA 10
(4) Performance and fire test standards that the extinguisher meets or exceeds [10:4.1.2]

13.6.1.3.2.1 Fire extinguishers manufactured prior to January 1, 1986, shall not be required to comply with 13.6.1.3.2. [10:4.1.2.1]

Table 13.6.1.2 Portable Fire Extinguishers Required

Occupancy Use	Where Required
Ambulatory health care occupancies	Yes
Apartment occupancies[a]	Yes
Assembly occupancies[b]	Yes
Business occupancies	Yes
Day-care occupancies	Yes
Detention and correctional occupancies[c,d]	Yes
Educational occupancies	Yes
Health care occupancies	Yes
Hotel and dormitory occupancies	Yes
Industrial occupancies	Yes
Lodging and rooming house occupancies	Yes
Mercantile occupancies	Yes
Occupancies in special structures	Yes
One- and two-family dwelling occupancies	No
Residential board and care occupancies	Yes
Storage occupancies[e]	Yes

[a]Portable fire extinguishers shall be permitted to be located at exterior locations or interior locations so that all portions of the buildings are within 75 ft (22.8 m) of travel distance to an extinguishing unit.
[b]Portable fire extinguishers are not required in seating or outdoor performance areas.
[c]Access to portable fire extinguishers shall be permitted to be locked.
[d]Portable fire extinguishers shall be permitted to be located at staff locations only.
[e]In storage areas where forklift, powered industrial truck, or cart operators are the primary occupants, fixed extinguishers, as specified in NFPA 10, need not be provided when:

(1) Use of vehicle-mounted extinguishers is approved by the AHJ.
(2) Each vehicle is equipped with a 10 lb, 40-A:80-B:C extinguisher affixed to the vehicle using a mounting bracket approved by the extinguisher manufacturer or the AHJ for vehicular use.
(3) Not less than two spare extinguishers of equal or greater rating are available onsite to replace a discharged extinguisher.
(4) Vehicle operators are trained in the proper operation and use of the extinguisher.
(5) Inspections of vehicle-mounted extinguishers are performed daily.

13.6.1.3.2.2 Halon extinguishers listed and labeled to UL 1093 shall be permitted to be used to comply with the requirements of Section 13.6 when installed, inspected and maintained in accordance with Section 13.6. [**10**:4.1.2.2]

13.6.1.3.3* An organization listing fire extinguishers used to comply with the requirements of Section 13.6 shall utilize a third-party certification program for portable fire extinguishers that meets or exceeds UL 1803, *Standard for Factory Follow-Up on Third Party Certified Portable Fire Extinguishers.* [**10**:4.1.3]

13.6.1.3.3.1 Fire extinguishers manufactured prior to January 1, 1989, shall not be required to comply with 13.6.1.3.3. [**10**:4.1.3.1]

13.6.1.3.3.2 Certification organizations accredited by the Standards Council of Canada shall not be required to comply with 13.6.1.3.3. [**10**:4.1.3.2]

13.6.1.3.3.3 Listed and labeled Class D extinguishing agents intended to be manually applied to combustible metal fires shall comply with the fire test requirements specified in ANSI/UL 711, CAN/ULC-S508, *Standard for Rating and Fire Testing of Fire Extinguishers.* [**10**:4.1.3.3]

13.6.1.3.4 Electrical Conductivity. Extinguishers listed for the Class C rating shall not contain an agent that is a conductor of electricity. [**10**:4.1.4]

13.6.1.3.4.1 In addition to successfully meeting the requirements of ANSI/UL 711, CAN/ULC-S508, *Standard for Rating and Fire Testing of Fire Extinguishers,* water-based agents shall be tested in accordance with ASTM D 5391, *Standard Test for Electrical Conductivity and Resistivity of a Flowing High Purity Water Sample.* [**10**:4.1.4.1]

13.6.1.3.4.2 Fire extinguishers containing water-based agents that have a conductivity higher than 1.00 µS/cm at 77°F (25°C) shall be considered a conductor of electricity and therefore shall not be rated Class C. [**10**:4.1.4.2]

13.6.1.3.4.3 Paragraphs 13.6.1.3.4.1 and 13.6.1.3.4.2 shall apply only to water-based extinguishers manufactured after August 15, 2002. [**10**:4.1.4.3]

13.6.1.4* Identification of Contents. A fire extinguisher shall have a label, tag, or stencil attached to it providing the following information:

(1) The content's product name as it appears on the manufacturer's Material Safety Data Sheet (MSDS)
(2) Listing of the hazardous material identification in accordance with *Hazardous Materials Identification System (HMIS), Implementational Manual* [in Canada, *Workplace Hazardous Materials Identification System* (WHMIS) *Reference Manual*] developed by the National Paint and Coatings Association
(3) List of any hazardous materials that are in excess of 1.0 percent of the contents
(4) List of each chemical in excess of 5.0 percent of the contents
(5) Information as to what is hazardous about the agent in accordance with the MSDS
(6) Manufacturer's or service agency's name, mailing address, and phone number
[**10**:4.2]

13.6.1.5* Instruction Manual.

13.6.1.5.1 The owner or the owner's agent shall be provided with a fire extinguisher instruction manual that details condensed instructions and cautions necessary to the installation, operation, inspection, and maintenance of the fire extinguisher(s). [**10**:4.3.1]

13.6.1.5.2 The manual shall refer to NFPA 10 as a source of detailed instruction. [**10**:4.3.2]

13.6.1.6 Obsolete Fire Extinguishers. The following types of fire extinguishers are considered obsolete and shall be removed from service:

(1) Soda acid
(2) Chemical foam (excluding film-forming agents)
(3) Vaporizing liquid (e.g., carbon tetrachloride)
(4) Cartridge-operated water
(5) Cartridge-operated loaded stream
(6) Copper or brass shell (excluding pump tanks) joined by soft solder or rivets
(7) Carbon dioxide extinguishers with metal horns
(8) Solid charge–type AFFF extinguishers (paper cartridge)

(9) Pressurized water fire extinguishers manufactured prior to 1971
(10) Any extinguisher that needs to be inverted to operate
(11) Any stored pressure extinguisher manufactured prior to 1955
(12) Any extinguishers with 4B, 6B, 8B, 12B, and 16B fire ratings
(13) Stored-pressure water extinguishers with fiberglass shells (pre-1976)
[10:4.4]

13.6.1.6.1* Dry chemical stored-pressure extinguishers manufactured prior to October 1984 shall be removed from service at the next 6-year maintenance interval or the next hydrotest, whichever comes first. [**10:**4.4.1]

13.6.1.6.1.1 Paragraph 13.6.1.6.1 shall not apply to wheeled-type dry chemical stored-pressure fire extinguishers. [**10:**4.4.1.1]

13.6.1.6.2* Any fire extinguisher that can no longer be serviced in accordance with the manufacturer's maintenance manual is considered obsolete and shall be removed from service. [**10:**4.4.2]

13.6.2 Selection of Portable Fire Extinguishers.

13.6.2.1 General Requirements. The selection of fire extinguishers for a given situation shall be determined by the applicable requirements of Sections 5.2 through 5.6 of NFPA 10 and the following factors:

(1) Type of fire most likely to occur
(2) Size of fire most likely to occur
(3) Hazards in the area where the fire is most likely to occur
(4) Energized electrical equipment in the vicinity of the fire
(5) Ambient temperature conditions
(6) Other factors *(see Section H.2 of NFPA 10)*
[**10:**5.1]

13.6.2.1.1 Portable fire extinguishers shall be installed as a first line of defense to cope with fires of limited size, except as required by 5.5.5 of NFPA 10. [**10:**5.1.1]

13.6.2.1.2 The selection of extinguishers shall be independent of whether the building is equipped with automatic sprinklers, standpipe and hose, or other fixed protection equipment. [**10:**5.1.2]

13.6.2.2 Classification of Fires. See 3.3.113.

13.6.2.3 Extinguisher Classification System.

13.6.2.3.1 The classification of fire extinguishers shall consist of a letter that indicates the class of fire on which a fire extinguisher has been found to be effective. [**10:**5.3.1]

13.6.2.3.1.1 Fire extinguishers classified for use on Class A or Class B hazards shall be required to have a rating number preceding the classification letter that indicates the relative extinguishing effectiveness. [**10:**5.3.1.1]

13.6.2.3.1.2 Fire extinguishers classified for use on Class C, Class D, or Class K hazards shall not be required to have a number preceding the classification letter. [**10:**5.3.1.2]

13.6.2.3.2 Fire extinguishers shall be selected for the class(es) of hazards to be protected in accordance with 13.6.2.3.2.1 through 13.6.2.3.2.5. *(For specific hazards, see Section 5.5 of NFPA 10.)* [**10:**5.3.2]

13.6.2.3.2.1* Fire extinguishers for the protection of Class A hazards shall be selected from types that are specifically listed and labeled for use on Class A fires. *(For halon agent–type extinguishers, see 13.6.2.3.2.6.)* [**10:**5.3.2.1]

13.6.2.3.2.2* Fire extinguishers for the protection of Class B hazards shall be selected from types that are specifically listed and labeled for use on Class B fires. *(For halon agent–type extinguishers, see 13.6.2.3.2.6.)* [**10:**5.3.2.2]

13.6.2.3.2.3* Fire extinguishers for the protection of Class C hazards shall be selected from types that are specifically listed and labeled for use on Class C hazards. *(For halon agent–type fire extinguishers, see 13.6.2.3.2.6.)* [**10:**5.3.2.3]

13.6.2.3.2.4* Fire extinguishers and extinguishing agents for the protection of Class D hazards shall be of the types specifically listed and labeled for use on the specific combustible metal hazard. [**10:**5.3.2.4]

13.6.2.3.2.5 Fire extinguishers for the protection of Class K hazards shall be selected from types that are specifically listed and labeled for use on Class K fires. [**10:**5.3.2.5]

13.6.2.3.2.6* Use of halon agent fire extinguishers shall be limited to applications where a clean agent is necessary to extinguish fire efficiently without damaging the equipment or area being protected, or where the use of alternative agents has the potential to cause a hazard to personnel in the area. [**10:**5.3.2.6]

13.6.2.3.2.6.1* Placement of portable fire extinguishers containing halogenated agents shall conform to minimum confined space volume requirement warnings contained on the fire extinguisher nameplates. [**10:**5.3.2.6.1]

13.6.2.3.2.7* Wheeled fire extinguishers shall be considered for hazard protection in areas in which a fire risk assessment has shown the following:

(1) High hazard areas are present
(2) Limited available personnel are present, thereby requiring an extinguisher that has the following features:
    (a) High agent flow rate
    (b) Increased agent stream range
    (c) Increased agent capacity
    [**10:**5.3.2.7]

13.6.2.4 Classification of Hazards.

13.6.2.4.1 Classifying Occupancy Hazard. Rooms or areas shall be classified as being light hazard, ordinary hazard, or extra hazard. [**10:**5.4.1]

13.6.2.4.1.1* Light Hazard. Light hazard occupancies shall be classified as locations where the quantity and combustibility of Class A combustibles and Class B flammables are low and fires with relatively low rates of heat release are expected. These occupancies consist of fire hazards having normally expected quantities of Class A combustible furnishings, and/or the total quantity of Class B flammables typically expected to be present is less than 1 gal (3.8 L) in any room or area. [**10:**5.4.1.1]

13.6.2.4.1.2* Ordinary Hazard. Ordinary hazard occupancies shall be classified as locations where the quantity and combustibility of Class A combustible materials and Class B flammables are moderate and fires with moderate rates of heat release are expected. These occupancies consist of fire hazards that only occasionally contain Class A combustible materials beyond normal anticipated furnishings, and/or the total quantity of Class B flammables typically expected to be present is from 1 gal to 5 gal (3.8 L to 18.9 L) in any room or area. [**10:**5.4.1.2]

13.6.2.4.1.3* Extra Hazard. Extra hazard occupancies shall be classified as locations where the quantity and combustibility of Class A combustible material are high or where high amounts of Class B flammables are present and rapidly developing fires with high rates of heat release are expected. These occupancies consist of fire hazards involved with the storage, packaging, handling, or manufacture of Class A combustibles, and/or the total quantity of Class B flammables expected to be present is more than 5 gal (18.9 L) in any room or area. [**10:**5.4.1.3]

13.6.2.4.1.4 Limited areas of greater or lesser hazard shall be protected as required. [**10:**5.4.1.4]

13.6.2.4.2* Selection by Occupancy. Fire extinguishers shall be provided for the protection of both the building structure and the occupancy hazards contained therein regardless of the presence of any fixed fire suppression systems. [**10:**5.4.2]

13.6.2.4.2.1 Required building protection shall be provided by fire extinguishers for Class A fires. [**10:**5.4.2.1]

13.6.2.4.2.2* Occupancy hazard protection shall be provided by fire extinguishers for such Class A, B, C, D, or K fire potentials as might be present. [**10:**5.4.2.2]

13.6.2.4.2.3 Fire extinguishers provided for building protection shall be permitted to also be considered for the protection of occupancies having a Class A fire potential. [**10:**5.4.2.3]

13.6.2.4.2.4 Buildings having an occupancy hazard subject to Class B or Class C fires, or both, shall have a standard complement of Class A fire extinguishers for building protection, plus additional Class B or Class C fire extinguishers, or both. [**10:**5.4.2.4]

13.6.2.4.2.5 Where fire extinguishers have more than one letter classification (such as 2-A:20-B:C), they shall be permitted to satisfy the requirements of each letter class. [**10:**5.4.2.5]

13.6.2.5 Selection for Specific Hazards.

13.6.2.5.1 Class B Fires.

13.6.2.5.1.1* Extinguishers for Pressurized Flammable Liquids and Pressurized Gas Fires.

13.6.2.5.1.1.1 Selection of fire extinguishers for this type of hazard shall be made on the basis of recommendations by manufacturers of this specialized equipment. [**10:**5.5.1.1.1]

13.6.2.5.1.1.2* Large capacity dry chemical extinguishers of 10 lb (4.54 kg) or greater and a discharge rate of 1 lb/sec (0.45kg/sec) or more shall be used to protect these hazards. [**10:**5.5.1.1.2]

13.6.2.5.2 Three-Dimensional Fires. Large capacity dry chemical extinguishers of 10 lb (4.54 kg) or greater and having a discharge rate of 1 lb/sec (0.45 kg/sec) or more shall be used to protect these hazards. [**10:**5.5.2]

13.6.2.5.3 Water-Soluble Flammable Liquid Fires (Polar Solvents). Aqueous film-forming foam (AFFF) and film-forming fluoroprotein foam (FFFP) types of fire extinguishers shall not be used for the protection of water-soluble flammable liquids, such as alcohols, acetone, esters, ketones, and so forth, unless specifically referenced on the fire extinguisher nameplate. [**10:**5.5.3]

13.6.2.5.4 Obstacle Fires. Selection of a fire extinguisher for this type of hazard shall be based on one of the following:

(1) Extinguisher containing a vapor-suppressing foam agent
(2)*Multiple extinguishers containing non-vapor-suppressing Class B agents intended for simultaneous application
(3) Larger capacity extinguishers of 10 lb (4.54 kg) or greater and a minimum discharge rate of 1 lb/sec (0.45 kg/sec) [**10:**5.5.4]

13.6.2.5.5* Class K Cooking Media Fires. Fire extinguishers provided for the protection of cooking appliances that use combustible cooking media (vegetable or animal oils and fats) shall be listed and labeled for Class K fires. [**10:**5.5.5]

13.6.2.5.5.1 Class K fire extinguishers manufactured after January 1, 2002, shall not be equipped with extended wand–type discharge devices. [**10:**5.5.5.1]

13.6.2.5.5.2 Fire extinguishers installed specifically for the protection of cooking appliances that use combustible cooking media (animal or vegetable oils and fats) without a Class K rating shall be removed from service. [**10:**5.5.5.2]

13.6.2.5.5.3* Where a hazard is protected by an automatic fire protection system, a placard shall be conspicuously placed near the extinguisher that states that the fire protection system shall be actuated prior to using the fire extinguisher. [**10:**5.5.5.3]

13.6.2.5.6* Electronic Equipment Fires. Fire extinguishers for the protection of delicate electronic equipment shall be selected from types specifically listed and labeled for Class C hazards. *(See 13.6.2.3.2.3.)* [**10:**5.5.6]

13.6.2.5.6.1* Dry chemical fire extinguishers shall not be installed for the protection of delicate electronic equipment. [**10:**5.5.6.1]

13.6.2.5.7 Areas Containing Oxidizers.

13.6.2.5.7.1 Only water-type extinguishers shall be installed in areas containing oxidizers, such as pool chemicals. [**10:**5.5.7.1]

13.6.2.5.7.2* Multipurpose dry chemical fire extinguishers shall not be installed in areas containing oxidizers, such as pool chemicals. [**10:**5.5.7.2]

13.6.2.5.8 Class D Combustible Metal Fires. Fire extinguishers or containers of Class D extinguishing agents provided for the protection of Class D fires shall be listed and labeled for Class D fires. [**10:**5.5.8]

13.6.2.5.8.1* Class D fire extinguishers and agents shall be compatible with the specific metal for which protection is provided. [**10:**5.5.8.1]

13.6.2.6 Selection for Specific Locations.

> Paragraph 13.6.2.6.1 was revised by a tentative interim amendment. (TIA). See page 1.

13.6.2.6.1* Where portable fire extinguishers are required to be installed, the following documents shall be reviewed for the occupancies outlined in their respective scopes:

(1) This *Code*
(2) NFPA 2, *Hydrogen Technologies Code*
(3) NFPA 22, *Standard for Water Tanks for Private Fire Protection*
(4) NFPA 30, *Flammable and Combustible Liquids Code*

(5) NFPA 30A, *Code for Motor Fuel Dispensing Facilities and Repair Garages*
(6) NFPA 33, *Standard for Spray Application Using Flammable or Combustible Materials*
(7) NFPA 40, *Standard for the Storage and Handling of Cellulose Nitrate Film*
(8) NFPA 45, *Standard on Fire Protection for Laboratories Using Chemicals*
(9) NFPA 51, *Standard for the Design and Installation of Oxygen–Fuel Gas Systems for Welding, Cutting, and Allied Processes*
(10) NFPA 51B, *Standard for Fire Prevention During Welding, Cutting, and Other Hot Work*
(11) NFPA 52, *Vehicular Gaseous Fuel Systems Code*
(12) NFPA 58, *Liquefied Petroleum Gas Code*
(13) NFPA 59, *Utility LP-Gas Plant Code*
(14) NFPA 59A, *Standard for the Production, Storage, and Handling of Liquefied Natural Gas (LNG)*
(15) *NFPA 72, National Fire Alarm and Signaling Code*
(16) NFPA 75, *Standard for the Fire Protection of Information Technology Equipment*
(17) NFPA 76, *Standard for the Fire Protection of Telecommunications Facilities*
(18) NFPA 96, *Standard for Ventilation Control and Fire Protection of Commercial Cooking Operations*
(19) NFPA 99, *Health Care Facilities Code*
(20) NFPA 99B, *Standard for Hypobaric Facilities*
(21) NFPA 101, *Life Safety Code*
(22) NFPA 102, *Standard for Grandstands, Folding and Telescopic Seating, Tents, and Membrane Structures*
(23) NFPA 115, *Standard for Laser Fire Protection*
(24) NFPA 120, *Standard for Fire Prevention and Control in Coal Mines*
(25) NFPA 122, *Standard for Fire Prevention and Control in Metal/Nonmetal Mining and Metal Mineral Processing Facilities*
(26) NFPA 130, *Standard for Fixed Guideway Transit and Passenger Rail Systems*
(27) NFPA 140, *Standard on Motion Picture and Television Production Studio Soundstages, Approved Production Facilities, and Production Locations*
(28) NFPA 150, *Standard on Fire and Life Safety in Animal Housing Facilities*
(29) NFPA 160, *Standard for the Use of Flame Effects Before an Audience*
(30) NFPA 232, *Standard for the Protection of Records*
(31) NFPA 241, *Standard for Safeguarding Construction, Alteration, and Demolition Operations*
(32) NFPA 301, *Code for Safety to Life from Fire on Merchant Vessels*
(33) NFPA 302, *Fire Protection Standard for Pleasure and Commercial Motor Craft*
(34) NFPA 303, *Fire Protection Standard for Marinas and Boatyards*
(35) NFPA 307, *Standard for the Construction and Fire Protection of Marine Terminals, Piers, and Wharves*
(36) NFPA 326, *Standard for the Safeguarding of Tanks and Containers for Entry, Cleaning, or Repair*
(37) NFPA 385, *Standard for Tank Vehicles for Flammable and Combustible Liquids*
(38) NFPA 400, *Hazardous Materials Code*
(39) NFPA 403, *Standard for Aircraft Rescue and Fire-Fighting Services at Airports*
(40) NFPA 407, *Standard for Aircraft Fuel Servicing*
(41) NFPA 408, *Standard for Aircraft Hand Portable Fire Extinguishers*
(42) NFPA 409, *Standard on Aircraft Hangars*
(43) NFPA 410, *Standard on Aircraft Maintenance*
(44) NFPA 418, *Standard for Heliports*
(45) NFPA 423, *Standard for Construction and Protection of Aircraft Engine Test Facilities*
(46) NFPA 484, *Standard for Combustible Metals*
(47) NFPA 495, *Explosive Materials Code*
(48) NFPA 498, *Standard for Safe Havens and Interchange Lots for Vehicles Transporting Explosives*
(49) NFPA 501A, *Standard for Fire Safety Criteria for Manufactured Home Installations, Sites, and Communities*
(50) NFPA 502, *Standard for Road Tunnels, Bridges, and Other Limited Access Highways*
(51) NFPA 505, *Fire Safety Standard for Powered Industrial Trucks Including Type Designations, Areas of Use, Conversions, Maintenance, and Operations*
(52) NFPA 655, *Standard for Prevention of Sulfur Fires and Explosions*
(53) NFPA 731, *Standard for the Installation of Electronic Premises Security Systems*
(54) NFPA 801, *Standard for Fire Protection for Facilities Handling Radioactive Materials*
(55) NFPA 804, *Standard for Fire Protection for Advanced Light Water Reactor Electric Generating Plants*
(56) NFPA 805, *Performance-Based Standard for Fire Protection for Light Water Reactor Electric Generating Plants*
(57) NFPA 820, *Standard for Fire Protection in Wastewater Treatment and Collection Facilities*
(58) NFPA 909, *Code for the Protection of Cultural Resource Properties — Museums, Libraries, and Places of Worship*
(59) NFPA 914, *Code for Fire Protection of Historic Structures*
(60) NFPA 1123, *Code for Fireworks Display*
(61) NFPA 1125, *Code for the Manufacture of Model Rocket and High Power Rocket Motors*
(62) NFPA 1126, *Standard for the Use of Pyrotechnics Before a Proximate Audience*
(63) NFPA 1141, *Standard for Fire Protection Infrastructure for Land Development in Wildland, Rural, and Suburban Areas*
(64) NFPA 1192, *Standard on Recreational Vehicles*
(65) NFPA 1194, *Standard for Recreational Vehicle Parks and Campgrounds*
(66) NFPA 1221, *Standard for the Installation, Maintenance, and Use of Emergency Services Communications Systems*
(67) NFPA 1901, *Standard for Automotive Fire Apparatus*
(68) NFPA 1906, *Standard for Wildland Fire Apparatus*
(69) NFPA 1925, *Standard on Marine Fire-Fighting Vessels*
(70) *NFPA 5000, Building Construction and Safety Code* [**10**:5.6.1]

13.6.2.6.2 In no case shall the requirements of the documents in 13.6.2.6.1 be less than those specified in Section 13.6 and Chapter 2. [**10**:5.6.2]

13.6.3 Installation of Portable Fire Extinguishers.

13.6.3.1 General.

13.6.3.1.1* Number of Extinguishers. The minimum number of fire extinguishers needed to protect a property shall be determined as outlined in 13.6.3. [**10**:6.1.1]

13.6.3.1.1.1 The installation of extinguishers shall be independent of whether the building is equipped with automatic sprinklers, standpipe and hose, or other fixed protection equipment. [**10**:6.1.1.1]

13.6.3.1.1.2 Additional extinguishers shall be permitted to be installed to provide more protection as necessary. [**10**:6.1.1.2]

13.6.3.1.1.3 Fire extinguishers having ratings less than those specified in Table 13.6.3.2.1.1 and Table 13.6.3.3.1.1 shall be permitted to be installed, provided they are not used in fulfilling the minimum protective requirements of this subsection, except as modified in 13.6.3.2.1.4, 13.6.3.2.1.5, and 13.6.3.3.1.1.1. [**10:**6.1.1.3]

13.6.3.1.2 Extinguisher Readiness. Portable fire extinguishers shall be maintained in a fully charged and operable condition and shall be kept in their designated places at all times when they are not being used. [**10:**6.1.2]

13.6.3.1.3 Placement.

13.6.3.1.3.1 Fire extinguishers shall be conspicuously located where they are readily accessible and immediately available in the event of fire. [**10:**6.1.3.1]

13.6.3.1.3.2 Fire extinguishers shall be located along normal paths of travel, including exits from areas. [**10:**6.1.3.2]

13.6.3.1.3.3 Visual Obstructions.

13.6.3.1.3.3.1 Fire extinguishers shall not be obstructed or obscured from view. [**10:**6.1.3.3.1]

13.6.3.1.3.3.2* In large rooms and in certain locations where visual obstructions cannot be completely avoided, means shall be provided to indicate the extinguisher location. [**10:**6.1.3.3.2]

13.6.3.1.3.3.3 Where signs are used to indicate fire extinguisher location, the signs shall comply with the following:

(1) They shall be located in close proximity to the extinguisher.
(2) They shall be visible from the normal path of travel. [**10:**6.1.3.3.3]

13.6.3.1.3.4* Portable fire extinguishers other than wheeled extinguishers shall be installed using any of the following means:

(1) Securely on a hanger intended for the extinguisher
(2) In the bracket supplied by the extinguisher manufacturer
(3) In a listed bracket approved for such purpose
(4) In cabinets or wall recesses [**10:**6.1.3.4]

13.6.3.1.3.5 Wheeled fire extinguishers shall be located in designated locations. [**10:**6.1.3.5]

13.6.3.1.3.6 Fire extinguishers installed in vehicles or under other conditions where they are subject to dislodgement shall be installed in approved strap-type brackets specifically designed for this application. [**10:**6.1.3.6]

13.6.3.1.3.7 Fire extinguishers installed under conditions where they are subject to physical damage (e.g., from impact, vibration, the environment) shall be protected against damage. [**10:**6.1.3.7]

13.6.3.1.3.8 Installation Height.

13.6.3.1.3.8.1 Fire extinguishers having a gross weight not exceeding 40 lb (18.14 kg) shall be installed so that the top of the fire extinguisher is not more than 5 ft (1.53 m) above the floor. [**10:**6.1.3.8.1]

13.6.3.1.3.8.2 Fire extinguishers having a gross weight greater than 40 lb (18.14 kg) (except wheeled types) shall be installed so that the top of the fire extinguisher is not more than 3½ ft (1.07 m) above the floor. [**10:**6.1.3.8.2]

13.6.3.1.3.8.3 In no case shall the clearance between the bottom of the hand portable fire extinguisher and the floor be less than 4 in. (102 mm). [**10:**6.1.3.8.3]

13.6.3.1.3.9 Label Visibility.

13.6.3.1.3.9.1 Extinguishers' operating instructions shall be located on the front of the extinguisher and shall be clearly visible. [**10:**6.1.3.9.1]

13.6.3.1.3.9.2 Hazardous materials identification systems (HMIS) labels, 6-year maintenance labels, hydrostatic test labels, or other labels shall not be located or placed on the front of the extinguisher. [**10:**6.1.3.9.2]

13.6.3.1.3.9.3 The restrictions of 13.6.3.1.3.9.2 shall not apply to original manufacturer's labels, labels that specifically relate to the extinguisher's operation or fire classification, or inventory control labels specific to that extinguisher. [**10:**6.1.3.9.3]

13.6.3.1.3.10 Cabinets.

13.6.3.1.3.10.1 Cabinets housing fire extinguishers shall not be locked, except where fire extinguishers are subject to malicious use and cabinets include a means of emergency access. [**10:**6.1.3.10.1]

13.6.3.1.3.10.2 The location of fire extinguishers as described in 13.6.3.1.3.3.2 shall be marked conspicuously. [**10:**6.1.3.10.2]

13.6.3.1.3.10.3 Fire extinguishers mounted in cabinets or wall recesses shall be placed so that the fire extinguisher's operating instructions face outward. [**10:**6.1.3.10.3]

13.6.3.1.3.10.4* Where fire extinguishers are installed in closed cabinets that are exposed to elevated temperatures, the cabinets shall be provided with screened openings and drains. [**10:**6.1.3.10.4]

13.6.3.1.3.10.5 Cabinets or wall recesses for fire extinguishers shall be installed such that the extinguisher mounting heights specified in 13.6.3.1.3.8.1 and 13.6.3.1.3.8.2 are met. [**10:**6.1.3.10.5]

13.6.3.1.3.11* Fire extinguishers shall not be exposed to temperatures outside of the listed temperature range shown on the fire extinguisher label. [**10:**6.1.3.11]

13.6.3.1.4 Antifreeze.

13.6.3.1.4.1 Fire extinguishers containing only plain water shall be protected to temperatures as low as -40°F (-40°C) by the addition of an antifreeze that is stipulated on the fire extinguisher nameplate. [**10:**6.1.4.1]

13.6.3.1.4.2 Calcium chloride solutions shall not be used in stainless steel fire extinguishers. [**10:**6.1.4.2]

13.6.3.1.5 Electronic Monitoring and Alarm System.

13.6.3.1.5.1 The connection to the electronic monitoring device shall be continuously supervised for integrity. [**10:**6.1.5.1]

13.6.3.1.5.2 The power source for the electronic monitoring device shall be supervised for continuity of power. [**10:**6.1.5.2]

13.6.3.2 Installations for Class A Hazards.

13.6.3.2.1 Fire Extinguisher Size and Placement for Class A Hazards.

13.6.3.2.1.1 Minimal sizes of fire extinguishers for the listed grades of hazards shall be provided on the basis of Table 13.6.3.2.1.1, except as modified by 13.6.3.2.1.4 and 13.6.3.2.1.5. [**10:**6.2.1.1]

Table 13.6.3.2.1.1 Fire Extinguisher Size and Placement for Class A Hazards

Criteria	Light Hazard Occupancy	Ordinary Hazard Occupancy	Extra Hazard Occupancy
Minimum rated single extinguisher	2-A	2-A	4-A
Maximum floor area per unit of A	3000 ft²	1500 ft²	1000 ft²
Maximum floor area for extinguisher	11,250 ft²	11,250 ft²	11,250 ft²
Maximum travel distance to extinguisher	75 ft	75 ft	75 ft

For SI units, 1 ft = 0.305 m; 1 ft² = 0.0929 m².
Note: For maximum floor area explanations, see E.3.3 of NFPA 10.
[**10:** Table 6.2.1.1]

13.6.3.2.1.2 The minimum number of extinguishers for Class A hazards shall be sufficient to meet the requirements of 13.6.3.2.1.2.1 through 13.6.3.2.1.2.3. [**10:**6.2.1.2]

13.6.3.2.1.2.1 The minimum number of fire extinguishers for Class A hazards for each floor of a building shall be determined by dividing the total floor area by the maximum area to be protected per extinguisher as determined by Table 13.6.3.2.1.1. *(See Annex E of NFPA 10.)* [**10:**6.2.1.2.1]

13.6.3.2.1.2.2 Fire extinguishers shall be located so that the maximum travel distances shall not exceed 75 ft (22.9 m), except as modified by 13.6.3.2.1.4. [**10:**6.2.1.2.2]

13.6.3.2.1.2.3 Where the quantity of extinguishers required to satisfy 13.6.3.2.1.2.2 exceeds the number calculated in 13.6.3.2.1.2.1, additional extinguishers shall be installed. [**10:**6.2.1.2.3]

13.6.3.2.1.3 Smaller fire extinguishers that are rated on Class B and Class C fires but do not have a minimum 1-A rating shall not be used to meet the requirements of 13.6.3.2.1. [**10:**6.2.1.3]

13.6.3.2.1.4 Fire extinguishers of lesser rating shall be permitted to be installed but shall not be considered as fulfilling any part of the requirements of Table 13.6.3.2.1.1, except as permitted in 13.6.3.2.1.4(A) and 13.6.3.2.1.4(B). [**10:**6.2.1.3.1]

(A) Up to two water-type extinguishers, each with 1-A rating, shall be permitted to be used to fulfill the requirements of one 2-A rated extinguisher. [**10:**6.2.1.3.1.1]

(B) Two 2½ gal (9.46 L) water-type extinguishers shall be permitted to be used to fulfill the requirements of one 4-A rated extinguisher. [**10:**6.2.1.3.1.2]

13.6.3.2.1.5 Up to one-half of the complement of fire extinguishers specified in Table 13.6.3.2.1.1 shall be permitted to be replaced by uniformly spaced 1½ in. (38 mm) hose stations for use by the occupants of the building. [**10:**6.2.1.4]

13.6.3.2.1.5.1 Where hose stations are so provided, they shall conform to NFPA 14, *Standard for the Installation of Standpipe and Hose Systems.* [**10:**6.2.1.4.1]

13.6.3.2.1.5.2 The location of hose stations and the placement of fire extinguishers shall be such that the hose stations do not replace more than every other fire extinguisher. [**10:**6.2.1.4.2]

13.6.3.2.1.6 Where the area of the floor of a building is less than that specified in Table 13.6.3.2.1.1, at least one fire extinguisher of the minimum size required shall be provided. [**10:**6.2.1.5]

13.6.3.2.1.7 The protection requirements shall be permitted to be fulfilled with fire extinguishers of higher rating, provided the travel distance to such larger fire extinguishers does not exceed 75 ft (22.9 m). [**10:**6.2.1.6]

13.6.3.3 Installations for Class B Hazards.

13.6.3.3.1 Spill Fires.

13.6.3.3.1.1 Minimum ratings of fire extinguishers for the listed grades of hazard shall be provided in accordance with Table 13.6.3.3.1.1 [**10:**6.3.1.1].

Table 13.6.3.3.1.1 Fire Extinguisher Size and Placement for Class B Hazards

Type of Hazard	Basic Minimum Extinguisher Rating	Maximum Travel Distance to Extinguishers	
		ft	m
Light (low)	5-B	30	9.14
	10-B	50	15.25
Ordinary (moderate)	10-B	30	9.14
	20-B	50	15.25
Extra (high)	40-B	30	9.14
	80-B	50	15.25

Note: The specified ratings do not imply that fires of the magnitudes indicated by these ratings will occur, but rather they are provided to give the operators more time and agent to handle difficult spill fires that have the potential to occur.
[**10:** Table 6.3.1.1]

13.6.3.3.1.1.1 Two or more fire extinguishers of lower rating shall not be used to fulfill the protection requirements of Table 13.6.3.3.1.1 except as permitted by 13.6.3.3.1.1.2 and 13.6.3.3.1.1.3. [**10:**6.3.1.1.1]

13.6.3.3.1.1.2 Up to three AFFF or FFFP fire extinguishers of at least 2½ gal (9.46 L) capacity shall be permitted to be used to fulfill extra hazard requirements. [**10:**6.3.1.1.2]

13.6.3.3.1.1.3 Two AFFF or FFFP fire extinguishers of at least 1.6 gal (6 L) capacity shall be permitted to be used to fulfill ordinary hazard requirements. [**10:**6.3.1.1.3]

13.6.3.3.1.2 Fire extinguishers of lesser rating, desired for small specific hazards within the general hazard area, shall be permitted to be installed but shall not be considered as fulfilling any part of the requirements of Table 13.6.3.3.1.1, unless permitted by 13.6.3.3.1.1.1 or 13.6.3.3.1.1.2. [**10:**6.3.1.2]

13.6.3.3.1.3 Fire extinguishers shall be located so that the maximum travel distances do not exceed those specified in Table 13.6.3.3.1.1. [**10:**6.3.1.3]

13.6.3.3.1.4 The protection requirements shall be permitted to be fulfilled with fire extinguishers of higher ratings, provided the travel distance to such larger fire extinguishers does not exceed 50 ft (15.25 m). [**10**:6.3.1.4]

13.6.3.3.2 Flammable Liquids of Appreciable Depth.

13.6.3.3.2.1 Portable fire extinguishers shall not be installed as the sole protection for flammable liquid hazards of appreciable depth where the surface area exceeds 10 ft^2 (0.93 m^2). [**10**:6.3.2.1]

13.6.3.3.2.2* Where personnel who are trained in extinguishing fires in the protected hazards are located on the premises and capable of responding immediately, the maximum surface area shall not exceed 20 ft^2 (1.86 m^2). [**10**:6.3.2.2]

13.6.3.3.2.3 For flammable liquid hazards of appreciable depth, a Class B fire extinguisher shall be provided on the basis of at least 2 numerical units of Class B extinguishing potential per 1 ft^2 (0.09 m^2) of flammable liquid surface of the largest hazard area. [**10**:6.3.2.3]

13.6.3.3.2.4 AFFF- or FFFP-type fire extinguishers shall be permitted to be provided on the basis of 1-B of protection per 1 ft^2 (0.09 m^2) of hazard. *(For fires involving water-soluble flammable liquids, see 5.5.3 of NFPA 10.)* [**10**:6.3.2.4]

13.6.3.3.2.5 Two or more fire extinguishers of lower ratings, other than AFFF- or FFFP-type fire extinguishers, shall not be used in lieu of the fire extinguisher required for the largest hazard area. [**10**:6.3.2.5]

13.6.3.3.2.6 Up to three AFFF- or FFFP-type fire extinguishers shall be permitted to fulfill the requirements, provided the sum of the Class B ratings meets or exceeds the value required for the largest hazard area. [**10**:6.3.2.6]

13.6.3.3.2.7 Travel distances for portable fire extinguishers shall not exceed 50 ft (15.25 m). *(See Annex E of NFPA 10.)* [**10**:6.3.2.7]

13.6.3.3.2.7.1 Scattered or widely separated hazards shall be individually protected. [**10**:6.3.2.7.1]

13.6.3.3.2.7.2 A fire extinguisher in the proximity of a hazard shall be located to be accessible in the presence of a fire without undue danger to the operator. [**10**:6.3.2.7.2]

13.6.3.3.3 Obstacle, Gravity/Three-Dimensional, and Pressure Fire Hazards.

13.6.3.3.3.1 Where hand portable fire extinguishers are installed or positioned for obstacle, gravity/three-dimensional, or pressure fire hazards, the actual travel distance to hazard shall not exceed 30 ft (1 m) unless otherwise specified *(See 5.6.1 of NFPA 10.)* [**10**:6.3.3.1]

13.6.3.3.3.2 Where wheeled fire extinguishers of 125 lb (56.7 kg) agent capacity or larger are installed or positioned for obstacle, gravity/three-dimensional, or pressure fire hazards, the actual travel distance to hazard shall not exceed 100 ft (30.5 m) unless otherwise specified. *(See 5.6.1 of NFPA 10.)* [**10**:6.3.3.2]

13.6.3.4* Installations for Class C Hazards.

13.6.3.4.1 Fire extinguishers with Class C ratings shall be required where energized electrical equipment can be encountered. [**10**:6.4.1]

13.6.3.4.2 The requirement in 13.6.3.4.1 shall include situations where fire either directly involves or surrounds electrical equipment. [**10**:6.4.2]

13.6.3.4.3 Because fire is a Class A or Class B hazard, the fire extinguishers shall be sized and located on the basis of the anticipated Class A or Class B hazard. [**10**:6.4.3]

13.6.3.5 Installations for Class D Hazards.

13.6.3.5.1* Fire extinguishers or extinguishing agents with Class D ratings shall be provided for fires involving combustible metals. [**10**:6.5.1]

13.6.3.5.2 Fire extinguishers or extinguishing agents (media) shall be located not more than 75 ft (22.9 m) of travel distance from the Class D hazard. *(See Section E.6 of NFPA 10.)* [**10**:6.5.2]

13.6.3.5.3* Portable fire extinguishers or extinguishing agents (media) for Class D hazards shall be provided in those work areas where combustible metal powders, flakes, shavings, chips, or similarly sized products are generated. [**10**:6.5.3]

13.6.3.5.4* Size determination shall be on the basis of the specific combustible metal, its physical particle size, area to be covered, and recommendations by the fire extinguisher manufacturer based on data from control tests. [**10**:6.5.4]

13.6.3.6 Installations for Class K Hazards.

13.6.3.6.1 Class K fire extinguishers shall be provided for hazards where there is a potential for fires involving combustible cooking media (vegetable or animal oils and fats). [**10**:6.6.1]

13.6.3.6.2 Maximum travel distance shall not exceed 30 ft (9.15 m) from the hazard to the extinguishers. [**10**:6.6.2]

13.6.3.6.3 All solid fuel cooking appliances (whether or not under a hood) with fire boxes of 5 ft^3 (0.14 m^3) volume or less shall have at least a listed 2-A rated water-type fire extinguisher or 1.6 gal (6 L) wet chemical fire extinguisher that is listed for Class K fires. [**10**:6.6.3]

13.6.4 Inspection, Maintenance, and Recharging.

13.6.4.1* General.

13.6.4.1.1 Responsibility. The owner or designated agent or occupant of a property in which fire extinguishers are located shall be responsible for inspection, maintenance, and recharging. *(See 13.6.4.1.2.)* [**10**:7.1.1]

13.6.4.1.2 Personnel.

13.6.4.1.2.1* Persons performing maintenance and recharging of extinguishers shall be certified. [**10**:7.1.2.1]

13.6.4.1.2.1.1 Persons training to become certified shall be permitted to perform maintenance and recharging of extinguishers under the direct supervision and in the immediate presence of a certified person. [**10**:7.1.2.1.1]

13.6.4.1.2.1.2 Certification requires that a person pass a test administered by an organization acceptable to the AHJ. [**10**:7.1.2.1.2]

13.6.4.1.2.1.3 The test shall at a minimum be based upon knowledge of the chapters and annexes of NFPA 10. [**10**:7.1.2.1.3]

13.6.4.1.2.1.4 The testing process shall permit persons to use NFPA 10 during the test. [**10**:7.1.2.1.4]

13.6.4.1.2.1.5 Persons passing the test required in 13.6.4.1.2.1.2 shall be issued a document or a certificate. [**10:**7.1.2.1.5]

13.6.4.1.2.1.6 The document or certificate shall be made available when requested by the AHJ. [**10:**7.1.2.1.6]

13.6.4.1.2.2* Persons performing maintenance and recharging of extinguishers shall be trained and shall have available the appropriate manufacturer's servicing manual(s), the correct tools, recharge materials, lubricants, and manufacturer's replacement parts or parts specifically listed for use in the fire extinguisher. [**10:**7.1.2.2]

13.6.4.1.2.3* Persons performing inspections shall not be required to be certified. [**10:**7.1.2.3]

13.6.4.1.3 Replacement While Servicing. Fire extinguishers removed from service for maintenance or recharging shall be replaced by a fire extinguisher suitable for the type of hazard being protected and shall be of at least equal rating. [**10:**7.1.3]

13.6.4.1.4 Tags or Labels.

13.6.4.1.4.1 Tags or labels intended for recording inspections, maintenance, or recharging shall be affixed so as not to obstruct the fire extinguisher use, fire extinguisher classification, or manufacturer's labels. [**10:**7.1.4.1]

13.6.4.1.4.2 Labels indicating fire extinguisher use or classification or both shall be permitted to be placed on the front of the fire extinguisher. [**10:**7.1.4.2]

13.6.4.2 Inspection.

13.6.4.2.1 Inspection Frequency.

13.6.4.2.1.1* Fire extinguishers shall be manually inspected when initially placed in service. [**10:**7.2.1.1]

13.6.4.2.1.2* Fire extinguishers and Class D extinguishing agents shall be inspected either manually or by means of an electronic monitoring device/system at intervals not exceeding 31 days. [**10:**7.2.1.2]

13.6.4.2.1.2.1 Fire extinguishers and Class D extinguishing agents shall be inspected at least once per calendar month. [**10:**7.2.1.2.1]

13.6.4.2.1.3* Fire extinguishers and Class D extinguishing agents shall be manually inspected daily or weekly when conditions exist that indicate the need for more frequent inspections. [**10:**7.2.1.3]

13.6.4.2.1.4 Extinguishers that are electronically monitored for location only, such as those monitored by means of a switch to indicate when the extinguisher is removed from its bracket or cabinet, shall be manually inspected in accordance with 13.6.4.2.2. [**10:**7.2.1.4]

13.6.4.2.2 Inspection Procedures. Periodic inspection or electronic monitoring of fire extinguishers shall include a check of at least the following items:

(1) Location in designated place
(2) No obstruction to access or visibility
(3) Pressure gauge reading or indicator in the operable range or position
(4) Fullness determined by weighing or hefting
(5) Condition of tires, wheels, carriage, hose, and nozzle for wheeled extinguishers
(6) Indicator for nonrechargeable extinguishers using push-to-test pressure indicators [**10:**7.2.2]

13.6.4.2.2.1* In addition to 13.6.4.2.2, fire extinguishers shall be visually inspected in accordance with 13.6.4.2.2.2 if they are located where any of the following conditions exists:

(1) High frequency of fires in the past
(2) Severe hazards
(3) Locations that make fire extinguishers susceptible to mechanical injury or physical damage
(4) Exposure to abnormal temperatures or corrosive atmospheres [**10:**7.2.2.1]

13.6.4.2.2.2 Where required by 13.6.4.2.2.1, the following inspection procedures shall be in addition to those addressed in 13.6.4.2.2:

(1) Verify that operating instructions on nameplates are legible and face outward
(2) Check for broken or missing safety seals and tamper indicators
(3) Examine for obvious physical damage, corrosion, leakage, or clogged nozzle [**10:**7.2.2.2]

13.6.4.2.2.3 Inspection Procedure for Containers of Class D Extinguishing Agent. Periodic inspection of containers of Class D extinguishing agent used to protect Class D hazards shall include verification of at least the following:

(1) Located in designated place
(2) No obstruction to access or visibility
(3) Lid is sealed
(4) Fullness by hefting or weighing
(5) No obvious physical damage to container [**10:**7.2.2.3]

13.6.4.2.3 Corrective Action. When an inspection of any fire extinguisher reveals a deficiency in any of the conditions in 13.6.4.2.2 or 13.6.4.2.2.2, immediate corrective action shall be taken. [**10:**7.2.3]

13.6.4.2.3.1 Rechargeable Fire Extinguishers. When an inspection of any rechargeable fire extinguisher reveals a deficiency in any of the conditions in 13.6.4.2.2(3), 13.6.4.2.2(4), 13.6.4.2.2 (5),or 13.6.4.2.2(1) through 13.6.4.2.2(3), the extinguisher shall be subjected to applicable maintenance procedures. [**10:**7.2.3.1]

13.6.4.2.3.2 Nonrechargeable Dry Chemical Fire Extinguisher. When an inspection of any nonrechargeable dry chemical fire extinguisher reveals a deficiency in any of the conditions listed in 13.6.4.2.2(3), 13.6.4.2.2(4),13.6.4.2.2(6), or 13.6.4.2.2.2(1) through 13.6.4.2.2.2(3), the extinguisher shall be removed from further use, discharged, and destroyed at the direction of the owner or returned to the manufacturer. [**10:**7.2.3.2]

13.6.4.2.3.3 Nonrechargeable Halon Agent Fire Extinguisher. When an inspection of any nonrechargeable fire extinguisher containing a halon agent reveals a deficiency in any of the conditions listed in 13.6.4.2.2(3), 13.6.4.2.2(4), 13.6.4.2.2(6), or 13.6.4.2.2.2(1) through 13.6.4.2.2.2(3), the extinguisher shall be removed from service, shall not be discharged, and shall be returned to the manufacturer, a fire equipment dealer, or a distributor to permit recovery of the halon. [**10:**7.2.3.3]

13.6.4.2.4 Inspection Record Keeping.

13.6.4.2.4.1 Manual Inspection Records.

13.6.4.2.4.1.1 Where manual inspections are conducted, records for manual inspections shall be kept on a tag or label attached to the fire extinguisher, on an inspection checklist maintained on file, or by an electronic method. [**10:**7.2.4.1.1]

13.6.4.2.4.1.2 Where manual inspections are conducted, the month and year the manual inspection was performed and the initials of the person performing the inspection shall be recorded. [**10:**7.2.4.1.2]

13.6.4.2.4.1.3 Personnel making manual inspections shall keep records of all fire extinguishers inspected, including those found to require corrective action. [**10:**7.2.4.1.3]

13.6.4.2.4.1.4 Records for manual inspection shall be kept to demonstrate that at least the last 12 monthly inspections have been performed. [**10:**7.2.4.1.4]

13.6.4.2.4.2 Electronic Inspection Records.

13.6.4.2.4.2.1 Where electronically monitored systems are employed for inspections, records shall be kept for fire extinguishers found to require corrective action. [**10:**7.2.4.2.1]

13.6.4.2.4.2.2 Records for electronic monitoring shall be kept to demonstrate that at least the last 12 monthly inspections have been performed. [**10:**7.2.4.2.2]

13.6.4.2.4.2.3 For electronically monitored fire extinguishers, where the extinguisher causes a signal at a control unit when a deficiency in any of the conditions listed in 13.6.4.2.2 occurs, record keeping shall be provided in the form of an electronic event log at the control panel. [**10:**7.2.4.2.3]

13.6.4.3 Extinguisher Maintenance.

13.6.4.3.1* Maintenance Procedures. Where required by another section of this *Code* or NFPA 10, maintenance procedures shall include the procedures detailed in the manufacturer's service manual and a thorough examination of the basic elements of the fire extinguisher, including the following:

(1) Mechanical parts of all fire extinguishers
(2) Extinguishing agent
(3) Expelling means
(4) Physical condition [**10:**7.3.1]

13.6.4.3.2 Annual External Examination of All Extinguishers.

13.6.4.3.2.1 Physical Condition. An annual external visual examination of all fire extinguishers shall be made to detect obvious physical damage, corrosion, or nozzle blockage; to verify that the operating instructions are present, legible, and facing forward, that the HMIS information is present and legible; and to determine if a 6-year interval examination or hydrostatic test is due. [**10:**7.3.2.1]

13.6.4.3.2.2* Seals or Tamper Indicators. At the time of the maintenance, the tamper seal of a rechargeable fire extinguisher shall be removed by operating the pull pin or locking device. [**10:**7.3.2.2]

13.6.4.3.2.2.1 After the applicable maintenance procedures are completed, a new listed tamper seal shall be installed. [**10:**7.3.2.2.1]

13.6.4.3.2.2.2 Seals or tamper indicators on nonrechargeable-type extinguishers shall not be removed. [**10:**7.3.2.2.2]

13.6.4.3.2.3* Boots, Foot Rings, and Attachments. All removable extinguisher boots, foot rings, and attachments shall be removed to accommodate thorough annual cylinder examinations. [**10:**7.3.2.3]

13.6.4.3.2.4 When subjected to temperatures at or above their listed rating, stored-pressure fire extinguishers that require a 12-year hydrostatic test shall be emptied and subjected to the applicable maintenance and recharge procedures on an annual basis. [**10:**7.3.2.4]

13.6.4.3.2.5 Corrective Action. When an external examination of any fire extinguisher reveals a deficiency, immediate corrective action shall be taken. [**10:**7.3.2.5]

13.6.4.3.3 Annual Internal Examination of Certain Types of Extinguishers.

13.6.4.3.3.1* Maintenance Intervals. Fire extinguishers shall be internally examined at intervals not exceeding those specified in Table 13.6.4.3.3.1. [**10:**7.3.3.1]

Table 13.6.4.3.3.1 Maintenance Involving Internal Examination

Extinguisher Type	Internal Examination Interval (years)
Stored-pressure loaded stream and antifreeze	1
Pump tank water and pump tank calcium chloride–based	1
Dry chemical, cartridge- and cylinder-operated, with mild steel shells	1*
Dry powder, cartridge- and cylinder-operated, with mild steel shells	1*
Wetting agent	1
Stored-pressure water	5
AFFF (aqueous film-forming foam)	3†
FFFP (film-forming fluoroprotein foam)	3†
Stored-pressure dry chemical, with stainless steel shells	5
Carbon dioxide	5
Wet chemical	5
Dry chemical stored-pressure, with mild steel shells, brazed brass shells, and aluminum shells	6
Halogenated agents	6
Dry powder, stored-pressure, with mild steel shells	6

*Dry chemical and dry powder in cartridge- or cylinder-operated extinguishers are examined annually.
†The extinguishing agent in liquid charge-type AFFF and FFFP extinguishers is replaced every 3 years, and an internal examination (teardown) is normally conducted at that time.
[**10:** Table 7.3.3]

13.6.4.3.3.2 Loaded Stream Charge. Stored-pressure types of fire extinguishers containing a loaded stream agent shall be disassembled on an annual basis and subjected to complete maintenance. [**10:**7.3.3.2]

13.6.4.3.3.2.1 The loaded stream charge shall be permitted to be recovered and re-used, provided it is subjected to agent analysis in accordance with the extinguisher manufacturer's instructions. [**10:**7.3.3.2.1]

13.6.4.3.3.2.2 When the internal maintenance procedures are performed during periodic recharging or hydrostatic testing, the 1-year requirement shall begin from that date. [**10:**7.3.3.2.2]

13.6.4.3.3.3 Cartridge- or Cylinder- Operated Extinguishers. The extinguishing agent of cartridge- or cylinder-operated extinguishers shall be internally examined annually. [**10**:7.3.3.3]

13.6.4.3.3.4 Wetting Agent Extinguishers. Wetting agent extinguishers shall be disassembled on an annual basis and subjected to complete maintenance. [**10**:7.3.3.4]

13.6.4.3.3.5 Pump Tank Extinguishers. Pump tank extinguishers shall be internally examined annually. [**10**:7.3.3.5]

13.6.4.3.3.6 Annual internal examination shall not be required for nonrechargeable fire extinguishers, carbon dioxide fire extinguishers, or stored-pressure fire extinguishers, except for those types specified in 13.6.4.3.3.2. [**10**:7.3.3.6]

13.6.4.3.4* Annual Maintenance Record Keeping.

13.6.4.3.4.1 Each fire extinguisher shall have a tag or label securely attached that indicates that maintenance was performed. [**10**:7.3.4.1]

13.6.4.3.4.1.1 The tag or label, as a minimum, shall identify the following:

(1) Month and year maintenance was performed
(2) Person performing the work
(3) Name of the agency performing the work [**10**:7.3.4.1.1]

13.6.4.3.4.2 Each extinguisher that has undergone maintenance that includes internal examination, except extinguishers identified in 13.6.4.3.3.3 and 13.6.4.3.3.5, shall have a verification-of-service collar located around the neck of the container. [**10**:7.3.4.2]

13.6.4.3.4.3 Verification-of-Service Collar (Maintenance or Recharging).

13.6.4.3.5 Corrective Action. When maintenance of any fire extinguisher reveals a deficiency, immediate corrective action shall be taken. [**10**:7.3.5]

13.6.4.3.6 Six-Year Internal Examination of Certain Types of Extinguishers. Every 6 years, stored-pressure fire extinguishers that require a 12-year hydrostatic test shall be emptied and subjected to the applicable internal and external examination procedures as detailed in the manufacturer's service manual and NFPA 10. [**10**:7.3.6]

13.6.4.3.6.1 When the applicable maintenance procedures are performed during periodic recharging or hydrostatic testing, the 6-year requirement shall begin from that date. [**10**:7.3.6.1]

13.6.4.3.6.2* The removal of agent from halon agent fire extinguishers shall only be done using a listed halon closed recovery system. [**10**:7.3.6.2]

13.6.4.3.6.3 Nonrechargeable fire extinguishers shall not be required to have a 6-year internal examination and shall not be hydrostatically tested but shall be removed from service at a maximum interval of 12 years from the date of manufacture. [**10**:7.3.6.3]

13.6.4.3.6.3.1 Nonrechargeable halon agent fire extinguishers shall be disposed of in accordance with 13.6.4.2.3.3. [**10**:7.3.6.3.1]

13.6.4.3.6.4 Corrective Action. When an internal examination of any fire extinguisher reveals a deficiency, immediate corrective action shall be taken. [**10**:7.3.6.4]

13.6.4.3.6.5* Six-Year Internal Examination Label. Fire extinguishers that pass the applicable 6-year requirement of 13.6.4.3.6 shall have the maintenance information recorded on a durable weatherproof label that is a minimum of 2 in. × 3½ in. (51 mm × 89 mm). [**10**:7.3.6.5]

13.6.4.3.6.5.1 The new label shall be affixed to the shell by a heatless process, and any previous 6-year internal examination labels shall be removed. [**10**:7.3.6.5.1]

13.6.4.3.6.5.2 These labels shall be of the self-destructive type when their removal from a fire extinguisher is attempted. [**10**:7.3.6.5.2]

13.6.4.3.6.5.3 The 6-year examination label shall, as a minimum, identify the following:

(1) Month and year the 6-year internal examination was performed
(2) Person performing the work
(3) Name of the agency performing the work [**10**:7.3.6.5.3]

13.6.4.4* Carbon Dioxide Hose Assembly Conductivity Test. A conductivity test shall be conducted annually on all carbon dioxide hose assemblies. [**10**:7.4]

13.6.4.4.1 Carbon dioxide hose assemblies that fail the conductivity test shall be replaced. [**10**:7.4.1]

13.6.4.4.2 Record Keeping for Conductivity Testing of Carbon Dioxide Hose Assemblies.

13.6.4.4.2.1 Carbon dioxide hose assemblies that pass a conductivity test shall have the test information recorded on a durable weatherproof label that has a minimum of ½ in. × 3 in. (13 mm × 76 mm). [**10**:7.4.2.1]

13.6.4.4.2.2 The label shall be affixed to the hose by means of a heatless process. [**10**:7.4.2.2]

13.6.4.4.2.3 The label shall include the following information:

(1) Month and year the test was performed, indicated by perforation such as is done by a hand punch
(2) Name or initials of person performing the and name of the agency performing the test [**10**:7.4.2.3]

13.6.4.5 Electronic Monitoring System Maintenance.

13.6.4.5.1 Electronic Monitoring. The components of the monitoring device/system shall be tested and maintained annually in accordance with the manufacturer's listed maintenance manual, with the following items as a minimum:

(1) Power supply inspection/battery change
(2) Obstruction sensor inspection
(3) Location sensor inspection
(4) Pressure indication inspection
(5) Connection continuity inspection *(see 13.6.4.5.1.1 and 13.6.4.5.1.2)*
[**10**:7.5.1]

13.6.4.5.1.1 One hundred percent of all units shall be tested upon initial installation or reacceptance with verification of receipt of signal at the control panel or a local alarm. [**10**:7.5.1.1]

13.6.4.5.1.2 Twenty percent of units shall be tested annually on a rotating basis so that all units are tested within a 5-year period. [**10**:7.5.1.2]

13.6.4.5.2 When used in conjunction with fire alarm systems, fire extinguisher electronic monitoring devices shall be inspected and maintained in accordance with *NFPA 72, National Fire Alarm and Signaling Code*, and 13.6.4.5.1. [**10**:7.5.2]

13.6.4.5.3 Corrective Action. When maintenance of any monitoring system reveals a deficiency, immediate corrective action shall be taken. [**10**:7.5.3]

13.6.4.6 Maintenance of Wheeled Extinguisher Hoses and Regulators.

13.6.4.6.1 Discharge hoses on wheeled-type fire extinguishers shall be completely uncoiled and examined for damage annually. [**10**:7.6.1]

13.6.4.6.2* Wheeled Unit Hoses. Discharge hoses on wheeled extinguishers shall be coiled in a manner to prevent kinks and to allow rapid deployment in accordance with the manufacturer's instructions. [**10**:7.6.2]

13.6.4.6.3 Pressure Regulators. Pressure regulators provided with wheeled-type fire extinguishers shall be tested annually for outlet static pressure and flow rate in accordance with the manufacturer's instructions. [**10**:7.6.3]

13.6.4.6.4 Corrective Action. When maintenance of any fire extinguisher hose or pressure regulator reveals a deficiency, immediate corrective action shall be taken. [**10**:7.6.4]

13.6.4.7 Extinguisher Recharging and Extinguishing Agents.

13.6.4.7.1* General.

13.6.4.7.1.1 All rechargeable-type fire extinguishers shall be recharged after any use or when the need is indicated by an inspection or servicing. [**10**:7.7.1.1]

13.6.4.7.1.2* When recharging is performed, the manufacturer's service manual shall be followed. *(For recharge agents, see 13.6.4.7.3.)* [**10**:7.7.1.2]

13.6.4.7.1.3* The amount of recharge agent shall be verified by weighing. [**10**:7.7.1.3]

13.6.4.7.1.3.1 For those fire extinguishers that do not have the gross weight marked on the nameplate or valve, a permanent label that indicates the gross weight shall be affixed to the cylinder. [**10**:7.7.1.3.1]

13.6.4.7.1.3.2 The added label containing the gross weight shall be a durable material of a pressure-sensitive, self-destruct type. *(For stored-pressure water-type extinguishers, see 13.6.4.7.3.10.)* [**10**:7.7.1.3.2]

13.6.4.7.1.3.3 Pump tank water and pump tank calcium chloride–based antifreeze types shall not be required to have weight marked. [**10**:7.7.1.3.3]

13.6.4.7.1.3.4* After recharging, a leak test shall be performed on stored-pressure and self-expelling types of fire extinguishers. [**10**:7.7.1.3.4]

13.6.4.7.1.3.5 In no case shall an extinguisher be recharged if it is beyond its specified hydrostatic test date. [**10**:7.7.1.3.5]

13.6.4.7.2 Extinguisher Recharging Frequency for Certain Types of Extinguishers.

13.6.4.7.2.1 Pump Tank. Every 12 months, pump tank water and pump tank calcium chloride–based antifreeze types of fire extinguishers shall be recharged with new chemicals or water as applicable. [**10**:7.7.2.1]

13.6.4.7.2.2 Wetting Agent. The agent in stored-pressure wetting agent fire extinguishers shall be replaced annually. [**10**:7.7.2.2]

13.6.4.7.2.2.1 Only the agent specified on the nameplate shall be used for recharging. [**10**:7.7.2.2.1]

13.6.4.7.2.2.2 The use of water or any other additives shall be prohibited. [**10**:7.7.2.2.2]

13.6.4.7.2.3 AFFF and FFFP.

13.6.4.7.2.3.1 The premixed agent in liquid charge–type AFFF and FFFP fire extinguishers shall be replaced at least once every 3 years. [**10**:7.7.2.3.1]

13.6.4.7.2.3.2 Only the foam agent specified on the extinguisher nameplate shall be used for recharge. [**10**:7.7.2.3.2]

13.6.4.7.2.3.3 The agent in nonpressurized AFFF and FFFP fire extinguishers that is subjected to agent analysis in accordance with manufacturer's instructions shall not be required to comply with 13.6.4.7.2.3.1. [**10**:7.7.2.3.3]

13.6.4.7.3* Recharge Agents.

13.6.4.7.3.1 Only those agents specified on the nameplate or agents proven to have equal chemical composition, physical characteristics, and fire-extinguishing capabilities shall be used. [**10**:7.7.3.1]

13.6.4.7.3.1.1 Agents listed specifically for use with that fire extinguisher shall be considered to meet these requirements. [**10**:7.7.3.1.1]

13.6.4.7.3.2* Mixing of Dry Chemicals. Multipurpose dry chemicals shall not be mixed with alkaline-based dry chemicals. [**10**:7.7.3.2]

13.6.4.7.3.3 Topping Off.

13.6.4.7.3.3.1 The remaining dry chemical in a discharged fire extinguisher shall be permitted to be re-used, provided that it is thoroughly checked for the proper type, contamination, and condition. [**10**:7.7.3.3.1]

13.6.4.7.3.3.2 Dry chemical found to be of the wrong type or contaminated shall not be re-used. [**10**:7.7.3.3.2]

13.6.4.7.3.4 Dry Chemical Agent Re-Use.

13.6.4.7.3.4.1 The dry chemical agent shall be permitted to be re-used, provided a closed recovery system is used and the agent is stored in a sealed container to prevent contamination. [**10**:7.7.3.4.1]

13.6.4.7.3.4.2 Prior to re-use, the dry chemical shall be thoroughly checked for the proper type, contamination, and condition. [**10**:7.7.3.4.2]

13.6.4.7.3.4.3 Where doubt exists with respect to the type, contamination, or condition of the dry chemical, the dry chemical shall be discarded. [**10**:7.7.3.4.3]

13.6.4.7.3.4.4 Dry Chemical Closed Recovery System.

(A) The system shall be constructed in a manner that does not introduce foreign material into the agent being recovered. [**10**:7.7.3.4.4.1]

(B) The system shall have a means for visual inspection of the recovered agent for contaminants. [**10**:7.7.3.4.4.2]

13.6.4.7.3.5 Dry Powder.

13.6.4.7.3.5.1 Pails or drums containing dry powder agents for scoop or shovel application for use on metal fires shall be kept full and sealed with the lid provided with the container. [**10:**7.7.3.5.1]

13.6.4.7.3.5.2 The dry powder shall be replaced if found damp. *(See A.13.6.4.7.3.)* [**10:**7.7.3.5.2]

13.6.4.7.3.6* Removal of Moisture. For all non-water types of fire extinguishers, any moisture shall be removed before recharging. [**10:**7.7.3.6]

13.6.4.7.3.7* Halogenated Agent. Halogenated agent fire extinguishers shall be charged with only the type and weight of agent specified on the nameplate. [**10:**7.7.3.7]

13.6.4.7.3.8 Halogenated Agent Re-Use.

13.6.4.7.3.8.1 The removal of Halon 1211 from fire extinguishers shall be done using only a listed halon closed recovery system. [**10:**7.7.3.8.1]

13.6.4.7.3.8.2 The removal of agent from other halogenated agent fire extinguishers shall be done using only a closed recovery system. [**10:**7.7.3.8.2]

13.6.4.7.3.8.3 The fire extinguisher shall be examined internally for contamination or corrosion or both. [**10:**7.7.3.8.3]

13.6.4.7.3.8.4 The halogenated agent retained in the system recovery cylinder shall be re-used only if no evidence of internal contamination is observed in the fire extinguisher cylinder. [**10:**7.7.3.8.4]

13.6.4.7.3.8.5 Halogenated agent removed from fire extinguishers that exhibits evidence of internal contamination or corrosion shall be processed in accordance with the fire extinguisher manufacturer's instructions. [**10:**7.7.3.8.5]

13.6.4.7.3.9* Carbon Dioxide.

13.6.4.7.3.9.1 The vapor phase of carbon dioxide shall be not less than 99.5 percent carbon dioxide. [**10:**7.7.3.9.1]

13.6.4.7.3.9.2 The water content shall be not more than 60 parts per million (ppm) by weight at −52°F (−47°C) dew point. [**10:**7.7.3.9.2]

13.6.4.7.3.9.3 Oil content shall not exceed 10 ppm by weight. [**10:**7.7.3.9.3]

13.6.4.7.3.10* Water Types. The amount of liquid agent shall be determined by using one of the following:

(1) Exact measurement by weight
(2) Exact measurement in volume
(3) Anti-overfill tube, if provided
(4) Fill mark on fire extinguisher shell, if provided
[**10:**7.7.3.10]

13.6.4.7.3.10.1 Only the agent specified on the extinguisher nameplate shall be used for recharge. [**10:**7.7.3.10.1]

13.6.4.7.3.10.2 Only additives identified on the original nameplate shall be permitted to be added to water type extinguishers. [**10:**7.7.3.10.2]

13.6.4.7.3.11 Wet Chemical and Water Mist Agent Re-Use.

13.6.4.7.3.11.1 Wet chemical and water mist agents shall not be re-used. [**10:**7.7.3.11.1]

13.6.4.7.3.11.2 If a wet chemical or water mist extinguisher is partially discharged, all remaining wet chemical or water mist shall be discarded. [**10:**7.7.3.11.2]

13.6.4.7.3.11.3 Wet chemical or water mist agent shall be discarded and replaced at the hydrostatic test interval. [**10:**7.7.3.11.3]

(A) Only the agent specified on the extinguisher nameplate shall be used for recharge. [**10:**7.7.3.11.3.1]

13.6.4.7.4 Recharging Expellant Gas for Stored-Pressure Fire Extinguishers.

13.6.4.7.4.1 Only standard industrial-grade nitrogen with a maximum dew point of −60°F (−51°C) in accordance with CGA G10.1, *Commodity Specification for Nitrogen*, shall be used to pressurize stored-pressure dry chemical and halogenated-type fire extinguishers that use nitrogen as a propellant. [**10:**7.7.4.1]

13.6.4.7.4.2 Halogenated-type fire extinguishers that require argon shall be pressurized with argon with a dew point of −65°F (−54°C) or lower. [**10:**7.7.4.2]

13.6.4.7.4.3 Compressed air shall be permitted to be used from special compressor systems capable of delivering air with a dew point of −60°F (−51°C) or lower. *(See Annex J of NFPA 10.)* [**10:**7.7.4.3]

13.6.4.7.4.3.1 The special compressor system shall be equipped with an automatic monitoring and alarm system to ensure that the dew point remains at or below −60°F (−51°C) at all times. [**10:**7.7.4.3.1]

13.6.4.7.4.3.2 Compressed air through moisture traps shall not be used for pressurizing even though so stated in the instructions on older fire extinguishers. [**10:**7.7.4.3.2]

13.6.4.7.4.3.3 Compressed air without moisture removal devices shall be permitted for pressurizing water extinguishers and foam hand extinguishers only. [**10:**7.7.4.3.3]

13.6.4.7.4.4* Class D, wet chemical, water mist, and halogenated agent fire extinguishers shall be repressurized only with the type of expellant gas referred to on the fire extinguisher label. [**10:**7.7.4.4]

13.6.4.7.4.5 A rechargeable stored-pressure-type fire extinguisher shall be pressurized only to the charging pressure specified on the fire extinguisher nameplate. [**10:**7.7.4.5]

13.6.4.7.4.5.1 The manufacturer's pressurizing adapter shall be connected to the valve assembly before the fire extinguisher is pressurized. [**10:**7.7.4.5.1]

13.6.4.7.4.5.2 A regulated source of pressure, set no higher than 25 psi (172 kPa) above the operating (service) pressure, shall be used to pressurize fire extinguishers. [**10:**7.7.4.5.2]

13.6.4.7.4.5.3 The gauge used to set the regulated source of pressure shall be calibrated at least annually. [**10:**7.7.4.5.3]

13.6.4.7.4.6* An unregulated source of pressure, such as a nitrogen cylinder without a pressure regulator, shall not be used. [**10:**7.7.4.6]

13.6.4.7.4.7* A fire extinguisher shall not be left connected to the regulator of a high-pressure source for an extended period of time. [**10:**7.7.4.7]

13.6.4.7.4.8 Recharge Record Keeping.

13.6.4.7.4.8.1 Each fire extinguisher shall have a tag or label attached that indicates the month and year recharging was performed, identifies the person performing the service, and identifies the name of the agency performing the work. [**10**:7.7.4.8.1]

13.6.4.7.4.8.2 Each extinguisher that has been recharged shall have a verification-of-service collar located around the neck of the container, except as identified in 13.6.4.10.4. [**10**:7.7.4.8.2]

13.6.4.8* Pressure Gauges.

13.6.4.8.1 Replacement pressure gauges shall have the correct indicated charging (service) pressure. [**10**:7.8.1]

13.6.4.8.2 Replacement pressure gauges shall be marked for use with the agent in the fire extinguisher. [**10**:7.8.2]

13.6.4.8.3 Replacement pressure gauges shall be compatible with the fire extinguisher valve body material. [**10**:7.8.3]

13.6.4.9 Prohibition on Uses of Extinguishers and Conversion of Fire Extinguisher Types.

13.6.4.9.1 Fire extinguishers shall not be used for any purpose other than that of a fire extinguisher. [**10**:7.9.1]

13.6.4.9.2 Fire extinguishers shall not be converted from one type to another, modified, or altered. [**10**:7.9.2]

13.6.4.9.3 Fire extinguishers shall not be converted to use a different type of extinguishing agent. [**10**:7.9.3]

13.6.4.10* Maintenance and Recharge Service Collar. Each extinguisher that has undergone maintenance that included internal examination or that has been recharged requiring the removal of the valve assembly shall have a verification-of-service collar located around the neck of the container. [**10**:7.10]

13.6.4.10.1 The collar shall contain a single circular piece of uninterrupted material forming a hole of a size that does not permit the collar assembly to move over the neck of the container unless the valve is completely removed. [**10**:7.10.1]

13.6.4.10.2 The collar shall not interfere with the operation of the fire extinguisher. [**10**:7.10.2]

13.6.4.10.3 The verification-of-service collar shall, as a minimum, identify the following:

(1) Month and year the recharging or internal examination was performed
(2) Name of the agency performing the work [**10**:7.10.3]

13.6.4.10.4 Service Collar Exemptions.

13.6.4.10.4.1 New extinguishers requiring an initial charge in the field (such as pressurized water, AFFF, FFFP, or wet chemical extinguishers) shall not be required to have a verification-of-service collar installed. [**10**:7.10.4.1]

13.6.4.10.4.2 Liquefied gas, halogenated agent, and carbon dioxide extinguishers that have been recharged without valve removal shall not be required to have a verification-of-service collar installed following recharge. [**10**:7.10.4.2]

13.6.4.10.4.3 Cartridge- and cylinder-operated extinguishers shall not be required to have a verification-of-service collar installed. [**10**:7.10.4.3]

13.6.4.11* Weight Scales. Weight scales used for the maintenance and recharge of fire extinguishers shall have the reading increments and the accuracy necessary to verify the charge weights required in the service manuals and on the nameplates. [**10**:7.11]

13.6.5 Hydrostatic Testing. For hydrostatic testing of portable fire extinguishers, see Chapter 8 of NFPA 10.

13.6.5.1 Condemning Extinguishers.

13.6.5.1.1 Fails Test or Examination. When a fire extinguisher cylinder, shell, or cartridge fails a hydrostatic pressure test or fails to pass a visual examination as specified in 8.4.2 of NFPA 10, it shall be condemned or destroyed by the owner or the owner's agent. [**10**:8.8.1]

13.6.5.1.1.1 When a cylinder is required to be condemned, the retester shall notify the owner in writing that the cylinder is condemned and that it cannot be reused. [**10**:8.8.1.1]

13.6.5.1.1.2 A condemned cylinder shall not be repaired. [**10**:8.8.1.2]

13.6.5.1.2 Marking Condemned Extinguishers.

13.6.5.1.2.1 Condemned cylinders shall be stamped "CONDEMNED" on the top, head, shoulder, or neck with a steel stamp. [**10**:8.8.2.1]

13.6.5.1.2.2 No person shall remove or obliterate the "CONDEMNED" marking. [**10**:8.8.2.2]

13.6.5.1.2.3 Minimum letter height shall be ⅛ in. (3 mm). [**10**:8.8.2.3]

13.7 Detection, Alarm, and Communications Systems.

13.7.1 General.

13.7.1.1 Where building fire alarm systems or automatic fire detectors are required by other sections of this *Code*, they shall be provided and installed in accordance with *NFPA 70*, *NFPA 72*, and Section 13.7.

13.7.1.2* Building Fire Alarm Systems. Protected premises fire alarm systems that serve the general fire alarm needs of a building or buildings shall include one or more of the following systems or functions:

(1) Manual fire alarm signal initiation
(2) Automatic fire alarm and supervisory signal initiation
(3) Monitoring of abnormal conditions in fire suppression systems
(4) Activation of fire suppression systems
(5) Activation of emergency control functions
(6) Activation of fire alarm notification appliances
(7) In-building fire emergency voice/alarm communications
(8) Guard's tour supervisory service
(9) Process monitoring supervisory systems
(10) Activation of off-premises signals
(11) Combination systems
[**72**:23.3.3.1]

13.7.1.3 All apparatus requiring rewinding or resetting to maintain normal operation shall be rewound or reset as promptly as possible after each test and alarm. [**72**:14.5.4]

13.7.1.4 The provisions of Section 13.7 shall apply only where specifically required by another section of this *Code*. [***101***:9.6.1.1]

13.7.1.4.1 Fire detection, alarm, and communications systems installed to make use of an alternative permitted by this *Code* shall be considered required systems and shall meet the provisions of this *Code* applicable to required systems. [*101:* 9.6.1.2]

13.7.1.4.2* To ensure operational integrity, the fire alarm system shall have an approved maintenance and testing program complying with the applicable requirements of Sections 13.4 and 13.7. [*101:* 9.6.1.4]

13.7.1.4.3* Fire alarm system impairment procedures shall comply with NFPA 72, *National Fire Alarm and Signaling Code.* [*101:* 9.6.1.5]

13.7.1.5* Impaired and Nuisance Alarm Prone Systems.

13.7.1.5.1 Impaired fire alarm systems shall include, but shall not be limited to, required systems that are not fully operational, are no longer monitored as required by the AHJ, or are under renovation or repair.

13.7.1.5.2 The system owner or designated representative shall immediately notify the AHJ in an approved manner when a fire alarm system is impaired.

13.7.1.5.3 The AHJ shall be authorized to require standby fire personnel or an approved fire watch in accordance with 1.7.16 at premises in which required fire alarm systems are impaired or classified as chronic nuisance alarm prone systems.

13.7.1.5.4 Fire alarm systems that have produced five or more nuisance alarms in a 365-day period shall be classified as chronic nuisance alarm prone systems.

13.7.1.5.5* The AHJ shall be authorized to require central station service be provided for chronic nuisance alarm prone systems.

13.7.1.5.6* Fire alarm supervising stations and fire alarm service companies shall immediately notify the AHJ when any of the following conditions exists:

(1) A fire alarm system is impaired.
(2) Required system monitoring is no longer being provided.
(3) Required testing, service, and maintenance is no longer being provided.
(4) A fire alarm system cannot be serviced or repaired to make it fully operational.
(5) A fire alarm system cannot be serviced or repaired to eliminate chronic nuisance alarms.

13.7.1.5.7 The system owner shall replace required fire alarm systems that cannot be serviced or repaired to eliminate system impairments or chronic nuisance alarms.

13.7.1.6* Nonrequired Coverage.

13.7.1.6.1 Detection installed for reasons of achieving specific fire safety objectives, but not required by any laws, codes, or standards, shall meet all of the requirements of this *Code*, with the exception of prescriptive spacing criteria of Chapter 17 of *NFPA 72.* [**72:** 17.5.3.3.1]

13.7.1.6.2 Where nonrequired detectors are installed for achieving specific fire safety objectives, additional detectors not necessary to achieve the objectives shall not be required. [**72:** 17.5.3.3.2]

13.7.1.7 Signal Initiation.

13.7.1.7.1 Where required by other sections of this *Code*, actuation of the fire alarm system shall occur by any or all of the following means of initiation, but shall not be limited to such means:

(1) Manual fire alarm initiation
(2) Automatic detection
(3) Extinguishing system operation [*101:* 9.6.2.1]

13.7.1.7.2 Manual fire alarm boxes shall be used only for fire-protective signaling purposes. Combination fire alarm and guard's tour stations shall be permitted. [*101:* 9.6.2.2]

13.7.1.7.3 A manual fire alarm box shall be provided as follows, unless modified by another section of this *Code*:

(1) For new alarm system installations, the manual fire alarm box shall be located within 60 in. (1525 mm) of exit doorways.
(2) For existing alarm system installations, the manual fire alarm box either shall be provided in the natural exit access path near each required exit or within 60 in. (1525 mm) of exit doorways.
[*101:* 9.6.2.3]

13.7.1.7.4 Manual fire alarm boxes shall be mounted on both sides of grouped openings over 40 ft (12.2 m) in width, and within 60 in. (1525 mm) of each side of the opening. [*101:*9.6.2.4]

13.7.1.7.5* Additional manual fire alarm boxes shall be located so that, on any given floor in any part of the building, no horizontal distance on that floor exceeding 200 ft (61 m) shall need to be traversed to reach a manual fire alarm box. [*101:*9.6.2.5]

13.7.1.7.6* For fire alarm systems using automatic fire detection or waterflow detection devices to initiate the fire alarm system in accordance with Chapters 11 through 43 of NFPA *101*, not less than one manual fire alarm box, located as required by the AHJ, shall be provided to initiate a fire alarm signal. [*101:* 9.6.2.6]

13.7.1.7.7* Manual fire alarm boxes shall be accessible, unobstructed, and visible. [*101:* 9.6.2.7]

13.7.1.7.8 Where a sprinkler system provides automatic detection and alarm system initiation, it shall be provided with an approved alarm initiation device that operates when the flow of water is equal to or greater than that from a single automatic sprinkler. [*101:* 9.6.2.8]

13.7.1.7.9 Where a total (complete) coverage smoke detection system is required by another section of this *Code*, automatic detection of smoke in shall be in accordance with shall be provided in all occupiable areas in environments that are suitable for proper smoke detector operation. [*101:* 9.6.2.9]

13.7.1.8 Smoke Alarms.

13.7.1.8.1 Where required by another section of this *Code*, single-station and multiple-station smoke alarms shall be in accordance with *NFPA 72* unless otherwise provided in 13.7.1.8.3, 13.7.1.8.4, 13.7.1.8.5, or 13.7.1.8.6. [*101:* 9.6.2.10.1]

13.7.1.8.2 Where automatic smoke detection is required by Chapters 11 through 43 of NFPA *101*, smoke alarms shall not be used as a substitute. [*101:* 9.6.2.10.2]

13.7.1.8.3* The interconnection of smoke alarms shall apply only to new construction as provided in 13.7.1.8.8. [*101:*9.6.2.10.3]

13.7.1.8.4 Smoke alarms and smoke detectors shall not be installed within an area of exclusion determined by a 10 ft (3.0 m) radial distance along a horizontal flow path from a stationary or fixed cooking appliance, unless listed for installation in close proximity to cooking appliances. Smoke alarms and smoke detectors installed between 10 ft (3.0 m) and 20 ft (6.1 m) along a horizontal flow path from a stationary or fixed cooking appliance shall be equipped with an alarm-silencing means or use photoelectric detection.

Exception: Smoke alarms or smoke detectors that use photoelectric detection shall be permitted for installation at a radial distance greater than 6 ft (1.8 m) from any stationary or fixed cooking appliance when the following conditions are met:

(1) The kitchen or cooking area and adjacent spaces have no clear interior partitions or headers and
(2) The 10 ft (3.0 m) area of exclusion would prohibit the placement of a smoke alarm or smoke detector required by other sections of NFPA 72.
[*72:* 29.8.3.4(4)]

13.7.1.8.5 Smoke alarms and smoke detectors shall not be installed within a 36 in. (910 mm) horizontal path from a door to a bathroom containing a shower or tub unless listed for installation in close proximity to such locations. [*72:* 29.8.3.4(6)]

13.7.1.8.6 System smoke detectors in accordance with *NFPA 72* and arranged to function in the same manner as single-station or multiple-station smoke alarms shall be permitted in lieu of smoke alarms. [*101:* 9.6.2.10.6]

13.7.1.8.7 Smoke alarms, other than battery-operated smoke alarms as permitted by other sections of this *Code*, shall be powered in accordance with the requirements of *NFPA 72*. [*101:* 9.6.2.10.7]

13.7.1.8.8* In new construction, where two or more smoke alarms are required within a dwelling unit, suite of rooms, or similar area, they shall be arranged so that operation of any smoke alarm shall cause the alarm in all smoke alarms within the dwelling unit, suite of rooms, or similar area to sound, unless otherwise permitted by the following:

(1) The requirement of 13.7.1.8.8 shall not apply where permitted by another section of this *Code*.
(2) The requirement of 13.7.1.8.8 shall not apply to configurations that provide equivalent distribution of the alarm signal. [*101:* 9.6.2.10.8]

13.7.1.8.9 The alarms described in 13.7.1.8.8 shall sound only within an individual dwelling unit, suite of rooms, or similar area and shall not actuate the building fire alarm system, unless otherwise permitted by the AHJ. [*101:* 9.6.2.10.9]

13.7.1.8.10 Smoke alarms shall be permitted to be connected to the building fire alarm system for the purpose of annunciation in accordance with *NFPA 72*. [*101:* 9.6.2.10.10]

13.7.1.9 Occupant Notification.

13.7.1.9.1 Occupant notification shall be provided to alert occupants of a fire or other emergency where required by other sections of this *Code*. [*101:* 9.6.3.1]

13.7.1.9.2 Occupant notification shall be in accordance with 13.7.1.9.3 through 13.7.1.9.10.2, unless otherwise provided in 13.7.1.9.2.1 through 13.7.1.9.2.4. [*101:* 9.6.3.2]

13.7.1.9.2.1* Elevator lobby, hoistway, and associated machine room smoke detectors used solely for elevator recall, and heat detectors used solely for elevator power shutdown, shall not be required to activate the building evacuation alarm if the power supply and installation wiring to such detectors are monitored by the building fire alarm system, and if the activation of such detectors initiates a supervisory signal at a constantly attended location. [*101:* 9.6.3.2.1]

13.7.1.9.2.2* Smoke detectors used solely for closing dampers or heating, ventilating, and air-conditioning system shutdown shall not be required to activate the building evacuation alarm, provided that the power supply and installation wiring to the detectors are monitored by the building fire alarm system, and the activation of the detectors initiates a supervisory signal at a constantly attended location. [*101:* 9.6.3.2.2]

13.7.1.9.2.3* Smoke detectors located at doors for the exclusive operation of automatic door release shall not be required to activate the building evacuation alarm, provided that the power supply and installation wiring to the detectors are monitored by the building fire alarm system, and the activation of the detectors initiates a supervisory signal at a constantly attended location. [*101:* 9.6.3.2.3]

13.7.1.9.2.4 Detectors in accordance with 22.3.4.3.1(2) and 23.3.4.3.1(2) of NFPA *101* shall not be required to activate the building evacuation alarm. [*101:* 9.6.3.2.4]

13.7.1.9.3 Where permitted by Chapters 11 through 43 of NFPA *101*, a presignal system shall be permitted where the initial fire alarm signal is automatically transmitted without delay to a municipal fire department, to a fire brigade (if provided), and to an on-site staff person trained to respond to a fire emergency. [*101:* 9.6.3.3]

13.7.1.9.4 Where permitted by Chapters 11 through 43 of NFPA *101*, a positive alarm sequence shall be permitted, provided that it is in accordance with *NFPA 72*. [*101:* 9.6.3.4]

13.7.1.9.5 Unless otherwise provided in 13.7.1.9.5.1 through 13.7.1.9.5.8, notification signals for occupants to evacuate shall be audible and visible signals in accordance with *NFPA 72* and ICC/ANSI A117.1, *American National Standard for Accessible and Usable Buildings and Facilities*, or other means of notification acceptable to the AHJ. [*101:* 9.6.3.5]

13.7.1.9.5.1 Areas not subject to occupancy by persons who are hearing impaired shall not be required to comply with the provisions for visible signals. [*101:* 9.6.3.5.1]

13.7.1.9.5.2 Visible-only signals shall be provided where specifically permitted in health care occupancies in accordance with Chapters 18 and 19 of NFPA *101*. [*101:* 9.6.3.5.2]

13.7.1.9.5.3 Existing alarm systems shall not be required to comply with the provision for visible signals. [*101:* 9.6.3.5.3]

13.7.1.9.5.4 Visible signals shall not be required in lodging or rooming houses in accordance with the provisions of Chapter 26 of NFPA *101*. [*101:* 9.6.3.5.4]

13.7.1.9.5.5 Visible signals shall not be required in exit stair enclosures. [*101:* 9.6.3.5.5]

13.7.1.9.5.6 Visible signals shall not be required in elevator cars. [*101:* 9.6.3.5.6]

13.7.1.9.5.7* Public mode visual notification appliances in accordance with *NFPA 72* shall not be required in designated areas as permitted by Chapters 11 through 43 of NFPA *101*, provided that they are replaced with approved alternative visible means. [*101:* 9.6.3.5.7]

13.7.1.9.5.8* Where visible signals are not required, as permitted by 13.7.1.9.5.7, documentation of such omission shall be maintained in accordance with 9.7.7 of NFPA *101*. [*101:* 9.6.3.5.8]

13.7.1.9.6 The general evacuation alarm signal shall operate in accordance with one of the methods prescribed by 13.7.1.9.6.1 through 13.7.1.9.6.3. [*101:* 9.6.3.6]

13.7.1.9.6.1 The general evacuation alarm signal shall operate throughout the entire building other than the locations described in 13.7.1.9.6.4 and 13.7.1.9.6.5. [*101:* 9.6.3.6.1]

13.7.1.9.6.2* Where total evacuation of occupants is impractical due to building configuration, only the occupants in the affected zones shall be initially notified, and provisions shall be made to selectively notify occupants in other zones to afford orderly evacuation of the entire building, provided that such arrangement is approved by the AHJ. [*101:* 9.6.3.6.2]

13.7.1.9.6.3 Where occupants are incapable of evacuating themselves because of age, physical or mental disabilities, or physical restraint, all of the following shall apply:

(1) The private operating mode as described in *NFPA 72* shall be permitted to be used.
(2) Only the attendants and other personnel required to evacuate occupants from a zone, area, floor, or building shall be required to be notified.
(3) Notification of personnel as specified in 13.7.1.9.6.3(2) shall include means to readily identify the zone, area, floor, or building in need of evacuation.
[*101:* 9.6.3.6.3]

13.7.1.9.6.4 The general evacuation signal shall not be required to operate in exit stair enclosures. [*101:* 9.6.3.6.4]

13.7.1.9.6.5 The general evacuation signal shall not be required to operate in elevator cars. [*101:* 9.6.3.6.5]

13.7.1.9.7 Audible alarm notification appliances shall be of such character and so distributed as to be effectively heard above the average ambient sound level that exists under normal conditions of occupancy. [*101:* 9.6.3.7]

13.7.1.9.8 Audible alarm notification appliances shall produce signals that are distinctive from audible signals used for other purposes in a given building. [*101:* 9.6.3.8]

13.7.1.9.9 Automatically transmitted or live voice evacuation or relocation instructions shall be permitted to be used to notify occupants and shall comply with either 13.7.1.9.9.1 or 13.7.1.9.9.2. [*101:* 9.6.3.9]

13.7.1.9.9.1 Automatically transmitted or live voice evacuation or relocation instructions shall be in accordance with *NFPA 72*. [*101:* 9.6.3.9.1]

13.7.1.9.9.2 Where permitted by Chapters 11 through 43 of NFPA *101*, automatically transmitted or live voice announcements shall be permitted to be made via a voice communication or public address system that complies with the following:

(1) Occupant notification, either live or recorded, shall be initiated at a constantly attended receiving station by personnel trained to respond to an emergency.
(2) An approved secondary power supply shall be provided for other than existing, previously approved systems.
(3) The system shall be audible above the expected ambient noise level.

(4) Emergency announcements shall take precedence over any other use.
[*101:* 9.6.3.9.2]

13.7.1.9.10 Unless otherwise permitted by another section of this *Code*, audible and visible fire alarm notification appliances shall comply with either 13.7.1.9.10.1 or 13.7.1.9.10.2. [*101:*9.6.3.10]

13.7.1.9.10.1 Audible and visible fire alarm notification appliances shall be used only for fire alarm system or other emergency purposes. [*101:* 9.6.3.10.1]

13.7.1.9.10.2 Emergency voice/alarm communication systems shall be permitted to be used for other purposes in accordance with *NFPA 72*. [*101:* 9.6.3.10.2]

13.7.1.10 Emergency Forces Notification.

13.7.1.10.1 Where required by another section of this *Code*, emergency forces notification shall be provided to alert the municipal fire department and fire brigade (if provided) of fire or other emergency. [*101:* 9.6.4.1]

13.7.1.10.2 Where emergency forces notification is required by another section of this *Code*, the fire alarm system shall be arranged to transmit the alarm automatically via any of the following means acceptable to the AHJ and shall be in accordance with *NFPA 72*:

(1) Auxiliary fire alarm system
(2) Central station fire alarm system
(3) Proprietary supervising station fire alarm system
(4) Remote supervising station fire alarm system
[*101:* 9.6.4.2]

13.7.1.10.3 For existing installations where none of the means of notification specified in 13.7.1.10.2(1) through 13.7.1.10.2(4) are available, an approved plan for notification of the municipal fire department shall be permitted. [*101:* 9.6.4.3]

13.7.1.10.4 For other than existing installations, where fire alarm systems are required to provide emergency forces notification, supervisory signals and trouble signals shall sound and be visibly displayed either at an approved, remotely located receiving facility or at a location within the protected building that is constantly attended by qualified personnel. [*101:* 9.6.4.4]

13.7.1.11 Fire Safety Functions.

13.7.1.11.1 Fire safety functions shall be installed in accordance with the requirements of *NFPA 72*. [*101:* 9.6.5.1]

13.7.1.11.2 Where required by another section of this *Code*, the following functions shall be actuated:

(1) Release of hold-open devices for doors or other opening protectives
(2) Stairwell or elevator shaft pressurization
(3) Smoke management or smoke control systems
(4) Unlocking of doors
(5) Elevator recall and shutdown
(6) HVAC shutdown
[*101:* 9.6.5.2]

13.7.1.12 Location of Controls. Operator controls, alarm indicators, and manual communications capability shall be installed at a convenient location acceptable to the AHJ. [*101:* 9.6.6]

13.7.1.13 Annunciation and Annunciation Zoning.

13.7.1.13.1 Where alarm annunciation is required by another section of this *Code*, it shall comply with 13.7.1.13.2 through 13.7.1.13.12. [*101:* 9.6.7.1]

13.7.1.13.2 Alarm Annunciation. Where required by other governing laws, codes, or standards, the location of an operated initiating device shall be annunciated by visible means. [**72:** 10.18.1.1]

13.7.1.13.2.1 Visible annunciation of the location of an operated initiating device shall be by an indicator lamp, alphanumeric display, printout, or other approved means. [**72:**10.18.1.1.1]

13.7.1.13.2.2 The visible annunciation of the location of operated initiating devices shall not be canceled by the means used to deactivate alarm notification appliances. [**72:**10.18.1.1.2]

13.7.1.13.3 Supervisory and Trouble Annunciation. Where required by other governing laws, codes, or standards, supervisory and/or trouble conditions shall be annunciated by visible means. [**72:**10.18.2.1]

13.7.1.13.3.1 Visible annunciation shall be by an indicator lamp, alphanumeric display, a printout, or other means. [**72:**10.18.2.1.1]

13.7.1.13.3.2 The visible annunciation of supervisory and/or trouble conditions shall not be canceled by the means used to deactivate supervisory or trouble notification appliances. [**72:**10.18.2.1.2]

13.7.1.13.4* Annunciator Access and Location.

13.7.1.13.4.1 All required annunciation means shall be readily accessible to responding personnel. [**72:**10.18.3.1]

13.7.1.13.4.2 All required annunciation means shall be located as required by the AHJ to facilitate an efficient response to the situation. [**72:**10.18.3.2]

13.7.1.13.5 Alarm Annunciation Display. Visible annunciators shall be capable of displaying all zones in alarm. [**72:**10.18.4]

13.7.1.13.5.1 If all zones in alarm are not displayed simultaneously, the zone of origin shall be displayed. [**72:**10.18.4.1]

13.7.1.13.5.2 If all zones in alarm are not displayed simultaneously, there shall be an indication that other zones are in alarm. [**72:**10.18.4.2]

13.7.1.13.6* Annunciation Zoning.

13.7.1.13.6.1 For the purpose of alarm annunciation, each floor of the building shall be considered as a separate zone. [**72:** 10.18.5.1]

13.7.1.13.6.2 For the purposes of alarm annunciation, a floor of the building is subdivided into multiple zones by fire or smoke barriers and the fire plan for the protected premises allows relocation of occupants from the zone of origin to another zone on the same floor, each zone on the floor shall be annunciated separately. [**72:**10.18.5.2]

13.7.1.13.6.3 Where the system serves more than one building, each building shall be annunciated separately. [**72:**10.18.5.3]

13.7.1.13.7 Alarm annunciation at the control center shall be by means of audible and visible indicators. [*101:* 9.6.7.2]

13.7.1.13.8 For the purposes of alarm annunciation, each floor of the building, other than floors of existing buildings, shall be considered as not less than one zone, unless otherwise permitted by 13.7.1.13.9.4, 13.7.1.13.9.5, 13.7.1.13.9.6 or as another section of this *Code*. [*101:* 9.6.7.3]

13.7.1.13.9 Where a floor area exceeds 22,500 ft^2 (2090 m^2), additional fire alarm zoning shall be provided, and the length of any single fire alarm zone shall not exceed 300 ft (91 m) in any direction, except as provided in 13.7.1.13.9.1 through 13.7.1.13.9.6 or otherwise modified by another section of this *Code*. [*101:* 9.6.7.4]

13.7.1.13.9.1 Where permitted by another section of this *Code*, fire alarm zones shall be permitted to exceed 22,500 ft^2 (2090 m^2), and the length of a zone shall be permitted to exceed 300 ft (91 m) in any direction. [*101:* 9.6.7.4.1]

13.7.1.13.9.2 Where the building is protected by an automatic sprinkler system in accordance with NFPA 13, the area of the fire alarm zone shall be permitted to coincide with the allowable area of the sprinkler system. [*101:* 9.6.7.4.2]

13.7.1.13.9.3 Where the building is protected by a water mist system in accordance with 9.8.1 and Table 9.8.1 of NFPA *101*, the area of the fire alarm zone shall be permitted to coincide with the allowable area of the water mist system. [*101:* 9.6.7.4.3]

13.7.1.13.9.4 Unless otherwise prohibited elsewhere in this *Code*, where a building not exceeding four stories in height is protected by an automatic water mist system in accordance with 9.7.3 of NFPA *101*, the water mist system shall be permitted to be annunciated on the fire alarm system as a single zone. [*101:* 9.6.7.4.4]

13.7.1.13.9.5 Unless otherwise prohibited by another section of this *Code*, where a building not exceeding four stories in height is protected by an automatic sprinkler system in accordance with NFPA 13, the sprinkler system shall be permitted to be annunciated on the fire alarm system as a single zone. [*101:*9.6.7.4.5]

13.7.1.13.9.6 Where the building is protected by an automatic sprinkler system in accordance with NFPA 13D or NFPA 13R, the sprinkler system shall be permitted to be annunciated on the fire alarm system as a single zone. [*101:*9.6.7.4.6]

13.7.1.13.10 A system trouble signal shall be annunciated by means of audible and visible indicators. in accordance with *NFPA 72*. [*101:* 9.6.7.5]

13.7.1.13.11 A system supervisory signal shall be annunciated by means of audible and visible indicators in accordance with *NFPA 72*. [*101:* 9.6.7.6]

13.7.1.13.12 Where the system serves more than one building, each building shall be annunciated separately. [*101:* 9.6.7.7]

13.7.1.13.13 Where permitted by another section of this *Code*, the alarm zone shall be permitted to coincide with the permitted area for smoke compartments. [*101:*9.6.7.8]

13.7.1.14 Carbon Monoxide (CO) Detection and Warning Equipment. Where required by another section of this *Code*, carbon monoxide (CO) detection and warning equipment shall be provided in accordance with NFPA 720, *Standard for the Installation of Carbon Monoxide (CO) Detection and Warning Equipment*. [*101:*9.12]

13.7.2 Where Required and Occupancy Requirements.

13.7.2.1 New Assembly Occupancies.

13.7.2.1.1 General.

13.7.2.1.1.1 New assembly occupancies with occupant loads of more than 300 and all theaters with more than one audience-viewing room shall be provided with an approved fire alarm system in accordance with Section 13.7 and 13.7.2.1, unless otherwise permitted by 13.7.2.1.1.2. [*101:* 12.3.4.1.1]

13.7.2.1.1.2 New assembly occupancies that are a part of a multiple occupancy protected as a mixed occupancy *(see 6.1.14)* shall be permitted to be served by a common fire alarm system, provided that the individual requirements of each occupancy are met. [*101:* 12.3.4.1.2]

13.7.2.1.2 Initiation.

13.7.2.1.2.1 Initiation of the required fire alarm system shall be by both of the following means:

(1) Manual means in accordance with 13.7.1.7.1(1), unless otherwise permitted by one of the following:
  (a) The requirement of 13.7.2.1.2.1(1) shall not apply where initiation is by means of an approved automatic fire detection system in accordance with 13.7.1.7.1(2) that provides fire detection throughout the building.
  (b) The requirement of 13.7.2.1.2.1(1) shall not apply where initiation is by means of an approved automatic sprinkler system in accordance with 13.7.1.7.1(3) that provides fire detection and protection throughout the building.
(2) Where automatic sprinklers are provided, initiation of the fire alarm system by sprinkler system waterflow, even where manual fire alarm boxes are provided in accordance with 13.7.2.1.2.1(1)
[*101:* 12.3.4.2.1]

13.7.2.1.2.2 The initiating device shall be capable of transmitting an alarm to a receiving station, located within the building, that is constantly attended when the assembly occupancy is occupied. [*101:* 12.3.4.2.2]

13.7.2.1.2.3* In new assembly occupancies with occupant loads of more than 300, automatic detection shall be provided in all hazardous areas that are not normally occupied, unless such areas are protected throughout by an approved, supervised automatic sprinkler system in accordance with Section 13.3. [*101:*12.3.4.2.3]

13.7.2.1.3 Notification. The required fire alarm system shall activate an audible and visible alarm in a constantly attended receiving station within the building when occupied for purposes of initiating emergency action. [*101:*12.3.4.3]

13.7.2.1.3.1 Positive alarm sequence in accordance with 13.7.1.9.4 shall be permitted. [*101:* 12.3.4.3.1]

13.7.2.1.3.2 Reserved.

13.7.2.1.3.3 Occupant notification shall be by means of voice announcements in accordance with 13.7.1.9.9, initiated by the person in the constantly attended receiving station. [*101:*12.3.4.3.3]

13.7.2.1.3.4 Occupant notification shall be by means of visible signals in accordance with 13.7.1.9.5, initiated by the person in the constantly attended receiving station, unless otherwise permitted by 13.7.2.1.3.5. [*101:* 12.3.4.3.4]

13.7.2.1.3.5* Visible signals shall not be required in the assembly seating area, or the floor area used for the contest, performance, or entertainment, where the occupant load exceeds 1000 and an approved, alternative visible means of occupant notification is provided. *(See 13.7.1.9.5.7.)* [*101:*12.3.4.3.5]

13.7.2.1.3.6 The announcement shall be permitted to be made via a voice communication or public address system in accordance with 13.7.1.9.9.2. [*101:* 12.3.4.3.6]

13.7.2.1.3.7 Where the AHJ determines that a constantly attended receiving station is impractical, both of the following shall be provided:

(1) Automatically transmitted evacuation or relocation instructions shall be provided in accordance with *NFPA 72, National Fire Alarm and Signaling Code.*
(2) The system shall be monitored by a supervising station in accordance with *NFPA 72.* [*101:* 12.3.4.3.7]

13.7.2.2 Existing Assembly Occupancies.

13.7.2.2.1 General.

13.7.2.2.1.1 Existing assembly occupancies with occupant loads of more than 300 and all theaters with more than one audience-viewing room shall be provided with an approved fire alarm system in accordance with Section 13.7 and 13.7.2.2, unless otherwise permitted by 13.7.2.2.1.2, 13.7.2.2.1.3, or 13.7.2.2.1.4. [*101:* 13.3.4.1.1]

13.7.2.2.1.2 Existing assembly occupancies that are a part of a multiple occupancy protected as a mixed occupancy *(see 6.1.14)* shall be permitted to be served by a common fire alarm system, provided that the individual requirements of each occupancy are met. [*101:* 13.3.4.1.2]

13.7.2.2.1.3 Voice communication or public address systems complying with 13.7.2.2.3.6 shall not be required to comply with Section 13.7. [*101:* 13.3.4.1.3]

13.7.2.2.1.4 The requirement of 13.7.2.2.1.1 shall not apply to existing assembly occupancies where, in the judgment of the AHJ, adequate alternative provisions exist or are provided for the discovery of a fire and for alerting the occupants promptly. [*101:* 13.3.4.1.4]

13.7.2.2.2 Initiation.

13.7.2.2.2.1 Initiation of the required fire alarm system shall be by both of the following means, and the system shall be provided with an emergency power source:

(1) Manual means in accordance with 13.7.1.7.1(1), unless otherwise permitted by one of the following:
  (a) The requirement of 13.7.2.2.2.1(1) shall not apply where initiation is by means of an approved automatic fire detection system in accordance with 13.7.1.7.1(2) that provides fire detection throughout the building.
  (b) The requirement of 13.7.2.2.2.1(1) shall not apply where initiation is by means of an approved automatic sprinkler system in accordance with 13.7.1.7.1(3) that provides fire detection and protection throughout the building.
(2) Where automatic sprinklers are provided, initiation of the fire alarm system by sprinkler system waterflow, even where manual fire alarm boxes are provided in accordance with 13.7.2.2.2.1(1)
[*101:* 13.3.4.2.1]

13.7.2.2.2.2 The initiating device shall be capable of transmitting an alarm to a receiving station, located within the building, that is constantly attended when the assembly occupancy is occupied. [*101:* 13.3.4.2.2]

13.7.2.2.2.3* In existing assembly occupancies with occupant loads of more than 300, automatic detection shall be provided in all hazardous areas that are not normally occupied, unless such areas are protected throughout by an approved automatic sprinkler system in accordance with Section 13.3. [*101:*13.3.4.2.3]

13.7.2.2.3 Notification. The required fire alarm system shall activate an audible alarm in a constantly attended receiving station within the building when occupied for purposes of initiating emergency action. [*101:* 13.3.4.3]

13.7.2.2.3.1 Positive alarm sequence in accordance with 13.7.1.9.4 shall be permitted. [*101:* 13.3.4.3.1]

13.7.2.2.3.2 A presignal system in accordance with 13.7.1.9.3 shall be permitted. [*101:* 13.3.4.3.2]

13.7.2.2.3.3 Occupant notification shall be by means of voice announcements in accordance with 13.7.1.9.9 initiated by the person in the constantly attended receiving station. [*101:*13.3.4.3.3]

13.7.2.2.3.4 Reserved.

13.7.2.2.3.5 Reserved.

13.7.2.2.3.6 The announcement shall be permitted to be made via a voice communication or public address system in accordance with 13.7.1.9.9.2. [*101:* 13.3.4.3.6]

13.7.2.2.3.7 Where the AHJ determines that a constantly attended receiving station is impractical, automatically transmitted evacuation or relocation instructions shall be provided in accordance with *NFPA 72, National Fire Alarm and Signaling Code.* [*101:* 13.3.4.3.7]

13.7.2.3 New Educational Occupancies.

13.7.2.3.1 General.

13.7.2.3.1.1 New educational occupancies shall be provided with a fire alarm system in accordance with Section 13.7 and 13.7.2.3. [*101:* 14.3.4.1.1]

13.7.2.3.1.2 The requirement of 13.7.2.3.1.1 shall not apply to buildings meeting all of the following criteria:

(1) Buildings having an area not exceeding 1000 ft^2 (93 m^2)
(2) Buildings containing a single classroom
(3) Buildings located not less than 30 ft (9.1 m) from another building
[*101:* 14.3.4.1.2]

13.7.2.3.2 Initiation.

13.7.2.3.2.1 General. Initiation of the required fire alarm system, other than as permitted by 13.7.2.3.2.3, shall be by manual means in accordance with 13.7.1.7.1(1). [*101:* 14.3.4.2.1]

13.7.2.3.2.2 Automatic Initiation. In buildings provided with automatic sprinkler protection, the operation of the sprinkler system shall automatically activate the fire alarm system in addition to the initiation means required in 13.7.2.3.2.1. [*101:*14.3.4.2.2]

13.7.2.3.2.3 Alternative Protection System. Manual fire alarm boxes shall be permitted to be eliminated in accordance with 13.7.2.3.2.3.1 or 13.7.2.3.2.3.2. [*101:* 14.3.4.2.3]

13.7.2.3.2.3.1* Manual fire alarm boxes shall be permitted to be eliminated where all of the following conditions apply:

(1) Interior corridors are protected by smoke detectors in accordance with Section 13.7.
(2) Auditoriums, cafeterias, and gymnasiums are protected by heat-detection devices or other approved detection devices.
(3) Shops and laboratories involving dusts or vapors are protected by heat-detection devices or other approved detection devices.
(4) Provision is made at a central point to manually activate the evacuation signal or to evacuate only affected areas. [*101:* 14.3.4.2.3.1]

13.7.2.3.2.3.2* Manual fire alarm boxes shall be permitted to be eliminated where both of the following conditions apply:

(1) The building is protected throughout by an approved, supervised automatic sprinkler system in accordance with Section 13.3.
(2) Provision is made at a central point to manually activate the evacuation signal or to evacuate only affected areas. [*101:* 14.3.4.2.3.2]

13.7.2.3.3 Notification.

13.7.2.3.3.1 Occupant Notification.

13.7.2.3.3.1.1 Occupant notification shall be accomplished automatically in accordance with 13.7.1.9. [*101:* 14.3.4.3.1.1]

13.7.2.3.3.1.2 The occupant notification required by 13.7.2.3.3.1.1 shall utilize an emergency voice/alarm communication system in accordance with 13.7.1.9 where the building has an occupant load of more than 100. [*101:* 14.3.4.3.1.2]

13.7.2.3.3.1.3 Positive alarm sequence shall be permitted in accordance with 13.7.1.9.4. [*101:* 14.3.4.3.1.3]

13.7.2.3.3.1.4 In accordance with 13.7.1.9.10.2, the emergency voice/alarm communication system shall be permitted to be used for other emergency signaling or for class changes. [*101:* 14.3.4.3.1.4]

13.7.2.3.3.1.5 To prevent students from being returned to a building that is burning, the recall signal shall be separate and distinct from any other signals, and such signal shall be permitted to be given by use of distinctively colored flags or banners. [*101:* 14.3.4.3.1.5]

13.7.2.3.3.1.6 If the recall signal required by 13.7.2.3.3.1.5 is electric, the push buttons or other controls shall be kept under lock, the key for which shall be in the possession of the principal or another designated person in order to prevent a recall at a time when there is an actual fire. [*101:* 14.3.4.3.1.6]

13.7.2.3.3.1.7 Regardless of the method of recall signal, the means of giving the recall signal shall be kept under lock. [*101:* 14.3.4.3.1.7]

13.7.2.3.3.2 Emergency Forces Notification. Emergency forces notification shall be accomplished in accordance with 13.7.1.10. [*101:* 14.3.4.3.2]

13.7.2.3.4 Carbon Monoxide Alarms and Carbon Monoxide Detection Systems.

13.7.2.3.4.1 Carbon monoxide alarms or carbon monoxide detectors in accordance with 13.7.1.14 shall be provided in new educational occupancies in the locations specified as follows:

(1) On the ceilings of rooms containing permanently installed fuel-burning appliances

(2) Centrally located within occupiable spaces served by the first supply air register from a permanently installed, fuel-burning HVAC system
(3) Centrally located within occupiable spaces adjacent to a communicating attached garage
[*101:* 14.3.4.4.1]

13.7.2.3.4.2 Carbon monoxide alarms and carbon monoxide detectors as specified in 13.7.2.3.4.1 shall not be required in the following locations:

(1) Garages
(2) Occupiable spaces with communicating attached garages that are open parking structures as defined in 3.3.183.23.3
(3) Occupiable spaces with communicating attached garages that are mechanically ventilated in accordance with the applicable mechanical code
[*101:* 14.3.4.4.2]

13.7.2.4 Existing Educational Occupancies.

13.7.2.4.1 General.

13.7.2.4.1.1 Existing educational occupancies shall be provided with a fire alarm system in accordance with Section 13.7 and 13.7.2.4. [*101:* 15.3.4.1.1]

13.7.2.4.1.2 The requirement of 13.7.2.4.1.1 shall not apply to buildings meeting all of the following criteria:

(1) Buildings having an area not exceeding 1000 ft^2 (93 m^2)
(2) Buildings containing a single classroom
(3) Buildings located not less than 30 ft (9.1 m) from another building
[*101:* 15.3.4.1.2]

13.7.2.4.2 Initiation.

13.7.2.4.2.1 General. Initiation of the required fire alarm system shall be by manual means in accordance with 13.7.1.7(1), unless otherwise permitted by one of the following:

(1) Manual fire alarm boxes shall not be required where permitted by 13.7.2.4.2.3.
(2) In buildings where all normally occupied spaces are provided with a two-way communication system between such spaces and a constantly attended receiving station from where a general evacuation alarm can be sounded, the manual fire alarm boxes shall not be required, except in locations specifically designated by the AHJ.
[*101:* 15.3.4.2.1]

13.7.2.4.2.2 Automatic Initiation. In buildings provided with automatic sprinkler protection, the operation of the sprinkler system shall automatically activate the fire alarm system in addition to the initiation means required in 13.7.2.4.2.1. [*101:* 15.3.4.2.2]

13.7.2.4.2.3 Alternative Protection System. Manual fire alarm boxes shall be permitted to be eliminated in accordance with 13.7.2.4.2.3.1 or 13.7.2.4.2.3.2. [*101:* 15.3.4.2.3]

13.7.2.4.2.3.1* Manual fire alarm boxes shall be permitted to be eliminated where all of the following conditions apply:

(1) Interior corridors are protected by smoke detectors using an alarm verification system as described in *NFPA 72, National Fire Alarm and Signaling Code.*
(2) Auditoriums, cafeterias, and gymnasiums are protected by heat-detection devices or other approved detection devices.
(3) Shops and laboratories involving dusts or vapors are protected by heat-detection devices or other approved detection devices.

(4) Provision is made at a central point to manually activate the evacuation signal or to evacuate only affected areas.
[*101:* 15.3.4.2.3.1]

13.7.2.4.2.3.2* Manual fire alarm boxes shall be permitted to be eliminated where both of the following conditions apply:

(1) The building is protected throughout by an approved, supervised automatic sprinkler system in accordance with Section 13.3.
(2) Provision is made at a central point to manually activate the evacuation signal or to evacuate only affected areas.
[*101:* 15.3.4.2.3.2]

13.7.2.4.3 Notification.

13.7.2.4.3.1 Occupant Notification.

13.7.2.4.3.1.1* Occupant notification shall be accomplished automatically in accordance with 13.7.1.9. [*101:* 14.3.4.3.1.1]

13.7.2.4.3.1.2 Reserved.

13.7.2.4.3.1.3 Positive alarm sequence shall be permitted in accordance with 13.7.1.9.4. [*101:* 15.3.4.3.1.3]

13.7.2.4.3.1.4 Where acceptable to the AHJ, the fire alarm system shall be permitted to be used for other emergency signaling or for class changes, provided that the fire alarm is distinctive in signal and overrides all other use. [*101:* 15.3.4.3.1.4]

13.7.2.4.3.1.5 To prevent students from being returned to a building that is burning, the recall signal shall be separate and distinct from any other signals, and such signal shall be permitted to be given by use of distinctively colored flags or banners. [*101:* 15.3.4.3.1.5]

13.7.2.4.3.1.6 If the recall signal required by 13.7.2.4.3.1.5 is electric, the push buttons or other controls shall be kept under lock, the key for which shall be in the possession of the principal or another designated person in order to prevent a recall at a time when there is an actual fire. [*101:* 15.3.4.3.1.6]

13.7.2.4.3.1.7 Regardless of the method of recall signal, the means of giving the recall signal shall be kept under lock. [*101:* 15.3.4.3.1.7]

13.7.2.4.3.2 Emergency Forces Notification.

13.7.2.4.3.2.1 Wherever any of the school authorities determine that an actual fire exists, they shall immediately call the local fire department using the public fire alarm system or other available facilities. [*101:* 15.3.4.3.2.1]

13.7.2.4.3.2.2 Emergency forces notification shall be accomplished in accordance with 13.7.1.10 where the existing fire alarm system is replaced. [*101:* 15.3.4.3.2.2]

13.7.2.5 New Day-Care Occupancies.

13.7.2.5.1 General. New day-care occupancies, other than day-care occupancies housed in one room having at least one door opening directly to the outside at grade plane or to an exterior exit access balcony in accordance with 14.10.3, shall be provided with a fire alarm system in accordance with Section 13.7 and 13.7.2.5. [*101:* 16.3.4.1]

13.7.2.5.2 Initiation. Initiation of the required fire alarm system shall be by manual means and by operation of any required smoke detectors and required sprinkler systems. *(See 13.7.2.5.5.)* [*101:*16.3.4.2]

13.7.2.5.3 Occupant Notification.

13.7.2.5.3.1 Occupant notification shall be in accordance with 13.7.1.9. [*101:* 16.3.4.3.1]

13.7.2.5.3.2 Positive alarm sequence shall be permitted in accordance with 13.7.1.9.4. [*101:* 16.3.4.3.2]

13.7.2.5.3.3 Private operating mode in accordance with 13.7.1.9.6.3 shall be permitted. [*101:* 16.3.4.3.3]

13.7.2.5.4 Emergency Forces Notification. Emergency forces notification shall be accomplished in accordance with 13.7.1.10. [*101:* 16.3.4.4].

13.7.2.5.5 Detection. A smoke detection system in accordance with 13.7.1 shall be installed in new day-care occupancies, other than those housed in one room having at least one door opening directly to the outside at grade plane or to an exterior exit access balcony in accordance with 14.10.3, and such system shall comply with both of the following:

(1) Detectors shall be installed on each story in front of the doors to the stairways and in the corridors of all floors occupied by the day-care occupancy.
(2) Detectors shall be installed in lounges, recreation areas, and sleeping rooms in the day-care occupancy. [*101:* 16.3.4.5]

13.7.2.6 Existing Day-Care Occupancies.

13.7.2.6.1 General. Existing day-care occupancies, other than day-care occupancies housed in one room, shall be provided with a fire alarm system in accordance with Section 13.7 and 13.7.2.6. [*101:* 17.3.4.1]

13.7.2.6.2 Initiation. Initiation of the required fire alarm system shall be by manual means and by operation of any required smoke detectors and required sprinkler systems. *(See 13.7.2.6.5.)* [*101:* 17.3.4.2]

13.7.2.6.3 Occupant Notification.

13.7.2.6.3.1 Occupant notification shall be in accordance with 13.7.1.9. [*101:* 17.3.4.3.1]

13.7.2.6.3.2 Positive alarm sequence shall be permitted in accordance with 13.7.1.9.4. [*101:* 17.3.4.3.2]

13.7.2.6.3.3 Private operating mode in accordance with 13.7.1.9.6.3 shall be permitted. [*101:* 17.3.4.3.3]

13.7.2.6.4 Emergency Forces Notification.

13.7.2.6.4.1 Emergency forces notification, other than for day-care occupancies with not more than 100 clients, shall be accomplished in accordance with 13.7.1.10. [*101:* 17.3.4.4.1]

13.7.2.6.4.2 Emergency forces notification shall be accomplished in accordance with 13.7.1.10 where the existing fire alarm system is replaced. [*101:* 17.3.4.4.2]

13.7.2.6.5 Detection. A smoke detection system in accordance with 13.7.1 shall be installed in existing day-care occupancies, other than those housed in one room or those housing clients capable of self-preservation where no sleeping facilities are provided, and such system shall comply with both of the following:

(1) Detectors shall be installed on each story in front of the doors to the stairways and in the corridors of all floors occupied by the day-care occupancy.
(2) Detectors shall be installed in lounges, recreation areas, and sleeping rooms in the day-care occupancy. [*101:* 17.3.4.5]

13.7.2.7 New Health Care Occupancies.

13.7.2.7.1 General. New health care occupancies shall be provided with a fire alarm system in accordance with Section 13.7 and 13.7.2.7. [*101:* 18.3.4.1]

13.7.2.7.2* Initiation.

13.7.2.7.2.1 Initiation of the required fire alarm systems shall be by manual means in accordance with 13.7.1.7 and by means of any required sprinkler system waterflow alarms, detection devices, or detection systems, unless otherwise permitted by 13.7.2.7.2.2 and 13.7.2.7.2.3. [*101:* 18.3.4.2.1]

13.7.2.7.2.2 Manual fire alarm boxes in patient sleeping areas shall not be required at exits if located at all nurses' control stations or other continuously attended staff location, provided that both of the following criteria are met:

(1) Such manual fire alarm boxes are visible and continuously accessible.
(2) Travel distances required by 13.7.1.7.5 are not exceeded. [*101:* 18.3.4.2.2]

13.7.2.7.2.3 The system smoke detector installed in accordance with 18.3.2.5.3(13) of NFPA *101* shall not be required to initiate the fire alarm system. [*101:* 18.3.4.2.3]

13.7.2.7.3 Notification. Positive alarm sequence in accordance with 13.7.1.9.4 shall be permitted. [*101:* 18.3.4.3]

13.7.2.7.3.1 Occupant Notification. Occupant notification shall be accomplished automatically in accordance with 13.7.1.9, unless otherwise modified by the following:

(1) Paragraph 13.7.1.9.2.3 shall not be permitted to be used.
(2)*In lieu of audible alarm signals, visible alarm-indicating appliances shall be permitted to be used in critical care areas.
(3) The provision of 18.3.2.5.3(13)(c) of NFPA *101* shall be permitted to be used. [*101:* 18.3.4.3.1]

13.7.2.7.3.2 Emergency Forces Notification.

13.7.2.7.3.2.1 Emergency forces notification shall be accomplished in accordance with 13.7.1.10, except that the provision of 18.3.2.5.3(13)(d) of NFPA *101* shall be permitted to be used. [*101:* 18.3.4.3.2.1]

13.7.2.7.3.2.2 Reserved.

13.7.2.7.3.3 Annunciation and Annunciation Zoning.

13.7.2.7.3.3.1 Annunciation and annunciation zoning shall be provided in accordance with 13.7.1.13, unless otherwise permitted by 13.7.2.7.3.3.2 or 13.7.2.7.3.3.3. [*101:* 18.3.4.3.3.1]

13.7.2.7.3.3.2 The alarm zone shall be permitted to coincide with the permitted area for smoke compartments. [*101:*18.3.4.3.3.2]

13.7.2.7.3.3.3 The provision of 13.7.1.13.9.2, which permits sprinkler system waterflow to be annunciated as a single building zone, shall be prohibited. [*101:* 18.3.4.3.3.3]

13.7.2.7.4 Fire Safety Functions. Operation of any activating device in the required fire alarm system shall be arranged to accomplish automatically any control functions to be performed by that device. *(See 13.7.1.11.)* [*101:* 18.3.4.4]

13.7.2.7.5 Detection.

13.7.2.7.5.1 General. Detection systems, where required, shall be in accordance with Section 13.7. [*101:* 18.3.4.5.1]

13.7.2.7.5.2 Detection in Spaces Open to Corridors. See 18.3.6.1 of NFPA *101*. [*101:* 18.3.4.5.2]

13.7.2.7.5.3* Nursing Homes. An approved automatic smoke detection system shall be installed in corridors throughout smoke compartments containing patient sleeping rooms and in spaces open to corridors as permitted in nursing homes by 18.3.6.1 of NFPA *101*, unless otherwise permitted by one of the following:

(1) Corridor systems shall not be required where each patient sleeping room is protected by an approved smoke detection system.
(2) Corridor systems shall not be required where patient room doors are equipped with automatic door-closing devices with integral smoke detectors on the room side installed in accordance with their listing, provided that the integral detectors provide occupant notification. [*101:* 18.3.4.5.3]

13.7.2.8 Existing Health Care Occupancies.

13.7.2.8.1 General. Existing health care occupancies shall be provided with a fire alarm system in accordance with Section 13.7 and 13.7.2.8. [*101:* 19.3.4.1]

13.7.2.8.2* Initiation.

13.7.2.8.2.1 Initiation of the required fire alarm systems shall be by manual means in accordance with 13.7.1.7 and by means of any required sprinkler system waterflow alarms, detection devices, or detection systems, unless otherwise permitted by 13.7.2.8.2.2 through 13.7.2.8.2.5. [*101:* 19.3.4.2.1]

13.7.2.8.2.2 Manual fire alarm boxes in patient sleeping areas shall not be required at exits if located at all nurses' control stations or other continuously attended staff location, provided that both of the following criteria are met:

(1) Such manual fire alarm boxes are visible and continuously accessible.
(2) Travel distances required by 13.7.1.7.5 are not exceeded. [*101:* 19.3.4.2.2]

13.7.2.8.2.3 The system smoke detector installed in accordance with 19.3.2.5.3(13) of NFPA *101* shall not be required to initiate the fire alarm system. [*101:* 19.3.4.2.3]

13.7.2.8.2.4 Fixed extinguishing systems protecting commercial cooking equipment in kitchens that are protected by a complete automatic sprinkler system shall not be required to initiate the fire alarm system. [*101:* 19.3.4.2.4]

13.7.2.8.2.5 Detectors required by 19.7.5.3 and 19.7.5.5 of NFPA *101* shall not be required to initiate the fire alarm system. [*101:* 19.3.4.2.5]

13.7.2.8.3 Notification. Positive alarm sequence in accordance with 13.7.1.9.4 shall be permitted in health care occupancies protected throughout by an approved, supervised automatic sprinkler system in accordance with NFPA 13. [*101:* 19.3.4.3]

13.7.2.8.3.1 Occupant Notification. Occupant notification shall be accomplished automatically in accordance with 13.7.1.9, unless otherwise modified by the following:

(1)*In lieu of audible alarm signals, visible alarm-indicating appliances shall be permitted to be used in critical care areas.
(2) Where visual devices have been installed in patient sleeping areas in place of an audible alarm, they shall be permitted where approved by the AHJ.
(3) The provision of 19.3.2.5.3(13)(c) of NFPA *101* shall be permitted to be used. [*101:* 19.3.4.3.1]

13.7.2.8.3.2 Emergency Forces Notification.

13.7.2.8.3.2.1 Emergency forces notification shall be accomplished in accordance with 13.7.1.10, except that the provision of 19.3.2.5.3(13)(d) of NFPA 101 shall be permitted to be used. [*101:* 19.3.4.3.2.1]

13.7.2.8.3.2.2 Smoke detection devices or smoke detection systems equipped with reconfirmation features shall not be required to automatically notify the fire department, unless the alarm condition is reconfirmed after a period not exceeding 120 seconds. [*101:* 19.3.4.3.2.2]

13.7.2.8.3.3 Reserved.

13.7.2.8.4 Fire Safety Functions. Operation of any activating device in the required fire alarm system shall be arranged to accomplish automatically any control functions to be performed by that device. *(See 13.7.1.11.)* [*101:* 19.3.4.4]

13.7.2.8.5 Detection.

13.7.2.8.5.1 Corridors. An approved automatic smoke detection system in accordance with Section 13.7 shall be installed in all corridors of limited care facilities, unless otherwise permitted by one of the following:

(1) Where each patient sleeping room is protected by an approved smoke detection system, and a smoke detector is provided at smoke barriers and horizontal exits in accordance with Section 13.7, the corridor smoke detection system shall not be required on the patient sleeping room floors.
(2) Smoke compartments protected throughout by an approved, supervised automatic sprinkler system in accordance with 13.3.2.12.8 shall be permitted. [*101:* 19.3.4.5.1]

13.7.2.8.5.2 Detection in Spaces Open to Corridors. See 19.3.6.1 of NFPA *101*. [*101:* 19.3.4.5.2]

13.7.2.9 New Ambulatory Health Care Occupancies.

13.7.2.9.1 General. New ambulatory health care facilities shall be provided with fire alarm systems in accordance with Section 13.7 and 13.7.2.9, except as modified by 13.7.2.9.2 through 13.7.2.9.4. [*101:* 20.3.4.1]

13.7.2.9.2 Initiation. Initiation of the required fire alarm systems shall be by manual means in accordance with 13.7.1.7 and by means of any detection devices or detection systems required. [*101:* 20.3.4.2]

13.7.2.9.3 Notification. Positive alarm sequence in accordance with 13.7.1.9.4 shall be permitted. [*101:* 20.3.4.3]

13.7.2.9.3.1 Occupant Notification. Occupant notification shall be accomplished automatically, without delay, in accordance with 13.7.1.9 upon operation of any fire alarm activating device. [*101:* 20.3.4.3.1]

13.7.2.9.3.2 Emergency Forces Notification.

13.7.2.9.3.2.1 Emergency forces notification shall be accomplished in accordance with 13.7.1.10. [*101:* 20.3.4.3.2.1]

13.7.2.9.3.2.2 Reserved.

13.7.2.9.4 Fire Safety Functions. Operation of any activating device in the required fire alarm system shall be arranged to accomplish automatically, without delay, any control functions required to be performed by that device. *(See 13.7.1.11.)* [*101:*20.3.4.4]

13.7.2.10 Existing Ambulatory Health Care Occupancies.

13.7.2.10.1 General. Existing ambulatory health care facilities shall be provided with fire alarm systems in accordance with Section 13.7 and 13.7.2.10, except as modified by 13.7.2.10.2 through 13.7.2.10.4. [*101:* 21.3.4.1]

13.7.2.10.2 Initiation. Initiation of the required fire alarm systems shall be by manual means in accordance with 13.7.1.7 and by means of any detection devices or detection systems required. [*101:* 21.3.4.2]

13.7.2.10.3 Notification. Positive alarm sequence in accordance with 13.7.1.9.4 shall be permitted. [*101:* 21.3.4.3]

13.7.2.10.3.1 Occupant Notification. Occupant notification shall be accomplished automatically, without delay, in accordance with 13.7.1.9 upon operation of any fire alarm activating device. [*101:* 21.3.4.3.1]

13.7.2.10.3.2 Emergency Forces Notification.

13.7.2.10.3.2.1 Emergency forces notification shall be accomplished in accordance with 13.7.1.10. [*101:* 21.3.4.3.2.1]

13.7.2.10.3.2.2 Smoke detection devices or smoke detection systems equipped with reconfirmation features shall not be required to automatically notify the fire department, unless the alarm condition is reconfirmed after a period not exceeding 120 seconds. [*101:* 21.3.4.3.2.2]

13.7.2.10.4 Fire Safety Functions. Operation of any activating device in the required fire alarm system shall be arranged to accomplish automatically, without delay, any control functions required to be performed by that device. *(See 13.7.1.11.)* [*101:* 21.3.4.4]

13.7.2.11 New Detention and Correctional Occupancies.

13.7.2.11.1 General. New detention and correctional occupancies shall be provided with a fire alarm system in accordance with Section 13.7 and 13.7.2.11, except as modified by 13.7.2.11.2 through 13.7.2.11.4.3. [*101:* :22.3.4.1]

13.7.2.11.2 Initiation. Initiation of the required fire alarm system shall be by manual means in accordance with 13.7.1.7, by means of any required detection devices or detection systems, and by means of waterflow alarm in the sprinkler system required by 13.3.2.13.1, unless otherwise permitted by the following:

(1) Manual fire alarm boxes shall be permitted to be locked, provided that staff is present within the area when it is occupied and staff has keys readily available to unlock the boxes.
(2) Manual fire alarm boxes shall be permitted to be located in a staff location, provided that both of the following criteria are met:
 (a) The staff location is attended when the building is occupied.
 (b) The staff attendant has direct supervision of the sleeping area.
 [*101:* 22.3.4.2]

13.7.2.11.3 Notification.

13.7.2.11.3.1 Occupant Notification. Occupant notification shall be accomplished automatically in accordance with 13.7.1.9, and the following also shall apply:

(1) A positive alarm sequence shall be permitted in accordance with 13.7.1.9.4.
(2)*Any smoke detectors required by this chapter shall be permitted to be arranged to alarm at a constantly attended location only and shall not be required to accomplish general occupant notification. [*101:* 22.3.4.3.2.1]

13.7.2.11.3.2 Emergency Forces Notification.

13.7.2.11.3.2.1 Fire department notification shall be accomplished in accordance with 13.7.1.10, unless otherwise permitted by one of the following:

(1) A positive alarm sequence shall be permitted in accordance with 13.7.1.9.4.
(2) Any smoke detectors required by this chapter shall not be required to transmit an alarm to the fire department.
(3) This requirement shall not apply where staff is provided at a constantly attended location that meets one of the following criteria:
 (a) It has the capability to promptly notify the fire department.
 (b) It has direct communication with a control room having direct access to the fire department.
 [*101:*22.3.4.3.2.1]

13.7.2.11.3.2.2 Where the provision of 13.7.2.11.3.2.1(3) is utilized, the fire plan, as required by 20.7.2.1.3, shall include procedures for logging of alarms and immediate notification of the fire department. [*101:* 22.3.4.3.2.2]

13.7.2.11.4* Detection. An approved automatic smoke detection system shall be in accordance with Section 13.7, as modified by 13.7.2.11.4.1 through 13.7.2.11.4.3, throughout all resident sleeping areas and adjacent day rooms, activity rooms, or contiguous common spaces. [*101:* 22.3.4.4]

13.7.2.11.4.1 Smoke detectors shall not be required in sleeping rooms with four or fewer occupants. [*101:* 22.3.4.4.1]

13.7.2.11.4.2 Other arrangements and positioning of smoke detectors shall be permitted to prevent damage or tampering, or for other purposes. [*101:* 22.3.4.4.2]

13.7.2.11.4.2.1 Other arrangements, as specified in 13.7.2.11.4.2, shall be capable of detecting any fire, and the placement of detectors shall be such that the speed of detection is equivalent to that provided by the spacing and arrangements required by the installation standards referenced in Section 13.7. [*101:* 22.3.4.4.2.1]

13.7.2.11.4.2.2 Detectors shall be permitted to be located in exhaust ducts from cells, behind grilles, or in other locations. [*101:* 22.3.4.4.2.2]

13.7.2.11.4.2.3 The equivalent performance of the design permitted by 13.7.2.11.4.2.2 shall be acceptable to the AHJ in accordance with the equivalency concepts specified in Section 1.4. [*101:* 22.3.4.4.2.3]

13.7.2.11.4.3* Smoke detectors shall not be required in Use Condition II open dormitories where staff is present within the dormitory whenever the dormitory is occupied. [*101:*22.3.4.4.3]

13.7.2.12 Existing Detention and Correctional Occupancies.

13.7.2.12.1 General. Existing detention and correctional occupancies shall be provided with a fire alarm system in accordance with Section 13.7 and 13.7.2.12, except as modified by 13.7.2.12.2 through 13.7.2.12.4.4. [*101:*23.3.4.1]

13.7.2.12.2 Initiation. Initiation of the required fire alarm system shall be by manual means in accordance with 13.7.1.7 and by means of any required detection devices or detection systems, unless otherwise permitted by the following:

(1) Manual fire alarm boxes shall be permitted to be locked, provided that staff is present within the area when it is occupied and staff has keys readily available to unlock the boxes.
(2) Manual fire alarm boxes shall be permitted to be located in a staff location, provided that both of the following criteria are met:
   (a) The staff location is attended when the building is occupied.
   (b) The staff attendant has direct supervision of the sleeping area.
   [*101:* 23.3.4.2]

13.7.2.12.3 Notification.

13.7.2.12.3.1 Occupant Notification. Occupant notification shall be accomplished automatically in accordance with 13.7.1.9, and the following also shall apply:

(1) A positive alarm sequence shall be permitted in accordance with 13.7.1.9.4.
(2)*Any smoke detectors required by this chapter shall be permitted to be arranged to alarm at a constantly attended location only and shall not be required to accomplish general occupant notification. [*101:* 23.3.4.3.1]

13.7.2.12.3.2 Emergency Forces Notification.

13.7.2.12.3.2.1 Fire department notification shall be accomplished in accordance with 13.7.1.10, unless otherwise permitted by one of the following:

(1) A positive alarm sequence shall be permitted in accordance with 13.7.1.9.4.
(2) Any smoke detectors required by this chapter shall not be required to transmit an alarm to the fire department.
(3) This requirement shall not apply where staff is provided at a constantly attended location that meets one of the following criteria:
   (a) It has the capability to promptly notify the fire department.
   (b) It has direct communication with a control room having direct access to the fire department.
   [*101:* 23.3.4.3.2.1]

13.7.2.12.3.2.2 Where the provision of 13.7.2.12.3.2.1(3) is utilized, the fire plan, as required by 20.7.2.1.3, shall include procedures for logging of alarms and immediate notification of the fire department. [*101:* 23.3.4.3.2.2]

13.7.2.12.4 Detection. An approved automatic smoke detection system shall be in accordance with Section 13.7, as modified by 13.7.2.12.4.1 through 13.7.2.12.4.4, throughout all resident housing areas. [*101:* 23.3.4.4]

13.7.2.12.4.1 Smoke detectors shall not be required in sleeping rooms with four or fewer occupants in Use Condition II or Use Condition III. [*101:* 23.3.4.4.1]

13.7.2.12.4.2 Other arrangements and positioning of smoke detectors shall be permitted to prevent damage or tampering, or for other purposes. [*101:* 23.3.4.4.2]

13.7.2.12.4.2.1 Other arrangements, as specified in 13.7.2.12.4.2, shall be capable of detecting any fire, and the placement of detectors shall be such that the speed of detection is equivalent to that provided by the spacing and arrangements required by the installation standards referenced in Section 13.7. [*101:* 23.3.4.4.2.1]

13.7.2.12.4.2.2 Detectors shall be permitted to be located in exhaust ducts from cells, behind grilles, or in other locations. [*101:* 23.3.4.4.2.2]

13.7.2.12.4.2.3 The equivalent performance of the design permitted by 13.7.2.12.4.2.2 shall be acceptable to the AHJ in accordance with the equivalency concepts specified in Section 1.4. [*101:* 23.3.4.4.2.3]

13.7.2.12.4.3* Smoke detectors shall not be required in Use Condition II open dormitories where staff is present within the dormitory whenever the dormitory is occupied and the building is protected throughout by an approved, supervised automatic sprinkler system in accordance with 13.3.2.14.2. [*101:* 23.3.4.4.3]

13.7.2.12.4.4 In smoke compartments protected throughout by an approved automatic sprinkler system in accordance with 13.3.2.14.2, smoke detectors shall not be required, except in corridors, common spaces, and sleeping rooms with more than four occupants. [*101:* 23.3.4.4.4]

13.7.2.13 New and Existing One- and Two-Family Dwellings.

13.7.2.13.1 Smoke alarms or a smoke detection system shall be provided in accordance with either 13.7.2.13.1.1 or 13.7.2.13.1.2, as modified by 13.7.2.13.1.3. [*101:* 24.3.4.1]

13.7.2.13.1.1* Smoke alarms shall be installed in accordance with 13.7.1.8 in all of the following locations:

(1) All sleeping rooms
(2)*Outside of each separate sleeping area, in the immediate vicinity of the sleeping rooms
(3) On each level of the dwelling unit, including basements
[*101:* 24.3.4.1.1]

13.7.2.13.1.2 Dwelling units shall be protected by an approved smoke detection system in accordance with Section 13.7 and equipped with an approved means of occupant notification. [*101:* 24.3.4.1.2]

13.7.2.13.1.3 In existing one- and two-family dwellings, approved smoke alarms powered by batteries shall be permitted. [*101:* 24.3.4.1.3]

13.7.2.13.2 Carbon Monoxide and Carbon Monoxide Detection Systems.

13.7.2.13.2.1 Carbon monoxide alarms or carbon monoxide detectors in accordance with 13.7.2.14 and 13.7.2.13.2 shall be provided in new one- and two-family dwellings where either of the following conditions exists:

(1) Dwelling units with communicating attached garages, unless otherwise exempted by 13.7.2.13.2.3
(2) Dwelling units containing fuel-burning appliances or fuel-burning fireplaces
[*101:* 24.3.4.2.1]

13.7.2.13.2.2* Where required by 13.7.2.13.2.1, carbon monoxide alarms or carbon monoxide detectors shall be installed in the following locations:

(1) Outside of each separate dwelling unit sleeping area in the immediate vicinity of the sleeping rooms

(2) On every occupiable level of a dwelling unit, including basements, and excluding attics and crawl spaces [*101:* 24.3.4.2.2]

13.7.2.13.2.3 Carbon monoxide alarms and carbon monoxide detectors as specified in 13.7.2.13.2.1(1) shall not be required in the following locations:

(1) In garages
(2) Within dwelling units with communicating attached garages that are open parking structures as defined by the building code
(3) Within dwelling units with communicating attached garages that are mechanically ventilated in accordance with the mechanical code [*101:* 24.3.4.2.3]

13.7.2.14 New and Existing Lodging or Rooming Houses.

13.7.2.14.1 General.

13.7.2.14.1.1 New and existing lodging or rooming houses, other than those meeting 13.7.2.14.1.2, shall be provided with a fire alarm system in accordance with Section 13.7. [*101:*26.3.4.1.1]

13.7.2.14.1.2 A fire alarm system in accordance with Section 13.7 shall not be required in existing lodging or rooming houses that have an existing smoke detection system meeting or exceeding the requirements of 13.7.2.14.5.1 where that detection system includes not less than one manual fire alarm box per floor arranged to initiate the smoke detection alarm. [*101:* 26.3.4.1.2]

13.7.2.14.2 Initiation. Initiation of the required fire alarm system shall be by manual means in accordance with 13.7.1.7, or by alarm initiation in accordance with 13.7.1.7.1 13.7.1.7.1(3) in buildings protected throughout by an approved automatic sprinkler system in accordance with 13.3.2.19. [*101:* 26.3.4.2]

13.7.2.14.3 Notification. Occupant notification shall be provided automatically in accordance with 13.7.1.9, as modified by 13.7.2.14.3.1 and 13.7.2.14.3.2. [*101:* 26.3.4.3]

13.7.2.14.3.1* Visible signals for the hearing impaired shall not be required where the proprietor resides in the building and there are five or fewer rooms for rent. [*101:* 26.3.4.3.1]

13.7.2.14.3.2 Positive alarm sequence in accordance with 13.7.1.9.4 shall be permitted. [*101:* 26.3.4.3.2]

13.7.2.14.4 Detection. (Reserved)

13.7.2.14.5 Smoke Alarms.

13.7.2.14.5.1 Approved smoke alarms, other than existing smoke alarms meeting the requirements of 13.7.2.14.5.3, shall be installed in accordance with 13.7.1.8 in every sleeping room. [*101:* 26.3.4.5.1]

13.7.2.14.5.2 In other than existing buildings, the smoke alarms required by 13.7.2.14.5.1 shall be interconnected in accordance with 13.7.1.8.3. [*101:* 26.3.4.5.2]

13.7.2.14.5.3 Existing battery-powered smoke alarms, rather than house electric-powered smoke alarms, shall be permitted where the facility has demonstrated to the AHJ that the testing, maintenance, and battery replacement programs will ensure reliability of power to the smoke alarms. [*101:* 26.3.4.5.3]

13.7.2.14.6 Carbon Monoxide Alarms and Carbon Monoxide Detection Systems.

13.7.2.14.6.1 Carbon monoxide alarms or carbon monoxide detectors in accordance with 13.7.1.14 and 13.7.2.14.6 shall be provided in new lodging or rooming houses where either of the following conditions exists:

(1) Lodging or rooming houses with communicating attached garages, unless otherwise exempted by 13.7.2.14.6.3
(2) Lodging or rooming houses containing fuel-burning appliances or fuel-burning fireplaces [*101:* 26.3.4.6.1]

13.7.2.14.6.2* Where required by 13.7.2.14.6.1, carbon monoxide alarms or carbon monoxide detectors shall be installed in the following locations:

(1) Outside of each separate sleeping area in the immediate vicinity of the sleeping rooms
(2) On every occupiable level, including basements, and excluding attics and crawl spaces [*101:* 26.3.4.6.2]

13.7.2.14.6.3 Carbon monoxide alarms and carbon monoxide detectors as specified in 13.7.2.14.6.1(1) shall not be required in the following locations:

(1) In garages
(2) Within lodging or rooming houses with communicating attached garages that are open parking structures as defined by the building code
(3) Within lodging or rooming houses with communicating attached garages that are mechanically ventilated in accordance with the mechanical code [*101:* 26.3.4.6.3]

13.7.2.15 New Hotels and Dormitories.

13.7.2.15.1 General. A fire alarm system in accordance with Section 13.7, except as modified by 13.7.2.15.2 through 13.7.2.15.6, shall be provided. [*101:* 28.3.4.1]

13.7.2.15.2 Initiation. The required fire alarm system shall be initiated by each of the following:

(1) Manual means in accordance with 13.7.1.7
(2) Manual fire alarm box located at the hotel desk or other convenient central control point under continuous supervision by responsible employees
(3) Required automatic sprinkler system
(4) Required automatic detection system other than sleeping room smoke detectors [*101:* 28.3.4.2]

13.7.2.15.3 Notification.

13.7.2.15.3.1* Occupant notification shall be provided automatically in accordance with 13.7.1.9. [*101:* 28.3.4.3.1]

13.7.2.15.3.2 Positive alarm sequence in accordance with 13.7.1.9.4 shall be permitted. [*101:* 28.3.4.3.2]

13.7.2.15.3.3* Guest rooms and guest suites specifically required and equipped to accommodate hearing-impaired individuals shall be provided with a visible notification appliance. [*101:* 28.3.4.3.3]

13.7.2.15.3.4 In occupiable areas, other than guest rooms and guest suites, visible notification appliances shall be provided. [*101:* 28.3.4.3.4]

13.7.2.15.3.5 Annunciation and annunciation zoning in accordance with 13.7.1.13 shall be provided in buildings three or more stories in height or having more than 50 guest rooms or guest suites. Annunciation shall be provided at a location readily accessible from the primary point of entry for emergency response personnel. [*101:* 28.3.4.3.5]

13.7.2.15.3.6 Emergency forces notification shall be provided in accordance with 13.7.1.10. [*101:* 28.3.4.3.6]

13.7.2.15.4 Detection. A corridor smoke detection system in accordance with Section 13.7 shall be provided in buildings other than those protected throughout by an approved, supervised automatic sprinkler system in accordance with 13.7.2.15. [*101:* 28.3.4.4]

13.7.2.15.5* Smoke Alarms. Smoke alarms shall be installed in accordance with 13.7.1.8 in every guest room and every living area and sleeping room within a guest suite. [*101:* 28.3.4.5]

13.7.2.15.6 Carbon Monoxide Alarms and Carbon Monoxide Detection Systems.

13.7.2.15.6.1 Carbon monoxide alarms or carbon monoxide detectors in accordance with 13.7.1.14 and 13.7.2.15.6 shall be provided in new hotels and dormitories where either of the following conditions exists:

(1) Guest rooms or guest suites with communicating attached garages, unless otherwise exempted by 13.7.2.15.6.3
(2) Guest rooms or guest suites containing a permanently installed fuel-burning appliance or fuel-burning fireplace
[*101:* 28.3.4.6.1]

13.7.2.15.6.2 Where required by 13.7.2.15.6.1, carbon monoxide alarms or carbon monoxide detectors shall be installed in the following locations:

(1) Outside of each separate guest room or guest suite sleeping area in the immediate vicinity of the sleeping rooms
(2) On every occupiable level of a guest room and guest suite
[*101:* 28.3.4.6.2]

13.7.2.15.6.3 Carbon monoxide alarms and carbon monoxide detectors as specified in 13.7.2.15.6.1(1) shall not be required in the following locations:

(1) In garages
(2) Within guest rooms or guest suites with communicating attached garages that are open parking structures as defined by the building code
(3) Within guest rooms or guest suites with communicating attached garages that are mechanically ventilated in accordance with the mechanical code
[*101:* 28.3.4.6.3]

13.7.2.15.6.4 Where fuel-burning appliances or fuel-burning fireplaces are installed outside guest rooms or guest suites, carbon monoxide alarms or carbon monoxide detectors shall be installed in accordance with the manufacturer's published instructions in the locations specified as follows:

(1) On the ceilings of rooms containing permanently installed fuel-burning appliances or fuel-burning fireplaces
(2) Centrally located within occupiable spaces served by the first supply air register from a permanently installed, fuel-burning HVAC system
(3) Centrally located within occupiable spaces adjacent to a communicating attached garage
[*101:* 28.3.4.6.4]

13.7.2.16 Existing Hotels and Dormitories.

13.7.2.16.1 General. A fire alarm system in accordance with Section 13.7, except as modified by 13.7.2.16.2 through 13.7.2.16.3.5, shall be provided in buildings, other than those where each guest room has exterior exit access in accordance with 14.10.3 and the building is three or fewer stories in height. [*101:* 29.3.4.1]

13.7.2.16.2 Initiation. The required fire alarm system shall be initiated by each of the following:

(1) Manual means in accordance with 13.7.1.7, unless there are other effective means to activate the fire alarm system, such as complete automatic sprinkler or automatic detection systems, with manual fire alarm box in accordance with 13.7.2.16.2(2) required
(2) Manual fire alarm box located at the hotel desk or other convenient central control point under continuous supervision by responsible employees
(3) Required automatic sprinkler system
(4) Required automatic detection system other than sleeping room smoke detectors
[*101:* 29.3.4.2]

13.7.2.16.3 Notification.

13.7.2.16.3.1 Occupant notification shall be provided automatically in accordance with 13.7.1.9. [*101:* 29.3.4.3.1]

13.7.2.16.3.2 Positive alarm sequence in accordance with 13.7.1.9.4, and a presignal system in accordance with 13.7.1.9.3, shall be permitted. [*101:* 29.3.4.3.2]

13.7.2.16.3.3 Reserved.

13.7.2.16.3.4 Reserved.

13.7.2.16.3.5 Reserved.

13.7.2.16.3.6* Where the existing fire alarm system does not provide for automatic emergency forces notification in accordance with 13.7.1.10, provisions shall be made for the immediate notification of the public fire department by telephone or other means in case of fire, and, where there is no public fire department, notification shall be made to the private fire brigade. [*101:* 29.3.4.3.6]

13.7.2.16.3.7 Where a new fire alarm system is installed or the existing fire alarm system is replaced, emergency forces notification shall be provided in accordance with 13.7.1.10. [*101:* 29.3.4.3.7]

13.7.2.16.4 Detection. (Reserved)

13.7.2.16.5* Smoke Alarms. An approved single-station smoke alarm shall be installed in accordance with 13.7.1.8 in every guest room and every living area and sleeping room within a guest suite. [*101:* 29.3.4.5]

13.7.2.16.5.1 The smoke alarms shall not be required to be interconnected. [*101:* 29.3.4.5.1]

13.7.2.16.5.2 Single-station smoke alarms without a secondary (standby) power source shall be permitted. [*101:* 29.3.4.5.2]

13.7.2.17 New Apartment Buildings.

13.7.2.17.1 General.

13.7.2.17.1.1 New apartment buildings four or more stories in height or with more than 11 dwelling units, other than those meeting the requirements of 13.7.2.17.1.2, shall be provided with a fire alarm system in accordance with Section 13.7, except as modified by 13.7.2.17.2 through 13.7.2.17.5. [*101:* 30.3.4.1.1]

13.7.2.17.1.2 A fire alarm system shall not be required in buildings where each dwelling unit is separated from other contiguous dwelling units by fire barriers *(see Section 12.7)* having a minimum 1-hour fire resistance rating, and where each dwelling unit has either its own independent exit or its own independent stairway or ramp discharging at the finished ground level. [*101:* 30.3.4.1.2]

13.7.2.17.2 Initiation.

13.7.2.17.2.1 Initiation of the required fire alarm system shall be by manual means in accordance with 13.7.1.7, unless the building complies with 13.7.2.17.2.2. [*101:* 30.3.4.2.1]

13.7.2.17.2.2 Initiation of the required fire alarm system by manual means shall not be required in buildings four or fewer stories in height, containing not more than 16 dwelling units, and protected throughout by an approved, supervised automatic sprinkler system installed in accordance with 13.3.2.17. [*101:* 30.3.4.2.2]

13.7.2.17.2.3 In buildings protected throughout by an approved, supervised automatic sprinkler system in accordance with 13.3.2.17, required fire alarm systems shall be initiated upon operation of the automatic sprinkler system. [*101:* 30.3.4.2.3]

13.7.2.17.3 Notification.

13.7.2.17.3.1 Occupant notification shall be provided automatically in accordance with Section 13.7, and both of the following shall also apply:

(1) Visible signals shall be installed in units designed for the hearing impaired.
(2) Positive alarm sequence in accordance with 13.7.1.9.4 shall be permitted.
[*101:* 30.3.4.3.1]

13.7.2.17.3.2 Annunciation, and annunciation zoning, in accordance with 13.7.1.13 shall be provided, unless the building complies with either 13.7.2.17.3.3 or 13.7.2.17.3.4. Annunciation shall be provided at a location readily accessible from the primary point of entry for emergency response personnel. [*101:* 30.3.4.3.2]

13.7.2.17.3.3 Annunciation, and annunciation zoning, shall not be required in buildings two or fewer stories in height and having not more than 50 dwelling units. [*101:* 30.3.4.3.3]

13.7.2.17.3.4 Annunciation, and annunciation zoning, shall not be required in buildings four or fewer stories in height containing not more than 16 dwelling units and protected throughout by an approved, supervised automatic sprinkler system installed in accordance with 13.3.2.17. [*101:* 30.3.4.3.4]

13.7.2.17.3.5 Emergency forces notification shall be accomplished in accordance with 13.7.1.10. [*101:* 30.3.4.3.5]

13.7.2.17.4 Detection. (Reserved)

13.7.2.17.5* Smoke Alarms. Smoke alarms shall be installed in accordance with 13.7.1.8 in every sleeping area, outside every sleeping area in the immediate vicinity of the bedrooms, and on all levels of the dwelling unit, including basements. [*101:* 30.3.4.5]

13.7.2.17.6 Carbon Monoxide Alarms and Carbon Monoxide Detection Systems.

13.7.2.17.6.1 Carbon monoxide alarms or carbon monoxide detectors in accordance with 13.7.1.14 and 13.7.2.17.6 shall be provided in new apartment buildings where either of the following conditions exists:

(1) Dwelling units with communicating attached garages, unless otherwise exempted by 13.7.2.17.6.3
(2) Dwelling units containing a permanently installed fuel-burning appliance or fuel-burning fireplace
[*101:* 30.3.4.6.1]

13.7.2.17.6.2 Where required by 13.7.2.17.6.1, carbon monoxide alarms or carbon monoxide detectors shall be installed in the following locations:

(1) Outside of each separate dwelling unit sleeping area in the immediate vicinity of the sleeping rooms
(2) On every occupiable level of a dwelling unit
[*101:* 30.3.4.6.2]

13.7.2.17.6.3 Carbon monoxide alarms and carbon monoxide detectors as specified in 13.7.2.17.6.1(1) shall not be required in the following locations:

(1) In garages
(2) Within dwelling units with communicating attached garages that are open parking structures as defined by the building code
(3) Within dwelling units with communicating attached garages that are mechanically ventilated in accordance with the mechanical code
[*101:* 30.3.4.6.3]

13.7.2.17.6.4 Where fuel-burning appliances or fuel-burning fireplaces are installed outside dwelling units, carbon monoxide alarms or carbon monoxide detectors shall be installed in accordance with the manufacturer's published instructions in the locations specified as follows:

(1) On the ceilings of rooms containing permanently installed fuel-burning appliances or fuel-burning fireplaces
(2) Centrally located within occupiable spaces served by the first supply air register from a permanently installed, fuel-burning HVAC system
(3) Centrally located within occupiable spaces adjacent to a communicating attached garage
[*101:* 30.3.4.6.4]

13.7.2.18 Existing Apartment Buildings.

13.7.2.18.1 General.

13.7.2.18.1.1 Existing apartment buildings four or more stories in height or with more than 11 dwelling units, other than those meeting the requirements of 13.7.2.18.1.2, shall be provided with a fire alarm system in accordance with Section 13.7, except as modified by 13.7.2.18.1.2 through 13.7.2.18.5. [*101:* 31.3.4.1.1]

13.7.2.18.1.2 A fire alarm system shall not be required where each dwelling unit is separated from other contiguous dwelling units by fire barriers *(see Section 12.7)* having a minimum ½-hour fire resistance rating, and where each dwelling unit has either its own independent exit or its own independent stairway or ramp discharging at the finished ground level. [*101:* 31.3.4.1.2]

13.7.2.18.2 Initiation.

13.7.2.18.2.1 Initiation of the required fire alarm system shall be by manual means in accordance with 13.7.1.7, unless the building complies with 13.7.2.18.2.2. [*101:* 31.3.4.2.1]

13.7.2.18.2.2 Initiation of the required fire alarm system by manual means shall not be required in buildings four or fewer stories in height, containing not more than 16 dwelling units, and protected throughout by an approved, supervised automatic sprinkler system installed in accordance with 13.7.2.18. [*101:* 31.3.4.2.2]

13.7.2.18.2.3 In buildings using Option 2 as defined by NFPA *101*, the required fire alarm system shall be initiated by the automatic fire detection system in addition to the manual initiation means of 13.7.2.18.2.1. [*101:* 31.3.4.2.3]

13.7.2.18.2.4 In buildings using Option 3 as defined by NFPA *101*, the required fire alarm system shall be initiated upon operation of the automatic sprinkler system in addition to the manual initiation means of 13.7.2.18.2.1. [*101:* 31.3.4.2.4]

13.7.2.18.2.5 In buildings using Option 4 as defined by NFPA *101*, the required fire alarm system shall be initiated upon operation of the automatic sprinkler system in addition to the manual initiation means of 13.7.2.18.2.1. [*101:* 31.3.4.2.5]

13.7.2.18.3 Notification.

13.7.2.18.3.1 Occupant notification shall be provided automatically in accordance with Section 13.7, and all of the following shall also apply:

(1) Visible signals shall be installed in units designed for the hearing impaired.
(2) Positive alarm sequence in accordance with 13.7.1.9.4 shall be permitted.
(3) Existing approved presignal systems shall be permitted in accordance with 13.7.1.9.3.
[*101:* 31.3.4.3.1]

13.7.2.18.3.2 An annunciator panel, whose location shall be approved by the AHJ, connected with the required fire alarm system shall be provided, unless the building meets the requirements of 13.7.2.18.3.3 or 13.7.2.18.3.4. [*101:* 31.3.4.3.2]

13.7.2.18.3.3 Annunciation shall not be required in buildings two or fewer stories in height and having not more than 50 rooms. [*101:* 31.3.4.3.3]

13.7.2.18.3.4 Annunciation shall not be required in buildings four or fewer stories in height containing not more than 16 dwelling units and protected throughout by an approved, supervised automatic sprinkler system installed in accordance with 13.3.2.18. [*101:* 31.3.4.3.4]

13.7.2.18.3.5 Emergency forces notification shall be accomplished in accordance with 13.7.1.10. [*101:* 31.3.4.3.5]

13.7.2.18.4 Detection.

13.7.2.18.4.1* In buildings using Option 2 as defined by NFPA *101*, a complete automatic fire detection system in accordance with 9.6.2.9 of NFPA *101* and 13.7.2.18.4.2 shall be required. [*101:* 31.3.4.4.1]

13.7.2.18.4.2 Automatic fire detection devices shall be installed as follows:

(1) Smoke detectors shall be installed in all common areas and work spaces outside the living unit, such as exit stairs, egress corridors, lobbies, storage rooms, equipment rooms, and other tenantless spaces in environments that are suitable for proper smoke detector operation.
(2) Heat detectors shall be located within each room of the living unit. [*101:* 31.3.4.4.2]

13.7.2.18.5 Smoke Alarms.

13.7.2.18.5.1* In buildings other than those equipped throughout with an existing, complete automatic smoke detection system, smoke alarms shall be installed in accordance with 13.7.1.8, as modified by 13.7.2.18.5.2, outside every sleeping area in the immediate vicinity of the bedrooms and on all levels of the dwelling unit, including basements. [*101:* 31.3.4.5.1]

13.7.2.18.5.2 Smoke alarms required by 13.7.2.18.5.1 shall not be required to be provided with a secondary (standby) power source. [*101:* 31.3.4.5.2]

13.7.2.18.5.3 In buildings other than those equipped throughout with an existing, complete automatic smoke detection system or a complete, supervised automatic sprinkler system in accordance with 13.3.2.18, smoke alarms shall be installed in every sleeping area in accordance with 13.7.1.8, as modified by 13.7.2.18.5.4. [*101:* 31.3.4.5.3]

13.7.2.18.5.4 Smoke alarms required by 13.7.2.18.5.3 shall be permitted to be battery powered. [*101:* 31.3.4.5.4]

13.7.2.19 New, Small (Not More Than 16 Residents) Residential Board and Care Occupancies.

13.7.2.19.1 General. A manual fire alarm system shall be provided in accordance with Section 13.7. [*101:* 32.2.3.4.1]

13.7.2.19.2 Occupant Notification. Occupant notification shall be provided automatically, without delay, in accordance with 13.7.1.9. [*101:* 32.2.3.4.2]

13.7.2.19.3 Smoke Alarms.

13.7.2.19.3.1 Approved smoke alarms shall be provided in accordance with 13.7.1.8. [*101:* 32.2.3.4.3.1]

13.7.2.19.3.2 Smoke alarms shall be installed on all levels, including basements but excluding crawl spaces and unfinished attics. [*101:* 32.2.3.4.3.2]

13.7.2.19.3.3 Additional smoke alarms shall be installed in all living areas, as defined in 3.3.21.5 of NFPA *101*. [*101:* 32.2.3.4.3.3]

13.7.2.19.3.4 Each sleeping room shall be provided with an approved smoke alarm in accordance with 13.7.1.8. [*101:* 32.2.3.4.3.4]

13.7.2.20 New, Large (More than 16 Residents) Residential Board and Care Occupancies.

13.7.2.20.1 General. A fire alarm system shall be provided in accordance with Section 13.7. [*101:* 32.3.3.4.1]

13.7.2.20.2 Initiation. The required fire alarm system shall be initiated by each of the following:

(1) Manual means in accordance with 13.7.1.7
(2) Manual fire alarm box located at a convenient central control point under continuous supervision of responsible employees
(3) Required automatic sprinkler system
(4) Required detection system
[*101:* 32.3.3.4.2]

13.7.2.20.3 Annunciator Panel. An annunciator panel, connected to the fire alarm system, shall be provided at a location readily accessible from the primary point of entry for emergency response personnel. [*101:* 32.3.3.4.3]

13.7.2.20.4 Occupant Notification. Occupant notification shall be provided automatically, without delay, in accordance with 13.7.1.9. [*101:* 32.3.3.4.4]

13.7.2.20.5 High-Rise Buildings. High-rise buildings shall be provided with an approved emergency voice communication/alarm system in accordance with 13.7.2.29.2. [*101:* 32.3.3.4.5]

13.7.2.20.6* Emergency Forces Notification. Emergency forces notification shall meet the following requirements:

(1) Emergency forces notification shall be accomplished in accordance with 13.7.1.10.
(2) Smoke detection devices or smoke detection systems shall be permitted to initiate a positive alarm sequence in accordance with 13.7.1.9.4 for not more than 120 seconds. [*101:* 32.3.3.4.6]

13.7.2.20.7 Smoke Alarms. Approved smoke alarms shall be installed in accordance with 13.7.1.8 inside every sleeping room, outside every sleeping area in the immediate vicinity of the bedrooms, and on all levels within a resident unit. [*101:* 32.3.3.4.7]

13.7.2.20.8 Smoke Detection Systems.

13.7.2.20.8.1 Corridors and spaces open to the corridors, other than those meeting the requirement of 13.7.2.20.8.3, shall be provided with smoke detectors that comply with *NFPA 72, National Fire Alarm and Signaling Code,* and are arranged to initiate an alarm that is audible in all sleeping areas. [*101:* 32.3.3.4.8.1]

13.7.2.20.8.2 Reserved.

13.7.2.20.8.3 Smoke detection systems shall not be required in unenclosed corridors, passageways, balconies, colonnades, or other arrangements with one or more sides along the long dimension fully or extensively open to the exterior at all times. [*101:* 32.3.3.4.8.3]

13.7.2.21 Existing, Small (Not More Than 16 Residents) Residential Board and Care Occupancies.

13.7.2.21.1 Fire Alarm Systems. A manual fire alarm system shall be provided in accordance with Section 13.7, unless the provisions of 13.7.2.21.1.1 or 13.7.2.21.1.2 are met. [*101:* 33.2.3.4.1]

13.7.2.21.1.1 A fire alarm system shall not be required where interconnected smoke alarms complying with 13.7.2.21.3, and not less than one manual fire alarm box per floor arranged to continuously sound the smoke detector alarms, are provided. [*101:* 33.2.3.4.1.1]

13.7.2.21.1.2 Other manually activated continuously sounding alarms acceptable to the AHJ shall be permitted in lieu of a fire alarm system. [*101:* 33.2.3.4.1.2]

13.7.2.21.2 Occupant Notification. Occupant notification shall be in accordance with 13.7.1.9. [*101:* 33.2.3.4.2]

13.7.2.21.3* Smoke Alarms.

13.7.2.21.3.1 Approved smoke alarms shall be provided in accordance with 13.7.1.8, unless otherwise indicated in 13.7.2.21.3.6 and 13.7.2.21.3.7. [*101:* 33.2.3.4.3.1]

13.7.2.21.3.2 Smoke alarms shall be installed on all levels, including basements but excluding crawl spaces and unfinished attics. [*101:* 33.2.3.4.3.2]

13.7.2.21.3.3 Additional smoke alarms shall be installed for living rooms, dens, day rooms, and similar spaces. [*101:* 33.2.3.4.3.3]

13.7.2.21.3.4 Reserved.

13.7.2.21.3.5 Smoke alarms shall be powered from the building electrical system and, when activated, shall initiate an alarm that is audible in all sleeping areas. [*101:* 33.2.3.4.3.5]

13.7.2.21.3.6 Smoke alarms in accordance with 13.7.2.21.3.1 shall not be required where buildings are protected throughout by an approved automatic sprinkler system, in accordance with 13.3.2.22.2, that uses quick-response or residential sprinklers, and are protected with approved smoke alarms installed in each sleeping room, in accordance with 13.7.1.8, that are powered by the building electrical system. [*101:* 33.2.3.4.3.6]

13.7.2.21.3.7 Smoke alarms in accordance with 13.7.2.21.3.1 shall not be required where buildings are protected throughout by an approved automatic sprinkler system, in accordance with 13.3.2.22.2, that uses quick-response or residential sprinklers, with existing battery-powered smoke alarms in each sleeping room, and where, in the opinion of the AHJ, the facility has demonstrated that testing, maintenance, and a battery replacement program ensure the reliability of power to the smoke alarms. [*101:* 33.2.3.4.3.7]

13.7.2.22 Existing, Large (More Than 16 Residents) Residential Board and Care Occupancies.

13.7.2.22.1 General. A fire alarm system in accordance with Section 13.7 shall be provided, unless all of the following conditions are met:

(1) The facility has an evacuation capability of prompt or slow.
(2) Each sleeping room has exterior exit access in accordance with 14.10.3.
(3) The building does not exceed three stories in height. [*101:* 33.3.3.4.1]

13.7.2.22.2 Initiation. The required fire alarm system shall be initiated by each of the following means:

(1) Manual means in accordance with 13.7.1.7, unless there are other effective means (such as a complete automatic sprinkler or detection system) for notification of fire as required
(2) Manual fire alarm box located at a convenient central control point under continuous supervision of responsible employees
(3) Automatic sprinkler system, other than that not required by another section of this *Code*
(4) Required detection system, other than sleeping room smoke alarms
[*101:* 33.3.3.4.2]

13.7.2.22.3 Reserved.

13.7.2.22.4 Occupant Notification. Occupant notification shall be provided automatically, without delay, by internal audible alarm in accordance with 13.7.1.9. [*101:* 33.3.3.4.4]

13.7.2.22.5 Reserved.

13.7.2.22.6 Emergency Forces Notification.

13.7.2.22.6.1* Where the existing fire alarm system does not provide for automatic emergency forces notification in accordance with 13.7.1.10, provisions shall be made for the immediate notification of the public fire department by either telephone or other means, or, where there is no public fire department, notification shall be made to the private fire brigade. [*101:* 33.3.3.4.6.1]

13.7.2.22.6.2 Where a new fire alarm system is installed, or the existing fire alarm system is replaced, emergency forces notification shall be provided in accordance with 13.7.1.10. [*101:* 33.3.3.4.6.2]

13.7.2.22.7 Smoke Alarms. Smoke alarms shall be provided in accordance with 13.7.2.22.7.1, 13.7.2.22.7.2, or 13.7.2.22.7.3. [*101:* 33.3.3.4.7]

13.7.2.22.7.1 Each sleeping room shall be provided with an approved smoke alarm in accordance with 13.7.1.8 that is powered from the building electrical system. [*101:* 33.3.3.4.7.1]

13.7.2.22.7.2 Existing battery-powered smoke alarms, rather than building electrical service–powered smoke alarms, shall be accepted where, in the opinion of the AHJ, the facility has demonstrated that testing, maintenance, and battery replacement programs ensure the reliability of power to the smoke alarms. [*101:* 33.3.3.4.7.2]

13.7.2.22.7.3 Sleeping room smoke alarms shall not be required in facilities having an existing corridor smoke detection system that complies with Section 13.7 and is connected to the building fire alarm system. [*101:* 33.3.3.4.7.3]

13.7.2.22.8 Smoke Detection Systems.

13.7.2.22.8.1 All living areas, as defined in 3.3.21.5 of NFPA *101*, and all corridors shall be provided with smoke detectors that comply with *NFPA 72, National Fire Alarm and Signaling Code*, and are arranged to initiate an alarm that is audible in all sleeping areas, as modified by 13.7.2.22.8.2 and 13.7.2.22.8.3. [*101:* 33.3.3.4.8.1]

13.7.2.22.8.2 Smoke detection systems shall not be required in living areas of buildings having a prompt or slow evacuation capability protected throughout by an approved automatic sprinkler system installed in accordance with 13.7.2.22.1. [*101:* 33.3.3.4.8.2]

13.7.2.22.8.3 Smoke detection systems shall not be required in unenclosed corridors, passageways, balconies, colonnades, or other arrangements with one or more sides along the long dimension fully or extensively open to the exterior at all times. [*101:* 33.3.3.4.8.3]

13.7.2.23 New Mercantile Occupancies.

13.7.2.23.1 General. New Class A mercantile occupancies shall be provided with a fire alarm system in accordance with Section 13.7. [*101:* 36.3.4.1]

13.7.2.23.2 Initiation. Initiation of the required fire alarm system shall be by any one of the following means:

(1) Manual means in accordance with 13.7.1.7.1(1)
(2) Approved automatic fire detection system in accordance with 13.7.1.7.1(2) that provides protection throughout the building, and the provision of 13.7.1.7.6 shall apply.
(3) Approved automatic sprinkler system in accordance with 13.7.1.7.1(3) that provides protection throughout the building, and the provision of 13.7.1.7.6 shall apply. [*101:* 36.3.4.2]

13.7.2.23.3 Notification.

13.7.2.23.3.1 Occupant Notification. During all times that the mercantile occupancy is occupied, the required fire alarm system, once initiated, shall perform one of the following functions:

(1) It shall activate an alarm in accordance with 13.7.1.9 throughout the mercantile occupancy.
(2) Positive alarm sequence in accordance with 13.7.1.9.4 shall be permitted. [*101:* 36.3.4.3.1]

13.7.2.23.3.2 Emergency Forces Notification. Emergency forces notification shall be provided and shall include notifying both of the following:

(1) Fire department in accordance with 13.7.1.10
(2) Local emergency organization, if provided [*101:* 36.3.4.3.2]

13.7.2.24 Existing Mercantile Occupancies.

13.7.2.24.1 General. Existing Class A mercantile occupancies shall be provided with a fire alarm system in accordance with Section 13.7. [*101:* 37.3.4.1]

13.7.2.24.2 Initiation. Initiation of the required fire alarm system shall be by one of the following means:

(1) Manual means in accordance with 13.7.1.7.1(1)
(2) Approved automatic fire detection system in accordance with 13.7.1.7.1(2) that provides protection throughout the building, and the provision of 13.7.1.7.6 shall apply.
(3) Approved automatic sprinkler system in accordance with 13.7.1.7.1(3) that provides protection throughout the building, and the provision of 13.7.1.7.6 shall apply. [*101:* 37.3.4.2]

13.7.2.24.3 Notification.

13.7.2.24.3.1 Occupant Notification. During all times that the mercantile occupancy is occupied, the required fire alarm system, once initiated, shall perform one of the following functions:

(1) It shall activate an alarm in accordance with 13.7.1.9 throughout the mercantile occupancy, and both of the following also shall apply:
  (a) Positive alarm sequence in accordance with 13.7.1.9.4 shall be permitted.
  (b) A presignal system in accordance with 13.7.1.9.3 shall be permitted.
(2) Occupant notification shall be made via a voice communication or public address system in accordance with 13.7.1.9.9.2 [*101:* 37.3.4.3.1]

13.7.2.24.3.2 Emergency Forces Notification. Emergency forces notification shall be provided and shall include notifying both of the following:

(1) Fire department in accordance with 13.7.1.10
(2) Local emergency organization, if provided [*101:* 37.3.4.3.2]

13.7.2.25 New Business Occupancies.

13.7.2.25.1 General. A fire alarm system in accordance with Section 13.7 shall be provided in all new business occupancies where any one of the following conditions exists:

(1) The building is three or more stories in height.
(2) The occupancy is subject to 50 or more occupants above or below the level of exit discharge.
(3) The occupancy is subject to 300 or more total occupants. [*101:* 38.3.4.1]

13.7.2.25.2 Initiation. Initiation of the required fire alarm system shall be by one of the following means:

(1) Manual means in accordance with 13.7.1.7.1(1)

(2) Approved automatic fire detection system in accordance with 13.7.1.7.1(2) that provides protection throughout the building and the provision of 13.7.1.7.6 shall apply.
(3) An approved automatic sprinkler system in accordance with 13.7.1.7.1(3) that provides protection throughout the building and the provision of 13.7.1.7.6 shall apply.
[*101:* 38.3.4.2]

13.7.2.25.3 Occupant Notification. During all times that the building is occupied *(see 7.2.1.1.3 of NFPA 101), the required fire alarm system, once initiated, shall perform one of the following functions:*

(1) It shall activate a general alarm in accordance with 13.7.1.9.
(2) A positive alarm sequence in accordance with 13.7.1.9.4 shall be permitted.
[*101:* 38.3.4.3]

13.7.2.25.4 Emergency Forces Notification. Emergency forces notification shall be provided and shall include notifying both of the following:

(1) Fire department in accordance with 13.7.1.10
(2) Approved local emergency organization, if provided
[*101:* 38.3.4.4]

13.7.2.26 Existing Business Occupancies.

13.7.2.26.1 General. A fire alarm system in accordance with Section 13.7 shall be provided in all existing business occupancies where any one of the following conditions exists:

(1) The building is three or more stories in height.
(2) The occupancy is subject to 100 or more occupants above or below the level of exit discharge.
(3) The occupancy is subject to 1000 or more total occupants.
[*101:* 39.3.4.1]

13.7.2.26.2 Initiation. Initiation of the required fire alarm system shall be by one of the following means:

(1) Manual means in accordance with 13.7.1.7.1(1)
(2) Approved automatic fire detection system in accordance with 13.7.1.7.1(2) that provides protection throughout the building and the provision of 13.7.1.7.6 shall apply.
(3) Approved automatic sprinkler system in accordance with 13.7.1.7.1(3) that provides protection throughout the building and the provision of 13.7.1.7.6 shall apply.
[*101:* 39.3.4.2]

13.7.2.26.3 Occupant Notification. During all times that the building is occupied *(see 7.2.1.1.3 of NFPA 101), the required fire alarm system, once initiated, shall perform one of the following functions:*

(1) It shall activate a general alarm in accordance with 13.7.1.9, and both of the following also shall apply:
 (a) Positive alarm sequence in accordance with 13.7.1.9.4 shall be permitted.
 (b) A presignal system in accordance with 13.7.1.9.3 shall be permitted.
(2) Occupant notification shall be permitted to be made via a voice communication or public address system in accordance with 13.7.1.9.9.2.
[*101:* 39.3.4.3]

13.7.2.26.4 Emergency Forces Notification. Emergency forces notification shall be accomplished in accordance with 13.7.1.10 when the existing fire alarm system is replaced. [*101:* 39.3.4.4]

13.7.2.27 New and Existing Industrial Occupancies.

13.7.2.27.1 General. A fire alarm system shall be required in accordance with Section 13.7 for new and existing industrial occupancies, unless the total occupant load of the building is under 100 persons and unless, of these, fewer than 25 persons are above or below the level of exit discharge. [*101:* 40.3.4.1]

13.7.2.27.2 Initiation. Initiation of the required fire alarm system shall be by any of the following means:

(1) Manual means in accordance with 13.7.1.7.1(1)
(2) Approved automatic fire detection system in accordance with 13.7.1.7.1(2) throughout the building, plus a minimum of one manual fire alarm box in accordance with 13.7.1.7.6
(3) Approved, supervised automatic sprinkler system in accordance with 13.7.1.7.1(3) throughout the building, plus a minimum of one manual fire alarm box in accordance with 13.7.1.7.6
[*101:* 40.3.4.2]

13.7.2.27.3 Notification.

13.7.2.27.3.1 The required fire alarm system shall meet one of the following criteria:

(1) It shall provide occupant notification in accordance with 13.7.1.9.
(2) It shall sound an audible and visible signal in a constantly attended location for the purposes of initiating emergency action.
[*101:* 40.3.4.3.1]

13.7.2.27.3.2 Positive alarm sequence in accordance with 13.7.1.9.4 shall be permitted. [*101:* 40.3.4.3.2]

13.7.2.27.3.3 Existing presignal systems in accordance with 13.7.1.9.3 shall be permitted. [*101:* 40.3.4.3.3]

13.7.2.27.3.4 In high hazard industrial occupancies, as described in 40.1.2.1.3 of NFPA *101*, the required fire alarm system shall automatically initiate an occupant evacuation alarm signal in accordance with 13.7.1.9. [*101:* 40.3.4.3.4]

13.7.2.28 New and Existing Storage Occupancies.

13.7.2.28.1 General. A fire alarm system shall be required in accordance with Section 13.7 for new and existing storage occupancies, except as modified by 13.7.2.28.1.1, 13.7.2.28.1.2, and 13.7.2.28.1.3. [*101:* 42.3.4.1]

13.7.2.28.1.1 Storage occupancies limited to low hazard contents shall not be required to have a fire alarm system. [*101:* 42.3.4.1.1]

13.7.2.28.1.2 Storage occupancies with ordinary or high hazard contents not exceeding an aggregate floor area of 100,000 ft^2 (9300 m^2) shall not be required to have a fire alarm system. [*101:* 42.3.4.1.2]

13.7.2.28.1.3 Storage occupancies protected throughout by an approved automatic sprinkler system in accordance with Section 13.3 shall not be required to have a fire alarm system. [*101:* 42.3.4.1.3]

13.7.2.28.2 Initiation. Initiation of the required fire alarm system shall be by any of the following means:

(1) Manual means in accordance with 13.7.1.7.1(1)
(2) Approved automatic fire detection system in accordance with 13.7.1.7.1(2) throughout the building, plus a minimum of one manual fire alarm box in accordance with 13.7.1.7.6

(3) Approved, supervised automatic sprinkler system in accordance with 13.7.1.7.1(3) throughout the building, plus a minimum of one manual fire alarm box in accordance with 13.7.1.7.6
[*101:* 42.3.4.2]

13.7.2.28.3 Notification.

13.7.2.28.3.1 The required fire alarm system shall meet one of the following criteria:

(1) It shall provide occupant notification in accordance with 13.7.1.9.
(2) It shall sound an audible and visible signal in a constantly attended location for the purposes of initiating emergency action.
[*101:* 42.3.4.3.1]

13.7.2.28.3.2 Positive alarm sequence in accordance with 13.7.1.9.4 shall be permitted. [*101:* 42.3.4.3.2]

13.7.2.28.3.3 Existing presignal systems in accordance with 13.7.1.9.3 shall be permitted. [*101:* 42.3.4.3.3]

13.7.2.28.3.4 In high hazard storage occupancies, the required fire alarm system shall automatically initiate an occupant evacuation alarm signal in accordance with 13.7.1.9. [*101:* 42.3.4.3.4]

13.7.2.29 Special Structures and High-Rise Buildings.

13.7.2.29.1 Detection, Alarm, and Communications Systems. Towers, as defined in 3.3.281 of NFPA *101*, designed for occupancy by not more than three persons shall be exempt from requirements for detection, alarm, and communications systems. [*101:* 11.3.3.4]

13.7.2.29.2 New High-Rise Buildings.

13.7.2.29.2.1* A fire alarm system using an approved emergency voice/alarm communication system shall be installed in accordance with Section 13.7 and NFPA *101*. [*101:* 11.8.4.1]

13.7.2.29.2.2 Two-way telephone service shall be in accordance with 13.7.2.29.2.2.1 and 13.7.2.29.2.2.2. [*101:* 11.8.4.2]

13.7.2.29.2.2.1 Two-way telephone communication service shall be provided for fire department use. This system shall be in accordance with *NFPA 72*. The communications system shall operate between the emergency command center and every elevator car, every elevator lobby, and each floor level of exit stairs. [*101:* 11.8.4.2.1]

13.7.2.29.2.2.2* The requirement of 13.7.2.29.2.2.1 shall not apply where the fire department radio system is approved as an equivalent system. [*101:* 11.8.4.2.2]

13.7.3 Fire Alarm Systems.

13.7.3.1 General.

13.7.3.1.1 Equipment.

13.7.3.1.1.1 Equipment constructed and installed in conformity with this *Code* shall be listed for the purpose for which it is used. [**72:**10.3.1]

13.7.3.1.1.2 System components shall be installed, tested, inspected, and maintained in accordance with the manufacturer's published instructions and this *Code*. [**72:** 10.3.2]

13.7.3.1.1.3* All devices and appliances that receive their power from the initiating device circuit or signaling line circuit of a control unit shall be listed for use with the control unit. [**72:**10.3.3]

13.7.3.1.1.4 All apparatus requiring rewinding or resetting to maintain normal operation shall be restored to normal as promptly as possible after each abnormal condition and maintained in normal condition for operation. [**72:**10.3.4]

13.7.3.1.1.5 Equipment shall be designed so that it is capable of performing its intended functions under the following conditions:

(1)*At 85 percent and at 110 percent of the nameplate primary (main) and secondary (standby) input voltage(s)
(2) At ambient temperatures of 0°C (32°F) and 49°C (120°F)
(3) At a relative humidity of 85 percent and an ambient temperature of 30°C (86°F) [**72:**10.3.5]

13.7.3.2 Documentation.

13.7.3.2.1 Approval and Acceptance. The AHJ shall be notified prior to installation or alteration of equipment or wiring. [**72:**10.20.2]

13.7.3.2.2 Minimum Required Documentation.

13.7.3.2.2.1 Where documentation is required by the enforcing authority, the following list shall represent the minimum documentation required for all fire alarm and emergency communications systems, including new systems and additions or alterations to existing systems:

(1) Written narrative providing intent and system description
(2) Riser diagram
(3) Floor plan layout showing location of all devices and control equipment
(4) Sequence of operation in either an input/output matrix or narrative form
(5) Equipment technical data sheets
(6) Manufacturers published instructions, including operation and maintenance instructions
(7) Battery calculations (where batteries are provided)
(8) Voltage drop calculations for notification appliance circuits
(9) Completed record of inspection and testing in accordance with 13.7.3.2.4.6 and 13.7.3.2.5.2
(10) Completed record of completion in accordance with 13.7.3.2.4.6 and 13.7.3.2.5.2
(11) Copy of site-specific software, where applicable
(12) Record (as-built) drawings
(13) Periodic inspection, testing, and maintenance documentation in accordance with 13.7.3.2.3.4
(14) Records, record retention, and record maintenance in accordance with Section 7.7 of *NFPA 72*
[**72:**7.2.1]

13.7.3.2.2.2 The person responsible for system design (layout) shall be identified on the system design documents. [**72:**7.2.2]

13.7.3.2.2.3 All fire alarm drawings shall use symbols described in NFPA 170, *Standard for Fire Safety and Emergency Symbols,* or other symbols acceptable to the AHJ. [**72:**7.2.3]

13.7.3.2.3 Completion Documentation.

13.7.3.2.3.1 The requirements of 13.7.3.2.3 shall apply only where required by other governing laws, codes, or standards; by other parts of *NFPA 72*; or by project specifications or drawings. [**72:**7.5.1]

13.7.3.2.3.2 Before requesting final approval of the installation, if required by the AHJ, the installing contractor shall furnish a written statement stating that the system has been installed in accordance with approved plans and tested in accordance with the manufacturer's published instructions and the appropriate NFPA requirements. [**72**:7.5.2]

13.7.3.2.3.3 All systems including new systems and additions or alterations to existing systems shall include the following documentation, which shall be delivered to the owner or the owner's representative upon final acceptance of the system:

(1) An owner's manual and manufacturer's published instructions covering all system equipment
(2) Record (as-built) drawings in accordance with 13.7.3.2.3.5
(3) A completed record of completion form in accordance with 13.7.3.2.3.6
(4) For software-based systems, record copy of the site-specific software in accordance with 13.7.3.2.3.7
[**72**:7.5.3]

13.7.3.2.3.4 Owner's manuals for emergency communications systems shall be in accordance with Section 24.8 of *NFPA 72*. [**72**:7.5.4]

13.7.3.2.3.5 Record Drawings (As-Builts).

13.7.3.2.3.5.1 Record drawings shall consist of current updated and shop drawings reflecting the actual installation of all system equipment, components, and wiring. [**72**:7.5.5.1]

13.7.3.2.3.5.2 A sequence of operations in input/output matrix or narrative form shall be provided with the record drawings to reflect actual programming at the time of completion. [**72**:7.5.5.2]

13.7.3.2.3.5.3 Where necessary, revised calculations in accordance with 7.4.10 of *NFPA 72* shall be provided depicting any changes due to installation conditions. [**72**:7.5.5.3]

13.7.3.2.3.5.4 Record drawings shall be turned over to the owner with a copy placed inside the documentation cabinet in accordance with Section 7.7 of *NFPA 72*. [**72**:7.5.5.4]

13.7.3.2.3.5.5 Record drawings shall include approval documentation resulting from variances, performance-based designs, risk analyses, and other system evaluations or variations. [**72**:7.5.5.5]

13.7.3.2.3.6 Record of Completion.

13.7.3.2.3.6.1 The record of completion shall be documented in accordance with 13.7.3.2.3.6 using either the record of completion forms, Figure 13.7.3.2.5.2(a) through Figure 13.7.3.2.5.2(l), or an alternative document that contains only the elements of Figure 13.7.3.2.5.2(a) through Figure 13.7.3.2.5.2(f) applicable to the installed system. [**72**:7.5.6.1]

13.7.3.2.3.6.2 The record of completion documentation shall be completed by the installing contractor and submitted to the enforcing authority and the owner at the conclusion of the job. The record of completion documentation shall be permitted to be part of the written statement required in 13.7.3.2.3.2 and part of the documents that support the requirements of 13.7.3.2.3.8. When more than one contractor has been responsible for the installation, each contractor shall complete the portions of the documentation for which that contractor has responsibility. [**72**:7.5.6.2]

13.7.3.2.3.6.3 The preparation of the record of completion documentation shall be the responsibility of the qualified and experienced person in accordance with 10.5.2 of *NFPA 72*. [**72**:7.5.6.3]

13.7.3.2.3.6.4 The record of completion documentation shall be updated to reflect all system additions or modifications and maintained in a current condition at all times. [**72**:7.5.6.4]

13.7.3.2.3.6.5 The updated copy of the record of completion documents shall be maintained in a documentation cabinet in accordance with 7.7.2 of *NFPA 72*. [**72**:7.5.6.5]

13.7.3.2.3.6.6 Revisions.

13.7.3.2.3.6.6.1 All fire alarm and/or signaling system modifications made after the initial installation shall be recorded on a revised version of the original completion documents. [**72**:7.5.6.6.1]

13.7.3.2.3.6.6.2 The revised record of completion document shall include a revision date. [**72**:7.5.6.6.2]

13.7.3.2.3.6.6.3 Where the original or the latest overall system record of completion cannot be obtained, a new system record of completion shall be provided that documents the system configuration as discovered during the current project's scope of work. [**72**:7.5.6.6.3]

13.7.3.2.3.6.7 Electronic Record of Completion.

13.7.3.2.3.6.7.1 Where approved by the AHJ, the record of completion shall be permitted to be filed electronically instead of on paper. [**72**:7.5.6.7.1]

13.7.3.2.3.6.7.2 If filed electronically, the record of completion document shall be accessible with standard software and shall be backed up. [**72**:7.5.6.7.2]

13.7.3.2.3.7 Site-specific software documentation shall be in accordance with 14.6.1.2 of *NFPA 72*. [**72**:7.5.7]

13.7.3.2.3.8 Verification of Compliant Installation.

13.7.3.2.3.8.1 Where required by the AHJ, compliance of the completed installation with the requirements of *NFPA 72*, as implemented via the referring code(s), specifications, and/or other criteria applicable to the specific installation, shall be certified by a qualified and impartial third-party organization acceptable to the AHJ. [**72**: 7.5.8.1]

13.7.3.2.3.8.2 Verification of compliant installation shall be performed according to testing requirements and procedures specified in 14.4.1 and 14.4.2 of *NFPA 72*. [**72**:7.5.8.2]

13.7.3.2.3.8.3 Verification shall ensure that:

(1) All components and functions are installed and operate per the approved plans and sequence of operation.
(2) All required system documentation is complete and is archived on site.
(3) For new supervising station systems, the verification shall also ascertain proper arrangement, transmission, and receipt of all signals required to be transmitted off-premises and shall meet the requirements of 14.4.1 and 14.4.2 of *NFPA 72*.
(4) For existing supervising station systems that are extended, modified, or reconfigured, the verification shall be required for the new work only, and reacceptance testing in accordance with Chapter 14 of *NFPA 72* shall be acceptable.
(5) Written confirmation has been provided that any required corrective actions have been completed
[**72**:7.5.8.3]

2015 Edition

13.7.3.2.3.9 Documentation of central station service shall be in accordance with 26.3.4 of *NFPA 72*. [**72:**7.5.9]

13.7.3.2.3.10 Documentation of remote station service shall be in accordance with 26.5.2 of *NFPA 72*. [**72:**7.5.10]

13.7.3.2.4 Inspection, Testing, and Maintenance Documentation.

13.7.3.2.4.1 Test plan documentation shall be provided in accordance with 14.2.10 of *NFPA 72*. [**72:**7.6.1]

13.7.3.2.4.2 Acceptance testing documentation shall be provided in accordance with 14.6.1 of *NFPA 72*. [**72:**7.6.2]

13.7.3.2.4.3 Reacceptance test documentation shall be provided in accordance with 14.6.1 of *NFPA 72*. [**72:**7.6.3]

13.7.3.2.4.4 Periodic inspection and testing documentation shall be provided in accordance with 14.6.2 through 14.6.4 of 14.6.1 of *NFPA 72*. [**72:**7.6.4]

13.7.3.2.4.5 Impairment documentation shall be provided in accordance with Section 10.21 of 14.6.1 of *NFPA 72*. [**72:**7.6.5]

13.7.3.2.4.6 Record of Inspection and Testing. The record of all inspections, testing, and maintenance as required by 14.6.2.4 of 14.6.1 of *NFPA 72* shall be documented using either the record of inspection and testing forms, Figure 13.7.3.2.5.2(g) through Figure 13.7.3.2.5.2(l), or an alternative record that includes all the applicable information shown in Figure 13.7.3.2.5.2(g) through Figure 13.7.3.2.5.2(l). [**72:**7.6.6]

13.7.3.2.5 Forms.

13.7.3.2.5.1 General.

13.7.3.2.5.1.1 The requirements of 13.7.3.2.5 shall apply only where required by other governing laws, codes, or standards; by other parts of this *Code*; or by project specifications or drawings. [**72:**7.8.1.1]

13.7.3.2.5.1.2 Where specific forms are required by other governing laws, codes, or standards; by other parts of *NFPA 72*; or by project specifications or drawings, form layouts and content that differ from those in 13.7.3.2.5 shall be permitted provided that the minimum required content is included. [**72:**7.8.1.2]

13.7.3.2.5.2 Forms for Record of Completion, Record of Inspection and Testing, and Risk Analysis. Unless otherwise permitted or required in 13.7.3.2.3.6, 13.7.3.2.4.6, or 13.7.3.2.5.1.2, Figure 13.7.3.2.5.2(a) through Figure 13.7.3.2.5.2(l) shall be used to document the record of completion and record of inspection and testing. [**72:**7.8.2]

13.7.3.3 Manually Actuated Alarm-Initiating Devices.

13.7.3.3.1 Manually actuated alarm-initiating devices for initiating signals other than for fire alarm shall be permitted if the devices are differentiated from manual for fire alarm boxes by a color other than red and labeling. [**72:**17.14.1]

13.7.3.3.2 Combination manual fire alarm boxes and guard's signaling stations shall be permitted. [**72:**17.14.2]

13.7.3.3.3 Manually actuated alarm-initiating devices shall be securely mounted. [**72:**17.14.3]

13.7.3.3.4 Manually actuated alarm-initiating devices shall be mounted on a background of contrasting color. [**72:**17.14.4]

13.7.3.3.5 The operable part of a manually actuated alarm-initiating device shall be not less than 42 in. (1.07 m) and not more than 48 in. (1.22 m) from the finished floor. [**72:**17.14.5]

13.7.3.3.6 Manually actuated alarm-initiating devices shall be permitted to be single action or double action. [**72:**17.14.6]

13.7.3.3.7* Listed protective covers shall be permitted to be installed over single- or double-action manually actuated alarm-initiating devices. [**72:**17.14.7]

13.7.3.3.8 Manual fire alarm boxes shall comply with 13.7.3.3.8.1 through 13.7.3.3.8.6. [**72:**17.14.8]

13.7.3.3.8.1 Manual fire alarm boxes shall be used only for fire alarm initiating purposes. [**72:**17.14.8.1].

13.7.3.3.8.2 Manual fire alarm boxes shall be installed so that they are conspicuous, unobstructed, and accessible. [**72:**17.14.8.2]

13.7.3.3.8.3* Unless installed in an environment that precludes the use of red paint or red plastic, manual fire alarm boxes shall be red in color. [**72:**17.14.8.3]

13.7.3.3.8.4 Manual fire alarm boxes shall be located within 5 ft (1.5 m) of each exit doorway on each floor. [**72:**17.14.8.4]

13.7.3.3.8.5* Additional manual fire alarm boxes shall be provided so that the travel distance to the nearest manual fire alarm box will not exceed 200 ft (61 m), measured horizontally on the same floor. [**72:**17.14.8.5]

13.7.3.3.8.6 Manual fire alarm boxes shall be mounted on both sides of grouped openings over 40 ft (12.2 m) in width, and within 5 ft (1.5 m) of each side of the grouped opening. [**72:**17.14.8.6]

13.7.3.3.9 When fire alarm systems are not monitored, an approved permanent sign shall be installed adjacent to each manual fire alarm box. The sign shall read as follows:

Local alarm only:

(1) Activate alarm

(2) Exit building

(3) Call fire department

13.7.3.4* Indication of Central Station Service. The prime contractor shall conspicuously indicate that the alarm system providing service at a protected premises complies with all the requirements of this *Code* through the use of a systematic follow-up program under the control of the organization that has listed the prime contractor. [**72:**26.3.4]

13.7.3.4.1 Documentation indicating *Code* compliance of the alarm system shall be issued by the organization that has listed the prime contractor. [**72:**26.3.4.1]

13.7.3.4.2 The documentation shall include, at a minimum, the following information:

(1) Name of the prime contractor involved with the ongoing *Code* compliance of the central station service
(2)*Full description of the alarm system as installed
(3) Issue and expiration dates of the documentation
(4) Name, address, and contact information of the organization issuing the document
(5) Identification of the AHJs for the central station service installation
[**72:**26.3.4.2]

SYSTEM RECORD OF COMPLETION

*This form is to be completed by the system installation contractor at the time of system acceptance and approval.
It shall be permitted to modify this form as needed to provide a more complete and/or clear record.
Insert N/A in all unused lines.
Attach additional sheets, data, or calculations as necessary to provide a complete record.*

Form Completion Date: _____   Supplemental Pages Attached: _____

1. PROPERTY INFORMATION
Name of property: _____
Address: _____
Description of property: _____
Name of property representative: _____
Address: _____
Phone: _____ Fax: _____ E-mail: _____

2. INSTALLATION, SERVICE, TESTING, AND MONITORING INFORMATION
Installation contractor: _____
Address: _____
Phone: _____ Fax: _____ E-mail: _____
Service organization: _____
Address: _____
Phone: _____ Fax: _____ E-mail: _____
Testing organization: _____
Address: _____
Phone: _____ Fax: _____ E-mail: _____
Effective date for test and inspection contract: _____
Monitoring organization: _____
Address: _____
Phone: _____ Fax: _____ E-mail: _____
Account number: _____ Phone line 1: _____ Phone line 2: _____
Means of transmission: _____
Entity to which alarms are retransmitted: _____ Phone: _____

3. DOCUMENTATION
On-site location of the required record documents and site-specific software: _____

4. DESCRIPTION OF SYSTEM OR SERVICE
This is a: ❏ New system   ❏ Modification to existing system   Permit number: _____
NFPA 72 edition: _____

4.1 Control Unit
Manufacturer: _____   Model number: _____

4.2 Software and Firmware
Firmware revision number: _____

4.3 Alarm Verification   ❏ This system does not incorporate alarm verification.
Number of devices subject to alarm verification: _____   Alarm verification set for _____ seconds

© 2014 National Fire Protection Association   NFPA 72 (p. 1 of 3)

FIGURE 13.7.3.2.5.2(a) System Record of Completion. [72: Figure 7.8.2(a)]

SYSTEM RECORD OF COMPLETION *(continued)*

5. SYSTEM POWER

5.1 Control Unit

5.1.1 Primary Power

Input voltage of control panel: _____ Control panel amps: _____

Overcurrent protection: Type: _____ Amps: _____

Branch circuit disconnecting means location: _____ Number: _____

5.1.2 Secondary Power

Type of secondary power: _____

Location, if remote from the plant: _____

Calculated capacity of secondary power to drive the system:

In standby mode (hours): _____ In alarm mode (minutes): _____

5.2 Control Unit

❑ This system does not have power extender panels

❑ Power extender panels are listed on supplementary sheet A

6. CIRCUITS AND PATHWAYS

Pathway Type	Dual Media Pathway	Separate Pathway	Class	Survivability Level
Signaling Line				
Device Power				
Initiating Device				
Notification Appliance				
Other (specify):				

7. REMOTE ANNUNCIATORS

Type	Location

8. INITIATING DEVICES

Type	Quantity	Addressable or Conventional	Alarm or Supervisory	Sensing Technology
Manual Pull Stations				
Smoke Detectors				
Duct Smoke Detectors				
Heat Detectors				
Gas Detectors				
Waterflow Switches				
Tamper Switches				

© 2014 National Fire Protection Association NFPA 72 (p. 2 of 3)

FIGURE 13.7.3.2.5.2(a) *Continued*

SYSTEM RECORD OF COMPLETION *(continued)*

9. NOTIFICATION APPLIANCES

Type	Quantity	Description
Audible		
Visible		
Combination Audible and Visible		

10. SYSTEM CONTROL FUNCTIONS

Type	Quantity
Hold-Open Door Releasing Devices	
HVAC Shutdown	
Fire/Smoke Dampers	
Door Unlocking	
Elevator Recall	
Elevator Shunt Trip	

11. INTERCONNECTED SYSTEMS

❏ This system does not have interconnected systems.

❏ Interconnected systems are listed on supplementary sheet _____ .

12. CERTIFICATION AND APPROVALS

12.1 System Installation Contractor

This system as specified herein has been installed according to all NFPA standards cited herein.

Signed:_____ Printed name:_____ Date:_____

Organization:_____ Title:_____ Phone:_____

12.2 System Operational Test

This system as specified herein has tested according to all NFPA standards cited herein.

Signed:_____ Printed name:_____ Date:_____

Organization:_____ Title:_____ Phone:_____

12.3 Acceptance Test

Date and time of acceptance test:_____

Installing contractor representative:_____

Testing contractor representative:_____

Property representative:_____

AHJ representative:_____

© 2014 National Fire Protection Association NFPA 72 (p. 3 of 3)

FIGURE 13.7.3.2.5.2(a) *Continued*

EMERGENCY COMMUNICATIONS SYSTEMS
SUPPLEMENTARY RECORD OF COMPLETION

This form is a supplement to the System Record of Completion. It includes systems and components specific to emergency communications systems.
This form is to be completed by the system installation contractor at the time of system acceptance and approval.
It shall be permitted to modify this form as needed to provide a more complete and/or clear record.
Insert N/A in all unused lines.

Form Completion Date: _____   Number of Supplemental Pages Attached: _____

1. PROPERTY INFORMATION
Name of property: _____
Address: _____

2. DESCRIPTION OF SYSTEM OR SERVICE
❏ Fire alarm with in-building fire emergency voice alarm communication system (EVAC)
❏ Mass notification system
❏ Combination system, with the following components:
   ❏ Fire alarm   ❏ EVACS   ❏ MNS   ❏ Two-way, in-building, emergency communications system
❏ Other (specify): _____
NFPA 72 edition: _____   Additional description of system(s): _____
_____

2.1 In-Building Fire Emergency Voice Alarm Communications System
Manufacturer: _____   Model number: _____
Number of single voice alarm channels: _____   Number of multiple voice alarm channels: _____
Number of speakers: _____   Number of speaker circuits: _____
Location of amplification and sound processing equipment: _____
_____
_____

Location of paging microphone stations:
Location 1: _____
Location 2: _____
Location 3: _____

2.2 Mass Notification System
2.2.1 System Type:
❏ In-building MNS–combination
❏ In-building MNS   ❏ Wide-area MNS   ❏ Distributed recipient MNS
❏ Other (specify): _____

© 2014 National Fire Protection Association   NFPA 72 (p. 1 of 3)

FIGURE 13.7.3.2.5.2(b) Emergency Communications System Supplementary Record of Completion. [72: Figure 7.8.2(b)]

EMERGENCY COMMUNICATIONS SYSTEMS
SUPPLEMENTARY RECORD OF COMPLETION *(continued)*

2. DESCRIPTION OF SYSTEM OR SERVICE *(continued)*

2.2.2 System Features:

❏ Combination fire alarm/MNS ❏ MNS autonomous control unit ❏ Wide-area MNS to regional national alerting interface
❏ Local operating console (LOC) ❏ Distributed-recipient MNS (DRMNS) ❏ Wide-area MNS to DRMNS interface
❏ Wide-area MNS to high power speaker array (HPSA) interface ❏ In-building MNS to wide-area MNS interface
❏ Other (specify): _____

2.2.3 MNS Local Operating Consoles

Location 1: _____
Location 2: _____
Location 3: _____

2.2.4 High Power Speaker Arrays

Number of HPSA speaker initiation zones: _____
Location 1: _____
Location 2: _____
Location 3: _____

2.2.5 Mass Notification Devices

Combination fire alarm/MNS visual devices: _____ MNS-only visual devices: _____
Textual signs: _____ Other (describe): _____
Supervision class: _____

2.2.6 Special Hazard Notification

❏ This system does not have special suppression predischarge notification.
❏ MNS systems DO NOT override notification appliances required to provide special suppression predischarge notification.

3. TWO-WAY EMERGENCY COMMUNICATIONS SYSTEMS

3.1 Telephone System

Number of telephone jacks installed: _____ Number of warden stations installed: _____
Number of telephone handsets stored on site: _____
Type of telephone system installed: ❏ Electrically powered ❏ Sound powered

3.2 Two-Way Radio Communications Enhancement System

Percentage of area covered by two-way radio service: Critical areas _____ % General building areas _____ %
Amplification component locations: _____
_____
Inbound signal strength _____ dBm Outbound signal strength _____ dBm
Donor antenna isolation is _____ dB above the signal booster gain.
Radio frequencies covered: _____
Radio system monitor panel location: _____

© 2014 National Fire Protection Association NFPA 72 (p. 2 of 3)

FIGURE 13.7.3.2.5.2(b) *Continued*

EMERGENCY COMMUNICATIONS SYSTEMS
SUPPLEMENTARY RECORD OF COMPLETION *(continued)*

3. **TWO-WAY EMERGENCY COMMUNICATIONS SYSTEMS** *(continued)*

   3.3 Area of Refuge (Area of Rescue Assistance) Emergency Communications Systems

   Number of stations: _____   Location of central control point: _____

   Days and hours when central control point is attended: _____

   Location of alternate control point: _____

   Days and hours when alternate control point is attended: _____

   3.4 Elevator Emergency Communications Systems

   Number of elevators with stations: _____   Location of central control point: _____

   Days and hours when central control point is attended: _____

   Location of alternate control point: _____

   Days and hours when alternate control point is attended: _____

   3.5 Other Two-Way Communications System

   Describe: _____

4. **CONTROL FUNCTIONS**

   This system activates the following control functions specific to emergency communications systems:

Type	Quantity
Mass Notification Override of Alarm Signaling Systems or Appliances	

See Main System Record of Completion for additional information, certifications, and approvals.

© 2014 National Fire Protection Association   NFPA 72 (p. 3 of 3)

FIGURE 13.7.3.2.5.2(b) *Continued*

POWER SYSTEMS
SUPPLEMENTARY RECORD OF COMPLETION

This form is a supplement to the System Record of Completion. It includes systems and components specific to power systems that incorporate generators, UPS systems, remote battery systems, or other complex power systems. This form is to be completed by the system installation contractor at the time of system acceptance and approval. It shall be permitted to modify this form as needed to provide a more complete and/or clear record. Insert N/A in all unused lines.

Form Completion Date: _____   Number of Supplemental Pages Attached: _____

1. PROPERTY INFORMATION
Name of property: _____

Address: _____

2. SYSTEM POWER

2.1 Control Unit

2.1.1 Primary Power

Input voltage of control panel: _____   Control panel amps: _____

Overcurrent protection: Type: _____   Amps: _____

Location (of primary supply panelboard): _____

Disconnecting means location: _____

2.1.2 Engine-Driven Generator

Location of generator: _____

Location of fuel storage: _____   Type of fuel: _____

2.1.3 Uninterruptible Power System

Equipment powered by UPS system: _____

Location of UPS system: _____

Calculated capacity of UPS batteries to drive the system components connected to it:

In standby mode (hours): _____   In alarm mode (minutes): _____

2.1.4 Batteries

Location: _____ Type: _____ Nominal voltage: _____ Amp/hour rating: _____

Calculated capacity of batteries to drive the system:

In standby mode (hours): _____   In alarm mode (minutes): _____

2.2 In-Building Fire Emergency Voice Alarm Communications System or Mass Notification System

2.2.1 Primary Power

Input voltage of EVACS or MNS panel: _____   EVACS or MNS panel amps: _____

Overcurrent protection: Type: _____   Amps: _____

Location (of primary supply panelboard): _____

Disconnecting means location: _____

© 2014 National Fire Protection Association   NFPA 72 (p. 1 of 2)

FIGURE 13.7.3.2.5.2(c) Power Systems Supplementary Record of Completion. [72:Figure 7.8.2(c)]

POWER SYSTEMS
SUPPLEMENTARY RECORD OF COMPLETION *(continued)*

2. SYSTEM POWER *(continued)*

2.2.2 Engine-Driven Generator

Location of generator: _____

Location of fuel storage: _____ Type of fuel: _____

2.2.3 Uninterruptible Power System

Equipment powered by UPS system: _____

Location of UPS system: _____

Calculated capacity of UPS batteries to drive the system components connected to it:

In standby mode (hours): _____ In alarm mode (minutes): _____

2.2.4 Batteries

Location: _____ Type: _____ Nominal voltage: _____ Amp/hour rating: _____

Calculated capacity of batteries to drive the system:

In standby mode (hours): _____ In alarm mode (minutes): _____

2.3 Notification Appliance Power Extender Panels

❏ This system does not have power extender panels.

2.3.1 Primary Power

Input voltage of power extender panel(s): _____ Power extender panel amps: _____

Overcurrent protection: Type: _____ Amps: _____

Location (of primary supply panelboard): _____

Disconnecting means location: _____

2.3.2 Engine Driven Generator

Location of generator: _____

Location of fuel storage: _____ Type of fuel: _____

2.3.3 Uninterruptible Power System

Equipment powered by UPS system: _____

Location of UPS system: _____

Calculated capacity of UPS batteries to drive the system components connected to it:

In standby mode (hours): _____ In alarm mode (minutes): _____

2.3.4 Batteries

Location: _____ Type: _____ Nominal voltage: _____ Amp/hour rating: _____

Calculated capacity of batteries to drive the system:

In standby mode (hours): _____ In alarm mode (minutes): _____

See Main System Record of Completion for additional information, certifications, and approvals.

© 2014 National Fire Protection Association　　　　　　　　　　　　　　　　　　　　　　NFPA 72 (p. 2 of 2)

FIGURE 13.7.3.2.5.2(c) *Continued*

NOTIFICATION APPLIANCE POWER PANEL
SUPPLEMENTARY RECORD OF COMPLETION

This form is a supplement to the System Record of Completion. It includes a list of types and locations of notification appliance power extender panels.
This form is to be completed by the system installation contractor at the time of system acceptance and approval.
It shall be permitted to modify this form as needed to provide a more complete and/or clear record.
Insert N/A in all unused lines.

Form Completion Date: _____   Number of Supplemental Pages Attached: _____

1. PROPERTY INFORMATION
Name of property: _____
Address: _____

2. NOTIFICATION APPLIANCE POWER EXTENDER PANELS

Make and Model	Location	Area Served	Power Source

See Main System Record of Completion for additional information, certifications, and approvals.

© 2014 National Fire Protection Association   NFPA 72

FIGURE 13.7.3.2.5.2(d) Notification Appliance Power Panel Supplementary Record of Completion. [72:Figure 7.8.2(d)]

INTERCONNECTED SYSTEMS
SUPPLEMENTARY RECORD OF COMPLETION

This form is a supplement to the System Record of Completion. It includes a list of types and locations of systems that are interconnected to the main system.
This form is to be completed by the system installation contractor at the time of system acceptance and approval.
It shall be permitted to modify this form as needed to provide a more complete and/or clear record.
Insert N/A in all unused lines.

Form Completion Date: _____   Number of Supplemental Pages Attached: _____

1. PROPERTY INFORMATION
Name of property: _____
Address: _____

2. INTERCONNECTED SYSTEMS

Description	Location	Purpose

See Main System Record of Completion for additional information, certifications, and approvals.

© 2014 National Fire Protection Association   NFPA 72

FIGURE 13.7.3.2.5.2(e) Interconnected Systems Supplementary Record of Completion. [72:Figure 7.8.2(e)]

FIRE PROTECTION SYSTEMS

DEVIATIONS FROM ADOPTED CODES AND STANDARDS
SUPPLEMENTARY RECORD OF COMPLETION

This form is a supplement to the System Record of Completion. It enables the designer and/or installer to document and justify deviations from accepted codes or standards. This form is to be completed by the system installation contractor at the time of system acceptance and approval. It shall be permitted to modify this form as needed to provide a more complete and/or clear record. Insert N/A in all unused lines.

Form Completion Date: _____   Number of Supplemental Pages Attached: _____

1. PROPERTY INFORMATION
Name of property: _____
Address: _____

2. DEVIATIONS FROM ADOPTED CODES OR STANDARDS

Description	Purpose

See Main System Record of Completion for additional information, certifications, and approvals.

© 2014 National Fire Protection Association   NFPA 72

FIGURE 13.7.3.2.5.2(f) Deviations from Adopted Codes and Standards Supplementary Record of Completion. [72:Figure 7.8.2(f)]

2015 Edition

SYSTEM RECORD OF INSPECTION AND TESTING

This form is to be completed by the system inspection and testing contractor at the time of a system test.
It shall be permitted to modify this form as needed to provide a more complete and/or clear record.
Insert N/A in all unused lines.
Attach additional sheets, data, or calculations as necessary to provide a complete record.

Inspection/Test Start Date/Time: _____   Inspection/Test Completion Date/Time: _____

Supplemental Form(s) Attached: _____ (yes/no)

1. PROPERTY INFORMATION

Name of property: _____
Address: _____
Description of property: _____
Name of property representative: _____
Address: _____
Phone: _____   Fax: _____   E-mail: _____

2. TESTING AND MONITORING INFORMATION

Testing organization: _____
Address: _____
Phone: _____   Fax: _____   E-mail: _____
Monitoring organization: _____
Address: _____
Phone: _____   Fax: _____   E-mail: _____
Account number: _____   Phone line 1: _____   Phone line 2: _____
Means of transmission: _____
Entity to which alarms are retransmitted: _____   Phone: _____

3. DOCUMENTATION

Onsite location of the required record documents and site-specific software: _____

4. DESCRIPTION OF SYSTEM OR SERVICE

4.1 Control Unit
Manufacturer: _____   Model number: _____

4.2 Software Firmware
Firmware revision number: _____

4.3 System Power
4.3.1 Primary (Main) Power
Nominal voltage: _____   Amps: _____   Location: _____
Overcurrent protection type: _____   Amps: _____   Disconnecting means location: _____

© 2014 National Fire Protection Association   NFPA 72 (p. 1 of 4)

FIGURE 13.7.3.2.5.2(g)   System Record of Inspection and Testing. [72:Figure 7.8.2(g)]

SYSTEM RECORD OF INSPECTION AND TESTING *(continued)*

4. DESCRIPTION OF SYSTEM OR SERVICE *(continued)*

4.3.2 Secondary Power

Type: _____ Location: _____

Battery type (if applicable): _____

Calculated capacity of batteries to drive the system:

In standby mode (hours): _____ In alarm mode (minutes): _____

5. NOTIFICATIONS MADE PRIOR TO TESTING

Monitoring organization	Contact: _____	Time: _____
Building management	Contact: _____	Time: _____
Building occupants	Contact: _____	Time: _____
Authority having jurisdiction	Contact: _____	Time: _____
Other, if required	Contact: _____	Time: _____

6. TESTING RESULTS

6.1 Control Unit and Related Equipment

Description	Visual Inspection	Functional Test	Comments
Control unit	❏	❏	
Lamps/LEDs/LCDs	❏	❏	
Fuses	❏	❏	
Trouble signals	❏	❏	
Disconnect switches	❏	❏	
Ground-fault monitoring	❏	❏	
Supervision	❏	❏	
Local annunciator	❏	❏	
Remote annunciators	❏	❏	
Remote power panels	❏	❏	
	❏	❏	

6.2 Secondary Power

Description	Visual Inspection	Functional Test	Comments
Battery condition	❏	❏	
Load voltage	❏	❏	
Discharge test	❏	❏	
Charger test	❏	❏	
Remote panel batteries	❏	❏	

© 2014 National Fire Protection Association

NFPA 72 (p. 2 of 4)

FIGURE 13.7.3.2.5.2(g) *Continued*

SYSTEM RECORD OF INSPECTION AND TESTING *(continued)*

6. TESTING RESULTS *(continued)*

6.3 Alarm and Supervisory Alarm Initiating Device

Attach supplementary device test sheets for all initiating devices.

6.4 Notification Appliances

Attach supplementary appliance test sheets for all notification appliances.

6.5 Interface Equipment

Attach supplementary interface component test sheets for all interface components.

Circuit Interface / Signaling Line Circuit Interface / Fire Alarm Control Interface

6.6 Supervising Station Monitoring

Description	Yes	No	Time	Comments
Alarm signal	❏	❏		
Alarm restoration	❏	❏		
Trouble signal	❏	❏		
Trouble restoration	❏	❏		
Supervisory signal	❏	❏		
Supervisory restoration	❏	❏		

6.7 Public Emergency Alarm Reporting System

Description	Yes	No	Time	Comments
Alarm signal	❏	❏		
Alarm restoration	❏	❏		
Trouble signal	❏	❏		
Trouble restoration	❏	❏		
Supervisory signal	❏	❏		
Supervisory restoration	❏	❏		

© 2014 National Fire Protection Association   NFPA 72 (p. 3 of 4)

FIGURE 13.7.3.2.5.2(g) *Continued*

SYSTEM RECORD OF INSPECTION AND TESTING *(continued)*

7. NOTIFICATIONS THAT TESTING IS COMPLETE

Monitoring organization	Contact: _____	Time: _____
Building management	Contact: _____	Time: _____
Building occupants	Contact: _____	Time: _____
Authority having jurisdiction	Contact: _____	Time: _____
Other, if required	Contact: _____	Time: _____

8. SYSTEM RESTORED TO NORMAL OPERATION

Date: _____ Time: _____

9. CERTIFICATION

This system as specified herein has been inspected and tested according to NFPA 72, 2013 edition, Chapter 14.

Signed: _____ Printed name: _____ Date: _____
Organization: _____ Title: _____ Phone: _____
Qualifications (refer to 10.5.3): _____

10. DEFECTS OR MALFUNCTIONS NOT CORRECTED AT CONCLUSION OF SYSTEM INSPECTION, TESTING, OR MAINTENANCE

_____
_____
_____
_____
_____
_____
_____
_____
_____
_____
_____
_____
_____
_____
_____
_____
_____

10.1 Acceptance by Owner or Owner's Representative:

The undersigned accepted the test report for the system as specified herein:

Signed: _____ Printed name: _____ Date: _____
Organization: _____ Title: _____ Phone: _____

© 2014 National Fire Protection Association

FIGURE 13.7.3.2.5.2(g) *Continued*

NOTIFICATION APPLIANCE
SUPPLEMENTARY RECORD OF INSPECTION AND TESTING

This form is a supplement to the System Record of Inspection and Testing.
It includes a notification appliance test record.
This form is to be completed by the system inspection and testing contractor at the time of the inspection and/or test.
It shall be permitted to modify this form as needed to provide a more complete and/or clear record.
Insert N/A in all unused lines.

Inspection/Test Start Date/Time: _____ Inspection/Test Completion Date/Time: _____

Number of Supplemental Pages Attached: _____

1. PROPERTY INFORMATION
Name of property: _____
Address: _____

2. NOTIFICATION APPLIANCE TEST RESULTS

Appliance Type	Location/Identifier	Test Results

© 2014 National Fire Protection Association NFPA 72 (p. 1 of 2)

FIGURE 13.7.3.2.5.2(h) Notification Appliance Supplementary Record of Inspection and Testing. [72:Figure 7.8.2(h)]

NOTIFICATION APPLIANCE
SUPPLEMENTARY RECORD OF INSPECTION AND TESTING *(continued)*

2. NOTIFICATION APPLIANCE TEST RESULTS *(continued)*

Appliance Type	Location/Identifier	Test Results

See main System Record of Inspection and Testing for additional information, certifications, and approvals.

© 2014 National Fire Protection Association

FIGURE 13.7.3.2.5.2(h) *Continued*

INITIATING DEVICE
SUPPLEMENTARY RECORD OF INSPECTION AND TESTING

This form is a supplement to the System Record of Inspection and Testing.
It includes an initiating device test record.
This form is to be completed by the system inspection and testing contractor at the time of the inspection and/or test.
It shall be permitted to modify this form as needed to provide a more complete and/or clear record.
Insert N/A in all unused lines.

Inspection/Test Start Date/Time: _____   Inspection/Test Completion Date/Time: _____

Number of Supplemental Pages Attached: _____

1. PROPERTY INFORMATION
Name of property: _____
Address: _____

2. INITIATING DEVICE TEST RESULTS

Device Type	Address	Location	Test Results

© 2014 National Fire Protection Association   NFPA 72 (p. 1 of 2)

FIGURE 13.7.3.2.5.2(i) Initiating Device Supplementary Record of Inspection and Testing. [72:Figure 7.8.2(i)]

INITIATING DEVICE
SUPPLEMENTARY RECORD OF INSPECTION AND TESTING *(continued)*

2. INITIATING DEVICE TEST RESULTS *(continued)*

Device Type	Address	Location	Test Results

See main System Record of Inspection and Testing for additional information, certifications, and approvals.

© 2014 National Fire Protection Association

FIGURE 13.7.3.2.5.2(i) *Continued*

MASS NOTIFICATION SYSTEM
SUPPLEMENTARY RECORD OF INSPECTION AND TESTING

This form is a supplement to the System Record of Inspection and Testing.
It includes a mass notification system test record.
This form is to be completed by the system inspection and testing contractor at the time of the inspection and/or test.
It shall be permitted to modify this form as needed to provide a more complete and/or clear record.
Insert N/A in all unused lines.

Inspection/Test Start Date/Time: _____   Inspection/Test Completion Date/Time: _____

Number of Supplemental Pages Attached: _____

1. PROPERTY INFORMATION
Name of property: _____
Address: _____

2. MASS NOTIFICATION SYSTEM

2.1 System Type
❑ In-building MNS—combination
❑ In-building MNS—stand alone   ❑ Wide-area MNS   ❑ Distributed recipient MNS
❑ Other (specify): _____

2.2 System Features
❑ Combination fire alarm/MNS   ❑ MNS ACU only   ❑ Wide-area MNS to regional national alerting interface
❑ Local operating console (LOC)   ❑ Direct recipient MNS (DRMNS)   ❑ Wide-area MNS to DRMNS interface
❑ Wide-area MNS to high-power speaker array (HPSA) interface   ❑ In-building MNS to wide-area MNS interface
❑ Other (specify): _____

3. IN-BUILDING MASS NOTIFICATION SYSTEM

3.1 Primary Power
Input voltage of MNS panel: _____   MNS panel amps: _____

3.2 Engine-Driven Generator   ❑ This system does not have a generator.
Location of generator: _____
Location of fuel storage: _____   Type of fuel: _____

3.3 Uninterruptible Power System   ❑ This system does not have a UPS.
Equipment powered by a UPS system: _____
Location of UPS system: _____
Calculated capacity of UPS batteries to drive the system components connected to it:
In standby mode (hours): _____   In alarm mode (minutes): _____

3.4 Batteries
Location: _____   Type: _____   Nominal voltage: _____   Amp/hour rating: _____
Calculated capacity of batteries to drive the system:
In standby mode (hours): _____   In alarm mode (minutes): _____
❑ Batteries are marked with date of manufacture.

© 2014 National Fire Protection Association   NFPA 72 (p. 1 of 2)

FIGURE 13.7.3.2.5.2(j) Mass Notification System Supplementary Record of Inspection and Testing. [72:Figure 7.8.2(j)]

MASS NOTIFICATION SYSTEM
SUPPLEMENTARY RECORD OF INSPECTION AND TESTING *(continued)*

4. MASS NOTIFICATION EQUIPMENT TEST RESULTS

Description	Visual Inspection	Functional Test	Comments
Functional test			
Reset/power down test			
Fuses			
Primary power supply			
UPS power test			
Trouble signals			
Disconnect switches			
Ground-fault monitoring			
CCU security mechanism			
Prerecorded message content			
Prerecorded message activation			
Software backup performed			
Test backup software			
Fire alarm to MNS interface			
MNS to fire alarm interface			
In-building MNS to wide-area MNS			
MNS to direct recipient MNS			
Sound pressure levels Occupied ❑ Yes ❑ No Ambient dBA:_____ Alarm dBA:_____ (attach supplementary notification appliance form(s) with locations, values, and weather conditions)			
System intelligibility Test method:_____ Score:_____ CIS value:_____ (attach supplementary notification appliance form(s) with locations, values, and weather conditions)			
Other (specify):			

See main System Record of Inspection and Testing for additional information, certifications, and approvals.

© 2014 National Fire Protection Association NFPA 72 (p. 2 of 2)

FIGURE 13.7.3.2.5.2(j) *Continued*

EMERGENCY COMMUNICATIONS SYSTEMS
SUPPLEMENTARY RECORD OF INSPECTION AND TESTING

This form is a supplement to the System Record of Inspection and Testing.
It includes systems and components specific to emergency communication systems.
This form is to be completed by the system inspection and testing contractor at the time of the inspection and/or test.
It shall be permitted to modify this form as needed to provide a more complete and/or clear record.
Insert N/A in all unused lines.

Inspection/Test Start Date/Time: _____   Inspection/Test Completion Date/Time: _____

Number of Supplemental Pages Attached: _____

1. PROPERTY INFORMATION

Name of property: _____

Address: _____

2. DESCRIPTION OF SYSTEM OR SERVICE

❑ Fire alarm with in-building fire emergency voice alarm communication system (EVAC)

❑ Mass notification system

❑ Combination system, with the following components:

   ❑ Fire alarm   ❑ EVACS   ❑ MNS   ❑ Two-way, in-building, emergency communication system

❑ Other (specify): _____

Additional description of system(s): _____

_____

2.1 In-Building Fire Emergency Voice Alarm Communication System

Manufacturer: _____ Model number: _____

Number of single voice alarm channels: _____ Number of multiple voice alarm channels: _____

Number of speakers: _____ Number of speaker circuits: _____

Location of amplification and sound processing equipment: _____

_____

_____

Location of paging microphone stations:

Location 1: _____

Location 2: _____

Location 3: _____

2.2 Mass Notification System

2.2.1 System Type:

❑ In-building MNS—combination

❑ In-building MNS   ❑ Wide-area MNS   ❑ Distributed recipient MNS

❑ Other (specify): _____

© 2014 National Fire Protection Association   NFPA 72 (p. 1 of 5)

FIGURE 13.7.3.2.5.2(k) Emergency Communications Systems Supplementary Record of Inspection and Testing. [72:Figure 7.8.2(k)]

FIRE PROTECTION SYSTEMS 1–167

**EMERGENCY COMMUNICATIONS SYSTEMS
SUPPLEMENTARY RECORD OF INSPECTION AND TESTING** *(continued)*

2. DESCRIPTION OF SYSTEM OR SERVICE *(continued)*

2.2.2 System Features:

❏ Combination fire alarm/MNS ❏ MNS autonomous control unit ❏ Wide-area MNS to regional national alerting interface
❏ Local operating console (LOC) ❏ Distributed-recipient MNS (DRMNS) ❏ Wide-area MNS to DRMNS interface
❏ Wide-area MNS to high-power speaker array (HPSA) interface ❏ In-building MNS to wide-area MNS interface
❏ Other (specify): _____

2.2.3 MNS Local Operating Consoles

Location 1: _____
Location 2: _____
Location 3: _____

2.2.4 High-Power Speaker Arrays

Number of HPSA speaker initiation zones: _____
Location 1: _____
Location 2: _____
Location 3: _____

2.2.5 Mass Notification Devices

Combination fire alarm/MNS visual devices: _____ MNS-only visual devices: _____
Textual signs: _____ Other (describe): _____
Supervision class: _____

2.2.6 Special Hazard Notification

❏ This system does not have special suppression pre-discharge notification
❏ MNS systems DO NOT override notification appliances required to provide special suppression pre-discharge notification

3. TWO-WAY EMERGENCY COMMUNICATION SYSTEMS

3.1 Telephone System

Number of telephone jacks installed: _____ Number of warden stations installed: _____
Number of telephone handsets stored on site: _____
Type of telephone system installed: ❏ Electrically powered ❏ Sound powered

3.2 Two-Way Radio Communications Enhancement System

Percentage of area covered by two-way radio service: Critical areas _____ % General building areas _____ %
Amplification component locations: _____

Inbound signal strength _____ dBm Outbound signal strength _____ dBm
Donor antenna isolation is _____ dB above the signal booster gain
Radio frequencies covered: _____
Radio system monitor panel location: _____

© 2014 National Fire Protection Association NFPA 72 (p. 2 of 5)

FIGURE 13.7.3.2.5.2(k) Continued

2015 Edition

EMERGENCY COMMUNICATIONS SYSTEMS
SUPPLEMENTARY RECORD OF INSPECTION AND TESTING *(continued)*

3. TWO-WAY EMERGENCY COMMUNICATIONS SYSTEMS *(continued)*

3.3 Area of Refuge (Area of Rescue Assistance) Emergency Communications Systems

Number of stations: _____ Location of central control point: _____

Days and hours when central control point is attended: _____

Location of alternate control point: _____

Days and hours when alternate control point is attended: _____

3.4 Elevator Emergency Communications Systems

Number of elevators with stations: _____ Location of central control point: _____

Days and hours when central control point is attended: _____

Location of alternate control point: _____

Days and hours when alternate control point is attended: _____

3.5 Other Two-Way Communication System

Describe: _____

4. TESTING RESULTS

4.1 Control Unit and Related Equipment

Description	Visual Inspection	Functional Test	Comments
Control unit	❏	❏	
Lamps/LEDs/LCDs	❏	❏	
Fuses	❏	❏	
Trouble signals	❏	❏	
Disconnect switches	❏	❏	
Ground fault monitoring	❏	❏	
Supervision	❏	❏	
Local annunciator	❏	❏	
Remote annunciators	❏	❏	
Remote power panels	❏	❏	
Other:	❏	❏	

4.2 Secondary Power

Description	Visual Inspection	Functional Test	Comments
Battery condition	❏	❏	
Load voltage	❏	❏	
Discharge test	❏	❏	
Charger test	❏	❏	
Remote panel batteries	❏	❏	

© 2014 National Fire Protection Association NFPA 72 (p. 3 of 5)

FIGURE 13.7.3.2.5.2(k) *Continued*

EMERGENCY COMMUNICATIONS SYSTEMS
SUPPLEMENTARY RECORD OF INSPECTION AND TESTING *(continued)*

4. TESTING RESULTS *(continued)*

4.3 Emergency Communications Equipment

Description	Visual Inspection	Functional Test	Comments
Control unit	❏	❏	
Lamps/LEDs/LCDs	❏	❏	
Fuses	❏	❏	
Secondary power supply	❏	❏	
Trouble signals	❏	❏	
Disconnect switches	❏	❏	
Ground fault monitoring	❏	❏	
Panel supervision	❏	❏	
System performance	❏	❏	
System audibility	❏	❏	
System intelligibility	❏	❏	
Other:	❏	❏	

4.4 Mass Notification Equipment

Description	Visual Inspection	Functional Test	Comments
Functional test	❏	❏	
Reset/Power down test	❏	❏	
Fuses	❏	❏	
Primary power supply	❏	❏	
UPS power test	❏	❏	
Trouble signals	❏	❏	
Disconnect switches	❏	❏	
Ground fault monitoring	❏	❏	
CCU security mechanism	❏	❏	
Prerecorded message content	❏	❏	
Prerecorded message activation	❏	❏	
Software backup performed	❏	❏	
Test backup software	❏	❏	
Fire alarm to MNS Interface	❏	❏	
MNS to fire alarm interface	❏	❏	
In-building MNS to wide-area MNS	❏	❏	
MNS to direct recipient MNS	❏	❏	

© 2014 National Fire Protection Association

NFPA 72 (p. 4 of 5)

FIGURE 13.7.3.2.5.2(k) *Continued*

EMERGENCY COMMUNICATIONS SYSTEMS
SUPPLEMENTARY RECORD OF INSPECTION AND TESTING *(continued)*

4. TESTING RESULTS *(continued)*

4.4 Mass Notification Equipment *(continued)*

Description	Visual Inspection	Functional Test	Comments
Sound pressure levels (attach report with locations, values, and weather conditions)	❏	❏	
System intelligibility ❏ CSI ❏ STI (attach report with locations, values, and weather conditions)	❏	❏	
Other:	❏	❏	

4.5 Two-Way Communication Equipment

Description	Visual Inspection	Functional Test	Comments
Phone handsets	❏	❏	
Phone jacks	❏	❏	
Off-hook indicator	❏	❏	
Call-in signal	❏	❏	
System performance	❏	❏	
System audibility	❏	❏	
System intelligibility	❏	❏	
Other:	❏	❏	

See main System Record of Inspection and Testing for additional information, certifications, and approvals.

© 2014 National Fire Protection Association

FIGURE 13.7.3.2.5.2(k) *Continued*

INTERFACE COMPONENT
SUPPLEMENTARY RECORD OF INSPECTION AND TESTING

This form is a supplement to the System Record of Inspection and Testing.
It includes an interface component test record for circuit interfaces, signaling line circuit interfaces, and fire alarm control interfaces.
This form is to be completed by the system inspection and testing contractor at the time of the inspection and/or test.
It shall be permitted to modify this form as needed to provide a more complete and/or clear record.
Insert N/A in all unused lines.

Inspection/Test Start Date/Time: _____   Inspection/Test Completion Date/Time: _____

Number of Supplemental Pages Attached: _____

1. PROPERTY INFORMATION
Name of property: _____
Address: _____

2. INTERFACE COMPONENT TEST RESULTS

Interface Component Type	Address	Location	Test Results

© 2014 National Fire Protection Association   NFPA 72 (p. 1 of 2)

FIGURE 13.7.3.2.5.2(l) Interface Component Supplementary Record of Inspection and Testing. [72:Figure 7.8.2(l)]

INTERFACE COMPONENT
SUPPLEMENTARY RECORD OF INSPECTION AND TESTING *(continued)*

2. INTERFACE COMPONENT TEST RESULTS *(continued)*

Interface Component Type	Address	Location	Test Results

See main System Record of Inspection and Testing for additional information, certifications, and approvals.

© 2014 National Fire Protection Association

NFPA 72 (p. 2 of 2)

FIGURE 13.7.3.2.5.2(1) *Continued*

13.7.3.4.3 The documentation shall be physically posted within 3 ft (1 m) of the control unit, and copies of the documentation shall be made available to the AHJs upon request. [**72:**26.3.4.3]

13.7.3.4.4 A central repository of issued documentation, accessible to the AHJ, shall be maintained by the organization that has listed the prime contractor. [**72:**26.3.4.4]

13.7.3.4.5* Alarm system service that does not comply with all the requirements of Section 26.3 of *NFPA 72* shall not be designated as central station service. [**72:**26.3.4.5]

13.7.3.4.6* For the purpose of Section 26.3 of *NFPA 72*, the subscriber shall notify the prime contractor, in writing, of the identity of the AHJs. [**72:**26.3.4.6]

13.7.3.4.7 The AHJs identified in 13.7.3.4.2(5) shall be notified of expiration or cancellation by the organization that has listed the prime contractor. [**72:**26.3.4.7]

13.7.3.4.8 The subscriber shall surrender expired or canceled documentation to the prime contractor within 30 days of the termination date. [**72:**26.3.4.8]

13.7.3.5 Automatic Fire Detection and Alarm Service.

13.7.3.5.1 Automatic fire detectors shall be located, maintained, and tested in accordance with *NFPA 72*.

13.7.4 Automatic Fire Detectors.

13.7.4.1 General Requirements.

13.7.4.1.1 The requirements of 13.7.4.1.1 through 13.7.4.1.5 shall apply to all initiating devices. [**72:**17.4.1]

13.7.4.1.2 Where subject to mechanical damage, an initiating device shall be protected. A mechanical guard used to protect a smoke, heat, or radiant energy–sensing detector shall be listed for use with the detector. [**72:**17.4.2]

13.7.4.1.3 Initiating devices shall be supported independently of their attachment to the circuit conductors. [**72:**17.4.3]

13.7.4.1.4 Initiating devices shall be installed in a manner that provides accessibility for periodic inspection, testing, and maintenance. [**72:**17.4.4]

13.7.4.1.5 Initiating devices shall be installed in all areas, compartments, or locations where required by other governing laws, codes, or standards. [**72:**17.4.5]

13.7.4.1.6 Duct Detector Installation.

13.7.4.1.6.1 Smoke detectors shall be installed, tested, and maintained in accordance with *NFPA 72*. [**90A:**6.4.4.1]

13.7.4.1.6.2 In addition to the requirements of 6.4.3 of NFPA 90A, *Standard for the Installation of Air-Conditioning and Ventilating Systems*, where an approved fire alarm system is installed in a building, the smoke detectors required by the provisions of Section 6.4 of NFPA 90A shall be connected to the fire alarm system in accordance with the requirements of *NFPA 72*. [**90A:**6.4.4.2]

13.7.4.1.6.2.1 Smoke detectors used solely for closing dampers or for heating, ventilating, and air-conditioning system shutdown shall not be required to activate the building evacuation alarm. [**90A:**6.4.4.2.1]

13.7.4.1.6.3 Where smoke detectors required by Section 6.4 of NFPA 90A are installed in a building not equipped with an approved fire alarm system as specified by 13.7.4.1.6.2, the following shall occur:

(1) Smoke detector activation required by Section 6.4 of NFPA 90A shall cause a visual and audible signal in a normally occupied area.
(2) Smoke detector trouble conditions shall be indicated visually or audibly in a normally occupied area and shall be identified as air duct detector trouble.
[**90A:**6.4.4.3]

13.7.4.1.6.4 Smoke detectors powered separately from the fire alarm system for the sole function of stopping fans shall not require standby power. [**90A:**6.4.4.4]

13.7.4.2 Requirements for Smoke and Heat Detectors.

13.7.4.2.1 Recessed Mounting. Unless tested and listed for recessed mounting, detectors shall not be recessed into the mounting surface. [**72:**17.5.1]

13.7.4.3 Location.

13.7.4.3.1* Unless otherwise modified by 17.6.3.2.2, 17.6.3.3.2, or 17.6.3.7 of *NFPA 72*, spot-type heat-sensing fire detectors shall be located on the ceiling not less than 4 in. (100 mm) from the sidewall or on the sidewalls between 4 in. and 12 in. (100 mm and 300 mm) from the ceiling. [**72:**17.6.3.1.3.1]

13.7.4.3.2 Unless otherwise modified by 17.6.3.2.2, 17.6.3.3.2, or 17.6.3.7 of *NFPA 72*, line-type heat detectors shall be located on the ceiling or on the sidewalls not more than 20 in. (510 mm) from the ceiling. [**72:**17.6.3.1.3.2]

13.7.4.3.3* Spot-Type Smoke Detectors.

13.7.4.3.3.1* Spot-type smoke detectors shall be located on the ceiling or, if on a sidewall, between the ceiling and 12 in. (300 mm) down from the ceiling to the top of the detector. [**72:**17.7.3.2.1]

13.7.4.3.3.2* To minimize dust contamination, smoke detectors, where installed under raised floors, shall be mounted only in an orientation for which they have been listed. [**72:**17.7.3.2.2]

13.7.4.3.3.3 On smooth ceilings, spacing for spot-type smoke detectors shall be in accordance with 13.7.4.3.3.3.1 through 13.7.4.3.3.3.4. [**72:**17.7.3.2.3]

13.7.4.3.3.3.1* In the absence of specific performance-based design criteria, one of the following requirements shall apply:

(1) The distance between smoke detectors shall not exceed a nominal spacing of 30 ft (9.1 m) and there shall be detectors within a distance of one-half the nominal spacing, measured at right angles from all walls or partitions extending upward to within the top 15 percent of the ceiling height.
(2)*All points on the ceiling shall have a detector within a distance equal to or less than 0.7 times the nominal 30 ft (9.1 m) spacing (0.7 *S*).
[**72:**17.7.3.2.3.1]

13.7.4.3.3.3.2 In all cases, the manufacturer's published instructions shall be followed. [**72:**17.7.3.2.3.2]

13.7.4.3.3.3.3 Other spacing shall be permitted to be used depending on ceiling height, different conditions, or response requirements. [**72:**17.7.3.2.3.3]

13.7.4.3.3.3.4 For the detection of flaming fires, the guidelines in Annex B of *NFPA 72* shall be permitted to be used. [**72**:17.7.3.2.3.4]

13.7.4.3.3.4* For solid joist and beam construction, spacing for spot-type smoke detectors shall be in accordance with 13.7.4.3.3.4.1 through 13.7.4.3.3.4.5. [**72**:17.7.3.2.4]

13.7.4.3.3.4.1 Solid joists shall be considered equivalent to beams for smoke detector spacing guidelines. [**72**:17.7.3.2.4.1]

13.7.4.3.3.4.2 For level ceilings, the following shall apply:

(1) For ceilings with beam depths of less than 10 percent of the ceiling height ($0.1\ H$), smooth ceiling spacing shall be permitted. Spot-type smoke detectors shall be permitted to be located on ceilings or on the bottom of beams.
(2) For ceilings with beam depths equal to or greater than 10 percent of the ceiling height ($0.1\ H$), the following shall apply:
   (a) Where beam spacing is equal to or greater than 40 percent of the ceiling height ($0.4\ H$), spot-type detectors shall be located on the ceiling in each beam pocket.
   (b) Where beam spacing is less than 40 percent of the ceiling height ($0.4\ H$), the following shall be permitted for spot detectors:
      i. Smooth ceiling spacing in the direction parallel to the beams and at one-half smooth ceiling spacing in the direction perpendicular to the beams
      ii. Location of detectors either on the ceiling or on the bottom of the beams
(3)*For beam pockets formed by intersecting beams, including waffle or pan-type ceilings, the following shall apply:
   (a) For beam depths less than 10 percent of the ceiling height ($0.1\ H$), spacing shall be in accordance with 13.7.4.3.3.4.2(1).
   (b) For beam depths greater than or equal to 10 percent of the ceiling height ($0.1\ H$), spacing shall be in accordance with 13.7.4.3.3.4.2(2)(2).
(4)*For corridors 15 ft (4.6 m) in width or less having ceiling beams or solid joists perpendicular to the corridor length, the following shall apply:
   (a) Smooth ceiling spacing shall be permitted.
   (b) Location of spot-type smoke detectors on ceilings, sidewalls, or the bottom of beams or solid joists
(5) For rooms of 900 ft^2 (84 m^2) or less, the following shall be permitted:
   (a) Use of smooth ceiling spacing
   (b) Location of spot-type smoke detectors on ceilings or on the bottom of beams
   [**72:** 17.7.3.2.4.2]

13.7.4.3.3.4.3* For sloping ceilings with beams running parallel up slope, the following shall apply:

(1) Spot-type detector(s) shall be located on the ceiling within beam pocket(s).
(2) The ceiling height shall be taken as the average height over slope.
(3) Spacing shall be measured along a horizontal projection of the ceiling.
(4) Smooth ceiling spacing shall be permitted within beam pocket(s) parallel to the beams.
(5) For beam depths less than or equal to 10 percent of the ceiling height ($0.1\ H$), spot-type detectors shall be located with smooth ceiling spacing perpendicular to the beams.
(6) For beam depths greater than 10 percent of the ceiling height ($0.1\ H$), the following shall apply for spacing perpendicular to the beams:
   (a) For beam spacing greater than or equal to 40 percent of the ceiling height ($0.4\ H$), spot-type detectors shall be located in each beam pocket.
   (b) For beam spacing less than 40 percent of the ceiling height ($0.4\ H$), spot-type detectors shall not be required in every beam pocket but shall be spaced not greater than 50 percent of smooth ceiling spacing. [**72**:17.7.3.2.4.3]

13.7.4.3.3.4.4* For sloping ceilings with beams running perpendicular across slope, the following shall apply:

(1) Spot-type detector(s) shall be located at the bottom of the beams.
(2) The ceiling height shall be taken as the average height over slope.
(3) Spacing shall be measured along a horizontal projection of the ceiling.
(4) Smooth ceiling spacing shall be permitted within beam pocket(s).
(5) For beam depths less than or equal to 10 percent of the ceiling height ($0.1\ H$), spot-type detectors shall be located with smooth ceiling spacing.
(6) For beam depths greater than 10 percent of the ceiling height ($0.1\ H$), spot-type detectors shall not be required to be located closer than ($0.4\ H$) and shall not exceed 50 percent of smooth ceiling spacing. [**72**:17.7.3.2.4.4]

13.7.4.3.3.4.5* For sloped ceilings with beam pockets formed by intersecting beams, the following shall apply:

(1) Spot-type detector(s) shall be located at the bottom of the beams.
(2) The ceiling height shall be taken as the average height over slope.
(3) Spacing shall be measured along a horizontal projection of the ceiling.
(4) For beam depths less than or equal to 10 percent of the ceiling height ($0.1\ H$), spot-type detectors shall be spaced with not more than three beams between detectors and shall not exceed smooth ceiling spacing.
(5) For beam depths greater than 10 percent of the ceiling height ($0.1\ H$), spot-type detectors shall be placed with not more than two beams between detectors, but shall not be required to be spaced closer than ($0.4\ H$), and shall not exceed 50 percent of smooth ceiling spacing. [**72**:17.7.3.2.4.5]

13.7.4.3.3.4.6 For sloped ceilings with solid joists, the detectors shall be located on the bottom of the joist. [**72**:17.7.3.2.4.6]

13.7.4.3.4 Air Sampling–Type Smoke Detector.

13.7.4.3.4.1 Each sampling port of an air sampling–type smoke detector shall be treated as a spot-type detector for the purpose of location and spacing. [**72**:17.7.3.6.1]

13.7.4.3.4.2 Maximum air sample transport time from the farthest sampling port to the detector shall not exceed 120 seconds. [**72**:17.7.3.6.2]

13.7.4.3.4.3* Sampling pipe networks shall be designed on the basis of, and shall be supported by, sound fluid dynamic principles to ensure required performance. [**72:**17.7.3.6.3]

13.7.4.3.4.4 Sampling pipe network design details shall include calculations showing the flow characteristics of the pipe network and each sample port. [**72:**17.7.3.6.4]

13.7.4.3.4.5 Air-sampling detectors shall give a trouble signal if the airflow is outside the manufacturer's specified range. [**72:**17.7.3.6.5]

13.7.4.3.4.6* The sampling ports and in-line filter, if used, shall be kept clear in accordance with the manufacturer's published instructions. [**72:**17.7.3.6.6]

13.7.4.3.4.7 Air-sampling network piping and fittings shall be airtight and permanently fixed. [**72:** 17.7.3.6.7]

13.7.4.3.4.8 Sampling system piping shall be conspicuously identified as "SMOKE DETECTOR SAMPLING TUBE — DO NOT DISTURB," as follows:

(1) At changes in direction or branches of piping
(2) At each side of penetrations of walls, floors, or other barriers
(3) At intervals on piping that provide visibility within the space, but no greater than 20 ft (6.1 m)
[**72:**17.7.3.6.8]

13.7.4.3.5* Projected Beam–Type Smoke Detectors.

13.7.4.3.5.1 Projected beam–type smoke detectors shall be located in accordance with the manufacturer's published instructions. [**72:**17.7.3.7.1]

13.7.4.3.5.2 The effects of stratification shall be evaluated when locating the detectors. [**72:**17.7.3.7.2]

13.7.4.3.5.3 The beam length shall not exceed the maximum permitted by the equipment listing. [**72:**17.7.3.7.3]

13.7.4.3.5.4 If mirrors are used with projected beams, the mirrors shall be installed in accordance with the manufacturer's published instructions. [**72:**17.7.3.7.4]

13.7.4.3.5.5 A projected beam–type smoke detector shall be considered equivalent to a row of spot-type smoke detectors for level and sloping ceiling applications. [**72:** 7.7.3.7.5]

13.7.4.3.5.6 Projected beam–type detectors and mirrors shall be mounted on stable surfaces to prevent false or erratic operation due to movement. [**72:**17.7.3.7.6]

13.7.4.3.5.7 The beam shall be designed so that small angular movements of the light source or receiver do not prevent operation due to smoke and do not cause nuisance or unintentional alarms. [**72:**17.7.3.7.7]

13.7.4.3.5.8* The light path of projected beam–type detectors shall be kept clear of opaque obstacles at all times. [**72:**17.7.3.7.8]

13.7.4.3.6* Protection During Construction.

13.7.4.3.6.1 Where detectors are installed for signal initiation during construction, they shall be cleaned and verified to be operating in accordance with the listed sensitivity, or they shall be replaced prior to the final commissioning of the system. [**72:**17.7.1.11.1]

13.7.4.3.6.2 Where detectors are installed but not operational during construction, they shall be protected from construction debris, dust, dirt, and damage in accordance with the manufacturer's recommendations and verified to be operating in accordance with the listed sensitivity, or they shall be replaced prior to the final commissioning of the system. [**72:**17.7.1.11.2]

13.7.4.3.6.3 Where detection is not required during construction, detectors shall not be installed until after all other construction trades have completed cleanup. [**72:**17.7.1.11.3]

13.7.4.3.7 Ceiling Tiles and Ceiling Assemblies. Where automatic detectors are installed, ceilings necessary for the proper actuation of the fire protection device in accordance with *NFPA 72* shall be maintained.

13.7.4.3.8 High Air Movement Areas.

13.7.4.3.8.1 Location. Smoke detectors shall not be located directly in the airstream of supply registers. [**72:**17.7.6.3.2]

13.7.4.3.8.2* Spacing.

13.7.4.3.8.2.1 Smoke detector spacing shall be reduced where the airflow in a defined space exceeds 8 minutes per air change (total space volume) (equal to 7.5 air changes per hour). [**72:**17.7.6.3.3.1]

13.7.4.3.8.2.2 Where spacing must be adjusted for airflow, spot-type smoke detector spacing shall be adjusted in accordance with Table 17.7.6.3.3.2 or Figure 17.7.6.3.3.2 of *NFPA 72* before making any other spacing adjustments required by this *Code*. [**72:**17.7.6.3.3.2]

13.7.4.4 Inspection, Testing, and Maintenance. The inspection, testing, and maintenance for fire alarm and fire detection systems shall be in accordance with Chapter 10 of *NFPA 72*.

13.7.4.5 Heat Detectors.

13.7.4.5.1 Fixed-Temperature, Rate-of-Rise, Rate-of-Compensation, Restorable Line, Spot Type (Excluding Pneumatic Tube Type). Heat test shall be performed with a listed and labeled heat source or in accordance with the manufacturer's published inspections. A test method for the installed equipment, shall be used that does not damage the nonrestorable fixed-temperature element of a combination rate-of-rise/fixed-temperature element detector. [**72:** Table 14.4.3.2, 17(d)1]

13.7.4.5.2 Fixed-Temperature, Nonrestorable Line Type. Heat test shall not be performed. Functionality shall be tested mechanically and electrically. Loop resistance shall be measured and recorded. Changes from acceptance test shall be investigated. [**72:** Table 14.4.3.2, 17(d)2]

13.7.4.5.3 Nonrestorable (General). Heat tests shall not be performed. Functionality shall be tested mechanically and electrically. [**72:** Table 14.4.3.2, 17(d)4]

13.7.4.5.4 Restorable Line Type, Pneumatic Tube Only. Heat tests shall be performed (where test chambers are in circuit), with a listed and labeled heat source or in accordance with the manufacturer's published instructions of the detector or a test with pressure pump shall be conducted. [**72:** Table 14.4.2.2, 17(d)5]

13.7.4.6 Smoke Detectors.

13.7.4.6.1 In Other Than One- and Two-Family Dwellings, System Detectors. Smoke detectors shall be tested in place to ensure smoke entry into the sensing chamber and an alarm response. Testing with smoke or listed and labeled product, acceptable to the manufacturer or in accordance with their published instructions, shall be permitted as acceptable test methods. Other methods listed in the manufacturer's published instructions that ensure smoke entry from the protected area, through the vents, into the sensing chamber shall be permitted. Any of the following tests shall be performed to ensure that each smoke detector is within its listed and marked sensitivity range:

(1) Calibrated test method
(2) Manufacturer's calibrated sensitivity test instrument
(3) Listed control equipment arranged for the purpose
(4) Smoke detector/control unit arrangement whereby the detector causes a signal at the control unit when its sensitivity is outside its listed sensitivity range
(5) Other calibrated sensitivity test method approved by the AHJ [**72:** Table 14.4.3.2, 17(h)(1)]

13.7.4.6.2 Projected Beam Type. The detector shall be tested by introducing smoke, other aerosol, or an optical filter into the beam path. [**72:**Table 14.4.3.2, 17(g)6]

13.7.4.6.3 A functional test shall be performed on all smoke detectors upon initial installation and at least annually as required by Table 13.7.3.2.4. [**72:**Table 14.4.5, 15(h)]

13.7.4.7* In other than one- and two-family dwellings, sensitivity of smoke detectors shall be tested in accordance with 13.7.4.7.1 through 13.7.4.7.7. [**72:**4.4.4.3]

13.7.4.7.1 Sensitivity shall be checked within 1 year after installation. [**72:**14.4.4.3.1]

13.7.4.7.2 Sensitivity shall be checked every alternate year thereafter unless otherwise permitted by compliance with 13.7.4.7.3. [**72:** 14.4.5.3.2]

13.7.4.7.3 After the second required calibration test, if sensitivity tests indicate that the device has remained within its listed and marked sensitivity range (or 4 percent obscuration light gray smoke, if not marked), the length of time between calibration tests shall be permitted to be extended to a maximum of 5 years. [**72:**14.4.4.3.3]

13.7.4.7.3.1 If the frequency is extended, records of nuisance alarms and subsequent trends of these alarms shall be maintained. [**72:**14.445.3.3.1]

13.7.4.7.3.2 In zones or in areas where nuisance alarms show any increase over the previous year, calibration tests shall be performed. [**72:**14.4.4.3.3.2]

13.7.4.7.4 To ensure that each smoke detector is within its listed and marked sensitivity range, it shall be tested using any of the following methods:

(1) Calibrated test method
(2) Manufacturer's calibrated sensitivity test instrument
(3) Listed control equipment arranged for the purpose
(4) Smoke detector/fire alarm control unit arrangement whereby the detector causes a signal at the fire alarm control unit where its sensitivity is outside its listed sensitivity range
(5) Other calibrated sensitivity test methods approved by the AHJ [**72:**14.4.4.3.4]

13.7.4.7.5 Unless otherwise permitted by 13.7.4.7.6, smoke detectors found to have a sensitivity outside the listed and marked sensitivity range shall be cleaned and recalibrated or be replaced. [**72:**14.4.4.3.5]

13.7.4.7.6 Smoke detectors listed as field adjustable shall be permitted to either be adjusted within the listed and marked sensitivity range, cleaned, and recalibrated, or be replaced. [**72:**14.4.4.3.6]

13.7.4.7.7 The detector sensitivity shall not be tested or measured using any device that administers an unmeasured concentration of smoke or other aerosol into the detector or smoke alarm. [**72:**14.4.4.3.7]

13.8 Other Fire Protection Systems. Where other fire protection systems are required to be installed by the provisions of this *Code*, or are installed with the approval of the AHJ as an alternative or equivalency, the design and installation of the system shall comply with the appropriate standards listed in Table 13.8. The system shall be tested and maintained in accordance with Section 10.4.

Table 13.8 Other Required Fire Protection Systems

Type of System	NFPA Standard
Low-, medium-, and high-expansion foam systems	NFPA 11, *Standard for Low-, Medium-, and High-Expansion Foam*
Carbon dioxide systems	NFPA 12, *Standard on Carbon Dioxide Extinguishing Systems*
Halon 1301 systems	NFPA 12A, *Standard on Halon 1301 Fire Extinguishing Systems*
Sprinklers in one- and two-family dwellings and manufactured homes	NFPA 13D, *Standard for the Installation of Sprinkler Systems in One- and Two-Family Dwellings and Manufactured Homes*
Sprinklers in residential occupancies up to and including four stories in height	NFPA 13R, *Standard for the Installation of Sprinkler Systems in Low-Rise Residential Occupancies*
Water spray systems	NFPA 15, *Standard for Water Spray Fixed Systems for Fire Protection*
Deluge foam-water sprinkler, foam-water spray systems, and closed-head foam-water sprinkler systems	NFPA 16, *Standard for the Installation of Foam-Water Sprinkler and Foam-Water Spray Systems*
Dry chemical extinguishing systems	NFPA 17, *Standard for Dry Chemical Extinguishing Systems*
Wet chemical extinguishing systems	NFPA 17A, *Standard for Wet Chemical Extinguishing Systems*
Water mist systems	NFPA 750, *Standard on Water Mist Fire Protection Systems*
Clean agent fire-extinguishing systems	NFPA 2001, *Standard on Clean Agent Fire Extinguishing Systems*
Aerosol extinguishing systems	NFPA 2010, *Standard for Fixed Aerosol Fire Extinguishing Systems*

13.9 Non-Listed Fire Protection or Suppression Devices and Equipment.

13.9.1 It shall be unlawful to market, sell, advertise, or distribute any device or equipment as suitable for fire protection or fire suppression purposes unless the device or equipment is listed for such purpose by a nationally recognized testing laboratory or as otherwise permitted by 13.9.2.

13.9.2 The requirements of 13.9.1 shall not apply where NFPA standards, other adopted standards, or the adopted code allow the use of non-listed fire protection or suppression equipment.

Chapter 14 Means of Egress

14.1 Application. Means of egress in new and existing buildings shall comply with this *Code* and NFPA *101, Life Safety Code.*

14.2 Exit Access Corridors. Corridors used as exit access and serving an area having an occupant load exceeding 30 shall be separated from other parts of the building by walls having not less than a 1-hour fire resistance rating in accordance with Section 12.7, unless otherwise permitted by the following:

(1) This requirement shall not apply to existing buildings, provided that the occupancy classification does not change.
(2) This requirement shall not apply where otherwise provided in Chapters 11 through 43 of NFPA *101*.

[*101:* 7.1.3.1]

14.3 Exits.

14.3.1 Where this *Code* requires an exit to be separated from other parts of the building, the separating construction shall meet the requirements of Section 8.2 of NFPA *101* and the following:

(1)*The separation shall have a minimum 1-hour fire resistance rating where the exit connects three or fewer stories.
(2) The separation specified in 14.3.1(1), other than an existing separation, shall be supported by construction having not less than a 1-hour fire resistance rating.
(3)*The separation shall have a minimum 2-hour fire resistance rating where the exit connects four or more stories, unless one of the following conditions exists:
  (a) In existing non-high-rise buildings, existing exit stair enclosures shall have a minimum 1-hour fire resistance rating.
  (b) In existing buildings protected throughout by an approved, supervised automatic sprinkler system in accordance with Section 13.3, existing exit stair enclosures shall have a minimum 1-hour fire resistance rating.
  (c) The minimum 1-hour enclosures in accordance with 28.2.2.1.2, 29.2.2.1.2, 30.2.2.1.2, and 31.2.2.1.2 of NFPA *101* shall be permitted as an alternative to the requirement of 14.3.1(3).
(4) Reserved.
(5) The minimum 2-hour fire resistance–rated separation required by 14.3.1(3) shall be constructed of an assembly of noncombustible or limited-combustible materials and shall be supported by construction having a minimum 2-hour fire resistance rating, unless otherwise permitted by 14.3.1(7).
(6)*Structural elements, or portions thereof, that support exit components and either penetrate into a fire resistance–rated assembly or are installed within a fire resistance–rated wall assembly shall be protected, as a minimum to the fire resistance rating required by 14.3.1(1) or 14.3.1(3).
(7) In Type III, Type IV, and Type V construction, as defined in NFPA 220, *Standard on Types of Building Construction (see 8.2.1.2 of* NFPA *101),* fire-retardant-treated wood enclosed in noncombustible or limited-combustible materials shall be permitted.
(8) Openings in the separation shall be protected by fire door assemblies equipped with door closers complying with 14.5.4.
(9)*Openings in exit enclosures shall be limited to door assemblies from normally occupied spaces and corridors and door assemblies for egress from the enclosure, unless one of the following conditions exists:
  (a) Vestibules that separate normally unoccupied spaces from an exit enclosure shall be permitted provided the vestibule is separated from adjacent spaces by corridor walls and related opening protectives as required for the occupancy involved but not less than a smoke partition in accordance with Section 8.4 of NFPA *101*.
  (b) In buildings of Type I or Type II construction as defined in NFPA 220, *Standard on Types of Building Construction (see 8.2.1.2 of* NFPA *101),* fire protection–rated door assemblies to normally unoccupied building service equipment support areas as addressed in Section 7.13 of NFPA *101* shall be permitted, provided the space is separated from the exit enclosure by fire barriers as required by 14.3.1(3).
  (c) Openings in exit passageways in mall buildings as provided in Chapters 36 and 37 of NFPA *101* shall be permitted.
  (d) In buildings of Type I or Type II construction, as defined in NFPA 220, *Standard on Types of Building Construction (see 8.2.1.2 of* NFPA *101),* existing fire protection–rated door assemblies to interstitial spaces shall be permitted, provided that such spaces meet all of the following criteria:
    i. The space is used solely for distribution of pipes, ducts, and conduits.
    ii. The space contains no storage.
    iii. The space is separated from the exit enclosure in accordance with Section 12.7.
  (e) Existing openings to mechanical equipment spaces protected by approved existing fire protection–rated door assemblies shall be permitted, provided that the following criteria are met:
    i. The space is used solely for non-fuel-fired mechanical equipment.
    ii. The space contains no storage of combustible materials.
    iii. The building is protected throughout by an approved, supervised automatic sprinkler system in accordance with Section 13.3.
(10) Penetrations into, and openings through, an exit enclosure assembly shall be limited to the following:
  (a) Door assemblies permitted by 14.3.1(9)
  (b)*Electrical conduit serving the stairway
  (c) Required exit doors
  (d) Ductwork and equipment necessary for independent stair pressurization
  (e) Water or steam piping necessary for the heating or cooling of the exit enclosure
  (f) Sprinkler piping
  (g) Standpipes

(h) Existing penetrations protected in accordance with 12.7.5
(i) Penetrations for fire alarm circuits, where the circuits are installed in metal conduit and the penetrations are protected in accordance with 12.7.5

(11) Penetrations or communicating openings shall be prohibited between adjacent exit enclosures.
(12) Membrane penetrations shall be permitted on the exit access side of the exit enclosure and shall be protected in accordance with 12.7.5.6.

[*101:* 7.1.3.2.1]

14.3.2 An exit enclosure shall provide a continuous protected path of travel to an exit discharge. [*101:* 7.1.3.2.2]

14.3.3* An exit enclosure shall not be used for any purpose that has the potential to interfere with its use as an exit and, if so designated, as an area of refuge. *(See also 14.6.3.)* [*101:*7.1.3.2.3]

14.4 Means of Egress Reliability.

14.4.1* Maintenance. Means of egress shall be continuously maintained free of all obstructions or impediments to full instant use in the case of fire or other emergency. [*101:* 7.1.10.1]

14.4.2 Furnishings and Decorations in Means of Egress.

14.4.2.1 No furnishings, decorations, or other objects shall obstruct exits or their access thereto, egress therefrom, or visibility thereof. [*101:* 7.1.10.2.1]

14.4.2.2 No obstruction by railings, barriers, or gates shall divide the means of egress into sections appurtenant to individual rooms, apartments, or other occupied spaces. Where the AHJ finds the required path of travel to be obstructed by furniture or other movable objects, the authority shall be permitted to require that such objects be secured out of the way or shall be permitted to require that railings or other permanent barriers be installed to protect the path of travel against encroachment. [*101:* 7.1.10.2.2]

14.4.2.3 Mirrors shall not be placed on exit door leaves. Mirrors shall not be placed in or adjacent to any exit in such a manner as to confuse the direction of egress. [*101:*7.1.10.2.3]

14.4.2.4 Every door opening and every principal entrance that is required to serve as an exit shall be designed and constructed so that the path of egress travel is obvious and direct. Windows that, because of their physical configuration or design and the materials used in their construction, have the potential to be mistaken for door openings shall be made inaccessible to the occupants by barriers or railings. [*101:* 7.2.1.1.2]

14.4.3 Impediments to Egress. Any device or alarm installed to restrict the improper use of a means of egress shall be designed and installed so that it cannot, even in case of failure, impede or prevent emergency use of such means of egress unless otherwise provided in 14.5.3 and Chapters 18, 19, 22, and 23 of NFPA *101.* [*101:* 7.1.9]

14.5 Door Openings.

14.5.1 Swing and Force to Open.

14.5.1.1* Swinging-Type Door Assembly Requirement. Any door assembly in a means of egress shall be of the side-hinged or pivoted-swinging type, and shall be installed to be capable of swinging from any position to the full required width of the opening in which it is installed, unless otherwise specified as follows:

(1) Door assemblies in dwelling units, as provided in Chapter 24 of NFPA *101,* shall be permitted.
(2) Door assemblies in residential board and care occupancies, as provided in Chapters 32 and 33 of NFPA *101,* shall be permitted.
(3) Where permitted in Chapters 11 through 43 of NFPA *101,* horizontal-sliding or vertical-rolling security grilles or door assemblies that are part of the required means of egress shall be permitted, provided that all of the following criteria are met:
  (a) Such grilles or door assemblies shall remain secured in the fully open position during the period of occupancy by the general public.
  (b) On or adjacent to the grille or door opening, there shall be a readily visible, durable sign in letters not less than 1 in. (25 mm) high on a contrasting background that reads as follows: THIS DOOR TO REMAIN OPEN WHEN THE SPACE IS OCCUPIED.
  (c) Door leaves or grilles shall not be brought to the closed position when the space is occupied.
  (d) Door leaves or grilles shall be operable from within the space without the use of any special knowledge or effort.
  (e) Where two or more means of egress are required, not more than half of the means of egress shall be equipped with horizontal-sliding or vertical-rolling grilles or door assemblies.
(4) Horizontal-sliding door assemblies shall be permitted under any of the following conditions:
  (a) Horizontal-sliding door assemblies in detention and correctional occupancies, as provided in Chapters 22 and 23 of NFPA *101,* shall be permitted.
  (b) Special purpose horizontally sliding accordion or folding door assemblies complying with 7.2.1.14 of NFPA *101* shall be permitted.
  (c) Unless prohibited by Chapters 11 through 43 of NFPA *101,* horizontal-sliding door assemblies serving a room or area with an occupant load of fewer than 10 shall be permitted, provided that all of the following criteria are met:
    i. The area served by the door assembly has no high hazard contents.
    ii. The door assembly is readily operable from either side without special knowledge or effort.
    iii. The force required to operate the door assembly in the direction of door leaf travel is not more than 30 lbf (133 N) to set the door leaf in motion and is not more than 15 lbf (67 N) to close the door assembly or open it to the minimum required width.
    iv. The door assembly complies with any required fire protection rating, and, where rated, is self-closing or automatic-closing by means of smoke detection in accordance with 14.5.4 and is installed in accordance with NFPA 80, *Standard for Fire Doors and Other Opening Protectives.*
    v. Corridor door assemblies required to be self-latching shall have a latch or other mechanism that ensures that the door leaf will not rebound into a partially open position if forcefully closed.
  (d) Where private garages, business areas, industrial areas, and storage areas with an occupant load not exceeding 10 contain only low or ordinary hazard contents, door openings to such areas and private

garages shall be permitted to be horizontal-sliding door assemblies.

(5) Where private garages, business areas, industrial areas, and storage areas with an occupant load not exceeding 10 contain only low or ordinary hazard contents, door openings to such areas and private garages shall be permitted to be vertical-rolling door assemblies.
(6) Revolving door assemblies complying with 7.2.1.10 of NFPA *101* shall be permitted.
(7) Existing fusible link–operated horizontal-sliding or vertical-rolling fire door assemblies shall be permitted to be used as provided in Chapters 39, 40, and 42 of NFPA *101*.

[*101:* 7.2.1.4.1]

14.5.1.2 Door Leaf Swing Direction. Door leaves required to be of the side-hinged or pivoted-swinging type shall swing in the direction of egress travel under any of the following conditions:

(1) Where serving a room or area with an occupant load of 50 or more, except under the following conditions:
 (a) Door leaves in horizontal exits shall not be required to swing in the direction of egress travel where permitted by 7.2.4.3.8.1 or 7.2.4.3.8.2 of NFPA *101*.
 (b) Door leaves in smoke barriers shall not be required to swing in the direction of egress travel in existing health care occupancies, as provided in Chapter 19 of NFPA *101*.
(2) Where the door assembly is used in an exit enclosure, unless the door opening serves an individual living unit that opens directly into an exit enclosure
(3) Where the door opening serves a high hazard contents area

[*101:* 7.2.1.4.2]

14.5.1.3 Door Leaf Encroachment.

14.5.1.3.1* During its swing, any door leaf in a means of egress shall leave not less than one-half of the required width of an aisle, a corridor, a passageway, or a landing unobstructed, unless both of the following conditions are met:

(1) The door opening provides access to a stair in an existing building.
(2) The door opening meets the requirement of 14.5.1.3.2.

[*101:* 7.2.1.4.3.1]

14.5.1.3.2 When fully open, any door leaf in a means of egress shall not project more than 7 in. (180 mm) into the required width of an aisle, a corridor, a passageway, or a landing, unless the door leaf is equipped with an approved self-closing device and is not required by the provisions of 14.5.1.2 to swing in the direction of egress travel. [*101:* 7.2.1.4.3.3]

14.5.1.3.3 Surface-mounted latch release hardware on the door leaf shall be exempt from being included in the maximum 7 in. (180 mm) projection requirement of 14.5.1.3.2, provided that both of the following criteria are met:

(1) The hardware is mounted to the side of the door leaf that faces the aisle, corridor, passageway, or landing when the door leaf is in the open position.
(2) The hardware is mounted not less than 34 in. (865 mm), and not more than 48 in. (1220 mm), above the floor.

[*101:* 7.2.1.4.3.2]

14.5.1.4 Screen Door Assemblies and Storm Door Assemblies. Screen door assemblies and storm door assemblies used in a means of egress shall be subject to the requirements for direction of swing that are applicable to other door assemblies used in a means of egress. [*101:* 7.2.1.4.4]

14.5.1.5 Door Leaf Operating Forces.

14.5.1.5.1 The forces required to fully open any door leaf manually in a means of egress shall not exceed 15 lbf (67 N) to release the latch, 30 lbf (133 N) to set the leaf in motion, and 15 lbf (67 N) to open the leaf to the minimum required width, unless otherwise specified as follows:

(1) The opening forces for interior side-hinged or pivoted-swinging door leaves without closers shall not exceed 5 lbf (22 N).
(2) The opening forces for existing door leaves in existing buildings shall not exceed 50 lbf (222 N) applied to the latch stile.
(3) The opening forces for horizontal-sliding door leaves in detention and correctional occupancies shall be as provided in Chapters 22 and 23 of NFPA *101*.
(4) The opening forces for power-operated door leaves shall be as provided in 7.2.1.9 of NFPA *101*.

[*101:* 7.2.1.4.5.1]

14.5.1.5.2 The forces specified in 14.5.1.5 shall be applied to the latch stile. [*101:* 7.2.1.4.5.2]

14.5.2 Locks, Latches, and Alarm Devices.

14.5.2.1 Door leaves shall be arranged to be opened readily from the egress side whenever the building is occupied. [*101:* 7.2.1.5.1]

14.5.2.2* The requirement of 14.5.2.1 shall not apply to door leaves of listed fire door assemblies after exposure to elevated temperature in accordance with the listing, based on laboratory fire test procedures. [*101:* 7.2.1.5.2]

14.5.2.3 Locks, if provided, shall not require the use of a key, a tool, or special knowledge or effort for operation from the egress side. [*101:* 7.2.1.5.3]

14.5.2.4 The requirements of 14.5.2.1 and 14.5.2.3 shall not apply where otherwise provided in Chapters 18 through 23 of NFPA *101*. [*101:* 7.2.1.5.4]

14.5.2.5 Key-Operated Locks.

14.5.2.5.1* Exterior door assemblies shall be permitted to have key-operated locks from the egress side, provided that all of the following criteria are met:

(1) This alternative is permitted in Chapters 11 through 43 of NFPA *101* for the specific occupancy.
(2) A readily visible, durable sign in letters not less than 1 in. (25 mm) high on a contrasting background that reads as follows is located on or adjacent to the door: THIS DOOR TO REMAIN UNLOCKED WHEN THE BUILDING IS OCCUPIED
(3) The locking device is of a type that is readily distinguishable as locked.
(4) A key is immediately available to any occupant inside the building when it is locked.

[*101:* 7.2.1.5.5.1]

14.5.2.5.2 The alternative provisions of 14.5.2.5.1 shall be permitted to be revoked by the AHJ for cause. [*101:* 7.2.1.5.5.2]

14.5.2.6 Electrically Controlled Egress Door Assemblies. Door assemblies in the means of egress shall be permitted to be electrically locked if equipped with approved, listed hardware that incorporates a built-in switch, provided that all of the following conditions are met:

(1) The hardware for occupant release of the lock is affixed to the door leaf.
(2) The hardware has an obvious method of operation that is readily operated in the direction of egress.
(3) The hardware is capable of being operated with one hand in the direction of egress.
(4) Operation of the hardware interrupts the power supply directly to the electric lock and unlocks the door assembly in the direction of egress.
(5) Loss of power to the hardware automatically unlocks the door assembly in the direction of egress.
(6) Hardware for new installations is listed in accordance with ANSI/UL 294.

[*101:* 7.2.1.5.6]

14.5.2.7 Where permitted in Chapters 11 through 43 of NFPA *101*, key operation shall be permitted, provided that the key cannot be removed when the door leaf is locked from the side from which egress is to be made. [*101:* 7.2.1.5.7]

14.5.2.8* Every door assembly in a stair enclosure serving more than four stories, unless permitted by 14.5.2.8.2, shall meet one of the following conditions:

(1) Re-entry from the stair enclosure to the interior of the building shall be provided.
(2) An automatic release that is actuated with the initiation of the building fire alarm system shall be provided to unlock all stair enclosure door assemblies to allow re-entry.
(3) Selected re-entry shall be provided in accordance with 14.5.2.8.1.

[*101:* 7.2.1.5.8]

14.5.2.8.1 Door assemblies on stair enclosures shall be permitted to be equipped with hardware that prevents re-entry into the interior of the building, provided that the following criteria are met:

(1) There shall be not less than two levels where it is possible to leave the stair enclosure to access another exit.
(2) There shall be not more than four stories intervening between stories where it is possible to leave the stair enclosure to access another exit.
(3) Re-entry shall be possible on the top story or next-to-top story served by the stair enclosure, and such story shall allow access to another exit.
(4) Door assemblies allowing re-entry shall be identified as such on the stair side of the door leaf.
(5) Door assemblies not allowing re-entry shall be provided with a sign on the stair side indicating the location of the nearest door opening, in each direction of travel, that allows re-entry or exit.

[*101:* 7.2.1.5.8.1]

14.5.2.8.2 The requirements of 14.5.2.8, except as provided in 14.5.2.8.3, shall not apply to the following:

(1) Existing installations in buildings that are not high-rise buildings as permitted in Chapters 11 through 43 of NFPA *101*.
(2) Existing installations in high-rise buildings as permitted in Chapters 11 through 43 of NFPA *101* where the occupancy is within a building protected throughout by an approved, supervised automatic sprinkler system in accordance with Section 13.3.
(3) Existing approved stairwell re-entry installations as permitted by Chapters 11 through 43 of NFPA *101*.
(4) Stair enclosures serving a building permitted to have a single exit in accordance with Chapters 11 through 43 of NFPA *101*.
(5) Stair enclosures in health care occupancies where otherwise provided in Chapter 18 of NFPA *101*.
(6) Stair enclosures in detention and correctional occupancies where otherwise provided in Chapter 22 of NFPA *101*.

[*101:* 7.2.1.5.8.2]

14.5.2.8.3 When the provisions of 14.5.2.8.2 are used, signage on the stair door leaves shall be required as follows:

(1) Door assemblies allowing re-entry shall be identified as such on the stair side of the door leaf.
(2) Door assemblies not allowing re-entry shall be provided with a sign on the stair side indicating the location of the nearest door opening, in each direction of travel, that allows re-entry or exit.

[*101:* 7.2.1.5.8.3]

14.5.2.9 If a stair enclosure allows access to the roof of the building, the door to the roof either shall be kept locked or shall allow re-entry from the roof. [*101:* 7.2.1.5.9]

14.5.2.10* A latch or other fastening device on a door leaf shall be provided with a releasing device that has an obvious method of operation and that is readily operated under all lighting conditions. [*101:* 7.2.1.5.10]

14.5.2.10.1 The releasing mechanism for any latch shall be located as follows:

(1) Not less than 34 in. (865 mm) above the finished floor for other than existing installations
(2) Not more than 48 in. (1220 mm) above the finished floor

[*101:* 7.2.1.5.10.1]

14.5.2.10.2 The releasing mechanism shall open the door leaf with not more than one releasing operation, unless otherwise specified in 14.5.2.10.3 and 14.5.2.10.4 or 14.5.2.10.6. [*101:* 7.2.1.5.10.2]

14.5.2.10.3* Egress door assemblies from individual living units and guest rooms of residential occupancies shall be permitted to be provided with devices, including automatic latching devices, that require not more than one additional releasing operation, provided that such device is operable from the inside without the use of a key or tool and is mounted at a height not exceeding 48 in. (1220 mm) above the finished floor. [*101:* 7.2.1.5.10.3]

14.5.2.10.4 Existing security devices permitted by 14.5.2.10.3 shall be permitted to have two additional releasing operations. [*101:* 7.2.1.5.10.4]

14.5.2.10.5 Existing security devices permitted by 14.5.2.10.3, other than automatic latching devices, shall be located not more than 60 in. (1525 mm) above the finished floor. [*101:* 7.2.1.5.10.5]

14.5.2.10.6 Two releasing operations shall be permitted for existing hardware on a door leaf serving an area having an occupant load not exceeding three, provided that releasing does not require simultaneous operations. [*101:* 7.2.1.5.10.6]

14.5.2.11 Where pairs of door leaves are required in a means of egress, one of the following criteria shall be met:

(1) Each leaf of the pair shall be provided with a releasing device that does not depend on the release of one leaf before the other.
(2) Approved automatic flush bolts shall be used and arranged such that the following criteria are met:
  (a) The door leaf equipped with the automatic flush bolts shall have no doorknob or surface-mounted hardware.
  (b) Unlatching of any leaf shall not require more than one operation.

[*101:* 7.2.1.5.11]

14.5.2.12* Devices shall not be installed in connection with any door assembly on which panic hardware or fire exit hardware is required where such devices prevent or are intended to prevent the free use of the leaf for purposes of egress, unless otherwise provided in 14.5.3. [*101:* 7.2.1.5.12]

14.5.3* Special Locking Arrangements.

14.5.3.1 Delayed-Egress Locking Systems.

14.5.3.1.1 Approved, listed, delayed-egress locking systems shall be permitted to be installed on door assemblies serving low and ordinary hazard contents in buildings protected throughout by an approved, supervised automatic fire detection system in accordance with Section 13.7 or an approved, supervised automatic sprinkler system in accordance with Section 13.3, and where permitted in Chapters 11 through 43 of NFPA *101*, provided that the following criteria are met:

(1) The door leaves shall unlock upon actuation of one of the following:
  (a) Approved, supervised automatic sprinkler system in accordance with Section 13.3
  (b) Not more than one heat detector of an approved, supervised automatic fire detection system in accordance with Section 13.7
  (c) Not more than two smoke detectors of an approved, supervised automatic fire detection system in accordance with Section 13.7
(2) The door leaves shall unlock upon loss of power controlling the lock or locking mechanism.
(3)*An irreversible process shall release the lock within 15 seconds, or 30 seconds where approved by the authority having jurisdiction, upon application of a force to the release device required in 14.5.2.10 under all of the following conditions:
  (a) The force shall not be required to exceed 15 lbf (67 N).
  (b) The force shall not be required to be continuously applied for more than 3 seconds.
  (c) The initiation of the release process shall activate an audible signal in the vicinity of the door opening.
  (d) Once the lock has been released by the application of force to the releasing device, relocking shall be by manual means only.
(4)*A readily visible, durable sign in letters not less than 1 in. (25 mm) high and not less than ⅛ in. (3.2 mm) in stroke width on a contrasting background shall be located on the door adjacent to the release device in the direction of egress, and shall read as follows:

  (a) PUSH UNTIL ALARM SOUNDS, DOOR CAN BE OPENED IN 15 SECONDS, for doors that swing in one direction of egress travel
  (b) PULL UNTIL ALARM SOUNDS, DOOR CAN BE OPENED IN 15 SECONDS, for doors that swing against the direction of egress travel
(5) The egress side of doors equipped with delayed-egress locks shall be provided with emergency lighting in accordance with Section 7.9 of NFPA *101*.

[*101:* 7.2.1.6.1.1]

14.5.3.1.2 The provisions of 14.5.3.2 for access-controlled egress door assemblies shall not apply to door assemblies with delayed-egress locking systems. [*101:* 7.2.1.6.1.2]

14.5.3.2* Access-Controlled Egress Door Assemblies. Where permitted in Chapters 11 through 43 of NFPA *101*, door assemblies in the means of egress shall be permitted to be equipped with an approved entrance and egress access control system, provided that all of the following criteria are met:

(1) A sensor shall be provided on the egress side, arranged to unlock the door leaf in the direction of egress upon detection of an approaching occupant.
(2) Door leaves shall automatically unlock in the direction of egress upon loss of power to the sensor or to the part of the access control system that locks the door leaves.
(3) Door locks shall be arranged to unlock in the direction of egress from a manual release device complying with all of the following criteria:
  (a) The manual release device shall be located on the egress side, 40 in. to 48 in. (1015 mm to 1220 mm) vertically above the floor, and within 60 in. (1525 mm) of the secured door openings.
  (b) The manual release device shall be readily accessible and clearly identified by a sign that reads as follows: PUSH TO EXIT.
  (c) When operated, the manual release device shall result in direct interruption of power to the lock — independent of the locking system electronics — and the lock shall remain unlocked for not less than 30 seconds.
(4) Activation of the building fire-protective signaling system, if provided, shall automatically unlock the door leaves in the direction of egress, and the door leaves shall remain unlocked until the fire-protective signaling system has been manually reset.
(5) The activation of manual fire alarm boxes that activate the building fire-protective signaling system specified in 14.5.3.2(4) shall not be required to unlock the door leaves.
(6) Activation of the building automatic sprinkler or fire detection system, if provided, shall automatically unlock the door leaves in the direction of egress, and the door leaves shall remain unlocked until the fire-protective signaling system has been manually reset.
(7) The egress side of access-controlled egress doors, other than existing access-controlled egress doors, shall be provided with emergency lighting in accordance with Section 14.13.

[*101:* 7.2.1.6.2]

14.5.3.3 Elevator Lobby Exit Access Door Assemblies Locking. Where permitted in Chapters 11 through 43 of NFPA *101*, door assemblies separating the elevator lobby from the exit access required by 14.9.1.6.1 shall be permitted to be electronically locked, provided that all the following criteria are met:

(1) The lock is listed in accordance with ANSI/UL 294, *Standard for Access Control System Units*.
(2) The building is protected throughout by a fire alarm system in accordance with Section 13.7.
(3) The building is protected throughout by an approved, supervised automatic sprinkler system in accordance with Section 13.3.
(4) Waterflow in the sprinkler system required by 14.5.3.3(3) is arranged to initiate the building fire alarm system.
(5) The elevator lobby is protected by an approved, supervised smoke detection system in accordance with Section 13.7.
(6) Detection of smoke by the detection system required by 14.5.3.3(5) is arranged to initiate the building fire alarm system and notify building occupants.
(7) Initiation of the building fire alarm system by other than manual fire alarm boxes unlocks the elevator lobby door assembly.
(8) Loss of power to the elevator lobby electronic lock system unlocks the elevator lobby door assemblies.
(9) Once unlocked, the elevator lobby door assemblies remain unlocked until the building fire alarm system has been manually reset.
(10) Where the elevator lobby door assemblies remain latched after being unlocked, latch-releasing hardware in accordance with 14.5.2.10 is affixed to the door leaves.
(11) A two-way communication system is provided for communication between the elevator lobby and a central control point that is constantly staffed.
(12) The central control point staff required by 14.5.3.3(11) is capable, trained, and authorized to provide emergency assistance.
(13) The provisions of 14.5.3.1 for delayed-egress locking systems are not applied to the elevator lobby door assemblies.
(14)*The provisions of 14.5.3.2 for access-controlled egress door assemblies are not applied to the elevator lobby door assemblies.

[*101:* 7.2.1.6.3]

14.5.3.4 Panic Hardware and Fire Exit Hardware.

14.5.3.4.1 Where a door assembly is required to be equipped with panic or fire exit hardware, such hardware shall meet all of the following criteria:

(1) It shall consist of a cross bar or a push pad, the actuating portion of which extends across not less than one-half of the width of the door leaf.
(2) It shall be mounted as follows:
   (a) New installations shall be not less than 34 in. (865 mm), nor more than 48 in. (1220 mm), above the floor.
   (b) Existing installations shall be not less than 30 in. (760 mm), nor more than 48 in. (1220 mm), above the floor.
(3) It shall be constructed so that a horizontal force not to exceed 15 lbf (66 N) actuates the cross bar or push pad and latches.

[*101:* 7.2.1.7.1]

14.5.3.4.2* Only approved fire exit hardware shall be used on fire-rated door assemblies. New panic hardware and new fire exit hardware shall comply with ANSI/UL 305 and ANSI/BHMA A156.3. [*101:* 7.2.1.7.2]

14.5.3.4.3 Required panic hardware and fire exit hardware, in other than detention and correctional occupancies as otherwise provided in Chapters 22 and 23 of NFPA *101*, shall not be equipped with any locking device, set screw, or other arrangement that prevents the release of the latch when pressure is applied to the releasing device. [*101:* 7.2.1.7.3]

14.5.3.4.4 Devices that hold the latch in the retracted position shall be prohibited on fire exit hardware, unless such devices are listed and approved for such a purpose. [*101:* 7.2.1.7.4]

14.5.4 Self-Closing Devices.

14.5.4.1* A door leaf normally required to be kept closed shall not be secured in the open position at any time and shall be self-closing or automatic-closing in accordance with 14.5.4.2, unless otherwise permitted by 14.5.4.3. [*101:* 7.2.1.8.1]

14.5.4.2 In any building of low or ordinary hazard contents, as defined in 3.3.142.2 and 3.3.142.3, or where approved by the AHJ, doors shall be permitted to be automatic-closing, provided that all of the following criteria are met:

(1) Upon release of the hold-open mechanism, the leaf becomes self-closing.
(2) The release device is designed so that the leaf instantly releases manually and, upon release, becomes self-closing, or the leaf can be readily closed.
(3) The automatic releasing mechanism or medium is activated by the operation of approved smoke detectors installed in accordance with the requirements for smoke detectors for door leaf release service in *NFPA 72*.
(4) Upon loss of power to the hold-open device, the hold-open mechanism is released and the door leaf becomes self-closing.
(5) The release by means of smoke detection of one door leaf in a stair enclosure results in closing all door leaves serving that stair.

[*101:* 7.2.1.8.2]

14.5.4.3 The elevator car doors and the associated hoistway enclosure doors at the floor level designated for recall in accordance with the requirements of 11.3.1 shall be permitted to remain open during Phase I Emergency Recall Operation. [*101:* 7.2.1.8.3]

14.6 Enclosure and Protection of Stairs.

14.6.1 Enclosures.

14.6.1.1 All inside stairs serving as an exit or exit component shall be enclosed in accordance with Section 14.3. [*101:* 7.2.2.5.1.1]

14.6.1.2 Inside stairs, other than those serving as an exit or exit component, shall be protected in accordance with Section 8.6 of NFPA *101*. [*101:* 7.2.2.5.1.2]

14.6.1.3 In existing buildings, where a two-story exit enclosure connects the story of exit discharge with an adjacent story, the exit shall be permitted to be enclosed only on the story of exit discharge, provided that not less than 50 percent of the number and capacity of exits on the story of exit discharge are independent of such enclosures. [*101:* 7.2.2.5.1.3]

14.6.2* Exposures.

14.6.2.1 Where nonrated walls or unprotected openings enclose the exterior of a stairway, other than an existing stairway, and the walls or openings are exposed by other parts of the building at an angle of less than 180 degrees, the building enclosure walls within 10 ft (3050 mm) horizontally of the nonrated wall or unprotected opening shall be constructed as required for stairway enclosures, including opening protectives. [*101:* 7.2.2.5.2.1]

14.6.2.2 Construction shall extend vertically from the ground to a point 10 ft (3050 mm) above the topmost landing of the stairs or to the roofline, whichever is lower. [*101:* 7.2.2.5.2.2]

14.6.2.3 The fire resistance rating of the separation extending 10 ft (3050 mm) from the stairs shall not be required to exceed 1 hour where openings have not less than a ¾-hour fire protection rating. [*101:* 7.2.2.5.2.3]

14.6.3* Usable Space. Enclosed, usable spaces, within exit enclosures shall be prohibited, including under stairs, unless otherwise permitted by 14.6.3.2. [*101:* 7.2.2.5.3]

14.6.3.1 Open space within the exit enclosure shall not be used for any purpose that has the potential to interfere with egress. [*101:* 7.2.2.5.3.1]

14.6.3.2 Enclosed, usable space shall be permitted under stairs, provided that both of the following criteria are met:

(1) The space shall be separated from the stair enclosure by the same fire resistance as the exit enclosure.
(2) Entrance to the enclosed, usable space shall not be from within the stair enclosure. *(See also 14.3.3.)*

[*101:* 7.2.2.5.3.2]

14.7* Exit Passageways.

14.7.1* General. Exit passageways used as exit components shall conform to the general requirements of Section 7.1 of NFPA *101* and to the special requirements of Section 14.7. [*101:* 7.2.6.1]

14.7.2 Enclosure. An exit passageway shall be separated from other parts of the building as specified in Section 14.3, and the following alternatives shall be permitted:

(1) Fire windows in accordance with 12.7.3 shall be permitted to be installed in the separation in a building protected throughout by an approved, supervised automatic sprinkler system in accordance with Section 13.3.
(2) Existing fixed wired glass panels in steel sash shall be permitted to be continued in use in the separation in buildings protected throughout by an approved, supervised automatic sprinkler system in accordance with Section 13.3.

[*101:* 7.2.6.2]

14.7.3 Stair Discharge. An exit passageway that serves as a discharge from a stair enclosure shall have not less than the same fire resistance rating and opening protective fire protection rating as those required for the stair enclosure. [*101:* 7.2.6.3]

14.7.4 Width.

14.7.4.1 The width of an exit passageway shall be sized to accommodate the aggregate required capacity of all exits that discharge through it, unless one of the following conditions applies:

(1)*Where an exit passageway serves occupants of the level of exit discharge as well as other stories, the capacity shall not be required to be aggregated.
(2) As provided in Chapters 36 and 37 of NFPA *101*, an exit passageway in a mall building shall be permitted to accommodate occupant loads independently from the mall

and the tenant spaces. *(See 36.2.2.7.2 and 37.2.2.7.2 of NFPA 101.)* [*101:* 7.2.6.4.1]

14.7.4.2 In new construction, the minimum width of any exit passageway into which an exit stair discharges, or that serves as a horizontal transfer within an exit stair system, shall meet the following criteria:

(1) The minimum width of the exit passageway shall be not less than two-thirds of the width of the exit stair.
(2) Where stairs are credited with egress capacity in accordance with 14.8.3.2, the exit passageway width shall be sized to accommodate the same capacity as the stair, with such capacity determined by use of the capacity factors in Table 14.8.3.1.

[*101:* 7.2.6.4.2]

14.8 Capacity of Means of Egress.

14.8.1 Occupant Load.

14.8.1.1 Sufficient Capacity.

14.8.1.1.1 The total capacity of the means of egress for any story, balcony, tier, or other occupied space shall be sufficient for the occupant load thereof. [*101:* 7.3.1.1.1]

14.8.1.1.2 For other than existing means of egress, where more than one means of egress is required, the means of egress shall be of such width and capacity that the loss of any one means of egress leaves available not less than 50 percent of the required capacity. [*101:* 7.3.1.1.2]

14.8.1.2* Occupant Load Factor. The occupant load in any building or portion thereof shall be not less than the number of persons determined by dividing the floor area assigned to that use by the occupant load factor for that use as specified in Table 14.8.1.2, Figure 14.8.1.2(a), and Figure 14.8.1.2(b). Where both gross and net area figures are given for the same occupancy, calculations shall be made by applying the gross area figure to the gross area of the portion of the building devoted to the use for which the gross area figure is specified and by applying the net area figure to the net area of the portion of the building devoted to the use for which the net area figure is specified. [*101:* 7.3.1.2]

Table 14.8.1.2 Occupant Load Factor

Use	(ft²[per] person)[a]	(m²[per] person)[b]
Assembly Use	-	-
Concentrated use, without fixed seating	7 net	0.65 net
Less concentrated use, without fixed seating	15 net	1.4 net
Bench-type seating	1 person/18 linear in.	1 person/455 linear mm
Fixed seating	Use number of fixed seats	Use number of fixed seats
Waiting spaces	See 12.1.7.2 and 13.1.7.2 of NFPA 101	See 12.1.7.2 and 13.1.7.2 of NFPA 101
Kitchens	100	9.3
Library stack areas	100	9.3
Library reading rooms	50 net	4.6 net

(continues)

Table 14.8.1.2 *Continued*

Use	(ft²[per] person)[a]	(m²[per] person)[b]
Swimming pools	50 (water surface)	4.6 (water surface)
Swimming pool decks	30	2.8
Exercise rooms with equipment	50	4.6
Exercise rooms without equipment	15	1.4
Stages	15 net	1.4 net
Lighting and access catwalks, galleries, gridirons	100 net	9.3 net
Casinos and similar gaming areas	11	1
Skating rinks	50	4.6
Business Use (other than below)	100	9.3
Concentrated Business Use[f]	50	4.6
Air traffic control tower observation levels	40	3.7
Day-Care Use	35 net	3.3 net
Detention and Correctional Use	120	11.1
Educational Use	-	-
Classrooms	20 net	1.9 net
Shops, laboratories, vocational rooms	50 net	4.6 net
Health Care Use	-	-
Inpatient treatment departments	240	22.3
Sleeping departments	120	11.1
Ambulatory health care	150	13
Industrial Use	-	-
General and high hazard industrial	100	9.3
Special-purpose industrial	NA	NA
Mercantile Use	-	-
Sales area on street floor[b,c]	30	2.8
Sales area on two or more street floors[c]	40	3.7
Sales area on floor below street floor[c]	30	2.8
Sales area on floors above street floor[c]	60	5.6
Floors or portions of floors used only for offices	See business use.	See business use.
Floors or portions of floors used only for storage, receiving, and shipping, and not open to general public	300	27.9

Table 14.8.1.2 *Continued*

Use	(ft²[per] person)[a]	(m²[per] person)[b]
Mall buildings[d]	Per factors applicable to use of space[e]	
Residential Use	-	-
Hotels and dormitories	200	18.6
Apartment buildings	200	18.6
Board and care, large	200	18.6
Storage Use	-	-
In storage occupancies	NA	NA
In mercantile occupancies	300	27.9
In other than storage and mercantile occupancies	500	46.5

NA: Not applicable. The occupant load is the maximum probable number of occupants present at any time.
[a]All factors are expressed in gross area unless marked "net."
[b]For the purpose of determining occupant load in mercantile occupancies where, due to differences in the finished ground level of streets on different sides, two or more floors directly accessible from streets (not including alleys or similar back streets) exist, each such floor is permitted to be considered a street floor. The occupant load factor is one person for each 40 ft² (3.7 m²) of gross floor area of sales space.
[c]For the purpose of determining occupant load in mercantile occupancies with no street floor, as defined in 3.3.250, but with access directly from the street by stairs or escalators, the floor at the point of entrance to the mercantile occupancy is considered the street floor.
[d]For any food court or other assembly use areas located in the mall that are not included as a portion of the gross leasable area of the mall building, the occupant load is calculated based on the occupant load factor for that use as specified in Table 14.8.1.2. The remaining mall area is not required to be assigned an occupant load.
[e]The portions of the mall that are considered a pedestrian way and not used as gross leasable area are not required to be assessed an occupant load based on Table 14.8.1.2. However, means of egress from a mall pedestrian way are required to be provided for an occupant load determined by dividing the gross leasable area of the mall building (not including anchor stores) by the appropriate lowest whole number occupant load factor from Figure 14.8.1.2(a) or Figure 14.8.1.2(b).
  Each individual tenant space is required to have means of egress to the outside or to the mall based on occupant loads calculated by using the appropriate occupant load factor from Table 14.8.1.2.
  Each individual anchor store is required to have means of egress independent of the mall.
[f]See A.14.8.1.2.
[*101:* Table 7.3.1.2]

14.8.1.3 Occupant Load Increases.

14.8.1.3.1 The occupant load in any building or portion thereof shall be permitted to be increased from the occupant load established for the given use in accordance with 14.8.1.2 where all other requirements of this *Code* are also met, based on such increased occupant load. [*101:* 7.3.1.3.1]

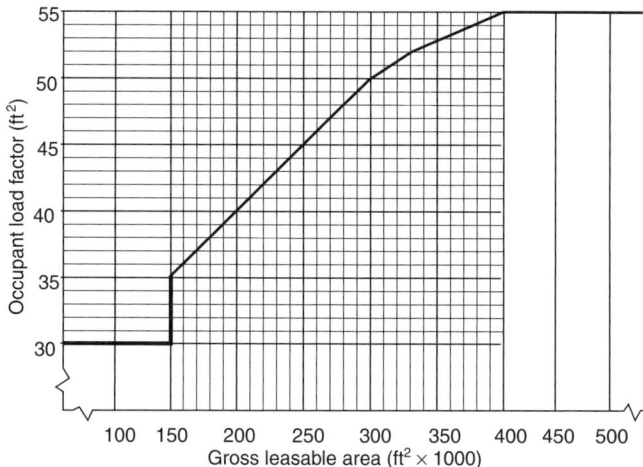

FIGURE 14.8.1.2(a) Mall Building Occupant Load Factors (U.S. Customary Units). [*101:* Figure 7.3.1.2(a)]

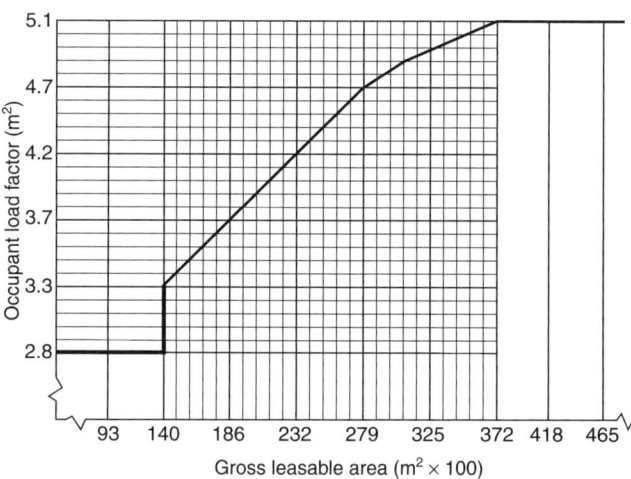

FIGURE 14.8.1.2(b) Mall Building Occupant Load Factors (SI Units). [*101:* Figure 7.3.1.2(b)]

14.8.1.3.2 The AHJ shall be permitted to require an approved aisle, seating, or fixed equipment diagram to substantiate any increase in occupant load and shall be permitted to require that such a diagram be posted in an approved location. [*101:* 7.3.1.3.2]

14.8.1.4 Exits Serving More than One Story. Where an exit serves more than one story, only the occupant load of each story considered individually shall be used in computing the required capacity of the exit at that story, provided that the required egress capacity of the exit is not decreased in the direction of egress travel. [*101:* 7.3.1.4]

14.8.1.5 Capacity from a Point of Convergence. Where means of egress from a story above and a story below converge at an intermediate story, the capacity of the means of egress from the point of convergence shall be not less than the sum of the required capacity of the two means of egress. [*101:* 7.3.1.5]

14.8.1.6 Egress Capacity from Balconies and Mezzanines. Where any required egress capacity from a balcony or mezzanine passes through the room below, that required capacity shall be added to the required egress capacity of the room in which it is located. [*101:* 7.3.1.6]

14.8.2 Measurement of Means of Egress.

14.8.2.1 The width of means of egress shall be measured in the clear at the narrowest point of the egress component under consideration, unless otherwise provided in 14.8.2.2 or 14.8.2.3. [*101:* 7.3.2.1]

14.8.2.2 Projections within the means of egress of not more than 4½ in. (114 mm) on each side shall be permitted at a height of 38 in. (965 mm) and below. In the case of stair and landing handrails forming part of a guard, in accordance with 7.2.2.4.4.3 of NFPA *101*, such projections shall be permitted at a height of 42 in. (1065 mm) and below. [*101:* 7.3.2.2]

14.8.2.3 In health care and ambulatory health care occupancies, projections shall be permitted in corridors in accordance with Chapters 18 through 21 of NFPA *101*. [*101:* 7.3.2.3]

14.8.3 Egress Capacity.

14.8.3.1 Egress capacity for approved components of means of egress shall be based on the capacity factors shown in Table 14.8.3.1, unless otherwise provided in 14.8.3.2. [*101:* 7.3.3.1]

Table 14.8.3.1 Capacity Factors

	Stairways (width per person)		Level Components and Ramps (width per person)	
Area	in.	mm	in.	mm
Board and care	0.4	10	0.2	5
Health care, sprinklered	0.3	7.6	0.2	5
Health care, nonsprinklered	0.6	15	0.5	13
High hazard contents	0.7	18	0.4	10
All others	0.3	7.6	0.2	5

[*101:* Table 7.3.3.1]

14.8.3.2* For stairways wider than 44 in. (1120 mm) and subject to the 0.3 in. (7.6 mm) width per person capacity factor, the capacity shall be permitted to be increased using the following equation:

$$C = 146.7 + \left(\frac{Wn - 44}{0.218}\right) \quad [14.8.3.2]$$

where:
 C = capacity, in persons, rounded to the nearest integer
 Wn = nominal width of the stair as permitted by 14.8.3.2 (in.) [*101:* 7.3.3.2]

14.8.3.3 The required capacity of a corridor shall be the occupant load that utilizes the corridor for exit access divided by the required number of exits to which the corridor connects, but the corridor capacity shall be not less than the required capacity of the exit to which the corridor leads. [*101:* 7.3.3.3]

14.8.3.4 Minimum Width.

14.8.3.4.1 The width of any means of egress, unless otherwise provided in 14.8.3.4.1.1 through 14.8.3.4.1.3, shall be as follows:

(1) Not less than that required for a given egress component in this chapter or 7 or Chapters 11 through 43 of NFPA *101*
(2) Not less than 36 in. (915 mm) where another part of this chapter and Chapters 11 through 43 of NFPA *101* do not specify a minimum width. [*101:* 7.3.4.1]

14.8.3.4.1.1* The width of exit access serving not more than six people, and having a length not exceeding 50 ft (15 m) shall meet both of the following criteria:

(1) The width shall be not less than 18 in. (455 mm), at and below a height of 38 in. (965 mm), and not less than 28 in. (710 mm) above a height of 38 in. (965 mm).
(2) A width of not less than 36 in. (915 mm) for new exit access, and not less than 28 in. (710 mm) for existing exit access, shall be capable of being provided without moving permanent walls.

[*101:* 7.3.4.1.1]

14.8.3.4.1.2 In existing buildings, the width of exit access shall be permitted to be not less than 28 in. (710 mm). [*101:* 7.3.4.1.2]

14.8.3.4.1.3 The requirement of 14.8.3.4.1 shall not apply to the following:

(1) Doors as otherwise provided for in 7.2.1.2 of NFPA *101*
(2) Aisles and aisle accessways in assembly occupancies as otherwise provided in Chapters 12 and 13 of NFPA *101*
(3) Industrial equipment access as otherwise provided in 40.2.5.2 of NFPA *101* [*101:* 7.3.4.1.3]

14.8.3.4.2 Where a single exit access leads to an exit, its capacity in terms of width shall be not less than the required capacity of the exit to which it leads. [*101:* 7.3.4.2]

14.8.3.4.3 Where more than one exit access leads to an exit, each shall have a width adequate for the number of persons it accommodates. [*101:* 7.3.4.3]

14.9 Number of Means of Egress.

14.9.1 General.

14.9.1.1 The number of means of egress from any balcony, mezzanine, story, or portion thereof shall be not less than two, except under one of the following conditions:

(1) A single means of egress shall be permitted where permitted in Chapters 11 through 43 of NFPA *101*.
(2) A single means of egress shall be permitted for a mezzanine or balcony where the common path of travel limitations of Chapters 11 through 43 of NFPA *101* are met.

[*101:* 7.4.1.1]

14.9.1.2 The number of means of egress from any story or portion thereof, other than for existing buildings as permitted in Chapters 11 through 43 of NFPA *101*, shall be as follows:

(1) Occupant load more than 500 but not more than 1000 — not less than 3
(2) Occupant load more than 1000 — not less than 4 [*101:* 7.4.1.2]

14.9.1.3 Accessible means of egress in accordance with 14.10.4 that do not utilize elevators shall be permitted to serve as any or all of the required minimum number of means of egress. [*101:* 7.4.1.3]

14.9.1.4 The occupant load of each story considered individually shall be required to be used in computing the number of means of egress at each story, provided that the required number of means of egress is not decreased in the direction of egress travel. [*101:* 7.4.1.4]

14.9.1.5 Doors other than the hoistway door; the elevator car door; and doors that are readily openable from the car side without a key, a tool, special knowledge, or special effort, shall be prohibited at the point of access to an elevator car. [*101:* 7.4.1.5]

14.9.1.6 Elevator Landing and Lobby Exit Access.

14.9.1.6.1 Each elevator landing and lobby shall have access to at least one exit. [*101:* 7.4.1.6.1]

14.9.1.6.2 The elevator landing and lobby exit access required by 14.9.1.6.1 shall not require the use of a key, a tool, special knowledge, or special effort, unless permitted by 14.9.1.6.3. [*101:* 7.4.1.6.2]

14.9.1.6.3 Doors separating the elevator lobby from the exit access required by 14.9.1.6.1 shall be permitted to be electronically locked in accordance with 14.5.3.3. [*101:* 7.4.1.6.3]

14.9.2 Spaces About Electrical Equipment.

14.9.2.1 600 Volts, Nominal, or Less. The minimum number of means of egress for working space about electrical equipment, other than existing electrical equipment, shall be in accordance with NFPA 70, Section 110.26(C). [*101:* 7.4.2.1]

14.9.2.2 Over 600 Volts, Nominal. The minimum number of means of egress for working space about electrical equipment, other than existing electrical equipment, shall be in accordance with NFPA 70, Section 110.33(A). [*101:* 7.4.2.2]

14.10 Arrangement of Means of Egress.

14.10.1 General.

14.10.1.1 Exits shall be located and exit access shall be arranged so that exits are readily accessible at all times. [*101:* 7.5.1.1]

14.10.1.1.1* Where exits are not immediately accessible from an open floor area, continuous passageways, aisles, or corridors leading directly to every exit shall be maintained and shall be arranged to provide access for each occupant to not less than two exits by separate ways of travel, unless otherwise provided in 14.10.1.1.3 and 14.10.1.1.4. [*101:* 7.5.1.1.1]

14.10.1.1.2 Exit access corridors shall provide access to not less than two approved exits, unless otherwise provided in 14.10.1.1.3 and 14.10.1.1.4. [*101:* 7.5.1.1.2]

14.10.1.1.3 The requirements of 14.10.1.1.1 and 14.10.1.1.2 shall not apply where a single exit is permitted in Chapters 11 through 43 of NFPA *101*. [*101:* 7.5.1.1.3]

14.10.1.1.4 Where common paths of travel are permitted for an occupancy in Chapters 11 through 43 of NFPA *101*, such common paths of travel shall be permitted but shall not exceed the limit specified. [*101:* 7.5.1.1.4]

14.10.1.2 Corridors shall provide exit access without passing through any intervening rooms other than corridors, lobbies, and other spaces permitted to be open to the corridor, unless otherwise provided in 14.10.1.2.1 and 14.10.1.2.2. [*101:* 7.5.1.2]

14.10.1.2.1 Approved existing corridors that require passage through a room to access an exit shall be permitted to continue to be used, provided that the following criteria are met:

(1) The path of travel is marked in accordance with Section 14.14.
(2) Doors to such rooms comply with 7.2.1 of NFPA *101*.
(3) Such arrangement is not prohibited by the applicable occupancy chapter in NFPA *101*. [*101:* 7.5.1.2.1]

14.10.1.2.2 Corridors that are not required to be fire resistance rated shall be permitted to discharge into open floor plan areas. [*101:* 7.5.1.2.2]

14.10.1.3 Remoteness shall be provided in accordance with 14.10.1.3.1 through 14.10.1.3.7. [*101:* 7.5.1.3]

14.10.1.3.1 Where more than one exit, exit access, or exit discharge is required from a building or portion thereof, such exits, exit accesses, or exit discharges shall be remotely located from each other and be arranged to minimize the possibility that more than one has the potential to be blocked by any one fire or other emergency condition. [*101:* 7.5.1.3.1]

14.10.1.3.2* Where two exits, exit accesses, or exit discharges are required, they shall be located at a distance from one another not less than one-half the length of the maximum overall diagonal dimension of the building or area to be served, measured in a straight line between the nearest edge of the exits, exit accesses, or exit discharges, unless otherwise provided in 14.10.1.3.3 through 14.10.1.3.5. [*101:* 7.5.1.3.2]

14.10.1.3.3 In buildings protected throughout by an approved, supervised automatic sprinkler system in accordance with Section 13.3, the minimum separation distance between two exits, exit accesses, or exit discharges, measured in accordance with 14.10.1.3.2, shall be not less than one-third the length of the maximum overall diagonal dimension of the building or area to be served. [*101:* 7.5.1.3.3]

14.10.1.3.4* In other than high-rise buildings, where exit enclosures are provided as the required exits specified in 14.10.1.3.2 or 14.10.1.3.3 and are interconnected by not less than a 1-hour fire resistance–rated corridor, exit separation shall be measured along the shortest line of travel within the corridor [*101:* 7.5.1.3.4]

14.10.1.3.5 In existing buildings, where more than one exit, exit access, or exit discharge is required, such exits, exit accesses, or exit discharges shall be exempt from the diagonal measurement separation distance criteria of 14.10.1.3.2 and 14.10.1.3.3, provided that such exits, exit accesses, or exit discharges are remotely located in accordance with 14.10.1.3.1. [*101:* 7.5.1.3.5]

14.10.1.3.6 In other than existing buildings, where more than two exits, exit accesses, or exit discharges are required, at least two of the required exits, exit accesses, or exit discharges shall be arranged to comply with the minimum separation distance requirement. [*101:* 7.5.1.3.6]

14.10.1.3.7 The balance of the exits, exit accesses, or exit discharges specified in 14.10.1.3.6 shall be located so that, if one becomes blocked, the others are available. [*101:* 7.5.1.3.7]

14.10.1.4 Interlocking or scissor stairs shall comply with 14.10.1.4.1 and 14.10.1.4.2. [*101:* 7.5.1.4]

14.10.1.4.1 New interlocking or scissor stairs shall be permitted to be considered only as a single exit. [*101:* 7.5.1.4.1]

14.10.1.4.2* Existing interlocking or scissor stairs shall be permitted to be considered separate exits, provided that they meet all of the following criteria:

(1) They are enclosed in accordance with Section 14.3.
(2) They are separated from each other by 2-hour fire resistance–rated noncombustible construction.
(3) No protected or unprotected penetrations or communicating openings exist between the stair enclosures.

[*101:* 7.5.1.4.2]

14.10.1.5* Exit access shall be arranged so that there are no dead ends in corridors, unless permitted by, and limited to the lengths specified in, Chapters 11 through 43 of NFPA *101*. [*101:* 7.5.1.5]

14.10.1.6 Exit access from rooms or spaces shall be permitted to be through adjoining or intervening rooms or areas, provided that such rooms or areas are accessory to the area served. Foyers, lobbies, and reception rooms constructed as required for corridors shall not be construed as intervening rooms. Exit access shall be arranged so that it is not necessary to pass through any area identified under Protection from Hazards in Chapters 11 through 43 of NFPA *101*. [*101:* 7.5.1.6]

14.10.2 Impediments to Egress. See also 7.1.9 of NFPA *101*, and 14.5.2. [*101:* 7.5.2]

14.10.2.1* Access to an exit shall not be through kitchens, storerooms other than as provided in Chapters 36 and 37 of NFPA *101*, restrooms, closets, bedrooms or similar spaces, or other rooms or spaces subject to locking, unless passage through such rooms or spaces is permitted for the occupancy by Chapters 18, 19, 22, or 23 of NFPA *101*. [*101:* 7.5.2.1]

14.10.2.2* Exit access and exit doors shall be designed and arranged to be clearly recognizable. [*101:* 7.5.2.2]

14.10.2.2.1 Hangings or draperies shall not be placed over exit doors or located so that they conceal or obscure any exit, unless otherwise provided in 14.10.2.2.2. [*101:* 7.5.2.2.1]

14.10.2.2.2 Curtains shall be permitted across means of egress openings in tent walls, provided that all of the following criteria are met:

(1) They are distinctly marked in contrast to the tent wall so as to be recognizable as means of egress.
(2) They are installed across an opening that is at least 6 ft (1830 mm) in width.
(3) They are hung from slide rings or equivalent hardware so as to be readily moved to the side to create an unobstructed opening in the tent wall that is of the minimum width required for door openings.

[*101:* 7.5.2.2.2]

14.10.3 Exterior Ways of Exit Access.

14.10.3.1 Exit access shall be permitted to be by means of any exterior balcony, porch, gallery, or roof that conforms to the requirements of this chapter and Chapter 7 of NFPA *101*. [*101:* 7.5.3.1]

14.10.3.2 The long side of the balcony, porch, gallery, or similar space shall be at least 50 percent open and shall be arranged to restrict the accumulation of smoke. [*101:* 7.5.3.2]

14.10.3.3 Exterior exit access balconies shall be separated from the interior of the building by walls and opening protectives as required for corridors, unless the exterior exit access balcony is served by at least two remote stairs that can be accessed without any occupant traveling past an unprotected opening to reach one of the stairs, or unless dead ends on the exterior exit access do not exceed 20 ft (6100 mm). [*101:* 7.5.3.3]

14.10.3.4 Exterior exit access shall be arranged so that there are no dead ends in excess of those permitted for dead-end corridors in Chapters 11 through 43 of NFPA *101*. [*101:* 7.5.3.4]

14.10.4 Accessible Means of Egress.

14.10.4.1* Areas accessible to people with severe mobility impairment, other than in existing buildings, shall have not less than two accessible means of egress, unless otherwise provided in 14.10.4.1.2 through 14.10.4.1.4. [*101:* 7.5.4.1]

14.10.4.1.1 Access within the allowable travel distance shall be provided to not less than one accessible area of refuge or one accessible exit providing an accessible route to an exit discharge. [*101:* 7.5.4.1.1]

14.10.4.1.2 A single accessible means of egress shall be permitted from buildings or areas of buildings permitted to have a single exit. [*101:* 7.5.4.1.2]

14.10.4.1.3 Accessible means of egress shall not be required in health care occupancies protected throughout by an approved, supervised automatic sprinkler system in accordance with Section 13.3. [*101:* 7.5.4.1.3]

14.10.4.1.4 Exit access travel along the accessible means of egress shall be permitted to be common for the distances permitted as common paths of travel. [*101:* 7.5.4.1.4]

14.10.4.2 Where two accessible means of egress are required, the exits serving such means of egress shall be located at a distance from one another not less than one-half the length of the maximum overall diagonal dimension of the building or area to be served. This distance shall be measured in a straight line between the nearest edge of the exit doors or exit access doors, unless otherwise provided in 14.10.4.2.1 through 14.10.4.2.3. [*101:* 7.5.4.2]

14.10.4.2.1 Where exit enclosures are provided as the required exits specified in 14.10.4.2 and are interconnected by not less than a 1-hour fire resistance–rated corridor, exit separation shall be permitted to be measured along the line of travel within the corridor. [*101:* 7.5.4.2.1]

14.10.4.2.2 The requirement of 14.10.4.2 shall not apply to buildings protected throughout by an approved, supervised automatic sprinkler system in accordance with Section 13.3. [*101:* 7.5.4.2.2]

14.10.4.2.3 The requirement of 14.10.4.2 shall not apply where the physical arrangement of means of egress prevents the possibility that access to both accessible means of egress will be blocked by any one fire or other emergency condition as approved by the AHJ. [*101:* 7.5.4.2.3]

14.10.4.3 Each required accessible means of egress shall be continuous from each accessible occupied area to a public way or area of refuge in accordance with 7.2.12.2.2 of NFPA *101*. [*101:* 7.5.4.3]

14.10.4.4 Where an exit stair is used in an accessible means of egress, it shall comply with 7.2.12 of NFPA *101* and either shall incorporate an area of refuge within an enlarged story-level landing or shall be accessed from an area of refuge. [*101:* 7.5.4.4]

14.10.4.5 To be considered part of an accessible means of egress, an elevator shall be in accordance with 7.2.12.2.4 of NFPA *101*. [*101:* 7.5.4.5]

14.10.4.6 To be considered part of an accessible means of egress, a smoke barrier in accordance with Section 12.9 with not less than a 1-hour fire resistance rating, or a horizontal exit in accordance with 7.2.4 of NFPA *101*, shall discharge to an area of refuge in accordance with 7.2.12 of NFPA *101*. [*101:* 7.5.4.6]

14.10.4.7 Accessible stories that are four or more stories above or below a story of exit discharge shall have not less than one elevator complying with 14.10.4.5, except as modified in 14.10.4.8. [*101:* 7.5.4.7]

14.10.4.8 Where elevators are required by 14.10.4.7, the smokeproof enclosure required by 7.2.12.2.4 of NFPA *101* shall not be required in buildings protected throughout by an approved, supervised automatic sprinkler system in accordance with NFPA 13. [*101:* 7.5.4.8]

14.10.4.9 An area of refuge used as part of a required accessible means of egress shall be in accordance with 7.2.12 of NFPA *101*. [*101:* 7.5.4.9]

14.11 Discharge from Exits.

14.11.1* Exit Termination. Exits shall terminate directly, at a public way or at an exterior exit discharge, unless otherwise provided in 14.11.1.2 through 14.11.1.4. [*101:* 7.7.1]

14.11.1.1 Yards, courts, open spaces, or other portions of the exit discharge shall be of required width and size to provide all occupants with a safe access to a public way. [*101:* 7.7.1.1]

14.11.1.2 The requirement of 14.11.1 shall not apply to interior exit discharge as otherwise provided in 14.11.2. [*101:* 7.7.1.2]

14.11.1.3 The requirement of 14.11.1 shall not apply to rooftop exit discharge as otherwise provided in 14.11.6. [*101:* 7.7.1.3]

14.11.1.4 Means of egress shall be permitted to terminate in an exterior area of refuge for detention and correctional occupancies as otherwise provided in Chapters 22 and 23 of NFPA *101*. [*101:* 7.7.1.4]

14.11.2 Exit Discharge Through Interior Building Areas. Exits shall be permitted to discharge through interior building areas, provided that all of the following are met:

(1) Not more than 50 percent of the required number of exit stairs serving normally occupied areas of each floor, and not more than 50 percent of the exit stair capacity required for normally occupied areas of each floor, shall discharge through areas on any level of discharge, except as otherwise permitted by one of the following:
  (a) One hundred percent of the exits shall be permitted to discharge through areas on any level of discharge in detention and correctional occupancies as otherwise provided in Chapters 22 and 23.
  (b) In existing buildings, the 50 percent limit on egress capacity shall not apply if the 50 percent limit on the required number of exits is met.
(2) Each level of discharge shall discharge directly outside at the finished ground level or discharge directly outside and provide access to the finished ground level by outside stairs or outside ramps.
(3) The interior exit discharge shall lead to a free and unobstructed way to the exterior of the building, and such way

shall be readily visible and identifiable from the point of discharge from the exit.
(4) The interior exit discharge shall be protected by one of the following methods:
   (a) The level of discharge shall be protected throughout by an approved automatic sprinkler system in accordance with Section 13.3, or the portion of the level of discharge used for interior exit discharge shall be protected by an approved automatic sprinkler system in accordance with Section 13.3 and shall be separated from the nonsprinklered portion of the floor by fire barriers with a fire resistance rating meeting the requirements for the enclosure of exits. *(See 14.3.1.)*
   (b) The interior exit discharge area shall be in a vestibule or foyer that meets all of the following criteria:
      i. The depth from the exterior of the building shall be not more than 10 ft (3050 mm), and the length shall be not more than 30 ft (9.1 m).
      ii. The foyer shall be separated from the remainder of the level of discharge by fire barriers with a minimum 1-hour fire resistance rating, and existing installations of wired glass in steel frames shall be permitted to be continued in use.
      iii. The foyer shall serve only as means of egress and shall include an exit directly to the outside.
(5) The entire area on the level of discharge shall be separated from areas below by construction having a fire resistance rating not less than that required for the exit enclosure, unless otherwise provided in 14.11.2(6).
(6) Levels below the level of discharge in an atrium shall be permitted to be open to the level of discharge where such level of discharge is protected in accordance with 8.6.7 of NFPA *101*.

[*101:* 7.7.2]

14.11.3 Arrangement and Marking of Exit Discharge.

14.11.3.1 Where more than one exit discharge is required, exit discharges shall be arranged to meet the remoteness criteria of 14.10.1.3. [*101:* 7.7.3.1]

14.11.3.2 The exit discharge shall be arranged and marked to make clear the direction of egress travel from the exit discharge to a public way. [*101:* 7.7.3.2]

14.11.3.3* Stairs and ramps that continue more than one-half story beyond the level of discharge shall be provided with an approved means to prevent or dissuade occupants from traveling past the level of discharge during emergency building evacuation. [*101:* 7.7.3.4]

14.11.4 Components of Exit Discharge. Doors, stairs, ramps, corridors, exit passageways, bridges, balconies, escalators, moving walks, and other components of an exit discharge shall comply with the detailed requirements of this chapter for such components. [*101:* 7.7.4]

14.11.5 Signs. See 10.11.3. [*101:* 7.7.5]

14.11.6 Discharge to Roofs. Where approved by the AHJ, exits shall be permitted to discharge to roofs or other sections of the building or an adjoining building where all of the following criteria are met:
(1) The roof/ceiling assembly construction has a fire resistance rating not less than that required for the exit enclosure.
(2) A continuous and safe means of egress from the roof is available.

[*101:* 7.7.6]

14.12 Illumination of Means of Egress.

14.12.1 General.

14.12.1.1* Illumination of means of egress shall be provided in accordance with Section 14.12 for every building and structure where required in Chapters 11 through 43 of NFPA *101*. For the purposes of this requirement, exit access shall include only designated stairs, aisles, corridors, ramps, escalators, and passageways leading to an exit. For the purposes of this requirement, exit discharge shall include only designated stairs, aisles, corridors, ramps, escalators, walkways, and exit passageways leading to a public way. [*101:* 7.8.1.1]

14.12.1.2 Illumination of means of egress shall be continuous during the time that the conditions of occupancy require that the means of egress be available for use, unless otherwise provided in 14.12.1.2.2. [*101:* 7.8.1.2]

14.12.1.2.1 Artificial lighting shall be employed at such locations and for such periods of time as are necessary to maintain the illumination to the minimum criteria values herein specified. [*101:* 7.8.1.2.1]

14.12.1.2.2* Unless prohibited by Chapters 11 through 43 of NFPA *101*, automatic lighting control devices shall be permitted to temporarily turn off the illumination within the means of egress, provided that each lighting control device complies with all of the following:

(1) In new installations, the lighting control device is listed.
(2) The lighting control device is equipped to automatically energize the controlled lights upon loss of normal power and is evaluated for this purpose.
(3) Illumination timers are provided and are set for a minimum 15-minute duration.
(4) The lighting control device is activated by any occupant movement in the area served by the lighting units.
(5) In new installations, the lighting control device is activated by activation of the building fire alarm system, if provided.
(6) The lighting control device does not turn off any lights relied upon for activation of photoluminescent exit signs or path markers.
(7) The lighting control device does not turn off any battery-equipped emergency luminaires, unit equipment, or exit signs.

[*101:* 7.8.1.2.2]

14.12.1.2.3* Energy-saving sensors, switches, timers, or controllers shall be approved and shall not compromise the continuity of illumination of the means of egress required by 14.12.1.2. [*101:* 7.8.1.2.3]

14.12.1.3 The floors and other walking surfaces within an exit and within the portions of the exit access and exit discharge designated in 14.12.1.1 shall be illuminated as follows:

(1) During conditions of stair use, the minimum illumination for new stairs shall be at least 10 ft-candle (108 lux), measured at the walking surfaces.
(2) The minimum illumination for floors and other walking surfaces, other than new stairs during conditions of stair use, shall be to values of at least 1 ft-candle (10.8 lux), measured at the floor.

(3) In assembly occupancies, the illumination of the walking surfaces of exit access shall be at least 0.2 ft-candle (2.2 lux) during periods of performances or projections involving directed light.
(4)*The minimum illumination requirements shall not apply where operations or processes require low lighting levels.

[*101:* 7.8.1.3]

14.12.1.4* Required illumination shall be arranged so that the failure of any single lighting unit does not result in an illumination level of less than 0.2 ft-candle (2.2 lux) in any designated area. [*101:* 7.8.1.4]

14.12.1.5 The equipment or units installed to meet the requirements of Section 14.14 also shall be permitted to serve the function of illumination of means of egress, provided that all requirements of Section 14.12 for such illumination are met. [*101:* 7.8.1.5]

14.12.2 Sources of Illumination.

14.12.2.1 Illumination of means of egress shall be from a source considered reliable by the AHJ. [*101:* 7.8.2.1]

14.12.2.2 Battery-operated electric lights and other types of portable lamps or lanterns shall not be used for primary illumination of means of egress. Battery-operated electric lights shall be permitted to be used as an emergency source to the extent permitted under Section 14.13. [*101:* 7.8.2.2]

14.13 Emergency Lighting.

14.13.1 General.

14.13.1.1* Emergency lighting facilities for means of egress shall be provided in accordance with Section 14.13 for the following:

(1) Buildings or structures where required in Chapters 11 through 43 of NFPA *101*
(2) Underground and limited access structures as addressed in Section 11.7 of NFPA *101*
(3) High-rise buildings as required by NFPA *101*
(4) Doors equipped with delayed-egress locks
(5) Stair shaft and vestibule of smokeproof enclosures, for which the following also apply:
  (a) The stair shaft and vestibule shall be permitted to include a standby generator that is installed for the smokeproof enclosure mechanical ventilation equipment.
  (b) The standby generator shall be permitted to be used for the stair shaft and vestibule emergency lighting power supply.
(6) New access-controlled egress doors in accordance with 14.5.3.2

[*101:* 7.9.1.1]

14.13.1.2 For the purposes of 14.13.1.1, exit access shall include only designated stairs, aisles, corridors, ramps, escalators, and passageways leading to an exit. For the purposes of 14.13.1.1, exit discharge shall include only designated stairs, ramps, aisles, walkways, and escalators leading to a public way. [*101:* 7.9.1.2]

14.13.1.3 Where maintenance of illumination depends on changing from one energy source to another, a delay of not more than 10 seconds shall be permitted. [*101:* 7.9.1.3]

14.13.2 Periodic Testing of Emergency Lighting Equipment.

14.13.2.1 Required emergency lighting systems shall be tested in accordance with one of the three options offered by 14.13.2.1.1, 14.13.2.1.2, or 14.13.2.1.3. [*101:* 7.9.3.1]

14.13.2.1.1 Testing of required emergency lighting systems shall be permitted to be conducted as follows:

(1) Functional testing shall be conducted monthly with a minimum of 3 weeks and a maximum of 5 weeks between tests, for not less than 30 seconds, except as otherwise permitted by 14.13.2.1.1(2).
(2) The test interval shall be permitted to be extended beyond 30 days with the approval of the AHJ.
(3) Functional testing shall be conducted annually for a minimum of 1½ hours if the emergency lighting system is battery powered.
(4) The emergency lighting equipment shall be fully operational for the duration of the tests required by 14.13.2.1.1(1) and 14.13.2.1.1(3).
(5) Written records of visual inspections and tests shall be kept by the owner for inspection by the AHJ.

[*101:* 7.9.3.1.1]

14.13.2.1.2 Testing of required emergency lighting systems shall be permitted to be conducted as follows:

(1) Self-testing/self-diagnostic battery-operated emergency lighting equipment shall be provided.
(2) Not less than once every 30 days, self-testing/self-diagnostic battery-operated emergency lighting equipment shall automatically perform a test with a duration of a minimum of 30 seconds and a diagnostic routine.
(3) Self-testing/self-diagnostic battery-operated emergency lighting equipment shall indicate failures by a status indicator.
(4) A visual inspection shall be performed at intervals not exceeding 30 days.
(5) Functional testing shall be conducted annually for a minimum of 1½ hours.
(6) Self-testing/self-diagnostic battery-operated emergency lighting equipment shall be fully operational for the duration of the 1½ hour test.
(7) Written records of visual inspections and tests shall be kept by the owner for inspection by the AHJ.

[*101:* 7.9.3.1.2]

14.13.2.1.3 Testing of required emergency lighting systems shall be permitted to be conducted as follows:

(1) Computer-based, self-testing/self-diagnostic battery-operated emergency lighting equipment shall be provided.
(2) Not less than once every 30 days, emergency lighting equipment shall automatically perform a test with a duration of a minimum of 30 seconds and a diagnostic routine.
(3) The emergency lighting equipment shall automatically perform annually a test for a minimum of 1½ hours.
(4) The emergency lighting equipment shall be fully operational for the duration of the tests required by 14.13.2.1.3(2) and 14.13.2.1.3(3).
(5) The computer-based system shall be capable of providing a report of the history of tests and failures at all times.

[*101:* 7.9.3.1.3]

14.14 Marking of Means of Egress.

14.14.1 General.

14.14.1.1 Where Required. Means of egress shall be marked in accordance with Section 14.14 where required in Chapters 11 through 43 of NFPA *101*. [*101:* 7.10.1.1]

14.14.1.2 Exits.

14.14.1.2.1* Exits, other than main exterior exit doors that obviously and clearly are identifiable as exits, shall be marked by an approved sign that is readily visible from any direction of exit access. [*101:* 7.10.1.2.1]

14.14.1.2.2* Horizontal components of the egress path within an exit enclosure shall be marked by approved exit or directional exit signs where the continuation of the egress path is not obvious. [*101:* 7.10.1.2.2]

14.14.1.3 Exit Stair Door Tactile Signage. Tactile signage shall be provided to meet the following criteria, unless otherwise provided in 14.14.1.4:

(1) Tactile signage shall be located at each exit door requiring an exit sign.
(2) Tactile signage shall read as follows: EXIT
(3) Tactile signage shall comply with ICC/ANSI A117.1, *American National Standard for Accessible and Usable Buildings and Facilities.*

[*101:* 7.10.1.3]

14.14.1.4 Existing Exemption. The requirements of 14.14.1.3 shall not apply to existing buildings, provided that the occupancy classification does not change. [*101:* 7.10.1.4]

14.14.1.5 Exit Access.

14.14.1.5.1 Access to exits shall be marked by approved, readily visible signs in all cases where the exit or way to reach the exit is not readily apparent to the occupants. [*101:* 7.10.1.5.1]

14.14.1.5.2* New sign placement shall be such that no point in an exit access corridor is in excess of the rated viewing distance or 100 ft (30 m), whichever is less, from the nearest sign. [*101:* 7.10.1.5.2]

14.14.1.6* Floor Proximity Exit Signs. Where floor proximity exit signs are required in Chapters 11 through 43 of NFPA *101*, such signs shall comply with 14.14.3, 14.14.4, 14.14.5, and 14.14.6 for externally illuminated signs and 14.14.7 for internally illuminated signs. Such signs shall be located near the floor level in addition to those signs required for doors or corridors. The bottom of the sign shall be not less than 6 in. (150 mm), but not more than 18 in. (455 mm), above the floor. For exit doors, the sign shall be mounted on the door or adjacent to the door, with the nearest edge of the sign within 4 in. (100 mm) of the door frame. [*101:* 7.10.1.6]

14.14.1.7* Floor Proximity Egress Path Marking. Where floor proximity egress path marking is required in Chapters 11 through 43 of NFPA *101*, an approved floor proximity egress path marking system that is internally illuminated shall be installed within 18 in. (455 mm) of the floor. Floor proximity egress path marking systems shall be listed in accordance with ANSI/UL 1994, *Standard for Luminous Egress Path Marking Systems.* The system shall provide a visible delineation of the path of travel along the designated exit access and shall be essentially continuous, except as interrupted by doorways, hallways, corridors, or other such architectural features. The system shall operate continuously or at any time the building fire alarm system is activated. The activation, duration, and continuity of operation of the system shall be in accordance with 7.9.2 of NFPA *101*. The system shall be maintained in accordance with the product manufacturing listing. [*101:* 7.10.1.7]

14.14.1.8* Visibility. Every sign required in Section 14.14 shall be located and of such size, distinctive color, and design that it is readily visible and shall provide contrast with decorations, interior finish, or other signs. No decorations, furnishings, or equipment that impairs visibility of a sign shall be permitted. No brightly illuminated sign (for other than exit purposes), display, or object in or near the line of vision of the required exit sign that could detract attention from the exit sign shall be permitted. [*101:* 7.10.1.8]

14.14.1.9 Mounting Location. The bottom of new egress markings shall be located at a vertical distance of not more than 6 ft 8 in. (2030 mm) above the top edge of the egress opening intended for designation by that marking. Egress markings shall be located at a horizontal distance of not more than the required width of the egress opening, as measured from the edge of the egress opening intended for designation by that marking to the nearest edge of the marking. [*101:* 7.10.1.9]

14.14.2 Directional Signs.

14.14.2.1 A sign complying with 14.14.3 with a directional indicator showing the direction of travel shall be placed in every location where the direction of travel to reach the nearest exit is not apparent. [*101:* 7.10.2.1]

14.14.2.2 Directional exit signs shall be provided within horizontal components of the egress path within exit enclosures as required by 14.14.1.2.2. [*101:* 7.10.2.2]

14.14.3 Sign Legend.

14.14.3.1* Signs required by 14.14.1 and 14.14.2 shall read as follows in plainly legible letters, or other appropriate wording shall be used:

EXIT

[*101:* 7.10.3.1]

14.14.3.2* Where approved by the AHJ, pictograms in compliance with NFPA 170, *Standard for Fire Safety and Emergency Symbols,* shall be permitted. [*101:* 7.10.3.2]

14.14.4* Power Source. Where emergency lighting facilities are required by the applicable provisions of Chapters 11 through 43 of NFPA *101* for individual occupancies, the signs, other than approved self-luminous signs and listed photoluminescent signs in accordance with 14.14.7.2, shall be illuminated by the emergency lighting facilities. The level of illumination of the signs shall be in accordance with 14.14.6.3 or 14.14.7 for the required emergency lighting duration as specified in 7.9.2.1 of NFPA *101*. However, the level of illumination shall be permitted to decline to 60 percent at the end of the emergency lighting duration. [*101:* 7.10.4]

14.14.5 Illumination of Signs.

14.14.5.1* General. Every sign required by 14.14.1.2, 14.14.1.5, or 14.14.8.1, other than where operations or processes require low lighting levels, shall be suitably illuminated by a reliable light source. Externally and internally illuminated signs shall be legible in both the normal and emergency lighting mode. [*101:* 7.10.5.1]

14.14.5.2* Continuous Illumination.

14.14.5.2.1 Every sign required to be illuminated by 14.14.6.3, 14.14.7, and 14.14.8.1 shall be continuously illuminated as required under the provisions of Section 14.12, unless otherwise provided in 14.14.5.2.2. [*101:* 7.10.5.2.1]

14.14.5.2.2* Illumination for signs shall be permitted to flash on and off upon activation of the fire alarm system. [*101:* 7.10.5.2.2]

14.14.6 Externally Illuminated Signs.

14.14.6.1* Size of Signs.

14.14.6.1.1 Externally illuminated signs required by 14.14.1 and 14.14.2, other than approved existing signs, unless otherwise provided in 14.14.6.1.2, shall read EXIT or shall use other appropriate wording in plainly legible letters sized as follows:

(1) For new signs, the letters shall be not less than 6 in. (150 mm) high, with the principal strokes of letters not less than ¾ in. (19 mm) wide.
(2) For existing signs, the required wording shall be permitted to be in plainly legible letters not less than 4 in. (100 mm) high.
(3) The word EXIT shall be in letters of a width not less than 2 in. (51 mm), except the letter I, and the minimum spacing between letters shall be not less than ⅜ in. (9.5 mm).
(4) Sign legend elements larger than the minimum established in 14.14.6.1.1(1) through 14.14.6.1.1(3) shall use letter widths, strokes, and spacing in proportion to their height. [*101:* 7.10.6.1.1]

14.14.6.1.2 The requirements of 14.14.6.1.1 shall not apply to marking required by 14.14.1.3 and 14.14.1.7. [*101:* 7.10.6.1.2]

14.14.6.2* Size and Location of Directional Indicator.

14.14.6.2.1 Directional indicators, unless otherwise provided in 14.14.6.2.2, shall comply with the following:

(1) The directional indicator shall be located outside of the EXIT legend, not less than ⅜ in. (9.5 mm) from any letter.
(2) The directional indicator shall be of a chevron type, as shown in Figure 14.14.6.2.1.
(3) The directional indicator shall be identifiable as a directional indicator at a distance of 40 ft (12 m).
(4) A directional indicator larger than the minimum established for compliance with 14.14.6.2.1(3) shall be proportionately increased in height, width, and stroke.
(5) The directional indicator shall be located at the end of the sign for the direction indicated. [*101:* 7.10.6.2.1]

14.14.6.2.2 The requirements of 14.14.6.2.1 shall not apply to approved existing signs. [*101:* 7.10.6.2.2]

FIGURE 14.14.6.2.1 Chevron-Type Indicator. [*101:* Figure 7.10.6.2.1]

14.14.6.3* Level of Illumination. Externally illuminated signs shall be illuminated by not less than 5 ft-candles (54 lux) at the illuminated surface and shall have a contrast ratio of not less than 0.5. [*101:* 7.10.6.3]

14.14.7 Internally Illuminated Signs.

14.14.7.1 Listing. Internally illuminated signs shall be listed in accordance with ANSI/UL 924, *Standard for Emergency Lighting and Power Equipment*, unless they meet one of the following criteria:

(1) They are approved existing signs.
(2) They are existing signs having the required wording in legible letters not less than 4 in. (100 mm) high.
(3) They are signs that are in accordance with 14.14.1.3 and 14.14.1.6. [*101:* 7.10.7.1]

14.14.7.2* Photoluminescent Signs. The face of a photoluminescent sign shall be continually illuminated while the building is occupied. The illumination levels on the face of the photoluminescent sign shall be in accordance with its listing. The charging illumination shall be a reliable light source as determined by the AHJ. The charging light source shall be of a type specified in the product markings. [*101:* 7.10.7.2]

14.14.8 Special Signs.

14.14.8.1 Sign Illumination.

14.14.8.1.1* Where required by other provisions of this *Code*, special signs shall be illuminated in accordance with 14.14.5, 14.14.6.3, and 14.14.7. [*101:* 7.10.8.1.1]

14.14.8.1.2 Where emergency lighting facilities are required by the applicable provisions of Chapters 11 through 43 of NFPA *101*, the required illumination of special signs shall additionally be provided under emergency lighting conditions. [*101:* 7.10.8.1.2]

14.14.8.2 Characters. Special signs, where required by other provisions of this *Code*, shall comply with the visual character requirements of ICC/ANSI A117.1, *American National Standard for Accessible and Usable Buildings and Facilities*. [*101:* 7.10.8.2]

14.14.8.3* No Exit.

14.14.8.3.1 Any door, passage, or stairway that is neither an exit nor a way of exit access and that is located or arranged so that it is likely to be mistaken for an exit shall be identified by a sign that reads as follows:

**NO
EXIT**

[*101:* 7.10.8.3.1]

14.14.8.3.2 The NO EXIT sign shall have the word NO in letters 2 in. (51 mm) high, with a stroke width of ⅜ in. (9.5 mm), and the word EXIT in letters 1 in. (25 mm) high, with the word EXIT below the word NO, unless such sign is an approved existing sign. [*101:* 7.10.8.3.2]

14.15 Secondary Means of Escape.

14.15.1 Secondary means of escape shall comply with NFPA *101*.

14.15.2 Where approved on secondary means of escape, security bars, grates, grilles, or similar devices shall be equipped with approved release mechanisms that are releasable from the inside without the use of a tool, a key, special knowledge, or force greater than that which it takes for normal operation of the door or window.

Chapter 15 Fire Department Service Delivery Concurrency Evaluation

15.1 Application.

15.1.1 The AHJ shall be permitted to require a proposed development in the jurisdiction undergo a fire department service delivery concurrency evaluation.

15.1.1.1 Proposed developments that would increase the fire department's service population by less than 1 percent or increase the fire department's total protected building square footage by less than 1 percent shall not be subject to a fire department service delivery concurrency evaluation.

15.2 Level of Service Objectives.

15.2.1 The fire department shall provide the developer with the current level of service standards for fire protection, emergency medical, prevention, and other operational services provided by the fire department.

15.2.2 The level of service for the proposed development shall not be less than the fire department's current level of service for fire protection, emergency medical, prevention, and other operational services.

15.2.2.1 The AHJ shall be permitted to approve a reduced level of service for the proposed development if a service mitigation plan has been adopted by the jurisdiction.

15.3 Evaluator Qualifications. The fire department service delivery concurrency evaluation shall be prepared by a person with qualifications acceptable to the AHJ.

15.4 Fire Department Service Delivery Concurrency Evaluation Documentation.

15.4.1 The fire department service delivery concurrency evaluation shall include, but not be limited to, the following:

(1) The current level of service for fire protection, emergency medical, and prevention services
(2) The post-development level of service for fire protection, emergency medical, and prevention services
(3) Mitigation recommendations if the level of service in the post-development condition falls below the current level of service
(4) Short- and long-term funding sources for implementation of the mitigation recommendations

15.4.2 The fire department service delivery concurrency evaluation shall be provided in a format approved by the AHJ.

15.4.3 The fire department service delivery concurrency evaluation shall utilize data sources and standards approved by the AHJ.

15.5 Independent Review. The AHJ shall be permitted to require an approved, independent third-party evaluation of the fire department service delivery concurrency evaluation at the expense of the developer.

15.6 Approval.

15.6.1 The AHJ shall make the final determination as to whether the level of service objectives have been met for the proposed development and, if applicable, the mitigation strategies are funded and appropriate.

15.6.2 If a fire department service delivery concurrency evaluation is required by the AHJ, development shall not proceed until the report has been accepted by the AHJ.

Chapter 16 Safeguarding Construction, Alteration, and Demolition Operations

16.1 General Requirements.

16.1.1 Structures undergoing construction, alteration, or demolition operations, including those in underground locations, shall comply with NFPA 241, *Standard for Safeguarding Construction, Alteration, and Demolition Operations*, and this chapter.

16.1.2 A fire protection plan shall be established where required by the AHJ.

16.1.3* In buildings under construction, adequate escape facilities shall be maintained at all times for the use of construction workers. Escape facilities shall consist of doors, walkways, stairs, ramps, fire escapes, ladders, or other approved means or devices arranged in accordance with the general principles of Chapter 14 and NFPA *101, Life Safety Code*, insofar as they can reasonably be applied to buildings under construction. [***101:*** 4.6.10.2]

16.1.4 Fire department access roads provided in accordance with 18.2.3 shall be provided at the start of a project and shall be maintained throughout construction.

16.1.5 Permanent fire department access road markings shall not be required until the building is complete or occupied for use.

16.2 Processes and Hazards.

16.2.1 Temporary Heating Equipment.

16.2.1.1* Temporary heating equipment shall be listed. [**241:**5.2.1]

16.2.1.2 Temporary heating equipment shall be installed in accordance with its listing, including clearance to combustible material, equipment, or construction. [**241:**5.2.2]

16.2.1.3 Temporary heating equipment shall be installed, used, and maintained in accordance with the manufacturer's instructions, except as otherwise provided in 16.2.1.4. [**241:**5.2.3]

16.2.1.4 Where instructions, as addressed in 16.2.1.3, are not available, temporary heating equipment shall be used in accordance with recognized safe practices. [**241:**5.2.4]

16.2.1.5 Temporary heating equipment shall be situated so that it is secured. [**241:**5.2.5]

16.2.1.6 Only personnel familiar with the operation of the temporary heating equipment shall be allowed to operate such devices. [**241:**5.2.6]

16.2.1.7* Temporary heating equipment, where utilized, shall be monitored for safe operation and maintained by properly trained personnel. [**241:**5.2.7]

16.2.1.8 Temporary heating equipment and devices noted to be damaged or considered to be a potential safety hazard shall not be used. [**241:**5.2.8]

16.2.1.9 Temporary heating equipment using exposed radiant heating wires shall not be used. [**241:**5.2.9]

16.2.1.10 Temporary electrical heating equipment shall be equipped with tip-over protection and overheat cutoffs. [**241:**5.2.10]

16.2.1.11 Chimney or vent connectors, where required from direct-fired heaters, shall be maintained at least 18 in. (460 mm) from combustibles and shall be installed in accordance with NFPA 211, *Standard for Chimneys, Fireplaces, Vents, and Solid Fuel–Burning Appliances*. [**241**:5.2.11]

16.2.1.12 Oil-fired heaters shall comply in design and installation features with Section 11.5. [**241**:5.2.12]

16.2.1.13 Fuel supplies for liquefied petroleum gas-fired heaters shall comply with NFPA 54, *National Fuel Gas Code*, and Chapter 69. [**241**:5.2.13]

16.2.1.14* Refueling operations shall be conducted in an approved manner. [**241**:5.2.14]

16.2.2 Waste Disposal.

16.2.2.1* Accumulations of combustible waste material, dust, and debris shall be removed from the structure and its immediate vicinity at the end of each work shift or more frequently as necessary for safe operations. [**241**:5.4.1]

16.2.2.2 Rubbish shall not be burned on the premises without first obtaining a permit from the AHJ. *(See Section 10.10.)* [**241**:5.4.2]

16.2.2.3 Materials susceptible to spontaneous ignition, such as oily rags, shall be stored in a listed disposal container. [**241**:5.4.3]

16.2.2.4 Trash chutes, where provided, shall comply with 16.2.2.4.1 through 16.2.2.4.6. [**241**:5.4.4]

16.2.2.4.1* A trash chute safety plan shall be submitted to and approved by the AHJ. [**241**:5.4.4.1]

16.2.2.4.2 Trash chutes used on the exterior of a building shall be of noncombustible construction, or protected in accordance with 16.2.2.4.3 through 16.2.2.4.6 if of combustible construction. [**241**:5.4.4.2]

16.2.2.4.3* The interior of combustible trash chutes shall be provided with not less than one temporary automatic sprinkler within a recess near the top of the chute. [**241**:5.4.4.3]

16.2.2.4.4 The temporary sprinkler required by 16.2.2.4.3 shall be protected by the recess as well as a listed sprinkler guard. [**241**:5.4.4.4]

16.2.2.4.5 The temporary sprinkler required by 16.2.2.4.3 shall be connected to any available water supply with a listed fire hose, or a flexible, commercial rubber hose, with a diameter of not less than ¾ in. (19 mm) and a listed flexible connector. [**241**:5.4.4.5]

16.2.2.4.6 The temporary sprinkler required by 16.2.2.4.3 shall be protected against freezing where required by the AHJ. [**241**:5.4.4.6]

16.2.3 Flammable and Combustible Liquids and Flammable Gases.

16.2.3.1 Storage.

16.2.3.1.1 Storage of flammable and combustible liquids shall be in accordance with Chapter 66, unless otherwise modified by 16.2.3. [**241**:5.5.1.1]

16.2.3.1.2* Storage of Class I and Class II liquids shall not exceed 60 gal (227 L) within 50 ft (15 m) of the structure. [**241**:5.5.1.2]

16.2.3.1.3 Storage areas shall be kept free of weeds, debris, and combustible materials not necessary to the storage. [**241**:5.5.1.3]

16.2.3.1.4 Open flames and smoking shall not be permitted in flammable and combustible liquids storage areas. [**241**:5.5.1.4]

16.2.3.1.5 Such storage areas shall be appropriately posted as "No Smoking" areas. [**241**:5.5.1.5]

16.2.3.1.6 Storage areas shall be appropriately posted with markings in accordance with NFPA 704, *Standard System for the Identification of the Hazards of Materials for Emergency Response*. [**241**:5.5.1.6]

16.2.3.2 Handling of Flammable and Combustible Liquids at Point of Final Use.

16.2.3.2.1 Handling of flammable and combustible liquids shall be in accordance with Chapter 66, except as modified by 16.2.3.2.2 through 16.2.3.2.4. [**241**:5.5.2.1]

16.2.3.2.2 Class I and Class II liquids shall be kept in approved safety containers. [**241**:5.5.2.2]

16.2.3.2.3 Means shall be provided to dispose of leakage and spills promptly and safely. [**241**:5.5.2.3]

16.2.3.2.4* Class I liquids shall be dispensed only where there are no open flames or other sources of ignition within the possible path of vapor travel. [**241**:5.5.2.4]

16.2.3.3 Storage and Handling of Combustible and Flammable Gases.

16.2.3.3.1 Storage and handling of combustible and flammable gases shall be in accordance with NFPA 54, *National Fuel Gas Code*, and Chapter 69. [**241**:5.5.3.1]

16.2.3.3.2 Open flames and smoking shall not be permitted in flammable gas storage areas. [**241**:5.5.3.2]

16.3 Fire Protection.

16.3.1 Fire Safety Program.

16.3.1.1 An overall construction or demolition fire safety program shall be developed.

16.3.1.2 All of the following items shall be addressed in the fire safety program:

(1) Good housekeeping
(2) On-site security
(3) Fire protection systems
  (a) For construction operations, installation of new fire protection systems as construction progresses
  (b) For demolition operations, preservation of existing fire protection systems during demolition
(4) Organization and training of an on-site fire brigade
(5) Development of a prefire plan with the local fire department
(6) Rapid communication
(7) Consideration of special hazards resulting from previous occupancies
(8) Protection of existing structures and equipment from exposure fires resulting from construction, alteration, and demolition operations

[**241**:7.1]

16.3.2 Owner's Responsibility for Fire Protection.

16.3.2.1* The owner shall designate a person who shall be responsible for the fire prevention program and who shall ensure that it is carried out to completion. [**241:**7.2.1]

16.3.2.1.1 The fire prevention program manager shall have the authority to enforce the provisions of NFPA 241 and other applicable fire protection standards. [**241:**7.2.1.1]

16.3.2.1.2 The fire prevention program manager shall have knowledge of the applicable fire protection standards, available fire protection systems, and fire inspection procedures. [**241:**7.2.1.2]

16.3.2.1.3 Inspection records shall be available for review by the AHJ. [**241:**7.2.1.3]

16.3.2.2 Where guard service is provided, the fire prevention program manager shall be responsible for the guard service. [**241:**7.2.2]

16.3.2.3* Prefire Plans.

16.3.2.3.1 Where there is public fire protection or a private fire brigade, the manager shall be responsible for the development of prefire plans in conjunction with the fire agencies. [**241:**7.2.3.1]

16.3.2.3.2 Prefire plans shall be updated as necessary. [**241:**7.2.3.2]

16.3.2.3.3 The prefire plan shall include provisions for on-site visits by the fire agency. [**241:**7.2.3.3]

16.3.2.4 Program Manager Responsibilities.

16.3.2.4.1 The manager shall be responsible for ensuring that proper training in the use of protection equipment has been provided. [**241:**7.2.4.1]

16.3.2.4.2 The manager shall be responsible for the presence of adequate numbers and types of fire protection devices and appliances and for their proper maintenance. [**241:**7.2.4.2]

16.3.2.4.3 The manager shall be responsible for supervising the permit system for hot work operations. *(See Section 5.1 of NFPA 241.)* [**241:**7.2.4.3]

16.3.2.4.4 A weekly self-inspection program shall be implemented, with records maintained and made available. [**241:**7.2.4.4]

16.3.2.4.5* Impairments to the fire protection systems or fire alarm, detection, or communications systems shall be authorized only by the fire prevention program manager. [**241:**7.2.4.5]

16.3.2.4.6 Temporary protective coverings used on fire protection devices during renovations, such as painting, shall be removed promptly when work has been completed in the area. [**241:**7.2.4.6]

16.3.2.5 Site Security.

16.3.2.5.1* Guard service shall be provided where required by the AHJ. [**241:**7.2.5.1]

16.3.2.5.2* Where guard service is provided, the guard(s) shall be trained in all of the following:

(1) Notification procedures that include calling the fire department and management personnel
(2) Function and operation of fire protection equipment
(3) Familiarization with fire hazards
(4) Use of construction elevators, where provided

[**241:**7.2.5.2]

16.3.2.5.3 Guards shall be informed of any special status of emergency equipment or hazards. [**241:**7.2.5.3]

16.3.2.5.4* Security fences shall be provided where required by the AHJ. [**241:**7.2.5.4]

16.3.2.5.5* Entrances (e.g., doors and windows) to the structure under construction, alteration, or demolition shall be secured where required by the AHJ. [**241:**7.2.5.5]

16.3.3* Fire Alarm Reporting.

16.3.3.1 There shall be a readily available public fire alarm box near the premises, telephone service to the responding fire department, or equivalent facilities. [**241:**7.4.1]

16.3.3.2 Instructions shall be issued for the immediate notification of the fire department in the case of a fire. Where telephone service is employed, the local fire department number and site address shall be conspicuously posted near each telephone. [**241:**7.4.2]

16.3.4 Access for Fire Fighting.

16.3.4.1 A suitable location at the site shall be designated as a command post and provided with plans, emergency information, keys, communications, and equipment, as needed. [**241:**7.5.1]

16.3.4.2 The person in charge of fire protection shall respond to the location command post whenever fire occurs. [**241:**7.5.2]

16.3.4.3 Where access to or within a structure or an area is unduly difficult because of secured openings or where immediate access is necessary for life-saving or fire-fighting purposes, the AHJ shall be permitted to require a key box to be installed in an accessible location. [**241:**7.5.3]

16.3.4.4 The key box shall be an approved type and shall contain keys to gain access as required by the AHJ. *(See Section 18.2.)* [**241:**7.5.4]

16.3.4.5 Stairs.

16.3.4.5.1 In all buildings over one story in height, at least one stairway shall be provided that is in usable condition at all times and that meets the requirements of NFPA *101*. [**241:**7.5.6.1]

16.3.4.5.2 This stairway shall be extended upward as each floor is installed in new construction and maintained for each floor still remaining during demolition. [**241:**7.5.6.2]

16.3.4.5.3 The stairway shall be lighted. [**241:**7.5.6.3]

16.3.4.5.4 During construction, the stairway shall be enclosed where the building exterior walls are in place. [**241:**7.5.6.4]

16.3.4.5.5 All exit stairs shall be provided with stair identification signs to include the floor level, stair designation, and exit path direction as required to provide for safe egress. [**241:**7.5.6.5]

16.3.5 Standpipes. In all new buildings in which standpipes are required or where standpipes exist in buildings being altered or demolished, such standpipes shall be maintained in conformity with the progress of building construction in such a manner that they are always ready for use. [**241:**7.6]

16.3.6* First-Aid Fire-Fighting Equipment.

16.3.6.1* The suitability, distribution, and maintenance of extinguishers shall be in accordance with Section 13.6. [**241**:7.7.1]

16.3.6.2 Wherever a toolhouse, storeroom, or other shanty is located in or adjacent to the building under construction or demolition, or where a room or space within that building is used for storage, a dressing room, or a workshop, at least one approved extinguisher shall be provided and maintained in an accessible location, unless otherwise permitted by 16.3.6.3. [**241**:7.7.2]

16.3.6.3 The requirement of 16.3.6.2 shall be permitted to be waived where the structure does not exceed 150 ft^2 (14 m^2) in floor area or is equipped with automatic sprinklers or other approved protection. [**241**:7.7.3]

16.3.6.4 At least one approved fire extinguisher also shall be provided in plain sight on each floor at each usable stairway as soon as combustible material accumulates. [**241**:7.7.4]

16.3.6.5 Suitable fire extinguishers shall be provided on self-propelled equipment. [**241**:7.7.5]

16.3.6.6* Free access to permanent, temporary, or portable first-aid fire equipment shall be maintained at all times. [**241**:7.7.6]

16.4 Safeguarding Construction and Alteration Operations.

16.4.1* Scaffolding, Shoring, and Forms.

16.4.1.1 Accumulations of unnecessary combustible forms or form lumber shall be prohibited. [**241**:8.2.1]

16.4.1.2 Combustible forms or form lumber shall be brought into the structure only when needed. [**241**:8.2.2]

16.4.1.3 Combustible forms or form lumber shall be removed from the structure as soon as stripping is complete. [**241**:8.2.3]

16.4.1.4 Those portions of the structure where combustible forms are present shall not be used for the storage of other combustible building materials. [**241**:8.2.4]

16.4.1.5* During forming and stripping operations, portable fire extinguishers or charged hose lines shall be provided to protect the additional combustible loading adequately. [**241**:8.2.5]

16.4.2 Temporary Separation Walls.

16.4.2.1 Protection shall be provided to separate an occupied portion of the structure from a portion of the structure undergoing alteration, construction, or demolition operations when such operations are considered as having a higher level of hazard than the occupied portion of the building. [**241**:8.6.2.1]

16.4.2.2 Walls shall have at least a 1-hour fire resistance rating. [**241**:8.6.2.2]

16.4.2.3 Opening protectives shall have at least a 45-minute fire protection rating. [**241**:8.6.2.3]

16.4.2.4* Nonrated walls and opening protectives shall be permitted when an approved automatic sprinkler system is installed. [**241**:8.6.2.4]

16.4.3 Fire Protection During Construction.

16.4.3.1 Water Supply.

16.4.3.1.1* A water supply for fire protection, either temporary or permanent, shall be made available as soon as combustible material accumulates. [**241**:8.7.2.1]

16.4.3.1.2 There shall be no delay in the installation of fire protection equipment. *(See A.16.4.1.5.)* [**241**:8.7.2.2]

16.4.3.1.3* Where underground water mains and hydrants are to be provided, they shall be installed, completed, and in service prior to commencing construction work on any structure. [**241**:8.7.2.3]

16.4.3.2 Sprinkler Protection.

16.4.3.2.1* If automatic sprinkler protection is to be provided, the installation shall be placed in service as soon as practicable. [**241**:8.7.3.1]

16.4.3.2.2 The details of installation shall be in accordance with NFPA 13. [**241**:8.7.3.2]

16.4.3.2.3 Where sprinklers are required for safety to life, the building shall not be occupied until the sprinkler installation has been entirely completed and tested so that the protection is not susceptible to frequent impairment caused by testing and correction, unless otherwise permitted by 16.4.3.2.4. [**241**:8.7.3.3]

16.4.3.2.4 The provision of 16.4.3.2.3 shall not prohibit occupancy of the lower floors of a building, even where the upper floors are in various stages of construction or protection, provided that both of the following conditions are satisfied:

(1) The sprinkler protection of the lower occupied floors has been completed and tested in accordance with 16.4.3.2.3.
(2) The sprinkler protection of the upper floors is supplied by entirely separate systems and separate control valves so that the absence or incompleteness of protection in no way impairs the sprinkler protection of the occupied lower floors.

[**241**:8.7.3.4]

16.4.3.2.5 The operation of sprinkler control valves shall be permitted only by properly authorized personnel and shall be accompanied by the notification of duly designated parties. [**241**:8.7.3.5]

16.4.3.2.6 Where the sprinkler protection is regularly turned off and on to facilitate connection of newly completed segments, the sprinkler control valves shall be checked at the end of each work shift to ascertain that protection is in service. [**241**:8.7.3.6]

16.4.3.3 Standpipes.

16.4.3.3.1 General.

16.4.3.3.1.1* The pipe size, hose valves, hose, water supply, and other details for new construction shall be in accordance with Section 13.2. [**241**:8.7.4.1.1]

16.4.3.3.1.2 On permanent Type II and Type III standpipes, hose and nozzles shall be provided and made ready for use as soon as the water supply is available to the standpipe, unless otherwise permitted by 16.4.3.3.1.3. [**241**:8.7.4.1.2]

16.4.3.3.1.3* In combined systems where occupant hose is not required, temporary hose and nozzles shall be provided during construction. [**241**:8.7.4.1.3]

16.4.3.3.2 Standpipe Installations in Buildings Under Construction.
Where required by the AHJ, in buildings under construction, a standpipe system, either temporary or permanent in nature, shall be installed in accordance with 16.4.3.3.2.1 through 16.4.3.3.2.10. [**241**:8.7.4.2]

16.4.3.3.2.1 The standpipes shall be provided with conspicuously marked and readily accessible fire department connections on the outside of the building at the street level and shall have at least one standard hose outlet at each floor. [**241**:8.7.4.2.1]

16.4.3.3.2.2 The pipe sizes, hose valves, hose, water supply, and other details for new construction shall be in accordance with NFPA 241. [**241**:8.7.4.2.2]

16.4.3.3.2.3 The standpipes shall be securely supported and restrained at each alternate floor. [**241**:8.7.4.2.3]

16.4.3.3.2.4* At least one approved hose valve for attaching fire department hose shall be provided at each intermediate landing or floor level in the exit stairway, as determined by the AHJ. [**241**:8.7.4.2.4]

16.4.3.3.2.5 Valves shall be kept closed at all times and guarded against mechanical injury. [**241**:8.7.4.2.5]

16.4.3.3.2.6 Hose valves shall have NH standard external threads for the valve size specified in accordance with NFPA 1963, *Standard for Fire Hose Connections*, unless modified by 16.4.3.3.2.7. [**241**:8.7.4.2.6]

16.4.3.3.2.7 Where local fire department connections do not conform to NFPA 1963, the AHJ shall designate the connection to be used. [**241**:8.7.4.2.7]

16.4.3.3.2.8* The standpipes shall be extended up with each floor and shall be securely capped at the top. [**241**:8.7.4.2.8]

16.4.3.3.2.9 Top hose outlets shall be not more than one floor below the highest forms, staging, and similar combustibles at all times. [**241**:8.7.4.2.9]

16.4.3.3.2.10 Temporary standpipes shall remain in service until the permanent standpipe installation is complete. [**241**:8.7.4.2.10]

16.4.4 Alteration of Buildings.

16.4.4.1 Where the building is protected by fire protection systems, such systems shall be maintained operational at all times during alteration.

16.4.4.2 Where alteration requires modification of a portion of the fire protection system, the remainder of the system shall be kept in service and the fire department shall be notified.

16.4.4.3 When it is necessary to shut down the system, the AHJ shall have the authority to require alternate measures of protection until the system is returned to service.

16.4.4.4 The fire department shall be notified when the system is shut down and when the system is returned to service.

16.4.4.5 All required exit components shall be maintained in accordance with this *Code* as deemed necessary by the AHJ.

16.4.4.6 Fire-resistive assemblies and construction shall be maintained.

16.5 Fire Safety During Demolition.

16.5.1 If a building intended to be demolished contains a sprinkler system, such system shall not be rendered inoperative without approval of the AHJ.

16.5.2 Demolition operations involving the use of cutting and welding shall be done in accordance with Chapter 41.

16.5.3 Combustible waste material shall not be burned at the demolition site unless approved by the AHJ. Combustible materials shall be removed from the site as often as necessary to minimize the hazards therefrom. *(See 16.2.2 and Section 10.10.)*

16.5.4 Where in the opinion of the AHJ the demolition site is of a hazardous nature, qualified personnel shall serve as an on-site fire watch.

16.6 Torch-Applied Roofing Systems.

16.6.1 Permits. Permits, where required, shall comply with Section 1.12.

16.6.2 Torch-applied roofing systems shall be installed in accordance with Chapter 9 of NFPA 241, *Standard for Safeguarding Construction, Alteration, and Demolition Operations*.

16.7 Tar Kettles.

16.7.1 General.

16.7.1.1 The provisions of Section 16.7 shall apply to any type of equipment including, but not limited to, chassis-mounted equipment used for preheating or heating tar, asphalt, pitch, or similar substances for roofs, floors, pipes, or similar objects.

16.7.1.2 Permits. Permits, where required, shall comply with Section 1.12.

16.7.1.3 Operating kettles shall not be located inside of or on the roof of any building.

16.7.1.4 Tar Kettle Location. The kettle shall be operated in a controlled area. The area shall be identified by the use of traffic cones, barriers, and other suitable means as approved by the AHJ.

16.7.1.5 Kettle Supervision.

16.7.1.5.1 An operating kettle shall be attended by a minimum of one employee who is knowledgeable of the operations and hazards.

16.7.1.5.2 The employee shall be within 25 ft (7.6 m) of the kettle and shall have the kettle within sight.

16.7.1.6 Fire Extinguishers.

16.7.1.6.1 Two approved 4-A:40-B:C fire extinguishers shall be provided and maintained within 25 ft (7.6 m) of the operating kettle.

16.7.1.6.2* A minimum of one approved 4-A:40-B:C fire extinguisher shall be provided and maintained on the roof in close proximity to the roofing operations while the roofing material is being applied.

16.7.1.6.3 Fire extinguishers shall be mounted in an accessible and visible or identified location.

16.7.1.7 Exits.

16.7.1.7.1 Roofing kettles shall not block exits, means of egress, gates, roadways, or entrances.

16.7.1.7.2 Kettles shall not be closer than 10 ft (3 m) from exits or means of egress.

16.7.2 Fuel System.

16.7.2.1 Fuel containers shall be constructed and approved for the use for which they were designed.

16.7.2.2 Liquefied petroleum gas (LP-Gas) containers, hose, regulators, and burners shall conform to the requirements in Chapter 69.

16.7.2.3 LP-Gas cylinders shall be secured to prevent accidental tipover.

16.7.2.4 Regulators shall be required on any cylinders.

16.7.2.5 Where, in the opinion of the AHJ, physical damage to the container is a danger, protection shall be provided to prevent such physical damage.

16.7.2.6 LP-Gas containers for roofing kettles shall not be used in any building.

16.7.3 Maintenance.

16.7.3.1 Roofing kettles and all integral working parts shall be in good working condition and shall be maintained free of excessive residue.

16.7.3.2 All piping used for pumping heated material to the roof shall be installed in a manner to prevent loss of heated material.

16.7.3.3 Flexible steel piping shall not be used on the vertical extension of piping systems.

16.7.3.4 Flexible steel piping shall be limited to those connections that are immediately adjacent to the pump kettle or discharge outlet.

16.7.3.5 No single length of flexible piping shall exceed 6 ft (1.8 m) in length, and all piping shall be able to withstand a pressure of at least four times the working pressure of the pump.

16.7.3.6 Roofing Kettle Doors.

16.7.3.6.1 All roofing kettles shall have doors permanently attached.

16.7.3.6.2 Roofing kettle doors shall be installed in a workmanlike manner and shall be provided with handles that allow them to be opened without the operator having to stand in front of same.

16.7.3.6.3 All kettles shall have an approved, working visible temperature gauge that indicates the temperature of the material being heated.

16.7.3.7 All kettle doors shall be tightly closed and latched when in transit.

16.7.4 Construction.

16.7.4.1 The materials and methods of construction of roofing kettles shall be acceptable to the AHJ.

16.7.4.2 Minimum Requirements.

16.7.4.2.1 Paragraph 16.7.4.2 shall apply to all roofing kettles or tar pots in excess of 1 gal (3.8 L) capacity.

16.7.4.2.2 No roofing kettle shall have a capacity in excess of 5 barrels (bbl).

16.7.4.2.3 Roofing kettles of 2 bbl capacity or less shall be constructed of steel sheet having a thickness of not less than 0.105 in. (No. 12 Manufacturers' Standard Gauge). Kettles of more than 2 bbl capacity shall be constructed of steel sheet having a thickness of not less than 0.135 in. (No. 10 Manufacturers' Standard Gauge). All supports, corners, and the top and bottom of the fire box shall be bound with angle iron or other reinforcements approved by the AHJ. All doors shall be hinged, closely fitted, and adequately latched. Fire boxes shall be of sufficient height from the ground or shall be provided with a system of shields or insulation to prevent heat damage to the street surface.

16.7.4.2.4 Lids that can be gravity operated shall be provided on all roofing kettles. The tops and covers of all kettles shall be constructed of steel sheet having a thickness of not less than 0.075 in. (1.90 mm) (No. 14 Manufacturers' Standard Gauge) that is close fitting and attached to the kettle with hinges that allow gravity to close the lid.

16.7.4.2.5 The chassis shall be substantially constructed and capable of carrying the load imposed upon it whether it is standing still or being transported.

16.7.4.2.6 Fuel containers, burners, and related appurtenances of roofing kettles in which LP-Gas is used for heating shall comply with all the requirements of Chapter 69.

16.7.4.2.7 Fuel containers that operate under air pressure shall not exceed 20 gal (76 L) in capacity and shall be subject to the approval of the AHJ.

16.7.4.2.8 All fuel containers shall be maintained in accordance with applicable NFPA codes and standards or shall be at least 10 ft (3 m) from the burner flame or at least 2 ft (0.6 m) therefrom when properly insulated from heat or flame.

16.8 Asbestos Removal.

16.8.1 Notification. The AHJ and the fire department shall be notified 24 hours prior to the commencement and closure of asbestos removal operations.

16.8.2 Permits. Permits, where required, shall comply with Section 1.12.

16.8.3 Signs. Approved signs shall be posted at the entrance, exit and exit access door, decontamination areas, and waste disposal areas for asbestos removal operations.

16.8.3.1 The signs shall state that asbestos is being removed from the area, that asbestos is a suspected carcinogen, and that proper respiratory protection is required.

16.8.3.2 Signs shall have a reflective surface, and lettering shall be a minimum of 2 in. (51 mm) high.

Chapter 17 Wildland Urban Interface

17.1 General. The planning, construction, maintenance, education, and management elements for the protection of life and property from wildfire shall meet the requirements of this chapter and NFPA 1144, *Standard for Reducing Structure Ignition Hazards from Wildland Fire*.

17.1.1 In cases in which the local jurisdiction declares that an area within the jurisdiction is a wildland urban interface as determined by an assessment tool based upon accepted fire services practices, or where new structures will be located in a wildland/urban interface or intermix area, the AHJ shall perform, or cause to be performed, a wildland fire hazard assessment of each structure ignition zone in the development to determine relative risk, the extent of wildland fire hazard, and applicable mitigation measures.

17.1.2* The structure assessment shall, as a minimum, include the following:

(1) Identification and documentation of the wildland fire hazards in the ignition zone(s) for each structure within wildland fire hazard areas, according to the elements and conditions in 17.1.4
(2) Determination of mitigation measures for vegetation, other combustibles, and the structure, including the periodic maintenance associated with such measures

(3) Establishment of priorities relative to mitigating the risks from wildland fire [1144:4.1.2]

17.1.3 The wildland fire hazard assessment shall be the basis for recommended mitigation measures relative to the vegetation, other combustibles, and structures on the site. [1144:4.1.3]

17.1.4* Structure Assessment Elements and Conditions. As a minimum, the structure assessment shall cover elements and conditions indicated in 17.1.5 through 17.1.9. [1144:4.2]

17.1.5 Overview of the Surrounding Environment. The structure assessment shall document the conditions of 17.1.5.1 through 17.1.5.5 in the assessment of the surrounding environment, as they will place the structure in the most risk from ignition by a wildland fire. [1144:4.2.1]

17.1.5.1* The structure assessment shall document the location of the structure in relation to predominant topographical features, such as flat open areas, ridges, saddles, steep slopes, natural chimneys like steep narrow draws, or small canyons, that will increase the ignition potential of the structure. [1144:4.2.1.1]

17.1.5.2* The structure assessment shall document local weather conditions, including wind, relative humidity, temperature, and fine fuel moisture content. [1144:4.2.1.2]

17.1.5.3* The structure assessment shall document nearby structures using the same criteria as the primary structure. [1144:4.2.1.3]

17.1.5.4* The structure assessment shall document any neighboring properties that could impact the ignition zone of the property being assessed. [1144:4.2.1.4]

17.1.5.5* The structure assessment shall document the structure's location on the slope relative to the structure's potential exposure to heat from a wildland fire. [1144:4.2.1.5]

17.1.6 From Chimney to Eaves. The structure assessment shall document the conditions of 17.1.6.1 through 17.1.6.6 to observe construction and vegetation as they place the structure in the most risk from ignition by a wildland fire. [1144:4.2.2]

17.1.6.1* The structure assessment shall document the type and construction of roofing materials. [1144:4.2.2.1]

17.1.6.2* The structure assessment shall document the condition of roofing materials and assemblies. [1144:4.2.2.2]

17.1.6.3* The structure assessment shall document all skylights in roof assemblies. [1144:4.2.2.3]

17.1.6.4* The structure assessment shall document the potential of roof gutters and areas where exterior walls meet roof or deck surfaces to collect litter on surfaces or in crevices. [1144:4.2.2.4]

17.1.6.5* The structure assessment shall document the construction materials of gutters, downspouts, and connectors. [1144:4.2.2.5]

17.1.6.6* The structure assessment shall document the materials and construction used in eaves of roof overhangs. [1144:4.2.2.6]

17.1.7 From Top of Exterior Wall to Foundation. The structure assessment shall document the conditions of 17.1.7.1 through 17.1.7.6 to observe construction and vegetation as they place the structure in the most risk from ignition by a wildland fire. [1144:4.2.3]

17.1.7.1* The structure assessment shall document the materials and construction used in exterior walls and exterior siding. [1144:4.2.3.1]

17.1.7.2 The structure assessment shall document the materials used for gutter downspouts and connectors on exterior walls. [1144:4.2.3.2]

17.1.7.3* The structure assessment shall document the materials used in windows and other openings in vertical surfaces. [1144:4.2.3.3]

17.1.7.4* The structure assessment shall document the location, size, and screening of ventilation openings. [1144:4.2.3.4]

17.1.7.5* The structure assessment shall document all attached accessory structures as part of the primary structure. [1144:4.2.3.5]

17.1.7.6* The structure assessment shall document areas next to or under a structure where combustible materials that present a source of flame exposure to the structure might collect. [1144:4.2.3.6]

17.1.8* From Foundation to the Immediate Landscaped Area. The structure assessment shall document the conditions of 17.1.8.1 through 17.1.8.5 to observe construction and vegetation, as they place the structure in the most risk from ignition by a wildland fire. [1144:4.2.4]

17.1.8.1* The structure assessment shall document all vegetative fuels and other combustible materials adjacent to and within 30 ft (9 m) of the structure for their potential to contribute to the intensity and spread of wildland fire. [1144:4.2.4.1]

17.1.8.2* The structure assessment shall document the presence and location of all heat and flame sources within 30 ft (9 m) of the primary structure. [1144:4.2.4.2]

17.1.8.3* The structure assessment shall document all projections attached to the primary structure. [1144:4.2.4.3]

17.1.8.4* The structure assessment shall document detached structures within 30 ft (9 m) of the primary structure that might be ignited by flames, radiant heat, or firebrands from wildland fires. [1144:4.2.4.4]

17.1.8.5* The structure assessment shall document vehicle parking areas within 30 ft (9 m) of any surface of the structure. [1144:4.2.4.5]

17.1.9 From the Immediate Landscaped Area to the Extent of the Structure Ignition Zone. The structure assessment shall document the conditions of 17.1.9.1 through 17.1.9.8 to observe construction and vegetation, as they place the structure in the most risk from ignition by a wildland fire. [1144:4.2.5]

17.1.9.1* The structure assessment shall document vegetation within the area between the outer edge of the immediate landscaped area and the extent of the structure ignition zone as potential fuel that can convey the fire to the structure. [1144:4.2.5.1]

17.1.9.2* The structure assessment shall document the species and location of trees and the separation of tree crowns within the area between the outer edge of the immediate landscaped area and the extent of the structure ignition zone. [1144:4.2.5.2]

17.1.9.3* The structure assessment shall document the presence and location of all heat and flame sources within the area between the outer edge of the immediate landscaped area and the extent of the structure ignition zone. [1144:4.2.5.3]

17.1.9.4* The structure assessment shall document detached structures within the area between the outer edge of the immediate landscaped area and the extent of the structure ignition zone that might be ignited by flames, radiant heat, or firebrands from wildland fires. [**1144:**4.2.5.4]

17.1.9.5* The structure assessment shall document vehicle parking areas within the area between the outer edges of the immediate landscaped area and the extent of the structure ignition zone. [**1144:**4.2.5.5]

17.1.9.6* The structure assessment shall document all projections attached to the primary structure that extend beyond the immediate landscaped area. [**1144:**4.2.5.6]

17.1.9.7 The structure assessment shall document all other factors that can affect the risk of ignition or the spread of wildland fire on improved property within the structure ignition zone, including the risk of structure fires spreading to vegetation. [**1144:**4.2.5.7]

17.1.9.8 Any structure that fails to comply with the requirements of Chapter 5 of NFPA 1144 shall be deemed to increase the risk of the spread of wildland fire to improved property and the risk of fires on improved property spreading to wildland fuels. [**1144:**4.2.5.8]

17.1.10 Development of Wildland Fire Hazard Mitigation Plan.

17.1.10.1 From the information gathered in each structure assessment, the AHJ shall require or cause to be developed a wildland fire hazard mitigation plan and schedule to address the wildland fire hazards identified in the specific structure ignition zone assessment. [**1144:**4.3.1]

17.1.10.2 The AHJ shall work with applicable agencies and organizations to resolve any conflicts between recommended wildland fire hazard mitigation measures and mitigation measures or objectives of other hazards. [**1144:**4.3.2]

17.1.10.3* This plan shall include, but not be limited to, the following:

(1) Specific mitigation recommendations based on the hazard assessment to reduce the ignition potential around and including the structure
(2) Construction modification or retrofit necessary to reduce the identified hazards as a minimum or to comply with the provisions of Chapter 5 of NFPA 1144
(3) Fuel modification recommendations as specified in Chapter 6 of NFPA 1144
(4) A hazard mitigation implementation and maintenance schedule approved by the AHJ [**1144:**4.3.3]

17.1.10.4* The history of wildland fire in the area under assessment shall be considered in determining required hazard mitigation plan. [**1144:**4.3.4]

17.1.10.5* The AHJ shall approve the mitigating measures relative to access, water supply, and construction based upon the structure assessment established in 17.1.2. [**1144:**4.3.5]

17.1.10.6 From the information gathered in each structure assessment, the AHJ shall require or cause to be developed a wildland fire hazard severity map of each residential development area addressed. [**1144:**4.3.6]

17.1.10.7 The map shall include, but not be limited to, the following data elements:

(1) Lot designations
(2) Structure locations on each lot
(3) Locations of wildland fire evacuation centers or safety zones
(4) Hazard severity for each lot
(5) Overlapping ignition zones [**1144:**4.3.7]

17.1.11 Mitigation Implementation and Enforcement.

17.1.11.1 The AHJ shall require the property owner to develop and comply with the approved wildland fire hazard mitigation plan and schedule according to 17.1.10.1. [**1144:**4.4.1]

17.1.11.2 No permit associated with construction shall be issued if the provisions of this *Code* are not addressed. [**1144:**4.4.2]

17.1.11.3 No permit associated with occupancy shall be issued until the provisions of this *Code* are satisfied. [**1144:**4.4.3]

17.2 Plans. The plans for construction and development within the wildland urban interface shall be submitted to the AHJ for review and approval.

17.3 Wildland Fire–Prone Areas.

17.3.1* Safeguards. Safeguards to prevent the occurrence of fires and to provide adequate fire protection and mitigation measures in hazardous fire areas shall be provided and maintained in accordance with Section 17.3.

17.3.2* Permits and Approvals. Permits for use of hazardous areas shall not be issued when public safety would be at risk, as determined by the AHJ. *(See Section 1.12 for additional requirements for permits.)*

17.3.3 Restricted Entry.

17.3.3.1 The AHJ shall determine and publicly announce when hazardous fire areas shall be closed to entry, and when such areas shall again be opened to entry.

17.3.3.2 Unauthorized persons shall not be permitted to enter or remain in closed hazardous fire areas.

17.3.3.3 Signs. Approved signs prohibiting entry by unauthorized persons shall be placed on every closed area and access point.

17.3.4 Use of Flammable Materials and Procedures.

17.3.4.1 Smoking. Lighting, igniting, or otherwise setting fire to any smoking material shall be prohibited unless within structures or smoking areas approved by the AHJ. *(See Section 10.9 for additional requirements on smoking.)*

17.3.4.2 Tracer Bullets, Tracer Charges, Rockets, and Model Aircraft.

17.3.4.2.1 Tracer bullets and tracer charges shall not be possessed, fired, or caused to be fired into or across hazardous fire areas.

17.3.4.2.2 Rockets, model planes, gliders, and balloons powered with an engine, propellant, or other feature liable to start or cause fire shall not be fired or projected into or across hazardous fire areas.

17.3.4.3 Explosives and Blasting. Explosives shall not be possessed, kept, stored, sold, offered for sale, given away, used, discharged, transported, or disposed of within hazardous fire areas except as permitted by the AHJ. *(See Chapter 65 for additional guidance.)*

17.3.4.4 Fireworks. Fireworks shall not be used or possessed in hazardous fire areas unless permitted by the AHJ. *(See Chapter 65 for additional guidance.)*

17.3.4.5 Apiaries. Lighted and smoldering material used in connection with smoking bees shall not be allowed in or upon hazardous fire areas except as permitted by the AHJ.

17.3.5 Clearance of Brush and Vegetative Growth.

17.3.5.1 Electrical Transmission Lines.

17.3.5.1.1 Clearance of brush and vegetative growth from electrical transmission and distribution line(s) shall be provided and maintained in accordance with 17.3.5.1.

17.3.5.1.2 A combustible-free space around poles and towers shall consist of a clearing of not less than 10 ft (3.05 m) in each direction from the outer circumference of the pole or tower during such periods of time as designated by the AHJ.

17.3.5.1.3 Trimming Clearance.

17.3.5.1.3.1 At the time of trimming, clearances not less than those established by Table 17.3.5.1.3.1 shall be provided.

Table 17.3.5.1.3.1 Minimum Clearances Between Vegetation and Electrical Lines at Time of Trimming

Line Voltage	Minimal Radial Clearance from Conductor	
	ft	m
2400–72,000	4	1.2
72,001–110,000	6	1.8
110,001–300,000	10	3.0
300,001 or more	15	4.6

17.3.5.1.3.2 The radial clearances in Table 17.3.5.1.3.1 are minimum clearances that shall be established at time of trimming between the vegetation and the energized conductors and associated live parts.

17.3.5.1.4 Clearances not less than those established by Table 17.3.5.1.4 shall be maintained during such periods of time as designated by the AHJ.

Table 17.3.5.1.4 Minimum Clearances Between Vegetation and Electrical Lines to Be Maintained

Line Voltage	Minimum Clearance	
	in.	mm
750–35,000	6	152
35,001–60,000	12	305
60,001–115,000	19	483
115,001–230,000	30.5	775
230,001–500,000	115	2920

17.3.5.1.4.1 The site-specific clearance achieved, at the time of pruning, shall vary based on species' growth rates, the utility company specific trim cycle, the potential line sway due to wind, line sway due to electrical loading and ambient temperature, and the tree's location in proximity to the high voltage lines.

17.3.5.1.4.2 The AHJ shall establish minimum clearances different than those specified by Table 17.3.5.1.4 when evidence substantiating such other clearances is submitted to the AHJ and approved.

17.3.5.1.5* Electrical Power Line Emergencies. During emergencies, the utility company shall perform the required work to the extent necessary to clear the hazard.

17.3.5.2 Structures.

17.3.5.2.1 Persons owning, leasing, controlling, operating, or maintaining buildings or structures in, upon, or adjoining hazardous fire areas, and persons owning, leasing, or controlling land adjacent to such buildings or structures, shall maintain an effective defensible space in accordance with 17.3.5.2.1.1 through 17.3.5.2.1.11.5.

17.3.5.2.1.1* Ground fuels, including native vegetation and plants used for landscaping within the defined landscaping zones, shall be treated or removed. [**1144:**6.2.1]

17.3.5.2.1.2 Live vegetation within the fuel modification area shall have dead material removed and shall be thinned and pruned in conformance with the wildland fire mitigation plan, as approved by the AHJ. [**1144:**6.2.2]

17.3.5.2.1.3 Dead and downed fuels within 30 ft (9 m) of all buildings shall be removed or treated to maintain the fuel modification area in conformance with the wildland fire mitigation plan, as approved by the AHJ. [**1144:**6.2.3]

17.3.5.2.1.4 Vegetation under trees within the fuel modification area shall be maintained at a height that will preclude ground fire from spreading in the tree crown. [**1144:**6.2.4]

17.3.5.2.1.5* Tree crowns within the structure ignition zone shall be spaced to prevent structure ignition from radiant heat. [**1144:**6.2.5]

17.3.5.2.1.6 The fuel modification plan shall include a maintenance element identifying and defining the responsibility for continued and periodic maintenance. [**1144:**6.2.6]

17.3.5.2.1.7 Chimneys and Flues.

17.3.5.2.1.7.1 Every fireplace and wood stove chimney and flue shall be provided with an approved spark arrester constructed of a minimum 12-gauge welded wire or woven wire mesh, with openings not exceeding ½ in. (12.7 mm). [**1144:**5.8.1]

17.3.5.2.1.7.2 Vegetation shall not be allowed within 10 ft (3 m) of a chimney outlet. [**1144:**5.8.2]

17.3.5.2.1.8* Accessory Structure(s). Accessory structures shall be constructed to meet the requirements of Chapter 5 of NFPA 1144 or shall be separated from the main structure by a minimum of 30 ft (9 m). [**1144:**5.9]

17.3.5.2.1.9 Mobile and Manufactured Homes.

17.3.5.2.1.9.1 Permanently located mobile and manufactured homes with an open space beneath shall have a skirt of noncombustible material or material that has a minimum fire-resistive rating of 20 minutes. [**1144:**5.10.1]

17.3.5.2.1.9.2 Any enclosed space beneath the mobile or manufactured home shall be vented according to 5.2.2 of NFPA 1144. [**1144:**5.10.2]

17.3.5.2.1.10 Vehicle Parking Areas. Vehicle parking areas within the immediate landscaped zone shall be maintained free of dry grasses and fine fuels that could be ignited by hot exhaust systems or firebrands. [1144:5.11]

17.3.5.2.1.11 Exterior Exposure Hazards.

17.3.5.2.1.11.1* Heat and flame sources that are unprotected or unsupervised shall not be permitted within 30 ft (9 m) of the primary structure. [1144:5.12.1]

17.3.5.2.1.11.2 Incinerators, outdoor fireplaces, permanent barbecues, and grills shall not be built, installed, or maintained in hazardous fire areas without prior approval of the AHJ. [1144:5.12.2]

17.3.5.2.1.11.3 Openings in incinerators, outdoor fireplaces, permanent barbecues, and grills shall be provided with an approved spark arrester, screen, or door. [1144:5.12.3]

17.3.5.2.1.11.4 Propane tanks and other flammable or combustible liquids storage shall conform to NFPA 58, *Liquefied Petroleum Gas Code*, and the wildland fire hazard mitigation plan required in 17.1.10. [1144:5.12.4]

17.3.5.2.1.11.5 Other combustible materials within 30 ft (9 m) of any structure shall be removed or stored in conformance with the wildland fire hazard mitigation plan as approved by the AHJ. [1144:5.12.5]

17.3.5.2.2 Where required by the AHJ because of extra hazardous conditions, additional areas shall be maintained to include additional defensible space from buildings or structures, trees adjacent to or overhanging a building shall be maintained free of deadwood, and the roof of a structure shall be free of leaves, needles, or other dead vegetative growth.

17.3.5.3 Roadways. Areas within 10 ft (3 m) on each side of portions of highways and private streets shall be cleared of combustible vegetation and other combustible growth. Single specimens of trees, shrubbery, or cultivated ground cover such as green grass, ivy, succulents, or similar plants used as ground covers shall be permitted to be exempt provided that they do not form a means of readily transmitting fire.

17.3.6 Unusual Circumstances. The AHJ shall determine that difficult terrain, danger of erosion, or other unusual circumstances could require additional safeguards.

17.3.7 Fire Roads, Firebreaks, and Emergency Access.

17.3.7.1 The provisions of 17.3.7 and Section 18.2 shall be used to determine the design, clearances, and provisions for emergency access (ingress and egress).

17.3.7.2 Unauthorized vehicles shall not be driven upon fire roads or firebreaks. Vehicles shall not be parked in a manner that obstructs the entrance to a fire road or firebreak.

17.3.7.3 Radio and television aerials, guy wires, and other obstructions shall not be installed or maintained on fire roads or firebreaks unless the vertical clearance is sufficient to allow the movement of fire and emergency apparatus.

17.3.7.4 Motorcycles, motor scooters, and motor vehicles shall not be operated within hazardous fire areas, except upon clearly established public or private roads.

17.3.8 Tampering with Fire Safety Equipment. See Section 10.7 for requirements on tampering with fire safety equipment.

17.3.9 Maintenance. See 4.5.8 for requirements on maintenance.

Chapter 18 Fire Department Access and Water Supply

18.1 General. Fire department access and water supplies shall comply with this chapter.

18.1.1 Application.

18.1.1.1 This chapter shall apply to public and privately owned fire apparatus access roads.

18.1.1.2 This chapter shall apply to public and privately owned fire hydrant systems.

18.1.2 Permits. Permits, where required, shall comply with Section 1.12.

18.1.3 Plans.

18.1.3.1 Fire Apparatus Access. Plans for fire apparatus access roads shall be submitted to the fire department for review and approval prior to construction.

18.1.3.2 Fire Hydrant Systems. Plans and specifications for fire hydrant systems shall be submitted to the fire department for review and approval prior to construction.

18.2 Fire Department Access.

18.2.1 Fire department access and fire department access roads shall be provided and maintained in accordance with Section 18.2.

18.2.2* Access to Structures or Areas.

18.2.2.1 Access Box(es). The AHJ shall have the authority to require an access box(es) to be installed in an accessible location where access to or within a structure or area is difficult because of security. The access box(es) shall be of an approved type listed in accordance with UL 1037.

18.2.2.2 Access to Gated Subdivisions or Developments. The AHJ shall have the authority to require fire department access be provided to gated subdivisions or developments through the use of an approved device or system.

18.2.2.3 Access Maintenance. The owner or occupant of a structure or area, with required fire department access as specified in 18.2.2.1 or 18.2.2.2, shall notify the AHJ when the access is modified in a manner that could prevent fire department access.

18.2.3 Fire Department Access Roads.

18.2.3.1 Required Access.

18.2.3.1.1 Approved fire department access roads shall be provided for every facility, building, or portion of a building hereafter constructed or relocated.

18.2.3.1.2 Fire department access roads shall consist of roadways, fire lanes, parking lot lanes, or a combination thereof.

18.2.3.1.3* The provisions of 18.2.3.1 through 18.2.3.2.2.1 shall be permitted to be modified by the AHJ where any of the following conditions exists:

(1) One- and two-family dwellings protected by an approved automatic sprinkler system in accordance with Section 13.1

(2) Existing one- and two-family dwellings
(3) Private garages having an area not exceeding 400 ft^2
(4) Carports having an area not exceeding 400 ft^2
(5) Agricultural buildings having an area not exceeding 400 ft^2
(6) Sheds and other detached buildings having an area not exceeding 400 ft^2

18.2.3.1.4 When fire department access roads cannot be installed due to location on property, topography, waterways, non-negotiable grades, or other similar conditions, the AHJ shall be authorized to require additional fire protection features.

18.2.3.2 Access to Building.

18.2.3.2.1 A fire department access road shall extend to within 50 ft (15 m) of at least one exterior door that can be opened from the outside and that provides access to the interior of the building.

18.2.3.2.1.1 Where a one- or two-family dwelling, or townhouse, is protected with an approved automatic sprinkler system that is installed in accordance with NFPA 13D or NFPA 13R, as applicable, the distance in 18.2.3.2.1 shall be permitted to be increased to 150 ft (46 m).

18.2.3.2.2 Fire department access roads shall be provided such that any portion of the facility or any portion of an exterior wall of the first story of the building is located not more than 150 ft (46 m) from fire department access roads as measured by an approved route around the exterior of the building or facility.

18.2.3.2.2.1 When buildings are protected throughout with an approved automatic sprinkler system that is installed in accordance with NFPA 13, NFPA 13D, or NFPA 13R, the distance in 18.2.3.2.2 shall be permitted to be increased to 450 ft (137 m).

18.2.3.3 Multiple Access Roads. More than one fire department access road shall be provided when it is determined by the AHJ that access by a single road could be impaired by vehicle congestion, condition of terrain, climatic conditions, or other factors that could limit access.

18.2.3.4 Specifications.

18.2.3.4.1 Dimensions.

18.2.3.4.1.1 Fire department access roads shall have an unobstructed width of not less than 20 ft (6.1 m).

18.2.3.4.1.2 Fire department access roads shall have an unobstructed vertical clearance of not less than 13 ft 6 in. (4.1 m).

18.2.3.4.1.2.1 Vertical clearance shall be permitted to be reduced, provided such reduction does not impair access by fire apparatus, and approved signs are installed and maintained indicating the established vertical clearance when approved.

18.2.3.4.1.2.2 Vertical clearances or widths shall be increased when vertical clearances or widths are not adequate to accommodate fire apparatus.

18.2.3.4.2 Surface. Fire department access roads shall be designed and maintained to support the imposed loads of fire apparatus and shall be provided with an all-weather driving surface.

18.2.3.4.3 Turning Radius.

18.2.3.4.3.1 The turning radius of a fire department access road shall be as approved by the AHJ.

18.2.3.4.3.2 Turns in fire department access roads shall maintain the minimum road width.

18.2.3.4.4 Dead Ends. Dead-end fire department access roads in excess of 150 ft (46 m) in length shall be provided with approved provisions for the fire apparatus to turn around.

18.2.3.4.5 Bridges.

18.2.3.4.5.1 When a bridge is required to be used as part of a fire department access road, it shall be constructed and maintained in accordance with nationally recognized standards.

18.2.3.4.5.2 The bridge shall be designed for a live load sufficient to carry the imposed loads of fire apparatus.

18.2.3.4.5.3 Vehicle load limits shall be posted at both entrances to bridges where required by the AHJ.

18.2.3.4.6 Grade.

18.2.3.4.6.1 The gradient for a fire department access road shall not exceed the maximum approved.

18.2.3.4.6.2* The angle of approach and departure for any means of fire department access road shall not exceed 1 ft drop in 20 ft (0.3 m drop in 6 m) or the design limitations of the fire apparatus of the fire department, and shall be subject to approval by the AHJ.

18.2.3.4.6.3 Fire department access roads connecting to roadways shall be provided with curb cuts extending at least 2 ft (0.61 m) beyond each edge of the fire lane.

18.2.3.4.7 Traffic Calming Devices. The design and use of traffic calming devices shall be approved by the AHJ.

18.2.3.5 Marking of Fire Apparatus Access Road.

18.2.3.5.1 Where required by the AHJ, approved signs, approved roadway surface markings, or other approved notices shall be provided and maintained to identify fire department access roads or to prohibit the obstruction thereof or both.

18.2.3.5.2 A marked fire apparatus access road shall also be known as a fire lane.

18.2.4* Obstruction and Control of Fire Department Access Road.

18.2.4.1 General.

18.2.4.1.1 The required width of a fire department access road shall not be obstructed in any manner, including by the parking of vehicles.

18.2.4.1.2 Minimum required widths and clearances established under 18.2.3.4 shall be maintained at all times.

18.2.4.1.3* Facilities and structures shall be maintained in a manner that does not impair or impede accessibility for fire department operations.

18.2.4.1.4 Entrances to fire department access roads that have been closed with gates and barriers in accordance with 18.2.4.2.1 shall not be obstructed by parked vehicles.

18.2.4.2 Closure of Accessways.

18.2.4.2.1 The AHJ shall be authorized to require the installation and maintenance of gates or other approved barricades across roads, trails, or other accessways not including public streets, alleys, or highways.

18.2.4.2.2 Where required, gates and barricades shall be secured in an approved manner.

18.2.4.2.3 Roads, trails, and other accessways that have been closed and obstructed in the manner prescribed by 18.2.4.2.1 shall not be trespassed upon or used unless authorized by the owner and the AHJ.

18.2.4.2.4 Public officers acting within their scope of duty shall be permitted to access restricted property identified in 18.2.4.2.1.

18.2.4.2.5 Locks, gates, doors, barricades, chains, enclosures, signs, tags, or seals that have been installed by the fire department or by its order or under its control shall not be removed, unlocked, destroyed, tampered with, or otherwise vandalized in any manner.

18.2.4.2.6 When authorized by the AHJ, public officers acting within their scope of duty shall be permitted to obtain access through secured means identified in 18.2.4.2.1.

18.3 Water Supplies.

18.3.1* An approved water supply capable of supplying the required fire flow for fire protection shall be provided to all premises upon which facilities, buildings, or portions of buildings are hereafter constructed or moved into the jurisdiction. The approved water supply shall be in accordance with Section 18.4.

18.3.1.1* Where no adequate or reliable water distribution system exists, approved reservoirs, pressure tanks, elevated tanks, fire department tanker shuttles, or other approved systems capable of providing the required fire flow shall be permitted.

18.4 Fire Flow Requirements for Buildings.

18.4.1* Scope.

18.4.1.1* The procedure determining fire flow requirements for buildings hereafter constructed or moved into the jurisdiction shall be in accordance with Section 18.4.

18.4.1.2 Section 18.4 shall not apply to structures other than buildings.

18.4.2 Definitions. See definitions 3.3.14.4, Fire Flow Area, and 3.3.119, Fire Flow.

18.4.3 Modifications.

18.4.3.1 Decreases in Fire Flow Requirements.

18.4.3.1.1* Fire flow requirements shall be permitted to be decreased by the AHJ for isolated buildings or a group of buildings in rural areas or suburban areas where the development of full fire flow requirements is impractical as determined by the AHJ.

18.4.3.1.2 The AHJ shall be authorized to establish conditions on fire flow reductions approved in accordance with 18.4.3.1.1 including, but not limited to, fire sprinkler protection, type of construction of the building, occupancy, development density, building size, and setbacks.

18.4.3.2 Increases in Fire Flow Requirements. The minimum required fire flow shall be permitted to be increased by the AHJ where conditions indicate an unusual susceptibility to group fires or conflagrations. An upward modification shall not be more than twice that required for the building under consideration.

18.4.4 Fire Flow Area.

18.4.4.1 General. The fire flow area shall be the total floor area of all floor levels of a building except as modified in 18.4.4.2.

18.4.4.2 Type I (443), Type I (332), and Type II (222) Construction. The fire flow area of a building constructed of Type I (443), Type I (332), and Type II (222) construction shall be the area of the three largest successive floors.

18.4.5 Fire Flow Requirements for Buildings.

18.4.5.1 One- and Two-Family Dwellings Not Exceeding 5000 ft^2 (464.5 m^2).

18.4.5.1.1 The minimum fire flow and flow duration requirements for one- and two-family dwellings having a fire flow area that does not exceed 5000 ft^2 (464.5 m^2) shall be 1000 gpm (3785 L/min) for 1 hour.

18.4.5.1.2* A reduction in required fire flow of 75 percent shall be permitted where the one- and two-family dwelling is provided with an approved automatic sprinkler system.

18.4.5.1.3* Where one- and two-family dwellings are proposed to be constructed in areas where water distribution systems providing fire flow were designed and installed prior to the effective date of this *Code*, the AHJ shall be authorized to accept the previously designed system fire flow where the one- and two-family dwellings are provided with approved automatic sprinkler systems.

18.4.5.1.4 A reduction in fire flow shall be permitted for building separation distance in accordance with 18.4.5.1.4 and Table 18.4.5.1.4.

Table 18.4.5.1.4 Permitted Fire Flow Reduction for Building Separation

Separation Distance Between Buildings on a Single Lot		Separation Distance to Lot Line or Easement[a]		Permitted Fire Flow Reduction
ft	m	ft	m	
>30 and ≤50	>9.1 and ≤15.2	>15 and ≤25	>4.6 and ≤7.6	25%
>50	>15.2	>25	>7.6	40%

[a]See 18.4.5.1.4.3.

18.4.5.1.4.1 Where multiple buildings are located on a single lot, the building separation distance shall be the distance between the buildings.

18.4.5.1.4.2 Where a building abuts a lot line, the building separation distance shall be the distance between the building and the lot line.

18.4.5.1.4.3 Where a building is contiguous to a public right of way or no-build easement, the separation distance shall be the distance between the building to the opposite side of the right of way or no-build easement.

18.4.5.1.4.4 Where multiple buildings are located on a single lot and abut a lot line, the building separation distance for determining fire flow reduction shall be the smallest of the two distances.

18.4.5.1.5* The reductions in 18.4.5.1.2, 18.4.5.1.3, and 18.4.5.1.4 shall not reduce the required fire flow to less than 500 gpm (1900 L/min).

18.4.5.2 One- and Two-Family Dwellings Exceeding 5000 ft^2 (464.5 m^2).

18.4.5.2.1 Fire flow and flow duration for dwellings having a fire flow area in excess of 5000 ft^2 (464.5 m^2) shall not be less than that specified in Table 18.4.5.2.1.

18.4.5.2.2 Required fire flow shall be reduced by 75 percent and the duration reduced to 1 hour where the one- and two-family dwelling is provided with an approved automatic sprinkler system.

18.4.5.2.3 A reduction in the required fire flow shall be permitted where a one- and two-family dwelling is separated from all lot lines in accordance with Table 18.4.5.1.4.

18.4.5.2.4 Required fire flow for one- and two-family dwellings protected by an approved automatic sprinkler system shall not exceed 2000 gpm (7571 L/min) for 1 hour.

18.4.5.2.5* The reductions in 18.4.5.2.2, and 18.4.5.2.3 shall not reduce the required fire flow to less than 500 gpm (1900 L/min) for 1 hour.

18.4.5.3 Buildings Other Than One- and Two-Family Dwellings.

18.4.5.3.1 The minimum fire flow and flow duration for buildings other than one- and two-family dwellings shall be as specified in Table 18.4.5.2.1.

18.4.5.3.2 Required fire flow shall be reduced by 75 percent when the building is protected throughout by an approved automatic sprinkler system. The resulting fire flow shall not be less than 1000 gpm (3785 L/min).

18.4.5.3.3 Required fire flow shall be reduced by 75 percent when the building is protected throughout by an approved automatic sprinkler system, which utilizes quick response sprinklers throughout. The resulting fire flow shall not be less than 600 gpm (2270 L/min).

18.4.5.3.4* Required fire flow for buildings protected by an approved automatic sprinkler system shall not exceed 2000 gpm (7571 L/min) for 2 hours.

18.4.5.3.5 Required fire flow for open parking structures that are not protected throughout by an approved automatic sprinkler system shall be reduced by 75 percent where all of the following conditions are met:

(1) The structure complies with the building code.
(2) The structure is of Type I or Type II construction.
(3) The structure is provided with a Class I standpipe system in accordance with NFPA 14. Class I standpipe systems of the manual dry type shall be permitted.
(4) The resulting fire flow is not less than 1000 gpm (3785 L/min).

18.4.5.4* Required Fire Flow and Automatic Sprinkler System Demand. For a building with an approved fire sprinkler system, the fire flow demand and the fire sprinkler system demand shall not be required to be added together. The water supply shall be capable of delivering the larger of the individual demands.

18.5 Fire Hydrants.

18.5.1 Fire Hydrant Locations and Distribution. Fire hydrants shall be provided in accordance with Section 18.5 for all new buildings, or buildings relocated into the jurisdiction unless otherwise permitted by 18.5.1.1 or 18.5.1.2.

18.5.1.1 Fire hydrants shall not be required where the water distribution system is not capable of providing a fire flow of greater than 500 gpm (1893 L/min) at a residual pressure of 20 psi (139.9 kPa).

18.5.1.2* Fire hydrants shall not be required where modification or extension of the water distribution system is deemed to be impractical by the AHJ.

18.5.1.3 The provisions of 18.5.1.1 and 18.5.1.2 shall not eliminate the fire flow requirements of Section 18.4.

18.5.1.4* The distances specified in Section 18.5 shall be measured along fire department access roads in accordance with 18.2.3.

18.5.1.5 Where fire department access roads are provided with median dividers incapable of being crossed by fire apparatus, or where fire department access roads have traffic counts of more than 30,000 vehicles per day, hydrants shall be placed on both sides of the fire department access road on an alternating basis, and the distances specified by Section 18.5 shall be measured independently of the hydrants on the opposite side of the fire department access road.

18.5.1.6 Fire hydrants shall be located not more than 12 ft (3.7 m) from the fire department access road.

18.5.2 Detached One- and Two-Family Dwellings. Fire hydrants shall be provided for detached one- and two-family dwellings in accordance with both of the following:

(1) The maximum distance to a fire hydrant from the closest point on the building shall not exceed 600 ft (122 m).
(2) The maximum distance between fire hydrants shall not exceed 800 ft (244 m).

18.5.3 Buildings Other than Detached One- and Two-Family Dwellings. Fire hydrants shall be provided for buildings other than detached one- and two-family dwellings in accordance with both of the following:

(1) The maximum distance to a fire hydrant from the closest point on the building shall not exceed 400 ft (76 m).
(2) The maximum distance between fire hydrants shall not exceed 500 ft (152 m).

18.5.4 Minimum Number of Fire Hydrants for Fire Flow.

18.5.4.1 The minimum number of fire hydrants needed to deliver the required fire flow for new buildings in accordance with Section 18.4 shall be determined in accordance with Section 18.5.4.

18.5.4.2 The aggregate fire flow capacity of all fire hydrants within 1000 ft (305 m) of the building, measured in accordance with 18.5.1.4 and 18.5.1.5, shall be not less than the required fire flow determined in accordance with Section 18.4.

18.5.4.3* The maximum fire flow capacity for which a fire hydrant shall be credited shall be as specified by Table 18.5.4.3. Capacities exceeding the values specified in Table 18.5.4.3 shall be permitted when local fire department operations have the ability to accommodate such values as determined by the fire department.

18.5.4.4 Fire hydrants required by 18.5.2 and 18.5.3 shall be included in the minimum number of fire hydrants for fire flow required by 18.5.4.

Table 18.4.5.2.1 Minimum Required Fire Flow and Flow Duration for Buildings

Fire Flow Area ft² (× 0.0929 for m²)					Fire Flow gpm† (× 3.785 for L/min)	Flow Duration (hours)
I(443), I(332), II(222)*	II(111), III(211)*	IV(2HH), V(111)*	II(000), III(200)*	V(000)*		
0–22,700	0–12,700	0–8200	0–5900	0–3600	1500	2
22,701–30,200	12,701–17,000	8201–10,900	5901–7900	3601–4800	1750	
30,201–38,700	17,001–21,800	10,901–12,900	7901–9800	4801–6200	2000	
38,701–48,300	21,801–24,200	12,901–17,400	9801–12,600	6201–7700	2250	
48,301–59,000	24,201–33,200	17,401–21,300	12,601–15,400	7701–9400	2500	
59,001–70,900	33,201–39,700	21,301–25,500	15,401–18,400	9401–11,300	2750	
70,901–83,700	39,701–47,100	25,501–30,100	18,401–21,800	11,301–13,400	3000	3
83,701–97,700	47,101–54,900	30,101–35,200	21,801–25,900	13,401–15,600	3250	
97,701–112,700	54,901–63,400	35,201–40,600	25,901–29,300	15,601–18,000	3500	
112,701–128,700	63,401–72,400	40,601–46,400	29,301–33,500	18,001–20,600	3750	
128,701–145,900	72,401–82,100	46,401–52,500	33,501–37,900	20,601–23,300	4000	4
145,901–164,200	82,101–92,400	52,501–59,100	37,901–42,700	23,301–26,300	4250	
164,201–183,400	92,401–103,100	59,101–66,000	42,701–47,700	26,301–29,300	4500	
183,401–203,700	103,101–114,600	66,001–73,300	47,701–53,000	29,301–32,600	4750	
203,701–225,200	114,601–126,700	73,301–81,100	53,001–58,600	32,601–36,000	5000	
225,201–247,700	126,701–139,400	81,101–89,200	58,601–65,400	36,001–39,600	5250	
247,701–271,200	139,401–152,600	89,201–97,700	65,401–70,600	39,601–43,400	5500	
271,201–295,900	152,601–166,500	97,701–106,500	70,601–77,000	43,401–47,400	5750	
Greater than 295,900	Greater than 166,500	106,501–115,800	77,001–83,700	47,401–51,500	6000	
		115,801–125,500	83,701–90,600	51,501–55,700	6250	
		125,501–135,500	90,601–97,900	55,701–60,200	6500	
		135,501–145,800	97,901–106,800	60,201–64,800	6750	
		145,801–156,700	106,801–113,200	64,801–69,600	7000	
		156,701–167,900	113,201–121,300	69,601–74,600	7250	
		167,901–179,400	121,301–129,600	74,601–79,800	7500	
		179,401–191,400	129,601–138,300	79,801–85,100	7750	
		Greater than 191,400	Greater than 138,300	Greater than 85,100	8000	

*Types of construction are based on NFPA 220.
†Measured at 20 psi (139.9 kPa).

Table 18.5.4.3 Maximum Fire Hydrant Fire Flow Capacity

Distance to Building[a]		Maximum Capacity[b]	
(ft)	(m)	(gpm)	(L/min)
≤ 250	≤ 76	1500	5678
> 250 and ≤ 500	> 76 and ≤ 152	1000	3785
> 500 and ≤ 1000	> 152 and ≤ 305	750	2839

[a]Measured in accordance with 18.5.1.4 and 18.5.1.5.
[b]Minimum 20 psi (139.9 kPa) residual pressure.

18.5.5 Testing and Maintenance.

18.5.5.1 Private water supply systems shall be tested and maintained in accordance with NFPA 25, *Standard for the Inspection, Testing, and Maintenance of Water-Based Fire Protection Systems*.

18.5.5.2 Public water supply systems providing fire flow shall be tested and maintained in accordance with ANSI/AWWA G200, *Standard for Distribution Systems Operation and Management*.

18.5.6 Accessibility. Fire hydrants and connections to other approved water supplies shall be accessible to the fire department.

18.5.7 Clear Space Around Hydrants.

18.5.7.1 A 36 in. (914 mm) clear space shall be maintained around the circumference of fire hydrants except as otherwise required or approved.

18.5.7.2 A clear space of not less than 60 in. (1524 mm) shall be provided in front of each hydrant connection having a diameter greater than 2½ in. (64 mm).

18.5.8 Protection. Where required by the AHJ, fire hydrants subject to vehicular damage shall be protected unless located within a public right of way.

18.5.9 Hydrants Out of Service. Where water supplies or fire hydrants are out of service for maintenance or repairs, a visible indicator acceptable to the AHJ shall be used to indicate that the hydrant is out of service.

18.5.10 Marking of Hydrants.

18.5.10.1 Fire hydrants shall be marked with an approved reflector affixed to the roadway surface where required by the AHJ.

18.5.10.2 Fire hydrants shall be marked with an approved flag or other device affixed to or proximate to the fire hydrant where required by the AHJ.

18.5.10.3* Where required by the AHJ, fire hydrants shall be color coded or otherwise marked with an approved system indicating the available flow capacity.

Chapter 19 Combustible Waste and Refuse

19.1 General.

19.1.1 Permits. Permits, where required, shall comply with Section 1.12.

19.1.2 Persons owning or having control of any property shall not allow any combustible waste material to accumulate in any area or in any manner that creates a fire hazard to life or property.

19.1.3 Combustible waste or refuse shall be properly stored or disposed of to prevent unsafe conditions.

19.1.4 Fire extinguishing capabilities approved by the AHJ including, but not limited to, fire extinguishers, water supply and hose, and earth-moving equipment shall be provided at waste disposal sites.

19.1.5 Burning debris shall not be dumped at a waste disposal site except at a remote location on the site where fire extinguishment can be accomplished before compacting, covering, or other disposal activity is carried out. *(See Section 10.10 for additional guidance.)*

19.1.6 Electrical Wiring.

19.1.6.1 Electrical wiring and equipment in any combustible fiber storage room or building shall be installed in accordance with the requirements of Section 11.1 and *NFPA 70, National Electrical Code,* for Class III hazardous locations.

19.1.6.2 The AHJ shall be responsible for designating the areas that require hazardous location electrical classifications and shall classify the areas in accordance with the classification system set forth in NFPA 70.

19.1.7 No Smoking.

19.1.7.1 No smoking or open flame shall be permitted in any area where combustible fibers are handled or stored or within 50 ft (15 m) of any uncovered pile of such fibers.

19.1.7.2 "No Smoking" signs shall be posted.

19.1.8 Vehicles or Conveyances Used to Transport Combustible Waste or Refuse.

19.1.8.1 Vehicles or conveyances used to transport combustible waste or refuse over public thoroughfares shall have all cargo space covered and maintained tight enough to ensure against ignition from external fire sources and the scattering of burning and combustible debris that can come in contact with ignition sources.

19.1.8.2 Transporting burning waste or refuse shall be prohibited.

19.1.8.3 Trucks or automobiles, other than mechanical handling equipment and approved industrial trucks as listed in NFPA 505, *Fire Safety Standard for Powered Industrial Trucks Including Type Designations, Areas of Use, Conversions, Maintenance, and Operations*, shall not enter any fiber storage room or building but shall be permitted to be used at loading platforms.

19.2 Combustible Waste and Refuse.

19.2.1 Rubbish Containers.

19.2.1.1 General. Rubbish containers kept outside of rooms or vaults shall not exceed 40.5 ft^3 (1.15 m^3) capacity.

19.2.1.1.1 Containers exceeding a capacity of 5⅓ ft^3 [40 gal (0.15 m^3)] shall be provided with lids.

19.2.1.1.2 Such containers and lids as described in 19.2.1.1.1 shall be constructed of noncombustible materials or nonmetallic materials complying with 19.2.1.2.

19.2.1.2 Nonmetallic Containers.

19.2.1.2.1* Nonmetallic rubbish containers exceeding a capacity of 5⅓ ft^3 [40 gal (0.15 m^3)] shall be manufactured of materials having a peak rate of heat release not exceeding 300 kW/m^2 at a flux of 50 kW/m^2 when tested in the horizontal orientation, at a thickness as used in the container but not less than of 0.25 in. (6 mm), in accordance with ASTM E 1354, *Test Method for Heat and Visible Smoke Release Rates for Materials and Products Using an Oxygen Consumption Calorimeter*.

19.2.1.2.2 Such containers shall be permanently labeled indicating capacity and peak rate of heat release.

19.2.1.3 Removal. Combustible rubbish stored in containers outside of noncombustible vaults or rooms shall be removed from buildings at least once each working day.

19.2.1.4 Rubbish Within Dumpsters. Dumpsters and containers with an individual capacity of 1.5 yd^3 [40.5 ft^3 (1.15 m^3)] or more shall not be stored in buildings or placed within 10 ft (3 m) of combustible walls, openings, or combustible roof eave lines.

19.2.1.4.1 Areas containing dumpsters or containers shall be protected by an approved automatic sprinkler system and enclosed with a fire resistance rating of 1 hour.

19.2.1.4.2 Structures of Types I and II fire-resistive construction used for dumpster or container storage shall be located not less than 10 ft (3 m) from openings and other buildings.

19.2.1.5 Commercial Rubbish-Handling Operations. Occupancies exclusively performing commercial rubbish handling or recycling shall maintain rubbish or product to be processed or recycled in one of the following ways:

(1) In approved vaults
(2) In covered metal or metal-lined receptacles or bins
(3) Completely baled and stacked in an orderly manner in an approved location

19.2.1.6 Approved metal receptacles with self-closing covers shall be provided for the storage or disposal of oil-soaked waste or cloths.

Chapter 20   Occupancy Fire Safety

20.1 Assembly Occupancies.

20.1.1 Application. New and existing assembly occupancies shall comply with Section 20.1 and NFPA *101*.

20.1.1.1 Permits. Permits, where required, shall comply with Section 1.12.

20.1.1.2 Indoor children's playground structures shall also comply with Section 10.19.

20.1.2 Flame-Retardant Requirements.

20.1.2.1 Combustible scenery of cloth, film, vegetation (dry), and similar materials shall comply with one of the following:

(1) They shall meet the flame propagation performance criteria contained in Test Method 1 or Test Method 2, as appropriate, of NFPA 701, *Standard Methods of Fire Tests for Flame Propagation of Textiles and Films*.
(2) They shall exhibit a heat release rate not exceeding 100 kW when tested in accordance with NFPA 289, *Standard Method of Fire Test for Individual Fuel Packages*, using the 20 kW ignition source. [*101:* 12.4.5.11.1; *101:* 13.4.5.11.1]

20.1.2.2 Foamed plastics (*see definition of cellular or foamed plastic in 3.3.41 of NFPA 101*) shall be permitted to be used if they exhibit a heat release rate not exceeding 100 kW when tested in accordance with NFPA 289, *Standard Method of Fire Test for Individual Fuel Packages*, using the 20 kW ignition source or by specific approval of the AHJ. [*101:* 12.4.5.11.2; *101:* 13.4.5.11.2]

20.1.2.3 Scenery and stage properties not separated from the audience by proscenium opening protection shall be of noncombustible materials, limited-combustible materials, or fire-retardant-treated wood. [*101:* 13.4.5.11.3]

20.1.2.4 In theaters, motion picture theaters, and television stage settings, with or without horizontal projections, and in simulated caves and caverns of foamed plastic, any single fuel package shall have a heat release rate not to exceed 100 kW where tested in accordance with one of the following:

(1) UL 1975, *Standard for Fire Tests for Foamed Plastics Used for Decorative Purposes*
(2) NFPA 289, *Standard Method of Fire Test for Individual Fuel Packages*, using the 20 kW ignition source [*101:* 12.4.5.11.4; *101:* 13.4.5.11.4]

20.1.3 Interior Finish.

20.1.3.1 General. Interior finish shall be in accordance with Section 12.5. [*101:* 12.3.3.1]

20.1.3.2 Corridors, Lobbies, and Enclosed Stairways. New and existing interior wall and ceiling finish materials complying with Section 12.5 shall be Class A or Class B in all corridors and lobbies and shall be Class A in enclosed stairways. [*101:* 12.3.3.2; *101:* 13.3.3.2]

20.1.3.3 Assembly Areas. New and existing interior wall and ceiling finish materials complying with Section 12.5 shall be Class A or Class B in general assembly areas having occupant loads of more than 300 and shall be Class A, Class B, or Class C in assembly areas having occupant loads of 300 or fewer. [*101:* 12.3.3.3; *101:* 13.3.3.3]

20.1.3.4 Screens. New and existing screens on which pictures are projected shall comply with requirements of Class A or Class B interior finish in accordance with Section 12.5. [*101:* 12.3.3.4; *101:* 13.3.3.4]

20.1.3.5 Interior Floor Finish.

20.1.3.5.1 New interior floor finish shall comply with Section 12.5. [*101:* 12.3.3.5.1]

20.1.3.5.2 New interior floor finish in exit enclosures and exit access corridors and in spaces not separated from them by walls complying with 12.3.6 of NFPA *101* shall be not less than Class II. [*101:* 12.3.3.5.2]

20.1.3.5.3 New interior floor finish shall comply with 12.5.8.1 or 12.5.8.2, as applicable. [*101:* 12.3.3.5.3]

20.1.3.5.4 Existing Interior Floor Finish. (Reserved) [*101:* 13.3.3.5]

20.1.4* Special Amusement Buildings.

20.1.4.1* General. Special amusement buildings, regardless of occupant load, shall meet the requirements for assembly occupancies in addition to the requirements of 20.1.4, unless the special amusement building is a multilevel play structure that is not more than 10 ft (3050 mm) in height and has aggregate horizontal projections not exceeding 160 ft² (15 m²). [*101:* 12.4.8.1; *101:* 13.4.8.1]

20.1.4.2* Automatic Sprinklers. Every special amusement building, other than buildings or structures not exceeding 10 ft (3050 mm) in height and not exceeding 160 ft² (15 m²) in aggregate horizontal projection, shall be protected throughout by an approved, supervised automatic sprinkler system installed and maintained in accordance with Section 13.3. [*101:* 12.4.8.2; *101:* 13.4.8.2]

20.1.4.3 Temporary Water Supply. Where the special amusement building required to be sprinklered by 20.1.4.2 is movable or portable, the sprinkler water supply shall be permitted to be provided by an approved temporary means. [*101:* 12.4.8.3; *101:* 13.4.8.3]

20.1.4.4 Smoke Detection. Where the nature of the special amusement building is such that it operates in reduced lighting levels, the building shall be protected throughout by an approved automatic smoke detection system in accordance with Section 13.7. [*101:* 12.4.8.4; *101:* 13.4.8.4]

20.1.4.5 Alarm Initiation. Actuation of any smoke detection system device shall sound an alarm at a constantly attended location on the premises. [*101:* 12.4.8.5, *101:* 13.4.8.5]

20.1.4.6 Illumination. Actuation of the automatic sprinkler system, or any other suppression system, or actuation of a smoke detection system having an approved verification or cross-zoning operation capability shall provide for the following:

(1) Increase in illumination in the means of egress to that required by Section 14.12
(2) Termination of any conflicting or confusing sounds and visuals [*101:* 12.4.8.6; *101:* 13.4.8.6]

20.1.4.7 Exit Marking.

20.1.4.7.1 Exit marking shall be in accordance with Section 14.14. [*101:* 12.4.8.7.1; *101:* 13.4.8.7.1]

20.1.4.7.2 Floor proximity exit signs shall be provided in accordance with 14.14.1.6. [*101:* 12.4.8.7.2; *101:* 13.4.8.7.2]

20.1.4.7.3* In special amusement buildings where mazes, mirrors, or other designs are used to confound the egress path, approved directional exit marking that becomes apparent in an emergency shall be provided. [*101:* 12.4.8.7.3; *101:* 13.4.8.7.3]

20.1.4.8 Interior Finish. Interior wall and ceiling finish materials complying with Section 12.5 shall be Class A throughout. [*101:* 12.4.8.8; *101:* 13.4.8.8]

20.1.5 Operating Features.

20.1.5.1 Means of Egress Inspection.

20.1.5.1.1 The building owner or agent shall inspect the means of egress to ensure it is maintained free of obstructions, and correct any deficiencies found, prior to each opening of the building to the public. [*101:* 12.7.1.1; *101:* 13.7.1.1]

20.1.5.1.2 The building owner or agent shall prepare and maintain records of the date and time of each inspection on approved forms, listing any deficiencies found and actions taken to correct them. [*101:* 12.7.1.2; *101:* 13.7.1.2]

20.1.5.1.3 Inspection of Door Openings. Door openings shall be inspected in accordance with 7.2.1.15 of NFPA *101*. [*101:* 12.7.1.3]

20.1.5.2 Special Provisions for Food Service Operations.

20.1.5.2.1 All devices in connection with the preparation of food shall be installed and operated to avoid hazard to the safety of occupants. [*101:* 12.7.2.1; *101:* 13.7.2.1]

20.1.5.2.2 All devices in connection with the preparation of food shall be of an approved type and shall be installed in an approved manner. [*101:* 12.7.2.2; *101:* 13.7.2.2]

20.1.5.2.3 Food preparation facilities shall be protected in accordance with Chapter 50 (NFPA 96) and shall not be required to have openings protected between food preparation areas and dining areas. [*101:* 12.7.2.3; *101:* 13.7.2.3]

20.1.5.2.4 Portable cooking equipment that is not flue-connected shall be permitted only as follows:

(1) Equipment fueled by small heat sources that can be readily extinguished by water, such as candles or alcohol-burning equipment, including solid alcohol, shall be permitted to be used, provided that precautions satisfactory to the AHJ are taken to prevent ignition of any combustible materials.
(2) Candles shall be permitted to be used on tables used for food service where securely supported on substantial noncombustible bases located to avoid danger of ignition of combustible materials and only where approved by the AHJ.
(3) Candle flames shall be protected.
(4) "Flaming sword" or other equipment involving open flames and flamed dishes, such as cherries jubilee or crêpes suzette, shall be permitted to be used, provided that precautions subject to the approval of the AHJ are taken.
(5) Listed and approved LP-Gas commercial food service appliances shall be permitted to be used where in accordance with Chapter 69. [*101:* 12.7.2.4; *101:* 13.7.2.4]

20.1.5.2.4.1 Permits. Permits, where required, shall comply with Section 1.12.

20.1.5.3 Open Flame Devices and Pyrotechnics. No open flame devices or pyrotechnic devices shall be used in any assembly occupancy, unless otherwise permitted by one of the following:

(1) Pyrotechnic special effect devices shall be permitted to be used on stages before proximate audiences for ceremonial or religious purposes, as part of a demonstration in exhibits, or as part of a performance, provided that both of the following criteria are met:
   (a) Precautions satisfactory to the AHJ are taken to prevent ignition of any combustible material.
   (b) Use of the pyrotechnic device complies with Section 65.3.
(2) Flame effects before an audience shall be permitted in accordance with Section 65.4.
(3) Open flame devices shall be permitted to be used in the following situations, provided that precautions satisfactory to the AHJ are taken to prevent ignition of any combustible material or injury to occupants:
   (a)*For ceremonial or religious purposes
   (b) On stages and platforms where part of a performance

(c) Where candles on tables are securely supported on substantial noncombustible bases and candle flame is protected

(4) The requirement of 20.1.5.3 shall not apply to heat-producing equipment complying with 11.2.2.
(5) The requirement of 20.1.5.3 shall not apply to food service operations in accordance with 20.1.5.2.
(6) Gas lights shall be permitted to be used, provided that precautions are taken, subject to the approval of the AHJ, to prevent ignition of any combustible materials. [*101:* 12.7.3; *101:* 13.7.3]

20.1.5.3.1 Permits. Permits, where required, shall comply with Section 1.12.

20.1.5.4 Furnishings, Decorations, and Scenery.

20.1.5.4.1* Fabrics and films used for decorative purposes, all draperies and curtains, and similar furnishings shall be in accordance with the provisions of 12.6.2. [*101:* 12.7.4.1; *101:* 13.7.4.1]

20.1.5.4.2 The AHJ shall impose controls on the quantity and arrangement of combustible contents in assembly occupancies to provide an adequate level of safety to life from fire. [*101:* 12.7.4.2; *101:* 13.7.4.2]

20.1.5.4.3* Exposed foamed plastic materials and unprotected materials containing foamed plastic used for decorative purposes or stage scenery shall have a heat release rate not exceeding 100 kW where tested in accordance with one of the following:

(1) UL 1975, *Standard for Fire Tests for Foamed Plastics Used for Decorative Purposes*
(2) NFPA 289, *Standard Method of Fire Test for Individual Fuel Packages*, using the 20 kW ignition source [*101:* 12.7.4.3; *101:* 13.7.4.3]

20.1.5.4.4 The requirement of 20.1.5.4.3 shall not apply to individual foamed plastic items and items containing foamed plastic where the foamed plastic does not exceed 1 lb (0.45 kg) in weight. [*101:* 12.7.4.4; *101:* 13.7.4.4]

20.1.5.5 Special Provisions for Exposition Facilities.

20.1.5.5.1 Permits. Permits, where required, shall comply with Section 1.12.

20.1.5.5.2 General. No display or exhibit shall be installed or operated to interfere in any way with access to any required exit or with the visibility of any required exit or required exit sign; nor shall any display block access to fire-fighting equipment. [*101:* 12.7.5.1; *101:* 13.7.5.1]

20.1.5.5.3 Materials Not on Display. A storage room having an enclosure consisting of a smoke barrier having a minimum 1-hour fire resistance rating and protected by an automatic extinguishing system shall be provided for combustible materials not on display, including combustible packing crates used to ship exhibitors' supplies and products. [*101:* 12.7.5.2; *101:* 13.7.5.2]

20.1.5.5.4 Exhibits.

20.1.5.5.4.1 Exhibits shall comply with 20.1.5.5.4.2 through 20.1.5.5.4.11. [*101:* 12.7.5.3.1; *101:* 13.7.5.3.1]

20.1.5.5.4.2 The travel distance within the exhibit booth or exhibit enclosure to an exit access aisle shall not exceed 50 ft (15 m). [*101:* 12.7.5.3.2; *101:* 13.7.5.3.2]

20.1.5.5.4.3 The upper deck of multilevel exhibits exceeding 300 ft^2 (28 m^2) shall have not less than two remote means of egress. [*101:* 12.7.5.3.3; *101:* 13.7.5.3.3]

20.1.5.5.4.4 Exhibit booth construction materials shall be limited to the following:

(1) Noncombustible or limited-combustible materials
(2) Wood exceeding ¼ in. (6.3 mm) nominal thickness
(3) Wood that is pressure-treated, fire-retardant wood meeting the requirements of NFPA 703, *Standard for Fire Retardant–Treated Wood and Fire-Retardant Coatings for Building Materials*
(4) Flame-retardant materials complying with one of the following:
   (a) They shall meet the flame propagation performance criteria contained in Test Method 1 or Test Method 2, as appropriate, of NFPA 701, *Standard Methods of Fire Tests for Flame Propagation of Textiles and Films*.
   (b) They shall exhibit a heat release rate not exceeding 100 kW when tested in accordance with NFPA 289, *Standard Method of Fire Test for Individual Fuel Packages*, using the 20 kW ignition source.
(5) Textile wall coverings, such as carpeting and similar products used as wall or ceiling finishes, complying with the provisions of 10.2.2 and 10.2.4 of NFPA *101*
(6) Plastics limited to those that comply with Sections 12.3.3 and 10.2 of NFPA *101*
(7) Foamed plastics and materials containing foamed plastics having a heat release rate for any single fuel package that does not exceed 100 kW where tested in accordance with one of the following:
   (a) UL 1975, *Standard for Fire Tests for Foamed Plastics Used for Decorative Purposes*
   (b) NFPA 289, *Standard Method of Fire Test for Individual Fuel Packages*, using the 20 kW ignition source
(8) Cardboard, honeycombed paper, and other combustible materials having a heat release rate for any single fuel package that does not exceed 150 kW where tested in accordance with one of the following:
   (a) UL 1975
   (b) NFPA 289, using the 20 kW ignition source [*101:* 12.7.5.3.4; *101:* 13.7.5.3.4]

20.1.5.5.4.5 Curtains, drapes, and decorations shall comply with 12.6.2. [*101:* 12.7.5.3.5; *101:* 13.7.5.3.5]

20.1.5.5.4.6 Acoustical and decorative material including, but not limited to, cotton, hay, paper, straw, moss, split bamboo, and wood chips shall be flame-retardant treated to the satisfaction of the AHJ. [*101:* 12.7.5.3.6; *101:* 13.7.5.3.6]

20.1.5.5.4.6.1 Materials that cannot be treated for flame retardancy shall not be used. [*101:* 12.7.5.3.6.1; *101:* 13.7.5.3.6.1]

20.1.5.5.4.6.2 Foamed plastics, and materials containing foamed plastics and used as decorative objects such as, but not limited to, mannequins, murals, and signs, shall have a heat release rate for any single fuel package that does not exceed 150 kW where tested in accordance with one of the following:

(1) UL 1975, *Standard for Fire Tests for Foamed Plastics Used for Decorative Purposes*
(2) NFPA 289, *Standard Method of Fire Test for Individual Fuel Packages*, using the 20 kW ignition source [*101:* 12.7.5.3.6.2; *101:* 13.7.5.3.6.2]

20.1.5.5.4.6.3 Where the aggregate area of acoustical and decorative materials is less than 10 percent of the individual floor or wall area, such materials shall be permitted to be used subject to the approval of the AHJ. [*101:* 12.7.5.3.6.3; *101:* 13.7.5.3.6.3]

20.1.5.5.4.7 The following shall be protected by automatic extinguishing systems:

(1) Single-level exhibit booths exceeding 300 ft^2 (28 m^2) and covered with a ceiling
(2) Each level of multilevel exhibit booths, including the uppermost level where the uppermost level is covered with a ceiling [*101:* 12.7.5.3.7; *101:* 13.7.5.3.7]

20.1.5.5.4.7.1 The requirements of 20.1.5.5.4.7 shall not apply where otherwise permitted by the following:

(1) Ceilings that are constructed of open grate design or listed dropout ceilings in accordance with NFPA 13, *Standard for the Installation of Sprinkler Systems*, shall not be considered ceilings within the context of 20.1.5.5.4.7.
(2) Vehicles, boats, and similar exhibited products having over 100 ft^2 (9.3 m^2) of roofed area shall be provided with smoke detectors acceptable to the AHJ.
(3)*The requirement of 20.1.5.5.4.7(2) shall not apply where fire protection of multilevel exhibit booths is consistent with the criteria developed through a life safety evaluation of the exhibition hall in accordance with 12.4.1 or 13.4.1 of NFPA *101*, subject to approval of the AHJ. [*101:* 12.7.5.3.7.1; *101:* 13.7.5.3.7.1]

20.1.5.5.4.7.2 A single exhibit or group of exhibits with ceilings that do not require sprinklers shall be separated by a distance of not less than 10 ft (3050 mm) where the aggregate ceiling exceeds 300 ft^2 (28 m^2). [*101:* 12.7.5.3.7.2; *101:* 13.7.5.3.7.2]

20.1.5.5.4.7.3 The water supply and piping for the sprinkler system shall be permitted to be of an approved temporary means that is provided by a domestic water supply, a standpipe system, or a sprinkler system. [*101:* 12.7.5.3.7.3; *101:* 13.7.5.3.7.3]

20.1.5.5.4.8 Open flame devices within exhibit booths shall comply with 20.1.5.3. [*101:* 12.7.5.3.8; *101:* 13.7.5.3.8]

20.1.5.5.4.9 Cooking and food-warming devices in exhibit booths shall comply with 20.1.5.2 and all of the following:

(1) Gas-fired devices shall comply with the following:
  (a) Natural gas-fired devices shall comply with Section 11.4.
  (b) The requirement of 20.1.5.5.4.9(1)(a) shall not apply to compressed natural gas where permitted by the AHJ.
  (c) The use of LP-Gas cylinders shall be prohibited.
  (d) Nonrefillable LP-Gas cylinders shall be approved for use where permitted by the AHJ.
(2) The devices shall be isolated from the public by not less than 48 in. (1220 mm) or by a barrier between the devices and the public.
(3) Multi-well cooking equipment using combustible oils or solids shall comply with Chapter 50.
(4) Single-well cooking equipment using combustible oils or solids shall meet all of the following criteria:
  (a) The equipment shall have lids available for immediate use.
  (b) The equipment shall be limited to 2 ft^2 (0.2 m^2) of cooking surface.
  (c) The equipment shall be placed on noncombustible surface materials.
  (d) The equipment shall be separated from each other by a horizontal distance of not less than 24 in. (610 mm).
  (e) The requirement of 20.1.5.5.4.9(4)(d) shall not apply to multiple single-well cooking equipment where the aggregate cooking surface area does not exceed 2 ft^2 (0.2 m^2).
  (f) The equipment shall be kept at a horizontal distance of not less than 24 in. (610 mm) from any combustible material.
(5) A portable fire extinguisher in accordance with Section 13.6 shall be provided within the booth for each device, or an approved automatic extinguishing system shall be provided. [*101:* 12.7.5.3.9; *101:* 13.7.5.3.9]

20.1.5.5.4.10 Combustible materials within exhibit booths shall be limited to a one-day supply. Storage of combustible materials behind the booth shall be prohibited. (*See 20.1.5.4.2 and 20.1.5.5.3.*) [*101:* 12.7.5.3.10; *101:* 13.7.5.3.10]

20.1.5.5.4.11 Plans for the exposition, in an acceptable form, shall be submitted to the AHJ for approval prior to setting up any exhibit. [*101:* 12.7.5.3.11; *101:* 13.7.5.3.11]

20.1.5.5.4.11.1 The plan shall show all details of the proposed exposition. [*101:* 12.7.5.3.11.1; *101:* 13.7.5.3.11.1]

20.1.5.5.4.11.2 No exposition shall occupy any exposition facility without approved plans. [*101:* 12.7.5.3.11.2; *101:* 13.7.5.3.11.2]

20.1.5.5.4.12 Vehicles. Vehicles on display within an exposition facility shall comply with 20.1.5.5.4.12.1 through 20.1.5.5.4.12.5. [*101:* 12.7.5.4; *101:* 13.7.5.4]

20.1.5.5.4.12.1 All fuel tank openings shall be locked and sealed in an approved manner to prevent the escape of vapors; fuel tanks shall not contain in excess of one-half their capacity or contain in excess of 10 gal (38 L) of fuel, whichever is less. [*101:* 12.7.5.4.1; *101:* 13.7.5.4.1]

20.1.5.5.4.12.2 At least one battery cable shall be removed from the batteries used to start the vehicle engine, and the disconnected battery cable shall then be taped. [*101:* 12.7.5.4.2; *101:* 13.7.5.4.2]

20.1.5.5.4.12.3 Batteries used to power auxiliary equipment shall be permitted to be kept in service. [*101:* 12.7.5.4.3; *101:* 13.7.5.4.3]

20.1.5.5.4.12.4 Fueling or defueling of vehicles shall be prohibited. [*101:* 12.7.5.4.4; *101:* 13.7.5.4.4]

20.1.5.5.4.12.5 Vehicles shall not be moved during exhibit hours. [*101:* 12.7.5.4.5; *101:* 13.7.5.4.5]

20.1.5.5.4.13 Prohibited Materials.

20.1.5.5.4.13.1 The following items shall be prohibited within exhibit halls:

(1) Compressed flammable gases
(2) Flammable or combustible liquids
(3) Hazardous chemicals or materials
(4) Class II or greater lasers, blasting agents, and explosives [*101:* 12.7.5.5.1; *101:* 13.7.5.5.1]

20.1.5.5.4.13.2 The AHJ shall be permitted to allow the limited use of any items specified in 20.1.5.5.4.13.1 under special circumstances. [*101:* 12.7.5.5.2; *101:* 13.7.5.5.2]

20.1.5.6 Crowd Managers.

20.1.5.6.1 Assembly occupancies shall be provided with a minimum of one trained crowd manager or crowd manager supervisor. Where the occupant load exceeds 250, additional trained crowd managers or crowd manager supervisors shall be provided at a ratio of 1 crowd manager or crowd manager supervisor for every 250 occupants, unless otherwise permitted by one of the following:

(1) This requirement shall not apply to assembly occupancies used exclusively for religious worship with an occupant load not exceeding 500.
(2) The ratio of trained crowd managers to occupants shall be permitted to be reduced where, in the opinion of the AHJ, the existence of an approved, supervised automatic sprinkler system and the nature of the event warrant. [*101:* 12.7.6.1; *101:* 13.7.6.1]

20.1.5.6.2* The crowd manager shall receive approved training in crowd management techniques. [*101:* 12.7.6.2; *101:* 13.7.6.2]

20.1.5.6.3 Duties and responsibilities for the crowd manager and crowd manager supervisor shall be documented within a written emergency plan as required by 12.7.13 of NFPA *101*. [*101:* 12.7.6.3; *101:* 13.7.6.3]

20.1.5.6.4* The training for the duties and responsibilities of crowd managers shall include the following:

(1) Understanding crowd manager roles and responsibilities
(2) Understanding safety and security hazards that can endanger public assembly
(3) Understanding crowd management techniques
(4) Introduction to fire safety and fire safety equipment
(5) Understanding methods of evacuation and movement
(6) Understanding procedures for reporting emergencies
(7) Understanding crowd management emergency response procedures
(8) Understanding the paths of travel and exits, facility evacuation and emergency response procedures and, where provided, facility shelter-in-place procedures
(9) Familiarization with the venue and guest services training
(10) Other specific event-warranted training [*101:* 12.7.6.4; *101:* 13.7.6.4]

20.1.5.6.5 The training for the duties and responsibilities of crowd manager supervisors shall include the following:

(1) The duties described in 20.1.5.6.4
(2) Understanding crowd manager supervisor roles and responsibilities
(3) Understanding of incident management procedures
(4) Understanding the facility evacuation plan
(5) Understanding the facility command structure [*101:* 12.7.6.5; *101:* 13.7.6.5]

20.1.5.7* Fire Detail. Fire details, if deemed necessary in any assembly occupancy, shall be determined by the AHJ.

20.1.5.8* Drills.

20.1.5.8.1 The employees or attendants of assembly occupancies shall be trained and drilled in the duties they are to perform in case of fire, panic, or other emergency to effect orderly exiting. [*101:* 12.7.7.1; *101:* 13.7.7.1]

20.1.5.8.2 Employees or attendants of assembly occupancies shall be instructed in the proper use of portable fire extinguishers and other manual fire suppression equipment where provided. [*101:* 12.7.7.2; *101:* 13.7.7.2]

20.1.5.8.3* In the following assembly occupancies, an audible announcement shall be made, or a projected image shall be shown, prior to the start of each program that notifies occupants of the location of the exits to be used in case of a fire or other emergency:

(1) Theaters
(2) Motion picture theaters
(3) Auditoriums
(4) Other similar assembly occupancies with occupant loads exceeding 300 where there are noncontinuous programs [*101:* 12.7.7.3; *101:* 13.7.7.3]

20.1.5.8.4 The requirement of 20.1.5.8.3 shall not apply to assembly occupancies in schools where used for nonpublic events. [*101:* 12.7.7.4; *101:* 13.7.7.4]

20.1.5.9 Smoking.

20.1.5.9.1 Smoking in assembly occupancies shall be regulated by the AHJ. [*101:* 12.7.8.1; *101:* 13.7.8.1]

20.1.5.9.2 In rooms or areas where smoking is prohibited, plainly visible signs shall be posted that read as follows:

NO SMOKING
[*101:* 12.7.8.2; *101:* 13.7.8.2]

20.1.5.9.3 No person shall smoke in prohibited areas that are so posted, unless permitted by the AHJ under both of the following conditions:

(1) Smoking shall be permitted on a stage only where it is a necessary and rehearsed part of a performance.
(2) Smoking shall be permitted only where the smoker is a regular performing member of the cast. [*101:* 12.7.8.3; *101:* 13.7.8.3]

20.1.5.9.4 Where smoking is permitted, suitable ashtrays or receptacles shall be provided in convenient locations. [*101:* 12.7.8.4; *101:* 13.7.8.4]

20.1.5.10 Seating.

20.1.5.10.1 Secured Seating.

20.1.5.10.1.1 Seats in assembly occupancies accommodating more than 200 persons shall be securely fastened to the floor, except where fastened together in groups of not less than three and as permitted by 20.1.5.10.1.2 and 20.1.5.10.2. [*101:* 12.7.9.1.1; *101:* 13.7.9.1.1]

20.1.5.10.1.2 Balcony and box seating areas that are separated from other areas by rails, guards, partial-height walls, or other physical barriers and have a maximum of 14 seats shall be exempt from the requirement of 20.1.5.10.1.1. [*101:* 12.7.9.1.2; *101:* 13.7.9.1.2]

20.1.5.10.2 Unsecured Seating.

20.1.5.10.2.1 Seats not secured to the floor shall be permitted in restaurants, night clubs, and other occupancies where fastening seats to the floor might be impracticable. [*101:* 12.7.9.2.1; *101:* 13.7.9.2.1]

20.1.5.10.2.2 Unsecured seats shall be permitted, provided that, in the area used for seating, excluding such areas as dance floors and stages, there is not more than one seat for each 15 ft^2 (1.4 m^2) of net floor area, and adequate aisles to reach exits are maintained at all times. [*101:* 12.7.9.2.2; *101:* 13.7.9.2.2]

20.1.5.10.2.3 Seating diagrams shall be submitted for approval by the AHJ to permit an increase in occupant load per 14.8.1.3. [*101:* 12.7.9.2.3; *101:* 13.7.9.2.3]

20.1.5.10.3 Festival Seating. Festival seating, as defined in 3.3.110, shall be prohibited within a building, unless otherwise permitted by one of the following:

(1) Festival seating shall be permitted in assembly occupancies having occupant loads of 250 or less.
(2) Festival seating shall be permitted in assembly occupancies where occupant loads exceed 250, provided that an approved life safety evaluation has been performed. *(See 10.15.3.)* [*101:* 12.2.5.4.1; *101:* 13.2.5.4.1]

20.1.5.10.4 Occupant Load Posting.

20.1.5.10.4.1 Every room constituting an assembly occupancy and not having fixed seats shall have the occupant load of the room posted in a conspicuous place near the main exit from the room. [*101:* 12.7.9.3.1; *101:* 13.7.9.3.1]

20.1.5.10.4.2 Approved signs shall be maintained in a legible manner by the owner or authorized agent. [*101:* 12.7.9.3.2; *101:* 13.7.9.3.2]

20.1.5.10.4.3 Signs shall be durable and shall indicate the number of occupants permitted for each room use. [*101:* 12.7.9.3.3; *101:* 13.7.9.3.3]

20.1.5.11 Clothing. Clothing and personal effects shall not be stored in corridors, and spaces not separated from corridors, unless otherwise permitted by one of the following:

(1) In new assembly occupancies, this requirement shall not apply to corridors, and spaces not separated from corridors, that are protected by an approved, supervised automatic sprinkler system in accordance with Section 13.3. [*101:* 12.7.12(1)]
(2) In existing assembly occupancies, this requirement shall not apply to corridors, and spaces not separated from corridors, that are protected by an approved automatic sprinkler system in accordance with Section 13.3. [*101:* 13.7.12(1)]
(3) This requirement shall not apply to corridors, and spaces not separated from corridors, that are protected by a smoke detection system in accordance with Section 13.3. [*101:* 12.7.12(2); *101:* 13.7.12(2)]
(4) This requirement shall not apply to storage in metal lockers, provided that the required egress width is maintained. [*101:* 12.7.12(3); *101:* 13.7.12(3)]

20.1.5.12 Projection Rooms.

20.1.5.12.1 Film or video projectors or spotlights utilizing light sources that produce particulate matter or toxic gases, or light sources that produce hazardous radiation, without protective shielding shall be located within a projection room complying with 12.3.2.1.2 of NFPA *101.* [*101:* 12.4.6.3; *101:* 13.4.6.3]

20.1.5.12.2 Every projection room shall be of permanent construction consistent with the building construction type in which the projection room is located and shall comply with the following:

(1) Openings shall not be required to be protected.
(2) The room shall have a floor area of not less than 80 ft^2 (7.4 m^2) for a single machine and not less than 40 ft^2 (3.7 m^2) for each additional machine.
(3) Each motion picture projector, floodlight, spotlight, or similar piece of equipment shall have a clear working space of not less than 30 in. (760 mm) on each side and at its rear, but only one such space shall be required between adjacent projectors. [*101:* 12.4.6.4; *101:* 13.4.6.4]

20.2 Educational Occupancies.

20.2.1 Application. New and existing educational occupancies shall comply with Section 20.2 and NFPA *101*.

20.2.2 Flexible Plan and Open Plan Buildings.

20.2.2.1 Flexible plan and open plan buildings shall comply with the requirements of 20.2.2 as modified by 20.2.2.2 through 20.2.2.5. [*101:* 14.4.3.1; *101:* 15.4.3.1]

20.2.2.2 Each room occupied by more than 300 persons shall have two or more means of egress entering into separate atmospheres. [*101:* 14.4.3.2; *101:* 15.4.3.2]

20.2.2.3 Where three or more means of egress are required, the number of means of egress permitted to enter into the same atmosphere shall not exceed two. [*101:* 14.4.3.3; *101:* 15.4.3.3]

20.2.2.4 Flexible plan buildings shall be permitted to have walls and partitions rearranged periodically only if revised plans or diagrams have been approved by the AHJ. [*101:* 15.4.3.4]

20.2.2.5 Flexible plan buildings shall be evaluated while all folding walls are extended and in use as well as when they are in the retracted position. [*101:* 14.4.3.5; *101:* 15.4.3.5]

20.2.3 Interior Finish.

20.2.3.1 General. Interior finish shall be in accordance with Section 12.5. [*101:* 14.3.3.1; *101:* 15.3.3.1]

20.2.3.2 Interior Wall and Ceiling Finish. New and existing interior wall and ceiling finish materials complying with Section 12.5 shall be permitted as follows:

(1) Exits — Class A [*101:* 14.3.3.2(1); *101:* 15.3.3.2(1)]
(2) In new educational occupancies other than exits — Class A or Class B [*101:* 14.3.3.2(2)]
(3) In existing educational occupancies, corridors and lobbies — Class A or Class B [*101:* 15.3.3.2(2)]
(4) Low-height partitions not exceeding 60 in. (1525 mm) and used in locations other than exits — Class A, Class B, or Class C [*101:* 14.3.3.2(3); *101:* 15.3.3.2(3)]

20.2.3.3 Interior Floor Finish.

20.2.3.3.1 New interior floor finish shall comply with Section 12.5. [*101:* 14.3.3.3.1]

20.2.3.3.2 New interior floor finish in exit enclosures and exit access corridors and spaces not separated from them by walls complying with 14.3.6 of NFPA *101* shall be not less than Class II. [*101:* 14.3.3.3.2]

20.2.3.3.3 New interior floor finish shall comply with 12.5.8.1 or 12.5.8.2, as applicable. [*101:* 14.3.3.3.3]

20.2.3.3.4 Existing Interior Floor Finish. (Reserved) [*101:* 15.3.3.3]

20.2.4 Operating Features.

20.2.4.1 Emergency Action Plan. Emergency action plans shall be provided in accordance with Section 10.8. [*101:* 14.7.1; *101:* 15.7.1]

20.2.4.2 Emergency Egress Drills.

20.2.4.2.1* Emergency egress drills shall be conducted in accordance with Section 10.5 and the applicable provisions of 20.2.4.2.3 as otherwise provided in 20.2.4.2.2. [*101:* 14.7.2.1; *101:* 15.7.2.1]

20.2.4.2.2 Approved training programs designed for education and training and for the practice of emergency egress to familiarize occupants with the drill procedure, and to establish conduct of the emergency egress as a matter of routine, shall be permitted to receive credit on a one-for-one basis for not more than four of the emergency egress drills required by 20.2.4.2.3, provided that a minimum of four emergency egress drills are completed prior to the conduct of the first such training and practice program. [*101:* :14.7.2.2; *101:* 15.7.2.2]

20.2.4.2.3 Emergency egress drills shall be conducted as follows:

(1) Not less than one emergency egress drill shall be conducted every month the facility is in session, unless both of the following criteria are met:
  (a) In climates where the weather is severe, the monthly emergency egress drills shall be permitted to be deferred.
  (b) The required number of emergency egress drills shall be conducted, and not less than four shall be conducted before the drills are deferred.
(2) All occupants of the building shall participate in the drill.
(3) One additional emergency egress drill, other than for educational occupancies that are open on a year-round basis, shall be required within the first 30 days of operation. [*101:* 14.7.2.3; *101:* 15.7.2.3]

20.2.4.2.4 All emergency drill alarms shall be sounded on the fire alarm system. [*101:* 14.7.2.4; *101:* 15.7.2.4]

20.2.4.3 Inspection.

20.2.4.3.1* It shall be the duty of principals, teachers, or staff to inspect all exit facilities daily to ensure that all stairways, doors, and other exits are in proper condition. [*101:* 14.7.3.1; *101:* 15.7.3.1]

20.2.4.3.2 Open plan buildings shall require extra surveillance to ensure that exit paths are maintained clear of obstruction and are obvious. [*101:* 14.7.3.2; *101:* 15.7.3.2]

20.2.4.3.3 Inspection of Door Openings. Door openings shall be inspected in accordance with 7.2.1.15 of NFPA *101.* [*101:* 14.7.3.3; *101:* 15.7.3.3]

20.2.4.4 Furnishings and Decorations.

20.2.4.4.1 Draperies, curtains, and other similar furnishings and decorations in educational occupancies shall be in accordance with the provisions of 12.6.2. [*101:* 14.7.4.1; *101:* 15.7.4.1]

20.2.4.4.2 Clothing and personal effects shall not be stored in corridors, unless otherwise permitted by one of the following:

(1) This requirement shall not apply to corridors protected by an automatic sprinkler system in accordance with Section 13.3.
(2) This requirement shall not apply to corridor areas protected by a smoke detection system in accordance with 13.7.1.4.
(3) This requirement shall not apply to storage in metal lockers, provided that the required egress width is maintained. [*101:* 14.7.4.2; *101:* 15.7.4.2]

20.2.4.4.3 Artwork and teaching materials shall be permitted to be attached directly to the walls in accordance with the following:

(1) In new educational occupancies, the artwork and teaching materials shall not exceed 20 percent of the wall area in a building that is not protected throughout by an approved, supervised automatic sprinkler system in accordance with Section 13.3. [*101:* 14.7.4.3(1)]
(2) In existing educational occupancies, the artwork and teaching materials shall not exceed 20 percent of the wall area in a building that is not protected throughout by an approved automatic sprinkler system in accordance with Section 13.3. [*101:* 15.7.4.3(1)]
(3) In new educational occupancies, the artwork and teaching materials shall not exceed 50 percent of the wall area in a building that is protected throughout by an approved, supervised automatic sprinkler system in accordance with Section 13.3. [*101:* 14.7.4.3(2)]
(4) In existing educational occupancies, the artwork and teaching materials shall not exceed 50 percent of the wall area in a building that is protected throughout by an approved automatic sprinkler system in accordance with Section 13.3. [*101:* 15.7.4.3(2)]

20.2.4.5 Unvented Fuel-Fired Heating Equipment. Unvented fuel-fired heating equipment, other than gas space heaters in compliance with NFPA 54/ANSI Z223.1, *National Fuel Gas Code,* shall be prohibited. [*101:* 14.5.2.2; *101:* 15.5.2.2]

20.3 Day-Care Occupancies.

20.3.1 Application. New and existing day-care occupancies shall comply with Section 20.3 and NFPA *101.*

20.3.1.1 In new day-care occupancies, where a facility houses more than one age group or self-preservation capability, the strictest requirements applicable to any group present shall apply throughout the day-care occupancy or building, as appropriate to a given area, unless the area housing such a group is maintained as a separate fire area. [*101:* 16.1.1.6]

20.3.1.2 In existing day-care occupancies, where a facility houses clients of more than one self-preservation capability, the strictest requirements applicable to any group present shall apply throughout the day-care occupancy or building, as appropriate to a given area, unless the area housing such a group is maintained as a separate fire area. [*101:* 17.1.1.6]

20.3.1.3 Places of religious worship shall not be required to meet the provisions of Section 20.3 where providing day care while services are being held in the building. [*101:* 16.1.1.7; *101:* 17.1.1.7]

20.3.1.4 General. Occupancies that include preschools, kindergartens, and other schools whose purpose is primarily educational for children 24 months of age or older, even though the children who attend such schools are of preschool age, shall comply with the provisions of Chapter 14 or Chapter 15 of NFPA *101,* as applicable. [*101:* 16.1.2.1; *101:* 17.1.2.1]

20.3.1.5 Adult Day-Care Occupancies.

20.3.1.5.1 Adult day-care occupancies shall include any building or portion thereof used for less than 24 hours per day to house more than three adults requiring care, maintenance, and supervision by other than their relative(s). [*101:* 16.1.2.2.1; *101:* 17.1.2.2.1]

20.3.1.5.2 Clients in adult day-care occupancies shall be ambulatory or semiambulatory and shall not be bedridden. [*101:* 16.1.2.2.2; *101:* 17.1.2.2.2]

20.3.1.5.3 Clients in adult day-care occupancies shall not exhibit behavior that is harmful to themselves or to others. [*101:* 16.1.2.2.3; *101:* 17.1.2.2.3]

20.3.2 General Requirements.

20.3.2.1 Unvented fuel-fired heating equipment, other than gas space heaters in compliance with NFPA 54/ANSI Z223.1, *National Fuel Gas Code*, shall be prohibited. [*101:* 16.5.2.2; *101:* 17.5.2.2]

20.3.2.2* Door Latches. Every door latch to closets, storage areas, kitchens, and other similar spaces or areas shall be such that clients can open the door from inside the space or area. [*101:* 16.2.2.2.4; *101:* 17.2.2.2.4]

20.3.2.3 Bathroom Doors. Every bathroom door lock shall be designed to allow opening of the locked door from the outside by an opening device that shall be readily accessible to the staff. [*101:* 16.2.2.2.5; *101:* 17.2.2.2.5]

20.3.2.4 Flexible Plan and Open Plan Buildings.

20.3.2.4.1 In new day-care occupancies, flexible plan and open plan buildings shall comply with the requirements of 20.3.2.4 as modified by 20.3.2.4.3 through 20.3.2.4.6. [*101:* 16.4.3.1]

20.3.2.4.2 In existing day-care occupancies, flexible plan and open plan buildings shall comply with the requirements of 20.3.2.4 as modified by 20.3.2.4.3 and 20.3.2.4.4. [*101:* :17.4.3.1]

20.3.2.4.3 Flexible plan buildings shall be permitted to have walls and partitions rearranged periodically only if revised plans or diagrams have been approved by the AHJ. [*101:* 16.4.3.2; *101:* 17.4.3.2]

20.3.2.4.4 Flexible plan buildings shall be evaluated while all folding walls are extended and in use as well as when they are in the retracted position. [*101:* 16.4.3.3; *101:* 17.4.3.3]

20.3.2.4.5 Each room occupied by more than 300 persons shall have two or more means of egress entering into separate atmospheres. [*101:* 16.4.3.4]

20.3.2.4.6 Where three or more means of egress are required from a single room, the number of means of egress permitted to enter into a common atmosphere shall not exceed two. [*101:* 16.4.3.5]

20.3.3 Interior Finish.

20.3.3.1 General. Interior finish shall be in accordance with Section 12.5. [*101:* 16.3.3.1; *101:* 17.3.3.1]

20.3.3.2 New Interior Wall and Ceiling Finish. New interior wall and ceiling finish materials complying with Section 12.5 shall be Class A in stairways, corridors, and lobbies; in all other occupied areas, new interior wall and ceiling finish shall be Class A or Class B. [*101:* 16.3.3.2]

20.3.3.3 Existing Interior Wall and Ceiling Finish. Existing interior wall and ceiling finish materials complying with Section 12.5 shall be Class A or Class B throughout. [*101:* 17.3.3.2]

20.3.3.4 Interior Floor Finish.

20.3.3.4.1 New interior floor finish shall comply with Section 12.5. [*101:* 16.3.3.3.1]

20.3.3.4.2 New interior floor finish in exit enclosures and exit access corridors and spaces not separated from them by walls complying with 14.3.6 of NFPA *101* shall be not less than Class II. [*101:* 16.3.3.3.2]

20.3.3.4.3 New interior floor finish shall comply with 12.5.8.1 or 12.5.8.2, as applicable. [*101:* 16.3.3.3.3]

20.3.3.4.4 Existing Interior Floor Finish. (Reserved) [*101:* 17.3.3.3]

20.3.4 Day-Care Homes.

20.3.4.1 Classification.

20.3.4.1.1 In new day-care homes, the requirements of 20.3.4 shall apply to day-care homes in which more than 3, but not more than 12, clients receive care, maintenance, and supervision by other than their relative(s) or legal guardian(s) for less than 24 hours per day, generally within a dwelling unit. *(See also 16.6.1.4 of NFPA 101.)* [*101:* 16.6.1.1.2]

20.3.4.1.2* In existing day-care homes, the requirements of Section 17.6 of NFPA *101* shall apply to existing day-care homes in which more than 3, but not more than 12, clients receive care, maintenance, and supervision by other than their relative(s) or legal guardian(s) for less than 24 hours per day, generally within a dwelling unit. An existing day-care home shall be permitted the option of meeting the requirements of Section 16.6 of NFPA *101* in lieu of Section 17.6 of NFPA *101*. Any existing day-care home that meets the requirements of Chapter 16 of NFPA *101* shall be judged as meeting the requirements of this chapter. *(See also 17.6.1.4 of NFPA 101.)* [*101:* 17.6.1.1.2]

20.3.4.1.3 In new day-care homes, where a facility houses more than one age group or one self-preservation capability, the strictest requirements applicable to any group present shall apply throughout the day-care home or building, as appropriate to a given area, unless the area housing such a group is maintained as a separate fire area. [*101:* 16.6.1.1.3]

20.3.4.1.4 In existing day-care homes, where a facility houses clients of more than one self-preservation capability, the strictest requirements applicable to any group present shall apply throughout the day-care home or building, as appropriate to a given area, unless the area housing such a group is maintained as a separate fire area. [*101:* 17.6.1.1.3]

20.3.4.1.5 Facilities that supervise clients on a temporary basis with a parent or guardian in close proximity shall not be required to meet the provisions of 20.3.4. [*101:* 16.6.1.1.4; *101:* 17.6.1.1.4]

20.3.4.1.6 Places of religious worship shall not be required to meet the provisions of 20.3.4 where operating a day-care home while services are being held in the building. [*101:* 16.6.1.1.5; *101:* 17.6.1.1.5]

20.3.4.2 Operating Features.

20.3.4.2.1* Emergency Action Plans. Emergency action plans shall be provided in accordance with Section 10.8. [*101:* 16.7.1; *101:* 17.7.1]

20.3.4.2.2 Emergency Egress and Relocation Drills.

20.3.4.2.2.1* Emergency egress and relocation drills shall be conducted in accordance with Section 10.5 and the applicable provisions of 20.3.4.2.2.2. [*101:* 16.7.2.1; *101:* 17.7.2.1]

20.3.4.2.2.2 Emergency egress and relocation drills shall be conducted as follows:

(1) Not less than one emergency egress and relocation drill shall be conducted every month the facility is in session, unless both of the following criteria are met:
   (a) In climates where the weather is severe, the monthly emergency egress and relocation drills shall be permitted to be deferred.
   (b) The required number of emergency egress and relocation drills shall be conducted, and not less than four shall be conducted before the drills are deferred.
(2) All occupants of the building shall participate in the drill.
(3) One additional emergency egress and relocation drill, other than for day-care occupancies that are open on a year-round basis, shall be required within the first 30 days of operation. [*101:* 16.7.2.2; *101:* 17.7.2.2]

20.3.4.2.3 Inspections.

20.3.4.2.3.1 Fire prevention inspections shall be conducted monthly by a trained senior member of the staff, after which a copy of the latest inspection report shall be posted in a conspicuous place in the day-care facility. [*101:* 16.7.3.1; *101:* 17.7.3.1]

20.3.4.2.3.2* It shall be the duty of site administrators and staff members to inspect all exit facilities daily to ensure that all stairways, doors, and other exits are in proper condition. [*101:* 16.7.3.2; *101:* 17.7.3.2]

20.3.4.2.3.3 Open plan buildings shall require extra surveillance to ensure that exit paths are maintained clear of obstruction and are obvious. [*101:* 16.7.3.3; *101:* 17.7.3.3]

20.3.4.2.3.4 Inspection of Door Openings. Door openings shall be inspected in accordance with 7.2.1.15 of NFPA *101*. [*101:* 16.7.3.4; *101:* 17.7.3.4]

20.3.4.2.3.5 Furnishings and Decorations.

20.3.4.2.3.5.1 Draperies, curtains, and other similar furnishings and decorations in day-care occupancies, other than in day-care homes, shall be in accordance with the provisions of 12.6.2. [*101:* 16.7.4.1; *101:* 17.7.4.1]

20.3.4.2.3.5.2 Clothing and personal effects shall not be stored in corridors, unless otherwise permitted by one of the following:

(1) This requirement shall not apply to corridors protected by an automatic sprinkler system in accordance with Section 13.3.
(2) This requirement shall not apply to corridor areas protected by a smoke detection system in accordance with Section 13.7.
(3) This requirement shall not apply to storage in metal lockers, provided that the required egress width is maintained. [*101:* 16.7.4.2; *101:* 17.7.4.2]

20.3.4.2.3.5.3 Artwork and teaching materials shall be permitted to be attached directly to the walls in accordance with the following:

(1) In new day-care homes, the artwork and teaching materials shall not exceed 20 percent of the wall area in a building that is not protected throughout by an approved, supervised automatic sprinkler system in accordance with Section 13.3. [*101:* 16.7.4.3(1)]
(2) In existing day-care homes, the artwork and teaching materials shall not exceed 20 percent of the wall area in a building that is not protected throughout by an approved automatic sprinkler system in accordance with Section 13.3. [*101:* 17.7.4.3(1)]
(3) In new day-care homes, the artwork and teaching materials shall not exceed 50 percent of the wall area in a building that is protected throughout by an approved, supervised automatic sprinkler system in accordance with Section 13.3. [*101:* 16.7.4.3(2)]
(4) In existing day-care homes, the artwork and teaching materials shall not exceed 50 percent of the wall area in a building that is protected throughout by an approved automatic sprinkler system in accordance with Section 13.3. [*101:* 17.7.4.3(2)]

20.3.4.2.3.5.4 The provision of 12.6.3 for cigarette ignition resistance of newly introduced upholstered furniture and mattresses shall not apply to day-care homes. [*101:* 16.7.4.4; *101:* 17.7.4.4]

20.3.4.2.3.6* Day-Care Staff. Adequate adult staff shall be on duty and alert at all times where clients are present. [*101:* 16.7.5; *101:* 17.7.5]

20.4 Health Care Occupancies.

20.4.1 Application. New and existing health care occupancies shall comply with Section 20.4, NFPA *101*, and NFPA 99.

20.4.2* Operating Features.

20.4.2.1 Evacuation and Relocation Plan and Fire Drills.

20.4.2.1.1 The administration of every health care occupancy shall have, in effect and available to all supervisory personnel, written copies of a plan for the protection of all persons in the event of fire, for their evacuation to areas of refuge, and for their evacuation from the building when necessary. [*101:* 18.7.1.1; *101:* 19.7.1.1]

20.4.2.1.2 All employees shall be periodically instructed and kept informed with respect to their duties under the plan required by 20.4.2.1.1. [*101:* 18.7.1.2; *101:* 19.7.1.2]

20.4.2.1.3 A copy of the plan required by 20.4.2.1.1 shall be readily available at all times in the telephone operator's location or at the security center. [*101:* 18.7.1.3; *101:* 19.7.1.3]

20.4.2.1.4 The provisions of Section 10.5 and 20.4.2.1.2 through 20.4.2.2.3 shall apply.

20.4.2.1.5* Fire drills in health care occupancies shall include the transmission of a fire alarm signal and simulation of emergency fire conditions. [*101:* 18.7.1.4; *101:* 19.7.1.4]

20.4.2.1.6 Infirm or bedridden patients shall not be required to be moved during drills to safe areas or to the exterior of the building. [*101:* 18.7.1.5; *101:* 19.7.1.5]

20.4.2.1.7 Drills shall be conducted quarterly on each shift to familiarize facility personnel (nurses, interns, maintenance engineers, and administrative staff) with the signals and emergency action required under varied conditions. [*101:* 18.7.1.6; *101:* 19.7.1.6]

20.4.2.1.8 When drills are conducted between 9:00 p.m. (2100 hours) and 6:00 a.m. (0600 hours), a coded announcement shall be permitted to be used instead of audible alarms. [*101:* 18.7.1.7; *101:* 19.7.1.7]

20.4.2.1.9 Employees of health care occupancies shall be instructed in life safety procedures and devices. [*101:* 18.7.1.8; *101:* 19.7.1.8]

20.4.2.2 Procedure in Case of Fire.

20.4.2.2.1* Protection of Patients.

20.4.2.2.1.1 For health care occupancies, the proper protection of patients shall require the prompt and effective response of health care personnel. [*101:* 18.7.2.1.1; *101:* 19.7.2.1.1]

20.4.2.2.1.2 The basic response required of staff shall include the following:

(1) Removal of all occupants directly involved with the fire emergency
(2) Transmission of an appropriate fire alarm signal to warn other building occupants and summon staff
(3) Confinement of the effects of the fire by closing doors to isolate the fire area
(4) Relocation of patients as detailed in the health care occupancy's fire safety plan [*101:* 18.7.2.1.2; *101:* 19.7.2.1.2]

20.4.2.2.2 Fire Safety Plan. A written health care occupancy fire safety plan shall provide for the following:

(1) Use of alarms
(2) Transmission of alarms to fire department
(3) Emergency phone call to fire department
(4) Response to alarms
(5) Isolation of fire
(6) Evacuation of immediate area
(7) Evacuation of smoke compartment
(8) Preparation of floors and building for evacuation
(9) Extinguishment of fire
(10) Location and operation of doors disguised with murals as permitted by 18.2.2.2.7 and 19.2.2.2.7 of NFPA *101*. [*101:* 18.7.2.2; *101:* 19.7.2.2]

20.4.2.2.3 Staff Response.

20.4.2.2.3.1 All health care occupancy personnel shall be instructed in the use of and response to fire alarms. [*101:* 18.7.2.3.1; *101:* 9.7.2.3.1]

20.4.2.2.3.2 All health care occupancy personnel shall be instructed in the use of the code phrase to ensure transmission of an alarm under the following conditions:

(1) When the individual who discovers a fire must immediately go to the aid of an endangered person
(2) During a malfunction of the building fire alarm system [*101:* 18.7.2.3.2; *101:* 19.7.2.3.2]

20.4.2.2.3.3 Personnel hearing the code announced shall first activate the building fire alarm using the nearest manual fire alarm box and then shall execute immediately their duties as outlined in the fire safety plan. [*101:* 18.7.2.3.3; *101:* 19.7.2.3.3]

20.4.2.3 Maintenance of Means of Egress.

20.4.2.3.1 Proper maintenance shall be provided to ensure the dependability of the method of evacuation selected. [*101:* 18.7.3.1; *101:* 19.7.3.1]

20.4.2.3.2 Health care occupancies that find it necessary to lock means of egress doors shall, at all times, maintain an adequate staff qualified to release locks and direct occupants from the immediate danger area to a place of safety in case of fire or other emergency. [*101:* 18.7.3.2; *101:* 19.7.3.2]

20.4.2.3.3* Where required by the AHJ, a floor plan shall be provided to indicate the location of all required means of egress corridors in smoke compartments having spaces not separated from the corridor by partitions. [*101:* 18.7.3.3; *101:* 19.7.3.3]

20.4.2.4* Smoking. Smoking regulations shall be adopted and shall include not less than the following provisions:

(1) Smoking shall be prohibited in any room, ward, or individual enclosed space where flammable liquids, combustible gases, or oxygen is used or stored and in any other hazardous location, and such areas shall be posted with signs that read NO SMOKING or shall be posted with the international symbol for no smoking.
(2) In health care occupancies where smoking is prohibited and signs are prominently placed at all major entrances, secondary signs with language that prohibits smoking shall not be required.
(3) Smoking by patients classified as not responsible shall be prohibited.
(4) The requirement of 20.4.2.4(3) shall not apply where the patient is under direct supervision.
(5) Ashtrays of noncombustible material and safe design shall be provided in all areas where smoking is permitted.
(6) Metal containers with self-closing cover devices into which ashtrays can be emptied shall be readily available to all areas where smoking is permitted. [*101:* 18.7.4; *101:* 19.7.4]

20.4.2.5 Furnishings, Mattresses, and Decorations.

20.4.2.5.1* Draperies, curtains, and other loosely hanging fabrics and films serving as furnishings or decorations in health care occupancies shall be in accordance with the provisions of 12.6.2 (*see 18.3.5.10 or 19.3.5.10 of* NFPA *101*), and the following also shall apply:

(1) Such curtains shall include cubicle curtains.
(2) Such curtains shall not include curtains at showers and baths.
(3) Such draperies and curtains shall not include draperies and curtains at windows in patient sleeping rooms in sprinklered smoke compartments.
(4) Such draperies and curtains shall not include draperies and curtains in other rooms or areas where the draperies and curtains comply with all of the following:
   (a) Individual drapery or curtain panel area does not exceed 48 ft^2 (4.5 m^2).
   (b) Total area of drapery and curtain panels per room or area does not exceed 20 percent of the aggregate area of the wall on which they are located.
   (c) Smoke compartment in which draperies or curtains are located is sprinklered in accordance with 13.3.2.12. [*101:* 19.7.5.1]

20.4.2.5.2 Newly introduced upholstered furniture within health care occupancies shall comply with one of the following provisions, unless otherwise provided in 20.4.2.5.3:

(1) The furniture shall meet the criteria specified in 12.6.3.1 and 12.6.3.2.1.
(2) The furniture shall be in a building protected throughout by an approved, supervised automatic sprinkler system in accordance with NFPA 13. [*101:* 18.7.5.2; *101:* 19.7.5.2]

20.4.2.5.3 The requirements of 20.4.2.5.2, 12.6.3.1, and 12.6.3.2.1 shall not apply to upholstered furniture belonging to the patient in sleeping rooms of existing nursing homes where the following criteria are met:

(1) A smoke detector shall be installed where the patient sleeping room is not protected by automatic sprinklers.
(2) Battery-powered single-station smoke detectors shall be permitted. [*101:* 19.7.5.3]

20.4.2.5.4 Newly introduced mattresses within health care occupancies shall comply with one of the following provisions, unless otherwise provided in 20.4.2.5.5:

(1) The mattresses shall meet the criteria specified in 12.6.3.2 and 12.6.3.2.2.
(2) The mattresses shall be in a building protected throughout by an approved, supervised automatic sprinkler system in accordance with NFPA 13. [*101:* 18.7.5.4; *101:* 19.7.5.4]

20.4.2.5.5 The requirements of 12.6.3.2, 12.6.3.2.2, and 20.4.2.5.4 shall not apply to mattresses belonging to the patient in sleeping rooms of existing nursing homes where the following criteria are met:

(1) A smoke detector shall be installed where the patient sleeping room is not protected by automatic sprinklers.
(2) Battery-powered single-station smoke detectors shall be permitted. [*101:* 19.7.5.5]

20.4.2.5.6 Combustible decorations shall be prohibited in any health care occupancy, unless one of the following criteria is met:

(1) They are flame-retardant or are treated with approved fire-retardant coating that is listed and labeled for application to the material to which it is applied.
(2)*The decorations meet the flame propagation performance criteria contained in Test Method 1 or Test Method 2, as appropriate, of NFPA 701, *Standard Methods of Fire Tests for Flame Propagation of Textiles and Films.*
(3) The decorations exhibit a heat release rate not exceeding 100 kW when tested in accordance with NFPA 289, *Standard Method of Fire Test for Individual Fuel Packages,* using the 20 kW ignition source.
(4)*The decorations, such as photographs, paintings, and other art, are attached directly to the walls, ceiling, and non-fire-rated doors in accordance with the following:

  (a) Decorations on non-fire-rated doors do not interfere with the operation or any required latching of the door and do not exceed the area limitations of 20.4.2.5.6(b), (c), or (d).
  (b) Decorations do not exceed 20 percent of the wall, ceiling, and door areas inside any room or space of a smoke compartment that is not protected throughout by an approved automatic sprinkler system in accordance with Section 13.3.
  (c) Decorations do not exceed 30 percent of the wall, ceiling, and door areas inside any room or space of a smoke compartment that is protected throughout by an approved supervised automatic sprinkler system in accordance with Section 13.3.
  (d) Decorations do not exceed 50 percent of the wall, ceiling, and door areas inside patient sleeping rooms having a capacity not exceeding four persons, in a smoke compartment that is protected throughout by an approved, supervised automatic sprinkler system in accordance with Section 13.3.

(5) In existing health care occupancies, they are decorations, such as photographs or paintings, in such limited quantities that a hazard of fire development or spread is not present. [*101:* 18.7.5.6; *101:* 19.7.5.6]

20.4.2.5.7 Soiled linen or trash collection receptacles shall not exceed 32 gal (121 L) in capacity and shall meet the following requirements:

(1) The average density of container capacity in a room or space shall not exceed 0.5 gal/ft^2 (20.4 L/m^2).
(2) A capacity of 32 gal (121 L) shall not be exceeded within any 64 ft^2 (6 m^2) area.
(3) Mobile soiled linen or trash collection receptacles with capacities greater than 32 gal (121 L) shall be located in a room protected as a hazardous area when not attended.
(4) Container size and density shall not be limited in hazardous areas. [*101:* 18.7.5.7.1; *101:* 19.7.5.7.1]

20.4.2.5.8* Containers used solely for recycling clean waste or for patient records awaiting destruction shall be permitted to be excluded from the limitations of 20.4.2.5.7 where all the following conditions are met:

(1) Each container is limited to a capacity of 96 gal (363 L) except as permitted by 20.4.2.5.8(2) or (3).
(2)*Containers with capacities greater than 96 gal (363 L) shall be located in a room protected as a hazardous area when not attended.
(3) Container size shall not be limited in hazardous areas.
(4) Containers for combustibles shall be labeled and listed as meeting the requirements of FM Approval Standard 6921; however, such testing, listing, and labeling shall not be limited to FM Approvals. [*101:* 18.7.5.7.2; *101:* 19.7.5.7.2]

20.4.2.5.9 The provisions of 19.2.1.1 through 19.2.1.2 applicable to soiled linen and trash receptacles shall not apply.

20.4.2.6 Portable Space-Heating Devices. Portable space-heating devices shall be prohibited in all health care occupancies, unless both of the following criteria are met:

(1) Such devices are permitted to be used only in nonsleeping staff and employee areas.
(2) The heating elements of such devices do not exceed 212°F (100°C). [*101:* 18.7.8; *101:* 19.7.8]

20.4.3 Interior Finish.

20.4.3.1 General. Interior finish shall be in accordance with Section 12.5. [*101:* 18.3.3.1; *101:* 19.3.3.1]

20.4.3.2 New Interior Wall and Ceiling Finish. Interior wall and ceiling finish materials complying with Section 12.5 shall be permitted throughout if Class A, except as indicated in 20.4.3.2.1 or 20.4.3.2.2. [*101:* 18.3.3.2]

20.4.3.2.1 New walls and ceilings shall be permitted to have Class A or Class B interior finish in individual rooms having a capacity not exceeding four persons. [*101:* 18.3.3.2.1]

20.4.3.2.2 New corridor wall finish not exceeding 48 in. (1220 mm) in height that is restricted to the lower half of the wall shall be permitted to be Class A or Class B. [*101:* 18.3.3.2.2]

20.4.3.2.3 Existing Interior Wall and Ceiling Finish. Existing interior wall and ceiling finish materials complying with Section 12.5 shall be permitted to be Class A or Class B. [*101:* 19.3.3.2]

20.4.3.3 Interior Floor Finish.

20.4.3.3.1 New interior floor finish shall comply with Section 12.5. [*101:* 18.3.3.3.1]

20.4.3.3.2 New interior floor finish in exit enclosures and exit access corridors and spaces not separated from them by walls complying with 18.3.6 of NFPA *101* shall be Class I or Class II. [*101:* 18.3.3.3.2]

20.4.3.3.3 New interior floor finish shall comply with 12.5.8.1 or 12.5.8.2, as applicable. [*101:* 18.3.3.3.3]

20.4.3.4 Interior Finish (Nonsprinklered Smoke Compartment Rehabilitation).

20.4.3.4.1 General. Interior finish within the modification area shall be in accordance with Section 12.5. [*101:* 18.4.4.6.1]

20.4.3.4.2 Interior Wall and Ceiling Finish. Newly installed interior wall and ceiling finish materials complying with Section 12.5 shall be permitted throughout nonsprinklered smoke compartments if the materials are Class A, except as otherwise permitted in 20.4.3.4.2.1 or 20.4.3.4.2.2. [*101:* 18.4.4.6.2]

20.4.3.4.2.1 Walls and ceilings shall be permitted to have Class A or Class B interior finish in individual rooms having a capacity not exceeding four persons. [*101:* 18.4.4.6.2.1]

20.4.3.4.2.2 Corridor wall finish not exceeding 48 in. (1220 mm) in height and restricted to the lower half of the wall shall be permitted to be Class A or Class B. [*101:* 18.4.4.6.2.2]

20.4.3.5 Interior Floor Finish.

20.4.3.5.1 Newly installed interior floor finish shall comply with Section 12.5. [*101:* 18.4.4.6.3.1]

20.4.3.5.2 The requirements for newly installed interior floor finish in exit enclosures and corridors not separated from them by walls complying with 19.3.5.7 of NFPA *101* shall be as follows:

(1) Unrestricted in smoke compartments protected throughout by an approved, supervised automatic sprinkler system in accordance with 19.3.5.7 of NFPA *101*
(2) Not less than Class I in smoke compartments not protected throughout by an approved, supervised automatic sprinkler system in accordance with 19.3.5.7 of NFPA *101* [*101:* 18.4.4.6.3.2]

20.4.3.5.3 Existing Interior Floor Finish. No restrictions shall apply to existing interior floor finish. [*101:* 19.3.3.3]

20.5 Residential Board and Care Occupancies.

20.5.1 Application. New and existing residential board and care occupancies shall comply with Section 20.5 and NFPA *101*.

20.5.2 Operating Features.

20.5.2.1 Emergency Action Plan.

20.5.2.1.1 The administration of every residential board and care facility shall have, in effect and available to all supervisory personnel, written copies of a plan for protecting all persons in the event of fire, for keeping persons in place, for evacuating persons to areas of refuge, and for evacuating persons from the building when necessary. [*101:* 32.7.1.1; *101:* 33.7.1.1]

20.5.2.1.2 The emergency action plan shall include special staff response, including the fire protection procedures needed to ensure the safety of any resident, and shall be amended or revised whenever any resident with unusual needs is admitted to the home. [*101:* 32.7.1.2; *101:* 33.7.1.2]

20.5.2.1.3 All employees shall be periodically instructed and kept informed with respect to their duties and responsibilities under the plan, and such instruction shall be reviewed by the staff not less than every 2 months. [*101:* 32.7.1.3; *101:* 33.7.1.3]

20.5.2.2 Resident Training.

20.5.2.2.1 All residents participating in the emergency action plan shall be trained in the proper actions to be taken in the event of fire. [*101:* 32.7.2.1; *101:* 33.7.2.1]

20.5.2.2.2 The training required by 20.5.2.2.1 shall include actions to be taken if the primary escape route is blocked. [*101:* 32.7.2.2; *101:* 33.7.2.2]

20.5.2.2.3 If a resident is given rehabilitation or habilitation training, training in fire prevention and the actions to be taken in the event of a fire shall be a part of the training program. [*101:* :32.7.2.3; *101:* 33.7.2.3]

20.5.2.2.4 Residents shall be trained to assist each other in case of fire to the extent that their physical and mental abilities permit them to do so without additional personal risk. [*101:* 32.7.2.4; *101:* 33.7.2.4]

20.5.2.3 Emergency Egress and Relocation Drills. Emergency egress and relocation drills shall be conducted in accordance with 20.5.2.3.1 through 20.5.2.3.6. [*101:* 32.7.3; *101:* 33.7.3]

20.5.2.3.1 Emergency egress and relocation drills shall be conducted not less than six times per year on a bimonthly basis, with not less than two drills conducted during the night when residents are sleeping, as modified by 20.5.2.3.5 and 20.5.2.3.6. [*101:* 32.7.3.1; *101:* 33.7.3.1]

20.5.2.3.2 The emergency drills shall be permitted to be announced to the residents in advance. [*101:* 32.7.3.2; *101:* 33.7.3.2]

20.5.2.3.3 The drills shall involve the actual evacuation of all residents to an assembly point, as specified in the emergency action plan, and shall provide residents with experience in egressing through all exits and means of escape required by this *Code*. [*101:* 32.7.3.3; *101:* 33.7.3.3]

20.5.2.3.4 Exits and means of escape not used in any drill shall not be credited in meeting the requirements of this *Code* for board and care facilities. [*101:* 32.7.3.4; *101:* 33.7.3.4]

20.5.2.3.5 Actual exiting from windows shall not be required to comply with 20.5.2.3; opening the window and signaling for help shall be an acceptable alternative. [*101:* 32.7.3.5; *101:* 33.7.3.5]

20.5.2.3.6 Residents who cannot meaningfully assist in their own evacuation or who have special health problems shall not be required to actively participate in the drill. Subsection 20.4.2 shall apply in such instances. [*101:* 32.7.3.6; *101:* 33.7.3.6]

20.5.2.4 Smoking.

20.5.2.4.1* Smoking regulations shall be adopted by the administration of board and care occupancies. [*101:* 32.7.4.1; *101:* 33.7.4.1]

20.5.2.4.2 Where smoking is permitted, noncombustible safety-type ashtrays or receptacles shall be provided in convenient locations. [*101:* 32.7.4.2; *101:* 33.7.4.2]

20.5.2.5* Furnishings, Bedding, and Decorations.

20.5.2.5.1 New draperies, curtains, and other similar loosely hanging furnishings and decorations in board and care facilities shall comply with 20.5.2.5.1.1 and 20.5.2.5.1.2. [*101:* 32.7.5.1; *101:* 33.7.5.1]

20.5.2.5.1.1 New draperies, curtains, and other similar loosely hanging furnishings and decorations in board and care facilities shall be in accordance with the provisions of 12.6.2, unless otherwise permitted by 20.5.2.5.1.2. [*101:* 32.7.5.1.1; *101:* 33.7.5.1.1]

20.5.2.5.1.2 In other than common areas, new draperies, curtains, and other similar loosely hanging furnishings and decorations shall not be required to comply with 20.5.2.5.1.1 where the building is protected throughout by an approved automatic sprinkler system installed in accordance with 13.3.2.21.2 for new small facilities, 13.3.2.21.1 for new large facilities, 13.3.2.22.2 for existing small facilities, or 13.3.2.22.1 for existing large facilities. [*101:* 32.7.5.1.2; *101:* 33.7.5.1.2]

20.5.2.5.2* New upholstered furniture within board and care facilities shall comply with 20.5.2.5.2.1 or 20.5.2.5.2.2. [*101:* 32.7.5.2; *101:* 33.7.5.2]

20.5.2.5.2.1 New upholstered furniture shall be tested in accordance with the provisions of 12.6.3.1(1) and 12.6.3.2.1. [*101:* 32.7.5.2.1; *101:* 33.7.5.2.1]

20.5.2.5.2.2 Upholstered furniture belonging to residents in sleeping rooms shall not be required to be tested, provided that a smoke alarm is installed in such rooms; battery-powered single-station smoke alarms shall be permitted in such rooms. [*101:* 32.7.5.2.2; *101:* 33.7.5.2.2]

20.5.2.5.2.3* Newly introduced mattresses within board and care facilities shall comply with 20.5.2.5.2.3.1 or 20.5.2.5.2.3.2. [*101:* 32.7.5.3; *101:* 33.7.5.3]

20.5.2.5.2.3.1 Newly introduced mattresses shall be tested in accordance with the provisions of 12.6.3.2 and 12.6.3.2.2. [*101:* 32.7.5.3.1; *101:* 33.7.5.3.1]

20.5.2.5.2.3.2 Mattresses belonging to residents in sleeping rooms shall not be required to be tested, provided that a smoke alarm is installed in such rooms; battery-powered single-station smoke alarms shall be permitted in such rooms. [*101:* 32.7.5.3.2; *101:* 33.7.5.3.2]

20.5.2.5.3 No stove or combustion heater shall be located to block escape in case of fire caused by the malfunction of the stove or heater. [*101:* 32.2.5.2.2; *101:* 33.2.5.2.2]

20.5.2.5.4 Unvented fuel-fired heaters shall not be used in any residential board and care facility. [*101:* 32.2.5.2.3; *101:* 33.2.5.2.3]

20.5.3 Interior Finish.

20.5.3.1 Small Facilities.

20.5.3.1.1 General. Interior finish shall be in accordance with Section 12.5. [*101:* 32.2.3.3.1; *101:* 33.2.3.3.1]

20.5.3.1.2 New Interior Wall and Ceiling Finish. New interior wall and ceiling finish materials complying with Section 12.5 shall be Class A, Class B, or Class C. [*101:* 32.2.3.3.2]

20.5.3.1.3 Existing Interior Wall and Ceiling Finish. Existing interior wall and ceiling finish materials complying with Section 12.5 shall be as follows:

(1) Class A or Class B in facilities other than those having prompt evacuation capability
(2) Class A, Class B, or Class C in facilities having prompt evacuation capability [*101:* 33.2.3.3.2]

20.5.3.1.4 Interior Floor Finish.

20.5.3.1.4.1 New interior floor finish shall comply with Section 12.5. [*101:* 32.2.3.3.3.1]

20.5.3.1.4.2 New interior floor finish shall comply with 12.5.8.1 or 12.5.8.2, as applicable. [*101:* 32.2.3.3.3.2]

20.5.3.1.4.3 Existing Interior Floor Finish. (Reserved) [*101:* 33.2.3.3.3]

20.5.3.2 Large Facilities.

20.5.3.2.1 General. Interior finish shall be in accordance with Section 12.5. [*101:* 32.3.3.3.1; *101:* 33.3.3.3.1]

20.5.3.2.2 New Interior Wall and Ceiling Finish. New interior wall and ceiling finish materials complying with Section 12.5 shall be in accordance with the following:

(1) Exit enclosures — Class A
(2) Lobbies and corridors — Class B
(3) Rooms and enclosed spaces — Class B [*101:* 32.3.3.3.2]

20.5.3.2.3 Existing Interior Wall and Ceiling Finish. Existing interior wall and ceiling finish materials complying with Section 12.5 shall be Class A or Class B. [*101:* 33.3.3.3.2]

20.5.3.2.4 Interior Floor Finish.

20.5.3.2.4.1 New interior floor finish shall comply with Section 12.5. [*101:* 32.3.3.3.3.1]

20.5.3.2.4.2 New interior floor finish in exit enclosures and exit access corridors and spaces not separated from them by walls complying with 32.3.3.6 of NFPA *101* shall be not less than Class II. [*101:* 32.3.3.3.3.2]

20.5.3.2.4.3 New interior floor finish shall comply with 12.5.8.1 or 12.5.8.2, as applicable. [*101:* 32.3.3.3.3.3]

20.5.3.2.4.4 Existing Interior Floor Finish. Existing interior floor finish, other than approved existing floor coverings, shall be Class I or Class II in corridors or exits. [*101:* 33.3.3.3.3]

20.5.3.3 Apartment Buildings Housing Board and Care Occupancies.

20.5.3.3.1 New Interior Finish.

20.5.3.3.1.1 The requirements of 20.9.3 shall apply only to the parts of means of egress serving the apartment(s) used as a residential board and care occupancy, as modified by 20.5.3.3.1.2. [*101:* 32.4.3.1.1]

20.5.3.3.1.2 If a new board and care occupancy is created in an existing apartment building, the requirements of 31.3.3 of NFPA *101* shall apply to the parts of the means of egress serving the apartment(s) used as a residential board and care occupancy. [*101:* 32.4.3.1.2]

20.5.3.3.2 Existing Interior Finish. The requirements of 20.9.3 shall apply only to the parts of means of egress serving the apartment(s) used as a residential board and care occupancy. [*101:* 33.4.3.1]

20.6 Ambulatory Health Care Centers.

20.6.1 Application. New and existing ambulatory health care centers shall comply with Section 20.6 and NFPA *101*.

20.6.2* Operating Features.

20.6.2.1 Evacuation and Relocation Plan and Fire Drills.

20.6.2.1.1 The administration of every ambulatory health care facility shall have, in effect and available to all supervisory personnel, written copies of a plan for the protection of all persons in the event of fire, for their evacuation to areas of refuge, and for their evacuation from the building when necessary. [*101:* 20.7.1.1; *101:* 21.7.1.2]

20.6.2.1.2 All employees shall be periodically instructed and kept informed with respect to their duties under the plan required by 20.6.2.1.1. [*101:* 20.7.1.2; *101:* 21.7.1.2]

20.6.2.1.3 A copy of the plan required by 20.6.2.1.1 shall be readily available at all times when the facility is open. [*101:* 20.7.1.3; *101:* 21.7.1.3]

20.6.2.1.4 The provisions of Section 10.6 and 20.6.2.1.5 through 20.6.2.2.3 shall apply.

20.6.2.1.5* Fire drills in ambulatory health care facilities shall include the simulation of emergency fire conditions. [*101:* 20.7.1.4; *101:* 21.7.1.4]

20.6.2.1.6 Patients shall not be required to be moved during drills to safe areas or to the exterior of the building. [*101:* 20.7.1.5; *101:* 21.7.1.5]

20.6.2.1.7 Drills shall be conducted quarterly on each shift to familiarize facility personnel (including but not limited to nurses, interns, maintenance engineers, and administrative staff) with the emergency action required under varied conditions. [*101:* 20.7.1.6; *101:* 21.7.1.6]

20.6.2.1.8 Employees of ambulatory health care facilities shall be instructed in life safety procedures and devices. [*101:* 20.7.1.7; *101:* 21.7.1.7]

20.6.2.2 Procedure in Case of Fire.

20.6.2.2.1* Protection of Patients.

20.6.2.2.1.1 For ambulatory health care facilities, the proper protection of patients shall require the prompt and effective response of ambulatory health care personnel. [*101:* 20.7.2.1.1; *101:* 21.7.2.1.1]

20.6.2.2.1.2 The basic response required of staff shall include the following:

(1) Removal of all occupants directly involved with the fire emergency
(2) Transmission of an appropriate fire alarm signal to warn other building occupants and summon staff
(3) Confinement of the effects of the fire by closing doors to isolate the fire area
(4) Relocation of patients as detailed in the facility's fire safety plan [*101:* 20.7.2.1.2; *101:* 21.7.2.1.2]

20.6.2.2.2 Fire Safety Plan. A written fire safety plan shall provide for the following:

(1) Use of alarms
(2) Transmission of alarms to fire department
(3) Response to alarms
(4) Isolation of fire
(5) Evacuation of immediate area
(6) Evacuation of smoke compartment
(7) Preparation of floors and building for evacuation
(8) Extinguishment of fire [*101:* 20.7.2.2; *101:* 21.7.2.2]

20.6.2.2.3 Staff Response.

20.6.2.2.3.1 All personnel shall be instructed in the use of and response to fire alarms. [*101:* 20.7.2.3.1; *101:* 21.7.2.3.1]

20.6.2.2.3.2 All personnel shall be instructed in the use of the code phrase to ensure transmission of an alarm under either of the following conditions:

(1) When the individual who discovers a fire must immediately go to the aid of an endangered person
(2) During a malfunction of the building fire alarm system [*101:* 20.7.2.3.2; *101:* 21.7.2.3.2]

20.6.2.2.3.3 Personnel hearing the code announced shall first activate the building fire alarm using the nearest fire alarm box and then shall execute immediately their duties as outlined in the fire safety plan. [*101:* 20.7.2.3.3; *101:* 21.7.2.3.3]

20.6.2.3 Maintenance of Exits.

20.6.2.3.1 Proper maintenance shall be provided to ensure the dependability of the method of evacuation selected. [*101:* 20.7.3.1; *101:* 21.7.3.1]

20.6.2.3.2 Ambulatory health care occupancies that find it necessary to lock exits shall, at all times, maintain an adequate staff qualified to release locks and direct occupants from the immediate danger area to a place of safety in case of fire or other emergency. [*101:* 20.7.3.2; *101:* 21.7.3.2]

20.6.2.4* Smoking. Smoking regulations shall be adopted and shall include not less than the following provisions:

(1) Smoking shall be prohibited in any room, ward, or compartment where flammable liquids, combustible gases, or oxygen is used or stored and in any other hazardous location, and such areas shall be posted with signs that read NO SMOKING or shall be posted with the international symbol for no smoking.
(2) In ambulatory health care facilities where smoking is prohibited and signs are placed at all major entrances, secondary signs with language that prohibits smoking shall not be required.
(3) Smoking by patients classified as not responsible shall be prohibited.
(4) The requirement of 20.6.2.4(3) shall not apply where the patient is under direct supervision.
(5) Ashtrays of noncombustible material and safe design shall be provided in all areas where smoking is permitted.
(6) Metal containers with self-closing cover devices into which ashtrays can be emptied shall be readily available to all areas where smoking is permitted. [*101:* 20.7.4; *101:* 21.7.4]

20.6.2.5 Furnishings, Mattresses, and Decorations.

20.6.2.5.1* Draperies, curtains, and other loosely hanging fabrics and films serving as furnishings or decorations in ambulatory health care occupancies shall be in accordance with the provisions of 12.6.2, and the following also shall apply:

(1) Such curtains shall include cubicle curtains.
(2) Such curtains shall not include curtains at showers. [*101:* 20.7.5.1; *101:* 21.7.5.1]

20.6.2.5.2 Newly introduced upholstered furniture shall comply with 12.6.3.1 and one of the following provisions:

(1) The furniture shall meet the criteria specified in 12.6.3.2.1.
(2) The furniture shall be in a building protected throughout by an approved, supervised automatic sprinkler system in accordance with NFPA 13. [*101:* 20.7.5.2; *101:* 21.7.5.2]

20.6.2.5.3 Newly introduced mattresses shall comply with 12.6.3.2 and one of the following provisions:

(1) The mattresses shall meet the criteria specified in 12.6.3.2.2.
(2) The mattresses shall be in a building protected throughout by an approved, supervised automatic sprinkler system in accordance with NFPA 13. [*101:* 20.7.5.3; *101:* 21.7.5.3]

20.6.2.5.4 Combustible decorations shall be prohibited, unless one of the following criteria is met:

(1) They are flame-retardant.
(2) The decorations meet the flame propagation performance criteria contained in Test Method 1 or Test Method 2, as appropriate, of NFPA 701, *Standard Methods of Fire Tests for Flame Propagation of Textiles and Films*.
(3) The decorations exhibit a heat release rate not exceeding 100 kW when tested in accordance with NFPA 289, *Standard Method of Fire Test for Individual Fuel Packages*, using the 20 kW ignition source.
(4)*The decorations, such as photographs, paintings, and other art, are attached directly to the walls, ceiling, and non-fire-rated doors in accordance with the following:
   (a) Decorations on non-fire-rated doors do not interfere with the operation or any required latching of the door and do not exceed the area limitations of 20.6.2.5.4(b) or (c).
   (b) Decorations do not exceed 20 percent of the wall, ceiling, and door areas inside any room or space of a smoke compartment that is not protected throughout by an approved automatic sprinkler system in accordance with Section 13.3.
   (c) Decorations do not exceed 30 percent of the wall, ceiling, and door areas inside any room or space of a smoke compartment that is protected throughout by an approved supervised automatic sprinkler system in accordance with Section 13.3. [*101:* 20.7.5.4; *101:* 21.7.5.4] [*101:* 20.7.5.4; *101:* 21.7.5.4]

20.6.2.5.5 Soiled Linen and Trash Receptacles.

20.6.2.5.5.1 Soiled linen or trash collection receptacles shall not exceed 32 gal (121 L) in capacity, and the following also shall apply:

(1) The average density of container capacity in a room or space shall not exceed 0.5 gal/ft^2 (20.4 L/m^2).
(2) A capacity of 32 gal (121 L) shall not be exceeded within any 64 ft^2 (6 m^2) area.
(3) Mobile soiled linen or trash collection receptacles with capacities greater than 32 gal (121 L) shall be located in a room protected as a hazardous area when not attended.
(4) Container size and density shall not be limited in hazardous areas. [*101:* 20.7.5.5.1; *101:* 21.7.5.5.1]

20.6.2.5.5.2* Containers used solely for recycling clean waste or for patient records awaiting destruction shall be permitted to be excluded from the requirements of 20.6.2.5.5.1 where all the following conditions are met:

(1) Each container shall be limited to a maximum capacity of 96 gal (363 L), except as permitted by 20.6.2.5.5.2(2) or (3).
(2) Containers with capacities greater than 96 gal (363 L) shall be located in a room protected as a hazardous area when not attended.
(3) Container size shall not be limited in hazardous areas.
(4) Containers for combustibles shall be labeled and listed as meeting the requirements of FM Approval Standard 6921, *Containers for Combustible Waste*; however, such testing, listing, and labeling shall not be limited to FM Approvals. [*101:* 20.7.5.5.2; *101:* 21.7.5.5.2]

20.6.2.5.5.3 The provisions of 19.2.1.1 through 19.2.1.2 applicable to soiled linen and trash receptacles shall not apply.

20.6.2.6 Portable Space-Heating Devices. Portable space-heating devices shall be prohibited in all ambulatory health care occupancies, unless both of the following criteria are met:

(1) Such devices are used only in nonsleeping staff and employee areas.
(2) The heating elements of such devices do not exceed 212°F (100°C). [*101:* 20.7.8; *101:* 21.7.8]

20.6.3 Interior Finish.

20.6.3.1 General. Interior finish shall be in accordance with Section 12.5. [*101:* 20.3.3.1; *101:* 21.3.3.1]

20.6.3.2 Interior Wall and Ceiling Finish.

20.6.3.2.1 Interior wall and ceiling finish material complying with Section 12.5 shall be Class A or Class B in exits and in exit access corridors. [*101:* 20.3.3.2.1; *101:* 21.3.3.2.1]

20.6.3.2.2 Interior wall and ceiling finishes shall be Class A, Class B, or Class C in areas other than those specified in 20.6.3.2.1. [*101:* 20.3.3.2.2; *101:* 21.3.3.2.2]

20.6.3.3 New Interior Floor Finish.

20.6.3.3.1 New interior floor finish shall comply with Section 12.5. [*101:* 20.3.3.3.1]

20.6.3.3.2 New interior floor finish in exit enclosures shall be Class I or Class II. [*101:* 20.3.3.3.2]

20.6.3.3.3 New interior floor finish shall comply with 12.5.8.1 or 12.5.8.2, as applicable. [*101:* 20.3.3.3.3]

20.6.3.4 Existing Interior Floor Finish. (Reserved) [*101:* 21.3.3.3]

20.7 Detention and Correctional Occupancies.

20.7.1 Application. New and existing detention and correctional occupancies shall comply with Section 20.7 and NFPA *101*.

20.7.2 Operating Features.

20.7.2.1 Attendants, Evacuation Plan, Fire Drills.

20.7.2.1.1 Detention and correctional facilities, or those portions of facilities having such occupancy, shall be provided with 24-hour staffing, and the following requirements also shall apply:

(1) Staff shall be within three floors or a 300 ft (91 m) horizontal distance of the access door of each resident housing area.
(2) For Use Condition III, Use Condition IV, and Use Condition V, the arrangement shall be such that the staff involved starts the release of locks necessary for emergency evacuation or rescue and initiates other necessary emergency actions within 2 minutes of alarm.
(3) The following shall apply to areas in which all locks are unlocked remotely in compliance with 22.2.11.8 or 23.2.11.8 of NFPA *101*:
  (a) Staff shall not be required to be within three floors or 300 ft (91 m) of the access door.
  (b) The 10-lock, manual key exemption of 22.2.11.8.2 or 23.2.11.8.2 of NFPA *101* shall not be permitted to be used in conjunction with the alternative requirement of 20.7.2.1.1(3)(a). [*101:* 22.7.1.1; *101:* 23.7.1.1]

20.7.2.1.2* Provisions shall be made so that residents in Use Condition III, Use Condition IV, and Use Condition V shall be able to notify staff of an emergency. [*101:* 22.7.1.2; *101:* 23.7.1.2]

20.7.2.1.3* The administration of every detention or correctional facility shall have, in effect and available to all supervisory personnel, written copies of a plan for the protection of all persons in the event of fire, for their evacuation to areas of refuge, and for evacuation from the building when necessary. [*101:* 22.7.1.3; *101:* 23.7.1.3]

20.7.2.1.3.1 All employees shall be instructed and drilled with respect to their duties under the plan. [*101:* 22.7.1.3.1; *101:* 23.7.1.3.1]

20.7.2.1.3.2 The plan shall be coordinated with, and reviewed by, the fire department legally committed to serve the facility. [*101:* 22.7.1.3.2; *101:* 23.7.1.3.2]

20.7.2.1.4 Employees of detention and correctional occupancies shall be instructed in the proper use of portable fire extinguishers and other manual fire suppression equipment. [*101:* 22.7.1.4; *101:* 23.7.1.4]

20.7.2.1.4.1 The training specified in 20.7.2.1.4 shall be provided to new staff promptly upon commencement of duty. [*101:* 22.7.1.4.1; *101:* 23.7.1.4.1]

20.7.2.1.4.2 Refresher training shall be provided to existing staff at not less than annual intervals. [*101:* 22.7.1.4.2; *101:* 23.7.1.4.2]

20.7.2.2* Combustible Personal Property. Books, clothing, and other combustible personal property allowed in sleeping rooms shall be stored in closable metal lockers or an approved fire-resistant container. [*101:* 22.7.2; *101:* 23.7.2]

20.7.2.3 Heat-Producing Appliances. The number of heat-producing appliances, such as toasters and hot plates, and the overall use of electrical power within a sleeping room shall be controlled by facility administration. [*101:* 22.7.3; *101:* 23.7.3]

20.7.2.4* Furnishings, Bedding, and Decorations.

20.7.2.4.1 Draperies and curtains, including privacy curtains, in detention and correctional occupancies shall be in accordance with the provisions of 12.6.2. [*101:* 22.7.4.1; *101:* 23.7.4.1]

20.7.2.4.2 Newly introduced upholstered furniture within detention and correctional occupancies shall meet the criteria specified in 12.6.3.1(2) and 12.6.3.2.1. [*101:* 23.7.4.2]

20.7.2.4.3* Newly introduced mattresses within detention and correctional occupancies shall meet the criteria specified in 12.6.3.2 and 12.6.3.2.2. [*101:* 23.7.4.3]

20.7.2.4.4 Combustible decorations shall be prohibited in any detention or correctional occupancy unless flame-retardant. [*101:* 22.7.4.4; *101:* 23.7.4.4]

20.7.2.4.5 Wastebaskets and other waste containers shall be of noncombustible or other approved materials. Waste containers with a capacity exceeding 20 gal (76 L) shall be provided with a noncombustible lid or lid of other approved material. [*101:* 22.7.4.5; *101:* 23.7.4.5]

20.7.2.5 Keys. All keys necessary for unlocking doors installed in a means of egress shall be individually identified by both touch and sight. [*101:* 22.7.5; *101:* 23.7.5]

20.7.2.6 Portable Space-Heating Devices. Portable space-heating devices shall be prohibited in all detention and correctional occupancies. [*101:* 22.7.6; *101:* 23.7.6]

20.7.2.7 Doors and door hardware in means of egress shall be inspected monthly by an appropriately trained person. The inspection shall be documented. [*101:* 22.7.7; *101:* 23.7.7]

20.7.3 Interior Finish.

20.7.3.1 General. Interior finish shall be in accordance with Section 12.5. [*101:* 22.3.3.1; *101:* 23.3.3.1]

20.7.3.2 New Interior Wall and Ceiling Finish. New interior wall and ceiling finish materials complying with Section 12.5 shall be Class A or Class B in corridors, in exits, and in any space not separated from corridors and exits by partitions capable of retarding the passage of smoke; and Class A, Class B, or Class C in all other areas. The provisions of 12.5.9.1 shall not apply to new detention and correctional occupancies. [*101:* 22.3.3.2]

20.7.3.3 Existing Interior Wall and Ceiling Finish. Existing interior wall and ceiling finish materials complying with Section 12.5 shall be Class A or Class B in corridors, in exits, and in any space not separated from corridors and exits by partitions capable of retarding the passage of smoke; and Class A, Class B, or Class C in all other areas. [*101:* 23.3.3.2]

20.7.3.4 New Interior Floor Finish.

20.7.3.4.1 New interior floor finish shall comply with Section 12.5. [*101:* 22.3.3.3.1]

20.7.3.4.2 Interior floor finish in exit enclosures and exit access corridors shall be not less than Class II. The provisions of 12.5.9.2 shall not apply to new detention and correctional occupancies. [*101:* 22.3.3.3.2]

20.7.3.4.3 New interior floor finish shall comply with 12.5.8.1 or 12.5.8.2, as applicable. [*101:* 22.3.3.3.3]

20.7.3.5 Existing Interior Floor Finish.

20.7.3.5.1 Existing interior floor finish complying with Section 12.5 shall be Class I or Class II in corridors and exits. [*101:* 23.3.3.3.1]

20.7.3.5.2 Existing floor finish material of Class A or Class B in nonsprinklered smoke compartments and Class A, Class B, or Class C in sprinklered smoke compartments shall be permitted to be continued to be used, provided that it has been evaluated based on tests performed in accordance with 12.5.4. [*101:* 23.3.3.3.2]

20.7.3.6 Interior Finish (Nonsprinklered Existing Building Renovations).

20.7.3.6.1 Interior Wall and Ceiling Finish. Interior wall and ceiling finish materials complying with Section 12.5 shall be Class A in corridors, in exits, and in any space not separated from corridors and exits by partitions capable of retarding the passage of smoke; and Class A, Class B, or Class C in all other areas. [*101:* 22.4.4.8.1]

20.7.3.6.2 Interior Floor Finish.

20.7.3.6.2.1 Interior floor finish shall comply with Section 12.5. [*101:* 22.4.4.8.2.1]

20.7.3.6.2.2 New interior floor finish in exit enclosures and exit access corridors shall be not less than Class I. [*101:* 22.4.4.8.2.2]

20.7.3.6.2.3 Interior floor finish shall comply with 12.5.8.1 or 12.5.8.2, as applicable. [*101:* 22.4.4.8.2.3]

20.8 Hotels and Dormitories.

20.8.1 Application. New and existing hotels and dormitories shall comply with Section 20.8 and NFPA *101*.

20.8.2 Operating Features.

20.8.2.1 Hotel Emergency Organization.

20.8.2.1.1* Employees of hotels shall be instructed and drilled in the duties they are to perform in the event of fire, panic, or other emergency. [*101:* 28.7.1.1; *101:* 29.7.1.1]

20.8.2.1.2* Drills of the emergency organization shall be held at quarterly intervals and shall cover such points as the operation and maintenance of the available first aid fire appliances, the testing of devices to alert guests, and a study of instructions for emergency duties. [*101:* 28.7.1.2; *101:* 29.7.1.2]

20.8.2.2 Emergency Duties. Upon discovery of a fire, employees shall carry out all of the following duties:

(1) Activation of the facility fire protection signaling system, if provided
(2) Notification of the public fire department
(3) Other action as previously instructed [*101:* 28.7.2; *101:* 29.7.2]

20.8.2.3 Drills in Dormitories. Emergency egress and relocation drills in accordance with Section 10.5 shall be held with sufficient frequency to familiarize occupants with all types of hazards and to establish conduct of the drill as a matter of routine. Drills shall be conducted during peak occupancy periods and shall include suitable procedures to ensure that all persons subject to the drill participate. [*101:* 28.7.3; *101:* 29.7.3]

20.8.2.4 Emergency Instructions for Residents or Guests.

20.8.2.4.1* A floor diagram reflecting the actual floor arrangement, exit locations, and room identification shall be posted in a location and manner acceptable to the AHJ on, or immediately adjacent to, every guest room door in hotels and in every resident room in dormitories. [*101:* 28.7.4.1; *101:* 29.7.4.1]

20.8.2.4.2* Fire safety information shall be provided to allow guests to make the decision to evacuate to the outside, to evacuate to an area of refuge, to remain in place, or to employ any combination of the three options. [*101:* 28.7.4.2; *101:* 29.7.4.2]

20.8.2.4.3 Emergency Action Plans. Emergency action plans in accordance with Section 10.8 shall be provided. [*101:* 28.7.5]

20.8.2.5 Contents and Furnishings.

20.8.2.5.1 New draperies, curtains, and other similar loosely hanging furnishings and decorations shall meet the flame propagation performance criteria contained in Test Method 1 or Test Method 2, as appropriate, of NFPA 701, *Standard Methods of Fire Tests for Flame Propagation of Textiles and Films*. [*101:* 28.7.6.1; *101:* 29.7.6.1]

20.8.2.5.2 Upholstered Furniture and Mattresses.

20.8.2.5.2.1 Newly introduced upholstered furniture shall meet the criteria specified in 12.6.3.1 and 12.6.3.2.2. [*101:* 28.7.6.2.1; *101:* 29.7.6.2.1]

20.8.2.5.2.2 Newly introduced mattresses shall meet the criteria specified in 12.6.3.2 and 12.6.3.2.2. [*101:* 28.7.6.2.2]

20.8.2.5.3 Furnishings or decorations of an explosive or highly flammable character shall not be used. [*101:* 28.7.6.3; *101:* 29.7.6.3]

20.8.2.5.4 Fire-retardant coatings shall be maintained to retain the effectiveness of the treatment under service conditions encountered in actual use. [*101:* 28.7.6.4; *101:* 29.7.6.4]

20.8.2.6 Fuel-Fired Heaters. Unvented fuel-fired heaters, other than gas space heaters in compliance with NFPA 54 shall not be used. [*101:* 28.5.2.2; *101:* 29.5.2.2]

20.8.3 Interior Finish.

20.8.3.1 General. Interior finish shall be in accordance with Section 12.5. [*101:* 28.3.3.1; *101:* 29.3.3.1]

20.8.3.2 New Interior Wall and Ceiling Finish. New interior wall and ceiling finish materials complying with Section 12.5 shall be permitted as follows:

(1) Exit enclosures — Class A
(2) Lobbies and corridors — Class A or Class B
(3) Other spaces — Class A, Class B, or Class C [*101:* 28.3.3.2]

20.8.3.3 Existing Interior Wall and Ceiling Finish. Existing interior wall and ceiling finish materials complying with Section 12.5 shall be permitted as follows:

(1) Exit enclosures — Class A or Class B
(2) Lobbies and corridors — Class A or Class B
(3) Other spaces — Class A, Class B, or Class C [*101:* 29.3.3.2]

20.8.3.4 New Interior Floor Finish.

20.8.3.4.1 New interior floor finish shall comply with Section 12.5. [*101:* 28.3.3.3.1]

20.8.3.4.2 New interior floor finish in exit enclosures and exit access corridors and spaces not separated from them by walls complying with 28.3.6.1 of NFPA *101* shall be not less than Class II. [*101:* 28.3.3.3.2]

20.8.3.4.3 New interior floor finish shall comply with 12.5.8.1 or 12.5.8.2, as applicable. [*101:* 28.3.3.3.3]

20.8.3.5 Interior Floor Finish (Existing Nonsprinklered Buildings). In nonsprinklered buildings, newly installed interior floor finish in exits and exit access corridors shall be not less than Class II in accordance with 12.5.8. [*101:* 29.3.3.3]

20.9 Apartment Buildings.

20.9.1 Application. New and existing apartment buildings shall comply with Section 20.9 and NFPA *101*.

20.9.2 Operating Features.

20.9.2.1 Emergency Instructions for Residents of Apartment Buildings. Emergency instructions shall be provided annually to each dwelling unit to indicate the location of alarms, egress paths, and actions to be taken, both in response to a fire in the dwelling unit and in response to the sounding of the alarm system. [*101:* 30.7.1; *101:* 31.7.1]

20.9.2.2 Fuel-Fired Heaters. Unvented fuel-fired heaters, other than gas space heaters in compliance with NFPA 54, shall not be used. [*101:* 30.5.2.2; *101:* 31.5.2.2]

20.9.3 Interior Finish.

20.9.3.1 General. Interior finish shall be in accordance with Section 12.5. [*101:* 30.3.3.1; *101:* 31.3.3.1]

20.9.3.2 New Interior Wall and Ceiling Finish. New interior wall and ceiling finish materials complying with Section 12.5 shall be permitted as follows:

(1) Exit enclosures — Class A
(2) Lobbies and corridors — Class A or Class B
(3) Other spaces — Class A, Class B, or Class C [*101:* 30.3.3.2]

20.9.3.3 Existing Interior Wall and Ceiling Finish. Existing interior wall and ceiling finish materials complying with Section 12.5 shall be permitted as follows:

(1) Exit enclosures — Class A or Class B
(2) Lobbies and corridors — Class A or Class B
(3) Other spaces — Class A, Class B, or Class C [*101:* 31.3.3.2]

20.9.3.4 New Interior Floor Finish.

20.9.3.4.1 New interior floor finish shall comply with Section 12.5. [*101:* 30.3.3.3.1]

20.9.3.4.2 New interior floor finish in exit enclosures and exit access corridors and spaces not separated from them by walls complying with 30.3.6 of NFPA *101* shall be not less than Class II. [*101:* 30.3.3.3.2]

20.9.3.4.3 New interior floor finish shall comply with 12.5.8.1 or 12.5.8.2, as applicable. [*101:* 30.3.3.3.3]

20.9.3.5 Existing Interior Floor Finish. In buildings utilizing Option 1 or Option 2, as defined in 31.1.1.1 of NFPA *101*, newly installed interior floor finish in exits and exit access corridors shall be not less than Class II in accordance with 12.5.8. [*101:* 31.3.3.3]

20.9.4 Contents and Furnishings.

20.9.4.1 Contents and furnishings shall not be required to comply with Section 12.6. [*101:* 30.7.2.1; *101:* 31.7.2.1]

20.9.4.2 Furnishings or decorations of an explosive or highly flammable character shall not be used outside of dwelling units. [*101:* 30.7.2.2; *101:* 31.7.2.2]

20.9.4.3 Fire-retardant coatings shall be maintained to retain the effectiveness of the treatment under service conditions encountered in actual use. [*101:* 30.7.2.3; *101:* 31.7.2.3]

20.10 Lodging or Rooming Houses.

20.10.1 Application. New and existing lodging or rooming houses shall comply with Section 20.10 and NFPA *101*.

20.10.2 Fuel-Fired Heaters. Unvented fuel-fired heaters, other than gas space heaters in compliance with NFPA 54, shall not be used. [*101:* 26.5.2.2]

20.10.3 Interior Finish.

20.10.3.1 General. Interior finish shall be in accordance with Section 12.5. [*101:* 26.3.3.1]

20.10.3.2 Interior Wall and Ceiling Finish. Interior wall and ceiling finish materials complying with Section 12.5 shall be Class A, Class B, or Class C. [*101:* 26.3.3.2]

20.10.3.3 Interior Floor Finish.

20.10.3.3.1 Newly installed interior floor finish shall comply with Section 12.5. [*101:* 26.3.3.3.1]

20.10.3.3.2 Newly installed interior floor finish shall comply with 12.5.8.1 or 12.5.8.2, as applicable. [*101:* 26.3.3.3.2]

20.10.4 Contents and furnishings shall not be required to comply with Section 12.6. [*101:* 26.7.1.1]

20.10.4.1 Furnishings or decorations of an explosive or highly flammable character shall not be used. [*101:* 26.7.1.2]

20.10.4.2 Fire-retardant coatings shall be maintained to retain the effectiveness of the treatment under service conditions encountered in actual use. [*101:* 26.7.1.3]

20.11 One- and Two-Family Dwellings and Manufactured Housing.

20.11.1 Application. New and existing one- and two-family dwellings shall comply with Section 20.11 and NFPA *101*.

20.11.2 Fuel-Fired Heaters. Unvented fuel-fired heaters shall not be used, unless they are listed and approved. [*101:* 24.5.1.2]

20.11.3 Interior Finish.

20.11.3.1 General. Interior finish shall be in accordance with Section 12.5. [*101:* 24.3.3.1]

20.11.3.2 Interior Wall and Ceiling Finish. Interior wall and ceiling finish materials complying with Section 12.5 shall be Class A, Class B, or Class C. [*101:* 24.3.3.2]

20.11.3.3 Interior Floor Finish. (Reserved) [*101:* 24.3.3.3]

20.11.4 Fire Protection of Floors. In new construction, floor assemblies shall be provided with a continuous membrane of gypsum wallboard having a nominal thickness of not less than ½ in. (13 mm), or equivalent, to protect the floor framing members from a fire exposure from below.

20.11.4.1 Protection in accordance with 20.11.4 shall not be required where the building is protected by an approved automatic sprinkler system installed in accordance with 13.3.1.2.

20.11.4.2 Protection in accordance with 20.11.4 shall not be required for floor assemblies located directly over a crawl space not intended for storage or fuel-fired equipment.

20.11.4.3 Portions of floor assemblies shall be permitted to be unprotected where the aggregate area of the unprotected portions does not exceed 80 ft^2 (7.4 m^2) per story and where fire blocking is installed along the perimeter of the unprotected portion to separate the unprotected portion from the remainder of the floor assembly.

20.11.4.4* Protection in accordance with 20.11.4 shall not be required in floor assemblies using wood joists with nominal dimensions not less than 2 in. (51 mm) in thickness by 10 in. (254 mm) in width, or other approved floor assemblies providing equivalent performance.

20.11.4.5 Protection in accordance with 20.11.4 shall not be required in floor assemblies using wood joist structural composite lumber that are compliant with ASTM D 5456 and that have dimensions not less than 1½ in. (38 mm) in thickness by 9¼ in. (235 mm) in width.

20.11.4.6 Penetrations by mechanical, plumbing, fire protection, and electrical systems through the membrane protection required by 20.11.4 shall not be required to be protected.

20.11.5 Manufactured Housing. New manufactured housing shall comply with Section 20.11 and NFPA 501, *Standard on Manufactured Housing*.

20.12 Mercantile Occupancies.

20.12.1 Application. New and existing mercantile occupancies shall comply with Section 20.12 and NFPA *101*.

20.12.2 Operating Features.

20.12.2.1 Emergency Plans. Emergency plans complying with Section 10.8 shall be provided in high-rise buildings. [*101:* 36.7.1; *101:* 37.7.1]

20.12.2.2 Drills. In every Class A or Class B mercantile occupancy, employees shall be periodically trained in accordance with Section 10.5. [*101:* 36.7.2; *101:* 37.7.2]

20.12.2.3 Extinguisher Training. Employees of mercantile occupancies shall be periodically instructed in the use of portable fire extinguishers. [*101:* 36.7.3; *101:* 37.7.3]

20.12.2.4 Food Service Operations. Food service operations shall comply with Chapter 50. [*101:* 36.7.4; *101:* 37.7.4]

20.12.3 Interior Finish.

20.12.3.1 General. Interior finish shall be in accordance with Section 12.5. [*101:* 36.3.3.1; *101:* 37.3.3.1]

20.12.3.2 Interior Wall and Ceiling Finish. Interior wall and ceiling finish materials complying with Section 12.5 shall be Class A, Class B, or Class C. [*101:* 36.3.3.2; *101:* 37.3.3.2]

20.12.3.3 Interior Floor Finish.

20.12.3.3.1 New interior floor finish shall comply with Section 12.5. [*101:* 36.3.3.3.1]

20.12.3.3.2 New interior floor finish in exit enclosures shall be Class I or Class II. [*101:* 36.3.3.3.2]

20.12.3.3.3 New interior floor finish shall comply with 12.5.8.1 or 12.5.8.2, as applicable. [*101:* 36.3.3.3.3]

20.12.3.3.4 Existing Interior Floor Finish. (Reserved) [*101:* 37.3.3.3]

20.13 Business Occupancies.

20.13.1 Application. New and existing business occupancies shall comply with Section 20.13 and NFPA *101*.

20.13.2 Operating Features.

20.13.2.1 Emergency Plans. Emergency plans complying with Section 10.8 shall be provided in high-rise buildings. [*101:* 38.7.1; *101:* 39.7.1]

20.13.2.2 Drills. In all business occupancy buildings occupied by more than 500 persons, or by more than 100 persons above or below the street level, employees and supervisory personnel shall be periodically instructed in accordance with Section 10.5 and shall hold drills periodically where practicable. [*101:* 38.7.2; *101:* 39.7.2]

20.13.2.3 Extinguisher Training. Designated employees of business occupancies shall be periodically instructed in the use of portable fire extinguishers. [*101:* 38.7.3; *101:* 39.7.3]

20.13.2.4 Food Service Operations. Food service operations shall comply with Chapter 50. [*101:* 38.7.4; *101:* 39.7.4]

20.13.3 Interior Finish.

20.13.3.1 General. Interior finish shall be in accordance with Section 12.5. [*101:* 38.3.3.1; *101:* 39.3.3.1]

20.13.3.2 Interior Wall and Ceiling Finish.

20.13.3.2.1 Interior wall and ceiling finish material complying with Section 12.5 shall be Class A or Class B in exits and in exit access corridors. [*101:* 38.3.3.2.1; *101:* 39.3.3.2.1]

20.13.3.2.2 Interior wall and ceiling finishes shall be Class A, Class B, or Class C in areas other than those specified in 20.13.3.2.1. [*101:* 38.3.3.2.2; *101:* 39.3.3.2.2]

20.13.3.3 Interior Floor Finish.

20.13.3.3.1 New interior floor finish shall comply with Section 12.5. [*101:* 38.3.3.3.1]

20.13.3.3.2 New interior floor finish in exit enclosures shall be Class I or Class II. [*101:* 38.3.3.3.2]

20.13.3.3.3 New interior floor finish shall comply with 12.5.8.1 or 12.5.8.2, as applicable. [*101:* 38.3.3.3.3]

20.13.3.3.4 Existing Interior Floor Finish. (Reserved) [*101:* 39.3.3.3]

20.14 Industrial Occupancies.

20.14.1 Application. New and existing industrial occupancies shall comply with Section 20.14 and NFPA *101*.

20.14.2 Permits. Permits, where required, shall comply with Section 1.12.

20.14.3 Interior Finish.

20.14.3.1 General. Interior finish shall be in accordance with Section 12.5. [*101:* 40.3.3.1]

20.14.3.2 Interior Wall and Ceiling Finish. Interior wall and ceiling finish materials complying with Section 12.5 shall be Class A, Class B, or Class C in operating areas and shall be as required by 7.1.4 of NFPA *101* in exit enclosures. [*101:* 40.3.3.2]

20.14.3.3 Interior Floor Finish.

20.14.3.3.1 Interior floor finish in exit enclosures and in exit access corridors shall be Class I or Class II in accordance with 12.5.8.4. [*101:* 40.3.3.3.1]

20.14.3.3.2 Interior floor finish in areas other than those specified in 20.14.3.3.1 shall not be required to comply with 12.5.8. [*101:* 40.3.3.3.2]

20.15 Storage Occupancies.

20.15.1 Application. New and existing storage occupancies shall comply with NFPA *101*, Chapter 34, appropriate codes or standards referenced in Chapter 2, and Section 20.15.

20.15.2 Permits. Permits, where required, shall comply with Section 1.12.

20.15.3 Interior Finish.

20.15.3.1 General. Interior finish shall be in accordance with Section 12.5. [*101:* 42.3.3.1]

20.15.3.2 Interior Wall and Ceiling Finish. Interior wall and ceiling finish materials shall be Class A, Class B, or Class C in accordance with 12.5 in storage areas and shall be as required by 7.1.4 of NFPA *101* in exit enclosures. [*101:* 42.3.3.2]

20.15.3.3 Interior Floor Finish.

20.15.3.3.1 Interior floor finish in exit enclosures and in exit access corridors shall be Class I or Class II. [*101:* 42.3.3.3.1]

20.15.3.3.2 Interior floor finish in areas other than those specified in 20.15.3.3.1 shall not be required to comply with 12.5.8. [*101:* 42.3.3.3.2]

> Paragraph 20.15.4 was revised by a tentative interim amendment. (TIA). See page 1.

20.15.4 Storage, Arrangement, Protection, and Quantities of Hazardous Commodities. The storage, arrangement, protection, and quantities of hazardous commodities shall be in accordance with the applicable provisions of the following:

(1) NFPA 13, *Standard for the Installation of Sprinkler Systems*
(2) NFPA 30, *Flammable and Combustible Liquids Code*
(3) NFPA 30B, *Code for the Manufacture and Storage of Aerosol Products*
(4) NFPA 400, *Hazardous Materials Code*, Chapter 14, for organic peroxide formulations
(5) NFPA 400, *Hazardous Materials Code*, Chapter 15, for oxidizer solids and liquids
(6) NFPA 400, **Hazardous Materials Code**, various chapters, depending on characteristics of a particular pesticide [*101:* 36.4.5.3]

20.15.5 Bulk Storage Elevators. Bulk storage elevators shall comply with 20.15.5 and NFPA 61, *Standard for the Prevention of Fires and Dust Explosions in Agricultural and Food Processing Facilities.*

20.15.5.1* Application. The requirements of 20.15.5 shall apply to all of the following:

(1) All facilities that receive, handle, process, dry, blend, use, mill, package, store, or ship dry agricultural bulk materials, their by-products, or dusts that include grains, oilseeds, agricultural seeds, legumes, sugar, flour, spices, feeds, and other related materials
(2) All facilities designed for manufacturing and handling starch, including drying, grinding, conveying, processing, packaging, and storing dry or modified starch, and dry products and dusts generated from these processes
(3) Those seed preparation and meal-handling systems of oilseed processing plants not covered by NFPA 36, *Standard for Solvent Extraction Plants* [**61:**1.1.1]

20.15.5.2 Subsection 20.15.5 shall not apply to oilseed extraction plants that are covered by NFPA 36. [**61:**1.1.2]

20.15.5.3 Applicability.

20.15.5.3.1 Unless otherwise noted, the provisions of 20.15.5 on bulk storage elevators shall not be applied to facilities, equipment, structures, or installations that were existing or approved for construction or installation prior to the effective date of this *Code*, except in those cases where it is determined by the AHJ that the existing situation involves a distinct hazard to life or adjacent property.

20.15.5.3.2 The requirements of Chapter 11 of NFPA 61 shall apply to all facilities.

20.15.6 Record Storage.

20.15.6.1 Records protection equipment, facilities, and records-handling techniques that provide protection from the hazards of fire shall comply with 20.15.6 and NFPA 232, *Standard for the Protection of Records.*

20.15.6.2* Because of the volume of records, 20.15.6.1 shall not cover large archives or records storage buildings.

20.15.7 Cellulose Nitrate Motion Picture Film Storage.

20.15.7.1 Application. The storage and handling of cellulose nitrate film records shall comply with 20.15.7 and NFPA 40, *Standard for the Storage and Handling of Cellulose Nitrate Film.*

20.15.7.2 Permits. Permits, where required, shall comply with Section 1.12.

20.15.8 High-Piled Storage.

20.15.8.1 Application. Buildings containing high-piled storage shall comply with Chapter 13, Chapter 34, and 20.15.8.

20.15.8.2 Permits. Permits, where required, shall comply with Section 1.12.

20.15.8.3 Fire Department Hose Connections.

20.15.8.3.1 When any portion of the high-piled combustible storage area is greater than 200 ft (61 m) from a fire department access door, Class I standpipe outlets connected to a system sized to deliver 250 gpm (946.4 L/min) at the most hydraulically remote outlet shall be provided in accordance with 20.15.8.3.

20.15.8.3.2 The outlet shall be permitted to be supplied from the sprinkler system and shall be hydraulically calculated.

20.15.8.3.3 Standpipe outlets shall be provided at each of the following locations:

(1) In each exit passageway at the entrance from the storage areas into the passageway
(2) At each intermediate landing between floor levels in every required exit stairway serving the storage area
(3) At exterior entrances into the storage

20.16 Special Structures and High-Rise Buildings.

20.16.1 Application.

20.16.1.1 New and existing special structures and high-rise buildings shall comply with NFPA *101.*

20.16.1.2 Motion picture and television production studio soundstages and approved production facilities shall comply with Chapter 32.

20.17 Historic Buildings and Cultural Resources.

20.17.1 Historic buildings shall comply with this *Code* or with the provisions of NFPA 914, *Code for Fire Protection of Historic Structures.*

20.17.2 Buildings that store or display cultural resources, including museum or library collections, or spaces within other buildings used for such culturally significant purposes, shall comply with this *Code* or with the provisions of NFPA 909, *Code for the Protection of Cultural Resource Properties — Museums, Libraries, and Places of Worship.*

20.17.3 The provisions of this *Code* relating to the construction, repair, alteration, enlargement, restoration, and moving of buildings or structures shall not be mandatory for the following:

(1) Existing buildings or structures identified and classified by the state or local government authority as historic buildings where such buildings comply with NFPA 914
(2)*Buildings or spaces within buildings that store or display cultural resources and comply with the provisions of NFPA 909

Chapter 21   Airports and Heliports

21.1 Hangars. The construction and protection of aircraft hangars from fire shall comply with this section; NFPA 409, *Standard on Aircraft Hangars*; NFPA 410, *Standard on Aircraft Maintenance*; and Sections 40.6 and 42.6 of NFPA *101*.

21.1.1 Permits. Permits, where required, shall comply with Section 1.12.

21.1.2 Fire Department Access. Fire department access roads shall be provided and maintained in accordance with Section 18.2 for all aircraft hangars.

21.1.3 Smoking.

21.1.3.1 Smoking shall be prohibited in aircraft hangars.

21.1.3.2 Smoking shall be in accordance with Section 10.9.

21.1.4* Means of Egress Provisions for Aircraft Servicing Hangars.

21.1.4.1 The requirements of Sections 40.1 through 40.5 of NFPA *101* shall be met, except as modified by 21.1.4.2 through 21.1.4.4. [*101:* 40.6.1]

21.1.4.2 The requirements for exits from aircraft servicing areas shall comply with 21.1.4.2.1 through 21.1.4.2.4. [*101:* 40.6.2]

21.1.4.2.1 There shall be not less than two means of egress from each aircraft servicing area. [*101:* 40.6.2.1]

21.1.4.2.2 Exits from aircraft servicing areas shall be provided at intervals not exceeding 150 ft (46 m) on all exterior walls. [*101:* 40.6.2.2]

21.1.4.2.3 Where horizontal exits are provided, doors shall be provided in the horizontal exit fire barrier at intervals not exceeding 100 ft (30 m). [*101:* 40.6.2.3]

21.1.4.2.4 Where dwarf, or "smash," doors are provided in doors that accommodate aircraft, such doors shall be permitted for compliance with 21.1.4.2.1 through 21.1.4.2.3. [*101:*40.6.2.4]

21.1.4.3 Means of egress from mezzanine floors in aircraft servicing areas shall be arranged so that the travel distance to the nearest exit from any point on the mezzanine does not exceed 75 ft (23 m), and such means of egress shall lead directly to a properly enclosed stair discharging directly to the exterior, to a suitable cutoff area, or to outside stairs. [*101:* 40.6.3]

21.1.4.4 Dead ends shall not exceed 50 ft (15 m) for other than high hazard contents areas and shall not be permitted for high hazard contents areas. [*101:* 40.6.4]

21.1.5* Means of Egress Provisions for Aircraft Storage Hangars.

21.1.5.1 The requirements of Sections 42.1 through 42.5 of NFPA *101* shall be met, except as modified by 21.1.5.1.1 through 21.1.5.1.3. [*101:* 42.6.1]

21.1.5.1.1 There shall be not less than two means of egress from each aircraft storage area. [*101:* 42.6.1.1]

21.1.5.1.2 Exits from aircraft storage areas shall be provided at intervals not exceeding 150 ft (46 m) on all exterior walls. [*101:* 42.6.1.2]

21.1.5.1.3 Where horizontal exits are provided, doors shall be provided in the horizontal exit fire barrier at intervals not exceeding 100 ft (30 m). [*101:* 42.6.1.3]

21.1.5.1.4 Where dwarf, or "smash," doors are provided in doors that accommodate aircraft, such doors shall be permitted for compliance with 21.1.5.1.1, 21.1.5.1.2, and 21.1.5.1.3. [*101:* 42.6.1.4]

21.1.5.2 Means of egress from mezzanine floors in aircraft storage areas shall be arranged so that the travel distance to the nearest exit from any point on the mezzanine does not exceed 75 ft (23 m), and such means of egress shall lead directly to a properly enclosed stair discharging directly to the exterior, to a suitable cutoff area, or to outside stairs. [*101:* 42.6.2]

21.1.5.3 Dead ends shall not exceed 50 ft (15 m) for other than high hazard contents areas and shall not be permitted for high hazard contents areas. [*101:* 42.6.3]

21.2 Terminals.

21.2.1 Application. Airport terminal buildings shall comply with the requirements of Section 21.2 and NFPA 415, *Standard on Airport Terminal Buildings, Fueling Ramp Drainage, and Loading Walkways*.

21.2.2 General.

21.2.2.1 Permits. Permits, where required, shall comply with Section 1.12.

21.2.2.2 Fire department access roads for all airport terminal buildings shall be provided and maintained in accordance with Section 18.2.

21.2.3 Smoking.

21.2.3.1 Smoking shall be prohibited in fuel ramp areas and loading walkways.

21.2.3.2 Smoking shall be in accordance with Section 10.9.

21.2.4 General.

21.2.4.1 Airport terminal buildings shall be of Type I, Type II, or Type IV construction, as defined in NFPA 220, *Standard on Types of Building Construction*.

21.2.4.2* Interior finish materials shall be limited to Class A or Class B regardless of the occupant load. [**415:**4.1.2]

21.2.4.3 Aircraft fueling facilities and ramps shall be designed in accordance with NFPA 407, *Standard for Aircraft Fuel Servicing*, and Chapter 5 of NFPA 415, *Standard on Airport Terminal Buildings, Fueling Ramp Drainage, and Loading Walkways*. [**415:**4.1.3]

21.2.4.4 Belowgrade areas and blind spaces in airport terminal buildings shall be protected against flammable fuel and vapor penetration or shall be mechanically ventilated to provide at least four complete air changes per hour. The mechanical ventilation system shall be installed in accordance with NFPA 91, *Standard for Exhaust Systems for Air Conveying of Vapors, Gases, Mists, and Noncombustible Particulate Solids*. [**415:**4.1.4]

21.2.4.5 Glazing Material–Covered Openings Facing the Ramp.

21.2.4.5.1 Openings covered with glazing material that have the lowest part of the glazing material not less than 7 ft (2.1 m) above each finished floor level shall not be required to comply with 21.2.4.5.3. [**415:**4.1.5.1]

21.2.4.5.2 Openings covered with glazing material listed for use in a fire barrier and installed in accordance with the listing shall not be required to comply with 21.2.4.5.3. [**415:**4.1.5.2]

21.2.4.5.3 Where potential fuel spill points are located less than 100 ft (30.5 m) horizontally from glazing material–covered openings in airport terminal building walls facing the airport ramp, they shall be provided with an automatically activated water spray system in accordance with 21.2.4.5.3.1 or an automatically activated, listed fire shutter system in accordance with 21.2.4.5.3.2. *(See Annex C of NFPA 415.)* [**415:**4.1.5.3]

21.2.4.5.3.1 Where an automatically activated water spray system(s) is provided, it shall be installed in accordance with NFPA 15, *Standard for Water Spray Fixed Systems for Fire Protection*. [**415:**4.1.5.3.1]

21.2.4.5.3.1.1 The system shall be designed to provide a density of at least 0.25 gpm/ft^2 [10.2 (L/min)/m^2] over the exterior surface area of the glazing material. [**415:**4.1.5.3.1.1]

21.2.4.5.3.1.2 Where multiple water spray systems are used, the water supply shall be capable of supplying all systems that could be expected to operate as a result of one fire incident. [**415:**4.1.5.3.1.2]

21.2.4.5.3.1.3 The detection system design analysis for the water spray system shall include consideration of false alarms and detector response time. [**415:**4.1.5.3.1.3]

21.2.4.5.3.2 Where an automatically activated, listed fire shutter is provided, it shall be installed in accordance with its listing. [**415:**4.1.5.3.2]

21.2.5 Heating, Ventilating, and Air Conditioning.

21.2.5.1 Heating, ventilating, and air-conditioning systems shall be installed in accordance with Section 11.2 and Section 11.5, as applicable.

21.2.5.2* Air supply intake and exhaust openings for air-conditioning or ventilating equipment serving the terminal building, if located on the ramp side, shall be not less than 10 ft (3 m) above the grade level of the ramp and shall be at least 50 ft (15 m) from any point of flammable vapor release. [**415:**4.2.2]

21.2.5.3* Openings to rooms that contain coal-, gas-, or oil-fired equipment or any other open-flame device and that face the ramp side of the terminal shall be above ramp grade and 50 ft (15 m) from any point of flammable vapor release. [**415:**4.2.3]

21.2.5.4 Stacks or chimneys from a boiler, heater, or incinerator shall terminate at least 20 ft (6.1 m) above ramp grade and above the roof of the building. Stacks or chimneys from boilers or heaters that use solid fuel or from any incinerator shall be fitted with double screening to control fly ash and sparks. Such stacks or chimneys shall be located so the outlet is at least 100 ft (30.5 m) horizontally from any aircraft position or point of flammable vapor release. [**415:**4.2.4]

21.2.5.5 Incinerators shall conform to the requirements of Chapter 4 of NFPA 82, *Standard on Incinerators and Waste and Linen Handling Systems and Equipment*. [**415:**4.2.5]

21.2.5.6 Exhaust hood ventilation systems for restaurant and flight kitchens shall conform to the applicable portions of Chapter 50. [**415:**4.2.6]

21.2.6 Exits.

21.2.6.1 Airport terminal building means of egress shall conform to the requirements of NFPA *101*, *Life Safety Code*. [**415:**4.3.1]

21.2.6.2* In addition to the exit signage requirements specified in NFPA *101*, doors serving as exits that discharge onto an airport ramp and are provided solely for the purpose of meeting emergency egress requirements from public areas shall be placarded "Emergency Exit Only" in letters at least 2 in. (50 mm) high. [**415:**4.3.2]

21.2.7 Fire Protection — Sprinkler Systems.

21.2.7.1* An airport terminal building with more than 12,000 ft^2 (1115 m^2) total floor area for the assembly portion of the occupancy shall be provided with an automatic sprinkler system installed in accordance with Section 13.3. [**415:**4.5.1.1]

21.2.7.2 Terminal buildings with less than 12,000 ft^2 (1115 m^2) total floor area for the assembly portion of the occupancy shall not be required to be provided with an automatic sprinkler system. [**415:**4.5.1.2]

21.2.7.3 Passenger-handling areas shall be classified as Ordinary Hazard Group 1 Occupancy, as defined in NFPA 13, for the purpose of sprinkler system design. [**415:**4.5.1.3]

21.2.7.4 Baggage, package, and mail-handling areas shall be classified as Ordinary Hazard Group 2 Occupancy, as defined in NFPA 13, for the purpose of sprinkler system design. [**415:**4.5.1.4]

21.2.7.5* Other areas of the airport terminal building shall be classified in accordance with Chapter 5 of NFPA 13, based on the occupancy of the area. [**415:**4.5.1.5]

21.2.7.6 Covered Plane-Loading Positions. Airport terminal buildings having canopy areas or roofed-over recesses at aircraft loading positions that, in effect, place the aircraft totally or substantially under such canopies or roofs shall have the canopies or roofs protected by automatic sprinkler systems in accordance with NFPA 409, *Standard on Aircraft Hangars*. [**415:**4.5.1.6]

21.2.8 Fire Alarm and Communications Systems. A fire alarm and communications system shall be installed as required by 13.7.2.1. [**415:**4.5.2]

21.2.8.1 Means to alert the public fire department or the airport fire station shall be available through manual fire alarm pull stations. Manual fire alarm services shall be installed in accordance with *NFPA 72*. [**415:**4.5.2.1]

21.2.8.2* Annunciation for all building fire alarm signals shall be provided near the front entrance of the building. [**415:**4.5.2.2]

21.2.8.3 If the public fire department has two-way voice communication with a constantly attended location, 21.2.8.2 shall not apply. [**415:**4.5.2.3]

21.2.9 Fire Hydrants. Fire hydrants shall be provided on both the ramp and the street sides of airport terminal buildings. Such hydrants shall be located so that no portion of the terminal building is more than 500 ft (152.4 m) from a hydrant. [**415**:4.5.3]

21.2.10 Standpipe and Hose Systems. Standpipe and hose systems shall be provided for all airport terminal buildings in excess of two stories [35 ft (10.7 m)] in height or 100 ft (30.5 m) in shortest horizontal dimension. Standpipe and hose systems shall be installed in accordance with Section 13.2. [**415**:4.5.4]

21.2.10.1 Class I standpipe systems shall be provided in buildings protected throughout by an approved automatic sprinkler system. Each 2½ in. (63.5 mm) hose connection shall be equipped with a 2½ in. × 1½ in. (63.5 mm × 38 mm) reducer and cap. [**415**:4.5.4.1]

21.2.10.2 Class III standpipe systems shall be provided in nonsprinklered buildings. Paragraphs 5.3.3.1 and 5.3.3.2 of NFPA 14, *Standard for the Installation of Standpipe and Hose Systems*, for Class III systems shall be applicable to this requirement. [**415**:4.5.4.2]

21.2.11 Portable Fire Extinguishers. Portable fire extinguishers shall be provided throughout the airport terminal building in accordance with Section 13.6. [**415**:4.5.6]

21.3 Rooftop Heliport Construction and Protection.

21.3.1 Application. Rooftop heliport construction and protection shall comply with Section 21.3 and NFPA 418, *Standard for Heliports*.

21.3.1.1 Section 21.3 shall not apply to ground level helicopter hangars. All hangars not covered by this section shall comply with NFPA 409.

21.3.1.2 Temporary landing sites and emergency evacuation facilities shall not be required to comply with Section 21.3.

21.3.2 General.

21.3.2.1 Permits. Permits, where required, shall comply with Section 1.12.

21.3.2.2 Fire Department Access. Fire department access roads for all buildings with a rooftop heliport shall be provided and maintained in accordance with Section 18.2.

21.3.2.3 Smoking.

21.3.2.3.1 Smoking shall be prohibited at rooftop heliports.

21.3.2.3.2 Smoking shall be in accordance with Section 10.9.

21.3.3 General Requirements — Land-Based Facilities.

21.3.3.1* Plans.

21.3.3.1.1 The design drawings for the construction and protection of the heliport shall be approved by the AHJ. [**418**:4.2.1]

21.3.3.1.2 The design of the heliport, including all the aeronautical components, shall be in accordance with FAA AC 150/5390-2B, *Heliport Design Advisory Circular*. [**418**:4.2.2]

21.3.3.1.3 The final approach and takeoff (FATO) area, the approach/departure path, and the touchdown and liftoff (TLOF) area shall be designated on the design drawings. [**418**:4.2.3]

21.3.3.2 Tank and Equipment Locations.

21.3.3.2.1 Storage, handling, and use of flammable and combustible liquids shall be in accordance with Chapter 66. [**418**:4.3.1]

21.3.3.2.2 Oxygen and other medical gases shall be stored and used in accordance with Section 9.4 of NFPA 99, *Health Care Facilities Code*. [**418**:4.3.2]

21.3.3.2.3 Aboveground flammable liquid storage tanks, compressed gas storage tanks, fuel storage tanks, and liquefied gas storage tanks shall be laterally located at least 50 ft (15.2 m) from the edge of the final approach and takeoff (FATO) area as defined in FAA AC 150/5390-2B, *Heliport Design Advisory Circular*. [**418**:4.3.3]

21.3.3.3 Fire-Fighting Access.

21.3.3.3.1 The heliport shall have at least two access points for fire-fighting/rescue personnel. The access points shall be located at least 90 degrees from each other as measured from the center of the landing pad (TLOF). [**418**:4.4.1]

21.3.3.3.2 Fences shall not prevent access by fire-fighting/rescue personnel. [**418**:4.4.2]

21.3.3.4 Fuel Spill Control. The landing pad shall be designed so that fuel spills are directed away from access/egress points and passenger holding areas. [**418**:4.5]

21.3.3.5 No Smoking.

21.3.3.5.1 No smoking shall be permitted within 50 ft (15.2 m) of the landing pad edge. [**418**:4.6.1]

21.3.3.5.2 NO SMOKING signs shall be erected at access/egress points to the heliport. [**418**:4.6.2]

21.3.3.6 Fueling System. Fueling systems shall be designed in accordance with Section 42.10. [**418**:4.7]

21.3.3.6.1 Fueling equipment shall not hinder or obstruct access to exits or fire-fighting equipment. [**418**:4.7.1]

21.3.3.6.2 Fueling equipment shall be located 25 ft (7.6 m) from hangars and fixed fire protection equipment. [**418**:4.7.2]

21.3.3.6.3 Fuel servicing equipment shall be designed to not penetrate the FATO and safety area obstruction clearance requirements in FAA AC 150/5390-2B, *Heliport Design Advisory Circular*. [**418**:4.7.3]

21.3.3.7* Means of Egress. At least two means of egress that lead to a public way shall be provided from the landing pad. [**418**:4.8]

21.3.3.7.1* The egress points shall be located at least 90 degrees from each other as measured from the center of the landing pad (TLOF). [**418**:4.8.1]

21.3.3.7.2 The egress points shall be located remotely from each other, not less than 30 ft (9.1 m) apart. [**418**:4.8.2]

21.3.3.7.3 No two egress points shall be located on the same side of the landing pad. [**418**:4.8.3]

21.3.4 Rooftop Landing Facilities.

21.3.4.1* Structural Support. Main structural support members that could be exposed to a fuel spill shall be made fire resistant using listed materials and methods to provide a fire-resistance rating of not less than 2 hours. [**418**:5.2]

21.3.4.2 Landing Pad Pitch. The rooftop landing pad shall be pitched to provide drainage at a slope of 0.5 percent to 2 percent. [**418**:5.3]

21.3.4.2.1 The pitch of the pad shall be designed to protect, at a minimum, the primary egress path, passenger holding area, rooftop hangar, and fire protection activation systems. [**418**:5.3.1]

21.3.4.2.2 Drainage flow shall not penetrate alternate egress points, stairways, ramps, hatches, and other openings not designed for drainage. [**418**:5.3.2]

21.3.4.2.3 The pitch of the pad shall not be required where the pad consists of a passive fire protection grid surface designed and listed for fuel catchment and containment. [**418**:5.3.3]

21.3.4.3 Landing Pad Construction Materials.

21.3.4.3.1 The rooftop landing pad surface shall be constructed of approved noncombustible, nonporous materials. [**418**:5.4.1]

21.3.4.3.2 The contiguous building roof covering within 50 ft (15.2 m) of the landing pad edge shall have a Class A rating. [**418**:5.4.2]

21.3.4.4* Means of Egress. Two means of egress from the rooftop landing pad to the building's egress system shall be provided. [**418**:5.5]

21.3.4.4.1* The egress points shall be located at least 90 degrees from each other as measured from the center of the landing pad (TLOF). [**418**:5.5.1]

21.3.4.4.2 The egress points shall be remotely located from each other, not less than 30 ft (9.1 m) apart. [**418**:5.5.2]

21.3.4.4.3 No two egress points shall be located on the same side of the rooftop landing pad. [**418**:5.5.3]

21.3.4.4.4* Means of egress from the landing pad shall not obstruct flight operations. [**418**:5.5.4]

21.3.4.5 Fire-Fighting Access. (Reserved)

21.3.4.6 Fire Protection. A foam fire-extinguishing system with either a fixed discharge outlet(s) in accordance with 21.3.4.6.3.1 or a hose line(s) in accordance with 21.3.4.6.4.1 shall be designed and installed to protect the rooftop landing pad, unless otherwise permitted by the following:

(1) A foam fire-extinguishing system shall not be required for heliports located on open parking structures or buildings that are not normally occupied.
(2) For H-1 heliports, two portable foam extinguishers, each having a rating of 20-A:160-B, shall be permitted to be used to satisfy the requirement of 21.3.4.6. [**418**:5.7]

21.3.4.6.1 Where trained personnel are not available, fixed fire protection outlet(s) shall be provided. [**418**:5.7.1]

21.3.4.6.2* The foam discharge rate for the fire-extinguishing system shall be 0.10 gpm/ft^2 (4.1 L/min·m^2) for aqueous film forming foam (AFFF). [**418**:5.7.2]

21.3.4.6.3 Fixed Systems.

21.3.4.6.3.1* The area of application of foam discharge for fixed discharge outlet systems shall be the entire rooftop landing pad. [**418**:5.7.3.1]

21.3.4.6.3.2 The duration of foam discharge for the fixed discharge outlet system shall be 5 minutes. [**418**:5.7.3.2]

21.3.4.6.3.2.1 The supply calculation method shall be performed in accordance with Chapter 6 of NFPA 409, *Standard on Aircraft Hangars*. [**418**:5.7.3.2.1]

21.3.4.6.4 Manual Fire-Fighting Equipment.

21.3.4.6.4.1* The area of application of foam discharge for hose line systems shall be the practical critical fire area for the category of the helicopter landing facility in accordance with Table 21.3.4.6.4.1. [**418**:5.7.4.1]

Table 21.3.4.6.4.1 Practical Critical Fire Areas for Hose Line Systems Only

Heliport Category	Helicopter Overall Length*	Practical Critical Fire Area	
		ft^2	m^2
H-1	Less than 50 ft (15.2 m)	375	34.8
H-2	50 ft (15.2 m) up to but not including 80 ft (24.4 m)	840	78.0
H-3	80 ft (24.4 m) up to but not including 120 ft (36.6 m)	1440	133.8

*Helicopter length, including the tail boom and the rotors.
[**418**: Table 5.7.4.1]

21.3.4.6.4.2 The duration of foam discharge for the hose line systems shall be 2 minutes. [**418**:5.7.4.2]

21.3.4.6.4.3 The supply calculation method shall be performed in accordance with Chapter 6 of NFPA 409, *Standard on Aircraft Hangars*. [**418**:5.7.4.3]

21.3.4.6.4.4 A fixed nozzle discharge outlet system shall be one of the following: fixed stationary nozzles around the perimeter, two or more oscillating monitors/nozzles, or in-deck nozzles within the perimeter of the deck. [**418**:5.7.4.4]

21.3.4.6.5 The water supply for the foam system shall be from a source approved by the AHJ. [**418**:5.7.5]

21.3.4.6.5.1 Fire pumps, if used, shall be installed in accordance with Section 13.4. [**418**:5.7.5.1]

21.3.4.6.5.2 Standpipes and hose stations, if used, shall be installed in accordance with Section 13.2. [**418**:5.7.5.2]

21.3.4.6.5.3 Where freezing is possible, freeze protection shall be provided. [**418**:5.7.5.3]

21.3.4.6.6 The foam components shall be installed in an area of the heliport and shall not penetrate the approach takeoff surface, transitional surfaces, and safety area as defined in FAA AC 150/5390-2B, *Heliport Design Advisory Circular*. [**418**:5.7.6]

21.3.4.6.7 At facilities where there is more than one rooftop landing pad, the supply of foam available shall be sufficient to cover an incident on at least one of the pads. [**418**:5.7.7]

21.3.4.6.8 Where fixed foam systems utilizing fixed deck nozzles or oscillating foam turrets, or both, are installed, system components shall be listed or approved. [**418**:5.7.8]

21.3.4.6.9 The foam concentrate for the fixed system or manual fire-fighting equipment shall be listed in accordance with UL 162, *Standard for Safety Foam Equipment and Liquid Concentrates,* and shall be on the qualified products list for MIL-F-24385, or equivalent. [**418**:5.7.9]

21.3.4.7 Activation of Systems.

21.3.4.7.1* The fixed discharge outlet system shall be activated manually. [**418**:5.8.1]

21.3.4.7.2* The activation shall be by manual pull stations located at each egress point from the rooftop landing pad. An additional manual pull station shall be located at an approved location inside the building from which the rooftop landing pad can be viewed. [**418**:5.8.2]

21.3.4.7.3 Where buildings are provided with a fire alarm system, the activation of the system shall be monitored by the building fire alarm system in accordance with *NFPA 72, National Fire Alarm and Signaling Code.* [**418**:5.8.3]

21.3.4.8 Fire Alarm. A means of communication shall be provided from the roof area to notify the fire department of emergencies. [**418**:5.9]

21.3.4.8.1 Where buildings are provided with a fire alarm system, a manual pull station shall be provided for each designated means of egress from the roof. *(See 21.3.4.4.)* [**418**:5.9.1]

21.3.5 Portable Fire Extinguishers.

21.3.5.1 Minimum Requirement. At least one portable fire extinguisher as specified in Table 21.3.5.1 shall be provided for each takeoff and landing area, parking area, and fuel storage area. [**418**:9.2]

Table 21.3.5.1 Minimum Ratings of Portable Fire Extinguishers for Heliport Categories

Heliport Category	Helicopter Overall Length*	Minimum Rating
H-1	Less than 50 ft (15.2 m)	4-A:80-B
H-2	50 ft (15.2 m) up to but not including 80 ft (24.4 m)	10-A:120-B
H-3	80 ft (24.4 m) up to but not including 120 ft (36.6 m)	30-A:240-B

*Helicopter length, including the tail boom and the rotors.
[**418**: Table 9.2]

21.3.5.2 Extinguishers Subject to Damage, Theft, or Tampering. Where the portable extinguisher cannot be maintained and safeguarded against damage, theft, or tampering, the portable fire extinguisher shall be omitted with the approval of the AHJ. [**418**:9.3]

Chapter 22   Automobile Wrecking Yards

22.1 General. Automobile wrecking yards shall be in accordance with this chapter.

22.2 Permits. Permits, where required, shall comply with Section 1.12.

22.3 Fire Department Access Roads. Fire department access roads shall be in accordance with Section 18.2.

22.4 Welding and Cutting. Welding and cutting operations shall be in accordance with Chapter 41.

22.5 Housekeeping. The yard shall be kept free of vegetation, debris, and any other material that is not necessary to the proper operation of the facility.

22.6 Fire Extinguishers. Fire extinguishers shall be placed and sized in accordance with Section 13.6.

22.7 Tire Storage. The storage of tires shall be in accordance with Chapters 33 and 34.

22.8 Burning Operations. Burning operations shall be in accordance with Section 10.10.

22.9 Motor Vehicle Fluids and Hazardous Materials.

22.9.1 General. The storage, use, and handling of motor vehicle fluids and hazardous materials shall be in accordance with Chapters 60 and 66.

22.9.2 Motor Vehicle Fluids.

22.9.2.1 Motor vehicle fluids shall be drained from salvage vehicles when such fluids are leaking.

22.9.2.2 Storage and handling of motor vehicle fluids shall be done in an approved manner.

22.9.2.3 Flammable and combustible liquids shall be stored and handled in accordance with Chapter 66.

22.9.3 Mitigation for Vehicle Fluid Leaks.

22.9.3.1 Supplies or equipment capable of mitigating leaks from fuel tanks, crankcases, brake systems, and transmissions shall be kept available on site.

22.9.3.2 Single-use plugging, diking, and absorbent materials shall be disposed of as hazardous waste and removed from the site in a manner approved by federal, state, and local requirements.

22.9.4 Air Bag Systems. Removed air bag systems shall be handled and stored in accordance with Chapter 60.

22.9.5 Lead-Acid Batteries.

22.9.5.1 Lead-acid batteries shall be removed from salvage vehicles when such batteries are leaking.

22.9.5.2 Lead-acid batteries that have been removed from vehicles shall be stored in an approved manner.

Chapter 23   Cleanrooms

23.1 General. All semiconductor facilities containing a cleanroom or a clean zone, or both, shall comply with this chapter and NFPA 318, *Standard for the Protection of Semiconductor Fabrication Facilities.*

23.2 Applicability. Unless otherwise noted in NFPA 318, the provisions of NFPA 318 shall not be applied to facilities, equipment, structures, or installations that were existing or approved for construction or installation prior to the effective date of this *Code,* except in those cases where it is determined by the AHJ that the existing situation involves a distinct hazard to life or adjacent property.

23.3 Permits. Permits, where required, shall comply with Section 1.12.

Chapter 24   Drycleaning

24.1 General.

24.1.1 Drycleaning plants shall comply with this chapter and NFPA 32, *Standard for Drycleaning Plants.*

24.1.2 Drycleaning plants or systems using solvents that have a flash point below 100°F (37.8°C) shall be prohibited.

24.2 Permits. Permits, where required, shall comply with Section 1.12.

Chapter 25   Grandstands and Bleachers, Folding and Telescopic Seating, Tents, and Membrane Structures

25.1 General.

25.1.1 The construction, location, protection, and maintenance of grandstands and bleachers, folding and telescopic seating, tents, and membrane structures shall meet the requirements of this chapter. Seating facilities located in the open air or within enclosed or semi-enclosed structures, such as tents, membrane structures, and stadium complexes, shall comply with this chapter, NFPA *101*, and , *Standard for Grandstands, Folding and Telescopic Seating, Tents, and Membrane Structures.*

25.1.2 Permits. Permits, where required, shall comply with Section 1.12.

25.1.3 Means of Egress.

25.1.3.1 Means of egress shall comply with the requirements of Chapter 14.

25.1.3.2 No guy wire or guy rope shall cross any means of egress at a height of less than 7 ft (2.1 m).

25.1.3.3 Tent stakes adjacent to any means of egress from any tent open to the public shall be railed off, capped, or covered so as not to present a hazard to the public.

25.1.3.4 New facilities shall comply with the means of egress provisions of NFPA *101* for the applicable occupancies.

25.1.3.5 Existing facilities shall comply with the means of egress provisions of NFPA *101* for the applicable occupancies.

25.1.4 Flammable Liquids and Gases.

25.1.4.1 The storage and handling of flammable liquids or gases shall be in accordance with the following applicable standards and chapters below:

(1) Chapter 66 for flammable and combustible liquids
(2) NFPA 54, *National Fuel Gas Code*
(3) Chapter 69 for liquefied petroleum gases and liquefied natural gases [*101:* 8.7.3.1]

25.1.4.2* No storage or handling of flammable liquids or gases shall be permitted in any location where such storage would jeopardize egress from the structure, unless otherwise permitted by 25.1.4.1. [*101:* 8.7.3.2]

25.1.4.3 Refueling of equipment with liquids having flash points below 100°F (38°C) shall not be permitted within the structure.

25.1.5 Fire Hazards.

25.1.5.1 The finished ground level enclosed by the structure, and the surrounding finished ground level not less than 10 ft (3050 mm) outside of the structure, shall be cleared of all flammable or combustible material and vegetation. [**5000:**32.3.5.1.1]

25.1.5.2 Where prohibited by the AHJ, smoking shall not be permitted in any temporary membrane structure. [*101:* 11.10.2.2]

25.1.5.3 Hay, straw, shavings, or similar combustible materials that have not been treated to make them flame retardant to a degree acceptable to the AHJ shall not be permitted within any structure used as an assembly occupancy.

Exception: Animal bedding and fodders in quantities approved by the AHJ.

25.1.5.4 Open Flame Devices and Pyrotechnics. Use of open flame devices and pyrotechnics shall comply with 20.1.5.3.

25.1.6 Extinguishment Requirements.

25.1.6.1 Enclosed stadiums, arenas, and similar structures shall be protected throughout by an approved, electrically supervised automatic sprinkler system in accordance with Section 13.3, unless otherwise permitted by the following:

(1) Where the ceiling or roof, whichever is lower, of the playing/activity area is more than 55 ft (16.7 m) above the floor, sprinklers shall not be required above the playing/activity area where permitted by the AHJ.
(2) Sprinklers shall not be required above seating areas that view the playing/activity area. [**5000:**32.3.5.2]

25.1.6.2 An enclosed area shall be protected by an approved sprinkler system in accordance with Section 13.3, unless such an area is one of the following:

(1) Enclosed stadiums, arenas, and similar structures
(2) Press boxes of less than 1000 ft² (93 m²)
(3) Storage facilities of less than 1000 ft² (93 m²), if enclosed with minimum 1-hour fire resistance–rated construction
(4) Enclosed areas underneath grandstands or bleachers that comply with 16.4.9.5 of *NFPA 5000* [**5000:**32.3.5.3]

25.1.6.3 Portable fire extinguishers shall be installed in assembly occupancies in accordance with Section 13.6, unless otherwise permitted by one of the following:

(1) The requirement of 25.1.6.3 shall not apply to seating areas.
(2) The requirement of 25.1.6.3 shall not apply to floor areas used for contests, performances, or entertainment.
(3) The requirement of 25.1.6.3 shall not apply to outside assembly occupancy areas.
(4) Portable extinguishers shall be permitted to be located in secure locations accessible to staff. [**5000:**16.3.5.3]

25.1.6.4 Fire-extinguishing equipment shall be maintained in accordance with Section 13.6.

25.1.6.5 Employees shall be trained to operate fire-extinguishing equipment and shall be required to exhibit their skill when requested by the AHJ.

25.1.7 Detection, Alarm, and Communications Systems. Detection, alarm, and communications systems shall comply with Section 13.7 where required by 13.7.2.1 or 13.7.2.2.

25.1.8* Fire Detail. See 1.7.17 for fire detail requirements.

25.1.9 Electrical Installations.

25.1.9.1 Electrical Systems. Electrical wiring and equipment shall be in accordance with Section 11.1, unless such installations are approved existing installations, which shall be permitted to be continued in service. [*101:* 9.1.2]

25.1.9.2 The electrical system shall be installed, maintained, and operated in a safe and professional manner. When in use, portable electrical systems shall be inspected daily by a qualified person representing the owner, and any defects found shall be corrected before the public is admitted.

25.1.9.3 The electrical system and equipment shall be isolated from the public by proper elevation or guarding, and all electrical fuses and switches shall be enclosed in approved enclosures. Cables on the ground in areas traversed by the public shall be placed in trenches or protected by approved covers.

25.1.10 Heating Devices.

25.1.10.1 Fired Heaters.

25.1.10.1.1 Heating devices shall comply with Sections 11.2 and 11.5.

25.1.10.1.2 Only labeled heating devices shall be used. [*101:* 11.9.5.1.1]

25.1.10.1.3 Fuel-fired heaters and their installation shall be approved by the AHJ. [*101:* 11.9.5.1.2]

25.1.10.1.4 Air-Conditioning, Heating, Ventilating Ductwork, and Related Equipment. Air-conditioning, heating, ventilating ductwork, and related equipment shall be in accordance with 11.2.1, as applicable, unless such installations are approved existing installations, which shall be permitted to be continued in service. [*101:* 9.2.1]

25.1.10.1.5 Ventilating or Heat-Producing Equipment. Ventilating or heat-producing equipment shall be in accordance with 11.2.2, as applicable, unless such installations are approved existing installations, which shall be permitted to be continued in service. [*101:* 9.2.2]

25.1.10.1.6 Containers for liquefied petroleum gases shall be installed not less than 5 ft (1.5 m) from any tent or temporary membrane structure and shall be in accordance with the provisions of Chapter 69.

25.1.10.1.7 Tanks shall be secured in the upright position and protected from vehicular traffic.

25.1.10.2 Electric Heaters.

25.1.10.2.1 Electric heaters shall comply with 25.1.10.2 and Section 11.5.

25.1.10.2.2 Only labeled heaters shall be permitted. [*101:* 11.9.5.2.1]

25.1.10.2.3 Electric heaters, their placement, and their installation shall be approved by the AHJ. [*101:* 11.9.5.2.2]

25.1.10.2.4 Heaters shall be connected to electricity by electric cable that is suitable for outside use and is of sufficient size to handle the electrical load. [*101:* 11.9.5.2.3]

25.1.11 Cooking. Cooking operations shall comply with Chapter 50.

25.1.12 Generators.

25.1.12.1 Generators and other internal combustion power sources shall be separated from temporary membrane structures and tents by a minimum of 5 ft (1.5 m) and shall be protected from contact by fencing, enclosure, or other approved means.

25.1.12.2 Fueling. Fuel tanks shall be of adequate capacity to permit uninterrupted operation during normal operating hours. Refueling shall be conducted only when not in use.

25.1.12.3 Fire Extinguishers. A minimum of one portable fire extinguisher with a rating of not less than 2-A:10-B:C shall be provided.

25.2 Tents.

25.2.1 General.

25.2.1.1 Tents shall be permitted only on a temporary basis. [*101:* 11.11.1.2]

25.2.1.2 Tents shall be erected to cover not more than 75 percent of the premises, unless otherwise approved by the AHJ. [*101:* 11.11.1.3]

25.2.2 Flame Propagation Performance.

25.2.2.1 All tent fabric shall meet the flame propagation performance criteria contained in Test Method 2 of NFPA 701, *Standard Methods of Fire Tests for Flame Propagation of Textiles and Films.* [*101:* 11.11.2.1]

25.2.2.2 One of the following shall serve as evidence that the tent fabric materials have the required flame propagation performance:

(1) The AHJ shall require a certificate or other evidence of acceptance by an organization acceptable to the AHJ.
(2) The AHJ shall require a report of tests made by other inspection authorities or organizations acceptable to the AHJ. [*101:* 11.11.2.2]

25.2.2.3 Where required by the AHJ, confirmatory field tests shall be conducted using test specimens from the original material, which shall have been affixed at the time of manufacture to the exterior of the tent. [*101:* 11.11.2.3]

25.2.3 Location and Spacing.

25.2.3.1 There shall be a minimum of 10 ft (3050 mm) between stake lines. [*101:* 11.11.3.1]

25.2.3.2 Adjacent tents shall be spaced to provide an area to be used as a means of emergency egress. Where 10 ft (3050 mm) between stake lines does not meet the requirements for means of egress, the distance necessary for means of egress shall govern. [*101:* 11.11.3.2]

25.2.3.3 Tents not occupied by the public and not used for the storage of combustible material shall be permitted to be erected less than 10 ft (3050 mm) from other structures where the AHJ deems such close spacing to be safe from hazard to the public. [*101:* 11.11.3.3]

25.2.3.4 Tents, each not exceeding 1200 ft^2 (112 m^2) in ground area and located in fairgrounds or similar open spaces, shall not be required to be separated from each other, provided that safety precautions meet the approval of the AHJ. [*101:* 11.11.3.4]

25.2.3.5 The placement of tents relative to other structures shall be at the discretion of the AHJ, with consideration given to occupancy, use, opening, exposure, and other similar factors. [*101:* 11.11.3.5]

25.2.4 Fire Hazards.

25.2.4.1 The finished ground level enclosed by any tent, and the finished ground level for a reasonable distance, but for not less than 10 ft (3050 mm) outside of such a tent, shall be cleared of all flammable or combustible material or vegetation that is not used for necessary support equipment. The clearing work shall be accomplished to the satisfaction of the AHJ prior to the erection of such a tent. The premises shall be kept free from such flammable or combustible materials during the period for which the premises are used by the public. [*101:* 11.11.4.1]

25.2.4.2 Smoking.

25.2.4.2.1 Smoking shall not be permitted in any tent, unless approved by the AHJ. [*101:* 11.11.4.2.1]

25.2.4.2.2 In rooms or areas where smoking is prohibited, plainly visible signs shall be posted that read as follows:

NO SMOKING

[*101:* 11.11.4.2.2]

25.2.5 Fire-Extinguishing Equipment. Portable fire-extinguishing equipment of approved types shall be furnished and maintained in tents in such quantity and in such locations as directed by the AHJ. [*101:* 11.11.5]

25.3 Grandstands.

25.3.1 Seating.

25.3.1.1 Where grandstand seating without backs is used indoors, rows of seats shall be spaced not less than 22 in. (560 mm) back-to-back. [*101:* 12.4.8.2.1]

25.3.1.2 The depth of footboards and seat boards in grandstands shall be not less than 9 in. (230 mm); where the same level is not used for both seat foundations and footrests, footrests independent of seats shall be provided. [*101:* 12.4.8.2.2]

25.3.1.3 Seats and footrests of grandstands shall be supported securely and fastened in such a manner that they cannot be displaced inadvertently. [*101:* 12.4.8.2.3]

25.3.1.4 Individual seats or chairs shall be permitted only if secured in rows in an approved manner, unless seats do not exceed 16 in number and are located on level floors and within railed-in enclosures, such as boxes. [*101:* 12.4.8.2.4]

25.3.1.5 The maximum number of seats permitted between the farthest seat in an aisle in grandstands and bleachers shall not exceed that shown in Table 25.3.1.5. [*101:* 12.4.8.2.5]

Table 25.3.1.5 Maximum Number of Seats Between Farthest Seat and an Aisle

Application	Outdoors	Indoors
Grandstands	11	6
Bleachers *[See 12.2.5.6.1.2 of 101]*	20	9

[*101:* Table 12.4.8.2.5]

25.3.2 Special Requirements — Wood Grandstands.

25.3.2.1 An outdoor wood grandstand shall be erected within not less than two-thirds of its height and, in no case, within not less than 10 ft (3050 mm) of a building, unless otherwise permitted by the following:

(1) The distance requirement shall not apply to buildings having minimum 1-hour fire resistance–rated construction with openings protected against the fire exposure hazard created by the grandstand.
(2) The distance requirement shall not apply where a wall having minimum 1-hour fire resistance–rated construction separates the grandstand from the building. [*101:* 12.4.8.3.1]

25.3.2.2 An outdoor wood grandstand unit shall not exceed 10,000 ft^2 (929 m^2) in ground area or 200 ft (61 m) in length, and the following requirements also shall apply:

(1) Grandstand units of the maximum size shall be placed not less than 20 ft (6100 mm) apart or shall be separated by walls having a minimum 1-hour fire resistance rating.
(2) The number of grandstand units erected in any one group shall not exceed three.
(3) Each group of grandstand units shall be separated from any other group by a wall having minimum 2-hour fire resistance–rated construction extending 24 in. (610 mm) above the seat platforms or by an open space of not less than 50 ft (15 m). [*101:* 12.4.8.3.2]

25.3.2.3 The finished ground level area or length required by 25.3.2.2 shall be permitted to be doubled where one of the following criteria is met:

(1) Where the grandstand is constructed entirely of labeled fire-retardant-treated wood that has passed the standard rain test, ASTM D 2898, *Standard Test Methods for Accelerated Weathering of Fire-Retardant-Treated Wood for Fire Testing*
(2) Where the grandstand is constructed of members conforming to dimensions for heavy timber construction [Type IV (2HH)] [*101:* 12.4.8.3.3]

25.3.2.4 The highest level of seat platforms above the finished ground level or the surface at the front of any wood grandstand shall not exceed 20 ft (6100 mm). [*101:* 12.4.8.3.4]

25.3.2.5 The highest level of seat platforms above the finished ground level, or the surface at the front of a portable grandstand within a tent or membrane structure, shall not exceed 12 ft (3660 mm). [*101:* 12.4.8.3.5]

25.3.2.6 The height requirements specified in 25.3.2.4 and 25.3.2.5 shall be permitted to be doubled where constructed entirely of labeled fire-retardant-treated wood that has passed the standard rain test, ASTM D 2898, or where constructed of members conforming to dimensions for heavy timber construction [Type IV (2HH)]. [*101:* 12.4.8.3.6]

25.3.3 Special Requirements — Portable Grandstands.

25.3.3.1 Portable grandstands shall conform to the requirements of Section 25.3 for grandstands and the requirements of 25.3.3.2 through 25.3.3.7. [*101:* 12.4.8.4.1]

25.3.3.2 Portable grandstands shall be self-contained and shall have within them all necessary parts to withstand and restrain all forces that might be developed during human occupancy. [*101:* 12.4.8.4.2]

25.3.3.3 Portable grandstands shall be designed and manufactured so that, if any structural members essential to the strength and stability of the structure have been omitted during erection, the presence of unused connection fittings shall make the omissions self-evident. [*101:* 12.4.8.4.3]

25.3.3.4 Portable grandstand construction shall be skillfully accomplished to produce the strength required by the design. [*101:* 12.4.8.4.4]

25.3.3.5 Portable grandstands shall be provided with base plates, sills, floor runners, or sleepers of such area that the permitted bearing capacity of the supporting material is not exceeded. [*101:* 12.4.8.4.5]

25.3.3.6 Where portable grandstands rest directly on a base of such character that it is incapable of supporting the load without appreciable settlement, mud sills of suitable material, having sufficient area to prevent undue or dangerous settlement, shall be installed under base plates, runners, or sleepers. [*101:* 12.4.8.4.6]

25.3.3.7 All bearing surfaces of portable grandstands shall be in contact with each other. [*101:* 12.4.8.4.7]

25.3.4 Spaces Underneath Grandstands. Spaces underneath a grandstand shall be kept free of flammable or combustible materials, unless protected by an approved, supervised automatic sprinkler system in accordance with Section 13.3 or unless otherwise permitted by the following:

(1) This requirement shall not apply to accessory uses of 300 ft² (28 m²) or less, such as ticket booths, toilet facilities, or concession booths where constructed of noncombustible or fire-resistive construction in otherwise nonsprinklered facilities.
(2) This requirement shall not apply to rooms that are enclosed in not less than 1-hour fire resistance–rated construction and are less than 1000 ft² (93 m²) in otherwise nonsprinklered facilities. [*101:* 12.4.8.5]

25.3.5 Guards and Railings.

25.3.5.1 Railings or guards not less than 42 in. (1065 mm) above the aisle surface or footrest or not less than 36 in. (915 mm) vertically above the center of the seat or seat board surface, whichever is adjacent, shall be provided along those portions of the backs and ends of all grandstands where the seats are more than 48 in. (1220 mm) above the floor or the finished ground level. [*101:* 12.4.8.6.1]

25.3.5.2 The requirement of 25.3.5.1 shall not apply where an adjacent wall or fence affords equivalent safeguard. [*101:* 12.4.8.6.2]

25.3.5.3 Where the front footrest of any grandstand is more than 24 in. (610 mm) above the floor, railings or guards not less than 33 in. (825 mm) above such footrests shall be provided. [*101:* 12.4.8.6.3]

25.3.5.4 The railings required by 25.3.5.3 shall be permitted to be not less than 26 in. (660 mm) high in grandstands or where the front row of seats includes backrests. [*101:* 12.4.8.6.4]

25.3.5.5 Cross aisles located within the seating area shall be provided with rails not less than 26 in. (660 mm) high along the front edge of the cross aisle. [*101:* 12.4.8.6.5]

25.3.5.6 The railings specified by 25.3.5.5 shall not be required where the backs of the seats in front of the cross aisle project 24 in. (610 mm) or more above the surface of the cross aisle. [*101:* 12.4.8.6.6]

25.3.5.7 Vertical openings between guardrails and footboards or seat boards shall be provided with intermediate construction so that a 4 in. (100 mm) diameter sphere cannot pass through the opening. [*101:* 12.4.8.6.7]

25.3.5.8 An opening between the seat board and footboard located more than 30 in. (760 mm) above the finished ground level shall be provided with intermediate construction so that a 4 in. (100 mm) diameter sphere cannot pass through the opening. [*101:* 12.4.8.6.8]

25.3.6 Maintenance of Outdoor Grandstands.

25.3.6.1 The owner shall provide for not less than annual inspection and required maintenance of each outdoor grandstand to ensure safe conditions. [*101:* 12.7.10.1]

25.3.6.2 At least biennially, the inspection shall be performed by a professional engineer, registered architect, or individual certified by the manufacturer. [*101:* 12.7.10.2]

25.3.6.3 Where required by the AHJ, the owner shall provide a copy of the inspection report and certification that the inspection required by 25.3.6.2 has been performed. [*101:* 12.7.10.3]

25.4 Folding and Telescopic Seating.

25.4.1 Seating.

25.4.1.1 The horizontal distance of seats, measured back-to-back, shall be not less than 22 in. (560 mm) for seats without backs, and the following requirements shall also apply:

(1) There shall be a space of not less than 12 in. (305 mm) between the back of each seat and the front of each seat immediately behind it.
(2) If seats are of the chair type, the 12 in. (305 mm) dimension shall be measured to the front edge of the rear seat in its normal unoccupied position.
(3) All measurements shall be taken between plumb lines. [*101:* 12.4.9.2.1]

25.4.1.2 The depth of footboards (footrests) and seat boards in folding and telescopic seating shall be not less than 9 in. (230 mm). [*101:* 12.4.9.2.2]

25.4.1.3 Where the same level is not used for both seat foundations and footrests, footrests independent of seats shall be provided. [*101:* 12.4.9.2.3]

25.4.1.4 Individual chair-type seats shall be permitted in folding and telescopic seating only if firmly secured in groups of not less than three. [*101:* 12.4.9.2.4]

25.4.1.5 The maximum number of seats permitted between the farthest seat in an aisle in folding and telescopic seating shall not exceed that shown in Table 25.3.1.5. [*101:* 12.4.9.2.5]

25.4.2 Guards and Railings.

25.4.2.1 Railings or guards not less than 42 in. (1065 mm) above the aisle surface or footrest or not less than 36 in. (915 mm) vertically above the center of the seat or seat board surface, whichever is adjacent, shall be provided along those portions of the backs and ends of all folding and telescopic seating where the seats are more than 48 in. (1220 mm) above the floor or the finished ground level. [*101:* 12.4.9.3.1]

25.4.2.2 The requirement of 25.4.2.1 shall not apply where an adjacent wall or fence affords equivalent safeguard. [*101:* 12.4.9.3.2]

25.4.2.3 Where the front footrest of folding or telescopic seating is more than 24 in. (610 mm) above the floor, railings or guards not less than 33 in. (825 mm) above such footrests shall be provided. [*101:* 12.4.9.3.3]

25.4.2.4 The railings required by 25.4.2.3 shall be permitted to be not less than 26 in. (660 mm) high where the front row of seats includes backrests. [*101:* 12.4.9.3.4]

25.4.2.5 Cross aisles located within the seating area shall be provided with rails not less than 26 in. (660 mm) high along the front edge of the cross aisle. [*101:* 12.4.9.3.5]

25.4.2.6 The railings specified by 25.4.2.5 shall not be required where the backs of the seats in front of the cross aisle project 24 in. (610 mm) or more above the surface of the cross aisle. [*101:* 12.4.9.3.6]

25.4.2.7 Vertical openings between guardrails and footboards or seat boards shall be provided with intermediate construction so that a 4 in. (100 mm) diameter sphere cannot pass through the opening. [*101:* 12.4.9.3.7]

25.4.2.8 An opening between the seat board and footboard located more than 30 in. (760 mm) above the finished ground level shall be provided with intermediate construction so that a 4 in. (100 mm) diameter sphere cannot pass through the opening. [*101:* 12.4.9.3.8]

25.4.3 Maintenance and Operation of Folding and Telescopic Seating.

25.4.3.1 Instructions in both maintenance and operation shall be transmitted to the owner by the manufacturer of the seating or his or her representative. [*101:* 12.7.11.1]

25.4.3.2 Maintenance and operation of folding and telescopic seating shall be the responsibility of the owner or his or her duly authorized representative and shall include the following:

(1) During operation of the folding and telescopic seats, the opening and closing shall be supervised by responsible personnel who shall ensure that the operation is in accordance with the manufacturer's instructions.
(2) Only attachments specifically approved by the manufacturer for the specific installation shall be attached to the seating.
(3) An annual inspection and required maintenance of each grandstand shall be performed to ensure safe conditions.
(4) At least biennially, the inspection shall be performed by a professional engineer, registered architect, or individual certified by the manufacturer. [*101:* 12.7.11.2]

25.5 Permanent Membrane Structures.

25.5.1 Application.

25.5.1.1 Use of Membrane Roofs. Membrane roofs shall be used in accordance with the following:

(1) Membrane materials shall not be used where fire resistance ratings are required for walls or roofs.
(2) Where every part of the roof, including the roof membrane, is not less than 20 ft (6100 mm) above any floor, balcony, or gallery, a noncombustible or limited-combustible membrane shall be permitted to be used as the roof in any construction type.
(3) With approval of the AHJ, membrane materials shall be permitted to be used where every part of the roof membrane is sufficiently above every significant fire potential, such that the imposed temperature cannot exceed the capability of the membrane, including seams, to maintain its structural integrity. [*101:* 11.9.1.2]

25.5.1.2 Testing. Testing of membrane materials for compliance with the requirements of Section 25.5 for use of the categories of noncombustible and limited-combustible materials shall be performed on weathered-membrane material as defined in 3.3.171.5 of NFPA *101*. [*101:* 11.9.1.3]

25.5.1.3 Flame Spread Index. The flame spread index of all membrane materials exposed within the structure shall be Class A in accordance with Section 12.5. [*101:* 11.9.1.4]

25.5.1.4 Roof Covering Classification. Roof membranes shall have a roof covering classification, as required by the applicable building codes, when tested in accordance with ASTM E 108, *Standard Test Methods for Fire Tests of Roof Coverings*; or ANSI/UL 790, *Test Methods for Fire Tests of Roof Coverings*. [*101:* 11.9.1.5]

25.5.1.5 Flame Propagation Performance.

25.5.1.5.1 All membrane structure fabric shall meet the flame propagation performance criteria contained in Test Method 2 of NFPA 701, *Standard Methods of Fire Tests for Flame Propagation of Textiles and Films*. [*101:* 11.9.1.6.1]

25.5.1.5.2 One of the following shall serve as evidence that the fabric materials have the required flame propagation performance:

(1) The AHJ shall require a certificate or other evidence of acceptance by an organization acceptable to the AHJ.
(2) The AHJ shall require a report of tests made by other inspection authorities or organizations acceptable to the AHJ. [*101:* 11.9.1.6.2]

25.5.1.5.3 Where required by the AHJ, confirmatory field tests shall be conducted using test specimens from the original material, which shall have been affixed at the time of manufacture to the exterior of the structure. [*101:* 11.9.1.6.3]

25.5.2 Tensioned-Membrane Structures.

25.5.2.1 The design, materials, and construction of the building shall be based on plans and specifications prepared by a licensed architect or engineer knowledgeable in tensioned-membrane construction. [*101:* 11.9.2.1]

25.5.2.2 Material loads and strength shall be based on physical properties of the materials verified and certified by an approved testing laboratory. [*101:* 11.9.2.2]

25.5.2.3 The membrane roof for structures in climates subject to freezing temperatures and ice buildup shall be composed of two layers separated by an air space through which heated air can be moved to guard against ice accumulation. As an alternative to the two layers, other approved methods that protect against ice accumulation shall be permitted. [*101:* 11.9.2.3]

25.5.2.4 Roof drains shall be equipped with electrical elements to protect against ice buildup that can prevent the drains from functioning. Such heating elements shall be served by on-site standby electrical power in addition to the normal public service. As an alternative to such electrical elements, other approved methods that protect against ice accumulation shall be permitted. [*101:* 11.9.2.4]

25.5.3 Air-Supported and Air-Inflated Structures.

25.5.3.1 General. In addition to the general provisions of 25.5.1, the requirements of 25.5.3 shall apply to air-supported and air-inflated structures. [*101:* 11.9.3.1]

25.5.3.2 Pressurization (Inflation) System. The pressurization system shall consist of one or more operating blower units. The system shall include automatic control of auxiliary blower units to maintain the required operating pressure. Such equipment shall meet the following requirements:

(1) Blowers shall be powered by continuous-rated motors at the maximum power required.
(2) Blowers shall have personnel protection, such as inlet screens and belt guards.
(3) Blower systems shall be weather protected.
(4) Blower systems shall be equipped with backdraft check dampers.
(5) Not less than two blower units shall be provided, each of which has capacity to maintain full inflation pressure with normal leakage.
(6) The blowers shall be designed to be incapable of overpressurization.
(7) The auxiliary blower unit(s) shall operate automatically if there is any loss of internal pressure or if an operating blower unit becomes inoperative.
(8) The design inflation pressure and the capacity of each blower system shall be certified by a professional engineer. [*101:* 11.9.3.2]

25.5.3.3 Standby Power System.

25.5.3.3.1* A fully automatic standby power system shall be provided. The system shall be either an auxiliary engine generator set capable of running the blower system or a supplementary blower unit that is sized for 1 times the normal operating capacity and is powered by an internal combustion engine. [*101:* 11.9.3.3.1]

25.5.3.3.2 The standby power system shall be fully automatic to ensure continuous inflation in the event of any failure of the primary power. The system shall be capable of operating continuously for a minimum of 4 hours. [*101:* 11.9.3.3.2]

25.5.3.3.3 The sizing and capacity of the standby power system shall be certified by a professional engineer. [*101:* 11.9.3.3.3]

25.5.4 Maintenance and Operation.

25.5.4.1 Instructions in both operation and maintenance shall be transmitted to the owner by the manufacturer of the tensioned-membrane, air-supported, or air-inflated structure. [*101:* 11.9.4.1]

25.5.4.2 Annual inspection and required maintenance of each structure shall be performed to ensure safety conditions. At least biennially, the inspection shall be performed by a professional engineer, registered architect, or individual certified by the manufacturer. [*101:* 11.9.4.2]

25.6 Temporary Membrane Structures.

25.6.1 Application.

25.6.1.1 Required Approval. Membrane structures designed to meet all the requirements of Section 25.6 shall be permitted to be used as temporary buildings subject to the approval of the AHJ. [*101:* 11.10.1.2]

25.6.1.2 Alternative Requirements. Temporary tensioned-membrane structures shall be permitted to comply with Section 25.2 instead of Section 25.6. [*101:* 11.10.1.3]

25.6.1.3 Roof Covering Classification. Roof membranes shall have a roof covering classification, as required by the applicable building codes, when tested in accordance with ASTM E 108 or ANSI/UL 790. [*101:* 11.10.1.4]

25.6.1.4 Flame Propagation Performance.

25.6.1.4.1 All membrane structure fabric shall meet the flame propagation performance criteria contained in Test Method 2 of NFPA 701, *Standard Methods of Fire Tests for Flame Propagation of Textiles and Films.* [*101:* 11.10.1.5.1]

25.6.1.4.2 One of the following shall serve as evidence that the fabric materials have the required flame propagation performance:

(1) The AHJ shall require a certificate or other evidence of acceptance by an organization acceptable to the AHJ.
(2) The AHJ shall require a report of tests made by other inspection authorities or organizations acceptable to the AHJ. [*101:* 11.10.1.5.2]

25.6.1.4.3 Where required by the AHJ, confirmatory field tests shall be conducted using test specimens from the original material, which shall have been affixed at the time of manufacture to the exterior of the structure. [*101:* 11.10.1.5.3]

25.6.2 Fire Hazards.

25.6.2.1 The finished ground level enclosed by any temporary membrane structure, and the finished ground level for a reasonable distance but for not less than 10 ft (3050 mm) outside of such a structure, shall be cleared of all flammable or combustible material or vegetation that is not used for necessary support equipment. The clearing work shall be accomplished to the satisfaction of the AHJ prior to the erection of such a structure. The premises shall be kept free from such flammable or combustible materials during the period for which the premises are used by the public. [*101:* 11.10.2.1]

25.6.2.2 Where prohibited by the AHJ, smoking shall not be permitted in any temporary membrane structure. [*101:* 11.10.2.2]

25.6.3 Fire-Extinguishing Equipment. Portable fire-extinguishing equipment of approved types shall be furnished and maintained in temporary membrane structures in such quantity and in such locations as directed by the AHJ. [*101:* 11.10.3]

25.6.4 Tensioned-Membrane Structures.

25.6.4.1 The design, materials, and construction of the building shall be based on plans and specifications prepared by a licensed architect or engineer knowledgeable in tensioned-membrane construction. [*101:* 11.10.4.1]

25.6.4.2 Material loads and strength shall be based on physical properties of the materials verified and certified by an approved testing laboratory. [*101:* 11.10.4.2]

25.6.4.3 The membrane roof for structures in climates subject to freezing temperatures and ice buildup shall be composed of two layers separated by an air space through which heated air can be moved to guard against ice accumulation. As an alternative to the two layers, other approved methods that protect against ice accumulation shall be permitted. [*101:* 11.10.4.3]

25.6.4.4 Roof drains shall be equipped with electrical elements to protect against ice buildup that can prevent the drains from functioning. Such heating elements shall be served by on-site standby electrical power in addition to the normal public service. As an alternative to such electrical elements, other approved methods that protect against ice accumulation shall be permitted. [*101:* 11.10.4.4]

25.6.5 Air-Supported and Air-Inflated Structures.

25.6.5.1 General. In addition to the general provisions of 25.6.1, the requirements of 25.6.5 shall apply to air-supported and air-inflated structures. [*101:* 11.10.5.1]

25.6.5.2 Pressurization (Inflation) System. The pressurization system shall consist of one or more operating blower units. The system shall include automatic control of auxiliary blower units to maintain the required operating pressure. Such equipment shall meet the following requirements:

(1) Blowers shall be powered by continuous-rated motors at the maximum power required.
(2) Blowers shall have personnel protection, such as inlet screens and belt guards.
(3) Blower systems shall be weather protected.
(4) Blower systems shall be equipped with backdraft check dampers.
(5) Not less than two blower units shall be provided, each of which has capacity to maintain full inflation pressure with normal leakage.
(6) The blowers shall be designed to be incapable of overpressurization.
(7) The auxiliary blower unit(s) shall operate automatically if there is any loss of internal pressure or if an operating blower unit becomes inoperative.
(8) The design inflation pressure and the capacity of each blower system shall be certified by a professional engineer. [*101:* 11.10.5.2]

25.6.5.3 Standby Power System.

25.6.5.3.1 A fully automatic standby power system shall be provided. The system shall be either an auxiliary engine generator set capable of running the blower system or a supplementary blower unit that is sized for 1 times the normal operating capacity and is powered by an internal combustion engine. [*101:* 11.10.5.3.1]

25.6.5.3.2 The standby power system shall be fully automatic to ensure continuous inflation in the event of any failure of the primary power. The system shall be capable of operating continuously for a minimum of 4 hours. [*101:* 11.10.5.3.2]

25.6.5.3.3 The sizing and capacity of the standby power system shall be certified by a professional engineer. [*101:* 11.10.5.3.3]

25.6.6 Maintenance and Operation.

25.6.6.1 Instructions in both operation and maintenance shall be transmitted to the owner by the manufacturer of the tensioned-membrane, air-supported, or air-inflated structure. [*101:* 11.10.6.1]

25.6.6.2 Annual inspection and required maintenance of each structure shall be performed to ensure safety conditions. At least biennially, the inspection shall be performed by a professional engineer, registered architect, or individual certified by the manufacturer. [*101:* 11.10.6.2]

Chapter 26 Laboratories Using Chemicals

26.1 General.

26.1.1 The handling or storage of chemicals in laboratory buildings, laboratory units, and laboratory work areas whether located above or below grade shall comply with this chapter. Construction and protection of new laboratories shall also comply with NFPA 45, *Standard on Fire Protection for Laboratories Using Chemicals.*

26.1.2 Chapter 26 shall apply to laboratory buildings, laboratory units, and laboratory work areas whether located above or below grade in which chemicals, as defined, are handled or stored. [**45:**1.1.1]

26.1.3 Chapter 26 shall not apply to the following:

(1)*Laboratories for which the following apply:
 (a) Laboratory units that contain less than or equal to 1 gal (4 L) of flammable or combustible liquid
 (b) Laboratory units that contain less than 75 scf (2.2 standard m^3) of flammable gas, not including piped-in low-pressure utility gas installed in accordance with NFPA 54, *National Fuel Gas Code*
(2)*Laboratories that are pilot plants
(3) Laboratories that handle only chemicals with a hazard rating of 0 or 1, as defined by NFPA 704, *Standard System for the Identification of the Hazards of Materials for Emergency Response,* for all of the following: health, flammability, and instability
(4) Laboratories that are primarily manufacturing plants
(5) Incidental testing facilities
(6) Physical, electronic, instrument, laser, or similar laboratories that use chemicals only for incidental purposes, such as cleaning
(7)*Hazards associated with radioactive materials, as covered by NFPA 801, *Standard for Fire Protection for Facilities Handling Radioactive Materials*
(8) Laboratories that work only with explosive material, as covered by NFPA 495, *Explosive Materials Code* [**45:**1.1.2]

26.1.4 Chapter 26 contains requirements, but not all-inclusive requirements, for handling and storage of chemicals where laboratory-scale operations are conducted and shall not cover the following:

(1) The special fire protection required when handling explosive materials *(See NFPA 495.)*
(2) The special fire protection required when handling radioactive materials [**45:**1.1.3]

26.1.5 Plans and Procedures.

26.1.5.1* Fire prevention, maintenance, and emergency action plans and procedures shall be established.

26.2 Permits. Permits, where required, shall comply with Section 1.12.

Chapter 27 Manufactured Home and Recreational Vehicle Sites

27.1 General.

27.1.1 Manufactured home and recreational vehicle sites shall meet the requirements of this chapter.

27.1.2 This chapter shall not apply to recreational vehicles as defined in NFPA 1192, *Standard on Recreational Vehicles*, or to park trailers as defined in RVIA/ANSI A.119.5, *Standard for Recreational Park Trailers*.

27.1.3 This chapter shall not cover the design of recreational vehicles or other forms of camping units or the operational and maintenance practices of recreational vehicle parks and campgrounds.

27.2 Manufactured Home Sites. The fire safety requirements for the installation of manufactured homes and manufactured home sites, including accessory buildings, structures, and communities, shall comply with NFPA 501A, *Standard for Fire Safety Criteria for Manufactured Home Installations, Sites, and Communities*.

27.3 Recreational Vehicle Parks and Campgrounds. The construction of recreational vehicle parks and campgrounds that offer temporary living sites for use by recreational vehicles and camping units shall comply with NFPA 1194, *Standard for Recreational Vehicle Parks and Campgrounds*.

Chapter 28   Marinas, Boatyards, Marine Terminals, Piers, and Wharves

28.1 Marinas, Boatyards, and Other Recreational Marine Facilities.

28.1.1 The construction and operation of marinas, boatyards, yacht clubs, boat condominiums, docking facilities associated with residential condominiums, multiple-docking facilities at multiple-family residences, and all associated piers, docks, and floats shall comply with NFPA 303, *Fire Protection Standard for Marinas and Boatyards*, and Section 28.1.

28.1.2 Section 28.1 shall not apply to private, non-commercial docking facility constructed or occupied for the use of the owners or residents of an associated single-family dwelling.

28.1.3 Section 28.1 also applies to support facilities and structures used for construction, repair, storage, hauling and launching, or fueling of vessels if fire on a pier would pose an immediate threat to these facilities, or if a fire at a referenced facility would pose an immediate threat to a docking facility. [**303**:1.1.1]

28.1.4 Section 28.1 applies to marinas and facilities servicing small recreational and commercial craft, yachts, and other craft of not more than 300 gross tons. [**303**:1.1.2]

28.1.5 No requirement in this chapter is to be construed as reducing applicable building, fire, and electrical codes. [**303**:1.1.4]

28.1.6 Fire Protection.

28.1.6.1 Portable Fire Extinguishers.

28.1.6.1.1 Placement.

28.1.6.1.1.1 Placement of portable fire extinguishers shall be in accordance with 13.6.2 unless otherwise permitted by 28.1.6.1.1.1.1, 28.1.6.1.1.1.2, and 28.1.6.1.1.1.3. [**303**:6.2.1.1]

28.1.6.1.1.1.1 Placement of portable fire extinguishers on piers and along bulkheads where vessels are moored or are permitted to be moored shall meet the following criteria:

(1) Extinguishers listed for Class A, Class B, and Class C fires shall be installed at the pier/land intersection on a pier that exceeds 25 ft (7.62 m) in length.
(2) Additional fire extinguishers shall be placed such that the maximum travel distance to an extinguisher does not exceed 75 ft (22.86 m). [**303**:6.2.1.1.1]

28.1.6.1.1.1.2 Fuel-Dispensing Areas.

(A) Portable fire extinguishers that meet the minimum requirements of 13.6.2 for extra (high) hazard type shall be installed on two sides of a fuel-dispensing area. [**303**:6.2.1.1.2.1]

(B) On piers or bulkheads where long fueling hoses are installed for fueling vessels, additional extinguishers installed on piers or bulkheads shall meet the requirements of 13.6.2 for extra (high) hazard type and 28.1.6.1.1.1.1. [**303**:6.2.1.1.2.2]

28.1.6.1.1.1.3 All extinguishers installed on piers shall meet the rating requirements set forth in 13.6.2 for ordinary (moderate) hazard type. [**303**:6.2.1.1.3]

28.1.6.1.2 Maintenance. All portable fire extinguishers shall be maintained in accordance with 13.6.3 and shall be clearly visible and marked. [**303**:6.2.2]

28.1.6.2* Fixed Fire-Extinguishing Systems.

28.1.6.2.1 Buildings on Piers.

28.1.6.2.1.1 Buildings in excess of 500 ft^2 (46 m^2) that are constructed on piers shall be protected by an approved automatic fire-extinguishing system unless otherwise permitted by 28.1.6.2.1.2 or 28.1.6.2.1.3. [**303**:6.3.1.1]

28.1.6.2.1.2 Buildings of Type I or Type II construction, as specified in NFPA 220, *Standard on Types of Building Construction*, and without combustible contents shall not be required to be protected by an automatic fire-extinguishing system. [**303**:6.3.1.2]

28.1.6.2.1.3* Existing facilities shall not be required to be protected by an automatic fire-extinguishing system where acceptable to the AHJ. [**303**:6.3.1.3]

28.1.6.2.2* Buildings Exceeding 5000 ft^2 (465 m^2).

28.1.6.2.2.1 Marina and boatyard buildings in excess of 5000 ft^2 (465 m^2) in total area shall be protected by an approved automatic fire-extinguishing system unless otherwise permitted by 28.1.6.2.2.2. [**303**:6.3.2.1]

28.1.6.2.2.2* Existing facilities shall not be required to be protected by an automatic fire-extinguishing system where acceptable to the AHJ. [**303**:6.3.2.2]

28.1.6.2.3 Combustible Piers and Substructures.

28.1.6.2.3.1 Combustible piers and substructures in excess of 25 ft (7.62 m) in width or in excess of 5000 ft^2 (465 m^2) in area, or within 30 ft (9.14 m) of other structures or superstructures required to be so protected, shall be protected in accordance with Section 4.3 of NFPA 307, *Standard for the Construction and Fire Protection of Marine Terminals, Piers, and Wharves*, unless otherwise permitted by 28.1.6.2.3.2, 28.1.6.2.3.3, or 28.1.6.2.3.4. [**303**:6.3.3.1]

28.1.6.2.3.2 Fixed piers shall not be required to be protected as specified in 28.1.6.2.3.1 where the vertical distance from the surface of mean high water level to the underside of the pier surface does not exceed 36 in. (914 mm). [**303**:6.3.3.2]

28.1.6.2.3.3 Floating piers shall not be required to be protected as specified in 28.1.6.2.3.1 where the vertical distance from the surface of the water to the underside of the pier surface does not exceed 36 in. (914 mm). [**303**:6.3.3.3]

28.1.6.2.3.4* Existing facilities shall not be required to be protected by an automatic fire-extinguishing system where acceptable to the AHJ. [**303**:6.3.3.4]

28.1.6.2.4 Indoor Rack Storage.

28.1.6.2.4.1* Where boats are stored on multilevel racks in buildings, an approved automatic fire-extinguishing system shall be installed throughout the building unless otherwise permitted by 28.1.6.2.4.2 or 28.1.6.2.4.3. [**303**:6.3.4.1]

28.1.6.2.4.2 An automatic fire-extinguishing system shall not be required for buildings less than 5000 ft^2 (465 m^2) having multilevel racks where provided with one of the following:

(1) An automatic fire detection and alarm system supervised by a central station complying with *NFPA 72*
(2) An automatic fire detection and alarm system supervised by a local protective signaling system complying with *NFPA 72*, if the provisions of 28.1.6.2.4.2(1) are not technically feasible
(3) A full-time watch service if the provisions of 28.1.6.2.4.2(1) are not technically feasible [**303**:6.3.4.2]

28.1.6.2.4.3* Existing facilities shall not be required to be protected by an automatic fire-extinguishing system where acceptable to the AHJ. [**303**:6.3.4.3]

28.1.6.2.5* An approved water supply shall be provided within 100 ft (30 m) of the pier/land intersection or fire department connection serving fire protection systems. [**303**:6.3.5]

28.1.6.2.6 Access between water supplies and pier/land intersections or fire department connections shall be by roadway acceptable to the AHJ. [**303**:6.3.6]

28.1.6.3* Fire Standpipe Systems.

28.1.6.3.1 Class I standpipe systems shall be provided for piers, bulkheads, and buildings where the hose lay distance from the fire apparatus exceeds 150 ft (45 m). [**303**:6.4.1]

28.1.6.3.2 Class I standpipes shall be provided in all buildings used for the rack storage of boats. [**303**:6.4.2]

28.1.6.3.3 Standpipe systems, where installed, shall be in accordance with Section 13.2, except for the provisions identified in 28.1.6.3.4 through 28.1.6.3.7. [**303**:6.4.3]

28.1.6.3.4 Hose racks, hoses, and standpipe cabinets shall not be required on piers and bulkheads. [**303**:6.4.4]

28.1.6.3.5 Supply piping for standpipes on piers and bulkheads shall be sized for the minimum flow rate for Class II systems. [**303**:6.4.5]

28.1.6.3.6 Manual dry standpipes shall be permitted. [**303**:6.4.6]

28.1.6.3.7 Flexible connections shall be permitted on floating piers where acceptable to the AHJ. [**303**:6.4.7]

28.1.6.4 Water supply and hoses or portable fire extinguishers and wheeled cart assemblies equipped with discharge nozzles capable of reaching all boats on the highest racks shall be provided. [**303**:6.5]

28.1.6.5 Hydrants and Water Supplies. Hydrants and water supplies for fire protection in marinas and boatyards shall be provided in accordance with Section 13.2, Section 13.3, and 13.5.1. [**303**:6.6]

28.1.6.6 Fire Detectors.

28.1.6.6.1 Fire detection devices and installation shall be in accordance with Section 13.7. [**303**:6.11.1]

28.1.6.6.2 Fire detectors shall be installed in the following interior or covered locations unless those locations are protected by a fixed automatic sprinkler system installed in accordance with NFPA 13:

(1) Rooms containing combustible storage or goods
(2) Rooms containing flammable liquid storage or use
(3) Rooms containing battery storage or maintenance
(4) Rooms containing paint and solvent storage or use
(5) Areas used for enclosed or covered storage of vessels
(6) Areas used for enclosed or covered maintenance of vessels
(7) Areas used for public assembly, dining, or lodging
(8) Kitchens and food preparation areas
(9) Dust bins and collectors
(10) Inside trash storage areas
(11) Rooms used for storing janitor supplies or linens
(12) Laundry rooms
(13) Furnace rooms [**303**:6.11.2]

28.1.7 Berthing and Storage.

28.1.7.1 Wet Storage and Berthing.

28.1.7.1.1 Each berth shall be arranged such that a boat occupying the berth can be removed in an emergency without the necessity of moving other boats. [**303**:7.1.1]

28.1.7.1.2 Access to all piers, floats, and wharves shall be provided for municipal fire-fighting equipment. [**303**:7.1.2]

28.1.7.1.3* Electrical lighting shall be provided to ensure adequate illumination of all exterior areas, piers, and floats. [**303**:7.1.3]

28.1.7.1.4 Electrical lighting shall not interfere with navigation or aids to navigation. [**303**:7.1.4]

28.1.7.1.5 Only listed 120/240 V ac electrical equipment shall be operated unattended. [**303**:7.1.5]

28.1.7.2 Dry Storage.

28.1.7.2.1 General.

28.1.7.2.1.1 Heaters.

28.1.7.2.1.1.1 The use of portable heaters in boat storage areas shall be prohibited except where necessary to accomplish repairs. [**303**:7.2.1.1.1]

28.1.7.2.1.1.2 Portable heaters used in accordance with 28.1.7.2.1.1.1 shall be used only when personnel are in attendance. [**303**:7.2.1.1.2]

28.1.7.2.1.1.3 Open flame heaters shall not be used in boat storage areas. [**303**:7.2.1.1.3]

28.1.7.2.1.2 Ladders long enough to reach the deck of any stored boat shall be provided and readily available. [**303**:7.2.1.2]

28.1.7.2.1.3 The use of blow torches or flammable paint remover shall be prohibited unless permitted by 8.7.1 of NFPA 303. [**303**:7.2.1.3]

28.1.7.2.1.4 The use of gasoline or other flammable solvents for cleaning purposes shall be prohibited. [**303**:7.2.1.4]

28.1.7.2.1.5 Where a boat is to be dry-stored for the season or stored indoors for an extended period of time, such as while awaiting repairs, the following precautions shall be taken:

(1) The vessel shall be inspected for any hazardous materials or conditions that could exist, and corrective action shall be taken.
(2) Liquefied petroleum gas (LPG) and compressed natural gas (CNG) cylinders, reserve supplies of stove alcohol or kerosene, and charcoal shall be removed from the premises or stored in a separate, designated safe area.
(3) All portable fuel tanks shall be removed from the premises or emptied and, if emptied, the cap shall be removed and the tank left open to the atmosphere.
(4)*Permanently installed fuel tanks shall be stored at least 95 percent full. [**303**:7.2.1.5]

28.1.7.2.1.6 No unattended electrical equipment shall be in use aboard boats. [**303**:7.2.1.6]

28.1.7.2.1.7 All storage areas shall be routinely raked, swept, or otherwise policed to prevent the accumulation of rubbish. [**303**:7.2.1.7]

28.1.7.2.1.8 Fire Department Access.

28.1.7.2.1.8.1 Access to boats stored outside shall be such that the hose-lay distance from the fire apparatus to any portion of the boat shall not exceed 150 ft (45 m). [**303**:7.2.1.8.1]

28.1.7.2.1.8.2 Access to buildings in which boats are stored shall be such that the hose-lay distance from the fire apparatus to all exterior portions of the building shall not exceed 150 ft (45 m). [**303**:7.2.1.8.2]

28.1.7.2.1.8.3 Wet standpipe systems shall be permitted to be used to meet the requirement in 28.1.7.2.1.8.1 or 28.1.7.2.1.8.2. [**303**:7.2.1.8.3]

28.1.7.2.2 Indoors.

28.1.7.2.2.1 When work is being carried out onboard a vessel in an unsprinklered storage building, management shall require an inspection of the vessel at the end of the day to ensure that no hazards resulting from the day's work are present. [**303**:7.2.2.1]

28.1.7.2.2.2 If a guard is employed, vessels addressed in 28.1.7.2.2.1 shall be included in the regular rounds. [**303**:7.2.2.2]

28.1.7.2.2.3 Class I flammable liquids shall not be stored in an indoor boat storage area. [**303**:7.2.2.3]

28.1.7.2.2.4 Work performed on boats stored indoors shall be performed by qualified personnel. [**303**:7.2.2.4]

28.1.7.2.2.5 Facility management shall maintain control over all personnel access to storage facilities and boats stored indoors. [**303**:7.2.2.5]

28.1.7.2.3 In-Out Dry Storage and Rack Storage.

28.1.7.2.3.1 Where boats are stored either inside or outside in single- or multiple-level racks, those boats shall have unimpeded vehicular access at one end, and equipment shall be available to remove any stored boat. [**303**:7.2.3.1]

28.1.7.2.3.2 Where boats are stored in multilevel racks, either inside or outside, for seasonal storage or for in-out operation, the following precautions shall be taken:

(1) Drain plugs shall be removed (in sprinklered buildings).
(2) Batteries shall be disconnected or the master battery switch turned off.
(3) Fuel tank valves shall be closed.
(4) For seasonal storage, the requirements of 28.1.7.2.1 shall apply. [**303**:7.2.3.2]

28.1.7.2.3.3 Repairs to boats that are on racks or that are inside an in-out dry storage building shall be prohibited. [**303**:7.2.3.3]

28.1.7.2.3.4 Portable power lines, such as drop cords, shall be prohibited from use on boats in an in-out dry storage building. [**303**:7.2.3.4]

28.1.7.2.3.5 The charging of batteries shall be prohibited in the in-out dry storage building. [**303**:7.2.3.5]

28.1.7.2.4* Battery Storage. Where due to size and weight the removal of batteries for storage or charging is impractical, batteries shall be permitted to remain onboard provided the following conditions are met:

(1) The battery compartment is arranged to provide adequate ventilation.
(2) A listed battery charger is used to provide a suitable charge.
(3) The power connection to the charger consists of a three-wire cord of not less than No. 14 AWG conductors connected to a source of 110 V to 125 V single-phase current, with a control switch and approved circuit protection device designed to trip at not more than 125 percent of the rated amperage of the charger.
(4) There is no connection on the load side of the charger to any other device except the battery, and the boat battery switch is turned off.
(5) The battery is properly connected to the charger, and the grounding conductor effectively grounds the charger enclosure.
(6) Unattended battery chargers are checked at intervals not exceeding 8 hours while in operation. [**303**:7.2.4]

28.1.8 Operational Hazards.

28.1.8.1* Conditions on Individual Boats.

28.1.8.1.1 The management shall have an inspection made of each boat received for major repair or storage as soon as practicable after arrival of a boat and before commencement of any work aboard. [**303**:8.1.1]

28.1.8.1.2 The inspection required in 28.1.8.1.1 shall include the following determinations:

(1) Presence of combustible vapors in any compartment
(2) General maintenance and cleanliness, and location of any combustible materials that require removal or protection for the safe accomplishment of the particular work involved
(3) Quantity, type, and apparent condition of fire-extinguishing equipment onboard
(4) Listed and appropriate shore power inlet(s) and ship-to-shore cable(s), when present [**303**:8.1.2]

28.1.8.1.3 The management shall, as a condition to accepting a boat received for major repair or storage, require the owner to correct any inadequacies found in 28.1.8.1.2 or to authorize management to do so. [**303**:8.1.3]

28.1.8.2 General Precautions.

28.1.8.2.1 Smoking in the working area shall be prohibited. [**303**:8.2.1]

28.1.8.2.2 Loose combustibles in the area of any hazardous work shall be removed. [**303**:8.2.2]

28.1.8.2.3 Unprotected battery terminals shall be covered to prevent inadvertent shorting from dropped tools or otherwise, and the ungrounded battery lead shall be disconnected. [**303**:8.2.3]

28.1.8.2.4 Personnel employed in the removal or installation of storage batteries shall be qualified. [**303**:8.2.4]

28.1.8.2.5 Where electric service is provided to boats in storage, the receptacle providing the power shall be protected with a ground-fault circuit-interrupter. [**303**:8.2.5]

28.1.8.2.6 The marina or boatyard operator shall post in a prominent location, or provide to boat operators using a marina or boatyard for mooring, repair, servicing, or storage, a list of safe operating procedures containing at least the following information:

(1) A prohibition against the use of any form of hibachis, charcoal, wood, or gas-type portable cooking equipment, except in specifically authorized areas that are not on the docks, on boats in the berthing area, or near flammables
(2) Procedures for disposal of trash
(3) Designation of nonsmoking areas
(4) Location of fire extinguishers and hoses
(5) Procedures for turning in a fire alarm
(6) Fueling procedures
(7)*Emergency contact information and marina address for notifying emergency services to respond to an incident [**303**:8.2.6]

28.1.8.2.7 The information on fueling procedures referred to in 28.1.8.2.6(6) shall include at least the following information:

(1) Procedures before fueling
  (a) Stop all engines and auxiliaries
  (b) Shut off all electricity, open flames, and heat sources
  (c) Check bilges for fuel vapors
  (d) Extinguish all smoking materials
  (e) Close access fittings and openings that could allow fuel vapors to enter the boat's enclosed spaces
  (f) Remove all personnel from the boat except the person handling the fueling hose
(2) Procedures during fueling
  (a) Maintain nozzle contact with fill pipe
  (b) Attend fuel-filling nozzle at all times
  (c) Wipe up spills immediately
  (d) Avoid overfilling
(3) Procedures after fueling and before starting engine
  (a) Inspect bilges for leakage or fuel odors
  (b) Ventilate until odors are removed [**303**:8.2.7]

28.2 Marine Terminals, Piers, and Wharves.

28.2.1 Section 28.2 shall apply to marine terminals as defined herein. Special use piers and wharf structures that are not marine terminals, such as public assembly, residential, business, or recreational occupancies that differ in design and construction from cargo handling piers, require special consideration. The general principles of NFPA 307 for the construction and fire protection of piers and wharves shall be applicable to such structures and shall comply with NFPA 307, *Standard for the Construction and Fire Protection of Marine Terminals, Piers, and Wharves*, and Section 28.2.

28.2.1.1 Marine terminals, piers, and wharves shall comply with 28.1.8.2.7.

28.2.2* Section 28.2 shall not apply to marinas and boatyards. *(See Section 28.1.)* [**307**:1.3.2]

28.2.3 Section 28.2 shall not apply to the handling of the following:

(1)*Flammable or combustible liquids in bulk *(See Chapter 66.)*
(2)*Liquefied gases in bulk *(See Chapter 69.)* [**307**:1.3.3]

28.2.4 Nothing in Section 28.2 shall supersede any of the regulations of governmental or other regulatory authority. [**307**:1.1.2]

28.3 Construction, Conversion, Repair, and Lay-Up of Vessels.

28.3.1* The construction, conversion, repair, or lay-up of vessels shall comply with NFPA 312, *Standard for Fire Protection of Vessels During Construction, Conversion, Repair, and Lay-Up*, and Section 28.3.

28.3.2 Nothing in Section 28.3 shall be construed as prohibiting the immediate dry-docking of a vessel whose safety is imperiled, as by being in a sinking condition or by being seriously damaged. [**312**:1.2.2]

28.3.3 In such cases, all necessary precautionary measures shall be taken as soon as practicable. [**312**:1.2.3]

28.3.4 The requirements of Section 28.3 shall not apply to situations where it is in conflict with or superseded by requirements of any government regulatory agency. [**312**:1.1.2]

Chapter 29 Parking Garages

29.1 General.

29.1.1 The protection of new and existing parking garages, as well as the control of hazards in open parking structures, enclosed parking structures, and basement and underground parking structures shall comply with this chapter and Section 42.8 of NFPA *101*.

29.1.2 Construction and protection of new parking garages shall also comply with NFPA 88A, *Standard for Parking Structures*.

29.1.3 Chapter 29 shall not apply to parking garages in one- and two-family dwellings.

Chapter 30 Motor Fuel Dispensing Facilities and Repair Garages

30.1 Motor Fuel Dispensing Facilities.

30.1.1 Application.

30.1.1.1 Motor fuel dispensing facilities, marine/motor fuel dispensing facilities, motor fuel dispensing facilities located inside buildings, and fleet vehicle motor fuel dispensing facilities shall comply with Sections 30.1 and 30.3 and NFPA 30A, *Code for Motor Fuel Dispensing Facilities and Repair Garages.*

30.1.1.2 This chapter shall not apply to refueling operations. *(For refueling operations, see Chapter 42.)*

30.1.1.3 Permits. Permits, where required, shall comply with Section 1.12.

30.1.2 Occupancy Classification. The occupancy classification of a motor fuel dispensing facility that is located inside a building or structure shall be a special purpose industrial occupancy as defined in NFPA *101*. [**30A:**7.3.1]

30.1.3 Means of Egress. In a motor fuel dispensing facility that is located inside a building or structure, the required number, location, and construction of means of egress shall meet all applicable requirements for special purpose industrial occupancies, as set forth in NFPA *101*. [**30A:**7.3.3]

30.1.4 Drainage. Where Class I or Class II liquids are dispensed, provisions shall be made to prevent spilled liquids from flowing into the interior of buildings. Such provisions shall be made by grading driveways, raising door sills, or other equally effective means. [**30A:**7.3.4]

30.1.5 Fixed Fire Protection.

30.1.5.1* For an unattended, self-serve, motor fuel dispensing facility, additional fire protection shall be provided where required by the AHJ. [**30A:**7.3.5.1]

30.1.5.2 Where required, an automatic fire suppression system shall be installed in accordance with the appropriate NFPA standard, manufacturers' instructions, and the listing requirements of the systems. [**30A:**7.3.5.2]

30.1.6 Fuel Dispensing Areas Inside Buildings.

30.1.6.1 The fuel dispensing area shall be separated from all other portions of the building by walls, partitions, floors, and floor–ceiling assemblies having a fire resistance rating of not less than 2 hours. [**30A:**7.3.6.1]

30.1.6.2 Interior finish shall be of noncombustible materials or of approved limited-combustible materials, as defined in this *Code* and NFPA 220. [**30A:**7.3.6.2]

30.1.6.3 Door and window openings in fire-rated interior walls shall be provided with listed fire doors having a fire protection rating of not less than 1½ hours. Doors shall be self-closing. They shall be permitted to remain open during normal operations if they are designed to close automatically in a fire emergency by means of listed closure devices. Fire doors shall be installed in accordance with NFPA 80. They shall be kept unobstructed at all times. [**30A:**7.3.6.3]

30.1.6.4 Openings for ducts in fire-rated interior partitions and walls shall be protected by listed fire dampers. Openings for ducts in fire-rated floor or floor–ceiling assemblies shall be protected with enclosed shafts. Enclosure of shafts shall be with wall or partition assemblies having a fire resistance rating of not less than 2 hours. Openings for ducts into enclosed shafts shall be protected with listed fire dampers. [**30A:**7.3.6.4]

30.1.6.5 The fuel dispensing area shall be located at street level, with no dispenser located more than 50 ft (15 m) from the vehicle exit to, or entrance from, the outside of the building. [**30A:**7.3.6.5]

30.1.6.6 The fuel dispensing area shall be limited to that required to serve not more than four vehicles at one time.

Exception: At a fleet vehicle motor fuel dispensing facility inside a building, where only Class II and Class III liquids are dispensed, the number of vehicles serviced at any one time shall be permitted to be increased to 12. [30A:7.3.6.6]

30.1.6.7* A mechanical exhaust system that serves only the fuel dispensing area shall be provided. This system shall meet all of the following requirements:

(1) The system shall be interlocked with the dispensing system so that airflow is established before any dispensing device can operate. Failure of airflow shall automatically shut down the dispensing system.
(2) The exhaust system shall be designed to provide air movement across all portions of the floor of the fuel dispensing area and to prevent the flowing of ignitible vapors beyond the dispensing area.
(3) Exhaust inlet ducts shall not be less than 3 in. (76 mm) or more than 12 in. (305 mm) above the floor. Exhaust ducts shall not be located in floors or penetrate the floor of the dispensing area. Exhaust ducts shall discharge to a safe location outside the building.
(4) The exhaust system shall provide ventilation at a rate of not less than 1 ft^3/min/ft^2 (0.3 m^3/min/m^2) of floor area, based on the fuel dispensing area.
(5) The exhaust system shall meet all applicable requirements of NFPA 91.

Exception: The provisions of 30.1.6.7 shall not apply to a fuel dispensing area located inside a building if two or more sides of the dispensing area are open to the building exterior. [30A:7.3.6.7]

30.1.6.8 The floor of the dispensing area shall be liquidtight. Where Class I liquids are dispensed, provisions shall be made to prevent spilled liquids from flowing out of the fuel dispensing area and into other areas of the building by means of curbs, scuppers, special drainage systems, or other means acceptable to the AHJ. [**30A:**7.3.6.8]

30.1.6.9* Oil drainage systems shall be equipped with approved oil/water traps or separators if they connect to public sewers or discharge into public waterways. [**30A:**7.3.6.9]

30.2 Repair Garages.

30.2.1 Application. The construction and protection of, as well as the control of hazards in, garages used for major repair and maintenance of motorized vehicles and any sales and servicing facilities associated therewith shall comply with Sections 30.2 and 30.3 and NFPA 30A.

30.2.1.1 Permits. Permits, where required, shall comply with Section 1.12.

30.2.2 Occupancy Classification. The occupancy classification of a repair garage shall be a special purpose industrial occupancy as defined in NFPA *101*. [**30A:**7.4.1]

30.2.3 General Construction Requirements. In major repair garages, where CNG-fueled vehicles, hydrogen-fueled vehicles, LNG-fueled vehicles, or LP-Gas-fueled vehicles are repaired, all applicable requirements of NFPA 52 or NFPA 58, whichever is applicable, shall be met. [**30A:**7.4.2]

30.2.4 Means of Egress. In a repair garage, the required number, location, and construction of means of egress shall meet all applicable requirements for special purpose industrial occupancies, as set forth in NFPA *101*. [**30A:**7.4.3]

30.2.5 Drainage. In areas of repair garages used for repair or servicing of vehicles, floor assemblies shall be constructed of noncombustible materials or, if combustible materials are used in the assembly, they shall be surfaced with approved, nonabsorbent, noncombustible material.

Exception: Slip-resistant, nonabsorbent, interior floor finishes having a critical radiant flux not more than 9.87 Btu/in.^{2} (0.45 W/cm^2), as determined by NFPA 253, shall be permitted. [30A: 7.4.4]

30.2.5.1 Floors shall be liquidtight to prevent the leakage or seepage of liquids and shall be sloped to facilitate the movement of water, fuel, or other liquids to floor drains. [**30A:**7.4.4.1]

30.2.5.2 In areas of repair garages where vehicles are serviced, any floor drains shall be properly trapped and shall discharge through an oil/water separator to the sewer or to an outside vented sump. [**30A:**7.4.4.2]

30.2.6 Pits, Belowgrade Work Areas, and Subfloor Work Areas.

30.2.6.1 Pits, belowgrade work areas, and subfloor work areas used for lubrication, inspection, and minor automotive maintenance work shall comply with the provisions of this chapter, in addition to other applicable requirements of NFPA 30A. [**30A:**7.4.5.1]

30.2.6.2 Walls, floors, and structural supports shall be constructed of masonry, concrete, steel, or other approved noncombustible materials. [**30A:**7.4.5.2]

30.2.6.3 In pits, belowgrade work areas, and subfloor work areas, the required number, location, and construction of means of egress shall meet the requirements for special purpose industrial occupancies in Chapter 40 of NFPA *101*. [**30A:**7.4.5.3]

30.2.6.4 Pits, belowgrade work areas, and subfloor work areas shall be provided with exhaust ventilation at a rate of not less than 1 ft^3/min/ft^2 (0.3 m^3/min/m^2) of floor area at all times that the building is occupied or when vehicles are parked in or over these areas. Exhaust air shall be taken from a point within 12 in. (0.3 m) of the floor. [**30A:**7.4.5.4]

30.2.7 Fixed Fire Protection. Automatic sprinkler protection installed in accordance with the requirements of Section 13.3 shall be provided in major repair garages, as herein defined, when any of the following conditions exist:

(1) The major repair garage is two or more stories in height, including basements, and any one of the floors exceeds 10,000 ft^2 (930 m^2).
(2) The major repair garage is one story and exceeds 12,000 ft^2 (1115 m^2).
(3) The major repair garage is servicing vehicles parked in the basement of the building. [**30A:**7.4.6]

30.2.8 Gas Detection System. Repair garages used for repair of vehicle engine fuel systems fueled by non-odorized gases, such as hydrogen and non-odorized LNG/CNG, shall be provided with an approved flammable gas detection system. [**30A:**7.4.7]

30.2.8.1 System Design. The flammable gas detection system shall be calibrated to the types of fuels or gases used by vehicles to be repaired. The gas detection system shall be designed to activate when the level of flammable gas exceeds 25 percent of the lower flammable limit (LFL). Gas detection shall also be provided in lubrication or chassis repair pits of repair garages used for repairing non-odorized LNG/CNG-fueled vehicles. [**30A:**7.4.7.1]

30.2.8.2 Operation. Activation of the gas detection system shall result in all of the following:

(1) Initiation of distinct audible and visual alarm signals in the repair garage
(2) Deactivation of all heating systems located in the repair garage
(3) Activation of the mechanical ventilation system, when the system is interlocked with gas detection [**30A:**7.4.7.2]

30.2.8.3 Failure of the Gas Detection System. Failure of the gas detection system shall result in the deactivation of the heating system and activation of the mechanical ventilation system and, where the ventilation system is interlocked with gas detection, shall cause a trouble signal to sound in an approved location. [**30A:**7.4.7.3]

30.2.8.4 The circuits of the detection system required by 30.2.8 shall be monitored for integrity in accordance with *NFPA 72*. [**30A:**7.4.7.4]

30.2.9* Heating, Ventilating, and Air-Conditioning.

30.2.9.1* Forced air heating, air-conditioning, and ventilating systems serving a fuel dispensing area inside a building or a repair garage shall not be interconnected with any such systems serving other occupancies in the building. Such systems shall be installed in accordance with NFPA 90A. [**30A:**7.5.1]

30.2.9.2 Return air openings in areas of repair garages used for the repair or servicing of vehicles or in a fuel dispensing area shall be not less than 18 in. (455 mm) above floor level measured to the bottom of the openings. [**30A:**7.5.2]

30.2.9.3 Combined ventilation and heating systems shall not recirculate air from areas that are below grade level. [**30A:**7.5.3]

30.2.9.4 Exhaust duct openings shall be located so that they effectively remove vapor accumulations at floor level from all parts of the floor area. [**30A:**7.5.4]

30.2.10 Heat-Producing Appliances.

30.2.10.1 Heat-producing appliances shall be installed in accordance with the requirements of 30.2.10. They shall be permitted to be installed in the conventional manner except as provided in 30.2.10. [**30A:**7.6.1]

30.2.10.2 Heat-producing appliances shall be of an approved type. Solid fuel stoves, improvised furnaces, salamanders, or space heaters shall not be permitted in areas of repair garages used for repairing or servicing of vehicles or in a fuel dispensing area.

Exception No. 1: Unit heaters, when installed in accordance with Chapter 7 of NFPA 30A, need not meet this requirement.

Exception No. 2: Heat-producing equipment for any lubrication room or service room where there is no dispensing or transferring of Class I or Class II liquids or LP-Gas, when installed in accordance with Chapter 7 of NFPA 30A, need not meet this requirement. [30A:7.6.2]

30.2.10.3 Heat-producing appliances shall be permitted to be installed in a special room that is separated from areas that are classified as Division 1 or Division 2, in accordance with Chapter 8 of NFPA 30A, by walls that are constructed to prevent the transmission of vapors, that have a fire resistance rating of at least 1 hour, and that have no openings in the walls that lead to a classified area within 8 ft (2.4 m) of the floor. Specific small openings through the wall, such as for piping and electrical conduit, shall be permitted, provided the gaps and voids are filled with a fire-resistant material to resist transmission of vapors. All air for combustion purposes shall be taken from outside the building. This room shall not be used for storage of combustible materials, except for fuel storage as permitted by the standards referenced in 30.2.10.9. [**30A:**7.6.3]

30.2.10.4 Heat-producing appliances using gas or oil fuel shall be permitted to be installed in a lubrication or service room where there is no dispensing or transferring of Class I liquids, including the open draining of automotive gasoline tanks, provided the bottom of the combustion chamber is at least 18 in. (455 mm) above the floor and the appliances are protected from physical damage. [**30A:**7.6.4]

30.2.10.5 Heat-producing appliances using gas or oil fuel listed for use in garages shall be permitted to be installed in lubrication rooms, service rooms, or fuel dispensing areas where Class I liquids are dispensed or transferred, provided the equipment is installed at least 8 ft (2.4 m) above the floor. [**30A:**7.6.5]

30.2.10.6* Where major repairs are conducted on CNG-fueled vehicles or LNG-fueled vehicles, open flame heaters or heating equipment with exposed surfaces having a temperature in excess of 750°F (399°C) shall not be permitted in areas subject to ignitible concentrations of gas. [**30A:**7.6.6]

30.2.10.7 Electrical heat-producing appliances shall meet the requirements of Chapter 8 of NFPA 30A. [**30A:**7.6.7]

30.2.10.8 Fuels used shall be of the type and quality specified by the manufacturer of the heating appliance. Crankcase drainings shall not be used in oil-fired appliances, unless the appliances are specifically approved for such use. [**30A:**7.6.8]

30.2.10.9 Heat-producing appliances shall be installed to meet the requirements of NFPA 31, *Standard for the Installation of Oil-Burning Equipment*; NFPA 54, *National Fuel Gas Code*; NFPA 82, *Standard on Incinerators and Waste and Linen Handling Systems and Equipment*; NFPA 90A, *Standard for the Installation of Air-Conditioning and Ventilating Systems*; and NFPA 211, *Standard for Chimneys, Fireplaces, Vents, and Solid Fuel–Burning Appliances*, as applicable, except as hereinafter specifically provided. [**30A:**7.6.9]

30.3 Operational Requirements. Operations conducted in motor fuel dispensing facilities and repair garages shall comply with Section 42.7.

Chapter 31 Forest Products

31.1* General. The storage, manufacturing, and processing of timber, lumber, plywood, veneers, and by-products shall be in accordance with this chapter and NFPA 664, *Standard for the Prevention of Fires and Explosions in Wood Processing and Woodworking Facilities*.

31.2 Permits. Permits, where required, shall comply with Section 1.12.

31.3 Protection of Storage of Forest Products.

31.3.1 Application.

31.3.1.1 The requirements of this chapter shall apply to the outside storage of the following:

(1) Lumber and wood panel products at retail and wholesale lumber storage yards
(2) Lumber and wood panel products at other than retail and wholesale storage yards
(3) Ties, poles, piles, posts, and other similar forest products at pressure-treating plant yards
(4) Outside storage of wood chips, hogged material, and wood by-products
(5) Logs

31.3.1.2 The requirements of this chapter shall not apply to forest products stored on piers and wharves as addressed in NFPA 307, *Standard for the Construction and Fire Protection of Marine Terminals, Piers, and Wharves*.

31.3.2 General Fire Protection. The requirements in this subsection shall apply to all facilities regulated by 31.3.3 through 31.3.8 except as modified by those subsections.

31.3.2.1 Operational Fire Prevention.

31.3.2.1.1* Combustible waste materials such as bark, sawdust, chips, and other debris shall not be permitted to accumulate in a quantity or location that constitutes an undue fire hazard.

31.3.2.1.2 Smoking shall be prohibited except in specified safe locations approved by the AHJ.

31.3.2.1.2.1 Signs that read "No Smoking" shall be posted in those areas where smoking is prohibited.

31.3.2.1.2.2 Signs indicating areas designated as safe for smoking shall be posted in those locations where smoking is permitted.

31.3.2.1.2.3 Smoking areas shall be provided with approved, noncombustible ash receptacles.

31.3.2.1.2.4 Smoking shall be specifically prohibited in and around railroad cars.

31.3.2.1.3 Access into yard areas by unauthorized persons shall be prohibited.

31.3.2.1.4 Storage areas shall be enclosed with a fence equipped with effective gates located as necessary to allow the entry of fire department apparatus.

31.3.2.1.5 Miscellaneous occupancy hazards such as vehicle storage and repair shops, cutting and welding operations, flammable liquid storage, liquefied petroleum gas storage, and similar operations shall be safeguarded in accordance with recognized good practice and this *Code*.

31.3.2.1.6 Vehicles and other power devices shall be of an approved type and shall be safely maintained and operated.

31.3.2.1.6.1* Vehicle fueling operations shall be conducted in specified safe locations, isolated from storage areas and principal operating buildings.

31.3.2.1.6.2 Diesel- or gasoline-fueled vehicles that operate on hogged material or chip piles, in log storage areas, or in lumber storage areas shall be equipped with fixed fire-extinguishing systems of a type approved for off-road vehicles.

31.3.2.1.7 All electrical equipment and installations shall conform to the provisions of Section 11.1.

31.3.2.1.8 Salamanders, braziers, open fires, and similar dangerous heating arrangements shall be prohibited.

31.3.2.1.9 Heating devices shall be limited to approved-type equipment installed in an approved manner.

31.3.2.1.10 Suitable safeguards shall be provided to minimize the hazard of sparks caused by equipment such as refuse burners, boiler stacks, vehicle exhausts, and locomotives.

31.3.2.1.10.1* Burning of shavings, sawdust, and refuse materials shall be conducted only in an approved, enclosed refuse burner equipped with an approved spark arrester and located at a safe distance from the nearest point of any yard. *(See Section 10.10.)*

31.3.2.1.10.2 The design and location of large burners presents special problems, and the AHJ shall be consulted.

31.3.2.1.11 Stacks from solid fuel-burning furnaces and boilers shall be equipped with spark-arresting equipment to prevent hot sparks from reaching the ground, and consideration shall be given to spark hazard in determining the height of such stacks.

31.3.2.1.12 Cutting, welding, or other use of open flames or spark-producing equipment shall not be permitted in the storage area unless by an approved permit system.

31.3.2.2 Exposure Protection. Exposure to the yard shall be protected in accordance with the requirements of 31.3.2.2.1 through 31.3.2.2.2.2.

31.3.2.2.1* Yard areas shall be separated from plant operations and other structures so that fire exposure into the yard is minimized.

31.3.2.2.1.1 Minimum separation shall be by means of a clear space permanently available for fire-fighting operations.

31.3.2.2.1.2 The width of the clear space shall be based on the severity of exposure, which varies with the area, height, occupancy, construction, and protection of the exposing structure and the type of stacking and height of adjacent stacks.

31.3.2.2.2* Forest, brush, and grass fire exposure shall be minimized by providing adequate clear space that is carefully kept free of combustible vegetation.

31.3.2.2.2.1 Clear space of a width at least equivalent to the fire department access road shall be provided for grass exposures, and clear space of a width not less than 100 ft (30 m) shall be provided for light brush exposures.

31.3.2.2.2.2 In forested areas, a wider clear space than in 31.3.2.2.2.1 shall be provided.

31.3.2.3* Fire Detection and Extinguishment. A reliable means for prompt transmission of fire alarms to public fire departments and plant emergency organizations shall be provided.

31.3.3 Outside Storage of Lumber and Wood Panel Products at Retail and Wholesale Storage Yards.

31.3.3.1 Application.

31.3.3.1.1 The requirements of 31.3.3 shall apply to the following areas:

(1) Retail lumberyards handling forest products and other building materials
(2) Wholesale lumber storage yards, including distribution, holding, and transshipment areas

31.3.3.1.2* The requirements of 31.3.4 shall apply to other than large outside wholesale and retail distribution yards.

31.3.3.2 General.

31.3.3.2.1* The fire hazard potential inherent in lumber storage operations with large quantities of combustible materials shall be controlled by a positive fire prevention program under the direct supervision of upper level management that shall include the following:

(1) Selection, design, and arrangement of storage yard areas and materials-handling equipment based upon proven fire prevention and protection principles
(2) Means for early fire detection, transmission of alarm, and fire extinguishment
(3) Fire department access roads to separate large stacks and provide access for effective fire-fighting operations
(4) Separation of yard storage from yard buildings and other exposing properties
(5) Effective fire prevention maintenance program, including regular yard inspections by trained personnel

31.3.3.2.2* Water supplies shall be provided in accordance with this *Code*.

31.3.3.3 Open Yard Storage.

31.3.3.3.1* Lumber stacks shall be on stable ground, and paved or surfaced with materials such as cinders, fine gravel, or stone.

31.3.3.3.2 The method of stacking shall be stable and in an orderly and regular manner.

31.3.3.3.3* The height of stacks shall not exceed 20 ft (6 m) with consideration for stability.

31.3.3.3.4 Where stacks are supported clear of the ground, 6 in. (150 mm) of clearance shall be provided for cleaning operations under the stacks.

31.3.3.3.5 Fire department access roads shall be spaced so that a grid system of not more than 50 ft × 150 ft (15 m × 46 m) is produced.

31.3.3.3.6 Fire department access roads shall comply with Section 18.2.

31.3.3.3.7 Stacking limits shall be designated to indicate yard area and alleyway limits in accordance with 31.3.3.3.7.1 or 31.3.3.3.7.2.

31.3.3.3.7.1 The stacking limits shall be designated with boundary posts having signs that indicate stacking limits unless otherwise permitted by 31.3.3.3.7.2.

31.3.3.3.7.2 Where yards have paved areas, painted boundary limits shall be permitted to be used to designate stacking limits.

31.3.3.4 Exposure Protection.

31.3.3.4.1 Exposure to the Yard.

31.3.3.4.1.1 Open yard stacking shall be located with not less than 15 ft (4.6 m) clear space to buildings.

31.3.3.4.1.2 Boundary posts with signs designating stacking limits shall be provided to designate the clear space to unsprinklered buildings in which hazardous manufacturing or other operations take place.

31.3.3.4.2* Exposure from the Yard.

31.3.3.4.2.1 Open yard stacking shall be located with not less than 15 ft (4.6 m) clear space to adjacent property lines.

31.3.3.4.2.2 Alternative forms of exposure protection shall be permitted where approved by the AHJ.

31.3.4 Outside Storage of Lumber and Wood Panel Products at Other Than Retail and Wholesale Storage Yards.

31.3.4.1* Application. The requirements of 31.3.4 shall apply to large yard storage areas containing lumber, wood panels, and other similar wood products not intended for retail or wholesale distribution at the site.

31.3.4.2* General. The fire hazard potential inherent in forest product storage operations with large quantities of combustible materials shall be controlled by a positive fire prevention program under the direct supervision of upper level management that shall include the following:

(1) Selection, design, and arrangement of storage yard areas and materials-handling equipment based on sound fire prevention and protection principles
(2) Means for early fire detection, transmission of alarm, and fire extinguishment
(3) Fire department access roads to separate large stacks and provide access for effective fire-fighting operations
(4) Separation of yard storage from mill or other plant operations and other exposing properties
(5) Effective fire prevention maintenance program, including regular yard inspections by trained personnel

31.3.4.3* Open Yard Storage.

31.3.4.3.1* Water supplies shall be provided in accordance with this *Code*.

31.3.4.3.2 Access to the plant and yard from public highways shall be provided by all-weather roadways capable of supporting fire department apparatus.

31.3.4.3.3 The storage site shall be reasonably level, on solid ground, and paved or surfaced with materials such as cinders, fine gravel, or stone.

31.3.4.3.4 Stack height shall be limited to 20 ft (6 m).

31.3.5 Outside Storage of Ties, Poles, Piles, Posts, and Other Similar Forest Products at Pressure-Treating Plant Yards.

31.3.5.1 Application.

31.3.5.1.1* The requirements of 31.3.5 shall apply to yard storage areas containing treated and untreated ties, poles, piles, posts, and other similar forest products in yards connected with pressure-treating plants.

31.3.5.1.2 The requirements of 31.3.5 shall not apply to pressure-treating buildings, processes, or storage of treating materials.

31.3.5.2* General. The fire hazard potential inherent in tie storage operations with large quantities of combustible materials shall be controlled by a positive fire prevention program under the direct supervision of upper level management that shall include the following:

(1) Selection, design, and arrangement of storage yard areas and materials-handling equipment based upon sound fire prevention and protection principles
(2) Means for early fire detection, transmission of alarm, and fire extinguishment
(3) Fire department access roads to separate large stacks and provide access for effective fire-fighting operations
(4) Separation of yard storage from mill buildings and other exposing properties
(5) Effective fire prevention maintenance program, including regular yard inspections by trained personnel

31.3.5.3* Tie Yard Protection.

31.3.5.3.1* Unobstructed alleyways of sufficient width for hand or cart fire hose laying operations shall be provided between piles.

31.3.5.3.1.1 Alleyways shall not be less than 2 ft (0.6 m) in width.

31.3.5.3.1.2 Where a minimum alleyway width of 4 ft (1.2 m) is provided, the length of the rows shall be not more than 100 ft (30 m).

31.3.5.3.1.3 Where an alleyway width less than 4 ft (1.2 m) is provided, the length of the rows shall be not more than 75 ft (23 m).

31.3.5.3.2* Water supplies shall be provided in accordance with this *Code*.

31.3.5.3.3 Access to the plant and yard from public highways shall be provided by all-weather roadways capable of supporting fire department apparatus.

31.3.5.3.4 The storage site shall be reasonably level, on solid ground, and paved or surfaced with materials such as cinders, fine gravel, or stone.

31.3.5.3.5* Stack heights shall be limited to 20 ft (6 m).

31.3.6 Outside Storage of Wood Chips and Hogged Material.

31.3.6.1* Application. The requirements of 31.3.6 shall apply to yard storage areas containing wood chips and hogged material.

31.3.6.2 General.

31.3.6.2.1* The fire hazard potential inherent in storage piles shall be controlled by a positive fire prevention program under the direct supervision of upper level management that shall include the following:

(1) Selection, design, and arrangement of storage yard areas and materials-handling equipment based upon sound fire prevention and protection principles
(2) Establishment of control over the various factors that lead to spontaneous heating, including provisions for monitoring the internal condition of the pile
(3) Means for early fire detection and extinguishment
(4) Fire department access roads around the piles and access roads to the top of the piles for effective fire-fighting operations
(5) Facilities for calling the public fire department and facilities needed by the fire department for fire extinguishment
(6) Effective fire prevention maintenance program, including regular yard inspections by trained personnel

31.3.6.2.2* The following items shall be addressed when establishing operating procedures:

(1) The storage site shall be reasonably level, solid ground, or shall be paved with blacktop, concrete, or other hard-surface material.
(2) Sites shall be cleaned before transferring wood products to the site.

(3) Operating plans for the buildup and reclaiming of the pile shall be based on a turnover time of not more than 1 year under ideal conditions.
(4)*Piles containing other than screened chips made from cleaned and barked logs shall be minimized.
(5)*The pile size shall be limited.
(6) Pile heights shall be kept low, particularly piles that inherently carry a larger percentage of fines and are subject to greater compaction.
(7) Thermocouples shall be installed during pile buildup, or other means for measuring temperatures within the pile shall be provided with regular (normally weekly) reports to management.
(8)*The pile shall be wetted regularly to help keep fines from drying out and help maintain the moisture content of the surface layer of the pile.

31.3.6.3* Pile Protection.

31.3.6.3.1* Piles shall be constructed with an access roadway to the top of the pile in order to reach any part of the pile.

31.3.6.3.2* Piles shall not exceed 60 ft (18 m) in height, 300 ft (90 m) in width, and 500 ft (150 m) in length.

31.3.6.3.2.1 Where pile height and width are such that all portions of the pile cannot be reached by direct hose streams from the ground, arrangements shall be made to provide firefighting service in these areas, and small fire stream supplies shall be available on the top of the pile for handling small surface fires and for wetting the pile in dry weather.

31.3.6.3.2.2 When more than one pile exists, they shall be subdivided by fire department access roads having not less than 30 ft (9 m) of clear space at the base of the piles.

31.3.6.3.2.3 Low barrier walls around piles shall be provided to clearly define pile perimeters, prevent creeping, and facilitate cleanup of fire department access roads.

31.3.6.3.3 Where suitable, a small, motorized vehicle amply equipped with portable extinguishing equipment or a water tank and pump shall be provided.

31.3.6.3.3.1 Lightweight ladders that can be placed against the side of the pile shall be placed at convenient locations throughout the yard for use by the plant emergency organization.

31.3.6.3.3.2 Training of the plant emergency organization also shall include procedures and precautions to be observed by yard crews employing power equipment in fighting internal fires.

31.3.6.3.4* Portable fire extinguishers for Class A fires shall be provided in accordance with Section 13.6 on all vehicles operating on the pile in addition to the normal Class B units for the vehicle.

31.3.6.3.5* Water supplies shall be provided in accordance with this *Code*.

31.3.6.3.6 All motor and switchgear enclosures shall be provided with approved, portable fire extinguishers suitable for the hazard involved in accordance with Section 13.6.

31.3.6.3.7* Power-operated, shovel-type or scoop-type vehicles, dozers, or similar equipment shall be available for use in moving stored material for fire fighting.

31.3.6.3.8 Temporary conveyors and motors on the surface or adjacent to the piles shall not be permitted.

31.3.6.3.9 Physical protection shall be provided to prevent heat sources such as steam lines, air lines, electrical motors, and mechanical drive equipment from becoming buried or heavily coated with combustible material.

31.3.6.3.10 Tramp metal collectors or detectors shall be required on all conveyor and blower systems.

31.3.6.4 Exposure Protection.

31.3.6.4.1* Incinerators or open refuse burning shall not be permitted in any area where sparks could reach the storage piles.

31.3.6.4.2* A clear space of not less than 15 ft (4.6 m) shall be maintained between piles and exposing structures, yard equipment, or stock, depending on the degree of exposure hazard.

31.3.6.4.3* Pile-to-pile clearance of not less than 30 ft (9 m) at the base of the pile shall be provided.

31.3.6.5 Emergency Action Plan. The facility shall have an emergency action plan for monitoring, controlling, and extinguishing spot fires.

31.3.7* Storage and Processing of Wood Chips, Hogged Material, Fines, Compost, and Raw Products at Yard Waste Recycling Facilities.

31.3.7.1 The storage and processing of wood chips, hogged material, fines, compost, and raw products produced from yard waste recycling facilities shall comply with 31.3.6 and 31.3.7.

31.3.7.2 When not protected by a fixed fire-extinguishing system in accordance with Chapter 13, piles shall not exceed 25 ft (7.6 m) in height, 150 ft (45 m) in width, and 250 ft (76.2 m) in length.

31.3.7.3 Static Pile Protection.

31.3.7.3.1 Static piles shall be monitored by an approved means to measure temperatures within the piles.

31.3.7.3.2 Internal pile temperatures shall be recorded weekly.

31.3.7.3.3 Records shall be kept on file at the facility and made available for inspection.

31.3.7.3.4 The facility shall have an operational plan indicating procedures and schedules for the inspection, monitoring, and restricting of excessive internal temperatures in static piles.

31.3.7.4 Fire Protection.

31.3.7.4.1 Conveyor tunnels and combustible enclosures that pass under a pile shall be protected with automatic sprinklers complying with Section 13.3.

31.3.7.4.2 Combustible or enclosed conveyor systems shall be protected with automatic sprinklers complying with Section 13.3.

31.3.8 Outside Storage of Logs.

31.3.8.1 Application.

31.3.8.1.1* The requirements of 31.3.8 shall apply to log yard storage areas containing saw, plywood veneer, or pulpwood logs stored in ranked piles commonly referred to as cold decks.

31.3.8.1.2 The requirements of 31.3.8 shall not apply to cordwood.

31.3.8.2* General. The fire hazard potential inherent in log storage operations with large quantities of combustible materials shall be controlled by a positive fire prevention program under the direct supervision of upper level management that shall include the following:

(1) Selection, design, and arrangement of storage yard areas and materials-handling equipment based on sound fire prevention and protection principles
(2) Means for early fire detection, transmission of alarm, and fire extinguishment
(3) Fire department access roads to separate large piles and provide access for effective fire-fighting operations
(4) Separation of yard storage from mill operations and other exposing properties
(5) Effective fire prevention maintenance program, including regular yard inspections by trained personnel

31.3.8.3* Log Yard Protection.

31.3.8.3.1 The storage site shall be reasonably level, on solid ground, and paved or surfaced with materials such as cinders, fine gravel, or stone.

31.3.8.3.2 Access to the plant and yard from public highways shall be provided by all-weather roadways capable of supporting fire department apparatus.

31.3.8.3.3* All sides of each cold deck shall be accessible by means of fire department access roads.

31.3.8.3.3.1 A fire department access road width of 1½ times the pile height but not less than 20 ft (6 m) shall be provided, with fire department access roads between alternate rows of two pile groups providing a clear space of at least 100 ft (30 m).

31.3.8.3.3.2* Each cold deck shall not exceed 500 ft (150 m) in length, 300 ft (90 m) in width, and 20 ft (6 m) in height.

31.3.8.3.3.3* Fire department access roads for access across each end, with a clear space of not less than 100 ft (30 m) to adjacent pile rows or other exposed property, shall be provided.

31.3.8.3.3.4* The size of cold decks shall be permitted to be increased where additional fire flow and fixed fire protection equipment is provided and the approval of the AHJ is obtained.

31.3.8.3.4 Water supplies shall be provided in accordance with this *Code*.

31.3.8.3.5 Dynamite shall never be used as a means to reclaim frozen log piles.

31.3.8.3.6* During dry weather, piles shall be wet down.

31.3.9 Wood Processing and Woodworking Facilities. Dust control shall be in accordance with NFPA 664 for combustible dust-producing operations that occupy areas of more than 5000 ft^2 (464 m^2), or to areas where dust-producing equipment requires an aggregate dust collection flow rate of more than 1500 ft^3/min (2549 m^3/hr).

Chapter 32 Motion Picture and Television Production Studio Soundstages and Approved Production Facilities

32.1 General. The design, construction, operation, and maintenance of soundstages and approved production facilities used in motion picture and television industry productions shall comply with NFPA 140, *Standard on Motion Picture and Television Production Studio Soundstages, Approved Production Facilities, and Production Locations*, and Chapter 32.

32.2 Permits. Permits, where required, shall comply with Section 1.12.

32.3 Housekeeping. Soundstages and approved production facilities shall maintain housekeeping in accordance with Chapters 10 and 19 where applicable.

32.4 Soundstages and Approved Production Facilities.

32.4.1 General. Section 32.4 shall apply to new and existing motion picture and television soundstages and approved production facilities. [**140**:4.1]

32.4.2 Permits. Where required by the AHJ, a permit shall be obtained for any of the activities that follow:

(1) Use of pyrotechnic special effects
(2) Use of open flames
(3) Welding
(4) Use of flammable or combustible liquids or gases
(5) Use of aircraft
(6) Presence of motor vehicles within a building
(7) Productions with live audiences
(8)*Change of use or change of occupancy classification [**140**:4.2]

32.4.3 Pyrotechnic Special Effects and Open Flames.

32.4.3.1* The use of pyrotechnic special effects and open flames shall be subject to the approval of the AHJ. [**140**:4.3.1]

32.4.3.2 When an audience is present, NFPA 1126, *Standard for the Use of Pyrotechnics Before a Proximate Audience*, shall be used to regulate any pyrotechnic use. [**140**:4.3.2]

32.4.3.3 When an audience is present, NFPA 160, *Standard for the Use of Flame Effects Before an Audience*, shall be used to regulate any flame effects use. [**140**:4.3.3]

32.4.4 Standby Fire Personnel.

32.4.4.1 Where required by the AHJ, standby fire personnel shall be provided for soundstages and approved production facilities where pyrotechnic special effects are used. [**140**:4.4.1]

32.4.4.2 Other Hazards. Where required by the AHJ, standby fire personnel shall be provided for hazardous operations, other than pyrotechnic special effects. [**140**:4.4.2]

32.4.5 Decorative Materials.

32.4.5.1 Foamed plastic materials used for decorative purposes, scenery, sets, or props shall have a heat release rate not exceeding 100 kW where tested in accordance with UL 1975, *Standard for Fire Tests for Foamed Plastics Used for Decorative Purposes*, or where tested in accordance with NFPA 289, *Standard Method of Fire Test for Individual Fuel Packages*, using the 20 kW ignition source. [**140**:4.5.1]

32.4.5.2 Combustible drapes, drops, and any other similar combustible hangings or vertically placed materials shall comply with one of the following options:

(1) The materials meet the requirements of NFPA 701, *Standard Methods of Fire Tests for Flame Propagation of Textiles and Films*.
(2) The materials exhibit a heat release rate not exceeding 100 kW when tested in accordance with NFPA 289, *Standard Method of Fire Test for Individual Fuel Packages*, using the 20 kW ignition source.
(3) The materials are present in such limited quantity that a hazard of fire development or spread is minimal.
(4)*The materials are considered by the AHJ to exhibit acceptable fire performance.

(5)*Approved interim measures are provided for the period during which the combustible materials are present. [**140**:4.5.2]

32.4.5.3 Cut greens shall be treated with an approved or listed fire retardant, and the process shall be repeated as often as necessary to maintain its effectiveness. [**140**:4.5.3]

32.4.6 Smoking.

32.4.6.1 Smoking shall be prohibited on soundstages and in approved production facilities unless otherwise provided in 32.4.6.2 or 32.4.6.3. [**140**:4.6.1]

32.4.6.2 Smoking shall be permitted when it is a necessary part of a performance, and only when the smoker is a member of the cast. [**140**:4.6.2]

32.4.6.3 Except where prohibited by the AHJ, smoking shall be permitted where all of the following conditions are met:

(1) The smoking area is outdoors.
(2) Hazardous materials are not present.
(3) Approved ash trays or receivers are provided.

[**140**:4.6.3]

32.4.7 Structural Loads.

32.4.7.1 Approved production facilities and soundstages shall be designed, constructed, or altered to sustain all structural load combinations in accordance with the local building code. [**140**:4.7.1]

32.4.7.2 Where the anticipated loads exceed those specified in the local building code for the purpose of suspending sets, ceilings, backings, and other heavy production set pieces, the building shall be designed and constructed for the additional loads. [**140**:4.7.2]

32.4.8 Electrical Requirements.

32.4.8.1 Electrical equipment shall be in accordance with Section 11.1. [**140**:4.8.1]

32.4.8.2* Soundstages and approved production facilities shall be provided with a minimum of 35 W/ft^2 (377 W/m^2) dedicated for production lighting and power. [**140**:4.8.2]

32.4.8.3 The electrical distribution equipment used shall comply with UL 1640, *Standard for Portable Power-Distribution Equipment*, and the provisions of Article 530 of *NFPA 70, National Electrical Code.* [*140:4.8.3*]

32.4.8.4 The wiring method to electrical distribution equipment shall comply with the provisions of Article 530 of *NFPA 70, National Electrical Code.* [**140**:4.8.4]

32.4.8.5 The location of portable, mobile, or stationary power-generating equipment shall be subject to the approval of the AHJ. [**140**:4.8.5]

32.4.8.6 Exterior penetrations shall be located near the predesignated location for portable and mobile power-generating equipment. [**140**:4.8.6]

32.4.8.7 Auxiliary power cables supplied from mobile generators or adjacent buildings shall not be routed through fire-rated windows and doors. [**140**:4.8.7]

32.4.8.8 Portable feeder cables shall be permitted to temporarily penetrate fire-rated walls, floors, or ceilings, provided that all of the following apply:

(1) The opening is of noncombustible material.

(2) When in use, the penetration is sealed with a temporary seal of a listed firestop material.
(3) When not in use, the opening shall be capped with a material of equivalent fire rating. [**140**:4.8.8]

32.4.8.9 Where the penetration utilizes a conduit, metal-threaded caps shall be attached to the pipe by means of chain or cable and shall effectively cap the conduit when not in use. [**140**:4.8.9]

32.4.8.10 The lighting equipment used shall comply with UL 1573, *Standard for Stage and Studio Luminaires and Connector Strips*, and the provisions of Article 530 of *NFPA 70, National Electrical Code.* [*140:4.8.10*]

32.4.9 Fire Department Access. Fire department access shall be maintained as required by the AHJ. [**140**:4.9]

32.4.10 Means of Egress.

32.4.10.1 Means of egress shall be in accordance with NFPA *101, Life Safety Code*. unless otherwise modified by 32.4.10.2 through 32.4.10.6. [**140**:4.10.1]

32.4.10.2 The maximum travel distance to an exit within the soundstage shall be 150 ft (45 m). [**140**:4.10.2]

32.4.10.3 Soundstages and approved production facilities shall have an aisle along the perimeter of the soundstage or facility as approved by the AHJ unless otherwise provided in 32.4.10.3.2. [**140**:4.10.3]

32.4.10.3.1 A clear unobstructed aisle height of 7 ft (2.1 m) shall be maintained. [**140**:4.10.3.1]

32.4.10.3.2 A soundstage or approved production facility with a gross area not exceeding 1500 ft^2 (139 m^2) shall be exempt from the perimeter aisle requirement of 32.4.10.3 provided there is a minimum of two means of egress. [**140**:4.10.3.2]

32.4.10.4 Emergency lighting shall be provided for the means of egress in accordance with NFPA *101, Life Safety Code.* [**140**:4.10.4]

32.4.10.5 Any door in a required means of egress from an area having an occupant load of 100 or more persons shall be permitted to be provided with a latch or lock only if it is panic hardware or fire exit hardware. [**140**:4.10.5]

32.4.10.6 Means of egress shall be kept clear of obstructions and tripping hazards. [**140**:4.10.6]

32.4.10.7 When an audience is present, an announcement shall be made notifying the audience of the following:

(1) The location of exits to be used in case of fire or other emergency
(2) The means that will be used to notify the audience of fire or other emergency [**140**:4.10.7]

32.4.11 Fire Protection.

32.4.11.1 Extinguishment Requirements.

32.4.11.1.1 Existing soundstages and existing approved production facilities equipped with automatic sprinkler systems shall maintain those systems in accordance with 13.3.3. [**140**:4.11.1.1]

32.4.11.1.2 A new soundstage or new approved production facility shall be equipped with an approved, supervised automatic sprinkler system. [**140**:4.11.1.2]

32.4.11.1.3 The automatic sprinkler system required by 32.4.11.1.2 shall be installed in accordance with Section 13.3, unless otherwise provided in 32.4.11.1.3.1 or 32.4.11.1.3.2. [**140**:4.11.1.3]

32.4.11.1.3.1* The requirements of NFPA 13 prohibiting obstructions to sprinkler discharge shall not be applicable if approved mitigation is employed. [**140**:4.11.1.3.1]

32.4.11.1.3.2* The requirements of NFPA 13 prohibiting obstructions to sprinkler discharge shall not be applicable if the building sprinkler system meets the design criteria for Extra Hazard, Group 2. [**140**:4.11.1.3.2]

32.4.11.1.4 The automatic sprinkler system required by 32.4.11.1.2 shall be maintained in accordance with 13.3.3. [**140**:4.11.1.4]

32.4.11.1.5 Portable fire extinguishers shall be installed and maintained in accordance with Section 13.6. [**140**:4.11.1.5]

32.4.11.2 Fire Alarm System. Fire alarm system notification appliances within soundstages and approved production facilities shall be permitted to be deactivated with the approval of the AHJ during videotaping, filming, or broadcasting of programs provided the following conditions exist:

(1) In the event of alarm system activation, notification appliances shall activate at a location that is constantly attended during the videotaping, filming, or broadcasting of programs.
(2) The attendants of the location identified in 32.4.11.2(1) shall be provided with a means of communicating with the fire command center for the building, where one is provided, and with the occupants of the soundstage to initiate emergency action.
(3) Deactivation of notification appliances shall cause activation of a visual signal at an approved location, which shall remain illuminated while notification appliances on the soundstage are deactivated.
(4) The visual signal shall be identified by a sign that shall read, "When Illuminated, Soundstage Fire Alarm System Notification Appliances Are Deactivated." [**140**:4.11.2]

32.4.12 Air Conditioning, Heating, and Ventilating. Air-conditioning, heating, and ventilating ductwork and related equipment shall be in good working order and in compliance with the requirements of the AHJ. [**140**:4.12]

32.5 Production Locations.

32.5.1 General. Section 32.5 shall apply to production locations. [**140**:5.1]

32.5.2 Permits. A permit shall be obtained, unless waived by the AHJ, for any of the following activities:

(1)*Use of the site as a production location
(2) Use of pyrotechnic special effects
(3) Use of open flames
(4) Welding
(5) Use of flammable or combustible liquids or gases
(6) Use of aircraft
(7) Presence of motor vehicles within a building [**140**:5.2]

32.5.3 Pyrotechnic Special Effects and Open Flames.

32.5.3.1 The use of pyrotechnic special effects and open flames shall be subject to the approval of the AHJ. [**140**:5.3.1]

32.5.3.2 When an audience is present, NFPA 1126 shall be used to regulate any pyrotechnic use. [**140**:5.3.2]

32.5.3.3 When an audience is present, NFPA 160 shall be used to regulate any flame effects use. [**140**:5.3.3]

32.5.4 Standby Fire Personnel.

32.5.4.1 Pyrotechnics. Standby fire personnel shall be required for production locations where pyrotechnic special effects are used, unless otherwise waived by the AHJ. [**140**:5.4.1]

32.5.4.2 Other Hazards. Where required by the AHJ, standby fire personnel shall be provided for hazardous operations, other than pyrotechnic special effects. [**140**:5.4.2]

32.5.5 Foamed Plastic Materials. Foamed plastic materials used for decorative purposes, scenery, sets, or props shall have a heat release rate not exceeding 100 kW when tested in accordance with UL 1975, *Fire Tests for Foamed Plastics Used for Decorative Purposes,* or where tested in accordance with NFPA 289, *Standard Method of Fire Test for Individual Fuel Packages,* using the 20 kW ignition source. [**140**:5.5]

32.5.6 Smoking.

32.5.6.1 Smoking shall be prohibited in production location buildings unless otherwise provided in 32.5.6.2 or 32.5.6.3. [**140**:5.6.1]

32.5.6.2 Smoking shall be permitted when it is a necessary part of a performance, and only when the smoker is a member of the cast. [**140**:5.6.2]

32.5.6.3 Except where prohibited by the AHJ, smoking shall be permitted where all of the following conditions are met:

(1) The smoking area is outdoors.
(2) Hazardous materials are not present.
(3) Approved ash trays or receivers are provided. [**140**:5.6.3]

32.5.7 Structural Loads.

32.5.7.1 Sets, scenery, and other equipment shall not impact the structural integrity of existing buildings. [**140**:5.7.1]

32.5.7.2 Additional loads applied onto the building shall require the approval of the AHJ. [**140**:5.7.2]

32.5.8 Electrical Requirements.

32.5.8.1 Electrical power connections made to the site electrical service shall be made by an approved electrician under permit from the AHJ. [**140**:5.8.1]

32.5.8.2 Portable cables shall be positioned to allow for emergency egress as approved by the AHJ. [**140**:5.8.2]

32.5.8.3* Auxiliary power cables supplied from mobile generators or adjacent buildings shall be permitted to be routed through fire-rated windows and doors with the approval of the AHJ. [**140**:5.8.3]

32.5.8.4 Where power from both mobile generators and site electrical services are used to energize equipment in the same proximate location at production locations, grounds for the two systems shall be bonded in accordance with *NFPA 70, National Electrical Code.* [**140**:5.8.4]

32.5.9* Fire Department Access. Fire department access shall be maintained as required by the AHJ. [**140**:5.9]

32.5.10* Means of Egress. The production location shall be provided with means of egress appropriate for the intended use as approved by the AHJ. [**140**:5.10]

32.5.11 Fire Protection.

32.5.11.1* Building areas used as production locations shall be designed, constructed, and maintained to protect the occupants not intimate with the initial fire development for the time needed to evacuate, relocate, or defend in place. [**140:**5.11.1]

32.5.11.2 Where an automatic sprinkler system is provided for compliance with 32.5.11.1, the automatic sprinkler system shall be installed in accordance with Section 13.3, unless otherwise provided in 32.5.11.4 or 32.5.11.5. [**140:**5.11.2]

32.5.11.3 In any production location building protected by an existing automatic sprinkler system, where solid- or hard-ceiling sets or platforms are introduced to create an obstruction to sprinkler discharge, the provisions of 32.5.11.4 or 32.5.11.5 shall be met. [**140:**5.11.3]

32.5.11.4* The requirements of NFPA 13 prohibiting obstructions to sprinkler discharge shall not be applicable if approved mitigation is employed. [**140:**5.11.4]

32.5.11.5* The requirements of NFPA 13 prohibiting obstructions to sprinkler discharge shall not be applicable if the building sprinkler system meets the design criteria for Extra Hazard, Group 2. [**140:**5.11.5]

32.5.11.6 Automatic sprinkler systems, where provided, shall be maintained in accordance with 13.3.3. [**140:**5.11.6]

32.5.11.7 Portable fire extinguishers shall be provided as required by the AHJ. [**140:**5.11.7]

32.5.11.8 Fire Hydrants and Fire Appliances. Hydrants, standpipes, and fire department connections (FDCs) shall not be obstructed, blocked, or rendered inoperable unless approved by the AHJ. [**140:**5.11.8]

32.6 Operating Features.

32.6.1 Waste or Refuse. Waste or refuse shall not be allowed to accumulate in any area or in any manner that creates a fire hazard. [**140:**6.1]

32.6.2 Flammable or Combustible Liquids.

32.6.2.1 The use, mixing, dispensing, and storage of flammable or combustible liquids shall be in accordance with this *Code* and the following codes, as applicable, unless otherwise permitted by 32.6.2.2:

(1) NFPA 30, *Flammable and Combustible Liquids Code (See Chapter 66.)*
(2) NFPA 58, *Liquefied Petroleum Gas Code (See Chapter 69.)* [**140:**6.2.1]

32.6.2.2 Approved flammable or combustible liquids and liquefied petroleum gases used for special effects shall be permitted. [**140:**6.2.2]

32.6.3 Welding. Welding shall be in accordance with NFPA 51, *Standard for the Design and Installation of Oxygen–Fuel Gas Systems for Welding, Cutting, and Allied Processes*, and NFPA 51B, *Standard for Fire Prevention During Welding, Cutting, and Other Hot Work. (See Chapter 41.)* [**140:**6.3]

32.6.4* Audience Life Safety. When an audience is present during productions, provisions for life safety and means of egress shall be subject to the approval of the AHJ. [**140:**6.4]

32.6.5 Emergency Services Notification. The production company shall provide a procedure acceptable to the AHJ for notifying the public emergency services of emergency incidents. [**140:**6.5]

Chapter 33   Outside Storage of Tires

33.1* General.

33.1.1 Facilities storing more than 500 tires outside shall be in accordance with Chapter 33.

33.1.2 Permits. Permits, where required, shall comply with Section 1.12.

33.1.3 Fire department access roads to separate tire piles and for effective fire-fighting operations shall be in accordance with Table 33.1.3.

33.1.4 Separation of yard storage from buildings, vehicles, flammable materials, and other exposures shall be in accordance with Table 33.1.3.

33.1.5 Trees, plants, and vegetation within the separation areas shall be managed in accordance with Section 10.13.

33.1.6 Ignition Sources.

33.1.6.1 Smoking shall be prohibited within the tire storage area.

33.1.6.2 Sources of ignition such as cutting and welding, heating devices, and open fires shall be prohibited within the tire storage area.

33.1.6.3 Safeguards shall be provided to minimize the hazard of sparks from equipment such as refuse burners, boiler stacks, and vehicle exhaust when such hazards are located near the tire storage area.

33.1.7 Piles of tires or altered tire material shall not be located beneath power lines or structures.

33.1.8 Piles of tires or altered tire material shall be at least 50 ft (15 m) from the perimeter fence.

33.1.9 Provisions for surface water drainage and measures to provide protection of pyrolitic oil runoff shall be directed around and away from the outdoor tire storage site to an approved location.

33.1.10 Tires shall be removed from rims immediately upon arrival at the storage site.

33.1.11 Tires shall not be stored on wetlands, flood plains, ravines, canyons, or steeply graded surfaces.

33.2 Individual Piles.

33.2.1 New Outside Tire Storage Sites and Piles.

33.2.1.1 New individual outside tire storage piles containing more than 500 tires shall be limited in volume to 125,000 ft^3 (3540 m^3).

33.2.1.2 The dimensions of new tire storage piles shall not exceed 10 ft (3 m) in height, 50 ft (15 m) in width, and 250 ft (75 m) in length.

33.2.1.3 Individual piles shall be separated in accordance with Table 33.1.3.

33.2.2 Existing Individual Piles.

33.2.2.1 Existing outside tire storage piles shall be in accordance with the provisions of 33.2.1 within 5 years of the adoption of this *Code*.

Table 33.1.3 Representative Minimum Exposure Separation Distances in Feet (Meters) for Tire Storage

Exposed Face Dimension		Pile Height												
ft	m	8 ft	2.4 m	10 ft	3 m	12 ft	3.7 m	14 ft	4.3 m	16 ft	4.9 m	18 ft	5.5 m	20 ft	6.1 m
25	7.6	56	17	62	19	67	20	73	22	77	23	82	25	85	26
50	15.2	75	23	84	26	93	28	100	30	107	33	113	34	118	36
100	30	100	30	116	35	128	39	137	42	146	44	155	47	164	50
150	45	100	30	116	35	128	39	137	42	146	44	155	47	164	50
200	61	100	30	116	35	128	39	137	42	146	44	155	47	164	50
250	75	100	30	116	35	128	39	137	42	146	44	155	47	164	50

33.2.2.2 Existing individual outside tire storage piles containing more than 500 tires shall be limited in volume to 250,000 ft^3 (7080 m^3).

33.2.2.3 Existing pile dimensions shall not exceed 20 ft (6 m) in height, 50 ft (15 m) in width, and 250 ft (75 m) in length.

33.2.2.4 Individual piles shall be separated in accordance with Table 33.1.3.

33.3 Emergency Response Plan.

33.3.1 The operator of the outside tire storage facility shall develop an emergency response plan and submit it for approval by the AHJ.

33.3.2 The AHJ shall retain a copy of the approved emergency response plan.

33.3.3 The operator of the outside tire storage facility shall keep a copy of the approved emergency response plan at the facility.

33.3.4 The AHJ shall be immediately notified of and approve any proposed changes to the emergency response plan.

33.4 Fire Control Measures. Measures to aid in the control of fire shall be in accordance with Section 33.4.

33.4.1 Manual Fire-Fighting Equipment.

33.4.1.1 At a minimum, the following items shall be maintained on site and in working order:

(1) One 2-A:10-B:C fire extinguisher
(2) One 2.5 gal (10 L) water extinguisher
(3) One 10 ft (3 m) long pike pole
(4) One rigid rake
(5) One round point shovel
(6) One square point shovel

33.4.1.2 One dry chemical fire extinguisher with a minimum rating of 4-A:40-B:C shall be carried on each piece of fuel-powered equipment used to handle scrap tires.

33.4.1.3 On-site personnel shall be trained in the use and function of this equipment to mitigate tire pile ignition.

33.4.2 An approved water supply capable of supplying the required fire flow to protect exposures and perform fire suppression and overhaul operations shall be provided.

33.4.3* The AHJ shall be permitted to require additional tools and equipment for fire control and the protection of life and property.

33.5 Site Access.

33.5.1 Access to the site and each tire storage yard and pile shall be in accordance with Section 18.2 and this section.

33.5.2 Accesses shall be maintained clear of combustible waste or vegetation and shall remain accessible to the fire department at all times.

33.6 Signs and Security. Access by unauthorized persons and security of the site shall be in accordance with Section 33.6.

33.6.1 Signs bearing the name of the operator, the operating hours, emergency telephone numbers, and site rules shall be posted at site entrances.

33.6.2 The facility shall have noncombustible fencing at least 10 ft (3 m) high with intruder controls on top, in accordance with local laws, around the entire perimeter of the property.

33.6.3 Access.

33.6.3.1 Access to the facility shall be in accordance with Section 18.2.

33.6.3.2 An attendant shall be on site at all times when the site is open.

33.7 Outdoor Storage of Altered Tire Material. Outdoor storage of altered tire material in the form of chunks, chips, or crumbs shall be protected in accordance with 33.7.1 through 33.7.5.

33.7.1 A 10 ft (3 m) fence shall be maintained around the altered tire material storage area.

33.7.2 Altered tire material piles shall be kept 50 ft (15 m) from perimeter fencing.

33.7.3 Potential ignition sources such as welding, smoking, or other open flame uses shall not be allowed within 20 ft (6 m) of the altered tire pile.

33.7.4 Individual altered tire material piles shall not be located on site in excess of 90 days.

33.7.5* Individual altered tire material piles shall be kept sheltered from precipitation.

Chapter 34   General Storage

34.1 General.

34.1.1 Application. This chapter shall apply to the indoor and outdoor storage of materials representing the broad range of combustibles, including plastics, rubber tires, and roll paper.

34.1.1.1 Storage configurations shall include palletized storage, solid-piled storage, and storage in bin boxes, on shelves, or on racks.

34.1.1.2 Chapter 34 shall not apply to the following:

(1) Storage of commodities that, with their packaging and storage aids, would be classified as noncombustible
(2) Unpackaged bulk materials such as grain, coal, or similar commodities but excluding wood chips and sawdust, which are addressed in Chapter 31
(3) Inside or outside storage of commodities covered by this *Code*, except where specifically mentioned herein (e.g., pyroxylin plastics)
(4) Storage of high-hazard materials covered by this *Code*, except where specifically mentioned herein
(5) Storage on plastic shelves on racks
(6)*Miscellaneous tire storage
(7) Combustible fiber storage, which is covered in Chapter 45

34.1.2 Permits. Permits, where required, shall comply with Section 1.12.

34.2 Classification of Commodities.

34.2.1 Commodity classification and the corresponding protection requirements shall be determined based on the makeup of individual storage units (i.e., unit load, pallet load). [**13**:5.6.1.1.1]

34.2.2 When specific test data of commodity classification by a nationally recognized testing agency are available, the data shall be permitted to be used in determining classification of commodities. [**13**:5.6.1.1.2]

34.2.3 Mixed Commodities.

34.2.3.1 Protection requirements shall not be based on the overall commodity mix in a fire area. [**13**:5.6.1.2.1]

34.2.3.2 Unless the requirements of 34.2.3.3 or 34.2.3.4 are met, mixed commodity storage shall be protected by the requirements for the highest classified commodity and storage arrangement. [**13**:5.6.1.2.2]

34.2.3.3 The protection requirements for the lower commodity class shall be permitted to be utilized where all of the following are met:

(1) Up to 10 pallet loads of a higher hazard commodity, as described in 34.2.5 and 34.2.6, shall be permitted to be present in an area not exceeding 40,000 ft² (3716 m²).
(2) The higher hazard commodity shall be randomly dispersed with no adjacent loads in any direction (including diagonally).
(3) Where the ceiling protection is based on Class I or Class II commodities, the allowable number of pallet loads for Class IV or Group A plastics shall be reduced to five. [**13**:5.6.1.2.3]

34.2.3.4 Mixed Commodity Segregation. The protection requirements for the lower commodity class shall be permitted to be utilized in the area of lower commodity class, where the higher hazard material is confined to a designated area and the area is protected to the higher hazard in accordance with the requirements of this *Code*. [**13**:5.6.1.2.4]

34.2.4 Pallet Types.

34.2.4.1 General. When loads are palletized, the use of wood or metal pallets, or listed pallets equivalent to wood, shall be assumed in the classification of commodities. [**13**:5.6.2.1]

34.2.4.2* Unreinforced Plastic Pallets. For Class I through Class IV commodities, when unreinforced polypropylene or unreinforced high-density polyethylene plastic pallets are used, the classification of the commodity unit shall be increased one class. [**13**.5.6.2.2]

34.2.4.2.1 Unreinforced polypropylene or unreinforced high-density polyethylene plastic pallets shall be marked with a permanent symbol to indicate that the pallet is unreinforced. [**13**:5.6.2.2.1]

34.2.4.3* For Class I through Class IV commodities, when reinforced polypropylene or reinforced high-density polyethylene plastic pallets are used, the classification of the commodity unit shall be increased two classes except for Class IV commodity, which shall be increased to a cartoned unexpanded Group A Plastic commodity. [**13**:5.6.2.3]

34.2.4.3.1 Pallets shall be assumed to be reinforced if no permanent marking or manufacturer's certification of non-reinforcement is provided. [**13**:5.6.2.3.1]

34.2.4.4 No increase in the commodity classification shall be required for Group A plastic commodities stored on plastic pallets. [**13**:5.6.2.4]

34.2.4.5 For ceiling-only sprinkler protection, the requirements of 34.2.4.2 and 34.2.4.3 shall not apply where plastic pallets are used and where the sprinkler system uses spray sprinklers with a minimum K-factor of 16.8 (240). [**13**:5.6.2.5]

34.2.4.6 The requirements of 34.2.4.2 through 34.2.4.7 shall not apply to nonwood pallets that have demonstrated a fire hazard that is equal to or less than wood pallets and are listed as such. [**13**:5.6.2.6]

34.2.4.7 For Class I through Class IV commodities stored on plastic pallets, when other than wood, metal, or polypropylene or high-density polyethylene plastic pallets are used, the classification of the commodity unit shall be determined by specific testing conducted by a national testing laboratory or shall be increased two classes. [**13**:5.6.2.7]

34.2.5* Commodity Classes.

34.2.5.1 Class I. A Class I commodity shall be defined as a noncombustible product that meets one of the following criteria:

(1) Placed directly on wood pallets
(2) Placed in single-layer corrugated cartons, with or without single-thickness cardboard dividers, with or without pallets
(3) Shrink-wrapped or paper-wrapped as a unit load with or without pallets [**13**:5.6.3.1]

34.2.5.2 Class II. A Class II commodity shall be defined as a noncombustible product that is in slatted wooden crates, solid wood boxes, multiple-layered corrugated cartons, or equivalent combustible packaging material with or without pallets. [**13**:5.6.3.2]

34.2.5.3 Class III.

34.2.5.3.1 A Class III commodity shall be defined as a product fashioned from wood, paper, natural fibers, or Group C plastics with or without cartons, boxes, or crates and with or without pallets. [**13**:5.6.3.3.1]

34.2.5.3.2 A Class III commodity shall be permitted to contain a limited amount (5 percent by weight or volume or less) of Group A or Group B plastics. [**13**:5.6.3.3.2]

34.2.5.4 Class IV.

34.2.5.4.1 A Class IV commodity shall be defined as a product, with or without pallets, that meets one of the following criteria:

(1) Constructed partially or totally of Group B plastics
(2) Consists of free-flowing Group A plastic materials
(3) Contains within itself or its packaging an appreciable amount (5 percent to 15 percent by weight or 5 percent to 25 percent by volume) of Group A plastics [**13**:5.6.3.4.1]

34.2.5.4.2 The remaining materials shall be permitted to be metal, wood, paper, natural or synthetic fibers, or Group B or Group C plastics. [**13**:5.6.3.4.2]

34.2.6 Classification of Plastics, Elastomers, and Rubber. Plastics, elastomers, and rubber shall be classified as Group A, Group B, or Group C. [**13**:5.6.4]

34.2.6.1 Group A. The following materials shall be classified as Group A:

(1) ABS (acrylonitrile-butadiene-styrene copolymer)
(2) Acetal (polyformaldehyde)
(3) Acrylic (polymethyl methacrylate)
(4) Butyl rubber
(5) EPDM (ethylene-propylene rubber)
(6) FRP (fiberglass-reinforced polyester)
(7) Natural rubber (if expanded)
(8) Nitrile-rubber (acrylonitrile-butadiene-rubber)
(9) PET (thermoplastic polyester)
(10) Polybutadiene
(11) Polycarbonate
(12) Polyester elastomer
(13) Polyethylene
(14) Polypropylene
(15) Polystyrene
(16) Polyurethane
(17) PVC (polyvinyl chloride — highly plasticized, with plasticizer content greater than 20 percent) (rarely found)
(18) SAN (styrene acrylonitrile)
(19) SBR (styrene-butadiene rubber) [**13**:5.6.4.1]

34.2.6.2 Group B. The following materials shall be classified as Group B:

(1) Cellulosics (cellulose acetate, cellulose acetate butyrate, ethyl cellulose)
(2) Chloroprene rubber
(3) Fluoroplastics (ECTFE — ethylene-chlorotrifluoro-ethylene copolymer; ETFE — ethylene-tetrafluoroethylene copolymer; FEP — fluorinated ethylene-propylene copolymer)
(4) Natural rubber (not expanded)
(5) Nylon (nylon 6, nylon 6/6)
(6) Silicone rubber [**13**:5.6.4.2]

34.2.6.3 Group C. The following materials shall be classified as Group C:

(1) Fluoroplastics (PCTFE — polychlorotrifluoroethylene; PTFE — polytetrafluoroethylene)
(2) Melamine (melamine formaldehyde)
(3) Phenolic
(4) PVC (polyvinyl chloride — flexible — PVCs with plasticizer content up to 20 percent)
(5) PVDC (polyvinylidene chloride)
(6) PVDF (polyvinylidene fluoride)
(7) PVF (polyvinyl fluoride)
(8) Urea (urea formaldehyde) [**13**:5.6.4.3]

34.2.6.4 Group A plastics shall be further subdivided as either expanded or nonexpanded. [**13**:5.6.4.4]

34.2.6.4.1 If a cartoned commodity is more than 40 percent (by volume) expanded plastic, it shall be protected as a cartoned expanded plastic. [**13**:5.6.4.4.1]

34.2.6.4.2 Exposed commodities containing greater than 25 percent by volume expanded plastic shall be protected as an exposed expanded plastic. [**13**:5.6.4.4.2]

34.2.7* Classification of Rolled Paper Storage. For the purposes of this *Code*, the classifications of paper described in 34.2.7.1 through 34.2.7.4 shall apply and shall be used to determine the sprinkler system design criteria. [**13**:5.6.5]

34.2.7.1 Heavyweight Class. Heavyweight class shall be defined so as to include paperboard and paper stock having a basis weight [weight per 1000 ft^2 (92.9 m^2)] of 20 lb (9.1 kg). [**13**:5.6.5.1]

34.2.7.2 Mediumweight Class. Mediumweight class shall be defined so as to include all the broad range of papers having a basis weight [weight per 1000 ft^2 (92.9 m^2)] of 10 lb to 20 lb (4.5 kg to 9.1 kg). [**13**:5.6.5.2]

34.2.7.3 Lightweight Class. Lightweight class shall be defined so as to include all papers having a basis weight [weight per 1000 ft^2 (92.9 m^2)] of less than 10 lb (4.5 kg). [**13**:5.6.5.3]

34.2.7.4 Tissue.

34.2.7.4.1 Tissue shall be defined so as to include the broad range of papers of characteristic gauzy texture, which, in some cases, are fairly transparent. [**13**:5.6.5.4.1]

34.2.7.4.2 For the purposes of this *Code*, tissue shall be defined as the soft, absorbent type, regardless of basis weight — specifically, crepe wadding and the sanitary class including facial tissue, paper napkins, bathroom tissue, and toweling. [**13**:5.6.5.4.2]

34.3 Building Construction.

34.3.1* Construction Type. Buildings used for storage of materials that are stored and protected in accordance with this chapter shall be permitted to be of any of the types described in NFPA 220, *Standard on Types of Building Construction*.

34.3.2 Fire-Fighting Access. Access shall be provided to all portions of the premises for fire-fighting purposes.

34.3.3* Emergency Smoke and Heat Venting.

34.3.3.1 Protection outlined in this chapter shall apply to buildings with or without smoke and heat vents.

34.3.3.2 Protection outlined in this chapter shall apply to buildings with or without draft curtains.

34.3.3.3 Where local codes require smoke and heat vents in buildings protected by early suppression fast response (ESFR) sprinklers, the vents shall be manually operated or have an operating mechanism with a standard response fusible element rated not less than 360°F (182°C).

34.4 Storage Arrangement.

34.4.1* Piling Procedures and Precautions.

34.4.1.1 Any commodities that are hazardous in combination with each other shall be stored so they cannot come into contact with each other.

34.4.1.2 Safe floor loads shall not be exceeded.

34.4.1.3 Where storing water-absorbent commodities, normal floor loads shall be reduced to take into account the added weight of water that can be absorbed during fire-fighting operations.

34.4.2 Commodity Clearance.

34.4.2.1 The clearance between top of storage and sprinkler deflectors shall conform to NFPA 13.

34.4.2.2* If the commodity is stored above the lower chord of roof trusses, not less than 1 ft (0.3 m) of clear space shall be maintained to allow wetting of the truss, unless the truss is protected with 1-hour fireproofing.

34.4.2.3 Storage clearance from ducts shall be maintained in accordance with NFPA 91, *Standard for Exhaust Systems for Air Conveying of Vapors, Gases, Mists, and Noncombustible Particulate Solids.*

34.4.2.4 The clearance between stored materials and unit heaters, radiant space heaters, duct furnaces, and flues shall not be less than 3 ft (0.9 m) in all directions or shall be in accordance with the clearances shown on the approval agency label.

34.4.2.5* Clearance shall be maintained to lights or light fixtures to prevent ignition.

34.4.2.6 Clearance shall be maintained around the path of fire door travel to ensure the door's proper operation and inspection.

34.4.2.7 Operation and inspection clearance shall be maintained around fire-extinguishing and fire protection equipment.

34.4.3 Aisles.

34.4.3.1 For the storage of commodities that expand with the absorption of water, such as roll paper, wall aisles not less than 24 in. (0.6 m) wide shall be provided.

34.4.3.2 Aisles shall be maintained to retard the transfer of fire from one pile to another and to allow convenient access for fire fighting, salvage, and removal of storage.

34.4.4 Flammable and Combustible Liquids. Storage of flammable or combustible liquids shall be in accordance with Chapter 60.

34.5 General Fire Protection.

34.5.1* Sprinkler Systems. Sprinkler systems installed in buildings used for storage shall be in accordance with Section 13.3.

34.5.2 High-Expansion Foam.

34.5.2.1 High-expansion foam systems installed in addition to automatic sprinklers shall be installed in accordance with NFPA 11, *Standard for Low-, Medium-, and High-Expansion Foam,* except where modified by other requirements in this chapter.

34.5.2.2 High-expansion foam used to protect idle pallets shall have a fill time of not more than 4 minutes.

34.5.2.3 High-expansion foam systems shall be automatic in operation.

34.5.2.4 Detectors for high-expansion foam systems shall be listed and shall be installed at the ceiling at not more than one-half the listed spacing in accordance with *NFPA 72.*

34.5.2.5 Detection systems, concentrate pumps, generators, and other system components essential to the operation of the system shall have an approved standby power source.

34.5.3 Manual Protection.

34.5.3.1 Portable Fire Extinguishers.

34.5.3.1.1 Portable fire extinguishers shall be provided in accordance with Section 13.6, unless 34.5.3.1.2 applies.

34.5.3.1.2 Where 1½ in. (38 mm) hose lines are available to reach all portions of areas with Class A fire loads, up to one-half of the portable fire extinguishers required by Section 13.6 shall be permitted to be omitted.

34.5.3.2 Hydrants. At locations without public hydrants, or where hydrants are not within 250 ft (75 m), private hydrants shall be installed in accordance with Section 13.5.

34.5.4 Fire Organization.

34.5.4.1 Arrangements shall be made to allow rapid entry into the premises by the municipal fire department, police department, or other authorized personnel in case of fire or other emergency.

34.5.4.2* Due to the unique nature of storage fires and the hazards associated with fighting such fires, facility emergency personnel shall be trained to have knowledge of the following:

(1) Pile and building collapse potential during fire-fighting and mop-up operations due to sprinkler water absorption, use of hose streams, and the undermining of piles by fire that is likely to cause material or piles to fall (especially roll tissue paper), resulting in injury
(2) Operation of sprinkler systems and water supply equipment
(3) Location of the controlling sprinkler valves so that the correct sprinkler system can be turned on or off as necessary
(4) Correct operation of emergency smoke and heat vent systems where they have been provided
(5) Use of material-handling equipment while sprinklers are operating to effect final extinguishment
(6) Procedure for summoning outside aid immediately in an emergency
(7) Maintenance of the security features of the premises
(8) Operation of foam systems, evacuation procedures, and safety precautions during all foam operations

34.5.4.3 A fire watch shall be maintained when the sprinkler system is not in service.

34.5.5 Alarm Service.

34.5.5.1 Automatic sprinkler systems and foam systems, where provided, shall have approved central station, auxiliary, remote station, or proprietary waterflow alarm service unless otherwise permitted by 34.5.5.1.1 or 34.5.5.1.2.

34.5.5.1.1 Local waterflow alarm service shall be permitted when recorded guard service also is provided.

34.5.5.1.2 Local waterflow alarm service shall be permitted where the storage facilities are occupied on a 24-hour basis.

34.5.5.2 Alarm service shall comply with *NFPA 72.*

34.5.6 Security Service. Security service, where provided, shall comply with NFPA 601, *Standard for Security Services in Fire Loss Prevention.*

34.6 Building Equipment, Maintenance, and Operations.

34.6.1 Industrial Trucks.

34.6.1.1 Power-operated industrial trucks and their use shall comply with NFPA 505, *Fire Safety Standard for Powered Industrial Trucks Including Type Designations, Areas of Use, Conversions, Maintenance, and Operations.*

34.6.1.2 Industrial trucks using liquefied petroleum gas (LP-Gas) or liquid fuel shall be refueled outside of the storage building at a location designated for the purpose.

34.6.2 Building Service Equipment. Electrical equipment shall be installed in accordance with the provisions of Section 11.1.

34.6.3 Cutting and Welding Operations.

34.6.3.1 Where welding or cutting operations are necessary, the requirements of Chapter 41 shall apply.

34.6.3.2* Welding, soldering, brazing, and cutting shall be permitted to be performed on building components or contents that cannot be removed, provided that no storage is located below and within 25 ft (7.6 m) of the working area and flameproof tarpaulins enclose the area.

34.6.3.3 During any of the operations identified in 34.6.3.2, all of the following shall apply:

(1) The sprinkler system shall be in service.
(2) Extinguishers suitable for Class A fires with a minimum rating of 2-A shall be located in the working area.
(3) Where inside hose lines are available, charged and attended inside hose lines shall be located in the working area.
(4) A fire watch shall be maintained during the operations specified in 34.6.3.2 and for not less than 30 minutes following completion of open-flame operation.

34.6.4 Waste Disposal.

34.6.4.1 Approved containers for rubbish and other trash materials shall be provided.

34.6.4.2 Rubbish, trash, and other waste material shall be disposed of at regular intervals.

34.6.5 Smoking.

34.6.5.1 Smoking shall be prohibited except in locations designated as smoking areas.

34.6.5.2 Signs that read "No Smoking" shall be posted in prohibited areas.

34.6.6* Maintenance and Inspection.

34.6.6.1 Fire walls, fire doors, and floors shall be maintained in functional condition at all times.

34.6.6.2* All water-based fire protection systems and the water supplies shall be inspected, tested, and maintained in accordance with NFPA 25.

34.6.7 Refrigeration Systems. Refrigeration systems, if used, shall be in accordance with ASHRAE 15, *Safety Code for Mechanical Refrigeration.*

34.6.8 Lighting. Where metal halide lighting is installed, it shall be selected, installed, and maintained such that catastrophic failure of the bulb shall not ignite materials below.

34.7 Protection of Rack Storage.

34.7.1 Application. Section 34.7 shall apply to the indoor storage of normal combustibles (Class I through Class IV) and plastics that are stored on racks.

34.7.2 Building Construction.

34.7.2.1 Fire protection of roof steel shall not be required when sprinkler systems are installed in accordance with Section 13.3.

34.7.2.2 Fire protection of steel building columns and vertical rack members that support the building shall not be required when ceiling sprinklers and in-rack sprinklers are installed in accordance with Section 13.3.

34.7.2.3 For sprinklered buildings with rack storage of over 15 ft (4.6 m) in height and only ceiling sprinklers installed, steel building columns within the rack structure and vertical rack members that support the building shall have a fire resistance rating not less than 1 hour, unless the installation meets the requirements of 16.1.4 of NFPA 13.

34.7.3 Storage Arrangement.

34.7.3.1* Rack Structure. Rack configurations shall be approved.

34.7.3.2* Rack Loading. Racks shall not be loaded beyond their design capacity.

34.7.3.3* Aisle Widths.

34.7.3.3.1 Aisle widths and depth of racks shall be determined by material-handling methods.

34.7.3.3.2 The width of aisles shall be considered in the design of the protection system.

34.7.3.3.3* Aisle widths shall be maintained by either fixed rack structures or control in placement of portable racks.

34.7.3.3.4 Any decrease in aisle width shall require a review of the adequacy of the protection system.

34.7.3.4 General Fire Protection.

34.7.3.4.1 High-Expansion Foam.

34.7.3.4.1.1* Where high-expansion foam systems are installed, they shall be automatic in operation and shall be in accordance with NFPA 11, except when modified by 34.7.3.4.

34.7.3.4.1.2 When high-expansion foam systems are used in combination with ceiling sprinklers, in-rack sprinklers shall not be required.

34.7.3.4.1.3 Detectors shall be listed and shall be installed in one of the following configurations:

(1) At one-half listed linear spacing [e.g., 15 ft × 15 ft (4.6 m × 4.6 m) rather than 30 ft × 30 ft (9.1 m × 9.1 m)] when the following conditions exist:
  (a) Detectors are installed at the ceiling only.
  (b) The clearance from the top of storage does not exceed 10 ft (3 m).
  (c) The height of storage does not exceed 25 ft (7.6 m).
(2) At the ceiling at listed spacing and on racks at alternate levels
(3) Where listed for rack storage installation and installed in accordance with ceiling detector listing to provide response within 1 minute after ignition using an ignition source equivalent to that used in a rack storage testing program

34.7.3.4.2 High-Expansion Foam Submergence.

34.7.3.4.2.1 The following requirements shall apply to storage of Class I, Class II, Class III, and Class IV commodities, as classified in Section 34.2, up to and including 25 ft (7.6 m) in height:

(1)*When high-expansion foam systems are used without sprinklers, the submergence time shall be not more than 5 minutes for Class I, Class II, or Class III commodities.
(2) When high-expansion foam systems are used without sprinklers, the submergence time shall be not more than 4 minutes for Class IV commodities.
(3) When high-expansion foam systems are used in combination with ceiling sprinklers, the submergence time shall be not more than 7 minutes for Class I, Class II, or Class III commodities.
(4) When high-expansion foam systems are used in combination with ceiling sprinklers, the submergence time shall be not more than 5 minutes for Class IV commodities.

34.7.3.4.2.2 The following requirements shall apply to storage of Class I, Class II, Class III, and Class IV commodities stored over 25 ft (7.6 m) high up to and including 35 ft (10.7 m) in height:

(1) Ceiling sprinklers shall be used in combination with the high-expansion foam system.
(2) The submergence time for the high-expansion foam shall be not more than 5 minutes for Class I, Class II, or Class III commodities.
(3) The submergence time for the high-expansion foam shall be not more than 4 minutes for Class IV commodities.

34.8 Protection of Rubber Tires.

34.8.1* Application.

34.8.1.1 Section 34.8 shall apply to new facilities with indoor storage of usable tires and to existing facilities being converted to the indoor storage of usable tires.

34.8.1.2 Existing buildings storing rubber tires shall be exempted from complying with Section 34.8.

34.8.1.3 This section shall not apply to scrap tire storage.

34.8.2 Building Arrangement.

34.8.2.1 Steel Columns. Steel columns shall be protected as follows unless protected in accordance with 16.1.4 of NFPA 13:

(1) For storage exceeding 15 ft to 20 ft (4.6 m to 6 m) in height, columns shall have 1-hour fireproofing.
(2) For storage exceeding 20 ft (6 m) in height, columns shall have 2-hour fireproofing for the entire length of the column, including connections with other structural members.

34.8.2.2 Fire Walls.

34.8.2.2.1 Four-hour fire walls shall be provided between the tire warehouse and tire manufacturing areas.

34.8.2.2.2 Fire walls shall be designed in accordance with NFPA 221, *Standard for High Challenge Fire Walls, Fire Walls, and Fire Barrier Walls*.

34.8.2.3* Travel Distance to Exits. Travel distance to exits shall be in accordance with NFPA *101*.

34.8.3 Storage Arrangement.

34.8.3.1 Piling Procedures.

34.8.3.1.1* Piles that are not adjacent to or located along a wall shall be not more than 50 ft (15 m) in width.

34.8.3.1.2 Tires stored adjacent to or along one wall shall not extend more than 25 ft (7.6 m) from the wall.

34.8.3.1.3 Where tires are stored on-tread, the dimension of the pile in the direction of the wheel hole shall be not more than 50 ft (15 m).

34.8.3.1.4 The width of the main aisles between piles shall be not less than 8 ft (2.4 m).

34.8.3.2 Clearances.

34.8.3.2.1 Storage clearance from roof structures shall be not less than 18 in. (470 mm) in all directions.

34.8.3.2.2 A clearance of not less than 24 in. (610 mm) shall be maintained around the path of fire door travel unless a barricade is provided.

34.8.3.2.3 Where protection in accordance with this chapter is provided, stored tires shall be segregated from other combustible storage by aisles not less than 8 ft (2.4 m) wide.

34.9 Protection of Roll Paper.

34.9.1 Application. Section 34.9 shall apply to new facilities with indoor storage of roll paper, and to existing facilities being converted to the indoor storage of roll paper, except for the following types of roll paper:

(1) Waxed paper
(2) Synthetic paper
(3) Palletized roll paper storage other than that stored on a single floor pallet or raised floor platform

34.9.2* Building Construction. The protection outlined in Section 34.9 shall apply to buildings with or without fireproofing or other modes of steel protection, unless modified by the requirements of 34.4.2.2.

34.9.3 Storage Arrangement. The floor load design shall take into account the added weight of water that could be absorbed by the commodity during fire-fighting operations.

34.10 Storage of Idle Pallets.

34.10.1* General. Idle pallets shall be stored outside or in a separate building designated for pallet storage, unless permitted by 34.10.2.

34.10.2 Indoor Storage. Idle pallets shall be permitted to be stored in a building used for other storage or other purpose if the building is sprinklered in accordance with Section 13.3.

34.10.3* Outdoor Storage. Idle pallets stored outside shall be stored in accordance with Table 34.10.3(a) and Table 34.10.3(b).

Table 34.10.3(a) Required Clearance Between Outside Idle Pallet Storage and Other Yard Storage

Pile Size	Minimum Distance	
	ft	m
Under 50 pallets	20	6
50–200 pallets	30	9
Over 200 pallets	50	15

34.10.4 Idle pallet stacks shall not exceed 15 ft (4.6 m) in height nor shall cover an area of greater than 400 ft^2 (37 m^2). Pallet stacks shall be arranged to form stable piles. A distance of not less than 8 ft (2.4 m) shall separate stacks. Piles shall be no closer than 8 ft (2.4 m) to any property line.

Table 34.10.3(b) Required Clearance Between Outside Idle Pallet Storage and Building

Wall Construction	Minimum Distance of Wall from Storage					
	Under 50 Pallets		50 to 200 Pallets		Over 200 Pallets	
	ft	m	ft	m	ft	m
Masonry with no openings	0	0	0	0	15	4.6
Masonry with wired glass in openings, outside sprinklers, and 1-hour doors	0	0	10	3	20	6
Masonry with wired or plain glass, outside sprinklers, and ¾-hour doors	10	3	20	6	30	9
Wood or metal with outside sprinklers	10	3	20	6	30	9
Wood, metal, or other	20	6	30	9	50	15

Chapter 35 Reserved

Chapter 36 Telecommunication Facilities and Information Technology Equipment

36.1 General.

36.1.1 Telecommunication facilities shall comply with NFPA 76, *Standard for the Fire Protection of Telecommunications Facilities.*

36.1.2 Information technology equipment and information technology equipment areas shall comply with NFPA 75, *Standard for the Protection of Information Technology Equipment.*

Chapter 37 Fixed Guideway Transit and Passenger Rail Systems

37.1 General.
Fixed guideway transit and passenger rail system facilities shall comply with NFPA 130, *Standard for Fixed Guideway Transit and Passenger Rail Systems.*

Chapter 38 Reserved

Chapter 39 Reserved

Chapter 40 Dust Explosion and Fire Prevention

40.1 General. Equipment, processes, and operations that involve the manufacture, processing, blending, repackaging, or handling of combustible particulate solids or combustible dusts regardless of concentration or particle size shall be installed and maintained in accordance with this chapter and the following standards as applicable:

(1) NFPA 61, *Standard for the Prevention of Fires and Dust Explosions in Agricultural and Food Processing Facilities*
(2) NFPA 69, *Standard on Explosion Prevention Systems*
(3) NFPA 85, *Boiler and Combustion Systems Hazards Code*
(4) NFPA 120, *Standard for Fire Prevention and Control in Coal Mines*
(5) NFPA 484, *Standard for Combustible Metals*
(6) NFPA 654, *Standard for the Prevention of Fire and Dust Explosions from the Manufacturing, Processing, and Handling of Combustible Particulate Solids*
(7) NFPA 655, *Standard for Prevention of Sulfur Fires and Explosions*
(8) NFPA 664, *Standard for the Prevention of Fires and Explosions in Wood Processing and Woodworking Facilities*

40.2 Permits. Permits, where required, shall comply with Section 1.12.

40.3 Fugitive Dust Control and Housekeeping.

40.3.1 Fugitive Dust Control.

40.3.1.1 Continuous suction to minimize the escape of dust shall be provided for processes where combustible dust is liberated in normal operation. [**654:**8.1.1]

40.3.1.2 The dust shall be conveyed to air-material separators. [**654:**8.1.2]

40.3.2 Housekeeping. All requirements of 40.3.2.1 through 40.3.2.3 shall be applied retroactively. [**654:**8.2]

40.3.2.1 Cleaning Frequency.

40.3.2.1.1* Where the facility is intended to be operated with less than the dust accumulation defined by the owner/operator's chosen criterion in Section 6.1 of NFPA 654, the housekeeping frequency shall be established to ensure that the accumulated dust levels on walls, floors, and horizontal surfaces such as equipment, ducts, pipes, hoods, ledges, beams, and above suspended ceilings and other concealed surfaces, such as the interior of electrical enclosures, does not exceed the threshold dust mass/accumulation. [**654:**8.2.1.1]

40.3.2.1.2 Where the facility is intended to be operated with less than the dust accumulation defined by the owner/

operator's chosen criterion in Section 6.1 of NFPA 654, a planned inspection process shall be implemented to evaluate dust accumulation rates and the housekeeping frequency required to maintain dust accumulations below the threshold dust mass/accumulation. [**654**:8.2.1.2]

40.3.2.1.3* Where the facility is intended to be operated with less than the dust accumulation defined by the owner/operator's chosen criterion in Section 6.1 of NFPA 654, the housekeeping procedure shall include specific requirements establishing time to clean local spills or short-term accumulation to allow the elimination of the spilled mass or accumulation from the calculations in Section 6.1 of NFPA 654. [**654**:8.2.1.3]

40.3.2.1.4* Where the facility is intended to be operated with more than the dust accumulation defined by the owner/operator's chosen criterion in Section 6.1 of NFPA 654, a documented risk evaluation acceptable to the AHJ shall be permitted to be conducted to determine the level of housekeeping consistent with any dust explosion and dust flash fire protection measures provided in accordance with Section 6.4 and 11.2.2 of NFPA 654. [**654**:8.2.1.4]

40.3.2.2 Cleaning Methods.

40.3.2.2.1 Surfaces shall be cleaned in a manner that minimizes the risk of generating a fire or explosion hazard. [**654**:8.2.2.1]

40.3.2.2.2 Vacuuming shall be the preferred method of cleaning. [**654**:8.2.2.2]

40.3.2.2.3 Where vacuuming is impractical, permitted cleaning methods shall include sweeping and water wash-down. [**654**:8.2.2.3]

40.3.2.2.4* Blow-downs using compressed air or steam shall be permitted to be used for cleaning inaccessible surfaces or surfaces where other methods of cleaning result in greater personal safety risk. Where blow-down using compressed air is used, the following precautions shall be followed:

(1) Vacuuming, sweeping, or water wash-down methods are first used to clean surfaces that can be safely accessed prior to using compressed air.
(2) Dust accumulations in the area after vacuuming, sweeping, or water wash-down do not exceed the threshold dust accumulation.
(3) Compressed air hoses are equipped with pressure relief nozzles limiting the discharge gauge pressure to 30 psi (207 kPa) in accordance with the OSHA requirements in 29 CFR 1910.242(b), "Hand and Portable Power Tools and Equipment, General."
(4) All electrical equipment potentially exposed to airborne dust in the area meets, as a minimum, the requirements of *NFPA 70, National Electrical Code*; NEMA12 as defined by NEMA 250; or the equivalent.
(5) All ignition sources and hot surfaces capable of igniting a dust cloud or dust layer are shut down or removed from the area. [**654**:8.2.2.4]

40.3.2.2.5* Housekeeping procedures shall be documented in accordance with the requirements of Sections 4.2 and 4.3 of NFPA 654. [**654**:8.2.2.5]

40.3.2.3 Portable Vacuum Cleaners.

40.3.2.3.1* Portable vacuum cleaners that meet the following minimum requirements shall be permitted to be used to collect combustible particulate solids:

(1) Materials of construction shall comply with 7.13.2 and 9.3.2 of NFPA 654.
(2) Hoses shall be conductive or static dissipative.
(3) All conductive components, including wands and attachments, shall be bonded and grounded.
(4) Dust-laden air shall not pass through the fan or blower.
(5) Electrical motors shall not be in the dust-laden air stream unless listed for Class II, Division 1 locations.
(6)*When liquids or wet material are picked up by the vacuum cleaner, paper filter elements shall not be used.
(7) Vacuum cleaners used for metal dusts shall meet the requirements of NFPA 484, *Standard for Combustible Metals*. [**654**:8.2.3.1]

40.3.2.3.2 In Class II electrically classified (hazardous) locations, vacuum cleaners shall be listed for the purpose and location or shall be a fixed-pipe suction system with remotely located exhauster and air-material separator installed in conformance with Section 7.13 of NFPA 654, and shall be suitable for the dust being collected. [**654**:8.2.3.2]

40.3.2.3.3 Where flammable vapors or gases are present, vacuum cleaners shall be listed for Class I and Class II hazardous locations. [**654**:8.2.3.3]

40.4 Ignition Sources.

40.4.1 Heat from Mechanical Sparks and Friction.

40.4.1.1 Risk Evaluation. A documented risk evaluation acceptable to the AHJ shall be permitted to be conducted to determine the level of protection to be provided according to this chapter. [**654**:9.1.1]

40.4.1.2 Foreign Materials.

40.4.1.2.1 Means shall be provided to prevent foreign material from entering the system when such foreign material presents an ignition hazard. [**654**:9.1.2.1]

40.4.1.2.2 Floor sweepings shall not be returned to any machine. [**654**:9.1.2.2]

40.4.1.2.3* Foreign materials, such as tramp metal, that are capable of igniting combustible material being processed shall be removed from the process stream by one of the following methods:

(1) Permanent magnetic separators or electromagnetic separators that indicate loss of power to the separators
(2) Pneumatic separators
(3) Grates or other separation devices [**654**:9.1.2.3]

40.4.1.3* Inherently Ignitible Process Streams.

40.4.1.3.1 Where the process is configured such that the pneumatic conveying, dust collection, or centralized vacuum cleaning system conveys materials that can act as an ignition source, means shall be provided to minimize the hazard. [**654**:9.1.3.1]

40.4.1.3.2 The means used to minimize the ignition source hazard specified in 40.4.1.3.1 shall be permitted to include protection measures identified in 7.1.1 and Section 10.1 of NFPA 654, as appropriate. [**654**:9.1.3.2]

40.4.1.4* Belt Drives. Belt drives shall be designed to stall without the belt's slipping, or a safety device shall be provided to shutdown the equipment if slippage occurs. [**654**:9.1.4]

40.4.1.5* Bearings.

40.4.1.5.1 Roller or ball bearings shall be used on all processing and transfer equipment. [**654**:9.1.5.1]

2015 Edition

40.4.1.5.2 Bushings shall be permitted to be used when a documented engineering evaluation shows that mechanical loads and speeds preclude ignition due to frictional heating. [**654:**9.1.5.2]

40.4.1.5.3 Lubrication shall be performed in accordance with the manufacturer's recommendations. [**654:**9.1.5.3]

40.4.1.6 Equipment. Equipment with moving parts shall be installed and maintained so that true alignment is maintained and clearance is provided to minimize friction. [**654:**9.1.6]

40.4.2 Electrical Equipment. All electrical equipment and installations shall comply with the requirements of Section 6.6 of NFPA 654. [**654:**9.2]

40.4.3 Static Electricity. The requirements of 40.4.3.1 through 40.4.3.1.4 shall be applied retroactively. [**654:**9.3]

40.4.3.1 For electrostatic hazard assessment purposes, MIE determination of dust clouds shall be based on a purely capacitive discharge circuit in accordance with ASTM E 2019, *Standard Test Method for Minimum Ignition Energy of a Dust Cloud in Air.* [**654:**9.3.1]

40.4.3.2* Conductive Components.

40.4.3.2.1 All system components shall be conductive. [**654:**9.3.2.1]

40.4.3.2.2 Nonconductive system components shall be permitted where all of the following conditions are met:

(1) Hybrid mixtures are not present.
(2) Conductive dusts are not handled.
(3) The MIE of the material being handled is greater than 3 mJ.
(4) The nonconductive components do not result in isolation of conductive components from ground.
(5)*The breakdown strength across nonconductive sheets, coatings, or membranes does not exceed 4 kV when used in high surface charging processes. [**654:**9.3.2.2]

40.4.3.2.3* Bonding and grounding with a resistance of less than 1.0×10^6 ohms to ground shall be provided for conductive components. [**654:**9.3.2.3]

40.4.3.3 Where belt drives are used, the belts shall be electrically conductive and have a resistance of less than 1.0×10^6 ohms to ground. [**654:**9.3.3]

40.4.3.4* Flexible Intermediate Bulk Containers (FIBCs). FIBCs shall be permitted to be used for the handling and storage of combustible particulate solids in accordance with the requirements in 40.4.3.4.1 through 40.4.3.4.7. [**654:**9.3.4]

40.4.3.4.1* Electrostatic ignition hazards associated with the particulate and objects surrounding or inside of the FIBC shall be included in the process hazard analysis required by Section 4.2 of NFPA 654. [**654:**9.3.4.1]

40.4.3.4.2 Type A FIBCs shall be limited to use with noncombustible particulate solids or combustible particulate solids having MIE >1000 mJ. [**654:**9.3.4.2]

40.4.3.4.2.1 Type A FIBCs shall not be used in locations where flammable vapors are present. [**654:**9.3.4.2.1]

40.4.3.4.2.2* Type A FIBCs shall not be used with conductive particulate solids. [**654:**9.3.4.2.2]

40.4.3.4.3 Type B FIBCs shall be permitted to be used where combustible dusts having MIE >3 mJ are present. [**654:**9.3.4.3]

40.4.3.4.3.1 Type B FIBCs shall not be used in locations where flammable vapors are present. [**654:**9.3.4.3.1]

40.4.3.4.3.2* Type B FIBCs shall not be used for conductive particulate solids. [**654:**9.3.4.3.2]

40.4.3.4.4 Type C FIBCs shall be permitted to be used with combustible particulate solids and in locations where flammable vapors having MIE >0.14 mJ are present. [**654:**9.3.4.4]

40.4.3.4.4.1 Conductive FIBC elements shall terminate in a grounding tab, and resistance from these elements to the tab shall be less than 10^8 ohms. [**654:**9.3.4.4.1]

40.4.3.4.4.2 Type C FIBCs shall be grounded during filling and emptying operations with a resistance to ground of less than 25 ohms. [**654:**9.3.4.4.2]

40.4.3.4.4.3 Type C FIBCs shall be permitted to be used for conductive particulate solids. [**654:**9.3.4.4.3]

40.4.3.4.5 Type D FIBCs shall be permitted to be used with combustible particulate solids and in locations where flammable vapor atmospheres having MIE >0.14 mJ are present. [**654:**9.3.4.5]

40.4.3.4.5.1 Type D FIBCs shall not be permitted to be used for conductive particulate solids. [**654:**9.3.4.5.1]

40.4.3.4.6* Type B, Type C, and Type D FIBCs shall be tested and verified as safe for their intended use by a recognized testing organization in accordance with the requirements and test procedures specified in IEC 61340-4-4, *Electrostatics — Part 4-4: Standard Test Methods for Specific Applications — Electrostatic Classification of Flexible Intermediate Bulk Containers*, before being used in hazardous environments. [**654:**9.3.4.6]

40.4.3.4.6.1 Intended use shall include both the product being handled and the environment in which the FIBC will be used. [**654:**9.3.4.6.1]

40.4.3.4.6.2 Materials used to construct inner baffles, other than mesh or net baffles, shall meet the requirements for the bag type in which they are to be used. [**654:**9.3.4.6.2]

40.4.3.4.6.3 Documentation of test results shall be made available to the AHJ. [**654:**9.3.4.6.3]

40.4.3.4.6.4 FIBCs that have not been tested and verified for type in accordance with IEC 61340-4-4, *Electrostatics — Part 4 4: Standard Test Methods for Specific Applications — Electrostatic Classification of Flexible Intermediate Bulk Containers*, shall be not be used for combustible dusts or in flammable vapor atmospheres. [**654:**9.3.4.6.4]

40.4.3.4.7* Deviations from the requirements in 40.4.3.4.1 through 40.4.3.4.6 for safe use of FIBCs shall be permitted upon expert review and a documented risk assessment acceptable to the AHJ. [**654:**9.3.4.7]

40.4.3.5 Rigid Intermediate Bulk Containers (RIBC).

40.4.3.5.1* Conductive RIBCs shall be permitted to be used for dispensing into any flammable vapor, gas, dust, or hybrid atmospheres provided that the RIBC is electrically grounded. [**654:**9.3.5.1]

40.4.3.5.2* Nonconductive RIBCs shall not be permitted to be used for applications, processes, or operations involving combustible particulate solids or where flammable vapors or gases are present unless a documented risk evaluation assessing the electrostatic hazards is acceptable to the AHJ. [**654:**9.3.5.2]

40.4.3.6 Particulate solids shall not be manually dumped directly into vessels containing flammable atmospheres (gases at a flammable concentration with an oxidant) or where displacement could cause a flammable atmosphere external to the vessel. [**654**:9.3.6]

40.4.3.7* Manual additions of solids through an open port or a manway into a vessel containing flammable atmospheres shall be permitted to be done in 50 lb (25 kg) batches or smaller, provided the requirements of 40.4.3.7.1 through 40.4.3.7.7 are satisfied. [**654**:9.3.7]

40.4.3.7.1* Conductive or static-dissipative components of the container shall be grounded. [**654**:9.3.7.1]

40.4.3.7.2 Direct emptying of powders from nonconductive plastic bags into a vessel that contains a flammable atmosphere shall be strictly prohibited. [**654**:9.3.7.2]

40.4.3.7.3 The use of nonconductive liners in grounded conductive or static-dissipative outer packaging shall be permitted, provided that the liner thickness is less than 0.08 in. (2 mm) and the liner cannot become detached during emptying. [**654**:9.3.7.3]

40.4.3.7.4* Loading chutes, receiving vessels, and auxiliary devices used for addition of bulk material shall be conductive and grounded. [**654**:9.3.7.4]

40.4.3.7.5* Personnel in the vicinity of openings of vessels that contain flammable atmospheres shall be grounded. [**654**:9.3.7.5]

40.4.3.7.6 Operators shall wear flame-resistant garments as specified in NFPA 2113, *Standard on Selection, Care, Use, and Maintenance of Flame-Resistant Garments for Protection of Industrial Personnel Against Flash Fire*, and any other personal protective equipment required for protection against flash fire hazards during charging operations. [**654**:9.3.7.6]

40.4.3.7.7* A documented risk evaluation acceptable to the AHJ shall be conducted to determine additional engineering and administrative controls necessary to protect against ignition of the flammable atmosphere. [**654**:9.3.7.7]

40.4.4 Cartridge-Actuated Tools. The requirements of 40.4.4.1 through 40.4.4.3 shall be applied retroactively. [**654**:9.4]

40.4.4.1 Cartridge-actuated tools shall not be used in areas where combustible material is produced, processed, or present unless all machinery is shut down and the area is cleaned and inspected to ensure the removal of all accumulations of combustible material. [**654**:9.4.1]

40.4.4.2 Accepted lockout/tagout procedures shall be followed for the shutdown of machinery. [**654**:9.4.2]

40.4.4.3 The use of cartridge-actuated tools shall be in accordance with 40.4.5.2. [**654**:9.4.3]

40.4.4.4 An inspection shall be made after the work is completed to ensure that no cartridges or charges are left in the area where they can enter equipment or be accidentally discharged after operation of the dust-producing or handling machinery is resumed. [**654**:9.4.4]

40.4.5 Open Flames and Sparks. The requirements of 40.4.5.1 through 40.4.5.3 shall be applied retroactively. [**654**:9.5]

40.4.5.1 Cutting and welding shall comply with the applicable requirements of NFPA 51B, *Standard for Fire Prevention During Welding, Cutting, and Other Hot Work*. [**654**:9.5.1]

40.4.5.2 Grinding, chipping, and other operations that produce either sparks or open-flame ignition sources shall be controlled by a hot work permit system in accordance with NFPA 51B. [**654**:9.5.2]

40.4.5.3 Smoking shall be permitted only in designated areas. [**654**:9.5.3]

40.4.6 Process and Comfort Heating Systems.

40.4.6.1* In areas processing combustible dust, process and comfort heating shall be provided by indirect means. [**654**:9.6.1]

40.4.6.2 Fired equipment shall be located outdoors or in a separate dust-free room or building. [**654**:9.6.2]

40.4.6.3 Air for combustion shall be taken from a clean outside source. [**654**:9.6.3]

40.4.6.4 Comfort air systems for processing areas containing combustible dust shall not be recirculated. [**654**:9.6.4]

40.4.6.5 Recirculating systems shall be permitted to be used provided that all of the following criteria are met:

(1) Only fresh makeup air is heated.
(2) The return air is filtered to prevent accumulations of dust in the recirculating system.
(3) The exhaust flow is balanced with fresh air intake. [**654**:9.6.5]

40.4.6.6 Comfort air shall not be permitted to flow from hazardous to nonhazardous areas. [**654**:9.6.6]

40.4.7* Hot Surfaces. In areas where a dust explosion hazard or dust flash fire hazard exists, the temperature of external surfaces, such as compressors; steam, water, or process piping; ducts; and process equipment shall be maintained below 80 percent (in degrees Celsius) of the lower of the dust surface ignition temperature or the dust-cloud ignition temperature. [**654**:9.7]

40.4.8 Industrial Trucks.

40.4.8.1 Where used, industrial trucks shall be listed or approved for the electrical classification of the area, as determined by Section 6.5 of NFPA 654, and shall be used in accordance with NFPA 505, *Fire Safety Standard for Powered Industrial Trucks Including Type Designations, Areas of Use, Conversions, Maintenance, and Operations*. [**654**:9.8.1]

40.4.8.2* Where industrial trucks, in accordance with NFPA 505, *Fire Safety Standard for Powered Industrial Trucks Including Type Designations, Areas of Use, Conversions, Maintenance, and Operations*, are not commercially available, a documented risk assessment acceptable to the AHJ shall be permitted to be used to specify the fire and explosion prevention features for the equipment used. [**654**:9.8.2]

40.5 Fire Protection.

40.5.1 General. Fire protection systems, where installed, shall be specifically designed to address building protection, process equipment, and the chemical and physical properties of the materials being processed. [**654**:10.1]

40.5.2 System Requirements. Fire protection systems required by this chapter shall comply with 40.5.2.1 through 40.5.2.10. [**654**:10.2]

40.5.2.1* Fire-extinguishing agents shall be compatible with the conveyed materials. [**654**:10.2.1]

40.5.2.2 Where fire detection systems are incorporated into pneumatic conveying dust collection, or centralized vacuum cleaning systems, an analysis shall be conducted to identify safe interlocking requirements for air-moving devices and process operations. [**654:**10.2.2]

40.5.2.3 Where fire-fighting water or wet product can accumulate in the system, vessel and pipe supports shall be designed to support the additional water weight. [**654:**10.2.3]

40.5.2.4 Detection Systems.

40.5.2.4.1 Where fire detection systems are incorporated into the pneumatic conveying, dust collection, or centralized vacuum cleaning system, the fire detection systems shall be interlocked to shut down any active device feeding materials to the pneumatic conveying, dust collection, or centralized vacuum cleaning system, on actuation of the detection system. [**654:**10.2.4.1]

40.5.2.4.2 Where spark or infrared detection and extinguishing systems are provided, the process shall be permitted to continue operating on activation of the detection system. [**654:**10.2.4.2]

40.5.2.4.3 Where a spark or infrared detection system actuates a diverter valve that sends potentially burning material to a safe location, the process shall be permitted to continue operating on activation of the detection system. [**654:**10.2.4.3]

40.5.2.5 Where the actuation of fire-extinguishing systems is achieved by means of electronic fire detection, the fire detection system, including control panels, detectors, and notification appliances, shall be designed, installed, and maintained in accordance with *NFPA 72*. [**654:**10.2.5]

40.5.2.6 All fire detection initiating devices shall be connected to the fire detection control panel via Style D or E circuits as described in *NFPA 72*. [**654:**10.2.6]

40.5.2.7 All fire detection notification appliances shall be connected to the fire detection control panel via Style Y or Z circuits as described in *NFPA 72*. [**654:**10.2.7]

40.5.2.8 System Releasing Devices.

40.5.2.8.1 All fire-extinguishing system releasing devices, solenoids, or actuators shall be connected to the fire detection control panel via Style Z circuits as described in *NFPA 72*. [**654:**10.2.8.1]

40.5.2.8.2 The supervision shall include the continuity of the extinguishing system releasing device, whether that device is a solenoid coil, a detonator (explosive device) filament, or other such device. [**654:**10.2.8.2]

40.5.2.9 All supervisory devices that monitor critical elements or functions in the fire detection and extinguishing system shall be connected to the fire detection control panel via Style D or E circuits as described in *NFPA 72*. [**654:**10.2.9]

40.5.2.10 Abort Gates and Abort Dampers.

40.5.2.10.1 All fire protection abort gates or abort dampers shall be connected to the fire detection control panel via Style Z circuits as described in *NFPA 72*. [**654:**10.2.10.1]

40.5.2.10.2 The supervision shall include the continuity of the abort gate or abort damper releasing device, whether that device is a solenoid coil, a detonator (explosive device) filament, or other such device. [**654:**10.2.10.2]

40.5.3 Fire Extinguishers.

40.5.3.1 Portable fire extinguishers shall be provided throughout all buildings in accordance with the requirements of Section 13.6. [**654:**10.3.1]

40.5.3.2* Personnel shall be trained to use portable fire extinguishers in a manner that minimizes the generation of dust clouds during discharge. [**654:**10.3.2]

40.5.4 Hoses, Nozzles, Standpipes, and Hydrants.

40.5.4.1 Standpipes and hose, where provided, shall comply with Section 13.2. [**654:**10.4.1]

40.5.4.2 Nozzles.

40.5.4.2.1* Portable spray hose nozzles that are listed or approved for use on Class C fires shall be provided in areas that contain dust, to limit the potential for generating unnecessary airborne dust during fire-fighting operations. [**654:**10.4.2.1]

40.5.4.2.2* Straight-stream nozzles shall not be used on fires in areas where dust clouds can be generated. [**654:**10.4.2.2]

40.5.4.2.3 Straight-stream nozzles or combination nozzles shall be permitted to be used to reach fires in locations that are otherwise inaccessible with the nozzles specified in 40.5.4.2.1. [**654:**10.4.2.3]

40.5.4.3 Private outside protection, including outside hydrants and hoses, where provided, shall comply with Section 13.3. [**654:**10.4.3]

40.5.5* Automatic Sprinklers.

40.5.5.1* Where a process that handles combustible particulate solids uses flammable or combustible liquids, a documented risk evaluation that is acceptable to the AHJ shall be used to determine the need for automatic sprinkler protection in the enclosure in which the process is located. [**654:**10.5.1]

40.5.5.2 Automatic sprinklers, where provided, shall be installed in accordance with Section 13.3. [**654:**10.5.2]

40.5.5.3 Where automatic sprinklers are installed, dust accumulation on overhead surfaces shall be minimized to prevent an excessive number of sprinkler heads from opening in the event of a fire. [**654:**10.5.3]

40.5.6 Spark/Ember Detection and Extinguishing Systems.
Spark/ember detection and extinguishing systems shall be designed, installed, and maintained in accordance with NFPA 69, *Standard on Explosion Prevention Systems*, and Section 13.7. [**654:**10.6]

40.5.7 Special Fire Protection Systems.

40.5.7.1 Automatic extinguishing systems or special hazard extinguishing systems, where provided, shall be designed, installed, and maintained in accordance with the following standards, as applicable:

(1) NFPA 11, *Standard for Low-, Medium-, and High-Expansion Foam*
(2) NFPA 12, *Standard on Carbon Dioxide Extinguishing Systems*
(3) NFPA 12A, *Standard on Halon 1301 Fire Extinguishing Systems*
(4) NFPA 15, *Standard for Water Spray Fixed Systems for Fire Protection*
(5) NFPA 16, *Standard for the Installation of Foam-Water Sprinkler and Foam-Water Spray Systems*

(6) NFPA 17, *Standard for Dry Chemical Extinguishing Systems*
(7) NFPA 25, *Standard for the Inspection, Testing, and Maintenance of Water-Based Fire Protection Systems*
(8) NFPA 750, *Standard on Water Mist Fire Protection Systems*
(9) NFPA 2001, *Standard on Clean Agent Fire Extinguishing Systems* [**654**:10.7.1]

40.5.7.2 The extinguishing systems shall be designed and used in a manner that minimizes the generation of dust clouds during their discharge. [**654**:10.7.2]

40.5.8 Alarm Service. Alarm service, if provided, shall comply with Section 13.7. [**654**:10.8]

40.5.9 Impairments of Fire Protection and Explosion Prevention Systems.

40.5.9.1* Impairments shall include anything that interrupts the normal intended operation of the fire protection or explosion prevention system. [**654**:10.9.1]

40.5.9.2* A written impairment procedure shall be followed for every impairment to the fire protection or explosion prevention system. [**654**:10.9.2]

40.5.9.3* Impairments shall be limited in size and scope to the system or portion thereof being repaired, maintained, or modified. [**654**:10.9.3]

40.5.9.4* Impairment notification procedures shall be implemented by management to notify plant personnel and the AHJ of existing impairments and their restoration. [**654**:10.9.4]

40.6 Training and Procedures.

40.6.1 Employee Training. The requirements of 40.6.2 and 40.6.3 shall be applied retroactively. [**654**:11.1]

40.6.2 Plan.

40.6.2.1 Operating and maintenance procedures shall be developed. [**654**:11.2.1]

40.6.2.2* Operating and maintenance procedures shall address personal protective equipment (PPE), including flame-resistant garments, in accordance with the workplace hazard assessment required by NFPA 2113, *Standard on Selection, Care, Use, and Maintenance of Flame-Resistant Garments for Protection of Industrial Personnel Against Flash Fire*. [**654**:11.2.2]

40.6.2.3 A written emergency response plan shall be developed for preventing, preparing for, and responding to work-related emergencies including but not limited to fire and explosion. [**654**:11.2.3]

40.6.2.4 The plans and procedures shall be reviewed annually and as required by process changes. [**654**:11.2.4]

40.6.3 Initial and Refresher Training.

40.6.3.1 Initial and refresher training shall be provided to employees who are involved in operating, maintaining, and supervising facilities that handle combustible particulate solids. [**654**:11.3.1]

40.6.3.2 Initial and refresher training shall ensure that all employees are knowledgeable about the following:

(1) Hazards of their workplace
(2) General orientation, including plant safety rules
(3) Process description
(4) Equipment operation, safe startup and shutdown, and response to upset conditions
(5) The necessity for proper functioning of related fire and explosion protection systems
(6) Equipment maintenance requirements and practices
(7) Housekeeping requirements
(8)*Emergency response plans [**654**:11.3.2]

40.6.4 Certification. The employer shall certify annually that the training and review required by 40.6.2 and 40.6.3 have been completed. [**654**:11.4]

40.6.5 Contractors and Subcontractors.

40.6.5.1 Owner/operators shall ensure that the requirements of 40.6.5.1.1 through 40.6.5.5 are met. [**654**:11.5.1]

40.6.5.1.1* Only qualified contractors possessing the requisite craft skills shall be employed for work involving the installation, repair, or modification of buildings (interior and exterior), machinery, and fire protection equipment. [**654**:11.5.1.1]

40.6.5.1.2 Contractors involved in the commissioning, repair, or modification of explosion protection equipment shall be qualified as specified in Chapter 15 of NFPA 69, *Standard on Explosion Prevention Systems*. [**654**:11.5.1.2]

40.6.5.2 Contractor Training.

40.6.5.2.1 Contractors operating owner/operator equipment shall be trained and qualified to operate the equipment and perform the work. [**654**:11.5.2.1]

40.6.5.2.2 Written documentation shall be maintained detailing the training that was provided and who received it. [**654**:11.5.2.2]

40.6.5.3 Contractors working on or near a given process shall be made aware of the potential hazards from and exposures to fire, explosion, or toxic releases. [**654**:11.5.3]

40.6.5.4* Contractors shall be trained and required to comply with the facility's safe work practices and policies, including but not limited to equipment lockout/tagout permitting, hot work permitting, fire system impairment handling, smoking, housekeeping, and use of personal protective equipment. [**654**:11.5.4]

40.6.5.5 Contractors shall be trained on the facility's emergency response and evacuation plan, including but not limited to emergency reporting procedures, safe egress points, and evacuation areas. [**654**:11.5.5]

40.7 Inspection and Maintenance.

40.7.1 General Requirements. The requirements of 40.7.1.1 through 40.7.1.3 shall be applied retroactively. [**654**:12.1]

40.7.1.1 An inspection, testing, and maintenance program shall be developed and implemented to ensure that the fire and explosion protection systems and related process controls and equipment perform as designed. [**654**:12.1.1]

40.7.1.2 The inspection, testing, and maintenance program shall include the following:

(1) Fire and explosion protection and prevention equipment in accordance with the applicable NFPA standards
(2) Dust control equipment
(3) Housekeeping
(4) Potential ignition sources
(5)*Electrical, process, and mechanical equipment, including process interlocks
(6) Process changes
(7) Lubrication of bearings [**654**:12.1.2]

2015 Edition

40.7.1.3 Records shall be kept of maintenance and repairs performed. [**654:**12.1.3]

40.7.2 Specific Requirements.

40.7.2.1 Maintenance of Material Feeding Devices.

40.7.2.1.1 Bearings shall be lubricated and checked for excessive wear on a periodic basis. [**654:**12.2.1.1]

40.7.2.1.2 If the material has a tendency to adhere to the feeder or housing, the components shall be cleaned periodically to maintain good balance and minimize the probability of ignition. [**654:**12.2.1.2]

40.7.2.2 Maintenance of Air-Moving Devices.

40.7.2.2.1 Fans and blowers shall be checked periodically for excessive heat and vibration. [**654:**12.2.2.1]

40.7.2.2.2 Maintenance, other than the lubrication of external bearings, shall not be performed on fans or blowers while the unit is operating. [**654:**12.2.2.2]

40.7.2.2.3 Bearings shall be lubricated and checked periodically for excessive wear. [**654:**12.2.2.3]

40.7.2.2.4* If the material has a tendency to adhere to the rotor or housing, the components shall be cleaned periodically to maintain good balance and minimize the probability of ignition. [**654:**12.2.2.4]

40.7.2.2.5* The surfaces of fan housings and other interior components shall be maintained free of rust. [**654:**12.2.2.5]

40.7.2.2.6 Aluminum paint shall not be used on interior steel surfaces. [**654:**12.2.2.6]

40.7.2.3 Maintenance of Air–Material Separators.

40.7.2.3.1 Means to Dislodge.

40.7.2.3.1.1 Air–material separation devices that are equipped with a means to dislodge particulates from the surface of filter media shall be inspected periodically as recommended in the manufacturers' instructions for signs of wear, friction, or clogging. [**654:**12.2.3.1.1]

40.7.2.3.1.2 These devices shall be adjusted and lubricated as recommended in the manufacturers' instructions. [**654:**12.2.3.1.2]

40.7.2.3.2 Air–material separators that recycle air (i.e., cyclones and filter media dust collectors) shall be maintained to comply with 6.1.3 of NFPA 654. [**654:**12.2.3.2]

40.7.2.3.3 Filter media shall not be replaced with an alternative type unless a thorough evaluation of the fire hazards has been performed, documented, and reviewed by management. [**654:**12.2.3.3]

40.7.2.4 Maintenance of Abort Gates and Abort Dampers. Abort gates and abort dampers shall be adjusted and lubricated as recommended in the manufacturers' instructions. [**654:**12.2.4]

40.7.2.5 Maintenance of Fire and Explosion Protection Systems.

40.7.2.5.1 All fire detection equipment monitoring systems shall be maintained in accordance with the requirements of 13.7.4.4. [**654:**12.2.5.1]

40.7.2.5.2 All fire-extinguishing systems shall be maintained pursuant to the requirements established in the standard that governs the design and installation of the system. [**654:**12.2.5.2]

40.7.2.5.3* All vents for the relief of pressure caused by deflagrations shall be maintained. [**654:**12.2.5.3]

40.7.2.5.4 All explosion prevention systems and inerting systems shall be maintained pursuant to the requirements of NFPA 69. [**654:**12.2.5.4]

Chapter 41   Welding, Cutting, and Other Hot Work

41.1 General.

41.1.1 Hot work shall comply with NFPA 51B, *Standard for Fire Prevention During Welding, Cutting, and Other Hot Work*, and this chapter.

41.1.2 Chapter 41 shall apply to the following hot work processes:

(1) Welding and allied processes
(2) Heat treating
(3) Grinding
(4) Thawing pipe
(5) Powder-driven fasteners
(6) Hot riveting
(7)*Torch-applied roofing in conjunction with the requirements of Section 16.6
(8) Similar applications producing or using a spark, flame, or heat [**51B:**1.3.1]

41.1.3 Chapter 41 shall not apply to the following:

(1) Candles
(2) Pyrotechnics or special effects
(3) Cooking operations
(4) Electric soldering irons
(5) Design and installation of gas cutting equipment and welding equipment covered in NFPA 51, *Standard for the Design and Installation of Oxygen–Fuel Gas Systems for Welding, Cutting, and Allied Processes*
(6) Additional requirements for hot work operations in confined spaces
(7) Lockout/tagout procedures during hot work [**51B:**1.3.2]

41.1.4 Acetylene cylinder charging plants shall comply with NFPA 51A, *Standard for Acetylene Cylinder Charging Plants.*

41.1.5 Permits.

41.1.5.1 Permits, where required, shall comply with Section 1.12.

41.1.5.2 Where an approved facility hot work permit program exists that meets the requirements of Chapter 41, the permit shall be permitted to be issued for an entire facility.

41.2 Responsibility for Hot Work.

41.2.1* Management. Management or a designated agent shall be responsible for the safe operations of hot work activity. [**51B:**4.1]

41.2.1.1 Management shall establish permissible areas for hot work. [**51B:**4.1.1]

41.2.1.2 Management shall designate a permit authorizing individual (PAI). [**51B:**4.1.2]

41.2.1.3 All equipment shall be examined to ensure it is in a safe operating condition. [**51B**:4.1.3]

41.2.1.4 When found to be incapable of reliable safe operation, the equipment shall be repaired by qualified personnel prior to its next use or be withdrawn from service and tagged out of service. [**51B**:4.1.4]

41.2.1.5 Management shall ensure that only approved apparatus, such as torches, manifolds, regulators or pressure-reducing valves, and acetylene generators, are used. [**51B**:4.1.5]

41.2.1.6 Management shall ensure that all individuals involved in the hot work operations, including contractors, are familiar with the provisions of Chapter 41. [**51B**:4.1.6]

41.2.1.6.1 Individuals involved in hot work operations shall be trained in the safe operation of their equipment and in the safe use of the process. [**51B**:4.1.6.1]

41.2.1.6.2 Individuals involved in hot work operations shall have an awareness of the inherent risks involved and understand the emergency procedures in the event of a fire. [**51B**:4.1.6.2]

41.2.1.7 Management shall advise all contractors about site-specific flammable materials, hazardous processes or conditions, or other potential fire hazards. [**51B**:4.1.7]

41.2.2 Permit Authorizing Individual (PAI). In conjunction with management, the PAI shall be responsible for the safe operation of hot work activities. [**51B**:4.2]

41.2.2.1* The PAI shall consider the safety of the hot work operator and fire watch with respect to personal protective equipment (PPE) for other special hazards beyond hot work. *(See 41.3.1.)* [**51B**:4.2.1]

41.2.2.2 The PAI shall determine site-specific flammable materials, hazardous processes, or other potential fire hazards that are present or likely to be present in the work location. [**51B**:4.2.2]

41.2.2.3 The PAI shall ensure the protection of combustibles from ignition by the following means:

(1)*Considering alternative methods to hot work
(2) Moving the work to a location that is free from combustibles
(3) If the work cannot be moved, moving the combustibles to a safe distance or having the combustibles properly shielded against ignition
(4) Scheduling hot work so that operations that could expose combustibles to ignition are not begun during hot work operations [**51B**:4.2.3]

41.2.2.4 If the criteria of 41.2.2.3(1) through 41.2.2.3(4) cannot be met, hot work shall not be performed. [**51B**:4.2.4]

41.2.2.5 The PAI shall determine that fire protection and extinguishing equipment are properly located at the site. [**51B**:4.2.5]

41.2.2.6 Where a fire watch is required *(see 41.3.5)*, the PAI shall be responsible for ensuring that a fire watch is at the site. [**51B**:4.2.6]

41.2.2.7* Where a fire watch is not required, the PAI shall make a final check ½ hour after the completion of hot work operations to detect and extinguish smoldering fires. [**51B**:4.2.7]

41.2.3 Hot Work Operator. The hot work operator shall handle equipment safely and use it as follows so as not to endanger lives and property:

(1) The operator shall have the PAI's approval before starting hot work operations.
(2) All equipment shall be examined to ensure it is in a safe operating condition, and, if found to be incapable of reliable safe operation, the equipment shall be repaired by qualified personnel prior to its next use or be withdrawn from service.
(3) The operator shall cease hot work operations if unsafe conditions develop and shall notify management, the area supervisor, or the PAI for reassessment of the situation. [**51B**:4.3]

41.2.4 Fire Watch.

41.2.4.1* The fire watch shall be trained to understand the inherent hazards of the work site and of the hot work. [**51B**:4.4.1]

41.2.4.2 The fire watch shall ensure that safe conditions are maintained during hot work operations. [**51B**:4.4.2]

41.2.4.3 The fire watch shall have the authority to stop the hot work operations if unsafe conditions develop. [**51B**:4.4.3]

41.2.4.4* The fire watch shall have fire-extinguishing equipment readily available and shall be trained in its use. [**51B**:4.4.4]

41.2.4.5 The fire watch shall be familiar with the facilities and procedures for sounding an alarm in the event of a fire. [**51B**:4.4.5]

41.2.4.6 The fire watch shall watch for fires in all exposed areas and try to extinguish them only when the fires are obviously within the capacity of the equipment available. If the fire watch determines that the fire is not within the capacity of the equipment, the fire watch shall sound the alarm immediately. [**51B**:4.4.6]

41.2.4.7* The fire watch shall be permitted to perform additional tasks, but those tasks shall not distract him or her from his or her fire watch responsibilities, except as outlined in Section 41.4. [**51B**:4.4.7]

41.2.5* Contractors. Before starting any hot work, contractors and their clients shall discuss the planned project completely, including the type of hot work to be conducted and the hazards in the area. [**51B**:4.5]

41.2.6 Mutual Responsibility. Management, contractors, the PAI, the fire watch, and the operators shall recognize their mutual responsibility for safety in hot work operations. [**51B**:4.6]

41.3 Fire Prevention Precautions.

41.3.1* Personal Protective Clothing. Clothing shall be selected to minimize the potential for ignition, burning, trapping hot sparks, and electric shock. [**51B**:5.1]

41.3.2 Permissible Areas.

41.3.2.1 General. Hot work shall be permitted only in areas that are or have been made fire safe. [**51B**:5.2.1]

41.3.2.2 Designated or Permit-Required Areas. Hot work shall be performed in either designated areas or permit-required areas. [**51B**:5.2.2]

41.3.2.2.1 Designated Areas.

41.3.2.2.1.1 In order for a location to be a designated area, the area shall meet the requirements in 41.3.4.2. [**51B:**5.2.2.1.1]

41.3.2.2.1.2 Prior to the start of any hot work in a designated area, at a minimum, the hot work operator shall perform the following:

(1) The location is verified as fire resistant.
(2) The requirements of 41.3.4.2(3) are met.
(3) Fire extinguishers are in working condition and readily available.
(4) Ventilation is working properly.
(5) Equipment is in working order. [**51B:**5.2.2.1.3]

41.3.2.2.1.3 Permanent areas designated for hot work shall be reviewed at least annually by the PAI. [**51B:**5.2.2.1.3]

41.3.2.2.2 Signs shall be posted designating hot work areas as deemed necessary by the PAI. [**51B:**5.2.2.2]

41.3.3* Nonpermissible Areas. Hot work shall not be permitted in the following areas:

(1) In areas not authorized by management
(2) In sprinklered buildings where sprinklers are impaired, unless the requirements of NFPA 25 are met
(3) In the presence of explosive atmospheres (i.e., where mixtures of flammable gases, vapors, liquids, or dusts with air exist)
(4) In the presence of uncleaned or improperly prepared equipment, drums, tanks, or other containers that have previously contained materials that could develop explosive atmospheres
(5) In areas with an accumulation of combustible dusts that could develop explosive atmospheres [**51B:**5.3]

41.3.4* Hot Work Permit.

41.3.4.1* Before hot work operations begin in a nondesignated location, a written hot work permit by the PAI shall be required. [**51B:**5.4.1]

41.3.4.2 Before a hot work permit is issued, the following conditions shall be verified by the PAI:

(1) The hot work equipment to be used shall be in satisfactory operating condition and in good repair.
(2) Where combustible materials, such as paper clippings, wood shavings, or textile fibers, are on the floor, the floor shall be swept clean for a radius of 35 ft (11 m) and the following criteria also shall be met:
  (a) Combustible floors shall be kept wet, covered with damp sand, or protected by a listed welding blanket, welding pad, or equivalent.
  (b) Where floors have been wet down, personnel operating arc welding equipment or cutting equipment shall be protected from possible shock.
(3)*All combustibles shall be relocated at least 35 ft (11 m) in all directions from the work site, and the following criteria also shall be met:
  (a) If relocation is impractical, combustibles shall be protected by a listed welding blanket, welding pad, or equivalent.
  (b) To prevent the entrance of sparks, the edges of covers at the floor shall be tight including at the point at which several covers overlap where a large pile is being protected.
(4) Openings or cracks in walls, floors, or ducts within 35 ft (11 m) of the site shall be covered or sealed with listed fire-rated or noncombustible material to prevent the passage of sparks to adjacent areas.
(5) Ducts and conveyor systems that might carry sparks to distant combustibles shall be shielded, or shut down, or both.
(6) If hot work is done near walls, partitions, ceilings, or roofs of combustible construction, they shall be protected by a listed welding curtain, welding blanket, welding pad, or equivalent.
(7) If hot work is done on one side of a wall, partition, ceiling, or roof, one of the following criteria shall be met:
  (a) Precautions shall be taken to prevent ignition of combustibles on the other side by relocating the combustibles.
  (b) If it is impractical to relocate combustibles, a fire watch shall be provided on the side opposite from where the work is being performed.
(8) Hot work shall not be attempted on a partition, wall, ceiling, or roof that has a combustible covering or insulation, or on walls or partitions of combustible sandwich-type panel construction.
(9) Hot work that is performed on pipes or other metal that is in contact with combustible walls, partitions, ceilings, roofs, or other combustibles shall not be undertaken if the work is close enough to cause ignition by conduction.
(10) Fully charged and operable fire extinguishers that are appropriate for the type of possible fire shall be available immediately at the work area.
(11) If existing hose lines are located within the hot work area defined by the permit, they shall be connected and ready for service but shall not be required to be unrolled or charged.
(12) The following shall apply to hot work done in close proximity to a sprinkler head:
  (a) A wet rag shall be laid over the sprinkler head and then removed at the conclusion of the welding or cutting operation.
  (b) During hot work, special precautions shall be taken to avoid accidental operation of automatic fire detection or suppression systems (e.g., special extinguishing systems or sprinklers).
(13) The operator and nearby personnel shall be suitably protected against dangers such as heat, sparks, and slag.
(14)*In instances where the scope of work and the tools used to conduct hot work result in possible travel of slag, sparks, spatter, or similar mobile sources of ignition farther than 35 ft (11 m), the PAI shall be permitted to extend the distances and areas addressed in 41.3.4.2(2) through 41.3.4.2(4).
(15)*In instances where the scope of work and tools used to conduct hot work are known to be incapable of generating slag, sparks, spatter or similar mobile sources of ignition capable of leaving the immediate area of the applied hot work, the PAI shall be permitted to do the following:
  (a) Reduce the distances and areas addressed in 41.3.4.2(2) through 41.3.4.2(4) to distances and areas that he or she considers fire safe for the intended operation.
  (b) Describe those distances and areas on the hot work permit. [**51B:**5.4.2]

41.3.4.3 The PAI shall determine the length of the period for which the hot work permit is valid. [**51B:**5.4.3]

41.3.4.4 The hot work permit shall not be valid for a period exceeding 24 hours. [**51B:**5.4.3.1]

41.3.4.5 The area shall be inspected by the PAI at least once per shift while the hot work permit is in effect to ensure that it is a fire-safe area. [**51B:**5.4.4]

41.3.5 Fire Watch.

41.3.5.1* A fire watch shall be required by the PAI when hot work is performed in a location where other than a minor fire might develop or where the following conditions exist:

(1)*Combustible materials in building construction or contents are closer than 35 ft (11 m) to the point of operation.
(2) Combustible materials are more than 35 ft (11 m) away from the point of operation but are easily ignited by sparks.
(3) Wall or floor openings within an 35 ft (11 m) radius expose combustible materials in adjacent areas, including concealed spaces in walls or floors.
(4) Combustible materials are adjacent to the opposite side of partitions, walls, ceilings, or roofs and are likely to be ignited. [**51B:**5.5.1]

41.3.5.2 A fire watch shall be maintained for at least ½ hour after completion of hot work operations in order to detect and extinguish smoldering fires. The duration of the fire watch shall be extended if the PAI determines the fire hazards warrant the extension. [**51B:**5.5.2]

41.3.5.3* More than one fire watch shall be required if combustible materials that could be ignited by the hot work operation cannot be directly observed by the initial fire watch. [**51B:**5.5.3]

41.3.6* Hot Tapping. Hot tapping or other cutting and welding on a flammable gas or liquid transmission or distribution utility pipeline shall be performed by a crew that is qualified to make hot taps. [**51B:**5.6]

41.3.7 Cylinders. Cylinder use and storage shall be in accordance with Chapter 63. [**51B:**5.7]

41.4 Sole Proprietors and Individual Operators.

41.4.1* Assignment of PAI and Fire Watch. In a site where hot work operations are not under the control of another authority, the individual hot work operator shall be permitted to serve as PAI and fire watch, provided that the operator is trained and follows the provisions of Chapter 41. [**51B:**6.1]

41.4.2 Written Hot Work Permit. A checklist shall be permitted to serve as the written hot work permit. [**51B:**6.2]

41.5 Public Exhibitions and Demonstrations.

41.5.1 Application. The provisions of Section 41.5 shall apply to oxy–fuel gas welding and cutting operations at public exhibitions, demonstrations, displays, and trade shows, referred to hereinafter as the "site," in order to promote the safe use of compressed gases in public gatherings. [**51B:**7.1]

41.5.2 Supervision. Installation and operation of welding, cutting, and related equipment shall be done by, or under the supervision of, a competent operator, to ensure the personal protection of viewers and demonstrators as well as the protection from fire of materials in and around the site and the building itself. [**51B:**7.2]

41.5.3 Site.

41.5.3.1 Location. Sites involving the use and storage of compressed gases shall be located so as not to interfere with egress during an emergency. [**51B:**7.3.1]

41.5.3.2 Design. The site shall be constructed, equipped, and operated in such a manner that the demonstration minimizes the possibility of injury to viewers. [**51B:**7.3.2]

41.5.4 Fire Protection.

41.5.4.1 Fire Extinguishers. Each site shall be provided with a portable fire extinguisher of appropriate size and type in accordance with NFPA 10, *Standard for Portable Fire Extinguishers.* [**51B:**7.4.1]

41.5.4.2 Shielding. The public, combustible materials, and compressed gas cylinders at the site shall be protected from flames, sparks, and molten metal. [**51B:**7.4.2]

41.5.4.3 Fire Department Notification. The fire department shall be notified in advance of the use of a site for public exhibitions, demonstrations, and trade shows. [**51B:**7.4.3]

41.5.5 Cylinders.

41.5.5.1 Gas Capacity Limitation.

41.5.5.1.1 Cylinders containing compressed gases for use at the site shall not be charged in excess of one-half their maximum permissible content. [**51B:**7.5.1.1]

41.5.5.1.2 Cylinders of nonliquefied gases and acetylene shall be charged to not more than one-half their maximum permissible charged gauge pressure [psi (kPa)]. [**51B:**7.5.1.2]

41.5.5.1.3 Cylinders of liquefied gases shall be charged to not more than one-half the maximum permissible capacity [lb (kg)]. [**51B:**7.5.1.3]

41.5.5.2 Storage.

41.5.5.2.1 Cylinders located at the site shall be connected for use. [**51B:**7.5.2.1]

41.5.5.2.2 A sufficient number of additional cylinders shall be permitted to be stored at the site to furnish approximately one day's consumption of each gas used. [**51B:**7.5.2.2]

41.5.5.2.3* Other cylinders shall be stored in an approved storage area, but not near a building exit. [**51B:**7.5.2.3]

41.5.5.3 Transporting Cylinders. Cylinders in excess of 40 lb (18 kg) total weight being transported to or from the site shall be carried on a hand truck or motorized truck. [**51B:**7.5.3]

41.5.5.4 Process Hose. Process hose shall be located and protected so that they will not be physically damaged. [**51B:**7.5.4]

41.5.5.5 Cylinder Valves. Cylinder valves shall be closed when equipment is unattended. [**51B:**7.5.5]

41.5.5.6 Valve Caps. If cylinders are designed to be equipped with valve protection caps, such caps shall be in place, except when the cylinders are in service or are connected and ready for service. [**51B:**7.5.6]

41.5.5.7 Cylinder Protection. Cylinders shall be secured so that they cannot be knocked over. [**51B:**7.5.7]

41.6 Arc Welding Equipment.

41.6.1 Installation. Electrical equipment shall be of an approved type and shall be installed and used in accordance with Section 11.1 and manufacturers' requirements.

41.6.2 Damaged cables shall be removed from service until repaired or replaced.

Chapter 42   Refueling

42.1 General. Chapter 42 shall apply to refueling of automotive vehicles, marine vessels, and aircraft.

42.2 Automotive Fuel Servicing.

42.2.1 Applicability.

42.2.1.1 Fueling processes at automotive service stations, service stations located inside buildings, and fleet vehicle service stations shall comply with NFPA 30A, *Code for Motor Fuel Dispensing Facilities and Repair Garages*, and Sections 42.2 through 42.8.

42.2.1.2 If approved by the AHJ, mobile fleet fueling at commercial, industrial, and governmental sites shall be conducted in accordance with 42.7.6.

42.2.1.3* Sections 42.2 through 42.8 shall not apply to those motor fuel dispensing facilities where only liquefied petroleum gas (LP-Gas), liquefied natural gas (LNG), or compressed natural gas (CNG) is dispensed as motor fuel. [**30A:**1.1.3]

42.2.2 General Requirements.

42.2.2.1 Permits. Permits, where required, shall comply with Section 1.12.

42.2.2.2 Plans and Specifications. Plans and specifications shall be submitted for review and approval prior to the installation or construction of a motor vehicle fuel dispensing station.

42.2.2.2.1 A site plan shall be submitted that illustrates the location of flammable and combustible liquids, LP-Gas or CNG storage vessels, and their spatial relation to each other, property lines, and building openings.

42.2.2.2.2 Aboveground and underground storage vessels shall be shown on plans.

42.2.2.2.3 For each type of fuel dispensing facility, plans and specifications shall also include, but not be limited to, the following:

(1) Type and design of underground and aboveground liquid storage tanks
(2) Quantity and types of liquids to be stored
(3) Location and design of the fuel dispensers and dispenser nozzles
(4) Distances from dispensers to tanks, property lines, and buildings
(5) Vehicle access
(6) Fire appliances
(7) Vehicle impact protection
(8) Method of storage and dispensing
(9) Overfill prevention
(10) Spill containment
(11) Vents
(12) Vapor recovery
(13) Other equipment and accessories
(14) Seismic design in accordance with the building code
(15) Secondary containment
(16) Design and specifications for related piping, valves, and fittings
(17) Location and classification of electrical equipment, including emergency fuel shutdown devices
(18) Specifications for fuel storage and venting components
(19) Other information as required by the AHJ

42.3 Storage of Liquids.

42.3.1 Scope. Section 42.3 shall apply to the storage of liquid fuels and to the storage of related materials, such as lubricating oils and greases, cleaning solvents, and windshield washer solvents. [**30A:**4.1]

42.3.2 General Requirements.

42.3.2.1 Liquids shall be stored in the following:

(1) Approved closed containers that do not exceed 60 gal (227 L) capacity and are located outside buildings
(2) Tanks or approved closed containers located inside motor fuel dispensing facilities or repair garages
(3) Aboveground tanks, underground tanks, and containers in accordance with the requirements of 42.3.3
(4) Tanks supplying marine service stations in accordance with 42.9.2. [**30A:**4.2.1]

42.3.2.2 A motor fuel dispensing facility located at a bulk plant shall be separated from areas in which bulk plant operations are conducted by a fence or other approved barrier. Dispensing devices at the motor fuel dispensing facility shall not be supplied by aboveground tanks located in the bulk plant. Storage tanks at motor fuel dispensing facilities shall not be connected by piping to aboveground tanks located in the bulk plant. [**30A:**4.2.2]

42.3.2.3 Class I liquids shall not be stored or handled in a building that has a basement or pit into which ignitible vapors can travel, unless the basement or pit is provided with ventilation that will prevent the accumulation of vapors. The ventilation system shall be capable of providing at least 1 ft^3/min of exhaust per ft^2 of floor area (0.3 m^3/min/m^2), but not less than 150 ft^3/min (4 m^3/min). [**30A:**4.2.3]

42.3.2.4 Where tanks are at an elevation that produces a gravity head on the dispensing device, the tank outlet shall be equipped with a device, such as a normally closed solenoid valve, positioned adjacent to and downstream from the valve specified in 22.13.1 of NFPA 30 that is installed and adjusted so that liquid cannot flow by gravity from the tank if the piping or hose fails when the dispenser is not in use. [**30A:**4.2.4]

42.3.3 Storage of Liquids.

42.3.3.1 Underground Tanks. Underground storage tanks shall meet all applicable requirements of Chapters 21 and 23 of NFPA 30. [**30A:**4.3.1]

42.3.3.2* Aboveground Storage Tanks. Except as modified by the provisions of this subsection, aboveground storage tanks shall meet all applicable requirements of Chapters 21 and 22 of NFPA 30. [**30A:**4.3.2]

42.3.3.2.1 The use of aboveground storage tanks at motor fuel dispensing facilities, fleet vehicle motor fuel dispensing facilities, and marine motor fuel dispensing facilities shall be permitted when installed in accordance with the requirements of this subsection and with all applicable requirements of Chapters 21, 22, and 27 of NFPA 30 and, for tanks other than tanks in vaults, when the specific installation has been approved by the AHJ. [**30A:**4.3.2.1]

42.3.3.2.2 Tanks designed and built for underground use shall not be installed for aboveground use. [**30A:**4.3.2.2]

42.3.3.2.3 Tanks storing liquid motor fuels at an individual site shall be limited to a maximum individual capacity of 12,000 gal (45,400 L) and aggregate capacity of 48,000 gal (181,700 L) unless such tanks are installed in vaults complying with 42.3.3.3, in which case the maximum individual capacity shall be permitted to be 15,000 gal (57,000 L). [**30A:**4.3.2.3]

42.3.3.2.4 Tanks shall be located in accordance with Table 42.3.3.2.4. [**30A:**4.3.2.4]

42.3.3.2.5 The maximum individual tank capacity of 12,000 gal (45,400 L), where indicated in Table 42.3.3.2.4, shall be permitted to be increased to 20,000 gal (75,700 L) for Class II and Class III liquids at a fleet vehicle motor fuel dispensing facility and an aggregate capacity of 80,000 gal (304,000 L). [**30A:**4.3.2.5]

42.3.3.2.6 At fleet vehicle motor fuel dispensing facilities, no minimum separation shall be required between the dispensing device and a tank in a vault, a protected aboveground tank, or a fire-resistant tank. [**30A:**4.3.2.6]

42.3.3.2.7 The provisions of this subsection shall not prohibit the dispensing of liquid motor fuels in the open from a fuel dispensing system supplied by an existing aboveground tank, not to exceed 6000 gal (22,710 L), located at commercial, industrial, government, or manufacturing establishments, and intended for fueling vehicles used in connection with their business. Such dispensing shall be permitted provided the following conditions are met:

(1) An inspection of the premises and operations has been made and approval has been granted by the AHJ.
(2) The tank is safeguarded against collision, spillage, and overfill to the satisfaction of the AHJ.
(3) The tank system is listed or approved for such aboveground use.
(4) The tank complies with requirements for emergency relief venting, the tank and dispensing system meet the electrical classification requirements of NFPA 30A, and the tank complies with the provisions of 42.3.2.4.
(5) The tank storage complies with Chapter 22 of NFPA 30. [**30A:**4.3.2.7]

42.3.3.2.8 Aboveground tanks shall be provided with spill control that meets the requirements of 66.21.7.1 and 66.22.11. Tank fill connections shall be provided with a noncombustible spill containment device.

Exception: Tanks installed in vaults that meet the requirements of 42.3.3.3 need not meet this requirement. [30A: 4.3.2.8]

42.3.3.3 Vaults for Aboveground Tanks.

42.3.3.3.1 Scope. Paragraph 42.3.3.3 shall apply to installation of aboveground tanks in vaults and design and installation of such vaults. [**30A:**4.3.3.1]

42.3.3.3.2 General. Aboveground tanks shall be permitted to be installed in vaults that meet the requirements of 42.3.3.3. Except as modified by the provisions of 42.3.3.3, vaults shall meet all other applicable provisions of NFPA 30A. Vaults shall be constructed and listed in accordance with UL 2245, *Standard for Below-Grade Vaults for Flammable Liquid Storage Tanks.*

Table 42.3.3.2.4 Minimum Separation Requirements for Aboveground Tanks

Tank Type	Individual Tank Capacity (gal)[a]	Minimum Distance (ft)				
		From the Nearest Important Building on the Same Property	From Nearest Fuel Dispensing Device[b]	From Lot Line That Is or Can Be Built Upon[c]	From the Nearest Side of Any Public Way	Between Tanks
Tanks in vaults[d]	0–15,000	0	0	0	0	Separate compartments required for each tank
Protected aboveground tanks	Less than or equal to 6,000	5	0	15	5	3
	6,001–12,000	15	0	25	15	3
Fire-resistant tanks	0–12,000	25	25	50	25	3
Other tanks meeting the requirements of NFPA 30	0–12,000	50	50	100	50	3

For SI units, 1 ft = 0.30 m; 1 gal = 3.8 L.
[a]See 42.3.3.2.3 and 42.3.3.2.5.
[b]See 42.3.3.2.6.
[c]Including the opposite side of a public way.
[d]The separation distances given for vaults are measured from the outer perimeter of the vault.
[**30A:** Table 4.3.2.4]

Vaults shall be permitted to be either above or below grade. [**30A:**4.3.3.2]

42.3.3.3.3* Construction and Installation of Storage Tank Vaults.

42.3.3.3.3.1 Construction Requirements. Vaults shall be designed and constructed in accordance with 42.3.3.3.3.1.1 through 42.3.3.3.3.1.4. [**30:**25.5.1]

42.3.3.3.3.1.1 The top of an abovegrade vault that contains a tank storing Class I liquid or Class II or Class III liquid stored at a temperature above its flash point shall be constructed of noncombustible material and shall be designed to be weaker than the walls of the vault to ensure that the thrust of any explosion occurring inside the vault is directed upward before destructive internal pressure develops within the vault. [**30A:**4.3.3.3.1.1]

42.3.3.3.3.1.2 The top of an at-grade or belowgrade vault that contains a tank storing Class I liquid or Class II or Class III liquid stored at a temperature above its flash point shall be designed to relieve or contain the force of any explosion occurring inside the vault. [**30A:**4.3.3.3.1.2]

42.3.3.3.3.1.3 Adjacent vaults shall be permitted to share a common wall. [**30:**25.5.1.3]

42.3.3.3.3.1.4 Where required, the vault shall be wind and earthquake resistant, in accordance with recognized engineering standards. [**30:**25.5.1.4]

42.3.3.3.3.2 Installation Requirements. Storage tank vaults shall be installed in accordance with the requirements of 42.3.3.3.3.2.1 and 42.3.3.3.3.2.2. [**30:**25.5.2]

42.3.3.3.3.2.1 Each vault and its tank shall be anchored to resist uplifting by groundwater or flooding, including when the tank is empty. [**30:**25.5.2.1]

42.3.3.3.3.2.2 Vaults that are not resistant to damage from the impact of a motor vehicle shall be protected by collision barriers. [**30:**25.5.2.2]

42.3.3.3.4 Tank Selection and Arrangement.

42.3.3.3.4.1 Tanks installed in storage tank vaults shall be listed for aboveground use. [**30:**25.3.1.4]

42.3.3.3.4.2 Each tank shall be in its own vault and shall be completely enclosed by the vault. [**30:**25.3.1.5]

42.3.3.3.4.3 Sufficient clearance between the tank and the vault shall be provided to allow for visual inspection and maintenance of the tank and its appurtenances. [**30:**25.3.1.6]

42.3.3.3.4.4 Backfill shall not be permitted around the tank. [**30:**25.3.1.7]

42.3.3.3.5 Tank Appurtenances.

42.3.3.3.5.1 Vent pipes that are provided for normal tank venting shall terminate outside the vault and at least 12 ft (3.6 m) above ground level and shall meet the requirements of 66.27.8.1. [**30A:**4.3.3.5.1]

42.3.3.3.5.2 Emergency vents shall be vaportight and shall be permitted to discharge inside the vault. Long-bolt manhole covers shall not be permitted for this purpose. [**30A:**4.3.3.5.2]

42.3.3.3.5.3 An approved means of overfill protection shall be provided for tanks. The use of ball float valves shall be prohibited. [**30A:**4.3.3.5.3]

42.3.3.3.5.4 Fill connections for vaults installed inside buildings shall comply with 66.22.13.4. [**30A:**4.3.3.5.4]

42.3.3.3.6 Ventilation Systems for Storage Tank Vaults. [**30:**25.10]

42.3.3.3.6.1 Vaults that contain tanks storing Class I liquids shall be ventilated at a rate of not less than 1 cfm/ft^2 of floor area (0.3 m^3/min/m^2), but not less than 150 cfm (4 m^3/min). [**30:**25.10.1]

42.3.3.3.6.2 Such ventilation shall operate continuously or shall be designed to operate upon activation of a vapor and liquid detection system. [**30:**25.10.2]

42.3.3.3.6.3 Failure of the exhaust airflow shall automatically shut down the dispensing system. [**30:**25.10.3]

42.3.3.3.6.4 The exhaust system shall be designed to provide air movement across all parts of the vault floor. [**30:**25.10.4]

42.3.3.3.6.5 Supply and exhaust ducts shall extend to within 3 in. (75 mm), but not more than 12 in. (300 mm) of the floor. [**30:**25.10.5]

42.3.3.3.6.6 The exhaust system shall be installed in accordance with the provisions of NFPA 91, *Standard for Exhaust Systems for Air Conveying of Vapors, Gases, Mists, and Noncombustible Particulate Solids*. [**30:**25.10.6]

42.3.3.3.7 Vapor and Liquid Detection Systems.

42.3.3.3.7.1 Each vault shall be provided with an approved vapor and liquid detection system that is equipped with on-site audible and visual warning devices with battery backup. [**30:**25.15.1]

42.3.3.3.7.2 The vapor detection system shall sound an alarm when the system detects vapors that reach or exceed 25 percent of the lower flammable limit of the liquid stored. [**30:**25.15.2]

42.3.3.3.7.3 Vapor detectors shall be located no higher than 12 in. (300 mm) above the lowest point in the vault. [**30:**25.15.3]

42.3.3.3.7.4 The liquid detection systems shall sound an alarm upon detection of any liquid, including water. [**30:**25.15.4]

42.3.3.3.7.5 Liquid detectors shall be located in accordance with the manufacturer's instructions. [**30:**25.15.5]

42.3.3.3.7.6 Activation of either vapor detection system or liquid detection system shall cause a signal to be sounded at an approved, constantly attended location within the facility serving the tanks or at an approved location. [**30:**25.15.6]

42.3.3.3.8 In lieu of the separation distance requirements given in 66.22.4, separation distances between the vault and any of the following shall be permitted to be reduced to 0 ft (0 m), as measured from the outer perimeter of the vault wall:

(1) Any property line that is or can be built upon
(2) The near and far sides of a public way
(3) The nearest important building on the same property [**30:**25.4]

42.3.3.3.9 Inspection and Maintenance of Storage Tank Vaults and Equipment. Vaults and their required equipment shall be maintained in accordance with the requirements of 42.3.3.3. [**30:**25.16]

42.3.3.4 Additional Requirements for Fire-Resistant Aboveground Storage Tanks.

42.3.3.4.1 Fire-resistant tanks shall be tested and listed in accordance with UL 2080, *Standard for Fire Resistant Tanks for Flammable and Combustible Liquids*.[**30:** 22.9.1]

42.3.3.4.2 Fire-resistant tanks shall also meet both of the following requirements:

(1) The construction that provides the required fire-resistive protection shall reduce the heat transferred to the primary tank in order to limit the temperature of the primary tank to an average maximum rise of 800°F (430°C) and a single point maximum rise of 1000°F (540°C) and to prevent release of liquid, failure of the primary tank, failure of the supporting structure, and impairment of venting for a period of not less than 2 hours when tested using the fire exposure specified in UL 2080.
(2) Reduction in sizing of the emergency vents in accordance with 22.7.3.5 of NFPA 30 shall not be permitted. [**30:**22.9.2]

42.3.3.5 Protected Tanks. Protected aboveground tanks shall be tested and listed in accordance with ANSI/UL 2085, *Standard for Protected Aboveground Tanks for Flammable and Combustible Liquids*. [**30:**22.10.1]

42.3.3.5.1 Protected tanks shall also meet both of the following requirements:

(1) The construction that provides the required fire-resistive protection shall reduce the heat transferred to the primary tank in order to limit the temperature of the primary tank to an average maximum rise of 260°F (144°C) and a single point maximum rise of 400°F (204°C) and to prevent release of liquid, failure of the primary tank, failure of the supporting structure, and impairment of venting for a period of not less than 2 hours when tested using the fire exposure specified in ANSI/UL 2085.
(2) Reduction in sizing of the emergency vents in accordance with 22.7.3.5 of NFPA 30 shall not be permitted. [**30:**22.10.2]

42.3.3.6 Additional Requirements for All Aboveground Tanks.

42.3.3.6.1 All openings shall be located above the maximum liquid level. [**30A:**4.3.6.1]

42.3.3.6.2 Means shall be provided for determining the liquid level in each tank, and this means shall be accessible to the delivery operator. [**30A:**4.3.6.2]

42.3.3.6.3 Means shall be provided to sound an audible alarm when the liquid level in the tank reaches 90 percent of capacity. Means shall also be provided either to automatically stop the flow of liquid into the tank when the liquid level in the tank reaches 98 percent capacity or to restrict the flow of liquid into the tank to a maximum flow rate of 2.5 gpm (9.5 L/min) when the liquid in the tank reaches 95 percent capacity. These provisions shall not restrict or interfere with the operation of either the normal vent or the emergency vent. [**30A:**4.3.6.3]

42.3.3.6.4 Means shall be provided to prevent the release of liquid by siphon flow. [**30A:**4.3.6.4]

42.3.3.6.5 Shutoff and check valves shall be equipped with a pressure-relieving device that will relieve the pressure generated by thermal expansion back to the tank. [**30A:**4.3.6.5]

42.3.3.6.6 Fuel shall not be dispensed from the tank by either gravity flow or pressurization of the tank. [**30A:**4.3.6.6]

42.3.3.7 Physical Protection for All Outside Aboveground Tanks.

42.3.3.7.1 Tanks that are not enclosed in vaults shall be enclosed with a chain link fence at least 6 ft (1.8 m) high. The fence shall be separated from the tanks by at least 10 ft (3 m) and shall have a gate that is secured against unauthorized entry.

Exception: Tanks are not required to be enclosed with a fence if the property on which the tanks are located has a perimeter security fence. [**30A:***4.3.7.1]*

42.3.3.7.2* Guard posts or other approved means shall be provided to protect tanks that are subject to vehicular damage. When guard posts are installed, the following design shall be acceptable:

(1) They shall be constructed of steel not less than 4 in. (100 mm) in diameter and shall be filled with concrete.
(2) They shall be spaced not more than 4 ft (1.2 m) on center.
(3) They shall be set not less than 3 ft (0.9 m) deep in a concrete footing of not less than 15 in. (380 mm) diameter. [**30A:**4.3.7.2]

42.3.3.8* Corrosion Protection. Any portion of a tank or its piping that is in contact with the soil shall have properly engineered, installed, and maintained corrosion protection that meets the requirements of 66.21.4.5. [**30A:**4.3.8]

42.3.3.9 Storage of Liquids Inside Buildings. Storage of flammable and combustible liquids in motor fuel dispensing facility buildings and in repair garage buildings shall meet the requirements of this subsection. [**30A:**4.3.9]

42.3.3.9.1 Class I, II, and IIIA Liquids in Tanks Not Exceeding 120 Gal (454 L) Capacity and in Containers.

42.3.3.9.1.1 The aggregate quantity of Class I liquids stored in a tank that does not exceed 120 gal (454 L) capacity and in containers shall not exceed 120 gal (454 L). Liquids in storage shall be maintained in tanks or in approved containers that are closed or are fitted with an approved dispensing device that meets the requirements of 42.7.2.4.1. [**30A:**4.3.9.1.1]

42.3.3.9.1.2 Except as permitted under 42.3.3.9.1.3, the aggregate quantity of Class II and Class IIIA liquids stored in a tank that does not exceed 120 gal (454 L) capacity and in containers shall not exceed 240 gal (908 L). The quantity for each class shall not exceed 120 gal (454 L). Liquids in storage shall be maintained in tanks or in approved containers that are closed or are fitted with an approved dispensing device that meets the requirements of 42.7.2.4.1. [**30A:**4.3.9.1.2]

42.3.3.9.1.3 Where there are no Class I liquids stored, the aggregate quantities of Class II liquids shall not exceed 240 gal (908 L). [**30A:**4.3.9.1.3]

42.3.3.9.2 Class I, II, and IIIA Liquids in Tanks Exceeding 120 Gal (454 L) Capacity. Where installation of a tank that exceeds 120 gal (454 L) capacity in accordance with 42.3.3.2 is not practical because of building or property limitations, the tank shall be permitted to be installed in a building if it is enclosed as described in 42.3.3.3 and if the installation is specifically approved by the AHJ. [**30A:**4.3.9.2]

42.3.3.9.3 Class IIIB Liquids. The quantity of Class IIIB liquids in storage shall not be limited. Class IIIB liquids shall be permitted to be stored in and dispensed from tanks and containers that meet the requirements of Chapter 9 and Chapters 21 through 23 of NFPA 30 as applicable. Tanks storing Class IIIB liquids inside buildings shall be permitted to be located at, below, or above grade. Adequate drainage shall be provided. Tanks and containers that contain only crankcase drainings shall be considered as containing Class IIIB liquids. [30A:4.3.9.3]

42.3.3.10 Temporary Storage of Liquid Fuels. Aboveground tanks used for dispensing of motor fuels shall not be required to be permanently installed when located on premises not normally accessible to the public provided that all of the following requirements are met:

(1) Approval of the AHJ shall be required prior to bringing the tank to a site in the jurisdiction. In reviewing a proposed installation, the condition of the tank, the site where the tank will be located, installation and testing procedures, and operational procedures shall be evaluated prior to approval.
(2) The approval shall include a definite time limit after which the tank shall be removed from the site and relocated to an approved location.
(3) The tank shall comply with 42.3.3 and all other applicable provisions of NFPA 30A and NFPA 30.
(4) A tank containing liquid shall not be moved unless it has been specifically investigated and approved for movement while full or partially full. [30A:4.3.10]

42.4 Piping for Liquids.

42.4.1 Scope. Section 42.4 shall apply to piping systems consisting of pipe, tubing, flanges, bolting, gaskets, valves, fittings, flexible connectors, the pressure-containing parts of other components such as expansion joints and strainers, and devices that serve such purposes as mixing, separating, snubbing, distributing, metering, controlling flow, or secondary containment of liquids and associated vapors. [30A:5.1]

42.4.2 General Requirements for All Piping Systems.

42.4.2.1 The design, fabrication, assembly, test, and inspection of the piping system shall meet the requirements of Section 66.27.

Exception No. 1: Where dispensing is from a floating structure or pier, approved oil-resistant flexible hose shall be permitted to be used between shore piping and the piping on the floating structure or pier and between separate sections of the floating structure to accommodate changes in water level or shoreline, provided that the hose is either resistant to or shielded from damage by fire.

Exception No. 2: Low melting point rigid piping shall be permitted to be used between underground shore piping and a floating structure or pier and on the floating structure or pier itself, provided that the piping is protected from physical damage and stresses arising from impact, settlement, vibration, expansion, contraction, or tidal action and provided that the hose is either resistant to or shielded from damage by fire exposure. [30A:5.2.1]

42.4.2.2 Piping shall be located so that it is protected from physical damage. Piping that passes through a dike wall shall be designed to prevent excessive stresses that could result from settlement or fire exposure. [30A:5.2.2]

42.4.2.3 Any portion of a piping system that is in contact with the soil shall be protected from corrosion in accordance with good engineering practice. [30A:5.2.3]

42.4.2.4 All piping inside buildings but outside the motor fuel dispensing area shall be enclosed within a horizontal chase or a vertical shaft used only for this piping. Vertical shafts and horizontal chases shall be constructed of materials having a fire resistance rating of not less than 2 hours. [30A:5.2.4]

42.4.2.5 Each fill pipe shall be identified by color code or other marking to identify the product for which it is used. The color code or marking shall be maintained in legible condition throughout the life of the installation. [30A:5.2.5]

42.4.2.6 Shutoff and check valves shall be equipped with a pressure-relieving device that will relieve any pressure generated by thermal expansion of the contained liquid back to the storage tank. [30A:5.2.6]

42.4.2.7 Piping components made of low melting point materials shall be permitted to be used without backfill with the following sumps:

(1) Belowgrade underground tank sumps that are fitted with a cover
(2) Belowgrade piping connection sumps that are fitted with a cover
(3) Containment sumps, under the following conditions:
   (a) The sump is monitored to detect any leaks.
   (b) Any leaks can be controlled.
   (c) The components are either resistant to or shielded from damage by fire exposure.
(4) Containment sumps, provided the piping components can successfully pass the test procedures described in API 607, *Fire Test for Soft-Seated Quarter-Turn Valves* [30A:5.2.7]

42.5 Fuel Dispensing Systems.

42.5.1 Scope. Section 42.5 shall apply to the system and components that dispense fuel into the tanks of motor vehicles and marine craft. [30A:6.1]

42.5.2 General Requirements.

42.5.2.1 Dispensing devices installed outside at motor fuel dispensing stations shall be located as follows:

(1) 10 ft (3 m) or more from property lines
(2) 10 ft (3 m) or more from buildings, other than canopies, having combustible exterior wall surfaces or buildings having noncombustible exterior wall surfaces that are not a part of a 1 hr fire-resistive assembly
(3) Such that all parts of the vehicle being served will be on the premises of the service station
(4) Such that the nozzle, when the hose is fully extended, will not reach within 5 ft (1.5 m) of building openings [30A:6.2.1]

42.5.2.2 Liquids shall not be dispensed by applying pressure to drums, barrels, and similar containers. Listed pumps taking suction through the top of the container or listed self-closing faucets shall be used. [30A:6.2.2]

42.5.2.3* Fuel dispensing systems, including dispensers, hoses, nozzles, breakaway fittings, swivels, flexible connectors, dispenser emergency shutoff valves, vapor recovery systems, and pumps that are used for alcohol-blended motor fuels shall be listed or approved for the specific purpose. [30A:6.2.3]

42.5.3 Requirements for Dispensing Devices.

42.5.3.1 Class I and Class II liquids shall be transferred from tanks by means of fixed pumps designed and equipped to allow control of the flow and prevent leakage or accidental discharge. [**30A:**6.3.1]

42.5.3.2 Dispensing devices for Class I and II liquids shall be listed. [**30A:**6.3.2]

42.5.3.2.1 Existing listed or labeled dispensing devices shall be permitted to be modified provided that the modifications made are "Listed by Report" by an approved testing laboratory or as otherwise approved by the AHJ. Modification proposals shall contain a description of the component parts used in the modification and the recommended methods of installation on specific dispensing devices. Modification proposals shall be made available to the AHJ upon request. [**30A:**6.3.2.1]

42.5.3.3 A control shall be provided that will permit the pump to operate only when a dispensing nozzle is removed from its bracket or normal position with respect to the dispensing device and the switch on this dispensing device is manually actuated. This control shall also stop the pump when all nozzles have been returned to their brackets or to their normal nondispensing position. [**30A:**6.3.3]

42.5.3.4 Dispensing devices shall be mounted on a concrete island or shall otherwise be protected against collision damage by means acceptable to the AHJ. Dispensing devices shall be securely bolted in place. If located indoors, dispensing devices shall also be located in a position where they cannot be struck by a vehicle that is out of control descending a ramp or other slope. Dispensing devices shall be installed in accordance with the manufacturers' instructions. [**30A:**6.3.4]

42.5.3.5 Dispensing devices used to fill portable containers with home heating fuels shall be located at least 20 ft (6 m) from any dispensing devices for motor fuels. [**30A:**6.3.5]

42.5.3.6 Inspections. Dispensing equipment shall be periodically inspected by a person who is knowledgeable in the operation of the equipment to verify that it is in proper working order and is not leaking. [**30A:**6.3.6]

42.5.3.6.1* Exterior Inspection. A visual inspection of the fuel dispenser and its associated hanging hardware (hose nozzle valve, hose, breakaway valve, and hose swivel) shall be conducted at least weekly and shall be documented. Documentation shall be available for review by the AHJ upon request. [**30A:**6.3.6.1]

42.5.3.6.2* Internal Dispenser Cabinet Inspection. An inspection of the fuel dispensing equipment that is located inside the dispenser cabinet shall be conducted. The interior of the fuel dispenser cabinet shall be inspected for signs of leaks, damage, corrosion, or weathering, with particular attention to the sump area and joints and castings of fluid handling components. The inspection shall be conducted at least monthly and shall be documented. Documentation shall be available for review by the AHJ upon request. [**30A:**6.3.6.2]

42.5.3.6.3 Maintenance When maintenance to dispensing devices is necessary and such maintenance is capable of causing accidental release or ignition of liquid, the following precautions shall be taken before such maintenance is begun:

(1) Only persons knowledgeable in performing the required maintenance shall perform the work.
(2) All electrical power to the dispensing devices, to the pump serving the dispensing devices, and to all associated control circuits shall be shut off at the main electrical disconnect panel.
(3) The emergency shutoff valve at the dispenser, if installed, shall be closed.
(4) All vehicular traffic and unauthorized persons shall be prevented from coming within 20 ft (6 m) of the dispensing device. [**30A:**6.3.6.3]

42.5.3.7 Motor vehicle traffic patterns at motor fuel dispensing facilities shall be designed to inhibit movement of vehicles that are not being fueled from passing through the dispensing area. [**30A:**6.3.7]

42.5.3.8 At unattended self-serve motor fuel dispensing facilities, coin- and currency–type devices shall be permitted only with the approval of the AHJ. [**30A:**6.3.8]

42.5.3.9 Where liquid is supplied to the dispensing device under pressure, a listed, rigidly anchored emergency shutoff valve incorporating a fusible link or other thermally actuated device, designed to close automatically in the event of severe impact or fire exposure, shall be installed in the supply line at the base of each individual island-type dispenser or at the inlet of each overhead dispensing device. The emergency shutoff valve shall be installed in accordance with the manufacturer's instructions. The emergency shutoff valve shall not incorporate a slip-joint feature.

Exception: As provided for in 42.5.3.10. [30A:6.3.9]

42.5.3.9.1 The automatic-closing feature of this valve shall be tested at the time of installation and at least once a year thereafter by manually tripping the hold-open linkage. Records of such tests shall be kept at the premises or shall be made available for inspection by the AHJ within 24 hours of a verbal or written request. [**30A:**6.3.9.1]

42.5.3.10 Where a suction-type dispensing system includes a booster pump or where a suction-type dispensing system is supplied by a tank in a manner that produces a gravity head on the dispensing device, a vacuum-actuated shutoff valve with a shear section or equivalent-type valve listed and labeled in accordance with UL 842, *Standard for Valves for Flammable Fluids*, shall be installed directly under the dispensing device. [**30A:**6.3.10]

42.5.4 Requirements for Remote/Submersible Pumps. Subsection 42.5.4 shall apply to systems for dispensing Class I and Class II liquids where the liquids are transferred from storage to individual or multiple dispensing devices by pumps located other than at the dispensing devices. [**30A:**6.4]

42.5.4.1 Pumps shall be listed and shall be designed or equipped so that no part of the system will be subjected to pressures above its allowable working pressure. [**30A:**6.4.1]

42.5.4.2 Each pump shall have installed on the discharge side a listed leak detection device that will provide an audible or visible indication if the piping or a dispenser is leaking. Each leak-detecting device shall be checked and tested at least annually according to the manufacturers' specifications to ensure proper installation and operation.

Exception: A leak detection device shall not be required if all piping is visible. [30A:6.4.2]

42.5.4.3 Pumps installed above grade outside of buildings shall be located not less than 10 ft (3 m) from lines of adjoining property that can be built upon and not less than 5 ft (1.5 m) from any building opening. Where an outside pump location is impractical, pumps shall be permitted to be installed inside buildings as provided for dispensers in 42.5.3.4 or in sumps as provided in

42.5.4.4. Pumps shall be anchored and protected against physical damage. [**30A**:6.4.3]

42.5.4.4 Sumps for subsurface pumps or piping manifolds of submersible pumps shall withstand the external forces to which they can be subjected without damage to the pump, tank, or piping. The sump shall be no larger than necessary for inspection and maintenance and shall be provided with a fitted cover. [**30A**:6.4.4]

42.5.5 Requirements for Dispensing Hose.

42.5.5.1 Listed hose assemblies shall be used to dispense fuel. Hose length at automotive motor fuel dispensing facilities shall not exceed 18 ft (5.5 m). Where hose length at marine motor fuel dispensing facilities exceeds 18 ft (5.5 m), the hose shall be secured so as to protect it from damage. [**30A**:6.5.1]

42.5.5.2 A listed emergency breakaway device designed to retain liquid on both sides of the breakaway point shall be installed on each hose dispensing Class I and II liquids. Such devices shall be installed and maintained in accordance with the manufacturer's instructions. [**30A**:6.5.2]

42.5.5.3 Where hose are attached to a hose-retrieving mechanism, the listed emergency breakaway device shall be installed between the point of attachment of the hose-retrieving mechanism to the hose and the hose nozzle valve.

Exception: Such devices shall not be required at marine motor fuel dispensing facilities. [30A:6.5.3]

42.5.6 Requirements for Fuel Delivery Nozzles.

42.5.6.1 An automatic closing–type hose nozzle valve, with a latch-open device and listed and labeled in accordance with ANSI/UL 842, *Standard for Valves for Flammable Fluids*, or ANSI/UL 2586, *Standard for Hose Nozzle Valves*, shall be provided on island-type dispensing devices used to dispense Class I or Class II liquids. [**30A**:6.6.1]

42.5.6.1.1 Any modification of the dispensing nozzle shall be listed or approved by the manufacturer of the nozzle. [**30A**:6.6.1.1]

42.5.6.2* At any installation where an automatic closing–type dispensing nozzle is used, the nozzle valve shall include a feature that causes or requires the closing of the hose nozzle valve before product flow can be resumed or before the hose nozzle valve can be replaced in its normal position in the dispenser. [**30A**:6.6.2]

42.5.6.3 Overhead-type dispensing devices shall be provided with a listed, automatic closing–type hose nozzle valve without a latch-open device.

Exception: A listed, automatic closing–type hose nozzle valve with a latch-open device shall be permitted to be used if the hose nozzle valve will close automatically in the event the valve is released from a fill opening or upon impact. [30A:6.6.3]

42.5.6.4 Dispensing nozzles used at marine motor fuel dispensing facilities shall be of the listed automatic closing–type hose nozzle valve without a latch-open device. [**30A**:6.6.4]

42.5.7 Emergency Electrical Disconnects. Fuel dispensing systems shall be provided with one or more clearly identified emergency shutoff devices or electrical disconnects. Such devices or disconnects shall be installed in approved locations but not less than 20 ft (6 m) or more than 100 ft (30 m) from the fuel dispensing devices that they serve. Emergency shutoff devices or electrical disconnects shall disconnect power to all dispensing devices; to all remote pumps serving the dispensing devices; to all associated power, control, and signal circuits; and to all other electrical equipment in the hazardous (classified) locations surrounding the fuel dispensing devices. When more than one emergency shutoff device or electrical disconnect is provided, all devices shall be interconnected. Resetting from an emergency shutoff condition shall require manual intervention and the manner of resetting shall be approved by the AHJ.

Exception: Intrinsically safe electrical equipment need not meet this requirement. [30A:6.7]

42.5.7.1 At attended motor fuel dispensing facilities, the devices or disconnects shall be readily accessible to the attendant. [**30A**:6.7.1]

42.5.7.2 At unattended motor fuel dispensing facilities, the devices or disconnects shall be readily accessible to patrons and at least one additional device or disconnect shall be readily accessible to each group of dispensing devices on an individual island. [**30A**:6.7.2]

42.5.8 Vapor Recovery Systems.

42.5.8.1 Dispensing devices that incorporate vapor recovery shall be listed. [**30A**:6.8.1]

42.5.8.2 Hose nozzle valves used on vapor recovery systems shall be listed for the purpose. [**30A**:6.8.2]

42.5.8.3 Means shall be provided in the vapor return path from each dispensing outlet to prevent the discharge of vapors when the hose nozzle valve is in its normal nondispensing position. [**30A**:6.8.3]

42.6 Building Construction Requirements. The construction of buildings and portions of buildings that are motor fuel dispensing facilities or repair garages shall comply with Chapter 30.

42.7 Operational Requirements.

42.7.1 Scope. Section 42.7 shall apply to those requirements that relate to the operation of motor fuel dispensing facilities and fuel dispensing systems. [**30A**:9.1]

42.7.2 Basic Requirements.

42.7.2.1* Inventory Control. Accurate daily inventory records shall be maintained and reconciled for all liquid fuel storage tanks for indication of possible leakage from tanks or piping. The records shall be kept on the premises or shall be made available to the AHJ for inspection within 24 hours of a written or verbal request. The records shall include, as a minimum and by product, daily reconciliation between sales, use, receipts, and inventory on hand. If there is more than one storage system serving an individual pump or dispensing device for any product, the reconciliation shall be maintained separately for each system. [**30A**:9.2.1]

42.7.2.2 Tank Filling and Bulk Delivery.

42.7.2.2.1 Delivery operations shall meet all applicable requirements of NFPA 385 and the requirements of 42.7.2.2.2 through 42.7.2.2.4. [**30A**:9.2.2.1]

42.7.2.2.2 The delivery vehicle shall be separated from any aboveground tank by at least 25 ft (7.6 m).

Exception No. 1: No minimum separation distance shall be required for tanks that are filled by gravity.

Exception No. 2: The required minimum separation distance shall be permitted to be reduced to 15 ft (4.6 m) where the fuel being delivered is not a Class I liquid. [30A:9.2.2.2]

42.7.2.2.3 The delivery vehicle shall be located so that all parts of the vehicle are on the premises when delivery is made.

Exception: This requirement shall not apply to existing fuel dispensing facilities and fuel dispensing facilities inside buildings. [30A:9.2.2.3]

42.7.2.2.4 Tank filling shall not begin until the delivery operator has determined that the tank has sufficient available capacity (ullage). [**30A:**9.2.2.4]

42.7.2.2.5 Tanks shall be filled through a liquidtight connection. [**30A:**9.2.2.5]

42.7.2.2.5.1 Where an aboveground tank is filled by means of fixed piping, either a check valve and shutoff valve with a quick-connect coupling or a check valve with a dry-break coupling shall be installed in the piping at a point where connection and disconnection is made between the tank and the delivery vehicle. This device shall be protected from tampering and physical damage. [**30A:**9.2.2.5.1]

42.7.2.2.5.2 Underground tanks and tanks in belowgrade vaults shall be filled through a liquidtight connection within a spill container. [**30A:**9.2.2.5.2]

42.7.2.3 Dispensing into Containers.

42.7.2.3.1* Class I or Class II liquids shall not be dispensed into portable containers unless the container is constructed of metal or is approved by the AHJ, has a tight closure, and is fitted with a spout or so designed that the contents can be poured without spilling. The hose nozzle valve shall be manually held open during the dispensing operation. [**30A:**9.2.3.1]

42.7.2.3.2 No sale or purchase of any Class I, Class II, or Class III liquids shall be made in containers unless such containers are clearly marked with the name of the product contained therein. [**30A:**9.2.3.2]

42.7.2.3.3 Portable containers of 12 gal (45 L) capacity or less shall not be filled while they are in or on a motor vehicle or marine craft. [**30A:**9.2.3.3]

42.7.2.4 Dispensing from a Tank That Does Not Exceed 120 Gal (454 L) and from Containers Inside Buildings. Dispensing of flammable and combustible liquids from a tank not exceeding 120 gal (454 L) capacity and from containers in a motor fuel dispensing facility or in a repair garage building shall meet the requirements of 42.7.2.4.1 and 42.7.2.4.2. *(See 42.3.3.9 for storage quantity limitations.)* [**30A:**9.2.4]

42.7.2.4.1 Not more than one container of Class I liquid shall be permitted to be provided with a dispensing pump inside a building at any one time. The number of tanks or containers of Class II or Class IIIA liquids fitted for dispensing at any one time shall not be limited, except as provided for in 42.3.3.9.2. The number of tanks or containers of Class IIIB liquids fitted for dispensing at any one time shall not be limited. [**30A:**9.2.4.1]

42.7.2.4.2 Class I, Class II, and Class IIIA liquids shall not be dispensed by applying pressure to tanks or containers. Listed pumps that take suction through the top of the tank or container or listed self-closing faucets shall be used. [**30A:**9.2.4.2]

42.7.2.5 Basic Fire Control.

42.7.2.5.1 Sources of Ignition. Smoking materials, including matches and lighters, shall not be used within 20 ft (6 m) of areas used for fueling, servicing fuel systems of internal combustion engines, or receiving or dispensing of Class I and Class II liquids. The motors of all equipment being fueled shall be shut off during the fueling operation except for emergency generators, pumps, and so forth, where continuing operation is essential. [**30A:**9.2.5.1]

42.7.2.5.2 Fire Extinguishers. Each motor fuel dispensing facility or repair garage shall be provided with fire extinguishers installed, inspected, and maintained as required by Section 13.6. Extinguishers for outside motor fuel dispensing areas shall be provided according to the extra (high) hazard requirements for Class B hazards, except that the maximum travel distance to an 80 B:C extinguisher shall be permitted to be 100 ft (30.48 m). [**30A:**9.2.5.2]

42.7.2.5.3 Fire Suppression Systems. Where required, automatic fire suppression systems shall be installed in accordance with the appropriate NFPA standard, manufacturers' instructions, and the listing requirements of the systems. [**30A:**9.2.5.3]

42.7.2.5.4* Signs. Warning signs shall be conspicuously posted in the dispensing area and shall incorporate the following or equivalent wording:

> **WARNING:** It is unlawful and dangerous to dispense gasoline into unapproved containers.
> No smoking.
> Stop motor.
> No filling of portable containers in or on a motor vehicle.
> Place container on ground before filling.
> Discharge your static electricity before fueling by touching a metal surface away from the nozzle.
> Do not re-enter your vehicle while gasoline is pumping.
> If a fire starts, **do not** remove nozzle — back away immediately.
> Do not allow individuals under licensed age to use the pump.
> [**30A:**9.2.5.4]

42.7.2.6 Waste Handling.

42.7.2.6.1 Crankcase drainings and waste liquids shall not be dumped into sewers, into streams, or on the ground. They shall be stored in approved tanks or containers outside any building, or in tanks installed in accordance with Chapters 4 and 5 of NFPA 30A, until removed from the premises.

Exception: As provided for in 42.3.3.9.3. [30A:9.2.6.1]

42.7.2.6.2 The contents of oil separators and traps of floor drainage systems shall be collected at sufficiently frequent intervals to prevent oil from being carried into sewers. [**30A:**9.2.6.2]

42.7.2.7 Housekeeping. The dispensing area and the area within any dike shall be kept free of vegetation, debris, and any other material that is not necessary to the proper operation of the motor fuel dispensing facility. [**30A:**9.2.7]

42.7.2.8 Fire Doors. Fire doors shall be kept unobstructed at all times. Appropriate signs and markings shall be used. [**30A:**9.2.8]

42.7.3 Operating Requirements for Full-Service Motor Fuel Dispensing Facilities. Each motor fuel dispensing facility shall have an attendant or supervisor on duty whenever the facility is open for business. The attendant or supervisor shall dispense liquids into fuel tanks or into containers, except as covered in 42.7.4 and 42.7.5. [**30A:**9.3]

42.7.4 Operating Requirements for Attended Self-Service Motor Fuel Dispensing Facilities.

42.7.4.1 "Self-service motor fuel dispensing facility" shall mean that portion of a property where liquids used as motor fuels are stored and dispensed from fixed, approved dispensing equipment into the fuel tanks of motor vehicles by persons other than the facility attendant and shall also include, where provided, facilities for the sale of other retail products. [**30A:**9.4.1]

42.7.4.2 There shall be at least one attendant on duty while the self-service facility is open for business. The attendant's primary function shall be to supervise, observe, and control the dispensing of Class I liquids while said liquids are being dispensed. [**30A:**9.4.2]

42.7.4.3 The responsibility of the attendant shall be as follows:

(1) Prevent the dispensing of Class I liquids into portable containers not in compliance with 42.7.2.3.1
(2) Prevent the use of hose nozzle valve latch-open devices that do not comply with 42.5.6.1
(3) Control sources of ignition
(4) Immediately activate emergency controls and notify the fire department of any fire or other emergency
(5) Handle accidental spills and fire extinguishers if needed [**30A:**9.4.3]

42.7.4.3.1 The attendant or supervisor on duty shall be mentally and physically capable of performing the functions and assuming the responsibility prescribed in 42.7.4. [**30A:**9.4.3.1]

42.7.4.4 Operating instructions shall be conspicuously posted in the dispensing area. [**30A:**9.4.4]

42.7.5 Operating Requirements for Unattended Self-Service Motor Fuel Dispensing Facilities.

42.7.5.1 Unattended self-service facilities shall be permitted, where approved by the AHJ. [**30A:**9.5.1]

42.7.5.2 Operating instructions shall be conspicuously posted in the dispensing area. The instructions shall include location of emergency controls and a requirement that the user stay outside of his/her vehicle and in view of the fueling nozzle during dispensing. [**30A:**9.5.2]

42.7.5.3 In addition to the warning signs specified in 42.7.2.5.4, emergency instructions shall be conspicuously posted in the dispenser area. The instructions shall incorporate the following or equivalent wording:

Emergency Instructions

In case of fire or spill

(1) Use emergency stop button.

(2) Report accident by calling (*specify local fire number*). Report location.

[**30A:**9.5.3]

42.7.5.4 A listed, automatic closing–type hose nozzle valve with latch-open device shall be provided. The hose nozzle valve shall meet the requirements of 42.5.6.2. [**30A:**9.5.4]

42.7.5.5 A telephone or other approved, clearly identified means to notify the fire department shall be provided on the site in a location approved by the AHJ. [**30A:**9.5.5]

42.7.5.6* Additional fire protection shall be provided where required by the AHJ. [**30A:**9.5.6]

42.7.6 Refueling from Tank Vehicles. The dispensing of Class I and Class II liquids in the open from a tank vehicle to a motor vehicle located at commercial, industrial, governmental, or manufacturing establishments and intended for fueling vehicles used in connection with their businesses shall be permitted only if all of the requirements of 42.7.6.1 through 42.7.6.7 have been met. [**30A:**9.6]

42.7.6.1 An inspection of the premises and operations shall be made and operations shall not be conducted unless approved by the AHJ. [**30A:**9.6.1]

42.7.6.2 The tank vehicle shall comply with the requirements of NFPA 385. [**30A:**9.6.2]

42.7.6.3 The dispensing hose shall not exceed 50 ft (15 m) in length. [**30A:**9.6.3]

42.7.6.4 The dispensing nozzle shall be a listed, automatic closing–type without a latch-open device. [**30A:**9.6.4]

42.7.6.5 Nighttime deliveries shall only be made in areas deemed adequately lighted by the AHJ. [**30A:**9.6.5]

42.7.6.6 The tank vehicle flasher lights shall be in operation while dispensing operations are in progress. [**30A:**9.6.6]

42.7.6.7 Expansion space shall be left in each fuel tank to prevent overflow in the event of temperature increase. [**30A:**9.6.7]

42.8 Additional Requirements for CNG, LNG, Hydrogen, and LPG.

42.8.1 Scope. Section 42.8 shall apply where CNG, LNG, compressed or liquefied hydrogen, or LP-Gas, or combinations of these, are dispensed as motor vehicle fuels along with Class I or Class II liquids that are also dispensed as motor vehicle fuels. [**30A:**12.1]

42.8.2 General Requirements.

42.8.2.1 The installation and use of CNG and LNG systems shall meet the requirements of NFPA 52 except as modified by Section 42.8. The installation and use of hydrogen systems shall meet the requirements of NFPA 2 except as modified by Section 42.8. The installation and use of LP-Gas systems shall meet the requirements of NFPA 58 except as modified by Section 42.8. [**30A:**12.2.1]

42.8.2.2 A means shall be provided that connects to the dispenser supply piping and that prevents flow in the event that the dispenser is displaced from its mounting. [**30A:**12.2.2]

42.8.2.3 Dispensing devices for CNG, LNG, hydrogen, and LP-Gas shall be listed. [**30A:**12.2.3]

42.8.2.4 Listed hose assemblies shall be used to dispense fuel. Hose length at automotive motor fuel dispensing facilities shall not exceed 18 ft (5.5 m). [**30A:**12.2.4]

42.8.3 Fuel Storage.

42.8.3.1 Aboveground tanks storing CNG or LNG shall be separated from any adjacent property line that is or can be built upon, any public way, and the nearest important building on the same property by not less than the distances given in Section 8.4 of NFPA 52. [**30A:**12.3.1]

42.8.3.2 Aboveground tanks storing hydrogen shall be separated from any adjacent property line that is or can be built upon, any public way, and the nearest important building on the same property by not less than the distances given in NFPA 2. [**30A:**12.3.2]

42.8.3.3 Aboveground tanks storing LP-Gas shall be separated from any adjacent property line that is or can be built upon, any public way, and the nearest important building on the same property by not less than the distances given in Section 6.3 of NFPA 58. [**30A:**12.3.3]

42.8.3.4* Aboveground tanks storing CNG, LNG, or LP-Gas shall be separated from each other by at least 20 ft (6 m) and from dispensing devices that dispense liquid or gaseous motor vehicle fuels by at least 20 ft (6 m).

Exception No. 1: This required separation shall not apply to tanks storing or handling fuels of the same chemical composition.

Exception No. 2: When both the gaseous fuel storage and dispensing equipment are at least 50 ft (15 m) from any other aboveground motor fuel storage or dispensing equipment, the requirements of NFPA 52 or NFPA 58, whichever is applicable, shall apply. [30A:12.3.4]

42.8.3.5 Aboveground storage tanks for the storage of CNG, LNG, or LP-Gas shall be provided with physical protection in accordance with 42.3.3.7. [**30A:** 12.3.5]

42.8.3.6 Horizontal separation shall not be required between aboveground tanks storing CNG, LNG, or LP-Gas and underground tanks containing Class I or Class II liquids, provided the structural limitations of the underground tanks are not exceeded. [**30A:**12.3.6]

42.8.4 Dispenser Installations Beneath Canopies. Where CNG or LNG dispensers are installed beneath a canopy or enclosure, either the canopy or enclosure shall be designed to prevent accumulation or entrapment of ignitable vapors or all electrical equipment installed beneath the canopy or enclosure shall be suitable for Class I, Division 2 hazardous (classified) locations. [**30A:**12.4]

42.8.5 Specific Requirements for LP-Gas Dispensing Devices.

42.8.5.1 Dispensing devices for LP-Gas shall meet all applicable requirements of Chapter 69 and NFPA 58. [**30A:**12.5.1]

42.8.5.2 Dispensing devices for LP-Gas shall be located as follows:

(1) At least 10 ft (3 m) from any dispensing device for Class I liquids
(2) At least 5 ft (1.5 m) from any dispensing device for Class I liquids where the following conditions exist:
   (a) The LP-Gas deliver nozzle and filler valve release no more than 0.1 oz (4 cm^3) of liquid upon disconnection.
   (b) The fixed maximum liquid level gauge remains closed during the entire refueling process. [**30A:**12.5.2]

42.8.6 Electrical Equipment.

42.8.6.1 All electrical wiring and electrical utilization equipment shall be of a type specified by, and shall be installed in accordance with, Section 11.1. [**30A:**12.6.1]

42.8.6.2* Table 42.8.6.2 shall be used to delineate and classify areas for the purpose of installation of electrical wiring and electrical utilization equipment. [**30A:**12.6.2]

42.9 Marine Fueling.

42.9.1 Scope.

42.9.1.1 Section 42.9 shall apply to that portion of a property where liquids used as fuels are stored, handled, and dispensed from equipment located on shore or from equipment located on piers, wharves, or floating docks into the fuel tanks of marine craft, including incidental activity, except as covered elsewhere in NFPA 30A or in other NFPA standards. [**30A:**11.1.1]

42.9.1.2 Section 42.9 shall not apply to the following:

(1) Bulk plant or terminal loading and unloading facilities
(2) Transfer of liquids utilizing a flange-to-flange closed transfer piping system
(3) Marine motor fuel dispensing facilities where liquids used as fuels are stored and dispensed into the fuel tanks of marine craft of 300 gross tons (272 metric tons) or more [**30A:**11.1.2]

42.9.1.3 For the purpose of Section 42.9, the word *pier* shall also mean dock, floating dock, and wharf. [**30A:**11.1.3]

42.9.1.4 Permits. Permits, where required, shall comply with Section 1.12.

42.9.2 Storage.

42.9.2.1 Liquids shall be stored in tanks or containers complying with 42.3.3. [**30A:**11.2.1]

42.9.2.2* Tanks that supply marine motor fuel dispensing facilities shall be located on shore or on a pier of the solid-fill type. Pumps that are not integral with the dispensing device shall also be located on shore or on a pier of the solid-fill type.

Exception: Tanks shall be permitted with the approval of the AHJ to be located on a pier, provided the installation meets all applicable requirements of Chapters 4 and 5 of NFPA 30A and 21.6.2 of NFPA 30 and the quantity stored does not exceed 1100 gal (4164 L) aggregate capacity. [30A:11.2.2]

42.9.2.3 Where a tank is at an elevation that produces a gravity head on the dispensing device, the tank outlet shall be equipped with a device, such as a normally closed solenoid valve, that will prevent gravity flow from the tank to the dispenser. This device shall be located adjacent to and downstream of the outlet valve specified by 66.22.13.1. The device shall be installed and adjusted so that liquid cannot flow by gravity from the tank to the dispenser if the piping or hose fails when the dispenser is not in use. [**30A:**11.2.3]

42.9.3 Piping Systems.

42.9.3.1 Piping shall be installed in accordance with all applicable requirements of Chapter 5 of NFPA 30A. [**30A:**11.3.1]

42.9.3.2 Piping systems shall be supported and protected against physical damage and stresses arising from impact, settlement, vibration, expansion, contraction, and tidal action. [**30A:**11.3.2]

42.9.3.3 Means shall be provided to ensure flexibility of the piping system in the event of motion of the pier. Flexible piping shall be of a type designed to withstand the forces and pressures exerted upon the piping. [**30A:**11.3.3]

42.9.3.4 Where dispensing is from a floating structure or pier, approved oil-resistant flexible hose shall be permitted to be used between shore piping and the piping on a floating structure or pier and between separate sections of the floating structure to accommodate changes in water level or shoreline, provided that the hose is either resistant to or shielded from damage by fire. [**30A:**11.3.4]

42.9.3.5 A valve to shut off the liquid supply from shore shall be provided in each pipeline at or near the approach to the pier and at the shore end of each marine pipeline adjacent to the point where each flexible hose is attached. [**30A:**11.3.5]

Table 42.8.6.2 Electrical Equipment Classified Areas for Dispensing Devices

Dispensing Device	Extent of Classified Area	
	Class I, Division 1	**Class I, Division 2**
Compressed natural gas (CNG)	Entire space within the dispenser enclosure	5 ft (1.5 m) in all directions from dispenser enclosure
Liquefied natural gas (LNG)	Entire space within the dispenser enclosure and 5 ft (1.5 m) in all directions from the dispenser enclosure	10 ft (3 m) in all directions from the dispenser enclosure
Liquefied petroleum gas (LP-Gas)	Entire space within the dispenser enclosure; 18 in. (46 cm) from the exterior surface of the dispenser enclosure to an elevation of 4 ft (1.22 m) above the base of the dispenser; the entire pit or open space beneath the dispenser and within 20 ft (6 m) horizontally from any edge of the dispenser when the pit or trench is not mechanically ventilated	Up to 18 in. (46 cm) above ground and within 20 ft (6 m) horizontally from any edge of the dispenser enclosure, including pits or trenches within this area when provided with adequate mechanical ventilation

[**30A:** Table 12.6.2]

42.9.4 Fuel Dispensing System.

42.9.4.1 All hose shall be listed. Where hose length exceeds 18 ft (5.5 m), the hose shall be secured so as to protect it from damage. [**30A:**11.4.1]

42.9.4.2 Dispensing nozzles shall be of the automatic-closing type without a latch-open device. [**30A:**11.4.2]

42.9.4.3 Dispensing devices shall be permitted to be located on open piers, on shore, or on piers of the solid-fill type and shall be located apart from other structures so as to provide room for safe ingress to and egress from marine craft. [**30A:**11.4.3]

42.9.4.4 Dispensing devices shall be located so that exposure to all other operational marina or pleasure boat berthing area facilities is minimized. Where tide and weather conditions permit, liquid fuel handling shall be outside the main berthing areas. Where located inside marina or pleasure craft berthing areas, fueling facilities shall be located so that, in case of fire aboard a marine craft alongside, the danger to other craft near the facility is minimized. [**30A:**11.4.4]

42.9.4.5 No vessel or marine craft shall be made fast to any other vessel or marine craft occupying a berth at a fuel dispensing location during fueling operations. [**30A:**11.4.5]

42.9.4.6 A marine motor fuel dispensing facility located at a bulk plant shall be separated by a fence or other approved barrier from areas in which bulk plant operations are conducted. Dispensing devices shall not be supplied by aboveground tanks located in the bulk plant. Marine motor fuel dispensing facility storage tanks shall not be connected by piping to aboveground tanks located in the bulk plant. [**30A:**11.4.6]

42.9.4.7 Each marine motor fuel dispensing facility shall have an attendant or supervisor on duty whenever the facility is open for business. The attendant's primary function shall be to supervise, observe, and control the dispensing of liquids. [**30A:**11.4.7]

42.9.5 Sources of Ignition.

42.9.5.1 All electrical components for dispensing liquids shall be installed in accordance with Chapter 8 of NFPA 30A. [**30A:**11.5.1]

42.9.5.2 All electrical equipment shall be installed and used in accordance with the requirements of Section 11.1 as it applies to wet, damp, and hazardous locations. [**30A:**11.5.2]

42.9.5.3 Clearly identified emergency electrical disconnects that are readily accessible in case of fire or physical damage at any dispensing unit shall be provided on each marine wharf. The disconnects shall be interlocked to shut off power to all pump motors from any individual location and shall be manually reset only from a master switch. Each such disconnect shall be identified by an approved sign stating EMERGENCY PUMP SHUTOFF in 2 in. (50 mm) red capital letters. [**30A:**11.5.3]

42.9.5.4 All electrical wiring for power and lighting shall be installed on the side of the wharf opposite from the liquid piping system. [**30A:**11.5.4]

42.9.5.5 Smoking materials, including matches and lighters, shall not be used within 20 ft (6 m) of areas used for fueling, servicing fuel systems for internal combustion engines, or receiving or dispensing of Class I liquids. Conspicuous NO SMOKING signs shall be posted within sight of the customer being served. [**30A:**11.5.5]

42.9.5.6 The motors of all equipment being fueled shall be shut off during the fueling operation, except for emergency generators, pumps, and so forth, where continuing operation is essential. [**30A:**11.5.6]

42.9.6 Electrical Installations.

42.9.6.1 Where excessive stray currents are encountered, piping handling Class I and Class II liquids shall be electrically isolated from the shore piping. [**30A:**8.5.1]

42.9.6.2* Pipelines on piers shall be bonded and grounded. Bonding and grounding connections on all pipelines shall be located on the pier side of hose riser insulating flanges, if used, and shall be accessible for inspection. [**30A:**8.5.2]

42.9.6.3 The fuel delivery nozzle shall be put into contact with the vessel fill pipe before the flow of fuel commences, and this bonding contact shall be continuously maintained until fuel flow has stopped, to avoid the possibility of electrostatic discharge. [**30A:**8.5.3]

42.9.6.4* Bonding and Grounding.

42.9.6.4.1* Pipelines on piers shall be bonded and grounded. Bonding and grounding connections on all pipelines shall be located on the pier side of hose riser insulating flanges, if used, and shall be accessible for inspection. [**30A:**11.6.1]

42.9.6.4.2 The fuel delivery nozzle shall be put into contact with the vessel fill pipe before the flow of fuel commences and this bonding contact shall be continuously maintained until fuel flow has stopped to avoid possibility of electrostatic discharge. [**30A:**11.6.2]

42.9.7 Fire Control.

42.9.7.1 Each marine motor fuel dispensing facility shall be provided with fire extinguishers installed, inspected, and maintained as required by Section 13.6. Extinguishers for marine motor fuel dispensing areas shall be provided according to the extra (high) hazard requirements for Class B hazards, except that the maximum travel distance to an 80 B:C extinguisher shall be permitted to be 100 ft (31 m). [**30A:**11.7.1]

42.9.7.2 Piers that extend more than 500 ft (152 m) in travel distance from shore shall be provided with a Class III standpipe that is installed in accordance with Section 13.2. [**30A:**11.7.2]

42.9.7.3 Materials shall not be placed on a pier in such a manner that they obstruct access to fire-fighting equipment or important piping system control valves. Where the pier is accessible to vehicular traffic, an unobstructed roadway to the shore end of the wharf shall be maintained for access by fire-fighting apparatus. [**30A:**11.7.3]

42.9.8 Containers and Movable Tanks.

42.9.8.1 The temporary use of movable tanks in conjunction with the dispensing of liquids into the fuel tanks of marine craft on premises not normally accessible to the public shall be permitted. Such installations shall only be made with the approval of the AHJ. [**30A:**11.8.1]

42.9.8.2* Class I or Class II liquids shall not be dispensed into a portable container unless the container is constructed of metal or is approved by the AHJ, has a tight closure, and is fitted with a spout or is so designed that the contents can be dispensed without spilling. [**30A:**11.8.2]

42.9.8.3 Portable containers of 12 gal (45 L) capacity or less shall not be filled while they are in or on a marine craft. [**30A:**11.8.3]

42.9.9 Cargo Tank Fueling Facilities. The provisions of 42.9.2 shall not prohibit the dispensing of Class II liquids in the open from a tank vehicle to a marine craft located at commercial, industrial, governmental, or manufacturing establishments when the liquid is intended for fueling marine craft used in connection with those establishments' businesses if the requirements of 42.9.9.1 through 42.9.9.7 are met. [**30A:**11.9]

42.9.9.1 An inspection of the premises and operations shall be made and approval granted by the AHJ. [**30A:**11.9.1]

42.9.9.2 The tank vehicle shall comply with the requirements of NFPA 385. [**30A:**11.9.2]

42.9.9.3 The dispensing hose shall not exceed 50 ft (15 m) in length. [**30A:**11.9.3]

42.9.9.4 The dispensing nozzle shall be a listed, automatic-closing type without a latch-open device. [**30A:**11.9.4]

42.9.9.5 Nighttime deliveries shall only be made in areas deemed adequately lighted by the AHJ. [**30A:**11.9.5]

42.9.9.6 The tank vehicle flasher lights shall be in operation while dispensing. [**30A:**11.9.6]

42.9.9.7 Fuel expansion space shall be left in each fuel tank to prevent overflow in the event of temperature increase. [**30A:**11.9.7]

42.9.10 Operating Requirements.

42.9.10.1 The following shall be the responsibilities of the attendant:

(1) Prevent the dispensing of Class I liquids into portable containers that do not comply with 42.9.8.2
(2) Be familiar with the dispensing system and emergency shutoff controls
(3) Ensure that the vessel is properly moored and that all connections are made
(4) Be within 15 ft (4.6 m) of the dispensing controls during the fueling operation and maintain a direct, clear, unobstructed view of both the vessel fuel filler neck and the emergency fuel shutoff control [**30A:**11.10.1]

42.9.10.2 Fueling shall not be undertaken at night except under well-lighted conditions. [**30A:**11.10.2]

42.9.10.3 During fueling operations, smoking shall be forbidden on board the vessel or marine craft and in the dispensing area. [**30A:**11.10.3]

42.9.10.4 Before opening the tanks of the vessel to be fueled, the following precautions shall be taken:

(1) All engines, motors, fans, and bilge blowers shall be shut down.
(2) All open flames and smoking material shall be extinguished and all exposed heating elements shall be turned off.
(3) Galley stoves shall be extinguished.
(4) All ports, windows, doors, and hatches shall be closed. [**30A:**11.10.4]

42.9.10.5 After the flow of fuel has stopped, the following shall occur:

(1) The fill cap shall be tightly secured.
(2) Any spillage shall be wiped up immediately.
(3) If Class I liquid has been delivered, the entire vessel or marine craft shall remain open.
(4) Bilge blowers shall be turned on and allowed to run for at least 5 minutes before starting any engines or lighting galley fires. If bilge blowers are not available, 10 minutes of ventilation shall be required. [**30A:**11.10.5]

42.9.10.6 No Class I liquids shall be delivered to any vessel having its tanks located below deck unless each tank is equipped with a separate fill pipe, the receiving end of which shall be securely connected to a deck plate and fitted with a screw cap. Such pipe shall extend into the tank. Vessels receiving Class II or Class IIIA liquids shall have the receiving end of the fill pipe securely connected to a deck plate and fitted with a screw cap. Such pipe shall be permitted to connect to a manifold system that extends into each separate tank. Each tank shall be provided with a suitable vent pipe that shall extend from the tank to the outside of the coaming or enclosed rails so that the vapors will dissipate away from the vessel. [**30A**:11.10.6]

42.9.10.7 Owners or operators shall not offer their vessel or marine craft for fueling unless the following conditions exist:

(1) The tanks being filled are properly vented to dissipate vapors to the outside atmosphere, and the fuel systems are liquidtight and vaportight with respect to all interiors.
(2) All fuel systems are designed, installed, and maintained in compliance with the specifications of the manufacturer of the vessel or marine craft.
(3) Communication has been established between the fueling attendant and the person in control of the vessel or craft receiving the fuel so as to determine the vessel's fuel capacity, the amount of fuel on board, and the amount of fuel to be taken on board.
(4) The electrical bonding and grounding systems of the vessel or craft have been maintained in accordance with the manufacturer's specifications. [**30A**:11.10.7]

42.9.10.8 A sign with the following legends printed in 2 in. (50 mm) red capital letters on a white background shall be conspicuously posted at the dispensing area:

Before Fueling:

(1) Stop all engines and auxiliaries.

(2) Shut off all electricity, open flames, and heat sources.

(3) Check all bilges for fuel vapors.

(4) Extinguish all smoking materials.

(5) Close access fittings and openings that could allow fuel vapors to enter enclosed spaces of the vessel.

During Fueling:

(1) Maintain nozzle contact with fill pipe.

(2) Wipe up spills immediately.

(3) Avoid overfilling.

(4) Fuel filling nozzle must be attended at all times.

After Fueling:

(1) Inspect bilges for leakage and fuel odors.

(2) Ventilate until odors are removed.
[**30A**:11.10.8]

42.10 Aircraft Fuel Servicing.

42.10.1 Application. Section 42.10 applies to the fuel servicing of all types of aircraft using liquid petroleum fuel in accordance with NFPA 407, *Standard for Aircraft Fuel Servicing.*

42.10.1.1 Section 42.10 does not apply to any of the following:

(1) In-flight fueling
(2) Fuel servicing of flying boats or amphibious aircraft on water
(3) Draining or filling of aircraft fuel tanks incidental to aircraft fuel system maintenance operations or manufacturing [**407**:1.1]

42.10.1.2 Permits. Permits, where required, shall comply with Section 1.12.

42.10.2 Design.

42.10.2.1 General.

42.10.2.1.1 Fueling Hose Apparatus. Nozzle receptacles and hose storage shall be arranged to avoid kinks and maintain the hose bend radius within the requirements of API BULL 1529, *Aviation Fueling Hose.* [**407**:4.1.1]

42.10.2.1.2 Electrostatic Hazards and Bonding.

42.10.2.1.2.1 A provision for bonding shall be incorporated in the design of fuel servicing vehicles or carts and systems to prevent differences in electrostatic potential in accordance with 42.10.5.4. [**407**:4.1.2.1]

42.10.2.1.2.2 The maximum resistance between the bonding cable clip and the fueling system framework shall not exceed 25 ohms. [**407**:4.1.2.2]

42.10.2.1.2.3 Bonding cables shall be constructed of conductive, durable, and flexible material. [**407**:4.1.2.3]

42.10.2.1.2.4 Bonding connections shall be electrically and mechanically firm. Jacks, plugs, clamps, and connecting points shall be clean, unpainted metal to provide a positive electrical connection. [**407**:4.1.2.4]

42.10.2.1.2.5 API BULL 1529 Type C hose (semiconductive) shall be used to prevent electrostatic discharges but shall not be used to accomplish required bonding. API BULL 1529 Type A hose that does not have a semiconductive cover shall not be used. Type F hose (hard wall) and Type CT hose (cold temperature) shall be permitted because they have semiconductive covers. [**407**:4.1.2.5]

42.10.2.1.2.6* The design of airport fueling systems shall incorporate the provision of a 30-second relaxation period between the filter separator, monitors, or other filtration devices discharging into tanks. [**407**:4.1.2.6]

42.10.2.1.2.6.1 Paragraph 42.10.2.1.2.6 shall not apply to the actual refueling of an aircraft. [**407**:4.1.2.6.1]

42.10.2.1.2.6.2 Paragraph 42.10.2.1.2.6 shall not apply to fuels with static dissipater additives. [**407**:4.1.2.6.2]

42.10.2.1.3 No Smoking Signs. Entrances to fueling areas shall be posted with "no smoking" signs. [**407**:4.1.3]

42.10.2.1.4 Aircraft Radar Equipment.

42.10.2.1.4.1 Surveillance radar equipment in aircraft shall not be operated within 300 ft (90 m) of any fueling, servicing, or other operation in which flammable liquids, vapors, or mist could be present. [**407**:4.1.4.1.1]

42.10.2.1.4.2 Weather-mapping radar equipment in aircraft shall not be operated while the aircraft in which it is mounted is undergoing fuel servicing. [**407**:4.1.4.1.2]

42.10.2.1.5* Ground Radar Equipment.

42.10.2.1.5.1 Antennas of airport flight traffic surveillance radar equipment shall be located so that the beam will not be directed toward any fuel storage or loading racks within 300 ft

(90 m). Aircraft fuel servicing shall not be conducted within this 300 ft (90 m) distance. [**407**:4.1.4.2.1]

42.10.2.1.5.2 Antennas of airport ground traffic surveillance radar equipment shall be located so that the beam will not be directed toward any fuel storage or loading racks within 100 ft (30 m). Aircraft fuel servicing or any other operations involving flammable liquids or vapors shall not be conducted within 100 ft (30 m) of such antennas. [**407**:4.1.4.2.2]

42.10.2.1.6 Emergency Fire Equipment Accessibility. Accessibility to aircraft by emergency fire equipment shall be considered in establishing aircraft fuel servicing positions. [**407**:4.1.5]

42.10.2.1.7 Portable Fire Extinguishers.

42.10.2.1.7.1* Portable extinguishers shall be provided in accordance with 42.10.2.4 and 42.10.5.13. [**407**:4.1.6.1]

42.10.2.1.7.2 Extinguishers shall conform to the requirements of Section 13.6. [**407**:4.1.6.2]

42.10.2.1.7.3* ABC multipurpose dry chemical fire extinguishers (ammonium phosphate) shall not be placed on aircraft fueling vehicles, airport fuel servicing ramps, or aprons, or at airport fuel facilities. [**407**:4.1.6.3]

42.10.2.2 Vehicle or Cart Lighting and Electrical Equipment.

42.10.2.2.1 Battery Compartments. Batteries that are not in engine compartments shall be securely mounted in compartments to prevent accidental arcing. The compartment shall be separate from fueling equipment. Suitable shielding shall be provided to drain possible fuel spillage or leakage away from the compartment. The compartment shall be provided with a vent at the top of the compartment. [**407**:4.3.7.1]

42.10.2.2.2 Wiring shall be of adequate size to provide the required current-carrying capacity and mechanical strength. Wiring shall be installed to provide protection from physical damage and from contact with spilled fuel either by its location or by enclosing it in metal conduit or other oil-resistant protective covering. All circuits shall have overcurrent protection. Junction boxes shall be weatherproofed. [**407**:4.3.7.2]

42.10.2.2.3 Spark plugs and other exposed terminal connections shall be insulated to prevent sparking in the event of contact with conductive materials. [**407**:4.3.7.3]

42.10.2.2.4* Motors, alternators, generators, and associated control equipment located outside of the engine compartment or vehicle cab shall be of a type listed for use in accordance with *NFPA 70* Class I, Division 1, Group D locations. [**407**:4.3.7.4]

42.10.2.2.5 Electrical equipment and wiring located within a closed compartment shall be of a type listed for use in accordance with *NFPA 70* Class I, Division 1, Group D locations. [**407**:4.3.7.5]

42.10.2.2.6 Lamps, switching devices, and electronic controls, other than those covered in 42.10.2.2.4 and 42.10.2.2.5, shall be of the enclosed, gasketed, weatherproof type. Other electrical components shall be of a type listed for use in accordance with *NFPA 70* Class I, Division 2, Group D locations. [**407**:4.3.7.6]

42.10.2.2.7 Electrical service wiring between a tractor and trailer shall be designed for heavy-duty service. The connector shall be of the positive-engaging type. The trailer receptacle shall be mounted securely. [**407**:4.3.7.7]

42.10.2.3 Cabinets. All cabinets housing vehicle auxiliary equipment shall have expanded metal flooring, perforated metal grating-type flooring, or open floor to facilitate air circulation within the enclosed space and to prevent the accumulation of fuel. [**407**:4.3.8]

42.10.2.4 Fire Extinguishers for Aircraft Fuel Servicing Vehicles or Carts.

42.10.2.4.1 Each aircraft fuel servicing tank vehicle shall have two listed fire extinguishers, each having a rating of at least 20-B:C with one extinguisher mounted on each side of the vehicle. [**407**:4.3.9.1]

42.10.2.4.2 One listed extinguisher having a rating of at least 20-B:C shall be installed on each hydrant fuel servicing vehicle or cart. [**407**:4.3.9.2]

42.10.2.4.3 Extinguishers shall be readily accessible from the ground. The area of the paneling or tank adjacent to or immediately behind the extinguisher(s) on fueling vehicles or carts shall be painted with a contrasting color. [**407**:4.3.9.3]

42.10.2.4.4 Extinguishers shall be kept clear of elements such as ice and snow. Extinguishers located in enclosed compartments shall be readily accessible, and their location shall be marked clearly in letters at least 2 in. (50 mm) high. [**407**:4.3.9.4]

42.10.2.5 Smoking Restrictions.

42.10.2.5.1 A "no smoking" sign shall be posted prominently in the cab of every aircraft fuel servicing vehicle. [**407**:4.3.11.1]

42.10.2.5.2 Smoking equipment such as cigarette lighters and ash trays shall not be provided. If a vehicle includes such equipment when initially procured, it shall be removed or rendered inoperable. [**407**:4.3.11.2]

42.10.2.6 Fuel Dispensing System.

42.10.2.6.1 The valve that controls the flow of fuel from an aircraft fuel servicing vehicle or cart to an aircraft shall have a deadman control(s) in accordance with the requirements of 4.1.7 of NFPA 407. [**407**:4.3.16.1]

42.10.2.6.2 The deadman flow control in the nozzle shall be permitted for overwing fueling. Notches or latches in the nozzle handle that could allow the valve to be locked open shall be prohibited. Each overwing servicing nozzle shall have a cable with a plug or clip for bonding to the aircraft. *(See 42.10.5.4.2.)* [**407**:4.3.16.2]

42.10.2.6.3 Nozzles for underwing fueling shall be designed to be attached securely to the aircraft adapter before the nozzle can be opened. Disengaging the nozzle from the aircraft adapter shall not be possible until the nozzle is fully closed. [**407**:4.3.16.3]

42.10.2.6.4 Fuel servicing pump mechanisms shall be designed and arranged so that failure or seizure does not cause rupture of the pump housing, a tank, or of any component containing fuel. Fuel pressure shall be controlled within the stress limits of the hose and plumbing by means of either an in-line pressure controller, a system pressure relief valve, or other suitable means. The working pressure of any system component shall equal or exceed any pressure to which it could be subjected. [**407**:4.3.16.4]

42.10.2.6.5 On tank full trailer or tank semitrailer vehicles, the use of a pump in the tractor unit with flexible connections to the trailer shall be prohibited unless one of the following conditions exists:

(1) Flexible connections are arranged above the liquid level of the tank in order to prevent gravity or siphon discharge in case of a break in the connection or piping.
(2) The cargo tank discharge valves required by 42.10.2.6.1 are arranged to be normally closed and to open only when the brakes are set and the pump is engaged. [**407**:4.3.16.5]

42.10.2.6.6 Hose shall be connected to rigid piping or coupled to the hose reel in a manner that prevents kinks or undue bending action or mechanical stress on the hose or hose couplings. [**407**:4.3.16.6]

42.10.2.6.7 Aircraft fuel servicing vehicles and carts shall have an integral system or device that prevents the vehicle or cart from being moved unless all fueling nozzles and hydrant couplers are properly stowed and mechanical lifts are lowered to their stowed position. [**407**:4.3.16.7]

42.10.2.6.8 Air Elimination. Aircraft fuel servicing tank vehicles having a positive displacement product pump shall be equipped with a product tank low level shutdown system that prevents air from being ingested into the fueling system. [**407**:4.3.16.8]

42.10.3 Airport Fuel Systems.

42.10.3.1 Design Approval. Work shall not be started on the construction or alteration of an airport fuel system until the design, plans, and specifications have been approved by the AHJ. [**407**:4.4.1]

42.10.3.2 System Approval. The AHJ shall inspect and approve the completed system before it is put into service. [**407**:4.4.2]

42.10.3.3 Fuel Storage Tanks.

42.10.3.3.1* Fuel storage tanks shall conform to the applicable requirements of NFPA 30. [**407**:4.4.4.1]

42.10.3.3.2 The AHJ shall determine the clearances required from runways, taxiways, and other aircraft movement and servicing areas to any aboveground fuel storage structure or fuel transfer equipment, with due recognition given to national and international standards establishing clearances from obstructions. Tanks located in designated aircraft movement areas or aircraft servicing areas shall be underground or mounded over with earth. Vents from such tanks shall be constructed in a manner to preclude collision hazards with operating aircraft. Aircraft operators shall be consulted regarding the height and location of such vents to avoid venting flammable vapors in the vicinity of ignition sources, including operating aircraft and automotive equipment permitted in the area. [**407**:4.4.4.2]

42.10.4 Fueling at Rooftop Heliports. Fueling on rooftop heliports shall be permitted only where approved by the AHJ. [**407**:4.5]

42.10.4.1 General Limitations.

42.10.4.1.1 In addition to the special requirements in Section 42.10, the heliport shall comply with the requirements of NFPA 418. [**407**:4.5.1.1]

42.10.4.1.2 Facilities for dispensing fuel with a flash point below 100°F (37.8°C) shall not be permitted at any rooftop heliport. [**407**:4.5.1.2]

42.10.4.2 Fueling Facilities.

42.10.4.2.1 In addition to the special requirements of Section 42.10, the fuel storage, piping, and dispensing system shall comply with the requirements of NFPA 30 and with applicable portions of NFPA 407 and this *Code*. [**407**:4.5.2.1]

42.10.4.2.2 The entire system shall be designed so that no part of the system is subjected to pressure above its working pressure. [**407**:4.5.2.2]

42.10.4.2.3 The fuel storage system shall be located at or below ground level. [**407**:4.5.2.3]

42.10.4.3 Pumps.

42.10.4.3.1 Pumps shall be located at or below ground level. Relay pumping shall not be permitted. [**407**:4.5.3.1]

42.10.4.3.2 Pumps installed outside of buildings shall be located not less than 5 ft (1.5 m) from any building opening. They shall be substantially anchored and protected against physical damage from collision. [**407**:4.5.3.2]

42.10.4.3.3 Pumps installed within a building shall be in a separate room with no opening into other portions of the building. The pump room shall be adequately ventilated. Electrical wiring and equipment shall conform to the requirements of *NFPA 70*, Article 515. [**407**:4.5.3.3]

42.10.4.4 Emergency Fuel Shutoff Stations.

42.10.4.4.1 A system shall be provided to completely shut off the flow of fuel in an emergency. The system shall shut off the fuel at the ground level. The emergency fuel shutoff controls shall be in addition to the normal operating controls for the pumps and deadman control. [**407**:4.5.9.1]

42.10.4.4.2 At least two emergency fuel shutoff stations located on opposite sides of the heliport at exitways or at similar locations shall be provided. An additional emergency fuel shutoff station shall be located at ground level and shall be near, but at least 10 ft (3 m) from, the pumps. [**407**:4.5.9.2]

42.10.4.4.3 Each emergency fuel shutoff station location shall be placarded EMERGENCY FUEL SHUTOFF in letters at least 2 in. (50 mm) high. The method of operation shall be indicated by an arrow or by the word PUSH or PULL, as appropriate. Any action necessary to gain access to the shutoff device (e.g., BREAK GLASS) shall be shown clearly. Lettering shall be of a color contrasting sharply with the placard background for visibility. Placards shall be weather resistant, shall be conspicuously located, and shall be positioned so that they can be seen readily from a distance of at least 25 ft (7.6 m). [**407**:4.5.9.3]

42.10.4.5 Fire Protection. Fire protection shall conform to the requirements of NFPA 418. [**407**:4.5.10]

42.10.4.6 Personnel Training. All heliport personnel shall be trained in the operation of emergency fuel shutoff controls and in the use of the available fire extinguishers. [**407**:4.5.11]

42.10.5 Operations.

42.10.5.1 General.

42.10.5.1.1* Only personnel trained in the safe operation of the equipment and fuels they use, the operation of emergency controls, and the procedures to be followed in an emergency shall be permitted to handle fuel. [**407**:5.1.1]

42.10.5.1.2 Where a valve or electrical device is used for isolation during maintenance or modification of the fuel system, it shall be tagged/locked. The tag/lock shall not be removed until the operation is completed. [**407**:5.1.2]

42.10.5.1.3 Aircraft fueling vehicles shall be marked with the name of the operator or the responsible organization. [**407**:5.1.3]

42.10.5.1.3.1 The marking shall be approved, legible signs on both sides of the exterior of the vehicle. [**407**:5.1.3.1]

42.10.5.1.4* The AHJ shall determine the suitability of fuel servicing vehicles utilizing tunnels, enclosed roadways, or the like. [**407**:5.1.4]

42.10.5.2* Prevention and Control of Spills.

42.10.5.2.1 Fuel servicing equipment shall comply with the requirements of NFPA 407 and this *Code* and shall be maintained in safe operating condition. Leaking or malfunctioning equipment shall be removed from service. [**407**:5.2.1]

42.10.5.2.2 Following fueling of an aircraft, all hoses shall be removed, including those from hydrant systems. All hoses shall also be properly stowed. [**407**:5.2.2]

42.10.5.2.3 Fuel nozzles shall not be dragged along the ground. [**407**:5.2.3]

42.10.5.2.4 Approved pumps, either hand operated or power operated, shall be used where aircraft are fueled from drums. Pouring or gravity flow shall not be permitted from a container with a capacity of more than 5 gal (19 L). [**407**:5.2.4]

42.10.5.2.5 Where a spill is observed, the fuel servicing shall be stopped immediately by release of the deadman controls. [**407**:5.2.5]

42.10.5.2.5.1 In the event that a spill continues, the equipment emergency fuel shutoff shall be actuated. [**407**:5.2.5.1]

42.10.5.2.5.2 In the event that a spill continues from a hydrant system, the system emergency fuel shutoff shall be actuated. [**407**:5.2.5.2]

42.10.5.2.5.3 The supervisor shall be notified immediately. [**407**:5.2.5.3]

42.10.5.2.5.4 Cleaning operations shall be performed by personnel trained in accordance with 42.10.5.1.1. [**407**:5.2.5.4]

42.10.5.2.5.5 Operation shall not be resumed until the spill has been cleared and conditions are determined to be safe. [**407**:5.2.5.5]

42.10.5.2.6 The airport fire crew shall be notified if a spill covers over 10 ft (3 m) in any direction or is over 50 ft^2 (5 m^2) in area, continues to flow, or is otherwise a hazard to persons or property. The spill shall be investigated to determine the cause, to determine whether emergency procedures were properly carried out, and to determine the necessary corrective measures. [**407**:5.2.6]

42.10.5.2.7 Transferring fuel by pumping from one tank vehicle to another tank vehicle within 200 ft (61 m) of an aircraft shall not be permitted. [**407**:5.2.7]

42.10.5.2.8 Not more than one tank vehicle shall be permitted to be connected to the same aircraft fueling manifold.

Exception: Where means are provided to prevent fuel from flowing back into a tank vehicle because of a difference in pumping pressure. [**407**:5.2.8]

42.10.5.3 Emergency Fuel Shutoff.

42.10.5.3.1 Access to emergency fuel shutoff control stations shall be kept clear at all times. [**407**:5.3.1]

42.10.5.3.2 A procedure shall be established to notify the fire department serving the airport in the event of a control station activation. [**407**:5.3.2]

42.10.5.3.3 If the fuel flow stops for any reason, it first shall be presumed that an emergency fuel shutoff system has been actuated. The cause of the shutoff shall be corrected before fuel flow is resumed. [**407**:5.3.3]

42.10.5.3.4 Emergency fuel shutoff systems shall be operationally checked at intervals not exceeding 6 months. Each individual device shall be checked at least once during every 12-month period. [**407**:5.3.4]

42.10.5.3.5 Suitable records shall be kept of tests required by 42.10.5.3. [**407**:5.3.5]

42.10.5.4* Bonding.

42.10.5.4.1 Prior to making any fueling connection to the aircraft, the fueling equipment shall be bonded to the aircraft by use of a cable, thus providing a conductive path to equalize the potential between the fueling equipment and the aircraft. The bond shall be maintained until fueling connections have been removed, thus allowing separated charges that could be generated during the fueling operation to reunite. Grounding during aircraft fueling shall not be permitted. [**407**:5.4.1]

42.10.5.4.2 In addition to the requirements in 42.10.5.4.1, where fueling overwing, the nozzle shall be bonded with a nozzle bond cable having a clip or plug to a metallic component of the aircraft that is metallically connected to the tank filler port. The bond connection shall be made before the filler cap is removed. If no plug receptacle or means for attaching a clip is available, the operator shall touch the filler cap with the nozzle spout before removing the cap in order to equalize the potential between the nozzle and the filler port. The spout shall be kept in contact with the filler neck until the fueling is completed. [**407**:5.4.2]

42.10.5.4.3* Where a funnel is used in aircraft fueling, it shall be kept in contact with the filler neck as well as the fueling nozzle spout or the supply container to avoid the possibility of a spark at the fill opening. Only metal funnels shall be used. [**407**:5.4.3]

42.10.5.4.4 Where a hydrant servicer or cart is used for fueling, the hydrant coupler shall be connected to the hydrant system prior to bonding the fuel equipment to the aircraft. [**407**:5.4.4]

42.10.5.4.5 Bonding and fueling connections shall be disconnected in the reverse order of connection. [**407**:5.4.5]

42.10.5.4.6 Conductive hose shall be used to prevent electrostatic discharge but shall not be used to accomplish required bonding. [**407**:5.4.6]

42.10.5.5 Operation of Aircraft Engines and Heaters.

42.10.5.5.1 Fuel servicing shall not be performed on a fixed wing aircraft while an onboard engine is operating. *(See 42.10.5.21.)*

Exception: In an emergency resulting from the failure of an onboard auxiliary power unit on a jet aircraft and in the absence of suitable ground support equipment, a jet engine mounted at the rear of the aircraft or on the wing on the side opposite the fueling point shall be permitted to be operated during fueling to provide power, provided that the operation follows written procedures approved by the AHJ. [407:5.5.1]

42.10.5.5.2 Combustion heaters on aircraft (e.g., wing and tail surface heaters, integral cabin heaters) shall not be operated during fueling operations. [**407**:5.5.2]

42.10.5.6 Use of Equipment Powered by Internal Combustion Engines Around Aircraft.

42.10.5.6.1 Equipment, other than that performing aircraft servicing functions, shall not be permitted within 50 ft (15 m) of aircraft during fuel servicing operations. [**407**:5.6.1]

42.10.5.6.2 Equipment performing aircraft servicing functions shall not be positioned within a 10 ft (3 m) radius of aircraft fuel system vent openings. [**407**:5.6.2]

42.10.5.6.3 During overwing aircraft fuel servicing where aircraft fuel system vents are located on the upper wing surface, equipment shall not be positioned under the trailing edge of the wing. [**407**:5.6.3]

42.10.5.6.4 All vehicles that have engines equipped with an exhaust after-treatment device, such as a DPF, that requires the filter to be cleaned at high temperature (regenerated) while installed on the vehicle shall meet the requirements of 42.10.5.6.4.1 through 42.10.5.6.4.7. [**407**:5.6.4]

42.10.5.6.4.1 DPF regeneration shall be performed only in area(s) designated by the AHJ. [**407**:5.6.4.1]

42.10.5.6.4.2 DPF regeneration shall not be performed within 100 ft (30 m) of any aircraft refueling operations. [**407**:5.6.4.2]

42.10.5.6.4.3* Vehicle Regeneration Area. [**407**:5.6.4.3]

42.10.5.6.4.3.1 The immediate area surrounding the DPF exhaust outlet shall be concrete or other high temperature–resistant material and shall be clear of any grass, soil, or flammable materials. [**407**:5.6.4.3.1]

42.10.5.6.4.3.2 The area shall be in a remote location that is a minimum of 100 ft (30 m) from the nearest aircraft parking location, airport terminal, or flammable storage or a minimum of 50 ft (15 m) from any other building. [**407**:5.6.4.3.2]

42.10.5.6.4.3.3 The area shall be clearly marked with a minimum 2 ft by 1 ft (61 cm by 30 cm) sign reading "Vehicle DPF Regeneration Area," which shall have letters at least 3 in. (75 mm) high and shall be of a color contrasting sharply with the sign background for visibility. [**407**:5.6.4.3.3]

42.10.5.6.4.4 The regeneration cycle shall be performed only by trained personnel, who shall remain with the vehicle until the regeneration cycle is complete. [**407**:5.6.4.4]

42.10.5.6.4.5 The vehicle shall be visually inspected for any signs of fluid leaks under or around the vehicle before regeneration is initiated. DPF regeneration shall not be initiated if there are any signs of any fluid leaks on or beneath the vehicle. [**407**:5.6.4.5]

42.10.5.6.4.6 Once a regeneration cycle is started, it shall be completed without interruption. [**407**:5.6.4.6]

42.10.5.6.4.7 After the regeneration process is successfully completed, the vehicle shall be permitted to return to normal service. Problems occurring during the regeneration cycle shall be corrected prior to the vehicle returning to normal service. [**407**:5.6.4.7]

42.10.5.6.4.8 Aircraft refueling operations shall not be initiated if the regenerative system indicates regeneration is required. [**407**:5.6.4.8]

42.10.5.7* Electrical Equipment Used on Aircraft Servicing Ramps.

42.10.5.7.1 Battery chargers shall not be connected, operated, or disconnected while fuel servicing is performed on the aircraft. [**407**:5.7.1]

42.10.5.7.2* Aircraft ground-power generators or other electrical ground-power supplies shall not be connected or disconnected while fuel servicing is performed on the aircraft. [**407**:5.7.2]

42.10.5.7.3 Electric tools or similar tools likely to produce sparks or arcs shall not be used while fuel servicing is performed on the aircraft. [**407**:5.7.3]

42.10.5.7.4 Photographic equipment shall not be used within 10 ft (3 m) of the fueling equipment or the fill or vent points of aircraft fuel systems. [**407**:5.7.4]

42.10.5.7.5 Other than aircraft fuel servicing vehicles, battery-powered vehicles that do not comply with the provisions of NFPA 407 shall not be operated within 10 ft (3 m) of fueling equipment or spills. *(See 42.10.5.6.)* [**407**:5.7.5]

42.10.5.7.6* Communication equipment located outside the cab of the vehicle and used during aircraft fuel servicing operations within 10 ft (3 m) of the fill or vent points of aircraft fuel systems shall be listed as intrinsically safe for Class I, Division 1, Group D hazardous (classified) locations in accordance with ANSI/UL 913, *Standard for Intrinsically Safe Apparatus and Associated Apparatus for Use in Class I, II, and III Division 1, Hazardous (Classified) Locations.* [**407**:5.7.6]

42.10.5.8 Open Flames on Aircraft Fuel Servicing Ramps.

42.10.5.8.1 Entrances to fueling areas shall be posted with "no smoking" signs. [**407**:5.8.1]

42.10.5.8.2 Open flames on aircraft fuel servicing ramps or aprons within 50 ft (15 m) of any aircraft fuel servicing operation or fueling equipment shall be prohibited. [**407**:5.8.2]

42.10.5.8.3 The category of open flames and lighted open-flame devices shall include, but shall not be limited to, the following:

(1) Lighted cigarettes, cigars, pipes
(2) Exposed flame heaters, liquid, solid, or gaseous devices, including portable and wheeled gasoline or kerosene heaters
(3) Heat-producing, welding, or cutting devices and blowtorches
(4) Flare pots or other open-flame lights [**407**:5.8.3]

42.10.5.8.4 The AHJ might establish other locations where open flames and open-flame devices shall not be permitted. [**407**:5.8.4]

42.10.5.8.5 Personnel shall not carry lighters or matches on their person while engaged in fuel servicing operations. [**407**:5.8.5]

42.10.5.8.6 Lighters or matches shall not be permitted on or in fueling equipment. [**407**:5.8.6]

42.10.5.9* Lightning Precautions.

42.10.5.9.1 Fuel servicing operations shall be suspended where lightning flashes are in the immediate vicinity of the airport. [**407**:5.9.1]

42.10.5.9.2 A written procedure shall be established to set the criteria for where fueling operations are to be suspended at each airport as approved by the fueling agent and the airport authority. [**407**:5.9.2]

42.10.5.10 Aircraft Fuel Servicing Locations.

42.10.5.10.1 Aircraft fuel servicing shall be performed outdoors. Aircraft fuel servicing incidental to aircraft fuel system maintenance operations shall comply with the requirements of NFPA 410, *Standard on Aircraft Maintenance.* [**407**:5.10.1]

42.10.5.10.2* Aircraft being fueled shall be positioned so that aircraft fuel system vents or fuel tank openings are not closer than 25 ft (7.6 m) to any terminal building, hangar, service building, or enclosed passenger concourse other than a loading walkway. Aircraft being fueled shall not be positioned so that the vent or tank openings are within 50 ft (15 m) of any combustion and ventilation air-intake to any boiler, heater, or incinerator room. [**407**:5.10.2]

42.10.5.10.3 Accessibility to aircraft by emergency fire equipment shall be established for aircraft fuel servicing positions. [**407**:5.10.3]

42.10.5.11 Aircraft Occupancy During Fuel Servicing Operations.

42.10.5.11.1 If passengers remain onboard an aircraft during fuel servicing, at least one qualified person trained in emergency evacuation procedures shall be in the aircraft at or near a door at which there is a passenger loading walkway, integral stairs that lead downward, or a passenger loading stair or stand. A clear area for emergency evacuation of the aircraft shall be maintained at not less than one additional exit. Where fueling operations take place with passengers onboard away from the terminal building, and stairways are not provided, such as during inclement weather (diversions), all slides shall be armed and the Aircraft Rescue and Fire Fighting (ARFF) services shall be notified to respond in standby position in the vicinity of the fueling activity with at least one vehicle. Aircraft operators shall establish specific procedures covering emergency evacuation under such conditions for each type of aircraft they operate. All "no smoking" signs shall be displayed in the cabin(s), and the no smoking rule shall be enforced. [**407**:5.11.1]

42.10.5.11.2 For each aircraft type, operators shall determine the areas through which it could be hazardous for boarding or deplaning passengers to pass while the aircraft is being fueled. Controls shall be established so that passengers avoid such areas. [**407**:5.11.2]

42.10.5.11.3 Passengers shall not be permitted to linger about the plane but shall proceed directly between the loading gate and the aircraft. [**407**:5.11.3]

42.10.5.12 Positioning of Aircraft Fuel Servicing Vehicles and Carts.

42.10.5.12.1 Aircraft fuel servicing vehicles and carts shall be positioned so that a clear path of egress from the aircraft for fuel servicing vehicles shall be maintained. [**407**:5.12.1]

42.10.5.12.2 The propulsion or pumping engine of aircraft fuel servicing vehicles or carts shall not be positioned under the wing of the aircraft during overwing fueling or where aircraft fuel system vents are located on the upper wing surface. Aircraft fuel servicing vehicles or carts shall not be positioned within a 10 ft (3 m) radius of aircraft fuel system vent openings. [**407**:5.12.2]

42.10.5.12.3 Parking brakes shall be set on all fuel servicing vehicles or carts before operators begin the fueling operation. [**407**:5.12.3]

42.10.5.13* Portable Fire Extinguishers.

42.10.5.13.1 During fueling operations, fire extinguishers shall be available on aircraft servicing ramps or aprons. [**407**:5.13.1]

42.10.5.13.2 Each aircraft fuel servicing tank vehicle shall have two listed fire extinguishers, each having a rating of at least 20-B:C, with one extinguisher mounted on each side of the vehicle. [**407**:5.13.2]

42.10.5.13.3 One listed fire extinguisher having a rating of at least 20-B:C shall be installed on each hydrant fuel servicing vehicle or cart. [**407**:5.13.3]

42.10.5.13.4 Where the open hose discharge capacity of the aircraft fueling system or equipment is more than 200 gpm (750 L/min), at least one listed wheeled extinguisher having a rating of not less than 80-B:C and a minimum capacity of 125 lb (55 kg) of agent shall be provided. [**407**:5.13.4]

42.10.5.13.5* Extinguishers shall be kept clear of elements such as ice and snow. Extinguishers located in enclosed compartments shall be readily accessible, and their location shall be marked clearly in letters at least 2 in. (50 mm) high. [**407**:5.13.5]

42.10.5.13.6* Fuel servicing personnel shall be trained in the use of the available fire extinguishing equipment they could be expected to use. [**407**:5.13.6]

42.10.5.14 Defueling.

42.10.5.14.1 The transfer of fuel from an aircraft to a tank vehicle through a hose generally is similar to fueling, and the same requirements shall apply. In addition, each operator shall establish procedures to prevent the overfilling of the tank vehicle, which is a special hazard when defueling *(see 4.3.21.7 of NFPA 407).* [**407**:5.14.1]

42.10.5.14.1.1 There shall be a procedure to eliminate air ingested during a defueling operation prior to the aircraft fuel servicing tank vehicle being reused. [**407**:5.14.1.1]

42.10.5.14.2 Where draining residual fuel from aircraft tanks incidental to aircraft fuel system maintenance, testing, manufacturing, salvage, or recovery operations, the procedures of NFPA 410 shall apply. [**407**:5.14.2]

42.10.5.15 Deadman Control Monitoring.

42.10.5.15.1 The fueling operator shall monitor the panel of the fueling equipment and the aircraft control panel during pressure fueling or shall monitor the fill port during overwing fueling. [**407**:5.15.1]

42.10.5.15.2 Fuel flow shall be controlled by use of a deadman control device. The use of any means that defeats the deadman control shall be prohibited. [**407**:5.15.2]

42.10.5.16* Aircraft Fueling Hose.

42.10.5.16.1 Aircraft fueling hose shall be inspected before use each day. The hose shall be extended as it normally would be for fueling and checked for evidence of blistering, carcass saturation or separation, cuts, nicks, or abrasions that expose reinforcement material, and for slippage, misalignment, or leaks at couplings. If coupling slippage or leaks are found, the cause of the problem shall be determined. Defective hose shall be removed from service. [**407**:5.16.1]

42.10.5.16.2 At least once each month the hose shall be completely extended and inspected as required in 42.10.5.16.1. The hose couplings and the hose shall be examined for a length approximately 12 in. (305 mm) adjacent to the couplings. Structural weakness shall be checked by pressing the hose in this area around its entire circumference for soft spots. Hoses that show evidence of soft spots shall be removed from service. The nozzle screens shall be examined for rubber particles. The presence of such particles indicates possible deterioration of the interior, and the hose shall be removed from service. With the hose still completely extended, it shall be checked at the working pressure of the fueling equipment to which it is attached. Any abnormal twisting or ballooning during this test indicates a weakening of the hose carcass, and the hose shall be removed from service. [**407**:5.16.2]

42.10.5.16.3 A hose assembly that has been subjected to abuse, such as severe end-pull, flattening or crushing by a vehicle, or sharp bending or kinking, shall be removed from service. The hose assembly that has been subjected to abuse shall be hydrostatically tested prior to use. *(See 4.2.2.1 of NFPA 407.)* [**407**:5.16.3]

42.10.5.16.4* If inspection shows that a portion of a hose has been damaged, the damaged portion shall be cut off and the undamaged portion recoupled. Two lengths of hose shall not be coupled together. Only couplings that are an exact match for the interior and exterior dimensions of the hose shall be used. Recoupled hose assemblies shall be hydrostatically tested. *(See 4.2.2.1 of NFPA 407.)* [**407**:5.16.4]

42.10.5.16.5 Before any hose assembly, new or recoupled, is placed in service, it shall be visually inspected for evidence of damage or deterioration. [**407**:5.16.5]

42.10.5.16.6 Kinks or short loops in fueling hose shall be avoided. [**407**:5.16.6]

42.10.5.16.7 Suitable records shall be kept of required inspections and hydrostatic tests. [**407**:5.16.7]

42.10.5.17 Maintenance of Aircraft Fuel Servicing Vehicles and Carts.

42.10.5.17.1 Aircraft fuel servicing vehicles or carts shall not be operated unless they are in proper repair and free of accumulations of grease, oil, or other combustibles. [**407**:5.17.1]

42.10.5.17.2 Leaking vehicles or carts shall be removed from service, defueled, and parked in a safe area until repaired. [**407**:5.17.2]

42.10.5.17.3 Maintenance and servicing of aircraft fuel servicing vehicles and carts shall be performed outdoors or in a building approved for the purpose. [**407**:5.17.3]

42.10.5.18 Parking Aircraft Fuel Servicing Tank Vehicles. Parking areas for unattended aircraft fuel servicing tank vehicles shall be arranged to provide the following:

(1) Dispersal of the vehicles in the event of an emergency
(2) A minimum of 10 ft (3 m) of clear space between parked vehicles for accessibility for fire control purposes
(3) Prevention of any leakage from draining to an adjacent building or storm drain that is not suitably designed to handle fuel
(4) A minimum of 50 ft (15 m) from any parked aircraft and buildings other than maintenance facilities and garages for fuel servicing tank vehicles [**407**:5.18]

42.10.5.19 Parking Aircraft Fuel Servicing Hydrant Vehicles and Carts. Parking areas for unattended aircraft fuel servicing hydrant vehicles or carts shall be arranged to provide the following:

(1) Dispersal of the vehicles in the event of an emergency
(2) Prevention of any leakage from draining to an adjacent building or storm drain that is not suitably designed to handle fuel [**407**:5.19]

42.10.5.20 Loading of Aircraft Fuel Servicing Tank Vehicles.

42.10.5.20.1 General Requirements.

42.10.5.20.1.1 Loading and Unloading.

42.10.5.20.1.1.1 Aircraft fuel servicing tank vehicles shall be loaded only at an approved loading rack. [**407**:5.20.1.1.1]

42.10.5.20.1.1.2 Aircraft fuel servicing tank vehicles shall not be loaded from a hydrant pit under emergency conditions unless permitted by the AHJ. [**407**:5.20.1.1.2]

42.10.5.20.1.2 Filling of the vehicle cargo tank shall be under the observation and control of a qualified and authorized operator at all times. [**407**:5.20.1.2]

42.10.5.20.1.3 The required deadman and automatic overfill controls shall be in normal operating condition during the filling operation. The controls shall not be blocked open or otherwise bypassed. [**407**:5.20.1.3]

42.10.5.20.1.4 The engine of the tank vehicle shall be shut off before starting to fill the tank. [**407**:5.20.1.4]

42.10.5.20.1.5 To prevent leakage or overflow from expansion of the contents due to a rise in atmospheric temperature or direct exposure to the sun, no cargo tank or compartment shall be loaded to the point where it is liquid full. [**407**:5.20.1.5]

42.10.5.20.2 Top Loading.

42.10.5.20.2.1 Where loading tank trucks through open domes, a bond shall be established between the loading piping and the cargo tank to equalize potentials. The bond connection shall be made before the dome is opened and shall be removed only after the dome is closed. [**407**:5.20.2.1]

42.10.5.20.2.2 Drop tubes attached to loading assemblies extending into the vehicle tank shall extend to the bottom of the tank and shall be maintained in that position until the tank is loaded to provide submerged loading and avoid splashing or free fall of fuel through the tank atmosphere. The flow rate into the tanks shall not exceed 25 percent of the maximum flow until the outlet is fully covered. [**407**:5.20.2.2]

42.10.5.20.2.3 The level in the tank shall be visually monitored at all times during top loading. [**407**:5.20.2.3]

42.10.5.20.3 Bottom Loading.

42.10.5.20.3.1 A bonding connection shall be made between the cargo tank and the loading rack before any fuel connections are made and shall remain in place throughout the loading operation. [**407**:5.20.3.1]

42.10.5.20.3.2 The operator shall initiate fuel flow by means of a deadman control device. [**407**:5.20.3.2]

42.10.5.20.3.3 The operator shall perform the precheck on each compartment shortly after flow has started, to ensure that the automatic high-level shutoff system is functioning properly. [**407**:5.20.3.3]

42.10.5.20.3.4 At least monthly the operator shall perform a check to ensure complete closure of the bottom-loading valve on the tank vehicle. [**407**:5.20.3.4]

42.10.5.21 Rapid Refueling of Helicopters.

42.10.5.21.1 Only turbine engine helicopters fueled with JET A or JET A-1 fuels shall be permitted to be fueled while an onboard engine is operating. Helicopters permitted to be fueled while an onboard engine is operating shall have all sources of ignition of potential fuel spills located above the fuel inlet port(s) and above the vents or tank openings. Ignition sources shall include, but shall not be limited to, engines, exhausts, auxiliary power units (APUs), and combustion-type cabin heater exhausts. [**407**:5.21.1]

42.10.5.21.2 Helicopter fueling while onboard engines are operating shall be permitted only under the following conditions:

(1) An FAA-licensed helicopter pilot shall be at the aircraft controls during the entire fuel servicing process.
(2)*Passengers shall be deboarded to a safe location prior to rapid refueling operations. Where the pilot in command deems it necessary for passengers to remain onboard for safety reasons, the provisions of 42.10.5.11.1 shall apply.
(3) Passengers shall not board or deboard during rapid refueling operations.
(4) Only designated personnel, properly trained in rapid refueling operations, shall operate the equipment. Written procedures shall include the safe handling of the fuel and equipment.
(5) All doors, windows, and access points allowing entry to the interior of the helicopter that are adjacent to, or in the immediate vicinity of, the fuel inlet ports shall be closed and shall remain closed during refueling operations.
(6) Fuel shall be dispensed into an open port from approved deadman-type nozzles, with a flow rate not to exceed 60 gpm (227 L/min), or it shall be dispensed through close-coupled pressure fueling ports. Where fuel is dispensed from fixed piping systems, the hose cabinet shall not extend into the rotor space. A curb or other approved barrier shall be provided to restrict the fuel servicing vehicle from coming closer than within 10 ft (3 m) of any helicopter rotating components. If a curb or approved barrier cannot be provided, fuel servicing vehicles shall be kept 20 ft (6 m) away from any helicopter rotating components, and a trained person shall direct fuel servicing vehicle approach and departure. [**407**:5.21.2]

42.10.5.22 Self-Service Fueling. Occupancy of the aircraft during self-service fueling shall be prohibited. [**407**:5.22]

42.11 Alternate Fuels.

42.11.1 Compressed Natural Gas (CNG) Vehicular Fuel Systems. The design and installation of CNG engine fuel systems on vehicles of all types shall comply with NFPA 52, *Vehicular Gaseous Fuel Systems Code*, and Section 42.11.

42.11.1.1* Scope.

42.11.1.1.1 Section 42.11 shall apply to the design, installation, operation, and maintenance of compressed natural gas (CNG) and liquefied natural gas (LNG) engine fuel systems on vehicles of all types and for fueling vehicle (dispensing) systems and associated storage, including the following:

(1) Original equipment manufacturers (OEMs)
(2) Final-stage vehicle integrator/manufacturer (FSVIM)
(3) Vehicle fueling (dispensing) systems [**52**:1.1.1]

42.11.1.1.2 Section 42.11 shall apply to the design, installation, operation, and maintenance of liquefied natural gas (LNG) engine fuel systems on vehicles of all types, to their associated fueling (dispensing) facilities, and to LNG to CNG facilities with LNG storage in ASME containers of 70,000 gal (265 m^3) or less. [**52**:1.1.2]

42.11.1.1.3* Vehicles and fuel supply containers complying with federal motor vehicle safety standards (FMVSSs) covering the installation of CNG fuel systems on vehicles and certified by the respective manufacturer as meeting these standards shall not be required to comply with Sections 4.4, 4.8, 4.9, and 4.10, and Chapter 6 of NFPA 52 (except Sections 6.9, 6.11, 6.12, 6.13, and 6.14 of NFPA 52). [**52**:1.1.3]

42.11.1.1.4 Section 42.11 shall include marine, highway, rail, off-road, and industrial vehicles. [**52**:1.1.4]

42.11.1.1.5 Vehicles that are required to comply with applicable federal motor vehicle safety standards covering the installation of LNG fuel systems on vehicles and that are certified by the manufacturer as meeting these standards shall not be required to comply with Chapter 9 of NFPA 52, except 9.12.8 of NFPA 52. [**52**:1.1.5]

42.11.2 Liquefied Petroleum Gas (LP-Gas).

42.11.2.1 Fuel dispensing facilities for vehicles using LP-Gas shall comply with NFPA 58, *Liquefied Petroleum Gas Code*, and 42.11.2.

42.11.2.2 Scope.

42.11.2.2.1* Chapter 11 of NFPA 58 applies to engine fuel systems on vehicles using LP-Gas in internal combustion engines, including containers, container appurtenances, carburetion equipment, piping, hose and fittings, and their installation. [**58**:11.1.1]

42.11.2.2.2* Chapter 11 of NFPA 58 applies to the installation of fuel systems supplying engines used to propel all motor vehicles. [**58**:11.1.2]

42.11.2.2.3 Chapter 11 of NFPA 58 applies to garaging of vehicles where such systems are installed. [**58**:11.1.3]

42.11.2.2.4 Permits. Permits, where required, shall comply with Section 1.12.

42.11.2.3 Training. Each person engaged in installing, repairing, filling, or otherwise servicing an LP-Gas engine fuel system shall be trained. [**58**:11.2]

42.11.2.4 Label Requirements.

42.11.2.4.1 Each over-the-road general-purpose vehicle powered by LP-Gas shall be identified with a weather-resistant, diamond-shaped label. [**58**:11.12.1.1]

42.11.2.4.2 The label shall be located on an exterior vertical or near vertical surface on the lower right rear of the vehicle (on the trunk lid of a vehicle so equipped but not on the bumper of any vehicle) inboard from any other markings. [**58:**11.12.1.2]

42.11.2.4.3 The label shall be a minimum of 4¾ in. (120 mm) long by 3¼ in. (83 mm) high. [**58:**11.12.1.3]

42.11.2.4.4* The marking shall consist of a border and the word PROPANE [1 in. (25 mm) minimum height centered in the diamond] in silver or white reflective luminous material on a black background. [**58:**11.12.1.4]

42.11.2.5 Industrial (and Forklift) Trucks Powered by LP-Gas.

42.11.2.5.1 Scope. Paragraph 42.11.2.5 applies to LP-Gas installation on industrial trucks (including forklift trucks), both to propel them and to provide the energy for their materials-handling attachments. [**58:**11.13.1]

42.11.2.5.2 Operations. The operation of industrial trucks (including forklift trucks) powered by LP-Gas engine fuel systems shall comply with 42.11.2.5.2.1 through 42.11.2.5.2.3. [**58:**11.13.4]

42.11.2.5.2.1 Industrial trucks shall be refueled outdoors. [**58:**11.13.4.1]

42.11.2.5.2.2 Where cylinders are exchanged indoors, the fuel piping system shall be equipped to minimize the release of fuel when cylinders are exchanged, in accordance with either of the following:

(1) Using an approved quick-closing coupling in the fuel line
(2) Closing the shutoff valve at the fuel cylinder and allowing the engine to run until the fuel in the line is exhausted [**58:**11.13.4.2]

42.11.2.5.2.3 Where LP-Gas–fueled industrial trucks are used in buildings or structures, the following shall apply:

(1) The number of fuel cylinders on such a truck shall not exceed two.
(2) The use of industrial trucks in buildings frequented by the public, including those times when such buildings are occupied by the public, shall require the approval of the AHJ.
(3) The total water capacity of the fuel cylinders on an individual truck shall not exceed 105 lb (48 kg) [nominal 45 lb (20 kg) propane capacity].
(4) Trucks shall not be parked and left unattended in areas occupied by or frequented by the public without the approval of the AHJ. If left unattended with approval, the cylinder shutoff valve shall be closed.
(5) In no case shall trucks be parked and left unattended in areas of excessive heat or near sources of ignition. [**58:**11.13.4.3]

42.11.2.6 General Provisions for Vehicles Having Engines Mounted on Them (Including Floor Maintenance Machines).

42.11.2.6.1 Scope.

42.11.2.6.1.1 Paragraph 42.11.2.6 applies to the installation of equipment on vehicles that supply LP-Gas as a fuel for engines installed on these vehicles. [**58:**11.14.1.1]

42.11.2.6.1.2 Vehicles include floor maintenance and any other portable mobile unit, whether the engine is used to propel the vehicle or is mounted on it for other purposes. [**58:**11.14.1.2]

42.11.2.6.2 General Requirements.

42.11.2.6.2.1 Industrial trucks (including forklift trucks) and other engines on vehicles operating in buildings other than those used exclusively to house engines shall have an approved automatic shutoff valve installed in the fuel system. [**58:**11.14.2.1]

42.11.2.6.2.2 The source of air for combustion shall be isolated from the driver and passenger compartment, ventilating system, or air-conditioning system on the vehicle. [**58:**11.14.2.2]

42.11.2.6.2.3 Non–self-propelled floor maintenance machinery (floor polishers, scrubbers, buffers) and other similar portable equipment shall be listed. [**58:**11.14.2.3]

42.11.2.6.2.3.1 A label shall be affixed to the machinery or equipment, with the label facing the operator, with the text denoting that the cylinder or portion of the machinery or equipment containing the cylinder shall be stored in accordance with Chapter 8 of NFPA 58. [**58:**11.14.2.3(A)]

42.11.2.6.2.3.2 The use of floor maintenance machines in buildings frequented by the public, including the times when such buildings are occupied by the public, shall require the approval of the AHJ. [**58:**11.14.2.3(B)]

42.11.2.7 Garaging of Vehicles. Where vehicles with LP-Gas engine fuel systems mounted on them, and general-purpose vehicles propelled by LP-Gas engines, are stored or serviced inside garages, the following conditions shall apply:

(1) The fuel system shall be leak-free.
(2) The container shall not be filled beyond the limits specified in Chapter 7 of NFPA 58.
(3) The container shutoff valve shall be closed when the vehicle or the engine is being repaired, except when the engine is required to operate. Containers equipped with an automatic shutoff valve as specified in 11.4.1.8 of NFPA 58 satisfy this requirement.
(4) The vehicle shall not be parked near sources of heat, open flames, or similar sources of ignition or near inadequately ventilated pits. [**58:**11.16]

42.11.3* Liquefied Natural Gas (LNG). Fuel dispensing facilities for marine, highway, rail, off-road, and industrial vehicles using LNG and LNG storage in ASME containers of 70,000 gal (265 m^3) or less shall comply with NFPA 52.

42.11.3.1 Permits. Permits, where required, shall comply with Section 1.12.

Chapter 43 Spraying, Dipping, and Coating Using Flammable or Combustible Materials

43.1 Application.

43.1.1* Operations involving the spray application of flammable and combustible materials shall comply with NFPA 33, *Standard for Spray Application Using Flammable or Combustible Materials*, and Section 43.1.

43.1.1.1* Section 43.1 shall apply to the spray application of flammable liquids, combustible liquids, or combustible powders either continuously or intermittently, by any of the following methods:

(1) Compressed air atomization

(2) Airless or hydraulic atomization
(3) Electrostatic application methods
(4) Fluidized bed application methods
(5) Electrostatic fluidized bed application methods
(6) Other acceptable application means [**33**:1.1]

43.1.1.2 Section 43.1 shall also apply to spray application of water-borne, water-based, and water-reducible materials that contain flammable or combustible liquids or that produce combustible deposits or residues. [**33**:1.1.3]

43.1.1.3 Section 43.1 shall not apply to the following:

(1)*Spray operations that use less than 1 L (33.8 fl oz) of flammable or combustible liquid in any 8-hour period
(2)*Spray application processes or operations that are conducted outdoors
(3)*Portable spraying equipment that is not used repeatedly in the same location
(4) Use of aerosol products in containers up to and including 1 L (33.8 oz) capacity that are not used repeatedly in the same location
(5) Spray application of noncombustible materials
(6) The hazards of toxicity or industrial health and hygiene [**33**:1.1]

43.1.1.4 Permits. Permits, where required, shall comply with Section 1.12.

43.1.2 Location of Spray Application Operations.

43.1.2.1* General. Spray application operations and processes shall be confined to spray booths, spray rooms, or spray areas, as defined in this *Code*. [**33**:4.1]

43.1.2.2 Locations in Other Occupancies. Spray application operations and processes shall not be conducted in any building that is classified as an assembly, educational, institutional, or residential occupancy, unless they are located in a room that is separated both vertically and horizontally from all surrounding areas by construction having a fire resistance rating of not less than 2 hours. The room shall be protected by an approved automatic sprinkler system designed and installed in accordance with Section 13.3. [**33**:4.2]

43.1.3 Construction and Design of Spray Areas, Spray Rooms, and Spray Booths.

43.1.3.1* Walls and Ceilings. Walls, doors, and ceilings that intersect or enclose a spray area shall be constructed of noncombustible or limited-combustible materials or assemblies and shall be securely and rigidly mounted or fastened. The interior surfaces of the spray area shall be smooth, designed and installed to prevent pockets that can trap residues, and designed to facilitate ventilation and cleaning. [**33**:5.1]

43.1.3.1.1 Air intake filters that are a part of a wall or ceiling assembly shall be listed as Class 1 or Class 2, in accordance with ANSI/UL 900, *Standard for Air Filter Units*. [**33**:5.1.1]

43.1.3.1.2 The floor of the spray area shall be constructed of noncombustible material, limited-combustible material, or combustible material that is completely covered by noncombustible material. [**33**:5.1.2]

43.1.3.1.3 Aluminum shall not be used for structural support members or the walls or ceiling of a spray booth or spray room enclosure. Aluminum also shall not be used for ventilation ductwork associated with a spray booth or spray room. Aluminum shall be permitted to be used for interior components, such as platforms, spray apparatus components, and other ancillary devices. [**33**:5.1.3]

43.1.3.1.4 If walls or ceiling assemblies are constructed of sheet metal, single-skin assemblies shall be no thinner than 0.0478 in. (1.2 mm), and each sheet of double-skin assemblies shall be no thinner than 0.0359 in. (0.9 mm). [**33**:5.1.4]

43.1.3.1.5 Structural sections of spray booths shall be permitted to be sealed with a caulk or sealant to minimize air leakage. [**33**:5.1.5]

43.1.3.1.6 Spray rooms shall be constructed of and separated from surrounding areas of the building by construction assemblies that have a fire resistance rating of 1 hour. [**33**:5.1.6]

43.1.3.1.7 Enclosed spray booths and spray rooms shall be provided with means of egress that meet the requirements of NFPA *101*. [**33**:5.1.7]

43.1.3.1.8 Spray booths that are used exclusively for powder coating shall meet the requirements of Section 43.6. They shall be permitted to be constructed of fire-retardant combustible materials where approved by the AHJ.

*Exception: Listed spray booth assemblies that are constructed of other materials shall be permitted. [**33**:5.1.8]*

43.1.3.2 Conveyor Openings. Conveyor openings that are necessary for transporting or moving work into and out of the spray area shall be as small as practical. [**33**:5.2]

43.1.3.3* Separation from Other Occupancies. Spray booths shall be separated from other operations by a minimum distance of 3 ft (915 mm) or by a partition, wall, or floor/ceiling assembly having a minimum fire resistance rating of 1 hour. Multiple connected spray booths shall not be considered as "other operations" except as provided for in Section 13.3 of NFPA 33. [**33**:5.3]

43.1.3.3.1 Spray booths shall be installed so that all parts of the booth are readily accessible for cleaning. [**33**:5.3.1]

43.1.3.3.2 A clear space of not less than 3 ft (915 mm) shall be maintained on all sides and above the spray booth. This clear space shall be kept free of any storage or combustible construction.

Exception No. 1: This requirement shall not prohibit locating a spray booth closer than 3 ft (915 mm) to or directly against an interior partition, wall, or floor/ceiling assembly that has a fire resistance rating of not less than 1 hour, provided the spray booth can be maintained and cleaned.

*Exception No. 2: This requirement shall not prohibit locating a spray booth closer than 3 ft (915 mm) to an exterior wall or a roof assembly, provided the wall or roof is constructed of noncombustible material and provided the spray booth can be maintained and cleaned. [**33**:5.3.2]*

43.1.3.4 Movement of Powered Vehicles. Powered vehicles shall not be moved into or out of a spray area or operated in a spray area unless the spray application operation or process is stopped and the ventilation system is maintained in operation.

*Exception: This requirement shall not apply to vehicles that are listed for the specific hazards of the spray area. [**33**:5.4]*

43.1.3.5 Vision and Observation Panels.

43.1.3.5.1 Panels for light fixtures or for observation shall be of heat-treated glass, laminated glass, wired glass, or hammered-wired glass and shall be sealed to confine vapors, mists, residues, dusts, and deposits to the spray area.

Exception: Listed spray booth assemblies that have vision panels constructed of other materials shall be permitted. [33:5.5.1]

43.1.3.5.2 Panels for light fixtures shall be separated from the fixture to prevent the surface temperature of the panel from exceeding 200°F (93°C). [33:5.5.2]

43.1.3.5.3 The panel frame and method of attachment shall be designed to not fail under fire exposure before the vision panel fails. [33:5.5.3]

43.1.3.5.4 Observation panels for spray booths that are used exclusively for powder coating processes shall be permitted to be constructed of fire-resistant combustible materials. [33:5.5.4]

43.1.3.6 Ventilation. Spray areas that are equipped with ventilation distribution or baffle plates or with dry overspray collection filters shall meet the requirements of 43.1.3.6.1 through 43.1.3.6.5. [33:5.6]

43.1.3.6.1 Distribution plates or baffles shall be constructed of noncombustible materials and shall be readily removable or accessible for cleaning on both sides. [33:5.6.1]

43.1.3.6.2 Filters shall not be used when applying materials known to be highly susceptible to spontaneous heating or spontaneous ignition. [33:5.6.2]

43.1.3.6.3 Supports and holders for filters shall be constructed of noncombustible materials. [33:5.6.3]

43.1.3.6.4 Overspray collection filters shall be readily removable or accessible for cleaning or replacement. [33:5.6.4]

43.1.3.6.5 Filters shall not be alternately used for different types of coating materials if the combination of the materials might result in spontaneous heating or ignition. *(See also Section 10.9 of NFPA 33.)* [33:5.6.5]

43.1.4 Electrical and Other Sources of Ignition.

43.1.4.1* General.

43.1.4.1.1 Electrical wiring and utilization equipment shall meet all applicable requirements of Articles 500, 501, 502, 505, and 516 of *NFPA 70* and all applicable requirements of this chapter.

Exception No. 1: Powered vehicles shall meet the requirements of 43.1.3.4.

Exception No. 2: Resin application operations shall meet the requirements of Chapter 17 of NFPA 33. [33:6.2.1]

43.1.4.1.2* For the purposes of this *Code*, the Zone system of electrical area classification shall be applied as follows:

(1) The inside of open or closed containers or vessels shall be considered a Class I, Zone 0 location.
(2) A Class I, Division 1 location shall be permitted to be alternatively classified as a Class I, Zone 1 location.
(3) A Class I, Division 2 location shall be permitted to be alternatively classified as a Class I, Zone 2 location.
(4) A Class II, Division 1 location shall be permitted to be alternatively classified as a Zone 21 location.
(5) A Class II, Division 2 location shall be permitted to be alternatively classified as a Zone 22 location. [33:6.2.2]

43.1.4.1.3 For the purposes of electrical area classification, the Division system and the Zone system shall not be intermixed for any given source of release. [33:6.2.3]

43.1.4.1.4 In instances of areas within the same facility classified separately, Class I, Zone 2 locations shall be permitted to abut, but not overlap, Class I, Division 2 locations. Class I, Zone 0 or Zone 1 locations shall not abut Class I, Division 1 or Division 2 locations. [33:6.2.4]

43.1.4.1.5* Open flames, spark-producing equipment or processes, and equipment whose exposed surfaces exceed the autoignition temperature of the material being sprayed shall not be located in a spray area or in any surrounding area that is classified as Division 2, Zone 2, or Zone 22.

Exception: This requirement shall not apply to drying, curing, or fusing apparatus covered by Section 43.4. [33:6.2.5]

43.1.4.1.6* Any utilization equipment or apparatus that is capable of producing sparks or particles of hot metal and that is located above or adjacent to either the spray area or the surrounding Division 2, Zone 2, or Zone 22 areas shall be of the totally enclosed type or shall be constructed to prevent the escape of sparks or particles of hot metal. [33:6.2.6]

43.1.4.2 Electrical Area Classification.

43.1.4.2.1* Class I Locations. A Class I location shall be any location where a flammable gas or vapor is present or might be present in the air in quantities sufficient to produce an explosive or ignitible mixture. [33:6.3.1]

43.1.4.2.1.1* Class I, Division 1 Locations. As defined in 500.5(B)(1) of *NFPA 70*, a Class I, Division 1 location shall be any location where one of the following conditions exists:

(1) An ignitible concentration of flammable gas or vapor can exist under normal operating conditions.
(2) An ignitible concentration of flammable gas or vapor can exist frequently because of repair or maintenance operations or because of leakage.
(3) Breakdown or faulty operation of equipment or processes might release an ignitible concentration of flammable gas or vapor and might also cause simultaneous failure of electrical equipment in such a way as to directly cause the electrical equipment to become a source of ignition. [33:6.3.1.1]

43.1.4.2.1.2* Class I, Division 2 Locations. As defined in 500.5(B)(2) of *NFPA 70*, a Class I, Division 2 location shall be any location where one of the following conditions exists:

(1) A flammable gas or a volatile flammable liquid is handled, processed, or used, but any flammable gas, vapor, or liquid is confined within a closed container or a closed system from which it can escape only in case of accidental rupture or breakdown of the container or system or in case of abnormal operation of the equipment.
(2) An ignitible concentration of flammable gas or vapor is normally prevented by positive mechanical ventilation but might exist because of failure or abnormal operation of the ventilating equipment.
(3) An ignitible concentration of flammable gas or vapor might occasionally be transmitted from an adjacent Class I, Division 1 location, unless such transmission is prevented by positive pressure ventilation from a source of clean air and effective safeguards against ventilation failure are provided. [33:6.3.1.2]

43.1.4.2.1.3* Class I, Zone 0 Locations. As defined in 505.5(B)(1) of *NFPA 70*, a Class I, Zone 0 location shall be any location where an ignitible concentration of flammable gas or vapor is present either continuously or for long periods of time. [**33**:6.3.1.3]

43.1.4.2.1.4* Class I, Zone 1 Locations. As defined in 505.5(B)(2) of *NFPA 70*, a Class I, Zone 1 location shall be any location where one of the following conditions exists:

(1) An ignitible concentration of flammable gas or vapor is likely to exist under normal operating conditions.
(2) An ignitible concentration of flammable gas or vapor might exist frequently because of repair or maintenance operations or because of leakage.
(3) Breakdown or faulty operation of equipment or processes might release an ignitible concentration of flammable gas or vapor and might also cause simultaneous failure of electrical equipment in such a way as to directly cause the electrical equipment to become a source of ignition.
(4) An ignitible concentration of flammable gas or vapor might occasionally be transmitted from an adjacent Class I, Zone 0 location, unless such transmission is prevented by positive pressure ventilation from a source of clean air and effective safeguards against ventilation failure are provided. [**33**:6.3.1.4]

43.1.4.2.1.5 Class I, Zone 2 Locations. As defined in 505.5(B)(3) of *NFPA 70*, a Class I, Zone 2 location shall be any location where one of the following conditions exists:

(1) An ignitible concentration of a flammable gas or vapor is not likely to exist under normal operating conditions, and if an ignitible concentration does exist, will exist only for a short period of time.
(2) A flammable gas or a volatile flammable liquid is handled, processed, or used, but any flammable gas, vapor, or liquid is confined within a closed container or a closed system from which it can escape only in case of accidental rupture or breakdown of the container or system or in case of abnormal operation of the equipment.
(3) An ignitible concentration of flammable gas or vapor is normally prevented by positive mechanical ventilation but might exist because of failure or abnormal operation of the ventilating equipment.
(4) An ignitible concentration of flammable gas or vapor might occasionally be transmitted from an adjacent Class I, Zone 1 location, unless such transmission is prevented by positive pressure ventilation from a source of clean air and effective safeguards against ventilation failure are provided. *(See also A.43.1.4.2.1.2.)* [**33**:6.3.1.5]

43.1.4.2.2 Class II Locations. A Class II location shall be any location that might be hazardous because of the presence of a combustible dust. [**33**:6.3.2]

43.1.4.2.2.1* Class II, Division 1 Locations. As defined in 500.5(C)(1) of *NFPA 70*, a Class II, Division 1 location shall be any location where one of the following conditions exists:

(1) Combustible dust is in the air in quantities sufficient to produce explosive or ignitible mixtures under normal operating conditions.
(2) Mechanical failure or abnormal operation of machinery or equipment might cause an explosive or ignitible mixture of combustible dust in air and might also provide a source of ignition through simultaneous failure of electrical equipment, operation of protection devices, or from other causes.
(3) Group E combustible dusts might be present in quantities sufficient to be hazardous. [**33**:6.3.2.1]

43.1.4.2.2.2* Class II, Division 2 Locations. As defined in 500.5(C)(2) of *NFPA 70*, a Class II, Division 2 location shall be any location where one of the following conditions exists:

(1) Combustible dust due to abnormal operations might be present in the air in quantities sufficient to produce explosive or ignitible mixtures.
(2) Combustible dust accumulations are present but are normally insufficient to interfere with the normal operation of electrical equipment or other apparatus, but could as a result of infrequent malfunctioning of handling or processing equipment become suspended in the air.
(3) Combustible dust accumulations on, in, or in the vicinity of the electrical equipment could be sufficient to interfere with the safe dissipation of heat from electrical equipment, or could be ignitible by abnormal operation or failure of electrical equipment. [**33**:6.3.2.2]

43.1.4.2.2.3* Zone 20. As defined in 506.5(B)(1) of *NFPA 70*, a Zone 20 location shall be any location where one of the following conditions exists:

(1) An ignitible concentration of combustible dust is present continuously.
(2) An ignitible concentration of combustible dust is present for long periods of time. [**33**:6.3.2.3]

43.1.4.2.2.4* Zone 21. As defined in 506.5(B)(2) of *NFPA 70*, a Zone 21 location shall be any location where one of the following conditions exists:

(1) An ignitible concentration of combustible dust is likely to exist occasionally under normal operating conditions.
(2) An ignitible concentration of combustible dust might exist frequently because of repair or maintenance operations or because of leakage.
(3) Equipment is operated or processes are carried on of such a nature that equipment breakdown or faulty operations could result in the release of an ignitible concentration of combustible dust and also cause simultaneous failure of electrical equipment in a mode to cause the electrical equipment to become a source of ignition.
(4) An ignitible concentration of combustible dust could be communicated from an adjacent Zone 20 location, unless communication is prevented by adequate positive pressure ventilation from a source of clean air and effective safeguards against ventilation failure are provided. [**33**:6.3.2.4]

43.1.4.2.2.5* Zone 22. As defined in 506.5(B)(3) of *NFPA 70*, a Zone 22 location shall be any location where one of the following conditions exists:

(1) An ignitible concentration of combustible dust is not likely to occur in normal operation, and if it does occur, will only persist for a short period.
(2) A combustible dust is handled, processed, or used, but the dust is normally confined within closed containers or closed systems from which it can escape only as a result of the abnormal operation of the equipment with which the dust is handled, processed, or used.
(3) An ignitible concentration of combustible dust could be communicated from an adjacent Zone 21 location, unless communication is prevented by adequate positive pressure ventilation from a source of clean air and effective safeguards against ventilation failure are provided. [**33**:6.3.2.5]

43.1.4.3 Electrical Devices in Spray Areas.

43.1.4.3.1 The spray area as defined in NFPA 33 shall be Class I, Division 1; Class I, Zone 1; Class II, Division 1; or Zone 21, whichever is applicable. [**33**:6.4.1]

43.1.4.3.2 Electrical wiring and utilization equipment that is located in the spray area and is not subject to deposits of combustible residues shall be suitable for Class I, Division 1; Class I, Zone 1; Class II, Division 1; or Zone 21 locations, whichever is applicable. [**33**:6.4.2]

43.1.4.3.3* Electrical wiring and utilization equipment that is located in the spray area and is subject to deposits of combustible residues shall be listed for such exposure and shall be suitable for Class I, Division 1; Class I, Zone 1; Class II, Division 1; or Zone 21 locations, whichever is applicable. [**33**:6.4.3]

43.1.4.4 Electrical Devices in Areas Adjacent to or Connected to Spray Areas. Electrical wiring and utilization equipment located in areas adjacent to or connected to the spray area, including but not limited to vestibules and tunnels, shall be classified in accordance with 43.1.4.4.1 through 43.1.4.4.5. [**33**:6.5]

43.1.4.4.1 Electrical wiring and utilization equipment located outside, but within 20 ft (6100 mm) horizontally and 10 ft (3050 mm) vertically, of an unenclosed spray area and not separated from the spray area by partitions extending to the boundaries of the area designated as Division 2, Zone 2; or Zone 22 in Figure 43.1.4.4.1 shall be suitable for Class I, Division 2; Class I, Zone 2; Class II, Division 2; or Zone 22 locations, whichever is applicable. [**33**:6.5.1]

43.1.4.4.2 If spray application operations are conducted within a closed-top, open-face or open-front booth or room, as shown in Figure 43.1.4.4.2, any electrical wiring or utilization equipment located outside the booth or room but within 3 ft (915 mm) of any opening shall be suitable for Class I, Division 2; Class I, Zone 2; Class II, Division 2; or Zone 22 locations, whichever is applicable. [**33**:6.5.2]

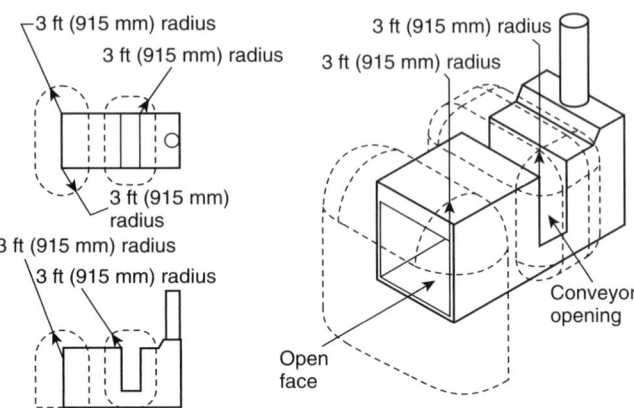

FIGURE 43.1.4.4.2 Class I, Division 2; Class I, Zone 2; Class II, Division 2; or Zone 22 Locations Adjacent to an Open-Face or Open-Front Spray Booth or Spray Room. [33:Figure 6.5.2]

43.1.4.4.3 If spray application operations are conducted within an open-top booth, any electrical wiring or utilization equipment located within the space 3 ft (915 mm) vertically from the top of the booth shall be suitable for Class I, Division 2; Class I, Zone 2; Class II, Division 2; or Zone 22 locations, whichever is applicable. In addition, any electrical wiring or utilization equipment located within 3 ft (915 mm) in all directions of openings other than the open top also shall be suitable for Class I, Division 2; Class I, Zone 2; Class II, Division 2; or Zone 22 locations, whichever is applicable. [**33**:6.5.3]

43.1.4.4.4 If spray application operations are confined to an enclosed spray booth or room, electrical area classification shall be as follows:

(1) The area within 3 ft (915 mm) of any opening shall be classified as Class I, Division 2; Class I, Zone 2; Class II, Division 2; or Zone 22 locations, whichever is applicable, as shown in Figure 43.1.4.4.4.
(2) Where exhaust air is recirculated and all requirements of 43.1.5.5 are met, both of the following shall apply:
   (a) The interior of any recirculation path from the secondary particulate filters up to and including the air supply plenum shall be classified as Class I, Division 2; Class I, Zone 2; Class II, Division 2; or Zone 22 locations, whichever is applicable.
   (b) The interior of fresh air supply ducts shall be unclassified.
(3) Where exhaust air is not recirculated, the interior of fresh air supply ducts and fresh air supply plenums shall be unclassified. [**33**:6.5.4]

43.1.4.4.5 Open containers, supply containers, waste containers, spray gun cleaners, and solvent distillation units that contain Class I liquids shall be located in areas ventilated in accordance with applicable requirements of 43.1.5. [**33**:6.5.5]

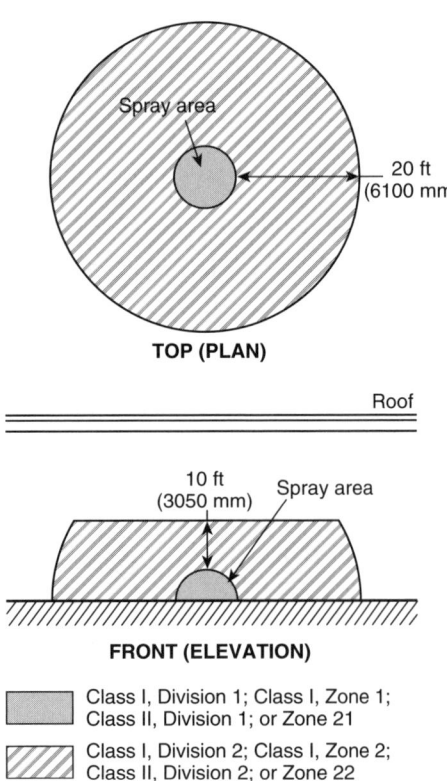

FIGURE 43.1.4.4.1 Electrical Area Classification for Unenclosed Spray Areas. [33:Figure 6.5.1]

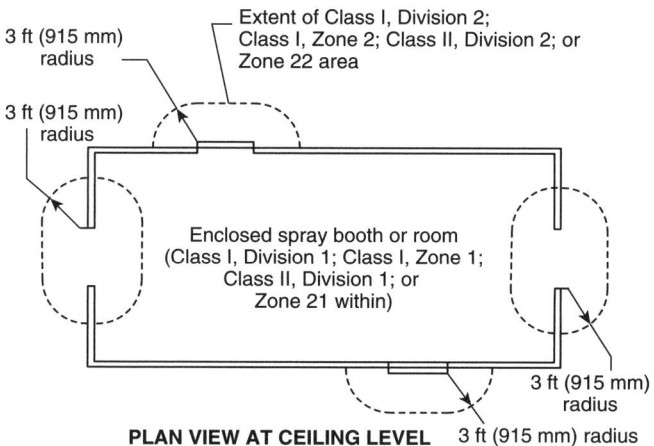

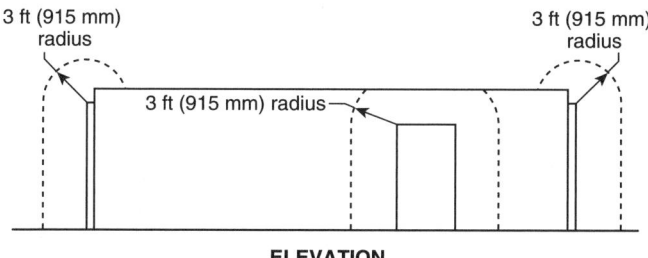

FIGURE 43.1.4.4.4 Class I, Division 2; Class I, Zone 2; Class II, Division 2; or Zone 22 Locations Adjacent to an Enclosed Spray Booth or Spray Room. [33:Figure 6.5.4]

43.1.4.4.5.1 Electrical area classification shall be as follows:

(1) The area within 3 ft (915 mm) in all directions from any such container or equipment and extending to the floor or grade level shall be classified as Class I, Division 1 or Class I, Zone 1, whichever is applicable.

(2) The area extending 2 ft (610 mm) beyond the Division 1 or Zone 1 location shall be classified as Class I, Division 2 or Class I, Zone 2, whichever is applicable.

(3) The area extending 5 ft (1525 mm) horizontally beyond the area described in 43.1.4.4.5.1(2) up to a height of 18 in. (460 mm) above the floor or grade level shall be classified as Class I, Division 2 or Class I, Zone 2, whichever is applicable.

(4) The area inside any tank or container shall be classified as Class I, Division 1 or Class I, Zone 0, whichever is applicable. [**33**:6.5.5.1]

43.1.4.4.5.2 Electrical wiring and utilization equipment installed in these areas shall be suitable for the location, as shown in Figure 43.1.4.4.5.2. [**33**:6.5.5.2]

43.1.4.5 Light Fixtures.

43.1.4.5.1 Light fixtures, like that shown in Figure 43.1.4.5.1, that are attached to the walls or ceiling of a spray area but that are outside any classified area and are separated from the spray area by glass panels that meet the requirements of 43.1.3.5 shall be suitable for use in unclassified locations. Such fixtures shall be serviced from outside the spray area. [**33**:6.6.1]

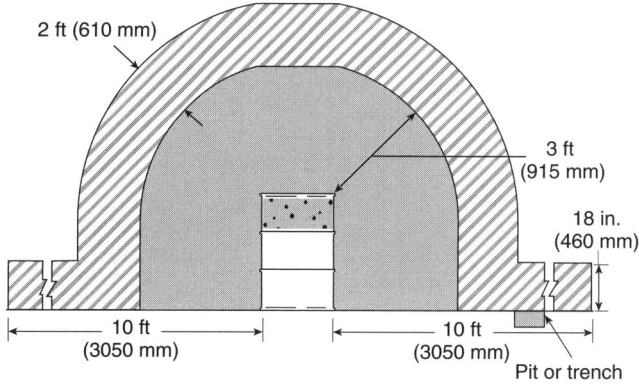

FIGURE 43.1.4.4.5.2 Electrical Area Classification for Class I Liquid Operations Around Open Containers, Supply Containers, Waste Containers, Spray Gun Cleaners, and Solvent Distillation Units. [33:Figure 6.5.5.2]

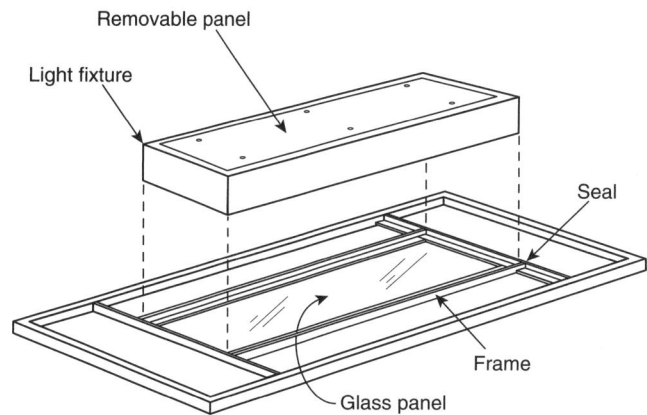

FIGURE 43.1.4.5.1 Example of a Light Fixture Mounted Outside of the Spray Area and Serviced from Outside the Spray Area. [33:Figure 6.6.1]

43.1.4.5.2 Light fixtures, like that shown in Figure 43.1.4.5.1, that are attached to the walls or ceiling of a spray area; that are separated from the spray area by glass panels that meet the requirements of 43.1.3.5; and that are located within a Class I, Division 2, a Class I, Zone 2, a Class II, Division 2; or a Zone 22 location shall be suitable for such location. Such fixtures shall be serviced from outside the spray area. [**33**:6.6.2]

43.1.4.5.3 Light fixtures, like that shown in Figure 43.1.4.5.3, that are an integral part of the walls or ceiling of a spray area shall be permitted to be separated from the spray area by glass panels that are an integral part of the fixture. Such fixtures shall be listed for use in Class I, Division 2; Class I, Zone 2; Class II, Division 2; or Zone 22 locations, whichever is applicable, and also shall be listed for accumulations of deposits of combustible residues. Such fixtures shall be permitted to be serviced from inside the spray area. [**33**:6.6.3]

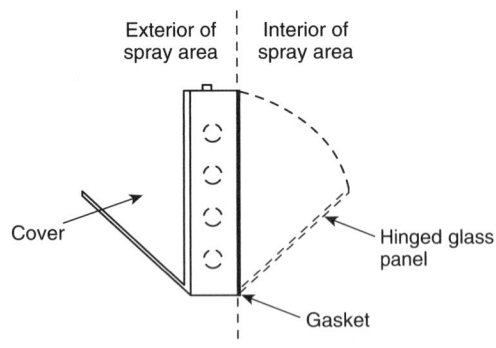

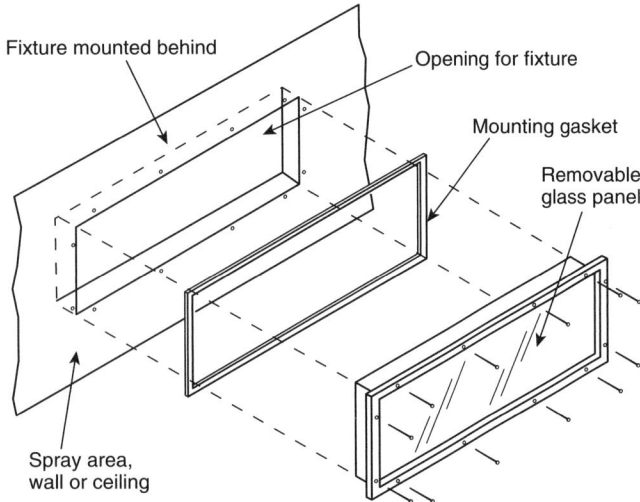

FIGURE 43.1.4.5.3 Examples of Light Fixtures That Are Integral Parts of the Spray Area and That Are Serviced from Inside the Spray Area. [33:Figure 6.6.3]

43.1.4.5.4 Light fixtures that are located inside the spray area shall meet the requirements of 43.1.4.3 and 43.1.4.6. [**33:**6.6.4]

43.1.4.6* Static Electricity. All electrically conductive objects in the spray area, except those objects required by the process to be at high voltage, shall be electrically connected to ground with a resistance of not more than 1 megohm (10^6 ohms). This requirement shall apply to containers of coating material, wash cans, guards, hose connectors, brackets, and any other electrically conductive objects or devices in the area. This requirement shall also apply to any personnel who enter the spray area. [**33:**6.7]

43.1.4.7 Flexible Power Cords. For automated equipment and robotic equipment, flexible power cords shall be permitted to be used in hazardous (classified) locations and shall be permitted to be connected to the fixed part of the electrical circuit, provided they meet all of the following conditions:

(1) They are approved for extra-hard usage.
(2) They are equipped with a grounding conductor that meets the requirements of Section 400.2 of *NFPA 70.*
(3) They are connected to terminals or conductors in an approved manner.
(4) They are supported by a positive mechanical clamp in such a manner that permits the cord to be readily replaced and prevents strain at the cord connections within the terminal enclosure.
(5) They are provided with explosionproof seals for liquid applications or dusttight seals for powder applications where the cord enters junction boxes, fittings, or enclosures.
(6) They are listed for deposits of combustible residues. [**33:**6.8]

43.1.4.8 Portable Electric Lights. Portable electric light fixtures shall not be used in any spray area while spray application operations are being conducted.

Exception: Where portable electric light fixtures are required for use in spaces that are not illuminated by fixed light fixtures within the spray area, they shall meet the requirements of 43.1.4.3.3. [33:6.9]

43.1.5 Ventilation.

43.1.5.1 General. Ventilating and exhaust systems shall be designed and installed in accordance with the applicable requirements of NFPA 91 except as amended by the requirements of 43.1.5. [**33:**7.1]

43.1.5.2 Performance Requirements. Each spray area shall be provided with mechanical ventilation that is capable of confining and removing vapors and mists to a safe location and is capable of confining and controlling combustible residues, dusts, and deposits. The concentration of the vapors and mists in the exhaust stream of the ventilation system shall not exceed 25 percent of the lower flammable limit. *(See Annex B of NFPA 33 for additional guidance on determining the lower flammable limit.)*

Exception: In confined spaces, where ventilation might not be capable of providing the necessary ventilation, a properly applied inerting procedure shall be permitted to be used. Such procedures shall meet the applicable requirements of NFPA 69 and shall be acceptable to the AHJ. [33:7.2]

43.1.5.2.1* Spray areas equipped with overspray collection filters shall have an effective means to ensure that the performance requirements of 43.1.5.2 are met. [**33:**7.2.1]

43.1.5.2.2 Powder Coating Systems. Powder coating systems also shall meet the requirements of Section 15.8 of NFPA 33. [**33:**7.2.2]

43.1.5.2.3 Mechanical ventilation shall be kept in operation at all times while spray operations are being conducted and for a sufficient time thereafter to allow the vapors from drying coated objects or material and residues to be exhausted. Where spray operations are conducted automatically without an attendant constantly on duty, the operating controls of the spray apparatus shall be arranged so that the spray apparatus cannot function unless the exhaust fans are operating. [**33:**7.2.3]

43.1.5.3* Make-Up Air. An adequate supply of clean make-up air shall be provided to compensate for the air exhausted from spray operations. The intake for this make-up air shall be located so that the air exhausted from spray operations is not recirculated. [**33:**7.3]

43.1.5.4 Routing of Exhaust Ducts. Air exhausted to the atmosphere from liquid spray operations shall be conducted by ducts directly to the outside of the building. Exhaust ducts shall follow the most direct route to the point of discharge but shall not penetrate a fire wall. The exhaust discharge shall be directed away from any fresh air intakes. The exhaust duct discharge point shall be at least 6 ft (1830 mm) from any exterior wall or roof. The exhaust duct shall not discharge in the direction of any combustible construction that is within 25 ft (7625 mm) of the exhaust duct discharge point, nor shall it discharge in the direction of any unprotected opening in any noncombustible or limited-combustible construction that is within 25 ft (7625 mm) of the exhaust duct discharge point. [**33**:7.4]

43.1.5.5 Recirculation of Exhaust.

43.1.5.5.1* Air exhausted from spray areas shall not be recirculated unless all of the following requirements are met:

(1) Recirculation shall be allowed only for unmanned spray operations and for cascading to subsequent unmanned spray operations.
(2) Solid particulates shall be removed from the recirculated air.
(3) The concentration of vapors in the exhaust airstream shall not exceed 25 percent of the lower flammable limit.
(4) Listed equipment shall be used to monitor the concentration of vapors in all exhaust airstreams.
(5) The equipment specified in 43.1.5.5.1(4) shall sound an alarm and shall automatically shut down the spray operation if the concentration of any vapor in the exhaust airstream exceeds 25 percent of the lower flammable limit.
(6) All equipment installed to process and remove contaminants from the air exhausted from spray operations shall be approved. [**33**:7.5.1]

43.1.5.5.2* The provisions of 43.1.5.5.1 shall not disallow recirculation of air to occupied spaces. However, other requirements addressing the toxicity and permissible exposure limits shall also apply. *(See ANSI/AIHA Z9.7, Recirculation of Air from Industrial Process Exhaust Systems.)* [**33**:7.5.2]

43.1.5.6* Manifolding of Exhaust Ducts. Individual spray booths shall be separately ducted to the building exterior.

Exception No. 1: Multiple cabinet spray booths whose combined frontal area does not exceed 18 ft² (1.7 m²) shall be permitted to be manifolded if the sprayed materials used will not react and cause ignition of the residue in the ducts.

Exception No. 2: Where treatment of exhaust is necessary for air pollution control or for energy conservation, ducts shall be permitted to be manifolded if all of the following conditions are met:

(1) The sprayed materials used will not react and cause ignition of the residue in the ducts.
(2) No nitrocellulose-based finishing material is used.
(3) An air-cleaning system is provided to reduce the amount of overspray carried into the duct manifold.
(4) Automatic sprinkler protection is provided at the junction of each booth exhaust with the manifold, in addition to the protection required by 43.1.7.
*(5) The installation is approved by the AHJ. [**33**:7.6]*

43.1.5.7* Materials of Construction. Exhaust plenums and exhaust ducts and fasteners shall be constructed of steel, except as allowed in 43.1.5.7.1, 43.1.5.7.2, and 43.1.5.7.3. [**33**:7.7]

43.1.5.7.1 For spray booths used exclusively for powder coating, ducts shall be permitted to be constructed of fire-retardant combustible materials. [**33**:7.7.1]

43.1.5.7.2 Concrete shall be permitted to be used. The interior surfaces of the concrete exhaust plenum or exhaust duct shall be smooth and sealed to facilitate cleaning. [**33**:7.7.2]

43.1.5.7.3 Other materials of construction shall be permitted to be used in cases where the conveyed materials are not compatible with steel. [**33**:7.7.3]

43.1.5.8* Support of Exhaust Ducts. Exhaust ducts shall be supported to prevent collapse under fire conditions. [**33**:7.8]

43.1.5.8.1 Duct supports shall be designed to carry the weight of the duct system itself, plus the anticipated weight of any residues. If sprinkler protection is provided inside the duct system, then the duct supports also shall be designed to carry the anticipated weight of any accumulation of sprinkler discharge. [**33**:7.8.1]

43.1.5.8.2 Hangers and supports shall be fastened securely to the building or to the structure to avoid vibration and stress on the duct system. [**33**:7.8.2]

43.1.5.8.3 Hangers and supports shall be designed to allow for expansion and contraction. [**33**:7.8.3]

43.1.5.8.4 Exhaust ducts shall not use building walls, floors, ceilings, or roofs as component parts. [**33**:7.8.4]

43.1.5.8.5 The provisions of 43.1.5.8.4 shall not disallow the use of concrete exhaust plenums or exhaust ducts where some or all of the plenum or duct is part of the concrete floor. [**33**:7.8.5]

43.1.5.9 Exhaust Duct Access Openings. Exhaust ducts shall be provided with doors, panels, or other means to facilitate inspection, maintenance, cleaning, and access to fire protection devices. [**33**:7.9]

43.1.5.10 Exhaust Fans and Drives.

43.1.5.10.1 The rotating element of the exhaust fan shall be nonferrous, or the fan shall be constructed so that a shift of the impeller or shaft will not permit two ferrous parts of the fan to rub or strike. There shall be ample clearance between the rotating element and fan casing to avoid a fire by friction, with necessary allowances being made for ordinary expansion and loading and to prevent contact between moving parts and the duct or fan housing. Fan blades shall be mounted on a shaft that is sufficiently heavy to maintain alignment even when the blades of the fan are heavily loaded. All bearings shall be of the self-lubricating type or shall be lubricated from a point outside the duct and preferably shall be located outside the duct and the booth. [**33**:7.10.1]

43.1.5.10.2 Electric motors that drive exhaust fans shall not be placed inside any spray area unless they meet the provisions of 43.1.4.3.3. [**33**:7.10.2]

43.1.5.10.3 Belts shall not enter any spray area unless the belt and pulley within the spray area are completely enclosed. [**33**:7.10.3]

43.1.5.11* Drying Areas. Freshly sprayed workpieces shall be dried only in spaces that are ventilated to prevent the concentration of vapors from exceeding 25 percent of the lower flammable limit. *(See also Section 43.4.)* [**33**:7.11]

43.1.6 Storage, Handling, and Distribution of Flammable and Combustible Liquids.

43.1.6.1* General. Storage, handling, and mixing of flammable and combustible liquids shall meet all the applicable requirements of NFPA 30 and 43.1.6. [**33**:8.1]

43.1.6.2 Storage in Process Areas.

43.1.6.2.1 The volume of Class I, Class II, and Class IIIA liquids stored in a storage cabinet shall not exceed 120 gal (454 L). [**33**:8.2.1]

43.1.6.2.1.1 The total aggregate volume of Class I, Class II, and Class IIIA liquids in a group of storage cabinets shall not exceed the maximum allowable quantity of flammable and combustible liquids per control area based on the occupancy where the cabinets are located, as set forth in Section 9.6 of NFPA 30, *Flammable and Combustible Liquids Code*. [**33**:8.2.1.1]

43.1.6.2.1.2 For industrial occupancies, the total aggregate volume of Class I, Class II, and Class IIIA liquids in a group of storage cabinets in a single area shall not exceed the maximum allowable quantity (MAQ) of flammable and combustible liquids per control area for industrial occupancies as set forth in Table 43.1.6.2.1.2. [**33**:8.2.1.2]

Table 43.1.6.2.1.2 Maximum Allowable Quantity of Flammable and Combustible Liquids per Control Area

	Liquid Classes	Quantity		Notes
		L	gal	
Flammable liquids	IA	115	30	1, 2
	IB & IC	460	120	1, 2
	IA, IB, IC combined	460	120	1, 2, 3
Combustible liquids	II	460	120	1, 2
	IIIA	1,265	330	1, 2

Source: Table 34.1.3.1 of *NFPA 5000, Building Construction and Safety Code*, 2009 edition.

Notes:
(1) Quantities are permitted to be increased 100 percent where all liquids are stored in approved flammable liquids storage cabinets or in safety cans. Where Note 2 also applies, the increase for both notes is permitted to be applied accumulatively.
(2) Quantities are permitted to be increased 100 percent in buildings equipped throughout with an automatic sprinkler system installed in accordance with NFPA 13, *Standard for the Installation of Sprinkler Systems*. Where Note 1 also applies, the increase for both notes is permitted to be applied accumulatively.
(3) Containing not more than the maximum allowable quantity per control area of Class IA, Class IB, or Class IC flammable liquids, individually. [**33**: Table 8.2.1.2]

43.1.6.2.2 The quantity of liquid located in the vicinity of spraying operations but outside of identified storage areas, such as storage cabinets, an inside liquid storage area, or a warehouse or outside of other specific process areas that are cut off by at least a 2-hour fire separation from the spraying operations shall not exceed the quantity given in either of the following, whichever is greater:

(1)*The amount required to supply spraying operations for one continuous 24-hour period
(2) The aggregate sum of the following:
  (a) 25 gal (95 L) of Class IA liquids in containers
  (b) 120 gal (454 L) of Class IB, Class IC, Class II, or Class III liquids in containers
  (c) 1585 gal (6000 L) of either of the following:
   i. Class IB, IC, II, or IIIA liquids in metal portable tanks or metal intermediate bulk containers, each not exceeding 793 gal (3000 L)
   ii. Class II or Class IIIA liquids in nonmetallic intermediate bulk containers, each not exceeding 793 gal (3000 L)
  (d) Twenty portable tanks or intermediate bulk containers, each not exceeding 793 gal (3000 L) of Class IIIB liquids [**33**:8.2.2]

43.1.6.2.3 The quantity of flammable and combustible liquids located in a spray area or in a mixing room adjacent to a spray area shall meet the requirements of 43.1.6.3. [**33**:8.2.3]

43.1.6.3 Mixing.

43.1.6.3.1 Dispensing or transfer of liquids from containers and filling of containers, including portable mixing tanks and "pressure pots," shall be done only in a spray area with the ventilation in operation or in a mixing room. [**33**:8.3.1]

43.1.6.3.2 Mixing rooms shall meet all of the following requirements:

(1) The mixing room shall meet the construction requirements of 43.1.3.
(2) The area of the mixing room shall not exceed 150 ft^2 (14 m^2).
(3) The mixing room shall be designed to contain a spill of the contents in the room.
(4) The mixing room used for mixing and dispensing operations shall be provided with continuous mechanical ventilation capable of providing air movement of not less than 1 ft^3/min per square foot of floor area (0.3 m^3/min/m^2) or 150 ft^3/min (4 m^3/min), whichever is greater. The ventilation system shall be in operation at all times.
(5) Dispensing and mixing rooms shall be classified, for purposes of electrical area classification, the same as enclosed spray booths, in accordance with 43.1.4.4.4.
(6) The mixing room shall be provided with an approved automatic fire protection system that meets all applicable requirements of 43.1.7.
(7) The mixing room shall be provided with portable fire extinguishers located in accordance with Section 13.6.

Exception: See 43.1.6.3.6. [*33:8.3.2*]

43.1.6.3.3 The amount of liquid permitted in a single spray area shall not exceed 60 gal (227 L). [**33**:8.3.3]

43.1.6.3.4 Where a separate mixing room is provided and the mixing room is located adjacent to or within 6 ft (1830 mm) of an adjacent spray area or areas, as shown in Figure 43.1.6.3.4(a) and Figure 43.1.6.3.4(b), the combined quantities of liquids located in the spray areas and the mixing room shall not exceed 120 gal (454 L).

Exception: See 43.1.6.3.6. [*33:8.3.4*]

43.1.6.3.5 Where a separate mixing room is provided and the mixing room is located more than 6 ft (1830 mm) from an adjacent spray area or areas, the quantity of liquid permitted in the mixing room shall not exceed 2 gal/ft^2 (80 L/m^2), up to a maximum of 300 gal (1135 L), as shown in Figure 43.1.6.3.5. The amount of liquid in the spray area shall not exceed 60 gal (227 L).

Exception: See 43.1.6.3.6. [*33:8.3.5*]

43.1.6.3.6 Where the quantities of liquids required or the floor area necessary to provide a suitable mixing room ex-

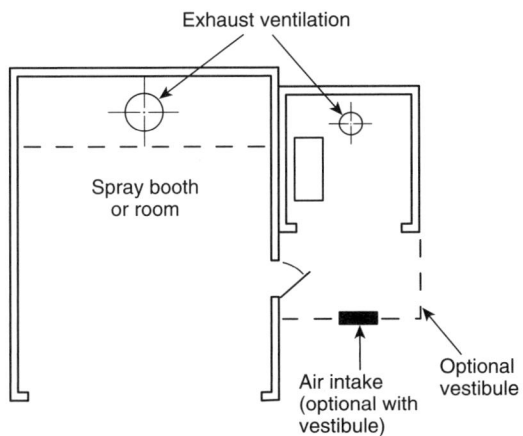

FIGURE 43.1.6.3.4(a) Mixing Room Within 6 ft (1830 mm) of Spray Area, Including Maximum Volume of Liquid Allowed. [33:Figure 8.3.4(a)]

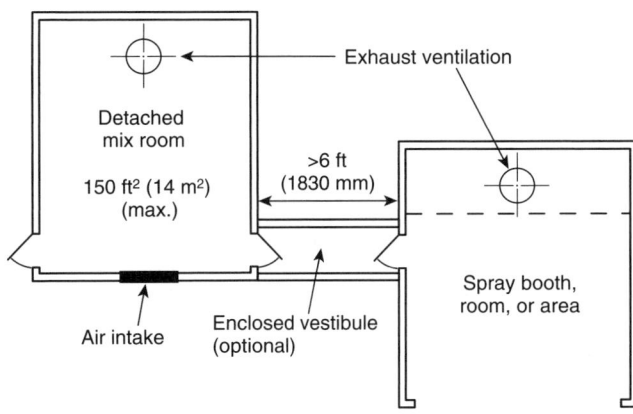

FIGURE 43.1.6.3.5 Mixing Room More Than 6 ft (1830 mm) from Spray Area, Including Maximum Volume of Liquid Allowed. [33:Figure 8.3.5]

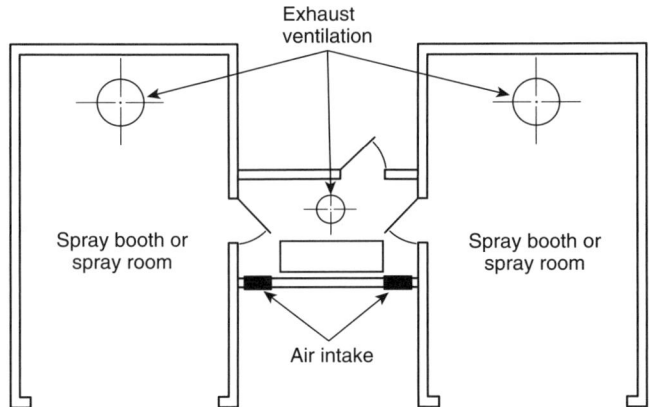

FIGURE 43.1.6.3.4(b) Mixing Room Within 6 ft (1830 mm) of Spray Area and with Direct Entry to Spray Area, Including Maximum Volume of Liquid Allowed. [33:Figure 8.3.4(b)]

ceeds the limits specified in 43.1.6.3.2 through 43.1.6.3.5, the mixing room shall meet all applicable requirements of NFPA 30. [**33**:8.3.6]

43.1.6.4 Distribution Systems — Piping.

43.1.6.4.1* Piping systems that convey flammable or combustible liquids between storage tanks, mixing rooms (paint kitchens), and spray areas shall be of steel or other material having comparable properties of resistance to heat and physical damage. Piping systems shall be properly bonded and grounded. [**33**:8.4.1]

43.1.6.4.2* Piping systems within the spray area shall be of steel or material having comparable heat and physical resistance where possible. Where tubing or hose is used, a shutoff valve shall be provided on the steel pipe at the connection. [**33**:8.4.2]

43.1.6.4.3* Tubing or hose shall be inspected and replaced as necessary. Replacement tubing or hose shall be that recommended by the equipment manufacturer. [**33**:8.4.3]

43.1.6.4.4 Where a pump is used to supply the liquid used in the spray application process, piping, tubing, hose, and other accessories shall be designed to withstand the maximum working pressure of the pump, or means shall be provided to limit the discharge pressure of the pump. [**33**:8.4.4]

43.1.6.4.5* Where a pump is used to supply the liquid used in the spray application process, an automatic means shall be provided to shut off the supply of liquid in event of fire. When pressurized tanks larger than 5 gal (19 L) are used to supply the liquid used in the spray application process, an automatic means shall be provided to shut off liquid flow at the tank outlet in the event of fire. [**33**:8.4.5]

43.1.6.4.6 All pressure tubing, hose, and couplings shall be inspected at regular intervals. With the hose extended, the hose and couplings shall be tested using the in-service maximum operating pressure. Any hose showing material deteriorations, signs of leakage, or weakness in its carcass or at the couplings shall be replaced. [**33**:8.4.6]

43.1.6.5 Distribution Systems — General.

43.1.6.5.1 Liquids shall be transported by means of closed containers, approved safety cans, or approved portable tanks or shall be transferred by means of a piping system. Open containers shall not be used for moving or storing liquids. [**33**:8.5.1]

43.1.6.5.2* Wherever liquids are transferred from one container to another, both containers shall be effectively bonded and grounded to dissipate static electricity. [**33**:8.5.2]

43.1.6.5.3 Containers that supply spray nozzles shall be of the closed type or shall be provided with metal covers that are kept closed. Containers that do not rest on the floor shall have supports or shall be suspended by wire cables. Containers that supply spray nozzles by gravity flow shall not exceed 10 gal (38 L) capacity. [**33**:8.5.3]

43.1.6.5.4 Original shipping containers shall not be subjected to air pressure for supplying spray nozzles. [**33**:8.5.4]

43.1.6.5.5 Containers that are pressurized to supply spray nozzles, air storage tanks, and coolers shall comply with all applicable requirements of the ASME *Boiler and Pressure Vessel Code*, Section VIII, for construction, tests, and maintenance.

Exception: The following need not meet this requirement:

(1) Pressure containers less than 6 in. (150 mm) in diameter
(2) Pressure containers that operate at less than a gauge pressure of 15 psi (1.03 kPa)
*(3) Siphon-type spray cups [**33**:8.5.5]*

43.1.6.5.6 If a heater is used to heat the liquid being sprayed, it shall be low-pressure steam, low-pressure hot water, or electric. If electric, it shall be approved and listed for the specific location in which it is used. *(See 43.1.4.)* Heaters shall not be located in spray booths or other locations subject to the accumulation of deposits of combustible residue. Agitators, if used, shall be driven by compressed air, water, low-pressure steam, or electricity. If the agitators are powered by an electric motor, the motor shall meet the requirements of 43.1.4. [**33**:8.5.6]

43.1.6.5.7 Methods for cleaning paint circulation systems shall meet the requirements of 7.3.7 of NFPA 30. [**33**:8.5.7]

43.1.6.5.8 Compressed air shall be permitted to be used for cleaning paint delivery hoses for individual applicators in a spray booth, provided both of the following requirements are met:

(1) The booth ventilation is operating.
(2) The maximum air pressure does not exceed the maximum working pressure of any component of the piping or hose system. [**33**:8.5.8]

43.1.7 Protection.

43.1.7.1* General. Spray areas, which include by definition any associated exhaust plenums and exhaust ductwork, any particulate filters, any solvent concentrator units, any recirculation air supply units, and mixing rooms, shall be protected with an approved automatic fire protection system. [**33**:9.1]

43.1.7.1.1 The automatic fire protection system shall be permitted to be, and shall be installed in accordance with, any of the following:

(1) An automatic water sprinkler system that meets all applicable requirements of NFPA 13
(2) An automatic foam water sprinkler system that meets all applicable requirements of NFPA 16
(3) A carbon dioxide extinguishing system that meets all applicable requirements of NFPA 12
(4) A dry chemical extinguishing system that meets all applicable requirements of NFPA 17
(5) A gaseous agent extinguishing system that meets all applicable requirements of NFPA 2001 [**33**:9.1.1]

43.1.7.1.2 The automatic fire protection system also shall meet all applicable requirements of 43.1.7.2 and 43.1.7.3. [**33**:9.1.2]

43.1.7.1.3 The fire alarm and fire protection system shall be supervised in accordance with *NFPA 72*. [**33**:9.1.3]

43.1.7.2 Continuous Spray Application Operations.

43.1.7.2.1 For continuous spray application operations, activation of the automatic fire protection system shall automatically accomplish all of the following:

(1) Activate a local alarm in the vicinity of the spraying operation
(2) Transmit an alarm signal to the facility's fire alarm system, if such a system is provided
(3) Shut down the coating material delivery system
(4) Shut down all spray application operations
(5) Stop any conveyors into and out of the spray area [**33**:9.2.1]

43.1.7.2.1.1 For continuous spray application operations, the additional requirements of 43.1.7.7, for automated powder application equipment, or 43.1.7.8, for automated liquid electrostatic spray application equipment, whichever is applicable, shall also apply. [**33**:9.2.1.1]

43.1.7.2.2 Emergency Shutdown. For continuous spray application operations, one or more manual emergency system shutdown stations shall be installed to serve each spray area. When activated, the stations shall accomplish at least the functions listed in 43.1.7.2.1(1) and 43.1.7.2.1(3) through 43.1.7.2.1(5). At least one such station shall be within ready access of operating personnel. If access to this station is likely to involve exposure to danger, an additional station shall be located adjacent to an exit from the area. [**33**:9.2.2]

43.1.7.3 Ventilation Systems. Air make-up systems and spray area exhaust systems shall remain functioning during any fire alarm condition.

Exception No. 1: Where the type of automatic fire protection system requires that ventilation be discontinued, air make-up systems and spray area exhaust systems shall be permitted to be shut down and dampers shall be permitted to close.

*Exception No. 2: For powder coating systems, the requirements of 43.1.7.7 shall be met instead of those of this paragraph. [**33**:9.3]*

43.1.7.4* Automatic Sprinkler Systems.

43.1.7.4.1* The automatic sprinkler system shall be a wet pipe system, a dry pipe system, a preaction system, or an open-head deluge system, whichever is most appropriate for the portion of the spray operation being protected. [**33**:9.4.1]

43.1.7.4.2 The automatic sprinkler system shall be designed for Extra Hazard (Group 2) occupancies, as defined in NFPA 13.

Exception No. 1: For spray application of styrene cross-link thermoset resins, Section 17.3 of NFPA 33 shall apply.

*Exception No. 2: Automatic sprinkler systems for powder coating operations shall be designed for Ordinary Hazard (Group 2), as defined in NFPA 13. [**33**:9.4.2]*

43.1.7.4.3 The water supply shall be sufficient to supply all sprinklers likely to open in any one fire incident without depleting the available water for use in hose streams. [**33**:9.4.3]

43.1.7.4.4 Where sprinklers are installed to protect spray areas and mixing rooms only, water shall be permitted to be supplied from domestic water systems, provided the domestic supply can meet the demand for the design criteria of 43.1.7.4.2. [**33**:9.4.4]

43.1.7.4.5 The sprinkler system shall be controlled by a separate, listed indicating valve(s), operable from floor level. [**33**:9.4.5]

43.1.7.4.6* Sprinkler systems protecting stacks or ducts shall meet all of the following requirements:

(1) Sprinklers shall be spaced no more than 12 ft (3.7 m) apart.
(2) If exhaust ducts are manifolded, a sprinkler shall be located in the manifold at the junction of each exhaust duct with the manifold.
(3) Sprinklers shall provide a minimum flow of 30 gpm (114 L/min) per head at a minimum of 15 psi (1 bar) pressure.
(4) Sprinklers shall be ordinary temperature rated, unless required to be higher due to operating temperatures measured in the ducts, in which case the operating temperature shall be at least 50°F (28°C) above the inside temperature of the duct. [**33**:9.4.6]

43.1.7.4.6.1 Stacks and exhaust ducts shall be provided with access openings for inspection and cleaning of sprinklers. [**33**:9.4.6.1]

43.1.7.4.6.2 Sprinkler systems protecting stacks and ducts that are subject to freezing shall be of a nonfreezing type or be a manually controlled open-head system. [**33**:9.4.6.2]

43.1.7.4.7 Sprinklers shall be protected against overspray residue, either by location or covering, so that they will operate quickly in event of fire. [**33**:9.4.7]

43.1.7.4.7.1 Sprinklers shall be permitted to be covered only by cellophane bags having a thickness of 0.003 in. (0.08 mm) or less or by thin paper bags. These coverings shall be replaced frequently so that heavy deposits of residue do not accumulate. [**33**:9.4.7.1]

43.1.7.4.7.2 Sprinklers that have been painted or coated by overspray or residues shall be replaced with new sprinklers. [**33**:9.4.7.2]

43.1.7.5* Automatic Carbon Dioxide, Dry Chemical, and Clean Agent Systems. The fire protection system shall be capable of discharging its contents into the entire protected area simultaneously, including the exhaust plenum and exhaust ductwork. [**33**:9.5]

43.1.7.6 Portable Fire Extinguishers. Portable fire extinguishers shall be provided and located in accordance with Section 13.6. [**33**:9.6]

43.1.7.7* Protection for Automated Powder Application Equipment.

43.1.7.7.1 Automated powder application equipment, both listed and unlisted, shall be further protected by listed optical flame detection, installed and supervised in accordance with *NFPA 72*. The optical flame detection shall, in event of ignition, react to the presence of flame within one-half (0.5) second and shall accomplish all of the following:

(1) Stop any conveyors into and out of the spray area
(2) Shut off ventilation
(3) Shut off application, transfer, and powder collection equipment
(4) Close segregation dampers in associated ductwork to interrupt airflows from application equipment to powder collectors
(5) Disconnect power to the high-voltage elements in the spray area and de-energize the system [**33**:9.7.1]

43.1.7.7.2 Automated powder application equipment that is unlisted shall be further protected by the following:

(1) In addition to meeting the requirements in 43.1.7.2.1 and 43.1.7.7.1, the optical flame detection system shall also activate the automatic fire protection system, if provided.
(2) Automatic electrostatic equipment enclosures inside the booth shall be protected with an approved automatic fire protection system. Activation of this system shall automatically accomplish the requirements of 43.1.7.2.1 and 43.1.7.7.1.
(3) Manual activation stations shall be installed. At least one such station shall be within ready access of operating personnel. If access to this station is likely to involve exposure to danger, an additional station shall be located adjacent to an exit from the area. These devices shall activate the fire protection system as specified in 43.1.7.1.1 for the affected automated zone, if applicable, and accomplish the requirements in 43.1.7.7.1.

*Exception: This requirement shall not apply to a closed-head wet pipe automatic sprinkler system. [**33**:9.7.2]*

43.1.7.8* Protection for Automated Liquid Electrostatic Spray Application Equipment.

43.1.7.8.1 Automated liquid electrostatic spray application equipment, both listed and unlisted, shall be further protected by listed optical flame detection, installed and supervised in accordance with *NFPA 72*. The optical flame detection shall, in event of ignition, react to the presence of flame within one-half (0.5) second and shall accomplish all of the following:

(1) Meet all of the requirements of 43.1.7.2.1
(2) Disconnect power to the high-voltage elements in the spray area and de-energize the system [**33**:9.8.1]

43.1.7.8.2 Automated liquid electrostatic spray application equipment that is unlisted shall be protected further by the following:

(1) In addition to meeting the requirements in 43.1.7.8.1, the optical flame detection system shall also activate one of the following over each zone in which fire has been detected:
  (a) An open head deluge system designed to discharge a minimum density of 0.6 gpm/ft^2 (24.4 mm/min)
  (b) A carbon dioxide extinguishing system
  (c) A dry chemical extinguishing system
  (d) A gaseous agent extinguishing system
(2) Manual activation stations shall be installed. At least one such station shall be within ready access of operating personnel. If access to this station is likely to involve exposure to danger, an additional station shall be located adjacent to an exit from the area. These devices shall activate the fire protection system as specified in 43.1.7.8.2(1) and accomplish the requirements of 43.1.7.2.1 and 43.1.7.8.1(2).
(3) A wet pipe sprinkler system shall also be provided throughout the spray booth. This system shall meet all the applicable requirements of NFPA 13 for Extra Hazard (Group 2) occupancies.
(4) Automatic electrostatic equipment enclosures inside the booth systems shall be protected with an approved automatic fire protection system. Activation of this system shall automatically accomplish the requirements of 43.1.7.2.1 and 43.1.7.8.1(2). [**33**:9.8.2]

43.1.8 Operations and Maintenance.

43.1.8.1* General. Maintenance procedures shall be established to ensure that all spray application apparatus and processes are operated and maintained in accordance with the manufacturers' specifications and the requirements of this *Code*. Maintenance shall be the responsibility of the users of the apparatus and processes. [**33:**10.1]

43.1.8.1.1* Spray application operations shall not be conducted outside predetermined spray areas. [**33:**10.1.1]

43.1.8.1.2 Inspection of extinguishing systems shall be conducted to ensure that the performance of the extinguishing system components will not be affected by overspray and residues. [**33:**10.1.2]

43.1.8.2* Combustible Deposits.

43.1.8.2.1 All spray areas shall be kept free of excessive accumulation of deposits of combustible residues. [**33:**10.2.1]

43.1.8.2.2 Combustible coverings (thin paper, plastic) and strippable coatings shall be permitted to be used to facilitate cleaning operations in spray areas. [**33:**10.2.2]

43.1.8.2.2.1 Where plastic covering is used, it shall be of a static dissipative nature or shall have a maximum breakdown voltage of 4 kV to prevent accumulation of a hazardous static electric charge. [**33:**10.2.2.1]

43.1.8.2.3 If residue accumulates to excess in booths, duct or duct discharge points, or other spray areas, all spraying operations shall be discontinued until conditions have been corrected. [**33:**10.2.3]

43.1.8.3 High-Pressure Hose Lines. High-pressure hose lines that convey flammable or combustible coating material in "airless" spray application operations shall be inspected frequently and shall be repaired or replaced as necessary. Hose lines and equipment shall be located so that, in the event of a leak or rupture, coating material will not be discharged into any space having a source of ignition. [**33:**10.3]

43.1.8.4 Maintenance Procedures.

43.1.8.4.1 Maintenance procedures shall be established to ensure that overspray collector filters are replaced before excessive restriction to airflow occurs. Overspray collectors shall be inspected after each period of use and clogged filters shall be discarded and replaced. [**33:**10.4.1]

43.1.8.4.2 At the close of the day's operation, all discarded overspray collector filters, residue scrapings, and debris contaminated with residue shall be removed immediately to a designated storage location, placed in a noncombustible container with a tight-fitting lid, or placed in a water-filled metal container. [**33:**10.4.2]

43.1.8.5* Waste Containers.

43.1.8.5.1 Approved waste containers shall be provided wherever rags or waste are impregnated with sprayed material, and all such rags or waste shall be deposited therein immediately after use. The contents of waste containers shall be placed in a designated storage location. [**33:**10.5.1]

43.1.8.5.2 Waste containers containing flammable liquids shall be located in ventilated areas that meet the requirements of 43.1.5. Such areas shall also meet the electrical area classification requirements of 43.1.4.4.5. [**33:**10.5.2]

43.1.8.5.3* Waste containers for flammable liquids shall be constructed of conductive materials and shall be bonded and grounded. [**33:**10.5.3]

43.1.8.5.4 Waste containers for flammable liquids shall be handled and stored in accordance with 43.1.6. [**33:**10.5.4]

43.1.8.6 Clothing. Employees' clothing contaminated with sprayed material shall not be left on the premises overnight unless kept in metal lockers. [**33:**10.6]

43.1.8.7 Cleaning Operations.

43.1.8.7.1 Scope. Paragraph 43.1.8.7 shall apply to the use of flammable or combustible liquids for the flushing and cleaning of equipment. [**33:**10.7.1]

43.1.8.7.2 Liquids. Class I and Class II liquids used in cleaning operations shall be in original shipping containers or in listed safety containers. [**33:**10.7.2]

43.1.8.7.3 Location. Cleaning operations using flammable or combustible liquids shall be conducted inside a spray area with ventilating equipment operating or in ventilated areas that meet the requirements of 43.1.5. Such areas shall also meet the electrical area classification requirements of 43.1.4.4.5. [**33:**10.7.3]

43.1.8.7.4* Equipment. Equipment using flammable or combustible liquids shall meet the requirements of 43.1.4.4.5 and shall be bonded and grounded. [**33:**10.7.4]

43.1.8.7.5 Manual Cleaning. Individual manual cleaning operations shall be limited to not more than 1 gal (4 L) of flammable or combustible liquid for each cleaning operator. [**33:**10.7.5]

43.1.8.7.6 Liquid Storage. Flammable and combustible liquids shall be handled and stored in accordance with 43.1.6. Containers used for handling, storage, or recovery of Class I liquids shall be constructed of conductive materials and shall be bonded and grounded. [**33:**10.7.6]

43.1.8.8 Solvent Distillation Units (Solvent Recyclers).

43.1.8.8.1 Scope.

43.1.8.8.1.1 Paragraph 43.1.8.8 shall apply to solvent distillation units having distillation chambers or still pots that do not exceed 60 gal (230 L) capacity and are used to recycle Class I, Class II, and Class IIIA liquids. [**30:**19.6.1.1]

43.1.8.8.1.2 Paragraph 43.1.8.8 shall not apply to research, testing, or experimental processes; to distillation processes carried out in petroleum refineries, chemical plants, or distilleries; or to distillation equipment used in dry cleaning operations. [**30:**19.6.1.2]

43.1.8.8.2 Equipment. Solvent distillation units shall be approved or shall be listed in accordance with ANSI/UL 2208, *Standard for Solvent Distillation Units*. [**30:**19.6.2]

43.1.8.8.3 Solvents. Solvent distillation units shall only be used to distill liquids for which they have been investigated and that are listed on the unit's marking or contained within the manufacturer's literature. [**30:**19.6.3]

43.1.8.8.3.1 Unstable or reactive liquids or materials shall not be processed unless they have been specifically listed on the system's markings or contained within the manufacturer's literature. [**30:**19.6.3.1]

43.1.8.8.4 Location.

43.1.8.8.4.1 Solvent distillation units shall be located and operated in locations in accordance with their approval or listing. [**30**:19.6.4.1]

43.1.8.8.4.2 Solvent distillation units shall not be used in basements. [**30**:19.6.4.2]

43.1.8.8.4.3 Solvent distillation units shall be located away from potential sources of ignition, as indicated on the unit's marking. [**30**:19.6.4.3]

43.1.8.8.5 Liquid Storage. Distilled liquids and liquids awaiting distillation shall be stored in accordance with NFPA 30. [**33**:10.8.5]

43.1.8.9* Spontaneous Ignition Hazards. The same spray booth shall not be alternately used for different types of coating materials if the combination of the materials is conducive to spontaneous ignition, unless all deposits of the first-used coating material are removed from the booth and exhaust ducts prior to spraying with the second coating material. [**33**:10.9]

43.1.8.10* Chlorinated Solvents. Coating materials containing chlorinated solvents shall not be used with spray application apparatus or fluid-handling equipment if the chlorinated solvent will come into contact with aluminum within a piping system, pump, enclosed container, or any enclosure that is capable of being pressurized by the potential reaction. This shall apply even if the container or system has been constructed with pressure relief devices. [**33**:10.10]

43.1.8.11 Smoking. Signs stating NO SMOKING OR OPEN FLAMES in large letters on contrasting color background shall be conspicuously posted at all spray areas and paint storage rooms. [**33**:10.11]

43.1.8.12* Hot Work. Welding, cutting, and other spark-producing operations shall not be permitted in or adjacent to spray areas until a written permit authorizing such work has been issued. The permit shall be issued by a person in authority following his or her inspection of the area to ensure that precautions have been taken and will be followed until the job is completed. [**33**:10.12]

43.2 Automated Electrostatic Spray Equipment. For information on the installation and use of automated electrostatic spray application apparatus, see Chapter 11 of NFPA 33.

43.3 Handheld Electrostatic Spray Equipment. For information on the installation and use of handheld electrostatic spray application apparatus, see Chapter 12 of NFPA 33.

43.4 Drying, Curing, or Fusion Processes. For information on drying, curing, or fusion apparatus used in connection with spray application of flammable and combustible materials, see Chapter 13 of NFPA 33.

43.5 Miscellaneous Spray Operations.

43.5.1 Vehicle Undercoating and Body Lining.

43.5.1.1 Spray undercoating or spray body lining of vehicles that is conducted in an area that has adequate natural or mechanical ventilation shall be exempt from the provisions of this *Code*, if all of the requirements of 43.5.1.1.1 through 43.5.1.1.4 are met. [**33**:14.1.1]

43.5.1.1.1 There shall be no open flames or spark-producing equipment within 20 ft (6100 mm) of the spray operation while the spray operation is being conducted. [**33**:14.1.1.1]

43.5.1.1.2 There shall be no drying, curing, or fusion apparatus in use within 20 ft (6100 mm) of the spray operation while the spray operation is being conducted. [**33**:14.1.1.2]

43.5.1.1.3 Any solvent used for cleaning procedures shall have a flash point not less than 100°F (37.8°C). [**33**:14.1.1.3]

43.5.1.1.4 The coating or lining materials used shall meet one of the following criteria:

(1) Be no more hazardous than UL Class 30-40, when tested in accordance with ANSI/UL 340, *Test for Comparative Flammability of Liquids*
(2) Not contain any solvent or component that has a flash point below 100°F (37.8°C)
(3) Consist only of Class IIIB liquids and not include any organic peroxide catalyst [**33**:14.1.1.4]

43.5.1.2 Noncomplying Undercoating Operations. Spray undercoating operations that do not meet the requirements of 43.5.1 shall meet all applicable requirements of this *Code* pertaining to spray finishing operations. [**33**:14.1.2]

43.5.2 Preparation Workstations. If spray finishing operations are performed at or in a preparation workstation, the preparation workstation shall be considered an unenclosed spray area and shall meet all requirements of an unenclosed spray area.

Exception: A preparation workstation that is designed and operated in accordance with 43.5.3 shall be considered a limited finishing workstation and not an unenclosed spray area. [**33**:14.2]

43.5.3 Limited Finishing Workstations. A limited finishing workstation shall be designed and operated in accordance with the requirements of 43.5.3.1 through 43.5.3.9. [**33**:14.3]

43.5.3.1 A limited finishing workstation shall be designed and constructed to have all of the following:

(1) A dedicated make-up air supply and air supply plenum
(2) Curtains or partitions that are noncombustible or limited combustible, as defined in 3.3.163 and 3.3.173.11 or that can successfully pass Test Method 2 of NFPA 701
(3) A dedicated mechanical exhaust and filtration system
(4)*An approved automatic extinguishing system that meets the requirements of 43.1.7 [**33**:14.3.1]

43.5.3.2 The amount of material sprayed in a limited finishing workstation shall not exceed 1 gal (3.8 L) in any 8-hour period. [**33**:14.3.2]

43.5.3.3 The limited finishing workstation shall meet all applicable requirements of 43.1.2 through 43.1.8 and Section 43.10. [**33**:14.3.3]

43.5.3.4 Curtains or partitions shall be fully closed during any spray application operations. [**33**:14.3.4]

43.5.3.5 The area inside the curtains or partitions shall be considered a Class I, Division 1; Class I, Zone 1; Class II, Division 1; or Zone 21 hazardous (classified) location, as defined by *NFPA 70*. [**33**:14.3.5]

43.5.3.5.1 A Class I, Division 2; Class I, Zone 2; Class II, Division 2; or Zone 22 hazardous (classified) location, as applicable, shall extend 3 ft (915 mm) both horizontally and vertically beyond the volume enclosed by the outside surface of the curtains or partitions as shown in Figure 43.5.3.5.1. [**33**:14.3.5.1]

43.5.3.5.2 For the purposes of this subsection, *interlocked* shall mean that the spray application equipment cannot be operated unless the exhaust ventilation system is operating and

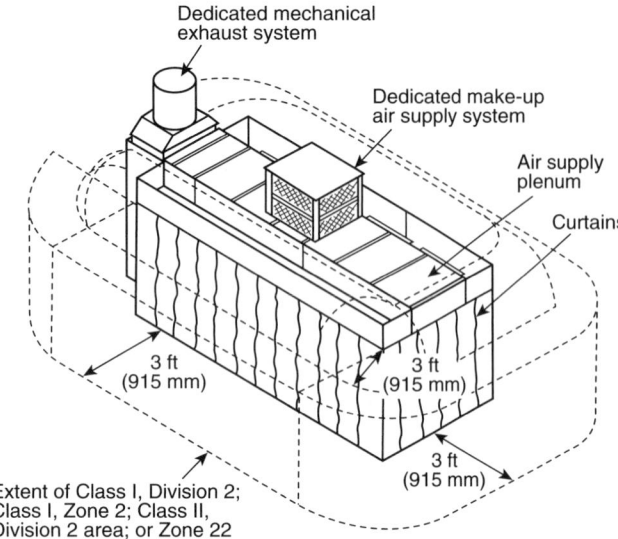

FIGURE 43.5.3.5.1 Class I, Division 2; Class I, Zone 2; Class II, Division 2; or Zone 22 Locations Adjacent to a Limited Finishing Workstation. [33:Figure 14.3.5.1]

functioning properly and spray application is automatically stopped if the exhaust ventilation system fails. [33:14.3.5.2]

43.5.3.6 Any limited finishing workstation used for spray application operations shall not be used for any operation that is capable of producing sparks or particles of hot metal or for operations that involve open flames or electrical utilization equipment capable of producing sparks or particles of hot metal. [33:14.3.6]

43.5.3.7 Drying, curing, or fusion apparatus shall be permitted to be used in a limited finishing workstation if they meet the requirements of Section 43.4 and the requirements of 43.5.3.7.1 through 43.5.3.7.3. [33:14.3.7]

43.5.3.7.1 When industrial air heaters are used to elevate the air temperature for drying, curing, or fusing operations, a high limit switch shall be provided to automatically shut off the drying apparatus if the air temperature in the limited finishing workstation exceeds the maximum discharge-air temperature allowed by the standard that the heater is listed to or 200°F (93°C), whichever is less. [33:14.3.7.1]

43.5.3.7.2* A means shall be provided to show that the limited finishing workstation is in the drying or curing mode of operation and that the limited finishing work station is to be unoccupied. [33:14.3.7.2]

43.5.3.7.3 Any containers of flammable or combustible liquids shall be removed from the limited finishing workstation before the drying apparatus is energized. [33:14.3.7.3]

43.5.3.8 Portable spot-drying, curing, or fusion apparatus shall be permitted to be used in a limited finishing workstation, provided that it is not located within the hazardous (classified) location defined in 43.5.3.5 when spray application operations are being conducted. [33:14.3.8]

43.5.3.9 Recirculation of exhaust air shall be permitted only if all provisions of 43.1.5.5 are met. [33:14.3.9]

43.6 Powder Coating. For information on the installation and use of powder coating application apparatus, see Chapter 15 of NFPA 33.

43.7 Organic Peroxides and Plural Component Coatings.

43.7.1* Scope. Section 43.7 shall apply to the spray application operations that involve the use of organic peroxide formulations and other plural component coatings.

Exception: As covered in Section 43.8. [33:16.1]

43.7.2 General. Spray application operations that involve the use of organic peroxide formulations and other plural component coatings shall be conducted in spray areas that are protected by approved automatic sprinkler systems that meet the requirements of 43.1.7. [33:16.2]

43.7.3 Prevention of Contamination. Measures shall be taken to prevent the contamination of organic peroxide formulations with any foreign substance. Only spray guns and related handling equipment that are specifically manufactured for use with organic peroxide formulations shall be used. Separate fluid-handling equipment shall be used for the resin and for the catalyst, and they shall not be interchanged. [33:16.3]

43.7.3.1 The wetted portions of equipment and apparatus that handle organic peroxide formulations shall be constructed of stainless steel (300 series), polyethylene, Teflon®, or other materials that are specifically recommended for the application. [33:16.3.1]

43.7.3.2* Measures shall be taken to prevent contamination of organic peroxide formulations with dusts or overspray residues resulting from the sanding or spray application of finishing materials. [33:16.3.2]

43.7.3.3 Spills of organic peroxide formulations shall be promptly removed so there are no residues. Spilled material shall be permitted to be absorbed by use of a noncombustible absorbent, which is then disposed of promptly in accordance with the manufacturer's recommendations. [33:16.3.3]

43.7.4 Storage of Organic Peroxides. Organic peroxide formulations shall be stored in accordance with the requirements of Chapter 70 and with the manufacturers' recommendations. [33:16.4]

43.7.5 Handling of Organic Peroxides. Measures shall be taken to prevent handling of organic peroxide formulations to avoid shock and friction, which can cause decomposition and violent reaction. [33:16.5]

43.7.6* Mixing of Organic Peroxides with Promoters. Organic peroxide formulations shall not be mixed directly with any cobalt compounds or other promoters or accelerators, due to the possibility of violent decomposition or explosion. To minimize the possibility of such accidental mixing, these materials shall not be stored adjacent to each other. [33:16.6]

43.7.7 Smoking. Smoking shall be prohibited, NO SMOKING signs shall be prominently displayed, and only nonsparking tools shall be used in any area where organic peroxide formulations are stored, mixed, or applied. [33:16.7]

43.7.8 Trained Personnel. Only designated personnel trained to use and handle organic peroxide formulations shall be permitted to use these materials. [33:16.8]

43.7.9 Material Safety Data Sheets. Where organic peroxide formulations are used, the material safety data sheet (MSDS) or its equivalent shall be consulted. [33:16.9]

43.8 Styrene Cross-Linked Composites Manufacturing (Glass Fiber–Reinforced Plastics).

43.8.1* Scope. Section 43.8 shall apply to manufacturing processes involving spray application of styrene cross-linked thermoset resins (commonly known as glass fiber–reinforced plastics) for hand lay-up or spray fabrication methods, that is, resin application areas, and where the processes do not produce vapors that exceed 25 percent of the lower flammable limit. [**33**:17.1]

43.8.2 Resin Application Equipment. The equipment and apparatus for spray application of the resin shall be installed and used in accordance with the requirements of Sections 43.7 and 43.8. [**33**:17.2]

43.8.3* Fire Protection. Resin application areas shall be protected in accordance with 43.1.7. If an automatic sprinkler system is utilized, it shall be permitted to be designed and installed in accordance with the requirements of NFPA 13 for at least Ordinary Hazard, Group 2 occupancies. [**33**:17.3]

43.8.4 Resin Storage. The quantity of flammable and combustible liquids located in the vicinity of resin application areas outside an inside storage room or storage cabinet in any one process area shall not exceed the greater of any of the following:

(1) A supply for one day
(2) The sum of 25 gal (95 L) of Class IA liquids in containers and 120 gal (454 L) of Class IB, IC, II, or III liquids in containers
(3) One approved portable tank not exceeding 660 gal (2500 L) of Class IB, IC, II, or III liquids [**33**:17.4]

43.8.5 Electrical and Other Hazards.

43.8.5.1 Electrical wiring and utilization equipment located in resin application areas that is not subject to deposits of combustible residues shall be installed in accordance with the requirements of *NFPA 70* for Ordinary Hazard locations. [**33**:17.5.1]

43.8.5.2 Electrical wiring and utilization equipment located in resin application areas that is subject to deposits of combustible residues shall be listed for such exposure and shall be suitable for Class I, Division 2 or Class I, Zone 2 locations if applicable as defined in 43.1.4.2.1.2. [**33**:17.5.2]

43.8.5.3* All metal parts of resin application areas, exhaust ducts, ventilation fans, spray application equipment, workpieces or containers that receive the spray stream, and piping that conveys flammable or combustible liquids shall be electrically grounded. [**33**:17.5.3]

43.8.5.4 Space heating appliances or other hot surfaces in resin application areas shall not be located where deposits or residues accumulate. [**33**:17.5.4]

43.8.6 Ventilation.

43.8.6.1 Mechanical ventilation shall be designed and installed throughout the resin application area in accordance with the requirements of 43.1.5.

Exception: Buildings that are not enclosed for at least three-quarters of their perimeter shall not be required to meet this requirement. [33:17.6.1]

43.8.6.2 Local ventilation shall be provided where personnel are under or inside of the workpiece being fabricated. [**33**:17.6.2]

43.8.7 Use and Handling.

43.8.7.1 The storage and use of organic peroxide formulations shall meet the requirements of Section 43.7. [**33**:17.7.1]

43.8.7.2 Excess catalyzed resin, while still in the liquid state, shall be drained into an open-top, noncombustible container. Enough water shall be added to the container to cover the contained resin by at least 2 in. (50 mm). [**33**:17.7.2]

43.8.7.3 In areas where chopper guns are used, paper, polyethylene film, or similar material shall be provided to cover the exposed surfaces of the walls and floor to allow the buildup of overchop to be removed. When the accumulated overchop has reached an average thickness of 2 in. (50 mm), it shall be disposed of after a minimum curing time of 4 hours.

Exception: A single day's accumulation of more than an average of 2 in. (50 mm) shall be permitted, provided that it is properly cured and disposed of before operations are resumed. [33:17.7.3]

43.8.7.3.1 Used paper, polyethylene film, or similar material shall be placed in a noncombustible container and disposed of when removed from the facility. [**33**:17.7.3.1]

43.9 Dipping, Coating, and Printing Processes.

43.9.1 Dipping, roll coating, flow coating, curtain coating, printing, cleaning, and similar processes, hereinafter referred to as "coating processes" or "processes," in which articles or materials are passed through tanks, vats, or containers, or passed over rollers, drums, or other process equipment that contain flammable or combustible liquids shall comply with NFPA 34, *Standard for Dipping, Coating, and Printing Processes Using Flammable or Combustible Liquids*, and Section 43.9. [**34**:1.1.1]

43.9.1.1 Section 43.9 shall also apply to cleaning processes that utilize a solvent vapor, such as vapor degreasing processes. [**34**:1.1.2]

43.9.1.2 Section 43.9 shall also apply to processes that use water-borne, water-based, and water-reducible materials that contain flammable or combustible liquids or that produce combustible deposits or residues. [**34**:1.1.3]

43.9.1.3 Section 43.9 shall not apply to processes that use only noncombustible liquids for processing and cleaning. This standard shall also not apply to processes that use only Class IIIB liquids for processing or cleaning, provided the liquids or mixtures thereof maintain their Class IIIB classification at their point of use. [**34**:1.1.4]

43.9.1.4 Section 43.9 shall not apply to processes that use a liquid that does not have a fire point when tested in accordance with ASTM D 92, *Standard Test Method for Flash and Fire Points by Cleveland Open Cup*, up to the boiling point of the liquid or up to a temperature at which the sample being tested shows an obvious physical change. [**34**:1.1.5]

43.9.1.5 Section 43.9 shall not apply to fluidized bed powder application. *(See Chapter 15 of NFPA 33, Standard for Spray Application Using Flammable or Combustible Materials.)* [**34**:1.1.6]

43.9.1.6* Section 43.9 shall not apply to quench tanks that are addressed in Chapter 51 of this *Code*.

43.9.2* Where unusual industrial processes are involved, the AHJ shall be permitted to require additional safeguards or modifications to the requirements of NFPA 34, provided equivalent safety is achieved.

43.10 Training.

43.10.1* General. All personnel involved in the spray application processes covered by this *Code* shall be instructed in the following:

(1) Potential safety and health hazards
(2) Operational, maintenance, and emergency procedures required
(3) Importance of constant operator awareness [**33**:18.1]

43.10.1.1 Personnel required to handle or use flammable or combustible materials shall be instructed in the safe handling, storage, and use of the materials, as well as emergency procedures. [**33**:18.1.1]

43.10.1.2* All personnel required to enter or to work within confined or enclosed spaces shall be instructed as to the nature of the hazard involved, the necessary precautions to be taken, and the use of protective and emergency equipment required. [**33**:18.1.2]

43.10.1.3 All personnel shall be instructed in the proper use, maintenance, and storage of all emergency, safety, or personal protective equipment that they might be required to use in their normal work performance. [**33**:18.1.3]

43.10.1.4 Documentation shall be employed to record the type and date of training provided to each individual involved in these processes. [**33**:18.1.4]

Chapter 44   Solvent Extraction

44.1 General. Solvent extraction plants shall comply with NFPA 36, *Standard for Solvent Extraction Plants*, and Chapter 44.

44.2 Application.

44.2.1 Chapter 44 shall apply to the following:

(1) The commercial scale extraction processing of animal and vegetable oils and fats by the use of Class I flammable hydrocarbon liquids, hereinafter referred to as "solvents" [**36**:1.1.1]
(2) Any equipment and buildings that are located within 100 ft (30 m) of the extraction process [**36**:1.1.2]
(3) The unloading, storage, and handling of solvents, regardless of distance from the extraction process [**36**:1.1.3]
(4) The means by which material to be extracted is conveyed from the preparation process to the extraction process [**36**:1.1.4]
(5) The means by which extracted desolventized solids and oil oils are conveyed from the extraction process [**36**:1.1.5]
(6) Preparation and meal finishing processes that are connected by conveyor to the extraction process, regardless of intervening distance [**36**:1.1.6]

44.2.2 Chapter 44 shall not apply to the following:

(1) The storage of raw materials or finished products [**36**:1.1.7]
(2) Extraction processes that use liquids that are miscible with water [**36**:1.1.8]
(3) Extraction processes that use flammable gases, liquefied petroleum gases, or nonflammable gases [**36**:1.1.9]

44.3 Permits. Permits, where required, shall comply with Section 1.12.

44.4 Special Requirements. The use of processes that employ oxygen-active compounds that are heat or shock sensitive, such as certain organic peroxides, shall be prohibited within the area defined in 44.2.1(2). [**36**:1.1.10]

Chapter 45   Combustible Fibers

45.1 General.

45.1.1 The storage, use, and handling of combustible fibers shall comply with the requirements of Chapter 45.

45.1.2* Chapter 45 shall not apply to buildings completely protected by an approved automatic fire-extinguishing system; however, this exclusion does not preclude the need for good housekeeping.

45.1.3 Permits. Permits, where required, shall comply with Section 1.12.

45.2 Electrical Wiring.

45.2.1 Electrical wiring and equipment in any combustible fiber storage room or building shall be installed in accordance with the requirements of *NFPA 70* for Class III hazardous locations.

45.2.2 The AHJ shall be responsible for designating the areas requiring hazardous location electrical classifications and shall classify the area in accordance with the classification system set forth in *NFPA 70*.

45.3 No Smoking.

45.3.1 No smoking or open flame shall be permitted in any area where combustible fibers are handled or stored, nor within 50 ft (15 m) of any uncovered pile of such fibers.

45.3.2 NO SMOKING signs shall be posted.

45.4 Vehicles and Material Handling Equipment. Trucks or automobiles, other than mechanical handling equipment and approved industrial trucks complying with NFPA 505, *Fire Safety Standard for Powered Industrial Trucks Including Type Designations, Areas of Use, Conversions, Maintenance, and Operations*, shall not enter any fiber storage room or building but shall be permitted to be used at loading platforms.

45.5 Loose Storage of Combustible Fibers.

45.5.1 Loose combustible fibers (not in bales or packages), whether housed or in the open, shall not be stored within 100 ft (30 m) of any building, except as hereinafter specified.

45.5.2 Quantities of loose combustible fibers up to 100 ft^3 (2.8 m^3) shall not be kept in any building unless stored in a metal or metal-lined bin that is equipped with a self-closing cover.

45.5.3 Rooms or Compartments for Quantities of Loose Combustible Fibers Ranging Between 100 ft^3 (2.8 m^3) and 500 ft^3 (14.2 m^3).

45.5.3.1 Quantities exceeding 100 ft^3 (2.8 m^3) of loose combustible fibers, but not exceeding 500 ft^3 (14.2 m^3), shall be permitted to be stored in rooms or compartments in which the floors, walls, and ceilings have a fire-resistance rating of not less than ¾ hour.

45.5.3.2 Each opening into such rooms or compartments from other parts of the building shall be equipped with an approved self-closing fire door.

45.5.4 Storage Vaults for Quantities of Loose Combustible Fibers Ranging Between 500 ft³ (14.2 m³) and 1000 ft³ (28.3 m³).

45.5.4.1 Quantities exceeding 500 ft³ (14.2 m³) of loose combustible fibers, but not exceeding 1000 ft³ (28.3 m³), shall be permitted to be stored in storage vaults enclosed with floors, walls, and ceilings that are 2-hour fire-resistance-rated fire barriers.

45.5.4.2 Such storage vaults shall be located outside of buildings or, if located inside, shall be protected with approved safety vents to the outside.

45.5.4.3 If such storage vaults are located inside a building, each opening into the storage vault from other parts of the building shall be protected on each side of the wall by an approved opening protective assembly having a fire resistance rating of 1½ hours.

45.5.4.4 If such storage vaults are located outside of buildings but have openings that expose other buildings (not sufficiently detached to be considered cutoff), each such opening shall be protected on each side of the wall by an approved opening protective assembly having a fire resistance rating of 1½ hours.

45.5.4.5 Roofs of outside vaults shall be of noncombustible material, but shall be permitted to be constructed so as to readily give way in case of an internal explosion.

45.5.5 Storage Vaults for Quantities of Loose Combustible Fibers Exceeding 1000 ft³ (28.3 m³).

45.5.5.1 Quantities exceeding 1000 ft³ (28.3 m³) of loose combustible fibers shall be permitted to be stored in storage vaults as indicated in 45.5.4.

45.5.5.2 The storage vault shall also be protected by an approved automatic sprinkler system designed and installed in accordance with Section 13.3.

45.5.6 Loose House.

45.5.6.1 Not more than 2500 ft³ (71 m³) of loose fibers shall be permitted to be stored in a detached loose house, with openings properly protected against the entrance of sparks.

45.5.6.2 The loose house shall be used for no other purpose.

45.6 Baled Storage.

45.6.1 Blocks or Piles.

45.6.1.1 No single block or pile shall contain more than 25,000 ft³ (708 m³) of combustible fibers, exclusive of aisles or clearances.

45.6.1.2 Blocks or piles of baled fiber shall be separated from adjacent storage by aisles not less than 5 ft (1.5 m) wide or by flash fire barriers consisting of continuous sheets of noncombustible material extending from the floor to a height of at least 1 ft (0.3 m) beyond the top of the piles and projecting not less than 1 ft (0.3 m) beyond the sides of the piles.

45.6.1.3 Baled cotton storage and combustibles shall be kept at least 4 ft (1.2 m) from fire door openings.

45.6.2 Sisal and Other Fibers.

45.6.2.1 Sisal and other fibers in bales bound with combustible tie ropes or jute and other fibers that are liable to swell when wet shall be stored in a manner that allows for expansion in any direction without endangering building walls, ceilings, or columns.

45.6.2.2 Not less than 3 ft (0.9 m) of clearance shall be left between walls and sides of piles, except that in storage compartments not more than 30 ft (9 m) in width, 1 ft (0.3 m) clearance at side walls shall be sufficient, provided that a center aisle not less than 5 ft (1.5 m) wide is maintained.

45.7 Storage of Hay, Straw, and Other Similar Agricultural Products.

45.7.1 Hay, straw, and other similar agricultural products shall not be stored adjacent to buildings or combustible material unless a cleared horizontal distance equal to the height of pile is maintained between such storage and combustible material and buildings.

45.7.2 Storage shall be limited to stacks of 100 tons (90,720 kg) each.

45.7.3 Either an approved 1-hour fire wall installed in accordance with NFPA 221, *Standard for High Challenge Fire Walls, Fire Walls, and Fire Barrier Walls*, or a clear space of 20 ft (6.1 m) shall be maintained between such stacks.

45.7.4 Unlimited quantities of hay, straw, and other agricultural products shall be permitted to be stored in or near farm buildings located outside of closely built areas.

45.8 Hazardous Materials. Combustible fibers shall not be stored in rooms or buildings with hazardous gases, flammable liquids, dangerous chemicals, or other similar materials.

Chapter 46   Reserved

Chapter 47   Reserved

Chapter 48   Reserved

Chapter 49   Reserved

Chapter 50   Commercial Cooking

50.1 Application.

50.1.1* The design, installation, operation, inspection, and maintenance of all public and private commercial cooking equipment shall comply with this chapter and NFPA 96, *Standard for Ventilation Control and Fire Protection of Commercial Cooking Operations*.

50.1.2 This chapter shall apply to residential cooking equipment used for commercial cooking operations. [**96:**1.1.2]

50.1.3 This chapter shall not apply to cooking equipment located in a single dwelling unit. [**96:**1.1.3]

50.1.4* This chapter shall not apply to facilities where all of the following are met:

(1) Only residential equipment is being used.
(2) Fire extinguishers are located in all kitchen areas in accordance with Section 13.6.
(3) The facility is not an assembly occupancy.
(4) The AHJ has approved the installation. [**96**:1.1.4]

50.2 General Requirements.

50.2.1 General.

50.2.1.1 Cooking equipment used in processes producing smoke or grease-laden vapors shall be equipped with an exhaust system that complies with all the equipment and performance requirements of this chapter. [**96**:4.1.1]

50.2.1.1.1* Cooking equipment that has been listed in accordance with ANSI/UL 197, *Standard for Commercial Electric Cooking Appliances*, or an equivalent standard for reduced emissions shall not be required to be provided with an exhaust system. [**96**:4.1.1.1]

50.2.1.1.2 The listing evaluation of cooking equipment covered by 50.2.1.1.1 shall demonstrate that the grease discharge at the exhaust duct of a test hood placed over the appliance shall not exceed 0.00018 oz/ft^3 (5 mg/m^3) when operated with a total airflow of 500 cfm (0.236 m^3/s). [**96**:4.1.1.2]

50.2.1.2 All such equipment and its performance shall be maintained in accordance with the requirements of this chapter during all periods of operation of the cooking equipment. [**96**:4.1.2]

50.2.1.3 The following equipment shall be kept in working condition:

(1) Cooking equipment
(2) Hoods
(3) Ducts (if applicable)
(4) Fans
(5) Fire-extinguishing equipment
(6) Special effluent or energy control equipment [**96**:4.1.3]

50.2.1.3.1 Maintenance and repairs shall be performed on all components at intervals necessary to maintain good working condition. [**96**:4.1.3.1]

50.2.1.4 All airflows shall be maintained. [**96**:4.1.4]

50.2.1.5 The responsibility for inspection, testing, maintenance, and cleanliness of the ventilation control and fire protection of the commercial cooking operations shall ultimately be that of the owner of the system, provided that this responsibility has not been transferred in written form to a management company, tenant, or other party. [**96**:4.1.5]

50.2.1.6* All solid fuel cooking equipment are required to comply with the requirements of Chapter 14 of NFPA 96. [**96**:4.1.6]

50.2.1.7 Multi-tenant applications shall require the concerted cooperation of design, installation, operation, and maintenance responsibilities by tenants and by the building owner. [**96**:4.1.7]

50.2.1.8 All interior surfaces of the exhaust system shall be accessible for cleaning and inspection purposes. [**96**:4.1.8]

50.2.1.9* Cooking equipment used in fixed, mobile, or temporary concessions, such as trucks, buses, trailers, pavilions, tents, or any form of roofed enclosure, shall comply with NFPA 96 or this chapter unless otherwise exempted by the AHJ in accordance with 1.3.2 of NFPA 96. [**96**:4.1.9]

50.2.2* Clearance.

50.2.2.1 Where enclosures are not required, hoods, grease removal devices, exhaust fans, and ducts shall have a clearance of at least 18 in. (457 mm) to combustible material, 3 in. (76 mm) to limited-combustible material, and 0 in. (0 mm) to noncombustible material. [**96**:4.2.1]

50.2.2.2 Where a hood, duct, or grease removal device is listed for clearances less than those required in 50.2.2.1, the listing requirements shall be permitted. [**96**:4.2.2]

50.2.2.3 Clearance Reduction.

50.2.2.3.1 Where a clearance reduction system consisting of 0.013 in. (0.33 mm) (28 gauge) sheet metal spaced out 1 in. (25 mm) on noncombustible spacers is provided, there shall be a minimum of 9 in. (229 mm) clearance to combustible material. [**96**:4.2.3.1]

50.2.2.3.2 Where a clearance reduction system consisting of 0.027 in. (0.69 mm) (22 gauge) sheet metal on 1 in. (25 mm) mineral wool batts or ceramic fiber blanket reinforced with wire mesh or equivalent spaced 1 in. (25 mm) on noncombustible spacers is provided, there shall be a minimum of 3 in. (76 mm) clearance to combustible material. [**96**:4.2.3.2]

50.2.2.3.3 Where a clearance reduction system consisting of a *listed* and *labeled* field-applied grease duct enclosure material, system, product, or method of construction specifically evaluated for such purpose in accordance with ASTM E 2336, the required clearance shall be in accordance with the listing. [**96**:4.2.3.3]

50.2.2.3.4 Zero clearance to limited-combustible materials shall be permitted where protected by one of the following:

(1) Metal lath and plaster
(2) Ceramic tile
(3) Quarry tile
(4) Other noncombustible materials or assembly of noncombustible materials that are listed for the purpose of reducing clearance
(5) Other materials and products that are listed for the purpose of reducing clearance [**96**:4.2.3.4]

50.2.3 Drawings. A drawing(s) of the exhaust system installation along with copies of operating instructions for subassemblies and components used in the exhaust system, including electrical schematics, shall be kept on the premises. [**96**:4.6]

50.2.4 AHJ Notification. If required by the AHJ, notification in writing shall be given of any alteration, replacement, or relocation of any exhaust or extinguishing system or part thereof or cooking equipment. [**96**:4.7]

50.3 Protection of Coverings and Enclosure Materials.

50.3.1 Measures shall be taken to prevent physical damage to any covering or enclosure material. [**96**:7.7.3.1]

50.3.2 Any damage to the covering or enclosure shall be repaired, and the covering or enclosure shall be restored to meet its intended listing and fire resistance rating and to be acceptable to the AHJ. [**96**:7.7.3.2]

50.3.3 In the event of a fire within a kitchen exhaust system, the duct, the enclosure, and the covering directly applied to the duct shall be inspected by qualified personnel to determine whether the duct, the enclosure, and the covering directly applied to the duct are structurally sound, capable of maintaining their fire protection functions, suitable for continued operation, and acceptable to the AHJ. [**96:**7.7.3.3]

50.3.4 Listed grease ducts shall be installed in accordance with the terms of the listing and the manufacturer's instructions. [**96:**7.7.3.4]

50.4 Fire-Extinguishing Equipment.

50.4.1 Prior to installation of any fire-extinguishing system, construction documents shall be reviewed and approved by the AHJ.

50.4.2 Permits. Permits, where required, shall comply with Section 1.12.

50.4.3 General Requirements.

50.4.3.1 Fire-extinguishing equipment for the protection of grease removal devices, hood exhaust plenums, and exhaust duct systems shall be provided. [**96:**10.1.1]

50.4.3.2* Cooking equipment that produces grease-laden vapors and that might be a source of ignition of grease in the hood, grease removal device, or duct shall be protected by fire-extinguishing equipment. [**96:**10.1.2]

50.4.4 Types of Equipment.

50.4.4.1 Fire-extinguishing equipment shall include both automatic fire-extinguishing systems as primary protection and portable fire extinguishers as secondary backup. [**96:**10.2.1]

50.4.4.2* A placard shall be conspicuously placed near each extinguisher that states that the fire protection system shall be activated prior to using the fire extinguisher. [**96:**10.2.2]

50.4.4.2.1 The language and wording for the placard shall be approved by the AHJ. [**96:**10.2.2.1]

50.4.4.3* Automatic fire-extinguishing systems shall comply with ANSI/UL 300, *Standard for Fire Testing of Fire Extinguishing Systems for Protection of Restaurant Cooking Areas*, or other equivalent standards and shall be installed in accordance with the requirements of the listing. [**96:**10.2.3]

50.4.4.3.1* In existing dry or wet chemical systems not in compliance with ANSI/UL 300, the fire-extinguishing system shall be made to comply with 50.4.4.3 when any of the following occurs:

(1) The cooking medium is changed from animal oils and fats to vegetable oils.
(2) The positioning of the cooking equipment is changed.
(3) Cooking equipment is replaced.
(4) The equipment is no longer supported by the manufacturer. [**96:**10.2.3.1]

50.4.4.3.2 Effective January 1, 2014, all existing fire-extinguishing systems shall meet the requirements of 50.4.4.3. [**96:**10.2.3.2]

50.4.4.4 Grease removal devices, hood exhaust plenums, exhaust ducts, and cooking equipment that are not addressed in ANSI/UL 300 or other equivalent test standards shall be protected with an automatic fire-extinguishing system(s) in accordance with the applicable NFPA standard(s), all local building and fire codes, and the fire extinguishing system's manufacturer's recommendations and shall be approved by the AHJ. [**96:**10.2.4]

50.4.4.5 Automatic fire-extinguishing equipment provided as part of listed recirculating systems shall comply with ANSI/UL 710B, *Outline of Investigation for Recirculating Exhaust System*. [**96:**10.2.5]

50.4.4.6 Automatic fire-extinguishing systems shall be installed in accordance with the terms of their listing, the manufacturer's instructions, and the following standards where applicable:

(1) NFPA 12
(2) NFPA 13
(3) NFPA 17
(4) NFPA 17A
(5) NFPA 750 [**96:**10.2.6]

50.4.4.7 Modifications to Existing Hood Systems.

50.4.4.7.1 Any abandoned pipe or conduit from a previous installation shall be removed from within the hood, plenum, and exhaust duct. [**96:**10.2.7.1]

50.4.4.7.2 Penetrations and holes resulting from the removal of conduit or piping shall be sealed with listed or equivalent liquidtight sealing devices. [**96:**10.2.7.2]

50.4.4.7.3 The addition of obstructions to spray patterns from the cooking appliance nozzle(s) such as baffle plates, shelves, or any modification shall not be permitted. [**96:**10.2.7.3]

50.4.4.7.4 Changes or modifications to the hazard after installation of the fire-extinguishing systems shall result in re-evaluation of the system design by a properly trained, qualified, and certified person(s). [**96:**10.2.7.4]

50.4.4.8 Fixed Baffle Hoods with Water Wash.

50.4.4.8.1 Grease removal devices, hood exhaust plenums, and exhaust ducts requiring protection in accordance with 50.4.3.1 shall be permitted to be protected by a listed fixed baffle hood containing a constant or fire-actuated water-wash system that is listed and in compliance with ANSI/UL 300 or other equivalent standards and shall be installed in accordance with the requirements of their listing. [**96:**10.2.8.1]

50.4.4.8.2 Each such area not provided with a listed water-wash extinguishing system shall be provided with a fire-extinguishing system listed for the purpose. [**96:**10.2.8.2]

50.4.4.8.3 The water for listed fixed baffle hood assemblies shall be permitted to be supplied from the domestic water supply when the minimum water pressure and flow are provided in accordance with the terms of the listing. [**96:**10.2.8.3]

50.4.4.8.4 The water supply shall be controlled by a supervised water supply control valve. [**96:**10.2.8.4]

50.4.4.8.5 The water wash in a fixed baffle hood specifically listed to extinguish a fire shall be activated by the cooking equipment extinguishing system. [**96:**10.2.8.5]

50.4.4.8.6 A water-wash system approved to be used for protection of the grease removal device(s), hood exhaust plenum(s), exhaust duct(s), or combination thereof shall include instructions and appropriate electrical interface for simultaneous activation of the water-wash system from an automatic fire-extinguishing system, where the automatic fire-extinguishing system is used for cooking equipment protection only. [**96:**10.2.8.6]

50.4.4.8.7 Where the fire-extinguishing system provides protection for the cooking equipment, hood, and duct, activation of the water wash shall not be required. [**96:**10.2.8.7]

50.4.4.8.7.1 Where the automatic fire extinguishing system in accordance with NFPA 17A provides protection for the hood and duct in a fixed baffle hood containing a water-wash system, the water-wash system shall be made inoperable or delayed for a minimum of 60 seconds upon operation of the automatic fire-extinguishing system. [**96:**10.2.8.7.1]

50.4.4.8.8 Grease removal devices, hood exhaust plenums, and exhaust ducts on fixed baffle hoods with water wash shall be permitted to be protected by a sprinkler system with an individual control valve if the design of the hood prevents the water from reaching the cooking appliances. [**96:**10.2.8.8]

50.4.4.9 Water-Based Fire-Extinguishing System.

50.4.4.9.1 The water required for listed automatic fire-extinguishing systems shall be permitted to be supplied from the domestic water supply where the minimum water pressure and flow are provided in accordance with the terms of the listing. The water supply shall be controlled by a supervised water supply control valve. [**96:**10.2.9.1]

50.4.4.9.2 Where the water supply is from a dedicated fire protection water supply in a building with one or more fire sprinkler systems, separate indicating control valves and drains shall be provided and arranged so that the hood system and sprinkler systems can be controlled individually. [**96:**10.2.9.2]

50.4.4.10 Water Valve Supervision. Valves controlling the water supply to listed fixed baffle hood assemblies, automatic fire-extinguishing systems, or both shall be listed indicating type of valve and shall be supervised open by one of the following methods:

(1) Central station, proprietary, or remote station alarm service
(2) Local alarm service that will cause the sounding of an audible signal at a constantly attended point
(3) Locking valves open
(4)*Sealing of valves and approved weekly recorded inspection [**96:**10.2.10]

50.4.5 Simultaneous Operation.

50.4.5.1 Fixed pipe extinguishing systems in a single hazard area *(see 3.3.44 of NFPA 96 for the definition of single hazard area)* shall be arranged for simultaneous automatic operation upon actuation of any one of the systems. [**96:**10.3.1]

50.4.5.1.1 Hoods installed end to end, back to back, or both, or sharing a common ductwork, and having a grease-producing appliance(s) located under one or more of the hoods shall be considered a single hazard area requiring simultaneous automatic fire protection in all hoods and ducts. [**96:**10.3.1.1]

50.4.5.1.2 Hoods installed end to end, back to back, or both that do not share a common exhaust and are separated by a wall(s) or other means to ensure that grease-laden vapors exhausted under one hood cannot propagate to the other hoods or exhaust systems shall not be required to comply with 50.4.5.1.1. [**96:**10.3.1.2]

50.4.5.2 Simultaneous operation shall not be required where the one fixed pipe extinguishing system is an automatic sprinkler system. [**96:**10.3.2]

50.4.5.2.1 Where an automatic sprinkler system is used in conjunction with a water-based fire-extinguishing system served by the same water supply, hydraulic calculations shall consider both systems operating simultaneously. [**96:**10.3.2.1]

50.4.5.3 Simultaneous operation shall be required where a dry or wet chemical system is used to protect common exhaust ductwork by one of the methods specified in NFPA 17 or NFPA 17A. [**96:**10.3.3]

50.4.6 Fuel and Electric Power Shutoff.

50.4.6.1 Upon activation of any fire-extinguishing system for a cooking operation, all sources of fuel and electric power that produce heat to all equipment requiring protection by that system shall automatically shut off. [**96:**10.4.1]

50.4.6.2 Steam supplied from an external source shall not be required to automatically shut off. [**96:**10.4.2]

50.4.6.3 Any gas appliance not requiring protection but located under ventilating equipment where protected appliances are located shall be automatically shut off upon activation of the extinguishing system. [**96:**10.4.3]

50.4.6.4 Shutoff devices shall require manual reset. [**96:**10.4.4]

50.4.7 Manual Activation.

50.4.7.1 A readily accessible means for manual activation shall be located between 42 in. and 48 in. (1067 mm and 1219 mm) above the floor, be accessible in the event of a fire, be located in a path of egress, and clearly identify the hazard protected. [**96:**10.5.1]

50.4.7.1.1 At least one manual actuation device shall be located a minimum of 10 ft (3 m) and a maximum of 20 ft (6 m) from the protected hood exhaust system(s) within the path of egress or at an alternative location acceptable to the AHJ. [**96:**10.5.1.1]

50.4.7.1.2 Manual activation using a cable-operated pull station shall not require more than 40 lb (178 N) of force, with a pull movement not to exceed 14 in. (356 mm) to activate the automatic fire-extinguishing equipment. [**96:**10.5.1.2]

50.4.7.2 The automatic and manual means of system activation external to the control head or releasing device shall be separate and independent of each other so that failure of one will not impair the operation of the other except as permitted by 50.4.7.3. [**96:**10.5.2]

50.4.7.3 The manual means of system activation shall be permitted to be common with the automatic means if the manual activation device is located between the control head or releasing device and the first fusible link. [**96:**10.5.3]

50.4.7.4 An automatic sprinkler system shall not require a manual means of system activation. [**96:**10.5.4]

50.4.7.5 The means for manual activation shall be mechanical or rely on electrical power for activation in accordance with 50.4.7.6. [**96:**10.5.5]

50.4.7.6 Electrical power shall be permitted to be used for manual activation if a standby power supply is provided or if supervision is provided in accordance with 50.4.9. [**96:**10.5.6]

50.4.7.7 Instruction shall be provided to employees regarding the proper use of portable fire extinguishers and the manual activation of fire-extinguishing equipment. [**96:**10.5.7]

50.4.8 System Annunciation.

50.4.8.1 Upon activation of an automatic fire-extinguishing system, an audible alarm or visual indicator shall be provided to show that the system has activated. [**96:**10.6.1]

50.4.8.2 Where a fire alarm signaling system is serving the occupancy where the extinguishing system is located, the activation of the automatic fire-extinguishing system shall activate the fire alarm signaling system. [**96:**10.6.2]

50.4.9 System Supervision.

50.4.9.1 Where electrical power is required to operate the fixed automatic fire-extinguishing system, the system shall be provided with a reserve power supply and be monitored by a supervisory alarm except as permitted in 50.4.9.2. [**96:**10.7.1]

50.4.9.2 Where fixed automatic fire-extinguishing systems include automatic mechanical detection and actuation as a backup detection system, electrical power monitoring and a reserve power supply shall not be required. [**96:**10.7.2]

50.4.9.3 System supervision shall not be required where a fire-extinguishing system(s) is interconnected or interlocked with the cooking equipment power source(s) so that if the fire-extinguishing system becomes inoperable due to power failure, all sources of fuel or electrical power that produce heat to all cooking equipment serviced by that hood shall automatically shut off. [**96:**10.7.3]

50.4.9.4 System supervision shall not be required where an automatic fire-extinguishing system, including automatic mechanical detection and actuation, is electrically connected to a listed fire-actuated water-wash system for simultaneous operation of both systems. [**96:**10.7.4]

50.4.10 Special Design and Application.

50.4.10.1 Hoods containing automatic fire-extinguishing systems are protected areas; therefore, these hoods are not considered obstructions to overhead sprinkler systems and shall not require floor coverage underneath. [**96:**10.8.1]

50.4.10.2 A single detection device, listed with the extinguishing system, shall be permitted for more than one appliance where installed in accordance with the terms of the listing. [**96:**10.8.2]

50.4.11 Review and Certification.

50.4.11.1 Where required, complete drawings of the system installation, including the hood(s), exhaust duct(s), and appliances, along with the interface of the fire-extinguishing system detectors, piping, nozzles, fuel and electric power shutoff devices, agent storage container(s), and manual actuation device(s), shall be submitted to the AHJ. [**96:**10.9.1]

50.4.11.2* Installation Requirements.

50.4.11.2.1 Installation of systems shall be performed only by persons properly trained and qualified to install the specific system being provided. [**96:**10.9.2.1]

50.4.11.2.2 The installer shall provide certification to the AHJ that the installation is in agreement with the terms of the listing and the manufacturer's instructions and/or approved design. [**96:**10.9.2.2]

50.4.12 Portable Fire Extinguishers.

50.4.12.1* Portable fire extinguishers shall be selected and installed in kitchen cooking areas in accordance with Section 13.6 and shall be specifically listed for such use. [**96:**10.10.1]

50.4.12.2 Class K fire extinguishers shall be provided for cooking appliance hazards that involve combustible cooking media (vegetable oils and animal oils and fats). [**96:**10.10.2]

50.4.12.3 Portable fire extinguishers shall be provided for other hazards in kitchen areas and shall be selected and installed in accordance with Section 13.6. [**96:**10.10.3]

50.4.12.4 Portable fire extinguishers shall be maintained in accordance with Section 13.6. [**96:**10.10.4]

50.5 Procedures for the Use, Inspection, Testing, and Maintenance of Equipment.

50.5.1 Operating Procedures.

50.5.1.1 Exhaust systems shall be operated whenever cooking equipment is turned on. [**96:**11.1.1]

50.5.1.2 Filter-equipped exhaust systems shall not be operated with filters removed. [**96:**11.1.2]

50.5.1.3 Openings provided for replacing air exhausted through ventilating equipment shall not be restricted by covers, dampers, or any other means that would reduce the operating efficiency of the exhaust system. [**96:**11.1.3]

50.5.1.4 Instructions for manually operating the fire-extinguishing system shall be posted conspicuously in the kitchen and shall be reviewed with employees by the management. [**96:**11.1.4]

50.5.1.5 Listed exhaust hoods shall be operated in accordance with the terms of their listings and the manufacturer's instructions. [**96:**11.1.5]

50.5.1.6 Cooking equipment shall not be operated while its fire-extinguishing system or exhaust system is nonoperational or impaired. [**96:**11.1.6]

50.5.1.6.1 Where the fire-extinguishing system or exhaust system is nonoperational or impaired, the systems shall be tagged as noncompliant, and the system owner or owner's representative shall be notified in writing of the impairment, and where required, the AHJ shall be notified. [**96:**11.1.6.1]

50.5.1.7 Secondary filtration and pollution control equipment shall be operated in accordance with the terms of its listing and the manufacturer's recommendations. [**96:**11.1.7]

50.5.1.8 Inspection and maintenance of "other equipment" allowed in 9.3.1 of NFPA 96 shall be conducted by properly trained and qualified persons at a frequency determined by the manufacturer's instructions or equipment listing. [**96:**11.1.8]

50.5.2 Inspection, Testing, and Maintenance of Fire-Extinguishing Systems.

50.5.2.1* Maintenance of the fire-extinguishing systems and listed exhaust hoods containing a constant or fire-activated water system that is listed to extinguish a fire in the grease removal devices, hood exhaust plenums, and exhaust ducts shall be made by properly trained, qualified, and certified person(s) acceptable to the AHJ at least every 6 months. [**96:**11.2.1]

50.5.2.2* All actuation and control components, including remote manual pull stations, mechanical or electrical devices, detectors, and actuators, shall be tested for proper operation during the inspection in accordance with the manufacturer's procedures. [**96:**11.2.2]

50.5.2.3 The specific inspection and maintenance requirements of the extinguishing system standards as well as the applicable installation and maintenance manuals for the listed system and service bulletins shall be followed. [**96**:11.2.3]

50.5.2.4* Fusible links of the metal alloy type and automatic sprinklers of the metal alloy type shall be replaced at least semiannually except as permitted by 50.5.2.6 and 50.5.2.7. [**96**:11.2.4]

50.5.2.5 The year of manufacture and the date of installation of the fusible links shall be marked on the system inspection tag. [**96**:11.2.5]

50.5.2.5.1 The tag shall be signed or initialed by the installer. [**96**:11.2.5.1]

50.5.2.5.2 The fusible links shall be destroyed when removed. [**96**:11.2.5.2]

50.5.2.6 Detection devices that are bulb-type automatic sprinklers and fusible links other than the metal alloy type shall be examined and cleaned or replaced annually. [**96**:11.2.6]

50.5.2.7 Fixed temperature-sensing elements other than the fusible metal alloy type shall be permitted to remain continuously in service, provided they are inspected and cleaned or replaced if necessary in accordance with the manufacturer's instructions, every 12 months or more frequently to ensure proper operation of the system. [**96**:11.2.7]

50.5.2.8 Where required, certificates of inspection and maintenance shall be forwarded to the AHJ. [**96**:11.2.8]

50.5.3 Inspection of Fire Dampers.

50.5.3.1 Actuation components for fire dampers shall be inspected for proper operation in accordance with the manufacturer's listed procedures. [**96**:11.3.1]

50.5.3.2 Replacement of Fusible Links.

50.5.3.2.1 Fusible links on fire damper assemblies shall be replaced at least semiannually or more frequently as necessary. [**96**:11.3.2.1]

50.5.3.2.2 Replacement shall be made by a certified person acceptable to the AHJ. [**96**:11.3.2.2]

50.5.3.3* Documentation Tag.

50.5.3.3.1 The year of manufacture and the date of installation of the fusible links shall be documented. [**96**:11.3.3.1]

50.5.3.3.2 The tag shall be signed or initialed by the installer. [**96**:11.3.3.2]

50.5.4* Inspection for Grease Buildup. The entire exhaust system shall be inspected for grease buildup by a properly trained, qualified, and certified person(s) acceptable to the AHJ and in accordance with Table 50.5.4. [**96**:11.4]

50.5.5 Inspection, Testing, and Maintenance of Listed Hoods Containing Mechanical, Water Spray, or Ultraviolet Devices. Listed hoods containing mechanical or fire-actuated dampers, internal washing components, or other mechanically operated devices shall be inspected and tested by properly trained, qualified, and certified persons every 6 months or at frequencies recommended by the manufacturer in accordance with their listings. [**96**:11.5]

50.5.6 Cleaning of Exhaust Systems.

50.5.6.1* If upon inspection, the exhaust system is found to be contaminated with deposits from grease-laden vapors, the contaminated portions of the exhaust system shall be cleaned by a properly trained qualified, and certified person(s) acceptable to the AHJ. [**96**:11.6.1]

Table 50.5.4 Schedule of Inspection for Grease Buildup

Type or Volume of Cooking	Inspection Frequency
Systems serving solid fuel cooking operations	Monthly
Systems serving high-volume cooking operations, such as 24-hour cooking, charbroiling, or wok cooking	Quarterly
Systems serving moderate-volume cooking operations	Semiannually
Systems serving low-volume cooking operations, such as churches, day camps, seasonal businesses, or senior centers	Annually

[**96**: Table 11.4]

50.5.6.2* Hoods, grease removal devices, fans, ducts, and other appurtenances shall be cleaned to remove combustible contaminants prior to surfaces becoming heavily contaminated with grease or oily sludge. [**96**:11.6.2]

50.5.6.3 At the start of the cleaning process, electrical switches that could be activated accidentally shall be locked out. [**96**:11.6.3]

50.5.6.4 Components of the fire suppression system shall not be rendered inoperable during the cleaning process. [**96**:11.6.4]

50.5.6.5 Fire-extinguishing systems shall be permitted to be rendered inoperable during the cleaning process where serviced by properly trained and qualified persons. [**96**:11.6.5]

50.5.6.6 Flammable solvents or other flammable cleaning aids shall not be used. [**96**:11.6.6]

50.5.6.7 Cleaning chemicals shall not be applied on fusible links or other detection devices of the automatic extinguishing system. [**96**:11.6.7]

50.5.6.8 After the exhaust system is cleaned, it shall not be coated with powder or other substance. [**96**:11.6.8]

50.5.6.9 When cleaning procedures are completed, all access panels (doors) and cover plates shall be restored to their normal operational condition. [**96**:11.6.9]

50.5.6.10 When an access panel is removed, a service company label or tag preprinted with the name of the company and giving the date of inspection or cleaning shall be affixed near the affected access panels. [**96**:11.6.10]

50.5.6.11 Dampers and diffusers shall be positioned for proper airflow. [**96**:11.6.11]

50.5.6.12 When cleaning procedures are completed, all electrical switches and system components shall be returned to an operable state. [**96**:11.6.12]

50.5.6.13 When an exhaust cleaning service is used, a certificate showing the name of the servicing company, the name of the person performing the work, and the date of inspection or cleaning shall be maintained on the premises. [**96**:11.6.13]

50.5.6.14 After cleaning or inspection is completed, the exhaust cleaning company and the person performing the work at the location shall provide the owner of the system with a written report that also specifies areas that were inaccessible or not cleaned. [**96**:11.6.14]

50.5.6.15 Where required, certificates of inspection and cleaning and reports of areas not cleaned shall be submitted to the AHJ. [**96**:11.6.15]

50.5.7 Cooking Equipment Maintenance.

50.5.7.1 Inspection and servicing of the cooking equipment shall be made at least annually by properly trained and qualified persons. [**96**:11.7.1]

50.5.7.2 Cooking equipment that collects grease below the surface, behind the equipment, or in cooking equipment flue gas exhaust, such as griddles or charbroilers, shall be inspected and, if found with grease accumulation, cleaned by a properly trained, qualified, and certified person acceptable to the AHJ. [**96**:11.7.2]

50.6 Minimum Safety Requirements for Cooking Equipment.

50.6.1 Cooking Equipment.

50.6.1.1* Cooking equipment shall be approved based on one of the following criteria:

(1) Listings by a testing laboratory
(2) Test data acceptable to the AHJ [**96**:12.1.1]

50.6.1.2 Installation.

50.6.1.2.1* All listed appliances shall be installed in accordance with the terms of their listings and the manufacturer's instructions. [**96**:12.1.2.1]

50.6.1.2.1.1 Solid fuel used for flavoring within a gas-operated appliance shall be in a solid fuel holder (smoker box) that is listed with the equipment. [**96**:12.1.2.1.1]

50.6.1.2.2* Cooking appliances requiring protection shall not be moved, modified, or rearranged without prior re-evaluation of the fire-extinguishing system by the system installer or servicing agent, unless otherwise allowed by the design of the fire-extinguishing system. [**96**:12.1.2.2]

50.6.1.2.2.1 A solid fuel holder shall not be added to an existing appliance until the fire-extinguishing system has been evaluated by the fire-extinguishing system service provider. [**96**:12.1.2.2.1]

50.6.1.2.3 The fire-extinguishing system shall not require re-evaluation where the cooking appliances are moved for the purposes of maintenance and cleaning, provided the appliances are returned to approved design location prior to cooking operations, and any disconnected fire-extinguishing system nozzles attached to the appliances are reconnected in accordance with the manufacturer's listed design manual. [**96**:12.1.2.3]

50.6.1.2.3.1 An approved method shall be provided that will ensure that the appliance is returned to an approved design location. [**96**:12.1.2.3.1]

50.6.1.2.4 All deep-fat fryers shall be installed with at least a 16 in. (406 mm) space between the fryer and surface flames from adjacent cooking equipment. [**96**:12.1.2.4]

50.6.1.2.5 Where a steel or tempered glass baffle plate is installed at a minimum 8 in. (203 mm) in height between the fryer and surface flames of the adjacent appliance, the requirement for a 16 in. (406 mm) space shall not apply. [**96**:12.1.2.5]

50.6.1.2.5.1 If the fryer and the surface flames are at different horizontal planes, the minimum height of 8 in. (203 mm) shall be measured from the higher of the two. [**96**:12.1.2.5.1]

50.6.2 Operating Controls. Deep-fat fryers shall be equipped with a separate high-limit control in addition to the adjustable operating control (thermostat) to shut off fuel or energy when the fat temperature reaches 475°F (246°C) at 1 in. (25.4 mm) below the surface. [**96**:12.2]

50.6.3 Commercial Kitchen Cooking Oil Storage Tank Systems. Commercial kitchen cooking oil storage tank systems shall comply with 66.19.7.

Chapter 51 Industrial Ovens and Furnaces

51.1 General.

51.1.1 Application. Industrial ovens and furnaces shall comply with this chapter and the applicable provisions of NFPA 86, *Standard for Ovens and Furnaces*.

51.1.2 Permits.

51.1.2.1 Permits, where required, shall comply with Section 1.12.

51.1.2.2 Applications for a permit shall be accompanied by plans for safe operation showing all essential details and calculations.

51.2 Location. Special consideration shall be given to the location of equipment using flammable liquids or when using gas fuels with a vapor density greater than air.

51.3 Safety Controls. Safety controls, as specified in NFPA 86, shall be sufficient in number and substantially constructed and arranged to maintain the required conditions of safety and prevent the development of fire and explosion hazards.

Chapter 52 Stationary Storage Battery Systems

52.1* **General.** Stationary storage battery systems having an electrolyte capacity of more than 100 gal (378.5 L) in sprinklered buildings or 50 gal (189.3 L) in unsprinklered buildings for flooded lead-acid, nickel-cadmium, and valve-regulated lead–acid (VRLA) batteries or 1000 lb (454 kg) for lithium-ion and lithium metal polymer batteries used for facility standby power, emergency power, or uninterrupted power supplies shall be in accordance with Chapter 52 and Table 52.1.

52.2 Permits.

52.2.1 Permits, where required, shall comply with Section 1.12.

52.2.2 Prior to installation, plans shall be submitted and approved by the AHJ.

Table 52.1 Battery Requirements

Requirement	Nonrecombinant Batteries		Recombinant Batteries		Other
	Flooded Lead-Acid	Flooded Nickel-Cadmium (Ni-Cd)	Valve-Regulated Lead–Acid (VRLA)	Lithium-Ion	Lithium Metal Polymer
Safety caps	Venting caps	Venting caps	Self-resealing flame-arresting caps	No caps	No caps
Thermal runaway management	Not required	Not required	Required	Not required	Required
Spill control	Required	Required	Not required	Not required	Not required
Neutralization	Required	Required	Required	Not required	Not required
Ventilation	Required	Required	Required	Not required	Not required
Signage	Required	Required	Required	Required	Required
Seismic control	Required	Required	Required	Required	Required
Fire detection	Required	Required	Required	Required	Required

52.3 Safety Features.

52.3.1 Safety Venting. Batteries shall be provided with safety venting caps as follows in 52.3.1.1 through 52.3.1.3.

52.3.1.1 Nonrecombinant Batteries. Vented lead-acid, nickel-cadmium, or other types of nonrecombinant batteries shall be provided with safety venting caps.

52.3.1.2 Recombinant Batteries. VRLA or other types of sealed, recombinant batteries shall be equipped with self-resealing flame-arresting safety vents.

52.3.1.3 Lithium-ion and lithium metal polymer batteries shall not require safety venting caps.

52.3.2 Thermal Runaway. VRLA, lithium-ion, and lithium metal polymer battery systems shall be provided with a listed device or other approved method to preclude, detect, and control thermal runaway.

52.3.3 Location and Occupancy Separation.

52.3.3.1 Battery systems shall be permitted in the same room as the equipment that they support.

52.3.3.2 Battery systems shall be housed in a noncombustible, locked cabinet or other enclosure to prevent access by unauthorized personnel unless located in a separate equipment room accessible only to authorized personnel.

52.3.3.3 In other than assembly, educational, detention and correction facilities, health care, ambulatory health care, day care centers, residential board and care, and residential occupancies, battery systems shall be located in a room separated from other portions of the building by a minimum of a 1-hour fire barrier.

52.3.3.4 In assembly, educational, detention and correction facilities, health care, ambulatory health care, day care centers, residential board and care, and residential occupancies, battery systems shall be located in a room separated from other portions of the building by a minimum of a 2-hour fire barrier.

52.3.4 Spill Control.

52.3.4.1 Rooms, buildings, or areas containing free-flowing liquid electrolyte in individual vessels having a capacity of more than 55 gal (208 L) or multiple vessels having an aggregate capacity exceeding 1000 gal (3785 L) shall be provided with spill control to prevent the flow of liquids to adjoining areas.

52.3.4.2* An approved method and materials for the control of a spill of electrolyte shall be provided that will be capable of controlling a spill from the single largest vessel.

52.3.4.3 VRLA, lithium-ion, lithium metal polymer, or other types of sealed batteries with immobilized electrolyte shall not require spill control.

52.3.5 Neutralization.

52.3.5.1* An approved method to neutralize spilled electrolyte shall be provided.

52.3.5.2 For nonrecombinant batteries and VRLA batteries, the method shall be capable of neutralizing a spill from the largest battery to a pH between 7.0 and 9.0.

52.3.5.3 Lithium-ion and lithium metal polymer batteries shall not require neutralization.

52.3.6* Ventilation. For flooded lead-acid, flooded nickel-cadmium, and VRLA batteries, ventilation shall be provided for rooms and cabinets in accordance with the mechanical code and one of the following:

(1) The ventilation system shall be designed to limit the maximum concentration of hydrogen to 1.0 percent of the total volume of the room during the worst-case event of simultaneous "boost" charging of all the batteries, in accordance with nationally recognized standards.
(2) Continuous ventilation shall be provided at a rate of not less than 1 ft^3/min/ft^2 (5.1 L/sec/m^2) of floor area of the room or cabinet.

52.3.6.1 Lithium-ion and lithium metal polymer batteries shall not require ventilation.

52.3.7 Environment. The battery environment shall be controlled or analyzed to maintain temperature in a safe operating range for the specific battery technology used.

52.3.8 Signs.

52.3.8.1 Doors or accesses into the following shall be provided with approved signs:

(1) Battery storage buildings
(2) Rooms containing stationary storage battery systems
(3) Other areas containing stationary storage battery systems

52.3.8.2 For rooms that contain Valve-Regulated Lead–Acid (VRLA), Lithium-Ion, or Lithium Metal Polymer batteries, the signs required by 52.3.8.1 shall state the following:

This room contains:
(1) Stationary storage battery systems
(2) Energized electrical circuits

52.3.8.3 For rooms that contain Flooded Lead-Acid or Flooded Nickel-Cadmium (Ni-Cd) batteries, the signs required by 52.3.8.1 shall state the following:

This room contains:
(1) Stationary storage battery systems
(2) Energized electrical circuits
(3) Corrosive battery electrolyte

52.3.8.4 Battery cabinets shall be provided with exterior labels that identify the manufacturer and model number of the system and electrical rating (voltage and current) of the contained battery system.

52.3.8.5 Signs shall be provided within battery cabinets to indicate the relevant electrical, chemical, and fire hazard.

52.3.9 Seismic Protection. In seismically active areas, battery systems shall be seismically braced in accordance with the building code.

52.3.10 Smoke Detection. An approved automatic smoke detection system shall be installed in such areas and supervised by an approved central, proprietary, or remote station service or a local alarm that will give an audible signal at a constantly attended location.

Chapter 53   Mechanical Refrigeration

53.1* General.

53.1.1 Applicability.

53.1.1.1* Refrigeration unit and system installations having a refrigerant circuit containing more than 220 lb (100 kg) of Group A1 or 30 lb (13.6 kg) of any other group refrigerant shall be in accordance with Chapter 53 and the mechanical code.

53.1.1.2 Temporary and portable installations shall be exempt from the requirements of this chapter when approved.

53.1.2 Permits and Plans.

53.1.2.1 Permits, where required, shall comply with Section 1.12.

53.1.2.2 Plans and specifications for devices and systems required by this chapter shall be submitted to the AHJ for review and approval prior to installation.

53.1.3 Reference Codes and Standards. Refrigeration systems shall be in accordance with ASHRAE 15 and the mechanical code. Refrigeration systems using ammonia as a refrigerant shall also comply with ANSI/IIAR 2, *Standard for Equipment, Design and Installation of Closed-Circuit Ammonia Mechanical Refrigerating Systems*.

53.2 Safety Features.

53.2.1 Emergency Pressure Control System. Refrigeration systems containing more than 6.6 lb (3 kg) of flammable, toxic, or highly toxic refrigerant or ammonia shall be provided with an emergency pressure control system in accordance with 53.2.1.1 and 53.2.1.2.

53.2.1.1 High and Intermediate Pressure Zones. Each high and intermediate pressure zone in a refrigeration system shall be provided with a single automatic valve providing a crossover connection to a lower pressure zone. Automatic crossover valves shall comply with 53.2.1.1.1 through 53.2.1.1.4.

53.2.1.1.1 Overpressure Limit Set Point for Crossover Valves. Automatic crossover valves shall be provided to automatically relieve excess system pressure to a lower pressure zone if the pressure in a high or intermediate pressure zone rises to within 90 percent of the set point for emergency pressure relief devices.

53.2.1.1.2 Manual Operation. Where required by the AHJ, automatic crossover valves shall be capable of manual operation.

53.2.1.1.3 System Design Pressure. Refrigeration system zones that are connected to a higher pressure zone by an automatic crossover valve shall be designed to safely contain the maximum pressure that can be achieved by interconnection of the two zones.

53.2.1.1.4 Automatic Emergency Stop. Operation of an automatic crossover valve shall cause all compressors on the affected system to immediately stop in accordance with the following:

(1) Dedicated pressure-sensing devices located immediately adjacent to crossover valves shall be permitted as a means for determining operation of a valve.
(2) To ensure that the automatic crossover valve system provides a redundant means of stopping compressors in an overpressure condition, high pressure cutout sensors associated with compressors shall not be used as a basis for determining operation of a crossover valve.

53.2.1.2 Low Pressure Zone.

53.2.1.2.1 Overpressure Limit Set Point for Emergency Stop. The lowest pressure zone in a refrigeration system shall be provided with a dedicated means of determining a rise in system pressure to within 90 percent of the set point for emergency pressure relief devices.

53.2.1.2.2 Automatic Emergency Stop. Activation of the overpressure sensing device shall cause all compressors on the affected system to immediately stop.

53.2.2 Treatment, Flaring, and Diffusion Systems for Refrigerant Discharge.

53.2.2.1 Required Systems. Unless the AHJ determines, upon review of an engineering analysis prepared at the expense of the owner, that a significant fire, health, or environmental hazard would not result from an atmospheric release, refrigeration systems that are designed to discharge refrigerant vapor to the atmosphere shall be provided with an approved treatment, flaring, or diffusion system where required by 53.2.2.1.1 through 53.2.2.1.3.

53.2.2.1.1 Toxic and Highly Toxic Refrigerants. Systems containing toxic or highly toxic refrigerants shall discharge vapor to the atmosphere only through an approved treatment system in accordance with Chapter 63 or flaring system in accordance with 53.2.2.2.

53.2.2.1.2 Flammable Refrigerants. Systems containing flammable refrigerants shall discharge vapor to the atmosphere in accordance with the following:

(1) For refrigerants having a density equal to or greater than the density of air, discharge shall be through an approved treatment system in accordance with or flaring system in accordance with 53.2.2.2.
(2) For refrigerants having a density less than the density of air, discharge to the atmosphere shall be permitted, provided that the point of discharge is located outside of the structure at not less than 15 ft (4.6 m) above the adjoining grade level and not less than 20 ft (6.1 m) from any window, ventilation opening, or exit.

53.2.2.1.3 Ammonia Refrigerant. Systems containing ammonia refrigerant shall discharge vapor to the atmosphere through a treatment system in accordance with 53.2.2.1, through a flaring system in accordance with 53.2.2.2, through an approved ammonia diffusion system in accordance with 53.2.2.3, or by other approved means except as follows:

(1) Discharge through a treatment, flaring, or diffusion system shall not be required for ammonia–water absorption unit systems installed outdoors serving a dwelling unit, provided that the discharge is shielded and dispersed.
(2) Discharge through a treatment, flaring, or diffusion system shall not be required for ammonia–water absorption unit systems containing less than 22 lb (10 kg) of ammonia and for which the ammonia circuit is located entirely outdoors.

53.2.2.2 Design of Flaring Systems.

53.2.2.2.1 Flaring systems for incineration of flammable, toxic, or highly toxic refrigerants or ammonia shall be designed to incinerate the entire discharge.

53.2.2.2.2 The products of refrigerant incineration shall not pose health or environmental hazards.

53.2.2.2.3 Incineration shall be automatic upon initiation of discharge, shall be designed to prevent blowback, and shall not expose structures or materials to threat of fire.

53.2.2.2.4 Standby fuel, such as LP-Gas, and standby power shall have the capacity to operate for one and one half the required time for complete incineration of refrigerant in the system.

53.2.2.3 Design of Ammonia Diffusion Systems.

53.2.2.3.1 Ammonia diffusion systems shall include a tank containing 1 gal of water for each pound of ammonia (4 L of water for each kg of ammonia) that will be released in 1 hour from the largest relief device connected to the discharge pipe.

53.2.2.3.2 The water used shall be prevented from freezing without the use of salt or chemicals by burial of the discharge pipe below frost depth or other approved means.

53.2.2.3.3 The discharge pipe from the pressure relief device shall distribute ammonia in the bottom of the tank, but no lower than 33 ft (10 m) below the maximum liquid level.

53.2.2.3.4 The tank shall contain the volume of water and ammonia, described in 53.2.2.3.1, without overflowing.

53.2.2.3.5 The tank shall be substantially constructed of not less than 1/8 in. (2.51 mm) (10 gauge) steel.

53.2.2.3.6 The horizontal dimensions of the tank shall be equal to or less than one half of the height.

53.2.2.3.7 The tank shall have a hinged cover or, if of the enclosed type, shall have a vent hole at the top.

53.2.2.3.8 Pipe connections shall be through the top of the tank.

53.2.3 Refrigeration Machinery Rooms. Where required by the mechanical code, refrigeration systems shall be provided with a refrigeration machinery room, which shall comply with 53.2.3.1 through 53.2.3.4.

53.2.3.1 Refrigerant Vapor Detection, Monitoring, Alarm, and Electrical Systems. Refrigeration machinery rooms shall have an approved refrigerant vapor detection, monitoring, and alarm system in accordance with 53.2.3.1.1 through 53.2.3.1.7 and the mechanical code.

53.2.3.1.1 Alarm Threshold. The refrigerant vapor detector shall activate approved visual and audible alarm signaling devices at one of the following refrigerant thresholds:

(1) At a value not greater than the corresponding TLV-TWA (or toxicity measure consistent therewith); not to exceed 25 percent of the lower flammable limit (LFL)
(2) For ammonia, at a concentration not exceeding 1000 parts per million

53.2.3.1.2 Location of Signaling Devices. Audible and visual alarm signaling devices shall be located inside the refrigeration machinery room and outside the room at each entrance into the room.

53.2.3.1.3 Audibility. Audible alarm signaling devices shall provide a sound level of at least 15 dB above the operating ambient noise sound pressure level of the space in which they are installed and shall provide approved, distinctive audible and visual alarms.

53.2.3.1.4* Emergency Shutoff Interface. Where the quantity of a Group A2, B2, A3, or B3 refrigerant, other than ammonia, in an independent circuit would exceed 25 percent of the LFL if released to the surrounding room, either of the following shall apply:

(1) Electrical equipment shall comply with the requirements of *NFPA 70* for Class I, Division 2.
(2) The refrigerant vapor detection system required by 53.2.3.1 shall automatically de-energize all electrical power within the space at vapor concentrations at or above 25 percent of the LFL.

53.2.3.1.5 Power and Supervision. Refrigerant vapor detection and alarm systems shall be powered and supervised as required for fire alarm systems in accordance with *NFPA 72*.

53.2.3.1.6 Monitoring and Annunciation. Refrigerant vapor detection and alarm systems shall transmit a signal to an approved location.

53.2.3.1.7 Installation and Maintenance. Detection and alarm systems shall be installed and maintained in accordance with the equipment manufacturers' specifications. *(Also see 53.3.2.1.)*

53.2.3.2* Prohibited Sources of Ignition. Open flames or devices having an exposed surface temperature exceeding 800°F

(427°C) shall be prohibited in refrigeration machinery rooms except as follows:

(1) Momentary temperature excursions such as electrical contacts in Group A1 and B1 systems shall be permitted.
(2) Open flames or devices having an exposed surface temperature exceeding 800°F (427°C) shall be permitted in refrigeration machinery rooms used exclusively for direct-fired absorption equipment.
(3) Existing nonconforming installations shall be permitted where approved by the AHJ, where the combustion system is interlocked with the refrigerant detection system to shut off at the permissible exposure limit (PEL).
(4) Direct-vented combustion equipment shall be permitted in accordance with the mechanical code.

53.2.3.3 Ventilation Systems.

53.2.3.3.1 Fans providing emergency purge ventilation for refrigerant escape from a refrigeration room shall have a clearly identified switch of the break-glass type providing on-only control immediately adjacent to, and outside of, each refrigerant machinery room means of egress.

53.2.3.3.2 An emergency purge control shall be provided with a manual reset only.

53.2.3.3.3 Purge fans shall also respond automatically to the refrigerant concentration detection system set to activate the ventilation system at the threshold levels set forth in 53.2.3.1.1.

53.2.3.3.4 Mechanical ventilation systems serving refrigeration rooms shall have switches to control the power to each fan.

53.2.3.3.5 The switches shall be key-operated or within a locked glass-covered or tamper-resistant enclosure at an approved location adjacent to and outside of the principal entrance to the refrigeration machinery room.

53.2.3.3.6 Keys necessary for operation of ventilation systems shall be located in a single approved location.

53.2.3.3.7 Switches controlling fans providing continuous ventilation shall be of the two-position, on/off type.

53.2.3.3.8 Switches controlling fans providing intermittent or emergency ventilation shall be of the three-position, automatic on/off type.

53.2.3.3.9 Switches shall be labeled identifying both the function and the specific fan being controlled.

53.2.3.3.10 Two colored and labeled indicator lamps responding to the differential pressure created by airflow shall be provided for each switch.

53.2.3.3.11 One lamp shall indicate flow, and the other shall indicate no flow.

53.2.3.3.12 Exhaust from mechanical ventilation systems in refrigeration rooms shall be discharged 20 ft (6.1 m) or more from a property line or openings into buildings.

53.2.3.3.13 Discharges capable of exceeding 25 percent of the LFL or 50 percent of the immediately dangerous to life and health (IDLH) value shall be equipped with approved treatment systems to reduce the discharge concentrations to these values or lower, except as provided in 53.2.3.3.13.1 and 53.2.3.3.13.2. *(Also see 53.2.2.1.)*

53.2.3.3.13.1 A treatment system shall not be required when an approved engineering analysis of plume dispersion demonstrates that the limiting value will not be exceeded at the property line.

53.2.3.3.13.2 A treatment system shall not be required for ventilation provided for an ammonia refrigeration system.

53.2.3.4 Electrical.

53.2.3.4.1 The refrigeration machinery room shall not be required to be classified as a hazardous location for electrical equipment except as provided in the mechanical code or *NFPA 70*.

53.2.3.4.2 Refrigeration machinery rooms used exclusively for direct-fired absorption equipment shall be permitted not to be classified as a hazardous location for electrical equipment in accordance with *NFPA 70*.

53.2.3.4.3 Electrical equipment and electrical installations in refrigeration machinery rooms shall comply with Section 11.1.

53.2.3.4.4 Where treatment, detection, or alarm systems are required, such systems shall be connected to a secondary source of power to automatically supply electrical power in the event of loss of power from the primary source.

53.2.3.4.5 A clearly identified switch of the break-glass type or with an approved tamper-resistant cover shall provide off-only control of refrigerant compressors, refrigerant pumps, and normally closed, automatic refrigerant valves located in the machinery room. In addition, this equipment shall be automatically shut off whenever the refrigerant vapor concentration in the machinery room exceeds the vapor detector's upper detection limit or 25 percent of the LFL, whichever is lower.

53.2.3.4.5.1 In machinery rooms where only nonflammable refrigerants are used, only compressors shall be required to be stopped by vapor detection or the cut-off switch. *(Also see 53.2.3.1.4.)*

53.2.4 Signs and Labels.

53.2.4.1 General. Refrigeration units or systems shall be provided with approved hazard identification signs in accordance with NFPA 704, *Standard System for the Identification of the Hazards of Materials for Emergency Response*; emergency operational signs, charts, and labels in accordance with the mechanical code, and the following:

(1) Name and address of the manufacturer or installer
(2) Type and total number of pounds of refrigerant contained in the system
(3) Field test pressure applied

53.2.4.2 Systems with More Than 110 lb (50 kg) of Refrigerant. Systems containing more than 110 lb (50 kg) of refrigerant shall be provided with signs having letters not less than ½ in. (12.7 mm) high, designating the following:

(1) Main shutoff valves to each vessel
(2) Mainstream or electrical controls
(3) Remote control switch
(4) Pressure-limiting device

53.3 Operations, Maintenance, and Testing.

53.3.1 Operations and Maintenance.

53.3.1.1 General. Refrigeration systems shall be operated and maintained in a safe and operable condition, free from accumulations of oil, dirt, waste, excessive corrosion, other debris, or leaks, and in accordance with ASHRAE 15 and the mechanical code. Ammonia refrigerator systems shall be maintained in accordance with ANSI/IIAR 7, *Developing Operating Procedures for Closed-Circuit Ammonia Mechanical Refrigerating Systems*.

53.3.1.2 Access to System. Refrigeration systems shall be maintained accessible to the fire department as required by the AHJ.

53.3.1.3 Storage in Machinery Rooms.

53.3.1.3.1 Flammable and combustible materials shall not be stored in refrigeration machinery rooms except for incidental materials necessary for the safe and proper operation and maintenance of the system.

53.3.1.3.2 Storage of materials in a refrigeration machinery room, including reserve supplies of refrigerants or refrigerant oils, shall be in accordance with other applicable chapters of this *Code*.

53.3.1.4 Changing of Refrigerant Type. Refrigerant types shall not be changed without prior notification and approval of the AHJ.

53.3.1.5 Records of Refrigerant Quantities. The person in charge of the premises on which a refrigeration unit or system subject to these regulations is installed or maintained shall keep a written record of refrigerant quantities brought onto and removed from the premises, which shall be made available to the AHJ upon request.

53.3.1.6 Permissible Refrigerant Discharges. Refrigerant shall be only permitted to be released to atmosphere in the following circumstances:

(1) Refrigeration systems operating at pressures below atmospheric and incorporating automatic purge cycles
(2) Incidental operation of automatic pressure relief valves resulting in minor release of the refrigerant charge
(3) Incidental minor releases associated with service operations after system pumpdown has been accomplished
(4) In an emergency

53.3.1.7 Notification of Fugitive Releases. Where required by the fire department, the fire department shall be notified upon discharges of refrigerant that are not in accordance with 53.3.1.6(1), (2), or (3).

53.3.2 Testing of Equipment.

53.3.2.1 Acceptance Testing. The following emergency devices or systems shall be tested to demonstrate their safety and effectiveness upon completion of the installation or alteration:

(1) Treatment and flaring systems
(2) Ammonia diffusion systems
(3) Fans and associated equipment intended to operate emergency purge ventilation systems
(4) Refrigerant vapor detection and alarm systems

53.3.2.2 Periodic Testing. The following emergency devices or systems shall be tested in accordance with the manufacturers' specifications at intervals not exceeding one year:

(1) Treatment and flaring systems
(2) Fans and associated equipment intended to operate emergency purge ventilation systems
(3) Refrigerant vapor detection and alarm systems

53.3.2.3 Records of Required Testing. A written record of required testing shall be maintained on the premises.

53.3.2.4 Testing Personnel Qualifications. Tests of emergency devices or systems required by Chapter 53 shall be conducted by persons trained in such testing.

Chapter 54   Ozone Gas–Generating Equipment

54.1 Scope.

54.1.1 Equipment having a maximum ozone-generating capacity of not less than ½ lb (0.23 kg) over a 24-hour period shall comply with Chapter 54 unless otherwise permitted by 54.1.2.

54.1.2 Chapter 54 shall not apply to ozone-generating equipment used in one- and two-family dwellings or lodging or rooming house occupancies.

54.2 Location.

54.2.1 General.

54.2.1.1 Ozone generators shall be located in approved cabinets or ozone generator rooms in accordance with Section 54.2 unless otherwise permitted by 54.2.1.2.

54.2.1.2 Ozone generators within approved pressure vessels located outside of buildings shall not be required to be located in a cabinet or ozone generator room.

54.2.2 Cabinets.

54.2.2.1 Ozone cabinets shall be constructed of approved materials compatible with ozone in accordance with nationally recognized standards.

54.2.2.2* Cabinets shall display an approved sign stating: OZONE GAS GENERATOR — HIGHLY TOXIC — OXIDIZER.

54.2.2.3 Cabinets shall be braced for seismic activity in accordance with the building code.

54.2.2.4 Cabinets shall be mechanically ventilated in accordance with all of the following:

(1) Not less than six air changes per hour shall be provided.
(2) Exhausted air shall be directed to a treatment system designed to reduce the discharge concentration of the gas to one-half of the immediately dangerous to life and health (IDLH) value at the point of discharge to the atmosphere.
(3) The average velocity of ventilation at makeup air openings with cabinet doors closed shall not be less than 200 ft/min (1.02 m/s).

54.2.3 Ozone Generator Rooms. Ozone generator rooms shall comply with all of the following:

(1) Not less than six air changes per hour shall be provided.
(2) Exhausted air shall be directed to a treatment system designed to reduce the discharge concentration of the gas to one-half of the IDLH value at the point of discharge to the atmosphere, or the ozone generator room shall be equipped with a continuous gas detection system that will shut off the ozone generator and sound a local alarm when concentrations above the permissible exposure limit occur.
(3) Ozone generator rooms shall not normally be occupied, and such rooms shall be kept free of combustible and hazardous material storage.

(4) Room access doors shall display an approved sign stating: OZONE GAS GENERATOR — HIGHLY TOXIC — OXIDIZER.

54.3 Piping, Valves, and Fittings.

54.3.1 General. Piping, valves, fittings, and related components used to convey ozone shall be in accordance with Section 54.3.

54.3.2 Secondary Containment.

54.3.2.1 Secondary containment, such as double-walled piping or exhausted enclosures, shall be provided for piping, valves, fittings, and related components, unless otherwise permitted by 54.3.2.3.

54.3.2.2 Secondary containment shall be capable of directing a sudden release to an approved treatment system.

54.3.2.3 Secondary containment shall not be required for welded stainless steel piping and tubing.

54.3.3 Materials. Materials shall be compatible with ozone and shall be rated for the design operating pressures.

54.3.4 Identification. Piping shall be identified: OZONE GAS — HIGHLY TOXIC — OXIDIZER.

54.4 Automatic Shutdown. Ozone generators shall be designed to automatically shut down when any one of the following occurs:

(1) The dissolved ozone concentration in the water being treated is above saturation when measured at the point where the water is exposed to the atmosphere.
(2) The process using generated ozone is shut down.
(3) The ventilation system for the cabinet or ozone generator room fails.
(4) The gas detection system fails.

54.5 Manual Shutdown. Manual shutdown controls shall be provided at the ozone generator and, if in a room, within 10 ft (3 m) of the main exit or exit access door.

Chapter 55 Reserved

Chapter 56 Reserved

Chapter 57 Reserved

Chapter 58 Reserved

Chapter 59 Reserved

Chapter 60 Hazardous Materials

60.1 General Requirements.

60.1.1 Applicability. Occupancies containing high hazard contents shall comply with this chapter in addition to other applicable requirements of this *Code*. [**5000:**34.1.1.1]

> Paragraph 60.1.2 was revised by a tentative interim amendment. (TIA). See page 1.

60.1.2 Subjects Not Regulated. Buildings, and portions thereof, containing high hazard contents limited to any of the following shall not be required to comply with this chapter:

(1) Flammable and combustible liquids associated with application of flammable finishes and complying with Chapter 43.
(2) Flammable and combustible liquids associated with wholesale and retail sales and storage in mercantile occupancies and complying with Chapter 66
(3) Class IIIA and Class IIIB combustible liquid solvents in closed systems employing listed cleaning equipment complying with Chapter 24
(4) Refrigerants and refrigerant oil contained within closed-cycle refrigeration systems complying with Chapter 53 and the building code
(5) Flammable and combustible liquid beverages in liquor stores and distributors without bulk storage
(6) High hazard contents stored or used in farm buildings or similar occupancies for on-premises agricultural use
(7) Corrosive materials in stationary batteries utilized for facility emergency power, uninterrupted power supply, or similar purposes, provided that the batteries are provided with safety venting caps and ventilation is provided in accordance with Chapter 52
(8) Corrosive materials displayed in original packaging in mercantile occupancies and intended for personal or household use or as building materials
(9) Aerosol products in storage or mercantile occupancies and complying with Chapter 61
(10) Flammable and combustible liquids storage tank buildings meeting the requirements of NFPA 30
(11) Flammable and combustible liquids storage tank vaults meeting the requirements of NFPA 30
(12) Flammable and combustible liquids process buildings meeting the requirements of NFPA 30
(13) Installation of fuel gas distribution systems and associated equipment in accordance with Section 11.4 and Chapter 69

[**5000:**34.1.1.2]

60.1.3 Applicability of Sections.

60.1.3.1 Quantities Not Exceeding the Maximum Allowable Quantities per Control Area. Storage, use, and handling of hazardous materials in quantities not exceeding maximum allowable quantities permitted in control areas set forth in Section 60.1.3.1 shall be in accordance with Section 60.1 through Section 60.5.

60.1.3.2 Quantities Exceeding the Maximum Allowable Quantities per Control Area. Storage, use, and handling of hazardous materials in quantities in excess of the maximum allowable quantities permitted in control areas set forth in 60.1.3.2 shall comply with Section 60.2 through Section 60.6.

60.1.3.3 Limited Applicability of this Chapter for Specific Material Classes. Chapter 60 shall apply in its entirety to all hazardous materials except where Chapters 61 through 73 of this *Code* specify that only certain sections of this chapter shall apply to a specific material classification category.

60.1.4 Facility Closure.

60.1.4.1 Where required by the AHJ, no facility storing hazardous materials listed in 1.1.1 of NFPA 400 shall close or abandon an entire storage facility without notifying the AHJ at least 30 days prior to the scheduled closing. [**400**:1.9.1]

60.1.4.2 The AHJ shall be permitted to reduce the 30-day period specified in 60.1.4.1 when there are special circumstances requiring such reduction. [**400**:1.9.2]

60.1.4.3 Facilities Out of Service.

60.1.4.3.1 Facilities Temporarily Out of Service. Facilities that are temporarily out of service shall continue to maintain a permit and be monitored and inspected. [**400**:1.9.3.1]

60.1.4.3.2 Facilities Permanently Out of Service. Facilities for which a permit is not kept current or that are not monitored and inspected on a regular basis shall be deemed to be permanently out of service and shall be closed in accordance with 60.1.4.4.1 through 60.1.4.4.2. [**400**:1.9.3.2]

60.1.4.4 Closure Plan.

60.1.4.4.1 Where required by the AHJ, the permit holder or applicant shall submit a closure plan to the fire department to terminate storage, dispensing, handling, or use of hazardous materials at least 30 days prior to facility closure. [**400**:1.9.4.1]

60.1.4.4.2 The plan shall demonstrate that hazardous materials that were stored, dispensed, handled, or used in the facility have been transported, disposed of, or reused in a manner that eliminates the need for further maintenance and any threat to public health and safety. [**400**:1.9.4.2]

60.1.5 Emergency Planning.

60.1.5.1 Emergency Action Plan. An emergency action plan, consistent with the available equipment and personnel, shall be established to respond to fire and other emergencies in accordance with requirements set forth in this Code. [**400**:1.10.1]

60.1.5.2 Activation. The facility responsible for an unauthorized release shall activate the emergency action element of the Hazardous Materials Management Plan. [**400**:1.10.2]

60.1.6 Hazardous Materials Management Plan (HMMP).

60.1.6.1* When required by the AHJ, new or existing facilities that store, use, or handle hazardous materials covered by this *Code* in amounts above the MAQ specified in 60.4.2.1.2 through 60.4.2.1.13 and 5.4.1.2 of NFPA 400 shall submit a hazardous materials management plan (HMMP) to the AHJ. [**400**:1.11.1]

60.1.6.2 The HMMP shall be reviewed and updated as follows:

(1) Annually
(2) When the facility is modified
(3) When hazardous materials representing a new hazard category not previously addressed are stored, used, or handled in the facility [**400**:1.11.2]

60.1.6.3 The HMMP shall comply with the requirements of Section 60.5. [**400**:1.11.3]

60.1.7* Hazardous Materials Inventory Statement (HMIS).

60.1.7.1 When required by the AHJ, a hazardous materials inventory statement (HMIS) shall be completed and submitted to the AHJ. [**400**:1.12.1]

60.2 Special Definitions.

60.2.1 Chemical Name. See 3.3.43.

60.2.2 Closed System Use. See 3.3.267.1.

60.2.3 Control Area. See 3.3.14.2.

60.2.4 Dispensing. See 3.3.86.

60.2.5 Flammable Solid. See 3.3.236.2.

60.2.6 Hazardous Material. See 3.3.173.4.

60.2.7 Health Hazard Material. See 3.3.173.6.

60.2.8 Highly Toxic Material. See 3.3.173.7.

60.2.9 Incompatible Material. See 3.3.173.9.

60.2.10 Liquid. See 3.3.164.

60.2.11 Open System Use. See 3.3.267.2.

60.2.12 Organic Peroxide. See 3.3.189.

60.2.12.1 Organic Peroxide Formulation. See 3.3.189.1.

60.2.12.1.1 Class I. See 3.3.189.1.1.

60.2.12.1.2 Class II. See 3.3.189.1.2.

60.2.12.1.3 Class III. See 3.3.189.1.3.

60.2.12.1.4 Class IV. See 3.3.189.1.4.

60.2.12.1.5 Class V. See 3.3.189.1.5.

60.2.13 Oxidizer. See 3.3.192.

60.2.13.1 Class 1. See 3.3.192.1.

60.2.13.2 Class 2. See 3.3.192.2.

60.2.13.3 Class 3. See 3.3.192.3.

60.2.13.4 Class 4. See 3.3.192.4.

60.2.14 Physical Hazard Material. See 3.3.173.12.

60.2.15 Pyrophoric Material. See 3.3.173.13.

60.2.16 Solid Material. See 3.3.237.

60.2.17 Toxic Material. See 3.3.173.14.

60.2.18 Unstable (Reactive) Material. See 3.3.173.15.

60.2.19 Use. See 3.3.267.

60.2.20 Water-Reactive Material. See 3.3.173.16.

60.3 Classification of Materials, Wastes, and Hazard of Contents.

60.3.1* Hazardous Material Classification. Materials shall be classified into one or more of the following categories of hazardous materials, based on the definitions found in Chapter 3:

(1) Corrosive solids, liquids, or gases
(2) Flammable solids
(3) Flammable gases
(4) Flammable cryogenic fluids
(5) Inert cryogenic fluids
(6) Inert gases
(7) Organic peroxide formulations
(8) Oxidizer solids or liquids
(9) Oxidizing gases
(10) Oxidizing cryogenic fluids
(11) Pyrophoric solids, liquids, or gases
(12) Toxic or highly toxic solids, liquids, or gases

(13) Unstable (reactive) solids, liquids, or gases
(14) Water-reactive solids or liquids [**400**:4.1]

60.3.2 Classification of High Hazard Contents.

60.3.2.1 General.

60.3.2.1.1 High hazard contents shall include materials defined as hazardous material in Chapter 3, whether stored, used, or handled. [**400**:4.2.1.1]

60.3.2.1.2 High hazard contents shall include those materials defined as hazardous material solids, liquids, or gases limited to the hazard categories specified in 1.1.1 of NFPA 400 and classified in accordance with 60.3.2.1.2.1 through 60.3.2.1.2.4 whether stored, used, or handled. [**400**:4.2.1.2]

60.3.2.1.2.1 High Hazard Level 1 Contents. High hazard Level 1 contents shall include materials that present a detonation hazard, including, but not limited to, the following hazard categories:

(1) Class 4 oxidizers
(2) Detonable pyrophoric solids or liquids
(3) Class 3 detonable and Class 4 unstable (reactive) solids, liquids, or gases
(4) Detonable organic peroxides [**400**:4.2.1.2.1]

60.3.2.1.2.2 High Hazard Level 2 Contents. High hazard Level 2 contents shall include materials that present a deflagration hazard or a hazard from accelerated burning limited to the following hazard categories:

(1) Combustible dusts stored, used, or generated in a manner creating a severe fire or explosion hazard
(2) Class I organic peroxides
(3) Class 3 solid or liquid oxidizers that are used or stored in normally open containers or systems or in closed containers or systems at gauge pressures of more than 15 psi (103.4 kPa)
(4) Flammable gases
(5) Flammable cryogenic fluids
(6) Nondetonable pyrophoric solids, liquids, or gases
(7) Class 3 nondetonable unstable (reactive) solids, liquids, or gases
(8) Class 3 water-reactive solids and liquids [**400**:4.2.1.2.2]

60.3.2.1.2.3 High Hazard Level 3 Contents. High hazard Level 3 contents shall include materials that readily support combustion or present a physical hazard limited to the following hazard categories:

(1) Flammable solids, other than dusts classified as high hazard Level 2, stored, used, or generated in a manner creating a high fire hazard
(2) Class II and Class III organic peroxides
(3) Class 2 solid or liquid oxidizers
(4) Class 3 solid or liquid oxidizers that are used or stored in normally closed containers or systems at gauge pressures of less than 15 psi (103.4 kPa)
(5) Class 2 unstable (reactive) materials
(6) Class 2 water-reactive solids, liquids, or gases
(7) Oxidizing gases
(8) Oxidizing cryogenic fluids [**400**:4.2.1.2.3]

60.3.2.1.2.4 High Hazard Level 4 Contents. High hazard Level 4 contents shall include materials that are acute health hazards limited to the following hazard categories:

(1) Corrosive solids, liquids, or gases
(2) Highly toxic solids, liquids, or gases

(3) Toxic solids, liquids, or gases [**400**:4.2.1.2.4]

60.3.3 Mixtures. Mixtures shall be classified in accordance with the hazards of the mixture as a whole by an approved, qualified organization, individual, or testing laboratory. [**400**:4.3]

60.3.4* Multiple Hazards. Hazardous materials that have multiple hazards shall conform to the code requirements for each applicable hazard category. [**400**:4.4]

60.3.5* Classification of Waste. Waste comprised of or containing hazardous materials shall be classified in accordance with 60.3.1 through 60.3.4 as applicable. [**400**:4.5]

60.4 Permissible Storage and Use Locations.

60.4.1* General.

60.4.1.1 Control Areas or Special Protection Required. Hazardous materials shall be stored and used in any of the following:

(1) In control areas complying with 60.4.2
(2) In occupancies complying with requirements for Protection Level 1, Protection Level 2, Protection Level 3, or Protection Level 4 in accordance with 60.4.3
(3) In outdoor areas complying with 60.4.4 [**400**:5.1.1]

60.4.1.2 Weather Protection Structures. Weather protection, when provided, shall comply with 6.2.7.2 of NFPA 400. [**400**:5.1.2]

60.4.1.3 High Hazard Contents. Occupancies in which high hazard contents are stored, used, or handled shall also comply with Chapter 6 of NFPA 400. [**400**:5.1.3]

60.4.2 Control Areas.

60.4.2.1 Hazardous materials shall be permitted to be stored and used in control areas in accordance with 60.4.2.1 and 60.4.2.2. [**400**:5.2.1]

60.4.2.1.1 General.

60.4.2.1.1.1 All occupancies shall be permitted to have one or more control area in accordance with 60.4.2. [**400**:5.2.1.1.1]

60.4.2.1.1.2 The quantity of hazardous materials in an individual control area shall not exceed the maximum allowable quantity (MAQ) for the applicable occupancy set forth in 60.4.2.1.2 through 60.4.2.1.13 except as modified by Table 60.4.2.1.1.3. [**400**:5.2.1.1.2]

60.4.2.1.1.3 For all occupancies not covered by 60.4.2.1.2 through 60.4.2.1.13, the MAQ of hazardous materials per control area shall be as specified in Table 60.4.2.1.1.3. [**400**:5.2.1.1.3]

> Tables 60.4.2.1.1.3, 60.4.2.1.2, 60.4.2.1.3, 60.4.2.1.4, 60.4.2.1.5, 60.4.2.1.6, 60.4.2.1.7, 60.4.2.1.8, and 60.4.2.1.10.1 were revised by a tentative interim amendment (TIA). See page 1.

60.4.2.1.2 Assembly Occupancies. The MAQ of hazardous materials per control area in assembly occupancies shall be as specified in Table 60.4.2.1.2. [**400**:5.2.1.2]

60.4.2.1.3 Educational Occupancies. The MAQ of hazardous materials per control area in educational occupancies shall be as specified in Table 60.4.2.1.3. [**400**:5.2.1.3]

60.4.2.1.4 Day-Care Occupancies. The MAQ of hazardous materials per control area in day-care occupancies shall be as specified in Table 60.4.2.1.4. [**400**:5.2.1.4]

Table 60.4.2.1.1.3 Maximum Allowable Quantity (MAQ) of Hazardous Materials per Control Area[a]

Material	Class	High Hazard Protection Level	Storage Solid Pounds	Storage Liquid Gallons (lb)	Storage Gas[b] scf (lb)	Use — Closed Systems Solid Pounds	Use — Closed Systems Liquid Gallons (lb)	Use — Closed Systems Gas[b] scf (lb)	Use — Open Systems Solid Pounds	Use — Open Systems Liquid Gallons (lb)
Physical Hazard Materials										
Combustible liquid	See note	See note	See note	See note	See note	See note	See note	See note	See note	See note
Combustible metals	See note	See note	See note	See note	See note	See note	See note	See note	See note	See note
Cryogenic fluid [**55:** Table 6.3.1]	Flammable	2	N/A	45[j,k]	N/A	N/A	45[j,k]	N/A	N/A	45[j,k]
	Oxidizing	3	N/A	45[c,d]	N/A	N/A	45[c,d]	N/A	N/A	45[c,d]
	Inert	N/A	N/A	NL	N/A	N/A	NL	N/A	N/A	NL
Explosives	See note	See note	See note	See note	See note	See note	See note	See note	See note	See note[l]
Flammable gas[l] [**55:** Table 6.3.1]	Gaseous	2	N/A	N/A	1000[c,d]	N/A	N/A	1000[c,d]	N/A	N/A
	Liquefied	2	N/A	N/A	(150)[c,d]	N/A	N/A	(150)[c,d]	N/A	N/A
	Liquefied Petroleum (LP)	See note	See note	See note	See note	See note	See note	See note	See note	See note
Flammable liquid	IA	See note	See note	See note	See note	See note	See note	See note	See note	See note
	IB and IC									
	Combination (IA, IB, IC)									
Flammable solid	N/A	3	125[c,d]	N/A	N/A	125[c,d]	N/A	N/A	25[c,d]	N/A
Inert gas	Gaseous	N/A	N/A	N/A	NL	N/A	N/A	NL	N/A	N/A
	Liquefied	N/A	N/A	N/A	NL	N/A	N/A	NL	N/A	N/A
Organic peroxide	UD	1	1[c,i]	(1)[c,i]	N/A	1/4[i]	(1/4)[i]	N/A	1/4[i]	(1/4)[i]
	I	1	5[c,d]	(5)[c,d]	N/A	1[c,d]	(1)[c,d]	N/A	1[c,d]	(1)[c,d]
	II	2	50[c,d]	(50)[c,d]	N/A	50[d]	(50)[d]	N/A	10[c,d]	(10)[c,d]
	III	3	125[c,d]	(125)[c,d]	N/A	125[d]	(125)[d]	N/A	25[c,d]	(25)[c,d]
	IV	N/A	NL	NL	N/A	NL	NL	N/A	NL	NL
	V	N/A	NL	NL	N/A	NL	NL	N/A	NL	NL
Oxidizer	4	1	1[g,l]	(1)[g,l]	N/A	¼[l]	(¼)[l]	N/A	¼[l]	(1/4)[l]
	3[j]	2 or 3	10[g,h]	(10)[g,h]	N/A	2[h]	(2)[h]	N/A	2[h]	(2)[h]
	2	3	250[g,h]	(250)[g,h]	N/A	250[h]	(250)[h]	N/A	50[h]	(50)[h]
	1	N/A	4,000[g,l]	(4,000)[g,i]	NA	4,000[g]	(4,000)	N/A	1,000[g]	(1,000)[g]
Oxidizing gas	Gaseous	3	N/A	N/A	1,500[g,h]	N/A	N/A	1,500[g,h]	N/A	N/A
	Liquefied	3	N/A	N/A	(150)[g,h]	N/A	N/A	(150)[g,h]	N/A	N/A
Pyrophoric		2	4[g,l]	(4)[g,l]	N/A	1[l]	(1)[l]	N/A	0	0
Pyrophoric Gas	Gaseous	2	N/A	N/A	50[g,l]	N/A	N/A	50[g,l]	N/A	N/A
	Liquefied	2	N/A	N/A	(4)[g,l]	N/A	N/A	(4)[g,l]	N/A	N/A
Unstable (reactive)	4	1	1[g,l]	(1)[g,l]	N/A	¼[l]	(¼)[l]	N/A	¼[l]	(¼)[h]
	3	1 or 2	5[g,h]	(5)[g,h]	N/A	1[h]	(1)[h]	N/A	1[h]	(1)[h]
	2	2	50[g,h]	(50)[g,h]	N/A	50[h]	(50)[h]	N/A	10[h]	(10)[h]
	1	N/A	NL	NL	N/A	NL	NL	N/A	NL	NL
Unstable (reactive) Gas	Gaseous									
	4 or 3 detonable	1	N/A	N/A	10[g,l]	N/A	N/A	10[g,l]	N/A	N/A
	3 nondetonable	2	N/A	N/A	50[g,h]	N/A	N/A	50[g,h]	N/A	N/A
	2	3	N/A	N/A	750[g,h]	N/A	N/A	750[g,h]	N/A	N/A
	1	N/A	N/A	N/A	NL	N/A	N/A	NL	N/A	N/A
Unstable (reactive) Gas[l]	Liquefied									
	4 or 3 detonable	1	N/A	N/A	(1)[g,l]	N/A	N/A	(1)[g,l]	N/A	N/A

Table 60.4.2.1.1.3 *Continued*

Material	Class	High Hazard Protection Level	Storage			Use — Closed Systems			Use — Open Systems	
			Solid Pounds	Liquid Gallons (lb)	Gas[b] scf (lb)	Solid Pounds	Liquid Gallons (lb)	Gas[b] scf (lb)	Solid Pounds	Liquid Gallons (lb)
	3 nondetonable	2	N/A	N/A	(2)[g,h]	N/A	N/A	(2)[g,h]	N/A	N/A
	2	3	N/A	N/A	[30][g,h]	N/A	N/A	[30][g,h]	N/A	N/A
	1	N/A	N/A	N/A	NL	N/A	N/A	NL	N/A	N/A
Water (reactive)	3	2	5[g,h]	(5)[g,h]	N/A	5[h]	(5)[h]	N/A	1[h]	(1)[h]
	2	3	50[g,h]	(50)[g,h]	N/A	50[h]	(50)[h]	N/A	10[h]	(10)[h]
	1	N/A	NL	NL	N/A	NL	NL	N/A	NL	NL
Corrosive	N/A	4	5,000[g,h]	500[g,h]	N/A	5,000[h]	500	N/A	1,000[h]	100[h]
Corrosive gas	Gaseous	4	N/A	N/A	810[g,h]	N/A	N/A	810[g,h]	N/A	N/A
	Liquefied		N/A	N/A	(150)[g,h]	N/A	N/A	(150)[g,h]	N/A	N/A
Highly toxic	N/A	4	10[g,h]	(10)[g,h]	N/A	10[h]	(10)[h]	N/A	3[h]	(3)[h]
Highly toxic gas	Gaseous	4	N/A	N/A	20[h,s]	N/A	N/A	20[h,s]	N/A	N/A
	Liquefied		N/A	N/A	(4)[h,s]	N/A	N/A	(4)[h,s]	N/A	N/A
Toxic	N/A	4	500[g,h]	(500)[g,h]	N/A	500[h]	(500)[h]	N/A	125[h]	(125)[h]
Toxic gas	Gaseous	4	N/A	N/A	810[g,h]	N/A	N/A	810[g,h]	N/A	N/A
	Liquefied		N/A	N/A	(150)[g,h]	N/A	N/A	(150)[g,h]	N/A	N/A

UD: Unclassified detonable
For SI units, 1 lb = 0.454 kg; 1 gal = 3.785 L; 1 scf = 0.0283 Nm^3.
N/A: Not applicable. NL: Not limited. NP: Not permitted.
Note: The hazardous material categories and MAQs that are shaded in this table are not regulated by Chapter 60 or NFPA 400 but are provided here for informational purposes. See Chapter 2 for the reference code or standard governing these materials and establishing the MAQs. In accordance with 1.1.1.2 of NFPA 400, materials having multiple hazards that fall within the scope of NFPA 400 shall comply with NFPA 400.
[a]Table values in parentheses correspond to the unit name in parentheses at the top of the column. The aggregate quantity in use and storage is not permitted to exceed the quantity listed for storage.
[b]Measured at NTP or 70°F (21°C) and 14.7 psia (101.3 kPa).
[c]Quantities are permitted to be increased 100 percent where stored or used in approved cabinets, gas cabinets, exhausted enclosures, gas rooms explosives magazines, or safety cans, as appropriate for the material stored, in accordance with this code. Where footnote d also applies, the increase for both footnote c and footnote d is permitted to be applied accumulatively.
[d]Maximum quantities are permitted to be increased 100 percent in buildings equipped throughout with an automatic sprinkler system in accordance with NFPA 13, *Standard for the Installation of Sprinkler Systems*. Where footnote c also applies, the increase for both footnote c and footnote d is permitted to be applied accumulatively.
[e]The permitted quantities are not limited in a building equipped throughout with an automatic sprinkler system in accordance with NFPA 13.
[f]A maximum quantity of 200 lb (91 kg) of solid or 20 gal (76 L) of liquid Class 3 oxidizer is permitted where such materials are necessary for maintenance purposes, operation, or sanitation of equipment. Storage containers and the manner of storage are required to be approved.
[g]Allowed only where stored or used in gas rooms or approved cabinets, exhausted gas cabinets or exhausted enclosures, as specified in this *Code*. [**5000:** Table 34.1.3.1]
[h]Conversion. Where quantities are indicated in pounds and when the weight per gallon of the liquid is not provided to the AHJ, a conversion factor of 10 lb/gal (1.2 kg/L) shall be used.
[i]Permitted only in buildings equipped throughout with an automatic sprinkler system in accordance with NFPA 13.
[j]None allowed in unsprinklered buildings unless stored or used in gas rooms or in approved gas cabinets or exhausted enclosures, as specified in this *Code*.
[k]With pressure-relief devices for stationary or portable containers vented directly outdoors or to an exhaust hood. [**55:** Table 6.3.1.1]
[l]Flammable gases in the fuel tanks of mobile equipment or vehicles are permitted to exceed the MAQ where the equipment is stored and operated in accordance with this *Code*. [**400:** Table 5.2.1.1.3]

Table 60.4.2.1.2 Maximum Allowable Quantities (MAQ) of Hazardous Materials per Control Area in Assembly Occupancies

Material	Class	Solid	Liquid[k]	Gas[a] (at NTP)
Flammable and combustible liquid[b,c]	See note	See note	See note	See note
Cryogenic fluid	Flammable	NA	10 gal	NA
	Oxidizing	NA	10 gal	NA
Explosives[d,e,f,g]	See note	See note	See note	See note
Flammable gas[c,h]	Gaseous	NP	NP	NP
	Liquefied	NP	20 lb	NA
Flammable solid	NA	5 lb	NA	NA
Oxidizers	4	NP	NP	NA
	3	10 lb[i]	1 gal[i]	NA
	2	250 lb	25 gal	NA
	1	4,000 lb	400 gal	NA
Oxidizing gas[h]	Gaseous	NA	NA	NP
	Liquefied	NA	NP	NA
Organic peroxides	I	NP	NP	NA
	II	NP	NP	NA
	III	1,500 lb	1,500 lb	NA
	IV	100,000 lb	100,000 lb	NA
	V	NL	NL	NA
Pyrophoric materials	NA	1 lb	1 lb	NP
Unstable reactives	4	¼ lb	¼ lb	NP
	3	1 lb	1 lb	NP
	2	10 lb	10 lb	NP[h]
	1	NL	NL	NP
Water-reactive	3	1 lb	1 lb	NA
	2	10 lb	10 lb	NA
	1	NL	NL	NA
Corrosives	NA	1,000 lb	100 gal	NP
Highly toxic	NA	3 lb	3 lb	NP[j]
Toxic	NA	125 lb	125 lb	NP[j]

For SI units, 1 lb = 0.454 kg; 1 gal = 3.785 L.
NTP: Normal temperature and pressure [measured at 70°F (21°C) and 14.7 psi (101 kPa)]. NA: Not applicable. NP: Not permitted. NL: Not limited.
Note: The hazardous material categories and MAQs that are shaded in this table are not regulated by Chapter 60 or NFPA 400 but are provided here for informational purposes. See Chapter 2 of NFPA 400 for the reference code or standard governing these materials and establishing the MAQs. In accordance with 1.1.1.2 of NFPA 400, materials having multiple hazards that fall within the scope of NFPA 400 shall comply with NFPA 400.
[a]Unlimited amounts of gas are permitted to be used for personal medical or emergency medical use.
[b]Storage in excess of 10 gal (38 L) of Class I and Class II liquids combined or 60 gal (227 L) of Class IIIA liquids is permitted where stored in safety cabinets with an aggregate quantity not to exceed 180 gal (681 L).
[c]Fuel in the tank of operating mobile equipment is permitted to exceed the specified quantity where the equipment is operated in accordance with this *Code*.
[d]The use of explosive materials required by federal, state, or municipal agencies while engaged in normal or emergency performance of duties is not required to be limited. The storage of explosive materials is required to be in accordance with the requirements of NFPA 495, *Explosive Materials Code*.
[e]The storage and use of explosive materials in medicines and medicinal agents in the forms prescribed by the official United States Pharmacopoeia or the National Formulary are not required to be limited.
[f]The storage and use of propellant-actuated devices or propellant-actuated industrial tools manufactured, imported, or distributed for their intended purposes are required to be limited to 50 lb (23 kg) net explosive weight.
[g]The storage and use of small arms ammunition, and components thereof, are permitted where in accordance with NFPA 495, *Explosive Materials Code*.
[h]Containers, cylinders, or tanks not exceeding 250 scf (7.1 m³) content measured at 70°F (21°C) and 14.7 psi (101 kPa) and used for maintenance purposes, patient care, or operation of equipment shall be permitted.
[i]A maximum quantity of 200 lb (91 kg) of solid or 20 gal (76 L) of liquid Class 3 oxidizer is permitted where such materials are necessary for maintenance purposes, operation, or sanitation of equipment. Storage containers and the manner of storage are required to be approved.
[j]Gas cylinders not exceeding 20 scf (0.57 m³) measured at 70°F (21°C) and 14.7 psi (101 kPa) are permitted in gas cabinets or fume hoods. [5000: Table 34.1.3.2(a)]
[k]Conversion. Where quantities are indicated in pounds and when the weight per gallon of the liquid is not provided to the AHJ, a conversion factor of 10 lb/gal (1.2 kg/L) shall be used.
[**400:** Table 5.2.1.2]

Table 60.4.2.1.3 Maximum Allowable Quantities (MAQ) of Hazardous Materials per Control Area in Educational Occupancies

Material	Class	Solid	Liquid[m]	Gas[a] (at NTP)
Flammable and combustible liquid[b,c]	See note	See note	See note	See note
Cryogenic fluid	Flammable Oxidizing	N/A N/A	10 10	N/A N/A
Explosives[d,e,f,g]	See note	See note	See note	See note
Flammable gas[c,h]	Gaseous Liquefied	NP NP	NP 20	NP N/A
Flammable solid	N/A	5 lb	N/A	N/A
Oxidizers	4 3 2 1	NP 10 lb[i] 250 lb 4,000 lb	NP 1 gal[i] 25 gal 400 gal	N/A N/A N/A NA
Oxidizing gas[h]	Gaseous Liquefied	N/A N/A	N/A NP	NP N/A
Organic peroxides	I II III IV V	NP NP 1,500 lb 100,000 lb NL	NP NP 1,500 lb 100,000 lb NL	N/A N/A N/A N/A N/A
Pyrophoric materials	N/A	1 lb	1 lb	NP
Unstable reactives	4 3 2 1	¼ lb 1 lb 10 lb NL	¼ lb 1 lb 10 lb NL	NP NP NP[h] NP
Water-reactive	3 2 1	1 lb 10 lb NL	1 lb 10 lb NL	N/A N/A N/A
Corrosives	N/A	1,000 lb	100 gal	NP
Highly toxic	N/A	3 lb	3 lb	NP[j]
Toxic	N/A	125 lb	125 lb	NP[j]

For SI units, 1 lb = 0.454 kg; 1 gal = 3.785 L; 1 ft^3 = 0.0283 m^3.
NTP: Normal temperature and pressure [measured at 70°F (21°C) and 14.7 psi (101 kPa)]. N/A: Not applicable. NP: Not permitted. NL: Not limited.
Note: The hazardous material categories and MAQs that are shaded in this table are not regulated by 60 or NFPA 400 but are provided here for informational purposes. See Chapter 2 of NFPA 400 for the reference code or standard governing these materials and establishing the MAQs. In accordance with 1.1.1.2 of NFPA 400, materials having multiple hazards that fall within the scope of NFPA 400 shall comply with NFPA 400.
[a]Unlimited amounts of gas are permitted to be used for personal medical or emergency medical use.
[b]Storage in excess of 10 gal (38 L) of Class I and Class II liquids combined or 60 gal (227 L) of Class IIIA liquids is permitted where stored in safety cabinets with an aggregate quantity not to exceed 180 gal (681 L).
[c]Fuel in the tank of operating mobile equipment is permitted to exceed the specified quantity where the equipment is operated in accordance with this *Code*.
[d]The use of explosive materials required by federal, state, or municipal agencies while engaged in normal or emergency performance of duties is not required to be limited. The storage of explosive materials is required to be in accordance with the requirements of NFPA 495, *Explosive Materials Code*.
[e]The storage and use of explosive materials in medicines and medicinal agents in the forms prescribed by the official United States Pharmacopoeia or the National Formulary are not required to be limited.
[f]The storage and use of propellant-actuated devices or propellant-actuated industrial tools manufactured, imported, or distributed for their intended purposes are required to be limited to 50 lb (23 kg) net explosive weight.
[g]The storage and use of small arms ammunition, and components thereof, are permitted where in accordance with NFPA 495, *Explosive Materials Code*.
[h]Containers, cylinders or tanks not exceeding 250 scf (7.1 m^3) content measured at 70°F (21°C) and 14.7 psi (101 kPa) and used for maintenance purposes, patient care, or operation of equipment shall be permitted.
[i]A maximum quantity of 200 lb (91 kg) of solid or 20 gal (76 L) of liquid Class 3 oxidizer is permitted where such materials are necessary for maintenance purposes, operation, or sanitation of equipment. Storage containers and the manner of storage are required to be approved.
[j]The permitted quantities are not limited in a building protected throughout by automatic sprinkler systems in accordance with NFPA 13, *Standard for the Installation of Sprinkler Systems*.
[k]Storage in laboratories only; additional 20 lb (9 kg) units are permitted where minimum 20 ft (6.1 m) separation is provided.
[l]Gas cylinders not exceeding 20 scf (0.57 m^3) measured at 70°F (21°C) and 14.7 psi (101 kPa) are permitted in gas cabinets or fume hoods.
[m]Conversion. Where quantities are indicated in pounds and when the weight per gallon of the liquid is not provided to the AHJ, a conversion factor of 10 lb/gal (1.2 kg/L) shall be used.
[**400**: Table 5.2.1.3]

Table 60.4.2.1.4 Maximum Allowable Quantities (MAQ) of Hazardous Materials per Control Area in Day-Care Occupancies

Material	Class	Solid	Liquid[k]	Gas[a] (at NTP)
Flammable and combustible liquid[b,c,l]	See note	See note	See note	See note
Cryogenic fluid	Flammable	N/A	10 gal	N/A
	Oxidizing	N/A	10 gal	N/A
Explosives[d,e,f,g]	See note	See note	See note	See note
Flammable gas[c,h]	Gaseous	NP	NP	NP
	Liquefied	NP	20 lb	N/A
Flammable solid	N/A	5 lb	N/A	N/A
Oxidizers	4	NP	NP	N/A
	3	10 lb[i]	1 gal[i]	N/A
	2	250	25	N/A
	1	4,000	400	N/A
Oxidizing gas[h]	Gaseous	N/A	N/A	NP
	Liquefied	N/A	NP	N/A
Organic peroxides	I	NP	NP	N/A
	II	NP	NP	N/A
	III	1,500	1,500	N/A
	IV	100,000 lb	100,000 lb	N/A
	V	NL	NL	N/A
Pyrophoric materials	N/A	1 lb	1 lb	NP
Unstable reactives	4	¼ lb	¼ lb	NP
	3	1 lb	1 lb	NP
	2	10 lb	10 lb	NP[h]
	1	NL	NL	NP
Water-reactive	3	1 lb	1 lb	N/A
	2	10 lb	10 lb	N/A
	1	NL	NL	N/A
Corrosives	N/A	1,000 lb	100 gal	NP
Highly toxic	N/A	3 lb	3 lb	NP[j]
Toxic	N/A	125 lb	125 lb	NP[j]

For SI units, 1 lb = 0.454 kg; 1 gal = 3.785 L.
NTP: Normal temperature and pressure [measured at 70°F (21°C) and 14.7 psi (101 kPa)]. N/A: Not applicable. NP: Not permitted. NL: Not limited.
Note: The hazardous material categories and MAQs that are shaded in this table are not regulated by NFPA 400 but are provided here for informational purposes. See Chapter 2 of NFPA 400 for the reference code or standard governing these materials and establishing the MAQs. In accordance with 1.1.1.2 of NFPA 400, materials having multiple hazards that fall within the scope of NFPA 400 shall comply with NFPA 400.
[a]Unlimited amounts of gas are permitted to be used for personal medical or emergency medical use.
[b]Storage in excess of 10 gal (38 L) of Class I and Class II liquids combined or 60 gal (227 L) of Class IIIA liquids is permitted where stored in safety cabinets with an aggregate quantity not to exceed 180 gal (681 L).
[c]Fuel in the tank of operating mobile equipment is permitted to exceed the specified quantity where the equipment is operated in accordance with this *Code*.
[d]The use of explosive materials required by federal, state, or municipal agencies while engaged in normal or emergency performance of duties is not required to be limited. The storage of explosive materials is required to be in accordance with the requirements of NFPA 495, *Explosive Materials Code*.
[e]The storage and use of explosive materials in medicines and medicinal agents in the forms prescribed by the official United States Pharmacopeia or the National Formulary are not required to be limited.
[f]The storage and use of propellant-actuated devices or propellant-actuated industrial tools manufactured, imported, or distributed for their intended purposes are required to be limited to 50 lb (23 kg) net explosive weight.
[g]Containers, cylinders, or tanks not exceeding 250 scf (7.1 m³) content measured at 70°F (21°C) and 14.7 psi (101 kPa and used for maintenance purposes, patient care, or operation of equipment shall be permitted.
[h]The permitted quantities are not limited in a building protected throughout by automatic sprinkler systems in accordance with NFPA 13, *Standard for the Installation of Sprinkler Systems*.
[i]A maximum quantity of 200 lb (91 kg) of solid or 20 gal (76 L) of liquid Class 3 oxidizer is permitted where such materials are necessary for maintenance purposes, operation, or sanitation of equipment. Storage containers and the manner of storage are required to be approved.
[j]Gas cylinders not exceeding 20 scf (0.57 m³) measured at 70°F (21°C) and 14.7 psi (101 kPa) are permitted in gas cabinets or fume hoods.
[k]Conversion. Where quantities are indicated in pounds and when the weight per gallon of the liquid is not provided to the AHJ, a conversion factor of 10 lb/gal (1.2 kg/L) shall be used.
[**400**: Table 5.2.1.4]

60.4.2.1.5 Health Care Occupancies. The MAQ of hazardous materials per control area in health care occupancies shall be as specified in Table 60.4.2.1.5. [**400**:5.2.1.5]

60.4.2.1.6 Ambulatory Health Care Occupancies. The MAQ of hazardous materials per control area in ambulatory health care occupancies shall be as specified in Table 60.4.2.1.6. [**400**:5.2.1.6]

60.4.2.1.7 Detention and Correctional Occupancies. The MAQ of hazardous materials per control area in detention and correctional occupancies shall be as specified in Table 60.4.2.1.7. [**400**:5.2.1.7]

60.4.2.1.8 Residential Occupancies. The MAQ of hazardous materials per control area in residential occupancies, including lodging and rooming houses, hotels, dormitories, apartments, and residential board and care facilities, shall be as specified in Table 60.4.2.1.8. [**400**:5.2.1.8]

Table 60.4.2.1.5 Maximum Allowable Quantities (MAQ) of Hazardous Materials per Control Area in Health Care Occupancies

Material	Class	Solid	Liquid[k]	Gas[a] (at NTP)
Flammable and combustible liquid[b,c]	See note	See note	See note	
Cryogenic fluid	Flammable	N/A	10	N/A
	Oxidizing	N/A	10	N/A
Explosives[d,e,f]	See note	See note	See note	See note
Flammable gas[c,g]	Gaseous	N/A	N/A	NP
	Liquefied	N/A	20	N/A
Flammable solid		5 lb	N/A	N/A
Oxidizers	4	NP	NP	N/A
	3	10 lb[h]	1 gal[h]	N/A
	2	250 lb	25 gal	N/A
	1	4,000 lb[i]	400 gal[i]	N/A
Oxidizing gas	Gaseous	N/A	N/A	NP[h]
	Liquefied	N/A	15 gal	N/A
Organic peroxides	I	NP	NP	N/A
	II	NP	NP	N/A
	III	1,500 lb	1,500 lb	N/A
	IV	100,000 lb	100,000 lb	N/A
	V	NL	NL	N/A
Pyrophoric materials	N/A	NP	NP	NP
Unstable reactives	4	NP	NP	NP
	3	NP	NP	NP
	2	10	10	NP[g]
	1	NL	NL	NP
Water-reactive	3	1 lb	1 lb	N/A
	2	10 lb	10 lb	N/A
	1	NL	NL	N/A
Corrosives	N/A	1,000 lb	100 gal	NP
Highly toxic	N/A	3 lb	3 lb	NP[j]
Toxic	N/A	125 lb	125 lb	NP[j]

For SI units, 1 lb = 0.454 kg; 1 gal = 3.785 L.
NTP: Normal temperature and pressure [measured at 70°F (21°C) and 14.7 psi (101 kPa)]. N/A: Not applicable. NP: Not permitted. NL: Not limited.
Note: The hazardous material categories and MAQs that are shaded in this table are not regulated by NFPA 400 but are provided here for informational purposes. See Chapter 2 of NFPA 400 for the reference code or standard governing these materials and establishing the MAQs. In accordance with 1.1.1.2 of NFPA 400, materials having multiple hazards that fall within the scope of NFPA 400 shall comply with NFPA 400.
[a]Unlimited amounts of gas are permitted to be used for personal medical or emergency medical use.
[b]Storage in excess of 10 gal (38 L) of Class I and Class II liquids combined or 60 gal (227 L) of Class IIIA liquids is permitted where stored in safety cabinets with an aggregate quantity not to exceed 180 gal (681 L).
[c]Fuel in the tank of operating mobile equipment is permitted to exceed the specified quantity where the equipment is operated in accordance with this code.
[d]The use of explosive materials required by federal, state, or municipal agencies while engaged in normal or emergency performance of duties is not required to be limited. The storage of explosive materials is required to be in accordance with the requirements of NFPA 495, *Explosive Materials Code*.
[e]The storage and use of explosive materials in medicines and medicinal agents in the forms prescribed by the official United States Pharmacopeia or the National Formulary are not required to be limited.
[f]The storage and use of propellant-actuated devices or propellant-actuated industrial tools manufactured, imported, or distributed for their intended purposes are required to be limited to 50 lb (23 kg) net explosive weight.
[g]Containers, cylinders, or tanks not exceeding 250 scf (7.1 m³) content measured at 70°F (21°C) and 14.7 psi (101 kPa) and used for maintenance purposes, patient care, or operation of equipment shall be permitted.
[h]A maximum quantity of 200 lb (91 kg) of solid or 20 gal (76 L) of liquid Class 3 oxidizer is permitted where such materials are necessary for maintenance purposes, operation, or sanitation of equipment. Storage containers and the manner of storage are required to be approved.
[i]The permitted quantities are not limited in a building protected throughout by automatic sprinkler systems in accordance with NFPA 13, *Standard for the Installation of Sprinkler Systems*.
[j]Gas cylinders not exceeding 20 scf (0.57 m³) measured at 70°F (21°C) and 14.7 psi (101 kPa) are permitted in gas cabinets or fume hoods.
[k]Conversion. Where quantities are indicated in pounds and when the weight per gallon of the liquid is not provided to the AHJ, a conversion factor of 10 lb/gal (1.2 kg/L) shall be used.
[**400**: Table 5.2.1.5]

Table 60.4.2.1.6 Maximum Allowable Quantities (MAQ) of Hazardous Materials per Control Area in Ambulatory Health Care Occupancies[a]

Material	Class	Solid	Liquid[k]	Gas[a] (at NTP)
Flammable and combustible liquid[b,c]	See note	See note	See note	See note
Cryogenic fluid	Flammable	N/A	10	N/A
	Oxidizing	N/A	10	N/A
Explosives[d,e,f]	See note	See note	See note	See note
Flammable gas[c,g]	Gaseous	N/A	N/A	NP
	Liquefied	N/A	N/A	N/A
Flammable solid	Liquefied Petroleum	N/A	N/A	(20)
	N/A	5	N/A	N/A
Oxidizers	4	NP	NP	NP
	3	10[h]	1[h]	NP
	2	250	25	NP
	1	4,000[i]	400[i]	NP
Oxidizing gas	Gaseous	N/A	N/A	NP[h]
	Liquefied	N/A	N/A	NP[h]
Organic peroxides	I	NP	NP	N/A
	II	NP	NP	N/A
	III	25	(25)	N/A
	IV	NL	NL	N/A
	V	NL	NL	N/A
Pyrophoric materials	N/A	NP	NP	NP
Unstable reactives	4	NP	NP	NP
	3	NP	NP	NP
	2	10	10	NP[g]
	1	NL	NL	NP
Water-reactive	3	1	(1)	N/A
	2	10	10	N/A
	1	NL	NL	N/A
Corrosives	N/A	1,000	100	NP
Highly toxic	N/A	3	(3)	NP[j]
Toxic	N/A	125	(125)	NP[j]

For SI units, 1 lb = 0.454 kg; 1 gal = 3.785 L.
NTP: Normal temperature and pressure [70°F (21°C) and 14.7 psi (101 kPa)]. N/A: Not applicable. NP: Not permitted. NL: Not limited.
Note: The hazardous material categories and MAQs that are shaded in this table are not regulated by NFPA 400 but are provided here for informational purposes. See Chapter 2 of NFPA 400 for the reference code or standard governing these materials and establishing the MAQs. In accordance with 1.1.1.2 of NFPA 400, materials having multiple hazards that fall within the scope of NFPA 400 shall comply with NFPA 400.
[a]Unlimited amounts of gas are permitted to be used for personal medical or emergency medical use.
[b]Storage in excess of 10 gal (38 L) of Class I and Class II liquids combined or 60 gal (227 L) of Class IIIA liquids is permitted where stored in safety cabinets with an aggregate quantity not to exceed 180 gal (681 L).
[c]Fuel in the tank of operating mobile equipment is permitted to exceed the specified quantity where the equipment is operated in accordance with this *Code*.
[d]The use of explosive materials required by federal, state, or municipal agencies while engaged in normal or emergency performance of duties is not required to be limited. The storage of explosive materials is required to be in accordance with the requirements of NFPA 495, *Explosive Materials Code*.
[e]The storage and use of explosive materials in medicines and medicinal agents in the forms prescribed by the official United States Pharmacopeia or the National Formulary are not required to be limited.
[f]The storage and use of propellant-actuated devices or propellant-actuated industrial tools manufactured, imported, or distributed for their intended purposes are required to be limited to 50 lb (23 kg) net explosive weight.
[g]Containers, cylinders, or tanks not exceeding 250 scf (7.1 m^3) content measured at 70°F (21°C) and 14.7 psi (101 kPa) and used for maintenance purposes, patient care, or operation of equipment shall be permitted.
[h]A maximum quantity of 200 lb (91 kg) of solid or 20 gal (76 L) of liquid Class 3 oxidizer is permitted where such materials are necessary for maintenance purposes, operation, or sanitation of equipment. Storage containers and the manner of storage are required to be approved.
[i]The permitted quantities are not limited in a building protected throughout by automatic sprinkler systems in accordance with NFPA 13, *Standard for the Installation of Sprinkler Systems*.
[j]Gas cylinders not exceeding 20 scf (0.57 m^3) measured at 70°F (21°C) and 14.7 psi (101 kPa) are permitted in gas cabinets or fume hoods.
[k]Conversion. Where quantities are indicated in pounds and when the weight per gallon of the liquid is not provided to the AHJ, a conversion factor of 10 lb/gal (1.2 kg/L) shall be used.
[**400:** Table 5.2.1.6]

Table 60.4.2.1.7 Maximum Allowable Quantities (MAQ) of Hazardous Materials per Control Area in Detention and Correctional Occupancies[a]

Material	Class	Solid	Liquid[k]	Gas[a] (at NTP)
Flammable and combustible liquid[b,c]	See note	See note	See note	See note
Cryogenic fluid	Flammable	N/A	10	N/A
	Oxidizing	N/A	10	N/A
Explosives[d,e,f,g]	See note	See note	See note	See note
Flammable gas[c,h]	Gaseous	N/A	N/A	NP
	Liquefied	N/A	N/A	(20)
	Liquefied Petroleum	N/A	N/A	(20)
Flammable solid	N/A	5	N/A	N/A
Oxidizers	4	NP	NP	N/A
	3	10[i]	1[i]	N/A
	2	250	25	N/A
	1	4000	400	N/A
Oxidizing gas[h]	Gaseous	N/A	N/A	NP
	Liquefied	N/A	N/A	N/A
Organic peroxides	I	NP	NP	N/A
	II	NP	NP	N/A
	III	25	(25)	N/A
	IV	NL	NL	N/A
	V	NL	NL	N/A
Pyrophoric materials	N/A	1	(1)	NP
Unstable reactives	4	¼	(¼)	NP
	3	1	(1)	NP
	2	10	10	NP[h]
	1	NL	NL	NP
Water-reactive	3	1	(1)	N/A
	2	10	(10)	N/A
	1	NL	NL	N/A
Corrosives	N/A	1,000	100	NP
Highly toxic	N/A	3	3	NP[j]
Toxic	N/A	125	125	NP[j]

For SI units, 1 lb = 0.454 kg; 1 gal = 3.785 L.
NTP: Normal temperature and pressure [measured at 70°F (21°C) and 14.7 psi (101 kPa)]. N/A: Not applicable. NP: Not permitted. NL: Not limited.
Note: The hazardous material categories and MAQs that are shaded in this table are not regulated by Chapter 60 or NFPA 400 but are provided here for informational purposes. See Chapter 2 of NFPA 400 for the reference code or standard governing these materials and establishing the MAQs. In accordance with 1.1.1.2 of NFPA 400, materials having multiple hazards that fall within the scope of NFPA 400 shall comply with NFPA 400.
[a]Unlimited amounts of gas are permitted to be used for personal medical or emergency medical use.
[b]Storage in excess of 10 gal (38 L) of Class I and Class II liquids combined or 60 gal (227 L) of Class IIIA liquids is permitted where stored in safety cabinets with an aggregate quantity not to exceed 180 gal (681 L).
[c]Fuel in the tank of operating mobile equipment is permitted to exceed the specified quantity where the equipment is operated in accordance with this *Code*.
[d]The use of explosive materials required by federal, state, or municipal agencies while engaged in normal or emergency performance of duties is not required to be limited. The storage of explosive materials is required to be in accordance with the requirements of NFPA 495, *Explosive Materials Code*.
[e]The storage and use of explosive materials in medicines and medicinal agents in the forms prescribed by the official United States Pharmacopeia or the National Formulary are not required to be limited.
[f]The storage and use of propellant-actuated devices or propellant-actuated industrial tools manufactured, imported, or distributed for their intended purposes are required to be limited to 50 lb (23 kg) net explosive weight.
[g]The storage and use of small arms ammunition, and components thereof, are permitted where in accordance with NFPA 495, *Explosive Materials Code*.
[h]Containers, cylinders, or tanks not exceeding 250 scf (7.1 m^3) content measured at 70°F (21°C) and 14.7 psi (101 kPa) and used for maintenance purposes, patient care, or operation of equipment shall be permitted.
[i]A maximum quantity of 200 lb (91 kg) of solid or 20 gal (76 L) of liquid Class 3 oxidizer is permitted where such materials are necessary for maintenance purposes, operation, or sanitation of equipment. Storage containers and the manner of storage are required to be approved.
[j]Gas cylinders not exceeding 20 scf (0.57 m^3) measured at 70°F (21°C) and 14.7 psi (101 kPa) are permitted in gas cabinets or fume hoods.
[k]Conversion. Where quantities are indicated in pounds and when the weight per gallon of the liquid is not provided to the AHJ, a conversion factor of 10 lb/gal (1.2 kg/L) shall be used.
[**400**: Table 5.2.1.7]

Table 60.4.2.1.8 Maximum Allowable Quantities of Hazardous Materials per Control Area in Residential Occupancies Consisting of Lodging and Rooming Houses, Hotels, Dormitories, Apartments, and Residential Board and Care Facilities

Material	Class	Solid	Liquid[1]	Gas[a] (at NTP)
Flammable and combustible liquid[b,c]	See note	See note	See note	See note
Cryogenic fluid	Flammable Oxidizing	N/A N/A	10 10	N/A N/A
Explosives[d,e,f,g]	See note	See note	See note	See note
Flammable gas[c,h]	Gaseous Liquefied[j]	N/A N/A	N/A N/A	NP (20)
Flammable solid	Liquefied Petroleum N/A	N/A 5 lb	N/A N/A	(20) N/A
Oxidizers	4 3 2 1	NP 10[i] 250 4000	NP 1[i] 25 400	N/A N/A N/A N/A
Oxidizing gas[h]	Gaseous Liquefied	N/A N/A	N/A 15	NP N/A
Organic peroxides	I II III IV V	NP NP 25 NL NL	NP NP (25) NL NL	N/A N/A N/A N/A N/A
Pyrophoric materials	N/A	1	(1)	NP
Unstable reactives	4 3 2 1	¼ 1 10 NL	(¼) (1) (10) NL	NP NP NP[h] NP
Water-reactive	3 2 1	1 10 NL	(1) (10) NL	N/A N/A N/A
Corrosives	N/A	1000	100	NP
Highly toxic	N/A	3	(3)	NP[k]
Toxic	N/A	125	(125)	NP[k]

For SI units, 1 lb = 0.454 kg; 1 gal = 3.785 L.

NTP: Normal temperature and pressure [measured at 70°F (21°C) and 14.7 psi (101 kPa)]. N/A: Not applicable. NP: Not permitted. NL: Not limited.

Note: The hazardous material categories and MAQs that are shaded in this table are not regulated by Chapter 60 or NFPA 400 but are provided here for informational purposes. See Chapter 2 of NFPA 400 for the reference code or standard governing these materials and establishing the MAQs. In accordance with 1.1.1.2 of NFPA 400, materials having multiple hazards that fall within the scope of NFPA 400 shall comply with NFPA 400.

[a]Unlimited amounts of gas are permitted to be used for personal medical or emergency medical use.
[b]Storage in excess of 10 gal (38 L) of Class I and Class II liquids combined or 60 gal (227 L) of Class IIIA liquids are permitted where stored in safety cabinets with an aggregate quantity not to exceed 180 gal (681 L).
[c]Fuel in the tank of operating mobile equipment is permitted to exceed the specified quantity where the equipment is operated in accordance with this *Code*.
[d]The use of explosive materials required by federal, state, or municipal agencies while engaged in normal or emergency performance of duties is not required to be limited. The storage of explosive materials is required to be in accordance with the requirements of NFPA 495, *Explosive Materials Code*.
[e]The storage and use of explosive materials in medicines and medicinal agents in the forms prescribed by the official United States Pharmacopeia or the National Formulary are not required to be limited.
[f]The storage and use of propellant-actuated devices or propellant-actuated industrial tools manufactured, imported, or distributed for their intended purposes are required to be limited to 50 lb (23 kg) net explosive weight.
[g]The storage and use of small arms ammunition, and components thereof, are permitted where in accordance with NFPA 495, *Explosive Materials Code*.
[h]Containers, cylinders, or tanks not exceeding 250 scf (7.1 m³) content measured at 70°F (21°C) and 14.7 psi (101 kPa) and used for maintenance purposes, patient care, or operation of equipment shall be permitted.
[i]A maximum quantity of 200 lb (91 kg) of solid or 20 gal (76 L) of liquid Class 3 oxidizer is permitted where such materials are necessary for maintenance purposes, operation, or sanitation of equipment. Storage containers and the manner of storage are required to be approved.
[j]Storage containers are not permitted to exceed 0.325 ft³ (0.0092 m³) capacity.
[k]Gas cylinders not exceeding 20 scf (0.57 m³) measured at 70°F (21°C) and 14.7 psi (101 kPa) are permitted in gas cabinets or fume hoods.
[l]Conversion. Where quantities are indicated in pounds and when the weight per gallon of the liquid is not provided to the AHJ, a conversion factor of 10 lb/gal (1.2 kg/L) shall be used.
[**400**: Table 5.2.1.8]

60.4.2.1.9 Mercantile Occupancies.
The MAQ of hazardous materials per control area in mercantile occupancies shall be as specified in Table 60.4.2.1.1.3, with increased quantities permitted where storage or display areas comply with 60.4.2.1.13. [**400**:5.2.1.9]

60.4.2.1.10 Business Occupancies.

60.4.2.1.10.1 The MAQ of hazardous materials per control area in business occupancies, other than laboratories, shall be as specified in Table 60.4.2.1.10.1. [**400**:5.2.1.10.1]

Table 60.4.2.1.10.1 Maximum Allowable Quantities (MAQ) of Hazardous Materials per Control Area in Business Occupancies

Material	Class	Solid	Liquid[j]	Gas[a,i] (at NTP)
Flammable and combustible liquid[b,c]	See note	See note	See note	See note
Cryogenic fluid	Flammable Oxidizing	N/A N/A	10 10	N/A N/A
Explosives[d,e,f,g]	See note	See note	See note	See note
Flammable gas[c]	Gaseous Liquefied Liquefied Petroleum	N/A N/A N/A	N/A N/A N/A	1000 (20) (20)
Flammable solid	N/A	5	N/A	N/A
Oxidizers	4 3 2 1	NP 10[h] 250 4000	NP 1[h] 25 400	NP NP NP NP
Oxidizing gas	Gaseous Liquefied	N/A N/A	N/A 15	1500 N/A
Organic peroxides	I II III IV V	NP NP 1500 100,000 NL	NP NP 1500 100,000 NL	N/A N/A N/A N/A N/A
Pyrophoric materials	N/A	1	(1)	10
Unstable reactives	4 3 2 1	¼ 1 10 NL	(¼) (1) (10) NL	2 10 750 NL
Water-reactive	3 2 1	1 10 NL	(1) (10) NL	N/A N/A N/A
Corrosives	N/A	1000	(100)	810
Highly toxic[i]	N/A	3	(3)	20
Toxic[i]	N/A	125	(125)	810

For SI units, 1 lb = 0.454 kg; 1 gal = 3.785 L; 1 scf = 0.0283 m³.
NTP: Normal temperature and pressure [measured at 70°F (21°C) and 14.7 psi (101 kPa)]. N/A: Not applicable. NP: Not permitted. NL: Not limited.
Note: The hazardous material categories and MAQs that are shaded in this table are not regulated by NFPA 400 but are provided here for informational purposes. See Chapter 2 of NFPA 400 for the reference code or standard governing these materials and establishing the MAQs. In accordance with 1.1.1.2 of NFPA 400, materials having multiple hazards that fall within the scope of NFPA 400 shall comply with NFPA 400.
[a]Unlimited amounts of gas are permitted to be used for personal medical or emergency medical use.
[b]Storage in excess of 10 gal (38 L) of Class I and Class II liquids combined or 60 gal (227 L) of Class IIIA liquids is permitted where stored in safety cabinets with an aggregate quantity not to exceed 180 gal (681 L).
[c]Fuel in the tank of operating mobile equipment is permitted to exceed the specified quantity where the equipment is operated in accordance with this *Code*.
[d]The use of explosive materials required by federal, state, or municipal agencies while engaged in normal or emergency performance of duties is not required to be limited. The storage of explosive materials is required to be in accordance with the requirements of NFPA 495, *Explosive Materials Code*.
[e]The storage and use of explosive materials in medicines and medicinal agents in the forms prescribed by the official United States Pharmacopeia or the National Formulary are not required to be limited.
[f]The storage and use of propellant-actuated devices or propellant-actuated industrial tools manufactured, imported, or distributed for their intended purposes are required to be limited to 50 lb (23 kg) net explosive weight.
[g]The storage and use of small arms ammunition, and components thereof, are permitted where in accordance with NFPA 495, *Explosive Materials Code*.
[h]A maximum quantity of 200 lb (91 kg) of solid or 20 gal (76 L) of liquid Class 3 oxidizer is permitted where such materials are necessary for maintenance purposes, operation, or sanitation of equipment. Storage containers and the manner of storage are required to be approved.
[i]Gas cylinders not exceeding 20 scf (0.57 m³) measured at 70°F (21°C) and 14.7 psi (101 kPa) are permitted in gas cabinets or fume hoods.
[j]Conversion. Where quantities are indicated in pounds and when the weight per gallon of the liquid is not provided to the AHJ, a conversion factor of 10 lb/gal (1.2 kg/L) shall be used.
[**400**: Table 5.2.1.10.1]

60.4.2.1.10.2 The MAQ of hazardous materials per control area in laboratories classified as business occupancies shall be as specified in Table 60.4.2.1.1.3. [**400**:5.2.1.10.2]

60.4.2.1.11 Industrial Occupancies. The MAQ of hazardous materials per control area in industrial occupancies shall be as specified in Table 60.4.2.1.1.3, with increased quantities permitted where storage areas comply with 60.4.2.1.13. [**400**:5.2.1.11]

60.4.2.1.12 Storage Occupancies. The MAQ of hazardous materials per control area in storage occupancies shall be as specified in Table 60.4.2.1.1.3, with increased quantities permitted where storage areas comply with 60.4.2.1.13. [**400**:5.2.1.12]

60.4.2.1.13 Special Quantity Limits for Mercantile, Industrial, and Storage Occupancies.

60.4.2.1.13.1 General. Where storage in mercantile, industrial, and storage occupancies is in compliance with all of the special controls set forth in 60.4.2.1.13.2, the MAQ of selected hazardous materials shall be permitted to be increased in accordance with 60.4.2.1.13.3. [**400**:5.2.1.13.1]

60.4.2.1.13.2 Special Controls Required for Increased Quantities. Where quantities of hazardous materials are increased in accordance with 60.4.2.1.13.3, such materials shall be stored in accordance with the following limitations:

(1) Storage and display of solids shall not exceed 200 lb/ft^2 (976.4 kg/m^2) of floor area actually occupied by solid merchandise.
(2) Storage and display of liquids shall not exceed 20 gal/ft^2 (76 L/m^2) of floor area actually occupied by liquid merchandise.
(3) Storage and display height shall not exceed 6 ft (1.8 m) above the finished floor.
(4) Individual containers less than 5 gal (19 L) or less than 25 lb (11 kg) shall be stored or displayed on pallets, racks, or shelves.
(5) Racks and shelves used for storage or display shall be in accordance with 60.5.1.13.
(6) Containers shall be listed or approved for the intended use.
(7) Individual containers shall not exceed 100 lb (45.4 kg) capacity for solids or a 10 gal (38 L) capacity for liquids.
(8) Incompatible materials shall be separated in accordance with 60.5.1.12.
(9) Except for surfacing, floors shall be of noncombustible construction.
(10) Aisles 4 ft (1.2 m) in width shall be maintained on three sides of the storage or display area.
(11) Hazard identification signs shall be provided in accordance with 60.5.1.8. [**400**:5.2.1.13.2]

60.4.2.1.13.3 Special Maximum Allowable Quantity Increases for Storage in Mercantile, Storage, and Industrial Occupancies. The aggregate quantity of nonflammable solid and nonflammable or noncombustible liquid hazardous materials permitted within a single control area of a mercantile, storage, or industrial occupancy shall be permitted to exceed the MAQ specified in Table 60.4.2.1.1.3, without complying with Protection Level 2, Protection Level 3, or Protection Level 4, provided that the quantities comply with Table 60.4.2.1.13.3(a) and Table 60.4.2.1.13.3(b) and that materials are displayed and stored in accordance with the special limitations in 60.4.2.1.13.2. [**400**:5.2.1.13.3]

Table 60.4.2.1.13.3(a) Maximum Allowable Quantity (MAQ) per Indoor and Outdoor Control Area for Selected Hazard Categories in Mercantile, Storage, and Industrial Occupancies

Hazard Category	Maximum Allowable Quantity[a,b]			
	Solids		Liquids	
	lb	kg	gal	L
Physical Hazard Materials: Nonflammable and Noncombustible Solids and Liquids				
Oxidizers				
Class 3	1,150	522	115	435
Class 2	2,250	1,021	225	852
Class 1	18,000[c]	8,165[c]	1,800[c]	6,814[c]

Note: Maximum quantities for hazard categories not shown are required to be in accordance with Table 60.4.2.1.1.3.
[a]Maximum quantities are permitted to be increased 100 percent in buildings that are sprinklered in accordance with NFPA 13, *Standard for the Installation of Sprinkler Systems*. Where footnote b also applies, the increase for both footnotes is permitted to be applied.
[b]Maximum quantities are permitted to be increased 100 percent where stored in approved storage cabinets in accordance with this *Code*. Where footnote a also applies, the increase for both footnotes is permitted to be applied.
[c]Quantities are not limited in buildings protected by an automatic sprinkler system complying with NFPA 13. [**5000**: Table 34.1.3.3.1(a)] [**400**: Table 5.2.1.13.3(a)]

60.4.2.2 Construction Requirements for Control Areas.

60.4.2.2.1 Number of Control Areas. The maximum number of control areas within a building shall be in accordance with Table 60.4.2.2.1. [**400**:5.2.2.1]

60.4.2.2.2 Where only one control area is present in a building, no special construction provisions shall be required. [**400**:5.2.2.2]

60.4.2.2.3 Where more than one control area is present in a building, control areas shall be separated from each other by fire barriers in accordance with Table 60.4.2.2.1. [**400**:5.2.2.3]

60.4.3 Protection Levels.

60.4.3.1 Where the quantity of hazardous materials in storage or use exceeds the MAQ for indoor control areas as set forth in 60.4.2, the occupancy shall comply with the requirements for Protection Level 1, Protection Level 2, Protection Level 3, or Protection Level 4, as required for the material in storage or use as defined in 6.2.2 through 6.2.5 of NFPA 400. [**400**:5.3.1]

60.4.3.2 Protection Level 5 shall apply to semiconductor fabrication facilities where required by the building code. [**400**:5.3.2]

60.4.3.3 Protection Level 1.

60.4.3.3.1 Buildings containing quantities of hazardous materials exceeding the MAQ of high hazard Level 1 contents permitted in control areas shall comply with applicable regulations for Protection Level 1, as set forth in the applicable sections of Chapter 6 and Chapters 11 through 21 of NFPA 400, and the building code. [**400**:5.3.3.1]

Table 60.4.2.1.13.3(b) Maximum Allowable Quantity (MAQ) per Indoor and Outdoor Control Area for Selected Hazard Categories in Mercantile and Storage Occupancies

Hazard Category	Maximum Allowable Quantity[a,b,c]			
	Solids		Liquids	
	lb	kg	gal	L
Physical Hazard Materials: Nonflammable and Noncombustible Solids and Liquids				
Unstable (reactive)				
Class 3	550	250	55	208
Class 2	1,150	522	115	435
Water-reactive				
Class 3	550	250	55	208
Class 2	1,150	522	115	435
Health Hazard Materials: Nonflammable and Noncombustible Solids and Liquids				
Corrosive	10,000	4,536	1,000	3,785
Highly toxic[d]	20	9	2	8
Toxic[d]	1,000	454	100	378

[a]Maximum quantities for hazard categories not shown are required to be in accordance with Table 60.4.2.1.1.3.
[b]Maximum quantities are permitted to be increased 100 percent in buildings that are sprinklered in accordance with NFPA 13, *Standard for the Installation of Sprinkler Systems*. Where footnote b also applies, the increase for both footnotes can be applied.
[c]Maximum quantities are permitted to be increased 100 percent where stored in approved storage cabinets in accordance with this *Code*. Where footnote a also applies, the increase for both footnotes is permitted to be applied. [**5000**: Table 34.1.3.3.1(b)]
[d]Toxic or highly toxic solids or liquids displayed in original packaging in mercantile or storage occupancies and intended for maintenance, operation of equipment, or sanitation when contained in individual packaging not exceeding 100 lb (45.4 kg) shall be limited to an aggregate of 1200 lb (544.3 kg) or 220 gal (832.8 L). The increases allowed by footnotes a, b, and c shall not apply to highly toxic solids and liquids. [**400**: Table 5.2.1.13.3(b)]

60.4.3.3.2 High hazard Level 1 contents shall include materials that present a detonation hazard as defined in 60.3.2.1.2.1. [**400**:5.3.3.2]

60.4.3.4 Protection Level 2.

60.4.3.4.1 Buildings, and portions thereof, containing quantities of hazardous materials exceeding the MAQ of high hazard Level 2 contents permitted in control areas shall comply with applicable regulations for Protection Level 2, as set forth in the applicable sections of Chapter 6 and Chapters 11 through 21 of NFPA 400, and the building code. [**400**:5.3.4.1]

60.4.3.4.2 High hazard Level 2 contents shall include materials that present a deflagration hazard or a hazard from accelerated burning as defined in 60.3.2.1.2.2. [**400**:5.3.4.2]

60.4.3.5 Protection Level 3.

60.4.3.5.1 Buildings, and portions thereof, containing quantities of hazardous materials exceeding the MAQ of high hazard Level 3 contents permitted in control areas shall comply with applicable regulations for Protection Level 3, as set forth in the applicable sections of Chapter 6 and Chapters 11 through 21 of NFPA 400, and the building code. [**400**:5.3.5.1]

60.4.3.5.2 High hazard Level 3 contents shall include materials that readily support combustion or present a physical hazard as defined in 60.3.2.1.2.3. [**400**:5.3.5.2]

60.4.3.6 Protection Level 4.

60.4.3.6.1 Buildings, and portions thereof, containing quantities of hazardous materials exceeding the MAQ of high hazard Level 4 contents permitted in control areas shall comply with applicable regulations for Protection Level 4, as set forth in the applicable sections of Chapter 6 and Chapters 11 through 21 of NFPA 400, and the building code. [**400**:5.3.6.1]

60.4.3.6.2 High hazard Level 4 contents shall include materials that are acute health hazards as defined in 60.3.2.1.2.4. [**400**:5.3.6.2]

60.4.3.7 Detached Building Required for High Hazard Level 2 and High Hazard Level 3 Materials. Buildings required to comply with Protection Level 2 or 3 and containing quantities of high hazard contents exceeding the quantity limits set forth in Table 60.4.3.7 shall be in accordance with 6.2.3.4 or 6.2.4.4 of NFPA 400, as applicable. [**400**:5.3.7]

60.4.4 Outdoor Areas.

60.4.4.1 Outdoor Control Areas.

60.4.4.1.1 General.

60.4.4.1.1.1 Hazardous materials shall be permitted to be stored or used in outdoor control areas in accordance with 60.4.4.1.2 and 60.4.4.1.3. [**400**:5.4.1.1.1]

60.4.4.1.1.2 Where storage or use is in an outdoor control area, compliance with the outdoor storage and use requirements in Chapters 11 through 21 of NFPA 400 shall not be required. [**400**:5.4.1.1.2]

Table 60.4.2.2.1 Design and Number of Control Areas

Floor Level	Maximum Allowable Quantity per Control Area (%)*	Number of Control Areas per Floor	Fire Resistance Rating for Fire Barriers† (hr)
Above grade			
>9	5.0	1	2
7–9	5.0	2	2
4–6	12.5	2	2
3	50.0	2	1
2	75.0	3	1
1	100.0	4	1
Below grade			
1	75.0	3	1
2	50.0	2	1
Lower than 2	NP	NP	N/A

NP: Not permitted. N/A: Not applicable.
*Percentages represent the MAQ per control area shown in Table 60.4.2.1.1.3, with all the increases permitted in the footnotes of that table.
†Fire barriers are required to include floors and walls, as necessary, to provide a complete separation from other control areas. [**400**: Table 5.2.2.1]

Table 60.4.3.7 High Hazard Level 2 and High Hazard Level 3 Materials — Detached Building Required

		Maximum Quantity Without a Detached Building	
Material	Class	Solids and Liquids (tons)	Gases scf (Nm³) [m³]*
Individual bulk compressed gas systems	N/A	N/A	15,000 (425)
Oxidizers	3	1,200	N/A
	2	2,000	N/A
Organic peroxides	II	25	N/A
	III	50	N/A
Unstable (reactive) materials	3, nondetonable	1	2,000 (57)
	2	25	10,000 (283)
Water-reactive materials	3	1	N/A
	2, deflagrating	25	N/A
Pyrophoric gases	N/A	N/A	2,000 (57)

For SI units, 1 ton = 0.9 met ton.
N/A: Not applicable.
*See Table 21.2.5 of NFPA 400. [**400**: Table 5.3.7]

60.4.4.1.2 Maximum Allowable Quantity per Outdoor Control Area. Maximum allowable quantities of hazardous materials in an outdoor control area shall be as specified in Table 60.4.2.1.13.3(a), Table 60.4.2.1.13.3(b), and Table 60.4.4.1.2. [**400**:5.4.1.2]

60.4.4.1.3 Number of Outdoor Control Areas.

60.4.4.1.3.1 A single outdoor control area shall be permitted on any property. [**400**:5.4.1.3.1]

60.4.4.1.3.2 Where a property exceeds 10,000 ft² (929 m²), a group of two outdoor control areas shall be permitted where approved and where each control area is separated by a minimum distance of 50 ft (15 m). [**400**:5.4.1.3.2]

60.4.4.1.3.3 Where a property exceeds 35,000 ft² (3252 m²), additional groups of outdoor control areas shall be permitted where approved, provided that each group is separated by a minimum distance of 300 ft (91 m). [**400**:5.4.1.3.3]

60.4.4.2 Outdoor Storage and Use Areas. Where the quantity of hazardous materials in outdoor storage or use exceeds the MAQ for outdoor control areas as set forth in Table 60.4.4.1.2, the outdoor area shall comply with the applicable outdoor requirements of Chapter 6 and Chapters 11 through 21 of NFPA 400. [**400**:5.4.2]

60.5 Fundamental Requirements.

60.5.1 General Requirements.

60.5.1.1 Applicability. Storage, use, and handling of hazardous materials in any quantity shall comply with 60.5.1. [**400**:6.1.1]

Table 60.4.4.1.2 Maximum Allowable Quantities of Hazardous Materials per Outdoor Control Area

		Storage			Use — Closed Systems			Use — Open Systems	
Material	Class	Solid Pounds	Liquid Gallons (lb)	Gas scf (lb)	Solid Pounds	Liquid Gallons (lb)	Gas scf (lb)	Solid Pounds	Liquid Gallons (lb)
Physical Hazard Materials									
Flammable gas									
Gaseous		N/A	N/A	3000	N/A	N/A	1500	N/A	N/A
Liquefied		N/A	N/A	(300)	N/A	N/A	(150)	N/A	N/A
Flammable solid		500	N/A	N/A	250	N/A	N/A	50	N/A
Organic peroxide	Detonable	1	(1)	N/A	¼	(¼)	N/A	¼	(¼)
Organic peroxide	I	20	20	N/A	10	(10)	N/A	2	2
	II	200	200	N/A	100	(100)	N/A	20	20
	III	500	500	N/A	250	(250)	N/A	50	50
	IV	NL	NL	N/A	NL	NL	N/A	NL	NL
	V	NL	NL	N/A	NL	NL	N/A	NL	NL
Oxidizer	4	2	(2)	N/A	1	(¼)	N/A	¼	(¼)
	3	40	(40)	N/A	20	(2)	N/A	2	(2)
	2	1000	(1000)	N/A	500	(250)	N/A	50	(50)
	1	NL	NL	N/A	NL	NL	N/A	NL	NL

Table 60.4.4.1.2 *Continued*

Material	Class	Storage			Use — Closed Systems			Use — Open Systems	
		Solid Pounds	Liquid Gallons (lb)	Gas scf (lb)	Solid Pounds	Liquid Gallons (lb)	Gas scf (lb)	Solid Pounds	Liquid Gallons (lb)
Oxidizing gas									
Gaseous		N/A	N/A	6000	N/A	N/A	6000	N/A	N/A
Liquefied		N/A	N/A	(600)	N/A	N/A	(300)	N/A	N/A
Pyrophoric		8	(8)	100	4	(4)	10	0	0
Unstable (reactive)	4	2	(2)	20	1	(1)	2	¼	(¼)
	3	20	(20)	200	10	(10)	10	1	(1)
	2	200	(200)	1000	100	(100)	250	10	(10)
	1	NL	NL	1500	NL	NL	NL	NL	NL
Water-reactive	3	20	(20)	N/A	10	(10)	N/A	1	(1)
	2	200	(200)	N/A	100	(100)	N/A	10	(10)
	1	NL	NL	N/A	NL	NL	N/A	NL	NL
Health Hazard Materials									
Corrosive		20,000	2000	N/A	10,000	1000	N/A	1000	100
Corrosive gas									
Gaseous		N/A	N/A	1620	— N/A	N/A	810	— N/A	N/A
Liquefied		N/A	N/A	(300)	— N/A	N/A	(150)	— N/A	N/A
Highly toxic		20	(20)	N/A	10	(10)	N/A	3	(3)
Highly toxic gas									
Gaseous		N/A	N/A	40*	— N/A	N/A	20*	— N/A	N/A
Liquefied		N/A	N/A	(8)*	— N/A	N/A	(4)*	— N/A	N/A
Toxic		1000	(1000)	N/A	500	50	N/A	125	(125)
Toxic gas									
Gaseous		N/A	N/A	1620	— N/A	N/A	810	— N/A	N/A
Liquefied		N/A	N/A	(300)	— N/A	N/A	(150)	— N/A	N/A

For SI units, 1 lb = 0.454 kg; 1 gal = 3.785 L; 1 scf = $0.0283 Nm^3$.

N/A: Not applicable. NL: Not limited.

Notes:
(1) Table values in parentheses correspond to the unit name in parentheses at the top of the column.
(2) For gallons of liquids, divide the amount in pounds by 10.
(3) The aggregate quantities in storage and use shall not exceed the quantity listed for storage.
(4) The aggregate quantity of nonflammable solid and nonflammable or noncombustible liquid hazardous materials allowed in outdoor storage per single property under the same ownership or control used for retail or wholesale sales is permitted to exceed the MAQ when such storage is in accordance with 60.4.2.1.13.3.

*Permitted only where stored or used in approved exhausted gas cabinets, exhausted enclosures, or fume hoods. [**400:** Table 5.4.1.2]

60.5.1.1.1* Storage of hazardous materials in quantities exceeding the maximum allowable quantity permitted in control areas set forth in Section 60.4 shall comply with Section 6.2 of NFPA 400 and the applicable material specific requirements in Chapters 11 through 21 of NFPA 400. [**400**:6.1.1.1]

60.5.1.1.2* The use, dispensing, and handling of hazardous materials in quantities exceeding the maximum allowable quantity (MAQ) permitted in control areas set forth in Section 60.4 shall comply with Section 6.3 of NFPA 400 and the applicable material specific requirements in Chapters 11 through 21 of NFPA 400. [**400**:6.1.1.2]

60.5.1.2* Material Safety Data Sheets (MSDS). Material safety data sheets (MSDS) shall be available on the premises for hazardous materials regulated by this code. When approved, MSDSs shall be permitted to be retrievable by electronic access. [**400**:6.1.2]

60.5.1.3 Release of Hazardous Materials.

60.5.1.3.1 Prohibited Releases. Hazardous materials shall not be released into a sewer, storm drain, ditch, drainage canal, lake, river, or tidal waterway; upon the ground, a sidewalk, a street, or a highway; or into the atmosphere, unless such release is permitted by the following:

(1) Federal, state, or local governing regulations
(2) Permits of the jurisdictional air quality management board
(3) National Pollutant Discharge Elimination System permit
(4) Waste discharge requirements established by the jurisdictional water quality control board
(5) Sewer pretreatment requirements for publicly or privately owned treatment works [**400**:6.1.3.1]

60.5.1.3.2 Control and Mitigation of Unauthorized Releases. Provisions shall be made for controlling and mitigating unauthorized releases. [**400**:6.1.3.2]

60.5.1.3.3 Records of Unauthorized Releases. Accurate records of the unauthorized release of hazardous materials shall be kept by the permittee. [**400**:6.1.3.3]

60.5.1.3.4* Notification of Unauthorized Releases. The fire department shall be notified immediately or in accordance with approved emergency procedures when an unauthorized release becomes reportable under state, federal, or local regulations. [**400**:6.1.3.4]

60.5.1.3.5 Container Failure. When an unauthorized release due to primary container failure is discovered, the involved primary container shall be repaired or removed from service. [**400**:6.1.3.5]

60.5.1.3.6 Overpack Containers. Overpack containers shall be permitted to be used as a means to provide protection for primary containers to be transported for repair or removal from service. [**400**:6.1.3.6]

60.5.1.3.7 Responsibility for Cleanup of Unauthorized Releases.

60.5.1.3.7.1 The person, firm, or corporation responsible for an unauthorized release shall institute and complete all actions necessary to remedy the effects of such unauthorized release, whether sudden or gradual, at no cost to the AHJ. [**400**:6.1.3.7.1]

60.5.1.3.7.2 When deemed necessary by the AHJ, cleanup of an unauthorized release shall be permitted to be initiated by the fire department or by an authorized individual or firm, and costs associated with such cleanup shall be borne by the owner, operator, or other person responsible for the unauthorized release. [**400**:6.1.3.7.2]

60.5.1.4* Personnel Training. Persons in areas where hazardous materials are stored, dispensed, handled, or used shall be trained in the hazards of the materials employed and actions required by the emergency plan. The level of training to be conducted shall be consistent with the responsibilities of the persons to be trained in accordance with 60.5.1.4.1 through 60.5.1.4.5. [**400**:6.1.4]

60.5.1.4.1 Awareness. The training provided for persons designated in 60.5.1.4 shall include awareness training in accordance with 60.5.1.4.1.1 through 60.5.1.4.1.3. [**400**:6.1.4.1]

60.5.1.4.1.1 Completion. Initial training shall be completed prior to beginning work in the work area. [**400**:6.1.4.1.1]

60.5.1.4.1.2 Hazard Communications. Training shall be provided prior to beginning work in the work area to enable personnel to recognize and identify hazardous materials stored, dispensed, handled, or used on site and where to find safety information pertaining to the hazards of the materials employed. [**400**:6.1.4.1.2]

60.5.1.4.1.3 Emergency Plan. Training shall be provided prior to beginning work in the work area to enable personnel to implement the emergency plan. [**400**:6.1.4.1.3]

60.5.1.4.2 Operations Personnel. Persons engaged in storing, using, or handling hazardous materials shall be designated as operations personnel and shall be trained in accordance with 60.5.1.4.1 and 60.5.1.4.2.1 through 60.5.1.4.2.6. [**400**:6.1.4.2]

60.5.1.4.2.1 Physical and Health Hazard Properties. Operations personnel shall be trained in the chemical nature of the materials, including their physical hazards and the symptoms of acute or chronic exposure as provided by the Material Safety Data Sheet (MSDS) furnished by the manufacturer or other authoritative sources. [**400**:6.1.4.2.1]

60.5.1.4.2.2 Dispensing, Using, and Processing. Operations personnel shall be trained in the use of specific safeguards applicable to the dispensing, processing, or use of the materials and equipment employed. [**400**:6.1.4.2.2]

60.5.1.4.2.3 Storage. Operations personnel shall be trained in the application of storage arrangements and site-specific limitations on storage for the materials employed. [**400**:6.1.4.2.3]

60.5.1.4.2.4 Transport (Handling). Operations personnel involved in materials handling shall be trained in the requirements for on-site transport of the materials employed. [**400**:6.1.4.2.4]

60.5.1.4.2.5 Actions in an Emergency. Operations personnel shall be trained in the necessary actions to take in the event of an emergency, including the operation and activation of emergency controls prior to evacuation. [**400**:6.1.4.2.5]

60.5.1.4.2.6 Changes. Training shall be provided whenever a new hazardous material is introduced into the work area that presents a new physical or health hazard, or when new information is obtained pertaining to physical or health hazards of an existing hazardous material that has not been included in previous training, and when there are changes in any of the following:

(1) Equipment

(2) Operations
(3) Hazardous materials [**400**:6.1.4.2.6]

60.5.1.4.3 Emergency Response Liaison.

60.5.1.4.3.1 Responsible persons shall be designated and trained to be emergency response (ER) liaison personnel. [**400**:6.1.4.3.1]

60.5.1.4.3.2 Emergency response liaison personnel shall do the following:

(1) Aid emergency responders in pre-planning responses to emergencies
(2) Identify locations where hazardous materials are located
(3) Have access to material safety data sheets
(4) Be knowledgeable in the site emergency response procedures [**400**:6.1.4.3.2]

60.5.1.4.4* Emergency Responders. Emergency responders shall be trained to be competent in the actions to be taken in an emergency event. [**400**:6.1.4.4]

60.5.1.4.4.1* Emergency Response Team Leader. Persons acting as ER team leaders shall be trained under the Incident Command System concept or equivalent. [**400**:6.1.4.4.1]

60.5.1.4.4.2* Response to Incipient Events. Responses to incidental releases of hazardous materials where the material can be absorbed, neutralized, or otherwise controlled at the time of release by employees in the immediate release area, or by maintenance personnel, shall not be considered emergency responses as defined within the scope of this *Code*. [**400**:6.1.4.4.2]

60.5.1.4.4.3* On-Site Emergency Response Team. When an onsite emergency response team is provided, emergency responders shall be trained in accordance with the requirements of the specific site emergency plan or as required by federal, state, or local governmental agencies. [**400**:6.1.4.4.3]

60.5.1.4.5 Training Mandated by Other Agencies. Training required by federal, state, or local regulations that is required based on the quantity or type of hazardous materials stored, dispensed, handled, or used shall be conducted in accordance with the requirements of and under the jurisdiction of the governing agency. [**400**:6.1.4.5]

60.5.1.4.6 Documentation. Training shall be documented and made available to the AHJ upon written request. [**400**:6.1.4.6]

60.5.1.5 Ignition Source Controls.

60.5.1.5.1 Smoking. Smoking shall be prohibited in the following locations:

(1) Within 25 ft (7.6 m) of outdoor storage areas, dispensing areas, or open use areas
(2) In rooms or areas where hazardous materials are stored or dispensed or used in open systems in amounts requiring a permit in accordance with Section 1.8 of NFPA 400 [**400**:6.1.5.1]

60.5.1.5.2 Open Flames and High-Temperature Devices. Open flames and high-temperature devices shall not be used in a manner that creates a hazardous condition. [**400**:6.1.5.2]

60.5.1.5.3 Energy-Consuming Equipment. Energy-consuming equipment with the potential to serve as a source of ignition shall be listed or approved for use with the hazardous materials stored or used. [**400**:6.1.5.3]

60.5.1.5.3.1* Powered Industrial Trucks. Powered industrial trucks shall be operated and maintained in accordance with Section 10.17. [**400**:6.1.5.3.1]

60.5.1.6 Systems, Equipment, and Processes. Processes, methods, specifications, equipment testing and maintenance, design standards, performance, installation, equipment design and construction, and other pertinent criteria shall be in accordance with this section. [**400**:6.1.6]

60.5.1.6.1 Design and Construction of Containers and Tanks. Containers, cylinders, and tanks shall be designed and constructed in accordance with approved standards. Containers, cylinders, tanks, and other means used for containment of hazardous materials shall be of an approved type. [**400**:6.1.6.1]

60.5.1.6.2 Piping, Tubing, Valves, and Fittings. Piping, tubing, valves, fittings, and related components used for hazardous materials shall be in accordance with the following:

(1) Piping, tubing, valves, fittings, and related components shall be designed and fabricated from materials compatible with the material to be contained and shall be of a strength and durability to withstand the pressure, structural and seismic stress, and exposure to which they are subject.
(2) Piping and tubing shall be identified in accordance with ASME A13.1 to indicate the material conveyed.
(3) Accessible manual valves, or fail-safe emergency shutoff valves operated by a remotely located manually or automatically activated shutdown control, shall be installed on supply piping and tubing at the following locations:
   (a) Point of use
   (b) Tank or bulk source
(4) Manual emergency shutoff valves and remotely located manually activated shutdown controls for emergency shutoff valves shall be identified, and the location shall be clearly visible, accessible, and indicated by means of a sign.
(5) Backflow prevention or check valves shall be provided when the backflow of hazardous materials could create a hazardous condition or cause the unauthorized discharge of hazardous materials.
(6) Liquids classified in accordance with NFPA 704, *Standard System for the Identification of the Hazards of Materials for Emergency Response*, shall be carried in pressurized piping above a gauge pressure of 15 psi (103 kPa) having a hazard ranking as follows:
   (a) Health hazard Class 3 or Class 4
   (b) Flammability Class 4
   (c) Instability Class 3 or Class 4
(7) The pressurized piping specified in 60.5.1.6.2(6) shall be provided with an approved means of leak detection and emergency shutoff or excess flow control in accordance with the following:
   (a) Where the piping originates from within a hazardous material storage room or area, the excess flow control shall be located within the storage room or area.
   (b) Where the piping originates from a bulk source, the excess flow control shall be located at the bulk source.
   (c) Piping for inlet connections designed to prevent backflow shall not be required to be equipped with excess flow control. [**400**:6.1.6.2]

60.5.1.6.3 Additional Regulations for Supply Piping for Health Hazard Materials. Supply piping and tubing for liquids or solids having a health hazard ranking of Class 3 or Class 4 in accordance with NFPA 704, *Standard System for the Identification of the Hazards of Materials for Emergency Response*, shall be in accordance with ASME B31.3 and the following:

(1) Piping and tubing utilized for the transmission of highly toxic, toxic, or highly volatile corrosive liquids shall have welded, threaded, or flanged connections throughout, except for connections located within a ventilated enclosure, or an approved method of drainage or containment.
(2) Piping and tubing shall not be located within corridors, within any portion of a means of egress required to be enclosed in fire resistance–rated construction, or in concealed spaces in areas not classified as Protection Level 1 through Protection Level 4 occupancies. [**400**:6.1.6.3]

60.5.1.6.4 Equipment, Machinery, and Alarms. Equipment, machinery, and required detection and alarm systems associated with the use, storage, or handling of hazardous materials shall be listed or approved. [**400**:6.1.6.4]

60.5.1.7 Empty Containers and Tanks. Empty containers and tanks previously used for the storage of hazardous materials shall be free from residual material and vapor as defined by DOT, the Resource Conservation and Recovery Act (RCRA), or other regulating authority or shall be maintained as specified for the storage of hazardous material. [**400**:6.1.7]

60.5.1.8 Signs.

60.5.1.8.1 General.

60.5.1.8.1.1 Design and Construction. Signs shall be durable, and the size, color, and lettering of signs shall be in accordance with nationally recognized standards. [**400**:6.1.8.1.1]

60.5.1.8.1.2 Language. Signs shall be in English as the primary language or in symbols permitted by this *Code*. [**400**:6.1.8.1.2]

60.5.1.8.1.3 Maintenance. Signs shall meet the following criteria:

(1) They shall not be obscured.
(2) They shall be maintained in a legible condition.
(3) They shall not be removed, unless for replacement. [**400**:6.1.8.1.3]

60.5.1.8.2 Hazard Materials Identification.

60.5.1.8.2.1 NFPA 704 Placard. Visible hazard identification signs in accordance with NFPA 704, *Standard System for the Identification of the Hazards of Materials for Emergency Response*, shall be placed at the following locations, except where the AHJ has received a hazardous materials management plan and a hazardous materials inventory statement in accordance with 60.1.6 and 60.1.7 and has determined that omission of such signs is consistent with safety:

(1) On stationary aboveground tanks
(2) On stationary aboveground containers
(3) At entrances to locations where hazardous materials are stored, dispensed, used, or handled in quantities requiring a permit
(4) At other entrances and locations designated by the AHJ [**400**:6.1.8.2.1]

60.5.1.8.2.2 Identification of Containers, Cartons, and Packages. Individual containers, cartons, or packages shall be conspicuously marked or labeled in accordance with nationally recognized standards. [**400**:6.1.8.2.2]

60.5.1.8.3 No Smoking Signs. Where "no smoking" is not applicable to an entire site or building, signs shall be provided as follows:

(1) In rooms or areas where hazardous materials are stored or dispensed or used in open systems in amounts requiring a permit in accordance with Section 1.8 of NFPA 400
(2) Within 25 ft (7.6 m) of outdoor storage, dispensing, or open-use areas [**400**:6.1.8.3]

60.5.1.9 Protection from Vehicles.

60.5.1.9.1 Guard posts or other approved means shall be provided to protect the following where subject to vehicular damage:

(1) Storage tanks and connected piping, valves, and fittings
(2) Storage areas containing tanks or portable containers except where the exposing vehicles are powered industrial trucks used for transporting the hazardous materials
(3) Use areas [**400**:6.1.9.1]

60.5.1.9.2 Where guard posts are installed, the posts shall meet the following criteria:

(1) They shall be constructed of steel not less than 4 in. (102 mm) in diameter and concrete filled.
(2) They shall be spaced not more than 4 ft (1.2 m) between posts on center.
(3) They shall be set not less than 3 ft (0.9 m) deep in a concrete footing of not less than a 15 in. (381 mm) diameter.
(4) They shall be set with the top of the posts not less than 3 ft (0.9 m) above ground.
(5) They shall be located not less than 5 ft (1.5 m) from the tank. [**400**:6.1.9.2]

60.5.1.10 Electrical Wiring and Equipment.

60.5.1.10.1 General. Electrical wiring and equipment shall be installed in accordance with Section 11.1. [**400**:6.1.10.1]

60.5.1.10.2 Static Accumulation. When processes or use conditions exist where flammable gases, dusts, or vapors can be ignited by static electricity, means shall be provided to prevent the accumulation of a static charge and to dissipate the static charge to ground. [**400**:6.1.10.2]

60.5.1.11 Protection from Light. Materials that are sensitive to light shall be stored in containers designed to protect them from such exposure. [**400**:6.1.11]

60.5.1.12 Separation of Incompatible Materials.

60.5.1.12.1 Incompatible materials in storage and storage of materials incompatible with materials in use shall be separated when the stored materials are in containers having a capacity of more than 5 lb (2.268 kg) or ½ gal (1.89 L). [**400**:6.1.12.1]

60.5.1.12.2 Separation shall be accomplished by one of the following methods:

(1) Segregating incompatible materials storage by a distance of not less than 20 ft (6.1 m)
(2) Isolating incompatible materials storage by a noncombustible partition extending not less than 18 in. (457 mm) above and to the sides of the stored material or by a noncombustible partition that interrupts the line of sight between the incompatible materials
(3) Storing liquid and solid materials in hazardous materials storage cabinets complying with 60.5.1.18

(4) Storing compressed gases in gas cabinets or exhausted enclosures complying with Chapter 21 of NFPA 400 [**400**:6.1.12.2]

60.5.1.12.3 Materials that are incompatible shall not be stored within the same cabinet or enclosure. [**400**:6.1.12.3]

60.5.1.13 General Storage.

60.5.1.13.1 Storage. The storage arrangement of materials shall be in accordance with this chapter and the material specific requirements of Chapters 11 through 21 of NFPA 400 as applicable. [**400**:6.1.13.1]

60.5.1.13.2 Shelf Storage. Shelving shall be constructed to carry the design loads and shall be braced and anchored in accordance with the seismic design requirements of the applicable building code. [**400**:6.1.13.2]

60.5.1.13.2.1 Shelf Construction.

60.5.1.13.2.1.1 Shelving shall be treated, coated, or constructed of materials that are compatible with the hazardous materials stored. [**400**:6.1.13.2.1.1]

60.5.1.13.2.1.2 Shelves shall be provided with a lip or guard where used for the storage of individual containers, except under either of the following conditions:

(1) Where storage is located in hazardous materials storage cabinets or laboratory furniture specifically designed for such use
(2) Where amounts of hazardous materials in storage do not exceed the quantity threshold for requiring a permit in accordance with Section 1.8 of NFPA 400 [**400**:6.1.13.2.1.2]

60.5.1.13.2.2 Shelf storage of hazardous materials shall be maintained in an orderly manner. [**400**:6.1.13.2.2]

60.5.1.14* Seismic Protection. Machinery and equipment utilizing hazardous materials in areas subject to seismic activity shall be seismically anchored in accordance with the building code. [**400**:6.1.14]

60.5.1.14.1 Shock Padding. Materials that are shock sensitive shall be padded, suspended, or otherwise protected against accidental dislodgement and dislodgement during seismic activity. [**400**:6.1.14.1]

60.5.1.15 Outdoor Storage and Use Areas. Outdoor storage and use areas for hazardous materials shall comply with the following:

(1) Outdoor storage and use areas shall be kept free of weeds, debris, and common combustible materials not necessary to the storage or use of hazardous materials.
(2) The area surrounding an outdoor storage and use area shall be kept clear of weeds, debris, and common combustible materials not necessary to the storage or use of hazardous materials for a minimum distance of 15 ft (4.5 m).
(3) Outdoor storage and use areas for hazardous materials shall be located not closer than 20 ft (6.1 m) from a property line that can be built upon, a street, an alley, or a public way, except that a 2-hour fire barrier wall, without openings and extending not less than 30 in. (762 mm) above and to the sides of the storage area, shall be permitted in lieu of such distance. [**400**:6.1.15]

60.5.1.16 Maintenance Required.

60.5.1.16.1* Equipment, machinery, and required detection and alarm systems associated with hazardous materials shall be maintained in an operable condition. [**400**:6.1.16.1]

60.5.1.16.2 Stationary tanks not used for a period of 90 days shall be safeguarded or removed in an approved manner. [**400**:6.1.16.2]

60.5.1.16.2.1 The tanks specified in 60.5.1.16.2 shall have the fill line, gauge opening, and pump connection secured against tampering. [**400**:6.1.16.2.1]

60.5.1.16.2.2 Vent lines shall be maintained. [**400**:6.1.16.2.2]

60.5.1.16.2.3* Tanks that are to be placed back in service shall be tested in an approved manner. [**400**:6.1.16.2.3]

60.5.1.16.3 The following shall apply to defective containers, cylinders, and tanks:

(1) They shall be removed from service, repaired, or disposed of in an approved manner.
(2) Overpack containers shall be permitted to be used as a means to provide protection for primary containers that are transported for repair or removal from service. [**400**:6.1.16.3]

60.5.1.16.4 Defective equipment or machinery shall be removed from service and repaired or replaced. [**400**:6.1.16.4]

60.5.1.16.5 Required detection and alarm systems that are defective shall be replaced or repaired. [**400**:6.1.16.5]

60.5.1.17 Testing.

60.5.1.17.1 The equipment, devices, and systems listed in 60.5.1.17.2.1 shall be tested at one of the intervals listed in 60.5.1.17.2.2. Written records of the tests conducted or maintenance performed shall be maintained. [**400**:6.1.17.1]

60.5.1.17.2 Testing shall not be required under the following conditions:

(1) Where approved written documentation is provided that testing will damage the equipment, device, or system and the equipment, device, or system is maintained as specified by the manufacturer
(2) Where equipment, devices, and systems fail in a fail-safe manner
(3) Where equipment, devices, and systems self-diagnose and report trouble, with records of the self-diagnosis and trouble reporting made available to the AHJ
(4) Where system activation occurs during the required test cycle for the components activated during the test cycle
(5) Where approved maintenance in accordance with 60.5.1.16.1 is performed not less than annually or in accordance with an approved schedule, in which case the testing requirements set forth in 60.5.1.17.2.1 and 60.5.1.17.2.2 are permitted to apply. [**400**:6.1.17.2]

60.5.1.17.2.1 Equipment, Devices, and Systems Requiring Testing. The following equipment, devices, and systems shall be tested in accordance with 60.5.1.17 and 60.5.1.17.2.2:

(1) Limit control systems for liquid level, temperature, and pressure required by 6.2.1.7 of NFPA 400
(2) Monitoring and supervisory systems required by 6.2.1.1 of NFPA 400 [**400**:6.1.17.2.1]

60.5.1.17.2.2 Testing Frequency. The equipment, systems, and devices listed in 60.5.1.17.2.1 shall be tested at one of the following frequencies:

(1) Not less than annually
(2) In accordance with the approved manufacturer's requirements

(3) In accordance with approved recognized industry standards
(4) In accordance with an approved schedule [**400**:6.1.17.2.2]

60.5.1.18 Hazardous Materials Storage Cabinets. When storage cabinets are used to increase maximum allowable quantities per control area or to otherwise comply with a specific provision in Section 60.5, such cabinets shall be in accordance with the following:

(1) Cabinets shall be constructed of metal.
(2) The interior of cabinets shall be treated, coated, or constructed of materials that are nonreactive with the hazardous material stored, and such treatment, coating, or construction shall include the entire interior of the cabinet.
(3) Cabinets shall be either listed as suitable for the intended storage or constructed in accordance with the following:
   (a) Cabinets shall be of steel having a thickness of not less than 0.044 in. (1.12 mm) (18 gauge).
   (b) The cabinet, including the door, shall be double-walled with 1½ in. (38.1 mm) airspace between the walls.
   (c) Joints shall be riveted or welded and shall be tightfitting.
   (d) Doors shall be well fitted, self-closing, and equipped with a self-latching device.
   (e) The bottoms of cabinets utilized for the storage of liquids shall be liquidtight to a minimum height of 2 in. (51 mm).
   (f) For requirements regarding electrical equipment and devices within cabinets used for the storage of hazardous liquids, compressed gases, or cryogenic fluids, see NFPA 70, *National Electrical Code*.
(4) Cabinets shall be marked in conspicuous lettering that reads as follows: HAZARDOUS — KEEP FIRE AWAY [**400**:6.1.18]

60.5.1.19 Installation of Tanks. Installation of tanks shall be in accordance with 60.5.1.19.1 through 60.5.1.19.2. [**400**:6.1.19]

60.5.1.19.1 Underground Tanks.

60.5.1.19.1.1 Underground tanks used for the storage of liquid hazardous materials shall be provided with secondary containment. [**400**:6.1.19.1.1]

60.5.1.19.1.2 In lieu of providing secondary containment for an underground tank, an aboveground tank in an underground vault complying with NFPA 30, *Flammable and Combustible Liquids Code*, shall be permitted. [**400**:6.1.19.1.2]

60.5.1.19.2 Aboveground Tanks. Aboveground stationary tanks installed outdoors and used for the storage of hazardous materials shall be located and protected in accordance with the requirements for outdoor storage of the particular material involved and in accordance with the requirements of Chapters 11 through 21 of NFPA 400. [**400**:6.1.19.2]

60.5.1.19.2.1 Aboveground tanks that are installed in vaults complying with NFPA 30, *Flammable and Combustible Liquids Code*, shall not be required to comply with location and protection requirements for outdoor storage. [**400**:6.1.19.2.1]

60.5.1.19.2.2 Aboveground tanks that are installed inside buildings and used for the storage of hazardous materials shall be located and protected in accordance with the requirements for indoor storage of the particular material involved. [**400**:6.1.19.2.2]

60.5.1.19.3 Marking. Aboveground stationary tanks shall be marked as required by 60.5.1.8.2.1. [**400**:6.1.19.2.3]

60.5.1.20 When required, fire alarm systems and smoke detection systems shall be installed in accordance with NFPA 72, *National Fire Alarm and Signaling Code*. [**400**:6.1.20]

60.5.2 Where permitted by Chapters 11 through 43 of NFPA 101, *Life Safety Code*, alcohol-based hand-rub dispensers shall be permitted provided they meet all of the following criteria:

(1) The maximum individual dispenser fluid capacity shall be as follows:
   (a) 0.32 gal (1.2 L) for dispensers in corridors and areas open to corridors
   (b) 0.53 gal (2.0 L) for dispensers in rooms or suites of rooms separated from corridors
(2) Where aerosol containers are used, the maximum capacity of the aerosol dispenser shall be 18 oz. (0.51 kg) and shall be limited to Level 1 aerosols as defined in NFPA 30B, *Code for the Manufacture and Storage of Aerosol Products*.
(3) Dispensers shall be separated from each other by horizontal spacing of not less than 48 in. (1220 mm).
(4) Not more than an aggregate 10 gal (37.8 L) of alcohol-based hand-rub solution or 1135 oz (32.2 kg) of Level 1 aerosols, or a combination of liquids and Level 1 aerosols not to exceed, in total, the equivalent of 10 gal (37.8 L) or 1135 oz (32.2 kg,) shall be in use outside of a storage cabinet in a single smoke compartment or fire compartment or story, whichever is less in area. One dispenser complying with 60.5.2(1) per room and located in that room shall not be included in the aggregated quantity.
(5) Storage of quantities greater than 5 gal (18.9 L) in a single smoke compartment or fire compartment or story, whichever is less in area, shall meet the requirements of NFPA 30, *Flammable and Combustible Liquids Code*.
(6) Dispensers shall not be installed in the following locations:
   (a) Above an ignition source for a horizontal distance of 1 in. (25 mm) to each side of the ignition source
   (b) To the side of an ignition source within a 1 in. (25 mm) horizontal distance from the ignition source
   (c) Beneath an ignition source within a 1 in. (25 mm) vertical distance from the ignition source
(7) Dispensers installed directly over carpeted floors shall be permitted only in sprinklered areas of the building.
(8) The alcohol-based hand-rub solution shall not exceed 95 percent alcohol content by volume.
(9) Operation of the dispenser shall comply with the following criteria:
   (a) The dispenser shall not release its contents except when the dispenser is activated, either manually or automatically by touch-free activation.
   (b) Any activation of the dispenser shall only occur when an object is placed within 4 in. (100 mm) of the sensing device.
   (c) An object placed within the activation zone and left in place shall not cause more than one activation.
   (d) The dispenser shall not dispense more solution than the amount required for hand hygiene consistent with label instructions.

(e) The dispenser shall be designed, constructed, and operated in a manner that ensures accidental or malicious activation of the dispensing device is minimized.

(f) The dispenser shall be tested in accordance with the manufacturer's care and use instructions each time a new refill is installed. [*101:* 8.7.3.3]

60.6 Emergency Action Planning, Fire Risk Control and Chemical Hazard Requirements for Industrial Processes. Emergency planning, fire risk control, and chemical hazard requirements associated with industrial processes where the quantities of materials in use require compliance with Protection Level 1, Protection Level 2, Protection Level 3, or Protection Level 4 based on materials exceeding the maximum allowable quantities (MAQ) in the following categories shall comply with the requirements of Chapter 7 of NFPA 400, *Hazardous Materials Code*:

(1) Unpackaged organic peroxide formulations that are capable of explosive decomposition in their unpackaged state
(2) Oxidizer Class 3 and Class 4: solids and liquids
(3) Pyrophoric solids, liquids, and gases
(4) Unstable reactive Class 3 and Class 4: solids, liquids, and gases
(5) Highly toxic solids, liquids, and gases
(6) Water-reactive liquids, Class 3

60.7 Performance Alternative. In lieu of complying with Chapter 60 in its entirety, occupancies containing high hazard Level 1 to high hazard Level 5 contents shall be permitted to comply with Chapter 10 of NFPA 400, *Hazardous Materials Code*.

Chapter 61   Aerosol Products

61.1 General Provisions.

61.1.1 Application.

61.1.1.1* The manufacture, storage, use, handling, and display of aerosol products shall comply with the requirements of Chapter 61; NFPA 30B, *Code for the Manufacture and Storage of Aerosol Products*; and Sections 60.1 through 60.4 of this *Code*.

61.1.1.2 Where the provisions of Chapter 61 or NFPA 30B conflict with the provisions of Chapter 60, the provisions of Chapter 61 and NFPA 30B shall apply.

61.1.1.3* Chapter 61 shall not apply to the storage and display of containers whose contents are comprised entirely of LP-Gas products. [**30B:**1.1.2]

61.1.1.4 Chapter 61 shall not apply to post-consumer processing of aerosol containers. [**30B:**1.1.3]

61.1.1.5* Chapter 61 shall not apply to containers that do not meet the definition of *Aerosol Container (see 3.3.2 of NFPA 30B)*. [**30B:**1.1.4]

61.1.1.5.1 Containers that contain a product that meets the definitions in 3.3.1 and 3.3.3 of NFPA 30B, but are larger than the limits specified in 3.3.2 of NFPA 30B, shall not be classified as aerosol products, and Chapter 61 shall not apply to the manufacture, storage, and display of such products. [**30B:**1.1.4.1]

61.1.2 Permits. Permits, where required, shall comply with Section 1.12.

61.1.3* Classification of Aerosol Products in Metal Containers of Not More Than 33.8 fl oz (1000 ml) and in Plastic or Glass Containers of Not More Than 4 fl oz (118 ml). See Annex E of NFPA 30B. [**30B:**1.7]

61.1.3.1 Aerosol products shall be classified by means of the calculation of their chemical or theoretical heats of combustion and shall be designated Level 1, Level 2, or Level 3 in accordance with 61.1.3.2 through 61.1.3.4 and Table 61.1.3.1. [**30B:**1.7.1]

Table 61.1.3.1 Aerosol Product Classification

If the chemical heat of combustion is		Aerosol Classification Level
>	≤	
0	20 kJ/g (8,600 Btu/lb)	1
20 kJ/g (8,600 Btu/lb)	30 kJ/g (13,000 Btu/lb)	2
30 kJ/g (13,000 Btu/lb)	—	3

[**30B:** Table 1.7.1]

61.1.3.1.1 In lieu of classification by means of the chemical heats of combustion, aerosol products shall be permitted to be classified by means of data obtained from properly conducted full-scale fire tests that utilize a 12-pallet test array. [**30B:**1.7.1.1]

Exception: This shall not apply to aerosol cooking spray products. (See 61.1.3.5.) [**30B:***1.7.1.1*]

61.1.3.1.2 The fire tests shall be conducted at an approved testing laboratory. *(See Annex C of NFPA 30B for information on the 12-pallet test array.)* [**30B:**1.7.1.2]

61.1.3.2 Level 1 Aerosol Products. Level 1 aerosol products shall be defined as those products with a total chemical heat of combustion that is less than or equal to 20 kJ/g (8600 Btu/lb). [**30B:**1.7.2]

61.1.3.3 Level 2 Aerosol Products. Level 2 aerosol products shall be defined as those products with a total chemical heat of combustion that is greater than 20 kJ/g (8600 Btu/lb), but less than or equal to 30 kJ/g (13,000 Btu/lb). [**30B:**1.7.3]

61.1.3.4 Level 3 Aerosol Products. Level 3 aerosol products shall be defined as those products with a total chemical heat of combustion that is greater than 30 kJ/g (13,000 Btu/lb). [**30B:**1.7.4]

61.1.3.5 Aerosol Cooking Spray Products. Aerosol cooking spray products shall be defined as those aerosol products designed to deliver a vegetable oil or a solid or nonflammable liquid to reduce sticking on cooking and baking surfaces or to be applied to food or both. These products have a chemical heat of combustion that is greater than 20 kJ/g (8600 Btu/lb) and contain not more than 18 percent by weight of flammable propellant. [**30B:**1.7.5]

61.1.3.5.1 If the aerosol cooking spray product has a chemical heat of combustion that does not exceed 20 kJ/g (8600 Btu/lb), it shall be considered a Level 1 aerosol product. [**30B:**1.7.5.1]

61.1.3.5.2 If the aerosol cooking spray product contains more than 18 percent by weight of flammable propellant, it shall be classified in accordance with its chemical heat of combustion, as set forth in Table 61.1.3.1. [**30B**:1.7.5.2]

61.1.4 Classification of Aerosol Products in Plastic Containers Greater Than 4 fl oz (118 ml) and Less Than 33.8 oz (1000 ml).

61.1.4.1 Plastic Aerosol 1 Products. Plastic aerosol 1 products shall be defined as those that meet one of the following criteria:

(1) The base product has no fire point when tested in accordance with ASTM D 92, *Standard Test Method for Flash and Fire Points by Cleveland Open Cup Tester*, and the propellant is nonflammable.
(2) The base product does not exhibit sustained combustion when tested in accordance with 49 CFR 173, Appendix H, "Method of Testing for Sustained Combustibility, or the *UN Recommendations on the Transport of Dangerous Goods*, and the propellant is nonflammable.
(3)*The base product contains not more than 20% by volume (15.8% by weight) of ethanol or propanol or mixtures thereof in an aqueous mix and the propellant is nonflammable.
(4)*The base product contains not more than 4% by weight of an emulsified liquefied flammable gas propellant within an aqueous base, said propellant to remain emulsified for the life of the product. Where such propellant is not permanently emulsified then the propellant shall be nonflammable. [**30B**:1.8.1]

61.1.4.2 Plastic Aerosol X Products. Plastic aerosol X products shall be defined as those that do not meet any of the criteria provided in 61.1.4.1. [**30B**:1.8.2]

61.1.5 Marking of Packages of Aerosol Products.

61.1.5.1 Manufacturers of aerosol products shall ensure that all cartons or packages of aerosol products are identified on at least one exterior side with the classification of the aerosol products contained therein, in accordance with 61.1.3 and 61.1.4. [**30B**: 1.9.1]

61.1.5.2 Cartons or packages containing aerosol products in metal containers or glass and plastic containers 4 fl oz (118 ml) or less shall be clearly marked as follows: [**30B**: 1.9.2]

Level _____ Aerosols

61.1.5.3 Cartons or packages containing aerosol products in plastic containers greater than 4 fl oz (118 ml) shall be clearly marked on the exterior of the carton as follows: [**30B**: 1.9.4]

Plastic Aerosol 1 (or X)

61.2 Basic Requirements.

61.2.1 Site Requirements. Distances between buildings used for the manufacture or storage of aerosol products and adjacent buildings or property lines that are or can be built upon shall be based on sound engineering principles. [**30B**:4.1]

61.2.2 Building Construction.

61.2.2.1 Openings in fire walls or fire barriers shall be kept to a minimum. [**30B**:4.2.1]

61.2.2.1.1 All openings (i.e., personnel doorways, ductwork, conveyor line, etc.) shall be protected with automatic-closing or self-closing fire doors or dampers. [**30B**:4.2.1.1]

61.2.2.1.2 Fire doors shall be installed in accordance with NFPA 80, *Standard for Fire Doors and Other Opening Protectives*. [**30B**:4.2.1.2]

61.2.2.1.3 Fire dampers shall be installed in accordance with manufacturer's instructions and NFPA 90A, *Standard for the Installation of Air-Conditioning and Ventilating Systems*. [**30B**:4.2.1.3]

61.2.2.2 Means of Egress.

61.2.2.2.1 Means of egress shall comply with applicable provisions of NFPA *101*. [**30B**:4.2.2.1]

61.2.2.2.2 The design and construction of conveyor lines and other physical obstacles, such as in the flammable propellant charging and pump rooms, shall not allow entrapment of personnel and shall provide for direct access to exits. [**30B**:4.2.2.2]

61.2.3 Electrical Installations.

61.2.3.1 All electrical equipment and wiring, including heating equipment, shall be installed in accordance with *NFPA 70*. [**30B**:4.3.1]

61.2.3.1.1 Electrical equipment and wiring in areas where flammable liquids or flammable gases are handled shall meet the additional requirements of Articles 500 and 501 of *NFPA 70*. [**30B**:4.3.1.1]

61.2.3.2 Aerosol product storage and display areas shall be considered unclassified for purposes of electrical installation. [**30B**:4.3.2]

61.2.4 Heating Equipment. Heating equipment shall be installed in accordance with the applicable requirements of the following:

(1) NFPA 31, *Standard for the Installation of Oil-Burning Equipment*
(2) NFPA 54, *National Fuel Gas Code*
(3) NFPA 58, *Liquefied Petroleum Gas Code*
(4) NFPA 85, *Boiler and Combustion Systems Hazards Code* [**30B**:4.4]

61.2.5 Flammable Liquids and Gases. Areas in which flammable liquids and flammable gases are handled or stored shall meet the applicable requirements of the following:

(1) Chapter 66 and NFPA 30, *Flammable and Combustible Liquids Code*
(2) Chapter 69 and NFPA 58, *Liquefied Petroleum Gas Code* [**30B**:4.5]

61.2.6 Fire Protection.

61.2.6.1 Automatic Sprinkler Systems. Installations of automatic sprinklers, where required by this *Code* and NFPA 30B, shall be installed in accordance with Section 13.3 and NFPA 13, *Standard for the Installation of Sprinkler Systems*, and the provisions of NFPA 30B. [**30B**:4.6.1]

61.2.6.1.1 Where the provisions of Chapter 61 and NFPA 13, *Standard for the Installation of Sprinkler Systems*, differ, the provisions of Chapter 61 shall prevail. [**30B**:4.6.1.1]

61.2.6.1.2 Where Chapter 61 does not address specific automatic sprinkler protection criteria, the provisions of NFPA 13, *Standard for the Installation of Sprinkler Systems*, shall prevail. [**30B**:4.6.1.2]

61.2.6.2 Standpipe and Hose System. Installations of standpipe and hose systems, where required by this *Code* and NFPA 30B, shall be designed and installed in accordance with Section 13.2 and NFPA 14 and with the provisions of NFPA 30B. Only combination or spray hose nozzles shall be used. [**30B:**4.6.2]

61.2.6.3 Portable Fire Extinguishers. Fire extinguishers shall be provided in accordance with Section 13.6. [**30B:**4.6.3]

61.2.6.4 Water Supplies.

61.2.6.4.1 In addition to the water supply requirements for automatic sprinkler systems, a minimum requirement for hose stream supply for combined inside and outside hose streams shall be provided in accordance with one of the following:

(1) 500 gpm (1900 L/min) for buildings protected with spray and/or control mode specific application (CMSA) sprinkler protection
(2) 250 gpm (950 L/min) for buildings protected with ESFR sprinkler protection
(3) 1000 gpm (3800 L/min) for buildings without automatic sprinkler protection [**30B:**4.6.4.1]

61.2.6.4.1.1 The water supply shall be sufficient to provide the required hose stream demand for a minimum duration of 2 hours, unless otherwise specified in 61.3.4.2. [**30B:**4.6.4.1.1]

61.2.6.4.1.2 The water supply system shall be designed and installed in accordance with Section 13.5 and NFPA 24, *Standard for the Installation of Private Fire Service Mains and Their Appurtenances.* [**30B:**4.6.4.1.2]

61.2.6.4.1.3 The water supply requirements shall be permitted as modified by the provisions of NFPA 30B. [**30B:**4.6.4.1.3]

61.2.6.4.2 Installations of fire pumps and tanks that are needed to supply the required fire protection water shall be installed in accordance with Section 13.4 and NFPA 20, *Standard for the Installation of Stationary Pumps for Fire Protection*, and NFPA 22, *Standard for Water Tanks for Private Fire Protection.* [**30B:**4.6.4.2]

61.2.7 Fire Alarms. Fire alarm systems shall be installed, tested, and maintained in accordance with applicable requirements of Section 13.7 and *NFPA 72*. [**30B:**4.7]

61.2.8 Sources of Ignition.

61.2.8.1 In areas where flammable gases or flammable vapors might be present, precautions shall be taken to prevent ignition by eliminating or controlling sources of ignition. [**30B:**4.8.1]

61.2.8.2 Sources of ignition shall include, but are not limited to, the following:

(1) Open flames
(2) Lightning
(3) Hot surfaces
(4) Radiant heat
(5) Smoking
(6) Cutting and welding
(7) Spontaneous ignition
(8) Frictional heat or sparks
(9) Static electricity
(10) Electrical arcs and sparks
(11) Stray currents
(12) Ovens, furnaces, and other heating equipment
(13) Automotive vehicles
(14) Material-handling equipment [**30B:**4.8.2]

61.3 Storage in Warehouses and Storage Areas.

61.3.1 Basic Requirements.

61.3.1.1 The protection criteria in Section 61.3 shall apply to the following:

(1) Level 1 aerosol products in metal containers not more than 33.8 fl oz (1000 ml) capacity, in accordance with 61.3.2
(2) Aerosol cooking spray products in metal containers not more than 33.8 fl oz (1000 ml) capacity, in accordance with 61.3.3
(3) Level 2 and Level 3 aerosol products in metal containers not more than 33.8 fl oz (1000 ml) capacity, in accordance with Section 6.4 of NFPA 30B
(4) Aerosol products in glass and plastic containers not more than 4 fl oz (118 ml) capacity, in accordance with Section 6.4
(5) Aerosol products in plastic containers greater than 4 fl oz (118 ml) capacity and not more than 33.8 fl oz (1000 ml) capacity, in accordance with Section 6.5 of NFPA 30B [**30B:**6.1.1]

61.3.1.2 All outer packaging of aerosol products, including cartons, trays, shrouds, or other packaging, shall be identified on at least one side with the classification of the aerosol products in accordance with Section 1.9 of NFPA 30B and with one of the following, whichever is appropriate:

(1) Level ____ Aerosols
(2) Aerosol Cooking Spray
(3) Plastic Aerosol 1 (or X) [**30B:**6.1.2]

61.3.1.3* Fire-retardant cartons shall not be considered an acceptable alternative to the protection requirements of 6 of NFPA 30B. [**30B:**6.1.3]

61.3.2* Storage of Level 1 Aerosol Products.

61.3.2.1 Level 1 aerosol products shall be considered equivalent to Class III commodities, as defined in NFPA 13. [**30B:**6.2.1]

61.3.2.2 In cases where the storage of Level 1 aerosol products is required to be protected, such storage shall be protected in accordance with the requirements for Class III commodities set forth in NFPA 13. [**30B:**6.2.2]

61.3.3 Storage of Aerosol Cooking Spray Products.

61.3.3.1 General.

61.3.3.1.1 Aerosol cooking spray products shall be permitted to be stored in a general-purpose warehouse. [**30B:**6.3.1.1]

61.3.3.1.2 Aerosol cooking spray products shall be permitted to be stored mixed with other higher hazard aerosols as long as the provided isolation, storage height restrictions, and protection are based on the highest hazard aerosol product present. [**30B:**6.3.1.2]

61.3.3.2 Fire Protection.

61.3.3.2.1 Encapsulated storage of cartoned aerosol cooking spray products shall be protected as uncartoned storage. [**30B:**6.3.2.1]

61.3.3.2.2 Stretch-wrapping of cartons of aerosol cooking spray products shall be protected as cartoned storage. [**30B:**6.3.2.2]

61.3.3.2.3 Wet-pipe automatic sprinkler protection shall be provided in accordance with Table 61.3.3.2.3(a) or Table 61.3.3.2.3(b) for cartoned aerosol cooking spray products stored in open frame racks without solid shelves or stored as palletized or solid pile storage. [**30B**:6.3.2.3]

61.3.3.2.4 Rack storage shall be arranged so that a minimum aisle width of 8 ft (2.4 m) is maintained between rows of racks and between racks and adjacent solid pile or palletized storage. [**30B**:6.3.2.4]

61.3.3.2.5 Solid pile and palletized storage shall be arranged so that no storage is more than 25 ft (7.6 m) from an aisle. Aisles shall be not less than 4 ft (1.2 m) wide. [**30B**:6.3.2.5]

61.3.3.2.6 Aerosol cooking spray product that is stored uncartoned shall be protected in accordance with Section 6.4 of NFPA 30B using the criteria for a Level 2 or Level 3 aerosol product, based on the product's chemical heat of combustion. [**30B**:6.3.2.6]

61.3.3.2.7 Protection criteria that are developed based on full-scale fire tests performed at an approved facility shall be considered an acceptable alternative to the protection criteria set forth in Table 61.3.3.2.3(a) or Table 61.3.3.2.3(b) [**30B**:6.3.2.7]

61.3.3.2.8 Storage in occupancies other than warehouses or mercantile occupancies, such as in assembly, business, educational, industrial, and institutional occupancies, shall be permitted up to a maximum of 1000 lb (454 kg) net weight. [**30B**:6.3.2.8]

61.3.3.2.9 Solid pile, palletized, or rack storage of aerosol cooking spray product shall be permitted in a general-purpose warehouse that is either unsprinklered or not protected in accordance with this *Code*, up to a maximum of 2500 lb (1135 kg). [**30B**:6.3.2.9]

61.3.4 Storage of Level 2 and Level 3 Aerosol Products.

61.3.4.1 The storage of Level 2 and Level 3 aerosol products shall be in accordance with 61.3.4. [**30B**: 6.4.1]

61.3.4.1.1 Level 2 aerosol products in containers whose net weight is less than 1 oz (28 g) shall be considered to be equivalent to cartoned unexpanded Group A plastics, as defined in NFPA 13. [**30B**: 6.4.1.1]

61.3.4.1.1.1 In cases where the storage of Level 2 aerosol products in containers whose net weight is less than 1 oz (28 g) is required to be protected, such storage shall be in accordance with the requirements set forth in NFPA 13 for cartoned unexpanded Group A plastics. [**30B**: 6.4.1.1.1]

61.3.4.2 Fire Protection — Basic Requirements.

61.3.4.2.1 Storage of Level 2 and Level 3 aerosol products shall not be permitted in basement areas of warehouses. [**30B**: 6.4.2.1]

61.3.4.2.1.1 Storage of Level 2 and Level 3 aerosol products shall be permitted as provided for in 6.3.3 of NFPA 30B. [**30B**: 6.4.2.1.1]

61.3.4.2.2* Encapsulated storage of cartoned Level 2 and Level 3 aerosol products shall be protected as uncartoned. [**30B**: 6.4.2.2]

61.3.4.2.2.1 Stretch-wrapping of cartons of aerosol products shall be permitted. [**30B**: 6.4.2.2.1]

61.3.4.2.2.2 Encapsulated storage of uncartoned Level 2 and Level 3 aerosol products on slip sheets or in trays shall be permitted. [**30B**: 6.4.2.2.2]

61.3.4.2.3 Level 2 and Level 3 aerosol products whose containers are designed to vent at gauge pressures of less than 210 psi (1450 kPa) shall not be stored. [**30B**: 6.4.2.3]

Table 61.3.3.2.3(a) Rack, Palletized and Solid Pile Storage of Cartoned Aerosol Cooking Spray Products (Metric Units)

Maximum Ceiling Height (m)	Maximum Storage Height (m)	Ceiling Sprinkler Protection Criteria			Hose Stream Demand (L/min)	Water Supply Duration (hr)
		Sprinkler Type/Nominal Orifice (L/min/bar$^{0.5}$)	Response/ Nominal Temperature Rating	Design (# sprinklers @ discharge pressure)		
9.1	7.6	ESFR-pendent K = 200	FR/Ordinary	12 @ 5.2 bar	950	1

[**30B**: Table 6.3.2.3(a)]

Table 61.3.3.2.3(b) Rack, Palletized and Solid Pile Storage of Cartoned Aerosol Cooking Spray Products (English Units)

Maximum Ceiling Height (ft)	Maximum Storage Height (ft)	Ceiling Sprinkler Protection Criteria			Hose Stream Demand (gpm)	Water Supply Duration (hr)
		Sprinkler Type/Nominal Orifice (gpm/psi$^{0.5}$)	Response/ Nominal Temperature Rating	Design (# sprinklers @ discharge pressure)		
30	25	ESFR-pendent K = 14.0	FR/Ordinary	12 @ 75 psi	250	1

[**30B**: Table 6.3.2.3(b)]

61.3.4.2.4 Noncombustible draft curtains shall extend down a minimum of 2 ft (0.61 m) from the ceiling and shall be installed at the interface between ordinary and high-temperature sprinklers. [**30B:** 6.4.2.4]

61.3.4.2.5 Storage of mixed commodities within or adjacent to aerosol product storage areas shall meet all applicable requirements of 6 of NFPA 30B. [**30B:** 6.4.2.5]

61.3.4.2.6 Storage of idle or empty pallets shall meet all applicable requirements of NFPA 13. [**30B:** 6.4.2.6]

61.3.4.2.7 Where required by Chapter 6 of NFPA 30B, wet-pipe automatic sprinkler protection shall be provided in accordance with Table 6.4.2.7(a) through Table 6.4.2.7(l) of NFPA 30B and Figure 6.4.2.7(a) through Figure 6.4.2.7(e) of NFPA 30B as designated in the corresponding table(s). Protection shall be based on the highest level of aerosol product present. No protection criteria have been established for the protection of palletized and solid piled storage of uncartoned Level 3 aerosol products. The tables are as follows:

(1) Table 6.4.2.7(a) of NFPA 30B Palletized and Solid Pile Storage of Cartoned Level 2 and Level 3 Aerosol Products (Metric Units)
(2) Table 6.4.2.7(b) of NFPA 30B Palletized and Solid Pile Storage of Cartoned Level 2 and Level 3 Aerosol Products (English Units)
(3) Table 6.4.2.7(c) of NFPA 30B Palletized and Solid Pile Storage of Uncartoned Level 2 Aerosol Products (Metric Units)
(4) Table 6.4.2.7(d) of NFPA 30B Palletized and Solid Pile Storage of Uncartoned Level 2 Aerosol Products (English Units)
(5) Table 6.4.2.7(e) of NFPA 30B Rack Storage of Cartoned Level 2 Aerosol Products (Metric Units)
(6) Table 6.4.2.7(f) of NFPA 30B Rack Storage of Cartoned Level 2 Aerosol Products (English Units)
(7) Table 6.4.2.7(g) of NFPA 30B Rack Storage of Cartoned Level 3 Aerosol Products (Metric Units)
(8) Table 6.4.2.7(h) of NFPA 30B Rack Storage of Cartoned Level 3 Aerosol Products (English Units)
(9) Table 6.4.2.7(i) of NFPA 30B Rack Storage of Uncartoned Level 2 Aerosol Products (Metric Units)
(10) Table 6.4.2.7(j) of NFPA 30B Rack Storage of Uncartoned Level 2 Aerosol Products (English Units)
(11) Table 6.4.2.7(k) of NFPA 30B Rack Storage of Uncartoned Level 3 Aerosol Products (Metric Units)
(12) Table 6.4.2.7(l) of NFPA 30B Rack Storage of Uncartoned Level 3 Aerosol Products (English Units) [**30B:**6.4.2.7]

61.3.4.2.7.1 The protection criteria in Tables 6.4.2.7(a) through 6.4.2.7(l) of NFPA 30B shall only be used with ceilings having a pitch of 2 in 12 or less. [**30B:**6.4.2.7.1]

61.3.4.2.7.2 Fire protection requirements for more demanding commodity and clearance situations shall be permitted to be used for less demanding situations. [**30B:**6.4.2.7.2]

61.3.4.2.7.3 The ordinary-temperature design criteria correspond to ordinary-temperature rated sprinklers and shall be used for sprinklers with ordinary- and intermediate-temperature classification. [**30B:**6.4.2.7.3]

61.3.4.2.7.4 The high-temperature design criteria correspond to high-temperature rated sprinklers and shall be used for sprinklers having a high-temperature rating. [**30B:**6.4.2.7.4]

61.3.4.2.8 Protection criteria that are developed based on full-scale fire tests performed at an approved test facility shall be considered an acceptable alternative to the protection criteria set forth in Table 6.4.2.7(a) through Table 6.4.2.7(l) of NFPA 30B. Such alternative protection criteria shall be subject to the approval of the AHJ. [**30B:**6.4.2.8]

61.3.4.2.9 Installation of in-rack sprinklers shall be in accordance with NFPA 13, *Standard for the Installation of Sprinkler Systems*, as modified by Table 6.4.2.7(e) through Table 6.4.2.7(l) of NFPA 30B. [**30B:**6.4.2.9]

61.3.4.2.9.1 The in-rack sprinkler water demand shall be based on the simultaneous operation of the most hydraulically remote sprinklers as follows:

(1) Sprinkler design parameters shall be in accordance with Table 6.4.2.7(a) through Table 6.4.2.7(l) of NFPA 30B, whichever is applicable.
(2) In-rack design flows indicated in Table 6.4.2.7(e) through Table 6.4.2.7(l) of NFPA 30B shall be provided, but in no case shall the end-sprinkler discharge be less than 10 psi (0.69 bar).
(3) Eight (8) sprinklers where only one level of in-rack sprinklers is provided.
(4) Twelve (12) sprinklers [six (6) sprinklers on two levels] where only two levels of in-rack sprinklers are provided.
(5) Eighteen (18) sprinklers [six (6) sprinklers on the top three levels] where more than two levels of in-rack sprinklers are provided. [**30B:**6.4.2.9.1]

61.3.4.2.9.2 Where in-rack sprinklers are not shielded by horizontal barriers, water shields shall be provided above the sprinklers or listed intermediate level/rack sprinklers shall be used. [**30B:**6.4.2.9.2]

61.3.4.2.9.3 When in-rack sprinklers are necessary to protect a higher hazard commodity that occupies only a portion of the length of a rack, the following shall apply:

(1) In-rack sprinklers shall be extended a minimum of 2.4 m (8 ft) or one bay, whichever is greater, in each direction along the rack on either side of the higher hazard.
(2) The in-rack sprinklers protecting the higher hazard shall not be required to be extended across the aisle. [**30B:**6.4.2.9.3]

61.3.4.2.9.4 Where a storage rack, due to its length, requires less than the number of in-rack sprinklers specified, only those in-rack sprinklers in a single rack need to be included in the calculation. [**30B:**6.4.2.9.4]

61.3.4.2.9.5* In-rack sprinklers shall be located at an intersection of the transverse and longitudinal flues while not exceeding the maximum spacing rules. [**30B:**6.4.2.9.5]

61.3.4.2.9.5.1 Where no transverse flues exist, in-rack sprinklers shall not exceed the maximum spacing rules. [**30B:**6.4.2.9.5.1]

61.3.4.2.9.6 A minimum 150 mm (6 in.) vertical clearance shall be maintained between the sprinkler deflectors and the top of the tier of storage. [**30B:**6.4.2.9.6]

61.3.4.2.9.7 Horizontal barriers used in conjunction with in-rack sprinklers to impede vertical fire development shall be constructed of minimum 22 ga sheet metal, 10 mm (⅜ in.) plywood, or similar material and shall extend the full length and depth of the rack. [**30B:**6.4.2.9.7]

61.3.4.2.9.7.1 Barriers shall be fitted within 50 mm (2 in.) horizontally around rack uprights. [**30B**:6.4.2.9.7.1]

61.3.4.2.10 Installations of hose connections shall meet the requirements of NFPA 13. [**30B**:6.4.2.10]

61.3.4.2.10.1 Subject to the approval of the AHJ, hose stations shall not be required to be installed in storage areas. [**30B**:6.4.2.10.1]

61.3.4.2.11 Storage height and building heights shall comply with Table 6.4.2.7(a) through Table 6.4.2.7(l) of NFPA 30B. [**30B**:6.4.2.11]

61.3.4.2.12 Solid shelving shall comply with 61.3.4.2.12.1 through 61.3.4.2.12.3. [**30B**:6.4.2.12]

61.3.4.2.12.1 Solid shelving that is installed in racks that contain Level 2 and Level 3 aerosol products shall be protected in accordance with Table 6.4.2.7(e) through Table 6.4.2.7(l) of NFPA 30B, whichever is applicable. [**30B**:6.4.2.12.1]

61.3.4.2.12.2 In addition to the in-rack sprinklers shown in Figure 6.4.2.7(a) through Figure 6.4.2.7(e) of NFPA 30B, whichever is applicable, a face sprinkler shall be provided directly below the solid shelf or the elevation of the solid shelf if the face sprinkler is located in a transverse flue. [**30B**:6.4.2.12.2]

61.3.4.2.12.3 The face sprinklers below the shelving required by 61.3.4.2.12.2 shall be not greater than 8 ft (2.4 m) apart as far as the solid shelving level extends. [**30B**:6.4.2.12.3]

61.3.4.2.13 Where spray sprinklers are utilized for ceiling protection, sprinkler spacing shall not exceed 100 ft^2 (9.3 m^2) unless otherwise permitted by 61.3.4.2.14. [**30B**:6.4.2.13]

61.3.4.2.14 Ordinary or intermediate temperature rated K = 25.2 extended-coverage spray sprinklers shall be permitted to be used for all density spray sprinkler design criteria in Table 6.4.2.7(a) through Table 6.4.2.7(l) of NFPA 30B when installed in accordance with their listing. [**30B**:6.4.2.14]

61.3.4.2.15 The ceiling heights in Table 6.4.2.7(e) through Table 6.4.2.7(l) of NFPA 30B shall be permitted to be increased by a maximum of 10 percent if an equivalent percent increase in ceiling sprinkler design density is provided. This shall only apply to spray sprinkler protection criteria. [**30B**:6.4.2.15]

61.3.4.2.16 Protection systems that are designed and developed based on full-scale fire tests performed at an approved test facility or on other engineered protection schemes shall be considered an acceptable alternative to the protection criteria set forth in Section 6.3 of NFPA 30B. Such alternative protection systems shall be approved by the AHJ. [**30B**:6.4.2.16]

61.3.4.2.17 Rack storage shall be arranged so that a minimum aisle width of 8 ft (2.4 m) is maintained between rows of racks and between racks and adjacent solid pile or palletized storage. [**30B**:6.4.2.17]

61.3.4.2.18 Where protection is provided by ESFR sprinklers, aisle width shall be not less than 4 ft (1.2 m). [**30B**:6.4.2.18]

61.3.4.2.19 Solid pile and palletized storage shall be arranged so that no storage is more than 25 ft (7.6 m) from an aisle. Aisles shall be not less than 4 ft (1.2 m) wide. [**30B**:6.4.2.19]

61.4 Mercantile Occupancies.

61.4.1 Plastic Aerosol X Products. Plastic aerosol X products shall be permitted to be stored in mercantile occupancies up to a maximum quantity of 100 lb (45 kg) net weight. [**30B**:7.1]

61.4.2 Sales Display Areas — Aerosol Product Storage Not Exceeding 8 ft (2.4 m) High.

61.4.2.1 Level 1 aerosol products and plastic aerosol 1 products in sales display areas shall not be limited. [**30B**:7.2.1]

61.4.2.2 Aerosol cooking spray products, Level 2 aerosol products, and Level 3 aerosol products shall be removed from combustible cartons, or the cartons shall be display-cut, when located in sales display areas. [**30B**:7.2.2]

61.4.2.2.1 Cartoned display of aerosol cooking spray products shall be permitted provided the area is protected in accordance with Table 6.3.2.3(a) or Table 6.3.2.3(b) of NFPA 30B, or the area is protected in accordance with Table 6.4.2.7(a) through Table 6.4.2.7(l) of NFPA 30B, or the maximum quantity of cartoned display complies with 61.4.2.3.1. [**30B**:7.2.2.1]

61.4.2.2.2 Cartoned display of Level 2 aerosol products and Level 3 aerosol products shall be permitted, provided the area is either protected in accordance with Table 6.4.2.7(a) through Table 6.4.2.7(l) of NFPA 30B or the maximum quantity of cartoned display complies with 61.4.2.3.1. [**30B**:7.2.2.1]

61.4.2.3 Aerosol cooking spray products, Level 2 aerosol products, and Level 3 aerosol products in sales display areas shall not exceed the maximum quantities given in 61.4.2.3.1 and 61.4.2.3.2 according to the protection provided. [**30B**:7.2.3]

61.4.2.3.1 In sales display areas that are nonsprinklered or whose sprinkler system does not meet the requirements of 61.4.2.3.2, the total aggregate quantity of aerosol cooking spray products, Level 2 aerosol products, and Level 3 aerosol products shall not exceed 2 lb/ft^2 (9.8 kg/m^2) of total sales display area, up to the quantities specified in Table 61.4.2.3.1. [**30B**:7.2.3.1]

Table 61.4.2.3.1 Maximum Quantity per Floor of Aerosol Cooking Spray Products, Level 2 Aerosol Products, and Level 3 Aerosol Products, and Aerosol Products in Plastic Containers

Floor	Max. Net Weight per Floor	
	lb	kg
Basement	Not Permitted	
Ground	2500	1135
Upper	500	227

[**30B**: Table 7.2.3.1]

61.4.2.3.1.1 No single 10 ft × 10 ft (3 m × 3 m) section of sales display area shall contain an aggregate quantity of more than 1000 lb (454 kg) net weight aerosol cooking spray products, Level 2 aerosol products, and Level 3 aerosol products. [**30B**:7.2.3.1.1]

61.4.2.3.2 In sales display areas that are sprinklered in accordance with NFPA 13, for at least Ordinary Hazard (Group 2) occupancies, the total aggregate quantity aerosol cooking spray products, Level 2 aerosol products, and Level 3 aerosol products shall not exceed 2 lb/ft^2 (9.8 kg/m^2) of total sales display area. [**30B:**7.2.3.2]

61.4.2.3.2.1 No single 10 ft × 10 ft (3 m × 3 m) section of sales display area shall contain an aggregate quantity of more than 1000 lb (454 kg) net weight of aerosol cooking spray products, Level 2 aerosol products, and Level 3 aerosol products. [**30B:**7.1.3.2.1]

61.4.2.4 Aerosol cooking spray products, Level 2 aerosol products, and Level 3 aerosol products shall be securely stacked to not more than 6 ft (1.8 m) high from base to top of the storage array unless on fixed shelving. [**30B:**7.2.4]

61.4.2.4.1 Shelving shall be of stable construction and storage shall not exceed 8 ft (2.4 m) in height. [**30B:**7.2.4.1]

61.4.3 Sales Display Areas — Aerosol Products Storage Exceeding 8 ft (2.4 m) High.

61.4.3.1 Storage and display of Level 1 aerosol products and plastic aerosol 1 products in sales display areas shall not be limited. [**30B:**7.3.1]

61.4.3.2 Uncartoned or display-cut (case-cut) aerosol cooking spray products, Level 2 aerosol products, and Level 3 aerosol products that are stored for display no more than 6 ft (1.8 m) above the floor shall be permitted where protection is installed in accordance with 61.4.3.3, based on the highest level of aerosol product in the array and the packaging method of the storage above 6 ft (1.8 m). [**30B:**7.3.2]

61.4.3.3 Protection.

61.4.3.3.1 The storage and display of aerosol cooking spray products in metal containers only shall be protected in accordance with Table 6.3.2.3(a) or Table 6.3.2.3(b) of NFPA 30B, or shall be protected in accordance with Table 6.4.2.7(a) through Table 6.4.2.7(l) of NFPA 30B. The storage and display of Level 2 and Level 3 aerosol products in metal containers only shall be protected in accordance with Table 6.3.2.7(a) through Table 6.3.2.7(l) of NFPA 30B, whichever is applicable. [**30B:**7.3.3.1]

61.4.3.3.1.1 Where in-rack sprinklers are required by Table 6.43.2.7(e) through Table 6.4.2.7(l) of NFPA 30B and where the aerosol cooking spray products, Level 2 aerosol products, and Level 3 aerosol products are stored for display below the 6 ft (1.8 m) level, the first tier of in-rack sprinklers shall be installed above the display, but not more than 6 ft (1.8 m) above the floor level. [**30B:**7.2.3.1.1]

61.4.3.3.2 Noncombustible draft curtains shall extend down a minimum of 2 ft (0.61 m) from the ceiling and shall be installed at the interface between ordinary and high-temperature sprinklers. [**30B:**7.3.3.2]

61.4.3.4 Storage and display of aerosol cooking spray products, Level 2 aerosol products, and Level 3 aerosol products shall not exceed 10,000 lb (4,540 kg) net weight within any 25,000 ft^2 (2,323 m^2) of sales display area. [**30B:**7.2.4]

61.4.3.4.1 Aerosol cooking spray products, Level 2 aerosol products, and Level 3 aerosol product display areas shall be separated from each other by a minimum of 25 ft (7.6 m). [**30B:**7.2.4.1]

61.4.3.5 The area of the design for the required ceiling sprinkler system shall extend 20 ft (6 m) beyond the area devoted to storage of aerosol cooking spray products or Level 2 aerosol product and Level 3 products. [**30B:**7.3.5]

61.4.3.6 Storage and display of aerosol cooking spray products, Level 2 aerosol products, and Level 3 aerosol products shall be separated from the storage of flammable and combustible liquids by a minimum distance of 25 ft (7.6 m) or by a segregating wall or noncombustible barrier. [**30B:**7.3.6]

61.4.3.6.1 Where aerosol cooking spray products, Level 2 aerosol products, and Level 3 aerosol products are stored within 25 ft (7.6 m) of flammable and combustible liquids, beneath the noncombustible barrier shall be liquidtight at the floor to prevent spilled liquids from flowing beneath the aerosol products. [**30B:**7.3.6.1]

61.4.3.7 The sales display area shall meet the requirements for mercantile occupancies in NFPA *101*. [**30B:**7.3.7]

61.4.4 Back Stock Storage Areas.

61.4.4.1 Where back stock areas are separated from sales display areas by construction having a minimum 1-hour fire resistance rating, storage of aerosol cooking spray products, Level 2 aerosol products, and Level 3 aerosol products shall meet the requirements of Chapter 6 of NFPA 30B. [**30B:**7.4.1]

61.4.4.2 Where back stock areas are not separated from sales display areas by construction having a minimum 1-hour fire resistance rating, the quantity of aerosol cooking spray products, Level 2 aerosol products, and Level 3 aerosol products in back stock areas shall be included in the total allowable quantities specified in 61.4.2.3 or 61.4.3.4. [**30B:**7.4.2]

61.4.4.2.1 Protection shall be provided in accordance with 61.4.3.3. [**30B:**7.3.2.1]

61.4.4.3 An additional quantity of aerosol cooking spray products, Level 2 aerosol products, and Level 3 aerosol products, up to a maximum of 500 lb (227 kg) net weight, shall be permitted in back stock areas where the additional quantities are stored in flammable liquid storage cabinets that meet the requirements of Section 9.5 of NFPA 30. [**30B:**7.4.3]

61.4.4.4 Storage of aerosol cooking spray products, Level 2 aerosol products, and Level 3 aerosol products in separate, inside flammable liquids storage rooms shall meet the requirements of 6.3.7 of NFPA 30B. [**30B:**7.4.4]

61.5 Operations and Maintenance.

61.5.1 Means of Egress. Means of egress and exits shall be maintained in accordance with NFPA *101*. [**30B:**8.1]

61.5.2 Powered Industrial Trucks.

61.5.2.1 The use and selection of powered industrial trucks shall comply with Section 10.17. [**30B:**8.2.1]

61.5.2.2 Only trained and authorized operators shall be allowed to operate powered industrial trucks. [**30B:**8.2.2]

61.5.2.3 Operator training shall be equivalent to that specified by ANSI/ASME B56.1, *Safety Standard for Low-Lift and High-Lift Trucks*. [**30B:**8.2.3]

61.5.2.4 Loads.

61.5.2.4.1 If the type of load handled presents a hazard of backward falls, the powered industrial truck shall be equipped with a vertical load backrest extension. [**30B:**8.2.4.1]

61.5.2.4.2 For loads that are elevated above the mast of the truck, the backrest extension shall reach at least halfway into the uppermost pallet load. [**30B**:8.2.4.2]

61.5.3 Control of Ignition Sources.

61.5.3.1 Sources of Ignition.

61.5.3.1.1 In areas where flammable gases or flammable vapors might be present, precautions shall be taken to prevent ignition by eliminating or controlling sources of ignition. Sources of ignition include, but are not limited to, the following:

(1) Open flames
(2) Lightning
(3) Hot surfaces
(4) Radiant heat
(5) Smoking
(6) Cutting and welding
(7) Spontaneous ignition
(8) Frictional heat or sparks
(9) Static electricity
(10) Electrical arcs and sparks
(11) Stray currents
(12) Ovens, furnaces, and other heating equipment
(13) Automotive vehicles
(14) Material-handling equipment [**30B**:8.3.1.1]

61.5.3.2 Smoking shall be strictly prohibited, except in designated smoking areas. [**30B**:8.3.2]

61.5.3.3* Welding, cutting, and similar spark-producing operations shall not be permitted in areas that contain aerosol products, until a written permit authorizing the work has been issued. [**30B**:8.3.3]

61.5.3.3.1 The permit shall be issued by a person in authority following an inspection of the area to assure that proper precautions have been taken and will be followed until completion of the work. [**30B**:8.3.3.1]

61.5.4 Aisles. Storage in aisles shall be prohibited so as to permit access for fire fighting, salvage, and removal of stored commodities. [**30B**:8.4]

61.5.5 Waste Disposal.

61.5.5.1 Filled or partly filled aerosol containers shall be separated from all other rubbish and trash. [**30B**:8.5.1]

61.5.5.1.1 Filled or partly filled aerosol containers shall be placed in noncombustible waste containers. [**30B**:8.5.1.1]

61.5.5.2 Filled or partly filled aerosol containers shall not be disposed of in compactors, balers, or incinerators that crush the container or heat its contents. [**30B**:8.5.2]

61.5.5.2.1 Equipment and facilities that are specifically designed for the disposal of aerosol containers shall be permitted to dispose of filled or partly filled aerosol containers. [**30B**:8.5.2.1]

61.5.6 Inspection and Maintenance.

61.5.6.1 A written and documented preventive maintenance program shall be developed for equipment, machinery, and processes that are critical to fire-safe operation of the facility. [**30B**:8.6.1]

61.5.6.2 Critical detection systems and their components, emergency trips and interlocks, alarms, and safety shutdown systems shall be inspected on a regularly scheduled basis, and any deficiencies shall be immediately corrected. [**30B**:8.6.2]

61.5.6.2.1 Items in this inspection schedule shall include, but are not limited to, the following:

(1) Gas detection systems
(2) Deflagration suppression systems
(3) Deflagration vent systems
(4) Ventilation and local exhaust systems
(5) Propellant charging room door interlocks
(6) Process safety devices
(7) Fire alarm systems [**30B**:8.6.2.1]

61.5.6.3 Maintenance. [**68**:11.10]

61.5.6.3.1 Vent closure maintenance shall be performed after every act of nature or process upset condition to ensure that the closure has not been physically damaged and there are no obstructions, including but not limited to, snow, ice, water, mud, or process material, that could lessen or impair the efficiency of the vent closure. [**68**:11.10.1]

61.5.6.3.2 An inspection shall be performed in accordance with 11.4.4 of NFPA 68, *Standard on Explosion Protection by Deflagration Venting*, after every process maintenance turnaround. [**68**:11.10.2]

61.5.6.3.3 If process material has a tendency to adhere to the vent closure, the vent closure shall be cleaned periodically to maintain vent efficiency. [**68**:11.10.3]

61.5.6.3.4 Process interlocks, if provided, shall be verified. [**68**:11.10.4]

61.5.6.3.5 Known potential ignition sources shall be inspected and maintained. [**68**:11.10.5]

61.5.6.3.6 Records shall be kept of any maintenance and repairs performed. [**68**:11.10.6]

61.5.7* Static Electricity. All process equipment and piping involved in the transfer of flammable liquids or gases shall be connected to a static-dissipating earth ground system to prevent accumulations of static charge. [**30B**:8.7]

Chapter 62   Reserved

Chapter 63   Compressed Gases and Cryogenic Fluids

63.1 General Provisions.

63.1.1 Application.

63.1.1.1* The installation, storage, use, and handling of compressed gases and cryogenic fluids in portable and stationary containers, cylinders, equipment, and tanks in all occupancies shall comply with the requirements of Chapter 63; NFPA 55, *Compressed Gases and Cryogenic Fluids Code*; and Sections 60.1 through 60.4 of this *Code*.

63.1.1.2 Where the provisions of Chapter 63 or NFPA 55 conflict with the provisions of Chapter 60, the provisions of Chapter 63 and NFPA 55 shall apply.

63.1.1.3 The requirements in this chapter shall apply to users, producers, distributors, and others who are involved with the storage, use, or handling of compressed gases or cryogenic fluids. [**55**:1.3]

63.1.1.4 Specific Applications. Chapter 63 shall not apply to the following:

(1)*Off-site transportation of materials covered by Chapter 63.
(2) Storage, use, and handling of radioactive gases in accordance with NFPA 801, *Standard for Fire Protection for Facilities Handling Radioactive Materials.*
(3)*Use and handling of medical compressed gases at health care facilities in accordance with NFPA 99, *Health Care Facilities Code.*
(4) Systems consisting of cylinders of oxygen and cylinders of fuel gas used for welding and cutting in accordance with NFPA 51, *Standard for the Design and Installation of Oxygen–Fuel Gas Systems for Welding, Cutting, and Allied Processes.*
(5)*Flammable gases used as a vehicle fuel when stored on a vehicle.
(6)*Storage, use, and handling of liquefied and nonliquefied compressed gases in laboratory work areas in accordance with NFPA 45, *Standard on Fire Protection for Laboratories Using Chemicals.*
(7) Storage, use, and handling of liquefied petroleum gases in accordance with NFPA 58, *Liquefied Petroleum Gas Code.*
(8) Storage, use, and handling of compressed gases within closed-cycle refrigeration systems complying with the mechanical code.
(9) Liquefied natural gas (LNG) storage at utility plants under NFPA 59A, *Standard for the Production, Storage, and Handling of Liquefied Natural Gas (LNG).*
(10) Compressed natural gas (CNG) and liquefied natural gas (LNG), utilized as a vehicle fuel in accordance with NFPA 52, *Vehicular Gaseous Fuel Systems Code.*
(11)*Compressed hydrogen gas (GH2), or liquefied hydrogen gas (LH2) generated, installed, stored, piped, used, or handled in accordance with NFPA 2, *Hydrogen Technologies Code*, when there are no specific or applicable requirements in NFPA 55.
(12) Nonflammable mixtures of ethylene oxide with other chemicals.
(13) Ethylene oxide in chambers 10 scf (0.283 Nm^3) or less in volume or for containers holding 7.05 oz (200 g) of ethylene oxide or less. [55:1.1.2]

63.1.2 Permits. Permits, where required, shall comply with Section 1.12.

63.1.2.1 The permit applicant shall apply for approval to close storage, use, or handling facilities at least 30 days prior to the termination of the storage, use, or handling of compressed or liquefied gases.

63.1.2.2 Such application shall include any change or alteration of the facility closure plan filed pursuant to 60.1.4.4.

63.1.2.3 This 30-day period shall be permitted to be waived by the AHJ if special circumstances require such waiver.

63.1.2.3.1 Permits shall not be required for routine maintenance.

63.1.2.3.2 For repair work performed on an emergency basis, application for permit shall be made within 2 working days of commencement of work.

63.1.3 General Definitions.

63.1.3.1 Absolute Pressure. See 3.3.1.

63.1.3.2 ASTM. See 3.3.17.

63.1.3.3 Automatic Emergency Shutoff Valve. See 3.3.18.

63.1.3.4 Bulk Hydrogen Compressed Gas System. See 3.3.254.1.

63.1.3.5 Bulk Inert Gas System. See 3.3.254.2.

63.1.3.6 Bulk Liquefied Hydrogen System. See 3.3.254.3.

63.1.3.7 Bulk Oxygen System. See 3.3.254.4.

63.1.3.8 Cathodic Protection. See 3.3.37.

63.1.3.9 Cathodic Protection Tester. See 3.3.38.

63.1.3.10 CGA. See 3.3.41.

63.1.3.11 Compressed Gas Container. See 3.3.69.3.

63.1.3.12 Compressed Gas System. See 3.3.254.6.

63.1.3.13 Continuous Gas Detection System. See 3.3.254.7.

63.1.3.14 Cryogenic Fluid. See 3.3.77.

63.1.3.14.1 Flammable Cryogenic Fluid. See 3.3.77.1.

63.1.3.14.2 Inert Cryogenic Fluid. See 3.3.77.2.

63.1.3.14.3 Oxidizing Cryogenic Fluid. See 3.3.77.3.

63.1.3.15 Cylinder. See 3.3.79.

63.1.3.16 Cylinder Containment Vessel. See 3.3.80.

63.1.3.17 Cylinder Pack. See 3.3.81.

63.1.3.18 Distributor. See 3.3.88.

63.1.3.19 Emergency Shutoff Valve. See 3.3.95.

63.1.3.20 Ethylene Oxide Drum. See 3.3.96.

63.1.3.21 Excess Flow Control. See 3.3.97.

63.1.3.22 Exhausted Enclosure. See 3.3.99.

63.1.3.23 Explosion Control. See 3.3.106.

63.1.3.24 Gallon. See 3.3.133.

63.1.3.25 Gas. See 3.3.135.

63.1.3.25.1 Compressed Gas. See 3.3.135.1.

63.1.3.25.2 Corrosive Gas. See 3.3.135.2.

63.1.3.25.3 Flammable Gas. See 3.3.135.3.

63.1.3.25.4 Flammable Liquefied Gas. See 3.3.135.4.

63.1.3.25.5 Highly Toxic Gas. See 3.3.135.5.

63.1.3.25.6 Inert Gas. See 3.3.135.6.

63.1.3.25.7 Irritant Gas. See 3.3.135.7.

63.1.3.25.8 Nonflammable Gas. See 3.3.135.11.

63.1.3.25.9 Other Gas. See 3.3.135.12.

63.1.3.25.10 Oxidizing Gas. See 3.3.135.13.

63.1.3.25.11 Pyrophoric Gas. See 3.3.135.14.

63.1.3.25.12 Toxic Gas. See 3.3.135.17.

63.1.3.25.13 Unstable Reactive Gas. See 3.3.135.18.

63.1.3.26 Gas Cabinet. See 3.3.136.

63.1.3.27 Gas Manufacturer/Producer. See 3.3.137.

63.1.3.28 Gas Room. See 3.3.138.

63.1.3.29 Gaseous Hydrogen System. See 3.3.139.

63.1.3.30 Hazard Rating. See 3.3.143.

63.1.3.31 Immediately Dangerous to Life and Health (IDLH). See 3.3.153.

63.1.3.32 Indoor Area. See 3.3.14.5.

63.1.3.33 ISO Module. See 3.3.160.

63.1.3.34 Liquid Oxygen Ambulatory Container. A container used for liquid oxygen not exceeding 0.396 gal (1.5 L) specifically designed for use as a medical device as defined by 21 USC Chapter 9, the United States Food, Drug and Cosmetic Act that is intended for portable therapeutic use and to be filled from its companion base unit which is liquid oxygen home care container.

63.1.3.35 Liquid Oxygen Home Care Container. A container used for liquid oxygen not exceeding 15.8 gal (60 L) specifically designed for use as a medical device as defined by 21 USC Chapter 9, the United States Food, Drug and Cosmetic Act that is intended to deliver gaseous oxygen for therapeutic use in a home environment.

63.1.3.36 Manual Emergency Shutoff Valve. See 3.3.168.

63.1.3.37 Mechanical Code. See 3.3.53.3.

63.1.3.38 Mobile Supply Unit. See 3.3.179.

63.1.3.39 Nesting. See 3.3.181.

63.1.3.40* Normal Temperature and Pressure (NTP). See 3.3.182.

63.1.3.41 OSHA. See 3.3.190.

63.1.3.42 Outdoor Area. See 3.3.14.8.

63.1.3.43 Permissible Exposure Limit (PEL). See 3.3.162.2.

63.1.3.44 Portable Tank. See 3.3.255.4.

63.1.3.45 Pressure Vessel. See 3.3.204.

63.1.3.46 Short-Term Exposure Limit (STEL). See 3.3.162.3.

63.1.3.47 Stationary Tank. See 3.3.255.6.

63.1.3.48 TC. See 3.3.258,

63.1.3.49 Treatment System. See 3.3.254.14.

63.1.3.50 Tube Trailer. See 3.3.261.

63.1.3.51 Valve Outlet Cap or Plug. See 3.3.268.3

63.1.3.52 Valve Protection Cap. See 3.3.268.4.

63.1.3.53 Valve Protection Device. See 3.3.268.5.

63.1.4 Hazardous Materials Classification.

63.1.4.1 Pure Gases. Hazardous materials shall be classified according to hazard categories as follows:

(1) Physical hazards, which shall include the following:
   (a) Flammable gas
   (b) Flammable cryogenic fluid
   (c) Oxidizing gas
   (d) Oxidizing cryogenic fluid
   (e) Pyrophoric gas
   (f) Unstable reactive (detonable) gas, Class 3 or Class 4
   (g) Unstable reactive (nondetonable) gas
   (h) Unstable reactive gas, Class 1 or Class 2
(2) Health hazards, which shall include the following:
   (a) Corrosive gas
   (b) Cryogenic fluids
   (c) Highly toxic gas
   (d) Toxic gas [**55**:5.1.1]

63.1.4.2 Other Hazards. Although it is possible that there are other known hazards, the classification of such gases is not within the scope of Chapter 63 and they shall be handled, stored, or used as an *other gas*. [**55**:5.1.2]

63.1.4.3 Mixtures. Mixtures shall be classified in accordance with the hazards of the mixture as a whole. [**55**:5.1.3]

63.1.4.4 Responsibility for Classification. Classification shall be performed by an approved organization, individual, or testing laboratory. [**55**:5.1.4]

63.1.4.4.1 Toxicity. The toxicity of gas mixtures shall be classified in accordance with CGA P-20, *Standard for the Classification of Toxic Gas Mixtures,* or by testing in accordance with the requirements of 29 CFR 1910.1000, DOT 49 CFR 173, or ISO 10298, *Determination of toxicity of a gas or gas mixture.* [**55**:5.1.4.1]

63.1.4.4.2 Flammability of Gas Mixtures. For gas mixtures other than those containing ammonia and nonflammable gases, flammability of gas mixtures shall be classified in accordance with CGA P-23, *Standard for Categorizing Gas Mixtures Containing Flammable and Nonflammable Components,* or by physical testing in accordance with the requirements of ASTM E 681, *Standard Test Method for Concentration Limits of Flammability of Chemicals (Vapors and Gases),* or ISO 10156, *Gases and gas mixtures — Determination of fire potential and oxidizing ability for the selection of cylinder valve outlets.* [**55**:5.1.4.2]

63.2 Building-Related Controls.

63.2.1 General.

63.2.1.1 Occupancy.

63.2.1.1.1 Occupancy Requirements. Occupancies containing compressed gases and cryogenic fluids shall comply with Section 63.2 in addition to other applicable requirements of NFPA 55. [**55**:6.1.1.1]

63.2.1.1.2 Occupancy Classification. The occupancy of a building or structure, or portion of a building or structure, shall be classified in accordance with the building code. [**55**:6.1.1.2]

63.2.2 Control Areas.

63.2.2.1 Construction Requirements. Control areas shall be separated from each other by fire barriers in accordance with Table 63.2.2.1. [**5000**:34.2.5.1.1]

63.2.2.2 Number of Control Areas. The maximum number of control areas within a building shall be in accordance with Table 63.2.2.1. [**5000**:34.2.5.2]

63.2.2.3 Where only one control area is present in a building, no special construction provisions shall be required. [**5000**:34.2.5.1.2]

63.2.2.4 Quantities Less Than or Equal to the MAQ. Indoor control areas with compressed gases or cryogenic fluids stored or used in quantities less than or equal to those shown in Table 63.2.3.1.1 shall be in accordance with 63.2.1, 63.2.3.1.6, 63.2.3.1.7, 63.2.7, 63.2.8, 63.2.12, 63.2.15, 63.2.16, and the applicable provisions of Chapters 1 through 5 and Chapters 7 through 15 of NFPA 55. [**55**:6.2.4]

Table 63.2.2.1 Design and Number of Control Areas

Floor Level	Maximum Allowable Quantity per Control Area (%)†	Number of Control Areas per Floor	Fire Resistance Rating for Fire Barriers‡ (hr)
Above grade			
>9	5	1	2
7–9	5	2	2
4–6	12.5	2	2
3	50	2	1
2	75	3	1
1	100	4	1
Below grade			
1	75	3	1
2	50	2	1
Lower than 2	NP	NP	N/A

NP: Not permitted.
N/A: Not applicable.
†Percentages represent the MAQ per control area shown in Table 60.4.2.1.1.3, with all of the increases permitted in the footnotes of that table.
‡Fire barriers are required to include floors and walls, as necessary, to provide a complete separation from other control areas. [**400:** Table 5.2.2.1]

63.2.3 Occupancy Protection Levels.

63.2.3.1 Quantity Thresholds for Compressed Gases and Cryogenic Fluids Requiring Special Provisions.

63.2.3.1.1 Threshold Exceedences. Where the quantities of compressed gases or cryogenic fluids stored or used within an indoor control area exceed those shown in Table 63.2.3.1.1, the area shall meet the requirements for Protection Levels 1 through 5 in accordance with the building code, based on the requirements of 63.2.3.2. [**55:**6.3.1.1]

63.2.3.1.2 Quantities Greater Than the MAQ. Building-related controls in areas with compressed gases or cryogenic fluids stored or used within an indoor area in quantities greater than those shown in Table 63.2.3.1.1 shall be in accordance with the requirements of Section 63.2. [**55:**6.3.1.2]

63.2.3.1.3 Aggregate Allowable Quantities. The aggregate quantity in use and storage shall not exceed the quantity listed for storage. [**55:**6.3.1.3]

63.2.3.1.4 Incompatible Materials. When the classification of materials in individual containers requires the area to be placed in more than one protection level, the separation of protection levels shall not be required providing the area is constructed to meet the requirements of the most restrictive protection level and that the incompatible materials are separated as required by 63.3.1.11.2. [**55:**6.3.1.4]

63.2.3.1.5 Multiple Hazards. Where a compressed gas or cryogenic fluid has multiple hazards, all hazards shall be addressed and controlled in accordance with the provisions for the protection level for which the threshold quantity is exceeded. [**55:**6.3.1.5]

63.2.3.1.6 Flammable and Oxidizing Gases.

63.2.3.1.6.1 Flammable and oxidizing gases shall not be stored or used in other than industrial and storage occupancies. [**55:**6.3.1.6.1]

63.2.3.1.6.2 Cylinders, containers, or tanks not exceeding 250 scf (7.1 Nm^3) content at normal temperature and pressure (NTP) and used for maintenance purposes, patient care, or operation of equipment shall be permitted. [**55:**6.3.1.6.2]

63.2.3.1.7 Toxic and Highly Toxic Compressed Gases. Except for containers or cylinders not exceeding 20 ft^3 (0.6 m^3) content at NTP stored or used within gas cabinets or exhausted enclosures of educational occupancies, toxic or highly toxic compressed gases shall not be stored or used in other than industrial and storage occupancies. [**55:**6.3.1.7]

63.2.3.2 Classification of Protection Levels. The protection level required shall be based on the hazard class of the material involved as indicated in 63.2.3.2.1 through 63.2.3.2.5. [**55:**6.3.2]

63.2.3.2.1 Protection Level 1. Occupancies used for the storage or use of unstable reactive Class 4 and unstable reactive Class 3 detonable compressed gases in quantities that exceed the quantity thresholds for gases requiring special provisions shall be classified Protection Level 1. [**55:**6.3.2.1]

63.2.3.2.2 Protection Level 2. Occupancies used for the storage or use of flammable, pyrophoric, and nondetonable, unstable reactive Class 3 compressed gases or cryogenic fluids in quantities that exceed the quantity thresholds for gases requiring special provisions shall be classified as Protection Level 2. [**55:**6.3.2.2]

63.2.3.2.3 Protection Level 3. Occupancies used for the storage or use of oxidizing and unstable reactive Class 2 compressed gases or cryogenic fluids in quantities that exceed the quantity thresholds for gases requiring special provisions shall be classified as Protection Level 3. [**55:**6.3.2.3]

63.2.3.2.4 Protection Level 4. Occupancies used for the storage or use of toxic, highly toxic, and corrosive compressed gases in quantities that exceed the quantity thresholds for gases requiring special provisions shall be classified as Protection Level 4. [**55:**6.3.2.4]

63.2.3.2.5 Protection Level 5. Buildings and portions thereof used for fabrication of semiconductors or semiconductor research and development and containing quantities of hazardous materials exceeding the maximum allowable quantities of high hazard level 5 contents permitted in control areas shall be classified as Protection Level 5. [**55:**6.3.2.5]

63.2.4 Gas Rooms. Where a gas room is used to increase the threshold quantity for a gas requiring special provisions or where otherwise required by the material- or application-specific requirements of Chapters 7 through 15 of NFPA 55, the room shall meet the requirements of 63.2.4.1 through 63.2.4.5. [**55:**6.44]

63.2.4.1 Pressure Control. Gas rooms shall operate at a negative pressure in relationship to the surrounding area. [**55:**6.4.1]

63.2.4.2 Exhaust Ventilation. Gas rooms shall be provided with an exhaust ventilation system. [**55:**6.4.2]

63.2.4.3 Construction. Gas rooms shall be constructed in accordance with the building code. [**55:**6.4.3]

63.2.4.4 Separation. Gas rooms shall be separated from other occupancies by a minimum of 1-hour fire resistance. [**55:**6.4.4]

63.2.4.5 Limitation on Contents. The function of compressed gas rooms shall be limited to storage and use of compressed gases and associated equipment and supplies. [**55:**6.4.5]

Table 63.2.3.1.1 Maximum Allowable Quantity (MAQ) of Hazardous Materials per Control Area (Quantity Thresholds for Gases Requiring Special Provisions)

Material	Class	High Hazard Protection Level	Storage Solid Pounds	Storage Liquid Gallons	Storage Gas[a] scf (lb)	Use — Closed Systems Solid Pounds	Use — Closed Systems Liquid Gallons	Use — Closed Systems Gas[a] scf (lb)	Use — Open Systems Solid Pounds	Use — Open Systems Liquid Gallons
Cryogenic fluid	Flammable	2	NA	45[b,c]	NA	NA	45[b,c]	NA	NA	45[b,c]
	Oxidizing	3	NA	45[d,e]	NA	NA	45[d,e]	NA	NA	45[d,e]
	Inert	NA	NA	NL	NA	NA	NL	NA	NA	NL
Flammable, gas[f]	Gaseous	2	NA	NA	1000[d,e]	NA	NA	1000[d,e]	NA	NA
	Liquefied	2	NA	NA	(150)[d,e]	NA	NA	(150)[d,e]	NA	NA
	LP	2	NA	NA	(300)[g,h,i]	NA	NA	(300)[g]	NA	NA
Inert gas	Gaseous	NA	NA	NA	NL	NA	NA	NL	NA	NA
	Liquefied	NA	NA	NA	NL	NA	NA	NL	NA	NA
Oxidizing gas	Gaseous	3	NA	NA	1500[d,e]	NA	NA	1500[d,e]	NA	NA
	Liquefied	3	NA	NA	(150)[d,e]	NA	NA	(150)[d,e]	NA	NA
Pyrophoric gas	Gaseous	2	NA	NA	50[d,j]	NA	NA	50[d,j]	NA	NA
	Liquefied	2	NA	NA	(4)[d,j]	NA	NA	(4)[d,j]	NA	NA
Unstable (reactive) gas	Gaseous									
	4 or 3 detonable	1	NA	NA	10[d,j]	NA	NA	10[d,j]	NA	NA
	3 nondetonable	2	NA	NA	50[d,e]	NA	NA	50[d,e]	NA	NA
	2	3	NA	NA	750[d,e]	NA	NA	750[d,e]	NA	NA
	1	NA	NA	NA	NL	NA	NA	NL	NA	NA
Unstable (reactive) gas	Liquefied									
	4 or 3 detonable	1	NA	NA	(1)[d,j]	NA	NA	(1)[d,j]	NA	NA
	3 nondetonable	2	NA	NA	(2)[d,e]	NA	NA	(2)[d,e]	NA	NA
	2	3	NA	NA	(150)[d,e]	NA	NA	(150)[d,e]	NA	NA
	1	NA	NA	NA	NL	NA	NA	NL	NA	NA
Corrosive gas	Gaseous	4	NA	NA	810[d,e]	NA	NA	810[d,e]	NA	NA
	Liquefied		NA	NA	(150)[d,e]	NA	NA	(150)[d,e]	NA	NA
Highly toxic gas	Gaseous	4	NA	NA	20[e,k]	NA	NA	20[e,k]	NA	NA
	Liquefied		NA	NA	(4)[e,k]	NA	NA	(4)[e,k]	NA	NA
Toxic gas	Gaseous	4	NA	NA	810[d,e]	NA	NA	810[d,e]	NA	NA
	Liquefied		NA	NA	(150)[d,e]	NA	NA	(150)[d,e]	NA	NA

NA: Not applicable within the context of NFPA 55 (refer to the applicable building or fire code for additional information on these materials).
NL: Not limited in quantity.
Notes:
(1) For use of control areas, see Section 6.2 of NFPA 55.
(2) Table values in parentheses or brackets correspond to the unit name in parentheses or brackets at the top of the column.
(3) The aggregate quantity in use and storage is not permitted to exceed the quantity listed for storage. In addition, quantities in specific occupancies are not permitted to exceed the limits in the building code.
[a]Measured at NTP [70°F (20°C) and 14.7 psi (101.3 kPa)].
[b]None allowed in unsprinklered buildings unless stored or used in gas rooms or in approved gas cabinets or exhausted enclosures, as specified in this code.
[c]With pressure-relief devices for stationary or portable containers vented directly outdoors or to an exhaust hood.
[d]Quantities are permitted to be increased 100 percent where stored or used in approved cabinets, gas cabinets, exhausted enclosures, gas rooms, as appropriate for the material stored. Where Footnote e also applies, the increase for the quantities in both footnotes is permitted to be applied accumulatively.
[e]Maximum quantities are permitted to be increased 100 percent in buildings equipped throughout with an automatic sprinkler system in accordance with NFPA 13, *Standard for the Installation of Sprinkler Systems*. Where Footnote d also applies, the increase for the quantities in both footnotes is permitted to be applied accumulatively.
[f]Flammable gases in the fuel tanks of mobile equipment or vehicles are permitted to exceed the MAQ where the equipment is stored and operated in accordance with the applicable fire code.
[g]See NFPA 58, *Liquefied Petroleum Gas Code*, and Chapter 69 for requirements for liquefied petroleum gas (LP-Gas). LP-Gas is not within the scope of NFPA 55 or Chapter 63.
[h]Additional storage locations are required to be separated by a minimum of 300 ft (92 m).
[i]In mercantile occupancies, storage of LP-Gas is limited to a maximum of 200 lb (91 kg) in nominal 1 lb (0.45 kg) LP-Gas containers.
[j]Permitted only in buildings equipped throughout with an automatic sprinkler system in accordance with NFPA 13.
[k]Allowed only where stored or used in gas rooms or in approved gas cabinets or exhausted enclosures, as specified in this code.
[**55:** Table 6.3.1.1]

63.2.5 Detached Buildings. Occupancies used for the storage or use of compressed gases, including individual bulk hydrogen compressed gas systems in quantities exceeding those specified in Table 63.2.5, shall be in detached buildings constructed in accordance with the provisions of the building code. [55:6.5]

Table 63.2.5 Detached Buildings Required Where Quantity of Material Exceeds Amount Shown

Gas Hazard	Class	Quantity of Material	
		scf	Nm³
Individual bulk hydrogen compressed gas systems	NA	15,000	425
Unstable reactive (detonable)	4 or 3	Quantity thresholds for gases requiring special provisions*	
Unstable reactive (nondetonable)	3	2,000	57
Unstable reactive (nondetonable)	2	10,000	283
Pyrophoric gas	NA	2,000	57

NA: Not applicable.
*See Table 63.2.3.1.1
[55: Table 6.5]

63.2.6 Weather Protection.

63.2.6.1 For other than explosive materials and hazardous materials presenting a detonation hazard, a weather protection structure shall be permitted to be used for sheltering outdoor storage or use areas, without requiring such areas to be classified as indoor storage or use. [55:6.6.1]

63.2.6.2 Weather protected areas constructed in accordance with 63.2.6.4 shall be regulated as outdoor storage or use. [55:6.6.2]

63.2.6.3 Weather protected areas that are not constructed in accordance with 63.2.6.4 shall be regulated as indoor storage or use. [55:6.6.2.1]

63.2.6.4 Buildings or structures used for weather protection shall be in accordance with the following:

(1) The building or structure shall be constructed of noncombustible materials.
(2) Walls shall not obstruct more than one side of the structure.
(3) Walls shall be permitted to obstruct portions of multiple sides of the structure, provided that the obstructed area does not exceed 25 percent of the structure's perimeter area.
(4) The building or structure shall be limited to a maximum area of 1500 ft² (140 m²), with increases in area allowed by the building code based on occupancy and type of construction.
(5) The distance from the structure constructed as weather protection to buildings, lot lines, public ways, or means of egress to a public way shall not be less than the distance required for an outside hazardous material storage or use area without weather protection based on the hazard classification of the materials contained.
(6) Reductions in separation distance shall be permitted based on the use of fire barrier walls where permitted for specific materials in accordance with the requirements of Chapters 7 through 11 of NFPA 55. [55:6.6.3]

63.2.7* Electrical Equipment. Electrical wiring and equipment shall be in accordance with this subsection and *NFPA 70*. [55:6.7]

63.2.7.1 Standby Power.

63.2.7.1.1 Where the following systems are required by NFPA 55 for the storage or use of compressed gases or cryogenic fluids that exceed the quantity thresholds for gases requiring special provisions, such systems shall be connected to a standby power system in accordance with *NFPA 70*:

(1) Mechanical ventilation
(2) Treatment systems
(3) Temperature controls
(4) Alarms
(5) Detection systems
(6) Other electrically operated systems [55:6.7.1.1]

63.2.7.1.2 The requirements of 63.2.7.1.1 shall not apply where emergency power is provided in accordance with 63.2.7.2 and *NFPA 70*. [55:6.7.1.2]

63.2.7.2 Emergency Power. When emergency power is required, the system shall meet the requirements for a Level 2 system in accordance with NFPA 110, *Standard for Emergency and Standby Power Systems*. [55:6.7.2]

63.2.8* Employee Alarm System. Where required by government regulations, an employee alarm system shall be provided to allow warning for necessary emergency action as called for in the emergency action plan required by 4.2.1.1 of NFPA 55, or for reaction time for safe egress of employees from the workplace or the immediate work area, or both. [55:6.8]

63.2.9 Explosion Control. Explosion control shall be provided as required by Table 63.2.9 in accordance with NFPA 68, *Standard on Explosion Protection by Deflagration Venting*, or NFPA 69, *Standard on Explosion Prevention Systems*, where amounts of compressed gases in storage or use exceed the quantity thresholds requiring special provisions. [55:6.9]

Table 63.2.9 Explosion Control Requirements

Material	Class	Explosion Control Methods	
		Barricade Construction	Explosion Venting or Prevention Systems
Flammable cryogenic fluid	—	Not required	Required
Flammable gas	Nonliquefied	Not required	Required
	Liquefied	Not required	Required
Pyrophoric gas	—	Not required	Required
Unstable reactive gas	4	Required	Not required
	3 (detonable)	Required	Not required
	3 (nondetonable)	Not required	Required

[55: Table 6.9]

63.2.10* Fire Protection Systems. Except as provided in 63.2.10.1, buildings or portions thereof required to comply with Protection Levels 1 through 5 shall be protected by an approved automatic fire sprinkler system complying with Section 13.3 and NFPA 13. [**55**:6.10]

63.2.10.1 Rooms or areas that are of noncombustible construction with wholly noncombustible contents shall not be required to be protected by an automatic fire sprinkler system. [**55**:6.10.1]

63.2.10.2 Sprinkler System Design.

63.2.10.2.1 When sprinkler protection is required, the area in which compressed gases or cryogenic fluids are stored or used shall be protected with a sprinkler system designed to be not less than that required by NFPA 13 for Ordinary Hazard Group 2. [**55**:6.10.2.1]

63.2.10.2.2 When sprinkler protection is required, the area in which the flammable or pyrophoric compressed gases or cryogenic fluids are stored or used shall be protected with a sprinkler system designed to be not less than that required by NFPA 13 for Extra Hazard Group 1. [**55**:6.10.2.2]

63.2.11 Lighting. Approved lighting by natural or artificial means shall be provided for areas of storage or use. [**55**:6.11]

63.2.12 Hazard Identification Signs.

63.2.12.1 Location. Hazard identification signs shall be placed at all entrances to locations where compressed gases are produced, stored, used, or handled in accordance with NFPA 704, *Standard System for the Identification of the Hazards of Materials for Emergency Response*. [**55**:6.12.1]

63.2.12.1.1 Ratings shall be assigned in accordance with NFPA 704. [**55**:6.12.1.1]

63.2.12.1.2 Rooms or cabinets containing compressed gases shall be conspicuously labeled as follows:

COMPRESSED GAS

63.2.12.1.3 The AHJ shall be permitted to waive 63.2.12.1.1 where consistent with safety. [**55**:6.12.1.2]

63.2.12.2 Application. Signage shall be provided as specified in 63.2.12.2.1 and 63.2.12.2.2. [**55**:6.11.2]

63.2.12.2.1 Signs. Signs shall not be obscured or removed. [**55**:6.12.2.1]

63.2.12.2.2 No Smoking. Signs prohibiting smoking or open flames within 25 ft (7.6 m) of area perimeters shall be provided in areas where toxic, highly toxic, corrosive, unstable reactive, flammable, oxidizing, or pyrophoric gases are produced, stored, or used. [**55**:6.12.2.2]

63.2.13 Spill Control, Drainage, and Secondary Containment. Spill control, drainage, and secondary containment shall not be required for compressed gases. [**55**:6.13]

63.2.14 Shelving.

63.2.14.1 Shelves used for the storage of cylinders, containers, and tanks shall be of noncombustible construction and designed to support the weight of the materials stored. [**55**:6.14.1]

63.2.14.2 In seismically active areas, shelves and containers shall be secured from overturning. [**55**:6.14.2]

63.2.15 Vent Pipe Termination. The termination point for piped vent systems serving cylinders, containers, tanks, and gas systems used for the purpose of operational or emergency venting shall be located to prevent impingement exposure on the system served and to minimize the effects of high temperature thermal radiation or the effects of contact with the gas from the escaping plume to the supply system, personnel, adjacent structures, and ignition sources. [**55**:6.15]

63.2.16 Ventilation. Indoor storage and use areas and storage buildings for compressed gases and cryogenic fluids shall be provided with mechanical exhaust ventilation or fixed natural ventilation, where natural ventilation is shown to be acceptable for the material as stored. [**55**: 6.16]

63.2.16.1 Compressed Air. The requirements of 63.2.16 shall not apply to cylinders, containers, and tanks containing compressed air. [**55**:6.16.1]

63.2.16.2 Ventilation Systems. In addition to the requirements of 63.2.16, ventilation systems shall be designed and installed in accordance with the requirements of the mechanical code. [**55**:6.16.2]

63.2.16.3 Mechanical Exhaust Ventilation. Where mechanical exhaust ventilation is provided, the system shall be operational during the time the building or space is occupied. [**55**:6.16.3]

63.2.16.4 Continuous Operation. When operation of ventilation systems is required, systems shall operate continuously unless an alternative design is approved by the AHJ. [**55**:6.16.3.1]

63.2.16.5 Ventilation Rate Mechanical exhaust or fixed natural ventilation shall be provided at a rate of not less than 1 scf/min/ft^2 (0.3048 Nm^3/min/m^2) of floor area over the area of storage or use. [**55**:6.16.3.2]

63.2.16.6 Shutoff Controls. Where powered ventilation is provided, a manual shutoff switch shall be provided outside the room in a position adjacent to the principal access door to the room or in an approved location. [**55**:6.16.3.3]

63.2.16.7 Manual Shutoff Switch. The switch shall be the break-glass or equivalent type and shall be labeled as follows:

WARNING:

VENTILATION SYSTEM EMERGENCY SHUTOFF [**55**:6.16.3.3.1]

63.2.16.8 Inlets to the Exhaust System.

63.2.16.8.1 The exhaust ventilation system design shall take into account the density of the potential gases released. [**55**:6.16.4.1]

63.2.16.8.2 For gases that are heavier than air, exhaust shall be taken from a point within 12 in. (305 mm) of the floor. The use of supplemental inlets shall be allowed to be installed at points above the 12 in. (305 mm) threshold level. [**55**:6.16.4.2]

63.2.16.8.3 For gases that are lighter than air, exhaust shall be taken from a point within 12 in. (305 mm) of the ceiling. The use of supplemental inlets shall be allowed to be installed at points below the 12 in. (305 mm) threshold level. [**55**:6.16.4.3]

63.2.16.8.4 The location of both the exhaust and inlet air openings shall be designed to provide air movement across all portions of the floor or ceiling of the room to prevent the accumulation of vapors within the ventilated space. [**55:**6.16.4.4]

63.2.16.9 Recirculation of Exhaust. Exhaust ventilation shall not be recirculated within the room or building if the cylinders, containers, or tanks stored are capable of releasing hazardous gases. [**55:**6.16.5]

63.2.16.10 Ventilation Discharge. Ventilation discharge systems shall terminate at a point not less than 50 ft (15 m) from intakes of air-handling systems, air-conditioning equipment, and air compressors. [**55:**6.16.6]

63.2.16.11 Air Intakes. Storage and use of compressed gases shall be located not less than 50 ft (15 m) from air intakes. For material-specific requirements, see 63.3.4 through 63.3.10. [**55:**6.16.7]

63.2.17 Gas Cabinets. Where a gas cabinet is required, is used to provide separation of gas hazards, or is used to increase the threshold quantity for a gas requiring special provisions, the gas cabinet shall be in accordance with the requirements of 63.2.17.1 through 63.2.17.5. [**55:**6.17]

63.2.17.1 Construction.

63.2.17.1.1 Materials of Construction. The gas cabinet shall be constructed of not less than 0.097 in. (2.46 mm) (12 gauge) steel. [**55:**6.17.1.1]

63.2.17.1.2 Access to Controls. The gas cabinet shall be provided with self-closing limited access ports or noncombustible windows to give access to equipment controls. [**55:**6.17.1.2]

63.2.17.1.3 Self-Closing Doors. The gas cabinet shall be provided with self-closing doors. [**55:**6.17.1.3]

63.2.17.2 Ventilation Requirements.

63.2.17.2.1 The gas cabinet shall be provided with an exhaust ventilation system designed to operate at a negative pressure relative to the surrounding area. [**55:**6.17.2.1]

63.2.17.2.2 Where toxic, highly toxic, pyrophoric, unstable reactive Class 3 or Class 4, or corrosive gases are contained, the velocity at the face of access ports or windows, with the access port or window open, shall be not less than 200 ft/min (61 m/min) average, with not less than 150 ft/min (46 m/min) at any single point. [**55:**6.17.2.2]

63.2.17.3 Fire Protection. Gas cabinets used to contain toxic, highly toxic, or pyrophoric gases shall be internally sprinklered. [**55:**6.17.3]

63.2.17.4 Quantity Limits. Gas cabinets shall contain not more than three containers, cylinders, or tanks. [**55:**6.17.4]

63.2.17.5 Separation of Incompatibles. Incompatible gases, as defined by Table 63.3.1.11.2, shall be stored or used within separate gas cabinets. [**55:**6.17.5]

63.2.18 Exhausted Enclosures.

63.2.18.1 Ventilation Requirements. Where an exhausted enclosure is required or used to increase the threshold quantity for a gas requiring special provisions, the exhausted enclosure shall be provided with an exhaust ventilation system designed to operate at a negative pressure in relationship to the surrounding area. [**55:**6.18.1]

63.2.18.1.1 Control Velocity at Access Openings. Where toxic, highly toxic, pyrophoric, unstable reactive Class 3 or Class 4, or corrosive gases are contained, the velocity at the face openings providing access shall be not less than 200 ft/min (61 m/min) average, with not less than 150 ft/min (46 m/min) at any single point. [**55:**6.18.1.1]

63.2.18.1.2 Separation of Incompatible Gases Within Enclosures. Cylinders, containers, and tanks within enclosures shall be separated in accordance with Table 63.3.1.11.2. [**55:**6.18.1.2]

63.2.18.1.3 Fire Protection. Exhausted enclosures shall be internally sprinklered. [**55:**6.18.1.3]

63.2.18.2 Separation. Incompatible gases, as defined by Table 63.3.1.11.2, shall be stored or used within separate exhausted enclosures. [**55:**6.18.2]

63.2.19* Source Valve. Bulk gas systems shall be provided with a source valve. [**55:**6.19]

63.2.19.1 The source valve shall be marked. [**55:**6.19.1]

63.2.19.2 The source valve shall be designated on the design drawings for the installation. [**55:**6.19.2]

63.3 Compressed Gases.

63.3.1 General. The storage, use, and handling of compressed gases in containers, cylinders, and tanks shall be in accordance with the provisions of Chapters 1 through 7 of NFPA 55. [**55:**7.1]

63.3.1.1 Compressed Gas Systems.

63.3.1.1.1 Design. Compressed gas systems shall be designed for the intended use and shall be designed by persons competent in such design. [**55:**7.1.1.1]

63.3.1.1.2 Installation. Installation of bulk compressed gas systems shall be supervised by personnel knowledgeable in the application of the standards for their construction and use. [**55:**7.1.1.2]

63.3.1.2 Insulated Liquid Carbon Dioxide Systems. Insulated liquid carbon dioxide systems shall be in accordance with Chapter 13 of NFPA 55. [**55:**7.1.2]

63.3.1.3* Insulated Liquid Nitrous Oxide Systems. (Reserved)

63.3.1.4* Listed and Approved Hydrogen Equipment.

63.3.1.4.1 Listed and approved hydrogen generating and consuming equipment shall be in accordance with the listing requirements and manufacturers' instructions. [**55:**7.1.4.1]

63.3.1.4.2 Such equipment shall not be required to meet the requirements of Chapter 7 of NFPA 55. [**55:**7.1.4.2]

63.3.1.5* Metal Hydride Storage Systems.

63.3.1.5.1 General Requirements.

63.3.1.5.1.1 Metal Hydride Storage System Requirements. The storage and use of metal hydride storage systems shall be in accordance with 63.3.1.5. [**55:**7.1.5.1.1]

63.3.1.5.1.2 Metal Hydride Systems Storing or Supplying Hydrogen. Those portions of the system that are used as a means to store or supply hydrogen shall also comply with Chapter 7 and Chapter 10 of NFPA 55 as applicable. [**55:**7.1.5.1.2]

63.3.1.5.1.3 Classification. The hazard classification of the metal hydride storage system, as required by 63.1.4.1 and 63.1.4.3, shall be based on the hydrogen stored without regard to the metal hydride content. [**55:**7.1.5.1.3]

63.3.1.5.1.4 Listed or Approved Systems. Metal hydride storage systems shall be listed or approved for the application and designed in a manner that prevents the addition or removal of the metal hydride by other than the original equipment manufacturer. [**55:**7.1.5.1.4]

63.3.1.5.1.5 Containers, Design, and Construction. Compressed gas cylinders, containers, and tanks used for metal hydride storage systems shall be designed and constructed in accordance with 63.3.1.6.1. [**55:**7.1.5.1.5]

63.3.1.5.1.6 Service Life and Inspection of Containers. Metal hydride storage system cylinders, containers, or tanks shall be inspected, tested, and requalified for service at not less than 5-year intervals. [**55:**7.1.5.1.6]

63.3.1.5.1.7 Marking and Labeling. Marking and labeling of cylinders, containers, tanks, and systems shall be in accordance with 63.3.1.6 and the requirements in 63.3.1.5.1.7.1 through 63.3.1.5.1.7.4. [**55:**7.1.5.1.7]

63.3.1.5.1.7.1 System Marking. Metal hydride storage systems shall be marked with the following:

(1) Manufacturer's name
(2) Service life indicating the last date the system can be used
(3) A unique code or serial number specific to the unit
(4) System name or product code that identifies the system by the type of chemistry used in the system
(5) Emergency contact name, telephone number, or other contact information
(6) Limitations on refilling of containers to include rated charging pressure and capacity [**55:**7.1.5.1.7.1]

63.3.1.5.1.7.2 Valve Marking. Metal hydride storage system valves shall be marked with the following:

(1) Manufacturer's name
(2) Service life indicating the last date the valve can be used
(3) Metal hydride service in which the valve can be used or a product code that is traceable to this information [**55:**7.1.5.1.7.2]

63.3.1.5.1.7.3 Pressure Relief Device Marking. Metal hydride storage system pressure relief devices shall be marked with the following:

(1) Manufacturer's name
(2) Metal hydride service in which the device can be used or a product code that is traceable to this information
(3) Activation parameters to include temperature, pressure, or both [**55:**7.1.5.1.7.3]

(A) Pressure Relief Devices Integral to Container Valves. The required markings for pressure relief devices that are integral components of valves used on cylinders, containers, and tanks shall be allowed to be placed on the valve. [**55:**7.1.5.1.7.3(A)]

63.3.1.5.1.7.4 Pressure Vessel Markings. Cylinders, containers, and tanks used in metal hydride storage systems shall be marked with the following:

(1) Manufacturer's name
(2) Design specification to which the vessel was manufactured
(3) Authorized body approving the design and initial inspection and test of the vessel
(4) Manufacturer's original test date
(5) Unique serial number for the vessel
(6) Service life identifying the last date the vessel can be used

(7) System name or product code that identifies the system by the type of chemistry used in the system [**55:**7.1.5.1.7.4]

63.3.1.5.1.8 Temperature Extremes. Metal hydride storage systems, whether full or partially full, shall not be exposed to artificially created high temperatures exceeding 125°F (52°C) or subambient (low) temperatures unless designed for use under the exposed conditions. [**55:**7.1.5.1.8]

63.3.1.5.1.9 Falling Objects. Metal hydride storage systems shall not be placed in areas where they are capable of being damaged by falling objects. [**55:**7.1.5.1.9]

63.3.1.5.1.10 Piping Systems. Piping, including tubing, valves, fittings, and pressure regulators, serving metal hydride storage systems shall be maintained gastight to prevent leakage. [**55:**7.1.5.1.10]

63.3.1.5.1.10.1 Leaking Systems. Leaking systems shall be removed from service. [**55:**7.1.5.1.10.1]

63.3.1.5.1.11 Refilling of Containers. The refilling of listed or approved metal hydride storage systems shall be in accordance with the listing requirements and manufacturers' instructions. [**55:**7.1.5.1.11]

63.3.1.5.1.11.1 Industrial Trucks. The refilling of metal hydride storage systems serving powered industrial trucks shall be in accordance with NFPA 2, *Hydrogen Technologies Code*. [**55:**7.1.5.1.11.1]

63.3.1.5.1.11.2 Hydrogen Purity. The purity of hydrogen used for the purpose of refilling containers shall be in accordance with the listing and the manufacturers' instructions. [**55:**7.1.5.1.11.2]

63.3.1.5.1.12 Electrical. Electrical components for metal hydride storage systems shall be designed, constructed, and installed in accordance with *NFPA 70, National Electrical Code*. [**55:**7.1.5.1.12]

63.3.1.5.2 Portable Containers or Systems.

63.3.1.5.2.1 Securing Containers. Containers, cylinders, and tanks shall be secured in accordance with 63.3.1.9.5. [**55:**7.1.5.2.1]

63.3.1.5.2.1.1 Use on Mobile Equipment. Where a metal hydride storage system is used on mobile equipment, the equipment shall be designed to restrain containers, cylinders, or tanks from dislodgement, slipping, or rotating when the equipment is in motion. [**55:**7.1.5.2.1.1]

63.3.1.5.2.1.2 Motorized Equipment. Metal hydride storage systems used on motorized equipment shall be installed in a manner that protects valves, pressure regulators, fittings, and controls against accidental impact. [**55:**7.1.5.2.1.2]

(A) Protection from Damage. Metal hydride storage systems, including cylinders, containers, tanks, and fittings, shall not extend beyond the platform of the mobile equipment. [**55:**7.1.5.2.1.2(A)]

63.3.1.5.2.2 Valves. Valves on containers, cylinders, and tanks shall remain closed except when containers are connected to closed systems and ready for use. [**55:**7.1.5.2.2]

63.3.1.6 Cylinders, Containers, and Tanks.

63.3.1.6.1 Design and Construction. Cylinders, containers, and tanks shall be designed, fabricated, tested, and marked (stamped) in accordance with regulations of DOT, Transport Canada (TC) *Transportation of Dangerous Goods Regulations*, or the ASME *Boiler and Pressure Vessel Code*, "Rules for the Construction of Unfired Pressure Vessels," Section VIII. [**55:**7.1.6.1]

63.3.1.6.2 Defective Cylinders, Containers, and Tanks.

63.3.1.6.2.1 Defective cylinders, containers, and tanks shall be returned to the supplier. [**55:**7.1.6.2.1]

63.3.1.6.2.2 Suppliers shall repair the cylinders, containers, and tanks, remove them from service, or dispose of them in an approved manner. [**55:**7.1.6.2.2]

63.3.1.6.2.3 Suppliers shall ensure that defective cylinders, containers, and tanks that have been repaired are evaluated by qualified individuals to verify that the needed repairs and any required testing has been performed and that those repaired or tested are in a serviceable condition before returning them to service. [**55:**7.1.6.2.3]

63.3.1.6.3 Supports. Stationary cylinders, containers, and tanks shall be provided with engineered supports of noncombustible material on noncombustible foundations. [**55:**7.1.6.3]

63.3.1.6.4 Cylinders, Containers, and Tanks Containing Residual Gas. Compressed gas cylinders, containers, and tanks containing residual product shall be treated as full except when being examined, serviced, or refilled by a gas manufacturer, authorized cylinder requalifier, or distributor. [**55:**7.1.6.4]

63.3.1.6.5 Pressure Relief Devices.

63.3.1.6.5.1 When required by 63.3.1.6.5.2, pressure relief devices shall be provided to protect containers and systems containing compressed gases from rupture in the event of overpressure from thermal exposure. [**55:**7.1.6.5.1]

63.3.1.6.5.2 Pressure relief devices to protect containers shall be designed and provided in accordance with CGA S-1.1, *Pressure Relief Device Standards – Part 1 – Cylinders for Compressed Gases,* for cylinders; CGA S-1.2, *Pressure Relief Device Standards – Part 2 – Cargo and Portable Tanks for Compressed Gases,* for portable tanks; and CGA S-1.3, *Pressure Relief Device Standards – Part 3 – Stationary Storage Containers for Compressed Gases,* for stationary tanks or in accordance with applicable equivalent requirements in the country of use. [**55:**7.1.6.5.2]

63.3.1.6.5.3 Pressure relief devices shall be sized in accordance with the specifications to which the container was fabricated. [**55:**7.1.6.5.3]

63.3.1.6.5.4 The pressure relief device shall have the capacity to prevent the maximum design pressure of the container or system from being exceeded. [**55:**7.1.6.5.4]

63.3.1.6.5.5 Pressure relief devices shall be arranged to discharge unobstructed to the open air in such a manner as to prevent any impingement of escaping gas upon the container, adjacent structures, or personnel. This requirement shall not apply to DOT specification containers having an internal volume of 2.0 scf (0.057 Nm^3) or less. [**55:**7.1.6.5.5]

63.3.1.6.5.6 Pressure relief devices or vent piping shall be designed or located so that moisture cannot collect and freeze in a manner that would interfere with operation of the device. [**55:**7.1.6.5.6]

63.3.1.7 Cathodic Protection. Where required, cathodic protection shall be in accordance with 63.3.1.7. [**55:**7.1.7]

63.3.1.7.1 Operation. Where installed, cathodic protection systems shall be operated and maintained to continuously provide corrosion protection. [**55:**7.1.7.1]

63.3.1.7.2 Inspection. Container systems equipped with cathodic protection shall be inspected for the intended operation by a cathodic protection tester. The frequency of inspection shall be determined by the designer of the cathodic protection system. [**55:**7.1.7.2]

63.3.1.7.2.1 The cathodic protection tester shall be certified as being qualified by the National Association of Corrosion Engineers, International (NACE). [**55:**7.1.7.2.1]

63.3.1.7.3 Impressed Current Systems. Systems equipped with impressed current cathodic protection systems shall be inspected in accordance with the requirements of the design and 63.3.1.5.1.12. [**55:**7.1.7.3]

63.3.1.7.3.1 The design limits of the cathodic protection system shall be available to the AHJ upon request. [**55:**7.1.7.3.1]

63.3.1.7.3.2 The system owner shall maintain the following records to demonstrate that the cathodic protection is in conformance with the requirements of the design:

(1) The results of inspections of the system
(2) The results of testing that has been completed [**55:**7.1.7.3.2]

63.3.1.7.4 Repairs, maintenance, or replacement of a cathodic protection system shall be under the supervision of a corrosion expert certified by NACE. [**55:**7.1.7.4]

63.3.1.7.4.1 The corrosion expert shall be certified by NACE as a senior corrosion technologist, a cathodic protection specialist, or a corrosion specialist or shall be a registered engineer with registration in a field that includes education and experience in corrosion control. [**55:**7.1.7.4.1]

63.3.1.8 Labeling Requirements.

63.3.1.8.1 Containers. Individual compressed gas containers, cylinders, and tanks shall be marked or labeled in accordance with DOT requirements or those of the applicable regulatory agency. [**55:**7.1.8.1]

63.3.1.8.2 Label Maintenance. The labels applied by the gas manufacturer to identify the liquefied or nonliquefied compressed gas cylinder contents shall not be altered or removed by the user. [**55:**7.1.8.2]

63.3.1.8.3 Stationary Compressed Gas Containers, Cylinders, and Tanks.

63.3.1.8.3.1 Stationary compressed gas containers, cylinders, and tanks shall be marked in accordance with NFPA 704. [**55:**7.1.8.3.1]

63.3.1.8.3.2 Markings shall be visible from any direction of approach. [**55:**7.1.8.3.2]

63.3.1.8.4 Piping Systems.

63.3.1.8.4.1 Except as provided in 63.3.1.8.4.2, piping systems shall be marked in accordance with ASME A13.1, *Scheme for the Identification of Piping Systems,* or other applicable standards as follows:

(1) Marking shall include the name of the gas and a direction-of-flow arrow.

(2) Piping that is used to convey more than one gas at various times shall be marked to provide clear identification and warning of the hazard.
(3) Markings for piping systems shall be provided at the following locations:
   (a) At each critical process control valve
   (b) At wall, floor, or ceiling penetrations
   (c) At each change of direction
   (d) At a minimum of every 20 ft (6.1 m) or fraction thereof throughout the piping run [**55**:7.1.8.4.1]

63.3.1.8.4.2 Piping within gas manufacturing plants, gas processing plants, refineries, and similar occupancies shall be marked in an approved manner. [**55**:7.1.8.4.2]

63.3.1.9 Security.

63.3.1.9.1 General. Compressed gas containers, cylinders, tanks, and systems shall be secured against accidental dislodgement and against access by unauthorized personnel. [**55**:7.1.9.1]

63.3.1.9.2* Security of Areas. Storage, use, and handling areas shall be secured against unauthorized entry. [**55**:7.1.9.2]

63.3.1.9.3 Administrative controls shall be allowed to be used to control access to individual storage, use, and handling areas located in secure facilities not accessible by the general public. [**55**:7.1.9.2.1]

63.3.1.9.4 Physical Protection.

63.3.1.9.4.1 Compressed gas containers, cylinders, tanks, and systems that could be exposed to physical damage shall be protected. [**55**:7.1.9.3.1]

63.3.1.9.4.2 Guard posts or other means shall be provided to protect compressed gas cylinders, containers, tanks, and systems indoors and outdoors from vehicular damage in accordance with Section 4.11 of NFPA 55. [**55**:7.1.9.3.2]

63.3.1.9.5 Securing Compressed Gas Containers, Cylinders, and Tanks. Compressed gas containers, cylinders, and tanks in use or in storage shall be secured to prevent them from falling or being knocked over by corralling them and securing them to a cart, framework, or fixed object by use of a restraint, unless otherwise permitted by 63.3.1.9.5.1 and 63.3.1.9.5.2. [**55**:7.1.9.4]

63.3.1.9.5.1 Compressed gas containers, cylinders, and tanks in the process of examination, servicing, and refilling shall not be required to be secured. [**55**:7.1.9.4.1]

63.3.1.9.5.2 At cylinder-filling plants, authorized cylinder requalifier's facilities, and distributors' warehouses, the nesting of cylinders shall be permitted as a means to secure cylinders. [**55**:7.1.9.4.2]

63.3.1.10 Valve Protection.

63.3.1.10.1 General. Compressed gas container, cylinder, and tank valves shall be protected from physical damage by means of protective caps, collars, or similar devices. [**55**:7.1.10.1]

63.3.1.10.1.1 Valve protection of individual valves shall not be required to be installed on individual cylinders, containers, or tanks installed on tube trailers or similar transportable bulk gas systems equipped with manifolds that are provided with a means of physical protection that will protect the valves from physical damage when the equipment is in use. Protective systems required by DOT for over the road transport shall provide an acceptable means of protection. [**55**:7.1.10.1.1]

63.3.1.10.1.1.1 Valve protection of individual valves shall not be required on cylinders, containers, or tanks that comprise bulk or non-bulk gas systems where the containers are stationary, or portable equipped with manifolds, that are provided with physical protection in accordance with Section 4.11 of NFPA 55 and 63.3.1.9.3 or other approved means. Protective systems required by DOT for over the road transport shall provide an acceptable means of protection. [**55**:7.1.10.1.1.1]

63.3.1.10.2 Valve-Protective Caps. Where compressed gas containers, cylinders, and tanks are designed to accept valve-protective caps, the user shall keep such caps on the compressed gas containers, cylinders, and tanks at all times, except when empty, being processed, or connected for use. [**55**:7.1.10.2]

63.3.1.10.3 Valve Outlet Caps or Plugs.

63.3.1.10.3.1 Gastight valve outlet caps or plugs shall be provided and in place for all full or partially full containers, cylinders, and tanks containing toxic, highly toxic, pyrophoric, or unstable reactive Class 3 or Class 4 gases that are in storage. [**55**:7.1.10.3.1]

63.3.1.10.3.2 Valve outlet caps and plugs shall be designed and rated for the container service pressure. [**55**:7.1.10.3.2]

63.3.1.11 Separation from Hazardous Conditions.

63.3.1.11.1 General.

63.3.1.11.1.1 Compressed gas containers, cylinders, tanks, and systems in storage or use shall be separated from materials and conditions that present exposure hazards to or from each other. [**55**:7.1.11.1]

63.3.1.11.2* Incompatible Materials. Gas cylinders, containers, and tanks shall be separated in accordance with Table 63.3.1.11.2. [**55**:7.1.11.2]

63.3.1.11.2.1 Subparagraph 63.3.1.11.2 shall not apply to gases contained within closed piping systems. [**55**:7.1.11.2.1]

63.3.1.11.2.2 The distances shown in Table 63.3.1.11.2 shall be permitted to be reduced without limit where compressed gas cylinders, tanks, and containers are separated by a barrier of noncombustible construction that has a fire resistance rating of at least 0.5 hour and interrupts the line of sight between the containers. [**55**:7.1.11.2.2]

63.3.1.11.2.3 The 20 ft (6.1 m) distance shall be permitted to be reduced to 5 ft (1.5 m) where one of the gases is enclosed in a gas cabinet or without limit where both gases are enclosed in gas cabinets. [**55**:7.1.11.2.3]

63.3.1.11.2.4 Cylinders without pressure relief devices shall not be stored without separation from flammable and pyrophoric gases with pressure relief devices. [**55**:7.1.11.2.4]

63.3.1.11.2.5 Spatial separation shall not be required between cylinders deemed to be incompatible in gas production facilities where cylinders are connected to manifolds for the purposes of filling, analysis of compressed gases or, manufacturing procedures, assuming the prescribed controls for the manufacture of gas mixtures are in place. [**55**:7.1.11.2.5]

Table 63.3.1.11.2 Separation of Gas Containers, Cylinders, and Tanks by Hazard Class

Gas Category	Other Gas	Unstable Reactive Class 2, Class 3, or Class 4		Corrosive		Oxidizing		Flammable		Pyrophoric		Toxic or Highly Toxic	
		ft	m	ft	m	ft	m	ft	m	ft	m	ft	m
Toxic or highly toxic	NR	20	6.1	20	6.1	20	6.1	20	6.1	20	6.1	—	—
Pyrophoric	NR	20	6.1	20	6.1	20	6.1	20	6.1	—	—	20	6.1
Flammable	NR	20	6.1	20	6.1	20	6.1	—	—	20	6.1	20	6.1
Oxidizing	NR	20	6.1	20	6.1	—	—	20	6.1	20	6.1	20	6.1
Corrosive	NR	20	6.1	—	—	20	6.1	20	6.1	20	6.1	20	6.1
Unstable reactive Class 2, Class 3, or Class 4	NR	—	—	20	6.1	20	6.1	20	6.1	20	6.1	20	6.1
Other gas	—	NR		NR		NR		NR		NR		NR	

NR: No separation required.
[55: Table 7.1.11.2]

63.3.1.11.3* Clearance from Combustibles and Vegetation. Combustible waste, vegetation, and similar materials shall be kept a minimum of 10 ft (3 m) from compressed gas containers, cylinders, tanks, and systems. [55:7.1.11.3]

63.3.1.11.3.1 A noncombustible partition without openings or penetrations and extending sides not less than 18 in. (457 mm) above and to the sides of the storage area shall be permitted in lieu of the minimum distance. [55:7.1.11.3.1]

63.3.1.11.3.2 The noncombustible partition shall be either an independent structure or the exterior wall of the building adjacent to the storage area. [55:7.1.11.3.2]

63.3.1.11.4 Ledges, Platforms, and Elevators. Compressed gas containers, cylinders, and tanks shall not be placed near elevators, unprotected platform ledges, or other areas where compressed gas containers, cylinders, or tanks could fall distances exceeding one-half the height of the container, cylinder, or tank. [55:7.1.11.4]

63.3.1.11.5 Temperature Extremes. Compressed gas containers, cylinders, and tanks, whether full or partially full, shall not be exposed to temperatures exceeding 125°F (52°C) or subambient (low) temperatures unless designed for use under such exposure. [55:7.1.11.5]

63.3.1.11.5.1 Compressed gas cylinders, containers, and tanks that have not been designed for use under elevated temperature conditions shall not be exposed to direct sunlight outdoors where ambient temperatures exceed 125°F (52°C). The use of a weather protected structure or shaded environment for storage or use shall be permitted as a means to protect against direct exposure to sunlight. [55:7.1.11.5.1]

63.3.1.11.6 Falling Objects. Compressed gas containers, cylinders, and tanks shall not be placed in areas where they are capable of being damaged by falling objects. [55:7.1.11.6]

63.3.1.11.7 Heating. Compressed gas containers, cylinders, and tanks, whether full or partially full, shall not be heated by devices that could raise the surface temperature of the container, cylinder, or tank to above 125°F (52°C). [55:7.1.11.7]

63.3.1.11.7.1 Electrically Powered Heating Devices. Electrical heating devices shall be in accordance with *NFPA 70*. [55:7.1.11.7.1]

63.3.1.11.7.2 Fail-Safe Design. Devices designed to maintain individual compressed gas containers, cylinders, or tanks at constant temperature shall be designed to be fail-safe. [55:7.1.11.7.2]

63.3.1.11.8 Sources of Ignition. Open flames and high-temperature devices shall not be used in a manner that creates a hazardous condition. [55:7.1.11.8]

63.3.1.11.9 Exposure to Chemicals. Compressed gas cylinders, containers, and tanks shall not be exposed to corrosive chemicals or fumes that could damage cylinders, containers, tanks, or valve-protective caps. [55:7.1.11.9]

63.3.1.11.10 Exposure to Electrical Circuits. Compressed gas containers, cylinders, and tanks shall not be placed where they could become a part of an electrical circuit. [55:7.1.11.10]

63.3.1.11.10.1* Electrical devices mounted on compressed gas piping, cylinders, containers, or tanks shall be installed, grounded, and bonded in accordance with the methods specified in *NFPA 70*. [55:7.1.11.10.1]

63.3.1.12 Service and Repair. Service, repair, modification, or removal of valves, pressure relief devices, or other compressed gas container, cylinder, or tank appurtenances shall be performed by trained personnel and with the permission of the container owner. [55:7.1.12]

63.3.1.13 Unauthorized Use. Compressed gas containers, cylinders, and tanks shall not be used for any purpose other than to serve as a vessel for containing the product for which it was designed. [55:7.1.13]

63.3.1.14 Containers, Cylinders, and Tanks Exposed to Fire. Compressed gas containers, cylinders, and tanks exposed to fire shall not be used or shipped while full or partially full until they are requalified in accordance with the pressure vessel code under which they were manufactured. [55:7.1.14]

63.3.1.15 Leaks, Damage, or Corrosion.

63.3.1.15.1 Removal from Service. Leaking, damaged, or corroded compressed gas containers, cylinders, and tanks shall be removed from service. [**55**:7.1.15.1]

63.3.1.15.2 Replacement and Repair. Leaking, damaged, or corroded compressed gas systems shall be replaced or repaired. [**55**:7.1.15.2]

63.3.1.15.3* Handling of Containers, Cylinders, and Tanks Removed from Service. Compressed gas containers, cylinders, and tanks that have been removed from service shall be handled in an approved manner. [**55**:7.1.15.3]

63.3.1.15.4 Leaking Systems. Compressed gas systems that are determined to be leaking, damaged, or corroded shall be repaired to a serviceable condition or shall be removed from service. [**55**:7.1.15.4]

63.3.1.16 Surfaces.

63.3.1.16.1 To prevent bottom corrosion, containers, cylinders, and tanks shall be protected from direct contact with soil or surfaces where water might accumulate. [**55**:7.1.16.1]

63.3.1.16.2 Surfaces shall be graded to prevent accumulation of water. [**55**:7.1.16.2]

63.3.1.17 Storage Area Temperature.

63.3.1.17.1 Compressed Gas Containers. Storage area temperatures shall not exceed 125°F (52°C). [**55**:7.1.17.1]

63.3.1.18 Underground Piping.

63.3.1.18.1 Underground piping shall be of welded construction without valves, unwelded mechanical joints, or connections installed underground. [**55**:7.1.18.1]

63.3.1.18.1.1 Valves or connections located in boxes or enclosures shall be permitted to be installed underground where such boxes or enclosures are accessible from above ground and where the valves or connections contained are isolated from direct contact with earth or fill. [**55**:7.1.18.1.1]

63.3.1.18.1.1.1 Valve boxes or enclosures installed in areas subject to vehicular traffic shall be constructed to resist uniformly distributed and concentrated live loads in accordance with the building code for areas designated as vehicular driveways and yards, subject to trucking. [**55**:7.1.18.1.1.1]

63.3.1.18.1.2* Piping installed in trench systems located below grade where the trench is open to above shall not be considered to be underground. [**55**:7.1.18.1.2]

63.3.1.18.2 Gas piping in contact with earth or other material that could corrode the piping shall be protected against corrosion in an approved manner. [**55**:7.1.18.2]

63.3.1.18.2.1 When cathodic protection is provided, it shall be in accordance with 63.3.1.7. [**55**:7.1.18.2.1]

63.3.1.18.3 Underground piping shall be installed on at least 6 in. (150 mm) of well-compacted bedding material. [**30**:27.6.5.1]

63.3.1.18.4 In areas subject to vehicle traffic, the pipe trench shall be deep enough to permit a cover of at least 18 in. (450 mm) of well-compacted backfill material and pavement. [**30**:27.6.5.2]

63.3.1.18.5 In paved areas where a minimum 2 in. (50 mm) of asphalt is used, backfill between the pipe and the asphalt shall be permitted to be reduced to 8 in. (200 mm) minimum. [**30**:27.6.5.3]

63.3.1.18.6 In paved areas where a minimum 4 in. (100 mm) of reinforced concrete is used, backfill between the pipe and the concrete shall be permitted to be reduced to 4 in. (100 mm) minimum. [**30**:27.6.5.4]

63.3.1.18.7 In areas not subject to vehicle traffic, the pipe trench shall be deep enough to permit a cover of at least 6 in. (150 mm) of well-compacted backfill material. [**30**:27.6.5.5]

63.3.1.18.8 A greater burial depth shall be provided when required by the manufacturer's instructions or where frost conditions are present. [**30**:27.6.5.6]

63.3.1.18.9 Piping within the same trench shall be separated horizontally by at least two pipe diameters. Separation shall not need to exceed 9 in. (230 mm). [**30**:27.6.5.7]

63.3.1.18.10 Two or more levels of pipes within the same trench shall be separated vertically by a minimum 6 in. (150 mm) of well-compacted bedding material. [**30**:27.6.5.8]

63.3.1.19 Cleaning and Purging of Gas Piping Systems.

63.3.1.19.1 General.

63.3.1.19.1.1 Piping systems shall be cleaned and purged in accordance with the requirements of 63.3.1.19 when one or more of the following conditions exist:

(1) When the system is installed and prior to being placed into service
(2) When there is a change in service
(3)*When there are alterations or repair of the system involving the replacement of parts or addition to the piping system and prior to returning the system to service
(4)*Where specified by the design standards or written procedures [**55**:7.1.19.1.1]

63.3.1.19.1.2 Cleaning and purging of the internal surfaces of piping systems shall be conducted by qualified individuals trained in cleaning and purging operations and procedures, including the recognition of potential hazards associated with cleaning and purging. [**55**:7.1.19.1.2]

63.3.1.19.1.3* A written cleaning or purging procedure shall be provided to establish the requirements for the cleaning and purging operations to be conducted. [**55**:7.1.19.1.3]

63.3.1.19.1.3.1* An independent or third-party review of the written procedure shall be conducted after the procedure has been written and shall:

(1) Evaluate hazards, errors, and malfunctions related to each step in the procedure
(2) Review the measures prescribed in the procedure for applicability
(3) Make recommendations for additional hazard mitigation measures if deemed to be necessary [**55**:7.1.19.1.3.1]

63.3.1.19.1.3.2 The completed written procedure shall be:

(1) Maintained on site by the facility owner/operator
(2) Provided to operating personnel engaged in cleaning or purging operations
(3) Made available to the AHJ upon request [**55**:7.1.19.1.3.2]

63.3.1.19.1.3.3 Where generic cleaning or purging procedures have been established, a job-specific operating procedure shall not be required. [**55**:7.1.19.1.3.3]

63.3.1.19.1.3.4 Generic procedures shall be reviewed when originally published or when the procedure or operation is changed. [**55:**7.1.19.1.3.4]

63.3.1.19.1.4 Written procedures to manage a change in process materials, technology, equipment, procedures, and facilities shall be established by the facility owner/operator. [**55:**7.1.19.1.4]

63.3.1.19.1.4.1 The management-of-change procedures shall ensure that the following topics are addressed prior to any change in the configuration or design of the piping system:

(1) The technical basis for the proposed change
(2) The safety and health implications
(3) Whether the change is permanent or temporary
(4) Whether modifications to the cleaning and purging procedures are required as a result of the changes identified [**55:**7.1.19.1.4.1]

63.3.1.19.1.4.2 When modifications to the cleaning and purging procedures are required, the written procedure shall be updated to incorporate any elements identified by the management-of-change procedures. [**55:**7.1.19.1.4.2]

63.3.1.19.1.5 Prior to cleaning or purging, piping systems shall be inspected and tested to determine that the installation, including the materials of construction, and method of fabrication, comply with the requirements of the design standard used and the intended application for which the system was designed. [**55:**7.1.19.1.5]

63.3.1.19.1.5.1 Inspection and testing of piping systems shall not be required to remove a system from service. [**55:**7.1.19.1.5.1]

63.3.1.19.1.5.2 Purging of piping systems shall not be required for systems that are utilized for operations designated by written operating procedures when systems are utilized in accordance with the requirements of the cleaning or purging procedure specified in 63.3.1.19.1.1. [**55:**7.1.19.1.5.2]

63.3.1.19.1.5.3* Personnel in the affected area(s), as determined by the cleaning or purging procedure, shall be informed of the hazards associated with the operational activity and notified prior to the initiation of any such activity. [**55:**7.1.19.1.5.3]

63.3.1.19.2* Cleaning. Piping system designs shall be documented to specify the requirements for the internal cleaning of the piping system prior to installation and initial use. [**55:**7.1.19.2]

63.3.1.19.2.1 The internal surfaces of gas piping systems shall be cleaned to ensure that the required standard of cleanliness specified by the design is met prior to placing the gas piping system into service. [**55:**7.1.19.2.1]

63.3.1.19.2.2* When piping systems are cleaned in stages during installation or assembly, the interior of the cleaned piping shall be protected against the infiltration of unwanted contaminants. [**55:**7.1.19.2.2]

63.3.1.19.3* Purging. Piping systems used to contain gases with a physical or health hazard in any of the categories specified by 63.1.4 shall be purged prior to being placed into service for initial use. [**55:**7.1.19.3]

63.3.1.19.3.1 Piping systems shall be purged to remove the internal contents preceding the following activities or operations to:

(1) activate or place a piping system into service
(2) deactivate or remove a piping system from service
(3) change the service of a piping system from one gas to another, except when such gas is supplied to a manifold or piping system designed for the purpose of filling or otherwise processing cylinders, containers, or tanks in a process with established procedures
(4) perform service, maintenance or modifications on a system where personnel or designated areas will potentially be exposed to the internal contents of the piping system
(5) perform hot work including but not limited to welding, cutting or brazing on the piping system. [**55:**7.1.19.3.1]

63.3.1.19.3.2 The termination point for the release of purged gases shall be in accordance with 63.2.15. [**55:**7.1.19.3.2]

63.3.1.19.3.2.1 The release of purged gases or mixtures containing any quantity of corrosive, toxic, or highly toxic gases shall be through a treatment system in accordance with the applicable requirements of 63.3.5.3.4 or 63.3.9.3. [**55:**7.1.19.3.2.1]

63.3.1.19.3.2.2 The termination point for the release of purged gases resultant from the purging of piping systems out of service, other than those in accordance with 63.3.1.19.3.2.1, shall not be required to be in accordance with 63.2.15 where the contained volume of the piping system when released to indoor areas does not result in a concentration in the room or area that exceeds any of the following limits or that will reduce the oxygen concentration in the room or area below a level of 19.5%:

(1) Ceiling limit
(2) Permissible exposure limit
(3) Short term exposure limit
(4) 25% of the lower flammable limit [**55:**7.1.19.3.2.2]

63.3.2 Storage.

63.3.2.1 General.

63.3.2.1.1 Applicability. The storage of compressed gas containers, cylinders, and tanks shall be in accordance with 63.3.2. [**55:**7.2.1.1]

63.3.2.1.2 Upright Storage Flammable Gas in Solution and Liquefied Flammable Gas. Cylinders, containers, and tanks containing liquefied flammable gases and flammable gases in solution shall be positioned in the upright position. [**55:**7.2.1.2]

63.3.2.1.2.1 Containers and Cylinders of 1.3 Gal (5 L) or Less. Containers with a capacity of 1.3 gal (5 L) or less shall be permitted to be stored in a horizontal position. [**55:**7.2.1.2.1]

63.3.2.1.2.2 Containers, Cylinders, and Tanks Designed for Horizontal Use. Containers, cylinders, and tanks designed for use in a horizontal position shall be permitted to be stored in a horizontal position. [**55:**7.2.1.2.2]

63.3.2.1.2.3 Palletized Containers, Cylinders, and Tanks. Containers, cylinders, and tanks, with the exception of those containing flammable liquefied compressed gases, that are palletized for transportation purposes shall be permitted to be stored in a horizontal position. [**55:**7.2.1.2.3]

63.3.2.1.3 Classification of Weather Protection as an Indoor Versus an Outdoor Area. For other than explosive materials and hazardous materials presenting a detonation hazard, a weather protection structure shall be permitted to be used for sheltering outdoor storage or use areas without requiring such areas to be classified as indoor storage. [**55:**7.2.1.3]

63.3.2.2 Material-Specific Regulations.

63.3.2.2.1 Indoor Storage. Indoor storage of compressed gases shall be in accordance with the material-specific provisions of 63.3.4 through 63.3.10. [**55:**7.2.2.1]

63.3.2.2.2 Exterior Storage.

63.3.2.2.2.1 General. Exterior storage of compressed gases shall be in accordance with the material-specific provisions of 63.3.4 through 63.3.10. [**55:**7.2.2.2.1]

63.3.2.2.2.2 Separation. Distances from property lines, buildings, and exposures shall be in accordance with the material-specific provisions of 63.3.4 through 63.3.10. [**55:**7.2.2.2.2]

63.3.3 Use and Handling.

63.3.3.1 General.

63.3.3.1.1 Applicability. The use and handling of compressed gas cylinders, containers, tanks, and systems shall be in accordance with 63.3.3.1. [**55:**7.3.1.1]

63.3.3.1.2 Controls.

63.3.3.1.2.1 Compressed gas system controls shall be designed to prevent materials from entering or leaving the process at an unintended time, rate, or path. [**55:**7.3.1.2.1]

63.3.3.1.2.2 Automatic controls shall be designed to be fail-safe. [**55:**7.3.1.2.2]

63.3.3.1.3 Piping Systems. Piping, tubing, fittings, and related components shall be designed, fabricated, and tested in accordance with the requirements of ANSI/ASME B31.3, *Process Piping*, or other approved standards. [**55:**7.3.1.3]

63.3.3.1.3.1 Integrity. Piping, tubing, pressure regulators, valves, and other apparatus shall be kept gastight to prevent leakage. [**55:**7.3.1.3.1]

63.3.3.1.3.2 Backflow Prevention. Backflow prevention or check valves shall be provided when the backflow of hazardous materials could create a hazardous condition or cause the unauthorized discharge of hazardous materials. [**55:**7.3.1.3.2]

63.3.3.1.4 Valves.

63.3.3.1.4.1 Valves utilized on compressed gas systems shall be designed for the gas or gases and pressure intended and shall be accessible. [**55:**7.3.1.4.1]

63.3.3.1.4.2 Valve handles or operators for required shutoff valves shall not be removed or otherwise altered to prevent access. [**55:**7.3.1.4.2]

63.3.3.1.5 Vent Pipe Termination.

63.3.3.1.5.1 Venting of gases shall be directed to an approved location. [**55:**7.3.1.5.1]

63.3.3.1.5.2 The termination point for piped vent systems serving cylinders, containers, tanks, and gas systems used for the purpose of operational or emergency venting shall be in accordance with 63.2.15. [**55:**7.3.1.5.2]

63.3.3.1.6 Upright Use.

63.3.3.1.6.1 Compressed gas cylinders, containers, and tanks containing flammable liquefied gas, except those designed for use in a horizontal position and those compressed gas cylinders, containers, and tanks containing nonliquefied gases, shall be used in a "valve end up" upright position. [**55:**7.3.1.6.1]

63.3.3.1.6.2 An upright position shall include a position in which the container, cylinder, or tank axis is inclined as much as 45 degrees from the vertical and in which the relief device is always in direct communication with the gas phase. [**55:**7.3.1.6.2]

63.3.3.1.7 Inverted Use. Cylinders, containers, and tanks containing nonflammable liquefied gases shall be permitted to be used in the inverted position when the liquid phase is used. [**55:**7.3.1.7]

63.3.3.1.7.1 Flammable liquefied gases at processing plants shall be permitted to use this inverted position method while transfilling. [**55:**7.3.1.7.1]

63.3.3.1.7.2 The container, cylinder, or tank shall be secured, and the dispensing apparatus shall be designed for use with liquefied gas. [**55:**7.3.1.7.2]

63.3.3.1.8 Containers and Cylinders of 1.3 Gal (5 L) or Less. Containers or cylinders with a water volume of 1.3 gal (5 L) or less shall be permitted to be used in a horizontal position. [**55:**7.3.1.8]

63.3.3.1.9 Transfer. Transfer of gases between containers, cylinders, and tanks shall be performed by qualified personnel using equipment and operating procedures in accordance with CGA P-1, *Safe Handling of Compressed Gases in Containers*. [**55:**7.3.1.9]

63.3.3.1.10 Use of Compressed Gases for Inflation. Inflatable equipment, devices, or balloons shall only be pressurized or filled with compressed air or inert gases. [**55:**7.3.1.10]

63.3.3.1.11 Emergency Shutoff Valves.

63.3.3.1.11.1 Accessible manual valves or automatic emergency shutoff valves shall be provided to shut off the flow of gas in case of emergency. [**55:**7.3.1.11.1]

63.3.3.1.11.1.1* Manual emergency shutoff valves or the device that activates an automatic emergency shutoff valve on a bulk source or piping system serving the bulk supply shall be identified by means of a sign. [**55:**7.3.1.11.1.1]

63.3.3.1.11.2 Emergency shutoffs shall be located at the point of use and at the tank, cylinder, or bulk source, and at the point where the system piping enters the building. [**55:**7.3.1.11.2]

63.3.3.1.12 Excess Flow Control.

63.3.3.1.12.1* Where compressed gases having a hazard ranking in one or more of the following hazard classes in accordance with NFPA 704 are carried in pressurized piping above a gauge pressure of 15 psi (103 kPa), an approved means of either leak detection with emergency shutoff or excess flow control shall be provided:

(1) Health hazard Class 3 or Class 4
(2) Flammability Class 4
(3) Instability Class 3 or Class 4 [**55:**7.3.1.12.1]

63.3.3.1.12.1.1 Excess Flow Control Location with Hazardous Material Storage. Where the piping originates from within a hazardous material storage room or area, the excess flow control shall be located within the storage room or area. [**55:**7.3.1.12.1.1]

63.3.3.1.12.1.2* Excess Flow Control Location with Bulk Storage. Where the piping originates from a bulk source, the excess flow control shall be located at the bulk source at a point immediately downstream of the source valve. [**55:**7.3.1.12.1.2]

63.3.3.1.12.2 The controls required by 63.3.3.1.12 shall not be required for the following:

(1) Piping for inlet connections designed to prevent backflow at the source
(2) Piping for pressure relief devices
(3) Where the source of the gas is not in excess of the quantity threshold indicated in Table 63.2.3.1.1 [55:7.3.1.12.2]

63.3.3.1.12.3 Location. The location of excess flow control shall be as specified in 63.3.3.1.12.1.1 and 63.3.3.1.12.1.2. [55:7.3.1.12.3]

63.3.3.1.12.3.1 Where piping originates from a source located in a room or area, the excess flow control shall be located within the room or area. [55:7.3.1.12.3.1]

63.3.3.1.12.3.2 Where piping originates from a bulk source, the excess flow control shall be as close to the bulk source as possible. [55:7.3.1.12.3.2]

63.3.3.1.12.4 Location Exemptions. The requirements of 63.3.3.1.12 shall not apply to the following:

(1) Piping for inlet connections designed to prevent backflow
(2) Piping for pressure relief devices
(3) Systems containing 430 scf (12.7 m^3) or less of flammable gas [55:7.3.1.12.4]

63.3.3.2 Material-Specific Regulations.

63.3.3.2.1 Indoor Use. Indoor use of compressed gases shall be in accordance with the requirements of 63.3.4 through 63.3.10. [55:7.3.2.1]

63.3.3.2.2 Exterior Use.

63.3.3.2.2.1 General. Exterior use of compressed gases shall be in accordance with the requirements of 63.3.4 through 63.3.10. [55:7.3.2.2.1]

63.3.3.2.2.2 Separation. Distances from property lines, buildings, and exposure hazards shall be in accordance with the material-specific provisions of 63.3.4 through 63.3.10. [55:7.3.2.2.2]

63.3.3.3 Handling.

63.3.3.3.1 Applicability. The handling of compressed gas containers, cylinders, and tanks shall be in accordance with 63.3.3.3. [55:7.3.3.1]

63.3.3.3.2 Carts and Trucks.

63.3.3.3.2.1 Containers, cylinders, and tanks shall be moved using an approved method. [55:7.3.3.2.1]

63.3.3.3.2.2 Where containers, cylinders, or tanks are moved by hand cart, hand truck, or other mobile device, such carts, trucks, or devices shall be designed for the secure movement of containers, cylinders, or tanks. [55:7.3.3.2.2]

63.3.3.3.3 Lifting Devices. Ropes, chains, or slings shall not be used to suspend compressed gas containers, cylinders, and tanks unless provisions at time of manufacture have been made on the container, cylinder, or tank for appropriate lifting attachments, such as lugs. [55:7.3.3.3]

63.3.4 Medical Gas Systems. Medical gas systems for health care shall be in accordance with NFPA 99, *Health Care Facilities Code*. [55:7.4]

63.3.5 Corrosive Gases.

63.3.5.1 General. The storage or use of corrosive compressed gases exceeding the quantity thresholds for gases requiring special provisions as specified in Table 63.2.3.1.1 shall be in accordance with Chapters 1 through 6 of NFPA 55 and 63.3.1 through 63.3.3 and 63.3.5. [55:7.5.1]

63.3.5.2 Distance to Exposures. The outdoor storage or use of corrosive compressed gas shall not be within 20 ft (6.1 m) of buildings not associated with the manufacture or distribution of corrosive gases, lot lines, streets, alleys, public ways, or means of egress. [55:7.5.2]

63.3.5.2.1 A 2-hour fire barrier wall without openings or penetrations and that extends not less than 30 in. (762 mm) above and to the sides of the storage or use area shall be permitted in lieu of the 20 ft (6.1 m) distance. [55:7.5.2.1]

63.3.5.2.1.1* Where a fire barrier is used to protect compressed gas systems, the system shall terminate downstream of the source valve. [55:7.5.2.1.1]

63.3.5.2.1.2 The fire barrier wall shall be either an independent structure or the exterior wall of the building adjacent to the storage or use area. [55:7.5.2.1.2]

63.3.5.2.1.3 The 2-hour fire barrier shall be located at least 5 ft (1.5 m) from any exposure. [55:7.5.2.1.3]

63.3.5.2.1.4 The 2-hour fire barrier wall shall not have more than two sides at approximately 90 degree (1.57 rad) directions or not more than three sides with connecting angles of approximately 135 degrees (2.36 rad). [55:7.5.2.1.4]

63.3.5.3 Indoor Use. The indoor use of corrosive gases shall be provided with a gas cabinet, exhausted enclosure, or gas room. [55:7.5.3]

63.3.5.3.1 Gas Cabinets. Gas cabinets shall be in accordance with 63.2.17. [55:7.5.3.1]

63.3.5.3.2 Exhausted Enclosures. Exhausted enclosures shall be in accordance with 63.2.18. [55:7.5.3.2]

63.3.5.3.3 Gas Rooms. Gas rooms shall be in accordance with 63.2.4. [55:7.5.3.3]

63.3.5.3.4 Treatment Systems. Treatment systems, except as provided for in 63.3.5.3.4.1, gas cabinets, exhausted enclosures, and gas rooms containing corrosive gases in use shall be provided with exhaust ventilation, with all exhaust directed to a treatment system designed to process the accidental release of gas. [55:7.5.3.4]

63.3.5.3.4.1 Treatment systems shall not be required for corrosive gases in use where provided with the following:

(1) Gas detection in accordance with 63.3.9.3.2.1.1
(2) Fail-safe automatic closing valves in accordance with 63.3.9.3.2.2 [55:7.5.3.4.1]

63.3.5.3.4.2 Treatment systems shall be capable of diluting, adsorbing, absorbing, containing, neutralizing, burning, or otherwise processing the release of corrosive gas in accordance with 63.3.9.3.4.1. [55:7.5.3.4.2]

63.3.5.3.4.3 Treatment system sizing shall be in accordance with 63.3.9.3.4. [55:7.5.3.4.3]

63.3.6 Flammable Gases.

63.3.6.1 Storage, Use, and Handling.

63.3.6.1.1 The storage or use of flammable gases exceeding the quantity thresholds for gases requiring special provisions as specified in Table 63.2.3.1.1 shall be in accordance with Chapters 1 through 6 of NFPA 55 and 63.3.1 through 63.3.3 and 63.3.6. [55:7.6.1.1]

63.3.6.1.2 Storage, use, and handling of gaseous hydrogen shall be in accordance with 63.3.6.1 and Chapter 10 of NFPA 55. [55:7.6.1.2]

63.3.6.2 Distance to Exposures. The outdoor storage or use of non-bulk flammable compressed gas shall be located from lot lines, public streets, public alleys, public ways, or buildings not associated with the manufacture or distribution of such gases in accordance with Table 63.3.6.2. [55:7.6.2]

63.3.6.2.1 Bulk hydrogen gas installations shall be in accordance with Chapter 10 of NFPA 55. [55:7.6.2.1]

63.3.6.2.1.1* Where a protective structure is used to protect compressed gas systems, the system shall terminate downstream of the source valve. [55:7.6.2.1.1]

63.3.6.2.1.2 The fire barrier wall shall be either an independent structure or the exterior wall of the building adjacent to the storage or use area. [55:7.6.2.1.2]

63.3.6.2.2 Bulk gas systems for flammable gases other than hydrogen shall be in accordance with Table 10.3.2.1(a), Table 10.3.2.1(b), or Table 10.3.2.1(c) of NFPA 55 where the quantity of flammable compressed gas exceeds 5000 scf (141.6 Nm^3). [55:7.6.2.2]

63.3.6.2.2.1 Where fire barriers are used as a means of distance reduction, fire barriers shall be in accordance with 10.3.2.4 of NFPA 55. [55:7.6.2.2.1]

63.3.6.2.2.2 Mobile acetylene trailer systems (MATS) shall be located in accordance with 15.2.2 of NFPA 55. [55:7.6.2.2.2]

63.3.6.2.3 The configuration of the protective structure shall be designed to allow natural ventilation to prevent the accumulation of hazardous gas concentrations. [55:7.6.2.3]

63.3.6.2.4 Storage and use of flammable compressed gases shall not be located within 50 ft (15.2 m) of air intakes. [55:7.6.2.4]

63.3.6.2.5 Storage and use of flammable gases outside of buildings shall also be separated from building openings by 25 ft (7.6 m). Fire barriers shall be permitted to be used as a means to separate storage areas from openings or a means of egress used to access the public way. [55:7.6.2.5]

63.3.6.3 Indoor Non-Bulk Hydrogen Compressed Gas System Location.

63.3.6.3.1 Hydrogen systems of less than 3500 scf (99 Nm^3) and greater than the MAQ, where located inside buildings, shall be in accordance with the following:

(1) In a ventilated area in accordance with the provisions of 63.2.16
(2) Separated from incompatible materials in accordance with the provisions of 7.1.11.2 of NFPA 55
(3) A distance of 25 ft (7.6 m) from open flames and other sources of ignition
(4) A distance of 50 ft (15 m) from intakes of ventilation, air-conditioning equipment, and air compressors located in the same room or area as the hydrogen system

   (a) The distance shall be permitted to be reduced to 10 ft (3.1 m) where the room or area in which the hydrogen system is installed is protected by a listed detection system per Article 500.7(K) of *NFPA 70, National Electrical Code*, and the detection system shuts down the fuel supply in the event of a leak that results in a concentration that exceeds 25 percent of the LFL.
   (b) Emergency shutoff valves shall be provided in accordance with 63.3.3.1.11.

(5) A distance of 50 ft (15 m) from other flammable gas storage
(6) Protected against damage in accordance with the provisions of 63.3.1.9.3. [55:7.6.3.1]

63.3.6.3.2 Systems Installed in One Room.

63.3.6.3.2.1 More than one system of 3500 scf (99 Nm^3) or less shall be permitted to be installed in the same room or area, provided the systems are separated by at least 50 ft (15 m) or a full-height fire-resistive partition having a minimum fire resistance rating of 2 hours is located between the systems. [55:7.6.3.2.1]

Table 63.3.6.2 Distance to Exposures for Nonbulk Flammable Gases

Maximum Amount per Storage Area (ft^3)	Minimum Distance Between Storage Areas (ft)	Minimum Distance to Lot Lines of Property That Can Be Built Upon (ft)	Minimum Distance to Public Streets, Public Alleys or Public Ways (ft)	Minimum Distance to Buildings on the Same Property		
				Less Than 2-Hour Construction	2-Hour Construction	4-Hour Construction
0–4225	5	5	5	5	0	0
4226–21,125	10	10	10	10	5	0
21,126–50,700	10	15	15	20	5	0
50,701–84,500	10	20	20	20	5	0
84,501–200,000	20	25	25	20	5	0

For SI units, 1 ft = 304.8 mm; 1 ft^3 = 0.02832 m^3.
Note: The minimum required distances shall not apply when fire barriers without openings or penetrations having a minimum fire resistive rating of 2 hours interrupt the line of sight between the storage and the exposure. The configuration of the fire barriers shall be designed to allow natural ventilation to prevent the accumulation of hazardous gas concentrations. [55: Table 7.6.2]

63.3.6.3.2.2 The separation distance between multiple systems of 3500 scf (99 Nm^3) or less shall be permitted to be reduced to 25 ft (7.6 m) in buildings where the space between storage areas is free of combustible materials and protected with a sprinkler system designed for Extra Hazard, Group 1 in accordance with the requirements of Section 6.10 of NFPA 55. [**55**:7.6.3.2.2]

63.3.6.3.2.3 The required separation distance between individual portable systems in the process of being filled or serviced in facilities associated with the manufacture or distribution of hydrogen and its mixtures shall not be limited by 63.3.6.3.2.1 or 63.3.6.3.2.2 when such facilities are provided with Protection Level 2 controls and the applicable requirements of Chapters 1 through 7 of NFPA 55. [**55**:7.6.3.2.3]

63.3.6.4 Ignition Source Control. Ignition sources in areas containing flammable gases shall be in accordance with 63.3.6.4. [**55**:7.6.4]

63.3.6.4.1 Static Producing Equipment. Static producing equipment located in flammable gas areas shall be grounded. [**55**:7.6.4.1]

63.3.6.4.2 No Smoking or Open Flame. Signs shall be posted in areas containing flammable gases stating that smoking or the use of open flame, or both, is prohibited within 25 ft (7.6 m) of the storage or use area perimeter. [**55**:7.6.4.2]

63.3.6.4.3 Heating. Heating, where provided, shall be by indirect means. Equipment used for heating applications in rooms or areas where flammable gases are stored or used shall be listed and labeled for use in hazardous environments established by the gases present and shall be installed in accordance with the conditions of the listing and the manufacturer's installation instructions. [**55**:7.6.4.3]

63.3.6.5 Electrical. Areas in which the storage or use of compressed gases exceeds the quantity thresholds for gases requiring special provisions shall be in accordance with *NFPA 70*. [**55**:7.6.5]

63.3.6.6 Maintenance of Piping Systems.

63.3.6.6.1 Maintenance of flammable gas system piping and components shall be performed annually by a qualified representative of the equipment owner. [**55**:7.6.6.1]

63.3.6.6.2 This maintenance shall include inspection for physical damage, leak tightness, ground system integrity, vent system operation, equipment identification, warning signs, operator information and training records, scheduled maintenance and retest records, alarm operation, and other safety-related features. [**55**:7.6.6.2]

63.3.6.6.3 Scheduled maintenance and retest activities shall be formally documented, and records shall be maintained a minimum of 3 years. [**55**:7.6.6.3]

63.3.7 Oxidizing Gases.

63.3.7.1 General. The storage or use of oxidizing compressed gases exceeding the quantity thresholds for gases requiring special provisions as specified in Table 63.2.3.1.1. shall be in accordance with Chapters 1 through 6 of NFPA 55 and 63.3.1 through 63.3.3 and 63.3.7. [**55**:7.7.1]

63.3.7.2 Distance to Exposures. The outdoor storage or use of oxidizing compressed gas shall be in accordance with Table 63.3.7.2. [**55**:7.7.2]

63.3.7.2.1 The distances shall not apply where fire barriers having a minimum fire resistance of 2 hours interrupt the line of sight between the container and the exposure. [**55**:7.7.2.1]

63.3.7.2.1.1* Where a fire barrier is used to protect compressed gas systems, the system shall terminate downstream of the source valve. [**55**:7.7.2.1.1]

63.3.7.2.1.2 The fire barrier wall shall be either an independent structure or the exterior wall of the building adjacent to the storage or use area. [**55**:7.7.2.1.2]

63.3.7.2.2 The fire barrier shall be at least 5 ft (1.5 m) from the storage or use area perimeter. [**55**:7.7.2.2]

63.3.7.2.3 The configuration of the fire barrier shall allow natural ventilation to prevent the accumulation of hazardous gas concentrations. [**55**:7.7.2.3]

63.3.8 Pyrophoric Gases.

63.3.8.1 General. Pyrophoric compressed gases exceeding the quantity thresholds for gases requiring special provisions as specified in Table 63.2.3.1.1 shall be stored and used in accordance with Chapters 1 through 6 of NFPA 55 and 63.3.1 through 63.3.3 and 63.3.8. [**55**:7.8.1]

63.3.8.2 Silane and Silane Mixtures. Silane and silane mixtures shall be stored, used, and handled in accordance with the provisions of ANSI/CGA G-13, *Storage and Handling of Silane and Silane Mixtures*. [**55**:7.8.2]

63.3.8.3 Distance to Exposures. The outdoor storage or use of pyrophoric compressed gas shall be in accordance with Table 63.3.8.3. [**55**:7.8.3]

63.3.8.3.1 The distances shall be allowed to be reduced to 5 ft (1.5 m) where fire barriers having a minimum fire resistance of 2 hours interrupt the line of sight between the container and the exposure. [**55**:7.8.3.1]

63.3.8.3.1.1* Where a fire barrier is used to protect compressed gas systems, the system shall terminate downstream of the source valve. [**55**:7.8.3.1.1]

63.3.8.3.1.2 The fire barrier shall be either an independent structure or the exterior wall of the building adjacent to the storage or use area. [**55**:7.8.3.1.2]

63.3.8.3.1.3 The fire barrier shall be at least 5 ft (1.5 m) from the storage or use area perimeter. [**55**:7.8.3.1.3]

63.3.8.3.1.4 The configuration of the fire barrier shall allow natural ventilation to prevent the accumulation of hazardous gas concentrations. [**55**:7.8.3.1.4]

63.3.8.3.2 Storage and use of pyrophoric gases outside buildings shall be separated from building openings by 25 ft (7.6 m). [**55**:7.8.3.2]

63.3.8.3.2.1 Fire barriers shall be permitted to be used as a means to separate storage areas from building openings that are used to access the public way. [**55**:7.8.3.2.1]

63.3.9 Toxic and Highly Toxic Gases.

63.3.9.1 General. The storage or use of toxic and highly toxic gases exceeding the quantity thresholds for gases requiring special provisions as specified in Table 63.2.3.1.1 shall be in accordance with Chapters 1 through 6 of NFPA 55 and 63.3.1 through 63.3.3 and 63.3.9. [**55**:7.9.1]

Table 63.3.7.2 Distance to Exposures for Oxidizing Gases

Quantity of Gas Stored (at NTP)		Distance to a Building Not Associated with the Manufacture or Distribution of Oxidizing Gases or to a Public Way or Property Line		Minimum Distance Between Storage Areas	
scf	Nm^3	ft	m	ft	m
0–50,000	0–1416	5	1.5	5	1.5
50,001–100,000	1417–2832	10	3.0	10	3.0
≤100,001	≤2833	15	4.6	15	4.6

[**55:** Table 7.7.2]

Table 63.3.8.3 Distance to Exposures for Pyrophoric Gases

Maximum Amount per Storage Area		Minimum Distance Between Storage Areas		Minimum Distance to Property Lines		Minimum Distance to Public Ways		Minimum Distance to Buildings on the Same Property					
								Less Than 2-Hour Construction		2-Hour Construction		4-Hour Construction	
scf	Nm^3	ft	m	ft	m	ft	m	ft	m	ft	m	ft	m
250	7.1	5	1.5	25	7.6	5	1.5	5	1.5	0	0	0	0
>250 to 2500	>7.1 to 71.0	10	3.0	50	15.2	10	3.0	10	3.0	5	1.5	0	0
>2500 to 7500	>71.0 to 212.4	20	6.0	100	30.5	20	6.0	20	6.0	10	3.0	0	0

[**55:** Table 7.8.3]

63.3.9.2 Ventilation and Arrangement.

63.3.9.2.1 Indoors. The indoor storage or use of highly toxic gases or toxic gases shall be provided with a gas cabinet, exhausted enclosure, or gas room. [**55:**7.9.2.1]

63.3.9.2.1.1 Gas cabinets shall be in accordance with 63.2.17. [**55:**7.9.2.1.1]

63.3.9.2.1.2 Exhausted enclosures shall be in accordance with 63.2.18. [**55:**7.9.2.1.2]

63.3.9.2.1.3 Gas rooms shall be in accordance with 63.2.4. [**55:**7.9.2.1.3]

63.3.9.2.2 Distance to Exposures. The outdoor storage or use of toxic or highly toxic compressed gases shall not be within 75 ft (23 m) of lot lines, streets, alleys, public ways or means of egress, or buildings not associated with such storage or use. [**55:**7.9.2.2]

63.3.9.2.2.1 A 2-hour fire barrier wall without openings or penetrations that extends not less than 30 in. (762 mm) above and to the sides of the storage or use area and that interrupts the line of sight between the storage or use area and the exposure shall be permitted in lieu of the 75 ft (23 m) distance. [**55:**7.9.2.2.1]

63.3.9.2.2.1.1* Where a fire barrier is used to protect compressed gas systems, the system shall terminate downstream of the source valve. [**55:**7.9.2.2.1.1]

63.3.9.2.2.1.2 The fire barrier wall shall be either an independent structure or the exterior wall of the building adjacent to the storage or use area. [**55:**7.9.2.2.1.2]

63.3.9.2.2.1.3 The 2-hour fire barrier wall shall be located at least 5 ft (1.5 m) from any exposure. [**55:**7.9.2.2.1.3]

63.3.9.2.2.1.4 The 2-hour fire barrier wall shall not have more than two sides at approximately 90 degree (1.5 rad) directions or more than three sides with connecting angles of approximately 135 degrees (2.36 rad). [**55:**7.9.2.2.1.4]

63.3.9.2.2.2 Where the storage or use area is located closer than 75 ft (23 m) to a building not associated with the manufacture or distribution of toxic or highly toxic compressed gases, openings in the building other than for piping shall not be permitted above the height of the top of the 2-hour fire barrier wall or within 50 ft (15 m) horizontally from the storage area, regardless of whether the openings are shielded by a fire barrier. [**55:**7.9.2.2.2]

63.3.9.2.3 Air Intakes. Storage and use of toxic and highly toxic compressed gases shall not be located within 75 ft (23 m) of air intakes. [**55:**7.9.2.3]

63.3.9.3 Treatment Systems. Except as provided in 63.3.9.3.1 and 63.3.9.3.2, gas cabinets, exhausted enclosures, and gas rooms containing toxic or highly toxic gases shall be provided with exhaust ventilation, with all exhaust directed to a treatment system designed to process accidental release of gas. [**55:**7.9.3]

63.3.9.3.1 Storage of Toxic or Highly Toxic Gases. Treatment systems shall not be required for toxic or highly toxic gases in storage where containers, cylinders, and tanks are provided with the controls specified in 63.3.9.3.1.1 through 63.3.9.3.1.3. [**55:**7.9.3.1]

63.3.9.3.1.1 Valve Outlets Protected. Valve outlets shall be equipped with outlet plugs or caps, or both, rated for the container service pressure. [**55:**7.9.3.1.1]

63.3.9.3.1.2 Handwheels Secured. Where provided, handwheel-operated valves shall be secured to prevent movement. [**55:**7.9.3.1.2]

63.3.9.3.1.3 Containment Devices Provided. Approved cylinder containment vessels or cylinder containment systems shall be provided at an approved location. [**55:**7.9.3.1.3]

63.3.9.3.2 Use of Toxic Gases. Treatment systems shall not be required for toxic gases in use where containers, cylinders, and tanks are provided with the controls specified in 63.3.9.3.2.1 and 63.3.9.3.2.2. [**55:**7.9.3.2]

63.3.9.3.2.1 Gas Detection.

63.3.9.3.2.1.1 A gas detection system with a sensing interval not exceeding 5 minutes shall be provided. [**55:**7.9.3.2.1.1]

63.3.9.3.2.1.2 The gas detection system shall monitor the exhaust system at the point of discharge from the gas cabinet, exhausted enclosure, or gas room. [**55:**7.9.3.2.1.2]

63.3.9.3.2.2 Fail-Safe Automatic Closing Valve. An approved automatic-closing fail-safe valve shall be located on or immediately adjacent to and downstream of active cylinder, container, or tank valves. [**55:**7.9.3.2.2]

63.3.9.3.2.2.1 The fail-safe valve shall close when gas is detected at the permissible exposure limit, short-term exposure limit (STEL), or ceiling limit by the gas detection system. [**55:**7.9.3.2.2.1]

63.3.9.3.2.2.2 For attended operations, a manual closing valve shall be permitted when in accordance with 63.3.9.3.4.3. [**55:**7.9.3.2.2.2]

63.3.9.3.2.2.3 For gases used at unattended operations for the protection of public health, such as chlorine at water or wastewater treatment sites, the automatic valve shall close if the concentration of gas detected by a gas detection system reaches one-half of the IDLH. [**55:**7.9.3.2.2.3]

63.3.9.3.2.2.4 The gas detection system shall also alert persons on-site and a responsible person off-site when the gas concentration in the storage/use area reaches the OSHA PEL, OSHA ceiling limit, or OSHA/STEL for the gas employed. [**55:**7.9.3.2.2.4]

63.3.9.3.3 Treatment System Design and Performance. Treatment systems shall be capable of diluting, adsorbing, absorbing, containing, neutralizing, burning, or otherwise processing stored or used toxic or highly toxic gas, or both. [**55:**7.9.3.3]

63.3.9.3.3.1 Where a total containment system is used, the system shall be designed to handle the maximum anticipated pressure of release to the system when it reaches equilibrium. [**55:**7.9.3.3.1]

63.3.9.3.3.2 Treatment systems shall be capable of reducing the allowable discharge concentrations to one-half the IDLH threshold at the point of discharge. [**55:**7.9.3.3.2]

63.3.9.3.4 Treatment System Sizing.

63.3.9.3.4.1 Worst-Case Release of Gas. Treatment systems shall be sized to process the maximum worst-case release of gas based on the maximum flow rate of release from the largest vessel utilized in accordance with 63.3.9.3.4.2. [**55:**7.9.3.4.1]

63.3.9.3.4.2 Largest Compressed Gas Vessel. The entire contents of the single largest compressed gas vessel shall be considered. [**55:**7.9.3.4.2]

63.3.9.3.4.3 Attended Operations — Alternative Method of System Sizing.

63.3.9.3.4.3.1 Where source containers, cylinders, and tanks are used in attended process operations, with an operator present at the enclosure where the activity occurs, the volume of the release shall be limited to the estimated amount released from the process piping system within a period not to exceed 5 minutes. [**55:**7.9.3.4.3.1]

63.3.9.3.4.3.2 Such process piping systems shall comply with the requirements of 63.3.9.3.4.3.2(A) through 63.3.9.3.4.3.2(E). [**55:**7.9.3.4.3.2]

(A) Local Exhaust. All gas transfer operations shall be conducted within a zone of local exhaust that is connected to a treatment system. [**55:**7.9.3.4.3.2(A)]

(B) Gas Detection. Gas detection shall be used to provide a warning to alert the operators to emission of gas into the zone of local exhaust, and the following requirements also shall apply:

(1) The system shall be capable of detecting gas at the permissible exposure limit (PEL) or the ceiling limit for the gas being processed.
(2) Activation of the gas detection system shall provide a local alarm. [**55:**7.9.3.4.3.2(B)]

(C) Process Shutdown. Operations involving the gas detected shall be shut down and leaks repaired. [**55:**7.9.3.4.3.2(C)]

(D) Piping System Construction. Piping systems used to convey gases shall be of all-welded construction throughout, with the exception of fittings used to connect cylinders, containers, or tanks, or any combination thereof, to the process system. [**55:**7.9.3.4.3.2(D)]

(E) Piping System Accessibility. Piping systems shall be designed to provide for readily accessible manual shutdown controls. [**55:**7.9.3.4.3.2(E)]

63.3.9.3.5 Rate of Release. The time release shall be in accordance with Table 63.3.9.3.5 for the type of container indicated. [**55:**7.9.3.5]

63.3.9.3.6* Maximum Flow Rate of Release.

63.3.9.3.6.1 For portable containers, cylinders, and tanks, the maximum flow rate of release shall be calculated based on

Table 63.3.9.3.5 Rates of Release

Container Type	Time Release	
	Nonliquefied Gases	Liquefied Gases
Cylinders without restrictive flow orifices	5 minutes	30 minutes
Portable tanks without restrictive flow orifices	40 minutes	240 minutes
All others	Based on peak flow from maximum valve orifice	Based on peak flow from maximum valve orifice

[**55:** Table 7.9.3.5]

assuming the total release from the cylinder or tank within the time specified. [**55:**7.9.3.6.1]

63.3.9.3.6.2* When portable containers, cylinders, or tanks are equipped with reduced flow orifices, the worst-case rate of release shall be determined by the maximum achievable flow from the valve based on the following formula:

[63.3.9.3.6.2]
$$CFM = (767 \times A \times P) \frac{(28.96/MW)^{1/2}}{60}$$

where:
CFM = standard cubic feet per minute of gas of concern under flow conditions
A = area of orifice in square inches (*See Table A.63.3.9.3.6 for areas of typical restricted flow orifices.*)
P = supply pressure of gas at NTP in pounds per square inch absolute
MW = molecular weight [**55:**7.9.3.6.2]

63.3.9.3.6.3 For mixtures, the average of molecular weights shall be used. [**55:**7.9.3.6.3]

63.3.9.4 Leaking Cylinders, Containers, and Tanks. When cylinders, containers, or tanks are used outdoors in excess of the quantities specified in Table 63.2.3.1.1 the column for unsprinklered areas (unprotected by gas cabinets or exhausted enclosures), a gas cabinet, exhausted enclosure, or containment vessel or system shall be provided to control leaks from leaking cylinders, containers, and tanks in accordance with 63.3.9.4.1 through 63.3.9.4.2.3. [**55:**7.9.4]

63.3.9.4.1 Gas Cabinets or Exhausted Enclosures. Where gas cabinets or exhausted enclosures are provided to handle leaks from cylinders, containers, or tanks, exhaust ventilation shall be provided that is directed to a treatment system in accordance with the provisions of 63.3.9.3. [**55:**7.9.4.1]

63.3.9.4.2 Containment Vessels or Systems. Where containment vessels or containment systems are provided, they shall comply with the requirements of 63.3.9.4.2.1 through 63.3.9.4.2.3. [**55:**7.9.4.2]

63.3.9.4.2.1 Performance. Containment vessels or containment systems shall be capable of fully containing or terminating a release. [**55:**7.9.4.2.1]

63.3.9.4.2.2 Personnel. Trained personnel capable of operating the containment vessel or containment system shall be available at an approved location. [**55:**7.9.4.2.2]

63.3.9.4.2.3 Location. Containment vessels or systems shall be capable of being transported to the leaking cylinder, container, or tank. [**55:**7.9.4.2.3]

63.3.9.5 Emergency Power.

63.3.9.5.1 General. Emergency power shall comply with the requirements of 63.3.9.5 in accordance with *NFPA 70*. [**55:**7.9.5.1]

63.3.9.5.2 Alternative to Emergency Power. Emergency power shall not be required where fail-safe engineering is provided for mechanical exhaust ventilation, treatment systems, and temperature control, and standby power is provided to alternative systems that utilize electrical energy. [**55:**7.9.5.2]

63.3.9.5.3 Where Required. Emergency power shall be provided for the following systems:

(1) Exhaust ventilation
(2) Treatment system
(3) Gas detection system
(4) Temperature control system
(5) Required alarm systems [**55:**7.9.5.3]

63.3.9.5.4 Level. Emergency power systems shall comply with the requirements for a Level 2 system in accordance with NFPA 110. [**55:**7.9.5.4]

63.3.9.6 Gas Detection. Except as provided in 63.3.9.6.1, a continuous gas detection system in accordance with the requirements of 63.3.9.6.2 through 63.3.9.6.6 shall be provided for the indoor storage or use of toxic or highly toxic compressed gases. [**55:**7.9.6]

63.3.9.6.1 Where Gas Detection Is Not Required. A gas detection system shall not be required for toxic gases where the physiological warning properties for the gas are at a level below the accepted PEL or the ceiling limit for the gas. [**55:**7.9.6.1]

63.3.9.6.2 Local Alarm. The gas detection system shall initiate a local alarm that is both audible and visible. [**55:**7.9.6.2]

63.3.9.6.3 Alarm Monitored. The gas detection system shall transmit a signal to a constantly attended control station for quantities exceeding one toxic or highly toxic compressed gas cylinder. [**55:**7.9.6.3]

63.3.9.6.4 Automatic Shutdown.

63.3.9.6.4.1 Activation of the gas detection system shall automatically shut off the flow of gas related to the system being monitored. [**55:**7.9.6.4.1]

63.3.9.6.4.2 An automatic shutdown shall not be required for reactors utilized for the production of toxic or highly toxic gases when such reactors are operated at gauge pressures less than 15 psi (103.4 kPa), constantly attended, and provided with readily accessible emergency shutoff valves. [**55:**7.9.6.4.2]

63.3.9.6.5 Detection Points. Detection shall be provided at the locations specified in 63.3.9.6.5.1 through 63.3.9.6.5.4. [**55:**7.9.6.5]

63.3.9.6.5.1 Treatment System Discharge. Detection shall be provided at the discharge from the treatment system. [**55:**7.9.6.5.1]

63.3.9.6.5.2 Point of Use. Detection shall be provided in the room or area in which the gas is used. [**55:**7.9.6.5.2]

63.3.9.6.5.3 Source. Detection shall be provided at the source cylinder, container, or tank used for delivery of the gas to the point of use. [**55:**7.9.6.5.3]

63.3.9.6.5.4 Storage. Detection shall be provided in the room or area in which the gas is stored. [**55:**7.9.6.5.4]

63.3.9.6.6 Level of Detection. The gas detection system shall detect the presence of gas at or below the PEL or the ceiling limit of the gas for those points identified in 63.3.9.6.5.2 and 63.3.9.6.5.3 and at not less than one-half the IDLH level for points identified in 63.3.9.6.5.1. [**55:**7.9.6.6]

63.3.9.7 Automatic Smoke Detection System. An automatic smoke detection system shall be provided for the indoor storage or use of highly toxic compressed gases in accordance with *NFPA 72*. [**55:**7.9.7]

63.3.10 Unstable Reactive Gases (Nondetonable). The storage or use of unstable reactive (nondetonable) gases exceeding the quantity thresholds for gases requiring special provisions as specified in Table 63.2.3.1.1 shall be in accordance with Chapters 1 through 6 of NFPA 55 and 63.3.1 through 63.3.3 and 63.3.10. [**55:**7.10]

63.3.10.1 Distances to Exposures for Class 2.

63.3.10.1.1 The outdoor storage or use of unstable reactive Class 2 compressed gas shall not be within 20 ft (6 m) of buildings, lot lines, streets, alleys, or public ways or means of egress. [**55:**7.10.1.1]

63.3.10.1.2 A 2-hour fire barrier wall without openings or penetrations shall be permitted in lieu of the 20 ft (6 m) distance required by 63.3.10.1.1. [**55:**7.10.1.2]

63.3.10.1.2.1* Where a fire barrier wall is used to protect compressed gas systems, the system shall terminate downstream of the source valve. [**55:**7.10.1.2.1]

63.3.10.1.2.2 The fire barrier wall shall be either an independent structure or the exterior wall of the building. [**55:**7.10.1.2.2]

63.3.10.1.2.3 The 2-hour fire barrier wall shall be located at least 5 ft (1.5 m) from any exposure. [**55:**7.10.1.2.3]

63.3.10.1.2.4 The 2-hour fire barrier wall shall not have more than two sides at approximately 90 degree (1.57 rad) directions or not more than three sides with connecting angles of approximately 135 degrees (2.36 rad). [**55:**7.10.1.2.4]

63.3.10.2 Distances to Exposures for Class 3.

63.3.10.2.1 The outdoor storage or use of unstable reactive Class 3 (nondetonable) compressed gas shall not be within 75 ft (23 m) of buildings, lot lines, streets, alleys, or public ways or means of egress. [**55:**7.10.2.1]

63.3.10.2.2 A 2-hour fire barrier wall without openings or penetrations, extending not less than 30 in. (762 mm) above and to the sides of the storage or use area, that interrupts the line of sight between the storage or use and the exposure shall be permitted in lieu of the 75 ft (23 m) distance specified by 63.3.10.2.1. [**55:**7.10.2.2]

63.3.10.2.2.1* Where a fire barrier wall is used to protect compressed gas systems, the system shall terminate downstream of the source valve. [**55:**7.10.2.2.1]

63.3.10.2.2.2 The fire barrier wall shall be either an independent structure or the exterior wall of the building adjacent to the storage or use area. [**55:**7.10.2.2.2]

63.3.10.2.2.3 The 2-hour fire barrier wall shall be located at least 5 ft (1.5 m) from any exposure. [**55:**7.10.2.2.3]

63.3.10.2.2.4 The 2-hour fire barrier wall shall not have more than two sides at approximately 90 degree (1.57 rad) directions or more than three sides with connecting angles of approximately 135 degrees (2.36 rad). [**55:**7.10.2.2.4]

63.3.10.3 Storage Configuration.

63.3.10.3.1 Unstable reactive Class 3 compressed gases stored in cylinders, containers, or tanks shall be arranged to limit individual groups of cylinders, containers, or tanks to areas not exceeding 100 ft^2 (9.3 m^2). [**55:**7.10.3.1]

63.3.10.3.2 Multiple areas shall be separated by aisles. [**55:**7.10.3.2]

63.3.10.3.3 Aisle widths shall not be less than the height of the cylinders, containers, or tanks or 4 ft (1.2 m), whichever is greater. [**55:**7.10.3.3]

63.3.10.4 Basements. Unstable reactive compressed gases shall not be stored in basements. [**55:**7.10.4]

63.3.10.5 Unstable Reactive Gases (Detonable).

63.3.10.5.1 Storage or Use.

63.3.10.5.2 Location. The location of storage areas shall be determined based on the requirements of the building code for explosive materials. [**55:**7.10.5.2]

63.4 Cryogenic Fluids.

63.4.1 General. This section shall apply to all cryogenic fluids, including those fluids regulated elsewhere in this *Code*, except that when specific requirements are provided in Sections 63.5, 63.7, or 63.11, those specific requirements shall apply as applicable. [**55:**8.1]

63.4.1.1 Storage, use, and handling of cryogenic fluids shall be in accordance with Sections 63.1, 63.2, and 63.4 as applicable. [**55:**8.1.1]

63.4.2* Containers — Design, Construction, and Maintenance. Containers employed for the storage or use of cryogenic fluids shall be designed, fabricated, tested, marked (stamped), and maintained in accordance with DOT regulations; Transport Canada (TC), *Transportation of Dangerous Goods Regulations*; the ASME *Boiler and Pressure Vessel Code*, "Rules for the Construction of Unfired Pressure Vessels"; or regulations of other administering agencies. [**55:**8.2]

63.4.2.1 Aboveground Tanks. Aboveground tanks for the storage of cryogenic fluids shall be in accordance with 63.4.2.1. [**55:**8.2.1]

63.4.2.1.1 Construction of the Inner Vessel. The inner vessel of storage tanks in cryogenic fluid service shall be designed and constructed in accordance with Section VIII, Division 1 of the ASME *Boiler and Pressure Vessel Code* and shall be vacuum jacketed in accordance with 63.4.2.1.2. [**55:**8.2.1.1]

63.4.2.1.2 Construction of the Vacuum Jacket (Outer Vessel).

63.4.2.1.2.1 The vacuum jacket used as an outer vessel for storage tanks in cryogenic fluid service shall be of welded steel construction designed to withstand the maximum internal and external pressure to which it will be subjected under operating conditions to include conditions of emergency pressure relief of the annular space between the inner vessel and the outer vessel. [**55**:8.2.1.2.1]

63.4.2.1.2.2 The jacket shall be designed to withstand a minimum collapsing pressure differential of 30 psi (207 kPa). [**55**:8.2.1.2.2]

63.4.2.1.2.3 Vacuum Level Monitoring.

63.4.2.1.2.3.1 A connection shall be provided on the exterior of the vacuum jacket to allow measurement of the pressure within the annular space between the inner vessel and the outer vessel. [**55**:8.2.1.2.3.1]

63.4.2.1.2.3.2 The connection shall be fitted with a bellows-sealed or diaphragm-type valve equipped with a vacuum gauge tube that is shielded to protect against damage from impact. [**55**:8.2.1.2.3.2]

63.4.2.2 Nonstandard Containers.

63.4.2.2.1 Containers, equipment, and devices that are not in compliance with recognized standards for design and construction shall be permitted if approved by the AHJ upon presentation of evidence that they are designed and constructed for safe operation. [**55**:8.2.2.1]

63.4.2.2.2 The following data shall be submitted to the AHJ with reference to the deviation from the standard with the application for approval:

(1) Type and use of container, equipment, or device
(2) Material to be stored, used, or transported
(3) Description showing dimensions and materials used in construction
(4) Design pressure, maximum operating pressure, and test pressure
(5) Type, size, and setting of pressure relief devices [**55**:8.2.2.2]

63.4.2.3 Foundations and Supports. Stationary tanks shall be provided with concrete or masonry foundations or structural steel supports on firm concrete or masonry foundations, and the requirements of 63.4.2.3.1 through 63.4.2.3.5 also shall apply. [**55**:8.2.3]

63.4.2.3.1 Excessive Loads. Stationary tanks shall be supported to prevent the concentration of excessive loads on the supporting portion of the shell. [**55**:8.2.3.1]

63.4.2.3.2 Expansion and Contraction. Foundations for horizontal containers shall be constructed to accommodate expansion and contraction of the container. [**55**:8.2.3.2]

63.4.2.3.3* Support of Ancilliary Equipment.

63.4.2.3.3.1 Foundations shall be provided to support the weight of vaporizers or heat exchangers. [**55**:8.2.3.3.1]

63.4.2.3.3.2 Foundations shall be designed to withstand soil and frost conditions as well as the anticipated seismic, snow, wind, and hydrostatic loading under operating conditions. [**55**:8.2.3.3.2]

63.4.2.3.4 Temperature Effects. Where drainage systems, terrain, or surfaces beneath stationary tanks are arranged in a manner that can subject stationary tank foundations or supports to temperatures below −130°F (−90°C), the foundations or supports shall be constructed of materials that are capable of withstanding the low-temperature effects of cryogenic fluid spillage. [**55**:8.2.3.4]

63.4.2.3.5 Corrosion Protection. Portions of stationary tanks in contact with foundations or saddles shall be painted to protect against corrosion. [**55**:8.2.3.5]

63.4.2.4 Pressure Relief Devices.

63.4.2.4.1 General.

63.4.2.4.1.1 Pressure relief devices shall be provided to protect containers and systems containing cryogenic fluids from rupture in the event of overpressure. [**55**:8.2.4.1.1]

63.4.2.4.1.2 Pressure relief devices shall be designed in accordance with CGA S-1.1, *Pressure Relief Device Standards — Part 1 — Cylinders for Compressed Gases*, and CGA S-1.2, *Pressure Relief Device Standards — Part 2 — Cargo and Portable Tanks for Compressed Gases*, for portable tanks; and CGA S-1.3, *Pressure Relief Device Standards — Part 3 — Stationary Storage Containers for Compressed Gases*, for stationary tanks. [**55**:8.2.4.1.2]

63.4.2.4.2 Containers Open to the Atmosphere. Portable containers that are open to the atmosphere and are designed to contain cryogenic fluids at atmospheric pressure shall not be required to be equipped with pressure relief devices. [**55**:8.2.4.2]

63.4.2.4.3 Equipment Other Than Containers. Heat exchangers, vaporizers, insulation casings surrounding containers, vessels, and coaxial piping systems in which liquefied cryogenic fluids could be trapped due to leakage from the primary container shall be provided with a pressure relief device. [**55**:8.2.4.3]

63.4.2.4.4 Sizing.

63.4.2.4.4.1 Pressure relief devices shall be sized in accordance with the specifications to which the container was fabricated. [**55**:8.2.4.4.1]

63.4.2.4.4.2 The pressure relief device shall have the capacity to prevent the maximum design pressure of the container or system from being exceeded. [**55**:8.2.4.4.2]

63.4.2.4.5 Accessibility. Pressure relief devices shall be located such that they are accessible for inspection and repair. [**55**:8.2.4.5]

63.4.2.4.5.1* ASME pressure relief valves shall be made to be tamper resistant in order to prevent adjusting of the set pressure by other than authorized personnel. [**55**:8.2.4.5.1]

63.4.2.4.5.2 Non-ASME pressure relief valves shall not be field adjusted. [**55**:8.2.4.5.2]

63.4.2.4.6 Arrangement.

63.4.2.4.6.1 Pressure Relief Devices. Pressure relief devices shall be arranged to discharge unobstructed to the open air in such a manner as to prevent impingement of escaping gas on personnel, containers, equipment, and adjacent structures or its entrance into enclosed spaces. [**55**:8.2.4.6.1]

63.4.2.4.6.2 Portable Containers with Volume Less Than 2.0 scf (0.057 Nm^3).

63.4.2.4.6.2.1 The arrangement of the discharge from pressure relief devices from DOT-specified containers with an internal water volume of 2.0 scf (0.057 Nm^3) or less shall be incorporated in the design of the container. [**55**:8.2.4.6.2.1]

63.4.2.4.6.2.2 Additional safeguards regarding placement or arrangement shall not be required. [**55**:8.2.4.6.2.2]

63.4.2.4.7 Shutoffs Between Pressure Relief Devices and Containers.

63.4.2.4.7.1 General. Shutoff valves installed between pressure relief devices and containers shall be in accordance with 63.4.2.4.7. [**55:**8.2.4.7.1]

63.4.2.4.7.2 Location. Shutoff valves shall not be installed between pressure relief devices and containers unless the valves or their use meet the requirements of 63.4.2.4.7.2.1 or 63.4.2.4.7.2.2. [**55:**8.2.4.7.2]

63.4.2.4.7.2.1 Security. Shutoff valves shall be locked in the open position, and their use shall be limited to service-related work performed by the supplier under the requirements of the ASME *Boiler and Pressure Vessel Code.* [**55:**8.2.4.7.2.1]

63.4.2.4.7.2.2 Multiple Pressure Relief Devices. Shutoff valves controlling multiple pressure relief devices on a container shall be installed so that either the type of valve installed or the arrangement provides the full required flow through the minimum number of required relief devices at all times. [**55:**8.2.4.7.2.2]

63.4.2.4.8 Temperature Limits. Pressure relief devices shall not be subjected to cryogenic fluid temperatures except when operating. [**55:**8.2.4.8]

63.4.3 Pressure Relief Vent Piping.

63.4.3.1 General. Pressure relief vent piping systems shall be constructed and arranged to direct the flow of gas to a safe location and in accordance with 63.4.3. [**55:**8.3.1]

63.4.3.2 Sizing. Pressure relief device vent piping shall have a cross-sectional area not less than that of the pressure relief device vent opening and shall be arranged so as not to restrict the flow of escaping gas. [**55:**8.3.2]

63.4.3.3 Arrangement. Pressure relief device vent piping and drains in vent lines shall be arranged so that escaping gas discharges unobstructed to the open air and does not impinge on personnel, containers, equipment, and adjacent structures or enter enclosed spaces. [**55:**8.3.3]

63.4.3.4 Installation. Pressure relief device vent lines shall be installed in a manner that excludes or removes moisture and condensation to prevent malfunction of the pressure relief device due to freezing or ice accumulation. [**55:**8.3.4]

63.4.3.5 Overfilling. Controls shall be provided to prevent overfilling of stationary containers. [**55:**8.3.5]

63.4.4 Marking.

63.4.4.1 General. Cryogenic containers and systems shall be marked in accordance with nationally recognized standards and in accordance with 63.4.4. [**55:**8.4.1]

63.4.4.1.1 Portable Containers.

63.4.4.1.1.1 Portable cryogenic containers shall be marked in accordance with CGA C-7, *Guide to the Preparation of Precautionary Labeling and Marking of Compressed Gas Containers.* [**55:**8.4.1.1.1]

63.4.4.1.1.2* All DOT-4L/TC-4LM liquid cylinders shall have product identification visible from all directions with minimum 2 in. (51 mm) high letters. [**55:**8.4.1.1.2]

63.4.4.1.2 Stationary Tanks. Stationary tanks shall be marked in accordance with NFPA 704. [**55:**8.4.1.2]

63.4.4.1.3 Identification Signs. Visible hazard identification signs shall be provided in accordance with NFPA 704 at entrances to buildings or areas in which cryogenic fluids are stored, handled, or used. [**55:**8.4.1.3]

63.4.4.2 Identification of Contents. Stationary containers shall be placarded with the identity of their contents to indicate the name of the material contained. [**55:**8.4.2]

63.4.4.3 Container Specification. Stationary containers shall be marked with the manufacturing specification and maximum allowable working pressure on a permanent nameplate. [**55:**8.4.3]

63.4.4.3.1 The nameplate shall be installed on the container in an accessible location. [**55:**8.4.3.1]

63.4.4.3.2 The nameplate shall be marked in accordance with nationally recognized standards. [**55:**8.4.3.2]

63.4.4.4 Identification of Container Connections.

63.4.4.4.1 Container inlet and outlet connections, liquid-level limit controls, valves, and pressure gauges shall be identified using one of the methods prescribed by 63.4.4.4.1.1 through 63.4.4.4.1.2. [**55:**8.4.4.1]

63.4.4.4.1.1 They shall be marked with a permanent tag or label identifying their function. [**55:**8.4.4.1.1]

63.4.4.4.1.2 They shall be identified by a schematic drawing that indicates their function and designates whether they are connected to the vapor or liquid space of the container. [**55:**8.4.4.1.2]

63.4.4.4.1.2.1 When a schematic drawing is provided, it shall be attached to the container and maintained in a legible condition. [**55:**8.4.4.1.2.1]

63.4.4.5 Identification of Piping Systems. Piping systems shall be identified in accordance with ASME A13.1, *Scheme for the Identification of Piping Systems.* [**55:**8.4.5]

63.4.4.6 Identification of Emergency Shutoff Valves. Emergency shutoff valves on stationary containers shall be identified, visible, and indicated by means of a sign. [**55:**8.4.6]

63.4.5 Medical Cryogenic Systems.

63.4.5.1 Bulk cryogenic fluid systems in medical gas applications at health care facilities shall be in accordance with Section 63.4, 63.1.1.4(3), and the material-specific requirements of Chapter 9 of NFPA 55 as applicable. [**55:**8.5.1]

63.4.5.1.1 Bulk cryogenic fluid systems shall be in accordance with the following provisions as applicable:

(1) Where located in a court, systems shall be in accordance with 63.4.13.2.7.2.
(2) Where located indoors, systems shall be in accordance with 63.4.14.11.1.
(3) Systems shall be installed by personnel qualified in accordance with CGA M-1, *Guide for Medical Gas Installations at Consumer Sites,* or ASSE 6015, *Professional Qualification Standard for Bulk Medical Gas Systems Installers.*
(4) Systems shall be installed in compliance with Food and Drug Administration Current Good Manufacturing Practices as found in 21 CFR 210 and 21 CFR 211. [**55:**8.5.1.1]

63.4.5.1.2 The following components of the bulk system shall be accessible and visible to delivery personnel during filling operations:

(1) Fill connection
(2) Top and bottom fill valves
(3) Hose purge valve
(4) Vent valve
(5) Full trycock valve
(6) Liquid level gauge
(7) Tank pressure gauge [**55:**8.5.1.2]

63.4.5.1.3 Bulk cryogenic fluid systems shall be anchored with foundations in accordance with the provisions of CGA M-1, *Guide for Medical Gas Installations at Consumer Sites.* [**55:**8.5.1.3]

63.4.5.1.4 Bulk cryogenic fluid systems shall consist of the following:

(1) One or more main supply vessel(s), whose capacity shall be determined after consideration of the customer usage requirements, delivery schedules, proximity of the facility to alternative supplies, and the emergency plan
(2) A contents gauge on each of the main vessel(s)
(3) A reserve supply sized for greater than an average day's supply, with the size of vessel or number of cylinders being determined after consideration of delivery schedules, proximity of the facility to alternative supplies, and the facility's emergency plan
(4) At least two main vessel relief valves and rupture discs installed downstream of a three-way (three-port) valve
(5) A check valve located in the primary supply piping upstream of the intersection with a secondary supply or reserve supply [**55:**8.5.1.4]

63.4.5.1.5 Bulk cryogenic fluid reserve supply systems consisting of either a second cryogenic fluid source or a compressed gas source shall include the following:

(1) When the reserve source is a compressed gas source, the reserve shall be equipped with the following:
   (a) A cylinder manifold having not less than three gas cylinder connections or as otherwise required for an average of one day's gas supply
   (b) A pressure switch to monitor the pressure in the cylinder manifold
(2) When the reserve source is a second cryogenic fluid vessel, the reserve tank shall be equipped with the following:
   (a) An actuating switch or sensor to monitor the internal tank pressure
   (b) A contents gauge to monitor the liquid level
(3) When the reserve source is either a cryogenic fluid or compressed gas source, a check valve shall be provided to prevent backflow into the reserve system [**55:**8.5.1.5]

63.4.5.1.6 Bulk cryogenic fluid systems shall include a fill mechanism consisting of the following components:

(1) A nonremovable product-specific fill connection in compliance with CGA V-6, *Standard Cryogenic Liquid Transfer Connection*
(2) A means to cap and secure the fill connection inlet
(3) A check valve to prevent product backflow from the fill inlet
(4) A fill hose purge valve
(5) Supports that hold the fill piping off the ground
(6) A secure connection between the bulk tank and the fill piping
(7) Supports as necessary to hold the fill line in position during all operations associated with the filling procedure [**55:**8.5.1.6]

63.4.5.1.7 Where vaporizers are required to convert cryogenic liquid to the gaseous state, the vaporizer units shall conform to the following:

(1) Be permitted to operate by either ambient heat transfer or external thermal source (e.g., electric heater, hot water, steam)
(2) Be designed to provide capacity for the customer's peak and average flow rates under local conditions, seasonal conditions for weather and humidity, and structures that obstruct air circulation flow and sunlight
(3) If switching is required as part of the system design, have piping and manual/automatic valving configured in such a manner that operating vaporizer(s) or sections of the vaporizer can be switched to nonoperating vaporizer or section of the vaporizer to de-ice through a valving configuration that ensures continuous flow to the facility through either or both vaporizers and/or sections of the vaporizer if valving switchover fails [**55:**8.5.1.7]

63.4.5.1.8 Where a vaporizer requires an external thermal source, the flow from the source of supply shall be unaffected by the loss of the external thermal source through either of the following:

(1) Reserve ambient heat transfer vaporizers capable of providing capacity for at least one day's average supply and piped so as to be unaffected by flow stoppage through the main vaporizer
(2) A reserve noncryogenic source capable of providing at least one day's average supply [**55:**8.5.1.8]

63.4.6 Security.

63.4.6.1 General. Cryogenic containers and systems shall be secured against accidental dislodgement and against access by unauthorized personnel in accordance with 63.4.6. [**55:**8.6.1]

63.4.6.2* Security of Areas. Areas used for the storage of containers and systems shall be secured against unauthorized entry. [**55:**8.6.2]

63.4.6.2.1 Administrative controls shall be allowed to be used to control access to individual storage areas located in secure facilities not accessible by the general public. [**55:**8.6.2.1]

63.4.6.3 Securing of Containers. Stationary containers shall be secured to foundations in accordance with the building code. [**55:**8.6.3]

63.4.6.3.1 Portable containers subject to shifting or upset shall be secured. [**55:**8.6.3.1]

63.4.6.3.2 Nesting shall be permitted as a means of securing portable containers. [**55:**8.6.3.2]

63.4.6.4 Securing of Vaporizers. Vaporizers, heat exchangers, and similar equipment shall be secured to foundations, and their connecting piping shall be designed and constructed to provide for the effects of expansion and contraction due to temperature changes. [**55:**8.6.4]

63.4.6.5 Physical Protection. Containers, piping, valves, pressure relief devices, regulating equipment, and other appurtenances shall be protected against physical damage and tampering. [**55:**8.6.5]

63.4.7 Separation from Hazardous Conditions.

63.4.7.1 General. Cryogenic containers and systems in storage or use shall be separated from materials and conditions that present exposure hazards to or from each other in accordance with . [**55:**8.7.1]

63.4.7.2* Stationary Cryogenic Containers. Stationary containers located outdoors shall be separated from exposure hazards in accordance with the minimum separation distances indicated in Table 63.4.7.2. [**55:**8.7.2]

Table 63.4.7.2 Minimum Separation Distance Between Stationary Cryogenic Containers and Exposures

Exposure	Minimum Distance	
	ft	m
(1) Buildings, regardless of construction type	1	0.3
(2) Wall openings	1	0.3
(3) Air intakes	10	3.1
(4) Property lines	5	1.5
(5) Places of public assembly (assembly occupancies)	50	15
(6) Nonambulatory patient areas	50	15
(7) Combustible materials, (e.g., paper, leaves, weeds, dry grass, debris)	15	4.5
(8) Incompatible hazardous materials	20	6.1
(9) Building exits	10	3.1

[**55:** Table 8.7.2]

63.4.7.2.1 Fire Barriers. A 2-hour fire barrier wall shall be permitted in lieu of the distances specified by Table 63.4.7.2 for items 1, 4, 7, 8 and 9, where in accordance with the provisions of 63.4.7.2.1.1 through 63.4.7.2.1.4. [**55:**8.7.2.1]

63.4.7.2.1.1 The fire barrier wall shall be without openings or penetrations. [**55:**8.7.2.1.1]

63.4.7.2.1.1.1 Penetrations of the fire barrier wall by conduit or piping shall be permitted provided that the penetration is protected with a firestop system in accordance with the building code. [**55:**8.7.2.1.1.1]

63.4.7.2.1.2 The fire barrier wall shall be either an independent structure or the exterior wall of the building adjacent to the storage system. [**55:**8.7.2.1.2]

63.4.7.2.1.3 The fire barrier wall shall be located not less than 5 ft (1.5 m) from any exposure. [**55:**8.7.2.1.3]

63.4.7.2.1.4 The fire barrier wall shall not have more than two sides at 90 degree (1.57 rad) directions or not more than three sides with connecting angles of 135 degrees (2.36 rad). [**55:**8.7.2.1.4]

63.4.7.2.1.4.1* The connecting angles between fire barrier walls shall be permitted to be reduced to less than 135 degrees (2.36 rad) for installations consisting of three walls when in accordance with 63.4.13.2.7.2. [**55:**8.7.2.1.4.1]

63.4.7.2.1.5 Where the requirement of 63.4.7.2.1.4 is met, the bulk system shall be a minimum distance of 1 ft (0.3 m) from the fire barrier wall. [**55:**8.7.2.1.5]

63.4.7.2.2 Point-of-Fill Connections. Point-of-fill connections serving stationary containers filled by mobile transport equipment shall not be positioned closer to exposures than the minimum distances in Table 63.4.7.2. [**55:**8.7.2.2]

63.4.7.2.3 Surfaces Beneath Containers. The surface of the area on which stationary containers are placed, including the surface of the area located below the point at which connections are made for the purpose of filling such containers, shall be compatible with the fluid in the container. [**55:**8.7.2.3]

63.4.7.3 Portable Cryogenic Containers. Portable containers used for cryogenic fluids located outdoors shall be separated from exposure hazards in accordance with Table 63.4.7.3. [**55:**8.7.3]

Table 63.4.7.3 Minimum Separation Distance Between Portable Cryogenic Containers and Exposures

Exposure	Minimum Distance	
	ft	m
Building exits	10	3.1
Wall openings	1	0.3
Air intakes	10	3.1
Property lines	5	1.5
Room or area exits	3	0.9
Combustible materials, (e.g., paper, leaves, weeds, dry grass, or debris)	15	4.5
Incompatible hazardous materials	20	6.1

[**55:** Table 8.7.3]

63.4.7.3.1 Non-bulk portable containers of liquefied hydrogen shall be separated from exposure hazards in accordance with Table 63.4.7.3.1. [**55:**8.7.3.1]

63.4.7.3.2 Fire Barriers. A 2-hour fire barrier wall shall be permitted in lieu of the distances specified by Table 63.4.7.3 or Table 63.4.7.3.1 when in accordance with the provisions of 63.4.7.3.2.1 through 63.4.7.3.2.4. [**55:**8.7.3.2]

63.4.7.3.2.1 The fire barrier wall shall be without openings or penetrations. [**55:**8.7.3.2.1]

63.4.7.3.2.1.1 Penetrations of the fire barrier wall by conduit or piping shall be permitted provided that the penetration is protected with a firestop system in accordance with the building code. [**55:**8.7.3.2.1.1]

63.4.7.3.2.2 The fire barrier wall shall be either an independent structure or the exterior wall of the building adjacent to the storage system. [**55:**8.7.3.2.2]

63.4.7.3.2.3 The fire barrier wall shall be located not less than 5 ft (1.5 m) from any exposure. [**55:**8.7.3.2.3]

63.4.7.3.2.4 The fire barrier wall shall not have more than two sides at approximately 90 degree (1.57 rad) directions or not more than three sides with connecting angles of approximately 135 degrees (2.36 rad). [**55:**8.7.3.2.4]

63.4.8 Electrical Wiring and Equipment.

63.4.8.1 General. Electrical wiring and equipment shall be in accordance with *NFPA 70* and 63.4.8. [**55:**8.8.1]

Table 63.4.7.3.1 Distance to Exposures for Non-Bulk Liquefied Hydrogen (LH$_2$)

Maximum Amount per Storage Area (gal)	Minimum Distance Between Storage Areas (ft)	Minimum Distance to Lot Lines of Property That Can Be Built Upon (ft)	Minimum Distance to Public Streets, Public Alleys, or Public Ways (ft)	Minimum Distance to Buildings on the Same Property		
				Less than 2-Hour Construction	2-Hour Construction	4-Hour Construction
0–39.7	5	5	5	5	0	0
39.8–186.9	10	10	10	10	5	0
187–448.7	10	15	15	20	5	0
448.8–747.8	10	20	20	20	5	0
>747.8	20	25	25	20	5	0

For SI units: 1 ft = 305 mm.

Notes:
(1) For requirements on minimum distance to air intakes, see 63.3.6.2.4.
(2) For requirements on minimum distance to building openings including exits, see 63.3.6.2.5.
(3) When 63.4.7.3.2 is used as a means of distance reduction, the configuration of the fire barriers should be designed to allow natural ventilation to prevent the accumulation of hazardous gas concentrations.
[55:Table 8.7.3.1]

63.4.8.2 Location. Containers and systems shall not be located where they could become part of an electrical circuit. [55:8.8.2]

63.4.8.3 Electrical Grounding and Bonding. Containers and systems shall not be used for electrical grounding. [55:8.8.3]

63.4.8.3.1 When electrical grounding and bonding is required, the system shall be in accordance with *NFPA 70*. [55:8.8.3.1]

63.4.8.3.2 The grounding system shall be protected against corrosion, including corrosion caused by stray electrical currents. [55:8.8.3.2]

63.4.9 Service and Repair. Service, repair, modification, or removal of valves, pressure relief devices, or other container appurtenances shall be in accordance with nationally recognized codes and standards. [55:8.9]

63.4.9.1 Containers. Containers that have been removed from service shall be handled in an approved manner. [55:8.9.1]

63.4.9.1.1 Testing. Containers out of service in excess of 1 year shall be inspected and tested as required under 63.4.9.1.2. [55:8.9.1.1]

63.4.9.1.2 Pressure Relief Device Testing. The pressure relief devices shall be tested for operability and to determine if they are set at the relief pressure required by the tank design. [55:8.9.1.2]

63.4.9.1.3 Containers that have previously been used for flammable cryogenic fluids and have been removed from service shall be purged with an inert gas to remove residual flammable gas and stored with all valves closed and the valve outlets plugged. [55:8.9.1.3]

63.4.9.2 Systems. Service and repair of containers or systems shall be performed by trained personnel in accordance with nationally recognized standards and with the permission of the container owner. [55:8.9.2]

63.4.10 Unauthorized Use. Containers shall not be used for any purpose other than to serve as a vessel for containing the product for which it is designated. [55:8.10]

63.4.11 Leaks, Damage, and Corrosion.

63.4.11.1 Leaking, damaged, or corroded containers shall be removed from service. [55:8.11.1]

63.4.11.2 Leaking, damaged, or corroded systems shall be replaced, repaired, or removed from service. [55:8.11.2]

63.4.12 Lighting. Where required by the AHJ, lighting, including emergency lighting, shall be provided for fire appliances and operating facilities such as walkways, control valves, and gates ancillary to stationary containers. [55:8.12]

63.4.13 Storage.

63.4.13.1 Indoor Storage.

63.4.13.1.1 Installation. Stationary containers indoors shall be installed in accordance with Chapters 9 and 11 of NFPA 55 or with ANSI/CGA P-18, *Standard for Bulk Inert Gas Systems at Consumer Sites*. [55:8.13.1.1]

63.4.13.1.2 Stationary Containers. Stationary containers shall be in accordance with 63.4.2. [55:8.13.1.2]

63.4.13.1.3 Cryogenic Fluids. Cryogenic fluids in stationary or portable containers stored indoors shall be stored in buildings, rooms, or areas constructed in accordance with the building code. [55:8.13.1.3]

63.4.13.1.4 Ventilation. Ventilation shall be in accordance with 63.2.16. [55:8.13.1.4]

63.4.13.2 Outdoor Storage.

63.4.13.2.1 General. Cryogenic fluids in stationary or portable containers stored outdoors shall be in accordance with 63.4.13.2. [55:8.13.2.1]

63.4.13.2.2 Access. Stationary containers shall be located to provide access by mobile supply equipment and authorized personnel. [55:8.13.2.2]

63.4.13.2.2.1 Where exit access is provided to serve areas in which equipment is installed, the minimum width shall be not less than 28 in. (710 mm). [55:8.13.2.2.1]

63.4.13.2.3 Physical Protection. Cryogenic fluid containers, cylinders, tanks, and systems that could be exposed to physical damage shall be protected. [**55:**8.13.2.3]

63.4.13.2.3.1 Guard posts or other means shall be provided to protect cryogenic fluid containers, cylinders, tanks, and systems indoors and outdoors from vehicular damage. *(See Section 4.11 of NFPA 55.)* [**55:**8.13.2.3.1]

63.4.13.2.4 Diked Areas Containing Other Hazardous Materials. Containers of cryogenic fluids shall not be located within diked areas with other hazardous materials. [**55:**8.13.2.4]

63.4.13.2.5* Areas Subject to Flooding. Stationary containers located in flood hazard areas shall be anchored to prevent flotation during conditions of the design flood as designated by the building code. [**55:**8.13.2.5]

63.4.13.2.5.1 Elevated Tanks. Structures supporting elevated tanks and tanks that are supported at a level above that designated in the design flood shall be anchored to resist lateral shifting due to flood and other hydrostatic effects. [**55:**8.13.2.5.1]

63.4.13.2.5.2 Underground Tanks. Underground tanks in flood hazard areas shall be anchored to prevent flotation, collapse, or lateral movement resulting from hydrostatic loads, including the effects of buoyancy, during conditions of the design flood. [**55:**8.13.2.5.2]

63.4.13.2.6 Drainage.

63.4.13.2.6.1 The area surrounding stationary and portable containers shall be provided with a means to prevent accidental discharge of fluids from endangering personnel, containers, equipment, and adjacent structures and from entering enclosed spaces in accordance with this *Code*. [**55:**8.13.2.6.1]

63.4.13.2.6.2 The stationary container shall not be placed where spilled or discharged fluids will be retained around the container. [**55:**8.13.2.6.2]

63.4.13.2.6.3 The provisions of 63.4.13.2.6.2 shall be permitted to be altered or waived where the AHJ determines that the container does not constitute a hazard after consideration of special features such as the following:

(1) Crushed rock utilized as a heat sink
(2) Topographical conditions
(3) Nature of occupancy
(4) Proximity to structures on the same or adjacent property
(5) Capacity and construction of containers and character of fluids to be stored [**55:**8.13.2.6.3]

63.4.13.2.6.4 The grade for a distance of not less than 50 ft (15.2 m) from where cryogenic fluid storage or delivery systems are installed shall be higher than the grade on which flammable or combustible liquids are stored or used. [**55:**8.13.2.6.4]

63.4.13.2.6.4.1* Drainage Control.

(A) Where the grade differential between the storage or delivery system and the flammable or combustible liquids storage or use area is not in accordance with 63.4.13.2.6.4, diversion curbs or other means of drainage control shall be used to divert the flow of flammable or combustible liquids away from the cryogenic system. [**55:**8.13.2.6.4.1(A)]

(B) The means of drainage control shall prevent the flow of flammable or combustible liquid to a distance not less than 50 ft (15.2 m) from all parts of the delivery system. [**55:**8.13.2.6.4.1(B)]

63.4.13.2.7 Outdoor Installations.

63.4.13.2.7.1 Enclosed Courts. Stationary containers shall not be installed within enclosed courts. [**55:**8.13.2.7.1]

63.4.13.2.7.2* Courts. Stationary containers shall be sited so that they are open to the surrounding environment except that encroachment by building walls of unlimited height shall be permitted when in accordance with the distances specified by Table 63.4.7.2 or the material-specific tables in Chapters 9 through 11 of NFPA 55. [**55:**8.13.2.7.2]

63.4.13.2.7.2.1* When exterior building walls encroach on the system to form a court, the system shall be located at a distance not less than the height of the wall from at least two court walls. [**55:**8.13.2.7.2.1]

63.4.13.2.7.2.2 The required distance between the exterior walls of the building forming the court and the container shall be determined independently without regard to fire barrier walls used to allow encroachment by fire exposure hazards. [**55:**8.13.2.7.2.2]

63.4.13.2.7.3 Fire Department Access. Fire department access roadways or other approved means shall be in accordance with Section 18.2. [**55:**8.13.2.7.3]

63.4.14 Use and Handling.

63.4.14.1 General. Use and handling of containers and systems shall be in accordance with 63.4.14. [**55:**8.14.1]

63.4.14.1.1 Operating Instructions. Operating instructions shall be provided for installations that require the operation of equipment. [**55:**8.14.1.1]

63.4.14.1.2 Attended Delivery. A qualified person shall be in attendance at all times cryogenic fluid is transferred from mobile supply units to a storage system. [**55:**8.14.1.2]

63.4.14.1.3 Inspection.

63.4.14.1.3.1 Cryogenic fluid storage systems shall be inspected and maintained by a qualified representative of the equipment owner as required by the material-specific requirements of Chapters 9 and 11 of NFPA 55. [**55:**8.14.1.3.1]

63.4.14.1.3.2* The interval between inspections other than those specified by material-specific requirements shall be based on nationally recognized good practices or standards. [**55:**8.14.1.3.1.1]

63.4.14.1.3.3 A record of the inspection shall be prepared and provided to the user or the AHJ upon request. [**55:**8.14.1.3.2]

63.4.14.1.4 Design.

63.4.14.1.4.1 Nationally Recognized Good Practices. Where nationally recognized good practices or standards have been established for the process employed, such practices and standards shall be followed. [**55:**8.14.1.4.1]

63.4.14.1.4.2 Piping Systems. Piping, tubing, fittings, and related components shall be designed, fabricated, and tested in accordance with the requirements of ANSI/ASME B31.3, *Process Piping*, or other approved standards and shall be in accordance with 63.4.14.2. [**55:**8.14.1.4.2]

63.4.14.1.5 Cleaning and Purging of Gas Piping Systems. Cleaning and purging of piping systems shall be in accordance with 63.3.1.19. [**55:**8.14.1.5]

63.4.14.2 Piping and Appurtenances.

63.4.14.2.1 Piping systems shall be designed for the use intended through the full range of pressure and temperature to which they will be subjected. [**55**:8.14.2.1]

63.4.14.2.2 Piping systems shall be designed and constructed to allow for expansion, contraction, vibration, settlement, and fire exposure. [**55**:8.14.2.2]

63.4.14.3 Joints. Joints in piping and tubing shall be in accordance with the requirements of ANSI/ASME B31.3, *Process Piping*, or other approved standards. [**55**:8.14.3]

63.4.14.4 Valves and Accessory Equipment. Valves and accessory equipment shall be acceptable for the intended use at the temperatures of the application and shall be designed and constructed to withstand the maximum pressure at the minimum temperature to which they will be subjected. [**55**:8.14.4]

63.4.14.5 Shutoff Valves on Containers. Shutoff valves shall be provided on all container connections, except for pressure relief devices. [**55**:8.14.5]

63.4.14.5.1 Shutoff valves for containers with multiple pressure relief devices shall be permitted in accordance with 63.4.2.4.7. [**55**:8.14.5.1]

63.4.14.5.2 Shutoff valves shall be accessible and located as close as practical to the container. [**55**:8.14.5.2]

63.4.14.6 Shutoff Valves on Piping.

63.4.14.6.1 Shutoff valves shall be installed in piping containing cryogenic fluids where needed to limit the volume of liquid discharged in the event of piping or equipment failure. [**55**:8.14.6.1]

63.4.14.6.2 Pressure relief valves shall be installed where liquid or cold gas can be trapped between shutoff valves in the piping system. *(See 63.4.2.4.)* [**55**:8.14.6.2]

63.4.14.7 Physical Protection and Support.

63.4.14.7.1 Aboveground piping systems shall be supported and protected from physical damage. [**55**:8.14.7.1]

63.4.14.7.2 Piping passing through walls shall be protected from mechanical damage. [**55**:8.14.7.2]

63.4.14.8 Corrosion Protection.

63.4.14.8.1 Aboveground piping that is subject to corrosion shall be protected against corrosion. [**55**:8.14.8.1]

63.4.14.8.2 Belowground piping shall be protected against corrosion. [**55**:8.14.8.2]

63.4.14.9 Cathodic Protection. Where required, cathodic protection shall be in accordance with 63.4.14.9. [**55**:8.14.9]

63.4.14.9.1 Operation. Where installed, cathodic protection systems shall be operated and maintained to continuously provide corrosion protection. [**55**:8.14.9.1]

63.4.14.9.2 Inspection.

63.4.14.9.2.1 Container systems equipped with cathodic protection shall be inspected for the intended operation by a cathodic protection tester. [**55**:8.14.9.2.1]

63.4.14.9.2.2 The cathodic protection tester shall be certified as being qualified by the National Association of Corrosion Engineers, International (NACE). [**55**:8.14.9.2.2]

63.4.14.9.3 Impressed Current Systems.

63.4.14.9.3.1 Systems equipped with impressed current cathodic protection systems shall be inspected in accordance with the requirements of the design and 63.4.14.9.2. [**55**:8.14.9.3.1]

63.4.14.9.3.2 The design limits shall be available to the AHJ upon request. [**55**:8.14.9.3.2]

63.4.14.9.3.3 The system owner shall maintain the following records to demonstrate that the cathodic protection is in conformance with the requirements of the design:

(1) The results of inspections of the system
(2) The results of testing that has been completed
[**55**:8.14.9.3.3]

63.4.14.9.4 Repairs, maintenance, or replacement of a cathodic protection system shall be under the supervision of a corrosion expert certified by NACE. [**55**:8.14.9.4]

63.4.14.9.4.1 The corrosion expert shall be certified by NACE as a senior corrosion technologist, a cathodic protection specialist, or a corrosion specialist or shall be a registered engineer with registration in a field that includes education and experience in corrosion control. [**55**:8.14.9.4.1]

63.4.14.10 Testing.

63.4.14.10.1 Piping systems shall be tested and proved free of leaks after installation as required by the codes and standards to which they are designed and constructed. [**55**:8.14.10.1]

63.4.14.10.2 Test pressures shall not be less than 150 percent of the maximum allowable working pressure when hydraulic testing is conducted or 110 percent when testing is conducted pneumatically. [**55**:8.14.10.2]

63.4.14.11 Material-Specific Requirements.

63.4.14.11.1 Indoor Use. Indoor use of cryogenic fluids shall be in accordance with the material-specific provisions of Chapters 9 and 11 of NFPA 55 or with ANSI/CGA P-18, *Standard for Bulk Inert Gas Systems at Consumer Sites*, and 63.4.14.2. [**55**:8.14.11.1]

63.4.14.11.2 Outdoor Use.

63.4.14.11.2.1 General. Outdoor use of cryogenic fluids shall be in accordance with the material-specific provisions of Chapters 9 and 11 of NFPA 55 or with ANSI/CGA P-18, *Standard for Bulk Inert Gas Systems at Consumer Sites*, and 63.4.14.2. [**55**:8.14.11.2.1]

63.4.14.11.2.2 Separation. Distances from property lines, buildings, and exposure hazards shall be in accordance with Table 63.4.7.2 and Table 63.4.7.3 and the material-specific provisions of Chapters 9 and 11 of NFPA 55 or with ANSI/CGA P-18, *Standard for Bulk Inert Gas Systems at Consumer Sites*. [**55**:8.14.11.2.2]

63.4.14.11.2.3 Emergency Shutoff Valves.

63.4.14.11.2.3.1* Accessible manual or automatic emergency shutoff valves shall be provided to shut off the cryogenic fluid supply in case of emergency. [**55**:8.14.11.2.3.1]

(A) Manual emergency shutoff valves or the device that activates an automatic emergency shutoff valve on a bulk source or piping systems serving the bulk supply shall be identified by means of a sign. [**55**:8.14.11.2.3.1(A)]

63.4.14.11.2.3.2 Emergency shutoff valves shall be located at the point of use, at the source of supply, and at the point where the system enters the building. [**55:**8.14.11.2.3.2]

63.4.14.11.3 Filling and Dispensing.

63.4.14.11.3.1 General. Filling and dispensing of cryogenic fluids shall be in accordance with 63.4.14.1.2. [**55:**8.14.11.3.1]

63.4.14.11.3.2 Dispensing Areas. Dispensing of cryogenic fluids associated with physical or health hazards shall be conducted in approved locations. [**55:**8.14.11.3.2]

63.4.14.11.3.2.1 Indoor Dispensing Areas. Dispensing indoors shall be conducted in areas constructed in accordance with the building code. [**55:**8.14.11.3.2.1]

63.4.14.11.3.2.2 Ventilation. Indoor areas in which cryogenic fluids are dispensed shall be ventilated in accordance with the requirements of 63.2.16 and the mechanical code. [**55:**8.14.11.3.2.2]

63.4.14.11.3.2.3 Piping Systems. Piping systems utilized for filling or dispensing of cryogenic fluids shall be designed and constructed in accordance with 63.4.14.2. [**55:**8.14.11.3.2.3]

63.4.14.11.3.3 Vehicle Loading and Unloading Areas. Loading and unloading areas shall be constructed in accordance with the requirements of Chapter 9 of NFPA 55 for liquid oxygen, Chapter 11 of NFPA 55 for liquid hydrogen, or ANSI/CGA P-18, *Standard for Bulk Inert Gas Systems at Consumer Sites*, for inert cryogenic fluids, as applicable. [**55:**8.14.11.3.3]

63.4.14.11.3.4* A noncombustible, delivery vehicle spill pad shall be provided when required by the material-specific requirements of Chapter 9 of NFPA 55 for liquid oxygen, Chapter 11 of NFPA 55 for liquid hydrogen, or ANSI/CGA P-18, *Standard for Bulk Inert Gas Systems at Consumer Sites*. [**55:**8.14.11.3.4]

63.4.14.11.3.4.1* A noncombustible spill pad shall be provided for delivery areas where bulk liquid helium is transferred from delivery vehicles. [**55:**8.14.11.3.4.1]

63.4.14.11.3.5 Filling Controls. A pressure gauge and full trycock valve shall be provided and shall be visible from the delivery point to allow the delivery operator to monitor the internal pressure and liquid level of stationary containers during filling. [**55:**8.14.11.3.5]

63.4.14.11.3.5.1 When the containers being filled are remote from the delivery point and pressure gauges or full trycock valves are not visible, redundant gauges and valves shall be installed at the filling connection. [**55:**8.14.11.3.5.1]

63.4.14.11.4 Handling.

63.4.14.11.4.1 Applicability. Handling of cryogenic containers shall be in accordance 63.4.14.11.4. [**55:**8.14.11.4.1]

63.4.14.11.4.2 Carts and Trucks.

63.4.14.11.4.2.1 Cryogenic containers shall be moved using an approved method. [**55:**8.14.11.4.2.1]

63.4.14.11.4.2.2 Where cryogenic containers are moved by hand cart, hand truck, or other mobile device, that device shall be designed for the secure movement of the container. [**55:**8.14.11.4.2.2]

63.4.14.11.4.3 Design. Carts and trucks used to transport cryogenic containers shall be designed to provide a stable base for the commodities to be transported and shall have a means of restraining containers to prevent accidental dislodgement. [**55:**8.14.11.4.3]

63.4.14.11.4.4 Closed Containers.

63.4.14.11.4.4.1 Pressurized containers shall be closed while being transported. [**55:**8.14.11.4.4.1]

63.4.14.11.4.4.2 Containers designed for use at atmospheric conditions shall be transported with appropriate loose-fitting covers in place to prevent spillage. [**55:**8.14.11.4.4.2]

63.5 Bulk Oxygen Systems.

63.5.1 Bulk oxygen systems shall comply with Chapter 9 of NFPA 55.

63.5.2 Cleaning and purging of piping systems shall be in accordance with 63.3.1.19. [**55:**9.4.1.9]

63.5.3 Cleaning of oxygen systems used in medical gas service shall be in accordance with NFPA 99, *Health Care Facilities Code*. *(See also 9.4.3.1 of NFPA 55.)* [**55:**9.4.1.9.1]

63.6 Bulk Gaseous Hydrogen Systems.

63.6.1 Bulk hydrogen compressed gas systems shall comply with NFPA 2, *Hydrogen Technologies Code*, and Chapter 10 of NFPA 55.

63.6.2 Cleaning and purging of piping systems shall be in accordance with 63.3.1.19. [**55:**10.2.3.2]

63.7 Bulk Liquefied Hydrogen Systems.

63.7.1 Bulk liquefied hydrogen systems shall comply with NFPA 2, *Hydrogen Technologies Code*, and Chapter 11 of NFPA 55.

63.7.2 Cleaning and purging of piping systems shall be in accordance with 63.3.1.19. [**55:**11.2.3.9]

63.8 Gas Generation Systems.

63.8.1 General. Gas generation systems shall comply with NFPA 2, *Hydrogen Technologies Code*, and Chapter 12 of NFPA 55.

63.8.2 Process purging and vents shall conform to the following:

(1) Pressure equipment and piping intended to be purged, pressure regulators, relief valves, and other potential sources of combustible gas shall be vented to the outside of the building in accordance with the applicable requirements of 63.2.15 or 63.3.1.19.
(2) The vent shall be designed to prevent entry of water or foreign objects.
(3) The vent gas shall be directed so as to not create additional hazards to the building openings, such as windows, doors, or HVAC intakes. [**55:**12.3.2.8.5.7]

63.9 Insulated Liquid Carbon Dioxide Systems.
Insulated liquid carbon dioxide systems shall comply with Chapter 13 of NFPA 55.

63.10 Storage, Handling, and Use of Ethylene Oxide for Sterilization and Fumigation.

63.10.1 General. Storage, handling, and use of ethylene oxide for sterilization and fumigation shall comply with Chapter 14 of NFPA 55.

63.10.2 Cleaning and Purging of Gas Piping Systems.

63.10.2.1 Cleaning and purging of piping systems shall be in accordance with 63.3.1.19. [**55:**14.4.1.3]

63.10.2.2 Piping and valves that have been used to transport ethylene oxide to or from a sterilizer to the emission control or release point shall be drained and purged in accordance with 63.3.1.19 prior to dismantling. [55:14.4.3.1]

63.11 Liquid Oxygen in Home Care.

63.11.1 General. The storage and use of liquid oxygen (LOX) in home care shall comply with Sections 63.4 and 63.11.

63.11.1.1 Gas equipment used in the home for health care shall conform to applicable requirements of NFPA 99, *Health Care Facilities Code*.

63.11.2 Information and Instructions. The seller of liquid oxygen shall provide the user with information in written form that includes, but is not limited to, the following:

(1) Manufacturer's instructions and labeling for storage and use of the containers
(2) Locating containers away from ignition sources, exits, electrical hazards, and high temperature devices in accordance with 63.11.3.2
(3) Restraint of containers to prevent falling in accordance with 63.11.3.3
(4) Requirements for handling containers in accordance with 63.11.3.4
(5) Safeguards for refilling of containers in accordance with 63.11.3.5

63.11.3 Containers. Containers of liquid oxygen in home care shall be in accordance with 63.11.3.1 through 63.11.3.5.

63.11.3.1* Containers shall be stored, used, and operated in accordance with the manufacturer's instructions and labeling.

63.11.3.2 Containers shall not be located in areas as follows:

(1) Where they can be overturned due to operation of a door
(2) Where they are in the direct path of egress
(3) Where they are subject to damage from falling objects
(4) Where they can become part of an electrical circuit
(5) Where open flames and high temperature devices could cause a hazard

63.11.3.3* Liquid oxygen home care containers shall be restrained by one of the following methods while in storage or use to prevent falling caused by contact, vibration, or seismic activity:

(1) Restraining containers to a fixed object with one or more restraints
(2) Restraining containers within a framework, stand, or assembly designed to resist container movement
(3) Restraining containers by locating a container against two points of contact

63.11.3.4 Containers shall be transported by use of a cart or hand truck designed for such use.

63.11.3.4.1 Liquid oxygen home care containers equipped with a roller base shall not be required to be transported by use of a cart or truck.

63.11.3.4.2 Liquid oxygen ambulatory containers shall be permitted to be hand carried.

63.11.3.5 The filling of containers shall be in accordance with 63.11.3.5.1 through 63.11.3.5.2:

63.11.3.5.1 Liquid oxygen home care containers shall be filled outdoors.

63.11.3.5.1.1* A drip pan compatible with liquid oxygen shall be provided under home care container filling and vent connections used during the filling process.

63.11.3.5.2 Liquid oxygen ambulatory containers shall be allowed to be filled indoors when the supply container is designed for filling such containers and written instructions are provided by the container manufacturer.

63.11.3.5.3* The use of open flames and high temperature devices shall be in accordance with the adopted fire prevention code.

63.11.4 Maximum Quantity. The maximum aggregate quantity of liquid oxygen allowed in storage and in use in a single dwelling unit shall be 31.6 gal (120 L).

63.11.4.1 The maximum aggregate quantity of liquid oxygen allowed in day care occupancies shall be limited by the maximum allowable quantity set forth in the adopted fire prevention code or building code.

63.11.4.2 Where individual sleeping rooms are separated from the remainder of the dwelling unit by fire barriers and horizontal assemblies having a minimum fire-resistance rating of 1 hour in accordance with the adopted building code, the maximum aggregate quantity per dwelling unit shall be allowed to be increased to a maximum of 31.6 gal (120 L) of liquid oxygen per sleeping room.

63.11.5 Smoking. Smoking shall be prohibited in rooms or areas where liquid oxygen is in use.

63.11.5.1* A sign stating "OXYGEN — NO SMOKING" shall be posted in the room or area where the liquid oxygen containers are stored or used.

Chapter 64 Corrosive Solids and Liquids

64.1 General.

64.1.1 The storage, use, and handling of corrosive solids and liquids shall comply with the requirements of Chapter 60.

64.1.2 The storage, use, and handling of corrosive solids and liquids in amounts exceeding the maximum allowable quantities permitted in control areas set forth in Chapter 60 shall comply with the requirements of NFPA 400, *Hazardous Materials Code*.

> Subsections 65.2.2 and 65.5.1 and Section 65.10 were deleted by a tentative interim amendment (TIA), and the remaining sections and subsections were renumbered as necessary. See page 1.

Chapter 65 Explosives, Fireworks, and Model Rocketry

65.1 General.

65.1.1 The storage, use, and handling of explosives, fireworks, and model rocketry shall comply with the requirements of this chapter, NFPA standards referenced within this chapter, and Sections 60.1 through 60.4 of this *Code*.

65.1.2 Where the provisions of this chapter or NFPA standards referenced herein conflict with the provisions of Chapter 60, the provisions of this chapter and referenced NFPA standards shall apply.

65.2 Display Fireworks.

65.2.1 The construction, handling, and use of fireworks intended solely for outdoor display as well as the general conduct and operation of the display shall comply with the requirements of NFPA 1123, *Code for Fireworks Display*.

65.2.2 Permits. Permits, where required, shall comply with Section 1.12.

65.3 Pyrotechnics Before a Proximate Audience.

65.3.1 The use of pyrotechnic special effects in the performing arts in conjunction with theatrical, musical, or any similar productions before a proximate audience, performers, or support personnel shall comply with NFPA 1126, *Standard for the Use of Pyrotechnics Before a Proximate Audience*.

65.3.2 Where any of the following conditions exist, they shall comply with NFPA 1126:

(1) Any indoor display of pyrotechnic special effects
(2) Any outdoor use of pyrotechnic special effects at distances less than those required by NFPA 1123
(3) The use of pyrotechnic special effects during any videotaping, audiotaping, or filming of any television, radio, or movie production if such production is before a proximate audience
(4) The rehearsal of any production in which pyrotechnic special effects are used

65.3.3 Permits. Permits, where required, shall comply with Section 1.12.

65.4 Flame Effects Before an Audience.

65.4.1 The use of flame effects before an audience shall comply with NFPA 160, *Standard for the Use of Flame Effects Before an Audience*.

65.4.2 Permits. Permits, where required, shall comply with Section 1.12.

65.5 Fireworks Manufacturing.

65.5.1 Permits. Permits, where required, shall comply with Section 1.12.

65.6 Model Rocketry. The design, construction, limitations of propellant mass and power, and reliability of model rocket motors and model rocket motor reloading kits and their components produced commercially for sale to or use by the public for purposes of education, recreation, and sporting competition shall comply with NFPA 1122, *Code for Model Rocketry*.

65.7 Rocketry Manufacturing.

65.7.1 The manufacture of model rocket motors designed, sold, and used for the purpose of propelling recoverable aero models shall comply with NFPA 1125, *Code for the Manufacture of Model Rocket and High Power Rocket Motors*.

65.7.2 Permits. Permits, where required, shall comply with Section 1.12.

65.8 High Power Rocketry.

65.8.1 The design, construction, limitations of propellant mass and power, and reliability of all high-power rocket motors and motor components produced commercially for sale to or use by the certified user for education, recreation, and sporting competition shall comply with NFPA 1127, *Code for High Power Rocketry*.

65.8.2 Permits. Permits, where required, shall comply with Section 1.12.

65.9 Explosives.

65.9.1 The manufacture, transportation, storage, sale, and use of explosive materials shall comply with NFPA 495, *Explosive Materials Code*, and NFPA 498, *Standard for Safe Havens and Interchange Lots for Vehicles Transporting Explosives*.

65.9.2 Permits.

65.9.2.1 Permits, where required, shall comply with Section 1.12.

65.9.2.2 A separate permit shall be required to conduct blasting operations.

Chapter 66   Flammable and Combustible Liquids

66.1 General.

66.1.1* The storage, handling, and use of flammable and combustible liquids, including waste liquids, as herein defined and classified, shall comply with this chapter; NFPA 30, *Flammable and Combustible Liquids Code*; and Sections 60.1 through 60.4 of this *Code*.

66.1.2 Where the provisions of this chapter or NFPA 30 conflict with the provisions of Chapter 60, the provisions of this chapter and NFPA 30 shall apply.

66.1.3 This chapter shall not apply to the following:

(1)*Any liquid that has a melting point of 100°F (37.8°C) or greater
(2)*Any liquid that does not meet the criteria for fluidity given in the definition of *liquid* in 3.3.30 of NFPA 30 and Chapter 4 of NFPA 30
(3) Any cryogenic fluid or liquefied gas, as defined in 3.3.135.8
(4)*Any liquid that does not have a flash point, but which is capable of burning under certain conditions
(5)*Any aerosol product
(6) Any mist, spray, or foam
(7)*Transportation of flammable and combustible liquids as governed by the U.S. Department of Transportation
(8)*Storage, handling, and use of fuel oil tanks and containers connected with oil-burning equipment
(9)*Use and installation of alcohol-based hand rub (ABHR) dispensers. *(See 60.5.2.)* [30:1.1.2]

66.1.4 Installations made in accordance with the applicable requirements of the following standards shall be deemed to be in compliance with this *Code*:

(1) NFPA 20, *Standard for the Installation of Stationary Pumps for Fire Protection*
(2) NFPA 30A, *Code for Motor Fuel Dispensing Facilities and Repair Garages*
(3) NFPA 31, *Standard for the Installation of Oil-Burning Equipment*
(4) NFPA 32, *Standard for Drycleaning Plants*
(5) NFPA 33, *Standard for Spray Application Using Flammable or Combustible Materials*

2015 Edition

(6) NFPA 34, *Standard for Dipping, Coating, and Printing Processes Using Flammable or Combustible Liquids*
(7) NFPA 35, *Standard for the Manufacture of Organic Coatings*
(8) NFPA 36, *Standard for Solvent Extraction Plants*
(9) NFPA 37, *Standard for the Installation and Use of Stationary Combustion Engines and Gas Turbines*
(10) NFPA 45, *Standard on Fire Protection for Laboratories Using Chemicals*
(11) NFPA 99, *Health Care Facilities Code*
(12) NFPA *101, Life Safety Code* [**30**:1.5.3]

66.1.5 Permits. Permits, where required, shall comply with Section 1.12.

66.2 Reserved.

66.3 Definitions.

66.3.1 (Reserved)

66.3.2 (Reserved)

66.3.3 General Definitions.

66.3.3.1 Alcohol-Based Hand Rub. See 3.3.10.

66.3.3.2 Area.

66.3.3.2.1 Fire Area. See 3.3.14.3.

66.3.3.2.2 Inside Liquid Storage Area. See 3.3.14.6.

66.3.3.3 Barrel. See 3.3.21.

66.3.3.4 Basement. See 3.3.22.

66.3.3.5 Boiling Point. See 3.3.27.

66.3.3.6* Boil-Over. See 3.3.28.

66.3.3.7 Building.

66.3.3.7.1* Important Building. See 3.3.29.7.

66.3.3.7.2 Storage Tank Building. See 3.3.29.11.

66.3.3.8 Chemical Plant. See 3.3.44.

66.3.3.9 Closed-Top Diking. See 3.3.51.

66.3.3.10 Container. Any vessel of 119 gal (450 L) or less capacity used for transporting or storing liquids. [**30**, 2012]

66.3.3.10.1 Closed Container. See 3.3.69.2.

66.3.3.10.2 Intermediate Bulk Container. See 3.3.69.6.

66.3.3.11 Control Area. For the purposes of this chapter, a building or portion of a building within which flammable and combustible liquids are allowed to be stored, dispensed, and used or handled in quantities that do not exceed the maximum allowable quantity (MAQ). [**30**, 2012]

66.3.3.12 Crude Petroleum. See 3.3.76.

66.3.3.13 Cryogenic Fluid. See 3.3.77.

66.3.3.14 Damage-Limiting Construction. See 3.3.82.

66.3.3.15 Distillery. See 3.3.87.

66.3.3.16 Fire Point. See 3.3.123.

66.3.3.17 Flash Point. See 3.3.129.

66.3.3.18* Fugitive Emissions. See 3.3.132.

66.3.3.19* Hazardous Material or Hazardous Chemical. Material presenting dangers beyond the fire problems relating to flash point and boiling point. [**30**, 2012]

66.3.3.20 Hazardous Materials Storage Locker. See 3.3.146.

66.3.3.21 Hazardous Reaction or Hazardous Chemical Reaction. See 3.3.147.

66.3.3.22 Heat Transfer Fluid (HTF). See 3.3.148.

66.3.3.23 High Hazard Level 2 Contents. Contents that present a deflagration hazard or a hazard from accelerated burning. For the purposes of this chapter, this includes Class I, Class II, or Class IIIA liquids that are used or stored in normally open containers or systems, or in closed containers or systems at gauge pressures 15 psi (103 kPa) or greater. [**30**, 2012]

66.3.3.24 High Hazard Level 3 Contents. Contents that readily support combustion or that present a physical hazard. For the purposes of this chapter, this includes Class I, Class II, or Class IIIA liquids that are used or stored in normally closed containers or in closed systems at gauge pressures of less than 15 psi (103 kPa). [**30**, 2012]

66.3.3.25 Incidental Liquid Use or Storage. See 3.3.156.

66.3.3.26 Liquid.

66.3.3.26.1 Combustible Liquid. See 3.3.164.1.

66.3.3.26.2* Flammable Liquid. See 3.3.164.2.

66.3.3.26.3 Stable Liquid. See 3.3.164.4.

66.3.3.27* Operating Unit (Vessel) or Process Unit (Vessel). See 3.3.187.

66.3.3.28 Operations. See 3.3.188.

66.3.3.29* Process or Processing. See 3.3.206.

66.3.3.30 Protection for Exposures. See 3.3.209.

66.3.3.31 Refinery. See 3.3.218.

66.3.3.32* Safety Can. See 3.3.222.

66.3.3.33 Storage Tank. See 3.3.255.7.

66.3.3.33.1 Aboveground Tank. See 3.3.255.2.

66.3.3.33.1.1 Protected Aboveground Tank. See 3.3.255.2.1.

66.3.3.33.2 Low-Pressure Tank. A storage tank designed to withstand an internal pressure above a gauge pressure of 1.0 psig (6.9 kPa) but not more than a gauge pressure of 15 psi (103 kPa) measured at the top of the tank. [**30**, 2012]

66.3.3.33.3 Portable Tank. See 3.3.255.4.

66.3.3.33.3.1* Nonmetallic Portable Tank. A portable tank, as herein defined, constructed of plastic, fiber, or a material other than metal. [**30**, 2012]

66.3.3.33.4 Secondary Containment Tank. See 3.3.255.5.

66.3.3.34 Unit Operation or Unit Process. See 3.3.263.

66.3.3.35 Vapor Pressure. See 3.3.269.

66.3.3.36 Vapor Processing Equipment. Those components of a vapor processing system designed to process vapors or liquids captured during transfer or filling operations. [**30**, 2012]

66.3.3.37* Vapor Processing System. See 3.3.254.15.

66.3.3.38 Vapor Recovery System. See 3.3.254.16.

66.3.3.39 Vent.

66.3.3.39.1 Emergency Relief Vent. See 3.3.94.

66.3.3.40* Warehouse.

66.3.3.40.1 General-Purpose Warehouse. See 3.3.272.1.

66.3.3.40.2 Liquid Warehouse. See 3.3.272.2.

66.4 Definition and Classification of Liquids.

66.4.1 Definitions Specific to Liquids. For the purposes of this chapter, the terms in this subsection shall have the definitions given. [**30:**4.2]

66.4.1.1* Boiling Point. See 3.3.27.

66.4.1.2 Combustible Liquid. See 3.3.164.1.

66.4.1.3 Flammable Liquid. See 3.3.164.2.

66.4.1.4* Flash Point. See 3.3.129.

66.4.1.5 Liquid. See 3.3.172.

66.4.1.6* Vapor Pressure. See 3.3.269.

66.4.2* Classification of Liquids. Any liquid within the scope of this *Code* and subject to the requirements of this *Code* shall be classified in accordance with this chapter. [**30:**4.3]

66.4.2.1 Flammable liquids, as defined in 3.3.164.2 and 66.4.1.3, shall be classified as Class I liquids and shall be further subclassified in accordance with the following:

(1) Class IA Liquid — Any liquid that has a flash point below 73°F (22.8°C) and a boiling point below 100°F (37.8°C)
(2) Class IB Liquid — Any liquid that has a flash point below 73°F (22.8°C) and a boiling point at or above 100°F (37.8°C)
(3) Class IC Liquid — Any liquid that has a flash point at or above 73°F (22.8°C), but below 100°F (37.8°C) [**30:**4.3.1]

66.4.2.2 Combustible liquids, as defined in 3.3.164.1 and 66.4.1.2, shall be classified in accordance with the following:

(1) Class II Liquid — Any liquid that has a flash point at or above 100°F (37.8°C) and below 140°F (60°C)
(2) Class III Liquid — Any liquid that has a flash point at or above 140°F (60°C)
   (a) Class IIIA Liquid — Any liquid that has a flash point at or above 140°F (60°C), but below 200°F (93°C)
   (b) Class IIIB Liquid — Any liquid that has a flash point at or above 200°F (93°C) [**30:**4.3.2]

66.4.3 Determination of Flash Point. The flash point of a liquid shall be determined according to the methods specified in 66.4.3.1 through 66.4.3.4. [**30:**4.4]

66.4.3.1 Except as specified in 66.4.3.1.1, the flash point of a liquid having a viscosity below 5.5 centiStokes at 104°F (40°C) or below 9.5 centiStokes at 77°F (25°C) shall be determined in accordance with ASTM D 56, *Standard Test Method for Flash Point by Tag Closed Cup Tester*. [**30:**4.4.1]

66.4.3.1.1 Cut-back asphalts, liquids that tend to form a surface film, and liquids that contain suspended solids shall not be tested in accordance with ASTM D 56, even if they otherwise meet the viscosity criteria. Such liquids shall be tested in accordance with 66.4.3.2. [**30:**4.4.1.1]

66.4.3.2 The flash point of a liquid having a viscosity of 5.5 centiStokes or more at 104°F (40°C) or 9.5 centiStokes or more at 77°F (25°C) or a flash point of 200°F (93.4°C) or higher shall be determined in accordance with ASTM D 93, *Standard Test Methods for Flash Point by Pensky-Martens Closed Cup Tester*. [**30:**4.4.2]

66.4.3.3 As an alternative, ASTM D 3278, *Standard Test Method for Flash Point of Liquids by Small Scale Closed Cup Apparatus*, shall be permitted to be used for paints, enamels, lacquers, varnishes, and related products and their components that have flash points between 32°F (0°C) and 230°F (110°C) and viscosities below 150 Stokes at 77°F (25°C). [**30:**4.4.3]

66.4.3.4 As an alternative, ASTM D 3828, *Standard Test Methods for Flash Point by Small Scale Closed Cup Tester*, shall be permitted to be used for materials other than those for which ASTM D 3278 is specifically required. [**30:**4.4.4]

66.5 Reserved.

66.6 Fire and Explosion Prevention and Risk Control.

66.6.1* Scope. This section shall apply to the hazards associated with storage processing, handling, and use of liquids. This section shall also apply when specifically referenced by another section. [**30:**6.1]

66.6.2 Reserved.

66.6.3* Management of Fire and Explosion Hazards. This chapter shall apply to the management methodology used to identify, evaluate, and control the hazards involved in the processing and handling of flammable and combustible liquids. These hazards include, but are not limited to, preparation, separation, purification, and change of state, energy content, or composition. [**30:**6.3]

66.6.4 Hazards Analysis.

66.6.4.1 General. Operations involving flammable and combustible liquids shall be reviewed to ensure that fire and explosion hazards are addressed by fire prevention, fire control, and emergency action plans.

Exception No. 1: Operations where liquids are used solely for on-site consumption as fuels.

Exception No. 2: Operations where Class II or Class III liquids are stored in atmospheric tanks or transferred at temperatures below their flash points.

Exception No. 3: Mercantile occupancies, crude petroleum exploration, drillings, and well servicing operations, and normally unoccupied facilities in remote locations. [**30:**6.4.1]

66.6.4.1.1* The extent of fire prevention and control that is provided shall be determined in consultation with the AHJ or by means of an engineering evaluation of the operation and application of sound fire protection and process engineering principles. This evaluation shall include, but not be limited to, the following:

(1) Analysis of the fire and explosion hazards of the operation
(2) Analysis of emergency relief from process vessels, taking into consideration the properties of the materials used and the fire protection and control measures taken
(3) Analysis of applicable facility design requirements in Chapters 17, 18, 19, 28, and 29 of NFPA 30
(4) Analysis of applicable requirements for liquid handling, transfer, and use, as covered in Chapters 17, 18, 19, 28, and 29 of NFPA 30
(5) Analysis of local conditions, such as exposure to and from adjacent properties and exposure to floods, earthquakes, and windstorms
(6) Analysis of the emergency response capabilities of the local emergency services [**30:**6.4.1.1]

66.6.4.1.2* Storage, processing, handling, and use of Class II and Class III liquids heated at or above their flash point shall follow the requirements for Class I liquids, unless an engineering evaluation conducted in accordance with Section 66.6 justifies following the requirements for some other liquid class. [**30**:6.4.1.2]

66.6.4.2 Management of Change. The hazards analysis shall be repeated whenever the hazards leading to a fire or explosion change significantly. Conditions that might require repeating a review shall include, but are not limited to, the following:

(1) When changes occur in the materials in process
(2) When changes occur in process equipment
(3) When changes occur in process control
(4) When changes occur in operating procedures or assignments [**30**:6.4.2]

66.6.5 Control of Ignition Sources.

66.6.5.1 General. Precautions shall be taken to prevent the ignition of flammable vapors by sources such as the following:

(1) Open flames
(2) Lightning
(3) Hot surfaces
(4) Radiant heat
(5) Smoking
(6) Cutting and welding
(7) Spontaneous ignition
(8)*Frictional heat or sparks
(9) Static electricity
(10) Electrical sparks
(11) Stray currents
(12) Ovens, furnaces, and heating equipment [**30**:6.5.1]

66.6.5.2 Smoking. Smoking shall be permitted only in designated and identified areas. [**30**:6.5.2]

66.6.5.3* Hot Work.

66.6.5.3.1 Welding, cutting, and similar spark-producing operations shall not be permitted in areas containing flammable liquids until a written permit authorizing such work has been issued. [**30**:6.5.3.1]

66.6.5.3.2 The permit shall be issued by a person in authority following inspection of the area to ensure that permit requirements have been implemented and will be followed until the job is completed. [**30**:6.5.3.2]

66.6.5.4* Static Electricity.

66.6.5.4.1 All equipment such as tanks, machinery, and piping shall be designed and operated to prevent electrostatic ignitions. [**30**:6.5.4.1]

66.6.5.4.2 All metallic equipment such as tanks, machinery, and piping where the potential exists for an ignitible mixture to be present shall be bonded and grounded. [**30**:6.5.4.2]

66.6.5.4.3 The bond and ground shall be physically applied or shall be inherently present by the nature of the installation. [**30**:6.5.4.3]

66.6.5.4.4 Any electrically isolated section of metallic piping or equipment shall be bonded and grounded to prevent hazardous accumulation of static electricity. [**30**:6.5.4.4]

66.6.5.4.5 All nonmetallic equipment and piping where the potential exists for an ignitable mixture to be present shall be designed and operated to prevent electrostatic ignition. [**30**:6.5.4.5]

66.6.5.5 Electrical Systems. Design, selection, and installation of electrical wiring and electrical utilization equipment shall meet the requirements of Section 66.7. [**30**:6.5.5]

66.6.6 Detection and Alarm Systems and Procedures.

66.6.6.1* An approved means for prompt notification of fire or emergency to those within the plant and to the available public or mutual aid fire department shall be provided. [**30**:6.6.1]

66.6.6.2 Those areas, including buildings, where a potential exists for a flammable liquid spill shall be monitored as appropriate. The following methods shall be permitted to be used:

(1) Personnel observation or patrol
(2) Process-monitoring equipment that would indicate a spill or leak could have occurred
(3) Provision of gas detectors to continuously monitor the area where facilities are unattended [**30**:6.6.2]

66.6.7 Fire Protection and Fire Suppression Systems.

66.6.7.1* This section identifies recognized fire protection and fire suppression systems and methods used to prevent or minimize the loss from fire or explosion in liquid-processing facilities. The application of one or a combination of these systems and methods as well as the use of fire-resistive materials shall be determined in accordance with this chapter. [**30**:6.7.1]

66.6.7.2 A reliable water supply or other suitable fire control agent shall be available in pressure and quantity to meet the fire demands indicated by the specific hazards of liquids-processing operations, storage, or exposure. [**30**:6.7.2]

66.6.7.3* Permanent connections between the fire water system and any process system shall be prohibited, to prevent contamination of fire water with process fluids. [**30**:6.7.3]

66.6.7.4 Where required by this chapter, hydrants, with or without fixed monitor nozzles, shall be provided in accordance with this *Code* and NFPA 24, *Standard for the Installation of Private Fire Service Mains and Their Appurtenances*. The number and placement shall depend on the hazards of the facility. [**30**:6.7.4]

66.6.7.5 Where the need is indicated by the hazards of liquid processing, storage, or exposure as determined by 66.6.4, fixed protection shall be provided. [**30**:6.7.5]

66.6.7.6 Where provided, fire control systems shall be designed, installed, and maintained in accordance with this *Code* and the following NFPA standards, as applicable:

(1) NFPA 11, *Standard for Low-, Medium-, and High-Expansion Foam*
(2) NFPA 12, *Standard on Carbon Dioxide Extinguishing Systems*
(3) NFPA 12A, *Standard on Halon 1301 Fire Extinguishing Systems*
(4) NFPA 13, *Standard for the Installation of Sprinkler Systems*
(5) NFPA 15, *Standard for Water Spray Fixed Systems for Fire Protection*
(6) NFPA 16, *Standard for the Installation of Foam-Water Sprinkler and Foam-Water Spray Systems*
(7) NFPA 17, *Standard for Dry Chemical Extinguishing Systems*
(8) NFPA 750, *Standard on Water Mist Fire Protection Systems*
(9) NFPA 2001, *Standard on Clean Agent Fire Extinguishing Systems* [**30**:6.7.6]

66.6.7.7 Where required by this chapter, standpipe and hose systems shall be installed in accordance with Section 13.2 and

NFPA 14, *Standard for the Installation of Standpipe and Hose Systems*, or hose connections from sprinkler systems using combination spray and straight stream nozzles shall be installed in accordance with NFPA 13. [**30**:6.7.7]

66.6.7.8* Where required by this chapter, listed portable fire extinguishers shall be provided in such quantities, sizes, and types as are needed for the specific hazards of operation and storage. [**30**:6.7.8]

66.6.7.9 Where provided, mobile foam apparatus and supplies of foam concentrate shall be appropriate to the specific hazards. [**30**:6.7.9]

66.6.8 Emergency Planning and Training.

66.6.8.1 A written emergency action plan that is consistent with available equipment and personnel shall be established to respond to fires and related emergencies. This plan shall include the following:

(1) Procedures to be followed in case of fire or release of liquids or vapors, such as sounding the alarm, notifying the fire department, evacuating personnel, and controlling and extinguishing the fire
(2) Procedures and schedules for conducting drills of these procedures
(3) Appointment and training of personnel to carry out assigned duties, including review at the time of initial assignment, as responsibilities or response actions change, and whenever anticipated duties change
(4) Procedures for maintenance and operation of (a) fire protection equipment and systems, (b) drainage and containment systems, and (c) dispersion and ventilation equipment and systems
(5) Procedures for shutting down or isolating equipment to reduce, mitigate, or stop the release of liquid or vapors, including assigning personnel responsible for maintaining critical plant functions or shutdown of plant processes and safe start-up following isolation or shutdown
(6) Alternate measures for the safety of occupants [**30**:6.8.1]

66.6.8.2 Personnel responsible for the use and operation of fire protection equipment shall be trained in the use of that equipment. Refresher training shall be conducted at least annually. [**30**:6.8.2]

66.6.8.3 Planning of effective fire control measures shall be co-ordinated with local emergency response agencies. [**30**:6.8.3]

66.6.8.4 Procedures shall be established to provide for safe shutdown of operations under emergency conditions and for safe start-up following cessation of emergencies. Provisions shall be made for training of personnel in shutdown and start-up procedures, and in activation, use, and deactivation of associated alarms, interlocks, and controls. Procedures shall also be established and provisions shall also be made for inspection and testing of associated alarms, interlocks, and controls. [**30**:6.8.4]

66.6.8.5 The emergency procedures shall be kept readily available in the operating areas and shall be updated when conditions change, as identified in 66.6.4.2. [**30**:6.8.5]

66.6.8.5.1 Where premises are likely to be unattended for considerable periods of time, a summary of the emergency plan shall be posted or located in a strategic and accessible location. [**30**:6.8.5.1]

66.6.9 Inspection and Maintenance.

66.6.9.1 All fire protection equipment shall be properly maintained, and periodic inspections and tests shall be done in accordance with both standard practice and the equipment manufacturers recommendations. Water-based fire protection systems shall be inspected, tested, and maintained in accordance with this *Code* and NFPA 25, *Standard for the Inspection, Testing, and Maintenance of Water-Based Fire Protection Systems*. [**30**:6.9.1]

66.6.9.2 Maintenance and operating practices shall be established and implemented to control leakage and prevent spillage of flammable and combustible liquids. [**30**:6.9.2]

66.6.9.3 Combustible waste material and residues in operating areas shall be kept to a minimum, stored in covered metal containers, and disposed of daily. [**30**:6.9.3]

66.6.9.4 Ground areas around facilities where liquids are stored, handled, or used shall be kept free of weeds, trash, or other unnecessary combustible materials. [**30**:6.9.4]

66.6.9.5 Aisles established for movement of personnel shall be kept clear of obstructions to permit orderly evacuation and ready access for manual fire-fighting activities. [**30**:6.9.5]

66.6.10 Management of Security. [**30**:6.10]

66.6.10.1 Scope. [**30**:6.10.1]

66.6.10.1.1 This section shall apply to the management methodology used to identify, evaluate, and control the security hazards involved in the processing and handling of flammable and combustible liquids. [**30**:6.10.1.1]

66.6.10.1.2 These hazards include, but are not limited to, vulnerability to terrorist or other malicious attacks. [**30**:6.10.1.2]

66.6.10.2 General. The methodology used shall incorporate a risk-based approach to site security and shall have the following objectives:

(1) Identification and evaluation of security risks
(2) Evaluation of the security performance of the facility
(3) Evaluation of protection for employees, the facility itself, the surrounding communities, and the environment. *(See Annex G of NFPA 30 for more detailed information.)* [**30**:6.10.2]

66.6.10.3 Specific Requirements. [**30**:6.10.3]

66.6.10.3.1 Operations involving flammable and combustible liquids shall be reviewed to ensure that security vulnerabilities identified during the security vulnerability analysis (SVA) are addressed in a facility security program, with corresponding fire prevention and emergency action plans and drills. [**30**:6.10.3.1]

66.6.10.3.2 The balance of physical, electronic, and personnel techniques used to respond to the SVA shall be determined by means of an engineering evaluation of the operation and application of sound security principles. This evaluation shall include, but not be limited to, the following:

(1) Assessing overall facility
(2) Evaluating vulnerabilities
(3) Assessing threats/consequences
(4) Assessing physical factors/attractiveness
(5) Identifying mitigation factors
(6) Conducting security assessment or gap analysis [**30**:6.10.3.2]

66.6.10.3.3 A written emergency action plan that is consistent with available equipment and personnel shall be established to respond to fires, security, and related emergencies. This plan shall include the following:

(1) Procedures to be followed such as initiating alarms, notifying appropriate agencies, evacuating personnel, and controlling and extinguishing the fire
(2) Procedures and schedules for conducting drills of these procedures
(3) Appointment and training of personnel to carry out assigned duties
(4) Maintenance of fire protection and response equipment
(5) Procedures for shutting down or isolating equipment to reduce the release of liquid
(6) Alternate measures for the safety of occupants [30:6.10.3.3]

66.6.10.3.4 Specific duties of personnel shall be reviewed at the time of initial assignment, as responsibilities or response actions change, and whenever anticipated duties change. [30:6.10.3.4]

66.6.10.3.5 The security management review conducted in accordance with this section shall be repeated under the following conditions:

(1) For an initial review of all new relevant facilities and assets
(2) When substantial changes to the threat or process occur
(3) After a significant security incident
(4) For periodic revalidation of the SVA [30:6.10.3.5]

66.7 Electrical Systems.

66.7.1 Scope. This chapter shall apply to areas where Class I liquids are stored or handled and to areas where Class II or Class III liquids are stored or handled at or above their flash points. [30:7.1]

66.7.2 Reserved.

66.7.3 General Requirements.

66.7.3.1 Electrical utilization equipment and wiring shall not constitute a source of ignition for any ignitible vapor that might be present under normal operation or because of a spill. Compliance with 66.7.3.2 through 66.7.3.7.1 shall be deemed as meeting the requirements of this section. [30:7.3.1]

66.7.3.2 All electrical utilization equipment and wiring shall be of a type specified by and installed in accordance with *NFPA 70, National Electrical Code.* [30:7.3.2]

66.7.3.3* Table 66.7.3.3 shall be used to delineate and classify areas for the purpose of installation of electrical utilization equipment and wiring under normal operating conditions. [30:7.3.3]

Table 66.7.3.3 Electrical Area Classifications

	NEC Class I		
Location	Division	Zone	Extent of Classified Area
Indoor equipment installed in accordance with 66.7.3 where flammable vapor–air mixtures can exist under normal operation	1	0	The entire area associated with such equipment where flammable gases or vapors are present continuously or for long periods of time
	1	1	Area within 5 ft of any edge of such equipment, extending in all directions
	2	2	Area between 5 ft and 8 ft of any edge of such equipment, extending in all directions; also, space up to 3 ft above floor or grade level within 5 ft to 25 ft horizontally from any edge of such equipment[1]
Outdoor equipment of the type covered in 66.7.3 where flammable vapor–air mixtures can exist under normal operation	1	0	The entire area associated with such equipment where flammable gases or vapors are present continuously or for long periods of time
	1	1	Area within 3 ft of any edge of such equipment, extending in all directions
	2	2	Area between 3 ft and 8 ft of any edge of such equipment, extending in all directions; also, space up to 3 ft above floor or grade level within 3 ft to 10 ft horizontally from any edge of such equipment
Tank storage installations inside buildings	1	1	All equipment located below grade level
	2	2	Any equipment located at or above grade level
Tank — aboveground, fixed roof	1	0	Inside fixed-roof tank
	1	1	Area inside dike where dike height is greater than the distance from the tank to the dike for more than 50 percent of the tank circumference
	2	2	Within 10 ft from shell, ends, or roof of tank; also, area inside dike up to top of dike wall
	1	0	Area inside of vent piping or vent opening

Table 66.7.3.3 *Continued*

Location	NEC Class I Division	NEC Class I Zone	Extent of Classified Area
	1	1	Within 5 ft of open end of vent, extending in all directions
	2	2	Area between 5 ft and 10 ft from open end of vent, extending in all directions
Tank — aboveground, floating roof			
With fixed outer roof	1	0	Area between the floating and fixed-roof sections and within the shell
With no fixed outer roof	1	1	Area above the floating roof and within the shell
Tank vault — interior	1	1	Entire interior volume, if Class I liquids are stored within
Underground tank fill opening	1	1	Any pit, box, or space below grade level, if any part is within a Division 1 or 2 or Zone 1 or 2 classified location
	2	2	Up to 18 in. above grade level within a horizontal radius of 10 ft from a loose fill connection and within a horizontal radius of 5 ft from a tight fill connection
Vent — discharging upward	1	0	Area inside of vent piping or opening
	1	1	Within 3 ft of open end of vent, extending in all directions
	2	2	Area between 3 ft and 5 ft of open end of vent, extending in all directions
Drum and container filling — outdoors or indoors	1	0	Area inside the drum or container
	1	1	Within 3 ft of vent and fill openings, extending in all directions
	2	2	Area between 3 ft and 5 ft from vent or fill opening, extending in all directions; also, up to 18 in. above floor or grade level within a horizontal radius of 10 ft from vent or fill opening
Pumps, bleeders, withdrawal fittings			
Indoor	2	2	Within 5 ft of any edge of such devices, extending in all directions; also, up to 3 ft above floor or grade level within 25 ft horizontally from any edge of such devices
Outdoor	2	2	Within 3 ft of any edge of such devices, extending in all directions; also, up to 18 in. above grade level within 10 ft horizontally from any edge of such devices
Pits and sumps			
Without mechanical ventilation	1	1	Entire area within a pit or sump if any part is within a Division 1 or 2 or Zone 1 or 2 classified location
With adequate mechanical ventilation	2	2	Entire area within a pit or sump if any part is within a Division 1 or 2 or Zone 1 or 2 classified location
Containing valves, fittings, or piping, and not within a Division 1 or 2 or Zone 1 or 2 classified location	2	2	Entire pit or sump
Drainage ditches, separators, impounding basins			
Outdoor	2	2	Area up to 18 in. above ditch, separator, or basin; also, area up to 18 in. above grade within 15 ft horizontally from any edge
Indoor			Same as pits and sumps

(continues)

Table 66.7.3.3 *Continued*

Location	NEC Class I		Extent of Classified Area
	Division	Zone	
Tank vehicle and tank car[2]			
Loading through open dome	1	0	Area inside of the tank
	1	1	Within 3 ft of edge of dome, extending in all directions
	2	2	Area between 3 ft and 15 ft from edge of dome, extending in all directions
Loading through bottom connections with atmospheric venting	1	0	Area inside of the tank
	1	1	Within 3 ft of point of venting to atmosphere, extending in all directions
	2	2	Area between 3 ft and 15 ft from point of venting to atmosphere, extending in all directions; also, up to 18 in. above grade within a horizontal radius of 10 ft from point of loading connection
Loading through closed dome with atmospheric venting	1	1	Within 3 ft of open end of vent, extending in all directions
	2	2	Area between 3 ft and 15 ft from open end of vent, extending in all directions; also, within 3 ft of edge of dome, extending in all directions
Loading through closed dome with vapor control	2	2	Within 3 ft of point of connection of both fill and vapor lines, extending in all directions
Bottom loading with vapor control or any bottom unloading	2	2	Within 3 ft of point of connections, extending in all directions; also, up to 18 in. above grade within a horizontal radius of 10 ft from point of connections
Storage and repair garage for tank vehicles	1	1	All pits or spaces below floor level
	2	2	Area up to 18 in. above floor or grade level for entire storage or repair garage
Garages for other than tank vehicles	Ordinary		If there is any opening to these rooms within the extent of an outdoor classified location, the entire room shall be classified the same as the area classification at the point of the opening
Outdoor drum storage	Ordinary		
Inside rooms or storage lockers used for the storage of Class I liquids	2	2	Entire room or locker
Indoor warehousing where there is no flammable liquid transfer	Ordinary		If there is any opening to these rooms within the extent of an indoor classified location, the classified location shall extend through the opening to the same extent as if the wall, curb, or partition did not exist
Office and rest rooms	Ordinary		If there is any opening to these rooms within the extent of an indoor classified location, the room shall be classified the same as if the wall, curb, or partition did not exist
Piers and wharves			See Figure 29.3.22 of NFPA 30.

For SI units, 1 in. = 25 mm; 1 ft = 0.3 m.

[1]The release of Class I liquids can generate vapors to the extent that the entire building, and possibly an area surrounding it, should be considered a Class I, Division 2, or Zone 2 location.

[2]When classifying extent of area, consideration should be given to the fact that tank cars or tank vehicles can be spotted at varying points. Therefore, the extremities of the loading or unloading positions should be used. [**30:** Table 7.3.3]

66.7.3.4 A classified area shall not extend beyond a floor, wall, roof, or other solid partition that has no openings within the classified area. [**30**:7.3.4]

66.7.3.5 The designation of classes, divisions, and zones shall be as defined in Chapter 5 of *NFPA 70*. [**30**:7.3.5]

66.7.3.6 The area classifications listed in Table 66.7.3.3 are based on the premise that all applicable requirements of this *Code* have been met. If this is not the case, the AHJ shall have the authority to classify the extent of the area. [**30**:7.3.6]

66.7.3.7* Where the provisions of 66.7.3.1 through 66.7.3.6 require the installation of electrical equipment suitable for Class I, Division 1 or 2, or Zone 1 or 2 locations, ordinary electrical equipment, including switchgear, shall be permitted to be used if installed in a room or enclosure that is maintained under positive pressure with respect to the classified area. [**30**:7.3.7]

66.7.3.7.1 Ventilation make-up air shall be taken from an uncontaminated source. [**30**:7.3.7.1]

66.8 Application of Area Classification. Area classification is used to assure that fixed electrical utilization equipment, electrical fixtures, and wiring are properly installed within Class I, Division 1; Class I, Zone 1; Class I, Division 2; or Class I, Zone 2 designated areas, as defined by Article 500 of *NFPA 70, National Electrical Code*. [**30**:7.4.1]

66.9 Storage of Liquids in Containers — General Requirements.

66.9.1 Scope.

66.9.1.1 This section shall apply to the storage of flammable and combustible liquids in:

(1) Drums or other containers that do not exceed 119 gal (450 L) individual capacity
(2) Portable tanks that do not exceed 660 gal (2500 L) individual capacity
(3) Intermediate bulk containers that do not exceed 793 gal (3000 L) [**30**:9.1.1]

66.9.1.2 This section shall also apply to limited transfer of liquids incidental thereto. [**30**:9.1.2]

66.9.1.3 This section shall also apply to overpack drums when used for temporary containment of containers that do not exceed 60 gal (230 L) capacity. Such overpack containers shall be treated as containers as defined in 66.3.3.10. [**30**:9.1.3]

66.9.1.4 This section shall not apply to the following:

(1) Containers, intermediate bulk containers, and portable tanks that are used in operations areas, as covered by Section 66.17
(2) Liquids in the fuel tanks of motor vehicles, aircraft, boats, or portable or stationary engines
(3) Beverages where packaged in individual containers that do not exceed 1.3 gal (5 L) capacity
(4) Medicines, foodstuffs, cosmetics, and other consumer products that contain not more than 50 percent by volume of water-miscible flammable or combustible liquids, with the remainder of the product consisting of components that do not burn and where packaged in individual containers that do not exceed 1.3 gal (5 L) capacity
(5) Liquids that have no fire point when tested in accordance with ASTM D 92, *Standard Test Method for Flash and Fire Points by Cleveland Open Cup*, up to the boiling point of the liquid or up to a temperature at which the liquid shows an obvious physical change
(6) Liquids with a flash point greater than 95°F (35°C) in a water-miscible solution or water-miscible dispersion with a water and noncombustible solids content of more than 80 percent by weight, and which does not sustain combustion when tested in accordance with "Method of Testing for Sustained Combustibility," in accordance with Title 49, Code of Federal Regulations, Part 173, Appendix H, or the UN publication *Recommendations on the Transport of Dangerous Goods*
(7) Distilled spirits and wines in wooden barrels or casks [**30**:9.1.4]

66.9.2 Reserved.

66.9.3 General Requirements.

66.9.3.1 The general requirements of this chapter shall be applicable to the storage of liquids in liquid storage areas as covered in Chapters 10 through 14 of NFPA 30, regardless of the quantities being stored.

Exception: Where more stringent requirements are set forth in Chapters 10 through 14 of NFPA 30, those requirements shall take precedence. [**30**:9.3.1]

66.9.3.2 For the purposes of Sections 66.9 through 66.16, unstable liquids shall be treated as Class IA liquids. [**30**:9.3.2]

66.9.3.3 Means of egress shall meet applicable requirements of NFPA *101, Life Safety Code*. [**30**:9.3.3]

66.9.3.3.1 Storage of liquids shall not physically obstruct a means of egress. [**30**:9.3.3.1]

66.9.3.4 For the purposes of this section and Chapters 10, 12, and 16 of NFPA 30, *protected storage* shall mean storage installed after January 1, 1997 that is protected in accordance with Section 66.16. All other storage shall be considered to be unprotected storage unless an alternate means of protection has been approved by the AHJ. [**30**:9.3.4]

66.9.3.5 Wood of at least 1 in. (25 mm) nominal thickness shall be permitted to be used for shelving, racks, dunnage, scuffboards, floor overlay, and similar installations. [**30**:9.3.5]

66.9.3.6 Class I liquids shall not be permitted to be stored in basements as defined in 3.3.23. [**30**:9.3.6]

66.9.3.7 Class II and Class IIIA liquids shall be permitted to be stored in basements as defined in 3.3.23, provided the basement is protected in accordance with Section 3.3.23. [**30**:9.3.7]

66.9.3.8 Class IIIB liquids shall be permitted to be stored in basements as defined in 3.3.23. [**30**:9.3.8]

66.9.3.9 Where containers, intermediate bulk containers, or portable tanks are stacked, they shall be stacked so that stability is maintained and excessive stress on container walls is prevented. [**30**:9.3.9]

66.9.3.9.1 Portable tanks and intermediate bulk containers stored more than one high shall be designed to stack securely, without the use of dunnage. [**30**:9.3.9.1]

66.9.3.9.2 Materials-handling equipment shall be capable of handling containers, portable tanks, and intermediate bulk containers that are stored at all storage levels. [**30**:9.3.9.2]

66.9.3.9.3* Power-operated industrial trucks used to move Class I liquids shall be selected, operated, and maintained in accordance with NFPA 505, *Fire Safety Standard for Powered Industrial Trucks Including Type Designations, Areas of Use, Conversions, Maintenance, and Operations.* [**30**:9.3.9.3]

66.9.3.10 Containers, intermediate bulk containers, and portable tanks in unprotected liquid storage areas shall not be stored closer than 36 in. (915 mm) to the nearest beam, chord, girder, or other roof or ceiling member. [**30**:9.3.10]

66.9.3.11 Liquids used for building maintenance, painting, or other similar infrequent maintenance purposes shall be permitted to be stored in closed containers outside of storage cabinets or inside liquid storage areas, if limited to an amount that does not exceed a 10-day supply at anticipated rates of use. [**30**:9.3.11]

66.9.3.12 Storage, handling, and use of Class II and Class III liquids heated at or above their flash point shall follow the requirements for Class I liquids, unless an engineering evaluation conducted in accordance with Section 66.6 justifies following the requirements for some other liquid class. *(See 66.6.4.1.2 and A.66.6.4.1.2.)* [**30**:9.3.12]

66.9.4 Acceptable Containers.

66.9.4.1* Only the following approved containers, intermediate bulk containers, and portable tanks shall be used for Class I, Class II, and Class IIIA liquids:

(1) Metal containers, metal intermediate bulk containers, and metal portable tanks meeting the requirements of and containing products authorized by the U.S. Department of Transportation Hazardous Materials Regulations in Title 49, Code of Federal Regulations, Parts 100–199, or by Part 6 of the UN *Recommendations on the Transport of Dangerous Goods*
(2) Plastic or metal consumer-use containers meeting the requirements of, and used within the scope of, one or more of the following specifications:
  (a) ASTM F 852, *Standard Specification for Portable Gasoline Containers for Consumer Use*
  (b) ASTM F 976, *Standard Specification for Portable Kerosene and Diesel Containers for Consumer Use*
(3) Nonmetallic or metallic commercial/industrial safety cans meeting the requirements of, and used with the scope of, one or more of the following specifications:
  (a) ANSI/UL 30, *Standard for Metal Safety Cans*
  (b) ANSI/UL 1313, *Standard for Nonmetallic Safety Cans for Petroleum Products*
  (c) FM Global *Approval Standard for Safety Containers and Filling, Supply, and Disposal Containers — Class Number 6051 and 6052*
(4) Plastic containers that meet requirements set by and contain products authorized by the following:
  (a) The U. S. Department of Transportation Hazardous Materials Regulations in Title 49, Code of Federal Regulations, Parts 100–199, or by Part 6 of the UN publication *Recommendations on the Transport of Dangerous Goods*
  (b) Items 256 or 258 of the *National Motor Freight Classification* (NMFC) for liquids that are not classified as hazardous by the U.S. Department of Transportation Hazardous Materials Regulations in Title 49, Code of Federal Regulations, Parts 100–199, or by Part 6 of the UN publication *Recommendations on the Transport of Dangerous Goods*
(5) Fiber drums that meet the following:
  (a) Requirements of Items 294 and 296 of the *National Motor Freight Classification* (NMFC), or Rule 51 of the *Uniform Freight Classification* (UFC), for Types 2A, 3A, 3B-H, 3B-L, or 4A
  (b) Requirements of, and containing liquid products authorized by, either the U.S. Department of Transportation Hazardous Materials Regulations in Title 49, Code of Federal Regulations, Chapter I, or by U.S. Department of Transportation exemption
(6)*Rigid nonmetallic intermediate bulk containers that meet requirements set by and contain products authorized by the following:
  (a) The U.S. Department of Transportation Hazardous Materials Regulations in Title 49, Code of Federal Regulations, Parts 100–199, or by Part 6 of the UN publication *Recommendations on the Transport of Dangerous Goods,* for Classes 31H1, 31H2, and 31HZ1
  (b) The *National Motor Freight Classification* (NMFC), or the International Safe Transit Association for liquids that are not classified as hazardous by the U.S. Department of Transportation Hazardous Materials Regulations in Title 49, Code of Federal Regulations, Parts 100–199, or by Part 6 of the UN publication *Recommendations on the Transport of Dangerous Goods*
(7) Glass containers up to the capacity limits stated in Table 66.9.4.3 and in accordance with U.S. Department of Transportation Hazardous Materials Regulations in Title 49, Code of Federal Regulations, Parts 100–199 [**30**:9.4.1]

66.9.4.1.1 For protected storage, rigid nonmetallic intermediate bulk containers, as described in 66.9.4.1(5), shall be subjected to a standard fire test that demonstrates acceptable inside storage fire performance and shall be listed and labeled. [**30**:9.4.1.1]

66.9.4.1.2 Medicines, beverages, foodstuffs, cosmetics, and other common consumer products, where packaged according to commonly accepted practices for retail sales, shall be exempt from the requirements of 66.9.4.1 and 66.9.4.3. [**30**:9.4.1.2]

66.9.4.2 Each portable tank or intermediate bulk container shall be provided with one or more devices installed in the top with sufficient emergency venting capacity to limit internal pressure under fire exposure conditions to a gauge pressure of 10 psi (70 kPa) or 30 percent of the bursting pressure of the portable tank, whichever is greater. [**30**:9.4.2]

66.9.4.2.1 The total venting capacity shall be not less than that specified in 22.7.3.2 or 22.7.3.4 of NFPA 30. [**30**:9.4.2.1]

66.9.4.2.2 At least one pressure-actuated vent having a minimum capacity of 6000 ft^3 (170 m^3) of free air per hour at an absolute pressure of 14.7 psi (101 kPa) and 60°F (15.6°C) shall be used. It shall be set to open at not less than a gauge pressure of 5 psi (35 kPa). [**30**:9.4.2.2]

66.9.4.2.3 If fusible vents are used, they shall be actuated by elements that operate at a temperature not exceeding 300°F (150°C). Where plugging of a pressure-actuated vent can occur, such as when used for paints, drying oils, and similar materials, fusible plugs or venting devices that soften to failure at a maximum of 300°F (150°C) under fire exposure shall be permitted to be used for the entire emergency venting requirement. [**30**:9.4.2.3]

66.9.4.3 The maximum allowable size of a container, intermediate bulk container, or metal portable tank for Class I, Class II, and Class IIIA liquids shall not exceed that specified in Table 66.9.4.3.

Exception: As provided for in 66.9.1, 66.9.4.3.1, 66.9.4.3.2, and 66.9.4.3.3. [30:9.4.3]

66.9.4.3.1 Class IB and Class IC water-miscible liquids shall be permitted to be stored in plastic containers up to 60 gal (230 L) in size, if stored and protected in accordance with Table 66.16.5.2.7. [**30**:9.4.3.1]

66.9.4.3.2 Class IA and Class IB liquids shall be permitted to be stored in glass containers of not more than 1.3 gal (5 L) capacity if the required liquid purity (such as American Chemical Society analytical reagent grade or higher) would be affected by storage in metal containers or if the liquid can cause excessive corrosion of a metal container. [**30**:9.4.3.2]

66.9.4.3.3 Leaking or damaged containers up to 60 gal (230 L) capacity shall be permitted to be stored temporarily in accordance with this section and Chapters 10 through 12 of NFPA 30, provided they are enclosed in overpack containers. [**30**:9.4.3.3]

66.9.4.3.3.1 To be considered protected storage as defined in 66.9.3.4 and in accordance with Section 66.16, an overpack container shall be constructed of the same material as the leaking or damaged container. [**30**:9.4.3.3.1]

66.9.4.3.3.2 Metal overpack containers shall be considered nonrelieving style containers. [**30**:9.4.3.3.2]

66.9.5* Flammable Liquids Storage Cabinets.

66.9.5.1 The volume of Class I, Class II, and Class IIIA liquids stored in an individual storage cabinet shall not exceed 120 gal (460 L). [**30**:9.5.1]

66.9.5.2 The total aggregate volume of Class I, Class II, and Class IIIA liquids in a group of storage cabinets shall not exceed the maximum allowable quantity of flammable and combustible liquids per control area based on the occupancy where the cabinets are located. [**30**:9.5.2]

66.9.5.3 Storage cabinets that meet at least one of the following sets of requirements shall be acceptable for storage of liquids:

(1) Storage cabinets designed and constructed to limit the internal temperature at the center of the cabinet and 1 in. (25 mm) from the top of the cabinet to not more than 325°F (163°C), when subjected to a 10-minute fire test that simulates the fire exposure of the standard time–temperature curve specified in NFPA 251, *Standard Methods of Tests of Fire*

Table 66.9.4.3 Maximum Allowable Size — Containers, Intermediate Bulk Containers (IBCs), and Portable Tanks

Container Type	Flammable Liquids			Combustible Liquids	
	Class IA	**Class IB**	**Class IC**	**Class II**	**Class IIIA**
Glass	1 pt (0.5 L)	1 qt (1 L)	1.3 gal (5 L)	1.3 gal (5 L)	5.3 gal (20 L)
Metal (other than drums) or approved plastic	1.3 gal (5 L)	5.3 gal (20 L)	5.3 gal (20 L)	5.3 gal (20 L)	5.3 gal (20 L)
Safety cans	2.6 gal (10 L)	5.3 gal (20 L)	5.3 gal (20 L)	5.3 gal (20 L)	5.3 gal (20 L)
Metal drum (e.g., UN 1A1/1A2)	119 gal (450 L)	119 gal (450 L)	119 gal (450 L)	119 gal (450 L)	119 gal (450 L)
Approved metal portable tanks and IBCs	793 gal (3000 L)	793 gal (3000 L)	793 gal (3000 L)	793 gal (3000 L)	793 gal (3000 L)
Rigid plastic IBCs (UN 31H1 or 31H2) and composite IBCs with rigid inner receptacle (UN31HZ1)	NP	NP	NP	793 gal (3000 L)	793 gal (3000 L)
Composite IBCs with flexible inner receptacle (UN31HZ2) and DOT/UN-approved flexible IBCs	NP	NP	NP	NP	NP
Non-bulk Bag-in-Box	NP	NP	NP	NP	NP
Polyethylene UN1H1 and UN1H2, or as authorized by DOT exemption	1.3 gal (5 L)	5.3 gal (20 L)*	5.3 gal (20 L)*	119 gal (450 L)	119 gal (450 L)
Fiber drum NMFC or UFC Type 2A; Types 3A, 3B-H, or 3B-L; or Type 4A	NP	NP	NP	119 gal (450 L)	119 gal (450 L)

NP: Not permitted for the container categories so classified unless a fire protection system is provided that is developed in accordance with 66.16.3.6 and is approved for the specific container and protection against static electricity is provided in accordance with 66.6.5.4.
*See 66.9.4.3.1. [**30**: Table 9.4.3]

Resistance of Building and Construction and Materials, shall be acceptable. All joints and seams shall remain tight and the door shall remain securely closed during the test.

(2) Metal storage cabinets constructed in the following manner shall be acceptable:

   (a) The bottom, top, door, and sides of the cabinet shall be at least No. 18 gauge sheet steel and shall be double-walled, with 1½ in. (38 mm) air space.
   (b) Joints shall be riveted, welded, or made tight by some equally effective means.
   (c) The door shall be provided with a three-point latch arrangement, and the door sill shall be raised at least 2 in. (50 mm) above the bottom of the cabinet to retain spilled liquid within the cabinet.

(3) Wooden cabinets constructed in the following manner shall be acceptable:

   (a) The bottom, sides, and top shall be constructed of exterior grade plywood that is at least 1 in. (25 mm) thick and of a type that will not break down or delaminate under fire conditions.
   (b) All joints shall be rabbetted and shall be fastened in two directions with wood screws.
   (c) Where more than one door is used, there shall be a rabbetted overlap of not less than 1 in. (25 mm).
   (d) Doors shall be equipped with a means of latching, and hinges shall be constructed and mounted in such a manner as to not lose their holding capacity when subjected to fire exposure.
   (e) A raised sill or pan capable of containing a 2 in. (50 mm) depth of liquid shall be provided at the bottom of the cabinet to retain spilled liquid within the cabinet.

(4) Listed storage cabinets that have been constructed and tested in accordance with 66.9.5.3(1) shall be acceptable. [**30**:9.5.3]

66.9.5.4* Storage cabinets shall not be required by this *Code* to be ventilated for fire protection purposes. [**30**:9.5.4]

66.9.5.4.1 If not ventilated, storage cabinet vent openings shall be sealed with the bungs supplied with the cabinet or with bungs specified by the cabinet manufacturer. [**30**:9.5.4.1]

66.9.5.4.2* If a storage cabinet is ventilated for any reason, the vent openings shall be ducted directly to a safe location outdoors or to a treatment device designed to control volatile organic compounds (VOCs) and ignitible vapors in such a manner that will not compromise the specified performance of the cabinet and in a manner that is acceptable to the AHJ. [**30**:9.5.4.2]

66.9.5.5* Storage cabinets shall include the following marking: [**30**:9.5.5]

FLAMMABLE
KEEP FIRE AWAY

66.9.5.5.1 The minimum letter height for FLAMMABLE (signal word) shall be 2.0 in. (50 mm) and the minimum letter height for KEEP FIRE AWAY (message) shall be 1.0 in. (25 mm). [**30**:9.5.5.1]

66.9.5.5.2 All letters shall be uppercase and in contrasting color to the background. [**30**:9.5.5.2]

66.9.5.5.3 The marking shall be located on the upper portion of the cabinet's front door(s) or frame. [**30**:9.5.5.3]

66.9.5.5.4 Use of other languages, the international symbol for "flammable" (a flame in a triangle), the international symbol for "keep fire away" (a burning match in "no" circle) shall be permitted. [**30**:9.5.5.4]

66.9.6 Maximum Allowable Quantities (MAQs) per Control Area.

66.9.6.1 General Occupancy Limits. The MAQs of liquids allowed in each control area shall not exceed the amounts specified in Table 66.9.6.1.

Table 66.9.6.1 MAQ of Flammable and Combustible Liquids per Control Area

	Liquid Class(es)	Quantity		Notes
		gal	L	
Flammable liquids	IA	30	115	1, 2
	IB and IC	120	460	1, 2
	IA, IB, IC combined	120	460	1, 2, 3
Combustible liquids	II	120	460	1, 2
	IIIA	330	1,265	1, 2
	IIIB	13,200	50,600	1, 2, 4

Notes:
(1) Quantities are permitted to be increased 100 percent where stored in approved flammable liquids storage cabinets or in safety cans in accordance with this *Code*. Where Note 2 also applies, the increase for both notes is permitted to be applied accumulatively.
(2) Quantities are permitted to be increased 100 percent in buildings equipped throughout with an automatic sprinkler system installed in accordance with NFPA 13. Where Note 1 also applies, the increase for both notes is permitted to be applied accumulatively.
(3) Containing not more than the maximum allowable quantity per control area of Class IA, Class IB, or Class IC flammable liquids, individually.
(4) Quantities are not limited in a building equipped throughout with an automatic sprinkler system installed in accordance with NFPA 13 and designed in accordance with the protection criteria contained in Section 66.16 of this *Code*. [**30**: Table 9.6.1]

Exception: As modified by 66.9.6.2 and Chapters 10 through 14 of NFPA 30. [30:9.6.1]

66.9.6.2 Special Occupancy Limits.

66.9.6.2.1 For the following occupancies, the MAQs per control area shall not exceed the amounts specified in Table 66.9.6.2.1:

(1) Assembly
(2) Ambulatory health care
(3) Business
(4) Day care
(5) Detention and correctional
(6) Educational
(7) Health care
(8) Residential [**30**:9.6.2.1]

66.9.6.2.2 For the occupancies specified in 66.9.6.2.1, storage in excess of 10 gal (38 L) of Class I and Class II liquids combined or in excess of 60 gal (227 L) of Class IIIA liquids shall be permitted where stored in flammable liquids storage cabi-

Table 66.9.6.2.1 MAQs — Special Occupancy Limits

Liquid Class(es)	Quantity	
	gal	L
I and II	10	38
IIIA	60	227
IIIB	120	454

[**30:** Table 9.6.2.1]

nets and where the total aggregate quantity does not exceed 180 gal (680 L). [**30:**9.6.2.2]

66.9.6.2.3 Fuel in the tanks of operating mobile equipment shall be permitted to exceed the quantities specified in Table 66.9.6.1, where the equipment is operated in accordance with this *Code*. [**30:**9.6.2.3]

66.9.6.2.4 For ambulatory health care, day care, educational, and health care occupancies, the MAQ for Class IIIB liquids shall be permitted to be increased 100 percent if the building is protected throughout with an automatic sprinkler system installed in accordance with Section 13.3 and NFPA 13. [**30:**9.6.2.4]

66.9.7 Control Areas.

66.9.7.1 For the purpose of this *Code*, a control area shall be a space within a building where quantities of liquids that do not exceed the maximum quantities allowed by Table 66.9.6.1 or Table 66.9.6.2.1 are stored. [**30:**9.7.1]

66.9.7.2 Control areas shall be separated from each other by fire barriers in accordance with Table 66.9.7.2. [**5000:**34.2.5.1.1]

Table 66.9.7.2 Design and Number of Control Areas

Floor Level	Maximum Allowable Quantity per Control Area (percent)*	Number of Control Areas per Floor	Fire Resistance Rating for Fire Barriers (hr)†
Above grade			
>9	5	1	2
7–9	5	2	2
4–6	12.5	2	2
3	50	2	1
2	75	3	1
1	100	4	1
Below grade			
1	75	3	1
2	50	2	1
Lower than 2	NP	NP	N/A

NP: Not permitted. N/A: Not applicable.
*Percentages represent the MAQ per control area shown in Table 66.9.6.1, with all of the increases permitted in the footnotes of that table.
†Fire barriers are required to include floors and walls, as necessary, to provide a complete separation from other control areas. [**5000:** Table 34.2.5.1.1]

66.9.7.3 Control areas located below grade that are considered basements, as defined in 3.3.22, shall not be utilized for the storage of Class I liquids. [**30:**9.7.3]

66.9.8 Classification of Occupancies That Exceed the MAQs of Liquids per Control Area.

66.9.8.1* Occupancy Classifications. Buildings and portions of buildings where liquids are stored shall be classified as Protection Level 2 or Protection Level 3, as established in this section, when the MAQs per control area are exceeded. [**30:**9.8.1]

66.9.8.1.1 Protection Level 2. Buildings and portions thereof storing quantities of liquids that are considered as High-Hazard Level 2 liquids and that exceed the maximum allowable quantities per control area shall be classified as Protection Level 2 occupancies. [**30:**9.8.1.1]

66.9.8.1.2 Protection Level 3. Buildings and portions thereof storing quantities of liquids that are considered as High-Hazard Level 3 liquids and that exceed the maximum allowable quantities per control area shall be classified as Protection Level 3 occupancies. [**30:**9.8.1.2]

66.9.8.2* Requirements for Specific Occupancies. Liquids stored in Protection Level 2 or Protection Level 3 occupancies shall meet the applicable requirements for storage in a Liquid Storage Room or Liquid Warehouse as defined in this *Code* and in *NFPA 5000, Building Construction and Safety Code*. [**30:**9.8.2]

66.9.9 Construction Requirements.

66.9.9.1 Storage areas shall be constructed to meet the fire resistance ratings specified in Table 66.9.9.1. Construction assemblies shall comply with the test specifications given in ASTM E 119. [**30:**9.9.1]

66.9.9.2 Openings in interior walls to adjacent rooms or buildings and openings in exterior walls with fire resistance ratings shall be provided with normally closed, listed fire doors with fire protection ratings that correspond to the fire resistance rating of the wall as specified in Table 66.9.9.2. [**30:**9.9.2]

66.9.9.2.1 Such doors shall be permitted to be arranged to stay open during material-handling operations if the doors are designed to close automatically in a fire emergency by provision of listed closure devices. [**30:**9.9.2.1]

66.9.9.2.2 Fire doors shall be installed in accordance with NFPA 80, *Standard for Fire Doors and Other Opening Protectives*. [**30:**9.9.2.2]

66.9.9.3 Exterior walls shall be constructed to provide ready access for fire-fighting operations by means of access openings, windows, or lightweight, noncombustible wall panels.

Exception: This requirement does not apply to liquid storage rooms totally enclosed within a building. [30:9.9.3]

66.9.10 Fire Protection.

66.9.10.1 Protected Storage. Fire protection requirements for protected storage shall meet the requirements of 66.9.10.2 and Section 66.16. [**30:**9.10.1]

66.9.10.2 Manual Fire Protection.

66.9.10.2.1 Portable fire extinguishers shall be provided in accordance with Section 13.6 and NFPA 10. [**30:**9.10.2.1]

Table 66.9.9.1 Fire Resistance Ratings for Liquid Storage Areas

Type of Storage Area	Fire Resistance Rating (hr)		
	Interior Walls[a], Ceilings, Intermediate Floors	Roofs	Exterior Walls
Liquid storage room			
Floor area ≤ 150 ft²	1	—	—
Floor area > 150 ft², but ≤ 500 ft²	2	—	—
Liquid warehouse[b,c,g]	4[d]	—	2[e], 4[f]

For SI units, 1 ft² = 0.09 m².

[a]Between liquid storage areas and any adjacent areas not dedicated to liquid storage.

[b]Fire resistance ratings for liquid warehouses storing only Class IIIB liquids, which are not heated above their flash point, are permitted to be reduced to 2 hours.

[c]Fire resistance ratings for liquid warehouses protected in accordance with Section 66.16 are permitted to be reduced to 2 hours.

[d]This shall be a fire wall as defined in NFPA 221, *Standard for High Challenge Fire Walls, Fire Walls, and Fire Barrier Walls*.

[e]For exposing walls that are located more than 10 ft (3 m) but less than 50 ft (15 m) from an important building or line of adjoining property that can be built upon.

[f]For exposing walls that are located 10 ft (3 m) or less from an important building or line of adjoining property that can be built upon.

[g]For accessory use areas in protected liquid warehouses, such as offices and restrooms, whose combined area is less than 10 percent of the area of the warehouse, no fire resistance rating shall be required for the interior walls and ceilings.

[**30**: Table 9.9.1]

Table 66.9.9.2 Protection Ratings for Fire Doors

Fire Resistance Rating of Wall as Required by Table 66.9.9.1 (hr)	Fire Protection Rating of Door (hr)
1	¾
2	1½
4	3*

*One fire door required on each side of interior openings for attached liquid warehouses. [**30**: Table 9.9.2]

66.9.10.2.2 Portable fire extinguishers shall meet the following requirements:

(1) At least one portable fire extinguisher having a capability of not less than 40:B shall be located outside of, but not more than 10 ft (3 m) from, the door opening into a liquid storage area.
(2) At least one portable fire extinguisher having a capability of not less than 40:B shall be located within 30 ft (9 m) of any Class I or Class II liquids located outside of a liquid storage area, or at least one portable fire extinguisher having a capacity of 80:B shall be located within 50 ft (15 m) of such a storage area. [**30**:9.10.2.2]

66.9.10.2.3 Where provided, hose connections supplied from sprinkler systems shall be installed in accordance with Section 13.3 and NFPA 13. [**30**:9.10.2.3]

66.9.10.2.4 Where provided, hose connections supplied by a standpipe system shall be installed in accordance with Section 13.2 and NFPA 14. [**30**:9.10.2.4]

66.9.10.2.5 Where provided, hose connections shall also meet the following requirements:

(1) Hose connections shall be provided in protected general-purpose warehouses and in protected liquid warehouses.
(2) Where preconnected hose is provided, it shall be either 1½ in. (38 mm) lined fire hose or 1 in. (25 mm) hard rubber hose, using combination spray and straight stream nozzles. [**30**:9.10.2.5]

66.9.10.2.6 Where hose connections are provided, the water supply shall be sufficient to meet the fixed fire protection demand plus a total of at least 500 gpm (1900 L/min) for inside and outside hose connections for at least 2 hours, unless otherwise specified in Section 66.16. [**30**:9.10.2.6]

66.9.11 Emergency Control Systems. (Reserved)

66.9.12 Electrical Systems.

66.9.12.1 Electrical area classification shall not be required for liquid storage areas where all containers, intermediate bulk containers, and portable tanks are sealed and are not opened, except as provided for in 66.9.12.2. [**30**:9.12.1]

66.9.12.2 For liquid storage rooms that are totally enclosed within the building, electrical wiring and utilization equipment for Class I liquid storage shall be Class I, Division 2 (Zone 2), and electrical wiring and utilization equipment in inside rooms used for the storage of Class II and Class III liquids shall be suitable for ordinary purpose.

Exception: Class I, Division 2 (Zone 2) requirements shall apply to Class II and Class III liquids when stored at temperatures above their flash points. [**30**:9.12.2]

66.9.13* Containment, Drainage, and Spill Control.

66.9.13.1 Storage areas shall be designed and operated to prevent the discharge of liquids to public waterways, public sewers, or adjoining property, unless such discharge has been specifically approved. [**30**:9.13.1]

66.9.13.1.1 Where the drainage system discharges to private or public sewers or waterways, the drainage system shall be equipped with traps and separators. [**30**:9.13.1.1]

66.9.13.2 Where individual containers exceed 10 gal (38 L), curbs, scuppers, drains, or other suitable means shall be provided to prevent flow of liquids under emergency conditions into adjacent building areas. [**30**:9.13.2]

66.9.13.3 Containment or drainage to an approved location shall be provided. [**30**:9.13.3]

66.9.13.3.1 Where a drainage system is used, it shall also have sufficient capacity to carry the expected discharge of water from fire protection systems. [**30**:9.13.3.1]

66.9.13.4 Where only Class IIIB liquids are stored, spill control, containment, and drainage shall not be required. [**30**:9.13.4]

66.9.13.5 Where only unsaturated polyester resins (UPRs) containing not more than 50 percent by weight of Class IC, Class II, or Class IIIA liquid constituents are stored and are protected in accordance with 66.16.5.2.11, spill control, containment, and drainage shall not be required. [**30**:9.13.5]

66.9.13.6 Where storage is protected in accordance with Section 66.16, spill control, containment, and drainage shall also meet the requirements of 66.16.8. [**30**:9.13.6]

66.9.14 Ventilation. Liquid storage areas where dispensing is conducted shall be provided with ventilation that meets the requirements of 66.18.6. [**30**:9.14]

66.9.15 Exhausted Enclosures. (Reserved)

66.9.16 Explosion Control.

66.9.16.1* Where Class IA liquids are stored in containers larger than 1 gal (4 L), areas shall be provided with a means of explosion control that meets the requirements of NFPA 69, *Standard on Explosion Prevention Systems*. An approved engineered damage limiting construction design shall also be permitted.

Exception: This shall not apply to a liquid storage room totally enclosed within a building. [30:9.16.1]

66.9.16.2* Where unstable liquids are stored, an approved engineered construction method that is designed to limit damage from a deflagration or detonation, depending on the liquid stored, shall be used. [**30**:9.16.2]

66.9.17 Separation from Incompatible Materials.

66.9.17.1 Except as provided for in 66.9.17.4, liquids shall be separated from incompatible materials where the stored materials are in containers having a capacity of more than 5 lb (2.268 kg) or ½ gal (1.89 L). [**30**:9.17.1]

66.9.17.1.1 Separation shall be accomplished by one of the following methods:

(1) Segregating incompatible materials storage by a distance of not less than 20 ft (6.1 m)
(2) Isolating incompatible materials storage by a noncombustible partition extending not less than 18 in. (460 mm) above and to the sides of the stored materials
(3) Storing liquid materials in flammable liquids storage cabinets in accordance with 66.9.5 [**30**:9.17.1.1]

66.9.17.2 Liquids shall be separated from Level 2 and Level 3 aerosols in accordance with Chapter 61 and NFPA 30B, *Code for the Manufacture and Storage of Aerosol Products*. [**30**:9.17.2]

66.9.17.3 The following shall apply where oxidizers are in segregated storage with flammable and combustible liquids:

(1) The oxidizer containers and flammable and combustible liquid containers shall be separated by at least 25 ft (7.6 m).
(2) The separation shall be maintained by dikes, drains, or floor slopes to prevent flammable liquid leakage from encroaching on the separation. [**400**:15.2.12.13.1]

66.9.17.4 Materials that are water-reactive, as described in NFPA 704, *Standard System for the Identification of the Hazards of Materials for Emergency Response*, shall not be stored in the same control area with liquids. [**30**:9.17.4]

66.9.18 Dispensing, Handling, and Use of Liquids in Storage Areas.

66.9.18.1 Dispensing, handling, and use of liquids shall meet all applicable requirements of Section 66.18. [**30**:9.18.1]

66.9.18.2 Dispensing of Class I liquids or Class II and Class III liquids at temperatures at or above their flash points shall not be permitted in storage areas that exceed 1000 ft^2 (93 m^2) in floor area unless the dispensing area is separated from the storage areas in accordance with Table 66.9.9.1 and meets all other requirements of 66.9.9. [**30**:9.18.2]

66.9.19 Outdoor Storage of Liquids. Storage of liquids outside of buildings shall meet the requirements of Section 66.14 or 66.15, whichever is applicable. [**30**:9.19]

66.10 Reserved.

66.11 Reserved.

66.12 Reserved.

66.13 Reserved.

66.14 Hazardous Materials Storage Lockers.

66.14.1* **Scope.** This section shall apply to the storage of liquids in movable, modular, prefabricated storage lockers, also known as hazardous materials storage lockers (hereinafter referred to as lockers), specifically designed and manufactured for storage of hazardous materials, in the following:

(1) Containers that do not exceed 119 gal (450 L) individual capacity
(2) Portable tanks that do not exceed 660 gal (2500 L) individual capacity
(3) Intermediate bulk containers that do not exceed 793 gal (3000 L) individual capacity [**30**:14.1]

66.14.2 Reserved.

66.14.3 General Requirements.

66.14.3.1 Lockers that are used as liquid storage rooms shall meet the requirements of Section 66.9. [**30**:14.3.1]

66.14.3.2 Lockers that are located outside shall meet the requirements of Sections 14.4 through 14.6 of NFPA 30. [**30**:14.3.2]

66.14.4 Design and Construction of Hazardous Materials Storage Lockers.

66.14.4.1 The design and construction of a locker shall meet all applicable local, state, and federal regulations and requirements and shall be subject to the approval of the AHJ. [**30**:14.4.1]

66.14.4.2 Movable prefabricated structures that have been examined, listed, or labeled by an organization acceptable to the AHJ for use as a hazardous materials storage facility shall be acceptable. [**30**:14.4.2]

66.14.4.3 Lockers shall not exceed 1500 ft^2 (140 m^2) gross floor area. [**30**:14.4.3]

66.14.4.4 Vertical stacking of lockers shall not be permitted. [**30**:14.4.4]

66.14.4.5 Where electrical wiring and equipment are required, they shall comply with Section 66.7 and 66.9.12. [**30**:14.4.5]

66.14.4.6 Where dispensing or filling is permitted inside a locker, operations shall comply with the provisions of Section 66.18. [**30**:14.4.6]

66.14.4.7 Ventilation shall be provided in accordance with 66.18.6. [**30**:14.4.7]

2015 Edition

66.14.4.8 Lockers shall include a spill containment system to prevent the flow of liquids from the structure under emergency conditions. [**30**:14.4.8]

66.14.4.8.1 The containment system shall have sufficient capacity to contain 10 percent of the volume of containers allowed in the locker or the volume of the largest container, whichever is greater. [**30**:14.4.8.1]

66.14.5 Designated Sites for Hazardous Materials Storage Lockers.

66.14.5.1 Lockers shall be located on a designated approved site on the property. [**30**:14.5.1]

66.14.5.2 The designated site shall be arranged to provide the minimum separation distances specified in Table 66.14.5.2 between individual lockers, from locker to property line that is or can be built upon, and from locker to nearest side of public ways or to important buildings on the same property. [**30**:14.5.2]

Table 66.14.5.2 Designated Sites

	Minimum Separation Distance (ft)		
Area of Designated Site[a] (ft²)	Between Individual Lockers	From Locker to Property Line That Is or Can Be Built Upon[b]	From Locker to Nearest Side of Public Way or to Important Buildings on Same Property[b,c]
≤100	5	10	5
>100 and ≤500	5	20	10
>500 and ≤1500[d]	5	30	20

For SI units, 1 ft = 0.3 m; 1 ft² = 0.09 m².
Note: If the locker is provided with a fire resistance rating of not less than 4 hours and deflagration venting is not required in accordance with 66.9.15, all distances required by Table 66.14.5.2 are permitted to be waived.
[a]Site area limits are intended to differentiate the relative size and thus the number of lockers that are permitted in one designated site.
[b]Distances apply to properties that have protection for exposures, as defined. If there are exposures and such protection for exposures does not exist, the distances should be doubled.
[c]When the exposed building has an exterior wall, facing the designated site, that has a fire resistance rating of at least 2 hours and has no openings to above grade areas within 10 ft (3 m) horizontally and no openings to below grade areas within 50 ft (15 m) horizontally of the designated area, the distances can be reduced to half of those shown in the table, except they should never be less than 5 ft (1.5 m).
[d]When a single locker has a gross single story floor area that will require a site area limit of greater than 1500 ft² (140 m²) or when multiple units exceed the area limit of 1500 ft² (140 m²), the AHJ should be consulted for approval of distances. [**30**: Table 14.5.2]

66.14.5.3 Once the designated site is approved, it shall not be changed without the approval of the AHJ. [**30**:14.5.3]

66.14.5.4 More than one locker shall be permitted on a designated site, provided that the separation distance between individual lockers is maintained in accordance with Table 66.14.5.2. [**30**:14.5.4]

66.14.5.5 Where the approved designated storage site is accessible to the general public, it shall be protected from tampering or trespassing. [**30**:14.5.5]

66.14.6 Storage Requirements.

66.14.6.1 Containers of liquid in their original shipping packages shall be permitted to be stored either palletized or solid piled. [**30**:14.6.1]

66.14.6.2 Unpackaged containers shall be permitted to be stored on shelves or directly on the floor of the locker. [**30**:14.6.2]

66.14.6.3 Containers over 30 gal (114 L) capacity storing Class I or Class II liquids shall not be stored more than two containers high. [**30**:14.6.3]

66.14.6.4 In all cases, the storage arrangement shall provide unrestricted access to and egress from the locker. [**30**:14.6.4]

66.14.6.5 Miscellaneous combustible materials, including but not limited to idle pallets, excessive vegetation, and packing materials, shall not be permitted within 5 ft (1.5 m) of the designated site approved for lockers. [**30**:14.6.5]

66.14.6.6 Warning signs for lockers shall be in accordance with applicable local, state, and federal regulations or with NFPA 704. [**30**:14.6.6]

66.15 Outdoor Storage.

66.15.1 Scope. This section shall apply to the storage of liquids outdoors in the following:

(1) Drums or other containers that do not exceed 119 gal (450 L) individual capacity
(2) Portable tanks that do not exceed 660 gal (2500 L) individual capacity
(3) Intermediate bulk containers that do not exceed 793 gal (3000 L) individual capacity [**30**:15.1]

66.15.2 Reserved.

66.15.3 General Requirements. Outdoor storage of liquids in containers, intermediate bulk containers, and portable tanks shall comply with Table 66.15.3 and with all applicable requirements of this section. [**30**:15.3]

66.15.3.1 Where two or more classes of liquids are stored in a single pile, the maximum quantity permitted in that pile shall be that of the most hazardous class of liquid present. [**30**:15.3.1]

66.15.3.2 No container, intermediate bulk container, or portable tank in a pile shall be more than 200 ft (60 m) from a minimum 20 ft (6 m) wide access way to permit approach of fire control apparatus under all weather conditions. [**30**:15.3.2]

66.15.3.3 The distances specified in Table 66.15.3 shall apply to properties that have protection for exposures as defined. If there are exposures and protection for exposures does not exist, the distance to the property line that is or can be built upon shall be doubled. [**30**:15.3.3]

66.15.3.4 Where total quantity stored does not exceed 50 percent of the maximum quantity per pile, as specified in Table 66.15.3, the distances to a property line that is or can be built upon and to streets, alleys, or public ways shall be permitted to be reduced by 50 percent but in no case to less than 3 ft (0.9 m). [**30**:15.3.4]

66.15.3.5 The storage area shall be graded in a manner to divert possible spills away from buildings or other exposures

Table 66.15.3 Storage Limitations for Outside Storage

Liquid Class	Containers		Portable Tanks and Metal IBCs		Rigid Plastic and Composite IBCs		Minimum Separation Distance (ft)		
	Maximum Quantity per Pile (gal)[a,b,c]	Maximum Storage Height (ft)	Maximum Quantity per Pile (gal)	Maximum Storage Height (ft)	Maximum Quantity per Pile (gal)[a,c]	Maximum Storage Height (ft)	Between Piles or Rack Sections	To Property Line That Is or Can Be Built Upon[b,d]	To Street, Alley, or Public Way[b]
IA	1,100	10	2,200	7	NP	NP	5	50	10
IB	2,200	12	4,400	14	NP	NP	5	50	10
IC	4,400	12	8,800	14	NP	NP	5	50	10
II	8,800	12	17,600	14	8,800	14	5	25	5
III	22,000	18	44,000	14	22,000	18	5	10	5

For SI units, 1 ft = 0.3 m; 1 gal = 3.8 L.
NP: Not permitted.
[a]See 66.15.3.1 regarding mixed-class storage.
[b]See 66.15.3.4 for smaller pile sizes.
[c]For storage in racks, the quantity limits per pile do not apply, but the rack arrangements should be limited to a maximum of 50 ft (15 m) in length and two rows or 9 ft (2.7 m) in depth.
[d]See 66.15.3.3 regarding protection for exposures. [30: Table 15.3]

or shall be surrounded by a curb at least 6 in. (150 mm) high. [30:15.3.5]

66.15.3.5.1 Where curbs are used, provisions shall be made to drain accumulations of groundwater or rainwater or spills of liquids. Drains shall terminate at a safe location and shall flow freely under fire conditions. [30:15.3.5.1]

66.15.3.6 When accessible to the public, the storage area shall be protected against tampering and trespassing. [30:15.3.6]

66.15.3.7 The storage area shall be kept free of weeds, debris, and other combustible materials not necessary to the storage for a distance of at least 10 ft (3 m) around the perimeter of the stored materials. [30:15.3.7]

66.15.3.8 The storage area shall be permitted to be protected from the weather by a canopy or roof that does not limit the dissipation of heat or dispersion of flammable vapors and does not restrict fire-fighting access and control. [30:15.3.8]

66.15.4 Outdoor Storage Adjacent to a Building.

66.15.4.1 A maximum of 1100 gal (4160 L) of liquids in containers, intermediate bulk containers, or portable tanks shall be permitted to be stored adjacent to a building under the same management, provided the following conditions apply:

(1) The adjacent building wall has an exterior fire resistance rating of 2 hours.
(2) The adjacent building wall has no openings at grade or above grade that are within 10 ft (3 m) horizontally of the storage.
(3) The adjacent building wall has no openings directly above the storage.
(4) The adjacent building wall has no openings below grade within 50 ft (15 m) horizontally of the storage. [30:15.4.1]

66.15.4.2 The provisions of 66.15.4.1(1) through (4) shall be permitted to be waived, subject to the approval of the AHJ, if the building in question is one story, is of fire-resistive or non-combustible construction, and is devoted principally to the storage of liquids. [30:15.4.2]

66.15.4.3 The quantity of liquid stored adjacent to a building that meets the conditions of 66.15.4.1(1) through (4) shall be permitted to exceed that permitted in 66.15.4.1, provided the maximum quantity per pile does not exceed 1100 gal (4160 L) and each pile is separated by a 10 ft (3 m) minimum clear space along the common wall. [30:15.4.3]

66.15.4.4 The quantity of liquid stored shall be permitted to exceed the 1100 gal (4160 L) quantity specified by 66.15.4.1 where a minimum distance equal to that specified by Table 66.15.3 for distance to property line shall be maintained between buildings and the nearest container or portable tank. [30:15.4.4]

66.15.4.5 Where the provisions of 66.15.4.1 cannot be met, a minimum distance equal to that specified by Table 66.15.3 for distance to property line shall be maintained between buildings and the nearest container or portable tank. [30:15.4.5]

66.16 Automatic Fire Protection for Inside Liquid Storage Areas.

66.16.1 Scope.

66.16.1.1* This section shall apply to automatic fire protection systems for all inside storage of flammable and combustible liquids in containers, intermediate bulk containers, and portable tanks as specified in 66.9.4. [30:16.1.1]

66.16.1.2* This section shall not apply to Class IA flammable liquids or to unstable flammable or combustible liquids. [30:16.1.2]

66.16.1.3 Storage of liquids that is protected in accordance with the applicable requirements of this section shall be considered protected, as defined in 66.16.2.2. All other storage shall be considered unprotected unless an alternate means of protection has been approved by the AHJ. [30:16.1.3]

66.16.2 Definitions Specific to Section 66.16. For the purpose of this section, the following terms shall have the definitions given. [**30:**16.2]

66.16.2.1 Protected Storage. Flammable and combustible liquids storage that is protected in accordance with this section. [**30:**16.2.2]

66.16.2.2* Relieving-Style Container. A metal container, a metal intermediate bulk container, or a metal portable tank that is equipped with at least one pressure-relieving mechanism at its top that is designed, sized, and arranged to relieve the internal pressure generated due to exposure to fire so that violent rupture is prevented. [**30:**16.2.3]

66.16.2.3* Unsaturated Polyester Resin (UPR). A resin that contains up to 50 percent by weight of Class IC, Class II, or Class III liquid, but no Class IA or Class IB liquid. [**30:**16.2.4]

66.16.2.4 Viscous Liquid. A liquid that gels, thickens, or solidifies when heated or whose viscosity at room temperature versus weight percent content of Class I, Class II, or Class III liquid is in the shaded portion of Figure 66.16.2.4. [**30:**16.2.5]

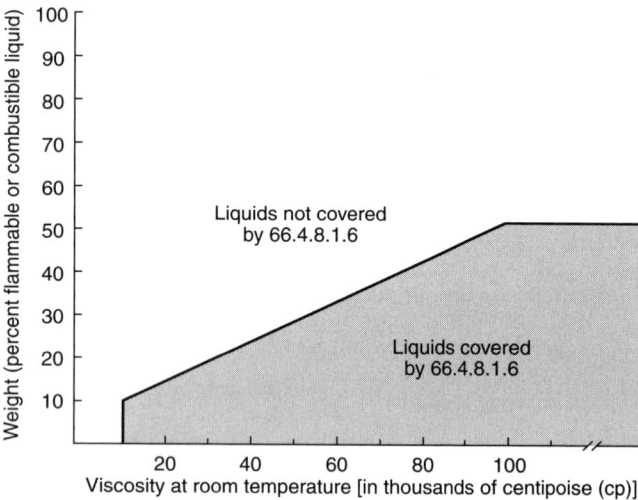

FIGURE 66.16.2.4 Viscous Liquid: Viscosity Versus Weight Percent Flammable or Combustible Component. [30: Figure 16.2.5]

66.16.2.5 Water-Miscible Liquid. A liquid that mixes in all proportions with water without the use of chemical additives, such as emulsifying agents. [**30:**16.2.6]

66.16.3 General Requirements.

66.16.3.1 Where different classes of liquids, container types, and storage configurations are stored in the same protected area, protection shall meet either of the following:

(1) Requirements of this section for the most severe storage fire hazard present
(2) Where areas are not physically separated by a barrier or partition capable of delaying heat from a fire in one hazard area from fusing sprinklers in an adjacent hazard area, the required protection for the more demanding hazard shall:

 (a) Extend 20 ft (6 m) beyond its perimeter, but not less than the required minimum sprinkler design area

 (b) Be provided with means to prevent the flow of burning liquid under emergency conditions into adjacent hazard areas
 (c) Provide containment and drainage as required by 66.16.8 [**30:**16.3.1]

66.16.3.2 Unless otherwise specified in this section, single-row racks shall not be more than 4.5 ft (1.4 m) in depth and double-row racks shall not be more than 9 ft (2.8 m) in depth. [**30:**16.3.2]

66.16.3.3 When applying the fire protection criteria of this section, a minimum aisle space of 6 ft (1.8 m) shall be provided between adjacent piles or adjacent rack sections, unless otherwise specified in the tables in 66.16.5. [**30:**16.3.3]

66.16.3.4 Viscous liquids, as defined in 66.16.2.4, shall be permitted to be protected using either of the following, as applicable:

(1) Criteria for a Class IIIB liquid in accordance with Figure 66.16.4.1(a) or Figure 66.16.4.1(b)
(2) Criteria for cartoned unexpanded Group A plastics in accordance with NFPA 13, *Standard for the Installation of Sprinkler Systems.* [**30:**16.3.4]

66.16.3.5 Protection systems that are designed and developed based on full-scale fire tests performed at an approved test facility or on other engineered protection schemes shall be considered an acceptable alternative to the protection criteria set forth in this section. Such alternative protection systems shall be approved by the AHJ. [**30:**16.3.5]

66.16.3.6 For relieving-style containers of greater than 6.6 gal (25 L) and up to 119 gal (450 L) capacity, the following shall apply:

(1) The pressure-relieving mechanism shall be listed and labeled in accordance with FM Global *Approval Standard for Plastic Plugs for Steel Drums,* Class Number 6083, or equivalent.
(2) The pressure-relieving mechanism shall not be painted, and cap seals, if used, shall be made of thermoplastic material.
(3) For metal containers greater than 6.6 gal (25 L) capacity, the pressure-relieving mechanism shall be unobstructed or an additional pressure-relieving mechanism shall be provided. [**30:**16.3.6]

66.16.3.7 To be considered protected by Table 66.16.5.2.9 and Table 66.16.5.2.10, rigid nonmetallic intermediate bulk containers shall be subjected to a standard fire test that demonstrates acceptable inside storage fire performance and shall be listed and labeled. [**30:**16.3.7]

66.16.4 Automatic Sprinkler and Foam-Water Sprinkler Fire Protection Systems.

66.16.4.1 Where automatic sprinkler systems or low-expansion foam-water sprinkler systems are used to protect storage of liquids, Figure 66.16.4.1(a), Figure 66.16.4.1(b), or Figure 66.16.4.1(c), whichever is applicable, and the appropriate table in 66.16.5 shall be used to determine protection criteria. [**30:**16.4.1]

66.16.4.1.1 Figure 66.16.4.1(a) shall be used for miscible and nonmiscible flammable and combustible liquids in metal containers, metal portable tanks, and metal intermediate bulk containers. [**30:**16.4.1.1]

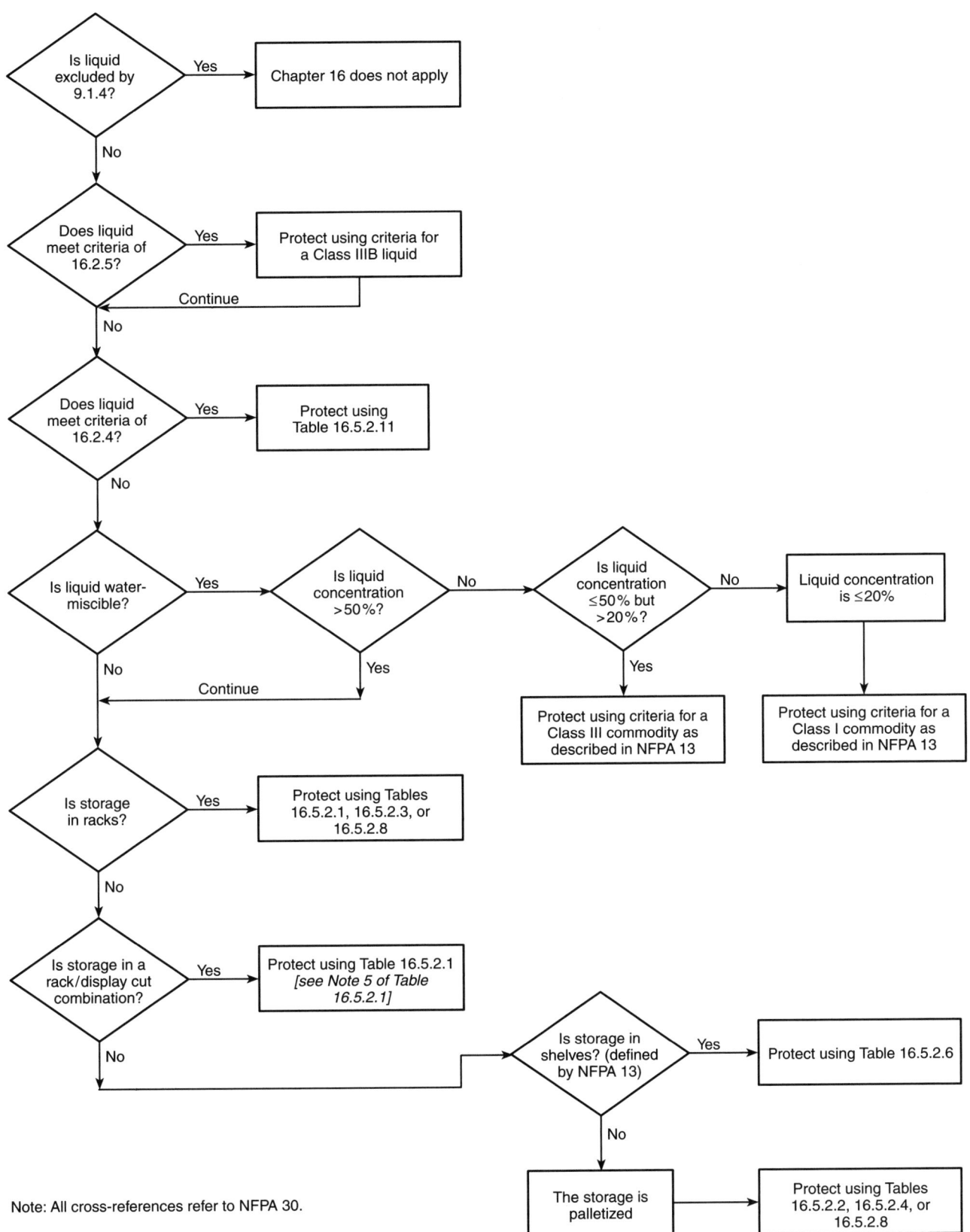

FIGURE 66.16.4.1(a) Fire Protection Criteria Decision Tree for Miscible and Nonmiscible Flammable and Combustible Liquids in Metal Containers. [30: Figure 16.4.1(a)]

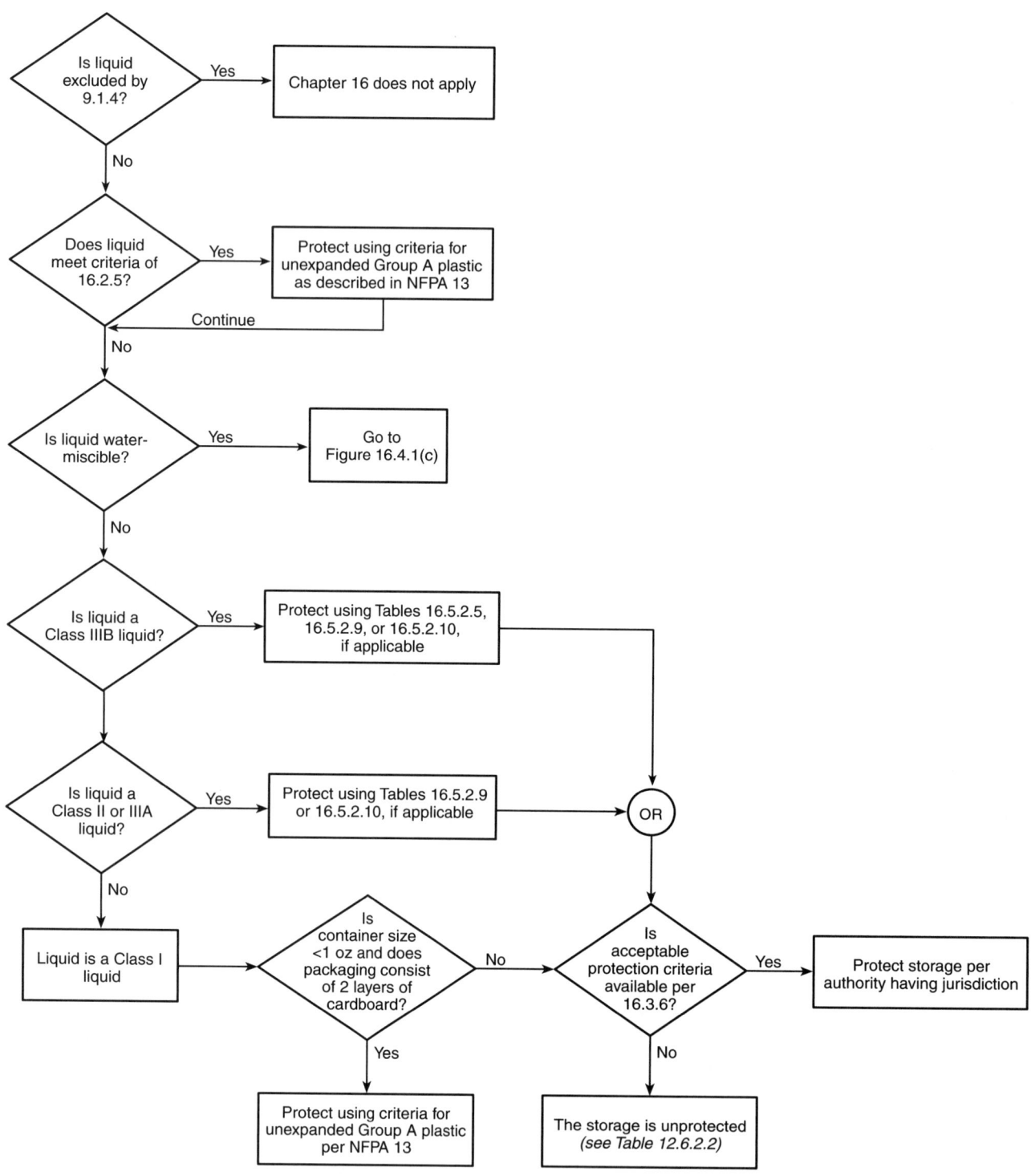

FIGURE 66.16.4.1(b) Fire Protection Criteria Decision Tree for Miscible and Nonmiscible Flammable and Combustible Liquids in Nonmetallic Containers. [30: Figure 16.4.1(b)]

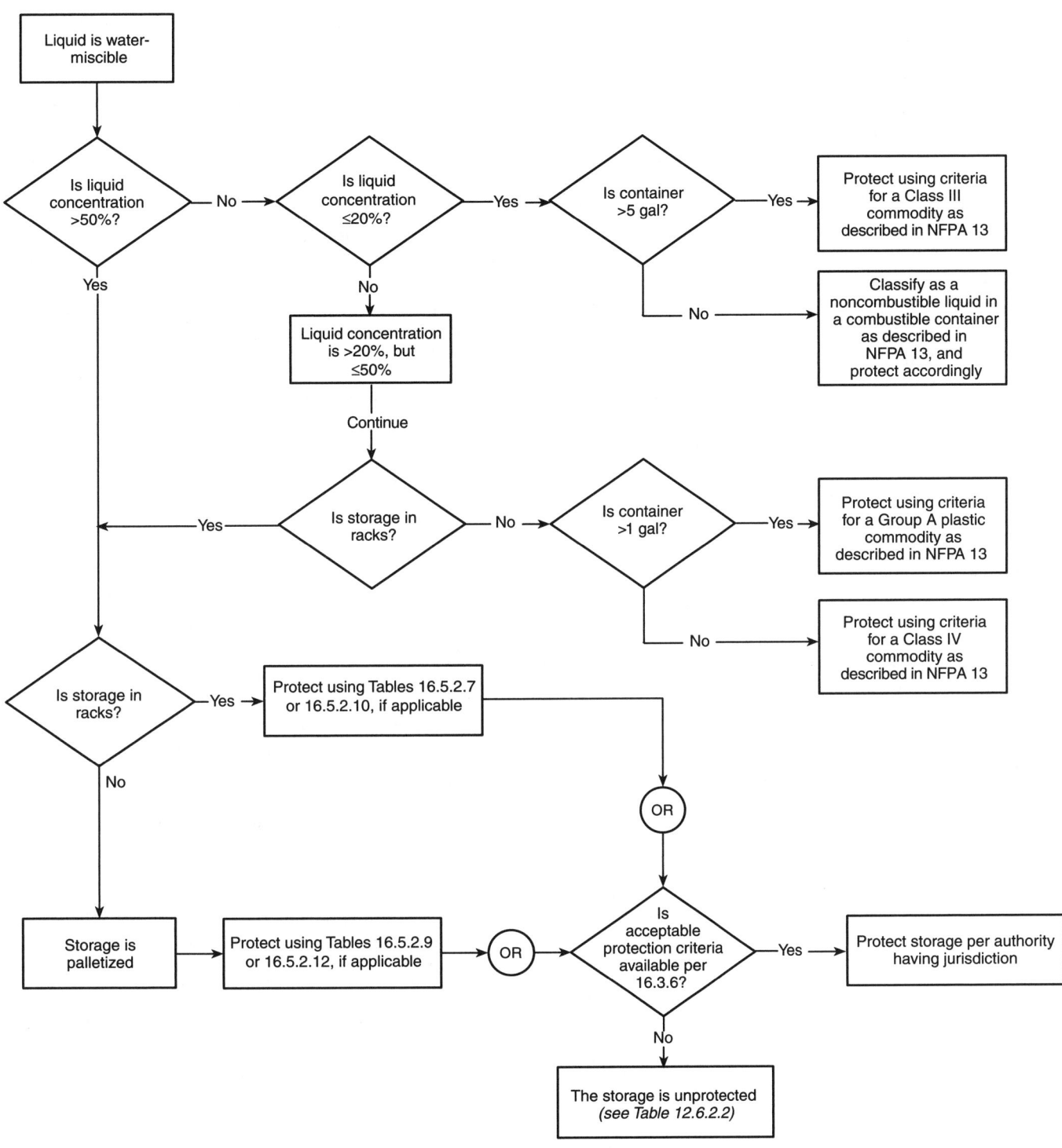

Note: For SI units, 1 gal = 3.8 L.
Note: All cross-references refer to NFPA 30.

FIGURE 66.16.4.1(c) Fire Protection Criteria Decision Tree for Miscible Flammable and Combustible Liquids in Nonmetallic Containers. [30: Figure 16.4.1(c)]

66.16.4.1.2 Figure 66.16.4.1(b) shall be used for miscible and nonmiscible flammable and combustible liquids in nonmetallic containers and in nonmetallic intermediate bulk containers. [**30**:16.4.1.2]

66.16.4.1.3 Figure 66.16.4.1(c) shall be used for water-miscible flammable and combustible liquids in nonmetallic containers and in nonmetallic intermediate bulk containers. [**30**:16.4.1.3]

66.16.4.2 Automatic sprinkler and foam-water fire protection systems shall be wet pipe, deluge, or preaction systems. [**30**:16.4.2]

66.16.4.2.1 If a preaction system is used, it shall be designed so that water or foam solution will immediately discharge from the sprinkler upon sprinkler actuation. [**30**:16.4.2.1]

66.16.4.2.2 A foam-water sprinkler system that meets any of the design criteria specified in the water sprinkler tables in this section shall be acceptable, provided that the system is installed in accordance with NFPA 16, *Standard for the Installation of Foam-Water Sprinkler and Foam-Water Spray Systems.* [**30**:16.4.2.2]

66.16.4.3 Water-based fire protection systems shall be inspected, tested, and maintained in accordance with NFPA 25. [**30**:16.4.3]

66.16.5 Fire Protection System Design Criteria.

66.16.5.1 General. Subsections 66.16.5.2.1 through 66.16.5.2.12 and their related tables, Table 66.16.5.2.1 through Table 66.16.5.2.12, shall be used to determine the protection criteria and storage arrangement for the applicable liquid class, container type, and storage configuration, as described in 66.16.5.2.1 through 66.16.5.2.12 and subject to the provisions of 66.16.5.1. [**30**:16.5.1]

66.16.5.1.1 Table 66.16.5.2.1 through Table 66.16.5.2.12 shall apply only to stable liquids. [**30**:16.5.1.1]

66.16.5.1.1.1 The protection criteria in Table 66.16.5.2.1 through Table 66.16.5.2.12 shall only be used with ceilings having a pitch of 2 in 12 or less. [**30**:16.5.1.1.1]

66.16.5.1.2 When foam or foam-water fire protection systems are provided, discharge densities shall be determined based on the listing criteria of the foam discharge devices selected, the foam concentrate, the specific liquids to be protected, and the criteria in the appropriate table in this section. Where the discharge densities given in the tables differ from those in the listing criteria for the discharge devices, the greater of the two shall be used. [**30**:16.5.1.2]

66.16.5.1.3 In-rack sprinklers shall be installed in accordance with the provisions of Section 13.3 and NFPA 13. In addition, the following modifications shall apply:

(1) In-rack sprinklers shall be laid out in accordance with 66.16.5.1.10 and 66.16.6, as applicable.
(2) Sprinklers in multiple-level in-rack sprinkler systems shall be provided with water shields unless they are separated by horizontal barriers or are specifically listed for installation without water shields.
(3) A vertical clear space of at least 6 in. (150 mm) shall be maintained between the sprinkler deflector and the top of the tier of storage.
(4) Sprinkler discharge shall not be obstructed by horizontal rack structural members.
(5) Where in-rack sprinklers are installed below horizontal barriers, the deflector shall be located a maximum of 7 in. (180 mm) below the barrier.
(6) Longitudinal and transverse flue spaces of at least 6 in. (150 mm) shall be maintained between each rack load. [**30**:16.5.1.3]

66.16.5.1.4 Ceiling sprinklers shall be installed in accordance with Section 13.3 and NFPA 13 and shall be permitted to have the following maximum head spacing:

(1) Classes I, II, and IIIA liquids: 100 ft^2 (9.3 m^2) per sprinkler
(2) Class IIIB liquids: 120 ft^2 (11.1 m^2) per sprinkler [**30**:16.5.1.4]

66.16.5.1.4.1 Ordinary or intermediate temperature–rated K-25 extended-coverage sprinklers shall be permitted to be used as standard response high temperature sprinklers at greater than 144 ft^2 (13 m^2) coverage, with 12 ft (3.7 m) minimum spacing and a maximum coverage area of 196 ft^2 (18 m^2) coverage. [**30**:16.5.1.4.1]

66.16.5.1.5 The ceiling heights given in Table 66.16.5.2.1 through Table 66.16.5.2.12, excluding Table 66.16.5.2.8, shall be permitted to be increased by a maximum of 10 percent if an equivalent percent increase in ceiling sprinkler design density is provided. [**30**:16.5.1.5]

66.16.5.1.6 Foam-water sprinkler systems shall be designed and installed in accordance with NFPA 16. [**30**:16.5.1.6]

66.16.5.1.6.1 Foam-water sprinkler systems shall have at least 15 minutes of foam concentrate, based on the required design flow rate. [**30**:16.5.1.6.1]

66.16.5.1.6.2* Foam-water sprinkler systems shall provide foam solution at the minimum required concentration with as few as four sprinklers flowing. [**30**:16.5.1.6.2]

66.16.5.1.7 When relieving style containers are used, both ¾ in. (20 mm) and 2 in. (50 mm) listed and labeled pressure-relieving mechanisms are required on containers greater than 6 gal (23 L) capacity. [**30**:16.5.1.7]

66.16.5.1.8 For the purposes of 66.16.5, a rigid nonmetallic intermediate bulk container is one that meets the maximum allowable capacity criteria of Table 66.9.4.3 and has been listed and labeled in accordance with UL 2368, *Standard for Fire Exposure Testing of Intermediate Bulk Containers for Flammable and Combustible Liquids,* or equivalent. [**30**:16.5.1.8]

66.16.5.1.9 For the purposes of 66.16.5, the following shall apply:

(1) 1 gal = 3.8 L; 1 ft = 0.3 m; 1 ft^2 = 0.09 m^2
(2) 1 gpm/ft^2 is equivalent to 40.7 L/min/m^2 or 40.7 mm/min
(3) A gauge pressure of 1 psi is equivalent to a gauge pressure of 6.9 kPa
(4) SR = standard response sprinkler; QR = quick response sprinkler; ESFR = early suppression fast response sprinkler; OT = ordinary temperature; HT = high temperature
(5) Where an ordinary-temperature sprinkler is indicated, an intermediate-temperature sprinkler shall be used where ambient conditions require. [**30**:16.5.1.9]

66.16.5.1.10 For the purposes of 66.16.5, the following shall apply to the in-rack sprinkler design layouts specified in Table 66.16.5.2.1 through Table 66.16.5.2.12:

(1) Layout 1, as referenced in Table 66.16.5.2.1, shall mean one line of in-rack sprinklers 8 ft (2.4 m) above the floor in the longitudinal flue space, with sprinklers spaced not more than 10 ft (3 m) on center.
(2) Layout 2, as referenced in Table 66.16.5.2.1, shall mean one line of in-rack sprinklers 6 ft (1.8 m) above the floor and one line of in-rack sprinklers 12 ft (3.6 m) above the floor in the longitudinal flue space, with sprinklers spaced not more than 10 ft (3 m) on center. Sprinklers shall be staggered vertically.
(3) Layout 3, as referenced in Table 66.16.5.2.1 and Table 66.16.5.2.1, shall mean one line of in-rack sprinklers in the longitudinal flue space at every storage level above the floor except above the top tier, with sprinklers spaced not more than 10 ft (3 m) on center. Sprinklers shall be staggered vertically, where more than one level of in-rack sprinklers is installed.
(4) Layout 4, as referenced in Table 66.16.5.2.1 and Table 66.16.5.2.3, shall mean one line of in-rack sprinklers in the longitudinal flue space at every other storage level, except above the top tier, beginning above the first storage level, with sprinklers spaced not more than 10 ft (3 m) on center. Sprinklers shall be staggered vertically where more than one level of in-rack sprinklers is installed.
(5) Layout 5, as referenced in Table 66.16.5.2.1, shall mean one line of in-rack sprinklers in the longitudinal flue space at every storage level above the floor except above the top tier and face sprinklers at the first storage level at each rack upright. In-rack sprinklers shall be spaced not more than 9 ft (2.7 m) on center and shall be staggered vertically, where more than one level of in-rack sprinklers is installed.
(6) Layout 6, as referenced in Table 66.16.5.2.1, shall mean one line of in-rack sprinklers in the longitudinal flue space at every other storage level above the first storage level except the top tier and face sprinklers at the first storage level at each rack upright. In-rack sprinklers shall be spaced not more than 10 ft (3 m) on center and shall be staggered vertically , where more than one level of in-rack sprinklers is installed.
(7) Layout 7, as referenced in Table 66.16.5.2.8, shall be as shown in Figure 66.16.6.4(a).
(8) Layout 8, as referenced in Table 66.16.5.2.8, shall be as shown in Figure 66.16.6.4(b) or Figure 66.16.6.4(c).
(9) Layout 9, as referenced in Table 66.16.5.2.8, shall be as shown in Figure 66.16.6.4(d) or Figure 66.16.6.4(e). [**30**:16.5.1.10]

66.16.5.1.11 The "Fire Test Ref." number given for each entry in Table 66.16.5.2.1 through Table 66.16.5.2.12 shall be used to identify in Section D.2 of NFPA 30 the information on the fire tests on which the protection criteria for that entry are based. [**30**:16.5.1.11]

66.16.5.1.12 The water supply shall be sufficient to meet the fixed fire protection demand plus a total of at least 500 gpm (1900 L/min) for inside and outside hose connections for at least 2 hours, unless otherwise specified in this chapter. [**30**:16.5.1.12]

66.16.5.2 Specific Design Criteria.

66.16.5.2.1 Table 66.16.5.2.1 shall apply to the following:

(1) Automatic sprinkler protection
(2) Single- or double-row rack storage
(3) Nonmiscible liquids and miscible liquids with concentration of flammable or combustible component greater than 50 percent by volume
(4) Metal containers, metal portable tanks, metal intermediate bulk containers
(5) Relieving- or nonrelieving-style containers [**30**:16.5.2.1]

66.16.5.2.2 Table 66.16.5.2.2 shall apply to the following:

(1) Automatic sprinkler protection
(2) Palletized or stacked storage
(3) Nonmiscible liquids and miscible liquids with concentration of flammable or combustible component greater than 50 percent by volume
(4) Metal containers, metal portable tanks, metal intermediate bulk containers
(5) Relieving- or nonrelieving-style containers [**30**:16.5.2.2]

66.16.5.2.3 Table 66.16.5.2.3 shall apply to the following:

(1) Foam water sprinkler protection
(2) Single- or double-row rack storage
(3) Nonmiscible liquids and miscible liquids with concentration of flammable or combustible component greater than 50 percent by volume
(4) Metal containers, metal portable tanks, metal intermediate bulk containers
(5) Relieving- or nonrelieving-style containers [**30**:16.5.2.3]

66.16.5.2.4 Table 66.16.5.2.4 shall apply to the following:

(1) Foam water sprinkler protection
(2) Palletized or stacked storage
(3) Nonmiscible liquids and miscible liquids with concentration of flammable or combustible component greater than 50 percent by volume
(4) Metal containers, metal portable tanks, metal intermediate bulk containers
(5) Relieving- or nonrelieving-style containers [**30**:16.5.2.4]

66.16.5.2.5 Table 66.16.5.2.5 shall apply to the following:

(1) Automatic sprinkler protection
(2) Single-, double-, or multiple-row rack storage
(3) Class IIIB nonmiscible liquids and Class IIIB miscible liquids with concentration of flammable or combustible component greater than 50 percent by volume
(4) Nonmetallic containers or intermediate bulk containers
(5) Cartoned or uncartoned [**30**:16.5.2.5]

66.16.5.2.6 Table 66.16.5.2.6 shall apply to the following:

(1) Automatic sprinkler protection
(2) Shelf storage
(3) Nonmiscible liquids and miscible liquids with concentration of flammable or combustible component greater than 50 percent by volume
(4) Nonrelieving-style metal containers [**30**:16.5.2.6]

66.16.5.2.7 Table 66.16.5.2.7 shall apply to the following:

(1) Automatic sprinkler protection
(2) Single- or double-row rack storage
(3) Water-miscible liquids with concentration of flammable or combustible component greater than 50 percent by volume
(4) Glass or plastic containers
(5) Cartoned or uncartoned
(6) Minimum 8 ft (2.4 m) aisle width [**30**:16.5.2.7]

Table 66.16.5.2.1 Design Criteria for Sprinkler Protection of Single- and Double-Row Rack Storage of Liquids in Metal Containers, Portable Tanks, and IBCs

Container Style and Capacity (gal)	Maximum Storage Height (ft)	Maximum Ceiling Height (ft)	Ceiling Sprinkler Protection				In-Rack Sprinkler Protection			Layout (See 66.16.5.1.10)	Notes	Fire Test Ref. [See NFPA 30: Table D.2(a)]
			Sprinkler		Design		Sprinkler		Discharge Flow (gpm)			
			Type	Response	Density (gpm/ft²)	Area (ft²)	Type	Response				
NONRELIEVING-STYLE CONTAINERS — LIQUID CLASSES IB, IC, II, IIIA												
≤1	16	30	K ≥ 11.2	QR (HT)	0.60	2000	K ≥ 5.6	QR(OT)	30	1	1, 2, 7	1
	20	30	K ≥ 11.2	SR or QR (HT)	0.60	2000	K ≥ 5.6	QR(OT)	30	2	1, 2, 7	2
≤5	25	30	K ≥ 8.0	SR or QR (HT)	0.30	3000	K ≥ 5.6	QR(OT)	30	3	1, 7	3
>5 and ≤60	25	30	K ≥ 11.2	SR (HT)	0.40	3000	K ≥ 5.6	QR or SR(OT)	30	5	1, 7	5
NONRELIEVING-STYLE CONTAINERS — LIQUID CLASS IIIB												
≤5	40	50	K ≥ 8.0	SR or QR (HT)	0.30	2000	K ≥ 5.6	QR(OT)	30	4	1, 3, 7	4
>5 and ≤60	40	50	K ≥ 8.0	SR (HT)	0.30	3000	K ≥ 5.6	QR(OT)	30	4	1, 3, 7	6
RELIEVING-STYLE CONTAINERS — LIQUID CLASSES IB, IC, II, IIIA												
≤5	14	18	K ≥ 11.2 pendent only	QR (HT)	0.65	2000	No in-rack sprinklers required			4		7
	25	30	K ≥ 8.0	SR or QR (HT)	0.30	3000	K ≥ 5.6	QR(OT)	30	4, 7	1, 5	8
>5 and ≤60	25	30	K ≥ 11.2	SR (HT)	0.60	3000	K ≥ 5.6	QR(OT)	30	6, 7	1	10
Portable tanks and IBCs	25	30	K ≥ 11.2	SR (HT)	0.60	3000	K ≥ 5.6	QR or SR(OT)	30	5, 7	1	12
RELIEVING-STYLE CONTAINERS — LIQUID CLASS IIIB												
≤ 5 gal	40	50	K ≥ 8.0	SR or QR (HT)	0.30	2000	K ≥ 5.6	QR(OT)	30	4, 7	1	9
>5 and ≤60	40	50	K ≥ 8.0	SR (HT)	0.30	3000	K ≥ 5.6	QR(OT)	30	4, 7	1, 3	11
Portable tanks and IBCs	40	50	K ≥ 8.0	SR (HT)	0.30	3000	K ≥ 5.6	QR(OT)	30	4, 7	1, 6	13

For SI units, 1 gal = 3.8 L, 1 ft = 0.3 m, 1 ft² = 0.09 m², 1 gpm/ft² = 40.7 L/min/m² = 40.7 mm/min.
For definitions of abbreviations used in the Response column, see 66.16.5.1.9(4). See also 66.16.5.1.9(5).
Notes:
(1) In-rack sprinkler design shall be based on the following:
  (a) Where one level of in-rack sprinklers is installed, the design shall include the 8 most hydraulically remote sprinklers
  (b) Where two levels of in-rack sprinklers are installed, the design shall include the 6 most hydraulically remote sprinklers on each level.
  (c) Where three or more levels of in-rack sprinklers are installed, the design shall include the 6 most hydraulically remote sprinklers on the top three levels.
(2) Protection for uncartoned or case-cut nonsolid shelf display up to 6.5 ft. (2 m) and storage above on pallets in racking and stored on shelf materials, including open wire mesh, or 2 in. × 6 in. (50 mm × 150 mm) wooden slats, spaced a minimum of 2 in. (50 mm) apart.
(3) Increase ceiling density to 0.60 if more than one level of storage exists above the top level of in-rack sprinklers.
(4) Double-row racks limited to maximum 6 ft (1.8 m) width.
(5) For K=8.0 and larger ceiling sprinklers, increase ceiling density to 0.60 over 2000 ft² if more than one level of storage exists above the top level of in-rack sprinklers.
(6) Reduce in-rack sprinkler spacing to maximum 9 ft (2.7 m) centers.
(7) The minimum in-rack discharge pressure shall not be less than 10 psi.
[**30**: Table 16.5.2.1]

Table 66.16.5.2.2 Design Criteria for Sprinkler Protection of Palletized and Stacked Storage of Liquids in Metal Containers, Portable Tanks, and IBCs

Container Style and Capacity (gal)	Maximum Storage Height (ft)	Maximum Ceiling Height (ft)	Sprinkler Type	Sprinkler Response	Design Density (gpm/ft²)	Design Area (ft²)	Notes	Fire Test Ref. [See Table D.2(b) of NFPA 30]
NONRELIEVING-STYLE CONTAINERS — LIQUID CLASSES IB, IC, II, IIIA								
≤5	4	18	K ≥ 8.0	SR or QR (HT)	0.21	1500	1	1
	5	18	K ≥ 8.0	SR or QR (HT)	0.30	3000	—	2
	6.5	30	K ≥ 11.2	QR (HT)	0.45	3000	—	3
>5 and ≤60	5	18	K ≥ 11.2	SR (HT)	0.40	3000	—	4
NONRELIEVING-STYLE CONTAINERS — LIQUID CLASS IIIB								
≤5	18	30	K ≥ 8.0	SR or QR (HT)	0.25	3000	—	5
>5 and ≤60	10	20	K ≥ 8.0	SR (HT)	0.25	3000	—	6
	18	30	K ≥ 8.0	SR (HT)	0.35	3000	—	7
RELIEVING-STYLE CONTAINERS — LIQUID CLASSES IB, IC, II, IIIA								
≤5	12	30	K ≥ 11.2 pendent only	QR (HT)	0.60	3000	2	8
>5 and ≤60	5	30	K ≥ 11.2	SR (HT)	0.40	3000	—	9
	6.5	30	K ≥ 11.2	SR (HT)	0.60	3000	3	10
Portable tanks and IBCs	1-high	30	K ≥ 8.0	SR (HT)	0.30	3000	—	14
	2-high	30	K ≥ 11.2	SR (HT)	0.60	3000	—	15
RELIEVING-STYLE CONTAINERS — LIQUID CLASS IIIB								
≤5	18	30	K ≥ 8.0	SR or QR (HT)	0.25	3000	—	11
>5 and ≤60	10	20	K ≥ 8.0	SR (HT)	0.25	3000	—	12
	18	30	K ≥ 8.0	SR (HT)	0.35	3000	—	13
Portable tanks and IBCs	1-high	30	K ≥ 8.0	SR (HT)	0.25	3000	—	16
	2-high	30	K ≥ 11.2	SR (HT)	0.50	3000	—	17

For SI units, 1 gal = 3.8 L, 1 ft = 0.3 m, 1 ft² = 0.09 m², 1 gpm/ft² = 40.7 L/min/m² = 40.7 mm/min.
For definitions of abbreviations used in the Response column, see 66.16.5.1.9(4). See also 66.16.5.1.9(5).
Notes:
(1) Minimum hose stream demand can be reduced to 250 gpm for 2 hours.
(2) Sprinklers must also be hydraulically calculated to provide a density of 0.80 gpm/ft² over 1000 ft².
(3) Drums must be placed on open slatted pallet, not nested, to allow pressure relief from drums on lower levels. [**30:** Table 16.5.2.2]

Table 66.16.5.2.3 Design Criteria for Foam-Water Sprinkler Protection of Single- or Double-Row Rack Storage of Liquids in Metal Containers, Portable Tanks, and IBCs

Container Style and Capacity (gal)	Maximum Storage Height (ft)	Maximum Ceiling Height (ft)	Ceiling Sprinkler Protection				In-Rack Sprinkler Protection				Notes	Fire Test Ref. [See NFPA 30: Table D.2(c)]
			Sprinkler		Design		Sprinkler		Discharge Flow (gpm)	Layout (See 66.16.5.1.10)		
			Type	Response	Density (gpm/ft²)	Area (ft²)	Type	Response				
NONRELIEVING-STYLE CONTAINERS — LIQUID CLASSES IB, IC, II, IIIA												
≤5	25	30	K ≥ 8.0	SR or QR (HT)	0.30	2000	K ≥ 5.6	QR or SR (OT)	30	3	1, 2, 4, 5	1
>5 and ≤60	25	30	K ≥ 8.0	SR (HT)	0.30	3000	K ≥ 5.6	QR or SR (OT)	30	3	1, 3, 4, 5	2
NONRELIEVING-STYLE CONTAINERS — LIQUID CLASS IIIB												
≤60	40	50	K ≥ 8.0	SR (HT)	0.30	2000	K ≥ 5.6	QR or SR (OT)	30	4	1, 5	3
RELIEVING-STYLE CONTAINERS — LIQUID CLASSES IB, IC, II, IIIA												
≤5	25	30	K ≥ 8.0	SR or QR (HT)	0.30	2000	K ≥ 5.6	QR or SR (OT)	30	4	1, 2, 4, 5	4
>5 and ≤60, portable tanks and IBCs	25	30	K ≥ 8.0	SR (HT)	0.30	3000	K ≥ 5.6		30	4	1, 3, 4, 5	5
RELIEVING-STYLE CONTAINERS — LIQUID CLASS IIIB												
≤60	40	50	K ≥ 8.0	SR (HT)	0.30	2000	K ≥ 5.6	QR or SR (OT)	30	4	1, 5	6

For SI units, 1 gal = 3.8 L, 1 ft = 0.3 m, 1 ft² = 0.09 m², 1 gpm/ft² = 40.7 L/min/m² = 40.7 mm/min.
For definitions of abbreviations used in the Response column, see 66.16.5.1.9(4). See also 66.16.5.1.9(5).
Notes:
(1) In-rack sprinkler design based on the 6 most hydraulically remote sprinklers in each of the upper three levels.
(2) Design area can be reduced to 1500 ft² when using a preprimed foam-water system installed in accordance with NFPA 16, *Standard for the Installation of Foam-Water Sprinkler and Foam-Water Spray Systems*, and maintained according to NFPA 25, *Standard for the Inspection, Testing, and Maintenance of Water-Based Fire Protection Systems*.
(3) Design area can be reduced to 2000 ft² when using a preprimed foam-water system installed in accordance with NFPA 16 and maintained according to NFPA 25.
(4) In-rack sprinkler hydraulic design can be reduced to three sprinklers operating per level, with three levels operating simultaneously, when using a preprimed foam-water sprinkler system designed in accordance with NFPA 16 and maintained in accordance with NFPA 25.
(5) The minimum in-rack sprinkler discharge pressure shall not be less than a gauge pressure of 10 psi.
[30: Table 16.5.2.3]

66.16.5.2.8 Table 66.16.5.2.8 shall apply to the following:
(1) Automatic sprinkler protection
(2) Single- or double-row rack storage or palletized storage
(3) Nonmiscible liquids and miscible liquids with concentration of flammable or combustible component greater than 50 percent by volume
(4) Relieving-style metal containers [**30**:16.5.2.8]

66.16.5.2.9 Table 66.16.5.2.9 shall apply to the following:
(1) Automatic sprinkler protection
(2) Palletized storage
(3) Class II and Class III nonmiscible and Class II and Class III miscible liquids
(4) Listed and labeled rigid nonmetallic intermediate bulk containers [**30**:16.5.2.9]

66.16.5.2.10 Table 66.16.5.2.10 shall apply to the following:
(1) Automatic sprinkler protection
(2) Single- or double-row rack storage
(3) Class II and Class III nonmiscible and Class II and Class III miscible liquids
(4) Listed and labeled rigid nonmetallic intermediate bulk containers [**30**:16.5.2.10]

66.16.5.2.11 Table 66.16.5.2.11 shall apply to the following:
(1) Automatic sprinkler protection
(2) Palletized or stacked storage
(3) Unsaturated polyester resins (UPRs) with not more than 50 percent by weight of Class IC, II, or IIIA liquid
(4) Metal containers; nonrelieving style allowed only up to 6 gal (23 L) [**30**:16.5.2.11]

66.16.5.2.12 Table 66.16.5.2.12 shall apply to the following:
(1) Automatic sprinkler protection
(2) Palletized or stacked storage
(3) Miscible liquids with concentration of flammable or combustible components no greater than 80 percent by volume
(4) Glass or plastic containers [**30**:16.5.2.12]

Table 66.16.5.2.4 Design Criteria for Foam-Water Sprinkler Protection of Palletized and Stacked Storage of Liquids in Metal Containers, Portable Tanks, and IBCs

Container Style and Capacity (gal)	Maximum Storage Height (ft)	Maximum Ceiling Height (ft)	Ceiling Sprinkler Protection				Notes	Fire Test Ref. [See Table D.2(d) of NFPA 30]
			Sprinkler		Design			
			Type	Response	Density (gpm/ft²)	Area (ft²)		
NONRELIEVING-STYLE CONTAINERS — LIQUID CLASSES IB, IC, II, IIIA								
≤5, cartoned	11	30	K ≥ 11.2	SR or QR (HT)	0.40	3000	1	1
≤5, uncartoned	12	30	K ≥ 8.0	SR or QR (HT)	0.30	3000	1	2
>5 and ≤60	5 (1-high)	30	K ≥ 8.0	SR (HT)	0.30	3000	1	3
RELIEVING-STYLE CONTAINERS — LIQUID CLASSES IB, IC, II, IIIA								
>5 and ≤60	6.5 (2-high)	30	K ≥ 8.0	SR (HT)	0.30	3000	2, 3	4
	10 (3-high)	33	K ≥ 11.2	SR (HT)	0.45	3000	2, 3	6
	13.75 (4-high)	33	K ≥ 11.2	SR (HT)	0.60	3000	2, 3	7
Portable tanks and IBCs	1- or 2-high	30	K ≥ 8.0	SR (HT)	0.30	3000		5

For SI units, 1 gal = 3.8 L, 1 ft = 0.3 m, 1 ft² = 0.09 m², 1 gpm/ft² = 40.7 L/min/m² = 40.7 mm/min.
For definitions of abbreviations used in the Response column, see 66.16.5.1.9(4). See also 66.16.5.1.9(5).
Notes:
(1) Design area can be reduced to 2000 ft² when using a pre-primed foam-water system installed in accordance with NFPA 16, *Standard for the Installation of Foam-Water Sprinkler and Foam-Water Spray Systems*, and maintained according to NFPA 25, *Standard for the Inspection, Testing, and Maintenance of Water-Based Fire Protection Systems*.
(2) Both ¾ in. (20 mm) and 2 in. (50 mm) listed pressure-relieving mechanisms are required on containers greater than 6 gal (23 L) capacity.
(3) Drums placed on open slatted pallet, not nested, to allow pressure relief from drums on lower levels. [**30:** Table 16.5.2.4]

Table 66.16.5.2.5 Design Criteria for Sprinkler Protection of Single-, Double-, and Multiple-Row Rack Storage of Class IIIB Liquids

Closed-Cup Flash Point (°F)	Container or IBC Capacity (gal)	Packaging	Maximum Storage Height (ft)	Maximum Ceiling Height (ft)	Minimum Aisle Width (ft)	Rack Depth (ft)	Sprinkler Protection		Fire Test Ref. [See Table D.2(e) of NFPA 30]
							Ceiling Sprinkler Type	Design	
≥200	≤5	Plastic containers, cartoned or uncartoned	Unlimited	Unlimited	4	Any	Any	See 66.16.6.1, Fire Protection System Design Scheme "A"	1 ≥
≥375	≤275	Flexible plastic liner within a composite continuously wound corrugated paperboard intermediate bulk container (See Special Note 1)	28	30	8	Any	Any	See 66.16.6.3, Fire Protection System Design Scheme "C"	2
≥375	≤6	Flexible plastic liner within a composite corrugated paperboard box	Unlimited	Unlimited	8	Any	Any	See 66.16.6.3, Fire Protection System Design Scheme "C"	2

For SI units, 1 gal = 3.8 L, 1 ft = 0.3 m, 200°F = 93°C, 375°F = 190°C.
Note: Construction of intermediate bulk container to be a minimum of 8 layers of paperboard, with a minimum nominal thickness of 1½ in. (38 mm) at the center of any side panel. [**30:** Table 16.5.2.5]

Table 66.16.5.2.6 Design Criteria for Sprinkler Protection of Shelf Storage of Liquids in Metal Containers

Container Style and Capacity (gal)	Maximum Storage Height (ft)	Maximum Ceiling Height (ft)	Ceiling Sprinkler Protection				Special Notes	Fire Test Ref. [See Table D.2(f) of NFPA 30]
			Sprinkler		Design			
			Type	Response	Density (gpm/ft^2)	Area (ft^2)		
≤1, nonrelieving style	6	18	K ≥ 5.6	SR or QR (HT)	0.19	1500	1, 2	1

For SI units, 1 gal = 3.8 L, 1 ft = 0.3 m, 1 ft^2 = 0.09 m^2, 1 gpm/ft^2 = 40.7 L/min/m^2 = 40.7 mm/min.
For definitions of abbreviations used in the Response column, see 66.16.5.1.9(4). See also 66.16.5.1.9(5).
Notes:
(1) Protection limited to mercantile shelving that is 2 ft (600 mm) or less in depth per side, with backing between each side.
(2) Minimum hose stream demand can be reduced to 250 gpm for 2 hours.
(3) The minimum aisle width shall not be less than 5 ft (1.5 m) [**30:** Table 16.5.2.6]

Table 66.16.5.2.7 Design Criteria for Sprinkler Protection of Single- and Double-Row Rack Storage of Water-Miscible Liquids in Glass or Plastic Containers

Container Style and Capacity	Maximum Storage Height (ft)	Maximum Ceiling Height (ft)	Ceiling Sprinkler Protection		Notes	Fire Test Ref. [See Table D.2(g) of NFPA 30]
			Ceiling Sprinkler Protection	In-Rack Sprinklers		
16 oz, cartoned	Unlimited	Unlimited	See 66.16.6.1, Fire Protection System Design Scheme "A"	See 66.16.6.1, Fire Protection System Design Scheme "A"	1, 2	3
≤1 gal, cartoned	Unlimited	Unlimited	See 66.16.6.2, Fire Protection System Design Scheme "B"	See 66.16.6.2, Fire Protection System Design Scheme "B"	1, 2	1
≤60 gal, cartoned or uncartoned	25	30	See 66.16.6.2, Fire Protection System Design Scheme "B"	See 66.16.6.2, Fire Protection System Design Scheme "B"	1, 2	2

For SI units, 1 gal = 3.8 L, 1 ft = 0.3 m.
Notes:
(1) Minimum aisle width in all cases is 8 ft (2.4 m).
(2) Maximum rack depth in all cases is 9 ft (2.7 m). [**30:** Table 16.5.2.7]

Table 66.16.5.2.8 Design Criteria for Single-Row Rack, Double-Row Rack, and Palletized Storage of Liquids in Relieving-Style Metal Containers

Container Style and Capacity (gal)	Maximum Storage Height (ft)	Maximum Ceiling Height (ft)	Ceiling Sprinkler Protection		In-Rack Sprinkler Protection			Layout (See 66.16.5.1.10 & 66.16.6.4)	Notes	Fire Test Ref. [Table D.2(h): See NFPA 30]
			Sprinkler Type	Design (Number of Sprinklers @ Stated Pressure)	Sprinkler Type	Sprinkler Response	Minimum Discharge Flow			
LIQUID CLASSES IB, IC, II, IIIA, IIIB **RACK STORAGE with MAXIMUM 6 ft RACK DEPTH and MINIMUM 7.5 ft AISLE WIDTH**										
≤5, cartoned or uncartoned	14	24	Pendent ESFR K ≥ 14.0 (OT)	12 @ 50 psi	K = 11.2	QR (OT) QR (OT)	36 gpm	7	1, 2, 3, 4, 5, 6, 7	1
	14	24	Pendent ESFR K ≥ 25.0 (OT)	12 @ 25 psi	No in-rack sprinklers required				2, 3, 4, 5, 6	2
LIQUID CLASSES IB, IC, II, IIIA, IIIB **RACK STORAGE with MAXIMUM 9 ft RACK DEPTH and 8 ft MINIMUM AISLE WIDTH**										
≤1, cartoned only	20	30	Pendent ESFR K ≥ 14.0 (OT)	12 @ 75 psi	No in-rack sprinklers required			—		3
≤1, cartoned only	25	30	Pendent ESFR K ≥ 14.0 (OT)	12 @ 50 psi	K = 8.0	QR (OT)	31 gpm	8	1, 2, 5, 7	4
≤5, cartoned or uncartoned	25	30	Pendent ESFR K ≥ 14.0 (OT)	12 @ 75 psi	K = 8.0	QR (OT)	44 gpm	9	1, 2, 5, 7	5
LIQUID CLASSES IB, IC, II, IIIA, IIIB PALLETIZED STORAGE with MINIMUM 7.5 ft AISLE WIDTH										
≤1, cartoned only	8	30	Pendent ESFR K ≥ 14.0 (OT)	12 @ 50 psi	—	—	—	—	—	6
≤5, cartoned or uncartoned	12	30	Pendent ESFR K ≥ 14.0 (OT)	12 @ 75 psi	—	—	—	—	—	7

For SI units, 1 gal = 3.8 L, 1 ft = 0.3 m, 1 psi = 6.9 kPa.
For definitions of abbreviations used in the Response column, see 16.5.1.9(4). See also 16.5.1.9(5).

Notes:
(1) The in-rack sprinkler water demand shall be based on the simultaneous operation of the most hydraulically remote sprinklers as follows:
  (a) Seven sprinklers where only one level of in-rack sprinklers is installed.
  (b) Fourteen sprinklers (seven on each of the two top levels) where more than one level of in-rack sprinklers is installed.
(2) The in-rack sprinkler water demand should be balanced with the ceiling sprinkler water demand at their point of connection.
(3) One-gallon and 1-quart containers are not required to be relieving style.
(4) Provide minimum 3 in. transverse flue at rack uprights.
(5) For Class IIIB liquids, see also Table 16.5.2.5.
(6) Racks can have open-mesh wire intermediate shelving on lower levels.
(7) The minimum in-rack sprinkler discharge pressure shall not be less than a gauge pressure of 10 psi.

[**30**:Table 16.5.2.8]

Table 66.16.5.2.9 Design Criteria for Sprinkler Protection of Palletized Storage of Class II and Class III Liquids in Listed and Labeled Rigid Nonmetallic IBCs

Maximum Capacity (gal)	Maximum Storage Height	Maximum Ceiling Height (ft)	Ceiling Sprinkler Protection				Notes	Fire Test Ref. [See Table D.2(i) of NFPA 30]
			Sprinkler		Design			
			Type	Response	Density (gpm/ft^2)	Area (ft^2)		
793	1-high	30	K ≥ 11.2	SR (HT)	0.45	3000	1, 2	1
793	2-high	30	K ≥ 11.2	SR (HT)	0.60	3000	1, 2, 3	2

For SI units, 1 gal = 3.8 L, 1 ft = 0.3 m, 1 gpm/ft^2 = 40.7 L/min/m^2 = 40.7 mm/min, 1 ft^2 = 0.9 m^2.
For definitions of abbreviations used in the Response column, see 66.16.5.1.9(4). See also 66.16.5.1.9(5).
Notes:
(1) Foam-water sprinkler protection shall be permitted to be substituted for water sprinkler protection, provided the same design criteria are used.
(2) Rigid nonmetallic intermediate bulk containers shall be listed and labeled in accordance with UL 2368, *Standard for Fire Exposure Testing of Intermediate Bulk Containers for Flammable and Combustible Liquids*; FM Class 6020, *Approval Standard for Intermediate Bulk Containers*; or an equivalent test procedure.
(3) The sprinkler operating gauge pressure shall be a minimum 30 psi (207 kPa).
[**30**: Table 16.5.2.9]

Table 66.16.5.2.10 Design Criteria for Sprinkler Protection of Single- and Double-Row Rack Storage of Class II and Class III Liquids in Listed and Labeled Rigid Nonmetallic IBCs

Maximum Capacity (gal)	Maximum Storage Height (ft)	Maximum Ceiling Height (ft)	Ceiling Sprinkler Protection		Notes	Fire Test Ref. [See Table D.2(j) of NFPA 30]
			Sprinkler Type	Design		
793	25	30	Standard spray	See 66.16.6.2, Fire Protection System Design Scheme "B"	1, 2, 3	1

For SI units, 1 gal = 3.8 L, 1 ft = 0.3 m.
Notes:
(1) Rigid nonmetallic intermediate bulk containers are listed and labeled in accordance with UL 2368, *Standard for Fire Exposure Testing of Intermediate Bulk Containers for Flammable and Combustible Liquids*, or an equivalent test procedure.
(2) Maximum rack depth is 9 ft (2.7 m).
(3) Minimum aisle width is 8 ft (2.4 m).
[**30**: Table 16.5.2.10]

Table 66.16.5.2.11 Design Criteria for Sprinkler Protection of Palletized or Stacked Storage of Unsaturated Polyester Resins in Metal Containers

Capacity (gal)	Maximum Storage Height (ft)	Maximum Ceiling Height (ft)	Ceiling Sprinkler Protection				Notes	Fire Test Ref. [See Table D.2(k) of NFPA 30]
			Sprinkler		Design			
			Type	Response	Density (gpm/ft^2)	Area (ft^2)		
>5 and <60	10	33	K ≥ 11.2	SR (HT or OT)	0.45	3000	1, 2, 3	1

For SI units, 1 gal = 3.8 L, 1 ft = 0.3 m, 1 ft^2 = 0.09 m^2, 1 gpm/ft^2 = 40.7 L/min/m^2 = 40.7 mm/min.
For definitions of abbreviations used in the Response column, see 66.16.5.1.9(4). See also 66.16.5.1.9(5).
Notes:
(1) Drums placed on open, slatted pallet, not nested, to allow pressure relief from drums on lower levels.
(2) Storage areas containing unsaturated polyester resin (UPR) should not be located in the same spill containment area or drainage path of other Class I or Class II liquids, unless protected as required for such other liquids.
(3) Both ¾ in. (20 mm) and 2 in. (50 mm) listed and labeled pressure-relieving devices are required on containers that exceed 6 gal (23 L) capacity. [**30**: Table 16.5.2.11]

Table 66.16.5.2.12 Design Criteria for Sprinkler Protection of Palletized or Stacked Storage of Miscible Liquids in Glass or Plastic Containers

Container Style and Capacity	Maximum Storage Height (ft)	Maximum Ceiling Height (ft)	Ceiling Sprinkler Protection				Notes	Fire Test Ref. [See Table D.2(l) of NFPA 30]
			Sprinkler		Design			
			Type	Response	Density (gpm/ft^2)	Area (ft^2)		
≤8 oz	5	38	K ≥ 11.2	QR (OT)	0.47	2000	—	P60 and P61

For SI units, 1 gal = 3.8 L, 1 ft = 0.3 m, 1 ft^2 = 0.09 m^2, 1 gpm/ft^2 = 40.7 L/min/m^2 = 40.7 mm/min.
For definitions of abbreviations used in the Response column, see 66.16.5.1.9(4). *[See also 66.16.5.1.9(5).]*
[**30:** Table 16.5.2.12]

66.16.6 Fire Protection System Design Schemes.

66.16.6.1 Fire Protection System Design Scheme A.

66.16.6.1.1 Horizontal barriers of plywood having a minimum thickness of ⅜ in. (10 mm) or of sheet metal of minimum 22 gauge thickness shall be installed in accordance with Figure 66.16.6.1.1(a), Figure 66.16.6.1.1(b), or Figure 66.16.6.1.1(c), whichever is applicable. All liquid storage shall be located beneath a barrier. *[See also 66.16.6.1.9 for liquids with flash points equal to or greater than 450°F (230°C).]* [**30:**16.6.1.1]

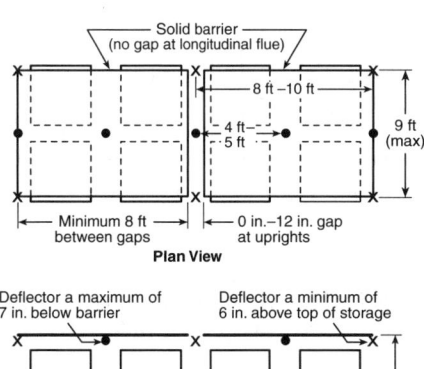

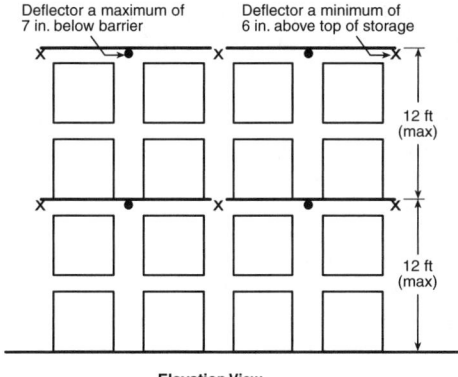

FIGURE 66.16.6.1.1(b) Double-Row Rack Sprinkler Layout for Design Scheme "A." [**30:** Figure 16.6.1.1(b)]

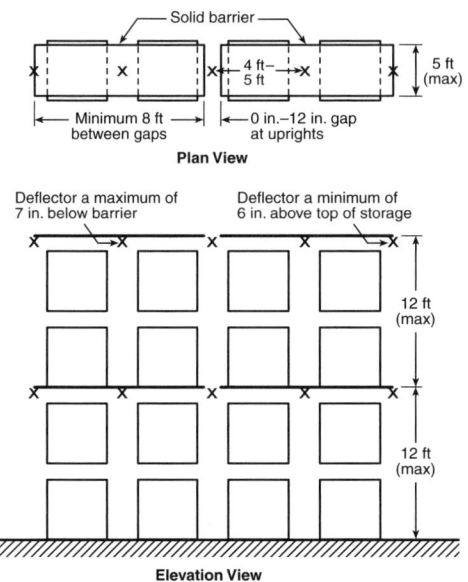

Notes: (1) For SI units, 1 in. = 25 mm; 1 ft = 0.3 m.
(2) X denotes K-8.0, ordinary, QR in-rack sprinkler.

FIGURE 66.16.6.1.1(a) Single-Row Rack Sprinkler Layout for Design Scheme "A." [**30:** Figure 16.6.1.1(a)]

66.16.6.1.2 In-rack sprinklers shall be installed in accordance with Figure 66.16.6.1.1(a), Figure 66.16.6.1.1(b), or Figure 66.16.6.1.1(c), whichever is applicable. [**30:**16.6.1.2]

66.16.6.1.3 Vertical barriers shall not be provided between in-rack sprinklers. [**30:**16.6.1.3]

66.16.6.1.4 In-rack sprinklers shall meet the following requirements:

(1) In-rack sprinklers shall be ordinary temperature–rated quick-response sprinklers and shall have a nominal K-factor equal to or greater than 8.0. Intermediate-temperature sprinklers shall be used where ambient conditions require.
(2) In-rack sprinklers shall be installed below each barrier level.
(3) In-rack sprinklers shall provide a minimum operating flow of 57 gpm out of each of the hydraulically most remote six sprinklers (three on two lines) if one barrier level is provided, or out of each of the hydraulically most remote eight sprinklers (four on two lines), if two or more barrier levels are provided. The minimum in-rack sprinkler discharge pressure shall not be less than a gauge pressure of 10 psi. [**30:**16.6.1.4]

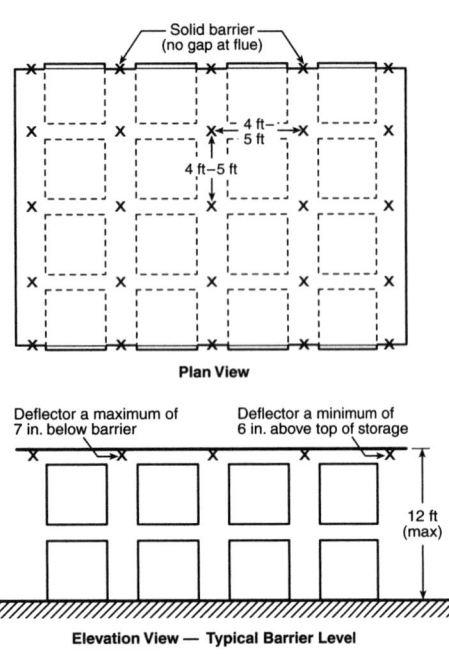

FIGURE 66.16.6.1.1(c) Multiple-Row Rack Sprinkler Layout for Design Scheme "A." [30: Figure 16.6.1.1(c)]

66.16.6.1.5* Where adjacent rack bays are not dedicated to storage of liquids, the barrier and in-rack sprinkler protection shall be extended at least 8 ft (2.4 m) beyond the area devoted to liquid storage. In addition, barrier and in-rack sprinkler protection shall be provided for any rack across the aisle within 8 ft (2.4 m) of the perimeter of the liquid storage in accordance with 66.16.6.1. [30:16.6.1.5]

66.16.6.1.6 Ceiling sprinkler demand shall not be included in the hydraulic calculations for in-rack sprinklers. [30:16.6.1.6]

66.16.6.1.7 Water demand at point of supply shall be calculated separately for in-rack and ceiling sprinklers and shall be based on the greater demand. [30:16.6.1.7]

66.16.6.1.8 Ceiling sprinklers shall meet the following requirements:

(1) Ceiling sprinkler protection shall be designed to protect the surrounding occupancy.
(2) Any sprinkler type shall be acceptable.
(3) If standard spray sprinklers are used, they shall be capable of providing not less than 0.20 gpm/ft² over 3000 ft² (8 mm/min over 270 m²).
(4) If the liquid storage does not extend to the full height of the rack, protection for commodities stored above the top horizontal barrier shall meet the requirements of Section 13.3 and NFPA 13 for the commodities stored, based on the full height of the rack. [30:16.6.1.8]

66.16.6.1.9 Barriers shall not be required for liquids with closed-cup flash points of 450°F (230°C) or greater. If barriers are omitted, the following shall apply:

(1) Ceiling sprinkler protection shall provide a minimum density of 0.3 gpm/ft² over the most hydraulically remote 2000 ft² (12 mm/min over 180 m²) using ordinary temperature, standard-response sprinklers. Sprinklers shall have a nominal K-factor equal to or greater than 8.0. Intermediate-temperature sprinklers shall be used where ambient conditions require.
(2) The ceiling sprinkler water demand and the in-rack water demand shall be balanced at their point of connection.
(3) The sprinklers located at the rack face shall be staggered vertically. [30:16.6.1.9]

66.16.6.1.10 A 500 gpm (1900 L/min) hose stream allowance shall be provided. [30:16.6.1.10]

66.16.6.2 Fire Protection System Design Scheme "B."

66.16.6.2.1 Horizontal barriers of plywood having a minimum thickness of ⅜ in. (10 mm) or of sheet metal of minimum 22 gauge thickness shall be installed in accordance with Figure 66.16.6.2.1(a), Figure 66.16.6.2.1(b), or Figure 66.16.6.2.1(c), whichever is applicable. All liquid storage shall be located beneath a barrier. [30:16.6.2.1]

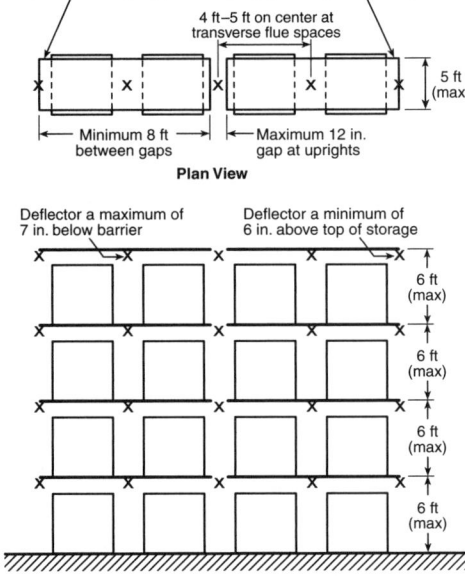

FIGURE 66.16.6.2.1(a) Single-Row Rack Sprinkler Layout for Design Scheme "B"— Sprinklers in Center of Rack. [30: Figure 16.6.2.1(a)]

66.16.6.2.2 In-rack sprinklers shall be installed in accordance with Figure 66.16.6.2.1(a), Figure 66.16.6.2.1(b), or Figure 66.16.6.2.1(c), whichever is applicable. [30:16.6.2.2]

66.16.6.2.3 Vertical barriers shall not be provided between in-rack sprinklers. [30:16.6.2.3]

66.16.6.2.4 In-rack sprinklers shall meet the following requirements:

(1) In-rack sprinklers shall be ordinary temperature–rated quick-response sprinklers and shall have a nominal K-factor equal to or greater than 8.0. Intermediate-temperature sprinklers shall be used where ambient conditions require.

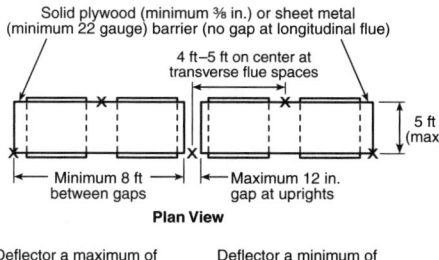

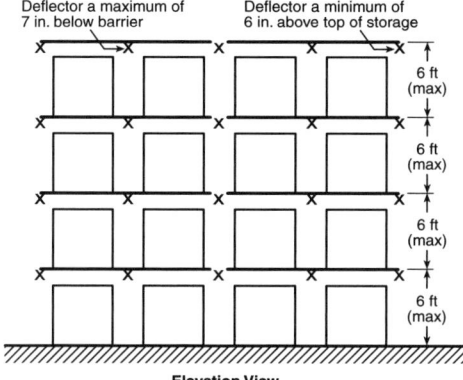

FIGURE 66.16.6.2.1(b) Single-Row Rack Sprinkler Layout for Design Scheme "B"— Sprinklers on Face of Rack. [30: Figure 16.6.2.1(b)]

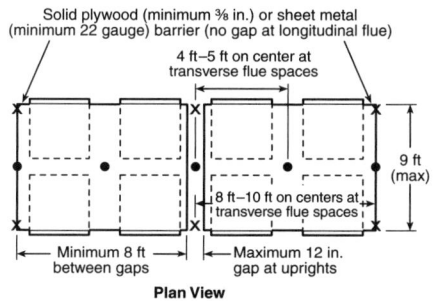

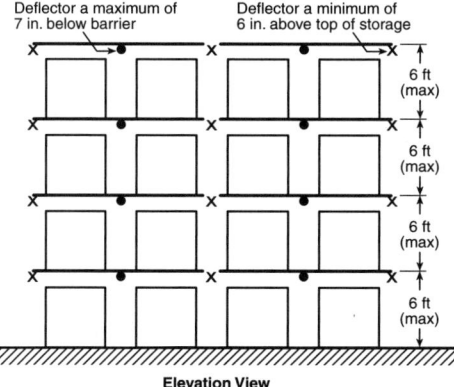

FIGURE 66.16.6.2.1(c) Double-Row Rack Sprinkler Layout for Design Scheme "B." [30: Figure 16.6.2.1(c)]

(2) In-rack sprinklers shall be installed below each barrier level.
(3) For containers that do not exceed 60 gal (230 L) capacity and where there is only one horizontal barrier, in-rack sprinklers shall provide a minimum discharge flow of 57 gpm out of each of the hydraulically most remote six sprinklers (three on two lines) if one barrier level is provided, or out of each of the hydraulically most remote eight sprinklers (four on two lines), if two or more barrier levels are provided. The minimum in-rack sprinkler discharge pressure shall not be less than a gauge pressure of 10 psi.
(4) For containers that exceed 60 gal (230 L) capacity, but do not exceed 793 gal (3000 L), in-rack sprinklers shall provide a minimum discharge flow of 57 gpm out of each of the hydraulically most remote 12 sprinklers, six each on two lines. The minimum in-rack sprinkler discharge pressure shall not be less than a gauge pressure of 10 psi. [**30**:16.6.2.4]

66.16.6.2.5 If there are adjacent rack bays that are not dedicated to storage of liquids, the barrier and in-rack sprinkler protection shall be extended beyond the area devoted to liquid storage as follows:

(1) For containers that do not exceed 1 gal (3.8 L) capacity, protection shall be extended at least 8 ft (2.4 m) beyond the area devoted to liquid storage. In addition, adjacent racks across the aisles on each side of the liquid storage shall be protected in accordance with Section 13.3 and NFPA 13 for the commodity stored.
(2) For containers that exceed 1 gal (3.8 L) capacity, but do not exceed 793 gal (3000 L), protection shall be extended at least 8 ft (2.4 m) beyond the area devoted to liquid storage. In addition, protection shall be provided to any rack across the aisle within 8 ft (2.4 m) of the perimeter of the liquid storage in accordance with 66.16.6.2. [**30**:16.6.2.5]

66.16.6.2.6 Ceiling sprinklers for containers that do not exceed 1 gal (3.8 L) capacity shall meet the following requirements:

(1) Ceiling sprinklers shall be designed to protect the surrounding occupancy.
(2) Ceiling sprinkler water demand shall not be included in the hydraulic calculations for the in-rack sprinkler protection.
(3) Water demand at the point of supply shall be calculated separately for in-rack and ceiling sprinklers and shall be based on the greater of the two.
(4) Any sprinkler type shall be acceptable for the ceiling sprinkler protection.
(5) If standard spray sprinklers are used, they shall be capable of providing not less than 0.20 gpm/ft^2 over 3000 ft^2 (8 L/min over 270 m^2).
(6) If the liquid storage does not extend to the full height of the rack, protection for commodities stored above the top horizontal barrier shall meet the requirements of Section 13.3 and NFPA 13 for the commodities stored, based on the full height of the rack. [**30**:16.6.2.6]

66.16.6.2.7 Ceiling sprinklers for containers that exceed 1 gal (3.8 L) capacity, but do not exceed 60 gal (230 L), shall meet the following requirements:

(1) Ceiling sprinkler protection shall provide a minimum density of 0.45 gpm/ft^2 (18.3 mm/min) over the most hydraulically remote 3000 ft^2 (270 m^2), using high-temperature, standard-response sprinklers of nominal K-factor of 11.2 or greater. Other types of sprinklers shall not be used.

(2) Ceiling sprinkler water demand and the in-rack sprinkler demand shall be balanced at the point of connection. [**30**:16.6.2.7]

66.16.6.2.8 Ceiling sprinklers for containers that exceed 60 gal (230 L) capacity, but do not exceed 793 gal (3000 L), shall meet the following requirements:

(1) Ceiling sprinklers shall be designed to provide a minimum density of 0.60 gpm/ft^2 over 3000 ft^2 (24 mm/min over the most remote 270 m^2), using high-temperature–rated, standard-response sprinklers of nominal K-factor of 11.2 or greater. Other types of sprinklers shall not be used.

(2) Ceiling sprinkler water demand and the in-rack sprinkler demand shall be balanced at the point of connection. [**30**:16.6.2.8]

66.16.6.2.9 A 500 gpm (1900 L/min) hose stream allowance shall be provided. [**30**:16.6.2.9]

66.16.6.3 Fire Protection System Design Scheme "C."

66.16.6.3.1 Horizontal barriers of plywood having a minimum thickness of ⅜ in. (10 mm) or of sheet metal of minimum 22 gauge thickness shall be installed in accordance with Figure 66.16.6.3.1(a), Figure 66.16.6.3.1(b), or Figure 66.16.6.3.1(c), whichever is applicable. All liquid storage shall be located beneath a barrier. [**30**:16.6.3.1]

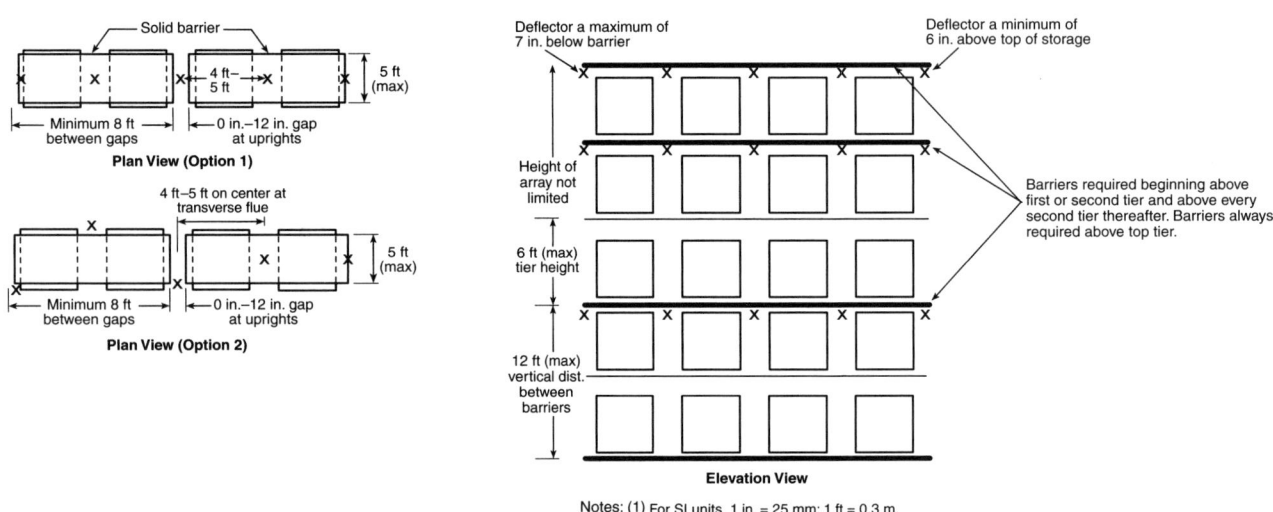

FIGURE 66.16.6.3.1(a) Single-Row Rack Sprinkler Layout for Design Scheme "C." [30: Figure 16.6.3.1(a)]

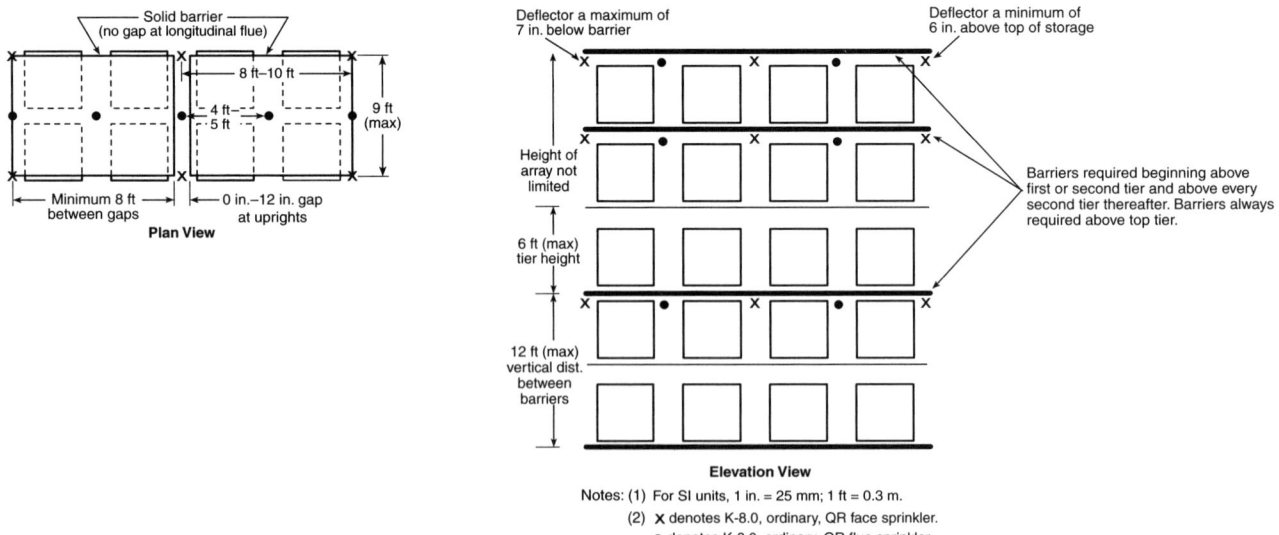

FIGURE 66.16.6.3.1(b) Double-Row Rack Sprinkler Layout for Design Scheme "C." [30: Figure 16.6.3.1(b)]

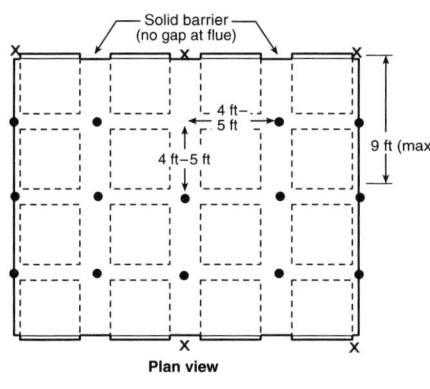
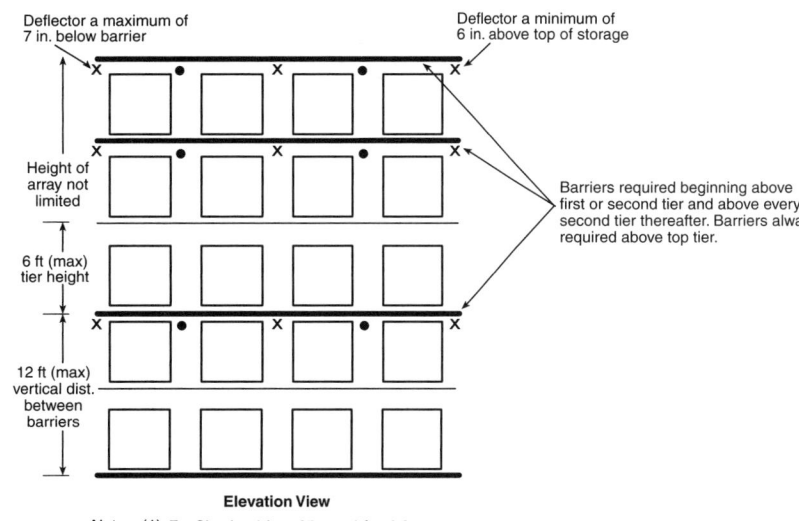

FIGURE 66.16.6.3.1(c) Multiple-Row Rack Sprinkler Layout for Design Scheme "C." [30: Figure 16.6.3.1(c)]

66.16.6.3.2 Vertical baffles shall not be installed between in-rack sprinklers. [**30**:16.6.3.2]

66.16.6.3.3 In-rack sprinklers shall meet the following requirements:

(1) In-rack sprinklers shall be ordinary temperature–rated, quick-response sprinklers. Sprinklers shall have a nominal K-factor equal to or greater than 8.0. An intermediate-temperature sprinkler shall be used where ambient conditions require.
(2) In-rack sprinklers shall be installed below each barrier level.
(3) In-rack sprinklers shall provide a minimum discharge flow of 30 gpm out of each of the hydraulically most remote six sprinklers (three on two lines), if one barrier level is provided, or out of each of the hydraulically most remote eight sprinklers (four on two lines), if two or more barrier levels are provided. The minimum in-rack sprinkler discharge pressure shall not be less than a gauge pressure of 10 psi. [**30**:16.6.3.3]

66.16.6.3.4 If there are adjacent bays of in-rack arrays that are not dedicated to storage of liquids, the barrier and in-rack sprinkler protection shall be extended at least 8 ft (2.4 m) beyond the area devoted to liquid storage. [**30**:16.6.3.4]

66.16.6.3.5 Ceiling sprinkler demand shall not be included in the hydraulic calculations for in-rack sprinklers. [**30**:16.6.3.5]

66.16.6.3.6 Water demand at point of supply shall be calculated separately for in-rack and ceiling sprinklers and shall be based on the greater demand. [**30**:16.6.3.6]

66.16.6.3.7 Ceiling sprinklers shall meet the following requirements:

(1) Ceiling sprinkler protection shall be designed to protect the surrounding occupancy.
(2) Any sprinkler type shall be acceptable.
(3) If standard spray sprinklers are used, they shall be capable of providing not less than 0.20 gpm/ft^2 over 3000 ft^2 (8 mm/min over 270 m^2).
(4) If the liquid storage does not extend to the full height of the rack, protection for commodities stored above the top horizontal barrier shall meet the requirements of Section 13.3 and NFPA 13 for the commodities stored, based on the full height of the rack. [**30**:16.6.3.7]

66.16.6.3.8 A 500 gpm (1900 L/min) hose stream allowance shall be provided. [**30**:16.6.3.8]

66.16.6.4 In-Rack Sprinkler Layouts for Table 66.16.5.2.8. Where indicated in Table 66.16.5.2.8, in-rack sprinklers shall be installed as follows:

(1) Where Layout 7 is required, in-rack sprinklers shall be installed in accordance with Figure 66.16.6.4(a),
(2) Where Layout 8 is required, in-rack sprinklers shall be installed in accordance with Figure 66.16.6.4(b) or Figure 66.16.6.4(c).
(3) Where Layout 9 is required, in-rack sprinklers shall be installed in accordance with Figure 66.16.6.4(d), or Figure 66.16.6.4(e), whichever is applicable. [**30**:16.6.4]

66.16.7 Water Supply. Water supplies for automatic sprinklers, other water-based protection systems, hose streams, and hydrants shall be capable of supplying the anticipated water flow demand for a minimum of 2 hours. [**30**:16.7]

66.16.8 Containment, Drainage, and Spill Control.

66.16.8.1 Containment or containment and drainage shall be provided in accordance with Figure 66.16.8.1, when protection systems are installed in accordance with the provisions of this section. [**30**:16.8.1]

66.16.8.2* Where control of the spread of liquid is required, means to limit the spread of liquid to an area not greater than the design discharge area of the ceiling sprinkler system shall be provided. [**30**:16.8.2]

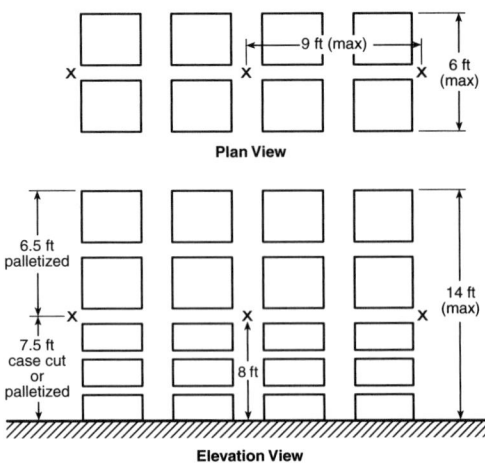

FIGURE 66.16.6.4(a) Double-Row Rack Sprinkler Layout G. [30: Figure 16.6.4(a)]

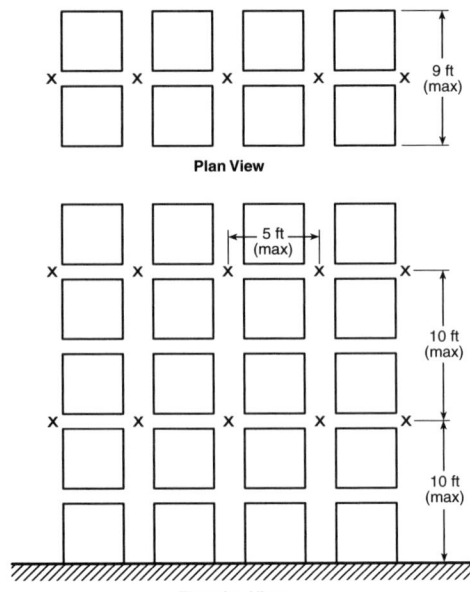

FIGURE 66.16.6.4(c) Double-Row Rack Sprinkler Layout I — Option #2. [30: Figure 16.6.4(c)]

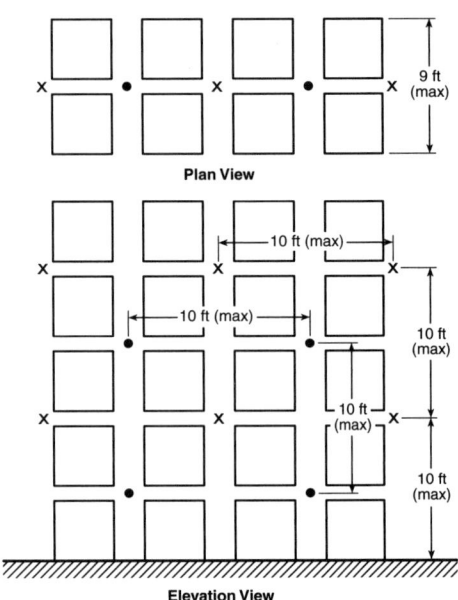

FIGURE 66.16.6.4(b) Double-Row Rack Sprinkler Layout I — Option #1. [30: Figure 16.6.4(b)]

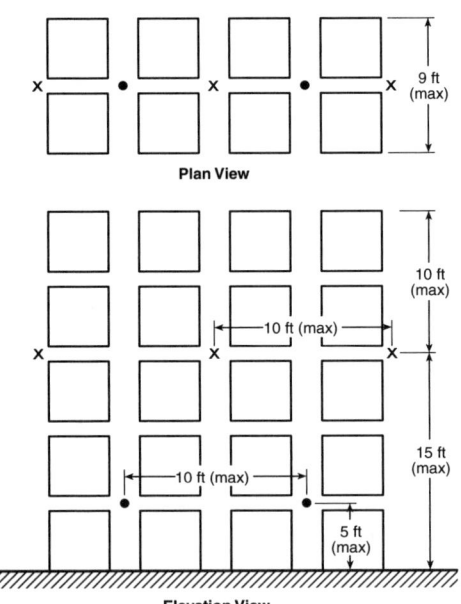

FIGURE 66.16.6.4(d) Double-Row Rack Sprinkler Layout H — Option #1. [30: Figure 16.6.4(d)]

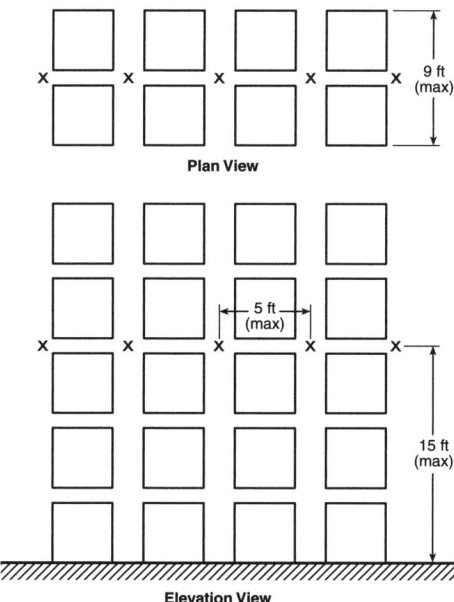

FIGURE 66.16.6.4(e) Double-Row Rack Sprinkler Layout H — Option #2. [30: Figure 16.6.4(e)]

66.16.9 Other Automatic Fire Protection Systems. Alternate fire protection systems, such as automatic water spray systems, automatic water mist systems, high-expansion foam systems, dry chemical extinguishing systems, alternate sprinkler system configurations, or combinations of systems shall be permitted if approved by the AHJ. Such alternate systems shall be designed and installed in accordance with the appropriate NFPA standard and with manufacturer's recommendations for the system(s) selected. [**30**:16.9]

66.17 Processing Facilities.

66.17.1 Scope.

66.17.1.1* This section shall apply where the processing of liquids is the principal activity, except as covered elsewhere in this *Code* or in other NFPA standards. *(See 66.1.4.)* [**30**:17.1.1]

66.17.1.2 Provisions of this chapter shall not prohibit the use of movable tanks for the dispensing of flammable or combustible liquids into fuel tanks of motorized equipment outside on premises not accessible to the public, where such use has the approval of the AHJ. [**30**:17.1.2]

66.17.2 Reserved.

66.17.3 General Requirements.

66.17.3.1 Liquid processing operations shall be located and operated so that they do not constitute a significant fire or explosion hazard to life, to property of others, or to important buildings or facilities within the same plant. [**30**:17.3.1]

66.17.3.2 Specific requirements shall depend on the inherent risk in the operations themselves, including the liquids being processed, operating temperatures and pressures, and the capability to control any liquid or vapor releases or fire incidents that could occur. [**30**:17.3.2]

66.17.3.3 The interrelationship of the many factors involved shall be based on good engineering and management practices to establish suitable physical and operating requirements. [**30**:17.3.3]

66.17.3.4 Process facilities shall comply with the applicable requirements for specific operations set forth in Sections 66.18, 66.19, 66.28, or 66.29. [**30**:17.3.4]

66.17.3.5 Process facilities shall comply with the applicable requirements for procedures and practices for fire and explosion prevention, protection, and control set forth in Section 66.6. [**30**:17.3.5]

66.17.3.6 Processing and handling of Class II and Class III liquids heated at or above their flash point shall follow the requirements for Class I liquids, unless an engineering evaluation conducted in accordance with Section 66.6 justifies following the requirements for some other liquid class. *(See 66.4.1.2 and A.66.6.4.1.2.)* [**30**:17.3.6]

66.17.3.7 When a process heats a liquid to a temperature at or above its flashpoint, the following shall apply:

(1) The process vessel shall be closed to the room in which it is located and vented to the outside of the building.
(2) If the vessel needs to be opened to add ingredients, the room ventilation shall meet the requirements of 66.17.11 and the process heating controls will be interlocked with the ventilation such that the process heat will shut down if the ventilation fails or is turned off.
(3) The process vessel shall be equipped with an excess temperature control set to limit excessive heating of the liquid and the subsequent release of vapors.
(4) If a heat transfer medium is used to heat the liquid and the heat transfer fluid can heat the liquid to its boiling point on failure of the process and excess temperature heat controls, a redundant excess temperature control shall be provided. [**30**:17.3.7]

66.17.4 Location of Process Vessels and Equipment.

66.17.4.1 Liquid-processing vessels and equipment shall be located in accordance with the requirements of this section. [**30**:17.4.1]

66.17.4.2 Processing vessels and buildings containing such processing vessels shall be located so that a fire involving the vessels does not constitute an exposure hazard to other occupancies. [**30**:17.4.2]

66.17.4.3 The minimum distance of a processing vessel to a property line that is or can be built upon, including the opposite side of a public way; to the nearest side of a public way; or to the nearest important building on the same property shall be determined by one of the following:

(1) In accordance with Table 66.17.4.3
(2) In accordance with an engineering evaluation of the process, followed by application of sound fire protection and process engineering principles [**30**:17.4.3]

66.17.4.3.1 Processing vessels used solely to process stable Class IIIB liquids shall be located in accordance with Table 22.4.1.6 of NFPA 30. [**30**:17.4.3.1]

66.17.4.4 Where process vessels are located in a building and the exterior wall facing the exposure (line of adjoining property that is or can be built upon or nearest important building on the same property) is greater than 25 ft (7.6 m) from the exposure and is a blank wall having a fire resistance rating of

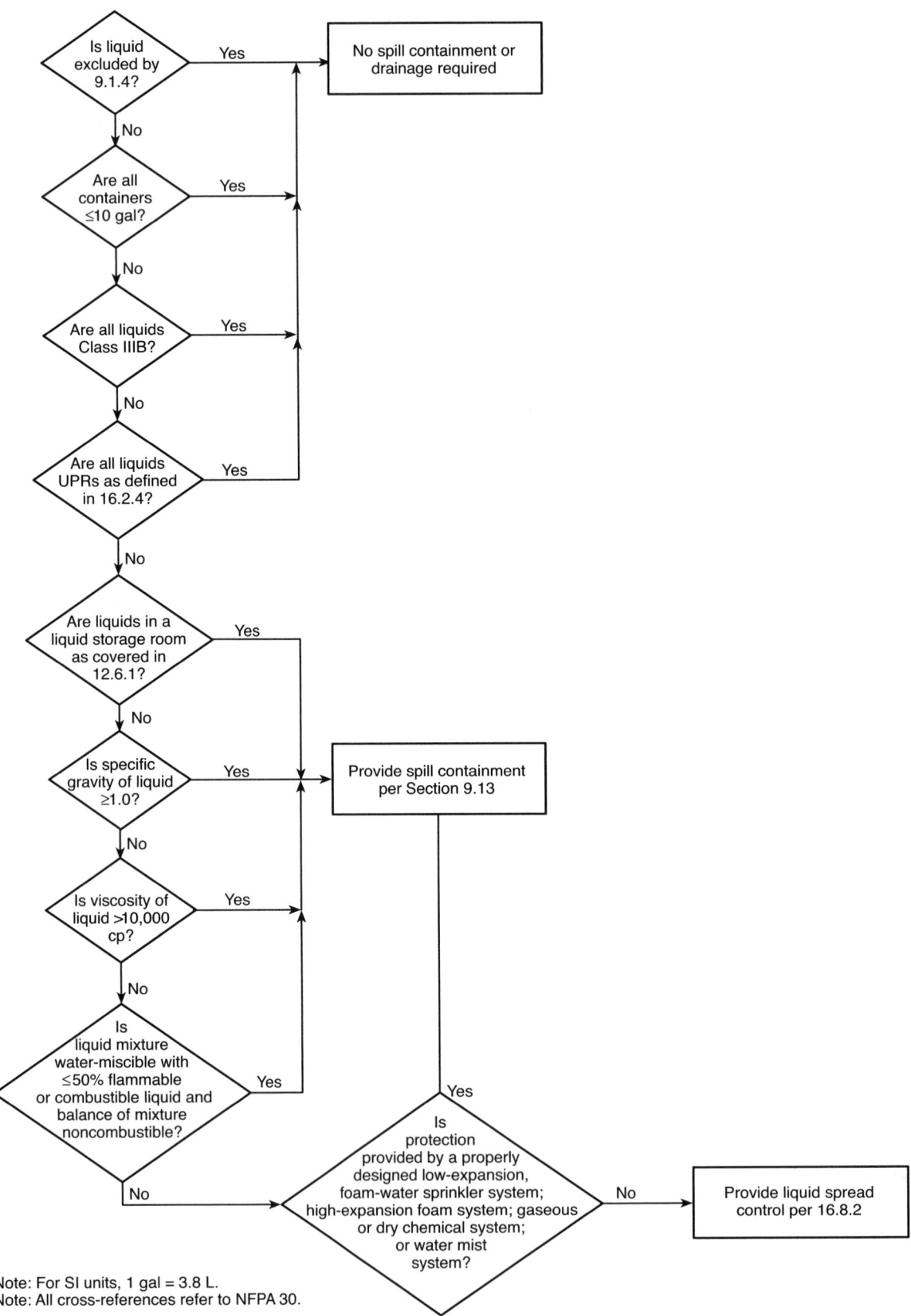

FIGURE 66.16.8.1 Spill Containment and Liquid Spread Control for Protected Storage. [30: Figure 16.8.1]

Table 66.17.4.3 Location of Process Vessels with Respect to Property Lines, Public Ways, and the Nearest Important Building on the Same Property — Protection for Exposures Is Provided

	Minimum Distance (ft)							
	From Property Line that Is or Can Be Built upon, Including Opposite Side of Public Way				From Nearest Side of Any Public Way or from Nearest Important Building on Same Property that Is Not an Integral Part of the Process			
	Stable Liquid Emergency Relief*		Unstable Liquid Emergency Relief*		Stable Liquid Emergency Relief*		Unstable Liquid Emergency Relief*	
Vessel Maximum Operating Liquid Capacity (gal)	Not Over 2.5 psi	Over 2.5 psi	Not Over 2.5 psi	Over 2.5 psi	Not Over 2.5 psi	Over 2.5 psi	Not Over 2.5 psi	Over 2.5 psi
275 or less	5	25	50	100	5	25	50	100
276 to 750	10	25	50	100	5	25	50	100
751 to 12,000	15	25	50	100	5	25	50	100
12,001 to 30,000	20	30	50	100	5	25	50	100
30,001 to 50,000	30	45	75	120	10	25	50	100
50,001 to 100,000	50	75	125	200	15	25	50	100
Over 100,000	80	120	200	300	25	40	50	100

For SI units, 1 gal = 3.8 L; 1 ft = 0.3 m; 1 psi = a gauge pressure of 6.9 kPa.
Note: Double all of above distances where protection for exposures is not provided.
*Gauge pressure. [**30**: Table 17.4.3]

not less than 2 hours, any greater distances required by Table 66.17.4.3 shall be permitted to be waived. If the exterior wall is a blank wall having a fire resistance rating of not less than 4 hours, all distances required by Table 66.17.4.3 shall be permitted to be waived. [**30**:17.4.4]

66.17.4.5 All the distances given in Table 66.17.4.3 shall be doubled where protection for exposures is not provided. [**30**:17.4.5]

66.17.4.6* Liquid-processing equipment, such as pumps, heaters, filters, and exchangers, shall not be located closer than 25 ft (7.6 m) to property lines where the adjoining property is or can be built upon or to the nearest important building on the same property that is not an integral part of the process. This spacing requirement shall be permitted to be waived where exposures are protected in accordance with 66.17.4.3. [**30**:17.4.6]

66.17.4.7 Processing equipment in which unstable liquids are handled shall be separated from unrelated plant facilities by either of the following:

(1) 25 ft (7.6 m) clear spacing
(2) A wall having a fire resistance rating of not less than 2 hours and explosion resistance consistent with the expected hazard [**30**:17.4.7]

66.17.5 Accessibility. Each process unit or building containing liquid-processing equipment shall be accessible from at least one side for fire fighting and fire control. [**30**:17.5]

66.17.6 Construction Requirements.

66.17.6.1 Process buildings or structures used for liquid operations shall be constructed consistent with the operations being conducted and with the classes of liquids handled. They shall be constructed to minimum Type II (000) construction, as defined in *NFPA 5000*, and shall be constructed in accordance with Table 66.17.6.1. [**30**:17.6.1]

Table 66.17.6.1 Minimum Separation Distances for Buildings or Structures Used for Liquid Handling and Operations

		Minimum Separation Distance (ft)	
Liquid Class	Minimum Type of Construction*	To Street, Alley, or Public Way	To Adjacent Property Line that Is or Can Be Built Upon
Class I liquids; unstable liquids of any class; liquids of any class heated above their flash points†	II (222)	5	10
	II (111)	5	25
	II (000)	10	50
Class II	II (111)	5	10
	II (000)	5	25
Class III	II (000)	5	10

For SI units, 1 ft = 0.3 m.
Note: Distances apply to properties that have protection for exposures, as defined in this code. If there are exposures for which protection does not exist, the distances should be doubled, in accordance with 66.17.6.3.
*Construction types are defined in NFPA 220, *Standard on Types of Building Construction*.
†For stable liquids of any class heated above their flash points, see 66.6.4.1.2 and A.66.6.4.1.2.

[**30**: Table 17.6.1]

66.17.6.2 Construction types shall be as defined in *NFPA 5000*. [**30**:17.6.2]

66.17.6.3 Where protection for exposures is not provided, the applicable distances given in Table 66.17.6.1 shall be doubled. [**30**:17.6.3]

66.17.6.4 For buildings or structures that are not provided with approved automatic sprinkler protection, the separation distances otherwise required by Table 66.17.6.1 shall be determined by an engineering evaluation of the process, but shall not be less than the separation distances required by Table 66.17.4.3. [**30**:17.6.4]

66.17.6.5 Buildings or structures used solely for blending, mixing, or dispensing of Class IIIB liquids at temperatures below their flash points shall be permitted to be constructed of combustible construction, subject to the approval of the AHJ. [**30**:17.6.5]

66.17.6.6 Buildings or structures used for processing or handling of liquids where the quantities of liquids do not exceed 360 gal (1360 L) of Class I and Class II liquids and 720 gal (2725 L) of Class IIIA liquids shall be permitted to be constructed of combustible construction, subject to the approval of the AHJ. [**30**:17.6.6]

66.17.6.7 Buildings or structures used for processing or handling of liquids protected with automatic sprinklers or equivalent fire protection systems shall be permitted to be constructed of combustible construction, subject to the approval of the AHJ. [**30**:17.6.7]

66.17.6.8* Load-bearing building supports and load-bearing supports of vessels and equipment capable of releasing quantities of liquids that could result in a fire capable of causing substantial property damage shall be protected by one or more of the following:

(1) Drainage to a safe location to prevent liquids from accumulating under vessels or equipment or around load-bearing supports
(2) Fire-resistive construction
(3) Fire-resistant protective coatings or systems
(4) Water spray systems designed and installed in accordance with NFPA 15, *Standard for Water Spray Fixed Systems for Fire Protection*
(5) Other alternate means acceptable to the AHJ [**30**:17.6.8]

66.17.6.9 Class I liquids shall not be handled or used in basements. [**30**:17.6.9]

66.17.6.9.1 Where Class I liquids are handled or used above grade within buildings with basements or closed pits into which flammable vapors can travel, such belowgrade areas shall be provided with mechanical ventilation designed to prevent the accumulation of flammable vapors. [**30**:17.6.9.1]

66.17.6.9.2 Means shall be provided to prevent liquid spills from running into basements. [**30**:17.6.9.2]

66.17.6.10* Smoke and heat venting shall be permitted to be used where it assists access for fire fighting. [**30**:17.6.10]

66.17.6.11* Areas shall have exit facilities arranged to prevent occupants from being trapped in the event of fire. [**30**:17.6.11]

66.17.6.11.1 Exits shall not be exposed by the drainage facilities described in 66.17.10. [**30**:17.6.11.1]

66.17.6.12 Aisles shall be maintained for unobstructed movement of personnel and fire protection equipment. [**30**:17.6.12]

66.17.6.13 Indoor areas where Class IA or unstable liquids are in use shall be designed to direct flame, combustion gases, and pressures resulting from a deflagration away from important buildings or occupied areas through the use of damage-limiting construction in accordance with NFPA 68, *Standard on Explosion Protection by Deflagration Venting*. [**30**:17.6.13]

66.17.6.13.1 The damage-limiting construction design shall be in accordance with recognized standards and shall be acceptable to the AHJ. *(See A.66.9.16.1.)* [**30**:17.6.13.1]

66.17.6.13.2 Where unstable liquids are in use, an approved engineered construction method that is designed to limit damage from an explosion (deflagration or detonation, depending on the characteristics of the liquid) shall be used. [**30**:17.6.13.2]

66.17.7 Reserved.

66.17.8 Reserved.

66.17.9 Electrical Systems. Electrical wiring and electrical utilization equipment shall comply with Section 66.7. [**30**:17.9]

66.17.10 Containment, Drainage, and Spill Control.

66.17.10.1* Emergency drainage systems shall be provided to direct liquid leakage and fire protection water to a safe location. [**30**:17.10.1]

66.17.10.2 Emergency drainage systems, if connected to public sewers or discharged into public waterways, shall be equipped with traps or separators. [**30**:17.10.2]

66.17.10.3 A facility shall be designed and operated to prevent the discharge of liquids to public waterways, public sewers, or adjoining property. [**30**:17.10.3]

66.17.11 Ventilation.

66.17.11.1 Enclosed processing areas handling or using Class I liquids, or Class II or Class III liquids heated to temperatures at or above their flash points, shall be ventilated at a rate sufficient to maintain the concentration of vapors within the area at or below 25 percent of the lower flammable limit (LFL). Compliance with 66.17.11.2 through 66.17.11.10 shall be deemed as meeting the requirements of this section. [**30**:17.11.1]

66.17.11.2* Ventilation requirements shall be confirmed by one of the following:

(1) Calculations based on the anticipated fugitive emissions *(see Annex F of NFPA 30 for calculation method)*.
(2) Sampling of the actual vapor concentration under normal operating conditions. Sampling shall be conducted at a 5 ft (1.5 m) radius from each potential vapor source extending to or toward the bottom and the top of the enclosed processing area. The vapor concentration used to determine the required ventilation rate shall be the highest measured concentration during the sampling procedure. [**30**:17.11.2]

66.17.11.3 A ventilation rate of not less than 1 $ft^3/min/ft^2$ (0.3 $m^3/min/m^2$) of solid floor area shall be considered as meeting the requirements of 66.17.11.1. [**30**:17.11.3]

66.17.11.4 Ventilation shall be accomplished by mechanical or natural means. [**30**:17.11.4]

66.17.11.5 Exhaust ventilation discharge shall be to a safe location outside the building. [**30**:17.11.5]

66.17.11.6 Recirculation of the exhaust air shall be permitted only when it is monitored continuously using a fail-safe system that is designed to automatically sound an alarm, stop recirculation, and provide full exhaust to the outside in the event that vapor–air mixtures in concentrations over one-fourth of the lower flammable limit are detected. [**30**:17.11.6]

66.17.11.7* Provision shall be made for introduction of make-up air in such a manner as to avoid short-circuiting the ventilation. [**30**:17.11.7]

66.17.11.8 Ventilation shall be arranged to include all floor areas or pits where flammable vapors can collect. [**30**:17.11.8]

66.17.11.9 Local or spot ventilation to control special fire or health hazards, if provided, shall be permitted to be utilized for up to 75 percent of the required ventilation. [**30**:17.11.9]

66.17.11.10 Where equipment such as dispensing stations, open centrifuges, plate and frame filters, and open vacuum filters is used in a building, the equipment and ventilation of the building shall be designed to limit flammable vapor–air mixtures under normal operating conditions to the interior of equipment and to not more than 5 ft (1.5 m) from equipment that exposes Class I liquids to the air. [**30**:17.11.10]

66.17.12 Reserved.

66.17.13 Reserved.

66.17.14* Process Equipment and Vessels. Equipment shall be designed and arranged to prevent the unintentional escape of liquids and vapors and to minimize the quantity escaping in the event of accidental release. [**30**:17.14]

66.17.15 Management of Operations Hazards.

66.17.15.1 This section shall apply to the management methodology used to identify, evaluate, and control the hazards involved in processing and handling of flammable and combustible liquids. These hazards include, but are not limited to, preparation; separation; purification; and change of state, energy content, or composition. [**30**:17.15.1]

66.17.15.2 Operations involving flammable and combustible liquids shall be reviewed to ensure that fire and explosion hazards resulting from loss of containment of liquids are provided with corresponding fire prevention and emergency action plans.

Exception No. 1: Operations where liquids are used solely for on-site consumption as fuels.

Exception No. 2: Operations where Class II or Class III liquids are stored in atmospheric tanks or transferred at temperatures below their flash points.

Exception No. 3: Mercantile occupancies, crude petroleum exploration, drillings, and well servicing operations, and normally unoccupied facilities in remote locations.
[30:17.15.2]

66.17.15.3 The extent of fire prevention and control that is provided shall be determined by means of an engineering evaluation of the operation and application of sound fire protection and process engineering principles. This evaluation shall include, but not be limited to, the following:

(1) Analysis of the fire and explosion hazards of the operation

(2) Analysis of emergency relief from process vessels, taking into consideration the properties of the materials used and the fire-protection and control measures taken
(3) Analysis of applicable facility design requirements in 66.17.3 through 66.17.4
(4) Analysis of applicable requirements in Sections 66.18, 66.19, 66.28, and 66.29 for liquid handling, transfer, and use
(5) Analysis of local conditions, such as exposure to and from adjacent properties and exposure to floods, earthquakes, and windstorms
(6) Analysis of the emergency response capabilities of the local emergency services [**30**:17.15.3]

66.17.15.4 A written emergency action plan that is consistent with available equipment and personnel shall be established to respond to fires and related emergencies. This plan shall include the following:

(1) Procedures to be followed in case of fire or release of liquids or vapors, such as sounding the alarm, notifying the fire department, evacuating personnel, and controlling and extinguishing the fire
(2) Procedures and schedules for conducting drills of these procedures
(3) Appointment and training of personnel to carry out assigned duties, which shall be reviewed at the time of initial assignment, as responsibilities or response actions change, and whenever anticipated duties change
(4) Procedures for maintenance of the following:
  (a) Fire protection equipment and systems
  (b) Drainage and containment systems
  (c) Ventilation equipment and systems
(5) Procedures for shutting down or isolating equipment to reduce, control, or stop the release of liquid or vapors, including assigning personnel responsible for maintaining critical plant functions or shutdown of plant processes and safe startup following isolation or shutdown
(6) Alternate measures for the safety of occupants [**30**:17.15.4]

66.17.15.5 The fire hazards management review conducted in accordance with 66.17.15.2 shall be repeated whenever the hazards leading to a fire or explosion change significantly. Conditions that might require repeating a review shall include, but are not limited to, the following:

(1) When changes occur in the materials in process
(2) When changes occur in process equipment
(3) When changes occur in process control
(4) When changes occur in operating procedures or assignments [**30**:17.15.5]

66.18 Dispensing, Handling, Transfer, and Use of Liquids.

66.18.1 Scope. This section applies where liquids are handled, dispensed, transferred, or used, including in process areas. [**30**:18.1]

66.18.2 Reserved.

66.18.3 General Requirements. Processing and handling of Class II and Class III liquids heated at or above their flash point shall follow the requirements for Class I liquids, unless an engineering evaluation conducted in accordance with Section 66.6 justifies following the requirements for some other liquid class. *(See 66.4.1.2 and A.66.6.4.1.2.)* [**30**:18.3]

66.18.4 Dispensing, Handling, Transfer, and Use.

66.18.4.1 Class I liquids shall be kept in closed tanks or containers when not actually in use. Class II and Class III liquids shall be kept in closed tanks or containers when not actually in use when the ambient or process temperature is at or above their flash points. [**30**:18.4.1]

66.18.4.2 Where liquids are used or handled, provisions shall be made to promptly and safely mitigate and dispose of leakage or spills. [**30**:18.4.2]

66.18.4.3 Class I liquids shall not be used outside closed systems where there are open flames or other ignition sources within the classified areas set forth in Section 66.7. [**30**:18.4.3]

66.18.4.4 Transfer of liquids among vessels, containers, tanks, and piping systems by means of air or inert gas pressure shall be permitted only under all of the following conditions:

(1) The vessels, containers, tanks, and piping systems shall be designed for such pressurized transfer and shall be capable of withstanding the anticipated operating pressure.
(2) Safety and operating controls, including pressure-relief devices, shall be provided to prevent overpressure of any part of the system.
(3) Only inert gas shall be used to transfer Class I liquids. Only inert gas shall be used to transfer Class II and Class III liquids that are heated above their flash points. [**30**:18.4.4]

66.18.4.4.1 Dispensing of Class I liquids from a container by means of air shall be permitted under the following conditions:

(1) The pressure shall be generated by means of a listed hand-operated device.
(2) Pressure shall not exceed a gauge pressure of 6 psi (41 kPa) and pressure relief shall be provided.
(3) The container shall not exceed 119 gal (450 L) and shall be capable of withstanding the maximum pressure generated by the device.
(4) The device shall be bonded and grounded or shall be demonstrated as not being capable of generating a static charge under any operating condition.
(5) The material of construction of the device shall be compatible with the liquid dispensed. [**30**:18.4.4.1]

66.18.4.5 Positive displacement pumps shall be provided with pressure relief that discharges back to the tank, pump suction, or other suitable location or shall be provided with interlocks to prevent overpressure. [**30**:18.4.5]

66.18.4.6 Piping, valves, and fittings shall meet the requirements of Section 66.27. [**30**:18.4.6]

66.18.4.7 Listed flexible connectors shall be permitted to be used where vibration exists. Approved hose shall be permitted to be used at transfer stations. [**30**:18.4.7]

66.18.4.8* The staging of liquids in containers, intermediate bulk containers, and portable tanks shall be limited to the following:

(1) Containers, intermediate bulk containers, and portable tanks that are in use
(2) Containers, intermediate bulk containers, and portable tanks that were filled during a single shift
(3) Containers, intermediate bulk containers, and portable tanks needed to supply the process for one continuous 24-hour period

(4) Containers, intermediate bulk containers, and portable tanks that are stored in accordance with Section 66.9 [**30**:18.4.8]

66.18.4.9 Class I, Class II, or Class IIIA liquids used in a process and staged in the process area shall not be filled in the process area.

Exception No. 1: Intermediate bulk containers and portable tanks that meet the requirements of Section 66.9.

Exception No. 2: Intermediate products that are manufactured in the process area. [**30**:18.4.9]

66.18.5 Incidental Operations.

66.18.5.1* This section shall apply to areas where the use, handling, and storage of liquids is only a limited activity to the established occupancy classification. [**30**:18.5.1]

66.18.5.2 Class I liquids or Class II and Class III liquids that are heated up to or above their flash points shall be drawn from or transferred into vessels, containers, or portable tanks as follows:

(1) From original shipping containers with a capacity of 5.3 gal (20 L) or less
(2) From safety cans
(3) Through a closed piping system
(4) From portable tanks or containers by means of a device that has antisiphoning protection and that draws through an opening in the top of the tank or container
(5) By gravity through a listed self-closing valve or self-closing faucet [**30**:18.5.2]

66.18.5.2.1 If hose is used in the transfer operation, it shall be equipped with a self-closing valve without a hold-open latch in addition to the outlet valve. Only listed or approved hose shall be used. [**30**:18.5.2.1]

66.18.5.2.2 Means shall be provided to minimize generation of static electricity. Such means shall meet the requirements of 66.6.5.4. [**30**:18.5.2.2]

66.18.5.2.3 Where pumps are used for liquid transfer, means shall be provided to deactivate liquid transfer in the event of a liquid spill or fire. [**30**:18.5.2.3]

66.18.5.3 Storage of liquids other than those governed by 66.18.5.4 and 66.18.5.5 shall comply with Section 66.9. [**30**:18.5.3]

66.18.5.4 The quantity of liquid located outside of identified storage areas, such as storage cabinets, other inside liquid storage areas, general-purpose warehouses, or other specific processing areas that are cut off from the general plant area by at least a 2-hour fire separation, shall meet the requirements of 66.18.5.4.1. [**30**:18.5.4]

66.18.5.4.1 The maximum quantity of liquids permitted for incidental operations in a single fire area shall not exceed the greater of the following:

(1)*The amount required to supply incidental operations for one continuous 24-hour period
(2) The aggregate sum of the following:
 (a) 25 gal (95 L) of Class IA liquids in containers
 (b) 120 gal (454 L) of Class IB, Class IC, Class II, or Class III liquids in containers
 (c) 1585 gal (6000 L) of any combination of the following:

  i. Class IB, IC, II, or IIIA liquids in metal portable tanks or metal intermediate bulk containers, each not exceeding 793 gal (3000 L)
  ii. Class II or Class IIIA liquids in nonmetallic intermediate bulk containers, each not exceeding 793 gal (3000 L)
 (d) 20 portable tanks or intermediate bulk containers each not exceeding 793 gal (3000 L) of Class IIIB liquids [**30**:18.5.4.1]

66.18.5.5 Where quantities of liquids in excess of the limits in 66.18.5.4.1 are necessary, storage shall be in tanks that meet all applicable requirements of Section 66.17, Sections 66.21 through 66.25, and Section 66.27. [**30**:18.5.5]

66.18.5.6 Areas in which liquids are transferred from one tank or container to another container shall be provided with the following:

(1) Separation from other operations where potential ignition sources are present by distance or by fire-resistant construction
(2) Drainage or other means to control spills
(3) Natural or mechanical ventilation that meets the requirements of 66.17.11 [**30**:18.5.6]

66.18.6 Ventilation for Dispensing Areas. Liquid storage areas where dispensing is conducted shall be provided with either a gravity system or a continuous mechanical exhaust ventilation system. Mechanical ventilation shall be used if Class I liquids are dispensed within the room. [**30**:18.6]

66.18.6.1 Exhaust air shall be taken from a point near a wall on one side of the room and within 12 in. (300 mm) of the floor, with one or more make-up inlets located on the opposite side of the room within 12 in. (300 mm) of the floor. [**30**:18.6.1]

66.18.6.2 The location of both the exhaust and inlet air openings shall be arranged to provide air movement across all portions of the floor to prevent accumulation of flammable vapors. [**30**:18.6.2]

66.18.6.3* Exhaust ventilation discharge shall be to a safe location outside the building. [**30**:18.6.3]

66.18.6.3.1 Recirculation of the exhaust air shall be permitted only when it is monitored continuously using a fail-safe system that is designed to automatically sound an alarm, stop recirculation, and provide full exhaust to the outside in the event that vapor-air mixtures in concentrations over one-fourth of the lower flammable limit are detected. [**30**:18.6.3.1]

66.18.6.4 If ducts are used, they shall not be used for any other purpose and shall comply with NFPA 91, *Standard for Exhaust Systems for Air Conveying of Vapors, Gases, Mists, and Noncombustible Particulate Solids*. [**30**:18.6.4]

66.18.6.4.1 If make-up air to a mechanical system is taken from within the building, the opening shall be equipped with a fire door or damper, as required in NFPA 91, *Standard for Exhaust Systems for Air Conveying of Vapors, Gases, Mists, and Noncombustible Particulate Solids*. [**30**:18.6.4.1]

66.18.6.4.2 For gravity systems, the make-up air shall be supplied from outside the building. [**30**:18.6.4.2]

66.18.6.5 Mechanical ventilation systems shall provide at least 1 cfm of exhaust air for each square foot of floor area (0.3 $m^3/min/m^2$), but not less than 150 cfm (4 m^3/min). [**30**:18.6.5]

66.18.6.5.1 The mechanical ventilation system for dispensing areas shall be equipped with an airflow switch or other equally reliable method that is interlocked to sound an audible alarm upon failure of the ventilation system. [**30**:18.6.5.1]

66.19 Specific Operations.

66.19.1 Scope. This section shall apply to the handling and use of flammable and combustible liquids in specific operations as herein described. [**30**:19.1]

66.19.2 Definitions Specific to Section 66.19.

66.19.2.1* Cooking Oil. Where used in this chapter, cooking oil shall be defined as a Class IIIB combustible liquid. This definition shall apply to both fresh, or new, cooking oil and waste, or used, cooking oil. [**30**:19.2.1]

66.19.3 Reserved.

66.19.4 Recirculating Heat Transfer Systems.

66.19.4.1 Scope.

66.19.4.1.1 This section shall apply only to recirculating heat transfer systems that use a heat transfer fluid that is heated up to or above its flash point under normal operation. [**30**:19.4.1.1]

66.19.4.1.2 This section shall not apply to process streams used as a means of heat transfer or to any heat transfer system of 60 gal (230 L) capacity or less. [**30**:19.4.1.2]

66.19.4.2* General Requirements. A heater or vaporizer for heat transfer fluid that is located inside a building shall meet all applicable requirements of Section 66.17. [**30**:19.4.2]

66.19.4.3* System Design.

66.19.4.3.1* Drainage shall be provided at strategic low points in the heat transfer system. Drains shall be piped to a safe location that is capable of accommodating the total capacity of the system or the capacity of that part of the system that is isolated. [**30**:19.4.3.1]

66.19.4.3.2* Where the heat transfer system expansion tank is located above floor level and has a capacity of more than 250 gal (950 L), it shall be provided with a low-point drain line that can allow the expansion tank to drain to a drain tank on a lower level. The drain line valve shall be operable from a safe location. [**30**:19.4.3.2]

66.19.4.3.3 A heat transfer fluid system shall not be used to provide direct building heat. [**30**:19.4.3.3]

66.19.4.3.4 All pressure-relief device outlets shall be piped to a safe location. [**30**:19.4.3.4]

66.19.4.4* Fuel Burner Controls and Interlocks. Oil- or gas-fired heaters or vaporizers shall be designed and installed in accordance with the applicable requirements of NFPA 31, *Standard for the Installation of Oil-Burning Equipment*, or NFPA 85, *Boiler and Combustion Systems Hazards Code*, whichever is applicable. Wood dust suspension-fired heaters or vaporizers shall be designed and installed in accordance with the applicable requirements of NFPA 85. [**30**:19.4.4]

66.19.4.5 Piping.

66.19.4.5.1* Piping shall meet all applicable requirements of Section 66.27. [**30**:19.4.5.1]

66.19.4.5.2 All pipe connections shall be welded. [**30**:19.4.5.2]

66.19.4.5.2.1 Welded, threaded connections shall be permitted to be used for piping 2 in. (50 mm) and smaller. [**30**:19.4.5.2.1]

66.19.4.5.2.2 Mechanical joints shall be permitted to be used at pump, valve, and equipment connections. [**30**:19.4.5.2.2]

66.19.4.5.3 New piping that is to be insulated with permanent insulation and existing piping that has been disturbed and is to be reinsulated with permanent insulation shall be covered with a closed-cell, nonabsorbent insulation material. [**30**:19.4.5.3]

66.19.4.5.3.1 Where all pipe joints are welded and where there are no other points in the system subject to leakage, such as at valves or pumps, other types of insulation shall be permitted. [**30**:19.4.5.3.1]

66.19.4.5.3.2 Where dams are formed around possible leak-producing areas, using metal "donut" flanges that are welded to the pipe or using a "donut" segment of nonabsorbent insulation sealed to the pipe to prevent migration of leakage into adjacent insulation, the piping from dam to dam shall be considered to be a closed system and other types of insulation shall be permitted. The area subject to leakage where the dam has been constructed shall be insulated with nonabsorbent insulation or a nonabsorbent insulation system. [**30**:19.4.5.3.2]

66.19.4.5.3.3 Where removable, reusable insulated covers are required for access, the covers shall be fabricated of flexible or rigid insulation that is encapsulated in a manner to provide a nonabsorbent insulation system to prevent absorption of leakage into the insulation. [**30**:19.4.5.3.3]

66.19.4.6 Fire Protection.

66.19.4.6.1* Automatic sprinkler protection meeting the requirements of Section 13.3 and NFPA 13, *Standard for the Installation of Sprinkler Systems* for Extra Hazard (Group I) Occupancies shall be provided for building areas containing a heat transfer system heater or vaporizer. [**30**:19.4.6.1]

66.19.4.6.2 An alternate fire protection system shall be permitted to be used, if approved by the AHJ. Such alternate system shall be designed and installed in accordance with the appropriate NFPA standard and with manufacturer's recommendations for the system selected. [**30**:19.4.6.2]

66.19.4.7 Operation.

66.19.4.7.1* Operations involving heat transfer fluid systems and equipment shall be reviewed to ensure that the fire and explosion hazards resulting from loss of containment of the fluid or failure of the system are provided with corresponding fire prevention and emergency action plans. [**30**:19.4.7.1]

66.19.4.7.2 Operators of heat transfer systems shall be trained in the hazards of improper operation of the system and leakage and shall be trained to recognize upset conditions that can lead to dangerous situations. [**30**:19.4.7.2]

66.19.4.7.3 Safety interlocks shall be inspected, calibrated, and tested annually or at other intervals established in accordance with other applicable standards to determine that they are in proper operating condition. [**30**:19.4.7.3]

66.19.5 Vapor Recovery and Vapor Processing Systems.

66.19.5.1 Scope.

66.19.5.1.1 This section shall apply to vapor recovery and vapor processing systems where the vapor source operates at pressures from vacuum up to and including a gauge pressure of 1.0 psi (6.9 kPa), or where there is a potential for vapor mixtures in the flammable range. [**30**:19.5.1.1]

66.19.5.1.2 This section shall not apply to the following:

(1) Marine systems that comply with U.S. Department of Transportation Regulations in Title 33, Code of Federal Regulations, Parts 154, 155, and 156, and U.S. Coast Guard Regulations in Title 46, Code of Federal Regulations, Parts 30, 32, 35, and 39
(2) Marine and automotive service station systems that comply with Chapter 30 and NFPA 30A, *Code for Motor Fuel Dispensing Facilities and Repair Garages* [**30**:19.5.1.2]

66.19.5.2 Overpressure Protection and Vacuum Protection. Tanks and equipment shall have independent venting for overpressure or vacuum conditions that could occur from malfunction of the vapor recovery or vapor processing system.

Exception: For tanks, venting shall comply with 66.21.4.3. [30:19.5.2]

66.19.5.3 Vent Location.

66.19.5.3.1 Vents on vapor processing systems shall be not less than 12 ft (3.7 m) from adjacent ground level, with outlets located and directed so that ignitible vapors will disperse to a concentration below the lower flammable limit before reaching any location that contains an ignition source. [**30**:19.5.3.1]

66.19.5.3.2 Vent outlets shall be located so that vapors will not be trapped by eaves or other obstructions and shall be at least 5 ft (1.5 m) from building openings and at least 15 ft (4.5 m) from powered ventilation air intake devices. [**30**:19.5.3.2]

66.19.5.3.3 Vapor processing equipment and their vents shall be located in accordance with 66.17.3. [**30**:19.5.3.3]

66.19.5.4 Vapor Collection Systems.

66.19.5.4.1 Vapor collection piping shall be designed to prevent trapping liquid. [**30**:19.5.4.1]

66.19.5.4.2 Vapor recovery and vapor processing systems that are not designed to handle liquid shall be provided with a means to eliminate any liquid that carries over to or condenses in the vapor collection system. [**30**:19.5.4.2]

66.19.5.5 Liquid Level Monitoring.

66.19.5.5.1* A liquid knock-out vessel used in the vapor collection system shall have means to verify the liquid level and a high liquid level sensor that activates an alarm. [**30**:19.5.5.1]

66.19.5.5.2 For unattended facilities, the high liquid level sensor shall initiate shutdown of liquid transfer into the vessel and shutdown of vapor recovery or vapor processing systems. [**30**:19.5.5.2]

66.19.5.6 Overfill Protection.

66.19.5.6.1 Storage tanks served by vapor processing or vapor recovery systems shall be equipped with overfill protection in accordance with 66.21.7.1. [**30**:19.5.6.1]

66.19.5.6.2 Overfill protection of tank vehicles shall be in accordance with applicable provisions of 66.28.11.1. [**30**:19.5.6.2]

66.19.5.7 Sources of Ignition.

66.19.5.7.1 Vapor Release. Tank or equipment openings provided for purposes of vapor recovery shall be protected against possible vapor release in accordance with 66.23.13.7 and 66.28.11.1.8.1. [**30**:19.5.7.1]

66.19.5.7.2* Electrical Area Classification. Electrical area classification shall be in accordance with Section 66.7. [**30**:19.5.7.2]

66.19.5.7.3* Static Electricity. Vapor collection and vapor processing equipment shall be protected against static electricity in accordance with 66.6.5.4. [**30**:19.5.7.3]

66.19.5.7.4* Spontaneous Ignition. Equipment shall be designed or written procedures established and implemented to prevent ignition where the potential exists for spontaneous ignition. [**30**:19.5.7.4]

66.19.5.7.5* Friction Heat or Sparks from Mechanical Equipment. Mechanical equipment used to move vapors that are in the flammable range shall be designed to prevent sparks or other ignition sources under both normal and equipment malfunction conditions. [**30**:19.5.7.5]

66.19.5.7.6* Flame Propagation. Where there is reasonable potential for ignition of a vapor mixture in the flammable range, means shall be provided to stop the propagation of flame through the vapor collection system. The means chosen shall prevent flame propagation under the conditions with which they will be used. [**30**:19.5.7.6]

66.19.5.7.7 Explosion Protection. Where used, explosion protection systems shall comply with NFPA 69. [**30**:19.5.7.7]

66.19.5.8 Emergency Shutdown Systems. Emergency shutdown systems shall be designed to fail to a safe position in the event of loss of normal system power (i.e., air or electric) or equipment malfunction. [**30**:19.5.8]

66.19.6 Solvent Distillation Units.

66.19.6.1 Scope.

66.19.6.1.1 This section shall apply to solvent distillation units having distillation chambers or still pots that do not exceed 60 gal (227 L) nominal capacity and are used to recycle Class I, Class II, or Class IIIA liquids. [**30**:19.6.1.1]

66.19.6.1.2 This section shall not apply to research, testing, or experimental processes; to distillation processes carried out in petroleum refineries, chemical plants, or distilleries; or to distillation equipment used in dry cleaning operations. [**30**:19.6.1.2]

66.19.6.2 Equipment. Solvent distillation units shall be approved or shall be listed in accordance with ANSI/UL 2208, *Standard for Solvent Distillation Units*. [**30**:19.6.2]

66.19.6.3 Solvents. Solvent distillation units shall only be used to distill liquids for which they have been investigated and that are listed on the unit's marking or contained within the manufacturers' literature. [**30**:19.6.3]

66.19.6.3.1 Unstable or reactive liquids or materials shall not be processed unless they have been specifically listed on the system's markings or contained within the manufacturer's literature. [**30**:19.6.3.1]

66.19.6.4 Location.

66.19.6.4.1 Solvent distillation units shall be located and operated in locations in accordance with their approval or listing. [**30**:19.6.4.1]

66.19.6.4.2 Solvent distillation units shall not be used in basements. [**30**:19.6.4.2]

66.19.6.4.3 Solvent distillation units shall be located away from potential sources of ignition, as indicated on the unit's marking. [**30**:19.6.4.3]

66.19.6.5 Liquid Storage. Distilled liquids and liquids awaiting distillation shall be stored in accordance with this *Code*. [**30**:19.6.5]

66.19.7 Cooking Oil Storage Tank Systems in Commercial Kitchens.

66.19.7.1 Scope.

66.19.7.1.1 This section shall apply to storage tank systems for cooking oil, as defined in 66.19.2.1, located in commercial kitchens where tank capacities are greater than 60 gal (227 L). [**30**:19.7.1.1]

66.19.7.1.2 This section shall apply to both fresh and waste cooking oil storage tank systems. [**30**:19.7.1.2]

66.19.7.1.3* Where there are conflicts between the requirements of this section and requirements of other sections of this code, the requirements of this section shall take precedence. [**30**:19.7.1.3]

66.19.7.2 Design and Construction of Cooking Oil Storage Tanks.

66.19.7.2.1 Materials of Construction. Tanks shall be constructed of materials of metallic or nonmetallic construction. [**30**:19.7.2.1]

66.19.7.2.1.1 Tanks and their appurtenances shall be constructed of materials compatible with cooking oil. [**30**:19.7.2.1.1]

66.19.7.2.1.2* For tanks storing waste cooking oil, the materials of construction of the tanks and their appurtenances shall be compatible with cooking oil at minimum temperatures of 140°F (60°C) continuous and 235°F (113°C) intermittent. [**30**:19.7.2.1.2]

66.19.7.2.2 Design Standards.

66.19.7.2.2.1* Metallic cooking oil storage tanks shall be listed in accordance with ANSI/UL 142, *Standard for Steel Aboveground Tanks for Flammable and Combustible Liquids*, or ANSI/UL 80, *Standard for Steel Tanks for Oil-Burner Fuels and Other Combustible Liquids*. [**30**:19.7.2.2.1]

66.19.7.2.2.2 Nonmetallic cooking oil storage tanks shall meet the following requirements:

(1) Tanks shall be listed for use with cooking oil, unless otherwise approved.
(2) Tanks shall not exceed 200 gal (757 L) per tank. [**30**:19.7.2.2.2]

66.19.7.2.3 Normal Venting.

66.19.7.2.3.1 The normal vent(s) shall be located above the maximum normal liquid level. [**30**:19.7.2.3.1]

66.19.7.2.3.2 The normal vent shall be at least as large as the largest filling or withdrawal connection. [**30**:19.7.2.3.2]

66.19.7.2.3.3 Where used, normal vents, including vent piping, that are smaller than 1.25 in. (32 mm) nominal inside diameter shall be tested to verify that internal tank pressures will remain below a gauge pressure of 0.5 psi (3.5 kPa) under maximum expected flow rates for tank filling and withdrawal. These tests shall be permitted to be conducted by a qualified outside agency or by the manufacturer, if certified by a qualified observer. [**30**:19.7.2.3.3]

66.19.7.2.3.4* Normal vents shall be permitted to discharge inside the building. [**30**:19.7.2.3.4]

66.19.7.2.4 Emergency Venting.

66.19.7.2.4.1 Cooking oil storage tanks shall be provided with emergency relief venting in accordance with Section 66.22. [**30**:19.7.2.4.1]

66.19.7.2.4.2* For nonmetallic cooking oil storage tanks, emergency relief venting by form of construction shall be permitted. This shall include the low melting point of the material of construction of the tank. [**30**:19.7.2.4.2]

66.19.7.2.4.3 For metallic cooking oil storage tanks, emergency relief venting by form of construction shall be prohibited. [**30**:19.7.2.4.3]

66.19.7.2.4.4 Emergency vents shall be permitted to discharge inside the building. [**30**:19.7.2.4.4]

66.19.7.2.5* Prevention of Overfilling of Cooking Oil Storage Tanks. Every cooking oil storage tank shall be provided with means to prevent an accidental overfill. Such means shall be automatic and fail-safe in nature. [**30**:19.7.2.5]

66.19.7.2.6 Tank Heating.

66.19.7.2.6.1* Electrical equipment used for heating cooking oil shall be listed to ANSI/UL 499, *Standard for Electrical Heating Appliances*, and shall comply with NFPA 70, *National Electric Code*. [**30**:19.7.2.6.1]

66.19.7.2.6.2* Electrical equipment used for heating cooking oil shall comply with NFPA 70, *National Electrical Code*, and shall be equipped with automatic means to limit the temperature of the oil to less than 140°F (60°C). [**30**:19.7.2.6.2]

66.19.7.2.6.3 Use of electrical immersion heaters in nonmetallic tanks shall be prohibited. [**30**:19.7.2.6.3]

66.19.7.3 Tank Installation and Testing.

66.19.7.3.1 Location of Cooking Oil Storage Tanks. Tanks shall be installed in locations appropriate for storage of foodstuffs or inventory and shall not be installed in areas designated as cooking areas. [**30**:19.7.3.1]

66.19.7.3.1.1* Tanks shall be spaced at least 3 ft (0.9 m) away from any cooking appliance or any surface heated to a temperature above 140°F (60°C) continuous and at least 6 ft (1.8 m) away from any open flame. [**30**:19.7.3.1.1]

66.19.7.3.1.2* Tanks shall not be installed under commercial kitchen ventilation hoods. [**30**:19.7.3.1.2]

66.19.7.3.1.3 Tanks shall not be required to be separated from one another. [**30**:19.7.3.1.3]

66.19.7.3.2 Foundations for and Anchoring of Cooking Oil Storage Tanks.

66.19.7.3.2.1 Tank supports shall be secured to the tank and to the floor to prevent the tank from tipping over. For a flat-bottom tank resting directly on the floor, the tank shall be secured to the floor to prevent the tank from tipping over. [**30**:19.7.3.2.1]

66.19.7.3.2.2 In areas subject to earthquakes, tank supports, the foundation, and anchoring shall meet the requirements of the applicable building code for the specific seismic zone. Engineering evaluation by a qualified, impartial outside agency shall be an acceptable method of meeting this requirement. [**30**:19.7.3.2.2]

66.19.7.3.2.3 Where a tank is located in areas subject to flooding, the method for anchoring the tank to the floor shall be capable of preventing the tank, either full or empty, from floating during a rise in water level up to the established maximum flood stage. Engineering evaluation by a qualified, impartial outside agency shall be an acceptable method of meeting this requirement. [**30**:19.7.3.2.3]

66.19.7.3.3 Tank Openings Other than Vents.

66.19.7.3.3.1 Each connection to the tank below the normal liquid level through which liquid can normally flow shall be provided with an internal or external valve located as close as possible to the shell of the tank, in accordance with Section 66.22. [**30**:19.7.3.3.1]

66.19.7.3.3.2* Connections to the tank above the normal liquid level through which liquid can normally flow shall not be required to have a valve, provided there exists a liquid-tight closure at the opposite end of the line. The liquidtight closure shall be in the form of a valve, a plug, or a coupling or fitting with positive shutoff. [**30**:19.7.3.3.2]

66.19.7.3.4 Field Testing.

66.19.7.3.4.1* As an alternate method to the testing requirements in Section 66.21, cooking oil storage tanks shall be tested for leaks at the time of installation by filling the tank with cooking oil to a liquid level above the highest tank seam or connection within the normal liquid level. Before the tank is placed in service, all leaks shall be corrected in an approved manner or the tank shall be replaced. [**30**:19.7.3.4.1]

66.19.7.3.4.2 An approved listing mark on a cooking oil storage tank shall be considered to be evidence of compliance with tank testing requirements. [**30**:19.7.3.4.2]

66.19.7.4 Fire Protection for Cooking Oil Storage Tanks.

66.19.7.4.1 Identification for Emergency Responders. A sign or marking that meets the requirements of NFPA 704, *Standard System for the Identification of the Hazards of Materials for Emergency Response*, or another approved system, shall be applied to each cooking oil storage tank in accordance with Section 66.21. Additional signage shall be applied to each tank identifying the contents of the tank as cooking oil, either fresh or waste. [**30**:19.7.4.1]

66.19.7.4.2* In areas where tanks are located, no additional ventilation shall be required beyond that required for comfort ventilation and provided that all cooking equipment is provided with exhaust systems in accordance with NFPA 96, *Standard for Ventilation Control and Fire Protection of Commercial Cooking Operations*. [**30**:19.7.4.2]

66.19.7.4.3 If ventilation is not provided as specified in 66.19.7.4.2, then the tank shall be vented to another room inside the building that meets these requirements, or the tank shall be vented to the outside of the building. [**30**:19.7.4.3]

66.19.7.5 Transfer Lines.

66.19.7.5.1* Design and Construction of Fresh Cooking Oil Transfer Lines. Transfer lines for fresh cooking oil shall be permitted to be constructed of metallic or nonmetallic materials that are compatible with cooking oil and food products. Nonmetallic transfer lines shall also meet the following requirements:

(1) Transfer lines in pressure applications shall be rated for a working gauge pressure of 100 psi (689 kPa) at 70°F (21°C), or the maximum output pressure of the transfer pump, whichever is higher.
(2) Transfer lines in suction applications shall be rated for full vacuum at 70°F (21°C).
(3) Transfer lines shall be rated for temperatures up to 120°F (49°C) continuous.
(4) The maximum nominal inside diameter shall be no larger than 1.25 in. (32 mm).
(5) Leakage shall be controlled through the use of check valves or antisiphon valves at points where the lines connect to the fresh oil tank. [30:19.7.5.1]

66.19.7.5.2* Design and Construction of Waste Cooking Oil Transfer Lines. Waste cooking oil transfer lines shall be permitted to be constructed of metallic or nonmetallic materials that are compatible with cooking oil. [30:19.7.5.2]

66.19.7.5.2.1 Transfer lines shall be rated for use with cooking oil at elevated temperatures of 275°F (135°C) continuous and 350°F (177°C) intermittent. [30:19.7.5.2.1]

66.19.7.5.2.2 Nonmetallic transfer lines shall be rated for working pressures up to 250 psi (1724 kPa) at 275°F (135°C). [30:19.7.5.2.2]

66.19.7.5.3 Flow Control. Cooking oil transfer lines shall be equipped with means to prevent unintended transfer or dispensing of cooking oil. These means shall be permitted to be in the form of momentary control switches, valves, check valves, antisiphon valves, plugs, couplings, fittings, or any combination thereof that are fail-safe in nature. [30:19.7.5.3]

66.19.7.5.4 Pressure Control. Pumping systems used to transfer cooking oil shall have means to prevent overpressurization of transfer lines. These means shall be in the form of relief valves, bypass valves, pressure sensor devices, or the pressure limitation of the pump itself. [30:19.7.5.4]

66.19.7.5.5 Installation of Cooking Oil Transfer Lines in Plenum-Rated Spaces. Cooking oil transfer lines installed in plenum-rated spaces shall be enclosed in noncombustible raceways or enclosures, or shall be covered with a material listed and labeled for installation within a plenum. [30:19.7.5.5]

66.19.7.5.6 Testing of Cooking Oil Transfer Lines. Cooking oil transfer lines shall be tested after installation and prior to use. Testing shall be with cooking oil at the normal operating pressures. Any leaks discovered in transfer lines as a result of testing shall be repaired or the transfer lines replaced prior to placing the transfer lines into service. [30:19.7.5.6]

66.20 Reserved.

66.21 Storage of Liquids in Tanks — Requirements for All Storage Tanks.

66.21.1 Scope. This section shall apply to the following:

(1) The storage of flammable and combustible liquids, as defined in 3.3.164.1 and 3.3.164.2 and Section 66.4, in fixed tanks that exceed 60 gal (230 L) capacity
(2) The storage of flammable and combustible liquids in portable tanks that exceed 660 gal (2500 L) capacity
(3) The storage of flammable and combustible liquids in intermediate bulk containers that exceed 793 gal (3000 L) capacity
(4) The design, installation, testing, operation, and maintenance of such tanks, portable tanks, and bulk containers [30:21.1]

66.21.2 Definitions Specific to Section 66.21. For the purpose of this section, the terms in this section shall have the definitions given. [30:21.2]

66.21.2.1 Compartmented Tank. A tank that is divided into two or more compartments intended to contain the same or different liquids. [30:21.2.1]

66.21.3 General Requirements.

66.21.3.1 Storage of Class II and Class III liquids heated at or above their flash point shall follow the requirements for Class I liquids, unless an engineering evaluation conducted in accordance with Section 66.6 and 66.21.6 justifies following the requirements for some other liquid class. [30:21.3.1]

66.21.3.2 Tanks shall be permitted to be of any shape, size, or type consistent with recognized engineering standards. Metal tanks shall be welded, riveted, and caulked, or bolted or constructed using a combination of these methods. [30:21.3.2]

66.21.3.3 Tanks designed and intended for aboveground use shall not be used as underground tanks. [30:21.3.3]

66.21.3.4 Tanks designed and intended for underground use shall not be used as aboveground tanks. [30:21.3.4]

66.21.3.5 Tanks shall be designed and built in accordance with recognized engineering standards for the material of construction being used. [30:21.3.5]

66.21.4 Design and Construction of Storage Tanks.

66.21.4.1 Materials of Construction. Tanks shall be of steel or other approved noncombustible material and shall meet the applicable requirements of 66.21.4.1.1 through 66.21.4.1.5. [30:21.4.1]

66.21.4.1.1 The materials of construction for tanks and their appurtenances shall be compatible with the liquid to be stored. In case of doubt about the properties of the liquid to be stored, the supplier, producer of the liquid, or other competent authority shall be consulted. [30:21.4.1.1]

66.21.4.1.2 Tanks shall be permitted to be constructed of combustible materials when approved. Tanks constructed of combustible materials shall be limited to any of the following:

(1) Underground installation
(2) Use where required by the properties of the liquid stored
(3) Aboveground storage of Class IIIB liquids in areas not exposed to a spill or leak of Class I or Class II liquid
(4) Storage of Class IIIB liquids inside a building protected by an approved automatic fire-extinguishing system [30:21.4.1.2]

66.21.4.1.3 Unlined concrete tanks shall be permitted to be used for storing liquids that have a gravity of 40° API or heavier. Concrete tanks with special linings shall be permitted to be used for other liquids, provided they are designed and constructed in accordance with recognized engineering standards. [**30**:21.4.1.3]

66.21.4.1.4 Tanks shall be permitted to have combustible or noncombustible linings. The selection, specification, and type of lining material and its required thickness shall be based on the properties of the liquid to be stored. When there is a change in the characteristics of the liquid to be stored, the compatibility of the lining and the liquid shall be verified. [**30**:21.4.1.4]

66.21.4.1.5 An engineering evaluation shall be made if the specific gravity of the liquid to be stored exceeds that of water or if the tank is designed to contain liquids at a liquid temperature below 0°F (-18°C). [**30**:21.4.1.5]

66.21.4.2 Design Standards for Storage Tanks.

66.21.4.2.1 Design Standards for Atmospheric Tanks.

66.21.4.2.1.1* Atmospheric tanks shall be designed and constructed in accordance with recognized engineering standards. Atmospheric tanks that meet any of the following standards shall be deemed as meeting the requirements of 66.21.4.2.1:

(1) API Specification 12B, *Bolted Tanks for Storage of Production Liquids*
(2) API Specification 12D, *Field Welded Tanks for Storage of Production Liquids*
(3) API Specification 12F, *Shop Welded Tanks for Storage of Production Liquids*
(4) API Standard 650, *Welded Steel Tanks for Oil Storage*
(5) UL 58, *Standard for Steel Underground Tanks for Flammable and Combustible Liquids*
(6) ANSI/UL 80, *Standard for Steel Tanks for Oil Burner Fuel*
(7) ANSI/UL 142, *Standard for Steel Aboveground Tanks for Flammable and Combustible Liquids*
(8) UL 1316, *Standard for Glass-Fiber Reinforced Plastic Underground Storage Tanks for Petroleum Products, Alcohols, and Alcohol-Gasoline Mixtures*
(9) ANSI/UL 1746, *Standard for External Corrosion Protection Systems for Steel Underground Storage Tanks*
(10) UL 2080, *Standard for Fire Resistant Tanks for Flammable and Combustible Liquids*
(11) ANSI/UL 2085, *Standard for Protected Aboveground Tanks for Flammable and Combustible Liquids* [**30**:21.4.2.1.1]

66.21.4.2.1.2 Except as provided for in 66.21.4.2.1.3 and 66.21.4.2.1.4, atmospheric tanks designed and constructed in accordance with Appendix F of API Standard 650, *Welded Steel Tanks for Oil Storage*, shall be permitted to operate at pressures from atmospheric to a gauge pressure of 1.0 psi (6.9 kPa). All other tanks shall be limited to operation from atmospheric to a gauge pressure of 0.5 psi (3.5 kPa). [**30**:21.4.2.1.2]

66.21.4.2.1.3 Atmospheric tanks that are not designed and constructed in accordance with Appendix F of API Standard 650, *Welded Steel Tanks for Oil Storage*, shall be permitted to operate at pressures from atmospheric to a gauge pressure of 1.0 psi (6.9 kPa) only if an engineering analysis is performed to determine that the tank can withstand the elevated pressure. [**30**:21.4.2.1.3]

66.21.4.2.1.4 Horizontal cylindrical and rectangular tanks built according to any of the standards specified in 66.21.4.2.1.1 shall be permitted to operate at pressures from atmospheric to a gauge pressure of 1.0 psi (6.9 kPa) and shall be limited to a gauge pressure of 2.5 psi (17 kPa) under emergency venting conditions. [**30**:21.4.2.1.4]

66.21.4.2.1.5 Low-pressure tanks and pressure vessels shall be permitted to be used as atmospheric tanks. [**30**:21.4.2.1.5]

66.21.4.2.1.6 Atmospheric tanks shall not be used to store a liquid at a temperature at or above its boiling point. [**30**:21.4.2.1.6]

66.21.4.2.2 Design Standards for Low-Pressure Tanks.

66.21.4.2.2.1 Low-pressure tanks shall be designed and constructed in accordance with recognized engineering standards. Low-pressure tanks that meet either of the following standards shall be deemed as meeting the requirements of 66.21.4.2.2:

(1) API 620, *Recommended Rules for the Design and Construction of Large, Welded, Low-Pressure Storage Tanks*
(2) ASME *Code for Unfired Pressure Vessels*, Section VIII, Division 1 [**30**:21.4.2.2.1]

66.21.4.2.2.2 Low-pressure tanks shall not be operated above their design pressures. [**30**:21.4.2.2.2]

66.21.4.2.2.3 Pressure vessels shall be permitted to be used as low-pressure tanks. [**30**:21.4.2.2.3]

66.21.4.2.3 Design Standards for Pressure Vessels.

66.21.4.2.3.1 Tanks with storage pressures above a gauge pressure of 15 psi (100 kPa) shall be designed and constructed in accordance with recognized engineering standards. Pressure vessels that meet any of the following standards shall be deemed as meeting the requirements of 66.21.4.2.3:

(1) Fired pressure vessels shall be designed and constructed in accordance with Section I (Power Boilers), or Section VIII, Division 1 or Division 2 (Pressure Vessels), as applicable, of the ASME *Boiler and Pressure Vessel Code.*
(2) Unfired pressure vessels shall be designed and constructed in accordance with Section VIII, Division 1 or Division 2, of the ASME *Boiler and Pressure Vessel Code.* [**30**:21.4.2.3.1]

66.21.4.2.3.2* Pressure vessels that do not meet the requirements of 66.21.4.2.3.1(1) or 66.21.4.2.3.1(2) shall be permitted to be used, provided they are approved by the AHJ. [**30**:21.4.2.3.2]

66.21.4.2.3.3 Pressure vessels shall not be operated above their design pressures. The normal operating pressure of the vessel shall not exceed the design pressure of the vessel. [**30**:21.4.2.3.3]

66.21.4.3 Normal Venting for Storage Tanks.

66.21.4.3.1 Storage tanks shall be vented to prevent the development of vacuum or pressure that can distort the tank or exceed the rated design pressure of the tank when the tank is filled or emptied or because of atmospheric temperature changes. Normal vents shall be located above the maximum normal liquid level. [**30**:21.4.3.1]

66.21.4.3.2* Normal venting shall be provided for primary tanks and each primary compartment of a compartmented tank. [**30**:21.4.3.2]

66.21.4.3.3 Normal vents shall be sized in accordance with either API Standard 2000, *Venting Atmospheric and Low-Pressure Storage Tanks*, or another approved standard. Alternatively, the normal vent shall be at least as large as the largest filling or withdrawal connection, but in no case shall it be less than 1.25 in. (32 mm) nominal inside diameter. [**30:**21.4.3.3]

66.21.4.3.4 Atmospheric storage tanks shall be vented to prevent the development of vacuum or pressure above the 1.0 psi (6.9 kPa) maximum operating pressure. [**30:**21.4.3.4]

66.21.4.3.5 Low-pressure tanks and pressure vessels shall be vented to prevent the development of pressure or vacuum that exceeds the rated design pressure of the tank or vessel. Means shall also be provided to prevent overpressure from any pump discharging into the tank or vessel when the pump discharge pressure can exceed the design pressure of the tank or vessel. [**30:**21.4.3.5]

66.21.4.3.6 If any tank or pressure vessel has more than one fill or withdrawal connection and simultaneous filling or withdrawal can be made, the vent size shall be based on the maximum anticipated simultaneous flow. [**30:**21.4.3.6]

66.21.4.3.7 For tanks equipped with vents that permit pressures to exceed a gauge pressure of 2.5 psi (17 kPa) and for low-pressure tanks and for pressure vessels, the outlet of all vents and vent drains shall be arranged to discharge in a manner that prevents localized overheating of or flame impingement on any part of the tank, if vapors from the vents are ignited. [**30:**21.4.3.7]

66.21.4.3.8 Tanks and pressure vessels that store Class IA liquids shall be equipped with venting devices that are closed, except when venting under pressure or vacuum conditions. [**30:**21.4.3.8]

66.21.4.3.9 Tanks and pressure vessels that store Class IB and Class IC liquids shall be equipped with venting devices or with listed flame arresters. When used, vent devices shall be closed, except when venting under pressure or vacuum conditions. [**30:**21.4.3.9]

66.21.4.3.10 Tanks of 3000 barrels (bbl) [126,000 gal or (475 m^3)] capacity or less that store crude petroleum in crude-producing areas and outside aboveground atmospheric tanks of less than 1000 gal (3785 L) capacity that contain other than Class IA liquids shall be permitted to have open vents. [**30:**21.4.3.10]

66.21.4.3.11* Flame arresters or venting devices required in 66.21.4.3.8 and 66.21.4.3.9 shall be permitted to be omitted on tanks that store Class IB or Class IC liquids where conditions are such that their use can, in case of obstruction, result in damage to the tank. [**30:**21.4.3.11]

66.21.4.3.12 Piping for normal vents shall be designed in accordance with Section 66.27. [**30:**21.4.3.12]

66.21.4.4* Tank Fill Pipes. Fill pipes that enter the top of a tank shall terminate within 6 in. (150 mm) of the bottom of the tank. Fill pipes shall be installed or arranged so that vibration is minimized.

Exception No. 1: Fill pipes in tanks whose vapor space under the expected range of operating conditions is not in the flammable range or is inerted need not meet this requirement.

Exception No. 2: Fill pipes in tanks handling liquids with minimal potential for accumulation of static charge need not meet this requirement, provided that the fill line is designed and the system is operated to avoid mist generation and to provide residence time downstream of filters or screens to allow dissipation of the generated static charge. [**30:**21.4.4]

66.21.4.5* Corrosion Protection.

66.21.4.5.1 Corrosion protection shall meet the requirements of 66.21.4.5.2 or 66.21.4.5.3, whichever is applicable. [**30:**21.4.5.1]

66.21.4.5.2 Internal Corrosion Protection for Metal Storage Tanks. Where tanks are not designed in accordance with standards of the American Petroleum Institute, the American Society of Mechanical Engineers, or Underwriters Laboratories Inc., or if corrosion is anticipated beyond that provided for in the design formulas or standards used, additional metal thickness or approved protective coatings or linings shall be provided to compensate for the corrosion loss expected during the design life of the tank. [**30:**21.4.5.2]

66.21.4.5.3 Internal Corrosion Protection for Nonmetallic Tanks. Where tanks are not designed in accordance with standards of the American Petroleum Institute, the American Society of Mechanical Engineers, ASTM International, or Underwriters Laboratories Inc., or if degradation is anticipated beyond that provided for in the design formulas or standards used, degradation shall be compensated for by providing additional tank material thickness or by application of protective coatings or linings, as determined by an engineering analysis. [**30:**21.4.5.3]

66.21.5 Testing Requirements for Tanks.

66.21.5.1 General. All tanks, whether shop-built or field-erected, shall be tested before they are placed in service in accordance with the requirements of the code under which they were built. [**30:**21.5.1]

66.21.5.1.1 An approved listing mark on a tank shall be considered to be evidence of compliance with 66.21.5.1. Tanks not so marked shall be tested before they are placed in service in accordance with the applicable requirements for testing in the codes listed in 66.21.4.2.1.1, 66.21.4.2.2.1, or 66.21.4.2.3.1 or in accordance with recognized engineering standards. Upon satisfactory completion of testing, a permanent record of the test results shall be maintained by the owner. [**30:**21.5.1.1]

66.21.5.1.2 Where the vertical length of the fill and vent pipes is such that, when filled with liquid, the static head imposed on the bottom of the tank exceeds a gauge pressure of 10 psi (70 kPa), the tank and its related piping shall be tested hydrostatically to a pressure equal to the static head thus imposed by using recognized engineering standards. [**30:**21.5.1.2]

66.21.5.1.3 Before the tank is initially placed in service, all leaks or deformations shall be corrected in an approved manner. Mechanical caulking shall not be permitted for correcting leaks in welded tanks except for pinhole leaks in the roof. [**30:**21.5.1.3]

66.21.5.1.4 Tanks to be operated at pressures below their design pressure shall be tested by the applicable provisions of 66.21.5.1.1 or 66.21.5.1.2 based upon the pressure developed under full emergency venting of the tank. [**30:**21.5.1.4]

66.21.5.2* Tightness Testing. In addition to the tests called for in 66.21.5.1, all tanks and connections shall be tested for tightness after installation and before being placed in service in accordance with 66.21.5.2.2 and 66.21.5.2.3, as applicable. Except for underground tanks, this test shall be made at operating pressure with air, inert gas, or water. [**30:**21.5.2]

66.21.5.2.1 Testing required by 66.21.5.2 shall not be required for a primary tank or an interstitial space that continues to maintain a factory-applied vacuum in accordance with the manufacturer's instructions. Such components shall be considered to be tight until such time that the vacuum is broken. Final tightness testing of an interstitial space shall not be required if the factory-applied vacuum is maintained until one of the following conditions is met:

(1) For aboveground tanks, the tank is set on the site at the location where it is intended to be installed.
(2) For underground tanks, backfill has been completed to the top of the tank. [**30**:21.5.2.1]

66.21.5.2.2 Air pressure shall not be used to test tanks that contain flammable or combustible liquids or vapors. *(See 66.27.7 for testing pressure piping.)* [**30**:21.5.2.2]

66.21.5.2.3 For field-erected tanks, the tests required by 66.21.5.1.1 or 66.21.5.1.2 shall be permitted to be considered the test for tank tightness. [**30**:21.5.2.3]

66.21.5.2.4 Horizontal shop-fabricated aboveground tanks shall be tested for tightness either hydrostatically or with air pressure at not less than a gauge pressure of 3 psi (20 kPa) and not more than a gauge pressure of 5 psi (35 kPa). [**30**:21.5.2.4]

66.21.5.2.5 Vertical shop-fabricated aboveground tanks shall be tested for tightness either hydrostatically or with air pressure at not less than a gauge pressure of 1.5 psi (10 kPa) and not more than a gauge pressure of 2.5 psi (17 kPa). [**30**:21.5.2.5]

66.21.5.2.6 Single-wall underground tanks and piping, before being covered, enclosed, or placed in use, shall be tested for tightness either hydrostatically or with air pressure at not less than a gauge pressure of 3 psi (20 kPa) and not more than a gauge pressure of 5 psi (35 kPa). [**30**:21.5.2.6]

66.21.5.2.7* Underground secondary containment tanks and horizontal aboveground secondary containment tanks shall have the primary (inner) tank tested for tightness either hydrostatically or with air pressure at not less than a gauge pressure of 3 psi (20 kPa) and not more than a gauge pressure of 5 psi (35 kPa). [**30**:21.5.2.7]

66.21.5.2.7.1 The interstitial space of such tanks shall be tested either hydrostatically or with air pressure at a gauge pressure of 3 to 5 psi (20 to 35 kPa), by vacuum at 5.3 in. Hg (18 kPa), or in accordance with the tank's listing or the manufacturer's instructions. These limits shall not be exceeded. [**30**:21.5.2.7.1]

66.21.5.2.7.2 The pressure or vacuum shall be held for not less than 1 hour or for the duration specified in the listing procedures for the tank. [**30**:21.5.2.7.2]

66.21.5.2.8 Vertical aboveground secondary containment-type tanks shall have their primary (inner) tank tested for tightness either hydrostatically or with air pressure at not less than a gauge pressure of 1.5 psi (10 kPa) and not more than a gauge pressure of 2.5 psi (17 kPa). [**30**:21.5.2.8]

66.21.5.2.8.1 The interstitial space of such tanks shall be tested either hydrostatically or with air pressure at a gauge pressure of 1.5 to 2.5 psi (10 to 17 kPa), by vacuum at 5.3 in. Hg (18 kPa), or in accordance with the tank's listing or manufacturer's instructions. These limits shall not be exceeded. [**30**:21.5.2.8.1]

66.21.5.2.8.2 The pressure or vacuum shall be held for not less than 1 hour or for the duration specified in the listing procedures for the tank. [**30**:21.5.2.8.2]

66.21.5.3* Periodic Testing. Each tank shall be tested when required by the manufacturer's instructions and applicable standards to ensure the integrity of the tank. [**30**:21.5.3]

66.21.6 Fire Prevention and Control.

66.21.6.1 General Requirements.

66.21.6.1.1 This section shall apply to the commonly recognized management techniques and fire control methods used to prevent or minimize the loss from fire or explosion in tank storage facilities. The wide range in size, design, and location of tank storage facilities shall preclude the inclusion of detailed fire prevention and control methods applicable to all such facilities. [**30**:21.6.1.1]

66.21.6.1.2 Tank storage facilities shall establish and implement fire prevention and control methods for life safety, for minimizing property loss, and for reducing fire exposure to adjoining facilities resulting from fire and explosion. Compliance with 66.21.6.2 through 66.21.6.6 shall be deemed as meeting the requirements of 66.21.6.1. [**30**:21.6.1.2]

66.21.6.2 Control of Ignition Sources. In order to prevent the ignition of flammable vapors in tank storage facilities, ignition sources shall be controlled in accordance with Section 66.6. [**30**:21.6.2]

66.21.6.3 Management of Fire Hazards. The extent of fire and explosion prevention and control procedures and measures provided for tank storage facilities shall be determined by an engineering evaluation of the installation and operation, followed by the application of recognized fire and explosion protection and process engineering principles. The evaluation shall include, but not be limited to, the following:

(1) Analysis of fire and explosion hazards of the facility
(2) Analysis of local conditions, such as exposure to and from adjacent properties, flood potential, or earthquake potential
(3) Fire department or mutual aid response [**30**:21.6.3]

66.21.6.4 Fire Control. Tank storage facilities for flammable and combustible liquids shall be reviewed to ensure that fire and explosion hazards resulting from loss of containment of liquids are provided with corresponding fire prevention and emergency action plans. *(See also 66.6.3.)* [**30**:21.6.4]

66.21.6.5 Emergency Planning and Training.

66.21.6.5.1* An emergency plan, consistent with the available equipment, resources, and personnel, shall be established and implemented to respond to fires and explosions, and other emergencies. This plan shall address the following:

(1) Procedures to be used in case of fire, explosion, or accidental release of liquid or vapor including, but not limited to, sounding the alarm, notifying the fire department, evacuating personnel, controlling and mitigating the explosion, and controlling and extinguishing the fire
(2) Appointing and training of personnel to carry out emergency response duties
(3) Maintenance of fire protection, spill control and containment, and other emergency response equipment
(4) Conducting emergency response drills
(5) Shutdown or isolation of equipment to control unintentional releases

(6) Alternative measures for the safety of personnel while any fire protection or other emergency response equipment is shut down or inoperative [**30**:21.6.5.1]

66.21.6.5.2 Personnel responsible for the use and operation of fire protection equipment shall be trained in the use of and be able to demonstrate knowledge of the use or operation of that equipment. Refresher training shall be conducted at least annually. [**30**:21.6.5.2]

66.21.6.5.3 Planning of effective fire control measures shall be coordinated with local emergency response agencies and shall include, but not be limited to, the identification of all tanks by location, contents, size, and hazard identification as required in 66.21.7.2.1. [**30**:21.6.5.3]

66.21.6.5.4 Procedures shall be established to provide for safe shutdown of tank storage facilities under emergency conditions and for safe return to service. These procedures shall provide requirements for periodic training of personnel and inspection and testing of associated alarms, interlocks, and controls. [**30**:21.6.5.4]

66.21.6.5.5 Emergency procedures shall be kept available in an operating area. The procedures shall be reviewed and updated whenever conditions change. [**30**:21.6.5.5]

66.21.6.5.6 Where tank storage facilities are unattended, a summary of the emergency plan shall be posted or located in a strategic location that is accessible to emergency responders. [**30**:21.6.5.6]

66.21.6.6 Inspection and Maintenance of Fire Protection and Emergency Response Equipment.

66.21.6.6.1* All fire protection and emergency response equipment shall be maintained, inspected, and tested in accordance with regulatory requirements, standard practices, and equipment manufacturers' recommendations. [**30**:21.6.6.1]

66.21.6.6.2 Maintenance and operating procedures and practices at tank storage facilities shall be established and implemented to control leakage and prevent spillage and release of liquids. [**30**:21.6.6.2]

66.21.6.6.3 Ground areas around tank storage facilities shall be kept free of weeds, trash, or other unnecessary combustible materials. [**30**:21.6.6.3]

66.21.6.6.4 Accessways established for movement of personnel shall be maintained clear of obstructions to permit evacuation and access for manual fire fighting and emergency response in accordance with regulatory requirements and the emergency plan. [**30**:21.6.6.4]

66.21.6.6.5 Combustible waste material and residues in operating areas shall be kept to a minimum, stored in covered metal containers, and disposed of daily. [**30**:21.6.6.5]

66.21.6.6.6 Personnel responsible for the inspection and maintenance of fire protection and emergency response equipment shall be trained and shall be able to demonstrate knowledge of the inspection and maintenance of that equipment. Refresher training shall be conducted as needed to maintain proficiency. [**30**:21.6.6.6]

66.21.7 Operation of Storage Tanks.

66.21.7.1* Prevention of Overfilling of Storage Tanks. Facilities with aboveground tanks larger than 1320 gal (5000 L) storing Class I or Class II liquids shall establish procedures or shall provide equipment, or both, to prevent overfilling of tanks. [**30**:21.7.1]

66.21.7.1.1 Facilities with aboveground tanks that receive and transfer Class I liquids from mainline pipelines or marine vessels shall establish and follow formal written procedures to prevent overfilling of tanks utilizing one of the following methods of protection:

(1) Tanks shall be gauged at intervals in accordance with established procedures by personnel continuously on the premises during product receipt. Acknowledged communication shall be maintained with the supplier so flow can be shut down or diverted in accordance with established procedures.
(2) Tanks shall be equipped with a high-level detection device that is either independent of any gauging equipment or incorporates a gauging and alarm system that provides electronic self-checking to indicate when the gauging and alarm system has failed. Alarms shall be located where personnel who are on duty throughout product transfer can arrange for flow stoppage or diversion in accordance with established procedures.
(3) Tanks shall be equipped with an independent high-level detection system that will automatically shut down or divert flow in accordance with established procedures. [**30**:21.7.1.1]

66.21.7.1.2 Alternatives to instrumentation described in 66.21.7.1.1(2) and 66.21.7.1.1(3) shall be allowed where approved as affording equivalent protection. [**30**:21.7.1.2]

66.21.7.1.3 Instrumentation systems covered in 66.21.7.1.1(2) and 66.21.7.1.1(3) shall be wired fail-safe, such that valid alarm conditions or system failures create an alarm condition that will notify personnel or automatically shut down or divert flow. [**30**:21.7.1.3]

66.21.7.1.3.1 Written instrumentation performance procedures shall be established to define valid alarm conditions and system failures in accordance with API 2350, *Overfill Protection for Storage Tanks in Petroleum Facilities*. [**30**:21.7.1.3.1]

66.21.7.1.3.2 System failure shall include but not be limited to the following:

(1) Loss of main electrical power
(2) Electrical break, short circuit, or ground fault in the level detection system circuit or the alarm and signal circuit
(3) Failure or malfunction of the level detection system control equipment or signaling devices [**30**:21.7.1.3.2]

66.21.7.1.4 Formal written procedures required by 66.21.7.1.1 shall include the following:

(1) Instructions covering methods to check for lineup and receipt of initial delivery to tank designated to receive shipment.
(2) Provision for training and monitoring the performance of operating personnel by supervisors.
(3) Schedules and procedures for inspection and testing of gauging equipment and high-level instrumentation and related systems. Inspection and testing intervals shall be approved but shall not exceed 1 year. [**30**:21.7.1.4]

66.21.7.1.5 An underground tank shall be equipped with overfill prevention equipment that will operate as follows either alert the transfer operator when the tank is no more than 90 percent full by triggering an audible and visual high-level alarm or automatically shut off the flow of liquid into the tank when the tank is no more than 95 percent full. [**30**:21.7.1.5]

66.21.7.1.5.1 Other methods of overfill protection shall be permitted as approved by the AHJ. [**30**:21.7.1.5.1]

66.21.7.1.6 Shop-fabricated aboveground atmospheric storage tanks, constructed to the recognized standards of 66.21.4.2.1.1, shall meet the requirements of 66.21.7.1.6.1 through 66.21.7.1.6.4 whenever the vertical length from the tank bottom to the top of the fill, normal vent, or emergency vent exceeds 12 ft (3.7 m). [**30**:21.7.1.6]

66.21.7.1.6.1 An approved means shall be provided to notify the tank filling operator of the pending completion of the tank fill operation at the fill connection. [**30**:21.7.1.6.1]

66.21.7.1.6.2 An approved means shall be provided to stop delivery of liquid to the tank prior to the complete filling of the tank. [**30**:21.7.1.6.2]

66.21.7.1.6.3 In no case shall these provisions restrict or interfere with the functioning of the normal vent or emergency vent. [**30**:21.7.1.6.3]

66.21.7.1.6.4 The manufacturer of the tank shall be consulted to determine if reinforcement of the tank is required. If reinforcement is deemed necessary, it shall be done. [**30**:21.7.1.6.4]

66.21.7.2 Identification and Security.

66.21.7.2.1 Identification for Emergency Responders. A sign or marking that meets the requirements of NFPA 704, *Standard System for the Identification of the Hazards of Materials for Emergency Response*, or another approved system, shall be applied to storage tanks containing liquids. The marking shall be located where it can be seen, such as on the side of the tank, the shoulder of an accessway or walkway to the tank or tanks, or on the piping outside of the diked area. If more than one tank is involved, the markings shall be so located that each tank can be identified. [**30**:21.7.2.1]

66.21.7.2.2* Security for Unsupervised Storage Tanks. Unsupervised, isolated aboveground storage tanks shall be secured and shall be marked to identify the fire hazards of the tank and the tank's contents to the general public. Where necessary to protect the tank from tampering or trespassing, the area where the tank is located shall be secured. [**30**:21.7.2.2]

66.21.7.3 Storage Tanks in Areas Subject to Flooding.

66.21.7.3.1 Water Loading.

66.21.7.3.1.1 The filling of a tank to be protected by water loading shall be started as soon as floodwaters are predicted to reach a dangerous flood stage. [**30**:21.7.3.1.1]

66.21.7.3.1.2 Where independently fueled water pumps are relied on, sufficient fuel shall be available at all times to permit continuing operations until all tanks are filled. [**30**:21.7.3.1.2]

66.21.7.3.1.3 Tank valves shall be locked in a closed position when water loading has been completed. [**30**:21.7.3.1.3]

66.21.7.3.2 Operating Instructions. Operating instructions or procedures to be followed in a flood emergency shall be established and implemented by personnel identified in 66.21.7.3.3. [**30**:21.7.3.2]

66.21.7.3.3 Personnel Training. Personnel responsible for activating and performing flood emergency procedures shall be trained in their implementation and shall be informed of the location and operation of valves and other controls and equipment necessary to effect the intent of these procedures. Personnel shall also be trained in the procedures required to place the facility back into service following a flood emergency. [**30**:21.7.3.3]

66.21.7.4 Removal from Service of Storage Tanks.

66.21.7.4.1* Closure of Aboveground Storage Tanks. Aboveground tanks taken out of service or abandoned shall be emptied of liquid, rendered vapor-free, and safeguarded against trespassing in accordance with NFPA 326, *Standard for the Safeguarding of Tanks and Containers for Entry, Cleaning, or Repair*, or in accordance with the requirements of the AHJ. [**30**:21.7.4.1]

66.21.7.4.2 Reuse of Aboveground Storage Tanks. Aboveground tanks shall be permitted to be reused for flammable or combustible liquids service provided they comply with applicable sections of this *Code* and are approved. [**30**:21.7.4.2]

66.21.7.4.3 Removal from Service of Underground Storage Tanks.

66.21.7.4.3.1 General. Underground tanks taken out of service or abandoned shall be emptied of liquid, rendered vapor-free, and safeguarded against trespassing in accordance with this section and in accordance with NFPA 326 or in accordance with the requirements of the AHJ. The procedures outlined in this section shall be followed when taking underground tanks temporarily out of service, closing them in place permanently, or removing them. *(See Annex C of NFPA 30 for additional information.)* [**30**:21.7.4.3.1]

66.21.7.4.3.2 Temporary Closure. Underground tanks shall be rendered temporarily out of service only when it is planned that they will be returned to active service, closed in place permanently, or removed within an approved period not exceeding 1 year. The following requirements shall be met:

(1) Corrosion protection and release detection systems shall be maintained in operation.
(2) The vent line shall be left open and functioning.
(3) The tank shall be secured against tampering.
(4) All other lines shall be capped or plugged. [**30**:21.7.4.3.2]

66.21.7.4.3.2.1 Tanks remaining temporarily out of service for more than 1 year shall be permanently closed in place or removed in accordance with 66.21.7.4.3.3 or 66.21.7.4.3.4, as applicable. [**30**:21.7.4.3.2.1]

66.21.7.4.3.3 Permanent Closure in Place. Underground tanks shall be permitted to be permanently closed in place if approved by the AHJ. All of the following requirements shall be met:

(1) All applicable AHJs shall be notified.
(2)*A safe workplace shall be maintained throughout the prescribed activities.
(3) All flammable and combustible liquids and residues shall be removed from the tank, appurtenances, and piping and shall be disposed of in accordance with regulatory requirements and industry practices, using a written procedure.
(4) The tank, appurtenances, and piping shall be made safe by either purging them of flammable vapors or inerting the potential explosive atmosphere. Confirmation that the atmosphere in the tank is safe shall be by testing of the atmosphere using a combustible gas indicator if purging, or an oxygen meter if inerting, at intervals in accordance with written procedures.

(5) Access to the tank shall be made by careful excavation to the top of the tank.
(6) All exposed piping, gauging and tank fixtures, and other appurtenances, except the vent, shall be disconnected and removed.
(7) The tank shall be completely filled with an inert solid material.
(8) The tank vent and remaining underground piping shall be capped or removed.
(9) The tank excavation shall be backfilled. [**30**:21.7.4.3.3]

66.21.7.4.3.4 Removal and Disposal. Underground tanks and piping shall be removed in accordance with the following requirements:

(1) The steps described in 66.21.7.4.3.3(1) through 66.21.7.4.3.3(5) shall be followed.
(2) All exposed piping, gauging and tank fixtures, and other appurtenances, including the vent, shall be disconnected and removed.
(3) All openings shall be plugged, leaving a ¼ in. (6 mm) opening to avoid buildup of pressure in the tank.
(4) The tank shall be removed from the excavated site and shall be secured against movement.
(5) Any corrosion holes shall be plugged.
(6) The tank shall be labeled with its former contents, present vapor state, vapor-freeing method, and a warning against reuse.
(7) The tank shall be removed from the site as authorized by the AHJ, preferably the same day. [**30**:21.7.4.3.4]

66.21.7.4.3.5 Temporary Storage of Removed Tanks. If it is necessary to temporarily store an underground tank that has been removed, it shall be placed in a secure area where public access is restricted. A ¼ in. (6 mm) opening shall be maintained to avoid buildup of pressure in the tank. [**30**:21.7.4.3.5]

66.21.7.4.3.6 Disposal of Tanks. Disposal of underground tanks shall meet the following requirements:

(1) Before a tank is cut up for scrap or landfill, the atmosphere in the tank shall be tested in accordance with 66.21.7.4.3.3(4) to ensure that it is safe.
(2) The tank shall be made unfit for further use by cutting holes in the tank heads and shell. [**30**:21.7.4.3.6]

66.21.7.4.3.7 Documentation. All necessary documentation shall be prepared and maintained in accordance with all federal, state, and local rules and regulations. [**30**:21.7.4.3.7]

66.21.7.4.3.8 Reuse of Underground Storage Tanks. Underground tanks shall be permitted to be reused for underground storage of flammable or combustible liquids provided they comply with applicable sections of this *Code* and are approved. [**30**:21.7.4.3.8]

66.21.7.5* Leak Detection and Inventory Records for Underground Storage Tanks. Accurate inventory records or a leak detection program shall be maintained on all Class I liquid storage tanks for indication of leakage from the tanks or associated piping. [**30**:21.7.5]

66.21.8 Inspection and Maintenance of Storage Tanks and Storage Tank Appurtenances.

66.21.8.1* Each storage tank constructed of steel shall be inspected and maintained in accordance with API Standard 653, *Tank Inspection, Repair, Alteration, and Reconstruction*, or STI SP001, *Standard for the Inspection of Aboveground Storage Tanks*, whichever is applicable. [**30**:21.8.1]

66.21.8.2 Each storage tank constructed of other materials shall be inspected and maintained in accordance with the manufacturer's instructions and applicable standards to ensure compliance with the requirements of this *Code*. [**30**:21.8.2]

66.21.8.3 Testing of storage tanks shall meet the requirements of 66.21.5. [**30**:21.8.3]

66.21.8.4 Each storage tank shall be maintained liquidtight. Each storage tank that is leaking shall be emptied of liquid or repaired in a manner acceptable to the AHJ. [**30**:21.8.4]

66.21.8.5 Each storage tank that has been structurally damaged, repaired, reconstructed, relocated, jacked, or damaged by impact, flood, or other trauma, or is suspected of leaking shall be inspected and tested in accordance with 66.21.5 or in a manner acceptable to the AHJ. [**30**:21.8.5]

66.21.8.6* Storage tanks and their appurtenances, including normal vents, emergency vents, overfill prevention devices, and related devices, shall be inspected and maintained to ensure that they function as intended in accordance with written procedures. [**30**:21.8.6]

66.21.8.7 Openings for gauging on storage tanks storing Class I liquids shall be provided with a vaportight cap or cover. Such covers shall be closed when not gauging. [**30**:21.8.7]

66.21.8.8* Facilities with aboveground storage tanks shall establish and implement a procedure to check for and remove water from the bottom of storage tanks that contain nonmiscible liquids. [**30**:21.8.8]

66.21.9 Change of Stored Liquid. Storage tanks that undergo any change of stored liquid shall be re-evaluated for compliance with Sections 66.21 through 66.25, as applicable. [**30**:21.9]

66.22 Storage of Liquids in Tanks — Aboveground Storage Tanks.

66.22.1 Scope. This chapter shall apply to the following:

(1) The storage of flammable and combustible liquids, as defined in 3.3.164.1 and 3.3.164.2 and Section 66.4, in fixed tanks that exceed 60 gal (230 L) capacity
(2) The storage of flammable and combustible liquids in portable tanks that exceed 660 gal (2500 L) capacity
(3) The storage of flammable and combustible liquids in intermediate bulk containers that exceed 793 gal (3000 L)
(4) The design, installation, testing, operation, and maintenance of such tanks, portable tanks, and bulk containers [**30**:22.1]

66.22.2 Definitions Specific to Section 66.22. For the purpose of this section, the terms in this section shall have the definition given. [**30**:22.2]

66.22.2.1 Fire-Resistant Tank. An atmospheric aboveground storage tank with thermal insulation that has been evaluated for resistance to physical damage and for limiting the heat transferred to the primary tank when exposed to a hydrocarbon fuel fire and is listed in accordance with UL 2080, *Standard for Fire Resistant Tanks for Flammable and Combustible Liquids*, or an equivalent test procedure. [**30**:22.2.1]

66.22.2.2 Floating Roof Tank. An aboveground storage tank that incorporates one of the following designs:

(1) A closed-top pontoon or double-deck metal floating roof in an open-top tank constructed in accordance with API Standard 650, *Welded Steel Tanks for Oil Storage*
(2) A fixed metal roof with ventilation at the top and roof eaves constructed in accordance with API Standard 650 and containing a closed-top pontoon or double-deck metal floating roof meeting the requirements of API Standard 650
(3) A fixed metal roof with ventilation at the top and roof eaves constructed in accordance with API Standard 650 and containing a metal floating cover supported by liquidtight metal floating devices that provide buoyancy to prevent the liquid surface from being exposed when half of the flotation is lost [**30**:22.2.2]

66.22.2.2.1 For the purposes of this section, an aboveground storage tank with an internal metal floating pan, roof, or cover that does not meet 66.22.2.2 or one that uses plastic foam (except for seals) for flotation, even if encapsulated in metal or fiberglass, shall meet the requirements for a fixed roof tank. [**30**:22.2.2.1]

66.22.2.3 Protected Aboveground Tank. An atmospheric aboveground storage tank with integral secondary containment and thermal insulation that has been evaluated for resistance to physical damage and for limiting the heat transferred to the primary tank when exposed to a hydrocarbon pool fire and is listed in accordance with ANSI/UL 2085, *Standard for Protected Aboveground Tanks for Flammable and Combustible Liquids*, or an equivalent test procedure. [**30**:22.2.3]

66.22.3 General Requirements. Storage of Class II and Class III liquids heated at or above their flash point shall follow the requirements for Class I liquids, unless an engineering evaluation conducted in accordance with Section 66.6 justifies following the requirements for some other liquid class. [**30**:22.3]

66.22.4* Location of Aboveground Storage Tanks.

66.22.4.1 Location with Respect to Property Lines, Public Ways, and Important Buildings.

66.22.4.1.1 Tanks storing Class I, Class II, or Class IIIA stable liquids whose internal pressure is not permitted to exceed a gauge pressure of 2.5 psi (17 kPa) shall be located in accordance with Table 66.22.4.1.1(a) and Table 66.22.4.1.1(b). Where tank spacing is based on a weak roof-to-shell seam design, the user shall present evidence certifying such construction to the AHJ upon request. [**30**:22.4.1.1]

66.22.4.1.2 Vertical tanks with weak roof-to-shell seams (*see 66.22.7.2*) that store Class IIIA liquids shall be permitted to be located at one-half the distances specified in Table 66.22.4.1.1(a), provided the tanks are not within the same diked area as, or within the drainage path of, a tank storing a Class I or Class II liquid. [**30**:22.4.1.2]

66.22.4.1.3 Tanks storing Class I, Class II, or Class IIIA stable liquids and operating at pressures that exceed a gauge pressure of 2.5 psi (17 kPa), or are equipped with emergency venting that will permit pressures to exceed a gauge pressure of 2.5 psi (17 kPa), shall be located in accordance with Table 66.22.4.1.3 and Table 66.22.4.1.1(b). [**30**:22.4.1.3]

66.22.4.1.4 Tanks storing liquids with boil-over characteristics shall be located in accordance with Table 66.22.4.1.4. Liquids with boil-over characteristics shall not be stored in fixed roof tanks larger than 150 ft (45 m) in diameter, unless an approved inerting system is provided on the tank. [**30**:22.4.1.4]

66.22.4.1.5 Tanks storing unstable liquids shall be located in accordance with Table 66.22.4.1.5 and Table 66.22.4.1.1(b). [**30**:22.4.1.5]

66.22.4.1.6 Tanks storing Class IIIB stable liquids shall be located in accordance with Table 66.22.4.1.6.

Exception: If located within the same diked area as, or within the drainage path of, a tank storing a Class I or Class II liquid, the tank storing Class IIIB liquid shall be located in accordance with 66.22.4.1.1.
[**30**:22.4.1.6]

66.22.4.1.7 Where two tank properties of diverse ownership have a common boundary, the AHJ shall be permitted, with the written consent of the owners of the two properties, to substitute the distances provided in 66.22.4.2 for the minimum distances set forth in 66.22.4.1.1. [**30**:22.4.1.7]

66.22.4.1.8 Where end failure of a horizontal pressure tank or vessel can expose property, the tank or vessel shall be placed with its longitudinal axis parallel to the nearest important exposure. [**30**:22.4.1.8]

66.22.4.2 Shell-to-Shell Spacing of Adjacent Aboveground Storage Tanks.

66.22.4.2.1* Tanks storing Class I, Class II, or Class IIIA stable liquids shall be separated by the distances given in Table 66.22.4.2.1. [**30**:22.4.2.1]

66.22.4.2.1.1 Tanks that store crude petroleum, have individual capacities not exceeding 3000 bbl (126,000 gal or 480 m^3), and are located at production facilities in isolated locations shall not be required to be separated by more than 3 ft (0.9 m). [**30**:22.4.2.1.1]

66.22.4.2.1.2 Tanks used only for storing Class IIIB liquids shall not be required to be separated by more than 3 ft (0.9 m) provided they are not within the same diked area as, or within the drainage path of, a tank storing a Class I or Class II liquid. If located within the same diked area as, or within the drainage path of, a tank storing a Class I or Class II liquid, the tank storing Class IIIB liquid shall be spaced in accordance with the requirements for Class IIIA liquids in Table 66.22.4.2.1. [**30**:22.4.2.1.2]

66.22.4.2.2 A tank storing unstable liquid shall be separated from any other tank containing either an unstable liquid or a Class I, II, or III liquid by a distance not less than one-half the sum of their diameters. [**30**:22.4.2.2]

66.22.4.2.3 Where tanks are in a diked area containing Class I or Class II liquids or in the drainage path of Class I or Class II liquids and are compacted in three or more rows or in an irregular pattern, greater spacing or other means shall be permitted to be required by the AHJ to make tanks in the interior of the pattern accessible for fire-fighting purposes. [**30**:22.4.2.3]

66.22.4.2.4 The minimum horizontal separation between an LP-Gas container and a Class I, Class II, or Class IIIA liquid storage tank shall be 20 ft (6 m). [**30**:22.4.2.4]

66.22.4.2.4.1 Means shall be provided to prevent Class I, Class II, or Class IIIA liquids from accumulating under adjacent LP-Gas containers by means of dikes, diversion curbs, or grading. [**30**:22.4.2.4.1]

Table 66.22.4.1.1(a) Location of Aboveground Storage Tanks Storing Stable Liquids — Internal Pressure Not to Exceed a Gauge Pressure of 2.5 psi (17 kPa)

		Minimum Distance (ft)	
Type of Tank	Protection	From Property Line That Is or Can Be Built Upon, Including the Opposite Side of a Public Way[a]	From Nearest Side of Any Public Way or from Nearest Important Building on the Same Property[a]
Floating roof	Protection for exposures[b]	½ × diameter of tank	⅙ × diameter of tank
	None	Diameter of tank but need not exceed 175 ft	⅙ × diameter of tank
Vertical with weak roof-to-shell seam	Approved foam or inerting system[c] on tanks not exceeding 150 ft in diameter[d]	½ × diameter of tank	⅙ × diameter of tank
	Protection for exposures[b]	Diameter of tank	⅓ × diameter of tank
	None	2 × diameter of tank but need not exceed 350 ft	⅓ × diameter of tank
Horizontal and vertical tanks with emergency relief venting to limit pressures to 2.5 psi (gauge pressure of 17 kPa)	Approved inerting system[b] on the tank or approved foam system on vertical tanks	½ × value in Table 66.22.4.1.1(b)	½ × value in Table 66.22.4.1.1(b)
	Protection for exposures[b]	Value in Table 66.22.4.1.1(b)	Value in Table 66.22.4.1.1(b)
	None	2 × value in Table 66.22.4.1.1(b)	Value in Table 66.22.4.1.1(b)
Protected aboveground tank	None	½ × value in Table 66.22.4.1.1(b)	½ × value in Table 66.22.4.1.1(b)

For SI units, 1 ft = 0.3 m.
[a]The minimum distance cannot be less than 5 ft (1.5 m).
[b]See definition 3.3.46 of NFPA 30, Protection for Exposures.
[c]See NFPA 69, *Standard on Explosion Prevention Systems*.
[d]For tanks over 150 ft (45 m) in diameter, use "Protection for Exposures" or "None," as applicable.
[**30:** Table 22.4.1.1(a)]

66.22.4.2.4.2 Where flammable or combustible liquid storage tanks are within a diked area, the LP-Gas containers shall be outside the diked area and at least 3 ft (0.9 m) away from the centerline of the wall of the diked area. [**30:**22.4.2.4.2]

66.22.4.2.5 If a tank storing a Class I, Class II, or Class IIIA liquid operates at pressures exceeding a gauge pressure of 2.5 psi (17 kPa) or is equipped with emergency relief venting that will permit pressures to exceed a gauge pressure of 2.5 psi (17 kPa), it shall be separated from an LP-Gas container by the appropriate distance given in Table 66.22.4.2.1. [**30:**22.4.2.5]

66.22.4.2.6 The requirements of 66.22.4.2.4 shall not apply where LP-Gas containers of 125 gal (475 L) or less capacity are installed adjacent to fuel oil supply tanks of 660 gal (2500 L) or less capacity. [**30:**22.4.2.6]

66.22.5 Installation of Aboveground Storage Tanks.

66.22.5.1 Tank Supports.

66.22.5.1.1 Tank supports shall be designed and constructed in accordance with recognized engineering standards. [**30:**22.5.1.1]

66.22.5.1.2 Tanks shall be supported in a manner that prevents excessive concentration of loads on the supported portion of the shell. [**30:**22.5.1.2]

66.22.5.1.3 In areas subject to earthquakes, tank supports and connections shall be designed to resist damage as a result of such shocks. [**30:**22.5.1.3]

66.22.5.2 Foundations for and Anchoring of Aboveground Storage Tanks.

66.22.5.2.1* Tanks shall rest on the ground or on foundations made of concrete, masonry, piling, or steel. [**30:**22.5.2.1]

66.22.5.2.2 Tank foundations shall be designed to minimize the possibility of uneven settling of the tank and to minimize corrosion in any part of the tank resting on the foundation. [**30:**22.5.2.2]

66.22.5.2.3 Where tanks storing Class I, Class II, or Class IIIA liquids are supported above their foundations, tank supports shall be of concrete, masonry, or protected steel.

Table 66.22.4.1.1(b) Reference Table for Use with Tables 66.22.4.1.1(a), 66.22.4.1.3, and 66.22.4.1.5

	Minimum Distance (ft)	
Tank Capacity (gal)	From Property Line that Is or Can Be Built Upon, Including the Opposite Side of a Public Way	From Nearest Side of Any Public Way or from Nearest Important Building on the Same Property
275 or less	5	5
276 to 750	10	5
751 to 12,000	15	5
12,001 to 30,000	20	5
30,001 to 50,000	30	10
50,001 to 100,000	50	15
100,001 to 500,000	80	25
500,001 to 1,000,000	100	35
1,000,001 to 2,000,000	135	45
2,000,001 to 3,000,000	165	55
3,000,001 or more	175	60

For SI units, 1 ft = 0.3 m; 1 gal = 3.8 L. [**30:** Table 22.4.1.1(b)]

Table 66.22.4.1.3 Location of Aboveground Storage Tanks Storing Stable Liquids — Internal Pressure Permitted to Exceed a Gauge Pressure of 2.5 psi (17 kPa)

		Minimum Distance (ft)	
Type of Tank	Protection	From Property Line that Is or Can Be Built Upon, Including the Opposite Side of a Public Way	From Nearest Side of Any Public Way or from Nearest Important Building on the Same Property
Any type	Protection for exposures*	1½ × value in Table 66.22.4.1.1(b) but not less than 25 ft	1½ × value in Table 66.22.4.1.1(b) but not less than 25 ft
	None	3 × value in Table 66.22.4.1.1(b) but not less than 50 ft	1½ × value in Table 66.22.4.1.1(b) but not less than 25 ft

For SI units, 1 ft = 0.3 m.
*See definition 3.3.46 of NFPA 30, Protection for Exposures. [**30:** Table 22.4.1.3]

*Exception: Single wood timber supports (not cribbing), laid horizontally, shall be permitted to be used for outside aboveground tanks if not more than 12 in. (300 mm) high at their lowest point. [**30:**22.5.2.3]*

Table 66.22.4.1.4 Location of Aboveground Storage Tanks Storing Boil-Over Liquids

		Minimum Distance (ft)	
Type of Tank	Protection	From Property Line that Is or Can Be Built Upon, Including the Opposite Side of a Public Way[a]	From Nearest Side of Any Public Way or from Nearest Important Building on the Same Property[a]
Floating roof	Protection for exposures[b]	½ × diameter of tank	⅙ × diameter of tank
	None	Diameter of tank	⅙ × diameter of tank
Fixed roof	Approved foam or inerting system[c]	Diameter of tank	⅓ × diameter of tank
	Protection for exposures[b]	2 × diameter of tank	⅔ × diameter of tank
	None	4 × diameter of tank but need not exceed 350 ft	⅔ × diameter of tank

For SI units, 1 ft = 0.3 m.
[a]The minimum distance cannot be less than 5 ft.
[b]See definition 3.3.46 of NFPA 30, Protection for Exposures.
[c]See NFPA 69, *Standard on Explosion Prevention Systems*. [**30:** Table 22.4.1.4]

66.22.5.2.4* Steel support structures or exposed piling for tanks storing Class I, Class II, or Class IIIA liquids shall be protected by materials having a fire resistance rating of not less than 2 hours.

Exception No. 1: Steel saddles do not need to be protected if less than 12 in. (300 mm) high at their lowest point.

*Exception No. 2: At the discretion of the AHJ, water spray protection in accordance with NFPA 15, Standard for Water Spray Fixed Systems for Fire Protection, or NFPA 13, is permitted to be used. [**30:**22.5.2.4]*

66.22.5.2.5 Where a tank is located in an area subject to flooding, provisions shall be taken to prevent tanks, either full or empty, from floating during a rise in water level up to the established maximum flood stage. *(See 66.21.7.3.)* [**30:**22.5.2.5]

66.22.6 Vent Piping for Aboveground Tanks. Piping for normal and emergency relief venting shall be constructed in accordance with Section 66.27. [**30:**22.6]

Table 66.22.4.1.5 Location of Aboveground Storage Tanks Storing Unstable Liquids

Type of Tank	Protection	Minimum Distance (ft)	
		From Property Line that Is or Can Be Built Upon, Including the Opposite Side of a Public Way	From Nearest Side of Any Public Way or from Nearest Important Building on the Same Property[a]
Horizontal and vertical tanks with emergency relief venting to permit pressure not in excess of a gauge pressure of 2.5 psi (17 kPa)	Tank protected with any one of the following: approved water spray, approved inerting,[a] approved insulation and refrigeration, approved barricade	Value in Table 66.22.4.1.1(b) but not less than 25 ft	Not less than 25 ft
	Protection for exposures[b]	2½ × value in Table 66.22.4.1.1(b) but not less than 50 ft	Not less than 50 ft
	None	5 × value in Table 66.22.4.1.1(b) but not less than 100 ft	Not less than 100 ft
Horizontal and vertical tanks with emergency relief venting to permit pressure over a gauge pressure of 2.5 psi (17 kPa)	Tank protected with any one of the following: approved water spray, approved inerting,[a] approved insulation and refrigeration, approved barricade	2 × value in Table 66.22.4.1.1(b) but not less than 50 ft	Not less than 50 ft
	Protection for exposures[b]	4 × value in Table 66.22.4.1.1(b) but not less than 100 ft	Not less than 100 ft
	None	8 × value in Table 66.22.4.1.1(b) but not less than 150 ft	Not less than 150 ft

For SI units, 1 ft = 0.3 m.
[a]See NFPA 69, *Standard on Explosion Prevention Systems*.
[b]See definition 3.3.46 of NFPA 30, Protection for Exposures. [**30:** Table 22.4.1.5]

Table 66.22.4.1.6 Location of Aboveground Storage Tanks Storing Class IIIB Liquids

Tank Capacity (gal)	Minimum Distance (ft)	
	From Property Line that Is or Can Be Built Upon, Including the Opposite Side of a Public Way	From Nearest Side of Any Public Way or from Nearest Important Building on the Same Property
12,000 or less	5	5
12,001 to 30,000	10	5
30,001 to 50,000	10	10
50,001 to 100,000	15	10
100,001 or more	15	15

For SI units, 1 ft = 0.3 m; 1 gal = 3.8 L. [**30:** Table 22.4.1.6]

66.22.7 Emergency Relief Venting for Fire Exposure for Aboveground Storage Tanks.

66.22.7.1 General.

66.22.7.1.1 Every aboveground storage tank shall have emergency relief venting in the form of construction or a device or devices that will relieve excessive internal pressure caused by an exposure fire. [**30:**22.7.1.1]

66.22.7.1.1.1 This requirement shall apply to each compartment of a compartmented tank, the interstitial space (annulus) of a secondary containment–type tank, and the enclosed space of tanks of closed-top dike construction. [**30:**22.7.1.1.1]

66.22.7.1.1.2 This requirement shall also apply to spaces or enclosed volumes, such as those intended for insulation, membranes, or weather shields, that are capable of containing liquid because of a leak from the primary vessel. The insulation, membrane, or weather shield shall not interfere with emergency venting. [**30:**22.7.1.1.2]

66.22.7.1.1.3 Tanks storing Class IIIB liquids that are larger than 12,000 gal (45,400 L) capacity and are not within the diked area or the drainage path of tanks storing Class I or

Table 66.22.4.2.1 Minimum Shell-to-Shell Spacing of Aboveground Storage Tanks

		Fixed or Horizontal Tanks	
Tank Diameter	Floating Roof Tanks	Class I or II Liquids	Class IIIA Liquids
All tanks not over 150 ft (45 m) in diameter	⅙ × sum of adjacent tank diameters but not less than 3 ft (0.9 m)	⅙ × sum of adjacent tank diameters but not less than 3 ft (0.9 m)	⅙ × sum of adjacent tank diameters but not less than 3 ft (0.9 m)
Tanks larger than 150 ft (45 m) in diameter:			
If remote impounding is provided in accordance with 66.22.11.1	⅙ × sum of adjacent tank diameters	¼ × sum of adjacent tank diameters	⅙ × sum of adjacent tank diameters
If open diking is provided in accordance with 66.22.11.2	¼ × sum of adjacent tank diameters	⅓ × sum of adjacent tank diameters	¼ × sum of adjacent tank diameters

Note: The "sum of adjacent tank diameters" means the sum of the diameters of each pair of tanks that are adjacent to each other. See also A.66.22.4.2.1. [**30**: Table 22.4.2.1]

Class II liquids shall not be required to meet the requirements of 66.22.7.1.1. [**30**:22.7.1.1.3]

66.22.7.1.2 For vertical tanks, the emergency relief venting construction referred to in 66.22.7.1.1 shall be permitted to be a floating roof, a lifter roof, a weak roof-to-shell seam, or another approved pressure-relieving construction. [**30**:22.7.1.2]

66.22.7.1.3 If unstable liquids are stored, the effects of heat or gas resulting from polymerization, decomposition, condensation, or self-reactivity shall be taken into account. [**30**:22.7.1.3]

66.22.7.1.4 If two-phase flow is anticipated during emergency venting, an engineering evaluation shall be conducted in order to size the pressure-relieving devices. [**30**:22.7.1.4]

66.22.7.2 Weak Roof-to-Shell Seam Construction. If used, a weak roof-to-shell seam shall be constructed to fail preferential to any other seam and shall be designed in accordance with API Standard 650, *Welded Steel Tanks for Oil Storage*. [**30**:22.7.2]

66.22.7.3 Pressure-Relieving Devices.

66.22.7.3.1* Where entire dependence for emergency relief venting is placed upon pressure-relieving devices, the total venting capacity of both normal and emergency vents shall be sufficient to prevent rupture of the shell or bottom of a vertical tank or of the shell or heads of a horizontal tank. [**30**:22.7.3.1]

66.22.7.3.2 Emergency relief vent devices shall be vaportight and shall be permitted to be any one of the following:

(1) Self-closing manway cover
(2) Manway cover provided with long bolts that permit the cover to lift under internal pressure
(3) Additional or larger relief valve or valves [**30**:22.7.3.2.1]

66.22.7.3.3 The outlets of all vents and vent drains on tanks equipped with emergency relief venting that permits pressures to exceed a gauge pressure of 2.5 psi (17.2 kPa) shall be arranged to discharge so that localized overheating of or flame impingement on any part of the tank will not occur if vapors from the vents are ignited. [**30**:22.7.3.9]

66.22.7.3.4 Each commercial tank venting device shall have the following information either stamped or cast into the metal body of the device or included on a metal nameplate permanently affixed to it.

(1) Start-to-open pressure
(2) Pressure at which the valve reaches the full open position
(3) Flow capacity at the pressure indicated by 66.22.7.3.4(2) [**30**:22.7.3.10]

66.22.7.4* Extension of Emergency Vent Piping. Piping to or from approved emergency vent devices for atmospheric and low-pressure tanks shall be sized to provide emergency vent flows that limit the back pressure to less than the maximum pressure permitted by the design of the tank. Piping to or from approved emergency vent devices for pressure vessels shall be sized in accordance with the ASME *Boiler and Pressure Vessel Code*. [**30**:22.7.4]

66.22.8 Fire Control.

66.22.8.1* A fire-extinguishing system in accordance with an applicable NFPA standard shall be provided or shall be available for vertical atmospheric fixed-roof storage tanks larger than 50,000 gal (190 m^3) capacity, storing Class I liquids, if located in a congested area where there is an unusual exposure hazard to the tank from adjacent property or to adjacent property from the tank. [**30**:22.8.1]

66.22.8.2 Fixed-roof tanks storing Class II or Class III liquids at temperatures below their flash points and floating-roof tanks storing any liquid shall not require protection when installed in accordance with this section. [**30**:22.8.2]

66.22.9 Additional Requirements for Fire-Resistant Aboveground Storage Tanks.

66.22.9.1 Fire-resistant tanks shall be tested and listed in accordance with UL 2080, *Standard for Fire Resistant Tanks for Flammable and Combustible Liquids*. [**30**:22.9.1]

66.22.10 Additional Requirements for Protected Aboveground Storage Tanks.

66.22.10.1 Protected aboveground tanks shall be tested and listed in accordance with ANSI/UL 2085, *Standard for Protected Aboveground Tanks for Flammable and Combustible Liquids*. [**30**:22.10.1]

66.22.11* Control of Spills from Aboveground Storage Tanks. Every tank that contains a Class I, Class II, or Class IIIA liquid shall be provided with means to prevent an accidental release of liquid from endangering important facilities and adjoining property or from reaching waterways. Such means shall meet the requirements of 66.22.11.1, 66.22.11.2, 66.22.11.3, or 66.22.11.4, whichever is applicable. [**30:**22.11]

66.22.11.1 Remote Impounding. Where control of spills is provided by drainage to a remote impounding area so that spilled liquid does not collect around tanks, the requirements of 66.22.11.1.1 through 66.22.11.1.4 shall apply. [**30:**22.11.1]

66.22.11.1.1 The drainage route shall have a slope of not less than 1 percent away from the tank for at least 50 ft (15 m) toward the impounding area. [**30:**22.11.1.1]

66.22.11.1.2 The impounding area shall have a capacity not less than that of the largest tank that drains into it.

Exception: Where compliance with 66.22.11.1.2 is not possible because there is not enough open area around the tanks, "partial" remote impounding for a percentage of the required capacity is permitted. The remainder of the volume required for spill control can be provided by open diking meeting the requirements of 66.22.11.2. [**30:**22.11.1.2]

66.22.11.1.3 The drainage route shall be located so that, if the liquid in the drainage system is ignited, the fire will not seriously expose tanks or adjoining property. [**30:**22.11.1.3]

66.22.11.1.4 The impounding area shall be located so that, when filled to capacity, the liquid will not be closer than 50 ft (15 m) from any property line that is or can be built upon or from any tank.

Exception: Where partial remote impounding as provided for in 66.22.11.1.2 is used, the liquid in the partial remote impounding area shall meet the requirements of 66.22.11.1.4. Tank spacing shall be determined based on the diked tank provisions of Table 66.22.4.2.1. [**30:**22.11.1.4]

66.22.11.2 Impounding Around Tanks by Open Diking. Where control of spills is provided by means of impounding by open diking around the tanks, such systems shall meet the requirements of 66.22.11.2.1 through 66.22.11.2.8. [**30:**22.11.2]

66.22.11.2.1 A slope of not less than 1 percent away from the tank shall be provided for at least 50 ft (15 m) or to the dike base, whichever is less. [**30:**22.11.2.1]

66.22.11.2.2* The volumetric capacity of the diked area shall not be less than the greatest amount of liquid that can be released from the largest tank within the diked area, assuming a full tank. [**30:**22.11.2.2]

66.22.11.2.2.1 To allow for volume occupied by tanks, the capacity of the diked area enclosing more than one tank shall be calculated after deducting the volume of the tanks, other than the largest tank, below the height of the dike. [**30:**22.11.2.2.1]

66.22.11.2.3 To permit access, the outside base of the dike at ground level shall be no closer than 10 ft (3 m) to any property line that is or can be built upon. [**30:**22.11.2.3]

66.22.11.2.4 Walls of the diked area shall be of earth, steel, concrete, or solid masonry designed to be liquidtight and to withstand a full hydrostatic head. [**30:**22.11.2.4]

66.22.11.2.4.1* Earthen walls 3 ft (0.9 m) or more in height shall have a flat section at the top not less than 2 ft (0.6 m) wide and shall have a slope that is consistent with the angle of repose of the material of which the wall is constructed. [**30:**22.11.2.4.1]

66.22.11.2.5 Where the average interior height of the walls of the diked area exceeds 6 ft (1.8 m), provisions shall be made for normal access; necessary emergency access to tanks, valves, and other equipment; and egress from the diked enclosure. The following requirements shall apply:

(1) Where the average height of a dike containing Class I liquids is over 12 ft (3.6 m) high, measured from interior grade, or where the distance between any tank and the top inside edge of the dike wall is less than the height of the dike wall, provisions shall be made for operation of valves and for access to tank roof(s) without entering below the top of the dike. These provisions shall be permitted to be met through the use of remote-operated valves, elevated walkways, or other arrangements.
(2) Piping passing through dike walls shall be designed to withstand imposed stresses as a result of settlement or fire exposure.
(3) The distance between the shell of any tank and the toe of the interior of the dike wall shall be not less than 5 ft (1.5 m). [**30:**22.11.2.5]

66.22.11.2.6 Each diked area containing two or more tanks shall be subdivided, preferably by drainage channels or at least by intermediate dikes, in order to prevent minor spills from a tank from endangering adjacent tanks within the diked area. [**30:**22.11.2.6]

66.22.11.2.6.1 The drainage channels or intermediate dikes shall be located between tanks so as to take full advantage of the space with due regard for the individual tank capacities. [**30:**22.11.2.6.1]

66.22.11.2.6.2 Intermediate dikes shall be not less than 18 in. (450 mm) in height. [**30:**22.11.2.6.2]

66.22.11.2.6.3 Subdivision shall be provided according to the requirements of 66.22.11.2.6.3.1, 66.22.11.2.6.3.2, 66.22.11.2.6.3.3, 66.22.11.2.6.3.4, or 66.22.11.2.6.3.5, whichever is applicable. [**30:**22.11.2.6.3]

66.22.11.2.6.3.1 Where stable liquids are stored in vertical cone roof tanks of weak roof-to-shell seam design or in floating roof tanks, one subdivision shall be provided for each tank greater than 10,000 bbl (420,000 gal or 1590 m^3) capacity. In addition, one subdivision shall be provided for each group of tanks [with no individual tank exceeding 10,000 bbl (420,000 gal or 1590 m^3) capacity] having an aggregate capacity not greater than 15,000 bbl (630,000 gal or 2385 m^3). [**30:**22.11.2.6.3.1]

66.22.11.2.6.3.2 Where crude petroleum is stored in producing areas in any type of tank, one subdivision shall be provided for each tank greater than 10,000 bbl (420,000 gal or 1590 m^3) capacity. In addition, one subdivision shall be provided for each group of tanks [with no individual tank exceeding 10,000 bbl (420,000 gal or 1590 m^3) capacity] having an aggregate capacity not greater than 15,000 bbl (630,000 gal or 2385 m^3). [**30:**22.11.2.6.3.2]

66.22.11.2.6.3.3 Where stable liquids are stored in tanks not covered in 66.22.11.2.6.3.1, one subdivision shall be provided for each tank greater than 2380 bbl (100,000 gal or 380 m^3) capacity. In addition, one subdivision shall be provided for each group of tanks [with no individual tank exceeding 2380 bbl (100,000 gal or 380 m^3) capacity] having an aggregate capacity not greater than 3750 bbl (150,000 gal or 570 m^3). [**30:**22.11.2.6.3.3]

66.22.11.2.6.3.4* Where unstable liquids are stored in any type of tank, one subdivision shall be provided for each tank.

Exception: Tanks that store unstable liquids and that are installed with drainage meeting the requirements of NFPA 15 need not meet this requirement. [30:22.11.2.6.3.4]

66.22.11.2.6.3.5 Whenever two or more tanks storing Class I liquids, any one of which is over 150 ft (45 m) in diameter, are located in a common diked area, intermediate dikes shall be provided between adjacent tanks to hold at least 10 percent of the capacity of the tank so enclosed, not including the volume displaced by the tank. [**30:**22.11.2.6.3.5]

66.22.11.2.7 Where provision is made for draining water from diked areas, such drains shall be controlled to prevent liquids from entering natural water courses, public sewers, or public drains. [**30:**22.11.2.7]

66.22.11.2.7.1 Control of drainage shall be accessible under fire conditions from outside the dike. [**30:**22.11.2.7.1]

66.22.11.2.8 Storage of combustible materials, empty drums, full drums, or barrels shall not be permitted within the diked area. [**30:**22.11.2.8]

66.22.11.3 Impounding Around Tanks by Closed-Top Diking. Where control of spills is provided by means of impounding by closed-top diking around the tanks, such systems shall meet all of the requirements of 66.22.11.4 or shall meet the requirements of 66.22.11.3.1 through 66.22.11.3.4. [**30:**22.11.3]

66.22.11.3.1* The volumetric capacity of the diked area shall not be less than the greatest amount of liquid that can be released from the largest tank within the diked area, assuming a full tank. [**30:**22.11.3.1]

66.22.11.3.2 To allow for volume occupied by tanks, the capacity of the diked area enclosing more than one tank shall be calculated after deducting the volume of the tanks, other than the largest tank, below the height of the dike. [**30:**22.11.3.2]

66.22.11.3.3 To permit access, the outside base of the dike at ground level shall be no closer than 10 ft (3 m) to any property line that is or can be built upon. [**30:**22.11.3.3]

66.22.11.3.4 Walls of the diked area shall be of steel, concrete, or solid masonry designed to be liquidtight and to withstand a full hydrostatic head. [**30:**22.11.3.4]

66.22.11.3.5 Where provision is made for draining water from diked areas, such drains shall be controlled to prevent liquids from entering natural water courses, public sewers, or public drains. [**30:**22.11.3.5]

66.22.11.3.5.1 Control of drainage shall be accessible under fire conditions from outside the dike. [**30:**22.11.3.5.1]

66.22.11.3.6 Storage of combustible materials, empty drums, full drums, or barrels shall not be permitted within the diked area. [**30:**22.11.3.6]

66.22.11.3.7 The capacity of the primary tank shall not exceed that given in 66.22.11.4.1. [**30:**22.11.3.7]

66.22.11.3.8 All piping connections to the tank shall be made above the normal maximum liquid level. [**30:**22.11.3.8]

66.22.11.3.9 The tank shall be capable of resisting the damage from the impact of a motor vehicle, or collision barriers shall be provided. [**30:**22.11.3.9]

66.22.11.3.10 Where the means of secondary containment is enclosed, it shall be provided with emergency venting in accordance with 66.22.7. [**30:**22.11.3.10]

66.22.11.3.11 Means shall be provided to establish the integrity of the secondary containment, in accordance with Section 66.21. [**30:**22.11.3.11]

66.22.11.3.12 Where the normal vent or the emergency vent device or both discharge outside the enclosure created by the closed-top diking, the tank within the enclosure shall comply with 66.22.11.4.4 and 66.22.11.4.5. [**30:**22.11.3.12]

66.22.11.3.13 Where the fill connection for the tank within the enclosure created by the closed-top diking is not located within the enclosure, the tank shall meet the requirements of 66.22.11.4.4 and 66.22.11.4.5. [**30:**22.11.3.13]

66.22.11.4 Secondary Containment–Type Aboveground Storage Tanks. Where a secondary containment–type tank is used to provide spill control, the tank shall meet all of the requirements of 66.22.11.4.1 through 66.22.11.4.10. [**30:**22.11.4]

66.22.11.4.1 The capacity of the listed primary tank for Classes I, II, and IIIA liquids shall not exceed 50,000 gal (189,000 L). [**30:**22.11.4.1]

66.22.11.4.2 All piping connections to the tank shall be made above the maximum liquid level. [**30:**22.11.4.2]

66.22.11.4.3 Means shall be provided to prevent the release of liquid from the tank by siphon flow. [**30:**22.11.4.3]

66.22.11.4.4 Means shall be provided for determining the level of liquid in the tank. This means shall be accessible to the delivery operator. [**30:**22.11.4.4]

66.22.11.4.5 Means shall be provided to prevent overfilling by sounding an alarm when the liquid level in the tank reaches 90 percent of capacity and by automatically stopping delivery of liquid to the tank when the liquid level in the tank reaches 95 percent of capacity. [**30:**22.11.4.5]

66.22.11.4.5.1 In no case shall these provisions restrict or interfere with the functioning of the normal vent or the emergency vent. [**30:**22.11.4.5.1]

66.22.11.4.6 Spacing between adjacent tanks shall comply with Table 66.22.4.2.1. [**30:**22.11.4.6]

66.22.11.4.7 The tank shall be capable of resisting the damage from the impact of a motor vehicle, or collision barriers shall be provided. [**30:**22.11.4.7]

66.22.11.4.8 Where the means of secondary containment is enclosed, it shall be provided with emergency venting in accordance with 66.22.7. [**30:**22.11.4.8]

66.22.11.4.9 Means shall be provided to establish the integrity of the secondary containment, in accordance with Section 66.21. [**30:**22.11.4.9]

66.22.11.4.10 The secondary containment shall be designed to withstand the hydrostatic head resulting from a leak from the primary tank of the maximum amount of liquid that can be stored in the primary tank. [**30:**22.11.4.10]

66.22.12 Equipment, Piping, and Fire Protection Systems in Remote Impoundment Areas and Diked Areas.

66.22.12.1* Location of Piping. Only piping for product, utility, or fire protection purposes directly connected to a tank or tanks within a single diked area shall be routed through a diked area, a remote impoundment area, a spillway draining to a remote impoundment area, or above a storage tank drainage area where the piping can be exposed to a fire.

Exception: Piping for other product lines and from adjacent tanks is permitted to be routed through such areas if engineering designs are provided to incorporate features to prevent the piping from creating an exposure hazard. [30:22.12.1]

66.22.12.2 Drainage.

66.22.12.2.1 Drainage shall be provided to prevent accumulation of any liquid under the piping by providing a slope of not less than 1 percent away from the piping for at least 50 ft (15 m). [30:22.12.2.1]

66.22.12.2.2 Corrosion-resistant piping and piping that is protected against corrosion shall be permitted to be buried where such drainage is not provided. [30:22.12.2.2]

66.22.12.3* Location of Equipment. If located in a remote impoundment area, a diked area, or a spillway draining to a remote impoundment area, process equipment, pumps, instrumentation, and electrical utilization equipment shall be located or protected so that a fire involving such equipment does not constitute an exposure hazard to the tank or tanks in the same area for a period of time consistent with emergency response capabilities. [30:22.12.3]

66.22.12.4 Fire Protection Systems. Hose connections, controls, and control valves for application of fire protection foam or water to tanks shall be located outside remote impoundment areas, diked areas, or spillways draining to a remote impoundment area. [30:22.12.4]

66.22.12.5 Combustible Materials. Structures such as stairways, walkways, instrumentation shelters, and supports for piping and equipment that are located in a remote impoundment area, diked area, or spillway draining to a remote impoundment area shall be constructed of noncombustible materials. [30:22.12.5]

66.22.13 Tank Openings Other Than Vents.

66.22.13.1 Each connection to an aboveground tank through which liquid can normally flow shall be provided with an internal or an external valve located as close as practical to the shell of the tank. [30:22.13.1]

66.22.13.2 Each connection below the liquid level through which liquid does not normally flow shall be provided with a liquidtight closure such as a valve, plug, or blind, or a combination of these. [30:22.13.2]

66.22.13.3 Openings for gauging on tanks storing Class I liquids shall be provided with a vaportight cap or cover. [30:22.13.3]

66.22.13.4 Filling and emptying connections for Class I, Class II, and Class IIIA liquids that are connected and disconnected shall be located outside of buildings at a location free from any source of ignition. [30:22.13.4]

66.22.13.4.1 Such connections shall be located not less than 5 ft (1.5 m) away from any building opening. [30:22.13.4.1]

66.22.13.4.2 Such connections for any liquid shall be closed and liquidtight when not in use and shall be properly identified. [30:22.13.4.2]

66.22.14 Aboveground Storage Tanks Located in Areas Subject to Flooding.

66.22.14.1 Vertical tanks shall be located so that the tops of the tanks extend above the maximum flood stage by at least 30 percent of their allowable storage capacity. [30:22.14.1]

66.22.14.2 Horizontal tanks that are located where more than 70 percent of the tank's storage capacity will be submerged at the established flood stage shall be secured by one of the following methods:

(1) Anchored to resist movement
(2) Attached to a foundation of steel and concrete or of concrete having sufficient weight to provide load for the tank when filled with liquid and submerged by flood water to the established flood stage
(3) Secured from floating by other means [30:22.14.2]

66.22.14.3 Tank vents or other openings that are not liquidtight shall extend above the maximum flood stage water level. [30:22.14.3]

66.22.14.4 A dependable water supply shall be used for filling an empty or partially filled tank.

Exception: Where filling the tank with water is impractical or hazardous because of the contents of the tank, the tank should be protected by other means against movement or collapse. [30:22.14.4]

66.22.14.5 Spherical or spheroid tanks shall be protected by any of the methods specified in 66.22.14. [30:22.14.5]

66.22.15 Collision Protection for Aboveground Storage Tanks. Where a tank is exposed to vehicular impact, protection shall be provided to prevent damage to the tank. [30:22.15]

66.22.16 Installation Instructions for Aboveground Storage Tanks. Factory-built aboveground tanks shall be provided with instructions for testing the tanks and for installation of the normal and emergency vents. [30:22.16]

66.22.17 Inspection and Maintenance of Aboveground Storage Tanks.

66.22.17.1 Inspection and maintenance of aboveground tanks shall meet the requirements of 66.21.8. [30:22.17.1]

66.22.17.2 Each aboveground steel tank shall be inspected and maintained in accordance with API 653, *Tank Inspection, Repair, Alteration, and Reconstruction*, or STI SP001, *Standard for Inspection of Aboveground Storage Tanks*, whichever is applicable. [30:22.17.2]

66.22.17.3 Each tank constructed of materials other than steel shall be inspected and maintained in accordance with manufacturers' instructions and applicable standards. [30:22.17.3]

66.22.17.4* Pontoons in external floating roof tanks shall be inspected, at intervals not exceeding 5 years, by visual and atmospheric testing methods to ensure that the pontoon covers are mechanically secured to the floating roof deck and to ensure the pontoons do not contain liquids or vapors resulting from leaks or corrosion holes in the pontoons. If liquids, or flammable vapor concentrations at or above 25 percent of the LFL are found, the liquids or vapors shall be safely removed and the source of the leak shall be repaired. The finding of vapors at levels below 25 percent of the LFL shall result either in the implementation of monitoring of the tank pontoons at least annually to assure that vapors in the flammable range are not achieved before corrective action is taken or removal of the tank from service. Rim vents, if any, shall also be inspected to ensure that they are not frozen open. [30:22.17.4]

66.23 Storage of Liquids in Tanks — Underground Tanks.

66.23.1 Scope. This section shall apply to the following:

(1) The storage of flammable and combustible liquids, as defined in 3.3.164.1 and 3.3.164.2, in fixed underground tanks
(2) The installation and operation of underground tanks [**30:**23.1]

66.23.2 Definitions Specific to Chapter 23. (Reserved)

66.23.3 General Requirements.

66.23.3.1 Class II and Class III Liquids at Elevated Temperatures. Storage of Class II and Class III liquids heated at or above their flash point shall follow the requirements for Class I liquids, unless an engineering evaluation conducted in accordance with Section 66.6 justifies following the requirements for some other liquid class. [**30:**23.3.1]

66.23.3.2 Installation. All underground tanks shall be installed in accordance with the manufacturer's instructions. [**30:**23.3.2]

66.23.3.3 Excavation. Excavation for underground tanks shall not undermine foundations of existing structures. [**30:**23.3.3]

66.23.3.4* Care in Handling of Tank. The tank shall not be damaged during delivery, unloading, and placement into the tank excavation. [**30:**23.3.4]

66.23.3.5* External Corrosion Protection for Underground Storage Tank. Underground tanks and their piping shall be protected by either of the following:

(1) A properly engineered, installed, and maintained cathodic protection system in accordance with recognized engineering standards of design
(2) Approved or listed corrosion-resistant materials or systems [**30:**23.3.5]

66.23.3.5.1* Selection of the type of protection to be employed shall be based upon the corrosion history of the area and the judgment of a qualified engineer.[**30:**23.3.5.1]

66.23.3.5.2* The AHJ shall be permitted to waive the requirements for corrosion protection where an engineering evaluation demonstrates that such protection is not necessary. [**30:**23.3.5.2]

66.23.4 Location of Underground Storage Tanks.

66.23.4.1 Underground tanks or tanks under buildings shall be located with respect to existing building foundations and supports so that the loads carried by the foundation are not transmitted to the tank. [**30:**23.4.1]

66.23.4.2 The distance from any part of a tank storing Class I liquids to the nearest wall of any basement or pit shall be not less than 1 ft (0.3 m) and to any property line that is or can be built upon shall not be less than 3 ft (0.9 m). [**30:**23.4.2]

66.23.4.3 The distance from any part of a tank storing Class II or Class III liquids to the nearest wall of any basement, pit, or property line shall be not less than 1 ft (0.3 m). [**30:**23.4.3]

66.23.5 Reserved.

66.23.6 Normal Venting for Underground Storage Tanks.

66.23.6.1* Tank venting systems shall be provided with sufficient capacity to prevent blowback of vapor or liquid at the fill opening while the tank is being filled. [**30:**23.6.1]

66.23.6.2 Vent piping shall be sized in accordance with Table 66.23.6.2, but shall not be less than 1.25 in. (32 mm) nominal inside diameter. [**30:**23.6.2]

Table 66.23.6.2 Nominal Vent Line Diameter in Inches

Maximum Flow (gpm)	Pipe Length*		
	50 ft	100 ft	200 ft
100	1.25	1.25	1.25
200	1.25	1.25	1.25
300	1.25	1.25	1.5
400	1.25	1.5	2
500	1.5	1.5	2
600	1.5	2	2
700	2	2	2
800	2	2	3
900	2	2	3
1000	2	2	3

For SI units, 1 in. = 25 mm; 1 ft = 0.3 m; 1 gal = 3.8 L.
*Assumes stated length of piping, plus 7 ells. [**30:** Table 23.6.2]

66.23.6.3 Where tank venting devices are installed in vent lines, their flow capacities shall be determined in accordance with 66.22.7.3.4. [**30:**23.6.3]

66.23.6.4 Piping for normal venting shall be designed in accordance with Section 66.27. [**30:**23.6.4]

66.23.7 Reserved.

66.23.8 Reserved.

66.23.9 Reserved.

66.23.10 Reserved.

66.23.11 Reserved.

66.23.12 Reserved.

66.23.13 Tank Openings Other than Vents.

66.23.13.1 Connections for all tank openings shall be liquidtight and vaportight. [**30:**23.13.1]

66.23.13.2 Openings for manual gauging, if independent of the fill pipe, shall be provided with a liquidtight and vaportight cap or cover. Covers shall be kept closed when not gauging. [**30:**23.13.2]

66.23.13.2.1 If inside a building, each such opening shall be protected against liquid overflow and possible vapor release by means of a spring-loaded check valve or other approved device. [**30:**23.13.2.1]

66.23.13.3 Fill and discharge lines shall enter tanks only through the top. [**30:**23.13.3]

66.23.13.4 Fill lines shall be sloped toward the tank. [**30:**23.13.4]

66.23.13.5 Underground tanks for Class I liquids having a capacity of more than 1000 gal (3800 L) shall be equipped with a tight fill device for connecting the fill hose to the tank. [**30**:23.13.5]

66.23.13.6 Filling, emptying, and vapor recovery connections for Class I, Class II, or Class IIIA liquids that are connected and disconnected shall be located outside of buildings at a location free from any source of ignition and not less than 5 ft (1.5 m) from any building opening or air intake. [**30**:23.13.6]

66.23.13.6.1 Such connections shall be closed and liquidtight and vaportight when not in use. [**30**:23.13.6.1]

66.23.13.6.2 Such connections shall be identified. [**30**:23.13.6.2]

66.23.13.7 Tank openings provided for purposes of vapor recovery shall be protected against possible vapor release by means of a spring-loaded check valve or dry-break connection, or other approved device, unless the opening is pipe-connected to a vapor processing system. [**30**:23.13.7]

66.23.13.7.1 Openings designed for combined fill and vapor recovery shall also be protected against vapor release unless connection of the liquid delivery line to the fill pipe simultaneously connects the vapor recovery line. [**30**:23.13.7.1]

66.23.13.7.2 All connections shall be vaportight. [**30**:23.13.7.2]

66.23.14 Underground Storage Tanks Located in Areas Subject to Flooding.

66.23.14.1* Tanks shall be anchored or shall be secured by approved means to resist movement when subjected to hydrostatic forces associated with high groundwater or floodwater. [**30**:23.14.1]

66.23.14.1.1 The design of the anchoring or securing method shall be based on the buoyancy of an empty tank that is fully submerged. [**30**:23.14.1.1]

66.23.14.1.2 Tank vents and other openings that are not liquidtight shall be extended above maximum flood stage water level. [**30**:23.14.1.2]

66.23.14.1.3 Each tank shall be so constructed and installed that it will safely resist external pressures if submerged. [**30**:23.14.1.3]

66.23.15 Reserved.

66.23.16 Installation Instructions for Underground Storage Tanks. Factory-built underground tanks shall be provided with instructions for testing and for installation of the normal vents. [**30**:23.16]

66.23.17 Inspection and Maintenance of Underground Storage Tanks.

66.23.17.1 Inspection and maintenance for underground tanks shall meet the requirements of 66.21.8. [**30**:23.17.1]

66.23.17.2 Overfill protection devices or systems shall be inspected and tested annually to ensure proper operation. [**30**:23.17.2]

66.24 Storage Tank Buildings.

66.24.1* Scope.

66.24.1.1 This section shall apply to installations of tanks storing Class I, Class II, and Class IIIA liquids in storage tank buildings. [**30**:24.1.1]

66.24.1.2 This section shall also apply to installations of aboveground storage tanks storing Class II, Class IIIA, or Class IIIB liquids in storage tank buildings where the liquids are heated at or above their flash points. In such cases, the liquids shall be regulated as Class I liquids unless an engineering evaluation conducted in accordance with Section 66.6 justifies following the requirements for some other liquid class. [**30**:24.1.2]

66.24.1.3 This section shall not apply to the following:

(1) Tanks covered by Sections 66.17, 66.18, and 66.19.
(2) A tank that has a canopy or roof that does not limit the dissipation of heat or dispersion of flammable vapors and does not restrict fire-fighting access and control. Such tanks shall comply with the provisions of this *Code*. [**30**:24.1.3]

66.24.2 Definitions Specific to Chapter 24. (Reserved)

66.24.3 Reserved.

66.24.4 Location of Storage Tank Buildings.

66.24.4.1 Tanks and associated equipment within the storage tank building shall be so located that a fire in the area shall not constitute an exposure hazard to adjoining buildings or tanks for a period of time consistent with the response and suppression capabilities of the fire-fighting operations available to the location. Compliance with 66.24.4.2 through 66.24.4.8 shall be deemed as meeting the requirements of 66.24.4.1. [**30**:24.4.1]

66.24.4.2 The minimum distance from exposed property lines and buildings for tank installations within structures having walls with a fire resistance rating of less than 2 hours shall be in accordance with Table 66.24.4.2. [**30**:24.4.2]

66.24.4.3 The capacity of any individual tank shall not exceed 100,000 gal (380 m^3) without the approval of the AHJ. [**30**:24.4.3]

66.24.4.4 Where protection for exposures is not provided, the distances given in Table 66.24.4.2 shall be doubled. The distances shall not be required to exceed 300 ft (90 m). [**30**:24.4.4]

66.24.4.5 Where a storage tank building has an exterior wall facing an exposure, the distances in Table 66.24.4.2 shall be permitted to be modified as follows:

(1) Where the wall is a blank wall having a fire resistance rating of not less than 2 hours, separation distance between the storage tank building and its exposure shall not be required to be greater than 25 ft (7.6 m).
(2) Where a blank wall having a fire resistance rating of not less than 4 hours is provided, the distance requirements of Table 66.24.4.2 shall not apply.
(3)*Where Class IA liquids or unstable liquids are stored, the exposing wall shall have explosion resistance in accordance with recognized engineering standards, and deflagration venting designed in accordance with NFPA 68 shall be provided in the nonexposing walls and roof. [**30**:24.4.5]

66.24.4.6 Other equipment associated with tanks, such as pumps, heaters, filters, and exchangers, shall not be located closer than 25 ft (7.6 m) to property lines where the adjoining property is or can be built upon or to the nearest important building on the same property that is not an integral part of the storage tank building. This spacing requirement shall not apply where exposures are protected as outlined in 66.24.4.2. [**30**:24.4.6]

Table 66.24.4.2 Location of Storage Tank Buildings with Respect to Property Lines, Public Ways, and the Nearest Important Building on the Same Property

Largest Tank — Operating Liquid Capacity (gal)	Minimum Distance from Property Line that Is or Can Be Built Upon, Including Opposite Side of Public Way (ft)				Minimum Distance from Nearest Side of Any Public Way or from Nearest Important Building on Same Property (ft)			
	Stable Liquid Emergency Relief		Unstable Liquid Emergency Relief		Stable Liquid Emergency Relief		Unstable Liquid Emergency Relief	
	Not over 2.5 psi	Over 2.5 psi	Not over 2.5 psi	Over 2.5 psi	Not over 2.5 psi	Over 2.5 psi	Not over 2.5 psi	Over 2.5 psi
Up to 12,000	15	25	40	60	5	10	15	20
12,001 to 30,000	20	30	50	80	5	10	15	20
30,001 to 50,000	30	45	75	120	10	15	25	40
50,001 to 100,000	50	75	125	200	15	25	40	60

For SI units, 1 gal = 3.8 L; 1 ft = 0.3 m; 1 psi = 6.9 kPa. [**30:** Table 24.4.2]

66.24.4.7 Tanks in which unstable liquids are stored shall be separated from potential fire exposures by a clear space of at least 25 ft (7.6 m) or by a wall having a fire resistance rating of not less than 2 hours. [**30:**24.4.7]

66.24.4.8 Each storage tank building and each tank within the building shall be accessible from at least two sides for fire fighting and fire control. [**30:**24.4.8]

66.24.4.9 Class I liquids and Class II or Class IIIA liquids heated above their flash points shall not be stored in basements. [**30:**24.4.9]

66.24.5 Construction of Storage Tank Buildings.

66.24.5.1 Storage tank buildings shall be constructed so as to maintain structural integrity for 2 hours under fire exposure conditions and to provide access and egress for unobstructed movement of all personnel and fire protection equipment. Compliance with 66.24.5.2 through 66.24.5.7 shall be deemed as meeting the requirements of 66.24.5.1. [**30:**24.5.1]

66.24.5.2* Buildings or structures shall be of at least 2-hour fire resistance rating. [**30:**24.5.2]

66.24.5.2.1 Noncombustible or combustible construction shall be permitted when protected by automatic sprinklers or equivalent protection subject to the approval of the AHJ. [**30:**24.5.2.1]

66.24.5.3 Where Class I liquids are stored above grade within buildings with basements or other belowgrade areas into which flammable vapors can travel, such belowgrade areas shall be provided with mechanical ventilation designed to prevent the accumulation of flammable vapors. Enclosed storage tank pits shall not be considered basements. [**30:**24.5.3]

66.24.5.4* Storage tank buildings where Class IA liquids are stored shall be designed to direct flame, combustion gases, and pressure resulting from a deflagration away from important buildings or occupied areas through the use of damage-limiting construction. The damage-limiting construction design shall be designed in accordance with NFPA 68 and shall be acceptable to the AHJ. [**30:**24.5.4]

66.24.5.5 Storage tank buildings where unstable liquids are stored shall be designed using an approved engineered construction method that is intended to limit damage from an explosion (deflagration or detonation, depending on the liquid). [**30:**24.5.5]

66.24.5.6* Access aisles not less than 3 ft (0.9 m) in width shall be provided and maintained from the exterior of the storage tank building into the building and around all storage tanks. [**30:**24.5.6]

66.24.5.7 A clear space of at least 3 ft (0.9 m) shall be maintained between the top of each tank and the building structure for buildings protected in accordance with 66.24.6.2.3. For buildings without fixed fire suppression systems, sufficient clear space shall be provided to allow for the application of hose streams to the top of the tank(s) for cooling purposes. [**30:**24.5.7]

66.24.6 Fire Protection for Storage Tank Buildings.

66.24.6.1 Manual Fire Control Equipment for Storage Tank Buildings.

66.24.6.1.1* Listed portable fire extinguishers shall be provided for facilities in such quantities, sizes, and types as could be needed for special storage hazards as determined in accordance with 66.21.6.1.2. [**30:**24.6.1.1]

66.24.6.1.2* Where the need is indicated in accordance with 66.21.6.3, water shall be utilized through standpipe and hose systems, or through hose connections from sprinkler systems using combination spray and straight stream nozzles to permit effective fire control. [**30:**24.6.1.2]

66.24.6.1.3 Where the need is indicated in accordance with 66.21.6.3, mobile foam apparatus shall be provided. [**30:**24.6.1.3]

66.24.6.2 Fixed Fire Control Equipment for Tank Buildings.

66.24.6.2.1 A reliable water supply or other suitable fire control agent shall be available in pressure and quantity to meet the fire demands indicated by special storage hazards or exposure as determined by 66.21.6.3. [**30:**24.6.2.1]

66.24.6.2.2* Hydrants, with or without fixed monitor nozzles, shall be provided in accordance with accepted practice. The number and placement shall depend on the hazard of the storage, or exposure, as determined by 66.21.6.3. [**30:**24.6.2.2]

66.24.6.2.3* Where the need is indicated by the hazards of storage or exposure as determined by 66.21.6.3, fixed protection shall be required utilizing approved foam, foam-water sprinkler systems, sprinkler systems, water spray systems, deluge systems, gaseous extinguishing systems, dry chemical extinguishing systems, fire-resistive materials, or a combination of these. [**30**:24.6.2.3]

66.24.6.2.3.1 When foam or foam-water fire protection systems are provided, discharge densities shall be determined based on the listing criteria for selected foam discharge devices, the foam concentrate, and the specific flammable or combustible liquids to be protected. [**30**:24.6.2.3.1]

66.24.6.2.4 If provided, fire control systems shall be designed, installed, and maintained in accordance with the following NFPA standards:

(1) NFPA 11, *Standard for Low-, Medium-, and High-Expansion Foam*
(2) NFPA 12, *Standard on Carbon Dioxide Extinguishing Systems*
(3) NFPA 12A, *Standard on Halon 1301 Fire Extinguishing Systems*
(4) NFPA 13, *Standard for the Installation of Sprinkler Systems*
(5) NFPA 15, *Standard for Water Spray Fixed Systems for Fire Protection*
(6) NFPA 16, *Standard for the Installation of Foam-Water Sprinkler and Foam-Water Spray Systems*
(7) NFPA 17, *Standard for Dry Chemical Extinguishing Systems*
(8) NFPA 25, *Standard for the Inspection, Testing, and Maintenance of Water-Based Fire Protection Systems* [**30**:24.6.2.4]

66.24.7 Reserved.

66.24.8 Electrical Systems for Storage Tank Buildings.

66.24.8.1 Installation of electrical utilization equipment and wiring shall meet the requirements of Section 66.7. [**30**:24.8.1]

66.24.8.2 Section 66.7 shall be used to determine the extent of classified locations for the purpose of installation of electrical equipment. [**30**:24.8.2]

66.24.8.2.1 In establishing the extent of a classified location, it shall not extend beyond a floor, wall, roof, or other solid partition that has no openings within the classified area. [**30**:24.8.2.1]

66.24.9 Containment, Drainage, and Spill Control from Storage Tank Buildings.

66.24.9.1 Drainage systems shall be designed to minimize fire exposure to other tanks and adjacent properties or waterways. Compliance with 66.24.9.2 through 66.24.9.6 shall be deemed as meeting the requirements of 66.24.9.1. [**30**:24.9.1]

66.24.9.2 The facility shall be designed and operated to prevent the discharge of flammable or combustible liquids to public waterways, public sewers, or adjoining property under normal operating conditions. [**30**:24.9.2]

66.24.9.3 Except for drains, solid floors shall be liquidtight and walls shall be liquidtight where they join the floor and for at least 4 in. (100 mm) above the floor. [**30**:24.9.3]

66.24.9.4 Openings to adjacent rooms or buildings shall be provided with noncombustible, liquidtight raised sills or ramps at least 4 in. (100 mm) in height or shall be otherwise designed to prevent the flow of liquids to the adjoining areas. [**30**:24.9.4]

66.24.9.4.1 An open-grated trench across the width of the opening inside of the room that drains to a safe location shall be permitted to be used as an alternative to a sill or ramp. [**30**:24.9.4.1]

66.24.9.5 Means shall be provided to prevent liquid spills from running into basements. [**30**:24.9.5]

66.24.9.6* The containment shall have a capacity not less than that of the largest tank that can drain into it. [**30**:24.9.6]

66.24.9.7 Emergency drainage systems shall be provided to direct flammable or combustible liquid leakage and fire-protection water to a safe location. [**30**:24.9.7]

66.24.9.8 Curbs, scuppers, or special drainage systems shall be permitted to be used. [**30**:24.9.8]

66.24.9.9 Emergency drainage systems, if connected to public sewers or discharged into public waterways, shall be equipped with traps or separators. [**30**:24.9.9]

66.24.10 Ventilation for Storage Tank Buildings.

66.24.10.1 Storage tank buildings storing Class I liquids or Class II or Class III liquids at temperatures at or above their flash points shall be ventilated at a rate sufficient to maintain the concentration of vapors within the building at or below 25 percent of the lower flammable limit. Compliance with 66.24.10.2 through 66.24.10.7 shall be deemed as meeting the requirements of 66.24.10.1. [**30**:24.10.1]

66.24.10.2* Ventilation shall be designed based on one of the following:

(1) Calculations based on the anticipated fugitive emissions *(See Annex E of NFPA 30 for calculation methods.)*
(2) Sampling of the actual vapor concentration under normal operating conditions
(3) Ventilation at a rate of not less than 1 cfm of exhaust air for each square foot of solid floor area (0.3 m^3/min/m^2) [**30**:24.10.2]

66.24.10.2.1 If vapor concentrations are confirmed by sampling, the sampling shall be conducted at a distance of a 5 ft (1.5 m) radius from each potential vapor source extending to or toward the bottom and the top of the enclosed storage area. The vapor concentration used to determine the required ventilation rate shall be the highest measured concentration during the sampling procedure. [**30**:24.10.2.1]

66.24.10.3 Ventilation shall be accomplished by natural or mechanical ventilation, with discharge or exhaust to a safe location outside the building. [**30**:24.10.3]

66.24.10.3.1 Recirculation of exhaust air shall be permitted only when it is monitored continuously using a fail-safe system that is designed to automatically sound an alarm, stop recirculation, and provide full exhaust to the outside in the event that vapor–air mixtures having concentrations over 25 percent of the lower flammable limit are detected. [**30**:24.10.3.1]

66.24.10.4* Provision shall be made for introduction of make-up air in such a manner as to avoid short-circuiting the ventilation. [**30**:24.10.4]

66.24.10.5 Ventilation shall be arranged to include all floor areas or pits where flammable vapors can collect. [**30**:24.10.5]

66.24.10.6 Where natural ventilation is inadequate, mechanical ventilation shall be provided and shall be kept in operation while flammable liquids are being handled. [**30**:24.10.6]

66.24.10.6.1 Local or spot ventilation, if provided, shall be permitted to be used for up to 75 percent of the required ventilation. [**30:**24.10.6.1]

66.24.10.7 Storage tank buildings with the interior grade more than 12 in. (300 mm) below the average exterior grade shall be provided with one of the following:

(1) Continuous mechanical ventilation in accordance with 66.24.10.2(3)
(2) A vapor detection system set to sound a warning alarm at a constantly attended location at 25 percent of the lower flammable limit, and to start the mechanical ventilation system [**30:**24.10.7]

66.24.11 Reserved.

66.24.12 Reserved.

66.24.13 Vents for Tanks Inside Storage Tank Buildings.

66.24.13.1 Vents for tanks inside tank buildings shall be designed to ensure that vapors are not released inside the building. Compliance with 66.24.13.2 through 66.24.13.6 shall be deemed as meeting the requirements of 66.24.13.1. [**30:**24.13.1]

66.24.13.2 Vents for tanks inside tank buildings shall be as required in 66.21.4.3 and 66.22.7. [**30:**24.13.2]

66.24.13.3 Emergency venting by the use of a weak roof-to-shell seam shall not be permitted. [**30:**24.13.3]

66.24.13.4 Automatic sprinkler systems designed in accordance with the requirements of Section 13.3 and NFPA 13 shall be accepted by the AHJ as equivalent to water spray systems for purposes of calculating the required airflow rates for emergency vents in 22.7.3.5 of NFPA 30, provided the density and coverage requirements of NFPA 15 are met. [**30:**24.13.4]

66.24.13.5 Vents shall terminate outside the building in accordance with 66.27.8.1. [**30:**24.13.5]

66.24.13.5.1 Emergency relief vents on protected aboveground tanks complying with UL 2085 containing Class II and Class III liquids shall be allowed to discharge inside the building. [**30:** 24.13.5.1]

66.24.13.6 Piping for normal and emergency relief venting shall meet the requirements of Section 66.27. [**30:**24.13.6]

66.24.14 Tank Openings Other than Vents for Tanks Inside Storage Tank Buildings.

66.24.14.1 Tank openings other than vents for tanks inside tank buildings shall be designed to ensure that flammable liquids or vapors are not released inside the building. Compliance with 66.24.14.2 through 66.24.14.9 shall be deemed as meeting the requirements of 66.24.14.1. [**30:**24.14.1]

66.24.14.2 All tank openings that are located at or below the maximum liquid level shall be liquidtight. Those that are located above the maximum liquid level shall be normally closed and shall be mechanically secured to prevent release of vapors. [**30:**24.14.2]

66.24.14.3 Each liquid transfer connection on any tank storing Class I or Class II liquids inside buildings shall be provided with one of the following:

(1) A normally closed, remotely activated valve
(2) An automatic-closing, heat-activated valve
(3) Another approved device [**30:**24.14.3]

66.24.14.4 Connections used for emergency disposal or to provide for quick cutoff of flow in the event of fire in the vicinity of the tank shall not be required to meet the requirement of 66.24.14.3. [**30:**24.14.4]

66.24.14.5 Each connection through which liquid can gravity flow from a tank inside a building shall be provided with an internal or an external valve located as close as practical to the shell of the tank. This valve shall be considered to be in compliance with 66.24.14.3. If a separate valve is used, both valves shall be located adjacent to each other. [**30:**24.14.5]

66.24.14.6* Openings for manual gauging of Class I or Class II liquids, if independent of the fill pipe, shall be provided with a vaportight cap or cover that shall be kept closed when not in use. [**30:**24.14.6]

66.24.14.6.1 Each such opening for any liquid shall be protected against liquid overflow and possible vapor release by means of a spring-loaded check valve or other approved device. [**30:**24.14.6.1]

66.24.14.7 The inlet of the fill pipe and the outlet of a vapor recovery line for which connections to tank vehicles and tank cars are made and broken shall be as follows:

(1) Located outside of buildings at a location free from any source of ignition
(2) Located not less than 5 ft (1.5 m) away from any building opening
(3) Closed tight and protected against tampering when not in use
(4) Identified [**30:**24.14.7]

66.24.14.8* Tanks storing Class I, Class II, or Class IIIA liquids inside buildings shall be equipped with a device, or other means shall be provided, to prevent overflow into the building. [**30:**24.14.8]

66.24.14.9 Tank openings provided for purposes of vapor recovery shall be protected against possible vapor release by means of a spring-loaded check valve or dry-break connection or other approved device, unless the opening is pipe-connected to a vapor processing system. [**30:**24.14.9]

66.24.14.9.1 Openings designed for combined fill and vapor recovery shall also be protected against vapor release unless connection of the liquid delivery line to the fill pipe simultaneously connects the vapor recovery line. [**30:**24.14.9.1]

66.24.14.9.2 All connections shall be vaportight. [**30:**24.14.9.2]

66.24.15 Detection and Alarm Systems for Storage Tank Buildings.

66.24.15.1 An approved means shall be provided to promptly notify those within the plant and the available public or mutual aid fire department of any fire or other emergency. [**30:**24.15.1]

66.24.15.2 Those areas, including buildings, where the potential exists for a flammable liquid spill shall be monitored as appropriate. Such methods shall include both of the following:

(1) Personnel observation or patrol
(2) Monitoring equipment that indicates a spill or leak has occurred in an unattended area [**30:**24.15.2]

66.24.16 Inspection and Maintenance for Storage Tank Buildings.

66.24.16.1 Combustible waste material and residues in operating areas shall be kept to a minimum, stored in covered metal containers, and disposed of daily. [**30**:24.16.1]

66.24.16.2 Storage of combustible materials and empty or full drums or barrels shall not be permitted within the storage tank building. [**30**:24.16.2]

66.25 Storage Tank Vaults.

66.25.1 Scope. This section shall apply to the design, construction, and installation of vaults for aboveground tanks. [**30**:25.1]

66.25.2 Definitions Specific to Section 66.25. (Reserved)

66.25.3 General Requirements.

66.25.3.1* Storage Tank Selection and Arrangement.

66.25.3.1.1 Aboveground tanks shall be permitted to be installed in vaults that meet the requirements of this section. [**30**:25.3.1.1]

66.25.3.1.2 Vaults shall be constructed and listed in accordance with UL 2245, *Standard for Below-Grade Vaults for Flammable Liquid Storage Tanks*. [**30**:25.3.1.2]

66.25.3.1.3 Except as modified by the provisions of this section, vaults shall meet all other applicable provisions of this *Code*. [**30**:25.3.1.3]

66.25.3.1.4 Tanks installed in storage tank vaults shall be listed for aboveground use. [**30**:25.3.1.4]

66.25.3.1.5 Each tank shall be in its own vault and shall be completely enclosed by the vault. [**30**:25.3.1.5]

66.25.3.1.6 Sufficient clearance between the tank and the vault shall be provided to allow for visual inspection and maintenance of the tank and its appurtenances. [**30**:25.3.1.6]

66.25.3.1.7 Backfill shall not be permitted around the tank. [**30**:25.3.1.7]

66.25.3.1.8 Dispensing devices shall be permitted to be installed on the tops of vaults. Dispensing devices used for motor fuels shall be installed in accordance with NFPA 30A, *Code for Motor Fuel Dispensing Facilities and Repair Garages*. [**30**:25.3.1.8]

66.25.3.1.9 At each entry point into the vault, a warning sign indicating the need for procedures for safe entry into confined spaces shall be posted. Each entry point shall be secured against unauthorized entry and vandalism. [**30**:25.3.1.9]

66.25.3.2 Storage Tank Appurtenances.

66.25.3.2.1 An approved means of overfill protection shall be provided for the tanks in the vaults. The use of ball float valves shall be prohibited. [**30**:25.3.2.1]

66.25.3.2.2 Fill connections for vaults installed inside buildings shall comply with 66.22.13.4. [**30**:25.3.2.2]

66.25.3.3 Vault Arrangement.

66.25.3.3.1 Vaults shall be permitted to be either above or below grade. [**30**:25.3.3.1]

66.25.4 Location of Storage Tank Vaults. In lieu of the separation distance requirements given in 66.22.4, separation distances between the vault and any of the following shall be permitted to be reduced to 0 ft (0 m), as measured from the outer perimeter of the vault wall:

(1) Any property line that is or can be built upon
(2) The near and far sides of a public way
(3) The nearest important building on the same property [**30**:25.4]

66.25.5* Construction and Installation of Storage Tank Vaults.

66.25.5.1 Construction Requirements. Vaults shall be designed and constructed in accordance with 66.25.5.1.1 through 66.25.5.1.4. [**30**:25.5.1]

66.25.5.1.1 The top of an abovegrade vault that contains a tank storing Class I liquid or Class II liquid stored at a temperature above its flash point shall be constructed of noncombustible material and shall be designed to be weaker than the walls of the vault to ensure that the thrust of any explosion occurring inside the vault is directed upward before destructive internal pressure develops within the vault. [**30**:25.5.1.1]

66.25.5.1.2 The top of an at-grade or belowgrade vault that contains a tank storing Class I liquid or Class II liquid stored at a temperature above its flash point shall be designed to relieve or contain the force of any explosion occurring inside the vault. [**30**:25.5.1.2]

66.25.5.1.3 Adjacent vaults shall be permitted to share a common wall. [**30**:25.5.1.3]

66.25.5.1.4 Where required, the vault shall be wind and earthquake resistant, in accordance with recognized engineering standards. [**30**:25.5.1.4]

66.25.5.2 Installation Requirements. Storage tank vaults shall be installed in accordance with the requirements of 66.25.5.2.1 and 66.25.5.2.2. [**30**:25.5.2]

66.25.5.2.1 Each vault and its tank shall be anchored to resist uplifting by groundwater or flooding, including when the tank is empty. [**30**:25.5.2.1]

66.25.5.2.2 Vaults that are not resistant to damage from the impact of a motor vehicle shall be protected by collision barriers. [**30**:25.5.2.2]

66.25.6 Reserved.

66.25.7 Reserved.

66.25.8 Reserved.

66.25.9 Containment, Drainage, and Spill Control for Storage Tank Vaults.

66.25.9.1 Means shall be provided to recover liquid from the vault. [**30**:25.9.1]

66.25.9.2 If a pump is used to meet this requirement, the pump shall not be permanently installed in the vault. [**30**:25.9.2]

66.25.9.3 Electric-powered portable pumps shall be approved for use in Class I, Division 1 locations, as defined in *NFPA 70*. [**30**:25.9.3]

66.25.10 Ventilation Systems for Storage Tank Vaults.

66.25.10.1 Vaults that contain tanks storing Class I liquids shall be ventilated at a rate of not less than 1 cfm/ft^2 of floor area (0.3 m^3/min/m^2), but not less than 150 cfm (4 m^3/min). [**30**:25.10.1]

66.25.10.2 Such ventilation shall operate continuously or shall be designed to operate upon activation of a vapor and liquid detection system. [**30**:25.10.2]

66.25.10.3 Failure of the exhaust airflow shall automatically shut down the dispensing system. [**30**:25.10.3]

66.25.10.4 The exhaust system shall be designed to provide air movement across all parts of the vault floor. [**30**:25.10.4]

66.25.10.5 Supply and exhaust ducts shall extend to within 3 in. (75 mm), but not more than 12 in. (300 mm) of the floor. [**30**:25.10.5]

66.25.10.6 The exhaust system shall be installed in accordance with the provisions of NFPA 91, *Standard for Exhaust Systems for Air Conveying of Vapors, Gases, Mists, and Noncombustible Particulate Solids*. [**30**:25.10.6]

66.25.11 Reserved.

66.25.12 Reserved.

66.25.13 Vents for Tanks Inside Storage Tank Vaults.

66.25.13.1 Vent pipes that are provided for normal tank venting shall terminate outside the vault and at least 12 ft (3.6 m) above ground level and shall meet the requirements of 66.27.8.1. [**30**:25.13.1]

66.25.13.2 Emergency vents shall be vaportight and shall be permitted to discharge inside the vault. Long-bolt manhole covers shall not be permitted for this purpose. [**30**:25.13.2]

66.25.14 Reserved.

66.25.15 Detection and Alarm Systems for Storage Tank Vaults.

66.25.15.1 Each vault shall be provided with an approved vapor and liquid detection system that is equipped with on-site audible and visual warning devices with battery backup. [**30**:25.15.1]

66.25.15.2 The vapor detection system shall sound an alarm when the system detects vapors that reach or exceed 25 percent of the lower flammable limit of the liquid stored. [**30**:25.15.2]

66.25.15.3 Vapor detectors shall be located no higher than 12 in. (300 mm) above the lowest point in the vault. [**30**:25.15.3]

66.25.15.4 The liquid detection system shall sound an alarm upon detection of any liquid, including water. [**30**:25.15.4]

66.25.15.5 Liquid detectors shall be located in accordance with the manufacturer's instructions. [**30**:25.15.5]

66.25.15.6 Activation of either the vapor detection system or the liquid detection system shall cause a signal to be sounded at an approved, constantly attended location within the facility serving the tanks or at an approved location. [**30**:25.15.6]

66.25.16 Inspection and Maintenance of Storage Tank Vaults and Equipment. Vaults and their required equipment shall be maintained in accordance with the requirements of this section. [**30**:25.16]

66.26 Reserved.

66.27 Piping Systems.

66.27.1 Scope.

66.27.1.1 This section shall apply to the design, installation, testing, operation, and maintenance of piping systems for flammable and combustible liquids or vapors. Such piping systems shall include but not be limited to pipe, tubing, flanges, bolting, gaskets, valves, fittings, flexible connectors, the pressure-containing parts of other components including but not limited to expansion joints and strainers, and devices that serve such purposes as mixing, separating, snubbing, distributing, metering, control of flow, or secondary containment. [**30**:27.1.1]

66.27.1.2 This section shall not apply to any of the following:

(1) Tubing or casing on any oil or gas wells and any piping connected directly thereto
(2) Motor vehicles, aircraft, boats, or piping that are integral to a stationary engine assembly
(3) Piping within the scope of any applicable boiler and pressure vessel code [**30**:27.1.2]

66.27.2 Definitions Specific to Section 66.27. For the purpose of this section, terms in this section shall have the definitions given. [**30**:27.2]

66.27.2.1 Corrosion Protection. A means to lessen or prevent the deterioration of the piping system from exposure to its contents or its environment. [**30**:27.2.1]

66.27.2.2 Flexible Connector. A connection joint in a piping system that allows differential movement of the piping system and limits system stress and mechanical damage. [**30**:27.2.2]

66.27.2.3 Leak. An unintended release of liquid or vapor from the piping system due to failure of the piping system. [**30**:27.2.3]

66.27.2.4 Low Melting Point Materials. Materials that melt at a low temperature, including but not limited to aluminum, copper, or brass; materials that soften on fire exposure, such as plastics; or nonductile materials, such as cast iron. [**30**:27.2.4]

66.27.2.5 Secondary Containment. Containment that is external to and separate from the primary piping system. [**30**:27.2.5]

66.27.3 General Requirements.

66.27.3.1 Performance Standards. The design, fabrication, assembly, test, and inspection of piping systems shall be suitable for the working pressures and structural stresses to be encountered by the piping system. Compliance with applicable sections of ASME B31, *Code for Pressure Piping*, and the provisions of this section shall be considered *prima facie* evidence of compliance with the foregoing provisions. [**30**:27.3.1]

66.27.3.2 Tightness of Piping. Piping systems shall be maintained liquidtight. A piping system that has leaks that constitute a hazard shall be repaired in a manner acceptable to the AHJ, or it shall be emptied of liquid, vapor freed, and no longer used. [**30**:27.3.2]

66.27.4 Materials of Construction for Piping Systems.

66.27.4.1 Materials Specifications. Pipe, valves, faucets, couplings, flexible connectors, fittings, and other pressure-containing parts shall meet the material specifications and pressure and temperature limitations of ASME B31, *Code for Pressure Piping*, except as provided for in 66.27.4.2, 66.27.4.3, and 66.27.4.4. [**30**:27.4.1]

66.27.4.2 Ductile Iron. Ductile (nodular) iron shall meet the specifications of ASTM A 395, *Standard Specification for Ferritic*

Ductile Iron Pressure-Retaining Castings for Use at Elevated Temperatures. [**30**:27.4.2]

66.27.4.3 Materials of Construction for Valves. Valves at storage tanks, as required by 66.22.13 and 66.24.14, and their connections to the tank shall be of steel or ductile iron, except as provided for in 66.27.4.3.1, 66.27.4.3.2, or 66.27.4.4. [**30**:27.4.3]

66.27.4.3.1 Valves at storage tanks shall be permitted to be other than steel or ductile iron where the chemical characteristics of the liquid stored are not compatible with steel or where the valves are installed internally to the tank. [**30**:27.4.3.1]

66.27.4.3.2* Valves installed externally to the tank shall be permitted to be other than steel or ductile iron if the material of construction has a ductility and melting point comparable to steel or ductile iron and is capable of withstanding the stresses and temperatures involved in fire exposure or the valves are otherwise protected from fire exposures, such as by materials having a fire resistance rating of not less than 2 hours. [**30**:27.4.3.2]

66.27.4.3.3 Cast iron, brass, copper, aluminum, malleable iron, and similar materials shall be permitted to be used on tanks described in 66.22.4.2.1.1 or on tanks storing Class IIIB liquids where the tanks are located outdoors and not within a diked area or drainage path of a tank storing a Class I, Class II, or Class IIIA liquid. [**30**:27.4.3.3]

66.27.4.4 Low Melting Point Materials.

66.27.4.4.1 Low melting point materials, as defined in 66.27.2.4, shall be compatible with the liquids being handled and shall be used within the pressure and temperature limitations of ASME B31, *Code for Pressure Piping*. [**30**:27.4.4.1]

66.27.4.4.2 Low melting point materials shall not be used as part of a tank's normal or emergency vent piping. [**30**:27.4.4.2]

66.27.4.4.3 Low melting point materials shall be permitted to be used underground. [**30**:27.4.4.3]

66.27.4.4.4 Low melting point materials shall be permitted to be used outdoors aboveground, outside a dike, outside a remote impounding area, or inside buildings, provided they meet one of the following conditions:

(1) They are resistant to damage by fire.
(2) They are located so that any leakage resulting from failure will not expose persons, important buildings, tanks, or structures.
(3) They are located where leakage can be controlled by operation of one or more accessible, remotely located valves. [**30**:27.4.4.4]

lp;&1q**66.27.4.4.5** Low melting point materials shall be permitted to be used within a dike or within a remote impounding area provided they meet one of the following:

(1) They are connected above the normal operating liquid level of the tank.
(2) They are connected below the normal operating liquid level of the tank and one of the following conditions is met:
   (a) The stored liquid is a Class IIIB liquid, the tank is located outdoors, and the piping is not exposed to a potential spill or leak of Class I, Class II or Class IIIA liquid.
   (b) The low melting point material is protected from fire exposure, such as by using materials that have a fire resistance of not less than 2 hours. [**30**:27.4.4.5]

66.27.4.4.6 Piping systems of these materials shall be designed and built in accordance with recognized standards of design for the particular materials chosen or with approved equivalent standards or shall be listed. [**30**:27.4.4.6]

66.27.4.5 Lining Materials. Piping, valves, and fittings shall be permitted to have combustible or noncombustible linings. [**30**:27.4.5]

66.27.4.6 Nonmetallic Piping.

66.27.4.6.1 Piping systems of nonmetallic materials, including piping systems incorporating secondary containment, shall be designed and built in accordance with recognized standards of design or approved equivalents and shall be installed in accordance with 66.27.4.4. [**30**:27.4.6.1]

66.27.4.6.2 Nonmetallic piping shall be built and used within the scope of their approvals or within the scope of UL 971, *Standard for Nonmetallic Underground Piping for Flammable Liquids*. [**30**:27.4.6.2]

66.27.4.6.3 Nonmetallic piping systems and components shall be installed in accordance with manufacturer's instructions. [**30**:27.4.6.3]

66.27.5 Pipe Joints.

66.27.5.1 Tightness of Pipe Joints.

66.27.5.1.1 Joints shall be made liquidtight and shall be welded, flanged, threaded, or mechanically attached. [**30**:27.5.1.1]

66.27.5.1.2* Joints shall be designed and installed so that the mechanical strength of the joint will not be impaired if exposed to a fire. [**30**:27.5.1.2]

66.27.5.1.3 Threaded joints shall be made with a suitable thread sealant or lubricant. [**30**:27.5.1.3]

66.27.5.1.4 Joints in piping systems handling Class I liquids shall be welded when located in concealed spaces within buildings. [**30**:27.5.1.4]

66.27.5.2 Flexible Connectors. Listed flexible connectors shall be permitted to be used where installed in accordance with 66.27.5.3. [**30**:27.5.2]

66.27.5.3 Friction Joints.

66.27.5.3.1 Pipe joints dependent upon the friction characteristics of combustible materials for mechanical continuity or liquidtightness of piping shall only be used outside of buildings above ground, except as provided for in 66.27.5.3.3, or below ground. [**30**:27.5.3.1]

66.27.5.3.2 Where such joints are used aboveground, either the piping shall be secured to prevent disengagement at the fitting or the piping system shall be so designed that any spill or leak resulting from disengagement will not expose persons, important buildings, or structures and can be controlled by remote valves. [**30**:27.5.3.2]

66.27.5.3.3 Pipe joints dependent on the friction characteristics of their components shall be permitted to be used inside buildings provided both of the following are met:

(1) They are located where leakage can be controlled by operation of an accessible, remotely located valve that is outside the fire risk area.
(2) The mechanical strength and liquidtightness of the joint is not dependent on the resiliency of a combustible material or component. [**30:**27.5.3.3]

66.27.6 Installation of Piping Systems.

66.27.6.1 General Requirements. Piping systems shall be supported and protected against physical damage, including damage from stresses arising from settlement, vibration, expansion, or contraction. The installation of nonmetallic piping shall be in accordance with the manufacturer's instructions. [**30:**27.6.1]

66.27.6.2* Load-Bearing Supports. Load-bearing piping supports that are located in areas with a high fire exposure risk shall be protected by one or more of the following:

(1) Drainage to a safe location to prevent liquid from accumulating under pipeways
(2) Fire-resistive construction
(3) Fire-resistant protective coatings or systems
(4) Water spray systems designed and installed in accordance with NFPA 15
(5) Other alternate means acceptable to the AHJ [**30:**27.6.2]

66.27.6.3 Pipe Penetrations. Piping that passes through or pierces a dike wall or the wall of a structure shall be designed to prevent damaging stresses and leakage due to settlement or fire exposure. [**30:**27.6.3]

66.27.6.4* Corrosion Protection. Aboveground piping systems that are subject to external corrosion shall be suitably protected. Underground piping systems shall be protected against corrosion in accordance with 66.23.3.5. [**30:**27.6.4]

66.27.6.5 Installation of Underground Piping. Underground piping shall be installed in accordance with 27.6.5 of NFPA 30.

66.27.6.6 Valves.

66.27.6.6.1 Piping systems shall contain valves to operate the system properly and to isolate the equipment in the event of an emergency. [**30:**27.6.6.1]

66.27.6.6.2 Piping systems in connection with pumps shall contain valves to properly control the flow of liquid both in normal operation and in the event of an emergency. [**30:**27.6.6.2]

66.27.6.6.3 Each connection to a piping system by which equipment such as tank cars, tank vehicles, or marine vessels discharges liquids into storage tanks shall be provided with a check valve for automatic protection against backflow if the piping arrangement is such that backflow from the system is possible. *(See also 66.22.13.1.)* [**30:**27.6.6.3]

66.27.6.7 Common Loading and Unloading Piping. If loading and unloading is done through a common pipe system, a check valve shall not be required. However, an isolation valve shall be provided. This valve shall be located so that it is accessible or shall be remotely operable. [**30:**27.6.7]

66.27.7 Testing of Piping Systems.

66.27.7.1 Initial Testing. Unless tested in accordance with the applicable sections of ASME B31, *Code for Pressure Piping*, all piping shall be tested before being covered, enclosed, or placed in use. [**30:**27.7.1]

66.27.7.1.1 Testing shall be done hydrostatically to 150 percent of the maximum anticipated pressure of the system or pneumatically to 110 percent of the maximum anticipated pressure of the system, and the test pressure shall be maintained while a complete visual inspection of all joints and connections is conducted. [**30:**27.7.1.1]

66.27.7.1.2 In no case shall the test pressure be less than a gauge pressure of 5 psi (35 kPa) measured at the highest point of the system, and in no case shall the test pressure be maintained for less than 10 minutes. [**30:**27.7.1.2]

66.27.7.2 Initial Testing of Secondary Containment Piping. The interstitial space of secondary containment–type piping shall be tested hydrostatically or with air pressure at a gauge pressure of 5 psi (35 kPa) or shall be tested in accordance with its listing or with the manufacturer's instructions. [**30:**27.7.2]

66.27.7.2.1 The pressure source shall be disconnected from the interstitial space to ensure that the test is being conducted on a closed system. [**30:**27.7.2.1]

66.27.7.2.2 The pressure shall be maintained for a minimum of 1 hour. [**30:**27.7.2.2]

66.27.7.3 Testing During Maintenance. Existing piping shall be tested in accordance with this subsection if the piping is leaking. [**30:**27.7.3]

66.27.7.3.1 Piping that could contain a Class I, Class II, or Class IIIA liquid or vapor shall not be tested using air. [**30:**27.7.3.1]

66.27.8 Vent Piping. Vent piping shall be designed, constructed, and installed in accordance with this section. [**30:**27.8]

66.27.8.1 Vent Piping for Aboveground Storage Tanks.

66.27.8.1.1 Where the outlets of vent pipes for tanks storing Class I liquids are adjacent to buildings or public ways, they shall be located so that vapors are released at a safe point outside of buildings and not less than 12 ft (3.6 m) above the adjacent ground level. [**30:**27.8.1.1]

66.27.8.1.2 Vapors shall be discharged upward or horizontally away from adjacent walls. [**30:**27.8.1.2]

66.27.8.1.3 Vent outlets shall be located so that vapors will not be trapped by eaves or other obstructions and shall be at least 5 ft (1.5 m) from building openings and at least 15 ft (4.5 m) from powered ventilation air intake devices. [**30:**27.8.1.3]

66.27.8.1.4 Manifolding of vent piping shall be prohibited except where required for special purposes such as vapor recovery, vapor conservation, or air pollution control. [**30:**27.8.1.4]

66.27.8.1.4.1 Where vent piping is manifolded, pipe sizes shall be capable of discharging, within the pressure limitations of the system, the vapors they are required to handle when all manifolded tanks are subject to the same fire exposure. [**30:**27.8.1.4.1]

66.27.8.1.5 Vent piping for tanks storing Class I liquids shall not be manifolded with vent piping for tanks storing Class II or Class III liquids unless positive means are provided to prevent the following:

(1) Vapors of Class I liquids from entering tanks storing Class II or Class III liquids
(2) Contamination
(3) Possible change in classification of the less volatile liquid
 [**30:**27.8.1.5]

66.27.8.1.6* Extension of Emergency Vent Piping. Piping to or from approved emergency vent devices for atmospheric and low-pressure tanks shall be sized to provide emergency vent flows that limit the back pressure to less than the maximum pressure permitted by the design of the tank. Piping to or from approved emergency vent devices for pressure vessels shall be sized in accordance with the ASME *Boiler and Pressure Vessel Code*. [**30**:27.8.1.6]

66.27.8.2 Vent Piping for Underground Tanks.

66.27.8.2.1* Vent pipes from underground tanks storing Class I liquids shall be located so that the discharge point is outside of buildings, higher than the fill pipe opening, and not less than 12 ft (3.6 m) above the adjacent ground level. [**30**:27.8.2.1]

66.27.8.2.2 Vent pipe outlets shall be located and directed so that vapors will not accumulate or travel to an unsafe location, enter building openings, or be trapped under eaves and shall be at least 5 ft (1.5 m) from building openings and at least 15 ft (4.5 m) from powered ventilation air intake devices. [**30**:27.8.2.2]

66.27.8.2.3 Vent pipes shall not be obstructed by devices provided for vapor recovery or other purposes unless the tank and associated piping and equipment are otherwise protected to limit back-pressure development to less than the maximum working pressure of the tank and equipment by the provision of pressure-vacuum vents, rupture discs, or other tank-venting devices installed in the tank vent lines. [**30**:27.8.2.3]

66.27.8.2.4 Vent outlets and devices shall be protected to minimize the possibility of blockage from weather, dirt, or insect nests. [**30**:27.8.2.4]

66.27.8.2.5 Vent piping shall be sized in accordance with Table 66.23.6.2. [**30**:27.8.2.5]

66.27.8.2.6 Vent pipes from tanks storing Class II or Class IIIA liquids shall terminate outside of the building and higher than the fill pipe opening. [**30**:27.8.2.6]

66.27.8.2.7 Vent outlets shall be above normal snow level. [**30**:27.8.2.7]

66.27.8.2.8 Vent pipes shall be permitted to be fitted with return bends, coarse screens, or other devices to minimize ingress of foreign material. [**30**:27.8.2.8]

66.27.8.2.9 Vent pipes and vapor return piping shall be installed without sags or traps in which liquid can collect. [**30**:27.8.2.9]

66.27.8.2.10 Condensate tanks, if utilized, shall be installed and maintained so that blocking of the vapor return piping by liquid is prevented. [**30**:27.8.2.10]

66.27.8.2.11 Vent pipes and condensate tanks shall be located so that they will not be subjected to physical damage. The tank end of the vent pipe shall enter the tank through the top. [**30**:27.8.2.11]

66.27.8.2.12 Where tank vent piping is manifolded, pipe sizes shall be such as to discharge, within the pressure limitations of the system, the vapors they could be required to handle when manifolded tanks are filled simultaneously. [**30**:27.8.2.12]

66.27.8.2.12.1 Float-type check valves installed in tank openings connected to manifolded vent piping to prevent product contamination shall be permitted to be used, provided that the tank pressure will not exceed that permitted by 23.5.3.2 of NFPA 30 when the valves close. [**30**:27.8.2.12.1]

66.27.8.2.13 Vent piping for tanks storing Class I liquids shall not be manifolded with vent piping for tanks storing Class II or Class III liquids unless positive means are provided to prevent the following:

(1) Vapors of Class I liquids from entering tanks storing Class II or Class III liquids
(2) Contamination
(3) Possible change in classification of the less volatile liquid [**30**:27.8.2.13]

66.27.9 Bonding and Grounding. Piping systems shall be bonded and grounded in accordance with 66.6.5.4. [**30**:27.9]

66.27.10* Identification and Marking of Piping Systems. Each loading and unloading riser shall be marked to identify the product for which it is to be used. [**30**:27.10]

66.27.11 Special Requirements for Marine Piping Systems.

66.27.11.1 Where piping is from a floating structure or pier, an approved flexible connector shall be permitted between the fixed shore piping and the piping on the floating structure or pier and between separate sections of the floating structure to accommodate changes in water level. [**30**:27.11.1]

66.27.11.2 The interior of the flexible connectors shall be compatible with the liquid handled. [**30**:27.11.2]

66.27.11.3 The exterior of the flexible connectors shall be resistant to or shielded from salt water and fresh water, ultraviolet radiation, physical damage, and damage by fire. [**30**:27.11.3]

66.27.11.4 The flexible connectors shall be suitable for the intended pressures and shall be tested in accordance with 66.27.7. [**30**:27.11.4]

66.27.12 Removal from Service of Piping Systems. Piping systems taken out of service or abandoned shall be temporarily or permanently closed in accordance with 66.27.12. [**30**:27.12]

66.27.12.1 Temporary Closure. (Reserved)

66.27.12.2 Permanent Closure in Place. (Reserved)

66.27.12.3 Permanent Removal. (Reserved)

66.28 Bulk Loading and Unloading Facilities for Tank Cars and Tank Vehicles.

66.28.1 Scope. This section shall apply to operations involving the loading or unloading of tank cars and tank vehicles. [**30**:28.1]

66.28.2 Reserved.

66.28.3 General Requirements.

66.28.3.1 Bonding and Grounding and Stray Currents.

66.28.3.1.1 Bonding for the control of static electricity shall not be required where the following conditions exist:

(1) Where tank cars and tank vehicles are loaded exclusively with products that do not have static-accumulating properties, such as asphalts (including cutback asphalts), most crude oils, residual oils, and water-soluble liquids
(2) Where no Class I liquids are handled at the loading facility and where the tank cars and tank vehicles loaded are used exclusively for Class II and Class III liquids at temperatures below their flash points
(3) Where tank cars and tank vehicles are loaded or unloaded through closed connections [**30**:28.3.1.1]

66.28.3.1.2* Loading and unloading facilities that are used to load liquids into tank vehicles through open domes shall be provided with a means for electrically bonding to protect against static electricity hazards. [**30**:28.3.1.2]

66.28.3.1.2.1 Such means shall consist of a metallic bond wire that is permanently electrically connected to the fill pipe assembly or to some part of the rack structure that is in electrical contact with the fill pipe assembly. [**30**:28.3.1.2.1]

66.28.3.1.2.2 The free end of this wire shall be provided with a clamp or an equivalent device for convenient attachment to some metallic part that is in electrical contact with the cargo tank of the tank vehicle. [**30**:28.3.1.2.2]

66.28.3.1.2.3 All parts of the fill pipe assembly, including, but not limited to, the drop tube, rack structure and piping, shall form a continuous electrically conductive path that is directed to ground through the rack assembly or by conductive wiring. [**30**:28.3.1.2.3]

66.28.3.1.3 Loading and unloading facilities that are used to transfer liquids into and from tank cars through open domes shall be protected against stray currents by permanently bonding the fill pipe to at least one rail and to the facility structure, if of metal. [**30**:28.3.1.3]

66.28.3.1.3.1 Multiple pipelines that enter the area shall be permanently bonded together. [**30**:28.3.1.3.1]

66.28.3.1.3.2 In areas where excessive stray currents are known to exist, all pipelines entering the area shall be provided with insulating sections to electrically isolate them from the facility piping.

Exception: These precautions need not be required where only Class II or Class III liquids, at temperatures below their flash points, are handled and where there is no probability that tank cars will contain vapors from previous cargoes of Class I liquids. [30:28.3.1.3.2]

66.28.4 Location of Loading and Unloading Facilities.

66.28.4.1 Tank vehicle and tank car loading and unloading facilities shall be separated from aboveground tanks, warehouses, other plant buildings, or the nearest line of adjoining property that can be built upon by a distance of at least 25 ft (7.6 m) for Class I liquids and for Class II and Class III liquids handled at temperatures at or above their flash points and at least 15 ft (4.6 m) for Class II and Class III liquids handled at temperatures below their flash points, measured from the nearest fill spout or transfer connection. [**30**:28.4.1]

66.28.4.2* These distances shall be permitted to be reduced if there is suitable protection for exposures. [**30**:28.4.2]

66.28.4.3 Buildings for pumps or shelters for personnel shall be permitted to be a part of the facility. [**30**:28.4.3]

66.28.5 Roofed Structures. A loading or unloading facility that has a canopy or roof that does not limit the dissipation of heat or dispersion of flammable vapors and does not restrict fire-fighting access and control shall be treated as an outdoor facility. [**30**:28.5]

66.28.6 Reserved.

66.28.7 Reserved.

66.28.8 Reserved.

66.28.9* Containment, Drainage, and Spill Control. Loading and unloading facilities shall be provided with drainage systems or other means to contain spills. [**30**:28.9]

66.28.10 Equipment.

66.28.10.1 Equipment such as piping, pumps, and meters used for the transfer of Class I liquids between storage tanks and the fill stem of the loading facility shall not be used for the transfer of Class II or Class III liquids unless one of the following conditions exists:

(1) Only water-miscible liquid mixtures are handled, and the class of the mixture is determined by the concentration of liquid in water.
(2) The equipment is cleaned between transfers. [**30**:28.10.1]

66.28.10.2 Remote pumps located in underground tanks shall have a listed leak detection device installed on the pump discharge side that will indicate if the piping system is not essentially liquidtight. [**30**:28.10.2]

66.28.10.2.1 This device shall be checked and tested at least annually according to the manufacturer's specifications to ensure proper installation and operation. [**30**:28.10.2.1]

66.28.11 Operating Requirements.

66.28.11.1 Loading and Unloading of Tank Vehicles.

66.28.11.1.1 Liquids shall be loaded only into cargo tanks whose material of construction is compatible with the chemical characteristics of the liquid. The liquid being loaded shall also be chemically compatible with the liquid hauled on the previous load unless the cargo tank has been cleaned. [**30**:28.11.1.1]

66.28.11.1.2 Before loading tank vehicles through open domes, a bonding connection shall be made to the vehicle or tank before dome covers are raised and shall remain in place until filling is completed and all dome covers have been closed and secured, unless one of the conditions of 66.28.3.1 exists. [**30**:28.11.1.2]

66.28.11.1.3 When transferring Class I liquids, or Class II or Class III liquids at temperatures at or above their flash points, engines of tank vehicles or motors of auxiliary or portable pumps shall be shut down during the making and breaking of hose connections. [**30**:28.11.1.3]

66.28.11.1.4 If loading or unloading is done without requiring the use of the motor of the tank vehicle, the motor shall be shut down throughout any transfer operations involving Class I liquids. [**30**:28.11.1.4]

66.28.11.1.5* Filling through open domes into tank vehicles that contain vapor–air mixtures within the flammable range or where the liquid being filled can form such a mixture shall be by means of a downspout that extends to within 6 in. (150 mm) of the bottom of the tank unless the liquid is not an accumulator of static electric charges. [**30**:28.11.1.5]

66.28.11.1.6 When top loading a tank vehicle with Class I or Class II liquids without a vapor control system, valves used for the final control of flow shall be of the self-closing type and shall be manually held open except where automatic means are provided for shutting off the flow when the vehicle is full. [**30**:28.11.1.6]

66.28.11.1.6.1 Automatic shutoff systems shall be provided with a manual shutoff valve located at a safe distance from the loading nozzle to stop the flow if the automatic system fails. [**30**:28.11.1.6.1]

66.28.11.1.6.2 When top loading a tank vehicle with vapor control, flow control shall be in accordance with 66.28.11.1.8 and 66.28.11.1.9. [**30**:28.11.1.6.2]

66.28.11.1.7 When bottom loading a tank vehicle, a positive means shall be provided for loading a predetermined quantity of liquid, together with a secondary automatic shutoff control to prevent overfill. [**30**:28.11.1.7]

66.28.11.1.7.1 The connecting components between the loading rack and the tank vehicle that are required to operate the secondary control shall be functionally compatible. [**30**:28.11.1.7.1]

66.28.11.1.7.2 The connection between the liquid loading hose or pipe and the tank vehicle piping shall be by means of a dry disconnect coupling. [**30**:28.11.1.7.2]

66.28.11.1.8 When bottom loading a tank vehicle that is equipped for vapor control, but when vapor control is not used, the tank shall be vented to the atmosphere, at a height not lower than the top of the cargo tank of the vehicle, to prevent pressurization of the tank. [**30**:28.11.1.8]

66.28.11.1.8.1 Connections to the facility's vapor control system shall be designed to prevent the escape of vapor to the atmosphere when the system is not connected to a tank vehicle. [**30**:28.11.1.8.1]

66.28.11.1.9 When bottom loading is used, reduced flow rates (until the fill opening is submerged), splash deflectors, or other devices shall be used to prevent splashing and to minimize turbulence. [**30**:28.11.1.9]

66.28.11.1.10 Metal or conductive objects, such as gauge tapes, sample containers, and thermometers, shall not be lowered into or suspended in a compartment while the compartment is being filled or immediately after cessation of pumping, in order to permit the relaxation of charge. [**30**:28.11.1.10]

66.28.11.1.11 Hose materials used for transfer shall be compatible with the liquids being handled. [**30**:28.11.1.11]

66.28.11.2 Loading and Unloading of Tank Cars.

66.28.11.2.1 Liquids shall be loaded only into tank cars whose material of construction is compatible with the chemical characteristics of the liquid. The liquid being loaded shall also be chemically compatible with the liquid hauled on the previous load unless the tank car has been cleaned. [**30**:28.11.2.1]

66.28.11.2.2* Filling through open domes into tank cars that contain vapor–air mixtures within the flammable range, or where the liquid being filled can form such a mixture, shall be by means of a downspout that extends to within 6 in. (150 mm) of the bottom of the tank unless the liquid is not an accumulator of static electric charges. [**30**:28.11.2.2]

66.28.11.2.3 When bottom loading is used, reduced flow rates (until the fill opening is submerged), splash deflectors, or other devices shall be used to prevent splashing and to minimize turbulence. [**30**:28.11.2.3]

66.28.11.2.4 Metal or conductive objects, such as gauge tapes, sample containers, and thermometers, shall not be lowered into or suspended in a compartment while the compartment is being filled or immediately after cessation of pumping, in order to permit the relaxation of charge. [**30**:28.11.2.4]

66.28.11.2.5 Hose materials used for transfer shall be compatible with the liquids being handled. [**30**:28.11.2.5]

66.28.11.3* Switch Loading. To prevent hazards due to a change in flash point of liquids, any tank car or tank vehicle that has previously contained a Class I liquid shall not be loaded with a Class II or Class III liquid unless proper precautions are taken. [**30**:28.11.3]

66.28.11.4 The person responsible for loading or unloading shall remain in attendance during the operation or be able to locally or remotely monitor and control the operation for the duration of the operation. [**30**:28.11.4]

*Exception: A responsible person shall not be required where a hazards analysis shows that the loading or unloading operation can be safely shut down in an emergency. [**30**:28.11.4]*

66.28.11.4.1* The responsible person shall be trained to recognize unsafe conditions and take appropriate actions. [**30**:28.11.4.1]

66.29 Wharves.

66.29.1 Scope.

66.29.1.1 This section shall apply to all wharves, as defined in 3.3.274, whose primary purpose is the bulk transfer of liquids. [**30**:29.1.1]

66.29.1.2 This section shall not apply to the following:

(1) Marine service stations, as covered in Chapter 30 and NFPA 30A
(2) Marinas and boatyards, as covered in Chapter 28 and NFPA 303
(3) Wharves that handle liquefied petroleum gas, as covered in Chapter 69 and NFPA 58, *Liquefied Petroleum Gas Code*, or liquefied natural gas, as covered in NFPA 59A, *Standard for the Production, Storage, and Handling of Liquefied Natural Gas (LNG)* [**30**:29.1.2]

66.29.2 Reserved.

66.29.3 General Requirements.

66.29.3.1 General-purpose wharves that handle bulk transfer of liquids and other commodities shall meet the requirements of Section 28.2 and NFPA 307, *Standard for the Construction and Fire Protection of Marine Terminals, Piers, and Wharves.* [**30**:29.3.1]

66.29.3.2 Incidental handling of packaged cargo of liquids and loading or unloading of general cargo, such as ships' stores, during transfer of liquids shall be conducted only when approved by the wharf supervisor and the senior officer of the vessel. [**30**:29.3.2]

66.29.3.3 Wharves at which liquid cargoes are to be transferred in bulk to or from tank vessels shall be at least 100 ft (30 m) from any bridge over a navigable waterway or from any entrance to or superstructure of a vehicular or railroad tunnel under a waterway. [**30**:29.3.3]

66.29.3.4 The termination of the loading or unloading fixed piping shall be at least 200 ft (60 m) from any bridge or from any entrance to or superstructure of a tunnel. [**30**:29.3.4]

66.29.3.5 The substructure and deck of the wharf shall be designed for the use intended. [**30**:29.3.5]

66.29.3.6 The deck of the wharf shall be permitted to be of any material that will afford the desired combination of flexibility, resistance to shock, durability, strength, and fire resistance. [**30**:29.3.6]

66.29.3.7 Heavy timber construction shall be permitted. [**30**:29.3.7]

66.29.3.8 Tanks used exclusively for ballast water or Class II or Class III liquids stored at temperatures below their flash points shall be permitted to be installed on a wharf designed to support the weight of the tank and its contents. [**30**:29.3.8]

66.29.3.9 Loading pumps capable of building up pressures that exceed the safe working pressure of cargo hose or loading arms shall be provided with bypasses, relief valves, or other arrangements to protect the loading facilities against excessive pressure. [**30**:29.3.9]

66.29.3.9.1 Relief devices shall be tested at least annually to determine that they function satisfactorily at their set pressure. [**30**:29.3.9.1]

66.29.3.10 All pressure hose and couplings shall be inspected at intervals recommended by the manufacturer for the service in which they are used. [**30**:29.3.10]

66.29.3.10.1 With the hose extended, the hose and couplings shall be tested using the in-service maximum operating pressure. [**30**:29.3.10.1]

66.29.3.10.2 Any hose showing material deterioration, signs of leakage, or weakness in its carcass or at the couplings shall be withdrawn from service and repaired or discarded. [**30**:29.3.10.2]

66.29.3.10.3 The hose materials used for transfer shall be compatible with the liquids being handled. [**30**:29.3.10.3]

66.29.3.11 Piping, valves, and fittings shall meet applicable requirements of Section 66.27 and shall also meet the following requirements:

(1) Flexibility of piping shall be assured by layout and arrangement of piping supports so that motion of the wharf structure resulting from wave action, currents, tides, or the mooring of vessels will not subject the piping to excessive strain.
(2) Pipe joints that depend on the friction characteristics of combustible materials or on the grooving of pipe ends for mechanical continuity of piping shall not be permitted.
(3) Swivel joints shall be permitted to be used in piping to which hose are connected and for articulated swivel-joint transfer systems, provided the design is such that the mechanical strength of the joint will not be impaired if the packing materials should fail, for example, by exposure to fire.
(4) Each line conveying Class I or Class II liquids leading to a wharf shall be provided with a readily accessible block valve located on shore near the approach to the wharf and outside of any diked area. Where more than one line is involved, the valves shall be identified as to their specific lines and grouped in one location.
(5) Means shall be provided for easy access to any cargo line valves that are located below the wharf deck. [**30**:29.3.11]

66.29.3.12 Pipelines on wharves that handle Class I or Class II liquids, or Class III liquids at temperatures at or above their flash points, shall be bonded and grounded. [**30**:29.3.12]

66.29.3.12.1 Insulating flanges or joints shall be installed for protection against stray currents. [**30**:29.3.12.1]

66.29.3.12.2 Bonding and grounding connections on all pipelines shall be located on the wharf side of insulating flanges, if used, and shall be accessible for inspection. [**30**:29.3.12.2]

66.29.3.12.3 Bonding between the wharf and the vessel shall not be required. [**30**:29.3.12.3]

66.29.3.13 Hose or articulated swivel-joint pipe connections used for cargo transfer shall be capable of accommodating the combined effects of change in draft and change in tide. Hose shall be supported to avoid kinking and damage from chafing. [**30**:29.3.13]

66.29.3.14 Mooring lines shall be kept adjusted to prevent surge of the vessel from placing stress on the cargo transfer system. [**30**:29.3.14]

66.29.3.15 Material shall not be placed on wharves in such a manner as to obstruct access to fire-fighting equipment or important pipeline control valves. [**30**:29.3.15]

66.29.3.16 Where the wharf is accessible to vehicle traffic, an unobstructed roadway to the shore end of the wharf shall be maintained for access of fire-fighting apparatus. [**30**:29.3.16]

66.29.3.17 Loading or unloading shall not commence until the wharf supervisor and the person in charge of the tank vessel agree that the tank vessel is properly moored and all connections are properly made. [**30**:29.3.17]

66.29.3.18 Mechanical work shall not be performed on the wharf during cargo transfer, except under special authorization based on a review of the area involved, methods to be employed, and precautions necessary. [**30**:29.3.18]

66.29.3.19 Sources of ignition shall be controlled during transfer of liquids. [**30**:29.3.19]

66.29.3.20 Vehicular traffic and mechanical work including, but not limited to, welding, grinding, and other hot work, shall not be performed during cargo transfer except as authorized by the wharf supervisor and the senior officer on the vessel. [**30**:29.3.20]

66.29.3.21 Smoking shall be prohibited at all times on the wharf during cargo transfer operations. [**30**:29.3.21]

66.29.3.22 For marine terminals handling flammable liquids and combustible liquids at temperatures at or above their flash points, Figure 66.29.3.22 shall be used to determine the extent of classified areas for the purpose of installation of electrical equipment. [**30**:29.3.22]

66.29.3.23 Where a flammable atmosphere can exist in the vessel cargo compartment, cargo transfer systems shall be designed to limit the velocity of the incoming liquid stream to 3 ft (0.9 m) per second until the compartment inlet opening is sufficiently submerged to prevent splashing. [**30**:29.3.23]

66.29.3.24 Filters, pumps, wire screens, and other devices that can produce static electric charges through turbulence shall be so located to allow a minimum of 30 seconds of relaxation time prior to discharging cargo into the compartment. [**30**:29.3.24]

66.29.3.25* Spill collection shall be provided around manifold areas to prevent spread of liquids to other areas of the wharf or under the wharf. [**30**:29.3.25]

66.29.3.26 Vapor seals shall be provided on all drain lines leaving the wharf. [**30**:29.3.26]

66.29.3.27 Where required, wharves shall have a system to isolate and shut down the loading operation in the event of

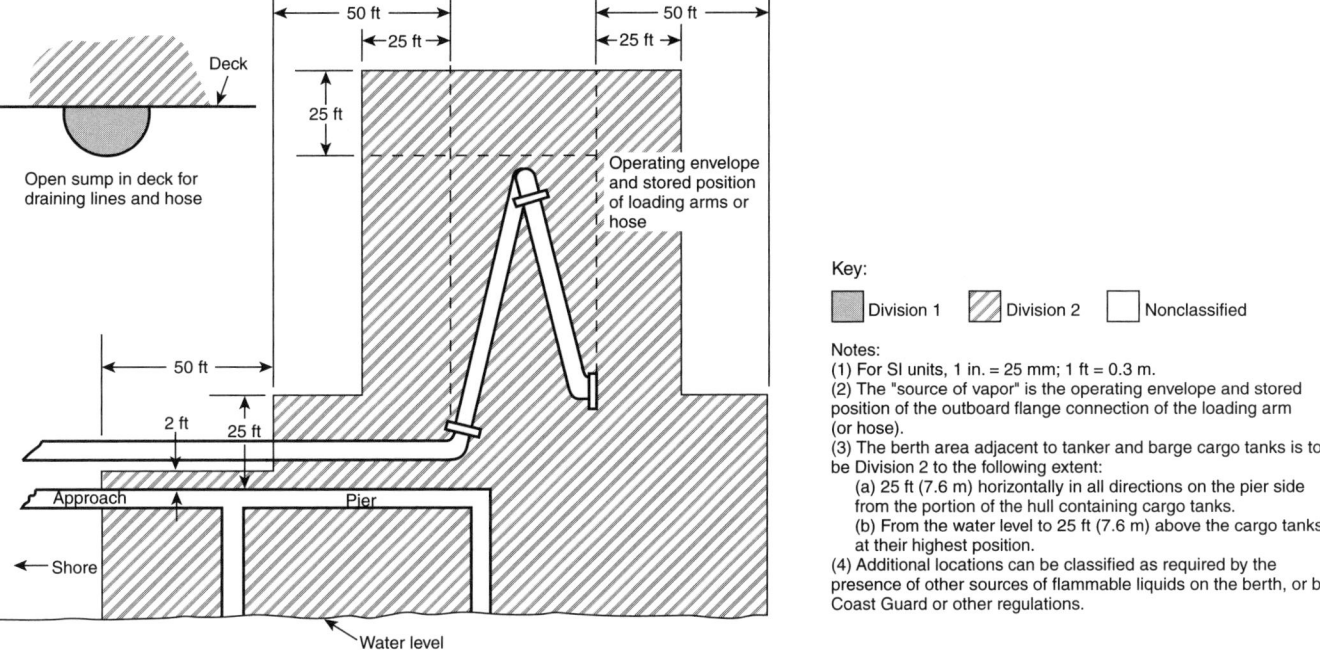

FIGURE 66.29.3.22 Area Classification for a Marine Terminal Handling Flammable Liquids. [30:Figure 29.3.22]

failure of a hose, loading arm, or manifold valve. This system shall meet all of the following requirements:

(1) If the protective system closes a valve on a gravity-fed or pipeline-fed loading system, it shall be designed to ensure the line is not subjected to damage from pressure surges.
(2) Emergency shutdown systems shall be permitted to be automatically or manually activated. [**30**:29.3.27]

66.29.3.27.1 Manually activated device(s) shall be identified and accessible during an emergency. [**30**:29.3.27.1]

66.29.3.28* Fire protection and emergency response equipment for wharves shall be related to the products being handled, emergency response capability, size, location, frequency of use, and adjacent exposures. [**30**:29.3.28]

66.29.3.28.1 Where a fire water main is provided, the main shall be permitted to be wet or dry. In all cases, isolation valves and fire department connections shall be provided at the wharf-to-shore connection. [**30**:29.3.28.1]

66.29.3.28.2 Where a fire water main is provided, hydrants and monitors shall also be provided so that effective fire water streams can be applied to any berth or loading manifold from two directions. [**30**:29.3.28.2]

66.29.3.28.3 Fire water pumps, fire hose, fire water mains, foam systems, and other fire suppression equipment shall be maintained and tested in accordance with NFPA 25, *Standard for the Inspection, Testing, and Maintenance of Water-Based Fire Protection Systems.* [**30**:29.3.28.3]

66.29.3.28.4 Where no fire water main is provided, at least two 150 lb (68 kg) dry chemical extinguishers shall be provided. The extinguishers shall be located within 50 ft (15 m) of pump or manifold areas and shall be easily reached along emergency access paths. [**30**:29.3.28.4]

Chapter 67   Flammable Solids

67.1 General.

67.1.1 The storage, use, and handling of flammable solids shall comply with the requirements of Chapter 60.

67.1.2 The storage, use, and handling of flammable solids in amounts exceeding the maximum allowable quantity permitted in control areas as set forth in Chapter 60 shall also comply with the requirements of NFPA 400, *Hazardous Materials Code.*

Chapter 68   Highly Toxic and Toxic Solids and Liquids

68.1 General.

68.1.1 The storage, use, and handling of highly toxic and toxic solids and liquids shall comply with Chapter 60.

68.1.2 The storage, use, and handling of highly toxic and toxic solids and liquids in amounts exceeding the maximum allowable quantity permitted in control areas as set forth in Chapter 60 shall also comply with the requirements of NFPA 400, *Hazardous Materials Code.*

Chapter 69   Liquefied Petroleum Gases and Liquefied Natural Gases

69.1 General Provisions.

69.1.1* Application.

69.1.1.1 The storage, use, and handling of liquefied petroleum gases (LP-Gas) shall comply with the requirements of this chapter; NFPA 58, *Liquefied Petroleum Gas Code*; and Sections 60.1 through 60.4 of this *Code*.

69.1.1.2 Where the provisions of Chapter 69 or NFPA 58 conflict with the provisions of Chapter 60, the provisions of this chapter and NFPA 58 shall apply.

69.1.1.3 Stationary Installations. Plans for stationary installations utilizing storage containers with aggregate water capacity exceeding 4000 gal (15.2 m^3), and all rooftop installations of ASME containers shall be submitted to the AHJ before the installation is started by the person or company that either installs or contracts to have the containers installed. *[See also 6.20.11.1(F) of NFPA 58.]* [**58:**4.3.1]

69.1.2 Permits. Permits, where required, shall comply with Section 1.12.

69.2 LP-Gas Equipment and Appliances.

69.2.1 Containers.

69.2.1.1 General.

69.2.1.1.1* Containers shall be designed, fabricated, tested, and marked (or stamped) in accordance with the regulations of the U.S. Department of Transportation (DOT); the ASME *Boiler and Pressure Vessel Code*, Section VIII, "Rules for the Construction of Unfired Pressure Vessels"; or the API-ASME *Code for Unfired Pressure Vessels for Petroleum Liquids and Gases*, except for UG-125 through UG-136. [**58:**5.2.1.1]

69.2.1.1.1.1 Used containers constructed to specifications of the Association of American Railroads shall not be installed. [**58:**5.2.1.1(A)]

69.2.1.1.1.2 Adherence to applicable ASME Code case interpretations and addenda that have been adopted and published by ASME 180 calendar days prior to the effective date of NFPA 58 shall be considered as compliant with the ASME Code. [**58:**5.2.1.1(B)]

69.2.1.1.1.3 Where containers fabricated to earlier editions of regulations, rules, or codes listed in 69.2.1.1.1, and of the Interstate Commerce Commission (ICC) *Rules for Construction of Unfired Pressure Vessels*, prior to April 1, 1967, are used, the requirements of Section 1.4 of NFPA 58 shall apply. [**58:**5.2.1.1(C)]

69.2.1.1.2 Containers that have been involved in a fire and show no distortion shall be requalified for continued service before being used or reinstalled. [**58:**5.2.1.2]

69.2.1.1.2.1 Cylinders shall be requalified by a manufacturer of that type of cylinder or by a repair facility approved by DOT. [**58:**5.2.1.2(A)]

69.2.1.1.2.2 ASME or API-ASME containers shall be retested using the hydrostatic test procedure applicable at the time of the original fabrication. [**58:**5.2.1.2(B)]

69.2.1.1.2.3 All container appurtenances shall be replaced. [**58:**5.2.1.2(C)]

69.2.1.1.2.4 DOT 4E specification (aluminum) cylinders and composite cylinders involved in a fire shall be permanently removed from service. [**58:**5.2.1.2(D)]

69.2.1.1.3 ASME paragraph U-68 or U-69 containers shall be permitted to be continued in use, installed, reinstalled, or placed back into service. Installation of containers shall be in accordance with all provisions listed in NFPA 58. (*See Section 5.2, Table 5.2.4.2 and Table 5.7.2.5(A), and Annex D of NFPA 58.*) [**58:**5.2.1.3]

69.2.1.1.4 Containers that show excessive denting, bulging, gouging, or corrosion shall be removed from service. [**58:**5.2.1.4]

69.2.1.1.5 Except for containers used in cargo tank vehicle service, ASME containers of 3000 gal (11.4 m^3) water capacity or less used to store anhydrous ammonia shall not be converted to LP-Gas fuel service. [**58:**5.2.1.5]

69.2.1.1.6 Repairs or alteration of a container shall comply with the regulations, rules, or code under which the container was fabricated. Repairs or alteration to ASME containers shall be in accordance with the ANSI/NB23 *National Board Inspection Code*. [**58:**5.2.1.6]

69.2.1.1.7 Field welding shall be permitted only on saddle plates, lugs, pads, or brackets that are attached to the container by the container manufacturer. [**58:**5.2.1.7]

69.2.1.1.8 Containers for general use shall not have individual water capacities greater than 120,000 gal (454 m^3). [**58:**5.2.1.8]

69.2.1.1.9 Containers in dispensing stations not located in LP-Gas bulk plants, industrial plants, or industrial applications shall have an aggregate water capacity not greater than 30,000 gal (114 m^3). [**58:**5.2.1.9]

69.2.1.1.10 Heating or cooling coils shall not be installed inside storage containers. [**58:**5.2.1.10]

69.2.1.1.11 ASME containers installed underground, partially underground, or as mounded installations shall incorporate provisions for cathodic protection and shall be coated with a material recommended for the service that is applied in accordance with the coating manufacturer's instructions. [**58:**5.2.1.11]

69.2.1.2 Portable Container Appurtenance Physical Damage Protection.

69.2.1.2.1 Cylinders shall incorporate protection against physical damage to cylinder appurtenances and immediate connections to such appurtenances when not in use by any of the following means:

(1) A ventilated cap
(2) A ventilated collar
(3) A cylinder valve providing inherent protection as defined by DOT in 49 CFR 173.301(h)(3) [**58:**5.2.6.1]

69.2.1.2.2 Protection of appurtenances of portable containers, skid tanks, and tanks for use as cargo tanks of more than 1000 lb (454 kg) water capacity [nominal 420 lb (191 kg) propane capacity] shall comply with 69.2.1.2.2.1 through 69.2.1.2.2.3. [**58:**5.2.6.2]

69.2.1.2.2.1 Appurtenance protection from physical damage shall be provided by recessing, by protective housings, or by location on the vehicle. [**58:**5.2.6.2(A)]

69.2.1.2.2.2 Appurtenance protection shall comply with the provisions under which the containers are fabricated. [**58:**5.2.6.2(B)]

69.2.1.2.2.3 Appurtenance protection shall be secured to the container in accordance with the ASME code under which the container was designed and built. [**58:**5.2.6.2(C)]

69.2.1.3 Containers with Attached Supports.

69.2.1.3.1 Vertical ASME containers of over 125 gal (0.5 m³) water capacity for use in permanent installations in stationary service shall be designed with steel supports that allow the container to be mounted on and fastened to concrete foundations or supports. [**58**:5.2.7.1]

69.2.1.3.1.1 Steel supports shall be designed to make the container self-supporting without guy wires and to withstand the wind and seismic (earthquake) forces anticipated at the site. [**58**:5.2.7.1(A)]

69.2.1.3.1.2 Steel supports shall be protected against fire exposure with a material having a fire resistance rating of at least 2 hours. [**58**:5.2.7.1(B)]

69.2.1.3.1.3 Continuous steel skirts having only one opening of 18 in. (460 mm) or less in diameter shall have 2-hour fire protection applied to the outside of the skirt. [**58**:5.2.7.1(C)]

69.2.1.3.2 ASME containers to be used as portable storage containers, including movable fuel storage tenders and farm carts for temporary stationary service (normally not more than 12 months duration at any location), shall comply with 69.2.1.3.2.1 through 69.2.1.3.2.4. [**58**:5.2.7.2]

69.2.1.3.2.1 The legs or supports, or the lugs for the attachment of legs or supports, shall be secured to the container in accordance with the ASME code under which the container was designed and built. [**58**:5.2.7.2(A)]

69.2.1.3.2.2 The attachment of a container to either a trailer or semi-trailer running gear, or the attachments to the container to make it a vehicle, so that the unit can be moved by a conventional over-the-road tractor, shall comply with the DOT requirements for cargo tank service. [**58**:5.2.7.2(B)]

69.2.1.3.2.3 The unit specified in 69.2.1.3.2.2 shall be approved for stationary use. [**58**:5.2.7.2(C)]

69.2.1.3.2.4 Movable fuel storage tenders, including farm carts, shall be secured to the trailer support structure for the service involved. [**58**:5.2.7.2(D)]

69.2.1.3.3 Portable tank design and construction of a full framework, skids, or lugs for the attachment of skids, and protection of fittings shall be in accordance with DOT portable tank specifications. The bottom of the skids shall be not less than 2 in. (50 mm) or more than 12 in. (300 mm) below the outside bottom of the tank shell. [**58**:5.2.7.3]

69.2.1.4 Container Marking.

69.2.1.4.1 Cylinders shall be marked as provided in the regulations, rules, or code under which they are fabricated. [**58**:5.2.8.1]

69.2.1.4.1.1 Where LP-Gas and one or more other compressed gases are to be stored or used in the same area, the cylinders shall be marked "Flammable" and either "LP-Gas," "Propane," or "Butane," or shall be marked in accordance with the requirements of 49 CFR, "Transportation." [**58**:5.2.8.1(A)]

69.2.1.4.1.2 When being transported, cylinders shall be marked and labeled in accordance with 49 CFR, "Transportation." [**58**:5.2.8.1(B)]

69.2.1.4.2* Cylinders shall be marked with the following information:

(1) Water capacity of the cylinder in pounds

(2) Tare weight of the cylinder in pounds, fitted for service [**58**:5.2.8.2]

69.2.1.4.3* The markings specified for ASME containers shall be on a stainless steel metal nameplate attached to the container, located to remain visible after the container is installed. [**58**:5.2.8.3]

69.2.1.4.3.1 The nameplate shall be attached in such a way as to minimize corrosion of the nameplate or its fastening means and not contribute to corrosion of the container. [**58**:5.2.8.3(A)]

69.2.1.4.3.2 Where the container is buried, mounded, insulated, or otherwise covered so the nameplate is obscured, the information contained on the nameplate shall be duplicated and installed on adjacent piping or on a structure in a clearly visible location. [**58**:5.2.8.3(B)]

69.2.1.4.3.3 Stationary ASME containers shall be marked with the following information:

(1) Service for which the container is designed (e.g., underground, aboveground, or both)
(2) Name and address of container supplier or trade name of container
(3) Water capacity of container in pounds or U.S. gallons
(4) MAWP in pounds per square inch
(5) Wording that reads "This container shall not contain a product that has a vapor pressure in excess of ___ psig at 100°F" (see Table 5.2.4.2 of NFPA 58)
(6) Outside surface area in square feet
(7) Year of manufacture
(8) Shell thickness and head thickness
(9) OL (overall length), OD (outside diameter), and HD (head design)
(10) Manufacturer's serial number
(11) ASME Code symbol
(12) Minimum design metal temperature ___°F at MAWP ___ psi
(13) Type of construction "W"
(14) Degree of radiography "RT-___" [**58**:5.2.8.3(C)]

69.2.1.4.3.4 In addition to the markings required by this Code, nameplates on cargo tanks shall include the markings required by the ASME *Boiler and Pressure Vessel Code* and the DOT. [**58**:5.2.8.3(D)]

69.2.1.4.4 Warning labels shall meet the following requirements:

(1) Warning labels shall be applied to all cylinders of 100 lb (45.4 kg) propane capacity or less that are not filled on site.
(2) Warning labels shall include information on the potential hazards of LP-Gas. [**58**:5.2.8.4]

69.2.1.4.5 All containers that contain unodorized LP-Gas products shall be marked "NOT ODORIZED." [**58**:5.2.8.5].

69.2.1.4.5.1 The marking shall have a contrasting background surrounded by a rectangular border in red letters and red border in the sizes shown in Table 69.2.1.4.5.1. [**58**:5.2.8.5(A)]

69.2.1.4.5.2 The markings shall be on both ends or on both sides of a container or on both sides and the rear of cargo tanks. [**58**:5.2.8.5(B)]

69.2.2 Container Appurtenances and Regulators. Container appurtenances and regulators shall be fabricated of materials

Table 69.2.1.4.5.1 "NOT ODORIZED" Label Size

Water Capacity		Letter Height		Border Width	
gal	m^3	in.	cm	in.	cm
≥499	≥1.89	4	10.0	½	1.3
49–498	0.19–1.88	1½	3.7	5/16	0.8
2.6–48	0.01–0.18	¾	1.8	¼	0.6
1–2.5	0.004–0.009	⅜	1.0	1/16	0.2

[58: Table 5.2.8.5(A)]

that are compatible with LP-Gas, shall be resistant to the action of LP-Gas under service conditions, and shall comply with Sections 5.7 and 5.8 of NFPA 58.

69.2.3 Piping (Including Hose), Fittings, and Valves. Piping (including hose), fittings, and valves shall comply with Section 5.9 of NFPA 58.

69.3 Installation of LP-Gas Systems.

69.3.1* Application. Section 69.3 shall apply to the following:

(1) Location and field installation of LP-Gas systems that use components, subassemblies, container assemblies, and container systems that are fabricated in accordance with Chapter 5 of NFPA 58
(2) Location of containers and liquid transfer systems
(3) Installation of container appurtenances and regulators
(4) Installation of piping (including flexible connectors and hose), hydrostatic relief valves, and piping service limitations
(5) Installation of equipment
(6) Testing of piping systems [**58:**6.1.1]

69.3.2 Location of Containers.

69.3.2.1 LP-Gas containers shall be located outside of buildings unless they are specifically allowed to be located inside of buildings. [**58:**6.2.1]

69.3.2.2 LP-Gas containers shall be allowed in buildings only for the following applications:

(1) Cylinders as specifically provided for in Section 6.20 of NFPA 58
(2) Containers of less than 125 gal (0.5 m^3) water capacity for the purposes of being filled in buildings or structures complying with Chapter 10 of NFPA 58
(3) Containers on LP-Gas vehicles complying with, and parked or garaged in accordance with, Chapter 9 of NFPA 58
(4) Containers used with LP-Gas portable engine fuel systems complying with 11.15.1 of NFPA 58
(5) Containers used with LP-Gas stationary engine fuel systems complying with Section 6.26 of NFPA 58
(6) Containers used with LP-Gas–fueled industrial trucks complying with 11.13.4 of NFPA 58
(7) Containers on LP-Gas–fueled vehicles garaged in accordance with Section 11.16 of NFPA 58
(8) Cylinders awaiting use, resale, or exchange when stored in accordance with Section 69.5 [**58:**6.2.2]

69.3.3 Container Separation Distances.

69.3.3.1 Aboveground Containers.

69.3.3.1.1* Containers installed outside of buildings, whether of the portable type replaced on a cylinder exchange basis or permanently installed and refilled at the installation, shall be located with respect to the adjacent containers, important building, group of buildings, or line of adjoining property that can be built upon, in accordance with Table 69.3.3.1.1, Table 69.3.4.1.2, 69.3.3.1.2 through 69.3.3.1.3, 69.3.3.3, 69.3.3.4.1 through 69.3.3.4.4, and 69.3.4.4.6 through 69.3.4.4.11. [**58:**6.3.1]

69.3.3.1.2 When the provisions of 6.28.3 through 6.28.5 of NFPA 58 are met, the minimum distance from an ASME container to a building shall be reduced by one-half for ASME containers of 2001 gal through 30,000 gal (7.6 m^3 through 114 m^3) water capacity. [**58:**6.3.1.2]

69.3.3.1.3 The 25 ft (7.6 m) minimum distance from aboveground ASME containers of 501 gal through 2000 gal (1.9 m^3 through 7.6 m^3) water capacity to buildings, a group of buildings, or the line of adjoining property that can be built upon shall be reduced to 10 ft (3 m) for a single ASME container of 1200 gal (4.5 m^3) or less water capacity where such container is at least 25 ft (7.6 m) from any other LP-Gas container of more than 125 gal (0.5 m^3) water capacity. [**58:**6.3.1.3]

69.3.3.2 Underground or Mounded ASME Containers.

69.3.3.2.1 Minimum distances for underground or mounded ASME containers of 2001 gal through 30,000 gal (7.6 m^3 through 114 m^3) water capacity, incorporating all the provisions of Section 6.28 of NFPA 58, shall be reduced to 10 ft (3 m). [**58:**6.3.2.1]

69.3.3.2.2 Distances for all underground and mounded ASME containers shall be measured from the container surface. [**58:**6.3.2.2]

69.3.3.2.3 No part of an underground or mounded ASME container shall be less than 10 ft (3 m) from a building or line of adjoining property that can be built upon. [**58:**6.3.2.3]

69.3.3.3 Minimum Separation Distances for ASME Containers.

69.3.3.3.1 The minimum separation distances specified in Table 69.3.3.1.1 between containers and buildings of other than wood-frame construction devoted exclusively to gas manufacturing and distribution operations shall be reduced to 10 ft (3 m). [**58:**6.3.3.1]

69.3.3.3.2 If the aggregate water capacity of a multicontainer installation is 501 gal (1.9 m^3) or more and the installation is comprised of individual containers, each with a water capacity of less than 125 gal (0.5 m^3), the minimum distance shall comply with Table 69.3.3.1.1 and 69.3.3.3.2.1 through 69.3.3.3.2.3. [**58:**6.3.3.2]

69.3.3.3.2.1 The aggregate capacity shall be used rather than the capacity per container. [**58:**6.3.3.2(A)]

69.3.3.3.2.2 If more than one such installation is made, each installation shall be separated from any other installation by at least 25 ft (7.6 m). [**58:**6.3.3.2(B)]

69.3.3.3.2.3 The minimum distances between containers shall not be applied to installations covered by 69.3.3.3.2. [**58:**6.3.3.2(C)]

69.3.3.4 Separation Distance Between Container Pressure Relief Valve and Building Openings.

69.3.3.4.1 Cylinders shall not be located and installed underneath any building unless the space is open to the atmosphere for 50 percent of its perimeter or more. [**58:**6.3.4.1]

69.3.3.4.2 ASME containers of less than 125 gal (0.5 m^3) water capacity shall be located and installed so that the discharge from pressure relief devices shall not terminate in or beneath any building. [**58:**6.3.4.2]

Table 69.3.3.1.1 Separation Distances Between Containers, Important Buildings, and Line of Adjoining Property That Can Be Built Upon

Water Capacity per Container		Minimum Distances					
		Mounded or Underground Containers[a]		Aboveground Containers		Between Containers[b]	
gal	m³	ft	m	ft	m	ft	m
<125[c]	<0.5[c]	10	3	0[d]	0[d]	0	0
125–250	0.5–1.0	10	3	10	3	0	0
251–500	>1.0–1.9	10	3	10	3	3	1
501–2,000	>1.9–7.6	10	3	25[e]	7.6	3	1
2,001–30,000	>7.6–114	50	15	50	15	5	1.5
30,001–70,000	>114–265	50	15	75	23		
70,001–90,000	>265–341	50	15	100	30	¼ of sum of diameters of adjacent containers	
90,001–120,000	>341–454	50	15	125	38		
120,001–200,000	>454–757	50	15	200	61		
200,001–1,000,000	>757–3785	50	15	300	91		
>1,000,000	>3785	50	15	400	122		

[a]See 69.3.3.2.1.
[b]See 69.3.3.4.5.
[c]See 69.3.3.4.4.
[d]See 69.3.3.4.1, 69.3.3.4.2, 69.3.3.4.3, and 69.3.3.4.4.
[e]See 69.3.3.1.3.
[58: Table 6.3.1.1]

69.3.3.4.3* The distance measured horizontally from the point of discharge of a container pressure relief valve to any building opening below the level of such discharge shall be in accordance with Table 69.3.3.4.3. [58:6.3.4.3]

69.3.3.4.4 The distance measured in any direction from the point of discharge of a container pressure relief valve, vent of a fixed maximum liquid level gauge on a container, and the container filling connection to exterior sources of ignition, openings into direct-vent (sealed combustion system) appliances, and mechanical ventilation air intakes shall be in accordance with Table 69.3.3.4.3. [58:6.3.4.4]

69.3.3.4.5 Access at the ends or sides of individual underground containers having a water capacity of 125 gal (0.5 m³) or more shall be provided in multicontainer installations to facilitate working with cranes or hoists. [58:6.3.4.5]

69.3.4 Other Container Location Requirements.

69.3.4.1 ASME Multi-Container Requirements.

69.3.4.1.1 Where storage containers having an aggregate water capacity of more than 4000 gal (15.2 m³) are located in heavily populated or congested areas, the siting provisions of 69.3.3.1.1 and Table 69.3.3.1.1 shall be permitted to be modified as indicated by the fire safety analysis described in 6.27.3 of NFPA 58. [58:6.4.1.1]

69.3.4.1.2 Aboveground multicontainer installations comprised of ASME containers having an individual water capacity of 12,000 gal (45 m³) or more and installed for use in a single location shall be limited to the number of containers in one group, with each group separated from the next group in accordance with the degree of fire protection provided in Table 69.3.4.1.2. [58:6.4.1.2]

69.3.4.1.3 Where the provisions of 6.28.3 and 6.28.4 of NFPA 58 are met, the minimum separation distance between groups of ASME containers protected by hose stream only shall be one-half the distances required in Table 69.3.4.1.2. [58:6.4.1.3]

69.3.4.2 Underground and Mounded ASME Containers.

69.3.4.2.1 Underground or mounded ASME containers shall be located in accordance with 69.3.4.2.2 and 69.3.4.2.3. [58:6.4.2.1]

69.3.4.2.2 Underground or mounded containers shall be located outside of any buildings. [58:6.4.2.2]

69.3.4.2.3 Buildings shall not be constructed over any underground or mounded containers. [58:6.4.2.3]

69.3.4.3 General Requirements.

69.3.4.3.1 The sides of adjacent containers shall be separated in accordance with Table 69.3.3.1.1 but shall not be separated by less than 3 ft (1 m). [58:6.4.3.1]

69.3.4.3.2 Where containers are installed parallel with ends in line, the number of containers in one group shall not be limited. [58:6.4.3.2]

69.3.4.3.3 Where more than one row of containers is installed, the adjacent ends of the containers in each row shall be separated by not less than 10 ft (3 m). [58:6.4.3.3]

69.3.4.4 Additional Container Installation Requirements.

69.3.4.4.1 Additional container installation requirements shall comply with 69.3.4.4.2 through 69.3.4.4.14 and 69.3.4.5. [58:6.4.4.1]

Table 69.3.3.4.3 Separation Distance Between Container Pressure Relief Valve and Building Openings

Container Type	Exchange or Filled on Site at the Point of Use	Distance Horizontally from Relief Valve Discharge to Opening Below Discharge		Discharge from Relief Valve, Vent Discharge, and Filling Connection to Exterior Source of Ignition, Openings into Direct-Vent Appliances, and Mechanical Ventilation Air Intakes	
		ft	m	ft	m
Cylinder	Exchange	3	0.9	5	1.5
Cylinder	Filled on site at the point of use	3	0.9	10	3.0
ASME	Filled on site at the point of use	5	1.5	10	3.0

[**58**: Table 6.3.4.3]

Table 69.3.4.1.2 Maximum Number of Containers in a Group and Their Separation Distances

Fire Protection Provided by	Maximum Number of Containers in One Group	Minimum Separation Between Groups	
		ft	m
Hose streams only (see 6.4.1.2 and 6.27.3.1 of NFPA 58)	6	50	15
Fixed monitor nozzles per 6.27.6.3 of NFPA 58	6	25	7.6
Fixed water spray per 6.27.6.1 of NFPA 58	9	25	7.6
Insulation per 6.27.5.1 of NFPA 58	9	25	7.6

[**58**: Table 6.4.1.2]

69.3.4.4.2 Containers shall not be stacked one above the other. [**58**:6.4.4.2]

69.3.4.4.3* Combustible materials shall not accumulate or be stored within 10 ft (3 m) of a container. [**58**:6.4.4.3]

69.3.4.4.4* The area under containers shall be graded or shall have dikes or curbs installed so that the flow or accumulation of flammable liquids with flash points below 200°F (93.4°C) is prevented. [**58**:6.4.4.4]

69.3.4.4.5 LP-Gas containers shall be located at least 10 ft (3 m) from the centerline of the wall of diked areas containing flammable or combustible liquids. [**58**:6.4.4.5]

69.3.4.4.6 The minimum horizontal separation between aboveground LP-Gas containers and aboveground tanks containing liquids having flash points below 200°F (93.4°C) shall be 20 ft (6 m). [**58**:6.4.4.6]

69.3.4.4.7 The requirements of 69.3.4.4.6 shall not apply where LP-Gas containers of 125 gal (0.5 m³) or less water capacity are installed adjacent to fuel oil supply tanks of 660 gal (2.5 m³) or less capacity. [**58**:6.4.4.7]

69.3.4.4.8 No horizontal separation shall be required between aboveground LP-Gas containers and underground tanks containing flammable or combustible liquids installed in accordance with NFPA 30. [**58**:6.4.4.8]

69.3.4.4.9* The minimum separation between LP-Gas containers and oxygen or gaseous hydrogen containers shall be in accordance with NFPA 55, *Compressed Gases and Cryogenic Fluids Code*. [**58**:6.4.4.9]

69.3.4.4.10 Where protective structures having a minimum fire resistance rating of 2 hours interrupt the line of sight between uninsulated portions of the oxygen or hydrogen containers and the LP-Gas containers, no minimum distance shall apply. [**58**:6.4.4.10]

69.3.4.4.11 The minimum separation between LP-Gas containers and liquefied hydrogen containers shall be in accordance with NFPA 55, *Compressed Gases and Cryogenic Fluids Code*. [**58**:6.4.4.11]

69.3.4.4.12 Where LP-Gas cylinders are to be stored or used in the same area with other compressed gases, the cylinders shall be marked to identify their content in accordance with ANSI/CGA C-7, *Guide to the Preparation of Precautionary Labeling and Marking of Compressed Gas Containers*. [**58**:6.4.4.12]

69.3.4.4.13 An aboveground LP-Gas container and any of its parts shall not be located within 6 ft (1.8 m) of a vertical plane beneath overhead electric power lines that are over 600 volts, nominal. [**58**:6.4.4.13]

69.3.4.4.14* Refrigerated LP-Gas containers shall be located within an impoundment in accordance with Section 12.5 of NFPA 58. [**58**: 6.4.4.14]

69.3.4.5* Structure Requirements.

69.3.4.5.1 Structures such as fire walls, fences, earth or concrete barriers, and other similar structures shall not be permitted around or over installed nonrefrigerated containers unless specifically allowed. [**58**:6.4.5.1]

69.3.4.5.2 Structures partially enclosing containers shall be permitted if designed in accordance with a sound fire protection analysis. [**58**:6.4.5.2]

69.3.4.5.3 Structures used to prevent flammable or combustible liquid accumulation or flow shall be permitted in accordance with 69.3.4.4.4. [**58**:6.4.5.3]

69.3.4.5.4 Structures between LP-Gas containers and gaseous hydrogen containers shall be permitted in accordance with 69.3.4.4.10. [**58**:6.4.5.4]

69.3.4.5.5 Structures such as fences shall be permitted in accordance with 6.19.4 of NFPA 58. [**58:**6.4.5.5]

69.3.5 Location of Transfer Operations.

69.3.5.1 Transfer of Liquids.

69.3.5.1.1* Liquid shall be transferred into containers, including containers mounted on vehicles, only outdoors or in structures specially designed for such purpose. [58:6.5.1.1]

69.3.5.1.2 The transfer of liquid into containers mounted on vehicles shall not take place within a building but shall be permitted to take place under a weather shelter or canopy. *(See 6.25.3.3 of NFPA 58.)* [58:6.5.1.2]

69.3.5.1.3 Structures housing transfer operations or converted for such use after December 31, 1972, shall comply with Chapter 10 of NFPA 58. [**58:**6.5.1.3]

69.3.5.1.4 The transfer of liquid into containers on the roofs of structures shall be permitted, provided that the installation conforms to the requirements specified in 6.6.7 and 6.20.11 of NFPA 58. [**58:**6.5.1.4]

69.3.5.1.5 The transfer hose shall not be routed in or through any building except those specified in 69.3.5.1.3. [**58:**6.5.1.5]

69.3.5.1.6 Filling of containers located outdoors in stationary installations in accordance with 69.3.3 shall be permitted to be filled at that location. [**58:**6.5.1.6]

69.3.5.2 Container Point of Transfer Location Requirements.

69.3.5.2.1 If the point of transfer of containers located outdoors in stationary installations is not located at the container, it shall be located in accordance with Table 69.3.5.2.1. [**58:**6.5.2.1]

69.3.5.2.2 Containers not located in stationary installations shall be filled at a location determined by the point of transfer in accordance with Table 69.3.5.2.1. [**58:**6.5.2.2]

69.3.5.3 Separation Distance from Point of Transfer.

69.3.5.3.1 If the point of transfer is a component of a system covered by Section 6.24 or Chapter 11 of NFPA 58, the requirements of parts A, B, and C of Table 69.3.5.2.1 shall not apply to the structure containing the point of transfer. [**58:**6.5.3.1]

69.3.5.3.2 If LP-Gas is vented to the atmosphere under the conditions stipulated in 7.3.1(5) of NFPA 58, the distances in Table 69.3.5.2.1 shall be doubled. [**58:**6.5.3.2]

69.3.5.3.3 If the point of transfer is housed in a structure complying with Chapter 10 of NFPA 58, and the common walls comply with 10.2.1 of NFPA 58, separation distances in Table 69.3.5.2.1 shall not be required where the common walls comply with 10.3.1.3 of NFPA 58. [**58:**6.5.3.3]

69.3.5.3.4 The distances in Table 69.3.5.2.1, parts B, C, D, E, F(2), and J, shall be reduced by one-half where the system incorporates the provisions of low emission transfer as provided in 6.28.5 of NFPA 58. [**58:**6.5.3.4]

69.3.6 Installation of Containers.

69.3.6.1 General Requirements.

69.3.6.1.1 Containers shall be positioned so that the pressure relief valve is in direct communication with the vapor space of the container. [**58:**6.6.1.1]

Table 69.3.5.2.1 Distance Between Point of Transfer and Exposures

Part	Exposure	Minimum Horizontal Distance ft	Minimum Horizontal Distance m
A	Buildings,[a] mobile homes, recreational vehicles, and modular homes with at least 1-hour fire-rated walls[b]	10[c]	3.1
B	Buildings[a] with other than at least 1-hour fire-rated walls[b]	25[c]	7.6[c]
C	Building wall openings or pits at or below the level of the point of transfer	25[c]	7.6[c]
D	Line of adjoining property that can be built upon	25[c]	7.6[c]
E	Outdoor places of public assembly, including schoolyards, athletic fields, and playgrounds	50[c]	15[c]
F	Public ways, including public streets, highways, thoroughfares, and sidewalks		
	(1) From points of transfer in LP-Gas dispensing stations and at vehicle fuel dispensers	10	3.1
	(2) From other points of transfer	25[c]	7.6[c]
G	Driveways[d]	5	1.5
H	Mainline railroad track centerlines	25	7.6
I	Containers[e] other than those being filled	10	3.1
J	Flammable and Class II combustible liquid[f] dispensers and the fill connections of containers	10[c]	3.1[c]
K	Flammable and Class II combustible liquid aboveground containers, and filling connections of underground containers	20	6.1

[a]For the purpose of the table, buildings also include structures such as tents and box trailers at construction sites.
[b]See ASTM E 119, *Standard Test Methods for Fire Tests of Building Construction and Materials*, or ANSI/UL 263, *Standard for Fire Tests for Building Construction and Materials*.
[c]See 69.3.5.3.4.
[d]Not applicable to driveways and points of transfer at vehicle fuel dispensers.
[e]Not applicable to filling connections at the storage container or to dispensing vehicle fuel dispenser units of 4000 gal (15.2 m^3) water capacity or less when used for filling containers not mounted on vehicles.
[f]NFPA 30 defines these as follows: Flammable liquids include those having a flash point below 100°F (37.8°C) and having a vapor pressure not exceeding 40 psia (276 kPa) at 100°F (37.8°C). Class II combustible liquids include those having a flash point at or above 100°F (37.8°C) and below 140°F (60°C).
[**58:** Table 6.5.2.1]

69.3.6.1.2 LP-Gas containers or systems of which they are a part that are installed within 10 ft (3m) of public vehicular thoroughfares shall be provided with a means of vehicular barrier protection. [**58**:6.6.1.2]

69.3.6.1.3 Field welding on containers shall be limited to nonpressure parts such as saddle plates, wear plates, or brackets installed by the container manufacturer. [**58**:6.6.1.3]

69.3.6.1.4* Aboveground containers shall be painted. [**58**:6.6.1.4]

69.3.6.1.5 Containers shall be installed so that all container operating appurtenances are accessible. [**58**:6.6.1.5]

69.3.6.1.6 Where necessary to prevent flotation due to possible high flood waters around aboveground or mounded containers, or high water table for those underground and partially underground, containers shall be securely anchored. [**58**:6.6.1.6]

69.3.6.2 Installation of Cylinders.

69.3.6.2.1 Cylinders shall be installed only aboveground and shall be set upon a firm foundation or otherwise be firmly secured. *(See 69.3.6.2.2.)* [**58**:6.6.2.1]

69.3.6.2.2 The cylinder shall not be in contact with the soil. [**58**:6.6.2.2]

69.3.6.2.3 Flexibility shall be provided in the connecting piping. *(See 69.3.6.2.4.)* [**58**:6.6.2.3]

69.3.6.2.4 Where flexible connectors are used, they shall comply with 6.9.6 of NFPA 58. [**58**:6.6.2.4]

69.3.7 Internal Valves.

69.3.7.1 The requirements of 69.3.7.2 through 69.3.7.5 shall be required for internal valves in liquid service that are installed in containers of over 4000 gal (15.2 m^3) water capacity by July 1, 2003. [**58**:6.11.1]

69.3.7.2 Internal valves shall be installed in accordance with 5.7.4.2 and Table 5.7.4.2 of NFPA 58 on containers of over 4000 gal (15.2 m^3) water capacity. [**58**:6.11.2]

69.3.7.3 Thermal Activation.

69.3.7.3.1 Automatic shutdown of internal valves in liquid service shall be provided using thermal (fire) actuation. [**58**:6.11.3.1]

69.3.7.3.2 The thermal sensing element of the internal valve shall be within 5 ft (1.5 m) of the internal valve. [**58**:6.11.3.2]

69.3.7.4 Remote Shutdown Station.

69.3.7.4.1 At least one remote shutdown station for internal valves in liquid service shall be installed not less than 25 ft (7.6 m) or more than 100 ft (30 m) from the liquid transfer point. [**58**:6.11.4.1]

69.3.7.4.2 This requirement shall be retroactive to all internal valves required by NFPA 58. [**58**:6.11.4.2]

69.3.7.5 Emergency remote shutdown stations shall be identified by a sign, visible from the point of transfer, incorporating the words "Propane — Container Liquid Valve Emergency Shutoff" in block letters of not less than 2 in. (51 mm) in height on a background of contrasting colors to the letters. [**58**:6.11.5]

69.3.8 Emergency Shutoff Valves.

69.3.8.1 On new installations and on existing installations, stationary container storage systems with an aggregate water capacity of more than 4000 gal (15.2 m^3) utilizing a liquid transfer line that is 1½ in. (39 mm) or larger, and a pressure equalizing vapor line that is 1¼ in. (32 mm) or larger, shall be equipped with emergency shutoff valves. [**58**:6.12.1]

69.3.8.2 An emergency shutoff valve shall be installed in the transfer lines of the fixed piping transfer system within 20 ft (6 m) of lineal pipe from the nearest end of the hose or swivel-type piping connections. [**58**:6.12.2]

69.3.8.3 When the flow is only into the container, a backflow check valve shall be permitted to be used in lieu of an emergency shutoff valve if installed in the piping transfer system downstream of the hose or swivel-type piping connections. [**58**:6.12.3]

69.3.8.4 The backflow check valve shall have a metal-to-metal seat or a primary resilient seat with metal back-up, not hinged with combustible material, and shall be designed for this specific application. [**58**:6.12.4]

69.3.8.5 Where there are two or more liquid or vapor lines with hoses or swivel-type piping connected of the sizes designated, an emergency shutoff valve or a backflow check valve, where allowed, shall be installed in each leg of the piping. [**58**:6.12.5]

69.3.8.6 Emergency shutoff valves shall be installed so that the temperature-sensitive element in the valve, or a supplemental temperature-sensitive element that operates at a maximum temperature of 250°F (121°C) that is connected to actuate the valve, is not more than 5 ft (1.5 m) from the nearest end of the hose or swivel-type piping connected to the line in which the valve is installed. [**58**:6.12.6]

69.3.8.7 Temperature-sensitive elements of emergency shutoff valves shall not be painted, nor shall they have any ornamental finishes applied after manufacture. [**58**:6.12.7]

69.3.8.8* The emergency shutoff valves or backflow check valves shall be installed in the fixed piping so that any break resulting from a pull will occur on the hose or swivel-type piping side of the connection while retaining intact the valves and piping on the plant side of the connection. [**58**:6.12.8]

69.3.8.9 Where emergency shutoff valves are required to be installed in accordance with 69.3.8.2, a means shall be incorporated to actuate the emergency shutoff valves in the event of a break of the fixed piping resulting from a pull on the hose. [**58**:6.12.9]

69.3.8.10 Emergency shutoff valves required by NFPA 58 shall be tested annually for the functions required by 5.12.2.3(2) and (3) of NFPA 58, and the results of the test shall be documented. [**58**:6.12.10]

69.3.8.11 Backflow check valves installed in lieu of emergency shutoff valves shall be checked annually for proper operation, and the results of the test shall be documented. [**58**:6.12.11]

69.3.8.12 All new and existing emergency shutoff valves shall comply with 69.3.8.12.1 through 69.3.8.12.3. [**58**:6.12.12]

69.3.8.12.1 Each emergency shutoff valve shall have at least one clearly identified and easily accessible manually operated remote emergency shutoff device. [**58**:6.12.12.1]

69.3.8.12.2 The shutoff device shall be located not less than 25 ft (7.6 m) or more than 100 ft (30 m) in the path of egress from the emergency shutoff valve. [**58**:6.12.12.2]

69.3.8.12.3 Where an emergency shutoff valve is used in lieu of an internal valve in compliance with 5.7.4.2(D)(2) of NFPA 58, the remote shutoff device shall be installed in accordance with 69.3.7.4 and 69.3.7.5. [**58**:6.12.12.3]

69.3.8.13 Emergency shutoff valves for railroad tank car transfer systems shall be in accordance with 6.19.2.6, 6.28.4, 7.2.3.7, and 7.2.3.8 of NFPA 58. [**58**:6.12.13]

69.3.9* Installation in Areas of Heavy Snowfall. In areas where the ground snow load is equal to or exceeds 175 psf (855 kg/m^2), piping, regulators, meters, and other equipment installed in the piping system shall be protected from the forces of accumulated snow. [**58**:6.16.1]

69.3.10 LP-Gas Systems in Buildings or on Building Roofs or Exterior Balconies.

69.3.10.1 Application.

69.3.10.1.1 Subsection 69.3.10 shall apply to the installation of the following LP-Gas systems in buildings or structures:

(1) Cylinders inside of buildings or on the roofs or exterior balconies of buildings
(2) Systems in which the liquid is piped from outside containers into buildings or onto the roof [**58**:6.20.1.1]

69.3.10.1.2 The phrase *cylinders in use* shall mean connected for use. [**58**:6.20.1.2]

69.3.10.1.2.1 The use of cylinders indoors shall be only for the purposes specified in 6.20.4 through 6.20.10 of NFPA 58. [**58**:6.20.1.2(A)]

69.3.10.1.2.2 The use of cylinders indoors shall be limited to those conditions where operational requirements make the indoor use of cylinders necessary and location outside is impractical. [**58**:6.20.1.2(B)]

69.3.10.1.2.3 The use of cylinders on roofs shall be limited to those conditions where operational requirements make the use of cylinders necessary and location other than on roofs of buildings or structures is impractical. [**58**:6.20.1.2(C)]

69.3.10.1.2.4 Liquid LP-Gas shall be piped into buildings or structures only for the purposes specified in 6.9.1.1(D) of NFPA 58. [**58**:6.20.1.2(D)]

69.3.10.1.3 Storage of cylinders awaiting use shall be in accordance with Chapter 8 of NFPA 58. [**58**:6.20.1.3]

69.3.10.1.4 Transportation of cylinders within a building shall be in accordance with 6.20.3.6 of NFPA 58. [**58**:6.20.1.4]

69.3.10.1.5 The following provisions shall be required in addition to those specified in Sections 6.2 and 6.3 of NFPA 58:

(1) Liquid transfer systems shall be in accordance with Chapter 7 of NFPA 58.
(2) Engine fuel systems used inside buildings shall be in accordance with Chapter 11 of NFPA 58.
(3) LP-Gas transport or cargo tank vehicles stored, serviced, or repaired in buildings shall be in accordance with Chapter 9 of NFPA 58. [**58**:6.20.1.5]

69.3.10.2 Additional Equipment Requirements for Cylinders, Equipment, Piping, and Appliances Used in Buildings, Building Roofs, and Exterior Balconies.

69.3.10.2.1 Cylinders shall be in accordance with the following:

(1) Cylinders shall not exceed 245 lb (111 kg) water capacity [nominal 100 lb (45 kg) propane capacity] each.
(2) Cylinders shall comply with other applicable provisions of Section 5.2 of NFPA 58, and they shall be equipped as provided in Section 5.7 of NFPA 58.
(3) Cylinders shall be marked in accordance with 5.2.8.1 and 5.2.8.2 of NFPA 58.
(4) Cylinders with propane capacities greater than 2 lb (0.9 kg) shall be equipped as provided in Table 5.7.4.1(D) of NFPA 58, and an excess-flow valve shall be provided for vapor service when used indoors.
(5) Cylinder valves shall be protected in accordance with 5.2.6.1 of NFPA 58.
(6) Cylinders having water capacities greater than 2.7 lb (1.2 kg) and connected for use shall stand on a firm and substantially level surface.
(7) Cylinders shall be secured in an upright position if necessary.
(8) Cylinders and the valve-protecting devices used with them shall be oriented to minimize the possibility of impingement of the pressure relief device discharge on the cylinder and adjacent cylinders. [**58**:6.20.2.1]

69.3.10.2.2 Manifolds and fittings connecting cylinders to pressure regulator inlets shall be designed for at least 250 psig (1.7 MPag) service pressure. [**58**:6.20.2.2]

69.3.10.2.3 Piping shall comply with Section 5.9 of NFPA 58 and shall have a pressure rating of 250 psig (1.7 MPag). [**58**:6.20.2.3]

69.3.10.2.4 Liquid piping and vapor piping at pressures above 125 psig (0.9 MPag) shall be installed in accordance with 6.9.3 of NFPA 58. [**58**:6.20.2.4]

69.3.10.2.5 Hose, hose connections, and flexible connectors shall comply with the following:

(1) Hose used at pressures above 5 psig (34 kPag) shall be designed for a pressure of at least 350 psig (2.4 MPag).
(2) Hose used at a pressure of 5 psig (34 kPag) or less and used in agricultural buildings not normally occupied by the public shall be designed for the operating pressure of the hose.
(3) Hose shall comply with 5.9.6 of NFPA 58.
(4) Hose shall be installed in accordance with 6.21.3 of NFPA 58.
(5) Hose shall be as short as practical, without kinking or straining the hose or causing it to be close enough to a burner to be damaged by heat.
(6) Hoses greater than 10 ft (3 m) in length shall be protected from damage. [**58**:6.20.2.5]

69.3.10.2.6* Portable heaters, including salamanders, shall comply with the following:

(1) Portable heaters shall be equipped with an approved automatic device to shut off the flow of gas to the main burner and to the pilot, if used, in the event of flame extinguishment or combustion failure.
(2) Portable heaters shall be self-supporting unless designed for cylinder mounting.
(3) Portable heaters shall not be installed utilizing cylinder valves, connectors, regulators, manifolds, piping, or tubing as structural supports.
(4) Portable heaters having an input of more than 50,000 Btu/hr (53 MJ/hr) shall be equipped with either a pilot that must be lighted and proved before the main burner can be turned on or an approved electric ignition system. [**58**:6.20.2.6]

69.3.10.2.7 The provisions of 69.3.10.2.6 shall not be applicable to the following:

(1) Tar kettle burners, hand torches, or melting pots
(2) Portable heaters with less than 7500 Btu/hr (8 MJ/hr) input if used with cylinders having a maximum water capacity of 2.7 lb (1.2 kg) and filled with not more than 16.8 oz (0.522 kg) of LP-Gas [**58:**6.20.2.7]

69.3.10.3 Buildings Under Construction or Undergoing Major Renovation.

69.3.10.3.1 Where cylinders are used and transported in buildings or structures under construction or undergoing major renovation and such buildings are not occupied by the public, the requirements of 69.3.10.3.2 through 69.3.10.3.10 shall apply. [**58:**6.20.4.1]

69.3.10.3.2 The use and transportation of cylinders in the unoccupied portions of buildings or structures under construction or undergoing major renovation that are partially occupied by the public shall be approved by the AHJ. [**58:**6.20.4.2]

69.3.10.3.3 Cylinders, equipment, piping, and appliances shall comply with 69.3.10.2. [**58:**6.20.4.3]

69.3.10.3.4 Heaters used for temporary heating shall be located at least 6 ft (1.8 m) from any cylinder. (*See 69.3.10.3.5 for an exception to this requirement.*) [**58:**6.20.4.4]

69.3.10.3.5 Integral heater-cylinder units specifically designed for the attachment of the heater to the cylinder, or to a supporting standard attached to the cylinder, and designed and installed to prevent direct or radiant heat application to the cylinder shall be exempt from the spacing requirement of 69.3.10.3.4. [**58:**6.20.4.5]

69.3.10.3.6 Blower-type and radiant-type units shall not be directed toward any cylinder within 20 ft (6.1 m). [**58:**6.20.4.6]

69.3.10.3.7 If two or more heater-cylinder units of either the integral or nonintegral type are located in an unpartitioned area on the same floor, the cylinder(s) of each such unit shall be separated from the cylinder(s) of any other such unit by at least 20 ft (6.1 m). [**58:**6.20.4.7]

69.3.10.3.8 If heaters are connected to cylinders manifolded together for use in an unpartitioned area on the same floor, the total water capacity of cylinders manifolded together serving any one heater shall not be greater than 735 lb (333 kg) [nominal 300 lb (136 kg) propane capacity]. If there is more than one such manifold, it shall be separated from any other by at least 20 ft (6.1 m). [**58:**6.20.4.8]

69.3.10.3.9 Where cylinders are manifolded together for connection to a heater(s) on another floor, the following shall apply.

(1) Heaters shall not be installed on the same floors with manifolded cylinders.
(2) The total water capacity of the cylinders connected to any one manifold shall not be greater than 2450 lb (1111 kg) [nominal 1000 lb (454 kg) propane capacity]
(3) Manifolds of more than 735 lb (333 kg) water capacity [nominal 300 lb (136 kg) propane capacity], if located in the same unpartitioned area, shall be separated from each other by at least 50 ft (15 m). [**58:**6.20.4.9]

69.3.10.3.10 Where compliance with the provisions of 69.3.10.3.6 through 69.3.10.3.9 is impractical, alternate installation provisions shall be allowed with the approval of the AHJ. [**58:**6.20.4.10]

69.3.10.4 Buildings Undergoing Minor Renovation When Frequented by the Public.

69.3.10.4.1 Cylinders used and transported for repair or minor renovation in buildings frequented by the public during the hours the public normally occupies the building shall comply with the following:

(1) The maximum water capacity of individual cylinders shall be 50 lb (23 kg) [nominal 20 lb (9.1 kg) propane capacity], and the number of cylinders in the building shall not exceed the number of workers assigned to the use of the propane.
(2) Cylinders having a water capacity greater than 2.7 lb (1.2 kg) shall not be left unattended. [**58:**6.20.5.1]

69.3.10.4.2 During the hours the building is not open to the public, cylinders used and transported within the building for repair or minor renovation and with a water capacity greater than 2.7 lb (1.2 kg) shall not be left unattended. [**58:**6.20.5.2]

69.3.10.5 Buildings Housing Industrial Occupancies.

69.3.10.5.1 Cylinders used in buildings housing industrial occupancies for processing, research, or experimental purposes shall comply with 69.3.10.5.1.1 and 69.3.10.5.1.2. [**58:**6.20.6.1]

69.3.10.5.1.1 If cylinders are manifolded together, the total water capacity of the connected cylinders shall be not more than 735 lb (333 kg) [nominal 300 lb (136 kg) propane capacity]. If there is more than one such manifold in a room, it shall be separated from any other by at least 20 ft (6.1 m). [**58:**6.20.6.1(A)]

69.3.10.5.1.2 The amount of LP-Gas in cylinders for research and experimental use in the building shall be limited to the smallest practical quantity. [**58:**6.20.6.1(B)]

69.3.10.5.2 The use of cylinders to supply fuel for temporary heating in buildings housing industrial occupancies with essentially noncombustible contents shall comply with the requirements in 69.3.10.3 for cylinders in buildings under construction. [**58:**6.20.6.2]

69.3.10.5.3 The use of fuel cylinders for temporary heating shall be permitted only where portable equipment for space heating is essential and a permanent heating installation is not practical. [**58:**6.20.6.3]

69.3.10.6 Buildings Housing Educational and Institutional Occupancies.

69.3.10.6.1 The use of cylinders in classrooms shall be prohibited unless they are used temporarily for classroom demonstrations in accordance with 69.3.10.8.1. [**58:**6.20.7.1]

69.3.10.6.2 Where cylinders are used in buildings housing educational and institutional laboratory occupancies for research and experimental purposes, the following shall apply:

(1) The maximum water capacity of individual cylinders used shall be 50 lb (23 kg) [nominal 20 lb (9.1 kg) propane capacity] if used in educational occupancies and 12 lb (5.4 kg) [nominal 5 lb (2 kg) propane capacity] if used in institutional occupancies.
(2) If more than one such cylinder is located in the same room, the cylinders shall be separated by at least 20 ft (6.1 m).

(3) Cylinders not connected for use shall be stored in accordance with Chapter 8 of NFPA 58.
(4) Cylinders shall not be stored in a laboratory room. [58:6.20.7.2]

69.3.10.7 Temporary Heating and Food Service Appliances in Buildings in Emergencies.

69.3.10.7.1 Cylinders shall not be used in buildings for temporary emergency heating purposes except when all of the following conditions are met:

(1) The permanent heating system is temporarily out of service.
(2) Heat is necessary to prevent damage to the buildings or contents.
(3) The cylinders and heaters comply with, and are used and transported in accordance with, 69.3.10.2 and 69.3.10.3.
(4) The temporary heating equipment is not left unattended.
(5) Air for combustion and ventilation is provided in accordance with NFPA 54, *National Fuel Gas Code*. [58:6.20.8.1]

69.3.10.7.2 When a public emergency has been declared and gas, fuel, or electrical service has been interrupted, portable listed LP-Gas commercial food service appliances meeting the requirements of 69.3.10.8.4 shall be permitted to be temporarily used inside affected buildings. [58:6.20.8.2]

69.3.10.7.3 The portable appliances used shall be discontinued and removed from the building at the time the permanently installed appliances are placed back in operation. [58:6.20.8.3]

69.3.10.8 Use in Buildings for Demonstrations or Training, and Use of Small Cylinders for Self-Contained Torch Assemblies and Food Service Appliances.

69.3.10.8.1 Cylinders used temporarily inside buildings for public exhibitions or demonstrations, including use in classroom demonstrations, shall be in accordance with the following:

(1) The maximum water capacity of a cylinder shall be 12 lb (5.4 kg) [nominal 5 lb (2 kg) propane capacity].
(2) If more than one such cylinder is located in a room, the cylinders shall be separated by at least 20 ft (6.1 m). [58:6.20.9.1]

69.3.10.8.2 Cylinders used temporarily in buildings for training purposes related to the installation and use of LP-Gas systems shall be in accordance with the following:

(1) The maximum water capacity of individual cylinders shall be 245 lb (111 kg) [nominal 100 lb (45 kg) propane capacity], but not more than 20 lb (9.1 kg) of propane shall be placed in a single cylinder.
(2) If more than one such cylinder is located in the same room, the cylinders shall be separated by at least 20 ft (6.1 m).
(3) The training location shall be acceptable to the AHJ.
(4) Cylinders shall be promptly removed from the building when the training class has terminated. [58:6.20.9.2]

69.3.10.8.3* Cylinders used in buildings as part of approved self-contained torch assemblies or similar appliances shall be in accordance with the following:

(1) Cylinders used in buildings shall comply with ANSI/UL 147A, *Standard for Nonrefillable (Disposable) Type Fuel Gas Cylinder Assemblies*.
(2) Cylinders shall have a maximum water capacity of 2.7 lb (1.2 kg). [58:6.20.9.3]

69.3.10.8.4 Cylinders used with commercial food service appliances shall be used inside restaurants and in attended commercial food catering operations in accordance with the following:

(1) Cylinders and appliances shall be listed.
(2) Commercial food service appliances shall not have more than two 10 oz (296 ml) nonrefillable butane gas cylinders, each having a maximum capacity of 1.08 lb (0.490 kg).
(3) Cylinders shall comply with ANSI/UL 147B, *Standard for Nonrefillable (Disposable) Type Metal Container Assemblies for Butane*.
(4) Cylinders shall be connected directly to the appliance and shall not be manifolded.
(5) Cylinders shall be an integral part of the listed, approved, commercial food service device and shall be connected without the use of a rubber hose.
(6) Storage of cylinders shall be in accordance with 8.3.1 of NFPA 58. [58:6.20.9.4]

69.3.10.9 Cylinders on Roofs or Exterior Balconies.

69.3.10.9.1 Where cylinders are installed permanently on roofs of buildings, the buildings shall be of fire-resistant construction or noncombustible construction having essentially noncombustible contents, or of other construction or contents that are protected with automatic sprinklers. [58:6.20.11.1]

69.3.10.9.1.1 The total water capacity of cylinders connected to any one manifold shall be not greater than 980 lb (445 kg) [nominal 400 lb (181 kg) propane capacity]. If more than one manifold is located on the roof, it shall be separated from any other by at least 50 ft (15 m). [58:6.20.11.1(A)]

69.3.10.9.1.2 Cylinders shall be located in areas where there is free air circulation, at least 10 ft (3 m) from building openings (such as windows and doors), and at least 20 ft (6.1 m) from air intakes of air-conditioning and ventilating systems. [58:6.20.11.1(B)]

69.3.10.9.1.3 Cylinders shall not be located on roofs that are entirely enclosed by parapets more than 18 in. (460 mm) high unless the parapets are breached with low-level ventilation openings not more than 20 ft (6.1 m) apart, or unless all openings communicating with the interior of the building are at or above the top of the parapets. [58:6.20.11.1(C)]

69.3.10.9.1.4 Piping shall be in accordance with 69.3.10.2.3 through 69.3.10.2.5. [58:6.20.11.1(D)]

69.3.10.9.1.5 Hose shall not be used for connection to cylinders. [58:6.20.11.1(E)]

69.3.10.9.1.6 The fire department shall be advised of each installation. [58:6.20.11.1(F)]

69.3.10.9.2 Cylinders having water capacities greater than 2.7 lb (1 kg) [nominal 1 lb (0.5 kg) LP-Gas capacity] shall not be located on decks or balconies of dwellings of two or more living units above the first floor unless they are served by exterior stairways. [58:6.20.11.2]

69.3.11 Installation of Appliances.

69.3.11.1 Installation of Patio Heaters.

69.3.11.1.1 Patio heaters utilizing an integral LP-Gas container greater than 1.08 lb (0.49 kg) propane capacity shall comply with 69.3.11.1.2 and 69.3.11.1.3. [58:6.21.2.1]

2015 Edition

69.3.11.1.2 Patio heaters shall be listed and used in accordance with their listing and the manufacturer's instructions. [58:6.21.2.2]

69.3.11.1.3 Patio heaters shall not be located within 5 ft (1.5 m) of exits from an assembly occupancy. [58:6.21.2.3]

69.3.11.2 Hose for Portable Appliances.

69.3.11.2.1 The requirements of 69.3.11 shall apply to hoses used on the low-pressure side of regulators to connect portable appliances. [58:6.21.3.1]

69.3.11.2.2 Where used inside buildings, the following shall apply:

(1) The hose shall be the minimum practical length and shall be in accordance with 69.3.10.2.5.
(2) The hose shall not extend from one room to another or pass through any partitions, walls, ceilings, or floors except as provided by 69.3.10.3.9.
(3) The hose shall not be concealed from view or used in concealed locations. [58:6.21.3.2]

69.3.11.2.3 Where installed outside of buildings, the hose length shall be permitted to exceed 10 ft (3.3 m) but shall be as short as practical. [58:6.21.3.3]

69.3.11.2.4 Hose shall be securely connected to the appliance. [58:6.21.3.4]

69.3.11.2.5 The use of rubber slip ends shall not be permitted. [58:6.21.3.5]

69.3.11.2.6 A shutoff valve shall be provided in the piping immediately upstream of the inlet connection of the hose. [58:6.21.3.6]

69.3.11.2.7 Where more than one such appliance shutoff is located near another, the valves shall be marked to indicate which appliance is connected to each valve. [58:6.21.3.7]

69.3.11.2.8 Hose shall be protected against physical damage. [58:6.21.3.8]

69.3.12 LP-Gas Systems on Vehicles (Other Than Engine Fuel Systems).

69.3.12.1* Application. Subsection 69.3.12 shall apply to the following:

(1) Nonengine fuel systems on all vehicles
(2) Installations served by exchangeable (removable) cylinder systems and by permanently mounted containers [58:6.24.1]

69.3.12.2 Nonapplication. Subsection 69.3.12 shall not apply to the following:

(1) Systems installed on mobile homes
(2) Systems installed on recreational vehicles
(3) Cargo tank vehicles, cargo tank vehicles (trailers and semitrailers), and similar units used to transport LP-Gas as cargo, which are covered by Chapter 9 of NFPA 58
(4) LP-Gas engine fuel systems on the vehicles, which are covered by Chapter 11 of NFPA 58 [58:6.24.2]

69.3.12.3 Container Installation Requirements.

69.3.12.3.1 Containers shall comply with 69.3.12.3.1.1 through 69.3.12.3.1.4. [58:6.24.3.1]

69.3.12.3.1.1 ASME mobile containers shall in accordance with one of the following:

(1) A MAWP of 312 psig (2.2 MPag) or higher where installed in enclosed spaces of vehicles
(2) A MAWP of 312 psig (2.2 MPag) or higher where installed on passenger vehicles
(3) A MAWP of 250 psig (1.7 MPag) or higher for containers where installed on the exterior of nonpassenger vehicles [58:6.24.3.1(A)]

69.3.12.3.1.2 LP-Gas fuel containers used on passenger-carrying vehicles shall not exceed 200 gal (0.8 m³) aggregate water capacity. [58:6.24.3.1(B)]

69.3.12.3.1.3 The capacity of individual LP-Gas containers on highway vehicles shall be in accordance with Table 69.3.12.3.1.3. [58:6.24.3.1(C)]

Table 69.3.12.3.1.3 Maximum Capacities of Individual LP-Gas Containers Installed on LP-Gas Highway Vehicles

Vehicle	Maximum Container Water Capacity	
	gal	m³
Passenger vehicle	200	0.8
Nonpassenger vehicle	300	1.1
Road surfacing vehicle	1000	3.8
Cargo tank vehicle	Not limited by NFPA 58	

[58:Table 6.24.3.1(C)]

69.3.12.3.1.4 Containers designed for stationary service only and not in compliance with the container appurtenance protection requirements of 5.2.6 of NFPA 58 shall not be used. [58:6.24.3.1(D)]

69.3.12.3.2 ASME containers and cylinders utilized for the purposes covered by 69.3.12 shall not be installed, transported, or stored (even temporarily) inside any vehicle covered by 69.3.12, except for ASME containers installed in accordance with 69.3.12.3.4.9, Chapter 9 of NFPA 58, or DOT regulations. [58:6.24.3.2]

69.3.12.3.3 The LP-Gas supply system, including the containers, shall be installed either on the outside of the vehicle or in a recess or cabinet vaportight to the inside of the vehicle but accessible from and vented to the outside, with the vents located near the top and bottom of the enclosure and 3 ft (1 m) horizontally away from any opening into the vehicle below the level of the vents. [58:6.24.3.3]

69.3.12.3.4 Containers shall be mounted securely on the vehicle or within the enclosing recess or cabinet. [58:6.24.3.4]

69.3.12.3.4.1 Containers shall be installed with road clearance in accordance with 11.8.3 of NFPA 58. [58:6.24.3.4(A)]

69.3.12.3.4.2 Fuel containers shall be mounted to prevent jarring loose and slipping or rotating, and the fastenings shall be designed and constructed to withstand, without permanent visible deformation, static loading in any direction equal to four times the weight of the container filled with fuel. [58:6.24.3.4(B)]

69.3.12.3.4.3 Where containers are mounted within a vehicle housing, the securing of the housing to the vehicle shall comply with this provision. Any removable portions of the housing or cabinet shall be secured while in transit. [**58**:6.24.3.4(C)]

69.3.12.3.4.4 Field welding on containers shall be limited to attachments to nonpressure parts such as saddle plates, wear plates, or brackets applied by the container manufacturer. [**58**:6.24.3.4(D)]

69.3.12.3.4.5 All container valves, appurtenances, and connections shall be protected to prevent damage from accidental contacts with stationary objects; from loose objects, stones, mud, or ice thrown up from the ground or floor; and from damage due to overturn or similar vehicular accident. [**58**:6.24.3.4(E)]

69.3.12.3.4.6 Permanently mounted ASME containers shall be located on the vehicle to provide the protection specified in 69.3.12.3.4.5. [**58**:6.24.3.4(F)]

69.3.12.3.4.7 Cylinders shall have permanent protection for cylinder valves and connections. [**58**:6.24.3.4(G)]

69.3.12.3.4.8 Where cylinders are located on the outside of a vehicle, weather protection shall be provided. [**58**:6.24.3.4(H)]

69.3.12.3.4.9 Containers mounted on the interior of passenger-carrying vehicles shall be installed in compliance with Section 11.9 of NFPA 58. Pressure relief valve installations for such containers shall comply with 11.8.5 of NFPA 58. [**58**:6.24.3.4(I)]

69.3.12.3.5 Cylinders installed on portable tar kettles alongside the kettle, on the vehicle frame, or on road surface heating equipment shall be protected from radiant or convected heat from open flame or other burners by the use of a heat shield or by the location of the cylinder(s) on the vehicle. In addition, the following shall apply:

(1) Cylinder valves shall be closed when burners are not in use.
(2) Cylinders shall not be refilled while burners are in use as provided in 7.2.3.2(B) of NFPA 58. [**58**:6.24.3.5]

69.3.12.4 Installation of Container Appurtenances.

69.3.12.4.1 Container appurtenances shall be installed in accordance with the following:

(1) Pressure relief valve installation on ASME containers installed in the interior of vehicles complying with Section 11.9 of NFPA 58 shall comply with 11.8.5 of NFPA 58.
(2) Pressure relief valve installations on ASME containers installed on the outside of vehicles shall comply with 11.8.5 of NFPA 58 and 69.3.12.3.3.
(3) Main shutoff valves on containers for liquid and vapor shall be readily accessible.
(4) Cylinders shall be designed to be filled in either the vertical or horizontal position, or if they are the universal type, they are permitted to be filled in either position.
(5) All container inlets, outlets, or valves installed in container inlets or outlets, except pressure relief devices and gauging devices, shall be labeled to designate whether they communicate with the vapor or liquid space.
(6) Containers from which only vapor is to be withdrawn shall be installed and equipped with connections to minimize the possibility of the accidental withdrawal of liquid. [**58**:6.24.4.1]

69.3.12.4.2 Regulators shall be installed in accordance with 6.8.2 of NFPA 58 and 69.3.12.4.2.1 through 69.3.12.4.2.5. [**58**:6.24.4.2]

69.3.12.4.2.1 Regulators shall be installed with the pressure relief vent opening pointing vertically downward to allow for drainage of moisture collected on the diaphragm of the regulator. [**58**:6.24.4.2(A)]

69.3.12.4.2.2 Regulators not installed in compartments shall be equipped with a durable cover designed to protect the regulator vent opening from sleet, snow, freezing rain, ice, mud, and wheel spray. [**58**:6.24.4.2(B)]

69.3.12.4.2.3 If vehicle-mounted regulators are installed at or below the floor level, they shall be installed in a compartment that provides protection against the weather and wheel spray. [**58**:6.24.4.2(C)]

69.3.12.4.2.4 Regulator compartments shall comply with the following:

(1) The compartment shall be of sufficient size to allow tool operation for connection to and replacement of the regulator(s).
(2) The compartment shall be vaportight to the interior of the vehicle.
(3) The compartment shall have a 1 in.^{2} (650 mm^2) minimum vent opening to the exterior located within 1 in. (25 mm) of the bottom of the compartment.
(4) The compartment shall not contain flame or spark-producing equipment. [**58**:6.24.4.2(D)]

69.3.12.4.2.5 A regulator vent outlet shall be at least 2 in. (51 mm) above the compartment vent opening. [**58**:6.24.4.2(E)]

69.3.12.5 Piping.

69.3.12.5.1 Piping shall be installed in accordance with 6.9.3 of NFPA 58 and 69.3.12.5.1.1 through 69.3.12.5.1.13. [**58**:6.24.5.1]

69.3.12.5.1.1 Steel tubing shall have a minimum wall thickness of 0.049 in. (1.2 mm). [**58**:6.24.5.1(A)]

69.3.12.5.1.2 A flexible connector shall be installed between the regulator outlet and the fixed piping system to protect against expansion, contraction, jarring, and vibration strains. [**58**:6.24.5.1(B)]

69.3.12.5.1.3 Flexibility shall be provided in the piping between a cylinder and the gas piping system or regulator. [**58**:6.24.5.1(C)]

69.3.12.5.1.4 Flexible connectors shall be installed in accordance with 6.9.6 of NFPA 58. [**58**:6.24.5.1(D)]

69.3.12.5.1.5 Flexible connectors longer than the length allowed in the *Code*, or fuel lines that incorporate hose, shall be used only where approved. [**58**:6.24.5.1(E)]

69.3.12.5.1.6 The piping system shall be designed, installed, supported, and secured to minimize the possibility of damage due to vibration, strains, or wear and to preclude any loosening while in transit. [**58**:6.24.5.1(F)]

69.3.12.5.1.7 Piping shall be installed in a protected location. [**58**:6.24.5.1(G)]

69.3.12.5.1.8 Where piping is installed outside the vehicle, it shall be installed as follows:

(1) Piping shall be under the vehicle and below any insulation or false bottom.
(2) Fastening or other protection shall be installed to prevent damage due to vibration or abrasion.

(3) At each point where piping passes through sheet metal or a structural member, a rubber grommet or equivalent protection shall be installed to prevent chafing. [**58**:6.24.5.1(H)]

69.3.12.5.1.9 Gas piping shall be installed to enter the vehicle through the floor directly beneath or adjacent to the appliance served. [**58**:6.24.5.1(I)]

69.3.12.5.1.10 If a branch line is installed, the tee connection shall be located in the main gas line under the floor and outside the vehicle. [**58**:66.24.5.1(J)]

69.3.12.5.1.11 Exposed parts of the fixed piping system either shall be of corrosion-resistant material or shall be coated or protected to minimize exterior corrosion. [**58**:6.24.5.1(K)]

69.3.12.5.1.12 Hydrostatic relief valves shall be installed in isolated sections of liquid piping as provided in Section 6.13 of NFPA 58. [**58**:6.24.5.1(L)]

69.3.12.5.1.13 Piping systems, including hose, shall be pressure tested and proven free of leaks in accordance with Section 6.14 of NFPA 58. [**58**:6.24.5.1(M)]

69.3.12.5.2 There shall be no fuel connection between a tractor and trailer or other vehicle units. [**58**:6.24.5.2]

69.3.12.6 Equipment Installation. Equipment shall be installed in accordance with Section 6.18 of NFPA 58 and 69.3.12.6.1 and 69.3.12.6.2. [**58**:6.24.6]

69.3.12.6.1 Installation shall be made in accordance with the manufacturer's recommendations and, in the case of approved equipment, as provided in the approval. [**58**:6.24.6.1]

69.3.12.6.2 Equipment installed on vehicles shall be protected against vehicular damage as provided for container appurtenances and connections in 69.3.12.3.4.5. [**58**:6.24.6.2]

69.3.12.7 Appliance Installation on Vehicles.

69.3.12.7.1 Paragraph 69.3.12.7 shall apply to the installation of all appliances on vehicles. It shall not apply to engines. [**58**:6.24.7.1]

69.3.12.7.2 All appliances covered by 69.3.12.7 installed on vehicles shall be approved. [**58**:6.24.7.2]

69.3.12.7.3 Where the device or appliance, such as a cargo heater or cooler, is designed to be in operation while the vehicle is in transit, means, such as an excess flow valve to stop the flow of gas in the event of a line break, shall be installed. [**58**:6.24.7.3]

69.3.12.7.4 Gas-fired heating appliances shall be equipped with shutoffs in accordance with 5.20.7(A) of NFPA 58 except for portable heaters used with cylinders having a maximum water capacity of 2.7 lb (1.2 kg), portable torches, melting pots, and tar kettles. [**58**:6.24.7.4]

69.3.12.7.5 Gas-fired heating appliances, other than ranges and illuminating appliances installed on vehicles intended for human occupancy, shall be designed or installed to provide for a complete separation of the combustion system from the atmosphere inside the vehicle. [**58**:6.24.7.5]

69.3.12.7.6* Where unvented-type heaters that are designed to protect cargo are used on vehicles not intended for human occupancy, provisions shall be made to provide air from the outside for combustion and dispose of the products of combustion to the outside. [**58**:6.24.7.6]

69.3.12.7.7 Appliances installed in the cargo space of a vehicle shall be readily accessible whether the vehicle is loaded or empty. [**58**:6.24.7.7]

69.3.12.7.8 Appliances shall be constructed or otherwise protected to minimize possible damage or impaired operation due to cargo shifting or handling. [**58**:6.24.7.8]

69.3.12.7.9 Appliances shall be located so that a fire at any appliance will not block egress of persons from the vehicle. [**58**:6.24.7.9]

69.3.12.7.10 A permanent caution plate shall be affixed to either the appliance or the vehicle outside of any enclosure, shall be adjacent to the container(s), and shall include the following instructions:

CAUTION:

(1) Be sure all appliance valves are closed before opening container valve.
(2) Connections at the appliances, regulators, and containers shall be checked periodically for leaks with soapy water or its equivalent.
(3) Never use a match or flame to check for leaks.
(4) Container valves shall be closed when equipment is not in use. [**58**:6.24.7.10]

69.3.12.7.11 Gas-fired heating appliances and water heaters shall be equipped with automatic devices designed to shut off the flow of gas to the main burner and the pilot in the event the pilot flame is extinguished. [**58**:6.24.7.11]

69.3.12.8 General Precautions.

69.3.12.8.1 Mobile units including mobile kitchens and catering vehicles that contain hotplates and other cooking equipment shall be provided with at least one approved portable fire extinguisher rated in accordance with Section 13.6 and NFPA 10 at not less than 10-B:C. [**58**:6.24.8.1]

69.3.12.8.2 Where fire extinguishers have more than one letter classification, they can be considered as meeting the requirements of each letter class. [**58**:6.24.8.2]

69.3.12.9 Parking, Servicing, and Repair.

69.3.12.9.1 Where vehicles with LP-Gas fuel systems used for purposes other than propulsion are parked, serviced, or repaired inside buildings, the requirements of 69.3.12.9.2 through 69.3.12.9.4 shall apply. [**58**:6.24.9.1]

69.3.12.9.2 The fuel system shall be leak-free, and the container(s) shall not be filled beyond the limits specified in Chapter 7 of NFPA 58. [**58**:6.24.9.2]

69.3.12.9.3 The container shutoff valve shall be closed, except that the container shutoff valve shall not be required to be closed when fuel is required for test or repair. [**58**:6.24.9.3]

69.3.12.9.4 The vehicle shall not be parked near sources of heat, open flames, or similar sources of ignition, or near unventilated pits. [**58**:6.24.9.4]

69.3.12.9.5 Vehicles having containers with water capacities larger than 300 gal (1.1 m^3) shall comply with the requirements of Section 9.7 of NFPA 58. [**58**:6.24.9.5]

69.3.13 Vehicle Fuel Dispenser and Dispensing Stations.

69.3.13.1 Application.

69.3.13.1.1 Subsection 69.3.13 includes the location, installation, and operation of vehicle fuel dispensers and dispensing stations. [**58**:6.25.1.1]

69.3.13.1.2 The provisions of 69.3.2 and 69.3.3, as modified by 69.3.13, shall apply. [**58:**6.25.1.2]

69.3.13.2 Location.

69.3.13.2.1 Location of vehicle fuel dispensers and dispensing stations shall be in accordance with Table 69.3.5.2.1. [**58:**6.25.2.1]

69.3.13.2.2 Vehicle fuel dispensers and dispensing stations shall be located away from pits in accordance with Table 69.3.5.2.1, with no drains or blow-offs from the unit directed toward or within 15 ft (4.6 m) of a sewer system's opening. [**58:**6.25.2.2]

69.3.13.3 General Installation Provisions.

69.3.13.3.1 Vehicle fuel dispensers and dispensing stations shall be installed in accordance with the manufacturer's installation instructions. [**58:**6.25.3.1]

69.3.13.3.2 Vehicle fuel dispensers and dispensing stations shall not be located within a building or structure, unless they comply with Chapter 10 of NFPA 58. [**58:**6.25.3.2]

69.3.13.3.3 Where a vehicle fuel dispenser is installed under a weather shelter or canopy, the area shall be ventilated and shall not be enclosed for more than 50 percent of its perimeter. [**58:**6.25.3.3]

69.3.13.3.4 Control for the pump used to transfer LP-Gas through the unit into containers shall be provided at the device in order to minimize the possibility of leakage or accidental discharge. [**58:**6.25.3.4]

69.3.13.3.5 An excess-flow check valve or a differential back pressure valve shall be installed in or on the dispenser at the point at which the dispenser hose is connected to the liquid piping. [**58:**6.25.3.5]

69.3.13.3.6 Piping and the dispensing hose shall be provided with hydrostatic relief valves in accordance with Section 6.13 of NFPA 58. [**58:**6.25.3.6]

69.3.13.3.7 Protection against trespassing and tampering shall be in accordance with 6.19.4 of NFPA 58. [**58:**6.25.3.7]

69.3.13.3.8 The container liquid withdrawal opening used with vehicle fuel dispensers and dispensing stations shall be equipped with one of the following:

(1) An internal valve fitted for remote closure and automatic shutoff using thermal (fire) actuation
(2) A positive shutoff valve that is located as close to the container as practical in combination with an excess-flow valve installed in the container, plus an emergency shutoff valve that is fitted for remote closure and installed downstream in the line as close as practical to the positive shutoff valve [**58:**6.25.3.8]

69.3.13.3.9 An identified and accessible remote emergency shutoff device for either the internal valve or the emergency shutoff valve required by 69.3.13.3.8(1) or (2) shall be installed not less than 3 ft (1 m) or more than 100 ft (30 m) from the liquid transfer point. [**58:**6.25.3.9]

69.3.13.3.10 Emergency shutoff valves and internal valves that are fitted for remote closure as required in this section shall be tested annually for proper operation. [**58:**6.25.3.10]

69.3.13.3.11 A manual shutoff valve and an excess-flow check valve shall be located in the liquid line between the pump and the dispenser inlet where the dispensing device is installed at a remote location and is not part of a complete storage and dispensing unit mounted on a common base. [**58:**6.25.3.11]

69.3.13.3.12 All dispensers shall be installed either on a concrete foundation or shall be part of a complete storage and dispensing unit mounted on a common base and installed in accordance with 6.6.3.1(G) of NFPA 58. [**58:**6.25.3.12]

69.3.13.3.13 Vehicle barrier protection (VBP) shall be provided for containers serving liquid dispensers where those containers are located within 10 ft of a vehicle thoroughfare or parking location. Such protection shall be either 69.3.13.3.13.1 or 69.3.13.3.13.2. [**58:**6.25.3.13]

69.3.13.3.13.1 Concrete filled guard posts constructed of steel not less than 4 in. (102 mm) in diameter, with the following characteristics:

(1) Spaced not more than 4 ft (1219 mm) between posts on center
(2) Set not less than 3 ft (900 mm) deep in a concrete footing of not less than 15 in. (380 mm) diameter
(3) Set with the top of the posts not less than 3 ft (900 mm) above ground
(4) Located not less than 3 ft (900 mm) from the protected installation [**58:**6.25.3.13(A)]

69.3.13.3.13.2 Equivalent protection in lieu of guard posts shall be a minimum of 3 ft (900 mm) in height and shall resist a force of 12,000 lb (53.375 N) applied 3 ft (900 mm) above the adjacent ground surface. [**58:**6.25.3.13(B)]

69.3.13.3.14 Where the dispenser is not mounted on a common base with its storage container and the dispensing unit is located within 10 ft of a vehicle thoroughfare, parking location, or a engine fuel filling station, the dispenser shall be provided with VBP. [**58:**6.25.3.14]

69.3.13.3.15 Dispensers shall be protected from physical damage. [**58:**6.25.3.15]

69.3.13.3.16 A listed quick-acting shutoff valve shall be installed at the discharge end of the transfer hose. [**58:**6.25.3.16]

69.3.13.3.17 An identified and accessible switch or circuit breaker shall be installed outside at a location not less than 20 ft (6.1 m) or more than 100 ft (30.5 m) from the dispensing device(s) to shut off the power in the event of a fire, an accident, or other emergency. [**58:**6.25.3.17]

69.3.13.3.18 The markings for the switches or breakers shall be visible at the point of liquid transfer. [**58:**6.25.3.18]

69.3.13.4 Installation of Vehicle Fuel Dispensers.

69.3.13.4.1 Hose shall comply with the following:

(1) Hose length shall not exceed 18 ft (5.5 m) unless approved by the AHJ.
(2) All hose shall be listed.
(3) When not in use, the hose shall be secured to protect the hose from damage. [**58:**6.25.4.1]

69.3.13.4.2 A listed emergency breakaway device shall be installed and shall comply with ANSI/UL 567, *Standard for Emergency Breakaway Fittings, Swivel Connectors, and Pipe-Connection Fittings for Petroleum Products and LP-Gas,* and be designed to retain liquid on both sides of the breakaway point, or other devices affording equivalent protection approved by the AHJ. [**58:**6.25.4.2]

69.3.13.4.3 Dispensing devices for LP-Gas shall be located as follows:

(1) Conventional systems shall be at least 10 ft (3.0 m) from any dispensing device for Class I liquids.
(2) Low-emission transfer systems in accordance with Section 6.28.5 of NFPA 58 shall be at least 5 ft (2 m) from any dispensing device for Class I liquids. [58:6.25.4.3]

69.4 LP-Gas Liquid Transfer.

69.4.1* Scope.

69.4.1.1 Section 69.4 applies to transfers of liquid LP-Gas from one container to another wherever this transfer involves connections and disconnections in the transfer system or the venting of LP-Gas to the atmosphere. [58:7.1.1]

69.4.1.2 Section 69.4 also applies to operational safety and methods for determining the quantity of LP-Gas permitted in containers. [58:7.1.2]

69.4.2 Operational Safety.

69.4.2.1 Transfer Personnel.

69.4.2.1.1 Transfer operations shall be conducted by qualified personnel meeting the provisions of Section 4.4 of NFPA 58. [58:7.2.1.1]

69.4.2.1.2 At least one qualified person shall remain in attendance at the transfer operation from the time connections are made until the transfer is completed, shutoff valves are closed, and lines are disconnected. [58:7.2.1.2]

69.4.2.1.3 Transfer personnel shall exercise caution to ensure that the LP-Gases transferred are those for which the transfer system and the containers to be filled are designed. [58:7.2.1.3]

69.4.2.2 Filling and Evacuating of Containers.

69.4.2.2.1 Transfer of LP-Gas to and from a container shall be accomplished only by qualified individuals trained in proper handling and operating procedures meeting the requirements of Section 4.4 of NFPA 58 and in emergency response procedures. [58:7.2.2.1]

69.4.2.2.2 When noncompliance with Section 5.2 and Section 5.7 of NFPA 58 is found, the container owner and user shall be notified in writing. [58:7.2.2.2]

69.4.2.2.3 Injection of compressed air, oxygen, or any oxidizing gas into containers to transfer LP-Gas liquid shall be prohibited. [58:7.2.2.3]

69.4.2.2.4 When evacuating a container owned by others, the qualified person(s) performing the transfer shall not inject any material other than LP-Gas into the container. [58:7.2.2.4]

69.4.2.2.5* Valve outlets on refillable cylinders of 108 lb (49 kg) water capacity [nominal 45 lb (20 kg) propane capacity] or less shall be equipped with a redundant pressure-tight seal or one of the following listed connections: CGA 790, CGA 791, or CGA 810, as described in CGA V-1, *Standard Compressed Gas Cylinder Valve Outlet and Inlet Connections*. [58:7.2.2.5]

69.4.2.2.6 Where redundant pressure seals are used, they shall be in place whenever the cylinder is not connected for use. [58:7.2.2.6]

69.4.2.2.7 Nonrefillable (disposable) and new unused cylinders shall not be required to be equipped with valve outlet seals. [58:7.2.2.7]

69.4.2.2.8 Containers shall be filled only after determination that they comply with the design, fabrication, inspection, marking, and requalification provisions of NFPA 58. [58:7.2.2.8]

69.4.2.2.9 Prior to refilling a cylinder that has a cylinder sleeve, the cylinder sleeve shall be removed to facilitate the visual inspection of the cylinder. [58:7.2.2.9]

69.4.2.2.10 "Single trip," "nonrefillable," or "disposable" cylinders shall not be refilled with LP-Gas. [58:7.2.2.10]

69.4.2.2.11 Containers shall comply with the following with regard to service or design pressure requirements:

(1) The service pressure marked on the cylinder shall be not less than 80 percent of the vapor pressure of the LP-Gas for which the cylinder is designed at 130°F (54.4°C).
(2) The maximum allowable working pressure (MAWP) for ASME containers shall be in accordance with Table 5.2.4.2 of NFPA 58. [58:7.2.2.11]

69.4.2.2.12 Transfer of refrigerated product shall be made only into systems that are designed to accept refrigerated product. [58:7.2.2.12]

69.4.2.2.13 A container shall not be filled if the container assembly does not meet the requirements for continued service. [58:7.2.2.13]

69.4.2.2.14 Transfer hoses larger than ½ in. (12 mm) internal diameter shall not be used for making connections to individual cylinders being filled indoors. [58:7.2.2.14]

69.4.2.3 Arrangement and Operation of Transfer Systems.

69.4.2.3.1 Public access to areas where LP-Gas is stored and transferred shall be prohibited, except where necessary for the conduct of normal business activities. [58:7.2.3.1]

69.4.2.3.2 Sources of ignition shall be turned off during transfer operations, while connections or disconnections are made, or while LP-Gas is being vented to the atmosphere. [58:7.2.3.2]

69.4.2.3.2.1 Internal combustion engines within 15 ft (4.6 m) of a point of transfer shall be shut down while such transfer operations are in progress, with the exception of the following:

(1) Engines of LP-Gas cargo tank vehicles, constructed and operated in compliance with Chapter 9 of NFPA 58, while such engines are driving transfer pumps or compressors on these vehicles to load containers in accordance with 6.5.2.2 of NFPA 58
(2) Engines for industrial (and forklift) trucks powered by LP-Gas used in buildings as provided in Section 11.13 of NFPA 58 [58:7.2.3.2(A)]

69.4.2.3.2.2 Smoking, open flame, portable electrical tools, and extension lights capable of igniting LP-Gas shall not be permitted within 25 ft (7.6 m) of a point of transfer while filling operations are in progress. [58:7.2.3.2(B)]

69.4.2.3.2.3 Metal cutting, grinding, oxygen–fuel gas cutting, brazing, soldering, or welding shall not be permitted within 35 ft (10.7 m) of a point of transfer while filling operations are in progress. [58:7.2.3.2(C)]

69.4.2.3.2.4 Materials that have been heated above the ignition temperature of LP-Gas shall be cooled before LP-Gas transfer is started. [**58**:7.2.3.2(D)]

69.4.2.3.2.5 Sources of ignition shall be turned off during the filling of any LP-Gas container on the vehicle. [**58**:7.2.3.2(E)]

69.4.2.3.3 Cargo tank vehicles unloading into storage containers shall be at least 10 ft (3.0 m) from the container and so positioned that the shutoff valves on both the truck and the container are readily accessible. [**58**:7.2.3.3]

69.4.2.3.4 The cargo tank vehicle shall not transfer LP-Gas into dispensing station storage while parked on a public way. [**58**:7.2.3.4]

69.4.2.3.5 Transfers to containers serving agricultural or industrial equipment requiring refueling in the field shall comply with 69.4.2.3.5.1 and 69.4.2.3.5.2. [**58**:7.2.3.5]

69.4.2.3.5.1* Where the intake of air-moving equipment is less than 50 ft (15 m) from a point of transfer, it shall be shut down while containers are being refilled. [**58**:7.2.3.5(A)]

69.4.2.3.5.2 Equipment employing open flames or equipment with integral containers shall be shut down while refueling. [**58**:7.2.3.5(B)]

69.4.2.3.6 During the time railroad tank cars are on sidings for loading or unloading, the following shall apply:

(1) A caution sign, with wording such as "STOP. TANK CAR CONNECTED," shall be placed at the active end(s) of the siding while the car is connected, as required by DOT regulations.
(2) Wheel chocks shall be placed to prevent movement of the car in either direction. [**58**:7.2.3.6]

69.4.2.3.7 Where a hose or swivel-type piping is used for loading or unloading railroad tank cars, it shall be protected as follows:

(1) An emergency shutoff valve shall be installed at the railroad tank car end of the hose or swivel-type piping where flow into or out of the railroad tank car is possible.
(2) An emergency shutoff valve or a backflow check valve shall be installed on the railroad tank car end of the hose or swivel piping where flow is only into the railroad tank car. [**58**:7.2.3.7]

69.4.2.3.8 Where cargo tank vehicles are filled directly from railroad tank cars on a private track with nonstationary storage tanks involved, the following requirements shall be met:

(1) Transfer protection shall be provided in accordance with 69.3.8.
(2) Ignition source control shall be in accordance with Section 6.23 of NFPA 58.
(3) Control of ignition sources during transfer shall be provided in accordance with 69.4.2.3.2.
(4) Fire extinguishers shall be provided in accordance with 9.4.7 of NFPA 58.
(5) Transfer personnel shall meet the provisions of 69.4.2.1.
(6) Cargo tank vehicles shall meet the requirements of 69.4.2.3.
(7) The points of transfer shall be located in accordance with 69.3.5.2.1 with respect to exposures.
(8) Provision for anchorage and breakaway shall be provided on the cargo tank vehicle side for transfer from a railroad tank car directly into a cargo tank vehicle.

(9) The provisions of Chapter 14 of NFPA 58 shall apply to all LP-Gas transfers performed in accordance with 69.4.2.3.8. [**58**:7.2.3.8]

69.4.2.3.9 Where cargo tank vehicles are filled from other cargo tank vehicles or cargo tanks, the following requirements shall apply:

(1) Transfer between cargo tanks or cargo tank vehicles where one is used as a bulk plant shall be temporary installations that comply with 4.3.2, 6.19.1, 6.19.2, 6.19.4 through 6.19.6 of NFPA 58, and 69.4.2.3.1.
(2) Arrangements and operations of the transfer system shall be in accordance with the following:
  (a) The point of transfer shall be in accordance with Table 69.3.5.2.1.
  (b) Sources of ignition within the transfer area shall be controlled during the transfer operation as specified in 69.4.2.3.2.
  (c) Fire extinguishers shall be provided in accordance with 9.4.7 of NFPA 58.
(3) Cargo tanks shall comply with the requirements of 69.4.2.2.8.
(4) Provisions designed either to prevent a pull-away during a transfer operation or to stop the flow of products from both cargo tank vehicles or cargo tanks in the event of a pull-away shall be incorporated.
(5) Off-truck remote shutoff devices that meet 49 CFR 173.315(n) requirements and are installed on the cargo tank vehicle unloading the product shall satisfy the requirements of 69.4.2.3.9.
(6) Cargo tank vehicle LP-Gas transfers that are for the sole purpose of testing, maintaining, or repairing the cargo tank vehicle shall be exempt from the requirements of 69.4.2.3.9. [**58**:7.2.3.9]

69.4.2.4 Hose Inspection.

69.4.2.4.1 Hose assemblies shall be observed for leakage or for damage that could impair their integrity before each use. [**58**:7.2.4.1]

69.4.2.4.2 The hose assemblies specified in 69.4.2.4.1 shall be inspected at least annually. [**58**:7.2.4.2]

69.4.2.4.3 Inspection of pressurized hose assemblies shall include inspection for the following:

(1) Damage to outer cover that exposes reinforcement
(2) Kinked or flattened hose
(3) Soft spots or bulges in hose
(4) Couplings that have slipped on the hose, are damaged, have missing parts, or have loose bolts
(5) Leakage other than permeability leakage [**58**:7.2.4.3]

69.4.2.4.4 Hose assemblies shall be replaced, repaired, or continued in service based on the results of the inspection. [**58**:7.2.4.4]

69.4.2.4.5 Leaking or damaged hose shall be immediately repaired or removed from service. [**58**:7.2.4.5]

69.4.3 Venting LP-Gas to the Atmosphere.

69.4.3.1 General. LP-Gas in either liquid or vapor form shall not be vented to the atmosphere unless it is vented under the following conditions:

(1) Venting of LP-Gas shall be permitted where the maximum flow from fixed liquid level, rotary, or slip tube gauges does not exceed that from a No. 54 drill orifice.

(2) Venting of LP-Gas between shutoff valves before disconnecting the liquid transfer line from the container shall be permitted.
(3) Venting of LP-Gas, where necessary, shall be permitted to be performed by the use of bleeder valves.
(4) Venting of LP-Gas shall be permitted for the purposes described in 69.4.3.1(1) and 69.4.3.1(2) within structures designed for container filling in accordance with Chapter 10 of NFPA 58.
(5) Venting of LP-Gas listed liquid transfer pumps using such vapor as a source of energy shall be permitted where the rate of discharge does not exceed the discharge from a No. 31 drill size orifice.
(6) Venting of LP-Gas for purging in accordance with 7.3.2 of NFPA 58 shall be permitted.
(7) Venting of LP-Gas shall be permitted for emergencies.
(8) Venting of LP-Gas vapor utilized as the pressure source in remote shutdown systems for internal valves and emergency shutoff valves shall be permitted. [**58:**7.3.1]

69.5 Storage of Cylinders Awaiting Use, Resale, or Exchange.

69.5.1 Scope.

69.5.1.1 The provisions of Section 69.5 apply to the storage of cylinders of 1000 lb (454 kg) water capacity or less, whether filled, partially filled, or empty, as follows:

(1) At consumer sites or dispensing stations, where not connected for use
(2) In storage for resale or exchange by dealer or reseller [**58:**8.1.1]

69.5.1.2 Section 69.5 does not apply to new or unused cylinders. [**58:**8.1.2]

69.5.1.3 Section 69.5 does not apply to cylinders stored at bulk plants. [**58:**8.1.3]

69.5.2 General Provisions.

69.5.2.1 General Location of Cylinders.

69.5.2.1.1 Cylinders in storage shall be located to minimize exposure to excessive temperature rises, physical damage, or tampering. [**58:**8.2.1.1]

69.5.2.1.2 Cylinders in storage having individual water capacity greater than 2.7 lb (1.1 kg) [nominal 1 lb (0.45 kg) LP-Gas capacity] shall be positioned so that the pressure relief valve is in direct communication with the vapor space of the cylinder. [**58:**8.2.1.2]

69.5.2.1.3 Cylinders stored in buildings in accordance with 69.5.3 shall not be located near exits, near stairways, or in areas normally used, or intended to be used, for the safe egress of occupants. [**58:**8.2.1.3]

69.5.2.1.4 If empty cylinders that have been in LP-Gas service are stored indoors, they shall be considered as full cylinders for the purposes of determining the maximum quantities of LP-Gas permitted by 69.5.3.1, 69.5.3.2.1, and 69.5.3.3.1. [**58:**8.2.1.4]

69.5.2.1.5 Cylinders shall not be stored on roofs. [**58:**8.2.1.5]

69.5.2.2 Protection of Valves on Cylinders in Storage.

69.5.2.2.1 Cylinder valves shall be protected as required by 69.2.1.2.1 and 69.4.2.2.5. [**58:**8.2.2.1]

69.5.2.2.2 Screw-on-type caps or collars shall be in place on all cylinders stored, regardless of whether they are full, partially full, or empty, and cylinder outlet valves shall be closed. [**58:**8.2.2.2]

69.5.2.2.3 Valve outlets on cylinders less than 108 lb (49 kg) water capacity [nominal 45 lb (20 kg) propane capacity] shall be plugged, capped, or sealed in accordance with 69.4.2.2.5. [**58:**8.2.2.3]

69.5.3 Storage Within Buildings.

69.5.3.1 General. Storage of cylinders in buildings shall be in accordance with Table 69.5.3.1(a) or Table 69.5.3.1(b) or the requirements of 69.5.3. [**58:**8.3.1]

69.5.3.2 Storage Within Buildings Frequented by the Public.

69.5.3.2.1 The quantity of LP-Gas in cylinders stored or displayed shall not exceed 200 lb (91 kg) in one location, with additional storage separated by 50 ft (15 m). The maximum quantity to be stored in one building shall not exceed 1000 lb (454 kg). [**58:**8.3.2.1]

69.5.3.2.1.1 Where the total quantity stored in a building exceeds 200 lb (91 kg), an approved sprinkler system that, at a minimum, meets the requirement of Section 13.3 and NFPA 13 for Ordinary Hazard (Group 2) shall be installed. [**58:**8.3.2.1(A)]

69.5.3.2.1.2 The sprinkler density shall be 0.300 gpm (12.2 L/min) over the most remote 2000 ft^2 (18.6 m^2) area, and the hose stream allowance shall be 250 gpm (946 L/min). [**58:**8.3.2.1(B)]

69.5.3.2.2 The cylinders shall not exceed a water capacity of 2.7 lb (1.1 kg) [nominal 1 lb (0.45 kg) LP-Gas]. [**58:**8.3.2.2]

69.5.3.2.3 In restaurants and at food service locations, storage of 10 oz (283 g) butane nonrefillable containers shall be limited to not more than 24 containers and 24 additional 10 oz (283 g) butane nonrefillable containers stored in another location within the building where constructed with at least 2-hour fire wall protection. [**58:**8.3.2.3]

69.5.3.3 Storage Within Buildings Not Frequented by the Public.

69.5.3.3.1 The maximum quantity of LP-Gas allowed in one storage location shall not exceed 735 lb (334 kg) water capacity [nominal 300 lb (136 kg) propane capacity]. [**58:**8.3.3.1]

69.5.3.3.2 Where additional storage locations are required on the same floor within the same building, they shall be separated by a minimum of 300 ft (91.4 m). [**58:**8.3.3.2]

69.5.3.3.3 Storage beyond the limitations described in 69.5.3.3.2 shall comply with 69.5.3.4. [**58:**8.3.3.3]

69.5.3.3.4 Cylinders carried as part of the service equipment on highway mobile vehicles shall not be part of the total storage capacity requirements of 69.5.3.3.1, where such vehicles are stored in private garages and carry no more than three cylinders with a total aggregate capacity per vehicle not exceeding 100 lb (45.4 kg) of propane. [**58:**8.3.3.4]

69.5.3.3.5 Cylinder valves shall be closed when not in use. [**58:**8.3.3.5]

69.5.3.4 Storage Within Special Buildings or Rooms.

69.5.3.4.1 The maximum quantity of LP-Gas stored in special buildings or rooms shall be 10,000 lb (4540 kg). [**58:**8.3.4.1]

69.5.3.4.2 Special buildings or rooms for storing LP-Gas cylinders shall not be located where the buildings or rooms adjoin the line of property occupied by schools, churches, hospitals, athletic fields, or other points of public gathering. [**58:**8.3.4.2]

Table 69.5.3.1(a) Maximum Allowable Storage Quantities of LP-Gas in Other Than Industrial, Storage, and Mercantile Occupancies

Occupancy	Assembly	Educational	Day Care	Health Care	Ambulatory Health Care	Detention and Correctional	One- and Two-Family Dwellings	Lodging or Rooming House	Hotel and Dormitory	Apartment	Residential Board and Care	Business
Maximum Allowable Quantity (MAQ):												
Storage (state units: lb, gal, etc.)	2 lb	2 lb	2 lb	2 lb	2 lb	2 lb	2 lb	2 lb	2 lb	2 lb	2 lb	2 lb
MAQ increases for:								Maximum 1 lb cylinders		1 lb cylinder		
Total (including cabinets)	2 lb	2 lb	2 lb	2 lb	2 lb	2 lb	2 lb	2 lb	2 lb	2 lb	2 lb	2 lb
Total for suppression	2 lb	2 lb	2 lb	2 lb	2 lb	2 lb	2 lb	2 lb	2 lb	2 lb	2 lb	2 lb
Total for both cabinets and suppression	0	2 lb	2 lb	2 lb	2 lb	2 lb	2 lb	2 lb	2 lb	2 lb	2 lb	2 lb
Attended catered food service per NFPA 58 in 10 oz maximum cylinders	15 lb	15 lb	15 lb	15 lb	15 lb	15 lb	15 lb	15 lb	15 lb	15 lb	15 lb	15 lb
			15 lb	15 lb	15 lb	15 lb	15 lb	15 lb	15 lb	15 lb	15 lb	15 lb
Additional 10 oz cylinders w/ 2-hr fire wall	15 lb	15 lb	15 lb	15 lb	15 lb	15 lb	15 lb	15 lb	15 lb	15 lb	15 lb	15 lb
Other												
Total (including threshold) for other	20 lb	20 lb	0	5 lb								
	Flame effects per NFPA 160. Additional 20 lb units with 20 ft (6 m) separation.	In labs, not in classrooms. Additional 20 lb units with 20 ft (6 m) separation.		In labs only. Additional 5 lb units with 20 ft separation						Amounts per dwelling		

[58: Table 8.3.1(a)]
For SI units, 1 lb = 0.45 kg, 1 oz = 0.028 kg.

69.5.3.4.3 The construction of all special buildings and rooms specified in 69.5.3.4.2 shall comply with Chapter 10 of NFPA 58 and the following:

(1) Vents to the outside only shall be provided at both the top and bottom of the building and shall be located at least 5 ft (1.5 m) from any building opening.
(2) The entire area shall be classified for purposes of ignition source control in accordance with Section 6.23 of NFPA 58. [58:8.3.4.3]

69.5.3.5 Storage Within Residential Buildings. Storage of cylinders within a residential building, including the basement or any storage area in a common basement of a multiple-family building and attached or detached garages, shall be limited to cylinders each with a maximum water capacity of 2.7 lb (1.2 kg) and shall not exceed 5.4 lb (2.4 kg) aggregate water capacity per each living space unit. [58:8.3.5]

69.5.4 Storage Outside of Buildings.

69.5.4.1* Location of Storage Outside of Buildings.

69.5.4.1.1 Storage outside of buildings for cylinders awaiting use or resale or that are part of a cylinder exchange point shall be located as follows:

Table 69.5.3.1(b) Maximum Allowable Storage Quantities of LP-Gas in Mercantile, Industrial, and Storage Occupancies

Occupancy	Mercantile	Industrial	Storage
Maximum Allowable Quantity (MAQ): Storage (state units: lb, gal, etc.)	200 lb (1 lb maximum/cylinder)	300 lb	300 lb
MAQ increases for: Total (including threshold) for cabinets	200 lb	300 lb	300 lb
Total (including threshold) for suppression	200 lb	300 lb	300 lb
Total (including threshold) for both cabinets and suppression	200 lb	300 lb	300 lb
Total (including threshold) for other (describe)	1000 lb Separation of groups of 200 lb by 50 ft and a sprinkler density of 0.300 gpm (1.1 L/min) over the most remote 2000 ft² (18.6 m²) area and 250 gpm (946 L/min) hose stream allowance	Additional 300 lb 300 ft separation	10,000 lb In special rooms or buildings per Chapter 10 of NFPA 58

[**58:** Table 8.3.1(b)]
For SI units, 1 lb = 0.45 kg; 1 gpm = 3.8 L/min; 1 ft = 0.3 m; 1 ft² = 0.09 m².

(1) At least 5 ft (1.5 m) from any doorway or opening in a building frequented by the public where occupants have at least two means of egress as defined by 3.3.176 and NFPA *101*
(2) At least 10 ft (3 m) from any doorway or opening in a building or sections of a building that has only one means of egress
(3) At least 20 ft (6.1 m) from any automotive service station fuel dispenser [**58:**8.4.1.1]

69.5.4.1.2 Distances from cylinders in storage outside of buildings shall be in accordance with Table 69.5.4.1.2 with respect to the following:

(1) Nearest important building or group of buildings
(2) Line of adjoining property that can be built upon
(3) Busy thoroughfares or sidewalks on other than private property
(4) Line of adjoining property occupied by schools, churches, hospitals, athletic fields, or other points of public gathering
(5) Dispensing station [**58:**8.4.1.2]

Table 69.5.4.1.2 Distances from Cylinders in Storage and Exposures

Quantity of LP-Gas Stored		Horizontal Distance to ...					
		(1) and (2)		(3) and (4)		(5)	
lb	kg	ft	m	ft	m	ft	m
≤720	≤227	0	0	0	0	5	1.5
721–2,500	>227–1,134	0	0	10	3	10	3
2,501–6,000	>1,134–2,721	10	3	10	3	10	3
6,001–10,000	>2,721–4,540	20	6.1	20	6.1	20	6.1
>10,000	>4,540	25	7.6	25	7.6	25	7.6

[**58:** Table 8.4.1.2]

69.5.4.1.3 Fire-Resistive Protective Structure.

(A) The distances in Table 69.5.4.1.2 shall be reduced to 0 where a 2-hour fire-resistive protective structure made of noncombustible materials is provided that breaks the line of sight of the storage and the building. [**58:**8.4.1.3(A)]

(B) For buildings with exterior walls rated 2-hour fire resistance and constructed of noncombustible materials not provided with eaves over the storage, the exterior wall shall be allowed in lieu of a protective structure to reduce the distance to 0. [**58:**8.4.1.3(B)]

69.5.4.1.4 Cylinders in the filling process shall not be considered to be in storage. [**58:**8.4.1.4]

69.5.4.2 Protection of Cylinders.

69.5.4.2.1* Cylinders at a location open to the public shall be protected by either of the following:

(1) An enclosure in accordance with 6.19.4.2 of NFPA 58
(2) A lockable ventilated enclosure of metal exterior construction [**58:**8.4.2.1]

69.5.4.2.2* Vehicular barrier protection (VBP) shall be provided where vehicle traffic is expected at the location. [**58:**8.4.2.2]

69.5.4.3 Alternate Location and Protection of Storage. Where the provisions of 69.5.4.1 and 69.5.4.2.1 are impractical at construction sites or at buildings or structures undergoing major renovation or repairs, alternative storage of cylinders shall be acceptable to the AHJ. [**58:**8.4.3]

69.5.5* Fire Protection and Electrical Area Classification.

69.5.5.1 Retail cylinder exchange locations shall be provided with at least one approved portable fire extinguisher having a minimum capacity of 10 lb (4.5 kg) dry chemical with an A:B:C rating complying with 69.5.5.3 on the premises where retail cylinder exchange cabinets are storing more than 720 lb (327 kg) of propane. [**58:**8.5.1]

69.5.5.2 Storage locations, other than those complying with 69.5.5.1, where the aggregate quantity of propane stored is in excess of 720 lb (327 kg), shall be provided with at least one approved portable fire extinguisher having a 40-B:C or 80-B:C rating and a minimum capacity of 18 lb (8.2 kg) dry chemical. [**58:**8.5.2]

69.5.5.3 The required fire extinguisher shall be located in accordance with 69.5.5.3.1 and 69.5.5.3.2. [**58**:8.5.3]

69.5.5.3.1 A 40-B:C fire extinguisher shall be located not more than 30 ft (10 m) from the propane storage location. [**58**:8.5.3.1]

69.5.5.3.2 An 80-B:C fire extinguisher shall be located not more than 50 ft (15 m) from the propane storage location. [**58**:8.5.3.2]

69.5.5.4 Where fire extinguishers have more than one letter classification, they shall be considered to satisfy the requirements of each letter class. [**58**:8.5.4]

69.5.5.5 The storage of cylinders awaiting resale shall be exempt from the electrical classification requirements of NFPA 58. [**58**:8.5.5]

69.5.6 Automated Cylinder Exchange Stations.

69.5.6.1 Cylinder exchange cabinets that include an automated vending system for exchanging cylinders shall comply with the requirements in 69.5.6.2 through 69.5.6.6. [**58**:8.6.1]

69.5.6.2 Electrical equipment installed in cylinder storage compartments shall comply with the requirements for Class I, Division 2 equipment in accordance with *NFPA 70, National Electrical Code*. [**58**:8.6.2]

69.5.6.3 Cabinets shall be designed such that cylinders can be placed inside only in the upright position. [**58**:8.6.3]

69.5.6.4 Door releases for access to stored cylinders shall be permitted to be pneumatic, mechanical, or electrically powered. [**58**:8.6.4]

69.5.6.5 A manual override control shall be permitted for use by authorized personnel. [**58**:8.6.5]

69.5.6.6 The vending system shall not be capable of returning to automatic operation after a manual override until the system has been inspected and reset by authorized personnel. [**58**:8.6.6]

69.6 Vehicular Transportation of LP-Gas.

69.6.1 Transportation in Portable Containers.

69.6.1.1 Transportation of Cylinders.

69.6.1.1.1 Cylinders having an individual water capacity not exceeding 1000 lb (454 kg) [nominal 420 lb (191 kg) propane capacity], when filled with LP-Gas, shall be transported in accordance with the requirements of 69.6.1. [**58**:9.3.2.1]

69.6.1.1.2 Cylinders shall be constructed as provided in 69.2.1 and equipped in accordance with Section 5.7 of NFPA 58 for transportation as cylinders. [**58**:9.3.2.2]

69.6.1.1.3 The quantity of LP-Gas in cylinders shall be in accordance with Chapter 7 of NFPA 58. [**58**:9.3.2.3]

69.6.1.1.4 Cylinder valves shall comply with the following:

(1) Valves of cylinders shall be protected in accordance with 69.2.1.2.1.
(2) Screw-on-type protecting caps or collars shall be secured in place.
(3) The provisions of 69.4.2.2.5 shall apply. [**58**:9.3.2.4]

69.6.1.1.5 The cargo space of the vehicle shall be isolated from the driver's compartment, the engine, and the engine's exhaust system. [**58**:9.3.2.5]

69.6.1.1.5.1 Open-bodied vehicles shall be considered to be in compliance with 69.6.1.1.5.

69.6.1.1.5.2 Closed-bodied vehicles having separate cargo, driver, and engine compartments shall be considered to be in compliance with 69.6.1.1.5. [**58**:9.3.2.5(B)]

69.6.1.1.5.3 Closed-bodied vehicles, such as passenger cars, vans, and station wagons, shall not be used for transporting more than 215 lb (98 kg) water capacity [nominal 90 lb (41 kg) propane capacity], but not more than 108 lb (49 kg) water capacity [nominal 45 lb (20 kg) propane capacity] per cylinder, unless the driver and engine compartments are separated from the cargo space by a vaportight partition that contains no means of access to the cargo space. [**58**:9.3.2.5(C)]

69.6.1.1.6 Cylinders and their appurtenances shall be determined to be leak-free before being loaded into vehicles. [**58**:9.3.2.6]

69.6.1.1.7 Cylinders shall be loaded into vehicles with flat floors or equipped with racks for holding cylinders. [**58**:9.3.2.7]

69.6.1.1.8 Cylinders shall be fastened in position to minimize the possibility of movement, tipping, and physical damage. [**58**:9.3.2.8]

69.6.1.1.9 Cylinders being transported by vehicles shall be positioned in accordance with Table 69.6.1.1.9. [**58**:9.3.2.9]

Table 69.6.1.1.9 Orientation of Cylinders on Vehicles

Propane Capacity of Cylinder			
lb	kg	Open Vehicles	Enclosed Spaces of Vehicles
≤45	≤20	Any position	
>45	>20	Relief valve in communication with the vapor space	
≤4.2	≤1.9		Any position
>4.2	>1.9		Relief valve in communication with the vapor space

[**58**:Table 9.3.2.9]

69.6.1.1.10 Vehicles transporting cylinders where the total weight is more than 1000 lb (454 kg), including the weight of the LP-Gas and the cylinders, shall be placarded as required by DOT regulations or state law. [**58**:9.3.2.10]

69.6.1.2 Fire Extinguishers.

69.6.1.2.1 Each truck or trailer transporting portable containers in accordance with 69.6.1.1 or 9.3.3 of NFPA 58 shall be equipped with at least one approved portable fire extinguisher having a minimum capacity of 18 lb (8.2 kg) dry chemical with a B:C rating. [**58**:9.3.5.1]

69.6.1.2.2 Where fire extinguishers have more than one letter classification, they shall be considered to satisfy the requirements of each letter class. [**58**:9.3.5.2]

69.6.2 Parking and Garaging Vehicles Used to Carry LP-Gas Cargo.

69.6.2.1 Application. Subsection 69.6.2 applies to the parking and garaging of vehicles used for the transportation of LP-Gas. [**58:**9.7.1]

69.6.2.2 Parking Outdoors.

69.6.2.2.1 Vehicles shall not be left unattended on any street, highway, avenue, or alley, except for necessary absences from the vehicle associated with drivers' normal duties, including stops for meals and rest stops during the day or night, except as follows:

(1) This requirement shall not apply in an emergency.
(2) This requirement shall not apply to vehicles parked in accordance with 69.6.2.2.3 and 69.6.2.2.4. [**58:**9.7.2.1]

69.6.2.2.2* Vehicles shall not be parked in congested areas. [**58:**9.7.2.2]

69.6.2.2.3 Where vehicles are parked off the street in uncongested areas, they shall be at least 50 ft (15 m) from any building used for assembly, institutional, or multiple residential occupancy. [**58:**9.7.2.3]

69.6.2.2.4 Where vehicles carrying portable containers or cargo tank vehicles of 3500 gal (13 m^3) water capacity or less are parked on streets adjacent to the driver's residence in uncongested residential areas, the parking locations shall be at least 50 ft (15 m) from a building used for assembly, institutional, or multiple residential occupancy. [**58:**9.7.2.4]

69.6.2.3 Parking Indoors.

69.6.2.3.1 Cargo tank vehicles parked in any public garage or building shall have LP-Gas liquid removed from the following:

(1) Cargo tank
(2) Piping
(3) Pump
(4) Meter
(5) Hose
(6) Related equipment [**58:**9.7.3.1]

69.6.2.3.2 Vehicles used to carry portable containers shall not be moved into any public garage or building for parking until all portable containers have been removed from the vehicle. [**58:**9.7.3.2]

69.6.2.3.3 The pressure in the delivery hose and related equipment shall be reduced to approximately atmospheric. [**58:**9.7.3.3]

69.6.2.3.4 All valves shall be closed before the vehicle is moved indoors. [**58:**9.7.3.4]

69.6.2.3.5 Delivery hose or valve outlets shall be plugged or capped before the vehicle is moved indoors. [**58:**9.7.3.5]

69.6.2.3.6 Vehicles carrying or containing LP-Gas shall only be parked in buildings complying with Chapter 10 of NFPA 58 and located on premises owned or under the control of the operator of such vehicles where the following provisions are met:

(1) The public shall be excluded from such buildings.
(2) Floor level ventilation shall be provided in all parts of the building where such vehicles are parked.
(3) Leaks in the vehicle LP-Gas systems shall be repaired before the vehicle is moved indoors.
(4) Primary shutoff valves on cargo tanks and other LP-Gas containers on the vehicle (except propulsion engine fuel containers) shall be closed and delivery hose outlets plugged or capped to contain system pressure before the vehicle is moved indoors.
(5) Primary shutoff valves on LP-Gas propulsion engine fuel containers shall be closed while the vehicle is parked.
(6) No LP-Gas container shall be located near a source of heat or within the direct path of hot air being blown from a blower-type heater.
(7) LP-Gas containers shall be gauged or weighed to determine that they are not filled beyond the maximum filling limit according to Section 7.4 of NFPA 58. [**58:**9.7.3.6]

69.6.2.3.7 Where vehicles are serviced or repaired indoors, the following shall apply:

(1) When it is necessary to move a vehicle into any building located on premises owned or operated by the operator of such vehicle for service on engine or chassis, the provisions of 69.6.2.3.6 shall apply.
(2) When it is necessary to move a vehicle carrying or containing LP-Gas into any public garage or repair facility for service on the engine or chassis, the provisions of 69.6.2.3.1 shall apply, or the driver or a qualified representative of an LP-Gas operator shall be in attendance at all times while the vehicle is indoors, and the following shall apply:
  (a) Leaks in the vehicle LP-Gas systems shall be repaired before the vehicle is moved indoors.
  (b) Primary shutoff valves on cargo tanks, portable containers, and other LP-Gas containers installed on the vehicle (other than propulsion engine fuel containers) shall be closed.
  (c) LP-Gas liquid shall be removed from the piping, pump, meter, delivery hose, and related equipment and the pressure therein reduced to approximately atmospheric before the vehicle is moved inside.
  (d) Delivery hose or valve outlets shall be plugged or capped before the vehicle is moved indoors.
  (e) No container shall be located near a source of heat or within the direct path of hot air blown from a blower or from a blower-type heater.
  (f) LP-Gas containers shall be gauged or weighed to determine that they are not filled beyond the maximum filling capacity in accordance with Section 7.4 of NFPA 58. [**58:**9.7.3.7]

69.6.2.3.8 If repair work or servicing is to be performed on a cargo tank vehicle system, all LP-Gas shall be removed from the cargo tank and piping, and the system shall be thoroughly purged before the vehicle is moved indoors. [**58:**9.7.3.8]

69.7 LP-Gases at Utility Plants. The design, construction, location, installation, and operation of refrigerated and non-refrigerated liquefied petroleum gas systems at utility gas plants shall be in accordance with NFPA 59, *Utility LP-Gas Plant Code.*

69.8 Liquefied Natural Gas (LNG) Facilities. The design, location, construction, and operation of liquefied natural gas facilities shall be in accordance with NFPA 59A, *Standard for the Production, Storage, and Handling of Liquefied Natural Gas (LNG).*

Chapter 70 Oxidizer Solids and Liquids

70.1 General.

70.1.1 The storage, use, and handling of oxidizer solids and liquids shall comply with the requirements of Chapter 60.

70.1.2 The storage, use, and handling of oxidizer solids and liquids in amounts exceeding the maximum allowable quantity permitted in control areas as set forth in Chapter 60 shall also comply with the requirements of NFPA 400, *Hazardous Materials Code*.

70.1.3 The display and storage of Class 1 through Class 3 oxidizer solids and liquids in mercantile, storage, or industrial occupancies where the general public has access to the material for sale, and to the storage of oxidizing solid and liquid materials in such occupancies in areas that are not accessible to the public, shall comply with the requirements of NFPA 400, *Hazardous Materials Code*.

Chapter 71 Pyrophoric Solids and Liquids

71.1 General.

71.1.1 The storage, use, and handling of pyrophoric solids and liquids shall comply with the requirements of Chapter 60.

71.1.2 The storage, use, and handling of pyrophoric solids and liquids in amounts exceeding the maximum allowable quantity permitted in control areas as set forth in Chapter 60 shall also comply with the requirements of NFPA 400, *Hazardous Materials Code*.

Chapter 72 Unstable (Reactive) Solids and Liquids

72.1 General.

72.1.1 The storage, use, and handling of unstable (reactive) solids and liquids shall comply with the requirements of Chapter 60.

72.1.2 The storage, use, and handling of unstable (reactive) solids and liquids in amounts exceeding the maximum allowable quantity permitted in control areas as set forth in Chapter 60 shall also comply with the requirements of NFPA 400, *Hazardous Materials Code*.

Chapter 73 Water-Reactive Solids and Liquids

73.1 General.

73.1.1 The storage, use, and handling of water-reactive solids and liquids shall comply with the requirements of Chapter 60.

73.1.2 The storage, use, and handling of water-reactive solids and liquids in amounts exceeding the maximum allowable quantity permitted in control areas as set forth in Chapter 60 shall also comply with the requirements of NFPA 400, *Hazardous Materials Code*.

Chapter 74 Ammonium Nitrate

74.1 General.

74.1.1 The storage, use, and handling of ammonium nitrate (solid oxidizer) shall comply with Chapter 60.

74.1.2 The storage of ammonium nitrate in the form of crystals, flakes, grains, or prills including fertilizer grade, dynamite grade, nitrous oxide grade, technical grade, and other mixtures containing 60 percent or more by weight of ammonium nitrate shall comply with NFPA 400, *Hazardous Materials Code*.

Chapter 75 Organic Peroxide Solids and Liquids

75.1 General.

75.1.1 The storage, use, and handling of organic peroxide solids and liquids shall comply with the requirements of Chapter 60.

75.1.2 The storage, use, and handling of organic peroxide solids and liquids in amounts exceeding the maximum allowable quantity permitted in control areas as set forth in Chapter 60 shall also comply with the requirements of NFPA 400, *Hazardous Materials Code*.

Annex A Explanatory Material

Annex A is not a part of the requirements of this NFPA document but is included for informational purposes only. This annex contains explanatory material, numbered to correspond with the applicable text paragraphs.

A.1.2 Consideration for life safety could include occupants, fire department personnel, fire brigade members, employees, responsible parties, and the general public.

A.1.3.2 This *Code* is partially composed of limited text references extracted from other NFPA codes and standards in an effort to bring together information useful during field inspections.

With respect to hazardous materials, provisions in Chapters 60, 61, 63, 65, 66, and 69, are partial extracts of materials from NFPA standards referenced in each of these chapters. These extracts are included in NFPA 1 to assist users of the document by providing ready access to provisions that could be routinely referenced by fire code enforcers. However, through their adoption by reference in NFPA 1, the NFPA standards identified in these chapters apply in their entirety.

A.1.3.6.2 A limited but reasonable time should be allowed for compliance with any part of this *Code* for existing buildings, commensurate with the magnitude of expenditure, disruption of services, and degree of hazard. Occupied existing buildings should comply with 10.3.3.

A.1.7.2 For additional information on qualifications of code enforcement personnel, see NFPA 1031, *Standard for Professional Qualifications for Fire Inspector and Plan Examiner*; NFPA 1033, *Standard for Professional Qualifications for Fire Investigator*; NFPA 1035, *Standard for Professional Qualifications for Fire and Life Safety Educator, Public Information Officer, and Juvenile Firesetter Intervention Specialist*; and NFPA 1037, *Standard for Professional Qualifications for Fire Marshal*.

A.1.7.6.1 The AHJ enforcing NFPA 1 may not have the technical expertise, required certifications, licensure, or legal authority to enforce all of the provisions and subject matter contained therein. As an example, Chapter 11 contains references to codes and standards that regulate specific building subsystems. These subsystems could be regulated by electrical, mechanical, plumbing, or other specialty enforcement officials with technical expertise or legal authority in the specific area of the subsystem. This paragraph authorizes the AHJ enforcing NFPA 1 to rely on the opinion and authority of these specialty enforcement officials in order to determine compliance.

A.1.7.17.3 Before each performance or the start of such activity, such individuals should inspect the required fire appliances provided to see that they are properly located and in good working order, and should keep diligent watch for fires during the time such place is open to the public or such activity is being conducted and take prompt measures for extinguishment of fires that can occur.

A.1.10.4.3 No additional information should be submitted to review by the Board of Appeals without the information submitted to the AHJ for their review prior to the hearing date. Additional information submitted after the filing of the appeal to the Board and AHJ should be made available to the Board and AHJ in a timeframe that permits adequate review before the hearing date.

A.1.12.6.13 Figure A.1.12.6.13 shows a sample permit.

A.1.13.5.2 The following is provided for information purposes only and has been provided by outside sources. Information concerning the noted services has not been independently verified, nor have the services been endorsed by the NFPA or any of its technical committees.

Examples of certification programs for fireworks displays include those conducted through the American Pyrotechnics Association (APA) and the Pyrotechnics Guild International (PGI). Both programs are recognized by several state fire marshals' offices throughout the United States. Authorities having jurisdiction should contact the applicable trade organizations or groups that cover each of the activities listed in 1.13.1 for information on recognized certification program(s).

A.1.13.5.4 An example of suggested requirements for licensing operators who perform fireworks displays can be found in Annex C, Suggested Requirements for Operator Licensing, of NFPA 1123, *Code for Fireworks Display*, 2010 edition.

A.2.1(1) For example, Chapter 2 references NFPA 10. Such reference does not mean that all buildings must be provided with portable fire extinguishers. Rather, portable fire extinguishers are mandatory only to the extent called for elsewhere in the *Code*.

A.3.2.1 Approved. The National Fire Protection Association does not approve, inspect, or certify any installations, procedures, equipment, or materials; nor does it approve or evaluate testing laboratories. In determining the acceptability of installations, procedures, equipment, or materials, the AHJ may base acceptance on compliance with NFPA or other appropriate standards. In the absence of such standards, said authority may require evidence of proper installation, proce-

---

Side 1
PERMIT
FOR CUTTING AND WELDING
WITH PORTABLE GAS OR ARC EQUIPMENT

Date _____
Building _____
Dept. _____ Floor _____
Work to be done _____
_____
Special precautions _____
_____
Is fire watch required? _____
The location where this work is to done has been examined, necessary precautions taken, and permission is granted for this work. (See other side.)
Permit expires _____
Signed _____
(Individual responsible for authorizing welding and cutting)
Time Started _____ Completed _____

FINAL CHECK
Work area and all adjacent areas to which sparks and heat might have spread [including floors above and below and on opposite side of wall(s)] were inspected 30 minutes after the work was completed and were found firesafe.

Signed _____
(Supervisor or Fire Watcher)

Side 2
ATTENTION
Before approving any cutting and welding permit, the fire safety supervisor or appointee shall inspect the work area and confirm that precautions have been taken to prevent fire in accordance with NFPA 51B.

PRECAUTIONS
❏ Sprinklers in service
❏ Cutting and welding equipment in good repair

WITHIN 35 FT (10.7 M) OF WORK
❏ Floors swept clean of combustibles
❏ Combustible floors wet down and covered with damp sand, metal, or other shields
❏ All wall and floor openings covered
❏ Covers suspended beneath work to collect sparks

WORK ON WALLS OR CEILINGS
❏ Construction noncombustible and without combustible covering
❏ Combustibles moved away from opposite side of wall

WORK ON ENCLOSED EQUIPMENT
(Tanks, containers, ducts, dust collectors, etc.)
❏ Equipment cleaned of all combustibles
❏ Containers purged of flammable vapors

FIRE WATCH
❏ To be provided during and 30 minutes after operation
❏ Supplied with extinguisher and small hose
❏ Trained in use of equipment and in sounding fire alarm

FINAL CHECK
❏ To be made 30 minutes after completion of any operation unless fire watch is provided

Signed _____
(Supervisor)

FIGURE A.1.12.6.13 Sample Permit.

dure, or use. The AHJ may also refer to the listings or labeling practices of an organization that is concerned with product evaluations and is thus in a position to determine compliance with appropriate standards for the current production of listed items.

A.3.2.2 Authority Having Jurisdiction (AHJ). The phrase "authority having jurisdiction," or its acronym AHJ, is used in NFPA documents in a broad manner, since jurisdictions and approval agencies vary, as do their responsibilities. Where public safety is primary, the AHJ may be a federal, state, local, or other regional department or individual such as a fire chief; fire marshal; chief of a fire prevention bureau, labor department, or health department; building official; electrical inspector; or others having statutory authority. For insurance purposes, an insurance inspection department, rating bureau, or other insurance company representative may be the AHJ. In many circumstances, the property owner or his or her designated agent assumes the role of the AHJ; at government installations, the commanding officer or departmental official may be the AHJ.

A.3.2.3 Code. The decision to designate a standard as a "code" is based on such factors as the size and scope of the document, its intended use and form of adoption, and whether it contains substantial enforcement and administrative provisions.

A.3.2.6 Listed. The means for identifying listed equipment may vary for each organization concerned with product evaluation; some organizations do not recognize equipment as listed unless it is also labeled. The AHJ should utilize the system employed by the listing organization to identify a listed product.

A.3.3.1 Absolute Pressure. Measured from this reference point, the standard atmospheric pressure at sea level is an absolute pressure of 14.7 psi (101.3 kPa). [**55**: A.3.3.1]

A.3.3.4 Aerosol Product. The base product can be dispensed from the container in such form as a mist, spray, foam, gel, or aerated powder. [**30B**: A.3.3.1]

A.3.3.7 Aisle Width. See Figure A.3.3.7. [**13**: A.3.9.3.1]

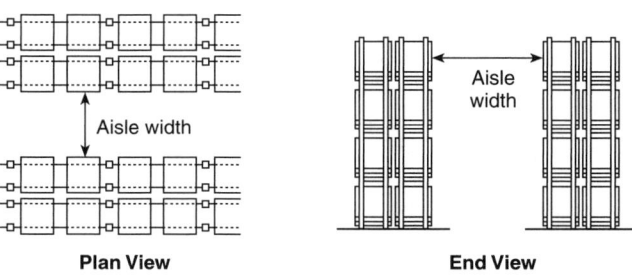

FIGURE A.3.3.7 Illustration of Aisle Width. [13:Figure A.3.9.3.1]

A.3.3.14.12 Spray Area. For the purpose of this *Code*, the AHJ can define the limits of the spray area in any specific case. The spray area in the vicinity of spray application operations will necessarily vary with the design and arrangement of the equipment and with the method of operation. Where spray application operations are strictly confined to predetermined spaces that are provided with adequate and reliable ventilation (such as a properly designed and constructed spray booth), the spray area ordinarily will not extend beyond this space. When spray application operations are *not* confined to an adequately ventilated space, then the spray area might extend throughout the room or building area where the spraying is conducted. [**33**: A.3.3.2.3]

A.3.3.19 Available Height for Storage. For new sprinkler installations, the maximum height of storage is the height at which commodities can be stored above the floor where the minimum required unobstructed space below sprinklers is maintained. For the evaluation of existing situations, the maximum height of storage is the maximum existing height if space between the sprinklers and storage is equal to or greater than required. [**13**: A.3.9.1.1]

A.3.3.20 Baled Cotton. See Table A.3.3.20.

The Joint Cotton Industry Bale Packaging Committee (JCIBPC) specifications for baling of cotton now requires that all cotton bales be secured with wire bands, polyester plastic strapping, or cold-rolled high tensile steel strapping, and then covered in fully coated or strip-coated woven polypropylene, polyethylene film, or burlap.

A.3.3.20.2 Densely Packed Baled Cotton. Experimental work by the U.S. Department of Agriculture, and others (Wakelyn and Hughs, 2002), investigated the flammability of cotton bales with a packing density of at least 22 lb/ft^3 (360 kg/m^2). The research showed that such cotton bales (densely packed cotton bales) did not undergo self-heating nor spontaneous combustion, and that the likelihood of sustained smoldering combustion internal to the cotton bale, creating a delayed fire hazard, was extremely low. The same research also showed that, when the cotton bales were exposed to smoldering cigarettes, matches, and open flames (including the gas burner ignition source used for the mattress tests, ASTM E 1590, *Standard Test Method for Fire Testing of Mattresses*, and California Technical Bulletin 129), the probability of initiating flaming combustion was at such a low level as not to qualify the densely packed cotton bales as flammable solids. These investigations resulted in harmonization between the U.S. Department of Transportation (49 CFR 172.102, note 137), the United Nations *Recommendations on the Transport of Dangerous Goods*, the International Maritime Organization (the International Maritime Dangerous Goods Code), and the International Civil Aviation Organization's Technical Instructions, with the removal of the flammable solid designation from densely packed cotton bales, complying with ISO 8115, *Cotton Bales — Dimensions and Density*, and the exemption of such cotton bales from the corresponding transportation hazardous materials regulations.

A.3.3.24.4 Valve-Regulated (VRLA). In VRLA batteries, the liquid electrolyte in the cells is immobilized in an absorptive glass mat (AGM cells or batteries) or by the addition of a gelling agent (gel cells or gelled batteries).

A.3.3.24.5 Vented (Flooded). Flooded lead-acid batteries have a provision for the user to add water to the cell and are equipped with a flame-arresting vent that permits the escape of hydrogen and oxygen gas from the cell in a diffused manner such that a spark, or other ignition source, outside the cell will not ignite the gases inside the cell.

A.3.3.27 Boiling Point. At the boiling point, the surrounding atmospheric pressure can no longer hold the liquid in the liquid state and the liquid boils. A low boiling point is indicative of a high vapor pressure and a high rate of evaporation. [**30**: A.4.2.1]

Table A.3.3.20 Typical Cotton Bale Types and Approximate Sizes

Bale Type	Dimensions		Average Weight		Volume		Density	
	in.	mm	lb	kg	ft³	m³	lb/ft³	kg/m³
Compressed, standard	57 × 29 × 23	1448 × 736 × 584	500	226.8	22.0	0.62	22.7	366
Gin, standard	55 × 31 × 21	1397 × 787 × 533	500	226.8	20.7	0.58	24.2	391
Compressed, universal	58 × 25 × 21	1475 × 635 × 533	500	226.8	17.6	0.50	28.4	454
Gin, universal	55 × 26 × 21	1397 × 660 × 533	500	226.8	17.4	0.49	28.7	463
Compressed, high density	58 × 22 × 21	1473 × 559 × 533	500	226.8	15.5	0.44	32.2	515
Densely packed baled cotton	55 × 21 × 27.6 to 35.4	1400 × 530 × 700 to 900	500	226.8	21.1	0.60	22.0	360

A.3.3.28 Boil-Over. Boil-over occurs when the residues from surface burning become more dense than the unburned oil and sink below the surface to form a hot layer, which progresses downward much faster than the regression of the liquid surface. When this hot layer, called a "heat wave," reaches water or water-in-oil emulsion in the bottom of the tank, the water is first superheated and then boils almost explosively, overflowing the tank. Oils subject to boil-over consist of components having a wide range of boiling points, including both light ends and viscous residues. These characteristics are present in most crude oils and can be produced in synthetic mixtures. [**30:** A.3.3.6]

A boil-over is an entirely different phenomenon from a slop-over or froth-over. Slop-over involves a minor frothing that occurs when water is sprayed onto the hot surface of a burning oil. Froth-over is not associated with a fire but results when water is present or enters a tank containing hot viscous oil. Upon mixing, the sudden conversion of water to steam causes a portion of the tank contents to overflow. [**30:** A.3.3.6]

A.3.3.29 Building. The term *building* is to be understood as if followed by the words *or portions thereof.* (*See also A.3.3.252, Structure.*) [*101:* A.3.3.36]

A.3.3.29.1 Airport Terminal Building. The term *terminal* is sometimes applied to airport facilities other than those serving passengers, such as cargo- and freight-handling facilities and fuel-handling facilities. These facilities are covered by other NFPA standards, such as NFPA 30. [**415:** A.3.3.4]

A.3.3.29.5 Existing Building. With respect to judging whether a building should be considered existing, the deciding factor is not when the building was designed or when construction started but, rather, the date plans were approved for construction by the appropriate AHJ. [*101:* A.3.3.36.5]

A.3.3.29.6 High-Rise Building. It is the intent of this definition that, in determining the level from which the highest occupiable floor is to be measured, the enforcing agency should exercise reasonable judgment, including consideration of overall accessibility to the building by fire department personnel and vehicular equipment. Where a building is situated on a sloping terrain and there is building access on more than one level, the enforcing agency might select the level that provides the most logical and adequate fire department access. [**5000:** A.3.3.68.10]

A.3.3.29.7 Important Building. Examples of important buildings include occupied buildings where egress within 2 minutes cannot be reasonably expected and control buildings that require presence of personnel for orderly shutdown of important or hazardous processes. Important buildings can also include unprotected storage where products from fire can harm the community or the environment or buildings that contain high-value contents or critical equipment or supplies. [**30:** A.3.3.8.1]

A.3.3.29.10 Special Amusement Building. Special amusement buildings include amusements such as a haunted house, a roller coaster–type ride within a building, a multilevel play structure within a building, a submarine ride, and similar amusements where the occupants are not in the open air. [*101:* A.3.3.36.10]

A.3.3.37 Cathodic Protection. This protection renders a metallic container or piping system or component negatively charged with respect to its surrounding environment. [**55:** A.3.3.16]

A.3.3.45 Chip. Chips are usually ¼ in. to 1¼ in. (6.4 mm to 31.8 mm) in size, with nothing finer than that which is retainable on a ¼ in. (6.4 mm) screen; however, blower and conveyor systems can create some fine dust particles after screening.

A.3.3.46 Cleaning Media. Cleaning methods that incorporate chemical washing techniques can include the use of chemical substances, usually liquid, capable of dissolving or dispersing a foreign substance or contaminants and can include techniques such as rinsing, heating, steaming, or vacuum with such techniques applied either individually or in combination with others. Air, inert gas, steam and water are acceptable cleaning media. [**55:** A.3.3.21]

A.3.3.57 Combustible Dust. Dusts traditionally were defined as material 420 µm or smaller (capable of passing through a U.S. No. 40 standard sieve). For consistency with other standards, 500µm (capable of passing through a U.S. No. 35 standard sieve) is now considered an appropriate size criterion. Particle surface area-to-volume ratio is a key factor in determining the rate of combustion. Combustible particulate solids with a minimum dimension more than 500 µm generally have a surface-to-volume ratio that is too small to pose a deflagration hazard. Flat platelet shaped particles, flakes, or fibers with lengths that are large compared to their diameter usually do not pass through a 500 µm sieve, yet could still pose a deflagration hazard. Many particulates accumulate electrostatic charge in handling, causing them to attract each other, forming agglomerates. Often agglomerates behave as if they were larger particles, yet when they are dispersed they present a significant hazard. Consequently, it can be inferred that any particulate that has a minimum dimension less than or equal to 500 µm could behave as a combustible dust if suspended in air or the process specific oxidizer. If the minimum dimension of the particulate is greater than 500 µm, it is unlikely that the material would be a combustible dust, as determined by test. The determination of whether a sample of combustible material presents a flash fire or explosion hazard could be based on a screening test methodology such as provided in the ASTM E 1226, *Standard Test Method for Explosibility of Dust Clouds*. Alternatively, a standardized test method such as ASTM E 1515, *Standard Test Method for Minimum Explosible Concentration of Combustible Dusts*, could be used to determine dust explosibility. [**654:** A.3.3.5]

There is some possibility that a sample will result in a false positive in the 20 L sphere when tested by the ASTM E 1226 screening test or the ASTM E 1515 test. This is due to the high energy ignition source overdriving the test. When the lowest ignition energy allowed by either method still results in a positive result, the owner/operator can elect to determine whether the sample is a combustible dust with screening tests performed in a larger scale (≤1 m³) enclosure, which is less susceptible to overdriving and thus will provide more realistic results. [**654:** A.3.3.5]

This possibility for false positives has been known for quite some time and is attributed to "overdriven" conditions that exist in the 20 L chamber due to the use of strong pyrotechnic igniters. For that reason, the reference method for explosibility testing is based on a 1 m³ chamber, and the 20 L chamber test method is calibrated to produce results comparable to those from the 1 m³ chamber for most dusts. In fact, the U.S. standard for 20 L testing (ASTM E 1226) states, "The objective of this test method is to develop data that can be correlated to those from the 1 m³ chamber (described in ISO 6184-1 and VDI 3673) …" ASTM E 1226 further states, "Because a number of factors (concentration, uniformity of dispersion, turbulence of ignition, sample age, etc.) can affect the test results, the test vessel to be used for routine work must be standardized using dust samples whose K_{St} and P_{max} parameters are known in the 1 m³ chamber." [**654:** A.3.3.5]

NFPA 68, *Standard on Explosion Protection by Deflagration Venting*, also recognizes this problem and addresses it stating that "the 20 L test apparatus is designed to simulate results of the 1 m³ chamber; however, the igniter discharge makes it problematic to determine K_{St} values less than 50 bar-m/sec. Where the material is expected to yield K_{St} values less than 50 bar-m/sec, testing in a 1 m³ chamber might yield lower values." [**654:** A.3.3.5]

Any time a combustible dust is processed or handled, a potential for deflagration exists. The degree of deflagration hazard varies, depending on the type of combustible dust and the processing methods used. [**654:** A.3.3.5]

A dust deflagration has the following four requirements:

(1) Combustible dust
(2) Dust dispersion in air or other oxidant
(3) Sufficient concentration at or exceeding the minimum explosible concentration (MEC)
(4) Sufficiently powerful ignition source such as an electrostatic discharge, an electric current arc, a glowing ember, a hot surface, welding slag, frictional heat, or a flame [**654:** A.3.3.5]

If the deflagration is confined and produces a pressure sufficient to rupture the confining enclosure, the event is, by definition, an "explosion." [**654:** A.3.3.5]

Evaluation of the hazard of a combustible dust should be determined by the means of actual test data. Each situation should be evaluated and applicable tests selected. The following list represents the factors that are sometimes used in determining the deflagration hazard of a dust:

(1) MEC
(2) MIE
(3) Particle size distribution
(4) Moisture content as received and as tested
(5) Maximum explosion pressure at optimum concentration
(6) Maximum rate of pressure rise at optimum concentration
(7) K_{St} (normalized rate of pressure rise) as defined in ASTM E 1226, *Standard Test Method for Explosibility of Dust Clouds*
(8) Layer ignition temperature
(9) Dust cloud ignition temperature
(10) Limiting oxidant concentration (LOC) to prevent ignition
(11) Electrical volume resistivity
(12) Charge relaxation time
(13) Chargeability [**654:** A.3.3.5]

It is important to keep in mind that as a particulate is processed, handled, or transported, the particle size generally decreases due to particle attrition. Consequently, it is often necessary to evaluate the explosibility of the particulate at multiple points along the process. Where process conditions dictate the use of oxidizing media other than air (nominally taken as 21 percent oxygen and 79 percent nitrogen), the applicable tests should be conducted in the appropriate process specific medium. [**654:** A.3.3.5]

A.3.3.58 Combustible Fiber. Combustible fibers can include cotton, sisal, henequen, ixtle, jute, hemp, tow, cocoa fiber, oakum, baled waste, baled wastepaper, kapok, hay, straw, excelsior, Spanish moss, or other like materials.

A.3.3.62 Combustible Waste. These materials include but are not limited to all combustible fibers, hay, straw, hair, feathers, down, wood shavings, turnings, all types of paper products, soiled cloth trimmings and cuttings, rubber trimmings and buffings, metal fines, and any mixture of the previously listed items, or any other salvageable combustible waste materials.

A.3.3.65 Common Path of Travel. Common path of travel is measured in the same manner as travel distance but terminates at that point where two separate and distinct routes become available. Paths that merge are common paths of travel. [***101:*** A.3.3.47]

A.3.3.66.1 Fire Compartment. Additional fire compartment information is contained in 8.2.2 of NFPA *101*. [***101:*** A.3.3.48.1]

In the provisions for fire compartments utilizing the outside walls of a building, it is not intended that the outside wall be specifically fire resistance rated, unless required by other standards. Likewise, it is not intended that outside windows or doors be protected, unless specifically required for exposure protection by another section of this *Code*, NFPA *101*, or by other standards. [*101*: A.3.3.48.1]

A.3.3.66.2 Smoke Compartment. Where smoke compartments using the outside walls or the roof of a building are provided, it is not intended that outside walls or roofs, or any openings therein, be capable of resisting the passage of smoke. Application of smoke compartment criteria where required elsewhere in NFPA *101*, should be in accordance with Section 8.5 of NFPA *101*. [*101*: A.3.3.48.2]

A.3.3.69.4 Container (Flammable or Combustible Liquid). The U.S. DOT defines *non-bulk packaging* as having up to 119 gal (450 L) capacity in 49 CFR 171.8. [**30**: A.3.3.12]

A.3.3.71 Conventional Pallets. See Figure A.3.3.71. [**13**: A.3.9.1.11]

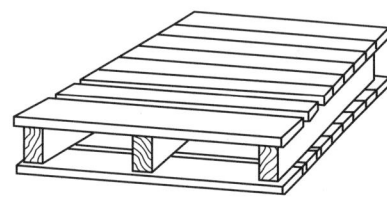

Conventional pallet

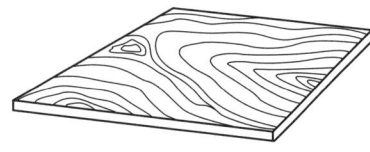

Solid flat bottom
wood pallet (slave pallet)

FIGURE A.3.3.71 Typical Pallets. [13:Figure A.3.9.1.11]

A.3.3.75 Corrosive Material. A chemical is considered to be corrosive if it destroys or irreversibly changes the structure of the tissue at the site of contact within a specified period of time using one of the *in vivo* or *in vitro* OECD test methods authorized in 49 CFR Part 173.137. For purposes of this code, this term does not refer to action on inanimate surfaces (e.g., steel or aluminum). Available testing data produced prior to September 30, 1995 from the test method in Appendix A to 49 CFR Part 173 in effect on October 1, 1994 can also be used to determine the corrosivity of a material. [**400**: A.3.3.61.2]

A.3.3.78 Cultural Resource Properties. Such properties include, but are not limited to, museums, libraries, historic structures, and places of worship. [**914**: A.3.3.16]

A.3.3.81 Cylinder Pack. Six-packs and twelve-packs are terms used to further define cylinder packs with a specific number of cylinders. The characteristic internal water volume of individual cylinders in a cylinder pack ranges from 1.52 ft^3 to 1.76 ft^3 (43 L to 50 L) or a water capacity of 95 lb to 110 lb (43 kg to 50 kg). [**55**: A.3.3.30]

A.3.3.84.4 Combination Detector. These detectors do not utilize a mathematical evaluation principle of signal processing more than a simple "or" function. Normally, these detectors provide a single response resulting from either sensing method, each of which operates independent of the other. These detectors can provide a separate and distinct response resulting from either sensing method, each of which is processed independent of the other. [**72**: A.3.3.66.4]

A.3.3.84.7 Fixed-Temperature Detector. The difference between the operating temperature of a fixed-temperature device and the surrounding air temperature is proportional to the rate at which the temperature is rising. The rate is commonly referred to as *thermal lag*. The air temperature is always higher than the operating temperature of the device. [**72**: A.3.3.66.7]

Typical examples of fixed-temperature sensing elements are as follows:

(1) *Bimetallic.* A sensing element comprised of two metals that have different coefficients of thermal expansion arranged so that the effect is deflection in one direction when heated and in the opposite direction when cooled.
(2) *Electrical Conductivity.* A line-type or spot-type sensing element in which resistance varies as a function of temperature.
(3) *Fusible Alloy.* A sensing element of a special composition metal (eutectic) that melts rapidly at the rated temperature.
(4) *Heat-Sensitive Cable.* A line-type device in which the sensing element comprises, in one type, two current-carrying wires separated by heat-sensitive insulation that softens at the rated temperature, thus allowing the wires to make electrical contact. In another type, a single wire is centered in a metallic tube, and the intervening space is filled with a substance that becomes conductive at a critical temperature, thus establishing electrical contact between the tube and the wire.
(5) *Liquid Expansion.* A sensing element comprising a liquid that is capable of marked expansion in volume in response to an increase in temperature. [**72**: A.3.3.66.7]

A.3.3.84.8 Flame Detector. Flame detectors are categorized as ultraviolet, single wavelength infrared, ultraviolet infrared, or multiple wavelength infrared. [**72**: A.3.3.66.8]

A.3.3.84.12 Multi-Criteria Detector. A multi-criteria detector is a detector that contains multiple sensing methods that respond to fire signature phenomena and utilizes mathematical evaluation principles to determine the collective status of the device and generates a single output. Typical examples of multi-criteria detectors are a combination of a heat detector with a smoke detector, or a combination rate-of-rise and fixed-temperature heat detector that evaluates both signals using an algorithm to generate an output such as pre-alarm or alarm. The evaluation can be performed either at the detector or at the control unit. Other examples are detectors that include sensor combinations that respond in a predictable manner to any combination of heat, smoke, carbon monoxide, or carbon dioxide. [**72**: A.3.3.66.12]

A.3.3.84.13 Multi-Sensor Detector. Typical examples of multi-sensor detectors are a combination of a heat detector with a smoke detector, or a combination rate-of-rise and fixed-temperature heat detector that evaluates both signals using an algorithm to generate an output such as pre-alarm or alarm. The evaluation can be performed either at the detector or at the control unit. Other examples are detectors that include sensor combinations that respond in a predictable manner to any combination of heat, smoke, carbon monoxide, or carbon dioxide. [**72**: A.3.3.66.13]

A.3.3.84.18 Rate Compensation Detector. A typical example of a rate compensation detector is a spot-type detector with a tubular casing of a metal that tends to expand lengthwise as it is heated and an associated contact mechanism that closes at a certain point in the elongation. A second metallic element inside the tube exerts an opposing force on the contacts, tending to hold them open. The forces are balanced in such a way that, on a slow rate-of-temperature rise, there is more time for heat to penetrate to the inner element, which inhibits contact closure until the total device has been heated to its rated temperature level. However, on a fast rate-of-temperature rise, there is not as much time for heat to penetrate to the inner element, which exerts less of an inhibiting effect so that contact closure is achieved when the total device has been heated to a lower temperature. This, in effect, compensates for thermal lag. [**72:** A.3.3.66.18]

A.3.3.84.19 Rate-of-Rise Detector. Typical examples of rate-of-rise detectors are as follows:

(1) *Pneumatic Rate-of-Rise Tubing.* A line-type detector comprising small-diameter tubing, usually copper, that is installed on the ceiling or high on the walls throughout the protected area. The tubing is terminated in a detector unit that contains diaphragms and associated contacts set to actuate at a predetermined pressure. The system is sealed except for calibrated vents that compensate for normal changes in temperature.
(2) *Spot-Type Pneumatic Rate-of-Rise Detector.* A device consisting of an air chamber, a diaphragm, contacts, and a compensating vent in a single enclosure. The principle of operation is the same as that described for pneumatic rate-of-rise tubing.
(3) *Electrical Conductivity–Type Rate-of-Rise Detector.* A line-type or spot-type sensing element in which resistance changes due to a change in temperature. The rate of change of resistance is monitored by associated control equipment, and an alarm is initiated when the rate of temperature increase exceeds a preset value. [**72:** A.3.3.66.19]

A.3.3.99 Exhausted Enclosure. Such enclosures include laboratory hoods, exhaust fume hoods, and similar appliances and equipment used to retain and exhaust locally the gases, fumes, vapors, and mists that could be released. Rooms or areas provided with general ventilation, in and of themselves, are not exhausted enclosures. [**55:** A.3.3.39]

A.3.3.100 Existing. See A.3.3.29.5, Existing Building. [***101:*** A.3.3.81]

A.3.3.102 Exit. Exits include exterior exit doors, exit passageways, horizontal exits, exit stairs, and exit ramps. In the case of a stairway, the exit includes the stair enclosure, the door to the stair enclosure, stairs and landings inside the enclosure, the door from the stair enclosure to the outside or to the level of exit discharge, and any exit passageway and its associated doors, if such are provided, so as to discharge the stair directly to the outside. In the case of a door leading directly from the street floor to the street or open air, the exit comprises only the door. [***101:*** A.3.3.83]

Doors of small individual rooms, as in hotels, while constituting exit access from the room, are not referred to as exits, except where they lead directly to the outside of the building from the street floor. [***101:*** A.3.3.83]

A.3.3.102.1 Horizontal Exit. Horizontal exits should not be confused with egress through doors in smoke barriers. Doors in smoke barriers are designed only for temporary protection against smoke, whereas horizontal exits provide protection against serious fire for a relatively long period of time in addition to providing immediate protection from smoke. (*See 7.2.4 of NFPA 101.*) [***101:*** A.3.3.83.1]

A.3.3.106 Explosion Control. NFPA 68, *Standard on Explosion Protection by Deflagration Venting,* provides guidance on the use of deflagration venting systems in buildings and other enclosures. The primary purpose of a venting system is to relieve the overpressure produced in an explosion to limit the potential damage to the building where the explosion occurs. Although some structural damage can be anticipated, the use of relief venting is expected to prevent massive building failure and collapse. In cases where detonation is probable, venting is often used in conjunction with barricade construction where the pressure-resistant portions of the building have been constructed to resist the pressures anticipated should an explosive event occur. Design of barricade systems is highly specialized and the subject of military standards applicable to the subject. NFPA 69, *Standard on Explosion Prevention Systems,* provides guidance on the use of suppression, ventilation systems, and the limiting of oxidants as a means to prevent the occurrence of an explosion. When relief vents are to be used as a means to provide explosion relief, the fundamental requirements of the building code for structural elements, including snow, wind, and seismic events, should be considered. In some instances, the requirements for wind resistance can impose more rigorous requirements on the relief vents than required by the engineering analysis used to determine the relief pressure. In such cases, users must demonstrate that the relief vents will not become airborne or release in such a manner as to create secondary hazards within or external to the building in which they are installed. Specific designs might require approval by the AHJ. [**55:** A.3.3.40]

A.3.3.107 Explosive Material. The term *explosive material* includes, but is not limited to, dynamite, black powder, pellet powder, initiating explosives, detonators, safety fuses, squibs, detonating cord, igniter cord, igniters, and Display Fireworks 1.3G (Class B, Special). The term *explosive* includes any material determined to be within the scope of Title 18, United States Code, Chapter 40, and also includes any material classified as an explosive, other than Consumer Fireworks 1.4G (Class C, Common), by the Hazardous Materials Regulations of the U.S. Department of Transportation (DOT) in 49 CFR. [**5000:** A.3.3.407.3]

The former classification system used by the DOT included the terms *high explosive* and *low explosive,* as further defined in 3.3.406.3.2 of *NFPA 5000.* These terms remain in use by the U.S. Bureau of Alcohol, Tobacco, and Firearms or explosives. Explosive materials classified as hazard Class 1 are further defined under the current system applied by DOT. Compatibility group letters are used in concert with division numbers to specify further limitations on each division noted. For example, the letter G (as in 1.4G) identifies substances or articles that contain a pyrotechnic substance and similar materials. UN/DOT Class 1 Explosives are defined as follows:

(1) Division 1.1 explosives are explosives that are a mass explosion hazard, which is a hazard that instantaneously affects almost the entire load.
(2) Division 1.2 explosives are explosives that are a projection hazard but not a mass explosion hazard.
(3) Division 1.3 explosives are explosives that are a fire hazard and either a minor blast hazard or a minor projection hazard, or both, but not a mass explosion hazard.

(4) Division 1.4 explosives are explosives that pose a minor explosion hazard and meet both of the following criteria:
  (a) The explosive effects are largely confined to the package, and no projection of fragments of appreciable size or range is to be expected.
  (b) An external fire cannot cause virtually instantaneous explosion of almost the entire contents of the package.
(5) Division 1.5 explosives are very insensitive explosives that are comprised of substances that are a mass explosion hazard, but are so insensitive that there is very little probability of initiation or of transition from burning to detonation under normal conditions of transport.
(6) Division 1.6 explosives are extremely insensitive articles that are not a mass explosion hazard, that are comprised of articles that contain only extremely insensitive detonating substances, and that demonstrate a negligible probability of accidental initiation or propagation. [*5000:* A.3.3.407.3]

A.3.3.112.2 Interior Finish. Interior finish is not intended to apply to surfaces within spaces such as those that are concealed or inaccessible. Furnishings that, in some cases, might be secured in place for functional reasons should not be considered as interior finish. [*101:* A.3.3.92.2]

A.3.3.112.3 Interior Floor Finish. Interior floor finish includes coverings applied over a normal finished floor or stair treads and risers. [*101:* A.3.3.92.3]

A.3.3.121 Fire Hydrant. See Figure A.3.3.121(a) and Figure A.3.3.121(b). [*25:* A.3.3.12]

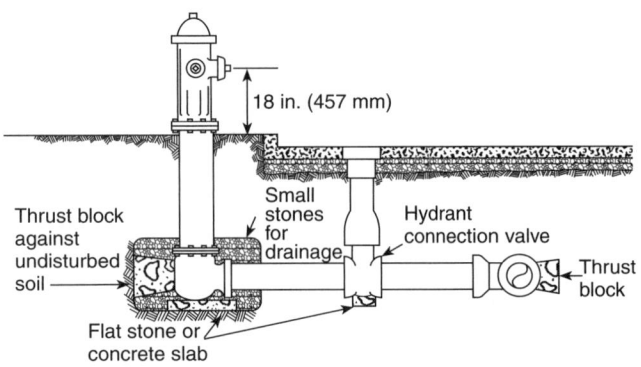

FIGURE A.3.3.121(a)   Typical Fire Hydrant Connection. [25:Figure A.3.3.12(a)]

A.3.3.122 Fire Lane. The traditional term *fire lane* is no longer utilized in this *Code*. However, a fire department access road that is marked and prohibits obstructions in accordance with 18.2.3.5 would meet the traditional intent of a fire lane.

A.3.3.126 Flame Spread. See Section 10.2 of NFPA *101*. [*101:* A.3.3.112]

A.3.3.129 Flash Point. Flash point is a direct measure of a liquid's ability to emit flammable vapors. The lower the flash point, the greater the risk of fire. Flash point is determined using one of several different test procedures and apparatus that are specified in Section 4.4 of NFPA 30. [*30:* A.4.2.4]

A liquid that has a flash point at or below ambient temperature is easy to ignite and will burn quickly. On ignition, the spread of flame over the surface of such a liquid will be rapid, because it is not necessary for the fire to expend energy heating the liquid to generate more vapor. Gasoline is a familiar example. A liquid with a flash point above ambient temperature presents less risk because it must be heated to generate enough vapor to become ignitible; it is more difficult to ignite and presents less potential for the generation and spread of vapor. A common example is home heating oil (Fuel Oil No. 2). Home heating oil must be atomized to a fine mist in order for it to be easily ignited. [*30:* A.4.2.4]

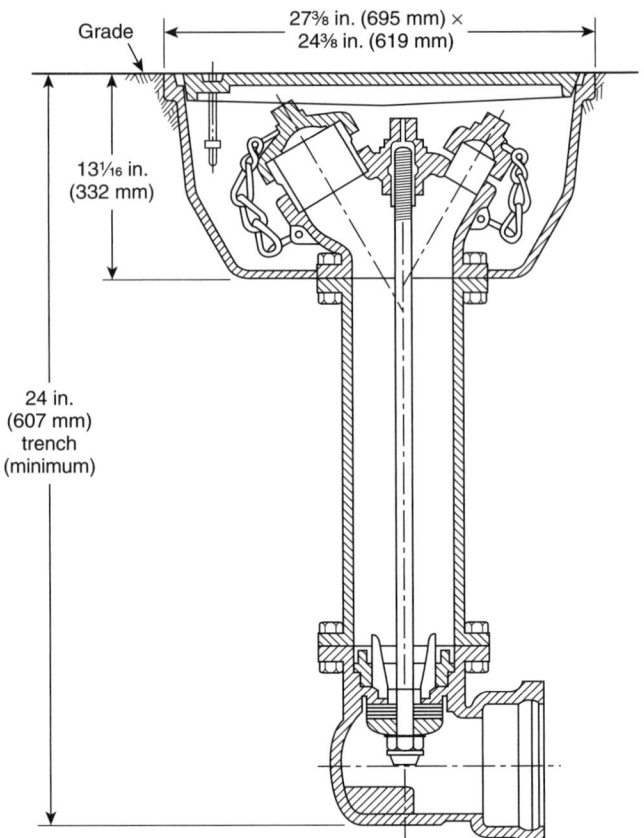

FIGURE A.3.3.121(b)   Flush-Type Hydrant. [25:Figure A.3.3.12(b)]

Certain solutions of liquids in water exhibit a flash point using the standard closed-cup test procedures but will not burn and could even extinguish a fire. To assist identifying such solutions, the following standards are helpful:

(1) ASTM D 4207, *Standard Test Method for Sustained Burning of Low Viscosity Liquid Mixtures by the Wick Test*
(2) ASTM D 4206, *Standard Test Method for Sustained Burning of Liquid Mixtures Using the Small Scale Open-Cup Apparatus* [*30:* A.4.2.4]

Liquid mixtures that do not sustain combustion for a specified time at a specified temperature are considered to be noncombustible. The tests described in the references listed in A.3.3.129(1) and A.3.3.129(2) provide additional data for determining proper storage and handling of such mixtures. In a confined space, such mixtures could still create an ignitible vapor–air mixture, depending on the amount of flammable liquid in the mixture and the quantity of the spill. [*30:* A.4.2.4]

Related to the flash point is the fire point. The fire point of a liquid is the temperature at which ignition of vapors will result in continued burning. As the term *flash point* suggests, the vapors generated at that temperature will flash but will not necessarily continue to burn. The difference between flash point and fire point has some significance when conducting flash point tests *[see 9.1.4(5) and 9.1.4(6) of NFPA 30]*. However, a closed-cup flash point is used to classify the liquid and characterize its hazard. [30: A.4.2.4]

For more information, see ASTM E 502, *Standard Test Method for Selection and Use of ASTM Standards for the Determination of Flash Point of Chemicals by Closed Cup Methods*, and the ASTM *Manual on Flash Point Standards and Their Use*. [30: A.4.2.4]

A.3.3.130.1 Gross Floor Area. Where the term *floor area* is used, it should be understood to be gross floor area, unless otherwise specified. [5000: A.3.3.34.8.1]

A.3.3.132 Fugitive Emissions. These include leaks from pump seals, valve packing, flange gaskets, compressor seals, process drains, and so forth. [30: A.3.3.22]

A.3.3.135.1 Compressed Gas. The states of a compressed gas are categorized as follows:

(1) Nonliquefied compressed gases are gases, other than those in solution, that are in a packaging under the charged pressure and are entirely gaseous at a temperature of 68°F (20°C).
(2) Liquefied compressed gases are gases that, in a packaging under the charged pressure, and are partially liquid at a temperature of 68°F (20°C). Cryogenic fluids represent a transient state of a gas that is created through the use of refrigeration. Cryogenic fluids cannot exist in the liquid form or partial liquid form at temperatures of 68°F (20°C); hence, they are not "compressed gases" as defined.
(3) Compressed gases in solution are nonliquefied gases that are dissolved in a solvent.
(4) Compressed gas mixtures consist of a mixture of two or more compressed gases contained in a packaging, the hazard properties of which are represented by the properties of the mixture as a whole. [55: A.3.3.49.1]

A.3.3.135.6 Inert Gas. Inert gases do not react readily with other materials under normal temperatures and pressures. For example, nitrogen combines with some of the more active metals such as lithium and magnesium to form nitrides, and at high temperatures it will also combine with hydrogen, oxygen, and other elements. The gases neon, krypton, and xenon are considered rare due to their scarcity. Although these gases are commonly referred to as inert gases, the formation of compounds is possible. For example, xenon combines with fluorine to form various fluorides and with oxygen to form oxides; the compounds formed are crystalline solids. [55: A.3.3.49.6]

A.3.3.135.10 Liquefied Petroleum Gas (LP-Gas). In the pure state propylene (Chemical Abstract Service 105-07-01) has a vapor pressure of 132.8 psig (915.72 kPa) at 70°F (21.1°C). The vapor pressure of commercial propane (Chemical Abstract Service 74-98-6) at 70°F 21.1°C) is 124 psig (855 kPa). Although commercial propane may contain a minor concentration of propylene as in impurity, propylene in the pure state does not meet the definition of LP-Gas. Propylene in the pure state is commonly found in use as an industrial fuel gas. *(See NFPA 51.)* [58: A.3.3.36]

A.3.3.135.12 Other Gas. A gas classified as an "other gas" might be a nonflammable gas or an inert gas. [55: A.3.3.49.9]

A.3.3.135.18 Unstable Reactive Gas. Unstable reactive materials are subdivided into five classifications. Class 4 materials are materials that in themselves are readily capable of detonation or explosive decomposition or explosive reaction at normal temperatures and pressures. They include the following:

(1) Materials that are sensitive to localized thermal or mechanical shock at normal temperatures and pressures
(2) Materials that have an instantaneous power density (product of heat of reaction and reaction rate) at 482°F (250°C) of 1000 W/mL or greater [55: A.3.3.49.14]

Class 3 materials are materials that in themselves are capable of detonation or explosive decomposition or explosive reaction but require a strong initiating source or heat under confinement before initiation. Class 3 materials include the following:

(1) Materials that have an instantaneous power density (product of heat of reaction and reaction rate) at 482°F (250°C) at or above 100 W/mL and below 1000 W/mL
(2) Materials that are sensitive to thermal or mechanical shock at elevated temperatures and pressures
(3) Materials that react explosively with water without requiring heat or confinement [55: A.3.3.49.14]

Class 2 materials are materials that readily undergo violent chemical change at elevated temperatures and pressures, including the following:

(1) Materials that have an instantaneous power density (product of heat of reaction and reaction rate) at 482°F (250°C) at or above 10 W/mL and below 100 W/mL
(2) Materials that react violently with water or form potentially explosive mixtures with water [55: A.3.3.49.14]

Class 1 materials are materials that in themselves are normally stable but that can become unstable at elevated temperatures and pressures, including the following:

(1) Materials that have an instantaneous power density (product of heat of reaction and reaction rate) at 482°F (250°C) at or above 0.01 W/mL and below 10 W/mL
(2) Materials that react vigorously with water, but not violently
(3) Materials that change or decompose on exposure to air, light, or moisture [55: A.3.3.49.14]

Class 0 materials are materials that in themselves are normally stable, even under fire conditions, including the following:

(1) Materials that have an instantaneous power density (product of heat of reaction and reaction rate) at 482°F (250°C) below 0.01 W/mL
(2) Materials that do not react with water
(3) Materials that do not exhibit an exotherm at temperatures less than or equal to 932°F (500°C) when tested by differential scanning calorimetry [55: A.3.3.49.14]

A.3.3.136 Gas Cabinet. Doors and access ports for exchanging cylinders and accessing pressure-regulating controls are permitted to be included as part of a gas cabinet. [55: A.3.3.50]

A.3.3.139 Gaseous Hydrogen System. The system includes stationary or portable containers, pressure regulators, pressure-relief devices, manifolds, interconnecting piping, and controls as required. [55: A.3.3.93.10]

A.3.3.142 Hazard of Contents. Hazardous materials are materials that present physical or health hazards and are regulated by the *Code*. The categories of materials classified as physical hazards, health hazards, or both have been established in concert with those categories identified by OSHA in 29 CFR that are used by preparers of Material Safety Data Sheets (MSDS). In some cases, the hazard categories are further subdivided into classes that have long been established by NFPA standards. For example, while OSHA recognizes flammable liquids as a broad class, including those that are combustible, such liquids are further categorized by building and fire codes with respect to degree of hazard under the system of classification used by NFPA to include Class I, Class II, and Class III liquids. They are further subdivided within these classes to Class IA, Class IB and so forth. A similar approach is used for materials in other categories where there are subcategories of hazard established by existing NFPA standards, including oxidizers, unstable reactives, organic peroxides, water reactives, and others. [**5000:** A.6.3.2]

Under the classification system used by OSHA, a hazardous material can have one or more physical or health hazards in categories not currently regulated by the *Code*; for example, irritants, sensitizers, radioactive materials, etiological agents, and others. This is not to say that these materials are not hazardous materials, but rather that the *Code* does not provide specific regulation for the hazard category represented. [**5000:** A.6.3.2]

The *Code* defines contents as either high hazard, low hazard, or ordinary hazard. The category of high hazard, which includes hazardous materials, is subdivided into groups in which the hazards of the groups are comparable, that is, high hazard Level 1-5. *(See also A.34.1.1 of NFPA 5000.)* [**5000:** A.6.3.2]

A.3.3.142.2 Low Hazard Contents. Chapter 42 of NFPA *101* recognizes storage of noncombustible materials as low hazard. In other occupancies, it is assumed that, even where the actual contents hazard is normally low, there is sufficient likelihood that some combustible materials or hazardous operations will be introduced in connection with building repair or maintenance, or some psychological factor might create conditions conducive to panic, so that the egress facilities cannot safely be reduced below those specified for ordinary hazard contents. [*101:* A.6.2.2.2]

A.3.3.142.3 Ordinary Hazard Contents. Ordinary hazard classification represents the conditions found in most buildings and is the basis for the general requirements of NFPA *101*. [*101:* A.6.2.2.3]

The fear of poisonous fumes or explosions is necessarily a relative matter to be determined on a judgment basis. All smoke contains some toxic fire gases but, under conditions of ordinary hazard, there should be no unduly dangerous exposure during the period necessary to escape from the fire area, assuming there are proper exits. [*101:* A.6.2.2.3]

A.3.3.143 Hazard Rating. The criteria for hazard rating are as defined in NFPA 704. [**55:** A.3.3.56]

A.3.3.147 Hazardous Reaction or Hazardous Chemical Reaction. These dangers might include, but are not limited to, toxic effects, reaction speed (including detonation), exothermic reaction, or production of unstable or reactive materials. [**30:** A.3.3.26]

A.3.3.149 Heliport. The term *heliport* applies to all sites used or intended to be used for the landing and takeoff of helicopters. [**418:** A.3.3.5]

A.3.3.153 Immediately Dangerous to Life and Health (IDLH). This level is established by the National Institute for Occupational Safety and Health (NIOSH). If adequate data do not exist for precise establishment of IDLH, an independent certified industrial hygienist, industrial toxicologist, or appropriate regulatory agency should make such determination. [**55:** A.3.3.58]

A.3.3.155 Incident Commander (IC). This position is equivalent to the on-scene incident commander as defined in OSHA 1910.120(8), Hazardous Waste Operations and Emergency Response. The IC has overall authority and responsibility for conducting incident operations and is responsible for the management of all incident operations at the incident site. [**472:** A.3.3.37]

A.3.3.160 ISO Module. The characteristic internal water volume of individual tubular cylinders is 43 ft^3 (1218 L) or a water capacity of 2686 lb (1218 kg). The frame of an ISO container module and its corner castings are specially designed and dimensioned to be used in multimodal transportation service on container ships, special highway chassis, and container-on-flatcar railroad equipment. [**55:** A.3.3.60]

A.3.3.162.1 Ceiling Limit. The ceiling limits utilized are to be those published in 29 CFR 1910.1000. [**5000:** A.3.3.371.1]

A.3.3.162.2 Permissible Exposure Limit (PEL). The maximum permitted time-weighted average exposures to be utilized are those published in 29 CFR 1910.1000. [**55:** A.3.3.55.2]

A.3.3.162.3 Short-Term Exposure Limit (STEL). STEL limits are published in 29 CFR 1910.1000. [**55:** A.3.3.55.3]

A.3.3.164.2 Flammable Liquid. For the purposes of this *Code*, a material with a Reid vapor pressure greater than an absolute pressure of 40 psi (276 kPa) is considered to be a gas and is, therefore, not within the scope of NFPA 30. See NFPA 58, *Liquefied Petroleum Gas Code*. [**30:** A.3.3.32.2]

A.3.3.173.7 Highly Toxic Material. While categorization is basically simple in application, the degree of hazard depends on many variables that should be carefully considered individually and in combination. Some examples include the following:

(1) Materials wherein the highly toxic component or mixtures thereof are inextricably bound and cannot be released so there is little or no potential for exposure
(2) Nonfriable solid hazardous materials existing in product forms and in the demonstrated absence of inhalable particles that might not present the same inhalation hazard as the chemical components existing in a friable state
(3) Mixtures of highly toxic materials with ordinary materials, such as water, that might not warrant classification as highly toxic [**400:** A.3.3.61.9.1]

Any hazard evaluation that is required for the precise categorization of highly toxic material is required to be performed by experienced, technically competent persons. [**400:** A.3.3.61.9.1]

A.3.3.173.9 Incompatible Material. Information on incompatible materials can be found in material safety data sheets (MSDS) or manufacturers' product bulletins. [**400:** A.3.3.61.5]

A.3.3.173.14 Toxic Material. While categorization is basically simple in application, the degree of hazard depends on many variables that should be carefully considered individually and in combination. Some examples include the following:

(1) Materials wherein the toxic component or mixtures thereof are inextricably bound and cannot be released so there is little or no potential for exposure
(2) Nonfriable solid hazardous materials existing in product forms and in the demonstrated absence of inhalable particles that might not present the same inhalation hazard as the chemical components existing in a friable state
(3) Mixtures of toxic materials with ordinary materials, such as water, that might not warrant classification as toxic

Any hazard evaluation that is required for the precise categorization of toxic material is required to be performed by experienced, technically competent persons.

A.3.3.173.15 Unstable (Reactive) Material. Unstable (reactive) material is classified as follows:

(1) Class 4 unstable (reactive) materials are those that, in themselves, are readily capable of detonation, explosive decomposition, or explosive reaction at normal temperatures and pressures and include, among others, materials that are sensitive to localized thermal or mechanical shock at normal temperatures and pressures.
(2) Class 3 unstable (reactive) materials are those that, in themselves, are capable of detonation, explosive decomposition, or explosive reaction, but that require a strong initiating source or that must be heated under confinement before initiation, and include, among others, materials that are sensitive to thermal or mechanical shock at elevated temperatures and pressures.
(3) Class 2 unstable (reactive) materials are those that readily undergo violent chemical change at elevated temperatures and pressures and include, among others, materials that exhibit an exotherm at temperatures less than or equal to 30°F (-1°C) when tested by differential scanning calorimetry.
(4) Class 1 unstable (reactive) materials are those that, in themselves, are normally stable, but that can become unstable at elevated temperatures and pressures and include among others, materials that change or decompose on exposure to air, light, or moisture and that exhibit an exotherm at temperatures greater than 30°F (-1°C), but less than or equal to 57°F (14°C), when tested by differential scanning calorimetry.

[*400:* A.3.3.61.10]

A.3.3.173.16 Water-Reactive Material. *Class 1 Water-Reactive Materials.* Materials whose heat of mixing is at or above 30 cal/g and less than 100 cal/g.

Class 2 Water-Reactive Materials. Materials whose heat of mixing is at or above 100 cal/g and less than 600 cal/g.

Class 3 Water-Reactive Materials. Materials whose heat of mixing is greater or equal to 600 cal/g. [*704:* Table F.2]

A.3.3.175 Maximum Allowable Quantity (MAQ). Quantities are permitted to exceed the MAQ when they are located in an area complying with Protection Levels 1–5 in accordance with the building code.

A.3.3.176 Means of Egress. A means of egress comprises the vertical and horizontal travel and includes intervening room spaces, doorways, hallways, corridors, passageways, balconies, ramps, stairs, elevators, enclosures, lobbies, escalators, horizontal exits, courts, and yards. [*101:* A.3.3.172]

A.3.3.179 Mobile Supply Unit. Examples include ISO modules, tube trailers, and cylinder packs. [**55:** A.3.3.72]

A.3.3.182 Normal Temperature and Pressure (NTP). There are different definitions of normal conditions. The normal conditions defined here are the ones most commonly used in the compressed gas and cryogenic fluid industry. [**55:** A.3.3.76]

A.3.3.183.1 Ambulatory Health Care Occupancy. It is not the intent that occupants be considered to be incapable of self-preservation just because they are in a wheelchair or use assistive walking devices, such as a cane, a walker, or crutches. Rather it is the intent to address emergency care centers that receive patients who have been rendered incapable of self-preservation due to the emergency, such as being rendered unconscious as a result of an accident or being unable to move due to sudden illness. [***101:*** A.3.3.190.1]

It is not the intent that the term *anesthesia* be limited to general anesthesia. [***101:*** A.3.3.190.1]

A.3.3.183.2 Apartment Building. The *Code* specifies that, wherever there are three or more living units in a building, the building is considered an apartment building and is required to comply with Chapter 30 or Chapter 31 of NFPA *101*, as appropriate. Townhouse units are considered to be apartment buildings if there are three or more units in the building. The type of wall required between units in order to consider them to be separate buildings is normally established by the AHJ. If the units are separated by a wall of sufficient fire resistance and structural integrity to be considered as separate buildings, then the provisions of Chapter 24 of NFPA *101*, apply to each townhouse. Condominium status is a form of ownership, not occupancy; for example, there are condominium warehouses, condominium apartments, and condominium offices. [***101:*** A.3.3.36.3]

A.3.3.183.3 Assembly Occupancy. Assembly occupancies might include the following:

(1) Armories
(2) Assembly halls
(3) Auditoriums
(4) Bowling lanes
(5) Club rooms
(6) College and university classrooms, 50 persons and over
(7) Conference rooms
(8) Courtrooms
(9) Dance halls
(10) Drinking establishments
(11) Exhibition halls
(12) Gymnasiums
(13) Libraries
(14) Mortuary chapels
(15) Motion picture theaters
(16) Museums
(17) Passenger stations and terminals of air, surface, underground, and marine public transportation facilities
(18) Places of religious worship
(19) Pool rooms
(20) Recreation piers
(21) Restaurants
(22) Skating rinks
(23) Special amusement buildings, regardless of occupant load
(24) Theaters
[***101:*** A.3.3.190.2]

Assembly occupancies are characterized by the presence or potential presence of crowds with attendant panic hazard in case of fire or other emergency. They are generally open or occasionally open to the public, and the occupants, who are present voluntarily, are not ordinarily subject to discipline or control. Such buildings are ordinarily occupied by able-bodied persons and are not used for sleeping purposes. Special conference rooms, snack areas, and other areas incidental to, and under the control of, the management of other occupancies, such as offices, fall under the 50-person limitation. [*101:* A.3.3.190.2]

Restaurants and drinking establishments with an occupant load of fewer than 50 persons should be classified as mercantile occupancies. [*101:* A.3.3.190.2]

For special amusement buildings, see 12.4.8 and 13.4.8 of NFPA *101*. [*101:* A.3.3.190.2]

A.3.3.183.5 Business Occupancy. Business occupancies include the following:

(1) Air traffic control towers (ATCTs)
(2) City halls
(3) College and university instructional buildings, classrooms under 50 persons, and instructional laboratories
(4) Courthouses
(5) Dentists' offices
(6) Doctors' offices
(7) General offices
(8) Outpatient Clinics (ambulatory)
(9) Town halls
 [*101:* A.3.3.190.3]

Doctors' and dentists' offices are included, unless of such character as to be classified as ambulatory health care occupancies. *(See 3.3.183.1.)*[*101:* A.3.3.190.3]

Birth centers should be classified as business occupancies if they are occupied by fewer than four patients, not including infants, at any one time; do not provide sleeping facilities for four or more occupants; and do not provide treatment procedures that render four or more patients, not including infants, incapable of self-preservation at any one time. For birth centers occupied by patients not meeting these parameters, see Chapter 18 or Chapter 19 of NFPA *101*, as appropriate. [*101:* A.3.3.190.3].

Service facilities common to city office buildings such as newsstands, lunch counters serving fewer than 50 persons, barber shops, and beauty parlors are included in the business occupancy group. [*101:* A.3.3.190.3]

City halls, town halls, and courthouses are included in the business occupancy group insofar as their principal function is the transaction of public business and the keeping of books and records. Insofar as they are used for assembly purposes, they are classified as assembly occupancies. [*101:* A.3.3.190.3]

A.3.3.183.6 Day-Care Home. A day-care home is generally located within a dwelling unit. [*101:* A.3.3.142.1]

A.3.3.183.7 Day-Care Occupancy. Day-care occupancies include the following:

(1) Adult day-care occupancies, except where part of a health care occupancy
(2) Child day-care occupancies
(3) Day-care homes
(4) Kindergarten classes that are incidental to a child day-care occupancy
(5) Nursery schools
 [*101:* A.3.3.190.4]

In areas where public schools offer only half-day kindergarten programs, many child day-care occupancies offer state-approved kindergarten classes for children who need full-day care. Because these classes are normally incidental to the day-care occupancy, the requirements of the day-care occupancy should be followed. [*101:* A.3.3.190.4]

A.3.3.183.8 Detention and Correctional Occupancy. Detention and correctional occupancies include the following:

(1) Adult and juvenile substance abuse centers
(2) Adult and juvenile work camps
(3) Adult community residential centers
(4) Adult correctional institutions
(5) Adult local detention facilities
(6) Juvenile community residential centers
(7) Juvenile detention facilities
(8) Juvenile training schools
 [*101:* A.3.3.190.5]

It is not the intent to classify as detention and correctional occupancies the areas of health care occupancies where doors are locked against patient egress where needed for the clinical needs of the patients. For example, a dementia treatment center can be adequately protected by the health care occupancies requirements of Chapter 19 of NFPA *101*. *[See 19.1.1.1.7, 19.2.2.2.2, 19.2.2.2.4(1), and 19.2.2.2.6 of NFPA 101.]* [*101:* A.23.1.1.1.6]

The one-resident threshold requirement of 23.1.1.1.6 of NFPA *101* is not meant to force a residential occupancy, where security is imposed on one or more occupants, to be reclassified as a detention and correctional occupancy. [*101:* A.23.1.1.1.6]

A.3.3.183.9 Dormitory. Rooms within dormitories intended for the use of individuals for combined living and sleeping purposes are guest rooms or guest suites. Examples of dormitories are college dormitories, fraternity and sorority houses, and military barracks. [*101:* A.3.3.65]

A.3.3.183.10 Educational Occupancy. Educational occupancies include the following:

(1) Academies
(2) Kindergartens
(3) Schools
 [*101:* A.3.3.190.6]

An educational occupancy is distinguished from an assembly occupancy in that the same occupants are regularly present. [*101:* A.3.3.190.6]

A.3.3.183.11 Health Care Occupancy. Health care occupancies include the following:

(1) Hospitals
(2) Limited care facilities
(3) Nursing homes
 [*101:* A.3.3.190.7]

Occupants of health care occupancies typically have physical or mental illness, disease, or infirmity. They also include infants, convalescents, or infirm aged persons. [*101:* A.3.3.190.6]

It is not the intent to consider occupants incapable of self-preservation because they are in a wheelchair or use assistive walking devices, such as a cane, a walker, or crutches. [*101:* A.3.3.190.7]

A.3.3.183.13 Hotel. So-called apartment hotels should be classified as hotels, because they are potentially subject to the same transient occupancy as hotels. Transients are those who occupy accommodations for less than 30 days. [*101:*A.3.3.145]

A.3.3.183.14 Industrial Occupancy. Industrial occupancies include the following:

(1) Drycleaning plants
(2) Factories of all kinds
(3) Food processing plants
(4) Gas plants
(5) Hangars (for servicing/maintenance)
(6) Laundries
(7) Power plants
(8) Pumping stations
(9) Refineries
(10) Sawmills
(11) Telephone exchanges
  [*101:*A.3.3.190.8]

In evaluating the appropriate classification of laboratories, the AHJ should treat each case individually, based on the extent and nature of the associated hazards. Some laboratories are classified as occupancies other than industrial; for example, a physical therapy laboratory or a computer laboratory. [*101:*A.3.3.190.8]

For laboratories within the scope of NFPA 45, the occupancies are defined in NFPA 45, Section 3.3, as follows:

(1) Noninstructional labs are considered industrial.
(2) Labs within the scope of NFPA 99 are considered health care.
(3) Instructional labs for grades 12 and below are considered educational.
(4) Labs for grades above grade 12 and Class D labs are business occupancies.
  [*5000:* A.3.3.445.8]

A.3.3.183.15 Limited Care Facility. Limited care facilities and residential board and care occupancies both provide care to people with physical and mental limitations. However, the goals and programs of the two types of occupancies differ greatly. The requirements in NFPA *101* for limited care facilities are based on the assumption that these are medical facilities, that they provide medical care and treatment, and that the patients are not trained to respond to the fire alarm; that is, the patients do not participate in fire drills but, rather, await rescue. *(See Section 18.7 of NFPA 101.)* [*101:* A.3.3.90.2]

The requirements for residential board and care occupancies are based on the assumption that the residents are provided with personal care and activities that foster continued independence, that the residents are encouraged and taught to overcome their limitations, and that most residents, including all residents in prompt and slow homes, are trained to respond to fire drills to the extent they are able. Residents are required to participate in fire drills. *(See Section 32.7 of NFPA 101.)* [*101:* A.3.3.90.2]

Persons with Alzheimer's and related illnesses might be located in a nursing home, limited care facility, or board and care facility. For such persons, it is the level of care provided, not the medical diagnosis, that matters for the purposes of determining whether the facility should meet the requirements for limited care. Where personal care is provided but medical or custodial care is not, the limited care definition does not typically apply. It is the intent of this definition that it not apply to persons not receiving medical or custodial care, provided they are able to assist in their own evacuation, regardless of their medical diagnosis. [*101:*A.3.3.90.2]

A.3.3.183.17 Mercantile Occupancy. Mercantile occupancies include the following:

(1) Auction rooms
(2) Department stores
(3) Drugstores
(4) Restaurants with fewer than 50 persons
(5) Shopping centers
(6) Supermarkets
  [*101:* A.3.3.190.9]

Office, storage, and service facilities incidental to the sale of merchandise and located in the same building should be considered part of the mercantile occupancy classification. [*101:*A.3.3.190.9]

A.3.3.183.19.3 Motor Fuel Dispensing Facility Located Inside a Building. The motor fuel dispensing facility can be either enclosed or partially enclosed by the building walls, floors, ceilings, or partitions or can be open to the outside. The motor fuel dispensing area is that area required for dispensing of fuels to motor vehicles. Dispensing of fuel at manufacturing, assembly, and testing operations is not included within this definition. [*30A:* A.3.3.11.5]

A.3.3.183.23 Parking Structure. A parking structure is permitted to be enclosed or open, use ramps, and use mechanical control push-button-type elevators to transfer vehicles from one floor to another. Motor vehicles are permitted to be parked by the driver or an attendant or are permitted to be parked mechanically by automated facilities. Where automated type parking is provided, the operator of those facilities is permitted either to remain at the entry level or to travel to another level. Motor fuel is permitted to be dispensed, and motor vehicles are permitted to be serviced in a parking structure in accordance with NFPA 30A. [*88A:* A.3.3.2]

A.3.3.183.25 Residential Board and Care Occupancy. The following are examples of facilities that are classified as residential board and care occupancies:

(1) Group housing arrangement for physically or mentally handicapped persons who normally attend school in the community, attend worship in the community, or otherwise use community facilities
(2) Group housing arrangement for physically or mentally handicapped persons who are undergoing training in preparation for independent living, for paid employment, or for other normal community activities
(3) Group housing arrangement for the elderly that provides personal care services but that does not provide nursing care
(4) Facilities for social rehabilitation, alcoholism, drug abuse, or mental health problems that contain a group housing arrangement and that provide personal care services but do not provide acute care
(5) Assisted living facilities
(6) Other group housing arrangements that provide personal care services but not nursing care
  [*101:* A.3.3.190.12]

A.3.3.183.26 Residential Occupancy. Residential occupancies are treated as separate occupancies in this *Code* as follows:

(1) One- and two-family dwellings (Chapter 24 of NFPA *101*)
(2) Lodging or rooming houses (Chapter 26 of NFPA *101*)

(3) Hotels, motels, and dormitories (Chapters 28 and 29 of NFPA *101*)
(4) Apartment buildings (Chapters 30 and 31 of NFPA *101*)
[*101:* A.3.3.190.13]

A.3.3.183.28 Storage Occupancy. Storage occupancies include the following:

(1) Barns
(2) Bulk oil storage
(3) Cold storage
(4) Freight terminals
(5) Grain elevators
(6) Hangars (for storage only)
(7) Parking structures
(8) Truck and marine terminals
(9) Warehouses
[*101:* A.3.3.190.15]

Storage occupancies are characterized by the presence of relatively small numbers of persons in proportion to the area. [*101:* A.3.3.190.15]

A.3.3.183.28.1 Mini-Storage Building. Mini-storage buildings are typically designed to accommodate relatively small transient tenants who are often private individuals or persons who own small businesses and need additional storage space that is generally very small in area to accommodate their short-term storage needs. This definition is not intended to apply to large warehouse buildings designed to be rented or leased to relatively large multiple tenants who are generally storing their wares in conjunction with their businesses. Garage units that are primarily intended for vehicular storage as part of a multi-family development are not intended to be classified as mini-storage buildings. [**5000:** A.3.3.68.13]

A.3.3.187 Operating Unit (Vessel) or Process Unit (Vessel). Unit operations include, but are not limited to, distillation, oxidation, cracking, and polymerization. [**30:** A.3.3.41]

A.3.3.189.1 Organic Peroxide Formulation. Terms such as *accelerator, catalyst, initiator, curing agent*, and so forth, are sometimes used to describe organic peroxide formulations. These terms are misleading because they can also refer to materials that are not or do not contain organic peroxides, some of which might present increased hazard when mixed with organic peroxides. [**400:** A.3.3.70]

A.3.3.192 Oxidizer. Examples of other oxidizing gases include bromine, chlorine, and fluorine. [**400:** A.3.3.72]

The classification of oxidizers is based on the technical committee's evaluation of available scientific and technical data, actual experience, and its considered opinion. Classification refers to the pure oxidizer. Gross contamination can cause oxidizers of all classes to undergo exothermic or explosive reaction, particularly if they also are subjected to confinement and heating. *(See B.5.2.2 through B.5.2.5 for oxidizer classifications.)* [**400:** A.3.3.72]

The classification of oxidizers is based on the degree to which an oxidizing chemical increases, if at all, the burning rate of available combustible fuels. Factors that can influence the burning rate of oxidizers are concentration, particle size, product form, product packaging, and packaging configuration. Examples of Class 1, 2, 3, and 4 chemical oxidizers are listed in B.5.2.2. The definition of the current classes and the oxidizers listed as typical of each Class in B.5.2.1 are based on the technical committee's evaluation of available data, experience, and results of tests done by the Bureau of Mines and GE Research in the 1970s. [**400:** A.3.3.72]

The definition of Class 1, 2, 3, and 4 oxidizers is subjective. Currently, there is no bench scale test method that adequately measures the burning rate of oxidizers for large scale storage. The UN's Recommendations on the Transport of Dangerous Goods includes a bench scale test method (Test O.1) to assign packing groups to solid oxidizers. Thirty grams (1.06 oz) of a mixture of the test substance and cellulose powder is ignited with a Nichrome wire. The time from ignition to the end of visible burning of the mixture is compared with the burning time of several different mixtures of potassium bromated (Class 3) and cellulose powder. The test does not characterize chemical reactivity or thermal stability. The test is not representative of packaged oxidizers. The determination of burning time is strongly dependent on test conditions, particle size, and the test operator's perception of the end of active burning. [**400:** A.3.3.72]

The Fire Protection Research Foundation (FPRF) published National Oxidizing Pool Chemicals Storage Fire Test Project in August 1998. The technical report includes literature abstracts, large-scale calorimetry test data, and intermediate scale rack storage tests. The peak rate of heat release of packaging and packaged oxidizers trichloroisocyanuric acid (Trichlor, Class 1) and calcium hypochlorite (available chlorine >68%, Class 3) are summarized in Table A.3.3.192. [**400:** A.3.3.72]

The Class 1 Trichlor did not increase the burning rate of the combustible packaging. Class 3 calcium hypochlorite (available chlorine >68%) caused a severe increase in the burning rate of the combustible packaging. In 2006, the FPRF published a report on the Development of an Enhanced Hazard Classification System for Oxidizers. The report includes a review of fire losses, historical test data, and current test methods for oxidizing materials used by transportation and environmental regulatory agencies. Two classification schemes with multiple test methods and performance-based criteria were proposed to distinguish between Class 1, 2, 3, and 4 oxidizers in a storage situation. [**400:** A.3.3.72]

Future FPRF effort is proposed to define an appropriate bench scale test, validated by medium scale free burn testing, for oxidizers. The goal of the enhanced classification system would be to prescribe tests and use performance-based criteria to define the different classes of oxidizers based on the degree of burning rate enhancement, chemical reactivity, and thermal stability. [**400:** A.3.3.72]

The FPRF completed a project that resulted in the development of a bench-scale test, validated by intermediate scale testing, for solid oxidizers. An enhanced classification system with prescribed tests and performance-based criteria to define the different classes of oxidizers based on the degree of burning rate enhancement was developed. [Buc, Elizabeth C., *Oxidizer Classification Research Project: Tests and Criteria*, Fire Protection Research Foundation, November 2009] [**400:** A.3.3.72]

A.3.3.200 Personal Care. Personal care involves responsibility for the safety of the resident while inside the building. Personal care might include daily awareness by management of the resident's functioning and whereabouts, making and reminding a resident of appointments, the ability and readiness for intervention in the event of a resident experiencing a crisis, supervision in the areas of nutrition and medication, and actual provision of transient medical care. [*101:* A.3.3.208]

Table A.3.3.192 Results of Large-Scale Calorimetry Tests with Packaging and Packaged Oxidizers on Wood Pallets

Oxidizer and Packaging	Total Weight with Pallets (lb)	Peak Convective HRR (kW)
40 cartons of empty HDPE 2 lb capacity containers	300	1736
40 cartons of pea gravel filled HDPE 2 lb capacity containers	1631	464
40 cartons of granular Trichlor in HDPE 2 lb capacity containers	1891	649
40 cartons of tablet form Trichlor in HDPE 2 lb capacity containers	1882	877
48 cartons of granular calcium hypochlorite in 1 lb capacity Surlin (plastic) bags	1468	6696
36 cartons of granular calcium hypochlorite in HDPE 1 lb capacity containers	1452	>16184

For SI units, 1 lb = 0.45 kg.
Source: FPRF, *National Oxidizing Pool Chemicals Storage Fire Test Project*, Aug. 1998.
[**400:** Table A.3.3.72]

A.3.3.203 Pier. The terms *pier* and *wharf* are used interchangeably. [**307:** A.3.3.13]

A.3.3.204 Pressure Vessel. Pressure vessels of any type can be subject to additional regulations imposed by various states or other legal jurisdictions. Users should be aware that compliance with DOT or ASME requirements might not satisfy all of the required regulations for the location in which the vessel is to be installed or used. Pressure vessels may be constructed to meet requirements of other regulatory agencies, including regulations for Transport, Canada (TC) or various ANSI standards that may be applicable for specific uses. [**400:** A.3.3.19.15]

A.3.3.206 Process or Processing. The sequence can include both physical and chemical operations, unless the term is modified to restrict it to one or the other. The sequence can involve, but is not limited to, preparation, separation, purification, or change in state, energy content, or composition. [**30:** A.3.3.45]

A.3.3.215 Rack. Some rack structures use solid shelves. Racks are permitted to be fixed, portable, or movable. Loading is permitted to be either manual, using lift trucks, stacker cranes, or hand placement, or automatic, using machine-controlled storage and retrieval systems. *[See Figure A.34.7.3.1(a) through Figure A.34.7.3.1(k).]*

A.3.3.215.2 Movable Racks. Movable racks can be moved back and forth only in a horizontal, two-dimensional plane. A moving aisle is created as abutting racks are either loaded or unloaded, then moved across the aisle to abut other racks.

A.3.3.215.4 Portable Racks. Portable racks can be arranged in any number of configurations.

A.3.3.216 Ramp. See 7.2.5 of NFPA *101*. [**101:** A.3.3.221]

A.3.3.222 Safety Can. Safety cans listed to ANSI/UL 30, *Standard for Metal Safety Cans,* are limited to 5 U.S. gal (19 L). ANSI/UL 1313, *Standard for Nonmetallic Safety Cans for Petroleum Products,* allows for capacities up to 5 Imperial gal (23 L). [**30:** A.3.3.48]

A.3.3.228 Signal.

A.3.3.228.1 Alarm Signal. Examples of alarm signals include outputs of activated alarm initiating devices, the light and sound from actuated alarm notification appliances, alarm data transmission to a supervising station, and so forth. [**72:** A.3.3.257.1]

A.3.3.228.2 Fire Alarm Signal. Examples include outputs from activated fire alarm initiating devices (manual fire alarm box, automatic fire detector, waterflow switch, etc.), the light and sound from actuated fire alarm notification appliances, fire alarm data transmission to a supervising station, and so forth. [**72:** A.3.3.257.5]

A.3.3.228.3 Supervisory Signal. Examples include activated supervisory signal-initiating device outputs, supervisory data transmissions to supervising stations, the light and sound from actuated supervisory notification appliances, a delinquency signal indicating a guard's tour supervisory condition, and so forth. [**72:** A.3.3.257.9]

The term *guard's tour supervisory signal,* associated with systems supporting guard's tour supervisory service, is a message indicating that a guard has activated a guard's tour reporting station (not in itself an indication of a supervisory condition). Guard's tour supervisory signals are not a subset of the general category of supervisory signals as used in this *Code.* [**72:** A.3.3.257.9]

A.3.3.228.4 Trouble Signal. Examples include off-normal outputs from integrity monitoring circuits, the light and sound from actuated trouble notification appliances, trouble data transmission to a supervising station, and so forth. [**72:** A.3.3.257.10]

A.3.3.231 Smoke Barrier. A smoke barrier, such as a wall, floor, or ceiling assembly, might be aligned vertically or horizontally. A smoke barrier might or might not have a fire resistance rating. Application of smoke barrier criteria where required elsewhere in the *Code* should be in accordance with Section 12.9.

A.3.3.233 Smoke Partition. A smoke partition is not required to have a fire resistance rating. [**101:** A.3.3.256]

A.3.3.236.1 Combustible Particulate Solid. Combustible particulate solids include dusts, fibers, fines, chips, chunks, flakes, and mixtures of these. A definition of this breadth is necessary because it is crucial to address the fact that there is attrition of the material as it is conveyed. Pieces and particles rub against each other and collide with the walls of the duct as they travel through the system. The rubbing and collision break down the material and produce a mixture of pieces and much finer particles, called dusts. Consequently, it is expected that every conveying system produces dusts, regardless of the starting size of the material, as an inherent by-product of the conveying process. [**69:** A.3.3.5]

A.3.3.236.2 Flammable Solid. Flammable solids include finely divided solid materials that, when dispersed in air as a cloud, could be ignited and cause an explosion. [**400:** A.3.3.45]

A.3.3.241 Spray Booth. Spray booths are manufactured in a variety of forms, including automotive refinishing, downdraft, open-face, traveling, tunnel, and updraft booths. This definition is not intended to limit the term *spray booth* to any particular design. The entire spray booth is part of the spray area. A spray booth is not a spray room. [**33:** A.3.3.14]

A.3.3.242 Spray Room. The entire spray room is considered part of the spray area. A spray booth is not a spray room. [**33:** A.3.3.15]

A.3.3.246.7 Miscellaneous Tire Storage. The limitations on the type and size of storage are intended to identify those situations where tire storage is present in limited quantities and incidental to the main use of the building. Occupancies such as aircraft hangars, automobile dealers, repair garages, retail storage facilities, automotive and truck assembly plants, and mobile home assembly plants are types of facilities where miscellaneous storage could be present. [**13:** A.3.9.4.4]

A.3.3.248.1 Occupiable Story. A story occupied by people on a regular basis. [***101:*** A.3.3.269.1]

A.3.3.250 Street Floor. Where, due to differences in street levels, there are two or more stories accessible from the street, each is a street floor. Where there is no floor level within the specified limits for a street floor above or below ground level, the building has no street floor.

A.3.3.252 Structure. The term *structure* is to be understood as if followed by the words *or portion thereof. (See also 3.3.29, Building.)* [***101:*** A.3.3.272]

A.3.3.254.4 Bulk Oxygen System. The bulk oxygen system terminates at the source valve, which is commonly the point where oxygen at service pressure first enters the supply line or a piece of equipment that utilizes the oxygen gas or liquid. The oxygen containers are either stationary or movable, and the oxygen is stored as a compressed gas or cryogenic fluid.

Bulk oxygen systems can be used to supply gas in either its compressed gaseous or liquefied form. Systems that may be used to supply both gaseous and liquid forms are referred to as hybrid systems. The following bulk oxygen systems are typical of those in use:

(1) When the primary supply of the gas as stored is from a compressed gaseous source that is used in the compressed and gaseous form, the bulk oxygen system is said to be a bulk compressed oxygen gas system.
(2) When the primary supply of the gas as stored is in a liquid form and the system is designed to transfer only liquid, the system is said to be a bulk liquefied oxygen system.
(3) When the primary supply of the gas as stored is in a liquid form and the system is designed to transfer or store the gas in a compressed gaseous form, with or without a feature that may also allow the subsequent transfer and use of liquid, the bulk oxygen system is said to be a hybrid bulk oxygen system. For the purposes of the application of the code, a hybrid system is viewed as a bulk liquefied oxygen system.

[**55:** A.3.3.15]

A.3.3.254.13 Standpipe System. This arrangement is accomplished by means of connections to water supply systems or by means of pumps, tanks, and other equipment necessary to provide an adequate supply of water to the hose connections. [**14:** A.3.3.15]

A.3.3.254.15 Vapor Processing System. Examples are systems using blower-assist for capturing vapors and refrigeration, absorption, and combustion systems for processing vapors. [**30:** A.3.3.56]

A.3.3.254.16 Vapor Recovery System. Examples are balanced-pressure vapor displacement systems and vacuum-assist systems without vapor processing. [**30:** A.3.3.57]

A.3.3.255.4 Portable Tank. (Compressed Gases and Cryogenic Fluids) A portable tank does not include any cylinder having less than 1000 lb (453.5 kg) water capacity, cargo tank, tank car tank, or trailers carrying cylinders of over 1000 lb (453.5 kg) water capacity. [**55:** A.3.3.94.1]

A.3.3.255.6 Stationary Tank. A stationary tank does not include a cylinder having less than 1000 lb (453.5 kg) water capacity. [**55:** A.3.3.82.2]

A.3.3.260 Traffic Calming Device. Traffic calming devices typically consist of, but are not limited to, speed bumps, speed humps, and traffic circles.

A.3.3.261 Tube Trailer. The characteristic internal water volume of individual tubular cylinders ranges from 43 ft^3 to 93 ft^3 (1218 L to 2632 L) or a water capacity of 2686 lb to 5803 lb (1218 kg to 2632 kg). [**55:** A.3.3.96]

A.3.3.267 Use. Examples of use include, but are not limited to, blending, mixing, reacting, distillation, heating or cooling, pumping, compressing, drying, screening, filling, loading and unloading, repackaging, scrubbing, absorbing, neutralizing, and incineration. [**400,** 2013]

A.3.3.267.1 Closed System Use. Examples of closed systems for solids and liquids include reaction process operations and product conveyed through a piping system into a closed vessel, system, or piece of equipment. [**400:** A.3.3.87.1]

A.3.3.267.2 Open System Use. Examples of open systems for solids and liquids include dispensing from or into open beakers or containers, and dip tank and plating tank operations. [**400:** A.3.3.87.2]

A.3.3.269 Vapor Pressure. Vapor pressure is a measure of the pressure that the liquid exerts against the atmosphere above it. Just as the atmosphere exerts pressure on the surface of the liquid, the liquid pushes back. Vapor pressure is normally less than atmospheric pressure and is a measure of the liquid's tendency to evaporate (i.e., to move from the liquid to the gaseous state). This tendency is also referred to as volatility, thus the use of the term *volatile* to describe liquids that evaporate very easily. The higher the vapor pressure, the greater the rate of evaporation and the lower the boiling point. Simply put, this means more vapors and increased fire risk. [**30:** A.4.2.6]

A.3.3.274 Wharf. The terms *wharf* and *pier* are used interchangeably. [**307:** A.3.3.24]

A.3.4.5 Design Specification. Design specifications include both hardware and human factors, such as the conditions produced by maintenance and training. For purposes of performance-based design, the design specifications of interest are those that affect the ability of the building to meet the stated goals and objectives. [**5000:** A.3.3.607.1]

A.3.4.7 Exposure Fire. An exposure fire usually refers to a fire that starts outside a building, such as a wildlands fire or vehicle fire, and that, consequently, exposes the building to a fire. [***101:*** A.3.3.88]

A.3.4.8 Fire Model. Due to the complex nature of the principles involved, models are often packaged as computer software. Any relevant input data, assumptions, and limitations needed to properly implement the model will be attached to the fire models. [*101:* A.3.3.101]

A.3.4.9 Fire Scenario. A fire scenario defines the conditions under which a proposed design is expected to meet the fire safety goals. Factors typically include fuel characteristics, ignition sources, ventilation, building characteristics, and occupant locations and characteristics. The term *fire scenario* includes more than the characteristics of the fire itself but excludes design specifications and any characteristics that do not vary from one fire to another; the latter are called assumptions. The term *fire scenario* is used here to mean only those specifications required to calculate the fire's development and effects, but, in other contexts, the term might be used to mean both the initial specifications and the subsequent development and effects (i.e., a complete description of fire from conditions prior to ignition to conditions following extinguishment). [*101:* A.3.3.105]

A.3.4.10 Fuel Load. Fuel load includes interior finish and trim. [*5000:* A.3.3.385.3]

A.3.4.14 Performance Criteria. Performance criteria are stated in engineering terms. Engineering terms include temperatures, radiant heat flux, and levels of exposure to fire products. Performance criteria provide threshold values used to evaluate a proposed design. [*101:* A.3.3.206]

A.3.4.15 Proposed Design. The design team might develop a number of trial designs that will be evaluated to determine whether they meet the performance criteria. One of the trial designs will be selected from those that meet the performance criteria for submission to the AHJ as the proposed design. [*101:* A.3.3.218]

The proposed design is not necessarily limited to fire protection systems and building features. It also includes any component of the proposed design that is installed, established, or maintained for the purpose of life safety, without which the proposed design could fail to achieve specified performance criteria. Therefore, the proposed design often includes emergency procedures and organizational structures that are needed to meet the performance criteria specified for the proposed design. [*101:* A.3.3.218]

A.4.1 The overall goals of this *Code* are presented in 4.1.1. These overall goals are treated in greater depth in 4.1.3 through 4.1.5. In each of these subsections, an overall goal for the subsection is defined, specific goals relating to the overall goal are presented next, and the objectives that relate to the specific goal follow. This format is intended to enhance the usability of the *Code*.

The subjects addressed in Chapter 4 are general in nature and supplement the provisions of Chapter 1, Administration. NFPA publication style dictates that Chapter 1 of all codes and standards is to include only title, scope, purpose, application, equivalency, units and formulas, and enforcement sections. All other general provisions are to be contained in Chapter 4, General Requirements, which follows Chapter 2, Referenced Publications, and Chapter 3, Definitions.

Chapter 4 provides general information about the *Code's* goals and objectives, inherent assumptions, options that can be applied for compliance with life safety and property protection requirements, and information regarding how the *Code* is applied *(see Sections 4.1 through 4.5)*. These goals and objectives establish the broad areas that this *Code* governs. They can be achieved via prescriptive-based options or performance-based options. Additionally, the goals and objectives can be reviewed to determine whether satisfactory conditions are being provided when equivalency options are being considered.

General administrative and application requirements that apply to all facilities and buildings are also included in this chapter *(see Section 4.5)*.

A.4.1.1 These highest level goals are intentionally general in nature. Each includes a broad spectrum of topics as shown in 4.1.3. The property protection goal is not just a goal unto itself, as it is also achieved in part as a result of designing to achieve the other stated goals. A reasonable level of safety is further defined by subsequent language in the *Code*. The facility/property owner or an insurance representative might also have other goals, which might necessitate more stringent objectives as well as more demanding criteria.

A.4.1.2 The objectives apply regardless of which option a user of the *Code* selects for a design — the performance-based option or the prescriptive-based option. The objectives are stated in more specific terms than the goals and tend to be more quantitative. The goals and objectives, taken together, form the broad, general targets at which a performance-based design can take aim. Specific criteria for design follow in Chapter 5.

A.4.1.3 The concept of providing for safety applies not only to safety during a fire, explosion, or hazardous materials incident, but also during the normal use of a building or facility. A reasonable level of safety should be provided for occupants in and individuals near the facility or building in question. The resultant design in addition to providing for occupant's safety also promotes the public welfare. Public welfare is also provided as a result of the mission continuity provisions of this *Code*.

A.4.1.3.1.1 The phrase *reasonably safe* from fire is defined by subsequent language in this *Code*, primarily in the objectives.

A.4.1.3.1.2.2 In many cases, the provisions of the *Code* to provide safety for occupants satisfies this goal for protection of emergency responders.

A.4.1.3.1.2.5 This provision addresses the fire safety objectives of operations addressed elsewhere in the *Code*, such as hot work, tar kettle operation, and so forth, that are not directly related to building construction and use.

A.4.1.3.2.1 The phrase *reasonably safe during normal use* is defined by subsequent language in this *Code*, primarily in the objectives. Certain requirements, such as heights of guards and stair dimensions, are provided to ensure that the occupants are safe during nonemergency use of the buildings. Failure to address these features could result in falls or other injuries to occupants in their normal day-to-day activities in the building.

A.4.1.3.2.2 For item 3, the phrase *external force* refers to the application of factors such as heat, water, shock, or other phenomenon onto hazardous materials that are sensitive to such factors and could react vigorously to produce unsafe conditions.

A.4.1.4.2.1 Ignition occurs when combustible materials come into contact with a source of heat of sufficient temperature and power for a requisite time in an atmosphere where oxygen is present. Combustible material does not necessarily ignite immediately upon contact with a source of heat.

A.4.1.4.2.2 Examples of specific conditions to avoid include, but are not limited to, flashover, fire spread beyond the item or room of fire origin, overheating of equipment, and overpressure of exterior walls.

A.4.1.5.1 This goal is applicable to certain buildings and facilities that have been deemed to be necessary to the continued welfare of a community. Depending on the nature of the critical mission provided by the building, various stakeholders, including community leaders, AHJs, and owners will identify the mission critical buildings. Mission critical areas should be identified and appropriately protected. The objectives for property protection and mission continuity are sometimes difficult to differentiate. Achieving the objectives for property protection could, to a certain extent, accomplish the objectives for mission continuity.

A.4.1.5.2 Examples of buildings and facilities that provide a public welfare role for a community could include hospitals, police and fire stations, evacuation centers, schools, water and sewerage facilities, and electrical generating plants. Also included are buildings and facilities with significant impact on the economic viability of the community. This objective is intended to ensure that such buildings and facilities are capable of providing essential services following a disaster since the community's well-being depends on such service being available.

A.4.2.1 Additional assumptions that need to be identified for a performance-based design are addressed in Chapter 5.

A.4.2.2 It is not assumed that a design scenario will be considered that simulates the hazards produced when unauthorized releases of hazardous materials occur simultaneously at different locations within a facility, unless it is reasonable to expect that a single incident, such as a fork lift accident or pipe failure, could be expected to create such a condition. However, when hazardous materials are in close proximity to one another, such as on a shelf or in adjacent storage cabinets, it could be reasonable to apply a design scenario where multiple releases of the hazardous materials occur simultaneously from these close proximity areas. In this case, it is not unreasonable to expect the shelf to collapse or a forklift to damage adjacent hazardous materials containers.

A.4.2.3 It is not assumed that a design scenario will be considered that simulates the hazards produced when a fire, explosion, or external force that creates a dangerous condition occurs at the same time that hazardous materials have been subject to an unauthorized release. This does not preclude considering a scenario where a fire or explosion occurs and impinges on hazardous materials that are in their normal storage, use, or handling conditions.

The phrase *external force that creates a dangerous condition* refers to the application of factors such as heat, water, shock, or other phenomenon onto hazardous materials that are sensitive to such factors and could react vigorously to produce unsafe conditions.

A.4.4.4 Fire alarms alert occupants to initiate emergency procedures, facilitate orderly conduct of fire drills, and initiate response by emergency services.

A.4.5.7 Examples of changes from one occupancy subclassification to another subclassification of the same occupancy could include a change from a Class B to a Class A mercantile occupancy. Hospitals and nursing homes are both health care occupancies and are defined separately, but they are not established as separate suboccupancies; thus, a change from one to the other does not constitute a change of occupancy subclassification.

For example, a building was used as a hospital but has been closed for 4 years. It is again to be used as a hospital. As long as the building was not used as another occupancy during the time it was closed, it would be considered an existing hospital.

Hotels and apartments, although both residential occupancies, are treated separately, and a change from one to the other constitutes a change of occupancy.

A.4.5.8.3 Examples of such features include automatic sprinklers, fire alarm systems, standpipes, and portable fire extinguishers. The presence of a life safety feature, such as sprinklers or fire alarm devices, creates a reasonable expectation by the public that these safety features are functional. When systems are inoperable or taken out of service but the devices remain, they present a false sense of safety. Also, before taking any life safety features out of service, extreme care needs to be exercised to ensure that the feature is not required, was not originally provided as an alternative or equivalent, or is no longer required due to other new requirements in the current *Code*. It is not intended that the entire system or protection feature be removed. Instead, components such as sprinklers, initiating devices, notification appliances, standpipe hose, and exit systems should be removed to reduce the likelihood of relying on inoperable systems or features. Conversely, equipment, such as fire or smoke dampers, that is not obvious to the public should be able to be taken out of service if no longer required by this *Code*. Where a door that is not required to be fire protection-rated is equipped with a fire protection listing label, it is not the intent of 4.5.8.3 to require such door to be self- or automatic-closing due merely to the presence of the label. [*101:* A.4.6.12.3]

A.4.5.8.4 In some cases, the requirements for new construction are less restrictive, and it might be justifiable to permit an existing building to use the less restrictive requirements. However, extreme care needs to be exercised when granting such permission, because the less restrictive provision might be the result of a new requirement elsewhere in the *Code*. For example, in editions of the *Code* prior to 1991, corridors in new health care occupancies were required to have a 1-hour fire resistance rating. Since 1991, such corridors have been required only to resist the passage of smoke. However, this provision is based on the new requirement that all new health care facilities be protected throughout by automatic sprinklers. *(See A.4.5.8.5.)* [*101:* A.4.6.7.4]

A.4.5.8.5 An example of what is intended by 4.5.8.4 and 4.5.8.5 follows. In a hospital that has 6 ft (1830 mm) wide corridors, such corridors cannot be reduced in width, even though the provisions for existing hospitals do not require 6 ft (1830 mm) wide corridors. However, if a hospital has 10 ft (3050 mm) wide corridors, they are permitted to be reduced to 8 ft (2440 mm) in width, which is the requirement for new construction. If the hospital corridor is 36 in. (915 mm) wide, it would have to be increased to 48 in. (1220 mm), which is the requirement for existing hospitals. [*101:* A.4.6.7.5]

A.4.5.9.1(1) Examples of such materials include steel, concrete, masonry, and glass. [**5000:** A.7.1.4.1.1(1)]

A.5.1 The performance option of this *Code* establishes acceptable levels of risk for facilities (i.e., buildings and other structures and the operations therewith associated) as addressed in Section 1.3. (Note that "facility" and "building" can be used interchangeably with facility being the more general term.) While the performance option of this *Code* does contain goals, objectives, and performance criteria necessary to provide for an acceptable level of risk, it does not describe how to meet these goals, objectives, and performance criteria. Design and engineering are needed to meet the provisions of Chapter 5. For fire protection designs, the *SFPE Engineering Guide to Performance-Based Fire Protection Analysis and Design of Buildings* provides a framework for these assessments.

Pre-construction design requirements address those issues, which have to be considered before the certificate of occupancy is issued for a facility.

A.5.1.3 Qualifications should include experience, education, and credentials that demonstrate knowledgeable and responsible use of applicable models and methods.

A.5.1.4 The *SFPE Engineering Guide to Performance-Based Fire Protection Analysis and Design of Buildings* outlines a process for using a performance-based approach in the design and assessment of building fire safety design and identifies parameters that should be considered in the analysis of a performance-based design. As can be seen this process requires the involvement of all stakeholders who have a share or interest in the successful completion of the project. The steps that are recommended by the *SFPE Engineering Guide to Performance-Based Fire Protection Analysis and Design of Buildings* for this process are shown in Figure A.5.1.4.

The guide specifically addresses building fire safety performance-based design. It might not be directly applicable to performance-based designs involving other systems and operations covered within this *Code*, such as hot work operations or hazardous materials storage. However, the various steps for defining, developing, evaluating, and documenting the performance-based design should still provide a useful framework for the overall design process.

The steps in the performance-based design process are as follows:

(1) *Step 1: Defining Project Scope.* The first step in a performance-based design is to define the scope of the project. Defining the scope consists of identifying and documenting the following:
 (a) Constraints on the design and project schedule
 (b) The stakeholders associated with project
 (c) The proposed building construction and features desired by the owner or tenant
 (d) Occupant and building characteristics
 (e) The intended use and occupancy of the building
 (f) Applicable codes and regulations
 An understanding of these items is needed to ensure that a performance-based design meets the stakeholders' needs.
(2) *Step 2: Identifying Goals.* Once the scope of the project is defined, the next step in the performance-based design process is to identify and document the fire safety goals of various stakeholders. Fire safety goals could include levels of protection for people and property, or they could provide for continuity of operations, historical preservation, and environmental protection. Goals could be unique for different projects, based on the stakeholders needs and desires. The stakeholders should discuss which goals are the most important for the project. In order to avoid problems later in the design process, all stakeholders should be aware of and agree to the goals prior to proceeding with the performance-based design process *(see Step 7)*.
(3) *Step 3: Defining Stakeholder and Design Objectives.* The third step in the design process is to develop objectives. The objectives are essentially the design goals that are further refined into tangible values that can be quantified in engineering terms. Objectives could include mitigating the consequences of a fire expressed in terms of dollar values, loss of life, or other impact on property operations, or maximum allowable conditions, such as extent of fire spread, temperature, spread of combustion products, and so forth.
(4) *Step 4: Developing Performance Criteria.* The fourth step in the design process is the development of performance criteria to be met by the design. These criteria are a further refinement of the design objectives and are numerical values to which the expected performance of the trial designs can be compared. Performance criteria could include threshold values for temperatures of materials, gas temperatures, carboxyhemoglobin (COHb) levels, smoke obscuration, and thermal exposure levels.
(5) *Step 5: Developing Design Scenarios.* Once the performance criteria have been established, the engineer will develop and analyze design alternatives to meet performance criteria. The first part of this process is the identification of possible scenarios and design scenarios. Fire scenarios are descriptions of possible fire events, and consist of fire characteristics, building characteristics (including facility operations), and occupant characteristics. The fire scenarios identified will subsequently be filtered (i.e., combined or eliminated) into a subset of design fire scenarios against which trial designs will be evaluated. Hazardous materials scenarios can be treated similarly.
(6) *Step 6: Developing Trial Design(s).* Once the project scope, performance criteria, and design scenarios are established, the engineer develops preliminary designs, referred to as trial designs, intended to meet the project requirements. The trial design(s) include proposed fire protection systems, construction features, and operation that are provided in order for a design to meet the performance criteria when evaluated using the design fire scenarios. The evaluation method should also be determined at this point. The evaluation methods used should be appropriate for the situation and agreeable to the stakeholders.
(7) *Step 7: Developing a Fire Protection Engineering Design Brief.* At this point in the process a fire protection engineering design brief should be prepared and provided to all stakeholders for their review and concurrence. This brief should document the project scope, goals, objectives, trial designs, performance criteria, design fire scenarios, and analysis methods. Documenting and agreeing upon these factors at this point in the design process will help avoid possible misunderstandings later.
(8) *Step 8: Evaluating Trial Designs.* Each trial design is then evaluated using each design scenario. The evaluation results will indicate whether the trial design will meet the performance criteria. Only trial design(s) that meet the performance criteria can be considered as final design proposals. Yet, the performance criteria can be revised with the stakeholders' approval. The criteria cannot be arbitrarily changed to ensure that a trial design meets a criterion, but can be changed based on additional analysis and the consideration of additional data.

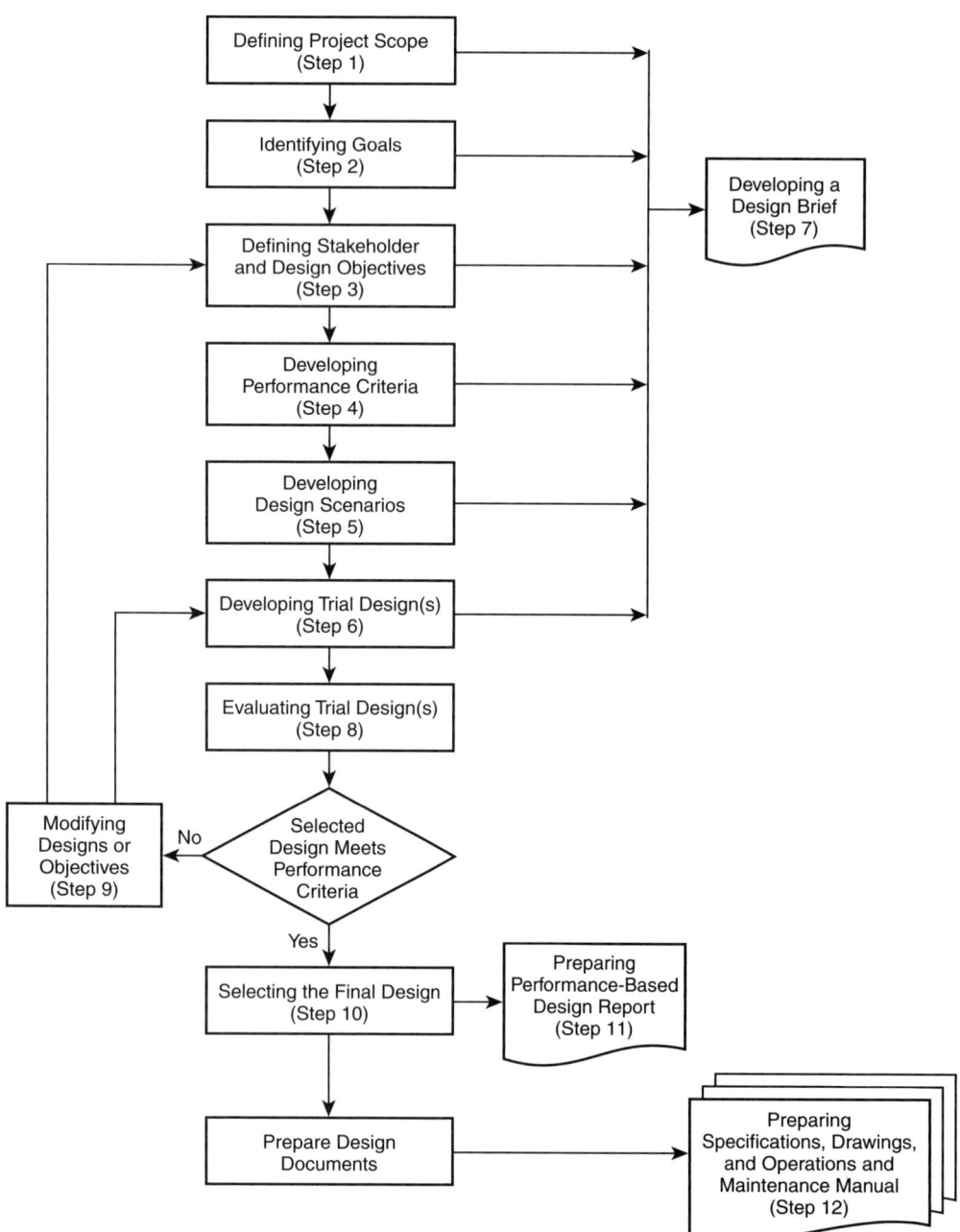

FIGURE A.5.1.4 Steps in the Performance-Based Analysis and the Conceptual Design Procedure for Fire Protection Design.

(9) *Step 9: Modifying Designs or Objectives.* If none of the trial designs evaluated comply with the previously agreed upon performance criteria, it could be necessary to either develop and evaluate new trial designs, or revisit the objectives and performance criteria previously agreed upon by the stakeholders to determine if stakeholder objectives and performance criteria should be modified.

(10) *Step 10: Selecting the Final Design.* Once an acceptable trial design is identified using the evaluation, it can be considered for the final project design. If multiple trial designs are evaluated, further analysis will be needed to select a final design. The selection of an acceptable trial design for the final design could be based on a variety of factors, such as financial considerations, timeliness of installation, system and material availability, ease of installation, maintenance and use, and other factors.

(11) *Step 11: Preparing Performance-Based Design Report.* Once the final design is identified, design documents need to be prepared. Proper documentation will ensure that all stakeholders understand what is necessary for the design implementation, maintenance, and continuity of the fire protection design. The documentation should include the fire protection engineering design brief, a performance design report, detailed specifications and

drawings, and a facility operations and maintenance manual.

(12) *Step 12: Preparing Specifications, Drawings, and Operations and Maintenance Manual.* The specifications and drawings portion of the performance-based design report convey to building and system designers and installing contractors how to implement the performance design. Specifications and drawings could include required sprinkler densities, hydraulic characteristics and spacing requirements, the fire detection and alarm system components and programming, special construction requirements including means of egress and location of fire-resistive walls, compartmentation, and the coordination of interactive systems. The detailed specifications are the implementation document of the performance-based design report. The detailed drawings will graphically represent the results of the performance design. The Operations and Maintenance (O&M) Manual clearly states the requirement of the facility operator to ensure that the components of the performance design are in place and operating properly. The O&M Manual describes the commissioning requirements and the interaction of the different systems' interfaces. All subsystems are identified, and inspection and testing regimes and schedules are created.

The O&M Manual also gives instruction to the facility operator on restrictions placed on facility operations. These limitations are based on the engineering assumptions made during the design and analysis. These limiting factors could include critical fire load, sprinkler design requirements, building use and occupancy, and reliability and maintenance of systems. The O&M Manual can be used to communicate to tenants and occupants these limits and their responsibilities as a tenant. It could also be used as a guide for renovations and changes. It also can be used to document agreements between stakeholders.

A.5.1.5 A third-party reviewer is a person or group of persons chosen by the AHJ to review proposed performance-based designs. Qualifications of the third-party reviewer should include experience, education, and credentials that demonstrate knowledgeable and responsible use of applicable models and methods.

A.5.1.8 See Step 12 of A.5.1.4 for a description of these documents.

A.5.1.9 Information that could be needed by the fire service arriving at the scene of a fire in a performance-based designed facility includes, but is not limited to, the following:

(1) Safe shutdown procedures of equipment and processes
(2) Facility personnel responsible for assisting the fire service
(3) Operating procedures required to maintain the effectiveness of the performance-based designed fire protection system: when it is and is not appropriate to alter, shut down, or turn off a design feature; assumptions that have to be maintained if a fire occurs; suggested fire-fighting tactics that relate to the specific nature of the performance-based design

The design specifications and O&M Manual documentation described in 5.1.8 should provide a guide for the facility owner and tenants to follow in order to maintain the required level of safety anticipated by the original design. It should also provide a guide for the AHJ to use in conducting ongoing inspections of the facility.

A.5.1.10 Continued compliance with the goals and objectives of the *Code* involves many factors. The building construction, including openings, interior finish, and fire- and smoke-resistive construction, and the building and fire protection systems need to retain at least the same level of performance as is provided for by the original design parameters. The use and occupancy should not change to the degree that assumptions made about the occupant characteristics, combustibility of furnishings, and existence of trained personnel are no longer valid. In addition, actions provided by other personnel, such as emergency responders, should not be diminished below the documented assumed levels. Also, actions needed to maintain reliability of systems at the anticipated level need to meet the initial design criteria.

Subsection 5.1.10 deals with issues that arise after the facility has been constructed and a certificate of occupancy has been issued. Therefore, any changes to the facility or the operations conducted therein, up to and including the demolition of the facility, that affect the assumptions of the original design are considered as part of the management of change.

The following is a process for evaluating performance-based facilities:

(1) Review of original design analysis and documentation as follows:
   (a) Assumptions
   (b) Input parameter values
   (c) Predictions and/or results of other calculations
(2) Review of design analysis and documentation for any subsequent renovations, additions, modifications, and so forth, as in Step 1 of A.5.1.4
(3) Review of the facility's operations and maintenance manual, including any and all revisions to it
(4) On-site inspection, involving the following:
   (a) Consideration of "prescriptive" issues (e.g., blocked egress paths, poor maintenance of systems)
   (b) Comparison of assumptions to specific, pertinent on-site conditions
   (c) Comparison of input parameter values to pertinent on-site conditions
   (d) Review of maintenance and testing documentation to ensure adherence to the schedules detailed in the facility's O&M Manual
(5) Reconciliation of discrepancies as follows:
   (a) Develop a list of discrepancies
   (b) Consultation with the facility owner and/or their representative
   (c) Preparation of a schedule that reconciles the discrepancies

A.5.1.11 Private fire inspection services can be used to meet this provision provided that they are qualified to assess the impact of changes on the performance-based design and assumptions.

A.5.2.2 The performance criteria in 5.2.2 define an acceptable level of performance that should be agreed upon by the stakeholders, including the owner and the AHJ. The acceptable level of performance can vary widely between different facilities based on a number of factors, including the existence of potential ignition sources, potential fuel loads present, reactivity and quantity of hazardous materials present, the nature of the operations conducted at the facility, and the characteristics and number of personnel likely to be present at the facility.

A.5.2.2.1 Many of the performance criteria related to safety from fire can also be found in the annex of NFPA *101, Life Safety Code.*

A.5.2.2.2 It is anticipated that the design provides protection for occupants who are not intimate with the initial unintentional detonation or deflagration of explosive materials, and individuals immediately adjacent to the property. It is recognized that employees should be trained and knowledgeable in the hazards of the materials present in the workplace. It is recognized that some of these individuals could experience psychological and physical injuries, such as hearing problems, on either a short- or long-term basis. However, the intent is that they do not experience thermal burns or loss of life or limb as a direct result of the explosion.

It is not the intent of the *Code* to provide protection against explosions caused by acts of terrorism. This would involve the introduction of an unknown quantity of explosives in an unknown location within or adjacent to a building. Where protection is needed against such acts of terrorism, the appropriate military and law enforcement agencies should be consulted.

A.5.2.2.3 Given the nature and variety of hazardous materials, more than one performance criterion for a specific facility could need to be developed. Criteria have to be developed for each hazardous material and possibly for different personnel; for example, higher levels of exposure can be tolerated by personnel that are in some way protected than those personnel having no protection. Development of performance criteria for hazardous materials should be developed by the facility owner and the facility's safety personnel in conjunction with the AHJ and the emergency response personnel expected to respond to an incident.

It is anticipated that the design provides protection for occupants inside or immediately adjacent to the facility who are not intimate with the initial unauthorized release of hazardous materials, or the initial unintentional reaction of hazardous materials. However, it is assumed that these individuals depart from the area of the incident in a time frame reasonable for their circumstances, based on their observation of the event, or some other form of notification.

It is also anticipated that employees and emergency response personnel are trained and aware of the hazardous materials present in the facility, and the potential consequences of their involvement in the incident, and take appropriate measures to ensure their own safety during search and rescue operations.

It is not the intent of the *Code* to provide protection against acts of terrorism involving the introduction of hazardous materials into a facility. This involves the introduction of an unknown quantity of materials in an unknown location within or adjacent to a building. Where protection is needed against such acts of terrorism, the appropriate military and law enforcement agencies should be consulted.

A.5.2.2.4 Each facility designed using a performance-based approach most likely has different levels of acceptable and unacceptable property damage. This reflects the unique aspects of the performance-based designed facility and the reasons for pursuing a performance-based design. Therefore, the definition of an acceptable and an unacceptable level of property damage results from discussions between the facility's owner, manager and engineer, the designer, (possibly) the insurance underwriter and field engineer, and the AHJ. There could be cases where a property damage criterion is not needed.

Note that the structural integrity performance criteria for property damage most likely differs from the structural integrity performance criteria for life safety. This reflects the difference in the associated objectives: a life safety criterion probably is more restrictive than one for property damage.

A.5.2.2.5 Each facility designed using a performance-based approach most likely has a different level of acceptable and unacceptable interruption of the facility's mission. This reflects the unique aspects of the performance-based designed facility and the reasons for pursuing a performance-based design. Therefore, the definition of an acceptable and an unacceptable interruption of the facility's mission results from discussions between the facility's owner, manager and engineer, the designer, (possibly) the insurance underwriter and field engineer, and the AHJ. There could be cases where a mission continuity criterion is not needed.

A.5.4 Many events can occur during the life of a facility; some have a higher probability of occurrence than others. Some events, though not typical, could have a devastating effect on the facility. A reasonable design should be able to achieve the goals, objectives, and performance criteria of this *Code* for any typical or common design scenario and for some of the nontypical, potentially devastating scenarios, up to some level commensurate with society's expectations as reflected in this *Code.*

The challenge in selecting design scenarios is finding a manageable number that are sufficiently diverse and representative so that, if the design is reasonably safe for those scenarios, it should then be reasonably safe for all scenarios, except for those specifically excluded as being unrealistically severe or sufficiently infrequent to be fair tests of the design.

A.5.4.1.2 The *SFPE Engineering Guide to Performance-Based Fire Protection Analysis and Design of Buildings* identifies methods for evaluating fire scenarios.

A.5.4.1.3 It is desirable to consider a wide variety of different design scenarios to evaluate the complete capabilities of the building or structure. Design scenarios should not be limited to a single or a couple of worst-case events.

A.5.4.2.1 An example of such a scenario for a health care occupancy involves a patient room with two occupied beds with a fire initially involving one bed and the room door open. This is a cursory example in that much of the explicitly required information indicated in 5.4.2.1 can be determined from the information provided in the example. Note that it is usually necessary to consider more than one scenario to capture the features and conditions typical of an occupancy.

A.5.4.2.2 Examples of such scenarios are a fire involving ignition of gasoline as an accelerant in a means of egress, clothing racks in corridors, renovation materials, or other fuel configurations that can cause an ultrafast fire. The means of egress chosen is the doorway with the largest egress capacity among doorways normally used in the ordinary operation of the building. The baseline occupant characteristics for the property are assumed. At ignition, doors are assumed to be open throughout the building.

A.5.4.2.3 An example of such a scenario is a fire in a storage room adjacent to the largest occupiable room in the building. The contents of the room of fire origin are specified to provide the largest fuel load and the most rapid growth in fire severity consistent with the normal use of the room. The adjacent occupiable room is assumed to be filled to capacity with occupants. Occupants are assumed to be somewhat impaired in whatever form is most consistent with the intended use of the building. At ignition, doors from both rooms are assumed to be open. Depending on the design, doorways connect the two rooms or they connect via a common hallway or corridor.

For purposes of this scenario, an occupiable room is a room that could contain people (i.e., a location within a building where people are typically found).

A.5.4.2.4 An example of such a scenario is a fire originating in a concealed wall- or ceiling-space adjacent to a large, occupied function room. Ignition involves concealed combustibles, including wire or cable insulation and thermal or acoustical insulation. The adjacent function room is assumed to be occupied to capacity. The baseline occupant characteristics for the property are assumed. At ignition, doors are assumed to be open throughout the building.

A.5.4.2.5 An example of such a scenario is a cigarette fire in a trash can. The trash can is close enough to room contents to ignite more substantial fuel sources but is not close enough to any occupant to create an intimate-with-ignition situation. If the intended use of the property involves the potential for some occupants to be incapable of movement at any time, then the room of origin is chosen as the type of room likely to have such occupants, filled to capacity with occupants in that condition. If the intended use of the property does not involve the potential for some occupants to be incapable of movement, then the room of origin is chosen to be an assembly or function area characteristic of the use of the property, and the trash can is placed so that it is shielded by furniture from suppression systems. At ignition, doors are assumed to be open throughout the building.

A.5.4.2.6 An example of such a scenario is a fire originating in the largest fuel load of combustibles possible in normal operation in a function or assembly room or in a process/manufacturing area, characteristic of the normal operation of the property. The configuration, type, and geometry of the combustibles are chosen so as to produce the most rapid and severe fire growth or smoke generation consistent with the normal operation of the property. The baseline occupant characteristics for the property are assumed. At ignition, doors are assumed to be closed throughout the building.

This scenario includes everything from a big couch fire in a small dwelling to a rack storage fire in combustible liquids stock in a big box retail store.

A.5.4.2.7 An example of such a scenario is an exposure fire. The initiating fire is the closest and most severe fire possible consistent with the placement and type of adjacent properties and the placement of plants and combustible adornments on the property. The baseline occupant characteristics of the property are assumed.

This category includes wildland/urban interface fires and exterior wood shingle problems, where applicable.

A.5.4.2.8 This scenario addresses a set of conditions with a typical fire originating in the building with any one passive or active fire protection system or feature being ineffective. Examples include unprotected openings between floors or between fire walls or fire barrier walls, rated fire doors that fail to close automatically or are blocked open, sprinkler system water supply that is shut off, fire alarm system that's nonoperative, smoke management system that is not operational, or automatic smoke dampers that are blocked open. This scenario should represent a reasonable challenge to the other building features provided by the design and presumed to be available.

The exemption from Fire Design Scenario 8 is applied to each active or passive fire protection system individually and requires two different types of information to be developed by analysis and approved by the AHJ. System reliability is to be analyzed and accepted. Design performance in the absence of the system is also to be analyzed and accepted, but acceptable performance does not require fully meeting the stated goals and objectives. It might not be possible to meet fully the goals and objectives if a key system is unavailable, and yet no system is totally reliable. The AHJ determines which level of performance, possibly short of the stated goals and objectives, is acceptable, given the very low probability (that is, the system's unreliability probability) that the system will not be available.

A.5.4.3.1 This scenario is intended to address facilities where explosives, and products containing explosives, are manufactured, stored, sold, or handled. From an overall safety standpoint, the operations being performed at these facilities should include stringent safety procedures that significantly reduce the likelihood of an explosion from occurring. However, if an explosion does occur, protection methods such as storage magazines, property set backs, deflagration, and explosion venting and containment need to be in place, as appropriate, to minimize potential injury and loss of life and property.

Where products containing explosives, such as pyrotechnic displays or fireworks, are stored, handled, or used in buildings, such as arenas, an explosion scenario should not result in significant injuries to occupants not intimate with the materials.

A.5.4.4 Design hazardous materials scenarios should explicitly account for the following:

(1) Occupant activities, training, and knowledge
(2) Number and location of occupants
(3) Discharge location and surroundings
(4) Hazardous materials' properties
(5) Ventilation, inerting, and dilution systems and conditions
(6) Normal and emergency operating procedures
(7) Safe shutdown and other hazard mitigating systems and procedures
(8) Weather conditions affecting the hazard
(9) Potential exposure to off-site personnel

Design hazardous materials scenarios should be evaluated as many times as necessary by varying the factors previously indicated. Design hazardous materials scenarios could need to be established for each different type of hazardous material stored or used at the facility.

A.5.4.4.4.2 This provision should be applied to each protection system individually and requires two different types of information to be developed by analysis and approved by the AHJ. System reliability is to be analyzed and accepted. Design performance in the absence of the system is also to be analyzed and accepted, but acceptable performance does not require fully meeting the stated goals and objectives. It might not be possible to meet fully the goals and objectives if a key system is unavailable, and yet no system is totally reliable. The AHJ determines which level of performance, possibly short of stated goals and objectives, is acceptable, given the very low probability (that is, the systems' unreliability probability) that the system will be unavailable.

A.5.4.5.1 An example of such a scenario would involve a fire or earthquake effectively blocking the principal entrance/exit but not immediately endangering the occupants. The full occupant load of the assembly space has to exit using secondary means.

A.5.6 The assessment of precision required in 5.7.2 requires a sensitivity and uncertainty analysis, which can be translated into safety factors.

Sensitivity Analysis. The first run a model user makes should be labeled as the base case, using the nominal values of the various input parameters. However, the model user should not rely on a single run as the basis for any performance-based fire safety system design. Ideally, each variable or parameter that the model user made to develop the nominal input data should have multiple runs associated with it, as should combinations of key variables and parameters. Thus, a sensitivity analysis should be conducted that provides the model user with data that indicates how the effects of a real fire could vary and how the response of the proposed fire safety design could also vary.

The interpretation of a model's predictions can be a difficult exercise if the model user does not have knowledge of fire dynamics or human behavior.

Reasonableness Check. The model user should first try to determine whether the predictions actually make sense, that is, they don't upset intuition or preconceived expectations. Most likely, if the results don't pass this test, an input error has been committed.

Sometimes the predictions appear to be reasonable but are, in fact, incorrect. For example, a model can predict higher temperatures farther from the fire than close to it. The values themselves could be reasonable, for example, they are not hotter than the fire, but they don't "flow" down the energy as expected.

A margin of safety can be developed using the results of the sensitivity analysis in conjunction with the performance criteria to provide the possible range of time during which a condition is estimated to occur.

Safety factors and margin of safety are two concepts used to quantify the amount of uncertainty in engineering analyses. Safety factors are used to provide a margin of safety and represent, or address, the gap in knowledge between the theoretically perfect model, that is, reality and the engineering models that can only partially represent reality.

Safety factors can be applied to either the predicted level of a physical condition or to the time at which the condition is predicted to occur. Thus, a physical or a temporal safety factor, or both, can be applied to any predicted condition. A predicted condition (that is, a parameter's value) and the time at which it occurs are best represented as distributions. Ideally, a computer fire model predicts the expected or nominal value of the distribution. Safety factors are intended to represent the spread of these distributions.

Given the uncertainty associated with data acquisition and reduction, and the limitations of computer modeling, any condition predicted by a computer model can be thought of as an expected or nominal value within a broader range. For example, an upper layer temperature of 1110°F (600°C) is predicted at a given time. If the modeled scenario is then tested (that is, full-scale experiment based on the computer model's input data), the actual temperature at that given time could be 1185°F or 1085°F (640°C or 585°C). Therefore, the temperature should be reported as 1110°F + 75°F, −25°F (600°C + 40°C, −15°C) or as a range of 1085°F to 1184°F (585°C to 640°C).

Ideally, predictions are reported as a nominal value, a percentage, or an absolute value. As an example, an upper layer temperature prediction could be reported as 1112°F (600°C), 86°F (30°C) or 1112°F (600°C), 5 percent. In this case, the physical safety factor is 0.05 (that is, the amount by which the nominal value should be degraded and enhanced). Given the state-of-the-art of computer fire modeling, this is a very low safety factor. Physical safety factors tend to be on the order of tens of percent. A safety factor of 50 percent is not unheard of.

Part of the problem in establishing safety factors is that it is difficult to state the percentage or range that is appropriate. These values can be obtained when the computer model predictions are compared to test data. However, using computer fire models in a design mode does not facilitate this since (1) the room being analyzed has not been built yet and (2) test scenarios do not necessarily depict the intended design.

A sensitivity analysis should be performed based on the assumptions that affect the condition of interest. A base case that uses all nominal values for input parameters should be developed. The input parameters should be varied over reasonable ranges, and the variation in predicted output should be noted. This output variation can then become the basis for physical safety factors.

The temporal safety factor addresses the issue of when a condition is predicted and is a function of the rate at which processes are expected to occur. If a condition is predicted to occur 2 minutes after the start of the fire, then this can be used as a nominal value. A process similar to that described for physical safety factors can also be employed to develop temporal safety factors. In this case, however, the rates (for example, of heat release and toxic product generation) will be varied instead of absolute values (for example, material properties).

The margin of safety can be thought of as a reflection of societal values and can be imposed by the AHJ for that purpose. Since the time for which a condition is predicted is most likely the focus of the AHJ (for example, the model predicts occupants have 5 minutes to safely evacuate), the margin of safety is characterized by temporal aspects and tacitly applied to the physical margin of safety.

Escaping the harmful effects of fire (or mitigating them) is, effectively, a race against time. When assessing fire safety system designs based on computer model predictions, the choice of an acceptable time is important. When an AHJ is faced with the predicted time of untenability, a decision needs to be made regarding whether sufficient time is available to ensure the safety of facility occupants. The AHJ is assessing the margin of safety. Is there sufficient time to get everyone out safely? If the AHJ feels that the predicted egress time is too close to the time of untenability, then the AHJ can impose an additional time that the designer has to incorporate into the system design. In other words, the AHJ can impose a greater margin of safety than that originally proposed by the designer.

A.5.7.1 The *SFPE Engineering Guide to Performance-Based Fire Protection Analysis and Design of Buildings* describes the documentation that should be provided for a performance-based design.

Proper documentation of a performance design is critical to the design acceptance and construction. Proper documentation also ensures that all parties involved understand what is necessary for the design implementation, maintenance, and continuity of the fire protection design. If attention to details is maintained in the documentation, then there should be little dispute during approval, construction, start-up, and use.

Poor documentation could result in rejection of an otherwise good design, poor implementation of the design, inadequate system maintenance and reliability, and an incomplete record for future changes or for testing the design forensically.

A.5.7.2 The sources, methodologies, and data used in performance-based designs should be based on technical references that are widely accepted and used by the appropriate professions and professional groups. This acceptance is often based on documents that are developed, reviewed, and validated under one of the following processes:

(1) Standards developed under an open consensus process conducted by recognized professional societies, codes or standards organizations, or governmental bodies
(2) Technical references that are subject to a peer review process and published in widely recognized peer-reviewed journals, conference reports, or other publications
(3) Resource publications such as the *SFPE Handbook of Fire Protection Engineering*, which are widely recognized technical sources of information

The following factors are helpful in determining the acceptability of the individual method or source:

(1) Extent of general acceptance in the relevant professional community. Indications of this acceptance include peer-reviewed publication, widespread citation in the technical literature, and adoption by or within a consensus document.
(2) Extent of documentation of the method, including the analytical method itself, assumptions, scope, limitations, data sources, and data reduction methods.
(3) Extent of validation and analysis of uncertainties. This includes comparison of the overall method with experimental data to estimate error rates as well as analysis of the uncertainties of input data, uncertainties and limitations in the analytical method, and uncertainties in the associated performance criteria.
(4) Extent to which the method is based on sound scientific principles.
(5) Extent to which the proposed application is within the stated scope and limitations of the supporting information, including the range of applicability for which there is documented validation. Factors such as spatial dimensions, occupant characteristics, and ambient conditions can limit valid applications.

In many cases, a method is built from and includes numerous component analyses. These component analyses should be evaluated using the same factors that are applied to the overall method as outlined in items (1) through (5).

A method to address a specific fire safety issue, within documented limitations or validation regimes, might not exist. In such a case, sources and calculation methods can be used outside of their limitations, provided that the design team recognizes the limitations and addresses the resulting implications.

The technical references and methodologies to be used in a performance-based design should be closely evaluated by the design team and the AHJ, and possibly by a third-party reviewer. The strength of the technical justification should be judged using criteria in items (1) through (5). This justification can be strengthened by the presence of data obtained from fire testing.

A.5.7.11 Documentation for modeling should conform to ASTM E 1472, *Standard Guide for Documenting Computer Software for Fire Models*, although most, if not all, models were originally developed before this standard was promulgated.

A.6.1.2.1 Assembly Occupancy. Assembly occupancies might include the following:

(1) Armories
(2) Assembly halls
(3) Auditoriums
(4) Bowling lanes
(5) Club rooms
(6) College and university classrooms, 50 persons and over
(7) Conference rooms
(8) Courtrooms
(9) Dance halls
(10) Drinking establishments
(11) Exhibition halls
(12) Gymnasiums
(13) Libraries
(14) Mortuary chapels
(15) Motion picture theaters
(16) Museums
(17) Passenger stations and terminals of air, surface, underground, and marine public transportation facilities
(18) Places of religious worship
(19) Pool rooms
(20) Recreation piers
(21) Restaurants
(22) Skating rinks
(23) Special amusement buildings, regardless of occupant load
(24) Theaters
[*101:* A.6.1.2.1]

Assembly occupancies are characterized by the presence or potential presence of crowds with attendant panic hazard in case of fire or other emergency. They are generally or occasionally open to the public, and the occupants, who are present voluntarily, are not ordinarily subject to discipline or control. Such buildings are ordinarily not used for sleeping purposes. Special conference rooms, snack areas, and other areas incidental to, and under the control of, the management of other occupancies, such as offices, fall under the 50-person limitation. [*101:* A.6.1.2.1]

Restaurants and drinking establishments with an occupant load of fewer than 50 persons should be classified as mercantile occupancies. [*101:* A.6.1.2.1]

Occupancy of any room or space for assembly purposes by fewer than 50 persons in another occupancy, and incidental to such other occupancy, should be classified as part of the other occupancy and should be subject to the provisions applicable thereto. [*101:* A.6.1.2.1]

For special amusement buildings, see 12.4.7 and 13.4.7 of NFPA *101, Life Safety Code*. [*101:* A.6.1.2.1]

A.6.1.3.1 Educational Occupancy. Educational occupancies include the following:

(1) Academies
(2) Kindergartens
(3) Schools
[*101:* A.6.1.3.1]

An educational occupancy is distinguished from an assembly occupancy in that the same occupants are regularly present. [*101:* A.6.1.3.1]

A.6.1.4.1 Day-Care Occupancy. Day-care occupancies include the following:

(1) Adult day-care occupancies, except where part of a health care occupancy
(2) Child day-care occupancies
(3) Day-care homes
(4) Kindergarten classes that are incidental to a child day-care occupancy
(5) Nursery schools
[*101:*A.6.1.4.1]

In areas where public schools offer only half-day kindergarten programs, many child day-care occupancies offer state-approved kindergarten classes for children who need full-day care. Because these classes are normally incidental to the day-care occupancy, the requirements of the day-care occupancy should be followed. [*101:* A.6.1.4.1]

A.6.1.5.1 Health Care Occupancy. Health care occupancies include the following:

(1) Hospitals
(2) Limited care facilities
(3) Nursing homes
[*101:*A.6.1.5.1]

Occupants of health care occupancies typically have physical or mental illness, disease, or infirmity. They also include infants, convalescents, or infirm aged persons. [*101:*A.6.1.5.1]

A.6.1.6.1 Ambulatory Health Care Occupancy. It is not the intent that occupants be considered to be incapable of self-preservation just because they are in a wheelchair or use assistive walking devices, such as a cane, a walker, or crutches. Rather, it is the intent to address emergency care centers that receive patients who have been rendered incapable of self-preservation due to the emergency, such as being rendered unconscious as a result of an accident or being unable to move due to sudden illness. [*101:*A.6.1.6.1]

A.6.1.7.1 Detention and Correctional Occupancy. Detention and correctional occupancies include the following:

(1) Adult and juvenile substance abuse centers
(2) Adult and juvenile work camps
(3) Adult community residential centers
(4) Adult correctional institutions
(5) Adult local detention facilities
(6) Juvenile community residential centers
(7) Juvenile detention facilities
(8) Juvenile training schools
[*101:*A.6.1.7.1]

See A.22.1.1.1.6 and A.23.1.1.1.6 of NFPA *101*. [*101:*A.6.1.7.1]

A.6.1.7.2 Chapters 22 and 23 of NFPA *101* address the residential housing areas of the detention and correctional occupancy as defined in 3.3.178.5 of NFPA *101*. Examples of uses, other than residential housing, include gymnasiums or industries. [*101:*A.6.1.7.2]

A.6.1.8.1.1 One- and Two-Family Dwelling Unit. The application statement of 24.1.1.1 of NFPA *101* limits each dwelling unit to being "occupied by members of a single family with not more than three outsiders." This *Code* and NFPA *101* do not define the term *family*. The definition of family is subject to federal, state, and local regulations and might not be restricted to a person or a couple (two people) and their children. The following examples aid in differentiating between a single-family dwelling and a lodging or rooming house:

(1) An individual or a couple (two people) who rent a house from a landlord and then sublease space for up to three individuals should be considered a family renting to a maximum of three outsiders, and the house should be regulated as a single-family dwelling in accordance with Chapter 24 of NFPA *101*.
(2) A house rented from a landlord by an individual or a couple (two people) in which space is subleased to four or more individuals, but not more than 16, should be considered and regulated as a lodging or rooming house in accordance with Chapter 26 of NFPA *101*.
(3) A residential building that is occupied by four or more individuals, but not more than 16, each renting from a landlord, without separate cooking facilities, should be considered and regulated as a lodging or rooming house in accordance with Chapter 26 of NFPA *101*.
[*101:*A.6.1.8.1.1]

A.6.1.8.1.3 Hotel. So-called apartment hotels should be classified as hotels, because they are potentially subject to the same transient occupancy as hotels. Transients are those who occupy accommodations for less than 30 days. [*101:*A.6.1.8.1.3]

A.6.1.8.1.4 Dormitory. Rooms within dormitories intended for the use of individuals for combined living and sleeping purposes are guest rooms or guest suites. Examples of dormitories include college dormitories, fraternity and sorority houses, and military barracks. [*101:*A.6.1.8.1.4]

A.6.1.9.1 Residential Board and Care Occupancy. The following are examples of facilities classified as residential board and care occupancies:

(1) Group housing arrangement for physically or mentally handicapped persons who normally attend school in the community, attend worship in the community, or otherwise use community facilities
(2) Group housing arrangement for physically or mentally handicapped persons who are undergoing training in preparation for independent living, for paid employment, or for other normal community activities
(3) Group housing arrangement for the elderly that provides personal care services but that does not provide nursing care
(4) Facilities for social rehabilitation, alcoholism, drug abuse, or mental health problems that contain a group housing arrangement and that provide personal care services but do not provide acute care
(5) Assisted living facilities
(6) Other group housing arrangements that provide personal care services but not nursing care
[*101:*A.6.1.9.1]

A.6.1.10.1 Mercantile Occupancy. Mercantile occupancies include the following:

(1) Auction rooms
(2) Department stores
(3) Drugstores
(4) Restaurants with fewer than 50 persons
(5) Shopping centers
(6) Supermarkets
[*101:*A.6.1.10.1]

Office, storage, and service facilities incidental to the sale of merchandise and located in the same building should be considered part of the mercantile occupancy classification. [*101:* A.6.1.10.1]

A.6.1.11.1 Business Occupancy. Business occupancies include the following:

(1) Air traffic control towers (ATCTs)
(2) City halls
(3) College and university instructional buildings, classrooms under 50 persons, and instructional laboratories
(4) Courthouses
(5) Dentists' offices
(6) Doctors' offices
(7) General offices
(8) Outpatient clinics (ambulatory)
(9) Town halls
[*101:* A.6.1.11.1]

Doctors' and dentists' offices are included, unless of such character as to be classified as ambulatory health care occupancies. *(See 3.3.188.1 of NFPA 101.)* [*101: A.6.1.11.1*]

Birth centers should be classified as business occupancies if they are occupied by fewer than four patients, not including infants, at any one time; do not provide sleeping facilities for four or more occupants; and do not provide treatment procedures that render four or more patients, not including infants, incapable of self-preservation at any one time. For birth centers occupied by patients not meeting these parameters, see Chapter 18 or Chapter 19 of NFPA *101*, as appropriate. [*101:* A.6.1.11.1]

Service facilities common to city office buildings, such as newsstands, lunch counters serving fewer than 50 persons, barber shops, and beauty parlors are included in the business occupancy group. [*101:* A.6.1.11.1]

City halls, town halls, and courthouses are included in this occupancy group, insofar as their principal function is the transaction of public business and the keeping of books and records. Insofar as they are used for assembly purposes, they are classified as assembly occupancies. [*101:* A.6.1.11.1]

A.6.1.12.1 Industrial Occupancy. Industrial occupancies include the following:

(1) Drycleaning plants
(2) Factories of all kinds
(3) Food processing plants
(4) Gas plants
(5) Hangars (for servicing/maintenance)
(6) Laundries
(7) Power plants
(8) Pumping stations
(9) Refineries
(10) Sawmills
(11) Telephone exchanges
[*101:* A.6.1.12.1]

In evaluating the appropriate classification of laboratories, the AHJ should treat each case individually, based on the extent and nature of the associated hazards. Some laboratories are classified as occupancies other than industrial; for example, a physical therapy laboratory or a computer laboratory. [*101:* A.6.1.12.1]

A.6.1.13.1 Storage Occupancy. Storage occupancies include the following:

(1) Barns
(2) Bulk oil storage
(3) Cold storage
(4) Freight terminals
(5) Grain elevators
(6) Hangars (for storage only)
(7) Parking structures
(8) Truck and marine terminals
(9) Warehouses
[*101:* A.6.1.13.1]

Storage occupancies are characterized by the presence of relatively small numbers of persons in proportion to the area. [*101:* A.6.1.13.1]

A.6.1.14.1.3 Examples of uses that might be incidental to another occupancy include the following:

(1) Newsstand (mercantile) in an office building
(2) Giftshop (mercantile) in a hotel
(3) Small storage area (storage) in any occupancy
(4) Minor office space (business) in any occupancy
(5) Maintenance area (industrial) in any occupancy
[*101:* A.6.1.14.1.3]

A.6.1.14.1.3(2) Examples of uses that have occupant loads below the occupancy classification threshold levels include the following:

(1) Assembly use with fewer than 50 persons within a business occupancy
(2) Educational use with fewer than 6 persons within an apartment building.
[*101:* A.6.1.14.1.3(2)]

A.6.1.14.4.5 Where the Code text states that the provision has applicability to the building, rather than just to the occupancy, the provision applies to the entire building, regardless of whether the separated occupancies form of protection is used. For example, the provision of 18.3.5.1 of NFPA *101* requires that the entire building housing a health care occupancy be sprinklered. Contrast that with the requirement of 20.3.4.1 of NFPA *101* which requires an ambulatory health care facility, and not the entire building, to be provided with a fire alarm system. [*101:* A.6.1.14.4.5]

A.10.1.2 It is the intent of this *Code* that all existing buildings comply with the referenced edition of NFPA *101*, *Life Safety Code*.

A.10.3.3 The AHJ should take into account the maintenance of required means of egress and fire protection systems during the construction, repair, alteration, or addition to the building. If necessary, alternative protection features can be required to ensure that no imminent hazards exist as the result of modifications.

A.10.4.2 Premises are deemed to be overcrowded when the occupant load exceeds the exit capacity or the posted occupant load.

A.10.4.3 This requirement is not necessarily intended to apply to facilities utilizing a "defend in place" strategy or other occupancies where total evacuation is not intended or desired (detention, health care, high rise). A written emergency response plan can clarify how a facility can conform to this requirement.

A.10.5 The purpose of emergency egress and relocation drills is to educate the participants in the fire safety features of the building, the egress facilities available, and the procedures to be followed. Speed in emptying buildings or relocating occupants, while desirable, is not the only objective. Prior to an evaluation of the performance of an emergency egress and relocation drill, an opportunity for instruction and practice should be provided. This educational opportunity should be presented in a nonthreatening manner, with consideration given to the prior knowledge, age, and ability of audience. [*101:*A.4.7]

The usefulness of an emergency egress and relocation drill, and the extent to which it can be performed, depends on the character of the occupancy. [*101:*A.4.7]

In buildings where the occupant load is of a changing character, such as hotels or department stores, no regularly organized emergency egress and relocation drill is possible. In such cases, the emergency egress and relocation drills are to be limited to the regular employees, who can be thoroughly schooled in the proper procedure and can be trained to properly direct other occupants of the building in case of emergency evacuation or relocation. In occupancies such as hospitals, regular employees can be rehearsed in the proper procedure in case of fire; such training is always advisable in all occupancies, regardless of whether regular emergency egress and relocation drills can be held. [*101:*A.4.7]

A.10.5.2 If an emergency egress and relocation drill is considered merely as a routine exercise from which some persons are allowed to be excused, there is a grave danger that, in an actual emergency, the evacuation and relocation will not be successful. However, there might be circumstances under which all occupants do not participate in an emergency egress and relocation drill, for example, infirm or bedridden patients in a health care occupancy. [*101:*A.4.7.2]

A.10.5.4 Fire is always unexpected. If the drill is always held in the same way at the same time, it loses much of its value. When, for some reason during an actual fire, it is not possible to follow the usual routine of the emergency egress and relocation drill to which occupants have become accustomed, confusion and panic might ensue. Drills should be carefully planned to simulate actual fire conditions. Not only should drills be held at varying times, but different means of exit or relocation areas should be used, based on an assumption that fire or smoke might prevent the use of normal egress and relocation avenues. [*101:*A.4.7.4]

A.10.5.6 The written record required by this paragraph should include such details as the date, time, participants, location, and results of that drill. [*101:*A.4.7.6]

A.10.6.1.3 This requirement should not be construed to forbid the owner, manager, or other person in control of the aforementioned building or premises from using all diligence necessary to extinguish such fire prior to the arrival of the fire department.

A.10.8.2.1 Items to be considered in preparing an emergency plan should include the following:

(1) Purpose of plan
(2) Building description, including certificate of occupancy
(3) Appointment, organization, and contact details of designated building staff to carry out the emergency duties
(4) Identification of events (man-made and natural) considered life safety hazards impacting the building
(5) Responsibilities matrix (role-driven assignments)
(6) Policies and procedures for those left behind to operate critical equipment
(7) Specific procedures to be used for each type of emergency
(8) Requirements and responsibilities for assisting people with disabilities
(9) Procedures for accounting for employees
(10) Training of building staff, building emergency response teams, and other occupants in their responsibilities
(11) Documents, including diagrams, showing the type, location, and operation of the building emergency features, components, and systems
(12) Practices for controlling life safety hazards in the building
(13) Inspection and maintenance of building facilities that provide for the safety of occupants
(14) Conducting fire and evacuation drills
(15) Interface between key building management and emergency responders
(16) Names or job titles of persons who can be contacted for further information or explanation of duties
(17) Post-event (including drill) critique/evaluation, as addressed in 5.14 of NFPA 1600, *Standard on Disaster/Emergency Management and Business Continuity Programs*
(18) Means to update the plan, as necessary
[*101:*A.4.8.2.1]

A.10.8.2.1(3) It is assumed that a majority of buildings will use a total evacuation strategy during a fire. It should be noted that evacuation from a building could occur for reasons other than a fire, but such other reasons are not the primary focus of the *Code*. As used herein, total evacuation is defined as the process in which all, or substantially all, occupants leave a building or facility in either an unmanaged or managed sequence or order. An alternative to total evacuation, is partial evacuation, which can be defined as the process in which a select portion of a building or facility is cleared or emptied of its occupants while occupants in other portions mostly carry on normal activity. In either case, the evacuation process can be ordered or managed in accordance with an established priority in which some or all occupants of a building or facility clear their area and utilize means of egress routes. This is typically done so that the more endangered occupants are removed before occupants in less endangered areas. Alternative terms describing this sequencing or ordering of evacuation are *staged evacuation* and *phased evacuation*. [*101:*A.4.8.2.1(3)]

Table A.10.8.2.1(3) illustrates options for extent of management and extent of evacuation. Some of the options shown might not be appropriate. As noted in Table A.10.8.2.1(3), either total or partial evacuation can include staged (zoned) evacuation or phased evacuation, which is referred to as managed or controlled evacuation. It should also be noted that the evacuation process might not include relocation to the outside of the building but might instead include relocation to an area of refuge or might defend the occupants in place to minimize the need for evacuation. [*101:*A.4.8.2.1(3)]

The different methods of evacuation are also used in several contexts throughout NFPA *101*. Though most of the methods of evacuation are not specifically defined or do not have established criteria, various sections of NFPA *101* promulgate them as alternatives to total evacuation. The following sections of NFPA *101* discuss these alternatives in more detail:

(1) Section 4.7 — Provides requirements for fire and relocation drills
(2) 7.2.12 — Provides requirements for area of refuge
(3) 7.2.4 — Provides requirements for horizontal exits
(4) 9.6.3.6 — Provides the alarm signal requirements for different methods of evacuation

Table A.10.8.2.1(3) Occupant Evacuation Strategies

Extent of Evacuation	Extent of Management	
	Managed Sequence	Unmanaged Sequence
Shelter in place	No movement — shelter in place upon direction	No movement — shelter in place per prior instruction
Relocation or partial evacuation	Managed or controlled partial evacuation In-building relocation on same floor In-building relocation to different floors Occupants of some floors leave building	Unmanaged movement
Total evacuation	Managed or controlled total evacuation	Unmanaged or uncontrolled total evacuation

[*101:* Table A.4.8.2.1(3)]

(5) 9.6.3.9 — Permits automatically transmitted or live voice evacuation or relocation instructions to occupants and requires them in accordance with *NFPA 72, National Fire Alarm and Signaling Code*

(6) 14.3.4.2.3 (also Chapter 15) — Describes alternative protection systems in educational occupancies

(7) 18.1.1.2/18.1.1.3/Section 18.7 (also Chapter 19) — Provide methods of evacuation for health care occupancies

(8) Chapters 22 and 23 — Provide methods of evacuation for detention and correctional occupancies, including the five groups of resident user categories

(9) Chapters 32 and 33 — Provide methods of evacuation for residential board and care occupancies

(10) 32.1.5/33.1.5 — For residential board and care occupancies, state that "no means of escape or means of egress shall be considered as complying with the minimum criteria for acceptance, unless emergency evacuation drills are regularly conducted"

(11) 40.2.5.2.2 — For industrial occupancies, states that "ancillary facilities in special-purpose industrial occupancies where delayed evacuation is anticipated shall have not less than a 2-hour fire resistance–rated separation from the predominant industrial occupancy and shall have one means of egress that is separated from the predominant industrial occupancy by 2-hour fire resistance–rated construction" [*101:* A.4.8.2.1(3)]

The method of evacuation should be accomplished in the context of the physical facilities, the type of activities undertaken, and the provisions for the capabilities of occupants (and staff, if available). Therefore, in addition to meeting the requirements of the *Code*, or when establishing an equivalency or a performance-based design, the following recommendations and general guidance information should be taken into account when designing, selecting, executing, and maintaining a method of evacuation:

(1) When choosing a method of evacuation, the available safe egress time (ASET) must always be greater than the required safe egress time (RSET).

(2) The occupants' characteristics will drive the method of evacuation. For example, occupants might be incapable of evacuating themselves because of age, physical or mental disabilities, physical restraint, or a combination thereof. However, some buildings might be staffed with people who could assist in evacuating. Therefore, the method of evacuation is dependent on the ability of occupants to move as a group, with or without assistance. For more information, see the definitions under the term *Evacuation Capability* in Chapter 3 of NFPA *101*.

(3) An alternative method of evacuation might or might not have a faster evacuation time than a total evacuation. However, the priority of evacuation should be such that the occupants in the most danger are given a higher priority. This prioritization will ensure that occupants more intimate with the fire will have a faster evacuation time.

(4) Design, construction, and compartmentation are also variables in choosing a method of evacuation. The design, construction, and compartmentation should limit the development and spread of a fire and smoke and reduce the need for occupant evacuation. The fire should be limited to the room or compartment of fire origin. Therefore, the following factors need to be considered:

  (a) Overall fire resistance rating of the building
  (b) Fire-rated compartmentation provided with the building
  (c) Number and arrangement of the means of egress

(5) Fire safety systems should be installed that complement the method of evacuation and should include consideration of the following:

  (a) Detection of fire
  (b) Control of fire development
  (c) Confinement of the effects of fire
  (d) Extinguishment of fire
  (e) Provision of refuge or evacuation facilities, or both

(6) One of the most important fire safety systems is the fire alarm and communication system, particularly the notification system. The fire alarm system should be in accordance with *NFPA 72, National Fire Alarm and Signaling Code*, and should take into account the following:

  (a) Initial notification of only the occupants in the affected zone(s) (e.g., zone of fire origin and adjacent zones)
  (b) Provisions to notify occupants in other unaffected zones to allow orderly evacuation of the entire building
  (c) Need for live voice communication
  (d) Reliability of the fire alarm and communication system

(7) The capabilities of the staff assisting in the evacuation process should be considered in determining the method of evacuation.

(8) The ability of the fire department to interact with the evacuation should be analyzed. It is important to determine if the fire department can assist in the evacuation or if fire department operations hinder the evacuation efforts.

(9) Evacuation scenarios for hazards that are normally outside of the scope of the *Code* should be considered to the extent practicable. (*See 4.3.1 of NFPA 101.*)
(10) Consideration should be given to the desire of the occupants to self-evacuate, especially if the nature of the building or the fire warrants evacuation in the minds of the occupants. Self-evacuation might also be initiated by communication between the occupants themselves through face-to-face contact, mobile phones, and so forth.
(11) An investigation period, a delay in the notification of occupants after the first activation of the fire alarm, could help to reduce the number of false alarms and unnecessary evacuations. However, a limit to such a delay should be established before a general alarm is sounded, such as positive alarm sequence as defined in *NFPA 72, National Fire Alarm and Signaling Code.*
(12) Consideration should be given to the need for an evacuation that might be necessary for a scenario other than a fire (e.g., bomb threat, earthquake).
(13) Contingency plans should be established in the event the fire alarm and communication system fail, which might facilitate the need for total evacuation.
(14) The means of egress systems should be properly maintained to ensure the dependability of the method of evacuation.
(15) Fire prevention policies or procedures, or both, should be implemented that reduce the chance of a fire (e.g., limiting smoking or providing fire-safe trash cans).
(16) The method of evacuation should be properly documented, and written forms of communication should be provided to all of the occupants, which might include sign postings throughout the building. Consideration should be given to the development of documentation for an operation and maintenance manual or a fire emergency plan, or both.
(17) Emergency egress drills should be performed on a regular basis. For more information, see Section 4.7 of NFPA *101*.
(18) The AHJ should also be consulted when developing the method of evacuation.

[*101:*A.4.8.2.1(3)]

Measures should be in place and be employed to sequence or control the order of a total evacuation, so that such evacuations proceed in a reasonably safe, efficient manner. Such measures include special attention to the evacuation capabilities and needs of occupants with disabilities, either permanent or temporary. For comprehensive guidance on facilitating life safety for such populations, go to www.nfpa.org. For specific guidance on stair travel devices, see ANSI/RESNA ED-1, *Emergency Stair Travel Devices Used by Individuals with Disabilities*. [*101:*A.4.8.2.1(3)]

In larger buildings, especially high-rise buildings, it is recommended that all evacuations — whether partial or total — be managed to sequence or control the order in which certain occupants are evacuated from their origin areas and to make use of available means of egress. In high-rise buildings, the exit stairs, at any level, are designed to accommodate the egress flow of only a very small portion of the occupants — from only one or a few stories, and within a relatively short time period — on the order of a few minutes. In case of a fire, only the immediately affected floor(s) should be given priority use of the means of egress serving that floor(s). Other floors should then be given priority use of the means of egress, depending on the anticipated spread of the fire and its combustion products, and for the purpose of clearing certain floors to facilitate eventual fire service operations. Typically, this means that the one or two floors above and below a fire floor will have secondary priority immediately after the fire floor. Depending on where combustion products move, for example, upward through a building with cool-weather stack effect, the next priority floors will be the uppermost occupied floors in the building. [*101:*A.4.8.2.1(3)]

Generally, in order to minimize evacuation time for most or all of a relatively tall building to be evacuated, occupants from upper floors should have priority use of exit stairs. For people descending many stories of stairs, this priority will maximize their opportunity to take rest stops without unduly extending their overall time to evacuate a building. Thus, the precedence behavior of evacuees should be that people already in an exit stair should normally not defer to people attempting to enter the exit stair from lower floors, except for those lower floors most directly impacted by a fire or other imminent danger. Notably, this is contrary to the often observed behavior of evacuees in high-rise building evacuations where lower floor precedence behavior occurs. (Similarly, in the most commonly observed behavior of people normally disembarking a passenger airliner, people within the aisle defer to people entering the aisle, so that the areas closest to the exit typically clear first.) Changing, and generally managing, the sequence or order within which egress occurs will require effectively informing building occupants and evaluating resulting performance in a program of education, training, and drills. [*101:*A.4.8.2.1(3)]

When designing the method of evacuation for a complex building, all forms of egress should be considered. For example, consideration could be given to an elevator evacuation system. An elevator evacuation system involves an elevator design that provides protection from fire effects so that elevators can be used safely for egress. See 7.2.13 and A.7.2.12.2.4 of NFPA *101* for more information. [*101:*A.4.8.2.1(3)]

For further guidance, see the following publications:

(1) *SFPE Engineering Guide to Human Behavior in Fire*, which provides information on occupant characteristics, response to fire cues, decision making in fire situations, and methods for predicting evacuation time
(2) *NFPA Fire Protection Handbook*, 20th edition, Section 1, Chapter 9, which provides good methodology for managing exposures and determining the method of evacuation
(3) *NFPA Fire Protection Handbook*, 20th edition, Section 20, which provides further commentary on methods of evacuation for different occupancies
(4) *SFPE Handbook of Fire Protection Engineering*, Section 3, Chapters 11–13, which provide an overview of some of the research on methods of evacuation and methods for predicting evacuation times

[*101:*A.4.8.2.1(3)]

A.10.8.2.3 Emergency action plans are a critical component of assuring life safety in buildings. Life safety is the result of an interaction of technical and social systems within the building and in the community. Gathering information to evaluate the performance and effectiveness of emergency action plans is important for verifying system performance and as a basis for improvement. Such reports should be retained by building management and used to inform the process for revision of the building emergency action plan. [*101:*A.4.8.2.3]

Following any drill or actual emergency or reported emergency occurring in the building, an after action report should be prepared by the building owner or designated representative to document the function of the building's life safety hardware, procedures, and occupant emergency organization. [*101:*A.4.8.2.3]

For ordinary drills and reported emergencies, areas of success and areas for improvement should be identified. [*101:*A.4.8.2.3]

For actual emergencies in the building, where there is major occupant movement, damage, or casualties, additional information should be collected. This includes questions concerning the event, as well as performance of life safety systems. It also identifies improvements in areas such as training, maintenance, interaction with local emergency response organizations, or occupant management. The reports from these significant events should be shared with the local emergency response organization. [*101:* A.4.8.2.3]

A.10.10.3.1 Areas for such use can include inhabited premises or designated campsites where such fires are built in a permanent barbecue, portable barbecue, outdoor fireplace, incinerator, or grill.

A.10.10.6.3 It is not the intent of this paragraph to allow the permanent installation of portable equipment unless it is permitted by its listing.

A.10.10.9.1 Areas for such use can include inhabited premises or designated campsites that maintain a defensible space in accordance with NFPA 1144, *Standard for Reducing Structure Ignition Hazards from Wildland Fire.*

A.10.11.1.1 Where a building is not routinely identified by a street address, other means of building identification such as building name or number should be permitted.

A.10.11.3 Figure A.10.11.3 shows an example of a stairway marking sign. [*101:* A.7.2.2.5.4]

FIGURE A.10.11.3 Example of a Stairway Marking Sign. [*101*: Figure A.7.2.2.5.4]

A.10.11.3.1.13 It is not the intent to require a sign that reads ROOF ACCESS, as such message might be misinterpreted by building occupants as an alternative egress route. However, signs that read ROOF ACCESS are not prohibited, as many such signs have been installed in existing buildings so as to make a requirement for removal impractical. Historically, the ROOF ACCESS sign has provided information for the fire department. Where there is no roof access, such information will be posted via a NO ROOF ACCESS sign. The absence of the NO ROOF ACCESS sign should be understood by the fire department to mean that roof access is possible. [*101:* A.7.2.2.5.4.1(M)]

A.10.11.3.3 Where environmental conditions (such as illumination levels and directionality or a complex visual field that draws a person's attention away from stair treads) lead to a hazardous reduction in one's ability to perceive stair treads, they should be made of a material that allows ready discrimination of the number and position of treads. In all cases, the leading edges of all treads should be readily visible during both ascent and descent. A major factor in injury-producing stair accidents, and in the ability to use stairs efficiently in conditions such as egress, is the clarity of the stair treads as separate stepping surfaces. [*101:* A.7.2.2.5.4.3]

For stair nosing marking, surface-applied material, such as adhesive-backed tape and magnetic strips, should not be used, as it is not durable under the scuffing from users' feet and, in coming loose, it creates a tripping hazard. While a carefully applied and consistently maintained coating is acceptable, contrasting color or photoluminescent material integral with the nosings is preferable because of its permanence. See also 7.1.6.4 and 7.2.2.3.6 of NFPA *101* for slip resistance uniformity requirements, as well as prohibition of projections on the treads. [*101:*A.7.2.2.5.4.3]

Guidance on the use of photoluminescent marking is provided by ASTM E 2030, *Guide for Recommended Uses of Photoluminescent (Phosphorescent) Safety Markings.* Additional marking, for example, at the side boundaries of the stair, should be applied in accordance with the guidance provided therein. [*101:* A.7.2.2.5.4.3]

A.10.11.3.4 Coatings and other applied markings, if used, should be durable for the expected usage, especially at end terminations of the marking and at changes in stair direction where usage is more extensive and hand forces are larger. [*101:* A.7.2.2.5.4.4]

A.10.12.2.1 Issues to be considered by the AHJ should include, but not be limited to, the availability of utilities to the building.

A.10.13.3 One example of acceptable fire retardance is for the individual decorative vegetation item to exhibit a maximum heat release rate of 100 kilowatts (kW) when tested in accordance with UL 1975, *Standard for Fire Tests for Foamed Plastics Used for Decorative Purposes,* or NFPA 289, *Standard Method of Fire Test for Individual Fuel Packages,* using the 20 kW ignition source. Another example of acceptable fire retardance is for the individual artificial Christmas trees, when exposed to the flames from 1 lb of shredded newspaper distributed around the tree, to meet the following three criteria:

(1) To have flames that do not extend more than 3 ft (0.9 m) above the tree
(2) To have no significant lateral flame spread away from the area affected by the ignition source
(3) To have no flaming droplets that continue flaming after reaching the floor

A.10.13.9.4 A method to check for dryness is to grasp a tree branch with a reasonably firm pressure and pull your hand to you, allowing the branch to slip through your grasp. If the needles fall off readily, the tree does not have adequate moisture content and should be removed.

A.10.14.3.1 Life safety evaluations are examples of performance-based approaches to life safety. In this respect, significant guidance in the form and process of life safety evaluations is provided by Chapter 5 of NFPA *101*, keeping in mind the fire safety emphasis in Chapter 5 of NFPA *101*. Performance criteria, scenarios, evaluation, safety factors, documentation, maintenance, and periodic assessment (including a warrant of fitness) all apply to the broader considerations in a life safety evaluation. A life safety evaluation deals not only with fire but also with storms, collapse, crowd behavior, and other related safety considerations for which a checklist is provided in A.10.14.3.3. Chapter 5 of NFPA *101* provides guidance, based on fire safety requirements, for establishing a documented case showing that products of combustion in all conceivable fire scenarios will not significantly endanger occupants using means of egress in the facility (for example, due to fire detection, automatic suppression, smoke control, large-volume space, or management procedures). Moreover, means of egress facilities plus facility management capabilities should be adequate to cope with scenarios where certain egress routes are blocked for some reason. [*101:*A.12.4.1.1]

In addition to making realistic assumptions about the capabilities of persons in the facility (e.g., an assembled crowd including many disabled persons or persons unfamiliar with the facility), the life safety evaluation should include a factor of safety of not less than 2.0 in all calculations relating to hazard development time and required egress time (the combination of flow time and other time needed to detect and assess an emergency condition, initiate egress, and move along the egress routes). The factor of safety takes into account the possibility that half of the egress routes might not be used (or be usable) in certain situations. [*101:*A.12.4.1.1]

Regarding crowd behavior, the potential hazards created by larger masses of people and greater crowd densities (which can be problematic during ingress, occupancy, and egress) demand that technology be used by designers, managers, and authorities responsible for buildings to compensate for the relaxed egress capacity provisions of Table 12.4.2.3 of NFPA *101*. In very large buildings for assembly use, the hazard of crowd crushes can exceed that of fire or structural failure. Therefore, the building designers, managers, event planners, security personnel, police authorities, and fire authorities, as well as the building construction authorities, should understand the potential problems and solutions, including coordination of their activities. For crowd behavior, this understanding includes factors of space, energy, time, and information, as well as specific crowd management techniques, such as metering. Published guidance on these factors and techniques is found in the *SFPE Handbook of Fire Protection Engineering*, Section 3, Chapter 13, pp. 3-342–3-366 (Proulx, G., "Movement of People"), and the publications referenced therein. [*101:*A.12.4.1.1]

Table 12.2.3.2 and Table 12.4.2.3 of NFPA *101* are based on a linear relationship between number of seats and nominal flow time, with not less than 200 seconds (3.3 minutes) for 2000 seats plus 1 second for every additional 50 seats up to 25,000. Beyond 25,000 total seats, the nominal flow time is limited to 660 seconds (11 minutes). Nominal flow time refers to the flow time for the most able group of patrons; some groups less familiar with the premises or less able groups might take longer to pass a point in the egress system. Although three or more digits are noted in the tables, the resulting calculations should be assumed to provide only two significant figures of precision. [*101:*A.12.4.1.1]

A.10.14.3.3 Factors to be considered in a life safety evaluation include the following:

(1) Nature of the events being accommodated, including the following:
  (a) Ingress, intra-event movement, and egress patterns
  (b) Ticketing and seating policies/practices
  (c) Event purpose (e.g., sports contest, religious meeting)
  (d) Emotional qualities (e.g., competitiveness) of event
  (e) Time of day when event is held
  (f) Time duration of single event
  (g) Time duration of attendees' occupancy of the building
(2) Occupant characteristics and behavior, including the following:
  (a) Homogeneity
  (b) Cohesiveness
  (c) Familiarity with building
  (d) Familiarity with similar events
  (e) Capability (as influenced by factors such as age, physical abilities)
  (f) Socioeconomic factors
  (g) Small minority involved with recreational violence
  (h) Emotional involvement with the event and other occupants
  (i) Use of alcohol or drugs
  (j) Food consumption
  (k) Washroom utilization
(3) Management, including the following:
  (a) Clear, contractual arrangements for facility operation/use as follows:
    i. Between facility owner and operator
    ii. Between facility operator and event promoter
    iii. Between event promoter and performer
    iv. Between event promoter and attendee
    v. With police forces
    vi. With private security services
    vii. With ushering services
  (b) Experience with the building
  (c) Experience with similar events and attendees
  (d) Thorough, up-to-date operations manual
  (e) Training of personnel
  (f) Supervision of personnel
  (g) Communications systems and utilization
  (h) Ratios of management and other personnel to attendees
  (i) Location/distribution of personnel
  (j) Central command location
  (k) Rapport between personnel and attendees
  (l) Personnel support of attendee goals
  (m) Respect of attendees for personnel due to the following:
    i. Dress (uniform) standards
    ii. Age and perceived experience
    iii. Personnel behavior, including interaction
    iv. Distinction between crowd management and control
    v. Management concern for facility quality (e.g., cleanliness)

vi. Management concern for entire event experience of attendees (i.e., not just during the occupancy of the building)

(4) Emergency management preparedness, including the following:
  (a) Complete range of emergencies addressed in operations manual
  (b) Power loss
  (c) Fire
  (d) Severe weather
  (e) Earthquake
  (f) Crowd incident
  (g) Terrorism
  (h) Hazardous materials
  (i) Transportation accident (e.g., road, rail, air)
  (j) Communications systems available
  (k) Personnel and emergency forces ready to respond
  (l) Attendees clearly informed of situation and proper behavior

(5) Building systems, including the following:
  (a) Structural soundness
  (b) Normal static loads
  (c) Abnormal static loads (e.g., crowds, precipitation)
  (d) Dynamic loads (e.g., crowd sway, impact, explosion, wind, earthquake)
  (e) Stability of nonstructural components (e.g., lighting)
  (f) Stability of movable (e.g., telescoping) structures
  (g) Fire protection
  (h) Fire prevention (e.g., maintenance, contents, housekeeping)
  (i) Compartmentation
  (j) Automatic detection and suppression of fire
  (k) Smoke control
  (l) Alarm and communications systems
  (m) Fire department access routes and response capability
  (n) Structural integrity
  (o) Weather protection
  (p) Wind
  (q) Precipitation (attendees rush for shelter or hold up egress of others)
  (r) Lightning protection
  (s) Circulation systems
  (t) Flowline or network analysis
  (u) Waywinding and orientation
  (v) Merging of paths (e.g., precedence behavior)
  (w) Decision/branching points
  (x) Route redundancies
  (y) Counterflow, crossflow, and queuing situations
  (z) Control possibilities, including metering
  (aa) Flow capacity adequacy
  (bb) System balance
  (cc) Movement time performance
  (dd) Flow times
  (ee) Travel times
  (ff) Queuing times
  (gg) Route quality
  (hh) Walking surfaces (e.g., traction, discontinuities)
  (ii) Appropriate widths and boundary conditions
  (jj) Handrails, guardrails, and other rails
  (kk) Ramp slopes
  (ll) Step geometries
  (mm) Perceptual aspects (e.g., orientation, signage, marking, lighting, glare, distractions)
  (nn) Route choices, especially for vertical travel
  (oo) Resting/waiting areas
  (pp) Levels of service (overall crowd movement quality)
  (qq) Services
  (rr) Washroom provision and distribution
  (ss) Concessions
  (tt) First aid and EMS facilities
  (uu) General attendee services
  [*101*: A.12.4.1.3]

A scenario-based approach to performance-based fire safety is addressed in Chapter 5 of NFPA *101*. In addition to using such scenarios and, more generally, the attention to performance criteria, evaluation, safety factors, documentation, maintenance, and periodic assessment required when the Chapter 5 of NFPA *101* option is used, life safety evaluations should consider scenarios based on characteristics important in assembly occupancies. These characteristics include the following:

(1) Whether there is a local or mass awareness of an incident, event, or condition that might provoke egress
(2) Whether the incident, event, or condition stays localized or spreads
(3) Whether or not egress is desired by facility occupants
(4) Whether there is a localized start to any egress or mass start to egress
(5) Whether exits are available or not available
[*101*: A.12.4.1.3]

Examples of scenarios and sets of characteristics that might occur in a facility follow. [*101*: A.12.4.1.3]

Scenario 1. Characteristics: mass start, egress desired (by management and attendees), exits not available, local awareness. [*101*: A.12.4.1.3]

Normal egress at the end of an event occurs just as a severe weather condition induces evacuees at the exterior doors to retard or stop their egress. The backup that occurs in the egress system is not known to most evacuees, who continue to press forward, potentially resulting in a crowd crush. [*101*: A.12.4.1.3]

Scenario 2. Characteristics: mass start, egress not desired (by management), exits possibly not available, mass awareness. [*101*: A.12.4.1.3]

An earthquake occurs during an event. The attendees are relatively safe in the seating area. The means of egress outside the seating areas are relatively unsafe and vulnerable to aftershock damage. Facility management discourages mass egress until the means of egress can be checked and cleared for use. [*101*: A.12.4.1.3]

Scenario 3. Characteristics: local start, incident stays local, egress desired (by attendees and management), exits available, mass awareness. [*101*: A.12.4.1.3]

A localized civil disturbance (e.g., firearms violence) provokes localized egress, which is seen by attendees, generally, who then decide to leave also. [*101*: A.12.4.1.3]

Scenario 4. Characteristics: mass start, egress desired (by attendees), incident spreads, exits not available, mass awareness. [*101*: A.12.4.1.3]

In an open-air facility unprotected from wind, precipitation, and lightning, sudden severe weather prompts egress to shelter, but not from the facility. The means of egress congest and block quickly as people in front stop once they are under shelter while people behind them continue to press forward, potentially resulting in a crowd crush. [*101*: A.12.4.1.3]

These scenarios illustrate some of the broader factors to be taken into account when assessing the capability of both building systems and management features on which reliance is placed in a range of situations, not just fire emergencies. Some scenarios also illustrate the conflicting motivations of management and attendees, based on differing perceptions of danger and differing knowledge of hazards, countermeasures, and capabilities. Mass egress might not be the most appropriate life safety strategy in some scenarios, such as Scenario 2. [*101:* A.12.4.1.3]

Table A.10.14.3.3 summarizes the characteristics in the scenarios and provides a framework for developing other characteristics and scenarios that might be important for a particular facility, hazard, occupant type, event, or management. [*101:* A.12.4.1.3]

A.10.14.11.3.1 Visitors to the crop maze should only use flashlights, chemical lights, or similar devices to illuminate their travel through the maze. Candles, gas-fired lanterns, cigarette lighters, or similar open flame or flame-producing devices are prohibited for use inside a crop maze at all times.

A.10.15 For additional guidance, see Chapter 34 for provisions for indoor and outdoor storage of material. Chapter 33 contains provisions for outside storage of tires.

A.10.18 See A.10.15.

A.10.19.1.2 The flame-retardant requirements for light-transmitting plastics can also be found in Chapter 48 of *NFPA 5000, Building Construction and Safety Code.*

A.11.1.5.2 See Table A.11.1.5.2.

A.11.1.7.1 Section 230.70 of *NFPA 70, National Electrical Code* (*NEC*), includes requirements for the location and marking of service disconnect means. *NFPA 70* applies to most public and private buildings, structures, yards, parking lots, and similar installations. It does not apply to certain electrical installations under the exclusive control of communications utilities or electric utilities, and other specific installations. *(See NFPA 70, Section 90.2.)* Multiple service disconnect means could be provided as allowed by *NFPA 70*.

A.11.3.3 Continued operation of solid-state elevator equipment is contingent on maintaining the ambient temperature in the range specified by the elevator manufacturer. If the machine room ventilation/air conditioning is connected to the general building system, and that system is shut down during a fire, the fire department might lose the use of elevators due to excessive heat in the elevator machine room. [*101:* A.9.4.5]

Table A.10.14.3.3 Life Safety Evaluation Scenario Characteristics Matrix

					Management		Occupants						
Scenario	Local Awareness	Mass Awareness	Incident Localized	Incident Spreads	Egress Desired	Egress Not Desired	Egress Desired	Egress Not Desired	Local Start	Mass Start	Exits Available	Exits Not Available	Other
1	X	—	—	—	X	—	X	—	—	X	—	X	—
2	—	X	—	—	—	X	—	—	—	X	—	X	—
3	—	X	X	—	X	—	X	—	X	—	X	—	—
4	—	X	—	X	—	—	X	—	—	X	—	X	—

[*101:* Table A.12.4.1.3]

Table A.11.1.5.2 Recommended Extension Cord Sizes for Portable Electric Tools

	Nameplate Ampere Rating											
	0–2.0		2.1–3.4		3.5–5.0		5.1–7.0		7.1–12.0		12.1–16.0	
Extension Cord Length (ft)	115 V	230 V	115 V	230 V	115 V	230 V	115 V	230 V	115 V	230 V	115 V	230 V
25	18	18	18	18	18	18	18	18	16	18	14	16
50	18	18	18	18	18	18	16	18	14	16	12	14
75	18	18	18	18	16	18	14	16	12	14	10	12
100	18	18	16	18	14	16	12	14	10	12	8	10
200	16	18	14	16	12	14	10	12	8	10	6	8
300	14	16	12	14	10	14	8	12	6	10	4	6
400	12	16	10	14	8	12	6	10	4	8	4	6
500	12	14	10	12	8	12	6	10	4	6	2	4
600	10	14	8	12	6	10	4	8	2	6	2	4
800	10	12	8	10	6	8	4	6	2	4	1	2
1000	8	12	6	10	4	8	2	6	1	4	0	2

Notes:
(1) Size is based on current equivalent to 150 percent of full load of tool and a loss in voltage of not over 5 volts.
(2) If voltage is already low at the source (outlet), voltage should be increased to standard, or a larger cord than listed should be used to minimize the total voltage drop.
[*70B:* Table 29.5.1]

A.11.5.1.5 Examples of portable devices not covered by NFPA 31 are blowtorches, melting pots, and weed burners. [**31**: A.1.1.5]

A.11.5.1.10.1 See Chapter 11 of NFPA 31 for additional requirements for oil-burning stoves, kerosene-burning room heaters, and kerosene-burning portable heaters. See Chapter 12 of NFPA 31 for additional requirements for used oil–burning appliances. See Chapter 13 of NFPA 31 for additional requirements for combination oil-and-gas–burning appliances. [**31**: A.4.5.1]

A.11.5.1.10.3 Where heavy oils are used, provisions should be made to maintain the oil within the recommended temperature range indicated in Table A.11.5.1.10.3 so that proper atomization is maintained. [**31**: A.4.5.3]

Table A.11.5.1.10.3 Recommended Temperature Range for Proper Atomization of Heavy Oils

Fuel No.	Viscosity in SSU at 100°F	Low Temperature Limit (°F)	High Temperature Limit (°F)
4	45	35*	50
	50	35*	65
	60	45*	85
	75	62	105
	100	80	125
5	150	100	145
	200	112	160
	300	130	180
	400	140	190
	500	150	200
6	1,000	170	225
	2,000	190	245
	3,000	205	260
	4,000	212	270
	5,000	218	275
	10,000	240	290

*At these temperatures, proper operation of the appliance might not be attained because of unsatisfactory atomization of the fuel. For this reason, the fuel oil should be kept at the high end of the recommended temperature range.
[**31**: Table A.4.5.3]

A.11.5.1.10.3(4) ANSI/UL 296A, *Standard for Waste Oil-Burning Air Heating Appliances*, specifies that a burner provided with preheating means for the fuel oil can be provided with an oil temperature interlock device to prevent delivery of the fuel oil to the firing portion of the burner until the fuel oil has reached a predetermined minimum temperature. On a burner that is not equipped with oil-preheating equipment, an oil temperature interlock device should not be provided on the burner and should be bypassed during any firing tests of the burner. [**31**: A.4.5.3(4)]

A.11.7.2.1 It is not the intent of this section to prohibit the installation or use of portable generators within outside structures such as lean-tos or sheds intended solely to provide weather protection for the generator.

A.11.8 NFPA 92, *Standard for Smoke Control Systems*, provides guidance in implementing systems using pressure differentials to accomplish one or more of the following:

(1) Maintain a tenable environment in the means of egress during the time required for evacuation
(2) Control and reduce the migration of smoke from the fire area
(3) Provide conditions outside the fire zone that assist emergency response personnel to conduct search and rescue operations and to locate and control the fire
(4) Contribute to the protection of life and reduction of property loss

A.11.10 Two-way radio communication enhancement systems provide for greater flexibility and safety for emergency responders during in-building operations.

A.11.12.2.1 Marking is needed to provide emergency responders with appropriate warning and guidance with respect to working around and isolating the solar electric system. This can facilitate identifying energized electrical lines that connect the solar modules to the inverter, which should not be cut when venting for smoke removal during fire-fighting operations.

A.11.12.2.1.3 Markings are intended to alert emergency responders to avoid inadvertent cutting through the conduits, raceways, or cable assemblies during fire-fighting operations.

A.11.12.2.1.3.2 Materials used for marking should be in compliance with ANSI/UL 969, *Marking and Labeling System Standard*.

A.11.12.2.1.6 Inverters are devices used to convert dc electricity from the solar system to ac electricity for use in the building's electrical system or the grid.

A.11.12.3.1 The zoning regulations of the jurisdiction setback requirements between buildings or property lines, and accessory structures may apply.

A.11.12.3.2 Though dirt with minor growth is not considered noncombustible, the AHJ might approve dirt bases as long as any growth is maintained under and around the installation to reduce the risk of ignition from the electrical system. This could be a serious consideration for large ground-mounted photovoltaic systems. Not only should the base be considered under the systems, but also around the systems to the point that the risk of fire from growth or other ignition sources will be reduced.

A.11.12.3.3 Security barriers are intended to protect individuals and animals from contact with energized conductors or other components.

A.12.2 Table A.12.2 provides a cross reference from the NFPA construction types to the model building codes.

A.12.2.1 Building construction types are defined in NFPA 220, *Standard on Types of Building Construction*. The following material is extracted verbatim from NFPA 220 and is included here as a convenience for users of this *Code*. Any requests for Formal Interpretations (FIs) or Tentative Interim Amendments (TIAs) on the following material should be directed to the Technical Committee on Building Construction. See Table A.12.2.1 for fire resistance ratings for each building construction type.

Type I and Type II Construction. Type I (442 or 332) and Type II (222, 111, or 000) construction shall be those types in which the fire walls, structural elements, walls, arches, floors, and roofs are of approved noncombustible or limited-combustible materials. [**220**:4.3.1]

Table A.12.2 Cross Reference of Building Construction Types

Code Source NFPA 220	I(442)	I(332)	II(222)	II(111)	II(000)	III(211)	III(200)	IV(2HH)	V(111)	V(000)
B/NBC	1A	1B	2A	2B	2C	3A	3B	4	5A	5B
IBC	—	IA	IB	IIA	IIB	IIIA	IIIB	IV	VA	VB
SBC	I	II	—	IV 1 hr	IV UNP	V 1 hr	V UNP	III	VI 1 hr	VI UNP
UBC	—	I FR	II FR	II 1 hr	II N	III 1 hr	III N	IV HT	V 1 hr	V N

B/NBC: BOCA/National Building Code.
FR: Fire resistive.
HT: Heavy timber.
IBC: International Building Code.
N: Nonrequirement.
SBC: Standard Building Code.
UBC: Uniform Building Code.
UNP: Unprotected.

Table A.12.2.1 Fire Resistance Ratings for Type I through Type V Construction (hr)

	Type I		Type II			Type III		Type IV	Type V	
	442	332	222	111	000	211	200	2HH	111	000
Exterior Bearing Walls[a]										
Supporting more than one floor, columns, or other bearing walls	4	3	2	1	0[b]	2	2	2	1	0[b]
Supporting one floor only	4	3	2	1	0[b]	2	2	2	1	0[b]
Supporting a roof only	4	3	1	1	0[b]	2	2	2	1	0[b]
Interior Bearing Walls										
Supporting more than one floor, columns, or other bearing walls	4	3	2	1	0	1	0	2	1	0
Supporting one floor only	3	2	2	1	0	1	0	1	1	0
Supporting roofs only	3	2	1	1	0	1	0	1	1	0
Columns										
Supporting more than one floor, columns, or other bearing walls	4	3	2	1	0	1	0	H	1	0
Supporting one floor only	3	2	2	1	0	1	0	H	1	0
Supporting roofs only	3	2	1	1	0	1	0	H	1	0
Beams, Girders, Trusses, and Arches										
Supporting more than one floor, columns, or other bearing walls	4	3	2	1	0	1	0	H	1	0
Supporting one floor only	2	2	2	1	0	1	0	H	1	0
Supporting roofs only	2	2	1	1	0	1	0	H	1	0
Floor-Ceiling Assemblies	2	2	2	1	0	1	0	H	1	0
Roof-Ceiling Assemblies	2	1½	1	1	0	1	0	H	1	0
Interior Nonbearing Walls	0	0	0	0	0	0	0	0	0	0
Exterior Nonbearing Walls[c]	0[b]	0[b]	0[b]	0[b]	0[b]	0[b]	0[b]	0[b]	0[b]	0[b]

Note: H = heavy timber members *(see NFPA 220 text for requirements)*.
[a]See *NFPA 5000*, 7.3.2.1.
[b]See *NFPA 5000*, Section 7.3.
[c]See 4.3.2.12, 4.4.2.3, and 4.5.6.8 of NFPA 220.
[**220:** Table 4.1.1]

Type III Construction. Type III (211 or 200) construction shall be that type in which exterior walls and structural elements that are portions of exterior walls are of approved noncombustible or limited-combustible materials, and in which fire walls, interior structural elements, walls, arches, floors, and roofs, are entirely or partially of wood of smaller dimensions than required for Type IV construction or are of approved noncombustible, limited-combustible, or other approved combustible materials. [**220:**4.4.1]

Type IV Construction. Type IV (2HH) construction shall be that type in which fire walls, exterior walls, and interior bearing walls and structural elements that are portions of such walls are of approved noncombustible or limited-combustible materials. Other interior structural elements, arches, floors, and roofs shall be of solid or laminated wood without concealed spaces and shall comply with the allowable dimensions of 4.5.5 of NFPA 220. [**220:**4.5.1]

Type V (111 or 000) Construction. Type V (111 or 000) construction shall be that type in which structural elements, walls, arches, floors, and roofs are entirely or partially of wood or other approved material. [**220:**4.6]

A.12.3.2 The scoping provision of 12.3.2 is extracted from *NFPA 5000, Building Construction and Safety Code,* but limited to new buildings that are three or more stories in height. Such threshold is reasonable from the fire inspection perspective.

A.12.3.3 Fire-resistive construction also includes fire-resistive coatings and sprayed fire-resistive materials, as well as membrane and through-penetration firestops and fire-resistive joint systems. It is important to conduct periodic inspections of fire-resistive construction, especially these elements and components that are directly visible or readily accessible for inspection.

Inspections of sprayed fire-resistive materials and coatings are especially important since they can be subject to delamination, removal, physical abuse, deterioration, and degradation over time. Periodic inspections should be able to identify apparent deficiencies, especially where they crumble or fall off when touched. When such conditions are identified, they should be further inspected or tested by qualified third parties to verify their integrity and effectiveness. Where they are found to be deficient, appropriate corrective action should be taken to restore them to their original condition.

A.12.4.1 See Annex K of NFPA 80, *Standard for Fire Doors and Other Opening Protectives,* for general information about fire doors. [**80:** A.1.1]

A.12.4.2 No fire test standard requirement currently exists to which fabric fire safety curtain assemblies can be tested. Only the curtain fabric is tested in accordance with ASTM E119, *Standard Test Methods for Fire Tests of Building Construction and Materials.* The perimeter and internal framework and all supporting, guide, and operating components used in specific applications are not tested. Variations in size of proscenium openings and the amount of side and head clearances available for individual stages dictate the number of variations in design of the assemblies. [**80:** A.1.1.1]

A.12.4.3 For requirements on their installation, see NFPA 82, *Standard on Incinerators and Waste and Linen Handling Systems and Equipment,* and NFPA 232, *Standard for the Protection of Records.* [**80:** A.1.1.2]

A.12.4.4 For requirements on the installation of hoistway doors for elevators and dumbwaiters, see the applicable sections of ASME A17.1, *Safety Code for Elevators and Escalators,* or CSA B44, *Safety Code for Elevators.* [**80:** A.1.1.3]

A.12.4.5 The fire performance evaluation of these assemblies is tested in accordance with ASTM E119, *Standard Test Methods for Fire Tests of Building Construction and Materials,* for horizontal access doors; NFPA 252, *Standard Methods of Fire Tests of Door Assemblies,* for fire doors and shutters; NFPA 257, *Standard on Fire Test for Window and Glass Block Assemblies,* for fire windows and glass block; and NFPA 288, *Standard Methods of Fire Tests of Horizontal Fire Door Assemblies Installed in Horizontal Fire Resistance-Rated Assemblies,* for doors in horizontal fire-rated assemblies. It is not the intent of this section to establish the degree of protection required or to constitute the approval of any product. These are determined by the AHJ. [**80:** A.1.1.4]

A.12.4.6.4.1 Field modifications beyond the scope of the prescriptive allowances permitted by 4.1.3.2 through 4.1.3.4 of NFPA 80 typically result in voiding the fire rating of the assembly. Paragraph 12.4.6.4.1 of NFPA 80 provides an alternative method whereby proposed modifications can be documented and presented to the labeling agency prior to work commencing. Where the proposed modification(s) are within the parameters of the manufacturer's procedures and will not degrade the fire resistance of the assembly, the labeling agency is permitted to authorize such modifications without a requirement for a subsequent field inspection. [**80:** A.5.1.4.1]

A.12.4.6.6 Doors, shutters, and windows are of no value unless they are properly maintained and closed or are able to close at the time of fire. A periodic inspection and maintenance program is generally the responsibility of the building owner. [**80:** A.5.2]

A.12.4.6.6.1 Hinges, catches, closers, latches, and stay rollers are especially subject to wear. [**80:** A.5.2.1]

A.12.4.6.6.2 Newer technology includes use of barcodes and other electronic devices. This section recognizes that completed and filed barcode reports should be considered signed by the inspector. [**80:** A.5.2.2]

A.12.4.6.6.2.2 In many cases, AHJs are not able to inspect each building in their jurisdiction each year. Inspection and testing records need to be retained during the intervening periods between the AHJ's formal visits to provide evidence that the inspections and testing were performed as required by this standard. Additionally, maintenance records documenting that the necessary corrective actions have been made in accordance with this standard should be stored with the inspection and testing records for the same period of time. Retaining the records for 7 years allows the AHJ the ability to look back over an extended period of time to verify that the fire door assemblies are being properly maintained. [**80:** A.5.2.2.2]

A.12.4.6.6.2.3 Installation of new fire door assemblies should be documented in the same manner and level of detail as the periodic inspections and testing of fire door assemblies required by 12.4.6.6.3 and 12.4.6.6.4. Records of new fire door assemblies should be retained with the periodic inspections and testing records for the facility. [**80:** A.5.2.2.3]

A.12.4.6.6.2.4(8) Each fire door assembly inspected and tested should be assigned a unique identifier code (e.g., door number as assigned by the facility) that can be used to track the assembly's compliance and maintenance records throughout the lifetime of its installation. Identifier codes could be a door assembly number, barcode, or other code that is unique to each fire door assembly. [**80:** A.5.2.2.4(8)]

A.12.4.6.6.2.4(9) To aid the AHJ during the review of the inspections and testing reports, the records should include a description of the type of fire door assembly as follows:

(1) Type 6: Swinging door with builders hardware
(2) Type 7: Swinging fire door with fire door hardware
(3) Type 8: Horizontally sliding fire door
(4) Type 9: Special purpose horizontally sliding accordion or folding door
(5) Type 10: Vertically sliding fire door
(6) Type 11: Rolling steel door
(7) Type 12: Fire shutter
(8) Type 13: Service counter fire door
(9) Type 14: Hoistway doors for elevators and dumbwaiter
(10) Type 15: Chute door
(11) Type 16: Access door
(12) Type 17: Fire window

[*80:* A.5.2.2.4(9)]

A.12.4.6.6.2.4(10) Functional operation of fire door assemblies should include testing of the closing device, complete closure of the fire door, and full engagement of latch(es) where required by door type. Functional testing of automatic-closing or power-operated fire door assemblies and electrically controlled latching hardware or release devices might need to be coordinated with the facility during other electrically controlled system tests. [*80:* A.5.2.2.4(10)]

A.12.4.6.6.2.5 Existing fire door assemblies that have been repaired should be inspected and tested immediately upon completion of the repair work to ensure that they are in compliance with this standard. [*80:* A.5.2.2.5]

A.12.4.6.6.3.1 Visual inspection and functional testing of fire door and fire window assemblies require the persons performing the inspections and testing to be thoroughly knowledgeable of the various components and systems that are used to create fire-rated assemblies. In the case of swinging doors with builders hardware, these assemblies are comprised of labeled and listed components from several manufacturers. Often, the listing of the door leaf determines which products are permitted to be installed on an assembly. Inspectors of swinging doors with builders hardware need be able to recognize which components can or cannot be used on specific assemblies, which requires training and experience on behalf of the persons performing the inspections. Additionally, AHJs need to be able to rely on the competency, expertise, experience, and knowledge of the fire door inspectors in their jurisdiction. [*80:* A.5.2.3.1]

A.12.4.6.6.3.2 Any fire door or fire window assembly or component that has a history of reoccurring failures should be evaluated for possible replacement or other corrective measures. [*80:* A.5.2.3.2]

A.12.4.6.6.3.6.2(12) Fusible links should not be coated with any materials such as fireproofing, drywall compound, or spray texturing. [*80:* A.5.2.3.6.2(12)]

A.12.4.6.6.3.8 Movable parts of the door assembly can include, but are not limited to, stay rollers, gears, and closing mechanisms. [*80:* A.5.2.3.8]

A.12.4.6.6.4.1 Doors subject to high-volume use and abuse might warrant an increased frequency of inspection. Components including, but not limited to, hinges, catches, closers, latches, and stay rollers are especially subject to wear. [*80:* A.5.2.4.1]

A.12.4.6.6.4.6 The determination of the time required for corrective action should be based on a risk analysis and availability of replacement materials. [*80:* A.5.2.4.6]

A.12.4.6.8 See Annex J of NFPA 80 for information regarding performance-based inspection, testing, and maintenance options for fire door assemblies. [*80:* A.5.4]

A.12.4.6.6.9.1 The determination of the time required for corrective action should be based on a risk analysis and availability of replacement materials. [*80:* A.5.5.1]

A.12.5 The requirements pertaining to interior finish are intended to restrict the spread of fire over the continuous surface forming the interior portions of a building. [*101:* A.10.2]

A.12.5.2 The requirements pertaining to interior finish are intended to restrict the spread of fire over the continuous surface forming the interior portions of a building. The presence of multiple paint layers has the potential for paint delamination and bubbling or blistering of paint. Testing (NFPA *Fire Technology*, August 1974, "Fire Tests of Building Interior Covering Systems," David Waksman and John Ferguson, Institute for Applied Technology, National Bureau of Standards) has shown that adding up to two layers of paint with a dry film thickness of about 0.007 in. (0.18 mm) will not change the fire properties of surface-covering systems. Testing has shown that the fire properties of the surface-covering systems are highly substrate dependent and that thin coatings generally take on the characteristics of the substrate. When exposed to fire, the delamination, bubbling, and blistering of paint can result in an accelerated rate of flame spread. [*101:* A.10.2.1]

A.12.5.2.5 Such partitions are intended to include washroom water closet partitions. [*101:* A.10.2.1.4]

A.12.5.3 Table A.12.5.3 provides a compilation of the interior finish requirements of the occupancy chapters (Chapters 12 through 42 of NFPA *101*). [*101:* A.10.2.2]

Table A.12.5.3 Interior Finish Classification Limitations

Occupancy	Exits	Exit Access Corridors	Other Spaces
Assembly — New			
>300 occupant load	A I or II	A or B I or II	A or B NA
≤300 occupant load	A I or II	A or B I or II	A, B, or C NA
Assembly — Existing			
>300 occupant load	A	A or B	A or B
≤300 occupant load	A	A or B	A, B, or C
Educational — New	A I or II	A or B I or II	A or B; C on low partitions* NA
Educational — Existing	A	A or B	A, B, or C
Day-Care Centers — New	A I or II	A I or II	A or B NA
Day-Care Centers — Existing	A or B	A or B	A or B
Day-Care Homes — New	A or B I or II	A or B	A, B, or C
Day-Care Homes — Existing	A or B	A, B, or C	A, B, or C

Table A.12.5.3 *Continued*

Occupancy	Exits	Exit Access Corridors	Other Spaces
Health Care — New	A NA I or II	A B on lower portion of corridor wall* I or II	A B in small individual rooms* NA
Health Care — Existing	A or B	A or B	A or B
Detention and Correctional — New (sprinklers mandatory)	A or B I or II	A or B I or II	A, B, or C NA
Detention and Correctional — Existing	A or B I or II	A or B I or II	A, B, or C NA
One- and Two-Family Dwellings and Lodging or Rooming Houses	A, B, or C	A, B, or C	A, B, or C
Hotels and Dormitories — New	A I or II	A or B I or II	A, B, or C NA
Hotels and Dormitories — Existing	A or B I or II*	A or B I or II*	A, B, or C NA
Apartment Buildings — New	A I or II	A or B I or II	A, B, or C NA
Apartment Buildings — Existing	A or B I or II*	A or B I or II*	A, B, or C NA
Residential Board and Care — *(See 32 and 33 of NFPA 101.)*			
Mercantile — New	A or B I or II	A or B	A or B NA
Mercantile — Existing			
Class A or Class B stores	A or B	A or B	Ceilings — A or B; walls— A, B, or C
Class C stores	A, B, or C	A, B, or C	A, B, or C
Business and Ambulatory Health Care — New	A or B I or II	A or B	A, B, or C NA
Business and Ambulatory Health Care — Existing	A or B	A or B	A, B, or C
Industrial	A or B I or II	A, B, or C I or II	A, B, or C NA
Storage	A or B I or II	A, B, or C	A, B, or C NA

Notes:
(1) Class A interior wall and ceiling finish — flame spread 0–25, (new applications) smoke developed 0–450.
(2) Class B interior wall and ceiling finish — flame spread 26–75, (new applications) smoke developed 0–450.
(3) Class C interior wall and ceiling finish — flame spread 76–200, (new applications) smoke developed 0–450.
(4) Class I interior floor finish — critical radiant flux, not less than 0.45 W/cm^2.
(5) Class II interior floor finish — critical radiant flux, not more than 0.22 W/cm^2, but less than 0.45 W/cm^2.
(6) Automatic sprinklers — where a complete standard system of automatic sprinklers is installed, interior wall and ceiling finish with a flame spread rating not exceeding Class C is permitted to be used in any location where Class B is required and with a rating of Class B in any location where Class A is required; similarly, Class II interior floor finish is permitted to be used in any location where Class I is required, and no critical radiant flux rating is required where Class II is required. These provisions do not apply to new detention and correctional occupancies.
(7) Exposed portions of structural members complying with the requirements for heavy timber construction are permitted.
*See corresponding chapters for details. [*101:* Table A.10.2.2]

A.12.5.3.2 This paragraph recognizes that traditional finish floors and floor coverings, such as wood flooring and resilient floor coverings, have not proved to present an unusual hazard. [*101:* A.10.2.2.2]

A.12.5.4 ASTM E 84, *Standard Test Method of Surface Burning Characteristics of Building Materials*, and UL 723, *Standard for Test for Surface Burning Characteristics of Building Materials*, are considered nationally recognized consensus standard test methods for determining the flame spread index and smoke developed index of building materials and are likely to yield equivalent test results. See also A.12.5.5.1. [*101:* A.10.2.3]

A.12.5.4.4 It has been shown that the method of mounting interior finish materials usually affects actual performance. The use of standard mounting methods will be helpful in determining appropriate fire test results. Where materials are tested in intimate contact with a substrate to determine a classification, such materials should be installed in intimate contact with a similar substrate. Such details are especially important for "thermally thin" materials. For further information, see ASTM E 84, *Standard Test Method for Surface Burning Characteristics of Building Materials*. [*101:* A.10.2.3.4]

Some interior wall and ceiling finish materials, such as fabrics not applied to a solid backing, do not lend themselves to a test made in accordance with ASTM E 84. In such cases, the large-scale test outlined in NFPA 701, *Standard Methods of Fire Tests for Flame Propagation of Textiles and Films*, is permitted to be used. [*101:* A.10.2.3.4]

In 1989, the NFPA Technical Committee on Fire Tests eliminated the so-called "small-scale test" from NFPA 701 because the results had been shown not to represent a fire performance that corresponded to what happened in real scale. Since then, NFPA 701 no longer contains a "small-scale test" but it now contains two tests (Test 1 and Test 2), which apply to materials as a function of their areal density. Thus NFPA 701 Test 1 applies to fabrics (other than vinyl-coated fabric blackout linings) having an areal density less than or equal to 21 oz/yd^2 (700 g/m^2) while NFPA 701 Test 2 applies to fabrics with an areal density greater than 21 oz/yd^2 (700 g/m^2), vinyl-coated fabric blackout linings, decorative objects and films. Representations that materials or products have been tested to the small-scale test in NFPA 701 normally refer to the pre-1989 small-scale test, which no longer exists and which does not represent acceptable fire performance. [*101:* A.10.2.3.4]

Prior to 1978, the test report described by ASTM E 84 included an evaluation of the fuel contribution as well as the flame spread rating and the smoke development value. However, it is now recognized that the measurement on which the fuel contribution is based does not provide a valid measure. Therefore, although the data are recorded during the test, the information is no longer normally reported. Classification of interior wall and ceiling finish thus relies only on flame spread index and smoke development value. [*101:* A.10.2.3.4]

The 450 smoke development value limit is based solely on obscuration. *(See A.12.5.5.1.)* [*101:* A.10.2.3.4]

A.12.5.4.7 The methodology specified in NFPA 265, *Standard Methods of Fire Tests for Evaluating Room Fire Growth Contribution of Textile or Expanded Vinyl Wall Coverings on Full Height Panels and Walls*, includes provisions for measuring smoke obscuration. Such measurement is considered desirable, but the basis for specific recommended values is not currently available. *(See A.12.5.5.1.)* [*101:* A.10.2.3.7]

A.12.5.5 Surface nonmetallic raceway products, as permitted by NFPA 70, *National Electrical Code*, are not interior finishes and are not subject to the provisions of Chapter 12. [*101:*A.10.2.4]

A.12.5.5.1 Previous editions of NFPA *101* have regulated textile materials on walls and ceilings using NFPA 255, *Standard Method of Test of Surface Burning Characteristics of Building Materials*. Full-scale room/corner fire test research has shown that flame spread indices produced by might not reliably predict all aspects of the fire behavior of textile wall and ceiling coverings. [*101:*A.10.2.4.1]

NFPA 265, *Standard Methods of Fire Tests for Evaluating Room Fire Growth Contribution of Textile or Expanded Vinyl Wall Coverings on Full Height Panels and Walls*, and NFPA 286, *Standard Methods of Fire Tests for Evaluating Contribution of Wall and Ceiling Interior Finish to Room Fire Growth*, both known as room-corner tests, were developed for assessing the fire and smoke obscuration performance of textile wall coverings and interior wall and ceiling finish materials, respectively. As long as an interior wall or ceiling finish material is tested by NFPA 265 or NFPA 286, as appropriate, using a mounting system, substrate, and adhesive (if appropriate) that are representative of actual use, the room-corner test provides an adequate evaluation of a product's flammability and smoke obscuration behavior. Manufacturers, installers, and specifiers should be encouraged to use NFPA 265 or NFPA 286, as appropriate— but not both — because each of these standard fire tests has the ability to characterize actual product behavior, as opposed to data generated by tests using NFPA 255, which only allows comparisons of one product's performance with another. If a manufacturer or installer chooses to test a wall finish in accordance with NFPA 286, additional testing in accordance with NFPA 255 is not necessary. [*101:*A.10.2.4.1]

The test results from NFPA 255 are suitable for classification purposes but should not be used as input into fire models, because they are not generated in units suitable for engineering calculations. Actual test results for heat, smoke, and combustion product release from NFPA 265, and from NFPA 286, are suitable for use as input into fire models for performance-based design. [*101:*A.10.2.4.1]

A.12.5.5.2 Expanded vinyl wall covering consists of a woven textile backing, an expanded vinyl base coat layer, and a non-expanded vinyl skin coat. The expanded base coat layer is a homogeneous vinyl layer that contains a blowing agent. During processing, the blowing agent decomposes, which causes this layer to expand by forming closed cells. The total thickness of the wall covering is approximately 0.055 in. to 0.070 in. (1.4 mm to 1.8 mm). [*101:*A.10.2.4.2]

A.12.5.5.3.1 See A.12.5.5.3.1.2. [*101:*A.10.2.4.3.1]

A.12.5.5.3.1.2 Both NFPA 286, *Standard Methods of Fire Tests for Evaluating Contribution of Wall and Ceiling Interior Finish to Room Fire Growth*, and ANSI/UL 1715, *Standard for Fire Test of Interior Finish Material*, contain smoke obscuration criteria. ANSI/UL 1040, *Standard for Fire Test of Insulated Wall Construction*, and FM 4880, *Approval Standard for Class I Insulated Wall or Wall and Roof/Ceiling Panels; Plastic Interior Finish Materials; Plastic Exterior Building Panels; Wall/Ceiling Coating Systems; Interior or Exterior Finish Systems*, do not. Smoke obscuration is an important component of the fire performance of cellular or foamed plastic materials. [*101:* A.10.2.4.3.1.2]

A.12.5.5.4 Light-transmitting plastics are used for a variety of purposes, including light diffusers, exterior wall panels, skylights, canopies, glazing, and the like. Previous editions of NFPA *101* have not addressed the use of light-transmitting plastics. Light-transmitting plastics will not normally be used in applications representative of interior finishes. Accordingly, ASTM E 84, *Standard Test Method for Surface Burning Characteristics of Building Materials*, or ANSI/UL 723, *Standard for Test for Surface Burning Characteristics of Building Materials*, can produce test results that might or might not apply. [*101:*A.10.2.4.4]

Light-transmitting plastics are regulated by model building codes such as, *NFPA 5000, Building Construction and Safety Code*. Model building codes provide adequate regulation for most applications of light-transmitting plastics. Where an AHJ determines that a use is contemplated that differs from uses regulated by model building codes, light-transmitting plastics in such applications can be substantiated by fire tests that demonstrate the combustibility characteristics of the light-transmitting plastics for the use intended under actual fire conditions. [*101:*A.10.2.4.4]

For additional information on light transmitting plastics, see Section 48.7 of *NFPA 5000*. [*101:*A.10.2.4.4]

A.12.5.7 Fire-retardant coatings need to be applied to surfaces properly prepared for the material, and application needs to be consistent with the product listing. Deterioration of coatings applied to interior finishes can occur due to repeated cleaning of the surface or painting over applied coatings. [*101:*A.10.2.6]

A.12.5.7.1 It is the intent of the *Code* to mandate interior wall and ceiling finish materials that obtain their fire performance and smoke developed characteristics in their original form. However, in renovations, particularly those involving historic buildings, and in changes of occupancy, the required fire performance or smoke developed characteristics of existing surfaces of walls, partitions, columns, and ceilings might have to be secured by applying approved fire-retardant coatings to surfaces having higher flame spread ratings than permitted. Such treatments should comply with the requirements of NFPA 703, *Standard for Fire Retardant–Treated Wood and Fire-Retardant Coatings for Building Materials*. When fire-retardant coatings are used, they need to be applied to surfaces properly prepared for the material, and application needs to be consistent with the product listing. Deterioration of coatings applied to interior finishes can occur due to repeated cleaning of the surface or painting over applied coatings, but permanency must be assured in some appropriate fashion. Fire-retardant coatings must possess the desired degree of permanency and be maintained so as to retain the effectiveness of the treatment under the service conditions encountered in actual use. [*101:*A.10.2.6.1]

A.12.5.8 The flooring radiant panel provides a measure of a floor covering's tendency to spread flames where located in a corridor and exposed to the flame and hot gases from a room fire. The flooring radiant panel test method is to be used as a basis for estimating the fire performance of a floor covering installed in the building corridor. Floor coverings in open building spaces and in rooms within buildings merit no further regulation, provided that it can be shown that the floor covering is at least as resistant to spread of flame as a material that meets the U.S. federal flammability standard 16 CFR 1630, "Standard for the Surface Flammability of Carpets and Rugs" (FF 1-70). All carpeting sold in the United States since 1971 is required to meet this standard and, therefore, is not likely to become involved in a fire until a room reaches or approaches flashover. Therefore, no further regulations are necessary for carpet, other than carpet in exitways and corridors. [*101:*A.10.2.7]

It has not been found necessary or practical to regulate interior floor finishes on the basis of smoke development. [*101:* A.10.2.7]

Full-scale fire tests and fire experience have shown that floor coverings in open building spaces merit no regulation beyond the U.S. federally mandated DOC FF 1-70 "pill test." This is because floor coverings meeting the pill test will not spread flame significantly until a room fire approaches flashover. At flashover, the spread of flame across a floor covering will have minimal impact on the already existing hazard. The minimum critical radiant flux of a floor covering that will pass the FF 1-70 test has been determined to be approximately 0.04 W/cm^2 (Tu, King-Mon and Davis, Sanford, Flame Spread of Carpet Systems Involved in Room Fires, NFSIR 76-1013, Center for Fire Research, National Bureau of Standards, June 1976). The flooring radiant panel is only able to determine critical radiant flux values to 0.1 W/cm^2. This provision will prevent use of a noncomplying material, which can create a problem, especially when the *Code* is used outside the United States where U.S. federal regulation FF 1-70 (16 CFR 1630) is not mandated. [*101:* A.10.2.7]

A.12.5.8.1 Compliance with 16 CFR 1630, "Standard for the Surface Flammability of Carpets and Rugs" (FFI-70), is considered equivalent to compliance with ASTM D 2859. [*101:* A.10.2.7.1]

A.12.5.8.2 The fire performance of some floor finishes has been tested, and traditional finish floors and floor coverings, such as wood flooring and resilient floor coverings, have not proved to present an unusual hazard. [*101:* A.10.2.7.2]

A.12.5.8.3 ASTM E 648, *Standard Test Method for Critical Radiant Flux of Floor Covering Systems Using a Radiant Heat Energy Source*, and NFPA 253, *Standard Method of Test for Critical Radiant Flux of Floor Covering Systems Using a Radiant Heat Energy Source*, are considered nationally recognized consensus standard test methods for determining the critical radiant flux from floor covering systems and are likely to yield equivalent test results. [*101:* A.10.2.7.3]

A.12.6.2 Testing per NFPA 701, *Standard Methods of Fire Tests for Flame Propagation of Textiles and Films*, applies to textiles and films used in a hanging configuration. If the textiles are to be applied to surfaces of buildings or backing materials as interior finishes for use in buildings, they should be treated as interior wall and ceiling finishes in accordance with Section 10.2 of NFPA *101*, and they should then be tested for flame spread index and smoke developed index values in accordance with NFPA 255, *Standard Method of Test of Surface Burning Characteristics of Building Materials*, or for flame spread and flashover in accordance with NFPA 265, *Standard Methods of Fire Tests for Evaluating Room Fire Growth Contribution of Textile or Expanded Vinyl Wall Coverings on Full Height Panels and Walls*. Films and other materials used as interior finish applied to surfaces of buildings should be tested for flame spread index and smoke developed index values in accordance with NFPA 255 or for heat and smoke release and flashover in accordance with NFPA 286, *Standard Methods of Fire Tests for Evaluating Contribution of Wall and Ceiling Interior Finish to Room Fire Growth*. [*101:* A.10.3.1]

The test results from NFPA 701 are suitable for classification purposes but should not be used as input into fire models, because they are not generated in units suitable for engineering calculations. [*101:* A.10.3.1]

A.12.6.3.1 The Class I requirement associated with testing per NFPA 260, *Standard Methods of Tests and Classification System for Cigarette Ignition Resistance of Components of Upholstered Furniture*, and the char length of not more than 1½ in. (38 mm) required with testing per NFPA 261, *Standard Method of Test for Determining Resistance of Mock-Up Upholstered Furniture Material Assemblies to Ignition by Smoldering Cigarettes*, are indicators that the furniture item or mattress is resistant to a cigarette ignition. A fire that smolders for an excessive period of time without flaming can reduce the tenability within the room or area of fire origin without developing the temperatures necessary to operate automatic sprinklers. The test results from NFPA 260 and from NFPA 261 are suitable for classification purposes but should not be used as input into fire models, because they are not generated in units suitable for engineering calculations. [*101:* A.10.3.2.1]

Until recently, NFPA 260 was equivalent to ASTM E 1353, *Standard Test Methods for Cigarette Ignition Resistance of Components of Upholstered Furniture*, and NFPA 261 was equivalent to ASTM E 1352, *Standard Test Method for Cigarette Ignition Resistance of Mock-Up Upholstered Furniture Assemblies*. However, that changed when NFPA 260 and NFPA 261 adopted the new NIST standard reference material (SRM 1196) as the igniting cigarette and ASTM E 1352 and ASTM E 1353 did not, meaning that ASTM E 1352 and ASTM E 1353 use commercial cigarettes that are low ignition propensity and have a low likelihood of properly assessing smoldering potential. [*101:* A.10.3.2.1]

A.12.6.3.2 The char length of not more than 2 in. (51 mm) required in 16 CFR 1632, "Standard for the Flammability of Mattresses and Mattress Pads (FF–4-72)," is an indicator that the mattress is resistant to a cigarette ignition. U.S. federal regulations require mattresses in the United States to comply with 16 CFR 1632. [*101:* A.10.3.2.2]

A.12.6.3.2.1 The intent of the provisions of 12.6.3.2.1 is as follows:

(1) The peak heat release rate of not more than 80 kW by a single upholstered furniture item was chosen based on maintaining a tenable environment within the room of fire origin, and the sprinkler exception was developed because the sprinkler system helps to maintain tenable conditions, even if the single upholstered furniture item were to have a peak rate of heat release in excess of 80 kW.
(2) The total energy release of not more than 25 MJ by the single upholstered furniture item during the first 10 minutes of the test was established as an additional safeguard to protect against the adverse conditions that would be created by an upholstered furniture item that released its heat in other than the usual measured scenario, and the following should also be noted:
   (a) During the test for measurement of rate of heat release, the instantaneous heat release value usually peaks quickly and then quickly falls off, so as to create a triangle-shaped curve.
   (b) In the atypical case, if the heat release were to peak and remain steady at that elevated level, as opposed to quickly falling off, the 80 kW limit would not ensure safety.
   (c) Only a sprinkler exception is permitted in lieu of the test because of the ability of the sprinkler system to control the fire.

[*101:* A.10.3.3]

Actual test results for heat, smoke, and combustion product release from ASTM E 1537, *Standard Test Method of Fire Testing of Upholstered Furniture*, might be suitable for use as input into fire models for performance-based design. Furthermore, California Technical Bulletin 133, "Flammability Test Procedure for Seating Furniture for Use in Public Occupancies," includes pass/fail criteria for a single upholstered furniture item of 80 kW peak heat release rate and 25 MJ total heat release over the first 10 minutes of the test. [*101:* A.10.3.3]

A.12.6.3.2.2 The intent of the provisions of 12.6.3.2.2 is as follows:

(1) The peak heat release rate of not more than 100 kW by a single mattress was chosen based on maintaining a tenable environment within the room of fire origin, and the sprinkler exception was developed because the sprinkler system helps to maintain tenable conditions, even if the single mattress were to have a peak rate of heat release in excess of 100 kW.

(2) The total energy release of not more than 25 MJ by the single mattress during the first 10 minutes of the test was established as an additional safeguard to protect against the adverse conditions that would be created by a mattress that released its heat in other than the usual measured scenario, and the following should also be noted:

   (a) During the test for measurement of rate of heat release, the instantaneous heat release value usually peaks quickly and then quickly falls off, so as to create a triangle-shaped curve.

   (b) In the atypical case, if the heat release were to peak and remain steady at that elevated level, as opposed to quickly falling off, the 100 kW limit would not ensure safety.

   (c) Only a sprinkler exception is permitted in lieu of the test because of the ability of the sprinkler system to control the fire.

[*101:* A.10.3.4]

Actual test results for heat, smoke, and combustion product release from ASTM E 1590, *Standard Test Method for Fire Testing of Mattresses*, might be suitable for use as input into fire models for performance-based design. Furthermore, California Technical Bulletin 129, "Flammability Test Procedure for Mattresses for Use in Public Buildings," includes pass/fail criteria for a single mattress of 100 kW peak heat release rate and 25 MJ total heat release over the first 10 minutes of the test. [*101:* A.10.3.4]

A.12.6.4 Christmas trees that are not effectively flame-retardant treated, ordinary crepe paper decorations, and pyroxylin plastic decorations might be classified as highly flammable. [*101:* A.10.3.5]

A.12.6.6 Neither UL 1975, *Standard for Fire Tests for Foamed Plastics Used for Decorative Purposes*, nor NFPA 289 is intended for evaluating interior wall and ceiling finish materials. [*101:* A.10.3.7]

Actual test results for heat, smoke, and combustion product release from UL 1975 or from NFPA 289 might be suitable for use as input into fire models intended for performance-based design. [*101:* A.10.3.7]

A.12.7.1(4) Walls in good condition with lath and plaster, or gypsum board of not less than ½ in. (13 mm) on each side, can be considered as providing a minimum ½-hour fire resistance rating. Additional information on archaic material assemblies can be found in Annex O of NFPA 914, *Code for Fire Protection of Historic Structures*. [*101:* A.8.3.1.1(4)]

A.12.7.2.1.1 Fire resistance–rated glazing complying with 12.7.2, where not installed in a door, is considered a wall, not an opening protective. [*101:* A.8.3.2.1.1]

A.12.7.3.2.1 Some door assemblies have been tested to meet the conditions of acceptance of ASTM E 119, *Standard Test Methods for Fire Tests of Building Construction and Materials*, or ANSI/UL 263, *Standard for Fire Tests of Building Construction and Materials*. Where such assemblies are used, the provisions of 12.7.2 should be applied instead of those of 12.7.3.2. [*101:* A.8.3.3.2]

A.12.7.3.2.3.1 In existing installations, it is important to be able to determine the fire protection rating of the fire door. However, steel door frames that are well set in the wall might be judged as acceptable even if the frame label is not legible. [*101:* A.8.3.3.2.3]

A.12.7.3.6 Some window assemblies have been tested to meet the conditions of acceptance of ASTM E 119 or ANSI/UL 263. Where such assemblies are used, the provisions of 12.7.2 should be applied instead of those of 12.7.3.6. [*101:* A.8.3.3.6]

A.12.7.4.2 Longer ratings might be required where opening protectives are provided for property protection as well as life safety. NFPA 80, *Standard for Fire Doors and Other Opening Protectives*, should be consulted for standard practice in the selection and installation of fire door assemblies and fire window assemblies.

Table 12.7.4.2. A vision panel in a fire door is not a fire window, and, thus, it is not the intent of the "NP" notations in the "Fire Window Assemblies" column of Table 12.7.4.2 to prohibit vision panels in fire doors. [*101:* A.8.3.4.2]

A.12.7.5.1 Firestop materials become systems when installed to the listed firestop system design from an accredited testing laboratory. Installation of firestop materials to the listed system should meet all limitations of the system. [*101:* A.8.3.5.1]

There are management system–based contractor approval or qualification programs offered by third-party, independent companies that quantifiably qualify a company to install firestop materials that become systems after proper installation. In each program, there is an industry firestop exam that gives the company a basis to appoint a "Designated Responsible Individual." [*101:* A.8.3.5.1]

Then, the third party firm audits the firestop company's product and systems documentation records in conjunction with the company's management system operational policies and procedures to verify company compliance does as it says it does. An audit also takes place on a project site to verify that the management system is working. [*101:* A.8.3.5.1]

Where the configuration of a penetrating item or group of items is such that a listed system is determined to be nonexistent and reconfiguration of the penetrations or fire resistance-rated assembly is determined to be impractical or impossible, alternative methods for maintaining the integrity of the required fire resistance rating of the assembly should be permitted to be established using an engineering analysis based on a comparison of listed systems prepared by a manufacturer's technical representative of the systems specified, by the laboratory that conducted the original test, or by a professional engineer. [*101:* A.8.3.5.1]

ASTM E 2174, *Standard Practice for On-Site Inspection of Installed Fire Stops*, provides guidance for the inspection of through-penetration firestop systems tested in accordance with ASTM E 814, *Standard Test Method for Fire Tests of Through-*

Penetration Fire Stops, and ANSI/UL 1479, *Standard for Fire Tests of Through-Penetration Firestops*. [*101*: A.8.3.5.1]

Independent inspection paid for by owner is in many specifications and referenced in this appendix using ASTM E 2174 and ASTM E 2393, *Standard Practice for On-Site Inspection of Installed Fire Resistive Joint Systems and Perimeter Fire Barriers*. As a result, there is an accreditation program available for firestop special inspection agencies. [*101*: A.8.3.5.1]

A.12.7.5.6.3(1)(c) Criteria associated with fireblocking can be found in the building code. [*101*: A.8.3.5.6.3(1)(c)]

A.12.8.1 Although a smoke partition is intended to limit the free movement of smoke, it is not intended to provide an area that would be free of smoke. [*101*: A.8.4.1]

A.12.8.2(2) An architectural, exposed, suspended-grid acoustical tile ceiling with penetrations for sprinklers, ducted HVAC supply and return-air diffusers, speakers, and recessed light fixtures is capable of limiting the transfer of smoke. [*101*: A.8.4.2(2)]

A.12.8.3.4 Gasketing of doors should not be necessary, as the clearances in NFPA 80 effectively achieve resistance to the passage of smoke if the door is relatively tight-fitting. [*101*: A.8.4.3.4]

A.12.8.6.2 An air-transfer opening, as defined in NFPA 90A, is an opening designed to allow the movement of environmental air between two contiguous spaces. [*101*: A.8.4.6.2]

A.12.9.1 Wherever smoke barriers and doors therein require a degree of fire resistance, as specified by requirements in the various occupancy chapters (Chapter 12 through Chapter 42 of NFPA *101*), the construction should be a fire barrier that has been specified to limit the spread of fire and restrict the movement of smoke. [*101*: A.8.5.1]

Although a smoke barrier is intended to restrict the movement of smoke, it might not result in tenability throughout the adjacent smoke compartment. The adjacent smoke compartment should be safer than the area on the fire side, thus allowing building occupants to move to that area. Eventually, evacuation from the adjacent smoke compartment might be required. [*101*: A.8.5.1]

A.12.9.2 To ensure that a smoke barrier is continuous, it is necessary to seal completely all openings where the smoke barrier abuts other smoke barriers, fire barriers, exterior walls, the floor below, and the floor or ceiling above. It is not the intent to prohibit a smoke barrier from stopping at a fire barrier if the fire barrier meets the requirements of a smoke barrier (that is, the fire barrier is a combination smoke barrier/fire barrier). [*101*: A.8.5.2]

A.12.9.4.1 For additional information on the installation of smoke-control door assemblies, see NFPA 105. [*101*: A.8.5.4.1]

A.12.9.4.4 Where, because of operational necessity, it is desired to have smoke barrier doors that are usually open, such doors should be provided with hold-open devices that are activated to close the doors by means of the operation of smoke detectors and other alarm functions. [*101*: A.8.5.4.4]

A.13.1.11 Such safeguards or fire safety equipment can include, but should not be limited to, automatic fire alarm systems, automatic sprinkler or water spray systems, standpipe and hose, fixed or portable fire extinguishers, breathing apparatus, manual or automatic covers, smoke and heat vents, and carbon dioxide, foam, halogenated, dry chemical, or other special fire-extinguishing systems.

A.13.2.2.4 Prior editions of the *Code* required stages to be protected by a Class III standpipe system in accordance with NFPA 14, *Standard for the Installation of Standpipe and Hose Systems*. NFPA 14 requires that Class II and Class III standpipes be automatic — not manual — because they are intended to be used by building occupants. Automatic standpipe systems are required to provide not less than 500 gpm (1890 L/min) at 100 psi (689 kN). This requirement often can be met only if a fire pump is installed. Installation of a fire pump presents an unreasonable burden for the system supplying the two hose outlets at the side of the stage. The revised wording of 13.2.2.4 offers some relief by permitting the hose outlets to be in accordance with NFPA 13. [*101*: A.12.4.5.12]

A.13.2.2.6 It is not the intent of 13.2.2.6 to permit the removal of portions of the existing standpipe system other than hose lines, and that such remaining system components be maintained and available for use by the fire department or other appropriate fire suppression personnel.

A.13.3.1.1 This *Code* contains requirements for automatic sprinkler protection that might not be required by other NFPA codes. These requirements are included in this *Code* from a property protection standpoint in an effort to reduce property damage due to fires as well as to reduce the costs of manual fire suppression in years to come.

A.13.3.1.6 Properly designed automatic sprinkler systems provide the dual function of both automatic alarms and automatic extinguishment. Dual function is not provided in those cases where early detection of incipient fire and early notification of occupants are needed to initiate actions in behalf of life safety earlier than can be expected from heat-sensitive fire detectors. [*101*: A.9.7.1.4]

A.13.3.1.8.1 *NFPA 72, National Fire Alarm and Signaling Code*, provides details of standard practice in sprinkler supervision. Subject to the approval of the AHJ, sprinkler supervision is also permitted to be provided by direct connection to municipal fire departments or, in the case of very large establishments, to a private headquarters providing similar functions. *NFPA 72* covers such matters. System components and parameters that are required to be monitored should include, but should not be limited to, control valves, water tank levels and temperatures, tank pressure, and air pressure on dry-pipe valves. [*101*: A.9.7.2.1]

Where municipal fire alarm systems are involved, reference should also be made to NFPA 1221, *Standard for the Installation, Maintenance, and Use of Emergency Services Communications Systems*. [*101*: A.9.7.2.1]

A.13.3.1.9 A diffuser in ceiling sheathing labeled by the manufacturer as "horizontal discharge" has directional vanes to move air further along the ceiling, and sprinklers located within the 2 ft 6 in. (0.8 m) radius should have an intermediate-temperature rating. [**13**: A.8.3.2.5]

A.13.3.2.6 Small loading docks, covered platforms, ducts, or similar small unheated areas can be protected by dry pendent sprinklers extending through the wall from wet sprinkler piping in an adjacent heated area. Where protecting covered platforms, loading docks, and similar areas, a dry pendent sprinkler should extend down at a 45 degree angle. The width of the area to be protected should not exceed 7½ ft (2.3 m). Sprinklers should be spaced not over 12 ft (3.7 m) apart. Exterior projections include, but are not limited to, exterior roofs, canopies, porte-cocheres, balconies, decks, or similar projections. *(See Figure A.13.3.2.6.)* [**13**: A.8.15.7]

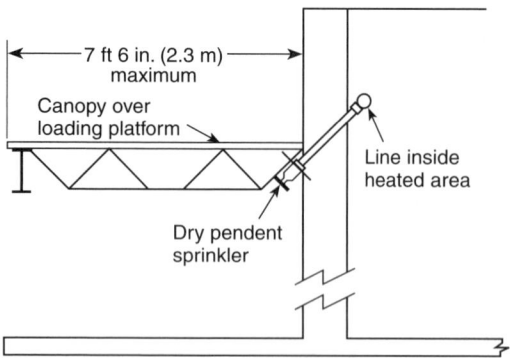

FIGURE A.13.3.2.6 Dry Pendent Sprinklers for Protection of Covered Platforms, Loading Docks, and Similar Areas. [13: Figure A.8.15.7]

A.13.3.2.6.2 Vehicles that are temporarily parked are not considered storage. Areas located at drive-in bank windows or porte-cocheres at hotels and motels normally do not require sprinklers where there is no occupancy above, where the area is entirely constructed of noncombustible or limited-combustible materials or fire retardant treated lumber, and where the area is not the only means of egress. However, areas under exterior ceilings where the building is sprinklered should be protected due to the occupancy above. [13: A.8.15.7.2]

A.13.3.2.6.5 Short-term transient storage, such as that for delivered packages, and the presence of planters, newspaper machines, and so forth, should not be considered storage or handling of combustibles. The presence of combustible furniture on balconies for occupant use should not require sprinkler protection. [13: A.8.15.7.5]

A.13.3.2.7.3(1) It is the intent to permit a single multipurpose room of less than 12,000 ft² (1115 m²) to have certain small rooms as part of the single room. These rooms could be a kitchen, office, equipment room, and the like. It is also the intent that an addition could be made to an existing building without requiring that the existing building be sprinklered, where both the new and existing buildings have independent means of egress and a fire-rated separation is provided to isolate one building from the other. [*101*: A.12.3.5.3(1)]

A school gymnasium with egress independent of, and separated from, the school would be included in this exception, as would a function hall attached to a church with a similar egress arrangement. [*101*: A.12.3.5.3(1)]

A.13.3.2.7.3(3) Examples of low fire hazard uses include spectator sporting events, concerts, and performances on platforms.

The following uses are not low fire hazard uses: concerts and performances on stages; tradeshows; exhibition and display of combustible items; displays of vehicles, boats, or similar items; or events using open flames or pyrotechnic effects. [*101*: A.12.3.5.3(3)]

A.13.3.2.9.1 It is the intent to permit use of the criteria of 8.2.1.3(1) of NFPA *101* to create separate buildings for purposes of limiting educational occupancy building area to not more than 12,000 ft² (1860 m²). [*101*: A.14.3.5.1]

A.13.3.2.11.1 In areas where the replenishment of water supplies is not immediately available from on-site sources, alternate provisions for the water-fill rate requirements of NFPA 13 and NFPA 22 that are acceptable to the AHJ should be provided. Appropriate means for the replenishment of these supplies from other sources, such as fire department tankers, public safety organizations, or other independent contractors should be incorporated into the overall fire safety plan of the facility. [*101*: A.18.3.5.1]

With automatic sprinkler protection required throughout new health care facilities and quick-response sprinklers required in smoke compartments containing patient sleeping rooms, a fire and its life-threatening byproducts can be reduced, thereby allowing the defend-in-place concept to continue. The difficulty in maintaining the proper integrity of life safety elements has been considered and it has been judged that the probability of a sprinkler system operating as designed is equal to or greater than other life safety features. [*101*: A.18.3.5.1]

A.13.3.2.11.4 The requirements for use of quick-response sprinklers intend that quick-response sprinklers be the predominant type of sprinkler installed in the smoke compartment. It is recognized, however, that quick-response sprinklers might not be approved for installation in all areas such as those where NFPA 13 requires sprinklers of the intermediate- or high-temperature classification. It is not the intent of the 13.3.2.11.4 requirements to prohibit the use of standard sprinklers in limited areas of a smoke compartment where intermediate- or high-temperature sprinklers are required. [*101*: A.18.3.5.6]

Residential sprinklers are considered acceptable in patient sleeping rooms of all health care facilities, even though not specifically listed for this purpose in all cases. [*101*: A.18.3.5.6]

Where the installation of quick-response sprinklers is impracticable in patient sleeping room areas, appropriate equivalent protection features acceptable to the AHJ should be provided. It is recognized that the use of quick-response sprinklers might be limited in facilities housing certain types of patients or by the installation limitations of quick-response sprinklers. [*101*: A.18.3.5.6]

A.13.3.2.11.5 This exception is limited to hospitals, as nursing homes and many limited care facilities might have more combustibles within the closets. The limited amount of clothing found in the small clothes closets in hospital patient rooms is typically far less than the amount of combustibles in casework cabinets that do not require sprinkler protection, such as nurse servers. In many hospitals, especially new hospitals, it is difficult to make a distinction between clothes closets and cabinet work. The exception is far more restrictive than similar exceptions for hotels and apartment buildings. NFPA 13 already permits the omission of sprinklers in wardrobes *[see 8.1.1(7) of NFPA 13]*. It is not the intent of 13.3.2.11.5 to affect the wardrobe provisions of NFPA 13. It is the intent that the sprinkler protection in the room covers the closet as if there were no door on the closet. *(See 8.5.3.2.3 of NFPA 13.)* [*101*: A.18.3.5.10]

A.13.3.2.11.6 For the proper operation of sprinkler systems, cubicle curtains and sprinkler locations need to be coordinated. Improperly designed systems might obstruct the sprinkler spray from reaching the fire or might shield the heat from the sprinkler. Many options are available to the designer including, but not limited to, hanging the cubicle curtains 18 in. (455 mm) below the sprinkler deflector; using a ½ in. (13 mm) diagonal mesh or a 70 percent open weave top panel that extends 18 in. (455 mm) below the sprinkler deflector; or designing the system to have a horizontal and minimum vertical distance that meets the requirements of NFPA 13. The test data that form the basis of the NFPA 13 requirements are from fire tests with sprinkler discharge that penetrated a single privacy curtain. [*101:* A.18.3.5.11]

A.13.3.2.12.6 It is not the intent to require existing standard sprinklers in existing sprinkler systems to be replaced with listed quick-response or listed residential sprinklers. It is the intent that new sprinkler systems installed in existing buildings comply with the requirements of Chapter 18 of NFPA *101*, including 18.3.5.6. [*101:* A.19.3.5.4]

A.13.3.2.12.8 It is intended that any valve that controls automatic sprinklers in the building or portions of the building, including sectional and floor control valves, be electrically supervised. Valves that control isolated sprinkler heads, such as in laundry and trash chutes, are not required to be electrically supervised. Appropriate means should be provided to ensure that valves that are not electrically supervised remain open. [*101:* A.19.3.5.7]

A.13.3.2.12.9 The provisions of 13.3.2.12.9(6) and (7) are not intended to supplant NFPA 13, which requires that residential sprinklers with more than a 10°F (5.6°C) difference in temperature rating not be mixed within a room. Currently there are no additional prohibitions in NFPA 13 on the mixing of sprinklers having different thermal response characteristics. Conversely, there are no design parameters to make practical the mixing of residential and other types of sprinklers. [*101:* A.19.3.5.8]

Residential sprinklers are considered acceptable in patient sleeping rooms of all health care facilities, even through not specifically listed for this purpose in all cases. [*101:* A.19.3.5.8]

A.13.3.2.12.11 This exception is limited to hospitals, as nursing homes and many limited care facilities might have more combustibles within the closets. The limited amount of clothing found in the small clothes closets in hospital patient rooms is typically far less than the amount of combustibles in casework cabinets that do not require sprinkler protection, such as nurse servers. In many hospitals, especially new hospitals, it is difficult to make a distinction between clothes closets and cabinet work. The exception is far more restrictive than similar exceptions for hotels and apartment buildings. NFPA 13 already permits the omission of sprinklers in wardrobes *[see 8.1.1(7) of NFPA 13]*. It is not the intent of 13.3.2.12.11 to affect the wardrobe provisions of NFPA 13. It is the intent that the sprinkler protection in the room covers the closet as if there were no door on the closet. *(See 8.5.3.2.3 of NFPA 13.)* [*101:* A.19.3.5.10]

A.13.3.2.12.12 For the proper operation of sprinkler systems, cubicle curtains and sprinkler locations need to be coordinated. Improperly designed systems might obstruct the sprinkler spray from reaching the fire or might shield the heat from the sprinkler. Many options are available to the designer including, but not limited to, hanging the cubicle curtains 18 in. (455 mm) below the sprinkler deflector; using ½ in. (13 mm) diagonal mesh or a 70 percent open weave top panel that extends 18 in. (455 mm) below the sprinkler deflector; or designing the system to have a horizontal and minimum vertical distance that meets the requirements of NFPA 13. The test data that forms the basis of the NFPA 13 requirements is from fire tests with sprinkler discharge that penetrated a single privacy curtain. [*101:* A.19.3.5.11]

A.13.3.2.14.1 Where the openings in ceilings or partitions are ¼ in. (6.3 mm) or larger in the smallest dimension, where the thickness or depth of the material does not exceed the smallest dimension of the openings, and where such openings constitute not less than 70 percent of the area of the ceiling or partition material, the disruption of sprinkler spray patterns is permitted to be disregarded. [*101:* A.23.3.5.2]

A.13.3.2.16.2 Although not required by NFPA *101*, the use of residential sprinklers or quick-response sprinklers is encouraged for new installations of sprinkler systems within dwelling units, apartments, and guest rooms. Caution should be exercised, as the system needs to be designed for the sprinkler being used. [*101:* A.29.3.5.3]

A.13.3.2.18.1 Although not required by NFPA *101*, the use of residential sprinklers or quick-response sprinklers is encouraged for new installations of sprinkler systems within dwelling units, apartments, and guest rooms. Caution should be exercised, because the system needs to be designed for the sprinkler being used. [*101:* A.31.3.5.2]

A.13.3.2.18.3 The provision of 13.3.2.18.3 differs from NFPA 13, *Standard for the Installation of Sprinkler Systems*, because fire data shows that in apartment fires where sprinklers were present, bathrooms were the area of origin in 1 percent of the total fires, and resulted in no civilian deaths, civilian injuries, or property loss. [*101:* A.31.3.5.4]

A.13.3.2.18.7 For example, if an Option 3 sprinkler system were being used to justify use of Class C wall finish in an exit enclosure, the sprinkler system would need to be extended into the exit enclosure, even if the rest of the requirements for Option 3 did not require the sprinklers in the exit enclosure. [*101:* A.31.3.5.11]

A.13.3.2.19.2.3 The decision to permit the use of the criteria from NFPA 13D in these occupancies is based on the following:

(1) The desire to obtain a level of fire suppression and control that is approximately equivalent to that delivered by residential facilities protected by such systems *(see A.1.1 in NFPA 13D)*
(2) The fact that potential fire exposure and challenge to the suppression system in a small lodging and rooming occupancy is of the same nature and no more severe than that found in residences

[*101:* A.26.3.6.2.3]

A.13.3.2.21.2.1 Where any provision requires the use of an automatic sprinkler system in accordance with 13.3.2.21.2, the provision of 13.3.2.21.2.2 is not permitted to be used. [*101:* A.32.2.3.5.1]

A.13.3.2.21.2.2 Where a facility utilizing the provision of 13.3.2.21.2.2 contains residents who can no longer comply with the 3-minute evacuation response, 33.1.8 of NFPA *101* requires the facility to comply with the requirements for new construction, including automatic sprinkler protection. (See also A.33.1.8 of NFPA *101*.) [*101:* A.32.2.3.5.2]

A.13.3.2.21.2.3.2 The decision to permit the use of the criteria from NFPA 13D in these occupancies is based on the following:

(1) The desire to obtain a level of fire suppression and control approximately equivalent to that delivered by residential facilities protected by such systems *(See A.1.1 in NFPA 13D.)*
(2) The fact that potential fire exposure and challenge to the suppression system in a small board and care facility are of the same nature and are no more severe than those found in residences

[*101:* A.32.2.3.5.3.2]

Chapter 13 permits the use of NFPA 13D and NFPA 13R outside of their scopes. This permission is based on a review of the occupancy and a recognition that the fires in board and care facilities are similar to those of other residential occupancies and that the level of protection is appropriate. The requirements of NFPA 13D and NFPA 13R have been supplemented with requirements for additional water supplies to compensate for the special needs of the board and care occupancy. [*101:* A.32.2.3.5.3.2]

NFPA 13D contains additional requirements for a piping system serving both sprinkler and domestic needs. [*101:* A.32.2.3.5.3.2]

A.13.3.2.22.1.1 It is intended that this requirement apply to existing small facilities that are converted to large facilities. [*101:* A.33.3.3.5.1]

Chapter 13 permits the use of NFPA 13D and NFPA 13R outside of their scopes. This permission is based on a review of the occupancy and a recognition that the fires in board and care facilities are similar to those of other residential occupancies and that the level of protection is appropriate. In some circumstances, such as those for impractical evacuation capabilities, the requirements of NFPA 13D and NFPA 13R have been supplemented with requirements for additional water supplies to compensate for the special needs of the board and care occupancy. [*101:* A.33.3.3.5.1]

A.13.3.2.22.2.1.1 The decision to permit the use of the criteria from NFPA 13D in these occupancies is based on the following:

(1) The desire to obtain a level of fire suppression and control approximately equivalent to that delivered by residential facilities protected by such systems *(See A.1.1 in NFPA 13D.)*
(2) The fact that potential fire exposure and challenge to the suppression system in a small board and care facility are of the same nature and are no more severe than those found in residences.

[*101:* A.32.2.3.5.3.1]

Chapter 13 permits the use of NFPA 13D and NFPA 13R outside of their scopes. This permission is based on a review of the occupancy and a recognition that the fires in board and care facilities are similar to those of other residential occupancies and that the level of protection is appropriate. In some circumstances, such as those for impractical evacuation capabilities, the requirements of NFPA 13D and NFPA 13R have been supplemented with requirements for additional water supplies to compensate for the special needs of the board and care occupancy. [*101:* A.33.2.3.5.3.1]

A.13.3.2.26.2 The enabling legislation adopting this *Code* should specify a specific date for compliance with 13.3.2.26.2. Building owners and managers should be notified of this requirement within 180 days of code adoption. The following items should be considered by the AHJ as guidance in evaluating compliance plans:

(1) Shortage of qualified contractors to install sprinkler systems
(2) Impact on owners and tenants as a result of existing conditions contained in lease agreements
(3) Environmental constraints resulting from contaminated material being removed from limited areas of the building during installation of sprinklers and attendant activity
(4) Available time to install sprinklers in the occupied spaces

(5) Financial constraints of owners being able to fund the cost of installing automatic sprinklers with associated costs
(6) Ability of the owner to coordinate general building remodeling with the actual sprinkler retrofit process

A.13.3.2.26.2.3 Examples of retrofit schedules can include the following:

(1) Plan submitted and approved within 1 year; 33 percent of square footage completed within 4 years; 66 percent of square footage completed within 8 years; 100 percent of square footage completed within 12 years.
(2) Plans submitted and approved with 1 year; all common areas completed within 4 years; 50 percent of remaining area completed within 8 years; 100 percent of remaining area completed within 12 years.
(3) An alternative schedule can be approved by the AHJ that does not have any intermediary stages but has to be 100 percent complete within 8 years.

A.13.3.2.27 For the purpose of the requirements in 13.3.2.27.1 through 13.3.2.27.3, combustibles include all combustible materials in storage as well as noncombustible materials that are enclosed, encapsulated, or packaged in combustible materials.

A.13.3.2.27.2 Portions of structures that are subdivided by fire walls can be considered to be separate buildings for the purpose of applying this *Code*. Fire walls by their definition have sufficient structural stability to maintain the integrity of the wall in the event of the collapse of the building construction on either side of the wall.

A.13.3.3.4.1.1 Any portion or all of the inspection, testing, and maintenance can be permitted to be contracted with an inspection, testing, and maintenance service. [**25:** A.4.1.1]

A.13.3.3.4.1.1(A) In order to ensure compliance, the owner should verify that windows, skylights, doors, ventilators, other openings and closures, concealed spaces, unused attics, stair towers, roof houses, and low spaces under buildings do not expose water-filled piping to freezing. This should occur prior to the onset of cold weather and periodically thereafter. [**25:** A.4.1.1.1]

A.13.3.3.4.1.1(C) Examples of designated representatives can include the occupant, management firm, or managing individual through specific provisions in the lease, written use agreement, or management contract. [**25:** A.4.1.1.3]

A.13.3.3.4.1.2 Other means of freeze protection for water-filled piping include heated valve enclosures, heat tracing, insulation, antifreeze solutions, or other methods are allowed by the applicable installation standard. Installation standards require heat tracing protecting fire protection piping against freezing to be supervised. [**25:** A.4.1.2]

A.13.3.3.4.1.3 The components are not required to be open or exposed. Doors, removable panels, or valve pits can be permitted to satisfy the need for accessibility. Such equipment should not be obstructed by features such as walls, ducts, columns, direct burial, or stock storage. [**25:** A.4.1.3]

A.13.3.3.4.1.5 Recalled products should be replaced or remedied. Remedies include entrance into a program for scheduled replacement. Such replacement or remedial product should be installed in accordance with the manufacturer's instructions and the appropriate NFPA installation standards. A recalled product is a product subject to a statute or administrative regulation specifically requiring the manufacturer, importer, distributor, wholesaler, or retailer of a product, or any combination of such entities, to recall the product, or a product voluntarily recalled by a combination of such entities. [**25:** A.4.1.5]

Needed corrections and repairs should be classified as an impairment, critical deficiency, or noncritical deficiency according to the effect on the fire protection system and the nature of the hazard protected. [**25:** A.4.1.5]

Impairments are the highest priority problem found during inspection, testing, and maintenance and should be corrected as soon as possible. The fire protection system cannot provide an adequate response to a fire, and implementation of impairment procedures outlined in 13.3.3.6 is required until the impairment is corrected. [**25:** A.4.1.5]

Critical deficiencies need to be corrected in a timely fashion. The fire protection system is still capable of performing, but its performance can be impacted and the implementation of impairment procedures might not be needed. However, special consideration must be given to the hazard in the determination of the classification. A deficiency that is critical for one hazard might be an impairment in another. [**25:** A.4.1.5]

Noncritical deficiencies do not affect the performance of the fire protection system but should be corrected in a reasonable time period so that the system can be properly inspected, tested, and maintained. [**25:** A.4.1.5]

Assembly occupancies, health care facilities, prisons, high-rise buildings, other occupancies where the life safety exposure is significant, or facilities that cannot be evacuated in a timely manner require special consideration. As an example, a nonfunctioning waterflow alarm might be considered a critical deficiency in a storage warehouse but an impairment in a hospital. [**25:** A.4.1.5]

High hazard occupancies where early response to a fire is critical also require special consideration. A small number of painted sprinklers could be considered an impairment for a system protecting a high hazard occupancy but might be considered a critical deficiency in a metal working shop. [**25:** A.4.1.5]

Classifications of needed corrections and repairs are shown in Table A.3.3.7 of NFPA 25. [**25:** A.4.1.5]

A.13.3.3.4.1.5.1 System deficiencies not explained by normal wear and tear, such as hydraulic shock, can often be indicators of system problems and should be investigated and evaluated by a qualified person or engineer. Failure to address these issues could lead to catastrophic failure. Examples of deficiencies that can be caused by issues beyond normal wear and tear are as follows:

(1) Pressure gauge deficiencies as follows:
  (a) Gauge not returning to zero
  (b) Gauge off scale
  (c) Gauge with bent needle
(2) Support devices deficiencies as follows:
  (a) Bent hangers and/or rods
  (b) Hangers pulled out/off structure
  (c) Indication of pipe or hanger movement such as the following:
    i. Hanger scrape marks on pipe, exposed pipe surface where pipe and hangers are painted
    ii. Firestop material damaged at pipe penetration of fire-rated assembly
(3) Unexplained system damage as follows:
  (a) Unexplained system damage beyond normal wear and tear
  (b) Bent or broken shafts on valves
  (c) Bent or broken valve clappers
  (d) Unexplained leakage at branch lines, cross main, or feed main piping
  (e) Unexplained leakage at closed nipples
  (f) Loose bolts on flanges and couplings
(4) Fire pump deficiencies as follows:
  (a) Fire pump driver out of alignment
  (b) Vibration of fire pump and/or driver
  (c) Unusual sprinkler system piping noises (sharp report, loud bang)

[**25:** A.4.1.5.1]

A.13.3.3.4.1.6 The inspections and tests specified in this *Code* do not address the adequacy of design criteria or the capability of the fire protection system to protect the building or its contents. It is assumed that the original system design and installation were appropriate for the occupancy and use of the building and were approved by all applicable AHJs. If no changes to the water supply or to the building or its use have transpired since it was originally occupied, no evaluation is required. If changes are contemplated, it is the owner's responsibility to arrange for the evaluation of the fire protection system(s). Where the inspections and tests specified in the *Code* have been contracted to a qualified inspection provider or contractor, it is not the role of the inspector or contractor to determine if any changes have been made or the subsequent evaluation of the fire protection system. The evaluation of any building changes should be conducted before any proposed change is incorporated and should utilize the appropriate installation standard and input from applicable AHJs. [**25:** A.4.1.6]

Fire protection systems should not be removed from service when the building is not in use; however, where a system that has been out of service for a prolonged period (such as in the case of idle or vacant properties) is returned to service, it is recommended that a responsible and experienced contractor be retained to perform all inspections and tests. [**25:** A.4.1.6]

A.13.3.3.4.1.7 See Annex E of NFPA 25 for an example of a hazard evaluation form. A hazard evaluation is not part of a system inspection. [**25:** A.4.1.7]

A.13.3.3.4.3.1 Inspection reports used for system inspections should contain an "Owner's Section" as shown in Figure A.13.3.3.4.3.1 that the property owner or designated representative should complete. Typical records include, but are not limited to, valve inspections; flow, drain, and pump tests; and trip tests of dry pipe, deluge, and preaction valves. [**25:** A.4.3.1]

Acceptance test records should be retained for the life of the system or its special components. Subsequent test records should be retained for a period of 1 year after the next test. The comparison determines deterioration of system performance or condition and the need for further testing or maintenance. [**25:** A.4.3.1]

A.13.3.3.4.3.1.1 Computer programs that file inspection and test results should provide a means of comparing current and past results and should indicate the need for corrective maintenance or further testing. [**25:** A.4.3.1.1]

A.13.3.3.4.3.3 See Section B.2 of NFPA 25 for information regarding sample forms. [**25:** A.4.3.3]

A.13.3.3.5.1.2 To help in the replacement of like sprinklers, unique sprinkler identification numbers (SINs) are provided on all sprinklers manufactured after January 1, 2001. The SIN accounts for differences in orifice size, deflector characteristics, pressure rating, and thermal sensitivity. [**25:** A.5.4.1.2]

Owner's Section

A. Is the building occupied? ☐ Yes ☐ No

B. Has the occupancy and hazard of contents remained the same since the last inspection? ☐ Yes ☐ No

C. Are all fire protection systems in service? ☐ Yes ☐ No

D. Has the system remained in service without modification since the last inspection? ☐ Yes ☐ No

E. Was the system free of actuation of devices or alarms since the last inspection? ☐ Yes ☐ No

Explain any "no" answers:

_____

_____

_____

_____

_____

Owner or Designated Representative (print)   Signature and Date

© 2014 National Fire Protection Association   NFPA 25

FIGURE A.13.3.3.4.3.1 Owner's Section on Inspection Report. [25:Figure A.4.3.1]

A.13.3.3.5.1.2.1 Old-style sprinklers are permitted to replace existing old-style sprinklers. Old-style sprinklers should not be used to replace standard sprinklers without a complete engineering review of the system. The old-style sprinkler is the type manufactured before 1953. It discharges approximately 40 percent of the water upward to the ceiling, and it can be installed in either the upright or pendent position. [25: A.5.4.1.2.1]

A.13.3.3.5.1.4 It is imperative that any replacement sprinkler have the same characteristics as the sprinkler being replaced. If the same temperature range, response characteristics, spacing requirements, flow rates, and K-factors cannot be obtained, a sprinkler with similar characteristics should be used, and the system should be evaluated to verify the sprinkler is appropriate for the intended use. With regard to response characteristics, matching identical Response Time Index (RTI) and conductivity factors is not necessary unless special design considerations are given for those specific values. [25: A.5.4.1.4]

A.13.3.3.5.1.5 A minimum of two sprinklers of each type and temperature rating installed should be provided. [25: A.5.4.1.5]

A.13.3.3.5.1.5.5 One sprinkler wrench design can be appropriate for many types of sprinklers, and multiple wrenches of the same design should not be required. [25: A.5.4.1.5.5]

A.13.3.3.5.1.5.6.1 The minimum information in the list contained in the spare sprinkler cabinet should be marked with the following:

(1) General description of the sprinkler, including upright, pendent, residential, ESFR, and so forth

(2) Quantity of sprinklers that is to be maintained in the spare sprinkler cabinet.

An example of the list is shown in Figure A.13.3.3.5.1.5.6.1. [25: A.5.4.1.5.6.1]

Sprinklers Contained in this Cabinet			
Sprinkler Identification, SIN	General Description	Temperature Rating, °F	Sprinkler Quantity Maintained
TY9128	Extended Coverage, K-25, upright	155	6
VK425	Concealed pendent residential	145	6
Issued: 10/3/05	Revised:		

FIGURE A.13.3.3.5.1.5.6.1 Sample List. [25:Figure A.5.4.1.5.6.1]

A.13.3.3.5.1.6 Corrosion-resistant or specially coated sprinklers should be installed in locations where chemicals, moisture, or other corrosive vapors exist. [25: A.5.4.1.6]

A.13.3.3.5.1.8.1 Typical sandwich bags purchased in a grocery store are generally plastic, not cellophane. Plastic bags have a tendency to shrink and adhere to the sprinkler prior to sprinkler activation, creating the potential for disruption of sprinkler spray patterns. Bags placed over sprinklers need to be true cellophane or paper. [**25:** A.5.4.1.8.1]

A.13.3.3.5.2 Conversion of dry pipe systems to wet pipe systems on a seasonal basis causes corrosion and accumulation of foreign matter in the pipe system and loss of alarm service. [**25:** A.5.4.2]

A.13.3.3.6.3.1 A clearly visible tag alerts building occupants and the fire department that all or part of the water-based fire protection system is out of service. The tag should be weather resistant, plainly visible, and of sufficient size [typically 4 in. × 6 in. (100 mm × 150 mm)]. The tag should identify which system is impaired, the date and time impairment began, and the person responsible. Figure A.13.3.3.6.3.1 illustrates a typical impairment tag. [**25:** A.15.3.1]

FIGURE A.13.3.3.6.3.1 Sample Impairment Tag. [25:Figure A.15.3.1]

A.13.3.3.6.3.2 An impairment tag should be placed on the fire department connection to alert responding fire fighters of an abnormal condition. An impairment tag that is located on the system riser only could go unnoticed for an extended period if fire fighters encounter difficulty in gaining access to the building or sprinkler control room. [**25:** A.15.3.2]

A.13.3.3.6.5 The need for temporary fire protection, termination of all hazardous operations, and frequency of inspections in the areas involved should be determined. All work possible should be done in advance to minimize the length of the impairment. Where possible, temporary feedlines should be used to maintain portions of systems while work is completed. [**25:** A.15.5]

Water-based fire protection systems should not be removed from service when the building is not in use. Where a system that has been out of service for a prolonged period, such as in the case of idle or vacant properties, is returned to service, qualified personnel should be retained to inspect and test the systems. [**25:** A.15.5]

A.13.3.3.6.5.2(4)(b) A fire watch should consist of trained personnel who continuously patrol the affected area. Ready access to fire extinguishers and the ability to promptly notify the fire department are important items to consider. During the patrol of the area, the person should not only be looking for fire, but making sure that the other fire protection features of the building such as egress routes and alarm systems are available and functioning properly. [**25:** A.15.5.2(4)(b)]

A.13.3.3.6.5.2(4)(c) Temporary water supplies are possible from a number of sources, including use of a large-diameter hose from a fire hydrant to a fire department connection, use of a portable tank and a portable pump, or use of a standby fire department pumper and/or tanker. [**25:** A.15.5.2(4)(c)]

A.13.3.3.6.5.2(4)(d) Depending on the use and occupancy of the building, it could be enough in some circumstances to stop certain processes in the building or to cut off the flow of fuel to some machines. It is also helpful to implement "No Smoking" and "No Hot Work" (cutting, grinding, or welding) policies while the system is out of service because these activities are responsible for many fire ignitions. [**25:** A.15.5.2(4)(d)]

A.13.3.3.6.6 Emergency impairments include, but are not limited to, system leakage, interruption of water supply, frozen or ruptured piping, equipment failure, or other impairments found during inspection, testing, or maintenance activities. [**25:** A.15.6]

A.13.3.3.6.6.2 When one or more impairments are discovered during inspection, testing, and maintenance activities the owner or owner's authorized representative should be notified in writing. See Figure A.13.3.3.6.6.2 for an example of written notification. [**25:** A.15.6.2]

A.13.3.3.6.7 Occasionally, fire protection systems in idle or vacant buildings are shut off and drained. When the equipment is eventually restored to service after a long period of not being maintained, it is recommended that a qualified person perform the work. The following is an example of a procedure:

(1) All piping should be traced from the extremities of the system to the main connections with a careful check for blank gaskets in flanges, closed valves, corroded or damaged sprinklers, nozzles or piping, insecure or missing hangers and insufficient support. Proper repairs or adjustments should be made and needed extensions or alterations for the equipment should be completed.

(2) An air test at low pressure (40 psi) should be conducted prior to allowing water to fill the system. When the piping has been proven tight by passing the air test, water can be introduced slowly into the system with proper precautions against damage by escape of water from previously undiscovered defects. When the system has been filled under normal service pressure, drain valve tests should be made to detect any closed valve that possible could have been overlooked. All available pipes should be flushed and an obstruction investigation completed to make sure that the system is clear of debris.

IMPAIRMENT NOTICE

DURING A RECENT INSPECTION OF YOUR FIRE PROTECTION SYSTEM(S), AN ***EMERGENCY IMPAIRMENT*** WAS DISCOVERED AND INDICATED ON THE INSPECTION REPORT. AS DEFINED BY NFPA 25, AN ***EMERGENCY IMPAIRMENT*** IS "A CONDITION WHERE A WATER-BASED FIRE PROTECTION SYSTEM OR PORTION THEREOF IS OUT OF ORDER DUE TO AN UNEXPECTED OCCURRENCE, SUCH AS A RUPTURED PIPE, OPERATED SPRINKLER, OR AN INTERRUPTION OF WATER SUPPLY TO THE SYSTEM." NFPA 25 FURTHER STATES, "EMERGENCY IMPAIRMENTS INCLUDE BUT ARE NOT LIMITED TO SYSTEM LEAKAGE, INTERRUPTION OF WATER SUPPLY, FROZEN OR RUPTURED PIPING, AND EQUIPMENT FAILURE."

WE RECOMMEND THAT IMMEDIATE STEPS BE TAKEN, AS DESCRIBED IN THE ATTACHED COPY OF CHAPTER 15 OF NFPA 25, TO CORRECT THE FOLLOWING IMPAIRMENT(S) TO YOUR FIRE PROTECTION SYSTEM(S):

[ ] CONTROL VALVE SHUT. SYSTEM OUT OF SERVICE.
[ ] LOW WATER PRESSURE DURING FLOW TEST. POSSIBLE OBSTRUCTION IN WATER SUPPLY OR PARTIALLY SHUT VALVE.
[ ] PIPE(S) FROZEN.
[ ] PIPE(S) LEAKING.
[ ] PIPE(S) ARE OBSTRUCTED.
[ ] SYSTEM PIPING OR PORTIONS OF SYSTEM PIPING ARE DISCONNECTED.
[ ] FIRE DEPT. CONNECTION MISSING OR DAMAGED OR OBSTRUCTED.
[ ] DRY PIPE VALVE CANNOT BE RESET.
[ ] DRY PIPE SYSTEM QUICK OPENING DEVICE IS OUT OF SERVICE.
[ ] SPRINKLERS ARE PAINTED, CORRODED, DAMAGED, OR LOADED.
[ ] FIRE PUMP IS OUT OF SERVICE.
[ ] DETECTION/ACTUATION SYSTEM IS OUT OF SERVICE.
[ ] OTHER: _____

FIGURE A.13.3.3.6.6.2 Sample Impairment Notice.

(3) Where the system was known to have been damaged by freezing or where other extensive damage may have occurred, a full hydrostatic test can be performed in accordance with NFPA 13 to determine whether the system integrity has been maintained.
(4) Dry-pipe valves, quick opening devices, alarm valves and all alarm connections should be examined, put in proper condition and tested.
(5) Fire pumps, pressure and gravity tanks, reservoirs and other water supply equipment should receive proper attention before being placed in service. Each supply should be tested separately; and then together if they are designed to work together.
(6) All control valves should be operated from the closed to fully open position and should be left sealed, locked or equipped with a tamper switch.
[25: A.15.7]

A.13.4.1.4 Because of the unique nature of fire pump units, the approval should be obtained prior to the assembly of any specific component. [20: A.4.2]

A.13.4.2 Special consideration needs to be given to fire pump installations installed belowgrade. Light, heat, drainage, and ventilation are several of the variables that need to be addressed. Some locations or installations might not require a pump house. Where a pump room or pump house is required, it should be of ample size and located to permit short and properly arranged piping. The suction piping should receive first consideration. The pump house should preferably be a detached building of noncombustible construction. A one-story pump room with a combustible roof, either detached or well cut off from an adjoining one-story building, is acceptable if sprinklered. Where a detached building is not feasible, the pump room should be located and constructed so as to protect the pump unit and controls from falling floors or machinery and from fire that could drive away the pump operator or damage the pump unit or controls. Access to the pump room should be provided from outside the building. Where the use of brick or reinforced concrete is not feasible, metal lath and plaster is recommended for the construction of the pump room. The pump room or pump house should not be used for storage purposes. Vertical shaft turbine–type pumps might necessitate a removable panel in the pump house roof to permit the pump to be removed for inspection or repair. Proper clearances to equipment should be provided as recommended by the manufacturer's drawings. [20: A.4.12]

A.13.4.2.1 A fire pump that is inoperative for any reason at any time constitutes an impairment to the fire protection system. It should be returned to service without delay. [20: A.4.12.1]

Rain and intense heat from the sun are adverse conditions to equipment not installed in a completely protective enclosure. At a minimum, equipment installed outdoors should be shielded by a roof or deck. [20: A.4.12.1]

A.13.4.2.1.1 Most fire departments have procedures requiring operation of a fire pump unit during an incident. Building designers should locate the fire pump room to be easily accessible during an incident. [20: A.4.12.1.1]

A.13.4.2.1.1.2 The purpose for the "Not Sprinklered" column in Table 13.4.2.1.1.2 is to provide guidance for unsprinklered buildings. This does not permit sprinklers to be omitted from pump rooms in fully sprinklered buildings. [20: A.4.12.1.1.2]

A.13.4.2.1.1.4 Equipment that increases the fire hazard (such as boilers) and is not related to fire protection systems should not be in a fire pump room. [20: A.4.12.1.1.4]

A.13.4.2.7 Pump rooms and pump houses should be dry and free of condensate. To accomplish a dry environment, heat might be necessary. [20: A.4.12.7]

A.13.4.3 Isolation valves and control valves are considered to be identical when used in conjunction with a backflow prevention assembly. [20: A.4.16]

A.13.4.4 Internal combustion engines necessarily embody moving parts of such design and in such number that the engines cannot give reliable service unless given diligent care. The manufacturer's instruction book covering care and operation should be readily available, and pump operators should be familiar with its contents. All of its provisions should be observed in detail. [20: A.11.6]

A.13.4.4.2 See NFPA 25, *Standard for the Inspection, Testing, and Maintenance of Water-Based Fire Protection Systems*, for proper maintenance of engine(s), batteries, fuel supply, and environmental conditions. [20: A.11.6.2]

A.13.4.4.4 Active systems that are permanently added to fuel tanks for removing water and particulates from the fuel can be acceptable, provided the following apply:

(1) All connections are made directly to the tank and are not interconnected with the engine or its fuel supply and return piping in any way.
(2) There are no valves or other devices added to the engine or its fuel supply and return piping in any way.

[**20:** A.11.6.4]

A.13.4.4.5 Proper engine temperature, in accordance with 11.2.8.2 of NFPA 20 and 13.4.4.5.1, maintained through the use of a supplemental heater has many benefits, as follows:

(1) Quick starting (a fire pump engine might have to carry a full load as soon as it is started)
(2) Reduced engine wear
(3) Reduced drain on batteries
(4) Reduced oil dilution
(5) Reduced carbon deposits, so that the engine is far more likely to start every time

[**20:** A.11.6.5]

A.13.4.5.1.2 It is recommended that the pilot lamp for signal service have operating voltage less than the rated voltage of the lamp to ensure long operating life. When necessary, a suitable resistor should be used to reduce the voltage for operating the lamp. [**20:** A.12.4.1.2]

A.13.4.5.1.4(1) The controller can set the signal trip point above the two-thirds level. But, higher than ¾ of nominal is not recommended to avoid false signals during normal battery aging. [**20:** A.12.4.1.4(1)]

A.13.4.5.1.6 This automatic reset function can be accomplished by the use of a silence switch of the automatic reset type or of the self-supervising type. [**20:** A.12.4.1.6]

A.13.4.5.2.3(3) The following signals should be monitored remotely from the controller:

(1) A common signal can be used for the following trouble indications: the items in 13.4.5.1.4(1) through 13.4.5.1.4(7) and loss of output of battery charger on the load side of the dc overcurrent protective device.
(2) If there is no other way to supervise loss of power, the controller can be equipped with a power failure circuit, which should be time delayed to start the engine upon loss of current output of the battery charger.
(3) The arrangement specified in A.13.4.5.2.3(3)(2) is only permitted where approved by the AHJ in accordance with Section 1.5 of NFPA 20 and allows, upon loss of the ac power supply, the batteries to maintain their charge, activates ventilation in case conditions require cooling the engine, and/or maintains engine temperature in case conditions require heating the engine. *(See also A.4.6.4 and A.11.4.2.1 of NFPA 20.)*

[**20:** A.12.4.2.3(3)]

A.13.4.6.1 In addition, representatives of the installing contractor, insurance company, and owner should be present. [**20:** A.14.2.1]

A.13.4.6.4 If a complete fire pump submittal package is available, it should provide for comparison of the equipment specified. Such a package should include an approved copy of the fire pump room general arrangement drawings, including the electrical layout, the layout of the pump and water source, the layout of the pump room drainage details, the pump foundation layout, and the mechanical layout for heat and ventilation. [**20:** A.14.2.4]

A.13.4.7 It is the intent to retain the record drawing, equipment manual, and completed test report for the life of the fire pump system. [**20:** A.14.3]

A.13.4.7.3 Consideration should be given to stocking spare parts for critical items not readily available. [**20:** A.14.3.3]

A.13.4.7.4(6) Recommended spare parts and lubricants should be stored on-site to minimize system impairment. [**20:** A.14.3.4(6)]

A.13.5.3 The installation of backflow prevention devices on services supplying water to existing fire protection systems can result in excessive pressure losses. Therefore, installation of backflow prevention devices to protect public health has to be accomplished with due regard for the implications on fire protection. The provisions of AWWA Manual 14, *Backflow Prevention and Cross Connection Control*, should be used as a guide for determining the appropriate protection for public health. Hydraulic calculations and water supply analysis should be conducted prior to installation to determine the impact on fire protection.

A.13.6.1.2 Employees expected or anticipated to use fire extinguishers should be instructed on the hazards of fighting fire, how to properly operate the fire extinguishers available, and what procedures to follow in alerting others to the fire emergency.

The intended application of footnote e in Table 13.6.1.2 is for warehouse areas that are generally unoccupied except by operators on forklifts or similar vehicles or occasional workers or maintenance personnel. The footnote is not intended to apply to office or process areas. Office and process areas have to be provided with fixed extinguishers in accordance with NFPA 10 and applicable provisions in this *Code*.

A.13.6.1.3.1 Listed and labeled halon portable fire extinguishers currently comply with Section 13.6 and have demonstrated compliance with the requirements of UL-1093, *Standard for Halogenated Agent Fire Extinguishers*, which also includes fire testing and rating criteria. As a result of the Montreal Protocol on Substances that Deplete the Ozone Layer, UL has withdrawn UL-1093. This does not imply that extinguishers that are listed and labeled to the requirements of UL-1093 are unsafe for use as fire extinguishers, nor does it mean that UL or the EPA is requiring halon extinguishers be removed from service. It does mean that UL will not accept new designs of halon extinguishers for testing or UL listing. It also means that no changes or updates are allowed to models that are currently listed and that had previously demonstrated compliance with UL 1093. [**10:** A.4.1.1]

Extinguisher manufacturers are allowed to manufacture their current design of UL-listed halon extinguishers with the UL listing mark until October 2014. Halon extinguishers currently in use will continue to be listed beyond the 2014 date and should be permitted to be used to comply with the requirements of NFPA 10 and this *Code* when installed, inspected, and maintained in accordance with NFPA 10 and this *Code*. [**10:** A.4.1.1]

A.13.6.1.3.2 AHJs should determine the acceptability and credibility of the organization listing or labeling fire extinguishers. Authorities should determine if the organization tests to all the requirements of NFPA 10. Factors such as the structure of the organization, its principal fields of endeavor, its reputation and established expertise, its involvement in the standards-writing process, and the extent of its follow-up service programs should all be assessed before recognition is given. [**10:** A.4.1.2]

The listing and labeling organization identification marking might be in the form of a symbol of the organization. The product category marking should identify the extinguisher, for example, "Carbon Dioxide Fire Extinguisher," "Dry Chemical Fire Extinguisher," or "Clean Agent Fire Extinguisher." Extinguisher ratings should indicate the classification of fire type, such as A, B, or C, and the associated fire size. An example of an extinguisher rating is 1-A: 5-B:C, which designates a Class A fire (wood) rating with an associated fire size of 1, as described in ANSI/UL711, CAN/ULC-S508, *Standard for Rating and Testing of Fire Extinguishers*; a Class B fire (flammable liquid) rating with an associated fire size of 5, as described in ANSI/UL711, CAN/ULC-S508; and a Class C compatible rating as described in ANSI/UL711, CAN/ULC-S508. [**10:** A.4.1.2]

A.13.6.1.3.3 AHJs should determine the thoroughness of the factory follow-up quality assurance program exercised by third-party certification organizations listing and labeling portable fire extinguishers. The specified factory follow-up standard provides a minimum basis for that determination. Application of the factory follow-up standard provides a reasonable assurance that portable fire extinguishers sold to the public continue to have the same structural reliability and performance as the fire extinguishers the manufacturer originally submitted to the listing and labeling organization for evaluation. [**10:** A.4.1.3]

A.13.6.1.4 Federal OSHA regulations require that manufacturers communicate information as to the type of chemicals in a product that can be hazardous and the level of hazard. This information is contained in the MSDS created for each chemical or mixture of chemicals and is summarized on labels or tags attached to the product. Additionally, state and local authorities have enacted similar acts and regulations requiring identification of chemicals and hazardous ingredients in products. MSDSs for fire extinguisher agents are available on request from fire equipment dealers or distributors or the fire equipment manufacturer. [**10:** A.4.2]

The identification of contents information enables determination of the type of chemicals contained in the fire extinguisher and helps to resolve complications arising from an unusual use of the agent. The HMIS (in Canada, the WHMIS) developed by the National Paint and Coatings Association uses a three-place format with numerical indexes from 0 to 4. The first place is for "toxic properties," the second place is for "flammability," and the third place is for "reactivity" with other chemicals. Most fire extinguishers have a 0 numerical index in the second and third places because they are nonflammable and relatively inert. [**10:** A.4.2]

Information on the HMIS can be obtained from Label Master, Inc., in Chicago, IL, or from the National Paint and Coatings Association in Washington, DC. Extinguisher contents information can be integrated into the standard fire extinguisher label in some form, or it can be on a separate label or tag. The following example is a typical chemical contents identification marking:

CONTENTS: ABC DRY CHEMICAL/HMIS 1-0-0 MUSCOVITE MICA, MONOAMMONIUM PHOSPHATE AMMONIUM SULFATE/NUISANCE DUST IRRITANT/CONTENTS UNDER PRESSURE [Manufacturer's Name, Mailing Address, Phone Number]

[**10:** A.4.2]

A.13.6.1.5 The manual can be specific to the fire extinguisher involved, or it can cover many types. [**10:** A.4.3]

A.13.6.1.6.1 The requirement in 13.6.1.6.1 brings the standard into line with the 1984 changes to UL 299, *Dry Chemical Fire Extinguishers*, and to UL 711, *Rating and Fire Testing of Fire Extinguishers*.

(1) *Hose.* The 1984 edition of UL 299 requires extinguishers rated 2A or higher or 20-B or higher to be equipped with a discharge hose. Before this change, almost all 5 lb extinguishers and many 10 lb extinguishers were equipped with a fixed nozzle on the outlet of the extinguisher valve and no hoses. These extinguishers, rated 2A to 4A and 10B to 60B are the ones used to comply with the installation requirements now contained in Chapter 6 of NFPA 10. To properly use one of these extinguishers, the user must keep it in the upright position, apply the dry chemical to the base of the fire, and sweep the discharge back and forth. The requirement for the addition of a hose to these extinguishers came out of the novice fire tests sponsored by Underwriters Laboratories (UL) and the Fire Equipment Manufacturers Association. The film footage of these tests shows that persons who had never used a fire extinguisher before often used both hands to operate these extinguishers, turning the extinguisher cylinder in a horizontal position while squeezing the handle and lever to open the valve. Sometimes they even inverted the extinguisher. The result of such actions is only a partial discharge of the extinguisher contents or possibly only the expellant gas and therefore no extinguishment of the fire. The addition of a hose also makes it much easier to direct the discharge at the base of the flames and to sweep the discharge from side to side. The requirement to add a hose makes it more likely that the extinguisher will be used in an upright position. In fact, it is almost impossible to do otherwise, since one hand opens the valve and the other hand, which holds the hose, directs the discharge stream to the fire. It is important to note that field modification of an extinguisher is generally not allowed since the modification might not have been evaluated to comply with the test requirements in the applicable UL extinguisher standards, and the extinguisher might not operate as intended. Thus, a fixed nozzle cannot simply be removed from an extinguisher and replaced with a hose and nozzle.

(2) *Minimum Discharge Time.* This requirement, found in the 1984 edition of UL 711, requires a minimum 13-second discharge duration for an extinguisher rated 2A or higher. The 13-second minimum requirement was the result of recommendations from the novice fire tests mentioned in A.13.6.1.6.1(1). Before 1984, almost all 2A-rated dry chemical extinguishers had discharge durations of only 8 to 10 seconds. The novice fire tests clearly showed that longer discharge duration resulted in an increased likelihood of extinguishment. The revision to UL 711 mandated a 50 percent to 60 percent increase in the minimum discharge duration for a 2A-rated dry chemical extinguisher. Modification of extinguishers with a nozzle/hose that gives different or longer discharge duration is not allowed. Such modification would not have been evaluated to comply with the test requirements in the applicable UL extinguisher standards, and the extinguisher might not operate as intended.

(3) *Pull Pins.* A revision to the extinguisher standards, including UL 299, required a maximum 30 lb of force to remove

a safety pin or pull pin from an extinguisher. This again came from the novice testing, in which some individuals could not physically remove the pin and actuate the extinguisher. The UL extinguisher standards also included a design requirement so the pin is visible from the front of the extinguisher unless noted by the operating instructions.

(4) *Operating Instructions/Marking.* The extinguisher standards, including the 1984 revision of UL 299, mandated the use of pictographic operating instructions and code symbols on all but Class D extinguishers and wheeled extinguishers. These requirements also came out of the novice fire tests, which showed many individuals taking too long to read and understand the written operating instructions. The novice tests actually developed the pictographic operating instructions and tested them on novice operators for effectiveness. The details of the number of instructions per pictogram came from the test program. The novice fire test was also the impetus to making the use code symbols for the various classes of fires more understandable. The new pictographic use code symbols were also mandated in 1984 as well as a uniform method of applying A, B, and C symbols to extinguishers with ABC or BC only ratings. The result was a uniform, consistent set of easily understood symbols that made the extinguisher more user friendly.

(5) *Service Manuals.* The extinguisher standards, including UL 299, for the first time mandated that extinguisher manufacturers have a service manual for their products. In addition, the 1984 edition of UL 299 required a reference to the service/maintenance manual on the extinguisher nameplate. Prior to 1984, service manuals were not required.

[**10:** A.4.4.1]

A.13.6.1.6.2 Fire extinguishers manufactured by companies that are no longer in business can remain in use if they meet the requirements of NFPA 10 and this *Code*, and are maintained in accordance with the manufacturer's service manual. When these extinguishers require recharging or maintenance and the required extinguishing agent or necessary repair parts are not available, the extinguishers should be removed from service. [**10:** A.4.4.2]

A.13.6.2.3.2.1 Examples of extinguishers for protecting Class A hazards are as follows:

(1) Water type
(2) Halogenated agent type *(For halogenated agent–type fire extinguishers, see 13.6.2.3.2.6.)*
(3) Multipurpose dry chemical type
(4) Wet chemical type

[**10:** A.5.3.2.1]

A.13.6.2.3.2.2 Examples of extinguishers for protecting Class B hazards are as follows:

(1) Aqueous film-forming foam (AFFF)
(2) Film-forming fluoroprotein foam (FFFP)
(3) Carbon dioxide
(4) Dry chemical type
(5) Halogenated agent type *(For halogenated agent–type fire extinguishers, see 13.6.2.3.2.6.)*

[**10:** A.5.3.2.2]

A.13.6.2.3.2.3 The use of dry chemical fire extinguishers on wet energized electrical equipment (such as rain-soaked utility poles, high-voltage switch gear, and transformers) could aggravate electrical leakage problems. The dry chemical in combination with moisture provides an electrical path that can reduce the effectiveness of insulation protection. The removal of all traces of dry chemical from such equipment after extinguishment is recommended. [**10:** A.5.3.2.3]

A.13.6.2.3.2.4 The following information pertains to Class D hazards:

(1) Chemical reaction between burning metals and many extinguishing agents (including water) can range from explosive to inconsequential, depending in part on the type, form, and quantity of metal involved. In general, the hazards from a metal fire are significantly increased when such extinguishing agents are applied. The advantages and limitations of a wide variety of commercially available metal fire extinguishing agents are discussed in NFPA 484, *Standard for Combustible Metals,* and in Section 6, Chapter 9, of the NFPA *Fire Protection Handbook.* The MSDS of the Class D hazard being protected or the extinguisher manufacturer should be consulted.

(2) The agents and fire extinguishers discussed in this section are of specialized types, and their use often involves special techniques peculiar to a particular combustible metal. A given agent will not necessarily control or extinguish all metal fires. Some agents are valuable in working with several metals; others are useful in combating only one type of metal fire. The AHJs should be consulted in each case to determine the desired protection for the particular hazard involved.

(3) Certain combustible metals require special extinguishing agents or techniques. See NFPA 484, , for additional information. If there is doubt, NFPA 484 or the NFPA *Fire Protection Guide to Hazardous Materials* should be consulted. (NFPA 49, *Hazardous Chemicals Data,* and NFPA 325, *Guide to Fire Hazard Properties of Flammable Liquids, Gases, and Volatile Solids,* have been officially withdrawn from the *National Fire Codes,* but the information is contained in the NFPA *Fire Protection Guide to Hazardous Materials.*)

(4) Reference should be made to the manufacturer's recommendations for use and special techniques for extinguishing fires in various combustible metals.

(5) Fire of high intensity can occur in certain metals. Ignition is generally the result of frictional heating, exposure to moisture, or exposure from a fire in other combustible materials. The greatest hazard exists when these metals are in the molten state or in finely divided forms of dust, turnings, or shavings.

[**10:** A.5.3.2.4]

The properties of a wide variety of combustible metals and the agents available for extinguishing fires in these metals are discussed in NFPA 484 and the NFPA *Fire Protection Handbook.* [**10:** A.5.3.2.4]

A.13.6.2.3.2.6 Halon agent is highly effective for extinguishing fire and evaporates after use, leaving no residue. Halon agent is, however, included in the Montreal Protocol list of controlled substances developed under the United Nations Environment Program. Where agents other than halon can satisfactorily protect the hazard, they should be used instead of halon. Halon use should be limited to extinguishment of unwanted fire; it should not be used for routine training of personnel. [**10:** A.5.3.2.6]

A.13.6.2.3.2.6.1 ANSI/UL 2129, CAN/ULC-S566, *Standard for Halocarbon Clean Agent Fire Extinguishers*, and CAN/ULC-S512, *Standard for Halogenated Agent Hand and Wheeled Fire Extinguishers*, require halocarbon and halogenated agent nameplates to provide safety guidelines for avoiding overexposure to agent vapors when the agents are discharged into confined spaces. The UL minimum volume requirement for confined spaces is based on exposure to the agent in the absence of a fire and does not include considerations for fire or agent decomposition products. [**10:** A.5.3.2.6.1]

A.13.6.2.3.2.7 Wheeled fire extinguishers are available in capacities of 33 gal (125 L) for foam units and range from 30 lb to 350 lb (13.6 kg to 158.8 kg) for other types of extinguishers. These fire extinguishers are capable of delivering higher agent flow rates and greater agent stream range than normal portable-type fire extinguishers. Wheeled fire extinguishers are capable of furnishing increased fire-extinguishing effectiveness for high hazard areas and have added importance where a limited number of people are available. [**10:** A.5.3.2.7]

A.13.6.2.4.1.1 Light hazard occupancies can include some buildings or rooms occupied as offices, classrooms, churches, assembly halls, guest room areas of hotels or motels, and so forth. This classification anticipates that the majority of content items are either noncombustible or so arranged that a fire is not likely to spread rapidly. Small amounts of Class B flammables used for duplicating machines, art departments, and so forth, are included, provided that they are kept in closed containers and safely stored. [**10:** A.5.4.1.1]

A.13.6.2.4.1.2 Ordinary hazard occupancies could consist of dining areas, mercantile shops and allied storage, light manufacturing, research operations, auto showrooms, parking garages, workshop or support service areas of light hazard occupancies, and warehouses containing Class I or Class II commodities as defined by NFPA 13. [**10:** A.5.4.1.2]

A Class I commodity is defined by NFPA 13 as a noncombustible product that meets one of the following criteria:

(1) Is placed directly on wooden pallets
(2) Is placed in single-layer corrugated cartons, with or without single-thickness cardboard dividers, with or without pallets
(3) Is shrink-wrapped or paper-wrapped as a unit load, with or without pallets
[**10:** A.5.4.1.2]

A Class II commodity is defined by NFPA 13 as a noncombustible product that is in slatted wooden crates, solid wood boxes, multiple-layered corrugated cartons, or equivalent combustible packaging material, with or without pallets. [**10:** A.5.4.1.2]

A.13.6.2.4.1.3 Extra hazard occupancies could consist of woodworking; vehicle repair; aircraft and boat servicing; cooking areas; individual product display showrooms; product convention center displays; and storage and manufacturing processes such as painting, dipping, and coating, including flammable liquid handling. Also included is warehousing or in-process storage of other than Class I and Class II commodities. [**10:** A.5.4.1.3]

A.13.6.2.4.2 Most buildings have Class A fire hazards. In any occupancy, there could be a predominant hazard as well as special hazard areas requiring supplemental protection. For example, a hospital will generally have need for Class A fire extinguishers covering patients' rooms, corridors, offices, and so forth, but will need Class B fire extinguishers in laboratories and where flammable anesthetics are stored or handled, Class C fire extinguishers in electrical switch gear or generator rooms, and Class K extinguishers in kitchens. [**10:** A.5.4.2]

A.13.6.2.4.2.2 If fire extinguishers intended for different classes of fires are grouped, their intended use should be marked conspicuously to aid in the choice of the proper fire extinguisher at the time of a fire. In an emergency, the tendency is to reach for the closest fire extinguisher. If this fire extinguisher is of the wrong type, users could endanger themselves and the property they are endeavoring to protect. Wherever possible, it is preferable to have only those fire extinguishers available that can be safely used on any type of fire in the immediate vicinity. [**10:** A.5.4.2.2]

A.13.6.2.5.1.1 Pressurized flammable liquids and pressurized gas fires are considered to be a special hazard. Class B fire extinguishers containing agents other than dry chemical are relatively ineffective on this type of hazard due to stream and agent characteristics. The system used to rate the effectiveness of fire extinguishers on Class B fires (flammable liquids in depth) is not applicable to these types of hazards. It has been determined that special nozzle design and rates of agent application are required to cope with such hazards. [**10:** A.5.5.1.1]

A.13.6.2.5.1.1.2 A three-dimensional Class B fire involves Class B materials in motion, such as pouring, running, or dripping flammable liquids, and generally includes vertical as well as one or more, horizontal surfaces. Fires of this nature are considered to be a special hazard. The system used to rate fire extinguishers on Class B fires (flammable liquids in depth) is not directly applicable to this type of hazard. The installation of fixed systems should be considered where applicable. [**10:** A.5.5.1.1.2]

A.13.6.2.5.4(2) Where multiple extinguishers are utilized, simultaneous discharge from multiple locations to eliminate any blind spots created by an obstacle should be employed. [**10:** A.5.5.4(2)]

A.13.6.2.5.5 Fire extinguishers for cooking media (vegetable or animal oils and fats) traditionally followed Table 6.3.1.1 of NFPA 10 for extra hazard, requiring a minimum 40-B -rated sodium bicarbonate or potassium bicarbonate dry chemical extinguisher. The evolution of high-efficiency cooking appliances and the change to hotter-burning vegetable shortening has created a more severe fire hazard. Testing has shown that wet chemical extinguishers have several times the cooking fire–extinguishing capability of a minimum 40-B rated sodium bicarbonate or potassium bicarbonate dry chemical extinguisher, which has prompted the creation of a new classification and a new listing test protocol. The test protocol is found in ANSI/UL 711, CAN/ULC-S508. [**10:** A.5.5.5]

See NFPA 96, *Standard for Ventilation Control and Fire Protection of Commercial Cooking Operations*, for further information. Persons in cooking areas need specific training on the use of extinguishers as an essential step for personal safety. Class K fire extinguishers equipped with extended wand–type discharge devices should not be used in a manner that results in subsurface injection of wet chemical extinguishing agents into hot cooking media. Subsurface injection causes a thermodynamic reaction comparable to an explosion. Class K fire extinguishers are no longer manufactured with extended wand–type discharge devices. [**10:** A.5.5.5]

A.13.6.2.5.5.3 Figure A.13.6.2.5.5.3(a) and Figure A.13.6.2.5.5.3(b) show the recommended wording for the Class K placard. Recommended size is 7⅝ in. × 11 in. (194 mm × 279 mm). [**10:** A.5.5.5.3]

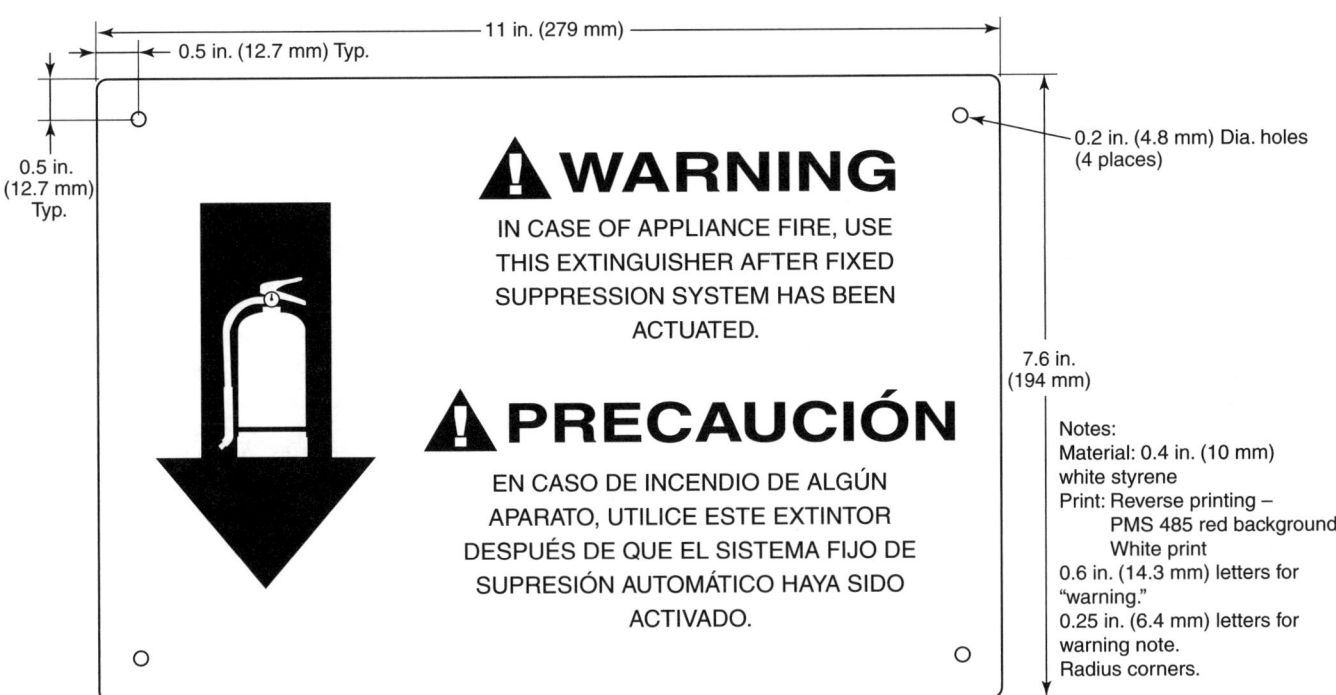

FIGURE A.13.6.2.5.5.3(a) Typical Class K Placard in English and Spanish. [10:Figure A.5.5.5.3(a)]

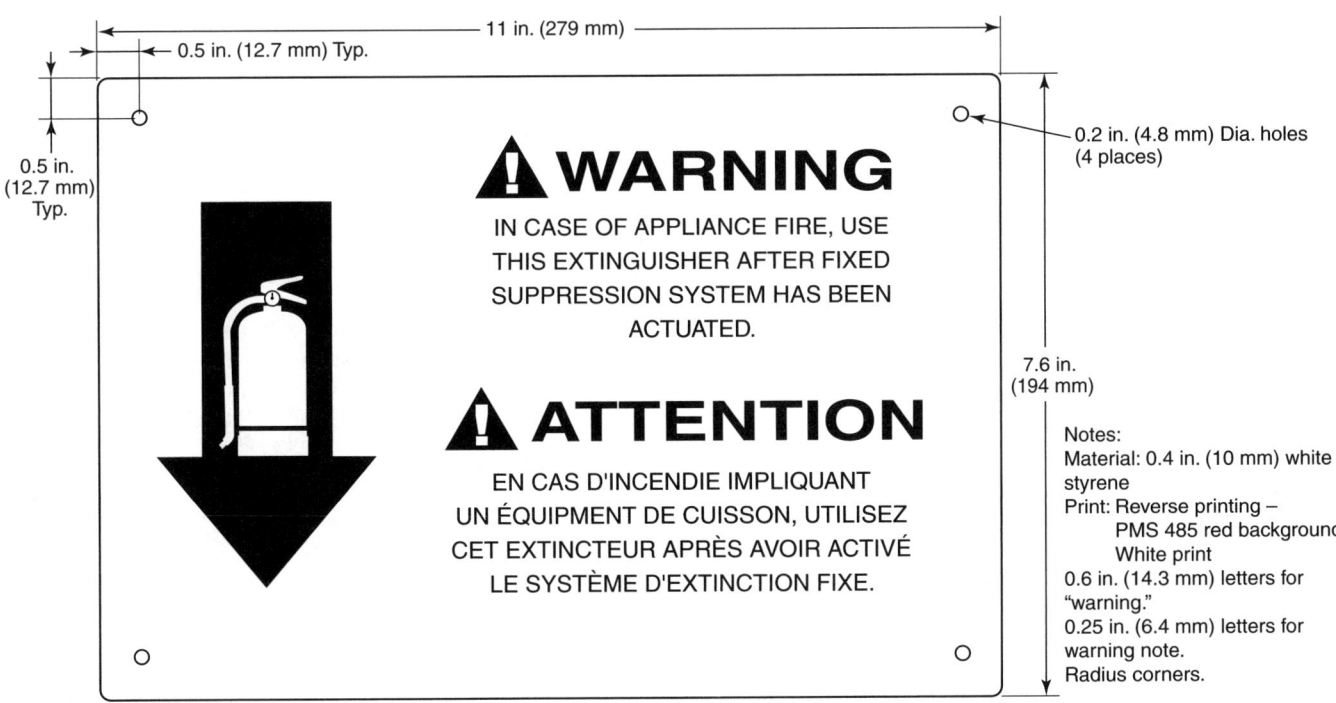

FIGURE A.13.6.2.5.5.3(b) Typical Class K Placard in English and French. [10:Figure A.5.5.5.3(b)]

A.13.6.2.5.6 Delicate electronic equipment includes, but is not limited to, data processing, computers, CAD, CAM, robotics, and reproduction equipment. Use of fire extinguishers containing other extinguishing agents can damage beyond repair both the equipment at the source of the fire and related equipment in the immediate vicinity of the fire. [**10:** A.5.5.6]

A.13.6.2.5.6.1 Dry chemical residue will probably not be able to be completely and immediately removed, and, in addition, multipurpose dry chemical exposed to temperatures in excess of 250°F (121°C) or relative humidity in excess of 50 percent can cause corrosion. [**10:** A.5.5.6.1]

A.13.6.2.5.7.2 A dry chemical fire extinguisher containing ammonium compounds should not be used on oxidizers that contain chlorine. The reaction between the oxidizer and the ammonium salts can produce the explosive compound nitrogen trichloride (NCl_3). [**10:** A.5.5.7.2]

A.13.6.2.5.8.1 Other nonlisted agents can be used if acceptable to the AHJ. Other nonlisted agents include specially dried sand, dolomite, soda ash, lithium chloride, talc, foundry flux, and zirconium silicate or other agents shown to be effective. Consult NFPA 484 for use and limitations of these agents and other non-listed alternatives. [**10:** A.5.5.8.1]

A.13.6.2.6.1 Where portable fire extinguishers are required to be installed, the following documents should be reviewed for the occupancies outlined in their respective scopes:

(1) NFPA 77, *Recommended Practice on Static Electricity*
(2) NFPA 402, *Guide for Aircraft Rescue and Fire-Fighting Operations*
(3) NFPA 610, *Guide for Emergency and Safety Operations at Motorsports Venues*
(4) NFPA 850, *Recommended Practice for Fire Protection for Electric Generating Plants and High Voltage Direct Current Converter Stations*
(5) NFPA 851, *Recommended Practice for Fire Protection for Hydroelectric Generating Plants*
(6) NFPA 921, *Guide for Fire and Explosion Investigations*
(7) NFPA 1452, *Guide for Training Fire Service Personnel to Conduct Dwelling Fire Safety Surveys*
[**10:** A.5.6.1]

A.13.6.3.1.1 The following items affect distribution of portable fire extinguishers:

(1) Area and arrangement of the building occupancy conditions
(2) Severity of the hazard
(3) Anticipated classes of fire
(4) Other protective systems or devices
(5) Distances to be traveled to reach fire extinguishers
[**10:** A.6.1.1]

In addition, the following factors should be considered:

(1) Anticipated rate of fire spread
(2) Intensity and rate of heat development
(3) Smoke contributed by the burning materials
(4) Accessibility of a fire to close approach with portable fire extinguishers
[**10:** A.6.1.1]

Wheeled fire extinguishers have additional agent and range and should be considered for areas where the additional protection is needed. Portable fire extinguishers offer the occupant a means to assist in evacuation of a building or occupancy. They are useful to knock down the fire if it occurs along the evacuation route. If possible, the individual property should be surveyed for actual protection requirements. [**10:** A.6.1.1]

A.13.6.3.1.3.3.2 Acceptable means of identifying the fire extinguisher locations could include arrows, lights, signs, or coding of the wall or column. [**10:** A.6.1.3.3.2]

A.13.6.3.1.3.4 In situations where it is necessary that fire extinguishers be provided temporarily, a good practice is to provide portable stands, consisting of a horizontal bar on uprights with feet, on which the fire extinguishers can be hung. [**10:** A.6.1.3.4]

A.13.6.3.1.3.10.4 Vented fire extinguisher cabinets should utilize tinted glass and should be constructed to prevent the entrance of insects and the accumulation of water. Vented fire extinguisher cabinets constructed in this manner lower the maximum internal temperature 10°F to 15°F (5.6°C to 8.3°C). [**10:** A.6.1.3.10.4]

A.13.6.3.1.3.11 The following precautions should be noted where fire extinguishers are located in areas that have temperatures outside the range of 40°F to 120°F (4°C to 49°C):

(1) AFFF and FFFP fire extinguishers cannot be protected against temperatures below 40°F (4°C) by adding an antifreeze charge because it tends to destroy the effectiveness of the extinguishing agent.
(2) Plain water fire extinguishers should not be protected against temperatures below 40°F (4°C) with ethylene glycol antifreeze. Calcium chloride solutions should not be used in stainless steel fire extinguishers.
(3) Fire extinguishers installed in machinery compartments, diesel locomotives, automotive equipment, marine engine compartments, and hot processing facilities can easily be subjected to temperatures above 120°F (49°C). Selection of fire extinguishers for hazard areas with temperatures above the listed limits should be made on the basis of recommendations by manufacturers of this equipment.

[**10:** A.6.1.3.11]

A.13.6.3.3.2.2 Where such personnel are not available, the hazard should be protected by fixed systems. [**10:** A.6.3.2.2]

A.13.6.3.4 Electrical equipment should be de-energized as soon as possible to prevent reignition. [**10:** A.6.4]

A.13.6.3.5.1 Where Class D fire hazards exist, it is common practice to place bulk quantities of extinguishing agent near the potential Class D hazard. Depending on the type of metal present, the Class D agent selected for the protection of the hazard might not be a listed fire-extinguishing agent. In the case of the production of lithium metal, the agent of choice is lithium chloride, which is feed stock to the electrolytic cell where the lithium metal is manufactured. The use of lithium chloride on a lithium fire will not poison the electrolytic cell so the cell would not have to be drained and relined with fire brick. There are several Class D agents that have been shown to be effective on specific Class D fires. Additional information on Class D agents is provided in NFPA 484. [**10:** A.6.5.1]

The operation of Class D fire extinguishers is much different from that of dry chemical extinguishers rated for Class A, B, or C. The extinguishing agent from a Class D extinguisher should be applied to avoid spreading the combustible metal material and/or suspending the metal product in the air, which can result in an explosion, by slowly applying the agent.

The application of a Class D agent on burning metals is intended to control the fire and assist in the formation of oxide crust that limits combustion. This is accomplished by first encircling the combustible metal material with the agent and then covering the burning metal in a smothering action. It is important to note that metal fires involving large quantities of metal beyond the incipient stage are nearly impossible to control or extinguish with a Class D agent. In most cases, the metal will continue to burn in a controlled fashion after application of the agent until it is completely oxidized. Disturbing the oxide crust can result in reignition and open burning if complete extinguishment, oxidation of the metal, or exclusion of oxygen has not occurred. Fires involving alkali earth metal and transitional metals will begin to form an oxide crust as they burn, which will limit open burning without the application of an extinguishing agent. Application of water or other extinguishing agents can result in an adverse reaction, including the potential for an explosion. Burning metals can also draw moisture from concrete or asphalt, which also maintains the potential for explosion. Large amounts of combustible metal materials involved in a fire can remain hot for some time and vigorously reignite if disturbed prior to complete extinguishment of the combustible metal materials. *(See A.13.6.2.3.2.4.)* [**10:** A.6.5.1]

A.13.6.3.5.3 See NFPA 484, *Standard for Combustible Metals, for additional information.* [**10:** A.6.5.3]

A.13.6.3.5.4 See NFPA 484, *Standard for Combustible Metals, for additional information.* [**10:** A.6.5.4]

A.13.6.4.1 Subsection 13.6.4 is concerned with the rules governing inspection, maintenance, and recharging of fire extinguishers. These factors are of prime importance in ensuring operation at the time of a fire. The procedure for inspection and maintenance of fire extinguishers varies considerably. Minimal knowledge is necessary to perform a monthly "quick check" or inspection in order to follow the inspection procedure as outlined in 13.6.4.2. [**10:** A.7.1]

A.13.6.4.1.2.1 Persons performing maintenance and recharging of extinguishers should meet one of the following criteria:

(1) Factory training and certification for the specific type and brand of portable fire extinguisher being serviced
(2) Certification by an organization acceptable to the AHJ
(3) Registration, licensure, or certification by a state or a local AHJ
[**10:** A.7.1.2.1]

Certification confirms that a person has fulfilled specific requirements as a fire extinguisher service technician and has earned the certification. For the purpose of Section 13.6, certification is the process of an organization issuing a document confirming that an applicant has passed a test based on the chapters and annexes of NFPA 10. The organization administering the test issues an official document that is relied upon as proof of passing the test. Ultimately, the document issued by the organization administering the test must be acceptable to the AHJ. Some AHJs do not rely on outside organizations and establish their own local licensing programs that include a test. [**10:** A.7.1.2.1]

A.13.6.4.1.2.2 Industrial facilities that establish their own maintenance and recharge facilities and that provide training to personnel who perform these functions are considered to be in compliance with this requirement. Examples include power generation, petrochemical, and telecommunications facilities. A letter from the facility management can be used as the certification document. [**10:** A.7.1.2.1.2]

A.13.6.4.1.2.3 This requirement is not intended to prevent service technicians from performing the inspections. [**10:** A.7.1.2.3]

A.13.6.4.2.1.1 Frequency of fire extinguisher inspections should be based on the need of the area in which fire extinguishers are located. The required monthly inspection is a minimum. [**10:** A.7.2.1.1]

A.13.6.4.2.1.2 Inspections should be performed on extinguishers 12 times per year, at least once per month. [**10:** A.7.2.1.2]

A.13.6.4.2.1.3 Inspections should be more frequent if any of the following conditions exist:

(1) High frequency of fires in the past
(2) Severe hazards
(3) Susceptibility to tampering, vandalism, or malicious mischief
(4) Possibility of or history of theft of fire extinguishers
(5) Locations that make fire extinguishers susceptible to mechanical injury
(6) Possibility of visible or physical obstructions
(7) Exposure to abnormal temperatures or corrosive atmospheres
(8) Characteristics of fire extinguishers, such as susceptibility to leakage

[**10:** A.7.2.1.3]

More frequent inspections could be enhanced through electronic monitoring of the fire extinguisher. [**10:** A.7.2.1.3]

A.13.6.4.2.2.1 Fire extinguishers in vehicles should be inspected at the beginning of a shift or whenever the vehicle is used. The inspection should ensure that the extinguisher is charged and ready for use. Extinguishers in compartments or trunks can become damaged or otherwise compromised because of weather exposure, other items in the compartment that are not secured, or other factors. [**10:** A.7.2.2.1]

A.13.6.4.3.1 The annual maintenance of a fire extinguisher requires the services of a trained and certified technician who has the proper tools, listed parts, and appropriate manufacturer's service manual. Maintenance of fire extinguishers should not be confused with inspection, which is a quick check of the extinguishers that is performed at least every 30 days. Because the detailed maintenance procedures for various extinguisher types and models differ, the procedures specified within service manuals need to be followed. [**10:** A.7.3.1]

The following list is a sample of maintenance procedures that should be followed to determine deficiencies that require additional attention to remediate the condition of the extinguisher as appropriate for rechargeable, stored-pressure, dry chemical, and halogenated agent hand portable fire extinguishers:

(1) Visually examine the extinguisher for damage by removing the extinguisher from the hanger, bracket, or cabinet, and visually examine the extinguisher for damage, including pressure gauge, cylinder dents, repairs, general corrosion, hose or nozzle threads, handles, and levers.
(2) Verify that the hanger, bracket, or cabinet is the proper one for the extinguisher.

(3) Verify that the hanger, bracket, or cabinet is secure, undamaged, and properly mounted.
(4) Verify that the nameplate operating instructions are legible and facing outward.
(5) Confirm that the extinguisher model is not subject to recall and is not obsolete.
(6) Verify the extinguisher records to determine internal examination and hydrostatic test intervals. Thoroughly examine the cylinder for dents, damage, repairs, or corrosion.
(7) Verify the pull pin functions properly and examine for damage or corrosion by removing the pull pin.
(8) Verify that the handle and levers are undamaged and operable.
(9) Verify that the valve stem is correctly extended and not corroded or damaged.
(10) Verify that the pressure gauge or indicator is in the operable range.
(11) Verify that the gauge-operating pressure corresponds with the nameplate instructions.
(12) Verify that the gauge face corresponds with the proper agent type.
(13) Verify that the gauge threads are compatible with the valve body material.
(14) Verify that the nozzle or hose assembly, or both, is unobstructed by, removing and examining the nozzle.
(15) Confirm that the nozzle and hose assembly are correct for the model of extinguisher.
(16) Verify that the hose and couplings are not cut, cracked, damaged, or deformed.
(17) Examine internal valve port surfaces and threads for signs of leakage or corrosion by removing the nozzle or hose assembly and reinstalling the nozzle and hose assembly securely after examination.
(18) Verify that the hose retention band is secure and properly adjusted.
(19) Weigh the extinguisher and verify that it corresponds to the weight listed on the nameplate.
(20) Reinstall the ring pin and install a new tamper seal.
(21) Clean exposed extinguisher surfaces to remove any foreign material.
(22) Record the maintenance on the extinguisher tag or label.
(23) Return the extinguisher to the hanger, bracket, or cabinet.
[10: A.7.3.1]

The following list is a sample of maintenance procedures that should be followed to determine deficiencies that require additional attention to remediate the condition of the extinguisher as appropriate for carbon dioxide hand portable fire extinguishers:

(1) Visually examine the extinguisher for damage by removing the extinguisher from the hanger or cabinet, and visually examine the extinguisher for damage, including cylinder dents, repairs, general corrosion, hose or nozzle threads, handles, and levers.
(2) Verify that the bracket or cabinet is the proper one for the extinguisher.
(3) Verify that the bracket or cabinet is secure, undamaged, and properly mounted.
(4) Verify that the nameplate operating instructions are legible and facing outward.
(5) Confirm that the extinguisher model is not subject to recall and is not obsolete.
(6) Verify the extinguisher records to determine hydrostatic test intervals.
(7) Verify the pull pin functions properly and examine for damage or corrosion by removing the pull pin.
(8) Examine the handle and levers to ensure that they are undamaged and operable.
(9) Verify that the valve stem is correctly extended and not corroded or damaged.
(10) Verify that the nozzle or hose assembly, or both, is unobstructed, by removing and examining the nozzle.
(11) Confirm that the nozzle and hose assembly are correct for the model of extinguisher.
(12) Verify that the hose and couplings are not cut, cracked, damaged, or deformed.
(13) Examine the discharge port for signs of leakage or corrosion by removing the nozzle or hose assembly and reinstalling the nozzle and hose assembly securely after examination.
(14) Conduct a conductivity test on the hose assembly.
(15) Affix the conductivity test label to hose assemblies that pass the conductivity test and replace hoses that fail the conductivity test.
(16) Verify that the safety assembly is not damaged or blocked.
(17) Verify that the hose retention band is secure and properly adjusted.
(18) Weigh the extinguisher to verify that it corresponds to the weight listed on the nameplate.
(19) Reinstall the ring pin and install a new tamper seal.
(20) Clean exposed extinguisher surfaces to remove any foreign material.
(21) Record the maintenance on the extinguisher tag or label.
(22) Return the extinguisher to the hanger, bracket, or cabinet.
[10: A.7.3.1]

The following list is a sample of maintenance procedures and checks that are commonly associated with pressurized water-type hand portable fire extinguishers:

(1) Visually examine the extinguisher for damage by removing the extinguisher from the hanger, bracket, or cabinet, and visually examine the extinguisher for damage, including pressure gauge, cylinder dents, repairs, general corrosion, hose or nozzle threads, handles, and levers.
(2) Verify that the hanger, bracket, or cabinet is the proper one for the extinguisher.
(3) Verify that the hanger, bracket, or cabinet is secure, undamaged, and properly mounted.
(4) Verify that the nameplate operating instructions are legible and facing outward.
(5) Confirm that the extinguisher model is not subject to recall and is not obsolete.
(6) Check the extinguisher records to determine hydrostatic test intervals.
(7) Verify that the pull pin functions properly and examine for damage or corrosion by removing the pull pin.
(8) Examine the handle and levers to ensure that they are undamaged and operable.
(9) Verify that the valve stem is correctly extended and not corroded or damaged.
(10) Verify that the pressure gauge is in the operable range.
(11) Verify that the gauge operating pressure corresponds with the nameplate instructions.

(12) Verify that the gauge face corresponds with the proper agent type.
(13) Verify that the gauge threads are compatible with the valve body material.
(14) Verify that the nozzle or hose assembly, or both, is unobstructed, by removing and examining the nozzle.
(15) Confirm that the nozzle and hose assembly are correct for the model of extinguisher.
(16) Verify that the hose and couplings are not cut, cracked, damaged, or deformed.
(17) Examine the internal valve port surfaces and threads for signs of leakage or corrosion by removing the nozzle or hose assembly and reinstalling the nozzle and hose assembly securely after examination.
(18) Verify that the hose retention band is secure and properly adjusted.
(19) Weigh the extinguisher to verify that it corresponds to the weight listed on the nameplate.
(20) Reinstall the ring pin and install a new tamper seal.
(21) Clean exposed extinguisher surfaces to remove any foreign material.
(22) Record the maintenance on the extinguisher tag or label.
(23) Return the extinguisher to the hanger, bracket, or cabinet.

[10: A.7.3.1]

The following list is a sample of maintenance procedures and checks that are commonly associated with cartridge-operated dry chemical and dry powder hand portable fire extinguishers:

(1) Visually examine the extinguisher for damage by removing the extinguisher from the hanger, bracket, or cabinet, and visually examine the extinguisher for damage, including pressure gauge, cylinder dents, repairs, general corrosion, hose or nozzle threads, handles, and levers.
(2) Verify that the hanger, bracket, or cabinet is the proper one for the extinguisher.
(3) Verify that the hanger, bracket, or cabinet is secure, undamaged, and properly mounted.
(4) Verify that the nameplate operating instructions are legible and facing outward.
(5) Confirm that the extinguisher model is not subject to recall and is not obsolete.
(6) Verify the extinguisher hydrostatic test records to determine the hydrostatic test interval.
(7) Invert the extinguisher and open the nozzle to ensure any pressure is relieved from the shell.
(8) Remove the cartridge guard and check the integral components for damage or corrosion.
(9) Unscrew the cartridge to examine the seal. (Replace the cartridge if the seal is punctured, damaged, or corroded.) Verify that the seal is not punctured, that it is the proper cartridge for that extinguisher, and that it has the proper manufacturer's seal.
(10) Install the shipping cap on the cartridge.
(11) Weigh the cartridge on a scale and verify the weight is within the tolerance specified in the manufacturer's service manual.
(12) Remove the discharge nozzle from its holder and lift the hose, breaking the tamper seal.
(13) Operate the puncture lever to verify proper operation.
(14) Check and clean the pressure relief vent in the cartridge receiver in accordance with manufacturer's service manual.
(15) Remove and examine the cartridge receiver gasket. Replace the gasket if brittle, compression set, cracked, cut, or missing.
(16) Lubricate the gasket in accordance with the manufacturer's manual and install.
(17) Slowly loosen the fill cap to relieve any trapped pressure and reinstall hand tight.
(18) Examine the hose, nozzle, and couplings for any damage.
(19) Operate the discharge nozzle to verify proper operation.
(20) Remove the nozzle tip in accordance with the manufacturer's service manual and verify the proper tip is installed and that it is not damaged. Install the nozzle tip in accordance with manufacturer's manual.
(21) Remove the discharge hose from the extinguisher and ensure that the hose is not obstructed.
(22) Examine the hose o-ring and replace if necessary.
(23) Verify that the hose connection is clean and not damaged.
(24) Install the hose on the extinguisher.
(25) Remove the fill cap and examine the threads and seating surfaces for any damage or corrosion.
(26) Verify that the pressure relief vent is not obstructed.
(27) Verify that the dry chemical agent is the correct type and that there are no foreign materials or caking.
(28) Examine and clean the fill cap, gasket, and indicator in accordance with manufacturer's manual.
(29) Lubricate and install the fill cap and gasket in accordance with manufacturer's manual.
(30) Secure the discharge hose in place and install the proper cartridge.
(31) Replace the cartridge guard and install new tamper seals.
(32) Record the maintenance on the extinguisher tag or label.
(33) Return the extinguisher to the hanger, bracket, or cabinet.

[10: A.7.3.1]

A.13.6.4.3.2.2 Where a safety seal or tamper indicator is missing, it can be evidence that the fire extinguisher has been used and therefore should be removed from service. Extreme caution should be exercised before replacing a tamper seal on a nonrechargeable fire extinguisher. [10: A.7.3.2.2]

A.13.6.4.3.2.3 Removable extinguisher boots and foot rings are those that are not put on by the extinguisher manufacturer with glue or welded. [10: A.7.3.2.3]

A.13.6.4.3.3.1 Persons performing maintenance operations usually come from two major groups:

(1) Fire extinguisher service agencies
(2) Trained industrial safety or maintenance personnel

[*101:* A.7.3.3.1]

Fire extinguishers owned by individuals are often neglected because a periodic follow-up program is not planned. It is recommended that such owners become familiar with their fire extinguishers so they can detect telltale warnings during inspection that suggest the need for maintenance. When maintenance is indicated, it should be performed by trained persons having proper equipment. *(See 13.6.4.1.2.2.)* [10: A.7.3.3.1]

The purpose of a well-planned and well-executed maintenance program for a fire extinguisher is to maximize the following probabilities:

(1) That the extinguisher will operate properly between the time intervals established for maintenance examinations in the environment to which it is exposed

(2) That the extinguisher will not constitute a potential hazard to persons in its vicinity or to operators or rechargers of fire extinguishers
[**10:** A.7.3.3.1]

Any replacement parts needed should be obtained from the manufacturer or a representative. [**10:** A.7.3.3.1]

A.13.6.4.3.4 In addition to the required tag or label, a permanent file record should be kept for each fire extinguisher. This file record should include the following information, as applicable:

(1) Maintenance date and the name of the person and the agency performing the maintenance
(2) Date of the last recharge and the name of the person and the agency performing the recharge
(3) Hydrostatic retest date and the name of the person and agency performing the hydrostatic test
(4) Description of dents remaining after passing of the hydrostatic test
(5) Date of the 6-year maintenance for stored-pressure dry chemical and halogenated agent types (*See 13.6.4.3.6.*)
[**10:** A.7.3.4]

It is recognized that an electronic bar coding system is often acceptable to the AHJ in lieu of a tag or label for maintenance record keeping. [**10:** A.7.3.4]

Under special circumstances or when local requirements are in effect, additional information can be desirable or required. [**10:** A.7.3.4]

A.13.6.4.3.6.2 Halon removed from a fire extinguisher is kept in a closed recovery/recharge system until disposition can be made as to whether to recharge the halon back into a fire extinguisher or return unsatisfactory halon to a manufacturer for proper disposal. A listed Halon 1211 closed recovery/recharge system has the following:

(1) Clear sight glass for monitoring the cleanliness of the Halon 1211
(2) A means of determining if the acceptable water content of the halon has been exceeded
(3) A means of mechanically filtering the Halon 1211 and removing excess water
[**10:** A.7.3.6.2]

Such a recovery system also has a motor-driven pump system that permits the transfer of halon into a fire extinguisher or supply container without the need to vent the receiving container to reduce its pressure before halon transfer. Closed recovery/recharge systems also include the plumbing, valves, regulators, and safety relief devices to permit convenient, quick transfer of the Halon 1211. [**10:** A.7.3.6.2]

A.13.6.4.3.6.5 Labels should be printed in black with a light blue background. [**10:** A.7.3.6.5]

A.13.6.4.4 Carbon dioxide hose assemblies have a continuous metal braid that connects to both couplings to minimize the static shock hazard. The reason for the conductivity test is to determine that the hose is conductive from the inlet coupling to the outlet orifice. A basic conductivity tester consists of a flashlight having an open circuit and a set of two wires with a conductor (clamps or probe) at each end. [**10:** A.7.4]

Figure A.13.6.4.4 provides a guide to the design of a conductivity test label. [**10:** A.7.4]

A.13.6.4.6.2 The following procedure permits rapid removal of the hose by one person without kinking of the hose and without obstruction of flow of the extinguishing agent:

FIGURE A.13.6.4.4 Conductivity Test Label. [**10:**Figure A.7.4]

(1) Form a loop over hose supports [*see Figure A.13.6.4.6.2(a)*].
(2) Follow with a reverse loop so that hose passes behind loop [*see Figure A.13.6.4.6.2(b)*].
(3) Repeat steps (1) and (2) until all hose is coiled on the support [*see Figure A.13.6.4.6.2(c)*].
(4) Adjust the coil so that the nozzle is in the downward position [*see Figure A.13.6.4.6.2(d)*]. Hose coiled in this manner pulls off free of twists.
(5) Place nozzle in holder with handle forward in the closed position [*see Figure A.13.6.4.6.2(e)*].
[**10:** A.7.6.2]

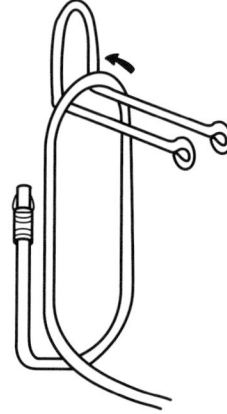

FIGURE A.13.6.4.6.2(a) Counterclockwise Loop. [**10:**Figure A.7.6.2(a)]

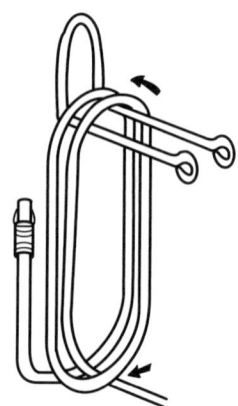

FIGURE A.13.6.4.6.2(b) Reverse Loop. [**10:**Figure A.7.6.2(b)

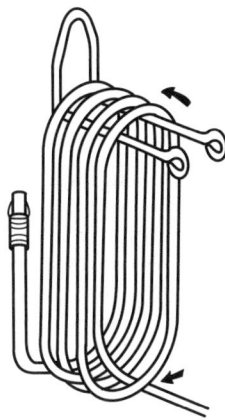

FIGURE A.13.6.4.6.2(c) Procedures in Figure A.13.6.4.6.2(a) and Figure A.13.6.4.6.2(b) Continued. [10:Figure A.7.6.2(c)]

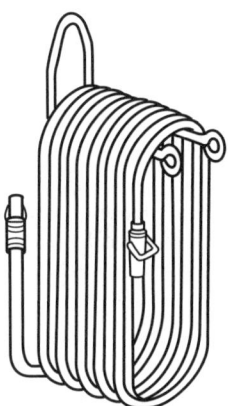

FIGURE A.13.6.4.6.2(d) Nozzle in Downward Position. [10:Figure A.7.6.2(d)]

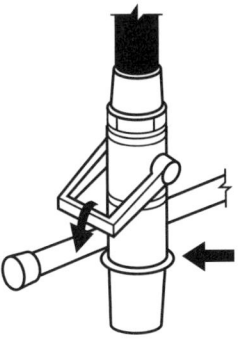

FIGURE A.13.6.4.6.2(e) Nozzle in Holder. [10:Figure A.7.6.2(e)]

A.13.6.4.7.1 General safety guidelines for recharging include the following:

(1) Make sure all pressure is vented from the fire extinguisher before attempting to remove the valve body or to fill the closure. (**Warning:** Do not depend on pressure-indicating devices to tell if the container is under pressure, because the devices could malfunction.)
(2) Use proper recharge materials when refilling a fire extinguisher. Mixing of some extinguishing agents can cause a chemical reaction, resulting in a dangerous pressure buildup in the container.
(3) The weight of agent as specified on the nameplate is critical. Overfilling could render the fire extinguisher dangerous or ineffective.
(4) Clean and properly lubricate all sealing components to prevent leakage after recharge.
(5) Check pressure-indicating device to ascertain that it is reading properly.
(6) Most manufacturers recommend the use of dry nitrogen as an expellant gas for stored-pressure fire extinguishers. Limiting charging pressure regulator setting to 25 psi (172 kPa) above service pressure, as 13.6.4.7.4, prevents gauge damage and loss of calibration. (**Warning:** Never connect the fire extinguisher to be charged directly to the high-pressure source. Connecting directly to the high-pressure source could cause the container to rupture, resulting in injury. Never leave a fire extinguisher connected to the regulator of a high-pressure source for an extended period of time. A defective regulator could cause the container to rupture due to excess pressure.)
(7) Use the manufacturer's recommended charging adapter to prevent damage to a valve and its components.
(8) When recharging separate expellant source fire extinguishers, make sure the filled enclosure is in place and tightened down. Replace all safety devices prior to installing replacement cartridges.
(9) Use only gas cartridges recommended by the manufacturer. Cartridge features such as pressure relief, puncturing capabilities, fill density, and thread compatibility are designed and approved to specific functional requirements.
(10) Use proper safety seals; other types, such as meter seals, could fail to break at the prescribed requirements.
(11) Regulators utilized on wheeled fire extinguishers are factory pinned at the operating pressure and should not be field adjusted.

[**10:** A.7.7.1]

A.13.6.4.7.1.2 Some manufacturers require that their fire extinguishers be returned to the factory for recharging. [**10:** A.7.7.1.2]

A.13.6.4.7.1.3 To determine the gross weight, the entire fire extinguisher should be weighed empty. The weight of the specified recharge agent should be added to that amount. [**10:** A.7.7.1.3]

A.13.6.4.7.1.3.4 The leak test required for stored-pressure and self-expelling types should be sufficiently sensitive to ensure that the fire extinguisher remains operable for at least 1 year. Any tamper indicators or seals need to be replaced after recharging. [**10:** A.7.7.1.3.4]

A.13.6.4.7.3 On properties where fire extinguishers are maintained by the occupant, a supply of recharging agents should be kept on hand. These agents should meet the requirements of 13.6.4.7.3. [**10:** A.7.7.3]

The intent of this provision is to maintain the efficiency of each fire extinguisher as produced by the manufacturer and as labeled by one or more of the fire testing laboratories. For example, the extinguishing agent and the additives used in the various types of dry chemical fire extinguishers vary in chemical composition and in particle size and, thus, in flow characteristics. Each fire extinguisher is designed to secure maximum efficiency with the particular formulation used. Changing the agent from that specified on the fire extinguisher nameplate could affect flow rates, nozzle discharge characteristics, and the quantity of available agent (as influenced by density) and would void the label of the testing laboratory. [10: A.7.7.3]

Certain recharging materials deteriorate with age, exposure to excessive temperature, and exposure to moisture. Storage of recharge agents for long periods of time should be avoided. [10: A.7.7.3]

Dry powder used for combustible metal fires (Class D) should not become damp, because the powder will not be free flowing. In addition, when dry powder contains sufficient moisture, a hazardous reaction could result when applied to a metal fire. [10: A.7.7.3]

A.13.6.4.7.3.2 Mixing multipurpose dry chemicals with alkaline-based dry chemicals could result in a chemical reaction capable of developing sufficient pressures to rupture a fire extinguisher. Substituting a different formulation for the one originally employed could cause malfunctioning of the fire extinguisher or result in substandard performance. [10: A.7.7.3.2]

A.13.6.4.7.3.6 Moisture within a non-water-type fire extinguisher creates a serious corrosion hazard to the fire extinguisher shell and also indicates that the extinguisher is probably inoperative. Moisture could possibly enter under the following conditions:

(1) After a hydrostatic test
(2) When recharging is being performed
(3) When the valve has been removed from the cylinder
(4) Where compressed air and a moisture trap are used for pressurizing non-water types
[10: A.7.7.3.6]

It is extremely important to remove any water or moisture from any fire extinguisher before recharging. Excess moisture in a dry chemical fire extinguisher causes the agent to cake and lump and become unusable. It also causes corrosion to the fire extinguisher shell and valve. In carbon dioxide and halogenated fire extinguishers, excess moisture combined with the extinguishing agent causes extremely corrosive acids to form. These acids can corrode the fire extinguisher shell and valve. [10: A.7.7.3.6]

A.13.6.4.7.3.7 If the fire extinguisher valve is removed for servicing, it is recommended that the fire extinguisher be purged with nitrogen or argon (as appropriate) or that a vacuum be drawn on the fire extinguisher cylinder prior to recharging. [10: A.7.7.3.7]

A.13.6.4.7.3.9 The preferred source of carbon dioxide for recharging fire extinguishers is from a low-pressure [300 psi at 0°F (2068 kPa at -17.8°C)] supply, supplied either directly or via dry cylinders used as an intermediary means. Dry ice converters should not be used to recharge carbon dioxide portable fire extinguishers. [10: A.7.4.3.9]

A.13.6.4.7.3.10 When stored-pressure fire extinguishers are recharged, overfilling results in improper discharge. [10: A.7.7.3.10]

A.13.6.4.7.4.4 Some Class D fire extinguishers are required to be pressurized with argon. [10: A.7.7.4.4]

A.13.6.4.7.4.6 The reason an unregulated source of pressure is not to be used is because the fire extinguisher has the potential to be overpressurized and possibly rupture. [10: A.7.7.4.6]

A.13.6.4.7.4.7 A defective regulator could cause the container to rupture due to excess pressure. [10: A.7.7.4.7]

A.13.6.4.8 If it becomes necessary to replace a pressure gauge on a fire extinguisher, in addition to knowing the charging pressure, it is important to know the type of extinguishing agent for which the gauge is suitable, as well as the valve body with which the gauge is compatible. This information often is available in the form of markings on the dial face. Where the marking is provided, the extinguishing agent is indicated by references such as "Use Dry Chemicals Only," while the valve body compatibility is indicated as follows:

(1) Gauges intended for use with aluminum or plastic valve bodies are marked with a line above the gauge manufacturer's code letter.
(2) Gauges intended for use with brass or plastic valve bodies are marked with a line below the manufacturer's code letter.
(3) Universal gauges that can be used with aluminum, brass, or plastic valve bodies are marked with lines above and below the manufacturer's code letter or by the absence of any line above or below the manufacturer's code letter.
[10: A.7.8]

Using the proper replacement gauge as to pressure range, extinguishing agent, and valve body compatibility is recommended to avoid or to reduce gauge-related problems. [10: A.7.8]

A.13.6.4.10 A number of states have regulations requiring an internal marking of an extinguisher that is used to verify if the extinguisher has been depressurized, if the valve has been removed, and if a complete maintenance has been performed. The verification-of-service collar design also requires that the valve be removed before the collar can be attached to the extinguisher. The collar provides the AHJs with a more convenient visual proof that the extinguisher has been disassembled and that maintenance most likely has been performed. [10: A.7.10]

All extinguishers are to have the valve removed for hydrostatic testing and are to be subsequently recharged before they are returned to service. To be valid, the date on the verification-of-service collar should always be the same as or more recent than the date on the hydrostatic test label. [10: A.7.10]

Figure A.13.6.4.10 provides a guide to the design of a verification-of-service collar. [10: A.7.10]

A.13.6.4.11 Weight scales used for weighing a fire extinguisher with a gross weight of 60 lb (27.2 kg) or less should permit readings to 0.25 lb (0.10 kg). Weight scales used for weighing extinguishers and cartridges should permit readings consistent with the tolerances identified on the nameplate of the extinguisher or cartridge. All scales should be calibrated (tested) for accuracy. Accuracy of weight scales should be demonstrated at least daily by the use of test weight(s) having a verified weight. The test method involves placing a test weight on the scale and reading the results. The following method should be used to calibrate weight scales daily or more frequently as needed:

(1) With nothing on the scale, "zero out" the weight scale by adjusting the weight scale calibration knob or wheel or

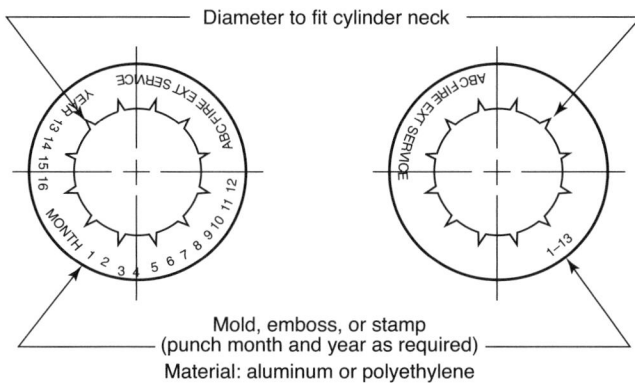

FIGURE A.13.6.4.10 Design of a Verification-of-Service Collar. [10:A.7.10]

tare/zero button so that it reads zero. A digital scale should be powered and allowed to stabilize before adjusting to read zero.
(2) Place the test weight(s) on the scale.
(3) Read the weight that is registered on the scale, and, if needed, adjust the scale by turning the calibration knob or wheel to show the weight of the test weight that is being tested. Some digital scales have an electronic push-button calibration feature to calibrate the weight during a test.
(4) Repeat the testing procedure two more times after any adjustment. The weight that is registered should be exactly the same. Weight scales that do not provide repeatable results within the tolerances specified in the manufacturer's literature should be repaired or replaced.

[10: A.7.11]

A.13.7.1.2 The following functions are included in Annex A to provide guidelines for utilizing building systems and equipment in addition to proprietary fire alarm equipment in order to provide life safety and property protection. Building functions that should be initiated or controlled during a fire alarm condition include, but should not be limited to, the following:

(1) Elevator operation consistent with ANSI/ASME A17.1/CSA B44, *Safety Code for Elevators and Escalators*
(2) Unlocking of stairwell and exit doors (see NFPA 80, *Standard for Fire Doors and Other Opening Protectives*, and NFPA 101, *Life Safety Code*)
(3) Release of fire and smoke dampers (see NFPA 90A, *Standard for the Installation of Air-Conditioning and Ventilating Systems*, and NFPA 90B, *Standard for the Installation of Warm Air Heating and Air-Conditioning Systems*)
(4) Monitoring and initiating of self-contained automatic fire extinguishing system(s) or suppression system(s) and equipment (see NFPA 11, *Standard for Low-, Medium-, and High-Expansion Foam*; NFPA 12, *Standard on Carbon Dioxide Extinguishing Systems*; NFPA 12A, *Standard on Halon 1301 Fire Extinguishing Systems*; NFPA 13, *Standard for the Installation of Sprinkler Systems*; NFPA 14, *Standard for the Installation of Standpipe and Hose Systems*; NFPA 15, *Standard for Water Spray Fixed Systems for Fire Protection*; NFPA 17, *Standard for Dry Chemical Extinguishing Systems*; NFPA 17A, *Standard for Wet Chemical Extinguishing Systems*; and NFPA 750, *Standard on Water Mist Fire Protection Systems*)

[**72:** A.23.3.3.1]

A.13.7.1.4.2 Records of conducted maintenance and testing and a copy of the certificate of compliance should be maintained. [*101:* A.9.6.1.4]

A.13.7.1.4.3 A fire watch should at least involve some special action beyond normal staffing, such as assigning an additional security guard(s) to walk the areas affected. Such individuals should be specially trained in fire prevention and in occupant and fire department notification techniques, and they should understand the particular fire safety situation for public education purposes. (*Also see NFPA 601, Standard for Security Services in Fire Loss Prevention.*) [*101:* A.9.6.1.6]

The term *out of service* in 13.7.1.4.3 is intended to imply that a significant portion of the fire alarm system is not in operation, such as an entire initiating device, signaling line, or notification appliance circuit. It is not the intent of the *Code* to require notification of the AHJ, or evacuation of the portion of the building affected, for a single nonoperating device or appliance. [*101:* A.9.6.1.5]

A.13.7.1.5 Requirements to address impaired fire alarm systems, and fire alarm systems prone to chronic nuisance alarms are provided in 13.7.1.5. In many situations, the problems can be corrected by ensuring the systems are maintained, serviced, and tested by an approved fire alarm service company. However, in some cases, the system problems may be attributed to aging for which suitable replacement parts are no longer available.

A.13.7.1.5.5 This paragraph allows the AHJ to require chronic nuisance alarm prone systems to comply with the *NFPA 72*, Section 26.3 requirements for central station service. Central station service, as compared to other supervising service, requires the system to be covered by a systematic follow-up program under the control of the organization that has listed the prime contractor. This will ensure that not only is the system being maintained, serviced, and periodically tested by an approved alarm service company, but it is also under an ongoing audit program by the company that listed the central station. Many jurisdictions that require central station service on fire alarm systems also communicate directly with the listing organization concerning the systems monitored in their jurisdiction.

A.13.7.1.5.6 It is not always practical for the AHJ to continually verify that required monitoring, testing, service, and maintenance are provided. It is also difficult for the AHJ to determine if older systems are no longer able to be serviced or repaired to keep them operational and resistant to nuisance alarms, particularly if spare parts are no longer available. Paragraph 13.7.1.5.6 requires the fire alarm companies to notify the AHJ when required services have been discontinued, or when systems can no longer be serviced and maintained in an operational condition, free from chronic nuisance alarms. It is not the intent of this paragraph to prevent system owners from getting a second opinion on the system status from another approved fire alarm service provider.

A.13.7.1.6 The requirement of 13.7.1.6 recognizes there will be instances where, for example, a facility owner would want to apply detection to meet certain performance goals and to address a particular hazard or need, but that detection is not required. Once installed, of course, acceptance testing, annual testing, and ongoing maintenance in accordance with this *Code* is expected. The intent of this section is to allow the use of a single detector, or multiple detectors provided for specific protection, with spacing to meet specific fire safety objectives as determined in accordance with 17.6.1.1 and 17.7.1.1 of *NFPA 72*. [**72:** A.17.5.3.3]

A.13.7.1.7.5 It is not the intent of 13.7.1.7.5 to require manual fire alarm boxes to be attached to movable partitions or to equipment, nor is it the intent to require the installation of permanent structures for mounting purposes only. [*101:*A.9.6.2.5]

A.13.7.1.7.6 The manual fire alarm box required by 13.7.1.7.6 is intended to provide a means to manually activate the fire alarm system when the automatic fire detection system or waterflow devices are out of service due to maintenance or testing, or where human discovery of the fire precedes automatic sprinkler system or automatic detection system activation. Where the fire alarm system is connected to a monitoring facility, the manual fire alarm box required by 13.7.1.7.6 should be connected to a separate circuit that is not placed "on test" when the detection or sprinkler system is placed on test. The manual fire alarm box should be located in an area that is accessible to occupants of the building and should not be locked. [*101:*A.9.6.2.6]

A.13.7.1.7.7 Manual fire alarm boxes can include those with key-operated locks for detention areas or psychiatric hospitals, manual fire alarm boxes in areas where explosive vapors or dusts might be a hazard, or manual fire alarm boxes in areas with corrosive atmospheres. The appearance of manual fire alarm boxes for special uses often differs from those used in areas of normal occupancy. Manual fire alarm boxes, such as those with locks, that are located in areas where the general public has limited access might need to have signage advising persons to seek assistance from staff in the event a fire is noted. [*101:*A.9.6.2.7]

A.13.7.1.8.3 *NFPA 72, National Fire Alarm and Signaling Code,* mandates smoke alarms in all sleeping rooms, and interconnection of smoke alarms is required for both new and existing installations. Per 13.7.1.8.1, the residential occupancy requirements determine whether smoke alarms are needed within sleeping rooms. Paragraph 13.7.1.8.3 limits the requirement for interconnection of smoke alarms to those in new construction. This *Code* does not intend to require compliant, existing smoke alarm installations to be interconnected. This *Code* is periodically revised to add retrospective requirements only where the need is clearly substantiated. [*101:*A.9.6.2.10.3]

A.13.7.1.8.8 A dwelling unit is that structure, area, room, or combination of rooms, including hotel rooms/suites, in which a family or individual lives. A dwelling unit includes living areas only and not common usage areas in multifamily buildings, such as corridors, lobbies, and basements. [*101:*A.9.6.2.10.8]

A.13.7.1.9.2.1 Elevator lobbies have been considered areas subject to unwanted alarms due to factors such as low ceilings and smoking. In the past several years, new features have become available to reduce this problem. These features are, however, not necessarily included in any specific installation. [*101:*A.9.6.3.2.1]

A.13.7.1.9.2.2 The concept addressed is that detectors used for releasing service, such as door or damper closing and fan shutdown, are not required to sound the building alarm. [*101:* A.9.6.3.2.2]

A.13.7.1.9.2.3 The concept addressed is that detectors used for releasing service, such as door or damper closing and fan shutdown, are not required to sound the building alarm. [*101:* A.9.6.3.2.3]

A.13.7.1.9.5.7 Visual notification appliances installed in large volume spaces, such as arenas, stadiums, malls and atriums, can be alternative devices which are not listed as visible notification appliances for fire alarm systems provided that the notification objective of the visual signal is reasonably achieved. Examples of alternative devices include, but are not limited to, scoreboards, message boards, and other electronic devices that meet the performance objectives of visible fire alarm appliances in large volume spaces. [*101:*A.9.6.3.5.7]

It is the intent to permit the omission of visible notification appliances as identified in 13.7.1.9.5.7 provided that the adjacent areas that have not been specifically designated as exempt are provided with visible notification as required by 13.7.1.9.5. [*101:*A.9.6.3.5.7]

A.13.7.1.9.5.8 Documentation should be maintained with the as-built drawings so that inspection and testing personnel understand that the visible appliances have been exempted from certain areas and, therefore, can note the deviation on the acceptance test documentation and ongoing inspection reports. This will provide inspection and testing personnel with necessary details regarding the omission of visible notification appliances. [*101:*A.9.6.3.5.8]

A.13.7.1.9.6.2 To approve an evacuation plan to selectively notify building occupants, the AHJ should consider several building parameters, including building compartmentation, detection and suppression system zones, occupant loads, and the number and arrangement of the means of egress.

In high-rise buildings, it is typical to evacuate the fire floor, the floor(s) above, and the floor immediately below. Other areas are then evacuated as the fire develops. [*101:*A.9.6.3.6.2]

A.13.7.1.13.4 The primary purpose of annunciation is to enable responding personnel to quickly and accurately determine the status of equipment or emergency control functions that might affect the safety of occupants. [**72:** A.10.18.3]

A.13.7.1.13.6 Fire alarm system annunciation should, as a minimum, be sufficiently specific to identify a fire alarm signal in accordance with the following:

(1) If a floor exceeds 22,500 ft^2 (2090 m^2) in area, the floor should be subdivided into detection zones of 22,500 ft^2 (2090 m^2) or less, consistent with the existing smoke and fire barriers on the floor.
(2) If a floor exceeds 22,500 ft^2 (2090 m^2) in area and is undivided by smoke or fire barriers, detection zoning should be determined on a case-by-case basis in consultation with the AHJ.
(3) Waterflow switches on sprinkler systems that serve multiple floors, areas exceeding 22,500 ft^2 (2090 m^2), or areas inconsistent with the established detection system zoning should be annunciated individually.
(4) In-duct smoke detectors on air-handling systems that serve multiple floors, areas exceeding 22,500 ft^2 (2090 m^2), or areas inconsistent with the established detection system zoning should be annunciated individually.
(5) If a floor area exceeds 22,500 ft^2 (2090 m^2), additional zoning should be provided. The length of any zone should not exceed 300 ft (91 m) in any direction. If the building is provided with automatic sprinklers throughout, the area of the alarm zone should be permitted to coincide with the allowable area of the sprinkler zone. [**72:** A.10.18.5]

A.13.7.2.1.2.3 The intent is to require detectors only in non-sprinklered hazardous areas that are unoccupied. When the building is occupied, the detectors in the unoccupied, unsprinklered hazardous areas will initiate occupant notification. If the building is unoccupied, the fire in the nonsprinklered hazardous area is not a life safety issue, and the detectors, upon activation, are not required to notify anyone. The signal from a detector is permitted to be sent to a control panel in an area that is occupied when the building is occupied, but that is unoccupied when the building is unoccupied, without the need for central station monitoring or the equivalent. [*101*: A.12.3.4.2.3]

A.13.7.2.1.3.5 Examples of devices that might be used to provide alternative visible means include scoreboards, message boards, and other electronic devices. [*101*: A.12.3.4.3.5]

A.13.7.2.2.2.3 The intent is to require detectors only in non-sprinklered hazardous areas that are unoccupied. Where the building is occupied, the detectors in the unoccupied, unsprinklered hazardous areas will initiate occupant notification. If the building is unoccupied, the fire in the nonsprinklered hazardous area is not a life safety issue, and the detectors, upon activation, are not required to notify anyone. The signal from a detector is permitted to be sent to a control panel in an area that is occupied when the building is occupied, but that is unoccupied when the building is unoccupied, without the need for central station monitoring or the equivalent. [*101*: A.13.3.4.2.3]

A.13.7.2.3.2.3.1 Occupied portions of the building should have access to a central point for manual activation of the evacuation signal. [*101*: A.14.3.4.2.3.1]

A.13.7.2.3.2.3.2 Occupied portions of the building should have access to a central point for manual activation of the evacuation signal. [*101*: A.14.3.4.2.3.2]

A.13.7.2.4.2.3.1 Occupied portions of the building should have access to a central point for manual activation of the evacuation signal. [*101*: A.15.3.4.2.3.1]

A.13.7.2.4.2.3.2 Occupied portions of the building should have access to a central point for manual activation of the evacuation signal. [*101*: A.15.3.4.2.3.2]

A.13.7.2.4.3.1.1 The audible occupant notification signal for evacuation of an educational occupancy building should be the distinctive three-pulse temporal pattern fire alarm evacuation signal that is required of new systems by *NFPA 72, National Fire Alarm and Signaling Code*.. The temporal pattern will help educate students to recognize the need to evacuate when they are in other occupancies. Existing fire alarm systems should be modified, as feasible, to sound the three-pulse temporal pattern. [*101*: A.15.3.4.3.1.1]

A.13.7.2.7.2 It is not the intent of this *Code* to require single-station smoke alarms that might be required by local codes to be connected to or to initiate the building fire alarm system. [*101*: A.18.3.4.2]

A.13.7.2.7.3.1(2) It is the intent of this provision to permit a visible fire alarm signal instead of an audible signal to reduce interference between the fire alarm and medical equipment monitoring alarms. [*101*: A.18.3.4.3.1(2)]

A.13.7.2.7.5.3 The requirement for smoke detectors in spaces open to the corridors eliminates the requirements of 18.3.6.1 (1)(c), (2)(b), and (5)(b) of NFPA *101* for direct supervision by the facility staff of nursing homes.[*101*: A.18.3.4.5.3]

A.13.7.2.8.2 It is not the intent of this *Code* to require single-station smoke alarms, which might be required by local codes, to be connected to or to initiate the building fire alarm system. [*101*: A.19.3.4.2]

A.13.7.2.8.3.1(1) It is the intent of this provision to permit a visible fire alarm signal instead of an audible signal to reduce interference between the fire alarm and medical equipment monitoring alarms. [*101*: A.19.3.4.3.1(1)]

A.13.7.2.11.3.1(2) The staff at the constantly attended location should have the capability to promptly initiate the general alarm function and contact the fire department or have direct communication with a control room or other location that can initiate the general alarm function and contact the fire department. [*101*: A.22.3.4.3.1(2)]

A.13.7.2.11.4 Examples of contiguous common spaces are galleries and corridors. [*101*: A.22.3.4.4]

A.13.7.2.11.4.3 An open dormitory is a dormitory that is arranged to allow staff to observe the entire dormitory area at one time. [*101*: A.22.3.4.4.3]

A.13.7.2.12.3.1(2) The staff at the constantly attended location should have the capability to promptly initiate the general alarm function and contact the fire department or have direct communication with a control room or other location that can initiate the general alarm function and contact the fire department.[*101*: A.23.3.4.3.1(2)]

A.13.7.2.12.4.3 An open dormitory is a dormitory that is arranged to allow staff to observe the entire dormitory area at one time. [*101*: A.23.3.4.4.3]

A.13.7.2.13.1.1 Paragraph 11.5.1.3 of *NFPA 72, National Fire Alarm and Signaling Code*, contains related requirements. They specify that, where the interior floor area for a given level of a dwelling unit, excluding garage areas, is greater than 1000 ft^2 (93 m^2), smoke alarms are to be installed as follows:

(1) All points on the ceiling are to have a smoke alarm within a distance of 30 ft (9.1 m), measured along a path of travel, or to have one smoke alarm per 500 ft^2 (46.5 m^2) of floor area, which is calculated by dividing the total interior floor area per level by 500 ft^2 (46.5 m^2).
(2) Where dwelling units include great rooms or vaulted/cathedral ceilings extending over multiple floors, smoke alarms located on the upper floor that are intended to protect the aforementioned area are permitted to be considered as part of the lower floor(s) protection scheme used to meet the requirements of A.13.7.2.13.1.1(1).

[*101*: A.24.3.4.1.1]

A.13.7.2.13.1.1(2) Paragraphs 11.5.1.1(2) and 11.5.1.2 of *NFPA 72, National Fire Alarm and Signaling Code*, contain related requirements. The requirement of 11.5.1.1(2) specifies that an alarm is to be installed outside of each separate dwelling unit sleeping area, within 21 ft (6.4 m) of any door to a sleeping room, with the distance measured along a path of travel. The requirement in 11.5.1.2 of *NFPA 72* specifies that, where the area addressed in 11.5.1.1(2) of *NFPA 72* is separated from the adjacent living areas by a door, a smoke alarm is to be installed in the area between the door and the sleeping rooms, and additional alarms are to be installed on the living area side of the door. [*101:*A.24.3.4.1.1(2)]

A.13.7.2.13.2.2 The placement requirements of NFPA 720, *Standard for the Installation of Carbon Monoxide (CO) Detection and Warning Equipment*, are modified specifically for one- and two-family dwellings as required by this *Code* and do not affect other regulations within a jurisdiction. [*101:*A.24.3.4.2.2]

A.13.7.2.14.3.1 The proprietor is the owner or owner's agent with responsible charge. [*101:*A.26.3.4.3.1]

A.13.7.2.14.6.2 The placement requirements of NFPA 720, *Standard for the Installation of Carbon Monoxide (CO) Detection and Warning Equipment*, are modified to accommodate lodging or rooming house occupancies that are part of multiple occupancy buildings (e.g., an on-call physicians' sleeping room in a hospital). The placement requirements of NFPA 720 are modified specifically for lodging or rooming houses as required by this *Code* and do not affect other regulations within a jurisdiction. [*101:*A.26.3.4.6.2]

A.13.7.2.15.3.1 Visible signaling appliances might be governed by provisions of federal regulations in 28 CFR 36, Appendix A, "Americans with Disabilities Act Accessibility Guidelines for Buildings and Facilities," Section 4.28, Alarms. [*101:*A.28.3.4.3.1]

A.13.7.2.15.3.3 A quantity of such rooms and suites might be required to be equipped to accommodate hearing-impaired individuals based on the total number of rooms in a transient lodging facility. *(See 28 CFR 36, Appendix A, "Americans with Disabilities Act Accessibility Guidelines for Buildings and Facilities.")* [*101:*A.28.3.4.3.3]

A.13.7.2.15.5 Caution needs to be exercised in locating smoke alarms with regard to their proximity to bathrooms, cooking facilities, and HVAC outlets in order to prevent nuisance alarms. [*101:*A.28.3.4.5]

A.13.7.2.16.3.6 The provision for immediate notification of the public fire department is intended to include, but is not limited to, all of the arrangements in 13.7.1.10.2. Other arrangements that depend on a clerk or other member of the staff to notify the fire department might also be permitted. In such cases, however, it is essential that a trained staff member and an immediately available means of calling the fire department are continuously available. If a telephone is to be used, it should not be of any type or arrangement that requires a coin or the unlocking of a device to contact the fire department. [*101:*A.29.3.4.3.6]

A.13.7.2.16.5 Caution needs to be exercised in locating smoke alarms with regard to their proximity to bathrooms, cooking facilities, and HVAC outlets in order to prevent nuisance alarms. [*101:*A.29.3.4.5]

A.13.7.2.17.5 Previous editions of NFPA *101* permitted the single-station smoke alarm required by 13.7.2.17.5 to be omitted from each apartment where a complete automatic smoke detection system was installed throughout the building. With such a system, when one detector is activated, an alarm is sounded throughout the building. Experience with complete smoke detection systems in apartment buildings has shown that numerous nuisance alarms are likely to occur. Where there is a problem with frequent nuisance alarms, occupants ignore the alarm, or the system is either disconnected or otherwise rendered inoperative. [*101:*A.30.3.4.5]

A.13.7.2.18.4.1 It is intended that a building compliant with Option 2 [, as defined in Chapter 31 of NFPA *101*,] function as described in the paragraph that follows. [*101:*A.31.3.4.4.1]

Occupants within a living unit become aware of a fire emergency, either through personal awareness or through being alerted by the smoke alarm(s) installed within the living unit. Other building occupants are alerted to the fire emergency by the building fire alarm system that is initiated by manual fire alarm boxes adjacent to the exits, heat detection within the living unit where the fire emergency exists, smoke detection in the common areas outside the living unit, or a combination thereof. The installation of system heat detectors versus smoke detectors within the living unit is intended to eliminate nuisance-type alarms and reduce occupant complacency from frequent false alarms. The installation of smoke detection within the living unit should only be contemplated after a careful analysis of the goals and with the approval of the AHJ. [*101:*A.31.3.4.4.1]

A.13.7.2.18.5.1 NFPA *101* provides adequate, balanced fire protection and takes into consideration the passive and active systems required in a given occupancy. The level of protection prescribed by *NFPA 72, National Fire Alarm and Signaling Code*, which includes smoke alarms in all sleeping rooms, without exception, does not necessarily take into consideration the complete protection package mandated by NFPA *101*. [*101:*A.31.3.4.5.1]

A.13.7.2.20.6 Positive alarm sequence applies only to emergency forces notification. Occupant notification is required to occur immediately upon activation of the detection device or system. [*101:*A.32.3.3.4.6]

A.13.7.2.21.3 Most often, smoke alarms sounding an alarm at 85 dBA or greater, installed outside the bedroom area, will meet the intent of this requirement. Smoke alarms remotely located from the bedroom might not be loud enough to awaken the average person. In such cases, it is recommended that smoke alarms be interconnected so that the activation of any smoke alarm will cause all smoke alarms to activate. [*101:*A.33.2.3.4.3]

NFPA *101* provides adequate, balanced fire protection and takes into consideration the passive and active systems required in a given occupancy. The level of protection prescribed by *NFPA 72, National Fire Alarm and Signaling Code*, which includes smoke alarms in all sleeping rooms, without exception, does not necessarily take into consideration the complete protection package prescribed by NFPA *101*. [*101:*A.33.2.3.4.3]

A.13.7.2.22.6.1 See A.13.7.2.16.3.6. [*101:*A.33.3.3.4.6.1]

A.13.7.2.29.2.1 The need for voice communication can be based on a decision regarding staged or partial evacuation versus total evacuation of all floors. The determination of need is a function of occupancy classification and building height. [*101:*A.11.8.4.1]

A.13.7.2.29.2.2 Public safety radio enhancement systems provide for greater flexibility and safety for emergency responders during in-building operations. This provision serves to facilitate adoption of *Code* language prescribing design, installation, testing, and maintenance criteria for in-building public safety radio enhancement systems. AHJs are directed to Chapter 24 of *NFPA 72 for details*.

A.13.7.3.1.1.3 This requirement does not apply to notification appliance circuits. [**72:**A.10.3.3]

A.13.7.3.1.1.5(1) The requirement of 13.7.3.1.1.5(1) does not preclude transfer to secondary supply at less than 85 percent of nominal primary voltage, provided the requirements of 10.6.7 of *NFPA 72* are met. [**72:** A.10.3.5(1)]

A.13.7.3.3.7 Protective covers, also called pull station protectors can be installed over manually actuated alarm initiating devices to provide mechanical protection, environmental protection, and to reduce the likelihood of accidental or malicious activation. The protective covers must be listed to ensure that they do not hinder the operation of the pull stations and to ensure that they meet accessibility requirements for activation by persons with physical disabilities. The *Code* explicitly permits installing them over single- or double-action devices. When installed over a double-action device, the assembly effectively becomes a triple-action device. Some units include battery-operated audible warning signals that have been shown to deter malicious activations. To be effective, it is important that the regular staff or occupants be aware of the sound and investigate immediately in order to catch someone who might otherwise activate the device without cause or to ensure that the device is activated if there is a legitimate reason. [**72:** A.17.14.7]

A.13.7.3.3.8.3 In environments where red paint or red plastic is not suitable, an alternative material, such as stainless steel, could be used as long as the box meets the requirements of 17.14.8.2 of *NFPA 72*. [**72:** A.17.14.8.3].

A.13.7.3.3.8.5 It is not the intent of 13.7.3.3.8.5 to require manual fire alarm boxes to be attached to movable partitions or to equipment, nor to require the installation of permanent structures for mounting purposes only. [**72:** A.17.14.8.5]

A.13.7.3.4 The terms *certificated* and *placarded*, which appeared in previous editions of *NFPA 72*, were considered by some to be too specific to two listing organizations and were replaced with more generic wording. The concept of providing documentation to indicate ongoing compliance of an installed system continues to be reflected by the current language. [**72:** A.26.3.4]

A.13.7.3.4.2(2) The record of completion *(see Chapter 10 of NFPA 72)* can be used to fulfill this requirement. [**72:** A.26.3.4.2(2)]

A.13.7.3.4.5 It is the prime contractor's responsibility to remove all compliance markings (certification markings or placards) when a service contract goes into effect that conflicts in any way with the requirements of 13.7.3.4. [**72:** A.26.3.4.5]

A.13.7.3.4.6 The prime contractor should be aware of statutes, public agency regulations, or certifications regarding alarm systems that might be binding on the subscriber. The prime contractor should identify for the subscriber which agencies could be an AHJ and, if possible, advise the subscriber of any requirements or approvals being mandated by these agencies. [**72:** A.26.3.4.6]

The subscriber has the responsibility for notifying the prime contractor of those private organizations that are being designated as an AHJ. The subscriber also has the responsibility to notify the prime contractor of changes in the AHJ, such as where there is a change in insurance companies. Although the responsibility is primarily the subscriber's, the prime contractor should also take responsibility for seeking out these private AHJs through the subscriber. The prime contractor is responsible for maintaining current records on the AHJ for each protected premises. [**72:** A.26.3.4.6]

The most prevalent public agency involved as an AHJ with regard to alarm systems is the local fire department or fire prevention bureau. These are normally city or county agencies with statutory authority, and their approval of alarm system installations might be required. At the state level, the fire marshal's office is most likely to serve as the public regulatory agency. [**72:** A.26.3.4.6]

The most prevalent private organizations involved as AHJs are insurance companies. Others include insurance rating bureaus, insurance brokers and agents, and private consultants. It is important to note that these organizations have no statutory authority and become AHJs only when designated by the subscriber. [**72:** A.26.3.4.6]

With both public and private concerns to satisfy, it is not uncommon to find multiple AHJs involved with a particular protected premises. It is necessary to identify all AHJs in order to obtain all the necessary approvals for a central station alarm system installation. [**72:** A.26.3.4.6]

A.13.7.4.3.1 Figure A.13.7.4.3.1 illustrates the proper mounting placement for detectors. [**72:** A.17.6.3.1.3.1]

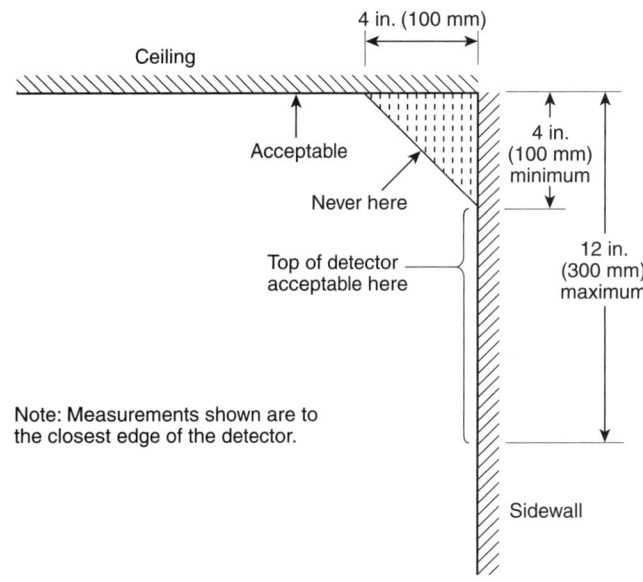

FIGURE A.13.7.4.3.1 Example of Proper Mounting for Heat Detectors. [72: Figure A.17.6.3.1.3.1]

A.13.7.4.3.3 In high-ceiling areas, such as atriums, where spot-type smoke detectors are not accessible for periodic maintenance and testing, projected beam–type or air sampling–type detectors should be considered where access can be provided. [**72:** A.17.7.3.2]

A.13.7.4.3.3.1 Refer to Figure A.13.7.4.3.3.1 for an example of proper mounting for detectors. Sidewall detectors mounted closer to the ceiling will respond faster. [**72:** A.17.7.3.2.1]

A.13.7.4.3.3.2 Figure A.13.7.4.3.3.2 illustrates under-floor mounting installations. [**72:** A.17.7.3.2.2]

A.13.7.4.3.3.3.1 The 30 ft (9.1 m) spacing is a guide for prescriptive designs. The use of such a spacing is based upon customary practice in the fire alarm community. [**72:** A.17.7.3.2.3.1]

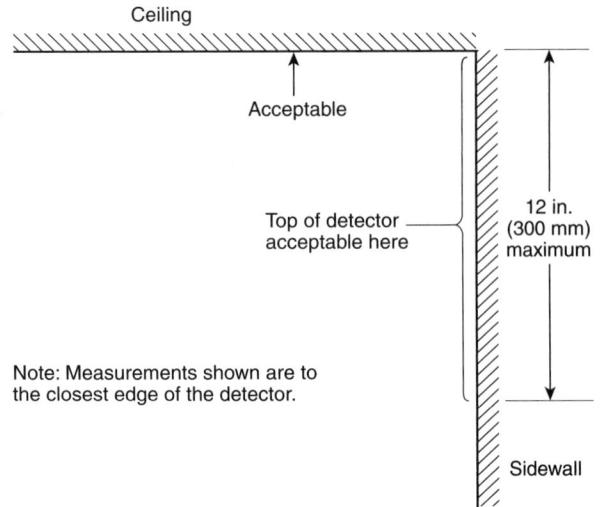

FIGURE A.13.7.4.3.3.1 Example of Proper Mounting of Smoke Detectors. [72: Figure A.17.7.3.2.1]

Where there are explicit performance objectives for the response of the smoke detection system, the performance-based design methods outlined in Annex B of *NFPA 72* should be used. For the purposes of this section, "nominal 30 ft (9.1 m)" should be determined to be 30 ft (9.1 m) ±5 percent [±18 in. (460 mm)]. [72: A.17.7.3.2.3.1]

A.13.7.4.3.3.3.1(2) This is useful in calculating locations in corridors or irregular areas *[see A.17.6.3.1.1 of NFPA 72 and Figure A.17.6.3.1.1(h) of NFPA 72]*. For irregularly shaped areas, the spacing between detectors can be greater than the selected spacing, provided the maximum spacing from a detector to the farthest point of a sidewall or corner within its zone of protection is not greater than 0.7 times the selected spacing (0.7S). [72: A.17.7.3.2.3.5]

A.13.7.4.3.3.4 Detectors are placed at reduced spacings at right angles to joists or beams in an attempt to ensure that detection time is equivalent to that which would be experienced on a flat ceiling. It takes longer for the combustion products (smoke or heat) to travel at right angles to beams or joists because of the phenomenon wherein a plume from a relatively hot fire with significant thermal lift tends to fill the pocket between each beam or joist before moving to the next beam or joist. [72: A.17.7.3.2.4]

Though it is true that this phenomenon might not be significant in a small smoldering fire where there is only enough thermal lift to cause stratification at the bottom of the joists, reduced spacing is still recommended to ensure that detection time is equivalent to that which would exist on a flat ceiling, even in the case of a hotter type of fire. [72: A.17.7.3.2.4]

A.13.7.4.3.3.4.2(3) The geometry and reservoir effect is a significant factor that contributes to the development of velocity, temperature, and smoke obscuration conditions at smoke detectors located on the ceiling in beam pocket areas or at the bottom of beams as smoke collected in the reservoir volume spills into adjacent pockets. The waffle- or pan-type ceiling created by beams or solid joists, although retarding the initial

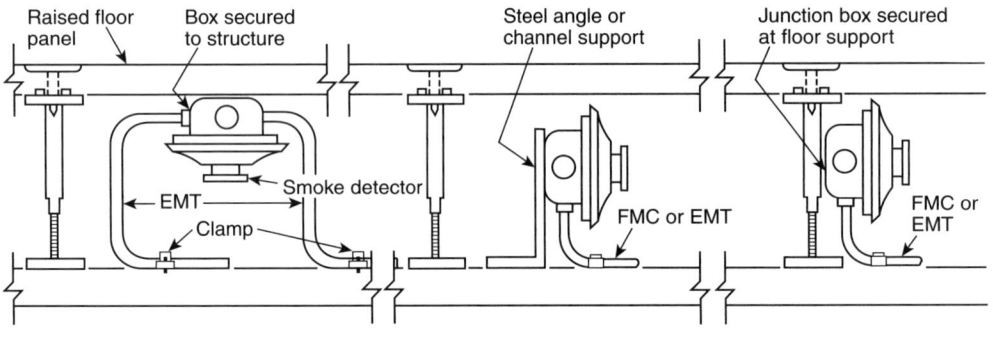

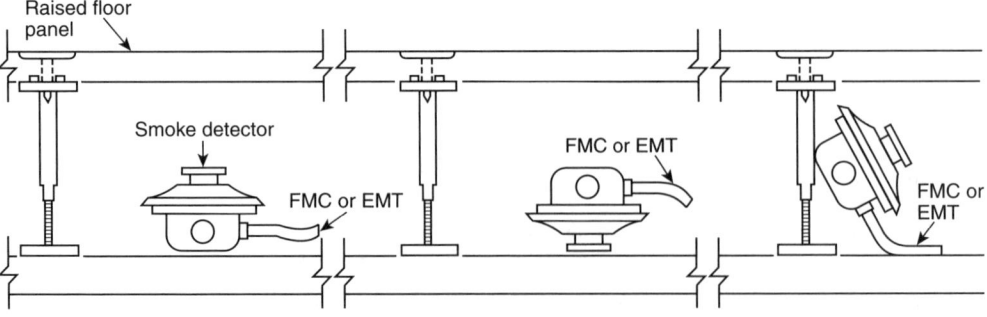

FIGURE A.13.7.4.3.3.2 Mounting Installations Permitted (*top*) and Not Permitted (*bottom*). [72: Figure A.17.7.3.2.2]

flow of smoke, results in increased optical density, temperature rise, and gas velocities comparable to unconfined smooth ceilings. [**72:** A.17.7.3.2.4.2(3)]

For waffle- or pan-type ceilings with beams or solid joists, an alternative smoke detector grid arrangement (such as a shifted grid), with detectors located to take advantage of the channeling effect due to the reservoirs created by the beam pockets, will improve detector response and might allow greater spacing. See Figure A.13.7.4.3.3.4.2(3)(a) and Figure A.13.7.4.3.3.4.2(3)(b) for an example of shifted grids. The alternative smoke detector grid arrangement and spacing should be justified by an engineering analysis comparing the alternative smoke detector grid arrangement with the performance of smoke detectors on a level ceiling of equal height using 30 ft (9.1 m) smoke detector spacing. [**72:** A.17.7.3.2.4.2(3)]

Figure A.13.7.4.3.3.4.2(3)(a) illustrates the reservoir and channeling effect that results from the deep beam configuration. The strongest gas flows occur in a direction perpendicular to the beam opposite the fire location. The weaker flow occurs in a directional 45 degrees off the beam grid; however, the reservoir effect accounts for higher concentrations of smoke eventually flowing from the strong area reservoirs into the weak area reservoirs. [**72:** A.17.7.3.2.4.2(3)]

Figure A.13.7.4.3.3.4.2(3)(b) is a generic example illustrating how a smoke detection grid using 30 ft (9.1 m) spacing can be shifted to take advantage of the channeling and reservoir effect to optimize detection response. In the circle, the fire is split into four beam bays that must fill with smoke before appreciable flows occur into the next adjoining eight beam bays. This represents the worst case scenario for smoke to reach the detectors on the circle. The three other fire locations shown require the fire to initially fill only one or two bays before spilling to adjacent bays. [**72:** A.17.7.3.2.4.2(3)]

A.13.7.4.3.3.4.2(4) Corridor geometry is a significant factor that contributes to the development of velocity, temperature, and smoke obscuration conditions at smoke detectors located along a corridor. This is based on the fact that the ceiling jet is confined or constrained by the nearby walls without opportunity for entrainment of air. For corridors of approximately 15 ft (4. m) in width and for fires of approximately 100 kW or greater, modeling has demonstrated that the performance of

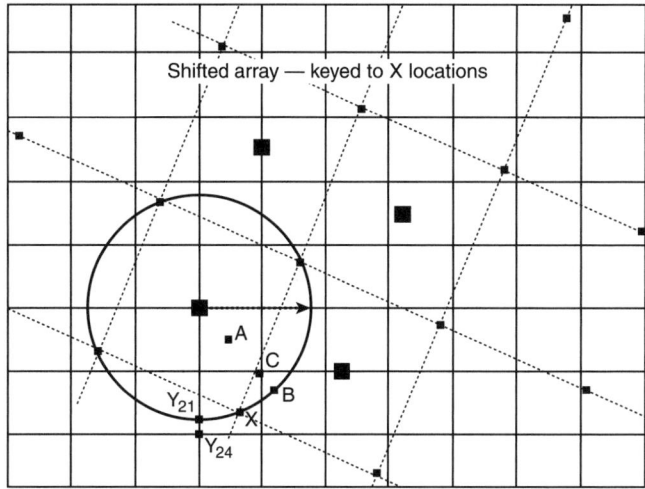

FIGURE A.13.7.4.3.3.4.2(3)(b) Shifted Smoke Detection Grid to Optimize Detection for Deep Beam Effects. [**72:** Figure A.17.7.3.2.4.2(3)(b)]

smoke detectors in corridors with beams has been shown to be comparable to spot smoke detector spacing on an unconfined smooth ceiling surface. [**72:** A.17.7.3.2.4.2(4)]

A.13.7.4.3.3.4.3 A smoke detector should be placed within each beam channel. Computer modeling has shown that parallel beams (upslope) are very effective at channeling smoke, and smoke spillover is rarely detectable in adjacent parallel pockets. [**72:** A.17.7.3.2.4.3]

A.13.7.4.3.3.4.4 Irregular area spacing guidance for level beam ceilings can be used. Computer modeling has shown that spot-type detectors should be located on the bottom of perpendicular beams. [**72:** A.17.7.3.2.4.4]

A.13.7.4.3.3.4.5 Computer modeling has shown that spot-type detectors should be located on the bottom of perpendicular beams and should be aligned with the center of pocket, as shown, in Figure A.13.7.4.3.3.4.5. [**72:** A.17.7.3.2.4.5]

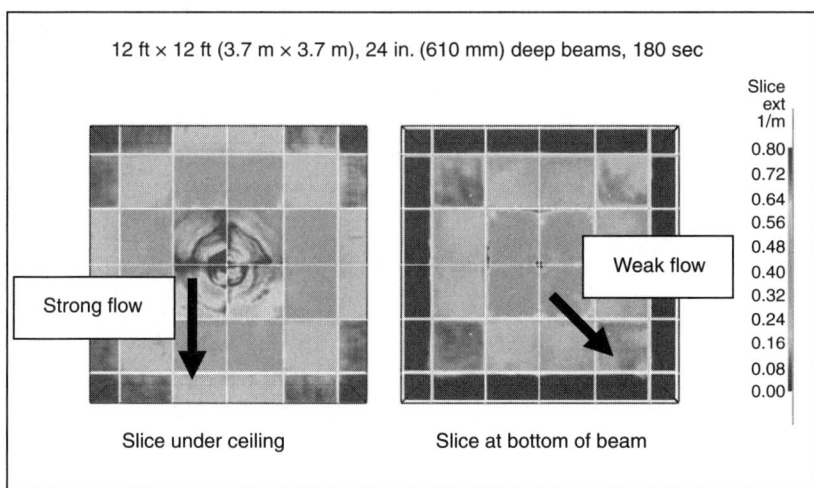

FIGURE A.13.7.4.3.3.4.2(3)(a) Reservoir and Channeling Effect of Deep Beams. [**72:** Figure A.17.7.3.2.4.2(3)(a)]

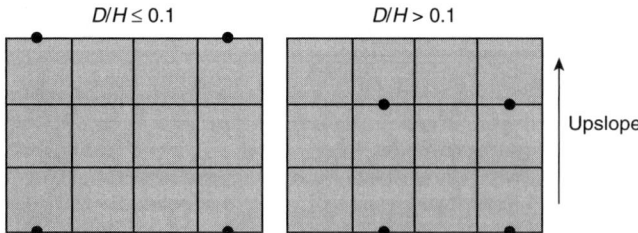

FIGURE A.13.7.4.3.3.4.5 Spot-Type Detector Spacing for Sloping Ceilings with Beam Pockets. [72: Figure A.17.7.3.2.4.5]

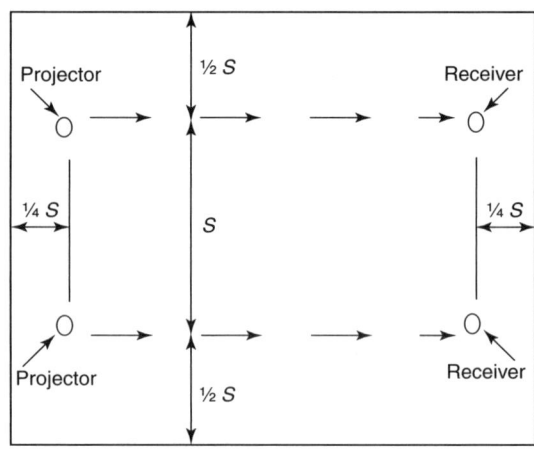

S = Selected detector spacing

FIGURE A.13.7.4.3.5 Maximum Distance at Which Ceiling-Suspended Light Projector and Receiver Can Be Positioned from End Wall Is One-Quarter Selected Spacing (S). [72: Figure A.17.7.3.7]

A.13.7.4.3.4.3 A single-pipe network has a shorter transport time than a multiple-pipe network of similar length pipe; however, a multiple-pipe system provides a faster smoke transport time than a single-pipe system of the same total length. As the number of sampling holes in a pipe increases, the smoke transport time increases. Where practicable, pipe run lengths in a multiple-pipe system should be nearly equal, or the system should be otherwise pneumatically balanced. [**72:** A.17.7.3.6.3]

A.13.7.4.3.4.6 The air sampling–type detector system should be able to withstand dusty environments by air filtering, electronic discrimination of particle size, or other listed methods or combinations thereof. The detector should be capable of providing optimal time delays of alarm outputs to eliminate nuisance alarms due to transient smoke conditions. The detector should also provide facilities for the connection of monitoring equipment for the recording of background smoke level information necessary in setting alert and alarm levels and delays. [**72:** A.17.7.3.6.6]

A.13.7.4.3.5 On smooth ceilings, a spacing of not more than 60 ft (18.3 m) between projected beams and not more than one-half that spacing between a projected beam and a sidewall (wall parallel to the beam travel) should be used as a guide. Other spacing should be determined based on ceiling height, airflow characteristics, and response requirements. [**72:** A.17.7.3.7]

In some cases, the light beam projector is mounted on one end wall, with the light beam receiver mounted on the opposite wall. However, it is also permitted to suspend the projector and receiver from the ceiling at a distance from the end walls not exceeding one-quarter the selected spacing (*S*). *(See Figure A.13.7.4.3.5)* [**72:** A.17.7.3.7]

A.13.7.4.3.5.8 Where the light path of a projected beam–type detector is abruptly interrupted or obscured, the unit should not initiate an alarm. It should give a trouble signal after verification of blockage. [**72:** A.17.7.3.7.8]

A.13.7.4.3.6 Construction debris, dust (especially gypsum dust and the fines resulting from the sanding of drywall joint compounds), and aerosols can affect the sensitivity of smoke detectors and, in some instances, cause deleterious effects to the detector, thereby significantly reducing the expected life of the detector. [**72:** A.17.7.1.11]

A.13.7.4.3.8.2 Smoke detector spacing depends on the movement of air within the room. [**72:** A.17.7.6.3.3]

A.13.7.4.7 Detectors that cause unwanted alarms should be tested at their lower listed range (or at 0.5 percent obscuration if unmarked or unknown). Detectors that activate at less than this level should be replaced. [**72:** A.14.4.4.3]

A.14.3.1(1) In existing buildings, existing walls in good repair and consisting of lath and plaster, gypsum wallboard, or masonry units can usually provide satisfactory protection for the purposes of this requirement where a 1-hour fire resistance rating is required. Further evaluation might be needed where a 2-hour fire resistance rating is required. Additional guidelines can be found in Annex O of NFPA 914, *Code for Fire Protection of Historic Structures*, and in the *SFPE Handbook of Fire Protection Engineering*. [***101:*** A.7.1.3.2.1(1)]

A.14.3.1(3) In existing buildings, existing walls in good repair and consisting of lath and plaster, gypsum wallboard, or masonry units can usually provide satisfactory protection for the purposes of this requirement where a 1-hour fire resistance rating is required. Further evaluation might be needed where a 2-hour fire resistance rating is required. Additional guidelines can be found in Annex O of NFPA 914 and in the *SFPE Handbook of Fire Protection Engineering*. [***101:*** A.7.1.3.2.1(3)]

A.14.3.1(6) It is not the intent to require the structural elements supporting outside stairs, or structural elements that penetrate within exterior walls or any other wall not required to have a fire resistance rating, to be protected by fire resistance–rated construction. [***101:*** A.7.1.3.2.1(6)]

A.14.3.1(9) Means of egress from the level of exit discharge is permitted to pass through an exit stair enclosure or exit passageway serving other floors. Doors for convenience purposes and unrelated to egress also are permitted to provide access to and from exit stair enclosures and exit passageways, provided that such doors are from corridors or normally occupied spaces. It is also the intent of this provision to prohibit exit enclosure windows, other than approved vision panels in doors, that are not mounted in an exterior wall. [***101:*** A.7.1.3.2.1(9)]

A.14.3.1(10)(b) Penetrations for electrical wiring are permitted where the wiring serves equipment permitted by the AHJ to be located within the exit enclosure, such as security systems, public address systems, and fire department emergency communications devices. [***101:*** A.7.1.3.2.1(10)(b)]

A.14.3.3 This provision prohibits the use of exit enclosures for storage or for installation of equipment not necessary for safety. Occupancy is prohibited other than for egress, refuge, and access. The intent is that the exit enclosure essentially be "sterile" with respect to fire safety hazards. [*101:* A.7.1.3.2.3]

A.14.4.1 A proper means of egress allows unobstructed travel at all times. Any type of barrier including, but not limited to, the accumulations of snow and ice in those climates subject to such accumulations is an impediment to free movement in the means of egress. Another example of an obstruction or impediment to full instant use of means of egress is any security device or system that emits any medium that could obscure a means of egress. It is, however, recognized that obstructions occur on a short-duration basis. In these instances, awareness training should be provided to ensure that blockages are kept to a minimum and procedures are established for the control and monitoring of the area affected. [*101:* A.7.1.10.1]

A.14.5.1.1 Where doors are subject to two-way traffic, or where their opening can interfere with pedestrian traffic, an appropriately located vision panel can reduce the chance of accidents. [*101:* A.7.2.1.4.1]

Swinging doors in horizontal- or vertical-rolling partitions complying with the following should be permitted in a means of egress where the following criteria are met:

(1) The door or doors comply with 14.5.1.
(2) The partition in which the doors are mounted complies with the applicable fire protection rating and closes upon smoke detection or power failure at a speed not exceeding 9 in./s (230 mm/s) and not less than 6 in./s (150 mm/s).
(3) The doors mounted in the partition are self-closing or automatic-closing in accordance with 14.5.4.1.

[*101:* A.7.2.1.4.1]

A.14.5.1.3.1 The requirements of 14.5.1.3 are not intended to apply to the swing of cross-corridor doors, such as smoke barrier doors and horizontal exits. Neither are the requirements intended to apply to doors from rooms that are typically unoccupied such as janitor's closets, electrical closets or telecommunications closets. [*101:* A.7.2.1.4.3.1]

A.14.5.2.2 Some fire door assemblies are listed for use with fire pins or fusible links that render the door leaf release inoperative upon exposure to elevated temperature during a fire. The door leaf release mechanism is made inoperative where conditions in the vicinity of the door opening become untenable for human occupancy, and such door opening no longer provides a viable egress path. [*101:* A.7.2.1.5.2]

A.14.5.2.5.1 Where the entrance consists of an exterior vestibule, the locking arrangement should be permitted on the egress side of either the interior or exterior door of the vestibule. [*101:* A.7.2.1.5.5.1]

A.14.5.2.8 It is intended that the re-entry provisions apply only to enclosed exit stairs, not to outside stairs. This arrangement makes it possible to leave the stairway at such floor if the fire renders the lower part of the stair unusable during egress or if the occupants seek refuge on another floor. [*101:* A.7.2.1.5.8]

A.14.5.2.10 Examples of devices that might be arranged to release latches include knobs, levers, and bars. This requirement is permitted to be satisfied by the use of conventional types of hardware, whereby the door is released by turning a lever, knob, or handle or by pushing against a bar, but not by unfamiliar methods of operation such as a blow to break glass.

It is also within the intent of this requirement that switches integral to traditional doorknobs, lever handles, or bars, and that interrupt the power supply to an electromagnetic lock, be permitted, provided that they are affixed to the door leaf. The operating devices should be capable of being operated with one hand and should not require tight grasping, tight pinching, or twisting of the wrist to operate. [*101:* A.7.2.1.5.10]

A.14.5.2.10.3 Examples of devices that, when used with a latch, can be arranged to require not more than one additional releasing operation include night latches, dead bolts, and security chains. [*101:* A.7.2.1.5.10.3]

A.14.5.2.12 Examples of devices prohibited by this requirement include locks, padlocks, hasps, bars, chains, or combinations thereof. [*101:* A.7.2.1.5.12]

A.14.5.3 None of the special locking arrangements addressed in 14.5.3 are intended to allow *credentialed egress, request to exit,* or similar provisions, where an occupant cannot leave the building without swiping a card through a reader. Where such an arrangement is desired to keep track of occupants, the swiping of cards needs to be procedural but not necessary for releasing the door lock or latch. Free egress needs to be available at all times. Another option to free egress is the use of a delayed-egress locking system. [*101:* A.7.2.1.6]

A.14.5.3.1.1(3) It is not the intent to require a direct physical or electrical connection between the door release device and the lock. It is the intent to allow door movement initiated by operating the door release device required in 14.5.2.10 as one option to initiate the irreversible process. [*101:* A.7.2.1.6.1.1(3)]

Several factors need to be considered in approving an increase in delay time from 15 seconds to 30 seconds. Some of those factors include occupancy, occupant density, ceiling height, fire hazards present, fire protection features provided, and the location of the delayed-egress locks. An example of a location where the increase on delay time might not be approved is at an exit stair discharge door. [*101:* A.7.2.1.6.1.1(3)]

A.14.5.3.1.1(4) In the event that the AHJ has permitted increased operation time, the sign should reflect the appropriate time. [*101:* A.7.2.1.6.1.1(4)]

A.14.5.3.2 It is not the intent to require doors that restrict access but that comply with 14.5.2.10 to comply with the access-controlled egress door provisions of 14.5.3.2. The term *access-controlled* was chosen when the requirements of 14.5.3.2 were first added to the *Code* to describe the function in which a door is electronically locked from the inside in a manner that restricts egress. It is not the *Code's* intent to prohibit methods of securing the door in a locked position from the outside with access control products, provided that the egress requirements of 14.5.3.2 are met. [*101:* A.7.2.1.6.2]

A.14.5.3.3(14) It is not the intent to prohibit elevator lobby doors from being equipped with card access systems for gaining access, for example, to tenant spaces. It is the access-controlled egress door system described in 14.5.3.2 that is prohibited from being installed on the same door as the lock addressed by 14.5.3.3. [*101:* A.7.2.1.6.3(14)]

A.14.5.3.4.2 The presence of fire exit hardware on a door does not imply the door is required to be a fire protection-rated door. [*101:* A.7.2.1.7.2]

A.14.5.4.1 Examples of doors designed to normally be kept closed include those to a stair enclosure or horizontal exit. [*101:* A.7.2.1.8.1]

A.14.6.2 The purpose of this provision is to protect the exterior wall of a stairway from fires in other portions of the building. If the exterior wall of the stair is flush with the building exterior wall, the fire would need to travel around 180 degrees in order to impact the stair. This has not been a problem in existing buildings, so no protection is required. However, if the angle of exposure is less than 180 degrees, protection of either the stair wall or building wall is required. [*101:* A.7.2.2.5.2]

Figure A.14.6.2(a), Figure A.14.6.2(b), and Figure A.14.6.2(c) illustrate the requirement, assuming nonrated glass on the exterior wall of the stair is used. [*101:* A.7.2.2.5.2]

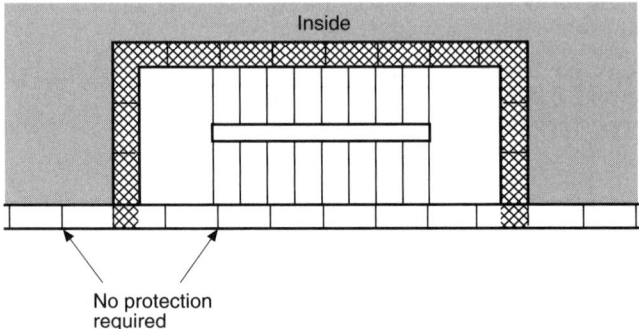

FIGURE A.14.6.2(a) Stairway with Nonrated Exterior Wall in Same Plane as Building Exterior Wall. [*101:* Figure A.7.2.2.5.2(a)]

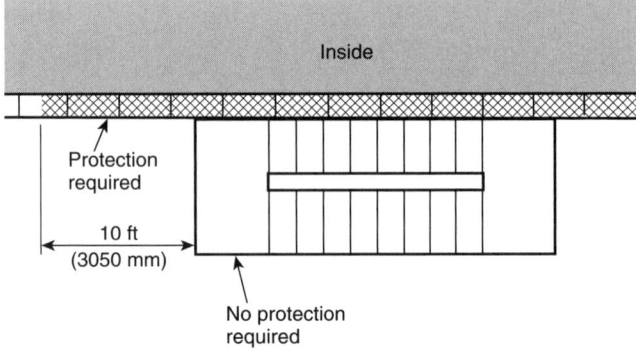

FIGURE A.14.6.2(b) Stairway with Unprotected Exterior Perimeter Protruding Past Building Exterior Wall. [*101:* Figure A.7.2.2.5.2(b)]

A.14.6.3 An example of a use with the potential to interfere with egress is storage. [*101:* A.7.2.2.5.3]

A.14.7 An exit passageway serves as a horizontal means of exit travel that is protected from fire in a manner similar to an enclosed interior exit stair. Where it is desired to offset exit stairs in a multistory building, an exit passageway can be used to preserve the continuity of the protected exit by connecting the bottom of one stair to the top of the stair that continues to the street floor. Probably the most important use of an exit passageway is to satisfy the requirement that at least 50 percent of the exit stairs discharge directly outside from multistory buildings *(see 7.7.2 of NFPA 101)*. Thus, if it is impractical to locate the stair on an exterior wall, an exit passageway can be

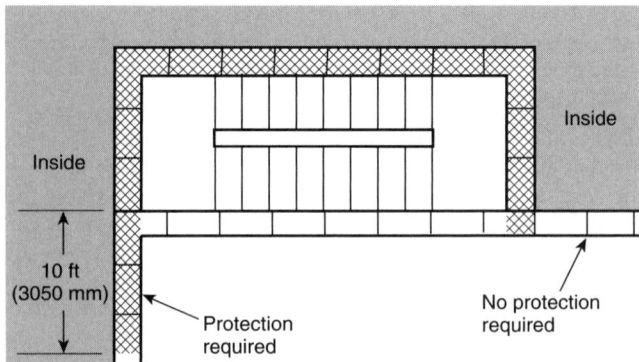

FIGURE A.14.6.2(c) Stairway with Nonrated Exterior Wall Exposed by Adjacent Exterior Wall of Building. [*101:* Figure A.7.2.2.5.2(c)]

connected to the bottom of the stair to convey the occupants safely to an outside exit door. In buildings of extremely large area, such as shopping malls and some factories, the exit passageway can be used to advantage where the travel distance to reach an exit would otherwise be excessive. [*101:* A.7.2.6]

A.14.7.1 Examples of building elements that might be arranged as exit passageways include hallways, corridors, passages, tunnels, underfloor passageways, or overhead passageways. [*101:* A.7.2.6.1]

A.14.7.4.1(1) Where an exit passageway serves occupants on the level of exit discharge as well as other floors, it should not be required that the occupant loads be added, thus increasing the width of the exit passageway. The situation is the same as that in which occupants from the level of exit discharge join occupants from upper floors for a few feet of horizontal travel through a stair enclosure. [*101:* A.7.2.6.4.1(1)]

A.14.8.1.2 The normal occupant load is not necessarily a suitable criterion, because the greatest hazard can occur when an unusually large crowd is present, which is a condition often difficult for AHJs to control by regulatory measures. The principle of this *Code* is to provide means of egress for the maximum probable number of occupants, rather than to attempt to limit occupants to a number commensurate with available means of egress. However, limits of occupancy are specified in certain special cases for other reasons. [*101:* A.7.3.1.2]

Suggested occupant load factors for components of large airport terminal buildings are given in Table A.14.8.1.2. However, the AHJ might elect to use different occupant load factors, provided that egress requirements are satisfied. [*101:* A.7.3.1.2]

Table A.14.8.1.2 Airport Terminal Occupant Load Factors

Airport Terminal Area	ft² (gross)	m² (gross)
Concourse	100	9.3
Waiting areas	15	1.4
Baggage claim	20	1.9
Baggage handling	300	27.9

[*101:* Table A.7.3.1.2]

The figure used in determining the occupancy load for mall shopping centers of varying sizes was arrived at empirically by surveying over 270 mall shopping centers, by studying mercantile occupancy parking requirements, and by observing the number of occupants per vehicle during peak seasons. [*101*: A.7.3.1.2]

These studies show that, with an increase in shopping center size, there is a decrease in the number of occupants per square foot of gross leasable area. [*101*: A.7.3.1.2]

This phenomenon is explained when one considers that, above a certain shopping center gross leasable area [approximately 600,000 ft^2 (56,000 m^2)], there exists a multiplicity of the same types of stores. The purpose of duplicate types of stores is to increase the choices available to a customer for any given type of merchandise. Therefore, when shopping center size increases, the occupant load increases as well, but at a declining rate. In using Table A.14.8.1.2, the occupant load factor is applied only to the gross leasable area that uses the mall as a means of egress. [*101*: A.7.3.1.2]

The value for concentrated business use is intended to address business use spaces with a higher density of occupants than would normally be expected in a general business occupancy. Where furnishings and floor layouts are arranged to maximize the number of occupants in the space, the value for concentrated business use should be applied. Examples of concentrated business use areas are call centers, trading floors, and data processing centers. [*101*: A.7.3.1.2]

A.14.8.3.2 The effective capacity of stairways has been shown by research to be proportional to the effective width of the stairway, which is the nominal width minus 12 in. (305 mm). This phenomenon, and the supporting research, were described in the chapter, "Movement of People," in the first, second, and third editions of the *SFPE Handbook of Fire Protection Engineering* and was also addressed in Appendix D of the 1985 edition of NFPA *101*, among several other publications. In 1988, this appendix was moved to form Chapter 2 of the 1988 edition of NFPA 101M, *Alternative Approaches to Life Safety*. (This document was later designated as NFPA 101A, *Guide on Alternative Approaches to Life Safety*, and this chapter remained in the document through the 1998 edition.) In essence, the effective width phenomenon recognizes that there is an edge or boundary effect at the sides of a circulation path. It has been best examined in relation to stairway width, where the edge effect was estimated to be 6 in. (150 mm) on each side, but a similar phenomenon occurs with other paths, such as corridors and doors, although quantitative estimates of their edge effect are not as well established as they have been for stairways, at least those stairways studied in Canada during the late 1960s through the 1970s in office building evacuation drills and in crowd movement in a variety of buildings with assembly occupancy. [*101*: A.7.3.3.2]

More recent studies have not been performed to determine how the edge effect might be changing (or has changed) with demographic changes to larger, heavier occupants moving more slowly, and thus swaying laterally, to maintain balance when walking. The impact of such demographic changes, which are significant and influential for evacuation flow and speed of movement on stairs, for example, has the effect of increasing the time of evacuation in a way that affects all stair widths, but will be most pronounced for nominal widths less than 56 in. (1422 mm). [*101*: A.7.3.3.2]

Without taking into account occupant demographic changes in the last few decades that affect evacuation performance, especially on stairs, the formula for enhanced capacity of stairways wider than 44 in. (1120 mm) assumes that any portion of the nominal width greater than 44 in. (1120 mm) is as effective proportionally as the effective width of a nominal 44 in. (1120 mm) stair, that is, 32 in. (810 mm). Thus, the denominator (0.218) in the equation is simply the effective width of 32 in. (810 mm) divided by the capacity of 147 persons that is credited, by the 0.3 in. (7.6 mm) capacity factor in Table A.14.8.3.2, to the corresponding nominal width, 44 in. (1120 mm). [*101*: A.7.3.3.2]

The resulting permitted stairway capacities, based on occupant load of single stories (in accordance with 7.3.1.4 of NFPA *101*), for several stairway widths are shown in Table A.14.8.3.2. [*101*: A.7.3.3.2]

Table A.14.8.3.2 Stairway Capacities

Permitted Capacity (no. of persons)	Nominal Width		Clear Width Between Handrails[a]		Effective Width	
	in.	mm	in.	mm	in.	mm
120[b]	36	915	28	710	24	610
147	44	1120	36	915	32	810
202	56	1420	48	1220	44	1120
257	68	1725	60	1525[c]	56	1420

[a]A reasonable handrail incursion of only 4 in. (100 mm), into the nominal width, is assumed on each side of the stair, although 7.3.3.2 of NFPA 101 permits a maximum incursion of 4½ in. (114 mm) on each side.
[b]Other *Code* sections limit the occupant load for such stairs more severely, (e.g., 50 persons in 7.2.2.2.1.2 of NFPA 101). Such lower limits are partly justified by the relatively small effective width of such stairs, which, if taken into account by Table 7.3.3.1 of NFPA 101, would result in a correspondingly low effective capacity of only 110 persons (24 divided by 0.218), or a more realistic capacity factor of 0.327, applicable to nominal width.
[c] A clear width of 60 in. (1525 mm) is the maximum permitted by the handrail reachability criteria of 7.2.2.4.1.2 of NFPA 101. Although some prior editions of the *Code* permitted wider portions of stairs [up to 88 in. (2240 mm), between handrails], such wider portions are less effective for reasonably safe crowd flow and generally should not be used for major crowd movement. To achieve the maximum possible, reasonably safe egress capacity for such stairs, retrofit of an intermediate — not necessarily central — handrail is recommended; for example, with an intermediate handrail located 36 in. (915 mm) from the closest side handrail. In this case, the effective capacity would be 358 persons for the formerly permitted, now retrofitted, stair. This is based on a retrofitted, effective width of about 78 in. (1980 mm) [subtracting 2 in. (51 mm) from each usable side of a handrail and assuming a 2 in. (51 mm) wide, retrofitted intermediate handrail]. [*101*: A.7.3.3.2]

A.14.8.3.4.1.1 The criteria of written, were intended to provide for minimum widths for small spaces such as individual offices. The intent is that these reductions in required width apply to spaces formed by furniture and movable walls so that accommodations can easily be made for mobility-impaired individuals. One side of a path could be a fixed wall, provided that the other side is movable. This does not exempt the door widths or widths of fixed-wall corridors, regardless of the number of people or length. The allowance for reduction in width has been expanded to include all exit accesses serving not more than six people where the travel length along the reduced-width path does not exceed 50 ft (15 m), regardless of occupancy or use of the space. [*101*: A.7.3.4.1.1]

Figure A.14.8.3.4.1.1(a) and Figure A.14.8.3.4.1.1(b) present selected anthropometric data for adults. The male and female figures depicted in the figures are average, 50th percentile, in size. Some dimensions apply to very large, 97.5 percentile, adults (noted as 97.5 P). [*101:*A.7.3.4.1.1]

A.14.10.1.1.1 See A.14.10.1.5. [*101:*A.7.5.1.1.1]

A.14.10.1.3.2 Figure A.14.10.1.3.2(a) through Figure A.14.10.1.3.2(e) illustrate the method of measurement intended by 14.10.1.3.2. [*101:*A.7.5.1.3.2]

A.14.10.1.3.4 Figure A.14.10.1.3.4 illustrates the method of measuring exit separation distance along the line of travel within a minimum 1-hour fire resistance–rated corridor. [*101:* A.7.5.1.3.4]

A.14.10.1.4.2 It is difficult in actual practice to construct scissor stairs so that products of combustion that have entered one stairway do not penetrate into the other. Their use as separate required exits is discouraged. The term *limited-combustible* is intentionally not included in 14.10.1.4.2. The user's attention is directed to the provisions for noncombustible and limited-combustible in 4.5.9 and 4.5.10, respectively. [*101:*A.7.5.1.4.2]

A.14.10.1.5 The terms *dead end* and *common path of travel* are commonly used interchangeably. Although the concepts of each are similar in practice, they are two different concepts. [*101:*A.7.5.1.5]

A common path of travel exists where a space is arranged so that occupants within that space are able to travel in only one direction to reach any of the exits or to reach the point at

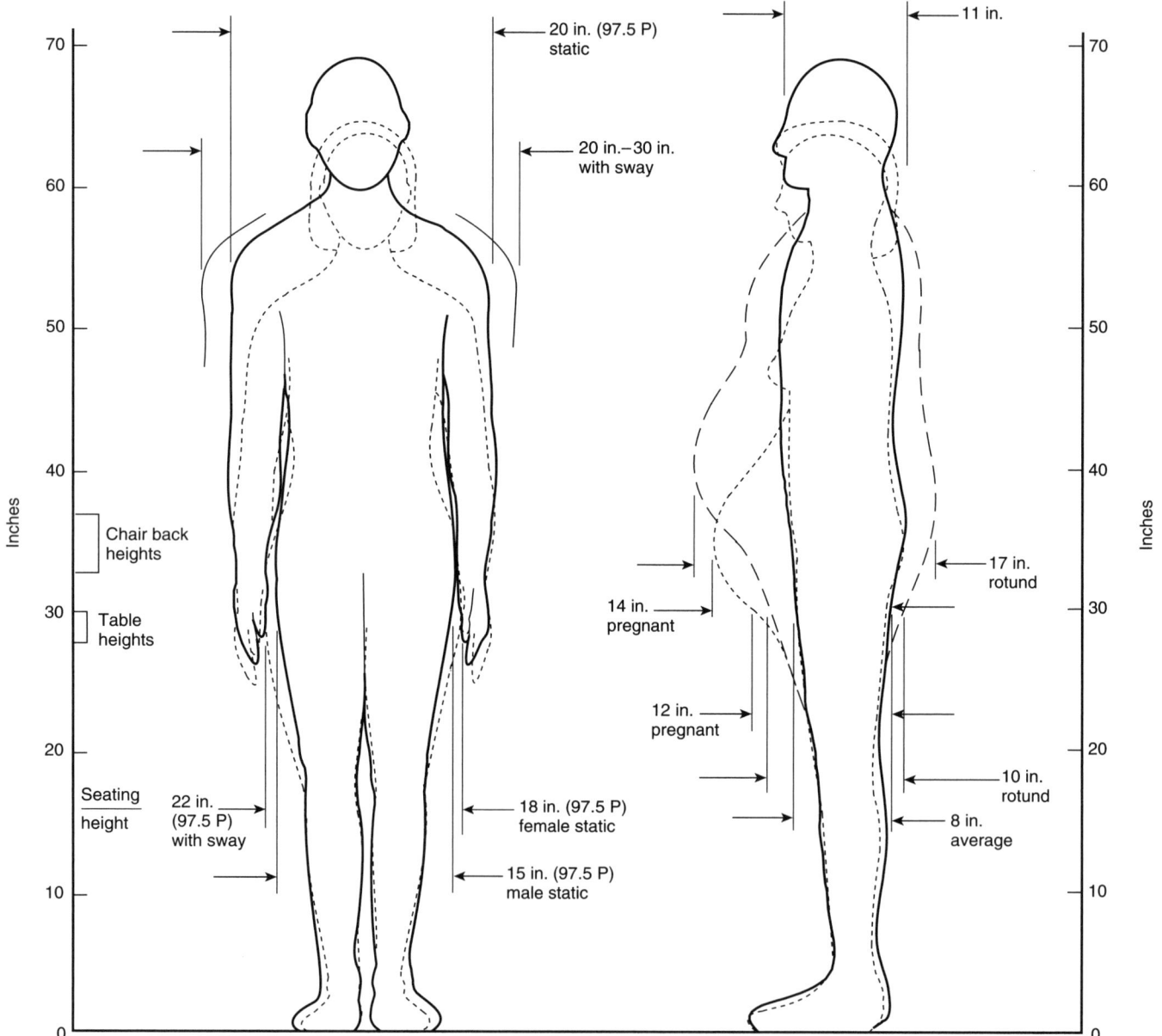

FIGURE A.14.8.3.4.1.1(a)   Anthropometric Data (in in.) for Adults; Males and Females of Average, 50th Percentile, Size; Some Dimensions Apply to Very Large, 97.5 Percentile (97.5 P), Adults. [*101:* Figure A.7.3.4.1.1(a)]

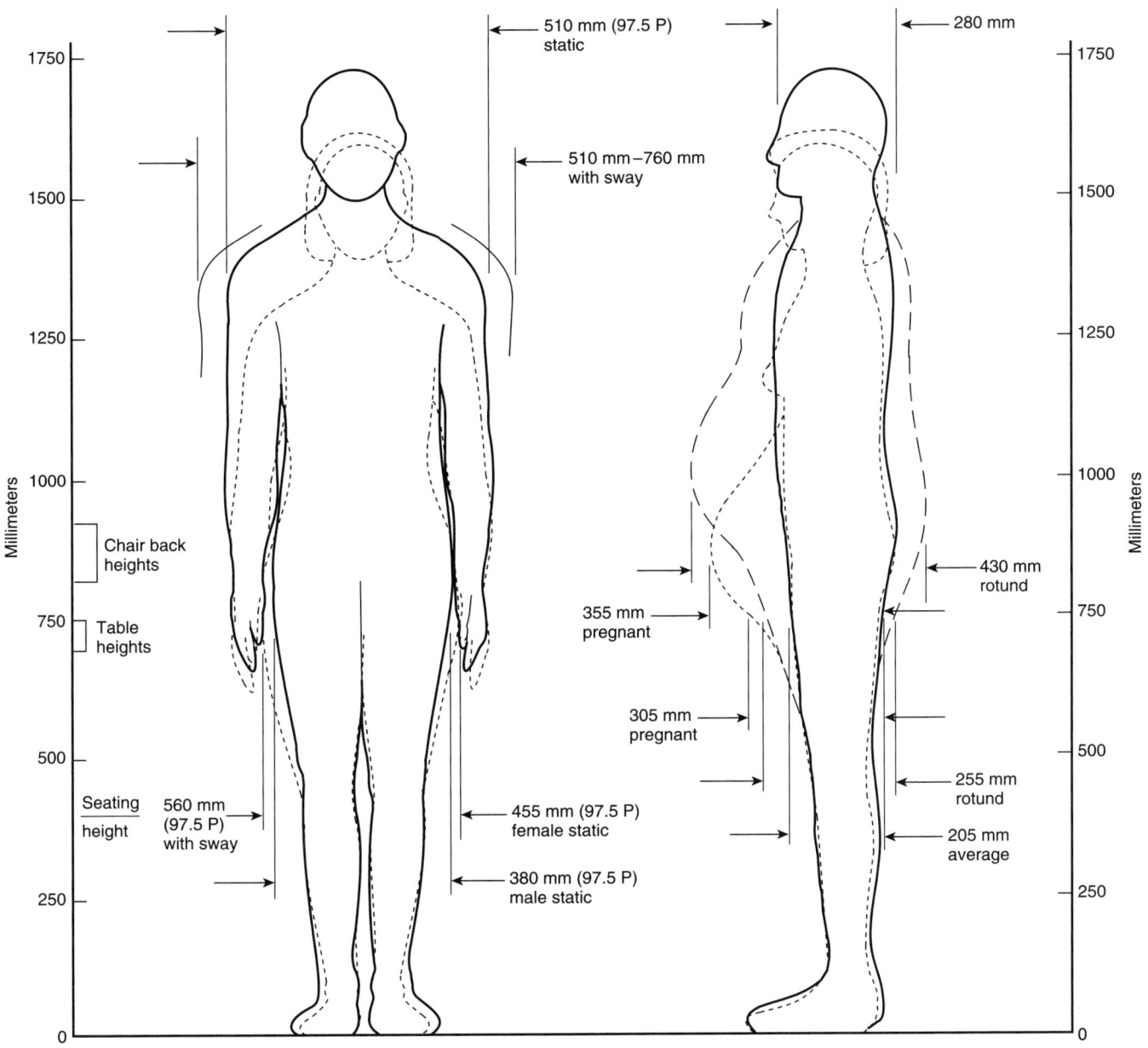

FIGURE A.14.8.3.4.1.1(b) Anthropometric Data (in mm) for Adults; Males and Females of Average, 50th Percentile, Size; Some Dimensions Apply to Very Large, 97.5 Percentile (97.5 P), Adults. [*101:* Figure A.7.3.4.1.1(b)]

which the occupants have the choice of two paths of travel to remote exits. Part (a) of Figure A.14.10.1.5 is an example of a common path of travel. [*101:* A.7.5.1.5]

While a dead end is similar to a common path of travel, a dead end can exist where there is no path of travel from an occupied space but can also exist where an occupant enters a corridor thinking there is an exit at the end and, finding none, is forced to retrace his or her path to reach a choice of exits. Part (b) of Figure A.14.10.1.5 is an example of such a dead-end arrangement. [*101:* A.7.5.1.5]

Combining the two concepts, Part (c) of Figure A.14.10.1.5 is an example of a combined dead-end/common path of travel problem. [*101:* A.7.5.1.5]

Common paths of travel and dead-end travel are measured using the same principles used to measure travel distance as described in Section 7.6 of NFPA *101*. Starting in the room shown in Part (d) of Figure A.14.10.1.5, measurement is made from the most remote point in the room, A, along the natural path of travel, and through the doorway along the centerline of the corridor to point C, located at the centerline of the corridor, which then provides the choice of two different paths to remote exits; this is common path of travel. The space between point B and point C is a dead end. *(See 3.3.65 for the definition of common path of travel.)* [*101:* A.7.5.1.5]

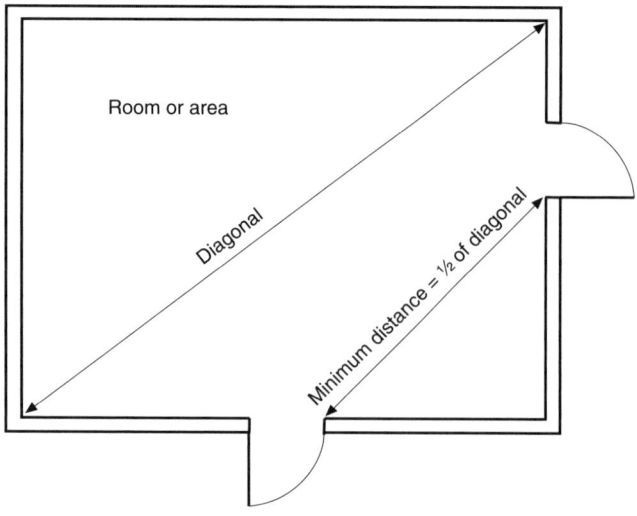

FIGURE A.14.10.1.3.2(a) Diagonal Rule for Exit Remoteness. [*101:* Figure A.7.5.1.3.2(a)]

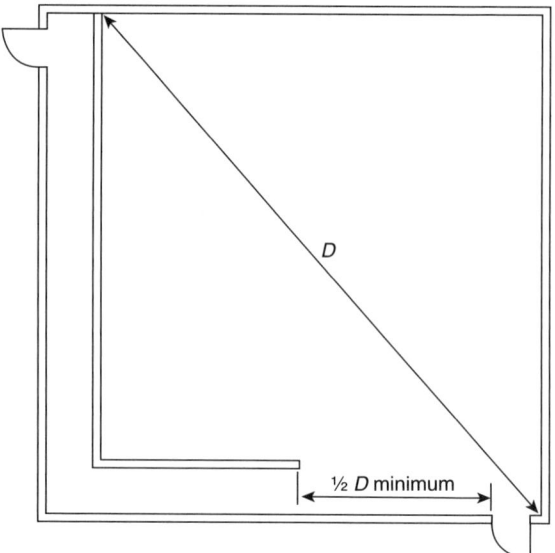

FIGURE A.14.10.1.3.2(c) Diagonal Rule for Exit and Access Remoteness. [*101:* Figure A.7.5.1.3.2(c)]

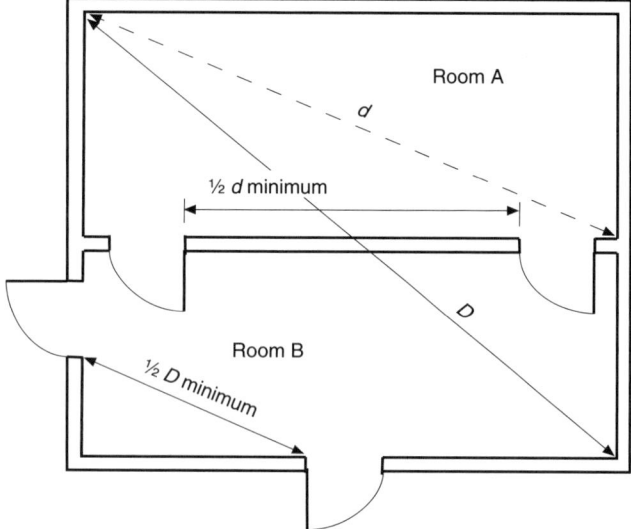

FIGURE A.14.10.1.3.2(b) Diagonal Rule for Exit and Exit Access Remoteness. [*101:* Figure A.7.5.1.3.2(b)]

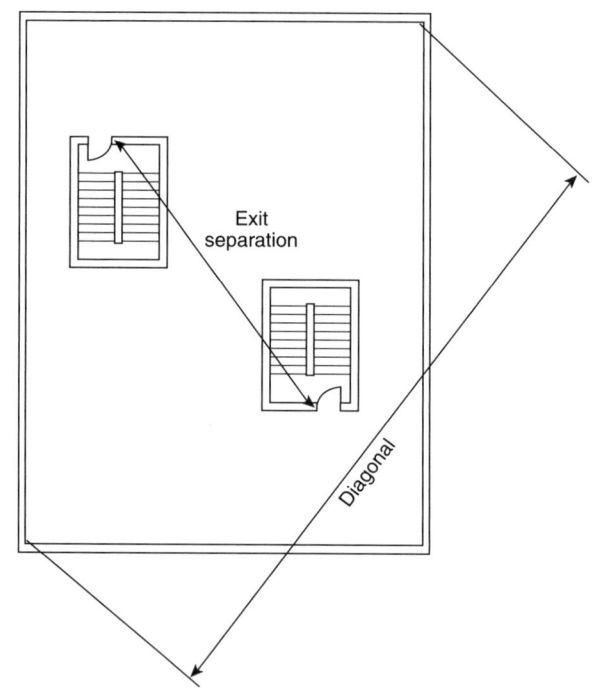

FIGURE A.14.10.1.3.2(d) Exit Separation and Diagonal Measurement of Area Served. [*101:* Figure A.7.5.1.3.2(d)]

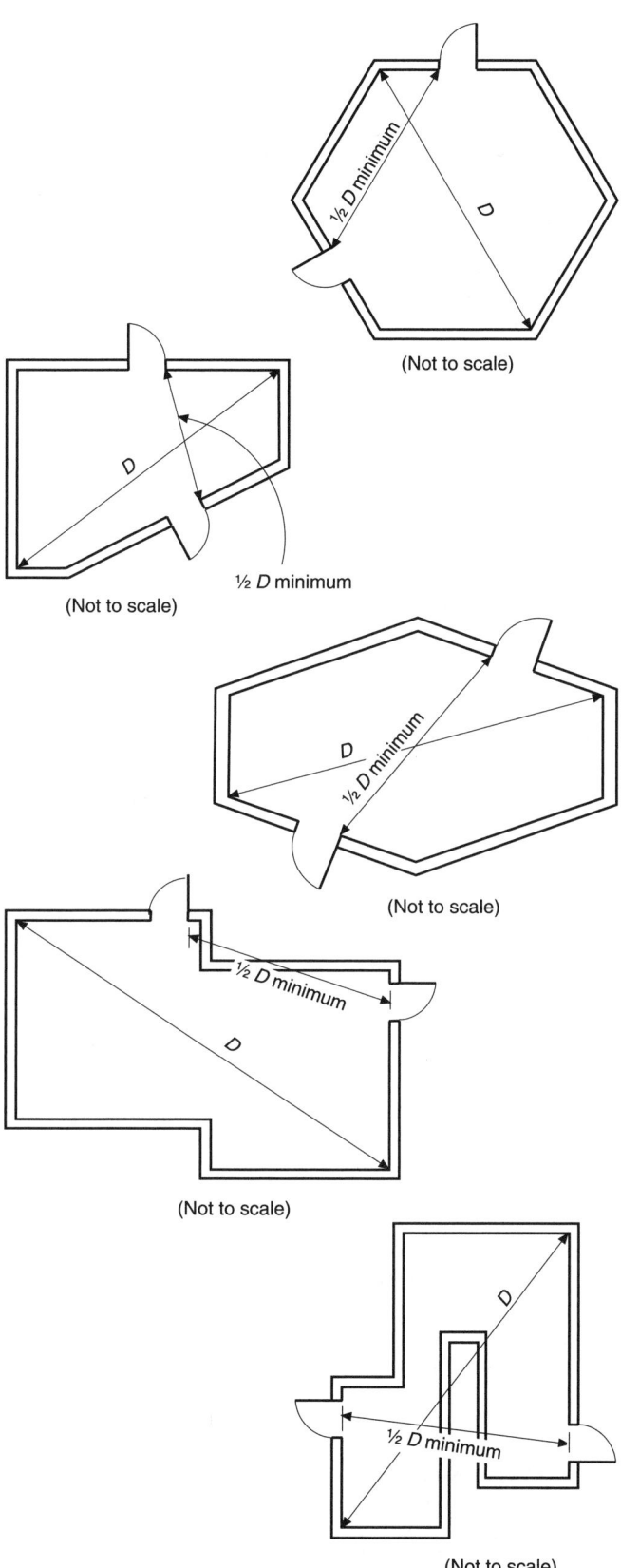

FIGURE A.14.10.1.3.2(e) Diagonal Measurement for Unusually Shaped Areas. [*101:* Figure A.7.5.1.3.2(e)]

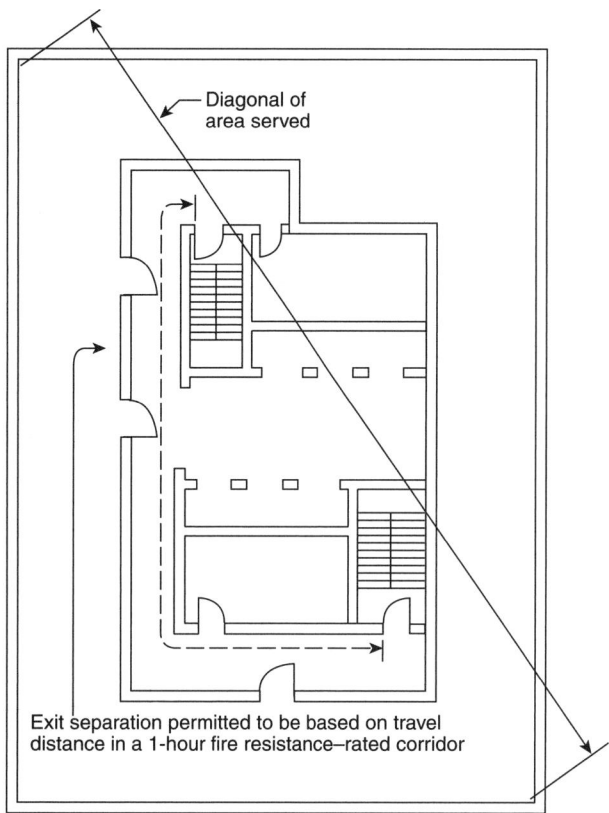

FIGURE A.14.10.1.3.4 Exit Separation Measured Along Corridor Path. [*101:* A.7.5.1.3.4]

A.14.10.2.1 It is not the intent that an area with equipment such as a beverage brewpot, microwave oven, and a toaster be considered a kitchen. [*101:* A.7.5.2.1]

A.14.10.2.2 Doors that lead through wall paneling, and that harmonize in appearance with the rest of the wall to avoid detracting from some desired aesthetic or decorative effect, are not acceptable, because casual occupants might not be aware of such means of egress even though it is visible. [*101:* A.7.5.2.2]

A.14.10.4.1 An accessible means of egress should comply with the accessible route requirements of ICC/ANSI A117.1, *American National Standard for Accessible and Usable Buildings and Facilities.* [*101:* A.7.5.4.1]

A.14.11.1 An exit from the upper stories in which the direction of egress travel is generally downward should not be arranged so that it is necessary to change to travel in an upward direction at any point before discharging to the outside. A similar prohibition of reversal of the vertical component of travel should be applied to exits from stories below the floor of exit discharge. However, an exception is permitted in the case of stairs used in connection with overhead or underfloor exit passageways that serve the street floor only. [*101:* A.7.7.1]

It is important that ample roadways be available from buildings in which there are large numbers of occupants so that exits will not be blocked by persons already outside. Two or more avenues of departure should be available for all but very small places. Location of a larger theater — for example, on a narrow dead-end street — might be prohibited by the AHJ

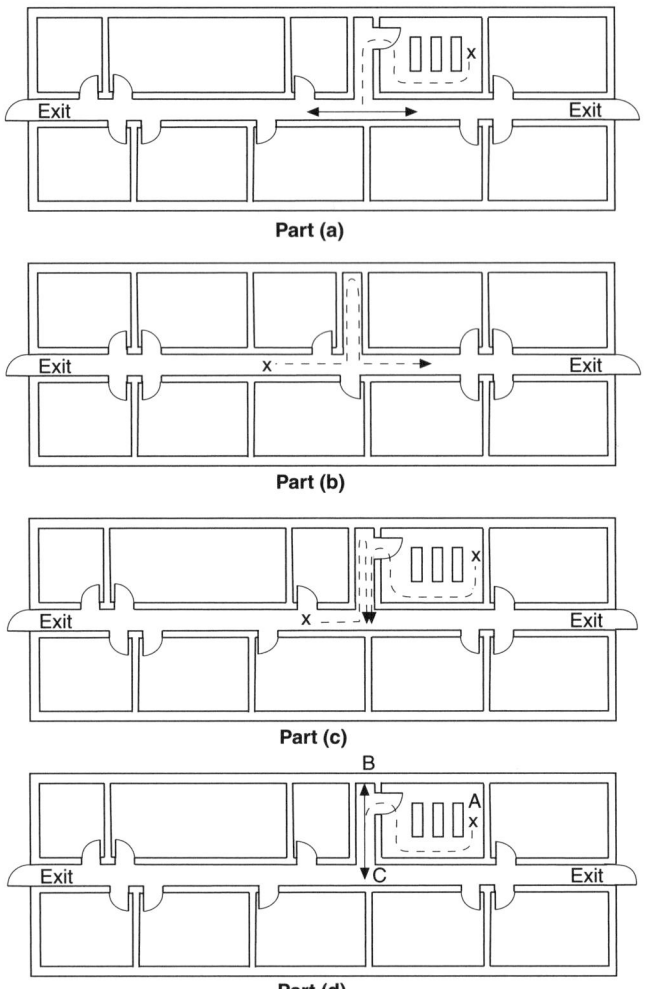

FIGURE A.14.10.1.5 Common Paths of Travel and Dead-End Corridors. [*101*: Figure A.7.5.1.5]

under this rule, unless some alternate way of travel to another street is available. [*101*: A.7.7.1]

Exterior walking surfaces within the exit discharge are not required to be paved and often are provided by grass or similar surfaces. Where discharging exits into yards, across lawns, or onto similar surfaces, in addition to providing the required width to allow all occupants safe access to a public way, such access also is required to meet the following:

(1) Provisions of 7.1.7 of NFPA *101* with respect to changes in elevation
(2) Provisions of 7.2.2 of NFPA *101* for stairs, as applicable
(3) Provisions of 7.2.5 of NFPA *101* for ramps, as applicable
(4) Provisions of 7.1.10 of NFPA *101* with respect to maintaining the means of egress free of obstructions that would prevent its use, such as snow and the need for its removal in some climates

[*101*: A.7.7.1]

A.14.11.3.3 Examples include partitions and gates. The design should not obstruct the normal movement of occupants to the exit discharge. Signs, graphics, or pictograms, including tactile types, might be permitted for existing exit enclosures where partitions or gates would obstruct the normal movement of occupants to the exit discharge. [*101*: A.7.7.3.4]

A.14.12.1.1 Illumination provided outside the building should be to either a public way or a distance away from the building that is considered safe, whichever is closest to the building being evacuated. [*101*: A.7.8.1.1]

A.14.12.1.2.2 Photoluminescent materials and battery-powered luminaires require some period of time to restore themselves to full operational capacity after being de-energized. [*101*: A.7.8.1.2.2]

Photoluminescent products rely on nearby luminaires to maintain their full capacity. When those luminaires are de-energized, the photoluminescent product will gradually deplete its capacity. Listed photoluminescent exit signs and path markers are restored to full rated capacity within one hour and there is no known limit to the number of times they can be discharged and recharged, nor any known degradation of overall capacity or lifetime as a result of discharge/charge cycles. [*101*: A.7.8.1.2.2]

De-energizing the normal (utility) power source will automatically begin the battery discharge cycle of emergency luminaires, unit equipment, and exit signs provided with battery backup. Once drained, these batteries will typically require between 24 to 72 hours, depending on the battery technology and charging circuitry design, to regain full capacity. Frequent discharge/charge cycles can reduce overall battery lifetime and, depending on battery technology, might also prematurely reduce overall battery capacity. [*101*: A.7.8.1.2.2]

A.14.12.1.2.3 A consideration for the approval of automatic, motion sensor–type lighting switches, controls, timers, or controllers is whether the equipment is listed as a fail-safe device for use in the means of egress. [*101*: A.7.8.1.2.3]

A.14.12.1.3(4) Some processes, such as manufacturing or handling of photosensitive materials, cannot be performed in areas provided with the minimum specified lighting levels. The use of spaces with lighting levels below 1 ft-candle (10.8 lux) might necessitate additional safety measures, such as written emergency plans, training of new employees in emergency evacuation procedures, and periodic fire drills. [*101*: A.7.8.1.3(5)]

A.14.12.1.4 Failure of a lighting unit is deemed to have occurred when the light output drops below 70 percent of its original level. [*101*: A.7.8.1.4]

A.14.13.1.1 Emergency lighting outside the building should provide illumination to either a public way or a distance away from the building that is considered safe, whichever is closest to the building being evacuated. [*101*: A.7.9.1.1]

A.14.14.1.2.1 Where a main entrance serves also as an exit, it will usually be sufficiently obvious to occupants so that no exit sign is needed. [*101*: A.7.10.1.2.1]

The character of the occupancy has a practical effect on the need for signs. In any assembly occupancy, hotel, department store, or other building subject to transient occupancy, the need for signs will be greater than in a building subject to permanent or semipermanent occupancy by the same people, such as an apartment house where the residents are presumed to be familiar with exit facilities by reason of regular use thereof. Even in a permanent residence-type building, however, there is need for signs to identify exit facilities such as outside stairs that are not subject to regular use during the normal occupancy of the building. [*101*: A.7.10.1.2.1]

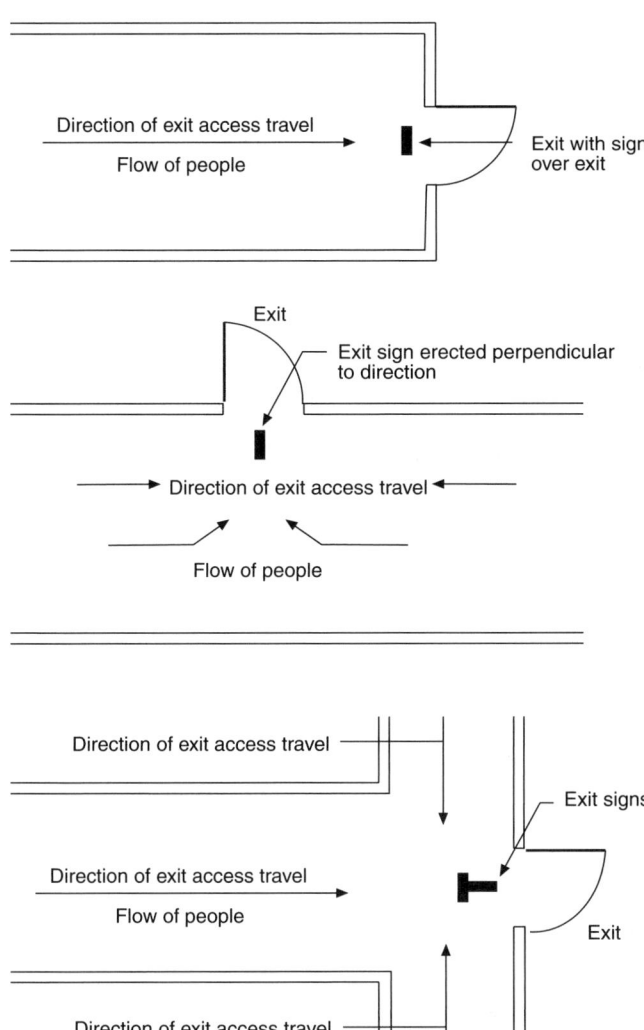

FIGURE A.14.14.1.2.1 Location of Exit Signs. [*101:* Figure A.7.10.1.2.1]

The requirement for the locations of exit signs visible from any direction of exit access is illustrated in Figure A.14.14.1.2.1. [*101:* A.7.10.1.2.1]

A.14.14.1.2.2 The direction of travel to the exit discharge within a stair enclosure with horizontal components in excess of the typical landings might need additional signage to be readily visible or obvious. Exit signs should be installed above doors through which the egress path leads. Directional exit signs should be installed where the horizontal egress path changes directions. The stairway marking signs required by 10.12.3, provided within the stair enclosure at each floor landing, indicate the vertical direction to exit discharge. [*101:* A.7.10.1.2.2]

A.14.14.1.5.2 For externally illuminated signs in accordance with 14.14.6 and internally illuminated signs listed without a marked viewing distance, the rated viewing distance should be considered to be 100 ft (30 m). Where placing signs at their rated viewing distance requires them to be placed above the line of sight, consideration should be given to increasing the size of the exit legend to compensate for the additional straight-line distance between the viewer and the sign. [*101:* A.7.10.1.5.2]

A.14.14.1.6 See 14.14.3. [*101:* A.7.10.1.6]

A.14.14.1.7 See 3.3.145.2 of NFPA *101* for the definition of *internally illuminated*. [*101:* A.7.10.1.7]

A.14.14.1.8 In stores, for example, an otherwise adequate exit sign could be rendered inconspicuous by a high-intensity illuminated advertising sign located in the immediate vicinity. [*101:* A.7.10.1.8]

Red is the traditional color for exit signs and is required by law in many places. However, at an early stage in the development of NFPA *101*, a provision made green the color for exit signs, following the concept of traffic lights in which green indicates safety and red is the signal to stop. During the period when green signs were specified by NFPA *101*, many such signs were installed, but the traditional red signs also remained. In 1949, the Fire Marshals Association of North America voted to request that red be restored as the required exit sign color, because it was found that the provision for green involved difficulties in law enactment that were out of proportion to the importance of safety. Accordingly, the 10th edition of NFPA *101* specified red where not otherwise required by law. The present text avoids any specific requirement for color on the assumption that either red or green will be used in most cases and that there are some situations in which a color other than red or green could actually provide better visibility. [*101:* A.7.10.1.8]

A.14.14.3.1 Where graphics are used, the symbols provided in NFPA 170, *Standard for Fire Safety and Emergency Symbols*, should be used. Such signs need to provide equal visibility and illumination and are to comply with the other requirements of Section 14.14. [*101:* A.7.10.3]

A.14.14.3.2 Pictograms are permitted to be used in lieu of, or in addition to, signs with text. [*101:* A.7.10.3.2]

A.14.14.4 It is not the intent of this paragraph to require emergency lighting but only to have the sign illuminated by emergency lighting if emergency lighting is required and provided. [*101:* A.7.10.4]

It is not the intent to require that the entire stroke width and entire stroke height of all letters comprising the word EXIT be visible per the requirements of 14.14.6.3 under normal or emergency lighting operation, provided that the sign is visible and legible at a 100 ft (30 m) distance under all room illumination conditions. [*101:* A.7.10.4]

A.14.14.5.1 See A.14.12.1.3(4). [*101:* A.7.10.5.1]

A.14.14.5.2 It is the intent to prohibit a freely accessible light switch to control the illumination of either an internally or externally illuminated exit sign. [*101:* A.7.10.5.2]

A.14.14.5.2.2 The flashing repetition rate should be approximately one cycle per second, and the duration of the off-time should not exceed ¼ second per cycle. During on-time, the illumination levels need to be provided in accordance with 14.14.6.3. Flashing signs, when activated with the fire alarm system, might be of assistance. [*101:* A.7.10.5.2.2]

A.14.14.6.1 Experience has shown that the word EXIT, or other appropriate wording, is plainly legible at 100 ft (30 m) if the letters are as large as specified in 14.14.6.1. [*101:* A.7.10.6.1]

A.14.14.6.2 Figure A.14.14.6.2 shows examples of acceptable locations of directional indicators with regard to left and right orientation. Directional indicators are permitted to be placed under the horizontal stroke of the letter T, provided that spacing of not less than ⅜ in. (9.5 mm) is maintained from the horizontal and vertical strokes of the letter T. [*101:* A.7.10.6.2]

EXIT>

<EXIT

<EXIT>

FIGURE A.14.14.6.2 Directional Indicators. [*101:* Figure A.7.10.6.2]

A.14.14.6.3 Colors providing a good contrast are red or green letters on matte white background. Glossy background and glossy letter colors should be avoided. [*101:* A.7.10.6.3]

The average luminance of the letters and background is measured in footlamberts or candela per square meter. The contrast ratio is computed from these measurements by the following formula:

$$\text{Contrast} = \frac{L_g - L_e}{L_g} \qquad [\text{A.14.14.6.3}]$$

Where L_g is the greater luminance and L_e is the lesser luminance, either the variable L_g or L_e is permitted to represent the letters, and the remaining variable will represent the background. The average luminance of the letters and background can be computed by measuring the luminance at the positions indicated in Figure A.14.14.6.3 by numbered spots. [*101:* A.7.10.6.3]

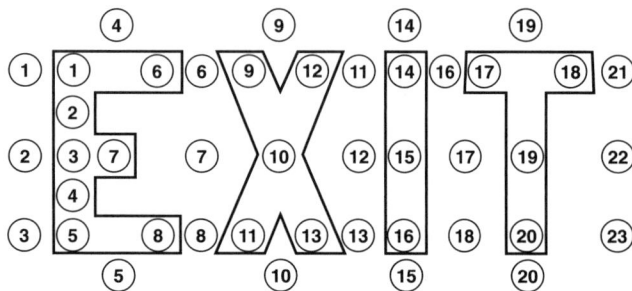

FIGURE A.14.14.6.3 Measurement of Exit Sign Luminance. [*101:* Figure A.7.10.6.3]

A.14.14.7.2 Photoluminescent signs need a specific minimum level of light on the face of the sign to ensure that the sign is charged for emergency operation and legibility in both the normal and emergency modes. Additionally, the type of light source (for example, incandescent, fluorescent, halogen, metal halide) is important. Each light source produces different types of visible and invisible light (for example, UV) that might affect the ability of some photoluminescent signs to charge and might also affect the amount of light output available during emergency mode. This type of sign would not be suitable where the illumination levels are permitted to decline. The charging light source should not be connected to automatic timers, because the continuous illumination of the sign is needed; otherwise, the sign illumination would not be available, because it would be discharged. [*101:* A.7.10.7.2]

A.14.14.8.1.1 Special signs require sufficient illumination in order for them to be readable at close proximity. They are not expected to be of a size or illumination level necessary to be readable from a distance, as is the case for an exit sign. [*101:* A.7.10.8.1.1]

A.14.14.8.3 The likelihood of occupants mistaking passageways or stairways that lead to dead-end spaces for exit doors and becoming trapped governs the need for exit signs. Thus, such areas should be marked with a sign that reads as follows:

NO EXIT

Supplementary identification indicating the character of the area, such as TO BASEMENT, STOREROOM, LINEN CLOSET, or the like, is permitted to be provided. [*101:* A.7.10.8.3]

A.16.1.3 See also NFPA 241. [*101:* A.4.6.10.2]

A.16.2.1.1 Examples of relevant test standards include, but are not limited to, the following:

(1) UL 647, *Standard for Unvented Kerosene-Fired Room Heaters and Portable Heaters*
(2) ANSI/UL 1278, *Standard for Moveable and Wall- or Ceiling-Hung Electric Room Heaters*

[**241:** A.5.2.1]

A.16.2.1.7 Misuse of temporary heating devices has resulted in numerous fires and millions of dollars in property loss. Temporary heating equipment, while operating, should be visually inspected every hour to ensure that combustibles have not blown or fallen over near the temporary heating device. During windy periods, it might be necessary to reduce the interval between inspections. Any object near the temporary heating device that is hot to the touch should be moved, or the temporary heating device should be relocated. The visual inspection also should ensure that the appliance is operating properly. Any appliance that is not operating properly should be turned off until repairs have been made. [**241:** A.5.2.7]

A.16.2.1.14 This might necessitate the removal of the heater prior to refueling. The appliance also should be allowed to cool prior to refueling. [**241:** A.5.2.14]

A.16.2.2.1 Failure to remove scrap and trash accumulations provides fuel for the rapid expansion of a fire that might otherwise be confined to a small area. These accumulations also provide a convenient fuel source for malicious fires. Open-topped dumpsters containing combustible materials should be emptied or moved to at least 35 ft (11 m) from combustible structures at the end of each work shift. [**241:** A.5.4.1]

A.16.2.2.4.1 An approved safety plan should include the following:

(1) A fire watch should be in accordance with Section 5.1 of NFPA 241.
(2) Adequate fire protection should include sprinklers, hose, extinguishers, or barriers as needed for the particular hazard present, including the construction of the chute.
(3) Protection of openings in exterior walls and protection of combustible exterior building surfaces should be adjacent to the chute.
(4) At the end of each work day, provisions should be made to assure that exposure fires are minimized. (*See 16.2.2.1.*)

(5) Trash chutes used in the interior of a building should be of noncombustible construction.
(6) The main artery of the chute should be as straight as practical to avoid accumulations or clogging within the chute.

[**241:** A.5.4.4.1]

A.16.2.2.4.3 The temporary sprinkler or sprinklers are not required to comply with NFPA 13, *Standard for the Installation of Sprinkler Systems.* Where trash chutes have a length exceeding 36 ft (11 m), intermittent levels of sprinkler protection should be provided at intervals not exceeding 36 ft (11 m). The use of fire retardant coatings can be substituted for sprinkler protection provided that the coating is compatible with the substrate, abrasion resistant, and approved by the AHJ. [**241:** A.5.4.4.3]

A.16.2.3.1.2 The reference to "structure" is intended to apply to those structures under construction, alteration, or demolition and not to temporary structures on the construction site. Additionally, existing properly protected storage within 50 ft (15 m) of the structure or inside an existing structure under alteration is not intended to be regulated by this provision. [**241:** A.5.5.1.2]

A.16.2.3.2.4 The vapors given off by flammable liquids generally have vapor densities greater than those of air. Therefore, these vapors tend to collect in low spots and travel at floor level. Being invisible, these vapors are difficult to detect without the aid of proper instruments designed specifically for the purpose. [**241:** A.5.5.2.4]

Proper ventilation is, therefore, important in the prevention of accidental ignition of these vapors. Proper ventilation can be accomplished by either natural or mechanical means. [**241:** A.5.5.2.4]

A.16.3.2.1 One person should be made responsible for the protection of property from fire. This person should ensure that the proper procedures for controlling fire hazards are established and should have full authority to enforce them. [**241:** A.7.2.1]

The responsible person should be appointed by the owner. Where an entirely new structure is being constructed, the owner should ensure that specifications for new buildings contain a clause stating that the "contractor will take all reasonable precautions against fire in accordance with good fire protection engineering practice." [**241:** A.7.2.1]

The responsibility for loss prevention is the owner's. However, loss prevention recommendations normally are accomplished by the contractor. To ensure that recommendations are carried out promptly, the owner's assistance might be needed. [**241:** A.7.2.1]

Fire prevention education should be a topic at contractor safety meetings ("tailgate talks") at least once a month. Topics that could be discussed include maintaining clear access to fire-fighting equipment, reinforcing cutting and welding procedures, flammable liquids use and storage, use of first aid fire-fighting equipment, roofing operations, and precautions for the use of temporary heating equipment. [**241:** A.7.2.1]

All fires should be investigated by the program manager, and necessary fire prevention improvements that are identified by the investigation should be communicated to all employees as soon as possible. [**241:** A.7.2.1]

A.16.3.2.3 Large-scale construction sites change rapidly as construction progresses. The prefire plan should be flexible to allow for different stages of construction. Critical stages that should be considered include access, installation of water mains and fire hydrants, framing/exterior shell, roofing, covering of interior partitions, installation of fixed fire protection, concrete form work, installation of building systems, and construction safety hazards. [**241:** A.7.2.3]

Since construction projects do change, the local fire department should be encouraged to visit the site on a regular basis. Prefire plan visits should be scheduled by the manager at least semiannually and when there have been major revisions to the fire prevention plan. Since municipal fire departments work rotating shifts, a series of prefire plan visits might be necessary to allow all responding fire fighters an opportunity to visit the site. In rural areas and smaller cities, the local fire department might be a volunteer organization or might have only a small career fire fighter crew on duty during the day. It might be necessary for the manager to schedule the prefire plan visit during the evening hours to meet the needs of the local fire department. [**241:** A.7.2.3]

A.16.3.2.4.5 See NFPA *101* for impairments to fire protection systems or fire alarm, detection, or communication systems where required by that code. In addition, see *NFPA 72* for impairments resulting to fire alarm equipment and NFPA 25 for impairments resulting to water-based fire protection equipment. [**241:** A.7.2.4.5]

A.16.3.2.5.1 Due to the growing threat of arson, guard service should be provided on major projects even where not required by the AHJ. The requirements for guard service also should be based on, but should not be limited to, the hazards at the site, the size of the risk, the difficulty of the fire-fighting situation, the exposure risk, and the physical security of the site. [**241:** A.7.2.5.1]

A.16.3.2.5.2 It is recommended that areas in buildings should be patrolled at all times when construction, alteration, and demolition operations are not in progress by a competent guard registered on an approved security tour supervision system (watch clock) with stations covering all parts of the building in accordance with NFPA 601, *Standard for Security Services in Fire Loss Prevention.* Guard rounds should include all parts of the buildings and outside areas where hazardous equipment or materials are located. Rounds should be conducted every ½ hour for 2 hours after suspension of work for the day and every hour thereafter during the night and nonworking days and should include tours of all accessible work areas. [**241:** A.7.2.5.2]

A.16.3.2.5.4 The requirements for security fencing should be based on, but should not be limited to, the hazards at the site, the size of the risk, the difficulty of the fire-fighting situation, the exposure risk, and the presence of guard service. [**241:** A.7.2.5.4]

A.16.3.2.5.5 Securing the openings (doors and windows) to the structure, where possible, reduces the chance of entry by unauthorized persons. This, in turn, reduces the chance of arson or accidental fires. It could, in some instances, eliminate the need for guard service or security fencing. It also helps prevent freezing or wind damage to fire protection equipment and prevents combustible material from being blown against heating devices and igniting. [**241:** A.7.2.5.5]

A.16.3.3 In large projects or tall structures, or both, the use of an audible device for an evacuation signal in case of fire or other emergency is recommended. [**241:** A.7.4]

A.16.3.6 Portable fire extinguishers, water pails, small hose lines, and 1.5 in. (38 mm) standpipe hose are considered first-aid fire-fighting equipment. To be effective, first-aid fire-fighting equipment should be used in the incipient stage of a fire. [**241:** A.7.7]

A.16.3.6.1 A suitable number and type of spare fire extinguishers should be provided on site for immediate replacement of discharged fire extinguishers. [**241:** A.7.7.1]

A.16.3.6.6 Clear and unobstructed access to all first-aid firefighting equipment should be maintained. Fire-fighting equipment also should be clearly visible from surrounding areas. If visibility to first-aid fire-fighting equipment is obstructed, signs in accordance with NFPA 170, *Standard for Fire Safety and Emergency Symbols*, should be installed to indicate the position of the fire-fighting equipment. [**241:** A.7.7.6]

A.16.4.1 Steel scaffolding or approved fire-retardant lumber and planking should be used on both the outside and inside of the structure. Construction materials (e.g., forms, shoring, bracing, temporary stairways, platforms, tool boxes, plan boxes, solvents, paints, tarpaulins, and similar items) should be of the noncombustible, fire-retardant, safety solvent, or high flash point type, as the case necessitates. A concerted effort should be made to attain as high a level of noncombustibility of materials as possible. *(See the definition of the term "fire retardant-treated wood" in the building code.)* [**241:** A.8.2]

A.16.4.1.5 The AHJ should be contacted regarding the adequacy of water supplies for hose lines. [**241:** A.8.2.5]

A.16.4.2.4 Construction tarpaulins would not be considered appropriate barriers or opening protectives. [**241:** A.8.6.2.4]

A.16.4.3.1.1 No minimum water supply is specified due to the wide range of construction types, sites, and sizes. However, unless combustibles are essentially nonexistent in the completed structure and occupancy, a minimum of 500 gpm (1893 L/min) should be provided. In most instances, the required supply is greater, and AHJs should be consulted. [**241:** A.8.7.2.1]

A.16.4.3.1.3 It is not intended to prohibit the construction of noncombustible structure foundation elements, such as foundations and footings, prior to the completion of underground water mains and hydrants. [**241:** A.8.7.2.3]

A.16.4.3.2.1 With proper scheduling and contracting, it is possible for the sprinkler installation to follow the building construction closely as it progresses. This is frequently done in multiple-story buildings to facilitate protection on the lower floors before the upper floors have been built. [**241:** A.8.7.3.1]

A.16.4.3.3.1.1 Threaded plugs should be inserted in fire department hose connections, and they should be guarded properly against physical damage. [**241:** A.8.7.4.1.1]

A.16.4.3.3.1.3 The intent of this provision is to permit the permanent standpipes to be used as temporary standpipes during construction. [**241:** A.8.7.4.1.3]

A.16.4.3.3.2.4 A substantial box, preferably of metal, in which a sufficient amount of hose to reach all parts of the floor, appropriate nozzles, spanner wrenches, and hose straps are kept should be maintained at the highest hose outlet. [**241:** A.8.7.4.2.4]

A.16.4.3.3.2.8 A supply of fire hose and nozzles should be ordered in advance so that it is available as soon as the standpipes are ready. Hose lines should be connected in areas where construction is in progress. [**241:** A.8.7.4.2.8]

A.16.7.1.6.2 Appropriate means should be provided to prevent portable fire extinguishers from damage and secured from falling when roofing operations are being conducted.

A.17.1.2 Figure A.17.1.2 and Table A.17.1.2 are examples of two different approaches to hazard assessment. [**1144:** A.4.1.2]

Figure A.17.1.2 is an example of an assessment guide with assessment information based on observation of the areas around the structure. This form, intended to be given to the resident, can be very useful by indicating the most serious hazards and the mitigation recommendation(s) that can be taken to reduce the ignition hazard. In this example, samples of the kind of information noted in an assessment are given as observations and suggestions for mitigation. [**1144:** A.4.1.2]

This example of an assessment guide is designed to help determine how vulnerable the structure will be during a wildland fire and to convey to the resident those items that should be corrected (mitigated) so that their home will have a better chance to survive a wildland fire. This form is offered as an example of the kind of tool that might be useful during a site visit as a guide for assessing the structure ignition zone. Remember, the following assessment items are for *prevention/mitigation* measures to be done *well in advance* of wildland fire season. [**1144:** A.4.1.2]

Figure A.17.1.2 is a form used to document observations, collect data, provide a hazard assessment, and give mitigation recommendations for the resident. From the mitigation recommendations, a mitigation plan and schedule is developed in accordance with 17.1.10. For more information on the use of this assessment form, refer to the course *Assessing Wildfire Hazards in the Home Ignition Zone*, available from the national Firewise Communities Program (www.firewise.org). [**1144:** A.4.1.2]

Table A.17.1.2 is a modified rating form based on the previous edition of NFPA 1144, *Standard for Reducing Structure Ignition Hazards from Wildland Fire*. Infrastructure elements of water supply, signage, and other fire suppression resources have been deleted, since the presence or absence of such resources does not modify the existing hazards of the structure. The table is presented only as an example of a rating system and should be modified to meet the environmental conditions of the area under consideration. For more information on creating an assessment system, consult *Wildland/Urban Interface Fire Hazards: A New Look at Understanding Assessment Methodologies Pamphlet*, produced by the national Firewise Communities Program (www.firewise.org). [**1144:** A.4.1.2]

A numeric rating form that will yield a hazard rating number can have a variety of uses, for example, determining relative hazards among several properties and mapping overall hazard ratings on a map. However, residents and homeowners often accept the rating number as finite and undertake mitigation measures that will merely reduce the rating rather than actually reduce the ignition potential of the structure. [**1144:** A.4.1.2]

A.17.1.4 It is critical to keep in mind that the ignition of the structure might occur from one or more of the following sources:

(1) Big flames (crown fire or intense surface fire). One objective of observation of the conditions and elements and subsequent mitigation recommendations is to keep crown fire and high intensity surface fire at a distance of 100–200 ft (30–60 m) or more from home and other potential hazards (flammables, buildings, etc.).
(2) Small flames (surface fire). Another objective is to keep small flames at a distance of 30 ft (9 m) or more from home(s) and flammable attachments (decks).
(3) Firebrands (embers). A final and essential objective is to eliminate beds of fine fuel and entry points for firebrands on and near home(s).

[**1144:** A.4.2]

ANNEX A 1–557

STRUCTURE ASSESSMENT GUIDE

Date of assessment: _22 Nov_ Property address: _70 Norris Rd._

Resident: _John and Jane Doe_ Property owner: _Same_

PRIMARY INFORMATION

Assessment Items	Mitigation Recommendations
1. OVERVIEW OF SURROUNDINGS	
How is the structure positioned in relationship to severe fire behavior? *The house is located near peak of a ridge at local map reference Q-4-12. The setbacks from the lot lines are approximately 15–20 ft. There is a slight sloping of the lot away from the house within 50 ft of the lot line on the north.*	*Since prevailing winds during fire season are most likely from the west-southwest, keep pine needles and leaf litter cleaned up on roadside berm.*
Type of construction: *Wood frame construction with brick façade on the front. Vinyl siding on back and two sides.*	
2. CHIMNEY TO EAVES	
Inspect the roof — noncombustible? shingles missing? shingles flat with no gaps? *Noncombustible roofing in good shape.*	*Inspect roof each spring for damage, especially after a hard winter or wind storm.*
Gutters — present? Noncombustible? *Aluminum gutters at all eaves. No overhanging limbs nearby. Pine needles and leaf litter not likely to collect in deep quantities.*	*Keep gutters free of pine needles and leaves. Check early spring and fall.*
Litter on roof, in gutters, and crevices? *Fairly clean. Not much of a concern. Easy to maintain.*	
3. TOP OF THE EXTERIOR WALL TO FOUNDATION	
Attic, eave, soffit vents, and crawl spaces: *Not much of a concern.*	
Inspect windows and screens — metal screens? Multi-paned windows? Picture windows facing vegetation? *Metal screens on all windows. Some windows on west side are double-paned. Some high vegetation near front windows. Low vegetation in rear.*	*Keep front bushes pruned and watered during fire season. Replace any missing or torn screens immediately, especially the front.*
Walls and attachments — noncombustible? Will they collect litter? *Not much of a concern.*	
Decks — combustible materials? *Wooden deck and privacy fence on south side. No skirting or screening beneath deck. Deck in good condition. Small vegetation around deck but overhanging tree limbs. Some collection of leaves and needles near deck and wooden stairs.*	*Prune trees closest to deck and privacy fence. Remove the pine needles and leaves. Store combustibles elsewhere — perhaps the shed in the backyard — especially during high fire danger periods. Put skirting or 1/4" wire mesh around deck openings.*

© 2014 National Fire Protection Association NFPA 1144 (p. 1 of 2)

FIGURE A.17.1.2 Structure Assessment—Guide Example with Notations. [1144:Figure A.4.1.2]

2015 Edition

STRUCTURE ASSESSMENT GUIDE (continued)

Assessment Items	Mitigation Recommendations
3. TOP OF THE EXTERIOR WALL TO FOUNDATION *(continued)*	
Fences. *Wooden stockade fence joins house on north side. Wooden fencing also on south side. Chain link in rear along lot line. Neighbor's wooden fence is less than 2–3 ft from their wooden fence — will allow leaves and embers to accumulate.*	*Keep wooden fence perimeter clear of dry leaves and other combustible materials like chairs, wood, etc. If the chance presents itself to use noncombustible materials to separate fence from house, you should consider it.*
Flammable material next to or under the structure. *None observed.*	
Combustible materials near or on the structure where walls meet roof or decking surfaces. *Plastic outdoor furniture pads on deck might pose problem from ember shower.*	*Keep combustible chair pads put away except when in use.*
Crawl space, attic vents, soffits. *All appear to be in excellent condition and protected.*	
Nooks and crannies and other small spaces. *All appear to be in excellent condition and protected.*	
4. FOUNDATION TO IMMEDIATE LANDSCAPED AREA	
Landscaped (managed) vegetation — separation distances, maintenance, plant selection? Firewise Landscaping Zones? *Lawn well cared for. Leaf and needle accumulation along east side (rear of property) with small stand of trees. Front and south side have mix of pine and other vegetation.*	*Be sure to keep these areas well tended, pine needles cleared and limbs pruned. Lawn needs to be kept green and mowed. Plants irrigated, pruned and raked — especially during high fire danger periods.*
Propane tanks. *No large ones. Outdoor grill small tank.*	*Make sure this area is kept clear of any combustibles — especially when using the grill.*
Vehicle and RV use and parking, including lawn mowers, etc. *Parking in front. Mower storage in shed which is 40–50 ft from NE corner of house. Plastic children's play house etc. near wooden fence along north side but over 30 ft from house.*	
5. IMMEDIATE LANDSCAPED AREA TO EXTENT OF THE HOME IGNITION ZONE	
Inspect vegetation clearance and crown separation. *Lot is rather small and the neighboring properties' vegetation is more dense than this one. Trees in back should pose little concern as prevailing winds will not communicate fire towards house.*	*Work with neighbors to improve all three lots to reduce the hazards on this corner. The neighbors behind this address and those on either side might benefit from some clearance that might take place but the separation of those properties appears to be sufficient.*

© 2014 National Fire Protection Association

NFPA 1144 (p. 2 of 2)

FIGURE A.17.1.2 *Continued*

Table A.17.1.2 Example of Structure Assessment Rating Form

Rating Values by Areas Assessed	Overview of Surrounding Environment (4.2.1)	From Chimney to Eaves (4.2.2)	From Top of the Exterior Wall to Foundation (4.2.3)	From Foundation to Immediate Landscaped Area (4.2.4)	From Immediate Landscaped Area to Extent of Structure Ignition Zone (4.2.5)
Topographical Features					
(1) Topographical features that adversely affect wildland fire behavior (4.2.1)	0–5				
(2) Areas with history of high fire occurrence (4.3.4)	0–5				
(3) Areas exposed to unusually severe fire weather and strong, dry winds (4.2.1.3)	0–5				
(4) Local weather conditions and prevailing winds (4.2.1.2)	0–5				
(5) Separation of structure on adjacent property that can contribute to fire spread/behavior (4.2.1.3)	0–5			0–5	0–5
Vegetation — Characteristics of predominant vegetation					
(1) Light (e.g., grasses, forbs, sawgrasses, and tundra) NFDRS Fuel Models A, C, L, N, S, and T	5			15	5
(2) Medium (e.g., light brush and small trees) NFDRS Fuel Models D, E, F, H, P, Q, and U	10			20	5
(3) Heavy (e.g., dense brush, timber, and hardwoods) NFDRS Fuel Models B, G, and O	15			25	15
(4) Slash (e.g., timber harvesting residue) NFDRS Fuel Models J, K, and L	15			30	20
Topography (4.2.1.1, 4.2.4, 4.2.5)					
(1) Slope 5–9%				1	1
(2) Slope 10–20%				4	2
(3) Slope 21–30%				7	3
(4) Slope 31–40%				10	6
(5) Slope >41%				15	10
Building Setback, relative to slopes of 30% or more (4.2.1.5, 5.1.3.2)					
(1) 30 ft (9.14 m) to slope	1				
(2) 30 ft (9.14 m) to slope	5				
Roofing Materials and Assembly, nonrated (4.2.2.1, 4.2.2.3)		50*			
Ventilation Soffits, without metal mesh or screening (4.2.3.4)		20			
Gutters, combustible (4.2.2.4, 4.2.2.5)		5			
Building Construction (predominant)† (4.2.4)					
(1) Noncombustible/fire-resistive/ignition-resistant siding and deck			Low		

(continues)

Table A.17.1.2 *Continued*

Rating Values by Areas Assessed	Overview of Surrounding Environment (4.2.1)	From Chimney to Eaves (4.2.2)	From Top of the Exterior Wall to Foundation (4.2.3)	From Foundation to Immediate Landscaped Area (4.2.4)	From Immediate Landscaped Area to Extent of Structure Ignition Zone (4.2.5)
(2) Noncombustible/fire-resistive/ignition-resistant siding and combustible deck			Medium		
(3) Combustible siding and deck			High		
Fences and Attachments, combustible (4.2.4.3)				15	
Placement of Gas and Electric Utilities					
(1) One underground, one aboveground	3				
(2) Both aboveground	5				
Fuel Modification within the structure ignition zone (4.2.4, 4.2.5)					
(1) 71–100 ft (21–30 m) of vegetation treatment from the structure(s)					5
(2) 30–70 ft (9–21 m) of vegetation treatment from the structure(s)				7	
(3) <30 ft (9 m) of vegetation treatment from the structure(s)				15	
No Fixed Fire Protection (NFPA 13, 13R, 13D sprinkler system)			5		
TOTALS (if numerical ranking is desired)					
Hazard Rating Scale (Compare with above totals)					
Slight Structure Ignition Hazards from Wildland Fire	0–14	0–14	0–14	0–14	0–14
Moderate Structure Ignition Hazards from Wildland Fire	15–29	15–29	15–29	15–29	15–29
Significant Structure Ignition Hazards from Wildland Fire	30–49	30–49	30–49	30–49	30–49
Severe Structure Ignition Hazards from Wildland Fire	50+	50+	50+	50+	50+

*Nonrated and combustible roof assemblies are predominantly structural exposures and severely increase the ignition hazard from wildland fire.

†The table provides both numerical and value rankings (low, medium, high). The user is urged to assign the value ranking of low, medium, or high based on the other ignition factors prevalent at the assessment site. For example, a deck made of combustible materials might rank low if it is small in size and the rest of the site is in a low fuel loading area that will not promote a large amount of firebrands. That same deck might rate high if it is in an area of high fuel loading that will promote numerous firebrands. Numeric values can be substituted as a local option. [**1144:** Table A.4.1.2]

A.17.1.5.1 Wildland fire dangers exist in flat land areas, as well as in mountainous terrain. In addition, property line limitations often preclude effective vegetation mitigation, and alternatives for mitigation are needed. [**1144:** A.4.2.1.1]

A.17.1.5.2 Local weather conditions or prevailing winds play a role in fire behavior (e.g., from which direction a fire is most likely to come, to the intensity and speed of fire travel, depending on the degree of slope), and the direction from which a wildland fire is most likely to approach the structure is an important exposure consideration. Sources of local weather records and fire weather history from the National Weather Service, National Oceanic and Atmospheric Administration (NOAA), local weather bureaus, or wildland fire agencies can be a valuable resource in assessing existing structures or in planning for new construction. [**1144:** A.4.2.1.2]

A.17.1.5.3 Adjacent ignitible structures (garages, carports, sheds, gazebos, utility cabinets) can contribute to heat intensity, flame contact, and fire spread from firebrands. [**1144:** A.4.2.1.3]

A.17.1.5.4 Overlapping zones could have a positive result in that the outermost extent of a structure ignition zone might be a neighboring parking lot or already treated vegetation area, such as a fuel modification. On the other hand, the overlap might include other private or public lands, which could make mitigation more difficult because it could involve state or federal agencies or absentee landowners who do little or no vegetation management or hazard mitigation. [**1144:** A.4.2.1.4]

A.17.1.5.5 Structure location on a slope increases the structure's exposure to heat (e.g., structure setback from the slope is sufficient to reduce its radiant heat exposure). Setback distances of the structure can be measured in accordance with A.5.1.3.2 of NFPA 1144. [**1144:** A.4.2.1.5]

A.17.1.6.1 All common coverings (composition shingles, tile, and, in many cases, metal) typically have a fire-resistive roofing classification adequate for interface fire protection if the covering material is tightly assembled to resist firebrand intrusion. [**1144:** A.4.2.2.1]

Untreated wood roofing is easily ignited and a major hazard. The only wood roof coverings that can be considered acceptable are wood shakes or shingles that have been treated at the factory by a pressure-impregnation fire-retardant process, tested for fire resistance, and certified with a fire-resistant roofing classification of Class A, Class B, or Class C. Pressure treated wood roofing looks very similar to the hazardous untreated wood roofing, and currently there is no permanent identification method. If in doubt, assume wood roofing is untreated unless documentation is provided. [**1144:** A.4.2.2.1]

A.17.1.6.2 Look for gaps in the roof covering that might allow small wind-blown firebrands to penetrate under the covering and ignite material below. [**1144:** A.4.2.2.2]

Some fire-resistive roof coverings are designed or installed with gaps that allow firebrand intrusion under the covering and have resulted in firebrand intrusion and ignition of the building under the roof covering. The worst example is roof coverings that allow combustible debris to blow under the covering or that allow rodents and birds to bring nesting material in under the roof covering. Clay (Spanish or straight barrel mission) tile roof covering can have this problem unless eave closures or "bird stops" are used to close the convex opening created by the shape of the tile at the eave. Metal tile roofing installed on top of old wood roofing left in place has been a problem. If you can see wood through gaps in metal tile roof covering, firebrands can penetrate and ignite the building. [**1144:** A.4.2.2.2]

A.17.1.6.3 Plastic skylights can melt from radiant heat or flaming embers or both. Deformation can result in large openings that can allow the entry of embers and other flaming materials. Skylights constructed of multilayered glazed panels or tempered glass provide increased protection from heat and embers. [**1144:** A.4.2.2.3]

A.17.1.6.4 The roof is the most vulnerable part of the structure and is subject to the collection of combustible vegetative litter (e.g., leaves, pine needles) or other debris and buildup that can be ignited by firebrands. Can litter build up and accumulate on surfaces next to combustible, perpendicular walls? Will combustible decking or roofing provide ember beds next to combustible, perpendicular walls? [**1144:** A.4.2.2.4]

Heat trapping under eaves does not occur until the wall supports flaming combustion as indicated by the portions of the wall that were protected (shaded) and did not char during experiments conducted by the USDA Forest Service Fire Sciences Lab in Missoula, MT. [**1144:** A.4.2.2.4]

A.17.1.6.5 Gutters and downspouts collect leaves and pine needles. Gutters and eave troughs made from combustible materials (e.g., wood, vinyl) are as vulnerable to firebrand collection as the roof and other parts of the structure. If leaf litter is allowed to gather in gutters, firebrands or embers can ignite the leaf litter, which in turn could ignite combustible eave materials or overhangs. If gutters are attached to combustible fascia boards, the fascia board should be considered as a possible fuel that can be ignited by fine fuels burning in the gutters. [**1144:** A.4.2.2.5]

Gutters that pose a fire threat from an approaching wildland fire are often pulled down by attending fire fighters. For the resident, an alternative might be to remove the gutters along the side(s) of the house most prone to the collection of leaves and needles and install a noncombustible drip line shown in Figure A.17.1.6.5. Removing gutters eliminates the collection of dry leaves and needles along the roof line and fascia board. Also reduced is the possibility of ice damage to the roof in the winter. The use of a

FIGURE A.17.1.6.5 Mitigating Risk of Leaf- and Needle-Filled Gutters. [1144: Figure A.4.2.2.5]

gravel bed for drip lines along the leeward side(s) of the house provides reduced ignition potential and reduced wind hazard, since the gravel would be less likely to be blown by high winds on the leeward elevations. The windward sides of the house can be landscaped with mulch (less impact damage in case of wind events) if protected with low volume sprinklers to raise the fine fuel moisture levels in times of high fire danger. [**1144:** A.4.2.2.5]

A.17.1.6.6 Eaves should be boxed to prevent flying embers from entering small spaces. [**1144:** A.4.2.2.6]

A.17.1.7.1 Identify the wall covering or siding (e.g., wood, vinyl, brick, stucco) and determine the possibility of litter buildup and accumulation on surfaces next to walls. Under low radiant heat levels, vinyl siding is damaged and falls off a wall, which can leave openings for firebrands exposing the interior of the home to ignition through eave vents and other possible openings. Vinyl is difficult to ignite by firebrands or radiant heat, but will sustain combustion when directly contacted by flames. [**1144:** A.4.2.3.1]

Hanging ½ in. (12.5 mm) or thicker drywall on the exterior wall studs prior to adding stucco, siding, and so forth can increase the fire rating. [**1144:** A.4.2.3.1]

A.17.1.7.3 Windows should be constructed of multi-paned or tempered glass that will resist fracture from intense heat in accordance with 5.7.1 of NFPA 1144, and window screens made from a material that will not allow hot firebrands to enter the home's interior in accordance with 5.7.2 of NFPA 1144. [**1144:** A.4.2.3.3]

A.17.1.7.4 Check attic, crawl space, eave, and soffit vents for appropriate protection (e.g., metal screening, noncombustible skirting) to prevent entry of firebrands. Roof turbine vents should be screened to prevent the entry of firebrands into attic spaces. [**1144:** A.4.2.3.4]

A.17.1.7.5 Examples of attached structures include decks, lean-to overhangs, patio covers, carports, balconies, fences, and similar structures that could be ignited by convection or firebrands. [**1144:** A.4.2.3.5]

A.17.1.7.6 Areas on, next to, or under a structure should be kept free of combustible fuel such as debris, vegetation, wooden furniture, brooms, welcome mats, furniture cushions, gasoline cans, firewood stacks, or piled construction materials. Look for combustible walkways, fencing, or decking attached to the structure, highly combustible fuels adjacent to the structure (e.g., junipers near decks and walkways), combustible materials (e.g., building materials, firewood) stored under decks or adjacent to the structure, animal nests among combustible structural fuels, and landscaping materials (e.g., bark mulch, ground cover plants) near the structure and surrounding plants that might support flaming combustion or that could easily be ignited by firebrands. [**1144:** A.4.2.3.6]

A.17.1.8 The structure ignition zone includes the spatially arranged traditional landscaping zones, but can exceed the extent of the property line. Figure A.17.1.8 illustrates the relationship of the structure and immediate landscaped area to the larger structure ignition zone. Within the immediate landscaped area [from the structure to approximately 30 ft (9 m)], often referred to as the defensible space, special consideration should be given that any combustible materials (e.g., plants, lawn furniture, litter, construction materials) should be removed or reduced to prevent their ignition, which in turn could ignite the structure. The total structure ignition zone includes any spatially arranged landscaping area and can exceed the extent of the property line. The level of risk of ignition within the total area of the ignition zone depends on the type of construction and is further influenced by slope, soils, and other site-specific conditions. [**1144:** A.4.2.4]

The AHJ should require the development of a landscape plan for the property. Such plans should address four zones around the property as follows:

(1) The most immediate landscaped area is the closest to the house and includes the area encircling the structure for at least 30 ft (9 m) on all sides. The landscaped vegetation within 30 ft (9 m) of structures should be irrigated as needed, cleared of dead vegetation, and/or planted with succulents and other plants (where appropriate) that are low in flammability potential. Plantings should be limited to carefully spaced, low-growing, low-flammability species, grasses, and lawns. Shrubs planted next to the structure should be of low flammability, no more than 18 in. (45 cm) in height, and not planted against the home. The planting bed should be noncombustible (e.g., stone, gravel, bare ground) or irrigated if combustible materials (e.g., bark mulch) are used.
All highly combustible plants, such as junipers and ornamental conifers, should be removed or trimmed and maintained to be ignition-resistant. Vegetation deposits (dry leaf and pine litter) that can support surface fire and flames should be removed regularly. Areas of vegetation (natural areas, undeveloped areas, landscaped areas, fields, etc.) that exist near the structure should be evaluated for the possibility of causing ignition of the structure.
(2) Progressing outward from the structure, the types and densities of vegetation should change to reduce the continuity of vegetation fuels. For example, plantings can be done in islands. Trees can be introduced into this zone with careful consideration of their flammability and continued maintenance to separate crowns and avoid ladder fuels. Tree placement should be planned so that the edge of the canopy of the tree when fully mature is no closer than 10 ft (3 m) to the edge of the structure.
(3) Progressing even farther from the structure, more medium-sized plants and well-spaced trees can be planted in well-spaced groupings to reduce exposure to wildland fire and help maintain privacy. The volume of vegetation (i.e., fuel) should be kept as low as possible or practical.
(4) The most distant area [100–200 ft (30–60 m)] from the structure determines the extent of the structure ignition zone. Plants in this furthermost area should be carefully pruned and thinned, and highly flammable vegetation removed. Particular attention should be paid to the types and densities of the vegetation in this area. For example, some vegetation and trees generate more firebrands than others and require additional thinning, removal, or replacement. [**1144:** A.4.2.4]

A.17.1.8.1 Vegetative fuels include live vegetation, mulch and landscaping materials, slash piles, composting piles, and firewood storage. [**1144:** A.4.2.4.1]

Flammable vegetation close enough to windows to provide intense radiant heat or flame contact should be pruned, moved, or substituted with smaller, lower flammability plants. Figure A.17.1.8.1(a) illustrates the use of low flammability plants separated by a gravel area next to the foundation. [**1144:** A.4.2.4.1]

FIGURE A.17.1.8 The Structure Ignition Zone. [1144:Figure A.4.2.4]

Mulch is an alternative to noncombustible landscaping materials such as gravel and rock. The size and texture of mulching materials affects its ignition and fire spread potential. Larger organic materials are preferable to smaller materials. [**1144:** A.4.2.4.1]

Landscaping with mulch can be acceptable if the mulch is protected with low volume sprinklers to raise the fine fuel moisture levels and offset its combustibility in times of high fire danger. The installation of sprinklers for areas using mulch for landscaping is shown in Figure A.17.1.8.1(b). [**1144:**A.4.2.4.1]

Figure A.17.1.8.1(c) describes the physical similarities of the NFDRS fuel models with fire behavior fuel models. See Annex B of NFPA 1144 for fuel model classifications. [**1144:** A.4.2.4.1]

FIGURE A.17.1.8.1(b) Use of Low Volume Sprinklers in Organic Material. [1144:Figure A.4.2.4.1(b)]

FIGURE A.17.1.8.1(a) Foundation Planting and Landscaping. [1144:Figure A.4.2.4.1(a)]

A.17.1.8.2 Typical heat and flame sources include, but are not limited to, propane heaters, barbecue cookers, and grills. [**1144:** A.4.2.4.2]

A.17.1.8.3 Attachments include, but are not limited to, permanent and temporary construction such as decks, fences, awnings, lean-to buildings; and flammable walkways, fencing, or decking attached to the home. [**1144:** A.4.2.4.3]

Physical Description Similarity Chart of NFDRS and FBO Fuel Models
NFDRS Models Realigned to Fuels Controlling Spread Under Severe Burning Conditions

NFDRS Fuel Models	Fire Behavior Fuel Models													Category
	1	2	3	4	5	6	7	8	9	10	11	12	13	
A Western Annuals	X													Grass
L Western Perennial	X													Grass
S Tundra	X					3rd			2nd					Grass
C Open Pine with Grass		X							2nd					Grass
T Sagebrush with Grass		X			3rd	2nd								Grass
N Sawgrass			X											Grass
B Mature Brush over 6 ft (1.8 m)				X										Shrub
O High Pocosin				X										Shrub
F Intermediate Brush					2nd	X								Shrub
Q Alaskan Black Spruce						X	2nd							Shrub
D Southern Rough						2nd	X							Shrub
H Short-Needle Closed (Normal Dead)								X						Timber
R Hardwood Litter (Summer)								X						Timber
U Western Long-Needle Pine									X					Timber
P Southern Long-Needle Pine									X					Timber
E Hardwood Litter (Fall)									X					Timber
G Short-Needle Closed (Heavy Dead)										X				Timber
K Light Slash											X			Slash
J Medium Slash												X		Slash
I Heavy Slash													X	Slash

Grass — Shrub — Timber — Slash

FIGURE A.17.1.8.1(c) Sample of a Physical Description Similarity Chart of NFDRS and FBO Fuel Models. [1144:Figure A.4.2.4.1(c)]

Figure A.17.1.8.3(a) shows a typical deck where combustible decking materials could result in the gathering of embers next to combustible walls and where the construction and design of decks, balconies, and porches with open spaces underneath could allow leaf and needle debris and embers to collect. [1144: A.4.2.4.3]

Figure A.17.1.8.3(b) illustrates one method of separating a combustible fence from the structure by the installation of a transitional section of noncombustible (iron) fencing. Similar use of masonry or stone can provide the same fire-resistant separation. [1144: A.4.2.4.3]

A.17.1.8.4 Examples of such structures include, but are not limited to, hot tubs, utility sheds, outbuildings, detached garages and carports, gazebos, trellises, auxiliary structures, stables, barns and other structures within 30 ft (9 m) of the primary structure, outdoor furniture, and recreational structures (e.g., children's playhouses, swing sets). In some cases, separation distances from lot lines might require the inclusion of neighboring residential structures in the assessment. [1144: A.4.2.4.4]

A.17.1.8.5 Parking vehicles on areas of dry grasses and fine fuels could result in ignition by hot exhaust systems or firebrands. Also, a fire that originates from a parked vehicle could present an exposure hazard to the primary structure or nearby vegetation. Any dry vegetation beneath the vehicle could cause ignition of the vehicle, which in turn could cause structure ignition; conversely, the ignition of the structure could cause ignition of the vehicle, which could present additional dangers to responding fire fighters. [1144: A.4.2.4.5]

A.17.1.9.1 Evaluation of the vegetative fuels should include the following:

(1) Can vegetative fuels lead surface fire and flames to the structure?

FIGURE A.17.1.8.3(a) Leaf Litter and Needles Collect in Small Spaces. *(Courtesy of Firewise Communities Program.)* [1144:Figure A.4.2.4.3(a)]

FIGURE A.17.1.8.3(b) Transition Fence Separates Combustible Fence from Structure. *(Courtesy of Firewise Communities Program. Photo by G. Johnston.)* [1144:Figure A.4.2.4.3(b)]

fire intensity and are dependent on the size, density, and species of trees and vegetation. [1144: A.4.2.5.2]

Consider using islands of trees that offer separation of trees from the structure and other combustibles. Figure A.17.1.9.2(a) illustrates the use of such planting islands that preserve key trees for aesthetics while providing shade and exposure separation from structures. Figure A.17.1.9.2(b) shows that small planting islands within an expanse of maintained lawn provides both separation and low flammability protection from ignition close the structure. [1144: A.4.2.5.2]

FIGURE A.17.1.9.2(a) Planting Islands Offer Exposure Protection, Preserve Aesthetics. *(Courtesy of Firewise Communities Program. Photo by G. Johnston.)* [1144:Figure A.4.2.5.2(a)]

FIGURE A.17.1.9.2(b) Small Planting Islands Within an Expanse of Maintained Lawn. *(Courtesy of Firewise Communities Program. Photo by D. Frazier.)* [1144:Figure A.4.2.5.2(b)]

(2) Have ladder fuels been eliminated within the structure ignition zone?
(3) Are tree crowns separated enough to prevent big flames from coming within 30 ft (9 m) of the structure?
[1144: A.4.2.5.1]

A.17.1.9.2 The location (placement) of trees and the separation between them is important to prevent ignition of the structure from radiant heat and to reduce the concentration of leaf fall and needle drop near the structure. Adequate separation and control of ignition potential are factors that affect

A.17.1.9.3 Typical heat and flame sources include, but are not limited to, propane- and charcoal-fired barbecue cookers, heaters, and grills. [**1144:** A.4.2.5.3]

A.17.1.9.4 Examples of such structures include, but are not limited to, hot tubs, utility sheds, outbuildings, detached garages and carports, gazebos, trellises, auxiliary structures, stables, barns and other structures between the immediate landscaped area and the extent of structure ignition zone, outdoor furniture, recreational structures (children's playhouses, swing sets). In some cases, separation distances from lot lines might require the inclusion of neighboring residential structures in the assessment. [**1144:** A.4.2.5.4]

A.17.1.9.5 See A.17.1.8.5. [**1144:** A.4.2.5.5]

A.17.1.9.6 Attachments include, but are not limited to, permanent and temporary construction such as decks, fences, awnings, and lean-to buildings. [**1144:** A.4.2.5.6]

A.17.1.10.3 Access and evacuation concerns along with fire suppression capabilities (such as fire station location, water supply, road widths, and grades) are important to overall fire protection and safety. Likewise, vegetation clearance and maintenance along private roadways, driveways, and water supplies are important elements in fire suppression and emergency evacuation. Since these elements do not relate specifically to reducing the ignition potential of the structure, these are covered in NFPA 1141, *Standard for Fire Protection Infrastructure for Land Development in Wildland, Rural, and Suburban Areas*; NFPA 1142, *Standard on Water Supplies for Suburban and Rural Fire Fighting*; and 17.3.5.3. [**1144:** A.4.3.3]

A.17.1.10.4 The frequency of wildland fire occurrence will affect the priorities of the mitigation measures and the periodic maintenance schedule of the property being assessed. [**1144:** A.4.3.4]

A.17.1.10.5 NFPA 1141, *Standard for Fire Protection Infrastructure for Land Development in Wildland, Rural, and Suburban Areas*, provides guidance on planning and installing fire protection infrastructure. [**1144:** A.4.3.5]

A.17.3.1 The unrestricted use of grass-, grain-, brush-, or forest-covered lands under the jurisdiction of the AHJ presents a potential hazard to life and property from fire and resulting erosion.

A.17.3.2 Possible uses include recreation (e.g., camping, hunting, hiking), construction, and seasonal habitation.

A.17.3.5.1.5 An emergency can include situations such as trees falling into power lines or trees' location in violation of Table 17.3.5.1.3.1.

A.17.3.5.2.1.1 Acceptable methods of fuel treatment include, but are not limited to, prescribed burning by qualified personnel, mowing, pruning, removing, substitution, mulching, converting to compost, and grazing. [**1144:** A.6.2.1]

Vegetation. Fire resistance in plants depends on many variables, including location, growing conditions, and maintenance. Plants should be chosen that are suitable for the geographic region and the location in the landscape, and plants with similar needs should be grouped to minimize care. Plant characteristics that reduce maintenance needs include the following:

(1) Drought-resistant
(2) Pest-resistant
(3) Native
(4) Noninvasive
(5) Slow-growing
(6) Wind-resistant
(7) Thriving without supplemental fertilizing
[**1144:** A.6.2.1]

High Flammability (fire-prone, fire-tolerant) Plants. Some plants burn readily because they are adapted to survive in firedependent ecosystems and can contain volatile compounds that support fire. Fire-prone plants have traits (i.e., adaptations) that help them to survive fire, such as thick bark or extensive roots. They often contain resins, oils, or waxes that ignite easily and burn intensely. Fire-prone plants will flame, not smolder, when preheated and ignited with a match. They should be removed from Zone 1 of the landscape, as illustrated in Figure A.17.1.8, Figure A.17.1.9.2(a), and Figure A.17.1.9.2(b). Where it is not practical or desirable to remove a fire-prone plant, surrounding it with open space or fireresistant plants can reduce the hazard. Typical characteristics of fire-prone plants include the following:

(1) Volatile resins, oils, or waxes, indicated by leaves that are aromatic when crushed
(2) Narrow leaves or needles (often evergreen)
(3) Waxy or fuzzy leaves
(4) Accumulation of fine, twiggy, dry, or dead material on the plant or on the ground under the plant
(5) Loose, papery, or thick bark
[**1144:** A.6.2.1]

Low Flammability Plants. In place of fire-prone plants, landscapers and homeowners should use low flammability plants, often referred to as fire-resistant plants. Although all plants will burn at some point, wildland fire researchers have shown that some types of plants, including many native plants, resist burning more than others. Additionally, some ornamental plants, when properly irrigated and maintained, are more resistant to fire than others. Low flammability plants are typically low fuel volume, non-oily, nonresinous plants that are also drought-resistant, have small thick leathery leaves, and produce very little dead plant material. Typical characteristics of fire-resistant plants include the following:

(1) High moisture content in leaves
(2) Low oil or resin content (not aromatic)
(3) Drought tolerance or drought resistance
(4) Minimal seasonal accumulation of dead vegetation, or accumulation of dead leaves that are somewhat resistant to fire because they hold moisture in the soil (large, flat leaves)
(5) Limited foliage and few dead branches
(6) Open or loose branching habit
(7) Easy maintenance and pruning
[**1144:** A.6.2.1]

A.17.3.5.2.1.5 Studies of structural ignition from radiant heat indicate that ignitions are unlikely to occur from burning vegetation beyond 120 ft (36.6 m) from a structure. Therefore, clearing of vegetation and thinning of trees to a distance of 120 ft (36.6 m) from a dwelling— as in a zoned Firewise landscape — will prevent ignition of a structure from the radiant heat from a flame front in a high-risk ecosystem (Cohen and Butler, 1996). [**1144:** A.6.2.5]

A tree crown spacing of 18 ft (5.5 m) for trees within the Zone 1 defensible space [within 30 ft (9 m) of a structure] will reduce radiant heat to at or below the level where ignition of wood occurs, with closer spacing of trees allowed in the zones further from the structure, as described in Table A.17.3.5.2.1.5. These tree-spacing recommendations apply equally to thinning of mature trees or planting of new trees in high- or extreme-risk areas. Tree spacing is measured between the outer edges of the crowns of mature trees, so new trees must be planted with spacing equivalent to the estimated diameter of the mature crown. [1144: A.6.2.5]

Table A.17.3.5.2.1.5 illustrates general clearance distances for tree crowns. However, these distances can be adjusted by the AHJ in consideration of species of trees and understory vegetation, slope of the property, the proximity to other neighboring structures, overlapping ignition zones, and other site-specific factors. [1144: A.6.2.5]

Table A.17.3.5.2.1.5 Recommended Tree Crown Spacing to Prevent Structural Ignition from Wildland Fire Radiant Heat

Zone	Distance from Structure	Recommended Tree Crown Spacing
1	0–30 ft (0–9 m)	18 ft (5.5 m)
2	30–60 ft (9–18 m)	12 ft (3.7 m)
3	60–100 ft (18–30 m)	6 ft (1.8 m)
4	Beyond 100 ft (30 m)	No restrictions

[1144: Table A.6.2.5]

A.17.3.5.2.1.8 Accessory structures include, but are not limited to, outbuildings, patio covers, gazebos, palapas, and similar outdoor structures. [1144: A.5.9]

A.17.3.5.2.1.11.1 Unprotected heat and flame sources include, but are not limited to, open burning without spark protection, barbecue pits, clay or stone fireplaces, and fire pits. Supervision of burning includes the presence of a source of water or other extinguishing equipment. [1144: A.5.12.1]

A.18.2.2 Access control devices take many forms such as remote opening devices, card keys, key codes, keys, and so forth.

A.18.2.3.1.3 The intent of 18.2.3.1.3 is to not require fire department access roads to detached gazebos and ramadas, independent buildings associated with golf courses, parks, and similar uses such as restrooms or snack shops that are 400 ft² (37 m²) or less in area, and detached equipment or storage buildings for commercial use that are 400 ft² (37 m²) or less in area.

A.18.2.3.4.6.2 The design limits of fire department apparatus should take into account mutual aid companies and other response agencies that might respond to emergencies.

A.18.2.4 Fire department access roads should be kept clear of obstructions such as parked vehicles, fences and other barriers, dumpsters, and excess vegetation. However, it should be understood that a severe snowstorm can make these roads temporarily inaccessible. In many parts of the country, the annual snowfall is of such magnitude that alternative arrangements such as temporary roads over the snow accumulation could be necessary.

A.18.2.4.1.3 These obstructions include those obscuring or interfering with fire department connections to sprinkler systems or standpipe systems or both.

A.18.3.1 See Section 18.4 for determining required fire flow.

A.18.3.1.1 NFPA 1141 and NFPA 1142 can serve as references for additional water supply and fire flow information.

A.18.4.1 Section 18.4 and the associated tables are only applicable for determining minimum water supplies for manual fire suppression efforts. Water supplies for fire protection systems are not addressed by this section. It is not the intent to add the minimum fire protection water supplies, such as for a fire sprinkler system, to the minimum fire flow for manual fire suppression purposes required by this section.

A.18.4.1.1 For the purpose of this section, a building subdivided by fire walls constructed in accordance with the building code is considered to be a separate building.

A.18.4.3.1.1 The intent of 18.4.3.1.1 is to provide some limited flexibility in those circumstances where there is no water supply available and the fire department's capabilities to deliver water via a tanker shuttle or drafting operation are also limited. The AHJ should consider establishing additional conditions, such as those contained in 18.4.3.1.2, prior to permitting decreased fire flow capability.

A.18.4.5.1.2 Approved automatic sprinkler systems for one- and two-family dwellings include those meeting the requirements of NFPA 13, *Standard for the Installation of Sprinkler Systems*, NFPA 13D, *Standard for the Installation of Sprinkler Systems in One- and Two-Family Dwellings and Manufactured Homes*, and NFPA 13R, *Standard for the Installation of Sprinkler Systems in Residential Occupancies up to and Including Four Stories in Height*.

A.18.4.5.1.3 Approved automatic sprinkler systems for one- and two-family dwellings include those meeting the requirements of NFPA 13, *Standard for the Installation of Sprinkler Systems*, NFPA 13D, *Standard for the Installation of Sprinkler Systems in One- and Two-Family Dwellings and Manufactured Homes*, and NFPA 13R, *Standard for the Installation of Sprinkler Systems in Residential Occupancies up to and Including Four Stories in Height*.

A.18.4.5.1.5 The fire flow reductions specified in 18.4.5.1.2, 18.4.5.1.3, and 18.4.5.1.4 are permitted to be combined. However, where the reductions are combined, the resulting required fire flow is not permitted to be reduced to less than 500 gpm (1900 L/min) for 1 hour.

A.18.4.5.2.5 The fire flow reductions specified in 18.4.5.2.2 and 18.4.5.2.3 are permitted to be combined. However, where the reductions are combined, the resulting required fire flow is not permitted to be reduced to less than 500 gpm (1900 L/min) for 1 hour.

A.18.4.5.3.4 The provision of 18.4.5.3.4 is intended to limit the required fire flow duration to not more than 2 hours where the building is sprinklered. The 2000 gpm (7571 L/min) limit is based on a 75% reduction of 8000 gpm (30,283 L/min), which is the maximum fire flow required by Table 18.4.5.2.1. The required 2-hour duration is consistent with the maximum hose stream duration requirements of NFPA 13, *Standard for the Installation of Sprinkler Systems.*

A.18.4.5.4 The fire sprinkler system demand is generally significantly less than the demands in Table 18.4.5.2.1, even after hose stream demands are applied. The sprinkler system demand can be a part of the overall flow available to a building site. There is no need to add these flow demands together, which would penalize the building owner that has decided to put fire sprinkler systems in place.

A.18.5.1.2 The conditions where a local jurisdiction might determine that a modification or extension of the water distribution system is deemed to be impractical are varied and should be evaluated on a case-by-case basis. Conditions that should be considered in determining if an extension is impractical should include, but not be limited to, the following:

(1) Distance required to extend the water distribution system
(2) Capability of the existing water distribution system to meet the fire flow demand
(3) Density and occupancy of the proposed development
(4) Potential additional future development in the area of the extension
(5) Other codes and standards, which might warrant extension of the water distribution system
(6) Future anticipated improvements to the water distribution system
(7) Buildings within a previously approved development

A.18.5.1.4 Fire department access roads are intended to include public streets provided they meet the requirements of 18.2.3.

A.18.5.4.3 It is not the intent of Table 18.5.4.3 to limit the actual fire flow capacity of a fire hydrant, only the fire flow capacity for which a fire hydrant is credited based on its distance from the building.

A.18.5.10.3 Color coding or stenciling a fire hydrant with the actual flow capacity are two methods to accomplish the capacity marking of fire hydrants when it is required by the AHJ. NFPA 291, *Recommended Practice for Fire Flow Testing and Marking of Hydrants*, specifies the following approach to hydrant marking for flow indication:

Classification of Hydrants. Hydrants should be classified in accordance with their rated capacities [at 20 psi (1.4 bar) residual pressure or other designated value] as follows:

(1) Class AA — Rated capacity of 1500 gpm (5680 L/min) or greater
(2) Class A — Rated capacity of 1000–1499 gpm (3785–5675 L/min)
(3) Class B — Rated capacity of 500–999 gpm (1900–3780 L/min)
(4) Class C — Rated capacity of less than 500 gpm (1900 L/min)

The tops and nozzle caps should be painted with the following capacity-indicating color scheme:

(1) Class AA — Light blue
(2) Class A — Green
(3) Class B — Orange
(4) Class C — Red paint.

The capacity colors should be of a reflective-type paint.

A.19.2.1.2.1 Nonmetallic or plastic rubbish containers should be limited in their combustibility and should be tested for heat release with the cone calorimeter, to the recognized standard of ASTM E 1354 referred to as the cone or oxygen consumption calorimeter. The cone calorimeter test standard does not indicate the exact conditions (heat flux and orientation) needed for testing. This test is intended to give detailed information as to how the fire performance of materials perform under actual fire conditions. The value of 300 kW/m^2 for peak rate of heat release of the rubbish container material corresponds to the value that Douglas fir wood emits under the same conditions. Rubbish containers are often manufactured of polyethylene [effective heat of combustion ca. 19,000 Btu/lb (45 MJ/kg)], which releases much more heat in a fire than the typical contents of the container, much of which is paper (effective heat of combustion ca. 6400 Btu/lb (15 MJ/kg)). For comparison purposes, Table A.19.2.1.2.1 shows peak heat release rates of a series of materials (34 plastics and Douglas fir wood) at an incident heat flux of 40 kW/m^2, in the horizontal orientation and at a thickness of 0.25 in. (6 mm) [Hirschler 1992]. For further comparison, a fire test conducted with a small ignition source on a 22.4 lb polyethylene rubbish container resulted in the release of 1.34 MW within 13.35 minutes of ignition (before it had to be manually extinguished) and caused flashover in the test room. The maximum a container can release is 300 kW/m^2 or maximum heat release rate. Douglas fir has a constant of 300 kW/m^2 where polyethylene has a peak heat release rate of 1268 kW/m^2. Nonmetallic containers such as polyethylene can represent more fuel than their contents (high density polyethylene 19,994 Btu/lb versus newsprint at 8000). A detailed review of listings or approvals is advised prior to acceptance.

A.20.1.4 Where a special amusement building is installed inside another building, such as within an exhibit hall, the special amusement building requirements apply only to the special amusement building. For example, the smoke detectors required by 20.1.4.4 are not required to be connected to the building's system. Where installed in an exhibit hall, such smoke detectors are also required to comply with the provisions applicable to an exhibit. [*101:*A.12.4.7; *101:*A.13.4.7]

A.20.1.4.1 The aggregate horizontal projections of a multilevel play structure are indicative of the number of children who might be within the structure and at risk from a fire or similar emergency. The word "aggregate" is used in recognition of the fact that the platforms and tubes that make up the multilevel play structure run above each other at various levels. In calculating the area of the projections, it is important to account for all areas that might be expected to be occupied within, on top of, or beneath the components of the structure when the structure is used for its intended function. [*101:* A.12.4.7.1; *101:*A.13.4.7.1]

A.20.1.4.2 See A.20.1.4.1. [*101:*A.12.4.7.2; *101:*A.13.4.7.2]

A.20.1.4.7.3 Consideration should be given to the provision of directional exit marking on or adjacent to the floor. [*101:* A.12.4.7.7.3; *101:*A.13.4.7.7.3]

A.20.1.5.3(3)(a) Securely supported altar candles in churches that are well separated from any combustible material are permitted. On the other hand, lighted candles carried by children wearing cotton robes present a hazard too great to be permitted. There are many other situations of intermediate hazard where the AHJ will have to exercise judgment. [*101:*A.12.7.3(3)(a); *101:* A.13.7.3(3)(a)]

A.20.1.5.4.1 Fabric applied over unused seating sections should meet the requirements of 20.1.5.4. [*101:* A.12.7.4.1; *101:*A.13.7.4.1]

A.20.1.5.4.3 The phrase "unprotected materials containing foamed plastic" is meant to include foamed plastic items covered by "thermally thin" combustible fabrics or paint. *(See A.12.5.4.4.)* [*101:*A.12.7.4.3; *101:*A.13.7.4.3]

A.20.1.5.5.4.7.1(3) See A.10.14.3.1. [*101:* A.12.7.5.3.7.1(3); *101:*A.13.7.5.3.7.1(3)]

A.20.1.5.6.2 Crowd managers and crowd manager supervisors need to clearly understand the required duties and responsibilities specific to the venue's emergency plan. The

Table A.19.2.1.2.1 Peak Rate of Heat Release of Materials in the Cone Calorimeter at an Incident Heat Flux of 40 kW/m^2, in the Horizontal Orientation, at a Thickness of 6 mm

	Material Description	Abbreviation	Peak Rate of Heat Release (kW/m^2)
1	Polytetrafluorethylene	PTFE	14
2	Poly(vinyl chloride) flexible 1	PVC Plenum 1	43
3	Poly(vinyl chloride) flexible 2	PVC Plenum 2	64
4	Poly(vinyl chloride) flexible 3	PVC Plenum 3	87
5	Polycarbonate 1	PolyCarb 1	429
6	Poly(vinyl chloride) flexible 4	PVC Plenum 4	77
7	Chlorinated PVC	CPVC	84
8	Poly(vinyl chloride) rigid computer housing	PVC computer	175
9	Poly(vinyl chloride) flexible wire FR	PVC flex FR	92
10	Poly(vinyl chloride) rigid low smoke	PVC low smoke	111
11	Cross linked polyethylene FR	XLPE FR	192
12	Poly(vinyl chloride) flexible wire semi FR	PVC Flex semi FR	142
13	Poly(vinyl chloride) rigid window	PVC window	183
14	Poly(vinyl chloride) flexible wire non FR	PVC Flex non FR	167
15	Poly(methyl methacrylate) FR Blend	PMMA FR	176
16	Polycarbonate 2	Polycarb 2	420
17	Polyphenylene Oxide FR Blend 1	PPO/PS 1	276
18	Polyphenylene Oxide FR Blend 2	PPO/PS 2	265
19	Acrylonitrile butadiene styrene FR 1	ABS FR 1	291
20	Acrylonitrile butadiene styrene FR 2	ABS FR 2	402
21	Poly(vinyl chloride) flexible bath curtain	PVC Flex Poor	237
22	Douglas fir	D Fir	221
23	Polystyrene FR	PS FR	334
24	Polyacetal	P Acetal	360
25	Polyurethane Flexible Foam non FR	PU	710
26	Poly(methyl methacrylate)	PMMA	665
27	Polyurethane Thermoplastic	TPU	221
28	Nylon	Nylon	1313
29	Acrylonitrile butadiene styrene	ABS	944
30	Polystyrene	PS	1101
31	Styrene acrylonitrile EPDM blend	EPDM SAN	956
32	Poly(butylene terephthalate)	PBT	1314
33	Poly(ethylene terephthalate)	PET	534
34	Polyethylene	PE	1408
35	Polypropylene	PP	1509

Source: Hirschler 1992. "Heat release from plastic materials", M.M. Hirschler, 12a, in "Heat Release in Fire," Elsevier, London, UK, Eds. V. Babrauskas and S.J. Grayson, 1992. pp. 375–422.

crowd management training program should include a clear appreciation of crowd dynamics factors including space, energy, time, and information, as well as specific crowd management techniques, such as metering. Training should involve specific actions necessary during normal and emergency operations, and include an assessment of people handling capabilities of a space prior to its use, the identification of hazards, an evaluation of projected levels of occupancy, the adequacy of means of ingress and egress and identification of ingress and egress barriers, the processing procedures such as ticket collection, and the expected types of human behavior. Training should also involve the different types of emergency evacuations and, where required by the emergency plan, relocation and shelter-in-place operations, and the challenges associated with each. [*101:*A.12.7.6.2; *101:*A.13.7.6.2]

A.20.1.5.6.4 In large facilities, crowd managers typically have a specific area of responsibility. In such facilities, the requirements of 20.1.5.6.4 might apply only to the crowd managers' area of responsibility. [*101:*A.12.7.6.4; *101:*A.13.7.6.4]

A.20.1.5.7 Because of the variety of types of places of assembly covered in this *Code*, no general requirement for patrols or fire watchers has been included. The NFPA 102 Committee fully recognizes the importance of this feature of fire protection, however, and believes that a system of well-trained patrols or fire watchers should be maintained in every place of assembly where fire hazards might develop. Such locations would include, among others, the spaces underneath grandstands and the areas inside and outside tents and air-supported structures. The fire watchers serve to detect incipient fires and to prevent an accumulation of materials that will carry fire. The number of such watchers required will, of course, vary for the different types of assembly occupancies, depending upon the combustibility of the construction and the number of persons accommodated. Provided with an adequate supply of portable fire extinguishing equipment located at readily accessible points, such a fire watch or detail should be able to prevent small fires from reaching serious proportions.

A.20.1.5.8 It is important that an adequate number of competent attendants are on duty at all times when the assembly occupancy is occupied. [*101:*A.12.7.7; *101:*A.13.7.7]

A.20.1.5.8.3 It is not the intent of this provision to require an announcement in bowling alleys, cocktail lounges, restaurants, or places of worship. [*101:*A.12.7.7.3; *101:*A.13.7.7.3]

A.20.2.4.2.1 The requirements are, of necessity, general in scope, as it is recognized that they apply to all types of educational occupancies as well as conditions of occupancies, such as truant schools; schools for the mentally handicapped, vision impaired, hearing impaired, and speech impaired; and public schools. It is fully recognized that no one code can meet all the conditions of the various buildings involved, and it will be necessary for site administrators to issue supplements to these requirements, but all supplements should be consistent with these requirements. [*101:*A.14.7.2.1; *101:*A.15.7.2.1]

A.20.2.4.3.1 Particular attention should be given to keeping all doors unlocked; keeping doors that serve to protect the safety of paths of egress closed and under no conditions blocked open, such as doors on stairway enclosures; keeping outside stairs and fire escape stairs free from all obstructions and clear of snow and ice; and allowing no accumulation of snow or ice or materials of any kind outside exit doors that might prevent the opening of the door or interfere with rapid escape from the building. [*101:*A.14.7.3.1; *101:*A.15.7.3.1]

Any condition likely to interfere with safe egress should be corrected immediately, if possible, or otherwise should be reported at once to the appropriate authorities. [*101:*A.14.7.3.1; *101:*A.15.7.3.1]

A.20.3.2.2 The purpose of this requirement is to prevent arrangements whereby a client can be trapped in a space or area. It is intended that this provision be broadly interpreted by the AHJ to include equipment such as refrigerators and freezers. [*101:*A.16.2.2.2.4; *101:*A.17.2.2.2.4]

A.20.3.4.1.2 Day-care homes do not provide for the full-time maintenance of a client. Day-care occupancies that provide a primary place of residence are addressed in other day-care occupancy chapters. *(See Chapters 24 through 33 of NFPA 101.)* [*101: A.17.6.1.1.2*]

A.20.3.4.2.1 The requirements are, of necessity, general in scope, because it is recognized that they apply to all types of day-care occupancies as well as conditions of occupancies, such as truant day-care occupancies; occupancies for the mentally handicapped, vision impaired, hearing impaired, and speech impaired; adult day-care; care of infants; and day-care occupancies. It is fully recognized that no one code can meet all the conditions of the various buildings involved, and it will be necessary for site administrators, through the written fire emergency response plan, to issue supplements to these requirements; however, all supplements should be consistent with these requirements. Additionally, it is recommended that fire safety be a part of the educational programs of the occupancy for clients. [*101:*A.16.7.1; *101:*A.17.7.1]

Fire emergency response plans need to be written and made available to all employees, including temporary or substitute staff, so that all employees know what is expected of them during a fire emergency. The elements needed in the written plan should be identified in coordination with the AHJ. [*101:*A.16.7.1; *101:*A.17.7.1]

The facility fire emergency response plan might be a module of a facility disaster plan that covers other emergencies. [*101:*A.16.7.1; *101:*A.17.7.1]

The proper safeguarding of clients during a fire emergency requires prompt and effective response by the facility employees in accordance with the fire emergency response plan. Duties covered under the plan should be assigned by position rather than by employee name. Such assignment ensures that, in the absence of an employee, the duties of the position will be performed by a substitute or temporary employee assigned to the position. Temporary or substitute employees should be instructed in advance regarding their duties under the plan for the position to which they are assigned. [*101:*A.16.7.1; *101:*A.17.7.1]

Written fire emergency response plans should include, but should not be limited to, information for employees regarding methods and devices available for alerting occupants of a fire emergency. Employees should know how the fire department is to be alerted. Even where automatic systems are expected to alert the fire department, the written plan should provide for backup alerting procedures by staff. Other responses of employees to a fire emergency should include the following:

(1) Removal of clients in immediate danger to areas of safety, as set forth in the plan
(2) Methods of using building features to confine the fire and its by-products to the room or area of origin
(3) Control of actions and behaviors of clients during removal or evacuation activities and at predetermined safe assembly areas

[*101:*A.16.7.1; *101:*A.17.7.1]

The written plan should state clearly the facility policy regarding the actions staff are to take or not take to extinguish a fire. It should also incorporate the emergency egress and relocation drill procedures set forth in 20.3.4.2.2. [*101:*A.16.7.1; *101:*A.17.7.1]

For additional guidance on emergency plans, see *NFPA 1600, Standard on Disaster/Emergency Management and Business Continuity Programs.* This standard establishes a common set of criteria for disaster management, emergency management, and business continuity programs. [*101:*A.16.7.1; *101:*A.17.7.1]

A.20.3.4.2.2.1 The requirements are, of necessity, general in scope, because it is recognized that they apply to all types of day-care occupancies as well as conditions of occupancies, such as truant day-care occupancies; day-care occupancies for the mentally handicapped, vision impaired, hearing impaired, and speech impaired. It is fully recognized that no one code can meet all the conditions of the various buildings involved, and it will be necessary for site administrators to issue supplements to these requirements, but all supplements should be consistent with these requirements. [*101:*A.16.7.2.1; *101:*A.17.7.2.1]

A.20.3.4.2.3.2 Particular attention should be given to keeping all doors unlocked; keeping doors that serve to protect the safety of paths of egress closed and under no conditions blocked open, such as doors on stairway enclosures; keeping outside stairs and fire escape stairs free from all obstructions and clear of snow and ice; and allowing no accumulation of snow or ice or materials of any kind outside exit doors that might prevent the opening of the door or interfere with rapid escape from the building. [*101:*A.16.7.3.2; *101:*A.17.7.3.2]

A.20.3.4.2.3.6 It is the intent that the requirement for adequate adult staff to be awake at all times when clients are present be applied to family day-care and group day-care homes that are operated at night, as well as day-care occupancies. [*101:*A.16.7.5; *101:*A.17.7.5]

A.20.4.2 Health care occupants have, in large part, varied degrees of physical disability, and their removal to the outside, or even their disturbance caused by moving, is inexpedient or impractical in many cases, except as a last resort. Similarly, recognizing that there might be an operating necessity for the restraint of the mentally ill, often by use of barred windows and locked doors, fire exit drills are usually extremely disturbing, detrimental, and frequently impracticable. [*101:*A.18.7; *101:*A.19.7]

In most cases, fire exit drills, as ordinarily practiced in other occupancies, cannot be conducted in health care occupancies. Fundamentally, superior construction, early discovery and extinguishment of incipient fires, and prompt notification need to be relied on to reduce the occasion for evacuation of buildings of this class to a minimum. [*101:*A.18.7; *101:*A.19.7]

A.20.4.2.1.5 Many health care occupancies conduct fire drills without disturbing patients by choosing the location of the simulated emergency in advance and by closing the doors to patients' rooms or wards in the vicinity prior to initiation of the drill. The purpose of a fire drill is to test and evaluate the efficiency, knowledge, and response of institutional personnel in implementing the facility fire emergency plan. Its purpose is not to disturb or excite patients. Fire drills should be scheduled on a random basis to ensure that personnel in health care facilities are drilled not less than once in each 3-month period. [*101:*A.18.7.1.4; *101:*A.19.7.1.4]

Drills should consider the ability to move patients to an adjacent smoke compartment. Relocation can be practiced using simulated patients or empty wheelchairs. [*101:*A.18.7.1.4; *101:*A.19.7.1.4]

A.20.4.2.2.1 Each facility has specific characteristics that vary sufficiently from other facilities to prevent the specification of a universal emergency procedure. The recommendations that follow, however, contain many of the elements that should be considered and adapted, as appropriate, to the individual facility. [*101:*A.18.7.2.1; *101:*A.19.7.2.1]

Upon discovery of fire, personnel should immediately take the following action:

(1) If any person is involved in the fire, the discoverer should go to the aid of that person, calling aloud an established code phrase, which provides for both the immediate aid of any endangered person and the transmission of an alarm.
(2) Any person in the area, upon hearing the code called aloud, should activate the building fire alarm using the nearest manual fire alarm box.
(3) If a person is not involved in the fire, the discoverer should activate the building fire alarm using the nearest manual fire alarm box.
(4) Personnel, upon hearing the alarm signal, should immediately execute their duties as outlined in the facility fire safety plan.
(5) The telephone operator should determine the location of the fire as indicated by the audible signal.
(6) In a building equipped with an uncoded alarm system, a person on the floor of fire origin should be responsible for promptly notifying the facility telephone operator of the fire location.
(7) If the telephone operator receives a telephone alarm reporting a fire from a floor, the operator should regard that alarm in the same fashion as an alarm received over the fire alarm system and should immediately notify the fire department and alert all facility personnel of the place of fire and its origin.
(8) If the building fire alarm system is out of order, any person discovering a fire should immediately notify the telephone operator by telephone, and the operator should then transmit this information to the fire department and alert the building occupants.

[*101:*A.18.7.2.1; *101:*A.19.7.2.1]

A.20.4.2.3.3 The purpose of this requirement is to provide a means for building designers, occupants, and operators to clearly designate approved egress corridors that can be identified even though physical or other obvious barriers might not be present to indicate their location. Floor plans used to satisfy this requirement might incorporate more than one function and more than one smoke compartment of the building, provided egress corridors are clearly identified where no fixed barriers are present. Such plans should be accessible to the AHJ but should not be required to be posted. [*101:*A.18.7.3.3; *101:*A.19.7.3.3]

A.20.4.2.4 The most rigid discipline with regard to prohibition of smoking might not be nearly as effective in reducing incipient fires from surreptitious smoking as the open recognition of smoking, with provision of suitable facilities for smoking. Proper education and training of the staff and attendants in the ordinary fire hazards and their abatement is unquestionably essential. The problem is a broad one, varying with different types and arrangements of buildings; the effectiveness of rules of procedure, which need to be flexible, depends in large part on the management. [*101:*A.18.7.4; *101:*A.19.7.4]

A.20.4.2.5.1 In addition to the provisions of 12.6.2, which deal with ignition resistance, additional requirements with respect to the location of cubicle curtains relative to sprinkler placement are included in NFPA 13. [*101:*A.18.7.5.1; *101:*A.19.7.5.1]

A.20.4.2.5.6(2) The user should verify that the products meet the referenced test methods of NFPA 701, and not the small-scale test procedure that was previously eliminated from NFPA 701. [*101:*A.18.7.5.6(2); *101:*A.19.7.5.6(2)]

A.20.4.2.5.6(4) The percentage of decorations should be measured against the area of any wall or ceiling, not the aggregate total of walls, ceilings, and doors. The door is considered part of the wall. The decorations must be located such that they do not interfere with the operation of any door, sprinkler, smoke detector, or any other life safety equipment. Other art might include hanging objects or three-dimensional items. [*101:*A.18.7.5.6(4); *101:*A.19.7.5.6(4)]

A.20.4.2.5.8 It is the intent that this provision allows recycling for bottles, cans, paper and similar clean items to use larger containers or have several adjacent containers and not be restricted to hazardous areas. Containers for medical records waiting shredding are often larger than 32 gallons. These containers are not to be included in the calculations and limitations of 20.4.2.5.7. There is no limit on the number of these containers as the FM Standard assures that the fire will not spread out of the container.

A.20.4.2.5.8(2) See 20.4.2.5.7(3).

A.20.5.2.4.1 Smoking regulations should include the following:

(1) Smoking should be prohibited in any room, compartment, or area where flammable or combustible liquids, combustible gases, or oxygen is used or stored and in any other hazardous location, and the following also should apply:

  (a) Such areas should be posted with signs that read NO SMOKING or the international symbol for no smoking.

  (b) In residential board and care facilities where smoking is totally prohibited and signs so indicating are placed at all major entrances, secondary signs with language that prohibits smoking are not required.

(2) Smoking by residents classified as not responsible with regard to their ability to safely use and dispose of smoking materials should be prohibited.

(3) Where a resident, as specified in A.20.5.2.4.1(2), is under direct supervision by staff or by a person approved by the administration, smoking might be permitted.

(4) Smoking materials should not be provided to residents or maintained by residents without the approval of the administration.

(5) Areas where smoking is permitted should be clearly identified.

(6) Ashtrays of noncombustible material and safe design should be provided and required to be used in all areas where smoking is permitted.

(7) Self-closing cover devices into which ashtrays can be emptied should be made available to all areas where smoking is permitted and should be required to be used.

[*101:*A.32.7.4.1; *101:*A.33.7.4.1]

A.20.5.2.5 The requirements applicable to draperies/curtains, upholstered furniture, and mattresses apply only to new draperies/curtains, new upholstered furniture, and new mattresses. The word *new* means unused, normally via procurement from the marketplace, either by purchase or donation, of items not previously used. Many board and care facilities allow residents to bring into the board and care home upholstered furniture items from the resident's previous residence. Such an item is not new and, thus, is not regulated. On the other hand, some of the larger board and care homes purchase contract furniture, as is done in hotels. Such new, unused furniture, whether purchased or received as a donation, is regulated by the requirements of 20.5.2.5.2. By federal law, mattresses manufactured and sold within the United States must pass testing per 16 CFR 1632 (FF4-72), *Standard for the Flammability of Mattresses and Mattress Pads.* [*101:*A.32.7.5; *101:*A.33.7.5]

A.20.5.2.5.2 New upholstered furniture within board and care homes should be tested for rates of heat release in accordance with 12.6.3.2.1. [*101:*A.32.7.5.2; *101:*A.33.7.5.2]

A.20.5.2.5.2.3 New mattresses within board and care homes should be tested for rates of heat release in accordance with 12.6.3.2.2. [*101:*A.32.7.5.3; *101:*A.33.7.5.3]

A.20.6.2 Ambulatory health care occupants have, in large part, varied degrees of physical disability, and their removal to the outside, or even their disturbance caused by moving, is inexpedient or impractical in many cases, except as a last resort. Similarly, recognizing that there might be an operating necessity for the restraint of the mentally ill, often by use of barred windows and locked doors, fire exit drills are usually extremely disturbing, detrimental, and frequently impracticable. [*101:*A.20.7; *101:*A.21.7]

In most cases, fire exit drills, as ordinarily practiced in other occupancies, cannot be conducted in ambulatory health care occupancies. Fundamentally, superior construction, early discovery and extinguishment of incipient fires, and prompt notification need to be relied on to reduce the occasion for evacuation of buildings of this class to a minimum. [*101:*A.20.7; *101:*A.21.7]

A.20.6.2.1.5 Many ambulatory health care occupancies conduct fire drills without disturbing patients by choosing the location of the simulated emergency in advance and by closing the doors in the vicinity prior to the initiation of the drill. The purpose of a fire drill is to test and evaluate the efficiency, knowledge, and response of personnel in implementing the facility fire emergency plan. Its purpose is not to disturb or excite patients. Fire drills should be scheduled on a random basis to ensure that personnel in ambulatory health care facilities are drilled not less than once in each 3-month period. [*101:*A.20.7.1.4; *101:*A.21.7.1.4]

Drills should consider the ability to move patients to an adjacent smoke compartment. Relocation can be practiced using simulated patients or empty wheelchairs. [*101:*A.20.7.1.4; *101:*A.21.7.1.4]

A.20.6.2.2.1 Each facility has specific characteristics that vary sufficiently from other facilities to prevent the specification of a universal emergency procedure. The recommendations that follow, however, contain many of the elements that should be considered and adapted, as appropriate, to the individual facility. [*101:*A.20.7.2.1; *101:*A.21.7.2.1]

Upon discovery of fire, personnel should immediately take the following action:

(1) If any person is involved in the fire, the discoverer should go to the aid of that person, calling aloud an established code phrase, which provides for both the immediate aid of any endangered person and the transmission of an alarm.

(2) Any person in the area, upon hearing the code called aloud, should activate the building fire alarm using the nearest manual fire alarm box.

(3) If a person is not involved in the fire, the discoverer should activate the building fire alarm using the nearest manual fire alarm box.

(4) Personnel, upon hearing the alarm signal, should immediately execute their duties as outlined in the facility fire safety plan.

(5) The telephone operator should determine the location of the fire as indicated by the audible signal.

(6) In a building equipped with an uncoded alarm system, a person on the floor of fire origin should be responsible for promptly notifying the facility telephone operator of the fire location.

(7) If the telephone operator receives a telephone alarm reporting a fire from a floor, the operator should regard that alarm in the same fashion as an alarm received over the fire alarm system and should immediately notify the fire department and alert all facility personnel of the place of fire and its origin.

(8) If the building fire alarm system is out of order, any person discovering a fire should immediately notify the telephone operator by telephone, and the operator should then transmit this information to the fire department and alert the building occupants.

[*101:*A.20.7.2.1; *101:*A.21.7.2.1]

A.20.6.2.4 The most rigid discipline with regard to prohibition of smoking might not be nearly as effective in reducing incipient fires from surreptitious smoking as the open recognition of smoking, with provision of suitable facilities for smoking. Proper education and training of the staff and attendants in the ordinary fire hazards and their abatement is unquestionably essential. The problem is a broad one, varying with different types and arrangements of buildings; the effectiveness of rules of procedure, which need to be flexible, depends in large part on the management. [*101:*A.20.7.4; *101:*A.21.7.4]

A.20.6.2.5.1 In addition to the provisions of 12.6.2, which deal with ignition resistance, additional requirements with respect to the location of cubicle curtains relative to sprinkler placement are included in NFPA 13. [*101:*A.20.7.5.1; *101:*A.21.7.5.1]

A.20.6.2.5.4(4) The percentage of decorations should be measured against the area of any wall or ceiling, not the aggregate total of walls, ceilings, and doors. The door is considered part of the wall. The decorations must be located such that they do not interfere with the operation of any door, sprinkler, smoke detector, or any other life safety equipment. Other art might include hanging objects or three-dimensional items. [*101:*A.21.7.5.4(4)]

A.20.6.2.5.5.2 It is the intent that this provision permits recycling of bottles, cans, paper and similar clean items that do not contain grease, oil, flammable liquids, or significant plastic materials using larger containers or several adjacent containers and not require locating such containers in a room protected as a hazardous area. Containers for medical records awaiting shredding are often larger than 32 gal (121 L). These containers are not to be included in the calculations and limitations of 20.6.2.5.5.1. There is no limit on the number of these containers, as FM Approval Standard 6921, *Containers for Combustible Waste*, ensures that the fire will not spread outside of the container. FM approval standards are written for use with FM Approvals. The tests can be conducted by any approved laboratory. The portions of the standard referring to FM Approvals are not included in this reference. [*101:*A.20.7.5.5.2; *101:*A.21.7.5.5.2]

A.20.7.2.1.2 This requirement is permitted to be met by electronic or oral monitoring systems, visual monitoring, call signals, or other means. [*101:*A.22.7.1.2; *101:*A.23.7.1.2]

A.20.7.2.1.3 Periodic, coordinated training should be conducted and should involve detention and correctional facility personnel and personnel of the fire department legally committed to serving the facility. [*101:*A.22.7.1.3; *101:*A.23.7.1.3]

A.20.7.2.2 Personal property provides combustible contents for fire development. Therefore, adequate controls are needed to limit the quantity and combustibility of the fuels available to burn to reduce the probability of room flashover. The provisions of 20.7.2.4 will not, by themselves, prevent room flashover if personal property controls are not provided. [*101:* A.22.7.2; *101:* A.23.7.2]

A.20.7.2.4 The type, quantity, and arrangement of furniture and other combustibles are important factors in determining how fast the fire will develop. Furnishings, including upholstered items and wood items, such as wardrobes, desks, and bookshelves, might provide sufficient fuel to result in room flashover, which is the full fire involvement of all combustibles within a room once sufficient heat has been built up within the room. [*101:*A.22.7.4; *101:*A.23.7.4]

A.20.7.2.4.3 Mattresses used in detention and correctional facilities should be evaluated with regard to the fire hazards of the environment. The potential for vandalism and excessive wear and tear also should be taken into account when evaluating the fire performance of the mattress. ASTM F1870, *Standard Guide for Selection of Fire Test Methods for the Assessment of Upholstered Furnishings in Detention and Correctional Facilities* provides guidance for this purpose. [*101:*A.23.7.4.3]

A.20.8.2.1.1 Employers are obligated to determine the degree to which employees are to participate in emergency activities. Regulations of the U.S. Department of Labor (OSHA) govern these activities and provide options for employers, from total evacuation to aggressive structural fire fighting by employee brigades. *(For additional information, see 29 CFR 1910, E and L, "OSHA Regulations for Emergency Procedures and Fire Brigades.")* [*101:*A.28.7.1.1; *101:*A.29.7.1.1]

A.20.8.2.1.2 Emergencies should be assumed to have arisen at various locations in the occupancy in order to train employees in logical procedures. [*101:*A.28.7.1.2; *101:*A.29.7.1.2]

A.20.8.2.4.1 Floor diagrams should reflect the actual floor arrangement and should be oriented with the actual direction to the exits. [*101:*A.28.7.4.1; *101:*A.29.7.4.1]

A.20.8.2.4.2 Factors for developing the fire safety information include such items as construction type, suppression systems, alarm and detection systems, building layout, and building HVAC systems. [*101:*A.28.7.4.2; *101:*A.29.7.4.2]

A.20.11.4.4 Materials such as wood I-Joist, wood or steel trusses, or cold formed steel would not typically be considered equivalent.

A.20.15.5.1 Examples of facilities covered by NFPA 61 include, but are not limited to, bakeries, grain elevators, feed mills, flour mills, milling, corn milling (dry and wet), rice milling, dry milk products, mix plants, soybean and other oilseed preparation operations, cereal processing, snack food processing, tortilla plants, chocolate processing, pet food processing, cake mix processing, sugar refining and processing, and seed plants. [*61:*A.1.1.1]

A.20.15.6.2 See NFPA 232, *Standard for the Protection of Records*, where large archives or records storage buildings are involved.

A.20.17.3(2) See also NFPA 914, *Code for Fire Protection of Historic Structures*.

A.21.1.4 For further information on aircraft hangars, see NFPA 409, *Standard on Aircraft Hangars*. [*101:*A.40.6]

A.21.1.5 For further information on aircraft hangars, see NFPA 409, *Standard on Aircraft Hangars*. [*101:*A.42.6]

A.21.2.4.2 Furniture, floor and wall coverings, and other furnishings in airport terminal occupancies, including passenger holding lounges, waiting areas, restaurant dining rooms, bars, and retail stores, should not be made of materials that have high combustibility, smoke-development characteristics, or both, for example, some plastic foams, latex-rubber foam, some plastics, and some synthetic fibers. Such materials have a tendency to release combustible gases at relatively low temperatures, making them easily ignitible. When burning, these materials also release high amounts of heat energy at rapid rates, thereby contributing greatly to fire propagation. [*415:*A.4.1.2]

Interior finish Class A and Class B are described in NFPA *101, Life Safety Code*. [*415:* A.4.1.2]

A.21.2.5.2 Examples of points of flammable vapor release are fuel tank vent openings and fuel hydrant pits. Air supply intake and exhaust openings for air-conditioning or ventilating equipment serving the terminal building should not be located on the ramp side of an airport terminal building. Fixed air-conditioning and ventilating equipment serving only aircraft should be in a room that has no openings communicating with the remainder of the terminal building. [**415:** A.4.2.2]

A.21.2.5.3 Rooms that contain coal-, gas-, or oil-fired equipment or any other open-flame device should not have openings on the ramp side of the building. Combustion and ventilation air should be supplied from the street side or the roof of the building or through a gravity louver from a nonhazardous area in the building. [**415:** A.4.2.3]

A.21.2.6.2 The hazards to persons from jet intakes and blast, noise, propellers, and so forth, on the ramp should be taken into consideration in locating emergency exit points leading to ramps from the airport terminal building. A means of notification of unauthorized usage (such as an alarm system) of these emergency exits may be desirable. [**415:** A.4.3.2]

A.21.2.7.1 The assembly portion of the terminal building can include areas such as the concourse waiting areas, baggage claim areas, and restaurants. The assembly portion should exclude kitchens, toilets, small office areas, and other areas not normally accessible to the public. [**415:** A.4.5.1]

A.21.2.7.5 The exposure to the airport terminal building from the airport ramp is significant. The number of building sprinklers operating from the exposure fire could be greater than the number of building sprinklers operating from an internal ignition source. [**415:** A.4.5.1.5]

A.21.2.8.2 If the public fire department is responding to the "street" side of the airport terminal building, timely access to the normal alarm receiving point might be limited by emergency conditions or distance. Planned radio communication with a constantly attended alarm-receiving point can assist in a more efficient response by the public fire department. The remote annunciator on the street side of the terminal building can provide building condition information not otherwise available. [**415:** A.4.5.2.2]

A.21.3.3.1 FAA AC 150/5390-2B, *Heliport Design Advisory Circular*, contains design and construction information on heliports. This advisory circular provides for adequate clearance between operating aircraft and buildings or structures located at the heliport. The FAA advisory circular should be consulted to ensure that adequate safe practice and facilities are maintained. [**418:** A.4.2]

A.21.3.3.7 The two means of egress can also be used for access to the landing pad for fire-fighting and/or rescue operations. Where doors accessing the interior of the building are locked, an approved means should be provided for entry of emergency responders. [**418:** A.4.8]

A.21.3.3.7.1 Figure A.21.3.3.7.1(a) and Figure A.21.3.3.7.1(b) are examples of acceptable configurations of egress points on landing pads. The geometry of the landing pad in Figure A.21.3.3.7.1(b) is such that it has no sides and does not comply with 21.3.3.7.3; however, it does comply with the 90-degree rule in 21.3.3.7.1. Figure A.21.3.3.7.1(c) is an example of an unacceptable configuration, due to both egress points being on the same side of the landing pad. [**418:** A.4.8.1]

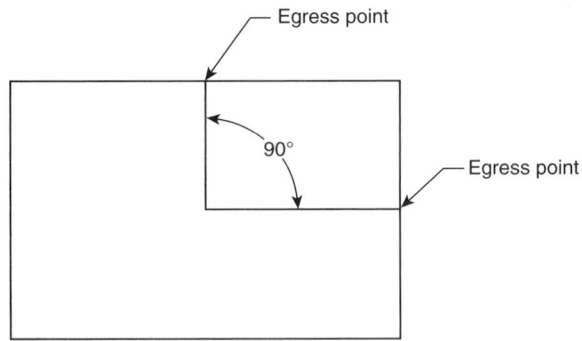

FIGURE A.21.3.3.7.1(a) Example of an Acceptable Configuration of Egress Points on a Landing Pad. [418:Figure A.4.8.1(a)]

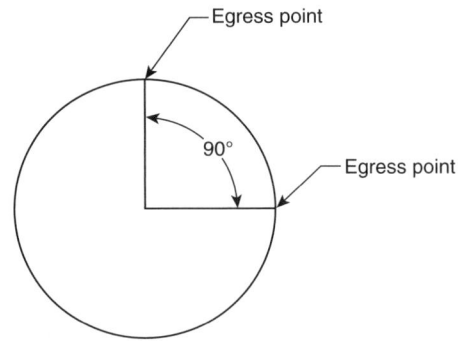

FIGURE A.21.3.3.7.1(b) Example of an Acceptable Configuration of Egress Points on a Landing Pad with No Sides. [418:Figure A.4.8.1(b)]

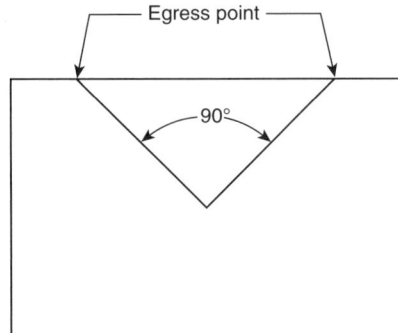

FIGURE A.21.3.3.7.1(c) Example of an Unacceptable Configuration of Egress Points on a Landing Pad. [418:Figure A.4.8.1(c)]

A.21.3.4.1 Where the landing pad is nonporous, fuel-tight, and provided with a proper drainage system, and where fuel cannot flow to support members, the main structural support members would not need to be fire rated. [**418:** A.5.2]

A.21.3.4.4 Design of the means of egress from a rooftop landing pad might involve a compromise among several different code requirements. Rooftop landing pads bring with them an inherent risk. The means of egress must be provided for safety to human life. Strict compliance with a code's requirement for rated stairways off the landing pad is not the intent of this standard. The intent of this standard is to provide a minimum safeguard to provide a reasonable degree of safety to all persons on the roof. The building's egress system is dictated by the adopted building code. Once those persons enter the building's egress system, they are away from the FATO area. [**418:** A.5.5]

A.21.3.4.4.1 See Figure A.21.3.3.7.1(a) through Figure A.21.3.3.7.1(c) for examples of acceptable configurations of egress points on landing pads. The geometry of the landing pad in Figure A.21.3.3.7.1(b) is such that it has no sides and cannot comply with 21.3.4.4.3; however, it does comply with the 90-degree rule in 21.3.4.4.1. Figure A.21.3.3.7.1(c) is not an acceptable configuration due to both egress points being on the same side of the landing pad. [**418:** A.5.5.1]

A.21.3.4.4.4 When considering the means of egress from the landing pad and for the rooftop, obstructions to the FATO need to be avoided since they can create unsafe flight conditions that have been shown to cause aircraft accidents. Exterior, open stairways leading to the building's egress system should not encroach into the FATO. [**418:** A.5.5.4]

A.21.3.4.6.2 Currently, the qualified products listed for MIL-F-24385 do not contain any fluoroprotein or protein foam products. [**418:** A.5.7.2]

A.21.3.4.6.3.1 Consideration should be given to the environmental conditions of the rooftop landing pad in the design of the system, including wind, exhaust fans, and other factors that affect the distribution of the foam on the rooftop landing pad. [**418:** A.5.7.3.1]

A.21.3.4.6.4.1 The area of application and the duration where using a hose line system is reduced because foam is applied efficiently and directly on the fire by trained personnel. [**418:** A.5.7.4.1]

A.21.3.4.7.1 Training on the operation of the fire protection system should be in accordance with Annex B of NFPA 418. [**418:** A.5.8.1]

A.21.3.4.7.2 It is acceptable for the rooftop landing pad to be viewed using video or other acceptable means. [**418:** A.5.8.2]

A.25.1.4.2 NFPA 58, *Liquefied Petroleum Gas Code*, permits portable butane-fueled appliances in restaurants and in attended commercial food catering operations where fueled by not in excess of two 10 oz (0.28 kg) LP-Gas capacity, nonrefillable butane containers having a water capacity not in excess of 1.08 lb (0.4 kg) per container. Containers are required to be directly connected to the appliance, and manifolding of containers is not permitted. Storage of cylinders is also limited to 24 containers, with an additional 24 permitted where protected by a 2-hour fire resistance–rated barrier. [***101:*** A.8.7.3.2]

A.25.1.8 Because of the variety of types of places of assembly covered by this *Code*, no general requirement for patrols or fire watchers has been included. The committee fully recognizes the importance of this feature of fire protection, however, and believes that a system of well-trained patrols or fire watchers should be maintained in every place of assembly where fire hazards might develop. Such locations would include, among others, the spaces underneath grandstands and the areas inside and outside tents and air-supported structures. The fire watchers serve to detect incipient fires and to prevent an accumulation of materials that will carry fire. The number of such watchers required will, of course, vary for the different types of assembly occupancies, depending upon the combustibility of the construction and the number of persons accommodated. Provided with an adequate supply of portable fire-extinguishing equipment located at readily accessible points, such a fire watch or detail should be able to prevent small fires from reaching serious proportions.

A.25.5.3.3.1 The requirements of 25.5.3.3.1 can be considered as a Class 4, Type 60 system per NFPA 110, *Standard for Emergency and Standby Power Systems*. [***101:*** A.11.9.3.3.1]

A.26.1.3(1) Either condition of 26.1.3(1) meeting the minimum quantity will bring the lab within the scope of Chapter 26. A school lab with a low pressure natural gas system supplying Bunsen burners (with less than the minimum quantities of combustible or flammable liquids and less than the minimum quantities of other flammable gases) is an example of a lab outside the scope of Chapter 26. [**45:** A.1.1.2(1)]

A.26.1.3(2) The hazards of pilot plants are primarily based on the process, the chemistry, and the equipment, not the laboratory environment. [**45:** A.1.1.2(2)]

A.26.1.3(7) NFPA 801, *Standard for Fire Protection for Facilities Handling Radioactive Materials*, provides direction for controlling hazards associated with radioactive materials. NFPA 801 should be used only for issues related to radioactive materials in a laboratory. All other nonradioactive, laboratory issues are covered by NFPA 45. [**45:** A.1.1.2(7)]

A.26.1.5.1 Laboratory buildings, laboratory units, and laboratory work areas need to have clearly developed plans for fire prevention, maintenance, and emergency procedures. Guidance of the development of these plans and procedures can be found in NFPA 45.

A.28.1.6.2 Where fixed fire-extinguishing system components are installed in areas subjecting these components to corrosion or other atmospheric damage, special considerations might be necessary. Corrosion-resistant types of pipe, fittings, and hangers or protective corrosion-resistant coatings should be used where corrosive conditions exist. [**303:** A.6.3]

A.28.1.6.2.1.3 Where clearly impractical for economic or physical reasons, the AHJ could permit the omission of an automatic fire-extinguishing system when considering water supply availability and adequacy and size of facility. [**303:** A.6.3.1.3]

A.28.1.6.2.2 It is not the intent of this paragraph to limit the types of fire protection systems to automatic sprinklers in order to comply with the requirements of 28.1.6.2.2. Other types of automatic fire-extinguishing systems, such as foam/water, expanded foam, or clean agents, can be used for compliance provided that the system is applicable to the hazard present; automatically provides for the detection, control, and extinguishment of fires involving the hazards that might be present in the building; and is acceptable to the AHJ. The combustibility of the boats in storage should be considered in determining the hazard classification for appropriate sprinkler system design. [**303:** A.6.3.2]

A.28.1.6.2.2.2 See A.28.1.6.2.1.3. [**303:** A.6.3.2.2]

A.28.1.6.2.3.4 See A.28.1.6.2.1.3. [**303:** A.6.3.3.4]

A.28.1.6.2.4.1 Compliance with the requirements of Chapter 12 of NFPA 13, *Standard for the Installation of Sprinkler*

Systems, for the protection of Group A plastics stored on solid shelves should be considered for the design and installation of automatic sprinkler systems provided for the protection of buildings housing boats stored on multilevel racks. The combustibility of the boats in storage should be considered in determining hazard classifications. Plan view configuration of the boats in storage should be reviewed to determine whether in-rack sprinklers are needed and to aid in the proper design of the in-rack portion of the sprinkler system. Sound engineering judgment is necessary in selecting sprinkler spacing, placement, and design criteria. [303: A.6.3.4.1]

A.28.1.6.2.4.3 See A.28.1.6.2.1.3. [303: A.6.3.4.3]

A.28.1.6.2.5 To comply with this requirement, water supplies can consist of a hydrant that is part of an approved water supply system, drafting hydrant, or drafting site. [303: A.6.3.5]

A.28.1.6.3 Where standpipe system components are installed in areas subjecting these components to corrosion or other atmospheric damage, special considerations might be necessary. Corrosion-resistant types of pipe, fittings, and hangers or protective corrosion-resistant coatings should be used where corrosive conditions exist. [303: A.6.4]

A.28.1.7.1.3 It is recommended that an auxiliary power supply be provided to ensure lighting in the event of a power failure. [303: A.7.1.3]

A.28.1.7.2.1.5(4) Where fuel tanks and fuel systems are susceptible to damage by certain fuel additives or fuel blends, special considerations might be required to prevent damage to tanks and fuel systems that could lead to fuel leaks. Such considerations might include, but are not limited to, completely emptying and purging the fuel tank and/or more frequent inspections to detect damage and leakage from the fuel tank and fuel system that are stored at least 95 percent full in accordance with the NFPA 303. [303: A.7.2.1.5(4)]

A.28.1.7.2.4 Batteries should be removed for storage and charging wherever practical. [303: A.7.2.4]

A.28.1.8.1 Marinas and boatyard owners and operators are encouraged to be familiar with the requirements of NFPA 302, *Fire Protection Standard for Pleasure and Commercial Motor Craft.* It is recommended that marina and boatyard owners and operators encourage vessel owners and occupants to practice proper fire prevention aboard moored and stored vessels. [303: A.8.1]

A.28.1.8.2.6(7) For the purpose of this requirement, the emergency contact information should only include the means to contact the fire department or emergency services and the marina or boatyard address. [303: A.8.2.6(7)]

A.28.2.2 See NFPA 303, *Fire Protection Standard for Marinas and Boatyards.* [307: A.1.3.2]

A.28.2.3(1) See NFPA 30, *Flammable and Combustible Liquids Code.* [307: A.1.3.3(1)]

A.28.2.3(2) See NFPA 59A, *Standard for the Production, Storage, and Handling of Liquefied Natural Gas (LNG),* or NFPA 58, *Liquefied Petroleum Gas Code.* [307: A.1.3.3(2)]

A.28.3.1 Many vessels undergoing construction, conversion, or repairs, and vessels laid up in a shipyard or elsewhere are readily vulnerable to fire, due to the quantity and character of combustible materials used in building. Long passageways, unenclosed stairways, hatches, and hoistways facilitate the rapid spread of fire throughout the vessel. Often the location of the vessel is isolated so that private protection is the main source of fire-fighting services. Even where major municipal protection is available, material damage or complete destruction before effective means of extinguishment are brought into action often results from the following:

(1) Possible delayed response, due either to late discovery of the fire or to the absence of means for quick notification
(2) Lack of special equipment in many municipal fire departments for combating shipboard fires
(3) An unfamiliarity with ship construction due to the transitory nature of the risk
[312: A.1.2]

A.30.1.5.1 Additional fire protection considerations can include items such as fixed suppression systems, automatic fire detection, manual fire alarm stations, transmission of alarms to off-site locations, and limiting volume delivered per transaction. [30A: A.7.3.5.1]

A.30.1.6.7 Natural ventilation can normally be expected to dissipate any fuel vapors before they reach ignitible concentrations if at least two sides of the dispensing area are open to the building exterior. [30A: A.7.3.6.7]

A.30.1.6.9 Oil/water separators might not be designed to remove or separate flammable or combustible liquids other than oil. [30A: A.7.3.6.9]

A.30.2.9 The ventilation requirements contained in this section do not consider exhaust emissions from motor vehicle engines. An appropriate professional should be consulted to determine precautions necessary to protect against this health hazard. [30A: A.7.5]

A.30.2.9.1 Manual control switches for supply and exhaust ventilating systems should be located close to the entrance to the area served. In buildings protected by automatic sprinklers or fire alarm systems, it is recommended that the necessary interlocks be provided to shut down supply and exhaust fans when the sprinklers or fire alarms operate. For service facilities for CNG-fueled vehicles and LNG-fueled vehicles, see NFPA 52. [30A: A.7.5.1]

A.30.2.10.6 Enclosed rooms or spaces storing CNG- or LNG-fueled vehicles should prohibit the transmission of gases to other areas of the building. Other areas outside of the enclosure, if not used for repairing or storing CNG- or LNG-fueled vehicles, can use other heating methods. Note that, according to A.1.1 of NFPA 52, CNG weighs about two-thirds as much as air and, therefore, as a gas, will rise in a room. LNG at a temperature of less than or equal to −170°F (−112°C) is heavier than ambient air [at 60°F (15°C)], but as the LNG's temperature rises, the gas becomes lighter than air. Determination of the potential for gas accumulation should be based on an engineering analysis. (Guidance for classification of hazardous locations is available in NFPA 497.) [30A: A.7.6.6]

A.31.1 Each individual property has its own special conditions of stock handling, exposure, and topography. For this reason, only basic fire protection principles are discussed herein and are intended to be applied with due consideration of all local factors involved. The AHJ should be consulted.

A.31.3.2.1.1 Good housekeeping should be maintained at all times, including regular and frequent cleaning of materials-handling equipment.

A.31.3.2.1.6.1 See NFPA 505, *Fire Safety Standard for Powered Industrial Trucks Including Type Designations, Areas of Use, Conversions, Maintenance, and Operations.*

A.31.3.2.1.10.1 See NFPA 82, *Standard on Incinerators and Waste and Linen Handling Systems and Equipment*, for small rubbish burners.

A.31.3.2.2.1 Saw mills, planing mills, treating plants, adzing mills, and similar buildings without blank walls should be separated from yard storage by a clear space in accordance with the recommendations of NFPA 80A, *Recommended Practice for Protection of Buildings from Exterior Fire Exposures.*

Unsprinklered manufacturing buildings and other large structures with combustible contents represent a severe exposure to yard storage, unless the exterior walls have the necessary fire resistance to act as a fire separation and are essentially absent of unprotected openings.

A.31.3.2.2.2 Weeds, grass, and similar vegetation should be prevented throughout the entire yard, and any vegetation growth should be sprayed as often as needed with an herbicide or ground sterilizer, or should be grubbed out. Dead weeds should be removed after destruction. Weed burners should not be used.

A.31.3.2.3 Where practical, some form of fixed system of alarm notification or communication equipment should be provided within the storage yard (e.g., telephones, radios).

Portable fire extinguishers suitable for the fire hazard involved should be provided at convenient, conspicuously accessible locations in the yard. Approved portable fire-extinguishing equipment should be located so that the travel distance to the nearest unit is not more than 75 ft (23 m). See Section 13.6. Approved fire extinguishers suitable for the fire hazard involved should be provided on all power vehicles and units, including haulage or private locomotives in the yard.

A.31.3.3.1.2 The type of operations at properties where the provisions of 31.3.4 apply vary widely. Retail lumber and building material operations are often characterized by large area buildings with minor outside storage areas. On the other hand, wholesale and distribution yards can involve large outside storage areas that present fire protection problems similar to mill yards.

A.31.3.3.2.1 Fire loss experience in lumberyards indicates that the following are the principal factors that allow lumberyard fires to reach serious proportions:

(1) Large, undivided stacks
(2) Congested storage conditions
(3) Delayed fire detection
(4) Inadequate fire protection
(5) Ineffective fire-fighting tactics

A.31.3.3.2.2 It is recognized that retail and wholesale lumber storage yards are normally located within municipal system boundaries, where the system should be capable of supplying not less than four 2½ in. (65 mm) hose streams simultaneously [1000 gpm (4000 L/min)]. Where large-scale fire-fighting operations can be expected, larger water supplies are needed. Where protection from municipal water supplies and hydrant systems is not provided or is not considered adequate by the AHJ, a yard fire hydrant system should be provided and installed in accordance with NFPA 24, *Standard for the Installation of Private Fire Service Mains and Their Appurtenances.*

A.31.3.3.3.1 Where the danger of underground fire is present, refuse-filled or sawdust-filled land should not be used.

A.31.3.3.3.3 Air-dried stickered stacks are subject to rapid-fire spread through the air spaces and should therefore be kept as low as practicable.

A.31.3.3.4.2 Because of the large quantities of material generally involved in lumberyard fires, some form of exposure protection for adjoining properties is recommended. Clear spaces or walls capable of providing fire barriers between yard storage and the exposed properties should be used. The responsibility for the protection of properties adjoining a lumberyard is often a joint responsibility to be worked out between the lumberyard and adjoining property owners. The AHJ should be consulted.

A.31.3.4.1 Each individual property has its own special conditions of yard use, material-handling methods, and topography. For this reason, only basic fire protection principles are discussed herein and are intended to be applied with due consideration of all local factors involved. The AHJ should be consulted.

A.31.3.4.2 Fire loss experience in lumber storage yards indicates that the following are the principal factors that allow lumberyard fires to reach serious proportions:

(1) Large, undivided stacks
(2) Congested storage conditions
(3) Delayed fire detection
(4) Inadequate fire protection
(5) Ineffective fire-fighting tactics

A.31.3.4.3 Refuse-filled or sawdust-filled land, swampy ground, or areas where the hazard of underground fire is present should not be used as a storage site.

A.31.3.4.3.1 For basic fire protection, the hydrant system should be capable of supplying not less than four 2½ in. (65 mm) hose streams simultaneously [1000 gpm (4000 L/min)] while maintaining a positive residual pressure in the fire protection hydrant system of not less than 20 psi (1.38 bar).

Where large-scale fire-fighting operations can be expected, larger water supplies with adequate mains are needed.

For early extinguishment with basic fire protection, hydrants should be spaced with sufficient 2½ in. (65 mm) hose attached to allow rapid hose laying to all parts of the stacking areas. For this reason, the hydrants should be spaced at about 250 ft (76 m) intervals so that any part of the yard can be reached with 250 ft (60 m) of hose. Hydrants preferably should be located at fire department access road intersections. A hydrant hose house with not less than 250 ft (60 m) of fire hose and auxiliary equipment should be provided at each hydrant. *(See NFPA 24.)*

A.31.3.5.1.1 Each individual property has its own special conditions of yard use, stock-handling methods, and topography. For this reason, only basic fire protection principles are discussed herein, and are intended to be applied with due consideration of all local factors involved. Ties, as used herein, include ties, poles, piles, posts, and other similar forest products. Treated ties are ties that are pressure impregnated with preservatives.

A.31.3.5.2 Fire loss experience in tie storage yards indicates that the following are the principal factors that allow fires to reach serious proportions:

(1) Large, undivided stacks
(2) Congested storage conditions

(3) Delayed fire detection
(4) Inadequate fire protection
(5) Ineffective fire-fighting tactics

A.31.3.5.3 Refuse-filled or sawdust-filled land, swampy ground, or areas where the hazard of underground fire is present should not be used as storage site.

A.31.3.5.3.1 With relatively open stacking (that is, stacking that allows for penetration of fire-extinguishing streams), sufficient alleyway width can usually be accomplished by providing a not-less-than 4 ft (1.2 m) alleyway width between alternate rows of tie stacks. *[See Figure A.31.3.5.3.1(a).]* Flat crib-style stacking without space between the stacks that forms solid packed rows should require a not-less-than 4 ft (1.2 m) alleyway width between each row. *[See Figure A.31.3.5.3.1(b).]*

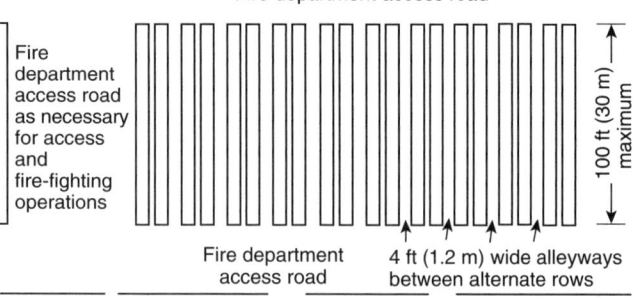

FIGURE A.31.3.5.3.1(a) Relatively Open Stacking Methods.

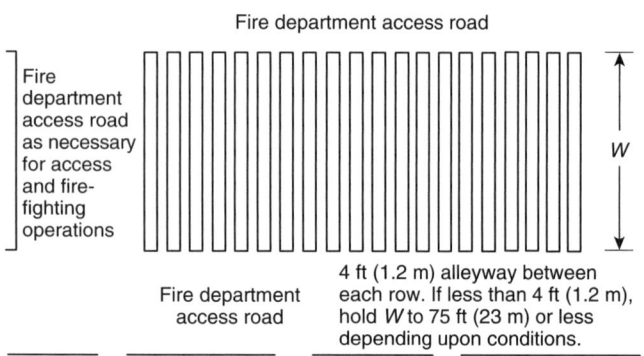

FIGURE A.31.3.5.3.1(b) Crib-Style Stacking into Solid Rows.

A.31.3.5.3.2 For basic fire protection, the hydrant system should be capable of supplying not less than four 2½ in. (65 mm) hose streams simultaneously [not less than 1000 gpm (4000 L/min)] while maintaining a positive residual pressure in the fire protection hydrant system of not less than 20 psi (1.38 bar).

Where large-scale fire-fighting operations can be expected, larger water supplies with adequate mains are needed.

For early extinguishment with basic fire protection, hydrants should be spaced with sufficient 2½ in. (65 mm) hose attached to allow rapid hose laying to all parts of the stacking areas. For this reason, hydrants should be spaced at about 250 ft (76 m) intervals so that any part of the yard can be reached with 200 ft (60 m) of hose. Hydrants preferably should be located at fire department access road intersections. A hydrant hose house with not less than 200 ft (60 m) of fire hose and auxiliary equipment should be provided at each hydrant. *(See NFPA 24.)*

A.31.3.5.3.5 Heights in excess of 20 ft (6 m) seriously restrict effective extinguishing operations.

A.31.3.6.1 Each individual property has its own special conditions of yard use, stock-handling methods, and topography. It is recognized that climate conditions, wood species, and the age of piles are all factors affecting fire safety. For these reasons, only basic fire protection principles are discussed herein, and are intended to be applied with due consideration of all local factors involved. Except for the surface layer, the moisture content of a pile of wood chips or hogged material is quite high, so surface fires do not generally penetrate more than a few inches into the pile. Fire tests indicate that, for areas of average humidity conditions, the flame propagation over the surface is relatively slow. These conditions allow ready extinguishment, provided that there is early detection and good access. It is expected that, in areas where long periods of low humidity prevail, faster surface flame spread can be anticipated, increasing the importance of early detection and good access.

A.31.3.6.2.1 Fire experience and fire tests indicate that two completely different types of fires can occur in storage piles — surface fires and internal fires. Fire prevention activities and fire protection facilities should, therefore, include preparations for coping with both situations.

Internal heating is a hazard inherent to long-term bulk storage of chips and hogged material that progresses to spontaneous combustion under certain pile conditions. Internal fires are difficult to detect and extinguish. Unless provisions are made for measuring internal temperatures, such fires can burn for long periods before emission of smoke at the surface indicates an internal fire.

Extinguishment then becomes a lengthy and expensive loss-control and operating problem requiring equipment and manpower to move large portions of the pile, either by digging out the burning portions or removing the unburned portions of the pile. Experience has shown that these conditions create very large losses, and special attention should be given to the prevention of spontaneous combustion and to pre-fire planning where evaluating how best to handle an imminent or actual fire in a particular pile.

A.31.3.6.2.2 Prevention of internal fires requires an understanding of the factors that cause exothermic oxidation so that steps can be taken to minimize this hazard and to provide means of monitoring temperature conditions inside the pile. Refuse and old chips should not be permitted in the chip pile base. The storage site should be thoroughly cleaned before starting a new pile.

The quality of chip supplies should be controlled in terms of percentage of fines. The concentration of fines should not be allowed during pile buildup.

Pneumatic systems produce an air classification of stored materials that should be recognized, and appropriate steps should be taken to minimize concentration of fines.

It is preferable to spread new stored materials in a relatively even layer over the pile.

Vehicles used on all piles should be of a type that minimizes compaction.

Veneer chip piles should be limited to 50 ft (15 m) in height.

A.31.3.6.2.2(4) For example, whole-tree chip piles containing bark, leaves, and other extraneous or hogged material can be subject to greater degrees of spontaneous heating and thermal degradation and should be reclaimed more frequently.

A.31.3.6.2.2(5) Fundamentally, several small piles are better than one large pile.

A.31.3.6.2.2(8) Minimizing the diffusion of water from wet, stored material into dry fires is important to reduce exothermic heating caused by adsorption effects. Maintaining surface moisture content is also important so as to reduce the hazard of surface fires during periods of hot, dry weather.

A.31.3.6.3 A high standard of housekeeping should be maintained around all potential heat sources.

Care should be exercised to prevent tramp metal from entering the piles, or sections of blower pipes from being buried in the piles.

A.31.3.6.3.1 For very large piles, two or more access roadways should be provided on opposite sides of the pile.

A.31.3.6.3.2 Narrow, low piles facilitate fire extinguishment.

A.31.3.6.3.4 Due to the size and configuration of piles, providing portable fire extinguishers within 75 ft (23 m) of travel distance to any point is not practical.

A.31.3.6.3.5 Fire hydrants connected to yard mains should be provided so that any part of the pile(s) can be reached by hose equipment provided in each hydrant hose house. Each hydrant hose house should be equipped with a complement of 2½ in. (65 mm) and 1½ in. (38 mm) hose, a 2½ in. (65 mm) and 1½ in. (38 mm) gated wye, and 1½ in. (38 mm) combination nozzles.

Hydrants should be spaced at about 250 ft (76 m) intervals so that any part of the yard can be reached with 200 ft (60 m) of hose.

Where pile configurations are such that all parts of the pile cannot be reached by the hose, a fire hose cart(s) equipped with an ample supply of hose and nozzles should be strategically placed in the storage area.

The amount of water needed to control a pile fire varies substantially depending on the size of the pile. Weather conditions, operating methods, geographic location, type of material stored, and the degree to which wetting can be employed affect the potential for a large area surface fire. Experience indicates that exposure to long periods of hot, dry weather with no regular surface wetting creates conditions under which fast-spreading surface fires, which require many hose streams for control depending on the size of the pile, can occur.

Likewise, the frequency of pile turnover and operating methods affect the potential for serious internal fires. Piles built using methods that allow a concentration of fines and piles stored for long periods of time with no turnover are subject to internal heating that, if undetected, can create intense internal fires.

A flow of not less than 500 gpm (2000 L/min) should be provided at any fire hydrant in the pile area. Additional flows should be provided as needed where conditions are likely to produce serious surface fires or large internal fires. Fire mains should be engineered to deliver the recommended gallonage plus allowance for operational uses and special extinguishing equipment at a residual pressure of 60 psi to 100 psi (4.1 bar to 6.9 bar) at the hydrants.

A.31.3.6.3.7 With the use of the equipment specified in 31.3.6.3.7, surface types of pile fires can usually be removed from the affected areas and extinguished.

Where deep-seated fires occur within the pile or under the pile in tunnels or other enclosures, this equipment is invaluable in breaking down the entire pile and spreading it out in a safe yard area, which allows fire fighters using hand hose lines or deluge units to extinguish both the pile and ground-spread stored material.

A.31.3.6.4.1 Experience indicates that radiated heat from exposing fires in storage piles does not ordinarily pose a serious ignition threat to other piles, provided that recommended clear spaces are maintained. Flying brands from exposing fires, especially during high winds, do present a hazardous ignition source. Upwind forest or brush fires can also present a problem in relation to flying sparks and brands.

A.31.3.6.4.2 Buildings or other structures near storage piles can pose a serious exposure hazard to the pile.

A.31.3.6.4.3 Greater clearance is desirable when piles are high and side slopes are greater than 60 degrees.

A.31.3.7 This type of chip has a much higher aliphatic hydrocarbon (sugar) content and spontaneously ignites readily. Lumber chips are debarked and thus lose the cambium layer associated with stored sugars. It is these sugars that start the bacterial decomposition that proceeds to spontaneous ignition.

A.31.3.8.1.1 Each individual property has its own special conditions for yard use, stock-handling methods, and topography. For this reason, only basic fire protection principles are discussed herein, and are intended to be applied with due consideration of all local factors involved.

A.31.3.8.2 Fire loss experience in outside storage of logs indicates that the following are the principal factors that allow log pile fires to reach serious proportions:

(1) Large, undivided piles
(2) Congested storage conditions
(3) Delayed fire detection
(4) Inadequate fire protection
(5) Ineffective fire-fighting tactics

A.31.3.8.3 Refuse-filled or sawdust-filled land, swampy ground, or areas where the hazard of underground fire is present should not be used as a storage site.

A.31.3.8.3.3 Where practical, greater widths should be provided to minimize the effects of radiated heat, particularly in high-piled yards.

A.31.3.8.3.3.2 Heights in excess of 20 ft (6 m) seriously restrict effective extinguishing operations, since successful extinguishment of log pile fires requires penetration of the pile from the side by hose streams.

A.31.3.8.3.3.3 See Figure A.31.3.8.3.3.3.

A.31.3.8.3.3.4 For basic fire protection, the hydrant system should be capable of supplying not less than four 2½ in. (65 mm) hose streams simultaneously [not less than 1000 gpm (4000 L/min)] while maintaining a positive residual pressure in the fire protection hydrant system of not less than 20 psi (1.38 bar).

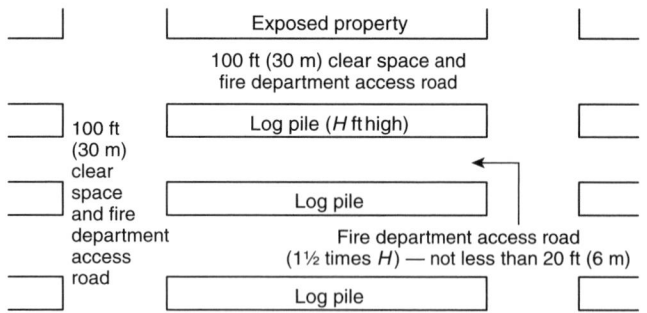

FIGURE A.31.3.8.3.3.3 Layout of Log Storage Yard.

Where large-scale fire-fighting operations can be expected, larger water supplies with adequate mains are needed.

For early extinguishment with basic fire protection, hydrants should be spaced with sufficient 2½ in. (65 mm) hose attached to allow rapid hose laying to all parts of the piling areas. For this reason, hydrants should be spaced at about 250 ft (76 m) intervals so that any part of the yard can be reached with 200 ft (60 m) of hose. Hydrants should be located at fire department access road intersections. A hydrant hose house with not less than 200 ft (60 m) of fire hose and auxiliary equipment should be provided at each hydrant. *(See NFPA 24.)*

A.31.3.8.3.6 The installation of a portable piping system equipped with irrigation or lawn-type sprinklers on the top of each log pile is recommended.

A.32.4.2(8) An example of a *change of use* would be a soundstage with audience facilities for 50 persons being used for a preview party for 500 persons. An example of a *change of occupancy classification* would be a soundstage without audience facilities being used for a preview party for 500 persons. [**140:** A.4.2(8)]

A.32.4.3.1 Particular attention needs to be given to combustible materials used in close proximity to pyrotechnic and open-flame special effects. On-site verification of the fire retardant properties of set components, furnishings, props, and other combustible materials is essential to ensure the safety of pyrotechnic and open-flame special effects. The provisions of 32.4.5 address the need to render drapes, greens, foamed plastics, and other combustible materials fire retardant. [**140:** A.4.3.1]

A comprehensive safety meeting should be conducted to define the intended scope of a special effect and establish appropriate safe areas. The safe areas need to be sized in consideration of the variable predictability of the materials used in the special effect. The safety meeting should include the participation of all persons who will be present during the special effect. The meeting discussion should also include consideration of the following:

(1) Conducting a test in an approved location of all devices and materials intended to be used in the special effect
(2) Excluding nonessential persons from the area of the effect until special effects personnel and a representative of the AHJ declare the area to be safe
(3) Evaluating the potential impact of the special effect on the uninvolved public
(4) Establishing an emergency plan that includes initial actions to take if the special effect exceeds its intended size, intensity, or duration
(5) Maintaining safe escape routes from the special effects area
(6) Developing methods of communication to be used during the special effect
(7) Identifying the individuals authorized to require that emergency actions be taken
(8) Specifying the licensing requirements for the individuals initiating the special effect
(9) Specifying the clothing to be worn by all special effects and safety personnel
(10) Evaluating the assignments and required abilities of all special effects and safety personnel
(11) Assigning the appropriate number of safety personnel to implement the plan
(12) Determining adequate and appropriate fire protection tailored to the materials used
(13) Establishing primary and backup methods of requesting additional fire suppression resources
(14) Identifying a definitive point when the special effect is complete

[**140:** A.4.3.1]

A.32.4.5.2(4) It is important that combustible drapes, drops, and similar materials exhibit adequate fire performance. The AHJ might be able to make a judgment of adequate fire performance without requiring testing of the materials. [**140:** A.4.5.2(4)]

A.32.4.5.2(5) Examples of interim measures that could be approved by the AHJ include, but are not limited to, the following:

(1) Providing a fire watch
(2) Removing the combustible materials at the end of the day's filming
(3) Keeping lighting and other heat-producing sources away from the combustible materials
(4) Providing baffles around heat-producing sources

[**140:** A.4.5.2(5)]

A.32.4.8.2 This requirement does not prohibit the use of mobile generators for auxiliary power. [**140:** A.4.8.2]

A.32.4.11.1.3.1 Paragraphs 32.4.11.1.3.1 and 32.4.11.1.3.2 recognize motion picture and television industry practices that require sets to change constantly and that sets are "temporary" construction not subject to building codes or standards. Solid ceilings that obstruct the stage sprinklers are "flown" (moved) in or out to permit special shooting angles or lighting requirements, often on a scene-by-scene basis. With temporary walls and ceilings, it would be impractical to install a sprinkler system in a constantly changing structure. Therefore, one or more of the following mitigation techniques should be used to compensate for the areas shielded from sprinkler spray by solid or hard ceilings or platforms:

(1) Approved and listed heat detectors or smoke detectors can be installed beneath such solid or hard ceilings in excess of 600 ft² (55.7 m²) in area and platforms in excess of 600 ft² (55.7 m²) in area and 3 ft (0.9 m) in height. Detectors should be connected to an approved and listed central, proprietary, or remote station service or to a local alarm that will provide an audible signal (i.e., a bell or horn) at a constantly attended location. The detector sys-

tem, including the alarm panel, is defined as a portable system because it is intended to be reinstalled when platforms or sets are changed. The detectors that are secured to standard outlet boxes and the listed fire alarm panels can be temporarily supported by sets, platforms, or pedestals. Spacing of detectors should be per manufacturers' requirements.

(2) The ceiling can be positioned to allow for the operation of the building's automatic fire sprinkler system after videotaping, filming, or broadcasting of programs has been completed for the day.

(3) A fire watch should be provided when the set is not in use.

(4) No combustible materials should be stored under any platforms. Consideration should be given to secure such covered areas with screen wire or other materials that will permit visual inspection and emergency access.

(5) Approved/listed fire retardants can be applied beneath combustible platforms.

(6) Approved/listed fire retardants can be applied to scenery, props, framework and deck of combustible platforms, and the hard-ceilings of combustible sets.

[140: A.4.11.1.3.1]

A.32.4.11.1.3.2 See A.32.4.11.1.3.1. [140: A.4.11.1.3.2]

A.32.5.2(1) The AHJ might waive the production location permit provided the AHJ is notified that the site is to be used as a production location. [140: A.5.2(1)]

A.32.5.8.3 The AHJ might approve the routing of power cables through fire-rated windows or doors if standby fire personnel or other approved safeguards are provided during such periods. [140: A.5.8.3]

A.32.5.9 The AHJ, when granting a permit to a production company to film on location should consider the placement of the support equipment. Typically, the production support vehicles are numerous, and unregulated placement of these vehicles could impede emergency access or egress. Additionally, the types of support vehicles need to be arranged so that a hazardous operation (e.g., fueling or special effects) is distant from sources of ignition and crew gathering areas (e.g., catering locations). The location permit should include a plot plan so the AHJ can adequately assess potential problems. [140: A.5.9]

A.32.5.10 Where a production company films *on location*, such activity might interfere with, or prevent, the normal use of the facility or area. As such, the facility being occupied as a production location is often used for a purpose different from that of its normal use. Where the production company filming causes the facility or area to curtail normal operations, the facility should not be required to meet the life safety provisions applicable to the normal occupancy. Rather, life safety features should be maintained consistent with provisions required for the temporary use. For example, consider a single story assembly occupancy building with occupant load of 600 persons that has three exits for compliance with the provision of NFPA *101*, that requires a minimum of three exits where the occupant load of a floor exceeds 500 persons. The assembly occupancy building is used as a production location for a total of 200 persons. The production crew presents, for approval of the AHJ, a plan to block off one of the three exits while maintaining compliance with the requirements for egress width, travel distance, common path of travel, and dead-end corridors. The AHJ approves the proposed means of egress as appropriate for the intended use as required by 32.5.10. [140: A.5.10]

A.32.5.11.1 The phrase "intimate with the initial fire development" refers to the person(s) at the ignition source or first materials burning, not to all persons within the same room or area. [140: A.5.11.1]

The occupant protection requirement of 32.5.11.1 is the same as that required for all occupancies by NFPA *101*. The activities associated with filming at a production location without an audience are characteristic of the occupancy classification of industrial occupancy. Industrial occupancies are not required by NFPA *101* to be sprinklered. The objective of protecting occupants not intimate with the initial fire development for the time needed to evacuate, relocate, or defend in place is accomplished for industrial occupancies by prescriptive provisions not dependent on sprinkler protection. [140: A.5.11.1]

Where production location filming occurs in a building area not provided with the life safety systems required for industrial occupancies (e.g., in a tower with a single means of egress provided by an unenclosed stair), sprinklers, a fire alarm system, or other mitigation techniques acceptable to the AHJ will need to be employed for compliance with 32.5.11.1. Where sprinklers are provided, see 32.5.11.2 and 32.5.11.6. [140: A.5.11.1]

A.32.5.11.4 See A.32.4.11.1.3.1. [140: A.5.11.4]

A.32.5.11.5 See A.32.4.11.1.3.1. [140: A.5.11.5]

A.32.6.4 Special attention should be focused on any possible obstructions to the means of egress. The means of egress and the marking of it might be confusing to the audience due to the numerous bright lights, scenery, video and film cameras, and other equipment in and around the soundstage. [140: A.6.4]

A.33.1 Fire service professionals who have managed major scrap tire piles believe that the best approach is to allow the tire pile to burn while protecting exposures like buildings, heavy equipment, and surrounding tire piles. Once the tire pile is in a smoldering stage, heavy equipment can be used to pull the pile apart and the tire material can be extinguished incrementally. For additional information, see "Rings of Fire: Fire Prevention & Suppression of Outdoor Tire Piles."

A.33.4.3 This can include but is not limited to the availability of earth-moving equipment or other approved means of controlling a fire.

A.33.7.5 Altered tire material piles have been known to spontaneously combust after a heavy precipitation. Investigators have considered anaerobic action and potential heat from oxidation of steel belts as the source of exothermic reaction.

A.34.1.1.2(6) The limitations on the type and size of storage are intended to identify those situations where tire storage is present in limited quantity and incidental to the main use of the building. Occupancies such as aircraft hangars, automobile dealers, repair garages, retail storage facilities, automotive and truck assembly plants, and mobile home assembly plants are types of facilities where miscellaneous tire storage could be present. The fire protection sprinkler design densities specified by NFPA 13 are adequate to provide protection for the storage heights indicated. Storage beyond these heights or areas presents hazards that are addressed by this *Code* and are outside the scope of NFPA 13.

A.34.2.4.2 For example, Class III will become Class IV, and Class IV will become a cartoned unexpanded Group A plastic commodity. [13: A.5.6.2.2]

A.34.2.4.3 For example, Class II will become Class IV, and Class III and Class IV will become a cartoned unexpanded Group A plastic commodity. [13: A.5.6.2.3]

A.34.2.5 See Table A.34.2.5.

Table A.34.2.5 Alphabetized Listing of Commodity Classes

Commodity	Commodity Class
Aerosols	
Cartoned or uncartoned — Level 1	Class III
Alcoholic Beverages	
Cartoned or uncartoned	
- Up to 20 percent alcohol in metal, glass, or ceramic containers	Class I
- Up to 20 percent alcohol in wood containers	Class II
Ammunition	
Small arms, shotgun — packaged, cartoned	Class IV
Appliances, Major (e.g., stoves, refrigerators)	
- Not packaged, no appreciable plastic exterior trim	Class I
- Corrugated, cartoned (no appreciable plastic trim)	Class II
Baked Goods	
Cookies, cakes, pies	
- Frozen, packaged in cartons[a]	Class II
- Packaged, in cartons	Class III
Batteries	
Dry cells (nonlithium or similar exotic metals)	
- Packaged in cartons	Class I
- Blister-packed in cartons	Class II
Automobile — filled[b]	Class I
Truck or larger — empty or filled[b]	Group A plastics
Beans	
Dried — packaged, cartoned	Class III
Boat Storage	
- Stored in racks	See Table A.5.6 of NFPA 13
Bottles, Jars	
Empty, cartoned	
- Glass	Class I
- Plastic PET (polyethylene terephthalate)	Class IV
Filled noncombustible powders	
- Plastic PET	Class II
- Glass, cartoned	Class I
- Plastic, cartoned [less than 1 gal (3.8 L)]	Class IV
- Plastic, uncartoned (other than PET), any size	Group A plastics
- Plastic, cartoned or exposed [greater than 1 gal (3.8 L)]	Group A plastics
- Plastic, solid plastic crates	Group A plastics
- Plastic, open plastic crates	Group A plastics
Filled noncombustible liquids	
- Glass, cartoned	Class I
- Plastic, cartoned [less than 5 gal (18.9 L)]	Class I

Table A.34.2.5 *Continued*

Commodity	Commodity Class
- Plastic, open or solid plastic crates[c]	Group A plastics
- Plastic, PET	Class I
Boxes, Crates	
- Empty, wood, solid walls	Class II
- Empty, wood, slatted	See Table A.5.6 of NFPA 13
Bread	
Wrapped cartoned	Class III
Butter	
Whipped spread	Class III
Candles	
Packaged, cartoned	
- Treat as expanded plastic	Group A plastics
Candy	
Packaged, cartoned	Class III
Canned Foods	
In ordinary cartons	Class I
Cans	
Metal — empty	Class I
Carpet Tiles	
Cartoned	Group A plastics
Cartons	
Corrugated	
- Unassembled (neat piles)	Class III
- Partially assembled	Class IV
Wax coated, single walled	Group A plastics
Cement	
Bagged	Class I
Cereals	
Packaged, cartoned	Class III
Charcoal	
Bagged — standard	Class III
Cheese	
- Packaged, cartoned	Class III
- Wheels, cartoned	Class III
Chewing Gum	
Packaged, cartoned	Class III
Chocolate	
Packaged, cartoned	Class III
Cloth	
Cartoned and not cartoned	
- Natural fiber, viscose	Class III
- Synthetic[d]	Class IV
Cocoa Products	
Packaged, cartoned	Class III
Coffee	
- Canned, cartoned	Class I
- Packaged, cartoned	Class III
Coffee Beans	
Bagged	Class III
Cotton	
Packaged, cartoned	Class III
Diapers	
- Cotton, linen	Class III
- Disposable with plastics and nonwoven fabric (in cartons)	Class IV
- Disposable with plastics and nonwoven fabric (uncartoned), plastic wrapped	Group A plastics

Table A.34.2.5 *Continued*

Commodity	Commodity Class
Dried Foods	
Packaged, cartoned	Class III
Fertilizers	
Bagged	
- Phosphates	Class I
- Nitrates	Class II
Fiberglass Insulation	
- Paper-backed rolls, bagged or unbagged	Class IV
File Cabinets	
Metal	
- Cardboard box or shroud	Class I
Fish or Fish Products	
Frozen	
- Nonwaxed, nonplastic packaging	Class I
- Waxed-paper containers, cartoned	Class II
- Boxed or barreled	Class II
- Plastic trays, cartoned	Class III
Canned	
- Cartoned	Class I
Frozen Foods	
Nonwaxed, nonplastic packaging	Class I
- Waxed-paper containers, cartoned	Class II
- Plastic trays	Class III
Fruit	
Fresh	
- Nonplastic trays or containers	Class I
- With wood spacers	Class I
Furniture	
Wood	
- No plastic coverings or foam plastic cushioning	Class III
- With plastic coverings	Class IV
- With foam plastic cushioning	Group A plastics
Grains — Packaged in Cartons	
- Barley	Class III
- Rice	Class III
- Oats	Class III
Ice Cream	Class I
Leather Goods	Class III
Leather Hides	
Baled	Class II
Light Fixtures	
Nonplastic — cartoned	Class II
Lighters	
Butane	
- Blister-packed, cartoned	Group A plastics
- Loose and in large containers (Level 3 aerosol)	See Table A.5.6 of NFPA 13
Liquor	
100 proof or less, 1 gal (3.8 L) or less, cartoned	
- Glass (palletized)[f]	Class IV
- Plastic bottles	Class IV
Marble	
Artificial sinks, countertops	
- Cartoned, crated	Class II

Table A.34.2.5 *Continued*

Commodity	Commodity Class
Margarine	
- Up to 50 percent oil (in paper or plastic containers)	Class III
- Between 50 percent and 80 percent oil (in any packaging)	Group A plastics
Matches	
Packaged, cartoned	
- Paper	Class IV
- Wood	Group A plastics
Mattresses	
- Standard (box spring)	Class III
- Foam (in finished form)	Group A plastics
Meat, Meat Products	
- Bulk	Class I
- Canned, cartoned	Class I
- Frozen, nonwaxed, nonplastic containers	Class I
- Frozen, waxed-paper containers	Class II
- Frozen, expanded plastic trays	Class II
Metal Desks	
- With plastic tops and trim	Class I
Milk	
- Nonwaxed-paper containers	Class I
- Waxed-paper containers	Class I
- Plastic containers	Class I
- Containers in plastic crates	Group A plastics
Motors	
- Electric	Class I
Nail Polish	
- 1 oz to 2 oz (29.6 ml to 59.1 ml) glass, cartoned	Class IV
- 1 oz to 2 oz (29.6 ml to 59.1 ml) plastic bottles, cartoned	Group A plastics
Nuts	
- Canned, cartoned	Class I
- Packaged, cartoned	Class III
- Bagged	Class III
Paints	
Friction-top cans, cartoned	
- Water-based (latex)	Class I
- Oil-based	Class IV
Paper Products	
- Books, magazines, stationery, plastic-coated paper food containers, newspapers, cardboard games, or cartoned tissue products	Class III
- Tissue products, uncartoned and plastic wrapped	Group A plastics
Paper, Rolled	
In racks or on side	Class III
- Medium- or heavyweight	
In racks	Class IV
- Lightweight	
Paper, Waxed	
Packaged in cartons	Class IV
Pharmaceuticals	
Pills, powders	
- Glass bottles, cartoned	Class II
- Plastic bottles, cartoned	Class IV

(continues)

Table A.34.2.5 *Continued*

Commodity	Commodity Class
Nonflammable liquids	
- Glass bottles, cartoned	Class II
Photographic Film	
- Motion picture or bulk rolls of film in polycarbonate, polyethylene, or metal cans; polyethylene bagged in cardboard boxes	Class II
- 35 mm in metal film cartridges in polyethylene cans in cardboard boxes	Class III
- Paper, in sheets, bagged in polyethylene, in cardboard boxes	Class III
- Rolls in polycarbonate plastic cassettes, bulk wrapped in cardboard boxes	Class IV
Plastic Containers (except PET)	
- Noncombustible liquids or semiliquids in plastic containers less than 5 gal (18.9 L) capacity	Class I
- Noncombustible liquids or semiliquids (such as ketchup) in plastic containers with nominal wall thickness of ¼ in. (6.4 mm) or less and larger than 5 gal (18.9) capacity	Class II
- Noncombustible liquids or semiliquids (such as ketchup) in plastic containers with nominal wall thickness greater than ¼ in. (6.4 mm) and larger than 5 gal (18.9 L) capacity	Group A plastics
Polyurethane	
- Cartoned or uncartoned expanded	Group A plastics
Poultry Products	
- Canned, cartoned	Class I
- Frozen, nonwaxed, nonplastic containers	Class I
- Frozen (on paper or expanded plastic trays)	Class II
Powders	
Ordinary combustibles — free flowing	
- In paper bags (e.g., flour, sugar)	Class II
PVA (polyvinyl alcohol) Resins	
PVC (polyvinyl chloride)	
- Flexible (e.g., cable jackets, plasticized sheets)	Class III
- Rigid (e.g., pipe, pipe fittings)	Class III
- Bagged resins	Class III
Rags	
Baled	
- Natural fibers	Class III
- Synthetic fibers	Class IV
Rubber	
- Natural, blocks in cartons	Class IV
- Synthetic	Group A plastics
Salt	
- Bagged	Class I
- Packaged, cartoned	Class II

Table A.34.2.5 *Continued*

Commodity	Commodity Class
Shingles	
- Asphalt-coated fiberglass	Class III
- Asphalt-impregnated felt	Class IV
Shock Absorbers	
- Metal dust cover	Class II
- Plastic dust cover	Class III
Signatures	
Books, magazines	
- Solid array on pallet	Class II
Skis	
- Wood	Class III
- Foam core	Class IV
Storage Container	
- Large container storage of household goods	See Table A.5.6 of NFPA 13
Stuffed Toys	
Foam or synthetic	Group A plastics
Syrup	
- Drummed (metal containers)	Class I
- Barreled, wood	Class II
Textiles	
Natural fiber clothing or textile products	Class III
Synthetics (except rayon and nylon) — 50/50 blend or less	
- Thread, yarn on wood or paper spools	Class III
- Fabrics	Class III
- Thread, yarn on plastic spools	Class IV
- Baled fiber	Group A plastics
Synthetics (except rayon and nylon) — greater than 50/50 blend	
- Thread, yarn on wood or paper spools	Class IV
- Fabrics	Class IV
- Baled fiber	Group A plastics
- Thread, yarn on plastic spools	Group A plastics
Rayon and nylon	
- Baled fiber	Class IV
- Thread, yarn on wood or paper spools	Class IV
- Fabrics	Class IV
- Thread, yarn on plastic spools	Group A plastics
Tobacco Products	
In paperboard cartons	Class III
Transformers	
Dry and oil filled	Class I
Vinyl-Coated Fabric	
Cartoned	Group A plastics
Vinyl Floor Coverings	
- Tiles in cartons	Class IV
- Rolled	Group A plastics
Wax-Coated Paper	
Cups, plates	
- Boxed or packaged inside cartons (emphasis on packaging)	Class IV
- Loose inside large cartons	Group A plastics

Table A.34.2.5 *Continued*

Commodity	Commodity Class
Wax	
Paraffin/petroleum wax, blocks, cartoned	Group A plastics
Wire	
- Bare wire on metal spools on wood skids	Class I
- Bare wire on wood or cardboard spools on wood skids	Class II
- Bare wire on metal, wood, or cardboard spools in cardboard boxes on wood skids	Class II
- Single- or multiple-layer PVC-covered wire on metal spools on wood skids	Class II
- Insulated (PVC) cable on large wood or metal spools on wood skids	Class II
- Bare wire on plastic spools in cardboard boxes on wood skids	Class IV
- Single- or multiple-layer PVC-covered wire on plastic spools in cardboard boxes on wood skids	Class IV
- Single, multiple, or power cables (PVC) on large plastic spools	Class IV
- Bulk storage of empty plastic spools	Group A plastics
Wood Products	
- Solid piles — lumber, plywood, particleboard, pressboard (smooth ends and edges)	Class II
- Spools (empty)	Class III
- Toothpicks, clothespins, hangers in cartons	Class III
- Doors, windows, wood cabinets, and furniture	Class III
- Patterns	Class IV

[a]The product is presumed to be in a plastic-coated package in a corrugated carton. If packaged in a metal foil, it can be considered Class I.
[b]Most batteries have a polypropylene case and, if stored empty, should be treated as a Group A plastic. Truck batteries, even where filled, should be considered a Group A plastic because of their thicker walls.
[c]As the openings in plastic crates become larger, the product behaves more like a Class III commodity. Conversely, as the openings become smaller, the product behaves more like a plastic.
[d]Tests clearly indicate that a synthetic or synthetic blend is considered greater than Class III.
[e]When liquor is stored in glass containers in racks, it should be considered a Class III commodity; where it is palletized, it should be considered a Class IV commodity. [**13**: Table A.5.6.3]

A.34.2.7 *Paper Classifications.* These classifications were derived from a series of large-scale and laboratory-type small-scale fire tests. It is recognized that not all paper in a class burns with exactly the same characteristics. [**13**: A.5.6.5]

Paper can be soft or hard, thick or thin, or heavy or light and can also be coated with various materials. The broad range of papers can be classified according to various properties. One important property is basis weight, which is defined as the weight of a sheet of paper of a specified area. Two broad categories of paper are recognized by industry — paper and paperboard. Paperboard normally has a basis weight of 20 lb (9.1 kg) or greater measured on a sheet 1000 ft^2 (92.9 m^2) sheet. Stock with a basis weight less than 20 lb/1000 ft^2 (9.1 kg/92.9 m^2) is normally categorized as paper. The basis weight of paper is usually measured on a sheet 3000 ft^2 (278.7 m^2) sheet. The basis weight of paper can also be measured on the total area of a ream of paper, which is normally the case for the following types of printing and writing papers:

(1) *Bond paper* — 500 sheets, 17 in. × 22 in. (432 mm × 559 mm) = 1300 ft^2 (120.8 m^2) per ream
(2) *Book paper* — 500 sheets, 25 in. × 38 in. (635 mm × 965 mm) = 3300 ft^2 (306.6 m^2) per ream
(3) *Index paper* — 500 sheets, 25½ in.× 30½ in. (648 mm × 775 mm) = 2700 ft^2 (250.8 m^2) per ream
(4) *Bristol paper* — 500 sheets, 22½ in. × 35 in. (572 mm × 889 mm) = 2734 ft^2 (254 m^2) per ream
(5) *Tag paper*— 500 sheets, 24 in. × 36 in. (610 mm × 914 mm) = 3000 ft^2 (278.7 m^2) per ream
[**13**: A.5.6.5]

For the purposes of this *Code*, all basis weights are expressed in lb/1000 ft^2 (kg/92.9 m^2) of paper. To determine the basis weight per 1000 ft^2 (92.9 m^2) for papers measured on a sheet of different area, the following formula should be applied:

$$\frac{\text{Basis weight}}{1000 \text{ ft}^2} = \text{basis weight} \times 1000 \text{ measured area}$$

Example: To determine the basis weight per 1000 ft^2 (92.9 m^2) of 16 lb (7.3 kg) bond paper:

$$\left(\frac{16 \text{ lb}}{1300 \text{ ft}^2}\right) 1000 = \frac{12.3 \text{ lb}}{1000 \text{ ft}^2}$$

Large- and small-scale fire tests indicate that the burning rate of paper varies with the basis weight. Heavyweight paper burns more slowly than lightweight paper. Full-scale roll paper fire tests were conducted with the following types of paper:

(1) *Linerboard* — 42 lb/1000 ft^2 (19.1 kg/92.9 m^2) nominal basis weight
(2) *Newsprint*— 10 lb/1000 ft^2 (4.5 kg/92.9 m^2) nominal basis weight
(3) *Tissue* — 5 lb/1000 ft^2 (2.3 kg/92.9 m^2) nominal basis weight
[**13**: A.5.6.5]

The rate of firespread over the surface of the tissue rolls was extremely rapid in the full-scale fire tests. The rate of fire spread over the surface of the linerboard rolls was slower. Based on the overall results of these full-scale tests, along with additional data from small-scale testing of various paper grades, the broad range of papers has been classified into three major categories as follows:

(1) *Heavyweight* — Basis weight of 20 lb/1000 ft^2 (9.1 kg/92.9 m^2) or greater
(2) *Mediumweight* — Basis weight of 10 lb to 20 lb/1000 ft^2 (4.5 kg to 9.1 kg/92.9 m^2)
(3) *Lightweight* — Basis weight of less than 10 lb/1000 ft^2 (4.5 kg/92.9 m^2) and tissues regardless of basis weight
[**13**: A.5.6.5]

The following SI units were used for conversion of English units:

(1) 1 lb = 0.454 kg
(2) 1 in. = 25.4 mm
(3) 1 ft = 0.3048 m; 1 ft^2 = 0.0929 m^2
[**13**: A.5.6.5]

The various types of papers normally found in each of the four major categories are provided in Table A.34.2.7. [**13:** A.5.6.5]

A.34.3.1 With protection installed in accordance with this *Code*, fire protection of overhead steel and steel columns might not be necessary. Consideration should be given to subdividing large area warehouses in order to reduce the amount of merchandise that could be affected by a single fire.

Walls or partitions are recommended to be provided to separate the storage area from mercantile, manufacturing, or other occupancies to prevent the possibility of transmission of fire or smoke between the two occupancies. Door openings should be equipped with automatic-closing fire doors appropriate for the fire resistance rating of the wall or partition.

A.34.3.3 Since most of the fire tests were conducted without heat and smoke venting and draft curtains, protection specified in NFPA 13 was developed without their use.

For guidance on smoke and heat venting, see NFPA 204, *Standard for Smoke and Heat Venting.*

Smoke removal is important to manual fire fighting and overhaul. Vents through eave-line windows, doors, monitors, or gravity or mechanical exhaust systems facilitate smoke removal after control of the fire is achieved.

Results of tests organized by the Fire Protection Research Foundation and the Retail Committee on Group A Plastics to study the interaction of sprinklers, vents, and draft curtains indicate that the impact of automatic vents on sprinkler performance is neutral when automatic sprinkler discharge is adequate for the hazard and that draft curtains are potentially negative. Test results show that the placement of sprinklers and the thermal sensitivity of sprinklers and vents should be considered. Care should be exercised in the placement of draft curtains. Where required to be installed, draft curtains should be aligned where possible with aisles or other clear spaces in storage areas. Draft curtains where positioned over storage could adversely affect sprinkler operations. The number of operating sprinklers increased and led to a fire that consumed more commodity compared to other tests with fires ignited away from the draft curtains.

A.34.4.1 Commodities that are particularly susceptible to water damage should be stored on skids, dunnage, pallets, or elevated platforms in order to maintain at least 4 in. (100 mm) clearance from the floor.

A.34.4.2.2 Protection for exposed steel structural roof members could be needed and should be provided as indicated by the AHJ.

A.34.4.2.5 Incandescent light fixtures should have shades or guards to prevent the ignition of commodity from hot bulbs where possibility of contact with storage exists.

A.34.5.1 Wet systems are recommended for storage occupancies. Dry systems are permitted only where it is impractical to provide heat. Preaction systems should be considered for storage occupancies that are unheated, particularly where in-rack sprinklers are installed or for those occupancies that are highly susceptible to water damage.

A.34.5.4.2 See Annex B of NFPA 13E.

A.34.6.3.2 The use of welding, cutting, soldering, or brazing torches in the storage areas introduces a severe fire hazard and, when possible, should be relocated to a designated area. The use of mechanical fastenings and mechanical saws or cutting wheels is recommended.

A.34.6.6 Periodic inspections of all fire protection equipment should be made in conjunction with regular inspections of the premises. Unsatisfactory conditions should be reported immediately and necessary corrective measures taken promptly.

A.34.6.6.2 All fire-fighting and safety personnel should realize the great danger in shutting off sprinklers once opened by heat from fire. Shutting off sprinklers to locate fire could cause a disaster. Ventilation, use of smoke masks, smoke removal equipment, and removal of material are more safe. *(See NFPA 1620, Standard for Pre-Incident Planning, for additional information.)*

Sprinkler water should be shut off only after the fire is extinguished or completely under the control of hose streams. Even then, rekindling is a possibility. To be ready for prompt valve reopening if fire rekindles, a person stationed at the valve, a fire watch, and dependable communications between them are needed until automatic sprinkler protection is restored.

Prefire emergency planning is important and should be done by management and fire protection personnel, and the action to be taken discussed and correlated with the local fire department personnel. The critical time during any fire is in the incipient stage, and the action taken by fire protection personnel upon notification of fire can allow the fire to be contained in its early stages.

Table A.34.2.7 Paper Classification

Heavyweight	Mediumweight	Lightweight	Tissue
Linerboards	Bond and reproduction	Carbonizing tissue	Toilet tissue
Medium	Vellum	Cigarette	Towel tissue
Kraft roll wrappers	Offset	Fruit wrap	
Milk carton board	Tablet	Onion skin	
Folding carton board	Computer		
Bristol board	Envelope		
Tag	Book		
Vellum bristol board	Label		
Index	Magazine		
Cupstock	Butcher		
Pulp board	Bag		
	Newsprint (unwrapped)		

[**13:** Table A.5.6.5]

Pre-emergency planning should incorporate the following:

(1) Availability of hand fire-fighting equipment for the height and type of commodity involved
(2) Availability of fire-fighting equipment and personnel trained for the type of storage arrangement involved
(3) Assurance that all automatic fire protection equipment, such as sprinkler systems, water supplies, fire pumps, and hand hose, is in service at all times

Sprinkler protection installed as required in this *Code* is expected to protect the building occupancy without supplemental fire department activity. Fires that occur in rack storage occupancies protected in accordance with this *Code* are likely to be controlled. Fire department activity can, however, minimize the extent of loss. The first fire department pumper arriving at a rack storage–type fire should connect immediately to the sprinkler system's fire department connection and start pumping operations.

In the test series for storage up to 25 ft (7.6 m), the average time from ignition to smoke obscuration in the test building was about 13 minutes. The first sprinkler operating time in these same fires averaged about 3 minutes. Considering response time for the waterflow device to transmit a waterflow signal, approximately 9 minutes remains between the time of receipt of a waterflow alarm signal at fire department headquarters and the time of smoke obscuration within the building as an overall average.

In the test series for storage over 25 ft (7.6 m), the visibility time was extended. If the fire department facility emergency personnel arrive at the building in time to have sufficient visibility to locate the fire, suppression activities with small hose lines should be started. (Self-contained breathing apparatus is recommended.) If, on the other hand, the fire is not readily visible, hose should be laid to exterior doors or exterior openings in the building and charged lines provided to these points, ready for ultimate mop-up operations. Manual fire-fighting operations in such a warehouse should not be considered a substitute for sprinkler protection.

Important: The sprinkler system should be kept in operation during manual fire-fighting and mop-up operations.

During the testing program, the installed automatic extinguishing system was capable of controlling the fire and reducing all temperatures to ambient within 30 minutes of ignition. Ventilation operations and mop-up were not started until this point. The use of smoke removal equipment is important.

Smoke removal capability should be provided. Examples of smoke removal equipment include the following:

(1) Mechanical air-handling systems
(2) Powered exhaust fans
(3) Roof-mounted gravity vents
(4) Perimeter gravity vents

Whichever system is selected, it should be designed for manual actuation by the fire department, thus allowing personnel to coordinate the smoke removal (ventilation) with mop-up operations.

See also NFPA 600, *Standard on Industrial Fire Brigades*, and Annex B of NFPA 13E and NFPA 1031, *Standard for Professional Qualifications for Fire Inspector and Plan Examiner*.

A.34.7.3.1 Rack storage as referred to in this *Code* contains commodities in a rack structure, usually steel. Many variations of dimensions are found. Racks can be single-row, double-row, or multiple-row, with or without solid shelves. The standard commodity used in most of the tests was 42 in. (1.07 m) on a side. The types of racks covered in this *Code* are as follows:

(1) Double-row racks, in which pallets rest on two beams parallel to the aisle. Any number of pallets can be supported by one pair of beams. *[See Figure A.34.7.3.1(a) through Figure A.34.7.3.1(d).]*
(2) Automatic storage-type rack, in which the pallet is supported by two rails running perpendicular to the aisle. *[See Figure A.34.7.3.1(e).]*
(3) Multiple-row racks more than two pallets deep, measured aisle to aisle, which include drive-in racks, drive-through racks, flow-through racks, and portable racks arranged in the same manner, and conventional or automatic racks with aisles less than 42 in. (1.07 m) wide. *[See Figure A.34.7.3.1(f) through Figure A.34.7.3.1(j).]*
(4) Movable racks, which are racks on fixed rails or guides. They can be moved back and forth only in a horizontal two-dimensional plane. A moving aisle is created as abutting racks are either loaded or unloaded, then moved across the aisle to abut other racks. *[See Figure A.34.7.3.1(k).]*
(5) Solid shelving, which are conventional pallet racks with plywood shelves on the shelf beams *[see Figure A.34.7.3.1(c) and Figure A.34.7.3.1(d)]*. These are used in special cases.
(6) Cantilever rack, in which the load is supported on arms that extend horizontally from columns. The load can rest on the arms or on the shelves supported by the arms. *[See Figure A.34.7.3.1(l).]*

Load depth in conventional or automatic racks should be considered a nominal 4 ft (1.22 m). *[See Figure A.34.7.3.1(b).]*

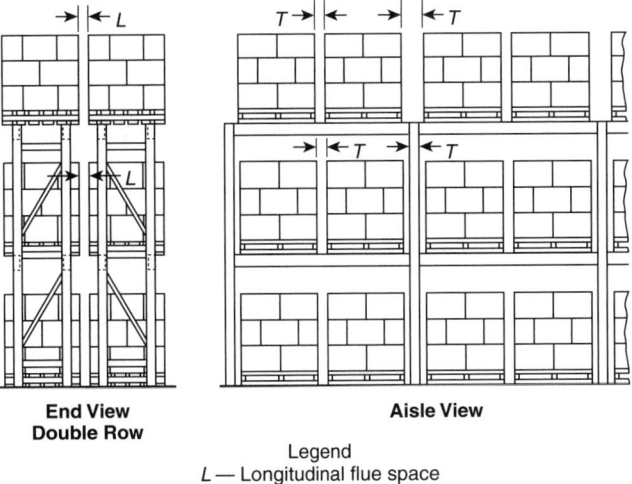

FIGURE A.34.7.3.1(a) Conventional Pallet Rack.

A.34.7.3.2 Fixed rack structures should be designed to facilitate removal or repair of damaged sections without resorting to flame cutting or welding in the storage area. Where sprinklers are to be installed in racks, rack design should anticipate the additional clearances necessary to facilitate installation of sprinklers. The rack structure should be anchored to prevent damage to sprinkler lines and supply piping in racks.

Rack structures should be designed for seismic conditions in areas where seismic resistance of building structure is required.

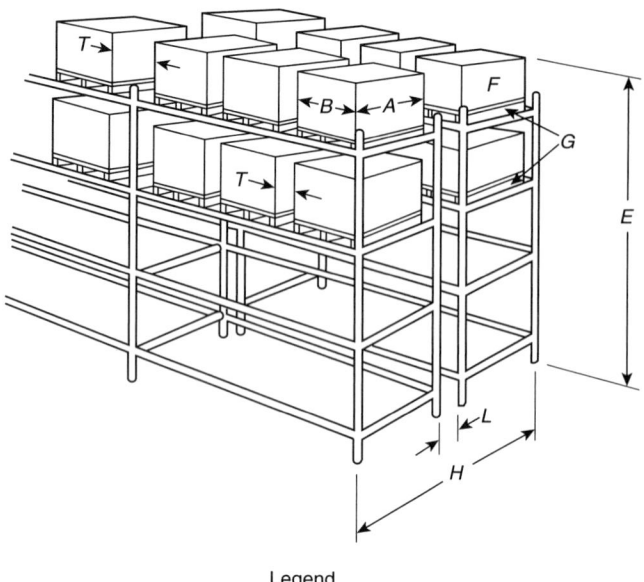

Legend
A — Load depth G — Pallet
B — Load width H — Rack depth
E — Storage height L — Longitudinal flue space
F — Commodity T — Transverse flue space

FIGURE A.34.7.3.1(b) Double-Row Racks Without Solid or Slatted Shelves.

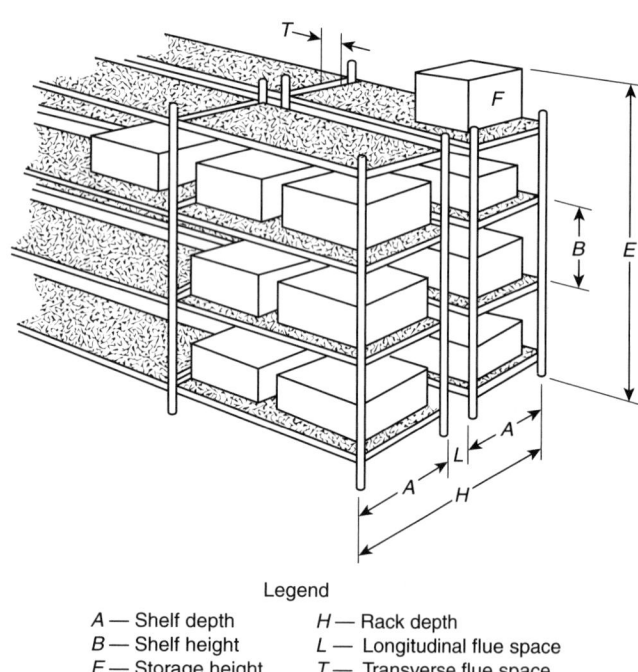

Legend
A — Shelf depth H — Rack depth
B — Shelf height L — Longitudinal flue space
E — Storage height T — Transverse flue space
F — Commodity

FIGURE A.34.7.3.1(c) Double-Row Racks with Solid Shelves.

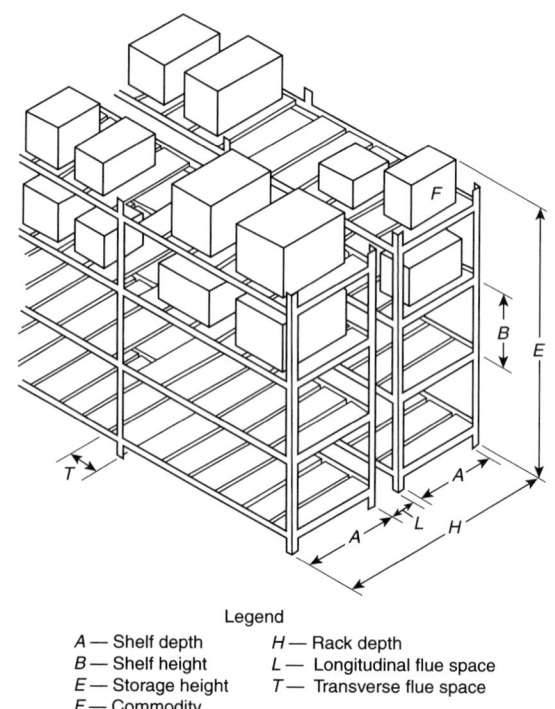

Legend
A — Shelf depth H — Rack depth
B — Shelf height L — Longitudinal flue space
E — Storage height T — Transverse flue space
F — Commodity

FIGURE A.34.7.3.1(d) Double-Row Racks with Slatted Shelves.

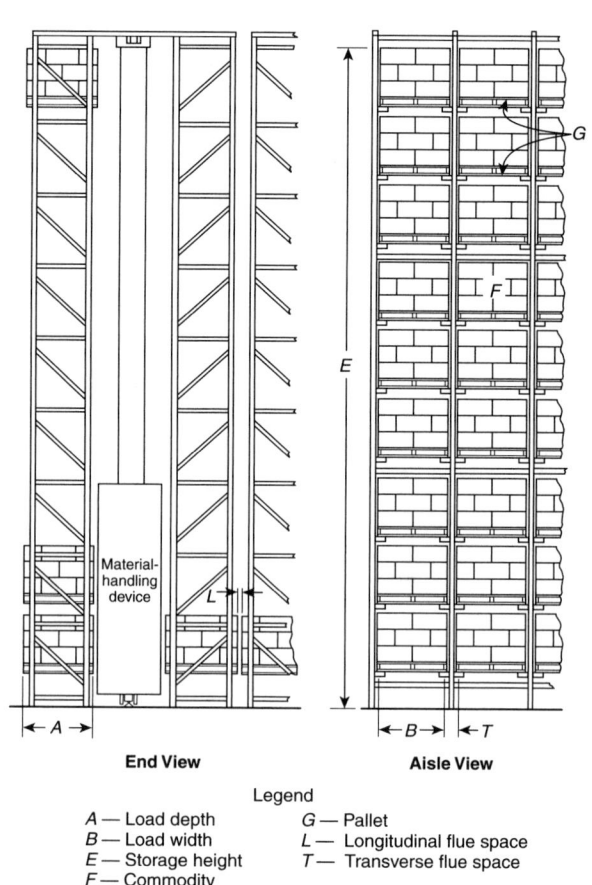

Legend
A — Load depth G — Pallet
B — Load width L — Longitudinal flue space
E — Storage height T — Transverse flue space
F — Commodity

FIGURE A.34.7.3.1(e) Automatic Storage-Type Rack.

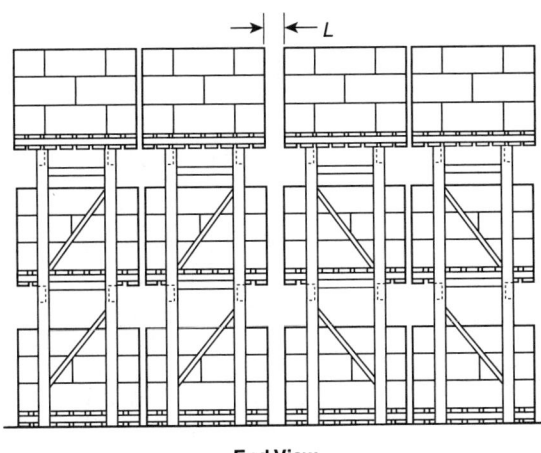

FIGURE A.34.7.3.1(f) Multiple-Row Rack to be Served by a Reach Truck.

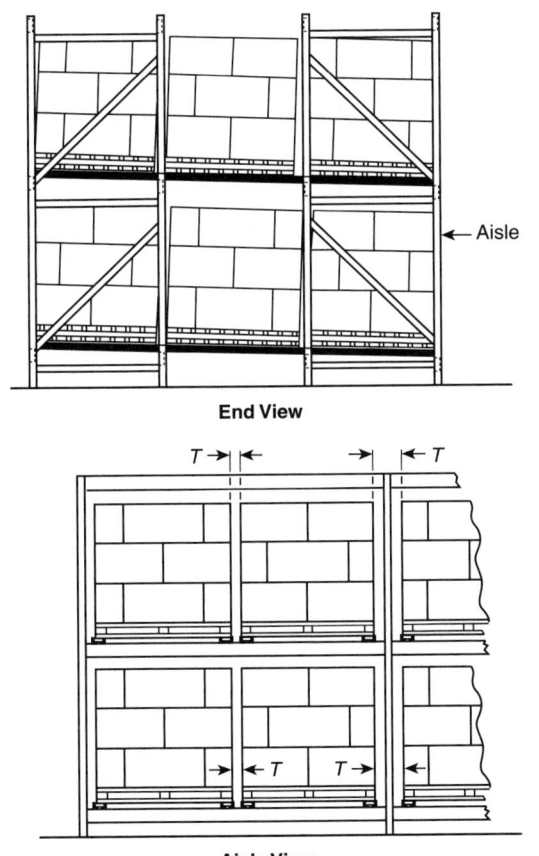

FIGURE A.34.7.3.1(g) Flow-Through Pallet Rack.

A.34.7.3.3 Storage in aisles can render protection ineffective and should be discouraged.

A.34.7.3.3.3 See Chapter 12 of NFPA 13.

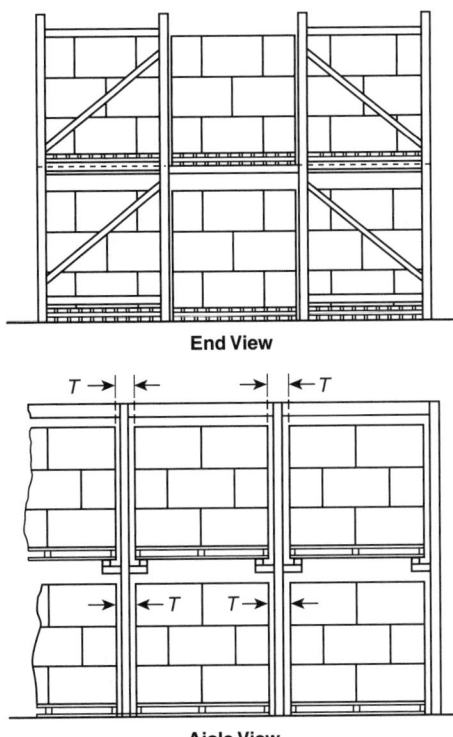

FIGURE A.34.7.3.1(h) Drive-In Rack — Two or More Pallets Deep (Fork Truck Drives into the Rack to Deposit and Withdraw Loads in the Depth of the Rack).

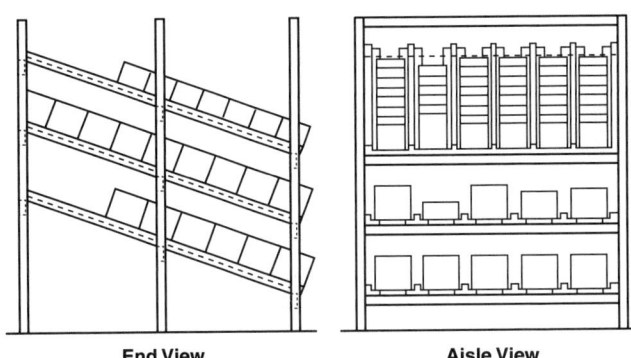

FIGURE A.34.7.3.1(i) Flow-Through Rack.

A.34.7.3.4.1.1 Detection systems, concentrate pumps, generators, and other system components essential to the operation of the system should have an approved standby power source.

A.34.7.3.4.2.1(1) Where high-expansion foam is contemplated as the protection media, consideration should be given to possible damage to the commodity from soaking and corrosion. Consideration also should be given to the problems associated with removal of foam after discharge.

A.34.8.1 Illustrations of some, but not necessarily all, tire storage arrangements are shown in Figure A.34.8.1(a) through Figure A.34.8.1(g).

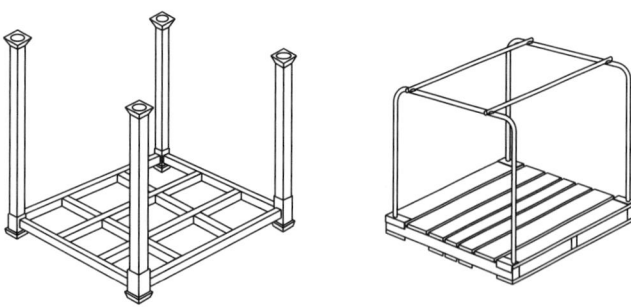

FIGURE A.34.7.3.1(j) Portable Racks.

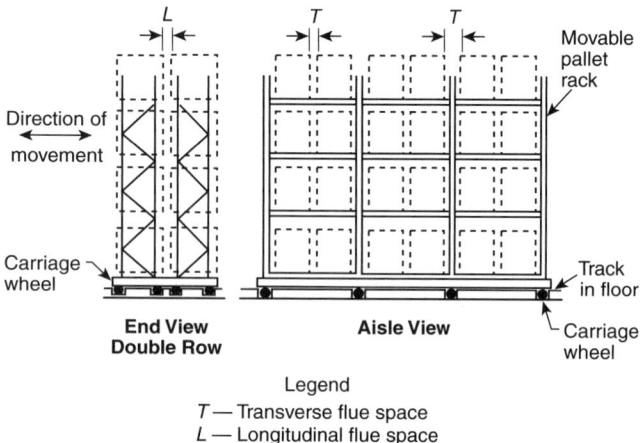

Legend
T — Transverse flue space
L — Longitudinal flue space

FIGURE A.34.7.3.1(k) Movable Rack.

A.34.8.2.3 NFPA *101* accurately reflects the travel distance requirements as follows:

(1) Tire storage is classified as ordinary hazard.
(2) Tire fires begin burning slowly. In combination with an acceptable automatic sprinkler system, this slower burning allows time for egress.
(3) Tire storage warehouses have a low occupant load.
(4) Large aisle widths [8 ft (2.4 m) minimum] required in 34.8.3.1.4 of this *Code* facilitate egress.

A.34.8.3.1.1 Limiting the pile length is not intended. *(See Figure A.34.8.3.1.1.)*

A.34.9.2 With protection installed in accordance with this *Code*, fire protection of overhead steel and steel columns is not necessary. However, some lightweight beams and joists can distort and necessitate replacement, particularly following fires involving plastic-wrapped rolls stored 20 ft (6.1 m) and higher.

A.34.10.1 Idle pallet storage introduces a severe fire condition. Stacking idle pallets in piles is the best arrangement of combustibles to promote rapid spread of fire, heat release, and complete combustion. After pallets are used for a short time in warehouses, they dry out and edges become frayed and splintered. In this condition they are subject to easy ignition from a small ignition source. Again, high piling increases considerably both the challenge to sprinklers and the probability of involving a large number of pallets when fire occurs. Therefore storing idle pallets outdoors where possible is preferable. A fire in idle plastic or wooden pallets is one of the greatest

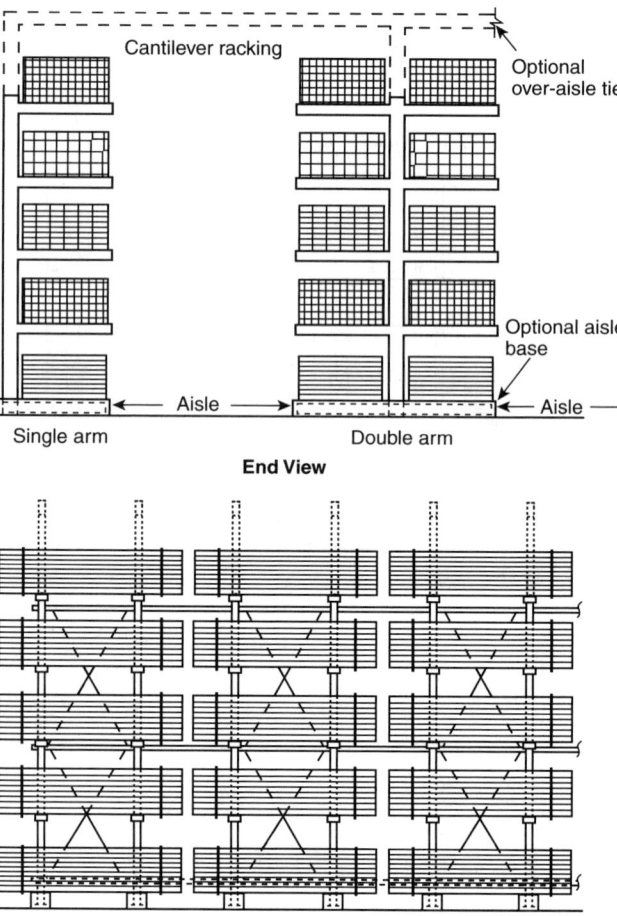

FIGURE A.34.7.3.1(l) Cantilever Rack.

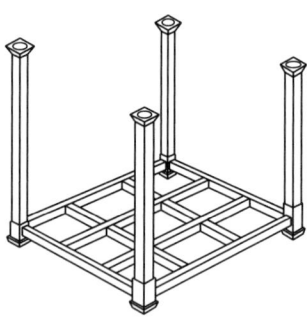

FIGURE A.34.8.1(a) Typical Open Portable Rack Unit.

challenges to sprinklers. The undersides of the pallets create a dry area on which a fire can grow and expand to other dry or partially wet areas. This process of jumping to other dry, closely located, parallel, combustible surfaces continues until the fire bursts through the top of the stack. Once this happens, very little water is able to reach the base of the fire. The only practical method of stopping a fire in a large concentration of pallets with ceiling sprinklers is by means of prewetting. In high stacks, prewetting cannot be done without abnormally high water supplies. The storage of idle pallets should not be permitted in an unsprinklered warehouse containing other storage.

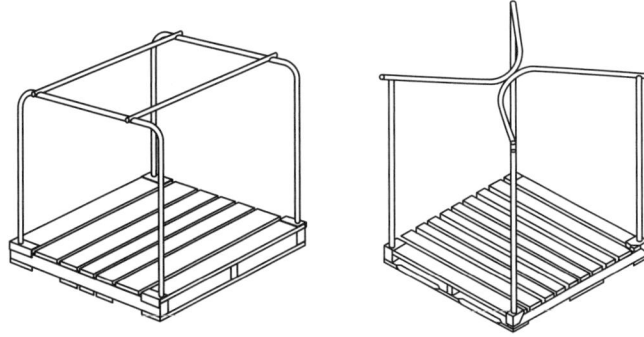

FIGURE A.34.8.1(b) Typical Palletized Portable Rack Units.

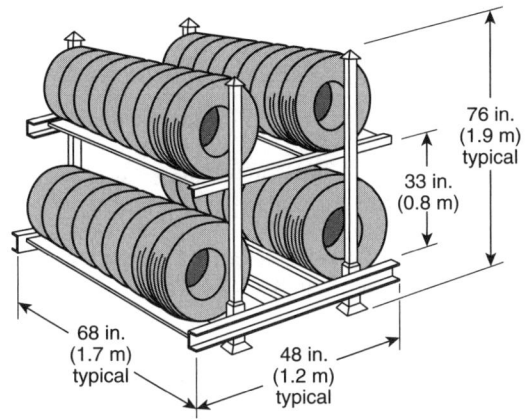

FIGURE A.34.8.1(c) Open Portable Tire Rack.

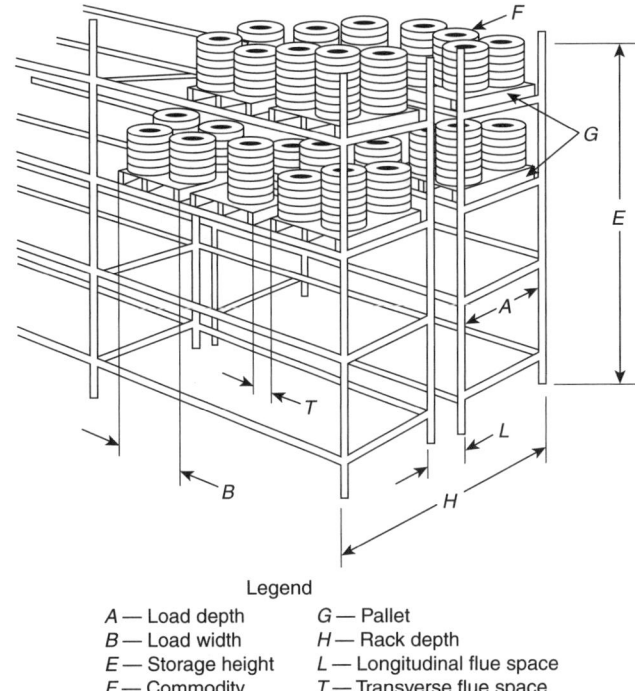

Legend
A — Load depth   G — Pallet
B — Load width   H — Rack depth
E — Storage height   L — Longitudinal flue space
F — Commodity   T — Transverse flue space

FIGURE A.34.8.1(d) Double-Row Fixed Rack Tire Storage.

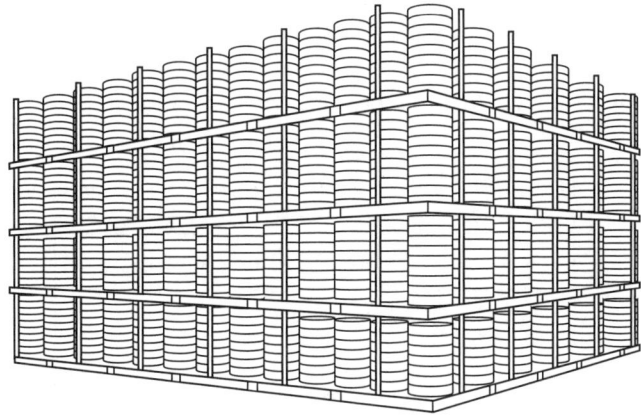

FIGURE A.34.8.1(e) Palletized Portable Rack On-Side Tire Storage Arrangement (Banded or Unbanded).

A.34.10.3 The practice that some materials are stored on pallets in an open yard is recognized. Since stacks of idle pallets present a severe fire problem, attention needs to be paid to the storage arrangements of the pallets. Manual outside open sprinklers generally are not a reliable means of protection unless property is attended to at all times by plant emergency personnel. Open sprinklers with a deluge valve are preferred.

A.40.3.2.1.1 Housekeeping for fugitive dusts is most important where the operational intent is that the dust accumulations are not normally present in the occupancy and the building has no deflagration protection features, such as damage limiting/explosion venting construction or classified electrical equipment, and additional personal protection from dust deflagration hazards is not provided. Factors that should be considered in establishing the housekeeping frequency include the following:

(1) Variability of fugitive dust emissions
(2) Impact of process changes and non-routine activities
(3) Variability of accumulations on different surfaces within the room (walls, floors, overheads)

[**654:** A.8.2.1.1]

A.40.3.2.1.3 Unscheduled housekeeping should be performed in accordance with Table A.40.3.2.1.3(a) to limit the time that a local spill or short-term accumulation of dust is allowed to remain before the local area is cleaned to less than the threshold dust mass/accumulation. Table A.40.3.2.1.3(b) shows approximate equivalent depths for the accumulation values in Table A.40.3.2.1.3(a) when the threshold dust mass/accumulation is 0.2 lb/ft^2 (1 kg/m^2). The owner/operator can use an approximate depth to facilitate communication of housekeeping needs. [**654:** A.8.2.1.3]

A.40.3.2.1.4 When the facility is intended to be operated with more than the dust accumulation defined by the owner/operator's chosen criterion in Section 6.1 of NFPA 654, additional protective measures are necessary. This is a concept similar to the maximum allowable quantities established in the building codes. [**654:** A.8.2.1.4]

FIGURE A.34.8.1(f) On-Tread, On-Floor Tire Storage Arrangement (Normally Banded).

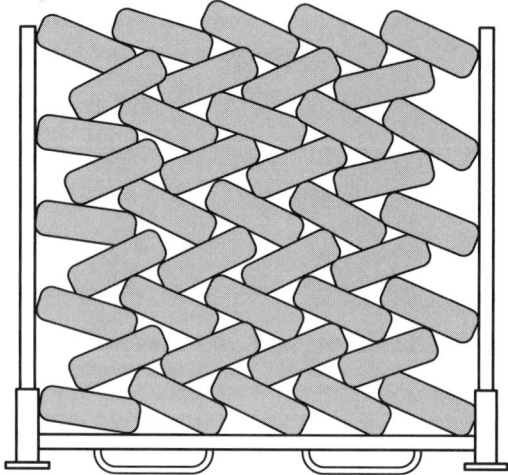

FIGURE A.34.8.1(g) Typical Laced Tire Storage.

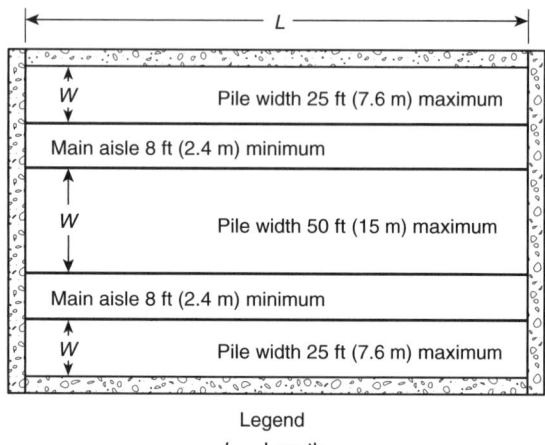

FIGURE A.34.8.3.1.1 Typical Tire Piling Arrangement.

A.40.3.2.2.4 All of the listed precautions might not be required for limited use of compressed air for cleaning minor accumulations of dust from machines or other surfaces between shifts. A risk assessment should be conducted to determine which precautions are required for the specific conditions under which compressed air is being used. [**654:** A.8.2.2.4]

A.40.3.2.2.5 Items that should be included in the housekeeping procedure include the following:

(1) A risk analysis that considers the specific characteristics of the dust being cleaned (particle size, moisture content, MEC, MIE) and other safety risks introduced by the cleaning methods used
(2) Personal safety procedures, including fall protection when working at heights
(3) PPE, including flame-resistant garments in accordance with the hazard analysis required by NFPA 2113, *Standard on Selection, Care, Use, and Maintenance of Flame-Resistant Garments for Protection of Industrial Personnel Against Flash Fire*
(4) Cleaning sequence
(5) Cleaning methods to be used
(6) Equipment, including lifts, vacuum systems, attachments, and so forth

[**654:** A.8.2.2.5]

A.40.3.2.3.1 If a large quantity of material is spilled in an unclassified area, the bulk material should be collected by sweeping, by shoveling, or with a portable vacuum cleaner listed as suitable for Class II locations. Vacuum cleaners meeting the requirements in 40.3.2.3.2 can be used to clean up residual material after the bulk of the spill has been collected. [**654:** A.8.2.3.1]

These requirements for portable vacuum cleaners should be applied to the use of vacuum trucks for combustible dust as well. However, there can be other safety issues concerning vacuum truck applications that are not covered within this section. Given that this application might represent a change from normal procedures, operators should also consider the guidance found in conducting a management of change evaluation. [**654:** A.8.2.3.1]

A.40.3.2.3.1(6) Liquids or wet material can weaken paper filter elements, causing them to fail, which can allow combustible dust to reach the fan and motor. [**654:** A.8.2.3.1(6)]

A.40.4.1.2.3 Specific attention should be paid to combustible particulate solids where they are introduced into the process stream. Some sources of particulate could include stone, tramp iron, other metallic contaminants, and already burning material. Before a risk management strategy is adopted, both the particulate and the process equipment have to be carefully evaluated. [**654:** A.9.1.2.3]

See Figure A.40.4.1.2.3(a) and Figure A.40.4.1.2.3(b) for examples of foreign material removal. [**654:** A.9.1.2.3]

A.40.4.1.3 If the particulate particle size range includes dusts that can attain concentrations capable of propagating a flame front through a fuel–air mixture, the risk management options in 40.4.1.3 are appropriate. Conversely, if the analysis indicates that the particle size and concentration do not predict a propagating flame front through the fuel–air mixture, the fire protection methods in Chapter 10 of NFPA 654 should be considered. [**654:** A.9.1.3]

A.40.4.1.4 Transmission of power by direct drive should be used, where possible, in preference to belt or chain drives. [**654:** A.9.1.4]

Table A.40.3.2.1.3(a) Unscheduled Housekeeping

Accumulation on the Worst Single Square Meter of Surface	Longest Time to Complete Unscheduled Local Cleaning of Floor-Accessible Surfaces	Longest Time to Complete Unscheduled Local Cleaning of Remote Surfaces
>1 to 2 times threshold dust mass/accumulation	8 hours	24 hours
>2 to 4 times threshold dust mass/accumulation	4 hours	12 hours
>4 times threshold dust mass/accumulation	1 hour	3 hours

[**654**: Table A.8.2.1.3(a)]

Table A.40.3.2.1.3(b) Unscheduled Housekeeping

Accumulation on the Worst Single Square Meter of Surface	Average Depth at 75 lb/ft³ (1200 kg/m³))	Average Depth at 30 lb/ft³ (481 kg/m³)
>0.2–0.4 lb/ft² (>1 to 2 kg/m²)	>1/32–1/16 in. (0.8-1.7 mm)	>5/64–5/32 in. (2.1–4.2 mm)
>0.4–0.8 lb ft² (>2 to 4 kg/m²)	>1/16–1/8 in. (1.7–3.3 mm)	>5/32 - 5/16 in. (4.2–8.3 mm)
>0.8 lb/ft² (>4 kg/m²)	>1/8 in. (>3.3 mm)	>5/16 in. (>8.3 mm)

[**654**: Table A.8.2.1.3(b)]

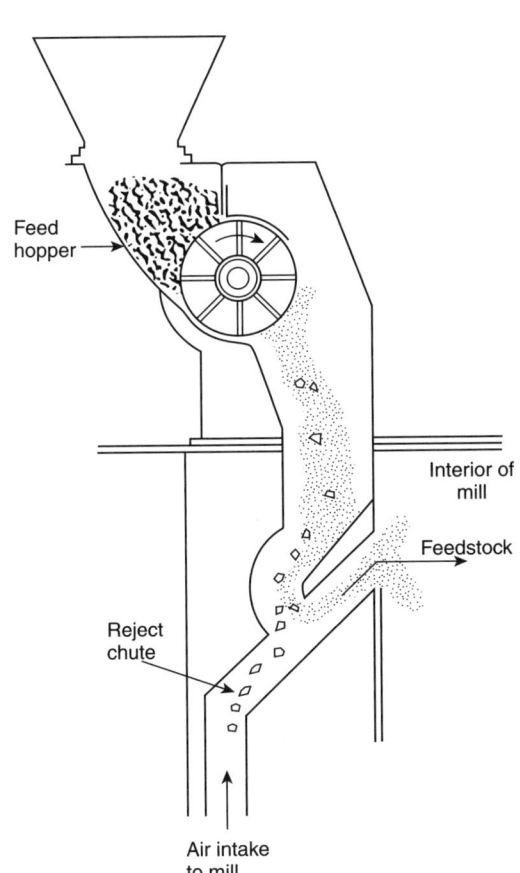

FIGURE A.40.4.1.2.3(a) Pneumatic Separator. [**654**: Figure A.9.1.2.3(a)]

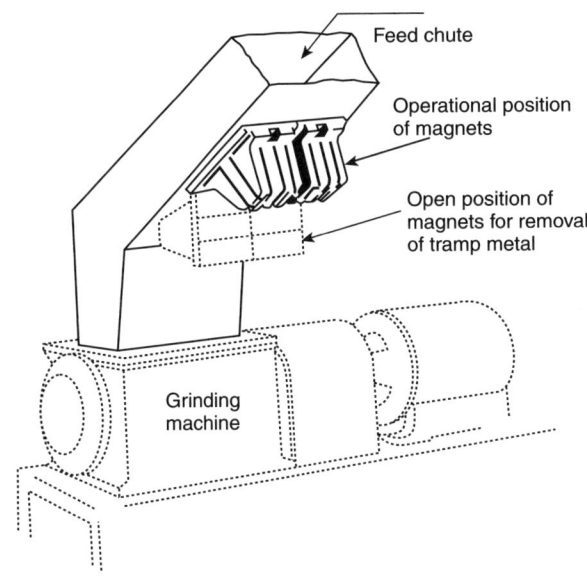

FIGURE A.40.4.1.2.3(b) Magnetic Separator. [**654**: Figure A.9.1.2.3(b)]

A.40.4.1.5 Consideration should be given to the potential for overheating caused by dust entry into bearings. Bearings should be located outside the combustible dust stream, where they are less exposed to dust and more accessible for inspection and service. Where bearings are in contact with the particulate solids stream, sealed or purged bearings are preferred. [**654**: A.9.1.5]

A.40.4.3.2 Bonding minimizes the potential difference between conductive objects. Grounding minimizes the potential difference between objects and ground. [**654**: A.9.3.2]

A.40.4.3.2.2(5) The potential for propagating brush discharges exists where nonconductive materials with breakdown voltages exceeding 4 kV are exposed to processes that generate strong surface charges such as pneumatic conveying. Such discharges do not occur where the breakdown voltage is less than 4 kV. [**654:** A.9.3.2.2(5)]

A.40.4.3.2.3 Where the bonding/grounding system is all metal, resistance in continuous ground paths is typically less than 10 ohms. Such systems include those having multiple components. Greater resistance usually indicates that the metal path is not continuous, usually because of loose connections or corrosion. A grounding system that is acceptable for power circuits or for lightning protection is more than adequate for a static electricity grounding system. [**654:** A.9.3.2.3]

A.40.4.3.4 A more detailed description of FIBC ignition hazards can be found in IEC 61340-4-4, *Electrostatics — Part 4-4: Standard Test Methods for Specific Applications — Electrostatic Classification of Flexible Intermediate Bulk Containers* (FIBC). [**654:** A.9.3.4]

A.40.4.3.4.1 Induction charging of ungrounded conductive objects, including personnel, should be addressed as part of the process hazard analysis. The process hazard analysis should also consider that higher rates of transfer into and out of the FIBC increase the rate of charge generation. Consideration should also be given to the possibility of surface (cone) discharges while the FIBC is being filled, regardless of FIBC type. For additional information on these phenomena, refer to NFPA 77, *Recommended Practice on Static Electricity*. The use of internal liners in FIBCs can introduce additional electrostatic ignition hazards and should be subject to expert review prior to use. [**654:** A.9.3.4.1]

A.40.4.3.4.2.2 For this application, conductive particulate solids typically are those materials having bulk resistivity $<10^6$ ohm-m. [**654:** A.9.3.4.2.2]

A.40.4.3.4.3.2 See A.40.4.3.4.2.2. [**654:** A.9.3.4.3.2]

A.40.4.3.4.6 Table A.40.4.3.4.6 provides a useful guide for the selection and use of FIBCs based on the MIE of product contained in the FIBC and the nature of the atmosphere surrounding it. [**654:** A.9.3.4.6]

A.40.4.3.4.7 In special cases it may be necessary to use a type of FIBC that is not permitted for the intended application based on the requirements of 40.4.3.4. For such cases, it might be determined that the FIBC is safe to use provided that filling or emptying rates are restricted in order to limit electrostatic charging. In the case of conductive combustible particulate solids, the use of a Type A FIBC might be acceptable provided that the maximum ignition energy from the FIBC or charged product within it is less than the MIE of the combustible particulate solids. [**654:** A.9.3.4.7]

A.40.4.3.5.1 Conductive containers are generally made from either metal or carbon-filled plastic having a volume resistivity less than 10^6 ohm-m. [**654:** A.9.3.5.1]

A.40.4.3.5.2 Induction charging of ungrounded conductive objects, including personnel, should be addressed as part of the risk evaluation and process hazard analysis when the use of nonconductive RIBC is being considered. The risk evaluation should also consider that higher rates of transfer into and out of the RIBC increase the rate of charge generation, which could result in the propagation of brush discharges or surface (cone) discharges while the RIBC is being filled. For additional information on these phenomena, refer to NFPA 77, *Recommended Practice on Static Electricity*. [**654:** A.9.3.5.2]

A.40.4.3.7 See NFPA 77, *Recommended Practice on Static Electricity*, for recommended practices on manual additions of solids into vessels containing flammable atmospheres, including recommended practices on the grounding of personnel. [**654:** A.9.3.7]

A.40.4.3.7.1 For example, metal chimes on fiber drums should be grounded. For uncoated fiber drums, grounding one chime might be sufficient. Where contact with a grounded operator is used to ground the container (such as with static-dissipative bags), it is important that gloves, if used, be static-dissipative and free of contaminants. [**654:** A.9.3.7.1]

A.40.4.3.7.4 Examples of auxiliary loading devices include shovels, scoops, and funnels. Conductive tools can be grounded through a properly grounded operator. See also A.40.4.3.7.1 for guidance related to grounding of containers. [**654:** A.9.3.7.4]

A.40.4.3.7.5 Where static-dissipative footwear is used for personnel grounding, the floor resistance to ground should be between 106 and 109 ohms. Care should be taken to ensure that deposits, residues, and coatings that build up over time do not impair grounding between the floor and personnel. [**654:** A.9.3.7.5]

A.40.4.3.7.7 A risk evaluation should address considerations such as container construction, properties of the solids, properties of the liquid, addition rate, material construction of the receiving vessel, agitating devices, and intensity of agitation. The risk evaluation should identify the necessary engineering and administrative controls to ensure that the potential charge accumulation during dumping of the contents will not produce a discharge that exceeds the MIE of the flammable atmosphere within the vessel. [**654:** A.9.3.7.7]

A.40.4.6.1 Heating by indirect means is less hazardous than by direct means and is therefore preferred. Improved protection can be provided for direct-fired dryers by providing an approved automatic spark detection and extinguishing system. [**654:** A.9.6.1]

A.40.4.7 This section does not apply to electrical equipment; that topic is addressed in 6.5.2 of NFPA 654. Dust layer and dust cloud ignition temperatures should be determined by ASTM E 2021, *Test Method for Hot-Surface Ignition Temperature of Dust Layers*; ASTM E 1491, *Test Method for Minimum Autoignition Temperature of Dust Clouds*; or other recognized test methods acceptable to the AHJ. Normally the minimum ignition temperature of a layer of a specific dust is lower than the minimum ignition temperature of a cloud of that dust; however, this is not universally true [see NFPA 499, *Recommended Practice for the Classification of Combustible Dusts and of Hazardous (Classified) Locations for Electrical Installations in Chemical Process Areas*]. The minimum ignition temperature typically decreases with increasing layer thickness, and testing up to maximum layer thickness to be expected on external surfaces is recommended. [**654:** A.9.7]

The ignition temperature of a layer of dust on hot surfaces could decrease over time if the dust dehydrates or carbonizes. For organic dusts that can dehydrate or carbonize, the temperature should not exceed the lower of the ignition temperature or 329°F (165°C). The ignition temperatures for many materials are shown in NFPA 499, *Recommended Practice for the Classification of Combustible Dusts and of Hazardous (Classified) Locations for Electrical Installations in Chemical Process Areas*. [**654:** A.9.7]

Table A.40.4.3.4.6 Use of Different Types of FIBCs

Bulk Product in FIBC	Surroundings		
MIE of Solids[a]	Nonflammable Atmosphere	Class II, Divisions 1 and 2 (1,000 mJ ≤ MIE >3 mJ)[a]	Class I, Divisions 1 and 2 (Gas Group C and D) or Class II, Divisions 1 and 2 (MIE ≤ 3 mJ)[a]
MIE > 1000 mJ	A, B, C, D	B, C, D	C, D[b]
1000 mJ ≥ MIE > 3 mJ	B, C, D	B, C, D	C, D[b]
MIE ≥ 3 mJ	C, D	C, D	C, D[b]

(1) Additional precautions usually are necessary when a flammable gas or vapor atmosphere is present inside the FIBC, e.g., in the case of solvent wet solids.
(2) Nonflammable atmosphere includes combustible particulate solids having a MIE >1000 mJ.
(3) FIBC Types A, B, and D are not suitable for use with conductive combustible particulate solids.
[a]Measured in accordance with ASTM E 2019, capacitive discharge circuit (no added inductance).
[b]Use of Type C and D is limited to Gas Groups C and D with MIE ≥ 0.14 mJ.
[**654:** Table A.9.3.4.6]

A.40.4.8.2 Diesel-powered front-end loaders suitable for use in hazardous locations have not been commercially available. The following provisions can be used to reduce the fire hazard from diesel-powered front-end loaders used in Class II hazardous areas as defined in Article 500 of NFPA 70, *National Electrical Code*:

(1) Only essential electrical equipment should be used, and wiring should be in metal conduit. Air-operated starting is preferred, but batteries are permitted to be used if they are mounted in enclosures rated for Type EX hazardous areas.
(2) Where practical, a water-cooled manifold and muffler should be used.
(3) Loaders that are certified to meet the Mine Safety and Health Administration (MSHA) criteria (formerly Schedule 31) found in 30 CFR 36, "Approved Requirements for Permissible Mobile Diesel-Powered Transportation Equipment," are also acceptable in lieu of A.40.4.8.2(1) and A.40.4.8.2(2).
(4) The engine and hydraulic oil compartments should be protected with fixed, automatic dry-chemical extinguishing systems.
(5) Loaders should have a high degree of maintenance and cleaning. Frequent cleaning (daily in some cases) of the engine compartment with compressed air could be necessary. Periodic steam cleaning also should be done.
(6) Loaders should never be parked or left unattended in the dust explosion hazard or dust fire hazard area.

[**654:** A.9.8.2]

A.40.5.2.1 Pneumatic conveying systems that move combustible particulate solids can be classified as water compatible, water incompatible, or water reactive. Inasmuch as water is universally the most effective, most available, and most economical extinguishing medium, it is helpful to categorize combustible particulate solids in relation to the applicability of water as the agent of choice. For details on use of water as an extinguishing agent, see Annex F of NFPA 654 for more information on use of water as extinguishing agent for combustible particulate solid. [**654:** A.10.2.1]

A.40.5.3.2 Extreme care should be employed in the use of portable fire extinguishers in facilities where combustible dusts are present. The rapid flow of the extinguishing agent across or against accumulations of dust can produce a dust cloud. When a dust cloud is produced, there is always a deflagration hazard. In the case of a dust cloud produced as a result of fire fighting, the ignition of the dust cloud and a resulting deflagration are virtually certain. [**654:** A.10.3.2]

Consequently, when portable fire extinguishers are used in areas that contain accumulated combustible dusts *(refer to A.6.2.3.1 of NFPA 654)*, the extinguishing agent should be applied in a manner that does not disturb or disperse accumulated dust. Generally, fire extinguishers are designed to maximize the delivery rate of the extinguishing agent to the fire. Special techniques of fire extinguisher use should be employed to prevent this inherent design characteristic of the fire extinguisher from producing an unintended deflagration hazard. [**654:** A.10.3.2]

A.40.5.4.2.1 A nozzle listed or approved for use on Class C fires produces a fog discharge pattern that is less likely than a straight stream nozzle to suspend combustible dust, which could otherwise produce a dust explosion potential. [**654:** A.10.4.2.1]

A.40.5.4.2.2 Fire responders should be cautioned when using straight stream nozzles in the vicinity of combustible dust accumulations that dust clouds can be formed and can be ignited by any residual smoldering or fire. [**654:** A.10.4.2.2]

A.40.5.5 Automatic sprinkler protection in air-material separators, silos, and bucket elevators should be considered. Considerations should include the combustibility of the equipment, the combustibility of the material, and the amount of material present. [**654:** A.10.5]

A.40.5.5.1 A risk evaluation should consider the presence of combustibles both in the equipment and in the area around the process. Considerations should include the combustibility of the building construction, the equipment, the quantity and combustibility of process materials, the combustibility of packaging materials, open containers of flammable liquids, and the presence of dusts. Automatic sprinkler protection in air-material separators, silos, and bucket elevators should be considered. [**654:** A.10.5.1]

A.40.5.9.1 Impairments can include isolating of fire pump controllers, closing of sprinkler system control valves, and isolating and disabling or disconnecting of detection, notification, and suppression systems. [**654:** A.10.9.1]

A.40.5.9.2 The impairment procedure consists of identifying the impaired system and alerting plant personnel that the protection system is out of service. [**654:** A.10.9.2]

A.40.5.9.3 The facility manager is responsible for ensuring that the condition causing the impairment is promptly corrected. [**654:** A.10.9.3]

A.40.5.9.4 When the impairment notification procedure is used, it provides for follow-up by the relevant authorities having jurisdiction. This follow-up helps to ensure that impaired fire and explosion protection systems are not forgotten. When the system is closed and reopened, most companies notify their insurance company, their broker, or the AHJ by telephone or other predetermined method. [**654:** A.10.9.4]

A.40.6.2.2 Where a dust explosion hazard or dust flash fire hazard exists, flame-resistant garments provide a measure of protection for exposed personnel. [**654:** A.11.2.2]

A.40.6.3.2(8) All plant personnel, including management, supervisors, and maintenance and operating personnel, should be trained to participate in plans for controlling plant emergencies. Trained plant fire squads or fire brigades should be maintained. [**654:** A.11.3.2(8)]

The emergency plan should contain the following elements:

(1) A signal or alarm system
(2) Identification of means of egress
(3) Minimization of effects on operating personnel and the community
(4) Minimization of property and equipment losses
(5) Interdepartmental and interplant cooperation
(6) Cooperation of outside agencies
(7) The release of accurate information to the public
[**654:** A.11.3.2(8)]

Emergency drills should be performed annually by plant personnel. Malfunctions of the process should be simulated and emergency actions undertaken. Disaster drills that simulate a major catastrophic situation should be undertaken periodically with the cooperation and participation of public fire, police, and other local community emergency units and nearby cooperating plants. [**654:** A.11.3.2(8)]

A.40.6.5.1.1 Qualified contractors should have proper credentials, which include applicable American Society of Mechanical Engineers (ASME) stamps and professional licenses. [**654:** A.11.5.1.1]

A.40.6.5.4 It is suggested that annual meetings be conducted with regular contractors to review the facility's safe work practices and policies. Some points to cover include to whom the contractors would report at the facility, who at the facility can authorize hot work or fire protection impairments, and smoking and nonsmoking areas. [**654:** A.11.5.4]

A.40.7.1.2(5) Process interlocks should be calibrated and tested in the manner in which they are intended to operate, with written test records maintained for review by management. Testing frequency should be determined in accordance with the AIChE *Guidelines for Safe Automation of Chemical Processes*. [**654:** 12.1.2(5)]

A.40.7.2.2.4 Periodic cleaning of components is especially important if the blower or fan is exposed to heated air. [**654:** A.12.2.2.4]

A.40.7.2.2.5 If rust is allowed to form on the interior steel surfaces, it is only a matter of time before an iron oxide (rust) becomes dislodged and is taken downstream, striking against the duct walls. In some cases, this condition could cause an ignition of combustibles within the duct. The situation worsens if aluminum paint is used. If the aluminum flakes off or is struck by a foreign object, the heat of impact could be sufficient to cause the aluminum particle to ignite, thereby initiating a fire downstream. [**654:** A.12.2.2.5]

A.40.7.2.5.3 For information on maintenance of deflagration venting, see NFPA 68, *Standard on Explosion Protection by Deflagration Venting*. [**654:** A.12.2.5.3]

A.41.1.2(7) There are more detailed, and in some cases more stringent, requirements for torch-applied roofing found in Section 16.6 and NFPA 241. [**51B:** A.1.3.1(7)]

A.41.2.1 The Technical Committee on Hot Work Operations (NFPA 51B) recognizes that management might not always have expertise in hot work and, therefore, would need a knowledgeable designated agent or contractor to act on its behalf. Examples of those who might not have the expertise can include owners of small retail shops, a small apartment complex manager, or a grocery store owner who has no knowledge of hot work safe practices. [**51B:** A.4.1]

Management should ensure that the contractor has evidence of financial responsibility, which can take the form of an insurance certificate or other document attesting to coverage or responsibility. [**51B:** A.4.1]

A.41.2.2.1 Other special hazards can include, but are not limited to, lead, noise, and radiation. Sometimes these special hazards require disposable outer garments that can catch fire. [**51B:** A.4.2.1]

A.41.2.2.3(1) Alternatives to hot work can include the following:

(1) Mechanical removal and relocation of frozen piping to a heated area
(2) Manual hydraulic shears
(3) Mechanical bolting
(4) Screwed, flanged, or clamped pipe
(5) Reciprocating saw
(6) Mechanical pipe cutter
(7) Approved self-drilling or compressed air-actuated fasteners
[**51B:** A.4.2.3(1)]

A.41.2.2.7 The inspection is usually made ½ hour after the completion of hot work to detect and extinguish possible smoldering fires. The inspector should be alert for circumstances that can require an extension of the final inspection interval. [**51B:** A.4.2.7]

A.41.2.4.1 The fire watch duties can be assigned to anyone who understands the hazard of the hot work being performed and the limitations placed on that hot work operation by the person issuing the hot work permit (PAI). The fire watch has the responsibility to make certain the hot work area is maintained in a fire-safe condition throughout performance of the hot work and has the authority to stop the hot work if unsafe conditions are observed. The fire watch must understand the basic hazards of any combustible construction involved with the hot work area, the fire exposure hazard hot work creates to occupancies adjacent to or below the hot work operation, the hazards associated with the occupancy, and the need to maintain proper isolation of all hot work operations from combustible or flammable materials. The fire watch should also be properly trained in use of manual, portable fire extinguishers and emergency notification procedures within the facility. The fire watch is not a replacement for proper planning to prevent conditions that allow a fire to develop, regardless of the firefighting equipment available and the capabilities of the individuals involved. [**51B:** A.4.4.1]

A.41.2.4.4 The fire watch should have experience with test fires. [**51B:** A.4.4.4]

A.41.2.4.7 These tasks might include moving partitions relating to the hot work, sweeping in the immediate area, and minimal assistance to the operator. [**51B:** A.4.4.7]

A.41.2.5 The trend toward outsourcing facility maintenance and renovations can influence the risks associated with hot work. A contractor may have the technical expertise to perform hot work but is not likely to have a full understanding of fire prevention or of the specific combustible hazards within a client property. Additional safeguards to be considered include, but are not limited to, how the hot work should be isolated to prevent fire hazards; who will be assigned as the fire watch for the hot work operations; the facility emergency notification procedures; available manual fire fighting tools (like portable fire extinguishers and small hose stations); identification of all areas where hot work is not allowed; connecting hot work equipment to existing utility systems (gas or electricity); and review of any requirements for completion of hot work by a certain time each day. [**51B:** A.4.5]

Hot work loss incidents involving contractors occur with regular frequency. For many of these incidents, facility management has not implemented a process for managing the fire hazards associated with the proposed contract work activity, views the contractor's personnel as the recognized subject matter expert, and is either ignorant of potential fire hazards with the planned contract activity or presumes the contractor is expert in all associated safety regulations and requirements and will address hazards accordingly. [**51B:** A.4.5]

A.41.3.1 At a work site, hazards other than hot work, such as radiation, lead, or noise, are often present. Any additional PPE donned for protection against these other hazards should also be appropriate for hot work. Heavier materials, such as woolen clothing or heavy cotton, are preferable to lighter materials because they are more difficult to ignite. Cotton clothing, if used for protection, should be chemically treated to reduce its combustibility. Clothing treated with flame-resistant materials can lose some of its protective characteristics after repeated washing or cleaning. Materials that can melt and cause severe burns should not be used as clothing when the wearer will be welding or cutting. [**51B:** A.5.1]

Sparks can lodge in rolled-up sleeves, pockets of clothing, or cuffs of overalls or trousers. Therefore, it is recommended that sleeves and collars be kept buttoned and pockets be eliminated from the front of clothing. Where pockets are present, they should be emptied of flammable or readily combustible materials. Trousers or overalls should not have cuffs and should not be turned up on the outside. Trousers should overlap shoe tops to prevent spatter from getting inside shoes. [**51B:** A.5.1]

Frayed clothing is particularly susceptible to ignition and burning and should not be worn when welding or cutting. [**51B:** A.5.1]

A.41.3.3 For additional information on cutting and welding of containers that have held flammable materials, see NFPA 326, *Standard for the Safeguarding of Tanks and Containers for Entry, Cleaning, or Repair*, and ANSI/AWS F-4.1, *Recommended Safe Practices for the Preparation for Welding and Cutting Containers and Piping*. [**51B:** A.5.3]

Additional consideration should be given when hot work is performed in areas near the storage of large quantities of exposed, readily ignitable materials such as bulk sulfur, baled paper, or cotton. For additional information on welding and cutting in storage areas, refer to Chapter 34 and NFPA 655, *Standard for Prevention of Sulfur Fires and Explosions*. [**51B:** A.5.3]

A.41.3.4 The decision tree in Figure A.41.3.4 can be used to determine if a hot work permit is necessary. [**51B:** A.5.4]

A.41.3.4.1 An example of a hot work permit is shown in Figure A.41.3.4.1. This permit can be modified to suit local conditions. [**51B:** A.5.4.1]

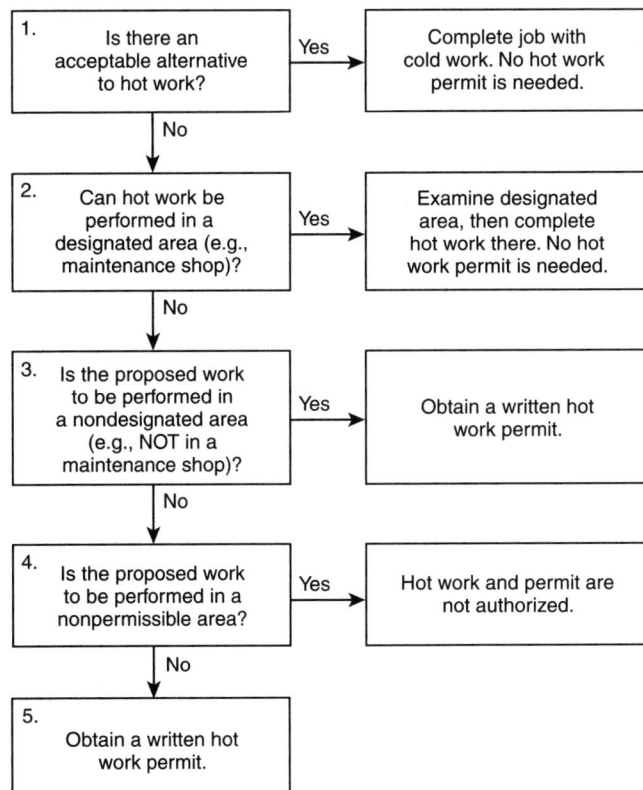

FIGURE A.41.3.4 Hot Work Permit Decision Tree. [**51B:** Figure A.5.4]

HOT WORK PERMIT
Seek an alternative/safer method if possible!

Before initiating hot work, ensure precautions are in place as required by NFPA 51B and ANSI Z49.1. Make sure an appropriate fire extinguisher is readily available.

This Hot Work Permit is required for any operation involving open flame or producing heat and/or sparks. This work includes, but is not limited to, welding, brazing, cutting, grinding, soldering, thawing pipe, torch-applied roofing, or chemical welding.

Date _____

Location/Building and floor _____

Work to be done _____

Time started _____ Time completed _____

THIS PERMIT IS GOOD FOR ONE DAY ONLY

Hot work by ❏ employee ❏ contractor

Name (print) and signature of person doing hot work _____

I verify that the above location has been examined, the precautions marked on the checklist below have been taken, and permission is granted for this work.

Name (print) and signature of permit-authorizing individual (PAI) _____

- ❏ Available sprinklers, hose streams, and extinguishers are in service and operable.
- ❏ Hot work equipment is in good working condition in accordance with manufacturer's specifications.
- ❏ Special permission obtained to conduct hot work on metal vessels or piping lined with rubber or plastic.

Requirements within 35 ft (11 m) of hot work
- ❏ Flammable liquid, dust, lint, and oily deposits removed.
- ❏ Explosive atmosphere in area eliminated.
- ❏ Floors swept clean and trash removed.
- ❏ Combustible floors wet down or covered with damp sand or fire-resistive/noncombustible materials or equivalent.
- ❏ Personnel protected from electrical shock when floors are wet.
- ❏ Other combustible storage material removed or covered with listed or approved materials (welding pads, blankets, or curtains; fire-resistive tarpaulins), metal shields, or noncombustible materials.
- ❏ All wall and floor openings covered.
- ❏ Ducts and conveyors that might carry sparks to distant combustible material covered, protected, or shut down.

Requirements for hot work on walls, ceilings, or roofs
- ❏ Construction is noncombustible and without combustible coverings or insulation.
- ❏ Combustible material on other side of walls, ceilings, or roofs is moved away.

Requirements for hot work on enclosed equipment
- ❏ Enclosed equipment is cleaned of all combustibles.
- ❏ Containers are purged of flammable liquid/vapor.
- ❏ Pressurized vessels, piping, and equipment removed from service, isolated, and vented.

Requirements for hot work fire watch and fire monitoring
- ❏ Fire watch is provided during and for a minimum of 30 min. after hot work, including any break activity.
- ❏ Fire watch is provided with suitable extinguishers and, where practical, a charged small hose.
- ❏ Fire watch is trained in use of equipment and in sounding alarm.
- ❏ Fire watch can be required in adjoining areas, above and below.
- ❏ Yes ❏ No Per the PAI/fire watch, monitoring of hot work area has been extended beyond the 30 min.

© 2008 National Fire Protection Association

NFPA 51B

FIGURE A.41.3.4.1 Sample of a Hot Work Permit. [51B:Figure A.5.4.1]

A.41.3.4.2(3) When hot work is performed at an elevated level, it should be noted that the sparks or slag can fall at a trajectory and land further than 35 ft (11 m) horizontally from a point directly under the hot work operator. [51B: A.5.4.2(3)]

A.41.3.4.2(14) Hot work operations that might fall into the category where the 35 Foot Rule could be enlarged include, but are not limited to, elevated hot work and windy areas. [51B: A.5.4.2(14)]

A.41.3.4.2(15) Hot work operations that might fall into the category where the 35 Foot Rule could be reduced include, but are not limited to, torch soldering, gas tungsten arc welding, heat gun operations, and handheld pen-type soldering. [51B: A.5.4.2(15)]

A.41.3.5.1 The decision tree in Figure A.41.3.5.1 can be used to determine if a fire watch is necessary. [51B: A.5.5.1]

A.41.3.5.1(1) Figure A.41.3.5.1(1)(a) and Figure A.41.3.5.1(1)(b) demonstrate the hot work 35 Foot Rule. [51B: A.5.5.1(1)]

A.41.3.5.3 An additional fire watch(es) might be necessary in certain situations, such as where hot work is performed near open shafts, or at elevated heights or where sparks can travel through spaces such as openings. [51B: A.5.5.3]

A.41.3.6 For hot tapping on a gas pipeline, see ANSI/ASME B31.8, *Gas Transmission and Distribution Piping Systems*. [51B: A.5.6]

A.41.4.1 A common example of a situation where Section 41.4 would apply is work performed in a single-dwelling home by a plumber sweating a pipe. Another example is the repair of a wrought iron railing used for steps in a single-dwelling home. A third example is welding performed on construction or agricultural equipment on site. The NFPA 51B committee recognizes that it is not always practical to have more than one individual present, and completing a job with one person is a common practice. The NFPA 51B committee stresses that it is always better to have more than one individual present to ensure fire safety, but realizes that it is not always practical to do so. [51B: A.6.1]

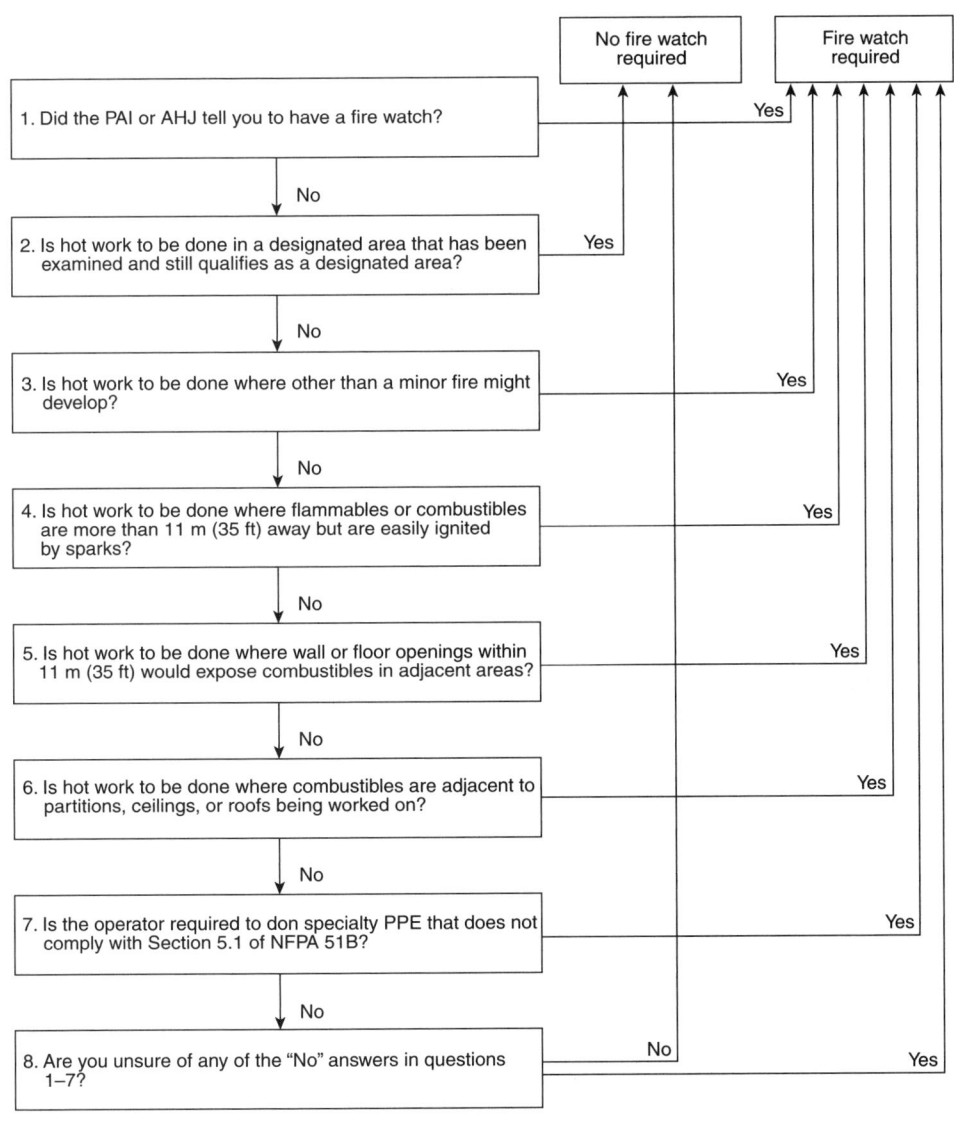

FIGURE A.41.3.5.1 Fire Watch Decision Tree. [51B:Figure A.5.5.1]

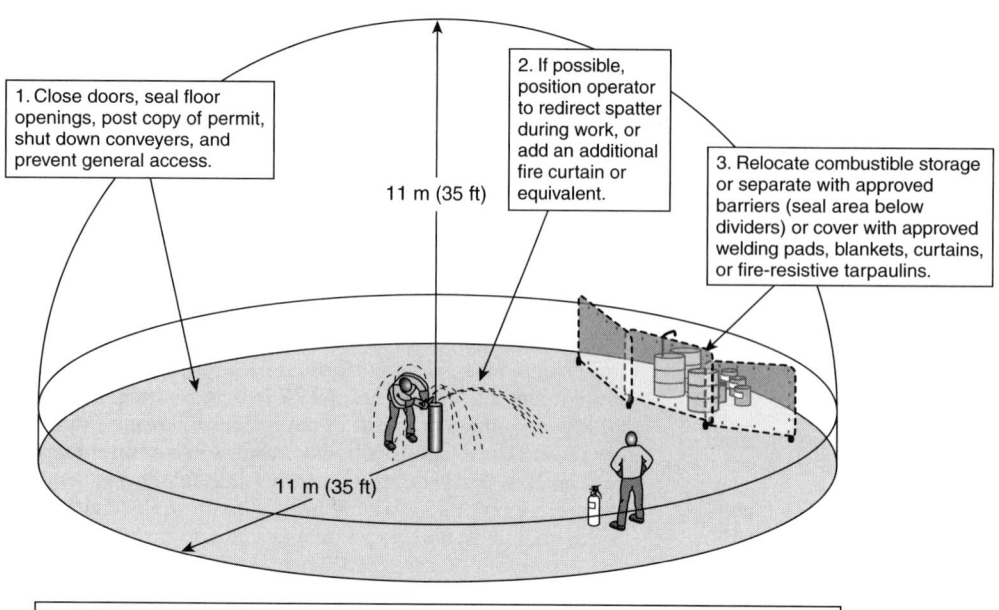

FIGURE A.41.3.5.1(1)(a) The 35 Foot Rule Illustrated. [51B:Figure A.5.5.1(1)(a)]

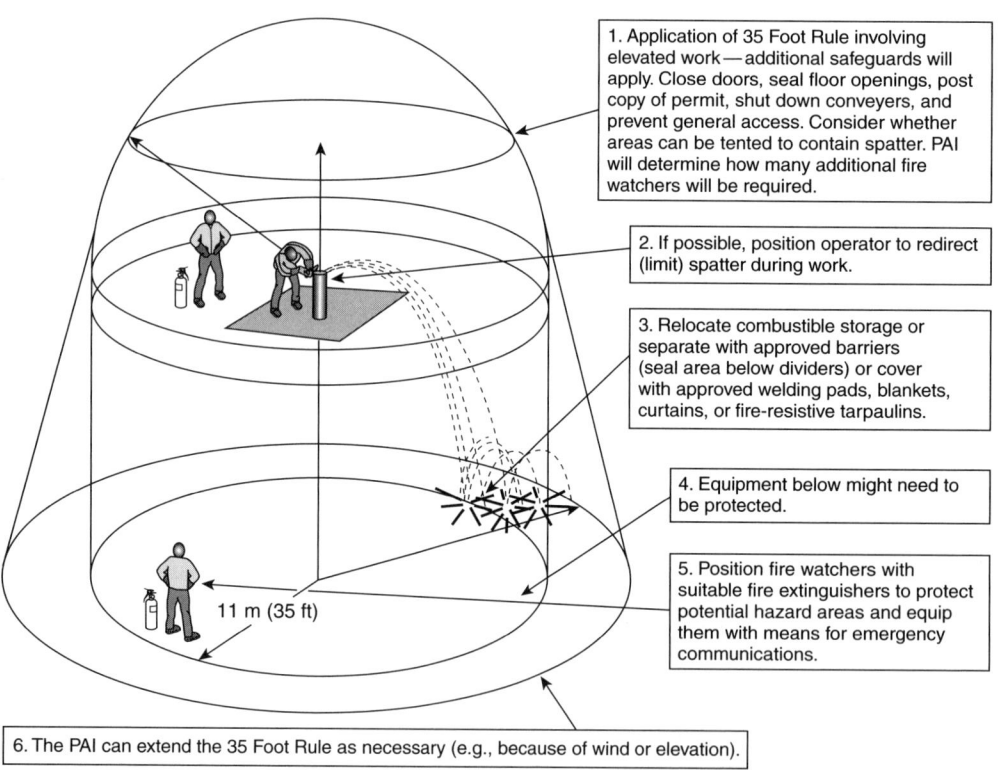

FIGURE A.41.3.5.1(1)(b) Example of Where Multiple Fire Watches Are Needed. [51B:Figure A.5.5.1(1)(b)]

A.41.5.5.2.3 The preferred location for cylinder storage is in an approved storage area outdoors. [**51B:** A.7.5.2.3]

A.42.2.1.3 See NFPA 52 and NFPA 58 for requirements for facilities where only these fuels are dispensed. [**30A:** A.1.1.3]

A.42.3.3.2 PEI RP200, *Recommended Practices for Installation of Aboveground Storage Systems for Motor Vehicle Fueling*, also provides information on this subject. [**30A:** A.4.3.2]

A.42.3.3.3.3 Some of the specifications for vault design and construction include the following:

(1) The walls and floor of the vault are to be constructed of reinforced concrete at least 6 in. (50 mm) thick.
(2) The top and floor of the vault and the tank foundation must be designed to withstand all anticipated loading, including loading from vehicular traffic, where applicable.
(3) The walls and floor of a belowgrade vault must be designed to withstand anticipated soil and hydrostatic loading.
(4) The vault must be liquidtight.
(5) The vault enclosure must have no openings except those necessary for access to, inspection of, and filling, emptying, and venting of the tank.
(6) The vault shall be provided with connections to permit ventilation to dilute, disperse, and remove any vapors prior to personnel entering the vault.
(7) The vault must be provided with a means for personnel entry.
(8) The vault must be provided with an approved means to admit a fire suppression agent.

[**30A:** A.4.3.3.3]

A.42.3.3.7.2 The top of the posts should be set not less than 3 ft (0.9 m) above ground and should be located not less than 5 ft (1.5 m) from the tank. Other approved means to protect tanks subject to vehicular damage include vehicle impact resistance testing such as that prescribed in ANSI/UL 2085, *Standard for Protected Aboveground Tanks for Flammable and Combustible Liquids*, for protected aboveground tanks. [**30A:** A.4.3.7.2]

A.42.3.3.8 Appropriate corrosion control standards include the following:

(1) STI RP 892-91, *Recommended Practice for Corrosion Protection of Underground Piping Networks Associated with Liquid Storage and Dispensing Systems*
(2) STI RP-01-69, *Recommended Practice for Control of External Corrosion of Underground or Submerged Metallic Piping Systems*
(3) STI RP 1632, *Cathodic Protection of Underground Petroleum Storage Tanks and Piping Systems*

[**30A:** A.4.3.8]

Other means of internal corrosion protection include protective coatings and linings and cathodic protection. [**30A:** A.4.3.8]

A.42.5.2.3 The following can be used to determine compliance with 42.5.2.3:

ANSI/UL 79 *Standard for Power-Operated Pumps for Petroleum Dispensing Products*

UL 87, *Standard for Power-Operated Pumps for Petroleum Dispensing Products*

UL Subject 87A, *Outline of Investigation for Power-Operated Dispensing Devices for Gasoline and Gasoline/Ethanol Blends with Nominal Ethanol Concentrations Up to 85 Percent (E0-E85)*

ANSI/UL 330, *Standard for Hose and Hose Assemblies for Dispensing Flammable Liquids*

ANSI/UL 567, *Standard for Emergency Breakaway Fittings, Swivel Connectors and Pipe-Connection Fittings for Petroleum Products and LP-Gas;*

ANSI/UL 842, *Standard for Valves for Flammable Fluids*

ANSI/UL 2586, *Standard for Hose Nozzle Valves.* [**30A:** A.6.2.3]

A.42.5.3.6.1 Useful forms for documentation can be found in PEI/RP500-05, *Recommended Practices for Inspection and Maintenance of Motor Fuel Dispensing Equipment*, and are available at www.pei.org/rp500. [**30A:** A.6.3.6.1]

A.42.5.3.6.2 See A.42.5.3.6.1. [**30A:** A.6.3.6.2]

A.42.5.6.2 The flow of fuel can be stopped by dispensers used in self-serve motor fuel dispensing facilities. The nozzle can be returned to the dispenser in the latched-open position. Subsequent activation of the dispenser would then immediately release fuel from the latched-open nozzle, creating a hazardous situation. [**30A:** A.6.6.2]

A.42.7.2.1 API RP 1621, *Recommended Practice for Bulk Liquid Stock Control at Retail Outlets*, provides information on this subject. [**30A:** A.9.2.1]

A.42.7.2.3.1 See Chapter 9 of NFPA 30 for further information. [**30A:** A.9.2.3.1]

A.42.7.2.5.4 The following language includes both the mandatory requirements and some optional text that could be used to comply with the requirements in 42.7.2.5.4:

WARNING

It is unlawful and dangerous to dispense gasoline into unapproved containers.
No smoking.
Stop motor.
No filling of portable containers in or on a motor vehicle.
Place container on ground before filling.
Discharge your static electricity before fueling by touching a metal surface away from the nozzle.
Before using pump, touch any metal on the car away from your vehicle's fuel filler with bare hand. This will discharge static electricity on your body. Failure to fully discharge may ignite gasoline vapors.
Do not re-enter your vehicle while gasoline is pumping. This can re-charge your body with static electricity. If you must re-enter your vehicle, discharge static electricity again before touching the pump nozzle.
If a fire starts, **do not** remove nozzle — back away immediately and tell attendant. If no attendant is on site, use the emergency shut-off button to stop pump.
Do not allow individuals under licensed age to use the pump.
Only persons of licensed age should use pump.
Keep children away from the pump area.
Do not allow children to use pump.

[**30A:** A.9.2.5.4]

A.42.7.5.6 Additional fire protection considerations can include fixed suppression systems, automatic fire detection, manual fire alarm stations, transmission of alarms to off-site locations, and limitation of the quantity of motor fuel delivered per transaction. [**30A:** A.9.5.6]

A.42.8.3.4 The selection of the 20 ft (6 m) separation distance between storage containers of different gaseous fuels is based on long-standing requirements in NFPA 2, NFPA 52, and NFPA 58. The separation distance between containers storing gaseous fuels and liquid motor fuel dispensers is based on the maximum 18-foot length of dispenser hose attached to the liquid fuel dispenser and the potential for a liquid pool fire to affect the gaseous fuel storage containers. [30A: A.12.3.4]

A.42.8.6.2 The designation of classes and divisions of classified locations is defined in Article 500 of *NFPA 70*. [30A: A.12.6.2]

A.42.9.2.2 Cases where the length of the supply line to dispensing devices would result in insufficient pressure for operational purposes or would increase the potential for leakage due to the increased number of fittings or exposure of the line can warrant location of the supply on the pier. [30A: A.11.2.2]

A.42.9.6.2 NFPA 77 contains information on this subject. [30A: A.8.5.2]

A.42.9.6.4 Where excessive stray currents are encountered, piping handling Class I and Class II liquids should be electrically isolated from the shore piping. This requirement prevents stray currents originating in the vessel's electrical system from causing an electrical arc or spark. [30A: A.11.6]

A.42.9.6.4.1 NFPA 77 contains information on this subject. [30A: A.11.6.1]

A.42.9.8.2 See Section 9.4 of NFPA 30 for further information. [30A: A.11.8.2]

A.42.10.2.1.2.6 The charge on the fuel can be reduced by the use of a static dissipater additive that increases the electrical conductivity of the fuel and thereby allows the charge to relax or dissipate more quickly, or by the use of a relaxation chamber that increases the residence time of the fuel downstream of the filter to at least 30 seconds, thereby allowing most of the charge to dissipate before the fuel arrives at the receiving tank. [407: A.4.1.2.6]

API RP 2003 recommends a 30-second relaxation time for loading tank trucks and refuelers. However, it has not been a common practice to require a similar relaxation time for aircraft refueling, primarily because of the relatively few electrostatic incidents that have occurred during aircraft fueling. *(For additional information on this topic, see CRC Report No. 583.)* [407: A.4.1.2.6]

In filling tank trucks or storage tanks, API RP 2003 recommends that at least 30 seconds of residence time be provided downstream of a filter in order to allow static charges generated in flowing fuel to relax before fuel enters the tank. [407: A.4.1.2.6]

The reason it is possible to fuel aircraft safely with low conductivity fuel without providing 30 seconds of relaxation time is due primarily to the difference in the geometry of aircraft tanks as compared with tank truck compartments. Flow into the aircraft normally is subdivided into several tanks simultaneously and also distributed into adjoining compartments of each tank by a multihole inlet. Bachman and Dukek (1972) conducted full-scale research using a simulated large aircraft tank and concluded that none of the tanks or compartments hold sufficient fuel to allow enough charges to accumulate and create large surface voltages. Slower fill rates per compartment also allow more charge to relax. [407: A.4.1.2.6]

Additionally, the inlet system of most aircraft tanks directs fuel towards the bottom of the tank to avoid splashing that generates more charge. Finally, while the hoses that connect the fueler to the aircraft provide only a few seconds of residence time for charge relaxation at high rates of flow, the actual relaxation volume in the system is significantly greater where a coated screen is used as a second stage water barrier. In this case, the vessel's volume after the first stage filter coalescer could represent an additional 15 seconds of residence time for charge relaxation. (The coated screen, unlike other water barriers, does not generate charge.) [407: A.4.1.2.6]

A flammable vapor space in the tank due to the presence of JET B or JP-4 fuels still constitutes a potential hazard. Therefore, to minimize the chance for static ignition, FAA regulations require that fueling be conducted at half of the rated flow where civil aircraft have used such fuels. [407: A.4.1.2.6]

A.42.10.2.1.5 The beam of radar equipment has been known to cause ignition of flammable vapor–air mixtures from inductive electric heating of solid materials or from electrical arcs or sparks from chance resonant conditions. The ability of an arc to ignite flammable vapor–air mixtures depends on the total energy of the arc and the time lapse involved in the arc's duration, which is related to the dissipation characteristics of the energy involved. The intensity or peak power output of the radar unit, therefore, is a key factor in establishing safe distances between the radar antenna and fueling operations, fuel storage or fuel loading rack areas, fuel tank truck operations, or any operations where flammable liquids and vapors could be present or created. [407: A.4.1.4.2]

Most commercially available weather-mapping airborne radar equipment operates at peak power outputs, varying from 25 kW to 90 kW. Normally this equipment should not be operated on the ground. Tests have shown that the beam of this equipment can induce energy capable of firing flash bulbs at considerable distances. If the equipment is operated on the ground for service checking or for any other reason, the beam should not be directed toward any of the hazards described in the previous paragraph that are located within 100 ft (30 m). (WARNING: Higher power radar equipment can require greater distances.) [407: A.4.1.4.2]

Airport surface detection radar operates under a peak power output of 50 kW. It is fixed rather than airborne equipment. [407: A.4.1.4.2]

Airborne surveillance radar of the type currently carried on military aircraft has a high peak power output. Aircraft carrying this type of radar can be readily distinguished by radomes atop or below the fuselage, or both. [407: A.4.1.4.2]

Aircraft warning radar installations are the most powerful. Most of these installations are, however, remotely located from the hazards specified in the first paragraph and therefore are not covered herein. Ground radar for approach control or traffic pattern surveillance is considered the most fire hazardous type of radar normally operating at an airport. The latter type of equipment has a peak power output of 5 MW. Where possible, new installations of this type of equipment should be located at least 500 ft (150 m) from any of the hazards described in the first paragraph. [407: A.4.1.4.2]

A.42.10.2.1.7.1 Carbon dioxide extinguishers should not be selected due to their limited range and effectiveness in windy conditions. [407: A.4.1.6.1]

A.42.10.2.1.7.3 Multipurpose dry chemical (ammonium phosphate) fire extinguishing agent is known to cause corrosion to aluminum aircraft components. Although the agent is capable of extinguishing fires on or near aircraft, it is likely that the agent will spread to other, uninvolved aircraft, causing damage from corrosion. [407: A.42.10.2.1.7.3]

A.42.10.2.2.4 Electrical equipment contained in aircraft fuel servicing vehicles or cart engine compartments and located 18 in. (460 mm) or more above ground can be permitted to be of the general purpose type. [**407:** A.4.3.7.4]

A.42.10.3.3.1 Where pressure tanks are used, details on construction, spacing, and location should be in accordance with industry good practice and approved by the AHJ. When AVGAS, MOGAS, or JET B turbine fuels are stored in bulk quantities in aboveground tanks, they should be stored in floating roof-type tanks. Covered floating roof tanks minimize the hazardous flammable vapor–air space above the liquid level. The vapor spaces of underground tanks storing fuels should not be interconnected. [**407:** A.4.4.4.1]

A.42.10.5.1.1 Records should be kept of personnel training. These records should be made available to the AHJ upon request. [**407:** A.5.1.1]

A.42.10.5.1.4 The use of tunnels or enclosed roadways is discouraged. Where there is no alternate route, and the fuel servicing vehicle requires the use of a tunnel or enclosed roadway, the AHJ should examine the following considerations:

(1) Length
(2) Clearances
(3) Fixed fire suppression or extinguishing systems
(4) Frequency of use
(5) Ventilation
(6) Overlying structures and operations
(7) Other traffic
(8) Fire department access
(9) Emergency egress
(10) Drainage
(11) Other conditions

[**407:** A.5.1.4]

A.42.10.5.2 The following actions are appropriate in the event of a fuel spill, although each spill should be treated as an individual case due to such variables as the size of the spill, type of flammable or combustible liquid involved, wind and weather conditions, equipment arrangement, aircraft occupancy, emergency equipment, and personnel available:

(1) The flow of fuel should be stopped, if possible. If the fuel is discovered leaking or spilling from fuel servicing equipment or hose, the emergency fuel shutoff should be operated at once. If the fuel is discovered leaking or spilling from the aircraft at the filler opening, vent line, or tank seams during fueling operations, fueling should be stopped immediately. Evacuation of the aircraft should be ordered when necessary. The aircraft then should be thoroughly checked for damage or entrance of flammable liquid or vapors into any concealed wing or fuselage area, and corrective action should be taken as necessary before it is returned to normal operational service.
(2) The airport fire crew should be notified if the spill presents a fire hazard. The only routine exceptions are for small spills. Supervisory personnel should be notified to ensure that operations in progress can be continued safely or halted until the emergency is past and that corrective measures can be taken to prevent recurrence of a similar accident.
(3) It could be necessary to evacuate the aircraft if the spill poses a serious fire exposure to the aircraft or its occupants. Walking through the liquid area of the fuel spill should not be permitted. Persons who have been sprayed with fuel or had their clothing soaked with fuel should go to a place of refuge, remove their clothing, and wash. Individuals whose clothing has been ignited should be wrapped in blankets, coats, or other items or should be told to or forced to roll on the ground.
(4) Mobile fueling equipment and all other mobile equipment should be withdrawn from the area or left as is until the spilled fuel is removed or made safe. No fixed rule can be made as fire safety varies with circumstances. Shutting down equipment or moving vehicles can provide a source of ignition if no fire immediately results from the spillage.
(5) Aircraft, automotive, or spark-producing equipment in the area should not be started before the spilled fuel is removed or made safe. If a vehicle or cart engine is running at the time of the spill, it normally is good practice to drive the vehicle away from the hazard area unless the hazard to personnel is judged too severe. Fuel servicing vehicles or carts in operation at the time of the spill should not be moved until a check is made to verify that any fuel hose that could have been in use or connected between the vehicle and the aircraft is safely stowed.
(6) If any aircraft engine is operating at the time of the spill, it normally is good practice to move the aircraft away from the hazard area unless air currents set up by operating power plants would aggravate the extent or the nature of the existing vapor hazard.
(7) If circumstances dictate that operating internal combustion engine equipment within a spill area that has not ignited should be shut down, engine speeds should be reduced to idle prior to cutting ignition in order to prevent backfire.
(8) The volatility of the fuel can be a major factor in the initial severity of the hazard created by a spill. Gasoline and other low flash point fuels at normal temperatures and pressures produce vapors that are capable of forming ignitible mixtures with the air near the surface of the liquid, whereas this condition does not normally exist with kerosene fuels (JET A or JET A-1) except where ambient temperatures are 100°F (38°C) or above or where the liquid has been heated to a similar temperature.
(9) Spills of gasoline and low flash point turbine fuels (JET B) greater than 10 ft (3 m) in any dimension and covering an area of over 50 ft^2 (5 m^2) or that are of an ongoing nature should be blanketed or covered with foam. The nature of the ground surface and the existing exposure conditions dictate the exact method to be followed. Such fuels should not be washed down sewers or drains. The decision to use a sewer or drain should be made only by the chief of the airport fire brigade or the fire department. If fuels do enter sewers, either intentionally or unintentionally, large volumes of water should be introduced to flush such sewers or drains as quickly as possible to dilute the flammable liquid content of the sewer or drain to the maximum possible extent. Normal operations involving ignition sources (including aircraft and vehicle operations) should be prohibited on surface areas adjacent to open drains or manholes from which flammable vapors could issue due to the introduction of liquids into the sewer system until it can be established that no flammable vapor–air mixture is present in the proximity. (NOTE: NFPA 415, *Standard on Airport Terminal Buildings, Fueling Ramp Drainage, and Loading Walkways*,

provides further information on aircraft fueling ramp drainage designs to control the flow of fuel that could be spilled on a ramp and to minimize the resulting possible danger.)

(10) Spills of kerosene grades of aviation fuels (JET A or JET A-1) greater than 10 ft (3 m) in any dimension and covering an area of over 50 ft^2 (5 m^2) or that are of an ongoing nature and that have not ignited should be blanketed or covered with foam if there is danger of ignition. If there is no danger of ignition, an absorbent compound or an emulsion-type cleaner can be used to clean the area. Kerosene does not evaporate readily at normal temperatures and should be cleaned up. Smaller spills can be cleaned up using an approved, mineral-type, oil absorbent.

(11) Aircraft on which fuel has been spilled should be inspected thoroughly to ensure that no fuel or fuel vapors have accumulated in flap well areas or internal wing sections not designed for fuel tankage. Any cargo, baggage, express, mail sacks, or similar items that have been wetted by fuel should be decontaminated before being placed aboard any aircraft.
[**407:** A.5.2]

A.42.10.5.4 Hydrocarbon fuels, such as aviation gasoline and JET A, generate electrostatic charge when passing through the pumps, filters, and piping of a fuel transfer system. (The primary electrostatic generator is the filter/separator that increases the level of charge on a fuel by a factor of 100 or more as compared with pipe flow.) Splashing, spraying, or free-falling of the fuel further enhances the charge. When charged fuel arrives at the receiving tank (cargo tank or aircraft fuel tank), one of two possible events will occur:

(1) The charge will relax harmlessly to ground.
(2) If the charge or the fuel is sufficiently high, a spark discharge can occur. Whether or not an ignition follows depends on the energy (and duration) of the discharge and the composition of the fuel/air mixture in the vapor space (i.e., whether or not it is in the flammable range).
[**407:** A.5.4]

The amount of charge on a fuel when it arrives at the receiving tank, and hence its tendency to cause a spark discharge, depends on the nature and amount of impurities in the fuel, its electrical conductivity, the nature of the filter media (if present), and the relaxation time of the system [i.e., the residence time of the fuel in the system between the filter (separator) and the receiving tank]. The time needed for this charge to dissipate is dependent upon the conductivity of the fuels; it could be a fraction of a second or several minutes. [**407:** A.5.4]

No amount of bonding or grounding prevents discharges from occurring inside of a fuel tank. Bonding ensures that the fueling equipment and the receiving tank (aircraft or fueler) are at the same potential and provides a path for the charges separated in the fuel transfer system (primarily the filter/separator) to combine with and neutralize the charges in the fuel. Also, in overwing fueling and in top loading of cargo tanks, bonding ensures that the fuel nozzle or the fill pipe is at the same potential as the receiving tank, so that a spark does not occur when the nozzle or fill pipe is inserted into the tank opening. For this reason, the bonding wire has to be connected before the tank is opened. [**407:** A.5.4]

Grounding during aircraft fueling or refueler loading is no longer required because of the following:

(1) Grounding does not prevent sparking at the fuel surface (*see* NFPA 77, *Recommended Practice on Static Electricity*).
(2) Grounding is not required by NFPA 77.
(3) The static wire might not be able to conduct the current in the event of an electrical fault in the ground support equipment connected to the aircraft and could constitute an ignition source if the wire fuses. If ground support equipment is connected to the aircraft or if other operations are being conducted that necessitate electrical earthing, then separate connections should be made for this purpose. Static electrical grounding points can have high resistance and, therefore, are unsuitable for grounding. For a more complete discussion of static electricity in fuels, see NFPA 77.
[**407:** A.5.4]

A.42.10.5.4.3 Ordinary plastic funnels or other nonconducting materials can increase static generation. The use of chamois as a filter is extremely hazardous. [**407:** A.5.4.3]

A.42.10.5.6.4.3 The size of the DPF regeneration area depends on the equipment being used (fleet size). The AHJ should designate the size and number of DPF regeneration pads and determine whether a centralized facility is advantageous. [**407:** A.5.6.4.3]

A.42.10.5.7 Electric hand lamps used in the immediate proximity of the fueling operation should be of the type approved for use in NFPA 70 Class I, Division 1, Group D hazardous locations. No supportable basis exists for requiring in the petroleum industry the use of approved, listed, or permitted two- or three-cell flashlights to avoid igniting Class I, Group D vapors. [**407:** A.5.7]

A.42.10.5.7.2 Aircraft ground-power generators should be located as far as practical from aircraft fueling points and tank vents to reduce the danger of igniting flammable vapors that could be discharged during fueling operations at sparking contacts or on hot surfaces of the generators. [**407:** A.5.7.2]

A.42.10.5.7.6 For further information on intrinsically safe apparatus, see ANSI/UL 913, FM Class 3610, ANSI/ISA 12.02.01, or ANSI/UL 60079-11. [**407:** A.5.7.6]

A.42.10.5.9 Establishing precise rules for fueling is impossible when the electrical storms are in the vicinity of the airport. The distance of the storm from the airport, the direction in which it is traveling, and its intensity are all factors to be weighed in making the decision to suspend fueling operations temporarily. Experience and good judgment are the best guides. Sound travels approximately $\frac{1}{5}$ mi/sec (322 m/sec). The approximate number of miles to the storm can be determined by counting the seconds between a flash of lightning and the sound of thunder and dividing by 5. [**407:** A.5.9]

A.42.10.5.10.2 The precautions in 42.10.5.10.2 are intended to minimize the danger of the ignition of any flammable vapors discharged during fueling and of fuel spills by sources of ignition likely to be present in airport terminal buildings. [**407:** A.5.10.2]

A.42.10.5.13 Portable fire extinguishers for ramps where fueling operations are conducted are intended to provide an immediate means of fire protection in an area likely to contain a high concentration of personnel and valuable equipment. The prominent and strategic positioning of portable fire extinguishers is essential in order for them to be of a maximum value in the event of an emergency. Extinguishers should not be located in probable spill areas. For normal, single parking configurations, extinguishers specified for protection of fuel servicing operations should be located along the fence, at terminal building egress points, or at emergency remote control stations of airport fixed-fuel systems. To provide accessibility from adjoining gates, particularly where more than one unit is specified, extinguishers can be permitted to be located approximately midway between gate positions. Where this is done, the maximum distance between extinguishers should not be over 200 ft (60 m). Where the specified extinguishers are not located along the fence but are brought into the servicing area prior to the fueling operation, they should be located upwind not over 100 ft (30 m) from the aircraft being serviced. For protection of fuel servicing of aircraft that are double parked or triple parked, extinguishers should be located upwind not over 100 ft (30 m) from the aircraft being serviced. [**407:** A.5.13]

A.42.10.5.13.5 During inclement weather, extinguishers not in enclosed compartments can be permitted to be protected by canvas or plastic covers. If icing occurs, the extinguisher should be sprayed with deicing fluid. [**407:** A.5.13.5]

A.42.10.5.13.6 Fuel servicing personnel should be given adequate training with extinguishers so that such equipment is used effectively in an emergency. Such training should be given on fires of the type that could be encountered on the job. To ensure prompt action in the event of a spill or other hazardous condition developing during fueling operations, aircraft servicing personnel also should be trained in the operation of emergency fuel shutoff controls. Each new fuel servicing employee should be given indoctrination training covering these and similar safety essentials that are related to the job. Follow-up and advanced training should be given as soon as the employee is sufficiently acquainted with the work to benefit from such training. Supervisors should be given training in the more technical aspects of fire safety so that they understand the reason for these and similar requirements and have an appreciation for the responsibility of a supervisor and the safety of an operation. [**407:** A.5.13.6]

A.42.10.5.16 Failure of an aircraft fueling hose in service is a potential source of fuel spillage and a potential fire hazard. The principal reasons for failure of aircraft fueling hoses include the following:

(1) Using damaged hoses
(2) Using aged hoses
(3) Exceeding pressure limits
(4) Improper installation

[**407:** A.5.16]

A.42.10.5.16.4 Splicing of a hose with couplings alters the design bend radius of the hose, creating two kinks when the hose is wound on a drum. [**407:** A.5.16.4]

A.42.10.5.21.2(2) If passengers remain onboard an aircraft during fuel servicing, at least one person trained in emergency evacuation procedures is required to be aboard *(see 42.10.5.11.1)*. It is not intended that the pilot in command perform this function. [**407:** A.5.21.2(2)]

A.42.11.1.1 Natural gas is a flammable gas. It is colorless, tasteless, and nontoxic. It is a light gas, weighing about two-thirds as much as air. As used in the systems covered by this standard, it tends to rise and diffuses rapidly in air when it escapes from the system.

Natural gas burns in air with a luminous flame. At atmospheric pressure, the ignition temperature of natural gas–air mixtures has been reported to be as low as 900°F (482°C). The flammable limits of natural gas–air mixtures at atmospheric pressure are about 5 percent to 15 percent by volume natural gas. [**52:** A.1.1]

Natural gas is nontoxic but can cause anoxia (asphyxiation) when it displaces the normal 21 percent oxygen in air in a confined area without adequate ventilation. [**52:** A.1.1]

The concentrations at which flammable or explosive mixtures form are much lower than the concentration at which asphyxiation risk is significant. [**52:** A.1.1]

NFPA 704, *Standard System for the Identification of the Hazards of Materials for Emergency Response*, rating is as follows:

(1) Health — 0
(2) Flammability — 4
(3) Reactivity — 0
(4) Special — None

[**52:** A.1.1]

Cryogenic fluids are gases that have been liquefied by having their temperature brought below –130°F (–90°C). They are typically stored at low pressures in vacuum jacketed containers. Some of the potential hazards of cryogenic fluids are the following:

(1) Extreme cold that freezes or damages human skin on contact and can embrittle metals
(2) Extreme pressure resulting from rapid vaporization of the fluid during a leak or release of the cryogenic fluid
(3) Asphyxiation resulting from a release of the cryogenic fluid that vaporizes and displaces air

[**52:** A.1.1]

Personnel handling cryogenic fluids should use the protective clothing prescribed on the material safety data sheet (MSDS). This clothing typically includes heavy leather gloves, aprons, and eye protection. [**52:** A.1.1]

A.42.11.1.1.3 Current DOT and TC specifications, exemptions, and specified permits do not address the use of cylinders that are approved for the transportation of natural gas to be used in CNG service. [**52:** A.5.4.4]

The following Compressed Gas Association publications are relevant cylinder inspection standards:

(1) CGA C-6, *Standards for Visual Inspection of Steel Compressed Gas Cylinders*
(2) CGA C-6.1, *Standards for Visual Inspection of High Pressure Aluminum Compressed Gas Cylinders*
(3) CGA C-6.2, *Guidelines for Visual Inspection and Requalification of Fiber Reinforced High Pressure Cylinders*
(4) CGA C-10, *Recommended Procedures for Changes of Gas Service for Compressed Gas Cylinders*

The following Compressed Gas Association publication is specified in ANSI/ISA NGV2, *Compressed Natural Gas Vehicle (NGV) Fuel Containers*, as appropriate for CNG container inspection:

CGA C-6.4, *Methods of External Visual Inspection of Natural Gas Vehicle (NGV) Fuel Containers and Their Installations*

[**52:** A.5.4.4]

A.42.11.2.2.1 Chapter 11 of NFPA 58 covers engine fuel systems for engines installed on vehicles for any purpose, as well as fuel systems for stationary and portable engines. [**58:** A.11.1.1]

A.42.11.2.2.2 Containers for engine fuel systems can be of the permanently installed or exchange type. [**58:** A.11.1.2]

A.42.11.2.4.4 See Figure A.42.11.2.4.4. [**58:** A.11.12.1.4]

FIGURE A.42.11.2.4.4 Example of Vehicle Identification Marking. [**58:**Figure A.11.12.1.4]

A.42.11.3 For information on on-site storage of LNG in ASME tanks larger than 70,000 gal (265 m³) and in tanks built to API or other standards, see NFPA 59A, *Standard for the Production, Storage, and Handling of Liquefied Natural Gas (LNG)*.

Prior to the time NFPA 52 was developed, the use of LNG as an aviation fuel, fueling site liquefaction facilities, and the use of residential LNG fueling facilities were not being considered actively. The NFPA 52 committee intends to provide coverage for these applications at the appropriate time.

A.43.1.1 The risk to life and property because of the fire and explosion hazards of spray application of flammable and combustible materials varies depending on the arrangement and operation of the particular process and on the nature of the material being sprayed. The principal hazards addressed in this *Code* are those of the materials being sprayed: flammable and combustible liquids and combustible powders, as well as their vapors, mists, and dusts, and the highly combustible deposits and residues that result from their use. Properly designed, constructed, and ventilated spray areas are able to confine and control combustible residues, dusts, or deposits and to remove vapors and mists from the spray area and discharge them to a safe location, thus reducing the likelihood of fire or explosion. Likewise, accumulations of overspray residues, some of which are not only highly combustible but also subject to spontaneous ignition, can be controlled. [**33:** A.1.1]

The control of sources of ignition in spray areas and in areas where flammable and combustible liquids or powders are handled, together with constant supervision and maintenance, is essential to safe spray application operations. The human element requires careful consideration of the location of spray application operations and the installation of fire extinguishing systems so that the potential for spread of fire to other property and damage to property by extinguishing agent discharge is reduced. [**33:** A.1.1]

A.43.1.1.1 Refer to Figure A.43.1.1.1 for assistance in determining whether Chapter 43 applies to a particular spray application process. [**33:** A.1.1.1]

A.43.1.1.3(1) There are many industrial applications that involve routine use of small quantities of flammable or combus-

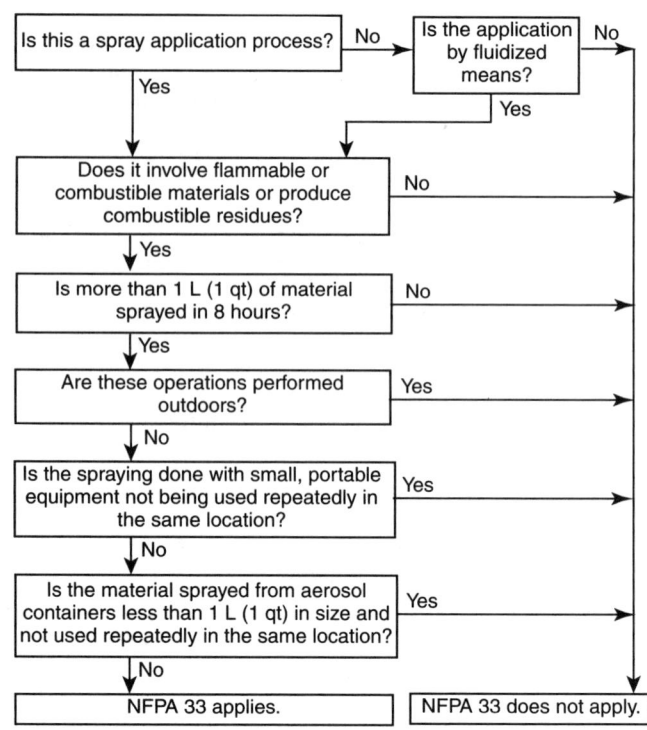

FIGURE A.43.1.1.1 Decision Tree — Does Chapter 43 Apply? [**33:**Figure A.1.1.1]

tible liquids (e.g., coatings, lubricants, adhesives) on a regular or periodic basis. An example would be touch-up of manufactured articles using aerosol containers or small, portable spray application equipment. The intent of this provision is to allow such use without having to comply with the requirements of Chapter 43. [**33:** A.1.1.4]

A.43.1.1.3(2) Chapter 43 does not cover spray application operations that are conducted outdoors on buildings, bridges, tanks, or similar structures. These situations occur only occasionally for any given structure and overspray deposits are not likely to present a hazardous condition. Also, the space where there might be an ignitible vapor–air or dust–air mixture is very limited due to atmospheric dilution. [**33:** A.1.1.5]

A.43.1.1.3(3) The occasional use of small portable spray equipment or aerosol spray containers is not likely to result in hazardous accumulations of overspray. Therefore, such operations are not within the scope of this *Code*. The following safeguards, however, should be observed:

(1) Adequate ventilation should be provided at all times, particularly where spray application is conducted in relatively small rooms or enclosures.
(2) Spray application should not be conducted in the vicinity of open flames or other sources of ignition. Either the spray operation should be relocated or the source of ignition should be removed or turned off.
(3) Containers of coating materials, thinners, or other hazardous materials should be kept tightly closed when not actually being used.
(4) Oily or coating-laden rags or waste should be disposed of promptly and in a safe manner at the end of each day's operations, due to the potential for spontaneous ignition

(5) The same fundamental rules for area cleanliness and housekeeping that are required for industrial spray application operations should be observed.
[**33:** A.1.1.6]

A.43.1.2.1 Fires involving spray application operations and processes can be expected to develop rapidly and to generate copious quantities of heat and smoke. In sprinklered buildings, such fires can also result in the operation of a greater-than-normal number of sprinklers. The following guidance is offered:

(1) Operations and equipment should be arranged and located so that there is adequate egress for personnel and adequate access for fire-fighting operations. Where spray application operations are extensive, they should be located in a separate building or in an area that is separated by fire-rated construction from all other operations or storage.
(2) Spray application operations that incorporate assembly lines or conveyor systems present special problems. If conveyor systems extend between separate buildings, a noncombustible or limited-combustible, sprinkler-protected enclosure or passageway might be of value. If conveyor systems pass through floors, the openings should be surrounded by deep [greater than 18 in. (460 mm)] draft curtains on the underside of the floor deck and might even be provided with automatic high-velocity spray nozzles arranged to create a counterdraft. If conveyor systems pass through fire walls or fire partitions, it will be difficult to reliably protect the openings by means of automatic-closing fire doors. One option is to provide a noncombustible or limited-combustible, sprinkler-protected tunnel on both sides of the opening.
(3) Rooms that house spray application operations should be separated from other occupancies or operations by construction that meets the requirements of 43.1.3.
(4) In sprinklered buildings where spray application operations occupy one portion of an open area, the spray application operations should be surrounded by noncombustible or limited-combustible draft curtains extending downward at least 18 in. (460 mm) from the ceiling, but deeper if practical. The draft curtains will aid in minimizing the number of sprinkler heads that open beyond the area of primary concern. Additional consideration might be given to the use of heat and smoke vents to aid in fire control.
(5) Sprinkler discharge should be drained to the outside of the building, to an internal drain system, or to some other suitable location. Properly designed and installed floor drains and scuppers of sufficient number and size to handle expected sprinkler discharge should be provided. Where spray application operations are located on an upper floor, they should not be located directly above goods or equipment that are subject to water damage. In addition, the floor should be made watertight and means should be provided to drain sprinkler discharge directly from the area.
(6) Spray application operations should not be located in a basement area.

[**33:** A.4.1]

A.43.1.3.1 Spray booths can be of a wide variety of shapes and sizes to accommodate the various industrial applications of spray application. Without the use of a spray booth, the spray area, as defined in 3.3.14.12, can constitute a considerable area, with all the requirements for a spray area then becoming applicable. It is important that only equipment suitable for specific purposes be utilized in connection with the handling and application of flammable or combustible liquids or powders. [**33:** A.5.1]

A.43.1.3.3 The "other" operations referred to in 43.1.3.3 are those that do not involve spray application processes. [**33:** A.5.3]

A.43.1.4.1 Because of the requirements for special safeguards, electrostatic apparatus; drying, curing, and fusing apparatus; and vehicle undercoating and body lining operations are covered in other chapters of NFPA 33. [**33:** A.6.2]

A.43.1.4.1.2 In the Division system, areas are classified as either Division 1 or Division 2, depending on whether ignitible gases or vapors are always present or likely to be present (Division 1) or whether ignitible gases or vapors are not normally present (Division 2). The Zone system identifies hazardous locations as Zone 0, Zone 1, or Zone 2, depending on whether the ignitible atmosphere will always be present (Zone 0), is likely to be present (Zone 1), or is not normally present (Zone 2). The Zone system is based on International Electrotechnical Commission (IEC) standards and was incorporated into NFPA 70 in 1996. [**33:** A.6.2.2]

A.43.1.4.1.5 There should be no open flames, hot surfaces, or spark-producing equipment in the spray area or in any area where they might be exposed to combustible residues. Open flames or spark-producing equipment should not be located where they can be exposed to deposits of combustible residues. Some residues can be ignited at low temperatures, such as those produced by steam pipes, incandescent light fixtures, and power tools. [**33:** A.6.2.5]

A.43.1.4.1.6 Areas that are above or adjacent to spray areas and where materials are located, stored, mixed, or processed should be ventilated. Equipment that is known to produce flame, sparks, or particles of hot metal, including light fixtures, that are adjacent to areas that are safe under normal operating conditions but which can become dangerous due to accident or careless operation should not be installed in such areas unless the equipment is totally enclosed or is separated from the area by partitions that will prevent the sparks or particles from entering the area. [**33:** A.6.2.6]

A.43.1.4.2.1 See NFPA 70. [**33:** A.6.3.1]

A.43.1.4.2.1.1 This classification usually includes the following locations:

(1) Where volatile flammable liquids are transferred from one container to another
(2) Interiors of spray booths and areas in the vicinity of spraying and painting operations where volatile flammable solvents are used
(3) Locations containing open tanks or vats of volatile flammable liquids
(4) Drying rooms or compartments for the evaporation of flammable solvents
(5) All other locations where ignitible concentrations of flammable vapors or gases are likely to occur in the course of normal operations

[**33:** A.6.3.1.1]

In some Division 1 locations, ignitible concentrations of flammable gases or vapors may be present continuously or for long periods of time. Examples include the following:

(1) The inside of vented tanks containing volatile flammable liquids
(2) Inadequately ventilated areas within spraying or coating operations using volatile flammable fluids
(3) The interior of an exhaust duct that is used to vent ignitible concentrations of vapors
[**33:** A.6.3.1.1]

A.43.1.4.2.1.2 This classification usually includes locations where volatile flammable liquids or ignitible vapors are used but that, in the judgment of the AHJ, would become hazardous only in case of an accident or of some unusual operating condition. The quantity of flammable material that might escape in case of accident, the adequacy of ventilating equipment, the total area involved, and the record of the industry or business with respect to explosions or fires are all factors that merit consideration in determining the classification and extent of each location. [**33:** A.6.3.1.2]

Piping without valves, checks, meters, and similar devices would not ordinarily introduce a hazardous condition even though used for flammable liquids. Depending on factors such as the quantity and size of the containers and ventilation, locations used for the storage of flammable liquids in sealed containers may be considered either hazardous (classified) or unclassified locations. See NFPA 30. [**33:** A.6.3.1.2]

A.43.1.4.2.1.3 This classification includes locations inside vented tanks or vessels that contain volatile flammable liquids; inside inadequately vented spraying or coating enclosures, where volatile flammable solvents are used; inside open vessels, tanks and pits containing volatile flammable liquids; and the interior of an exhaust duct that is used to vent ignitible concentrations of vapors. [**33:** A.6.3.1.3]

It is not good practice to install electrical equipment in Zone 0 locations except when the equipment is essential to the process or when other locations are not feasible. *[See NFPA 52, 505.5(A) IN No. 2.]* If it is necessary to install electrical systems in a Zone 0 location, it is good practice to install intrinsically safe systems as described by NFPA 70, Article 504. [**33:** A.6.3.1.3]

A.43.1.4.2.1.4 Normal operation is considered the situation when plant equipment is operating within its design parameters. Minor releases of flammable material might be part of normal operations. Minor releases include the releases from mechanical packings on pumps. Failures that involve repair or shutdown (such as the breakdown of pump seals and flange gaskets, and spillage caused by accidents) are not considered normal operation. [**33:** A.6.3.1.4]

This classification usually includes locations where volatile flammable liquids are transferred from one container to another; areas in the vicinity of spraying and painting operations where flammable solvents are used; adequately ventilated drying rooms or compartments for evaporation of flammable solvents; inadequately ventilated pump rooms for volatile flammable liquids; … and other locations where ignitible concentrations of flammable vapors or gases are likely to occur in the course of normal operation but not classified Zone 0. [**33:** A.6.3.1.4]

A.43.1.4.2.2.1 Dusts containing magnesium or aluminum are particularly hazardous, and the use of extreme precaution is necessary to avoid ignition and explosion. [**33:** A.6.3.2.1]

A.43.1.4.2.2.2 The quantity of combustible dust that may be present and the adequacy of dust removal systems are factors that merit consideration in determining the classification and may result in an unclassified area. [**33:** A.6.3.2.2]

Where products are handled in a manner that produces low quantities of dust, the amount of dust deposited may not warrant classification. [**33:** A.6.3.2.2]

A.43.1.4.2.2.3 As a guide to classification of Zone 20, 21, and 22 locations, refer to ANSI/ISA-61241 (12.10.05), *Electrical Apparatus for Use in Zone 20, Zone 21 and Zone 22 Hazardous (Classified) Locations — Classification of Zone 20, Zone 21, and Zone 22 Hazardous (Classified) Locations*. [**33:** A.6.3.2.3]

Zone 20 classification includes locations inside dust containment systems; inside hoppers, silos, cyclones and filter houses, dust transport systems, except some parts of belt and chain conveyors, etc.; inside blenders, mills, dryers, bagging equipment, etc. [**33:** A.6.3.2.3]

A.43.1.4.2.2.4 This classification usually includes locations outside dust containment and in the immediate vicinity of access doors subject to frequent removal or opening for operation purposes when internal combustible mixtures are present; locations outside dust containment in the proximity of filling and emptying points, feed belts, sampling points, truck dump stations, belt dump over points, etc. where no measures are employed to prevent the formation of combustible mixtures; locations outside dust containment where dust accumulates and where due to process operations the dust layer is likely to be disturbed and form combustible mixtures; locations inside dust containment where explosive dust clouds are likely to occur (but neither continuously, nor for long periods, nor frequently) as, for example, silos (if filled and/or emptied only occasionally) and the dirty side of filters if large self-cleaning intervals are occurring. *(See also A.43.1.4.2.2.3.)* [**33:** A.6.3.2.4]

A.43.1.4.2.2.5 Zone 22 locations usually include outlets from bag filter vents, because in the event of a malfunction there can be emission of combustible mixtures; locations near equipment that has to be opened at infrequent intervals or equipment that from experience can easily form leaks where, due to pressure above atmospheric, dust will blow out; pneumatic equipment, flexible connections that can become damaged, etc.; storage locations for bags containing dusty product, since failure of bags can occur during handling, causing dust leakage; and locations where controllable dust layers are formed that are likely to be raised into explosive dust/air mixtures. Only if the layer is removed by cleaning before hazardous dust–air mixtures can be formed is the area designated non-hazardous. [**33:** A.6.3.2.5]

Locations that normally are classified as Zone 21 can fall into Zone 22 when measures are employed to prevent the formation of explosive dust–air mixtures. Such measures include exhaust ventilation. The measures should be used in the vicinity of (bag) filling and emptying points, feed belts, sampling points, truck dump stations, belt dump over points, etc. *(See also A.43.1.4.2.2.3.)* [**33:** A.6.3.2.5]

A.43.1.4.3.3 Equipment that is listed for both Class I, Division 1; Class I, Zone 1; Class II, Division 1; and Zone 21 locations and is also listed for accumulation of deposits of combustible residues can be installed in the spray area. *(See NFPA 70.)* [**33:** A.6.4.3]

A.43.1.4.6 During operation of any electrostatic equipment, electrically conductive isolated objects within the process area are influenced by the process and can become charged to voltages that result in spark discharges capable of igniting flammable or combustible substances. Objects commonly involved in such incidents include workpieces on conveyor racks that have fouled contact points; solvent containers or tools placed on nonconducting paint residues, cardboard, or wooden rests; spray booth components such as loose floor grates; and human beings insulated from ground by rubber footwear, paint residue accumulations on floors, and gloves. [**33:** A.6.7]

Even in spray painting environments where there is no electrostatic equipment in operation but where sticky, electrically nonconductive paint residues have accumulated on the floor, a significant hazard is associated with static electrification of human bodies that results from walking across such a floor. As few as two or three steps can produce sufficient voltage on the body of a worker to create an incendive spark when he or she approaches a grounded object. If this spark occurs in a flammable vapor such as is found surrounding a solvent container or a freshly painted object, a fire results. See NFPA 77 for additional information. [**33:** A.6.7]

A.43.1.5.2.1 Acceptable means to comply with 43.1.5.2.1 include, but are not limited to, visible gauges, audible alarms, approved interlocks, or an effective inspection program. [**33:** A.7.2.1]

A.43.1.5.3 All spray areas require make-up air, and since the air exhausted from spray application operations is normally contaminated and can be recirculated only under rigidly controlled conditions, the source of the make-up air should be given careful consideration. When the capacity of the ventilating fan is low and the area where the exhaust system is located is large, sufficient make-up air often can be provided by natural infiltration of air through building walls, windows, doors, and so forth. In general, if the volume of the room or building where the exhaust system is located is not equal to at least 20 times the volumetric capacity of the fans (three air changes per hour), then additional make-up air should be provided. Outside air should be tempered and might have to be dehumidified or chilled for proper operation of the spray application apparatus. Automatic controls, including a high temperature limit switch, fan interlocks, and safety shutoff valves, should be provided for safe operation. [**33:** A.7.3]

The method of distributing the make-up air requires careful consideration. If the velocities and distribution of air through baffles, filters, and registers have not been carefully designed, the spray application operation can be inefficient. The velocity of the air through filters, and so forth, should not exceed 200 ft/min (60 m/min). Higher velocities can disrupt spray application operations due to turbulent airflow in the vicinity of the spray apparatus. This turbulence can also cause a properly designed exhaust system to fail to confine and remove vapors or to fail to confine and control residues, dusts, and deposits. [**33:** A.7.3]

In some heating arrangements, forced make-up or replacement air directly compensating for the contaminated air exhausted from spray application operations is used in place of or to augment general area heating and ventilation. [**33:** A.7.3]

With the many variables that can be encountered in heating and ventilating systems, it generally is advisable to engage the services of a qualified ventilating engineer to obtain a safe and efficient installation. [**33:** A.7.3]

The features that should be considered include the following:

(1) Location of sources of heat to comply with 43.1.4
(2) Locating air intakes to prevent recalculation of contaminated air, and equipping air intakes with appropriate screens or filters
(3) Automatic temperature and proportioning controls, including an independent excess temperature limit control
(4) A safety system interlocked with the heater to automatically provide for its safe ignition and to minimize the hazards that might result from failure of its proper operating cycle, proper pressure of fuel supply, ventilation, and electrical power
(5) An interlock between the spray booth exhaust system and the make-up air system to ensure that both systems are operable and provide a proper balance of supply and replacement air
(6) In the case of direct-fired units, operating controls that ensure that concentrations of unburned fuel or products of combustion, if inhaled, are kept to levels that are safe for operating personnel

[**33:** A.7.3]

A.43.1.5.5.1 If air exhausted from the spray area is permitted to be recirculated, as provided for in 43.1.5.5.1, it is critical for effective monitoring that sensors be protected from obstruction and contamination. See *NFPA 72* for recommended maintenance and calibration procedures. [**33:** A.7.5.1]

A.43.1.5.5.2 If recirculated air is used for make-up air for occupied spaces, including spray areas, spray booths, spray rooms, and other process areas, the requirements for decontamination and maximum allowable concentrations of solvents are far more stringent than those required by this *Code* for fire and explosion prevention. Refer to appropriate occupational safety and health and industrial hygiene standards for permissible exposure limits. One such standard is ANSI/AIHA Z9.7, *Recirculation of Air from Industrial Process Exhaust Systems*. [**33:** A.7.5.2]

A.43.1.5.6 Exhaust systems should be individually ducted to the outside of the building. Where treatment of the exhaust airstream is necessary to satisfy environmental regulations or where energy conservation measures are used, this might not be practical, and manifolding of the exhaust ducts might be necessary. It should be understood that manifolding of exhaust ducts increases the fire hazard. A fire starting in one booth can spread through the exhaust system and involve other spray areas. Heat exchangers, which are sometimes used to preheat exhaust air before it enters an incinerator, are subject to fires from the spontaneous ignition of residue that collects on heat exchanger surfaces. [**33:** A.7.6]

A.43.1.5.7 For ducts for powder coating systems, the strength of the materials of construction should be considered, since the duct might have to contain the pressure of a deflagration. *(See NFPA 68, Standard on Explosion Protection by Deflagration Venting.)* [**33:** A.7.7]

A.43.1.5.8 The designer of the exhaust ducts and fasteners should refer to appropriate design guides, such as the SMACNA *Round Industrial Duct Construction Standards* and the SMACNA *Rectangular Industrial Duct Construction Standards*, published by the Sheet Metal and Air Conditioning Contractors National Association. [**33:** A.7.8]

A.43.1.5.11 If there are other operations that give off ignitible vapors in the vicinity of a spray application operation, they should be provided with independent mechanical ventilation. [**33:** A.7.11]

A.43.1.6.1 For large spray operations, coatings, thinners, and solvents can be stored in one of the following locations:

(1) Underground storage tanks
(2) Aboveground storage tanks
(3) Separate buildings
(4) Separate dedicated rooms within the facility
[**33:** A.8.1]

In some cases, liquids are pumped to a mixing room or paint kitchen, where they are mixed and then pumped to the spray area. For smaller operations, separate storage and mixing areas might not be justified. However, it is desirable to minimize the fire loading in or near the spray area by one or a combination of the following methods:

(1) Flammable liquid storage cabinets
(2) A protected enclosed metal structure
(3) Use of metal containers with limitations on the quantity of liquid located near the spray area
[**33:** A.8.1]

A.43.1.6.2.2(1) The intent of this requirement is to allow the quantities of flammable and combustible liquids needed to safely and efficiently operate for the actual operating hours in any 24-hour period. As an example, if the facility operates only 8 hours out of 24 (i.e., a single shift) and uses 50 gal (190 L) of liquid during that time, then 50 gal (190 L) is the allowable quantity for the continuous 24-hour period. If the facility increases operations to two shifts, then the allowable quantity doubles to 100 gal (380 L). [**33:** A.8.2.2(1)]

A.43.1.6.4.1 NFPA 77 provides information on bonding and grounding. [**33:** A.8.4.1]

A.43.1.6.4.2 Valves should be kept shut when spray application operations are not being conducted, to minimize the release of coating material in the event of fire. [**33:** A.8.4.2]

A.43.1.6.4.3 If plastic tubing leaks within shielded areas, such as within color changers, the resulting spray fire will destroy all tubing, releasing large quantities of coating material in an area that cannot be reached by the booth protection system. Automatic protection systems should be provided for these areas. [**33:** A.8.4.3]

A major cause of fire in automatic electrostatic spray booths has been the replacement of original equipment plastic tubing with other types of tubing. Such replacement tubing, particularly if conductive coatings are used, is susceptible to the development of pinhole leaks. [**33:** A.8.4.3]

A.43.1.6.4.5 The severity and extent of the many fires in spray application operations has been substantially increased when rubber or plastic supply hose were burned off, resulting in the entire contents of the supply system being added to the fire. By limiting the amount of fuel available, the magnitude of the fire can be held to more manageable limits. The shutoff should be accomplished by means of an interlock with a fire detection system or the automatic fire extinguishing system for the spray area. This shutoff is normally accomplished by shutting the distribution pumps. In some cases, it is also advisable to limit the flow from the solvent piping system. This can be accomplished with properly specified check valves in the pipe "drops." [**33:** A.8.4.5]

A.43.1.6.5.2 NFPA 77 provides information on static protection. [**33:** A.8.5.2]

A.43.1.7.1 As indicated in 43.1.6, it is not advisable to keep large quantities of flammable or combustible liquids in areas that expose personnel or important property to injury or loss. The primary reason is that fires in flammable liquids are difficult to extinguish by the usual methods, and if large quantities are involved, they can spread the fire by flowing over large areas. For fires in small amounts of flammable or combustible liquids, hand extinguishers or large extinguishers on wheels especially designed for such fires are effective. If large quantities of liquids are to be protected, suitable automatic equipment should be provided and special attention should be given to proper dikes, curbs, and drains to prevent the flow to other property. [**33:** A.9.1]

For the extinguishment of fire in spray residues, handheld fire extinguishers suitable for fire in ordinary combustibles or hose streams are effective. [**33:** A.9.1]

Regardless of the level of filtration, residues will accumulate in the exhaust ductwork. Because the ductwork is part of the spray area, it must be protected in accordance with 43.1.7. This includes the ductwork from a water-wash booth. [**33:** A.9.1]

Because the particulate filters will accumulate paint residue, they must be protected. The solvent concentrator units, by their design, contain high concentrations of solvent, so they also must be protected. Also, the most commonly used solvent concentrators use activated carbon as the adsorption media. This media is highly combustible, especially with high levels of solvents absorbed. Ketone solvents pose an even greater risk. [**33:** A.9.1]

Because suppression media other than water might damage the carbon bed, water-based suppression systems (wet pipe sprinklers, preaction sprinklers, dry pipe sprinklers, and open-head deluge systems) are recommended for this application. [**33:** A.9.1]

The recirculated air supply unit must be protected because of the filter media it contains. Also, many large air supply units have gas-fired heaters to heat outside make-up air. [**33:** A.9.1]

Air supply ducts from the particulate filter to the air supply unit and from the air supply unit to the spray booth are not normally protected, since all particulates have been filtered. [**33:** A.9.1]

The choice of the automatic fire protection system should always be based on good engineering practice. Generally, for most spray areas, automatic sprinklers are considered most appropriate *(see A.43.1.7.4)*. However, consideration must be given to how much water is likely to flow and to how much water is to be contained. [**33:** A.9.1]

Dry chemical extinguishing systems are most appropriate for small spray application operations (e.g., automotive refinishing, furniture refinishing, and similar processes) that utilize dry filters to capture overspray. These systems provide economical adequate protection. They are a viable alternative for any facility without sufficient water supply to support an automatic sprinkler system. [**33:** A.9.1]

Carbon dioxide or clean agent extinguishing systems should be used for open area protection only after careful consideration. Holding the required concentration of agent for the period of time needed for extinguishment in a spray booth environment can be difficult. In addition, total flooding with carbon dioxide in normally or potentially occupied areas presents serious health concerns. The time delay required prior to discharge can allow a fire time to grow and spread. Carbon dioxide and clean agent systems, however, are an appropriate choice for protecting electrostatic equipment enclosures inside or immediately outside the spray area. [**33:** A.9.1]

A.43.1.7.4 Spray application operations should be located only in buildings that are completely protected by an approved system of automatic sprinklers. If the operations are located in unsprinklered buildings, sprinklers should be installed to protect spray application processes where practical. Because of the rapidity and intensity of fires that involve spray operations, the available water should be ample to simultaneously supply all sprinkler heads likely to open in one fire without depleting the available water for use by hose streams. Noncombustible draft curtains can be used to limit the number of sprinklers that will open. [33: A.9.4]

Even when areas adjacent to coating operations are considered under reasonably positive fire control by adequate automatic sprinkler protection, damage is possible if operations are conducted on floors above those containing contents that are highly susceptible to water damage. Waterproofing and drainage of spray room floors can assist in reducing water damage on floors below. Proper drainage of the large volume of water frequently necessary to extinguish spray finishing room fires often presents considerable difficulty. [33: A.9.4]

Automatic sprinklers in spray areas, including the interior of spray booths and exhaust ducts, should be wet pipe, preaction, or deluge system so that water can be placed on the fire in the shortest possible time. Automatic sprinklers in spray booths and exhaust ducts should be of the lowest practical temperature rating. The delay in application of water with ordinary dry pipe sprinklers can permit a fire to spread so rapidly that final extinguishment is difficult without extensive resulting damage. [33: A.9.4]

The location of the sprinkler heads inside spray booths should be selected with care to avoid heads being placed in the direct path of spray and yet afford protection for the entire booth interior. When sprinkler heads are in the direct path of spray, even one day's operation can result in deposits on the sprinkler heads that insulate the fusible link or choke open head orifices to the extent that sprinklers cannot operate efficiently. [33: A.9.4]

Automatic sprinklers should also be located so that areas subject to substantial accumulations of overspray residue are protected. Generally, sprinklers are located no more than 4 ft (1220 mm) from side walls of booths and rooms and from dry overspray collectors (where applicable). Sprinklers in booths or rooms should be on Extra Hazard occupancy spacing of 90 ft^2 (8.4 m^2). [33: A.9.4]

All sprinkler systems in spray areas should be controlled by an accessible control valve, preferably an OS&Y valve. [33: A.9.4]

Use of water as the extinguishing agent for solvent and coating material fires might, in some cases, cause problems with splashing and "floating" of flaming liquids and residues. This possibility should be included with the other factors that are normally considered in the selection of an extinguishing agent. In addition, water from sprinkler or deluge systems, after coming into contact with coating materials, residues, or solvents, might have to be collected and treated as hazardous waste. [33: A.9.4]

A.43.1.7.4.1 Paragraph 43.1.7.4.1 lists four types of automatic sprinkler systems and requires that the one "most appropriate for the portion of the spray area being protected" be used. Generally, an open-head deluge system provides the highest level of protection, given that all sprinklers in the protected area flow simultaneously. This type of system is most appropriate for large, down-draft, water-wash spray booths when protecting automatic electrostatic spray application zones. [33: A.9.4.1]

Wet pipe automatic sprinkler systems are appropriate for protecting spray booths that utilize nonelectrostatic application processes or operations using listed electrostatic application processes. Wet pipe systems are also generally used to protect exhaust plenums (eliminator or scrubber sections), exhaust ducts, and air recirculation filter houses. [33: A.9.4.1]

Dry pipe systems have been included because some exhaust duct designs include sections that are subject to freezing. [33: A.9.4.1]

Preaction systems have been included because some spray application processes and equipment can be damaged by unwanted water discharge. This damage can be disruptive and costly. Powder spray booths and solvent concentrator (air pollution abatement) systems are examples of systems where it is appropriate to use a preaction system. [33: A.9.4.1]

A.43.1.7.4.6 Water supply requirements for most industrial paint spray operations should be adequate to supply all automatic sprinklers in the spray area. Loss experience has shown that fires starting in the exhaust duct can spread to the spray booth and that fires starting in the booth can spread to the exhaust duct. [33: A.9.4.6]

Sprinklers or sprinkler systems protecting stacks or ducts should be of a type not subject to freezing. Automatic systems are preferred, but manual systems are also acceptable. Nonfreeze or dry-type sprinkler systems can be used in ducts subject to freezing. For some industries, such as the automotive industry, manually operated open-head systems have proved to be effective protection for ducts and stacks. [33: A.9.4.6]

A.43.1.7.5 This discharge is typically accomplished by means of a piping network from the fire protection system into all parts of the spray area. To avoid potential flashback of an unextinguished fire, modular fire protection units should not be used to protect areas with ducts or plenums, or areas that exceed the listing of the system. They might, however, be suited for smaller open spray areas that fall within the limits of the listing. [33: A.9.5]

A.43.1.7.7 During the first few seconds in the development of a fire in a dry powder spray booth, the following observations can be made:

(1) *Conventional structure equipment (spray booth connected to enclosed collector by ductwork)*
    (a) Airborne powder in the spray plumes of the gun(s) burns vigorously as long as the gun feeder(s) continues to supply powder. Flames from about 2 ft to 6 ft (600 mm to 1800 mm) in length might extend from the guns but do not intrude into the interior of the guns. These flames do not extend into the exhaust ductwork if adequate airflow has been provided to maintain maximum powder concentration in the exhaust stream below the minimum explosive concentration (MEC). The flames are extinguished almost instantly if their supply of airborne fuel is interrupted by shutting down the gun feeders.
    (b) Deposits of powder that have accumulated on the interior surfaces of the spray enclosure are not readily ignited, even by direct exposure to flames for a few seconds.

(c) If a fire in a powder spray booth has been sustained for an appreciable period of time (10- to 60-second delays have been observed), propagation proceeds as follows:

    i. Heat exposure effects of the fire, acting on the deposits of overspray powder that have accumulated on the interior surfaces of the spray enclosure, will modify a layer on the surface of the deposits to form an extremely fragile, tissue-thin structure of powder grains that have been softened only enough to adhere to adjacent grains but not enough to flow together and form a film. This is called a *sintered structure*. In response to the effects of vibration and rapidly fluctuating temperature (flickering of flames, etc.), this structure will break into a "mud-cracked" pattern, and individual platelets in some regions will curl up, presenting their edges to the fire-involved atmosphere. Exposure to this environment's heat and turbulence will char and dislodge platelets to form airborne glowing embers comparable to those formed by burning piles of autumn leaves. These embers, if drawn through exhaust ductwork to the powder collector, could ignite the collector, resulting in an explosion.

    ii. If this sequence is interrupted within the first few seconds of a fire's history, then ember formation and propagation by this mechanism can be stopped. The requirements of 43.1.7.7 are directed toward this result.

(2) *Integrated spray booth/"open" collector*

  (a) Fire in the spray plumes of the guns is identical to that found in A.43.1.7.7(1). Because there is no exhaust ductwork and no enclosed collector, however, the conditions necessary for generation of an explosion do not exist and the risk is confined only to conventional fire considerations. If powder feed to the spray guns is sustained after ignition and if the exhaust fan is kept in operation, enough heat can be delivered to the region of the cartridge filters to result in ignition of the filters and collected residues, which will then be sustained as a "deep-seated" fire producing large quantities of smoke but limited heat.

  (b) Attempts to extinguish "deep-seated" fires with carbon dioxide and dry chemical extinguishers have yielded disappointing results. Although flame is promptly knocked down, continued production of smoke and ultimate reflash should be expected. The most satisfactory results have been yielded by thoroughly soaking the filter cartridges and residues with water.

[**33:** A.9.7]

A.43.1.7.8 Unlike powder application systems, the make-up air and exhaust systems for a liquid application system have to continue to function, unless there is a compelling reason to shut them down. [**33:** A.9.8]

A.43.1.8.1 The materials used in spray application processes can create serious fire hazards. For example, the vapors and mists created by the atomization of flammable and combustible liquids can form explosive mixtures in air. In addition, deposits of residues can ignite spontaneously or be easily ignited. Finally, fires involving flammable and combustible liquids or combustible residues can spread rapidly and can produce intense heat and smoke. Properly designed equipment can do much to lessen these hazards but cannot eliminate them. These inherent characteristics should make it obvious that supervision of operations, maintenance of equipment, and daily cleaning are essential to a safe operation. [**33:** A.10.1]

It is important that some type of periodic inspection be conducted and recorded as part of the maintenance procedures. It is also important that any inspections of spray application equipment be conducted by competent and reliable personnel who have knowledge of the equipment and the inherent characteristics of the materials used. [**33:** A.10.1]

The frequency of the inspections depends on the individual components of the spray application process. For example, it might be acceptable to check sprinkler control valves or other control mechanisms for approved fire protection systems on a weekly or even monthly basis. However, this frequency would not be acceptable for ensuring adequate airflow through collector filters of a spray booth. At a minimum, that should be done at the beginning of each operating shift. Similarly, the buildup of residues would also need to be checked on a per-shift basis. Individual plant operations might dictate that either of these items (airflow and residue buildup) be checked every few hours. [**33:** A.10.1]

A.43.1.8.1.1 The use of the term *predetermined* is intended to convey the idea that one cannot arbitrarily locate or conduct spray application operations without thought to the hazards and special requirements that such operations demand. Requirements regarding electrical equipment and ventilation are of primary concern. This *Code* also specifies requirements that can vary based on the type of equipment used, the type of material being spray applied, and even the type of operation. Any spray application operation should also consider the storage, handling, and distribution of the coating materials used in the process. Certainly there are other factors, but these examples should adequately explain the need for predetermining the spray area and why operations should be confined to those areas. [**33:** A.10.1.1]

A.43.1.8.2 In the spray finishing of any workpiece, there is frequently a portion of the spray that does not deposit directly on the object or material being coated but does deposit on adjacent surfaces as residue material. This is referred to as *overspray*. Many of these residues are highly combustible, igniting at very low temperatures or spontaneously, resulting in fast-spreading fires. To limit the duration and intensity of fires, the accumulation of deposits has to be minimized and controlled as much as practical. The accumulation of residues represents one of the most significant challenges to fire control. [**33:** A.10.2]

Cleaning. The interior of spray booths, exhaust fan blades, and exhaust ducts should be cleaned regularly to avoid the accumulation of residues. Either spray operators should be allowed ample time for this cleaning, or a special maintenance crew should be provided for cleaning at the close of each day's operation. If equipment is so designed that during cleanup hose streams or fixed water nozzles can be used in ducts and spray booths without water damage to building and contents, cleaning operations are greatly facilitated. Many plants have found that by coating the interior of spray booths with a suitable soap-like or water-soluble material immediately after cleaning, adhesive spray deposits can be removed on the following day with the use of water streams. Other materials, such as plastics that can be readily peeled off the interior of the spray booth, can also be used to facilitate cleaning of the overspray residue. [**33:** A.10.2]

Properly maintained water-wash booths offer lower fire loading than dry booths. To maintain this advantage, it is necessary to perform regular and scheduled maintenance. This maintenance schedule should be recorded and the records filed. When the nozzles, jets or orifices, eliminator packs, and strainer screens become fouled with accumulated sludge or overspray, combustible residues will be deposited on the interior of the exhaust duct and fan blades. The nozzles, jets, orifices, and eliminator packs should be inspected each work shift. Strainer screens should be removed and cleaned each work shift. [**33:** A.10.2]

The booth interior, exhaust stack, and fan blades should be checked periodically, and accumulations of overspray and dirt should be removed as required. Exhaust ducts or stacks should not be entered for cleaning or repairs unless they are free from flammable vapors and have been thoroughly wet down. [**33:** A.10.2]

A.43.1.8.5 Many fires have originated from the spontaneous ignition of fabric and waste impregnated with coating materials. When sprayed articles are rubbed with rags or waste, all unclean rags and waste should be immediately placed in approved waste cans and removed from the premises at least daily at the close of each shift. When employees change clothes on plant premises, soiled clothing should be kept in metal lockers provided in a segregated dressing room. [**33:** A.10.5]

A.43.1.8.5.3 See NFPA 77 for information on bonding and grounding. [**33:** A.10.5.3]

A.43.1.8.7.4 See NFPA 77 for information on bonding and grounding. [**33:** A.10.7.4]

A.43.1.8.9 Bleaching compounds, such as hydrogen peroxide, hypochlorites, perchlorates, or other oxidizing compounds, can cause fires when in contact with organic finishing materials. Hence, if bleaching compounds are to be used in spray booths, the booths should be thoroughly cleaned and used only for that purpose. The alternate use of spray booths for bleaching compounds and other finishing materials or the alternate use of lacquers containing nitrocellulose and other types of finishing materials containing drying oils, such as varnishes, oil-based stains, air-drying enamels, primers, and so forth, without first thoroughly removing all traces of deposits can result in a spontaneous ignition fire. [**33:** A.10.9]

A.43.1.8.10 Stricter environmental regulation has given rise to the increased use of chlorinated solvents, such as 1,1,1-trichloroethane and methylene chloride. These solvents are not photochemically reactive and, therefore, can be useful in helping to meet standards regarding volatile organic compound emissions. However, these solvents have a well-documented characteristic of being chemically reactive with aluminum. The reaction that occurs is unpredictable both in terms of when it will occur and to what degree it will proceed. In most situations there is no apparent reaction. Other situations have noted effects ranging from simple corrosion to catastrophic explosion-like failure accompanied by considerable shrapnel and a fireball. Understanding and controlling the subsequent hazard is hindered by this unpredictability. Although there is some understanding of the actual reaction, the following factors acting as independent variables have been found to have an effect on the initiation and rate of reaction:

(1) Heat
(2) Pressure
(3) Ratio of aluminum surface area to volume of solvent, presence of moisture (condensation), aluminum alloy content, metal content of the coating, and the introduction of other solvents or materials

[**33:** A.10.10]

Therefore, the only assuredly safe condition is to keep these materials separate. [**33:** A.10.10]

It is important to realize that aluminum has been used as a primary material for spray equipment construction over many years. Incorporating these solvents into existing spray systems cannot be done safely without first determining the construction material of the equipment and then replacing those components where contact with aluminum and chlorinated solvent will occur within a pressurizable device (e.g., pumps, heaters, piping, fluid valves, and spray gun cups). [**33:** A.10.10]

A.43.1.8.12 If repairs or changes are to be made to equipment, care should be taken to see that all residue deposits are removed and the area wet down with water beforehand in order to avoid a fire. During such repairs, no spraying should be conducted, all flammable and combustible liquids and portable combustible material should be removed from the vicinity, and suitable fire extinguishers should be kept readily available. [**33:** A.10.12]

The use of welding or cutting torches should be prohibited except under the supervision of a competent person familiar with the fire hazards involved. *(See NFPA 51B.)* [**33:** A.10.12]

A.43.5.3.1(4) For dry chemical fire protection systems, it might be prudent to double the quantity of agent and its flow-rate, compared to a similar size fully enclosed spray booth to achieve the desired degree of protection. This is due to the relatively unenclosed nature of a limited finishing workstation compared to a traditional spray booth. [**33:** A.14.3.1(4)]

This recommendation is based on a white paper provided by the Fire Equipment Manufacturers' Association titled "Recommendations for Protection of Curtained Limited Finishing Workstations." [**33:** A.14.3.1(4)]

A.43.5.3.7.2 A means of showing that the limited finishing workstation is in the drying or curing mode of operation can be, but is not limited to, having the lighting of the workstation go out, use of a flashing light or strobe, or use of an audible device. [**33:** A.14.3.7.2]

A.43.7.1 Organic peroxides are a group of chemicals that are used as catalysts (chain reaction initiators) in the polymerization of plastics monomers and resins. Commercially, they are available as numerous formulations that differ not only in chemical species but also in concentration, type, and amount of diluent. [**33:** A.16.1]

The rapidly expanding reinforced styrene–polyester composites industry is one of the larger users of organic peroxide formulations. The formulations are used to catalyze (harden) the styrene–polyester resin. Frequently, the resin mixture and the catalyst are spray-applied to the reinforcing matrix using an automatic proportioning spray applicator. The most widely used catalyst systems are formulations of methyl ethyl ketone peroxide (MEKP), in varying concentration with different diluents, usually dibutyl phthalate. For transportation purposes, the U.S. Department of Transportation classifies these formulations as "organic peroxides" or "flammable liquids." [**33:** A.16.1]

For purposes of storage and warehousing, NFPA 400 classifies these materials using a five-tiered system, depending on their relative hazard as packaged for shipment. Thus, NFPA 400 recognizes that the different formulations available differ widely in fire hazard. In many cases, the "active oxygen," a measure of the material's catalytic activity and one measure of its reactivity hazard, has been reduced, thus reducing any explosion hazard. [**33:** A.16.1]

The following precautions are recommended:

(1) Organic peroxide formulations should be stored in a cool, dry location that is separated from the work area. The formulations should not be stored with materials with which they might not be compatible. Storage quantity limitations and fire protection requirements are contained in NFPA 400.
(2) The amount of organic peroxide formulation kept in the work area should be limited to that needed for a single day's use. Any formulation remaining at the end of a workday should be returned to the storage area.
(3) All necessary precautions, as recommended by the supplier, should be taken when organic peroxide formulations are used. Good housekeeping should be strictly observed, and spills should be immediately cleaned. Spilled material or material (such as resin) that has been contaminated with organic peroxide formulations has to be properly disposed of immediately. Trained personnel and safe operating procedures are essential for safe operation. The user should refer to the material safety data sheet (MSDS) or its equivalent for safety and handling information for the specific formulation being used.

[**33:** A.16.1]

A.43.7.3.2 Such mixing can result in a spontaneous fire or explosion. [**33:** A.16.3.2]

A.43.7.6 The chemical and thermal stability of organic peroxide formulations is markedly reduced by contact or contamination with strong acids or bases, sulfur compounds, amines, and reducing agents of any type. Decomposition gases or vapors produced by some organic peroxide formulations can present a fire or explosion hazard. For example, the decomposition of benzoyl peroxide produces highly flammable vapors. [**33:** A.16.6]

Heat, including heat from fire exposure, is an important factor in the decomposition of organic peroxide formulations. Some formulations decompose quietly when exposed to a slow, gradual increase in temperature. However, these same formulations can decompose violently or even explode when subjected to a rapid, excessive increase in temperature, such as from fire exposure. [**33:** A.16.6]

In general, an organic peroxide that is formulated with a diluent into a dilute solution or paste burns more slowly than the concentrated or pure material and is less sensitive to shock or impact. [**33:** A.16.6]

A.43.8.1 The reinforced styrene–polyester composites industry uses a variety of fabrication techniques to manufacture a wide range of useful products. Most of these products are fabricated with polyester- or vinyl ester–based resins and a fiber reinforcement, most commonly glass fiber. The resins contain a monomer, usually styrene, and are mixed with a catalyst to initiate curing. Other volatile organic chemicals used include the organic peroxide formulations, such as methyl ethyl ketone peroxide (MEKP), used to cure the resin, and various dyes and admixtures. [**33:** A.17.1]

Open molding is the predominant molding method, with mold sizes ranging from less than 1 ft^2 (0.1 m^2) to very large structures, such as boat hulls over 100 ft (30 m) in length. The two most widely used application methods are hand lay-up and spray-up. In the hand lay-up fabrication method, a glass fiber mat is saturated with the resin by direct spray application or by manual application of the liquid resin. The spray-up fabrication method employs a "chopper gun" that simultaneously applies catalyzed resin and chopped glass fiber to a mold. In addition, many operations use a spray-applied polyester resin gelcoat, as for in-mold coating. Products produced by this industry include boats, bathtubs and shower enclosures, sinks and lavatories, underground storage tanks, auto and truck bodies, recreational vehicles, pollution control equipment, piping, and other specialized parts. [**33:** A.17.1]

A.43.8.3 The determination by the Technical Committee on Finishing Processes that Ordinary Hazard (Group 2) sprinkler design density is sufficient for protecting spray application of styrene cross-linked thermoset resins (commonly known as glass fiber–reinforced plastics) is based on the following factors:

(1) Although the styrene monomer that is a component in unsaturated polyester resin is a Class I flammable liquid by definition, actual burn tests reveal that the resin does not readily ignite and burns slowly when it does ignite.
(2) Tests of resin application areas have shown that the processes do not produce vapors that exceed 25 percent of the lower flammable limit (LFL). Resin application tests have also indicated that the maximum levels of vapor concentrations are about 690 parts per million (ppm) for spray application. The tests were conducted in an enclosed area with no ventilation. This concentration is much less than 25 percent of the LFL, which is 11,000 ppm for styrene.

[**33:** A.17.3]

A.43.8.5.3 NFPA 77 contains information on static electricity. [**33:** A.17.5.3]

A.43.9.1.6 See NFPA 86, *Standard for Ovens and Furnaces*.

A.43.9.2 Section 43.9 anticipates conditions of average use.

A.43.10.1 The safety of a spray application process depends on the employees who operate it and the knowledge and understanding they have of the process and equipment involved. Therefore, it is important to maintain an effective and ongoing training program for all employees involved in such work. New employees should be effectively trained before being assigned to a job. After the initial training, employees should receive periodic retraining to ensure their knowledge and understanding of normal process procedures as well as with emergency procedures or changes in procedures. Safe work habits are developed; they do not occur naturally. [**33:** A.18.1]

All training should be provided by qualified personnel knowledgeable in the processes and operations involved. Appropriate training should be provided for all employees involved in or affected by spray application processes. This includes, but is not limited to, operating, supervisory, housekeeping, and maintenance personnel. [**33:** A.18.1]

A.43.10.1.2 Any work requiring entry of employees into confined spaces should be conducted in accordance with a written procedure that is rigidly followed. This procedure should include, but not be limited to, the following:

(1) Analysis of confined space atmosphere for flammable, combustible, toxic, or oxygen-deficient conditions
(2) Rescue, fire, and emergency procedures
(3) Locking and tagging procedures for all power and process hazard sources
(4) Ventilation
(5) Personal protective equipment
(6) Proper tools and electrical equipment
(7) Written entry authorization by a qualified responsible individual
[33: A.18.1.2]

A.45.1.2 The use of automatic sprinkler protection in accordance with NFPA 13 is recommended for all storage of combustible fibers.

A.50.1.1 These requirements include, but are not limited to, all manner of cooking equipment, exhaust hoods, grease removal devices, exhaust ductwork, exhaust fans, dampers, fire-extinguishing equipment, and all other auxiliary or ancillary components or systems that are involved in the capture, containment, and control of grease-laden cooking effluent. [96: A.1.1.1]

A.50.1.4 This judgment should take into account the type of cooking being performed, the items being cooked, and the frequency of cooking operations. Examples of operations that might not require compliance with Chapter 50 include the following:

(1) Day care centers warming bottles and lunches
(2) Therapy cooking facilities in health care occupancies
(3) Churches and meeting operations that are not cooking meals that produce grease-laden vapors
(4) Employee break rooms where food is warmed
[96: A.1.1.4]

A.50.2.1.1.1 See ANSI/UL 710B. [96: A.4.1.1.1]

A.50.2.1.6 When solid fuel is burned in cooking operations, increased quantities of carbon, creosote, and grease-laden vapors are produced that rapidly contaminate surfaces, produce airborne sparks and embers, and are subject to significant flare-ups. Also, solid fuel cooking requires fuel storage and handling and produces ash that requires disposal. For these reasons, solid fuel cooking operations are required to comply with Chapter 14 of NFPA 96. [96: A.4.1.6]

A.50.2.1.9 The AHJ can exempt temporary facilities, such as a tent, upon evaluation for compliance to the applicable portions of NFPA 96 or this *Code*.

Although it might not be practical to enforce all requirements of NFPA 96 in temporary facilities, the AHJ should determine that all necessary provisions that affect the personal safety of the occupants are considered. [96: A.4.1.9]

A.50.2.2 See Figure A.50.2.2(a) through Figure A.50.2.2(h) for clarification of the appropriate clearances required in 50.2.2. [96: A.4.2]

A.50.4.3.2 Examples of cooking equipment that produce grease-laden vapors include, but are not limited to, deep fat fryers, ranges, griddles, broilers, woks, tilting skillets, and braising pans. [96: A.10.1.2]

A.50.4.4.2 NFPA 10, Annex A, provides recommendations for placards. [96: A.10.2.2]

A.50.4.4.3 ANSI/UL 300 primarily addresses the method of fire testing for self-contained chemical extinguishing systems commonly referred to as pre-engineered systems. ANSI/UL 300 has been identified as a baseline for testing fire-extinguishing systems intended for the protection of commercial cooking–related hazards. Additional equivalent testing standards can and have been written for other types of fire-extinguishing systems not considered pre-engineered that demonstrate equivalent fire testing severity to the ANSI/UL 300 test standard. Current examples include, but are not limited to, ANSI/UL 199, UL Subject 199B, UL Subject 199E, and ANSI/UL 710B. [96: A.10.2.3]

A.50.4.4.3.1 A change from rendered animal fat to cooking oil likely will increase auto-ignition temperatures, and a change to insulated energy-efficient cooking equipment that does not allow ease of cooling likely will result in difficulties sustaining extinguishment with systems not complying with UL 300 or equivalent standards. [96: A.10.2.3.1]

A.50.4.4.10(4) An approved weekly recorded inspection could consist of a log of entries that would display the date and time of each inspection and the initials of the person(s) conducting the visual inspection. Attaching the log to a clipboard and mounting it near the valve in question serves as a convenient reminder of the need to conduct the inspection. [96: A.10.2.10(4)]

A.50.4.11.2 Although training and qualification might be available elsewhere, the manufacturer of the equipment being installed should be considered an appropriate source of training and qualification. [96: A.10.9.2]

A.50.4.12.1 The system used to rate extinguishers for Class B fires (flammable liquids in depth) does not take into consideration the special nature of heated grease fires. Cooking-grease fires are a special hazard requiring agents that saponify (make a soap foam layer to seal the top surface of the grease) for this application. [96: A.10.10.1]

A.50.5.2.1 It is recommended that such training and qualification be performed by the manufacturer of the equipment being inspected and serviced. The various electrical, mechanical, and filtration components of the systems should be inspected and tested as required to ensure that they continue to function according to original design. [96: A.11.2.1]

A.50.5.2.2 It is not intended that actual discharge of agent occur to test all components, but where pressure from the discharging agent or from compressed gas actuators is needed to activate control components, an alternate means for testing those components should be provided and used. [96: A.11.2.2]

A.50.5.2.4 The date of manufacture marked on fusible metal alloy sensing elements does not limit when they can be used. These devices have unlimited shelf life. The intent of 50.5.2.4 is to require semiannual replacement of fusible metal alloy sensing elements that have been installed in environments that subject them to contaminant loading, such as grease in restaurant hoods and ducts, that could adversely affect their proper operation. [96: A.11.2.4]

A.50.5.3.3 See A.50.5.2.4. [96: A.11.3.3]

A.50.5.4 The primary focus of an inspection for cleanliness is to establish whether the volume of grease buildup within the exhaust system warrants cleaning and to determine whether adequate access is available throughout the exhaust system to remove the grease buildup. [96: A.11.4]

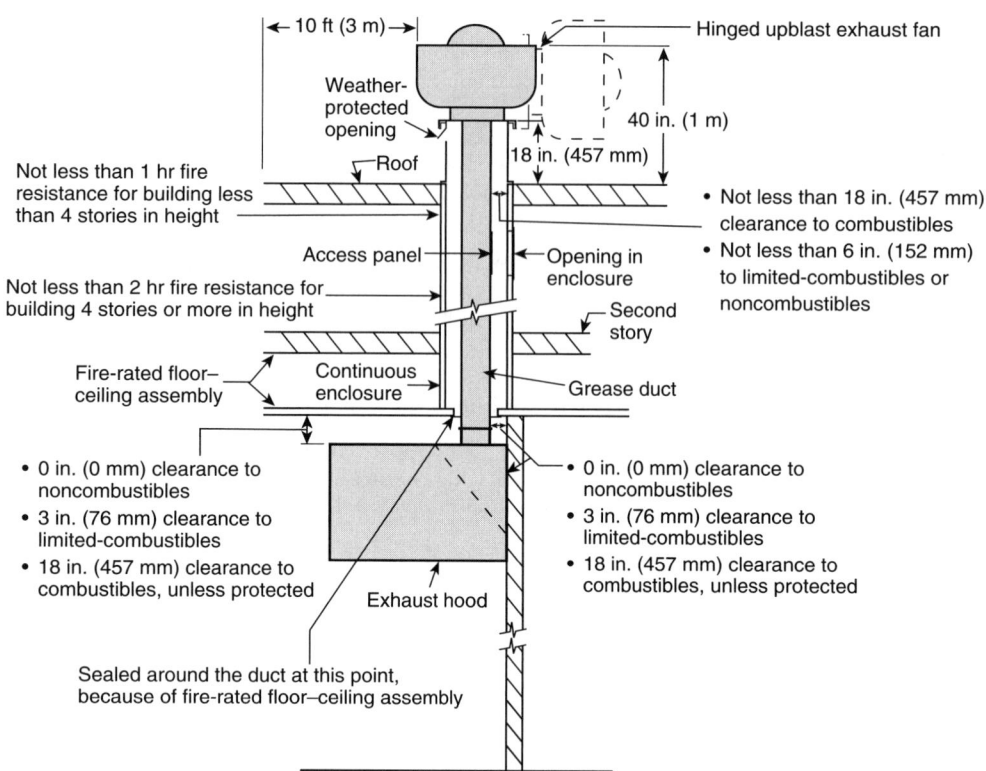

FIGURE A.50.2.2(a) Typical Section View for Building with Two Stories or More with Fire-Rated Floor–Ceiling Assembly. [96:Figure A.4.2(a)]

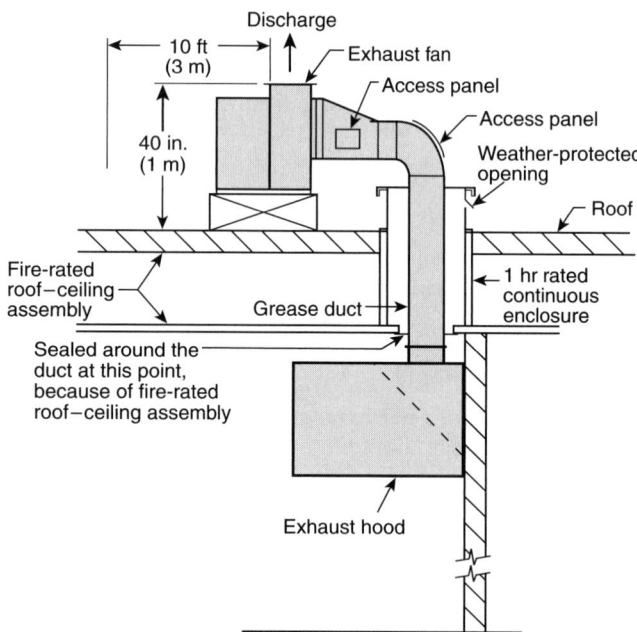

FIGURE A.50.2.2(b) Typical Section View for One-Story Building with Fire-Rated Roof–Ceiling Assembly. [Clearances given in Figure A.50.2.2(a) apply also to this drawing.] [96:Figure A.4.2(b)]

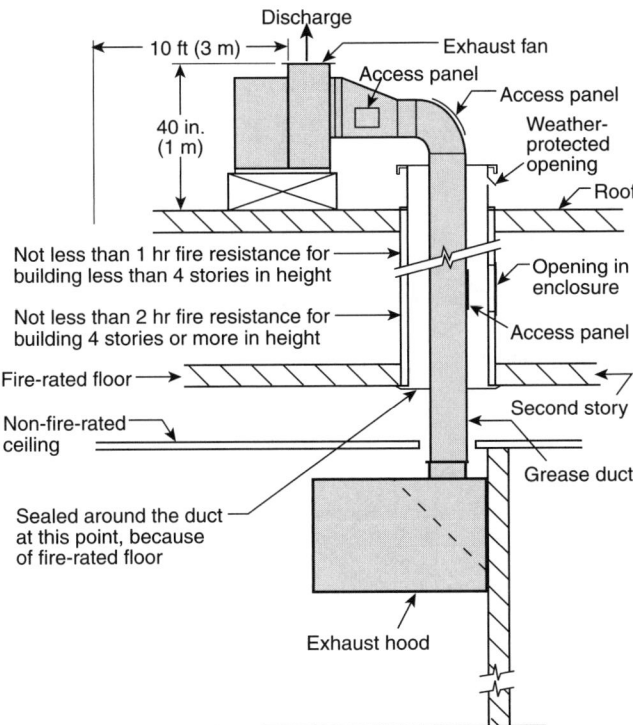

FIGURE A.50.2.2(c) Typical Section View for Building with Two Stories or More with Non-Fire-Rated Ceiling and Fire-Rated Floor. [Clearances given in Figure A.50.2.2(a) apply also to this drawing.] [96:Figure A.4.2(c)]

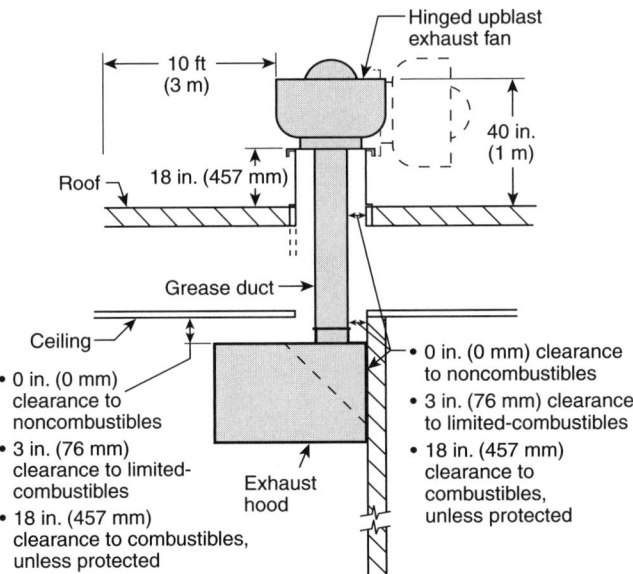

Note: Enclosure is not required in 1-story building where roof–ceiling assembly does not have a fire resistance rating.

FIGURE A.50.2.2(d) Typical Section View for One-Story Building Without Fire-Rated Roof–Ceiling Assembly. [96:Figure A.4.2(d)]

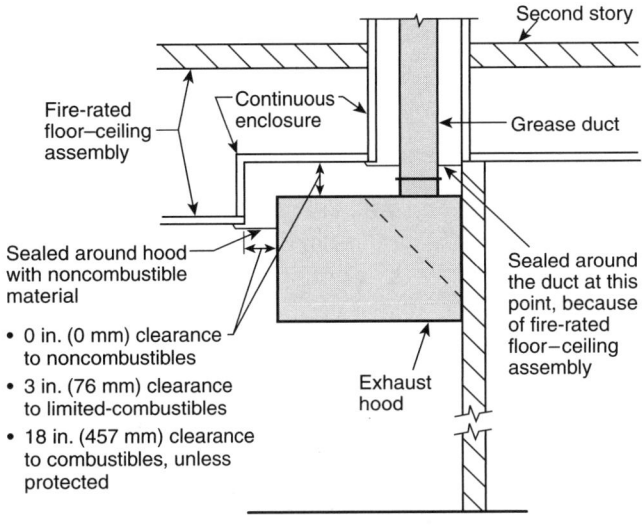

TYPICAL SECTION VIEW
(For building with 2 or more stories with fire-rated floor–ceiling assembly)

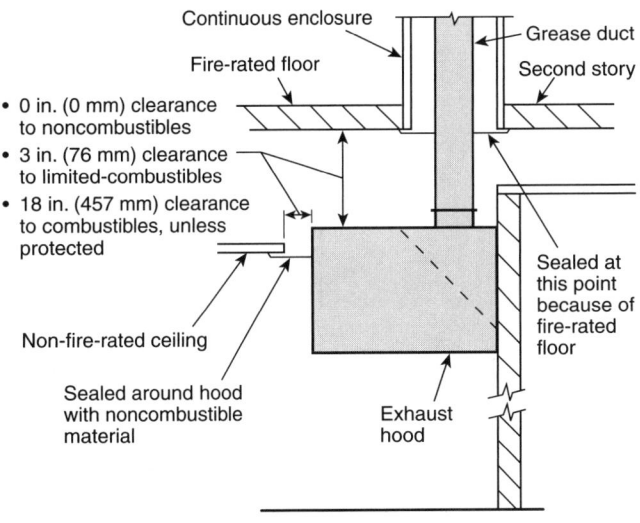

TYPICAL SECTION VIEW
(For building with 2 or more stories with non-fire-rated ceiling and fire-rated floor)

FIGURE A.50.2.2(e) Detail Drawings Showing Hoods Penetrating Ceilings. [96:Figure A.4.2(e)]

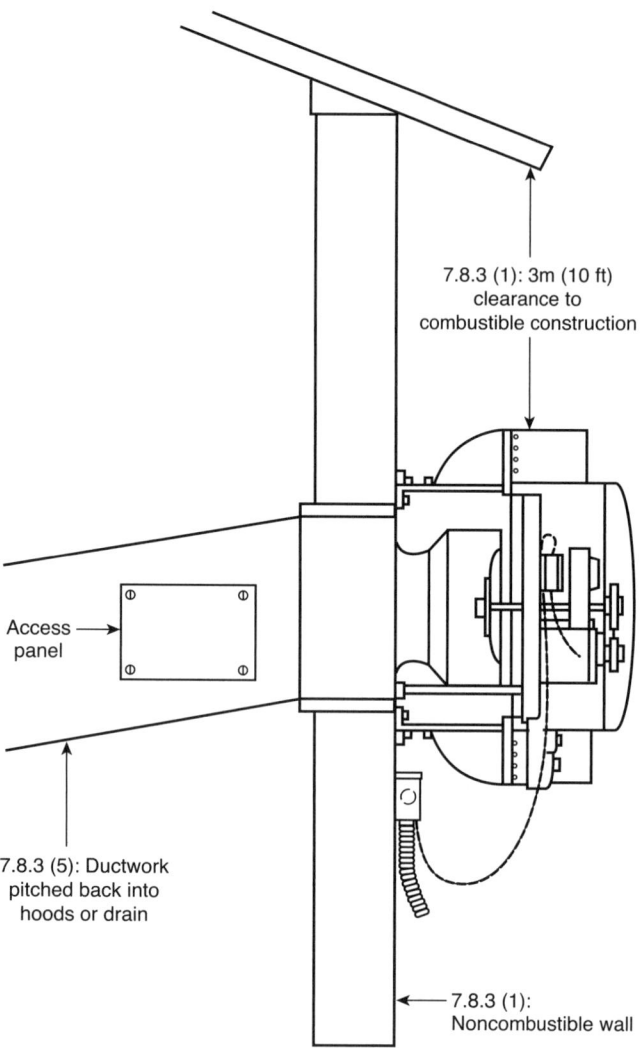

FIGURE A.50.2.2(f) Wall Mounted Fan. [96:Figure A.4.2(f)]

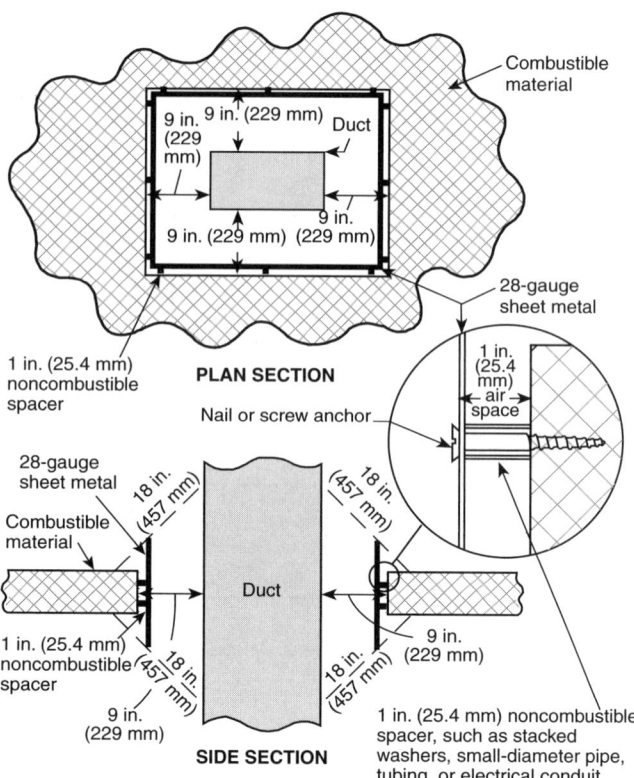

FIGURE A.50.2.2(g) Example of Clearance Reduction System: 9 in. (229 mm) Clearance to Combustible Material. [96:Figure A.4.2(g)]

A.50.5.6.1 A good operating practice is for cleaning personnel of commercial kitchen exhaust systems to have personal protective equipment (PPE) and height access equipment. The following items should be considered as a minimum:

(1) Eye protection
(2) Hand protection
(3) Head protection
(4) Foot protection
(5) Respiratory protection
(6) Fall protection
(7) Ladders
(8) Lock-out/tag-out kit
[96: A.11.6.1]

Preparation. The fan should be turned off, locked out, and tagged out. Open flames should be extinguished, and switches/breakers serving the appliance and cooking area outlets should be locked out. If the switches/breakers are not capable of being locked out and tagged out, any solid-fuel cooking appliances should be extinguished and the solid fuel removed. [96: A.11.6.1]

Removal or Covering of Equipment. Food products, cookware, and cooking support equipment that can be removed should be removed from the cleaning area. Equipment that cannot be removed should be covered. [96: A.11.6.1]

Cleaning Methods. The following methods for cleaning surfaces covered with grease and contaminants been proved to be effective:

(1) Manual cleaning by scraping, grinding, or scrubbing
(2) Chemical cleaning with agents and water
(3) Pressure washing with pressurized water or pressurized water and agents
(4) Steam cleaning with pressurized steam
[96: A.11.6.1]

Waste Water and Solid Waste. Water and agents used in the cleaning process and solid waste should be collected for disposal. [96: A.11.6.1]

A.50.5.6.2 Hoods, grease removal devices, fans, ducts, and other appurtenances should be cleaned to remove combustible contaminants to a minimum of 0.002 in. (50 μm). [96: A.11.6.2]

When to clean: A measurement system of deposition should be established to trigger a need to clean. [96: A.11.6.2]

The method of measurement is a depth gauge comb, shown in Figure A.50.5.6.2, which is scraped along the duct surface. For example, a measured depth of 0.078 in. (2000 μm) indicates the need to remove the deposition risk. The system would also include point measurement in critical areas. For example, 0.125 in. (3175 μm) in a fan housing requires cleaning. [96: A.11.6.2]

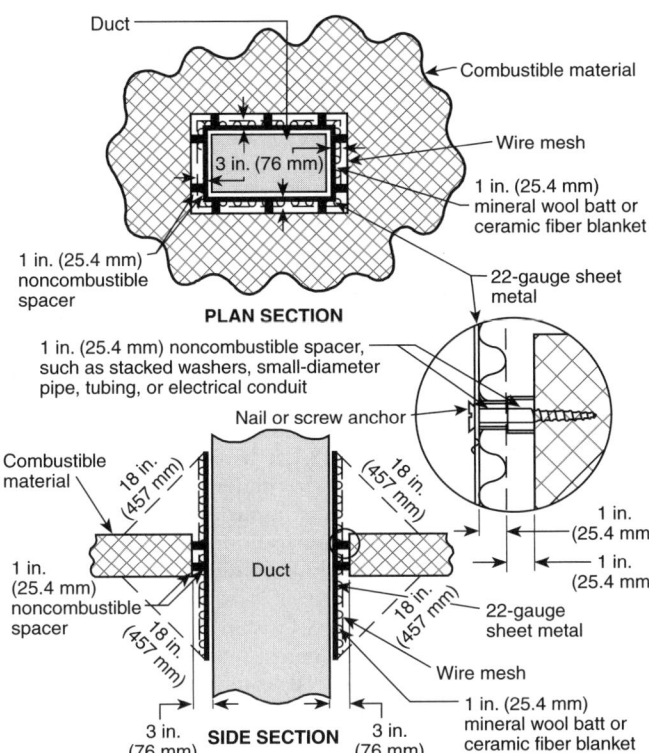

FIGURE A.50.2.2(h) Example of Clearance Reduction System: 3 in. (76 mm) Clearance to Combustible Material. [96:Figure A.4.2(h)]

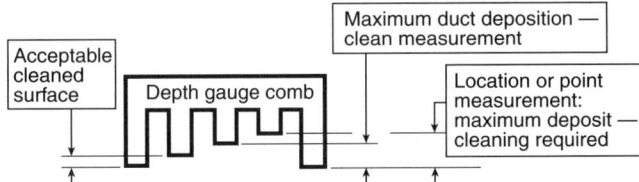

FIGURE A.50.5.6.2 Depth Gauge Comb. [96:Figure A.11.6.2]

A.50.6.1.1 Cooking appliances that are designed for permanent installation, including, but not limited to, ranges, ovens, stoves, broilers, grills, fryers, griddles, and barbecues, should be installed in accordance with the manufacturer's installation instructions.

(1) Commercial electric cooking appliances should be listed and labeled in accordance with ANSI/UL 197.
(2) Microwave cooking appliances should be listed and labeled in accordance with ANSI/UL 923.
(3) Oil-burning stoves should be listed and labeled in accordance with ANSI/UL 896.
(4) Wood-fired cooking appliances should be listed and labeled in accordance with ANSI/UL 737, UL Subject 2162, or UL Subject 2728, depending on exact appliance type.
(5) Gas-fired cooking appliances should be listed and labeled in accordance with ANSI Z83.11.
(6) Gas-wood-fired cooking appliances should be listed and labeled in accordance with ANSI Z83.11, ANSI/UL 737, and/or UL Subject 2162, depending on exact appliance type. [96: A.12.1.1]

A.50.6.1.2.1 Gas-fueled appliances should be installed to the requirements of NFPA 54 or NFPA 58. [96: A.12.1.2.1]

A.50.6.1.2.2 The effectiveness of an automatic extinguishing system is affected by the placement of the nozzles. For this reason, it is essential that cooking appliances be situated in the area in which they were when the extinguishing equipment was designed and installed. If an appliance is moved from under the equipment for cleaning or any other reason, it should be returned to its original position prior to initiation of a cooking operation. [96: A.12.1.2.2]

When appliances are on wheels or casters for ease of cleaning, it is important that the appliance be placed in its design position to ensure that the fire-extinguishing system will be effective. An approved method should ensure that the appliance is returned to its appropriate position before cooking takes place. Channels, markings, or other approved methods assist in ensuring proper placement. [96: A.12.1.2.2]

A.52.1 The requirements in Chapter 52 supersede all the hazardous material designations, permits, and requirements in Chapter 60.

A.52.3.4.2 Methods of achieving this protection can include, but are not limited to, the following:

(1) Liquidtight sloped or recessed floors in indoor locations or similar areas in outdoor locations
(2) Liquidtight floors in indoor locations or similar areas in outdoor locations provided with liquidtight raised or recessed sills or dikes
(3) Sumps and collection systems
(4) Spill containment systems such as that described in A.52.3.5.1

A.52.3.5.1 One method to determine compliance with the neutralization requirements of this subsection is found in Underwriters Laboratories Subject 2436 *Outline of Investigation for Spill Containment For Stationary Lead Acid Battery Systems*. Subject 2436 investigates the liquid tightness, level of electrolyte absorption, pH neutralization capability, and flame spread resistance of spill containment systems.

A.52.3.6 Information on battery room ventilation can be found in IEEE 1635/ASHRAE 21, *Guide to Battery Room Ventilation and Thermal Management*.

A.53.1 See the mechanical code for refrigerant group descriptions.

A.53.1.1.1 Refrigerant safety groups are established by ANSI/ASHRAE 34, *Designation and Safety Classification of Refrigerants*. Safety groups are based on the relative safety with respect to toxicity and flammability. The classification groups include a letter designation that indicates the toxicity (A is "lower toxicity" and B is "higher toxicity") and a number that indicates flammability (1 indicates no flame propagation in air when tested by prescribed methods at specified conditions, 2 is "lower flammability," and 3 is "higher flammability").

A.53.2.3.1.4 See A.53.1.1.1.

A.53.2.3.2 See A.53.1.1.1.

A.54.2.2.2 NEMA 250, *Enclosures for Electrical Equipment*, is intended for use as a guide in the design, fabrication, testing, and use of equipment regulated by Chapter 54.

A.60.1.6.1 See Annex D for a model Hazardous Materials Management Plan (HMMP).

A.60.1.7 See Annex D for a model Hazardous Materials Inventory Statement (HMIS).

A.60.3.1 The categorization and classification of hazardous materials enables the code user to determine the applicability of requirements based on hazard category and class related to the physical and health hazards of materials. The current definitions found in Chapter 3 have been developed using a compilation of criteria found in NFPA codes and standards, requirements of the U.S. Department of Transportation, and in some cases definitions established by OSHA in 29 CFR. [**400**: A.4.1]

A system known as Globally Harmonized System of Classification and Labeling of Chemicals (GHS) has been developed based on standards for classification published by the United Nations (UN) Subcommittee of Experts on the GHS. The United States continues its efforts to incorporate the GHS in its federal regulatory scheme. OSHA plans to issue a final rule to harmonize its Hazard Communication Standard (29 CFR 1910.1200) with the GHS in August 2011. [**400**: A.4.1]

It is anticipated by the Committee that over time, the GHS will be reviewed for applicability and possible integration into the regulatory scheme developed in NFPA 400 for hazardous materials storage, handling, and use. The evolution of this system of classification will be facilitated by the changes associated with classification, labeling, and Safety Data Sheets. It is not anticipated that the GHS will be fully implemented immediately within NFPA 400, recognizing the historical basis that exists for some of the classifications of materials, such as flammable and combustible liquids. [**400**: A.4.1]

A.60.3.4 Where a conflict exists between applicable requirements, an analysis should be made and the proper applicable requirement should be implemented or conformed to subject to the approval of the AHJ. [**400**: A.4.4]

A.60.3.5 The safe handling, collection, and disposal of hazardous waste can be accomplished only if the physical, chemical, and hazardous properties of its components are known and that information is properly applied. The categorization of a material as waste is normally under the purview of the user. In some cases the waste might be contaminated or "off spec" material, or material where the concentration of the hazardous components has been diluted. In other cases the waste might consist of cleaning materials that have become contaminated with a hazardous material. [**400**: A.4.5]

The classifiers of waste are cautioned that the classification of hazardous waste under the requirements of the Environmental Protection Agency (EPA) or Department of Transportation (DOT) for labeling required for shipping purposes might not correspond to the system of classification incorporated into 60.3.1. In addition, some judgment is needed to apply the *Code* in circumstances where the waste material is not in a form that is normally encountered when the hazardous material employed is in its virgin state. For example, a material that might not have been hazardous in its pure form might become hazardous when it becomes contaminated as use occurs. A tank of water used for rinsing parts on a plating line will eventually become contaminated by the materials that are being rinsed from parts as they travel through the line. If the concentration of the material being rinsed from parts becomes high enough, the content of hazardous materials in the rinse tank might be present in a concentration sufficient enough to cause the waste rinse water to be classified as hazardous. See Section B.5 of NFPA 400 for examples on the classification of dilute solutions of common corrosive materials. In many cases the waste material could be a mixture of materials that must be classified in accordance with the requirements of 60.3.3. [**400**: A.4.5]

A.60.4.1 Section 60.4 introduces the concepts of control areas and maximum allowable quantities (MAQ). The purpose is to permit limited amounts of hazardous contents in occupancies having minimum controls without triggering the more restrictive Protection Level 1 through Protection Level 4 building requirements. The maximum allowable quantities in Table 60.4.2.1.1.3, Table 60.4.2.1.2 through Table 60.4.2.1.8, and Table 60.4.2.1.10.1 are based on demonstrated need and historical safe storage and use of hazardous contents. Subsection 60.4.3, however, establishes additional controls for occupancies exceeding the hazardous contents limits prescribed for control areas. [**400**: A.5.1]

All of the hazardous materials within the scope of 1.1.1 of NFPA 400 are high hazard contents, see 60.3.2.1.1. However, not all of the hazardous materials categories are placed into High Hazard Levels 1–4 requiring Protection Levels 1–4 are considered to be high hazard contents and some of these materials have been recognized as being of low or ordinary hazards, depending on their nature in a fire. In some cases, Class 1 unstable (reactive) materials, Class 1 water-reactive materials, and Class IV and Class V organic peroxides, do not have a maximum allowable quantity (MAQ) and, therefore, are not required to comply with the requirements for Protection Level 1 through Protection Level 4. Figure A.60.4.1 helps to illustrate the conditions under which the protection level requirements are applicable. [**400**: A.5.1]

A.60.5.1.1.1 Outdoor control areas are not classified with protection levels. [**400**: A.6.1.1.1]

A.60.5.1.1.2 Outdoor control areas are not classified with protection levels. [**400**: A.6.1.1.2]

A.60.5.1.2 *Readily available* can mean access to the product manufacturer's or user's paper or electronic copies of MSDSs. [**400**: A.6.1.2]

A.60.5.1.3.4 There might be additional regulations that must be complied with to notify other agencies. [**400**: A.6.1.3.4]

A.60.5.1.4 The hazard potential of a facility is not dependent on any single factor. Physical size, number of employees, and the quantity and the nature of the hazardous materials are important considerations. The level of training can vary with the complexity of the facility under consideration. [**400**: A.6.1.4]

A.60.5.1.4.4 Emergency responders can include on-site personnel that have been designated and trained to respond to emergencies, persons from the public sector such as fire department personnel, or persons from the private sector that can be contracted or otherwise engaged to perform emergency response duties. *(See Annex I of NFPA 400.)* [**400**: A.6.1.4.4]

A.60.5.1.4.4.1 OSHA describes an Incident Command System as a standardized on-scene incident management concept designed specifically to allow responders to adopt an inte-

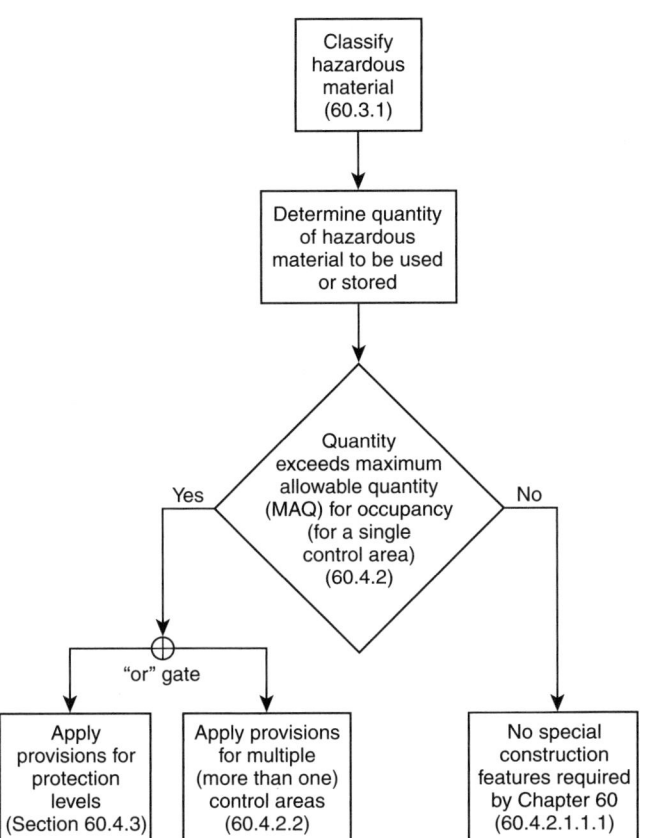

FIGURE A.60.4.1 Application of Chapter 60 Requirements for Hazardous Materials. [400:Figure A.5.1]

grated organizational structure equal to the complexity and demands of any single incident or multiple incidents without being hindered by jurisdictional boundaries. [**400:** A.6.1.4.4.1]

A.60.5.1.4.4.2 Responses to releases of hazardous materials where there is no potential safety or health hazard such as fire, explosion, or chemical exposure are not considered emergency responses as defined within the context of this *Code*. [**400:** A.6.1.4.4.2]

A.60.5.1.4.4.3 Emergency response training will vary depending on the level of emergency response required and by the requirements of the governmental agency. [**400:** A.6.1.4.4.3]

A.60.5.1.5.3.1 The approved powered industrial trucks addressed in NFPA 505, *Fire Safety Standard for Powered Industrial Trucks Including Type Designations, Areas of Use, Conversions, Maintenance, and Operations*, are trucks that are listed by a testing laboratory for the use intended and should be tested and labeled in accordance with ANSI/UL 558, *Standard for Safety Industrial Trucks, Internal Combustion Engine-Powered*, or ANSI/UL 583, *Standard for Safety Electric Battery-Powered Industrial Trucks*. [**505:**1.3.3]

A.60.5.1.14 For seismic requirements and the seismic zone in which the material is located, see the building code. [**400:** A.6.1.14]

A.60.5.1.16.1 Maintenance procedures are an important part of any mechanical integrity program. They should contain information on which equipment is covered; what tests and inspections are to be performed; how to perform the tests and inspections in accordance with recognized industry standards and manufacturer's recommendations; what constitutes acceptance of the measured parameters; corrective actions to be taken if the equipment does not meet requirements; and the frequency of the testing and inspection. For examples of additional guidance, refer to *Guidelines for Mechanical Integrity Systems* (AIChE/CCPS); *Guidelines for Safe and Reliable Instrumented Protective Systems* (AIChE/CCPS); and *Guidelines for Writing Effective Operating and Maintenance Procedures* (AIChE/CCPS). [**400:** A.6.1.16.1]

A.60.5.1.16.2.3 Testing can include visual inspection, x-ray, spark testing, pressure testing, leak testing, or other nondestructive methods. [**400:** A.6.1.16.2.3]

A.61.1.1.1 Chapter 61 provides minimum acceptable requirements for fire prevention and protection in facilities that manufacture and store aerosol products and in mercantile occupancies where aerosol products are displayed and sold. As explained in A.5.1 of NFPA 30B, the hazards presented by each stage of the manufacturing process will vary, depending on the flammability of the base product and on the flammability of the propellant. Considerable judgment will be required of the designer and of the AHJ to provide an adequate level of fire protection. *(See also Annex B of NFPA 30B, Mechanism of Fire Growth in Aerosol Containers.)* [**30B:** A.1.2]

A.61.1.1.3 See NFPA 58, *Liquefied Petroleum Gas Code*. [**30B:** A.1.1.2]

A.61.1.1.5 Chapter 61 does not apply to products that can be dispensed as aerosolized sprays that are not packaged in aerosol containers as defined in 3.3.2 of NFPA 30B. Chapter 61 is not applicable to other applications such as industrial spray adhesives that are dispensed from large [5–125 gal (18.9 L–475 L)] pressurized gas cylinders. There is no assurance that the protection specified in Chapter 61 will be adequate. [**30B:** A.1.1.4]

A.61.1.3 Tests have shown that aerosol products in plastic containers with a heat of combustion of 10.5 kJ/g have been adequately protected as determined by fire tests. See Annex C of NFPA 30B for a description of the testing of aerosol products in plastic containers. [**30B:** A.1.7]

A.61.1.4.1(3) Fire testing with alcohol and water at this percentage in plastic bottles has been successful. Small-scale burn tests of aerosol products in plastic containers have shown the aerosol with a nonflammable propellant to behave the same as the aerosol with no propellant. [**30B:** A.1.8.1(3)]

A.61.1.4.1(4) A fire test with a formula of this type using liquefied petroleum gas was successful. An emulsion, in an aerosol product, would be a mixture of two or more liquids in which one is present as droplets, of microscopic or ultramicroscopic size, distributed throughout the other. Emulsions are formed from the component liquids either spontaneously or, more often, by mechanical means, such as agitation, provided that the liquids that are mixed have no (or a very limited) mutual solubility. Emulsions are stabilized by agents that form films at the surface of the droplets (e.g., soap molecules) or that impart to them a mechanical stability (e.g., colloidal carbon or bentonite). Colloidal distributions or suspension of one or more liquid(s) with another will have a shelf life that varies with the efficiency of the recipe used. [**30B:** A.1.8.1(4)]

A.61.3.1.3 At the present time there have been no fire-retardant packaging systems tested that have demonstrated substantial mitigation of the fire hazards presented by aerosol products. [**30B:** A.6.1.3]

A.61.3.2 Fire tests and fire experience show that Level 1 aerosol products present relatively the same fire hazards as Class III commodities, as these are defined and described in NFPA 13. In some cases, the AHJ or applicable fire or building regulations might require storage of such materials to be protected from fire. If fire protection is by means of automatic sprinklers, then the requirements of NFPA 13 should be used as a design basis. [**30B:** A.6.2]

A.61.3.4.2.2 Fire testing has not been performed on encapsulated pallets of cartoned aerosol products; however, this type of protection should be appropriate for this condition, based on testing of uncartoned aerosol products. [**30B:** A.6.3.2.2]

A.61.3.4.2.9.5 In-rack sprinklers have proven to be the most effective way to fight fires in rack storage. To accomplish this, however, in-rack sprinklers must be located where they will operate early in a fire as well as direct water where it will do the most good. Simply maintaining a minimum horizontal spacing between sprinklers does not achieve this goal, because fires in rack storage develop and grow in transverse and longitudinal flues, and in-rack sprinklers do not operate until flames actually impinge on them. To ensure early operation and effective discharge, in-rack sprinklers in the longitudinal flue of open-frame racks must be located at transverse flue intersections. The commodity loads shown in Figure 6.3.2.7(a) through Figure 6.3.2.7(e) of NFPA 30B are typically 1.2 m (4 ft) cubes. Accounting for flue spaces and vertical clear space between loads, this puts the in-rack sprinklers shown in the figures approximately 1.4 m (4.5 ft) apart horizontally when they are between each load and approximately 2.7 m (9 ft) apart horizontally when they are spaced at every other load. If the length or width of loads exceeds 1.2 m (4 ft), in-rack sprinklers should still be positioned at flue intersections, but additional sprinklers may be necessary between the loads. [**30B:** A.6.3.9.2.5]

A.61.5.3.3 See NFPA 51B, *Standard for Fire Prevention During Welding, Cutting, and Other Hot Work*, for further information. [**30B:** A.8.3.3]

A.61.5.7 See NFPA 77, *Recommended Practice on Static Electricity*, for further information. [**30B:** A.8.7]

A.63.1.1.1 See A.1.3.2.

A.63.1.1.4(1) For regulations on the transportation of gases, see 49 CFR 100–185 (Transportation) and *Transportation of Dangerous Goods Regulations*. [**55:** A.1.1.2(1)]

A.63.1.1.4(3) Bulk compressed gas and cryogenic fluid system installations are intended to be covered by the requirements of this *Code*. Instrumentation and alarms that are attendant to the system and designed to interface with the application in the health care facility are to be retained within the purview of NFPA 99, *Health Care Facilities Code*. [**55:** A.1.1.2(3)]

Refer to Section 63.11 for requirements for liquid oxygen (LOX) in home health care.

A.63.1.1.4(5) For information, see NFPA 52, *Vehicular Gaseous Fuel Systems Code*, or NFPA 58, *Liquefied Petroleum Gas Code*. [**55:** A.1.1.2(5)]

A.63.1.1.4(6) The storage and use of compressed gases outside the boundaries of laboratory work areas are covered by NFPA 55. [**55:** A.1.1.2(6)]

A.63.1.1.4(11) NFPA 55 is used as the source document for the fundamental requirements for compressed hydrogen gas (GH2), or liquefied hydrogen gas (LH2) system installations. Correlation between NFPA 55 and NFPA 2, *Hydrogen Technologies Code*, is the responsibility of the two technical committees involved. The installation requirements for bulk GH2 or LH2 are viewed as fundamental provisions. On the other hand, use-specific requirements for designated applications such as vehicular fueling are not resident in NFPA 55 and are under the purview of the NFPA 2 Technical Committee. Where there are specific provisions or controls included in NFPA 55, the specific controls of NFPA 55 will govern except that modifications made to provisions that have been extracted can be followed when the modifications have been made within NFPA's extract procedure as indicated in the *Manual of Style for NFPA Technical Committee Documents*. [**55:** A.1.1.2(11)]

A.63.1.3.40 Normal Temperature and Pressure (NTP). There are different definitions of normal conditions. The normal conditions defined here are the ones most commonly used in the compressed gas and cryogenic fluid industry. [**55:** A.3.3.76]

A.63.2.7 Electrical and electronic equipment and wiring for use in hazardous locations as defined in Article 500 of NFPA 70, *National Electrical Code*, should meet the requirements of Articles 500 and 501 of *NFPA 70*. Note that Article 505 also details requirements for this equipment and wiring in hazardous locations and uses a zone classification method rather than the division method of Article 500. [**55:** A.6.7]

A.63.2.8 Under the requirements of 29 CFR 1910.38 established by OSHA regulations, employers must establish an employee alarm system that complies with 29 CFR 1910.165. The requirements of 29 CFR 1910.165 for the employee alarm system include, but are not limited to, systems that are capable of being perceived above ambient noise or light levels by all employees in the affected portions of the workplace. Tactile devices may be used to alert those employees who would not otherwise be able to recognize the audible or visual alarm. The alarm system can be electrically powered or powered by pneumatic or other means. State, local, or other governmental regulations might also establish requirements for employee alarm systems. [**55:** A.6.8]

A.63.2.10 The intent of this section is to require a water-based fire extinguishing system to keep vessels containing compressed gases cool in the event of an exposure fire, thereby minimizing the likelihood of a release and associated consequences. Accordingly, alternative fire extinguishing systems, such as dry-chemical or gaseous agent systems, should not be substituted. [**55:** A.6.10]

A.63.2.19 Figure A.63.2.19 shows three possible locations of the source valve. [**55:** A.6.19]

A.63.3.1.3 For information on insulated nitrous oxide systems, see CGA G-8.1, *Standard for Nitrous Oxide Systems at Consumer Sites*. [**55:** A.7.1.3]

A.63.3.1.4 The compressed gas system equipment referenced is intended to include fuel cell applications, generation of hydrogen from portable or transportable hydrogen generation equipment, batteries, and similar devices and equipment that utilize hydrogen for the purpose of power generation. It does not include hydrogen production facilities intended to produce hydrogen used for distribution or repackaging operations operated by gas producers, distributors, and repackagers. [**55:** A.7.1.4]

ANNEX A

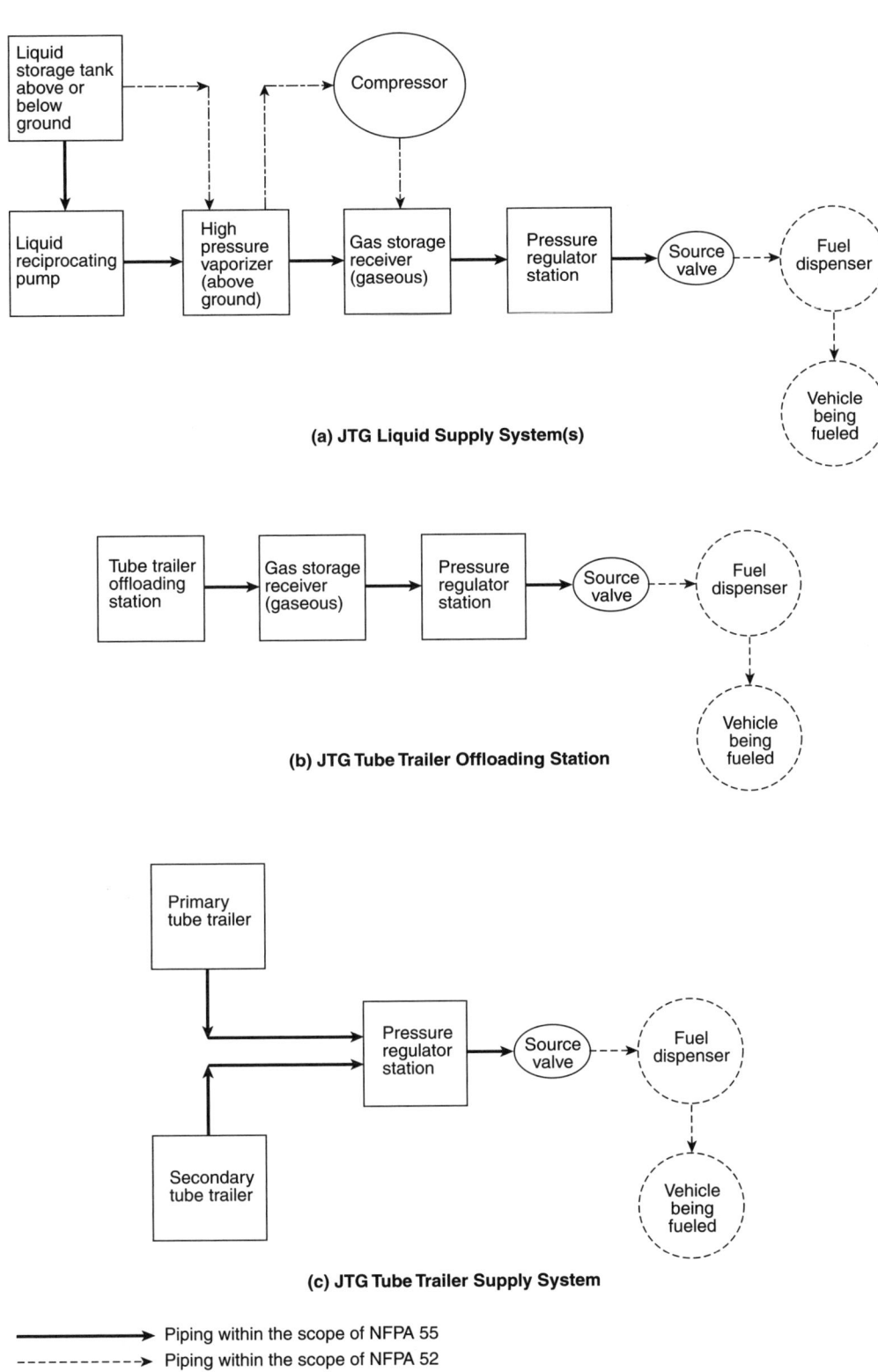

FIGURE A.63.2.19 Three Examples of Source Valve Locations. [55: Figure A.6.19]

A.63.3.1.5 Numerous metal hydrides are currently being tested for gaseous hydrogen storage applications. While certain Class D extinguishing agents have been effective on some metal hydride materials, they have not been tested on the wide range of hydrides. It is crucial to understand any adverse chemical reactions between the hydride and the agent prior to using the fire suppressant. Additionally, it is important to understand that the application should be limited to small incipient stage fires. Larger fires would require the use of personal protective equipment in the application of the extinguishing agent. [55: A.7.1.5]

A.63.3.1.9.2 The goal of this requirement is to prevent unauthorized personnel or those unfamiliar with gas storage systems from tampering with the equipment as well as to prevent the inadvertent or unauthorized removal or use of compressed gases from storage areas. Where the compressed gases are located in an area open to the general public, a common practice is to fence and lock the storage or use area, with access restricted to supplier and user personnel. When the storage or use area is located within the user's secure area and is not accessible by the general public, it is not always necessary to fence or otherwise secure the individual gas storage or use areas. Personnel access patterns may still mandate that the system be fenced, as determined by the supplier and the user. [55: A.7.1.9.2]

A.63.3.1.11.2 Figure A.63.3.1.11.2 is a schematic showing the separation distances required by 63.3.1.11.2. [55: A.7.1.11.2]

A.63.3.1.11.3 Clearance is required from combustible materials to minimize the effects of exposure fires to the materials stored or used. The requirement to separate the materials from vegetation should not be interpreted to mean that the area is maintained free of all vegetation. In some settings, gas systems are located on grounds that are maintained with formal landscaping. Some judgment must be exercised to determine whether the vegetation poses what might be viewed as an exposure hazard to the materials stored. Cut lawns, formal landscaping, and similar vegetation do not ordinarily present a hazard and should be allowed. On the other hand, tall, dry grass or weeds and vegetation that fringes on the border of an urban–wildland interface might be viewed as a hazard. [55: A.7.1.11.3]

A.63.3.1.11.10.1 Electrical devices can include pressure transducers, signal transmitters, shutoff controls, and similar devices. Some of these devices may be nonincendive and suitable for use in hazardous areas. Flammability of gases is not the only concern with respect to electrical circuits, because piping serving systems in use can act as conductors of electrical energy, exposing unrelated portions of the system to electrical hazards if improperly installed. [55: A.7.1.11.10.1]

A.63.3.1.15.3 The gas supplier should be consulted for advice under these circumstances. [55: A.7.1.15.3]

A.63.3.1.18.1.2 Underground piping systems are those systems that are buried and in contact with earth fill or similar materials. Piping located in open-top or grated-top trenches is not considered to be underground although it may be below grade. [55: A.7.1.18.1.2]

A.63.3.1.19.1.1(3) The replacement of parts in a system to repair leaks, the addition of gaskets, and similar routine maintenance is not intended to establish the need for cleaning of the entire piping system. Conversely, when a piping system is extended, or when the system needs to be rendered safe for maintenance purposes, purging the system before disassembly will likely be required as will internal cleaning if new piping or materials of construction are introduced. [55: A.7.1.19.1.1(3)]

A.63.3.1.19.1.1(4) Cleaning and purging of piping systems can be conducted as individual functions, i.e., just cleaning or just purging, or in combination as required to satisfy the requirements of the procedures. [55: A.7.1.19.1.1(4)]

A.63.3.1.19.1.3 It is not intended that a new written procedure be required each time the activity occurs within a facility. [55: A.7.1.19.1.3]

A.63.3.1.19.1.3.1 The review of the written procedures should not be performed solely by the same person or persons responsible for developing the procedures. It can be performed by an independent person or group within the company or department or by a third-party consultant. [55: A.7.1.19.1.3.1]

A.63.3.1.19.1.5.3 The notification is given to warn personnel that such procedures are about to occur so that they will be out of zones potentially affected by the cleaning or purging procedure. The intended notification is to be commensurate with the operation to be conducted and the timing of the notification should be relevant to the activity conducted so that personnel in the area can respond in a timely manner. Notification could consist of sounding of an audible and/or visible alarm, or it could consist of an announcement over a public address system, private network, radio, or similar and reliable means of electronic transmission. [55: A.7.1.19.1.5.3]

Verbal notification can be used in operations where the piping system is limited to the area occupied by those that will

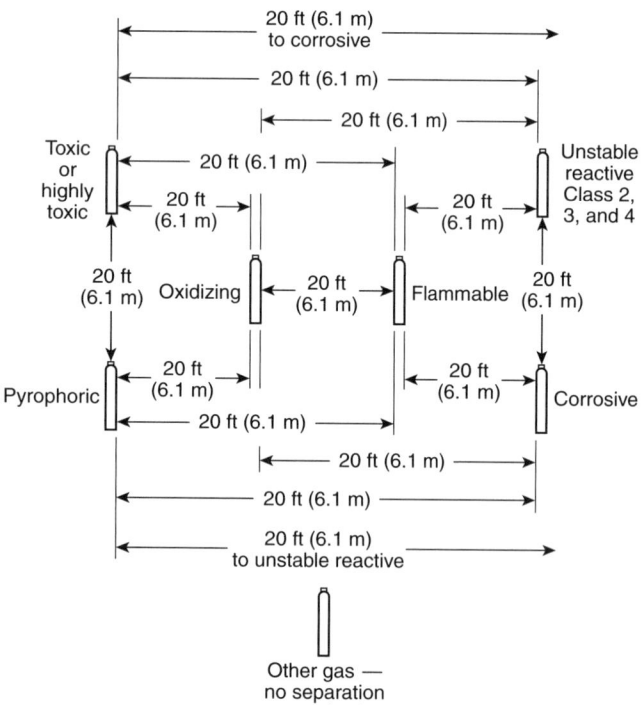

FIGURE A.63.3.1.11.2 Separation of Gas Cylinders by Hazard. [55:Figure A.7.1.11.2]

be conducting the cleaning or purging procedures and related operating personnel. These areas are frequently found in occupancies where the gas used to charge the piping system is supplied from portable containers, as well as those areas where the piping system is primarily located in the occupied work area. [55: A.7.1.19.1.5.3]

A.63.3.1.19.2 For additional information on cleaning techniques used for stainless steel parts and equipment, see ASTM A380, *Standard Practice for Cleaning, Descaling, and Passivation of Stainless Steel Parts, Equipment, and Systems*. [55: A.7.1.19.2]

A.63.3.1.19.2.2 During construction, visual inspection should be performed on sections of pipe as the piping system is assembled to ensure that no gross contamination is left in the pipe. When the standard of cleanliness is high, fabrication techniques should be utilized that do not introduce contamination into the pipe. Examples of these techniques can include, but are not limited to, constant inert gas purging, or assembly in a particulate controlled environment. The use of piping and components with a high quality interior surface finish, and materials of construction all have an effect on the ability to maintain a high degree of cleanliness. Cleaning after construction can typically be accomplished by applying one or more of the following methods:

(1) pigging
(2) mechanical scraping
(3) high velocity gas flow
(4) liquid washing
(5) use of cleaning media
(6) application of high vacuum
(7) solvent cleaning
(8) water washing
(9) steam cleaning.

[55: A.7.1.19.2.2]

A.63.3.1.19.3 Purging can be accomplished by continuous media or gas flow, evacuation or vacuum, or repeated pressurizing and venting cycles commonly referred to as pulse or cycle purging. In some cases purge procedures can involve more than one type of purging technique. Purging can be accomplished by manual or automatic means. The use of automated purge panels or manifold systems operated by a programmable logic controller is common as a means to enhance the results of a purging process where high purity gas delivery systems are employed. [55: A.7.1.19.3]

A.63.3.3.1.11.1.1 In operations where an automatic emergency shutoff valve is activated by a control system that is operated from a remote station or by remote station software, the software system should be designed to provide a visual indication of the emergency shutdown control system. The visual emergency shutdown function should be able to be identified by trained operators and recognizable to emergency response personnel. [55: A.7.3.1.11.1.1]

A.63.3.3.1.12.1 An approved means of leak detection and emergency shutoff is one way of meeting the requirements for excess flow control. [55: A.7.3.1.12.1]

A.63.3.3.1.12.1.2 When distributed systems are employed, the excess flow control system located at the bulk source may be sized to operate at a release rate greater than any single point of use or branch connection. Additional points of excess flow control may be required throughout the system in order to provide shutdown in the event of a failure in any single system branch. Such systems will generally be designed to operate when flow exceeds the capacity of the point(s) of use served. [55: A.7.3.1.12.1.2]

A.63.3.5.2.1.1 Portions of the system upstream of the source valve include the containers or bulk supply as well as control equipment designed to control the flow of gas into a piping system. The piping system downstream of the source valve is protected by excess flow control should failure occur in the piping system and is not required to be protected by the fire barrier. The fire barrier serves to protect those portions of the system that are the most vulnerable along with the necessary controls used to operate the system. [55: A.7.5.2.1.1]

A.63.3.6.2.1.1 See A.63.3.5.2.1.1. [55: A.7.6.2.1.1]

A.63.3.7.2.1.1 See A.63.3.5.2.1.1. [55: A.7.7.2.1.1]

A.63.3.8.3.1.1 See A.63.3.5.2.1.1. [55: A.7.8.3.1.1]

A.63.3.9.2.2.1.1 See A.63.3.5.2.1.1. [55: A.7.9.2.2.1.1]

A.63.3.9.3.6 The areas for typical restricted flow orifices are shown in Table A.63.3.9.3.6. [55: A.7.9.3.6]

Table A.63.3.9.3.6 Typical Orifice Areas

Orifice Diameter		Area	
in.	cm	in.^{2}	cm^2
0.006	0.015	2.83×10^{-5}	1.83×10^{-4}
0.010	0.025	7.85×10^{-5}	5.06×10^{-4}
0.014	0.036	1.54×10^{-4}	9.93×10^{-4}

[55: Table A.7.9.3.6]

A.63.3.9.3.6.2 The formula has been taken from industry publications including the Scott Specialty Gases *Design and Safety Handbook*. It is based on estimated flow rates for air at 70°F (21°C) discharging to normal atmospheric pressure through an average shape and quality orifice. It can be assumed to be ±15 percent accurate. Correction factors have been built into the formula as presented in 63.3.9.3.6.2 to accommodate the use of gases other than air (e.g., use of specific gravity data). [55: A.7.9.3.6.2]

A.63.3.10.1.2.1 See A.63.3.5.2.1.1. [55: A.7.10.1.2.1]

A.63.3.10.2.2.1 See A.63.3.5.2.1.1. [55: A.7.10.2.2.1]

A.63.4.2 Pressure vessels of any type can be subject to additional regulations imposed by various states or other legal jurisdictions. Users should be aware that compliance with DOT or ASME requirements might not satisfy all the required regulations for the location in which the vessel is to be installed or used. [55: A.8.2]

A.63.4.2.3.3 Vaporizers or heat exchangers used to vaporize cryogenic fluids can accumulate a large load of ice during operation. Additional requirements to be considered in the design include snow load for the area where the installation is located as well as the requirements for seismic conditions. The operating conditions of systems vary, and the designer has a responsibility to consider all the loads that might be imposed. Foundations that could be used to support delivery vehicles as well might require special consideration relevant to live loads as well as for the dead loads imposed by the equipment itself. [55: A.8.2.3.3]

A.63.4.2.4.5.1 Pressure relief valves typically are spring-loaded valves where the relief pressure is set by adjustment of a spring. Valves should be made to be tamper resistant in order to prevent adjustment by other than authorized personnel typically found at a retest facility. An ASME pressure relief valve is designed to comply with the requirements of the ASME *Boiler and Pressure Vessel Code* and typically is equipped with a wire and lead seal to resist tampering. [**55:** A.8.2.4.5.1]

A.63.4.4.1.1.2 An example of this identification is 360 degree wraparound tape. [**55:** A.8.4.1.1.2]

A.63.4.6.2 The purpose of this requirement is to prevent unauthorized personnel or those unfamiliar with cryogenic storage systems from tampering with the equipment. Where the bulk storage system is located in an area open to the general public, a common practice is to fence the system and lock it, with access restricted to supplier personnel and sometimes user personnel. When the bulk storage system is located within the user's secure area and is not open to the general public, it is not always necessary to fence the bulk storage system. Personnel access patterns may still mandate that the system be fenced, as determined by the supplier and the user. [**55:** A.8.6.2]

A.63.4.7.2 It is not uncommon to have inert cryogenic fluids used to provide stage effects for theatrical performances that are conducted within assembly occupancies. The fluids are sometimes placed within these occupancies with special controls, including ventilation systems, fire detection systems, monitors for oxygen deficiency, warning signs, and remote fill indicating devices that indicate tank volume when a remote filling point is provided and stationary tanks are involved. Such installations are normally permitted on a case-by-case basis under the requirements of Section 1.5 of NFPA 55. [**55:** A.8.7.2]

Clearance is required from combustible materials to minimize the effects of exposure fires to the materials stored or used. The requirement to separate the materials from vegetation should not be interpreted to mean that the area is maintained free of all vegetation. In some settings, gas systems are located on grounds that are maintained with formal landscaping. Some judgment must be exercised to determine whether the vegetation poses what might be viewed as an exposure hazard to the materials stored. Cut lawns, formal landscaping, and similar vegetation do not ordinarily present a hazard, and should be allowed. On the other hand, tall, dry grass or weeds and vegetation that fringes on the border of an urban–wildland interface might be viewed as a hazard. [**55:** A.8.7.2]

A.63.4.7.2.1.4.1 See Figure A.63.4.13.2.7.2.1, which addresses bulk cryogenic systems located in a courtyard. This figure also applies to the case where any or all of the three walls are constructed as fire barrier walls. [**55:** A.8.7.2.1.4.1]

A.63.4.13.2.5 Flood hazard areas typically are identified on either (1) the special flood hazard area shown on the flood insurance rate map or (2) the area subject to flooding during the design flood and shown on a jurisdiction's flood hazard map or otherwise legally designated. [**55:** A.8.13.2.5]

A.63.4.13.2.6.4.1 The intent of these provisions is to make certain that the cryogenic installation is not exposed to the potential of a pool fire from the release of flammable or combustible liquids. Cryogenic fluids are not diked in order that they are allowed to dissipate should leakage occur. Studies conducted by NASA (NSS 1740.16, *Safety Standard for Hydrogen and Hydrogen Systems*, 1997) show that the use of dikes around liquid hydrogen storage facilities serves to prolong ground-level flammable cloud travel and that the dispersion mechanism is enhanced by vaporization-induced turbulence. The travel of spilled or leaked cryogenic fluid to distances greater than a few feet (meters) from the source given the nature of the typical leak is considered to be implausible due to the character of cryogenic fluids and their ability to quickly absorb heat from the surrounding environment. [**55:** A.8.13.2.6.4.1]

A.63.4.13.2.7.2 The placement of stationary containers is limited with respect to exposure hazards. Table 63.4.7.2 establishes the minimum separation distance between a building and any stationary tank at 1 ft (0.3 m). Additional limitations are placed on wall openings, air intakes, and other exposures. The material-specific tables for liquid hydrogen and liquid oxygen specify increased distances according to the type of construction adjacent to the tank. A problem arises when courtyards are configured so as to interrupt the free movement of air around a tank where an asphyxiation hazard, a flammable hazard, or an oxygen-enriched environment can be created. [**55:** A.8.13.2.7.2]

Placement of stationary containers proximate to the wall of the building served is allowable providing the minimum separation distances for exposure hazards are met. When additional walls encroach on the installation to form a court, the focus of concern shifts away from the exposure hazards associated with the building itself to the hazards associated with personnel due to hazardous atmospheres that can be created due to the lack of free air movement and ventilation. [**55:** A.8.13.2.7.2]

By specifying the minimum distance between the tank and the encroaching walls that form the court, the circulation of adequate air is ensured. Placing the tank at not less than the height of two of the three encroaching walls results in creating an opening such that the angular dimension between the top of two of the three encroaching walls and the point over which the tank is placed is not greater than 45 degrees, thereby allowing the circulation of air through the space in which the tank is installed. [**55:** A.8.13.2.7.2]

A.63.4.13.2.7.2.1 The separation distances shown in Figure A.63.4.13.2.7.2.1 are required to provide for ventilation in the space in order to avoid creating a confined space. Chapter 8 of NFPA 55 is a generic chapter used to establish minimum requirements for all cryogens. Material-specific requirements for oxygen, hydrogen, or other gases might require greater separation distances based on the type of construction or the related exposure. For example, wall number 3 shown in Figure A.63.4.13.2.7.2.1 could be an exterior building wall, and the gas could be hydrogen. Refer to Table 63.4.7.2 of this *Code*, and Table 9.3.2 and Table 11.3.2.2 of NFPA 55 for specific details regarding building walls, wall openings, air intakes, and similar conditions. [**55:** A.8.13.2.7.2.1]

A.63.4.14.1.3.2 CGA P-18, *Standard for Bulk Inert Gas Systems at Consumer Sites*, recommends periodic inspection intervals for inert gas systems. [**55:** A.8.14.1.3.1.1]

A.63.4.14.11.2.3.1 In operations where an automatic emergency shutoff valve is activated by a control system that is operated from a remote station or by remote station software, the software system should be designed to provide a visual indication of the emergency shutdown control system. The visual emergency shutdown function should be able to be identified by trained operators and recognizable to emergency response personnel. [**55:** A.8.14.11.2.3.1]

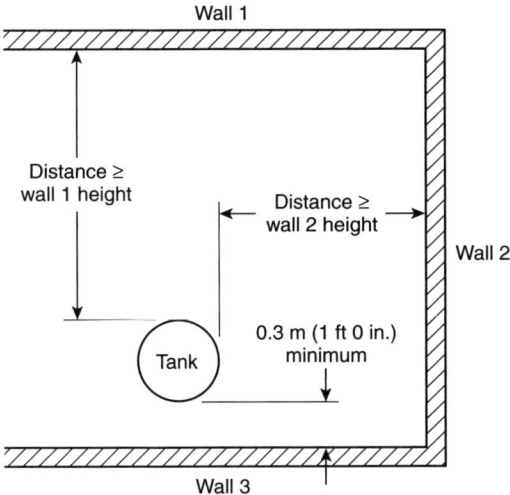

FIGURE A.63.4.13.2.7.2.1 Bulk Cryogenic System Located in a Courtyard. [55:Figure A.8.13.2.7.2.1]

A.63.4.14.11.3.4 The inert cryogens, nitrogen abd argon, do require the installation of a noncombustible spill pad, because they do not typically condense oxygen from the air in sufficient quantities to pose a hazard during transfer. [55: A.8.14.11.3.4]

A.63.4.14.11.3.4.1 The noncombustible spill pad is provided for liquid helium transfer operations, because the cryogen is at a temperature that is sufficiently low enough to liquefy oxygen, presenting a hazard when in contact with combustible surfaces. [55: A.8.14.11.3.4.1]

A.63.11.3.1 The seller has a responsibility to provide written instructions to the user in accordance with 63.11.2. In fulfilling this responsibility the seller should explain to the user the use of the equipment being delivered and precautions that are to be taken. The seller's written instructions are intended to make the user aware of the hazards of the material and to provide recommendations that will address the location, restraint, movement, and refill of ambulatory containers when these containers are to be refilled by the user. However, the user has the responsibility to receive, read, and understand the written material regarding storage and use of liquid oxygen and the containers and equipment that is furnished by the seller. In addition to specific information or instructions provided by the seller or equipment manufacturer regarding the storage or use of the equipment and of the liquid oxygen or the containers used, the user remains responsible to see that the containers are used or maintained in accordance with the seller's instructions to ensure that they are as follows:

(1) Located and maintained in accordance with the requirements of 63.11.3.2
(2) Restrained in accordance with the requirements of 63.11.3.3
(3) Handled or transported in accordance with the requirements of 63.11.3.4
(4) When liquid oxygen ambulatory containers are to be refilled by the user, that the containers are refilled in accordance with the requirements of 63.11.3.5 and the manufacturer's instructions

A.63.11.3.3 Two points of contact can be provided by using elements of a room or furnishings in the room such as the walls of a corner of a room or a wall and a furnishing or object such as a table or a desk.

A.63.11.3.5.1.1 Drip pans or similar containment devices are used in order to protect against liquid oxygen spillage from coming into contact with combustible surfaces, including asphalt thereby elevating the potential for ignition.

A.63.11.3.5.3 Oxygen is not a flammable gas, and ignition of the gas itself is not the primary hazard. When oxygen is present in concentrations that exceed normal ambient concentrations of approximately 21 percent (by volume), ordinary combustible materials can be ignited more easily, and when combustion occurs, the combustion is more vigorous. As a general rule, the higher the concentration of oxygen present, the more likely ignition of ordinary combustibles will occur if ignition sources are present, and the more rapid the combustion process. Fire prevention codes frequently contain general statements cautioning against the use of open flames, and warnings are designed to prevent a hazardous condition caused by ignition sources. On the other hand, these codes assume that the normal ambient atmosphere is present, and they do not typically warn of the hazards of an oxygen-enriched atmosphere, which represents a condition out of the ordinary.

A.63.11.5.1 A sign prohibiting smoking in areas where oxygen is used may be provided by the seller. However, the posting of the sign within the user's premises and observing the prohibitions and precautionary information printed on the sign remains the responsibility of the user.

A.66.1.1 See A.1.3.2.

A.66.1.3(1) Liquids that are solid at 100°F (37.8°C) or above, but are handled, used, or stored at temperatures above their flash points, should be reviewed against pertinent sections of this *Code*. [**30:** A.1.1.2(1)]

A.66.1.3(2) The information in A.66.1.3(1) also applies here. [**30:** A.1.1.2(2)]

A.66.1.3(4) Certain mixtures of flammable or combustible liquids and halogenated hydrocarbons either do not exhibit a flash point using the standard closed-cup test methods or will exhibit elevated flash points. However, if the halogenated hydrocarbon is the more volatile component, preferential evaporation of this component can result in a liquid that does have a flash point or has a flash point that is lower than the original mixture. In order to evaluate the fire hazard of such mixtures, flash point tests should be conducted after fractional evaporation of 10, 20, 40, 60, or even 90 percent of the original sample or other fractions representative of the conditions of use. For systems such as open process tanks or spills in open air, an open-cup test method might be more appropriate for estimating the fire hazard. [**30:** A.1.1.2(4)]

A.66.1.3(5) See NFPA 30B, *Code for the Manufacture and Storage of Aerosol Products*. [**30:** A.1.1.2(5)]

A.66.1.3(7) Requirements for transportation of flammable and combustible liquids can be found in NFPA 385, *Standard for Tank Vehicles for Flammable and Combustible Liquids*, and in the U.S. Department of Transportation's Hazardous Materials Regulations, Title 49, Code of Federal Regulations, Parts 100–199. [**30:** A.1.1.2(7)]

A.66.1.3(8) See NFPA 31, *Standard for the Installation of Oil-Burning Equipment.* [**30:** A.1.1.2(8)]

A.66.1.3(9) Requirements for the use and installation of alcohol-based hand rubs are covered in this *Code* and NFPA *101, Life Safety Code.* [**30:** A.1.1.2(9)]

A.66.3.3.6 See A.3.3.28.

A.66.3.3.7.1 See A.3.3.29.7.

A.66.3.3.18 See A.3.3.132.

A.66.3.3.19 Hazardous Material or Hazardous Chemical. These dangers can arise from, but are not limited to, toxicity, reactivity, instability, or corrosivity. [**30:** A.3.3.24]

A.66.3.3.26.2 See A.3.3.164.2.

A.66.3.3.27 See A.3.3.187.

A.66.3.3.29 See A.3.3.206.

A.66.3.3.32 See A.3.3.222.

A.66.3.3.33.3.1 Nonmetallic Portable Tank. Permissible nonmetallic portable tanks for shipping Class I, Class II, and Class IIIA liquids are governed by hazardous materials transportation regulations promulgated by the United Nations (UN) and the U.S. Department of Transportation (DOT). Small tanks for Class IIIB liquids are not governed by either UN or DOT hazardous materials regulations. Fiber portable tanks for Class IIIB liquids include composite designs consisting of a multi-ply corrugated box with a rigid or flexible inner plastic bladder. [**30:** A.3.3.51.4.1]

A.66.3.3.37 See A.3.3.254.15.

A.66.3.3.40 Warehouse. Warehousing operations referred to in these definitions are those operations not accessible to the public and include general-purpose, merchandise, distribution, and industrial warehouse–type operations. [**30:** A.3.3.62]

A.66.4.1.1 See A.3.3.27.

A.66.4.1.4 See A.3.3.129.

A.66.4.1.6 See A.3.3.269.

A.66.4.2 The classification of liquids is based on flash points that have been corrected to sea level, in accordance with the relevant ASTM test procedures. At high altitudes, the actual flash points will be significantly lower than those either observed at sea level or corrected to atmospheric pressure at sea level. Allowances could be necessary for this difference in order to appropriately assess the risk. [**30:** A.4.3]

Table A.66.4.2 presents a comparison of the definitions and classification of flammable and combustible liquids, as set forth in Chapter 66 of this *Code*, with similar definitions and classification systems used by other regulatory bodies. [**30:** A.4.3]

The Hazardous Materials Regulations of the U.S. Department of Transportation (DOT), as set forth in the 49 CFR 173.120(b)(2) and 173.150(f), provide an exception whereby a flammable liquid that has a flash point between 37.8°C (100°F) and 60.5°C (141°F) and does not also meet the definition of any other DOT hazard class can be reclassified as a combustible liquid [i.e., one having a flash point above 60.5°C (141°F)] for shipment by road or rail within the United States. [**30:** A.4.3]

A.66.6.1 These provisions might not provide adequate protection for all operations involving hazardous materials or chemical reactions, nor do they consider health hazards resulting from exposure to such materials. [**30:** A.6.1]

A.66.6.3 The evaluation for management of fire hazards should consider probability of an ignitible mixture, the presence of a credible ignition source, and consequences of an ignition. Where the risk is unacceptable to the AHJ, explosion protection in accordance with NFPA 69, *Standard on Explosion Prevention Systems,* or deflagration venting in accordance with NFPA 68, *Standard on Explosion Protection by Deflagration Venting,* or a combination of the two should be provided. See also *Guidelines for Chemical Process Quantitative Risk Analysis,* 2nd edition, from the Center for Chemical Process Safety/American Institute of Chemical Engineers. [**30:** A.6.3]

A.66.6.4.1.1 The wide range in size, design, and location of liquid-processing facilities precludes the inclusion of detailed fire and hazard prevention and control systems and methods applicable to all such facilities. The user should seek further guidance from documents such as NFPA 551, *Guide for the Evaluation of Fire Risk Assessments.* [**30:** A.6.4.1.1]

A.66.6.4.1.2 Storage, processing, handling, and use of Class II and Class III liquids at temperatures above the flash point can produce ignitible vapors if the liquid is released or vessels are vented. Class I liquid requirements address such events to minimize the likelihood of ignition and the consequences if ignition occurs, thus becoming a benchmark for design features when Class II and III liquids are handled above the flash point. However, their characteristics differ from those of Class I liquids. For example, the extent of travel of the Class II and III vapors is limited by the quick condensation of released vapors as they cool to lower temperatures. This might justify a more limited electrical area classification, different ventilation, elimination of explosion venting, and so forth. In addition, the process handling these Class II and III heated liquids may incorporate safety design features that accomplish the intent of NFPA 30, that is to address the hazards of released vapors. Further, the more restrictive building construction requirements in Table 17.6.1 of NFPA 30 might not be necessary for a particular process involving Class II, and III liquids heated above the flash point. The option of conducting an engineering evaluation in accordance with Section 66.6 was included to allow the use of alternative designs to address the level of hazards identified. [**30:** A.6.4.1.2]

A.66.6.5.1(8) With respect to frictional heat or sparks, it is recognized that there is a need to control sources of ignition, including mechanical sparks from hand tools, that have sufficient energy to ignite flammable vapors. Studies, anecdotes, codes, and referenced standards (e.g., API 2214, *Spark Ignition Properties of Hand Tools*) show that there is a potential for hand tool sparks to ignite flammable vapors from a limited number of chemicals and under certain unique conditions. These include flammable liquids with low minimum ignition energies, operations in which flammable or combustible liquids are heated, and atypical spark generation that can occur between specific types of hand tools and struck surfaces (i.e., thermite reactions or impact of steel tools on quartzitic materials). Even spark-resistant tools might not provide suitable protection against ignition. For example, hard metal particles can become imbedded in the relatively soft metal of spark-resistant tools, and these particles can cause sparks when the tools are used. [**30:** A.6.5.1(8)]

NFPA 30 requires analyses, such as job safety analyses or activity hazard analyses, of the hazards and risks of a given task

Table A.66.4.2 Comparative Classification of Liquids

Agency	Agency Classification	Agency Flash Point		NFPA Definition	NFPA Classification	NFPA Flash Point	
		°F	°C			°F	°C
ANSI Z129.1	Flammable	<141	<60.5	Flammable	Class I	<100	<37.8
				Combustible	Class II	≥100 to <140	≥37.8 to <60
					Class IIIA	≥140 to <200	≥60 to <93
	Combustible	≥141 to <200	≥60.5 to <93	Combustible	Class IIIA	≥140 to <200 ≥	≥60 to <93
DOT	Flammable	<141	<60.5	Flammable	Class I	<100	<37.8
				Combustible	Class II	≥100 to <140	≥37.8 to <60
					Class IIIA	≥140 to <200	≥60 to <93
	Combustible	≥141 to <200 ≥	≥60.5 to <93	Combustible	Class IIIA	≥140 to <200	≥60 to <93
DOT HM-181 Domestic Exemption*	Flammable	<100	<37.8	Flammable	Class I	<100	<37.8
	Combustible	≥100 to <200	≥37.8 to <93	Combustible	Class II	≥100 to <140	≥37.8 to <60
					Class IIIA	≥140 to <200	≥60 to <93
UN	Flammable	<141	<60.5	Flammable	Class I	<100	<37.8
				Combustible	Class II	≥100 to <140	≥37.8 to <60
					Class IIIA	≥140 to <200	≥60 to <93
	Combustible	≥141 to <200	≥60.5 to <93	Combustible	Class II	≥100 to <140	≥37.8 to <60
					Class IIIA	≥140 to <200	≥60 to <93
OSHA	Flammable	<100	<37.8	Flammable	Class I	<100	<37.8
	Combustible†	≥100	≥37.8	Combustible	Class II	≥100 to <140	≥37.8 to <60
					Class IIIA	≥140 to <200	≥60 to <93
					Class IIIB†	≥200	≥93

*See A.66.4.3.
†See 29 CFR 1910.106 for Class IIIB liquid exemptions. [30: Table A.4.3]

and the application of appropriate protective measures to prevent or mitigate the hazards and risks. This includes identification and mitigation of ignition risk from multiple sources, including hand tools. Due to the complexity of the numerous operations involving flammable liquids, NFPA 30 cannot address all conditions in which spark-resistant tools should be made mandatory, might be advisable, or are unnecessary to help control the ignition risk of any given operation. [30: A.6.5.1(8)]

It is recognized that the adoption of the new Globally Harmonized System for labeling by the U.S. Occupational Safety and Health Administration (29 CFR 1910.1200, Appendix C) creates a generalized mandate for the use of spark-resistant tools. However, based on available technical information, this mandate goes beyond what is considered necessary for fire safety, given the fact that it applies to liquids that present little risk of ignition unless heated to or above their flash points. *(See A.66.6.4.1.2.)* [30: A.6.5.1(8)]

A.66.6.5.3 See NFPA 51B, *Standard for Fire Prevention During Welding, Cutting, and Other Hot Work*. [30: A.6.5.3]

A.66.6.5.4 The prevention of electrostatic ignition in equipment is a complex subject. Refer to NFPA 77, *Recommended Practice on Static Electricity*, for guidance. [30: A.6.5.4]

A.66.6.6.1 One method of complying with this requirement could be through the installation of an automatic and/or manual fire alarm system as covered in *NFPA 72, National Fire Alarm and Signaling Code*. [30: A.6.6.1]

A.66.6.7.1 Other recognized fire prevention and control factors, involving construction, location, and separation, are addressed elsewhere in Section 66.6. [30: A.6.7.1]

A.66.6.7.3 Permanent connections to process water lines from the fire water system present an opportunity for contamination of the fire water with process fluids. Incidents have occurred where fire water was contaminated with flammable process liquids, with subsequent increased fire damage and, in some cases, injury. Temporary connections are permitted to meet extraordinary needs, as in turnaround and inspection periods, tank cleaning, and so forth. However, care should be taken to address the potential for contamination. Where such use occurs frequently enough to justify a more robust arrangement, double block-and-bleed valves, removable spool pieces, or other means should be used to assure that no contamination can occur. Check valves alone are not sufficient. [30: A.6.7.3]

Use of utility water sources, such as boiler feedwater, that are not contaminated, is acceptable for use as a supplemental fire water supply. [30: A.6.7.3]

A.66.6.7.8 NFPA 10, *Standard for Portable Fire Extinguishers*, provides information on the suitability of various types of extinguishers. [30: A.6.7.8]

A.66.7.3.3 For additional information, see NFPA 497, *Recommended Practice for the Classification of Flammable Liquids, Gases, or Vapors and of Hazardous (Classified) Locations for Electrical Installations in Chemical Process Areas.* [**30:** A.7.3.3]

A.66.7.3.7 NFPA 496, *Standard for Purged and Pressurized Enclosures for Electrical Equipment*, provides details for these types of installations. [**30:** A.7.3.7]

A.66.9.3.9.3 Section 5.1 of NFPA 505, *Fire Safety Standard for Powered Industrial Trucks Including Type Designations, Areas of Use, Conversions, Maintenance, and Operations,* states"In locations used for the storage of flammable liquids in sealed containers or liquefied or compressed flammable gases in containers, approved power-operated industrial trucks designated as Types CNS, DS, ES, GS, LPS, GS/CNS, or GS/LPS shall be permitted to be used where approved by the AHJ." Compared to the above types, industrial trucks that are designated DY and EE have significantly less potential for igniting flammable vapors (such as might result from a spill of Class I liquid) and should be used in inside liquid storage areas where conditions warrant. [**30:** A.9.3.9.3]

A.66.9.4.1 It is not the intent of 66.9.4 to regulate containers and packaging systems for Class IIIB liquids, except as required for protected storage in accordance with Chapter 16 of NFPA 30. [**30:** A.9.4.1]

A.66.9.4.1(6) The term *rigid nonmetallic intermediate bulk container* is used to describe intermediate bulk containers that have a plastic vessel that serves as the primary liquid-holding component. This vessel can be enclosed in or encased by an outer structure consisting of a steel cage, a single-wall metal or plastic enclosure, a double wall of foamed or solid plastic, or a paperboard enclosure. These are often called *composite IBCs*, which is the term used by the U.S. Department of Transportation (DOT) to describe them. The term *rigid nonmetallic intermediate bulk container* also denotes an all-plastic single-wall IBC that might or might not have a separate plastic base and for which the containment vessel also serves as the support structure. IBCs that have an outer liquidtight metal structure are considered to be metal IBCs or metal portable tanks by DOT and are defined in 66.9.4.1(1). [**30:** A.9.4.1(6)]

A.66.9.5 The requirements in 66.9.5 are based on hazards associated with fixed flammable liquids storage cabinets. They do not address potential hazards associated with mobile storage cabinets (i.e., cabinets with integral wheels) such as the following:

(1) Increased risk of spills
(2) Potential for tipover or blockage of egress
(3) Maintenance of vent and grounding integrity
(4) Variable condition of exposed floor surfaces under the cabinet
[**30:** A.9.5]

A.66.9.5.4 Venting of storage cabinets has not been demonstrated to be necessary for fire protection purposes. Additionally, venting a cabinet could compromise the ability of the cabinet to adequately protect its contents from involvement in a fire, because cabinets are not generally tested with any venting. Therefore, venting of storage cabinets is not recommended. [**30:** A.9.5.4]

However, it is recognized that some jurisdictions might require storage cabinets to be vented and that venting can also be desirable for other reasons, such as health and safety. In such cases, the venting system should be installed so as to not affect substantially the desired performance of the cabinet during a fire. Means of accomplishing this can include thermally actuated dampers on the vent openings or sufficiently insulating the vent piping system to prevent the internal temperature of the cabinet from rising above that specified. Any make-up air to the cabinet should also be arranged in a similar manner. [**30:** A.9.5.4]

If vented, the cabinet should be vented from the bottom with make-up air supplied to the top. Also, mechanical exhaust ventilation is preferred and should comply with NFPA 91, *Standard for Exhaust Systems for Air Conveying of Vapors, Gases, Mists, and Noncombustible Particulate Solids.* Manifolding the vents of multiple storage cabinets should be avoided. [**30:** A.9.5.4]

A.66.9.5.4.2 A "safe location" should be selected as the location of a vent discharge to minimize the potential for ignitible vapors to travel to a source of ignition after discharge from the vent. Electrical equipment that does not meet the requirements for hazardous locations can serve as an ignition source. The Technical Committee advises that vent discharge locations should consider such factors as the following:

(1) Characteristics of the exhausted material (vapor density, toxicity, velocity of discharge, etc.)
(2) Proximity to potential ignition sources
(3) Building openings such as doors, windows, air intakes, and so forth
(4) Dispersion characteristics (distance to discharge within the flammable range, direction of discharge, atmospheric conditions, and the influence of building and neighboring buildings on discharged vapors)
(5) Likelihood of vapor accumulation following discharge, such as accumulation under building eaves
(6) Likelihood of sufficient discharge volume to allow an ignitible concentration to reach an ignition source
[**30:** A.9.5.4.2]

Historically, NFPA 30 has provided prescriptive guidance, often based on area classification requirements, and results have been acceptable. Closer distances should be accepted only if an analysis by a qualified person justifies closer distances. Similarly, the specified distances might not be acceptable for all installations, thus the guidance provided above. [**30:** A.9.5.4.2]

A.66.9.5.5 ANSI Z535.2.2007, *Environmental and Facility Safety Signs,* Section 9.2, was used to determine the letter height, based on a safe viewing distance of 25 ft (7.5 m). Markings can be reflective to improve visibility. See ASTM D 4956, *Standard Specification for Retroreflective Sheeting for Traffic Control,* for more information on providing reflective surfaces. If international symbols are used, they should be a minimum of 2.0 in. (50 mm) in size. [**30:** A.9.5.5]

A.66.9.8.1 The Protection Level classifications are taken from *NFPA 5000, Building Construction and Safety Code.* Protection Levels 1, 4, and 5 do not apply to the storage of flammable and combustible liquids and are therefore not extracted here. [**30:** A.9.8.1]

A.66.9.8.2 See *NFPA 5000, Building Construction and Safety Code,* for additional requirements. [**30:** A.9.8.2]

A.66.9.13 Spill containment can be accomplished by any of the following:

(1) Noncombustible, liquidtight raised sills, curbs, or ramps of suitable height at exterior openings

(2) Noncombustible, liquidtight raised sills, curbs, or ramps of suitable height, or other flow-diverting structures at interior openings
(3) Sloped floors
(4) Open-grate trenches or floor drains that are connected to a properly designed drainage system
(5) Wall scuppers that discharge to a safe location or to a properly designed drainage system
(6) Other means that are acceptable to the AHJ

[**30:** A.9.13]

Where sills, curbs, or ramps are used, the appropriate height will depend on a number of factors, including the maximum expected spill volume, the floor area, and the existence of any drainage systems. Historically, curbs and sills have been 4 in. (100 mm) high. [**30:** A.9.13]

A variety of curb, sill, and ramp heights can be used to obtain the desired containment volume. As a guide, 1 ft^2 of water at a depth of 1 in. equals 0.6 gal (1 m^2 of water @ 25 mm = 25 L). Once the total quantity of liquid containment has been established, the necessary curb, sill, or ramp height can then be calculated. [**30:** A.9.13]

Where open-grate trenches are used, the volume of the trench should be able to contain the maximum expected spill volume or otherwise be connected to a properly designed drainage system. [**30:** A.9.13]

It should be noted that these containment and drainage provisions address only fire protection concerns. Consult the appropriate environmental regulations for other restrictions that could apply. [**30:** A.9.13]

A.66.9.16.1 Release of a Class IA liquid into a room or enclosure can result in the evolution of large quantities of flammable vapor. The ignition of this flammable mixture can result in a significant pressure rise, the production of hot combustion gases, and flame. Failure to adequately design a room or building for this type of event can result in the failure of the room or building walls and/or roof and the uncontrolled release of the hot combustion gases, flames, and pressure. An acceptable method of protection against this type of event is the use of damage-limiting construction consisting of a combination of pressure-relieving construction and pressure-resistant construction as described in NFPA 68, *Standard on Explosion Protection by Deflagration Venting*. [**30:** A.9.16.1]

A.66.9.16.2 Unstable liquids can create deflagration or detonation hazards. A complete engineering review of the type of explosion event that might be produced by an unstable liquid is needed to define the necessary protection measures. Protection measures for detonations require construction features such as barricades. [**30:** A.9.16.2]

A.66.14.1 Environmental concerns have dictated special handling of hazardous materials, chemicals, and wastes. Some of these have flammable and combustible liquid characteristics, in addition to their environmental and health problems, thus causing some questions as to how they should be stored and handled. [**30:** A.14.1]

Several manufacturers have met this problem by designing and manufacturing movable, modular prefabricated storage lockers, working diligently with various building officials and AHJs. This results in a product that is intended to meet governmental standards and regulations for hazardous materials storage. Several municipalities have passed model ordinances covering the design, construction, and location of hazardous materials storage lockers. Design features can include, but are not limited to, the following:

(1) Secondary spill containment sumps
(2) Deflagration venting
(3) Ventilation requirements, including mechanical ventilation where dispensing operations are expected
(4) Electrical equipment for hazardous locations in accordance with *NFPA 70, National Electrical Code*
(5) Static electricity control
(6) Fire suppression systems (dry chemical or sprinklers)
(7) Heavy structural design for the following:
  (a) Security provisions
  (b) Doors that lock and permit pallet loading
  (c) Wind load, snow load, and storage load conditions
  (d) Anchorage provisions
  (e) Skid design, permitting relocation using lift trucks
(8) Fire-related exterior walls, if required
(9) Interior partitions to segregate incompatible materials
(10) Size limits to limit quantities that can be stored within preassembled or ready-to-assemble designs
(11) Nonsparking floors
(12) Shelving, if required
(13) Heating or cooling units, if needed
(14) Corrosion protection as required
(15) Employee safety provisions (eye/face wash)
(16) NFPA 704, *Standard System for the Identification of the Hazards of Materials for Emergency Response*, hazard symbols

[**30:** A.14.1]

Features provided are determined by specific storage requirements and needs of the owner, keeping in mind applicable regulations and ordinances that apply and the approval requirements of the AHJ. [**30:** A.14.1]

Several testing laboratories have developed internal procedures for the examination, testing, and listing or labeling of hazardous materials storage lockers submitted by manufacturers. [**30:** A.14.1]

A.66.16.1.1 See Annex E of NFPA 30 for limitations of the protection criteria of Table 16.5.2.1 through Table 16.5.2.12 of NFPA 30, particularly for intermediate bulk containers and portable tanks having capacities greater than 60 gal (230 L). [**30:** A.16.1.1]

Protected storage allowed under previous editions of NFPA 30 can be continued if the class of liquids stored, the quantity of liquids stored, fire protection, and building configuration remain unchanged. Table A.66.16.1.1(a) and Table A.66.16.1.1(b), reprinted here from the 1993 edition of NFPA 30, can be used as a reference for storage arrangements in previously approved, protected, inside liquid storage areas. [**30:** A.16.1.1]

For certain liquids such as ketones, esters, and alcohols, the minimum required densities established in the listing criteria for foam discharge devices are often higher than the general densities specified for protection of flammable and combustible liquids. When determining the design criteria for extinguishing systems using foam, it is important to ensure that the listing criteria, which are typically based on empirical data from fire tests, are not overlooked. Otherwise, the fire protection system design can be inadequate for proper protection. [**30:** A.16.1.1]

Early suppression fast-response (ESFR) sprinklers have been tested for protection of liquids only to the extent reflected in the tables in Section 16.5 of NFPA 30. Any other use of ESFR sprinklers for protection of liquids should be based on an engineering analysis that evaluates the potential failure of the sprinkler system based on a rapid-growth fire or a large pool fire that would operate more sprinklers than are accommodated by the design area. The use of ESFR protection, particularly without provisions for the control of spread of liquid, presents the possibility of a liquid pool fire that could exceed the limited design operating area of an ESFR system. [30: A.16.1.1]

The information in Table 16.5.2.1 through Table 16.5.2.12 of NFPA 30 was developed from full-scale fire tests. Where only one K-factor sprinkler is allowed, this was the only size proven to provide fire control. Where a choice of K-factors is allowed by the tables, each was able to provide fire control; however, the larger K-factor sprinklers sometimes demonstrated better fire control and further limited fire damage. Where only one response-type of sprinkler is allowed, this is the only type of sprinkler proven to provide fire control. Where a choice of response characteristics (SR or QR) is allowed by the tables, each was able to provide fire control; however, the QR sprinklers sometimes demonstrated better fire control and further limited fire damage. [30: A.16.1.1]

In the testing involving metal containers, only steel containers were tested. Other metal containers, such as aluminum, have not been tested. [30: A.16.1.1]

A.66.16.1.2 To date, there has been no full-scale testing to determine appropriate fire protection design criteria for Class IA liquids or unstable liquids. [30: A.16.1.2]

A.66.16.2.2 Table A.66.16.2.2 provides examples of commonly used metal containers that are considered either relieving style or nonrelieving style for use in developing protected storage arrangements in accordance with Table 16.5.2.1 through Table 16.5.2.12 of NFPA 30. [30: A.16.2.3]

A.66.16.2.3 Unsaturated polyester resins (UPRs) are high molecular weight unsaturated polymers dissolved in a reactive monomer, usually styrene, in concentrations of 50 percent or less by weight. UPRs are combined with reinforcements such as fiberglass and/or fillers to produce a wide range of products. Examples of such products include automobile parts, bathroom tubs and shower stalls, cultured marble, and many products for architectural, recreational, construction, and corrosion-resistant applications. UPRs are normally packaged in 55 gal (208 L) drums. The U.S. Department of Transportation classification for UPRs is "UN 1866, Resin Solution"; however, it should be noted that this classification includes many materials that are not unsaturated polyester resins. [30: A.16.2.4]

A.66.16.5.1.6.2 Most fire tests using foam-water protection schemes have been conducted with immediate foam solution discharge from the operating sprinklers. If an appreciable delay is encountered before properly proportioned foam is discharged, control of the fire might not be established. One method of accomplishing immediate foam solution discharge is by using an in-line balanced pressure (ILBP) proportioning system. [30: A.16.5.1.6.2]

A.66.16.6.1.5 The 8 ft (2.4 m) separation distance required in 66.16.6.1.5 is measured from the face of liquid storage in one rack to the face of liquid storage and/or other storage across the aisle in an adjacent rack. Rack designers, code officials, and plan reviewers are cautioned to the fact that many rack storage arrangements involve the storage of pallets that

Table A.66.16.1.1(a) Storage Arrangements for Protected Palletized or Solid Pile Storage of Liquids in Containers and Portable Tanks

Liquid Class	Storage Level	Maximum Storage Height (ft)		Maximum Quantity per Pile (gal)		Maximum Quantity* (gal)	
		Containers	Portable Tanks	Containers	Portable Tanks	Containers	Portable Tanks
IA	Ground floor	5	—	3,000	—	12,000	—
	Upper floors	5	—	2,000	—	8,000	—
	Basement	NP	NP	—	—	—	—
IB	Ground floor	6½	7	5,000	20,000	15,000	40,000
	Upper floors	6½	7	3,000	10,000	12,000	20,000
	Basement	NP	NP	—	—	—	—
IC	Ground floor	6½†	7	5,000	20,000	15,000	40,000
	Upper floors	6½†	7	3,000	10,000	12,000	20,000
	Basement	NP	NP	—	—	—	—
II	Ground floor	10	14	10,000	40,000	25,000	80,000
	Upper floors	10	14	10,000	40,000	25,000	80,000
	Basement	5	7	7,500	20,000	7,500	20,000
III	Ground floor	20	14	15,000	60,000	55,000	100,000
	Upper floors	20	14	15,000	60,000	55,000	100,000
	Basement	10	7	10,000	20,000	25,000	40,000

For SI units, 1 ft = 0.3 m; 1 gal = 3.8 L.
NP: Not permitted.
*Applies only to cut-off rooms and attached buildings.
†These height limitations can be increased to 10 ft for containers of 5 gal capacity or less. [30: Table A.16.1.1(a)]

Table A.66.16.1.1(b) Storage Arrangements for Protected Rack Storage of Liquids in Containers and Portable Tanks

Liquid Class	Type Rack	Storage Level	Maximum Storage Height of Containers (ft)	Maximum Quantity of Containers (gal)*†
IA	Double row or single row	Ground floor Upper floors Basement	25 15 NP	7,500 4,500 —
IB IC	Double row or single row	Ground floor Upper floors Basement	25 15 NP	15,000 9,000 —
II	Double row or single row	Ground floor Upper floors Basement	25 25 15	24,000 24,000 9,000
III	Multirow, double row, or single row	Ground floor Upper floors Basement	40 20 20	55,000 55,000 25,000

For SI units, 1 ft = 0.3 m; 1 gal = 3.8 L.
NP: Not permitted.
*Maximum quantity allowed on racks in cut-off rooms and attached buildings.
†Maximum quantity allowed per rack section in liquid warehouses.
[**30**: Table A.16.1.1(b)]

overhang the face of the rack. Therefore, although the structural rack members might be arranged to have an 8 ft (2.4 m) aisle between the racks, the distance between the face of the stored materials in the racks could be less than 8 ft (2.4 m) when the racks are filled with pallets. This will not be in compliance with the requirements of 66.16.6.1.5, unless the barrier and in-rack sprinkler protection is extended. [**30**: A.16.6.1.5]

A.66.16.8.2 Subsection 66.16.8 requires that control of liquid spread be provided to prevent a pool fire on the floor from spreading and opening more sprinkler heads than the design of the sprinkler system anticipates. For example, if the sprinkler system is designed to provide 0.45 gpm/ft² over 3000 ft² (18 mm/min over 280 m²), 66.16.8.2 requires that the spread of liquid also be limited to 3000 ft² (280 m²). Various means are available to achieve this control. [**30**: A.16.8.2]

Typical methods use trench or spot drains that divide the floor of the storage area into rectangles having areas equal to or less than the design area of the sprinkler system. Drains are centered under racks, and the floor is sloped toward the drain trenches with a minimum slope of 1 percent. The floor is made highest at the walls. See Figure A.66.16.8.2(a) and Figure A.66.16.8.2(b). Trenches are arranged as described in NFPA 15, *Standard for Water Spray Fixed Systems for Fire Protection*, and as shown in Figure A.66.16.8.2(c). Note particularly the dimensions of the trenches, and note that the solid covering spans one-third of the width on either side of the open grate and the open grate spans the middle third. Spot drains can be similarly arranged. Another method, shown in Figure A.66.16.8.2(d), uses spot drains located at building columns, where the area between any four columns does not exceed the design area of the sprinkler system. The floor is sloped to direct water flow to the drains. [**30**: A.16.8.2]

Connections to the drains are provided at trapped sumps, arranged as described in NFPA 15. See Figure A.66.16.8.2(e). To provide a safety factor, the drain pipes are sometimes sized to carry 150 percent of anticipated sprinkler discharge. The following equation can be used to calculate the flow of the drain pipe:

$$F = 1.5DA \quad \text{[A.66.16.8.2]}$$

where:
F = flow (gpm or L/min)
D = sprinkler design density (gpm/ft² or L/min/m²)
A = sprinkler design area (ft² or m²)
[**30**: A.16.8.2]

Additional information can be found in *Guidelines for Safe Warehousing of Chemicals*, Center for Chemical Process Safety, American Institute of Chemical Engineers. [**30**: A.16.8.2]

A.66.17.1.1 Facilities designed in accordance with Chapter 17 of NFPA 30 do not use the maximum allowable quantity and control area concepts found in the building code. [**30**: A.17.1.1]

A.66.17.4.6 Equipment operated at gauge pressures that exceed 1000 psi (6900 kPa) might require greater spacing. [**30**: A.17.4.6]

A.66.17.6.8 API 2218, *Fireproofing Practices in Petroleum and Petrochemical Processing Plants*, contains guidance on selecting and installing fire-resistant coatings to protect exposed steel supports from a high-challenge fire exposure. It also contains a general discussion on determining need for such protection and estimating the extent of the area exposed. [**30**: A.17.6.8]

A.66.17.6.10 NFPA 204, *Standard for Smoke and Heat Venting*, provides information on this subject. [**30**: A.17.6.10]

A.66.17.6.11 NFPA *101, Life Safety Code*, provides information on this subject. [**30**: A.17.6.11]

A.66.17.10.1 This might require curbs, scuppers, or special drainage systems to control the spread of fire. Annex A of NFPA 15, *Standard for Water Spray Fixed Systems for Fire Protection*, provides information on this subject. [**30**: A.17.10.1]

A.66.17.11.2 Equipment in enclosed processing areas can deteriorate over time, and periodic evaluation should be conducted to ensure that leakage rates have not increased or that the ventilation rate is adequate for any increase in leakage rates. [**30**: A.17.11.2]

A.66.17.11.7 NFPA 91, *Standard for Exhaust Systems for Air Conveying of Vapors, Gases, Mists, and Noncombustible Particulate Solids*, and NFPA 90A, *Standard for the Installation of Air-Conditioning and Ventilating Systems*, provide information on this subject. [**30**: A.17.11.7]

A.66.17.14 Where the vapor space of equipment is usually within the flammable range, the probability of explosion damage to the equipment can be limited by inerting, by providing an explosion suppression system, or by designing the equipment to contain the peak explosion pressure that can be modified by explosion relief. Where the special hazards of operation, sources of ignition, or exposures indicate a need, consideration should be given to providing protection by one or more of the above means. [**30**: A.17.14]

See NFPA 68, *Standard on Explosion Protection by Deflagration Venting*, and NFPA 69, *Standard on Explosion Prevention Systems*,

Table A.66.16.2.2 Common Relieving- and Nonrelieving-Style Metal Containers

Container Type	Relieving Style	Nonrelieving Style
≤1 qt[a]	All	N/A
>1 qt and ≤6 gal[a]	Metal containers with plastic cap, or flexible or rigid plastic spout with plastic cap	Metal containers with steel spout and steel screw cap
≤1 gal, friction lid	Metal containers with metal friction-fit covers (e.g., paint can lid)	N/A
1 gal and ≤6 gal (lug cover)	Metal containers with metal covers held in place with a mechanical friction-fit (e.g., lug-type) closure mechanism	N/A
>6 gal and ≤60 gal[b,c] (drums)	Metal containers, tight or open-head (drums) having at least one 2 in. plastic plug (Note: Cap seals, if used, need to be plastic and nonmetallic)	Open head metal containers with steel covers having no steel flange openings; or open head and tight head metal containers with steel flange openings where only steel plugs and/or cap seals are used
>60 gal and ≤793 gal	Metal portable tanks or metal intermediate bulk containers with at least one relief device conforming to the design, construction, and capacity of the container's section	N/A

For SI units, 1 gal = 3.8 L.
N/A: Not applicable.
[a]All containers ≤1 qt are considered relieving style because their failure is inconsequential.
[b]In full-scale fire tests, where containers were provided with both ¾ in. (19 mm) and 2 in. (50 mm) relieving vent openings and, in some cases, both vents were obstructed by pallet slats, rupture of containers did not occur. Because it is not possible to determine if all conceivable obstruction scenarios were represented, where drums are stacked more than one high, provide an additional ¾ in. (19 mm) or 2 in. (50 mm) pressure-relieving mechanism.
[c]The use of plastic plugs instead of steel plugs (bungs) in a steel drum in order to achieve a relieving-style container should contemplate the following issues in order to assure the safe storage of liquids:
(1) The compatibility of the plastic plug materials and gaskets with the liquids being stored.
(2) The stability and shelf life of the liquids being stored as the plastic plugs can admit water vapor, oxygen, and light.
(3) The difference in expansion coefficients for plastic plugs and steel drums for those drums subject to temperature variations and hot or cold conditions.
(4) The tooling issues involved with the use of plastic plugs as the torque levels are different from those levels used for steel plugs.
(5) The training of fill line operators in order to avoid cross-threading and/or the stripping of threads.
(6) The voiding of the United Nations (UN) rating on the steel drum by installing plastic plugs. If the user needs to install a plug other than the one originally provided by the container manufacturer, then the user should contact the manufacturer to ensure that the UN rating will still be valid. [30: Table A.16.2.3]

for additional information on various methods of mitigating losses from explosions. [30: A.17.14]

A.66.18.4.8 The process area is not intended to be a storage area for liquid containers. However, it is recognized that containers will be brought into the process area either for transfer of liquids to the process or for dispensing liquids from the process to the containers. [30: A.18.4.8]

The amount of liquid in containers in the process area should be limited as much as possible. Full containers should not be stored in the process area but can be staged there. Only the amount of liquid needed for one continuous 24-hour period should be brought into the process area in full containers. Partial containers can remain in the process area as long as they do not increase the hazard present. Containers that were filled in the process area can remain there during the shift that they were filled but should be relocated to the appropriate storage area before the end of the workday or shift in the case of 24-hour-a-day operations. [30: A.18.4.8]

A.66.18.5.1 Incidental operations are operations that utilize liquids only as a limited activity to that which establishes the occupancy classification. Examples include automobile assembly, assembly of electronic equipment, furniture manufacturing, and areas within refineries, distilleries, and chemical plants where the use of liquids is incidental, such as in maintenance shops, offices, or vehicle repair shops. Some more detailed descriptions follow:

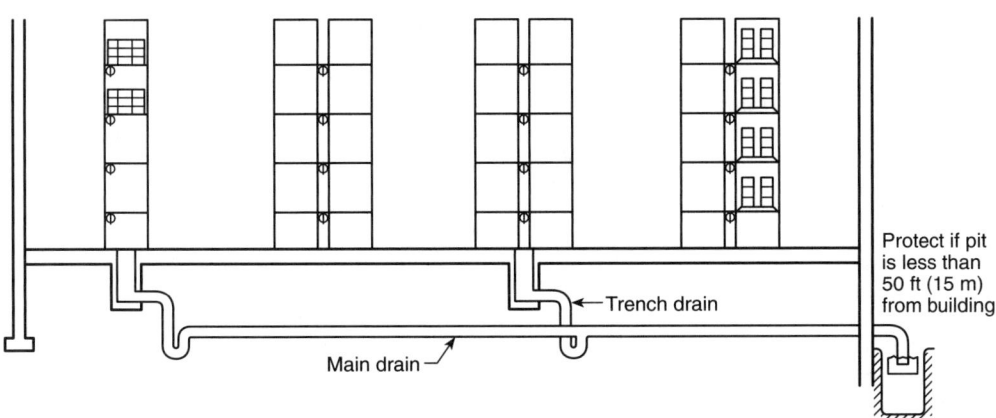

FIGURE A.66.16.8.2(a) General Scheme for Warehouse Spill Control of Liquids. [30: Figure A.16.8.2(a)]

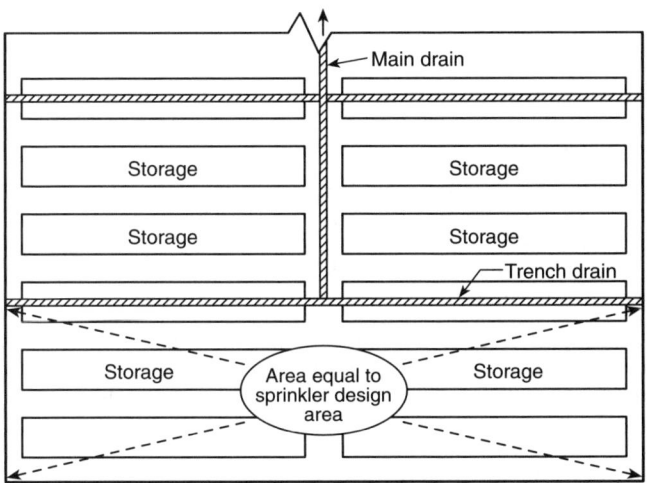

FIGURE A.66.16.8.2(b) Plan View of Warehouse Spill Control of Liquids. [30: Figure A.16.8.2(b)]

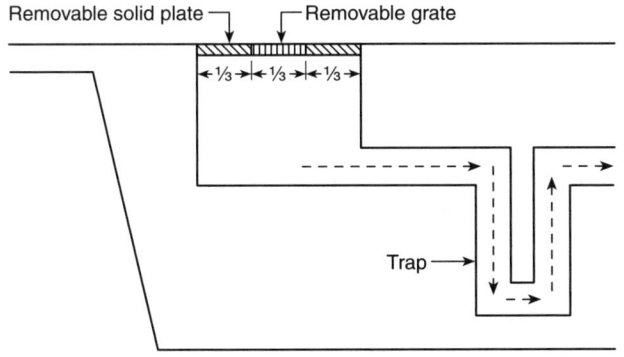

FIGURE A.66.16.8.2(c) Details of Drainage Trench Design. [30: Figure A.16.8.2(c)]

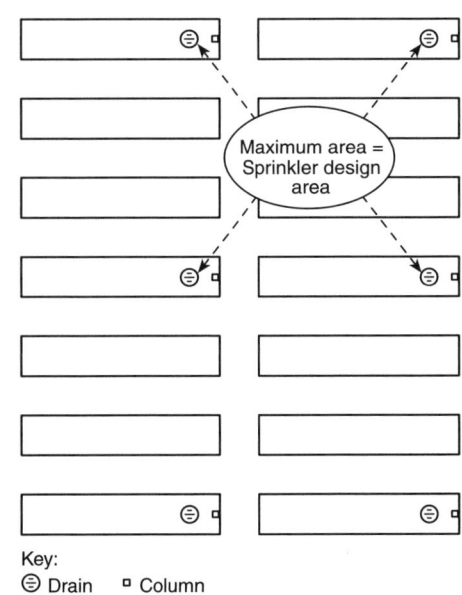

FIGURE A.66.16.8.2(d) Typical Arrangement of Floor Drains. [30: Figure A.16.8.2(d)]

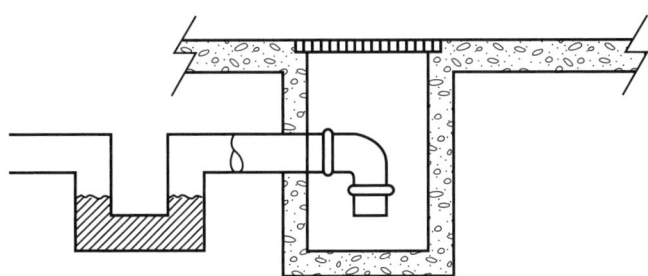

FIGURE A.66.16.8.2(e) Details of Liquid-Seal Trap. [30: Figure A.16.8.2(e)]

(1) *Vehicle Assembly.* Vehicle assembly operations usually involve both process and incidental use of liquids. An example of a process operation would be paint storage and mixing utilized for application of the vehicle primer, color coats, and clear coats. For these operations, the requirements of Chapter 17 of NFPA 30 apply. Examples of incidental use would be sealer deck wipedown operations, windshield washer solvent dispensing, brake fluid filling, and final line paint repair operations. These operations might be continuous. However, the quantities of liquids used and the vapor exposures are significantly reduced from larger volume usage found within vehicle body component paint mixing and storage operations.

(2) *Assembly of Electrical Equipment.* Examples of incidental use of liquids in these types of occupancies might include "photoresist" coating operations, "softbaking" operations, wave solder operations, and wipedown operations.

(3) *Chemical Plant Maintenance Shop.* Incidental use of liquids is commonplace in maintenance shops located within a chemical plant. Examples are cutting oils used in a machine shop, Class II solvents for degreasing, and Class I and II paint solvents and fuels associated with automotive and industrial truck repair.

(4) *Cleaning and Sanitation.* Under provisions established by the U.S. Food and Drug Administration (FDA) in 21 CFR, "GMP for Medical Devices," Class I and Class II liquids can be used for cleaning and sanitation purposes. Limited quantities are used to remove manufacturing materials, mold release compounds, and other contaminants not intended to be on the final product. An example would be the use of isopropyl alcohol (IPA), transferred to a cleaning wipe via a plunger-type liquid-dispensing container. The cleaning wipe is then used to remove manufacturing materials not intended to be on the final product. The key point here is not that the liquid is not part of the final product, but that limited quantities of liquid are used and the use is incidental to the manufacturing operation that produces the product.

[**30:** A.18.5.1]

A.66.18.5.4.1(1) The intent of this requirement is to allow the quantities of flammable and combustible liquids needed to safely and efficiently operate for the actual operating hours in any 24-hour period. As an example, if the facility operates only 8 hours out of 24 (i.e., a single shift) and uses 50 gal (190 L) of liquid during that time, then 50 gal (190 L) is the allowable quantity for the continuous 24-hour period. If the facility increases operations to two shifts, then the allowable quantity doubles to 100 gal (380 L). [**30:** A.18.5.4.1(1)]

A.66.18.6.3 A "safe location" should be selected as the location of a vent discharge to minimize the potential for ignitible vapors to travel to a source of ignition after discharge from the vent. Electrical equipment that does not meet the requirements for hazardous locations can serve as an ignition source. The Technical Committee advises that vent discharge locations should consider such factors as the following:

(1) Characteristics of the exhausted material (vapor density, toxicity, velocity of discharge, etc.)
(2) Proximity to potential ignition sources
(3) Building openings such as doors, windows, air intakes, and so forth.
(4) Dispersion characteristics (distance to discharge within the flammable range, direction of discharge, atmospheric conditions, and the influence of building and neighboring buildings on discharged vapors)
(5) Likelihood of vapor accumulation following discharge, such as accumulation under building eaves
(6) Likelihood of sufficient discharge volume to allow an ignitible concentration to reach an ignition source

[**30:** A.18.6.3]

Historically, NFPA 30 has provided prescriptive guidance, often based on area classification requirements, and results have been acceptable. Closer distances should be accepted only if an engineering study by a qualified engineer justifies closer distances. Similarly, the specified distances might not be acceptable for all installations, thus the guidance provided above. [**30:** A.18.6.3]

A.66.19.2.1 Cooking oil is a Class IIIB liquid with a high flash point typically above 500°F (260°C). Because of its high flash point, cooking oil presents a lower fire hazard than Class IIIB liquids having flash points lower than 500°F (260°C). Fresh, or new, cooking oil is supplied to the user for cooking operations. As the oil becomes degraded through repeated use, it must be replaced with fresh oil. This waste, or used, cooking oil is recovered from the cooking appliance and temporarily stored for offsite removal. To maintain fluidity in the transfer process, the waste oil is heated to approximately 100°F (38°C), well below the flash point temperature. [**30:** A.19.2.1]

A.66.19.4.2 Mist explosions have occurred when heat transfer fluid that is above its boiling point has been released in an enclosed area. Consideration should be given to locating heaters or vaporizers either in a detached building or in a room with damage-limiting construction. [**30:** A.19.4.2]

A.66.19.4.3 The system should be interlocked to stop circulation of the heat transfer fluid through the system and to shut off the system heater or vaporizer in the event of a fire, abnormally low pressure in the system, or operation of an approved heat detection system. Where the refractory inside the heater or vaporizer can retain enough heat to cause either breakdown of the heat transfer fluid or tube fouling if fluid circulation through the unit is stopped, circulation could have to be continued. In the event of a confirmed fire, it is desirable to subdivide the piping system by means of interlocked safety shutoff valves. A practical way of accomplishing this is to isolate all secondary circulating loops from the primary loop that runs into and out of the vaporizer or heater. [**30:** A.19.4.3]

A well-marked remote emergency shutoff switch or electrical disconnect should be provided to shut down the entire system in the event of an emergency. This should be located either in a constantly attended location or at a location that would be accessible in the event of a leak or a fire. [**30:** A.19.4.3]

If there are any process or utility lines running in or through rooms or areas containing parts of the heat transfer system, consideration should be given to providing emergency shutoff valves. They should be located so they are readily accessible in the event of a fire. [**30:** A.19.4.3]

Where the liquid level in the system expansion tank is maintained by an automatically actuated supply pump taking suction from the heat transfer fluid storage tank, an interlock should be provided to shut down the supply pump when a high level indicator is actuated, regardless of whether the pump is in automatic or manual mode. [**30:** A.19.4.3]

A.66.19.4.3.1 Heat transfer fluid systems have the potential for releasing large quantities of heated flammable or combustible liquid. Low point drains piped to a safe location provide the ability to remove heat transfer fluid from a breached piping system in order to minimize the total quantity of fluid released. An engineering analysis should be used to determine the location and design of low-point drains. The engineering analysis should consider system inventory, the amount of heat transfer fluid that can be released in a specific fire area, the exposure created by a release, and the fire protection provided. [**30:** A.19.4.3.1]

A.66.19.4.3.2 Where possible, the drain tank(s) should be located below the lowest system drain opening to permit gravity flow. Breather vents should be provided based on the maximum emptying or filling rates. [**30:** A.19.4.3.2]

A.66.19.4.4 If stack gas from a heater or vaporizer is recovered to provide auxiliary heat for other equipment (e.g., rotary dryers), suitable dampers, isolation gates, burner control logic, or other means should be provided to ensure that all equipment is properly purged and will operate in a safe manner. The control logic should anticipate all possible operating modes of the individual pieces of equipment, whether operating singly or together, to ensure safe startup and shutdown under normal or upset conditions. [**30:** A.19.4.4]

Instrumentation and interlocks should be provided to sound an alarm and to automatically shut down the fuel source to the heater or vaporizer when any of the following conditions are detected:

(1) Low flow of heat transfer fluid through the heat exchange tubes of the heater, as measured at the discharge.
(2) High temperature or pressure of the fluid at the heater or vaporizer outlet. The high-temperature interlock should be set at or below the manufacturer's maximum recommended bulk fluid temperature.
(3) Low pressure at the heater or vaporizer outlet or elsewhere in the system. This interlock could require a bypass to allow for startup.
(4) Low fluid level in the expansion tank.
(5) Low liquid level in the vaporizer.
(6) Sprinkler system flow in any area containing the heat transfer equipment or piping.

[**30:** A.19.4.4]

Alarm set points should be provided at levels below or above the automatic shutoff setpoints to monitor the above-mentioned variables and provide an opportunity for operators to correct the problem before conditions reach an unsafe level. [**30:** A.19.4.4]

A.66.19.4.5.1 Where possible, piping should be run underground, outside, or in floor trenches. Overhead routing of heat transfer fluid piping should be minimized. [**30:** A.19.4.5.1]

A.66.19.4.6.1 Historical records show that fires involving heat transfer fluids can be very severe and long lasting. It is recommended that automatic sprinkler or deluge protection be provided throughout all building areas potentially exposed to a heat transfer fluid spill fire. [**30:** A.19.4.6.1]

A.66.19.4.7.1 Some factors that should be considered as part of such a review include the following:

(1) Infiltration of material being heated into the heat transfer system. In this case, the system should be shut down and the internal leak point found and repaired as soon as possible.
(2) Leaks in the system. Any leak should be corrected promptly regardless of how small. Corrections should be permanent, such as repacking valve stems and replacing leaky gaskets. Any heat transfer fluid released as a result of a leak or operation of a safety valve should be cleaned up immediately if it is or can come in contact with a hot surface. Other spills can be cleaned up at the first available opportunity.
(3) Pipe or equipment insulation that is soaked with heat transfer fluid. In this case, the cause of the leak should be corrected promptly and the insulation replaced with clean, dry insulation.
(4) High temperature anywhere in the system. In this case, operating procedures should specify shutdown of the heater or vaporizer fuel supply as soon as the temperature of the heat transfer fluid exceeds the manufacturer's recommended maximum bulk fluid temperature. Any corrective actions taken to correct a high temperature condition should only be done with the heat source shut off.

[**30:** A.19.4.7.1]

A.66.19.5.5.1 If the liquid knock-out vessel utilizes a pump for automatic liquid removal, consideration should be given to a low-level alarm and shutdown to avoid running the pump dry, resulting in a potential source of ignition. [**30:** A.19.5.5.1]

A.66.19.5.7.2 Electrical enclosures that need to be opened frequently for maintenance (i.e., enclosures housing vapor processing system controls) have a higher potential for mechanical damage that could render the enclosures unable to contain an explosion. Additional inspection could be needed to ensure the integrity of the enclosure. [**30:** A.19.5.7.2]

A.66.19.5.7.3 NFPA 77, *Recommended Practice on Static Electricity*, and API RP 2003, *Protection Against Ignition Arising Out of Static, Lightning, and Stray Currents*, can be used as a reference for protections against static ignition. [**30:** A.19.5.7.3]

A.66.19.5.7.4 Spontaneous ignition can be a problem in the following:

(1) Facilities where pyrophoric deposits can accumulate from the handling of oxygen-deficient vapors containing sulfur compounds or asphaltic materials. When air is introduced into the system, the pyrophoric materials can react, resulting in potential ignition and fire.
(2) Facilities that handle fluids in such a way that mixing of hypergolic or otherwise incompatible materials can occur. Such mixing could occur with fluids remaining in the vapor recovery system from prior loading activities.
(3) Facilities handling oxygenated hydrocarbons in carbon absorption units. Higher heats of absorption for these types of vapors can potentially lead to overheated carbon beds and increase the chance that an oxidation reaction can be initiated. (For further information, refer to API Report, "An Engineering Analysis of the Effects of Oxygenated Fuels on Marketing Vapor Recovery Equipment.")

[**30:** A.19.5.7.4]

A.66.19.5.7.5 U.S. Coast Guard Regulations in Title 33, Code of Federal Regulations, Part 154, Section 154.826(b), (c), and (d), can be used as a reference for vapor mover designs that minimize the potential for ignition. [**30:** A.19.5.7.5]

A.66.19.5.7.6 The potential for ignition in the vapor collection system needs to be evaluated on a case-by-case basis. If ignition occurs, flame propagation in piping systems containing vapor mixtures in the flammable range normally starts with low-speed burning (deflagration). As the flame moves through the piping, it accelerates and, within a short distance, can reach supersonic speeds (detonation). Initial low-speed flame propagation can be stopped by flame arresters, liquid seals, or automatic fast-acting valve systems where designed, operated, and tested within the requirements of NFPA 69, *Standard on Explosion Prevention Systems*. Flame propagation can also be stopped for both deflagrations and detonations by use of detonation arresters tested in accordance with U.S. Department of Transportation Coast Guard Regulations of the 33 CFR 154, Appendix A, or other procedures acceptable to the AHJ, or automatic fast-acting valve systems tested under the appropriate conditions. [30: A.19.5.7.6]

A.66.19.7.1.3 The goal of 66.19.7 is to consolidate in one location all requirements for commercial kitchen cooking oil storage and operations. There are a number of chapters in NFPA 30 that apply to these systems, including chapters on storage tanks and piping systems, transferring and dispensing of liquids, and so forth. Many of these requirements are more applicable to industrial or process situations and commercial kitchen cooking oil storage and use was not anticipated. All applicable chapters have been assessed in detail. Those specific requirements in this section that are in potential conflict with other sections of this code have been identified, and alternate methods or exceptions have been developed where appropriate. This approach eliminates the need to add exceptions throughout the existing code, improving ease of use particularly for fire officials. [30: A.19.7.1.3]

A.66.19.7.2.1.2 Waste oil is drained from commercial cooking equipment via a transfer pump and transfer lines to a waste oil storage tank. The oil might be as hot as 375°F (190°C), still well below the oil's flash point. Experience shows that the oil loses significant heat in the transfer process. The maximum temperature of waste cooking oil entering the storage tank is typically below 235°F (113°C). The storage tank should be constructed of materials compatible with cooking oil in that temperature range. [30: A.19.7.2.1.2]

A.66.19.7.2.2.1 Existing steel tanks listed for flammable and combustible liquids are considered acceptable for waste oil use. These tank standards contain design and construction requirements that would not meet food code requirements, making the tanks unacceptable for storage of liquid food products (i.e., fresh cooking oil). [30: A.19.7.2.2.1]

A.66.19.7.2.3.4 High flash point cooking oils do not create ignitable vapors when stored under the conditions specified in 66.19.7. [30: A.19.7.2.3.4]

A.66.19.7.2.4.2 Nonmetallic tanks will melt above the liquid level as an external exposure fire progresses, venting the vapor space of the tank. [30: A.19.7.2.4.2]

A.66.19.7.2.5 Although generally not required for tanks storing Class IIIB liquids, overfill protection is considered necessary for cooking oil storage tanks to prevent inadvertent spillage. [30: A.19.7.2.5]

A.66.19.7.2.6.1 The prohibition of electrical immersion heaters in nonmetallic tanks eliminates a primary ignition source for the oil stored in the tank. [30: A.19.7.2.6.1]

A.66.19.7.2.6.2 The temperature limitation of 140°F (60°C) corresponds to ASTM C 1055 (ISO 13732-1) restrictions for maximum allowable temperatures of nonmetallic industrial surfaces for human contact. [30: A.19.7.2.6.2]

A.66.19.7.3.1.1 The kitchen cooking area has historically been an area where fires occur. Tanks should, therefore, be located away from the kitchen cooking area. [30: A.19.7.3.1.1]

A.66.19.7.3.1.2 The area beneath the ventilation hood is another area of potential accidental ignition. [30: A.19.7.3.1.2]

A.66.19.7.3.3.2 An example of a fitting with a positive shutoff is a spring-loaded check valve or a hydraulic quick-coupling with a spring-loaded poppet. [30: A.19.7.3.3.2]

A.66.19.7.3.4.1 Cooking oil storage tanks are atmospheric tanks with open vents. The requirement in Section 66.21 to pressurize the tank for leak testing would be difficult to achieve in the field, due to tank construction and configuration. It is also desirable to prevent water contamination of the cooking oil. A more appropriate test would be to fill the tank with cooking oil to cover all connections and seams below the normal liquid level. [30: A.19.7.3.4.1]

A.66.19.7.4.2 Supplemental ventilation, as is required for cooking operations, is not needed for cooking oil storage tanks. [30: A.19.7.4.2]

A.66.19.7.5.1 Waste oil lines are generally pumped until there is little residual oil remaining in the lines. Fresh cooking oil lines are likely to contain residual oil after fill and removal operations. Restricting the fresh oil line size to 1.25 in. (32 mm) maximum inside diameter limits the amount of oil in the line. Additionally, the requirement for check valves or antisiphon valves on the lines at points where the lines connect to the tank eliminates the possibility of a compromised line siphoning the contents of the tank. To the extent possible, transfer lines should avoid being routed over seating areas. These requirements are designed to minimize fire risk by limiting cooking oil quantities in transfer lines that could become involved in a fire. In buildings protected by automatic fire sprinklers, the need to add sprinklers in previously unprotected spaces (assuming the transfer lines are located in these spaces) should be considered in accordance with the requirements of NFPA 13, *Standard for the Installation of Sprinkler Systems*. [30: A.19.7.5.1]

A.66.19.7.5.2 The temperature and pressure ratings for the waste oil lines are consistent with the maximum expected conditions. [30: A.19.7.5.2]

A.66.21.4.2.1.1 Atmospheric tanks include tanks of compartmented design and tanks that incorporate secondary containment. [30: A.21.4.2.1.1]

A.66.21.4.2.3.2 Such pressure vessels are generally referred to as "state special." [30: A.21.4.2.3.2]

A.66.21.4.3.2 Normal venting is not required for the interstitial space of a secondary containment tank. [30: A.21.4.3.2]

A.66.21.4.3.11 Liquid properties that justify omitting such devices include, but are not limited to, condensation, corrosiveness, crystallization, polymerization, freezing, or plugging. When any of these conditions exist, consideration should be given to heating, use of devices that employ special materials of construction, use of liquid seals, or inerting. See NFPA 69, *Standard on Explosion Prevention Systems*. [30: A.21.4.3.11]

A.66.21.4.4 In Exception No. 2, examples of liquids with minimal potential for accumulation of static charge include crude oil, asphalt, and water-miscible liquids. For additional information, see NFPA 77, *Recommended Practice on Static Electricity*. [30: A.21.4.4]

A.66.21.4.5 Other means of internal corrosion protection include protective coatings and linings and cathodic protection. [30: A.21.4.5]

A.66.21.5.2 See PEI RP200, *Recommended Practices for Installation of Aboveground Storage Systems for Motor Vehicle Fueling*, and STI R 931, *Double Wall AST Installation and Testing Instructions*, for additional requirements to test secondary containment tanks. [**30:** A.21.5.2]

A.66.21.5.2.7 Underground double-wall tanks can be considered to be a type of secondary containment. The terms "double-wall tank" and "jacketed tank" are sometimes used to describe underground secondary containment tanks. [**30:** A.21.5.2.7]

A.66.21.5.3 For information on testing of underground tanks, see NFPA 329, *Recommended Practice for Handling Releases of Flammable and Combustible Liquids and Gases.* For information on testing aboveground tanks, see API 653, *Tank Inspection, Repair, Alteration, and Reconstruction.* [**30:** A.21.5.3]

A.66.21.6.5.1 Resources include, but are not limited to, the following:

(1) Mutual aid
(2) Water supply
(3) Extinguishing agent supply
[**30:** A.21.6.5.1]

A.66.21.6.6.1 See NFPA 25, *Standard for the Inspection, Testing, and Maintenance of Water-Based Fire Protection Systems,* or other specific fire protection system standards. [**30:** A.21.6.6.1]

A.66.21.7.1 Further guidance is given in API 2350, *Overfill Protection for Storage Tanks in Petroleum Facilities.* [**30:** A.21.7.1]

A.66.21.7.2.2 Protection from tampering or trespassing might include one or more of the following: appropriate fencing around isolated tanks in remote areas; "No Trespassing" signs; warning signs indicating the fire hazard of the tank or its contents; locked or secured access to stairways and ladders; locked or secured hatches, valves, and so forth. [**30:** A.21.7.2.2]

A.66.21.7.4.1 For further information, see API 2015, *Safe Entry and Cleaning of Petroleum Storage Tanks;* and API 2016, *Guidelines and Procedures for Entering and Cleaning Petroleum Storage Tanks.* [**30:** A.21.7.4.1]

A.66.21.7.4.3.3(2) Special training might be required. [**30:** A.21.7.4.3.3(2)]

A.66.21.7.5 See NFPA 329, *Recommended Practice for Handling Releases of Flammable and Combustible Liquids and Gases,* for information on testing methods. [**30:** A.21.7.5]

A.66.21.8.1 Regular inspections of aboveground storage tanks, including shop fabricated aboveground storage tanks, performed in accordance with national standards, provide a means to ensure system maintenance. Acceptable standards include, but are not limited to, the following:

(1) API 653, *Tank Inspection, Repair, Alteration, and Reconstruction*
(2) STI SP001, *Standard for Inspection of Aboveground Storage Tanks*
(3) API 12R1, *Setting, Maintenance, Inspection, Operation, and Repair of Tanks in Production Service*
(4) API 2350, *Overfill Protection for Storage Tanks in Petroleum Facilities*
[**30:** A.21.8.1]

A.66.21.8.6 For additional information, see API 653, *Tank Inspection, Repair, Alteration, and Reconstruction,* API RP 2350, *Overfill Protection for Storage Tanks in Petroleum Facilities,* and PEI RP600, *Recommended Practices for Overfill Prevention for Shop-Fabricated Aboveground Tanks.* [**30:** A.21.8.6]

A.66.21.8.8 The accumulation of water in the bottom of a tank encourages microbial activity that hampers operations and increases the risk of product release. It is imperative that tank owners and operators routinely monitor the tank bottom for accumulation of water and establish a procedure for when and how the water is to be removed. Additional information can be found in API 1501, *Filtration and Dehydration of Aviation Fuels,* API RP 1621, *Bulk Liquid Stock Control at Retail Outlets,* and API Standard 2610, *Design, Construction, Operation, Maintenance, and Inspection of Terminal and Tank Facilities.* Other sources of information are ASTM D 6469, *Standard Guide for Microbial Contamination in Fuels and Fuel Systems,* the National Oilheat Research Alliance *Oilheat Technician's Manual,* and the STI publication *Keeping Water Out of Your Storage System.* [**30:** A.21.8.8]

A.66.22.4 See PEI RP200, *Recommended Practices for Installation of Aboveground Storage Systems for Motor Vehicle Fueling,* for additional information. [**30:** A.22.4]

A.66.22.4.2.1 Where more than two tanks are involved, the sum of the diameters of each possible pair of tanks is calculated. For example, assume four tanks in a common diked area, numbered 1 through 4 clockwise from tank #1. The diameter of each pair of tanks is summed, as follows: 1 and 2, 1 and 3, 1 and 4, 2 and 3, 2 and 4, and 3 and 4. [**30:** A.22.4.2.1]

A.66.22.5.2.1 Appendix E of API Standard 650, *Welded Steel Tanks for Oil Storage,* and Appendix B of API 620, *Recommended Rules for the Design and Construction of Large, Welded, Low-Pressure Storage Tanks,* provide information on tank foundations. [**30:** A.22.5.2.1]

A.66.22.5.2.4 For further information, see ASTM E 119, *Standard Test Methods for Fire Tests of Building Construction and Materials,* and ANSI/UL 1709, *Standard for Rapid Rise Fire Tests of Protection Materials for Structural Steel.* [**30:** A.22.5.2.4]

A.66.22.7.3.1 An engineering evaluation should be performed whenever two-phase flow is anticipated. The objective of the engineering evaluation determining emergency vent requirements and design of the relief system is to protect against catastrophic failure resulting in unacceptable risk to persons or to the facility. Factors that should be included in the evaluation are as follows:

(1) Properties of the materials including evaluated influence of two-phase flow and thermally induced instability. See the following references from the Design Institute for Emergency Relief Systems of the Center for Chemical Process Safety/American Institute of Chemical Engineers:
    (a) Fisher, H. G. and Forrest, H. S., "Protection of Storage Tanks from Two-Phase Flow Due to Fire Exposure"
    (b) Houser, J., et al., "Vent Sizing for Fire Considerations: External Fire Duration, Jacketed Vessels, and Heat Flux Variations Owing to Fuel Consumption"
    (c) *Guidelines for Pressure Relief and Effluent Handling Systems*
(2) Rate of heat input to the tank and contents. Computer models such as PLGS (supported by the UK Health and Safety Executive) can be useful in making the analysis.
(3) Fire duration. For pool fires this analysis can be based on burning rate and pool depth. Computer programs can be useful in making this analysis.

[**30:** A.22.7.3.1]

A.66.22.7.4 Vent sizing formulae and prescriptive vent sizes, such as those established by ANSI/UL 142, *Standard for Steel Aboveground Tanks for Flammable and Combustible Liquids*, are typically based on the direct installation of a venting device on to a tank with a nipple not exceeding 12 in. (300 mm). When the outlet of a vent must be extended to a remote location, such as for tanks located in buildings, which require vent discharges to be located outside, a significant reduction in vent flow can occur unless the size of the vent and connecting piping is increased. In such cases, the size of vents and vent pipe extensions should be calculated to ensure that a tank will not be over-pressurized during a fire exposure. [30: A.22.7.4]

A.66.22.8.1 Protection against fire or explosion required for large flammable liquid storage tanks should consider the use of fixed, semi-fixed, or portable protection system designed in conformance with good engineering practice such as those described in NFPA 11, *Standard for Low-, Medium-, and High-Expansion Foam*, NFPA 15, *Standard for Water Spray Fixed Systems for Fire Protection*, and NFPA 69, *Standard on Explosion Prevention Systems*. Ordinary combustibles (such as wood) would be subject to radiant heat unpiloted ignition from a burning tank, when such exposures are located a distance of less than about 150 percent of the tank diameter (assuming no wind effects). Exposure from adjacent property to the tanks would depend on the specific products and storage arrangement and may require some engineering analysis based on the occupancy and its exposure potential. [30: A.22.8.1]

A.66.22.11 "Accidental release" includes but is not limited to the following:

(1) Leakage from the tank shell
(2) Overfill
(3) Leakage from piping connected to the tank
 [30: A.22.11]

A.66.22.11.2.2 An aboveground storage tank dike is normally sized to contain the entire contents of the largest single tank within it. Some designs incorporate sufficient freeboard (additional capacity) to accommodate precipitation or fire-fighting water. The amount of this freeboard is usually governed by local conditions. [30: A.22.11.2.2]

A.66.22.11.2.4.1 Diked areas for tanks containing Class I liquids located in extremely porous soils might require special treatment to prevent seepage of hazardous quantities of liquids to low-lying areas or waterways in case of spills. [30: A.22.11.2.4.1]

A.66.22.11.2.6.3.4 Because unstable liquids will react more rapidly when heated than when at ambient temperatures, subdivision by drainage channels is the preferred method. [30: A.22.11.2.6.3.4]

A.66.22.11.3.1 See 66.22.11.2.2. [30: A.22.11.3.1]

A.66.22.12.1 As noted in the exception, engineering designs that can reduce exposure hazards include use of sealed sleeve piping and secondary containment piping to prevent leakage and the use of remotely controlled isolation valves on product lines to stop the flow of liquids when the piping is subjected to fire exposure. [30: A.22.12.1]

A.66.22.12.3 Methods of preventing an exposure hazard include intermediate diking, drainage, or fire protection features such as water spray systems, monitors, or fire-resistive coatings. High integrity pumps or equipment also constitute a method of limiting exposure hazards. [30: A.22.12.3]

A.66.22.17.4 An explosion hazard can exist due to flammable liquids or vapors within the pontoon. Ignition can be caused by lightning strikes or general maintenance activities. Lightning protection systems and other means of tank grounding cannot prevent sparking caused by lightning across gaps such as those between pontoon covers and the tank roof, between the tank wall and the roof, or at shunts. Such sparks can serve as a source of ignition causing a fire or explosion that can result in sufficient overpressure to throw portions of the pontoon assembly completely away from the tank with subsequent, partial, or complete loss of the tank due to fire. Caution is particularly advisable where tanks with vapor-containing pontoons are located within lightning-prone areas. [30: A.22.17.4]

A.66.23.3.4 Dropping or rolling the tank into the hole can break a weld, puncture or damage the tank, or scrape off the protective coating of coated tanks. See PEI RP100, *Recommended Practices for Installation of Underground Liquid Storage Systems*. [30: A.23.3.4]

A.66.23.3.5 See UL 1316, *Standard for Glass-Fiber-Reinforced Plastic Underground Storage Tanks for Petroleum Products, Alcohols, and Alcohol-Gasoline Mixtures*; UL 1746, *Standard for External Corrosion Protection Systems for Steel Underground Storage Tanks*; and STI ACT-100, *Specification for External Corrosion Protection of FRP Composite Steel Underground Tanks*, F894. [30: A.23.3.5]

A.66.23.3.5.1 See API RP 1615, *Installation of Underground Petroleum Storage Systems*, for further information. [30: A.23.3.5.1]

A.66.23.3.5.2 Acceptable design standards for cathodic protection systems include the following:

(1) API RP 1632, *Cathodic Protection of Underground Petroleum Storage Tanks and Piping Systems*
(2) CAN/ULC-S603.1, *Standard for External Corrosion Protection Systems for Steel Underground Tanks for Flammable and Combustible Liquids*
(3) STI-P3, *Specification and Manual for External Corrosion Protection of Underground Steel Storage Tanks*
(4) NACE RP-0169, *Recommended Practice, Control of External Corrosion on Underground or Submerged Metallic Piping Systems*
(5) NACE RP-0285, *Recommended Practice, Corrosion Control of Underground Storage Tank Systems by Cathodic Protection*
(6) ANSI/UL 1746, *Standard for External Corrosion Protection Systems for Steel Underground Storage Tanks*, Part 1
(7) STI RP 892, *Recommended Practice for Corrosion of Underground Piping Networks Associated with Liquid Storage and Dispensing Systems*
 [30:23.3.5.2]

A.66.23.6.1 The required venting capacity depends upon the filling or withdrawal rate, whichever is greater, and the vent line length. Unrestricted vent piping sized in accordance with Table 66.23.6.2 will prevent back pressure development in tanks from exceeding a gauge pressure of 2.5 psi (17.2 kPa). [30: A.23.6.1]

A.66.23.14.1 Anchoring can be accomplished using nonmetallic straps or metallic straps that are separated from the tank shell by inert insulating dielectric material. The straps should be connected to a bottom hold-down pad or deadman anchors. For additional information, see reference to API RP 1615, *Installation of Underground Petroleum Storage Systems*; PEI RP100, *Recommended Practices for Installation of Underground Liq-*

uid Storage Systems; and STI RP R011, *Recommended Practice for Anchoring of Steel Underground Storage Tanks*. [**30:** A.23.14.1]

Previous editions of NFPA 30 included provisions for the use of water ballast as a means to weight a tank to prevent movement during a flood. In anticipation of a flood event, water could be used to fill the tank to reduce buoyancy. While this approach remains technically viable for existing tanks that are not properly secured to prevent movement, the use of water as a means of providing ballast is no longer considered an acceptable basis of design for new tank installations. [**30:** A.23.14.1]

It is not the intent of this section to prohibit the use of water as ballast in underground tanks during system installation and prior to the initial introduction of the stored liquid. [**30:** A.23.14.1]

A.66.24.1 Section 66.24 provides an approach that allows considerable flexibility for compliance without compromising fire safety, while fostering ingenuity in application of fire safety principles to achieve the intended objectives, outlined in the performance criteria set out at the beginning of each subsection. Each subsection has been written with the first sentence outlining the performance criteria that, if implemented, would achieve compliance with that subsection. In order to clarify the intent of each performance criterion, the subsequent paragraphs constitute one method of achieving compliance with the intent envisioned in the performance requirements. It is recognized that other combinations of requirements can also be used to meet the intent of the performance criteria, provided such requirements are acceptable to the AHJ. [**30:** A.24.1]

A.66.24.4.5(3) See NFPA 68, *Standard on Explosion Protection by Deflagration Venting*, for information on deflagration venting. [**30:** A.24.4.5(3)]

A.66.24.5.2 See NFPA 220, *Standard on Types of Building Construction*. [**30:** A.24.5.2]

A.66.24.5.4 See NFPA 68, *Standard on Explosion Protection by Deflagration Venting*, for information on deflagration venting. [**30:** A.24.5.4]

A.66.24.5.6 The purpose of the access aisles is to provide for ease of maintenance and emergency operations. [**30:** A.24.5.6]

A.66.24.6.1.1 NFPA 10, *Standard for Portable Fire Extinguishers*, provides information on the suitability of various types of extinguishers. [**30:** A.24.6.1.1]

A.66.24.6.1.2 See NFPA 13, *Standard for the Installation of Sprinkler Systems*, and NFPA 14, *Standard for the Installation of Standpipe and Hose Systems*. [**30:** A.24.6.1.2]

A.66.24.6.2.2 See NFPA 24, *Standard for the Installation of Private Fire Service Mains and Their Appurtenances*, for information on this subject. [**30:** A.24.6.2.2]

A.66.24.6.2.3 See NFPA 13, *Standard for the Installation of Sprinkler Systems*; NFPA 15, *Standard for Water Spray Fixed Systems for Fire Protection*; and NFPA 16, *Standard for the Installation of Foam-Water Sprinkler and Foam-Water Spray Systems*, for information on these subjects. [**30:** A.24.6.2.3]

For certain fuel types, such as ketones, esters, and alcohols, the minimum required densities established in the listing criteria for foam discharge devices are often higher than the general densities specified for protection of flammable and combustible liquids. When determining the design criteria for extinguishing systems using foam, it is important to ensure that the listing criteria, which are typically based on empirical data from fire tests, are not overlooked. Otherwise, the fire protection system design can be inadequate for proper protection. [**30:** A.24.6.2.3]

A.66.24.9.6 Annex A of NFPA 15, *Standard for Water Spray Fixed Systems for Fire Protection*, provides information on this subject. [**30:** A.24.9.6]

A.66.24.10.2 Equipment in enclosed storage areas can deteriorate over time and periodic evaluation should be conducted to assure that leakage rates have not increased or that the ventilation rate is adequate for any increase in leakage rates. [**30:** A.24.10.2]

A.66.24.10.4 Local or spot ventilation might be needed for the control of special fire or health hazards. NFPA 91, *Standard for Exhaust Systems for Air Conveying of Vapors, Gases, Mists, and Noncombustible Particulate Solids*, and NFPA 90A, *Standard for the Installation of Air-Conditioning and Ventilating Systems*, provide information on this subject. [**30:** A.24.10.4]

A.66.24.14.6 Substitutes for manual gauging include, but are not limited to, heavy-duty flat gauge glasses; magnetic, hydraulic, or hydrostatic remote reading devices; and sealed float gauges. [**30:** A.24.14.6]

A.66.24.14.8 Suitable devices include, but are not limited to, a float valve; a pre-set meter on the fill line; a low head pump incapable of producing overflow; or a liquidtight overflow pipe, sized at least one pipe size larger than the fill pipe, that discharges by gravity back to the outside source of liquid or to an approved location. [**30:** A.24.14.8]

A.66.25.3.1 Inspections are recommended for shop fabricated aboveground tanks. One guide is SP001, *Standard for Inspection of Aboveground Storage Tanks*, which is published by the Steel Tank Institute. In addition, the tank owner might desire to conduct additional inspections to ensure the ongoing integrity of tanks and equipment. Because the interior of a vault will ordinarily remain dry and temperature-moderated, environmental effects on tanks and equipment inside vaults will be reduced as compared to aboveground tanks that are not protected from weather exposure. Accordingly, inspection and maintenance frequencies for exterior surfaces of tanks and piping in vaults are typically less critical than for aboveground tanks installed outdoors. Nevertheless, inspection and maintenance of emergency vents and overfill prevention devices are still necessary. [**30:** A.25.3.1]

Clearance between the shell of a tank or equipment in a vault and the interior vault wall should be sufficient to accommodate visual inspections and maintenance that might be needed. In addition, consideration should be given to the need for inspection and maintenance of tank interior surfaces that may be impacted by internal corrosion. [**30:** A.25.3.1]

Clearance should be adequate to permit the following:

(1) Entry into the vault interior by an inspector or maintenance worker
(2) Access to manipulate, repair, or replace any equipment or fittings in the vault
(3) Access within the vault to visually inspect, either by direct sight or with the aid of an optical vision extension tools, interior vault surfaces and exterior surfaces of tanks and equipment, to determine the source of any leakage that may occur, and to conduct any needed repairs

[**30:** A.25.3.1]

Because vaults are designed to provide for entry by inspectors or maintenance workers, consideration should also be given to providing access for rescue by emergency responders who might be called upon to rescue an individual from a vault. Such consideration can include providing a minimum access hatch dimension of 36 in. (915 mm) and a minimum dimension for walkways in vault interior spaces of 30 in. (760 mm) to permit an emergency responder with an SCBA to maneuver and providing, in some cases, a second means of access to the vault interior. [**30:** A.25.3.1]

A.66.25.5 Some of the specifications for vault design and construction include the following:

(1) The walls and floor of the vault are to be constructed of reinforced concrete at least 6 in. (50 mm) thick.
(2) The top and floor of the vault and the tank foundation must be designed to withstand all anticipated loading, including loading from vehicular traffic, where applicable.
(3) The walls and floor of a belowgrade vault must be designed to withstand anticipated soil and hydrostatic loading.
(4) The vault must be liquidtight.
(5) The vault enclosure must have no openings except those necessary for access to, inspection of, and filling, emptying, and venting of the tank.
(6) The vault must be provided with connections to permit ventilation to dilute, disperse, and remove any vapors prior to personnel entering the vault.
(7) The vault must be provided with a means for personnel entry.
(8) The vault must be provided with an approved means to admit a fire suppression agent.
[**30:** A.25.5]

A.66.27.4.3.2 For further information, see ASTM E 119, *Standard Test Methods for Fire Tests of Building Construction and Materials,* and ANSI/UL 1709, *Standard for Rapid Rise Fire Tests of Protection Materials for Structural Steel.* [**30:** A.27.4.3.2]

A.66.27.5.1.2 It is expected that some joints might leak under fire conditions but will not come apart. [**30:** A.27.5.1.2]

A.66.27.6.2 API 2218, *Fireproofing Practices in Petroleum and Petrochemical Processing Plants,* contains guidance on selecting and installing fire-resistant coatings to protect exposed steel supports from a high-challenge fire exposure. It also contains a general discussion on determining need for such protection and estimating the extent of the area exposed. [**30:** A.27.6.2]

A.66.27.6.4 Buried steel piping should be coated with a suitable material and should be cathodically protected. Galvanized steel pipe, by itself and without other corrosion protection methods, is not acceptable for underground piping. Steel swing joints and stainless steel flexible connectors should also be made corrosion resistant when in contact with the soil. Thus, such fittings should also be coated and cathodically protected when installed between nonmetallic, compatible tanks and piping, such as fiberglass-reinforced plastic. [**30:** A.27.6.4]

A.66.27.8.1.6 Vent sizing formulae and prescriptive vent sizes, such as those established by ANSI/UL 142, *Standard for Steel Aboveground Tanks for Flammable and Combustible Liquids,* are typically based on the direct installation of a venting device onto a tank. When the outlet of a vent must be extended to a remote location, such as for tanks located in buildings, which require vent discharges, to be located outside, a significant reduction in vent flow can occur unless the size of the vent and connecting piping is increased. In such cases, the size of vents and vent pipe extensions should be calculated to ensure that a tank will not be overpressurized during a fire exposure. [**30:** A.27.8.1.6]

A.66.27.8.2.1 API RP 500, *Recommended Practice for Classification of Locations for Electrical Installations at Petroleum Facilities Classified as Class I, Division 1 and Division 2,* and API RP 505, *Recommended Practice for Classification of Locations for Electrical Installations at Petroleum Facilities Classified as Class I, Zone 0, Zone 1, and Zone 2,* establish a 10 ft (3 m) classified zone around most tank vents that are potential sources of ignitible vapors. However, neither document provides specific distances for a belowgrade tank. Applying these strategies to 66.27.8.2.1 resulted in a minimum height for these tank vents of 10 ft (3 m) above grade. Since the majority of these vents exist at retail service station tanks, and since vehicles and other publicly introduced ignition sources could be located close to the vent, an additional 2 ft (0.6 m) was added to the minimum height as a safety factor to ensure the vehicle does not introduce a potential ignition source into the vapor space surrounding the vent. This results in a total height for the vent stack from a belowgrade tank of 12 ft (3.6 m). [**30:** A.27.8.2.1]

A.66.27.10 Where loading and unloading risers for Class II or Class IIIA liquids are located in the same immediate area as loading and unloading risers for Class I liquids, consideration should be given to providing positive means, such as different pipe sizes, connection devices, special locks, or other methods designed to prevent the erroneous transfer of Class I liquids into or from any container or tank used for Class II or Class IIIA liquids. Note that such consideration might not be necessary for water-miscible liquids, where the class is determined by the concentration of liquid in water, or where the equipment is cleaned between transfers. [**30:** A.27.10]

A.66.28.3.1.2 The use of nonconductive materials in the fill pipe assembly should be avoided to prevent any electrical discontinuity in the piping of the system. Serious accidents have occurred when nonconductive materials, such as plastic or rubber hose, have been used in the fill pipe assembly. [**30:** A.28.3.1.2]

A.66.28.4.2 Use of fixed fire protection systems, dikes, fire-rated barriers, or a combination of any of these can provide suitable protection from exposures. [**30:** A.28.4.2]

A.66.28.9 The intent of this requirement is to prevent the spread of uncontrolled, spilled liquid from traveling beyond the loading or unloading area and exposing surrounding equipment and buildings. [**30:** A.28.9]

A.66.28.11.1.5 NFPA 77, *Recommended Practice on Static Electricity,* provides additional information on static electricity protection. [**30:** A.28.11.1.5]

A.66.28.11.2.2 NFPA 77 provides additional information on static electricity protection. [**30:** A.28.11.2.2]

A.66.28.11.3 The term *switch loading* describes a situation that warrants special consideration. [**30:** A.28.11.3]

When a tank is emptied of a cargo of Class I liquid, a mixture of vapor and air is left, which can be, and often is, within the flammable range. When such a tank is refilled with a Class I liquid, any charge that reaches the tank shell will be bled off by the required bond wire. Also, there will be no flammable mixture at the surface of the rising oil level because the Class I liquid produces at its surface a mixture too rich to be ignitible. This is the situation commonly existing in tank vehicles in gasoline service. If, as occasionally happens, a static charge does accumulate on the surface sufficient to produce a spark, it occurs in a too-rich, nonignitible atmosphere and thus causes no harm. [**30:** A.28.11.3]

A very different situation arises if the liquid is "switch loaded," that is, when a Class II or Class III liquid is loaded into a tank vehicle that previously contained a Class I liquid. [**30:** A.28.11.3]

Class II or Class III liquids are not necessarily more potent static generators than the Class I liquid previously loaded, but the atmosphere in contact with the rising oil surface is not enriched to bring it out of the flammable range. If circumstances are such that a spark should occur either across the oil surface or from the oil surface to some other object, the spark occurs in a mixture that can be within the flammable range, and an explosion can result. [**30:** A.28.11.3]

It is emphasized that bonding the tank to the fill stem is not sufficient; a majority of the recorded explosions have occurred when it was believed the tank had been adequately bonded. The electrostatic potential that is responsible for the spark exists inside the tank on the surface of the liquid and cannot be removed by bonding. Measures to reduce the chance of such internal static ignition can be one or more of the following:

(1) Avoid spark promoters. Conductive objects floating on the oil surface increase the charge of sparking to the tank wall. Metal gauge rods or other objects projecting into the vapor space can create a spark gap as the rising liquid level approaches the projection. A common precaution is to require that fill pipes (downspouts) reach as close to the bottom of the tank as practicable. Any operation such as sampling, taking oil temperature, or gauging that involves lowering a conductive object through an opening into the vapor space on the oil should be deferred until at least 1 minute after flow has ceased. This will permit any surface charge to relax.

(2) Reduce the static generation by one or more of the following:
   (a) Avoid splash filling and upward spraying of oil where bottom filling is used.
   (b) Employ reduced fill rates at the start of filling through downspouts, until the end of the spout is submerged. Some consider 3 ft/sec (0.9 m/sec) to be a suitable precaution.
   (c) Where filters are employed, provide relaxation time in the piping downstream from the filters. A relation time of 30 seconds is considered by some to be a suitable precaution.
(3) Eliminate the flammable mixture before switch loadings by gas freeing or inerting.
[**30:** A.28.11.3]

See NFPA 77, *Recommended Practice on Static Electricity*, and NFPA 385, *Standard for Tank Vehicles for Flammable and Combustible Liquids*, for further information. [**30:** A.28.11.3]

A.66.28.11.4.1 Emergency and safety procedures include, but are not limited to, the following:

(1) Procedures for bonding and grounding the tank vehicle
(2) Proper use of portable extinguishers
(3) Procedures for recognizing and eliminating sources of ignition
(4) Procedures for recognizing and understanding contingency plans for handling a spill or leak
(5) Procedures for notifying the appropriate agencies in an emergency
[**30:** A.28.11.4.1]

A.66.29.3.25 Where practical, the collection basin should be drained to a remote location. [**30:** A.29.3.25]

A.66.29.3.28 Because of the many variables involved, exact requirements cannot be provided. However, Table A.66.29.3.28 provides guidance on the level of fire protection typically provided at wharves and marine terminals handling flammable liquids. [**30:** A.29.3.28]

Table A.66.29.3.28 Typical Fire Protection for Wharves and Marine Terminals

Locations	Water Demand (gpm)	Hydrant Monitors[a] (gpm)	Hose Reels	Fire Extinguisher Dry Chemical 30 lb	Fire Extinguisher Dry Chemical 150 lb Wheeled	International Shore Connection	Emergency Equipment Lockers	Monitors and Hose Foam Concentrate Required (gal)	Fire Boat Connection
Barge terminals	500–1000	Two 500	Two 1¼	2	NR	NR	1	100[b]	NR
Tankers 20,000 DWT and under	1000–2000	Two 500	Two 1¼	2	1	1	1	300[b]	2
20,001–70,000 DWT	2000	Two 1000	Four 1¼[c]	2	2[d]	2	1	2000	2
70,001 DWT and over	2000[e]	Two 1000	Four 1¼[c]	3	2[d]	2	1	2000[f]	2
Sea islands	2000–4000[e]	Three 1000	Four 1¼[c]	4	2	3	2	3000	2

For SI units, 1 gpm = 3.8 L/min; 1 gal = 3.8 L; 1 lb = 0.45 kg.
NR: Not required.
[a]A minimum of two 1½ in. (38 mm) hydrant outlets should be provided at each monitor riser.
[b]Can be provided by onshore mobile equipment.
[c]One hose reel at each berth should have foam capability.
[d]The proximity of adjacent berths can reduce total required.
[e]Under-dock systems are optional. Add water for under-dock system (0.16 × area).
[f]Under-dock systems are optional. Add foam for under-dock system (0.16 × 0.3 × 30 × area).
[**30:** Table A.29.3.28]

A.69.1.1 See A.1.3.2.

A.69.2.1.1.1 Prior to April 1, 1967, regulations of the U.S. Department of Transportation were promulgated by the Interstate Commerce Commission. In Canada, the regulations of the Canadian Transport Commission apply and are available from the Canadian Transport Commission, Union Station, Ottawa, Canada. [**58**: A.5.2.1.1]

Construction of containers to the API-ASME *Code for Unfired Pressure Vessels for Petroleum Liquids and Gases* has not been authorized after July 1, 1961. [**58**: A.5.2.1.1]

A.69.2.1.4.2 The tare weight is the cylinder weight plus the weight of all permanently attached valves and other fittings but does not include the weight of protecting devices that are removed in order to load the cylinder. [**58**: A.5.2.8.2]

A.69.2.1.4.3 Head design refers to the shape of the head. Shapes include hemispherical, semi-ellipsoidal, and others. *(Refer to the API-ASME Code for Unfired Pressure Vessels for Petroleum Liquids and Gases for more information.)* [**58**: A.5.2.8.3]

A.69.3.1 Section 6.4 of NFPA 58 includes general provisions that are applicable to most stationary systems. Sections 6.5 through 6.13 of NFPA 58 extend and modify Section 6.4 of NFPA 58 for systems installed for specific purposes. [**58**: A.6.1.1]

A.69.3.3.1.1 When applying Table 69.3.3.1.1 to cylinders, which have their capacities expressed in pounds, the first table entry, <125 gal (<0.5 m^3), includes all cylinders. Cylinders have a maximum capacity of 1000 lb or 119 gal (454 kg or 3.8 m^3) (water capacity). [**58**: A.6.3.1]

The "Line of Adjoining Property that can be built upon" refers to the property boundaries of the plot adjacent to the one upon which the tank is located. This is illustrated in Figure A.69.3.3.1.1 taking into consideration a condition that involves property on the other side of a street, highway, navigable waterway, or other right of way. The minimum distance limitation is from the tank to the property line where that property line is common to plots of ground of different ownership and would also apply between the tank and the property line of the far side of a street or other public right of way. [**58**: A.6.3.1]

A.69.3.3.4.3 Building openings in the context of 69.3.3.4.3 are any opening that communicates air from the exterior to the interior of the building, including windows, doors, or dryer vent terminations below the level of the relief valve discharge. [**58**: A.6.3.4.2]

A.69.3.4.4.3 Clearance is required between combustible materials and propane containers in order to minimize the effects of fires on the container. The requirement to maintain separation between the container and stored combustible materials is needed so that an accumulation of materials that may represent a hazard to the container does not occur. The term "stored" is intended to denote materials that are purposely placed. Vegetation of any type located near or under the container is not considered to be a hazard. [**58**: A.6.4.4.3]

A.69.3.4.4.4 For information on flash point see NFPA 30 [**58**: A.6.4.4.4]

A.69.3.4.4.9 Also see NFPA 51 for oxygen systems. [**58**: A.6.4.4.9]

A.69.3.4.4.14 Because of the anticipated flash of some nonrefrigerated LP-Gases when released to the atmosphere, dikes normally serve no useful purpose for these nonrefrigerated installations. [**58**: A.6.4.4.14]

A.69.3.4.5 The presence of such structures can create significant hazards, such as the following:

(1) Pocketing of escaping gas
(2) Interference with application of cooling water by fire departments
(3) Redirection of flames against containers
(4) Impeding the egress of personnel in an emergency

[**58**: A.6.4.5]

A.69.3.5.1.1 It is the intent to allow transfer of liquid into containers in open areas under canopies or roofs where 50 percent or more of the perimeter is not enclosed. [**58**: A.6.5.1.1]

A.69.3.6.1.4 Generally, a light-reflecting color paint is preferred unless the system is installed in an extremely cold climate. [**58**: A.6.6.1.4]

A.69.3.8.8 Anchorage can be accomplished by the use of concrete bulkheads or equivalent anchorage or by the use of a weakness or shear fitting. [**58**: A.6.12.8]

A.69.3.9 Gas leaks have resulted from snow or ice accumulations on gas systems, and snow or ice shedding from roofs onto gas systems. In these incidents, external fires have occurred and in some cases gas has migrated into or under buildings, resulting in interior fires or explosions. Selection of appropriate methods of protection should be based upon the installation and anticipated snow and or ice loading. Possible methods of protection include the following:

(1) Minimizing the extent of above-ground piping.
(2) Locating above-ground piping, regulators, and meters above anticipated snow accumulations.
(3) Locating above-ground piping, regulators and meters on the gable end of buildings, rather than under eaves, to prevent damage from snow or ice shedding off of roofs.
(4) Protecting above-ground piping, regulators, and meters with extended roof overhangs or dedicated covers.
(5) Adding additional support above-ground piping, regulators and meters to withstand anticipated snow or ice loading.

[**58**: A.6.16]

A.69.3.10.2.6 The requirement for a pilot or an electronic ignition system became effective for heaters with inputs over 50,000 Btu/hr manufactured on or after May 17, 1967. [**58**: A.6.20.2.6]

A.69.3.10.8.3 The weight of the cylinders will be affected by the specific gravity of the LP-Gas. Weights varying from 16.0 oz to 16.8 oz (454 g to 476 g) are recognized as being within the range of what is nominal. [**58**: A.6.20.9.3]

A.69.3.12.1 Typical non-engine fuel systems include those on commercial, industrial, construction, and public service vehicles such as trucks, semitrailers, trailers, portable tar kettles, road surface heating equipment, mobile laboratories, clinics, and mobile cooking units (such as catering and canteen vehicles). [**58**: A.6.24.1]

A.69.3.12.7.6 Requirements for the design of containers are located in Section 5.2 of NFPA 58. Requirements for container appurtenances are located in Section 5.3 of NFPA 58. [**58**: A.6.24.7.6]

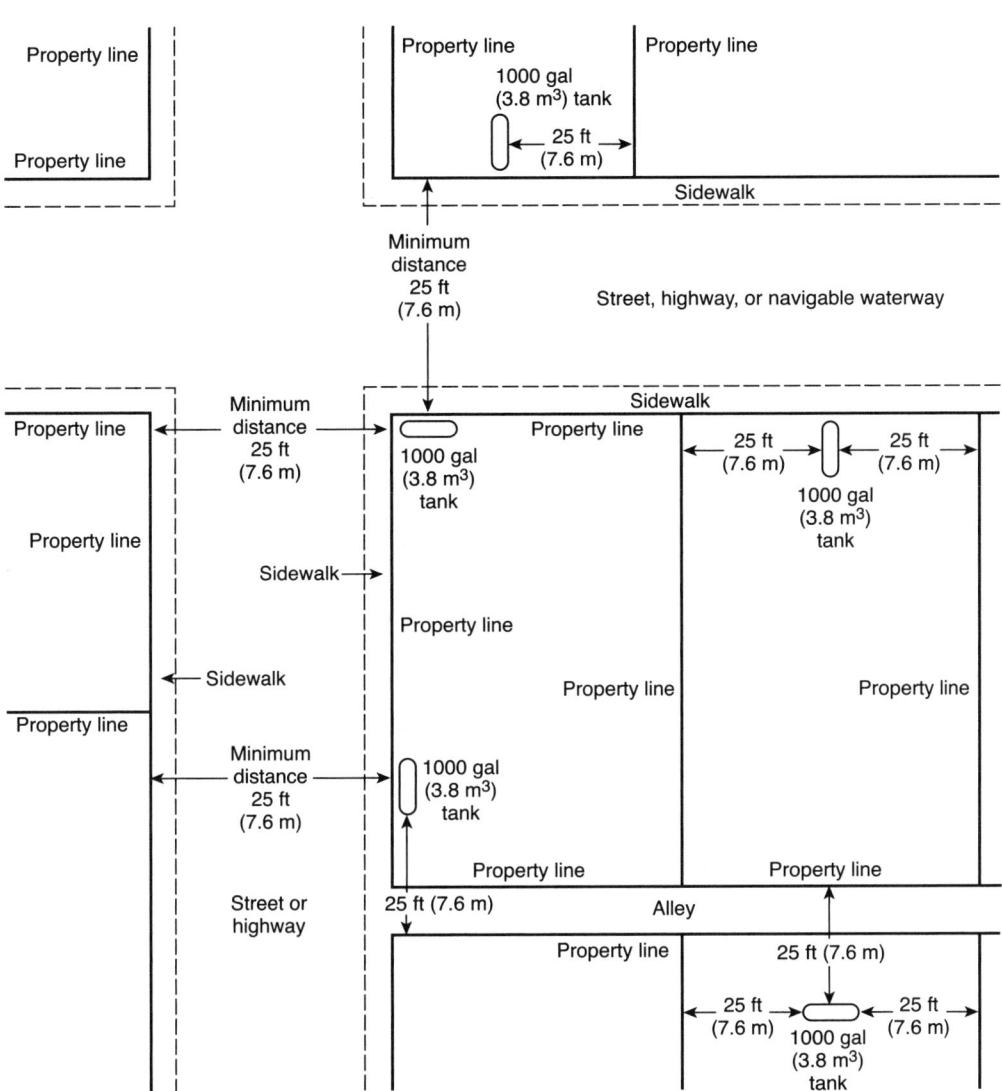

FIGURE A.69.3.3.1.1 Illustration of Separation Distances from Containers to the Line of Adjoining Property that can be Built Upon. [58:Figure A.6.3.1]

A.69.4.1 Ignition source control at transfer locations is covered in Section 6.22 of NFPA 58. Fire protection is covered in Section 6.26 of NFPA 58. [**58:** A.7.1]

A.69.4.2.2.5 Examples of an effective seal are a POL plug or cap. Listed quick-closing couplings with CGA V-1 connection numbers 790 (fork lift ACME connection), 791 (portable cylinder ACME/POL connection), and 810 (socket/plug quick connection) have secondary seals. Therefore, plugs or caps for these connections are not required or recommended. [**58:** A.7.2.2.5]

A.69.4.2.3.5.1 Air-moving equipment includes large blowers on crop dryers, space heaters, and some central heating equipment. Equipment employing open flames includes flame cultivators, weed burners, and tar kettles. [**58:** A.7.2.3.5(A)]

A.69.5.4.1 The filling process in 69.5.4.1.4 refers to the time period beginning when a cylinder or cylinders are brought to a dispensing station to be filled and ending when the last cylinder is filled and all the cylinders are removed from the filling area. This is meant to define a continuous process, with the cylinders being unattended for only brief periods, such as operator breaks or lunch. [**58:** A.8.4.1]

A.69.5.4.2.1 The shelves should be made of any material with a flame spread index, in accordance with ASTM E 84, *Standard Test Method for Surface Burning Characteristics of Building Materials*, or UL 723, *Standard for Test for Surface Burning Characteristics of Building Materials*, of less than 25 and should be of sufficient strength to support the cylinders. [**58:** A.8.4.2.1]

A.69.5.4.2.2 Only minimal VBP, such as either parking bumpers (minimum of 6 inches above grade) or sidewalks (minimum of 6 inches above grade), may be needed for cylinder exchange cabinets. The storage cabinets associated with cylinder exchange may provide limited protection against physical damage to the stored cylinders. Examples of such protection include, but are not limited to:

(1) Guard rails
(2) Steel bollards

(3) Raised sidewalks (minimum of 6 in. in height)
(4) Fencing
(5) Ditches
(6) Berms (not to exceed 50% of the container perimeter)
(7) Jersey barriers
(8) Parking bumpers (minimum of 6 in. in height)
(9) Fencing/Gates
[**58:** A.8.4.2.2]

A.69.5.5 See 6.26.4.4 of NFPA 58. [**58:** A.8.5]

A.69.6.2.2.2 The term "congested area" is intended to describe situations where access to the vehicle during an emergency would be impeded or where moving the vehicle away from an emergency would be prevented. [**58:** A.9.7.2.2]

Annex B   Hazardous Materials Classifications

This annex is not a part of the requirements of this NFPA document but is included for informational purposes only.

B.1 Scope. Annex B provides information, explanations, and examples to illustrate and clarify the hazard categories contained in Chapter 60. The hazard categories are based upon Title 29 of the Code of Federal Regulations. Where numerical classifications are included, they are in accordance with nationally recognized standards. Annex B should not be used as the sole means of hazardous materials classification.

B.2 Hazard Categories.

B.2.1 Physical Hazards.

B.2.1.1 Explosives and Blasting Agents.

B.2.1.1.1 High Explosives. Can be detonated by means of blasting cap when unconfined. Examples: dynamite, TNT, nitroglycerine, C-3, and C-4.

B.2.1.1.2 Low Explosives. Can be deflagrated when confined. Examples: black powder, smokeless powder, propellant explosives, and display fireworks.

B.2.1.1.3 Blasting Agents. Oxidizer and liquid fuel slurry mixtures. Example: ammonium nitrate combined with fuel oil.

B.2.1.2 Compressed Gases.

B.2.1.2.1 Flammable. Examples: acetylene, carbon monoxide, ethane, ethylene, hydrogen, and methane.

B.2.1.2.2 Oxidizing. Examples: oxygen, ozone, oxides of nitrogen, chlorine, and fluorine. Chlorine and fluorine do not contain oxygen but reaction with flammables is similar to that of oxygen.

B.2.1.2.3 Corrosive. Examples: ammonia, hydrogen chloride, and fluorine.

B.2.1.2.4 Highly Toxic. Examples: arsine, cyanogen, fluorine, germane, hydrogen cyanide, hydrogen selenide, nitric oxide, phosphine, and stibene.

B.2.1.2.5 Toxic. Examples: chlorine, hydrogen fluoride, hydrogen sulfide, silicon tetrafluoride, and phosgene.

B.2.1.2.6 Inert (Chemically Unreactive). Examples: argon, helium, krypton, neon, nitrogen, and xenon.

B.2.1.2.7 Pyrophoric. Examples: diborane, dichloroborane, phosphine, and silane.

B.2.1.2.8 Unstable (Reactive). Examples: butadiene (unstabilized), ethylene oxide, and vinyl chloride.

B.2.1.3 Flammable and Combustible Liquids.

B.2.1.3.1 Flammable Liquids.

B.2.1.3.1.1 Class I-A liquids include those having flash points below 73°F (22.8°C) and having a boiling point below 100°F (37.8°C).

B.2.1.3.1.2 Class I-B liquids include those having flash points below 73°F (22.8°C) and having a boiling point at or above 100°F (37.8°C).

B.2.1.3.1.3 Class I-C liquids include those having flash points at or above 73°F (22.8°C) and below 100°F (37.8°C).

B.2.1.3.2 Combustible Liquids.

B.2.1.3.2.1 Class II liquids include those having flash points at or above 100°F (37.8°C) and below 140°F (60°C).

B.2.1.3.2.2 Class III-A liquids include those having flash points at or above 140°F (60°C) and below 200°F (93.3°C).

B.2.1.3.2.3 Class III-B liquids include those liquids having flash points at or above 200°F (93.3°C).

B.2.1.4 Flammable Solids.

B.2.1.4.1 Organic Solids. Examples: camphor, cellulose nitrate, and naphthalene.

B.2.1.4.2 Inorganic Solids. Examples: decaborane, lithium amide, phosphorous heptasulfide, phosphorous sesquisulfide, potassium sulfide, anhydrous sodium sulfide, and sulfur.

B.2.1.4.3 Combustible Metals (Except Dusts and Powders). Examples: cesium, magnesium, and zirconium.

B.2.1.4.4 Combustible Dusts and Powders (Including Metals). Examples: wood sawdust, plastics, coal, flour, and powdered metals (few exceptions).

B.2.1.5 Oxidizers.

B.2.1.5.1 Gases. Examples: oxygen, ozone, oxides of nitrogen, fluorine, and chlorine (reaction with flammables is similar to that of oxygen).

B.2.1.5.2 Liquids. Examples: bromine, hydrogen peroxide, nitric acid, perchloric acid, and sulfuric acid.

B.2.1.5.3 Solids. Examples: chlorates, chromates, chromic acid, iodine, nitrates, perchlorates, and peroxides.

B.2.1.5.4 Examples of Liquid and Solid Oxidizers According to Hazard.

B.2.1.5.4.1 Class 4. Examples: ammonium perchlorate (particle size greater than 15 microns), ammonium permanganate, guanidine nitrate, hydrogen peroxide solutions (greater than 91 percent), and tetranitromethane.

B.2.1.5.4.2 Class 3. Examples: ammonium dichromate, calcium hypochlorite (over 50 percent by weight), chloric acid (10 percent maximum concentration), hydrogen peroxide solutions (greater than 52 percent up to 91 percent), mono-(trichloro)-tetra-(monopotassium dichloro)-penta-s-triazinetrione, nitric acid, fuming (more than 86 percent concentration), perchloric acid solutions (60 percent to 72 percent by weight), potassium bromate, potassium chlorate, potassium dichloro-s-triazinetrione (potassium dichloroisocyanurate), sodium bromate, sodium chlorate, sodium chlorite (over 40 percent by weight), and sodium dichloro-s-triazinetrione (sodium dichloroisocyanurate).

B.2.1.5.4.3 Class 2. Examples: barium bromate, barium chlorate, barium hypochlorite, barium perchlorate, barium permanganate, 1-bromo-3-chloro-5, 5-dimethylhydantoin, calcium chlorate, calcium chlorite, calcium hypochlorite (50 percent or less by weight), calcium perchlorate, calcium permanganate, chromium trioxide (chromic acid), copper chlorate, halane (1,3-dichloro-5, 5-dimethylhydantoin), hydrogen peroxide (greater than 27.5 percent up to 52 percent), lead perchlorate, lithium chlorate, lithium hypochlorite (more than 39 percent available chlorine), lithium perchlorate, magnesium bromate, magnesium chlorate, magnesium perchlorate, mercurous chlorate, nitric acid (more than 40 percent but less than 86 percent), perchloric acid solutions (more than 50 percent but less than 60 percent), potassium perchlorate, potassium permanganate, potassium peroxide, potassium superoxide, silver peroxide, sodium chlorite (40 percent or less by weight), sodium perchlorate, sodium perchlorate monohydrate, sodium permanganate, sodium peroxide, strontium chlorate, strontium perchlorate, thallium chlorate, trichloro-s-triazinetrione (trichloroisocyanuric acid), urea hydrogen peroxide, zinc bromate, zinc chlorate, and zinc permanganate.

B.2.1.5.4.4 Class 1. Examples: all inorganic nitrates (unless otherwise classified), all inorganic nitrites (unless otherwise classified), ammonium persulfate, barium peroxide, calcium peroxide, hydrogen peroxide solutions (greater than 8 percent up to 27.5 percent), lead dioxide, lithium hypochlorite (39 percent or less available chlorine), lithium peroxide, magnesium peroxide, manganese dioxide, nitric acid (40 percent concentration or less), perchloric acid solutions (less than 50 percent by weight), potassium dichromate, potassium percarbonate, potassium persulfate, sodium carbonate peroxide, sodium dichloro-s-triazinetrione dihydrate, sodium dichromate, sodium perborate (anhydrous), sodium perborate monohydrate, sodium perborate tetrahydrate, sodium percarbonate, sodium persulfate, strontium peroxide, and zinc peroxide.

B.2.1.6 Organic Peroxides. Examples of organic peroxides according to hazard: Unclassified. Unclassified organic peroxides are capable of detonation and are regulated in accordance with Chapter 75.

B.2.1.6.1 Class I. Examples: acetyl cyclohexane sulfonyl 60-65 percent concentration by weight, fulfonyl peroxide, benzoyl peroxide over 98 percent concentration, t-butyl hydroperoxide 90 percent, t-butyl peroxyacetate 75 percent, t-butyl peroxyisopropylcarbonate 92 percent, diisopropyl peroxydicarbonate 100 percent, di-n-propyl peroxydicarbonate 98 percent, and di-n-propyl peroxydi-carbonate 85 percent.

B.2.1.6.2 Class II. Examples: acetyl peroxide 25 percent, t-butyl hydroperoxide 70 percent, t-butyl peroxybenzoate 98 percent, t-butyl peroxy-2-ethylhex-anoate 97 percent, t-butyl peroxyisobutyrate 75 percent, t-butyl peroxyisopropylcarbonate 75 percent, t-butyl peroxypivalate 75 percent, dybenz-oyl peroxydicarbonate 85 percent, di-sec-butyl peroxydicarbonate 98 percent, di-sec-butyl peroxydicarbonate 75 percent, 1,1-di-(t-butylperoxy)-3,5,5-trimethyecyclohexane 95 percent, di-(2-ethyhexyl) peroxydicarbonate 97 percent, 2,5-dymethyl-2-5 di (benzoylperoxy) hexane 92 percent, and peroxyacetic acid 43 percent.

B.2.1.6.3 Class III. Examples: acetyl cyclohexane sulfonal peroxide 29 percent, benzoyl peroxide 78 percent, benzoyl peroxide paste 55 percent, benzoyl peroxide paste 50 percent peroxide/50 percent butylbenzylphthalate diluent, cumene hydroperoxide 86 percent, di-(4-butylcyclohexyl) peroxydicarbonate 98 percent, t-butyl peroxy-2-ethylexanoate 97 percent, t-butyl peroxyneodecanoate 75 percent, decanoyl peroxide 98.5 percent, di-t-butyl peroxide 99 percent, 1,1-di-(t-butylperoxy)-3,5,5-trimethylcyclohexane 75 per-cent, 2,4-dichlorobenzoyl peroxide 50 percent, diisopropyl peroxydi-carbonate 30 percent, 2,-5-dimethyl-2,5-di- (2-ethylhexanolyperoxy)-hexane 90 percent, 2,5-dimethyl-2,5-di- (t-butylperoxy) hexane 90 percent, and methyl ethyl ketone peroxide 9 percent active oxygen diluted in dimethyl phthalate.

B.2.1.6.4 Class IV. Examples: benzoyl peroxide 70 percent, benzoyl peroxide paste 50 percent peroxide/15 percent water/35 percent butylphthalate diluent, benzoyl peroxide slurry 40 percent, benzoyl peroxide powder 35 percent, t-butyl hydroperoxide 70 percent, t-butyl peroxy-2-ethylhexanoate 50 percent, decumyl peroxide 98 percent, di-(2-ethylhexal) peroxydicarbonate 40 percent, laurel peroxide 98 percent, p-methane hydroperoxide 52.5 percent, methyl ethyl ketone peroxide 5.5 percent active oxygen and methyl ethyl ketone peroxide 9 percent active oxygen diluted in water and glycols.

B.2.1.6.5 Class V. Examples: benzoyl peroxide 35 percent, 1,1-di-t-butyl peroxy 3,5,5-trimethylcyclohexane 40 percent, 2,5-di-(t-butyl peroxy) hexane 47 percent, and 2,4-pentanedione peroxide 4 percent active oxygen.

B.2.1.7 Pyrophoric Materials.

B.2.1.7.1 Gases. Examples: diborane, phosphine, and silane.

B.2.1.7.2 Liquids. Examples: diethyl aluminum chloride, diethyl beryllium, diethyl phosphine, diethyl zinc, dimethyl arsine, triethyl aluminum etherate, thriethyl bismuthine, thriethyl boron, trimethyl aluminum, and trimethyl gallium.

B.2.1.7.3 Solids. Examples: cesium, hafnium, lithium, white or yellow phosphorus, plutonium, potassium, rubidium, sodium, and thorium.

B.2.1.8 Examples of Unstable (Reactive) Materials According to Hazard. Classification by degree of hazard must be in accordance with Chapter 71.

B.2.1.8.1 Class 4. Examples: acetyl peroxide, dibutyl peroxide, dinitrobenzene, ethyl nitrate, peroxyacetic acid, and picric acid (dry) trinitrobenzene.

B.2.1.8.2 Class 3. Examples: hydrogen peroxide (greater than 52 percent), hydroxylamine, nitromethane, paranitroaniline, perchloric acid, and tetrafluoroethylene monomer.

B.2.1.8.3 Class 2. Examples: acrolein, acrylic acid, hydrazine, methacrylic acid, sodium perchlorate, styrene, and vinyl acetate.

B.2.1.8.4 Class 1. Examples: acetic acid, hydrogen peroxide 35 percent to 52 percent, paraldehyde, and tetrahydrofuran.

B.2.1.9 Examples of Water-Reactive Materials According to Hazard. Classification by degree of hazard must be in accordance with Chapter 73.

B.2.1.9.1 Class 3. Examples: aluminum alkyls such as triethylaluminum, isobutylaluminum, and trimethylaluminum; bromine pentafluoride, bromine trifluoride, chlorodiethylaluminium, and diethylzinc.

B.2.1.9.2 Class 2. Examples: calcium carbide, calcium metal, cyanogen bromide, lithium hydride, methyldichlorosilane, potassium metal, potassium peroxide, sodium metal, sodium peroxide, sulfuric acid, and trichlorosilane.

B.2.1.9.3 Class 1. Examples: acetic anhydride, sodium hydroxide, sulfur monochloride, and titanium tetrachloride.

B.2.1.10 Cryogenic Fluids. All of the cryogenics listed will exist as compressed gases when they are stored at ambient temperatures.

B.2.1.10.1 Flammable. Examples: carbon monoxide, deuterium (heavy hydrogen), ethylene, hydrogen, and methane.

B.2.1.10.2 Oxidizing. Examples: fluorine, nitric oxide, and oxygen.

B.2.1.10.3 Corrosive. Examples: fluorine and nitric oxide.

B.2.1.10.4 Inert (Chemically Unreactive). Examples: argon, helium, krypton, neon, nitrogen, and xenon.

B.2.1.10.5 Highly Toxic. Examples: fluorine and nitric oxide.

B.2.2 Health Hazards.

B.2.2.1 Highly Toxic and Toxic Materials.

B.2.2.1.1 Highly Toxic Materials.

B.2.2.1.1.1 Gases. Examples: arsine, chlorine trifluoride, cyanogen, diborane, fluorine, germane, hydrogen cyanide, nitric oxide, nitrogen dioxide, ozone, phosphine, hydrogen selenide, and stibene.

B.2.2.1.1.2 Liquids. Examples: acrolein, acrylic acid, 2-chloroethanol (ethylene chlorohydrin), hydazine, hydrocyanic acid, 2-methylaziridine (propylenimine), 2-methyllactonitrile (acetone cyanohydrin), methyl ester isocyanic acid (methyl isocyanate), nicotine, tetranitromethane, and tetraethylstannane (tetraethyl tin).

B.2.2.1.1.3 Solids. Examples: (acetato) phenylmercury (phenyl mercuric acetate), 4-aminopyridine, arsenic pentoxide, arsenic trioxide, calcium cyanide, 2-choloroacetophenone, aflatoxin B, decaborane (14), mercury (II) bromide (mercuric bromide), mercury (II) chloride (corrosive mercury chloride), pentachlorophenol, methyl parathion, phosphorus (white), and sodium azide.

B.2.2.1.2 Toxic Materials.

B.2.2.1.2.1 Gases. Examples: boron trichloride, boron trifluoride, chlorine, hydrogen fluoride, hydrogen sulfide, phosgene, and silicon tetrafluoride.

B.2.2.1.2.2 Liquids. Examples: acrylonitrile, allyl alcohol, alpha-chlorotoluene, aniline, 1-chloro-2, 3-epoxypropane, chloroformic acid (allyl ester), 3-chloropropene (allyl chloride), o-cresol, crotonaldehyde, dibromomethane, diisopropylamine, diethyl ester sulfuric acid, dimethyl ester sulfuric acid, 2-furaldehyde (furfural), furfuryl alcohol, phosphorus chloride, phosphoryl chloride (phosphorus oxychloride), and thionyl chloride.

B.2.2.1.2.3 Solids. Examples: acrylamide, barium chloride, barium (II) nitrate, benzidine, p-benzoquinone, beryllium chloride, cadmium chloride, cadmium oxide, chloroacetic acid, chlorophenylmercury (phenyl mercuric chloride), chromium (VI) oxide (chromic acid, solid), 2,4-dinitrotoluene, hydroquinone, mercury chloride (calomel), mercury (II) sulfate (mercuric sulfate), osmium tetroxide, oxalic acid, phenol, P-phenylenediamine, phenylhydrazine, 4-phenylmorpholine, phosphorus sulfide, potassium fluoride, potassium hydroxide, selenium (IV) disulfide, and sodium fluoride.

B.2.2.2 Radioactive Materials. (Reserved)

B.2.2.3 Corrosives.

B.2.2.3.1 Acids. Examples: chromic, formic, hydrochloric (muriatic greater than 15 percent), hydrofluoric, nitric (greater than 6 percent), perchloric, and sulfuric (4 percent or more).

B.2.2.3.2 Bases (Alkalis). Examples: hydroxides — ammonium (greater than 10 percent), calcium, potassium (greater than 1 percent), sodium (greater than 1 percent), and certain carbonates — potassium.

B.2.2.3.3 Other Corrosives. Examples: bromine, chlorine, fluorine, iodine, and ammonia.

Note: Corrosives that are oxidizers, e.g., nitric acid, chlorine, fluorine; or are compressed gases, e.g., ammonia, chlorine, fluorine; or are water-reactive, e.g., concentrated sulfuric acid, sodium hydroxide, are physical hazards in addition to being health hazards.

B.2.2.4 Carcinogens, Irritants, Sensitizers, and Other Health Hazard Materials. (Reserved)

B.3 Evaluation of Hazards.

B.3.1 Degree of Hazard. The degree of hazard present depends upon many variables that should be considered individually and in combination. Some of the variables are as follows in B.3.1.1 through B.3.1.3.

B.3.1.1 Chemical Properties of the Material. Chemical properties of the material determine self-reactions and reactions that can occur with other materials. Generally, materials within subdivisions of hazard categories exhibit similar chemical properties. However, materials with similar chemical properties can present very different hazards. Each individual material should be researched to determine its hazardous properties and then considered in relation to other materials that it could contact and the surrounding environment.

B.3.1.2 Physical Properties of the Material. Physical properties, such as whether a material is a solid, liquid, or gas at ordinary temperatures and pressures, considered along with chemical properties determines requirements for containment of the material. Specific gravity (weight of a liquid compared to water) and vapor density (weight of a gas compared to air) are both physical properties that are important in evaluating the hazards of a material.

B.3.1.3 Amount and Concentration of the Material.

B.3.1.3.1 General. The amount of material present and its concentration must be considered along with physical and chemical properties to determine the magnitude of the hazard. Hydrogen peroxide, for example, is used as an antiseptic and a hair bleach in low concentrations (approximately 8 percent in water solution). Over 8 percent, hydrogen peroxide is classed as an oxidizer and is toxic. Above 90 percent, it is a Class 4 oxidizer "that can undergo an explosive reaction when catalyzed or exposed to heat, shock, or friction," a definition that incidentally also places hydrogen peroxide over 90 percent concentration in the unstable (reactive) category. Small amounts at high concentrations can present a greater hazard than large amounts at low concentrations.

B.3.1.3.2 Mixtures. Gases — toxic and highly toxic gases include those gases that have an LC_{50} of 2000 parts per million (ppm) or less when rats are exposed for a period of 1 hour or less. To maintain consistency with the definitions for these materials, exposure data for periods other than 1 hour must be normalized to 1 hour. To classify mixtures of compressed gases that contain one or more toxic or highly toxic components, the LC_{50} of the mixture must be determined. Mixtures that contain only two components are binary mixtures. Those that contain more than two components are multicomponent mixtures. When two or more hazardous substances (components) having an LC_{50} below 2000 ppm are present in a mixture, their combined effect, rather than that of the individual substances (components), must be considered. In the absence of information to the contrary, the effects of the hazards present must be considered as additive. Exceptions to the above rule can be made when there is a good reason to believe that the principal effects of the different harmful substances (components) are not additive.

For binary mixtures where the hazardous component is diluted with a nontoxic gas such as an inert gas, the LC_{50} of the mixture is estimated by use of the following formula:

$$LC_{50m} = \frac{1}{\left(\dfrac{C_i}{LC_{50i}}\right)} \qquad [\text{B.3.1.3.2a}]$$

For multicomponent mixtures where more than one component has a listed LC_{50}, the LC_{50} of the mixture is estimated by use of the following formula:

$$LC_{50m} = \frac{1}{\left(\dfrac{C_{i1}}{LC_{50i1}}\right) + \left(\dfrac{C_{i2}}{LC_{50i2}}\right) + \left(\dfrac{C_{in}}{LC_{50e}}\right)} \qquad [\text{B.3.1.3.2b}]$$

where:
LC_{50m} = LC_{50} of the mixture in parts per million (ppm).
C = concentration of component (i) in decimal percent. The concentration of the individual components in a mixture of gases is to be expressed in terms of percent by volume.
LC_{50i} = LC_{50} of component (i). The LC_{50} of the component is based on a 1-hour exposure. LC_{50} data that are for other than 1-hour exposures must be normalized to 1 hour by multiplying the LC_{50} for the time determined by the factor indicated in Table B.3.1.3.2. The preferred mammalian species for LC_{50} data is the rat, as specified in the definitions of toxic and highly toxic in Chapter 3. If data for rats are unavailable, and in the absence of information to the contrary, data for other species can be utilized. The data must be taken in the following order of preference: rat, mouse, rabbit, guinea pig, cat, dog, and monkey.
i_n = component 1, component 2, and so on to the nth component.

Examples:

A. What is the LC_{50} of a mixture of 15 percent chlorine, 85 percent nitrogen? The 1-hour (rat) LC_{50} of pure chlorine is 293 ppm.

LC_{50m} = 1 / (0.15 / 293) or 1953 ppm. Therefore the mixture is toxic.

Table B.3.1.3.2 Normalization Factor

Time (hours)	Multiply By
0.5	0.7
1.0	1.0
1.5	1.2
2.0	1.4
3.0	1.7
4.0	2.0
5.0	2.2
6.0	2.4
7.0	2.6
8.0	2.8

B. What is the LC_{50} of a mixture of 15 percent chlorine, 15 percent fluorine, and 70 percent nitrogen? The 1-hour (rat) LC_{50} of chlorine is 293 ppm. The 1-hour (rat) LC_{50} of fluorine is 185 ppm.

LC_{50m} = 1 / (0.15 / 293) + (0.15 / 185) or 755 ppm. Therefore the mixture is toxic.

C. Is the mixture of 1 percent phosphine in argon toxic or highly toxic? The 4-hour (rat) LC_{50} is 11 ppm.

LC_{50m} = 1 / [0.01 / (11 × 2)] or 2200 ppm. Therefore the mixture is neither toxic nor highly toxic. Note that the 4-hour LC_{50} of 11 ppm was normalized to 1 hour by use of Table B.3.1.3.2.

B.3.1.3.3 Actual Use, Activity, or Process Involving the Material. The definition of handling, storage, and use in closed systems refers to materials in packages or containers. Dispensing and use in open containers or systems describes situations where a material is exposed to ambient conditions or vapors are liberated to the atmosphere. Dispensing and use in open systems, then, are generally more hazardous situations than handling, storage, or use in closed systems. The actual use or process can include heating, electric or other sparks, catalytic or reactive materials, and many other factors that could affect the hazard and must therefore be thoroughly analyzed.

B.3.1.3.4 Surrounding Conditions. Conditions such as other materials or processes in the area, type of construction of the structure, fire protection features (e.g., fire walls, sprinkler systems, alarms, etc.), occupancy (use) of adjoining areas, normal temperatures, exposure to weather, etc., must be taken into account in evaluating the hazard.

B.3.2 Evaluation Questions. The following are sample evaluation questions:

(1) What is the material? Correct identification is important; exact spelling is vital. Check labels, MSDS, ask responsible persons, etc.
(2) What are the concentration and strength?
(3) What is the physical form of the material? Liquids, gases, and finely divided solids have differing requirements for spill and leak control and containment.
(4) How much material is present? Consider in relation to permit amounts, exempt amounts (from Group H Occupancy requirements), amounts that require detached storage, and overall magnitude of the hazard.
(5) What other materials (including furniture, equipment, and building components) are close enough to interact with the material?
(6) What are the likely reactions?

(7) What is the activity involving the material?
(8) How does the activity impact the hazardous characteristics of the material? Consider vapors released or hazards otherwise exposed.
(9) What must the material be protected from? Consider other materials, temperature, shock, pressure, etc.
(10) What effects of the material must people and the environment be protected from?
(11) How can protection be accomplished? Consider the following:
   (a) Proper containers and equipment
   (b) Separation by distance or construction
   (c) Enclosure in cabinets or rooms
   (d) Spill control, drainage, and containment
   (e) Control systems — ventilation, special electrical, detection and alarm, extinguishment, explosion venting, limit controls, exhaust scrubbers, and excess flow control
   (f) Administrative (operational) controls — signs, ignition source control, security, personnel training, established procedures, storage plans, and emergency action plans

Evaluation of the hazard is a strongly subjective process; therefore, the person charged with this responsibility must gather as much relevant data as possible so that the decision is objective and within the limits prescribed in laws, policies, and standards.

It could be necessary to cause the responsible persons in charge to have tests made by qualified persons or testing laboratories to support contentions that a particular material or process is or is not hazardous. See 1.4.2.

B.4 Reference Publications. (Reserved)

B.5 Oxidizers and Organic Peroxides.

B.5.1 General. This annex provides information, explanations, and examples to illustrate and clarify the hazard categories contained in Chapter 70 and Chapter 75 of this *Code*. The hazard categories are based on 29 CFR. Where numerical classifications are included, they are in accordance with nationally recognized standards.

B.5.2 Oxidizers.

B.5.2.1 General. The oxidizers on the following lists are typical for their class. Each oxidizer is undiluted unless a concentration is specified.

Unless concentration is specified, undiluted material is referenced. The following lists of oxidizers are provided to clarify how the NFPA Hazardous Chemicals Committee has classified typical oxidizers. The lists are not all-inclusive and are amended to reflect typical oxidizers used.

B.5.2.2 Class 1 Oxidizers. The following are typical Class 1 oxidizers:

(1) All inorganic nitrates (unless otherwise classified)
(2) All inorganic nitrites (unless otherwise classified)
(3) Ammonium persulfate
(4) Barium peroxide
(5) Calcium hypochlorite (nominal 80 percent, maximum 81 percent) blended with magnesium sulfate heptahydrate (nominal 20 percent, minimum 19 percent) having an available chlorine of less than or equal to 66 percent and a total water content of at least 17 percent.
(6) Calcium peroxide
(7) Hydrogen peroxide solutions (greater than 8 percent up to 27.5 percent)
(8) Lead dioxide
(9) Lithium hypochlorite (39 percent or less available chlorine)
(10) Lithium peroxide
(11) Magnesium peroxide
(12) Manganese dioxide
(13) Nitric acid (40 percent concentration or less)
(14) Perchloric acid solutions (less than 50 percent by weight)
(15) Potassium dichromate
(16) Potassium percarbonate
(17) Potassium persulfate
(18) Sodium carbonate peroxide
(19) Sodium dichloro-s-triazinetrione dihydrate (sodium dicholorisocyanurate dihydrate)
(20) Sodium dichromate
(21) Sodium perborate (anhydrous)
(22) Sodium perborate monohydrate
(23) Sodium perborate tetrahydrate
(24) Sodium percarbonate
(25) Sodium persulfate
(26) Strontium peroxide
(27) Trichloro-s-triazinetrione [trichloroisocyanuric acid (TCCA; trichlor), all physical forms]
(28) Zinc peroxide [**400:** G.3.2]

B.5.2.3 Class 2 Oxidizers. The following are typical Class 2 oxidizers:

(1) Barium bromate
(2) Barium chlorate
(3) Barium hypochlorite
(4) Barium perchlorate
(5) Barium permanganate
(6) 1-Bromo-3-chloro-5,5-dimethylhydantoin (BCDMH)
(7) Calcium chlorate
(8) Calcium chlorite
(9) Calcium hypochlorite (50 percent or less by weight unless covered by other formulations in B.5.2)
(10) Calcium perchlorate
(11) Calcium permanganate
(12) Chromium trioxide (chromic acid)
(13) Copper chlorate
(14) Halane (1,3-dichloro-5,5-dimethylhydantoin)
(15) Hydrogen peroxide (greater than 27.5 percent up to 52 percent)
(16) Lead perchlorate
(17) Lithium chlorate
(18) Lithium hypochlorite (more than 39 percent available chlorine)
(19) Lithium perchlorate
(20) Magnesium bromate
(21) Magnesium chlorate
(22) Magnesium perchlorate
(23) Mercurous chlorate
(24) Nitric acid (more than 40 percent but less than 86 percent)
(25) Nitrogen tetroxide
(26) Perchloric acid solutions (more than 50 percent but less than 60 percent)
(27) Potassium perchlorate
(28) Potassium permanganate
(29) Potassium peroxide
(30) Potassium superoxide

(31) Silver peroxide
(32) Sodium chlorite (40 percent or less by weight)
(33) Sodium perchlorate
(34) Sodium perchlorate monohydrate
(35) Sodium permanganate
(36) Sodium peroxide
(37) Strontium chlorate
(38) Strontium perchlorate
(39) Thallium chlorate
(40) Urea hydrogen peroxide
(41) Zinc bromate
(42) Zinc chlorate
(43) Zinc permanganate [**400:** G.3.3]

B.5.2.4 Class 3 Oxidizers. The following are typical Class 3 oxidizers:

(1) Ammonium dichromate
(2) Calcium hypochlorite (over 50 percent by weight unless covered in other formulations in B.5.2)
(3) Calcium hypochlorite (over 50 percent by weight)
(4) Chloric acid (10 percent maximum concentration)
(5) Hydrogen peroxide solutions (greater than 52 percent up to 91 percent)
(6) Mono-(trichloro)-tetra-(monopotassium dichloro)-penta-s-triazinetrione
(7) Nitric acid, fuming (more than 86 percent concentration)
(8) Perchloric acid solutions (60 percent to 72 percent by weight)
(9) Potassium bromate
(10) Potassium chlorate
(11) Potassium dichloro-s-triazinetrione (potassium dichloro-isocyanurate)
(12) Sodium bromate
(13) Sodium chlorate
(14) Sodium chlorite (over 40 percent by weight)
(15) Sodium dichloro-s-triazinetrione anhydrous (sodium dichloroisocyanurate anhydrous) [**400:** G.3.4]

B.5.2.5 Class 4 Oxidizers. The following are typical Class 4 oxidizers:

(1) Ammonium perchlorate (particle size greater than 15 microns)
(2) Ammonium permanganate
(3) Guanidine nitrate
(4) Hydrogen peroxide solutions (greater than 91 percent)
(5) Tetranitromethane

Ammonium perchlorate less than 15 microns is classified as an explosive and, as such, is not covered by NFPA 400. (*See NFPA 495.*) [**400:** G.3.5]

B.5.3 Typical Organic Peroxide Formulations.

B.5.3.1 General. The assignment of the organic peroxide formulation classifications shown in the tables in this annex are based on the container sizes shown. A change in the container size could affect the classification.

For an alphabetical listing of typical organic peroxide formulations, see Table B.5.3.1. [**400:** F.1]

Table B.5.3.1 Typical Organic Peroxide Formulations

| Organic Peroxide | Concentration | Diluent | Recommended Maximum Temperatures[1] | | | | Hazard Identification[2] | | | Class | Container |
| | | | Control | | Emergency | | | | | | |
			°F	°C	°F	°C	Health	Flammability	Reactivity		
t-Amyl hydroperoxide	88	Water					3	3	2	III	55 gal (208 L)
t-Amyl peroxyacetate	60	OMS					2	3	2	III	5 gal (19 L)
t-Amyl peroxybenzoate	96	—					2	3	2	II	5 gal (19 L)
t-Amyl peroxy-2-ethylhexanoate	96	—	68	20	77	25	0	3	2	III	55 gal (208 L)
t-Amyl peroxyneodecanoate	75	OMS	32	0	50	10	1	3	2	III	5 gal (19 L)
t-Amyl peroxypivalate	75	OMS	50	10	59	15	1	3	2	III	5 gal (19 L)
t-Butyl cumyl peroxide	95	—					2	2	2	IV	55 gal (208 L)
n-Butyl-4,4-di(t-butyl peroxy) valerate	98	—					2	3	2	II	5 gal (19 L)
t-Butyl hydroperoxide	90	Water and t-BuOH					3	3	3	I	5 gal (19 L)
t-Butyl hydroperoxide[3]	70	DTBP and t-BuOH					3	3	3	II	55 gal (208 L)
t-Butyl hydroperoxide[3]	70	Water					3	2	2	IV	55 gal (208 L)
t-Butyl monoperoxymaleate	98	—					2	3	3	I	50 @ 1 lb (50 @ 0.5 kg)
t-Butyl peroxyacetate	75	OMS					1	3	3	I	5 gal (19 L)
t-Butyl peroxyacetate	60	OMS					1	3	3	I	5 gal (19 L)
t-Butyl peroxybenzoate	98	—					1	3	3	II	5 gal (19 L)
t-Butyl peroxy-2-ethylhexanoate	97	—	68	20	77	25	1	3	3	III	5 gal (19 L)
t-Butyl peroxy-2-ethylhexanoate	97	—	68	20	77	25	1	3	3	II	55 gal (208 L)
t-Butyl peroxy-2-ethylhexanoate	50	DOP or OMS	86	30	95	35	1	2	2	IV	5 gal (19 L)
t-Butyl peroxy-2-ethylhexanoate	50	DOP or OMS	86	30	95	35	1	2	2	III	55 gal (208 L)

(*continues*)

Table B.5.3.1 *Continued*

Organic Peroxide	Concentration	Diluent	Control °F	Control °C	Emergency °F	Emergency °C	Health	Flammability	Reactivity	Class	Container
t-Butylperoxy 2-ethylhexyl carbonate	95	—					1	3	2	III	5 gal (19 L)
t-Butyl peroxyisobutyrate	75	OMS	59	15	68	20	2	3	3	II	5 gal (19 L)
t-Butylperoxy isopropyl carbonate	92	OMS					1	3	3	I	5 gal (19 L)
t-Butylperoxy isopropyl carbonate	75	OMS					1	3	3	II	5 gal (19 L)
t-Butyl peroxyneodecanoate	75	OMS	32	0	50	10	2	3	2	III	5 gal (19 L)
t-Butyl peroxypivalate	75	OMS	32	0	50	10	2	3	3	II	5 gal (19 L)
t-Butyl peroxypivalate	45	OMS	32	0	50	10	2	2	2	IV	5 gal (19 L)
Cumyl hydroperoxide	88	Cumene					3	2	2	III	55 gal (208 L)
Cumyl peroxyneodecanoate	75	OMS	14	−10	32	0	1	3	2	III	5 gal (19 L)
Cumyl peroxyneoheptanoate	75	OMS	32	0	50	10	2	3	2	III	5 gal (19 L)
Diacetyl peroxide	25	DMP	68	20	77	25	2	3	3	II	5 gal (19 L)
1,1-Di(t-amylperoxy) cyclohexane	80	OMS or BBP					2	3	2	III	5 gal (19 L)
Dibenzoyl peroxide	98	—					1	3	4	I	1 lb (0.5 kg)
Dibenzoyl peroxide	78	Water					1	2	3	II	25 lb (11 kg)
Dibenzoyl peroxide	75	Water					1	2	2	III	25 lb (11 kg)
Dibenzoyl peroxide	70	Water					1	2	2	IV	25 lb (11 kg)
Dibenzoyl peroxide (paste)	55	Plasticizer	T[4]				1	2	2	III	350 lb (160 kg)
Dibenzoyl peroxide (paste)	55	Plasticizer and water	T				1	2	2	IV	350 lb (160 kg)
Dibenzoyl peroxide (paste)	50	Plasticizer	T				1	2	2	III	380 lb (170 kg)
Dibenzoyl peroxide (paste)	50	Plasticizer and water	T				1	2	2	IV	380 lb (170 kg)
Dibenzoyl peroxide (slurry)	40	Water and plasticizer	T				1	2	2	IV	380 lb (170 kg)
Dibenzoyl peroxide (slurry)	40	Water					1	2	2	IV	5 gal (19 L)
Dibenzoyl peroxide (powder)	35	Dicalcium phosphate dihydrate or calcium sulfate dihydrate					1	0	0	V	100 lb (45 kg)
Dibenzoyl peroxide (powder)	35	Starch					1	2	2	IV	100 lb (45 kg)
Di (4-t-butylcyclohexyl) peroxydicarbonate	98	—	86	30	95	35	1	3	2	III	88 lb (40 kg)
Di-t-butyl peroxide[3]	99	—					1	3	2	III	55 gal (208 L)
2,2-Di(t-butylperoxy) butane	50	Toluene					1	3	3	I	1 gal (4 L)
1,1-Di(t-butylperoxy) cyclohexane	80	OMS or BBP					1	3	3	II	5 gal (19 L)
Di-sec-butyl peroxydicarbonate	98	—	−4	−20	14	−10	1	3	3	II	1 gal (4 L)
Di-sec-butyl peroxydicarbonate	75	OMS	−4	−20	14	−10	1	3	3	II	5 gal (19 L)
Di(2-t-butylperoxy-iso-propyl) benzene	96	—					1	2	2	III	100 lb (45 kg)
Di(2-t-butylperoxyiso-propyl) benzene	40	Clay					1	1	0	V	100 lb (45 kg)
Di(butylperoxy) phthalate	40	DBP					2	2	2	IV	30 gal (110 L)
1,1-Di(t-butylperoxy)-3,3,5-trimethyl- cyclohexane	75–95	—					2	3	3	II	5 gal (19 L)
1,1-Di(t-butylperoxy)-3,3,5-trimethyl-cyclohexane	40	Calcium carbonate					1	1	1	V	100 lb (45 kg)
Dicetyl peroxydicarbonate	85	—	86	30	95	35	1	2	2	IV	44 lb (20 kg)
Dicumyl peroxide	98	—					2	2	2	IV	55 gal (208 L)
Dicumyl peroxide	40	Clay or calcium carbonate					1	1	1	V	100 lb (45 kg)

Table B.5.3.1 *Continued*

Organic Peroxide	Concentration	Diluent	Recommended Maximum Temperatures[1]				Hazard Identification[2]			Class	Container
			Control		Emergency		Health	Flammability	Reactivity		
			°F	°C	°F	°C					
Didecanoyl peroxide	98	—	86	30	95	35	1	3	2	III	50 lb (23 kg)
Di-2,4-dichlorobenzoyl peroxide	50	DBP and silicone		T			1	2	2	III	5 gal (19 L)
Di(2-ethylhexyl) peroxydicarbonate	97	—	−4	−20	14	−10	1	3	3	II	1 gal (4 L)
Di(2-ethylhexyl) peroxydicarbonate	40	OMS	5	−15	23	−5	1	2	2	IV	5 gal (19 L)
Diisopropyl peroxydicarbonate	99	—	5	−15	23	−5	2	3	4	I	10 lb (4.5 kg)
Diisopropyl peroxydicarbonate	30	Toluene	14	−10	32	0	2	3	2	III	5 lb (2.3 kg)
Di-*n*-propyl peroxydicarbonate	98	—	−13	−25	5	−15	2	3	4	I	1 gal (4 L)
Di-*n*-propyl peroxydicarbonate	85	OMS	−13	−25	5	−15	2	3	4	I	1 gal (4 L)
Dilauroyl peroxide	98	—					1	2	2	IV	110 lb (50 kg)
2,5-Dimethyl-2,5-di (benzoylperoxy)hexane	95	—					2	3	3	II	4 @ 5 lb (4 @ 2.3 kg)
2,5-Dimethyl-2,5-di (*t*-butylperoxy)hexane	92	—					2	3	2	III	30 gal (110 L)
2,5-Dimethyl-2,5-di (*t*-butylperoxy)hexane	47	Calcium carbonate or silica					1	1	1	V	100 lb (45 kg)
2,5-Dimethyl-2,5-di (2-ethylhexanoylperoxy) hexane	90	—	68	20	77	25	0	3	2	III	5 gal (19 L)
2,5-Dimethyl-2,5-dihydroperoxyhexane	70	Water					2	3	3	II	100 lb (45 kg)
Ethyl- 3,3-di(*t*-amylperoxy) butyrate	75	OMS					1	3	2	III	5 gal (19 L)
Ethyl- 3,3-di(*t*-butylperoxy) butyrate	75	OMS					2	2	2	III	5 gal (19 L)
Ethyl- 3,3-di(*t*-butylperoxy) butyrate	40	Clay or calcium silicate					1	3	2	V	100 lb (45 kg)
p-Menthyl hydroperoxide	54	Alcohols and ketones					3	2	2	IV	55 gal (208 L)
Methyl ethyl ketone peroxide	9.0% AO	DMP					3	2	2	III	5 gal (19 L)
Methyl ethyl ketone peroxide	5.5% AO	DMP					3	2	2	IV	5 gal (19 L)
Methyl ethyl ketone peroxide	9.0% AO	Water and glycols					3	2	2	IV	5 gal (19 L)
Methyl ethyl ketone peroxide and Cyclohexanone peroxide mixture	9.0% AO	DMP					3	2	2	III	5 gal (19 L)
2,4-Pentanedione peroxide	4.0% AO	Water and solvent					2	1	1	IV	5 gal (19 L)
Peroxyacetic acid, Type E, stabilized	43	Water, HOAc, and H_2O_2					3	2	3	II	30 gal (110 L)

[1]These columns refer to temperatures in the Department of Transportation (DOT) Organic Peroxides Table. Refer to document 49 CFR 173.225 for details.

[2]The column refers to NFPA 704, *Standard System for the Identification of the Hazards of Materials for Emergency Response*, hazard ratings for health, flammability, and reactivity. See NFPA 704 for details.

[3]See NFPA 30, *Flammable and Combustible Liquids Code*, for additional storage requirements.

[4]T — Temperature control should be considered to reduce fire hazard depending on packaging size and recommendations in manufacturers' literature.

Note: Diluents: AO — Active oxygen; BBP — Butyl benzyl phthalate; DBP — Dibutyl phthalate; DMP — Dimethyl phthalate; DOP — Dioctyl phthalate; DTBP — Di-tertiary-butyl peroxide; HOAc — Acetic acid; H_2O_2 — Hydrogen peroxide; OMS — Odorless mineral spirits; *t*-BuOH — Tertiary butanol.

[**400**: Table F.1]

B.5.3.2 Class I Formulations.

B.5.3.2.1 Fire Hazard Characteristics. Class I formulations present a deflagration hazard through easily initiated, rapid explosive decomposition. Class I includes some formulations that are relatively safe only under closely controlled temperatures. Either excessively high or low temperatures can increase the potential for severe explosive decomposition. [**400:** F.2.1]

B.5.3.2.2 Fire-Fighting Information. The immediate area should be evacuated and the fire should be fought from a remote location. Some damage to structures from overpressure can be expected should a deflagration occur. [**400:** F.2.2]

B.5.3.2.3 Typical Class I Formulations. See Table B.5.3.2.3. [**400:** F.2.3]

B.5.3.3 Class II Formulations.

B.5.3.3.1 Fire Hazard Characteristics. Class II formulations present a severe fire hazard similar to Class I flammable liquids. The decomposition is not as rapid, violent, or complete as that produced by Class I formulations. As with Class I formulations, this class includes some formulations that are relatively safe when under controlled temperatures or when diluted. [**400:** F.3.1]

B.5.3.3.2 Fire-Fighting Information. Fires should be fought from a safe distance, because a hazard exists from rupturing containers. [**400:** F.3.2]

B.5.3.3.3 Typical Class II Formulations. See Table B.5.3.3.3. [**400:** F.3.3]

B.5.3.4 Class III Formulations.

B.5.3.4.1 Fire Hazard Characteristics. Class III formulations present a fire hazard similar to Class II combustible liquids. They are characterized by rapid burning and high heat liberation due to decomposition. [**400:** F.4.1]

B.5.3.4.2 Fire-Fighting Information. Caution should be observed due to possible unexpected increases in fire intensity. [**400:** F.4.2]

B.5.3.4.3 Typical Class III Formulations. See Table B.5.3.4.3. [**400:** F.4.3]

B.5.3.5 Class IV Formulations.

B.5.3.5.1 Fire Hazard Characteristics. Class IV formulations present fire hazards that are easily controlled. Reactivity has little effect on fire intensity. [**400:** F.5.1]

B.5.3.5.2 Fire-Fighting Information. Normal fire-fighting procedures can be used. [**400:** F.5.2]

B.5.3.5.3 Typical Class IV Formulations. See Table B.5.3.5.3. [**400:** F.5.3]

B.5.3.6 Class V Formulations.

B.5.3.6.1 Fire Hazard Characteristics. Class V formulations do not present severe fire hazards. Those that do burn do so with less intensity than ordinary combustibles. [**400:** F.6.1]

B.5.3.6.2 Fire-Fighting Information. Fire-fighting procedures need primarily consider the combustibility of containers. [**400:** F.6.2]

B.5.3.6.3 Typical Class V Formulations. See Table B.5.3.6.3. [**400:** F.6.3]

Table B.5.3.2.3 Typical Class I Formulations

			Recommended Maximum Temperatures[1]				Hazard Identification[2]			
			Control		Emergency					
Organic Peroxide	Concentration	Diluent	°F	°C	°F	°C	Health	Flammability	Reactivity	Container
t-Butyl hydroperoxide	90	Water & *t*-BuOH					3	3	3	5 gal (19 L)
t-Butyl monoperoxymaleate	98	—					2	3	3	50 @ 1 lb (50 @ 0.5 kg)
t-Butyl peroxyacetate	75	OMS					1	3	3	5 gal (19 L)
t-Butyl peroxyacetate	60	OMS					1	3	3	5 gal (19 L)
t-Butylperoxy isopropyl carbonate	92	OMS					1	3	3	5 gal (19 L)
Dibenzoyl peroxide	98	—					1	3	4	1 lb (0.5 kg)
2,2-Di(*t*-butylperoxy) butane	50	Toluene					1	3	3	1 gal (4 L)
Diisopropyl peroxydicarbonate	99	—	5	−15	23	−5	2	3	4	10 lb (4.5 kg)
Di-*n*-propyl peroxydicarbonate	98	—	−13	−25	5	−15	2	3	4	1 gal (4 L)
Di-*n*-propyl peroxydicarbonate	85	OMS	−13	−25	5	−15	2	3	4	1 gal (4 L)

[1]These columns refer to temperatures in the Department of Transportation (DOT) Organic Peroxides Table. Refer to document 49 CFR 173.225 for details.

[2]The column refers to NFPA 704, *Standard System for the Identification of the Hazards of Materials for Emergency Response*, hazard ratings for health, flammability, and reactivity. See NFPA 704 for details.

Note: Diluents: OMS — Odorless mineral spirits; *t*-BuOH — Tertiary butanol.

[**400:** Table F.2.3]

Table B.5.3.3.3 Typical Class II Formulations

Organic Peroxide	Concentration	Diluent	Control °F	Control °C	Emergency °F	Emergency °C	Health	Flammability	Reactivity	Container
t-Amyl peroxybenzoate	96	—					2	3	2	5 gal (19 L)
n-Butyl- 4,4-di(t-butylperoxy) valerate	98	—					2	3	2	5 gal (19 L)
t-Butyl hydroperoxide	70	DTBP and t-BuOH					3	3	3	55 gal (208 L)
t-Butyl peroxybenzoate	98	—					1	3	3	5 gal (19 L)
t-Butyl peroxy-2-ethyl-hexanoate	97	—	68	20	77	25	1	3	3	55 gal (208 L)
t-Butyl peroxyisobutyrate	75	OMS	59	15	68	20	2	3	3	5 gal (19 L)
t-Butylperoxy isopropyl carbonate	75	OMS					1	3	3	5 gal (19 L)
t-Butyl peroxypivalate	75	OMS	32	0	50	10	2	3	3	5 gal (19 L)
Diacetyl peroxide	25	DMP	68	20	77	25	2	3	3	5 gal (19 L)
Dibenzoyl peroxide	78	Water					1	2	3	25 lb (11 kg)
1,1-Di(t-butylperoxy) cyclohexane	80	OMS or BBP					1	3	3	5 gal (19 L)
Di-sec-butyl peroxydicarbonate	98	—	−4	−20	14	−10	1	3	3	1 gal (4 L)
Di-sec-butyl peroxydicarbonate	75	OMS	−4	−20	14	−10	1	3	3	5 gal (19 L)
1,1-Di(t-butylperoxy)-3,3,5-trimethyl-cyclohexane	75–95	—					2	3	3	5 gal (19 L)
Di(2-ethylhexyl) peroxydicarbonate	97	—	−4	−20	14	−10	1	3	3	1 gal (4 L)
2,5-Dimethyl-2,5-di(benzoylperoxy) hexane	95	—					2	3	3	4 @ 5 lb (4 @ 2.3 kg)
2,5-Dimethyl-2,5-dihydroperoxy hexane	70	Water					2	3	3	100 lb (45 kg)

[1]These columns refer to temperatures in the Department of Transportation (DOT) Organic Peroxides Table. Refer to document 49 CFR 173.225 for details.
[2]The column refers to NFPA 704, *Standard System for the Identification of the Hazards of Materials for Emergency Response*, hazard ratings for health, flammability, and reactivity. See NFPA 704 for details.
Note: Diluents: BBP — Butyl benzyl phthalate; DMP — Dimethyl phthalate; DTBP — Di-tertiary-butyl peroxide; OMS — Odorless mineral spirits; t-BuOH — Tertiary butanol.
[**400**: Table F.3.3]

Table B.5.3.4.3 Typical Class III Formulations

Organic Peroxide	Concentration	Diluent	Recommended Maximum Temperatures[1]				Hazard Identification[2]			Container
			Control		Emergency		Health	Flammability	Reactivity	
			°F	°C	°F	°C				
t-Amyl hydroperoxide	88	Water					3	3	2	55 gal (208 L)
t-Amyl peroxyacetate	60	OMS					2	3	2	5 gal (19 L)
t-Amyl peroxy-2-ethylhexanoate	96	—	68	20	77	25	0	3	2	55 gal (208 L)
t-Amyl peroxyneodecanoate	75	OMS	32	0	50	10	1	3	2	5 gal (19 L)
t-Amyl peroxypivalate	75	OMS	50	10	59	15	1	3	2	5 gal (19 L)
t-Butyl peroxy-2-ethylhexanoate	97	—	68	20	77	25	1	3	3	5 gal (19 L)
t-Butyl peroxy-2-ethylhexanoate	50	DOP or OMS	86	30	95	35	1	2	2	55 gal (208 L)
t-Butyl peroxy-2-ethylhexyl carbonate	95	—					1	3	2	5 gal (19 L)
t-Butyl peroxyneodecanoate	75	OMS	32	0	50	10	2	3	2	5 gal (19 L)
Cumyl hydroperoxide	88	Cumene					3	2	2	55 gal (208 L)
Cumyl peroxyneodecanoate	75	OMS	14	−10	32	0	1	3	2	5 gal (19 L)
Cumyl peroxyneoheptanoate	75	OMS	32	0	50	10	2	3	2	5 gal (19 L)
1,1-Di(t-amylperoxy) cyclohexane	80	OMS or BBP					2	3	2	5 gal (19 L)
Dibenzoyl peroxide	75	Water					1	2	2	25 lb (11 kg)
Dibenzoyl peroxide (paste)	55	Plasticizer	T[4]				1	2	2	350 lb (160 kg)
Dibenzoyl peroxide (paste)	50	Plasticizer	T				1	2	2	380 lb (170 kg)
Di(4-t-butylcyclohexyl) peroxydicarbonate	98	—	86	30	95	35	1	3	2	88 lb (40 kg)
Di-t-butyl peroxide[3]	99	—					1	3	2	55 gal (208 L)
Di(2-t-butylperoxy-isopropyl) benzene	96	—					1	2	2	100 lb (45 kg)
Didecanoyl peroxide	98	—	86	30	95	35	1	3	2	50 lb (23 kg)
Di-2,4-dichlorobenzoyl peroxide	50	DBP and silicone	T				1	2	2	5 gal (19 L)
Diisopropyl peroxydicarbonate	30	Toluene	14	−10	32	0	2	3	2	5 lb (2.3 kg)
2,5-Dimethyl-2,5-di(t-butylperoxy) hexane	92	—					2	3	2	30 gal (110 L)
2,5-Dimethyl-2,5-di(2-ethyl hexanoylperoxy) hexane	90	—		20		25	0	3	2	5 gal (19 L)
Ethyl-3,3-di (t-amylperoxy) butyrate	75	OMS					1	3	2	5 gal (19 L)
Ethyl-3,3-di (t-butylperoxy) butyrate	75	OMS					2	2	2	5 gal (19 L)
Methyl ethyl ketone peroxide	9.0% AO	DMP					3	2	2	5 gal (19 L)
Methyl ethyl ketone peroxide and Cyclohexanone peroxide mixture	9.0% AO	DMP					3	2	2	5 gal (19 L)

[1]These columns refer to temperatures in the Department of Transportation (DOT) Organic Peroxides Table. Refer to document 49 CFR 173.225 for details.

[2]The column refers to NFPA 704, *Standard System for the Identification of the Hazards of Materials for Emergency Response*, hazard ratings for health, flammability, and reactivity. See NFPA 704 for details.

[3]Also a flammable liquid; see NFPA 30, *Flammable and Combustible Liquids Code*, for storage requirements.

[4]T — Temperature control should be considered to reduce fire hazard depending on packaging size and recommendations in manufacturers' literature.

Note: Diluents: AO — Active oxygen; BBP — Butyl benzyl phthalate; DBP — Dibutyl phthalate; DMP — Dimethyl phthalate; DOP — Dioctyl phthalate; OMS — Odorless mineral spirits.

[**400**: Table F.4.3]

Table B.5.3.5.3 Typical Class IV Formulations

Organic Peroxide	Concentration	Diluent	Recommended Maximum Temperatures[1]				Hazard Identification[2]			Container
			Control		Emergency		Health	Flammability	Reactivity	
			°F	°C	°F	°C				
t-Butyl cumyl peroxide	95	—					2	2	2	55 gal (208 L)
t-Butyl hydroperoxide	70	Water					3	2	2	55 gal (208 L)
t-Butyl peroxy-2-ethylhexanoate	50	DOP or OMS	86	30	95	35	1	2	2	5 gal (19 L)
t-Butyl peroxypivalate	45	OMS	32	0	50	10	2	2	2	5 gal (19 L)
Dibenzoyl peroxide	70	Water					1	2	2	25 lb (11 kg)
Dibenzoyl peroxide (paste)	55	Plasticizer and water	T				1	2	2	350 lb (160 kg)
Dibenzoyl peroxide (paste)	50	Plasticizer and water	T				1	2	2	380 lb (170 kg)
Dibenzoyl peroxide (slurry)	40	Water and plasticizer	T				1	2	2	380 lb (170 kg)
Dibenzoyl peroxide (slurry)	40	Water					1	2	2	5 gal (19 L)
Dibenzoyl peroxide (powder)	35	Starch					1	2	2	100 lb (45 kg)
Di(t-butylperoxy) phthalate	40	DBP					2	2	2	30 gal (110 L)
Dicetyl peroxydicarbonate	85	—	86	30	95	35	1	2	2	44 lb (20 kg)
Dicumyl peroxide	98	—					2	2	2	55 gal (208 L)
Di(2-ethylhexyl) peroxydicarbonate	40	OMS	5	−15	23	−5	1	2	2	5 gal (19 L)
Dilauroyl peroxide	98	—					1	2	2	110 lb (50 kg)
p-Menthyl hydroperoxide	54	Alcohols and ketones	T				3	2	2	55 gal (208 L)
Methyl ethyl ketone peroxide	55% AO	DMP					3	2	2	5 gal (19 L)
Methyl ethyl ketone peroxide	9.0% AO	Water and glycols					3	2	2	5 gal (19 L)
2,4-Pentanedione peroxide	4.0% AO	Water and solvent					2	1	1	5 gal (19 L)

[1]These columns refer to temperatures in the Department of Transportation (DOT) Organic Peroxides Table. Refer to document 49 CFR 173.225 for details.
[2]The column refers to NFPA 704, *Standard System for the Identification of the Hazards of Materials for Emergency Response*, hazard ratings for health, flammability, and reactivity. See NFPA 704 for details.
[4]T — Temperature control should be considered to reduce fire hazard depending on packaging size and recommendations in manufacturers' literature.
Note: Diluents: BP — Dibutyl phthalate; DMP — Dimethyl phthalate; DOP— Dioctyl phthalate; OMS — Odorless mineral spirits; AO — Active oxygen.
[**400:** Table F.5.3]

Table B.5.3.6.3 Typical Class V Formulations

Organic Peroxide	Concentration	Diluent	Recommended Maximum Temperatures[1]				Hazard Identification[2]			Container
			Control		Emergency		Health	Flammability	Reactivity	
			°F	°C	°F	°C				
Dibenzoyl peroxide (powder)	35	Dicalcium phosphate dihydrate or Calcium sulfate dihydrate					1	0	0	100 lb (45 kg)
Di(2-t-butylperoxy-isopropyl) benzene	40	Clay					1	1	0	100 lb (45 kg)
1,1-Di(t-butylperoxy)-3,3,5-trimethyl-cyclohexane	40	Calcium carbonate					1	1	1	100 lb (45 kg)
Dicumyl peroxide	40	Clay or calcium carbonate					1	1	1	100 lb (45 kg)
2,5-Dimethyl-2,5-di(t-butylperoxy) hexane	47	Calcium carbonate or silica					1	1	1	100 lb (45 kg)
Ethyl-3,3-di(t-butylperoxy) butyrate	40	Clay or calcium silicate					1	3	2	100 lb (45 kg)

[1]These columns refer to temperatures in the Department of Transportation (DOT) Organic Peroxides Table. Refer to document 49 CFR 173.225 for details.
[2]The column refers to NFPA 704, *Standard System for the Identification of the Hazards of Materials for Emergency Response*, hazard ratings for health, flammability, and reactivity. See NFPA 704 for details.
AO — Active oxygen.
[**400**: Table F.6.3]

Annex C Sample Ordinance Adopting the NFPA 1, *Fire Code*

This annex is not a part of the requirements of this NFPA document but is included for informational purposes only.

C.1 The following sample ordinance is provided to assist a jurisdiction in the adoption of this *Code* and is not part of this *Code*.

ORDINANCE NO. _____

An ordinance of the *[jurisdiction]* adopting the *[year]* edition of NFPA 1, *Fire Code*, 2015 edition; and documents listed in Chapter 2 of that *Code*; prescribing regulations governing conditions hazardous to life and property from fire or explosion; providing for the issuance of permits and collection of fees; repealing Ordinance No. _____ of the *[jurisdiction]* and all other ordinances and parts of ordinances in conflict therewith; providing a penalty; providing a severability clause; and providing for publication; and providing an effective date.

BE IT ORDAINED BY THE *[governing body]* **OF THE** *[jurisdiction]*:

SECTION 1 That the NFPA 1, *Fire Code*, 2015 edition, and documents adopted by Chapter 2, three (3) copies of which are on file and are open to inspection by the public in the office of the *[jurisdiction's keeper of records]* of the *[jurisdiction]*, are hereby adopted and incorporated into this ordinance as fully as if set out at length herein, and from the date on which this ordinance shall take effect, the provisions thereof shall be controlling within the limits of the *[jurisdiction]*. The same are hereby adopted as the *Code* of the *[jurisdiction]* for the purpose of prescribing regulations governing conditions hazardous to life and property from fire or explosion and providing for issuance of permits and collection of fees.

SECTION 2 Any person who shall violate any provision of this code or standard hereby adopted or fail to comply therewith; or who shall violate or fail to comply with any order made thereunder; or who shall build in violation of any detailed statement of specifications or plans submitted and approved thereunder; or fail to operate in accordance with any certificate or permit issued thereunder; and from which no appeal has been taken; or who shall fail to comply with such an order as affirmed or modified by a court of competent jurisdiction, within the time fixed herein, shall severally for each and every such violation and noncompliance, respectively, be guilty of a misdemeanor, punishable by a fine of not less than $ _____ nor more than $_____ or by imprisonment for not less than _____ days nor more than _____ days or by both such fine and imprisonment. The imposition of one penalty for any violation shall not excuse the violation or permit it to continue; and all such persons shall be required to correct or remedy such violations or defects within a reasonable time; and when not otherwise specified the application of the above penalty shall not be held to prevent the enforced removal of prohibited conditions. Each day that prohibited conditions are maintained shall constitute a separate offense.

SECTION 3 Additions, insertions, and changes — that the [year] edition of NFPA 1, *Fire Code*, 2015 edition, is amended and changed in the following respects:

[List Amendments]

SECTION 4 That ordinance No. _____ of *[jurisdiction]* entitled *[fill in the title of the ordinance or ordinances in effect at the present time]* and all other ordinances or parts of ordinances in conflict herewith are hereby repealed.

SECTION 5 That if any section, subsection, sentence, clause, or phrase of this ordinance is, for any reason, held to be invalid or unconstitutional, such decision shall not affect the validity or constitutionality of the remaining portions of this ordinance. The *[governing body]* hereby declares that it would have passed this ordinance, and each section, subsection, clause, or phrase hereof, irrespective of the fact that any one or more sections, subsections, sentences, clauses, and phrases be declared unconstitutional.

SECTION 6 That the *[jurisdiction's keeper of records]* is hereby ordered and directed to cause this ordinance to be published.

[NOTE: An additional provision may be required to direct the number of times the ordinance is to be published and to specify that it is to be in a newspaper in general circulation. Posting may also be required.]

SECTION 7 That this ordinance and the rules, regulations, provisions, requirements, orders, and matters established and adopted hereby shall take effect and be in full force and effect *[time period]* from and after the date of its final passage and adoption.

Annex D Hazardous Materials Management Plans and Hazardous Materials Inventory Statements

This annex is not a part of the requirements of this NFPA document unless specifically adopted by the AHJ.

D.1 Scope. Hazardous materials inventory statements (HMIS) and hazardous materials management plans (HMMP), which are required by the AHJ pursuant to Chapter 60, shall be provided for hazardous materials in accordance with Annex D.

Exception No. 1: Materials that have been satisfactorily demonstrated not to present a potential danger to public health, safety, or welfare, based upon the quantity or condition of storage, when approved.

Exception No. 2: Chromium, copper, lead, nickel, and silver need not be considered hazardous materials for the purposes of this annex unless they are stored in a friable, powdered, or finely divided state. Proprietary and trade secret information shall be protected under the laws of the state or AHJ.

D.2 Hazardous Materials Inventory Statements (HMIS).

D.2.1 When Required. A separate HMIS shall be provided for each building, including its appurtenant structures, and each exterior facility in which hazardous materials are stored. The hazardous materials inventory statement shall list by hazard class all hazardous materials stored. The hazardous materials inventory statement shall include the following information for each hazardous material listed:

(1) Hazard class.
(2) Common or trade name.
(3) Chemical name, major constituents, and concentrations if a mixture. If a waste, the waste category.
(4) Chemical Abstract Service number (CAS number) found in 29 Code of Federal Regulations (CFR).
(5) Whether the material is pure or a mixture, and whether the material is a solid, liquid, or gas.
(6) Maximum aggregate quantity stored at any one time.
(7) Storage conditions related to the storage type, temperature, and pressure.

D.2.2 Changes to HMIS. An amended HMIS shall be provided within 30 days of the storage of any hazardous materials that changes or adds a hazard class or that is sufficient in quantity to cause an increase in the quantity that exceeds 5 percent for any hazard class.

D.3 Hazardous Materials Management Plan (HMMP).

D.3.1 General. Applications for a permit to store hazardous materials shall include an HMMP standard form or short form in accordance with Section D.3 and shall provide a narrative description of the operations and processes taking place at the facility. *(See Figure D.3.1.)*

D.3.2 Information Required. The HMMP standard form shall include the information in D.3.2.1 through D.3.2.9.

D.3.2.1 General Information. General information, including business name and address, emergency contacts, business activity, business owner or operator, SIC code, number of employees and hours, Dunn and Bradstreet number, and signature of owner, operator, or designated representative.

D.3.2.2 General Site Plan. A general site plan drawn at a legible scale that shall include, but not be limited to, the location of buildings, exterior storage facilities, permanent access ways, evacuation routes, parking lots, internal roads, chemical loading areas, equipment cleaning areas, storm and sanitary sewer accesses, emergency equipment, and adjacent property uses. The exterior storage areas shall be identified with the hazard class and the maximum quantities per hazard class of hazardous materials stored. When required by the AHJ, information regarding the location of wells, flood plains, earthquake faults, surface water bodies, and general land uses within 1 mile (1.6 km) of the facility boundaries shall be included.

D.3.2.3 Building Floor Plan. A building floor plan drawn to a legible scale that shall include, but not be limited to, hazardous materials storage areas within the building and shall indicate rooms, doorways, corridors, means of egress, and evacuation routes. Each hazardous materials storage facility shall be identified by a map key that lists the individual hazardous materials, their hazard class, and quantity present for each area.

> # SAMPLE FORMAT
> # HAZARDOUS MATERIALS MANAGEMENT PLAN (HMMP) INSTRUCTIONS
>
> ## SECTION I — FACILITY DESCRIPTION
>
> ### 1.1 Part A
>
> 1. Fill out Items 1 through 11 and sign the declaration.
> 2. Only Part A of this section is required to be updated and submitted annually, or within 30 days of a change.
>
> ### 1.2 Part B — General Facility Description (Site Plan)
>
> 1. Provide a site plan on 8½ in. by 11 in. (215 mm by 279 mm) paper, using letters on the top and bottom margins and numbers on the right and left side margins, showing the location of all buildings, structures, chemical loading areas, parking lots, internal roads, storm and sanitary sewers, wells, and adjacent property uses. Indicate the approximate scale, northern direction and date the drawing was completed.
> 2. List all special land uses within 1 mile (1.609 km).
>
> ### 1.3 Part C — Facility Storage Map (Confidential Information)
>
> 1. Provide a floor plan of each building on 8½ in. by 11 in. (215 mm by 279 mm) paper, using letters on the top and bottom margins and numbers on the right and left side margins, with approximate scale and northern direction, showing the location of each storage area. Mark map clearly "Confidential — Do Not Disclose" for trade-secret information as specified by federal, state, and local laws.
> 2. Identify each storage area with an identification number, letter, name, or symbol.
> 3. Show the following:
>   (a) Accesses to each storage area.
>   (b) Location of emergency equipment.
>   (c) The general purpose of other areas within the facility.
>   (d) Location of all aboveground and underground tanks to include sumps, vaults, belowgrade treatment systems, piping, etc.
> 4. **Map key.** Provide the following on the map or in a map key or legend for each storage area:
>   (a) A list of hazardous materials, including wastes.
>   (b) Hazard class of each hazardous waste.
>   (c) The maximum quantity for hazardous materials.
>   (d) Include the contents and capacity limit of all tanks at each area and indicate whether they are above or below ground.
>   (e) List separately any radioactives, cryogens, and compressed gases for each facility.
>   (f) Trade-secret information shall be listed as specified by federal, state, and local laws.
>
> ## SECTION II — HAZARDOUS MATERIALS INVENTORY STATEMENT (HMIS)
>
> ### 2.1 Part A — Declaration
>
> Fill out all appropriate information.
>
> ### 2.2 Part B — Inventory Statement
>
> 1. You must complete a separate inventory statement for all waste and nonwaste hazardous materials. List all hazardous materials in alphabetical order by hazard class.
> 2. Inventory Statement Instructions.
>
> | Column | Information Required |
> |---|---|
> | 1 | Provide hazard class for each material. |
> | 2 | **Nonwaste.** Provide the common or trade name of the regulated material.
Waste. In lieu of trade names, you may provide the waste category. |
> | 3 | Provide the chemical name and major constituents and concentrations, if a mixture. |
> | 4 | Enter the chemical abstract service number (CAS number) found in 29 CFR. For mixtures, enter the CAS number of the mixture as a whole if it has been assigned a number distinct from its constituents. For a mixture that has no CAS number, leave this item blank or report the CAS numbers of as many constituent chemicals as possible. |
> | 5 | Enter the following descriptive codes as they apply to each material. You may list more than one code, if applicable.
P = Pure
M = Mixture
S = Solid
L = Liquid
G = Gas |
> | 6 | Provide the maximum aggregate quantity of each material handled at any one time by the business. For underground tanks, list the maximum volume [in gallons (liters)] of the tank.
Enter the estimated average daily amount on site during the past year. |
> | 7 | Enter the units used in Column 6 as:
Lb = Pounds
Ga = Gallons
Cf = Cubic Feet |
> | 8 | Enter the number of days that the material was present on site (during the last year). |
>
> © 2014 National Fire Protection Association
>
> NFPA 1 (p. 1 of 8)

FIGURE D.3.1 Sample Format of Hazardous Materials Management Plan (HMMP) Instructions.

Column	Information Required
9	Enter the storage codes below for type, temperature, and pressure:

Type

- A = Aboveground Tank
- B = Belowground Tank
- C = Tank Inside Building
- D = Steel Drum
- E = Plastic or Nonmetallic Drum
- F = Can
- G = Carboy
- H = Silo
- I = Fiber Drum
- J = Bag
- K = Box
- L = Cylinder
- M = Glass Bottle or Jug
- N = Plastic Bottles or Jugs
- O = Tote Bin
- P = Tank Wagon
- Q = Rail Car
- R = Other

Temperature

- 4 = Ambient
- 5 = Greater than Ambient
- 6 = Less than Ambient, but not Cryogenic [less than –150°F (–101.1°C)]
- 7 = Cryogenic conditions [less than –150°F (–101.1°C)]

Pressure

- 1 = Ambient (Atmospheric)
- 2 = Greater than Ambient (Atmospheric)
- 3 = Less than Ambient (Atmospheric)

10   For each material listed, provide the SARA Title III hazard class as listed below. You may list more than one class. These categories are defined in 40 CFR 370.3.

Physical Hazard

- F = Fire
- P = Sudden Release of Pressure
- R = Reactivity

Health Hazard

- I = Immediate (Acute)
- D = Delayed (Chronic)

11   **Waste Only.** For each waste, provide the total estimated amount of hazardous waste handled throughout the course of the year.

SECTION III — SEPARATION AND MONITORING

3.1 Part A — Aboveground

Fill out Items 1 through 6, or provide similar information for each storage area shown on the facility map. Use additional sheets as necessary.

3.2 Part B — Underground

1. Complete a separate page for each underground tank, sump, vault, belowgrade treatment system, etc.
2. Check the type of tank and method(s) that applies to your tank(s) and piping, and answer the appropriate questions. Provide any additional information in the space provided or on a separate sheet.

SECTION IV — WASTE DISPOSAL

Check all that apply and list the associated wastes for each method checked.

SECTION V — RECORD KEEPING

Include a brief description of your inspection procedures. You are also required to keep an inspection log and recordable discharge log, which are designed to be used in conjunction with routine inspections for all storage facilities or areas. Place a check in each box that describes your forms. If you do not use the sample forms, provide copies of your forms for review and approval.

SECTION VI — EMERGENCY RESPONSE PLAN

1. This plan should describe the personnel, procedures, and equipment available for responding to a release or threatened release of hazardous materials that are stored, handled, or used on site.
2. A check or a response under each item indicates that a specific procedure is followed at the facility, or that the equipment specified is maintained on site.
3. If the facility maintains a more detailed emergency response plan on site, indicate this in Item 5. This plan shall be made available for review by the inspecting jurisdiction.

SECTION VII — EMERGENCY RESPONSE TRAINING PLAN

1. This plan should describe the basic training plan used at the facility.
2. A check in the appropriate box indicates the training is provided or the records are maintained.
3. If the facility maintains a more detailed emergency response training plan, indicate this in Item 4. This plan shall be made available for review by the inspecting jurisdiction.

© 2014 National Fire Protection Association

FIGURE D.3.1 *Continued*

HAZARDOUS MATERIALS MANAGEMENT PLAN
SECTION I: FACILITY DESCRIPTION

Part A — General Information

1. Business Name: _____ Phone: _____
   Address: _____

2. Person Responsible for the Business:

Name	Title	Phone
_____	_____	_____

3. Emergency Contacts:

Name	Title	Home Number	Work Number
_____	_____	_____	_____
_____	_____	_____	_____

4. Person Responsible for the Application/Principal Contact:

Name	Title	Phone
_____	_____	_____

5. Property Owner:

Name	Address	Phone
_____	_____	_____

6. Principal Business Activity: _____
7. Number of Employees: _____
8. Number of Shifts: _____
9. Hours of Operation: _____
10. SIC Code: _____
11. Dunn and Bradstreet Number: _____
12. Declaration:
    I certify that the information above and on the following parts is true and correct to the best of my knowledge.

    Signature: _____ Date: _____
    Print Name: _____ Title: _____
    (Must be signed by owner/operator or designated representative)

Part B — General Facility Description/Site Plan

(Use grid format in Part C)

Special land uses within 1 mile (1.609 km): _____
_____
_____

© 2014 National Fire Protection Association NFPA 1 (p. 3 of 8)

FIGURE D.3.1 *Continued*

SECTION I: FACILITY DESCRIPTION (Continued)

Part C — Facility Map
(Use grid format below)

	A	B	C	D	E	F	G	H	I	J	K	L	M	N	
1															1
2															2
3															3
4															4
5															5
6															6
7															7
8															8
9															9
10															10
11															11
12															12
13															13
14															14
15															15
16															16
17															17
	A	B	C	D	E	F	G	H	I	J	K	L	M	N	

BUSINESS NAME _____ DATE _____

ADDRESS _____ CITY _____ PAGE ____ OF ____

SECTION II: HAZARDOUS MATERIALS INVENTORY STATEMENT

Part A — Declaration

1. Business Name: _____
2. Address: _____
3. Declaration:
   Under penalty of perjury, I declare the above and subsequent information, provided as part of the hazardous materials inventory statement, is true and correct.

Signature: _____ Date: _____

Print Name: _____ Title: _____

(Must be signed by owner/operator or designated representative)

© 2014 National Fire Protection Association

FIGURE D.3.1 *Continued*

SECTION II: HAZARDOUS MATERIALS INVENTORY STATEMENT (Continued)

Part B—Hazardous Materials Inventory Statement

(1) Hazard Class	(2) Common/ Trade Name	(3) Chemical Name, Components, and Concentration	(4) Chemical Abstract Service No.	(5) Physical State

(6) Maximum Quantity on Hand at Any Time	(7) Units	(8) Days on Site	(9) Storage Code (Type, Pressure, Temperature)	(10) SARA Class	(11) Annual Waste Throughput

SECTION III: SEPARATION, SECONDARY CONTAINMENT, AND MONITORING

Part A—Aboveground Storage Areas

Storage Area Identification (as shown on facility map): _____

1. Storage Type:
    - ____ Original Containers
    - ____ Inside Machinery
    - ____ 55 gal (208.2 L) Drums or Storage Shed
    - ____ Pressurized Vessel
    - ____ Safety Cans
    - ____ Bulk Tanks
    - ____ Outside Barrels
    - ____ Other: _____

2. Storage Location:
    - ____ Inside Building
    - ____ Secured
    - ____ Outside Building

3. Separation:
    - ____ All Materials
    - ____ Compatible
    - ____ Separation by 20 ft (6.1 m)
    - ____ One-Hour Separation Wall/Partition
    - ____ Approved Cabinets
    - ____ Other: _____

© 2014 National Fire Protection Association

FIGURE D.3.1 *Continued*

SECTION III: SEPARATION, SECONDARY CONTAINMENT, AND MONITORING *(Continued)*

4. Secondary Containment:
   - _____ Approved Cabinet
   - _____ Tray
   - _____ Vaulted Tank
   - _____ Double-Wall Tank
   - _____ Secondary Drums
   - _____ Bermed, Coated Floor
   - _____ Other: _____

5. Monitoring:
   - _____ Visual
   - _____ Continuous
   - _____ Other: _____

   Attach specifications if necessary

6. Monitoring Frequency:
   - _____ Daily
   - _____ Weekly
   - _____ Other: _____

   Attach additional sheets as necessary

Part B—Underground

Single-Wall Tanks and Piping

Tank Area Identification (as shown on facility map): _____

1. _____ Backfill Vapor Wells
   Model and Manufacturer: _____
   Continuous or Monthly Testing: _____
2. _____ Groundwater Monitoring Wells
3. _____ Monthly Precision Tank Test
4. _____ Piping
   Monitoring Method: _____
   Frequency: _____
5. _____ Other: _____

Double-Wall Tanks and Piping

Tank Area Identification (as shown on facility map): _____

1. Method of monitoring the annular space: _____
2. Frequency: ❑ Continuous ❑ Daily ❑ Weekly ❑ Other: _____
3. List the type of secondary containment for piping: _____
4. List method of monitoring the secondary containment for piping: _____
5. Are there incompatible materials within the same vault? ❑ Yes ❑ No
   If yes, how is separate secondary containment provided? _____

Note: If you have continuous monitoring equipment, you shall maintain copies of all service and maintenance work. Such reports shall be made available for review on site, and shall be submitted to the fire prevention bureau upon request.

Attach additional sheets as necessary

SECTION IV: WASTE DISPOSAL

- _____ Discharge to the Sanitary Sewer—
  Wastes: _____

- _____ Licensed Waste Hauler—
  Wastes: _____

- _____ Pretreatment—
  Wastes: _____

- _____ Recycle—
  Wastes: _____

© 2014 National Fire Protection Association

NFPA 1 (p. 6 of 8)

FIGURE D.3.1 *Continued*

SECTION IV: WASTE DISPOSAL *(Continued)*

_____ Other—
  Describe Method: _____
  Wastes: _____

_____ No Waste

SECTION V: RECORD KEEPING

Description of our inspection program: _____
_____
_____

_____ We will use the attached sample forms in our inspection program.
_____ We will not use the sample forms. We have attached a copy of our own forms.

SECTION VI: EMERGENCY RESPONSE PLAN

1. In the event of an emergency, the following shall be notified:
    A. On-Site Responders:

Name	Title	Phone

    B. Method of Notification to Responder:
        _____ Automatic Alarm   _____ Verbal
        _____ Manual Alarm   _____ Other: _____
        _____ Phone
    C. Agency and Phone Number: _____
        Fire Department: _____
        State Office of Emergency: _____
        Services: _____
        Other: _____

2. Designated Local Emergency Medical Facility:

Name	Address	Phone (24 hours)

3. Mitigation Equipment:
    A. Monitoring Devices:
        _____ Toxic or Flammable Gas Detection
        _____ Fluid Detection
        _____ Other: _____
    B. Spill Containment:
        _____ Absorbents   _____ Other: _____
    C. Spill Control and Treatment
        _____ Vapor Scrubber   _____ Mechanical Ventilation
        _____ Pumps/Vacuums   _____ Secondary Containment
        _____ Neutralizer   _____ Other: _____

© 2014 National Fire Protection Association

FIGURE D.3.1 *Continued*

SECTION VI: EMERGENCY RESPONSE PLAN (Continued)

4. Evacuation:
   - _____ Immediate area evacuation routes posted
   - _____ Entire building evacuation procedures developed
   - _____ Assembly areas preplanned
   - _____ Evacuation maps posted
   - _____ Other: _____

5. Supplemental hazardous materials emergency response plan on site.
   Location: _____
   Responsible Person: _____
   Phone: _____

SECTION VII: EMERGENCY RESPONSE TRAINING PLAN

1. Person responsible for the emergency response training plan:

Name	Title	Phone

2. Training Requirements:
   A. All employees trained in the following as indicated:
      - _____ Procedures for internal alarm/notification
      - _____ Procedures for notification of external emergency response organizations
      - _____ Location and content of the emergency response plan
   B. Chemical handlers are trained in the following as indicated:
      - _____ Safe methods for handling and storage of hazardous materials
      - _____ Proper use of personal protective equipment
      - _____ Locations and proper use of fire- and spill-control equipment
      - _____ Specific hazards of each chemical to which they may be exposed
   C. Emergency response team members are trained in the following:
      - _____ Procedures for shutdown of operations
      - _____ Procedures for using, maintaining, and replacing facility emergency and monitoring equipment

3. The following records are maintained for all employees:
   - _____ Verification that training was completed by the employee
   - _____ Description of the type and amount of introductory and continuing training
   - _____ Documentation on and description of emergency response drills conducted at the facility

4. A more comprehensive and detailed emergency response training plan is maintained on site.
   Location: _____
   Responsible Person: _____
   Phone: _____

© 2014 National Fire Protection Association

FIGURE D.3.1 *Continued*

D.3.2.4 Hazardous Materials Handling. Information showing that activities involving the handling of hazardous materials between the storage areas and manufacturing processes on site are conducted in a manner to prevent the accidental release of such materials.

D.3.2.5 Chemical Compatibility and Separation. Information showing procedures, controls, signs, or other methods used to ensure separation and protection of stored materials from factors that could cause accidental ignition or reaction of ignitable, reactive, or incompatible materials in each area.

D.3.2.6 Monitoring Program. Information including, but not limited to, the location, type, manufacturer's specifications, if applicable, and suitability of monitoring methods for each storage facility when required.

D.3.2.7 Inspection and Record Keeping. Schedules and procedures for inspecting safety and monitoring and emergency equipment. The permittee shall develop and follow a written inspection procedure acceptable to the AHJ for inspecting the facility for events or practices that could lead to unauthorized discharges of hazardous materials. Inspections shall be conducted at a frequency appropriate to detect problems prior to a discharge. An inspection check sheet shall be developed to be used in conjunction with routine inspections. The check sheet shall provide for the date, time, and location of inspection; note problems and dates and times of corrective actions taken; and include the name of the inspector and the countersignature of the designated safety manager for the facility.

D.3.2.8 Employee Training. A training program appropriate to the types and quantities of materials stored or used shall be conducted to prepare employees to safely handle hazardous materials on a daily basis and during emergencies. The training program shall include the following:

(1) Instruction in safe storage and handling of hazardous materials, including maintenance of monitoring records
(2) Instruction in emergency procedures for leaks, spills, fires, or explosions, including shutdown of operations and evacuation procedures
(3) Record-keeping procedures for documenting training given to employees

D.3.2.9 Emergency Response. A description of facility emergency procedures is to be provided.

D.3.3 HMMP Short Form — Minimal Storage Site. A facility shall qualify as a minimal storage site if the quantity of each hazardous material stored in one or more facilities in an aggregate quantity for the facility is 500 lb (227 kg) or less for solids, 55 gal (208.2 L) or less for liquids, or 200 ft^3 (5.7 m^3) or less at NTP for compressed gases and does not exceed the threshold planning quantity as listed in 40 CFR 355 Sections 302 and 304. The applicant for a permit for a facility that qualifies as a minimal storage site shall be permitted to file the short form HMMP. Such plan shall include the following components:

(1) General facility information
(2) A simple line drawing of the facility showing the location of storage facilities and indicating the hazard class or classes and physical state of the hazardous materials being stored
(3) Information describing that the hazardous materials will be stored and handled in a safe manner and will be appropriately contained, separated, and monitored

(4) Assurance that security precautions have been taken, employees have been appropriately trained to handle the hazardous materials and react to emergency situations, adequate labeling and warning signs are posted, adequate emergency equipment is maintained, and the disposal of hazardous materials will be in an appropriate manner

D.4 Maintenance of Records. Hazardous materials inventory statements and hazardous materials management plans shall be maintained by the permittee for a period of not less than 3 years after submittal of updated or revised versions. Such records shall be made available to the AHJ upon request.

Annex E Fire Fighter Safety Building Marking System

This annex is not a part of the requirements of this NFPA document unless specifically adopted by the AHJ.

E.1 Fire Fighter Safety Building Marking System (FFSBMS).

E.1.1 General.

E.1.1.1 The fire fighter safety building marking system provides basic building information for fire fighters responding to the building or structure.

E.1.1.2 Where required by the AHJ, buildings and structures shall have the fire fighter safety building marking system sign installed.

E.1.2 Sign.

E.1.2.1 The approved fire fighter safety building marking system sign shall be placed in a position to be plainly legible and visible from the street or road fronting the property or as approved by the fire department.

E.1.2.2 The fire fighter safety building marking system sign shall consist of the following:

(1) White reflective background with black letters
(2) Durable material
(3) Arabic numerals or alphabet letters
(4) Permanently affixed to the building or structure in an approved manner

E.1.2.3 The fire fighter safety building marking system shall be a Maltese cross as shown in Figure E.1.2.3.

FIGURE E.1.2.3 Sample Sign for Fire Fighter Safety Building Marking System.

E.1.2.4 The minimum size of the fire fighter safety building marking system sign and lettering shown in Figure E.1.2.4

shall be in accordance with the following or as approved by the fire department:

(1) *A* shall be 5 in. × 5 in.
(2) *B* shall be 1¼ in.
(3) *C* shall be 2½ in.
(4) Letters shall be 1 in. height with a stroke of ¼ in.

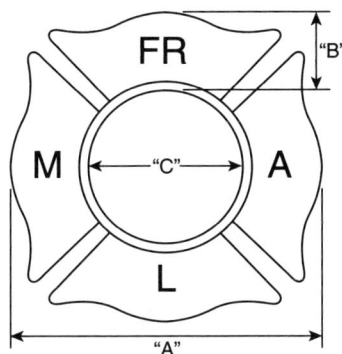

FIGURE E.1.2.4 Dimensions for Fire Fighter Safety Building Marking System Signs.

E.1.3 Ratings.

E.1.3.1 Ratings shall be determined by the construction type, hazards of contents, automatic fire sprinkler systems and standpipe systems, occupancy/life safety, and special hazards in accordance with this section.

E.1.3.1.1 Where multiple ratings occur within a classification category, a determination shall be made by the AHJ of the rating that shall be based on the greatest potential risk for the specific category. *(See Note 1 in E.2.1.)*

E.1.3.2 Construction Type. The construction type shall be designated by assigning the appropriate lettering to the top of the Maltese cross as follows:

(1) FR — Fire-resistive construction
(2) NC — Noncombustible construction
(3) ORD — Ordinary construction
(4) HT — Heavy timber construction
(5) C — Combustible construction

E.1.3.3 Hazards of Contents. The hazards of contents shall be rated by determining its hazard and assigning the appropriate rating to the left of the Maltese cross as follows *(see Note 2 in E.2.2)*:

L — Low hazard. Low hazard contents shall be classified as those of such low combustibility that no self-propagating fire therein can occur.

M — Moderate hazard. Moderate hazard contents shall be classified as those that are likely to burn with moderate rapidity or to give off a considerable volume of smoke.

H — High hazard. High hazard contents *(see Note 3 in E.2.3)* shall be classified as those that are likely to burn with extreme rapidity or from which explosions are likely.

E.1.3.4 Automatic Fire Sprinkler and Standpipe System. The automatic fire sprinkler system and standpipe system shall be rated by determining its level of protection and assigning the appropriate rating to the right of the Maltese cross. If multiple systems are provided, all systems shall be included in the Maltese cross as follows:

(1) A — Automatic fire sprinkler system installed throughout
(2) P — Partial automatic fire sprinkler system or other suppression system installed
(3) S — Standpipe system installed
(4) N — None

E.1.3.5 Occupancy/Life Safety Issues. The occupancy/life safety type shall be rated by determining the level of difficulty in evacuating occupants from the building and the occupancy type by assigning the appropriate rating to the bottom of the Maltese cross as follows:

(1) L — Business, industrial, mercantile, residential, and storage occupancies
(2) M — Ambulatory health care, assembly, educational, and day care occupancies
(3) H — Detention and correction facilities, health care, and board and care occupancies

E.1.3.6 Special Designations. The special hazards can be assigned to the center of the Maltese cross *(see Note 4 in E.2.4)*.

E.1.4 Installation and Maintenance.

E.1.4.1 Fire departments that implement the fire fighter safety building marking system (FFSBMS) shall provide written instructions to the owner/operator of a facility equipped with a fire fighter safety building marking system sign regarding the information to be included on the sign, and the fire department shall perform annual inspections to verify continued compliance with the information shown on the sign *(see Note 5 in E.2.5)*.

E.1.4.2 Installation and maintenance of the sign shall be the responsibility of the owner/operator.

E.1.4.3 The fire department shall enact procedures to identify changes of occupancy that could establish a need to update information on the sign and shall notify the owner/operator when changes are necessary.

E.1.5 Training.

E.1.5.1 Training shall be provided to all fire department personnel responding to buildings using the FFSBMS sign.

E.2 Notes. The following notes are explanatory and are not part of the mandatory text for Annex E.

E.2.1 Note 1. An example of the greatest potential risk for construction type where an FR and an NC are present, the ranking on the FFSBMS sign would be NC.

E.2.2 Note 2. Hazard of contents are described as follows:

Low hazard recognizes storage of noncombustible materials as low hazard. In other occupancies it is assumed that, even where the actual contents hazard is normally low, there is sufficient likelihood that some combustible materials or hazardous operations will be introduced in connection with building repair or maintenance, or some psychological factor might create conditions conducive to panic, so that the egress facilities cannot safely be reduced below those specified for ordinary hazard contents.

Moderate hazard classification represents the conditions found in most buildings and is the basis for the general requirements of this *Code*.

The fear of poisonous fumes or explosions is necessarily a relative matter to be determined on a judgment basis. All smoke contains some toxic fire gases but, under conditions of moderate hazard, there should be no unduly dangerous exposure during the period necessary to escape from the fire area, assuming there are proper exits.

E.2.3 Note 3. High hazard contents include occupancies where flammable liquids are handled or used or are stored under conditions involving possible release of flammable vapors; where grain dust, wood flour or plastic dust, aluminum or magnesium dust, or other explosive dusts are produced; where hazardous chemicals or explosives are manufactured, stored, or handled; where cotton or other combustible fibers are processed or handled under conditions producing flammable flyings; and other situations of similar hazard.

E.2.4 Note 4. The center of the fire fighter safety building marking system sign has been left empty to permit the local jurisdiction space to provide for additional information that they may wish to add. The NFPA 704 marking system can be incorporated into the center of the fire fighter safety building marking system sign if all the applicable provisions of NFPA 704 are met including lettering size and so forth.

E.2.5 Note 5. The intent of this provision is to verify that the information on the FFSBMS sign is correct on a regular basis. Fire departments responding to facilities equipped with a FFSBMS sign should verify signage and preplans annually. Other means of verifying the information on the FFSBMS sign could include mailings, outside consultants, and community service programs.

Annex F Informational References

Sections F.1.1 and F.2 were revised by a tentative interim amendment. (TIA). See page 1.

F.1 Referenced Publications. The documents or portions thereof listed in this annex are referenced within the informational sections of this code and are not part of the requirements of this document unless also listed in 2 for other reasons.

F.1.1 NFPA Publications. National Fire Protection Association, 1 Batterymarch Park, Quincy, MA 02169-7471.

NFPA 2, *Hydrogen Technologies Code*, 2011 edition.

NFPA 10, *Standard for Portable Fire Extinguishers*, 2013 edition.

NFPA 11, *Standard for Low-, Medium-, and High-Expansion Foam*, 2010 edition.

NFPA 13, *Standard for the Installation of Sprinkler Systems*, 2013 edition.

NFPA 13D, *Standard for the Installation of Sprinkler Systems in One- and Two-Family Dwellings and Manufactured Homes*, 2013 edition.

NFPA 13E, *Recommended Practice for Fire Department Operations in Properties Protected by Sprinkler and Standpipe Systems*, 2010 edition.

NFPA 13R, *Standard for the Installation of Sprinkler Systems in Residential Occupancies up to and Including Four Stories in Height*, 2013 edition.

NFPA 14, *Standard for the Installation of Standpipe and Hose Systems*, 2013 edition.

NFPA 15, *Standard for Water Spray Fixed Systems for Fire Protection*, 2012 edition.

NFPA 16, *Standard for the Installation of Foam-Water Sprinkler and Foam-Water Spray Systems*, 2011 edition.

NFPA 20, *Standard for the Installation of Stationary Pumps for Fire Protection*, 2013 edition.

NFPA 22, *Standard for Water Tanks for Private Fire Protection*, 2013 edition.

NFPA 24, *Standard for the Installation of Private Fire Service Mains and Their Appurtenances*, 2013 edition.

NFPA 25, *Standard for the Inspection, Testing, and Maintenance of Water-Based Fire Protection Systems*, 2014 edition.

NFPA 30, *Flammable and Combustible Liquids Code*, 2015 edition.

NFPA 30A, *Code for Motor Fuel Dispensing Facilities and Repair Garages*, 2015 edition.

NFPA 30B, *Code for the Manufacture and Storage of Aerosol Products*, 2015 edition.

NFPA 31, *Standard for the Installation of Oil-Burning Equipment*, 2011 edition.

NFPA 33, *Standard for Spray Application Using Flammable or Combustible Materials*, 2011 edition.

NFPA 45, *Standard on Fire Protection for Laboratories Using Chemicals*, 2011 edition.

NFPA 51, *Standard for the Design and Installation of Oxygen–Fuel Gas Systems for Welding, Cutting, and Allied Processes*, 2013 edition.

NFPA 51B, *Standard for Fire Prevention During Welding, Cutting, and Other Hot Work*, 2014 edition.

NFPA 52, *Vehicular Gaseous Fuel Systems Code*, 2013 edition.

NFPA 55, *Compressed Gases and Cryogenic Fluids Code*, 2013 edition.

NFPA 58, *Liquefied Petroleum Gas Code*, 2014 edition.

NFPA 59A, *Standard for the Production, Storage, and Handling of Liquefied Natural Gas (LNG)*, 2013 edition.

NFPA 68, *Standard on Explosion Protection by Deflagration Venting*, 2013 edition.

NFPA 69, *Standard on Explosion Prevention Systems*, 2014 edition.

NFPA 70®, *National Electrical Code®*, 2014 edition.

NFPA 72®, *National Fire Alarm and Signaling Code*, 2013 edition.

NFPA 77, *Recommended Practice on Static Electricity*, 2014 edition.

NFPA 80, *Standard for Fire Doors and Other Opening Protectives*, 2013 edition.

NFPA 80A, *Recommended Practice for Protection of Buildings from Exterior Fire Exposures*, 2012 edition.

NFPA 82, *Standard on Incinerators and Waste and Linen Handling Systems and Equipment*, 2014 edition.

NFPA 86, *Standard for Ovens and Furnaces*, 2015 edition.

NFPA 90A, *Standard for the Installation of Air-Conditioning and Ventilating Systems*, 2015 edition.

NFPA 91, *Standard for Exhaust Systems for Air Conveying of Vapors, Gases, Mists, and Noncombustible Particulate Solids*, 2010 edition.

NFPA 92, *Standard for SmokeControl Systems*, 2012 edition.

NFPA 96, *Standard for Ventilation Control and Fire Protection of Commercial Cooking Operations*, 2014 edition.

NFPA 99, *Health Care Facilities Code*, 2015 edition.

NFPA *101®*, *Life Safety Code®*, 2015 edition.

NFPA 101A, *Guide on Alternative Approaches to Life Safety*, 2013 edition.

NFPA 102, *Standard for Grandstands, Folding and Telescopic Seating, Tents, and Membrane Structures*, 2011 edition.

NFPA 105, *Standard for Smoke Door Assemblies and Other Opening Protectives*, 2013 edition.

NFPA 110, *Standard for Emergency and Standby Power Systems*, 2013 edition.

NFPA 170, *Standard for Fire Safety and Emergency Symbols*, 2012 edition.

NFPA 204, *Standard for Smoke and Heat Venting*, 2012 edition.

NFPA 220, *Standard on Types of Building Construction*, 2015 edition.

NFPA 232, *Standard for the Protection of Records*, 2012 edition.

NFPA 241, *Standard for Safeguarding Construction, Alteration, and Demolition Operations*, 2013 edition.

NFPA 252, *Standard Methods of Fire Tests of Door Assemblies*, 2012 edition.

NFPA 257, *Standard on Fire Test for Window and Glass Block Assemblies*, 2012 edition.

NFPA 259, *Standard Test Method for Potential Heat of Building Materials*, 2013 edition.

NFPA 260, *Standard Methods of Tests and Classification System for Cigarette Ignition Resistance of Components of Upholstered Furniture*, 2013 edition.

NFPA 261, *Standard Method of Test for Determining Resistance of Mock-Up Upholstered Furniture Material Assemblies to Ignition by Smoldering Cigarettes*, 2013 edition.

NFPA 265, *Standard Methods of Fire Tests for Evaluating Room Fire Growth Contribution of Textile or Expanded Vinyl Wall Coverings on Full Height Panels and Walls*, 2011 edition.

NFPA 286, *Standard Methods of Fire Tests for Evaluating Contribution of Wall and Ceiling Interior Finish to Room Fire Growth*, 2011 edition.

NFPA 288, *Standard Methods of Fire Tests of Floor Fire Door Assemblies Installed Horizontally in Fire Resistance–Rated Floor Systems*, 2012 edition.

NFPA 289, *Standard Method of Fire Test for Individual Fuel Packages*, 2013 edition.

NFPA 291, *Recommended Practice for Fire Flow Testing and Marking of Hydrants*, 2013 edition.

NFPA 302, *Fire Protection Standard for Pleasure and Commercial Motor Craft*, 2015 edition.

NFPA 303, *Fire Protection Standard for Marinas and Boatyards*, 2011 edition.

NFPA 326, *Standard for the Safeguarding of Tanks and Containers for Entry, Cleaning, or Repair*, 2010 edition.

NFPA 329, *Recommended Practice for Handling Releases of Flammable and Combustible Liquids and Gases*, 2010 edition.

NFPA 385, *Standard for Tank Vehicles for Flammable and Combustible Liquids*, 2012 edition.

NFPA 400, *Hazardous Materials Code*, 2013 edition.

NFPA 409, *Standard on Aircraft Hangars*, 2011 edition.

NFPA 415, *Standard on Airport Terminal Buildings, Fueling Ramp Drainage, and Loading Walkways*, 2013 edition.

NFPA 418, *Standard for Heliports*, 2011 edition.

NFPA 495, *Explosive Materials Code*, 2013 edition.

NFPA 496, *Standard for Purged and Pressurized Enclosures for Electrical Equipment*, 2013 edition.

NFPA 497, *Recommended Practice for the Classification of Flammable Liquids, Gases, or Vapors and of Hazardous (Classified) Locations for Electrical Installations in Chemical Process Areas*, 2012 edition.

NFPA 499, *Recommended Practice for the Classification of Combustible Dusts and of Hazardous (Classified) Locations for Electrical Installations in Chemical Process Areas*, 2013 edition.

NFPA 505, *Fire Safety Standard for Powered Industrial Trucks Including Type Designations, Areas of Use, Conversions, Maintenance, and Operations*, 2013 edition.

NFPA 600, *Standard on Industrial Fire Brigades*, 2010 edition.

NFPA 601, *Standard for Security Services in Fire Loss Prevention*, 2010 edition.

NFPA 654, *Standard for the Prevention of Fire and Dust Explosions from the Manufacturing, Processing, and Handling of Combustible Particulate Solids*, 2013 edition.

NFPA 655, *Standard for Prevention of Sulfur Fires and Explosions*, 2012 edition.

NFPA 701, *Standard Methods of Fire Tests for Flame Propagation of Textiles and Films*, 2010 edition.

NFPA 703, *Standard for Fire Retardant–Treated Wood and Fire-Retardant Coatings for Building Materials*, 2015 edition.

NFPA 704, *Standard System for the Identification of the Hazards of Materials for Emergency Response*, 2012 edition.

NFPA 720, *Standard for the Installation of Carbon Monoxide (CO) Detection and Warning Equipment*, 2015 edition.

NFPA 801, *Standard for Fire Protection for Facilities Handling Radioactive Materials*, 2013 edition.

NFPA 914, *Code for Fire Protection of Historic Structures*, 2010 edition.

NFPA 1031, *Standard for Professional Qualifications for Fire Inspector and Plan Examiner*, 2014 edition.

NFPA 1033, *Standard for Professional Qualifications for Fire Investigator*, 2014 edition.

NFPA 1035, *Standard for Professional Qualifications for Fire and Life Safety Educator, Public Information Officer, and Juvenile Firesetter Intervention Specialist*, 2010 edition.

NFPA 1037, *Standard for Professional Qualifications for Fire Marshal*, 2012 edition.

NFPA 1122, *Code for Model Rocketry*, 2013 edition.

NFPA 1123, *Code for Fireworks Display*, 2014 edition.

NFPA 1127, *Code for High Power Rocketry*, 2013 edition.

NFPA 1141, *Standard for Fire Protection Infrastructure for Land Development in Wildland, Rural, and Suburban Areas*, 2012 edition.

NFPA 1142, *Standard on Water Supplies for Suburban and Rural Fire Fighting*, 2012 edition.

NFPA 1144, *Standard for Reducing Structure Ignition Hazards from Wildland Fire*, 2013 edition.

NFPA 1221, *Standard for the Installation, Maintenance, and Use of Emergency Services Communications Systems*, 2013 edition.

NFPA 1600®, *Standard on Disaster/Emergency Management and Business Continuity Programs*, 2013 edition.

NFPA 1620, *Standard for Pre-Incident Planning*, 2010 edition.

NFPA 2113, *Standard on Selection, Care, Use, and Maintenance of Flame-Resistant Garments for Protection of Industrial Personnel Against Flash Fire*, 2012 edition.

NFPA 5000®, *Building Construction and Safety Code®*, 2015 edition.

NFPA *Fire Protection Guide to Hazardous Materials*, 2010 edition.

NFPA *Fire Protection Handbook*, 19th edition, 2003.

NFPA *Fire Technology*, August 1974, "Fire Tests of Building Interior Covering Systems."

SFPE *Engineering Guide*.

SFPE *Handbook of Fire Protection Engineering*, 3rd edition, 2002.

F.1.2 Other Publications.

F.1.2.1 AIChE Publications. American Institute of Chemical Engineers, Three Park Avenue, New York, NY 10016-5991.

Guidelines for Safe Warehousing of Chemicals, 1998.

Guidelines for Pressure Relief and Effluent Handling Systems, 1998.

Testing the Suitability of FIBCs for Use in Flammable Atmospheres.

F.1.2.2 ANSI Publications. American National Standards Institute, Inc., 25 West 43rd Street, 4th Floor, New York, NY 10036.

ICC/ANSI A117.1, *American National Standard for Accessible and Usable Buildings and Facilities*, 2009.

ANSI/CMA Z129.1, *American National Standard for Hazardous Industrial Chemicals - Precautionary Labeling*, 2006.

ANSI/FM 4950, *Evaluating Welding Pads, Welding Blankets and Welding Curtains for Hot Work Operations*, 2007.

ANSI/AIHA Z9.7, *Recirculation of Air from Industrial Process Exhaust Systems*, 2007.

ANSI/ISA 12.02.01, *Electrical Apparatus for use in Class I, Zones 0, 1 & 2 Hazardous (Classified) Locations - Intrinsic Safety*, 2002.

ANSI/ISA 61241, (12.10.02), *Electrical Apparatus for Use in Zone 20, Zone 21 and Zone 22 Hazardous (Classified) Locations - General Requirements*, 2006.

ANSI Z83.11, *Gas Food Service Equipment*, 2006.

F.1.2.3 API Publications. American Petroleum Institute, 1220 L Street NW, Washington, DC 20005-4070.

"An Engineering Analysis of the Effects of Oxygenated Fuels on Marketing Vapor Recovery Equipment."

API 12R1, *Setting, Maintenance, Inspection, Operation, and Repair of Tanks in Production Service.*

API 620, *Recommended Rules for the Design and Construction of Large, Welded, Low-Pressure Storage Tanks*, 11th Edition, 2012.

API Standard 650, *Welded Steel Tanks for Oil Storage*, 11th Edition, 2011.

API 653, *Tank Inspection, Repair, Alteration, and Reconstruction*, 4th edition, 2012.

API 1501, *Filtration and Dehydration of Aviation Fuels*, 1st Edition, 1965.

API RP 1615, *Installation of Underground Petroleum Storage Systems*, 6th Edition, 2011

API 2015, *Cleaning Petroleum Storage Tanks*, 6th edition, reaffirmed 2016.

API 2218, *Fireproofing Practices in Petroleum and Petrochemical Processing Plants*, 2nd Edition, 1999.

API 2350, *Overfill Protection for Storage Tanks in Petroleum Facilities*, 4th Edition, 2012.

API RP 1621, *Bulk Liquid Stock Control at Retail Outlets*, 2001.

API 2003, *Protection Against Ignition Arising Out of Static, Lightning, and Stray Currents*, 7th Edition, 2008.

F.1.2.4 ASHRAE Publications. American Society of Heating, Refrigerating and Air Conditioning Engineers, Inc., 1791 Tullie Circle, NE, Atlanta, GA 30329-2305.

ANSI/ASHRAE 34, *Designation and Safety Classification of Refrigerants*, 2010.

F.1.2.5 ASME Publications. American Society of Mechanical Engineers, Two Park Avenue, New York, NY 10016-5990.

Boiler and Pressure Vessel Code.

ASME A17.1/CSA B44, *Safety Code for Elevators and Escalators*, 2007.

ANSI/ASME B31.8, *Gas Transmission and Distribution Piping Systems*, 2010.

F.1.2.6 ASTM Publications. ASTM International, 100 Barr Harbor Drive, P.O. Box C700, West Conshohocken, PA 19428-2959.

ASTM *Manual on Flash Point Standards and Their Use.*

ASTM A380/A380M, *Standard Practice for Cleaning, Descaling, and Passivation of Stainless Steel Parts, Equipment, and Systems*, 2013.

ASTM D 2859, *Standard Test Method for Ignition Characteristics of Finished Textile Floor Covering Materials*, 2006, (2011).

ASTM D 4206, *Standard Test Method for Sustained Burning of Liquid Mixtures using the Small-Scale Open Cup Apparatus*, 1996 (2007).

ASTM D 4207, *Standard Test Method for Sustained Burning of Low Viscosity Liquid Mixtures by the Wick Test, withdrawn*, last edition 1991.

ASTM D 6469, *Standard Guide for Microbial Contamination in Fuels and Fuel Systems*, 2012.

ASTM E 84, *Standard Test Method of Surface Burning Characteristics of Building Materials*, 2013.

ASTM E 119, *Standard Test Methods for Fire Tests of Building Construction and Materials*, 2012a.

ASTM E 502, *Standard Test Method for Selection and Use of ASTM Standards for the Determination of Flash Point of Chemicals by Closed Cup Methods*, 2007e1.

ASTM E 814, *Standard Test Method for Fire Tests of Through Penetration Fire Stops*, 2011a.

ASTM E 1226, *Standard Test Method for Explosibility of Dust Clouds*, 2010.

ASTM E 1352, *Standard Test Method for Cigarette Ignition Resistance of Mock-Up Upholstered Furniture Assemblies*, 2008a.

ASTM E 1353, *Standard Test Methods for Cigarette Ignition Resistance of Components of Upholstered Furniture*, 2008ae1.

ASTM E 1354, *Standard Test Method for Heat and Visible Smoke Release Rates for Materials and Products Using an Oxygen Consumption Calorimeter*, 2013.

ASTM E 1472, *Standard Guide for Documenting Computer Software for Fire Models*, 2007 (Withdrawn).

ASTM E 1491, *Test Method for Minimum Autoignition Temperature of Dust Clouds*, 2006.

ASTM E 1537, *Standard Test Method for Fire Testing of Upholstered Furniture*, 2012.

ASTM E 1590, *Standard Test Method for Fire Testing of Mattresses*, 2012.

ASTM E 2019, *Standard Test Method for Minimum Ignition Energy of a Dust Cloud in Air*, 2003 (2007).

ASTM E 2021, *Standard Test Method for Hot-Surface Ignition of Dust Layers*, 2009.

ASTM E 2030, *Guide for Recommended Uses of Photoluminescent (Phosphorescent) Safety Markings*, 2009a.

ASTM E 2174, *Standard Practice for On-Site Inspection of Installed Fire Stops*, 2010ae1.

F.1.2.7 AWS Publications. American Welding Society, 550 NW LeJeune Road, Miami, FL 33126.

ANSI/AWS F-4.1, *Safe Practices for the Preparation of Containers and Piping for Welding and Cutting*, 2007.

F.1.2.8 AWWA Publications. American Water Works Association Inc., 6666 West Quincy Avenue, Denver, CO 80235.

AWWA M14, *Recommended Practice for Backflow Prevention and Cross-Connection Control*, 2004 edition.

F.1.2.9 CGA Publications. Compressed Gas Association, 14501 George Carter Way, Suite 103, Chantilly, VA 20151.

CGA C-6 (C-6.3), *Standards for Visual Inspection of Steel Compressed Gas Cylinders*, 2007.

CGA C-6.1, *Standards for Visual Inspection of High Pressure Aluminum Compressed Gas Cylinders*, 2006.

CGA C-6.2, *Guidelines for Visual Inspection and Requalification of Fiber Reinforced High Pressure Cylinders*, 2009.

CGA C-10, *Recommended Procedures for Changes of Gas Service for Compressed Gas Cylinders*, 2005.

F.1.2.10 CSFM Publications. California State Fire Marshal Publications, Office of the State Fire Marshal, 1131 S Street, Sacramento, CA 95811.

"Rings of Fire: Fire Prevention & Suppression of Waste Tire Piles," 2005.

F.1.2.11 FAA Publications. Federal Aviation Administration, U.S. Department of Transportation, 800 Independence Avenue, SW, Washington, DC 20591.

FAA A/C 150/5390-2B, *Heliport Design*, 2004.

F.1.2.12 ICAO Publications. International Civil Aviation Organization, Document Sales Unit, 999 University Street, Montréal, Quebec, Canada, H3C 5H7. icaohq@icao.int

Technical Publications.

F.1.2.13 IEC Publications. International Electrotechnical Commission, 3, rue de Varembé, P.O. Box 131, CH-1211 Geneva 20, Switzerland.

IEC 61340-4-4, *Electrostatics—Part 4-4: Standard Test Methods for Specific Applications — Electrostatic Classification of Flexible Intermediate Bulk Containers (FIBC)*, 2005.

F.1.2.14 IMO Publications. International Maritime Organization, 4 Albert Embankment, London SE1 7SR, U.K., publications-sales@imo.org.

IM Dangerous Goods Code, 2007.

F.1.2.15 ISO Publications. International Organization for Standardization 1, ch. de la Voie-Creuse, case postale 56, CH-1211 Geneva 20, Switzerland.

ISO 8115, *Cotton Bales — Dimensions and Density,* 1986.

F.1.2.16 PEI Publications. Petroleum Equipment Institute, P.O. Box 2380, Tulsa, OK 74101-2380.

PEI RP100, *Recommended Practices for Installation of Underground Liquid Storage Systems,* 2011.

PEI RP200, *Recommended Practices for Installation of Aboveground Storage Systems for Motor Vehicle Fueling,* 2008.

F.1.2.17 Scott Specialty Gases Publications. Scott Specialty Gases, 6141 Easton Road, Box 310, Plumsteadville, PA 18949.

Design and Safety Handbook, 2006.

F.1.2.18 California Department of Consumer Affairs Publications. Bureau of Home Furnishings and Thermal Insulation, 3485 Orange Grove Avenue, North Highlands, CA 95660-5595.

Technical Bulletin CA TB 129, *Flammability Test Procedure for Mattresses for Use in Public Buildings,* 1992.

F.1.2.19 STI Publications. Steel Tank Institute, 570 Oakwood Road, Lake Zurich, IL 60047.

STI P3, *Specification and Manual for External Corrosion Protection of Underground Steel Storage Tanks.*

STI RP 01-69, *Recommended Practice for Control of External Corrosion of Underground or Submerged Metallic Piping Systems.*

STI RP 892-91, *Recommended Practice for Corrosion Protection of Underground Piping Networks Associated with Liquid Storage and Dispensing Systems.*

STI RP 1632, *Cathodic Protection of Underground Petroleum Storage and Piping Systems.*

STI SP001, *Standard for Inspection of Aboveground Storage Tanks*

STI R 931, *Double Wall AST Installation and Testing Instructions.*

STI RP R011, *Recommended Practice for Anchoring of Steel Underground Storage Tanks.*

Keeping Water Out of Your Storage System.

F.1.2.20 Transport Canada Publications. Transport Canada, 330 Sparks Street, Ottawa, Ontario K1A 0N5. webfeedback@tc.gc.ca

Transportation of Dangerous Goods Regulations.

F.1.2.21 UL Publications. Underwriters Laboratories Inc., 333 Pfingsten Road, Northbrook, IL 60062-2096.

ANSI/UL 30, *Standard for Metal Safety Cans,* 1995, revised 2009.

ANSI/UL 142, *Standard for Steel Aboveground Tanks for Flammable and Combustible Liquids,* 2006, revised 2010.

ANSI/UL 197, *Standard for Commercial Electric Cooking Appliances,* 2010.

ANSI/UL 199, *Standard for Automatic Sprinklers for Fire-Protection Service,* 2005, revised 2008.

ANSI/UL 263, *Standard for Fire Tests of Building Construction and Materials* 2003, revised 2011.

ANSI/UL 296A, *Standard for Waste Oil-Burning Air-Heating Appliances,* 2010.

ANSI/UL 299, *Dry Chemical Fire Extinguishers,* 2002, revised 2009.

ANSI/UL 300, *Fire Testing of Fire Extinguishing Systems for Protection of Commercial Cooking Equipment,* 2005, revised 2010.

ANSI/UL 711, *Standard for Rating and Fire Testing of Fire Extinguishers,* 2004, revised 2009.

ANSI/UL 723, *Standard for Test for Surface Burning Characteristics of Building Materials,* 2008, revised 2010.

ANSI/UL 737, *Standard for Fireplace Stoves,* 2011.

ANSI/UL 896, *Standard for Oil-Burning Stoves,* 1993.

ANSI/UL 913, *Standard for Intrinsically Safe Apparatus and Associated Apparatus for Use in Class I, II, and III Division 1, Hazardous (Classified) Locations,* 2006, revised 2011.

ANSI/UL 923, *Standard for Microwave Cooking Appliances,* 2008.

ANSI/UL 969, *Standard for Marking and Labeling Systems,* 1995, revised 2008.

ANSI/UL 1040, *Standard for Fire Test of Insulated Wall Construction,* 1996, revised 2007.

ANSI/UL 1313, *Nonmetallic Safety Cans for Petroleum Products,* 1993, revised 2007.

ANSI/UL 1479, *Standard for Fire Tests of Through-Penetration Firestops,* 2003, revised 2010.

ANSI/UL 1709, *Standard for Rapid Rise Fire Tests of Protection Materials for Structural Steel,* 2011.

ANSI/UL 1715, *Standard for Fire Test of Interior Finish Material,* 1997, revised 2008.

ANSI/UL 1746, *Standard for External Corrosion Protection Systems for Steel Underground Storage Tanks,* 2007.

UL 1975, *Standard for Fire Tests for Foamed Plastics Used for Decorative Purposes,* 2006.

ANSI/UL 2085, *Standard for Protected Aboveground Tanks for Flammable and Combustible Liquids*, 1997, revised 2010.

ANSI/UL 2129, *Halocarbon Clean Agent Fire Extinguishers*, 2005, revised 2011.

UL Subject 199B, *Outline of Investigation for Control Cabinets for Automatic Sprinkler Systems Used for Protection of Commercial Cooking Equipment*, 2006.

UL Subject 199E, *Outline of Investigation for Fire Testing of Sprinklers and Water Spray Nozzles for Protection of Deep Fat Fryers*, 2004.

UL Subject 2162, *Outline of Investigation for Commercial Wood-Fired Baking Ovens*, 2004.

UL Subject 2436, *Outline of Investigation for Spill Containment For Stationary Lead Acid Battery Systems*, 2006.

UL Subject 2728, *Outline of Investigation for Pellet Fuel Burning Cooking Appliances*, 2009.

F.1.2.22 United Nations Publications. United Nations Publications, United Nations Plaza, Room DC2–853, New York, NY 10017.

UN Recommendations on the Transport of Dangerous Goods, 2011.

F.1.2.23 U.S. Government Publications. U.S. Government Printing Office, 732 North Capitol St., NW, Washington, DC 20401.

Title 16, Code of Federal Regulations, Part 1500, Commercial Practices, Chapter 11.

Title 16, Code of Federal Regulations, Part 1630, *Standard for the Surface Flammability of Carpets and Rugs*.

Title 16, Code of Federal Regulations, Part 1632, *Standard for the Flammability of Mattresses and Mattress Pads*.

Title 18, Code of Federal Regulations, "Importation, Manufacture, Distribution and Storage of Explosive Materials."

Title 29, Code of Federal Regulations, Part 1910, OSHA Regulations for Emergency Procedures and Fire Brigades.

Title 29, Code of Federal Regulations, Part 1910.38.

Title 29, Code of Federal Regulations, Part 1910.100.

Title 29, Code of Federal Regulations, Part 1910.165.

Title 33, Code of Federal Regulations, Part 154.

Title 49, Code of Federal Regulations, U.S. Department of Transportation, Hazardous Materials Regulations.

Title 49, Code of Federal Regulations, Parts 100–179, Transportation.

Title 49, Code of Federal Regulations, Parts 100–199.

Title 49, Code of Federal Regulations, Part 172.102.

Title 49, Code of Federal Regulations, Part 173.225.

Title 49, Code of Federal Regulations, Part 173, Appendix A.

F.1.2.24 Other Publications. Bachman, K. C., and W. G. Dudek, *Static Electricity in Fueling Superjets*, 1972. Exxon Research and Engineering Co. Brochure, Linden, NJ.

Blue Book.

Britton, *Avoiding Static Ignition Hazards*.

BOCA/National Building Code.

CRC Report NO. 583.

CSA B44, *Safety Code for Elevators and Escalators*.

Fisher, H. G. and Forrest, H. S., "Protection of Storage Tanks from Two-Phase Flow Due to Fire Exposure."

Hirschler, 1992: "Heat release from plastic materials."

Fire Equipment Manufacturers' Association, "Recommendations for Protection of Curtained Limited Finishing Workstations."

FM 4880, *Approval Standard for Class I Insulated Wall or Wall and Roof/Ceiling Panels; Plastic Interior Finish Materials; Plastic Exterior Building Panels; Wall/Ceiling Coating Systems; Interior or Exterior Finish Systems*.

FM Data Sheet 7–76, "Operations and Maintenance."

Houser, J. et al, "Vent Sizing for Fire Considerations: External Fire Duration, Jacketed Vessels, and Heat Flux Variations Owing to Fuel Consumption."

NACE RP-0169, *Recommended Practice, Control of External Corrosion on Underground or Submerged Metallic Piping Systems*.

NACE RP-0285, *Recommended Practice, Corrosion Control of Underground Storage Tank Systems by Cathodic Protection*.

NASA, NSS 1740.16, *Safety Standard for Hydrogen and Hydrogen Systems*.

International Building Code.

Standard Building Code.

Uniform Building Code.

Oilheat Research Alliance, *Oilheat Technicians's Manual*.

P. J. Wakelyn and S. E. Hughs, "Evaluation of the Flammability of Cotton Bales," *Fire and Materials* Volume 26, pages 183–189 (2002).

SMACNA Rectangular Industrial Duct Construction Standards.

SMACNA Round Industrial Duct Construction Standards.

Specifications and Standards (Marine Standards).

"Cotton Ginners Handbook," Agricultural Handbook Number 503, W. S. Anthony and W. D. Mayfield, editors, 1994.

ULC-S603, *Standard for Galvanic Corrosion Protection Systems for Steel Underground Tanks for Flammable and Combustible Liquids*.

F.2 References for Extracts. The following documents are listed here to provide reference information, including title and edition, for extracts given throughout the nonmandatory sections of this code as indicated by a reference in brackets [ ] following a section or paragraph. These documents are not a part of the requirements of this document unless also listed in Chapter 2 for other reasons.

NFPA 10, *Standard for Portable Fire Extinguishers*, 2013 edition.

NFPA 13, *Standard for the Installation of Sprinkler Systems*, 2013 edition.

NFPA 14, *Standard for the Installation of Standpipe and Hose Systems*, 2013 edition.

NFPA 20, *Standard for the Installation of Stationary Pumps for Fire Protection*, 2013 edition.

NFPA 25, *Standard for the Inspection, Testing, and Maintenance of Water-Based Fire Protection Systems*, 2014 edition.

NFPA 30, *Flammable and Combustible Liquids Code*, 2015 edition.

NFPA 30A, *Code for Motor Fuel Dispensing Facilities and Repair Garages*, 2015 edition.

NFPA 30B, *Code for the Manufacture and Storage of Aerosol Products*, 2015 edition.

NFPA 31, *Standard for the Installation of Oil-Burning Equipment*, 2011 edition.

NFPA 33, *Standard for Spray Application Using Flammable or Combustible Materials*, 2011 edition.

NFPA 45, *Standard on Fire Protection for Laboratories Using Chemicals*, 2011 edition.

NFPA 51B, *Standard for Fire Prevention During Welding, Cutting, and Other Hot Work*, 2014 edition.

NFPA 52, *Vehicular Gaseous Fuel Systems Code*, 2013 edition.

NFPA 55, *Compressed Gases and Cryogenic Fluids Code*, 2013 edition.

NFPA 58, *Liquefied Petroleum Gas Code*, 2014 edition.

NFPA 61, *Standard for the Prevention of Fires and Dust Explosions in Agricultural and Food Processing Facilities*, 2013 edition.

NFPA 69, *Standard on Explosion Prevention Systems*, 2014 edition.

NFPA 70®, *National Electrical Code®*, 2014 edition.

NFPA 70B, *Recommended Practice for Electrical Equipment Maintenance*, 2013 edition.

NFPA 72®, *National Fire Alarm and Signaling Code*, 2013 edition.

NFPA 80, *Standard for Fire Doors and Other Opening Protectives*, 2013 edition.

NFPA 88A, *Standard for Parking Structures*, 2015 edition.

NFPA 96, *Standard for Ventilation Control and Fire Protection of Commercial Cooking Operations*, 2014 edition.

NFPA 99, *Health Care Facilities Code*, 2015 edition.

NFPA *101®*, *Life Safety Code®*, 2015 edition.

NFPA 102, *Standard for Grandstands, Folding and Telescopic Seating, Tents, and Membrane Structures*, 2011 edition.

NFPA 140, *Standard on Motion Picture and Television Production Studio Soundstages, Approved Production Facilities, and Production Locations*, 2013 edition.

NFPA 220, *Standard on Types of Building Construction*, 2015 edition.

NFPA 241, *Standard for Safeguarding Construction, Alteration, and Demolition Operations*, 2013 edition.

NFPA 303, *Fire Protection Standard for Marinas and Boatyards*, 2011 edition.

NFPA 307, *Standard for the Construction and Fire Protection of Marine Terminals, Piers, and Wharves*, 2011 edition.

NFPA 312, *Standard for Fire Protection of Vessels During Construction, Conversion, Repair, and Lay-Up*, 2011 edition.

NFPA 400, *Hazardous Materials Code*, 2013 edition.

NFPA 407, *Standard for Aircraft Fuel Servicing*, 2012 edition.

NFPA 415, *Standard on Airport Terminal Buildings, Fueling Ramp Drainage, and Loading Walkways*, 2013 edition.

NFPA 418, *Standard for Heliports*, 2013 edition.

NFPA 472, *Standard for Competence of Responders to Hazardous Materials/Weapons of Mass Destruction Incidents*, 2013 edition.

NFPA 654, *Standard for the Prevention of Fire and Dust Explosions from the Manufacturing, Processing, and Handling of Combustible Particulate Solids*, 2013 edition.

NFPA 914, *Code for Fire Protection of Historic Structures*, 2010 edition.

NFPA 1144, *Standard for Reducing Structure Ignition Hazards from Wildland Fire*, 2013 edition.

NFPA 5000®, *Building Construction and Safety Code®*, 2015 edition.

Index

Copyright © 2014 National Fire Protection Association. All Rights Reserved.

The copyright in this index is separate and distinct from the copyright in the document that it indexes. The licensing provisions set forth for the document are not applicable to this index. This index may not be reproduced in whole or in part by any means without the express written permission of NFPA.

-A-

Aboveground tanks .... *see* Tanks
Absolute pressure (definition) 3.3.1, A.3.3.1
Access, fire-fighting/emergency ...... 1.1.1(8), 18.1, 18.2, A.18.2.2 to A.18.2.4.1.3
   Aircraft fuel servicing 42.10.2.1.6
   Aircraft hangars 21.1.2
   Airport terminal buildings 21.2.2.2
   Automobile wrecking yards 22.3
   Construction sites 16.3.4, 16.3.6.6, A.16.3.6.6
   Cryogenic fluids storage containers 63.4.13.2.7.3
   Electrical service disconnect 11.1.7, A.11.1.7.1
   Elevator fire service keys 11.3.6.3.1
   Fire hydrants and water supply connections 18.5.6
   Fire protection equipment, access to 13.1.4, 13.1.11, 13.3.3.4.1.3, A.13.1.11, A.13.3.3.4.1.3
   Flammable and combustible liquids processing and storage 66.6.9.5, 66.9.9.3, 66.14.6.4, 66.17.5, 66.17.6.10, 66.17.6.12, 66.21.6.6.4, 66.24.5.6, A.66.17.6.10, A.66.24.5.6
   Forest products, storage of ...... 31.3.3.3.5, 31.3.3.3.6, 31.3.4.2(3), 31.3.4.3.2, 31.3.5.2(3), 31.3.5.3.3, 31.3.6.2.1(4), 31.3.8.3.2, 31.3.8.3.3, A.31.3.8.3.3
   Gated communities 18.2.2.2
   Heliports, roof-top 21.3.2.2, 21.3.3.3
   Marinas, boatyards, piers, and wharves 28.1.6.2.6, 28.1.7.2.1.8, 28.1.7.2.3.1
   Marine motor fuel dispensing facilities 42.9.7.3
   Motion picture production soundstages, facilities, and locations 32.4.9, 32.5.9, A.32.5.9
   Permits .... Table 1.12.8(a)
   Photovoltaic systems 11.12.2.2
   Special outdoor events, carnivals, and fairs 10.14.2
   Storage occupancies 34.3.2, 34.4.3.2, 34.5.4.1
   Tires, outside storage of 33.5, 33.6.3
   Wildland fire-prone areas 17.3.7
Access, limiting 1.7.11.3
   Tires, outside storage of 33.6
   Wildland fire-prone areas 17.3.3
Access boxes 11.3.6.3.1, 16.3.4.3, 16.3.4.4, 18.2.2.1
   Definition 3.3.2
Additions .... 1.3.6.3 ; *see also* Buildings, Under construction
   Definition 3.3.3
Aerosol products .... 60.1.2(9), Chap. 61
   Classification of .... 61.1.3, 61.1.4, A.61.1.3, A.61.1.4.1(3), A.61.1.4.1(4)
   Cooking spray products .... 61.1.3.5, 61.3.3, 61.4.2.2 to 61.4.2.4, 61.4.3.2, 61.4.3.3.1, 61.4.3.4 to 61.4.3.6
   Definition 3.3.4, A.3.3.4
   Marking of 61.1.5, 61.3.1.2
   Mercantile occupancies 61.4
   Operations and maintenance 61.5, A.61.5.3.3, A.61.5.7
   Permits .... Table 1.12.8(a), 61.1.2, 61.5.3.3, A.61.5.3.3
   Plastic aerosol X products 61.1.4.2, 61.4.1
   Spray operations, use in .... 43.1.1.2(4)
   Storage .... 61.2 to 61.4, 66.9.17.2, A.61.3.1.3 to A.61.3.4.2.9.5
Agricultural products, storage of 45.7
Air bag systems 22.9.4
Air conditioning .... *see* Heating, ventilating, and air conditioning (HVAC) systems

Aircraft fuel servicing .... 21.2.3.3, 42.10, A.42.10.2.1.2.6 to A.42.10.5.21.2(2)
   Bonding 42.10.5.4, A.42.10.5.4
   Defueling 42.10.5.14
   Heliports, rooftop 21.3.3.4, 21.3.3.6, 42.10.4
   Internal combustion engine equipment near 42.10.5.6, A.42.10.5.6.4.3
   Occupancy of aircraft during fueling 42.10.5.11
   Open flames 42.10.5.8
   Operation of aircraft engines and heaters 42.10.5.5
   Permit requirements .... Table 1.12.8(a)
   Spills, prevention and control of 42.10.5.2, A.42.10.5.2
Aircraft hangars .... Table 1.12.8(a), 21.1, A.21.1.4, A.21.1.5
Air-inflated structures 25.5.3, 25.6.5, A.25.5.3.3.1
Airport (aerodrome) .... Chap. 21
   Definition 3.3.5
   Fuel systems 42.10.3, A.42.10.3.3.1
   Radar equipment 42.10.2.1.4, 42.10.2.1.5, A.42.10.2.1.5
Airport ramps 21.2.3.3, 21.2.3.5, 21.2.5.2, 42.10.5.7, 42.10.5.8, A.21.2.5.2, A.42.10.5.7
   Definition 3.3.6
Airport terminal buildings .... 21.2, A.21.2.3.2 to A.21.2.7.2
   Definition 3.3.29.1, A.3.3.29.1
   Permits .... Table 1.12.8(a), 21.2.2.1
Air sampling–type detectors 13.7.4.3.4, A.13.7.4.3.4.3, A.13.7.4.3.4.6
   Definition 3.3.84.1
Air-supported structures 25.5.3, 25.6.5, A.25.5.3.3.1
Air-transfer openings 12.8.6, 12.9.5, A.12.8.6.2
Aisles
   Aerosol products storage 61.5.4
   Compressed gases, storage, handling, and use 63.3.10.3.2, 63.3.10.3.3
   Flammable and combustible liquids storage, handling, and use 66.17.6.12, 66.24.5.6, A.66.24.5.6
   Hazardous materials .... 60.4.2.1.13.2(10)
   Soundstages 32.4.10.3
   Storage occupancies 34.4.3, 34.7.3.3, 34.8.3.1.4, 34.8.3.2.3, A.34.7.3.3
   Width
      Compressed gases, storage, handling, and use 63.3.10.3.3
      Definition 3.3.7, A.3.3.7
      Flammable and combustible liquids storage, handling, and use 66.24.5.6, A.66.24.5.6
      Storage occupancies 34.4.3.1, 34.7.3.3, 34.8.3.1.4, 34.8.3.2.3, A.34.7.3.3
Alarms
   Definition 3.3.8
   Door .... 14.5.2, A.14.5.2.2 to A.14.5.2.12
   Waterflow .... 11.9.5(6), 34.5.5.1
Alarm signals .... *see* Signals
Alarm systems ... 13.7, A.13.7.1.2 to A.13.7.1.4.7; *see also* Notification; Waterflow alarms
   Aerosol products storage, handling, and use 61.2.7
   Airports 21.2.7, A.21.2.7.2
   Assembly occupancies 20.1.4.5
   Central station .... *see* Central station fire alarm systems
   Compressed gas 63.2.8, 63.3.9.6.2, 63.3.9.6.3, A.63.2.8
   Construction sites 16.3.3, A.16.3.3
   Cooking equipment .... 50.4.4.10, 50.4.8, 50.4.9, A.50.4.4.10(4)
   Cryogenic fluids 63.2.8, A.63.2.8

Definition (fire alarm system) 3.3.254.10
Detection and 13.7.1.7.1, 13.7.1.7.6, 13.7.1.7.8, 13.7.1.7.9,
    13.7.3.5, A.13.7.1.7.6
Dust explosion and fire prevention 40.5.8
Emergency command center 11.9.5
Extinguishers, portable fire 13.6.3.1.5, 13.6.4.5.1.1,
    13.6.4.5.1.2, 13.6.4.7.4.3.1
Fire pumps .... 13.4.3, 13.4.5, A.13.4.3, A.13.4.5.1.2 to
    A.13.4.5.2.3(3)
Flammable and combustible liquids operations 66.6.6,
    66.24.15, A.66.6.6.1
Forest products ... 31.3.2.3, 31.3.3.3.2.1(2), 31.3.4.2(2), 31.3.5.2(2),
    31.3.8.2(2), A.31.3.2.3
Hazardous material storage and use 60.5.1.6.4, 60.5.1.16.1,
    60.5.1.16.5, 60.5.1.20, A.60.5.1.16.1
Health care occupancies .. 20.4.2.2.1.2 to 20.4.2.2.3.3, 20.6.2.2.1.2,
    20.6.2.2.2, 20.6.2.2.3, A.20.6.2.2.1
Heliports, roof-top 21.3.4.7.3, 21.3.4.8
Hot work operations 41.2.4.5
Impaired and nuisance alarm prone systems 13.7.1.4.3,
    13.7.1.5, A.13.7.1.4.3, A.13.7.1.5, A.20.6.2.2.1
Inspection, testing, and maintenance 10.2.5, 13.7.3.2.4
Integrity, monitoring for 13.7.1.4.2, A.13.7.1.4.2
Manual fire alarm boxes ....see Manual fire alarm boxes
Marinas and boatyards 28.1.6.2.4.2
Motion picture and television soundstages 32.4.11.2
Permit requirements .... Table 1.12.8(a)
Refrigerant machinery rooms 53.2.3.1, 53.2.3.4.4, A.53.2.3.1.4
Seasonal buildings 10.12.2, 10.12.3, A.10.12.2.1
Spray application operations 43.1.7.2.1
Storage occupancies 34.5.5
Tents, membrane structures, grandstands, and folding/telescopic
    seating 25.1.7
Vacant buildings 10.12.2, 10.12.3, A.10.12.2.1
Zoning 13.7.1.13, A.13.7.1.13.4, A.13.7.1.13.6
Alcohol-based hand rub 60.5.2
    Definition 3.3.10
Alleyways 18.2.4.2.1
    Definition 3.3.11
Alterations ....see Construction
Alternate fuels .... 42.8, 42.11, A.42.8.3.4, A.42.8.6.2, A.42.11.1.1 to
    A.42.11.3
Alternative calculation procedure (definition) 3.4.1
Alternatives to code 1.4, 1.11.1
    Definition 3.3.12
Ambulatory health care occupancies 20.6, A.20.6.2
    Alarm systems 13.7.2.9, 13.7.2.10
    Battery systems, location of 52.3.3.4
    Christmas tree provisions .... Table 10.13.1.1
    Definition 3.3.183.1, 6.1.6.1, A.3.3.191.1, A.6.1.6.1
    Emergency plans 10.8.1, 20.6.2.1, 20.6.2.2.2, A.20.6.2.1.5
    Extinguishers, portable fire .... Table 13.6.1.2
    Fire fighter safety building marking system (FFSBMS) .. E.1.3.5(2)
    Flammable and combustible liquids storage . 66.9.6.2.1, 66.9.6.2.2,
        66.9.6.2.4
    Hazardous materials storage and use 60.4.2.1.6
    Multiple occupancies ..... Table 6.1.14.4.1(a), Table 6.1.14.4.1(b)
Ammonia refrigerant 53.2.2.1.3, 53.2.2.2, 53.2.2.3
Ammonium nitrate .... Table 1.12.8(a), Chap. 74
Amusement parks .... Table 1.12.8(a); see also Special amusement
    buildings
Analysis
    Sensitivity 5.7.7, 5.7.8
        Definition 3.4.2.1
    Uncertainty 5.5.3.3
        Definition 3.4.2.2
Annunciation 13.7.1.13, A.13.7.1.13.4, A.13.7.1.13.6
ANSI/ASME (definition) 3.3.13
Apartment buildings 20.9
    Board and care occupancies, housing 20.5.3.3
    Christmas tree provisions .... Table 10.13.1.1
    Definition 3.3.183.2, 6.1.8.1.5, A.3.3.183.2

Detection, alarm, and communication systems 13.7.2.17,
    13.7.2.18, A.13.2.17.5, A.13.7.2.18.4.1, A.13.7.2.18.5.1
Extinguishers, portable fire .... Table 13.6.1.2
Hazardous materials storage and use 60.4.2.1.8
Multiple occupancies .... Table 6.1.14.4.1(b)
Sprinkler systems .... 13.3.2.17, 13.3.2.18, A.13.3.2.18.1 to
    A.13.3.2.18.7
Apiaries 17.3.4.5
Appeals
    Board of 1.10, A.1.10.4.3
        Definition 3.3.26
    Means of 1.10.4, A.1.10.4.3
Application of code 1.3, A.1.3.2, A.1.3.6.2
Approvals .... 1.12, A.1.12.6.13; see also Permits
    Fire department service delivery concurrency evaluation 15.6
    Fire protection systems 13.1.1, 13.7.3.2.1, 50.2.4, 50.4.11,
        A.50.4.11.2
    Fire pumps 13.4.1.4, A.13.4.1.4
    Refrigerant type, changing 53.3.1.4
    Wildland fire-prone areas, use of 17.3.2, A.17.3.2
Approved (definition) 3.2.1, A.3.2.1
Arc welding equipment 41.6
Areas ......see also Control areas; Fire areas; Fire flow area; Floor area;
        Indoor areas; Inside liquid storage areas; Outdoor
        areas; Permissible areas; Sales display area; Spray areas
    Back stock area
        Aerosol products 61.4.4
        Definition 3.3.14.1
    Organic peroxide storage area (definition) 3.3.14.7
    Of refuge 20.7.2.1.3, A.20.7.2.1.3
    Smoking area 10.9.2
        Definition 3.3.14.11
    Sub-floor work area, repair garage 30.2.6, 30.2.9.3
Arson 10.1.5, A.16.3.2.5.1
Artificial barricades ....see Barricades
Artwork 20.2.4.4.3, 20.3.4.2.3.5.3
Asbestos removal .... Table 1.12.8(a), 16.8
ASME (definition) 3.3.15
ASME containers or tanks 69.2.1.1.1, 69.2.1.1.2.2, 69.2.1.1.3,
    69.2.1.1.5, 69.2.1.1.6, 69.2.1.1.11, 69.2.1.3.1, 69.2.1.3.2,
    69.3.12.3.1.1, 69.3.12.3.2, 69.3.12.3.4.6, A.69.2.1.1.1
    Definition 3.3.69.1
    Markings 69.2.1.4.3.3, 69.2.1.4.3.4
    Separation distances 69.3.3.3, 69.3.3.4, A.69.3.3.4.3
Asphyxiant gas, simple .... Table 1.12.8(b), A.42.11.1.1
    Definition 3.3.135.16
Assemblies, fire-resistant .... 12.3, A.12.3.2, A.12.3.3; see also Fire
        barriers; Fire door assemblies
Assembly occupancies .... 20.1, A.20.1.4 to A.20.1.5.8.3
    Battery systems, location of 52.3.3.4
    Christmas tree provisions .... Table 10.13.1.1
    Definition 3.3.183.3, 6.1.2.1, A.3.3.183.3, A.6.1.2.1
    Detection, alarm, and communication systems 13.7.2.1, 13.7.2.2,
        A.13.7.2.1.2.3, A.13.7.2.1.3.5, A.13.7.2.2.2.3
    Emergency plans 10.8.1
    Extinguishers, portable fire .... Table 13.6.1.2, 25.1.6.3
    Fire fighter safety building marking system
        (FFSBMS) .... E.1.3.5(2)
    Flammable and combustible liquids storage 66.9.6.2.1,
        66.9.6.2.2
    Hazardous materials storage and use 60.4.2.1.2
    Means of egress, occupant load .... Table 14.8.1.2
    Multiple occupancies ..... Table 6.1.14.4.1(a), Table 6.1.14.4.1(b)
    Permits .... Table 1.12.8(a), 20.1.1.1, 20.1.5.2.4.1, 20.1.5.3.1
    Sprinkler systems 13.3.2.7, 13.3.2.8, 20.1.4.2, 20.1.4.6,
        A.13.3.2.7.3(1), A.13.3.2.7.3(3), A.20.1.4.2
    Standpipe systems 13.2.2.4, A.13.2.2.4
    Tents and membrane structures 25.1.5.3, 25.1.6.3, A.25.1.8
Assumptions, fire protection .... 4.2, A.4.2.1 to A.4.2.3
ASTM (definition) 3.3.17
Atmospheric tanks 66.21.4.2.1, 66.22.8.1, A.66.21.4.2.1.1,
    A.66.22.8.1
Attached buildings (definition) 3.3.29.3

Attendants .... *see* Staff
Attics
  Sprinklers for .... 13.3.1.9(5), Table 13.3.1.9(b), 13.3.2.6.3(2), 13.3.2.21.2.7, 13.3.2.22.1.4, 13.3.2.22.4
  Storage in 10.18.6
Audience
  Life safety 32.6.4, A.32.6.4
  Pyrotechnics, use of .... *see* Pyrotechnics before a proximate audience
Authority having jurisdiction .... 1.7, 4.5.1, A.1.7.2 to A.1.7.17.3; *see also* Approvals
  Certificate of fitness requirement 1.13, A.1.13.5.2, A.1.13.5.4
  Definition 3.2.2, A.3.2.2
  Liability 1.9
  Performance-based design, role in .... 5.1.3 to 5.1.8, 5.4.1.1, 5.4.1.2, 5.4.1.3.1, 5.4.2.8, 5.4.4.4.2, 5.5.1.2, 5.7.2.1, A.5.1.3 to A.5.1.8, A.5.4.1.2, A.5.4.2.8, A.5.4.4.4.2
  Plan review 1.14
  Technical assistance 1.15, 5.1.5, A.5.1.5
Automatic-closing doors 12.8.3.5, 12.9.4.4, 13.7.1.9.2.3, 14.5.4, 30.1.6.3, A.12.9.4.4, A.13.7.1.9.2.3, A.14.5.4.1
Automatic emergency shutoff valves 63.3.3.1.11, 69.3.13.3.10, 69.3.13.3.16, A.63.3.3.1.11.1.1
  Cryogenic fluids, outdoor use 63.4.14.11.2.3, A.63.4.14.11.2.3.1
  Definition 3.3.18
Automatic fire detectors 13.7.1.1, 13.7.3.5, 13.7.4
  Definition 3.3.84.2
Automatic fire extinguishing or suppression system operation detectors (definition) 3.3.84.3
Automatic fire extinguishing system .... *see* Extinguishing systems
Automatic sprinkler systems .... *see* Sprinkler systems
Automobile wrecking yards .... Table 1.12.8(a), Chap. 22
Automotive fuel servicing .... *see* Motor fuel dispensing facilities
Available height for storage (definition) 3.3.19, A.3.3.19

-B-

Backflow prevention devices .... 13.5.3.1, 63.3.3.1.3.2, 69.3.8.3 to 69.3.8.5, 69.3.8.8, A.69.3.8.8
Back stock areas
  Aerosol products 61.4.4
  Definition 3.3.14.1
Balconies 14.11.4
  Cooking grills or hibachis on 10.10.6, A.10.10.6.3
  LP-Gas systems on 69.3.10, A.69.3.10.2.6, A.69.3.10.8.3
  Means of egress 14.8.1.6, 14.9.1.1
  Sprinkler systems 13.3.2.6, A.13.3.2.6
Baled cotton 45.6.1.3
  Block (definition) 3.3.20.1
  Definition 3.3.20, A.3.3.20
  Densely packed .... Table A.3.3.20
    Definition 3.3.20.2, A.3.3.20.2
  Fire-packed (definition) 3.3.20.3
  Naked cotton bales (definition) 3.3.20.4
Baled storage, combustible fibers 45.6
Barrels (bbl) (definition) .... 3.3.21; *see also* Containers
Barricades
  Fire department access roads 18.2.4.1.4, 18.2.4.2
  Tampering with 10.7.3
Barriers
  Emergency scene 1.8.4, 1.8.5
  Fire .... *see* Fire barriers
  Photovoltaic system security barriers 11.12.3.3, A.11.12.3.3
  Smoke .... *see* Smoke barriers
Basement parking structures 29.1.1
  Definition 3.3.183.23.1
Basements
  Aerosol products, storage of 61.3.4.2.1
  Definition 3.3.22

Flammable and combustible liquids storage, handling, and use ... 66.9.3.6 to 66.9.3.8, Table 66.9.7.2, 66.17.6.9
Sprinkler systems 13.3.2.2
Unstable reactive compressed gases 63.3.10.4
Batteries
  Boat storage and .... 28.1.7.2.3.2(2), 28.1.7.2.3.5, 28.1.7.2.4, 28.1.8.2.3, 28.1.8.2.4, A.28.1.7.2.4
  Exposition facilities, vehicles at 20.1.5.5.4.12.2, 20.1.5.5.4.12.3
  Fire pumps 13.4.4.9
  Lithium-ion 52.1, 52.3.1.3, 52.3.4.3, 52.3.5.3, 52.3.6.1, 52.3.8.2
    Definition 3.3.24.1
  Lithium metal polymer 52.1, 52.3.1.3, 52.3.4.3, 52.3.5.3, 52.3.6.1, 52.3.8.2
    Definition 3.3.24.2
  Motor vehicle fuel dispensing facilities, use at 42.10.2.2.1
  Nickel cadmium (NiCad) 52.1, 52.3.1.1, 52.3.6, 52.3.8, A.52.3.6
    Definition 3.3.24.3
  Nonrecombinant .... Table 52.1, 52.3.1.1
  Recombinant .... Table 52.1, 52.3.1.2
  Salvage vehicles, removal from 22.9.5
  Valve-regulated (VRLA) 52.1, 52.3.1.2, 52.3.2, 52.3.4.3, 52.3.5.2, 52.3.6, A.52.3.6
    Definition 3.3.24.4, A.3.3.24.4
  Vented (flooded) 52.1, 52.3.1, 52.3.6, 52.3.8.3, A.52.3.6
    Definition 3.3.24.5, A.3.3.24.5
Battery systems
  Definition 3.3.23
  Permits .... Table 1.12.8(a), 52.2
  Stationary systems .... Chap. 52
Bedding .... *see also* Furnishings; Mattresses
  Board and care occupancies 20.5.2.5, A.20.5.2.5
  Detention and correctional occupancies 20.7.2.4, A.20.7.2.4
Blasting 17.3.4.3
Blasting agents B.2.1.1.3
Bleachers .... *see* Grandstands
Board and care occupancies, residential .... *see* Residential board and care occupancies
Board of appeals 1.10, A.1.10.4.3
  Definition 3.3.26
Boatyards .... 28.1, A.28.1.6.2 to A.28.1.8.2.6(7)
Boiling point (definition) 3.3.27, A.3.3.27
Boil-over 66.22.4.1.4
  Definition 3.3.28, A.3.3.28
Bonding, electrical
  Aircraft fuel servicing 42.10.2.1.2, 42.10.5.4, A.42.10.2.1.2.6, A.42.10.5.4
  Cryogenic fluid containers and systems 63.4.8.3
  Dust explosion and fire prevention 40.4.3.2.3, A.40.4.3.2.3
  Flammable and combustible liquid piping systems 66.27.9
  Marine motor fuel dispensing facilities ..... 42.9.6.4, 42.9.10.7(4), A.42.9.6.4
  Spray application operations ... 43.1.8.5.3, 43.1.8.7.4, A.43.1.8.5.3, A.43.1.8.7.4
  Tank cars and tank vehicles, loading and unloading of .. 66.28.3.1, A.66.28.3.1.2
  Wharves, pipelines on 66.29.3.12
Bridges 14.11.4, 18.2.3.4.5
Building codes 10.1.3
  Definition 3.3.53.1
Buildings ... *see also* Apartment buildings; Existing buildings; Historic buildings; Special amusement buildings
  Attached (definition) 3.3.29.3
  Under construction .... 4.5.6, 5.3.3(8), 10.3.3, 11.1.6, Chap. 16, 69.3.10.3, 69.3.10.4, A.10.3.3
  Definition 3.3.29, A.3.3.29
  Detached .... *see* Detached storage
  Emergency services buildings, sprinkler systems for 13.3.2.3
  Fire flow requirements for .... 18.4, A.18.4.1 to A.18.4.5.4
  Important .... *see* Important buildings

Loose house 45.5.6
    Definition .... see Storage occupancies
Mini-storage .... see Storage occupancies
On piers 28.1.6.2.1, A.28.1.6.2.1.3
Safety during building use 4.1.3.2, 5.4.5, A.4.1.3.2.1, A.5.4.5.1
Satellite (definition) 3.3.29.9
Seasonal 10.12, A.10.12.2.1
Storage tank .... 66.24, A.66.24.1 to A.66.24.14.8
    Definition 3.3.29.11
Vacant .... 5.3.3(6), 10.12, A.10.12.2.1
Wildland fire–prone areas .... 17.3.5.2, A.17.3.5.2.1.1 to A.17.3.5.2.1.11.1
Building services .... Chap. 11
    Design/installation 4.4.6
    Equipment rooms, storage in 10.18.5
    Storage occupancies 34.6.2
Bulk compressed gas systems, individual .... Table 60.4.3.7
Bulk cryogenic systems 63.4.5.1, 63.4.7.2.1.4.1, A.63.4.7.2.1.4.1
Bulk hydrogen compressed gas systems 63.2.5, 63.3.6.2.1, 63.6, A.63.3.6.2.1.1
    Definition 3.3.254.1
Bulk inert gas systems 63.4.13.1.1, 63.4.14.11.1, 63.4.14.11.2.1, 63.4.14.11.2.2, 63.4.14.11.3.3, 63.4.14.11.3.4, A.63.4.14.1.3.2, A.63.4.14.11.3.4
    Definition 3.3.254.2
Bulk liquefied hydrogen gas systems 63.7
    Definition 3.3.254.3
Bulk loading/unloading facilities for tank cars/vehicles .... 66.28, A.66.28.3.1.2 to A.66.28.11.4.1
Bulk merchandising retail buildings
    Definition 3.3.183.4
    Multiple occupancies ..... Table 6.1.14.4.1(a), Table 6.1.14.4.1(b)
    Sprinkler systems 13.3.2.23.3, 13.3.2.24.2
Bulk oxygen systems 63.5
    Definition 3.3.254.4, A.3.3.254.4
Bulk plants or terminals
    Definition 3.3.34
    Motor fuel dispensing facility at .... 42.3.2.2, 42.9.1.2(1)
Bulk storage .... 34.1.1.2(2)
    Elevators 20.15.5, A.20.15.5.1
    Tires 13.3.2.27.5
Burners, kerosene 11.5.2
Burning, open .... see Open fires
Burn-it (definition) 3.3.35
Bury-it (definition) 3.3.36
Business occupancies 20.13
    Christmas tree provisions .... Table 10.13.1.1
    Definition 3.3.183.5, 6.1.11.1, A.3.3.183.5, A.6.1.11.1
    Detection, alarm, and communication systems 13.7.2.25, 13.7.2.26
    Extinguishers, portable fire .... Table 13.6.1.2, 20.13.2.3
    Fire fighter safety building marking system (FFSBMS) .... E.1.3.5(1)
    Flammable and combustible liquids storage 66.9.6.2.1, 66.9.6.2.2
    Hazardous materials storage and use 60.4.2.1.10
    Means of egress, occupant load .... Table 14.8.1.2
    Multiple occupancies .... 6.1.14.1.3, Table 6.1.14.4.1(a), Table 6.1.14.4.1(b), A.6.1.14.1.3
Bus repair garages .... see Repair garages

-C-

Calculation procedure, alternative (definition) 3.4.1
Campgrounds 27.3
Candles .... see Open flames
Canopies .... see also Outdoor areas
    Airports 21.2.6.6
    CNG or LNG motor fuel dispensing facilities 42.8.4
    Flammable and combustible liquids storage 66.15.3.8
    Permit requirements .... Table 1.12.8(a)
    Sprinkler systems 13.3.2.6, A.13.3.2.6
Carbon dioxide extinguishing systems .... Table 13.8, 43.1.7.5, 43.1.7.8.2(1), 66.6.7.6, 66.24.6.2.4, A.43.1.7.5
Carbon dioxide portable fire extinguishers .... Table 13.6.4.3.3.1, 13.6.4.4, 13.6.4.7.3.9, 13.6.4.10.4.2, A.13.6.4.4, A.13.6.4.7.3.9
Carbon dioxide systems, insulated liquid 63.3.1.2, 63.9
Carbon monoxide alarms or detection systems 13.7.1.14
    Apartment buildings 13.7.2.17.6
    Hotels and dormitories 13.7.2.15.6
    Lodging or rooming houses 13.7.2.14.6, A.13.7.2.14.6.2
    One- and two-family dwellings 13.7.2.13.2, A.13.7.2.13.2.2
Cargo tank fueling facilities 42.9.9
Cargo vehicles, LP-Gas 69.6, A.69.6.2.2.2
Carnivals .... Table 1.12.8(a), 10.14, A.10.14.3.1 to A.10.14.11.3.1
Cartoned storage .... see Storage
Cartridge-actuated tools 40.4.4
Cathodic protection ... 63.3.1.7, 63.3.1.18.2.1, 63.4.14.9, 66.23.3.5(1), 69.2.1.1.11, A.42.3.3.8, A.66.21.4.5, A.66.23.3.5.2, A.66.27.6.4
    Definition 3.3.38, A.3.3.38
Cathodic protection tester 63.3.1.7.2.1, 63.4.14.9.2.2
    Definition 3.3.38
Ceiling limit (definition) 3.3.162.1, A.3.3.162.1
Ceilings
    Detector installation .... 13.7.4.3.1, 13.7.4.3.3.1, 13.7.4.3.3.3, 13.7.4.3.3.4.2 to 13.7.4.3.3.4.6, 13.7.4.3.7, A.13.7.4.3.1, A.13.7.4.3.3.1, A.13.7.4.3.3.3.1, A.13.7.4.3.3.4.2(3) to A.13.7.4.3.3.4.5
    Finish .... see Interior finish
Ceiling tiles and ceiling assemblies
    Hot work operations .... 41.3.4.2(6) to (9), 41.3.5.2(4)
    Sprinkler systems 13.3.3.3
Cellulose nitrate film .... Table 1.12.8(a), Table 1.12.8(d), 20.15.7
Cellulose nitrate plastic .... Table 1.12.8(a)
Central station fire alarm systems 13.7.3.4, A.13.7.3.4
    Definition 3.3.254.5
Certificate of fitness 1.13, A.1.13.5.2, A.1.13.5.4
    Definition 3.3.39
Certificate of occupancy 1.7.14
Certification, annual, for performance-based design features 5.1.11, A.5.1.11
CFR (definition) 3.3.40
CGA (definition) 3.3.41
Chemical heat of combustion
    Aerosol products .... Table 61.1.3.1, 61.1.3.2 to 61.1.3.5, 61.1.3.3.2.6
    Definition 3.3.42
Chemical name (definition) 3.3.43
Chemical plants 43.1.8.8.1.2, 66.19.6.1.2, A.66.18.5.1
    Definition 3.3.44
Chemicals
    Hazardous (definition) .... see Hazardous chemicals
    Peroxide forming (definition) 3.3.199
Chips (wood)
    Definition 3.3.45, A.3.3.45
    Outside storage of .... 31.3.1.1(4), 31.3.2.1.1, 31.3.2.1.6.2, 31.3.6, 31.3.7, A.31.3.2.1.1, A.31.3.6.1 to A.31.3.6.4.3, A.31.3.7
Christmas trees 10.13, A.10.13.3, A.10.13.9.4
Chutes, rubbish or laundry .... 11.6, Table 12.7.4.2, 16.2.2.4, A.16.2.2.4.1, A.16.2.2.4.3
Circuits, initiating device 13.7.3.1.1.3, A.13.7.3.1.1.3
    Definition 3.3.158
Class A fires
    Definition 3.3.113.1

Extinguishers for .... 13.6.2.3.1.1, 13.6.2.3.2.1, 13.6.2.4.2.1 to 13.6.2.4.2.5, 13.6.3.2, A.13.6.2.3.2.1, A.13.6.2.4.2.2
Class B fires
  Definition 3.3.113.2
  Extinguishers for 13.6.2.3.1.1, 13.6.2.3.2.2, 13.6.2.4.2.2, 13.6.2.4.2.4, 13.6.2.4.2.5, 13.6.2.5.1, 13.6.3.3, A.13.6.2.3.2.2, A.13.6.2.4.2.2, A.13.6.2.5.1.1, A.16.3.3.2.2
Class C fires
  Definition 3.3.113.3
  Extinguishers for 13.6.2.3.1.2, 13.6.2.3.2.3, 13.6.2.4.2.2, 13.6.2.4.2.4, 13.6.2.4.2.5, 13.6.2.5.6, 13.6.3.4, A.13.6.2.3.2.3, A.13.6.2.4.2.2, A.13.6.2.5.6, A.13.6.3.4
Class D fires
  Definition 3.3.113.4
  Extinguishers for .... 13.6.2.3.1.2, 13.6.2.3.2.4, 13.6.2.4.2.2, 13.6.2.5.8, 13.6.3.5, 13.6.4.2.1.2, 13.6.4.2.1.3, 13.6.4.2.2.3, 13.6.4.7.4.4, A.13.6.2.3.2.4, A.13.6.2.4.2.2, A.13.6.2.5.8.1, A.13.6.3.5.1 to A.13.6.3.5.4, A.13.6.4.2.1.2, A.13.6.4.2.1.3, A.13.6.4.7.4.4
Class K fires
  Definition 3.3.113.5
  Extinguishers for 13.6.2.3.1.2, 13.6.2.3.2.5, 13.6.2.4.2.2, 13.6.2.5.5, 13.6.3.6, A.13.6.2.4.2.2
Clean agent extinguishing systems ...... Table 13.8, 43.1.7.5, 66.6.7.6, A.43.1.7.5
Cleaning, cooking equipment 50.5.6, A.50.5.6.1, A.50.5.6.2
Cleaning media A.63.3.1.19.2.2
  Definition 3.3.46, A.3.3.46
Cleaning solvents 43.1.8.7, A.43.1.8.7.4
Cleanrooms .... Table 1.12.8(a), Chap. 23
  Definition 3.3.48
  Permits 23.3
Clean zones 23.1
  Definition 3.3.47
Clearance
  Brush, wildland urban interface .... 17.3.5, A.17.3.5.1.5 to A.17.3.5.2.1.11.1
  Ceiling sprinklers, from storage .... 10.18.3.2 to 10.18.3.4, 34.4.2.1, 34.4.2.2, A.34.4.2.2
  Cooking equipment 50.2.2, A.50.2.2
  Ducts, from storage 34.4.2.3
  Heaters, from storage 34.4.2.4
  Idle pallet storage 34.10.3, A.34.10.3
  Tire storage 34.8.3.2
Clear space 13.1.4, 18.5.7
  Definition 3.3.49
Closed containers 42.3.2.1, 43.1.6.5.1
  Definition 3.3.69.2
Closed system use (definition) 3.3.267.1, A.3.3.267.1
Closed-top diking 66.22.11.3
  Definition 3.3.51
Clothes dryers 11.5.1.11
  Definition 3.3.52
Clothing storage
  Assembly occupancies 20.1.5.11
  Day-care occupancies 20.3.4.2.3.5.2
  Detention and correctional occupancies 20.7.2.2, A.20.7.2.2
  Educational occupancies 20.2.4.4.2
  Spray application operations 43.1.8.6
Coating processes .... Table 1.12.8(a), 13.3.3.5.1.6, 43.9, A.13.3.3.5.1.6, A.43.9.1.6, A.43.9.2
Code
  Application 1.3, A.1.3.2, A.1.3.6.2
  Building code 10.1.3
    Definition 3.3.53.1
  Compliance 10.1.3
  Conflicts 1.3.3
  Definition 3.2.3, A.3.2.3
  Electrical code (definition) 3.3.53.2
  Enforcement 1.6
    Assistance 1.7.4
  Interference with 1.7.9
  Liability 1.9
  Equivalencies, alternatives, and modifications 1.4, 1.11.1, 4.5.1.2, 4.5.2, 4.5.3, 5.3.5
  Interpretations 1.7.3
  Life Safety Code 10.1.2, A.10.1.2
  Mechanical code (definition) 3.3.53.3
  Plumbing code (definition) 3.3.53.4
  Purpose 1.2
  Sample ordinance adopting .... Annex C
  Scope 1.1
  Severability 1.3.7
  Violations 1.16, 10.1.5
Cold deck 31.3.8.3.3, A.31.3.8.3.3
  Definition 3.3.54
Column (paper) (definition) 3.3.55
Combustible dusts .... Chap. 40, B.2.1.4.4
  Definition 3.3.57, A.3.3.57
  Hot work operations .... 41.3.3(5)
  Permits .... Table 1.12.8(a), 40.2
Combustible fibers .... *see* Fibers, combustible
Combustible liquids .... 60.1.2, Table 60.4.2.1.1.3, Chap. 66
  In buildings under construction 16.2.3, A.16.2.3.1.2, A.16.2.3.2.4
  Classification of 66.4.2, A.66.4.2, B.2.1.3
  Containers .... *see* Containers
  Definition 3.3.164.1, 66.4.2.2
  Electrical equipment and systems .....*see* Electrical equipment and systems
  Fire prevention and risk control .... 66.6, A.66.6.1 to A.66.6.7.8
  Handling, dispensing, transfer, and use of ... 66.18, A.66.18.4.8 to A.66.18.6.3
  Motion picture production soundstages, facilities, and locations ...... 32.4.2(4), 32.5.2(5), 32.6.2
  Operations .... 66.17.15, 66.21.7, A.66.21.7.1 to A.66.21.7.5
  Permits .... Table 1.12.8(a), Table 1.12.8(d), 32.4.2(4), 32.5.2(5), 66.1.5
  Piping systems .... 66.27, A.66.27.4.3.2 to A.66.27.10
  Processing facilities .... 66.17, A.66.17.1.1 to A.66.17.14
  Recirculating heat transfer systems .... 66.19.4, A.66.19.4.2 to A.66.19.4.7.1
  Solvent distillation units 66.19.6
  Specific occupancies, storage and use in .... Tables 60.4.2.1.2 to 60.4.2.1.8, Table 60.4.2.1.10.1
  Spray applications ....*see* Spray applications, of flammable and combustible materials
  Storage of .... 34.4.4, 43.1.6, 43.1.8.7.6, 66.9, 66.21 to 66.25, A.43.1.6.1 to A.43.1.6.5.2, A.66.9.4.1 to A.66.9.16.2, A.66.21.4.2.1.1 to A.66.25.5 *see also* Tanks
  Tank cars/vehicles, loading and unloading of .... 66.28, A.66.28.3.1.2 to A.66.28.11.4.1
  Vapor recovery and vapor processing systems .... 66.19.5, A.66.19.5.5.1 to A.66.19.5.7.6
  Wharves 66.29, A.66.29.3.5, A.66.29.3.28
  Wildland/urban interface, storage in 17.3.5.2.1.11.4
Combustible (material) (definition) 3.3.56
Combustible material storage ....*see* Storage
Combustible particulate solid (definition) .... 3.3.236.1, A.3.3.236.1; *see also* Combustible dusts
Combustible refuse ....*see* Refuse, combustible
Combustible vegetation ....*see* Vegetation, combustible
Combustible waste ....*see* Waste, combustible
Combustion (definition) 3.3.63
Command center, emergency 11.9
Commodities
  Classification of .... 34.2, A.34.2.4.2 to A.34.2.7
    Paper, rolled 34.2.7, A.34.2.7
    Plastics, elastomers, and rubber 34.2.6
  Definition 3.3.64
  Mixed 34.2.3

Common path of travel 14.10.1.1.4, A.14.10.1.5
   Definition 3.3.65, A.3.3.65
Communications systems .... 13.7, A.13.7.1.2 to A.13.7.1.4.7
   Airports 21.2.7, A.21.2.7.2
   Emergency command center 11.9.4, 11.9.5
   Special outdoor events, carnivals, and fairs 10.14.9
   Tents, membrane structures, grandstands, and folding/telescopic
      seating 25.1.7
   Two-way radio communication enhancement system 11.10,
      A.11.10
Compartmented tanks (definition) 66.21.2.1
Compartments
   Fire 3.3.67.1, 12.5.9.2, 60.5.2, A.3.3.67.1
   Smoke 3.3.67.2, 12.5.9.2, 60.5.2, A.3.3.67.2
Compatible materials (definition) 3.3.173.2
Compliance options 4.3
Compost, storage at yard waste recycling facilities 31.3.7,
   A.31.3.7
Compressed air 63.2.16.1
Compressed gas ...... Chap. 63, B.2.1.2; *see also* Hazardous materials;
   specific gases
   Building-related controls .... 63.2, A.63.2.7 to A.63.2.19
   Compressed natural gas (CNG) vehicular fuel 30.2.10.6,
      42.8, 42.11.1, A.30.2.10.6, A.42.8.3.4, A.42.8.6.2,
      A.42.11.1.1
   Definition 3.3.135.1, A.3.3.135.1
   Inflation, use for 63.3.3.1.10
   Liquefied (definition) .... 3.3.135.1.3 *see also* specific gases
   Mixtures 63.1.4.3, 63.1.4.4
      Definition 3.3.135.1.1
   Nonliquefied (definition) 3.3.135.1.4
   Permits .... Table 1.12.8(a), Table 1.12.8(b), 63.1.2
   In solution (definition) 3.3.135.1.2
Compressed gas containers 63.3.1.6
   Boat storage and .... 28.1.7.2.1.5(2)
   Definition 3.3.69.3
   Leaking 63.3.1.15, 63.3.9.4, A.63.3.1.15.3
   Metal hydride storage systems .... 63.3.1.5.1.5 to
      63.3.1.5.1.11, 63.3.1.5.2
   Weather protection 63.2.6
Compressed gas systems
   Compressed natural gas (CNG) vehicular fuel 30.2.10.6,
      42.11.1, A.30.2.10.6, A.42.11.1.1
   Definition 3.3.254.6
Concealed spaces, storage in 10.18.6
Conditions, existing (definition) 3.3.101
Connectors, flexible 66.27.5.2
   Definition 66.27.2.2
Construction
   Aerosol products, buildings for 61.2.2
   Airport terminal buildings 21.2.3.1
   Buildings under ....*see* Buildings
   Damage-limiting 66.17.6.13
      Definition 3.3.82
   Detectors, protection of 13.7.4.3.6, A.13.7.4.3.6
   Documents 1.7.12.3, 1.14, 13.1.1, 50.4.1
      Definition 3.3.68
   Fire safety features 12.2.2
   Flammable and combustible liquids storage 66.9.9, 66.14.4,
      66.17.6, 66.21.4.1, 66.24.5, 66.25.5.1, 66.27.4,
      A.66.17.6.8 to A.66.17.6.11, A.66.24.5.2 to A.66.24.5.6,
      A.66.27.4.3.2
   Gas rooms 63.2.4.3
   Hazardous materials control areas 60.4.2.2
   Heliports, roof-top .... 21.3, A.21.3.3.1 to A.21.3.3.7.1
   Historic buildings and cultural resources .... 20.17.3, A.20.17.3(2)
   Marine vessels 28.3, A.28.3.1
   Motor fuel dispensing facilities 42.6
   Occupancy during 4.5.6.1
   Permits .... Table 1.12.8(a)
   Repair garages 30.2.3
   Roofing kettles 16.7.4

   Safeguards during .... 5.3.3(8), Chap. 16
   Spray areas, spray rooms, and spray booths 43.1.3,
      A.4.1.3.1, A.43.1.3.3
   Storage occupancies 34.3, 34.7.2, 34.9.2, A.34.3.1,
      A.34.3.3, A.34.9.2
   Types of construction 12.2.1, A.12.2.1
      Airport terminal buildings 21.2.3.1
      Fire fighter safety building marking system (FFSBMS) .. E.1.3.2
      Storage occupancies 34.3.1, A.34.3.1
Contained, Use Condition V .... 13.3.2.13.1, 20.7.2.1.1(2),
   20.7.2.1.2, A.20.7.2.1.2
   Definition 3.3.183.8.1.5
Containers ......*see also* ASME containers or tanks; Closed containers;
   Intermediate bulk containers; Tanks
   Aerosol products, disposal of 61.5.5
   Combustible liquids ....*see* Combustible liquids
   Compressed gas ....*see* Compressed gas containers
   Cryogenic fluids .... 63.4, A.63.4.2 to A.63.4.14.11.3.4.1
      Definition 3.3.69.5
   Definition 3.3.69, 66.3.3.10
   Flammable and combustible liquids .... 16.18.5.4.1(2),
      43.1.6.3.1, 43.1.6.5, Table 66.7.3.3, 66.9, 66.14.6.1 to
      66.14.6.3, 66.15, 66.18.4.1, 66.18.4.4, 66.18.4.8,
      66.18.4.9, 66.18.5.2, 66.18.5.6, A.43.1.6.5.2, A.66.9.4.1 to
      A.66.9.16.2, A.66.18.4.8
      Definition 3.3.69.4, A.3.3.69.4
   Hazardous materials .... 60.4.2.1.13.2(6), 60.5.1.3.5, 60.5.1.3.6,
      60.5.1.6.1, 60.5.1.7, 60.5.1.8.2.2, 60.5.1.16.3
   Liquid oxygen ....*see* Oxygen
   Location 69.5.2.1
   LP-Gas ....*see* LP-Gas containers
   Portable
      Cryogenic fluids 63.4.2.4.6.2, 63.4.4.1.1, 63.4.7.3,
         A.63.4.4.1.1.2
      Fuel .... 42.5.3.5, 42.7.2.3, 42.7.4.3(1), 42.9.8,
         A.42.7.2.3.1, A.42.9.8.2
      LP-Gas .... 69.2.1.2, 69.5, A.69.5.4.1 to A.69.5.5
      Metal hydride storage systems 63.3.1.5.2
   Relieving-style .... 66.16.3.6, 66.16.5.2.1 to 66.16.5.2.4,
      66.16.5.2.8
      Definition 66.16.2.2, A.66.16.2.2
   Waste and refuse .... 19.2.1, 20.4.2.5.7 to 20.4.2.5.9,
      20.6.2.5.5, 20.7.2.4.5, 34.6.4.1, 43.1.8.5, A.19.2.1.2.1,
      A.20.4.2.5.8, A.20.6.2.5.5.2, A.43.1.8.5
Containment .... 21.3.4.2.3; *see also* Secondary containment; Spillage
   Primary (definition) 3.3.205
   Vessels 63.3.9.4.2
Contents ....*see* Furnishings
Continuous gas detection system .... 54.2.3(2), 63.3.9.6
   Definition 3.3.254.7
Control areas .... 60.4.1.1, 60.4.2, 60.4.4.1, 63.2.2, 66.9.6 to 66.9.8,
   73.1.2, 75.1.2, A.66.9.8.1, A.66.9.8.2
   Definition 3.3.14.2, 66.3.3.11
Controllers, fire pump .... 13.4.5, A.13.4.5.1.2 to A.13.4.5.2.3(3)
Controls
   Emergency ....*see* Emergency controls
   Ovens and furnaces 51.3
Conventional pallets ....*see* Pallets, conventional
Conveyors 11.3.5
   Aerosol products, buildings for 61.2.2.2
   Dust explosion and fire prevention ...... 40.4.1 to 40.4.3, 40.5.2.1,
      40.5.2.2, 40.5.2.4.1, A.40.4.1.2.3 to A.40.4.3.7.7,
      A.40.5.2.1
   Forest products, storage of 31.3.6.3.8, 31.3.7.4
   Hot work operations .... 41.3.4.2(5)
   Spray areas .... 43.1.3.2, 43.1.7.7.1(1)
Cooking equipment
   Assembly occupancies 20.1.5.2, 20.1.5.5.4.9
   Business occupancies 20.13.2.4
   Clearances 50.2.2, A.50.2.2
   Commercial .... Chap. 50
   Concession stands 10.14.8, 50.2.1.9, A.50.2.1.9

Extinguishing systems for 50.6.1.2.2, 50.6.1.2.3
Grills, location of 10.10.6, 10.10.8, 17.3.5.2.1.11.2, 17.3.5.2.1.11.3, A.10.10.6.3
Health care occupancies 13.7.2.8.2.4
LP-Gas 69.3.10.7, 69.3.10.8.4, 69.3.12.8, 69.5.3.2.3
Mercantile occupancies 20.12.2.4
Permit requirements . . . . Table 1.12.8(a)
Portable . . . . 10.18.7, 20.1.5.2.4, 28.1.8.2.6(1)
Smoke alarm and smoke detector installation 13.7.1.8.4
Sprinkler systems 13.3.3.5.1.7
Tents, membrane structures, grandstands, and folding/telescopic seating 25.1.11, 50.2.1.9, A.50.2.1.9
Ventilation of . . . . *see* Duct systems
Cooking fires . . . . 10.10, A.10.10.3.1 to A.10.10.9.1
Definition 3.3.72
Cooking media fires, Class K fire extinguishers for 13.6.2.5.5, A.13.6.2.5.5
Cooking oil
Definition 66.19.2.1
Fires, extinguishers for 13.6.2.5.5.2
Storage tanks, commercial kitchen . . . . 50.6.3, 66.19.7, A.66.19.7.1.3 to A.66.19.7.5.2
Cords
Extension 11.1.3.1, 11.1.5, A.11.1.5.2
Flexible 43.1.4.7
Cordwood 31.3.8.1.2
Definition 3.3.73
Core (definition) 3.3.79
Correctional occupancies . . . . *see* Detention and correctional occupancies
Corridors, exit access . . . . Table 12.7.4.2, 14.2, 14.10.1.5, 14.11.4, A.14.10.1.5
Corrosion protection . . . . *see also* Cathodic protection
Definition 66.27.2.1
Piping systems
Cryogenic fluids 63.4.2.3.5, 63.4.14.8
Flammable and combustible liquids 66.27.6.4, A.66.27.6.4
Tanks 42.3.3.8, 66.21.4.5, 66.22.12.2.2, 66.23.3.5, A.42.3.3.8, A.66.21.4.5, A.66.23.3.5
Corrosive gas . . . . Table 60.4.2.1.1.3, Table 60.4.4.1.2, 63.1.4.1(2)(a), Table 63.2.3.1.1, Table 63.3.1.11.2, 63.3.5, A.63.3.5.2.1.1, B.2.1.2.3; *see also* Compressed gas
Definition 3.3.135.2
Permit amounts for . . . . Table 1.12.8(b), Table 1.12.8(d)
Corrosive material . . . . Table 60.4.4.1.2, B.2.2.3; *see also* Corrosive gas; Corrosives (solids and liquids)
Cryogen . . . . Table 1.12.8(c)
Definition 3.3.173.3, A.3.3.80
Corrosives (solids and liquids) . . . . Table 1.12.8(c), Table 1.12.8(d), 60.1.2, Table 60.4.2.1.1.3, Tables 60.4.2.1.2 to 60.4.2.1.8, Table 60.4.2.1.10.1, Table 60.4.2.1.13.3(b), Chap. 64, B.2.1.10.3; *see also* Hazardous materials
Cotton . . . . *see* Baled cotton
Covered mall buildings . . . . *see* Mall buildings
Covered plane-loading positions 21.2.6.6
Crop maze . . . . Table 1.12.8(a), 10.14.11, A.10.14.11.3.1
Crowd managers 20.1.5.6, A.20.1.5.6.2, A.20.1.5.6.4
Crude petroleum 66.22.4.2.1.1, 66.22.11.2.6.3.2
Definition 3.3.76
Cryogenic fluids . . . . Table 60.4.2.1.1.3, Tables 60.4.2.1.2 to 60.4.2.1.8, Table 60.4.2.1.10.1, 63.1, 63.2, 63.4, A.63.1.1.1 to A.63.1.3.40, A.63.2.7 to A.63.2.19, A.63.4.2 to A.63.4.14.11.3.4.1, B.2.1.10; *see also* Hazardous materials
Building-related controls . . . . 63.2, A.63.2.7 to A.63.2.19
Definition 3.3.77
Flammable . . . . Table 1.12.8(c), B.2.1.10.1
Definition 3.3.83.1
Inert . . . . 60.3.1(5), 63.4.14.11.3.3, A.63.4.7.2, B.2.1.10.4
Definition 3.3.77.2
Medical 63.4.5

Oxidizing . . . . Table 1.12.8(c), B.2.1.10.2
Definition 3.3.77.3
Permits . . . . Table 1.12.8(a), Table 1.12.8(c), Table 1.12.8(d), 63.1.2
Cryogenic fluids containers . . . . 63.4, A.63.4.2 to A.63.4.14.11.3.4.1
Definition 3.3.69.5
Cultural resource properties . . . . 20.17, A.20.17.3(2)
Definition 3.3.78, A.3.3.78
Cutting and welding . . . . *see* Hot work operations
Cylinder containment system 63.3.9.3.1.3
Definition 3.3.254.8
Cylinder containment vessel 63.3.9.3.1.3
Definition 3.3.80
Cylinder pack (definition) 3.3.81, A.3.3.81
Cylinders . . . . *see also* Containers
Compressed gas . . . . *see* Compressed gas containers
Definition 3.3.79
Hot work operations 41.3.7, 41.5.5
LP-Gas . . . . *see* LP-Gas containers

-D-

Damage-limiting construction 66.17.6.13
Definition 3.3.82
Dampers
Fire 30.1.6.4, 50.5.3, 50.5.5, 50.5.6.11, 61.2.2.1.3, A.50.5.3.3
Smoke . . . . 12.8.6.2 to 12.8.6.4, 12.9.5, A.12.8.6.2
Data conversion (definition) 3.4.3
Data sources, performance-based design 5.1.6
Day-care homes . . . . 20.3.4, A.20.3.4.1.2 to A.20.3.4.2.3.6
Definition 3.3.183.6, A.3.3.183.6
Detection, alarm, and communication systems 13.7.2.6
Multiple occupancies . . . . Table 6.1.14.4.1(a), Table 6.1.14.4.1(b)
Day-care occupancies . . . . 20.3, A.20.3.2.2 to A.20.3.4.2.3.6
Adult care 20.3.1.5
Battery systems, location of 52.3.3.4
Christmas tree provisions . . . . Table 10.13.1.1
Definition 3.3.183.7, 6.1.4.1, A.3.3.183.7, A.6.1.4.1
Detection, alarm, and communication systems 13.7.2.5
Emergency plans 10.8.1
Extinguishers, portable fire . . . . Table 13.6.1.2
Fire fighter safety building marking system (FFSBMS) . . . . E.1.3.5(2)
Flammable and combustible liquids storage 66.9.6.2.1, 66.9.6.2.2, 66.9.6.2.4
Hazardous materials storage and use 60.4.2.1.4
Means of egress, occupant load . . . . Table 14.8.1.2
Multiple occupancies . . . . Table 6.1.14.4.1(a), Table 6.1.14.4.1(b)
Sprinkler systems 13.3.2.29
Dead-end access roads 18.2.3.4.4
Dead-end corridors 14.10.1.5, 21.1.4.4, 21.1.5.3, A.14.10.1.5
Decorations 12.5.5.5, 12.6.1
Ambulatory health care occupancies . . . . 20.6.2.5, A.20.6.2.5.1 to A.20.6.2.5.5.2
Apartment buildings 20.9.4
Assembly occupancies 20.1.5.4, A.20.1.5.4.1, A.20.1.5.4.3
Board and care occupancies 20.5.2.5, A.20.5.2.5
Day-care occupancies 20.3.4.2.3.5
Detention and correctional occupancies 20.7.2.4, A.20.7.2.4
Educational occupancies 20.2.4.4
Health care occupancies . . . . 20.4.2.5, A.20.4.2.5.1 to A.20.4.2.5.8(2)
Hotels and dormitories 20.8.2.5

In means of egress 14.4.2
Motion picture production soundstages, facilities,
and locations .... 32.4.5, 32.5.5, A.32.4.5.2(4),
A.32.4.5.2(5)
Dedicated smoke control systems (definition) 3.3.254.9
Deep fat fryers 50.6.1.2.4, 50.6.1.2.5, 50.6.2
Defend-in-place 5.2.2.6, 32.5.11.1, A.32.5.11.1
Definitions .... Chap. 3, 6.1.2 to 6.1.14, 63.1.3, 66.3.3, 66.4,
66.16.2, 66.21.2, 66.27.2, A.6.1.2.1 to A.6.1.13.1,
A.66.4.1.1 to A.66.4.2, A.66.16.2.2, A.66.16.2.3
Deflagration
Definition 3.3.83
Unstable (reactive) solids and liquids, storage of 66.17.6.13
Delayed-egress locks .... 14.5.3.1, A.14.5.3.1.1(3),
A.14.5.3.1.1.(4)
Deluge systems .... Table 13.8
Flammable and combustible liquids storage, handling,
and use 66.16.4.2, 66.24.6.2.3, A.66.24.6.2.3
Spray application equipment 43.1.7.8.2
Demolition, safeguards during .... 5.3.3(8), 16.5
Design ....*see* Performance-based design; Prescriptive-based design
Designated area ....*see* Permissible areas
Design fire scenarios ....*see* Fire scenarios (design)
Design specifications (definition) 3.4.5, A.3.4.5
Design team (definition) 3.4.6
Detached storage 60.4.3.7
Compressed gases 63.2.5
Definition 3.3.246.3
Detection systems ...... 13.7, A.13.7.1.2 to A.13.7.1.4.7; *see also* Flame
detection systems; Gas detection systems; Smoke
detectors
Alarm systems and 13.7.3.5
Battery systems, stationary storage .... Table 52.1, 52.3.10
Cooking equipment 50.4.10.2, 50.5.6.7
Dust explosion and fire prevention ... 40.5.2.2, 40.5.2.4 to 40.5.2.7
Emergency command center .... 11.9.5(2)
Flammable and combustible liquids storage, handling,
and use 66.6.6, 66.21.7.5, 66.24.15, 66.25.15,
A.66.6.6.1, A.66.21.7.5
Forest products storage, handling, and use 31.3.2.3,
31.3.3.2.1(2), 31.3.4.2(2), 31.3.5.2(2), 31.3.6.2.1(3),
31.3.8.2(2), A.31.3.2.3
Hazardous material storage and use 60.5.1.6.4,
60.5.1.16.1, 60.5.1.16.5, 60.5.1.20, A.60.5.1.16.1
Inspection, testing, and maintenance 13.7.3.5.1,
13.7.4.4 to 13.7.4.7, A.13.7.4.7
Marinas and boatyards 28.1.6.2.4.2, 28.1.6.6
Permits .... Table 1.12.8(a)
Rack storage 34.7.3.4.1.3
Refrigerant vapor detection 53.2.3.1, 53.2.3.4.4,
A.53.2.3.1.4
Spray application operations .... 43.1.7.7.1, 43.1.7.7.2(1),
43.1.7.8.1, 43.1.7.8.2(1)
Detectors
Air sampling–type ....*see* Air sampling–type detectors
Automatic fire ....*see* Automatic fire detectors
Automatic fire extinguishing or suppression system operation
(definition) 3.3.84.3
Combination (definition) 3.3.84.4, A.3.3.84.4
Definition 3.3.984
Electrical conductivity heat (definition) 3.3.84.5,
A.3.3.90.7, A.3.3.90.19
Fire-gas (definition) 3.3.84.6
Fixed-temperature 13.7.4.5.1, 13.7.4.5.2
Definition 3.3.84.7, A.3.3.84.7
Flame (definition) 3.3.84.8, A.3.3.84.8
Gas .... 66.6.6.2(3)
Definition 3.3.84.9
Heat ....*see* Heat detectors
Line-type 13.7.4.3.2, 13.7.4.5
Definition 3.3.84.11
Multi-criteria (definition) 3.3.84.12, A.3.3.84.12

Multi-sensor (definition) 3.3.84.13, A.3.3.84.13
Other (definition) 3.3.84.14
Pneumatic rate-of-rise (definition) 3.3.84.15,
A.3.3.84.19
Projected beam-type ....*see* Projected beam-type detectors
Radiant energy-sensing 13.7.4.1.2
Definition 3.3.84.17
Rate compensation 13.7.4.5.1
Definition 3.3.84.18, A.3.3.84.18
Rate-of-rise 13.7.4.5.1
Definition 3.3.84.19, A.3.3.84.19
Restorable line 13.7.4.5.1
Smoke ....*see* Smoke detectors
Spark/ember (definition) 3.3.84.21
Spot-type ....*see* Spot-type detectors
Detention and correctional occupancies .... 20.7, A.20.7.2.1.2 to
A.20.7.2.4.3
Battery systems, location of 52.3.3.4
Christmas tree provisions .... Table 10.13.1.1
Definition 3.3.183.8, 6.1.7.1, A.3.3.183.8, A.6.1.7.1
Detection, alarm, and communication systems 13.7.2.11,
13.7.2.12, A.13.7.2.11.3.1(2) to A.13.7.2.11.4.3,
A.13.7.2.12.3.1(2), A.13.7.2.12.4.3
Emergency plans 10.8.1, 20.7.2.1.3, A.20.7.2.1.3
Extinguishers, portable fire .... Table 13.6.1.2
Fire fighter safety building marking system
(FFSBMS) .... E.1.3.5(3)
Flammable and combustible liquids
storage 66.9.6.2.1, 66.9.6.2.2
Hazardous materials storage and use 60.4.2.1.7
Means of egress, occupant load .... Table 14.8.1.2
Multiple occupancies ..... Table 6.1.14.4.1(a), Table 6.1.14.4.1(b)
Nonresidential uses 6.1.7.2, A.6.1.7.2
Sprinkler systems 13.3.2.13, 13.3.2.14, A.13.3.2.14.1
Standpipe systems 13.2.2.5
Detention and correctional use conditions 13.3.2.13.1,
13.7.2.7.2.3, 13.7.2.8.2.1, 13.7.2.8.2.3, 13.7.2.11.4.3,
13.7.2.12.4.1, 13.7.2.12.4.3, 20.7.2.1.1(2), 20.7.2.1.2,
A.13.7.2.7.2.3, A.13.7.2.8.2.3, A.13.7.2.11.4.3,
A.13.7.2.12.4.3, A.20.7.2.1.2
Definition 3.3.183.8.1
Detonation
Definition 3.3.85
High hazard level 1 contents 60.3.2.1.2.1
Dipping and coating processes 43.9, A.43.9.1.6, A.43.9.2
Directional signs and indicators 14.14.2
Discharge, unauthorized ....*see* Unauthorized discharge
Dispensing (definition) 3.3.86
Dispensing areas
Cryogenic fluids 63.4.14.11.3, A.63.4.14.11.3.4
Flammable and combustible liquids 66.9.14, 66.9.18,
66.14.4.6, 66.18, 66.25.3.1.8, A.66.18.4.8 to A.66.18.6.3
Fuel dispensing, inside buildings 30.1.6, 30.3, 42.2.1.1,
42.3.2.1, 42.3.3.9, A.30.1.6.7, A.30.1.6.9
Dispensing stations ....*see* Motor fuel dispensing facilities
Dispensing systems and devices ....*see* Fuel dispensing systems and
devices
Distilleries 66.19.6
Definition 3.3.87
Distributors (definition) 3.3.88
Documentation ....*see* Records
Doors ....*see also* Opening protectives
Access-controlled 14.5.3.2, A.14.5.3.2
Aerosol products, buildings for 61.2.2.1.2
Alarms .... 14.5.2, A.14.5.2.2 to A.14.5.2.12
Combustible fiber storage room or building 45.5.3.2
Day-care occupancies 20.3.2.2, 20.3.2.3, 20.3.4.2.3.4,
A.20.3.2.2
Educational occupancies 20.2.4.3.3
Elevator lobby exit .... 14.5.3.3, A.14.5.3.3(14)
Fire door assemblies ....*see* Fire door assemblies

Flammable and combustible liquids inside storage
    areas 66.9.9.2
Gas cabinets 63.2.17.1.3
Kettle 16.7.3.6
As means of egress .... 14.5, 14.10.2.2, 14.11.4, A.14.5.1.1 to
    A.14.5.1.3.1, A.14.10.2.2
As means of escape 4.5.6.2.2
Motor vehicle fuel dispensing facilities 30.1.6.3, 42.7.2.8
Panic hardware and fire exit hardware 14.5.3.4, 32.4.10.5,
    A.14.5.3.4.2
Performance-based design option .... 5.3.4(3)
Screen and storm assemblies 14.5.1.4
Self-closing ....see Self-closing doors
Smoke barriers 12.9.4, A.12.9.4.1, A.12.9.4.4
Smoke partitions 12.8.3, A.12.8.3.4
Soundstages and approved production facilities 32.4.10.5
Storage occupancies 34.6.6.1
Swing and force to open 14.5.1, A.14.5.1.1, A.14.5.1.3.1
Dormitories .... 20.8, A.20.8.2.1.1 to A.20.8.2.4.2
Christmas tree provisions .... Table 10.13.1.1
Definition 3.3.183.9, 6.1.8.1.4, A.3.3.183.9, A.6.1.8.1.4
Detection, alarm, and communication systems 13.7.2.15,
    13.7.2.16, A.13.7.2.15.3.1 to A.13.7.2.15.5,
    A.13.7.2.16.3.6, A.13.7.2.16.5
Extinguishers, portable fire .... Table 13.6.1.2
Hazardous materials storage and use 60.4.2.1.8
Multiple occupancies ..... Table 6.1.14.4.1(a), Table 6.1.14.4.1(b)
Sprinkler systems 13.3.2.15, 13.3.2.16, A.13.3.2.16.2
DOT
Definition 3.3.90
LP-Gas containers 69.2.1.1.1, 69.2.1.1.2.1, 69.2.1.1.2.4,
    69.2.1.3.3, A.69.2.1.1.1
Drainage systems
Compressed gases and cryogenic fluids 63.2.13, 63.4.13.2.6,
    A.63.4.13.2.6.4.1
Cryogenic fluids containers 63.4.13.2.6, A.63.4.13.2.6.4.1
Flammable and combustible liquids storage, handling,
    and use ...... Table 66.7.3.3, 66.9.13, 66.16.8, 66.17.6.8,
    66.17.10, 66.18.5.6(2), 66.22.11.1, 66.22.11.2.6,
    66.22.11.2.7.1, 66.22.11.3.5, 66.22.12.2, 66.24.9, 66.25.9,
    66.28.9, A.66.9.13, A.66.16.8.2, A.66.17.6.8, A.66.17.10.1,
    A.66.22.11.2.6.3.4, A.66.24.9.6, A.66.28.9
Motor vehicle fuel dispensing facilities 30.1.4, 30.1.6.9,
    A.30.1.6.9
Pump room or house 13.4.2.7, A.13.4.2.7
Repair garages 30.2.5
Tires, outside storage of 33.1.9
Drills .... see Fire drills
Driveways (definition) .... 3.3.91; see also Clear space; Fire
    department access roads
Drums .... see Tanks, portable
Dry chemical extinguishing systems .... Table 13.8, 43.1.7.5,
    43.1.7.8.2(1), 50.4.5.3, 66.6.7.6, 66.16.9, 66.24.6.2.3,
    66.24.6.2.4, A.43.1.7.5, A.66.24.6.2.3
Dry chemical portable fire extinguishers 13.6.4.2.3.2,
    Table 13.6.4.3.3.1, 13.6.4.7.3.2 to 13.6.4.7.3.4.4,
    13.6.4.7.4.1, A.13.6.4.7.3.2, Table A.66.29.3.28
Drycleaning plants .... Table 1.12.8(a), Chap. 24
Dry pipe sprinkler systems 13.3.3.5.2, A.13.3.3.5.2
Dry powder portable fire extinguishers .... Table 13.6.4.3.3.1,
    13.6.4.7.3.5
Duct systems
Air-handling ductwork 11.2.1, 12.9.5, 25.1.10.1.4
Openings for 12.7.5.7, 12.9.5
Cooking equipment .... 50.2.1.3(3), 50.2.2.1, 50.2.2.2, 50.3.3,
    50.4.3, 50.4.4.4, 50.4.4.8.1, 50.4.4.8.6, 50.4.5.3,
    50.4.11.1, 50.5.6.2, A.50.4.3.2, A.50.5.6.2
Detector installation 13.7.4.1.6
Dust explosion and fire prevention 40.4.7, A.40.4.7
Flammable and combustible liquids storage,
    handling, and use 66.18.6.4, 66.25.10.5
Heaters, from storage 34.4.2.4

Hot work operations .... 41.3.4.2(4), 41.3.4.2(5)
Motor vehicle fuel dispensing facilities 30.1.6.4
Spray application operations .... 43.1.5.4, 43.1.5.6 to
    4.3.1.5.9, A.43.1.5.6
Sprinkler temperature ratings for .... Table 13.3.1.9(a),
    Table 13.3.1.9(c)
Dumbwaiters 11.3.5, 12.4.4, A.12.4.4
Dumpsters, rubbish within 19.2.1.4
Dusts
Combustible .... see Combustible dusts
Explosion prevention .... Table 1.12.8(a), Chap. 40
Wood processing and woodworking facilities 31.3.9
Dwellings, one- and two-family ...... see One- and two-family dwellings
Dwelling units
Definition 3.3.92
Doors .... 14.5.1.1(1)
Smoke alarm installation 13.7.1.8.8, 13.7.1.8.9,
    A.13.7.1.8.8

-E-

Educational occupancies 20.2, A.20.2.4.2.1,
    A.20.2.4.3.1
Battery systems, location of 52.3.3.4
Christmas tree provisions .... Table 10.13.1.1
Definition 3.3.183.10, 6.1.3.1, A.3.3.183.10,
    A.6.1.3.1
Detection, alarm, and communication systems 13.7.2.3,
    13.7.2.4, A.13.7.2.3.2.3.1, A.13.7.2.3.2.3.2,
    A.13.7.2.4.2.3.1 to A.13.7.2.4.3.1.1
Extinguishers, portable fire .... Table 13.6.1.2
Fire fighter safety building marking system
    (FFSBMS) .... E.1.3.5(2)
Flammable and combustible liquids storage 66.9.6.2.1,
    66.9.6.2.2, 66.9.6.2.4
Hazardous materials storage and use 60.4.2.1.3
Incidental instruction 6.1.3.3
LP-Gas use in 69.3.10.6
Means of egress .... Table 14.8.1.2, 20.2.2.2, 20.2.2.3,
    20.2.4.3, A.20.2.4.3.1
Multiple occupancies ..... Table 6.1.14.4.1(a), Table 6.1.14.4.1(b)
Other occupancies associated with 6.1.3.2
Sprinkler systems 13.3.2.9, 13.3.2.10, A.13.3.2.9.1
Egress, means of ....see Means of egress
Elastomers 34.2.6
Electrical code (definition) 3.3.53.2
Electrical conductivity heat detectors (definition) 3.3.84.5,
    A.3.3.90.7, A.3.3.90.19
Electrical equipment and systems ....see also Batteries; Lighting;
    Wiring
Aerosol products, buildings for 61.2.3
Boat storage facilities 28.1.7.2.1.6, 28.1.8.2.5
Combustible fiber storage rooms or buildings 45.2
Compressed gases and cryogenic fluids 63.2.7,
    63.3.1.5.1.12, 63.3.1.11.7.1, 63.3.6.5, 63.4.8, A.63.2.7
Detention and correctional occupancies 20.7.2.3
Disconnects
    Emergency disconnects, fuel dispensing systems 42.5.7
    Fire department access 11.1.7, A.11.1.7.1
    Photovoltaic systems 11.12.2.1.1
Dust explosion and fire prevention .... 40.4.2, 40.7.1.2(5),
    A.40.7.1.2(5)
Equipment rooms, storage in 10.18.5.1
Fibers, combustible, storage and handling 19.1.6.1
Fires .... see Class C fires, extinguishers for
Fire safety 11.1, A.11.1.5.2, A.11.1.7.1
Flammable and combustible liquids storage, handling,
    and use 66.6.5.5, 66.7, 66.9.12, 66.14.4.5, 66.17.9,
    66.24.8, A.66.7.3.3, A.66.7.3.7
Forest products storage 31.3.2.1.7
Hazardous materials areas 60.5.1.10
Means of egress for spaces about 14.9.2

Motion picture production soundstages, facilities, and
    locations 32.4.8, 32.5.8, A.32.4.8.2, A.32.5.8.3
Motor vehicle fuel dispensing facilities 42.5.7, 42.8.6,
    42.9.5.1 to 42.9.5.4, 42.9.6, 42.10.2.2, 42.10.5.7,
    A.42.9.6.2, A.42.9.6.4, A.42.10.2.2.4, A.42.10.5.7
Oil-burning appliances, for 11.5.1.9
Performance-based design features 5.3.2
Photovoltaic systems .... 11.12, A.11.12.2.1 to A.11.12.3.3
Refrigeration, mechanical .... 53.2.3.2(1), 53.2.3.4
Special outdoor events, carnivals, and fairs 10.14.7
Spray application operations .... 43.1.4, 43.1.7.7.1(5), 43.8.5,
    A.43.1.4.1 to A.43.1.4.6, A.43.8.5.3
Tents, membrane structures, grandstands, and folding/telescopic
    seating 25.1.9, 25.1.10.2
Transmission lines
    Clearance of brush from 17.3.5.1, A.17.3.5.1.5
    Tire piles, locations of 33.1.7
Waste and refuse, handling of combustible 19.1.6
Electronic equipment fires ....*see* Class C fires
Electrostatic spray application equipment ......*see* Spray applications,
    of flammable and combustible materials
Elevator machine rooms 11.3.3, 13.7.1.9.2.1, A.11.3.3,
    A.13.7.1.9.2.1
Elevators .... 10.2.5, 10.8.2.1(4), 11.3, A.11.3.3
Bulk storage 20.15.5, A.20.15.5.1
Fire fighters' emergency operations 11.3.1
Hoistway doors 12.4.4, 14.9.1.5, A.12.4.4
Hoistways .... Table 12.7.4.2, 13.7.1.9.2.1, A.13.7.1.9.2.1
Lobbies .... Table 12.7.4.2, 14.9.1.6
    Exit access door .... 14.5.3.3, A.14.5.3.3(14)
    Smoke and heat detectors for 13.7.1.9.2.1,
    A.13.7.1.9.2.1
Means of egress 14.9.1.5
Standardized fire service keys 11.3.6
Testing 10.2.5, 11.3.4
Ember detectors ....*see* Spark/ember detectors
Emergency
Definition 3.3.93
Egress drills ....*see* Fire drills
Reporting of 10.6, A.10.6.1.3
Response records 1.11.3
Emergency action plans 10.2.5, 10.8, A.10.8.2.3
Compressed gases or cryogenic fluids storage
    and use 63.2.8, A.63.2.8
Day-care occupancies 20.3.4.2.1, A.20.3.4.2.1
Educational occupancies 20.2.4.1
Flammable and combustible liquids storage, handling,
    and use 66.6.4.1, 66.6.8.1, 66.6.10.3.1, 66.6.10.3.3,
    66.17.15.2, 66.17.15.4, 66.19.4.7.1, 66.21.6.4,
    A.66.6.4.1.1
Hazardous materials 60.1.5.1, 60.6
Hotels and dormitories 20.8.2.4.3
Laboratories using chemicals 26.1.5, A.26.1.5.1
Residential board and care occupancies 20.5.2.1, 20.5.2.2.1,
    20.5.2.3.3
Special outdoor events, carnivals, and fairs .... 10.14.3.5.2(16)
Wood chips and hogged material, outside storage of 31.3.6.5
Emergency command center 11.9
Emergency controls 13.7.1.12
Compressed gas shutoff 63.3.3.1.11, A.63.3.3.1.11.1.1
Electric power shutoff
    Cooking equipment 50.4.6
    Fuel dispensing systems 42.5.7
Fuel shutoff
    Aircraft refueling 42.10.4.4, 42.10.5.3
    Cooking equipment 50.4.6
    LP-Gas 69.3.8, A.69.3.8.8
Ozone-gas generating equipment 54.4, 54.5
Refrigeration systems 53.2.1, 53.2.3.3, 53.2.3.4.5
Spray application operations 43.1.7.2.2
Vapor recovery/processing systems 66.19.5.8
Emergency evacuation and relocation drills ....*see* Fire drills

Emergency evacuation and relocation plans 20.4.2.1,
    20.6.2.1, A.20.4.2.1.5, A.20.6.2.1.5
Emergency forces notification ....*see* Notification
Emergency instructions
Apartment building residents 20.9.2.1
Hotel and dormitory residents/guests 20.8.2.4,
    A.20.8.2.4.1, A.20.8.2.4.2
Emergency lighting .... 5.3.4(11), 14.13, A.14.13.1.1
Fire pump areas 13.4.2.5
Soundstages and approved production
    facilities 32.4.10.4
Emergency organization
Hotels 20.8.2.1, 20.8.2.4, A.20.8.2.1.1, A.20.8.2.1.2,
    A.20.8.2.4.1, A.20.8.2.4.2
Storage occupancies 34.5.4, A.34.5.4.2
Wood chips and hogged material, storage of 31.3.6.3.3.2
Emergency plans .... 10.2.5, 10.8, A.10.8.2.1 to A.10.8.2.3; *see also*
    Emergency action plans
Ambulatory health care occupancies 20.6.2.1,
    20.6.2.2.2, A.20.6.2.1.5
Detention and correctional occupancies 10.8.1,
    20.7.2.1.3, A.20.7.2.1.3
Dust explosion and fire prevention 40.6.2, A.40.6.2.2
Flammable and combustible liquids storage, handling,
    and use 66.6.4.1, 66.6.8, 66.6.10.3.1, 66.6.10.3.3,
    66.17.15.2, 66.17.15.4, 66.19.4.7.1, 66.21.6.4, 66.21.6.5,
    A.66.6.4.1.1, A.66.21.6.5.1
Hazardous materials 60.1.5, 60.1.6, 60.5.1.4.1.3,
    60.6, A.60.1.6.1, D.3
Health care occupancies 10.8.1, 20.4.2.1,
    20.4.2.2.2, A.20.4.2.1.5
Mercantile occupancies 20.12.2.1
Residential board and care occupancies 10.8.1,
    20.5.2.1, 20.5.2.2.1, 20.5.2.3.3
Storage operations A.34.6.6.2
Tires, outside storage of 33.3
Emergency power .... 10.2.5, 11.7.2 to 11.7.5, 11.9.5(7),
    63.2.7.2, 63.3.9.5, A.11.7.2.1
Emergency relief vents ....*see* Venting
Emergency responder protection 5.2.2.7
Emergency scene
Barriers 1.8.4, 1.8.5
Control of 1.8.2
Emergency services, buildings housing 13.3.2.3
Emergency shutoff valves ....*see also* Automatic emergency shutoff
    valves; Manual emergency shutoff valves
Cryogenic containers, stationary 63.4.4.6
Definition 3.3.95
LP-Gas containers 69.3.8, A.69.3.8.8
Emissions, fugitive ....*see* Fugitive emissions
Enclosed parking structures 29.1.1
Definition 3.3.183.23.2
Enclosures ....*see also* Exhausted enclosures
Exit .... 14.3, A.14.3.1(1) to 14.3.1(10)(b)
Exit passageways 14.7.2
Rubbish chutes and laundry chutes 11.6.1
Stairs 14.5.2.8, 14.6, 14.7.3, A.14.5.2.8, A.14.6.2, A.14.6.3
Energy-consuming equipment 60.5.1.5.3, A.60.5.1.5.3.1
Equipment rooms, storage in 10.18.5
Equivalency to code 1.4, 1.11.1, 5.3.5
Escalators 14.11.4
Escape, means of ....*see* Means of escape
Ethylene oxide 63.10
Ethylene oxide drum (definition) 3.3.96
Evacuation .... 1.7.16, 5.2.2.6, 10.2.5, 10.4, 10.8.2.1(3),
    A.10.4.2, A.10.4.3, A.10.8.2.1(3); *see also* Fire drills
Aircraft 42.10.5.11
Ambulatory health care occupancies 20.6.2.1,
    20.6.2.2.1.2, 20.6.2.2.2, A.20.6.2.1.5

Compressed gases or cryogenic fluids storage
and use 63.2.8, A.63.2.8
Detention and correctional occupancies 20.7.2.1,
A.20.7.2.1.2, A.20.7.2.1.3
Flammable and combustible liquids operations 66.6.9.5,
66.21.6.6.4
Health care occupancies 20.4.2.1, 20.4.2.2.1.2,
20.4.2.2.2, A.20.4.2.1.5
Motion picture production locations 32.5.11.1,
A.32.5.11.1
Residential board and care facilities 13.3.2.22.1.1.2,
13.3.2.22.1.2, 13.3.2.22.2.1.1 to 13.3.2.22.2.1.5,
13.3.2.22.2.2, 13.7.2.22.8.2, A.13.3.2.22.2.1.1
Storage occupancies .... 34.5.4.2(8)
Excess flow control 63.3.3.1.12, A.63.3.3.1.12.1
Definition 3.3.97
Excess flow valves .... 69.3.10.2.1(4), 69.3.12.7.3, 69.3.13.3.8
Definition 3.3.98
Exhausted enclosures 63.2.18, 63.3.5.3.2
Definition 3.3.99, A.3.3.99
Exhaust systems
Compressed gases and cryogenic fluids 63.2.4.2,
63.2.16, 63.2.17.2.1, 63.2.18, 63.3.9.3.4.3.2(A),
63.3.9.4.1
Cooking equipment 50.2.2.1, 50.2.3, 50.2.4, 50.3.3,
50.4.4.4, 50.4.4.8, 50.4.11.1, 50.5.2.1, 50.5.4, 50.5.6,
A.50.5.2.1, A.50.5.4, A.50.5.6.1, A.50.5.6.2
Flammable and combustible liquids storage, handling,
and use .... 66.17.11.5 to 66.17.11.7, 66.24.10.3,
66.25.10, A.66.17.11.7
Motor vehicle fuel dispensing facilities 30.1.6.7,
A.30.1.6.7
Repair garages 30.2.9.4
Spray application operations 43.1.5, 43.5.3.1,
43.5.3.9, A.43.1.5.2.1 to A.43.1.5.11, A.43.5.3.1(4)
Exhibits .... 20.1.5.5.2, 20.1.5.5.4, A.20.1.5.5.4.7.1(3)
Hot work 41.5, A.41.5.5.2.3
LP-Gas, use of 69.3.10.8, A.69.3.10.8.3
Permit requirements .... Table 1.12.8(a)
Existing (definition) 3.3.100, A.3.3.100
Existing buildings 1.3.6.2, 10.1.1, 10.1.2, 11.3.6.2,
11.3.6.3, A.1.3.6.2, A.10.1.2
Definition 3.3.29.5, A.3.3.29.5
Existing conditions .... 1.3.1, 1.3.2.4, A.13.3.2.26.2(2)
Definition 3.3.101
Exit access .... 14.2, 14.10, A.14.10.1.1.1 to A.14.10.4.1
Definition .... 3.3.103 see also Means of egress
Elevator lobby .... 14.5.3.3, A.14.5.3.3(14)
Exterior ways 14.10.3
Marking of means of egress 14.14.1.5, A.14.14.1.5.2
Protectives, minimum ratings for .... Table 12.7.4.2
Width of 14.8.3.4, A.14.8.3.4.1.1
Exit discharge 14.7.3, 14.11, A.14.11.1, A.14.11.3.3
Definition 3.3.104
Exit passageways 14.7, 14.11.4, A.14.7
Exits ...... 14.3, A.14.3.1(1) to 14.3.1(10)(b); see also Means of egress
Airport terminal buildings 21.2.5, A.21.2.5.2
Ambulatory health care occupancies 20.6.2.3
Definition 3.3.102, A.3.3.102
Educational occupancies 20.2.4.3, A.20.2.4.3.1
Enclosures .... 14.3, A.14.3.1(1) to 14.3.1(10)(b)
Flammable and combustible liquids processing areas 66.17.6.11,
A.66.17.6.11
Health care occupancies 20.4.2.3, A.20.4.2.3.3
Horizontal .... see Horizontal exits
Maintenance of .... see Inspection, testing, and maintenance
Mirrors on 14.4.2.3
Obstruction of 14.4.1, A.14.4.1
Soundstages and approved production facilities 32.4.10.2
Storage occupancies 34.8.2.3, A.34.8.2.3
Explosion control
Compressed gases or cryogenic fluids storage and use 63.2.9

Definition 3.3.106, A.3.3.106
Flammable and combustible liquids storage, handling,
and use 66.9.16, A.66.9.16.1, A.66.9.16.2
Explosions
Definition 3.3.105
Dust explosions, prevention of .... Chap. 40
Flammable and combustible liquids 66.6.3, 66.6.4,
66.9.16, 66.19.5.7.7, A.66.6.3, A.66.6.4.1.1, A.66.6.4.1.2,
A.66.9.16.1, A.66.9.16.2
Investigations 1.7.11.1
Organic peroxides, mixing of 43.7.5, 43.7.6, A.43.7.6
Performance-based design option
Design scenarios 5.4.3, A.5.4.3.1
Performance criteria 5.2.2.2, A.5.2.2.2
Property protection 4.1.4, A.4.1.4.2.1, A.4.1.4.2.2
Safety from 4.1.3, A.4.1.3
Explosive materials .... Table 60.4.2.1.1.3, Tables 60.4.2.1.2 to
60.4.2.1.8, Table 60.4.2.1.10.1, 65.9, 65.10.2.5, B.2.1.1;
see also Hazardous materials
Definition 3.3.107, A.3.3.107
Permits .... Table 1.12.8(a), Table 1.12.8(d), 65.9.2
For repairs or alterations 4.5.6.3
Wildland fire-prone areas 17.3.4.3
Exposition facilities ..... 20.1.5.5, A.20.1.5.5.4.7.1(3); see also Exhibits
Exposure fires .... 5.4.2.7, 5.4.4.2, 16.3.1.2(8), 66.22.7.1.1,
A.5.4.2.7, A.16.2.2.4.1, A.21.2.6.5, A.63.2.10,
A.63.3.1.11.3, A.63.4.7.2, A.66.19.7.2.4.2
Definition 3.4.7, A.3.4.7
Exposures, protection for .... see Protection for exposures
Extension cords 11.1.3.1, 11.1.5, A.11.1.5.2
Extinguishers, portable fire .... 13.6, A.13.6.1.2 to A.13.6.4.11
Aerosol products storage, handling, and use 61.2.6.3
Aircraft fuel servicing 42.10.5.13, A.42.10.5.13
Airport terminal buildings 21.2.10
Antifreeze in 13.6.3.1.4
Assembly occupancies .... 20.1.5.5.4.9(5), 25.1.6.3
Automobile wrecking yards 22.6
Buildings under construction 16.3.6, 16.7.1.6,
A.16.3.6, A.16.7.1.6.2
Business occupancies 20.13.2.3
Cabinets for 13.6.3.1.3.10, A.13.6.3.1.3.10.4
Classification, ratings, and performance 13.6.2.3,
A.13.6.2.3.2.1 to A.13.6.2.3.3.2.7
Concession stands 10.14.5
Cooking equipment 50.4.4.1, 50.4.4.2, 50.4.12,
A.50.4.4.2, A.50.4.12.1
Detention and correctional occupancies 20.7.2.1.4
Dust explosion and fire prevention 40.5.3, A.40.5.3.2
Flammable and combustible liquids storage, handling,
and use 66.6.7.8, 66.9.10.2, 66.24.6.1.1, A.66.6.7.8,
A.66.24.6.1.1, Table A.66.29.3.28
Forest products, storage of 31.3.6.3.3, 31.3.6.3.4,
A.31.3.6.3.4
Heliports 21.3.5
Hot work operations .... 41.3.4.2(10), 41.5.4.1
Identification of contents 13.6.1.4, A.13.6.1.4
Inspection, testing, and maintenance 13.6.4, 13.6.5,
A.13.6.4.1 to A.13.6.4.11
Installation .... 13.6.3, 13.6.3.1.1 to A.13.6.3.5.4
Listing and labeling 13.6.1.3, 13.6.3.1.3.9,
A.13.6.1.3.1 to A.13.6.1.3.3
LP-Gas systems and containers .... 69.3.12.8, 69.5.5.1 to
69.5.5.4, 69.6.1.2
Marinas and boatyards 28.1.6.1, 28.1.6.4
Membrane structures 25.1.6.3, 25.1.12.3, 25.6.3
Mercantile occupancies 20.12.2.3
Motion picture production soundstages, facilities,
and locations 32.4.11.1.5, 32.5.11.7
Motor vehicle fuel dispensing facilities 42.7.2.5.2,
42.7.4.3(5), 42.9.7.1, 42.10.2.1.7, 42.10.2.4,
A.42.10.2.1.7.1, A.42.10.2.1.7.3
Parade floats 10.16.2

Recharging 13.6.4.1.1, 13.6.4.1.2.2, 13.6.4.2.3.1,
  13.6.4.3.2.2, 13.6.4.3.4.3, 13.6.4.7, 13.6.4.10,
  A.13.6.4.3.2.2, A.13.6.4.7.1 to A.13.6.4.7.4.7, A.13.6.4.10
Selection of .... 13.6.2, A.13.6.2.3.2.1 to A.13.6.2.5.8.1
Special outdoor events, carnivals, and fairs 10.14.5, 10.14.10.4
Spray application operations 43.1.7.6
Storage occupancies .... 34.5.3.1, 34.6.3.3(2)
Tampering with 10.7
Tar kettles 16.7.1.6, A.16.7.1.6.2
Tents 25.1.6.3, 25.1.12.3, 25.2.5
Tires, outside storage of 33.4.1.1, 33.4.1.2
Waste disposal sites 19.1.4
Extinguishing systems
 Aerosol products storage, handling, and use 61.2.6,
  61.4.3.3, 61.4.3.5
 Airports 21.2.3.5.3, 21.2.6, A.21.2.6
 Assembly occupancies 20.1.5.5.4.7,
  A.20.1.5.5.4.7.1(3)
 Automatic fire .... 50.4.4, A.50.4.4.2 to
  A.50.4.4.10(4)
 Buildings under construction 16.4.2.4, 16.4.3,
  A.16.4.2.4, A.16.4.3.1.1 to A.16.4.3.3.2.8
 Combustible fibers, storage vaults for 45.1.2,
  45.5.5.2, A.45.1.2
 Cooking equipment .... 50.2.1.3(5), 50.2.4, 50.4,
  50.5.6.5, 50.6.1.2.2, 50.6.1.2.3, A.50.4.3.2 to A.50.4.12.1
 Dust explosion and fire prevention .... 40.5, A.40.5.2.1 to
  A.40.5.9.4
 Flammable and combustible liquids storage, handling,
  and use ...... 66.6.7, 66.16.4 to 66.16.7, 66.16.9, 66.22.8,
  66.29.3.28, A.66.6.7.1 to A.66.6.7.3.7, A.66.16.5.1.6.2,
  A.66.16.6.1.5, A.66.22.8.1, A.66.29.3.28
 Forest products .... 31.3.2.1.6.2, 31.3.2.3, 31.3.3.2.1(2),
  31.3.4.2(2), 31.3.5.2(2), 31.3.6.2.1(3), 31.3.6.2.1(5),
  31.3.7.4, 31.3.8.2(2), A.31.3.2.3
 Heliports, roof-top .... 21.3.4.6, 21.3.4.7, A.21.3.4.6.2 to
  A.21.3.4.6.4.1, A.21.3.4.7.1, A.21.3.4.7.2
 Hot work operations .... 41.2.2.5, 41.2.4.4, 41.3.4.2(12),
  A.41.2.4.4
 Marinas and boatyards 28.1.6.2, A.28.1.6.2
 Motor vehicle fuel dispensing facilities 30.1.5, 42.7.2.5.3,
  42.9.7.2, A.30.1.5.1
 Non-listed devices and equipment 13.9
 Permit requirements .... Table 1.12.8(a)
 Repair garages 30.2.7
 Spray application operations 43.1.7.1, 43.1.7.7.2,
  43.1.7.8.2, 43.5.3.1(4), 43.8.3, A.43.1.7.1, A.43.5.3.1(4),
  A.43.8.3
 Storage occupancies .... 34.5.1, 34.5.2, 34.5.4.2(8),
  34.5.5.1, 34.6.3.3(1), 34.7.2, 34.7.3.4, A.34.5.1,
  A.34.7.3.4.1.1, A.34.7.3.4.2.1(1)
 Tents, membrane structures, grandstands, and folding/telescopic
  seating 25.1.6
 Waste disposal sites 19.1.4
 Wharves and marine terminals 66.29.3.28, A.66.29.3.28
Extra hazard occupancies .... *see* High hazard contents

-F-

Facilities
 Definition 3.3.108
 Hazardous materials storage facility
  Closure of 60.1.4
  Definition 3.3.145
Fail-safe 60.5.1.17.2, 66.17.11.6
 Automatic closing valves .... 63.3.5.3.4.1(2), 63.3.9.3.2.1.2
 Compressed gas containers and systems 63.3.1.11.7.2,
  63.3.3.1.2.2, 63.3.5.3.4.1(2), 63.3.9.3.2.1.2, 63.3.9.5.2
 Definition 3.3.109
 Emergency shutoff valves .... 60.5.1.6.2(3)
Fairs .... Table 1.12.8(a), 10.14, A.10.14.3.1 to A.10.14.11.3.1

Fans
 Dust explosion and fire prevention 40.7.2.2,
  A.40.7.2.2.4, A.40.7.2.2.5
 Exhaust .... 50.2.1.3(4), 50.2.2.1, 50.5.6.2, A.50.5.6.2
Festival seating .... 13.3.2.7.1(4), 13.3.2.8.1(4), 20.1.5.10.3
 Definition 3.3.110
Fiberboard/fiber containers .... *see* Containers
Fibers, combustible .... 19.1.6.1, 19.1.7, 34.1.1.2(7), Chap. 45; *see also*
  Baled cotton
 Definition 3.3.58, A.3.3.58
 Permits .... Table 1.12.8(a), Table 1.12.8(d), 45.1.3
Film, cellulose nitrate .... Table 1.12.8(a), 20.15.7
Fines (wood)
 Definition 3.3.111
 Yard waste recycling facilities, storage at 31.3.7, A.31.3.7
Finish .... *see* Interior finish
Fire alarm systems ....*see* Alarm systems
Fire areas 10.10.3.1, A.10.10.3.1, A.11.8,
  A.13.3.2.30, E.2.2
 Ambulatory health care occupancies .... 20.6.2.2.1.2(3)
 Day-care occupancies 20.3.1.1, 20.3.1.2,
  20.3.4.1.3, 20.3.4.1.4
 Definition 3.3.14.3
 Flammable and combustible liquids storage, handling,
  and use 66.18.5.4.1, A.66.19.4.3.1
 Health care occupancies 20.4.2.2.1.2
 Helicopter landing facilities 21.3.4.6.4.1,
  A.21.3.4.6.4.1
 Storage, general 34.2.3
 Wildland fire-prone areas 17.3.1, 17.3.3.1, 17.3.3.2,
  17.3.4.2 to 17.3.4.5, 17.3.5.2.1, 17.3.7.4, A.17.3.1
Fire barriers 12.3, 12.7, 12.9.3, A.12.3.2, A.12.3.3,
  A.12.7.1(4) to A.12.7.5.6.3(1)(c)
 Aerosol products, buildings for 61.2.2.1
 Combustible fibers, storage vaults for 45.5.4.1
 Cryogenic fluids storage and use 63.4.7.2.1,
  63.4.7.3.2, A.63.4.7.2.1.4.1
 Flammable and combustible liquids storage 66.9.7.2
 Hazardous materials control areas 60.4.2.2.3
 Toxic and highly toxic gases, storage and
  use areas 63.3.9.2.2.1, A.63.3.9.2.2.1.1
 Unstable reactive gases, storage and use areas 63.3.10.1.2
Fireblocking .... 12.7.5.6.3(1)(c), A.12.7.5.6.3(1)(c)
Firebreaks 17.3.7
Fire compartments .... *see* Compartments
Fire conditions, performance design criteria 5.2.2.1, A.5.2.2.1
Fire control
 Flammable and combustible liquids storage, handling,
  and use ... 66.21.6, 66.22.8, A.66.21.6.5.1, A.66.21.6.6.1,
  A.66.22.8.1
 Motor vehicle fuel dispensing facilities 42.7.2.5,
  42.9.7, A.42.7.2.5.4
 Tires, outside storage of 33.4, A.33.4.3
Fire dampers .... *see* Dampers
Fire department access roads 16.1.4, 16.1.5, 18.1.1.1,
  18.2.3, 18.2.4, 22.3, 28.1.6.2.6, A.18.2.3.1.3,
  A.18.2.3.4.6.2, A.18.2.4
 Definition 3.3.117
 Forest products, storage of 31.3.3.3.5, 31.3.3.3.6,
  31.3.4.2(3), 31.3.5.2(3), 31.3.5.3.3, 31.3.6.2.1(4),
  31.3.8.3.2, 31.3.8.3.3, A.31.3.8.3.3
Fire department connections 13.1.12, 13.2.3.4.1,
  13.3.3.6.3.2, 16.4.3.3.2.1, 16.4.3.3.2.7, 28.1.6.2.5,
  28.1.6.2.6, 32.5.11.8, 66.29.3.28.1, A.13.3.3.6.3.2,
  A.13.3.3.6.5.2(4)(c), A.18.2.4.1.3, A.28.1.6.2.5
Fire department operations .... *see also* Access,
  fire-fighting/emergency; Emergency scene
 Fire fighter safety building marking system (FFSBMS) ... Annex E
 Liability 1.9
 Obstruction of 1.8.3
Fire department service delivery concurrence evaluation ... Chap. 15
Fire detail .... *see* Fire watch

Fire door assemblies . . . . 12.4, 12.7.3, Table 12.7.4.2, 12.7.4.3,
   12.7.4.4, 34.6.6.1, A.12.4.1 to A.12.4.6.9.1, A.12.7.3.2 to
   A.12.7.3.6
   Aerosol products, buildings for 61.2.2.1.2
   Combustible fiber storage room or building 45.5.3.2
   Definition 3.3.118
   Flammable and combustible liquids inside liquid
      storage areas 66.9.9.2
   Motor vehicle fuel dispensing facilities and repair
      garages 30.1.6.3, 42.7.2.8
Fire drills . . . . 5.3.3(2), 10.2.5, 10.5, 10.8.2.1(5), A.10.5
   Ambulatory health care occupancies 20.6.2.1,
      A.20.6.2.1.5
   Assembly occupancies 20.1.5.8, A.20.1.5.8
   Board and care occupancies 20.5.2.3
   Business occupancies 20.13.2.2
   Day-care occupancies 20.3.4.2.2, A.20.3.4.2.2.1
   Detention and correctional occupancies 20.7.2.1.3.1
   Dormitories 20.8.2.3
   Educational occupancies 20.2.4.2, A.20.2.4.2.1
   Flammable and combustible liquids storage, handling,
      and use . . . . 66.17.15.4(2)
   Health care occupancies 20.4.2.1, A.20.4.2.1.5
   Hotels 20.8.2.1, A.20.8.2.1.1, A.20.8.2.1.2
   Mercantile occupancies 20.12.2.2
Fire escapes 4.5.6.2.2
Fire exit hardware 14.5.3.4, 32.4.10.5, A.14.5.3.4.2
Fire fighter safety building marking system (FFSBMS) . . . . Annex E
Fire flow
   Buildings, requirements for . . . . 18.4, A.18.4.1 to A.18.4.5.4
   Definition 3.3.119
   Hydrants, requirements for 18.5.4, A.18.5.4.3
Fire flow area . . . . 18.4.5.1.1, 18.4.5.2.1, Table 18.4.5.2.1
   Definition 3.3.14.4
Fire-gas detectors (definition) 3.3.84.6
Fire hazards
   Definition . . . . 3.3.120 *see also* Ignition sources
   Flammable and combustible liquids 66.6.3, 66.6.4,
      A.66.6.3, A.66.6.4.1.1, A.66.6.4.1.2
Fire hydrants . . . . 18.1.1.2, 18.1.3.2, 18.5, A.18.5.1.2 to
      A.18.5.10.3
   Airport terminal buildings 21.2.8
   Buildings under construction 16.4.3.1.3,
      A.16.4.3.1.3
   Definition 3.3.121, A.3.3.121
   Dust explosion and fire prevention 40.5.4.3
   Flammable and combustible liquids storage, handling,
      and use 66.6.7.4, 66.16.7, 66.24.6.2.2, A.66.24.6.2.2,
      Table A.66.29.3.28
   Forest products, storage of A.31.3.4.3.1,
      A.31.3.5.3.2, A.31.3.6.3.5, A.31.3.8.3.3.4
   Indoor storage 34.5.3.2
   Marinas and boatyards 28.1.6.5
   Motion picture production soundstages, facilities,
      and locations 32.5.11.8
   Obstructions 13.1.3
   Outdoor storage 34.5.3.2
   Permit requirements . . . . Table 1.12.8(a)
   Private . . . . Table 1.12.8(a), 18.1.1.2, 18.1.3.2,
      18.5.5.1
Fire lanes . . . . 3.3.128, A.3.3.128; *see also* Fire department access roads
Fire model 5.7.11, 5.7.12, A.5.7.11
   Definition 3.4.8, A.3.4.8
Fire personnel, standby 1.7.17, 10.14.4, A.1.7.17.3
Fireplaces
   Outdoor . . . . 5.3.3(4), 10.10.8, 17.3.5.2.1.11.2,
      17.3.5.2.1.11.3
   Sprinkler temperature ratings in area of . . . . Table 13.3.1.9(c)
   Wildland/urban interface 17.3.5.2.1.7,
      17.3.5.2.1.11.2

Fire point . . . . 66.9.1.4(5)
   Definition 3.3.123
Fire protection assumptions . . . . 4.2, A.4.2.1 to A.4.2.3
Fire protection markings . . . . 5.3.3(5), 10.11, A.10.11.1.1 to
      A.10.11.3.4
Fire protection systems and equipment . . . . 10.8.2.1(6),
      Chap. 13; *see also* Extinguishers, portable fire;
      Extinguishing systems; Fire pumps; Standpipe systems
   Aerosol products storage, handling, and use 61.2.6,
      61.3.1.3, 61.3.2.2, 61.3.3.2, 61.3.4.2, 61.4.3.3, 61.4.3.5,
      A.61.3.1.3, A.61.3.4.2.2
   Airport terminal buildings 21.2.3.5.3, 21.2.6,
      A.21.2.6
   Buildings, fire flow requirements for . . . . 18.4, A.18.4.1 to
      A.18.4.5.4
   Buildings under construction 10.3.3, 16.3, A.10.3.3,
      A.16.3.2.1 to A.16.3.6.6
   Combustible fibers, storage vaults for 45.1.2, 45.5.5.2,
      A.45.1.2
   Compressed gases and cryogenic fluids 63.2.10, 63.2.17.3,
      63.2.18.1.3, A.63.2.10
   Definition 3.3.254.11
   Design/installation 4.4.6
   Dust explosion and fire prevention . . . . . . 40.5, 40.7.1.2(1), 40.7.2.5,
      A.40.5.2.1 to A.40.5.9.4, A.40.7.2.5.3
   Flammable and combustible liquids storage, handling,
      and use . . . . 66.6.7, 66.9.10, 66.16, 66.17.15.4(4),
      66.19.4.6, 66.21.6, 66.22.8 to 66.22.10, 66.22.12.4,
      66.24.6, 66.29.3.28, A.66.6.7.1 to A.66.6.7.3.7,
      A.66.16.1.1 to A.66.16.8.2, A.66.19.4.6.1, A.66.21.6.5.1,
      A.66.21.6.6.1, A.66.22.8.1, A.66.24.6.1.1 to A.66.24.6.2.3,
      A.66.29.3.28
   Heliports, roof-top . . . . 21.3.4.6, 21.3.4.7, A.21.3.4.6.2 to
      A.21.3.4.6.4.1, A.21.3.4.7.1, A.21.3.4.7.2
   Hot work operations . . . . 41.2.2.5, 41.2.4.4, 41.3.4.2(12),
      41.5.4, A.41.2.4.4
   Inspection, testing, and maintenance . . . . *see* Inspection, testing,
      and maintenance
   LP-Gas systems and containers 69.5.5, 69.6.1.2, A.69.5.5
   Manual . . . . *see* Manual fire suppression equipment
   Marinas and boatyards 28.1.6, A.28.1.6.2, A.28.1.6.3
   Motion picture production soundstages, facilities,
      and locations 32.4.11, 32.5.11, A.32.4.11.1.3.1,
      A.32.4.11.1.3.2, A.32.5.11.1 to A.32.5.11.5
   Motor vehicle fuel dispensing facilities 30.1.5, 42.7.2.5.2,
      42.7.2.5.3, 42.7.4.3(5), 42.7.5.6, 42.9.7.1, 42.9.7.2,
      42.10.2.1.6, 42.10.2.1.7, 42.10.2.4, 42.10.4.5, A.30.1.5.1,
      A.42.7.5.6, A.42.10.2.1.7.1, A.42.10.2.1.7.3
   Non-listed devices and equipment 13.9
   Performance-based design features
      Annual certification 5.1.11, A.5.1.11
      Fire service, information transfer to 5.1.9, A.5.1.9
      Maintenance 5.1.10, A.5.1.10
      Operations and maintenance (O & M) manual . . . 5.1.8, A.5.1.8
      Retained prescriptive elements 5.3.1
   Repair garages 30.2.7
   Seasonal buildings 10.12.2, 10.12.3, A.10.12.2.1
   Spray application operations . . . . 43.1.7, 43.5.3.1(4), 43.8.3,
      A.43.1.7.1 to A.43.1.7.8, A.43.5.3.1(4), A.43.8.3
   Storage occupancies 34.5, 34.6.3.3, 34.6.6.2, 34.7.2,
      A.34.5.1, A.34.5.4.2, A.34.6.6.2
   Tampering with 10.7, 17.3.8
   Tents, membrane structures, grandstands, and folding/telescopic
      seating 25.1.6
   Vacant buildings 10.12.2, 10.12.3, A.10.12.2.1
   Wharves and marine terminals 66.29.3.28,
      A.66.29.3.28
Fire pumps . . . . 11.9.5(8), 13.4, 61.2.6.4.2, A.13.4.1.4 to
      A.13.4.7.4(6)
   Controllers . . . . 13.4.5, A.13.4.5.1.2 to
      A.13.4.5.2.3(3)
   Foam extinguishing systems 21.3.4.6.5.1

Inspection, testing, and maintenance .... 13.4.4, 13.4.6 to 13.4.9, A.13.4.4, A.13.4.6.1 to A.13.4.7.4(6)
Permit requirements .... Table 1.12.8(a)
Fire reporting 10.6.1, A.10.6.1.3
Fire-resistant assemblies .... 12.3, A.12.3.2, A.12.3.3; *see also* Fire barriers; Fire door assemblies
   Tank buildings 66.24.6.2.3, A.66.24.6.2.3
   Tanks 66.22.9
Fire retardant 12.5.7, 32.4.5.3, A.12.5.7
   Definition 3.3.124
Fires .... *see also* Exposure fires
   Classifications
      Definitions 3.3.113
      Extinguishers selected and distributed for .... 13.6.2.3, 13.6.2.4, A.13.6.2.3.2.1 to A.13.6.2.3.3.2.7, A.13.6.2.4.1.1 to A.13.6.2.4.2.2
   Investigations 1.7.11.1
   Open .... *see* Open fires
   Property protection 4.1.4, A.4.1.4.2.1, A.4.1.4.2.2
   Recreational 10.10.1.1, 10.10.4.3
      Definition 3.3.217
   Safety from .... 4.1.3.1, A.4.1.3.1.1 to A.4.1.3.1.2.5
Fire safety, general .... Chap. 10
Fire safety equipment ..... *see* Fire protection systems and equipment
Fire scenarios (definition) 3.4.9, A.3.4.9
Fire scenarios (design) 5.4, A.5.4
   Assumptions 4.2.2.2, 4.2.3, A.4.2.3
   Definition 3.4.9.1
Fire service, information transfer to 5.1.9, A.5.1.9
Fire source, single 4.2.1, A.4.2.1
Firestop systems and devices 12.7.5.1, 12.7.5.6.2, A.12.7.5.1
Fire walls .... 12.3, 12.7.5, 34.6.6.1, 34.8.2.2, 45.7.3, 61.2.2.1, A.12.3.2, A.12.3.3, A.12.7.5.1, A.12.7.5.6.3(1)(c), A.18.4.1.1
Fire watch 1.7.17, 16.5.4
   Assembly occupancies 20.1.5.7, 25.1.8, A.20.1.5.7, A.25.1.8
   Construction, alteration, and demolition operations .. A.16.2.2.4.1
   Definition 3.3.125
   Fire protection systems, impaired .... 13.3.3.6.5.2(4)(b), 13.7.1.5.3, A.13.3.3.6.5.2(4)(b)
   Hot work operations .... 41.2.2.6, 41.2.2.7, 41.2.4, 41.3.5, 41.4.1, A.41.2.2.7, A.41.2.4.1 to A.41.2.4.7, A.41.3.5.1, A.41.3.5.3, A.41.4.1
   Storage occupancies .... 34.5.4.3, 34.6.3.3(4)
   Tents, membrane structures, grandstands, and folding/telescopic seating 25.1.8, A.25.1.8
Fire windows .... 12.4, 12.7.3, Table 12.7.4.2, 12.9.4.5, A.12.4.1 to A.12.4.6.9.1, A.12.7.3.2 to A.12.7.3.6
Fitness
   Certificate of .... *see* Certificate of fitness
   Warrant of 4.5.5
Fixed guideway transit and passenger rail systems .... Chap. 37
Fixed-temperature detectors 13.7.4.5.1, 13.7.4.5.2
   Definition 3.3.84.7, A.3.3.84.7
Flame detection systems .... 43.1.7.7.1, 43.1.7.7.2(1), 43.1.7.8.1, 43.1.7.8.2(1)
Flame detectors (definition) 3.3.84.8, A.3.3.84.8
Flame effects before an audience .... Table 1.12.8(a), 32.4.3.3, 32.5.3.3, 65.4
Flame spread 4.1.4.2.2, A.4.1.4.2.2
   Definition 3.3.126, A.3.3.126
Flame spread index (definition) 3.3.127
Flammable cryogenic fluid .... Table 1.12.8(c), B.2.1.10.1
   Definition 3.3.77.1
Flammable gas .... Table 60.4.2.1.1.3, Table 60.4.4.1.2, 63.1.4.1(1), 63.1.4.4.2, Table 63.2.3.1.1, 63.2.3.1.6, Table 63.2.9, 63.2.10.2.2, Table 63.3.1.11.2, 63.3.6, A.63.3.6.2.1.1, B.2.1.2.1; *see also* Compressed gas; Hazardous materials
   Aerosol products and 61.2.5

In buildings under construction 16.2.3, A.16.2.3.1.2, A.16.2.3.2.4
Definition 3.3.135.3
Dust explosion and fire prevention 40.4.3.5, 40.4.3.6, A.40.3.5.1, A.40.3.5.2
Liquefied gas .... Table 60.4.4.1.2
   Definition .... 3.3.135.4 *see also* Liquefied natural gas (LNG)
Motion picture production soundstages, facilities, and locations .... 32.4.2(4), 32.5.2(5)
Permits .... Table 1.12.8(b), Table 1.12.8(d), 32.4.2(4), 32.5.2(5)
Refrigerants 53.2.2.1.2, 53.2.2.2
Specific occupancies, storage and use in .... Tables 60.4.2.1.2 to 60.4.2.1.8, Table 60.4.2.1.10.1
Tents, membrane structures, grandstands, and folding/telescopic seating 25.1.4, A.25.1.4.2
Vacuum cleaner operation and 40.3.2.3.3
Flammable liquids .... 60.1.2, Table 60.4.2.1.1.3, Chap. 66; *see also* Hazardous materials
   Aerosol products and 61.2.5
   In buildings under construction 16.2.3, A.16.2.3.1.2, A.16.2.3.2.4
   Classification of 66.4.2, A.66.4.2, B.2.1.3
   Cleaning solvents 43.1.8.7, A.43.1.8.7.4
   Containers .... *see* Containers
   Definition 3.3.164.2, 66.4.2.1, A.3.3.164.2
   Electrical equipment and systems ..... *see* Electrical equipment and systems
   Fire prevention and risk control .... 66.6, A.66.6.1 to A.66.6.7.8
   Fires .... *see* Class B fires
   Handling, dispensing, transfer, and use of .... 66.18, A.66.18.4.8 to A.66.18.6.3
   Marinas and boatyards, use and storage at 28.1.7.2.1.3, 28.1.7.2.1.4, 28.1.7.2.2.3
   Motion picture production soundstages, facilities, and locations .... 32.4.2(4), 32.5.2(5), 32.6.2
   Motor fuel dispensing facilities and systems .... 42.3, 42.5, 42.9.2, A.42.3.3.2 to A.42.3.3.8, A.42.5.2.3 to A.42.5.6.2, A.42.9.2.2
   Operations .... 66.17.15, 66.21.7, A.66.21.7.1 to A.66.21.7.5
   Permits .... Table 1.12.8(a), Table 1.12.8(c), Table 1.12.8(d), 32.4.2(4), 32.5.2(5), 66.1.5
   Piping systems .... 66.27, A.66.27.4.3.2 to A.66.27.10
   Processing facilities .... 66.17, A.66.17.1.1 to A.66.17.14
   Recirculating heat transfer systems .... 66.19.4, A.66.19.4.2 to A.66.19.4.7.1
   Solvent distillation units 66.19.6
   Solvent extraction .... Chap. 44
   Specific occupancies, storage and use in .... Tables 60.4.2.1.2 to 60.4.2.1.8, Table 60.4.2.1.10.1
   Spray applications .... *see* Spray applications, of flammable and combustible materials
   Storage of .... 34.4.4, 43.1.6, 43.1.8.7.6, 66.9, 66.21 to 66.25, A.43.1.6.1 to A.43.1.6.5.2, A.66.9.4.1 to A.66.9.16.2, A.66.21.4.2.1.1 to A.66.25.5 *see also* Tanks
   Tank cars/vehicles, loading and unloading of .... 66.28, A.66.28.3.1.2 to A.66.28.11.4.1
   Tents, membrane structures, grandstands, and folding/telescopic seating 25.1.4, A.25.1.4.2
   Vapor recovery and vapor processing systems .... 66.19.5, A.66.19.5.5.1 to A.66.19.5.7.6
   Wharves 66.29, A.66.29.3.5, A.66.29.3.28
   Wildland/urban interface, storage in 17.3.5.2.1.11.4
Flammable materials
   For repairs or alterations 4.5.6.3
   Wildland fire-prone areas 17.3.4

Flammable solids .... Table 1.12.8(d), Table 60.4.2.1.1.3,
Tables 60.4.2.1.2 to 60.4.2.1.8, Table 60.4.2.1.10.1, Table
60.4.4.1.2, Chap. 67, B.2.1.3; *see also* Hazardous
materials
    Definition 3.3.236.2, A.3.3.236.2
Flammable vapors 40.3.2.3.3, 40.4.3.4.4, 40.4.3.4.5, 40.4.3.5,
A.40.3.5.1, A.40.3.5.2; *see also* Flammable gas
    Definition 3.3.128
    Detection systems 53.2.3.1, 66.25.15, A.53.2.3.1.4
Flash point
    Classification of liquids and 66.4.2, A.66.4.2
    Definition 3.3.129, A.3.3.129
    Determination of 66.4.3
    Drycleaning solvents 24.1.2
    Inert gas use and 66.18.4.4
    Spray operations 43.5.1.1.3
Fleet vehicle motor fuel dispensing facilities .... *see* Motor fuel
dispensing facilities
Flexible connectors 66.27.5.2
    Definition 66.27.2.2
Flexible intermediate bulk containers 40.4.3.4, A.40.4.3.4
Flexible plan buildings 20.2.2, 20.3.2.4
Floating roof tanks .... Table 66.7.3.3, 66.22.2.2,
Table 66.22.4.1.1(a), Table 66.22.4.1.4, 66.22.8.2
Flooding, tanks in areas subject to 66.22.14, 66.23.14,
66.25.5.2.1, A.66.23.14.1
Floor area
    Gross (definition) 3.3.130.1, A.3.3.130.1
    Net (definition) 3.3.130.2
Floors
    Hazardous materials storage and use areas .... 60.4.2.1.13.2(9)
    Hot work operations .... 41.3.4.2(2), 41.3.4.2(4),
41.3.5.1(3)
    Interior finish .... *see* Interior finish
    One- and two-family dwellings 20.11.4,
A.20.11.4.4
    Openings in 4.4.5
    Storage occupancies 34.6.6.1
    Under-floor detector mounting 13.7.4.3.3.2,
A.13.7.4.3.3.2
    Under-floor storage 10.18.6
Flow control, excess .... *see* Excess flow control
Foam agent portable fire extinguishers 13.6.2.5.3,
Table 13.6.4.3.3.1, 13.6.4.7.2.3, 13.6.4.10.4.1
Foam extinguishing systems .... Table 13.8
    Flammable and combustible liquids storage, handling,
and use 66.6.7.6, 66.6.7.9, 66.16.4, 66.16.5.1.2,
66.16.5.1.6, 66.16.5.2.3, 66.16.5.2.4, 66.16.9, 66.24.6.1.3,
66.24.6.2.3, 66.24.6.2.4, A.66.16.5.1.6.2, A.66.24.6.2.3,
Table A.66.29.3.28
    Heliports, rooftop .... 21.3.4.6, A.21.3.4.6.2 to
A.21.3.4.6.4.1
    Storage occupancies .... 34.5.2, 34.5.4.2(8), 34.5.5.1, 34.7.3.4,
A.34.7.3.4.1.1, A.34.7.3.4.2.1(1)
Folding and telescopic seating .... Table 1.12.8(a), 25.1, 25.4,
A.25.1.4.2, A.25.1.8
Food service operations .... *see* Cooking equipment
Forecasting (definition) 3.3.131
Forest products .... Chap. 31
Forms, construction 16.4.1, A.16.4.1
Free egress, Use condition I (definition) 3.3.183.8.1.1
Fruit ripening process, permit for .... Table 1.12.8(a)
Fuel delivery nozzles 42.5.6, 42.7.5.4, 42.7.6.4, 42.9.4.2,
42.9.9.4, 42.10.2.1.1, 42.10.2.6.3, 42.10.5.2.3, A.42.5.6.2
Fuel dispensing areas .... *see* Dispensing areas
Fuel dispensing stations .... *see* Motor fuel dispensing facilities
Fuel dispensing systems and devices
    Compressed natural gas 42.8, 42.11.1, A.42.8.3.4,
A.42.8.6.2, A.42.11.1.1
    LNG 42.8, 42.11.3, A.42.8.3.4, A.42.8.6.2, A.42.11.3

    LP-Gas 42.8, 42.11.2, 69.3.13, A.42.8.3.4, A.42.8.6.2,
A.42.11.2.2.1 to A.42.11.2.4.4
    Motor vehicle fuel dispensing facilities 42.5, 42.9.4,
42.10.2.6, A.42.5.2.3 to A.42.5.6.2
Fueled equipment, storage of 10.18.7
Fuel load (definition) 3.4.10, A.3.4.10
Fuel tanks .... *see* Tanks
Fugitive dust control .... 40.3, A.40.3.2.1.1 to A.40.3.2.3.1(6)
Fugitive emissions .... 66.17.11.2(1), 66.24.10.2(1)
    Definition 3.3.132, A.3.3.132
Fundamental requirements 4.4, A.4.4.4
Furnishings 12.5.5.5, 12.6, A.12.6.2
    Ambulatory health care occupancies 20.6.2.5,
A.20.6.2.5.1 to A.20.6.2.5.5.2
    Apartment buildings 20.9.4
    Assembly occupancies 20.1.5.4, A.20.1.5.4.1,
A.20.1.5.4.3
    Board and care occupancies 20.5.2.5, A.20.5.2.5
    Day-care occupancies 20.3.4.2.3.5
    Detention and correctional occupancies 20.7.2.4,
A.20.7.2.4
    Educational occupancies 20.2.4.4
    Health care occupancies .... 20.4.2.5, A.20.4.2.5.1 to
A.20.4.2.5.8(2)
    Hotels and dormitories 20.8.2.5
    In means of egress 14.4.2
Fuses, covered .... *see* Covered fuses

-G-

Gallon (definition) 3.3.133
Garages
    Definition 3.3.134
    Flammable and combustible liquids tank
vehicles .... Table 66.7.3.3
    LP-Gas cargo vehicles 69.6.2, A.69.6.2.2.2
    LP-Gas fueled vehicles 42.11.2.7
    LP-Gas systems on vehicles 69.3.12.9
    Repair .... *see* Repair garages
Gas
    Compressed .... *see* Compressed gas
    Cooking equipment 10.18.7
    Corrosive .... *see* Corrosive gas
    Flammable .... *see* Flammable gas
    Highly toxic .... *see* Highly toxic gas
    Irritant (definition) 3.3.135.7
    Liquefied .... *see* Liquefied gas
    Nonflammable (definition) 3.3.135.11
    Other (definition) 3.3.135.12, A.3.3.135.12
    Oxidizing .... *see* Oxidizing gas
    Ozone-gas generating equipment .... Chap. 54
    Permit amounts for .... Table 1.12.8(b)
    Pyrophoric .... *see* Pyrophoric gas
    Scavenged (definition) 3.3.135.15
    Simple asphyxiant .... Table 1.12.8(b), A.42.11.1.1
    Definition 3.3.135.16
    Toxic .... *see* Toxic gas
    Unstable reactive .... *see* Unstable (reactive) gas
Gas cabinets 63.2.17, 63.3.5.3.1, 63.3.9.4.1
    Definition 3.3.136, A.3.3.136
    Ozone 54.2.2
Gas detection systems 30.2.8, 63.3.9.3.2.1,
63.3.9.3.4.3.2(B), 63.3.9.6
    Compressed gas 63.3.9.6, 63.3.9.7
    Continuous gas detection system .... 54.2.3(2), 63.3.9.6
    Definition 3.3.254.7
Gas detectors .... 66.6.6.2(3)
    Definition 3.3.84.9
Gaseous extinguishing systems .... 43.1.7.8.2(1), 66.24.6.2.3,
A.66.24.6.2.3
Gaseous hydrogen systems 63.3.6.2.1, 63.6,
A.63.3.6.2.1.1
    Definition 3.3.139, A.3.3.139
Gas-fired vehicles .... *see* Motor vehicles

Gas-fueled heating appliances .... *see* Heating equipment and appliances
Gas manufacturer/producer (definition) 3.3.137
Gas rooms 63.2.4, 63.3.5.3.3
   Definition 3.3.138
Gas turbines 11.7.1
Gated communities, access to 18.2.2.2
General requirements .... Chap. 4
General storage .... *see* Storage occupancies
Generators
   Aircraft ground-power 42.10.5.7.2, A.42.10.5.7.2
   Membrane structures 25.1.12
   Ozone-gas generating equipment .... Chap. 54
   Portable 11.7.2, A.11.7.2.1
   Stationary .... 11.7.1, 11.7.3 to 11.7.5, 11.9.5(9)
Glass fiber reinforced plastics .... 43.8, A.43.8.1 to A.43.8.5.3
Goals 4.1.1, A.4.1.1
   Compliance options 4.3
   Performance-based design 5.1.2
   Property protection 4.1.1, 4.1.4.1, A.4.1.1
   Public welfare 4.1.5.1, A.4.1.5.1
   Safety-during-building-use 4.1.3.2.1, A.4.1.3.2.1
   Safety-from-fire 4.1.3.1.1, A.4.1.3.1.1
   Safety-from-hazardous materials 4.1.3.3.1
Grandstands .... Table 1.12.8(a), 25.1, 25.3, A.25.1.4.2, A.25.1.8
Grease removal devices 50.2.2.1, 50.2.2.2, 50.4.3, 50.4.4.4, 50.4.4.8.1, 50.4.4.8.6, 50.5.6.2, A.50.4.3.2, A.50.5.6.2
Grounding
   Cryogenic fluid containers and systems 63.4.8.3
   Dust explosion and fire prevention 40.4.3.2.3, 40.4.3.4.4.1, 40.4.3.4.4.2, 40.4.3.7.5, A.40.4.3.2.3, A.40.4.3.7.5
   Flammable and combustible liquid piping systems 66.27.9
   Marine motor fuel dispensing facilities .... 42.9.6.4, 42.9.10.7(4), A.42.9.6.4
   Spray application operations 43.1.4.6, 43.1.8.5.3, 43.1.8.7.4, A.43.1.4.6, A.43.1.8.5.3, A.43.1.8.7.4
   Tank cars and tank vehicles, loading and unloading of 66.28.3.1, A.66.28.3.1.2
   Wharves, pipelines on 66.29.3.12
Ground kettles (definition) 3.3.140
Guard service .... 16.3.2.5.1 to 16.3.2.5.3, 28.1.6.2.4.2(3), 28.1.7.2.2.2, 34.5.6, A.16.3.2.5.1, A.16.3.2.5.2
Guide (definition) 3.2.4

-H-
Halogenated agent extinguishers .... 13.6.2.3.2.6, 13.6.4.2.3.3, Table 13.6.4.3.3.1, 13.6.4.3.6.2, 13.6.4.3.6.3.1, 13.6.4.7.3.7, 13.6.4.7.3.8, 13.6.4.7.4.1, 13.6.4.7.4.2, 13.6.4.7.4.4, 13.6.4.10.4.2, A.13.6.2.3.2.6, A.13.6.4.3.6.2, A.13.6.4.3.7, A.13.6.4.7.4.4
Halon 1301 extinguishing systems ... Table 13.8, 66.6.7.6, 66.24.6.2.4
Handling (definition) 3.3.141
Hangars .... *see* Aircraft hangars
Hay, straw, and other agricultural products, storage of 45.7
Hazard of contents .... *see also* High hazard contents; Low hazard contents; Ordinary hazard contents
   Definition A.3.3.142
   Fire fighter safety building marking system (FFSBMS) E.1.3.3, E.2.2
Hazardous chemicals .... 20.1.5.5.4.13.1(3); *see also* Hazardous materials; specific chemicals
   Definition 66.3.3.19, A.66.3.3.19
Hazardous materials .... 20.1.5.5.4.13.1(3), Chap. 60; *see also* specific materials
   Automobile wrecking yards 22.9
   Classification .... 60.3, 63.1.4, A.60.3.1 to A.60.3.5, Annex B

Combustible fiber storage and 45.8
Containers .... *see* Containers
Control areas .... *see* Control areas
Definition 3.3.173.4, 66.3.3.19, A.66.3.3.19
General storage 60.5.1.13
Incidents
   Assumptions 4.2.3, A.4.2.3
   Investigation 1.7.11.1
   Safety, design for 5.2.2.3, A.5.2.2.3
Inventory statements 60.1.7, A.60.1.7, D.2
Management plans D.3
Maximum allowable quantities .... *see* Maximum allowable quantities
Mixtures 60.3.3
Multiple hazards 60.3.4, A.60.3.4
Notification of unauthorized discharge 10.6.3
Outdoor storage and use 60.4.4, 60.5.1.15
Performance-based design option 5.1.12
   Design scenarios 5.4.4, A.5.4.4
   Performance criteria 5.2.2.3, A.5.2.2.3
Permissible storage and use locations 60.4, A.60.4.1
Permits .... Table 1.12.8(a)
Property protection 4.1.4.2.4
Protection 60.4.3, 60.5.1.9
Release of 1.7.11.1, 53.3.1.6, 53.3.1.7, 60.5.1.3, A.60.5.1.3.4
   For repairs or alterations 4.5.6.3
Safety from 4.1.3.3, A.4.1.3.3.2.2
Shelf storage 60.5.1.13.2
Single release, assumption of 4.2.2, A.4.2.2
Specific occupancies, allowable storage and use in .... 60.4.2.1.1 to 60.4.2.1.13
Storage cabinets 60.5.1.18
Storage of hazardous commodities 20.15.4
Weather protection 60.4.1.2
Hazardous materials storage facilities
   Closure of 60.1.4
   Definition 3.3.145
Hazardous materials storage lockers 66.14, A.66.14.1
   Definition 3.3.146
Hazardous production materials (HPM) (definition) 3.3.173.5
Hazardous reaction or hazardous chemical reaction (definition) 3.3.147, A.3.3.147
Hazard rating (definition) 3.3.143, A.3.3.143
Health care occupancies .... 20.4, A.20.4.2; *see also* Ambulatory health care occupancies
   Battery systems, location of 52.3.3.4
   Christmas tree provisions .... Table 10.13.1.1
   Cryogenic systems 63.4.5
   Definition 3.3.183.11, 6.1.5.1, A.3.3.183.11, A.6.1.5.1
   Detection, alarm, and communication systems .... 13.7.2.7, 13.7.2.8, A.13.7.2.7.2 to A.13.7.2.7.5.3, A.13.7.2.8.2, A.13.7.2.8.3.1(1)
   Emergency plans 10.8.1, 20.4.2.1, 20.4.2.2.2, 20.6.2.1, 20.6.2.2.2, A.20.4.2.1.5, A.20.6.2.1.5
   Extinguishers, portable fire .... Table 13.6.1.2
   Fire fighter safety building marking system (FFSBMS) E.1.3.5
   Flammable and combustible liquids storage 66.9.6.2.1, 66.9.6.2.2, 66.9.6.2.4
   Hazardous materials storage and use 60.4.2.1.5
   Means of egress .... Table 14.8.1.2, Table 14.8.3.1, 20.4.2.3, 20.6.2.3, A.20.4.2.3.3
   Multiple occupancies .... Table 6.1.14.4.1(a), Table 6.1.14.4.1(b)
   Sprinkler systems .... 13.3.2.11, 13.3.2.12, Table 14.8.3.1, A.13.3.2.11.1 to A.13.3.2.11.6, A.13.3.2.12.6 to A.13.3.2.12.12
Health hazard materials .... 63.1.4.1(2), B.2.2; *see also* Hazardous materials
   Definition 3.3.173.6
   Supply piping for 60.5.1.6.3

Heat detectors .... 13.7.2.18.4.2(2), 13.7.4.3.2, 13.7.4.5
   Definition 3.3.84.10
Heating, ventilating, and air conditioning (HVAC)
      systems .... 11.2, 11.9.5(4)
   Airport terminal buildings 21.2.3.4, 21.2.4, A.21.2.4.2,
      A.21.2.4.3
   Battery rooms and cabinets .... Table 52.1, 52.3.6,
      A.52.3.6
   Compressed gases and cryogenic fluids 63.2.16, 63.2.18,
      63.3.9.2, A.63.3.9.2.2.1.1
   Cryogenic fluid containers and systems 63.4.13.1.4,
      63.4.14.11.3.2.2
   Elevator machine rooms 11.3.3, A.11.3.3
   Flammable and combustible liquids storage, handling,
      and use 66.7.3.7.1, 66.9.5.4, 66.9.14, 66.14.4.7,
      66.17.11, 66.18.5.6(3), 66.18.6, 66.24.10, 66.25.10,
      A.66.9.5.4, A.66.17.11.2, A.66.17.11.7, A.66.18.6.3,
      A.66.24.10.2, A.66.24.10.4 *see also* subhead: Spray
      applications, of flammable and combustible materials
   Gas cabinets 63.2.17.2
   Gas rooms 63.2.4.2
   Pump room or house 13.4.2.6
   Refrigerant machinery rooms 53.2.3.3
   Repair garages 30.2.9, A.30.2.9
   Smoke dampers 12.9.5, 13.7.1.9.2.2,
      A.13.7.1.9.2.2
   Smoke detectors, shutdown by 13.7.1.9.2.2,
      A.13.7.1.9.2.2
   Soundstages and approved production facilities 32.4.12
   Spray applications, of flammable and combustible
      materials .... 43.1.3.6, 43.1.5, 43.1.6.3.2(4), 43.1.7.3,
      43.1.7.7.1(2), 43.5.3.1, 43.5.3.9, 43.8.6, A.43.1.5.2.1 to
      A.43.1.5.11, A.43.5.3.1(4)
   Sprinkler systems for 13.3.3.5.1.7
   Tents, membrane structures, grandstands, and folding/telescopic
      seating 25.1.10.1.4, 25.1.10.1.5
Heating equipment and appliances
   Aerosol products, buildings for 61.2.4
   Aircraft 42.10.5.5
   Compressed gases and cryogenic fluids 63.3.1.11.7,
      63.3.6.4.3
   Dust explosion and fire prevention 40.4.6,
      A.40.4.6.1
   Electric 25.1.10.2
   Escape blocked by 20.5.2.5.3
   Fire pumps 13.4.2.3
   Forest products, storage of 31.3.2.1.8,
      31.3.2.1.9
   Installation .... 11.5, A.11.5.1.5 to
      A.11.5.1.10.3(4)
   Kerosene burners 11.5.2
   LP-Gas .... 69.3.10.2.6, 69.3.10.3.4 to 69.3.10.3.10,
      69.3.10.7, 69.3.11.1, 69.3.12.7.4 to 69.3.12.7.6,
      A.69.3.10.2.6, A.69.3.12.7.6
   Oil- and gas-fueled .... Table 1.12.8(a), 11.5.2, 25.1.10.1,
      66.19.4.4, A.66.19.4.4
   Oil stoves 11.5.2
   Patio heaters 10.10.7
   Permits 11.5.1.8
   Portable 11.5.3, 20.4.2.6, 20.6.2.6, 20.7.2.6, 28.1.7.2.1.1,
      69.3.10.2.6, A.69.3.10.2.6
   Spray application operations 43.5.3.7.1, 43.8.5.4
   Sprinkler temperature ratings for .... Table 13.3.1.9(a),
      Table 13.3.1.9(c)
   Stored commodities, clearance from 34.4.2.4
   Temporary .... 16.2.1, 69.3.10.3.4, 69.3.10.7, A.16.2.1.1 to
      A.16.2.1.14
   Tents, membrane structures, grandstands, and folding/telescopic
      seating 25.1.10
   Tires, outside storage of 33.1.6.2
   Unvented fuel-fired 20.2.4.5, 20.3.2.1, 20.5.2.5.4, 20.8.2.6,
      20.9.2.2, 20.10.2, 20.11.2, 69.3.12.7.6, A.69.3.12.7.6
   Vents 11.5.4
Heat-producing appliances
   Detention and correctional appliances 20.7.2.3
   LP-Gas 69.3.10.2.6, A.69.3.10.2.6
   Repair garages 30.2.10, A.30.2.10.6
   Tents, membrane structures, grandstands, and folding/telescopic
      seating 25.1.10.1.5
Heat transfer fluid (HTF) 66.19.4.1.1, 66.19.4.2, 66.19.4.3.3,
      A.66.19.4.2
   Definition 3.3.148
Heat transfer systems, recirculating .... 66.19.4, A.66.19.4.2 to
   A.66.19.4.7.1
Heliports
   Definition 3.3.149, A.3.3.149
   Rapid refueling of helicopters 42.10.5.21,
      A.42.10.5.21.2(2)
   Rooftop
      Construction and protection .... 21.3, A.21.3.3.1 to
      A.21.3.4.7.2
      Fueling at 42.10.4
      Permit requirements .... Table 1.12.8(a),
      21.3.2.2
High air movement areas, smoke detectors in 13.7.4.3.8,
   A.13.7.4.3.8.2
High hazard contents 13.6.2.4.1.3, A.13.6.2.4.1.3,
   E.2.3; *see also* Hazardous materials
   Classification of 60.3.2
   Definition 3.3.142.1
   Extinguishers, portable fire .... Table 13.6.3.2.1.1
   Industrial occupancies .... Table 6.1.14.4.1(a),
      Table 6.1.14.4.1(b), 13.7.2.27.3.4
   Level 2 .... 60.3.2.1.2.2
      Definition 3.3.142.1.2, 66.3.3.23
   Level 3 .... 60.3.2.1.2.3
      Definition 3.3.142.1.3, 66.3.3.24
   Level 4 .... 60.3.2.1.2.4
      Definition 3.3.142.1.4
   Level 1 (definition) 3.3.142.1.1
   Level 5 (definition) 3.3.142.1.5
   Means of egress, capacity .... Table 14.8.3.1
   Performance-based design option 5.1.12, 60.7
   Storage occupancies .... Table 6.1.14.4.1(a),
      Table 6.1.14.4.1(b), 13.7.2.28.1.2, 13.7.2.28.3.4,
      34.1.1.2(4)
Highly toxic gas .... 1, Table 60.4.4.1.2, 63.1.4.1(2)(c),
   Table 63.2.3.1.1, 63.2.3.1.7, Table 63.3.1.11.2, 63.3.9,
   A.63.3.9.2.2.1.1 to A.63.3.9.3.6.2, B.2.1.2.4, B.2.2.1.1; *see
   also* Compressed gas
   Definition 3.3.135.5
   Ozone-gas generating equipment .... Chap. 54
   Permit amounts for .... Tables 1.12.8(b) to (d)
   Refrigerants 53.2.2.1.1, 53.2.2.2
   Specific occupancies, storage and use in .... Table 60.4.2.1.1.3
Highly toxic materials (solids and liquids) .... Table 60.4.2.1.1.3,
   Tables 60.4.2.1.2 to 60.4.2.1.8, Table 60.4.2.1.10.1, Table
   60.4.2.1.13.3(b), Table 60.4.4.1.2, Chap. 68, B.2.1.10.5,
   B.2.2.1.1.2, B.2.2.1.1.3; *see also* Hazardous materials
   Definition 3.3.173.7, A.3.3.173.7
   Permit amounts for .... Table 1.12.8(c), Table 1.12.8(d)
Highly volatile liquids .... 60.5.1.6.3(1)
   Definition 3.3.164.3
High-piled storage .... Table 1.12.8(a), 13.3.2.27.1, 20.15.8
   Definition 3.3.246.4
High-powered rocketry .... *see* Rockets, model
High-rise buildings 20.16
   Definition 3.3.29.6, A.3.3.29.6
   Detection, alarm, and communication systems 13.7.2.20.5,
      13.7.2.29.2, A.13.7.2.29.2.1, A.13.7.2.29.2.2
   Emergency plans 10.8.1, 20.12.2.1, 20.13.2.1
   Sprinkler systems 13.3.2.16.1, 13.3.2.22.1.3,
      13.3.2.26, A.13.3.2.26.2

Standpipe systems 13.2.2.3
High-temperature devices 60.5.1.5.2
Historic buildings .... 4.5.2, 20.17, A.20.17.3(2)
Hogged material
  Definition 3.3.150
  Outside storage of .... 31.3.1.1(4), 31.3.2.1.6.2, 31.3.6,
    31.3.7, A.31.3.6.1 to A.31.3.6.4.3, A.31.3.7
Hoods, commercial cooking .... 50.2.1.3(2), 50.2.2.1,
    50.2.2.2, 50.4.3, 50.4.4.4, 50.4.4.7, 50.4.4.8, 50.4.5.1.1,
    50.4.5.1.2, 50.4.10.1, 50.4.11.1, 50.5.5, 50.5.6.2,
    A.50.4.3.2, A.50.5.6.2
Horizontal exits
  Aircraft hangars 21.1.4.2.3, 21.1.5.1.3
  Definition 3.3.102.1, A.3.3.102.1
  Doors in .... 14.5.1.1(4), 14.5.1.1(7)
  Protectives, minimum ratings for .... Table 12.7.4.2
Hose lines 13.2.2.4, 13.2.2.6, 16.4.1.5, 21.3.4.6, 34.5.3.1.2,
    34.6.3.3(3), 41.3.4.2(11), 66.9.10.2.3 to 66.9.10.2.6,
    66.16.7, A.13.2.2.4, A.13.2.2.6, A.16.3.6, A.16.4.1.5,
    A.16.4.3.3.2.8, A.21.3.4.6.4.1, A.31.3.6.3.7, A.34.6.6.2,
    Table A.66.29.3.28; see also Standpipe systems
Hospitals (definition) ... 3.3.183.12; see also Health care occupancies
Hotels .... 20.8, A.20.8.2.1.1 to A.20.8.2.4.2
  Christmas tree provisions .... Table 10.13.1.1
  Definition 3.3.183.13, 6.1.8.1.3, A.3.3.183.13, A.6.1.8.1.3
  Detection, alarm, and communication systems 13.7.2.15,
    13.7.2.16, A.13.7.2.15.3.1 to A.13.7.2.15.5,
    A.13.7.2.16.3.6, A.13.7.2.16.5
  Extinguishers, portable fire .... Table 13.6.1.2
  Hazardous materials storage and use 60.4.2.1.8
  Multiple occupancies .... Table 6.1.14.4.1(a),
    Table 6.1.14.4.1(b)
  Sprinkler systems 13.3.2.15, 13.3.2.16,
    A.13.3.2.16.2
Hot work operations 10.10.9.1, 40.4.5.1, 40.4.5.2,
    Chap. 41, A.10.10.9.1
  Aerosol products storage, handling, and use .... 61.2.8.2(6),
    61.5.3.1.1(6), 61.5.3.3, A.61.5.3.3
  Automobile wrecking yards 22.4
  Contractors 41.2.5, A.41.2.5
  Demolition sites 16.5.2
  Flammable and combustible liquids storage, handling,
    and use .... 66.6.5.1(6), 66.6.5.3, A.66.6.5.3
  Forest products, storage of 31.3.2.1.12
  Motion picture production soundstages, facilities, and
    locations .... 32.4.2(3), 32.5.2(4), 32.6.3
  Permits .... Table 1.12.8(a), 32.4.2(3), 32.5.2(4), 40.4.5.2,
    41.1.5, 41.2.1.1, 41.2.1.2, 41.2.2, 41.3.2 to 41.3.4, 41.4.2,
    43.1.8.12, 61.5.3.3, A.41.2.2.1 to A.42.2.2.7, A.41.3.3,
    A.41.3.4, A.43.1.8.12, A.61.5.3.3
  Personal protective clothing .... 41.3.1, 41.3.4.2(13),
    A.41.3.1
  Sole proprietors and individual owners 41.4,
    A.41.4.1
  Spray application operations 43.1.8.12,
    A.43.1.8.12
  Storage occupancies 34.6.3, A.34.6.3.2
  Tires, outside storage of 33.1.6.2, 33.7.3
Housekeeping
  Automobile wrecking yards 22.5
  Dust explosion and fire prevention .... 40.3.2, 40.7.1.2(3),
    A.40.3.2.1.1 to A.40.3.2.1.4
  Motion picture and television soundstages 32.3
  Motor vehicle fuel dispensing facilities 42.7.2.7
Hydrants .... see Fire hydrants
Hydrogen .... 63.3.6.1.2, A.42.11.1.1; see also Compressed gas
  Gas generation systems 63.8
  Loading and unloading areas 63.4.14.11.3.3,
    63.4.14.11.3.4, A.63.4.14.11.3.4
Hydrogen containers 69.3.4.5.4
  Non-bulk portable 63.4.7.3.1
  Separation of .... 69.3.4.4.9 to 69.3.4.4.11

Hydrogen equipment, listed and approved 63.3.1.4,
  A.63.3.1.4
Hydrogen systems .... 63.3.1.4, A.63.1.1.4(11), A.63.3.1.4,
  A.63.4.13.2.6.4.1, A.63.4.13.2.7.2
  Gaseous 63.3.6.2.1, 63.6, A.63.3.6.2.1.1
    Definition 3.3.139 A.3.3.139
  Liquefied 63.7
  Metal hydride storage systems 63.3.1.5,
    A.63.3.1.5
Hydrogen vehicle fuel 42.8, A.42.8.3.4, A.42.8.6.2

-I-

Ignition sources 4.1.4.2.1, A.4.1.4.2.1
  Acrosol products storage, handling, and use 61.2.8,
    61.5.3, A.61.5.3.3
  Compressed gases and cryogenic fluids 63.3.1.11.8,
    63.3.6.4
  Dust explosion and fire prevention .... 40.4, 40.7.1.2(4),
    A.40.4.1.2.3 to A.40.4.8.2
  Flammable and combustible liquids storage, handling,
    and use .... 66.6.5, 66.18.5.6(1), 66.19.5.7, 66.21.6.2,
    A.66.6.5.1(8) to A.66.6.5.4, A.66.19.5.7.2 to A.66.19.5.7.6
  Hazardous materials, in areas with 60.5.1.5, A.60.5.1.5.3.1
  Motor vehicle fuel dispensing facilities 42.7.2.5.1,
    42.7.4.3(3), 42.9.5
  Outdoor storage
    Forest products .... 31.3.2.1, A.31.3.2.1.1 to
      A.31.3.2.1.10.1
    Tires 33.1.6, 33.7.3
  Refrigeration machinery rooms 53.2.3.2, A.53.2.3.2
  Spray application, flammable and combustible
    liquids ..... 43.1.4, 43.1.8.5 to 43.1.8.12, 43.5.3.6, 43.7.5
    to 43.7.7, 43.8.5, A.43.1.4.1 to A.43.1.4.6, A.43.1.8.5 to
    A.43.1.8.12, A.43.7.6, A.43.8.5.3
  Sprinkler system impairment program .... 13.3.3.6.5.2(4)(d),
    A.13.3.3.6.5.2(4)(d)
Illumination of means of egress .... 4.3.3.2.3, 5.3.4(10), 14.12,
    14.14.5, 14.14.6, 20.1.4.6, 65.10.3.14.7, A.14.12.1.1 to
    A.14.12.1.4, A.14.14.5.1 to A.14.14.5.2.2, A.14.14.6.1 to
    A.14.14.6.3; see also Emergency lighting
Immediately dangerous to life and health (IDLH) 53.2.3.3.13,
    54.2.2.4(2)
  Definition 3.3.153, A.3.3.153
Imminent danger .... 1.3.2.4.3, 1.7.7.5, 1.7.15(3), 1.7.16, 1.16.5,
    10.3.2(2), 11.1.2.2
  Definition 3.3.154
Impeded egress, Use Condition IV .... 13.3.2.13.1, 20.7.2.1.1(2),
    20.7.2.1.2, A.20.7.2.1.2
  Definition 3.3.183.8.1.4
Important buildings
  Definition 3.3.29.7, A.3.3.29.7
  Flammable and combustible liquids storage, handling,
    and use 66.14.5.2, 66.17.3.1, 66.17.4.3,
    66.17.4.4, 66.17.4.6, 66.17.6.13, 66.22.4.1, Table
    66.24.4.2, 66.24.4.6, 66.24.5.4, 66.25.4(3),
    66.27.4.4.4(2), 66.27.5.3.2, A.66.17.4.6, A.66.24.5.4
  LP-Gas storage, handling, and use 69.3.3.1.1,
    69.5.4.1.2, A.69.3.3.1.1
  Motor fuel dispensing facilities .... Table 42.3.3.2.4,
    42.3.3.3.8(3), 42.8.3.1 to 42.8.3.3
Incapacitation (definition) 3.4.11
Incidental liquid use or storage (definition) 3.3.156
Incident commanders
  Definition 3.3.155, A.3.3.155
  Duties and powers 1.8
  Liability 1.9
Incinerators .... 5.3.3(4), 10.10, 11.6, 12.4.3, A.10.10.3.1 to
    A.10.10.9.1, A.12.4.3
  Forest products, storage of 31.3.2.1.10,
    A.31.3.2.1.10.1

Refrigerant flaring systems 53.2.2
Tires, outside storage of 33.1.6.3
Wildland fire-prone areas 17.3.5.2.1.11.2
Incompatible materials
   Definition 3.3.173.9, A.3.3.173.9
   Flammable and combustible liquids, separation of 66.9.17
   Hazardous materials, separation of 60.5.1.12
Independent review 1.15, 5.1.5, 15.5, A.5.1.5
Indicating valves 43.1.7.4.5
   Definition 3.3.268.1
Indoor areas
   Definition 3.3.14.5
   Hazardous materials 60.4.2.2, 60.4.3
Industrial occupancies 20.14
   Christmas tree provisions .... Table 10.13.1.1
   Definition 3.3.183.14, 6.1.12.1, A.3.3.183.14, A.6.1.12.1
   Detection, alarm, and communication systems 13.7.2.27
   Extinguishers, portable fire .... Table 13.6.1.2
   Fire fighter safety building marking system
      (FFSBMS) .... E.1.3.5(1)
   Hazardous materials storage and use 60.4.2.1.11,
      60.4.2.1.13, 60.6
   LP-Gas use in 69.3.10.5
   Means of egress, occupant load .... Table 14.8.1.2
   Motor vehicle fuel dispensing facilities ...*see* Motor fuel dispensing facilities
   Multiple occupancies .... 6.1.14.1.3, Table 6.1.14.4.1(a),
      Table 6.1.14.4.1(b), A.6.1.14.1.3
   Sprinkler systems 13.3.2.30
Industrial ovens and furnaces .... Table 1.12.8(a), Chap. 51,
   61.2.8.2(12), 61.5.3.1.1(12), 66.6.5.1(12)
Industrial trucks 10.17, 42.11.2.5
   Aerosol products storage, handling, and use 61.5.2
   Combustible fiber storage room or building 45.4
   Dust explosion and fire prevention 40.4.8,
      A.40.4.8.2
   Flammable and combustible liquids storage, handling,
      and use 66.9.3.9.3, A.66.9.3.9.3
   Hazardous materials, in areas with 60.5.1.5.3.1,
      A.60.5.1.5.3.1
   Metal hydride storage systems 63.3.1.5.1.11.1
   Spray areas 43.1.3.4
   Storage occupancies 34.6.1
Inert cryogenic fluid .... *see* Cryogenic fluids
Inert gas .... Table 1.12.8(b), Table 63.2.3.1.1, 66.18.4.4,
   B.2.1.2.6
   Bulk inert gas systems .... *see* Bulk inert gas systems
   Definition 3.3.135.6, A.3.3.135.6
Information technology equipment .... Chap. 36
Infrared detection systems 40.5.2.4.2, 40.5.2.4.3
Initiating device circuits 13.7.3.1.1.3, A.13.7.3.1.1.3
   Definition 3.3.158
Input data specification 5.5.3, 5.7.7
   Definition 3.4.12
Inside liquid storage areas .... Table 66.7.3.3, 66.9.3,
   66.9.8.2, 66.9.9, 66.9.12.1, 66.9.13, 66.9.14, 66.9.16,
   66.9.18.2, 66.16, A.66.9.3.9.3, A.66.9.8.2, A.66.9.13,
   A.66.9.16.1, A.66.9.16.2, A.66.16.1.1 to A.66.16.8.2
   Definition 3.3.14.6
Inspection, testing, and maintenance .... 4.5.8, A.4.5.8.3 to
   A.4.5.8.5
   Aerosol products storage, handling, and use 61.5.6
   Aircraft fuel servicing 42.10.5.16, 42.10.5.17,
      A.42.10.5.16
   Alarm systems 10.2.5, 13.7.3.2.4, 13.7.3.5.1
   Alternatives, test of 1.4.7
   Authority having jurisdiction, inspections by 1.7.7,
      1.7.13, 1.11.2
   Ceiling tiles and ceiling assemblies 13.3.3.3,
      13.7.4.3.7
   CNG and LNG vehicle fuel dispensing 42.11.1.1.1,
      42.11.1.1.2

   Compressed gases storage and use 63.3.1.6.2,
      63.3.1.8.2
   Construction and installation, inspection of 1.7.13
   Cooking equipment extinguishing and exhaust
      systems ...... 50.2.1.5, 50.4.4.10(4), 50.5, A.50.4.4.10(4),
      A.50.5.2.1 to A.50.5.6.2
   Cryogenic fluids storage 63.4.14.1.3, 63.4.14.9,
      63.4.14.10, A.63.4.14.1.3.2
   Day-care occupancies 20.3.4.2.3, A.20.3.4.2.3.2
   Detection systems .... 13.7.3.5.1, 13.7.4.4 to 13.7.4.7,
      A.13.7.4.7
   Dust explosion and fire prevention 40.4.3.4.6, 40.7,
      A.40.4.3.4.6, A.40.7.1.2(5) to A.40.7.2.5.3
   Emergency command center 11.9.6
   Emergency lighting 14.13.2
   Emergency plans 10.2.5
   Equipment rooms 10.18.5.2
   Exits
      Ambulatory health care occupancies 20.6.2.3
      Day-care occupancies 20.3.4.2.3.2, 20.3.4.2.3.3,
         A.20.3.4.2.3.2
      Educational occupancies 20.2.4.3, A.20.2.4.3.1
      Health care occupancies 20.4.2.3, A.20.4.2.3.3
   Extinguishers, portable fire 13.6.4, 13.6.5, 28.1.6.1.2,
      A.13.6.4.1 to A.13.6.4.11
   Fire department access 18.2.4.1.3, A.18.2.4.1.3
   Fire doors and other opening protectives 12.4.6,
      A.12.4.6.4.1 to A.12.4.6.9.1
   Fire fighter safety building marking system (FFSBMS) E.1.4
   Fire protection systems 10.2.5, 10.12.3, 13.1.1, 13.1.5,
      13.3.3, 18.5.5, 18.5.7, 18.5.9, 34.6.6.2, A.13.3.3.4.1.1 to
      A.13.3.3.6.7, A.34.6.6.2
   Fire pumps .... 13.4.4, 13.4.6 to 13.4.9, A.13.4.4, A.13.4.6.1 to
      A.13.4.7.4(6)
   Fire-resistive construction 12.3.2, 12.3.3, A.12.3.2,
      A.12.3.3
   Flammable and combustible liquids storage, handling,
      and use .... 66.6.9, 66.16.4.3, 66.17.15.4(4), 66.21.5,
      66.21.6.6, 66.21.8, 66.22.10.1, 66.22.17, 66.23.17,
      66.24.16, 66.25.16, 66.27.7, A.66.21.5.2, A.66.21.5.3,
      A.66.21.6.6.1, A.66.21.8.1, A.66.22.17.4
   Folding and telescopic seating 25.4.3
   Forest products, outside storage of .... 31.3.3.2.1(5),
      31.3.4.2(5), 31.3.5.2(5), 31.3.7.3.4, 31.3.8.2(5)
   Grandstands 25.3.6
   Hazardous material storage and use 60.5.1.16, 60.5.1.17,
      A.60.5.1.16.1, A.60.5.1.16.2.3
   Heating, ventilating, and air conditioning systems 12.9.5.4
   Interior finishes 12.5.4, 12.5.8, A.12.5.4, A.12.5.8
   Laboratories using chemicals 26.1.5, A.26.1.5.1
   Membrane structures 25.5.4, 25.6.6
   Motor fuel dispensing devices 42.5.3.6, 42.5.3.9.1,
      A.42.5.3.6.1, A.42.5.3.6.2
   Other enforcement officials, inspections by 1.7.6,
      A.1.7.6.1
   Owner/occupant requirements 10.2.3, 13.3.3.4.1.1,
      A.13.3.3.4.1.1
   Performance-based design features 5.1.10, A.5.1.10
   Private fire service mains 13.5.4
   Refrigeration, mechanical 53.3
   Roofing kettles 16.7.3
   Rubbish chutes, laundry chutes, and incinerators 11.6.2
   Seasonal and vacant buildings 10.12.3
   Smoke control 10.2.5, 11.8, A.11.8
   Smoke dampers 12.9.5.4
   Sprinkler systems .... 13.3.3, A.13.3.3.4.1.1 to
      A.13.3.3.6.7
   Standpipe systems 13.2.3
   Stationary generators and standby power systems 11.7.5
   Storage occupancies 34.6.6, A.34.6.6
   Tank vehicles, refueling from 42.7.6.1

INDEX

Wildland fire-prone areas 17.3.9
Wiring, temporary 11.1.6.3.3
Institutional occupancies .... *see also* specific occupancies
   LP-Gas use in 69.3.10.6
Interior finish 12.5, A.12.5
   Airport terminal buildings 21.2.3.2, A.21.2.3.2
   Ambulatory health care centers 20.6.3
   Apartment buildings 20.9.3
   Assembly occupancies 20.1.3, 20.1.4.8
   Business occupancies 20.13.3
   Ceiling .... 12.5.2.1 to 12.5.2.4, 12.5.3.1, 12.5.4 to 12.5.6, 12.5.9.1, A.12.5.4 to A.12.5.5.4
      Ambulatory health care centers 20.6.3.2
      Apartment buildings 20.9.3.2, 20.9.3.3
      Assembly occupancies 20.1.3.2, 20.1.3.3, 20.1.4.8
      Business occupancies 20.13.3.2
      Daycare occupancies 20.3.3.2, 20.3.3.3
      Definition 3.3.112.1
      Detention and correctional occupancies 20.7.3.2, 20.7.3.3
      Educational occupancies 20.2.3.2
      Health care occupancies 20.4.3.2, 20.4.3.4.2
      Hotels and dormitories 20.8.3.2, 20.8.3.3
      Industrial occupancies 20.14.3.2
      Lodging or rooming houses 20.10.3.2
      Mercantile occupancies 20.12.3.2
      One- and two-family dwellings 20.11.3.2
      Residential board and care occupancies 20.5.3.1.2, 20.5.3.1.3, 20.5.3.2.2, 20.5.3.2.3
      Storage occupancies 20.15.3.2
   Daycare occupancies 20.3.3
   Definition 3.3.112.2, A.3.3.112.2
   Detention and correctional occupancies 20.7.3
   Educational occupancies 20.2.3
   Floor 12.5.3.2, 12.5.6.2, 12.5.8, 12.5.9.2, 20.6.3.3, A.12.5.3.2, A.12.5.8
      Apartment buildings 20.9.3.4, 20.9.3.5
      Assembly occupancies 20.1.3.5
      Business occupancies 20.13.3.3
      Daycare occupancies 20.3.3.4
      Definition 3.3.112.3, A.3.3.112.3
      Detention and correctional occupancies 20.7.3.4
      Educational occupancies 20.2.3.3
      Health care occupancies 20.4.3.3, 20.4.3.5
      Hotels and dormitories 20.8.3.4, 20.8.3.5
      Industrial occupancies 20.14.3.3
      Lodging or rooming houses 20.10.3.3
      Mercantile occupancies 20.12.3.3
      Residential board and care occupancies 20.5.3.1.4, 20.5.3.2.4
      Storage occupancies 20.15.3.3
   Fuel dispensing areas, inside buildings 30.1.6.2
   Health care occupancies 20.4.3
   Hotels and dormitories 20.8.3
   Industrial occupancies 20.14.3
   Lodging or rooming houses 20.10.3
   Mercantile occupancies 20.12.3
   One- and two-family dwellings 20.11.3
   Residential board and care occupancies 20.5.3
   Storage occupancies 20.15.3
   Wall .... 12.5.2.1 to 12.5.2.4, 12.5.3.1, 12.5.4 to 12.5.6, 12.5.9.1, A.12.5.4 to A.12.5.5.4
      Ambulatory health care centers 20.6.3.2
      Apartment buildings 20.9.3.2, 20.9.3.3
      Assembly occupancies 20.1.3.2, 20.1.3.3, 20.1.4.8
      Business occupancies 20.13.3.2
      Daycare occupancies 20.3.3.2, 20.3.3.3
      Definition 3.3.112.4
      Detention and correctional occupancies 20.7.3.2, 20.7.3.3
      Educational occupancies 20.2.3.2
      Health care occupancies 20.4.3.2, 20.4.3.4.2
      Hotels and dormitories 20.8.3.2, 20.8.3.3
      Industrial occupancies 20.14.3.2
      Lodging or rooming houses 20.10.3.2
      Mercantile occupancies 20.12.3.2
      One- and two-family dwellings 20.11.3.2
      Residential board and care occupancies 20.5.3.1.2, 20.5.3.1.3, 20.5.3.2.2, 20.5.3.2.3
      Storage occupancies 20.15.3.2
Intermediate bulk containers (IBCs) .... 16.18.5.4.1(2), 66.9, 66.15, 66.16.5.2.1 to 66.16.5.2.5, 66.16.5.2.9, 66.16.5.2.10, 66.18.4.8, 66.18.4.9, A.66.9.4.1 to A.66.9.16.2, A.66.18.4.8
   Definition 3.3.69.6
   Flexible 40.4.3.4, A.40.4.3.4
   Rigid 40.4.3.5, A.40.4.3.5.1, A.40.4.3.5.2
Internal combustion power sources 10.14.10, 11.5.1.5, A.11.5.1.5
Irritant gas (definition) 3.3.135.7
Isolated storage (definition) 3.3.246.5
ISO module (definition) 3.3.160, A.3.3.160

-J-

Joints
   Fire/smoke partitions and barriers 12.7.5.8, 12.8.5, 12.9.7
   Flammable and combustible liquids pipe 66.27.5, A.66.27.5.1.2
Jurisdiction (definition) 3.3.161

-K-

Kerosene burners 11.5.2
Kettles
   Ground (definition) 3.3.140
   Patch (definition) 3.3.196
   Tar .... Table 1.12.8(a), 16.7, 69.3.12.3.5, A.16.7.1.6.2
Key boxes .... *see* Access boxes
Keys 20.7.2.5

-L-

Labeled
   Definition 3.2.5
   Equipment, devices, and materials 10.1.7
Laboratories using chemicals .... Table 1.12.8(a), Chap. 26
Ladders .... 4.5.6.2.2, 5.3.4(6), 28.1.7.2.1.2, 31.3.6.3.3.1
Laundry chutes .... *see* Chutes, rubbish or laundry
Leak detection .... 60.5.1.6.2(7)
   Compressed gas 63.3.1.12.1, A.63.3.3.1.12.1
   Flammable and combustible liquids 66.21.7.5, 66.28.10.2, A.66.21.7.5
Leaks .... *see also* Leak detection; Spillage
   Compressed gas containers 63.3.1.15, 63.3.9.4, A.63.3.1.15.3
   Cryogenic fluid containers 63.4.11
   Definition 66.27.2.3
   Flammable and combustible liquids .... 66.6.6.2(2), 66.6.9.2, 66.6.9.4.3.3, 66.6.9.17.3, 66.6.9.17.10.1, 66.6.9.17.18.4.2, 66.6.9.19.4.5.3, 66.6.9.19.4.7.2, 66.6.9.19.4.7.3.4.1, 66.6.9.19.4.7.5.1(5), 66.6.9.19.4.7.5.6, 66.21.4.1.2, 66.21.4.5.1.3, 66.21.6.6.3, 66.21.8.4, 66.21.8.5, 66.22.7.1.1.2, 66.22.11.4.10, 66.22.17.4, 66.24.9.7, 66.24.15.2(2), 66.27.2.3, 66.27.3.2, 66.27.4.4.4, 66.27.4.4.5(2), 66.27.5.3.2, 66.27.5.3.3, 66.27.6.3, 66.27.7.3, 66.29.10.2, A.66.22.17.4
   LP-Gas .... 69.3.12.5.1.13, 69.3.12.7.10, 69.3.12.9.2, 69.3.13.3.4, 69.4.2.4.1, 69.4.2.4.3(5), 69.4.2.4.5, 69.6.1.1.6, 69.6.2.3.6, 69.6.2.3.7(2)
Liability 1.9
Life safety .... 4.1.3, A.4.1.3; *see also* Means of egress
   Appropriateness of safeguards 4.4.2
   Of audience 32.6.4, A.32.6.4
   Authority having jurisdiction, role of .... *see* Authority having jurisdiction
   Building use, safety during 4.1.3.2, 5.4.5, A.4.1.3.2.1, A.5.4.5.1

2015 Edition

Evaluation, special outdoor events, carnivals,
and fairs 10.14.3, A.10.14.3.1, A.10.14.3.3
Fire fighter safety building marking system (FFSBMS) ... Annex E
Multiple safeguards 4.4.1
Safety from fire .... 4.1.3.1, A.4.1.3.1.1 to
A.4.1.3.1.2.5
Life Safety Code 10.1.2, A.10.1.2
Light hazard occupancies .... *see* Low hazard contents
Lighting
Christmas tree lights 10.13.5, 10.13.6
Compressed gases and cryogenic fluids 63.2.11
Cryogenic fluid containers and systems 63.4.12
Emergency .... *see* Emergency lighting
Fire pump areas 13.4.2.4, 13.4.2.5
Hazardous materials areas 60.5.1.11
Marinas, boatyards, piers, and wharves 28.1.7.1.3,
A.28.1.7.1.3
Means of egress illumination .... *see* Means of egress
Motor vehicle fuel dispensing facilities 42.10.2.2,
A.42.10.2.2.4
Spray application areas
Fixtures 43.1.4.5
Portable lights 43.1.4.8
Sprinkler temperature ratings in area of .... Table 13.3.1.9(c)
Storage occupancies 34.6.8
Temporary .... 11.1.6.3.1 to 11.1.6.3.3
Lightning precautions, aircraft fuel servicing 42.10.5.9,
A.42.10.5.9
Limited access structures .... 10.8.1, 13.3.2.25, 14.13.1.1(2)
Limited care facilities (definition) 3.3.183.15,
A.3.3.183.15; *see also* Health care occupancies
Limited-combustible (material) 4.5.10
Definition 3.3.173.10
Limits
Ceiling (definition) 3.3.162.1, A.3.3.162.1
Permissible exposure limit (PEL) (definition) 3.3.162.2,
A.3.3.162.2
Short-term exposure limit (STEL) (definition) 3.3.162.3,
A.3.3.162.3
Line-type detectors 13.7.4.3.2, 13.7.4.5
Definition 3.3.84.11
Liquefied gas
Definition 3.3.135.8
Hydrogen systems 63.7
Liquefied natural gas (LNG) ......*see* Liquefied natural gas (LNG)
Liquefied petroleum ....*see* LP-Gas
Liquefied hydrogen systems 63.7
Liquefied natural gas (LNG) 69.8
Definition 3.3.135.9
Vehicular fuel 30.2.10.6, 42.8, 42.11.3, A.30.2.10.6,
A.42.8.3.4, A.42.8.6.2, A.42.11.3
Liquid-fired vehicles ....*see* Motor vehicles
Liquid fuel-burning appliances .... Table 1.12.8(a), 11.5.1.1,
11.5.1.9, 11.5.1.10, A.11.5.1.10.1 to A.11.5.1.10.3(4)
Liquid oxygen containers ....*see* oxygen
Liquids ....*see also* Combustible liquids; Flammable liquids; Inside
liquid storage areas; Stable liquids; Unstable (reactive)
materials (solids and liquids); Warehouses, Liquid
Classification 66.4.2, A.66.4.2
Definition 3.3.164
Flash point ....*see* Flash point
Highly volatile .... 60.5.1.6.3(1)
Definition 3.3.164.3
Incidental liquid use or storage (definition) 3.3.156
Storage room ....*see* Inside liquid storage areas
Viscous 6.16.3.4
Definition 66.16.2.4
Liquid storage cabinets 66.9.5, A.66.9.5
Listed
Definition 3.2.6, A.3.2.6
Equipment, devices, and materials 10.1.7
Lockers 12.5.2.6, 12.6.7

Locks and latches .... 14.5.2, A.14.5.2.2 to A.14.5.2.12
Construction sites 16.3.4.3, 16.3.4.4
Day-care occupancies 20.3.2.2, 20.3.2.3,
A.20.3.2.2
Detention and correctional occupancies 20.7.2.1.1,
20.7.2.5
Elevator lobby exit access .... 14.5.3.3, A.14.5.3.3(14)
Fire apparatus access roads or fire lanes 18.2.4.2.5
Lodging or rooming houses 20.10
Christmas tree provisions .... Table 10.13.1.1
Definition 3.3.183.16, 6.1.8.1.2
Detection, alarm, and communication systems 13.7.2.14,
A.13.7.2.14.3.1, A.13.7.2.14.6.2
Extinguishers, portable fire .... Table 13.6.1.2
Hazardous materials storage and use 60.4.2.1.8
Multiple occupancies .... Table 6.1.14.4.1(a),
Table 6.1.14.4.1(b)
Sprinkler systems 13.3.2.19, A.13.3.2.19.2.3
Logs
Definition 3.3.165
Outside storage of .... 31.3.1.1(5), 31.3.2.1.6.2, 31.3.8,
A.31.3.8.1.1 to A.31.3.8.3.6
Loose house 45.5.6
Definition 3.3.166
Low hazard contents E.2.2
Definition 3.3.142.2, A.3.3.142.2
Extinguishers, portable fire 13.6.2.4.1.1,
Table 13.6.3.2.1.1, 13.6.3.4.1.1, A.13.6.2.4.1.1,
A.13.6.3.4.1.1
Storage occupancies .... Table 6.1.14.4.1(a),
Table 6.1.14.4.1(b), 13.7.2.28.1.1
Low melting point materials 42.4.2.7, 66.27.4.4
Definition 66.27.2.4
Low-pressure tanks 66.21.4.2.2
Definition 66.3.3.33.2
LP-Gas .... Chap. 69
Containers .... *see* LP-Gas containers
Definition 3.3.135.10, A.3.3.135.10
Equipment and appliances .... 20.1.5.2.4(5), 69.3.9,
69.3.10.2, 69.3.10.7, 69.3.10.8.4, 69.3.11, 69.3.12.6 to
69.3.12.8, A.69.3.9, A.69.3.10.2.6, A.69.3.12.7.6
Motion picture production soundstages, facilities, and
locations, use at 32.6.2.2
Permits .... Table 1.12.8(a), Table 1.12.8(d), 69.1.2
Piping, fittings, and valves .... 69.2.3, 69.3.9, 69.3.10.2.3 to
69.3.10.2.5, 69.3.12.5, A.69.3.9
Systems ....*see* LP-Gas systems
Tar kettles, use with 16.7.2, 16.7.4.2.6, 69.3.12.3.5
Transfer operations, location of 69.3.5, 69.4,
A.69.3.5.1.1, A.69.4.1 to A.69.4.2.3.5.1
Utility plants, at 69.7
Vehicular fuel 42.8, 42.11.2, 69.3.13, A.42.8.3.4,
A.42.8.6.2, A.42.11.2.2.1 to A.42.11.2.4.4
Vehicular transportation of 69.6, A.69.6.2.2.2
Wildland/urban interface, tanks in 17.3.5.2.1.11.4
LP-Gas containers .... 69.2, A.69.2.1.1.1 to A.69.2.1.4.3
Appurtenances 69.2.1.2, 69.2.2, 69.3.12.4
ASME ....*see* ASME containers or tanks
On balconies 69.3.10, A.69.3.10.2.6, A.69.3.10.8.3
Boat storage and .... 28.1.7.2.1.5(2)
In buildings 69.3.10, 69.5.2.1.3, 69.5.2.1.4, 69.5.3,
A.69.3.10.2.6, A.69.3.10.8.3
Definition 3.3.69.7
Exchange stations, automated 69.5.6
Filling and evacuating 69.4.2.2, A.69.4.2.2.5
Fire protection for 69.6.1.2
Installation .... 69.3.1 to 6.9.3.4, 69.3.6, A.69.3.1 to
A.69.3.4.5, A.69.3.6.1.4
Location .... 69.3.2 to 6.9.3.4, A.69.3.3.1.1 to
A.69.3.4.5
Marking 69.2.1.1.1, 69.2.1.4, A.69.2.1.1.1,
A.69.2.1.4.2, A.69.2.1.4.3

INDEX

Outside storage .... 69.5.4, A.69.5.4.1 to A.69.5.4.2.2
Portable .... 69.2.1.2, 69.5, A.69.5.4.1 to A.69.5.5
Refrigerated 69.3.4.4.14, A.69.3.4.4.14
On roofs 69.3.10, A.69.3.10.2.6, A.69.3.10.8.3
Special storage buildings 69.5.3.4
Storage of containers awaiting use or resale .... 69.5, A.69.5.4.1 to A.69.5.5
Tents, membrane structures, grandstands, and folding/telescopic seating 25.1.4.1, 25.1.10.1.6
Underground .... Table 69.3.3.1.1, 69.3.3.2, 69.3.3.4.5, 69.3.4.2
Vehicle (other than engine fuel system) 69.3.12.3
Vehicular transportation of 69.6.1

LP-Gas systems
In buildings, on roofs, or on balconies 69.3.10, A.69.3.10.2.6, A.69.3.10.8.3
Fire protection 69.5.5, 69.6.1.2, A.69.5.5
Installation of .... 69.3, A.69.3.1 to A.69.3.12.7.6
Snowfall, systems in areas of heavy 69.3.9, A.69.3.9
Tampering, protection against 69.3.13.3.7
On vehicles (other than engine fuel systems) 69.3.12, A.69.3.12.1, A.69.3.12.7.6

Lumber
Definition 3.3.167
Storage, manufacturing, and processing of .... Chap. 31

Lumber yards .... Table 1.12.8(a), 31.3.1 to 31.3.4, A.31.3.2.1.1 to A.31.3.4.3.1

-M-

Maintenance .... *see* Inspection, testing, and maintenance
Make-up air 43.1.5.3, 66.7.3.7.1, 66.17.11.7, 66.18.6.4.1, 66.24.10.4, A.43.1.5.3, A.66.17.11.7, A.66.24.10.4

Mall buildings
Extinguishing systems 13.3.2.23.4
Multiple occupancies .... Table 6.1.14.4.1(a), Table 6.1.14.4.1(b)
Occupant load factor .... Fig. 14.8.1.2(a), Fig. 14.8.1.2(b)
Permit requirements .... Table 1.12.8(a)

Manual emergency shutoff valves
Cryogenic fluids, outdoor use 63.4.14.11.2.3, A.63.4.14.11.2.3.1
Definition 3.3.168

Manual fire alarm boxes .... 13.7.1.7.1 to 13.7.1.7.7, 13.7.3.3, 14.5.3.2(5), A.13.7.1.7.5 to A.13.7.1.7.7, A.13.7.3.3.7 to A.13.7.3.3.8.5, A.20.6.2.2.1
Airports 21.2.7.1
Ambulatory health care occupancies 13.7.2.9.2, 13.7.2.10.2, 20.6.2.2.3.3
Apartment buildings 13.7.2.17.2, 13.7.2.18.2
Assembly occupancies 13.7.2.1.2.1, 13.7.2.2.2.1
Business occupancies .... 13.7.2.25.2(1), 13.7.2.26.2(1)
Construction sites 16.3.3.1
Day-care occupancies 13.7.2.5.2, 13.7.2.6.2
Definition 3.3.169
Detention and correctional occupancies 13.7.2.11.2, 13.7.2.12.2
Educational occupancies 13.7.2.3.2.1, 13.7.2.3.2.3, 13.7.2.4.2.1, 13.7.2.4.2.3, A.13.7.2.3.2.3.1, A.13.7.2.3.2.3.2, A.13.7.2.4.2.3.1, A.13.7.2.4.2.3.2
Health care occupancies 13.7.2.7.2, 13.7.2.8.2, A.13.7.2.7.2, A.13.7.2.8.2
Heliports, rooftop 21.3.4.7.2, 21.3.4.8.1, A.21.3.4.7.2
Hotels and dormitories 13.7.2.15.2, 13.7.2.16.2
Industrial occupancies 13.7.2.27.2
Mercantile occupancies 13.7.2.23.2, 13.7.2.24.2
Residential board and care occupancies 13.7.2.19.1, 13.7.2.20.2, 13.7.2.21.1, 13.7.2.22.2
Storage occupancies 13.7.2.28.2

Manual fire suppression equipment .... 20.7.2.1.4, 33.4.1, 43.1.7.7.2(3), 43.1.7.8.2(2), 50.4.7; *see also* Extinguishers, portable fire
Heliports, rooftop 21.3.4.6.4, A.21.3.4.6.4.1
Storage tank buildings, flammable and combustible liquids storage 66.24.6.1, A.66.24.6.1.1, A.66.24.6.1.2

Manual pull stations .... *see* Manual fire alarm boxes
Manufactured homes sites 27.1, 27.2
Manufactured housing .... 17.3.5.2.1.9, 20.11.5, 27.1.1, 27.2; *see also* One- and two-family dwellings
Marinas .... 28.1, A.28.1.6.2 to A.28.1.8.2.6(7)
Marine motor fuel dispensing facilities .... Table 1.12.8(a), 28.1.6.1.1.2, 28.1.8.2.6(6), 28.1.8.2.7, 42.3.2.1(4), 42.5.6.4, 42.9, A.42.9.2.2 to A.42.9.8.2; *see also* Motor fuel dispensing facilities
Definition 3.3.183.19.2
Marine piping, flammable and combustible liquids 66.27.11
Marine terminals .... 28.2, A.28.2.2 to A.28.2.3(2)
Definition 3.3.171
Marine vessels 1.3.5
Construction, repair, and lay-up of 28.3, A.28.3.1
Definition 3.3.172
Marking .... *see also* Signs
Aerosol products 61.1.5, 61.3.1.2
Central station fire alarm systems 13.7.3.4, A.13.7.3.4
Compressed gas containers, cylinders, and tanks 63.3.1.5.1.7, 63.3.1.6.1, 63.3.1.8
Compressed gas ventilation system 63.2.16.7
Cryogenic containers and systems 63.2.16.7, 63.4.4, A.63.4.4.1.1.2
Disconnecting means 11.1.7.3
Extinguishers, portable fire .... 13.6.1.3, 13.6.1.4, 13.6.3.1.3.9, 13.6.4.1.4, 13.6.4.2.4.1.1, 13.6.4.3.4.1, 13.6.4.3.4.2, 13.6.4.3.6.5, 13.6.5.1.2, A.13.6.1.3.1 to A.13.6.1.3.3, A.13.6.1.4, A.13.6.4.3.6.5
Fire alarm systems 13.7.3.4, A.13.7.3.4
Fire apparatus access road or fire lane 18.2.3.5
Fire fighter safety building marking system (FFSBMS) ... Annex E
Fire hydrants 18.5.10, A.18.5.10.3
Fire protection .... 5.3.3(5), 10.11, A.10.11.1.1 to A.10.11.3.4
Flammable and combustible liquid piping systems 66.27.10, A.66.27.10
Flammable and combustible liquids storage cabinets 66.9.5.5, A.66.9.5.5
Flammable and combustible liquids storage tanks 66.21.7.2, A.66.21.7.2.2
Hazardous materials tanks 60.5.1.19.3
LP-Gas containers 69.2.1.1.1, 69.2.1.4, A.69.2.1.1.1, A.69.2.1.4.2, A.69.2.1.4.3
LP-Gas fuel dispensing stations 69.3.13.3.18
LP-Gas fueled vehicles 42.11.2.4, A.42.11.2.4.4
Means of egress .... 14.11.3, 14.14, A.14.1.4.1.2.1 to A.14.14.8.3, A.14.11.3.3
Motor fuel dispensing facility fill pipes 42.4.2.5
Photovoltaic systems 11.12.2.1, A.11.12.2.1
Sprinkler systems, impairment of 13.3.3.6.3, A.13.3.3.6.3.1, A.13.3.3.6.3.2

Materials
Compatible (definition) 3.3.173.2
Corrosive .... *see* Corrosive material
Hazardous .... *see* Hazardous materials
Health hazard .... *see* Health hazard materials
Highly toxic .... *see* Highly toxic materials
Hogged .... *see* Hogged material
Incompatible .... *see* Incompatible materials
Physical hazard .... *see* Physical hazard materials
Toxic .... *see* Toxic materials
Unstable (reactive) .... *see* Unstable (reactive) materials
Water-reactive .... *see* Water-reactive materials

Material safety data sheet (MSDS) 43.7.9, 60.5.1.2, A.60.5.1.2
   Definition 3.3.174
Mattresses ...... 12.6.3, A.12.6.3.1 to A.12.6.3.2.2; *see also* Furnishings
   Ambulatory health care occupancies .... 20.6.2.5, A.20.6.2.5.1 to A.20.6.2.5.5.2
   Day-care homes 20.3.4.2.3.5.4
   Detention and correctional occupancies 20.7.2.4.3, A.20.7.2.4.3
   Health care occupancies .... 20.4.2.5, A.20.4.2.5.1 to A.20.4.2.5.8(2)
   Hotels or dormitories 20.8.2.5.2.2
   Residential board and care occupancies 20.5.2.5.2.3, A.20.5.2.5.2.3
Maximum allowable quantities .... Table 1.12.8(d), 60.1.3.1, 60.4.2.1.1.2, 60.4.2.1.1.3, 60.4.2.1.2 to 60.4.2.1.13, 66.9.6
   Definition 3.3.175, A.3.3.175
   Storage and use in amounts exceeding 60.1.3.2, 73.1.2, 75.1.2
Maze, crop 10.14.11, A.10.14.11.3.1
Means of egress .... 4.4.3, Chap. 14; *see also* Doors; Exits; specific occupancies
   Accessible 14.9.1.3, 14.10.4, A.14.10.4.1
   Aerosol products, buildings for 61.2.2.2, 61.5.1
   Aircraft hangars 21.1.4, 21.1.5, A.21.1.4, A.21.1.5
   Airport terminal buildings 21.2.5, A.21.2.5.2
   Arrangement of .... 14.10, A.14.10.1.1.1 to A.14.10.4.1
   Awareness of egress system 4.4.3.2
   Buildings under construction 10.3.3, 16.1.3, 16.3.4.5, 16.7.1.7, A.10.3.3, A.16.1.3
   Capacity of .... 5.3.4(8), 14.8, A.14.8.1.2 to A.14.8.3.4.1.1
   Combustible materials storage 10.18.4
   Definition 3.3.176, A.3.3.176
   Exterior ways of exit access 14.10.3
   Heliports, roof-top 21.3.3.7, 21.3.4.4, A.21.3.3.7, A.21.3.4.4
   Illumination .... *see* Illumination of means of egress
   Impediments to egress .... 4.5.6.3, 5.3.4(9), 14.4.1, 14.4.3, 14.10.2, A.14.4.1
   Marking of .... 5.3.4(12), 14.14, 20.1.4.7, A.14.1.4.1.2.1 to A.14.14.8.3, A.20.1.4.7.3
   Motion picture production soundstages, facilities, and locations 32.4.10, 32.5.10, A.32.5.10
   Motor vehicle fuel dispensing facilities 30.1.3
   Number of 14.9
   Performance-based design option 5.3.4
   Permits .... Table 1.12.8(a)
   Reliability 14.4, A.14.4.1
   Repair garages 30.2.4
   Roof 11.12.2.2.1
   Tents, membrane structures, grandstands, and folding/telescopic seating 25.1.3
   Unobstructed egress 4.4.3.1
   Width of .... 14.8.2, Table 14.8.3.1, 14.8.3.4, A.14.8.3.4.1.1
Means of escape 5.3.4, 14.15
   Buildings under construction 4.5.6.2, 16.1.3, A.16.1.3
   Definition 3.3.177
Measurement, units of 1.5
Mechanical code (definition) 3.3.53.3
Medical cryogenic systems 63.4.5
Medical gas systems 11.11, 63.3.4
Membrane penetrations .... 12.7.5.6, 12.9.6.1, A.12.7.5.6.3(1)(c)
Membrane structures
   Permanent .... Table 1.12.8(a), 25.1, 25.5, A.25.1.4.2, A.25.1.8, A.25.5.3.3.1
   Temporary .... Table 1.12.8(a), 25.1, 25.6, A.25.1.4.2, A.25.1.8

Mercantile occupancies 13.3.2.23, 13.3.2.24, 20.12
   Aerosol products 61.4
   Christmas tree provisions .... Table 10.13.1.1
   Class A (definition) 3.3.183.17.1
   Class B (definition) 3.3.183.17.2
   Class C (definition) 3.3.183.17.3
   Definition 3.3.183.17, 6.1.10.1, A.3.3.191.17, A.6.1.10.1
   Detection, alarm, and communication systems 13.7.2.23, 13.7.2.24
   Extinguishers, portable fire .... Table 13.6.1.2, 20.12.2.3
   Fire fighter safety building marking system (FFSBMS) .... E.1.3.5(1)
   Flammable and combustible liquids 66.17.15.2
   Hazardous materials storage and use 60.4.2.1.9, 60.4.2.1.13
   Means of egress, occupant load .... Table 14.8.1.2
   Multiple occupancies .... 6.1.14.1.3, Table 6.1.14.4.1(a), Table 6.1.14.4.1(b), A.6.1.14.1.3
   Sprinkler systems 13.3.2.23.3, 13.3.2.24.2
Metal hydride storage systems 63.3.1.5, A.63.3.1.5
Metals, combustible .... B.2.1.4.3; *see also* Class D fires
Mezzanines
   Definition 3.3.178
   Means of egress 14.8.1.6, 14.9.1.1, 21.1.4.3, 21.1.5.2
Mini-storage buildings .... *see* Storage occupancies
Mixed occupancies .... 6.1.14.1.1(1), 6.1.14.3
   Definition 3.3.183.18, 6.1.14.2.2
Mixing rooms 13.3.3.5.1.8, 43.1.6.3, 43.1.7.1, A.13.3.3.5.1.8.1, A.43.1.7.1
Mobile homes 17.3.5.2.1.9
Mobile storage unit, consumer fireworks 65.10.3.12, A.65.10.3.12
Mobile supply units
   Cryogenic fluids 63.4.14.1.2
   Definition 3.3.179, A.3.3.179
Model rocketry .... *see* Rockets, model
Modifications, code 1.4, 4.5.1.2, 4.5.2
Motion picture production soundstages, facilities, and locations .... Table 1.12.8(a), 20.16.1.2, Chap. 32
Motor fuel dispensing facilities .... 30.1, 30.3, Chap. 42, A.30.1.5.1 to A.30.1.6.9
   Aircraft .... *see* Aircraft fuel servicing
   Alternate fuels .... 42.8, 42.11, A.42.8.3.4, A.42.8.6.2, A.42.11.1.1 to A.42.11.3
   Definition 3.3.183.19
   Fleet vehicle motor fuel dispensing facilities 42.2.1.1, 42.2.1.2, 42.3.3.2.6
   Definition 3.3.183.19.1
   Forest products storage, manufacturing, and processing 31.3.2.1.6.1, A.31.3.2.1.6.1
   Located inside buildings 30.1.6, 30.3, 42.2.1.1, 42.3.2.1, 42.3.3.9, A.30.1.6.7, A.30.1.6.9
   Definition 3.3.183.19.3, A.3.3.183.19.3
   Marine .... *see* Marine motor fuel dispensing facilities
   Permits .... Table 1.12.8(a), 30.1.1.3, 42.2.2.1, 42.9.1.4, 42.11.2.2.4, 42.11.3.1
   Piping 42.4
   Storage requirements .... 42.3, A.42.3.3.2 to A.42.3.3.8
Motor vehicle fluids 22.9
   Definition 3.3.180
Motor vehicles .... 1.3.5; *see also* Salvage vehicles
   Aerosol products storage, handling, and use .... 61.2.8.2(13), 61.5.3.1.1(13)
   Air bag systems 22.9.4
   Alternative fuels .... *see* Compressed gas systems; LP-Gas systems
   Combustible fiber storage room or building, use in/near 45.4
   Cryogenic fluids, loading and unloading of 63.4.14.11.3.3
   Exposition facilities .... Table 1.12.8(a), 20.1.5.5.4.12
   Forest products, storage of 31.3.2.1.6, 31.3.2.1.10, A.31.3.2.1.6.1, A.31.3.2.1.10.1

Fueled equipment, storage of 10.18.7
Hazardous materials areas, protection of 60.5.1.9
Motion picture production soundstages, facilities, and
  locations .... 32.4.2(6), 32.5.2(7)
Spray application, undercoating and body lining 43.5.1
Tanks/vaults, collision protection for 66.22.15,
  66.25.5.2.2
Waste or refuse transport 19.1.8
Wrecking yards .... Table 1.12.8(a), Chap. 22
Moving walks 14.11.4
Multilevel play structures 20.1.4.1, A.20.1.4.1
Multiple occupancies .... 1.3.4, 6.1.14, A.6.1.14.1.3 to
  A.6.1.14.4.5
  Definition 3.3.183.20, 6.1.14.2.1
Multiplug adapters 11.1.3

-N-

Natural barricades .... *see* Barricades
Nesting 63.3.1.9.5.2, 63.4.6.3.2
  Definition 3.3.181
No exit, marking of 14.14.8.3, A.14.14.8.3
Noncombustible material .... 4.5.9, A.4.5.9(1)
  Definition 3.3.173.11
  Photovoltaic system base 11.12.3.2, A.11.12.3.2
Nondedicated smoke control systems (definition) 3.3.254.12
Nonflammable cryogens .... Table 1.12.8(c)
Nonflammable gas (definition) 3.3.135.11
Normal temperature and pressure (NTP) (definition) 3.3.182,
  A.3.3.182, A.63.1.3.40
Notice of violations, penalties 1.16
Notification
  Emergency forces .... 10.14.9, 13.7.1.10, 32.6.5, 42.7.4.3(4),
    42.7.5.5, 53.3.1.7, 60.5.1.3.4, A.60.5.1.3.4
  Occupant notification 4.4.4, 13.7.1.9, A.4.4.4,
    A.13.7.1.9.2.1 to A.13.7.1.9.6.2
Nozzles, dust control and 40.5.4.2, A.40.5.2.2,
  A.40.5.4.2.1
Nursing homes .... *see also* Health care occupancies
  Definition 3.3.183.21
  Smoke detection systems 13.7.2.7.5.3,
    A.13.7.2.7.5.3

-O-

Objectives 4.1.2, A.4.1, A.4.1.2
  Compliance options 4.3
  Fire department service 15.2
  Performance-based design 5.1.2
  Property protection 4.1.4.2, A.4.1.4.2.1, A.4.1.4.2.2
  Public welfare 4.1.5.2, A.4.1.5.2
  Safety-during-building-use 4.1.3.2.2
  Safety-from-fire 4.1.3.1.2, A.4.1.3.1.2.2,
    A.4.1.3.1.2.5
  Safety-from-hazardous materials 4.1.3.3.2,
    A.4.1.3.3.2.2
Occupancies .... *see also* specific occupancies, e.g., Assembly
    occupancies
  Certificate of occupancy 1.7.14
  Changes of .... Table 1.12.8(a), 4.5.7, 10.2.2, 10.3.4,
    13.3.3.4.1.6, 13.3.3.4.1.7, 32.4.2(8), A.4.5.7,
    A.13.3.3.4.1.6, A.13.3.3.4.1.7, A.32.4.2(8)
  Classification of .... Chap. 6, E.1.3.5
  Definition 3.3.183
  Multiple 1.3.4
Occupancy, conditions for 4.5.4, 10.3, A.10.3.3
Occupancy fire safety .... Chap. 20
Occupant characteristics (definition) 3.4.13
Occupant load 14.8.1, 14.8.3.3, 14.9.1.2, 14.9.1.4,
  A.14.8.1.2
  Assembly occupancies, posting in 20.1.5.10.3
  Definition 3.3.184

Occupant notification 4.4.4, 13.7.1.9, A.4.4.4,
  A.13.7.1.9.2.1 to A.13.7.1.9.6.2
**Occupant protection, performance-based design
  option** 5.2.2.6, 5.2.2.8
Occupant responsibilities 10.2
  Extinguishers, portable fire 13.6.4.1.1
  Fire reporting requirements 10.6.1.3, A.10.6.1.3
Occupiable story (definition) 3.3.248.1
Oil, cooking .... *see* Cooking oil
Oil burners .... *see* Liquid fuel-burning appliances
Oil-fueled heating appliances .... *see* Heating equipment and
  appliances
Oil stoves 11.5.2
One- and two-family dwellings 20.11, A.20.11.4.4
  Access to 18.2.3.2.1.1
  Christmas tree provisions .... Table 10.13.1.1
  Definition 3.3.183.22, 6.1.8.1.1, A.6.1.8.1.1
  Detection, alarm, and communication systems 13.7.2.13,
    A.13.7.2.13.1.1 to A.13.7.2.13.2.2
  Extinguishers, portable fire .... Table 13.6.1.2
  Fire flow requirements 18.4.5.1, 18.4.5.2,
    A.18.4.5.1.2 to A.18.4.5.2.5
  Fire hydrants for 18.5.2
  Multiple occupancies .... Table 6.1.14.4.1(a),
    Table 6.1.14.4.1(b)
  Photovoltaic systems 11.12.2.2.2
  Sprinkler systems .... 13.3.2.20, Table 13.8, 18.2.3.2.1.1,
    18.4.5.1.2, 18.4.5.1.3, 18.4.5.2.2, 18.4.5.2.4, A.18.4.5.1.2,
    A.18.4.5.1.3
One- and two-family dwelling units (definition) 3.3.183.22.1,
  6.1.8.1.1, A.6.1.8.1.1; *see also* Dwelling units
Open fires .... 5.3.3(4), 10.10, A.10.10.3.1 to A.10.10.9.1
  Automobile wrecking yards 22.8
  Permit requirements .... Table 1.12.8(a)
  Tires, outside storage of 33.1.6.2
Open-flame devices .... 5.3.3(4)
  Assembly occupancies 20.1.5.3, 20.1.5.5.4.8,
    A.20.1.5.3(3)(a)
  Hazardous materials, in areas with 60.5.1.5.2
  Marinas and boatyards, use at 28.1.7.2.1.3
Open flames .... 10.1.6, 10.10, 10.13.7, A.10.10.3.1 to
  A.10.10.9.1
  Aerosol products storage, handling, and use .... 61.2.8.2(1),
    61.5.3.1.1(1)
  Aircraft fuel servicing 42.10.5.8
  Buildings under construction 16.2.3.1.4
  Compressed gases and cryogenic fluids 63.3.6.4.2
  Dust explosion and fire prevention 40.4.5
  Fibers, combustible, storage and handling 19.1.7
  Forest products, storage of 31.3.2.1.12
  Motion picture production soundstages, facilities,
    and locations .... 32.4.2(2), 32.4.3, 32.5.2(3),
    32.5.3, A.32.4.3.1
  Motor fuel dispensing facilities .... 42.9.10.4(2)
  Permit requirements .... Table 1.12.8(a), 32.4.2(2)
  Refrigerant machinery rooms 53.2.3.2, A.53.2.3.2
  Spray application operations 43.1.4.1.5, 43.5.3.6,
    A.43.1.4.1.5
  Tents and temporary membrane structures 25.1.5.4
  Tires, outside storage of 33.7.3
Opening protectives .... *see also* Fire door assemblies; Fire windows
  Combustible fiber storage room or building 45.5.3.2,
    45.5.4.3, 45.5.4.4
  Fire barriers .... 12.7.3, 12.7.4, A.12.7.3.2 to
    A.12.7.3.6, A.12.7.4.2
  Fuel dispensing areas, inside buildings 30.1.6.3
  Smoke barriers and partitions 12.8.3, 12.9.4,
    A.12.8.3.4, A.12.9.4.1, A.12.9.4.4
  Temporary separation walls 16.4.2.3, 16.4.2.4,
    A.16.4.2.4
Openings
  Aerosol products, buildings for 61.2.2.1
  Airport ramps, openings facing 21.2.3.5

2015 Edition

Compressed gases and cryogenic fluids 63.3.9.2.2.2
Conveyor, spray areas 43.1.3.2
Door .... 14.5, A.14.5.1.1 to A.14.5.1.3.1
Exit enclosures .... 14.3.1, A.14.3.1(1) to 14.3.1(10)(b)
Flammable and combustible liquids storage, handling, and use 66.9.9.2, 66.22.13, 66.23.13, 66.24.14, A.66.24.14.6, A.66.24.14.8
Hot work operations .... 41.3.4.2(4), 41.3.5.1(3)
Smoke barriers 12.9.6
Vertical .... 4.4.5 *see also* Penetrations
   For conveyors, elevators, and dumbwaiters 11.3.5
   Marking of shaftways 10.11.2
   Protectives, minimum ratings for .... Table 12.7.4.2
   Rubbish chutes and laundry chutes .... *see* Chutes, rubbish or laundry

Open parking structures 13.3.2.5, 13.3.2.15.5, 13.3.2.17.7, 18.4.5.3.5, 29.1.1
   Definition 3.3.183.23.3
Open plan buildings 20.2.2, 20.3.2.4, 20.3.4.2.3.3
Open system use (definition) 3.3.267.2, A.3.3.267.2
Operating or process unit (vessel) .... 66.6.4.1.1(2), 66.17.4.1 to 66.17.4.5, 66.17.14, 66.18.4.4, 66.18.5.2, 66.21.4.2.3, A.66.17.14, A.66.21.4.2.3.2
   Definition 3.3.187, A.3.3.187
Operating pressure (definition) 3.3.186
Operations and maintenance (O & M) manual 5.1.8, A.5.1.8
Operations (definition) 3.3.188
Operators, responsibilities of .... *see* Owners, responsibilities of
Ordinance adopting code, sample .... Annex C
Ordinary hazard contents E.2.2
   Definition 3.3.142.3, A.3.3.142.3
   Extinguishers, portable fire .... 13.6.2.4.1.2, Table 13.6.3.2.1.1, A.13.6.2.4.1.2
   Storage occupancies .... Table 6.1.14.4.1(a), Table 6.1.14.4.1(b), 13.7.2.28.1.2
Organic coatings .... *see* Coating processes
Organic peroxide .... 44.4, Table 60.4.2.1.1.3, Table 60.4.3.7, Table 60.4.4.1.2, Chap. 75; *see also* Hazardous materials
   Definition 3.3.189
   Permits .... Table 1.12.8(a), Table 1.12.8(d)
   Peroxide-forming chemical (definition) 3.3.199
   Specific occupancies, storage and use in .... Tables 60.4.2.1.2 to 60.4.2.1.8, Table 60.4.2.1.10.1
   Spray application of .... 43.7, 43.8.7, A.43.7.1 to A.43.7.6
   Storage, use, and handling 75.1.2
   Storage area (definition) 3.3.14.7
Organic peroxide formulations B.2.1.6, B.5.1, B.5.3
   Class I B.5.3.2
     Definition 3.3.189.1.1
   Class II B.5.3.3
     Definition 3.3.189.1.2
   Class III B.5.3.4
     Definition 3.3.189.1.3
   Class IV B.5.3.5
     Definition 3.3.189.1.4
   Class V B.5.3.6
     Definition 3.3.189.1.5
   Definition 3.3.189.1, A.3.3.189.1
OSHA (definition) 3.3.190
Outdoor areas 60.4.1.2, 60.4.4, 63.2.6
   Definition 3.3.14.8
Outdoor storage .... 10.15, Chap. 34, A.10.15; *see also* Yards
   Compressed gases 63.2.6
   Cryogenic fluid containers .... 63.4.13.2, A.63.4.13.2.5 to A.63.4.13.2.7.2.1
   Flammable and combustible liquids 66.9.19, 66.15
   Forest products .... Chap. 31
   Hazardous materials .... *see* Hazardous materials

LP-Gas portable containers .... 69.5.4, A.69.5.4.1 to A.69.5.4.2.2
Tires .... *see* Tires
Ovens and furnaces .... *see* Industrial ovens and furnaces
Overcrowded 10.4.2, A.10.4.2
   Definition 3.3.191
Owners, responsibilities of 10.2, 13.1.2, 13.2.3.2
   Buildings under construction .... 16.3.2, A.16.3.2.1 to A.16.3.2.5.5
   Extinguishers, portable fire 13.6.4.1.1
   Fire reporting requirements 10.6.1.3, A.10.6.1.3
   Hot work 41.4, A.41.4.1
   Marine vessels, fueling of 42.9.10.7
   Private fire service mains 13.5.4.1
   Sprinkler systems .... 13.3.3.3.4.1, A.13.3.3.3.4.1.1 to A.13.3.3.3.4.1.9.2
Oxidizers .... Table 60.4.2.1.1.3, Table 60.4.2.1.13.3(a), Table 60.4.3.7, Table 60.4.4.1.2, 66.9.17.3, Chap. 70; *see also* Hazardous materials
   Class 1 .... B.2.1.5.4.4, B.5.2.2
     Definition 3.3.192.1
   Class 2 .... B.2.1.5.4.3, B.5.2.3
     Definition 3.3.192.2
   Class 3 .... B.2.1.5.4.2, B.5.2.4
     Definition 3.3.1920.3
   Class 4 .... B.2.1.5.4.1, B.5.2.5
     Definition 3.3.192.4
   Classification of B.2.1.5, B.5.1
   Definition 3.3.192, A.3.3.192
   Detached storage .... *see* Detached storage
   Fire protection 13.6.2.5.7, A.13.6.2.5.7.2
   Permits .... Table 1.12.8(a), Table 1.12.8(c), Table 1.12.8(d)
   Specific occupancies, storage and use in .... Tables 60.4.2.1.2 to 60.4.2.1.8, Table 60.4.2.1.10.1
Oxidizing cryogenic fluid .... Table 1.12.8(c), B.2.1.10.1
   Definition 3.3.77.3
Oxidizing gas .... Table 60.4.2.1.1.3, Table 60.4.4.1.2, 63.1.4.1(1), Table 63.2.3.1.1, 63.2.3.1.6, Table 63.3.1.11.2, 63.3.7, A.63.3.7.2.1.1, B.2.1.2.2, B.2.1.5.1; *see also* Compressed gas; Hazardous materials
   Definition 3.3.135.13
   Permit amounts for .... Tables 1.12.8(b) to (d)
   Specific occupancies, storage and use in .... Tables 60.4.2.1.2 to 60.4.2.1.8, Table 60.4.2.1.10.1
Oxygen
   Home care, liquid oxygen in .... 63.11, A.63.11.3.1 to A.63.11.5.1
   Liquid oxygen ambulatory containers 63.11.2, 63.11.3, A.63.11.3.1, A.63.11.3.3
     Definition 63.1.3.34
   Liquid oxygen home care containers .... 63.11.2, 63.11.3, A.63.11.3.1 to A.6.11.3.5.5.1
     Definition 63.1.3.35
Oxygen-fuel gas systems 41.5, A.41.5.5.2.3
Ozone-gas generating equipment .... Chap. 54
Ozone generators 54.2.1.1, 54.2.1.2, 54.2.3, 54.4, 54.5
   Definition 3.3.193

-P-

Packaging
   Definition 3.3.194
Palletized storage .... 34.1.1.1, 34.2.3.3, 34.2.4, 34.2.5, 34.9.1(3), A.34.2.4.2, A.34.2.4.3, A.34.2.5, Fig. A.34.8.1(b), Fig. A.34.8.1(e)
   Aerosol products .... 61.3.3.2.3 to 61.3.3.2.5, 61.3.3.2.9, 61.3.4.2.7, 61.3.4.2.17, 61.3.4.2.19
   Compresses gases and cryogenic fluids 63.3.2.1.2.3
   Definition 3.3.246.10
   Flammable and combustible liquids .... 66.14.6.1, 66.14.6.5, 66.16.5.2.2(2), 66.16.5.2.4(2), 66.16.5.2.8(2), 66.16.5.2.9(2), 66.16.5.2.11(2), 66.16.5.2.12(2)

Flammable and combustible liquids inside liquid
storage areas 66.16.5.2.2, 66.16.5.2.4, 66.16.5.2.8,
66.16.5.2.9, 66.16.5.2.11, 66.16.5.2.12
Hazardous materials .... 60.4.2.1.13.2(4)
Idle pallets 34.5.2.2, 34.10, 61.3.4.2.6,
A.34.10.1, A.34.10.3
Pallets, conventional .... Fig. A.34.7.3.1(a)
Definition 3.3.71, A.3.3.71
Panic hardware 14.5.3.4, 32.4.10.5, A.14.5.3.4.2
Paper
Column (definition) 3.3.55
Core (definition) 3.3.74
Definition 3.3.195
Storage, rolled paper 34.1.1, 34.2.7, 34.9,
A.34.1.1.2(6), A.34.2.7, A.34.9.2
Tissue 34.2.7.4
Parade floats .... Table 1.12.8(a), 10.16
Parking areas
Wildland/urban interface 17.3.5.2.1.10
Parking structures 13.3.2.5, 13.3.2.15.5,
13.3.2.17.7, Chap. 29
Basement and underground 29.1.1
Definition 3.3.183.23.1
Definition 3.3.183.23, A.3.3.183.23
Fire flow for 18.4.5.3.5
LP-Gas cargo vehicles 69.6.2, A.69.6.2.2.2
LP-Gas fueled vehicles 42.11.2.7
LP-Gas systems on vehicles 69.3.12.9
Partitions .... 41.3.4.2(6) to (9), A.14.8.3.4.1.1; *see also* Smoke
partitions
Passenger rail systems .... Chap. 37
Patch kettles (definition) 3.3.196
Patio heaters 10.10.7
Penalties, for code violation 1.16
Penetrations .... 12.7.5, A.12.7.5.1, A.12.7.5.6.3(1)(c)
Exit enclosures .... 14.3.1, A.14.3.1(1) to 14.3.1(10)(b)
Smoke barriers 12.9.6
Smoke partitions 12.8.4
Performance-based design .... 1.4, 4.3.2, 4.5.3, Chap. 5
Definitions 3.4
Design scenarios 5.4, A.5.4
Documentation requirements .... 5.7, A.5.7.1 to A.5.7.11
Evaluation 5.1.5, 5.5, 5.7.13, A.5.1.5
High hazard contents 5.1.12, 60.7
Performance criteria .... *see* Performance criteria
Pre-construction design requirements 5.1, A.5.1
Retained prescriptive elements 4.3.2.2, 5.3, 5.7.10
Safety factors 5.6, 5.7.9, A.5.6
Warrant of fitness 4.5.5.1
Performance criteria 5.2, A.5.2.2
Definition 3.4.14, A.3.4.14
Permissible areas 41.2.1.1, 41.3.2
Designated area 41.3.2.2
Definition 3.3.14.9.1
Nonpermissible areas 41.3.3, A.41.3.3
Permit-required area 41.3.2.2
Definition 3.3.14.9.2
Permissible exposure limit (PEL) (definition) 3.3.162.2,
A.3.3.170.2
Permit-required area .... *see* Permissible areas
Permits ..... 1.12, A.1.12.6.13; *see also* Maximum allowable quantities;
specific occupancies
Aerosol products 61.1.2, 61.5.3.3, A.61.5.3.3
Aircraft hangars 21.1.1
Asbestos removal .... Table 1.12.8(a), 16.8.2
Automobile wrecking yards .... Table 1.12.8(a), 22.2
Commercial cooking equipment 50.4.2
Compressed gas 63.1.2
Crop maze 10.14.11.1
Cryogenic fluids 63.1.2
Definition 3.3.198

Dust explosion and fire prevention 40.4.3.4.4.3,
40.4.3.4.5, 40.4.3.4.7, A.40.4.3.4.7
Explosives, fireworks, and model rocketry 65.2.3,
65.3.3, 65.4.2, 65.5.2, 65.7.2, 65.8.2, 65.9.2
Fibers, combustible 45.1.3
Fire protection systems 13.1.1.1
Fire pumps 13.4.1.2
Forest products 31.2
Hazardous materials .... *see* Hazardous materials
Hot work operations .... *see* Hot work operations
Industrial occupancies 20.14.2
Industrial ovens and furnaces 51.1.2
Laboratories using chemicals 26.2
Misrepresentation, effect of 1.12.5
Motion picture and television production soundstages, facilities,
and locations .... 32.2, 32.4.2, 32.5.2, A.32.4.2(8),
A.32.5.2(1)
Motor fuel dispensing facilities .... *see* Motor fuel dispensing
facilities
Refrigeration, mechanical 53.1.2
Revocation or suspension of 1.12.7
Special outdoor events, carnivals, and fairs .... Table 1.12.8(a),
10.14.1, 10.14.11.1, 10.16.1
Spraying, dipping, and coating operations 43.1.1.4
Storage .... Table 1.12.8(a), 10.18.2, 34.1.2
Tents, membranes, grandstands, and folding/telescopic
seating 25.1.2
Tires, outside storage of 33.1.2
Waste and refuse 19.1.1
Wildland fire–prone areas 17.3.2, A.17.3.2
Peroxide-forming chemicals (definition) 3.3.199
Personal care (definition) 3.3.200, A.3.3.2090
Pesticides 20.15.4
Definition 3.3.201
Petroleum, crude .... *see* Crude petroleum
Photovoltaic systems .... 11.12, A.11.12.2.1 to A.11.12.3.3
Physical hazard materials ... 63.1.4.1(1); *see also* Hazardous materials
Definition 3.3.181.12
Physical hazards .... B.2.1; *see also* Organic peroxide; Oxidizers
Definition 3.3.202
Piers .... Chap. 28, 42.9.1.3, 42.9.2.2, 42.9.7.2, 42.9.7.3,
A.42.9.2.2
Definition 3.3.203, A.3.3.203
Flammable and combustible liquids, bulk
transfer of ....
.... Table 66.7.3.3, 66.29, A.66.29.3.5, A.66.29.3.28
Pipes and piping
Compressed gases and cryogenic fluids 63.2.15,
63.3.1.5.1.10, 63.3.1.8.4, 63.3.1.19, A.63.3.1.19.1.1 to
A.63.3.1.19.3
Cryogenic fluids 63.4.14.1.4.2, 63.4.14.2,
63.4.14.11.3.2.3
Flammable and combustible liquids 43.1.6.4, 66.18.4.4,
66.18.4.6, 66.18.5.2, 66.19.4.5, 66.19.5.4.1, 66.22.11.4.2,
66.22.12.1, 66.27, 66.29.3.11 to 66.29.3.13, A.43.1.6.4.1
to A.43.1.6.4.5, A.66.19.4.5.1, A.66.22.12.1, A.66.27.4.3.2
to A.66.27.10
Hazardous materials 60.5.1.6.2, 60.5.1.6.3
Hot tapping of pipeline 41.3.6, A.41.3.6
Hot work operations .... 41.3.4.2(9)
LP-Gas equipment and appliances 69.2.3, 69.3.1,
69.3.9, 69.3.12.5, 69.3.13.3.6, A.69.3.1, A.69.3.9
Motor vehicle fuel dispensing facilities 42.4, 42.9.3,
42.9.7.3
Ozone-gas generating equipment 54.3
Tar kettles .... 16.7.3.2 to 16.7.3.5
Pits, repair garages 30.2.6, 30.2.9.3
Plans .... 1.7.12; *see also* Emergency plans
Construction operations
Prefire plans for 16.3.2.3, A.16.3.2.3

Waste chutes, safety plans for 16.2.2.4, A.16.2.2.4.1
Wildland/urban interface 17.2
Fire department access 18.1.3.1
Fire hydrants 18.1.3.2
Forest products, outside storage of 31.3.6.5, 31.3.7.3.4
Hazardous materials storage and handling 60.1.5, 60.1.6, 60.5.1.4.1.3, 60.6, A.60.1.6.1, D.3
Heliports 21.3.3.1, A.21.3.3.1
Laboratories using chemicals 26.1.5, A.26.1.5.1
Motor vehicle fuel dispensing facilities 42.2.2.2
Refrigeration, mechanical 53.1.2
Review of 1.14
Wildland/urban interface
    Construction plans for 17.2
    Hazard mitigation plan .... 17.1.10, A.17.1.10.3 to A.17.1.10.5
Plastic containers .... see Containers
Plastics .... 20.1.5.5.4.4(6)
    Cellulose nitrate plastic .... Table 1.12.8(a), Table 1.12.8(d)
    Foamed or cellular .... 10.19.1.1(3), 12.5.5.3, 20.1.2.2, 20.1.2.4, 20.1.5.4.3, 20.1.5.5.4.4(7), 20.1.5.5.4.6.2, 32.4.5.1, 32.5.5, A.12.5.5.3.1, A.20.1.5.4.3
    Indoor children's play structures 10.19.1.1, 10.19.1.2, A.10.19.1.2
    Light-transmitting .... 10.19.1.1(2), 10.19.1.2, 12.5.5.4, A.10.19.1.2, A.12.5.5.4
    Pyroxylin .... Table 1.12.8(a)
    Storage .... 34.1.1, 34.2.4.3, 34.2.6, A.34.1.1.2(6), A.34.2.4.3
Play structures 20.1.1.2
    Indoor playground structures 10.19, A.10.19.1.2
    Multilevel 20.1.4.1, A.20.1.4.1
Plumbing code (definition) 3.3.53.4
Plural component coverings .... 43.7, A.43.7.1 to A.43.7.6
Pneumatic rate-of-rise detectors (definition) 3.3.84.15, A.3.3.84.19
Poles, outside storage of .... 31.3.1.1(3), 31.3.5, A.31.3.5.1.1 to A.31.3.5.3.5
Portable cooking .... see Cooking equipment
Portable tanks .... see Tanks
Posts, outside storage of .... 31.3.1.1(3), 31.3.5, A.31.3.5.1.1 to A.31.3.5.3.5
Powder coating 43.1.3.1.8, 43.1.5.2.2, 43.1.7.2.1.1, 43.1.7.3, 43.1.7.7, 43.6, A.43.1.7.7
Power .... see Emergency power; Standby power
Preaction sprinkler systems 66.16.4.2
Premises identification 10.11.1, A.10.11.1.1
Prepackaged fireworks merchandise .... see Fireworks
Prescriptive-based design 4.3.1, 4.3.2.2, 5.3, 5.7.10
Pressure-treating plants .... 31.3.5, A.31.3.5.1.1 to A.31.3.5.3.5
Pressure vessels 66.21.4.2.3, A.66.21.4.2.3.2
    Definition 3.3.204, A.3.3.204
Pressurization system, membrane structures 25.5.3.2, 25.6.5.2
Primary containment (definition) 3.3.205
Private fire hydrants .... see Fire hydrants
Private fire service mains 13.5.1, 13.5.4
Private water supply systems 18.5.5.1
Processes or processing ...... see also specific processes, e.g. Oxidizers
    Definition 3.3.206, A.3.3.206
    Dust explosion and fire prevention .... 40.4, 40.7.1.2, 40.7.2, A.40.4.1.2.3 to A.40.4.8.2, A.40.7.1.2(5), A.40.7.2.2.4 to A.40.7.2.5.3
Process unit (vessel) .... see Operating or process unit (vessel)
Projected beam-type detectors 13.7.4.3.5, 13.7.4.6.2, A.13.7.4.3.5
    Definition 3.3.84.16

Projection rooms 20.1.5.12
Projection screens 20.1.3.4
Property protection 4.1.1, 4.1.4, A.4.1.1, A.4.1.4.2.1, A.4.1.4.2.2
    Appropriateness of safeguards 4.4.2
    Multiple safeguards 4.4.1
    Performance-based design option 5.2.2.4, A.5.2.2.4
Proposed design (definition) 3.4.15, A.3.4.15
Proprietary information (definition) 3.3.208
Protected above ground tanks .... see Tanks
Protected storage .... see Storage
Protection for exposures
    Definition 3.3.209
    Forest products, storage of .... 31.3.2.2, 31.3.3.4, 31.3.6.4, A.31.3.2.2.1, A.31.3.2.2.2, A.31.3.3.4.2, A.31.3.6.4.1 to A.31.3.6.4.3
    Wildland/urban interface 17.3.5.2.1.11, A.17.3.5.2.1.11.1
Public fire education 1.7.18
Public way (definition) .... 3.3.210; see also Roadways
Public welfare 4.1.5, 5.2.2.5, A.4.1.5.1, A.4.1.5.2, A.5.2.2.5
Pumps, fire .... see Fire pumps
Pumps, fuel
    Aircraft fueling 42.10.5.2.4, 42.10.5.2.7
    Remote/submersible 42.5.4
    Rooftop heliports 42.10.4.3
Pump tank fire extinguishers .... Table 13.6.4.3.3.1, 13.6.4.3.3.5, 13.6.4.7.1.3.3, 13.6.4.7.2.1
Purging
    Bulk gaseous hydrogen systems 63.6.2
    Bulk liquefied hydrogen systems 63.7.2
    Bulk oxygen systems 63.5.2
    Cryogenic fluids 63.4.9.1.3, 63.4.14.1.5
    Definition 3.3.211
    Ethylene oxide 63.10.2
    Flammable and combustible liquids .... 66.21.7.4.3.3.3(4)
    Fuel tanks .... A.28.1.7.2.1.5(4)
    Gas generation systems 63.8.2
    Gas piping systems .... 63.3.1.19, 63.3.10.2, 63.4.14.1.5, A.63.3.1.19.1 to A.63.3.1.19.3
    LP-Gas .... 69.4.3.1(6), 69.6.2.3.8
    Refrigerants .... 53.2.3.3.1 to 53.2.3.3.3, 53.3.1.6(1), 53.3.2.1(3), 53.3.2.2(2)
Purpose of code 1.2, A.1.2
Pyrophoric gas ..... Table 60.4.2.1.1.3, Table 60.4.3.7, 63.1.4.1(1)(e), Table 63.2.3.1.1, Table 63.2.9, 63.2.10.2.2, Table 63.3.1.11.2, 63.3.8, A.63.3.8.3.1.1, B.2.1.2.7, B.2.1.7.1; see also Compressed gas; Hazardous materials
    Definition 3.3.135.14
    Permit amounts for .... Table 1.12.8(b), Table 1.12.8(d)
Pyrophoric material B.2.1.7
    Definition 3.3.173.13
    Outside control areas .... Table 60.4.4.1.2
Pyrophorics (solids and liquids) .... Table 60.4.2.1.1.3, Tables 60.4.2.1.2 to 60.4.2.1.8, Table 60.4.2.1.10.1, Chap. 71, B.2.1.7.2, B.2.1.7.3
    Definition 3.3.212
    Permit amounts for .... Table 1.12.8(d)
Pyrotechnic articles .... Table 1.12.8(a), 20.1.5.3, A.20.1.5.3(3)(a)
Pyrotechnic devices 25.1.5.4
Pyrotechnics before a proximate audience .... Table 1.12.8(a), 32.4.3.2, 32.5.3.2, 65.3
Pyrotechnic special effects .... 32.4.2(1), 32.4.3, 32.4.4.1, 32.5.2(2), 32.5.3, 32.5.4.1, A.32.4.3.1
Pyroxylin plastics .... Table 1.12.8(a)

-Q-

Quality assurance 12.3.2, A.12.3.2, A.13.6.1.3.3
    Definition 3.3.213

Quality assurance program 12.3.2, A.12.3.2, A.13.6.1.3.3
   Definition 3.3.214

-R-

Racks
   Definition 3.3.215, A.3.3.215
   Double-row racks .... A.34.7.3.1, Fig. A.34.8.1(d)
      Definition 3.3.215.1
   Movable racks A.34.7.3.1
      Definition 3.3.215.2, A.3.3.215.2
   Multiple-row racks A.34.7.3.1
      Definition 3.3.215.3
   Portable racks .... Figs. A.34.8.1(a) to (e)
      Definition 3.3.215.4, A.3.3.215.4
   Single-row racks A.34.7.3.1
      Definition 3.3.215.5
Rack storage .... 34.1.1.1, 34.1.1.2(5), 34.7, A.34.7.3.1 to
      A.34.7.3.4.2.1(1)
   Aerosol products 61.3.3.2.3, 61.3.3.2.4, 61.3.3.2.9,
      61.3.4.2.9, 61.3.4.2.12.1, 61.3.4.2.12.2, 61.41.3.3.1.1
   Boats 28.1.6.2.4, 28.1.7.2.3, A.28.1.6.2.4.3,
      A.28.6.2.4.1
   Flammable and combustible liquids inside liquid
      storage areas 66.16.3.3, 66.16.5.1.3, 66.16.5.1.10,
      66.16.5.2.1, 66.16.5.2.3, 66.16.5.2.5, 66.16.5.2.7,
      66.16.5.2.8, 66.16.5.2.10, 66.16.6, A.66.16.6.1.5
   Hazardous materials .... 60.4.2.1.13.2(5)
Radar equipment, airports 42.10.2.1.4, 42.10.2.1.5, A.42.10.2.1.5
Radiant energy-sensing detectors 13.7.4.1.2
   Definition 3.3.84.17, 13.7.4.1.2
Rail systems, fixed guideway transit and passenger .... Chap. 37
Ramps 14.11.4
   Airport .... see Airport ramps
   Definition 3.3.216, A.3.3.216
   As means of escape 4.5.6.2.2
   Performance-based design option .... 5.3.4(5)
   Width of .... Table 14.8.3.1
Rate compensation detectors 13.7.4.5.1
   Definition 3.3.84.18, A.3.3.84.18
Rate-of-rise detectors 13.7.4.5.1
   Definition 3.3.84.19, A.3.3.84.19
Recirculating heat transfer systems .... 66.19.4, A.66.19.4.2 to
      A.66.19.4.7.1
Recommended practice (definition) 3.2.7
Records and reports 1.11
   Aerosol products storage, handling, and use 61.5.6.1
   Board of appeals 1.10.5
   Construction documents 1.7.12.3, 1.14, 13.1.1
      Definition 3.3.68
   Cooking equipment
      Exhaust system 50.2.3, 50.2.4, 50.4.11, 50.5.3.3,
         50.5.6.13 to 50.5.6.15, A.50.4.11.2, A.50.5.3.3
      Water valve supervision .... 50.4.4.10(4),
         A.50.4.4.10(4)
   Cryogenic fluids storage 63.4.14.1.3.3
   Dust explosion and fire prevention 40.3.4.6.3,
      40.7.1.3
   Fire department service delivery concurrence evaluation 15.4
   Fire drills 10.5.6, A.10.5.6
   Fire protection systems 13.3.3.4.3, 13.6.4.2.4,
      13.6.4.3.4, 13.7.3.2, A.13.3.3.4.3.1 to A.13.3.3.4.3.3,
      A.13.6.4.3.4
      Construction documents for 13.1.1
      Testing and maintenance 13.1.5, 13.6.4.4.2
   Fire-resistive construction, maintenance of 12.3.3.3.2
   Fires and other emergencies, reporting of 10.6, A.10.6.1.3
   Flammable and combustible liquids storage 66.21.7.1.1,
      66.21.7.1.3.1, 66.21.7.1.4, 66.21.7.4.3.7, 66.21.7.5,
      A.66.21.7.5
   Hazardous materials 60.5.1.3.3, 60.5.1.4.6, D.2,
      D.3.2.7, D.4

   Owners and occupants, of 10.2.5, 10.2.6
   Performance-based design 5.1.4, 5.1.6, 5.1.12.3, 5.7,
      A.5.1.4, A.5.7.1 to A.5.7.11
   Refrigerant quantities 53.3.1.5, 53.3.2.3
   Spray application staff, training of 43.10.1.4
Record storage 12.4.3, 20.15.6, A.12.4.3,
      A.20.15.6.2
Recreational fires 10.10.1.1, 10.10.4.3
   Definition 3.3.217
Recreational vehicle parks 27.3
Reduced flow valves (definition) 3.3.268.2
References .... 1.3.2, Chap. 2, Annex F
Refineries 16.19.6.1.2, 43.1.8.8.1.2, 63.3.1.8.4.2,
      A.6.1.12.1, A.66.18.5.1
   Definition 3.3.218
Refrigeration, mechanical .... Table 1.12.8(a), 13.3.3.5.2.2,
      34.6.7, Chap. 53, 60.1.2(4)
Refueling .... Chap. 42
Refuge, areas or 20.7.2.1.3, A.20.7.2.1.3
Refuse, combustible ... 10.12.1, Chap. 19; see also Waste, combustible
   Definition 3.3.61
Registered design professional (definition) 3.3.219
Relocatable power taps 11.1.4
   Definition 3.3.220
Relocation area ...... 5.2.2.6, 10.2.5, 10.5.5, 10.8.2.1(3), A.10.8.2.1(3)
Relocation drills .... see Fire drills
Remote pumping systems 42.5.4
Repair garages .... 30.2, 30.3, A.30.2.9 to A.30.2.10.6
   Construction 30.2.3
   Flammable and combustible liquids tank
      vehicles in .... Table 66.7.3.3
   LP-Gas cargo vehicles 69.6.2.3.7, 69.6.2.3.8
   LP-Gas fueled vehicles 42.11.2.7
   LP-Gas systems on vehicles 69.3.12.9
   Major repair garage ... 30.2.1, 30.2.3, 30.2.7, 30.2.10.6, A.30.2.10.6
      Definition 3.3.183.24.1
   Minor repair garage (definition) 3.3.183.24.2
   Permit requirements .... Table 1.12.8(a)
Repairs to structure ... 10.1.4, 10.2.4; see also Inspection, testing, and
      maintenance
Reports .... see Records and reports
Residential board and care occupancies .... 20.5, A.20.5.2.4.1 to
      A.20.5.2.5.2.3
   Battery systems, location of 52.3.3.4
   Christmas tree provisions .... Table 10.13.1.1
   Definition 3.3.183.25, 6.1.9.1, A.3.3.183.25, A.6.1.9.1
   Detection, alarm, and communication systems .... 13.7.2.19 to
      13.7.2.23, A.13.7.2.20.6 to A.13.7.2.22.6.1
   Doors .... 14.5.1.1(2)
   Emergency plans 10.8.1, 20.5.2.1
   Extinguishers, portable fire .... Table 13.6.1.2
   Fire fighter safety building marking system
      (FFSBMS) .... E.1.3.5(3)
   Hazardous materials storage and use 60.4.2.1.8
   Means of egress, capacity .... Table 14.8.3.1
   Multiple occupancies .... Table 6.1.14.4.1(a),
      Table 6.1.14.4.1(b)
   Sprinkler systems .... 13.3.2.21, 13.3.2.22, 13.7.2.20.2(3),
      13.7.2.21.3.6, 13.7.2.21.3.7, 13.7.2.22.2(3), 13.7.2.22.8.2,
      A.13.3.2.21.2.1 to A.13.3.2.22.2.1.1
Residential occupancies .... see also Specific occupancies
   Battery systems, location of 52.3.3.4
   Board and care facilities .... see Residential board and care
      occupancies
   Definitions 3.3.183.26, 6.1.8.1, A.3.3.183.26,
      A.6.1.8.1.1
   Fire fighter safety building marking system
      (FFSBMS) .... E.1.3.5(1)
   Flammable and combustible liquids storage 66.9.6.2.1
   Hazardous materials storage and use 60.4.2.1.8
   LP-Gas storage in 69.5.3.5

Multiple occupancies .... Table 6.1.14.4.1(a), Table 6.1.14.4.1(b)
    Sprinkler temperature ratings for specific areas of .... Table 13.3.1.9(c)
Resins, spray application of .... 43.8, A.43.8.1 to A.43.8.5.3
Retail buildings, bulk merchandising
    Definition 3.3.183.4
    Sprinkler systems 13.3.2.23.3, 13.3.2.24.2
Rigid intermediate bulk containers 40.4.3.5, A.40.3.5.1, A.40.3.5.2
Roadways
    Fire department access roads ..... *see* Fire department access roads
    Wildland fire-prone areas 17.3.5.3, 17.3.7
Rockets, model .... 65.6 to 65.8
    Permit requirements .... Table 1.12.8(a)
    Wildland fire-prone areas 17.3.4.2
Roofing kettles .... *see* Kettles
Roofing systems, torch-applied .... Table 1.12.8(a), 16.6, 41.1.2(7), A.41.1.2(7)
Roofs .... *see also* Canopies
    Access to .... 11.12.2.2.1 to 11.12.2.2.3, 14.11.6
    Combustible fibers, storage vaults for 45.5.4.5
    Heliports, rooftop .... *see* Heliports, rooftop
    Hot work operations .... 41.3.4.2(6) to (9)
    LP-Gas systems on 69.3.10, A.69.3.10.2.6, A.69.3.10.8.3
    Membrane structures 25.5.1.1, 25.5.1.4, 25.6.1.3
    Photovoltaic systems on .... 11.12.2.2.1 to 11.12.2.2.3
    Sprinkler systems
        Exterior spaces under roof, sprinkler systems for 13.3.2.6, 21.2.6.6, A.13.3.2.6
        Sprinkler temperature ratings .... Table 13.3.1.9(b)
Roof tanks .... Table 66.7.3.3, 66.22.2.2, 66.22.8.2
Rooming houses .... *see* Lodging or rooming houses
Rooms .... *see also* Gas rooms
    Equipment rooms, storage in 10.18.5
    Liquid storage .... *see* Inside liquid storage areas
Rows (definition) 3.3.221
Rubber, storage of .... 34.2.6; *see also* Tire storage
Rubbish, combustible .... 16.2.2, 34.6.4, A.16.2.2.1 to A.16.2.2.4.3; *see also* Waste, combustible
Rubbish chutes; .... *see* Chutes, rubbish or laundry
Rubbish-handling operations, commercial .... Table 1.12.8(a)

-S-

Safe location (definition) 3.4.16
Safety .... *see* Life safety
Safety cans .... 43.1.6.5.1, 66.9.4.1(3), 66.18.5.2(2)
    Definition 3.3.222, A.3.3.222
Safety factor (definition) 3.4.17
Safety margin (definition) 3.4.18
Sales display area
    Definition 3.3.14.10
Salvage vehicles 22.9.2.1, 22.9.5.1
    Definition 3.3.224
Satellite buildings (definition) 3.3.29.9
Scaffolding, shoring, and forms 16.4.1, A.16.4.1
Scavenged gas (definition) 3.3.135.15
Scene .... *see* Emergency scene
Scope of code 1.1
Seasonal buildings 10.12, A.10.12.2.1
Seating
    In assembly occupancies 20.1.5.10
    Festival .... 13.3.2.7.1(4), 13.3.2.8.1(4), 20.1.5.10.3
        Definition 3.3.110
    Folding and telescopic .... Table 1.12.8(a), 25.1, 25.4, A.25.1.4.2, A.25.1.8
    Grandstands 25.1, 25.3, A.25.1.4.2, A.25.1.8
Secondary containment 66.22.11.3.10, 66.22.11.3.11
    Definition 66.27.2.5

Secondary containment tanks 66.22.11.4
    Definition 3.3.255.5
Security service .... *see* Guard service
Segregated storage (definition) 3.3.246.11
Seismic protection
    Battery systems .... Table 52.1, 52.3.9
    Compressed gases and cryogenic fluids storage 63.2.14.2
    Hazardous materials storage and use 60.5.1.14, A.60.5.1.14
    Tank storage, flammable and combustible liquids 66.22.5.1.3
Self-closing (definition) 3.3.225
Self-closing doors 12.8.3.5, 12.9.4.4, 14.5.4, 30.1.6.3, 45.5.3.2, 63.2.17.1.3, A.12.9.4.4, A.14.5.4.1
Self-service stations
    Aircraft fueling 42.10.5.22
    Attended 42.7.4
    Unattended 42.5.3.8, 42.5.7.2, 42.7.5, A.42.7.5.6
Semiconductor fabrication facilities .... *see* Cleanrooms
Sensitivity analysis .... *see* Analysis
Separated occupancies .... 6.1.14.1.1(2), 6.1.14.4
    Definition 3.3.183.27, 6.1.14.2.3
Separation of hazards
    Aerosol products 61.4.3.6, 61.4.4.1, 61.4.4.2
    Compressed gases and cryogenic fluids .... 63.2.17.5, 63.2.18.1.2, 63.2.18.2, 63.3.1.11, 63.3.3.2.2.2, 63.4.7, 63.4.14.11.2.2, A.63.3.1.11.2 to A.6.3.3.1.11.10.1, A.63.4.7.2
    Definition 3.3.226
    Flammable and combustible liquids storage .... 66.9.17, Table 66.17.6.1, 66.17.6.4, 66.22.4, 66.23.4, 66.24.4, 66.25.4, A.66.22.4, A.66.24.4.5(3)
    Gas rooms 63.2.4.4
    Hazardous materials storage and use 60.5.1.12
    LP-Gas containers 69.3.3, A.69.3.3.1.1, A.69.3.3.4.3
    Spray booths 43.1.3.3
    Tires, outdoor storage of .... 33.1.3 to 33.1.5, 33.2.1.3, 33.2.2.4
Shaftways .... *see* Openings, vertical
Shall (definition) 3.2.8
Shelter-in-place .... 10.8.2.1(3), A.10.8.2.1(3)
Shelving, solid 61.3.4.2.12, A.28.1.6.2.4.1, A.34.7.3.1
    Definition 3.3.238
Shop drawings (definition) 3.3.227
Shoring, construction 16.4.1, A.16.4.1
Short-term exposure limit (STEL) (definition) 3.3.162.3, A.3.3.162.3
Should (definition) 3.2.9
Signals
    Alarm (definition) 3.3.228.1, A.3.3.228.1
    Fire alarm signal .... 13.3.1.8.2, 13.7.1.7, A.13.7.1.7.5 to A.13.7.1.7.7
        Definition 3.3.228.2, A.3.3.228.2
    Supervisory signals 13.3.1.8.1, A.13.3.1.8.1
        Definition 3.3.228.3, A.3.3.228.3
    Trouble 13.7.1.10.4, 13.7.1.13.10, 13.7.4.3.4.5, 30.2.8.3, A.13.7.4.3.5.8
        Definition 3.3.228.4, A.3.3.228.4
Signs .... *see also* Marking
    Aircraft fuel servicing 42.10.2.1.3
    Airports 21.2.5.2, A.21.2.5.2
    Ambulatory health care occupancies .... 20.6.2.4(1)
    Asbestos removal 16.8.3
    Assembly occupancies 20.1.5.9.2, 20.1.5.10.4
    Battery systems, location of .... Table 52.1, 52.3.8
    Buildings under construction 16.2.3.1.5
    Combustible fibers, handling or storage of 45.3.2
    Compressed gases and cryogenic fluids 63.2.12, 63.3.6.4.2, 63.4.4.6, 63.11.5.1, A.63.11.5.1
    Cooking media fires, extinguishers for 13.6.2.5.5.3, A.13.6.2.5.5.3
    Cryogenic containers and systems 63.4.4.1.3
    Doors .... 14.5.1.1(3), 14.5.2.5.1(2), 14.5.3.1(5), 14.5.3.1(6), 14.5.3.2(3)

INDEX

Egress direction 14.14.2
Emergency fuel shutoff stations 42.10.4.4.3
Exit discharge 14.11.5
Fibers, combustible, storage and handling 19.1.7.2
Fire fighter safety building marking system (FFSBMS) E.1.2
Flammable and combustible liquids storage tank
    vaults 66.25.3.1.9
Forest products, storage of 31.3.2.1.2.1,
    31.3.2.1.2.2
Hazardous materials .... 60.4.2.1.13.2(11),
    60.5.1.8, 60.5.1.8.3
Hazardous material storage lockers 66.14.6.6
Health care occupancies .... 20.4.2.4(1)
Heliports, roof-top 21.3.3.5.2
Hot work operations 41.3.2.2.2
Marinas and boatyards 28.1.8.2.6, 28.1.8.2.7,
    A.28.1.8.2.6(7)
Means of egress 14.14, 20.1.4.7, A.14.1.4.1.2.1
    to A.14.14.8.3, A.20.1.4.7.3
Motor fuel dispensing facilities 42.7.2.5.4,
    42.7.5.3, 42.9.5.3, 42.9.5.5, 42.9.10.8, 42.10.2.5.1,
    A.42.7.2.5.4
No exit 14.14.8.3, A.14.14.8.3
No smoking .... 10.9.3 see also Smoking
Ozone-gas generating equipment 54.2.2.2,
    54.2.3(4), 54.3.4, A.54.2.2.2
Photovoltaic systems 11.12.2.1.5
Refrigeration systems 53.2.4
Shaftways 10.11.2
Spray application operations 43.1.8.11, 43.7.7
Sprinkler system information 13.3.3.4.1.9, A.13.3.3.4.1.9
Stair identification 10.11.3, A.10.11.3
Storage occupancies 34.6.5.2
Tents 25.2.4.2.2
Tires, outside storage of 33.6.1
Wildland fire-prone areas, restricted entry to 17.3.3.3
Silane and silane mixtures 63.3.8.2
Simple asphyxiant gas .... Table 1.12.8(b), A.42.11.1.1
    Definition 3.3.135.16
Single fire source, assumption of 4.2.1, A.4.2.1
Sisal, baled storage of 45.6.2
SI units 1.5
Smoke alarms 13.7.1.8, A.13.7.1.8.8, A.17.7.1.8.3
    Apartment buildings 13.7.2.17.5, 13.7.2.18.5,
    A.13.7.2.17.5, A.13.7.2.18.5.1
    Definition 3.3.230
    Hotels and dormitories 13.7.2.15.5, 13.7.2.16.5,
    A.13.7.2.15.5, A.13.7.2.16.5
    Lodging or rooming houses 13.7.2.14.5
    One- and two-family dwelling 13.7.2.13.1, A.13.7.2.13.1.1
    Residential board and care occupancies 13.7.2.19.3,
    13.7.2.20.7, 13.7.2.21.3, 13.7.2.22.7, 20.5.2.5.2.3.2,
    A.13.7.2.21.3
    Stock or equipment trailers 10.14.6
Smoke barriers .... 12.7.4.2, 12.9, A.12.7.4.2, A.12.9.1 to
    A.12.9.4.4
    Definition 3.3.231, A.3.3.231
Smoke compartments .... see Compartments
Smoke control systems .... 10.2.5, 11.8, 11.9.5(11),
    12.9.5.3(2), A.11.8
    Dedicated (definition) 3.3.254.9
    Nondedicated (definition) 3.3.254.12
Smoke dampers .... see Dampers
Smoke detectors .... 13.7.1.7.9, 13.7.1.8.2, 13.7.1.8.4 to
    1.3.7.1.8.6, 13.7.4.6; see also Detection systems
    Ambulatory health care occupancies 13.7.2.10.3.2.2
    Apartment buildings 13.7.2.18.4.2, 13.7.2.18.5.3
    Assembly occupancies .... 20.1.4.4 to 20.1.4.6
    Battery systems, location of 52.3.10
    Compressed gas 63.3.9.7
    Day-care occupancies 13.7.2.5.5, 13.7.2.6.5
    Definition 3.3.84.20

    Detention and correctional occupancies .... 13.7.2.11.3.2.1(2),
    13.7.2.11.4, 13.7.2.12.3.2.1(2), 13.7.2.12.4, A.13.7.2.11.4,
    A.13.7.2.12.4.3
    Hazardous material storage and use 60.5.1.20
    Health care occupancies 13.7.2.7.2.3, 13.7.2.7.5,
    13.7.2.8.2.3, 13.7.2.8.2.5, 13.7.2.8.3.2.2, 13.7.2.8.5.1,
    A.13.7.2.7.5.3
    Hotels and dormitories 13.7.2.15.4
    Lodging or rooming houses 13.7.2.14.1.2
    One- and two-family dwellings 13.7.2.13.1,
    A.13.7.2.13.1.1
    Residential board and care occupancies 13.7.2.20.8,
    13.7.2.22.8
    Smoke dampers, closing of 12.8.6.4, 12.9.5.7,
    13.7.1.9.2.2, A.13.7.1.9.2.2
Smoke partitions .... 12.7.4.2, 12.8, A.12.7.4.2, A.12.8.1 to
    A.12.8.6.2
    Definition 3.3.233, A.3.3.233
Smoke ventilation, photovoltaic systems 11.12.2.2.1,
    11.12.2.2.3.3
Smoking .... 5.3.3(3), 10.9
    Aerosol products storage, handling, and use .... 61.2.8.2(5),
    61.5.3.1.1(5), 61.5.3.2
    Aircraft fuel servicing 42.10.2.1.3
    Aircraft hangars 21.1.3
    Airport terminal buildings 21.2.2.3
    Ambulatory health care occupancies 20.6.2.4,
    A.20.6.2.4
    Assembly occupancies 20.1.5.9
    Board and care occupancies 20.5.2.4, A.20.5.2.4.1
    Buildings under construction 16.2.3.1.4, 16.2.3.1.5
    Combustible fibers, handling or storage of 45.3
    Compressed gases and cryogenic fluids 63.2.12.2.2,
    63.3.6.4.2, 63.11.5, A.63.11.5.1
    Definition 3.3.234
    Dust explosion and fire prevention 40.4.5.3
    Fibers, combustible, storage and handling 19.1.7
    Flammable and combustible liquids storage,
        handling, and use .... 66.6.5.1(5), 66.6.5.2
    Forest products, storage of 31.3.2.1.2
    Hazardous materials, in areas with 60.5.1.5.1,
    60.5.1.8.3
    Health care occupancies 20.4.2.4, A.20.4.2.4
    Heliports, roof-top 21.3.2.3, 21.3.3.5
    Marinas, boatyards, piers, and wharves 28.1.8.2.1
    Motion picture production soundstages, facilities,
        and locations 32.4.6, 32.5.6
    Motor fuel dispensing facilities 42.7.2.5.1, 42.9.5.5,
    42.9.10.4(2), 42.10.2.5
    Spray application operations 43.1.8.11, 43.7.7
    Storage occupancies 34.6.5
    Temporary membrane structures 25.1.5.2, 25.6.2.2
    Tents 25.1.5.2, 25.2.4.2
    Tires, outside storage of 33.1.6.1, 33.7.3
    Wildland fire-prone areas 17.3.4.1
Smoking areas 10.9.2
    Definition 3.3.14.11
Solid material (definition) 3.3.237
Solids
    Combustible particulate solid (definition) 3.3.236.1,
    A.3.3.236.1 see also Combustible dusts
    Flammable .... see Flammable solids
Solid shelving .... see Shelving, solid
Solvent distillation units 43.1.8.8, 66.19.6
Solvent extraction plants .... Chap. 44
    Permits .... Table 1.12.8(a), 44.3
Solvents .... 60.1.2(3)
    Chlorinated 43.1.8.10, A.43.1.8.10
    Cleaning 43.1.8.7, 43.5.1.1.3, 50.5.6.6,
    A.43.1.8.7.4
Soundstages .... Table 1.12.8(a), 20.16.1.2, Chap. 32

2015 Edition

Spark arresters 10.10.8.3, 17.3.5.2.1.7.1, 17.3.5.2.1.11.3, 31.3.2.1.11
Spark/ember detectors 40.5.2.4.2, 40.5.2.4.3, 40.5.6
   Definition 3.3.84.21
Sparks .... 40.4.1, 40.4.5, A.40.4.1.2.3 to A.40.4.1.5
   Aerosol products storage, handling, and use 61.2.8.2, 61.5.3.1.1, 61.5.3.3, A.61.5.3.3
   Airport terminals 21.2.4.4
   Combustible fibers, loose storage of 43.5.6.1
   Flammable and combustible liquids .... 66.6.5.1, 66.6.5.3.1, 66.19.5.7.5, A.66.6.5.1(8), A.66.19.5.7.5
   Forest products storage .... 31.3.2.1.10 to 31.3.2.1.12
   Hot work .... 41.1.2(8), 41.3.1, 41.3.4.2, 41.3.5.1, 41.3.5.2
   LP-Gas systems .... 69.3.12.4.2.4(4)
   Refueling operations 42.10.2.2.3, 42.10.5.4.3, 42.10.5.7.3
   Spray operations 43.1.4.5, 43.1.4.6, 43.1.8.12, 43.5.1.1.1, 43.5.3.6
   Tire storage 31.3.6.4.1, 33.1.6.3
Special amusement buildings 10.8.1, 20.1.4, A.20.1.4
   Definition 3.3.29.10, A.3.3.29.10
Special outdoor events .... Table 1.12.8(a), 10.14, A.10.14.3.1 to A.10.14.11.3.1
Special structures 6.1.1.2, 13.7.2.29, 20.16, A.13.7.2.29.2.1, A.13.7.2.29.2.2.2
   Extinguishers, portable fire .... Table 13.6.1.2
   LP-Gas storage in 69.5.3.4
Special uses
   Definition 3.3.267.3
   Manual fire alarm boxes for A.13.7.1.7.7
   Piers and wharves 28.2.1
Spillage .... *see also* Leaks
   Aerosol products 61.4.3.6.1
   Aircraft fuel servicing 21.3.3.4, 42.10.5.2, A.42.10.5.2
   Compressed gases and cryogenic fluids 63.2.13
   Electrolyte .... Table 52.1, 52.3.4, 52.3.5, A.52.3.4.2, A.52.3.5.1
   Flammable and combustible liquids .... 66.6.6.2, 66.6.9.2, 66.9.4.3.3, 66.9.13, 66.14.4.8, 66.15.3.5, 66.16.8, 66.17.6.8, 66.17.10, 66.18.4.2, 66.18.5.6(2), 66.21.6.6.2, 66.21.7.5, 66.22.11, 66.22.12, 66.25.9, 66.28.9, A.66.9.13, A.66.16.8.2, A.66.17.6.8, A.66.17.10.1, A.66.21.7.5, A.66.22.11, A.66.22.12.1, A.66.22.12.3, A.66.28.9
   Hazardous materials .... 66.14.4.8 *see also* Hazardous materials, Release of
   Motor vehicle fuel dispensing facilities .... 42.7.4.3(5)
Spontaneous ignition 16.2.2.3
   Aerosol products storage, handling, and use .... 61.2.8.2(7), 61.5.3.1.1(7)
   Flammable and combustible liquids storage, handling, and use .... 66.6.5.1(7), 66.19.5.7.4, A.66.19.5.7.4
   Spray application, flammable and combustible liquids 43.1.8.9, A.43.1.8.9
Spot-type detectors 13.7.4.3.1, 13.7.4.3.3, 13.7.4.3.8.2.2, 13.7.4.5.1, A.13.7.4.3.1, A.13.7.4.3.3
   Definition 3.3.84.22, A.3.3.84.19
Spray applications, of flammable and combustible materials ... Chap. 43; *see also* Spray areas; Spray booths; Spray rooms
   Drying, curing, or fusion processes 43.4, 43.5.3.7, 43.5.3.8, A.43.5.3.7.2
   Drying areas 43.1.5.11, A.43.1.5.11
   Electrical equipment and systems .... 43.1.4, 43.1.7.7.1(5), 43.8.5, A.43.1.4.1 to A.43.1.4.6, A.43.8.5.3
   Electrostatic equipment
      Automated 43.1.7.8, 43.2, A.43.1.7.8
      Handheld 43.3
   Fire protection systems and equipment .... 43.1.7, A.43.1.7.1 to A.43.1.7.8
   High-pressure hose lines 43.1.8.3
   Ignition sources .... 43.1.4, A.43.1.4.1 to A.43.1.4.6
   Limited finishing workstations 43.5.3, A.43.5.3.1, A.43.5.3.7.2
   Location of 43.1.2, A.43.1.2.1
   Operations and maintenance .... 43.1.8, A.43.1.8.1 to A.43.1.8.12
   Organic peroxides and plural component coatings .... 43.7, A.43.7.1 to A.43.7.6
   Outdoor .... 43.1.1.2(2)
   Overspray collectors 43.1.8.4
   Permits .... Table 1.12.8(a), 43.1.8.12, A.43.1.8.12
   Portable spraying equipment or aerosol product use .... 43.1.1.2(3)
   Preparation workstations 43.5.2
   Storage, handling and distribution of flammable and combustible liquids .... 43.1.6, A.43.1.6.1 to A.43.1.6.5.2
   Styrene cross-linked composites manufacturing .... 43.8, A.43.8.1 to A.43.8.5.3
   Vehicle undercoating and body lining 43.5.1
   Ventilation .... 43.1.3.6, 43.1.5, 43.1.6.3.2(4), 43.1.7.7.1(2), 43.8.6, A.43.1.5.2.1 to A.43.1.5.11
Spray areas 43.1.3, A.4.1.3.1, A.43.1.3.3
   Definition 3.3.14.12, A.3.3.14.12
   Electrical devices in or adjacent to 43.1.4.3, 43.1.4.4, 43.1.4.7, 43.1.4.8, A.43.1.4.3.3
   Extinguishing systems 43.1.7.1, A.43.1.7.1
   Flammable and combustible liquids in .... 43.1.6.2, A.43.1.6.2.2(1)
   Sprinklers in 13.3.3.5.1.8, A.13.3.3.5.1.8.1
   Static electricity 43.1.4.6, A.43.1.4.6
   Ventilation 43.1.5.2, A.43.1.5.2.1
Spray booths .... 43.1.3, 43.1.4.4.2 to 43.1.4.4.4, 43.1.7.7.2(2), 43.1.7.8.2, A.4.1.3.1, A.43.1.3.3
   Definition 3.3.241, A.3.3.241
   Permit requirements .... Table 1.12.8(a)
Spray rooms 43.1.3, 43.1.4.4.2, 43.1.4.4.4, A.4.1.3.1, A.43.1.3.3
   Definition 3.3.242, A.3.3.242
   Permit requirements .... Table 1.12.8(a)
Sprinklers
   Alteration or painting of 13.3.3.5.1.6, A.13.3.3.5.1.6
   In spray areas 13.3.3.5.1.8, A.13.3.3.5.1.8.1
   Penetrations for 12.9.6.4
   Quick-response or residential, use of listed 13.3.2.11.4, 13.3.2.15.5, 13.3.2.17.6, 13.3.3.5.1.4, 13.7.2.21.3.6, 13.7.2.21.3.7, 18.4.5.3.3, A.13.3.2.11.4, A.13.3.3.5.1.4
   Spare, stock of 13.3.3.5.1.5, A.13.3.3.5.1.5
   Temperature ratings 13.3.1.9, A.13.3.1.9
Sprinkler systems .... 11.9.5(6), 13.3, Table 13.8, 14.5.3.2(6), A.13.3.3.1.1 to A.13.3.3.6.7; *see also* Deluge systems; Extinguishing systems
   Aerosol products storage, handling, and use .. 61.2.6.1, 61.2.6.4.1, 61.3.3.2.3, 61.3.4.2.7, 61.3.4.2.9 to 6.3.4.2.15, 61.4.3.3.1, 61.4.3.3.2, 61.4.3.5, A.61.3.4.2.9.5
   Airports 21.2.6, A.21.2.6
   Alarm and detection initiation .... 13.7.1.7.8 *see also* Waterflow alarms
   Apartment buildings .... 13.3.2.17, 13.3.2.18, A.13.3.2.18.1 to A.13.3.2.18.7
   Assembly occupancies .... *see* Assembly occupancies
   Canopies and exterior roofs 13.3.2.6, 21.2.6.6, A.13.3.2.6
   Combustible fibers, storage of 45.5.5.2
   Compressed gases and cryogenic fluids 63.2.10, A.63.2.10
   Construction, during 16.4.2.4, 16.4.3.2, A.16.4.2.4, A.16.4.3.2.1
   Cooking equipment 13.3.3.5.1.7, 50.4.5.2, 50.4.7.4, 50.4.10.1
   Day-care occupancies 13.3.2.29
   Demolition of buildings and 16.5.1
   Detention and correctional occupancies 13.3.2.13, 13.3.2.14, A.13.3.2.14.1
   Dust explosion and fire prevention 40.5.5, A.40.5.5

Educational occupancies 13.3.2.9, 13.3.2.10, A.13.3.2.9.1
Fire department access and 18.2.3.2.1.1, 18.2.3.2.2.1
Fire fighter safety building marking system (FFSBMS) E.1.3.4
Fire flow and 18.4.5.1.2, 18.4.5.1.3, 18.4.5.2.2, 18.4.5.2.4,
    18.4.5.3.2 to 18.4.5.3.5, 18.4.5.4, A.18.4.5.1.2,
    A.18.4.5.1.3, A.18.4.5.3.4, A.18.4.5.4
Flammable and combustible liquids storage, handling,
    and use 66.6.7.6, 66.6.7.7, 66.6.9.1, 66.9.6.2.4,
    66.9.10.2.3, 66.16.4 to 66.16.7, 66.16.9, 66.17.6.7,
    66.19.4.6, 66.24.6.1.2, 66.24.6.2.3, 66.24.6.2.4,
    66.24.13.4, A.66.16.5.1.6.2, A.66.16.6.1.5, A.66.19.4.6.1,
    A.66.24.6.1.2, A.66.24.6.2.3
Forest products, storage of 31.3.7.4
Health care occupancies .... see Health care occupancies
High rise buildings 13.3.2.16.1, 13.3.2.22.1.3, 13.3.2.26,
    A.13.3.2.26.2
Hotels and dormitories 13.3.2.15, 13.3.2.16, A.13.3.2.16.2
Hot work operations .... 41.3.3(2), 41.3.4.2(12)
Impairment .... 13.1.8 to 13.1.10, 13.3.3.4.1.4, 13.3.3.4.1.10,
    13.3.3.6, 16.5.1, A.13.3.3.6.3.1 to A.13.3.3.6.7
Industrial occupancies 13.3.2.30
Inspection, testing, and maintenance 13.3.3,
    A.13.3.3.4.1.1 to A.13.3.3.6.7
Interior finish and 12.5.9
Marinas and boatyards 28.1.6.6.2
Mercantile occupancies 13.3.2.23.3, 13.3.2.24.2
Motion picture production soundstages, facilities, and
    locations .... 32.4.11.1.1 to 32.4.11.1.4, 32.5.11.2
    to 32.5.11.6, A.32.4.11.1.3.1, A.32.4.11.1.3.2, A.32.5.11.4,
    A.32.5.11.5
One- and two-family dwellings .... 13.3.2.20, Table 13.8,
    18.2.3.2.1.1, 18.4.5.1.2, 18.4.5.1.3, 18.4.5.2.2, 18.4.5.2.4,
    A.18.4.5.1.2, A.18.4.5.1.3
Repair garages 30.2.7
Residential board and care occupancies ...... see Residential board
    and care occupancies
Spray application operations 43.1.7.1.1, 43.1.7.4,
    43.1.7.8.2(3), 43.8.3, A.43.1.7.4, A.43.8.3
Storage occupancies .... see Storage occupancies
Tents, membrane structures, grandstands, and folding/telescopic
    seating 25.1.6.1, 25.1.6.2
Ventilating systems 13.3.3.5.1.7
Stable liquids 66.22.4.1.6, 66.22.4.2.1, 66.22.11.2.6.3.1,
    66.22.11.2.6.3.3, A.66.22.4.2.1
Definition 3.3.164.4
Staff, training of
Ambulatory health care occupancies 20.6.2.1.2,
    20.6.2.1.7, 20.6.2.1.8, 20.6.2.2, A.20.6.2.2.1
Business occupancies 20.13.2.2, 20.13.2.3
Day-care occupancies 20.3.4.2.3.6, A.20.3.4.2.3.6
Detention and correctional occupancies 20.7.2.1,
    A.20.7.2.1.2, A.20.7.2.1.3
Dust explosion and fire prevention 40.5.3.2, 40.6,
    A.40.5.3.2, A.40.6.2.2 to A.40.6.5.4
Fire fighter safety building marking system (FFSBMS) E.1.5
Flammable and combustible liquids storage, handling,
    and use 43.10.1.1, 66.6.8, 66.17.15.4, 66.21.6.5,
    A.66.21.6.5.1
Hazardous materials, handling of 53.3.2.4, 60.5.1.4,
    A.60.5.1.4, D.3.2.8
Health care occupancies 20.4.2.1.2, 20.4.2.1.7,
    20.4.2.1.9, 20.4.2.2, A.20.4.2.2.1
Heliports 42.10.4.6, A.21.3.4.7.1
Hotels 20.8.2.1, A.20.8.2.1.1, A.20.8.2.1.2
LP-Gas liquid transfer 69.4.2.1
Maintenance of fire extinguishers 13.6.4.1.2,
    A.13.6.4.1.2.1 to A.13.6.4.1.2.3
Mercantile occupancies 20.12.2.2, 20.12.2.3
Motor fuel dispensing facilities 42.7.3, 42.7.4,
    42.9.10.1, 42.11.2.3
Spray application operations 43.7.8, 43.10,
    A.43.10.1
Storage occupancies 34.5.4.2, A.34.5.4.2
Tank operation 66.21.7.3.3
Tire storage 33.4.1.3
Wood chips and hogged material, storage of 31.3.6.3.3.2
Stages
Scenery, assembly occupancies 20.1.2, 20.1.5.4,
    A.20.1.5.4.1, A.20.1.5.4.3
Sprinkler systems 13.3.2.7.5, 13.3.2.8.5
Standpipe systems 13.2.2.4, A.13.2.2.4
Stairways .... 11.9.5(5), 14.11.4
Buildings under construction 16.3.4.5
Doors, reentry through 14.5.2.8, A.14.5.2.8
Enclosure and protection of 14.5.2.8, 14.6, 14.7.3,
    A.14.5.2.8, A.14.6.2, A.14.6.3
Exit discharge 14.7.3
Interior finish 20.1.3.2
Interlocking or scissor 14.10.1.4, A.14.10.1.4.2
Marking 10.11.3, A.10.11.3
As means of escape 4.5.6.2.2
Performance-based design option .... 5.3.4(4)
Protectives, minimum ratings for .... Table 12.7.4.2
Width of .... Table 14.8.3.1, 14.8.3.2, A.14.8.3.2
Stakeholder (definition) 3.4.20
Standard cubic foot (scf) (definition) 3.3.243
Standard (definition) 3.2.10
Standard temperature and pressure (definition) 3.3.244
Standby fire personnel 1.7.17, 10.14.4, 13.7.1.5.3,
    32.4.4, 32.5.4, A.1.7.17.3
Standby power .... 11.7.2 to 11.7.5, 11.9.5(7), 50.4.7.6,
    A.11.7.2.1
Compressed gases and cryogenic fluids 63.2.7.1
Membrane structures 25.5.3.3, 25.6.5.3,
    A.25.5.3.3.1
Standpipe systems 13.2, A.13.2.2.4, A.13.2.2.6
Aerosol products storage, handling, and use 61.2.6.2
Airports 21.2.9
Buildings under construction 16.3.5, 16.4.3.3,
    A.16.4.3.3.1.1 to A.16.4.3.3.2.8
Definition 3.3.254.13, A.3.3.254.13
Detention and correctional occupancies 13.2.2.5
Dust explosion and fire prevention 40.5.4.1
Fire fighter safety building marking system (FFSBMS) E.1.3.4
Flammable and combustible liquids storage, handling,
    and use 66.6.7.7, 66.9.10.2.4, 66.24.6.1.2, A.66.24.6.1.2
Heliports, roof-top 21.3.4.6.5.2
Hot work operations .... 41.3.4.2(11)
Marinas, boatyards, piers, and wharves 28.1.6.3,
    A.28.1.6.3
Marine motor fuel dispensing facilities 42.9.7.2
Motion picture production soundstages, facilities, and
    locations 32.5.11.8
Permit requirements .... Table 1.12.8(a)
Storage occupancies 20.15.8.3
Static electricity
Aerosol products storage, handling, and use .... 61.2.8.2(9),
    61.5.3.1.1(9), 61.5.7, A.61.5.7
Compressed gases and cryogenic fluids 63.3.6.4.1
Dust explosion and fire prevention .... 40.4.3, A.40.4.3.2 to
    A.40.4.3.7.7
Flammable and combustible liquids storage, handling,
    and use .... 66.6.5.1(9), 66.6.5.4, 66.19.5.7.3,
    A.66.6.5.4, A.66.19.5.7.3
Hazardous materials storage and use 60.5.1.10.2
Spray application operations 43.1.4.6, A.43.1.4.6
Stationary tanks .... see Tanks
Stop work 1.7.15
Storage .... see also High-piled storage; Inside liquid storage areas;
    Outdoor storage; Tanks; Warehouses
Aerosol products .... 61.2.3.2, 61.3, 61.4, A.61.3.1.3 to
    A.61.3.4.2.9

Aircraft storage hangars 21.1.5, A.21.1.5
Ammonium nitrate .... Chap. 74
Automotive fuel servicing .... 42.2.2.2.2, 42.3, A.42.3.3.2 to A.42.3.3.8
Available height for storage (definition) 3.3.19, A.3.3.19
Baled, combustible fibers .... 45.6 see also Baled cotton
Boats .... 28.1.6.2.4, 28.1.7, A.28.1.6.2.4.1, A.28.1.6.2.4.3, A.28.1.7.1.3 to A.28.1.7.2.4
Bulk .... see Bulk storage
Cartoned (definition) 3.3.246.2
Cellulose nitrate motion picture film 20.15.7
Clothing .... see Clothing storage
Combustible materials .... Table 1.12.8(a), 10.18, A.10.18
Compressed gas 63.2.4, 63.2.5, 63.2.17, 63.3.2, 63.3.6.1, 63.3.9.3.1
Corrosive solids and liquids .... Chap. 64
Cryogenic fluids .... 63.4, A.63.4.2 to A.63.4.14.11.3.4.1
Detached .... see Detached storage
Exhibit booths 20.1.5.5.4.10
Exposition facilities 20.1.5.5.3
Flammable and combustible liquids .... Chap. 66
Flammable solids .... Chap. 67
Forest products .... Chap. 31
Of fueled equipment 10.18.7
Hay, straw, and other agricultural products 45.7
Hazardous materials .... see Hazardous materials
Highly toxic and toxic solids and liquids .... Chap. 68
High-piled .... see High-piled storage
Incidental liquid use or storage (definition) 3.3.156
Isolated (definition) 3.3.246.5
Organic peroxide .... 43.7.4, 43.8.7.1, Chap. 75
Oxidizers .... see Oxidizers
Oxygen-fuel gas cylinders and containers 41.5.5.2
Permits .... Table 1.12.8(a), 10.18.2, 34.1.2
Protected (definition) 66.16.2.1
Pyrophoric solids and liquids .... Chap. 71
Records 20.15.6, A.20.15.6.2
Refrigerant machinery rooms 53.3.1.3
Resins 43.8.4
Segregated (definition) 3.3.246.11
Tires .... see Tire storage
Unstable (reactive) solids and liquids .... Chap. 72
Waste and rubbish, combustible 19.1.6.1, 19.1.7
Water-reactive solids and liquids .... Chap. 73
Wildland/urban interface 17.3.5.2.1.11.4, 17.3.5.2.1.11.5
Yards .... see Yards
Storage aids (definition) .... 3.3.247; see also Palletized storage
Storage cabinets .... see also Gas cabinets
Hazardous materials 60.5.1.18
Liquid 66.9.5, A.66.9.5
Storage occupancies .... 20.15, Chap. 34, A.20.15.5.1, A.20.15.6.2
Christmas tree provisions .... Table 10.13.1.1
Definition 3.3.183.28, 6.1.13.1, A.3.3.183.28, A.6.1.13.1
Detection, alarm, and communication systems 13.7.2.28
Extinguishers, portable fire .... Table 13.6.1.2
Fire fighter safety building marking system (FFSBMS) .... E.1.3.5(1)
Hazardous materials 20.15.4, 60.4.2.1.12, 60.4.2.1.13
Mini-storage buildings 13.3.2.27.4
Definition 3.3.183.28.1, A.3.3.183.28.1
Multiple occupancies .... 6.1.14.1.3, Table 6.1.14.4.1(a), Table 6.1.14.4.1(b), A.6.1.14.1.3
Permits .... Table 1.12.8(a), 20.15.2, 20.15.7.2, 20.15.8.2
Sprinkler systems .... 10.18.3.2 to 10.18.3.4, 13.3.2.27, 13.7.2.28.1.3, 20.15.8.3.2, 34.2.4.5, 34.4.2.1, 34.4.2.2, 34.5.1, 34.5.4.2, 34.5.5.1, 34.6.3.3(1), 34.7.2, 34.7.3.4.1.2, 34.7.3.4.2, A.13.3.2.27, A.34.4.2.2, A.34.5.1, A.34.5.4.2, A.34.7.3.4.2.1(1)

Storage tank buildings .... Table 66.7.3.3, 66.24, A.66.24.1 to A.66.24.14.8
Definition 3.3.29.11
Storage tanks .... see Tanks
Stored electrical energy systems 11.7.4, 11.7.5.3
Story
Definition 3.3.248
Means of egress, number of 14.9.1.1, 14.9.1.2
Occupiable (definition) 3.3.258.1
Street (definition) .... 3.3.249; see also Roadways
Street floor (definition) 3.3.250, A.3.3.250
Structural element (definition) 3.3.251
Structural failure, occupant protection from 5.2.2.8
Structural integrity 4.1.4.2.3
Structures .... see also Buildings
Access to .... see Access, fire-fighting/emergency
Definition 3.3.252, A.3.3.252
Special 20.16
Styrene cross-linked composites manufacturing ..... 43.8, A.43.8.1 to A.43.8.5.3
Sub-floor work areas, repair garages 30.2.6, 30.2.9.3
Submersible pumping systems 42.5.4
Summarily abate (definition) 3.3.253
Supervision
Alarm systems 13.7.1.5.6, A.13.7.1.5.6
Cooking equipment alarm systems .... 50.4.4.10, 50.4.9, A.50.4.4.10(4)
Extinguishing system releasing devices 40.5.2.8
Fire pump valves 13.4.3, A.13.4.3
Sprinkler systems 13.3.1.8, A.13.3.1.8.1
Supervisory signals .... see Signals
Suppression systems .... see Extinguishing systems
Systems .... see also specific systems
Definition 3.3.254
Design/installation 4.4.6

-T-

Tank cars .... Table 66.7.3.3, 66.28, A.66.28.3.1.2 to A.66.28.11.4.1
Tanks
Aboveground
Alternative fuels 42.8.3, A.42.8.3.4
Cryogenic fluids 63.4.2.1, 63.4.13.2.5.1
Definition 3.3.255.2
Hazardous materials 60.5.1.19.2, 60.5.1.19.3
Motor vehicle fuel dispensing facilities .... 42.2.2.2.2, 42.3.2.1, 42.3.3.2 to 42.3.3.10, 42.7.2.2.5.1, A.42.3.3.2 to A.42.3.3.8
Fire-resistant 42.3.3.4
Protection .... 42.3.3.5 to 42.3.3.8, A.42.3.3.7.2, A.42.3.3.8
Vaults 42.3.3.3, A.42.3.3.3.3
Aboveground storage
In areas subject to flooding 66.22.14
Definition 3.3.255.1
Fire control 66.22.8, A.66.22.8.1
Fire-resistant 66.22.9
Flammable and combustible liquids storage ..... Table 66.7.3.3, 66.21, 66.22, A.66.21.4.2.1.1 to A.66.21.8.8, A.66.22.4 to A.66.22.17.4
Floating roof tanks .... see Floating roof tanks
Inspection, testing, and maintenance 66.22.10.1, 66.22.17, A.66.22.17.4
Installation 66.22.5, 66.22.16, A.66.22.5.2.1, A.66.25.5.2.4
Location of 66.22.4, A.66.22.4
Openings other than vents 66.22.13
Protected .... Table 66.22.4.1.1(a), 66.22.8 to 66.22.10, 66.22.12.4, 66.22.15, A.66.22.8.1
Definition 3.3.255.2.1

Spill control and impounding 66.22.11, 66.22.12, A.66.22.11, A.66.22.12.1, A.66.22.12.3
   Vaults 66.25, A.66.25.3.1, A.66.25.5
   Venting 66.22.4.2.5, 66.22.6, 66.22.7, 66.22.11.3.12, A.66.22.7.3.1, A.66.22.7.4
  ASME .... *see* ASME containers or tanks
  Cargo 42.9.9
  Compartmented (definition) 66.21.2.1
  Compressed gas .... 63.3.1.5.1.5 to 63.3.1.5.1.7, 63.3.1.6
  Cooking oil storage, commercial kitchen .... 50.6.3, 66.19.7, A.66.19.7.1.3 to A.66.19.7.5.2
  Cryogenic fluids 63.4.2, 63.4.4.1.2, 63.4.7.2, A.63.4.2, A.63.4.7.2
  Flammable and combustible liquids .... 16.18.5.4.1(2), Table 66.7.3.3, 66.9, 66.15, 66.18.4.1, 66.18.4.4, 66.18.4.8, 66.18.4.9, 66.18.5.2, 66.18.5.6, 66.19.5.2, 66.19.5.6, 66.21 to 66.25, 66.27.8.2, A.66.9.4.1 to A.66.9.16.2, A.66.18.4.8, A.66.21.4.2.1.1 to A.66.25.5, A.66.27.8.2.1
  Fuel
   Aircraft fuel 42.10.3.3, A.42.10.3.3.1
   Boat storage and .... 28.1.7.2.1.5, A.28.1.7.2.1.5(4)
   Fire pump fuel supply 13.4.4.4, A.13.4.4.4
   Generators 25.1.12.2
   Heliports 21.3.3.2
   Motor vehicle 42.5.1, 42.7.3, 42.7.4.1
  Hazardous materials 60.1.2, 60.5.1.6.1, 60.5.1.7, 60.5.1.16.2, 60.5.1.16.3, 60.5.1.19, A.60.5.1.16.2.3
  Motor vehicle fuel dispensing facilities .... 42.3, 42.7.2.2.4, 42.7.2.2.5, 42.9.2, 42.9.8, A.42.3.3.2 to A.42.3.3.8, A.42.9.2.2, A.42.9.8.2
  Operation .... 66.21.7, A.66.21.7.1 to A.66.21.7.5
  Portable 42.9.8, 43.1.6.5.1, A.42.9.8.2
  Definition 3.3.255.4, A.3.3.255.4
   Flammable and combustible liquids .... 16.18.5.4.1(2), Table 66.7.3.3, 66.9, 66.15, 66.16.5.2.1 to 66.16.5.2.4, 66.18.4.8, 66.18.4.9, 66.18.5.2, A.66.9.4.1 to A.66.9.16.2, A.66.18.4.8
   Mixing tanks 43.1.6.3.1
   Nonmetallic (definition) 66.3.3.33.3.1, A.66.3.3.33.3.1
  Secondary containment 66.22.11.4
   Definition 3.3.255.5
  Stationary (definition) 3.3.255.6, A.3.3.2655.6
  Storage (definition) ...... 3.3.255.7 *see also* subhead: Aboveground storage
  Underground .... 42.2.2.2.2, 42.3.2.1(3), 42.3.3.1 *see also* LP-Gas containers
   Cryogenic fluids 63.4.13.2.5.2
   Flammable and combustible liquids storage ... 66.21.3.3, 66.21.3.4, 66.21.4.1.2(1), 66.21.7.1.5, 66.21.7.4.3, 66.23, 66.27.8.2, A.66.21.7.4.3.3(2), A.66.23.3.4 to A.66.23.14.1, A.66.27.8.2.1
   Hazardous materials 60.5.1.19.1
   LP-Gas 69.3.4.4.8
   Water supply 61.2.6.4.2
Tank vehicles .... 42.7.2.2, 42.7.6, 42.9.9, 42.10.5.17 to 42.10.5.20, Table 66.7.3.3, 66.28, A.66.28.3.1.2 to A.66.28.11.4.1
Tar kettles .... *see* Kettles
TC (Transport Canada) (definition) 3.3.258
Technical assistance 1.15, 5.1.5, 10.1.4, A.5.1.5
Telecommunication facilities .... Chap. 36
Telephones, two-way 13.7.2.29.2.2, A.13.7.2.29.2.2.2
Television production soundstages, facilities, and locations .... Table 1.12.8(a), 20.16.1.2, Chap. 32
Temporary heating equipment .... *see* Heating equipment and appliances
Temporary wiring 11.1.6
  Definition 3.3.256
Tensioned-membrane structures 25.5.2, 25.6.4

Tents 25.1, 25.2, A.25.1.4.2, A.25.1.8
  Permits .... Table 1.12.8(a), 25.1.2
Terminal buildings, airport .... *see* Airport terminal buildings
Testing .... *see* Inspection, testing, and maintenance
Ties, outside storage of .... 31.3.1.1(3), 31.3.5, A.31.3.5.1.1 to A.31.3.5.3.5
Tires .... *see also* Tire storage
  Rubber (definition) 3.3.257.1
  Scrap 33.4.1.2
  Definition 3.3.267.2
Tire storage .... 34.1.1, 34.8, A.34.1.1.2(6), A.34.8.1 to A.34.8.3.1.1
  Banded .... Fig. A.34.8.1(e), Fig. A.34.8.1(f)
  Definition 3.3.246.1
  Bulk storage
   Automobile wrecking yards 22.7
   Sprinkler systems for 13.3.2.27.5
  Laced .... Fig. A.34.8.1(g)
  Definition 3.3.246.6
  Miscellaneous .... 34.1.1.2(6), A.34.1.1.2(6)
  Definition 3.3.246.7, A.3.3.246.7
  On-side .... Fig. A.34.8.1(e)
  Definition 3.3.246.8
  On-tread .... 34.8.3.1.3, Fig. A.34.8.1(f)
  Definition 3.3.246.9
  Outside storage .... Table 1.12.8(a), Chap. 33
Title of code 1.1.2
Torch-applied roofing systems .... Table 1.12.8(a), 16.6, 41.1.2(7), A.41.1.2(7)
Torches, use of .... *see* Hot work
Towers 13.7.2.29.1
Townhouses .... *see also* Apartment buildings
  Photovoltaic systems in 11.12.2.2.2
Toxic gas .... Table 60.4.2.1.1.3, Table 60.4.4.1.2, 63.1.4.1(2)(d), 63.1.4.4.1, Table 63.2.3.1.1, 63.2.3.1.7, Table 63.3.1.11.2, 63.3.9, A.63.3.9.2.2.1.1 to A.63.3.9.3.6.2, B.2.1.2.5, B.2.2.1.2.1; *see also* Compressed gas
  Definition 3.3.135.17
  Permit amounts for .... Table 1.12.8(b), Table 1.12.8(d)
  Refrigerants 53.2.2.1.1, 53.2.2.2
Toxic materials (solids and liquids) .... Table 60.4.2.1.1.3, Tables 60.4.2.1.2 to 60.4.2.1.8, Table 60.4.2.1.10.1, Table 60.4.2.1.13.3(b), Table 60.4.4.1.2, Chap. 68, B.2.2.1.2.2, B.2.2.1.2.3; *see also* Hazardous materials
  Definition 3.3.173.14, A.3.3.173.14
  Permit amounts for .... Table 1.12.8(d)
Tracer bullets and tracer charges 17.3.4.2
Trade secrets 1.7.11.4
Trade shows .... *see* Exhibits
Traffic calming devices 18.2.3.4.7
  Definition 3.3.260, A.3.3.260
Training
  Board and care occupancy residents, of 20.5.2.2
  Staff .... *see* Staff, training of
Treated finishes 12.6.1
Treatment systems (definition) 3.3.254.14
Trouble signals .... *see* Signals
Truck repair garages .... *see* Repair garages
Tube trailers 63.3.1.10.1.1
  Definition 3.3.261, A.3.3.261
Turbines, gas 11.7.1
Turning radius, access roads 18.2.3.4.3
Two-family dwellings .... *see* One- and two-family dwellings
Two-way radio communication enhancement system 11.10, A.11.10

-U-

Unauthorized discharge .... 10.6.3, 60.5.1.6.2(5), 63.3.3.1.3.2, D.3.2.7
  Definition 3.3.262
Uncertainty analysis .... *see* Analysis

Underground structures
    Emergency plans 10.8.1
    Parking structures 29.1.1
        Definition 3.3.183.23.1
    Sprinkler systems 13.3.2.25
Underground tanks ....*see* Tanks
Unit operation or process (definition) 3.3.264
Units of measurement 1.5
Unit (vessel), operating or process ......*see* Operating or process unit (vessel)
Unsaturated polyester resins (UPRs) 66.9.3.5, 66.16.5.2.11
    Definition 66.16.2.3, A.66.16.2.3
Unstable (reactive) gas .... Table 60.4.2.1.1.3, 63.1.4.1(1), Table 63.2.3.1.1, Table 63.2.9, Table 63.3.1.11.2, 63.3.10, A.63.3.10.1.2.1, A.63.3.10.2.2.1, B.2.1.2.8; *see also* Compressed gas; Hazardous materials
    Definition 3.3.135.18, A.3.3.135.18
    Permit amounts for .... Table 1.12.8(b), Table 1.12.8(d)
Unstable (reactive) materials (solids and liquids) .... Table 60.4.2.1.1.3, Table 60.4.2.1.13.3(b), Table 60.4.3.7, Table 60.4.4.1.2, Chap. 72; *see also* Hazardous materials
    Containers, storage of liquids in 66.9.3.2, 66.9.16.2, A.66.9.16.2
    Definition 3.3.173.15, A.3.3.173.15
    Indoor storage 66.16.1.2, A.66.16.1.2
    Permit amounts for .... Table 1.12.8(d)
    Processing facilities .... Table 16.17.4.3, 66.17.4.7, Table 66.17.6.1, 66.17.6.13
    Solvent distillation units 66.19.6.3.1
    Specific occupancies, storage and use in .... Tables 60.4.2.1.2 to 60.4.2.1.8, Table 60.4.2.1.10.1
    Storage tank buildings .... Table 66.24.4.2, 66.24.4.5(3), 66.24.4.7, 66.24.5.5, A.66.24.4.5(3)
    Tank storage 66.22.4.1.5, 66.22.4.2.2, 66.22.7.1.3, 66.22.11.2.6.3.4, A.66.22.11.2.6.3.4
Untenable conditions, occupant protection from 5.2.2.6
Use
    Closed system use (definition) 3.3.267.1, A.3.3.267.1
    Definition 3.3.273, 3.3.278, A.3.3.273
    Incidental liquid use or storage (definition) 3.3.164
    Open system use (definition) 3.3.267.2, A.3.3.267.2
    Special uses .... *see* Special uses
Utilities 11.4
Utility plants, LP-Gas at 69.7

-V-

Vacant buildings .... 5.3.3(6), 10.12, A.10.12.2.1
Vacuum cleaners .... 40.3.2.2.2 to 40.3.2.2.4, 40.3.2.3, A.40.3.2.2.4
Vacuum systems, medical 11.11
Valve-regulated batteries .... *see* Batteries
Valves .... *see also* Emergency shutoff valves; Excess flow valves
    Compressed gas systems 63.3.1.5.1.7.2, 63.3.1.5.2.2, 63.3.3.1.4
    Cryogenic fluid piping systems .... 63.4.14.4 to 6.4.14.6
    Fire pump valves, supervision of 13.4.3, A.13.4.3
    Flammable and combustible liquids piping systems 66.27.4.3, 66.27.4.5, 66.27.6.6, 66.29.3.11, A.66.27.4.3.2
    Hazardous materials 60.5.1.6.2
    Indicating 43.1.7.4.5
        Definition 3.3.268.1
    LP-Gas systems and equipment 69.2.3, 69.3.7, 69.3.8, 69.3.13.3.8, 69.3.13.3.10, 69.5.2.2, A.69.3.8.8
    Outlet cap or plug 63.3.1.10.2, 63.3.8.9.3.1.1
        Definition 3.3.268.3
    Ozone gas-generating equipment 54.3
    Protection cap 63.3.1.10.2
        Definition 3.3.268.4
    Protection device 63.3.1.10
        Definition 3.3.268.5

    Reduced flow (definition) 3.3.268.2
    Sprinkler systems 13.3.3.4.1.8
Vapor pressure (definition) 3.3.269, A.3.3.269
Vapor processing equipment (definition) 66.3.3.36
Vapor processing systems .... 66.19.5, A.66.19.5.5.1 to A.66.19.5.7.6
    Definition 3.3.254.15, A.3.3.254.15
Vapor recovery systems .... 42.5.8, 66.19.5, A.66.19.5.5.1 to A.66.19.5.7.6
    Definition 3.3.254.16, A.3.3.254.16
Vapors, flammable .... *see* Flammable vapors
Vaults
    Combustible fiber storage 45.5.4
    Doors 12.4.3, A.12.4.3
    Flammable and combustible liquids, aboveground tanks for ... Table 66.7.3.3, 66.25, A.66.25.3.1, A.66.25.5
    Motor vehicle fuel dispensing facility tank 42.3.3.3, A.42.3.3.3.3
Vegetation, combustible .... 5.3.3(7), 10.12.1, 10.13, 17.3.5, 25.1.5.1, 33.5.2, 63.3.1.11.3, 66.6.9.4, 66.15.3.7, 66.21.6.6.3, A.10.13.3, A.10.13.9.4, A.17.3.5.1.5 to A.17.3.5.2.1.11.1, A.63.3.1.11.3
Vehicles .... *see* Motor vehicles
Vented batteries .... *see* Batteries
Ventilation systems ...... *see* Heating, ventilating, and air conditioning (HVAC) systems
Venting .... *see also* Vents
    Compressed gases and cryogenic fluids 63.2.16, 63.3.3.1.5
    Emergency relief vents .... 42.3.2.7(4), 66.19.7.2.4, Table 66.22.4.1.1(a), Table 66.22.4.1.5, 66.22.4.2.5, 66.22.6, 66.22.7, Table 66.24.4.2, 66.24.13.5.1, 66.24.13.6, A.66.19.7.2.4.2, A.66.22.7.3.1, A.66.22.7.4
        Definition 3.3.94
    Flammable and combustible liquids .... Table 66.7.3.3, 66.9.4.2, 66.19.7.2.3, 66.19.7.2.4, 66.22.4.2.5, 66.22.6, 66.22.7, 66.22.11.3.12, 66.23.6, 66.24.13, 66.27.8, A.66.19.7.2.3.4, A.66.19.7.2.4.2, A.66.22.7.3.1, A.66.22.7.4, A.66.23.6.1, A.66.27.8.1.6, A.66.27.9.2.1
        Processing areas 66.17.6.10, A.66.17.6.10
        Storage tanks 66.21.4.3, A.66.21.4.3.2, A.66.21.4.3.11
    Vapor recovery/processing systems 66.19.5.2, 66.19.5.3
    LP-Gas 69.3.5.3.2, 69.4.3
Vents .... *see also* Venting
    Emergency smoke and heat .... 34.3.3, 34.5.4.2(4), A.34.3.3
    Heating equipment and appliances 11.5.4
Verification method (definition) 3.4.22
Vertical openings .... *see* Openings, vertical
Vessels, marine .... *see* Marine vessels
Vessels, pressure .... *see* Pressure vessels
Vessels, process .... *see* Operating or process unit (vessel)
Violations of code 1.16, 10.1.5
Viscous liquids 6.16.3.4
    Definition 66.16.2.4

-W-

Walls
    Fire .... *see* Fire walls
    Fire barrier .... 12.7.2, 12.7.5, A.12.7.2.1.1, A.12.7.5.1, A.12.7.5.6.3(1)(c)
    Hot work operations .... 41.3.4.2(4), 41.3.4.2(6) to (9), 41.3.5.1(4), 41.3.5.2(3)
    Interior finish .... *see* Interior finish
    Temporary separation, construction site 16.4.2, A.16.4.2.4
Warehouses
    Definition A.66.3.3.40
    General-purpose .... 66.9.10.2.5(1)
        Definition 3.3.272.1

Liquid .... Table 66.7.3.3, 66.9.8.2, 66.9.10.2.5(1), A.66.9.8.2, A.66.16.8.2
    Definition 3.3.272.2
Warrant of fitness 4.5.5
Waste, combustible .... Chap. 19, 43.1.8.5, A.43.1.8.5
    Aerosol containers 61.5.5
    Buildings under construction .... 16.2.2, A.16.2.2.1 to A.16.2.2.4.3
    Commercial rubbish-handling operations 19.2.1.5
    Definition 3.3.62, A.3.3.632
    Demolition sites 16.5.3
    Flammable and combustible liquids storage, handling, and use 66.9.9.3, 66.9.9.4, 66.15.3.7, 66.19.7.5.2, 66.21.6.6.3, 66.21.6.6.5, A.66.19.7.5.2
    Forest products, storage of 31.3.2.1.1, 31.3.7, A.31.3.2.1.1, A.31.3.7
    Motion picture production soundstages, facilities, and locations 32.6.1
    Motor vehicle fuel dispensing facilities 42.7.2.6
    Storage occupancies 34.6.4
    Vacant buildings 10.12.1
Waste, hazardous materials 60.3.5, A.60.3.5
Water capacity (definition) 3.3.273
Waterflow alarms .... 11.9.5(6), 13.7.1.7.6, 34.5.5.1, A.13.7.1.7.6
Water-miscible liquids .... 44.2.2(2), 66.9.1.4, 66.9.4.3.1, 66.16.5.2.1 to 66.16.5.2.8, 66.16.5.2.10, 66.16.5.2.12, A.66.21.4.4
    Bulk loading and unloading facilities for tank cars and vehicles 66.28.10.1
    Definition 66.16.2.5
    Fire protection criteria decision trees .... 66.16.4.1.1 to 66.16.4.1.3
    Piping systems A.66.27.10
Water mist extinguishing systems .... Table 13.8, 66.16.9
Water mist portable fire extinguishers 13.6.4.7.3.11, 13.6.4.7.4.4, A.13.6.4.7.4.4
Water-reactive materials .... Table 60.4.2.1.1.3, Tables 60.4.2.1.2 to 60.4.2.1.8, Table 60.4.2.1.10.1, Table 60.4.2.1.13.3(b), Table 60.4.3.7, Table 60.4.4.1.2, 66.9.17.4, Chap. 73, B.2.1.9; *see also* Hazardous materials
    Definition 3.3.173.16, A.3.3.173.16
    Permit amounts for .... Table 1.12.8(d)
Water spray systems .... Table 13.8
    Airport terminal buildings 21.2.3.5.3
    Cooking equipment 50.5.5
    Flammable and combustible liquids storage, handling, and use ...... 66.6.7.6, 66.16.9, 66.17.6.8(4), 66.24.6.2.3, 66.24.6.2.4, A.66.24.6.2.3
Water supplies .... 13.5, Chap. 18, A.13.5.3; *see also* Fire hydrants
    Aerosol products storage, handling, and use 61.2.6.4
    Assembly occupancies 20.1.4.3
    Buildings under construction 16.4.3.1, A.16.4.3.1.1, A.16.4.3.1.3
    Fire flow requirements for buildings .... 18.4, A.18.4.1 to A.18.4.5.4
    Flammable and combustible liquids storage, handling, and use 66.6.7.2, 66.6.7.3, 66.9.10.2.6, 66.16.7, 66.24.6.2.1, A.66.6.7.3
    Foam extinguishing systems 21.3.4.6.5
    Forest products, storage of 31.3.3.2.2, 31.3.4.3.1, 31.3.5.3.2, 31.3.6.3.5, 31.3.8.3.4, A.31.3.3.2.2, A.31.3.4.3.1, A.31.3.5.3.2, A.31.3.6.3.5
    Marinas, boatyards, piers, and wharves 28.1.6.2.5, 28.1.6.2.6, 28.1.6.4, 28.1.6.5, A.28.1.6.2.5
    Permits, fire flow water supply system .... Table 1.12.8(a)
    Private 18.5.5.1
    Spray application operations 43.1.7.4.3
    Sprinkler systems .... 13.3.3.6.5.2(4)(c), 43.1.7.4.3, A.13.3.3.6.5.2(4)(c)
    Storage occupancies 34.6.6.2, A.34.6.6.2
    Tires, outside storage of 33.4.2

Welding and cutting .... *see* Hot work operations
Wet chemical extinguishing systems .... Table 13.8, 50.4.5.3
Wet chemical portable fire extinguishers .... Table 13.6.4.3.3.1, 13.6.4.7.3.11, 13.6.4.7.4.4, 13.6.4.10.4.1, A.13.6.4.7.4.4
Wet pipe sprinkler systems 66.16.4.2
Wetting agent portable fire extinguishers .... Table 13.6.4.3.3.1, 13.6.4.3.3.4, 13.6.4.7.2.2
Wharves .... Chap. 28; *see also* Piers
    Definition 3.3.274, A.3.3.274
    Flammable and combustible liquids, bulk transfer of .... Table 66.7.3.3, 66.29, A.66.29.3.5, A.66.29.3.28
Wheeled fire extinguishers .... 13.6.1.6.1.1, 13.6.2.3.2.7, 13.6.3.1.3.5, 13.6.3.3.3.2, 13.6.4.2.2(5), 13.6.4.6, A.13.6.2.3.2.7, A.13.6.4.6.2
Wildland fire–prone areas .... 17.3, A.17.3.1 to A.17.3.5.2.11.1
    Permits .... Table 1.12.8(a), 17.3.2, A.17.3.2
Wildland/urban interface .... Chap. 17
    Construction and development plants 17.2
    Definition 3.3.275
    Fire-prone areas .... 17.3, A.17.3.1 to A.17.3.5.2.11.1
    Hazard mitigation plan .... 17.1.10, A.17.1.10.3 to A.17.1.10.5
    Structure assessment .... 17.1.4 to 17.1.9, A.17.1.2 to A.17.1.9.6
Windowless structures .... *see* Limited access structures
Windows .... *see also* Opening protectives
    Fire windows .... *see* Fire windows
    Motor fuel dispensing facilities 30.1.6.3
    Sprinkler temperature ratings .... Table 13.3.1.9(b)
Wiring .... *see also* Electrical equipment and systems
    For oil-burning appliances 11.5.1.9
    Permanent 11.1.2
    Photovoltaic systems 11.12.2.1.3, 11.12.2.2.4, A.11.12.2.1.3
    Temporary 11.1.6
    Definition 3.3.256
Wood .... *see also* Logs
    Cordwood 31.3.8.1.2
    Definition 3.3.73
    Lumber .... *see also* Lumber yards
    Definition 3.3.167
    Storage, manufacturing, and processing of .... Chap. 31
Wood chips, storage of .... 31.3.6, A.31.3.6.1 to A.31.3.6.4.3
Wood panels
    Definition 3.3.276
    Outside storage of .... Chap. 31
Wood processing and woodworking facilities .... Table 1.12.8(a), 13.3.2.28, 31.1, 31.3.9, A.31.1
Wrecking yards .... Table 1.12.8(a), Chap. 22
Written notice (definition) 3.3.277

-Y-

Yards
    Automobile wrecking .... Table 1.12.8(a), Chap. 22
    Exit discharge 14.11.1.1
    Storage .... *see also* Baled cotton; Outdoor storage
    Definition 3.3.246.12
    Forest products storage .... Chap. 31

-Z-

Zoned egress, Use condition II 13.3.2.13.1, 13.7.2.7.2.3, 13.7.2.8.2.1, 13.7.2.8.2.3, 13.7.2.11.4.3, 13.7.2.12.4.1, 13.7.2.12.4.3, A.13.7.2.7.2.3, A.13.7.2.8.2.3, A.13.7.2.11.4.3, A.13.7.2.12.4.3
    Definition 3.3.183.8.1.2
Zoned impeded egress, Use condition III .... 13.3.2.13.1, 13.7.2.8.2.1, 13.7.2.12.4.1, 20.7.2.1.1(2), 20.7.2.1.2, A.20.7.2.1.2
    Definition 3.3.183.8.1.3
Zoning, alarm 13.7.1.13, A.13.7.1.13.4, A.13.7.1.13.6

Sequence of Events for the Standards Development Process

As soon as the current edition is published, a Standard is open for Public Input

Step 1: Input Stage

- Input accepted from the public or other committees for consideration to develop the First Draft
- Committee holds First Draft Meeting to revise Standard (23 weeks)
  Committee(s) with Correlating Committee (10 weeks)
- Committee ballots on First Draft (12 weeks)
  Committee(s) with Correlating Committee (11 weeks)
- Correlating Committee First Draft Meeting (9 weeks)
- Correlating Committee ballots on First Draft (5 weeks)
- First Draft Report posted

Step 2: Comment Stage

- Public Comments accepted on First Draft (10 weeks)
- If Standard does not receive Public Comments and the Committee does not wish to further revise the Standard, the Standard becomes a Consent Standard and is sent directly to the Standards Council for issuance
- Committee holds Second Draft Meeting (21 weeks)
  Committee(s) with Correlating Committee (7 weeks)
- Committee ballots on Second Draft (11 weeks)
  Committee(s) with Correlating Committee (10 weeks)
- Correlating Committee First Draft Meeting (9 weeks)
- Correlating Committee ballots on First Draft (8 weeks)
- Second Draft Report posted

Step 3: Association Technical Meeting

- Notice of Intent to Make a Motion (NITMAM) accepted (5 weeks)
- NITMAMs are reviewed and valid motions are certified for presentation at the Association Technical Meeting
- Consent Standard bypasses Association Technical Meeting and proceeds directly to the Standards Council for issuance
- NFPA membership meets each June at the Association Technical Meeting and acts on Standards with "Certified Amending Motions" (certified NITMAMs)
- Committee(s) and Panel(s) vote on any successful amendments to the Technical Committee Reports made by the NFPA membership at the Association Technical Meeting

Step 4: Council Appeals and Issuance of Standard

- Notification of intent to file an appeal to the Standards Council on Association action must be filed within 20 days of the Association Technical Meeting
- Standards Council decides, based on all evidence, whether or not to issue the Standards or to take other action

Committee Membership Classifications[1,2,3,4]

The following classifications apply to Committee members and represent their principal interest in the activity of the Committee.

1. M   *Manufacturer:* A representative of a maker or marketer of a product, assembly, or system, or portion thereof, that is affected by the standard.
2. U   *User:* A representative of an entity that is subject to the provisions of the standard or that voluntarily uses the standard.
3. IM   *Installer/Maintainer:* A representative of an entity that is in the business of installing or maintaining a product, assembly, or system affected by the standard.
4. L   *Labor:* A labor representative or employee concerned with safety in the workplace.
5. RT   *Applied Research/Testing Laboratory:* A representative of an independent testing laboratory or independent applied research organization that promulgates and/or enforces standards.
6. E   *Enforcing Authority:* A representative of an agency or an organization that promulgates and/or enforces standards.
7. I   *Insurance:* A representative of an insurance company, broker, agent, bureau, or inspection agency.
8. C   *Consumer:* A person who is or represents the ultimate purchaser of a product, system, or service affected by the standard, but who is not included in (2).
9. SE   *Special Expert:* A person not representing (1) through (8) and who has special expertise in the scope of the standard or portion thereof.

NOTE 1: "Standard" connotes code, standard, recommended practice, or guide.

NOTE 2: A representative includes an employee.

NOTE 3: While these classifications will be used by the Standards Council to achieve a balance for Technical Committees, the Standards Council may determine that new classifications of member or unique interests need representation in order to foster the best possible Committee deliberations on any project. In this connection, the Standards Council may make such appointments as it deems appropriate in the public interest, such as the classification of "Utilities" in the National Electrical Code Committee.

NOTE 4: Representatives of subsidiaries of any group are generally considered to have the same classification as the parent organization.

Submitting Public Input / Public Comment through the Electronic Submission System (e-Submission):

As soon as the current edition is published, a Standard is open for Public Input.

Before accessing the e-Submission System, you must first sign-in at www.NFPA.org. *Note: You will be asked to sign-in or create a free online account with NFPA before using this system*:

a. Click in the gray Sign In box on the upper left side of the page. Once signed-in, you will see a red "Welcome" message in the top right corner.
b. Under the Codes and Standards heading, Click on the Document Information pages (List of Codes & Standards), and then select your document from the list or use one of the search features in the upper right gray box.

OR

a. Go directly to your specific document page by typing the convenient short link of www.nfpa.org/document#, (Example: NFPA 921 would be www.nfpa.org/921) Click in the gray Sign In box on the upper left side of the page. Once signed in, you will see a red "Welcome" message in the top right corner.

To begin your Public Input, select the link The next edition of this standard is now open for Public Input (formally "proposals") located on the Document Information tab, the Next Edition tab, or the right-hand Navigation bar. Alternatively, the Next Edition tab includes a link to Submit Public Input online

At this point, the NFPA Standards Development Site will open showing details for the document you have selected. This "Document Home" page site includes an explanatory introduction, information on the current document phase and closing date, a left-hand navigation panel that includes useful links, a document Table of Contents, and icons at the top you can click for Help when using the site. The Help icons and navigation panel will be visible except when you are actually in the process of creating a Public Input.

Once the First Draft Report becomes available there is a Public comment period during which anyone may submit a Public Comment on the First Draft. Any objections or further related changes to the content of the First Draft must be submitted at the Comment stage.

To submit a Public Comment you may access the e-Submission System utilizing the same steps as previous explained for the submission of Public Input.

For further information on submitting public input and public comments, go to: http://www.nfpa.org/publicinput

Other Resources available on the Doc Info Pages

Document information tab: Research current and previous edition information on a Standard

Next edition tab: Follow the committee's progress in the processing of a Standard in its next revision cycle.

Technical committee tab: View current committee member rosters or apply to a committee

Technical questions tab: For members and Public Sector Officials/AHJs to submit questions about codes and standards to NFPA staff. Our Technical Questions Service provides a convenient way to receive timely and consistent technical assistance when you need to know more about NFPA codes and standards relevant to your work. Responses are provided by NFPA staff on an informal basis.

Products/training tab: List of NFPA's publications and training available for purchase.

Community tab: Information and discussions about a Standard

Information on the NFPA Standards Development Process

I. Applicable Regulations. The primary rules governing the processing of NFPA standards (codes, standards, recommended practices, and guides) are the NFPA *Regulations Governing the Development of NFPA Standards (Regs)*. Other applicable rules include NFPA *Bylaws*, NFPA *Technical Meeting Convention Rules*, NFPA *Guide for the Conduct of Participants in the NFPA Standards Development Process*, and the NFPA *Regulations Governing Petitions to the Board of Directors from Decisions of the Standards Council*. Most of these rules and regulations are contained in the *NFPA Standards Directory*. For copies of the *Directory*, contact Codes and Standards Administration at NFPA Headquarters; all these documents are also available on the NFPA website at "www.nfpa.org."

The following is general information on the NFPA process. All participants, however, should refer to the actual rules and regulations for a full understanding of this process and for the criteria that govern participation.

II. Technical Committee Report. The Technical Committee Report is defined as "the Report of the responsible Committee(s), in accordance with the Regulations, in preparation of a new or revised NFPA Standard." The Technical Committee Report is in two parts and consists of the First Draft Report and the Second Draft Report. (See *Regs* at 1.4)

III. Step 1: First Draft Report. The First Draft Report is defined as "Part one of the Technical Committee Report, which documents the Input Stage." The First Draft Report consists of the First Draft, Public Input, Committee Input, Committee and Correlating Committee Statements, Correlating Input, Correlating Notes, and Ballot Statements. (See *Regs* at 4.2.5.2 and Section 4.3) Any objection to an action in the First Draft Report must be raised through the filing of an appropriate Comment for consideration in the Second Draft Report or the objection will be considered resolved. [See *Regs* at 4.3.1(b)]

IV. Step 2: Second Draft Report. The Second Draft Report is defined as "Part two of the Technical Committee Report, which documents the Comment Stage." The Second Draft Report consists of the Second Draft, Public Comments with corresponding Committee Actions and Committee Statements, Correlating Notes and their respective Committee Statements, Committee Comments, Correlating Revisions, and Ballot Statements. (See *Regs* at Section 4.2.5.2 and 4.4) The First Draft Report and the Second Draft Report together constitute the Technical Committee Report. Any outstanding objection following the Second Draft Report must be raised through an appropriate Amending Motion at the Association Technical Meeting or the objection will be considered resolved. [See *Regs* at 4.4.1(b)]

V. Step 3a: Action at Association Technical Meeting. Following the publication of the Second Draft Report, there is a period during which those wishing to make proper Amending Motions on the Technical Committee Reports must signal their intention by submitting a Notice of Intent to Make a Motion. (See *Regs* at 4.5.2) Standards that receive notice of proper Amending Motions (Certified Amending Motions) will be presented for action at the annual June Association Technical Meeting. At the meeting, the NFPA membership can consider and act on these Certified Amending Motions as well as Follow-up Amending Motions, that is, motions that become necessary as a result of a previous successful Amending Motion. (See 4.5.3.2 through 4.5.3.6 and Table1, Columns 1-3 of *Regs* for a summary of the available Amending Motions and who may make them.) Any outstanding objection following action at an Association Technical Meeting (and any further Technical Committee consideration following successful Amending Motions, see *Regs* at 4.5.3.7 through 4.6.5.3) must be raised through an appeal to the Standards Council or it will be considered to be resolved.

VI. Step 3b: Documents Forwarded Directly to the Council. Where no Notice of Intent to Make a Motion (NITMAM) is received and certified in accordance with the Technical Meeting Convention Rules, the standard is forwarded directly to the Standards Council for action on issuance. Objections are deemed to be resolved for these documents. (See *Regs* at 4.5.2.5)

VII. Step 4a: Council Appeals. Anyone can appeal to the Standards Council concerning procedural or substantive matters related to the development, content, or issuance of any document of the Association or on matters within the purview of the authority of the Council, as established by the *Bylaws* and as determined by the Board of Directors. Such appeals must be in written form and filed with the Secretary of the Standards Council (See *Regs* at 1.6). Time constraints for filing an appeal must be in accordance with 1.6.2 of the *Regs*. Objections are deemed to be resolved if not pursued at this level.

VIII. Step 4b: Document Issuance. The Standards Council is the issuer of all documents (see Article 8 of *Bylaws*). The Council acts on the issuance of a document presented for action at an Association Technical Meeting within 75 days from the date of the recommendation from the Association Technical Meeting, unless this period is extended by the Council (See *Regs at* 4.7.2). For documents forwarded directly to the Standards Council, the Council acts on the issuance of the document at its next scheduled meeting, or at such other meeting as the Council may determine (See *Regs* at 4.5.2.5 and 4.7.4).

IX. Petitions to the Board of Directors. The Standards Council has been delegated the responsibility for the administration of the codes and standards development process and the issuance of documents. However, where extraordinary circumstances requiring the intervention of the Board of Directors exist, the Board of Directors may take any action necessary to fulfill its obligations to preserve the integrity of the codes and standards development process and to protect the interests of the Association. The rules for petitioning the Board of Directors can be found in the *Regulations Governing Petitions to the Board of Directors from Decisions of the Standards Council* and in 1.7 of the *Regs*.

X. For More Information. The program for the Association Technical Meeting (as well as the NFPA website as information becomes available) should be consulted for the date on which each report scheduled for consideration at the meeting will be presented. For copies of the First Draft Report and Second Draft Report as well as more information on NFPA rules and for up-to-date information on schedules and deadlines for processing NFPA documents, check the NFPA website (www.nfpa.org/aboutthecodes) or contact NFPA Codes & Standards Administration at (617) 984-7246.

STAY UP-TO-DATE.
JOIN NFPA® TODAY!

YES Please enroll me as a member of NFPA for the term checked below. Activate all benefits, and ship
Member Kit including the *Benefits Guide* and other resources to help me make the most of my NFPA membership.
allow three to four weeks for the kit to arrive.

ING INFORMATION:

_____ Title _____

ization _____

ess _____

_____ State _____ Zip/Postal Code _____

try _____

e _____ E-mail _____

Priority Code: 8J-MIS-1Z

SE ANSWER THE FOLLOWING QUESTIONS:

itle *(check one)*
- rchitect, Engineer, Consultant, Contractor (C17)
- cilities Safety Officer (F14)
- re Chief, Other Fire Service (A11)
- oss Control, Risk Manager (L11)
- spector, Building Official, Fire Marshal (F03)
- wner, President, Manager, Administrator (C10)
- ther (please specify): (G11) _____

e of Organization *(check one)*
- rchitecture, Engineering, Contracting (A14)
- ommercial Firm (Office, Retail, Lodging, Restaurant) (G13)
- lectrical Services, Installation (J11)
- ire Service, Public and Private (AA1)
- overnment (C12)
- ndustrial Firm (Factory, Warehouse) (C11)
- nstitutional (Health Care, Education, Detention, Museums) (B11)
- nsurance, Risk Management (B12)
- Jtilities (G12)
- Other (please specify): (G11) _____

TERMS AND PAYMENT:

❏ 1 year ($165)
❏ 2 years ($300) **SAVE $30**
❏ 3 years ($430) **SAVE $65**

Annual membership dues include a $45 subscription to *NFPA Journal®*. Regular membership in NFPA is individual and non-transferable. NFPA Journal is a registered trademark of the National Fire Protection Association, Quincy, MA 02169. Voting privileges begin after 180 days of individual membership. Prices subject to change.

PAYMENT METHOD:

Check One:

❏ **Payment Enclosed** *(Make check payable to NFPA.)*
❏ **Purchase Order** *(Please attach this form to your P.O.)*
❏ **Bill Me Later** *(Not available on International memberships.)*

Charge My: ❏ VISA   ❏ MasterCard   ❏ AmEx   ❏ Discover

Card # _____

Expiration Date _____

Name on Card _____

Signature _____

International members: Please note prepayment is required on all International orders. Be sure to enclose a check or select your preferred credit card option.

EASY WAYS TO JOIN

- 1-800-593-6372, Outside the U.S. +1-508-895-8301
- NFPA Membership Services Center,
  11 Tracy Drive, Avon, MA 02322-9908
- line: nfpa.org
- 1-800-344-3555
  Outside the U.S. call +1-617-770-3000

100% MONEY-BACK GUARANTEE
If anytime during your first year you decide membership is not for you, let us know and you'll receive a 100% refund of your dues.

"Member-Only" Benefits
Keeps You Up-To-Date!

FREE! Technical Support — Technical Support by Phone/Email. Get fast, reliable answers to all code-related questions—from electrical safety for employee workplaces to carbon dioxide extinguishing systems—from NFPA's team of fire protection specialists.

NFPA Journal® — THE journal of record for fire protection, this bi-monthly publication will keep you abreast of the latest fire prevention and safety practices, as well as new technologies and strategies for protecting life and property from fire.

NFPA Update — This easy-to-read monthly e-newsletter will keep you up-to-date on important association programs such as the annual meeting; bring you times of interest from NFPA's regional offices; and alert you to nationwide events and opportunities you won't want to miss.

NFPA News — From new standards for dry cleaning plants to warning equipment for household carbon monoxide, this monthly online update keeps you abreast of additions of changes that could impact how you do you work.

NFPA Standards Directory — The NFPA Standards Directory is your complete guide to NFPA's code-making process. Simply access your online NFPA member profile for document revision guidelines, the revision cycle schedule, and forms for submitting Proposals and Comments. Your online NFPA member profile and access to the NFPA Standards Directory is automatically generated once you join NFPA.

FREE! Section Membership — Share YOUR expertise with others in any of 16 industry-specific sections covering your own field of interest.

Member Kit — Includes Membership Certificate, Pin, Decals, ID Card, and Camera-ready Logo Art. Display the NFPA member logo proudly on your business correspondence, literature, website, and vehicles.

10% Discounts — Save hundreds of dollars each year on the many products and services listed in the NFPA Catalog, including codes and standards publications, handbooks, training videos, and other education materials to increase your knowledge and skills.

Voting Rights — Your chance to help shape the future direction of fire prevention codes and standards. Voting rights go into effect 180 days from the start of individual membership.

Conference Invitation— Invitation to the NFPA Conference and Expo. Attend this important meeting at discounted rates as a member of NFPA.

Join NFPA today!
www.nfpa.org

NFPA® and NFPA Journal® are registered trademarks of the National Fire Protection Association, Quincy, MA 02169-7471